County Court Note Book

Volumes I-X

and

Ancestral Proofs and Probabilities

Numbers 1-4

Edited by

Milnor Ljungstedt

With an Introduction by

Mary K. Meyer

Genealogical Librarian,
Maryland Historical Society

CLEARFIELD COMPANY

Originally Published
Bethesda, Maryland
County Court Note-Book, 1921-1931
Ancestral Proofs and Probabilities, 1935-1936

Reprinted with
New Introduction and Indexes to Volumes I and X
Genealogical Publishing Co., Inc.
Baltimore, 1972

Library of Congress Cataloging in Publication Data
Main entry under title:

The County court note-book, volumes I-X.

The first work, originally published Oct. 1921-Dec. 1931, is reprinted with new introd. and indexes to volumes I and X. Ancestral proofs and probabilities is a reprint of the 4 numbers published 1935-36 and originally compiled for the County court note-book.

1. U. S.—Genealogy—Periodicals. 2. Maryland—Genealogy—Periodicals. 3. Virginia —Genealogy—Periodicals. I. Ljungstedt, Milnor, 1858-1942, ed. II. Ljungstedt, Milnor, 1858-1942, ed. Ancestral proofs & probabilities. 1972. III. Title: Ancestral proofs and probabilities.

CS42.C62 929'.1'0973 77-173265
ISBN 0-8063-0505-3

Reprinted for
Clearfield Company, Inc. by
Genealogical Publishing Co., Inc.
Baltimore, Maryland
1995

Made in the United States of America

INTRODUCTION

Hannah Milnor (Robinson) Ljungstedt was born in Boston, Massachusetts in 1858 and remained a proper Bostonian with the proper New England regard for genealogy until the end of her life in 1942. In 1896 she married Carl Olaf Alex Ljungstedt after which she did a great deal of moving about.

Mrs. Ljungstedt's many years of residence in Maryland placed her in a position where she could conduct genealogical researches in the original court records of several states with some ease. In 1921 she began publication of The County Court Note-Book in order to make available to the public the mass of material she had collected.

After ten years of publication and many discouragements the Note-Book was discontinued. But the editor still had a great deal of unpublished material in her possession and in 1935 she began a new series, Ancestral Proofs and Probabilities. As this series was actually a continuation of The Note-Book it is included in this publication.

This rare and little known work includes material from numerous states: Maryland, Virginia, West Virginia, Georgia, the Carolinas, Delaware, Kentucky, and Pennsylvania. It contains references to New Englanders found in the court records of other states, Virginia head rights, Maryland's "next-of-kin", and Newcastle County, Delaware's tax list of 1776, to name only a few of the subjects covered. A more complete list of subjects can be found in Volume IX, page 30.

There was some confusion in the pagination of the first two volumes of The Note-Book as originally published as well as confusion in the pagination of the two indexes for Volume I. The confusion has been eliminated with this printing by renumbering the pages of Volume I and collating the indexes accordingly and by renumbering the pages of Volume II to correspond with its index. An index to Volume X which was not a part of the original publication but published and sold separately after the series had been discontinued has also been included in this printing.

No attempt has been made to list the abbreviations used by Mrs. Ljungstedt in her work as they are not uniform throughout. The majority can be easily recognized although others may take some thought.

The reader is cautioned to check every variation of the spelling of a surname in which he is interested. Many of the records in this work were created at a very early day when few people could read or write and county clerks took great delight in conjuring up fanciful spellings for ordinary names.

Mrs. Ljungstedt made every effort to reference all material which she published. She belonged to the early school of scientific genealogy and was a contributing editor of The American Genealogist under the editorship of Donald Lines Jacobus. She was also contributing editor to the Genealogical Society of Pennsylvania Publications as well as honorary member of that Society.

The constant genealogist will find the editorials a source of amusement as well as of pain as the Editor is confronted with much the same problems as exist in the genealogical field today. The careful genealogist will gain much by reading each volume rather than merely scanning the indexes for his own family name. In so doing, he will find notices of genealogical works published in the 1920's of which he may be unaware, articles not included in the name index, and tips on the location of little known source material which in many instances are as timely today as they were fifty years ago.

(Mrs.) Mary K. Meyer
Genealogical Librarian
Maryland Historical Society

GUIDE TO THE INDEX

In order to obtain the full use of this work, the reader should note that there is a separate index for each volume of The County Court Note-Book.

There is no index for the supplemental Ancestral Proofs and Probabilities; the entries are for the most part arranged alphabetically.

The page number underscored or accompanied by an asterisk indicates that the name will be found more than once on the page.

The reader should consider every possible spelling of the name in which he is interested. Many of the records in this work were created at a very early day when many people could not read, write or spell and county clerks did little better than the average person.

The indexes for Volumes II and III are printed together following Volume III.

The

County Court Note-Book

A Little Bulletin of History and Genealogy.

Vol. 1. Bethesda, Montgomery Co., Md., October, 1921 .No. 1.

The WEBBS

Although WEBB is not considered a common name, there are an amazing number of them in the early records. They are in CONNECTICUT, DELAWARE, PENNSYLVANIA, the Eastern Shore of MARYLAND and VIRGINIA; the JAMES RIVER, especially about ISLE of WIGHT and NORFOLK; and farther South. Many were Quakers.

Abner Webb m. Prudence Baker, 1780. Conn. Mar.

Ann Webb of Bristol, Eng., binds herself to Simon Stephens for four years, to pay her passage. Sam Webb a wit. 10 Oct. 1679, Dor. Co. Md., v. 4, p.

Ann Webb m. John Wright 1798, Caroline Co. [Wright Ancestry.]

Anne Webb, will [ab. 1800] I. W., Va., xvi-185.

Antho. Webb, under John Sharp. L. O. 1664.

Armiger Webb, Norf. Va., Tax Lists, 1787 et seq.

Augustus Webb, Dor. Co., Md., Transquakin hd., Census 1776.

Benj. Webb son of Jonas and Ann, Dela., 1748, [Sussex, Wills.]

Catharine Webb and Chas S. Boush, Norf. Va., M. L. B., 17 Oct. 1822.

Chas. Webb, under James Akin, L. O. v-434, 1665.

Chas. Webb, under Wm. Boren [?], Stafford Co., Va. L. O. v-526, 1666.

Charles Webb, bond of £100 to Mary, wid. of Geo. Smith, in connection with the div. of the estate of Dorman Laughland. Charles Webb having m. Sarah, dau. of Laughland, and Mary Smith being the other dau. N-n Co., Va., xix-322. 13 Feby. 1715-16.

Charles Webb's hrs. were Charity Griffeth, Mary, Grace and Wm. Webb. Charity Webb, admx. N-n Co., xxxviii-216 12 July 1737.

Charles Webb, buys 300 acres. I. W. ixD, 1742.

Christian Webb under Stevens, Rappahannock River. L. O. vol. v. 1662.

Daniel Webb's cattle-mark. N-n Co. Va., 12 May 1731.

Ebenezer Webb, 1772, Windham, Conn. [Windham Hist'y. p.57.]

Edgar Webb, Shipwright, m. Elizabeth.. iii-344 Talbot, Co. Md.*

Edmond Webb, under Scarborough. Acco. Co., Va., i-81, 17 Nov. 1664.

Edmund Webb was in Talbot Co., Md., 1659, 1682, 1684.

Edmund Webb, will. Dau. Elizabeth Camp [?], land called Bowlton; dau. Mary Webb, under 16; sons Edmond and William. William Webb of Talbott, oath as extr. Annap. wills 11 Nov. 1685, Prob. ab 1 Jany. 1685.

Edward Webb, Hening, i-86, 23 May 1609.

Edward Webb, L. O. v-102, 1662.

Edward Webb, of Hog Island, par. Lowne's Creek Surry, Va., i-257, 1665.

Edward Web, from Edmond Palmer and wf. Alce, tract on Deep Run. I. W. iii-287 ab., Sept 1673.

Edward Webb, [wf Hannah] conveys right to land to John Williams. Ackn by Wm. Webb and wf. I. W. iii-352. 6 Apr. 1677.

Edward Webb. Appears in a list of that part of the est. of John Burnell, bel. to Alice Shapley in Barbadoes. I. W. 689.

Edward Webb, cattle-marks, N-n Co., Va., 1701.

Edward Webb appears in records under Wm. Webb, whose father-in-law was John Adolph, 1701 N-n Co. Va.

Edward Webb lived on 100 a. bel. to John Robins, near Cherrystones Crk. N-n xix-31. 1707.

Edward Webb in Talbott Co., Md., near

*Note: For some of these Talbott Co., notes the Editor owes acknowledgement to Dr. Thos. Edw'd Sears of Baltimore.

Mile End....Talbott Co., R. R. Md. 1723.

Elisha and Ann Webb conveyance to Geo. Smith. Wor. Co., Md., B-242. 1747.

Elizabeth x Webb a wit. to Robert Dunster's will. I. W. i-74. 17 May 1656. [Date of record.]

Elizabeth Webb, 100 a. Nansemond Co., Va. In the Upper Psh. in the woods, behind Tucker's Neck, beginning in sight of the church path. L. O. vii-7 5 Sept. 1679.

Elizabeth Webb, 75 a. Nansemond Co. L. O. viii-665. 1705.

Ezra Webb, m. Hannah Nott., 1763. Conn. Mar.

Foster Webb of New Kent and John Webb, (wf Judith) of Hanover Co. See deed from Isaac Davis. Alb. Va., 1769.

Francis Webb came to New Kent with Thos. Merriditih under Merriditih's ctf. L.O. v-61. 1656.

Francis Webb, Farnham Psh., Rappanhannock Co., 100 a., Pocossin Crk. Rap. i-108. 6 Aug. 1667.

Francis Webb, from Hudson and wf. Dorothy, 100 a., Rap. vol. 1668-1672. p.108.

Frances Webb was dau of Thomas, a svt. Acco. 1670. See Thos.

Francis Webb, planter, Rappa., Co., to Richard Holl [?] 100 a., Rappa. 1-454. 5 July 1671.

George Webb, Jr., and Hannah Fleming. Gchland, Va., M. L. B. 1756.

George Webb, Wattson's Lott, 1726. Q. A. Co., R. R. 1760, p.-83.

George Webb, Webb's Plains. Queen A. Co., Md., R. R. 1760.

George Webb and Miss Peggy Cheshire, Norf., Va., Co. M. L. B. 7 Dec. 1769.

George Webb and Judith Fleming. Gchland, Va., M. L. B. 1785.

George Webb, m. Catherine Veale. Norf. Mar. Ret. 25 June 1788.

George Webb, seaman, Norfolk Co., Va Tax Lists, 1792 et seq.

George Y. Webb, m. Miss Eliza Ann H Bell, Norf., Va., Mar. Ret. 22 Apr. 1823

Giles Webb, Lower Norf. Co., Va., ab 1648 vol. B.

Giles Webb, Rappanhannock Co. Va., 1654 vol. 1656-64, 19-20.

Mr. Giles Webb, Rappa., Co., ab 1669 Rappa. Co., vol. 1668-1672.

Giles Webb's cattlemark, Rappa., Co. Va., 1661. Vol. 1656-1664.

Grace Webb, m. John Woodward, 6 Aug 1741. Talbott Co., Md.

Grace Webb, m. (2) George Rule. See Talbott mar.

Grace Webb, Tred Avon Mtg. Md., iii-16-19 -21-23.

Hannah Webb certifies to the age of a boy. Surry, Va., ii-37 3 Oct. 1673.

Hannah the dau. of John Webb, cattlemarks. N-n Co. Va., 1685. vol. iv.

Hannah Webb, wid. of John Webb, gets letters of admn., N-n Co. Va., xii-437. 29 May 1689.

Hannah Webb chooses Phillip Jacob for gdn. N-n Co 12 Sept. 1721.

Hannah Webb, orphan [of John Webb] inv. of her est. Includes pistols, holsters and a carbine. Dixon x Knight gdn. N-n Co., xxvi-157 10 Sept 1728.

Hannah Webb, Jonas Webb receipts to Knight for whole est., of sister Hannah dec'd. N-n Co. xxvi-228. 14 Apr. 1730. [See Jonas Webb, d. 1748. See Sussex Co., Dela., Wills.]

Henry Webb, of Boston, N. E. 1660. [See Maryland Wills.]

Henry Webb, depn. Age 22. N-n Co. xii-473, 29 Nov. 1689.

Henry Webb, N-n Co. [wf Esther] to John Marshall. 100 a. bet. Occahanock and Nuswattox Crk. N-n Co. Va. xii-403. 1705.

Isaac Webb, 1680-81. Sussex Co. Dela. [Some Record of. p.21.]

Jacob Webb from William Webb, Wor. Co. Md. B-98, 1747.

Mr. James Webb's est. I. W., Va., ii-140. 1 Mch. 1675-6.

James Webb, left a wid. Elizabeth, dau. of Col. Thos. Godwyn. I. W. ii-39. 15 Mch. 1675-6.

James Webb, wit. to deed from Barnabe Mackinnie and wf to Richard Exum. I. W. iv-340. 9 Dec. 1701.

James Webb, legacy from Samuel Bridger. I. W., Va., ii-564. 1704. Capt. James Webb, power to him from Samuel Furment. I. W., v-100. 17 Jany. 1708.

James Webb, will, 250 a., to Wm. Wilkinson and wf., with reversion to Giles Webb, Richard Webb. Remainder est. to Wilkinson and wf and makes them extrs. I. W., vi-22. 19 Jany. 1719-28 Mch. 1720.

James Webb, m. Penelope Butt. Solomon Butt sec. Norf. Co. Va., 19 Apr. 1744. M. L. B.

Mr. James Webb, Norf. Co. Tax List 1754.

James Webb, Norf., Co. 50 a., Swamp land on the "Green sea." adj. Solomon Butt. L. O. xxxi-511. 10 July 1755.

James Webb (and Maj. Willis Wilson) 909 a. swamp land. L. O. xxxiv-169. 5 Feby. 1757.

James Webb and Rasha Butt, Norf., Co., Va., 1779 a. swamp land. L. O. xxxiv-807, 1761.

James Webb and Mrs. Cephia [Sophia?]

Langley, Norf. Co. Va., M. L. B. 24 Dec. 1767.

James Webb from Jacob Sikes, land and pltn. where he now lives. [Original deed.] Norf., Co., Va. 23 Jany. 1767.

James Webb, Oath of fidelity etc. Talbott Co. Md., 1778.

James Webb, Jr., and Mrs. Sarah Shields Norf., Co., Va. M. L. B. 9 Nov. 1779.

James Webb, Fluvanna Co., Va., from Anthony Haden, same, 200 a., Fluvanna Co., Va. i-323. 4 Apr. 1781.

James Webb, 150 a., adj., other lands of Webb's, Norf., Co. Va. L. O.——54. 21 June 1784.

James Webb, Sr., and James Webb, Jr., Norf., Co. Tax List, 1784.

James Webb, Norf., Co., 150 a., adj., pat'd land and other Webb land. L. O. x-28[illegible] 23 Nov. 1787.

James Webb, went to Fairfield Co., from Fluvanna Co. Va., [bef. 1800.] Fluv., Va., iii-510.

Jane Webb, svt., entered under Col. Edm. Scarburgh. N-n Co., Va., v-9. 29 May 1654.

Jane Webb, under John Evans. N-n Co. Va., viii-92, 28 Feby 1660.

Jane Webb petitions for freedom of her child being born in lawful wedlock. N-n Co., xxiv-178-185. 11 Sept. 1722.

Jane Webb, cattle-mark, N-n vi (. . .) N-n, Va., 27 Jany. 1725.

Jeptha Webb from Bartho'w Slattery, Wor. Co., Md. M-233, 1786.

John Webbe, carpenter, Dep'n., 23 yrs., of age, was bldg., house for Capt. Thorowgood. Lower Norf., Co. A-7, 4 Mch. 1638.

John Webb's house to be used for Court and prison. N-n Co., Va., viii-190. 28 Sept. 1655.

(To be Continued.)

Note: The Editor desiresto apologize for the occasional lack of exact references. This list was copied from card indces whch were made some time ago for general use in connection with note-books and not for publicaiton.

Note: For those not familiar with the abreviations used the following explanation is given: L. O., Virginia State Land Office. N-n Co., Northampton Co. I. W., Isle of Wight Co. Rappa., Rappahannock Co. Acco., Accomack Co. M. L. B. Marriage license bonds. Mar. Ret. Marriage returns by ministers.

The following marriages are from the Court records of FREDERICK COUNTY, MARYLAND. (Note: Frederick County was formed in 1748 from the northern and western part of Prince George's:

Miranda Fischer to John Shipman, 1822.

Miranda Frizzle to Thos. Fossett, 1828.

Maranda Frushour (?) to John Mathias, 1840.

Miranda Gillis to Nimrod Conaway, 1829.

Marinda Jones to Jas. W. Thomas, 1850.

Miranda Liesher to Geo. T. Syes, 1847.

Miranda Henry to John A. Collins, 1823.

Maronda Burrier to James Fread, 1824.

Miranda Browning to Jesse Penn, 1836.

Maranda Carlisle to Jacob Larue, 1831.

Mirando O. Devilbiss to Geo. W. Devilbiss, 1842.

Miranda Richards to Lloyd Hyatt, 1827.

Miranda Steele to Arthur Etzler, 1834.

Miranda Waters to Eli Hyatt, 1818.

Mary Miranda Weller to Alfred A. Troxell, 1851.

Miranda Nelson to Joshua Selman, 1822.

Meranda Owings to John Evans, 1800.

Miranda Perry to Burgess Nelson, 1820.

Miranda Phillips to Darius Eader, 1823.

Miranda Poole to Samuel Shipley, 1831.

Miranda Poole to Moses Denman, 1844.

Miranda Peters to Wm. S. Sowders, 1846.

Miranda Pool to Amos Poole, 1847.

There was a small volume published in 1906, printed for the Representative Committee of the Yearly Meeting of the Society of Friends held in Philadelphia, which is little known outside of Eastern Pennsylvania searchers. Its title is "A List of the Records of the Meetings Constituting the Yearly Meeting of the Society of Friends," held as stated above. It gives in a brief form what might be called the genealogy of these meetiings, when they were established and when laid down, and also gives a list of the existing records. It is feared that the volume cannot now be had, but it can be seen in the library of the Historical Society at Philadelphia, or in the libraries of the principal Quaker meetings. It should be added that these records, owing no doubt to a somewhat recent endeavor to collect the earlier volumes at some central depository, are not always where the book places them. It is advisable to write to the Clerk of the local Meeting for direct information, and laso for permission to examine the records. This is required, even though the records themselves may be in Philadelphia.

The County Court Note-Book

An every-other-monthly devoted to abstracts from the County Court and other records, prior to 1800, and with a department of notes and queries.*

MILNOR LJUNGSTEDT, Editor and Publisher. Bethesda, R. 1, Md.

Published every other month. Subscription, one dollar a year, in advance.

VOL. 1. October, 1921. No. 1.

FOREWORD

The Editor and Publisher of this Bulletin proposes to tell you why the Bulletin is being brought out, and something about the material it will publish.

The Editor has been for some years exploring, with a certain amount of methodical patience, the records of the County Courts of a large section of those States immediately north and south of the Mason and Dixon line, as well as parts of New Jersey, and earlier counties of Kentucky and West Virginia.

In this work the Editor has collected a large amount of data which is of no particular use to her or her friends and clients, but which, as touching certain families, is rather comprehensive. It is proposed to publish this material, as much at one time as can conveniently be included in one copy of this Bulletin. The families include such farspread names as WILSON and WILLIAMS; THOMPSON, CUNNINGHAM, ROGERS and HUGHES; PANCOASTS, MOHLERS and MUSGRAVES; and unusual names, of which MOURNING is a good example.

Every item published will have an exact reference. Nearly all the Court notes are from the original manuscript volumes of the Clerk's Offices. Some few have been gathered from published material.

A second section of the Bulletin will be devoted to "NOTES and QUERIES." Part of the object of this Bulletin is to advertise...in this section to advertise for long-lost "missing links." Any subscriber may send in any inquiry upon genealogical or historical subjects. Such an inquiry will be published in the next following issue, if received in time, and the answer if desired, sent to the inquirer direct. The Editor retains the right to print the answer. All answers must give some exact reference and some date, even if only approximate. The statement unaccompanied by any reference, that JOHN SMITH married MARY JONES and had a son PETER, is not desired. Some clue to the decade, at least, can usually be found.

The Editor desires very much to make this department of use to the many searchers who are not within reach of the more important quarterly and yearly publications.

The Editor wishes to state explicitly, that inquiries and answers will appear, even if other material has to be crowded out.

A third section will give historical notes, odds and ends of interest, drawn from original sources.

A section will be devoted to "BOOK NOTES." The Editor will be glad to receive notices of recent or proposed genealogical or historical books, especially local histories. One of the main aims of the Bulletin is to advertise just such material.

A fifth and most important section... the Editor desires to take you into editorial confidence.... will be the advertising proper. The advertising, with the subscriptions, must pay the cost of publishing and make the Bulletin not only possible, but of the greatest use. Co-operation is so sadly lacking among experts of every kind, that the Editor would like to help along a bit. For this reason the cards of professional genealogists will be published at the lowest possible rate. Whatever this rate will be fixed at, it is proposed to make it much below the usual commercial rates ....to subscribers, be it understood.

The Editor hopes in a later issue to include a list to be called "Where to Stay... and How to Get There." The Editor will give the addresses of a few hotels and boarding houses which she has sampled and knows are satisfactory...routes to out-of-the-way court-houses will also be given.

The Editor, in short, desires you to believe that this Bulletin is intended to be friendly and helpful...and that she is quite willing to tell all she knows...with reservations!

If sufficient subscriptions are received, the COUNTY COURT NOTE-BOOK will be continued. The price will be one dollar a year. For "NOTES and QUERIES," a small tax for postage and paper will be made, probably about ten cents. The rate for genealogists' cards will be fixed later.

The Editor feels that she cannot close this explanatory preface, without expressing her thanks to the many Clerks of Courts and their Deputies who have receiv-

*Abstracts of wills are made to 1830.

ed her with courtesy, helped her in her work, and asked her to come again!

The following toast was given at a celebration at Savannah, Georgia, 22 Dec. 1826, by a "numerous party" of natives of New England..."Sons of Pilgrims."

"GEORGIA: Here we have pitched our tents, here we have built our altars, here we have had born to us sons and daughters, —it is a goodly land to live in. We will cherish and support its laws." From the Niles Register, v. xxxi, p. 353.

"SAM'L CALDWEL may remember the end of the 19th line of Carrollsburg, where he was almost knocked down by an Axe which flew off its handle." Deposition, Frederick, Md. Court records. W. R. 15, 1797.

"JNO. SANEISHES (?) to Polly Dust in mistake." From Jefferson Co. Va., Mar. Ret'ns. 1807.

Will of J...., R....."N. B. If any one of them [his sons] shall Commit a Crime worthy of Forty Shillings, from the age of fifteen to twenty-one years, he shall not have any part of what I leave. This every Master shall note down to them in or under his Charge four times a year at least..." Prince William Co., Va., 1783.

SEARCHERS who dislike to read through old Orphans' Court and other Minutes, which so often have no indices, will be interested to learn that the Editor on a recent visit to the Court-House of Montgomery County, Md., discovered in the "Tower Room," the missing index of the first volume of Orphans' Court records of that county.

It is to be regretted that the Committee which controls the very attractive and hisorically valuable D. A. R. monthly, does not care to apportion more space to the Genealogical Department, of which Mrs. Mamsburgh is the able Editor. Many magazines publish historical material.....a few ought to give liberal space to Notes and Queries.

PRINCE WILLIAM BONDS

The following list of EXECUTORS' BONDS (including a few administrators' bonds) is taken from an early book in PRINCE WILLIAM COUNTY, Virginia, which has but a partial index. The first name is that of the decedent; the executor or executors come next, followed by the securities.

Thomas Davis; Judith Davis, extx; Edward Emms, Joseph Thurman, sec. 27 Aug. 1753.

Pembroke Oden; Mary Oden, admx., Wm. Rookard, Thomas Boggess, esc. 22 Oct. 1753.

William Farrow; Ann Farrow, John Graham, Gent., Alex. Frarow, extrs.; Geo. Johnston, Gent., Thomas Machen, sec. 25 Mch. 1754.

James Anderson; Samuel X. Organ extr., Wm. Colclough, Aaron Fletcher, sec. 25 Mch. 1754.

John Smith; John Smith, extr.; John Wright, Vincent Garner, sec. 22 Apr. 1754.

Wm. Baylis; John and Wm. Baylis, extrs.; Anthony Seale, John Linton, Jr., Hugh West, Jr., sec. 27, May 1754.

Thomas Colvert; Sarah Colvert, admx.; John Colvert, Thomas Reeves, sec. 25, June 1754.

Wm. Hogan; Margaret Hogan, extx.; Wm. Hogan, James Hogan, sec. 23, Sept 1754. [The next bond has been torn out. The decedent was Bland.]

Lewis Reno; Thos. and Lewis Reno, extrs. Nath'l Overall, Thomas Machen, sec. 27, Jany. 1755.

Denis Conyers; Sam'l and John Conyers, extrs.; Thos. Mitchell, Henry Boatman, sec. 24, Mch. 1755.

Thomas Stribling; Francis and Tallioferro Stribling, extrs.; Henry Peyton, sec. 25, Mch. 1755.

Wm. Davis; Ellen and Isaac Davis, extrs.; Benj. Grayson, Gent., Geo. Britt, sec. 28 Apr. 1755.

Agatha Thornton; Thomas Thornton, extr; Duff Green, sec. 22, Sept. 1755.

James Bland; Mary and Benj. Bland, extrs. Edward Gawtkins, Wm. Carr, sec. 22 Mch. 1756.

James Moss; Mathew x Moss, extr.; Wm. Foster, sec.

Thomas Stone; John Stone, extr.; John Wright, Jeremiah Darnell, 23 Aug. 1756.

John Peake; Lucy and Wm. Peake, extrs.; Edw'd Humston, Rich'd Rixey, Geo. Clavert, sec. 23, Aug. 1756.

Sarah Tacket; Wm. Tacket, extr; Sam'l Jones, Wm. Spillar, sec. 22, Nov. 1756.

Wm. Creel; John Creel, extr; Yelverton Peyton, Isaac Foster, sec. 23, May 1757.

Alex'r Edwards; Mary Edwards, extr; John Dawkins, Wm. Wyatt, sec. 23, May 1757.

John Baylis, Wm. Blackwell, Foushee Tebbs, Wm. Baylis, Gent., give bonds. [Name of decedent not given, and no date. Probably same as next.]

Richard Blackburn, Gent.; John Baylis, extr; Wm. Eustace, Wm. Grant, Gent, sec. 27, July 1757.

Mary Sinclair; John Sinclair, Francis Tennil, extrs.; Anthony x Lathan, Edward x Wilburn, [Milburn?] sec. 24 Oct. 1757.

Benj. Bullitt, Jr., Thoms Bullitt, Cuthbert Bullitt, extrs; Thomas Harrison, Cuthbert Harrison, John McMillion, sec. 28, Nov. 1757.

(To be continued.)

NOTES AND QUERIES

KEITH-CORDER: Parentage etc., of SMITH KEITH, born 25 April, 1817 in Fauquier Co. Va., married 20 Dec. 1838, presumably at "Flint Hill", Rappahannock Co. Va., Miss MARGARET CORDER; died 2 September 1876, at Leavenworth, Kansas. Address F. B. C. care COUNTY COURT NOTE-BOOK.

BOWDOIN: Some time before 1700, JOHN BOWDOIN, a son of PIERRE BOWDOIN, then of Boston, came to the Eastern Shore of Virginia, buying land and settling in Northampton County. His wife was SUSANNA. The maiden name and parentage of SUSANNA is greatly desired. Please address the Editor.

MUSGROVE-[SIMPSON?] William Musgrove of FAIRFAX and LOUDOUN counties, Virginia, died about 1778, Revolutionary service, is supposed to to have married a daughter of Gilbert Simpson. Definite information wanted. V.M.H. COUNTY COURT NOTE-BOOK.

BURFORD: DANIEL BURFORD of Amherst County, Va., who died before 1790 had a wife MARY. He seems to have married but once. The maiden name of MARY BURFORD, is greatly desired with exact references. The name of DANIEL BURFORD'S mother is also desired. The inquirer will gladly reciprocate. Address P. S. C. care COUNTY COURT NOTE-BOOK.

FLOYD-DAVIS. Wanted: the record of the marriage of WILLIAM FLOYD of Amherst Co. Va., and ABADIAH DAVIS This marriage took place some time prior to 1750. Date given as 1747, but no authority. Please address P. S. C. as above.

FLOYD of BUCKINGHAM Co. Va. Any information touching him prior to 1800, is greatly desired. BUCKINGHAM Court-house was destroyed by fire in 1868, and practically all records burned. The information asked for may be in private hands. Address P. S. C. as above.

WANTED: Any SAUL or SOLL ROBINSON born circa 1730 or 1735, New England New York, New Jersey, Delaware or Pennsylvania. Will gladly reciprocate in kind. Address the Editor.

GIBSON: About 1795, ANDREW GIBSON, then residing in WINCHESTER, FREDERICK, Co. Va., a merchant or trader of some means, went farther south (tradition says to GEORGIA) with a large quantity of goods and two negro servants. Nothing more was ever heard of him. Tradition says he was murdered. Andrew Gibson was the brother of John Gibson, of Rockbridge Co., a man of education and considerable property and his (Andrew's) sons were citizens of prominence. Definite information, however slight, is greatly desired as to the death of the father. A reasonable amount will be paid for any clue. Address S. G. G. Care COUNTY COURT NOTE-BOOK.

DAVENPORT: In 1778, ABRAHAM DAVENPORT, second of his name, married in Montgomery Co. Maryland, FRANCES WILLIAMS, an orphan. Wanted: the names of her parents. Address the editor.

PANCOAST-MOHLER. In 1815 WILLIAM (HARDING) PANCOAST married ~~JANE~~ (BARNET) MOHLER, possibly in or near Sheperdstown, West Virginia. The record of this marrige is greatly desired, also the parentage of WILLIAM (HARDING) PANCOAST, who appears to have been of LOUDOUN Co. Va. Address the Editor.

VIRGINIA RECORDS

Persons intending to visit the COUNTY COURTS of VIRGINIA in order to examine the records, are advised to apply first to the State Librarian, Dr. H. S. McIlwaine, at Richmond, for information as to what records are in existence and where they are to be found.

The records of HENRICO COUNTY, for example, are at the State Library, in the Archives Department. They are incomplete, and some of them have been very seriously damaged by dampness, worms, etc. The Library is having the most dilapiated volumes repaired by experts.

The Library has also copies of the early records of a number of counties. A list of these will be given in a later issue.

Further than this, the Library has lists of the records still to be found in the counties, and the condition of the volumes. These lists are being made and turned in from time to time by an unofficial but interested searcher, who is glad to return in this way some of the courtesy extended to her by the Library itself.

BOOK NOTES

THE PLIGRIM SPIRIT. "A new and notable piece of American dramatic literature has come out of the celebration of the tercentenary of the landing of the Pilgrims. It is by George Pierce Baker, Professor of Dramatic Literature at Harvard University; it is called the 'Pilgrim Spirit,' and it was performed a dozen times during July and August by the people of Plymouth, Massachusetts, before audiences which aggregated about one hundred thousand persons.

"It has been called a 'pageant'.... It is no more specifically a Pageant than any of Shaksespeare's Chronicle histories. It is an historical drama, built about an idea, with a beginning, a middle, and an end.... a deeply moving play of human conflict and sacrifice, tied as closely to the America of to-day and to-morrow as to the America of three hundred years ago........"

Mr. Hagedorn's fine review of the play is too long to give here....but the final paragraph must be quoted.

"There is a clash of cymbals. Up the steep slope out of the sea, literally 'over the top' leap, as if in answer, the flags of the Allies and are borne forward.

"Once more the voice of the Rock is heard [a voice has at intervals been proceeding from the close vicinity of the canopied stone]

"THE PATH OF THE MAYFLOWER MUST FOREVER BE KEPT FREE."

If there could be a more magnificently fine ending than this, I know not what it could be.

"Professor Baker's 'Pilgrim Spirit' (I again quote Mr. Hadgedorn) has the sincerity, the simplicity, the beauty, and the imaginative quality which we associate with lasting literature."

The extracts above are from the OUTLOOK. The "Pilgrim Spirit" is earnestly commended to those who have not read it.....or who had not the good fortune to see it. If there be a descendant, in South Carolina or California, in Minnesota or Texas, of that wonderful band, if he can read this drama without a thrill of glorious pride in race and ancestry....**can there be such?**

The Editor.

Miss MILDRED MAUPIN HOLLADAY, of Portsmouth, Vinrginia, is gathering material for a small volume about the HOLLADAYS, GODWINS, and allied families.

Miss Holladay is a descendant of Col. THOMAS GODWIN, of ISLE of WIGHT and NANSEMOND counties, and of Col. ANTHONY HOLLADAY of ISLE of WIGHT County. As the greater part of the early GODWIN records of NANSEMOND were destroyed by the Court-House fire of 1866, Miss Holladay would be glad to receive any data touching the family, prior to that time. Fortunately, about 1856, Miss Holladay's father had copies made of the GODWIN wills in the direct line. Miss Holladay has recently permitted the Clerk of the Nansemond Court to copy these copies, so that by that much the lacking records of the Clerk's Office are supplied.

It is interesting to note that Mr. Holladay leaves on record the statement that some of the records were missing in 1856 having been destroyed by a previous fire.

It will be a matter of regret to many to learn that the publication of the ROBINSON GENEALOGY, for which Mr. Chas. E. ROBINSON of Newport, R. I., has been gathering material for many years, has been deferred for the present, by the decision of the ROBINSON GENEALOGICAL SOCIETY, at its meeting in Plymouth, Mass., in August last. Mr. ROBINSON is now the President emeritus. The President is N. Winthrop Robinson, of Dorchester, and the Secretary is Miss Emma J. C. Robinson, of Gloucester.

Mrs. PAULINE STEWART CROSLEY is gathering material, with the assistance of Mrs. MILNOR LJUNGSTEDT, for a forthcoming book about the FLOYDS and Stewarts of VIRGINIA. Mrs. Crosley is a Georgian by birth, but a Virginian by descent. Her life as the wife of an officer of the United States Navy, Capt. Walter Selwyn Crosley, whose details have taken him to all parts of the globe, to many of which she has accompanied him, has made her cosmopolitan in taste and experience, and has given her a view-point which does not admit of sectionalism.

Travel and cosmopolitan life have not, however, destroyed Mrs. Crosley's affection for the State in which she was born, nor for the State in which she grew up, attending school at one of the best of the noted schools of Virginia. So that it is with a real desire to gather up and give out, as has never been done before, the records of the past as they touch all Virginians of the name FLOYD or STEWART (and with these the allied families of DAVIS, DANIELS and CUNNINGHAM) that she undertakes this work.

Nor will this collection be limited to Virginia. It will include these families in Maryland, in Delaware, in the older parts of Kentucky and West Virgina, and in the southern and eastern counties of Pennsylvania....those counties which gave so many staunch Presbyterian families to the Valley of Virginia, and to the regions of the southwest.

The publication....which will possibly be in two volumes, will not undertake to construct any "family tree" or "trees", but will give in catalogue form all the wills, deeds and marriages, as well as other material gleaned from the Order Books of the Courts, of the families named above. It will be necessary, in order to keep the book within a reasonable expense, to give these wills and deeds in a brief abstract, but full references will accompany each item, so that copies may be had on application to the Clerks of the Courts concerned. As a matter of fact, the abstracts will usually prove to be all that is required.

It is hoped that this work will be ready for the public in about a year; those who have searched early civil and ecclia tic records will appreciate the unavoidable delays.

The FLOYDS and STEWARTS of VIRGINIA will not be Mrs. Crosley's first entrance into the light of publication, as she is the author of "INTIMATE LETTERS FROM PETROGRAD," a forcible, readable vivid, yet restrained account of the first stages of the Russian revolution as she and her husband witnessed it while in Petrograd, where Capt. Crosley was stationed as Naval Attache to the American Embassy, and where she accompanied him. The full description of their escape from Petrograd, and from Finland, is particularly interesting, as the newspaper accounts at the time could not be satisfactory, owing to the pecular political conditions.

This book of Mrs. Crosley's has been listed by a committee of Russians charged with the selection of the most distinctive literature of that extraordinary period, as among the best. It has the warm endorsement of Baron Rosen, formerly Russian Ambassador to the United States, and has been the text for much discussion among those students of Russian conditions who are trying to understand "What's What" in that unhappy country, especially among those who have a concern, as the Friends say, to be of help.

The Editor.

From the Press of the EASTERN SHORE HERALD, Eastville, Virginia.

The
County Court Note-Book

A Little Bulletin of History and Genealogy.

Vol. I. **December, 1921.** **No. 2.**

THE NAME MOURNING

The Editor has a friend whose great-grandmother's baptismal name was MOURNING. The Editor asked an Attorney of the county where the record was found, what could be the origin of so unusual a name. The answer was that it was given as a matter of sentiment to commemorate the early death of the child's mother. He recollected but one other use of the same name, and then it was borne by an old negro woman of the same county, probably an ex-slave. The Editor was interested and began to collect notes; they are given below. It will be seen that there is a family of MOURNINGS who appeared very early, indeed, in the records of tidewater Virginia. They appear to have been Irish, and the name, from contemporary evidence, would seem to have been pronounced MOORNING. The spelling MORING (unquestionably of the same name) appears occasionally. There was also an early family of MOURNINGS in Pennsylvania.

MOURNING: Slave of Richard Cock. Surry Co., Va. 1678. x-195.

MOURNING BURGH: sister of Elizabeth and dau. of Wm. Burgh. (Elizabeth m. Thos. Jordan, 1679.) Nanse., Va., Quaker Records.

MOURNING BRAY was the relict of Thomas Pettus and wf of James Bray, York Co., Va., 26 Oct. 1693.*

SARAH MORNING: wit. to mar. Nanse., Va., Quaker Records. 16-2-1704.

Mrs. MOURING, wf. of Capt. James Bray, dec'd. 1710, Bruton Psh. Records, Va.

MOURNING EXUM: dau. of Jeremiah. I. W. Co., Va., 3 Sept. 1712. vi-21.

MOURNING ENGLAND: b. 1 Apr. 1718. St. Peter's Psh. New Kent Co., Va.

MOURNING SCOTT, wit. Nanse., Va., Quaker Records, p. 178. 1723. [She was an heir of Richard Exum.]

ANN MOURNING COLEMAN; dau. of Thos. Christian. See his will, 1736. (Va.)

MOURNING WILLIAMSON: wf. of Francis. I. W. Co., Va., 1736. viii-170.

MOURNING ELEY: dau. Robert Eley. I. W. Co., Va., 1738. viii-234.

ELIZABETH MOURNING: dau. Dennis and Mary Mourning. b. 1740. Bruton Psh. Va., Records.

MOURNING x GRAY. I. W. Co., Va., 1740. viii-.

MOURNING WILLIAMSON: gr. dau. of Francis Williamson. 1743. I. W. Co. Va., viii-476.

JOHN MORING: son of Dennis and Mary Mroing. 1748. Bruton Psh, Va., Records.

MORNING: negro girl. b. 1749. Nanse., Va., Quaker Records.

MORNING HARDY: wit. to nun-cup. will of Elizabeth Robertson. 1751. Surry Co., Va., iii-737.

MARY MORNING: dau. of Henry Parish. See his will. 1753. (Va.)

MORNING BASDEL: dau. of Hannah Basdel. Cumb., Co., Va., 1753.

LEONARD JAMES MOURNING WALLER: see will of John Waller. 1753-4. Spots. Co., Va. B-109.**

MOURNING FLEMING: wf of Daniel Fleming. See his will. Louisa Co., Va. 23 Mch 1754.
[MOURNING SLISH was their daughter.]

ANN MOURNING x COLEMAN. 1756. Goochland Co., Va.

THOMAS MOURNING served as a soldier from Hanover Co., Va., 1758. S. L. O.

MOURNING HOLDSWORTH: dau. of Thomas Clary. See will. Sussex Co., Va., 26 June 1763. A-305.

MURNING SLISH: mentioned in will of

*From Stanard's Notes, Va. State Library.

**From Mr. Torrence's Spots. Abstracts.

Robert Fleming. Louisa Co., Va., 17 July 1763.

JOHN and MOUNING CONNELLY: have son John and dau. Nelley. Bruton Psh, Va., Records. 1766, 1768.

ELIZABETH MOURNING and Wm. Smith. Penna. Ma. Li. 1 Dec. 1766.

(To be continued.)

THE WEBBS.

(Continued from October number)

John Webb, mariner: 50 a. in Accomacke, on the maine river of that plantation—lines of Capt. Clemont Dilke and Geo. Medcalfe. L. O. i-85. 13 Dec. 1627.

John Webbe was in Lower Norfolk Co., Va., 1638. A-7.

John Webb was in N-n Co., Va., 1638. ix-111.

John Webb in case. Lower Norf. Co., Va., 4 Jany 1640. A-31.

John Webb, was dec'd. Lower Norf., Va., 15 Nov. 1641. A-56.

John Webb, dep'n. Age 35. Lower Norf. Co., Va., 12 Apr. 1641. A-38.

John Webb, dec'd referred to. Lower Norf. Co., Va., 26 May 1642. A-56.

John Webb, dec'd. Cornelius Loyd, admr. Norf. Co., Va., 1646 B-14.

John Webb "lately come from Barbadoes." Compensation asked for sufferings. State Papers, p. 304. 6 June 1650 and 29 June 1650.

John Webb; wit. to will of Lewis White. Dep'n. age ab. 27 yrs. Was present when Mr. Wm. Johnson "made the above will.". N-n Co., Va., v-122, 7 July and 28 Oct. 1756.

John Webb, wit. to sale of negro by Francis Pott. N-n Co., Va., vii-78. 1 Dec. 1657.

John x Webb, depn. N-n Co., viii-63. 28 Feby 1659.

John Webb; legacy under will of John Pennell. Pennell appoints his now svt John Webb overseer over the other svts., etc. N-n Co., Va., ix-82. 18 Dec. 1660.

John Webb, carpenter, James Lindsey, admr. 18 Jany 1660.

John Webb, a tithable. N-n Co., Va. 25 June 1662. viii-138. [He lived in the same tithing district as John Custis and other notables.]

John Webb, wit. to John Cole's assignment. N-n Co., Va. ix-172. 1662.

John Webb was gdn. of John Pannell, son of Mr. John Pannell. John Robins, Gent., and Francis Pettit, pltr, security. N-n Co., Va. ix-166. 20 Jany 1662.

John Webb ackn. rec't of est. of John Pennell in his custody. Signs, further bond. N-n Co., Va. ix-168. 19 Jany 1662.

John Webb, wit. to Dolby's deed. N-n Co., Va. ix-162. 1663.

John Webb, pltr. Bond that he deliver John Panell's property to him at 18, according to the will of John Panwell [sic]. Div'n of est. follows. N-n Co., Va. vii-208. 28 July 1664. His joint bond on the est. on p.166 et seq. "The new Mansion House where the said John Webb dwelleth" mentioned.

John Webb, a tithable. N-n Co., Va. 29 Aug. 1664.

John Webb, under John Dolby. (Dolby's patent, 1000 a.) L. O. v-190. 10 Sept 1664.

John Webb, under Thos, Tover, Northumberland Co., Va., (N-n Co.?) L. O. v-299. 1664.

John Webb, ctf for 450 a. N-n Co., Va. viii-200. 28 Oct. 1664.

John Webb, in county acc't N-n Co., Va., x-2 28 Feby 1664.

John Webb, a tithe. N-n Co., Va. x-14. 1665.

John Webb of N-n Co., Va., pltr. to Rich'd. Nottingham, a cow and calf. N-n Co. ix-217. 10 May 1665.

John Webb, an appr'r. N-n Co., Va., x-13. 28 Aug. 1665.

John Webb's svt. N-n Co., Va., x-18. 28 Dec. 1665.

John Webb and wf. Hannah x Webb, convey negro woman, Ann Rodriggues, to Will Kendall. N-n Co., Va., vii-8. 29 Dec. 1665.

John Webb's cattle-marks. N-n Co., Va., iv-227. 1665.

John Webb to appraise an est. N-n Co., Va., x-5. 27 June 1665.

Mr. John Webb, grand juror. N-n Co., Va., x-25. 10 Apr. 1666.

John Webb, pltr. to John Robins. 200 a. N-n Co., Va. vii-9. 8 Jany 1666.

John Webb, Samuel England, The Arundell, tithes. N-n Co., Va., x-41. 9 Sept 1667.

John Webb, 200 a. from Wm. Williamson. Wit. Robert Hill and Abraham x Johnson. Rappa. Co., Va., 22 Feby 1667. (Vol. has no number.)

John Webb, depn. Age ab. 40. Case of Capt. Custis' svt. N-n Co., Va., 1 Dec. 1668 ix-51.

Mr. John Webb a juror. N-n Co., Va., x-47. 30 Mch 1668, also 1 Dec. 1668.

John Webb, tithable. Tho: Arundell with him. N-n Co., Va., 1668. A juror, 1668.

John Webb, 6 tithes. N-n Co., Va., x-112. Aug. 1671. a juror, 1672.

John Webb, juror, N-n Co., Va., 1673. x-217.

John Webb, lower part Co., of N-n. pltr. to Tnos. Shepheard, 100 a. on a branch issuing out of main Cherristones Crk., Consideration, 3500 lbs. Part of purchase in 1666 fr. Mr. John Robins. Wf. Hannar rel. dower. N-n Co., Va., xi-51. 27 Sept. 1673.

John Wibb [sic] with Davis and Langworthy, gets pat. for 1900 a. New Kent. __Machumps Crk—so., side York Riv. 38 head rights, names given. L. O. vi-504. 15 Dec. 1673.

John Webb, Poss'r. of 100 a. Mattapony hd., 437 a., part of 600 pat., to Alex. Williams, 1673. Som Co., R. R., Md. Date supposed to be 1723.

John Webb and John Rea. 1700 a., on Machumps Crk. upper part of New Kent Co., Va. 14 head rights. L. O. vi-619. (ab. 1674.)

John Webb, tithable. John Hale and Hen. More, with him. N-n Co., Va., 1674. ix-272.

John Webb assigns right to land. Hannah Webb rel. dower. N-n Co., Va., xi-37. 1674.

John Webb, (wf. Hannah) to Daniel Neech, land in N-n Co., 9,000 lbs. tob. Wit. John Robins, Chas, Holden. N-n Co., Va., xi-72. 1674.

John Webb, grand juror. N-n Co., Va., xi-255. 28 Apr. 1674.

John Webb, one titnable. N-n Co., Va., x-73. 1675. Also 1676. Also 1677 and 1678.

John Webb, juror. N-n Co., Va., xii-45. 28 June 1675.

John Webb on committee, 1676 and 1677. Vol. i, Tred Avon Mtg., Md., p. 4 and p. 10.

John Webb builds a boat for use of friends in the ministry; travels to Va., etc. Is to be paid. Tred Avon, vol. i-15, 1678.

John Webb marries out, Tred Avon, vol. i. Ab. 1726. Is a wit. 1724. vol. vi-43. Tred Avon.

John Webb, Talbot Co., Md. Will. Mother Anne Webb, Banbury, Oxfordshire, Eng.; Elizabeth Sharpe, wf of William; Solloman Thomas, Petuxon Riv.; Robert Day, Petuxon Riv.; House of Richard Johns upon the Clifts mentioned. Friend Wm. Sharpe of Talbot Co. extr. Wit. Wheatly, Underwood. Annap. Wills. x-113. 23-7th-1678. [No date of probate.]

(To be continued.)

AN INTERESTING LIBRARY

FROM the Inventory and Appraisement of the personal estate of JOHN ROBINSON, deceased, of Harts Bottom taken the 7th and 8th days of July in the year One Thousand Eight Hundred and Twenty-Six On file in ROCKBRIDGE COUNTY, Virginia, Clerk's Office.*

Large Bible; Dictionary Crockett; Salms Geography; Don Quixote, 4 vols.; Arabian Tales, 4 vols.; Plutarch Lives, 6 vols.; Jefferson's Notes; Paine's Writings; Miranda's Expedition; Rob Roy, 2 vols.; Fables and Dialogues of the Dead; Parks Travels; Burns Poems; Revirie [sic] 2 vols.; Burk's Virginia; 2d and 3d vols.; Milliots Gen. History of Green [?] 4th vol.; Beauties of Spectator, 2 vols.; American War by Snowden; Lees Memoirs; Ready Reckner; Village Memoirs; Charles Goodville [sic] 1 vol.; Travels Cariat [?] Jr., Hale's Contemplation; Cordural De Retz; Glass Cookery; Sentimental Journey; Dodsley's Fables; Military Exercise; Senecas Morals; Chesterfield's Letters, 2d, 3d and 4th; Goodwin's Political Justice, 2 vols.; Zimmerman on Solitude; Morses Geography; Memiors Gen'l Jackson; Life Doctor Franklin; Taylor's Orator; School Master's Assistant; Millenium Hall; Tinnins Letters, 2 vols.; Irish Rebellion; Johnstone Lives, 3 vols.; Manners and Customs 2 vols.; Burns Poems, 4 vols.; Letters from the South, 2 vols.; Aphorisms cover torn off; Mountain Muse; Glass Journal; Freeman's Poems; Johnstons Table Talk; Memtors of Napoleon; Clerks Magazine; 3 vols. Sterns Sermons; Henry's Meditations; Cabinet of Boneparte; Livis Travels, 2 vols.; Blue Lights; Purvis Attempt; Watts Lyric Poems; Milliot's Frame; Thompson's Travels; History of Rome; Lewis Letters; Life of Washington; American Farrier; Wesley's Poems; Village Curate; Mason on Self Knowledge; Watson's Apology; Jennings View; Noble Slaves; History of America; Crises by Thos. Paine; Johnston's Meditations; Magazines, Pamphlets, old Almanacks. and 25 Curran's Speeches. (Other books on the list of sales include the Newgate Calendar and the Chaplet of Comus.)

*JOHN ROBINSON, whose inventory includes these books, was a native of County Armagh, Ireland; served in the Revolution, and by his will left his property to Washington College, Rockbridge County, Va., now known as Washington & Lee University. He specifically provided for a chair of Geology and Agriculture, and also for certain medals. A monument on the campus, to his memory, bears the sentence, "Honor to him to whom Honor is."

The spelling of the titles is evidently as the Clerk found it in the original inventory.

The County Court Note-Book

An every-other-monthly devoted to abstracts from the County Court and other records, prior to 1800, and with a department of notes and queries.*

MILNOR LJUNGSTEDT, Editor and Publisher. Bethesda, Route, 1, Maryland.

Published every other month. Subscription, one dollar a year, in advance.

VOL I. December, 1921. No. 2.

THE EDITOR'S LETTER.

"Now, what I want is, Facts...You can only form the minds of reasoning animals upon Facts—Stick to Facts, Sir!" (Dickens. Hard Times. p. 7.)

The Editor confessess to a sort of agreement with Mr. Gradgrind, far from lovable as he is, and much as he has been condemned. It is, perhaps, a case of the point of view—Mr. Gradgrind may be intrinsically right, but right at the wrong time.

The Editor "admires" facts—to drop into a dear New England colloquialism. The Editor even loves facts. The beautiful consecutiveness of the alphabet—the fact that two and two make four and can't make anything else—these are so restfully definite. It is strange to the Editor that anything doubtful about figures or ancestors can hold any charm.

Our ancestors were our ancestors, and it is too late to talk about changing them now. Kings and princes; peasants and pirates; they are with us forever. The Editor does think that if a person's ancestor had to be a king, he might at least be a respectable one. But so many of the kings who pose as ancestors aren't so very respectable. However, that seems to depend on the contemporiary point of view. The Editor bears a personal grudge against one of hers—he was one of the very worst of them all. And the shocking thought comes occasionally—how much of that detestable person am I?

The Editor is merely aiming at this—take your ancestors philosophically. They didn't know anything about you—and they didn't know you were going to know about them, dig them out of their royal tombs and lowly graves, and exhibit them to the eyes of a modern world in their unveiled skin and bones, so to speak. Treat them kindly, but exactly. If I were an ancestor I should hate to have my dates mixed-up, and my wives made into my daughters or even my granddaughters. The best we can now do for them is to be frank when we can, and respectfully reticent when we can't.

OCCASIONAL.

Heard in Dorchester County, Maryland. "Lawed en lawed en lawed tell they both busted."

The "Land Book" or land tax-list of Bedford Co., Penna., includes this name: "TOSCAPE DEATH alias HERMAN HUSBANDS." 1774.

A modern genealogy, that of the MACK FAMILY, published in Connecticut, has this:. ISAAC ROBINSON, b. Leyden 1610, d. 1704; son of JOHN ROBINSON who came in the MAYFLOWER, 1620. Most New Englanders who are interested in research work know that there was not one ROBINSON on the MAYFLOWER.

An early Virginia head right: DENNIS OMOLIGON. N-n Co., x.49. 1668. Another: HANS NICOLAY. Acco. Co., 1663. In Talbot Co., Md. Census 1776. RICHARD LINKORN, 2 in family.

The old records of ANN ARUNDEL Co., MARYLAND, contain the rates on tobacco, etc., as published by sea-captains about to sail. JOSEPH PENHALLOW, Commander of the Ship "PATRIDGE" publishes his rates in 1736, 1738 and 1739.

Mr. DAVIS, the Register of Wills for Prince George's county, Maryland, has recently discovered in the attic of the Courthouse, and has placed with the other records in his office, ADMINISTRATION ACCOUNTS, Liber S. I., No. 1, beginning 1777, and ending 19 October 1790. The volume contains 451 pp. and has an index.

A Pedigree is a Ladder by which we mount into past ages, and on any round of which we find a convenient resting-place for staying to look about us. (London Athenaeum.)

CONCERNING CERTAIN MISSING RECORDS

The STATE LIBRARY of VIRGINIA, through the Librarian, Dr. McIlwaine, writes that one of the most serious obstacles encountered by genealogists and local historians working in the material to be found in the offices of the Clerks of the County Courts in Virginia, is the fact that in many of the Counties there are very serious breaks in the records. These breaks are to be accounted for in various ways. The Librarian believes that no one thing has caused more of these losses than the thoughtless action of Federal troops during the Civil War, or, he explains, rather of individuals among the troops, who sometimes carried away with them invaluable court records to their homes in the north and west.

Such volumes have probably, by this time, been widely distributed. Many of them have come into the hands of persons who would not be indisposed to return them to the Courts where they belong if these persons could realize the inconvenience which the absence of such records entails.

While to the average northerner of intelligence an deducation, the theft or destruction of any record is an atrocity which cannot be sufficiently condemned, and the Editor believes this to apply especially to old New England, it is feared the present possessors of missing volumes are as thoughtless as the original souvenir hunters. It is in this belief that this note is written, urging such as may possess any of these records, or may know where any of them are to be found, that they use their best endeavors to have them returned to the Court-houses from which they disappeared so many years ago.

The Editor adds to the above the information that a number of the missing records have been gratuitously returned, sometimes, no doubt, by persons who have accidentally discovered them in their old collections. In one case, however, the County paid one hundred dollars for a volume.

Being a New Englander herself, the Editor prints this appeal for her good friends in Virginia, and trusts that it will be taken in just the spirit in which she sends it out.

It has been stated that the missing records of NEWCASTLE COUNTY, Delaware, were probably lost when they were removed by wagon from the Court-house at New-Castle to Wilmington. A record on p. 253, vol. E2, 1783, Wilmington Clerk's Office, referring to a deed from James Dunn to Henry Darby, as supposed to have been destroyed by the British, says: **"When they took the Records belonging to the aforesaid County of New Castle in September Anno Dom'i 1777."** The Editor gives this as interesting but is inclined to think that the circumstantial account of the removal by wagon is more apt to be true—and the possible loss through haste and carelessness. It is known that the early and almost priceless wills were stuffed in a barrel when rescued within recent years by a well-known Judge.

From an old record book in ISLE of WIGHT Co., Va. PETER VASSER and wf. Margaret, son and heir of JOHN VASSER, 150 a. now in poss'n of JOHN BELL, upon the Maine Crk of Warrisquaike Bay —lying next behind the land of Nathaniell Floyd—on a Back Creek parting them two —which Creek runs up near the Maine Creeke—which land was granted to my foresd father JOHN VASSER—1635. 9 Oct. 1700. iv-316.

Mr. FRANCIS B. CULVER, genealogist and a member of the Maryland Historical Society, of Baltimore, has recently acquired from the heirs of the late Kirk Browne, the well-known Quaker genealogist of Baltimore, the very valuable collection of copies of Quaker records, and of Maryland and Virginia family data, which Mr. Brown had accumulated in more than a generation of research work.

Mr. Brown was the custodian of the records of the Park Avenue (Hixite) Meeting, Baltimore. (At a later date the Editor intends to give a list of the local meetings which belong or did belong to the Baltimore Yearly Meeting.)

Mr. Culver has also found time to compile certain family records which will be of special interest to Kentuckians—being the story of the "BLOODED HORSES OF COLONIAL DAYS," comprised in a paper of unusual historical value recently read before the Historical Society. Mr. Culver's contribution is a deserved—if somewhat tardy honor—to a number of our noblest and most blue-blooded Americans

PRINCE WILLIAM, VA., BONDS

(Continued from October number)

Benj. Grayson; Thos. Harrison, James Nisbett, Benj. Grayson, Spence Grayson, extrs. Jas. Douglas, Wm. Elzey. Geo. Johnstone, and Wm. Ashmore, sec. 27 Mch 1758.

Gabriel Muffett [?], Edward Gwatkins, Wm. More, extrs. Wm. Ellzey, Wm. Carr, sec. 27 Mch 1758.

George Mason; Benj. Mason, extr; Benj. Mason, Wm. Elzey, Francis Jackson, sec. 28 Mch 1758.

James Peters; Mary Peters, extx; Wm. Roussau, Rodham Tullors [?] sec. 22 May 1758.

Jefrey Johnson; Jeoffrey and Moses Johnson, extrs; John Bell, Samuel Earle, sec. 28 Aug 1758.

John Ambrose; Elizabeth Ambrose, Wm. Obanion, extrs; Elias Edmonds, Jeremisa Darnell, sec. 27 Nov. 1758.

Edward Emms, Elizabeth Emms, Wm. Kincheloe, Isaac Davis, extrs; John Baylis, Gent. sec. 27 Nov. 1758.

George Seaton; Wm. Conway, extr; Joseph Blackwell, sec. 27 Nov. 1758.

Robert Sinclair; Margaret x Sinclair, extr; Wm. Dawkins, sec. 27 Nov 1758.

John Graham; John Graham, extr; Wm. Seal, Newman Matthis, sec. 26 Mch 1759.

Ebenezer Wross; Sarah Cocker, extx; Mason Bennit, Thos. Reeve, sec. 25 June 1759.

George Seaton; James Seaton, extr; Bertrand Ewell, Howson Kenner, Gent., sec. 27 Aug. 1759.

Mathew Moss; Edward Moss, extr; Thos. Thornxorn, John Reeve, sec. 22 Oct. 1759.

Robert Hughs; William Hughs, extr; Richard Jarvis, Redman Grigsby, sec. 28 Nov 1759.

Robert Wickliff; Elizabeth Wickliff, extx; William Tebbs, Elijah Wickliff, sec. 26 May 1760.

William Lashbrooke; Mary Lashbrooke, James Bridges, extrs; James Bridges, Benj. Rush, Jun'r, sec. 24 June 1760.

George Bigby, Edward Gawtkins, Archibald Bigby, extrs.; Wm. Ellzey, Thos, Attwell, sec. 23 Feby 1761.

John Foley; Rosannah Foly, James Foly, extrs; John Baylis, Gent., John Peake, sec. 25 May 1761.

William Spiller; Wm. Tackitt, extr; John Baylis, Lynaugh Helm, Peter Glascock, sec. 25 May 1761.

Dixey Ward; Rebecca x Ward, extx; John Jackson, Thos. Reno, sec. 23 June 1761.

(To be continued.)

NOTES AND QUERIES

KEITH-CORDER: Parentage, etc., of SMITH KEITH, born 25 April, 1817 in Fauquier Co. Va., married 20 Dec. 1838, presumably at "Flint Hill," Rappahannock Co., Va., Miss MARGARET CORDER; died 2 September 1876, at Leavenworth, Kansas. F. B. C.

BOWDOIN: Some time before 1700, JOHN BOWDOIN, a son of PIERRE BOWDOIN, then of Boston, came to the Eastern Shore of Virginia, buying land and settling in Northampton County. His wife was SUSANNA. The maiden name and parentage of SUSANNA is greatly desired. Please address the Editor.

MUSGROVE-[SIMPSON?] William Musgrove of FAIRFAX and LOUDOUN counties, Virginia, died about 1778, is supposed to have married a daughter of GILBERT SIMPSON. Definite information wanted. V.M.H.

BURFORD: DANIEL BURFORD of Amherst County, Va., who died before 1790 had a wife MARY. He seems to have married but once. The maiden name of MARY BURFORD, is greatly desired with exact references. The name of DANIEL BURFORD'S mother is also desired. The inquirer will gladly reciprocate. P. S. C.

FLOYD-DAVIS: Wanted the record of the marriage of WILLIAM FLOYD of Amherst Co., Va., and ABADIAH DAVIS This marrige took place some time prior to 1750. Date given as 1747, but no authority. P. S. C.

FLOYD of BUCKINGHAM Co., Va. Any information touching him prior to 1800, is greatly desired. Buckingham Courthouse was destroyed by fire in 1868, and practically all records burned. The information asked for may be in private hands. P. S. C.

WANTED: Any SAUL or SOLL ROBINSON born circa 1730 or 1735, New England, New York, New Jersey, Delaware or Pennsylvania. Will gladly reciprocate in kind. Address the Editor.

GIBSON: About 1795, ANDREW GIBSON, then residing in WINCHESTER, FREDERICK Co., Va., a merchant or trader of some means, went farther south (tradition says to GEORGIA) with a large quantity of goods and two negro servants. Nothing more was ever heard of him. Tradition says he was murdered. Andrew Gibson was the brother of John Gibson, of Rockbridge Co., a man of education and considerable property and his (Andrew's) sons were citizens of prominence. Definite information, however slight, is greatly desired as to the death of the father. A reasonable amount will be paid for any clue. Address S. G. G.

PANCOAST-MOHLER. In 1815, WILLIAM (HARDING) PANCOAST married LYDIA (BARNET) MOHLER possibly in or near Shepherdstown, West Virginia. The record of this marriage is greatly desired, also the parentage of WILLIAM (HARDING) PANCOAST, who appears to have been of LOUDOUN Co., Va. Address the Editor.

SCARBURGH-CHARLTON: It is claimed by some writers that the wife of Lt. Col. EDMUND SCARBURGH (second of his name) was MARY CHARLTON. It is known that her name was MARY and that they were married before 1640, but there is nothing in the court records of Northampton or Accomack counties, Virginia to show what her family name was. Any **authentic** tradition will be greatly appreciated. Address the Editor.

CALVERT: A reasonable amount will be be paid for the names (with authority) of the children of REUBEN CALVERT, who died in Prince William Co., Virginia, 1778. A son, THOMAS, is mentioned in 1794. E. F. O'G.

ROBINSON: Gov. LUCIUS ROBINSON of N. Y., is said to have been of the fifth generation from ISAAC ROBINSON, son of ISAAC ROBINSON of Barnstable, Mass., who was the son of JOHN ROBINSON, the Pilgrim pastor (who died in Leyden, 1625.) No proof is given of this statement. References are greatly desired by a descendant of the same line. Mrs. E. R. C.

ROBINSON-WADE: The marriage record of SAUL or SOLL ROBINSON, and MIRIAM WADE, both of Chester county, Penna., is wanted. A reasonable amount will be paid. This record is possibly in some WADE or PHILLIPS family. Address the Editor.

MUSGRAVE-CAIN (KEAN KEANE KAIN) Circa 1800, JOSEPH MUSGRAVE of Chester Co., Penna., married a widow KEAN or CAIN. It is believed her forename was CATHERINE. Both were Presbyterians. The record of this marriage is wanted. H. H.

LITTLETON JOHNSTON, born in Virginia, 1756, m. LUCY CHILDS IN N. C., 1781. Parents of both very much desired. Oldest son named LARKIN CHEW JOHNSTON. M. L. H.

FLOYD: JOHN BURFORD FLOYD was b. in Virginia, 1771, m. in Oglethorpe Co. Ga., died Ga., 1836. Wanted: names of his parents. M. L. H.

DAVENPORT: In 1778, ABRAHAM DAVENPORT, second of his name, married in Montgomery Co, Maryland, FRANCES WILLIAMS, an orphan. Wanted: the names of her parents. Address the Editor.

MILNOR: Wanted: an old Bible containing the record of the family of ISAAC MILNOR of Philada. About thirty years ago this Bible was in Buffalo, N. Y. Address the Editor.

TAUL: ARTHUR THOMAS TAUL m. MARY ANN JOHNSON in Montgomery Co., Md. His will was probated in 1812 in Clark (formerly Fayette Co.,) Ky. The date of the marriage is wanted, also the parents of both parties. Bessie Taul Conkwright.

DUTY: Wanted the address of any one with this surname, especially of any person descending from pre-Revolutionary DUTYS. F. B. H.

HAYS: A WILLIAM HAYS of Penna., settled in Virginia in the 18th century, m a TAYLOR. Was this WILLIAM HAYS the same as a person of the same name living in Virginia, in Mecklenburg, Lee or Princess Anne Co., and father of a large family, including Dr. JOHN W. who d. in N. C., and CLAYTON, who went to TEXAS? F. B. H.

EARL-WATTS: A very early immigrant of the name of EARL came to Virginia and married a WATTS, tradition says she was a niece of Sir Isaac Watts, the hymnologist. Any direct information or reliable tradition concerning them is very much wanted. F. B. H.

WANTED: Five dollars will be paid for information with, proof, concerning the parentage of SAMUEL WEBB who m. JANE WYRE (WEIR) at Christ Church, Philada., 21 Oct. 1731. Information is also desired as to GEORGE WEIR, of Chester Co., Pa., the father of JANE WYRE (WEIR). WEBB removed to Harford Co., Md., before 1740. J. B. T.

WANTED: In the year 1832 an artist in New York or Philada., possibly the younger Sully, painted at the request of an eminent Episcopal divine, whose name cannot be recalled, a St. Joseph and the Holy Child. The models for the picture were the late Rev. JOHN PALMER ROBINSON and his baby son. The daughter of the little son is most anxious to trace this painting and to secure a photograph. If it be still in existence it is probably in the possession of some Episcopal churchman in Philada., Baltimore, or on tshe Eastern Shore of Maryland. Editor (who knows is probably the only living person who knows the history of this painting.

MICHAEL DARLEY settled in Alexandria, Va., about 1780. Wanted: his previous residence; also family name of wife (Caroline).

WODDWARD: Wanted the parentage of AMON WOODWARD, b. Prince George's Co., Md., 1793. Was an officer U. S. A. War of 1812; married (1) Sarah Martin; (2) Barbara Lowe.,F. B. C.

BOOK NOTES

The Editor has received a copy of the REGISTER of the ANCESTORS of DORR EUGENE FELT and AGNES (McNULTY) FELT, compiled by Alfred L. Holman, and printed for private distribution. This is one of the very best of this style of genealogy. It is remarkably clear, and made up with a wonderful and most admirable exactness. The compiler makes no statement he cannot prove. The notation of the generations is good, and the use of the numerical system of foot-notes is of the greatest advantage to the careful reader.

Mr. FELT is the inventor of the comptograph and the comptometer, which the Editor sincerely wishes she could understand.

In the note as to the STEWART-FLOYD volumes which are being prepared (see October issue) the DAVISES were casually listed as among the other families to be catalogued. The Editor believes that the many DAVISES will be interested to know that so far as possible any and every DAVIS prior to 1800, within the geographical bounds mentioned, will be given in the catalogue form which has been decided upon. And there are a great many more DAVISES than FLOYDS, and more DAVISES than STEWARTS. The various spellings, DAVIS, DAVISS, and DAVIES will all be given.

An index to the wills of St. MARY'S COUNTY, Maryland, has been compiled by Mrs. Geo. W. Hodges, and will be published by the Carter Braxton Chapter. D. A. R., 3526, Roland avenue, Baltimore, Md.

The Editor is advised that only a limited number will be published, and advanced orders are solicited. The price will be $12.50.

From the Press of the EASTERN SHORE HERALD, Eastville, Virginia.

The

County Court Note-Book

A Little Bulletin of History and Genealogy.

Vol. I. March, 1922. No. 3.

THE NAME MOURNING

(Continued from December number)

ANN MOURNING COLEMAN of Goochland was a wit. for James Christian. Amherst, Va., Ct. Orders. Date ab. 1768.

MOURNING CLARY was the dau. of Bird Clary, Sussex, Va. E-237, 1769.

MOURNING DUGAL, wf. of Dugal McDugal, P. E., Va. C-212, 216. 17, 18 July 1769.

MOURNING TATOM or TATUM, wf. of Stephen. Spots. Abstr. p. 286. 1771.

WILLIAM MORNING, wit. to will of Robert Owen. Sussex, Va., E-351. 1772. (Perhaps Moring?)

MOURNING FLEMING and William Lowe John Park(??), Louisa, Va. M. L. B. 2 Dec. 1773.

THOMAS MOURNING of Hanover Co., Va. Fr. and Ind. war. Ct. Mch. 1780.

MOURNING BAILEY, gr. dau. of Nicholas Hiles. Hen. 1781.

MOURNING PIGG. 1782. Hist. Orange Co., Va.

NICHOLAS MOURNING, Amherst, Va., Tax list. 1782. Also 1783. (Also spelled MORNAN.)

KATY MOURNING m. Isaac Ramsbottom, 16 Jany. 1783. Hen., Va., M. L. B.

"MORNING" ROBERTS and Elizabeth Harding. Alb., Va. M. L. B. 21 Dec. 1785.

MOURNING PARKE was the mother of John Fleming. See will of John Fleming. Hanover, Va. 1785-1793.

MOURNING CLARK and Robt. Mansfield. Alb., Va. M. L. B. 1785.

"MORNIN" CHRISTIAN, Sp., and Drury Christian, Bach. Amherst, Va. M. L. B.

SALLY MOURNING and William Chandler. Hen., Va. M. L. B. 28 July 1785.

MOURNING MATTHEWS m. Edward Hannah. I. W. Mar. Ret. 28 July 1785.

BARNETT MORNING, Tax list, Bot., Va. 1786.

MOURNING ROBERTS, JOSEPH x ROBERTS, ELIZABETH x ROBERTS, wits. to William Shelton's will. Alb., Va., 1787.

RODGER MORNING, Bot., Va., Tax list. 1787. Also 1788.

MORNING was a slave child of EASTER, slave of David Shelton, see his will. Louisa, Va., 189-1787.

MOURNING JORDAN, I. W. Tax list, 1789.

MORNING, negro slave of David Shelton. Hanover, Va. 1789.

MOURNING RYAN and Hopper Ward. Gchld, Va., M. L. B., 22 Jany. 1790.

MITCHEL MORNING and Elizabeth Rudder. Norf., Va. 1 July 1790. M. L. B. (Note: The sig. to this bond appears to be *Monery.*)

MOURNING WADE, Spr., and John Bailey, Bach. Am., Va., M. L. B. 28 Dec. 1791. Jacob PettyJohn certifies that MOURNING WADE, his half-sister, was b. 18 June 1770.

MOURNING WINN was the wf. of John Hix. See will of Thomas Winn. Lunenb., Va. iii-75.

MORNING WINN, son of John Winn. Lunenb., Va. iv-83, 17 Aug. 1793.

MOURNING BALLARD m. Joseph Morelan, Bedford Co., Va. Upper Goose Crk. Mtg. 1794.

MOURNING LIPSCOMB, King Wm. Co., St. John's Psh., to John Liscomb . . . son of Charles, same Co. . . . refers in deed to MOURNING LIPSCOMB being sec. for John Lipscomb for latter's admn. on Mrs. Frances Quarles' est. King Wm., Va. "i" 290. 28 July 1794.

MOURNING HUDSON and Levin Landrum, Chest. Co., Va., 1794. M. L. B.

MOURNING JOHNSON, wit. to mar. of Jason Moreland and Martha Tullis. 1796. (County?)

MOURNING, negro girl left by will of Charles Burrus to dau. Permelia Burrus. Amherst, Va. ab. 1796-1797.

MOURNING LIPSCOMB, wit. to deed of Hilliard and wf. King Wm., Va., "vi" 142. 1798.
MOURNING, negro slave of William Smith. Fauq., Va. iii-111. 1798.

(To be continued)

THE WEBBS

(Continued from December number)

John Webb, wf. Hannah. Letters of admn. granted her. N-n Co., Va., 1689.
John Webb, a juror. Essex Co., Va., i-71. 1693.
John Webb, Sr. See Essex Co., Va., i-123. 1693.
Mr. John Webb's svt. Same p. 128.
John Webb, sexton, St. Paul's Psh., Hanover Co., Va., 1705.
John Webb and wf. Smart, extrs., petn. for divn. of est. of Thomas Hunt. 16 Aug. 1722.
John Webb, Quaker, admr. of Wm. Elston. Talbot Co., Md. viii-483. 1727. ix-27. 1728.
John Webb; Inv. his est. John Webb, Jr., a purchaser at sale. N-n Co., Va., 25 May 1728.
John Webb, Quaker, admr. of Hannah Neale. Talbot Co., Md. xiii-292. 1735.
John Webb m. Ann Devotion. Conn. Mar. 1746.
John Webb; Jonathan Noale, Jr. Trustee. (Neale?) See Silvester's Addition. Queen Anne R. R., Md. 1760.
John Webb in Windham, Conn. 1760. See Hist'y Windham, p. 47.
John Webb. Webb's Chance, pat. 1702. See Queen Anne Co., Md. R. R. 1760.
John Webb and wf. Martha, St. Anne's psh. Alb. Co., Va., to Richard Melton, 400 a. Alb. Co., Va., iii-79, 1761.
John x Web, wf. Martha, Alb., Va., to Thomas Tilman, same. 84 a. Bremer Crk. Alb. Co., Va., iii-183. 1762.
John Webb and wf. Judith, Hanover Co., Va., and Foster Webb, Gent., of New Kent Co., Va., to Isaac Davis, Gent., Alb. Co., Va., 797 a. on James Riv. Alb. Co., Va. v-66. 3 Mch. 1769. [Foster Webb is mentioned first.]
John Webb, Jr., m. Zipporah Robinson. Conn. Mar. 1772.
John Webb. Three of this name were on the prison ship Jersey. (Amer. Prisoners of the Revolution.)
John Webb. Transquakin hd., Census, Dor. Co., Md. 1776.
John Webb and Mrs. Elizabeth Theaton, wid. Norf. Co., Va. M. L. B. 5 Feby. 1779.
John Webb, dec'd. Report on dower, div'n, &c. Widow, Alice; Chn: Rachel m. Thos. Daniel; Joshua, Hessey, John, William. Sussex Co., Dela. E-270, 271, 1789 and 1793.
John Webb; master Brig Recovery, 1790; Brig Nancy, and the Harriet. Norwich History (Conn.) pp. 488, 495, 496, 498.
John Webb m. Mary Hancock. Wor. Co., Md. i-4. 1797.
John C. Webb and Elizabeth I. Bussies(?), Norf. Co., Va. M. L. B. 9 May 1817.
John C. Webb, Norf. Co., Va. Will. All property to wf. Elizabeth. Wit.: Scott, Hall, Sr., Wallace. Norf. v-105. 2 Jany. 1823—17 Feby. 1823.
JONAS WEBB, bro. of Hannah. See Hannah Webb. N-n Co., 1730.
JONAS WEBB, d. 1748; m. Ann ——. Had chn. Benj., John, Jonas, "Leedleton." Sussex Co., Dela., wills.
JOSEPH WEBB, a wit. with Henry Custis. Acco., Va., vi-20. 26 Jany. 1676.
JOSEPH WEBB; makes oath that he was in His Majesty's service agt. the late Rebellion, that he was 40 days in the service. A ctf. is granted him. Acco. vii-20. 16 Oct. 1678.
Mr. JOSEPH WEBB and Mrs. Ann Michaell, extx. of Mr. John Michaell . . . a difference between them. Acco. 21 June 1687.
Mr. JOSEPH WEBB appears to have left the country, Acco. vi-154. 20 Feby. 1688.
JOSEPH WEBB m. Mahitable Not. 1748-9. Ct. Mar.
JOSEPH WEBB m. Abigail Chester. 1774. Ct. Mar.
Lt. JOSEPH WEBB, taken prisoner during expedition agt. Quebec. 1775. N. E. H. G. Reg. vi-185.
JOYCE WEBB m. Robert Chilcoat. 1781. Balto., Md.
LAURENCE SMITH WEBB and Kesiah Wood. 23 Jany. 1794. Bertie Co., N. C. M. L. B. (N. C. H. and G. Reg.)
LITTLETON (Leedleton) WEBB, son of Jonas and Ann., Sussex, Dela. wills, 1748.
MARK WEBB, Little Neck, St. Martin's Riv., Somerset Co., Md. 1715, 1716.
MARTHA WEBB and Mary Robinson, "greatest creditors," est. of Mr. John Robinson, gent. Kent, Md. iv-329. 1742.
MARY WEBB, wid. of Isaac of Kent Co., Md. (Dela.?) d. 1687. Sussex Records, p. 137.
MARY WEBB, dau. of John and Mary, b. 1697. Charles Psh., York Co., Va.
MARY WEBB, admx. of Richard Webb, dec. (who was a church warden). Upper Psh. Nanse. Co. 1760.
MARY WEBB. I. W. Vestry Bk. 1728.

MARY WEBB m. Francis Chaplin. 14 Dec. 1742. Talbot, Md. Mar.

MARY WEBB, wid., James Webb's heirs; Joshua Clark, and Mary Jadwin for Robt. Jadwin's heirs, are the representatives of property rights in *Lyford*, a tract of 1000 a., Queen Anne Co., Md. Rent Roll. 1760.

MARY WEBB and William Earl. Chowan Co., N. C. M. L. B. 9 Sept. 1779. (N. C. H. and G. Reg.)

(To be continued)

NEW ENGLANDERS AND OTHERS IN EARLY VIRGINIA RECORDS

Mr. EDGAR ALLERTON, of N. E. N-n, iii-24 25 Feby. 1645.

JAMES BERRY "being in New England" Thomas Hunt gives notice as to stray cattle, etc. N-n iii-39. 29 June 1646. (This Berry was probably a settler on the Eastern Shore of Virginia, associated with Thomas Hunt, —— Bibbe, and John Floyd.)

THOMAS ALCOTT, of N. E. mcht. N-n iii-102. 17 Mch. 1647.

ISAAC ALLERTON of N. E. appears many times in the records of N-n county *circa* 1648.

WILLIAM CLAWSON—saith that Pattricke Cudgeley (?) a trader amonge the Indyans is nowe well and in health att foart Hoarekill the Sweede forte. (See a letter to the Commander of Forte Horrekill in Dillawar baye.) N-n iii-174 16 June 1649.

WILLIAM CROSSE of N. E. mariner. N-n v-35 28 Apr 1650.

WILLIAM STRANGWIDGE (?) of Boston, marriner. N-n v-36. 28 Apr. 1650.

WILLIAM WESTEROUS (?) of N. E. Mcht, sells to John Stringer one-eighth of goode Shipp called the Swallowe of Nershanen (?) in N. E. N-n iii-214 7 May 1650.

WILLIAM PAYNE of Ipswich in N. E. Mcht, power to Willm Strangwidge. (sig. Willm Payne.) N-n iv-197 9 Oct. 1652.

Mr. SAMLL MAVERICKE, Mr. ROBERT KNIGHT, and Mr. NATHLL GARDNER, three principall merchants liveing in Boston in New England. N-n iv-162 28 Feby. 1652.

DANIEL SELKIRK, Mcht of Boston, N. E. N-n iv-165 22 Sept. 1653. (This name is SELLICK, and appears again as below.)

Mr. DANIEL SELLICKE Mcht of Boston, Mass., left a widow Susanna, who intended marriage with Mr. Robert Tillghman. See her agreement as to property. N-n v-48 15 Feby. 1654.

Mrs. SELLICKE sells a bark called the RETURNE, John Lambert, master. N-n vii-17 (ab.) 1 May 1655.

SUSANNA SELLICKE, wid. of Mr. Daniel Sellicke, m. Mr. Robert Tilghman ab. 29 May 1655. N-n v-48.

EDWARD GIBONS, a letter to (or from?) him, dated Boston the 9th of the fifth month 1654. N-n v-33.

Capt. WILLIAM HAWLEY of Maryland. N-n v-28 1 Sept. 1654.

WILLIAM KENDALL was the atty of WILLIAM PAYNE of Ipswich of N. E. mcht. N-n v-24 28 Aug. 1654.

WILLIAM SCOTT of Maryland. N-n v-7 29 Apr. 1654.

Mr. PARKER of Maryland. N-n v-8 29 Apr. 1654.

(To be continued)

THE PEDIGREE OF MOSES

(Tabulated by W. B. Powell)

MOSES was the son of Amram and Jochabed; Amram was the son of Kohath; Kohath was the son of Levi; Levi was the son of Jacob and Leah; Jacob was the son of Isaac and Rebekah; Isaac was the son of Abraham and Sarah; Abraham was the son of TERAH.

Rebekah was the daughter of Bethuel; Bethuel was the son of Nahor and Milcah; Nahor was the son of TERAH.

Sarah was the daughter of Haran; Haran was the son of TERAH.

Milcah was the daughter of Haran; Haran was the son of TERAH.

Leah was the daughter of Laban; Laban was the son of Bethuel; Bethuel was the son of Nahor and Milcah; Nahor was the son of TERAH.

Milcah was the daughter of Haran; Haran was the son of TERAH.

Jochabed, the mother of MOSES, was the daughter of Levi; Levi was the son of Jacob and Leah; Jacob was the son of Isaac and Rebekah; Isaac was the son of Abraham and Sarah; Abraham was the son of TERAH.

Rebekah was the daughter of Bethuel who was the son of Nahor and Milcah; Nahor was the son of TERAH.

Milcah was the daughter of Haran; Haran was the son of TERAH.

Sarah was the daughter of Haran; Haran was the son of TERAH.

Leah was the daughter of Laban, who was the son of Bethuel; Bethuel was the son of Nahor and Milcah; Nahor was the son of TERAH.

Milcah was the daughter of Haran who was the son of TERAH.

The County Court Note-Book

An every-other-monthly devoted to abstracts from the County Court and other records, prior to 1800*, and with a department of notes and queries.

MILNOR LJUNGSTEDT, Editor and Publisher. Bethesda, Route 1, Maryland

Published every other month. Subscription, one dollar a year, in advance.

VOL. I. March, 1922 No. 3

THE PARIS POSTMAN

(In place of an editorial the Editor takes from that otherwise dismal novel by Rolland . . . the three or four volumes of *Jean-Christophe*, considered by critics to be of a greatness . . . the following sympathetic and philosophical study of a family. It seems to the Editor it must be true, but whether true or not in actual detail, it is true in a large way, and the Editor hopes it will appeal to some who have not read it, or have overlooked it in the interminable length of *Jean-Christophe's* journey in the world, as it has appealed to her.

Some liberties have been taken with the text—the Editor believes she has held closer to the spirit of the original.)

The postman, who is named Hurteloup, comes in with a registered letter. Answering some question or other, he explains that he is from Avallon, and that he belongs to one of the oldest families in Burgundy; he has family papers going back to "1200 and some-" thing." . . . "One of his ancestors had " been a crusader with Phillippe Auguste; " another had been Minister of State under " Henri II. In the seventeenth century the " family had begun to decay. At the time " of the Revolution they were ruined and " lost themselves in the ocean of the people. " Now, they were coming to the surface as " the result of honest labor and the physical " and moral vigor of Hurteloup, the post-" man, and his fidelity to his race.

" Hurteloup had a hobby—it was the col-" lection of historical and genealogical docu-" ments relating to his family and their " province. In his off hours he would go to " the archives and copy old papers. When-" ever he did not understand them, he asked " one of the residents on his beat to ex-" plain—a Chartist or Sorbonne student. " His illustrious ancestry had not turned " his head; he spoke of it with a laugh, with-" out embarrassment, without indignation at " the hardness of fate. And when Olivier " looked at him he felt the mysterious ebb " and flow of the life of human families, " which for centuries sweeps gloriously in " the open; for centuries disappears under " ground, and thence comes bubbling forth " again, having gathered fresh energy from " the depths of the earth itself.

" And to Olivier the people seemed to be " an immense reservoir into which plunge " the rivers of the past, while the rivers of " the future spring forth ever and again, " and though they bear new names, are " sometimes the same as those of old."

On account of a change in printers, the February NOTE-BOOK has been slipped over and dated as of March. Still further delay is due to the illness of the Editor. It is hoped that the fourth number (May) can be brought out on time.

The Editor takes pleasure in stating that the COUNTY COURT NOTE-BOOK will begin in the May number to publish a list of "MARRIAGES BY INFERENCE." This is a part of the material which will appear more fully in the DICTIONARY CATALOGUE of FLOYDS and STEWARTS, which will be published later by Mrs. Pauline Stewart Crosley and Mrs. Ljungstedt. Mrs. Crosley has consented to permit a part of this very valuable collection to appear primarily in the NOTE-BOOK. The title chosen for these marriages is brief and convenient. They are those which are shown by the various court records other than marriage license bonds, licenses, and marriage returns. The material is drawn from Virginia and other States, but excludes Maryland, for which State Mrs. George W. Hodges has done similar work. Mrs. Hodges has many thousands of marriage notes—part of them have been purchased by the State of Maryland, and are now included in the records at the State Land Office.

OCCASIONAL

"Portobake in Maryland." L. Norf. D-117. 25 Nov. 1657.

Among the presentments made by the grand jury to the Hustings Court of Fredericksburg, Va., in 1795, is one against the very high price of bread—"it being in undue proportion to [the] price of flour—and very injurious to the poor." (See Fredericksburg Court records.)

* Wills are abstracted to 1830.

These are to certifye....that R.... B.... desyreing to marry with J.... F....'s mayd servant conditioned betweene the said R.... and J.... F.... that R.... B.... should furnish J.... F.... with a suffict man servant or a Boye of xiiij years or a mayd servant a suffict hand to serve in her stead to bee bought when shippinge came in out of the shippinge next comeinge in about XPmas [or E....?] And this is all I can remember. N-n iii-168 Recorded 12 Mch. 1648.

OLD HOUSES

(The Editor, having read with some interest an article in a recent Forestry magazine stating that the oldest frame building in the United States is a Friends' meeting-house in Maryland, was led to call the attention of a prominent authority, residing in Boston, to the matter, and has received this very interesting statement. As the subject seems quite within the province of the NOTE-BOOK, it is given below. Others will agree with the Editor in appreciation of what some reviewer calls "the scholarly care and moderation" of the writer.)

There is apt to be a considerable degree of ignorance in any one part of the country concerning the antiquities of the other parts, and perhaps a few words concerning merely a few of the many old houses of New England will be of interest.

One of New England's very earliest houses must certainly be that which is said to have been built by Jonathan Fairbanks, in Dedham, Massachusetts, about the year 1638. It has all the ear-marks of great antiquity (as antiquity goes in this country), and suggests more nearly than any other the early type of English cottage architecture, especially in the framing of the garret.

The same date, 1638, is claimed for the John Balch house at Beverly, Massachusetts. These two houses still stand in a very vigorous old age. The Balch house is now in process of restoration and the Fairbanks house is much in need of it, and somewhat in need of repairs also, but on the whole very well looked after by the Fairbanks Family Association.

The Whipple house at Ipswich, Massachusetts, is claimed to be of 1638-42.

All of the above-mentioned houses are of wood. The oldest house of stone seems to be that of Henry Whitfield, built in Guilford, Connecticut, in 1639. This house has been altered and much restored and probably bears but slight resemblance to the original, but was a "mansion" of many rooms.

The Thomas Hart house, at Ipswich, is given the date 1642. It certainly looks old enough for that date, and until very recently had some colored work, probably as part of its original scheme of decoration.

For the wooden Iron Works house in Saugus, the date 1642-45 is claimed, and with much show of probability. This house is believed to have been built as the residence of the superintendent of the Iron Works, one of the first industries established in New England.

For the Noyes house in Newbury, Massachusetts, the date 1646 is given, and 1648 for the Blake house in Dorchester.

The date of all the houses mentioned so far has been a matter for considerable discussion. Most antiquarians, however, would be willing to concede the approximate accuracy of the figures given.

The date of the Scotch-Boardman house, in Saugus, is one of the best established in New England. There seems to be no manner of doubt that it was in 1651 that there was erected on the town line, between Lynn and Boston, a house of four rooms, for the purpose of housing a number of Scotchmen captured by Cromwell at the battle of Dunbar, and sent to New England to work as indentured servants until after the lapse of a stated number of years they should have earned their freedom. The fact that the house stood right on the town line (which passed through the front door, the entry, staircase, and "stack of chimneys" beyond) made it necessary to mention the building in each of the town perambulations, and not until late in the 18th century did the letters "B." and "L." disappear from the old door, where they had so long remained as a sort of town bond. This house and the Iron Works house had the structural overhang of the second story—one of the most interesting features to be found in any old houses of America.

This house was one of the first to be owned by the Society for the Preservation of New England Antiquities. The society now owns other buildings of great age, such as the Cooper-Austin house, in Cambridge, built about 1657; the Swett-Ilsley house in Newbury (already standing in 1670); the Eleazer Arnold house, Lincoln, R. I. (date about 1687).

The writer closes his most interesting article (much of which has had to be omitted for want of space) by the statement that there are many hundred more old houses in New England with fair evidence for their great antiquity. He gives this very brief list as sufficient to arouse the interest of the reader to the fact that probably every section of our country has work of which it may justly be proud, and in praising it to others it will always be well to do so in a spirit of modesty, for the best each section has, is, as a general rule, little better than the best in another section, and they all find their artistic ancestry in Europe, and, generally, in Old England.

PRINCE WILLIAM BONDS

(Continued from December number)

John Lattimore; Sarah x Lattimore, extx.; Bertrand Ewell, George Colvert, Jr., sec. 25 Aug. 1761.

Richard Hazelrig; Wm. x James, Abel x Hazelrig, extrs.; Thos. Falner[?], Patrick Hamrick, sec. 22 Feby. 1762.

Rich'd Crupper; Geo. Calvert, Jacob Calvert, extrs.; Wm. Bennett, John Reeves, sec. 22 Feby. 1762.

George Brett; Simon Luttrell, John Brett, extrs.; Wm. Carr, Elijah Wickliffe, sec. 23 Feby. 1761.

John Bland; Patience Bland, extx.; Edward Gwatkins, Benj. Bland, sec. 7 June 1762.

James Cullins; James Cullins, extr.; Thomas Thornton, Peter Glascock, sec. 7 June 1762.

John McMillion; John McMillion, extr.; Burr Harrison, Wm. Bennett, sec. 22 Feby 1762.

Griffin Mathis; Newman Mathis, extr.; James Bridges, Jone Reve, sec. 2 May 1763.

Thomas Hart; Leonard Hart, extr.; John Peyton, John Lumsden, sec. 6 June 1763.

Wm. Spikeman; Mary Reeves, Wm. Wilson, extrs.; Edward Gwatkins, Benj. Bristow, sec. 5 Sept. 1763.

Elijah Wickliff; Rovert Wickliff, Daniel Kincheloe, extrs.; Isaac Davis, Wm. Tyler, sec. 5 Mch. 1764.

Patrick Hamrick; Patrick Hamrick, extr.; James Bridges, sec. 2 Apr. 1764.

William Baylis; John Baylis, extr.; John Graham, sec. 10 May 1764.

David Wise; John Hedges, extr.; John Graham, John Linton, James Triplett, sec. 3 Sept. 1764.

John Johnson; John Ship, extr.; James Hawkins, John Wake, sec. 3 Sept. 1764.

John Diskis (??) Bridgar Haynes, extr.; Benja. Rush, sec. 1 Oct. 1764.

William Rookard; Thos. Arrington, extr.; George Colvert, Jr., John Rookard, sec. 3 Dec. 1764.

Charles Wells; Mary x Wells, extx.; Samuel Wells, James Grinstead, sec. 4 Mch. 1765.

John Baylis; Jane Baylis, extx.; Wm. Brent, James Nisbett, Thomas Blackburn, sec. 9 Oct. 1765.

John Coster (Coffer?); Mary Coster(?), extx.; Wm. Carr, sec. 7 July 1766.

Judith Barr; William Barr, extr.; Henry Lee, Wm. Elzey, sec. 7 Oct. 1766.

(To be continued)

NOTES AND QUERIES

KEITH-CORDER: Parentage, etc., of SMITH KEITH, born 25 April, 1817, in Fauquier Co., Va., married 20 Dec. 1838, presumably at "Flint Hill," Rappahannock Co., Va., Miss MARGARET CORDER; died 2 September 1876, at Leavenworth, Kansas. F. B. C.

BURFORD: DANIEL BURFORD of Amherst County, Va., who died before 1790 had a wife MARY. He seems to have married but once. The maiden name of MARY BURFORD is greatly desired with exact references. The name of DANIEL BURFORD'S mother is also desired. The inquirer will gladly reciprocate. P. S. C.

FLOYD-DAVIS: Wanted the record of the marriage of WILLIAM FLOYD of Amherst Co., Va., and ABADIAH DAVIS. This marriage took place some time prior to 1750. Date given as 1747, but no authority. P. S. C.

WANTED: Any SAUL or SOLL ROBINSON born *circa* 1730 or 1735, New England, New York, New Jersey, Delaware, or Pennsylvania. Will gladly reciprocate in kind. Address the Editor.

PANCOAST-MOHLER: In 1815, WILLIAM (HARDING) PANCOAST married LYDIA (BARNET) MOHLER, possibly in or near Shepherdstown, West Virginia. The record of this marriage is greatly desired, also the parentage of WILLIAM (HARDING) PANCOAST, who appears to have been of Loudoun Co., Va. Address the Editor.

CALVERT: A reasonable amount will be paid for the names (with authority) of the children of REUBEN CALVERT, who died in Prince William Co., Virginia, 1778. A son, THOMAS, is mentioned in 1794. E. F. O'G.

ROBINSON: Gov. LUCIUS ROBINSON of New York is said to have been of the fifth generation from ISAAC ROBINSON, son of ISAAC ROBINSON of Barnstable, Mass., who was the son of JOHN ROBINSON, the Pilgrim pastor (who died in Leyden, 1625). No proof is given of this statement. References are greatly desired by a descendant of the same line. Mrs. E. R. C.

ROBINSON-WADE: The marriage record of SAUL or SOLL ROBINSON, and MIRIAM WADE, both of Chester County, Pa., is wanted. A reasonable amount will be paid. This record is possibly in some WADE or PHILLIPS family. Address the Editor.

LITTLETON JOHNSTON, born in Virginia, 1756; m. LUCY CHILDS in North Carolina, 1781. Parents of both very much desired. Oldest son named LARKIN CHEW JOHNSTON. M. L. H.

FLOYD: JOHN BURFORD FLOYD was b. in Virginia, 1771; m. in Oglethorpe Co., Ga.; died, Ga., 1836. Wanted: names of his parents. M. L. H.

DAVENPORT: In 1778, ABRAHAM DAVENPORT, second of his name, married in Montgomery Co., Maryland, FRANCES WILLIAMS, an orphan. Wanted: the names of her parents. Address the Editor.

TAUL: ARTHUR THOMAS TAUL m. MARY ANN JOHNSON in Montgomery Co., Md. His will was probated in 1812 in Clark (formerly Fayette) Co., Ky. The date of the marriage is wanted, also the parents of both parties. Bessie Taul Conkwright.

DUTY: Wanted the address of any one with this surname, especially of any person descending from pre-Revolutionary DUTYS. F. B. H.

HAYS: A WILLIAM HAYS of Pennsylvania settled in Virginia in the 18th century; m. a TAYLOR. Was this WILLIAM HAYS the same as a person of the same name living in Virginia, in Mecklenburg, Lee, or Princess Anne Co., and father of a large family, including Dr. John W., who d. in North Carolina, and CLAYTON, who went to Texas? F. B. H.

EARL-WATTS: A very early immigrant of the name of EARL came to Virginia and married a WATTS; tradition says she was a niece of Sir Isaac Watts, the hymnologist. Any direct information or reliable tradition concerning them is very much wanted. F. B. H.

WANTED: Five dollars will be paid for information, with proof, concerning the parentage of SAMUEL WEBB, who m. JANE WYRE (WEIR) at Christ Church, Philadelphia, 21 Oct. 1731. Information is also desired as to GEORGE WEIR, of Chester Co., Pa., the father of JANE WYRE (WEIR). WEBB removed to Harford Co., Md., before 1740. J. B. T.

DARLEY: MICHAEL DARLEY settled in Alexandria, Va., about 1780. Wanted: his previous residence; also family name of wife (Caroline). Mrs. C.

WOODWARD: Wanted the parentage of AMON WOODWARD, b. Prince Georges Co., Md., 1793. Officer, War 1812; m. (1) Sarah Martin; (2) Barbara Lowe. F. B. C.

MUSGROVE: Who was the wife of WILLIAM MUSGROVE of Loudoun Co., Va.? Who was the wife of GILBERT SIMPSON? Dates 1777 and prior. V. M. H.

GIBSON: Wanted the record of the death of ANDREW GIBSON, who was in Winchester, Virginia, in 1795, and went to Georgia. S. G. G.

$5.00 REWARD: JAMES STEELE came from England about 1788, and afterwards lived in Pittsburgh. He m. —— PORTER, of Virginia. Had one child, Robert P. Steele, b. 1791. Ancestry wanted of James Steele's wife. F. B. L.

$5.00 REWARD for proof of ancestry of SARAH REED, of Virginia, b. 1770; m. (1) —— KEMP, said to have had plantation near James River. Daus. Belinda and Caroline. Married (2) THOMAS HARTLEY, said to have been Kemp's partner. Chn.: ROBERT H., MARTHA S., JAMES REED; WILLIAM T., JANE, and SARAH REED. HARTLEYS lived for a time in Pittsburgh. SARAH REED said to have been connected with Washingtons. F. B. L.

CAIN: Information wanted of GEORGE CATHEY CAIN, b. North Carolina, 15 Apr. 1813; probably son of ROBERT CAIN, whose wife was perhaps b. HOOKER or MAXWELL. C. A. B.

CARR-COLE: Would like any clue to ancestry of RACHEL CARR, supposed dau. of JOHN and ELIZABETH (WHITE) CARR. She m. AQUILA COLE of Frankfort, Ky. C. A. B.

COLE: AQUILA COLE lived near Frankfort, Ky., about 1800; was son of SALATHIEL and grandson of THOMAS COLE, of Va., or Penna. The COLES came to Kentucky with BOONES, or shortly after. Any information appreciated. C. A. B.

ZACHARY: What was the maiden name of wife of PETER ZACHARY, and date of marriage? Caroline Co., Va. M. L. H.

FINLEY: JAMES FINLEY, son of JOHN FINLEY and MARTHA BERKLEY, his wife, served with South Carolina Revolutionary troops. Wanted: his residence in South Carolina and place of death in Virginia. Mrs. C. S. P.

DAWKINS: WILLIAM DAWKINS died Georgia, 1800. Married CYNTHIA ——. Information wanted as to his and his wife's family. M. L. H.

TAYLOR: Did ZACHARY TAYLOR, Caroline Co., Va., get his name from the SACHARY family? M. L. H.

EUBANK-EWBANKS: THOMAS EUBANK d. Talbott Co., Md., 1732. Wanted: names of his parents and further information concerning THOMAS. Wife was MARTHA. What was her maiden name? K. D. S.

FRANKLIN: THOMAS, ROBERT, JOHN, EDWARD (brothers), were in Augusta County, Va., 1745-1776. What were the parents' names and where did the brothers remove from (to Virginia)? K. D. S.

HASKINS-WOMACK: REBECCA HASKINS and BYRD WOMACK, of Virginia, were married 1800. Who were their parents? Mrs. T. A.

BOOK NOTES

The HILLS OF WILKES COUNTY, GEORGIA, AND ALLIED FAMILIES. This volume ready for delivery March 10th. 300 pp. Price, $5.00 and postage. Address Lodowick J. Hill, 495 Courtland Street, Atlanta, Georgia.

This will be a very valuable work, as it will include the Pope, Walton, Wootten, McKimmie, Exum, Colquitt, Colhoun, Richardson, Barrow, and other well-known families of the South.

The Editor has just had the pleasure of reading a manuscript volume, compiled for private distribution, entitled the ROBINSON FAMILY HISTORY. Mr. Ellsworth D. Robinson, of Pittsburgh, has had the work done, and it is an unusually interesting volume, owing to the fact that a large part of it is the history of the immigrant ancestor and his ancestry, written many years ago by a closely related descendant. The highly romantic story, as given by this descendant, is undoubtedly based upon fact, and it is to be regretted that it lacks the dates and references which the modern genealogist demands. There is enough detail given, however, to make the work of proof quite possible, and it would be an unusually interesting task, as the line runs back to a Scotch family, said to be descended from a James, King of Scotland.

The second part of the compilation is charmingly written and also gives a framework of facts which will be valuable to others of the same line.

An index to the wills of St. Mary's County, Maryland, has been compiled by Mrs. Geo. W. Hodges, and will be published by the Carter Braxton Chapter, D. A. R., 3526 Roland Avenue, Baltimore, Md.

The Editor is advised that only a limited number will be published, and advanced orders are solicited. The price will be $12.50.

Copies of the Baltimore Sun articles on Maryland and Virginia families may be obtained from

Mrs. Blanche L. Hayes,
3526 Roland Avenue,
Baltimore, Md.

MR. FRANK POLLARD BROWN, 15 Bosworth St., Boston, Mass., specializes in early American stamps. Persons owning old stamps, especially of the issues between 1847 and 1857, would do well to correspond with him.

GENEALOGISTS AND OTHERS INTERESTED IN RESEARCH WORK

MR. FRANCIS B. CULVER,
2203 North Charles St.,
Baltimore, Md.

Researches in genealogy and heraldry for early families of Maryland, Pennsylvania, and Virginia. Historical biographies compiled and authentic coats of arms emblazoned.

MR. ALFRED L. HOLMAN,
GENEALOGIST,
2036 Indiana Avenue,
Chicago, Ill.

Refers, by special permission, to Mr. Geo. B. Utley, Librarian, Newberry Library.

MRS. EDITH ROBERTS RAMSBURGH,
The Portner,
Washington, D. C.

Heraldry and genealogy. Compiler of family records. Historical and genealogical research.

MRS. GEORGE W. HODGES,
Gloucester Apartments,
Annapolis, Md.

Special facilities for genealogical and historical work.

Research work, literary and historical, Congressional Library. Address

Mrs. D. S. Ward,
1865 Mintwood Avenue,
Washington, D. C.

Any person interested in the early records of Stafford, King George, Lancaster, Northumberland, Westmoreland Counties, Virginia, and desiring careful, detailed searches, may join in a very simple co-operative plan by addressing M. L., County Court Note-Book.

Twenty-five cents each will be paid for ten copies of the October NOTE-BOOK. Editor.

JUDD & DETWEILER (INC.), PRINTERS, WASHINGTON, D. C.

The

County Court Note-Book

A Little Bulletin of History and Genealogy.

Vol. I. **May, 1922.** **No. 4.**

MARRIAGES BY INFERENCE *

(*For explanation of this title, see March* NOTE-BOOK.)

MATHEW MOORE and ELIZABETH PIGOT, dau. of Capt. Fancis Pigot, N-n Co. xiv-224 ab. 1633.

JOHN WILLIAMS and ELIZABETH COOPER, N-n Co., vii-10, ab. 1647.

JEFFREY x MINSHALL and FRANCES CARLSLEY, mar. contract. N-n Co. iv-48. 18 May 1650.

CHARLES SCARBRAGH [sic] and KATHRYNE BARLOWE, mar. contract, N-n Co., vii-20, (about?) 27 May 1654.

ABRAHAM MORGAN and ANN SHAWE, N-n Co. vii-21, bef. 4 Nov. 1654.

......EDWARDS, late citizen and freeman of London, mar. KATHRYNE HEMLOCKE, wid. of Mr. EDWARD HEMLOCKE (see depn. of John Edwards' son of Edwards), N-n Co., 30 Apr. 1655. [Date of depn.]

Capt. EDWARD STREETER (?) and the wid. of Col. Thomas Burbage, L. Norf. D-29, ab. 17 Nov. 1656.

RICHARD POOLE and the wid. of Thomas Workman. L. Norf. D-15, bef. 17 Nov. 1656. (Note: ANN, wid. of THOMAS WORKMAN mar. Natha. HAYES ab. 1656.)

WILLIAM CORNIX (?) and the wid. of THOMAS NEEDHAM. L. Norf. D-50, bef. 15 Jany. 1656.

WILLIAM NORWOOD and MARY ROOKE (?) L. Norf. D-52, bef. 15 Jany. 1656.

RICHARD HANBY, Shoemaker, and MARIA CHILCOTT, single woman. Mar. contract. N-n vii-8, 20 Aug. 1656.

Mr. WM. SMARTE and MARY ANDREWS, wid. of Lt. Col. Wm. Andrews. N-n vii-57, bef. 25 June 1656.

GEORGE HINCKS and wid. of EDWARD LILLY. L. Norf. D-65, bef. 20 Mch. 1656.

GEORGE BEASELEY and WM. BASNETT'S dau. L. Norf. D-67, bef. 20 Mch. 1656.

JOHN SMYTH and REBECCA SAVAGE, wid. of Thomas Savage. N-n v-142, bef. (?) 1656.

GEORGE HEIGHAN and the wid. of Mr. JOHN FERNEYHAUGH. L. Norf. D-81, bef. 5 July 1657.

RICHARD MARKHAM gives notice by setting up his name, at the C. H. door, of intended marriage with FRANCES YEATES. L. Norf. D-90. 18 Aug. 1657.

ROBERT RUSSELL and JANE HINSON, wid. L. Norf. D-88, bef. 17 Aug. 1657.

EDMUND COOPER and ELENOR CLUER (??) L. Norf. D-125, ab. 15 Feby. 1657.

JOHN STRATTON and the wid. of Mr. THO. CASON [CARSON, CAUSON] L. Norf. D-98, bef. 26 Oct. 1867.

Mr. WILLIAM GOUGE [GEORGE?] and the wid. of ROBERT KINSEY. L. Norf. D-97, bef. 20 Oct. 1657.

FRANCIS DOUGHTY, minister, and ANN EATON, mar. contract. N-n vii-48, 8 June 1657.

STEPHEN FISHER, pltr., and ROBERTA ANDREWS wid, Mar. contract. N-n vii-48, 20 Apr. 1657.

JOHN WATFORD and THOMAS DIER'S wid. L. Norf. D-146, ab. 15 June 1658.

JOSIAS TOWNSENDE and the wid. of EDWARD ROBINSON. L. Norf. D-146, ab. 1655.

EDWARD ROBINSON and the wid. of Mr. PLOMER (PLOMER BRAY??) L. Norf. D-147, ab. 1658.

HENRY COOCEE [COURCY??] and ELIZABETH JOLLY, dau. of JOHN. L. Norf. D-147, bef. 15 June 1658.

Mr. STANNAWAY (?) and ELIZABETH PERRY, wid. L. Norf. D-172, bef. 20 Oct. 1658.

THO. LOVELL and the wid. of THO. HORNE. L. Norf. D-176, ab. 15 Nov. 1658.

DARBY SEXTON and the dau. of THOMAS CHEELEY. [This name has various spellings.] (Her father-in-law was JOHN HENLEY.) L. Norf. D-161, bef. 16 Aug. 1658.

NATHL. GIBBS and the wid. of WM. WATTS. L. Norf. D-164, ab. 15 Sept. 1658.

(To be continued.)

THE NAME MOURNING

(Continued from March number.)

MOURNING LIPSCOMB [a man], King Wm. Co. Va., from John Peerse and wf. Elizabeth, 150 a. in the psh. of St. Johns. K. Wm. "1" 179. 26 Aug. 1794.

SALLY MOURNING m. Edmund Caston (?) Car. Co. Va., mar. 18 July 1795.

"MOURNAN," negro slave of John B. Trent. Amherst Co. Va., ab. 1800.

MOURNING SLAUGHTER was one of the seven sisters of George Slaughter. She was mar. to Wharton Quarles. K. Wm. "13" 493, bef. 17 Mch. 1800.

See also "2" 25. Also "1" 25, K. Wm. records.

MOURNING, a negro willed by James ROBINSON of Greensv. Co., Va. 1801.

MOURNING LIPSCOMB and THOMAS LIPSCOMB, Jr., were extrs of John Langley Allen. K. Wm., "9"-45. 1802.

MOURNING SHELTON, dau. of Henry, mar. John White, bef. 1802. (See Wood's Hist'y Alb. Co.)

MOURNING SADLER mar. Stephen Benson. Gchld Co., Va. Mar. Li. Bonds, 1804.

MOURNING, a negro slave of Henry Christian, who d. 1804-5. Amherst Co., Va.

MOURNING TIMBERLAKE. From Campbell Co. Friends' Mtg. to Ohio. Ab. 1805. (See Friends' Records.)

MOURNING MURRAY, sp., mar. Allen Davis. Am. Co., Va. 1806.

MOURNING T. MALLORY and James x Moseley. Gchld. Co., Va., M. L. B. 22 Feby. 1806.

MOURNING x BLALOCK and Robert Edwards. Gchld Co., Va., M. L. B. 1810.

MOURNING MITCHELL and Walter Williams. Am. Co., Va., M. L. B. 1811.

MOURNING LIPSCOMB'S wf. was Jane K. Wm. "15" 334. 1814.

MOURNING, a negro slave left by Thomas Wilson, Sr., to dau.. Nancy Wilson, wf. of Aaron. Henry Co., Va. 2-137. 1816-1817.

MOURNING JORDAN was wf. of Joseph. (See N. C. H. & G. Reg. ii.5. Chowan Co. 1819.)

MOURNING M. DAVIS from Henry Davis, St. John's Psh., K. Wm. Co., Va. K. Wm. "12" 498. 1 Nov. 1820. [This was a man.] See also "17" 113, 1821.

MOURNING RIDDICK, wf. of Willis Riddick, Perq. Co., N. C. (See N. C. H. & G. Reg. iii-348. 7 Nov. 1829.)

MOURNING CHRISTIAN, her will. Am. Co., Va. 1837. Her negro slave Suckey had child MORNING. [Sic.]

MOURNING FAMILY: The following notes were contributed by Mrs. R. L. Bucker, of Kentucky—

Roger MOURNING, b. Ulster, Ireland, 1739. Emigrated 1775. Enlisted 1776. Died 10 Oct. 1827. His first wife's name not given. He had two chn. by first wf. JOHN and SALLY. Married (2) Jane Kennedy from Penna., also from Ulster. Had seven chn. by second marriage. Youngest b. 1793. All moved to Kentucky. (The marriages of these children are given, but without dates.)

(Concluded.)

THE WEBBS

(Continued from March number.)

MARY MARGARET WEBB, b. 25 Nov. 1712, d. 14 Nov. 1781., m. WILLIAM ROBINSON, b. 11 June 1704, d. 1 Feby. 1778. (Contributed by a correspondent. From a Robinson Bible.)

MATTHEW WEBB had wf. Ann. I. W. iii-406. 1 Jany. 1770.

MATTHIAS WEBB'S wf. was Ann. I. W. 1777.

MELCHIZADECK x WEBB, wit. to will of John Day. I. W. vi-172. 26 Sept. 1725.

NAPTHALI WEBB m. Mary Mudge. 1751. Ct. Mar.

NICH: WEBB, wit. . . . assignment pat. by Wm. Waters. Acco. i-39. 11 Nov. 1663.

PARK WEBB, pltr. mar. GRACE. . . . Had chn. Ann, James, Elizabeth. (See Talbot Co., Md. xviii-498.) 1741. (Annap. records.) (See also Talbot Co., xxv-7.) 1748. (Annap. records.)

PARK WEBB, Shadwell's Addition, Queen A. Rent Roll, p. 50. (M. H. Soc.) 1760. See also Talbot Co. Accts., xxv-7, Annapolis L. O.

PARK WEBB, Tred Avon Mtg. Md. Records, vol. viii.

PARK WEBB and Edward Neall (Quakers) extrs of Mary Wiles. . . .

PARK WEBB, Oaths of allegiance, Talbot Co., Md. 1778.

PETER WEBB mar. SARAH. . . . She adm. his est., 1719. Talbot Co., Md. (Records at Annap.)

PETER WEBB, Tred Avon Mtg. Records. vol. viii. Also vol. iii.

PETER WEBB, son of PETER and SARAH WEBB, was born 1, 14, 1760. Tred Avon Mtg. Recds. vi-2.

PETER WEBB, Sr. and Jr., Talbot Co., Md. Oaths of allegiance. 1778.

PETER WEBB mar. Sarah Trippe. Dor. Co. Md., M. L. 22 Feby. 1793.

PETER WEBB mar. Mary Trippe, Dor. Co., Md., Mar. Li. 10 May 1796.

REBECCA WEBB, extx will of Richard Webb, pltr., Talbot Co., Md. iii-119. 14 June 1720.

RICHARD WEBB, an early settler in Barbadoes. N. E. H-G. xxxix-138, ab. 1638. (?)

RICHARD WEBB died 1665. Hist'y Col. New Haven.

RICHARD WEBB, original, unrecorded will. Son Richard; son John; 300 a, called Redford, bought of Wm. Berry; reversion to dau. Mary Webb; (chn. are under sixteen); wf., Wm. Southbee, Thos. Taylor, extrs. Friend Margaret Berry to take dau. John Wootters (?) and Wm. x Hill wit. John Wootters (Wootten?), age 35, and Wm. x Hill, age 40, attest ("all attestation that can be saving an oath") as to will. Codicil provides for son if wf. should have one; if a dau., to have a maintenance. 17 Dec. 1677. Annap., Md. Wills.

RICHARD WEBB, will. Mary Webb, extx John Dennis, sec. Som. Co., Md. 1709. Annap. Records.

RICHARD WEBB, overseer of Thomas Moyses [sic] will. Surry Co., Eng. No. 244. 1597.

RICHARD WEBB, member of Virginia Company. Hening, 1-86. 23 May 1609.

RICHARD WEBB: The Early Settlers index at Annapolis shows a svt of this name transp. 1658; an immigrant, 1661 (i. e., he brought himself in); another in Somerset Co., Md., from Virginia, 1671; a svt. in Chas. Co., Md. 1675; and one transp. in 1677, county not given.

(To be continued.)

NEW ENGLANDERS AND OTHERS IN EARLY VIRGINIA RECORDS.

WILLIAM FOXE, late of N. E.; Thomas Baxter, sometime an inhabitant of N. E. N-n v-150 2 Nov. 1654.

PEDIGREENE [*sic*] WHITE of N. E. N-n v-97 29 May 1656.

Mr. THOMAS TODD was of Elizabeth City, Va. N-n iv-217 30 Jany. 1653.

Mr. JOHN LORD of N. E. N-n v-116 28 Feby. 1654.

JOHN THORNDIKE, of Salem, N. E. N-n v-121 20 Nov. 1655.

Mr. WILLIAM BRENTON, of N. E. Mcht. N-n v-135 1 May 1655.

Mr. RICHARD LORD, Mcht. of N. E. N-n vii-13 28 Mch. 1655.

WILLIAM FLERDE (?), Tanner, City of Westchester (?), mentioned in will of Wm. Mellinge. N-n Co., Va. i-46. 26 Oct. 1635.

SUSAN GRACE mentioned in will of NICHOLAS WHITE, bound on a voyage to N. E. about 1639. White's uncle, Samuel White, lived in *Blackwall*, London. N-n Co., Va., i-151. 1639.

James Standish, N-n Co., Va. ii-33. 23 Nov. 1640.

SAMUEL ANDREWS, of London, Mcht. now resident in N. E. N-n Co., Va. vii-40, 27 June 1646.

NICH: PERQ. (This name is given as Nicholas Parker, Parque, Nichola Parque. The Editor does not know what it originally was.) "The said PERQ (or PERG) is a Frenchman." N-n iii-133, 1 Feby. 1647.

THOS. FALKNER deposes (1640) that Maj. Edw. Gibbons tended Thos. Maior his svt. (?) at Marblehead in N. E., when he was at Boston. N-n ii-168. 12 Mch. 1648.

"LLAUS DEO BOSTON in New England 24th of July 1649" (heading of a record.) N-n iii-191 29 Nov. 1649.

JOHN FISHER'S voyage to the South River of New England ("Delaware Bay.") N-n iv-41 10 Aug. 1651.

Capt. JOHN JACOB, a High Germayne of Frankendell in the Palatinate who in the year 1651, &c., &c. N-n iv-162. Feby. 1652.

JOHN HOLLAND, of Dorchester in N. E., Mcht., power of atty to Mr. Jno. Custice. N-n iv-107 29 Sept. 1652. He is deceased before this date.

RA: BARLOWE deposes. . . . being at a house in Elizabeth County (where Robert Parker then lived) where had lived lately Mr. ANTHONY WEST. . . . N-n iv-102. 23 Sept. 1652.

WILLIAM DARVALL, Co. of Kent, Penna., paid by Capt. JOHN NELLSON Mcht., Boston, Massachusetts. Land eight miles from Lewes. Deed Book D, 4. p. 108. 10-3-1687.*

EDWARD BELLAMY, of Gray's Inn, in the County of Middx., bro. and hr. of JOHN BELLAMY, formerly of the psh. of St. Olave, Hart street, London, and Nathaniel Puckle, of Philada. [Deed between] Land near Lewes. 4-20-1702. Deed Book D, 4, p. 127.*

JOHN LANGDON, Province of Massachusetts Bay, N. E., Gentleman, and WILLIAM SCARLETT (wf. Judith) late of the psh. of St. James, Island of Jamaica. (Slaves bought from SCARLETT.) Deed Book D, 4. p. 157. 4-6-1715.*

ISAAC SAVAGE of Boston, in N. E., tallow-chandler, bro. and hr.-at-law of John Savage, late of STAFFORD, Gent., power to William MacWilliams, the younger, of Fredsb'g., Spots. Co., Va., to convey property, &c. Wit: Robert Massey, Thomas Abercrombie. P-157, 23 July 1757.

*Contributed from Sussex Co. Dela. records.

The County Court Note-Book

An every-other-monthly devoted to abstracts from the County Court and other records, prior to 1800*, and with a department of notes and queries.

MILNOR LJUNGSTEDT, Editor and Publisher. Bethesda, Route 1, Maryland.

Published every other month. Subscription, one dollar a year, in advance.

Vol. I. May, 1922. No. 4.

SENTIMENT . . . or SENSIBILITY?

The Editor grew up in an age of scrap-books, and little lockets with enclosed curls; some of the curls were nearly golden, some were brown and some were gray; in an age when one never put any other book atop the BIBLE, and never stepped upon a grave. The Editor thinks this must have been inherited tradition. . . . she cannot distinctly remember ever having been told not to do these things.

This was not the environment of funeral wreaths preserved under glass, nor of photographic prints at the head of the grave. A rosebud or two may have been put by, or a bit of English heather, until a succeeding and less remembering generation burned them; the broad white ribbon sent by the Masonic order may yet be in the granddaughter's possession; but there was nothing out of taste, it seems to the Editor looking back, except when a chance in-law discussed too early the division of the household treasures.

But, somehow, the dead, once dead, became wrapped in a garment of tremendous respect. One closed the blinds and walked softly; the clothes they had worn, the letters they had written, the books they had owned, were gently handled and forever treasured.

And the graves were the FAMILY, and those able to do so, made provision for their care in perpetuity.

* * * * * * * *

At sixteen this Editor was patiently scratching the dust from inscriptions on ancestral stones, yet the stones were not hers. Another inherited instinct. The Editor still remembers:

Abel his offering accepted is
His body to the grave his soul to bliss
In October's twentieth and no more
The yeare was 1644.

While on the other half of the square topping stone she read:

Submit submitted to her Heaavenly King
Being a flower of that Eternal Spring
Nigh three yeares old she died in Heven to wait
The yeare was 1648.

So . . . when the Editor happened upon the first desecrated burying-ground it is difficult for her to put into words the shock, the over-powering horror and disgust which came upon her. That first graveyard is very dim in her recollection, she regrets to say she believes it was in the old county from which her own forbears hailed, for after some years she made a closer examination and identification of what was undoubtedly the same ground.

But the first neglected and desecrated burial place which the Editor clearly identifies is the old Northern Methodist churchyard in LEESBURG, LOUDOUN COUNTY, VIRGINIA. . . .

The Editor finds she has not space in this number of the NOTE-BOOK for an article touching upon similar conditions in many counties, conditions which she wishes to bring to the attention of her readers. This editorial will, therefore, be continued in the next number.

OCCASIONAL.

A RECORDE BOOKE cost 1200 lb of tobacco. (Acco. Co., Va. xiv-74. 4 May 1714.)

SAMUEL FRENCH is summoned for greate offence . . . takeing and carryinge away the County Records & the High Sheriff's books out of the Court House of this County * * * (Northampton Co., Va., xvii-70. 11 Feby. 1695.)

REVOLUTIONARY SERVICE: NATHAN DAVIS served on guard. LYDIA McGEE was wf. of GEORGE McGEE, a soldier in the Continental service. (Shenan. Co., Va. Ct. 28 Aug. 1728.)

The *STATE OF FRANKLIN:* JOHN NELSON of the County of WASHINGTON, and STATE of FRANKLIN . . . gives power to friend William Tyler of *Shanando* County, Virginia, to acknowledge and convey a deed to 140 a. to Spencer Breeding. Wit: John Barnett and Joseph Barnes. (Shenan. Co., Va. F-410. 17 Jany. 1780.)

PALMER'S ISLAND: The Court (at Jamestown) declares that PALMER'S ISLAND is within the limits of VIRGINIA, and out of the limits of MARYLAND. (N-n Co., Va., iv-22. 21 May 1651.)

"Its Ordred a Dore a table and Convenient Cences be made for the Jury room in the Courthouse." (Car. Co., Va., 1st Order Book, p. 389. 14 Jany. 1736.)

EARTHQUAKES: "16 m. after 2 O'clock afternoon supposed to be an Earthquake." (Sussex Co., Va. E-461 21 Feby 1774)

"Between the Hours of 3 and 5 o'clock. Supposed to be an Earthquake." (Sussex Co., Va., 29 (19?) Dec. 1789.)

The mention of a brick kiln in the records of Northampton Co., Va., (ii-177), as early as 28 Oct. 1642, may throw some light on the disputed question of "English brick."

WHAT YOU CAN FIND AT ANNAPOLIS.

(Note: The Biennial Reports of the Commissioner of the Land Office at Annapolis, Maryland, give a most useful detailed list of all the records which are there at the command of the historian and genealogical searcher. The limits of this bulletin permit only a brief extract of from the lists of the earlier volumes.)

WILL BOOKS, ETC.

41 Will Books; (from the earliest dates of probate to 1777).

47 vols. Testamentary Proceedings (records of the probate court).

175 vols. of Inventories, Accounts, Balance Books, &c.

1920 Original Wills.

220 vols. of Chancery Records (1668 to 1852); 35 of these have been indexed. The others have individual indexes.

2172 vols. of Land Records from the various counties.

291 vols of Patents, Warrants, &c.

49 Rent Rolls (under the Proprietor.)

53 Colonial Maryland Debt Books. (These serve as a sort of index to the Rent Rolls, as they give the individual names. The Rent Rolls are indexed only under properties.)

In addition to the above, the State of Maryland is leading the way in the matter of the classification and official preservation of individual records touching early marriages. Mrs. GEORGE W. HODGES, of Annapolis, has for some years been listing those marriages which are incidentally proved by references in the mass of county material filed in the Land Office. The State Legislature having previously authorized the acquisition of 10,000 references, has during the recent session provided for the inclusion in the budget of an appropriation for 10,000 more, their card-indexing, and, necessarily, the continuance of this invaluable work.

It gives the Editor the greatest pleasure to say that through the kind co-operation of Mrs. HODGES (above referred to) the COUNTY COURT NOTE-BOOK will in July, begin the publication of "MARYLAND'S NEXT OF KIN." The old law or custom which ruled the Deputy Commissary and the Probate Court, required that the two nearest of kin should sign each inventory. It is unnecessary to say here how valuable this material is.

It is regretted that these lists cannot be alphabetized, to do so would greatly delay their publication. At some future time the material will be re-issued in book form, suitably arranged or indexed.

PRINCE WILLIAM, VA., BONDS.

Allan Macrae; John Lee, Thomas Lawson, extrs.; Wm. Carr, Thomas Blackburn, sec. 1 Dec. 1766.

James Douglass, Gent.; Wm. Carr, Alex. Henderson, John Riddle, extrs.; Robert Brent, Thomas Lawson, sec. 1 Dec. 1766.

George Harper; Betty Harper, extx.; Richard Evans, Wm. Carr, sec. 1 Dec. 1766.

Thomas Thornton; Lettice Thornton, extr.; John Peyton, Cuthbert Bullett, sec. 7 Dec. 1767.

William Foster; Wm. Foster, extr.; James Bridges, Alex. Davidson, Wm. Wyatt, sec. 7 Dec. 1767.

Richard Wright; Mary Ann Wright [sig. Maryan], Wm. Wright, Joseph Wright, extrs.; Wm. Moore, Jeremiah Moore, sec. 7 Dec. 1767.

Edward Gwatkins; John Gwatkins, James Gwatkins, extrs.; Wm. Bennett, Geo. Calvert, sec. 8 Dec. 1767.

John Renoe; Lewis Reno, Elender Reno, extrs.; Lynaugh Helm, John Graham, sec 10 Mch. 1768.

Robert Foster; Sarah Foster, extx.; Wm. Davis [sig.] Wm. Foster, Thos. Leachman, sec. 2 May 1768.

William Triplett; James Triplett, extr.; Foushee Tebbs, sec. 1 Aug. 1768.

John Gwatkin; James Gwatkin, Wm. Moore, extrs.; Wm. Moore, Geo. Bigbie, Simon Luttrell, sec. 5 Sept. 1768.

William White; Ann White, extx.; Wm. Carr, Thos. Moss, Wm. Finch, sec. 3 Oct. 1768.

Joseph Kelley; Esther Kelley, extx.; Hugh Brent, John Matison, sec. 3 Oct. 1768.

John Dalton; Rachel Dalton, James Dalton, extrs.; Wm. Carr and Wm. Bennett, sec. 7 Nov. 1768.

Thomas Arrington; Peggy x Arrington, extx.; James x Johnson, sec. 7 Mch. 1769.

Samuel Stone; Sarah Stone, extx.; Isaac Davis, sec. 3 July 1769.

Elizabeth Bridges English; John Bridges, extr.; James Bridges, sec. 2 Oct. 1769.

Thomas Reno; Lewis Reno, Jr., extr.; Wm. Davis, Valentine Clevinger, sec. 2 Oct. 1769.

Margaret Helm; Lynaugh Helm, John Moffett, extrs.; Wm. Alexander, sec. 2 Oct. 1769.

Thomas Thornton; Charles Thornton, extr.; Thomas Attwell, Hugh Brent, sec. 5 Mch. 1770.

Benjamin Wilkinson; Elizabeth Wilkinson, extx.; Thomas Lawson, Henry Lee, sec. 7 Mch. 1770.

Susannah Cooper; John x Smith, extr.; Giles Carter, sec. 7 Jany. 1771.

Cuthbert McMillian; John McMillian, extr.; Cuthbert McMillian, Gent., sec. 6 May 1771.

Robert Foster; Wm. Foster, extr.; John Hooe, sec. 4 June 1771.

Daniel Marr; Daniel Bradford, extr.; Cuthbert Bullitt, sec. 1 July 1771.

John Cook; Evan Williams, Elizabeth Cook, extrs.; Wm. Cocke [sic.] Wm. Grayson Israel Folsom, Chas. Adams, sec. 5 Aug. 1771.

Normand Drummond; Thos. Harrison, Jr., George Florence, Jr., extrs., Cuthbert Harrison, Wm. Purcell, sec. 2 Sept. 1771.

George Calvert; Obed Calvert, Thos. Stone, Esther Calvert, extrs.; Foushee Tebbs, Thomas Blackburn, sec. 2 Dec. 1771.

William Ashmore; Betty Ashmore, extx.; Francis Triplett, Chas. Gallahue, sec. 2 Dec. 1771.

Israel Folsom; Kesia Folsom, extx.; Daniel Kincheloe, Charles Adams, Wm. Davis, Hubbard Prine (?) sec. 2 Mch. 1772.

James Tebbs; Mary Tebbs, extr.; Wm. Grayson, Thos. Chapman, sec. 4 May 1772.

Lydia Byrn; Wm. Brown, extr.; John Hooe, Anthony Seal, sec. 5 May 1772.

Jacob Calvert; Sarah /x Calvert, Francis Calvert, extrs.; Wm. Farrow, George Colvert (Deep Hole [Farm]) sec. 1 June 1772.

(To be continued.)

NOTES AND QUERIES.

TAUL: ARTHUR THOMAS TAUL m. MARY ANN JOHNSON in Montgomery Co., Md. His will was probated in 1812, in Clark (formerly Fayette) Co., Ky. Wanted: the date of marriage, also the names of his parents. B. T. C. Ky.

MAYHEW:- Wanted: any information as to Capt. HILLIARD MAYHEW of New Bedford, Mass., especially the name of his first wife, and date of marriage, also the name of his mother, and date of the marriage of his parents. [Note: The Mayhew "Tree" gives no wives.] Mrs. V. N-C.

GODWIN: Who was THOMAS GODWIN, whose wife was Ann, who administered his estate about ten years before *Col.* THOMAS GODWIN died. Both of ISLE OF WIGHT Co., Va. Col. Thomas died about 1676. M. M. H. V.

FLOYD-DAVIS: Wanted the record of the marriage of WILLIAM FLOYD of Amherst Co., Va., and ABADIAH DAVIS. This marriage took place some time prior to 1750. Date given as 1747, but no authority. P. S. C.

WANTED: Any SAUL or SOLL ROBINSON born *circa* 1730 or 1735, New England, New York, New Jersey, Delaware, or Pennsylvania. Will gladly reciprocate in kind. Address the Editor.

ROBINSON-WADE: The marriage record of SAUL or SOLL ROBINSON, and MIRIAM WADE, both of Chester County, Pa., is wanted. A reasonable amount will be paid. This record is possibly in some WADE or PHILLIPS family. Address the Editor.

WANTED: Five dollars will be paid for information, with proof, concerning the parentage of SAMUEL WEBB, who m. JANE WYRE (WEIR) at Christ Church, Philadelphia, 21 Oct. 1731. Information is also desired as to GEORGE WEIR, of Chester Co., Pa., the father of JANE WYRE (WEIR). WEBB removed to Harford Co., Md., before 1740. J. B. T.

WOODWARD: Wanted the parentage of AMON WOODWARD, b. Prince Georges Co., Md., 1793. Officer, War 1812; m. (1) Sarah Martin; (2) Barbara Lowe. F. B. C. M.

MUSGROVE: Who was the wife of WILLIAM MUSGROVE of Loudoun Co., Va.? Who was the wife of GILBERT SIMPSON? Dates 1777 and prior. V. M. H. M.

GIBSON: Wanted the record of the death of ANDREW GIBSON, who was in Winchester, Virginia, in 1795, and went to Georgia. S. G. G. W. V.

$5.00 REWARD: JAMES STEELE came from England about 1788, and afterwards lived in Pittsburgh. He m. —— PORTER, of Virginia. Had one child, Robert P. Steele, b. 1791. Ancestry wanted of James Steele's wife. F. B. L. N. Y.

$5.00 REWARD for proof of ancestry of SARAH REED, of Virginia, b. 1770; m. (1) —— KEMP, said to have had plantation near James River. Daus. Belinda and Caroline. Married (2) THOMAS HARTLEY, said to have been Kemp's partner. Chn. (Robert H., Martha S., James Reed; William T., Janes, and Sarah Reed.) HARTLEYS lived for a time in Pittsburgh. Sarah Reed said to have been connected with Washingtons. F. B. L. N. Y.

CAIN: Information wanted of GEORGE CATHEY CAIN, b. North Carolina, 15 Apr. 1813; probably son of ROBERT CAIN, whose wife was perhaps b. HOOKER or MAXWELL. C. A. B. C.

CARR-COLE: Would like any clue to ancestry of RACHEL CARR, supposed dau. of JOHN and ELIZABETH (WHITE) CARR. She m. AQUILA COLE of Frankfort, Ky. C. A. B. C.

COLE: AQUILA COLE lived near Frankfort, Ky., about 1800; was son of SALATHIEL and grandson of THOMAS COLE, of Va., or Penna. The COLES came to Kentucky with BOONES, or shortly after. Any information appreciated. C. A. B. C.

ZACHARY: What was the maiden name of wife of PETER ZACHARY, and date of marriage? Caroline Co., Va. M. L. H. C.

FINLEY: JAMES FINLEY, son of JOHN FINLEY and MARTHA BERKLEY, his wife, served with South Carolina Revolutionary troops. Wanted: his residence in South Carolina and place of death in Virginia. Mrs. C. S. P.

DAWKINS: WILLIAM DAWKINS died Georgia, 1800. Married CYNTHIA ——. Information wanted as to his and his wife's family. M. L. H. G.

TAYLOR: Did ZACHARY TAYLOR, Caroline Co., Va., get his name from the ZACHARY family? M. L. H. G.

ENBANK-EWBANKS: THOMAS EUBANK d. Talbott Co., Md., 1732. Wanted: names of his parents and further information concerning THOMAS. Wife was MARTHA. What was her maiden name? K. D. S. A.

SHANKLIN: THOMAS, ROBERT, JOHN, EDWARD (brothers), were in Augusta Co., Va., 1745-1776. What were the parents' names and where did the brothers remove from (to Virginia)? K. D. S. A.

HASKINS-WOMACK: REBECCA HASKINS and BYRD WOMACK, of Virginia, were married 1800. Who were their parents? Mrs. T. A. A.

FENWICK COLONY, N. J. ELIZABETH DIXON, wife of WILLIAM DIXON, of Talbot Co., Md., sister of John Gary, of The Cliffs, Calvert Co., Md., bequeathes to her eldest son, JOHN HARWOOD, (son of Robert Harwood her first husband) "all that tract or parcel of land in Fenwick Collony in Ned Jersey, being in quantity 800 a. . . . . which my brother JOHN GARY bought of THOMAS HUTCHINSON of Beverly, Tanner." He is to have the land "out of all that two thousand acres of land which the said HUTCHINSON bought of JOHN FENWICK." (From a record of the S. L. O. Annap., 30 Oct. 1696.) WANTED: information as to JOHN GARY'S connection with FENWICK COLONY prior to his settlement in Calvert Co., Md., M. R. H. M.

BOOK NOTES.

The HILLS OF WILKES COUNTY, GEORGIA, and ALLIED FAMILIES. Compiled by LODOWICK JOHNSON HILL, Sr., of Atlanta, Georgia. (John-Dallis Company, Publishers.)

The Editor has received from the publishers this very interesting and well-gotten up volume. It is a mine of information; so generous in its scope that it will interest many people who are not kin or even "Virginia cousins" to the HILLS. It is a book that one can read, and the lack of unproved and controversional assertion increases the reader's respect for the ability of the compiler.

The volume includes data concerning thirty-one families; among them the Calhouns, the Jordans, the Popes, Lanes, Lewises and Lipscombs.

KITH AND KIN. An unusually interesting volume under this name will soon be published by Mrs. John Russell Sampson, 3505 Brook Road, Richmond, Virginia. "It "will contain a full account of the settlement in America of each family, and some "mention of their background across the "Atlantic; of persecutions and escapes; of "Colonial and Revolutionary service; of "Indian captures and rescues; of romances "and run-away marriages; of some Royal "Descents; of service in Legislatures and "Congress and a list of 300 names (with "each pedigree) in the ministry, ministers, "wives of Ministers and Missionaries." Seventy-four families are mentioned. Among these the Editor notes familiar Pennsylvania stock.

Attention is invited to a small Quarterly which has appeared in an historical field where every such beginning should be most strongly encouraged.

Mr. FOLKS HUXFORD, of Homerville, Georgia, has begun the publication of the SOUTH GEORGIA HISTORICAL and GENEALOGICAL QUARTERLY, the first number of which was issued in January last. Mr. Huxford cannot be too highly commended for his effort to preserve the history and the tradition of his section, and to give it out in such a form that it may be available to many, and be added to, enlarged upon and preserved in quarters where such material is appreciated.

Mr. Huxford promises that very useful section of a periodical of this kind, a department of Notes and Queries.

GENERAL INFORMATION.

Visitors to STAFFORD C. H., Va., would do well to write the Postmaster, Mr. E. S. Moore, for information as to a place to stay. Mr. Moore is a very helpful official.

Any person interested in the early records of STAFFORD, KING GEORGE, LANCASTER, NORTHUMBERLAND, MIDDLESEX or WESTMORELAND counties, VIRGINIA, and desiring careful, detailed search, may join in a very simple, co-operative plan by addressing the Editor of the COUNTY COURT NOTE-BOOK.

Twenty-five cents each will be paid for ten copies of the October, and ten copies of the December NOTE-BOOK.—Editor.

ACME PRINTING CO., INC., 708 13th Street N. W., Washington, D. C.

The

County Court Note-Book

A Little Bulletin of History and Genealogy.

Vol. I. **July, 1922.** **No. 5.**

MARYLAND'S NEXT OF KIN *

(*From inventories at the State Land Office, Annapolis, Md.*)

THOMAS DORSETT; inv. John Dorsett, Pr. Geo's Co. 25 June 1718. i-v.

MARY and SAMUEL CHENEY; inv. Rich'd Cheney, A. A. Co. 8 July 1718. i-17.

Capt. CHARLES WHITEHEAD; inv. Col. John Thomas of Balto. Co. 13 Mch. 1718. i-19.

JOSEPH PAGE; inv. Wm. Robinson, Balto. Co., 1718. i-21.

ELINOR and JOHN MARTIN; inv. John Martin, Balto. Co. 23 June 1718. i-25.

JOHN YATE, brother; inv. George Yate, Balto. Co. 10 June 1718. i-27.

JOHN POWELL; inv. George Powell, Q. A. Co. 17 Jan. 1717. i-31.

ALICE RICH, HENRY OLDSUM, HENRY WILLIAMS; inv. Henry Williams, Q. A. Co. [1717.] i-35.

WILLIAM WRENCH, WILLIAM WRENCH; inv. Robert Farrah, Q. A. Co. 1718. i-38.

T. T. GREENFIELD; inv. John Hanes, St. Marys Co. 15 May 1718. i-39.

JOSHUA DORSEY, JOHN DORSEY, son of E. DORSEY; inv. Nicholas Dorsey, Balto. Co. 4 July 1718. i-40.

RICHARD WOOTTERS; SARAH WOOTTERS; inv. John Wooters, Q. A. Co. 1718. i-43.

THOMAS WELSH; inv. John Kelly, Q. A. Co. 20 Dec. 1717. i-45.

FRANCES LOWE; BARBARY HIDDON; inv. John Miller, St. Marys Co. 22 Feby 1717. i-49.

TOBIAS and TIMOTHY TOLLE; inv. John Grant, St. Marys Co. 12 May 1718. i-50.

DANIEL St. THOMAS JENIFER and HENRY LOWE; inv. John Silence, St. Marys Co. 11 Mch. 1717-18. i-51.

THOMAS MORRIS, "a relation"; inv. Nathaniel Freman, Chas. Co. 18 Dec. 1717. i-60.

GEORGE and RICHARD BRETT; inv. Martha Booker, Chas. Co. 23 Apr. 1718 i-65.

HENRY BRITT and SARAH BRITT; inv. William Brett, Chas. Co. 10 Apr. 1718. i-71.

JOHN PARRY; inv. Andrew Norton, mcht. Chas. Co. 24 Mch. 1717-18. i-73.

WILLIAM SMITH; inv. 'William Smith, Chas. Co. 10 June 1718. i-75.

CATHERINE BOTELER; inv. Ann Lingan, Calvert Co. 4 June 1718. i-83.

PHIL. HOSKINS and ROBERT HANSON; inv. Mary Hoskins, Chas. Co. 16 June 1718. i-90.

MAGNE KING; inv. George Siddall, Dor. Co. 14 Nov. 1718. i-93.

JOHN HUCHESON, aged 23 yrs., "son of deceased"; inv. Mr. John Hucheson. 18 Mch. 1717. i-101. [County not stated.]

WILLIAM HAWKINS and JOHN GRAY; inv. Stephen White, Balto. Co. 6 Mch. 1717. i-103.

ALEXANDER HEATHMAN; St. Mary's Co. 25 Feby. 1717. "No kindred here but his children." i-104.

JEREMIAH HARRIS approved inv. of Thomas Pritchett of Smiths Island, Som. Co. 1717-18. i-107.

JOHN COBB; inv. Samuell Cobb, Som. Co. 9 Nov. 1717. i-108.

JOHN McCLESTER approves inv. Margaret McClester, Stepney Psh., Som. Co. 27 June 1717-18. i-108.

MICHAEL ROBSON; inv. Isaac Ironshear, Som. Co., 1717-18. i-110.

JOSEPH ALFORD; inv. John Halpen, Dor. Co. 27 Jan. 1717. i-112.

WILLIAM MURRAH, Dor. Co. 1717-18. "No kindred in ye country." i-113.

MARY MILLMAN; inv. Thomas Millman, Dor. Co. 18 Jan. 1717. i-114.

JOHN and JAMES NOELL; inv. Septimus Noell, Talb. Co. 28 May 1717. i-115.

THOMAS and MARY ROYALL; inv. Manass Morris, Dor. Co. 10 Aug. 1717. i-120.

JOHN DAWSON, JOHN TOMPSON, EDWARD NEWTON, "allow this appraisement as being nearest in kin"; inv. Joseph Thompson, Dor. Co. 23 Feb. 1717. i-121.

EZEKIELL GREENE and JAMES INGLISH; inv. Matthew Neal; Dor. Co. 21 Feb. 1717-18. i-122.

WALTER TATCHYORN and RICHARD BUSICK; inv. Harmon Peterson, Dor. Co. 27 Nov. 1717. i-124.

ELIZABETH ALFORD and RACHEL ALFORD; inv. Cecily Bourks, Dor. Co. 30 Nov. 1717. i-126.

SOLOMON and MARGARET BRYAN; inv. Jeane Tales, Talb. Co. 6 Aug. 1715. i-128.

ROBERT and CHARLES PAUL; inv. Charles Paul, Dor. Co. 19 June 1717. i-129.

EDWARD BILLETON, JOHN TOMLINSON; inv. William Wetherell, Dor. Co. 3 Feb. 1717. i-131.

MARY FISHER and THOMAS VICKERS; inv. John Vicars, Dor. Co. 22 Feb. 1717. i-132.

GEORGE STAPLE and WILLIAM TAYLOR; inv. Dorothy Taylor, Dor. Co. 20 June 1717. i-134.

HENRY LEAKE; inv. Robert Lake, Dor. Co. 30 Nov. 1717. i-135.

RICHARD PEARSON, Sen.; JOSEPH MERCHANT; inv. Alexander Wall, Dor. Co. 28 Sept. 1717. i-136.

GEORGE DASHSELL and CHARLES BALLARD; inv. Alexander Knox, Som. Co. 29 June 1717. i-137.

CHARLES UNGLE and PHIL. FEDDEMAN; inv. Henry Beckworth, Sen., Dor. Co. 16 Jan. 1717. i-143.

(To be continued.)

MARRIAGES BY INFERENCE *

(The first twenty marriages are from the records of NEW NORFOLK and LOWER NORFOLK counties, Virginia. NEW NORFOLK was formed in 1636 from ELIZABETH CITY county. LOWER NORFOLK county was formed in 1637. It covered what is now PRINCESS ANNE, and for the year 1636, NEW NORFOLK included what is now NANSEMOND. For convenience the name NEW NORFOLK, which was in use but a short time, has not been used. After 1691, when the county was again divided, its name became NORFOLK.

The records of LOWER NORFOLK county, among the earliest in the country, are, with the exception of one volume of NORTHAMPTON records, the most difficult to read of any in Virginia. Not only are the early scribes' hands frequently undecipherable except after long study, but the records themselves, through exposure to damp and generations of careless usage, are in a very bad condition. Thanks to the new swamp land interests of the county, one volume has been repaired to an extent, and another is promised to be....too late, however, to replace important historical and genealogical material now gone forever.)

Mr. JOHN MARTIN and GRACE DIER, relict of John; (she renounces her husband's will and "flies to her thirds"). D-257, about 14 Mch. 1659.

JOHN BRAY and JEANNE BEASELEY, widow. Banns set up. D-524. 14 Mch. 1659.

ROGER HAYWARD and KATHERINE REINS (REYNE) widow of John; about 17 Dec. 1660. D-266, D-272.

JOHN LAWRENCE and the widow of John STRATTON; before Oct. 1659. D-224 (She was also the widow of Theo. Carson.)

THOMAS BRIDGES and the relict of Mr. Geo. BATEMAN. D-271. Before 17 Dec. 1660. (She was also the relict of John HOLMES. D.-282.)

Mr. GEORGE COLEBOUGH (COLELOUGH?) and the widow of Mr. Symon OVERZEE; before 18 June 1661. D-305.

Coll. LAMBARD and DOROTHY MASON sett up their names at the C. H. doore....first publication of banns, about 23 May 1661. D-301.

THOMAS LOWELL and the relict and extx. of Thomas HORN; before 18 June 1661. D-308.

PLOMER BRAY and the relict and admx. of Simon BARROWES; before 5 Nov. 1660. D-266. (The widow's name was MARY; see D312.)

Mr. WALTER BREWER and the widow of Mr. Thomas SAYRES; before 15 Feb. 1659. D-243.

JOHN MANING and LIDIA RICHARDSON, "banns set up at Court doore"; 16 Apr 1660. D-253.

RICHARD CHURCH and MARY SAWYER, dau. of Thomas; before 15 June 1666. E-3.

JOHN OKEHAM and the relict of Mr. John MARTIN; before 15 Oct. 1666. E-8.

MORIS FITZGARRELL and the relict of Roger HOWARD; before 15 June 1669. E-33.

JOHN SWAYNE and MARY WISE, widow of Nicholas; about 17 Jan. 1669. E-43.

JAMES BROWNE and the relict and extx. of Capt. Thos. BROWNE; before 15 Feb. 1670-71. E-59.

JOHN FERREBY and the relict of William ELLIS; before 15 April 1671. E-61.

MOSES LINTON, Jr., and the relict of John MARTIN; about 15 Apr. 1671.

WILLIAM SIMPSON and the relict and admx. of James JACKSON; before 15 June 1671. E-64.

THOMAS ENDRIDGE, Jr., and the relict of John BRIGHT; before 16 June 1671. E-66.

JAMES HOMEY and MARGARET DIXON, of St. Stephen's Psh., King and Queen Co. K. Wm. "14"-423; before 20 May 1704.

WILLIAM TALIAFERO and MARY PENNINGTON HICKMAN, dau. of John and [Martha]; before 20 Nov. 1794. K. Wm. "11"-405.

JOHN KING and NANCY DABNEY; mar. contract; about July Court, 1796. K. Wm. "11"-342.

JOHN ROSE (of Amherst) and CATHARINE ROSE; before 27 Feb. 1797. K. Wm. "1"-328.

JOSEPH HILLYARD and ANN HILL, dau. of John Hill, Gent.; before 1 Apr. 1797. K. Wm. "1"-195.

JOSEPH GWATHMEY and MARY HILL, dau. of John Hill, Gent.; before 1 Apr. 1797; K. Wm. "1"-195.

THOMAS HODGE (of Westmoreland Co.) and MARY ROSE; before 27 Feb. 1797; K. Wm. "11"-328. [HODGE dec'd at this date.]

LEONARD TUNSTALL and MARY CAMIN (?) GARLICK, dau. of Camin (?) Garlick; before 1 Mch. 1799; K. Wm. "3"-235.

JAMES JONES (of King and Queen) and JANE SLAUGHTER; before 17 Mch. 1800; K. Wm. "13"-493.

WILLIAM TANDY BURRUS (of Orange) and MARTHA SLAUGHTER; before 17 Mch. 1800; K. Wm. "13"-493.

WHARTON QUARLES and MOURNING SLAUGHTER; before 17 Mch. 1800; K. Wm. "13"-493.

SAMUEL MEREDITH and ELIZABETH SLAUGHTER; before 17 Mch. 1800; K. Wm. "13"-493.

AMBROSE EDWARDS, Junr., and ANN SLAUGHTER; before 17 Mch. 1800; K. Wm. "13"-493.

JOHN DREWRY and SARAH SLAUGHTER; before 17 Mch. 1800; K. Wm. "13"-493.

WILLIAM RICHARDSON and ANN ABBETT; before 17 Jan. 1814; K. Wm. "15"-317.

CHARLES HILL BRAXTON and BETSY POPE GRYMES; before 7 May 1814; K. Wm. "15"-343.

ANDREW WADE and ANN HENRY RICHARDSON; dau. of Ann Richardson wf. of Wm. Richardson; before 17 Jan. 1814; K. Wm. "15"-317.

FRANCIS W. RICHESON and ELIZABETH RAGSDALE, dau. of DRURY and BARBARA; before 2 Jan. 1815; K. Wm. "15"-277.

JOHN HUXTER DRURY and MARY WILSON REINS, dau. of Robert; before 16 Apr. 1816; K. Wm. "15"-198.

ROBERT C. WASLEY and ANN B. MITVHELL, dau. of James; before 1 Sept. 1817; K. Wm. "11."

RICHARD GIBSON and the widow of Thos. HOLMES; before 12 June 1690; Staff Orders i-65.

THOMAS WATTS and FRANCES NORGRAVE, dau. of Capt. John Norgrave; before 7 Apr. 1670; Staff Orders i-43.

(To be continued.)

THE WEBBS

(Continued from May number.)

RICHARD WEBB, a h. r. under Moseley and Hull, Rappa. Co., Va. L. O. 1-229. 1662.

RICHARD WEBB, h. r. under Wm. Perrie, Rappa. Co., Va. L. O. v-154. 1 June 1663.

RICHARD WEBB h. r. under Thos. Sherwood, who had 880 a., n. side Carolina Riv. No county mentioned. Va. L. O. v- . . . 25 Sept. 1663.

RICHARD WEBB, h. r. under John Bruerton (?), in Westmoreland Co., Va. L. O. 389. 1664.

RICHARD WEBB was a pltr. in New Haven Colony. He d. 1665. . . .

RICHARD WEBB, h. r. under Moses Davis and Thos. Biggins. New Kent. Co., Va. L. O. v-416. 1665.

RICHARD WEBB, h. r. under Henry Smith. Acco., Va. iii-36. 16 Aug. 1667.

RICHARD WEBB, svt. of Henry Smith, died. Acco. iii-106. 4 Feby. 1668.

RICHARD WEBB, of Calvert Co., Md., to Thomas Wall. Refers to grant, 20 Aug. 1668, to RICHARD WEBB, of land in Little Choptank Riv., on Fishing Creek. . . . being 100 a. called *SNAKE POINT*. Wit. Daniel Clarke and Edward Sauvage. Dor. Co., Md., T-79. 28 Oct. 1669.

RICHARD WEBB, svt. to Mr. Edward Revell, age 17. Acco., Va. iii-190. 8 Apr. 1670.

RICHARD WEBB mar. Elizabeth [Parrot] His chn. were Mary, b. 1670; Richard, b. 1673; John, b. 1676; Elizabeth, b. 1677. Tred Avon Mtg. Rec'ds. Md. iv-133.

RICHARD WEBB mar. Mary Jeferies. Son Richard b. 5 Feby. 1672. Som. Co., Md. Records. vol. D. B., I. K. L. p. 276.

RICHARD WEBB, of Talbot Co., Md. Will. Legacies to Sarah Young, Elizabeth Young, Wm. Young, chn. of Wm. Young. *Midel* Plantation mentioned. John Sergeant, Wm. Clearsmon, Francisco Ferdinando Goyer, John Sergeant's wf., mentioned. Wm. Young extr. Wit: Goyer, Cheasmon (?), Sergent. Annap. Wills, vol. 8, 9, 10. p. 22 of 10. 4 Sept. 1678, 18 Jany. 1678, 18 Feby. 1678-9.

RICHARD WEBB had 200 a. Som. Co., Md. Surveyed 1683; called *Mortilack* (Mattapony hd).

RICHARD WEBB; his conveyance of 100 a. to Richard Gadsby ref. to in deed by Richard Reynolds and wf. Elizabeth. I. W., Va. iv-216. 9 Feby 1685-6.

(To be continued.)

The County Court Note-Book

An every-other-monthly devoted to abstracts from the County Court and other records, prior to 1800, and with a department of notes and queries.

MILNOR LJUNGSTEDT, Editor and Publisher. Bethesda, Route 1, Maryland.

Published every other month. Subscription, one dollar a year, in advance.

Vol. I. July, 1922. No. 5

"YET THE DEAD ARE THERE"

The NORTHERN METHODIST CEMETERY at LEESBURG, VIRGINIA, that is to say, the burial-ground that surrounded the church of that denomination (now taken down), as the Editor saw it some years ago was a sad and sorry place. One fine table tomb covered a gaping hole where the masonry of the tomb had fallen in. Other stones were partly hid in weeds and trash; the spot was unfenced and open to all manner of abominations. But the worst and most shocking condition was the location of a chicken yard on a part of the actual churchyard. Here the old headstones and the chicken coops neighbored each other, shoulder to shoulder, and the hens and their flocks scratched above forgotten dust . . . forgotten to their descendants, but with names and dates still preserved in the faithful stone.

Part of the church land had been sold, it seems, to a buyer who built his house nearby and enclosed a number of the graves in his chicken "park."

* * * * *

Turning from LEESBURG, the writer recalls but one other visit to a neglected VIRGINIA cemetery, and that one in ORANGE, she believes. The sight of neglected and desecrated tombs is painful anywhere, but especially so in the negihborhood of a church, in an old county, where tradition still lives, and where the children of the county have peopled many States.

Many are the family burial places of VIRGINIA which are, if not absolutely lost, but mere tangles of briar, honeysuckle, wild rose and poison oak; tramped over by cattle, rooted by hogs, and handy shelters for chickens and wandering dogs.

In the County of ISLE of WIGHT, in the corner of the field on which the Clerk's Office stands, is the grave of a Revolutionary officer. The present owner ploughs about it, perhaps he burns the brush occasionally; in time the site will be lost.

On the Eastern Shore of VIRGINIA are the graves of one of our foremost early families. Near the site of Arlington, a few miles below Cape Charles City, the Colonial Dames have rebuilt two tombs. They left them with a slight wire enclosure. That is now broken down, and plain traces of hogs and cattle are to be found in the surrounding weeds and brush.

The family buried here have two other known burial places. One of these is at Wilsonia Neck. Here there was a fine table tomb, with a long inscription. Shortly before the writer's visit the slab had slipped off the supporting legs and was lying on the ground. A tree had apparently grown up through one bricked-in tomb, carrying up with it portions of the mason work. As in other places a hog-pen bordered the plot on one side.

The burial plot of the same family at Deep Creek is enclosed in an iron fence, but the gate cannot be closed, and only a part of the stones can be found on account of the growth of vines and brush and trees.

Another of the old families . . . one of the oldest in America . . . lies in another forlorn and neglected spot, the stones lying at angles upon the ground, and the place overgrown and inaccessible. In this case the Editor is informed that the owners will not sell the fifty-foot square to the descendants, who now live in a northern city, the fifty-foot square which holds their lineal ancestry, and so . . . nothing is done.

* * * * *

If all this is sad to the sentimentalist, how is it when a city of the size of CHESTER, Pennsylvania, allows an old churchyard to fall into a condition of squalor which it is difficult to justly describe. Worn-out baby carriages and sick chickens about graves which still put up some show of dignity in their iron railings and stones, and which are on the property of an active church organization, and, furthermore, are but a few hundred yards from a sacred circle which it has been proposed to draw about the early Colonial centre . . . the spot where the eminent ancestor of a prominent present-day litterateur and historian took his official seat, on ground which belonged at one time to the family of this Editor.

It is really unbelievable, and the Editor recalls the pathetic earnestness with which a Deaconess of the Church (which is Episcopal), begged that some statement of these conditions might be sent out.

It seems strange that men who honor Chester for the memory of WILLIAM PENN and their own forbears, should not have a present civic pride in its condition.

The Editor is "doing her bit."

* * * * *

Four other cemeteries in the same State should be touched upon, but there is not room in this present issue of THE NOTE-BOOK.

The Editor had read with great pleasure the statement that the County Commissioners of FREDERICK COUNTY, VIRGINIA, have finally decided to have the old marriage register copied. The Clerk is to be congratulated on putting this through. It is regrettably too late to save certain illegible margins, but the missing names or parts of names can usually be found in an old church register, which is now in private hands. Further information may be had from the Editor.

The COUNTY COURT NOTE-BOOK will begin in SEPTEMBER the publication of an extremely valuable list of names from the earliest legislation of MARYLAND. This will be a list of persons naturalized, by particular acts from about the year 1670 and on.

This list has been compiled by Mrs. George W. Hodges, of the Baltimore Chapter, D. A. R., who has most generously given the Editor permission to make use of her notes.

It is probable that this material, as well as the NEXT OF KIN will be alphabetized and republished later. At present it seems advisable to give both lists without arrangement rather than delay them indefinitely.

The Editor turns sadly to record the passing over of one of the few of the Clerks of the old school now left in Virginia.

Mr. Albert Sterling Edwards, for fifty-two years the Clerk of SURRY county, Virginia, died on the 31st of May. Mr. Edwards was most unusual in his love for and his care of his records. He peculiarly felt that they were *his* records, and this fact sometimes brought him into a "difference" with his visitors. But any one who knew him well, who had heard him say as he did to this writer: "I love my books . . . why, they . . . talk to me," would understand his jealousy for his ancient volumes.

Mr. Edwards told this writer that when he first came to the office the absolutely priceless old volumes were piled on a brick floor in the corner of the old Clerk's Office, now used as a Confederate Museum. The damage done then can never be repaired, but most of the records are intact, or have been carefully copied, and two of the old volumes still bear on their beautiful covers the embossed arms of England.

Mr. Edwards' death was, no doubt, hastened by the recent burning of the Courthouse Fortunately the records were in a small but secure fireproof room.

ERRATA in May number: The last line of the last item on page 3, of the MAY number, should give this reference: Staff., Va., P-157, 23 July 1757.

On page 1, third item, the name CARSKEY should be CARSLEY.

OCCASIONAL

Capt. GEO. NICH. HACK "petitions that he hath omitted by inadvertence to set down the ages of his children by which means the certain ages of his children could not be known." [Capt. Hack omitted his son Spencer from his list of tithables.] Acco. x-221. 5 Feb. 1696.

The question of brick: JAMES HUMPHERY deposes that "He durst not put bricks in the *Quicksillver* [which appeared to have been a small boat used between the vessel and the shore], notwithstanding wee had a great many to unload for fear Mr. Parker would be angry for twas not his bargain to put anything in her but accomadacion for himself & his Company." Acco. viii-65. 17 Mch. 1678.

PRINCE WILLIAM, VA., BONDS

(Continued from May number.)

Lydia Byrn; George Ash, one of the extrs.; Jesse Efell and Thomas Bird, sec. 6 July 1772.

Joseph Smith; Jane Smith, extx.; Charles Stuart, Vester x Moss, sec. 5 Oct. 1772.

James Carberry; Jas. Gwatkin, extr.; Francis Jackson and Hugh Brent, sec. 1 Feb. 1773.

Wm. Parsons, Senr.; Lydia Parsons, extx.; Josphua Ratcliff, Elijah Wood, sec. 2 Aug. 1773.

Samuel King; James King, extr.; Thomas Bland, John Dowell, sec. 4 Oct. 1773.

George Reeve; Asa x Reeve, extr.; John Hooe, John x Reeve, sec. 7 Feb. 1774.

Christopher Linch; Mary x Linch, extx.; Robert Lawson, sec. 5 Sept. 1774.

Lewis Reno; Lewis Reno, Thomas Reno and David Reno, extrs. John McMillian, sec. 3 Oct. 1774.

John Peyton; Seth, Valentine and John Peyton, extrs.; John Linton, John Brett, Timothy Peyton, sec. 7 Nov. 1774.

Thos. Falner; John Hooe, extr.; Howson Hooe, sec. 7 Nov. 1774. [The next form is not filled out as to decedent or extr.] Daniel Barnet, Jacob Marshall and James Foley give bond.

Wm. Hornbuckle; Solomon Hornbuckle, extr.; Wm. Lindsay, sec. 7 Mch. 1775.

Elizabeth Highlander; Wm. Carter and John Higgerson, extrs.; Jas. Grimstead, John Earls, sec. 3 Apr. 1775.

Henry Whiting; Humphrey-Frances-Ann-Whiting, extx. [sig. is *H. Frances Whiting*]; Mathew Whiting, sec. 2 Oct. 1775.

Mary O'Brian; John Gunyon, extr.; Jesse Ewell, sec. 8 Nov. 1775.

Samuel Jones; Wm. Alexander, James Gwatkin, extrs.; Cuthbert Harrison, sec. 6 May 1776.

James Calk; William Calk, extr.; James Grimstead, Joshua Bott, sec. 5 Aug. 1776.

Mary Cannon; Valentine Peyton, extr.; John Brett, sec. 7 Oct. 1776.

William Milton, Jr.; Fanny Milton, extx.; Scarlet Maden, John See Wright, Jr., sec. 1 Sept. 1777.

Charles Gallahue; John McQuillian, extr.; John Murray, sec. 1 Sept. 1777.

Thomas Newman; Elizabeth x and Thomas Newman, extrs.; Alexander Brown, sec. 6 Oct. 1777.

Joshua Owens; John and Elizabeth Owens, extrs.; John Linton and John Simms, sec. 6 Oct. 1777.

Jacob Foley; Mary x Foley, extr.; John Simms, Benj. Cooper, sec. 6 Oct. 1777.

Benjamin Carpenter; Sarah x Carpenter, extx.; Samuel x Bryn, Benj. x Cooper, sec. 6 Oct. 1777.

Jonathan Hoof; Mary x Hoof, extx.; Timothy Peyton, sec. 6 Apr. 1778.

Henry Hampton; Geo. Newman Brown; Wm. Hampton and Henry Hampton, extrs.; Hugh Brent, Robert Warren, Thomas Thornton, sec. 4 May 1778.

Charles Thornton; Robert Warren, extr.; Valentine Peyton, sec. 4 May 1778.

Henry Wilson; Henry Wilson and Benj. Wiginton, extrs.; Thos. Bland and Eli Cleveland, sec. 6 July 1778.

Caleb Smith; Sarah and James Smith, extrs.; Robert Warren, sec. 7 Sept. 1778.

Thomas Dagg; Wm. Powell, Jr., extr.; John Linton, sec. 8 Dec. 1778.

Thos. Hogan; Thos. Hogan, extr.; Geo. Greene, sec. 1 Mch. 1779.

Zephaniah Crook; Mary Haden x Crook, extx.; Anthony Whitehead, sec. 1 Mch. 1779.

Rob't Dale; Eliz'th Dale, Luke x Hanks and Robt. Warren, extrs.; Alex'r Keith and Robt Brown, sec. 30 May 1779.

Rich'd Foote; Margaret Foote, extx.; Lynaugh Helm and Wm. Alexander, sec. 3 May 1779.

William Foster; Thos. Leachman, extr.; Leonard Leachman and James Rose, sec. 5 July 1779.

George Reeve; Jane x Reeve and Wm. x Reeve, extrs.; Robt Warren, sec. 2 Aug 1779.

Francis Tennell; Margaret Tennell and Bernard Hooe, extrs.; Benj. Tennell, John Peyton, sec. 5 Oct. 1779.

Sam. Peachy; Ann Peachy, extx.; Thos. Lawson, sec. 7 Feb. 1780.

Cuthbert Harrison; Seth Harrison, Wm. Alexander, extrs.; Cuthbert Bullitt, Gent., sec. 7 Feb. 1780.

Jno. Hutchinson; Robt Hutchinson, extr.; Ben. Hutchinson, sec. 6 Mch. 1780.

John Cheshire; Sithe x Cheshire, extx.; John and Wm. Lynn, sec. [Date probably 6 Mch. 1780.]

Geo. Thomas; Eleanor x Thomas, extx.; Mark Matthew Mankin and Geo. Maddox, sec. 5 Feb. 1781.

Mary Foley; Benj'n x Cooper, extr.; Jas. Gwatkin, sec. 5 Mch. 1781.

Joshua Botts; Benj. Gaines, extr.; Joseph and Aaron Botts, sec. 5 Mch. 1781.

Mary Reeve; Thomas x Chapman, extr.; John Brett and Henry Peyton, sec. 5 Mch. 1781.

Henry Peyton, Gt.; James Ewell, extr.; Thomas Blackburn, sec. 6 Aug. 1781.

Henry Peyton, Gt.; John Peyton, Jr., an extr.; John McMillian, Alex. Keith, sec. [No date. The two bonds appear to refer to the same estate.]

(To be concluded.)

OUR ANCESTRAL RECORDS IN ENGLAND

(Mr. E. Dwelly, Fleet, England, has been good enough to answer the Editor's request for detailed information as to the form and matter of English records, by sending the following interesting statement as to one class of these records, but little known to the average American searcher. Each issue of THE NOTE-BOOK will contain a paragraph describing other records. This information coming at first-hand from an English authority, is of unusual value.)

BISHOP'S TRANSCRIPTS. From 1597 two copies of his register were to be made on Easter Day by every incumbent of a parish church; one to be sent to his Bishop, and one to the Archdeacon, so that should the original Register be destroyed or lost by any means there might still be two chances of the contents being preserved. As no fine was levied by the Order in Council which required these copies to be made, it was shamefully disregarded, and now, as a result, the Bishops' series are all very incomplete and the Archdeacons' practically non-existent. Very many of those which still survive, however (about two in every five), supply the years missing from the original Parish Registers, which, in many cases, may commence at any date from 1538, the correct commencement of the records, to 1750.

Gaps in English (and American) pedigrees can more often than is generally known, be filled in from these Transcripts.

Mr. Dwelly is making the first systematic attempt to copy and print them, and is now publishing or has published the Transcripts of the diocese of Wells, Somerset.

NOTES AND QUERIES

MAYHEW: Wanted any information as to Capt. HILLIARD MAYHEW of New Bedford, Mass., especially the name of his first wife, and date of marriage, also the name of his mother, and date of the marriage of his parents. [Note: The Mayhew "Tree" gives no wives.] Mrs. V. N-C.

GODWIN: Who was THOMAS GODWIN, whose wife was Ann, who administered his estate about ten years before *Col.* THOMAS GODWIN died. Both of ISLE OF WIGHT Co., Va. Col. Thomas died about 1676. M. M. H. V.

ROBINSON: A Robinson from Ireland, a widower, whose fore-name is unknown, came to New York about 1781, with two young sons, one of them but a few months old, named CORNELIUS. The father married again soon after his arrival. CORNELIUS was sent to an aunt in South Carolina, his brother remained in New York. A half-brother, younger than CORNELIUS, removed to Missouri. WANTED: The Christian name of the father and brothers, and record of the father's New York marriage. A reasonable amount will be paid for this information. J. A. S. K.

ROBINSON-FELL: It is stated that a JOHN ROBINSON, "son of John Robinson, of Middlesex county, Virginia," married LUCY FELL of Baltimore. No date or reference is given. Proof is greatly desired. M. L. M.

ROBINSON-COLE: HANNAH ROBINSON, Chester county, Penna., or Philada., is said to have married THOMAS COLE, 1790-1800, and had three daughters. One married THOMAS RAWLINGS; one married a PALMER. Five Dollars will be paid for definite information with authority as to the descendants of these marriages. M. L. M.

JOHN WILSON, of Chester county, Penna., married about 1760, ISABELLA (KENNEDY) DANIEL, widow. Wanted: the parentage of JOHN WILSON, also information as to when he removed from Chester county to Virginia. E. C. W. N. C.

FLOYD-DAVIS: Wanted the record of the marriage of WILLIAM FLOYD of Amherst Co., Va., and ABADIAH DAVIS. This marriage took place some time prior to 1750. Date given as 1747, but no authority. P. S. C.

DWELLEY: Wanted information as to place (in Somerset, England?) whence JOHN DWELLEY came who first appears at Hingham, Massachusetts, in 1654. Cannot find his name among list of emigrants, or those having license "to go beyond the seas," in Public Record Office, London. E. D. E.

WANTED: Any SAUL or SOLL ROBINSON born *circa* 1730 or 1735, New England, New York, New Jersey, Delaware, or Pennsylvania. Will gladly reciprocate in kind. Address the Editor.

FINLEY: JAMES FINLEY, son of JOHN FINLEY and MARTHA BERKLEY, his wife, served with South Carolina Revolutionary troops. Wanted: his residence in South Carolina and place of death in Virginia. Mrs. C. S. P.

EUBANK-EWBANKS: THOMAS EUBANK d. Talbott Co., Md., 1732. Wanted: names of his parents and further information concerning THOMAS. Wife was MARTHA. What was her maiden name? K. D. S. A.

SHANKLIN: THOMAS, ROBERT, JOHN, EDWARD (brothers), were in Augusta Co., Va., 1745-1776. What were the parents' names and where did the brothers remove from (to Virginia)? K. D. S. A.

UNDERWOOD: Wanted the ancestors of FANNIE UNDERWOOD, who married WILLIAM POUND; said to be the granddaughter of WILLIAM UNDERWOOD of Virginia, a member of the House of Burgesses in 1652. M. B. C. W.

LYON: Wanted the ancestry of ANN LYON who married RICHARD POUND, son of the above WILLIAM and FANNIE POUND. M. B. C. W.

HALE: Wanted the ancestry of JOHN HALE, of Franklin Co., Va., who married ELIZABETH SAUNDERS, dau. of Capt. Edward or Ebenezer Saunders and wife Theodosia. M. B. C. W.

BOOK NOTES

Three new genealogies, the BOONE, STOWELL and QUINBY families are announced by the Tuttle Company, of Rutland, Vermont. It is stated that Hazel Atterbury Speaker, who has compiled the BOONE FAMILY, has traced more than five thousand BOONES and descendants of twenty-two allied families. The volume includes a biography of DANIEL BOONE, written by Mr. Crump, of Independence, Missouri, a direct descendant. From personal knowledge of the migrations of the BOONES from New Jersey, through Pennsylvania, Maryland, Virginia, Kentucky, North Carolina, the Editor believes that no more interesting family exists as a genealogical study, and the fact that an apparently entirely distinct family of the same name is in Maryland, and was as strongly Catholic as the other BOONES were Quaker, makes the study of the two lines as they neighbor each other still more unusual.

PUBLICATIONS OF VALUE TO HISTORIANS AND GENEALOGISTS

GENERAL INFORMATION.

If any *subscriber* will ask the Editor, enclosing a stamped, self-addressed envelope, she will be glad to give information as to Courts, where they are, how to get there, and where to stay . . . when the Editor knows. Non-subscribers may receive the same information upon payment of a fee of twenty-five cents.

GENEALOGISTS AND OTHERS INTERESTED IN RESEARCH WORK

Any person interested in the early records of STAFFORD, KING GEORGE, LANCASTER, NORTHUMBERLAND, MIDDLESEX or WESTMORELAND counties, VIRGINIA, and desiring careful, detailed search, may join in a very simple, co-operative plan by addressing the Editor of the COUNTY COURT NOTE-BOOK.

Twenty-five cents each will be paid for ten copies of the October, and ten copies of the December NOTE-BOOK.—Editor.

ACME PRINTING CO., INC., 708 13th Street N. W., Washington, D. C.

The

County Court Note-Book

A Little Bulletin of History and Genealogy.

Vol. I. September, 1922. No. 6.

NEW ENGLANDERS AND OTHERS IN EARLY VIRGINIA RECORDS

(Third Instalment.)

RICHARD CHAPMAN, of London, mariner. L. Norf. B-166. 15 Feby. 1650.

ROBERT CUSTICE, bound to N. E. with Mr. John Holland. N-n, iv-64. 30 Mch. 1652.

Mr. AUGUSTINE HARMAN appears before notaries at New Amsterdam. N-n, v-62 (date 1652), recorded Jany., 1654.

Mr. PHILLIP PARKER, letter of att'y from MARGARET SANDERS, of London. N-n v-1 28 Mch. 1654.

Mr. AUGUSTINE HERMAN, a Bohemian German, permitted a plantation in Northampton Co. N-n, vi-17. 20 Nov. 1655.

WILLIAM CHICHESTER was master of the Catch *Hopewell*, of Boston, N. E. L. Norf. C-159. 1655 (A later entry states that he was of Salem.)

Mr. WILLIAM SMART, of Bristoll, mcht. (Reference to former exchange of land at Rappahannock.) N-n, v-140. 28 Feby. 1655.

JOHN HUDSON, of Nansimon County, gives power to John Badham. N-n, vii-51. 21 Jany. 1655.

JANE ELTONHEAD, of the Province of Maryland. N-n, vii. 13 Sept. 1656.

JOHN THORNDICKE, of Salem, N. E. N-n, vii-21. 13 Sept. 1656.

NICHOLAS DANISON or DAVISON, mcht, of Charlestowne, in N. E. N-n, vii-22. 13 Sept. 1656.

JOHN GIFFORD, of Boston. N-n, vii-22. 13 Sept. 1656.

JOHN RICHARDS, of Boston, N. E., mcht. Also Thomas Lake and John Scottowe. N-n, vii-23. 28 Oct. 1656.

Mr. WILLIAM PARKER, citizen and draper of London; power to bro. PHILLIP PARKER, mcht, in Virginia. Wit.: .... Geo. Warde. N-n, vii-35. 20 Augt. 1656.

RALPH EARLE, Sr., Portch-mouth, upon Roade Island, sells a mare coult to John Spires. N-n, vii-63. Recorded 10 Feby. 1656.

DANIELL LANE was Master of the Ketch *Dolphin* of Salem. L. Norf. C-221-44. 17 Nov. 1656.

SAMUEL ANDREWS, of London, mcht, now resident in N. E. N-n, vii-40. 27 June 1656.

JOHN RICHARDS (RICKARDS?), of Boston, N. E., mcht. Also Lake and Scottowe (as above). N-n, vii-23. 13 Sept. 1656.

LEWIS READE, of Somersett County, Maryland. N-n, v-125. 29 May 1656.

JOSEPH and ROBERT PAYNE, of Norwich, England. N-n, vii-53. 17 Sept. 1656.

ROBERT PARKER, power to Mr. RICHARD CORNELIUS, of the towne and county of South'ton, mcht. (Signed by Robert and Jane Parker.) N-n, v-107. 21 May 1656.

ROBERT PARKER, of Southampton; power to Rich. Baylie and John Parker of Virginia. N-n, ix-13. 24 Sept. 1657.

RICHARD PERQ (PERG?), mcht, late of New Haven; is agent of Mr. George Passemer, and Mr. George Fryer, mchts of Madera; Mr. Thos. Lake, Mr. Josuar Scotto (?), and Mr. Rickards, of N. E., administrators of Maj. Gen. Edward Gibbon. N-n, vii-73. 28 Dec. 1657.

JOHN CRABTREE, of Boston, N. E. N-n, vii-79. 1 Dec. 1657.

ISAAKE ALLERTON, Sr., of New Haven in N. E., mcht. Power to Thomas Hall. N-n, vii-54. 1 June 1657.

THOMAS HALL, of New Amsterdam, power to John Custis, mcht. N-n, vii-59. 1 June 1657.

MARY MURREN, of (......?) Maryland; extx. of Demetrius Murren [also written Marrine] The widow seems to have married Drought (?). L. Norf. D-167. 16 Sept. 1658.

WILLIAM PAIN, of Boston, mcht. N-n, ix-50. 1659.

NICHOLAS DAVISON, of Charlestown in Massachusetts Colony, mcht. N-n, ix-54. 1659.

EDWARD CURTIS, mariner, of the parish of Stepney, Middlesex County, England; power to Matthew Battell (?) of Surrey County, Virginia. Sur. i-145. 8 Mch. 1659.

EDWARD CURTIS, of Ratcliffe, near London, mariner; power. Sur. i-176. 1661.

Mr. NICHOLAS BOOTE, of the Manhatan. L. Norf. D-317 15 Oct. 1661.

Mr. NICHOLAS HART, of Rhode Island, in N. E. L. Norf. D-338. 26 July 1661.

Mr. RICHARD BANCKS, of London. Power to Col. John Custis, and Mr. John Custis, Jr. Acco., vi-62. 1677.

JOHN and SAMUEL HANSON were merchants of Barbadoes Acco., vi-268. 13 July 1681.

JOSEPH TOWNSEND, of Boston, N. E. N-n, xiv-12. 30 May 1681.

MARRIAGES BY INFERENCE *

(Continued from the July number.)

[The first twenty marriages are from the records of STAFFORD COUNTY, VIRGINIA. Stafford County was formed in 1664, from WESTMORELAND COUNTY. These counties are included in what is known as the Northern Neck of Virginia. The records of Stafford are incomplete. Fortunately the first Order Book has been recovered within very recent date.]

EDWARD WATTS and the relict and extr. of Jacob HUBBARD; before 14 Mch. 1689-90. Orders i-39.

ELIZABETH HOLMES, widow of Richard, and . . . NICKSON; before 10 Mch. 1689-90. Orders i-16.

WILLIAM BURTON and MARTHA FOLIO, widow of Thomas; before 11 Mch. 1690. Orders i-125

RICHARD NICKSON and ELIZABETH HOLMES, widow of Thomas; before 10 Mch. 1689-90. Orders i-16, 132.

MARGARET MASON, widow and relict of EDWARD, mar. . . . FARROW before 12 Mch. 1690. Orders i-129.

JOSEPH SMITH and ANN BROWN, dau. of Joseph; about 14 Mch. 1785. S-174.

PETER HANSBOROUGH and BETTY BROWN, dau. of Joseph; about 14 Mch 1785. S-173.

JAMES DONEAL, Jr., and THEODOCIA CONYERS, dau. of Henry, Gent.; before 12 Jan. 1757. P-137

JANE AUSTINE, dau. of Charles, mar. . . . LAMKIN; after 1698. P-229.

EDWARD PAYNE of Fairfax Co., and ANNE HOLLAND CONYERS, dau. of Henry; before 7 Sept. 1758. P-192.

Mr. JOHN THORNTON and BEHETHLAND GILSON; before 5 Feby 1762. O-462.

RANDALL DAVENPORT and the wid. of GERRARD FOORD. Orders-139.

MARTIN SCARLET and the relict of WILLIAM GREEN; before 13 Mch. 1689-90. Orders i-.

Capt. ZACHARIAS BRAZIER and Mrs. ELIZABETH BUCKNER, wid. mar. contract. P-241. 5 Nov. 1759.

RICHARD MARTIN and [probably] JANE RUSSELL, wid. of John. Z-214; before 30 Dec. 1763.

ELIZABETH HANSUN [HANKINS or HAWKINS?] wid. of Daniel, mar. . . . COLEMAN. Orders i-380; before 8 Nov. 1693.

HENRY MEREST (?) and the relict. of JOHN [or JONAH] REVET, Sr. Orders i-47; before 13 Sept. 1693.

Mr. JOSEPH NEWTON and the wid. of JAMES PRICE. Orders i-331; before 8 Mch. 1692-3.

THOMAS THOMPSON and the wid. of JOHN PEAKE, Sr. Orders i-332; before 8 Feby. 1692.

RICE HOOE and MARY MASSEY, wid. of [Sigismund]. [She was extx. of Gerrard Lowther.] Orders i-208; about 10 Feby. 1691-2.

SAMUEL WHITSON and ELIZABETH SKEELE, "wid. and relict" of John Skeele. Orders i-123; before 11 Mch. 1690.

Dr. EDWARD MADDOCKE and FRANCES NORGRAVE, wid. of Capt. JOHN NORGRAVE. Orders i-86; before or about 8 July 1690.

FRANCIS DADE and FRANCES TOWNSHEND, dau. of Robert. Orders i-98. 10 Sept. 1690.

SAMPSON DARRELL and MARGARET NORGRAVE, dau. of Capt. John Norgrave. Orders i-43; before 7 Apr. 1690.

DAVID JOHNSON and HANNAH CRAIG, wid. of Alexander Craig. Sussex Co., Dela. M-208; before 1780 (?).

JOHN THARP and LEAH MORRIS, Sussex Co., Dela. N-414; before (?) 28 Dec. 1786.

JACOB THOMAS (afterwards of Chester Co., Pa.), and SARAH RUSSELL. Sussex Co., Dela. B-346; 1768.

JACOB WHITE and MARY CRAIG. Sussex Co., Dela. I-216; before 8 Aug. 1759.

JOHN TODD and [MARTHA] WILLSON, wid. of James Willson. Chester Co., Pa Orphans' Court, vi-2; before 17 Mch. 1752.

JAMES DOWNING and MARY DYER, wid. of Peter Dyer. Rock'm Co., Va. C-78; before 13 Feby. 1749.

JOHN GIBSON and CATHARINE CLOVERFIELD. Rock'm Co. OO-363; before 17 Sept. 1799.

JOHN CROOKSHANKS and MARY CLOVERFIELD. Rck'm. OO-363; before 17 Sept. 1799.

JOHN HEISE and ANNA MARIA HAAS, dau. of John. Shenan. Co., Va. D-443; before 15 Apr. 1793.

WILLIAM POPE and ANN BURGESS, wid., Surry Co., Va. I-463; before 4 Nov. 1684.

JEMIMA ODELL and . . . JOB, the dau. of James Job. Shenan. Co., Va. F-461; before 1806.

ELIZABETH GREGG, wid. of John GREGG, and . . . ADAMS. Pr. Wm. Co., Va. U-339; before 16 June 1784.

GALVAN DE BERNOUX; marriage contract with ELIZABETH MURRAY referred to. Pr. Wm. Co. Z-409; 9 Aug. 1784.

THOMAS HARWOOD and ANN WYTHE, wid. of Thomas Wythe, Sr. Mar. Li. E. C. Co., Va 7 Sept. 1695. [From a copy.]

Mr. JAMES WALLACE, Clerk, and the wid. [ANN] of Mr. Thos. Wythe; before 18 Nov. 1697. [From a copy.]

WILLIAM LOURY and FRANCES HAND, wid. of Richard. E. C. Co. [From a copy.]

FRANCES HILL dau. of JOHN HILL, Gent, and THOMAS WALKER. K. Wm. Co., Va. "I"-195; before 1 Apr. 1797.

JOHN BRIAN and CYNTHIA L. GRESHAM, dau. of Lumpkin Gresham. K. Wm. Co. "15"-430; before 30 Apr. 1830.

WILLIAM CHANCE, Jr., and ESTER AYRES, wid. of Richard Hill Ayres. Acco. Co., Va. xviii-76; about 5 Mch. 1723.

GEORGE POUNCEY and SARAH WEST, wid. of Benoni West. Acco. Co. xix-14; about 9 Jan. 1724.

THOMAS HAZARD (Prov. of R. I.), and MARY BOWDOIN, dau. of Peter [son of John, son of Pierre]. N-n Co., Va. M. L. B. 15 Nov. 1746.

WILLIAM KENDALL, Sr., and SARAH MATHEWS, wid. Marriage contract. N-n Co. xiv-109. 6 June 1684. Ackn. by SARAH KENDALL. 1 Dec. 1684.

Mr. SAMUEL PALMER and Mrs. SARAH KENDALL, wid. of Col. William. N-n Co. xiv-251; about 29 Mch. 1690. [See also xviii-64; xvii-192; 203; 244; 175.]

(To be continued.)

MARYLAND'S NEXT OF KIN *

(Continued from the July number.)

THOMAS COCKAYNE, EDW'D LUDDINGHAM; inv. John Luddingham, Talbot Co.; 15 Feby 1717-18; i-145.

JOHN KING, Jr., SARAH GRAYSON; inv. Andrew Skinner, Talbot Co.; 13 Mch. 1717; i-146.

JOSEPH HARRISON; inv. Robert Harrison, Talbot Co.; 21 Mch. 1717; i-150.

RICHARD BRUFF, FRA: ARMSTRONG; inv. Michaell Russell, Talbot Co.; 30 Mch. 1718; i-153.

EZEBELL [sic] PALMER, ELIZABETH DOBSON; inv. Jacob Palmer, of Talbot Co.; 8 Mch. 1717; i-157.

DOROTHY MILLER, ELIZABETH HIGGENS; inv. Henry Woolman, of Talbot Co.; 12 Mch. 1717; i-161.

MARY RUMSEY, CATHERINE WOOD; inv. Charles Rumsey, of Cecil Co.; 30 Jany. 1717; i-164.

ZACH. GRAY, MATTHEW ASHLEY; inv. Zechariah Gray, of A. A. Co.;. 31 Mch. 1718; i-175.

JOSEPH BOYS, DANIEL DOYS (?); inv. Joseph Boyce, of Somerset Co.; 1718; i-176.

JAMES SMITH, JOHN ROACH; inv. George Smith, of Som. Co.; 5 Dec. 1717; i-180.

MICHAEL ROACH, SAMUEL ROACH; inv. John Roach; Sen.; 15 May 1718; i-181.

ABRAHAM HYWAY [sic]; inv. Thomas Hiway; [no county given]; 16 Nov. 1716; i-182.

SAMUEL POWELL WILLIAM POWELL; inv. Thos. Powell, of Som. Co.; 14 June 1718; i-184.

RANDOLPH MITCHELL, JOHN WHITE; inv. John Moor, of Som. Co.; 12 Apr. 1718; i-185.

THOMAS DASHFIELD, BENJ. WAILES; inv. Thomas Taylor, of Som. Co.; 11 Jany. 1718; i-186.

THOMAS JUKES, ROBERT MALVEN; inv. John Stevens, of Som. Co.; 22 Apr. 1718; i-186.

RICHARD and EZEKIELL GREEN; inv. Alex. Gibbons, of Som. Co.; 10 Nov. 1716; i-187.

DEPUTY COM'RY, of Cecil Co., "am allowed £154, 4sh. 10d. for disburstments; the Remainder belongs to his Wife as Sole Heir." (?) Mezick, of Som. Co.; 6 Aug. 1718; i-218.

JOHN NICHOLSON; inv. John Nicholson, Sen., of A. A. Co.; 26 Mch. 1718; i-189.

EDWARD and JOHN CARSLAKE; inv. Reynold Thropsher, of Talbot Co.; 5 May 1718; i-190.

"The WIFE of the Dec. being all the Relations"; inv. William Thomas of St. M. Co.; 7 Jany. 1716; i-191.

MATTHEW and ELIZABETH CUNNINGHAM; inv. Thomas Shaw, of Som. Co.; 26 Oct. 1717; i-192.

WM. WHITTINGTON, for THOS. SANDFORD; inv. Wm. Powell, of Som. Co.; 12 Jany 1718; i-194.

WILLIAM HOLLAND; inv. John Phelps, of St. M. Co.; 19 Sept. 1718; i-197.

THOMAS HYNSON WRIGHT; inv. Solomon Wright, of Q. A. Co.; 2 May 1717; i-202.

JAMES WILKINSON; inv. Wm. Wilkinson, of Balto. Co.; 28 June 1718; i-205.

PHIL COALE, JOHN TALBOTT; inv. Edward Talbot, of Balto. Co.; 21 Oct. 1718.

WILLIAM and ELIZABETH POWELL; inv. John Powell of Som. Co.; 26 July 1718; i-212.

JOFFREY [sic] and DANIEL LONG; inv. John Long, of Som. Co.; 29 July 1718; i-213.

(To be continued.)

The County Court Note-Book

An every-other-monthly devoted to abstracts from the County Court and other records, prior to 1800, and with a department of notes and queries.

MILNOR LJUNGSTEDT, Editor and Publisher. Bethesda, Route 1, Maryland.

Published every other month. Subscription, one dollar a year, in advance.

Volume I. September, 1922 No. 6

"YET THE DEAD ARE THERE"

(Continued from July number.)

The counties of WESTMORELAND and WASHINGTON, of the Keystone State, are, to judge by their courthouses and other buildings at the county seats, extremely wealthy. The cost of the two courthouses, the Editor was informed, was above two million. Both are large buildings with interior stairways and corridors of a magnificence suited for a State Capitol. The entrance staircase of the building in Greensburgh (Westmoreland County) is especially fine and appears on post cards which have been sent far and wide. This building has the best provision for the preservation of the early taxlists and the comfort of the searcher of any the Editor recollects. Tables, chairs, electric lighting are all provided in a very attractive mezzanine story.

Greensburgh has also a church for which a lady, a member of the congregation, gave $100,000.

Washington, "Little Washington," the county-seat of Washington County, is the home of an old college. So many of the students and professors went to the World War that the college either did close, or seriously considered it.

Yet both of these towns, these cities, have cemeteries which are a disgrace to civilization. Especially the old cemetery at Washington.

The Editor photographed four cemeteries, and has called the attention of many supposedly interested persons to the conditions. But it appears to be useless. The people who neglect and insult the memory of their ancestors are unworthy of ancestors. And in these western Pennsylvania graveyards lie the forbears of the south and west, and southwest and northwest. Even the monument to St. Clair, of which the towns people are very proud, is backed by a neglected wilderness partly occupied as a children's playground. It seems to be the commonly accepted idea that the best thing to do with an old cemetery is to let the children play there. Should not the children respect the dead? Should old grave-stones be gathered up and piled in a corner so that the children may have a swing and a hop-scotch ground?

The Editor believes it is a mistake to destroy sentiment. This mistake is only too clearly shown by a picture, both photographic and mental, which the Editor has of one particular cemetery. Several stray dogs were using it, and a worn-out, cast away spring mattress decorated the plots nearest the street.

In the fine old German cemetery in Greensburgh, where there are some wonderfully well-cut stones still in excellent condition, a child had constructed a playhouse with broken slabs.

In the German cemetery at Washington, the stones had been loosened by frost, but were otherwise not in bad condition, but a handy hole in the fence next to the yard of the abutting residence, permitted the usual rambling dog, and other abominations. The Editor does not mean that a dog is an abomination, but a dog in a graveyard is just that.

It is only fair to say that these conditions are as they were a few years ago. It is barely possible they have been improved.

The Editor has no great love for a cemetery like Mt. Auburn, or Laurel Hill, or Hollywood; they lack some appeal difficult to characterize; it is to a friendly, cheerful place like the Old Granary Burying Ground, which many others than Bostonians know, that one turns as to a chapter of history and genealogy bound in living green, and shelved in the heart of a great city, near all that it chronicles.

Posterity and strangers hurry by the crowded way but many stop, and through the railings read the lettering to the honored past. The friendly trees shelter both the quick and the dead; book lovers at the window of the Athenæum lift their eyes from a page writ by the very hands beneath the turf below them; from other windows eyes of casual business soften perhaps to thought . . . for the DEAD are THERE, and the DEAD are OURS.

OCCASIONAL

From an early estate account: "To dyett lodging and Washinge his Daughter for 12 months . . ." N-n Co., Va., xiii-220. 29 Mch. 1682.

The following marriage contract is in the records of SUSSEX County, Virginia, about 1766. "WHEREAS AUGUSTINE CLAIBORNE hath now and is likely to have a numerous issue by the said MARY [his wife] . . . in case the said AUGUSTINE CLAIBORNE shall survive the said MARY his now wife, and he be about taking another wife . . ." before he enters into such second marriage he is to convey to MARY'S children all the land, &c., &c.

BALDWIN PEARCE does not wish his wife to wear mourning; objects to "vain ceremony and empty pageantry," and suggests a gold medal "with some inscription and device suitable to the melancholy occasion" [of his death and burial]. Petersburg, Va., Corporation Court, 1798.

The CITY of BOSTON, a town of Massachusetts of which we occasionally hear, has been rather recently investigating prices at its restaurants, and courageously giving the results to the public. This encourages the Editor to publish the following:

The Mary-Virginia Tea Room [somewhere in Virginia]; 1 [piece] Chocolate cake and milk . . . 40c. Both were very good.

PRINCE WILLIAM, VA., BONDS

(Continued from July Number.)

Charles Cornwell; Ezekiel and Francis Cornwell, extrs.; Wm. x Lynn, Ben x Thomas, sec. 5 Nov. 1781.

Anthony Seale; John Seale, Anthony Seale, Wm. x Brown, extrs.; Bernard Hooe, John Hooe, sec. 5 Nov. 1781.

Henry Cooper; Sarah Cooper, Chas Johnston, extrs.; Wm. Randolph, Wm. Cornwell, sec. 3 Dec. 1781.

Fras. Jackson; Samuel Jackson, Jr., Wm. x Fielder, extrs.; John McMilliam, Stephen Howison, sec. 7 Jany. 1782.

Wm. Landrum; Sarah Ann x Landrum, extx.; Richard Graham, John Hooe, Gent., sec. 3 June 1782.

William Whitledge; Wm. Whitledge, extr.; Thomas Whiteledge, John Oreas, sec. 5 Aug. 1782.

John Reeves; Daniel x Obrien, extr.; Asa x Reeves, John x Crook, sec. 5 Aug. 1782.

James Scott Clark; John Scott, extr.; Cuthbert Bullitt, sec. 2 Nov. 1782.

Truman Higgs; Benj. Mattison, extr.; William Fewell, Geo. Jackson, James Hamrick, sec. 2 Dec. 1782.

John Murray, Gent.; Eliz'th Murray, extr.; Jesse Ewell, sec. 3 Mch. 1783.

John Delgran; Joanna x Delgarn, Jno. x Delgarn, extrs.; Wm. Carr, Richard Graham, sec. 1783. [Month and day not given.]

Wm. Tackett; Lewis Reno, Wm. Tackett, extrs.; John Seewright, Jr., Cuth[bert] Bullitt, Esq., sec. 8 Apr. 1783.

Thomas Smoot; Elizabeth Smoot, extx.; James Ewell, Notley Smoot, sec. 7 July 1783.

John Delgarne; Joanna Delgarne, James Delgarne, extrs.; Valentine Peyton, Gent, Geo. Tainie, sec. 4 Aug. 1783.

Daniel O'Neal; Wm. McDaniel [extr.?]; James Gwatkins, sec. 1 Sept. 1783.

Ann Harrison; Sitha [Seth] Harrison, extx.; Wm. Alexander, sec. 1 Dec. 1783.

William Tenison; Nathal Wickliff, Mary Tenison, extrs.; Isaac Wickliff, John Jordan, sec. Dec. 1783.

Fanny Shute; Scarlett Madden, extr.; John Cannon, sec. 3 May, 1784.

Sarah Scott; Wm. Scott, extr.; Cleon Moore, sec. Sept. 1784.

Lydia Musgrove Ismenger; Mark (?) Matthew Mankin, extr.; Stephen Lee, sec. 3 Aug. 1784.

Foushee Tebbs, Gentl.; Willoughby Tebbs, extr.; Wm. Tebbs, sec. 7 Mch. 1785.

Giles Carter; Wm. Carter, Sam'l Carter, David Carter, extrs.; John Hedges, sec. 7 Mch. 1785.

Thomas Chapman; Wm. Carr, Gent., extr.; Cuthbert Bullitt, sec.. 5 Apr. 1785.

John Cheshire; Stephen Howison, extr.; Cuthbert Bullitt, sec. 5 Apr. 1785.

George Kitchen; Wm. B. Harrison, extr.; Robt. Brown, sec. 6 Apr. 1785.

Foushee Tebbs, Gent.; Samuel Tebbs, extr ; Cuthbert Bullitt, sec. 4 July 1785.

Joseph Pettey; Presly Petty, admr.; Redman Grigsby, Mark Tharp, sec. 6 Sept. 1785.

Samuel Jackson; John Jackson, George Jackson, extrs.; John Calvert, John Redman, James Grinstead, sec. 6 Mch. 1786.

Vallentine Peyton; Burr Peyton, extr.; John Linton, John Cannon, sec. 6 Mch. 1786.

John Hoskins; James Lowe, John Jordan, extrs.; David Bland, John Curry, sec. 6 Mch. 1786.

John Grayham; Timothy Holtzclaw, James Graham, Joseph Barker, extrs ; Wm. Brown, Wm. Matthis, sec. 4 Sept. 1786.

John Burroughs; Mary Burroughs, extx.; John Hammitt, Philip Spitter, sec. 5 Sept. 1786.

(Concluded.)

OUR ANCESTRAL RECORDS IN ENGLAND

(Second article.)

Contributed by Mr. E. Dwelly, of England.

PARISH REGISTERS. Parish Registers and wills form the backbone of every English pedigree. The following brief tabulation of the laws regarding Registers will assist American searchers to understand the value and the limits of these records:

1535. Registration was first introduced by Sir Thomas Cromwell, but met with so much opposition that it had to be abandoned.
1538. The project succeeded and the Registers commenced.
1555. Sponsors' names added to baptismal records.
1597. All existing Registers to be copied into parchment books, and two transcripts sent, one to the Bishop of the Diocese, and one to the Archdeacon, on Easter Day of each year.
1645. Dates of births and deaths to be added to dates of baptisms and burials.
1653. Registrar ("register") to be elected by parishioners.
1654. Civil marriages by magistrates ordered; legalized in 1660.
1711. Printed register books with ruled and numbered pages ordered.
1735. All records to be in English in future.
1752. All dates to be recorded in "New Style."
1753. Hardwicke's Marriage Act, until the passing of which, marriage without either banns or license were valid, although called "irregular."
1783. Duty of 3d. in each entry till repealed in 1794.

[The NOTE-BOOK will publish further articles upon this subject. Mr. Dwelly's notes upon the Quaker records of England are especially interesting.]

On Application by ELIZABETH SANDERS wife of ROGER SANDERS who by a Certificate of Col Thomas Price appears to be a soldier for and during the war in the Maryland line and it appearing that she needs assistance toward the support of a family of 15 young children. Ordered that the Clerk draw an order on the Treas. of the Western Shore in her favor for the sum of 15 pounds by way of assistance to her in the support of her family for one year from this date. Minute Book, Aug. Court, 1782, Fred. Co., Md.

NOTES AND QUERIES

HAMER-HICKS: Wanted; the ancestry of WILLIAM HAMER, b. Maryland, settled Anson County, N. C. Also of his wife, FRANCES HICKS. T. A. A.

FOWKE, FOULKE, FOOKS: Persons interested in the ancestry of any branch of this family should communicate with HERBERT C. FOOKS, 723 Munsey Building, Baltimore, Md.

PALMER: Five dollars will be paid for authoritative information as to the ancestry of MARTIN PALMER, of Charlotte Co., Va., father of CHILIAN PALMER. W. B. P. A.

ELLEGOOD or ELLIGOOD: MARGARET ELLEGOOD was the aunt of Peter Bowdoin; see his will in Northampton County, Va. Can any one supply her maiden name? E. G. W. M.

ROBINSON: Wanted information as to SAUL ROBINSON who died in Worcester County, Maryland, about twenty-five years ago. Who was he? M. L. M.

TOWNSEND: Was "SAUL" TOWNSEND of Worcester County, really SOLOMON? There was at the same time a SOLOMON TOWNSEND, Senior and Junior. M. L. M.

ROBINSON-FELL: Wanted authority for the statement that LUCY FELL, of Baltimore, married JOHN, a son of JOHN ROBINSON, of Middlesex County, Va. No date or reference given in published statements. M. L. M.

WILSON: When did JOHN WILSON, of Chester County, Pa., who married ISABELLA (KENNEDY) DANIEL, about 1760, remove to Virginia? When did he come to this country? E. C. W. N. C.

PATTEN: Wanted the parentage of THOMAS PATTEN, of Cecil County, Maryland; name of his wife; his will. One of the daughters of PATTEN was born 1782. A. B. S. R.

HOOKER: Would like any notes on HOOKERS of NORTH CAROLINA, VIRGINIA or MARYLAND, before 1800. C. A. B. C.

CAIN: Wanted parentage of GEORGE CATHEY CAIN; born in NORTH CAROLINA, 1813. Supposed son of ROBERT CAIN; mother probably a MAXWELL, HOOKER, or CATHEY. FIVE DOLLARS reward for information with authority. C. A. B. C.

CARR-COLE: Reward of FIVE DOLLARS for authoritative information of locality from which either family emigrated to KENTUCKY. Pre-emption warrant of land in MERCER CO., KENTUCKY, granted 1795, to AQUILA and ELIJAH COLE. AQUILA COLE lived near FRANKFORT, KENTUCKY; married *circa* 1800, RACHEL, dau. of JOHN and ELIZABETH (WHITE) CARR. C. A. B. C.

"HENRY CECILL borne on his Lordships "Mannor of Patuxent the 4th Nov., being "Wednesday about half an hour after two "o'clock in the morning A.D. 1696, and his "brother twinn named ISAAC CECILL was "borne half an hour after being one o'clock "the same morning and they were Christened "the same morning about 11 o'clock by Mr. "Jones, Minister of the Home Church, be- "longing to Christ Church Parish in Calvert "Co." Deeds, A, 318, P. G. Co., Md.

BOOK AND PUBLISHER'S NOTES.

THE PALMER ANCESTRY AND GENEALOGY, containing 30,000 PALMERS, classified and systematically arranged in several volumes, will be published before long. The compiler, Dr. Byron S. PALMER, of Palmyra, New York, is most anxious to receive all possible information as to any branch of this family.

Dr. PALMER writes the Editor that the books will not be published as a means to private gain, but with the sole intention to record and preserve for all of his name, all that is known of the PALMERS of this country.

The Editor of the South Georgia Quarterly writes that he has secured the Georgia militia rolls from 1793 to 1838, including muster rolls of about ten companies who served in the Indian wars of that section. The latter will shortly be published.

THE CATALOGUE RAISONNÉ of all the ROBINSONS (and ROBERTSONS) of America, which is being compiled by a descendant of Capt. JOSEPH ROBINSON, a Philadelphia sea captain of the first quarter of the nineteenth century, will become, in due course, the property of the Pennsylvania Genealogical Society.

The compiler has been able to add recently a large quantity of New York material, and also to prove the descent of a very remarkable Maryland ROBERTSON branch of the house of STROWAN.

The compiler regrets to state that the CATALOGUE RAISONNÉ is not available for current research work, except in very special cases.

If sufficient subscriptions are received to warrant the undertaking, the compiler of the above catalogue will publish an abstract of the SCOTCH records concerning the CLAN DONNACHIE, to which the House of Strowan belongs. Recent publications, not usually available, have brought the various branches of this family of ROBERTSONS down to modern times. As they are represented all over this country under the name of ROBINSON as well as ROBERTSON, the compiler believes that the paper which it is proposed to publish, in simple folder form, will be found valuable. The price will be one dollar. Address the Editor.

The DECEMBER NOTE-BOOK will begin the publication of persons naturalized by Particular Acts in the State of Maryland. This list from Bacon's Laws of Maryland, 1637-1763, is of great value and interest. Through the kind co-operation of Mrs. Geo. W. Hodges this material will be made available.

GENERAL INFORMATION.

The RURAL HILL TEA ROOM, Accomac C. H., Va., is most delightfully located on the road to Cape Charles. Address Mrs. Bell for further information.

Visitors to WEST CHESTER, the county-seat of CHESTER Co., Penna., can get excellent and reasonably priced meals at the OVERTOWN, which is situated above the bank. Sometimes the hostess, who is a member of the Society of Friends, can also provide rooming facilities.

If any *subscriber* will ask the Editor, enclosing a stamped, self-addressed envelope, she will be glad to give information as to Courts, where they are, how to get there, and where to stay . . . when the Editor knows. Non-subscribers may receive the same information upon payment of a fee of twenty-five cents.

Persons desiring information as to the old County of Ohio, Virginia, (now West Virginia), please address the Editor.

Any person interested in the early records of STAFFORD, KING GEORGE, LANCASTER, NORTHUMBERLAND, MIDDLESEX or WESTMORELAND counties, VIRGINIA, and desiring careful, detailed search, may join in a very simple, co-operative plan by addressing the Editor of the COUNTY COURT NOTE-BOOK.

PUBLICATIONS OF VALUE TO HISTORIANS AND GENEALOGISTS

Persons desiring the records of RALEIGH, N. C., NASHVILLE, Tenn., and DOVER, Dela., examined; please address the Editor.

GENEALOGISTS AND OTHERS INTERESTED IN RESEARCH WORK

Twenty-five cents each will be paid for ten copies of the October, and ten copies of the December NOTE-BOOK.—Editor.

ACME PRINTING CO., INC., 708 13th Street N. W., Washington, D. C.

The

County Court Note-Book

A Little Bulletin of History and Genealogy

Vol. I **November, 1922** **No. 7**

SHIPS IN PORT

(See page 5)

The Catch *Adventure*, of Hull; Mr. James, Se'r Com'dr. Acco. vi-102. 7 Apr 1678.

Ship *Affryca*, at the Port of Susquehanna, upp the bay of Chesapiogue. N-n i-34. 4 May 1635.

Shipp *Americay*, William Barker, age about 36, master and part owner. Richard Orchar [Archer?] master in 1637. L. Norf. B-170.

Ship *Amity*, John Tully, master. Brit. State Papers. 24 Nov 1653.

The *Ann* from Boston. N-n v-130. 29 Jany 1655.

Ship *Barbadoes Merchant*, of Liverpool; Robert Middleton, master. Acco. xii-20. 5 Apr 1698.

Ship *Barbadoes*, William Fletcher, commander. Acco. 1699. xii-81.

The *Batchelour's Delight*, a vessel lately cast away. Robert Greeneway, master. Acco. 19 Mch 1680. viii-214.

Bark called *The Beginning*, of Block Island, N. E. Surry, Va. i-253. 1664.

Shippe *Beginning*, of Biddeford in England. N-n. 1681.

Ship *Blessing*. This vessel appears in two N-n records, ii-359, 368, April, 1645, Paul Sympson, commander. She also appears (Ship *Blissing*) in the L. Norf. records. D-392. Court of 15 Dec 1663, James Gilbert, master. At the time of this record the Quakers had held a meeting on board (Mr. John Porter, the speaker) and were fined by the Court.

Ship *Brittainia*. Bryant Hanly [or Hanley], age about 37, deposes that Henry Kelly came with him in this ship, Capt. Peirce, master, and that the "merchant's name was Grenslott." That they took ship near a place called Ballyhack in Waterford river, Ireland... believes it was about 30 years since they came. James Gahagan testifies that it was reported that said Kelly was "Kidnapt." K. Geo. i-502 3 May 1728.

The *Carolus Secundus* was a vessel cast away about 1675. N-n xiv.

(To be continued)

MARRIAGES BY INFERENCE*

(Continued from September number)

The first twenty marriages are from the records of SURRY COUNTY, VIRGINIA. Surry county was formed in 1652 from James City county. Its records are remarkably complete and among the most interesting of any of the early counties.

AR: ALLEN and CATHERINE BAKER, daughter of Laurence; i(2)-290; before 18 Mch 1681.

ROGER ARCHER and MARY CLAY, relict of Mr. John Clay, Sr., of Isle of Wight county; i(2)-241; before or about 31 May 1678.

WILLIAM ARCHER and the relict and admx of WILLIAM DUKE; i(2)-238; before 25 Jany 1678.

JOHN BATTELL and MARGARET SOWSBY; "2"-2; before 1 July 1684.

RICHARD BLOW and ELIZABETH BARROW [Blow d. 1686]; "2"-13; 5 May 1685.

THOMAS BLUNT and PRISCILLA BROWNE, dau of William Browne, Sr. See Browne's will, iv-305; before 4 Dec 1704.

THOMAS BLUNT and PRISCILLA JORDAN, relict and extx of River Jordan; Orders ii-237; 1703.

Mr. GEORGE BRANCH, Jr., and SUSANNA CORKER, eldest daughter of Capt. William Corker, dec.; Orders i-157 (also ii-674); before 15 Apr 1737.

THOMAS *alias* SACKFORD BREWSTER of Sackford Hall, Suffolk, Gent., and ELIZABETH WATKINS, admx of John; i-63; about or before 22 Apr 1655.

WILLIAM CHAMBERS and MARGERY JARRETT, wid of Richard; Orders i-48; before 3 Mch 1673.

FRANCIS CLEMENTS and LYDIA BLIGHTON, admx of George; iii-81; about 28 Apr 1711.

JUDETH CORKER, dau. of Capt. William, and... CLAY [Clay was then dec.]; i(2)-140; before 1677.

WILLIAM COCKER (?) and MARY WHITE, relict of William; Orders i-173; 15 Sept 1677.

JOHN DENFIELD [DUNFORD] and [MARY] WARREN, relict and admx of John; Orders i-72; about 3 Sept 1674.

WILLIAM DUKE and the widow of WILLIAM BIRD; Orders i-17; see also i-16; before 29 Sept 1672.

Mr. SION HILL and the relict of JOHN SPILTIMBER; i(2)-129; before or about 12 May 1697. See also Orders i-134.

WILLIAM HARE and MARY CARTER, widow of George; Orders i-19; 7 Jany 1672.

JOHN HODGE and the relict of JOHN COOPER; i(2); before 15 June 1677.

WILLIAM LYLE and JUDAH HUDSON, only dau and heir of Rowland Hudson; i(2); before 27 July 1679.

DANIELL ROOME and MARY HILL, *orphant;* i-275; about 4 Sept 1666.

JOHN HILL and SARAH HOLLENSWORTH; Henry Co., Va., Mar. Ret. 1783.

WILLIAM MOSELEY, Jr., and the "sole heiress of" Mr. RICHARD POOLE; S. L. O., Va., viii-64; before 21 Apr 1690.

GEORGE READ, Esq., of Newcastle, Dela., N-520; before 2 Apr 1788.

GENERAL WILLIAM RUSSELL and ELIZABETH CAMPBELL; Wash'n county, Va. ii-106, 107; before 1796. (Their children were: Elizabeth Henry Russell and Jean Robertson Russell.)

JONATHAN SHIPLEY of the bridge Towne in the Island of Barbadoes, and ELLES [ELLICE] BURNELL, dau of John. I. W. co., Va. iv-23; before 17 May 1689.

FRANCIS SMITH and ELIZABETH HENRY RUSSELL. Wash'n Co., Va., before or about 28 Feby 1806. iii-10.

PETER STEPHENS and BARBARA [probably dau of Robert WILLSON.] Fred'k Co., Va. xi-331; about 4 Mch 1767.

FRANCIS THORNTON and ALICE SAVAGE, dau of Anthony, Gent. K. Geo. county, Va. i-453; before 1675(?).

THOMAS WALKER and FRANCES HILL, dau of John Hill, Gent. K. Wm. "8"-194; before 1 Apr 1797. [Walker then deceased.]

ROBERT WILSON and MARY CALVERT, widow of Robert. Fred'k Co., Va. xix-92; about or before 16 June 1780.

LEWIS YATES and FRANCES HOLTZCLAW. Fauquier co., Va. iii-293; about 1801.

(To be continued)

MARYLAND'S NEXT OF KIN*

(Continued from September number)

GEORGE TRUIT, Jr.; inv. Philip Trewets [sic] of Som. Co.; 29 June 1718.

* Copyright by Mrs. George W. Hodges.

EPH. WILSON, JOB SHARRY ("Approved on by us"); inv. Randell Revell, of Som. Co.; 2 Aug. 1718; i-215.

HENRY WALTER, only brother to the deceased; inv. John Walter; 17 July 1718. [No co. given.]

NEHEMIAH and JOHN MEZICK; inv. Julin (?) Mezick, of Som. Co.; 6 Aug 1718; i-218.

KATHERINE BILLINGS, ROSE WHITE, "approvers"; inv. Michael Clifton, of Som. Co.; 9 Aug 1718; i-219.

THOMAS and GEORGE DASHIELL; inv. JOHN Winder, of Som. Co.; 4 Aug. 1718.

SUSANNA JONES; inv. Isaac Carington, of Som. Co.; 30 Mch 1718; i-220.

JOHN EVANS, "approver"; inv. William Evans, of Som. Co.; 4 June 1718; i-221.

THOS. WILSON, JOHN PILES; inv. Maj. Josiah Wilson, of P. G. Co.; 24 July 1718; i-222.

ARNOLD ELZEY and CHARLES BALLARD; inv. Samuel Worthington, of Som. Co.; 26 May 1718; i-230.

JOHN CHESHIRE, ANTONY GOTT; inv. Richard Gott, of A. A. Co.; 1718; i-241.

WILLIAM WORTHINGTON; inv. John Ingram of A. A. Co.; 21 Apr 1718; i-241.

JOHN DICKENSON, MARY CASIE; son and dau of John Dickenson, of Talbot Co.; inv. July 1718; i-252.

JAMES BERRY and DANIEL POWELL; inv. John Pitt of Talbot Co., 6 Feby 1717; i-257.

THOMAS WORTHINGTON; inv. Henry Waters, of A. A. Co.; 14 July 1718; i-261.

WILLIAM DISNEY, STEPHEN WARMAN; inv. George Miller, of A. A. Co.; 12 May 1718; i-263.

THOMAS EDMONDSON, EDMONDSON STEVENS; inv. William Stevens of Talbot Co.; 4 Feby 1717; i-264.

JOSEPH WOODWARD; inv. James Arthur Whiteley (of Dor. Co. ?), 22 Jany 1717; i-269.

ELIZABETH OCHAIN; inv. Manass Ochain, 1718; i-271.

SAMUEL DICKENSON, EDWARD HARDING; inv. David Fairbanks; 26 Mch 1718; i-271.

THOMAS HOPKINS, BENJAMIN KIMMONT; inv. Francis Kimmont of Talbot Co.; 15 April 1718.

WILLIAM HALL; inv. Robert Hall of Talbot Co.; 1 July 1718; i-274.

CHARLES and MARY FEAY; inv. William Feay, of Talbot Co.; 30 May 1717; i-276.

RICHARD HOLMES, EVE HOLMES; inv. Anne Watts, 25 Apr 1718; i-277.

ROBERT HANSON, A. CONTEE; inv. John Rogers, of Chas. Co.; 19 Sept 1718; i-279.

JOSEPH DOUGLASS, DOUGLASS GIFFERD; inv. William Herbert, of Chas. Co.; 12 Aug 1718; i-281.

GEORGE DENT, DOUGLASS GIFFORD; inv. Sarah Harbert of Chas. Co.; 8 Oct 1718; i-288.

THOMAS OWEN, BOWLING SPEAKE; inv. Joseph Gardiner, of Chas. Co.; 7 Oct 1718; i-291.

FRANCIS WITLY, JAMES CAHOW; inv. William Hardy, of Chas. Co.; 8 Oct 1718; i-295.

CHARLES and SUSANNAH YATES; inv. George Dreyden, of Chas. Co.; 26 Aug 1718; i-296.

WILLIAM COOMBES, JOHN READ, JAMES MARTIN; inv. William Read, of St. Mary's Co.; 3 June 1718; i-297.

JANE TANSON (?); inv. Michael Wellman, of St. Mary's Co.; 25 April 1718; i-299.

WILLIAM and FRANCIS HARBERT; inv. William Herbert, of St. Mary's Co.; 22 July 1718; i-302.

(To be continued)

THE WEBBS

(Continued from July number)

RICHARD WEBB was a servant to Mr. Edward Revell; age about 17. Acco. iii-190. 8 Apr 1670.

RICHARD WEBB m. MARY JEFERIES. Son Richard born 1 Feby 1672. Som., Md. May, 1672.

RICHARD WEB, h. r. under Col. Lemuel Mason. L. Norf. E-106. 19 Feby 1673-4.

RICHARD WEBB, wit. to will of Peter Beach, Staff., Va. Z-144. 20 Apr 1702.

RICHARD WEBB, Penna. Assembly. Pènna. Arch. vol. ix, 2d series. 1705.

RICHARD WEBB m. Rebecca Parrot, dau. of Wm. Tred Avon Mtg. Records, Md. i-302-304. 1700.

RICHARD WEB; lines between his land and the land of Mrs. Mary Hill and Mr. Forbis processioned. I. W. Vestry Book, Va., p. 5. Richard *Weeb* a processioner, p. 31. 1728. Also p. 24, 1727.

RICHARD WEBB; *MORTILACK,* Mattapony hd., was surveyed for him in 1683. Som. Md. R. R. 1723.

RICHARD WEBB had 250 acres of *TRUEBRIDGE,* Pocomoke hd., Som. R. R. 1723. [Note: The Debt Book of 1735 gives John Webb Trubridge and Winter Quarter.]

RICHARD WEBB; *WEBB'S HOPE* surveyed for him. See Calvert, Md., R. R. 1723 [date of roll].

RICHARD WEBB, Som. Co. Will. Eldest son William Webb, 100 acres called Littell Tract; second son Richard Webb; youngest son Mark Webb, 100 acres, part of Smith's Choice; dau. Mary, extx; dau. Anna. Bro-in-law John Tull overseer and trustee. Wit: Rich'd Holland, Mary Quillen. Annap., Md. Wills 18-293. 9 Dec 1723.

RICHARD WEBB; *SNAKEPOINT* east side of Fishing Creek surveyed for him. Dor. R. R. Md. 1635.

RICHARD WEBB an appraiser of the estate of William Thomas. I. W., Va., vii-75. 23 Mch 1728.

RICHARD WEBB was in King and Queen county, Va., 1733. See Stratton Major Parish.

RICHARD WEBB, wit. to will of Thomas Davis, I. W., Va., viii-23. 15 Aug 1734. Probate 23 Sept 1734.

RICHARD WEBB, see Henry Kea's estate account. I. W., Va., viii-66. 1735.

(To be continued)

FRIENDS' MEMORIALS

The following information is taken from a small volume, published in 1875, entitled as above, the Friends whose biographies are given in brief having been members of the Baltimore Yearly Meeting, which included certain Pennsylvania meetings.

ANN MOORE, b. Penna., 16th 9th 1710, in 1753 removed with her husband and family to Maryland, and settled within the compass of Gunpowder particular meeting. She died in Baltimore, the 11th 11th 1783. This testimony (of which only the mere personal record is given here) was signed by the Clerks of Gunpowder Meeting, John Wilson and Mary Parrish.

JOSEPH BERRY, son of James and Sarah Berry, of Talbot county, Maryland, died 22d 10th 1783, age 51. He was buried in Friends' burying ground at Tuckaho. Tristram Needles was Clerk of the Third-Haven Meeting, to which Joseph Berry belonged. JAMES BERRY, his brother, died 24th 1st 1785, age about 56, and was buried at Third-Haven.

JUDITH HOLLINGSWORTH, dau. of Isaac and Hannah Hollingsworth, of New Castle county, Delaware, was born 21st 12th 1776. She married 19th 4th 1797, David Preston. About 1806 they removed to Maryland and settled within the compass of Little Falls Preparative meeting. She died 29th 8th 1835.

DEBORAH PLEASANTS was born at Beaver Dam, Goochland county, Virginia, 25th 11th 1763. She was the daughter of Thomas and Elizabeth Pleasants, and married William Stabler of Petersburg, Virginia, in her 26th year. They removed to Leesburg, Loudoun county, Virginia. In 1793 they removed again to near Sandy Spring, Maryland. Her husband died 1806. She died 27th 6th 1845.

(To be continued)

The County Court Note-Book

An every-other-monthly devoted to abstracts from the County Court and other records, prior to 1800, and with a department of notes and queries.

MILNOR LJUNGSTEDT, Editor and Publisher. Bethesda, Route 1, Maryland.

Published every other month. Subscription, two dollars a year, in advance. Special rates on renewals.

VOL. I NOVEMBER, 1922 No. 7

ON COMPENSATION AND THE MARKET VALUE OF AN ANCESTOR

The Editor's earliest distinct recollection of earning money has no genealogical or literary association whatever. It was a case of taking childhood's most objectionable medicine, castor oil, and the Editor's dear and utterly unsystematic father had offered her twenty-five cents as an inducement to obey directions and take the hated dose. The Editor must confess she has no recollection of earning the then tremendous sum offered.

The next test of her earning ability was the offer by an in-law of five cents if she, the Editor, would keep still, that is, keep her tongue still one-half hour. A contemporary book bears on its fly-leaf, "Uncle... may I talk now?"

But the third adventure into high finance was more suitable to these pages. The Editor was actually paid one dollar for copying for the said in-law, the record of the MILNORS in the family Bible. Dear Family Bible! The Editor wishes she had it now, with its fascinating Apochrypha and equally fascinating pictures.

To the foregoing list might be added the offer of the Editor's grandfather that he would give her an apple and she could give him a rose if she didn't cry before church time. But this seems more in the nature of a wager and shockingly out of place in a minister's household on a Sunday morning; the Editor still reserves her opinion as to its propriety. Grandfathers of those days had no idea of what small, active, nervously temperamental children had to put up with on a Sunday! The day when every kind of a delightful plan or scheme came crowding upon the mind released from English history, partial payments, Audubon's mocking-bird (for parsing); and the mysteries of the solar system as set forth in the then geography, and visualized by a head master not above performing slow circles on the platform to explain the movements of the members of the stellar universe. Such a day, when the possibly "practicable" churn (made in Germany and costing one cent) could not be bought before Monday, nor could the tangled mysteries of the old streets be explored as on crowded week-days. There were so many ways of going to any one place!

Such was the Sunday of a child of the Victorian!

All this, my Reader, is not strictly connected with the Editor's subject.

The Editor is not absolutely a "professional," yet she is enough of one to make a few comments on the curious limitations of ancestral aspirants. The dear soul who desires a king or a duke, or even a member of the House of Burgesses in her line, often has so little realization, if any, that the *search* for these desired and distinguished folk justly requires recompense as much as does the night watchman who walks his lonely beat for years, yet never finds a burglar!

So the employer of the searcher consigns him or her to the dangers and discomforts of the rail, with or without Pullmans (mostly without); to the cross-country Fords and the impossible "Inns," and thinks it sufficient to pay for *results* only.

A case in which the end only is supposed to justify the means.

While it is regrettably true that there is much unreasonable overcharging in this work, especially in small county seats,... and the Editor personally knows of a payment of twenty-five dollars for a perfectly worthless piece of *mis*information constructed by fitting together two distinct and unrelated chancery records... and while much guesswork is willingly paid for... yet the Editor believes that the average client does not realize the patient intelligence which very many searchers, indeed, the greater number, give to the lines they are working upon. Eminently conscientious as to time; doing one-night stands at all sorts of personal inconvenience and discomfort; facing dirt and other insanitary conditions which really cannot be described, but are enough to appal the bravest; the Editor believes the service is worthy of the expenditure. Contingent pay should be ruled out; and a fair rate for personal service should always be added to actual subsistence and railroad fares.

Quite apropos is the following which comes to the Editor in all good faith from a correspondent of education and intelligence. Names have been changed by the Editor.

An Indiana banker having had unhappy results with professional genealogists is offering two dollars and fifty cents for each ancestor. The proposition as further explained by the Editor's correspondent, is that two dollars and fifty cents will be given for the name of the wife of a certain John Smith, who was living, we may say, in the county of Smithkins, Virginia, shortly before 1800. And two dollars and fifty cents more is offered for any proved ancestor of the aforesaid John Smith and all the information obtainable about said ancestor. This offer to hold good up to twenty-five dollars, "that is, twelve names." The decision as to whether the ancestor be proven, and the two dollars and fifty cents honorably earned, to rest with the employer. It will be seen from this that for the... say thirty-two ancestors of 1700, one might acquire the sum of eighty dollars.

The early records of seaboard counties contain many references to vessels and their masters. Sometimes these entries are in the form of long "Protests" against the force of "wind and wave"; two remarkably fine accounts of shipwrecks, one as good as Stevenson's best, are in two counties bordering on Hampton Roads. The NOTE-BOOK hopes to print one of these later. The value of the brief entries given on page one of this issue lies merely in their contribution to contemporary shipping lists, and to information as to masters, mostly from England or New England. Sometimes the names of vessels give very good clues as to family. The *Martha and Miriam,* Capt. John Wade of Chester, Penna., master, was named after the captain's wife and daughter. There are probably many vessels thus distinguished.

OCCASIONAL

Revolutionary War rates in Shenandoah County, Va., from Minute Book B. 1 June 1781. Dinner, £9; Supper or Breakf't, £6; Lodging, £3.

Martin Shaner and wife Catherine, county of *Hawkins,* Territory *south of the Ohio,* to William C. Williams of Shenandoah, two lots in Woodstock... Wit. Allen, Lee and Williams. Shenan. H-371, 28 April 1792.

Henry Nelson, county of Washington and *Territory of United States south of Ohio,* conveys land in Shenandoah county, corner to William Nelson. Shenan. i-429, 8 Sept 1794.

It being proved that MARY McDONALD was married to ANGLES [sic] McDONALD who died in the Continental Army... the same is ordered to be Certified. Loudoun Co., Va., Orders II-469. 12 Apr 1785.

From a coroner's verdict in Surry, Va. Ann A.... wife to John A...., "runs away, as was her wonted used and custom, and so comes to her death." ii-1677.

WHEREAS Comfort X. was Psented by the Grand Jury for swearing and Cursing to the value of Six oaths and curses &c... on the 7th day of March being on the Sabboth day [her attys] made it appeare to this Co'rt that the 7th day of March was not the Sabboth day & pray'd that for their false presentm't that she may be discharged from the Sd Pstm't & the Co'rt proceeded to Judgm't & ware of that oppi'on & ordered that She be discharged from the Sd Psentm't paying Charges [&c., &c.] Acco. xviii-62. 6 Aug 1723.

With this number the COUNTY COURT NOTE-BOOK closes the first year of its existence. The Editor regrets very much that it is found necessary to raise the subscription price to two dollars a year. Renewals may be made at one dollar and fifty cents, if received before January fifteenth.

The Editor has tried to be of as much use as possible, and if, in covering so much ground, the abstracted records seem a bit dry (resembling somewhat an evaporated fruit, which is all there, but needs water) it is hoped that the intelligence of the NOTE-BOOK'S readers will grasp the situation and make use of the material offered as one well-known genealogist does, as a sort of index. The Editor herself considers her pages as merely guideposts to historical and genealogical by-ways.

The Editor just naturally hates to "quit" and hopes her subscribers will not only renew but bring in others. The NOTE-BOOK has enough material on hand to be bigger and better. It won't be bigger... it may be better.

The next NOTE-BOOK will contain EARLY MARYLAND NATURALIZATIONS; KING GEORGE COUNTY (Va.) BONDS; and extracts from QUAKER MEMORIALS.

KNOW ALL MEN by these presents that I THOMAS FARRILL of Washington county in the State of Maryland, late Deputy Field Commissary of Millitary Stores in the Service of the United States of America is scized in fee simple of and in a Certain tract or parcell of Land lying & being in the State of Massachusetts Bay Called & commondly known by the name of Deer Island which said Islands lays in the Bay of Passamacadie and west of the River St. Croix NOW therefore know ye that the said Thomas Farrill for divers good causes & considerations him thereunto moving hath made ordained and Authorized, constituted and appointed and by these presents doth make ordain Authorize and appoint Daniel Cresap Jr. of the County of Washington in the State of Maryland & James Chasey, John Lawless and John Fountain. all of the said Island called Deer Island as above or either of them true and lawful Attorneys of him the said THOMAS FARRELL & in his name to convey & make over to a Certain Col. Thomas Cresap of Washington County in the State of Maryland all the Right & Claim of him the said FARRILL... to the above Described Island... In witness whereof the said THOMAS FARRILL hath hereunto set his hand & seal this 18th day of April in the year of our Lord 1783. THOMAS FARRILL. (Seal) In the Presence of Charles Prather, And'w Bruce, John I. Jacob. Deeds Lib. C, p. 48, Hagerstown, Md.

[*Contributed by Mrs. Geo. W. Hodges.*]

OUR ANCESTRAL RECORDS IN ENGLAND

(Second article continued)

Contributed by Mr. E. Dwelly, of England.

PARISH REGISTERS. Curious and interesting ordinances concerning the Registers, other than those given in a previous article, are found in the English records.

In 1667, burials in wool were ordered. In 1678 this was strongly enforced. These "woollen" acts were not repealed until 1814.

In 1698, duties on all entries (in Registers) were imposed for five years. As stated in the former article, a duty of 3d. was imposed in 1783, and only repealed in 1794.

In 1812 all Registers were placed under control of the Registrar-General, books of new and uniform design being insisted on.

In 1831, a list of existing Registers was compiled. This list shows their deficiency and their careless treatment.

In 1837, civil registration commenced, since which date a certificate of the birth, marriage or death of any individual in Great Britain can be obtained from Somerset House, London. Records of residents in Scotland can similarly be obtained in the Register House, Edinburgh.

A pamphlet could be filled with interesting information concerning Parish Registers. Space will permit only the most useful items.

Baptisms: "Half-baptized" refers to children privately baptized, as those in danger of death, and is generally followed at a later date by "publickly christened" or "received into the Church." Illegitimacy was frankly recorded; also the unequal social position of parents, such as when the father was of gentle birth, the mother not. *"Spurious"* is the curious term used when, vice versa, the mother was gentle, the father not. These terms were not, however, always used in their literal sense. *"Patre incognito"* is a common form in some registers.

(Further articles will be published later, including a very interesting account of the Scottish records, their removal and return.)

NOTES AND QUERIES

BRUFF-GOLDSBOROUGH: Rachel Bruff m. sometime about the middle of the 18th century FOSTER (Nicholas 3 Nicholas 2 Nicholas 1) GOLDSBOROUGH. List of her children wanted, dates and to whom married; also her ancestry. Was she descended from BRUFF of Bruff's Island, Talbot Co., Md.?

FOSTER GOLDSBOROUGH received by father's will tract called "Hog Island," Dorchester Co., also "Goose Pond" and other small lots.

Who was REBECCA, second wife of NICHOLAS GOLDSBOROUGH (4)? Has anyone an authentic list of his children? E. J. A. C.

RICHARD THOMPSON m. MAGDALEN BOUCHELLE, 1706, 4, 18, and they had had a daughter Margaret, born 1718, 5, 20. ABEL VAN BARKLO m. CATHERINE HERMAN, 1715, 6, 7, and they had a daughter, Margaret, b. 1719, 10, 8.

ANDREW GRAVENRAET m. MARGARET (...?) a descendant of AUGUSTINE HARMAN. Did he marry one of the Margarets above? C. H. B. T.

TEN DOLLARS will be paid for *authentic* record of ancestor of JAMES FOWKE (FOWKES, FOOKS) of Northampton and Accomack counties, Virginia, immigrant about 1660. H. C. F. M.

MARGARET (SAVAGE) ELLIGOOD was the sister of SUSANNA BOWDOIN, wife of JOHN BOWDOIN, of Northampton Co., Va. Can any one give definite information as to SUSANNA BOWDOIN, whether she was a full sister or only a half-sister of MARGARET ELLIGOOD? M. L. M.

THOMAS SAVAGE, father of MARGARET ELLIGOOD, died about 1708. Full list of children wanted, and name of wife. M. L. M.

PALMER: Five dollars will be paid for authoritative information as to the ancestry of MARTIN PALMER, of Charlotte Co., Va., father of Chilian Palmer. W. B. P. A.

ROBINSON: Who was SAUL ROBINSON who died in Worcester Co., Md., about twenty-five years ago? M. L. M.

ROBINSON-FELL: Is there any authority for the statement that LUCY FELL, of Baltimore, married JOHN ROBINSON, of Middlesex Co., Va.? M. L. M.

HOOKER: Would like any notes on HOOKERS of North Carolina, Virginia, or Maryland, before 1800. C. A. B. C.

CAIN: Wanted, parentage of GEORGE CATHEY CAIN; born North Carolina, 1813. Five dollars will be paid for information with authority. C. A. B. C.

CARR-COLE: Five dollars for authoritative information of locality from which either family emigrated to Kentucky. AQUILA COLE m. *circa* 1800, RACHEL CARR, dau. of John and Elizabeth (White) Carr. C. A. B. C.

MASON: What was the maiden name of MARGARET MASON, widow of EDWARD, of Stafford Co., Va., who married (2) ABRAHAM FARROW shortly after 1700? Mrs. W. W.

HART: The will of VALENTINE HART, 1792 or 3, in Rockbridge county, Va., names four persons: Valentine, Jr., Leonard, Moses and one other. What became of this MOSES HART and whom did he marry? E. J. C. A.

ROBINSON-WILCOX: Information is very much desired as to the marriage record of JOHN ROBINSON and EUNICE WIL-

COX. This marriage occurred somewhere in eastern New York, probably about 1770. E. D. R. P.

WILLIAM ROBINSON, born 1704, m. MARY MARGARET WEBB. Both, probably from the Northern Neck of Virginia. Wanted: parents of both. G. F. R. I.

ROBINSON: Fore-name unknown; had son CORNELIUS who went to a Southern State. The father came from Ireland to New York about 1780. Information greatly desired. J. A. S. K.

FROM THE TOMB OF SUSANNA ROBINSON, ST. PAUL'S CHURCHYARD, NORFOLK, VIRGINIA

To the memory of Susanna Robinson
Born ----------------1769
Died September 30th, 1826
This stone is erected
By her affectionate relatives
Age did not chill her heart
Nor misfortune embitter it.
And when deprived by death
Of nearly all allied to her by blood,
She dispensed her kindness
To the deserving and unfortunate stranger.
But her charity like her religion
Was unostentatious
And the indigent felt without knowing
The hand which ministered to them.
In every relation of life
A kind heart made her indulgent,
And a strong mind just.
Affable to her equals, kind to her dependents,
A practical Christian,
She had every quality to endear her to this world
And fit her for a better,
The hope of which cheered in solitude
And solaced her in death.
When dust like hers returns to nature's bourn,
We feel in truth that we have cause to mourn.
Departed virtue ever leaves behind
A fond remembrance in the grateful mind.

Interesting facts, as sometimes portrayed in the preamble of an old deed.

This INDENTURE made 15th Aug. in the year of Our Lord one thousand seven hundred and sixty-seven, Between Petrus Eltinge of the Precinct of the Wallkill in the County of Ulster and the Province of New York yeoman and Elizabeth his wife of the one part and Mary Elmendorph widow of Petrus Edmiondus Elmendorph late of the town of Kingston in the County of Ulster aforesaid Merchant deceased of the other part, WHEREAS Rudolphus Eytinge late of Potomack in the Colony of Maryland deceased died without issue, and intestate seized of and in the six several certain Tracts Pieces or Parcells of land hereinafter particularly mentioned and described and whereas the said Petrus Eltinge is full Cousin and heir at law of the said Rudolphus Eltinge deceased [then follows the usual conveyance]. Frederick Co., Md., Liber L, p. 28.

BOOK NOTICES

The FIRST PARISHES OF THE PROVINCE OF MARYLAND. A most interesting and valuable work under this title has been prepared by Percy G. Skirven of Baltimore, well-known for his previous publications on Maryland history. The present volume will give historical sketches of the ten counties and thirty parishes of the province in 1692 (at the time of the establishment of the Church of England), and will also contain a large map in colors, showing the boundaries of the counties and parishes. This map throws newly discovered light on the geographical situation prior to 1706, which has been more or less obscure.

The book is the fruit of years of laborious research on the part of Mr. Skirven, of which this Editor has some personal knowledge, and the information brought together is of the greatest importance and will be of inestimable value to the historian, the genealogist, and the antiquarian, as well as to the student of Church history.

Publication, it is understood, depends on the response received by the publishers to their advance announcement.

The Reverend Benjamin Ancell, M. A., member of the Virginia Historical Society, the Society of the Sons of the American Revolution, etc., is preparing a genealogical list of the descendants of Mistress Katherine Banks, of Canterbury, England, who married (1) Joseph Royall, of Henrico County, Virginia, and (2) Henry Isham, of the same county. The number of her descendants already compiled through the Royall, Perrin, Randolph, and Eppes families (her only Isham son died without issue) is more than eleven thousand. The compiler hopes that all who know themselves to be of such ancestry will co-operate to make this a still more complete historical list of an honourable lineage.

Address Rev. BENJAMIN ANCELL, D. D., Mahan School, Yangchow, China.

GENERAL INFORMATION

Persons wishing to stay at SURRY C. H., Va., are advised to wait until the new Court House is finished. At present the Clerk's Office is moved into the "fire-proof"... a not very large room and difficult to heat in wintry weather.

The Courthouses in STAFFORD and KING GEORGE are both being rebuilt, and searchers will find it inconvenient in both offices to examine records and do any writing. The Clerk at King George hopes to have his office finished before the remainder of the building, and will, no doubt, answer any inquiry for information as to when the records will be again properly housed.

Persons interested in the old county of OHIO, Virginia, or in the records at RALEIGH, N. C., or at EDENTON, N. C., please address the Editor.

Also anyone who wishes detailed search in RICHMOND, NORTHUMBERLAND, LANCASTER, MIDDLESEX, or ESSEX counties, Virginia.

Also in DOVER, Delaware.

PUBLICATIONS OF VALUE TO HISTORIANS AND GENEALOGISTS

Twenty-five cents each will be paid for ten copies of the October, and ten copies of the December NOTE-BOOK.—Editor.

GENEALOGISTS AND OTHERS INTERESTED IN RESEARCH WORK

Columbian Ptg. Co., Inc.

Index to Volume I

Abbett, 35
Abercrombie, 27
Adams, 30, 43
Adolph, 1
Akin, 1
Alcott, *19
Alexander, 30, *38, 45
Alford, 33, 34
Allen, 26, 49, 53
Allerton, *19, 41
Ambrose, 14
Anderson, 5
Andrews, *25, 27, 41
Archer, *49
Armstrong, 43
Arrington, 22, 29
Arundell, *10
Ash, 37
Ashley, 43
Ashmore, 14, 30
Attwell, 14, 30
Austine, 42
Ayres, 43

Badham, 41
Bailey, 17
Baker, 1, 49
Ballard, 17, 34, 50
Bancks, 42
Banks, 55
Barker, 45, 49
Barlowe, 25, 27
Barnes, 28
Barnett, 28, 37
Barr, 22
Barrow, 22, 49
Barrowes, 34
Basdell, 9
Basnett, 25
Bateman, 34
Battell, 41
Baxter, 27
Baylie, 41
Baylis, *5, *14, 22
Beach, 51
Beaseley, 25, 51
Beckwith, 34
Bell, 2, 13, 14
Bellamy, 27
Bennett, 14, 22, *29
Benson, 26
Berkeley, 23
Bernoux, de, 43
Berry, 19, 27, 50, 51
Bibbe, 19
Bigby, 14, 29
Biggins, 35
Billeton, 34
Billings, 50
Blackburn, 5, 22, 29, 30, 38
Blackwell, 5, 14
Blalock, 26
Bland, 5, 22, 37, 38, 45
Blighton, 49
Blow, 49
Blunt, 49
Boatman, 5
Boggess, 5
Booker, 33
Boone, 39
Boote, 42
Boren, 1
Boteler, 33
Bott, 38
Botts, 38
Bouchelle, 49
Bourkes, 34
Boush, 1
Bowdoin, 6, 14, 43, 54
Boyce, Boys, *43
Bradford, 30
Branch, 49
Braxton, 35
Bray, 9, *34
Brazier, 42
Breeding, 28
Brent, 19; *29, 30, 38
Brenton, 27
Brett, 19, *33, 37, *38
Brewer, 34
Brewster, 49
Brian, 43
Bridger, 2
Bridges, 14, 22, 29, 30, 34
Bright, 34
Bristow, 19
Britt, 5, 33
Brown, 30, 34, *38, *42, *45, 49
Browning, 3
Bruce, 45
Bruff, 43, 54
Bryan, 34
Buckner, 42
Bullett, 6, 29, 30, 38
Bullitt, 45
Burbage, 25
Burford, 6, 14, 22
Burgess, 42
Burgh, 9
Burnell, 42
Burrier, 3
Burroughs, 45
Burrus, 17, 35
Burton, 42
Busick, 34
Bussies, 18
Butt, *2
Byrn, 30, 37, 38

Cahow, 51
Cain, 15, 23, 31, 46, 54
Caldwell, 5
Calk, 38
Calvert, see Colvert
Calvert, *22, 29, *30, 45, 50
Camp, 1
Campbell, 50
Cannon, 38, *45
Carberry, 37
Carlisle, 3
Carpenter, 38
Carr, 5, 14, *22, 23, *29, 31, 45, 46, 54
Carrington, 50
Carslake, 43
Carsley, 25, 37
Carson, 34
Carter, 30, 37, 45, 50
Casie, 50
Cason, 25
Caston, 26
Cathey, 23, 31, 54
Cecil, 47
Chambers, 49
Chance, 43
Chandler, 17
Chaplin, 19
Chapman, 30, 38, 41, 45
Charlton, 15
Chasey, 53
Cheasman, 35
Cheney, 33
Cheshire, 2, 38, 40, 45
Chesley, 25
Chester, 18
Chichester, 41
Chilcoat, Chilcott, 18, 25
Childs, 15
Christian, 9, *17, *26
Church, 34
Claiborne, 45
Clark, 17, 19, 35, 45
Clary, 9, 17
Clavert, 5
Clawson, 19
Clay, *49
Clearsman, 35
Clements, 50
Cleveland, 38
Clevinger, 30
Clifton, 50
Cloverfield, 42
Cluer, 25
Cobb, 33
Cock, 9, 30
Cockayne, 43
Cocker, 14, 50
Coffer, 22
Cole, Coale, 10, 23, 31, 39, 43, 46, 54
Colebaugh, 34
Coleblough, 34
Coleclough, 5, 34

Coleman, *9, 17, 42
Colhoun, 24
Collins, 3
Colquitt, 24
Colvert, see Calvert
Colvert, 5, *22, 30
Com'ry, see Mezick
Conelly, 10
Connaway, 3
Contee, 50
Conway, 14
Conyers, 5, 42
Coocee, 25
Cook, 30
Coombes, 51
Cooper, *25, 30, *38, 45, 50
Corder, 6, 14, 22
Corker, 50, 59
Cornelius, 41
Cornix, 25
Cornwell, *5
Coster, 22
Courcy, 25
Crabtree, 41
Craig, 42
Creel, 5
Cresap, 53
Crook, 38, 45
Crookshanks, 42
Crosse, 19
Crupper, 25
Cudgely, 19
Cullins, 22
Cunningham, 4, 7, 43
Curry, 45
Curtis, 41, 42
Custis, 10, 18, 27, 41

Dabney, 35
Dade, 42
Dagge, 38
Dale, 38
Dalton, 29
Daniel, Daniels, 7, 39
Danison, 41
Darby, 13
Darley, 16, 23
Darnell, 5, 14
Darrell, 42
Darvall, 27
Dashfield, 43
Dashill, Dashsell, 34, 50
Davenport, 5, 15, 23, 42
Davidson, 29
Davis, 2, *5, 11, 14, 16, 18, *22, *26, 28, *29, *30, 35, 39, 51, 67
Davison, 41
Dawkins, 5, 14, 23, 31
Dawson, 33
Day, 11, 26
De Bernoux, 43
Delgarn, 45
Denfield, 50
Denman, 3
Dennis, 27
Dent, 51
Devilbiss, 3
Devotion, 18
Dickenson, *50
Dier, 25, 34
Dilke, 10
Diskis, 22
Disney, 42
Dixon, 31, 34
Dobson, 43
Dolby, 10
Doneal, 42
Dorsett, 33
Dorsey, 33
Doughty, 25
Douglas, 14, 29, *51
Dowell, 37
Downing, 42
Doys, 43
Dreyden, 51
Drought, 41
Drummond, 30
Drury, Drewry, *35
Dugal, 17
Duke, 49, 50
Dunford, 50
Dunn, 13
Dunster, 2
Dust, 5
Duty, 15, 23
Dwelley, 39
Dyer, 42

Eader, 2
Earle, Earles, 14, 15, 19, 23, 37, 41
Eaton, 25
Edmond, 14
Edmondson, 50
Edwards, 5, 25, 26, 35
Efell, 37
Ellegood, Elligood, 46, 54
Ellis, 34
Elmendorph, 55
Elston, 18
Eltinge, 55
Eltonhead, 41
Ely, 9
Elzey, *14, 22, 42
Emms, 5, 14
Endridge, 34
England, 9, 10
English, 30, 34
Eppes, 55
Etzler, 3
Eubanks, Ewbanks, 23, 31, 39
Eustace, 5
Evans, 3, 29, 50
Ewell, 14, 22, *38, *45
Exum, 2, 9, 24
Eytinge, 55

Fairbanks, 50
Falkner, 27
Falner, 22, 37
Farrah, 34
Farrill, 53
Farrow, 5, 30, 42, 54
Feay, 50
Feddeman, 34
Fell, 39, 46
Felt, 16
Ferneyhaugh, 25
Ferreby, 34
Fewell, 45
Fielder, 45
Finch, 29
Finley, 23, 31, 39
Fisher, Fischer, 3, 25, 27, 34
Fitzgarrell, 34
Fleming, *2, 9, *17
Flerde, 27
Fletcher, 5, 14
Florence, 30
Floyd, 6, 7, 13, 14, 15, 19, 22, 23, 30, 39
Foley, 14, 37, *38
Folis, 42
Folsom, *30
Fookes, Fooks, 46, 54
Foord, 42
Foote, 38
Forbis, 51
Fossett, 3
Foster, 5, *29, 30, 38
Foulke, 46
Fountain, 53
Fowke, 46, 54
Fox, 27
Franklin, 24
Fread, 3
Freeman, 33
French, 28
Frizzle, 3
Frushour, 3
Fryer, 41
Furment, 2

Gadsby, 35
Gahagan, 49
Gaines, 38
Gallahue, 30, 38
Gardiner, Gardner, 19, 43
Garlick, 35
Garner, 5
Gary, 31

George, 25
Gibbons, Gibons, 41, 43
Gibbs, 25
Gibson, 6, 14, 23, 30, 35, 42
Gifferd, 51
Gifford, 41
Gilbert, 49
Gillis, 3
Gilson, 42
Glascock, 14, 22
Godwin, 2, 7, 30, 39
Godwyn, 2
Goldsborough, 54
Gott, 50
Gouge, 25
Goyer, 35
Grace, 27
Graham, 5, 14, 22, 29, *45
Grant, 5, 33
Gravenraet, 54
Gray, 9, 33, 43
Grayson, 5, 14, 30, 43
Green, Greene, 5, 34, 38, 42, 43
Greenfield, 33
Greenway, 49
Gregg, 43
Gresham, 43
Griffith, 1
Grigsby, 14, 45
Grimstead, Grinstead, 22, 37, 38, 45
Grymes, 35
Gunyon, 38
Gwathmey, 35
Gwatkin, Gwatkins, 5, 14, *22, *29, 37, 38, 45

Haas, 42
Haden, 3, 38
Hale, 11, 39
Hall, 18, *41, 50
Halpen, 33
Hamer, 46
Hammitt, 45
Hampton, 38
Hamrick, *22, 45
Hanby, 25
Hancock, 18
Hand, 43
Hanes, 33
Hankins, 42
Hanks, 38
Hanley, 49
Hannah, 17
Hansburgh, 42
Hanson, 33, *42, 50
Harbert, *51
Harding, 17, 50
Hardy, 9, 51
Hare, 50
Harman, 41, 54
Harper, 29
Harris, 33
Harrison, 6, 14, 22, 30, *38, 43, *45
Hart, 22, 42, 54
Hartley, 23, 31
Harwood, 31, 43
Haskins, 24, 31
Hawkins, 22, 33, 42
Hawley, 19
Hays, 15, 23, 25
Haynes, 22, 23
Hayward, 34
Hazard, 43
Hazelrig, 22
Heathman, 33
Hedges, 22, 45
Heighan, 25
Heise, 42
Helm, 14, 29, 30, 38
Hemlock, 25
Henderson, 29
Henley, 25
Henry, 3
Herbert, *51
Herman, 41, 54
Hickman, 35
Hicks, 46
Hiddon, 33
Higgens, 43
Higgerson, 37
Higgs, 45
Highlander, 37
Hiles, 17
Hill, 10, 24, 27, *35, 43, *50, 51
Hillyard, 35
Hinckes, 25
Hinson, 25
Hiway, Hyway, *43
Hix, 17
Hodge, 35, 42
Hogan, 5, 38
Holden, 11
Holdsworth, 9
Holl, 2
Holladay, 7
Holland, 27, 41, 43, 51
Hollensworth, Hollingsworth, 50, 51
Holmes, 34, 35, 42, 50
Holtzclaw, 45, 50
Homey, 34
Hooe, *30, *37, 38, 42, 45
Hoof, 38
Hooker, 46, 54
Hopkins, 50
Horn, 25, 34
Hornbuckle, 37
Hoskins, 33, 45
Howard, 34
Howison, *45
Hubbard, 42
Hucheson, 33
Hudson, 17, 41, 50
Hughes, 4, 14
Humphery, 37
Humston, 5
Hunt, 18, 19
Husbands, 12
Hutchinson, 31, 33, 38
Hyatt, *3

Inglish, 34
Ingram, 50
Ironshear, 33
Isham, 47

Jackson, 14, 34, 37, 45
Jacob, 2, 27, 53
Jadwin, 19
James, 49
Jarrett, 49
Jarvis, 14
Jeferies, 35, 51
Jeffrey, 25
Jenifer, 33
Job, 43
Johnson, *10, 14, 17, 22, 25, 29, 30, 42, 45
Johnstone, 5, 14, 15, 23
Jolly, 25
Jones, 3, *5, 35, 38, *45, 49
Jordan, 9, 17, 26, 31, *45, 49
Jukes, 43

Kea, 51
Keane, 15
Keith, 6, 14, 22, 38
Kelly, 29, 33, 49
Kemp, 22, 31
Kendall, 10, 19, 43
Kennedy, 39, 46
Kenner, 14
Kimmont, 50
Kincheloe, 14, 22, 30
King, 33, 34, 37, 43
Kinsey, 25
Kitchen, 45
Knight, 2, 19
Knox, 34

Lake, 34, *41
Lambert, Lambardt, 19, 34
Lamkin, 42
Landrum, 17, 45
Lane, 31, 41
Langdon, 27
Langworthy, 11

Larue, 3
Lashbrook, 14
Lathan, 6
Lattimore, 22
Laughland, 1
Lawless, 53
Lawrence, 34
Lawson, 29, 30, 37, 38
Leake, 34
Lee, 22, 29, 30, 53
Lewis, 31
Liesher, 3
Lilly, 25
Linck, 37
Lindsay, 10, 37
Lingan, 33
Linkhorn, 12
Linton, 5, 22, 34, 37, *38
Lipscomb, 17, 18, *26, 31
Long, 43
Lord, *27
Lovell, 25
Lowe, 17, *33, 45
Lowell, 34
Lowry, 43
Lowther, 42
Loyd, 10
Luddingham, 43
Lumsden, 22
Luttrell, 22, 29
Lyle, 42
Lynn, 38, 45
Lyon, 39

McClester, 33
Macrae, 29
McDaniel, 45
McDonald, 53
McDugal, 17
McGee, 28
McKimmie, 24
Mackinnie, 2
McMilliam, 45
McMillian, McMillion, 6, 22, 30, 37, 38
McQuillian, 38
McWilliams, 27
Machen, 5
Mack, 12
Madden, Maden, 38, 45
Maddocke, 42
Maddox, 38
Major, 27
Mallory, 26
Malvern, 43
Maning, 34
Mankin, 38, 45
Mansfield, 17
Markham, 25
Marr, 30
Marrine, 41
Marshall, 2, 37
Martin, 33, 34, 42, 51
Mason, 14, 34, 42, 51, 54
Massey, 27, 42
Mathias, 3
Mathis, 14, 22
Matison, 29
Matthews, Mathews, 17, 43
Matthis, 14, 22, 45
Mattison, 45
Mavericke, 19
Mayhew, 30, 39
Medcalfe, 10
Melling, 27
Melton, 18
Merchant, 34
Meredith, 2, 35
Merest, 42
Mezick, 43, 50
Michael, 18
Middleton, 49
Milburn (?), 6
Miller, 33, 43, 50
Millman, 33
Milner, 15
Milton, 38
Minshall, 25
Mitchell, 5, 26, 35, 43
Moffett, 14, 30
Mohler, 4, 6, 15, 22
Moreland, 17
Monery, 17
Moore, 25, *29, 43, 45, 51
More, 11, 14
Moreland, 17
Morgan, 25
Moring, 9, 17
Mornan, 17
Morris, 33, 42
Moseley, 26, 50
Moss, 5, 14, 29, 37
Mouring, 17
Mourning, Morning, 9, *17
Moyses, 27
Mudge, 26
Muffett, 14
Murrah, 33
Murray, 26, 33, 38, 43, 45
Murren, 41
Musgrave, 4, 15
Musgrove, 6, 14, 23, 30, 45

Neale, 18, 26, 34
Neeck, 11
Needham, 25
Needles, 51
Nelson, 3, 27, 53
Newman, 38
Newton, 33, 42
Nicholson, 43
Nickson, *42
Nicolay, 12
Nisbett, 14, 22
Noale, 18
Noell, 33
Norgrave, 35, *42
Norton, 33
Norwood, 25
Not, Nott, 2, 18
Nottingham, 10

Obanion, 14
O'Brien, 38, 45
Ochain, 50
Odell, 43
Oden, 5
Okeham, 34
Oldsum, 33
Omoligon, 12
O'Neal, 45
Orchar, 49
Oreas, 45
Organ, 49
Overall, 5
Overzee, 34
Owen, 17, 51
Owens, 38
Owings, 3

Page, 33
Pain, Payne, 19, *41, 42
Palmer, 1, 39, *43, 46, 54
Pancoast, 4, 6, 15, 22
Panell, 10
Parish, 9, 51
Parke, *17
Parker, 19, 37, *41
Parrott, 35, 51
Parry, 33
Parsons, 37
Passemer, 41
Patten, 46
Paul, 34
Payne, see Pain
Peachy, 38
Peake, 5, 14, 42
Pearce, 45
Pearson, 34
Peerse, 26
Penhallow, 12
Penn, 3
Pennell, 10
Perg, 41
Perq, 27
Perrie, 35
Perrin, 47
Perry, 3, 25
Peters, 3, 4
Peterson, 34
Pettit, 10
Pettus, 9
Petty, 45

Pettyjohn, *17
Peyton, 5, 22, 29, 37, *38, 45
Phelps, 43
Phillips, 3
Pigg, 17
Pigot, 25
Piles, 50
Pitt, 50
Pleasants, 43
Plomer, 25
Poole, *3, 25, 50
Pope, 24, 31, 42
Porter, 23, 30
Pott, 10
Pouncey, *43
Pound, 39
Powell, 33, 38, 43, 50
Prather, 53
Preston, 51
Price, 42, 46
Prine, 30
Pritchett, 33
Puckle, 27
Purcell, 30

Quarles, 17, 26, 35
Quillan, 51
Quimby, 39

Ragsdale, 35
Ramsbottom, 17
Randolph, 45, 55
Ratcliffe, 37
Rawlins, 39
Rea, 11
Read, 41, 51
Redman, 45
Reed, 23, 31
Reeve, *14, 22, 37, 38
Reeves, 5, *22, 45
Reins, 34, 35
Reno, 5, 14, 29, 30, 37, 45
Reve, 22
Revell, 35, 50, 51
Revet, 42
Reyne, 34
Reynolds, 35
Rich, 33
Richards, Rickards, *1, 3, 41
Richardson, 24, 34, 35
Richeson, 35
Riddick, 26
Riddle, 29
Rixey, 5
Roach, 43
Roberts, *17
Robertson, see Robinson
Robertson, 9, 47
Robins, 1, 10, *11
Robinson, see Robertson
Robinson, 6, 7, 11, 14, 15, *18, *22, 23, 24, *25, *26, 30, *39, *46, 47, *54, *55
Robson, 51
Rogers, 4
Rookard, 5, 22
Rooke, 25
Roome, 50
Rose, 35, 54
Rossau, 14
Royall, 33, 55
Rudder, 17
Rule, 2
Rumsey, 43
Rush, 14, 22
Russell, 25, *42, 43, 50
Ryan, 17

Sadler, 26
Sanders, 41, 46
Sandford, 43
Saneishes (?), 5
Saunders, 39
Savage, 25, 27, 35, 42, 45, 50, 54
Sawyer, 34
Sayres, 34
Scarburgh, 3, 15, 25
Scarlett, 27, 42
Scott, 9, 18, 19, *45
Scottowe, 41
Seale, 5, 14, 30, 45
Seaton, 14
Seewright, 45
Selkirke, 19
Sellicke, 19
Sellman, 3
Sergeant, 35
Sexton, 25
Shaner, 53
Shanklin, 31, 39
Shapley, 1
Sharpe, 1, 11
Sharry, 50
Shaw, 25, 43
Shelton, *17, 26
Shepheard, 11
Sherwood, 35
Shields, 3
Ship, 22
Shipley, 3, 50
Shute, 45
Siddall, 33
Sikes, 3
Silence, 33
Simms, 38
Simpson, 6, 14, 23, 30, 34, 49
Sinclair, 5, 14
Skeele, 42
Skinner, 43
Slatterly, 3
Slaughter, 26, 35
Slish, 2
Smart, 25, 41
Smith, 1, 2, *5, 10, 30, 33, 35, 37, 38, 42, 43, 50
Smoot, 45
Smythe, 25
Southbee, 27
Sowders, 3
Sowsby, 49
Speake, 51
Spikeman, 22
Spillar, 5
Spiller, 14
Spiltimber, 42
Spires, 41
Spitter, 45
Stabler, 51
Stannaway, 25
Staple, 34
Steele, 3, 23, 30
Stephens, 1, 50
Stevens, 43, 50
Stewart, see Stuart
Stewart, 7
Stone, *5, *30
Stowell, 39
Strangwidge, 19
Stratton, 25, 34
Streeter, 25
Stribling, 5
Stringer, 19
Stuart, see Stewart
Stuart, 37
Swayne, 34
Syes, 3
Sympson, 49

Tackitt, 5 (?), 14, 45
Tainie, 45
Talbot, 43
Tales, 34
Taliafero, 35
Tanson, 51
Tatchyorn, 34
Tatum, 17
Taul, 15, 23, 30
Taylor, 23, 27, 31, 34, 43
Tebbs, 5, 14, 29, *30, *45
Tenison, 45
Tennell, Tennil, 5, 38
Tharp, 2, 5
Thomas, 3, 11, 33, 42, 43, 51
Thompson, 4, 33, 38, 41, 54
Thorndike, 27, 41
Thornton, *5, 22, *29, 30, *38, 50
Thornton (?), 14, 42
Thorowgood, 3

Thropsher, 43
Thurman, 5
Tilghman, Tilman, 18, *19
Timberlake, 26
Todd, 27, 42
Tolle, 33
Tomlinson, 34
Tover, 10
Townsend, 25, *42, *46
Townshend, Townsend, *2, 6
Trent, 26
Trewets, 50
Triplett, 22, 29, 30
Tripp, 26
Troxell, 3
Truit, 50
Tull, 51
Tullis, 17
Tullors, 14
Tully, 41
Tunstall, 35
Tyler, 22, 28

Underwood, 11, 39
Ungle, 34

Valentine, 37
Van Barklo, 54
Vasser, 13
Veale, 2
Vester, 37
Vickers, 34

Wade, 15, 17, 23, 35, 53
Wailes, 43
Wake, 22
Walker, 43, 50
Wall, 34, 35
Wallace, 18, 43
Waller, 9
Walters, 50
Walton, 24
Ward, 14, 17, 41
Warman, 50
Warren, *38, 50
Wasley, 35
Waters, 3, 26, 50
Watford, 25
Watkins, 49
Watts, 15, 25, 35, 42, 50
Webb, 1, 2, 3, *10, *11, 15, *18, 23, *26, 30, 35, 51, 55
Weir, 15, 23, 30
Weller, 3
Wellman, 51
Wells, 22
Welsh, 33
West, 5, 27, 43
Westerous, 19
Wetherell, 34
Wheatley, 11
White, 10, 26, *27, 29, 33, 42, 43, 46, 51
Whitehead, 33, 38
Whitely, 50
Whiting, 37
Whitledge, 45
Whitson, 42
Whittington, 43
Wickliff, 14, *22
Wigginton, 38
Wilburne, 6
Wilcox, 54
Wiles, 26
Wilkinson, 2, 30, 43
Williams, 1, 4, 6, 11, 15, 25, 26, 33, 53
Williamson, 9, 10
Willson, 2, 4, 22, 26, 38, 39, 42, 46, *50, 51
Winder, 50
Winn, 17
Wise, 23, 24
Witley, 51
Womack, 24, 31
Wood, 18, 37, 43
Woodward, 2, 16, 23, 30, 50
Woolman, 43
Wooten, 24
Wooters, 27, 33
Workman, 25
Worthington, *50
Wrench, 33
Wright, 1, *5, *29, 38, 43
Wross, 14
Wyatt, *5, 29
Wyre, 15, 23, 30
Wythe, 43

Yate, 33
Yeates, 25
Young, 35

Zachary, *23, 31

The

County Court Note-Book

A Little Bulletin of History and Genealogy

Vol. II **February, 1923** **No. 1**

NEW ENGLANDERS AND OTHERS IN EARLY VIRGINIA RECORDS

(Fourth instalment)

Mr. EDWARD ASHLEY of N. E. N-n, xvii-191. 29 Sept 1692. (Called of Boston in a later record.)

JAMES ADLINGTON, JOHN ROBINSON, and JOHN x TROWALL, all of Boston in N. E., Mchts; power to John Burroughs of N-n, Va. N-n, xv-263. 5 Dec 1685.

PETER BRACKET of Brantbrye (?) in N. E., power to Thomas Luund [sic] of Boston in N. E., Mcht. Wmld, 1-114. 20 Aug 1658. (A later record calls him of Brantoye (?), County of Suffolk, in N. E., Mcht., and he gives power to Mr. Robert Slye of Matapony, Md. ii-51. 20 Sept 1660.)

[Mr.] WILLIAM BRENTON, of Boston in New England; power to Mr. Daniel Hute [Hutt], master of the *Mayflower*. Wit: Thomas Michell, John Lee. Wmld, ii-38. 17 Sept. 1658.

WILLIAM BRENTON, of Newport on Road Island, Mcht, in the province of Providence plantacons in New England in America; power to Capt. James Cudworth [Gent.] of Newport, aforesaid. Wmld, ii-52. 12 Sept 1661.

CHRISTOPHER BUTLER from Kent Co., son of William Butler. Acco., x-115; 1693.

ROBERT BRONSDON (?) of Boston in N. E., Mcht; power to Capt. Edmund Febuarry of Salem, marriner. Wit: Jonathan Very, James Cox. I. W. iv-9; 26 Sept 1688.

JOHN CLARKE, of Boston, Mariner; power to father, Christopher Clarke, of Boston, mariner. N-n, xiv-36. 12 Mch 1680. Mortgages a dwelling-house on Back streete in Boston, which he bought of Thomas Savage, Jr., of Boston. N-n, xiv. 12 Mch 1680.

ROBERT CLARKE, of Wapping, County of Middex [Eng.], mariner; power to George Durant, of London, mariner. Wmld, ii-19; 11 Jany 1657.

JOHN CLARKE, of Boston, N. E., mariner; JOSEPH TOWNSEND of same place, Mcht; MALACHY PEALE, of Westmoreland [Co., Va.] Mcht; and JOHN BAGWELL, of Rappa. Co. [Va.] Mcht; join in a bond. N-n, "At a private court;" xiii-136. 8 Feby 1680.

TILNEY COACHMAN, of Barbadoes. E. C. Co., Va. Ab. 1692.

BETHIALL [sic] x COLE, widow of Mr. Alexander COLE of the towne of Salem in the county of Essex in N. E., marriner. She gives power to Mr. EDMUND FENDRYEAR [sic] of the towne of Salem... Shipmaster. Wit: Jonathan Very, James Cox. I. W. iv-10. 9 Sept 1688.

SEBASTIAN DELASTATIUS, a Frenchman; formerly appointed Constable and now "disabled by Act of Parliament." Acco., x-243; 2 June 1697.

JONE ELZEY, of Old England, widow. N-n viii-20. 28 June 1658. She was in England in 1660. See N-n viii-81. John Parker was her attorney. Mrs. ELZEY had a grandson Robert Parker, of Southampton, who gives power to Richard Baylie and John Parker of Va. N-n, ix-13. 24 Sept 1657.

(To be continued)

A LIST OF PERSONS NATURALIZED BY PARTICULAR ACTS

From Bacon's Laws of Maryland *

(Contributed by Mrs. George W. Hodges)

PETER ACHILLIS, 1674; 25.
JOHN ALWARD, of Charles county, 1682; 11.
ABRAHAM AMBROSE, 1694; 4.
MIUNTS ANDERSON, 1674; 12.
PETER ANLETON, 1683; 4.
CORNELIUS ARENSON, 1674; 12.
ISAAC DE BARRETTE, 1669; 4.
BARBARA DE BARRETTE, wife of GARRET VANSWERINGEN; 4.
PETER BYARD (?), 1684; 8.
STEPHEN BEENSON, Dorchester county, 1671; 1.
MICHAEL BELLICAINE, Sr., of Cecil county, 1700; 9.
MICHAEL BELLICAINE, Jr., CHRISTOPHER BELLICAINE, JAMES BELLICAINE, his sons, 1700; 9.
SAMUEL BERRY, carpenter, Kent county, 1713; 16.
PAULE BERTE (or BARTEAUD) and wife MARY; 6.
WILLIAM BLACKENSTEIN, St. Mary's county, 1682; 14.
LEWIS BLANEY, 1681; 10.
FRANCIS RUDOLPH BODIEN, Chirurgeon, of Kent county, and his children, 1727; 12.

* The figures other than dates refer to chapters.

HENRY BOUQUET (col.), 1762; 29.
CORNELIUS BOYS, 1681; 9.
ANTHONY BRISPOE, 1674; 25.
JAMES BROORD, of Kent county, 1702; 6.
JAMES, JOHN, and SOLOMON BROORD, his sons, 1702; 6.
DERRICK BROWN, 1686; 5.
LEWIS DE ROCH BRUNE, 1694; 4.
HERMAN VAN BURKELE; 4.
LEONARD CAMPERSON, 1695; 10.
MATTHEW CARTWRIGHT, St. Mary's county, 1671; 10.
LAURENCE CHRISTIAN, 1674; 12.
ANDREW CLEMENTS, 1674; 12.
WILLIAM CODY, Taylor, of Charles county, and his children, 1711; 20.
DERRICK COLIEMAN, planter, Cecil county, 1702; 6.
OLIVER COLKE, 1674; 12.
CORNELIUS COMEGYS, the elder; his wife, MILLEMENTY COMEGYS; and their children, CORNELIUS the younger, ELIZABETH and HANNAH COMEGYS, 1671; 29.

(To be continued)

MARRIAGES BY INFERENCE*

(Continued from November number)

(The first twenty marriages are from the records of Isle of Wight county, Virginia. The county was an "original shire," formed in 1634. It was first called Warrosquyoake. Parts of Upper Norfolk and of Nansemond were added to it later. Its records are very early, but incomplete. One volume contains a deed of date earlier than the erection of the county, and is, so far as the Editor knows, the earliest record to be found in County record books.)

JOHN APPLEWHAITE m. ANNE MARSHALL, dau. of Humphrey, before 18 Dec 1711. I. W. ii-533.

JOHN BRIDGER m. the widow of Christopher DICKENSON, before 10 May 1735. viiiW-66.

NATHAN BAGNALL m. ANN WILKINSON, dau. of Richard; before 13 April 1741. viiiW-418.

JOHN BATTEL m. SARAH BROWNE, dau. of Samuel; before 17 Oct 1739. viiiW-273.

GEORGE BRANCH, son of George, of Surry, m. ANN ENGLAND, dau. of Francis of I. W. [who was gr. fa. of George Branch] before 26 Mch 1687. iv-10.

WILLIAM x COOK m. JOANE ROPER, one of the daus. of Hugh Roper, of Burneham, Somersett county, before 1664 (?). iii-32.

JUSTINIAN COOPER, Gent., m. ANNE HARRIS, wid. of James; before 29 Sept 1629. i-103.

GEORGE CRIPPS m. JOYCE ENGLAND, wid. of Francis; between 13 May 1677 and 26 Mch 1687. iv-10.

Mr. PHILLIPE COCHIN (CODIN) (?) m. MARY GREENE, widow of Mr. THOMAS GREENE; before 24 Apr 1689. iv-17.

WILLIAM CARVER, Lower Psh, I. W., m. JEANE MOORE, dau. of John; about 1692. iv-40.

JOHN COUNCELLINGE m. the relict of Richard JEFFERIES; about Oct 1666. ii-13.

RALP [sic] CHANNELL m. GRACE PERRY, widow of Phillip, about Oct 1669. ii-22.

WILLIAM COLLINS m. ANN WILDS, widow of Thomas. About June 1675. ii-35.

JOHN DRAKE m. MARY BROWNE, dau. of Samuel; before 17 Oct 1739. viiiW-274.

JOHN DUPRA m. LUCY LITTLE, dau. of Robert, before 29 Mch 1736. viiiW-136.

PATIENCE GODWIN m. JAMES GREGORY; See Woodleys of I. W. p. 4.

SARAH JARRELL, dau. of Thomas, m. —— PARKER; before 1741. viiiW-391.

ROBERT JOHNSON m. MARTHA JONES, dau. of Thomas; before 23 Nov 1737. viiiW-172.

RICHARD JORDAN m. REBECAH RATCLIFF; before 8th 8th 1713. ii-638.

WILLIAM LAWRANCE *probably* m. PENELOPE BROWNE, dau. of SAMUEL; before 17 Oct 1739. viiiW-276.

THOMAS LOWE m. GRACE JONES, "an orphant"; before 16 Aug 1673. L. Norf., Va. E-98.

EVAN LEWIS m. MARY HAYES, dau. of John [Jonathan (?)]; P. A. xix-670 (2d series); before 29th 2d 1720.

CHARLES LEWIS m. SUSANNAH GROMARRIN, dau. of "Gillee"; Hening, viii-644; before Feby 1772.

WILLIAM MARSHALL m. MARY PARKER; 12 May 1660. N-n, Va. ix-92.

MARYLAND'S NEXT OF KIN*

(Continued from November number)

WILLIAM DOXCEY; inv. Thomas Doxcey of St. Mary's county; 29 Apr 1718; i-308.

OSWALD DASH, MARY BULL; inv. Richard Reeder of St. Mary's county; 4 July 1718; i-308.

CHARLES ASHCOM, JOHN ASHCOM; inv. Winifred Ashcom of St. Mary's county; 29 May 1718; i-309.

JOHN BLACKISTON, WILLIAM COODE [sic]; inv. John Code of St. Mary's county; 21 May 1718; i-315.

WILLIAM MATHEWS, JOHN CRAYCROFT; inv. Anne Hoskins of Charles county; 12 Aug 1718; i-316.

JOSHUA MAYOR, ROBERT STEWARD, JAMES STEWARD; inv. Charles Steward of A. A. county; i-318.

RICHARD BLUNT, ROBERT BLUNT; inv. Robert Blunt of Kent Island, Q. A. county; 12 Sept 1718; i-318.

BENJAMIN LAWRENCE; "There is no more kindred but young children"; inv. John Lawrence of Q. A. county; 30 June 1718; i-333.

ELIZABETH MONROE, JOSEPH EARLE; inv. Dunkin Monroe of Q. A. county; 2 May 1718; i-334.

ELIZABETH COURSEY, JOHN HAWKINS; inv. John Hawkins of Q. A. county; 1718; i-336.

GERARD SLYE, WILLIAM COODE; inv. Kenelyne Chesyldine of St. Mary's county; 19 May 1718; i-339.

THOMAS CHAIRES, JAMES CHAIRES; inv. John Chaires of Q. A. county; 1718; i-343.

ROBERT HANDON, THOMAS STONE; inv. Philip Hoskins, of Charles county; 12 Aug 1718; i-345.

ANN *FAULKUM,* JOHN *FAULKUM;* inv. Peter *Falkiner,* Sr., of Q. A. county; 27 Nov 1719; i-349.

JOHN NICHOLSON, THOMAS NICHOLSON; inv. John Nicholson of Q. A. county; 2 June 1718; i-354.

J—— EARLE, JO. EARLE; inv. Peter Denny of Q. A. county; 12 Aug 1718; i-355.

WALTER HAMON, ANN HAMON; inv. Richard Hamon of Q. A. county; 14 June 1718; i-345.

JOHN CUSSEEN, THOMAS REEVES; inv. William Cusseen of Charles county; 27 May 1718; i-358.

HENRY YOUNG, FRANCIS YOUNG, "sons of the dec."; inv. George Young of Calvert county; 24 July 1718; i-361.

FRANCIS YOUNG, "being the dec's brother"; inv. George Young, Jr., of Calvert county; 24 July 1718; i-364.

JOHN HODSON, MARY FOSTER; inv. John Ennalls of Dor. county; 13 Oct 1718; i-365.

ALEXANDER WARFIELD; inv. of John Warfield of A. A. county; 29 July 1718; i-367.

BENJ. DAVIS; inv. Sarah Davis, admx. of Maurice Davis of Cecil county; 14 Mch 1717-18; i-374.

(To be continued)

THE WEBBS

(Continued from November number)

RICHARD WEBB, assee of Edward Loftis, sues John Ayrs for a bill. L. Norf. vol. v., no p. 15 May 1688.

RICHARD WEBB, intends marriage. Cliffs Mtg., Md., p. 23. 29-1-1700.

RICHARD WEBB, pd. as a wit. Capt. John Hatton's will. L. Norf. Va. vi-pt. 1, fo. 256. 15 Sept. 1702.

RICHARD WEBB, Jr. Possessor of *SMITH'S CHOICE,* Poquadenorton n. side St. Martin's Riv.; surv. 1679 for John White and assigned to Ambrose White. 100 a. possessed by RICHARD WEBB, Jr., and 100 a. by John Tull. [John Tull was Webb's bro.-in-law. See his will.] Som. Co. Rent Roll.

RICHARD WEBB, of Phila. Co., Penna., yeoman. Pat. for 415 acres Chester Co. State Ld. Rec'ds, H'burg, Penna. A2-358. 11 Sept 1702.

RICHARD and JOHN WEBB, committee. Tred Avon Mtg. Records. i-359. 1703.

RICHARD WEBB, 200 a. Nanse R. R. Va., 1704. (Mss. at L. C.)

RICHARD WEBB, Sr., Somerset Co., will; very sick and weak; 250 a. of *TURBRIDGE,* so. side Pocomoke river, to two youngest sons, John and Mark; son Richard; dau. Sarah; dau. Elizabeth; dau. Mary; Elizabeth Lowder; wf. Mary; chn. John, Elizabeth, and Mark are under age. Wits: Mark Gendron, Dan'l x Quillian, Robert Heath (Weath?). Annap. Wills, 12-254. 13 Nov 1707; 9 Mch 1707-8.

RICHARD WEBB and wf. REBECCA, and John Baggs and wf. Hannah, of Talbot county, pltrs., to Joseph Blackwell, of Dor. county; one-half of *EDMONDSON'S RESERVE* (200 a.) left by Wm. Parrot, of Talbot county to daus. Rebecca and Hannah Parrot. Dor., Md. vi-131. 2 Mch 1708.

RICHARD WEBB, of Talbot county, pltr.; legacy to Tuckahow Mtg.; wf. Rebecca; mother Eliza. Meares; James, Richard and Park Webb, sons of bro. John Webb, and "Rebecca Carvich"; equal division among the four; to Richard Webb, son of bro. John, 150 acres *HIGH FIELDS ADDITION* (where I now live), also *BARRY'S RANGE,* 130 acres. Wf. Rebecca, extx. Wits.; Berry-Dudley, Dudley, Bowes. Annap. Wills, Md. xv-119; 6 11th 1718; 16 June 1719.

RICHARD WEBB; grant of 214 acres, escheated land, Upper Psh., Nanse, Va., westward side so. br. Nanse river. S. L. O. x-53; 19 Dec 1711.

RICHARD and THOMAS WEBB wits. to will of John Davis; I. W. ii-581; 31 Dec 1713.

RICHARD WEBB, wit. to Reubin Gledhill's will. I. W., Va., ii-592; 19 Feb 1714-15.

RICHARD WEBB was a vestryman of the Upper Parish of Nansemond Co., Va. See Stanard's Notes, 1758.

RICHARD WEBB'S wife was Ann. I. W., Va., 1760.

RICHARD WEBB; patent for 290 acres, on a branch of Nansemond river, binding on Jeremish Godwin, Webb, Dr. Temble, Edw'd Moore, Wm. Ward. [Presumably Nansemond county, Va.] S. L. O. 33-287, 30 June 1760.

RICHARD WEBB and Miss Sally Bressie; Thomas Bressie, sec. Norfolk, Va., M. L. B. 28 Nov 1792.

RICHARD WEBB and Delila Cale. Chowan county, N. C., M. L. B. 22 Aug 1797. (N. C. H. and G. Reg.)

RICHARD WEBB in St. Bride's parish, Norf. county, Va. Tax Lists 1794-1809.

RICHARD WEBB in Orange county, Va. 4 Nov 1812. iv-520.

RICHARD WEBB [son of George] and Jane Schute. Norf., Va., M. L. B., 1 Apr 1815.

(To be continued)

The County Court Note-Book

An every-other-monthly devoted to abstracts from County Court and other records, prior to 1800, and with a department of notes and queries.

MILNOR LJUNGSTEDT, Editor and Publisher. Bethesda, Route 1, Maryland.

Published six times a year. Subscription, two dollars a year, in advance. Special rates on renewals. Advertising rates moderate.

VOL. II FEBRUARY, 1923 NO. 1

A FRIENDLY WORD FOR SOME ANCESTORS

The Editor is probably the only living American of colonial descent who has an ancestor so poor that the town gave him land. It is true that he ended his career as a member of a Provincial Assembly, and was probably a man of probity and other respectable qualities, even if he were not a king of finance, or lord of many acres tilled by others hands than his own. Among his descendants have been several near-geniuses, also a Member of Congress and this Editor, so that you never can tell what may happen to your forbears as personages of American history. The simple soldier of the Revolution you are looking for and stopping short when you find him or his parents, because he did not happen to own a "Shirley" or a "Westover," a "Manor" in New England or New York, or a "great house" somewhere else; and because you are afraid he might have descended from a "redemptioner" or an "indentured servant," or nobody else in particular, may have been the grandson of even an American grandfather of many holdings, and also many sons, to whose younger sons fell the younger sons' portion, or no portion at all, after the custom of the time.

The fact that the ancestor you find could not sign his name...could neither read or write...has many sides to it. Somebody says, or the Editor has evolved it from her experience, that whatever is worth having, is worth going for, and that folk in general do usually go after what they want. The boy who wants an education, gets it. If his heart was satisfied with labor in his father's fields, and hog and hominy at night, and a bed of straw, he had it. If he preferred the frontier, the new discoveries of adventure, all he needed was a stout heart, a pair of serviceable legs (or a horse), a good knife and gun. He learned the sign language of the sun and wind, as well as of the Indian,—no chance here for lettering. Had he been the eldest son of wealthy or high parentage (not always synonymous) he might have been sent home to England to acquire the polite amount of education and the customary vices of his peers; but had he been the younger son of the same family, the Editor judges that a Dame's school, or possibly an indentured Irishman, would have been his means to a very simple form of the "three R's."

And even if it were that no such great or little opening to learning was before him, he was, after all, a man, and, in time, an ancestor. Had he known how posterity would view him ...well, had he known, it might not have helped him to bear what he had to bear, for he had no easy time of it, that ancestor. He did for posterity, either as a leader or in the ranks, what nine-tenths of that posterity could not possibly do for itself.

The Editor does not suggest that you weep over his grave (though you might try to find the forgotten spot), or erect a monument, but that you admit him into that brave and often tragic assembly of AMERICAN PIONEERS, with or without a title and a "signet of arms," and even without Revolutionary service.

And, anyhow, some learned and optimistic professor says that all of us, or most of us, of English descent share the blood of the Saxon Egbert. The Editor will discuss this another time; she offers it now merely by way of encouragement.

This FEBRUARY NOTE-BOOK should have been as of JANUARY. But the Editor has a sort of affection for February...not only is it so much nearer spring, but if it hadn't been for February there would not have been any Editor. For her great-grandparents were married in Philadelphia in February, and so were her grandparents, and so was the Editor herself, she might as well add. As can readily be seen, sentiment for the past and for forbears is one of the Editor's weak points.

This FEBRUARY issue would also have contained an extract from a letter written in Boston in 1863, in which the writer (a Philadelphian), quotes from another letter just received from Washington. This quoted letter was from the Editor's father, then in charge of the headquarters for transport, supplies, &c., at the old Sixth street wharf in Washington. And the letter said that President LINCOLN had spent the entire day on the wharf, waiting for news from the front... then somewhere about the James...there having been a great battle.

But, alas, the old letter cannot be found.

Not long ago the Editor was in Harrodsburg, Kentucky. She had to catch a train back to Lexington and the taxi was at the door of the Clerk's office. "Have we time enough?" The chauffeur thought we had. So we drove down the street, and turned a corner, and bumped along a rough and unpaved road, and in the sunsetting or nearly twilight stopped beside a stone wall. The Editor climbed the wall and stood before the LINCOLN cabin...in a forlorn and desolate enclosure. The Editor approached the closed door, she had no special wish to enter, and laid her hand upon the door-jamb. And then, after a minute or two, the Editor turned about and re-climbed the wall. The last remaining light served for the camera, and also for Fort Harrod, the site of which lies a few yards beyond. All of that will be found in every good history of the frontier, or in manuscripts at Madison, Wisconsin. But what is not written is how an American of the Editor's kind feels before the closed door of the cabin which was LINCOLN'S home.

OCCASIONAL

STAFFORD COURTHOUSE, Va. The stocks are to be brought from the old Courthouse over Potomack River to the new Courthouse. Orders i-Ct. 7 Oct 1691.

ROGER MOY and ANN MOY bind themselves [for service] until they have satisfied John Stringer, practitioner in physic... N-n., Va. ii-27; 26 Nov 1639.

SAMPSON DARRELL [who m. a dau. of Capt. John Norgrave] petitions the Court for a Cow and a Signet of Arms which was left by will of Capt. John Norgrave to one (either) of his children. Darrell complains that the widow yet unjustly keeps and detaines the Cow and Signet of Arms and prays that the Court order that they be delivered. Staff., Va., Orders i-86. 1690.

JOHN NELSON takes oath as 1st Lieut., Militia; sworn again as Lieut., 1782. WILLIAM TYLER, oath as 2d Lieut., Shenan, Va., B... 27 Apr. 1781.

ANGUS McDONALD, age about 21, Deposition: That William Holdbrook, Jr., lately in his Majestie's service, died at Fort Cumberland and was ordered to be buried by the Deponent, but that the Deponent found him just buried. That he knew nothing of any Will made by the said Holdbrook when he was in his Majestie's Service. Staff., Va., P-66; 14 Oct 1755.

JAMES SIMMONS, a soldier in Capt. John Grigory's Co., had chn. Willis and Jane. Norf., Va., Orders, 1777.

JOHN DOSS was a soldier in the Continental Service, and had one child. Wife was JUDITH; 24 Nov 1777; Cumb. Co., Va.

EXECUTORS' AND GUARDIANS' BONDS

The following bonds are recorded on 39 pages of Deed Book 3, KING GEORGE County, Virginia.

Richard Elkins, gdn of William Lampton; 1726.
Thomas Gough, gdn of John Willis; 1728.
Elizabeth Sullivant, admx of Owen Sullivant; 1729.
Martin Gollathan, extr of Christopher Pritchett; 1730.
William Taliaferro, gdn of Katherine Rymer; 1731.
William Alsup, extr of Margaret Boyle; 1732.
Thomas Reids, gdn of William Thatcher; 1735.
Henry Head, gdn of John Grimsley; 1735.
Edward Turberville, admr of Rush Hudson; 1735.
William Mumford, admr of Richard Price; 1735.
Daniel McCarty, gdn of Nicholas and Elizabeth Smith; 1735.
Ann Naylor and Hannah Bronaugh, extrs of John Naylor; 1735.
Ann Naylor, gdn of Arrabin [sic] Moor; 1735.
Thomas Bartlett, gdn of John Boddington; 1735.
John Tiller, admr of William Hudson; 1735.
Thomas Turner, admr of Isarel [sic] Illingsworth; 1735.
Rosammond Tucker, admr of Joseph Tucker; 1735.
Margaret Gill, admx of Richard Gill; 1735.
Sarah Rosser, extx of Richard Rosser; 1735.
Hugh French, extr of Daniel French; 1736.
Martha Wharton, Samuel Wharton, and William Wharton, extrs of John Wharton; 1736.
Alice Dickason, extx of Thomas Dickason; 1736.
Margaret Grant, admx of William Grant; 1736.
Jonathan Gibson, admr of Sarah Gibson; 1736.
Sarah Keer (?), admx of Peter Keer; 1736.
Mary Butler, admx of Elias Powell; 1736.
William Harrison, gdn of George Harrison; 1736.
Sarah Jones, admx of John Jones; 1736.
Ann Stribling, admx of John Stribling; 1737.
Agatha Wing, admx of Joseph Wing, 1737.
Elizabeth Brown, admx of John Brown; 1737.
John Edwards, gdn of William Patishall; 1737.
Anthony Strother, gdn of Elizabeth Strother; 1738.

WANTED: Numbers 1, 2, 3, and 5, Vol. I, County Court Note-Book.

OUR ANCESTRAL RECORDS IN ENGLAND AND SCOTLAND

(Third article)

Contributed by Mr. E. Dwelly, of England.

SCOTTISH RECORDS. Most of the ancient records of Scotland are now in the General Register House, Edinburgh. Many were taken to England by Edward I and his successors, and about ninety or one hundred hogsheads full were sent back by sea from London to Scotland in the beginning of 1661. One of the ships, containing eighty-five hogsheads, became a total wreck and these records were lost.

Scottish records are of two kinds: historical, such as Parliament, Privy Council, Exchequer, and Monastic Records—all in charge of the Curator of the Historical Department. The others relate to transactions of the people and are under the care of the Deputy Keeper of Records.

The following are the chief sources of information available for the genealogist:

SASINE Records,—Feu-charters, Transfers of land, &c., from 1599.

BURGH Registers from 1681; these concern the holdings of land and buildings in the sixty-five Royal Burghs.

RECORD of RETOURS,—Proof of right to inheritance claimed by the heirs on the death of a predecessor. These records contain the particulars of descent of a large number of families.

WILLS in the various Provincial Depositories; 1539, in Dumblane, is the earliest date, but the series is incomplete. Here are also inventories and similar material.

There are many other sets of records. The list is too long to give in the space permitted in the NOTE-BOOK, but among the most interesting and valuable may be mentioned the records of forfeited estates (rebellions of 1689, 1715, 1745); tax-rolls from 1543 to 1649; entail registers; oaths of allegiance (from 1661); registration of arms; and the parish registers previous to 1855. These commence about the middle of the 16th century, but are very incomplete.

(Further articles will be published later.)

SOME KENNEDY-WILSON NOTES

In a recent very charmingly written collection of family records, there are some errors which can best be corrected by giving the abstracts from the original court records. The publication in question is entitled "KITH and KIN," and contains a great deal of material concerning Pennsylvania-Virginia families.

DAVID KENNEDY received a warrant for land in Chester county, Penna., 4 May 1734. This was for 500 acres. He received an additional warrant for 40 acres, 29 Oct 1743. And a third warrant for 76 acres, 6 Apr 1776. See vol. xxiv, p. 83, Penna. Arch. (3d series).

DAVID KENNEDY, of Londonderry, Chester county, Penna. Will. He leaves his wf. Margaret £100 (mentioned in marriage contract); to his son Montgomery one pound; sons Samuel, DAVID, and John, £10 each; son Joseph, £80, on condition he returns within five years after the testator's decease; daughters Agnes Finley, ISABEL WILSON, £40 each; daughter Jean Fryer, £60; for use of the Jersey College, ten pounds. Extrs are to sell all estate. Sons Samuel and John Kennedy and son-in-law Michael Finley, extrs. Wit: Sam'l Creswell, Archibald Fleming, Hugh Hamilton.

Signed, 9 Mch 1773; probate 23 Feby 1774. Letters granted to sons, the third extr being absent. See Abstract of Chester county wills at Penna. Gen. Society.

SAMUEL KENNEDY, Whiteland Tshp., and JOHN KENNEDY, Lancaster Borough, practitioners of physick, extrs of the will of DAVID KENNEDY, late of Londenderry, Chester Co., yeoman, to Alexander Gibson; 475 acres, granted to DAVID KENNEDY, 1739. (Reference made to provisions of will.)

The Orphans' Court records, of Chester county, show that ISABELLA DANIEL was granted letters of administration on the estate of JOHN DANIEL, and gave bond 22 Nov 1759. Her securities were DAVID KENNEDY and MONTGOMERY KENNEDY. (Docket No. 1814.)

On the 17 Mch 1761, JOHN WILLSON and ISABELLA his wife, appear on the records of the same court as administrators of JOHN DANIEL deceased. Previously, on the 18 Dec 1760, ISABELLA WILSON, and apparently Montgomery Kennedy and Michael Finley are appointed guardians of John Daniel's children, John, David, Andrew, and Robert. John Daniel had also a son Samuel, the eldest. This son, Samuel, is mentioned in the will of James Daniel, of Londongrove.

It does not appear necessary to give the will of WILLIAM WILSON of Berkeley county, Va. (now W. Va.), but it might be well to note that his name was William Wilson, not WILLIAM MONTGOMERY WILSON, and that he had a daughter ISABELLA WILSON, who has probably been mistaken for ISABELLA KENNEDY-DANIEL-WILSON above. Col. David Kennedy, who appears in the records of Frederick county, Va., I believe, was, of course, the *son* of David Kennedy of Chester county.

JOHN WILSON, first of Chester county, Penna., the father of WILLIAM WILSON, of Berkeley, appears to have died in Berkeley county in 1789. Letters of administration are granted on his estate. William Willson was administrator, and Samuel Parks, security.

THE EDITOR.

NOTES AND QUERIES

GIRARDIN - GERDINE: Was Dr. JOHN GIRARDIN of Georgia, who changed his name to GERDINE, of the same family as LOUIS E. GIRARDIN, professor of modern languages and other studies at William and Mary, about 1805. Dr. JOHN had a son Dr. LOUIS GERDINE. Mrs. H. J. S. C.

PALMER: TWENTY - FIVE DOLLARS will be paid for authoritative information as to the parents, grandparents, and great-grandparents of MARTIN PALMER of Charlotte and Halifax counties, Virginia. He was father of Luke, Isham, Martin, Jr., and possibly others. Information as to his wife also desired. Martin Palmer was probably in the Revolutionary Army. W. B. P. A.

ROBINSON: WANTED—The ancestry of WILLIAM ROBINSON of Monongalia county, Va., who had sons Maj. William and Maj. Benjamin of Harrison county. G. F. R. I.

SAULE: WANTED—Information as to an immigrant from Ireland, before 1770, named SAULE. Also any information as to a SAULE-BUTLER marriage, or a ROBINSON-SAULE marriage, between 1700 and 1770. M. L. M.

TEN DOLLARS will be paid for *authentic* record of the ancestor of JAMES FOWKE (FOWKES, FOOKES) of Northampton and Accomack counties, Virginia; immigrant about 1660. H. C. F. M.

THOMAS SAVAGE (3d generation) had daughter MARGARET ELLIGOOD. PETER BOWDOIN of Northampton calls MARGARET ELLIGOOD his aunt. Was his mother (SUSANNA) a daughter of THOMAS SAVAGE or a stepdaughter? Was she half-sister to MARGARET by another mother? M. L. M.

GEORGE CATHEY was in North Carolina before 1800; did one of his daughters marry a CAIN? If so, what was his fore-name, and her name? C. A. B. C.

MASON: What was the maiden name of MARGARET MASON, who was wife of EDWARD and afterward married ABRAHAM FARROW, in Stafford county, Va.? Mrs. W. W. I.

HART: What became of MOSES HART, of Rockbridge county, Va., and whom did he marry? E. J. C. A.

ROBINSON-WILCOX: Can anyone give the marriage record of JOHN ROBINSON (perhaps ROBERTSON) whose wife was EUNICE WILCOX. This marriage occurred in eastern New York, probably about 1770. E. D. R. P.

WEBB: Who was MARY MARGARET WEBB, said to have married WILLIAM ROBINSON about 1730, in Virginia. G. R. F. I.

WILSON-KENNEDY: Information wanted as to date when JOHN WILSON of Chester county, Penna., who married ISABELLA DANIEL, born KENNEDY, left Chester county and removed to Virginia, where he died in 1789. E. C. W. N. C.

HOPKINS-GIBSON: Who were the parents of SARAH HOPKINS who married ANDREW GIBSON about 1775, or a few years before that. The marriage was probably in Pennsylvania. E. C. W. N. C.

HALL: Was DURHAM HALL, of N. C., in the Revolution, and was he son of CLEMENT HALL, who died 1758? M. L. H. G.

BOOTH: Who were the parents of THOMAS BOOTH (1777-1843) who died Clarke Co., Ga., 1843. M. L. H. G.

BOOK NOTICES AND GENERAL INFORMATION

In commemoration of the approaching Tercentenary of Maryland, it is proposed to publish a Tercentenary History. The first volume will comprise the historical narrative; the remaining one (or two) will cover the biographical material. The Committee has made the very wise choice of Mr. Francis B. Culver for Chairman of the Sub-committee on Colonial Biographies (1634-1775). No abler man could be found for this valuable work.

Attention is invited to the original registers of English parishes and the contemporary transcripts of these registers made for the Bishops of the Diocese, which Mr. Edward Dwelly is publishing. These registers are of special interest to Americans on account of the large immigration from Somerset county, to which the registers appertain. Somerset county is on the south of Bristol Channel; Devon, Dorset, and Gloucester touch its borders; Cornwall and Land's End are to the southwest; and the great shipping port of Bristol lies near the mouth of the Severn, partly in Somerset, partly in Gloucester. Mr. Dwelly is the compiler and publisher of the Gaelic Dictionary, for which the English Government has granted him a special pension.

THE HARTS. Mrs. C. D. CHENAULT, of Lexington, Kentucky, has for several years been collecting material touching the southern branches of the HART family, and writes the Editor that she is now preparing to publish a Hart book.

Mr. CHARLES SHEPARD II, of Washington, D. C., in association with Mr. MILTON THOMAS, is about to bring out a very valuable piece of work; this is a list of some 500 inscriptions from the cemeteries of RENSSELAER COUNTY, N. Y. The material is new, the compilers stating that these inscriptions are not to be found in any other publication. The edition (mimeographed) will be limited, and will be sold only by subscription. The price first fixed was twenty dollars, but as there has been a greater demand for the work than was anticipated, the publisher (Mr. Charles Shepard, 2153 California street, Washington, D. C.) states that if twenty subscriptions are received sufficiently early, the price will be reduced to $10. Subscribers at $20 will, of course, receive the benefit of the reduction if it be found possible to make it. Early subscription is urged. For further information address Mr. Shepard.

FOOKS, FOOKES, FOWKES, FFOULKES, &c. Mr. Herbert C. Fooks, Munsey Building, Baltimore, will be very glad to hear from anyone interested in any branch of this family, but especially in the FOOKES or FOWKES of the Eastern Shore of Maryland and Virginia.

ROBINSON. Mr. Charles Edward Robinson, of Newport, R. I., writes the Editor that he has completed the final pages of his MSS. of the Descendants of Pastor JOHN ROBINSON, of Leyden, and that it has been turned in to the publication committee. The Editor learns in other quarters that any delay in publication will be due to the question of expense. It is to be hoped that everyone interested in this line—than which there is none more honorable in this country—will either send in subscriptions or advance in some way the means for publication.

The NOTE-BOOK is informed that the Paris Chapter of the D. A. R. (Bourbon Co., Kentucky) intends to place a tablet in the local Courthouse in commemoration of the Revolutionary soldiers who died in that county. Mrs. William B. Ardery, of Roccliggan, Paris, is chairman of the committee having the matter in hand, and is making every effort to identify and record the service of such soldiers. This should interest many families of Pennsylvania and Kentucky, whose sons fared farther west.

By writing to Mrs. A. S. EDWARDS, of Surry C. H., Va., information can be had as to a convenient and comfortable place to stay (after April 15th).

Visitors to WEST CHESTER, the county seat of CHESTER Co., Penna., can get excellent and reasonably priced meals at the OVERTOWN, which is situated above the bank. Sometimes the hostess, who is a member of the Society of Friends, can also provide rooming facilities.

It is encouraging to note how more and more the women who are doing research work are taking up the exact and tedious side of it —the systematic listing and abstracting of one or more specific classes of records. Mrs. Ardery, of Paris, Kentucky, writes the Editor that she has, for her own use, made a complete abstract of all estates settled in Bourbon county, from 1785 to 1840. It is to be hoped that Mrs. Ardery will be persuaded to publish this in some available form.

PUBLICATIONS, ETC., OF VALUE TO HISTORIANS AND GENEALOGISTS

GENEALOGISTS AND OTHERS INTERESTED IN RESEARCH WORK

Reasonable price will be paid for numbers 1, 2, 3, and 5, COUNTY COURT NOTE-BOOK, 1921-1922. Address Editor.

The

County Court Note-Book

A Little Bulletin of History and Genealogy

Vol. II April, 1923 No. 2

SHIPS IN PORT

(Second instalment)

The *Benedict,* John Pitt, master. P. R. O. 33-xix. 1702.

Barq *Benjamin.* N-n v-127. 29 Jany 1655.

The *Bennett,* Sam'll Parramore, master. P. R. O. 33-xix. 1702.

The *"Bird Galley,"* Capt. Jos: Dunn, Commander. Dor. Co. Md. See Inv. and Accts, Annap. i-15. 13 June 1718.

Ship *Cesar* from Bristol, Peter Wade, captain. Norf. Corp. Ct. Records.

The "Hoy" *Content,* John Trombell, master. N-n iii-31, 30 Apr 1646.

Ship *Daniell* of Dublin. Acco., Va. 1666, also 1667.

Ship *Delight* of Bristol; Capt. Benj. T... (?) and Mr. Warren were her masters. L. Norf., Va., 25 Nov 1657.

Sloop *Diamond,* of Acco., Va. Dep'n as to the death of Arthur Thorne by being swept overboard by the boom. Acco., Va. xi-393. 4 Aug 1706.

Sloop *Dolphin,* see will of John Thomas, mate. Capt. Thos. Watts, master. N-n, Va. xxi-193. 1722-1729.

Ketch *Dolphin,* of Salem; Daniel Lane, master. L. Norf., Va. D-27. 17 Nov 1756.

Sloop *Dove,* Emanuell Long, master. Acco., Va. xiv-79. 7 Sept 1714.

Ship *Dove,* Robert Pitt, master. Acco., Va. iii-44. 23 Apr 1667.

Ship *Dover;* N-n, Va. v-132. 21 Jany 1655.

Barque *Dolphin,* of N. E. L. Norf., Va. 1662. D-350.

Sloop *Dolphin,* bound for Barbadoes; Capt. Thomas Watts, Comdr. N-n, Va. xxiiiR-193. 6 Apr 1722.

Brigantine *Dragon,* wrecked; Z... both Collins, master. N-n, Va. xviii-181. 6 Dec 1703.

Ship *Dragonier,* Thos: Gallope, *gunner.* L. Norf., Va. D-220, 230. 17 Oct 1659.

His Majesty's Ship *Dunbarton;* Capt. Sam'l Rowe, Commdr. Acco., Va. ix-118. 1 July 1687.

Ship *Edward* of London. N-n, Va. v-142. 15 May 1655.

Brigantine *Eagle* of Exon. John Chappell, master, gives power to Richard Drummond. Acco., Va. xi-594. 13 Dec 1712.

Ship *Eagle;* Eusebius Esterbrook, master. Acco., Va. ix-140. 1 Sept 1688.

(To be continued)

MORE OR LESS DISTINCTIVE FORENAMES OF THE COLONIAL ERA

(Of all the unusual given names with which the colonists endowed their daughters, the names in this list seem to the collector the most unusual. The spelling varies.)

ELISHEBA ANDREWS, the granddaughter of William Andrews, Sr.; N-n, Va. 22 Feby 1654, v-85, and 21 May 1655, v-47. She was a wit. in 1664.

ELISHEBA REVERDY, wf of Peter, and only grandchild of George Traveller. N-n, Va. xi-13. 20 Jany 1669.

ELISHA or ALISHA RUSSELL. See wills of Luke and Barbara Billington, her parents. Rappa., Va. i-57, 76. 1671-1674. (This name probably Alicia.)

ELISHEBA REVERDY was also granddaughter of Alicia Custis. See N-n records, 1676-7.

ELISHA FRESHWATER, N-n xv-170. 26 Oct 1685. She was the dau. of George Freshwater. N-n, Va., xv-372. 19 Mch 1687.

ELISHA BAKER was the dau. of William, see his will. N-n, Va., xviii-55. 1700. Also xviii-54. 12 Aug 1700.

ELISHEBA VAULX, wid. of James, late of York Co., Va. m... Frank. before 29 Sept 1709. N-n, Va., xviii-490.

ELISHA STRINGER was dau. of Grace Harmanson. N-n, Va., xviii-514. 28 Feby 1709-10. Her father was Thomas Harmanson. N-n xix-138. She was wf of Jacob. N-n xxiiiR-206. 1724.

ELISHE SAVAGE was dau. of Elkenton [sic]. N-n, Va. xxiiiR-46. 21 Aug 1719.

ELISHABA BENTHALL. N-n, Va. M. L. B. 1724.

ELISHE GODWIN, wf of Daniel. Context shows this name to be Alicia. N-n, Va. xxivR-277. 5 June 1731.

ELESHE HARMANSON, M. L. B., N-n, Va. 1740.

ELISHE DUPARKS... see will of Margaret Ellegood. N-n, Va. 28 Apr 1750. Original will.

ELISHE NELSON, widow of John. N-n, Va. xxviiiR-430. 10 July 1753.

ELISHE HUNT, dau. of Azariah Hunt. N-n, Va. M. L. B. 1757.

ELISHE KENDALL, a widow. N-n, Va. M. L. B. 1758.
ELISHE JACOB, dau. of Esau Jacob, m. Abraham Boswell. N-n, Va. M. L. B. 1763.
ELISHE TOWNSEND, dau. of Solomon. Wor., Md. bet. 1769-1783.

The very pretty Irish name of Ellice may be allied to the foregoing. Maryland genealogies have turned it into "Elise." (N-n, Va., 1661.)

(To be continued)

MARRIAGES BY INFERENCE*

(Continued from February number)

The first fifteen marriages are from the records of NORTHAMPTON county, Virginia. Northampton county covers about half of the "original shire" of ACCAWMACK, formed in 1634. The name was changed to NORTHAMPTON in 1642-3, and in 1663 the upper half of the county was cut off and given the name of ACCOMACK. NORTHAMPTON county is said to have the earliest continuous records in the country. The bound Court records are made continuous by the substitution of two or three "Court Minutes" for missing "Court Orders." Volumes of Orphans' Court records are, however, unquestionably gone. The county possesses a remarkable number of marriage license bonds. The following marriages are taken, however, from miscellaneous records. The bonds have been copied by Mr. Stratton Nottingham, and published.

EDMUND ALLEN and ANNE BAGWELL, wid. of John; xv-324; before 29 Dec 1687.
JAMES ANSELL m. SARAH PANEWELL, wid. of John. She was a dau. of Henry Mathews. N-n. iv—; 1 May 1692.
ROBERT ANDREWS and ELIZABETH SHEPHEARD, dau. of John and Elizabeth. xvi-39; before 27 July 1696.
GARRETT ANDERSON and AMY PRITCHETT, wid. ii-147; before 1647.
ARTHUR ARMITRADINGE probably married CHRISTIAN GRANGER, dau. of Nicholas; iii-94; before or about Oct 1647.
HENRY ALLEN and ELIZABETH ATKINSON, wid. of James; N-n xviii-60; before 28 Mch 1700.
WILLIAM ANDREWS mar. contract with ELIZABETH TRAVELLER; v-47; 17 Jany 1651.
HENRICH ABLE and SOPHIA VANWEKER (?) dau. of HENRICK of Ulrick in the Netherlands. xiii-75; before 3 Mch 1679.
JOHN ADOLPH and MILLICENT DIXON, wid. of Christopher; xii-64; before 29 July 1675.
RALPH ARNELL and MARY TIPSHOTT, wid. of William; xv-125; before 30 Mch 1685.
JOHN AYRES, mariner, and MARY HILL, dau. of Richard. xiv-184; before 28 Sept 1688.
JOSEPH BENTHALL, Jr., and . . . SMOTHERS, wid. of John. xviii-92; before 28 Feby 1701.

* Copyright, Mrs. Pauline Stewart Crosley, 1923.

WILLIAM BREWER and JOANE x MILLS, a widow. xiv-293; 20 Apr 1691.
GEORGE BELL and HANNAH BRICKHOUSE; xv-400; before 19 Nov 1688.
DANIEL BENTHALL and ELIZABETH GASCOINE, widow of Henry; xvii-169; about 30 May 1692.
EDM'D McVEAGH m. ALICE DICKINSON, about or before 1703. P. A. xix-409 (2d series).
WILLIAM MALLORY m. MARY GIBSON; before 27 Jany 1800. Fauq., Va., iii-227.
DANIEL McMURPH [Y] m. SUSANNAH CROSSLE, dau. of William, late of Ireland; about or before 1804. Fredsburg, Va. vol. A.
HENRY x MUSGROVE and NANCY BURDIT; Franklin co., Va., M. L. B. 4 Jany 1798.
ROBERT MUSGRAVES m. BETTY JOHNSTON; about 1794. Washn. co., Va.
LIDDY MUSGROVE m. WILLIAM DUNN; 7 Oct 1788. Washn. Co., Va., Mar. Ret.
THOMAS McGUIRE m. ELIZABETH PARKER, widow of John; before or about 1765. Berkeley Co., W. Va., v-32.
WILLIAM McWILLIAMS, Esq., of Fredsbg., m. DOROTHY BRAYNE BENGER (?), dau. of John of Spottsylvania co. Staff. co., Va., L-238. (Ctf. by minister.)
JOHN NICOLL, Esq., of Conway Hatch, Middlesex county, m. MARGARET LOWTHER, dau. of Anthony and Margaret, of Maske, county of York; before 23d 7bre 1731. P. A. i-34 (3d series).
JEREMY OSBORN m. ELIZ'TH DAY; about or before 1703. P. A. xix-409 (2d series).
WILLIAM NEWSUM m. the relict and admx. of THO: HUNT; before 5 May 1674. Surry county, Va. Orders i-54.
BOWEN PRICE m. ELIZABETH POPE, dau. of Jane; before 23 Apr 1752. Wmld. co., Va. 11-428.
COLWELL PETTYPOOL m. MARY GROMARRIN, dau. of "Gillee" of Henrico; before Feby 1772. Hening viii-644.
EDWARD PERKINS m. ELIZABETH SNOWDEN, widow of Thomas of Penna.; before Mch 1703-4. N. C. H. & G. Reg. i-143.
HEZEKIAH POLLARD and ELIZABETH TRIMMER; mar. contract; 20 July 1799. K. Wm., Vo. "9"-35.
JAMES ROBBIN m. ELIZABETH NUGENT, widow of Edward; before 5 Feby 1796. Fauq., Va., ii-400.
THOMAS SYMONS of J. C. Co., Va., m. DOROTHY CASTLE before 8 June 1639. S. L. O. i-678.
JOSEPH WILLIAMSON m. ANN BROWN; 6 Sept. 1781. Lunenb., Va., Mar. Ret. ii-92.
HENRY WHITE m. MARY CROSHAW, dau. of Joseph; about 22 Mch 1659. York, Va., iii-90.
Capt. NATHL WEST m. MARTHA MACON, wid. of Mr. Gideon Macon; before 20 July 1703. K. Wm., Va., "5"-37.

(To be continued)

MARYLAND'S NEXT OF KIN*

(Continued from February number)

JAMES NOELL, BAZELL NOELL; inv. John Noell of Dor. county; 20 June 1718; i-375.

RICHARD WARFIELD, ALEXANDER WARFIELD; inv. Benjamin Warfield of A. A. county; 5 Aug 1718; i-377.

JAMES NOELL, BAZELL NOELL; inv. James Noell, Sr., of Dor. county; 21 Aug 1718; i-384.

ALLEN THOMAS; inv. William Thomas of Dor. county; 13 June 1716; i-386.

MORDECAI PRICE; inv. Mary Price of A. A. county; 9 July 1718; i-388.

KATHERINE BOTELER; inv. Edward Boteler of Calvert county; 31 May 1718; i-393.

THOMAS WALL; inv. Joseph Wall of Dor. county; 10 Oct 1717; i-399.

JOHN and JOSEPH PORTER; inv. Francis Porter of Talbot county; 19 June 1718; i-400.

JOHN HELLEN, PETER HELLEN; inv. David Hellen of Calvert county; 9 Oct 1718; i-403.

RICHARD BROWN; inv. Thomas Davis of St. Mary's county; 30 July 1718; "To May Davis' wearing apparill, 7. 3. 9." i-407.

MATTHEW GUIBERT, THOMAS CLARKE; inv. Thomas Barber of St. Mary's county; 19 Sept 1718; i-411.

JOHN REED, MARGARET REED; inv. John Reed of Charles county; 22 Feby 1717; i-414.

JOHN BROKE [sic] and DOROTHY SMITH of Calvert county; inv. of Roger Brooke of Prince George's county; 2 Dec 1718; i-414.

EDWARD PARISH, aged about 48 years, "being [asked] what he knows of the finding of An Inv. of Anthony Holland's Estate among the papers of Mord'c. Price dec. exc. of the sd Holland, Declares that he himself looking among the papers of sd Price did find the very Inventory, and that Mary Price admix of the said Mord'c. Price afirmed to him that [the] Inv. which he found was a Copy of the Inv. Exhibited into the County's office. Edward Parish being one of the people called Quakers makes his solemn afirmitation [sic] according to Law. 13 Nov 1718." Benjamin Holland being aged about 44 yrs. Acknowledged the same 14 Nov 1718. Inv. ANTHONY HOLLAND of A. A. county, 11 Aug 1703. i-422.

JOHN CROCKETT; inv. of Solomon Sparrow of A. A. county; 3 Sept 1718; i-425.

JOHN JONES; inv. Morgan Jones of A. A. county; 1718. i-432.

RICHARD MAKINGS; inv. Richard Meakings of Dor. county; 12 Dec 1718. i-434.

(To be continued)

THE WEBBS

(Continued from February number)

RICHARD WEBB, a member of the Virginia Company. Hening, i-86. 23 May 1609.

RICHARD WEBB, purchaser of 1,000 acres of William Penn, about 1682. Penna. Arch. i-41 (3d series).

RICHARD WEBB, wife and family; ctf. from Mailsworth Quarterly Mtg. to Phila. Mo'ly Mtg. P. G. Pub. vi-73, 95, 205. 28-12-1700. Removes to Concord Mtg. 1705.

RICHARD WEBB, died 1719. Came from City of Gloucester, Eng., to Philada., 1700, and four years later removed to Birmingham, Chester county. His wf. was Elizabeth, a "noted minister among Friends." Their chn. were: William, Mary, Esther, Sarah, Daniel, Benjamin, Elizabeth, and James. Histy Chester and Delaware counties, p. 534.

RICHARD WEBB was in King and Queen County, Va., 1733. See Strattoon Major Parish records.

RICHARD WEBB; warrant for 250 acres, Chester county, Penna. P. A. xix-576. 20th 11th 1713.

RICHARD WEBB, J. P., Penna. P. A. ix (2d series). 30 May 1715.

RICHARD WEBB; Newport Parish, I. W. Will, wf. Mary; chn. that lives now with me; dau. Martha has had her portion. Wf. and Joseph Webb, extrs. Wit: Carey, Glover, Sam'l Webb. I. W., Va., xW-152. 6 Feby 1745-6; 9 Feby 1748. [Widow m. —— Pollard before 9 Feby 1748.]

ROB'T WEBB: Eliz: x Bannister gives bond as guardinesse Robert Hill and Charles Barecraft, sec. Surry, Va., i-81. 3 Jany 1655. See also 1-100. 1656. Robert was of age 7 Jany 1657. i-114.

ROBERT WEBB, of London, Gent. and wf Elizabeth; power to Patrick Robinson. P. A. xix-120 (2d series). 31 Dec 1689.

ROBERT WEBB m. Eliz'th Barber, widow dau. of Jno. Langhurst. Before 31 Dec 1689 P. A. xix-383. (2d series.)

ROBERT WEBB, of Talbott county, Md., to Wm. Wildey, Jr., of London. (Appears to be Webb's contract as a factor.) John Pope and D [?] Kerwan, wit. Dor. Co., Md. v-10. 29 Oct 1691.

ROBERT WEBB was in Essex county, Va., 1692. See i-12.

ROBERT WEBB, Marshal of the Court of Vice-Admiralty. P. A. ix-633. 1693.

ROBERT WEBB, a tithable. Surry, Va. iv-21. 1694. Also 1702. iii-44. [Note: Surry volume numbering not consecutive.]

ROBERT WEBB, Som. Co., Md. Will. Bro. John Webb; mother, Mrs. Cattebra (?) Webb, extx. Wit. Mr. Math. Scarborough, John Scarborough. Annap. Wills. xiii-328. 12 Oct 1710-29 Sept 1711. Mother assigns extrship to son John Webb. 14 May 1711.

ROBERT WEBB; inv. Annap. Records, xxxviiiA-208. 1711.

(Continued on page 7)

The County Court Note-Book

An every-other-monthly devoted to abstracts from County Court and other records, prior to 1800, and with a department of notes and queries.

MILNOR LJUNGSTEDT, Editor and Publisher. Bethesda, Route 1, Maryland.

Published six times a year. Subscription, two dollars a year, in advance. Special rates on renewals. Advertising rates moderate.

Vol. II APRIL, 1923 No. 2

CRITICISM AND CRITICISM

Some time last year there was published in a prominent historical and genealogical magazine of standing, and also in the genealogical edition of one of the finest newspapers in America (some of us think it is the finest), a long and apparently carefully worked out article touching upon the birth and the marriages of the immigrant JOHN WASHINGTON. To a careful reader there were apparent certain inaccuracies in dates, probably errors on the part of the original copyist (for later admissions showed that the paper had been made up from previously published matter and from copies made by others, not the writer); and there was also one very weak point in the argument which any one with a familiar knowledge of the usages of old courts would have at once turned down as evidence ... but otherwise it read well. As to the question of dates, it is quite evident no one made the absurd mistake of deliberately falsifying any such, as the answer to the article claims. Inexperienced persons find it difficult at times to distinguish the old 1's from 7's, or 7's from 9's. Very recently a gentleman of distinguished ability has insisted on transmuting the absurd horizontal "8" of the old scribes into a "5"!

Quite lately a voluminous answer has been put forth to the statement published as above, which answer is, no doubt, correct, with possibly a few of the errors that are always made in this class of work. One mistake commonly made by an untrained copyist is to translate the "X" mark into an initial. Another is to take it for granted that the Clerk who did the original copying (in America) copied the "X" marks in all cases. It is quite evident the Clerk at Westmoreland did not. In some ways he was a bit unusual. But these are small matters.

What is to be regretted is that the writer of the second article did not content himself with that moderation and restraint which make any scholarly statement so much the more forcible. Abusive adjectives add nothing to evidence.

The Editor must further confess that she cannot see any appositeness in dragging in the percentage of colonial illegitimacy in New England. New England apparently plays the part of a counter-irritant to the sensitive skin of some other colonies. It's a pity. Any one who is textually familiar with the ancient records of certain sections (if a mere 250 years can be considered ancient) understands conditions as they were then entirely too well to comment upon them elsewhere, and especially too well to do anything but smile at many published statements. Though often it takes some patience to "get away with" the smile.

But one must really be permitted a certain amusement at this: "A study of Hening's Stat- "utes ... for the seventeenth century, impresses "one with the spiritual loyalty to the church "of the settlers and their immediate descend- "ants ... and with the solidity of their charac- "ter in general." The Editor does not question the "solidity" ... it is much in evidence, but for the "spiritual loyalty" begs to call the writer's attention to the Rev. Hugh Jones's "Present State ... " p. 97. The Editor is practicing the reticence she admires in not giving a quotation.

The Editor thought there was a nice Latin "quote" something to the effect that "Time conquers all [that]" ... but she can't find it. It sounds as if it ought to be, however, and if the Editor were not incurably honest, she would invent it.

The English were just as loyal to their Church as to their King and their homes, probably because of that dear English view (which the Editor quite understands) that it was *their* Church; but while Hening's Statutes were in the making the Quakers were fighting for their very lives and property and right to marry as they chose; the Presbyterians ... well, I don't exactly know what the Presbyterians were doing, but they were certainly not showing spiritual loyalty! The Quakers were English (and Irish) it is true; but the Presbyterians were Scotch, Scotch-Irish, Irish, and Ulster-Irish as some prefer to name them ... and they surely enjoyed "differences!"

They had a kind of spiritual loyalty, a grand, fighting kind, but it wasn't exactly always to the English church. It was a solid, sordid age outside of Court circles and high fashion; little glamor hangs about it to those who have read, but time only adds to the dignity of the high souls who gave up home and country for freedom, and who, when they found that freedom not altogether one of thought, moved still further on and faced another wilderness.

OCCASIONAL

From an old family burial-place, King William C. H., Va. "ELIZABETH, consort of Wm. B. LIPSCOMB, daughter of SAMUEL and ELIZABETH MEREDITH. Born [illegible] 1799; died [illegible] 1839; leaving a husband and three sons."

THOMAS JONES gets certificate for 150 acres, for himself, ELIZABETH his first wife, KATHERINE his last wife. N-n, Va., ii-98. 13 Sept 1641.

MARKE HAMMOND gets certificate for 250 acres; [50 acres] for ANN DENNIS his first wife; [50 acres] for MARY CLARKE his now wyfe. N-n, Va., ii-97. 13 Sept 1641.

JAMES LONGO presented for working on Christmas and for planting corne the last solemn fast, being the 8th of May last. Acco., Va., x-32; 16 June 1691.

THOMAS ROWLAND, Jr., is presented by the Grand Jury of Stafford county, Va., for wishing that the Justices would all Swear themselves to the devil, *Provided they might get some rain.* Staff., Va. Orders i-207. 10 Feby 1691-2.

WILLIAM DAVIS, Gent., appointed and took oath as Ensign in Howson Hooe, Gent's, Company. Pr. Wm. Va. Orders, p. 206. 7 July 1762.

ROBERT FOSTER takes oath as Ensign in Capt. Daniel Kincheloe's Company. Pr. Wm. Orders, p. 102. 4 May 1762.

ERRATA

Page 2 of *November* NOTE-BOOK; George Read, Esq., of Newcastle, Dela., *and Gertrude Till, wid. of Thomas.* Sussex Co., Dela., N-520; before 2 Apr 1788.

WANTED: Numbers 1, 2, 3, and 5, Vol. I, County Court Note-Book. A reasonable price will be paid for these numbers, or a full subscription for the current year will be given in exchange.

The Editor regrets that the fourth article contributed by Mr. Dwelly on the subject of records in Great Britain is crowded out of the present number, certain new material having recently been collected which it seems desirable to publish. With Mr. Dwelly's kind collaboration the NOTE-BOOK will publish before long, either in electrotype form, or on a supplemental sheet, a list of the curious abbreviations and compound letters used by the old scribes.

PIONEERS OF BOURBON COUNTY, KENTUCKY, DYING BETWEEN 1786 AND 1800

(Note: Bourbon county was formed in 1786 from Fayette county, and was then a part of Virginia.)

Compiled by Mrs. Julia Spencer Ardery.

James Alexander, Hammonds Alkire, James Allen, Charles Allison, George Anderson, Jacob Andrews, James Armstrong;

John Baseman, Robert Bell, Charles Bevins, James Black, John Black, William Boyd, Abel Brown, Alexander Brown, James Brown, James Brush, John Burton, Andrew Burns;

Cussenberry Champ, Robert Clark, John Clarkson, Robert Clifford, Joseph Cogswell, John Congleton, John Constant, Elijah Collins, John Cook, Andrew Couchman, Thomas Craig, James Curry, Moses Cusenberry;

Thomas Daisy, James Donald, John Douglass, Samuel Douglass, James Dudley, Robert Duffield, Joseph Duncan, John Dunlap, Thomas Dowden;

Robert Edmiston, [Haden] Edwards, Edward Elliott, William Evans;

John Fearn, John Fencher, Jacob Fight, James Folker, John Forqueran, Peter Forqueran, Robert Franklin, Jacob Furnace;

William Galloway, Ramey Gilberts, Samuel Gilledon, Daniel Gillespie, Nathaniel Gist, John Glasgow, Jeremiah Godman, William Gosney, John Green, Amos Griffith, Manassa Griffith, William Griffeth, Stephen Grimes;

Thomas Hamilton, William Hamilton, Jacob Hawker, Nathaniel Hayden, Alexander Henderson, Daniel Hendricks, Peter Hendricks, Joshua Higgins, John Hinkson, Ebenezer Homans, John Hornback, Simon Hornback, Ulrich Huffstetter, Ralph Hughes, John Hughland, Conrad Humble, Gabriel Hutsell;

Francis S. Jacob, John Jacobs, Henry Jacoby, John Jackson, Samuel Jameson, John T. Jenifee, David Jolly, Thomas Jones, John Jones;

John Kannebrook, Isaac Keller, John Kennedy, Joseph Kennedy, David Kenny, David Kinkead, Joseph Kinkead, John Kirkpatrick, Henry Kuykendall.

(To be continued)

WILLS PROBATED AND ADMINISTRATIONS GRANTED IN PRINCE WILLIAM COUNTY, VIRGINIA, 1752-1753

From Order Book Covering Those Years

(Note: Many Prince William books are missing, thought to have been carried off during the civil war. Two volumes have been returned, and it is hoped that others will be found. There is no record of wills between 1744 and 1778. This is a great loss. The list given below to a very slight extent helps to bridge the gap. Other lists will follow.)

JOHN HOLTZCLAW; Jacob Holtzclaw, extr. Jacob Holtzclaw and Joseph Hitt give bonds. 22 June 1752. p. 8.

JOHN OWENS; l. a. to widow, Frances; John Diskin and James Grimes, sec. 22 June 1752. p. 8.

JOHN FLORENCE; will presented by Elizabeth Florence, extx. Thomas and Joseph Faulkner, sec. 27 July 1752. p. 26.

JAMES NOLAND; Wilmouth Noland, his admx, brings in acct of estate. 27 July 1752. p. 27.

JOHN SMITH; inv. and appraisement his estate returned. 28 July 1752. p. 34.

JOHN PURCELL; John Sims and wf Jane are his admrs. 29 July 1752. p. 49.

HENRY MACHEN; will presented by Grace and Thomas Machen, extrs, and proved. Humphrey Pope and Rodham Tullos, sec. 24 Aug 1752. p. 60.

JOSEPH HACKLY; admn on his estate granted John Hackley; George Johnston, sec. 24 Aug 1752. p. 61.

JOSEPH CRUMP; his will presented by William Blackwell, one of the extrs, and proved by Robert Slaughter, Gent., and Richard Gray. John Wright, sec. 25 Aug 1752. p. 67.

ISAAC SUTTLE; will presented by Joseph and Jane Suttle, extrs. ISAAC, Benjamin Suttle, and John Arnold, sec. 23 Oct 1752. p. 69.

(WILLIAM MASON'S inventory returned. 23 Oct. 1752. p. 70.)

THOMAS WELSH; will proved by John Garner and Parish Garner, two of the witnesses, who make oath to Jane Garner's sig. as wit. Joseph Blackwell and John Butler refuse extrship. L. a. to John Garner and John Welsh. 23 Oct 1752. p. 71.

BENJAMIN BROWN; will presented by James Bayley and Richard Cundiff, extrs. Ann Brown one of extrs, refuses. John Barton, wit., makes oath, also to sig. of William Barton, another wit. Henry Peyton, sec. 27 Nov 1752. p. 74.

MARY DAWKINS; will presented and proved by Benjamin Neale, one of the wit. who also makes oath to sig, of Thomas Young, a wit. William Dodson extr mentioned in will being dead admn granted to Sarah Dodson. William Stamps sec. 27 Nov 1752. p. 75.

WILLIAM WHEELAND; will presented and proved by George Roberts and William Hardy, two of the wit. Charles Dick, admr. 27 Nov 1752. p. 77.

(To be continued)

NOTES AND QUERIES

GIRARDIN - GERDINE: Was Dr. JOHN GIRARDIN of Georgia, who changed his name to GERDINE, of the same family as LOUIS E. GIRARDIN, professor of modern languages and other studies at William and Mary, about 1805. Dr. JOHN had a son Dr. LOUIS GERDINE. Mrs. H. J. S. C.

PALMER: TWENTY - FIVE DOLLARS will be paid for authoritative information as to the parents, grandparents, and great-grandparents of MARTIN PALMER of Charlotte and Halifax counties, Virginia. He was father of Luke, Isham, Martin, Jr., and possibly others. Information as to his wife also desired. Martin Palmer was probably in the Revolutionary Army. W. B. P. A.

SAULE: WANTED—Information as to an immigrant from Ireland, before 1770, named SAULE. Also any information as to a SAULE-BUTLER marriage, or a ROBINSON-SAULE marriage, between 1700 and 1770. M. L. M.

TEN DOLLARS will be paid for *authentic* record of the ancestor of JAMES FOWKE (FOWKES, FOOKES) of Northampton and Accomack counties, Virginia; immigrant about 1660. H. C. F. M.

THOMAS SAVAGE (3d generation) had daughter MARGARET ELLIGOOD. PETER BOWDOIN of Northampton calls MARGARET ELLIGOOD his aunt. Was his mother (SUSANNA) a daughter of THOMAS SAVAGE or a stepdaughter? Was she half-sister to MARGARET by another mother? M. L. M.

MARGARET ROBINSON of Wilmington, Dela., or of Phila., m. *circa* 1800, a Baptist minister named YOUNG. Information greatly desired as to her descendants. M. L. M.

DAVIS, LEWIS, Jr., and AARON BROWN, settled in Giles county, Tenn., about 1811. Who was DAVIS BROWN'S wife and did LEWIS BROWN, Sr., serve in the Revolution? E. J. A. C.

ANDREWS: Wanted, the ancestry of DAVID ANDREWS, who m. ELIZA BROWN, dau. of DAVID. E. J. A. C.

BROWN and PORTRESS (PORTEUS or POYTHRESS): Who were the parents of REBECCA BROWN who m. WILLIS PORTRESS of Giles county, Tenn. Also who were the parents of WILLIS PORTRESS, of whose ancestry nothing is known. E. J. A. C.

HENRY POPE died in Halifax county, N. C., in 1764, leaving wife TABITHA, and children Burwell, Willis, John, Henry Augustine, and Wiley. Who were the parents of TABITHA POPE? L. J. H. G.

HALL-HICKS: Would appreciate any information as to the families of DURHAM HALL and FRANCES HICKS. A dau. married THOMAS BOOTH in 1817, who died in Clarke county, Georgia. M. L. H. G.

BRIDGER: Who were the parents and where were they from, of JAMES BRIDGER, the explorer, so prominent in early western life. Bridger was born in Richmond, Va., in 1804, and was in Missouri in 1820. M. M. H. V.

SAULE: Who was ELEZEZER SAULE of New York, living before 1800. M. L. M.

BOOK AND OTHER NOTES

The KEENERS and ALLIED FAMILIES. This is a history of Melchoir Keener and his granddaughter, Anna Maria. Ready for distribution about 1 May 1923. For information, write Mrs. L. P. Wilson, 2608 Keyworth avenue, Baltimore, Maryland.

It gives the Editor sincere pleasure to say that Mrs. VIRGINIA EDWARDS SAVEDGE, of Alliance, Surry county, Virginia, will make researches in the old records of her county, and will also furnish any desired copies.

Mrs. Edwards is the daughter of the late Mr. Albert Sterling Edwards, who was Clerk of the Surry Court for over fifty years. She is probably more familiar with the old Surry records (which date back to 1652) than any one in the county, having assisted her father in his work and been trained by him in the reading of the very difficult old Clerks' hands in which these early records are written.

Miss Susan S. Towles is the President of the newly organized Henderson Historical Society, Henderson, Kentucky, and Mrs. Thixton is the Vice-President. Mrs. Thixton writes that the Society is copying early material on file in their Courthouse, regarding Transylvania, and the Richard Henderson purchase and sale, and the founding of the town.

In a letter written by Miss Julia S. White, of Guilford [Friends'] College, N. C., she states that their records consist of marriage, birth, and death data. They have no wills and only deeds to church property. The further statement is made that they have records for Friends from all over North Carolina and for South Carolina and Georgia. Searches are made for a moderate fee; the initial payment should be prepaid.

The Editor has received positive information from the daughter of a former Rector of St. George's, Accomack county, Virginia, that the Register of this parish was in existence some years ago, and that, at her father's death, it passed into the hands of one of the vestry. It would seem this Register might be still in Accomack, and could be found.

Mr. George T. Edson, of Filley, Nebraska, is the Editor of a very interesting and valuable little paper, called the STEWART CLAN MAGAZINE. It contains a great deal of information, especially valuable to northern STEWARTS. Is issued monthly, and the subscription is one dollar a year. Mr. Edson is a descendant of John Alden.

Mr. STRATTON NOTTINGHAM, now of Onancock, Virginia, who is more familiar with the old Eastern Shore records than any one now resident there, writes the Editor that he can still undertake a limited amount of research work in Accomack and Northampton counties. Mr. Nottingham's present engagements do not permit him to give more than a portion of his time to research, but it is probable he can be of assistance to those readers of the NOTE-BOOK in cases where a familiarity with the old script is absolutely essential.

THE WEBBS

(Continued from page 3)

ROBERT WEBB of Surry, Va. Patent for 280 acres, north side Raccoon Swamp, Surry. S. L. O. x-362. 24 Jany 1717.

ROBERT WEBB, Jr., Surry county; patent for 295 acres, south side Nottoway river. S. L. O. xi-268. 5 Sept 1723. Also 175 acres, parish of Southwark. x-350. 22 Jany 1717.

ROBERT WEBB to his daughter-in-law, Sarah Pirkins; original deed. Norfolk county, Va. 1732.

ROBERT x WEBB and wf Elizabeth to Robert Rose. Deed. Norfolk, Va. 1 Aug 1737.

ROBERT WEBB, the younger. Surry county, Va., iii-46. About 1739.

ROBERT WEBB was in Albemarle Psh, Surry, Va. 1743. (See Psh Records.)

ROBERT WEBB, Jr., was a "processioner," Albemarle Psh, Surry, 1743. (See Parish records.)

ROBERT WEBB, Sr. and Jr., were on the tax-list of Norfolk co., Va., 1754. [Robert, Sr., probably died about 1761.]

ROBERT WEBB'S estate; widow, Agnes; William Webb an heir; Peter Rose admr [extr?] Norfolk Co., Va., Audits, i-56. 1761.

ROBERT WEBB in Sussex county, Va. 1767.

ROBERT WEBB and Ann Davenport. Tyrrel county, N. C. M. L. B. 28 Apr. 1767. N. C. H. & G. Reg. iii-108.

ROBERT WEBB, a pilot. Virginia navy, Amer. Rev. Va. Mags. i-65. [1776].

ROBERT WEBB of Baltimore, m. Sabina Willcox: Chn: James, Sabina and Mary Ann. See Chart of Jenkins Family. No dates.

RUTH WEBB m. Absalom Swift. St. Luke's, Q. A., Md. 1743.

SAMUEL WEBB in Somerset county, Md. Annapolis Records. 1709.

SAMUEL and THOMAS WEBB in the estate acc't of Wm. English (Inglish) I. W. viii-505. 1744.

(To be continued)

GENEALOGISTS AND OTHERS INTERESTED IN RESEARCH WORK

PUBLICATIONS, ETC., OF VALUE TO HISTORIANS AND GENEALOGISTS

COLUMBIAN PRINTING CO., INC., WASHINGTON, D. C.

The

County Court Note-Book

A Little Bulletin of History and Genealogy

Vol. II June, 1923 No. 3

NEW ENGLANDERS AND OTHERS IN EARLY VIRGINIA RECORDS

(Fifth instalment)

RALPH ALLEN, of London, Mcht; power; 29 Aug 1664. N-n, Va. ix-204.

JOHN ALMERY, mariner, of *Pascatqua* in N. E. 3 Mch 1702. Acco., Va. xii-142.

THOMAS BOYS' will mentions that he left, living not far from Newport, in the Isle of Wight, sisters and his son, about 32, born in I. W. Wmld. O.i-85. 1 Aug 1656.

Mr. JARVIS BALLARD, of Boston, N. E., Mcht. Also JOHN CLARKE, of Boston, N. E., marriner. 29 Dec 1681. N-n xiii-198.

JOHN BARKER of Sussex county, [Penna.?] Acco. ix-180. 19 Mch 1689.

"Mr. [Wm] BURTON being gon to Pensilvania." Acco. xiv-40. 6 May 1712.

NATH'L BROWNE of Lancaster [Va?] assigns title to land. N-n xi-17. 1670.

JOB CHANDLER and wf Anne, of *Portobake* in Maryland, refer to Mrs. Sarah Yardley of Lynhaven as "our mother," now deceased. L. Norf. D-117. 25 Nov 1657.

SAMUEL CHANDLER, of London, Mcht. N-n ii-212. Feby 1642.

Mr. RICHARD CORNELIUS of the towne and county of South'ton, Mcht. Power to Robert and Jane Parker. Wit. Jno. Elsye, Geo. Parker. N-n, v-107. 21 May 1656.

PETER COLLIER, *Clarke,* formerly of Fransworth, Lanc. county, Eng. N-n xviii-31. 29 Dec 1699.

JOSHUA CURLE of Elizabeth City county. N-n xviii-58. 28 Jany 1700.

JNO. CAMPBELL, JOS'E APPLETON, JNO. MARTIALL and JAMES BOWDOIN, all of Boston, send power to JOHN BOWDOIN of Smith's Island, N-n, Mcht, their "trusty friend." Acco. xiv-33. 7 Feby 1711.

WILLIAM CHRISTIAN of the City of Bristol. N-n vii-22. 27 Sept 1667.

JOHN x CREW of Sussex, Penna., power to Holden and Marsh. N-n xiv-178. 28 May 1688.

JOHN COLE, a marinor in Boston. Acco. xvi-322. 1727.

SUSANNA x DAVIS; dep'n relative to JOHN BELLAMY (who went to the Whorekills) and a young man who wanted to go with him. This was Henry Suttwell (?) a svt of William Baker. N-n xv-161. 28 July 1685.

ROBERT DRUMMOND and wf Elizabeth, of Sussix, Penna. Acco. xvi-34. 1717.

JOHN EDWARDS, of Boston, in N. E. Age about 27. Sig. "Jno. Edwards." Acco. x-128. 19 June 1694.

SAMUEL ELDRIDGE of St. Michael, Barbadoes; power to James Gibson. Acco. xix-126. 1 Oct 1728.

SIMON EDGILL, of Philada., Mcht. Power to Isaac Morris of Sommersett county. Acco. ix-270. 1736.

(To be continued)

MARRIAGES BY INFERENCE*

(Continued from April number)

The following marriages are from the records of ACCOMACK county, Virginia. ACCOMACK was formed in 1663 from NORTHAMPTON county, being the upper half of the narrow peninsula which includes these two Virginia counties ... the Eastern Shore of Virginia. The remainder of the State is referred to in the records and by the Accomackians as the "Western Shore" or the "continent" of Virginia.

ROBERT ABOT, son of John, and ELIZABETH HILL, widow of Robert; about 1689. vi-506.

JOHN ABDILL and ELIZABETH EYERS; before 1713. xi-110.

NATHAN ADASON and BRIDGET BRADFORD, dau. of William; before 28 Apr 1722; xvi-163.

MASON ABBOTT and ELIZABETH PARREMORE; before 1721. xvi-176.

WILLIAM ANDREWS and MARY GORE, widow of Daniel; about 4 Apr 1722. xviii-41.

NATHANIEL ANDREWS and ELIZABETH PITTS; widow of Robert, Gent.; (no date found); xviii-47. [Long before 1731 ... see xix-243.]

WILLIAM ANDREWS and ANN WARD, widow of THOMAS; about 1718; xvii-12.

JOHN ABBOT, Sr., and ANN GRAY, widow; marriage contract; 21 Jany 1688. vi-511.

ARTHUR ARMITRADINGE and ROSE KELLAM, dau. of Richard; about 18 June 1673. v-12.

RICHARD ARMITRADING and ELIZA-

BETH CHANCEY, dau of. Henry, [Sig. is *Henre Chance.*] 2 Apr 1706. xi-391.

JAMES ADKINS [probably] mar. ELIZABETH ESHAM, dau. of Daniel and Gertrude Esham; before 8 Dec 1697. xi-186.

JOHN BARNES and FRANCES SACKER, widow; about 3 May 1672. vi-102.

EDMOND BROWNE and MARTHA DAVIS, in the Psh Church of St. Mary Newington, Butts, Surry, England; before 27 June 1677. viii-174.

JOSEPH x BELLOTE and dau. of Andrew Stuart. dec'd. 5 Aug 1712. xi-586.

EDMUND BAILY and HANNAH SCARBURGH, dau. of Maj. Edmund; before 4 May 1713. xi-598.

NATHANIEL BRADFORD and JONE FRANKLING of Northumberland county; see dep'n 4 Aug 1713. xi-603.

JOHN BAGWELL and TABITHA SCARBURGH, dau. of Charles; before 6 July 1733. xi-633.

HENRY BROWN and ELLEN SOUTHLAND, widow of Alexander; before or about 1 Apr 1663. i-2.

(To be continued)

MARYLAND'S NEXT OF KIN*

(Continued from April number)

JOHN WHITE, JOHN NICHOLSON; inv. Robert Munday of Queen Anns county; 27 Aug 1718. i-436.

JOHN ROWE, WILLIAM MOUNTEINE; inv. John Tootall, Queen Ann's county; 30 Aug 1718. i-438.

MARY C. ATTON; inv. William Catton of A. A. county; 24 Feby 1718-9. i-441.

CHRIS. HENDRICKSONS, MARY HENDRICKSONS; inv. John Jobson of Cecil county, 1718; i-442.

JOHN and MATT WALLACE; inv. Oliver Wallace of Cecil county; 16 Sept 1717. i-443.

WILLIAM BREWER; inv. Joseph Brewer of A. A. county, 12 Dec. 1718. i-448.

WILLIAM and SUSANNA JUMP; inv. William Vaughan, of Dor. county, 14 Dec 1717. i-449.

FRANCIS RICHARDS, "exc."; inv. James Lord of Calvert county, 12 May 1718. i-451.

FRANCIS HOLSTEEN, wid. and admx; inv. Andrew Holsteen of Talbot county; 7 June 1718; i-453.

CALEB SPRIGNELL and ELIZABETH EVENS; inv. Christopher Sprignell of Talbot county; 15 Aug. 1718. i-454.

THOMAS ALDRISS and SARAH MERIDEY; inv. Thomas Aldriss of A. A. county; 22 Dec 1718; i-459.

PATRICK CREAGH; inv. Mary (?) Craugh of A. A. county, 21 Jany 1718. i-462.

NATH'L CHEW; inv. Samuel Chew of A. A. county; 6 Jany 1718. i-464.

SAMUEL and NATH'L CHEW; inv. John Chew of A. A. county; 5 Jany 1718. i-470.

THOMAS and JAMES BISCOE; inv. John Biscoe of St. Mary's county; 19 Nov 1718. i-474.

WILLIAM SWALE and MARY BARRON; inv. George Ervain (?) of St. Mary's county; 1718. i-477.

HENRY HORNE, exc.; inv. Phillip Ragon of St. Mary's county; 2 Dec 1718. i-478.

RICHARD DUCKETT and BENJ. JACOBS; inv. George Westoll of Balto. county; 23 Mch 1718. i-479.

GEORGE TRUITT; inv. James Truitt, Sr., of Somerset county. 20 Nov 1718. i-483.

(To be continued)

A LIST OF PERSONS NATURALIZED BY PARTICULAR ACTS

From Bacon's Laws of Maryland *

(Contributed by Mrs. George W. Hodges)

(Continued from February number)

HESTER CORDEA, 1674; 12.

MARK CORDEA of St. Mary's county, 1671; 10.

MATTHIAS de COSTA, St. Mary's county, 1671; 28.

JOSEPH CRISMAND, planter, of Charles county, 1712; 24.

MICHAEL CURTIS, of St. Mary's county, 1695; 25.

BENJAMIN DAFFOUR, planter, of A. A. county, 1708; 14.

CHRISTOPHER DANGERMAN, sadler, of Calvert county, 1705; 7.

DANIEL DANISON, Sr., of Calvert county, and DANIEL DANISON, Jr., 1694; 35.

JASPER DAUNTRESS, 1684; 8.

JOHN DEBRUTER, of Balto. county. 1700; 6.

JOHN and WILLIAM, his sons, together with other sons and daus. of the said Dubruter, the father, born in this Province. 1700. 6.

JOHN DELAMAIRE, 1674; 12.

ANTHONY DEMOUDERER, of Anne Arundel county, 1671; 10.

JOHN DESJARDINS, 1674; 12.

ALEXANDER DHYNIOSSA and wife Margaretta, Foster's Island, Talbot county, 1671; 10.

ALEXANDER, JOHANNES, PETER, MARIA, JONATHAN, CHRISTIAN and BAR[B]ARA, sons and daughters of said ALEXANDER and MARGARETTA, 1671; 10.

PETER DOWDEE, a Frenchman, living in Somerset county, 1698; 10.

JACOB DYHATTOWAY, 1674; 25.

CLAUDIUS DUTITREE, 1694; 4.

JOHN EDGAR, Somerset county, 14 May 1696; 6.

JOHN ELEXON, of Kent county, 19 Apr 1671; 10.

HENRY ENLOES, Baltimore county, 6 June 1674; 12.

* The figures other than dates refer to chapters.

MATHEW ERRICKSON, Kent county, 13 May 1682; 10.
PETER FERDINANDO and his children, St. Mary's county, 18 Oct 1694; 4.
ALEXANDER FORBAS, Talbot county, 19 Oct 1695; 25.
NICHOLAS FOUNTAIN, Somerset county, 19 Apr 1671; 10.
PETER FOWCATE, Baltimore county; 18 Sept 1681; 9.
STEPHEN FRANCIS, "an Italian," A. A. county, 11 June 1697; 9.

THE WEBBS

(Continued from April number)

SOUTHEY WEBB and Ann Miles. M. L. B., N-n co., Va, 1795.
SOLOMON WEBB [deed] to John Blades; Wor. co., Md. K-518, 1776.
SOLOMON WEBB, Jr. [deed] to Ezekiel Coston; Wor. co., Md., L-368. 1784.
SCARBURGH WEBB; will presented by Thomas Blake. Acco. Orders, 1717-1719, f. 19. 2 Sept 1718. (Inv. 17 Feby 1718. f. 66.)
SCARBOROUGH x WEBB; will; sor Thomas; son John; dau. Elizabeth; [minors] Patience Webb; bro-in-law John Dicks; Sarah Harrison a gray mare running in Mme. West's Neck; son Scarborough. John Dicks and Thos. Blake extrs. Wit: John Morrogh, Mason Abbott, John Lewis. Acco., xvi-55. 16 May 1718-2 Sept 1718.
SCARBURGH WEBB; deed from Mr. Henry Custis and wf Tabitha Scarburgh Custis. Acco. xiv-58. 5 May 1713.
SCARBURGH WEBB, son of Thomas Web. Concerning a heifer. 2 Aug 1798. Acco.
Capt. SILAS WEBB and Elizabeth Hews. Mar. 1st Baptist Ch., Phila. Pa. Arch. (Second) viii-775. 13 Aug 1794.
SARAH WEBB, St. Bride's Psh tax-list, Norfolk county, Va. 1805. (Sarah Webb also appears in Kidd's tax-list, for Portsmouth and Elizabeth River, same county, 1800.)
SARAH WEBB taxed for land, St. Bride's Psh, Norf. county, 1799. (She appears in the tax-lists of this parish in various lists from 1794 to 1805.)
SARAH WEBB and Timothy Banger; mar. 1st Baptist Ch, Phila. See Pa. Arch. (second) viii-775. 20 Nov 1794.
SARAH x WEBB, of N-n, widow; to Matthew Floyd, Jr., 130 acres whereon I now dwell. Sarah and Dorman Webb among wit. N-n, Va., xviii-203. 12 Nov 1740.
SARAH WEBB and Peter Walker; mar. St. Paul's, Phila, Pa. Arch. (second) ix-444. 1 July 1760.
SARAH WEBB petitions for comm'n to prove bounds of tract in the freshes of Nanticoke, called *BARNSTABLE*. Dor., Md. viii-61. 1728 or 1729.
SARAH WEBB, wid. of Talbot county, Md., to Lambroch [Lambert?] Flowers, consideration £30; all that tract called *PHILLIP'S RANGE*... n. e. branch Gt. Choptank... mouth of Phillips Creek... Wit. Kennerley, John Stevens, Wray. Ackn. in person. Dor. ii-140. 14 Nov 1722.
SARAH WEBB, admx of Henry King. Talbot 1721. iii-469. (Annap. Records.)
SARAH WEBB, admx of Peter Webb. Talbot county, ii-314. 21 Sept 1719. (Annap. Records.)
SARAH WEBB a wit. Tred Avon Mtg records, vi-25. 1718.
SARAH WEBB, h. r. under Wm. Roberts. Acco 18 Apr 1672. iv-85.
SARAH WEBB was a svt of John Lewis. Acco. iii-43. 16 Dec 1667.
SAMUEL WEBB, will. See I. W. county, Va., 1763 also about 1800.
SAMUEL WEBB, on tax-list, Pr. A. county, Va., 1788.
SAMUEL WEBB on tax-list, I. W. county, Va., 1782.
SAMUEL WEBB, wit. to a deed by Shemuel Godwin and wf Esther; I. W. county, xvi-192. 1780.
SAMUEL WEBB signs declaration; Hist'y Westchester co., N. Y. p. 248. 13 Apr 1775.
SAMUEL WEBB, Windham, Ct. 1760. See Windham Hist'y. (Webb published the Native American; was a native of Windham. See also Hist'y Norwich, Conn. In 1760 he was a selectman.)
SAMUEL WEBB, tanner and currier, from Thomas Renshaw, part of *GILES* and *WEBSTER'S DISCOVERY*. Balto., Md. deeds. xxii-205. 29 Apr 1751.
SAMUEL WEBB mar. Belinda Elliott. St. Paul's, Balto. 1787. See Md. Mar.
SYLVESTER WEBB had wf Abigail. She is buried in Sussex county, Dela. Died 17 Dec 1785, age 25. Some Rec'ds Sus. Co. (Turner) p. 160.
SYLVESTER WEBB a wit. to Wm. Wheeler's will. Sus., Dela. D-14. 1783.
STEPHEN WEBB, age 25. Muster of men over the water at Smith's plntn James City, Va. 1624. (Mss. at L. C.)
STEVEN WEBB, a tenant of the Virginia Company. Va. Mags. xvii-2, p. 145. 22 Nov 1626.
STEPHEN WEBB had son Robert, b. 16 Nov 1636; also son William b. 14 Feby 1645. "Beinge found in an old Bible and subscribed by their father's owne hand." Recorded 3 Jany 1655. Surry i-75. Va.
Mr. STEPHEN WEBB, Burgess, J. C. county, Va. Hening i-239. 1642-3.
STEPHEN WEBB; lease to him by George Powell. Surry, 1642. i-176.
STEPHEN WEBB; wit. to deed by Edward Prince; I. W. county, i-97. 1646.
STEPHEN WEBB under Corbyn in Lancaster county, Va. L. O. 1658, v-144.
STEPHEN WEBB, Windham, Ct. 1772. See Hist'y Windham.
THOMAS WEBB mentioned in will of Arthur Shore, Wmld, Va., wills. p. 3. 1663-1664.

(To be continued)

The County Court Note-Book

An every-other-monthly devoted to abstracts from County Court and other records, prior to 1800, and with a department of notes and queries.

MILNOR LJUNGSTEDT, Editor and Publisher. Bethesda, Route 1, Maryland.

Published six times a year. Subscription, two dollars a year, in advance. Special rates on renewals. Advertising rates moderate.

VOL. II JUNE, 1923 No. 3

THE COUNTY COURT

Occasionally some one asks the Editor *"Why the County Court?"* Such an inquiry comes, of course, from some reader who is not familiar with the old county records and does not know their scope.

It seems to the Editor that the following extracts from Haymond's History of Harrison County will serve as an editorial and give valuable information in far better shape than the Editor could paraphrase it.

> The institution of the County Courts originated in Virginia as early as 1623-4 . . . they were first called Monthly Courts . . . In 1642-43 the style of Monthly Courts was changed to that of County Courts . . . and thenceforward their duties, powers, and jurisdiction was continuously enlarged by the colonial assembly . . . As early as 1645 they had matured into Courts of general jurisdiction in law and equity . . . Previous to 1661-2 the judges of the County Courts had been styled *Commissioners* of the Monthly Courts and afterwards *Commissioners* of the County Courts; but at that time it was enacted that they should take the oath of a Justice of the Peace and be called *Justices of the Peace*.
>
> The functions of these tribunals have ever since been so important that their institution may well be considered as a part of the constitution both of the colonial and present form of government. No material change was introduced by the war of the revolution in their general powers and duties of any kind.
>
> The County Court was the medium through which small disputes were settled and breaches of the peace were tried, roads laid out, mills established, bridges built, licenses granted, taxes levied and collected, deeds, wills, and marriages recorded, and all things conducted that entered into the home life of the settlers and tended to establish law and order and organize self-government.

To the above it may be added that vestry records and certain church records are found in some courts, and that while the foregoing is written as specially of Virginia, the county courts of other colonies exercised similar functions.

It is probable that this article was written prior to the change made shortly after 1900 in the title of the courts of Virginia. In some counties the abolishment of the old Monthly Court has resulted in its place being taken for the purpose of social gathering together by what are variously called "Social Courts," "Horse Courts," and even "Watermelon Courts." "Social Court" in Caroline county, Virginia, is a very important day. The Editor helped sweep the Clerk's Office the day after "Social Court," so that she feels she can speak with authority. This was at a time when janitors' services had ceased, owing to war conditions.

OCCASIONAL

A case in which RICHARD ROBINSON appears is dismissed, because the "Court is not satisfied that [Thomas] Lingo [the witness] is sixteen, nor of his partaking of the Sacrament of Baptism." N-n, Va. xvii-216. 30 Dec 1692.

JNO. WILLIAMS made answer "that his wife should be hanged before ever she should come downe of her knees or submitt to the Court, without it bee to god." N-n, Va. v-15. 28 June 1654.

JUSTICES refuse to sett on account of differences with the Clerk [of the Court]. L. Norf., Va. 4 Jany 1668-9. E-29.

The COURT comments on persons having "unnecessarily brought dogs to a burial." Surry, Va. i-376. 1670.

The COURT being informed that Jackson Allen of this County have set three of his negroes free; ORD: that he be sum'd to app'r at the next court to Shew Cause why they should not be sold according to an Act of Assembly in that case made and provided. Shen. Co., Va. Minute Book B. 28 May 1776.

JOHN BALL, WILLIAM BALL, LAURENCE PARKER, and JOHN WASHINGTON are included in the list of taxables on Duck Creek, New Castle county, the Three Lower counties, 1693. Misc. Papers at Harrisburg.

JOSEPH SEARS, enlisted 1775. Histy Westchester Co., N. Y., p. 277.

EETHAN [sic] SEERS, taken prisoner at Ft. Montgomery about 1777. Histy Orange Co., N. Y., p. 577.

MORE OR LESS DISTINCTIVE FORE-NAMES OF THE COLONIAL ERA

(And some later notes.)

MARIENE x WILLIAMS, a wit., N-n, Va. ix-210. 1658.
MARIAM HAEY (?) m. Hugh Kunneloe (?) N-n, Va. ix-92. 14 Oct 1660.
MARRIAM FRUM (? name uncertain) Acco, Va. C122-8. 1667.
MERIAM WINDER, dau. of John and Bridgett. Som., Md. b. 27 Mch 1673. (Vol. D. B. I. K. L.)
MERIAM SMITH, admr of James Smith, Som, Md. x-391. 1695.
MARIAM BELSHER; admx of John Belsher. Henrico, Va. 1708.
MIRIAM WHITE, b. 1712. Conn.
MIRIAM ROBINSON, m. Roger Barratt. See p. 20, Barratt's Chapel and Methodism. See also Col. Fams. iii-31. Barratt was b. 1728.
MIRIAM BUTLER of Orange co., m. William Eagen after 1728. N. Y. H. S. xiv-303. See also Histy Orange Co.
MARIAN JACKSON m. James Penington 1729. St. Luke's. Q. A. county, Md.
MARIAM WRIGHT, wf of Benjamin, of Burlington county, N. J. Will probated 1730. See N. J. wills, 527. Benjamin had also a dau. MERRIAM.
MERIHAM WRIGHT m. Aaron Owen, Ct. Mar. 11 Jany 1733.
MIRIAM TRUEBLOOD, dau. of John. See his will. N. C. wills, p. 381.
MIRIAM AIKING, dau. of James, of Talbot co., Md., mariner. xiv-163. 1735.
MIRIAM HARDFIELD, wf of Matthew, had dau. Mary Dyer b. 11 Feby 1738. St. Peter's Psh Reg. New Kent, Va.
MIRIAM LURRY, wf of William. See his will, N. C. wills, p. 226. 1746.
MIRIAM WILSON, dau. of Isaac. See his will 1749-1751. N. C. wills. p. 416.
MARIAM LOUGE, dau. of David Louge and Ann (Lockwood). b. 1750-1-2. St. Martin's Psh, Wor. county, Md.
MIRIAM (MARIAM) DALY, dau. and extx of Martha Short, wid. of Adam. N. C. Co., Dela. wills. G-481. 1748-1751.
MIRIAM ANDREWS, wid. and extx of William. N. C. Co., Dela. wills, G-109. 1747-1748.

PIONEERS OF BOURBON COUNTY, KENTUCKY, DYING BETWEEN 1786 AND 1800

Compiled by Mrs. Julia Spencer Ardery.

(Continued from April number)

George Lail, Matthias Lair, William Lamey, Robert Lamme, James M. Laughlin, David Leer, William Logan, Edmund Lyne;

John McCann, William McClelland, Jr., William McClannahan, Nathaniel McClintook, Andrew McClure, William McClure, Archibald McConnell, George McCullough, James McCutchen, Enos McDaniel, David McNay, John McNay, Samuel McNay, Joseph McNay, John McMullen, James McMillan, Arthur McNickle, Edward McShain;

George Mauck, John Maxwell, Samuel Maxwell, George Martin, Daniel Matheney, Robert Marney, George Mason, Lewis Masquerier, Thomas Metheny, Barnabas Miller, John Mitchell, Adam Mitts, Thomas Moore, Jacob Moore, John Morrison, James Morin, William Monroy, Thomas Moss;

Benjamin Y. Neal, Charles Nelson, Samuel Nesbitt, Jeremiah Nisbitt, Stephen Newell, Joseph Norris;

Benjamin Ogle;

John Palmer, John Parks, William Patton, Joseph Payne, Robert Perry, Timothy Peyton, Elijah Phillips, Jenkin Phillips, George Price;

James Quiett;

Joshua Rawlings, George Reading, George Redmon, Thomas Reynolds, William Rickey, Philip Ritchey, Henry Ross, Archibald Ruddle, John Ruddle, Isaac Ruddells, Jr., Thomas Ruder.

(To be continued)

LAND TAX BOOK FOR THE YEAR 1788, OHIO COUNTY, NOW WEST VIRGINIA, FORMERLY VIRGINIA

(For the history of the erection of this county, see County Bulletin, Virginia State Library. The county is an interesting one on account of its connection with the West Augusta District of Virginia, and because it was on the highway to the west for both Pennsylvanians and Virginians.)

John Atkison, 324 acres; [Note: the word *acres* is to be understood as following the figures in the remainder of this list.]
Benjamin Biggs, 190 and 186; John Been, 300; William Bonner, 239; Samuel Bruce, 400; Samuel Beek, 400; Samuel Beck, Jr., 145; Henry Barton, 310; William Brown, 245; William Beard, 530 and 400;

David Chambers, 100; Robert Carny, 220; Israel Cocks, 258; Peter Cocks, 200; Daniel Callander, 400; James Curtice, 360; Abraham Chaplin, 190; John Connal, 346;

William Dunlap, 200; John Duke, 400;

Andrew Fants, 380 and 320; Agnus Findley, 400; (this is perhaps Angus);

Samuel Glass, 400; John Grier (Grien?) 353; Samuel Grayham, 315 and 220; Hugh Gellaraid (?), 100; William Gorral (Garral?) 190;

George Hamond, 50; Derick Hoagland, 304; Hezekiah Hyatt, 21, 10 and 137; James Harris, 400; Charles Hedges, 230; George Humphries, 400; John Humphries, 385; Aaron Hedges, 190; Joushua [sic] Hurd, 260; Benjamin Hammit, 372; Solomon Hedges, 249; Daniel Harris, 273; Joseph Hedges, 300; Silas Hedges, 337 and 384; William Holmes, 50; Abediah [probably Obediah] Holmes, 100;

Peter Kellar, 320; John Kid, 113;

Moses Lin, 69; William Logan, 150; Jobe L... [this may be Lucas or Luies], 100;

John McColloh, 600; Abraham McColloh, 300; Edward Morgan, 300 and 400; Samuel McColloh, 295; William McMaham, 400, 400 and 330; Levi Mills, 221 and 400; Robert More, 400; John Morgan, 352; John Mitchel, 60 and 400; George McColloh, Jr., 300; James Millar, 740; David McClure, 300; Daniel Morgan, 400 and 135; George McNab, 116; George McCollah, 300; Levi Mills, 184.

(To be continued)

WILLS PROBATED AND ADMINISTRATIONS GRANTED IN PRINCE WILLIAM COUNTY, VIRGINIA, 1754-1757

From the Second Remaining Order Book

WILLIAM FARROW; will presented by Ann Farrow [widow]; John Graham, Gent., and Alexander Farrow, extrs. Proved by Elizabeth Graham, Lewise Woodyard, Mary Jenkinson, wit. Ctf. for probate granted. 25 Mch 1754. p. 4.

JOHN FARROW; admn his estate granted John Summers and wf Elizabeth; John Metcalf and William Thorn, sec. 25 Mch 1754. p. 5.

JAMES ANDERSON; will presented by Samuel Orgain, extr; proved by oaths of John Neavill, Jr., and Harry Neavill, two of the wit. 25 Mch 1754. p. 6.

WILLIAM CHAMBLIN; admn his est. granted John Goar; Henry Poulson and Aaron Chamblin, sec. [25 Mch 1754]. p. 8.

JOHN SMITH; will presented by John Smith, extr; proved by wit. Ctf. granted for probate. 22 Apr 1754. p. 36.

(ROBERT MARSHALL; Thomas Barnet and wf Juduth are summoned to *shew* cause why they detain a will of Robert Marshall, dec'd. 22 Apr 1754. p. 39.)

WILLIAM BAILIS; will presented by John and William Baylis, two of his extrs, and proved by wit. Ctf. for probate granted. 27 May 1754. p. 65.

WILLIAM GALLAHUE; admn granted to Ann Gallahue, widow; Richard Kenner, Nathaniel Overall, George Calvert, Jr., sec.

ROBERT MARSHALL; admn on his est. granted Margaret Marshall, his widow; Simon Lutterall, Isaac Farrow and William Rookard, sec. 25 June 1754, p. 113.

THOMAS CALVERT *als* HARRISON; will presented by widow, Sarah Calvert and Thomas Calvert, the other extr refusing, and the widow refusing to abide by said will, admn with will annexed granted said Sarah. Thomas Reeves, John Calvert, sec. 25 June 1754. p. 117.

FRANCIS WATTS; admn of his estate granted Thomas Watts; Thomas Conway and John Conner, sec. 23 Sept 1754. p. 137.

WILLIAM HOGAN; his will presented by Margaret Hogan, extx; proved by Bailey Johnson and Hanah Johnson, two of wit. Ctf. for probate granted 23 Sept 1754. p. 139.

(Daniel Hogan summoned to appear and contest proof of father's will if he thinks fit.)

ROBERT MARSHALL; admn his est. granted Robert and Thomas Marshall; sec., John Peyton, Jr., John Simms, Scarlet Madden.

MARGARET MARSHALL; admn on her est. granted Simon Lutterell. Sec. William Anderson. 24 Sept 1754. p. 153.

HENRY WATKINS; will presented by widow, Ann Watkins and proved by John Adams and William Linton, wit. Ctf. for l. a. granted widow. 26 Nov. 1754. p. 179.

(To be continued)

EXTRACTS FROM VOLUME MARKED "RECORDS OF LAND CAUSES, 1809-1819," FAUQUIER COUNTY, VIRGINIA

These records, which are found in many courts, appear to have been of cases involving land titles which were heard before some district superior court. They contain many depositions, giving the ages of the deponents, the dates when they or others came into the county or country, wills, deeds, and so forth. Sometimes the record of the deed in its proper volume has been lost. The same is true of the wills.

JOHN x CORBIN, of Prince William county, to William Pickett of Prince George [sic] (colony of Virginia) 398 acres on Great Run in P. W. county, granted by Thomas, Lord Fairfax, to John Corbin, father of the said John, 10 June 1728. Proved in P. W. by wit. 29 Nov 1748.

JOHN x CORBIN, Jr., of King George county, (wf Frances) to William Pickett, same; £100, 298 acres in P. W. county, near Watry Mountain, pat. by John Corbin, dec'd, grandfather to said John, Jr., who died intest. and the said land descended to John Corbin, now senior, and by him 100 acres was given to said John Corbin, Jr., his son. Ackn in P. W. 27 July 1752.

JOHN x CORBIN, Brunswick psh, King George; love and affection to son John Corbin, Jr., "one moiety or third" part of that tract whereon "my Father John Corbin lived"... said land being in the psh of Hanover, P. W. county, on the north side of Rappahannock river. Proved by wit. P. Wm. court, 25 July 1748.

JOHN x MILLER, depn; upwards of 90 years; he knew the chn of John Corbin, among others John Corbin who was his eldest son; that John Corbin the elder died upwards of 60 years ago... deponent was a chain carrier when the land was surveyed. [Dep'n about 1808.]

WILLIAM PICKETT, depn; about 68; was a boy of about 9 or 10 when he came with his father from the lower country where he lived to the place his father purchased of Corbin in Fauquier. (Depn 8 Apr 1808.)

WILLIAM MILLER; depn; age about 68; came to live in neighborhood about 46 years ago; when he first came he worked with William Pickett, uncle to pltff's [John Scott's] wife. Depn 26 Aug 1808.

JAMES SPENNY, age about 80. Depn; came to this country to live in the year previous to Braddock's defeat. Depn 21 Aug 1809.

NOTES AND QUERIES

PALMER: TWENTY-FIVE DOLLARS will be paid for authoritative information as to the parents, grandparents and greatgrandparents of MARTIN PALMER of Charlotte and Halifax counties, Virginia. He was the father of Luke, Isham, Martin, Jr., and possibly others. Information as to his wife is also desired. W. B. P. A.

SAULE: Wanted information as to an immigrant from Ireland (a Quaker) about 1717, named JOHN SAUL[E]. Also any information as to a SAULE-BUTLER marriage, or a ROBINSON-SAULE marriage, between 1700 and 1770. M. L. M.

TEN DOLLARS will be paid for *authentic* record of the ancestor of JAMES FOWKE (FOWKES, FOOKES) of Northampton and Accomack counties Virginia; immigrant about 1660. H. C. F. M.

ELLIGOOD - SAVAGE - BOWDOIN, &c. PETER BOWDOIN of Northampton county, Virginia, calls MARGARET ELLIGOOD his "aunt." His mother is understood to have been SUSANNA; how was she related to MARGARET ELLIGOOD? M. L. M.

BRIDGER: Who were the parents and where from, of JAMES BRIDGER, the explorer, so prominent in early western life? Bridger was born in Richmond, Va., in 1804, and was in Missouri in 1820. M. M. H. V.

COOK: Wanted the ancestry of HENRY COOK and his wife REBECCA STONE of Giles county, Tenn., earlier of Virginia. The son, James Madison Cook married Mary Elizabeth, dau. of Willis Portress and Rebecca Brown. Would like to correspond with others interested in these families, and will pay reasonable rates for genealogical data concerning them. E. J. A. C.

BOOK AND OTHER NOTES

The ALLERTON BOOK CO., 142 East 59th street, New York, is bringing out the AMERICAN EXPLORERS SERIES... the "first-hand records of Lewis and Clark, Champlain, De Soto, Tonty, Hennepin, La Salle and others." These books at a reasonable price and of convenient size, should be in demand by students of our earliest days.

The Editor had the pleasure recently of examining the last bulletin (No. 3) of the Fauquier Historical Society (Fauquier County, Virginia.) Mr. Horner, the Secretary of this Society, is giving his own time to the most painstaking research of the county records, and the Society can well be proud of its publication. If all societies would follow the example of this one, fewer records would be buried under the dust of ages.

Mrs. MARGARET TURNER KELLER, 3738 Kanawha street, Chevy Chase, D. C., is preparing for early publication the court records of the Maryland and Virginia families of TURNER, STONE, LOWE, HAWKINS, DAWSON, and HYATT.

The STEWART CLAN MAGAZINE, published in Filley, Nebraska, by Mr. George T. Edson, is a very nice piece of work. The May number contains an excellent reproduction of a page from an old Haverhill Bible.

The Northampton County Chapter of the D. A. R. (Virginia) at its May meeting, adopted resolutions, joining with other patriotic organizations, appealing to the A. P. V. A. for the restoration and preservation of the old Court-House at Eastville. While the building referred to is not of extreme age (as ages go in America) it is a very good example of the small, simple court-house, of colonial days. It is built on good lines, and well built, otherwise it could never have stood as it has for years, windowless, doorless, without a particle of care. The Chapter is to be congratulated on trying to wake to active life an organization which has quite a name.

Mrs. Gilmore Kendall (who was a Miss Wise) presented the Chapter with the old County Court Seal, which probably had been long in her possession.

The KENNE FAMILY HISTORY and GENEALOGY. Dr. Elias Jones, who wrote the history of DORCHESTER COUNTY, MARYLAND, has completed his book about the KEENES and it will soon be brought out. As the edition is limited, it is suggested that orders should be sent in promptly. Address ELIAS JONES, 511 West Pratt street, Baltimore, Maryland. The price of the volume delivered will be five dollars.

PLACES TO STAY

Columbian Printing Co., Inc., Washington, D. C.

The

County Court Note-Book

A Little Bulletin of History and Genealogy

Vol. II | August, 1923 | No. 4

SHIPS IN PORT

(Third instalment)

Ship *Expedition;* Edward Harvard (Haward?) master. L. Norf. 1661.

Sloop *Experiment;* Jonathan Ellegood, master. Acco., Va. Naval Entries and Clearances. 6 Oct 1781.

Barque, formerly called *Expedition;* sold by Henry Hudson, mcht, of Maryland. [Also called a frigott.] L. Norf. 1664. D-401.

Shipp *Expedition;* Peter Howell, master. L. Norf., Va. 15 Dec 1663. D-390.

Brigantine *Endeavour;* Geo. Jeffereys, owner. Acco., Va. xii-142. 3 Mch 1702.

The *Endeavour;* John Hunkins (?) of Pascatqua in N. E., master. Acco., Va. xii-142. 3 Mch 1702.

Ship *Europe* of Whitehaven; John Robinson, master. Norf. Corp. Ct., Va. 1758.

Ship *Elizabeth and Kathrine;* William Robinson, master. 1714.

Ship *Edward* of London; N-n, Va. v-142. Ct. 15 May 1655.

Shipp *Exon* (?) Mr. Tho: Averell (?) master. L. Norf. Va., 25 Nov 1657. D-113.

Ship *Ellinor* of London; Mr. Rich: Ingle, master. N-n, Va. ii-136. 26 Apr 1642.

Sloop *Elizabeth;* Nathaniel Owen, master. Acco., Va. xvii-8. 7 Jany 1717.

Elizabeth and Anne; from Liverpool and Williamsburg [Va.] Capt. Edwd Trafford. Brought rebel prisoners taken in the Scotch uprising. Cal. Va. State Papers. i-185. 14 Jany 1716.

Ship *Friendship* of Kingston-upon-Hull; Jonathan Waterland, master. Acco., Va. 11 Sept 1764.

Ship *Francis and Mary;* formerly King David. Thos: Alexander assigns his interest in her. L. Norf., Va. 2 July 1659. D-342. See also D-227. 17 Oct 1659.

Ship *Francis and Mary;* Capt. Francis Emperor and Mr. Thos. Alexander part owners. L. Norf., Va. 15 Dec 1657. D-108.

Sloop *Francis;* John Pitt, master. Built in Bermudas, 1778. Acco., Va. Naval Entries and Clearances. 21 Sept 1780.

Ketch *Fortune* of Virginia; Mrs. Katherine Cooper and Mr. Thos. Daines owned one-quarter each. The Ketch was to be employed for Mrs. Dorothy and Susanna Cooper, orphans. L. Norf., Va. 16 Nov 1657. D-102.

Pinnace Fortune is sold by Jenrien (?) Blanck, an inhabitant of Amsterdam, to Mrs. Anna Scarlet. "Towe of ye Prince his flagge" included. N-n, Va., iv-113. 29 May 1652.

"Shipp or Vessell called the *Fortune* of Boston." N-n, Va. xv-279. 30 May 1687.

Schr *Flying Fish;* Jonathan Copes, Master, Acco., Va. Naval Entries and Clearances. 5 Dec 1780.

Ship ye *"Fenix;"* Capt. Church. L. Norf., Va. 1661.

Sloop *Fortune;* John West, skipper. Cal. Va. State Papers. i-92. 2 June 1705.

Ketch *Grosser's Adventure* of Hull; James Senior, master. Acco., Va. viii-64. 17 Mch 1678. Also viii-21. 16 Oct 1678. Also vii-142.

(To be continued)

REVOLUTIONARY AND MILITARY NOTES FROM THE ORDER BOOKS OF WEST VIRGINIA COUNTIES

Ordered that CATHERINE LINDSEY wife of DAVID LINDSEY, a soldier in the Continental Service be allowed One Hundred Pounds "for her support and four children for the present year." Berkeley county, ORDERS, vol. iv, p. 129. 16 May 1780.

JOHN GRANTHAM to be appointed an Ensign in a Company of Militia of this [Berkeley] county, commanded by Captain John McCormack (?) p. 198. 20 Sept 1780.

WILLIAM GRANTHAM appointed Lieutenant in the same company. p. 198. 20 Sept 1780.

WILLIAM JOHNS to be appointed Lieutenant in a company of militia commanded by Alexander Porterfield. p. 184. 17 Aug 1780.

Ordered that ELEANOR REASONER, wife of JOHN REASONER, a soldier in the Continental Service be "allowed her eighty pounds for support and two children for the present year." ORDERS, vol. iv, p. 131. 16 May 1780.

BARBARA SUSONG, wife of ANDREW SUSONG, a Soldier in the Continental Service to be allowed one hundred and twenty pounds for her support for the year. p. 131. 16 May 1780.

ELIZABETH KENNY, wife of RICHARD, a soldier in the Continental Service to be allowed twelve pounds ten shillings for her support for the year. p. 3. Aug 1779.

CATHERINE SMITH, wife of ROBERT, a Soldier in the Continental Service to be allowed twenty-five pounds for her support for the year. p. 2. Aug 1779.

AMOS NICHOLS, recommended for Captain of Militia of this county [Berkeley] p. 12. Aug 1779.

BARBARAH ALDICK, wife of (——) ALDICK, a Soldier in the Continental Service, to be allowed twenty pounds for her support for the year. p. 43. 21 Sept 1779.

CATHERINE MOODY, wife of WILLIAM, a Soldier in the Continental Service to be allowed Twenty pounds for her support for the year. p. 43. 21 Sept 1779.

MARY COVEY [CAVEY?] wife of DAURETT (?) COVEY to be allowed Twenty pounds for her support for the year. p. 42. 21 Sept 1779.

MARY KINSELL, wife of LEWIS, a Soldier in the Continental Service to be allowed Thirty pounds for her support for the year. p. 84. 16 Nov 1779.

MARY McDONALD, wife of JOHN, to be allowed Thirty pounds for her support for the year. p. 85. 17 Nov 1779.

CHRISTIANA PENNYBAKER, wife of JACOB, to be allowed Forty pounds for her support for the year. p. 86. 17 Nov 1779.

(To be continued)

MARRIAGES BY INFERENCE*

(Continued from June number)

The following marriages are all from KING WILLIAM COUNTY, Virginia. King William was formed in 1702 from King and Queen county. The Clerk's Office was burned in 1885, in the night. Early in the morning the then Clerk went down and took a look at the still smoking ruins. It is said he then went back home and to bed. About twelve o'clock a by-stander, observing some volumes still holding together, got a long pole and dragged them out and poured water on them. In this way a few records were saved. The Editor has this information from an eye-witness. These records with the backs burned off and the leaves consequently all loose, were placed in a box and remained there perhaps twenty years. The new Clerk then got an appropriation from the county, bought some temporary binders and set two boys at work pasting the leaves in by their unburned edges, that is to say, their front edges. No effort was made to arrange them chronologically so that the rather puzzling result is about seventeen large binders, each volume containing an assortment of wills and deeds from 1702 to 1880 or later. At the most, only three early volumes are represented, but their value is great.

JAMES ADAMS and ELIZABETH JOHNS, dau. of Richard. v. "6"-69. Before 12 Jany 1703.

EDWARD BURGESS probably m. CATHARINE STANDBRIDGE, a widow. Before or about Jany 1705. v. "11"-227.

WILLIAM BURROUGHS and MARY HIGGASON, dau. of John. Before or about 26 Sept 1706. v-"11"-

JOSEPH BICKLEY, of King and Queen, and [Mrs.] SARAH GISSEDGE. (Marriage contract.) v. "11"-111. 30 Sept 1703.

HUMPHREY BROOKE and SARAH PAGE, dau. of Robert. (Marriage contract.) 7 Feby 1799. v. "9"-187.

NANCY BAKER, wid. of Thomas, m. ... DABNEY. Before or about June Ct, 1794. v. "1"-297.

SAMUEL COLEMAN and CHRISTIAN FOSTER, dau. of Joseph. About 1787. v. "2"-61.

THOMAS DOUGLAS and FRANCES JONES, Jr., dau. of Frances Jones. (Intended marriage.) 1 June 1811. v. "4"-211.

ANDERSON DUGAR and FANNY ELLETT, dau. of Thomas. Before 28 Feby 1799. v. "9"-30.

THOMAS FAIRFAX and MARY AYLETT, dau. of William. Before 1798. v. "16"-21.

FALVEY FRAZER and LUCY MADISON. (Marriage contract.) 10 Jany 1799. v. "11"-314.

GEORGE B. FLEET and CATHERINE LIPSCOMB. Before 25 Aug 1819. v. "5"-135.

JANE FRAZER, widow of John G. Frazer, m. ... LIPSCOMB. Before 1810. v. "4"-176.

EZEKIEL FIELD and CATY GATEWOOD. Before 13 June 1803. v. "1"-424.

JOSEPH GWATHMEY and MARY HILL, dau. of John Hill, Gent. [She perhaps married before.] Before 1 Apr 1797. v. "8"-194.

Mr. RICHARD GISSEDGE and Mrs. SARAH SHELTON, widow. Before 30 Sept 1703. [At this date Gissedge was dead.] v. "11"-111.

ORLANDO JONES and MARTHA [WEST?] dau. of Nathaniel and Martha West. Before 1706-7. v. "11"-155.

DANIEL LIPSCOMB, parish of St. John's, and JANE FRAZER, same. (Marriage contract.) 3 Nov 1792. v. "1"-359.

GEORGE LIPSCOMB and ANN LIPSCOMB. (Marriage contract.) 16 Sept 1785. v. "11"-284.

JOHN LEWIS and ELIZABETH MITCHELL, dau. of James. About or before 1811. v. "4"-225.

Mr. GEDION MACON (late of New Kent, dec'd) m. MARTHA WOODWARD, dau. of William. Before 1695. v. "5"-37.

REUBEN MADISON and JUDITH LIPSCOMB. Before 30 July 1804. v. "9"-112.

FREDERICK NOEL and SENECA GARNETT, dau. of *Achiles*. Before 28 May 1797. v. "11"-324.

ROBERT PYNES and ANNE FOSTER. Before 11 Mch 1793. v. "1"-303.

DAVID POWERS and JANE, the dau. of John Foard. About 20 July 1703. v. "12"-344.
BENJAMIN PYNES and SARAH FOSTER. Before 11 Mch 1793. v. "1"-303.
CHARLES PRIGG and ANN ELLETT dau. of Thomas. Before 28 Feby 1799. v. "9"-30.
JOSIAS RANDLE m. JANE JOHNS, dau. of RICHARD. Before 12 Jany 1703. [Randle was then deceased.] v. "6"-69.
JOHN RANDLE and MARY JOHNS, dau. of Richard. Before 12 Jany 1703. v. "6"-69.

(To be continued)

MARYLAND'S NEXT OF KIN*

(Continued from June number)

FRANCIS COMPTON, Charles co. John Beale who married the Excx makes oath that he knows of no relative of the deceased capable of being shearers in ye destrubution of ye Dec's Estate. 12 May 1718. 1-488.
RICHARD HARRISON, brother of ye whole blood; inv. Elizabeth Hagall, of Charles county; 16 Oct 1718. i-490.
SIBIA DURRANT; inv. Anthony Durrant of Baltimore county. 26 July 1718. i-492.
LUKE WHEELER and MARY JESSUP; inv. Thomas Lawton of St. Mary's county (Mary Jemmyma Lawton, extx.) 10 Mch 1718-19. i-496.
JEMIME LAUGHTON; Mary Jessup, admx of Joseph Jessup of St. Mary's county. 10 Mch 1718-19. i-498.
GEORGE MORDICK, son; inv. Joseph Murdick of Talbot county. 2 Mch 1718. i-504.
"Presents appraisement FORST; TURBUTT not presents but had notice," inv. William Skinner; of Talbot county; 2 Mch 1718; i-505.
JOHN GARRETT; inv. Elizabeth Garret of Balto. county; 1718; i-507.
WILLIAM WRITE, A.... BROWN; inv. Signey Brown of Som. county; Dec. 1718; i-509.
NATHANIEL WALE, ELIAS WALE; inv. Edward Wale of Som. county; 3 Feb 1718-19; i-510.
HENRY DARNALL, Jr., CHARLES DIGGS, JAMES BOWLES, NICHO. LOWE; inv. Henry Lowe; 10 Oct 1718; i-512. of St. Mary's county.
BRIAN SHIELD; inv. Bryan Shield of Queen Ann county; 1718; i-515.
THOMAS DILLON, CHARLES DILLON; inv. Lawrence Dillon, of St. Mary's county; 21 Mch 1718; i-523.
ABRAHAM HIGHWAY; inv. Jacob Highway of Som. county; 5 Mch 1718; i-524.
MARY DELLOHUNT; inv. Thomas Finckes of Chas. county; 14 Nov 1718; i-528.
MARY JESUP; inv. Thomas Lawton of St. Mary's county; 10 Mch 1718; i-529.
"No kindred qualified." inv. JOHN GREEN of Talbot county; 10 Jany 1718; i-531.
SCHOLFIELD and RICHARD BEDDER; inv. William Bedder, Sen., of Som. county; 1718; i-532.
CHARLES KING; admr; inv. Edward Hall of St. Mary's county; 19 Mch 1718-19.
FRANCIS WILLISON, ANNE WILLINSON; inv. *Alld'x* Willinson of Som. county; 28 Jany 1717. i-530.

(End of first volume of inventories, Annapolis. To be continued.)

THE WEBBS

(Continued from June number)

THOMAS WEBB; died 10 Feby 1686. (Also HENRY WEBB, same day) York Hampton Psh Reg. Va.
TAPLEY WEBB; a magistrate of Norfolk county, Va. K. Wm. "15." 1816.
TERENCE WEBB; suit. Norf., Va. vii-50. 1704.
THOMAS WEB; member of the Virginia Company under second charter. Hening i-84. 23 May 1609.
THOMAS WEBB; agreement with Ambrose Bennet; Bennet to erect a mill. I. W., Va. iii-426. 29 Apr 1650.
Mr. THOMAS WEBB; mcht of London. N-n, Va. viii-114. 29 Nov 1661.
THOMAS WEBB, son of WILLIAM; receives a legacy by will of Robert Davis. L. Norf. 21 Apr 1661. See also 16 June 1662. D-346.
Mr. THOMAS WEB; case of a servant's passage. [This is Mr. WEBB of London.] N-n, Va. viii-154. 28 June 1662. Same. case 2 Mch 1662. N-n, Va. viii-163.
THOS. WEBB; power to *Booller* to take possession of Webb's mill. I. W. Va. iii-12. 25 Feby 1663.
THOS. WEBB, Westmoreland, Va. H. r. under Alexander. S. L. O. v-162. 1664.
Mr. THOMAS WEBB; brother to Mr. Devorax Browne. Acco., Va. i-89. 16 Jany 1664.
THOS. WEBB; a witness. Acco., Va. i-82. 10 Aug 1664.
THOS. WEBB; a witness to power from Ralph Allen of London. N-n, Va. ix-204. 29 Aug 1664.
THOMAS WEBBE, son of Thomas Webbe, lately dec'd, gets a colt and other legacies from Mathew x Gething of N-n county. N-n, Va. xi-4. 21 Aug 1665. (See Gething's will.)
THOS. WEBBE, orphant; left to the care of Mathew Gethings and his wife and having been given by said Gethings a mare colt, &c., and [that] being all the estate that the said orphant hath... "Itt beinge meane & Inconsiderable for a free Education; yett Ellenor Gethings the Relict & ex'x of Mathew Gethings & for the affection she beares to the said orphant... preferred to take him without diminution of the principall or increase [of his estate.]" N-n, Va. 28 Jany 1668. x-60.

(To be continued)

The County Court Note-Book

An every-other-monthly devoted to abstracts from County Court and other records, prior to 1800, and with a department of notes and queries.

MILNOR LJUNGSTEDT, Editor and Publisher. Bethesda, Route 1, Maryland.

Published six times a year. Subscription, two dollars a year, in advance, must begin with the year. Special rates on renewals. Advertising rates moderate.

VOL. II AUGUST, 1923 No. 4

ON CONDITIONS

An editorial in chapters.

The Editor visited CUMBERLAND COUNTY, Virginia, a few years ago in search of records. This is the county where the Clerk of the Court and his brother are on trial for the shooting of the Baptist minister. The incident was the result of a long-standing semi-political feud in which the Clerk of the Court represents one faction.

It is quite interesting to come into close touch with such communities. A certain thrill of underlying excitement accompanies the knowledge that one is sitting in friendly company with a reputable citizen who is armed against another more or less reputable citizen —according to the point of view. The Editor spent three weeks at Cumberland Courthouse and had this experience. The Editor being of an analytical or argumentative turn of mind ... as one may choose to call it ... would really like to know what she would have done had the shooting begun then. She has a vague idea that she would have fired one of the invaluable records at the shooter ... had he been the other man. Her friendly companion was a little man and old ... quite old.

The office of the Clerk of the Cumberland County Court, as it was while these political incidents were earlier in the happening, and as it may be now, is what the Editor would wish to describe. The office is a small brick building, containing one good-sized room, and set off by itself (the one redeeming feature in the usual run of Clerks' offices) with four large windows, a double front door, and the usual large soft-coal stove. The Editor, being argumentative and not over-timid, remembers that she tried in vain to convince the Clerk's brother that no stove would burn properly with the upper door and the lower door open at the same time. It was several years before the chance discovery of an article on how to burn soft coal convinced the Editor that there was a good deal she didn't know.

The west wall of the office leaked badly, and the floor was sagged under the weight of some modern steel cases. Several panes were out of the windows ... not a bad thing in summer. The leaky west wall, of plastered brick, was lined with a very high, old-time wooden pigeonhole case with wider cupboards underneath. Thanks to this projection the Editor was able to explore. As a result of the damp the silver-fish and other "critters" had done some remarkable work with the marriage bonds. The Editor collected the peculiar papier-maché-like remains. One of the record books (a volume of deeds) also showed a most beautiful and perfect specimen of a fan-growing fungus. The fungus, of course, had destroyed the record.

The Editor, with the assistance of the deputy, a young and intelligent girl, explored the pigeonholes. The deputy was much younger than the Editor and could clumb with more facility. Indifferent hands of many searchers had left marriage bonds, chancery cases, judgments, executions and the like in sad confusion. The Editor made rough assortments of these papers, placing them in groups of pigeonholes with the sincere hope that those following her would at least keep to the rank and file. Several rats' nests had to be cleared out.

After a thorough examination of the matters in the Clerk's Office, the Editor received permission to visit the jail. The Sheriff sent the key and an old lawyer escorted her.

The jail of Cumberland county is a small stone building in two stories, with, the Editor thinks, four rather small rooms on each floor. One of the upper rooms had been given over to the papers the Clerk had no use for ... or the county, either. The floor was thickly spread with them ... perhaps six inches deep on an average. A long plank on the inside and one against the outside wall furnished a couple of shelves. One of these held a row of bound volumes. In the corner a small wooden pigeonhole case, moved there it is supposed at the time of the change in the court system, was filled with judgments, executions, &c., and rats' nests. Among these small, folded, tightly wrapped and usually carefully endorsed papers are such records as Mr. Charles E. Kemper has shown in the pages of WILLIAM AND MARY to be of high historical value.

The Editor's immediate search was for certain personal tax-lists. There were many "land-books" or their remains. A useful small boy worked faithfully for the sum of fifty cents and he and the Editor together made a discovery. The first ORDER BOOK of CUMBERLAND COUNTY was supposed to be lost. No one knew anything about it, and no one cared, apparently, though it seems to be customary among some searchers to walk and talk darkly and secretly as to what they find or want to find. It does remind the Editor of the house dog, otherwise friendly, endeavoring to secrete his last bone beyond even the sight of his best friend.

Just before closing the search, however, the small boy handed the Editor the missing first ORDER BOOK. Fifteen pages gone from the front, and more from the back ... but it was and is the record that all counties treasure. The Editor removed it to the Clerk's Office.

* * * * * * *

A quite different picture is presented by the Clerk's Office in the old county of SURRY. But the Editor must leave this description, with others, for another issue.

This AUGUST NOTE-BOOK has been delayed by the absence of the Editor on a quest in a very different section... yet among historical and genealogical material that touches upon a long and varied frontier. The Editor has had the great privilege and great pleasure of spending two weeks at the Wisconsin State Historical Library in Madison. Three weeks more were taken up in a somewhat meandering route by way of the older counties of West Virginia, Chicago, Pittsburgh, Harrisburg, and several old Pennsylvania counties. Part of the material... that touching French and Indian War service, and Revolutionary service, will be published in the NOTE-BOOK.

The Editor wishes she had time and ability to give an idea of what the Draper Collection, at the Wisconsin Historical Library, means to the historical and genealogical searcher. It is a collection so wonderful in its scope that only a personal examination can give a clear sense of its value.

The manuscripts are under the immediate care of Dr. Louise Phelps Kellogg (widely known as an historian and as having received the Justin Winsor prize for her thesis on Colonial Charters), and the courtesy and help given by Dr. Kellogg as well as the Assistant Director of the Library, Miss Nunns, and Mrs. Levi and Miss Kasten, could well be emulated in certain more eastern libraries.

At present the lack of sufficient calendars makes the work of research somewhat slow and tedious. The Society is about starting on a second calendar of these manuscripts and will, no doubt, within a few years, have the work well advanced. The Editor will write more in detail as to the collection at another time.

The Durrett papers at the Chicago University are hardly in shape as yet for examination. It is hoped they will soon be bound, backed, and calendared.

PIONEERS OF BOURBON COUNTY, KENTUCKY, DYING BETWEEN 1786 AND 1800

Compiled by Mrs. Julia Spencer Ardery.

(Continued from June number)

Richard Sampson, Reuben Sanford, James Scott, John Scott, John Scouce, Thomas Scouce, Christian Shanks, Daniel Shawhan, Samuel Slater, Peter Smelzer, James M. Smith, John Smith (2), Jacob Smith,

Thomas Smith, George Stephenson, John Stokes, Thomas Strother, James Stuart, Peter Stuart, John Summers.

John Talbott, Frederick Tarr, Jone Tate, James Thomas, Joseph Thompson, John Thornhill, Joshua Thurman, Edward Todd, Samuel Todd, Thomas Trundle, David Trimble, Edward Tucker, Jonathan Tucker, Jesse Turner.

Reuben Underwood.

John Wood, Aldrew Wallace, Edward Waller, Benjamin Ward, Isaac Ward, James Warson, Wm. Cook Weaklin [Weakland], James Webb, Wm. E. Webb, Michael Welch, John West, James Whaley, John Whitledge,

John Wickersham, John Williams, Benjamin Wills, John Wilson, Owen Winn, Atwell Worrel.

Samuel Young.

CERTAIN RECORDS OF SOMERSET AND WORCESTER COUNTY, MARYLAND

[Note: The Editor discovered some years ago that there are records in Worcester County, Maryland, which apparently belong to its parent county of Somerset. The following extracts from a Maryland Act explain the matter, at least in part.]

An Act to Provide for Recording Certain Wills in the Register's Office of Worcester County.

WHEREAS it is represented to this general Assembly by the petition of the Register of Wills of Worcester County, and certified by the Orphans Court of said County, that a number of Wills, anterior to the division of Somerset and erection of Worcester County aforesaid, are in a ruinous and imperfect state and that a new record, made from the original Wills in the said office would be of great utility; THEREFORE... the Justices of the Orphans Court of Worcester County are hereby empowered and required to cause to be recorded... in good leather bound books to which fair and regular Alphabets shall be prepared, all such Wills filed in the office of the Register of Wills of said County, and which have not been recorded, as... in their judgment may deem necessary and proper... And be it ENACTED that this Act shall continue in force untill the first day of May Eighteen hundred and eleven, and no longer.

In the Record of the proceedings of the Orphans Court of Worcester County, 18 May 1808, the following Order is entered:

It is Ordered that the Register Record in Books of the description mentioned in said Act, all Wills in said Office of date Anterior to the year 1743...

WILLS PROBATED AND ADMINISTRATIONS GRANTED IN PRINCE WILLIAM COUNTY, VIRGINIA, 1754-1757

From the Second Remaining Order Book

(Continued from June number)

LEWIS RENO; will presented by Lewis and Thomas Reno, extrs; proved by witnesses and ctf granted for probate. (Isaac Farrow one of the appraisers of the estate.) 27 Jany 1755. p. 181.

DENNIS CONYERS; will presented by Samuel and John Conyers, extrs. Ctf granted for probate. 24 Mch 1755. p. 187.

THOMAS STRIBLING, Gent.; will presented by Francis and Talliaferro Stribling, two of the extrs. Proved by Anthony Teale (?), gent., and Margaret Sinclair, and ctf for probate granted. 25 Mch 1755. p. 194.

(SARAH CONYERS disclaims all benefit under will of husband, Dennis. 28 Apr 1755. p. 220.)

WILLIAM DAVIS; will presented by Isaac and Ellen Davis, extrs. proved by witnesses and ctf for probate granted. 28 Sept 1755. p. 220.

WILLIAM OAKLY; admn his estate granted Jemima Oakly his widow. John Hopper and William Bridges, sec. 28 Apr 1755. p. 221.

WALTER SNAILS; admn his estate granted Francis Jackson; Benj. Bridges, sec. 26 May 1755. p. 232.

JOHN CANTERBURRY; Elizabeth Canterburry was his extx. See Ct 28 May 1755. p. 255.

THOMAS SCOTT; admn his estate granted to Mary Scott his widow, Richard Crupper and George Calvert, Jr., sec. 28 July 1755. p. 264.

MARY HALL; Edward Hall granted admn on her estate. John Keely and Henry Cooper, sec. 26 Aug. 1755. p. 278.

AGATHA THORNTON; her will presented by Thomas Thornton, extr, and proved by witnesses: Henry *Holtzclaw* and John Brown. Ctf granted for probate. 22 Sept 1755. p. 308. *(End of this volume.)*

From the same volume are the following military appointments.

WILLIAM BAILIS; oath as militia officer. 28 May 1754. p. 72.

JOSEPH NEVILL; oath as militia officer. 25 Mch 1755. p. 191.

FRANCIS STRIBLING; oath as militia officer. (Lieutenant.) 25 Aug 1755. p. 270.

WILLIAM CARR; oath as Lieutenant militia. 25 Aug 1755. p. 270.

JOHN JAMES; oath as officer; 26 Aug 1755. p. 279.

THOMAS FALKNER; oath as officer; 26 Aug 1755. p. 280.

JOHN HOOE, sworn Lieutenant. 22 Sept 1755. p. 313.

WILLIAM BARR; sworn ensign. 22 Sept 1755. p. 313.

GEORGE CALVERT, younger; patroler. 24 Nov 1755. p. 15.

WILLIAM FARROW; oath as militia officer; 27 Oct 1755. p. 9.

JOHN FARROW; patroler. 22 Nov 1756. p. 244.

JOHN CALVERT; patroler. 22 Nov 1756. p. 244.

OBED CALVERT; patroler. 22 Nov. 1756. p. 244.

GEORGE CALVERT, the younger; patroler. 22 Nov. 1756. p. 244. [Presumably a reappointment.]

NOTES AND QUERIES

BOLTON-CHAPMAN: Five dollars will be paid for authoritative information as to the State and county in which can be found the marriage of MATTHEW BOLTON and MARY CHAPMAN in 1788. Bolton was from Virginia but may have married in another State. F. P. B. L.

ANDREWS: Wanted, the ancestry of DAVID ANDREWS, who married ELIZA BROWN, dau. of DAVIS BROWN. DAVIS BROWN settled in Giles county, Tennessee, about 1811. E. J. A. C.
[This query erroneously gave the name DAVID BROWN instead of DAVIS, in the April NOTE-BOOK.]

COOK: Wanted, the ancestry of HENRY COOK and his wife MARTHA STONE, of Giles county, Tennessee, earlier of Virginia. [See June NOTE-BOOK.] E. J. A. C.

COOK: Who were the parents of JOHN THOMSON (or THOMPSON) COOK (whose wife was Grace Shute) of Franklin, Tennessee. John Thompson Cook had a brother HENRY COOK (whose wife was Martha Stone) of Giles county, Tennessee. Would like to correspond with members of this family. E. J. A. C.

LIGON: Would like to know the ancestors of RICHARD LIGON and his wife ALICE JETER, of Nottoway county, Virginia. ALICE (JETER) LIGON was the aunt of Jeremiah Jeter, the Baptist divine of Richmond. A son of the LIGONS went to Kentucky in 1846. L. W. T. K.

CHENOWETH: A reward is offered for the given names of the parents and grandparents of WILLIAM CHENOWETH who married SARAH BAXTER about 1793 at Hamstead, Carroll county, Maryland... then Baltimore county. The CHENOWETHS lived at Hamstead and died there between 1805 and 1825. C. C. H. I.

SAULE: JOHN SAULE, an Irish Quaker, came to Pennsylvania about 1717. Did he survive and leave a family? Will pay for satisfactory information. M. L. M.

ROBINSON-SAULE: Wanted, proof of a marriage between a ROBINSON and a SAULE, before 1750. M. L. M.

FOWKE, FOWKES, FOOKES: Who was the father of James FOWKE of the Eastern Shore of Virginia; immigrant about 1660. H. C. F. M.

BOOK AND OTHER NOTES

Mrs. MARGARET TURNER KELLER, 3738 Kanawha street, Chevy Chase, D. C., is preparing for early publication the court records of the Maryland-Virginia families of TURNER, STONE, LOWE, HAWKINS, DAWSON, and HYATT. Mrs. Keller will be glad to hear from persons interested in these families.

The STEWART CLAN MAGAZINE, published in Filley, Nebraska, by Mr. George T. Edson, is continuing the publication of northern Stewart families. It is an interesting, valuable and well-printed paper.

In the June number of this NOTE-BOOK the reference to the KEENE FAMILY HISTORY contains a regrettable misprint. The name should be KEENE and not KENNE. Orders for the publication should be sent to Dr. Elias Jones, 511 West Pratt street, Baltimore, Maryland.

The WISCONSIN STATE HISTORICAL SOCIETY is preparing to publish its calendar of the KENTUCKY MANUSCRIPTS of the Draper collection. It is thought this calendar can be brought out in 1924. The Editor understands that the price will be a pro rata one and early subscriptions will be advantageous. The value of the work cannot be overestimated. Examination of the already published PRESTON PAPERS calendar will give an idea of its great usefulness.

The EDITOR or Mrs. PAULINE STEWART CROSLEY (now in Seattle, Washington) will be glad to receive conditional subscriptions (names only) to the forthcoming FLOYDS and STEWARTS of VIRGINIA (and neighboring colonies); THEIR CATALOGUE. It is probable that this compilation will be put out in two volumes, either of which can be sold separately. The price for the two volumes will not be over fifteen dollars, and it is hoped that sufficient subscriptions will be received to enable the compilers to print at a much less cost. The work will include the DAVISES of the same section; the CUNNINGHAMS; BURFORDS and some other intermarried families. It will also include fifteen hundred or two thousand marriages such as are now being published in the NOTE-BOOK. The FLOYD-STEWART material has been gathered from Church registers; from county courts; from State Land Offices; and from such publications as are considered reliable references. Few genealogies will be worked out. The books will be in dictionary catalogue form and the data given may be accepted as fact.

The D. A. R. Library in Washington (which year by year grows more valuable to the searcher) has a copy of a very interesting manuscript list called "genealogical Sources," which was presented to the Library by Mrs. George W. Hodges. This is a list of such material in the Maryland Historical Society, and, the Editor is informed, was compiled by Mr. Robert F. Hays, Jr., under the direction of the former Librarian, Mr. McCreary, now dead. The MSS. is, unfortunately, not up to date, but, nevertheless, is of great value, especially account of its arrangement under counties. Searchers intending to visit the M. H. S. would do well to consult this list in Washington. It must be added that only members of the Society are, as a rule, permitted access to its manuscript collections.

The JOHN BELL CHAPTER, D. A. R., of Madison, Wisconsin, with the co-operation of the State Historical Society of Wisconsin and the Wisconsin Archeological Society, has recently erected a Marker on the WISCONSIN HEIGHTS BATTLEFIELD, which lies about two miles southwest of the bridge at Sauk City. The marker commemorates the last Indian war within the limits of what is now Wisconsin. The Sauk Chieftain, Black Hawk, and his band were overtaken at that spot by the Wisconsin and Illinois troops on the 21st July, 1832. At the close of the "war" treaties were made ceding all the land in southern Wisconsin to the United States, and soon thereafter immigration began, largely from New York and New England. The first United States Land Offices were opened in 1834; the government land was purchased by the settlers for the most part at $1.25 an acre. (This information kindly furnished by Dr. Louise Phelps Kellogg of the Wisconsin Historical Society, who was one of the speakers on the occasion; Gov. Blaine and Joseph Schafer, Superintendent of the State Library, also delivered addresses.)

If anyone desiring specialized searches of the Draper MSS. will address the Editor she will be glad to give them the name of a reliable person.

PLACES TO STAY

Visitors to WEST CHESTER, the county seat of CHESTER Co., Penna., can get excellent and reasonably priced meals at the OVERTOWN, which is situated above the bank. Sometimes the hostess, who is a member of the Society of Friends, can also provide rooming facilities.

By writing to Mrs. A. S. EDWARDS, of Surry C. H., Va., information can be had as to a convenient and comfortable place to stay.

Ladies visiting Madison, Wisconsin, will find the City Y. W. C. A. comfortable and reasonable. The cafeteria is one of the very best and reasonable in price.

The Central "Y" at Harrisburg has also a limited number of rooms for transients, and is a very attractive place. It is located opposite Capitol Park.

From personal experience the Editor recommends the Ft. Dearborn Hotel, Chicago, and its excellent cafeteria.

COLUMBIAN PRINTING CO., INC., WASHINGTON, D. C.

The

County Court Note-Book

A Little Bulletin of History and Genealogy

Vol. II — October, 1923 — No. 5

NEW ENGLANDERS AND OTHERS IN EARLY VIRGINIA RECORDS

(*Sixth instalment*)

OBEDIAH COOKSON, County of Suffolk and Province of the Massachusetts Bay in New England, Merchant; gives power to John Wise of Accomack. Acco. xx-95. 27 Jany 1731.

JOHN EDWARDS; his deposition: age about 22 . . . is the legitimate son of Mr. Edwards, late citizen and freeman of London; his mother's name being Kathryne Edwards, widow, the late wife of Mr. Edw. Hemlocke, dec'd, and he was in Silver-Street at the corner house over ag't the church of the same parish . . . &c., &c. N-n, vii-18. 30 Apr 1655.

ARGOLL SIMONS; Robert Foster deposes that Simons is son of Jno. and Anne Simons, and said John (dec'd) lived in Sussex county, in the Territoryes of Penna. N-n —— p. 464. 29 July 1689.

GEORGE GORHAM, citizen and Mcht Tailor of London, age about 28; WILLIAM TURNER, citizen & wool packer of London, age about 40; HENRY BEALE, the Elder, citizen & Mcht Tailor of London . . . JOHN HODGSON, of Accomack River in Virginia, Mcht, then living in St. Mary Ax, London. Acco. ii-152. 1669.

ROBERT GLENDALL, late of Elizabeth City County, Va. N-n, xvii-455. 28 Jany 1697.

Mr. THO: GIBSON of Littlewood street, London; Rich'd Gibson's draft upon him. L. Norf. v-246. 24 Oct 1692.

RICHARD HOPKINS, Marriner, of the City of Bristol, England, had an estate of 500 acres in the County. Acco. ix-176. 19 Feby 1689.

EDWARD HARPER, of Somerset, Maryland, formerly of N-n; son and heir of Francis and Elizabeth Harper. N-n, xi-194. 6 Dec 1679.

RICHARD LEE (wife Judith) of Northumberland county, Va., gives power to Capt. Hancock Nickless to ackn. a deed for 850 acres. This deed recites that one Smith sold to Coll. William Kendall, and Kendall by will left one moiety to his daughter, Mrs. Mary Lee and her heirs; from the said Mary Lee descended to the said Richard. Acco. xx-71. 17 Apr 1731.

Mr. WM. PAYNE of Lancaster county, was made guardian of Catherine Barker. Acco. xviii-82. 8 July 1724.

Mr. GEORGE PURCHAS, of King William county, Va., came from Pensilvana. Cal. Va. St. Pa. i-114. 1707.

ROBERT MASON, planter, Cople Parish, Wmld, was heir of Joseph Baker, *Calbert* county, Md. Wmld, v-519. 30 May 1716.

BENJAMIN ROLFE, Notary and Tabellion Publick . . . dwelling at Boston in N. E., certifies that John Ballantine, Esq., before whom power of att'y was executed, is one of His Majesty's Justices of the Peace in the County of Suffolk . . . Acco. xx-96. 1731.

HANNAH WALDRON, of Marblehead in the County of Essex and Province of the Massachusetts Bay in New England, widow; "admin'x to the estate of my late husband, Joseph Waldron, deceased," gives power to her brother, Samuel Parker, of Marblehead, aforesaid, Joyner, but now resident in Maryland. Wit: Ezek. Goldthwait; Mich'l Nolen, Mich. S. Nolan. Acco. xx-96. 23 July 1731.

(*To be continued*)

A LIST OF PERSONS NATURALIZED BY PARTICULAR ACTS

From Bacon's Laws of Maryland *

(*Contributed by Mrs. George W. Hodges*)

(*Continued from June number*)

HENRY FREEMAN, Calvert county; 6 June 1674; 12.

MATTHEW FREEMAN, see "Matthiason," Cecil county. 22 May 1695; 10.

RUTGERTSON GARRETS, Baltimore county. 19 Apr 1671; 10.

CHRISTIAN GEIFT, City of Annapolis. 5 Aug 1721; 5.

PETER GOLLEY, Dorchester county. 22 May 1695; 10.

JOHN GOUTTEE, Dorchester county. 22 May 1695; 10.

JOHN and JOSEPH GOUTTEE, his sons.

ARNOLDUS de la GRANGE, Baltimore county. 26 Sept 1684; 8.

HENRY GREEN, of Talbot county. 6 June 1674. 14.

* The figures other than dates refer to chapters.

ALBERT GREENING of Anne Arundel county. 28 Feby 1721. 15.
JOSHUA GUIBERT of St. Mary's county. 15 Nov 1678. 12.
SAMUEL GUICHARD of Anne Arundel county. 15 Nov 1712. 17.
ANNA HACK of Cecil county, widow of Dr. George Hack, an early settler; also GEORGE and PETER HACK, her sons. 1 May 1666. 7.
HANS HENSON, Kent county. 20 Oct 1671. 29.
THOMAS HARVEY "and his children," of Calvert county. 3 June 1715. 2.
HENRY HENDERSON. 6 June 1674. 12.
JOHN HENDRICKSON, "a Native of Rotterdam in Holland," of Kent county. 16 June 1730. Also his sons and daughters: JOHN, SAMUEL, RACHEL, MARY, MILDRED, MARGARET, MARTHA, REBECKAH, HANNAH, and RUTH. 11.
AUGUSTINE HARMAN, "of Prague, in the Kingdom of Bohemia," of Cecil county, and the sons and daughters of the said Augustine: EPHRAIM, GEORGIUS, CASPARUS, ANNA, MARGARITTA, JUDITH and FRANCINA. 1 May 1666. 7.
GUSTAVUS HESSELIUS, of Prince George's county, "and his Children." 5 Aug 1721. 5.
JOHN FRANCIS HOLLAND of Baltimore county. 15 Apr 1707. 10.
JEOFFREY JACOBSON. 6 June 1674. 12.
JOHN JARBO, "of Dyon in the Realm of France," of St. Mary's county. 1 May 1666. 7.

MARRIAGES BY INFERENCE*

(Continued from August number)

WILLIAM BAILEY and ISABELLA RIPPEY, dau. of Samuel. Cumb. co., Pa. Before 16 Dec 1800. BB-83.
JOHN BARNHART and SUSANNA HALDIMAN. Before 10 Aug 1800. Dauphin co. Pa. B-60.
THOMAS BURCHANEL [sic] and ANNE WOOD, dau. of Enoch. Before 6 Sept 1831. Fayette co., Pa. i-332.
JOHN BURTNEY (of Ireland) and MARGARET STEELE. Before 18 Jany 1821. Alleg. co., Pa. ii-230.
CHARITY CALVERT, wid. of Thomas, late of E. Pennsbury Tshp, and —— MILLER. Before 20 Nov 1782. Cumb. co., Pa. O. C. ii-157.
ISAAC DEHAVEN, of Scott county, and REBECCA STEEL. 1 Jany 1801. Draper Mss. 17CC42.
JAMES DUGAN and JENNY STEELE. Before 18 Jany 1821. Alleg. co. Pa. ii-230.
DEWITT (?) ERFORD and MAGDALENE RUPLEY, dau. of Jacob. Before 6 July 1789. Cumb. Co., Pa. E-284.
CAPT. MICHAEL ERSKINE from Penna., and MARGARET (HANDLEY) PAWLEY, a widow. 1785. Draper Mss. 8ZZ30.

DANIEL FRANK and DOROTHY RUPLEY, dau. of Jacob. Before 6 July 1789. Cumb. co., Pa. E-284.
JOHN E. FINLEY, son of Rev'd James Finley and wf Hannah, b. 26 July 1753, d. 7 Jany 1810; married ELIZABETH RUSTON, dau. of Job (b. 16 Sept 1759), in 1782. Draper Mss. 12ZZ322.
ADAM FONDERACE and MARGARET RUPLEY. Before 6 July 1789. Cumb. co. Pa. E-284.
MARGARET HAYS, dau. of William, m. —— KIRKPATRICK. Before 12 Apr 1793. Cumb. co., Pa. E-320.
ESTHER HAYS, dau. of William, m. —— MATHEWS. Before 12 Apr 1793. Cumb. co., Pa. E-320.
SAMUEL HENRY and HANNAH GRAY. (George Gray was her half-bro.) Before 7 Jany 1801. Dauphin co., Pa. B-149.
JOSEPH HILL and MARY JEMMISON, dau. of David. See his will, 1814. Fayette co., Pa. i-188.
GEORGE HAMIL and MARY RIPPEY, dau. of Samuel, of Shippensburg, Pa. Before 16 Dec 1800. Cumb. co. Pa. BB-83.
ROBERT HUTCHINSON and MARY LOVE, dau. of Hugh. Before 1819. Fayette co., Pa. i-196.
JOHN JACK and MARGARET WILKINS, one of the daus. of Peter, late of Cumberland. Before 24 Aug 1762. Cumb. co., Pa. O. C. Docket i-70.
—— JORDAN and AGNES STEELE, a widow. 1800, Cumb. Pa. F-207.
JOHN KEITH and JENNY MATTHEWS, dau. of James, (Woodford co., Ky.?) 18 Dec 1800. Draper Mss. 17CC42.
JOHN LITTLE and SARAH SAMPLE. Before 3 Sept 1792. Cumb. co., Pa.
JOHN MARTIN, of Ireland, and NANCY STEELE. Before 18 Jany 1821. Alleg. co. Pa. ii-230.
GEN'L GEORGE MATHEWS and —— PAUL. Draper Mss. 8ZZ37.
CHRISTOPHER MOHR and MARIA MARGARET REIGEL, dau. of William. Before 11 Jany 1779. Northumb. co., Pa. O. C. Docket i-18.

(To be continued)

THE WEBBS

(Continued from August number)

THOMAS x WEBB; age about 27. Acco., Va. 17 May 1669. iii-144.
THOMAS WEBB; orphan; cattle-marks. Thomas is in the tuition of Daniel Neech. N-n, Va. 1670. iv-1.
THOMAS WEBB, a svt to Capt. John West, binds his dau. FRANCES to Mrs. Kathrin Scarborough Acco. Va. iii-190. 8 Apr 1670.
THOMAS x WEBB; depn; age about 40. [From this depn it appears that that Capt. John West had made at least one trip to Nevis.] Acco., Va. 20 July 1671. iv-14.

THOMAS x WEBB; freed by John West but agrees to serve West and binds his dau. to West's dau. till she come of age. West is to give her a colt, &c. Acco., Va. 17 Sept 1672. iv-140.

THOMAS WEBB has a difference with the church wardens. Acco., Va. 20 Feby 1673. v-83.

THOMAS x WEBB discharges John West from all contracts and John West discharges Webb from all obligations. Mary Scarburgh a wit., also Wm. Towers. Acco., Va. 6 Feby 1674. v-246.

THOMAS WEBB; one tithable. Acco., Va. 1675. v-325.

THOMAS x WEBB; overseer for James *Fowset;* depn, age about 40. Acco., Va. 8 July 1675. v-300.

THOMAS WEBB; depn. Age about 30. Acco., Va. 19 July 1676. vii-17.

THOMAS WEBB, an orphan; cattle-marks. N-n, Va. 25 June 1677. vol. iv.

THOMAS WEBB, a tithable. N-n, Va. 1677. x-189.

THOMAS WEBB; head right under Dan'll Neech. N-n, Va. xii-284. 29 Aug. 1678.

THOMAS WEBB [died about August, 1679]. Admn on his estate granted to Teigue O'deare, gdn of Teigure Aboghell. N-n, Va. 28 Aug 1679. xiii-45. Revoked 28 Oct 1679 (xiii-45) Aboghell "having no right to any part of the estate intended for said WEBB if he had lived to be twenty-one."

THOMAS WEBB; a delinquent tithable. Acco., Va. 16 July and 4 Sept 1679. viii-96, 110.

THOMAS WEBB; appears in tax-lists to 1689. Acco., Va.

THOMAS WEBB, a delinquent soldier. Acco., Va. ix-89. 7 Sept 1685.

THOMAS WEBB and Daniel Webb, his son, arrived in the Bristoll Merchant. 10-9th mo. 1685. See records at Penn. Gen. Soc.

THOMAS WEBB died 10 Feby 1686. Also Henry Webb, same day. York-Hampton Psh. Reg. Va.

THOMAS WEBB m. Elizabeth Jones, wid. of Nicholas, about 9 Oct 1688. Annap. Records xiv-103.

THOMAS x WEBB, planter; love and respects to Katherine Mason, my goddaughter, dau. to William Mason, carpenter . . . gives a cow. Acco., Va. 18 Sept 1688. vi-481.

THOMAS WEBB; age about 50. Acco., Va. x-34. 17 June 1691.

THOMAS WEBB; two tithables; Acco. ix-227. 1691.

Mr. THOMAS WEBB, a grand juror. Essex, Va. 1692. i-8.

THO. WEBB had one tithe. Acco., Va. 1692.

THOMAS WEBB; patent for 206 acres, "Westward side of the seashore." Princess Anne county, Va. 29 Apr 1693. S. L. O. viii-269.

THOMAS WEBB was the son of William Webb and Mary *Taberer,* dau. of Thomas. I. W. county, Va. 1694. ii-351.

THOMAS WEBB, a headright under Goodridge. 1701 [?] N. C. H. & G. i-305.

THOMAS WEBB m. Mary Doe, admx of Samuel, about 2 Dec 1702. Acco., Va. xii-134.

THOMAS WEBB, a minor orphan and heir to Tho. Webb, dec. Patent for land. 1710. S. L. O. iv-30.

THOMAS WEBB and wf Charity, to Richard West, a water gristmill. Wit: Green, Wm. x Everett, Robt Bracewell. 24 Sept 1711. I. W. co. v-197.

THOMAS WEBB d. 1714. St. Paul's Reg., Kent co., Md.

THOMAS WEBB was grandson of Thomas *Taberer.* See I. W. co., Va., xD-215.

THOMAS WEBB asks that Ralph Doe be his gdn. 3 Aug 1725. Acco., Va. xix-34.

THOMAS WEBB, a witness. 28 Jany 1736. K. Geo. co., Va. i-421.

THOMAS WEBB, son of Ann Webb. Born 28 Mch 1738. Farnham Psh Reg. W. & M. xiii.

THOMAS x WEBB, of Acco., pltr, to Rodulphus Scott; 72 acres near the head of Deep Creek Branch. 28 Oct 1740. Acco., Va. Deeds i-195.

THOMAS WEBB, Acco., Va. Will. Wf Rachel, extx; son William; godson Custis McCloud; John Kitson, Sr., or John Kitson, Jr., to have charge of education of son if wife fails, &c. Wife's three daughters; Kezia Townsend, Elizabeth McCloud, Peggy McCloud; Reuben Rogers' three chn, Sarah, Leah and Rachel. Prayer-books ordered. Acco. Va. 1754-1757.

THOMAS WEBB, Census, Southwark. Philada. Three free white males over 16; three free white females over 16. 1790.

THOMAS WEBB (and Jas. Owen) ship carpenters, Southwark, Philada. county. Two white males over 16; four white females over 16. Census, 1790.

THOMAS WEBB, Norfolk, Va. tax-list. 1792.

THOMAS WEBB; was son of Ezekiel, son of William, son of Richard, Married Esther Paxson and had chn: Matilda, Mary, Esther, Jane, Ezekiel, Henry, Thomas, William. (William born 1820.) Histy Chester and Delaware counties, Pa. p. 534.

THOMAS V. WEBB m. Miss Elizabeth Forsyth. 2 June 1819. Norf. Va., M. L. B.

Mr. THOMAS V. WEBB m. Mrs. Elizabeth Webb. 29 Jany 1821. Norf. Va., Mar. returns.

THOMAS WEBB, Harrison co., W. Va. Will. Wf Sarah; sons, Daniel, James, Nathan; daus. Sarah, Jane, Phebe, Mary Davisson, "Prudent" Arnold, Nancy Robinson; Sarah's dau. Nancy; son Jonas; sons Thomas and David; dau. Elizabeth Johnson. Chn under age to live with mother. Wife, L. E. Davission Thomas Webb, Jr. extrs. Wit: John and David Davisson. Sig. THOS. WEBB. 17 June 1820. Har. co. W. Va. ii-346. Inventory returned 2 Nov. 1820. p. 351.

(*To be continued*)

The County Court Note-Book

An every-other-monthly devoted to abstracts from County Court and other records, prior to 1800, and with a department of notes and queries.

MILNOR LJUNGSTEDT, Editor and Publisher. Bethesda, Route 1, Maryland.

Published six times a year. Subscription, two dollars a year, in advance, must begin with the year. Special rates on renewals. Advertising rates moderate.

VOL. II OCTOBER, 1923 No. 5

ON CONDITIONS

An editorial in chapters

In a previous chapter the Editor referred to SURRY, Virginia. Here the conditions are vastly different from those in the county previously touched upon. A Clerk of another kind came into office some fifty-three years ago. Would there were more of his type... but they are rapidly passing. Here was a young gentleman, scarcely more than a lad, who was born with an appreciation of ancient records and with that conscientious care for them which is so often lacking, even among searchers. This Clerk found, as he told the Editor, the ancient volumes piled upon the brick floor in a corner of the small, old building which is now used as a Confederate museum. Naturally, by that time, dampness and the bookworm had done irreparable mischief. But our young caretaker rescued the volumes and in course of time those that were seriously damaged and no longer fit to handle were copied by himself or under his direction; others were re-bound, and in further due course all were placed in a fireproof vault. When the Courthouse lately burned, the records were safe, although in the same building and under the same roof.

Two of these old Surry books are of great beauty and still bear upon their covers the royal arms of royal England.

With such a Clerk the love for his records grew with the years, and to this writer he admitted, almost with a kind of shyness, that he loved his books, and added, *"they talk to me."* It is to be hoped that fifty years from now the volumes he loved will be in existence.

The only drawback to the present "fire-proof," as it was when the writer last visited it, is the lack of sufficient heat. While steam heat in many offices is rapidly disintegrating the paper of the records, the soft coal fire of the Surry office not only makes a black dust but insufficiently heats the room. When the writer was in Surry on a former visit this fire was tended, on occasion, by the sole and only prisoner in the jail. This prisoner was a six-foot mulatto, really about seven-eighths white, with a most amiable and friendly countenance. He was entirely without mentality, other than that of a very small child. The Clerk explained that he was kept in jail for his own safety... he could not be worked on the roads or anywhere outside, as he would simply wander off. The County had no other place for him, so the jail was his home, and he was made useful to a certain extent, carrying coal, etc. The writer well remembers the childlike smile which spread over the face of this poor derelict when she gave him a small amount for tobacco.

But the "fire-proof," in spite of the attractive fire, was impossible, so the Editor took refuge in the Clerk's Office at the end of the Clerk's table.

Court was in session, the presentation of a case had just finished, and the Judge had to write his instructions. There was no place but the jury room, and the jury room was as cold as outdoors, so the Judge also took refuge in the Clerk's Office, at one side of the long table. All interested persons departed and in the quiet of the office it grew darker and darker as the short winter's day came to an end. What should this writer do? If she could not see, certainly the Judge could not see! There was no judicial precedent within the writer's knowledge and a Judge intent on his instructions might be dangerous. It might be contempt of Court to ask him if he could write in the dark, or even *lèse-majesté.* The writer made her own precedent. She got the big Rochester lamp down, found some matches and lighted it, and set it on the table near the Judge. The Judge murmured "Thank you," and continued on the instructions. Evidently the Editor was safe. Presently it grew toward supper time so she quietly withdrew and left the Judge to follow when he got good and hungry... or the lamp gave out.

And supper or dinner with Judge, Commonwealth's Attorney, Opposing Counsel, and so on, is quite interesting. Occasionally one can discuss the evidence. In this case, the learned counsel in a most learned and impassioned address to the jury, apparently all about whether a separator or something of that sort was really meant to work or not, in which address he laid great stress on the proved fact that the smokepipe didn't fit, forgot to give the exact size of the open space about the pipe... which was most evidently a very bad ommission and left an opening of doubt for the Opposing Counsel to wriggle through. The Editor called attention to this, as a matter of some seriousness.

But that case could not compare with the "Moonshine" trial in Washington county... which is another story.

With the next number, December, the second year of the COUNTY COURT NOTE-BOOK closes. Single-handed the Editor has begun it and run it. It will continue. Prompt renewals will assist the Editor and save unnecessary correspondence.

OCCASIONAL

What is a "Weltch Chimney?" (Editor.) N-n co. Va. ii-3 10 Feby 1644.

"Irish Neck" was in Westmoreland county, Virginia. See will of James Butler, 1749-1752.

(In a County Clerk's Office.) Dissatisfied citizen who has arrived at the post office just too late: "Afraid to say what his birthday was for fear the Postmaster would close the Post Office."

From an interrogatory in the NORTHAMPTON COUNTY, Virginia, records. "Whether you did not heare Eliza the wife of the said Phillip Parker [say to] Margaret Teackle that her father was suddanily to be marryed to Capt. Wallop descd his Kinswoman and what a proud woman she was and wore fringes at the binding of her petticoate..." x-161. Court of 12 Sept 1695.

Capt. GILES BRENT: petn... being seated on the south side of the Potomecke River... nevertheless Lord Baltimore hath given instructions to his surveyor... to issue grants out of Maryland for land belonging to the petitioner... Ct. at St. Maries. 4 Oct 1648. See ORDERS 1-17. Westmoreland, Va.

From St. Peter's Register, Talbot county, Md. p. 91.

JOHN BOOTH of Cumberland, Ship Carpintr departed this life 28th day of September Ano. Do. 1719. JOHN BLINDELL of Cumberland, Ship Carpintr, departed this life the 30th day of September Ano. Do. 1719.

"Lewis Chavalier alis Knight of Accomack County, Virginia, Marchant Tayler." Acco. xi-263. 1 Apr 1701.

George Nicholas Hack is accused of having a book entitled a "Bull from the Pope" or "The Pope's Bull." Acco. ix-171. 21 Nov 1689.

A Soldier's Will: MOSES x BLAND directs that he is to be buried at the "Burying Place at Fort Augusta at the Discretion of my Good Captain Shippen." All cash and other effects to Marg't Reid daughter of James Reid. James Reid to be sole executor. Wit: McAllister, Boyle, Hains. Cumb. co., Pa. A-54. 1758.

While in Madison this summer, the Editor realized, mainly because of her surroundings in the pleasant and beautiful Historical Library, that she really knew very little in any particular way about the settlement and founding of Wisconsin. So she asked Miss (Dr.) Kellogg if she would write her a brief paragraph to be shared with others through the medium of the NOTE-BOOK. Miss Kellogg was good enough to do so, and to put in a nutshell for such readers as the Editor herself, not deep students or learned historians, the beginnings of her State.

Miss Kellogg's work as an historian is well known. She is now head of the Manuscript Department of the Wisconsin State Library.

The list of MARYLAND'S NEXT OF KIN is omitted from this number but will appear in December.

WISCONSIN BEGINNINGS

Contributed by Louise Phelps Kellogg, Ph. D., B. L., of the Wisconsin Historical Society.

Just fourteen years after the Pilgrims landed on the shores of Massachusetts Bay, a French explorer, Jean Nicolet, had penetrated a thousand miles inland and met the Indians then dwelling on Green Bay, an inlet of Lake Michigan. Thenceforward for a century and a quarter the land we now know as WISCONSIN was a part of the colonial empire of the French monarchs, governed from Versailles, and garrisoned at small primitive waterside forts by officers and troops wearing the uniform of Louis XIV and Louis XV. Throughout this land, lying at the head of the Mississippi Valley, French explorers, fur traders, and missionaries came and went. Two or three small settlements grew up around the forts, and a primitive agriculture was developed. For the most part, however, the fur trade was the dependence of the French inhabitants. When, at the close of the French and Indian War (1763), Wisconsin became part of the British empire, the chief change was in the uniformed officers and heads of the fur companies. The French-speaking traders as *voyageurs* and *engagés* continued to come and go, and the small settlements at Green Bay and Prairie du Chien continued to speak the French language, while owning allegiance to George III. Nor was this condition changed after the American Revolution; although ceded to the United States by the Treaty of Paris, this region continued to be occupied by fur traders until the close of the War of 1812. In 1816, the United States sent garrisons and built forts in this territory, which was a part, successively, of the Territories of Indiana and Illinois; and when the latter became a State was annexed to Michigan. In 1836 Wisconsin Territory was erected and the tide of American emigration set in that direction. For twelve years it poured in with a flood, chiefly from New York and New England. In 1848 the State was admitted to the Union, with a population of nearly 300,000. This year (1923) the State is celebrating its seventy-fifth birthday, coincident with the two hundred and fiftieth anniversary of the discovery of the Mississippi River.

Credit for the Frederick county notes in this issue is due to Mrs. GEORGE W. HODGES, of Annapolis, who possesses in a remarkable degree the ability to recognize the value of material often overlooked by others. Mrs. Hodges' work on Maryland records is well known, especially her collection of marriages, which had been acquired by the State.

WILLS PROBATED AND ADMINISTRATIONS GRANTED IN PRINCE WILLIAM COUNTY, VIRGINIA, 1755-1757

(*From the third remaining Order Book*)

The previous article in this series was wrongly headed 1754-1767. It should have read 1753-1755.

BENJAMIN SEBASTIAN, Gent. Certificate of probate on account of, against William Brent ordered. (?) p. 10. Ct 27 Oct 1755.

JAMES BLAND; will presented by Mary and Benjamin Bland, extrs. Proved by John Metcalf, Edward Gwatkin and Margaret Gwatkin. p. 50. Ct Mch 1756.

WILLIAM RUSSELL; admn of his estate granted to William Russell; Parish Garner and John Conyers, security. Ct Mch 1756. p. 52.

JAMES TOWERS; admn on his estate granted to Mathew Steele. Ct Mch 1756. p. 52.

THOMAS MITCHELL; Charity Mitchell, his widow, summoned to shew if she will accept of the admn of her deceased husband's estate. Ct Mch 1756. p. 53.

WADDINGTON SPILLER; will proved by George Mason and John Summers. Ct 24 May 1756. p. 71.

THOMAS MITCHELL; admn granted to Allan Macrae and Matthew Steele. John Baylis, Gent., and Thomas Machen, security. Ct 24 May 1756. p. 71.

HUMPHREY POPE; admn on his estate granted Bertrand Ewell, Gent. Lynaugh Helm, William Ashmore, Darby Gallahue and John Peyton, security. Ct 24 May 1756. p. 73.

JOHN CARR; admn on his estate to William Carr. George Brent, Gent., security. Ct 25 May 1756. p. 75.

JAMES BELFARE; admn granted to Sarah, his widow. Henry Churchill, Esq., security. Ct 28 June 1756. p. 113.

JAMES MOSS; will presented by Mathew Moss, extr. Proved by John Adams and Edward Moss. Ct 23 Aug 1756. p. 184.

WILLIAM JONES; admn on his estate granted to Solomon Jones. Charles Chinn and James Young, security. Ct 23 Aug 1756. p. 184.

THOMAS STONE; will presented by John Stone, extr. Proved by John Wright and Jeremiah Darnall. Ct 23 Aug 1756. p. 185.

THOMAS DALLAS; will proved by John Peyton and Redman Grigsby. Ct 25 Oct 1756. p. 236.

THOMAS DALLAS; admn his estate granted Violett Dallas, his widow. John Sias and Thomas Davis, security. Ct 25 Oct 1756. p. 237.

THOMAS STAMPS, Jr.; admn granted to Lidia Stamps, his widow. Joseph Duncan and John Duncan, Jr., security. Ct 22 Nov 1756. p. 239.

SARAH TACKETT; her will presented by William Tackett, extr. Proved by William Farrow and John Metcalf. Ct. 22 Nov 1756. p. 242.

WILLIAM GREEN; admn on his estate granted to William Carr. William Ellzey, Gent., security. Ct 22 Nov 1756. p. 242.

WILLIAM SPILLER; admn on his estate granted to William Spiller his son. George Dodson and William Tackett, security. Ct 28 Nov 1757. p. 256.

JOHN HAMRICK; admn on his estate granted to Sarah Hamrick, his widow. Richard Melton and Thomas Stone, security. Ct 28 Nov 1757. p. 257.

(*To be continued*)

NOTES FROM FREDERICK COUNTY, MARYLAND

The Court orders payments to the wives of certain recruits from Frederick county. March Court, 1779. (From the records of the County Court.)

Mrs. ANN GRAY, wife of RICHARD GRAY, in the Continental service, and her two children.

Mrs. MARY LEWIS, whose husband is in the Continental service; three children.

Mrs. LEVY, wife of DAVID LEVY; six children.

Mrs. POLHOUSE, wife of THOMAS POLHOUSE; four children.

Mrs. ZIMMERMAN, wife of JOHN ZIMMERMAN; two children.

Mrs. HILL, wife of CASMER HILL; two children.

The record states that the above men were soldiers in Col. Weltner's Regiment.

THE AGES OF SOME FREDERICK COUNTY (MARYLAND) ORPHANS

The following are shown by the records of Frederick county to have been minors at the dates given.

JESSE ALLISON, age 17 in Aug. 1764.
JOHN ALLISON, age 16, June 1765.
HENRY ALLISON, age 12, August, 1771.
WILLIAM ALLISON, age 13, Mch, 1770.
ANN MARY ARNOLD, age 8, Apr 1777.
SARAH ALLEN, age 8, 6 Mch 1778.
EDWARD BULLEN, age 14, 1757.
RICHARD BRADCUT, age 10, 1763.
SARAH BROWN, age 6, 1763.
DAVID BURCHAM, age 3, June, 1775.
EDMUND BUTTS, age 7 mos. Jany 1785.
JOHN BRADDOCK, age 12, June 1775.
JOSEPH BRADDOCK, age 10, June 1777.
THOMAS BRADDOCK, age 8, June 1779.
ANN BRADDOCK, age 5, June 1776.
WILLIAM BLAIR, age 10, 10 Apr 1777.
JOHN BENNETT, age — April 1778.
WILLIAM BRAWNER, age 16, Aug 1773.
JACOB BARRINGER, age — Dec 1773.
JOHN BROWN, age 15, 15 May 1777 (9?).

NOTES AND QUERIES

KEITH: John Keith, born ab. 1710, Balto. co., Md. In 1743 had wf KATHERINE, and about this date moved to Frederick and then Hampshire co., Va. About 1777 to southwestern Penna. Maiden name of Katherine Keith wanted.

LAWSON: John Lawson, schoolmaster, Balto. Co., Md, 1728. Died 1767. Parentage, and name and parentage of wife wanted.

TAYLOR: John Taylor, Balto. co., Md., 1659; wife Margaret. Wife's maiden name wanted. Also maiden name of son Arthur Taylor's wife, Margaret. (1670.)

HARRIOTT (HARRATT, HERRIOT, &c.) Ambrose Harriott came to Balto. Co. Md. 1673; died before 1690, probably in Kent co. Had chn. Oliver and Unity. Whom did Ambrose marry? His son Oliver had a son Richard; b. about 1707; died 1777. Wife Mary, 1744. What was her maiden name? A. L. K. S. D.

GRAVENRATE: Margaret, widow of Andrew Gravenrate, who afterwards married Jacob Grantham, was perhaps a Margaret Thompson or Ross of Cecil county, Md. Ten dollars will be paid for proof of her parentage. C. H. B. T. D.

HAMMON: John Hammon, whose first signature is Johan Hammon, appears to have removed from Frederick county, Maryland, to the Valley of Virginia, *circa* 1778. A reasonable amount will be paid for information concerning him or his wife, EVE; dates of birth, marriage and death desired. M. L. M.

BOLTON-CHAPMAN: Five dollars will be paid for authoritative information as to the State and county in which the marriage is recorded of MATTHEW BOLTON and MARY CHAPMAN, 1788. Bolton was from Virginia, but may have been married elsewhere. F. P. B. L.

RICHARD LIGON: Would like to know the ancestors of Richard Ligon and his wife Alice Jeter, of Nottoway county, Va. Ligon's son Matthew went to Kentucky, 1846. Two other sons, James and Samuel, went south. Susan Lipscomb, of Nottoway, was a daughter. L. W. T. K.

SOLOMON ROBINSON, perhaps of the Eastern Shore of Maryland, but later of Chester county, Penna., died during the Revolution between 1775 and 1780. Entered in some records as SAUL or SOL. Any information concerning him will gladly be received and paid for. M. L. M.

NEWS AND NOTES

Mrs. C. W. AVERY, of Washington, D. C., is listing the tombstones of old FAIRFAX COUNTY, VIRGINIA, and is including the lately formed ARLINGTON county, as well as ALEXANDRIA. Mrs. Avery has over 4,000 records from Fairfax county alone. This is a fine piece of work. A great deal could be done, in this way, if done at once, to save the names of our ancestry.

Mr. ROBERT F. HAYES, Jr., for many years with the Maryland Historical Society, has resigned, and has taken up not only research work, but the collection and sale of books and pamphlets concerning Maryland and Virginia. In connection with this, Mr. Hayes has started a very excellent thing—a genealogical and historical circulating library. Rare and valuable books may be obtained from him on very liberal terms, and after use may be returned. This scheme is strongly recommended to the readers of the NOTE-BOOK. The Editor had thought of it a long time ago, and hopes it will receive general attention. Mr. Hayes' address is 3526 Roland avenue, Baltimore.

Mrs. Mynna Thurston's pamphlet on Col. Thomas Cresap, the Maryland Pioneer who cut the first path for the National Highway, contains interesting illustrations as well as valuable directions for tourists. It costs fifty cents and is for sale by Mr. Hayes, who is sole agent.

PALMER: Dr. Byron S. Palmer, Palmyra, New York, will be glad to hear from anyone interested in a comprehensive Palmer book. Dr. Palmer is gathering data from all the eastern states, and has information concerning many lines. This information he intends to publish and wishes to make it as complete as possible.

If anyone desiring specialized searches of the Draper MSS. will address the Editor she will be glad to give them the name of a reliable and entirely competent lady.

PLACES TO STAY

Visitors to WEST CHESTER, the county seat of CHESTER Co., Penna., can get excellent and reasonably priced meals at the OVERTOWN, which is situated above the bank. Sometimes the hostess, who is a member of the Society of Friends, can also provide rooming facilities.

Ladies visiting Madison, Wisconsin, will find the City Y. W. C. A. comfortable and reasonable. The cafeteria is one of the very best and reasonable in price.

The Central "Y" at Harrisburg has also a limited number of rooms for transients, and is a very attractive place. It is located opposite Capitol Park.

From personal experience the Editor recommends the Ft. Dearborn Hotel, Chicago, and its excellent cafeteria.

There is a good and comfortable boarding house in Snow Hill, Md. Ask the Editor.

WANTED: Numbers 1, 2, 3, and 5, Vol. I, County Court Note-Book. A reasonable price will be paid for these numbers, or a full subscription for the current year will be given in exchange.

GENEALOGISTS AND OTHERS INTERESTED IN RESEARCH WORK

Mr. FRANCIS B. CULVER,
2203 North Charles Street,
Baltimore, Md.

Researches in genealogy and heraldry for early families of Maryland, Pennsylvania, and Virginia. Historical biographies compiled and authentic coats of arms emblazoned.

Mr. ALFRED L. HOLMAN,
Genealogist
2036 Indiana Avenue
Chicago, Ill.

Refers by special permission to Mr. George B. Utley, Librarian Newberry Library.

Mrs. GEORGE W. HODGES,
Gloucester Apartments,
Annapolis, Maryland.

Special facilities for genealogical and historical work.

EDWARD DWELLY,

Record Searcher and Genealogist.

Wellington Avenue, Fleet, Hants, England.

Searches undertaken with care in ENGLAND. Special facilities for Somerset, Devon, and records in London. Index of 303,000 Somerset names. A few copies of "DWELLY'S PARISH RECORDS" (Registers and Bishops' Transcripts of Registers for Somerset, and inscriptions for Devon and Somerset, England), still to be had.

CHARLES SHEPARD II,
Genealogist and Antiquarian.
Suite 609, 2153 California Street,
Washington, D. C.

Author of works on Bowen, Coward, Dole, Martin, Rochester, Shepard, and Wildes families; Rensselaer Co., N. Y., wills, tombstone inscriptions, etc. Agents throughout New England and other states.

"Problems of More Than Ordinary Difficulty"

Mrs. LETITIA P. WILSON,
2608 Keyworth Avenue,
Baltimore, Maryland.

Special facilities for genealogical and historical work.

Mrs. FRANCIS H. MARKELL,
Frederick, Maryland.
Genealogical Research.

Refers by permission to Mr. Frank E. Norwood, president Frederick County Historical Society, Frederick, Maryland.

Mrs. WILLIAM HYDE TALBOTT
Rockville, Maryland,

Genealogical and historical research. Special facilities for all western and southern Maryland.

Miss CORDELIA JACKSON,
2815 Q Street N. W.,
Washington, D. C.

Historical and genealogical reasearch at the Library of Congress.

Mrs. VIRGINIA EDWARDS SAVEDGE
Alliance, Surry County, Virginia.

Historical and genealogical research in the records of Surry county.

RESEARCH WORK
In BOURBON and adjoining counties of Kentucky.
JULIA SPENCER ARDERY,
Rocclicgan, Paris, Ky.

PUBLICATIONS, ETC., OF VALUE TO HISTORIANS AND GENEALOGISTS

The GENERAL INDEX of WILLS of ST. MARYS COUNTY, MARYLAND, compiled by Mrs. George W. Hodges, has been published by the CARTER BRAXTON CHAPTER, D. A. R., also

The GENERAL INDEX of WILLS of ANNE ARUNDEL COUNTY, MARYLAND. A limited number only will be sold. Price $12.50. For information as to both volumes address Mrs. LETITIA P. WILSON, Regent, 2608 Keyworth avenue, Baltimore, Md.

An INDEX of NORTHAMPTON and ACCOMACK records from 1632 to about 1710 is available to readers of the NOTE-BOOK. Fee $3.00. Address the Editor.

Mr. FRANK POLLARD BROWN is a buyer of all old U. S. stamps of the period 1845-1856; also of old Confederate stamps, issue of 1861-63. Those on the original envelopes are worth much more than when removed. Write Mr. Brown, 15 Bosworth street, Boston, Mass.

Copies of the BALTIMORE SUN articles on Maryland and Virginia families may be obtained from Mrs. BLANCHE L. HAYES, 3526 Roland avenue, Baltimore, Md.

Reasonable price will be paid for numbers 1, 2, 3, and 5, COUNTY COURT NOTE-BOOK, 1921-1922. Address Editor.

COLUMBIAN PRINTING CO., INC., WASHINGTON, D. C.

The

County Court Note-Book

A Little Bulletin of History and Genealogy

Vol. II | December, 1923 | No. 6

REVOLUTIONARY AND MILITARY NOTES FROM ORDER BOOKS AND ORPHANS' COURT RECORDS

RALEIGH MARTIN, a soldier in the Continental service; his depositions ordered to be filed. Ohio co. W. Va. Ct 7 Sept 1778.

CATRINE SMITH, wife of SAMUEL SMITH, a regular enlisted soldier in the Virginia Regt, to be allowed £7 10 sh. to support herself and three small children for the ensuing six months. Ohio co. W. Va. Ct 3 Aug 1778.

MARY OGLE, wife of JACOB OGLE, dec'd, killed in the service of the United States, a Militia soldier of this county, to be allowed the sum of twenty-five pounds to enable her to support herself and six small children for the ensuing year. Ohio co. W. Va. Ct May 1778.

SARAH CLARK, wife of HEZEKIAH CLARK, a regular enlisted soldier in the 13th Virginia Regt, be allowed fifteen pounds for her own support and two small children for one year. Ohio co. W. Va. Ct May 1778.

MATTHEW FOWLER proves that he Served as a Corporall in the Old Virginia Regt before 1763. Ct 6 Mch 1780. Ohio Co., W. Va.

BATHSHEBA RANDLE, Heiress-at-Law to DAVID RANDLE who was killed in the field of Battle, proved that said DAVID RANDLE served as a Lieutenant in the Regular Service in the year 1763. Ct 6 Mch 1780. Ohio co., W. Va.

JAMES PARK proved service as Serjant, Regular Service. 1763. Ohio co. W. Va. Ct 6 Mch 1780.

AUGUSTINE WADE produces proof that he was a private soldier in the 6th Maryland Regt, and was wounded. Pension ordered. Washington co., Md. O. C. 12 June 1787.

HANNAH CRAWFORD, widow and relict of the late Col. WILLIAM CRAWFORD, who was killed by Indians at Sandusky, states that she is still a widow and prays further allowance of pension. So ordered. Fayette co., Penna. O. C. Docket ii-145. Apr. 1814.

CORNELIUS DARNEL, of Tennessee. Was born Charles county, Md. 15 Apr 1762. Was drafted, 1781, in the Revolutionary service from Washington co., Penna. Draper Mss. 26V192.

EDWARD O'NEIL, of Middleton Tshp, Cumb. Co., Pa. Age 29. A pensioner. Discharged 1 Nov 1783. O. C. Docket ii-379.

ARON PENWELL [PENIVELL?], W. Pennsborough Tshp; a private, 7th Batt'n Militia. Wounded and pension granted. Cumberland co. Penna. O. C. Docket ii-381.

JOHN FITZSUMONS; Benjamin Alison, Surgeon, certifies that he was a Private Soldier in Col. James Potter's Batt'n of Militia, and was wounded in the Right arm at Piscataqua in N. J., on 1 Feby 1777, and that his time of service ended the 28th Mch 1777. Half-pay ordered. O. C. Docket i-11. Sept 1778. Northumberland Co., Penna.

HENRY DOUGHERTY, private; Lt. Col. James Murray and Benjamin Allison, Surgeon, certify that he was so badly wounded at Piscataquay, N. J., as to render him incapable of labour. His service ended 28 Mch 1777. Pension ordered. p. 11. Sept 1778. Northumberland Co., Penna.

MARRIAGES BY INFERENCE*

(Continued from October number)

(The following marriages are from the records of Northampton county, Va.)

JNO. SMYTH and REBECCA SAVAGE, wid. of Thomas. About 1 Mch 1656. v-142.

Mr. EPHRAIM SAVAGE and the wid. of Obediah WALKER, late of N. E. dec'd. [Obediah Walker appears to have been bro. of Capt. Nathaniel Walker, also of N. E.] Before 27 Apr 1683. xv-26.

WM. SPADY and a dau. of Thomas x DUPARKES. Before 1702. xviii-135.

GEORGE SMITH and MARY LAUGHLAND, dau. of Dorman Laughland. Before 13 Feby 1715-16. xix-322.

Mr. THOMAS SAVAGE and ELITIA HARMANSON, dau. of Thomas Harmanson, Sr. Before 26 Mch 1696. xviii-112.

EDWARD SMITH and ANN JOHNSON, widow of John. Before 24 Jany 1659.

WM. SMARTE and MARY ANDREWS, wid. of Lt. Col. Wm. Andrews. Before 20 June 1657. vii-70.

CHARLES SCARBRAGH and KATHRYNE BARLOWE. Mar. contract, 27 May 1654. vii-20.

Mr. THOS. SPRIGG and KATHRYNE ROPER, wid. of Capt. Wm. Roper, 1-3 Mch 1650. iv-14.

EDWARD SMITH and the "wife" of JOHN JOHNSON. Before or about 29 Apr 1658. viii-13.

CHARLES SOMERVILLE and FRANCES BURT, wid. of John. About 30 May 1692. xvii-174.

WILLIAM SCOTTE, Sr. and ANN DAVIS, [mother-in-law of Gawton Hunt and Wm. Kendall, Jr.] About 29 Nov 1709. xviii-503.

WILLIAM SCOTT and ELIZABETH HANBY. Before 22 Aug 1682. xiii-296.

JOHN SENIOR and the widow of Sampson WEBSTER. Before 25 July 1696. xvii-409.

DIGBY SEYMOUR and ROSE CHRISTIAN. 10 Feby 1736. M. L. B.

JOHN SEVERNE and ELIZABETH CHAPMAN. Mar. contract. 5 Oct 1654. v-48.

GEORGE SMYTH and Tho: WARD'S widow. Before 28 Apr 1653. iv-175.

JOHN SMALL and SARAH MASMAN, dau. of Henry, Sr. Before 28 Feby 1697. xvii-470.

THOMAS SELLBY and ANN RICKARDS, the widow of Michael Rickards, Sr. Before 29 July 1690. xvii-56, 57.

JOHN SHEPHEARD and ELIZABETH JORDAN, dau. of William and Dorothy. Before 27 July 1696. xvi-39.

THOMAS STAYTON and ELIZABETH DRUMMOND, dau. of Hill Drummond. Before 2 June 1736. (N-n Land Causes.)

(To be continued)

MARYLAND'S NEXT OF KIN *

(Continued from August number)

HENRY ENNALLS, ROGER WOOLFORD; inv. Col. Thos. Ennalls of Dor. county. 21 Oct 1718. ii-4.

RICHARD WARFIELD and ALEXANDER WARFIELD; inv. John Warfield of A. A. county. 28 Feby 1718. ii-22.

OTHO and WILLIAM COURSEY; inv. Col. William Coursey of Q. A. county. ii-23. [No date given.]

EMANUELL and SILVANUS MARRIOTT; inv. John Marriott of A. A. county. 11 May 1719. ii-28.

JOHN STOKES and RICHARD SMITHERS; inv. George Wells of Baltimore county. 1 May 1717. ii-31.

JOSEPH LAWRENCE and CHRISTOPHER HAMMOTT; inv. Henry Lawrence of St. Mary's county. 24 Feby 1713. ii-42.

BENJAMIN BATTEL and SAM: PEELE; inv. Thomas Hood of A. A. county. ii-43. [No date given.]

JAMES BOWLES, RICHARD HOPEWELL and CHARLES KING; inv. Henry Spink of St. Mary's county. 3 June 1719. ii-46.

JOHN NICHOLSON and RICHARD TODD; inv. Richard Todd of A. A. county. 3 June 1719. ii-50.

UPSHUR KING, WILLIAM, JOHN and RISTEN BOZMAN, sons of the deceased, "creditors and of kinn;" inv. John Bozman of Som. county. 7 Dec 1716. ii-53.

JOHN CORNWELL; inv. HENRY WEBB of Som. county. 9 Aug 1719. ii-58.

JOHN and JAMES MARTIN; inv. James Martin of Charles county. 23 Mch 1718. ii-60.

JOHN BOREING and THOMAS SHEREDIN... "approved by us"; inv. Joseph Horne of Baltimore county. 23 Jany 1718-19. ii-64.

NICHOLAS PAUL; inv. Edward Paul. [County not given.] 1 Nov 1718. ii-65.

JOHN KILLAM, Sen. and JAMES TAYLOR; inv. William Killam of Som. county. 15 Apr 1719. ii-66.

PETER JOHNSON; inv. Robert Johnson, Sen., of Som. county. 20 Apr 1719. ii-67.

THOMAS DASHIELL; inv. Robert Dashiell. [No county given.] 8 May 1719. ii-70.

MARY HUCKINS and SARAH GOLORTH (?); inv. Robert Miller, of Talbot county. 28 May 1718. ii-78.

WILLIAM RINGGOLD... "I do prove of the appraisement." Inv. Rowland White of Talbot county; 28 May 1718. ii-79.

SAMUEL EASON; inv. John Eason, Jr. of Talbot county. 11 May 1719. ii-81.

(To be continued)

THE WEBBS

(Continued from October number)

WILLIAM WEBB, citizen and grocer; St. Giles, London. Mentions Elizabeth Webb, dau. of bro. Richard; William, son of bro. Nicholas; dau. of bro. Nicholas; bro. Thomas; bro. Henry; bro. John; Sister Mary Parkwood; sister Eliz. Hall. [Also other names] John Burdett a wit. Cant. Wills, No. 1057. 2 Sept 1620.

WM. WEBB desires to be made a freeman. Winthrop's New Eng. ii-447. 25 May 1636.

WILLIAM WEBB writes from London. N-n, Va. ii-214. 20 July 1642. See also ii-183.

WINKLEFFIELD WEBB. N-n, Va. ii-328. 20 Sept. 1644.

WILLIAM WEBB, svt to Robert Davis, L. Norf. 14 Mch 1655. D-255.

WILLIAM WEBB, dec'd. Soldier in American expedition. Brit. State Papers. 455. 1656.

WILLIAM WEBB, pltr, from Herbert Smith, pltr. Land upon upper Machodeck R. 3 Sept 1656. Wmld, Va. i-39. He buys a "Pcell of Land more or less" from Herbert Smith. 31 Mch 1657. Wmld. Orders i-73.

WILLIAM WEBB, a head right under Streater, Westmoreland co., Va. 19 Sept 1657. S. L. O. v-143.

WILLIAM WEBB, head right under Pullams, New Kent, Va. 1658. S. L. O. v-151.

WILLIAM WEBB'S cattle-mark. 2 Nov 1658. Wmld, i-117.

WILLIAM WEBB is certified to be younger bro. to Stephen Webb, lately dec'd; and that William Webb was uncle to Robert Webb, dec'd, son and heir to Stephen, dec'd; and that William Webb was his only brother and they were born in Bushly, Worcester Co. That William Webb and wife and family lived in Tewksbury, and that William and Stephen were sons of Stephen and wife Ane. 1659. Surry, Va. i-139.

WILLIAM WEBB, mcht, power to son William Webb. Geo. Joyne a wit. 1659. Surry, vol. i.

WILLIAM WEBB, a member of the Appamattox vestry. 3 July 1661. Wmld, ii-49.

WILLIAM WEBB is left a legacy by Robert Davis for the use of his son Thomas Webb, 1662. L. Norf. D-346. He was one of Davis' extrs., see D-350. 15 Aug 1662.

WILLIAM WEBB has 580 acres with William Pulliam, in New Kent, south side Narrows, York river. Twelve persons, no names. 16 Sept 1662. S. L. O. Va. iv-408.

WILLIAM WEBB with Henry Hunt; under John Lewis, Poropotanke Crk. 1663. S. L. O. Va. v-278.

WILLIAM WEBB, head right under John Martin. 16 Oct 1664. L. Norf. D. 407.

WILLIAM WEBB and Edward Witherington. Jacob Lucas assigns land to them. 7 Sept 1667. Wmld, Va. i-320.

WILLIAM WEBB, of Tewkesbury, Gloucester, Shoomaker; power to Lott Ricketts of Bristol, Mcht; refers to Webb's plntns in Virginia. Wit: Rich: Hill, Conway Whitehouse. 4 Oct 1667. Surry, Va. i-327.

WILLIAM WEBB; in 1673; with wf Ann, in 1665; in 1674, transported; also in 1675; 1678, an immigrant. See Maryland Early Settlers List.

WILLIAM WEBB; 400 acres in Westmoreland Co. 26 Sept 1668. S. L. O. Va. vi-180.

WILLIAM WEBB of Tewksbury, conveys land to Richard Briggs. 1669. Surry, Va. i-358.

WILLIAM WEBB of Linnhaven; power to Robert Bray. 12 June 1669. L. Norf, Va., E-53.

WILLIAM WEBB of Westmoreland, from Francis Gray; 100 acres, consideration 3,000 lbs tobacco. Wit: Edward Daning, John Bowing. 11 Dec 1669. Wmld, Va., i-358.

WILLIAM WEBB, Wmld, Va. Will. Son William; William, eldest son of Geo. Campion; wf Joane, extx, Wit. George Stow, John Sands. 4 Jany 1669—25 May 1670. Wmld, Va. i-357.

WILLIAM WEBB appears in Isle of Wight co., Va. about 1670 (ii-104); as an appraiser of Thomas Elm's estate (about 1683; ii-254); of Robert Hodges' estate (about 1686, ii-272); mentioned as a planter, 1675 (iii-350); appraiser of Lt. Col. Nicholas Hill's estate 1679-80 (ii-227).

WILLIAM WEBB and wf Hannah, acknowledge a deed releasing interest in land on Deep Run. [The deed is made in the name of EDWARD WEBB, who was the grantee about 1669, see iii-287.] I. W. co., 1677. iii-352.

WILLIAM WEBB, I. W. from Jno. x Bynam and wf Rosamond of Surry; 100 acres in Surry on west side of Branch. Wit: Robt Ruffin, Sam'll Thompson. 22 Oct 1681. Surry i(2)-297.

WILLIAM WEBB, son of Samuell and Jone; Bap. 16 Mch 1682. Pitcombe Psh, Som. Co. England. Jone, dau. of same, Bap. 26 Mch 1684; Sebell, dau. of same, Bap. 19 Feby 1689. (From Pitcombe Psh Reg. Som. Co., Eng.)

WILLIAM WEBB, a tithable, with Tho. Bently, Jr. 1691. Surry, iii.

WILLIAM WEBB, Jr., an appraiser estate of Robert Fenn. 9 Mch 1693, I. W., Va. iv-26.

WILLIAM WEBB, Jr. constable in place of Richard Gray. Oct 1694. I. W. Va. iv (reverse)-53.

WILLIAM WEBB m. Mary Taberer, dau. of Thomas. Before 17 Sept 1695. I. W., Va. iv-223.

WILLIAM WEBB appears as an appraiser of Thos. Davis' est. (met at Webb's house) 1696; and of Jno. Jenning's est. 10 Jany 1696. I. W., Va. ii-370 and ii-372.

WILLIAM WEBB and William Webb, Jr. appear in Robert Kae's account for teaching. About 1697-8. I. W. ii-386(?)

WILLIAM WEBB'S land mentioned in Lawrence Washington's will. N. E. H.-G. xliii-81. 1697-8.

WILLIAM WEBB. Will. Eldest dau. Hannah Webb; dau. Elizabeth, "all land in the Forrest;" cozen Ann Maiders, Jr.; Cozen Robert Marcey; Cousin Ann Maider's chn; Thomas Redman; Robert Redman and Robert Levell (Sevell?) extrs; Wit: John Wineter (?); Geo. Maisey, Francis Readman. 20 Mch 1698—25 May 1698. Wmld, Va. ii-156. [Note: the then Clerk at Wmld had not decided on any system of spelling.]

WILLIAM WEBB, Jr., wf. Mary. His will. 1699-1700. I. W. ii-246.

WILLIAM WEBB, Jr. Will. Youngest cousin Mary Ricketts; wf Mary. Wit: Tayler, Gray. 19 Sept 1699—10 June 1700. I. W., Va. ii-226.

WILLIAM WEBB; his cattle-mark recorded by his father-in-law, John Adolph. 23 May 1701. N-n, Va. iv-

WENTWORTH WEBB, son of John and Mary. Born 23 Mch 1699. D. 23 Oct 1701. Charles Psh. Reg., York co., Va.

WILLIAM WEBB. Will. Dau. Dashell under 16; wf Katherine and son Wm. Webb (a minor) extrs. Wit: Sherwood, Feddeman, Riggby, Rungy, (?) 9 Oct 1704—23 Jany 1704. Annap. Md. Wills. iii-467.

(To be concluded)

The County Court Note-Book

An every-other-monthly devoted to abstracts from County Court and other records, prior to 1800, and with a department of notes and queries.

MILNOR LJUNGSTEDT, Editor and Publisher. Bethesda, Route 1, Maryland.

Published six times a year. Subscription, two dollars a year, in advance; must begin with the year. *Renewals one dollar and a half.* Advertising rates moderate.

VOL. II DECEMBER, 1923 No. 6

THE END OF ANOTHER YEAR

The COUNTY COURT NOTE-BOOK is two years old. The Editor feels rather pleased about her experiment. It is true that in her early days she considered herself as liable to be a poet, rather than a mere collector of dates and things. But, on the whole, dates and things are more satisfactory. There isn't anything to criticize about them if you exercise a wise discretion in your collecting and do not give out indigestible material. If, however, you write poetry, rhymed or unrhymed, there is always somebody, including yourself, who will be actively critical or passively uninterested. Besides, as somebody says, when you write verse or speak French, you don't write or say what you want to, but what you have to. How very different are facts and dates. Being facts and dates they are fixed and immutable as time, and neither your personal desire or personal grammar has any control over them.

The Editor is pleased because her subscription list, though far from extensive, includes these:

The New Hampshire Historical Society; the Essex Institute; the Massachusetts Historical Society; the New England Historic-Genealogical Society; the Antiquarian Society of America; the Connecticut State Library; the New York Historical Society and the New York State Library; the Long Island Historical Society; the New York Biographical and Genealogical Society; the New York City Library, as well as the Public Libraries of St. Louis, Los Angeles, Detroit, Indianapolis and others; the Pennsylvania and Virginia State Libraries; the Pennsylvania Historical Society; the Missouri and Wisconsin Historical Societies and a number of others; and the State Society of the Sons of the Revolution in California.

The Editor is very proud of that list, as also of the names of many of her subscribers. Emerson says, "A good pride is worth five hundred dollars a year." The Editor wishes that this list were worth just about one hundred dollars more than it is, so that she could go collecting and forget the printer. If each of her subscribers would bring in just three-eighths of a subscriber apiece it would be as satisfactory as two hundred and fifty-six proved ancestors. The fun of ancestor hunting is the hunting. But for the joy of the search one needs to forget both printer and pocketbook.

* * * * * * *

The NOTE-BOOK will be as good as the Editor can make it... perhaps some day it may grow to sixteen pages. There is plenty of material collected and to collect. The Editor bespeaks your friendly interest.

OCCASIONAL

Is this somebody's ancestor? HATHEN-FETTAPLACE [or PACE] CHANDLER. He was the son of John, and will be found in Acco., Va., xvi-356. 23 Jany 1728. CHANDLER is elsewhere spelled CHAINLOR and CHANLER.

From a modern genealogy: THOMAS ANDERSON, of Dinwiddie Co., Va., married "Miss Kehrenhappuck." [No date given.]

"LEWIS CHAVALIER alis KNIGHT of Accomack County, Virginia, Marchant Tayler." Acco., Va., xi-263, 1 Apr 1701.

"The Minister of this Parish shall not be liable to Delapedations or Repairs." Strataton Major Psh Vestry Book, King and Queen co., Va. 1750.

ROBERT HUGHS, Prince William co., Taylor, to Howson Hooe, St. Paul's Psh, Stafford co.; 200 acres in King George county, Va., consideration, two negroes four foot high. K. Geo., Va. i-19. 11 Aug 1753.

A remarkable number of members of a family, either by blood or marriage, is shown by the record of a suit to force the division of certain property left by one JAMES DAY, who was the owner of land in MONTGOMERY COUNTY, Maryland, and elsewhere, and who, in his will (dated 14 Mch 1837) gave his wife certain real estate during her widowhood, providing that should she die or marry again, the property should be sold and the proceeds divided among all his children. The wife's name was SARAH. The suit was brought in 1866, and is entitled JAMES W. DAY and wife SARAH W.; Jackson Day and wife Servilla; John Boyer and wife Elizabeth; Elman G. Burdette and wife Elizabeth; Samuel Hopkins and wife Louisa; Luther Day; James E. Day; Washington L. Day; Servilla A. W. Day; Venisa A. S. Day; Sarah W. Day; James S. Kemp; Columbus S. W. Kemp (all of Montgomery county); Franklin Day and wife Ellen M., of Washington county, Md.; Aquilla Day of Carroll county, Md.; Rufus K. Day and wife Ann; Belt Norwood and wife Sarah Ann; Madison L. Day and wife Frances; Thomas Etchison and wife Sarah A.; Perry Stockman and wife Matilda; Harrison Etchison and wife Ann R. (the foregoing of Frederick county, Md.); Dorsey Etchison and wife Rachel A.; Greenbury Baker and wife Hessey Baker; William H. Baker and wife Jemima; Angelina Baker; Isaac Moxley and wife Margaret (these of Montgomery county); Ann Hammond and Emeline Gillis of Indiana; Hamilton I. Day of Baltimore; Thomas Day and wife Leah of Frederick county, Maryland, ... *plaintiffs;* and Franklin H. Mullinix, Robert M., Emma M., the infant children of Caroline Mullinix, a daughter of said JAMES DAY who married Robert B. Mullinix (all residing in Howard county, Maryland) are the *defendants.*

Court ordered sale and division. Judg. Rec. E. B. P. 2, p. 261. Montg. co., Md.

THE GRAVEYARD AT ASHLAND, KENTUCKY

Mrs. Chenault, of Lexington, Ky., kindly contributes the following. (Ashland, the home of Henry Clay, is now owned by McDonnells.)

In Memory of MARY ERWIN, who departed this life the 26th day of April in the year of our Lord, 1824. Supposed to be 80 years of age.

In Memory of MARGARET ERWIN, who departed this life the 2nd Nov. in the year of our Lord 1818. Aged 70 years.

In Memory of WILLIAM GIBSON, Sr., born 17th June, 1751, and departed this life, 13th of March, 1823, aged 71 years.

ANNIE GIBSON. Consort of WILLIAM GIBSON [no dates legible].

In Memory of MARGARET JANE, daughter of JANE ELIZABETH GIBSON, who was born on the 10th of May, A. D. 1823, and departed this life on the 10th day of July A. D. 1842.

WILLIAM GIBSON, Senior, son of —— Who was born in October 1746 Departed this life Nov 1824.

(Three other stones bear the names of DOWNING, THOMPSON and CARLISLE.)

WILLS PROBATED AND ADMINISTRATIONS GRANTED IN PRINCE WILLIAM COUNTY, VIRGINIA, 1755-1757

(*From the third remaining Order Book*)

THOMAS SHIRLEY; will presented by Mary Shirley, his widow. Proved by oaths of James Hawkins and Sarah Shirley. Ct 28 Nov 1757. p. 258.

DAVID McCAUL; admn on his estate granted to Allan Macrae. William Ellzey and Bertrand Ewell, security. Ct 28 Nov 1757. p. 258.

JAMES FEARNSLY; admn on his estate granted to Sarah, his widow. Joseph Blackwell, Gent., and William Miller, security. Ct 28 Mch 1757. p. 266.

THOMAS DOOLITTLE; admn on his estate granted to Absolom Raimey. Francis Burgess and Joseph Kelly, security. Ct 28 Mch 1757. p. 270.

ROMERT HAMRICK; admn on his estate granted to Elizabeth Hamrick his widow. Samuel Stone and John Smith, security. Ct 23 May 1757. p. 272.

RICHARD MARSHALL; admn on his estate granted to Thomas Marshall. Richard Crupper, security. Ct 23 May 1757. p. 273.

EBENEZER MOSS; will presented by Deborah Moss, widow, and proved by Foushee Tebbs and Thomas Machen. Ct 23 May 1757. p. 275.

WILLIAM CREEL; will presented by John Creel, one of the extrs, Anne Creel, another of the extrs, refusing to act. Proved by oaths of Benjamin Neale and Mary Edwards. Ct 23 May 1757. p. 275.

ALEXANDER EDWARDS; will presented by Mary Edwards, extx, Proved by Benjamin and Ann Neale. Ct. 23 May 1757. p. 277.

(*End of this volume of Orders.*)

SARAH (S. D.) DIXON, of Fred'k co., Maryland. Will. To good friend John Trammel all my Lands that I have or ought to have in "Carolinia" and all my Land in Maryland and all my Land in Pennsylvania ... also all the Remains of my Worl[d]ey Asteate both Rail & Personal. [Also makes him sole executor.] Wit: John Young, George x Fox, Richard Tinnix (?), William x Willson. Fred'k, Md. G. M. 1-254. 19 Apr 1782—14 Aug 1782.

FRIENDS' MEMORIALS

(*See November number,* 1922)

JOHN BARTLETT, son of Joseph and Martha Bartlett of Maryland, died 26th 8th 1784, age 42, and was buried at Third-Haven.

JOHN MALSBY, born in Pennsylvania, 17th 9th 1753. His parents removed with their family to Maryland, and settled within the compass of Gunpowder Meeting. In 1778 he removed within the verge of Pipe Creek Meeting, and soon after entered into a marriage state with Mary Starr. In 1783, he removed to Baltimore Town, and died 10th 9th 1785.

SUSANNA BROWN was born 7th month 1701, the daughter of John and Hannah Churchman of Nottingham [Chester co.] Penna. She was wife of William Brown. She died 25th 8th 1790.

WILLIAM MATTHEWS, the son of William and Mary Matthews, was born in Stafford county, Va., 19th 6th 1732. William Matthews, Sr., died about 1739, and Mary Matthews died about 1746. William, Jr., died 7th 5th 1792, and was buried in York Town [Penna?]

MARGARET MATTHEWS, daughter of William and Mary, was born in Frederick co., Maryland, 2d 2d 1739-40. She married Joseph Elgar in 1771, and later removed within the verge of Warrington Meeting. In 1807 she became a member of York Meeting. Joseph Elgar died 1811. She died 29th 3d 1821, "as one falling asleep."

WILLIAM WILSON, born in Kent co., Delaware, 1739, died 15th 7th 1795, and was buried at Westland, Washington co., Penna. He lived in that county.

MERCY SHREVE, dau. of Caleb and Abigail, born Mansfield, Burlington co., N. J., 15th 12th 1763. She married 1808, Jeremiah Brown, and removed to Lancaster co., Penna., where she died 24th 10th 1823.

COLONIAL FORENAMES

(*See March,* 1922, *and April and June,* 1923.)

MERRIAM BELSHER m. Alexander Manatear. Overwh. Psh Reg. Va. 24 Dec 1751.

MIRIAM CASE m. Joseph Atwell, Bloomfield (Windsor), Conn. Mar. 1754.

MIRIAM HAVEN, b. 27 Dec 1760, m. David Stewart. See Stewarts of Londonderry, N. H.

MIRIAM BARNES, widow. Westchester co. N. Y. N. Y. G. and B. liv-44. 1762.

MIRIAM PETERS, dau. of Valentine Hewlett and Ruth Peters, Hemstead, L. I. Born 18 Apr 1762. N. Y. G. and B. liv-42.

MIRIAM TILTON m. Edmund Williams. Monmouth Co., N. J. 1762.

MIRIAM BARNES, Jr. Spinster. N. Y. G. and B. liv-44. 1762.

MIRIAM DAWES and Gerrard Hopkins. Pa. Arch. (2)ix-451. St. Paul's, Philada. 6 July 1764.

MIRIAM RICHARDSON, wf of Samuel. Fredk, Md. 1764. Her will mentions gr. dau. Henrietta MIRIAM Chew and MIRIAM Walter; also MIRIAM Richardson.

MIRIAM KELLY and Joseph Potts. St. Paul's, Philada. Pa. Arch. ix-452. 25 July 1765.

MIRIAM HUNNICUTT m. John Pleasants. Burleigh Mo'ly Mtg. Pr. Geo. Co. Va. 1769.

MIRIAM BURR m. Alpheus Brown. Bloomfield, Conn. 1771.

MARRIAM PERRY m. Peter Coffin. Nantucket Mar. N. E. H. G. xli-164. 1773.

MIRIAM TYLOR m. William Powell. N. H. Mar. 1773. New Haven. Conn. Mar.

MIRIAM ROBINSON m. Roger Barret. See will of Samuel Robinson. Philada. 1774. (See NOTE-BOOK for June, 1923.)

MIRIAM HALL m. Samuel Abbey. Mansfield, Conn. Mar. 1775.

MARIAM MALERY m. Edmund Smith. Fairhaven, Conn. 1778. See 6th book, Conn. Mar.

MIRIAM SARGEANT m. Edy Trap, 1778. Mansfield (Windham). Conn. Mar.

MIRIAM WALLER, dau. of George, of Stafford, Va. (d. before or about 1779) m. Paul Hoye. Was of Montg. co., Md, 18 May 1780. See Staff., S-5.

MARIAMME TRUEMAN STODDART m. Wm. Tyler. Charles co., Md., 1779. See Maryland Mar.

MIRIAM LEWIS, dau. of David, of Alb. co., Va., m. Col. Gabriel Madison. [No date given, but David Lewis died in Alb. in 1779.] Draper Mss. 8ZZ66.

MIRIAN BENNET, dau. of Pernal and Mariam[?] b. 20 Feby 1779. See Some Records Sussex Co. Married Thomas R. Norman, 7 June 1798. See p. 340.

MIRIAM EASTHAM m. Joel Lewis, b. Alb. co., Va. [No date, but Micajah Lewis, bro. of Joel was killed in the Rev., 1781.] Draper Mss, HZZ66.

MIRIAM WHEELER, was wife of William. See his will. Sussex, Dela, 1783. D-14. (There was a dau. MIRIAM WHEELER.)

MIRIAM JORDAN and James Evans. M. L. B. Chowan co., N. C. 19 Feby 1785. N. C. H. G. i-246.

MIRIAM TERRELL, dau. of Jonathan and Margaret. B. 11-2-1786. Our Quaker Friends, p. 21. (Cedar Crk Mo'ly Mtg, Hanover co., Va.)

THE AGES OF SOME FREDERICK COUNTY (MARYLAND) ORPHANS

(*See October number*)

ANTHONY ADAMS, age 6, 2 Mch 1786.
GEORGE ALLEN, age 17, Nov 1775.
MICHAEL COKER, age 11 in 1761.
ELIZABETH COKER, age 13 in 1754.
HENRY CHAP, age 3 in 1770.
AMBROSE COOKE, age 8 in 1766.
JOHN COOK, age 10 in 1764.
ZACHARIAH COOKE, age 14 in 1760.
MOSES COLEMAN, age 12 in 1763.
JOHN CAMMILL, age 3 in 1773.
SARAH CROSWELL, age 14 in 1760.
HUGH COPELAND, age 13 in Nov 1769.
JAMES CUMMING, age 13 in Nov 1775.
HENRY CONROD, age 11 in Nov 1778.
WILLIAM DOWNING, age 9 in 1761.
JOSIAS DOWNING, age 9 in 1764.
JOHN DOWNING, age 13 in 1760.
SAMUEL DUNN, age 13 in 1763.
ARTHUR DUNN, age 12 in 1764.
JAMES DUNN, age 14 in Nov 1771.
CATHERINE DAVISON, age 10 in 1774.
ELIZABETH DAVIS, age 12 the 1 Sept 1772.

NOTES AND QUERIES

HAMMON: Information wanted as to JOHN (JOHAN) HAMMON, who bought land in Frederick county, Maryland, in 1764. His wife was EVE. What was her last name? Did Hammon and wife come from Pennsylvania? Information with full references will be paid for. Mrs. J. H. H. T.

WADE: TWENTY-FIVE dollars will be paid for reliable information, must be from civil or church records, or early Bible, as to Capt. JOHN WADE, of Chester or Marcus Hook, Penna. Dates of birth and death, parentage, marriage and children. Date of death and place where he died especially desired. Proportionate payment for part information. Mrs. C. A. D. I.

LIGON-JETER: Who were the ancestors of RICHARD LIGON and his wife OLIVE JETER, of Nottoway county, Virginia. OLIVE (JETER) LIGON was aunt of Rev. Jeremiah Jeter of Richmond. L. W. T. K. (In a previous number the name OLIVE was wrongly given as ALICE.)

JOHN LAWSON, Jr., married SARAH HARRATT, in 1764, Baltimore county, Md. Sarah was supposed to have been daughter of RICHARD HARRATT. Proof wanted.

CHARLES CROOK died Baltimore county, Md., 1749. He was son of James. Did Charles marry and leave children? Who were they?

JAMES and ALLEN CROOK appear in Fairfax county, Va., about 1782. Allen was a soldier in the Revolution. Who were the parents of these Crooks?

McCARTY. JAMES McCARTY was in Fairfax county, Va., 1782. Had wife Ann; chn: Thomas (m. 1777), Nancy (m. James Crook about 1780), Elizabeth and Cornelius. Wanted: parentage of James McCarty, and maiden name and parentage of his wife.

BOSLEY; JAMES BOSLEY died Baltimore county, Md., about 1761. What were the names of his children (he had twelve). Was one of them Ann McCarty, wife of James?

ROBERTSON: THOMAS ROBERTSON, born 22 May 1744; married RACHEL ROBERTSON (no relationship known), born 2 June 1745. Probably lived in Penna. or Maryland, but prior to the Revolution moved to Caswell county, N. C. Thomas m. (2) Mary English. Moved to Tennessee before 1789. Parentage of Thomas and Rachel wanted.

SMALLWOOD. JAMES SMALLWOOD of Charles county, Maryland, had wife Esther in 1664. What was her maiden name? A. L. K. S. D.

UNDERWOOD: Wanted, the ancestors of FANNIE UNDERWOOD, who married WILLIAM POUND; said to be granddaughter of William Underwood of Virginia, a member of the House of Burgesses in 1652. M. B. C. W.

NEWS AND NOTES

Mrs. AUGUSTA B. FOTHERGILL, of Richmond, Virginia, states that the JONES record which she has for some time been engaged in compiling, will be ready for distribution by the first of April, 1924. It is entitled PETER JONES—RICHARD JONES. The price will be ten dollars.

It is thought now that the volume of FLOYDS, STEWARTS, DAVISES, and other allied pioneer families which Mrs. Crosley and Mrs. Ljungstedt hope soon to publish, may be brought within the scope of one volume of not over five hundred pages, and that the price can be fixed at not over ten dollars. Advance orders are desirable.

Miss Hattie M. Scott, of Frankfort, Kentucky, who is very familiar with Kentucky records, has kindly contributed to the NOTE-BOOK some interesting and valuable material. It is unfortunately crowded out of this issue but will appear in the next. Miss Scott is a member of the Kentucky State Historical Society, and specializes in early court records and military and other grants.

The WOMEN'S AUXILIARY of the AMERICAN SCENIC and HISTORIC PRESERVATION SOCIETY deserves high credit for the restoration of the James Monroe house in New York city. It is not only fitting that the home of a man so connected with American history should be preserved, but many of us will be grateful that houses of a distinct and beautiful type should be so restored and cared for that an occasional American may realize that we really have a bit of a background. The other society "with the long name" in New England, and this with the still longer name, set an example that it could be wished a certain other section would follow. The bulletins of the S. P. N. E. A. are in themselves a grammar of artistic restoration.

PLACES TO STAY

GENEALOGISTS AND OTHERS INTERESTED IN RESEARCH WORK

PUBLICATIONS, ETC., OF VALUE TO HISTORIANS AND GENEALOGISTS

COLUMBIAN PRINTING CO., INC., WASHINGTON, D. C.

The

County Court Note-Book

A Little Bulletin of History and Genealogy

Vol. III — January, 1924 — No. 1

NOTES FROM KENTUCKY RECORDS

(*Contributed by Miss Hattie M. Scott, of Frankfort, Kentucky*)

BEVERLY PREWITT, son of Jas. and Delphine Prewitt; born in Va.; died Jefferson co., Ky., 9 Dec 1855, aged 74.

AARON QUISENBERRY, son of Aaron Quisenberry; born in Va.; died Jefferson co., Ky., 16 June 1857, aged 76.

JOHN L. DUVALL; born in Penna.; died Bullitt co., Ky, 28 Oct 1859, aged 88.

JAMES C. PENDLETON, son of James and Sarah Pendleton; born in Virginia; died 22 Feby 1855, in Bullitt co., Ky, aged 62.

MARY ARMSTRONG, widow; dau. of John and Betty Wilson; born in Maryland; died Franklin co., Ky, aged 64.

WILLIAM ARMSTRONG, son of Rich. and Peggy Armstrong; born in Penna.; died Franklin co., Ky, 29 Apr 1860, aged 79.

SUSAN BENNETT, widow, dau. of John and Elizabeth Wade; born Rockbridge co., Va.; died Franklin co., Ky, 15 Apr 1854, aged 80.

J. W. BENNETT, son of John and Susan Bennett; born Franklin co.; died same co. 14 Dec 1860, aged 60.

MESHACK BROCK; born Virginia; died Franklin co., Ky, 10 Aug 1860, aged 86.

HENRY CRUTCHER, son of Henry and Martha Crutcher; born Caroline co., Va.; died Franklin co., Ky, 11 Apr 1852, aged 72.

ELLEN CLARKE, dau. of Hezekiah and Ellen Brown; born Virginia; died Franklin co., Ky, 1856, aged 93. [Hezekiah Brown in his will, 1819, names wife Sarah, dau. Milly Clarke, and son Hezekiah Brown.]

LOUISE CRUMBAUGH, widow; dau. David and Cassandra Flournoy; born in Maryland; died Franklin co., Ky, 15 Nov 1852, aged 73.

BENJ. COX, son of John and Eliz. Cox; born Penna., died Franklin co., Ky, 15 Nov 1855, aged 75.

NANCY CRUTCHER, dau. of Abraham and ...Chambers; born Virginia; died Franklin co. Ky, Nov 1857, aged 70.

THOMAS CHISM, widower, son of John Chism; born Culpeper co., Va.; died Franklin co., Ky., 16 Oct 1857, aged 91.

JAMES CONOVER, son of John Conover; born Trenton, N. J.; died Franklin co., Ky, 5 Oct 1860, aged 78. [This name was at first signed "Cownover."]

REUBEN DANIEL, widower, son of Jacob and Mary Daniel; born Caroline co., Va.; died Franklin co. Ky, 23 Nov 1857, aged 84.

REBECCA DAUGHERTY, widow; born Maryland; died Franklin co., Ky, 2 Aug 1860, aged 89.

BENNETT EDWARDS, widower; son of Uriah and Betsey Edwards; born Virginia; died Franklin co., Ky, 16 Feby 1853, aged 70.

SIMEON EDWARDS, widower; born So. Carolina; died Franklin co., Ky, 29 May 1853, aged 70.

MARY FENWICK; dau. of John and Sara Ready; born St. Mary's co., Md, died Franklin co., Ky, 26 June 1852, aged 78.

CORNELIUS FENWICK, widower; born Maryland; died Franklin co. Ky, 7 May 1856, aged 94.

(*To be continued*)

MARRIAGES BY INFERENCE*

(*Continued from December number*)

FRANCIS CRISP and ANNE HARMAN, dau. of William; York, Va. About 1669. iii-275.

EZEKIEL COLLINS and ESTHER TOWNSEND, dau. of Charles; Sussex, Dela. Before 1788. M-496.

THOMAS CARTER [of S. C.] and MARY CHAMBERS, dau. of William; Fred'k, Va. 2 Oct 1787. xxi-741.

DAVID CARTER and MARY BUTLER, dau. of Joseph; Pr. Wm, Va. Before 22 Sept 1788. H-50.

DANIEL COLE and CONSTANCE (CONSTANT) KING, dau. of William; Pr. Wm, Va. Before 25 July 1741. E-521.

HUGH COLHOUN and MARY SHORT, widow, See will of Thomas Short, N. C. co., Dela. Before 1793. N 1-349.

GEORGE CLARKE and ANEY SMITH; Lunenb., Va. 27 Dec 1781. Mar. Ret. (Vol. iii of records.)

SUSANNA CAIN, dau. of James, and... WADE. Sussex, Va. Before 1765. E-239.

THOMAS CORPREW and ANN DURANT; before 3 Aug, 1745. N. C. H. G. Reg. i-118.

COOPER CHANCELLOR and MARY HORE; Fauq., Va. Before 1811. xviii-238.

JOHN FILSON and JEMIMAH BUTT; Berk., W. Va. 22 May 1799. M. L. B.

JOHN GOOD and NANCY KING, a dau. of William; Pr. Wm., Va. Before 25 July 1741. E-521.

JOHN SAVAGE, Gent. and MARY ROBINS, Sp. Mar. contract. 16 Dec 1667. vii-24.

JACOB STRINGER and ELESHA HARMANSON, dau. of Thomas. Before 10 Mch 1724. xxiiiR-206.

JONATHAN STOTT [SCOTT?] and AMYAH(?) JACOB, before 10 Sept 1702. xviii-172.

SIMON THOMAS and REBECCA HANBY, dau. of Richard. Before 22 Aug 1682. xiii—.

LAWRENCE TEIGUE [?] and MARY KATHERINE VAN HAMELL, dau. of Derick and Sophia. See 8 Sept 1679. xiii-59.

JOHN TANKRED and SARAH SMART, dau. of William. Before 26 July 1708. xviii-437.

Mr. ROBERT TILLGHMAN and Mrs. SUSANNA SELLICK, widow of Daniel Sellick, Mcht. Before 1 May 1655. v-134.

ROBERT TOMPSON and SANNIKA[?] TYSON, widow of John. About 28 July 1691, N-n xiv-296.

SUSANNAH TILNEY, dau. of John Tilney, and... DIXON, Before 31 May 1701. N-n xviii-68.

ANN TILNEY, dau, of John Tilney, and... DRUMMOND. Before 31 May 1701. N-n xviii-68.

JOHN TILNEY and ANN MOORE. Before 28 Feby 1709-10. N-n xviii-515.

JOHN TOWNSEND and ELIZ: WHEATLY. 20 May 1660. N-n ix-92.

JOHN TOWNSEND and ELIZA: DANFORD. 9 Feby 1661. N-n ix-114.

(To be continued)

MARYLAND'S NEXT OF KIN *

(Continued from December number)

WILLIAM and NICHOLAS FIELDER; inv. William Fielder of St. Mary's county; 7 Feby 1718. ii-82.

PAUL BUSEY, JOHN BUSEY; inv. Paul Busey, Sen., of Prince George's co., 2 Feby 1718-19. ii-83.

THOMAS HEBB, Jr., JOSEPH HEBB; inv. William Hebb of St. Mary's county, 23 Apr 1719. ii-87.

SARAH BEAN, PHILIP CLARK; inv. John Bean of St. Mary's county; 2 June 1719. ii-92.

FRANCIS WEAVER, WILLIAM MEADCALF[?]; inv. Francis Spinks of St. Mary's county; 7 Apr 1719. ii-94.

THOMAS and JOHN SHANKS; inv. John Shanks of St. Mary's county; 14 June 1719. ii-96.

CHARLES TAYLOR; inv. Henry Taylor of St. Mary's county; 4 Apr 1719. ii-96.

PHIL. FEDDEMAN, ELIZABETH KING; inv. Henry Frith of Talbot county; 26 Jany 1718. ii-97.

JOHN START and JACOB GIBSON, "in behalf of my wife;" inv. John Start of St. Mary's county; 1 June 1719. ii-99.

ROBERT WISEMAN, EDWARD BELLDING; inv. Francis Miles of St. Mary's county; 1 June 1719. ii-102.

THOMAS TURNER, HENRY NEALE; inv. James Neale of Charles county; 17 Apr 1719. ii-105.

JOHN and RICHARD HARRISON; inv. Capt. Joseph Harrison of Charles county; 4 May 1719. ii-110.

EDWARD PHILLPOTT; inv. Edward Phillpott of Charles county; 31 Oct 1718. ii-111.

RICHARD and JAMES SMITH; inv. Hannah Wilson of Charles county; 8 Apr 1719. ii-118.

ELIZABETH and JAMES MUNKESTER; inv. William Munkester of Charles county; 24 Mch 1718. ii-119.

CHRISTO. GRANGER and VOL. CARTER "approve;" inv. George Mathas of Kent Island in Queen Ann's county; 9 May 1719. ii-121.

WILLIAM and JOHN POWELL; inv. Richard Powell of Anne Arundell county; 5 Jany 1718. ii-126.

RICHARD and ALEXANDER WARFIELD; inv. Benjamin Warfield of Anne Arundel county; 28 Feby 1718. ii-127.

JAMES and ELIZABETH DOBSON; inv. John Newman of Talbot county; 11 Feby 1718. ii-131.

(To be continued)

THE WEBBS

WILLIAM WEBB'S widow, ANN, gets letters of admn for herself and child. John Webb to appraise the estate. N-n, Va. xviii-545. 28 Sept 1710.

WILLIAM WEBB, son of William, son of Richard; b. 3 Nov 1710; m. 23 Sept 1732, Elizabeth Hooper, dau. of Daniel. Chn: William, Stephen, Rebecca, Ezekiel, Jane. Histy Chester and Dela. counties, Penna. p. 554.

WILLIAM WEBB, of Bristol, Gt. Brit., marriner, residing in Maryland; will. Dau. Anne, wf of John Hodges of Bristol; son William; dau. Elizabeth Webb; wf Sarah Webb; Wit: Lock, Holland, Heath. [Sig. "Will Webb."] Annap. Wills, xiii-143. 20 Oct 1710—24 Nov 1710.

WILLIAM WEBB. Will. 215 acres to son Richard, reversion to younger son; son William; remainder estate to wf Mary, Thomas Webb, Wm. Webb, Susanah Webb, Joseph Webb; "for Matthew, Richard and Elizabeth have had their parts." Wf Mary and son Thomas extrs. Wit: Ougbourne, Munger, Kae. I. W., Va. ii-575. 16 June 1708—25 Jany 1713.

WILLIAM WEBB, son of Lorrance and Mabel Webb. Born 14 Nov 1718. York-Hampton Psh Reg. Va.

WILLIAM WEBB'S heir: *MERCHANT'S FOLLY* is possessed by Geo. Haddaway for... Talbot co., Md, Rent Roll. 1722.

"One WEBB in Northumberland co., Va." appears on Somerset co., Md. Rent Roll. 1723.

WILLIAM WEBB, an Assemblyman in Penna. 1724-1736. See Penna. Arch. ix-2d ser.

WILLIAM WEBB; account current his estate. Orphan Samuel Webb mentioned; also "Burying John Webb." I. W., Va. vii-186. 22 May 1727.

WILLIAM WEBB, warrantee for 600 acres. Chester co., Penna. Penna. Arch. xxiv-103. 3d ser. 10 Sept 1736.

WILLIAM WEBB from John Tull. Newington Green, 118 acres. Alienation Alphabet, Som. Co., Md. 8 Apr 1740. In the Rent Roll for Worcester co., 1744 (fo. 36), William Webb has 100 acres of *SMITH'S CHOICE*. Also 118 acres of *NEWINGTON GREEN* (fo. 46).

WILLIAM WEBB, a Justice in Penna. 1741. Penna. Arch ix, 2d ser.

WILLIAM and ELIZABETH WEBB; son John b. 1745 [1746?] York-Hamp. Psh Reg. Va.

WILLIAM WEBB, wit to John Graves' will. Spots. co., Va. 1747.

WILLIAM WEBB, in Virginia, 1747. List of Emigrant Ministers.

WILLIAM WEBB, wit to deed. Original deed in Nansemond co., Va. 1749. [The records of Nansemond county were burned in 1866. A few early original papers are there and a few copies.]

WILLIAM x WEBB conveys part of tract pat. to Wintworth Webb, dec'd, 1747, and conveyed by "William Webb to Abraham Webb." Alb. Co., Va. i-127. 1749.

WILLIAM WEBB records judgment agt Tho. Keley. (Joseph Robenett one of security?) Fred'k co., Md. B-322. 21 Nov 1750.

WILLIAM WEBB, tanner, Balto. from Charles Carroll of A. A. co., Md. extr of James. (Recites former agreement with Samuel Webb that a certain tract called Saint Annes should be conveyed to his *brother* William Webb.) Balto. Md. xxii-207. 12 Sept 1751.

WILLIAM WEBB, a member of the vestry of Appomatox Psh, Va. See Wmld co., ii-49. [1752?]

WILLIAM WEBB, Wor. Co. Md. Inv. Solomon Webb and William Tull sign as kin, Margaret Webb makes oath. Annap. Inv. lxiii-12. 10 Dec 1752.

WILLIAM WEBB, foreman of jury. Fredk, Md. Minute Book. Nov. Ct 1752.

WILLIAM WEBB, in a suit agt Samuel Jackson. Pr. Wm. Va. Orders [2] 95. 30 May 1754. Another suit 1753.

WILLIAM WEBB, son of Richard and Elizabeth; died 1753. Was a member of the Assembly and Justice. M. 22 Jany 1709-10, Rebecca Harlan, dau. of George. Chn: Wm., b. 1710; Ezekiel. Histy Chester and Dela. counties, Penna. p. 534.

WILLIAM WEBB; 124 acres [Nansemond county.] S. L. O., Va. 10 Sept 1755.

WILLIAM WEBB; a Gentleman Justice of the County Court. Fredk, Md. H-722. 18 Mch 1755. See also H-1, 21 Aug 1753.

WILLIAM WEBB'S wife was Mildred. Richard Webb a wit to deed. I. W. co., Va. 1761.

WILLIAM WEBB, of the 45th Regiment, to Rebecca Neilson, widow. N. Y. B. & G. xiv-121. 3 June 1767. (Presbytn Church.)

WILLIAM WEBB, inv. and appraisement. I. W., Va. xivW-98. 13 Apr 1771.

WILLIAM WEBB, Q. A. co., Md. Inventory. Mary Webb and James x Webb sign as kin. John Dwiggens, extr. Annap. Records, cx-291. 8 May 1772.

WILLIAM WEBB m. Lydia Cowgill. Talbot co. 1772.

WILLIAM WEBB of Caroline co., Md. See Annapolis Records, lxi-347. (Admns.) 1773.

WILLIAM WEBB; oath of allegiance, 23 June, 14 July, 1777. Also 2 Aug 1779. See Penna. Arch. iii-6. iii-35.

WILLIAM WEBB, paymaster Penna. State Navy. Penna. Arch. iii-621. 1 Mch 1777. Order on him to pay wages. i-154. 2d ser. 12 May 1777.

WILLIAM WEBB and Comfort Holson. Car. Co., Md. Mar. Li. 19 Dec 1780. (Contributed.)

WILLIAM WEBB, a notary public. Penna. Arch. iii-609. 23 July 1781.

WILLIAM WEBB, owner of part of Webb's Chance. Car. co., Md. tax-list. 1783.

WILLIAM WEBB and Mary James. Chowan Co., N. C. Mar. Li. Bond. N. C. H. & G. i-249. 10 Jany 1790.

WILLIAM WEBB and Sally Bailey. Norf., Va. M. L. B. 18 Dec 1792.

WILLIAM WEBB on Norf, Va. tax-lists. 1789, 1790, 1792.

WILLIAM WEBB and Rachel Diggins. Car. co., Md. Mar. Li. 20 Aug 1795.

WILSON WEBB and Rebecca Wilson. Perquimans co., N. C. M. L. B. N. C. H. G. Reg. iii-422. 3 Sept 1795.

WILLIAM WEBB and Catharine Evans. Fred'k co., Va. Mar. returns. 3 Aug 1799.

WILLIAM WEBB'S estate; William Webb makes oath to inventory. Wash'n co., Md. C-443. 19 Feby 1807.

WILLIAM WEBB; Fred'k co. Md. Will. Wf Mary; eldest son George; 2d son Thomas; 3d son Evan; youngest son Washington; dau. Ann Ogley "hath highly offended and disobliged me by her late improvident marriage"... leaves her interest on $1000, with reversion of principal to her chn. Wf Mary and son George extrs. Wit: Moore, Cooke, Garber. Codicil: negro girl to be freed at 33. Fred'k co. R. H. S. 1-121. 15 Aug 1814—20 Nov 1815.

ZACHARIAH WEBB; Pr. Wm. Va. Orders [1]. 1753. Suit, 1754. One of the extrs of Thomas Young. 26 May 1756.

ZACHARIAH WEBB and Mrs. Mary Wallis. Perq. co., N. C. M. L. B. N. C. H. G. iii-412. 6 Feby 1758.

ZACHARIAH WEBB; a grant. N. C. H. G. i-22. 1782.

ZACHARIAH WEBB and Sarah Cheshire. Chowan co., N. C. M. L. B. 23 Apr 1795. N. C. H. G. i-246.

ZEPORAH WEBB and John Ross. Har. co., W. Va. Mar. record. 13 Oct 1795.

The County Court Note-Book

An every-other-monthly devoted to abstracts from County Court and other records, prior to 1800, and with a department of notes and queries.

MILNOR LJUNGSTEDT, Editor and Publisher. Bethesda, Route 1, Maryland.

Published six times a year. Subscription, two dollars a year, in advance; must begin with the year. *Renewals one dollar and a half.* Advertising rates moderate.

VOL. III JANUARY, 1924 No. 1

FOR 1924

The NOTE-BOOK will continue to publish the MARRIAGES BY INFERENCE. These marriages, of which the Editor has collected some thousands, will finally appear as an appendix to the FLOYDS and STEWARTS; THEIR CATALOGUE. The title is not a particularly good one, since it may be considered that if John Smith says his daughter Mary is the wife of Peter Jones, the marriage may be more than inferred. However, it was difficult to think of a heading which would cover the various evidences. It was more the intention to cover those alliances which are not shown by actual licenses, marriage license bonds, or marriage returns. Possibly Mrs. Hodges' title for her Maryland Marriages, "Marriage References," is a better one. If the Editor newly acquires somebody's old cat or turned-out kitten, she usually waits until a name just comes to her. Perhaps a happier name would have been thought of had she waited in this case.

With reference to the accuracy of these marriage statements, whenever individual deduction comes into play, there is a chance for differing opinion, and some chance for error. The Editor has used her best judgment and worked her conscience overtime. One case has been called to her attention, fortunately before publication, in which a man refers to his step-grandfather as his grandfather. This is most unusual and resulted in throwing out the supposed correct family name of the man's mother, who was the step-daughter and not the daughter of the "grandfather."

Mrs. George W. Hodges will contribute the NEXT OF KIN and NATURALIZATIONS; both of them extremely valuable.

Miss Scott, of Frankfort, will contribute Kentucky material, also of great value and somewhat unusual.

Revolutionary and other military material will be given more place.

The WEBBS will come to at least a temporary end with this Number. The Editor has more Webbs, but she is decidedly tired of them. The Editor never dreamed when she started in some years ago to identify the parents of a certain WEBB ROBINSON, ex-Confederate soldier from North Carolina, then in Virginia, with a shadowy tradition of descent from the "wise and tolerant" Pilgrim Pastor, that there were so many WEBBS in the world, and a later search revealed that most of them were named RICHARD. Why all the DAVISES are named SAMUEL and THOMAS, and all the WEBBS who aren't RICHARDS are WILLIAMS, is something that nobody now knows, but the Editor supposes it could be found out, and suggests it as a subject for philosophic research.

As the Editor has received some inquiries as to the abbreviations used in the NOTE-BOOK—and they are rather puzzling at times—it may not be amiss at the beginning of the year to explain some of them. The counties of Virginia can usually be identified by those familiar with them, though it may be well to state that "N-n" is Northampton; "S-n," Southampton; "I. W.," Isle of Wight; "J. C." and "E. C.," James City and Elizabeth City, respectively—both are counties. "Nanse" is Nansemond; "Hen.," Henrico; "Ldn." is Loudoun; "Shenan.," Shenandoah; "Fluv.," Fluvanna; "Acco.," Accomack, and so on.

"Annap Rec." are Annapolis Records, the county (and State) records which are in the Maryland State Land Office; they include not only all matters relating to lands, but the records of the Provincial Court, the Chancery causes, and wills, inventories and accounts. The testamentary material is recorded there up to 1775; since then at the county-seats.

"S. L. O." is the State Land Office at Richmond, Va. This contains all land patent records, surveys, and a good deal of material relating to soldiers' warrants, &c.

"S. L." is the Richmond State Library at Richmond, where there is a great deal of value in the way of tax-lists, copies of county records, &c. (See partial list in this issue.)

"P. A." stands for Pennsylvania Archives. A good list of what can be found in one or more series of this publication has been printed in one of the volumes of the American Historical Review.

The abbreviations for the counties of Penna., Maryland and Delaware are fairly clear. It should be noted that both Delaware and Virginia have a Sussex county, and Maryland and Virginia a Frederick county. (This explanation is not written for those who are familiar with the section!)

Persons unfamiliar with old Virginia records are, it is most likely, much troubled with the duplication of names of counties as names for parishes, especially when the parishes and counties don't in the least coincide. Sometime when the Editor finds out all she doesn't know now, she will try to give a list of this differing and troublesome nomenclature... she has been hoping that somebody would get out a Bulletin of Parishes, as clear and valuable as the County Bulletin of the Virginia State Library.

OCCASIONAL

ANTHONY CARPENTER claims that whereas he came into the country of Virginia free, it is his dew to have fifty acres. N-n, Va., vii-4. 4 Feby 1655.

The Clerk of AUGUSTA county, Va., is to write to the Clerk of ORANGE county, Va., for lists of tithables of Augusta county now in the office of the Clerk of Orange county. [This (from the context) appears to have been in connection with courts-martial, probably of settlers not reporting for military service.] Draper Mss. 1QQ35. 25 May 1747.

Those who have suddenly happened on deeds to land in the West Florida district, recorded in some western Pennsylvania county, and like the Editor knew nothing about the aforesaid district, will find this interesting. EAST and WEST FLORIDA DISTRICT, The Eastern District lay between the Appalachicola and Pearl rivers; the western district, called New Feliciana, lay between the Mississippi and Pearl rivers. Draper Mss. 12ZZ186.

The following is apropos of the recent editorial on Surry records, Va. The Clerk of the Court, William Hill, makes this entry, concerning the books and papers then in the office: "Three old books in folio without covers being Pte torne and lost." i(2)-45. 1673.

THOMAS MATTOCKS, son of ALEXANDER and ELIZABETH MATTOCKS, was baptized in the yeare 1651, about the latter end of the Summer, but the precise Day & Month is not remembered by mee. THO. TEACKLE.

The said THOMAS MATTOCKS When baptized was not above two months old if soe much as is supposed by THO: TEACKLE. Acco., Va. ii-64. 3 Aug 1668.

MANUSCRIPT MATERIAL IN THE VIRGINIA STATE LIBRARY

In 1919 the Archivist of Virginia, with the approval of the Librarian, Dr. H. R. McIlwaine, prepared for specific use at that time, but not for official publication, a list of the material in the Archives Department. The Editor possesses a copy of this list and the following epitome, with some omissions, it is thought will be found valuable to searchers. It may answer some of the innumerable questions with which the Library officers are assailed, before they are asked. The figures used are usually in round hundreds or thousands.

BOUNTY WARRANTS, 16,000, filed and indexed;

CONFEDERATE RECORDS (at that date about 140,000 index cards prepared);

GEORGE ROGERS CLARKE PAPERS, filed but unindexed; 21,000;

GOVERNOR and COUNCIL JOURNALS, 1776 to 1835; 78 volumes;

HENRICO COUNTY RECORDS (all prior to 1781); 23 volumes;

HENRICO COUNTY DEEDS, WILLS, &c., 1695-1808; 970 pieces;

MILITIA AND OTHER MILITARY RECORDS, 300,000 pieces;

SOCIETY of the CINCINNATI, papers from 1783 to 1810, 220 papers;

PERSONAL PROPERTY BOOKS OF THE CITIES AND COUNTIES OF VIRGINIA; about 12,700 "books," estimated to make over 1600 volumes when bound. These lists cover the period between 1782 and 1863. [Note: the list does not mention the "land books" (tax-lists) which it is thought are now in the custody of the Library.]

PETITIONS TO THE GENERAL ASSEMBLY, 25,000. [In 1919 nearly 20,000 had been indexed by localities.]

REJECTED CLAIMS for Revolutionary Bounty Land, about 12,000.

STATE LAND OFFICE, Letters to the Registers of; about 2400.

TRANSCRIPTS, 38 vols.

WAR OF 1812, manuscript muster and pay rolls, 26 vols.

REGISTER OF JUSTICES, 17,000.

MILITIA RECORDS, 75,000 pieces.

ILLINOIS REVOLUTIONARY MATERIAL; 202 pieces.

MISCELLANEOUS REVOLUTIONARY MUSTER AND PAY ROLLS of the "Western Country;" 32 pieces.

MISCELLANEOUS PIECES OF MANUSCRIPT not yet arranged in the Archives room, estimated at 300,000 pieces.

REVOLUTIONARY AND MILITARY NOTES

TIMOTHY LENNINGTON, a Serjeant in the 2d Batt'l'n Penna. Militia; Col. James Murray certifies that he was badly wounded 11 Dec 1777 at the battel of the Gulph. His service ended 13 Jany 1778. Pension ordered. O. C. Docket i. p. 12. Sept 1778. Northumberland Co., Penna.

MICHAEL CAMPBELL, Private, 3d Batt'l'n North'd Co. Militia; widow Sarah produces certificate of Col. Peter Holsterman and Robert Reynolds, Capt'n, that said Michael was in actual service 13 June 1778, when he was killed by the Savages. Pension ordered. p. 21. 11 Jany 1779. Northumberland Co., Penna.

ROB'T McWILLIAMS, a militia-man in Capt. Arthur Tagert's company of Northumb'd Militia; John Chattam certifies that on or nr the 12 Dec 1777. McWilliams (under his command), was killed near the Gulph Mill in Philadelphia County, in action with the British Army. Ctf is dated 14 Jany 1781. Entered under Court of 27 Aug. 1779. p. 27. (McWilliams left a wife and three children, the eldest only seven.) Northumberland Co., Penna.

Major WM. LOWTHER appears and proves that he was in the volunteer service under the command of General George Rogers Clark in the year 1781, and obtained a Major's Commission and acted in that capacity from 21st June to 11th August ensuing... that his obtaining a discharge was occasioned by sickness... Ordered certified. Harrison co., W. Va. Ct 18 Apr 1786.

JAMES McDEAD proves that he entered as a substitute in the regular service in room of Uriah Gardee in 1780 and continued twenty-one months and was discharged by Major Snead of the light infantry. Ordered certified. Harrison co. W. Va. Ct 20 Apr 1788.

ADAM O'BRYAN proves that he served nine months as a spy. Harrison co. W. Va. Ct 20 Apr 1788.

JOHN WILSON Commissioned as Captain of Militia and sworn into his commission. Harrison co., W. Va. Ct 17 Nov 1785.

THOMAS BECKLY: It is proven to the satisfaction of the Court that he lost a certificate that was liquidated by the Court of Claims of Monongalia county. Harrison co., W. Va. Ct [3 Aug?] 1784.

JOHN STACKHOUSE, a militia soldier, came into Court and proved to the satisfaction of the same that he was captivated [sic] at Col. Archibald Locken's (?) Depot on the Ohio River in the year 1781, and that he was captivated on the 1st day of August in said year and returned to the mouth of Grave Creek on the East side of the Ohio on the 16th day of July 1784. Harrison co., W. Va., Ct 22 Sept 1784.

LAND TAX BOOK FOR THE YEAR 1788, OHIO COUNTY, WEST VIRGINIA

(*See June number,* 1923)

(Note: It is not clear, at present, whether this is a complete list of land owners, or only those taken by the collector of one district.)

Robert More, 400 acres; John Morgan, 352; John Mitchel, 60 and 400; George McColloh, Jr., 300; James Millar, 740; David McClure, 300; Daniel Morgan, 400 and 135; George McNab, 116; George McCollah, 300;

Levi Mills, 184; Benjamin Ogle, 400; Alexander Ogle, 330; Baldwin Persons, 400 and 250; John Pattison, 400; Charles Tray(?), 481; Lewis Pearce, 192; Reason Pumpry, 400 and 400; Jacob Pyatt, 220;

Hambelton Reed, 200 and 107; Edward Robison, 400; Aaron Robison, 460; Nicholas Rogges [Rogers?], 230; Van Swaringen, 370 and 227; Jonah Seaman, 300; Zachariah Sprig, 300 and 150; George Smith, 400; John Span, 400;

George Stevenson, 342; John Tilton, 400 and 353; Morgan Vanmatre, 400 and 100; Larance [?] Vanhuskerk, 400; W. I. A. I. Vanmatre, 100; John Vanmatre, 300; Abraham Van matre, 100; Larance Vanmatre, Jr., 350; John Vanbuskerk, 424 and 172;

Larance Vanbuskirk, 70; Daniel Vanmatre, 150; Archabeld Wood, 400; David Williamson, 500; Charles Wells, 400; Robert Woods, 320; Abslom Wells, 400 and 100; William Warpinbay, 100; John Wilson, 560;

Ebnezar Zean, 400, 285 and 54; Jonathan Zeane, 145; Elezebeth I. G. Zeane, 293.

Moses Chaplin certifies to the foregoing lists, as "Clk: O. C."

A LIST OF PERSONS NATURALIZED BY PARTICULAR ACTS

From Bacon's Laws of Maryland.*

(*Contributed by Mrs. George W. Hodges*)
(*Continued from October number*)

ANDREW IMBERT, Queen Anne's county; 8 Oct 1694. 4.

ALBERT JOHNSON of Talbot county; 13 May 1682. 10.

BERNARD JOHNSON of Calvert county; "Cooper;" 19 Apr 1671. 1.

CORNELIUS JOHNSON of Somerset county; 6 June 1674. 12.

JOHN JOHNSON of Talbot county; 6 June 1674. 14.

SIMON JOHNSON 6 Nov 1682. 4.

PETER JOHNSON of St. Mary's county; 8 May 1669. 4.

JEAN JOURDAIN of St. Mary's county; 8 May 1669. 4.

HERMAN KINKEL of Cecil county; "a Dutchman," and his children. 22 Apr 1720. 2.

JUSTUS ENGLEHEAD KITCHEN, "Planter," of Anne Arundell county; 17 December 1708. 14.

JOHN LAMEE, "Weaver," of Dorchester county, and his children. Nov 1713. 16.

JOHN LAVIELE, "a Frenchman," of Calvert county. 22 Apr 1720. 2.

JOSEPH LAZEAR of Prince George's county, "with his children." 5 Aug 1721. 5.

JOHN LECOUNT of Dorchester county; also MOSES, PHILIP and ANTHONY LECOUNT of same county; Sons of Anthony and Hester Lecompt," and HESTER and KATHERINE LECOUNT, "dau's of Anthony and Hester Lecompt." 6 June 1674. 12. [See Wills i, p. 262.]

JOHN LEDERER of Calvert county; 19 Apr 1671. 10.

ARNOLD LIVERS, "Taylor," of Prince George's county; 3 May 1704. 2.

JACOB LOCKERMAN of Dorchester county; 15 Nov 1678. 13.

JACOB LOOTON, of St. Mary's county; 13 May 1682. 9.

PETER MANNADOE, "a Frenchman and his children;" of Cecil county; 22 Apr 1720. 2.

ROLAND MAUS, of Baltimore county; 17 Nov 1682. 15.

(*To be continued*)

* The figures other than dates refer to chapters.

THE AGES OF SOME FREDERICK COUNTY (MARYLAND) ORPHANS

JOHN ELLIS, age 14, Sept 1772.
ANDREW EVERHART, age 15, June 1777.
WILLIAM FRANCIS, age 12, 1759.
SAMUEL FRANCIS, age 7, 1764.
THOMAS FOSSETT, age 17, 1756.
NOAH FLEEHARTY, age 9, June 1770.
JAMES FLEEHARTY, age 10, Mch 1772.
JACOB FOUT, age 17, 1766.
JAMES FARRELL, age 2, Mch 1781.
STEPHEN FLEEHARTY, age 13, Jany 1776.
ELIZ'H FOX, age 12, 26 July 1771.
WILLIAM GYLES, age 16, 1756.
ELISABETH GYLES, age 12, 1755.
SAMUEL GATES, age 10, 1761.
JOHN GATES, age 7, 1765.
ROBERT GATES, age 5, 1767.
EDW'D BLACK GOUGH, age 12, 1762.
DAVID GLASTER, age 3, 1773.
JOHN GRANT, age 10, Feby 1769.
JOSEPH GREEN, age 8, Oct 1772.
JOHN GAMBOL, age 7, Aug 1776.
WILLIAM GAMBOL, age 4, Aug 1779.
FRANCIS GAREY, age 13, Nov 1773.
ADAM GROSE, age 17, 27 Aug 1772.
DOROTHY SPEAK GREEN, age 8, Mch 1779.
HEZEKIAH CLEM'S GREEN, age 4, Dec 1782.
SARAH GREEN, age 2, Dec 1784.
HENRY GROSE, age 15, Aug 1776.
THOMAS GRAHAM, age 9 mos., Feby 1791.
SIMON HARDIN, age 7 or 8 in 1761 or 1762.
ELIZABETH HENN, age 12 in 1753.
JONAS HAMMOND, age 1 in 1770.
WILLIAM HARE, age 14 in 1757.
DEVORAN[x?] HARE, age 11 in 1760.
ROBERT HARE, age 15 in 1756.
BENJAMIN HOWARD, age 4 in 1768.
SARAH HARE, age 4 in 1764.
CATHRINE HARTLINE, age 1 yr, in 1768.
JOHN HUGHS, age 17 in 1767.
WILLIAM HUNT, age 16 in Nov 1767.

NOTES AND QUERIES

JAMES SMALLWOOD, son of James Smallwood, of Charles co., Md., died in 1723. What was the maiden name of his wife, Mary? JOHN SMALLWOOD died in 1770. Whom did he marry? JAMES SMALLWOOD had wife Jemima in 1760. He moved to Frederick county, Va., about 1768, where he died about 1783. Who was his wife Jemima?

MOSES CAWOOD, in Frederick co., Va., about 1769, married a widow Jemima Berry, née Smallwood. Who were her parents? A. L. K. S. D.

GIBSON: Can any reader of the NOTE-BOOK tell me anything of FRANCIS and GIBBY GIBSON, whose tomb-stones are in James City, Virginia, dated 1634, or of JOHN GIBSON who m. ELIZABETH WILLCOCK, in Middlesex co., Virginia, 1708? S. C. K.

HAMMON: Would like to hear from any descendant of JOHAN or JOHN HAMMON and wife EVE, at one time resident and owning land in Frederick county, Md., and afterwards perhaps in Augusta county, Virginia. EVE HAMMON died in Georgia. Was JOHN HAMMON an immigrant into this country in 1764? Mrs. J. H. H. T.

WADE: Twenty-five dollars will be paid for reliable information from church or civil records, or early Bible, as to Capt. JOHN WADE, of Chester or Marcus Hook (Lower Chichester), Penna. Was he lost at sea with his vessel as claimed by tradition, or captured by the British about 1775-6? Was THOMAS WADE his son, and was he also lost about 1782? C. A. D. I.

"SAUL" ROBISON: Who was "SAUL" (perhaps SOL) ROBINSON who died in Worcester county about twenty or thirty years ago? M. L. M.

PALMER: Dr. Byron S. Palmer, of Palmyra, New York, will be glad to hear from any PALMERS who are interested in the name.

LYON: Wanted, the ancestry of ANN LYON who married RICHARD POUND son of William and Fannie (Underwood) Pound, of Virginia.

HALE: Wanted, the ancestry of JOHN HALE, of Franklin co., Va., who married ELIZABETH SAUNDERS, dau. of Capt. Edward or Ebenezer Saunders and wife Theodosia. M. B. C. W.

PLACES TO STAY

Visitors to WEST CHESTER, the county seat of CHESTER Co., Penna., can get excellent and reasonably priced meals at the OVERTOWN, which is situated above the bank. Sometimes the hostess, who is a member of the Society of Friends, can also provide rooming facilities.

Ladies visiting Madison, Wisconsin, will find the City Y. W. C. A. comfortable and reasonable. The cafeteria is one of the very best and reasonable in price.

The Central "Y" at Harrisburg has also a limited number of rooms for transients, and is a very attractive place. It is located opposite Capitol Park.

Visitors at FAIRFAX COURTHOUSE, Virginia, can get excellent meals at Mrs. Mitchell's, a short way down the street from the courthouse enclosure.

Columbian Printing Co., Inc., Washington, D. C.

The

County Court Note-Book

A Little Bulletin of History and Genealogy

Vol. III March, 1924 No. 2

NEW ENGLANDERS AND OTHERS IN EARLY VIRGINIA RECORDS

(*Seventh instalment*)

JOHN BOYS, of the Citie of London, Mcht. (Then resident in Ireland.) Acco. ii-32. 1 Dec 1665.

MARMADUKE CHERRIEHOLME, late of Virginia, now resident in Charles Towne in the County of Middx in New England, Chirurgeon. Will. Refers to father, Thos. Cherrieholme, late of Wakefield, in Yorkshire, England, apothecary; friend Bartholomew Greene, of Charlestowne, Mariner. Wit: Fosdick, Younge, Stevens, Leman. I. W. ii-311. 19 Nov 1690—9 Sept 1691.

JOHN COLLOME, late of Plymouth, Devon, England. Col. Isaac Allerton, being a creditor, asks admn of his estate. Staff., Va. i-42. 7 Apr 1690.

Mr. NICHOLAS DAVISON of New England. N-n, viii-65. 27 Mch 1660.

JOHN DANIELL; bond from Joseph Townsend of Boston, Mcht. N-n, xi-266. 16 May 1679.

LIVIN DENWOOD of Maryland, buys land in Accomack, Va. Acco. ix-250. 1692. (Mr. Livinge Denwood, of Somersett county, Md. N-n, xvii-509. 1698.)

Maj. EDW. GIBBONS; Thos. Ffalkner deposes that Maj. Gibbons tended [sic] Thos. Maior his debt at Marblehead in N. E. when he was at Boston... (1640). N-n, iii-168. 16 Mch 1648.

JONAH GROOS of Hartford, *Conatteat,* in N. E. Acco. xvi-18. 1715-16.

JESSEY HUNT, of New York, Marriner, to Luke Luker (Lukens?) of Accomack, planter. Acco. Deeds iii-476. 26 May 1767.

RICHARD HAMBY, of Patuxon, Maryland; power to Thos. Stratton. N-n, ix-15. 1657.

Mr. WM. HEMSLEY, of Talbot County, Maryland; Daniel Jenifer, Gent. and wife Ann, of Accomack, give him power to acknowledge deed to 500 acres in Chester River, Md. Acco. vi-193. 12 Feby 1679.

SAMUEL PAINE, of Chickahommony River in the Parish of Wallingford; power to him from Samuel Andrews of London. N-n, ix-32. 28 Sept 1658.

JOHN PROCTER, age about 40. In North Carolina, Bath county, where he testifies as to Robert Watson's will. (Levi Truwhitt was Clerk of Bath county.) Acco xi-317. 6 July 1703.

JOHN PAYNE and son Robert, of Norwich, England. N-n vii-66. 16 Apr 1657. See also vii-53.

THOMAS PREESON, of Leverpool, Marriner. N-n xv-416. 29 May 1689.

RICHARD PERG (PERY?), Mcht, late of New Haven. Agent of Mr. George Passemer and Mr. George Fryer. N-n vii-73; 30 Nov 1651.

GEORGE PARKE [PARKER] came from New England, trading. Acco viii-331. 4 Jany 1682.

ABELL PORTER of Boston, N. E. Acco ix-127. 26 Apr 1684.

HENRY RANDOLPH to RICHARD ATTKINS, Somersett county, Mcht. 5 cowes and an Indian Boy. Surry i-22. About 1654.

HUGH RYDING, Gent., of Westdeby [*sic*] in England was heir to Mr. Thomas Ryding. Acco ix-36. 7 Feby 1783.

THOMAS ROWSE, of London, Mcht, power to Gerrard Ffowke. Wmld ii-51; 6 Oct 1656.

LEWIS READE of Somersett county, Marriner. N-n v-125; 15 Dec 1656.

ANN RIDLEY leaves property to cousin Susannah McMurph[y] of Georgia, wife of Daniel and dau. of Wm. Crosle, late of Ireland. Freds'burg records, about 1804.

JOSEPH ROTCH, marriner of N. E.; power to Nicholas Bowdoin, I. W. county, Va. I. W. D-266. 6 Feby 1742-3.

MARYLAND'S NEXT OF KIN *

(*Continued from January number*)

SAML ABBOTT and WILLIAM SHARNAHAM; inv. MARGARET RAGLACE, widow, of Talbot county; 26 June 1719. ii-132.

WM. COMPTON; inv. John Compton of Charles county; 18 May 1719. ii-135.

WILLIAM PRATHER, bro. of dec'd, and Katherine Prather, widow; inv. John Prather of Pr. Geo's county; 3 June 1719. ii-136.

JOHN and NICHOLAS DAVIS, sons of dec'd; inv. Nicholas Davis, Sen'r, of Prince George's county; 6 Mch 1717-18. ii-139.

WILLIAM LOVE and JOHN MARRETT; inv. William Marrett of Dorchester county; 8 May 1719. ii-146.

WILLIAM ROBINSON and MICHAEL TODD; inv. of William Insley of Dorchester county; 4 May 1719. ii-149.

JOHN RUMBLY and JOHN WILLY; inv. of James Cannon of Dorchester county. 6 May 1719. ii-150.

JONAS and ABILLE DAWSON; inv. Anne Dawson of Dorchester county; 1 July 1719; ii-152.

ANTHONY and SARAH HADDER; inv. Warren Hadder of Sumersett county; 1 Aug 1719. ii-153.

CHARLES and JAMES KING; inv. John King of St. Maries county; 31 July 1719. ii-155.

ELIZABETH CARBERRY, JOSHUA and MATHEW GUIBERT; inv. Joshua Turner of St. Mary's county; 4 May 1718. ii-157.

WILLIAM JONES, admr.; inv. Morgan Jones of Anne Arundel county; 4 Sept 1719. ii-158.

CHARLES and MARY WHITE; inv. William White of Somersett county; 10 Feby 1718-19. ii-159.

THOS. and GEORGE AISQUITH; inv. of Col. William Aisquith of St. Mary's county; 8 June 1719. ii-161.

ANNE WINSER and CHARLES YOUNG; inv. William Bounds of Sumersett county; 30 Aug 1718. ii-163.

ANDREW THOMSON and JOHN BENSON ("Approved on by us"); inv. John Browne of Somersett county; 25 June 1719. ii-164.

THOMAS HALBROOK, admr; inv. Thomas Halbrook of Sumersett county; 9 Feby 1718. ii-167.

WM. HARRISS and RICHARD HARRISS; inv. Joseph Austin of Sumersett county; 28 May 1718. ii-168.

HUGH NELSON and BENJAMIN SCOOLFIELD; inv. John Bratten of Sumersett county; 16 Apr 1719. ii-169.

WILLIAM GRILFIN; inv. Joseph Wouldhave of Sumersett county; 10 June 1719. ii-172.

WILLIAM GRILFIN; inv. Benjamin Woulhaven[?] of Sumersett county; 10 June 1719. ii-173.

ELIZABETH ALLIN; inv. Abraham Richards of Sumersett county; 7 Aug 1719. ii-174.

(To be continued)

MARRIAGES BY INFERENCE*

(Continued from January number)

LAWRENCE ABINGTON and LIDIA BROOKES, dau of Henry Brookes. Wmld, Va. About 20 Feby 1657. O. i-101.

HENRY ALLEN and MARY...; dau of Mary Powell, wf of Stephen Powell. I. W. About 1693. iv-66.

DAVID ANDREW, Jr. and MARY FLOOD, the widow of John Flood. [Mary Creede?] Surry, Va. About or before 25 July 1679. See also fo. 233, 14 Aug 1679.

SAMUEL ALDRED and widow of Richard CARY. Staff, Va. P-267. After 29 Nov 1682.

DAVID ANDERSON and widow of John HALLOWES, Wmld, Va. i-__ Before 11 July 1659.

GEORGE ATKINS and ANN PINNER, wid of Richard. About 15 Apr 1667. L. Norf E-13.

JOHN ATHWORTH and wid of RICH. SELBY. About 16 Aug 1671. L. Norf E-68.

SIMON ARNOLD and PRUDENT WEBB, dau of Thomas Webb. Har. Co., W. Va. Before 17 June 1780. ii-346.

JOSEPH BELL and ANNE WARRINGTON, probably wid of Alexander. Acco. Before 3 Jany 1721-2. xviii-38.

WILLIAM BURTON, Sr., and MARY SNEAD, wid of Robert. Acco. Before 4 Dec 1728. xvi-341.

JOHN BLAKE and SARAH RATCLIFF. Acco, Va. Land Causes. 5 Nov. 1692.

HENRY BIGGS and ELIZABETH KEITH. Pr. Wm. Land Causes. p. 268. Before 22 Dec 1785.

OWEN BRADIE [of Ffx co.] and HANOVER AUBREY, eldest dau of John. Pr. Wm Va. Land Causes, p. 143. Before 16 Nov 1767.

EDWARD BRYAN and CHRISTIAN COUNCELL, dau of Hodges Councell. I. W., Va. Before 10 Apr 1699. ii-409. [In another will the name is given as *Briand.*]

JOHN BARNES and ANNE JONES, dau of John *Johnes,* Sr. I. W. Va. Before 8 July 1697. ii-385.

JOHN BAID and SUSANAH FRAME, dau of James. Fayette co., Penna. Before 14 Jany 1796. B-337.

RICHARD BAYLEY and MARY JONES. Acco. Before 8 Feby 1664. ii-5.

(To be continued)

A LIST OF PERSONS NATURALIZED BY PARTICULAR ACTS

From Bacon's Laws of Maryland.*

(Contributed by Mrs. George W. Hodges)

(Continued from January number)

ANDREW MATSON, Cecil county; 6 Nov 1682. 1.

HENRY MATTHEWS, Baltimore county; 6 Jany 1674. 12.

MATTHIAS MATTHIASON (*alias* Freeman), Cecil county; 22 May 1695. 10.

DANIEL MAYNADIER (Rev) "and his children," of Talbot county; 30 Oct 1727. 14.

PETER MILLS, of St. Mary's county; 19 April 1671. 10.

PETER MAIZE de MOIGNE; 6 Nov 1683. 1.

NICHOLAS de la MONTAGNE, of Cecil county; 18 Oct 1694. 4.

PETER MONTGOMERY, Charles county, "Planter and his children;" 30 Oct 1727. 23.

CHRISTOPHER MOUNTS, Cecil county; "born of Dutch parents;" 9 May 1700. 9.

* The figures other than dates refer to chapters.

MARTIN MUGENBOURG, Cecil county; 6 June 1674. 12.
ANDREW MULLOCK [see Poulson], Cecil county; 6 Nov 1682. 4.
JOHN SAMUEL MYNSKIE, City of Annapolis, "Blacksmith;" 30 Oct 1727. 18. CATHERINE MYNSKI, his Wife, and SUSANNA MYNSKIE, his Daughter. [Same date.]
JAMES NEALE, Charles county; 1 May 1666. 8. His four children: HENRIETTA MARIA, JAMES, DOROTHY, and ANTHONY NEALE, "born in Spain of ANNA NEALE his Wife, during his Residence there as a Merchant and also employed there by the King, and the Duke of York, in sveral emergent affairs, as by Commissions herewith produced, might appear, &c."
AMBROSE NELSON, Baltimore county; 15 Nov 1712. 24.
WILLIAM MENGFINGER, St. Mary's county. 19 Apr 1671. 1.
JOHN MOWERS, 6 June 1674; 12.
JOHN OETH, Anne Arundel county. 28 Feby 1721. 15.
JOHN OLDSON, Baltimore county; 9 June 1692. 71.
PETER OLDSON, Cecil county; 17 Sept 1681. 10.
SEBASTIAN OLEY, Anne Arundel county; 25 Mch 1702. 6.

(*To be continued*)

THE AGES OF SOME FREDERICK COUNTY (MARYLAND) ORPHANS

(*Continued from January number*)

JOHN HENDRY INGLE, 13 in July, 1765.
JOHN JONES, 9 in July, 1769.
MARY JONES, 3 in May 1770.
ZACHARIAH JONES, 8 in Jan., 1769.
PARMENAS JOHNSON, 9 in 1764.
CHARLES JOHNSON, 7 in 1766.
ANN JOHNSON, ... (before Nov. Ct 1759).
MARTIN KERN, 7 in 1767.
SIMON KEIZER, 4 in Dec 1775.
FRED'K KELLOR, 16 in June 1775.
ELEANOR KENNEDY, 14 in Apr 1773.
RICHARD LOFLIN, 15 in 1756.
JOHN LARKIN, 10 in Mch 1768.
JOHN LARKIN ... Aug. Ct 1763.
ADAM LANE, 6 in Aug 1787.
MARY LANE, 6 in Aug 1782.
ELISABETH MAUGRIGE, age 5, 1761.
JANE MATHEWS, age 11, 1757.
MATHEW MOCKBEE, age 15, Aug 1763.
JEREMIAH MOCKBEE, age 11, Aug. 1768.
KEZIAH MOCKBEE, age 2, Aug 1772.
MARY MOCKBEE, age 5, Aug 1768.
JOHN McCULLOCH, age 12, Apr 1769.
DANIEL McCULLOCH, age 7, May 1774.
Wm. McKINSEY, age 8, Nov 1777.
SARAH MEDCALF, age 4, Aug 1773.
NEAL MORRIS, age 7, Oct 1779.
ADAM MILHOUSE, age 14, Sept 1773.
CHARLES MILLS, age 8, June 1779.
JOHN MEYRICK, age 5, Jany 1782.

(*To be continued*)

NOTES FROM NORTHAMPTON COUNTY, VIRGINIA

(*Record books and loose papers*)

AT A COURT...held for Gloucester county on Tuesday the 20th day of May 1707. In a suit in Chancery between JOHN CLARKE and ANNE his wife complainant and RICHARD HUBBARD and WILLIAM MILLER Respondts Wherein the said Complainants...set forth...[that] JOHN CLARKE and ANNE his wife formerly ANNE SINCOE...that yo'r Oratrix was formerly married to one RICHARD SINCOE of this County dec'ed who dyed intestate and left behind him yo'r Oratrix his widow & three Children WILLIAM, ANNE and SARAH and a considerable estate...and yo'r Oratrix then petitioning for administracon of the said estate it was granted by this Court to her and one RICHARD HUBBARD and WILLIAM MILLER became security...and did...enter into...bond...After which one of the said children to wit the said WILLIAM departed this life being very young and not of age to make a will...and some time after administration [was] granted to yo'r Oratrix she...did intermarry with...JOHN [CLARKE] after which...the said HUBBARD and MILLER ...came to yo'r Orator and Oratrix and [in a] threatening manner demanded security... Fearing that...she and her children should want bread [HUBBARD & MILLER having threatened to take the estate from her] she persuaded her husband...to enter into such bond...[The petition which is somewhat damaged then relates suit brought by the security and the arrest of the orators, &c.]

Another paper in the same suit mentions that Wm. SEGRAVE married ANN, daughter of RICH'D SINCOE and wife ANNE, now the wife of JOHN CLARKE. [ANN SEGRAVE was but twenty years of age in 1717.]

MARY X FITCHETT, wife of NEHEMIAH FITCHETT, formerly widow of JOHN POWELL, late of Savage's Neck, Northampton, planter, assigns [with her husband] all right to five hundred acres which were given after the expiration of a certain term of years by will of JOHN SAVAGE Gent., deceased, to his daughter FRANCES, deceased, and her heirs, which FRANCES was the mother of JOHN POWELL, and died leaving no other son. v. xviii-368.

JOHN TOMPKINS and JOHN KENDALL give bond to HANCOCK CUSTIS, infant son and heir at law of JOHN CUSTIS, late of said county, Gent., deceased, for £500, the CONDITION being That WHEREAS a marriage is intended between JOHN TOMPKINS and ANN CUSTIS *widow of above named* JOHN CUSTIS, dec'd, who by will directed that should his widow marry she should give bond to keep the Houses and plantations at Hungars in good repair [this being the bond]. vol. xviii-372. 25 Feby 1747.

The County Court Note-Book

An every-other-monthly devoted to abstracts from County Court and other records, prior to 1800, and with a department of notes and queries.

MILNOR LJUNGSTEDT, Editor and Publisher. Bethesda, Route 1, Maryland.

Published six times a year. Subscription, two dollars a year, in advance; must begin with the year. *Renewals one dollar and a half.* Advertising rates moderate.

VOL. III MARCH, 1924 No. 2

THE OLD CHURCH

AN APPEAL

I have a few minutes before the taxi comes to take me to the station and I sit and wait upon the steps of the old church.

The occasional, indifferent traffic of the small town passes by.

The main church door, under whose arch I am, is closed; there is a side entrance open. I have been inside and have taken pictures of the golden windows and the gray windows and the small, old font, and the pathetic organ.

On either hand are the old churchyard and what was once the rectory garden. Box planted many a year ago, scrubby in places, and showing gaps, borders the narrow walks. Cheerful hens scratch under it; the mocking bird and the cardinal bird are somewhere in the trees.

There comes to me a picture of the past, of the brides who have stepped across this threshold, of the soldiers in gray whose bearers strained to a careful level as they carried their burdens to quiet sleep in the once beautiful graveyard far in the rear.

In the church itself, with its cracked and weather-stained walls; its broken and patched windows; its rusty stoves; its dingy altar cloth; I seem to see in the slanting sunbeams the belles and beaux of the 50's, of the pleasant years before the war. How charming is the picture! Curls, bonnets, and mits; rustling skirts quite filling the aisle (sure, the bridal party must have gone to the chancel rail in Indian file!); curled and raven locks upon the men, with fine rolling collars and (am I not right?) most beautiful of waistcoats, all worn with a grace and dignity long forgotten; and even in the gay gossip of the after church, a charm of sociability and friendliness which to us... looking back, is a part of Sunday morning service... all this is as if it had never been. Not ten families, it may be, of the old congregation are still in town, and of these, some have drifted into the flourishing Baptist, Methodist, Reformed Presbyterian, and other evangelical folds. Of some families, all are dead, others have moved away.

Forgotten are the brides; forgotten are the soldiers in gray, except for some perfunctory annual decoration; forgotten is the lonely church. Once a fortnight, maybe, a student from somewhere comes to read the service, and a child of fourteen is the organist.

The beautiful churchyard is open to all, including dogs and the neighbors' chickens. It is a place and house of desolation.

A LITTLE OF EVERYTHING

The Editor is pleased to state that with the MAY issue there will begin the publication of the "head rights" in "old volume five," Virginia STATE LAND OFFICE. When "old volume five" was recopied into volumes four and five, the copyist omitted the "head rights." There is no index to the old volume and the Editor believes these "head rights" have never been published. She has, at some personal trouble, arranged for copies of the lists as they appear under the individual patents. It will not be possible to index them (the Editor's expenses are much beyond her subscription list) but they will be easy reading.

Rights of indexing are reserved.

GUILFORD COLLEGE, North Carolina, is the repository of Friends' records for the southern meetings, exclusive of those which are within the confines of the Philadelphia Yearly Meeting of the same branch of Friends. Only two records of these southern meetings are known to be in existence outside of those at the College. It is hoped to secure these.

The Library is equipped with a small fireproof, and the volumes are carefully arranged. Miss KATHARINE CRENSHAW RICKS, the now Librarian, was, when the Editor visited the College in February, engaged in classifying and shelf-listing a mass of periodical literature which had been allowed to accumulate without proper arrangement. It is hoped that before long some check-list of the Friends' records may be had in printed form.

If persons desiring searches in ROWAN COUNTY, N. C., will send a self-addressed envelope to the Editor, she will give them the name of a local searcher.

DANIEL BOONE'S cabin home is in Rowan county, said to be the original.

Mrs. PENELOPE JOHNSON ALLEN, of St. Elmo, Tennessee, a well-known officer of the State D. A. R., is doing unusually good work in the South in the way of copying certain valuable lists as they appear in court records. Later the Editor may be able to give this information more in detail. Systematic work, for the benefit of others as well as for themselves, is rather rare among searchers. For this reason, the Editor takes the unauthorized liberty of mentioning Miss De Saussure, of Charleston, South Carolina, for her remarkable ability in this line. Miss De Saussure furnished the Editor with a list of volumes in one of the old Charleston offices, which was of the greatest help. The Editor remembers this lady as among a few who have generously contributed to another's work.

The Editor has found a name for the quaint row of one-story, white-painted cabins or cottages which southern lawyers have for generations occupied and still occupy, about the Courthouse quadrangles. The Editor has learned that in one State, at least, the row is called "Lawyer's Range." The term "range" sounds odd to the Editor, but is reminiscent, it must be, of the dormitories of the University of Virginia.

Mr. FRED. S. OLDS, Collector for the Raleigh, North Carolina, Commission, has ready for the press his abstracts of North Carolina Wills which will follow in date the volume of wills already much in use, prepared by Mr. ... (the Editor forgets the name and doesn't know where her notes are). Mr. Olds, however, has been able to find and abstract a number of early wills not included in the previous publication.

Mr. Olds' work as a collector is quite beyond any poor praise by this Editor, as is the whole Commission, its work, and the placement of that work. The Historical Commission has five hundred boxes of marriage bonds, all those now in existence except as to two counties. The Editor asked a clerk in a local court how Mr. Olds got these bonds without any direct authority of law. The clerk answered, "Oh, he just says 'I'll take these to Raleigh with me and give you a receipt'!"

These bonds are now carefuly alphabetized as to the first letter, and have been and are being repaired. When a particularly poor bond is taken out for repairing (by the best known processes) a card bearing all the necessary information is typewritten and substituted in the bond's place.

The work of the Commission is so utterly admirable in every way that it cannot justly be written up in this brief and informal manner. At some later date the Editor will enlarge upon it, but must here express her grateful thanks for the most helpful courtesy, as well as for the comfort and convenience of good light, good chairs, good tables, and plenty of room.

A return visit will be made to both North and South Carolina capitals.

The GEORGIA ARCHIVES DEPARTMENT is four years old. It has done a large amount of good work in that time, and is still doing it. Miss BLAIR, the active executive head of the Department, is wisely doing as much as she can in a simple and inexpensive way for, the Editor judges, immediate results. Instead of waiting for the purchase of expensive cards and index cases, or for the carrying of each index into a completed form, a very great number of index slips have been written off in pencil on inexpensive paper, for current use and later copying, and through these much of the valuable material which is often held back for slow and expensive index or calendering in other collections is made immediately available. Touching upon the growth of the Department (which will be shown later in an article kindly prepared by Miss Blair herself), but four days before the Editor's visit, ten or eleven volumes of early conveyances had been found in the Capitol and added to the records already on the shelves.

The Editor had intended to devote this number largely to Georgia, but returned so late that she has found it impossible to get it in shape, more especially as some of her notes are yet hovering on the Georgia-South Carolina line, loath to leave.

The MAY number of the NOTE-BOOK will also include an important contribution from Mr. Dwelly, who has kindly furnished for the readers of the NOTE-BOOK a matrix made from specially cast type showing the more common contractions formerly in use by scriveners. From this matrix an electrotype is being made for the May issue.

Mr. Dwelly's last volume of PARISH RECORDS (the third of North Petherton, England) has just been received. These registers are being annotated by Mr. Dwelly with the contemporary Transcripts made for the Bishop of Wells.

The church referred to in the article on the Editorial page of this issue is the Protestant Episcopal Church of Trinity, in Abbeville, South Carolina. It was once the church of the parish.

Miss ADELAIDE L. FRIES, Archivist of the Moravian Church in America, Southern Province, is translating and editing the records in her care, which date from 1752 to the present day. Volume two, RECORDS OF THE MORAVIANS IN NORTH CAROLINA, will soon appear from the press of the North Carolina Historical Commission. These records are full of colonial and national history.

The Southeastern Express Company having lost the Editor's entire subscription list, the Editor will be most grateful if those subscribers who have not paid this year's subscription will kindly say so and send in the amount due.

From the PUBLIC LEDGER, Philadelphia, Penna., 25 March 1836.

MARRIED: On Monday, 21st inst. [March, 1836] by John Swift, Mayor, BERNARD H. BUCKNER, Esq., of Washington co., Miss., to Miss FANNY, daughter of DAVID HIGGINBOTHAM, Esq., of Albemarle county, Virginia.

DIED: On the 18th ult. [February, 1836] in New Orleans, Mr. Wm. B. Hendel, printer, a native of Carlisle, Cumberland county, Pa. The deceased has a wife and child in Philadelphia.

COLONIAL FORENAMES

ARGILLUS MERRIL was grandson (?) of Hannah Stockley. Acco. 30 Nov 1739. xxiiW-202.

ARCHELAUS MITCHELL, a tithable. Amherst, Va., Tax list, 1782, S. L.

ARCHELAUS ROSSON m. Henrietta Warren. Orange county, Va. 1798. Va. Mags. xxvii-345.

ARCHELAUS SCOTT, one of Capt. Daniel Smith's company of militia, in Fincastle county, Va. Probably about 1782. See Draper Mss. 4XX61.

ARCHELAUS THOMPSON. Amherst county, Va., taxlist. 1786. S. L.

ARGILAUS TAYLOR and wife Mary, had dau. Artemisia. Shen. county, Va. Mar. Rec. The dau. was b. 17 July 1774.

ARCHELAUS WOODMAN desires to be made a freeman. Winthrop's N. E. p. 448. 17 May 1637.

(Note: The N. E. H.—G. xxxix-62, says that Hercules Woodman went by the name of Archelaus in America. Date 1635. Several "Hercules" are, therefore, given below.)

HERCULES BRIDGES. His attorney, Geo. Wiscombe, confesses judgment for him to Anthony West. York county, Va. [ii-]-71. 1647.

HERCULES RYDER, wit. to a deed by Alexander Stuart. Fred'k county, Va., i-263. 1745.

HERCULES SHEPARD, of Accomack county, pltr, from Richard x Hill, Jr., pltr. 500 acres. Acco. vi-217. 20 Oct 1679.

HERCULES SHEPHEARD, a deed. Acco. vi-322. 25 Dec 1682.

REVOLUTIONARY AND MILITARY NOTES

PATRICK MARTIN was a soldier in the independent Company of Fr. Nicholson at Fort King George... "WHEREAS the Witnesses to his will may be People belonging to the said Company and cannot be absent from His Majesty's service there so long as to go to any Precinct Court, to prove the sd Will"... Nicholson orders that John Barnwell and Joseph Palmeter summon the witnesses and take their testimony in the usual form.... Whereupon Lt. Charles Huddy, William Prout-ting, Sjt, and Joseph Ball physician (being also of sd Independent Company at Fort King George receive instructions in connection with the matter.) Vol. 1722-24, pp. 193, &c, 26 July 1723 and 24 Aug. 1723. (Records in the Office of the Probate Judge, Charleston, S. C.)

THE MILITIA OFFICERS of GREENE county, Georgia, 4 July 1799. Lt. Col. Wm. Melton; Maj. Reuben De Jernatt, Capt. Robert Harper, Capt. David Flenniken, Capt. Robt Mettor [? perhaps Melton?], Capt. Wm. Wiggins, Capt. Benj. Posey, Capt. Wm. Colvert, Capt. Bird Terrill, Capt. Allin Stewart, Capt. Wm. Stewart, Lt. Henry English, Lt. Royall Jenkins, Lt. John Butler, Lt. Jesse Tucker, Lt. Shad'k Kimbrough, Lt. Jacobus Watts, Lt. Wm. Kimbrough, Lt. Whitmill Boums [?], Lt. Wm. Stephens and Lt. John Harrison.

"I THOMAS WILLIAM JENKINS, Signifying the Son of William Jenkins Malster and Storekeeper of the Town of Usk in the County of Monmouth South Wales and Nephew to Walter Jenkins Esq High Sheriff for the City of Bristol in England..." One of the witnesses to this will is Thomas Richard Davis; the testator's daughter, Susannah, is wife of James Corbet, and among his children, one is mentioned (Mary Jenkins) as being in London. Saint Mark's Parish, S. C. 6 Aug 1786. Kershaw co., S. C., A-34.

THESE ARE TO CERTIFY unto all whom it may Concern that the Bearer hereof a descendant of East Indians Born in London, five feet two Inches high, mutch pitted with the small Pox, Black strait hair, Named John Calais, hath resided in Charles Town in South Carolina for Six Years Past, is a freeman & is entitled to the Rights & Priviledges of a British Subject, having here Paid Scot & Lot & that he hath now Shipped himself as Cook on Board the Brit Spy, William Lyford Mastr. for Bristol. G [illegible] under my Notorial [illegible] of office at Charles Town afsd [illegible] first day of October 1759. Jno. Remington. Recorded 28 Febry 1766.

(From Misc. Record Book, Archives Dept., Atlanta, Ga.)

FRANCIS LEWIS TANEY, of Montgomery county, Maryland, to ALICE TANEY of St. Mary's county, Maryland; for the natural love and affection which he hath for his sister, the aforesaid Alice Taney and the sum of fifty pounds current money of this State ... by and with the consent and approbation of her husband Raphael Taney... conveys to sd Alice Taney all his part or moiety of a Tract of Land Scituate in the fork of Littel River... in Wilkes county, Georgia. late the property of Henry Taney. dec'd... 230 acres. Wit: Geo. French, Thos. Turner. Sig. Frans Lews Taney. 26 Aug 1794. Oglethorpe co., Ga. A-137.

ORDERED that the will of EDWARD POWELL be probated "By Virtue of the affidavits sent in the Commissions from the counties of Sussex and Maclenburg, Virginia." Minute Book i, 30 Mch 1798. Clerk's Office, Sup. Ct., Oglethorpe co., Ga.

ORDERED that the Widow of Cap: JOHN SLOANE who was killed in the Service of his Country; the Widow of Ninian STEEL, who was also killed, and JOSEPH WASSON who was wounded in the Service of his Country. be recommended to the General Assembly to obtain an Annuity. Rowan co, Records, N. C., Minutes, p. 372. 7 Aug 1783.

NOTES FROM KENTUCKY RECORDS

(Contributed by Miss Hattie M. Scott, of Frankfort, Kentucky)

REUBEN FORD, Sr., son of David Ford; b. Richmond [Va.]; d. 7 Apr 1856, aged 72.

LUCY FRENCH, dau. Moses and Sarah Dear; b. Virginia; d. 17 Sept 1860, aged 78.

WILLIAM and MARY GOODE, the parents of Elizabeth Johnson; b. Chesterfield county, Virginia; d. 1855, aged 87.

JAMES GAINES, married; b. Woodford county [Ky?]; son Wm. and Jane Gaines; d. 21 June 1860, aged 70.

Dr. WM. GAYLE, son of Wm. and Margaret Gayle; b. Virginia; d. 6 June 1860, aged 70.

FRANCIS GRAHAM, "Gentleman," the father of Catherine Samuel; b. Botetourt county, Virginia; d. 1855, aged 70.

EUNICE E. HALE, dau. John and Wade Carter; b. Pr. Wm county, Virginia; d. 20 Mch 1855, aged 50.

THORNTON HALE, son of Thomas and Catherine Hale; b. Pr. Wm county Virginia; d. 22 Feby 1857, aged 57.

ELIJAH HARROD, married; son of John and Nancy Harrod; d. 20 Oct 1852, aged 53.

THOMAS HALL, married; b. Virginia, son of Wm. and N. Hall; d. 8 Feby 1859, aged 84.

BERRYMAN HOLDER; born in Virginia; son of B. and A. Holder; d. 10 Sept 1859, aged 90 [70?].

MARY HAWKINS, widow; b. Virginia, dau. of Anthony and Mary Crockett; d. 31 Mch 1856, aged 76.

C. A. B. HARRISON, widow; born Culpeper county, Va. dau John and Eliz. Pendleton; d. 18 Aug 1852, aged 63.

FRANCES JACKSON; b. Charlotte county, Virginia; dau. Isaac and Sarah Gore; d. 2 Oct 1856, aged 74. (Franky Gore [Goar] m. Reuben Jacson, 31 Mch 1804. H. M. S.)

ELIZABETH JETT, widow; b. Scott county, Ky. dau. George and Mary Swetnam; d. 21 July 1859, aged 60.

MATTHEW JETT; b. Culpeper county, Va. Son of Wm. and Susan Jett; d. 15 Mch 1854, aged 75.

ELIZABETH JOHNSON, widow; dau William and Mary Goode; b. Chesterfield county, Va.; d. 30 Aug 1855, aged 30.

NOTES AND QUERIES

WANTED: WILLIAM PAYNE; b. Round Tower, Virginia; dates of birth, marriage and death; and to whom married, and when.

ELIZABETH CHANCELLOR; she was daughter of John, who was third son of Richard and Catherine (Cooper) Chancellor; when was she born, when married and when did she die? F. L. B. C.

ROE: Mrs. Chas. R. Keith, of Richmond, Kentucky, will be glad to hear from any ROE descended from the ROES of New York; or of any SHIPMAN or KIRTLAND (KIRKLAND) who traces back to Saybrook, Connecticut.

KEITH: Wanted, ancestry of MARTIN H. KEITH and ELIZABETH (BETSY) BLOCK, who married, probably in Alabama, about 1826. The KEITHS lived in Tallodega, Alabama. Elizabeth (Block) Keith was a Methodist. Her brother Jack was a Baptist preacher. A. D. R. K.

ANDREW GIBSON appears in the records of the State Land Office, Richmond, Virginia, as assigning his rights to a certain tract of surveyed land to JAMES CAMPBELL. This was in Berkeley county at the time, 1787. Wanted further information as to ANDREW GIBSON. Will be paid for. M. L. M.

WADE: Twenty-five dollars will be paid for reliable information from church or civil records, or contemporary Bible, as to Capt. JOHN WADE, sometime of Chester or Marcus Hook, Penna. Was THOMAS WADE his son? M. L. M.

HALE: Wanted, the ancestry of JOHN HALE, of Franklin county, Virginia, who married ELIZABETH SAUNDERS. M. B. C. W.

AARON COPPOCK, of Pennsylvania, went to Newberry District (perhaps to what was then Ninety Six District) South Carolina. Which AARON COPPOCK was this? M. L. M.

Dr. BYRON S. PALMER, of Palmyra, New York, will be glad to hear of any PALMERS who are interested in the name.

GENERAL INFORMATION

The GRACE STREET CAFETERIA, 717 East Grace street, Richmond, Virginia, is excellent. Good cooking, moderate prices, and convenient to Library and Land Office.

Searchers going to Charleston, S. C., will find that a very comfortable and economical way to live there for a short time, at least, is to take a room in one of the old houses and board at a cafeteria. Mrs. McKinley, 62 Society street, can take care of one or two ladies, and the cafeteria is in the next block. Both are within walking distance of the "Fire-Proof Building" and of the old churches.

The YARBOROUGH, in Raleigh, is good, reasonably priced, and near the Historical Commission. The Red Cross has a very good cafeteria near by, though it is higher priced than other similar places.

Columbia, S. C., has several excellent cafeterias and small cafes. The Y. W. C. A. has a cafeteria and, the Editor thinks, rooms. It is within walking distance of the Historical Commission (in the Capitol), but not very near.

Information as to other places will be given subscribers, if desired, upon receipt of a stamped, self-addressed envelope.

GENEALOGISTS AND OTHERS INTERESTED IN RESEARCH WORK

Mr. FRANCIS B. CULVER,
2203 North Charles Street,
Baltimore, Md.

Researches in genealogy and heraldry for early families of Maryland, Pennsylvania, and Virginia. Historical biographies compiled and authentic coats of arms emblazoned.

Mr. ALFRED L. HOLMAN,
Genealogist
2036 Indiana Avenue
Chicago, Ill.

Refers by special permission to Mr. George B. Utley, Librarian Newberry Library.

Mrs. GEORGE W. HODGES,
Gloucester Apartments,
Annapolis, Maryland.

Special facilities for genealogical and historical work.

EDWARD DWELLY, F. S. A. Scot., F. S. G.
Record Searcher and Genealogist.

Church Road, West Ewell, Surrey, England.

All kinds of research work carefully undertaken. Special facilities for Somerset and Devon families and for records in London. Daily attendance at Somerset House, British Museum and Public Record Office when necessary without extra charge, London being only 9 miles distant.

A few sets of "Dwelly's Parish Records" (Registers, Monument Inscriptions, &c., for Devon and Somerset—12 vols.) still in stock.

Access to slip indices containing over 3 million names. State your difficulty in pedigree and send for free suggestions and booklet.

CHARLES SHEPARD II,
Genealogist and Antiquarian.
Suite 609, 2153 California Street,
Washington, D. C.

Author of works on Bowen, Coward, Dole, Martin, Rochester, Shepard, and Wildes families; Rensselaer Co., N. Y., wills, tombstone inscriptions, etc. Agents throughout New England and other states.

"Problems of More Than Ordinary Difficulty"

Mrs. LETITIA P. WILSON,
3905 Gwynn Oak Avenue,
Baltimore, Maryland.

Special facilities for genealogical and historical work.

Mrs. FRANCIS H. MARKELL,
Frederick, Maryland.
Genealogical Research.

Refers by permission to Mr. Frank E. Norwood, president Frederick County Historical Society, Frederick, Maryland.

Mrs. WILLIAM HYDE TALBOTT
Rockville, Maryland,

Genealogical and historical research. Special facilities for all western and southern Maryland.

MISS HATTIE M. SCOTT,
GENEALOGIST.
402 Shelby Street, Frankfort, Ky.

Research in early Kentucky Court Records, State Historical Society, State Library, State Deeds, Kentucky and Virginia Military and Preemption Land Grants a specialty.

Member of Kentucky State Historical Society and of the Daughters of the American Revolution.

ROBERT F. HAYES, Jr.
3526 Roland Avenue, Baltimore, Md.

Formerly with the Maryland Historical Society.

RESEARCHES — HISTORICAL, BIOGRAPHICAL AND GENEALOGICAL.

Copies of the BALTIMORE SUN articles on Maryland and Virginia families.

PUBLICATIONS, ETC., OF VALUE TO HISTORIANS AND GENEALOGISTS

The GENERAL INDEX of WILLS of ST. MARYS COUNTY, MARYLAND, compiled by Mrs. George W. Hodges, has been published by the CARTER BRAXTON CHAPTER, D. A. R., also

The GENERAL INDEX of WILLS of ANNE ARUNDEL COUNTY, MARYLAND. A limited number only will be sold. Price $12.50. For information as to both volumes address Mrs. LETITIA P. WILSON, Regent, 3905 Gwynn Oak Avenue, Baltimore, Md.

An INDEX of NORTHAMPTON and ACCOMACK records from 1632 to about 1710 is available to readers of the NOTE-BOOK. Fee $3.00. Address the Editor.

Reasonable price will be paid for numbers 1, 2, 3, and 5, COUNTY COURT NOTE-BOOK, 1921-1922. Address Editor.

COLUMBIAN PRINTING CO., INC., WASHINGTON, D. C.

The

County Court Note-Book

A Little Bulletin of History and Genealogy

Vol. III May, 1924 No. 3

VIRGINIA IMMIGRANTS

From "Old volume 5," State Land Office. See note on page 20.

THOMAS DAVIS, Warwick county, 1655;
Head rights: Thomas Morgan, Mary Goodman, Jno. Gullam, Phillip Baker, Phillip Parker, Rob. Reeves.

Major MILES CAREY, Warwick county, 1655;
Head rights: Tho. Wilkinson, John Thomas, Margaret May, John Tistull(?).

Lt. Coll. THOMAS SWAN, Surry county, 1655;
Head rights: Margarett Delton, Sarah Coe, Susanna Coe, Thomas Smith, Rich. Jacksall, Jno. Sinckler, Jane Sinckler, Jno. Douglas, Mary Hawkins, Tegh, an Irish boy, James Leward, Michaell White, Jno. Long, Jno. Lewis, Jno. and James Pelloone, Wm. Sanford, and an Irish woman.

JOHN DORMAN, Northampton county, 1655;
Head rights: Sarah DORMAN, Wm. Hickman, Mary Overton, Ellenor Higgenson, James Murhead, Wm. Jones, Giles Pickfrizell, Job Edmunds, Eliz. Holliday, Anne Haies, Rog. Amolachan [O'Mulligan?], Elizabeth Haies, Tho. Younge, Marg: Cornelius, John Toole, James and Grace Adwicke.

WM. WRIGHT, [county not mentioned], 1655;
Head rights: Wm. WRIGHT, Dorothy Hall, Alexander Flaminge, Marie Owen.

ROBERT CASTLE, James City County, 1655;
Head rights: John Nayler, Wm. Franklin, Kath. Browninge, Mary Cobb, Rob. Whitefare, John Hayall.

PHILLIP CHARLES, [county not given], 1656;
Head rights: Thos. Beggon, Eliz. Marin, Hugh H.... [?]

SOUTHEY LITTLETON, Northampton county, 1656;
Head rights: Richd Smith, Geo. Daw, Sam. Lucas, Tho. Buffield, Rob. Max, Dick of the Frigot, Elinr Glover, Dorothy Slaughter, Fra. Rowles, Geo. Butcher, Phillip Gardner, Jno. Jackson, Richd Johns, Margaret Alen, Eliz. Bond, Tho. Newton, Geo. Freshwater, Tho. Blacklock and his wife and child, Gabriell Powell, Mathew Pippinge, Step. Corson, Richd Pickeringe, Sanders Wilson, Thomas Hogg, Mathew Wardell, Xpher Donoh, Richd Conner and Daniel, Irishmen, Jno. Pryer, Dan. Baker, Will Fisher, John Wyse, Mary Fleetwood, Wm. Smith, Geo. Smith, Mathy Bennet, Wm. Clerke, Richd Smith, Jno Symons, Jno. Munday, Tho. Fowler, Richd Skinner, John Johnson.

JOHN SYMONS, (county not mentioned), 1656;
Head rights: John Aggor [Hadger?], John Morehead, Elizabeth Hatly, Mary Finch.

FRANCIS HUTCHINS, Nansemond county, 1656;
Head rights: Elizabeth Pye, Daniell Murrey, Mary Misomer[?] Armagall Greenwood.

Capt. THOMAS GODWIN, Nansemond county, 1655;
Head rights: four persons, only one mentioned by name, Dorothy Loyd.

JOHN WYSE, Northampton county, 1655;
Head rights: Nohah[?] Hobs, Lawrence Hillyer, Hannah WISE, Wently Mackclayne.

GEORGE TRUETT, Northampton county, 1655;
Head rights: Alice Watson, John Omarwrare[?], Mackwm. Owen, John Huntley, James Oger, Thomas Jones.

WILLIAM GOWERS, Northampton county, 1656;
Head rights: 6 negroes.

MARY LEWIS, Northampton county, 1656;
Head rights: Kath. Merifell, Anne Jones, Mary Allvit, Jno. Mackmillian, and four negroes.

JOHN DYER, Lower Norfolk county, 1655;
Head rights: James Cole, Wm. Jackson.

(*To be continued*)

MARYLAND'S NEXT OF KIN *

(*Continued from March number*)

JOSEPH VANSWERINGEN; inv. of William Bladen of Anne Arundel county; 6 Aug 1719. ii-176.

ELIZABETH WHITEATS WELLMAN; inv. Micael [sic] Wellman (no county given). 1719. ii-179.

RICHARD POWER; inv. Margaret Lanyott [?] of St. Mary's county. 4 Mch 1717. ii-190.

CHARLES KING, JOSEPH HOPEWELL; inv. William Cretchett of St. Mary's county. 17 Aug 1719, ii-194.

WM. and JOSEPH LAWRENCE; inv. Robert Hammett of St. Mary's county. 31 July 1719. ii-196.

RICHARD and LEWES HASELER; inv. William Haseler, of St. Mary's county. 23 July 1719. ii-198.

CHARLES BOWEN Sr., and Jr.; inv. David Bowen, of Calvert county, 18 Aug 1719. ii-205.

JAMES MULLIKEN, LUKE BARNARD; inv. James Mulliken, Sr., of Prince George's county. 22 May 1718, ii-212.

JAMES and ELINOR ROBINS; inv. Thomas Robins of Prince George's county. 21 July 1719. ii-214.

JOHN GREEN "approves"; inv. John Humbleton, of Prince George's county. 21 July 1719. ii-216.

SAMUEL SWERENGEN, SAMUEL FARMER; inv. Thomas Clarke, of Prince George's county. 19 June 1719. ii-217.

ANNE VINCENT, wife of John Vincent, dau. and only kin; inv. John Denegoe of Charles county. 13 July 1719. ii-224.

Z. DIVARD[?]; inv. Edward Brusbank, of Kent county. 28 Nov 1719. ii-225.

BIGGER and MARY HEAD; inv. William Head, Prince George's county, 15 Aug 1719. ii-230.

JOSEPH DOUGLASS and DOUGLASS GELFARD; inv. Capt. William Herbert of Charles county. 8 July 1719. ii-234.

ELIZABETH BARNABY and ELIAS SMITH; inv. William Smith of Charles county. 15 July 1719. ii-234.

ROGER and JANE YOPP; inv. Charles Yopp of Charles county. 22 Apr 1719. ii-235.

THOMAS and NATHAN WELLS; inv. Thomas Wells, Sr., of Prince George's county. 2 May 1719. ii-236.

PHILEMON LLOYD, Esq., "brother to the deceased;" inv. Col. Edward Lloyd of Talbot county. 27 Aug 1719. iii-1-40.

ELIZABETH PEARCE and ABIGALL HOLLINS; inv. Jonathan Beck of Cecill county. 8 Dec 1718. iii-40.

JEREMIAH BARRACLOUGH, "son of the deceased;" inv. Jeremiah Barraclough of Q. A. county. 1 June 1717. iii-43.

THOMAS VAUGHOP, GEORGE CLARKE; inv. Peter Watts, St. Mary's county. 14 Aug 1719. iii-44.

FRANCES NICLES, AUDRY TAYLARD; inv. Kenelyne [Kenelm] Cheseldine, St. Mary's county; 15 June 1719. iii-46.

THOMAS BRUKE, Jr., "Uncle LEONARD BROOKE adm."; inv. Richard Brooke, St. Mary's county. 6 Aug 1719, iii-54.

ELIZABETH DAWSON, JOHN HIGINS; inv. Turlogh Higgins of Talbot county. 3 July 1718. iii-60.

DANIEL and JOHN SHERWOOD; inv. Philip Sherwood of Talbot county. 2 Nov 1719. iii-60.

JOHN DIVYOR, JAMES HOGILL; inv. William Divier of Talbot county. 28 Apr. 1718. iii-61.

ROBERT HUTCHINS, brother, and admr.; inv. Francis Hutchins of St. Mary's county; 27 Oct 1719. iii-62.

ROBERT BRYNE; inv. Edward Bryne of Talbot county. 11 Oct 1718. iii-63.

JAMES DICKINSON; inv. Wm. Disckinson [sic] of Talbot county. 29 June 1719. iii-64.

(*To be continued*)

MARRIAGES BY INFERENCE*

(*Continued from March number*)

The following marriages are from the records of NORTHAMPTON county, Virginia. (See NOTE-BOOK for April, 1923.)

JAMES ANCELL and ANN SHEPARD, extx of Thomas. Before 29 Sept 1710. xix-205.

JONATHAN BELL and FRANCES POWELL, wid. of John. Before 30 May 1709. xix-71.

JOHN CLARKE and ANNE SINCOE, wid. of Richard. Before 20 May 1707. (From old loose papers.)

GILES COOK of Geo'town, Kent county, Md. and MARGARET SAVAGE, dau. of Thomas, Gent., and Esther. Before 10 Aug 1756. xix-327.

JAMES COX and ANNE MARY WILKINS, dau. of John. Before 23 Jany 1760. xix-433. [She was then dec'd.]

BENJAMIN DUNTON and MARGARET WIDGEON. See 17 Oct 1715. xix-321.

—— EDMUNDS and SARAH BENSON, wid. of John. Before 6 Feby 1762. xix-506.

PETER NORLY ELLEGOOD, Gent., and MARGARET SAVAGE, dau. of Thomas [She was b. about 1693.] Before 1742. xviii-205.

LITTLETON EYRE and BRIDGET HARMANSON, dau. of Col. George Harmanson. Before 12 June 1759. xix-418.

NEHEMIAH FITCHETT and MARY POWELL, wid of John, late of Savage's Neck, pltr. Before 11 Nov 1747. xviii-368.

ROBERT FOSTER and ANN KNIT[E], wid. of John. Before or about 1713. xix-283.

BENJAMIN GRIFFITH and MARY BACKER [BAKER], wid. of William. 5 July 1709. xix-84.

LEONARD HALL and ANN DUPARKS. Before 29 Sept 1709. xix-96.

PATRICK HARMANSON and ELISHE KENDALL, wid. of George. About 10 July 1758. xix-399.

GAWTON HUNT and ANN PARKS, dau. of Charles. Before 21 Feby 1709-10. xix-143.

THOMAS JAMES and REBECKAH MADDUX, wid. of Thomas. About Apr 1715. xix-317.

JOHN KENDALL, Gent., and ELIZABETH HARMANSON. Before 12 Oct 1754. xix-238.

Lt. Col. WILLIAM KENDALL and (1) —— LARRINGTON, wid. of Mr. Thomas Larrington. (See Kendall's will.) xv-224.

WILLIAM KENDALL and JOAN PARKS, dau. of Charles. Before 21 Feby 1709-10. xix-143.

WILLIAM KENDALL, Sr., and SORROWFULL MARGARET [CUSTIS]. Before or about 27 July 1709. xix-82.

HANCOCK LEE and MARY KENDALL, dau. of Lt. Col. William Kendall. (See Kendall's will.) xv-224.

STEPHEN MAXFIELD prob. m. SUSANNA LITTLETON, widow. Before 1710. xix-222.

GABRIEL x POWELL and a dau. of William Lawrence. Before 11 Oct 1678. (Old loose papers.)

JOSEPH SEWARD, of Surry co., Va., and SUSANNA ALLEN, Sp., of Williamsburg. (Draft of mar. contract.) 4 Dec [year?] (Old loose papers.)

WILLIAM SEGRAVE and ANN SINCOE (b. 1697), dau. of Richard and Ann. Before 20 May 1707. (Old loose papers.)

WILLIAM STARKE and MARY WHITBY, wid. After 13 Feby 1711. (Old loose papers.)

PETER TEMPLE and MARY LUDLOW, dau. of Thomas. Before 18 June 1716. (Old loose papers.)

(To be continued)

NOTES FROM KENTUCKY RECORDS

(Contributed by Miss Hattie M. Scott, of Frankfort, Kentucky)

JEREMIAH KENDALL, b. Caroline county, Virginia; son of Thomas and Nancy Kendall; d. [ab. 185-] aged 76.

BEN LONG; b. Virginia, son of James and Eliz. Long; d. 10 July 1860, aged 70.

JOHN LEWIS, lawyer and teacher; b. Virginia, son of Zachariah and Ann Lewis; d. 15 Aug 1859; aged 75.

MARY R. McDANIEL, widow, born Culpeper county, Virginia; dau. of Samuel and Catherine Wise; d. 10 Oct 1857, aged 69.

ANN MORRIS, dau. of Harry and E. Innis; b. Virginia; d. 13 July 1859, aged 73. [Married John Morris, Oct. 1802.]

NIMROD MASON, b. Virginia; son of Lewis and Agatha Mason; d. 30 Apr 1859, aged 90.

MARY ROBB, b. Hagerstown, Md.; dau. of John and Susan Neat; d. 1856, aged 65.

M. NOEL, son of John and Barbary Noel; b. Virginia; d. 13 Oct 1859, aged 62.

SUSAN PAGE, widow; b. Virginia; dau. of John and Rachel Page; d. Sept 1857, aged 80.

ELIZABETH PERRY, b. Virginia; dau. of Bevin and Susan Abbott; d. June 1857, aged 56.

CHARLES PENN, farmer; b. Maryland, son of Benjamin and Rebecca (Ryan) Penn; d. 24 Dec. 1859, aged 70.

WILLIAM PARKER, b. Virginia; son of John and Mary Parker; d. 18 Oct 1859, aged 93.

MARGARET QUINN, dau. of Thomas L. and Deborah Judge. Born N. J.; d. Nov 1859, aged 34.

CATHERINE RODGERS, b. Richmond, Va.; dau. of —— Austin; d. 12 Jany 1856, aged 76.

MARY O. SULLINGER, widow; b. Virginia; dau. of Alex and Penelope Macey; d. Mch 1852, aged 63.

JAMES SULLIVAN, b. Essex county, Va.; son of James and Elizabeth Sullivan; d. 25 Mch 1855, aged 87.

(To be continued)

COLONIAL FORENAMES

VIRLINDA SANDERS, wf of James Sanders. N-n ix-92, 1660.

VIRLINDA COTTON: Thomas Harmanson, Sr., deposes... that he came to Northampton county, Va., about 46 years before... that there was a young woman named VERLINDA COTTON reputed dau. of Mr. William Cotton, Clarke, and was afterwards reputed to be marryed to Mr. Thomas Burdett then a dweller in Maryland. N-n xvii-366. 10 Feby 1695.

VERLINDA x GOUGH, wf of Francis Gough. Staff., Va. P-179. 10 Feby 1785.

VIRLINDA WILLIAMS, wf of William, Sr. See Fredk, Md. E-831. 25 Aug 1755.

VIRLINDER x MOORE, wf of Augustis Moore. Fayette, Penna. B-136, (Deeds). 28 Apr 1789.

VERLINDER x BEALL. Will. Pr. Geo's, Md. 1-357. 1744-1745.

VERLINDA x BEALL, wf of Thomas Beall of Samuel, Alleg. Co., Md. Hamp. co., W. Va. xi- 8 Feby 1798.

VIOLINDA ATHEY and Dennis Bridges (Married). Ldn co., Va. 1805 or 1806.

WILMOT TILFAITE, a poor woman. N-n xii-243. 1 Mch 1677.

WILLMOT or WILMOT was wf of Richard Hill, Jr., formerly of Accomack, Va.; in 1678, of Somerset co., Md. Acco. vi-127. 11 Nov 1678.

WILMOUTH HARDING, dau. of Henry and Wilmouth; Overwh. Psh Reg., Va. Born 14 Apr 1741.

WILLMOUTH GEORGE, dau. of Nicholas and Margaret; Overwh. Psh Reg., Va. Born 4 Mch 1751.

WILMOUTH WITHERS, d. 21 Aug 1744. (Same record.) [i]-27, 27 July 1752.

WILMOUTH NOLAND, admx of James, exhibits acct. Pr. Wm, Va. Orders.

WILMOUTH HARDING, wf of Henry. Staff. co., Va. P-89. 14 Oct 1755.

WILMOUTH HARDEN, wf of Henry Harden, Sr., Shenan. co., Va. C-439. 1780.

SHIPPED by the Grace of God in good order and well conditioned by Richard Splatt, in and upon the good Ship called the *Friend,* whereof is Master, under God for the present Voyage, William Robinson, and now riding at Anchor in the harbour of Charles City [South Carolina], and by God's grace bound for Barbados, to say Two Cases qts 21 sides Bacon, on my proper account, being marked & numbered as in the Margent, and are to be delivered in the like good order, and well conditioned, at the aforesaid Port of Barbados (the danger of the Seas only accepted) unto Mr. Richard Dearsley, or to his assigns, he or they paying Freight for the said Goods, Thirty Shillings for the whole with Primage and Avarage accustomed. In Witness whereof the Master or Purser of the said Ship hath affirmed to three Bills of Lading, all of this tenor and date, the one of which Bills being accomplished the other to stand void. And so God send the Good Ship to her desired Port in safety. Amen.

Dated in Charles City, the 15 day of April Anno 1723—

In Sids and Contents unknown etc

Wm. Robinson

etc Chas. Hart Scety.

Recorded April 4th, 1724 (Indorsed, vizt April 4th, 1724)

So Carolina (Charleston, S. C., records.)

The County Court Note-Book

An every-other-monthly devoted to abstracts from County Court and other records, prior to 1800, and with a department of notes and queries.

MILNOR LJUNGSTEDT, Editor and Publisher. Bethesda, Route 1, Maryland.

Published six times a year. Subscription, two dollars a year, in advance; must begin with the year. *Renewals one dollar and a half.* **Advertising rates moderate.**

VOL. III MAY, 1924 NO. 3

AS I REMEMBER

Where did the rhythm of life swing more tunefully than off on the plantation on the Chattahoochee? The odor of pine and the slippery walk on pine needles exhilarated me. The lady of the manor, my aunt, never lost her dignity as I romped about her, exuberant with freedom and with the intoxication of the surroundings.

Columbus, Georgia, the early home, was soon to be a thing of the past, hence the plantation life. I came into the STEWART home while it was yet in Columbus, so, fortunately, I have the precious recollection of life there, also.

The picture of the plantation life which appeals most to me is that of dear old Aunt Rhoda, the aristocratic type of the long gone but not forgotten ancient slave. I was an event in her life—no one accorded me quite so much of courtly respect as she did. The other negroes from the "Quarter," with few exceptions, were of a younger generation, and even then had lost some of that distinction of the high bred "mammies," for freedom had gotten into their bones, but they were respectful and affectionate. To Aunt Rhoda I was a kind of a fairy princess; she wanted to serve and I enjoyed being served. I took so naturally to it that I smile now as I recall my childish impressions; I sat on a high chair, swinging my feet, while Aunt Rhoda, spick and span, in calico and apron, remained standing before me, questioning my wishes, listening to my experiences in the big city. I felt more and more important as I found that I had a listener whom I could astound.

Aunt Rhoda had been a slave and a devoted one. Grandfather had built for her and her son a double log cabin, consisting of two rooms, separated by a wide passageway, open at either end. A door from each room opened into this passageway. In this entrance way the water bucket, with its shining brass hoops, was always full of cold, fresh well water; a gourd for a dipper hung nearby—the sweetest and cleanest of dippers.

Aunt Rhoda's bedroom had a large open fireplace in which she cooked for me, in the hot ashes, sweet potatoes wrapped in wet brown paper, or eggs in the same way, and made me "Johnny cake." Jelly made of the wild grapes, spread on "Johnny cake," was the dessert; after that a drink from Aunt Rhoda's gourd. I admired as high decoration the fireplace crane and the iron kettle which hung from it, and after the meal, stood with folded hands and looked around the room at the walls covered with pictures cut from papers and magazines. Now and then a fancy colored one met my approval; then only was my temperamental side touched.

I loved to linger near "The Quarters," where I often went with the kind aunt, always ready to be pulled in any direction by me. At night, the quilts in the making were hung in a frame suspended from the ceiling. After the day's work was done, the darkies gathered for a neighborly visit, the women sitting around the frame to quilt, and the men standing behind the women, singing the melodious plantation songs. What is work or money in so sequestered a life?

Supper, with the negroes, meant Johnny cake and bacon . . . and the appetizing odor sent my hungry feet prancing back to the house, where, however, old Aunt Rena, also a former slave, fed us with hot rolls, fine hominy, and a gloriously baked ham, with the best coffee in the world, served in the daintiest of cups, at the shocking hour of eight, for no one was in a hurry for meals or bed. After supper we all joined for a grand peeling of sugar cane, around a roaring fire, such as pine can make . . . and there the family sat and talked the simplest, sometimes wierdest talk, no one ever aggressive or argumentative.

Our nearest neighbor was three miles away, but at night no one cared to visit. The roads were sandy, dark, and lonesome. The nearest little village, quaint and quiet, was seven miles away, and no "movies," telephones, or radios to make time fly.

Not far from our home was the negro church, and when baptizing time came (the nearby stream was dammed for the purpose), the excitement became intense. It took stalwart darkies to hold the ebony maids who were to be plunged in the pool. I always did think it was the cold water, more than religion, which caused the hysterical state. After "Religion," one had to keep out of the path, for if white or colored stood in the way, the strong arms of the converted would embrace and carry one 'round and 'round in one mad whirl. "Getting Religion" was a c-u-r-i-o-u-s thing. I dodged many a time, and my eyes, I know, grew big with fear, while I peeped from a nearby window or door.

There were other meetings which brought entertainment; the barbecue a year after the burial of a friend or one of their kin; marriages . . . for some reason I missed one of these, perhaps none took place while I was about.

Farewell, sweet childhood days! The plantation family lie in the old burial plot, now made modern by progressives . . . it hurts to see the buried Past molested . . . When I saw that change I bowed my head and passed on by . . . after all, resignation is the philosophy of life.

P. S. C.

"Dear Mrs. Lj——:

"How kind of you to let me talk out the pent-up sentiments that germinated in youth. Something within me responded to my surroundings. Today I regard myself as fortunate to have been a part of the fleeting old South..."

This note explains why Mrs. Pauline Stewart Crosley has written for the Editor, at the latter's request, in a friendly and unstudied way, an article on Georgia plantation life as a child remembers it, which the Editor gladly presents in place of an editorial.

The EDITOR is very pleased to say that upon her list of subscribers she now has the BOSTON ATHENAEUM, the STATE LAND OFFICE of MARYLAND, and the STATE LIBRARY of NORTH CAROLINA.

Many years ago quite a small little lad applied to the choir-master of an historic church to have his voice tried. He was accepted, and in three weeks was a full-fledged chorister. His pay was seventy-five cents a week. As he laid the first pay envelope in the family hand, beaming with delighted pride he exclaimed, *"There, D——, isn't that worth while?"*

When the Editor *brashly* promised that the "head rights" from "old volume five," Virginia State Land Office, would be easy reading, she had in mind the printed form they are now assuming in the NOTE-BOOK. The reading of the original is quite another matter. The Editor herself did not do this copying, but she is perfectly familiar with the script of the record and has given her best judgment as to some of the entries. However, as a sort of satisfaction to herself and the copyist she has obtained permission to present in fac-simile some of the more curious names. These fac-similes will appear in a later issue. The Editor is not above adding, that if one knows the name, *sometimes* it is easy to recognize. If an apology be needed for any of the readings, it may be added that when an English Clerk of the Court undertook to turn an Irish name into English script, a certain latitude may be allowed him as well as the later reader. Some of these immigrants could not speak English. (See records of Northampton county, Virginia... "of two Irishmen one is noted as being able to speak English.")

OCCASIONAL

The Sheriff of P——m county talking in the confidence of the Clerk's Office: *"Me and him just meets and parts. He done one of the most presumptionest things ever was."*

The Quakers inform the Court that they Constantly meet at their meeting-house built for that use neare Gilford... and on Thursday either at the house of Sarah Coe, Widow, or at the house of Georg Johnson, dec., and our monthly and quarterlie meteings at Geo. Johnson's house. JOHN DRUMMOND signs. Acco., Va. ix-242. 22 June 1692.

Inventory of Capt. ROBT PITTS includes: 1 Book called The Waggoner, being bothe old and muck broke; also six *occany* [alchemy?] spoones. There is also an account of Porke carried to Barbadoes for severall persons. 8 Oct 1668. See Acco., Va., iv-170. Court 16 Dec 1672.

COURT RECORDS: Capt MASON, a justice, and Major WASHINGTON and Mr. HUTT to "take notice" of them. Wmld, Va. iii-16. 28 Oct 1663.

FIFTY DOLLARS REWARD and no questions asked, will be paid for the contents of a khaki-covered mailing case, mislaid, lost, or stolen, at Trenton, S. C., or between Trenton and Columbia, S. C., while in transit to Abbeville, S. C., via the Southern Railroad, in care of the Southeastern Express Company. EDITOR.

A criticism received by the Editor from a Southern friend concerned her statements as to the North Carolina records. The EDITOR thinks it only just to say, having in mind her paragraph in the MARCH issue, which was misunderstood, that she visited only six of the older North Carolina counties; that of these there were two at least in which the conditions could not be said by anyone to be conducive to the preservation of valuable papers. The Editor has no wish to go into details but will add that there are counties in Georgia, and at least one county in South Carolina, and counties in Virginia where the records are rapidly being destroyed by unsuitable housing and careless handling. All such records should be removed to a *suitable* fireproof State repository.

That *all* central repositories are better than any county, cannot be said.

Another objection to centralization (which centralization the Editor's friendly critic was not impressed by) is the chance there is for favoritism and discrimination. It is more than irritating to have records of a very wide interest given by will or otherwise to societies or libraries where they are available only to the select among the members.

As to preservation, it may be said, on the whole, to be six of one and half a dozen of the other. But certainly the Historical Commission of North Carolina is doing fine work. Other Southern States are also making good, and if their respective Legislatures could be convinced that an old will book may be as valuable as the Acts of a session... and may have downright good history in it, as well as titles to swamp lands... well... if they just could!

In connection with the above, the article which Miss BLAIR, of the Department of Archives and History of Georgia, has been good enough to write for the NOTE-BOOK, will be found of interest.

DEPARTMENT OF ARCHIVES AND HISTORY OF THE STATE OF GEORGIA

The law creating the Department of Archives and History for the State of Georgia went into effect January 1, 1919, and there was immediately turned over to the State Historian, whose office had been provided for in the same bill, some 6,000 bound manuscript volumes and 250,000 loose papers. These records, dating from 1732, relate to every phase of the State's history, but owing to the several changes in the seat of government, to the fact that the Capital was twice surrendered to hostile military forces, and to the long years of neglect, many valuable documents are missing. The greater part of the material originated in two offices—the office of the Secretary of State and the Executive Office, though the department is the depository of all non-current records of the various state-house offices.

Among the more important of the book series are Conveyances of Property, 1751-1802; Mortgages, 1755-1822; Wills, 1754-1777; Journals of the House of Representatives, 1781-1861; Journals of the Upper House of Assembly, 1765-1772; Journals of the Executive Council, 1777-1789; Minutes of the Executive Department, 1790-1924; Governor's Letter Books, 1786-1897; Appointments of Civil Officers, 1754-1827. Unique single volumes are Registrations of Cattle Brands, 1755-1793, and the General Account of All Monies and Effects Received and Expended by the Trustees of the Colony of Georgia in America, 1732-1854. This last mentioned book is a work of art, being the original record kept by the Secretary of the Board of Trustees, Harman Verelst, who was an artist and engraver, and the painter of the portrait of Tomochichi, the old Indian Mico accompanying General Oglethorpe to England on his first return from the infant Colony. Among the loose papers those claiming first attention, perhaps, are the certificates of service issued the soldiers of the Revolution by their commanding officers in order that the men might receive from the State Government the bounty land grants since payment in currency was not possible.

In addition to the sorting, cataloging, and arranging of all materials, the work of the Department includes the following compilations: Roster of the Revolution; of the War of 1812; of the General Assembly, 1777-1924; judges and solicitors of all Courts from time of creation to present; state-house officials, 1777-1924; heads of the various state institutions from establishment to date; U. S. Senators and Members of Congress, 1789-1924; civil service records (all state and Federal offices) for all Georgians, 1743-1924; World War casualties; an index to the Colonial will books; et cetera; several of which have been published, either as separate records or as a part of the 1923 edition of the State's Official and Statistical Register, which is a biennial publication of the Department.

RUTH BLAIR, Secretary.

A CUSTIS LINE?

From Boogher's Gleanings, p. 329. A Bible Record.

JOHN CUSTIS m. Anne Kendall, 5 Mch 1732; son JOHN, b. 7 July 1734; dau. Mary-Brown, b. 9 Jany 1736; dau. Peggy, b. 16 July 1738;

JOHN CUSTIS d. 27 Dec 1738; Hannah Custis, b. 25 July 1740; d. 31 Aug 1740; JOHN CUSTIS, b. 10 Apr 1743; Hannah Custis, b. 19 Mch 1745; d. 27 Jany 1751;

Col. JOHN CUSTIS d. 1 Dec 1746, age 40;

JOHN CUSTIS, 2d of name and 3d son of above JOHN, dec'd, d. 24 Aug 1747.

JOHN THOMPKINS m. ANNE CUSTIS, 25 Feby 1747.

* * * * * * *

From the Records of Northampton county, Virginia. (Vol. xviii-371, 372.)

Bond of JOHN TOMPKINS, 25 Feby 1747.

WHEREAS a marriage is intended between JOHN TOMPKINS and ANN CUSTIS, *widow of*... JOHN CUSTIS, dec'd, and JOHN CUSTIS dec'd, by will directed that should his widow marry she is to give bond to keep the houses and plantations at Hungars in good repair... &c., &c.

THE AGES OF SOME FREDERICK COUNTY (MARYLAND) ORPHANS

(Continued from March number)

SAMUEL NASH, of age in Aug 1777.

MARY NORRIS, of age in Feby 1774.

CORNELIUS NORNS[?], of age in Mch 1773.

SAML NORNS[?], of age in Mch 1775.

NEAL NORNS or MORNS, of age in Oct 1779. [These names very uncertain.]

ISAAC PRESTON, of age in 1758.

MARY PRICE, of age in 1767.

ELIAS PEARCE, of age in Mch 1766.

JACOTT PETT, of age in Oct 1770.

WILLIAM PARKS, of age in Nov 1775.

JOHN REESLING, of age in 1754.

JOSEPH ROBERTS, of age in 1761.

WILLIAM ROBERT, of age in 1764.

MARGARET RIDDLE, of age in 1756.

JOHN ROBERTS, of age in 1758.

ELEANOR RYAN, of age in 1765.

RICHARD RHODDY, of age in 1777.

ISAAC RUE, of age in Nov 1771.

FRANCIS ROSE, of age in Dec 1775.

MOSES SCAGGS, of age in 1769.

REBECCA SMITH, of age in Feby 1764.

ADAM STULL, of age Christmas, 1766.

CATHERINE SINCLER, of age in Mch 1771.

SAMUEL SMITH, of age Christmas, 1768.

ADAM STROUP, of age in July 1772.

CHRIS. SPECK, of age in Nov 1771.

CHRISTIANA SHAVER, of age in Nov 1778.

JACOB SHOAT, of age in Mch 1780.

HERBERT SHOEMAKER, of age 20 July 1780.

GEORGE SUPPERT[?], of age 1 Mch 1777.
ELVIN SPRIGG, of age in May 1778.

Note: An error has been made in copying the list of these orphans, an error made by the Editor in copying her own notes. The date given in each and every case is that when the orphan *would be of age*...and *not* the date of the age as given. For example: Elvin Sprigg was fourteen when brought before the Court. He was of age, if living, in May 1778, having been born, therefore, in May 1757. The list was rather difficult to understand as to dates, but appears to have been made out in the early part of 1763.

The PRESBYTERY of HANOVER...have agreed to establish...a public Academy near Timber Ridge Meeting House in Augusta County [Virginia], Mr. William Graham to be the Rector. The trustees are Rev. John Brown, James Waddell, Charles Cummins, William Irwin and the Rector; with General Andrew Lewis, Col. William Flemming, Mr. Thomas Stewart, Mr. John Gratten, Mr. Samuel Lyle, Col. William Preston, Col. William Christian, Mr. Sampson Matthews, Col. John Bowyer, Maj'r Samuel McDowell, Cap. Alexander Stewart, Cap. William McKee, Mr. John Houston, Cap. Charles Campbell, Cap. George Maffett, Mr. William McPheeters, Mr. William Ward, and Cap. John Lewis at the Warm Springs. 8 Sept 1776. Draper Mss. 7ZZ-7.

NOTES AND QUERIES

JAMES BRIDGER, western explorer: Born in Richmond, Va., 1804; was in Missouri in 1820. Who were his parents and where were they from? M. M. H. V.

WHITLEY: Were Paul, Solomon and Jonathan Whitley, of Rockbridge county, Va., brothers? Parents' names desired. Paul's will in Botetourt county, Va., mentions N. C. land. Evidence desired of removal of his son Thomas from N. C. or Va. to St. Louis, where he died, 1820.

HILL: Robert Hill, b. 1764, Frederick county, Md., there m. (1) Elinor Highfield in 1786; (2) Amelia Fitzgerald in 1790. Names of their parents desired.

TAYLOR: Who were parents of Elizabeth Taylor (b. 1759, St. Mary's county, Md.) and her brother, Rev. Caleb Jarvis Taylor, who about 1790 removed to Mason county, Ky.

CHISHOLM or CHISUM: Names desired of chn of John Chisum of Amelia and Halifax counties, Va., and his wife, Elinor Gillington (or Gillentine), dau. of Nicholas of Amelia. John, Obadiah and Elijah are believed to have been sons. Further information of both Chisum or Chisholm and Gillentine. E. T. C. N. Y.

EWING: Malinda Ewing (wf of Robert) of middle Tennessee, first of Virginia; was a cousin of Finas Ewing, one of the founders of Cumberland Presbyterian Church; had half-brothers John, Rheuben, James. James Ewing died in the Alamo, San Antonio, Texas. Who were the parents of Malinda Ewing? Mrs. C. A. K. K.

RICHARD WRIGHT m. Elizabeth, dau. of William and Frances Wigginton, of Westmoreland county, Va., would be glad to hear from WRIGHT or WIGGINTON families interested.
Jas. W. Wigginton, 432 F st., San Diego, Cal.

ROBERTSON or ROBINSON: Ancestry wanted of Philip Robertson who m. a Miss Proctor. One dau. Matilda m. Jas. Twyman, Anderson county, Ky. J. W. W. C.

HENRY TOWLES m. Ann Stockley, Accomack, Va., about 1668-9. Record of this marriage desired, also information as to Ann's parents. Was her father Francis or John? M. T. V.

THOMAS SCAG was a Virginia immigrant, 1654. Information concerning him very much desired.

SKAGS-MOREDOCK; James(?) Skaggs m. ...Moredock, *circa* 1787; had sons named James, Abraham, Gideon and dau. who m. Hankins. Further information desired.

MYERS: (German settler in Maryland, 1760). Sons Esquire Lawrence, Phillip, Henry, Michael. Full information desired as to HENRY and MICHAEL...also as to their parents, the settlers. H. V. C. T.

TWENTY-FIVE DOLLARS will be paid for detailed information as to Capt. JOHN WADE, of Chester or Marcus Hook, Penna. His parents, name of his wife, his children, date of his death, &c., &c. M. L. M.

GENERAL INFORMATION

Searchers going to Charleston, S. C., will find that a very comfortable and economical way to live there for a short time, at least, is to take a room in one of the old houses and board at a cafeteria. Mrs. McKinley, 62 Society street, can take care of one or two ladies, and the cafeteria is in the next block. Both are within walking distance of the "Fire-Proof Building" and of the old churches.

The YARBOROUGH, in Raleigh, is good, reasonably priced, and near the Historical Commission. The Red Cross has a very good cafeteria near by, though it is higher priced than other similar places.

Columbia, S. C., has several excellent cafeterias and small cafes. The Y. W. C. A. has a cafeteria and, the Editor thinks, rooms. It is within walking distance of the Historical Commission (in the Capitol), but not very near.

FIFTY DOLLARS REWARD!
FIFTY DOLLARS REWARD!

See page 21

PUBLICATIONS, ETC., OF VALUE TO HISTORIANS AND GENEALOGISTS

The GENERAL INDEX of WILLS of ST. MARYS COUNTY, MARYLAND, compiled by Mrs. George W. Hodges, has been published by the CARTER BRAXTON CHAPTER, D. A. R., also

The GENERAL INDEX of WILLS of ANNE ARUNDEL COUNTY, MARYLAND. A limited number only will be sold. Price $12.50. For information as to both volumes address Mrs. LETITIA P. WILSON, Regent, 3905 Gwynn Oak Avenue, Baltimore, Md.

Reasonable price will be paid for numbers 1, 2, 3, and 5, COUNTY COURT NOTE-BOOK, 1921-1922. Address Editor.

Columbian Printing Co., Inc., Washington, D. C.

The

County Court Note-Book

A Little Bulletin of History and Genealogy

Vol. III | July, 1924 | No. 4

SHIPS IN PORT

(*Fourth instalment*)

Ship or pinke of Maryland, the *Grace*. N-n, Va., vii-55. 1 June 1657.

The *Gordon*, a snow; Daniel Allan, master. Henrico, Va., 1748.

Ship the *Goodwill*, of Bristoll; Mr. Peter Wraxall, commander. N-n, Va. x-22. 1665.

Ship *Good Speed;* mentioned by Scharf in his History of Maryland as bringing rebel prisoners, 18 Oct 1716.

The *Golden Faulkon*, Capt. Hunter; she seems to have belonged to Col. Edmund Scarburgh, as the Court orders her delivery to him. N-n, Va., viii-82. 1660. (Also 1662, viii-128.)

The *Gabriell & Ellinor;* Mr. Edward Moore, *maister;* Timothy Rose, part owner. N-n, Va., ii-224. 24 Feby 1642. Also ii-229, 235.

"Shipp'd by the Grace of God in good Order and well Condition'd, by Mr. Jno. Person in and upon the good ship called the *Hannah*, whereof is Master, under God, for this present Voyage, Samll Barnes..." [Barnes signs.] I. W., Va., viiiD-611. 28 Apr 1741.

Shipp *Harrison*, Capt. Thos. Posford. I. W., Va. ii-530. 1710-11.

Ship *Happy Adventure;* Acco., Va., i-58. 16 Feby 1663.

Sloop *Henry;* Samuel Wintworth, master (his wife was probably Mary Calcoat.) I. W., Va. viiiD-1739.

The *Henery & Ann*, of Manokin, Md. John Harrison, master. Acco., Va. ix-225. 1691.

The *Hobbyhorse*. N-n, Va. iv-162, 28 Feby 1652. Also iv-164.

The *Honnybarrell;* Jacob Derrickson, late master; skipper Abraham Johnson, of Graft, in Holland. N-n, Va. iv-121. 25 May 1652.

Ship *Hope als Hopewell;* N-n, Va. v-132. 30 Jany 1654.

Ketch *Hopewell*, of Boston in New England; Will: Chichester, master. L. Norf. Va. 1655.

Ship *The Hope of Lancaster;* Robert Pearson, master. Acco, Va. 1681 and 1683.

Ship *Hopeful Adventure;* Capt. Richard Husband, commdr; Wm. Earle, quartermaster. N-n, Va. iv-126. 16 Oct 1652. v-148. 8 June 1655. v-149. 28 May 1655. Also 13 June.

Ship *Humphra & Elizabeth;* Capt. Robt Fox, commdr. I. W., Va. iii-5. 18 Feby 1663-4.

Ship *Isaiah & Benjamin*. Rappa., Va. 1670.

The *James & Ann of London;* Thomas Fry, commdr. N-n, Va. xviii-191. 28 Mch 1704.

The *James & John*[?]; Capt. John Warner. L. Norf., Va. D-299. 4 Apr 1661.

Sloop *James & John;* owned by John White. E. C. co., Va. 1750.

The *James;* Capt. John Tully, master. N-n, Va. 29 June 1672. x-142.

The *Jamaica Mcht;* John Blake, commdr, Va. St. Pa. i-141. 1710.

Ship *John*, of Topsham; John Shepheard, master. N-n, Va. xv-442. 29 July 1689.

The *John & Barbara;* [William Barker, master?] L. Norf., Va. B-170. 1636.

The *Jono. & Mary;* Danll of St. Thomas Jenifer, master. P. R. O. 33-xix. 1702.

MARRIAGES BY INFERENCE*

(*Continued from May number*)

The following are from the records of ACCOMACK county, Virginia. For explanation of the formation of this county, see NOTE-BOOK for APRIL, 1923.

JOHN ARLENTON and CHARITY CHANDLER, dau. of John. Before 1728. xvi-356.

MASON ABBOTT and ELIZABETH PARREMORE, sister of John and Thomas Parremore. See deed 2 May 1721. xvi-176.

WILLIAM ANDREWS, Gent. and MARY GORE, widow of Daniel. Before or about 28 Aug 1753. Deeds ii-454.

JOHN ABBOT, Jr., and ANNE MASON, sole heir of Robert, dec'd. [Her mother was TEMPERANCE.] Before 18 Dec 1693. xi-38. (See also ix-199. 2 June 1719.)

NATHANIEL BRADFORD and ALICE SMITH, dau. of Richard. See deed 2 Mch 1724. xvi-231. (A bond of Nathaniel Bradford, Sr., to give to his son "my heire and the heire of the sd Smith" 800 acres, in consideration of the marriage will be found i-77. 18 Oct 1664.)

NATHANIEL BRADFORD and ELIZABETH [PARKER], dau. of George. Before 4 Mch 1711. xiv-36. (See also xvi-218, xiv-33, xiv-61.)

THOMAS BLAIR and ANNE McKEMIE, dau. of Francis. Before 3 Oct 1721. xiv-287.

EDMUND BAYLY and TABITHA SCARBURGH, wid. of JOHN. See 26 Dec 1749. Deeds ii-236-7.

EDMUND BAYLY and MARY BAYLY, wid. of Charles. Before 6 Feby 1717-18. xvi-43.

THOMAS BAYLY and ANNE DRUMMOND, dau. of Richard. Before 25 Apr 1764. Diii-295.
CHARLES BAYLY or BAILY and MARY SCARBOROW, dau. of Charles, Esq. Before 7 July 1716. xvi-22.
CHARLES BAYLY and ANNE SIMPSON, dau. of John. Before or about 15 Feby 1763. Diii-224.
RICHARD BAYLY and MARY JONES, sister of Richard Jones, Before 16 Jany 1664. ii-5.
RICHARD BAILEY, Jr., Gent., and URSILLIA [sic] SCARBURGH, dau. of Edmund, of Occahannock, Gent. About? 14 Sept 1693. xi-22.
THOMAS BUD[?] and JOANE BRADFORD, wid. of Nathaniel. Before 17 Sept 1691. x-42.
THOMAS BUDD and ANNA DANELA MIDDLETON, dau. of Thomas. Before 1707. xi-442. The name or names Anna Danela will be found spelled in various ways. The form here given appears to have been intended.
WILLIAM BARNES and ELIZABETH LEATHERBURY, wid. of Charles. Before 21 Mch 1693. x-125.
WILLIAM BARNS and SUSANNA PARKER, dau. of Sacker Parker. Before 3 July 1738. ix-107.
JOHN BALDWIN and PATIENCE MERCY, extx of William. Before 27 May 1755. xxvW-282.
Mr. JEARVIS BAGALE and BRIDGET SAVAGE, wid. of Griffith. 13 Jany 1684. (Probably before this date?) ix-56.
JOHN BOWEN, Wor. Co., and SARAH FOOKS. Before 2 Oct 1761. Diii-162.
EDWARD BELL and MARY BLOCKSON, wid. of Nicholas. Before 5 Apr 1720. xvi-104.
NICHOLAS BOOT and ANNE HACK, wid. of Dr. George Hack. Before 6 Mch 1667. iii-30.
FRANCIS BENSTON and ANN SMITH, wid. of Thomas. Before 2 Aug 1710. xiv-8.
NICHOLAS BLOXSOM and MARY WATSON, whose mother was ELIZABETH... See 5 Apr 1720. xvi-104.
ABRAHAM BANCKS probably m. SARAH NIBLET, See record 16 Mch 1699. xi-253.
GEORGE CORBIN and LOVE WARD, dau. of THOMAS Ward. See 19 Nov 1759. Diii-97.

(To be continued)

MARYLAND'S NEXT OF KIN*

(Continued from May number)

JAMES and ELIZABETH DOBSON; inv. Edward Pinders of Talbot cty. 11 Feby 1718. iii-69.
THOMAS and JAMES HOPKINS; inv. Robert Hopkins of Talbot cty. 2 July 1718. iii-70.
SAMUEL and EDWARD NEAL; inv. Jonathan Neal of Talbot cty. 6 June 1719. iii-73.
HENRY MUNK and ONER[?] MUNK; inv. John Maden of Kent cty; 4 Sept 1719. iii-75.

JOSEPH HARDEN; inv. John Love of Talbot cty. 24 Mch 1718. iii-77.
EDWARD HARDING and WALTER JENKINS; inv. Thomas Jenkins of Talbot cty. 12 Aug 1719. iii-78.
SOLOMON CLAYTON and WILLIAM FINNEY; inv. of Mary Smithson, "Gentlewoman," of Talbot cty. 25 May 1719. iii-81.
ELIZABETH MEARS, "my mother;" inv. Richard Webb of Talbot cty. 28 Sept 1719. iii-84.
GEORGE DENT and DOUGLAS GIFFERD; inv. of Sarah Harbert of Charles cty. 13 Nov 1719. iii-97-178.
MARY PLOOMER [PLUMMER?]; inv. Thomas Bruff of Talbot cty. 9 June 1718. iii-98.
MATHEW BREEDING; inv. Isabella Dryden of Charles cty. 6 July 1719. iii-101.
JOHN & DANIEL BOULTON; inv. Christopher Gould of Queen Anne's cty. 1 Apr 1719. iii-102.
THOMAS ELDERINGTON and ALICE COMETON[?]; inv. Newton Barber of Q. A. cty. 18 May 1719. iii-104.
PRISCILLA FREEBORN and ANNE THOMAS; inv. Richard Freeborn of Baltimore cty. 18 May 1719. iii-106.
RICHARD & THOMAS DORNELE [DARNEILLE?] inv. John Bennand of "Tuckhoe" Q. A. cty. 18 Apr 1719. iii-107.
THOMAS HYNSON WRIGHT and SOLOMON WRIGHT; inv. Nathaniel Wright, Q. A. cty. 6 Aug 1719. iii-109.
THOMAS MOUNSEER; inv. William Mounseer of Q. A. cty. 3 June 1719. iii-115.
ROBERT KING; inv. Rev. John Henry of Som. cty. 6 Sept 1718. iii-116.
RICHARD THOMPSON; inv. John Thompson of Cecill cty. 25 July 1719. iii-123.
ANNE SMITH and HENRY ATWOOD; inv. William Smith of A. A. Cty. 21 July 1719. iii-128.
WILLIAM BESWICK; inv. Thomas Beswick of Talbot cty. 26 Mch 1716. iii-130.
RICHARD BENNETT; inv. William Sweatman of Q. A. cty. 30 Oct 1719. iii-141.
WILLIAM DARE; inv. William Dare, Sr., of Cecill cty. 30 Oct 1719. iii-146.
ROBERT WILSON and HANNAH MALOYE[?]; inv. William Wilson of Kent Island, Q. A. cty. 5 Sept 1719. iii-150.

(To be continued)

KING GEORGE COUNTY, VIRGINIA, PROBATES AND ADMINISTRATIONS

There is no will record in King George county prior to 1751. The previous volume or volumes are missing. But the ORDER BOOKS are complete for the period covered by the lost will records, and the following abstracts are made from those volumes. What is given in this issue is from the second volume of ORDERS. The abstracts will be continued until the entire period is covered.

WILLIAM SMITH; L. a. to Margery Smith, his widow. Wm. Rowley, Jr., and John Grant, sec. ii-248. 3 Apr 1741.
JAMES BROWN; L. a. to Francis Thornton. Harry Turner, sec. Jeremiah Brown, heir-at-law. ii-248. 3 Apr 1741.

GEORGE LEWIS; George Pain presents petn praying admn on Lewis' estate. ii-265. 2 Oct 1741.

ROWLAND THORNTON, Gent.; will presented by Francis Thornton, one of his executors. Proved by John Moore and William Mackay. ii-269. 5 Mch 1741.

WILLIAM THACHER; L. a. to Elizabeth Thacher. Samuel Reid, sec. ii-269. 5 Mch 1741.

JOSEPH CROUCH; L. a. to Widow Crouch. Richard Elkins, sec. ii-269. 5 Mch 1741.

GEORGE KEEVEY; L. a. to Richard Keevey. Henry Drake, sec. ii-270. 5 Mch 1741.

THOMAS GREENSTREET; will presented by Mary Greenstreet, extx. Proved by Daniel White, Jr., Thomas White and Thomas Theed. ii-271. 2 Apr 1742.

GEORGE LEWIS; L. a. to George Paine. John White, sec. 2 Apr 1742. ii-271.

THOMAS AMMON; L. a. to Sarah Ammon; Henry Drake and Thomas Thompson, sec. 7 May 1742. ii-283.

GEORGE WILKINSON; L. a. to Stephen Bowen; James Strother, sec. 5 Nov 1742. ii-309.

WILLIAM ROBINSON, Gent., his will presented by Maxmilian Robinson, Gent., his extr; proved by John Minton and Joseph Minton. 3 Dec 1742. ii-312.

WILLIAM THORNTON, Gent. Will presented by Francis Thornton and William Thornton, his extrs; proved by Elias Sharp and John Hobby[?]. 4 Mch 1742. ii-319.

ROBERT MONGUMRAY [sic]; L. a. to Thomas Turner; Harry Turner, sec. 4 Mch 1742. ii-319.

BENJAMIN PALMER; L. a. to Margaret Palmer; James Grant, sec. 4 Mch 1742. ii-320.

AUGUSTINE WASHINGTON; will presented by Lawrence Washington one of the extrs; proved by Anthony Strother, James Thompson, Thomas Turner; Jonathan Sydenham, sec. 6 May 1743. ii-330.

JOHN KENYON; his will presented by Jane and Abraham Kenyon, extrs; proved by James Somervell and William Clark. 6 May 1743. ii-330. John Taylor; William Clark sec. for extrs.

WILLIAM TAYLOR; L. a. to Elizabeth Taylor; Anthony Strother, sec. 6 May 1743. ii-330.

(*To be continued*)

VIRGINIA IMMIGRANTS

From "Old Volume 5," State Land Office

GEORGE ABBOT, Gent., Nansemond county, 1656.

Head rights: Ann Warburton, William Adams, Francis Croffa, Thomas Perry, Robert Bayly, John Jones, Tho. Dowde, John Bowinge, John, an Irishman, Margaret, an Irish woman ("woeman"), Robert Murry, Tho. Ingan, Eliz: his wife, Wm. Moore and one negro.

Lt. Coll. ROBERT ABRALL, New Kent county, [Date not given.]

Head rights: James Tyler, Mary Rodes, Davies Otley, Roger Patter, Robert Mallett. Robert Wade, Eliza: Ware, Tho. Parker, Jane Roper, Jacob Kickerly, Georg Mosse, Tho. Dissey, Jane Evans, John O'Kelly, Edward Cooke, Edmond Thacker, Jenkin Yearkey, Tho. Cocny[?].

ANTHONY ARNELL, New Kent county, 1657.

Head rights: John Roberts, Mary Evans, Tho. Kirby, John Dibbin, Wm. Tucker, Mary Raffey [or Rassey], John Hohne, Tho. Daniell, Rich. Budworll, Wm. Adiggin[?].

WILLIAM ALLEN, New Kent county, 1657.

Head rights: Georg Moore, Tho. Smith, Wm. Cox, Darey Murley, Horatio Vere.

THOMAS BEST & CHRISTOPHER ASHLY, Nansemond county, 1656.

Head rights: Jane Gittins, Wm. Grant.

ROBERT BAYLY, Northampton county, 1655.

Head rights: Richard Perry, Jacobin Trenis, Wm. Trenis, Lydia Easterfeild.

THOMAS BUSBIE, Surry county, 1656.

Head rights: Peeter Spicer, Eliza: Paine, Wm. Gray, Jane Barker, Anth. Hulburt, THOMAS BUSBY, Rich: Ballard, Cicily More.

JNO: BROMFIELD, James City county, 1656.

Head rights: Abraham Sinckler [St. Clair], Wm. Mosse, Sarah Allyson, Rebecca Bradshew, Francis Chambers, Sarah Allyson, Morgan Williams, Rob. Paddison, Mathew Burrowes, Margaret Hilton.

THOMAS BELL, *Gloster* county, 1656.

Head rights: Wm. Watts.

JNO. BILLIOTT, Northampton county, 1656.

Head rights: An Smith, Knora Nimcahoe [?], Derreman Machoone, Elizabeth Winn, Susuan Dowdridge, Alice Deane, Robert Bright, Mary Fawne, Charity Jenkins, Morrice Whitsorrell, Sarah Greene, Jno. Twoale, Dennis Modekann[?], Edmd. Brockhum, Mary Liefford, Joane Newes, Mary Joanes, Ann Winn, Xph. Cox, Ann Benhowe [Benbow?]

Mr. MARTIN BAKER, New Kent county, 1656.

Head rights: Robert West, William West, Mary West, Henry West, John Sill, Geo. Fisher, Adam Miles, Margarett Turner, Nicholas Porter, Adam Miles, John Midleton, Tho: Jackson, Tho. Stacy, Margaret Turner, John Vaultier, Mathew Wilson, Elizabeth Porter, David Ritch, Jno. Smith, Robert Woodby, Nich. Porter, James Turner, Wm. Sansom.

RICHARD BARNEHOUSE, Gent., James City county, 1656.

Head rights: Eliz: Bakone, Jno. Spencer, Edwd. Shinger, Tho. Jenkins, Robert Shoare, Wm. Squire, Hugh Lowell.

THO: BINNS, Surry county, (date not given).

Head rights: Phillip Weyfield, Judith Ballard, Peeter Knowles, Wm. Pryde, Wm. Aman, Rebecca Bullifant, Wm. Sincklar.

HENRY BERRY, Lancaster county, 1656.

Head rights: Jno. Humphreys, Peeter Hamlin, Ralph Perry.

Mr. WM. BLACKEY, New Kent county, 1656.

Head rights: Joseph Stowell, Poare [Peare?] Leasure, Jno. Lace [Lacey], Michaell Lovett, Abra: Griffton, Margarett Colbert, Jno. Proude, Edmund Machin, Jno. Dringe, Ro. Tard, Henry Prother, James Tox, Tho. Abbott, Edward Goodson, Henry Wassell, Wm. French, Rich. Carrott, Jno. Lavington, Eliz: Stokes.

(*To be continued*)

The County Court Note-Book

An every-other-monthly devoted to abstracts from County Court and other records, prior to 1800, and with a department of notes and queries.

MILNOR LJUNGSTEDT, Editor and Publisher. Bethesda, Route 1, Maryland.

Published six times a year. Subscription, two dollars a year, in advance; must begin with the year. *Renewals one dollar and a half.* Advertising rates moderate.

VOL. III JULY, 1924 No. 4

BY WAY OF SAYING SOMETHING

The thermometer registers a scant fifth of a degree short of ninety on this porch. The EDITOR has a lot of things she would like to say, but she feels sure that she would be led into some persiflage which no doubt, many of her serious-minded friend subscribers would consider unbecoming in the serious-minded editor of an epitome of dates. Some of them don't understand that if you are awfully in earnest about everything in the world, except bridge, and parties and fruit punches, you just can't stand it during a longish life if you don't acquire the art of... being inconsequential!

Besides, the Editor can't think of anything but her lost notes which were in that lost package, and her annotated County Bulletin, her charts, and her subscription list... not to mention the pink bathrobe (which was a bargain), the blue jersey dress which can't be had anywhere, and she does wish that every subscriber and correspondent south of the line would fall upon the Southeastern Express Company and tell them how to run an express business. Even the *petite vitesses* of the Continent get you your luggage in time, and are most polite about it. The Editor is sure that if they lost one thing consigned to the *petitest* of *vitesses* they would be heartbroken over it. She cannot discover in the Southeastern Express Company the slightest atom of remorse. They, figuratively, shrug their shoulders and say... *"It is lost. We acknowledge it. We pay. What can you ask more?"* The Editor hopes for your sympathy.

Conditions in various county-seats should be touched upon... but will be laid by for cooler weather. However, King George county, Va., has a pretty new little courthouse, of good style, and still the same helpful Clerk. But the Clerk's Office is unbearably hot... no provision having been made for ventilating fans or awnings.

One of the most picturesque, and not altogether inconvenient Clerk's offices... perhaps it is the most picturesque... is at Warsaw, Richmond country. The Clerk gives it a date of about 1740. The thick walls make even a hot day bearable, and it opens front and back. It should be preserved for all time. Even the slates, hand riven and weather-worn, protest against change. But the searcher is advised to stay overnight at Montross, at Mrs. Walker's, or at King George, at Mrs. Mason's. Or at Tappahannock.

The Editor is continuing the paging of the PRINCE WILLIAM Orders and Minute books, but owning to an error, volume five was taken up instead of volume four... another visit will be required for the omitted volume. It is pleasant to be able to state that the Clerk at Prince William (Manassas) is regaining his health. The Editor is grateful for some useful advice received from the Commonwealth's attorney.

The Editor asks that her correspondents will kindly not send her original material. It places a considerable responsibility on the Editor, as well as some expense of postage.

OCCASIONAL

"The Quakers live all in Cameron [parish] "or the Upper Parish, and scarcely one man "of them ever came to Church in my time "except Elisha Hall." (Misc. papers at L. C.) Fairfax, Va. tithables, 1749. [This paper also mentions the building of a church at *Rocky Run.*]

Records of Scott cty, Kentucky, show that the heirs of HANCOCK LEE were Pamela, Mary W., Fanny, Elizabeth, and Anna G. Lee of Fauquier cty, Va.; Thomas Lee and wf Mary; Hancock and wf Susan; and John A. Lee of Woodford cty, Kentucky; and Henry Richards and wf Emeline (born Lee) of Bath cty, Va. See Draper Mss. 5J-25. 27 Dec 1821.

Confidences of the Clerk's Office: Judge, signing his decision: "I don't know whether that's strictly correct or not [as to law], *but that's what it ought to be."*

Bashful young man comes for a marriage license: Clerk: *"Nobody in the office but me and he actually called me into the back office."*
A Georgia county.

Also Georgia: "If you say this bale of cot- "ton is yours, you're a liar and if you want "anything else I'm prepared to give it. There "wasn't no language nor cussin' nor nothin', "just that. We set up all night, me on one "side of the bale and him on the other. In "the morning he wasn't in a good humor [the "fellow that had bought the bale.]" X—— county.

FIFTY DOLLARS REWARD and no questions asked, will be paid for the contents of a khaki-covered mailing case, mislaid, lost, or stolen, between Trenton and Columbia, S. C., or in Columbia, while in transit to Abbeville, S. C., via the Southern Railroad, in care of the Southeastern Express Company. EDITOR.

A LIST OF PERSONS NATURALIZED BY PARTICULAR ACTS

From Bacon's Laws of Maryland *

(Contributed by Mrs. Geo. W. Hodges)

(Continued from January number)

OTHO OTHOSON, of Cecil cty. 3 Oct 1704. 85.

PETER OWERARD, of the City of Annapolis, sadler. 15 Nov 1712. 24.

DANIEL PACKET, of Anne Arundel cty, laborer. 15 Nov 1712. 24.

DANIEL PACQUET, Anne Arundel cty, labourer, 11 Nov 1709. 10.

DAVID PAGET, of Queen Anne's cty, pltr. 3 Nov 1711. 8.

MAUDLIN PAGET, "wife of David," and "their children." 3 Nov 1711. 8.

JAMES and JOHN PARANDIER, of Charles cty, 22 Apr 1720. 2.

JAMES PEANE, MAGDALEN PEANE, his wife; ANNE PEANE, their daughter, of St. Mary's cty. 15 Nov 1678. 13.

CHRISTIAN PETERS, of Cecil cty. a "Native of Germany," 8 Aug 1729. 1.

CORNELIUS PETERSON, of Cecil cty, 6 June 1674. 12.

HANS PETERSON, of Baltimore cty, "from Holland." 6 June 1674. 12.

MATHIAS PETERSON; PETER PETERSON, his son, and other chn., of Talbot cty. 19 Apr 1671. 10.

MATHIAS PETERSON, & "his children," of Talbot cty. 6 June 1683. 4.

ANDREW POULSON (alias Mullock), of Cecil cty. 6 June 1674. 12.

STEPHEN RAFHOON, planter, and his children, of Talbot cty. 3 Nov 1711, 20.

WILLIAM RAYMAN, of the City of Annapolis. 24 Oct 1728, 14.

ONORIO RAZOLINI, of the City of Annapolis. 8 Aug 1732. 7.

STEPHEN RICH, of Queen Anne's cty, carpenter, "and his children." 14 Nov 1713. 16.

JAMES RICHARD, of Baltimore cty. 4 June 1744. 10.

HANS JACOB de RING, of Baltimore cty. 19 Apr 1671. 10.

JAMES ROBERT, of Calvert cty, pltr. 22 Nov. 1708. 10.

CHARLES de le ROCHE, of St. Mary's cty, 8 May 1669. 4.

ROBERT ROELANDS, 8 May 1669. 4.

(To be continued)

* Figures other than dates refer to chapters.

The TRUSTEES of the Methodist Episcopal Church in Georgia, in 1788, were:
Nathaniel Allen,
Richard Hunt,
John Harkelford,
John Tollet,
Robert Brown,
William Hanson,
Peter Stubbs,

Thomas Carter, late of Wilkes cty, conveys to them all that lately erected House known by the name of Beaverdam Preaching House ...with one acre of land... "also the Priviledges of the nearest Spring." Wilkes Cty, Ga. FF-79. 17 May 1788.

COLONIAL AND REVOLUTIONARY AND OTHER MILITARY NOTES

DAVID SHAFFERS sells to MICAJAH WILLIAMSON one bounty of land given him (sd David Shaffer) for his service as a militia soldier. Wilkes cty, Ga. Vol. CC [page gone] 16 Feby 1782.

JOHN DIVINES, a soldier in the first Georgia State Reg't, commanded by Colo. John Clark... gives power to obtain Bounty on Land due him for his services as a Soldier. Wilkes cty, Ga. [Unbacked vol.] p. 130. 9 Feby 1790.

CALEP [*Sic*] HARMON; receipt for pay at Fort Lewis. June-Nov. 1757. Draper 6QQ-102.

WILLIAM ROACH, acct agt Commonwealth; ordered certified. Ffx cty, Va. Orders. 22 Sept 1789.

WILLIAM HARMAN; Jeremiah Archer testifies, 31 Jany 1817, that in Sept 1814, he saw HARMAN lying dead at the "Eleven Mile Creek from Black Rock"; that he died of common sickness without a wound, to the knowledge of the deponent. Fayette cty, Penna. i-170. 31 Jany 1817.

RALPH JUSTICE, Captn of Troop of Horse; Thomas Hall, Captn of a Company of Foot; Joseph Hickman, Ensign; William Sturgis, Lieut't of a Company of Foot, took the oaths of Government as also the Test. Acco. cty, Va. Orders xxii0-192. 25 Sept 1739.

JOHN LONG, of the cty of Hawkins, Tenn., certifies that he was a soldier in Shelby's Regt, at the Battle of King's Mtn. Draper 31S-260. 19 Feby 1823.

HENRY BLEVINS, Hawkins cty, Penn., certifies that he was a private, Capt. Elliott's Company, Shelby's Reg't, King's Mountain. Draper, 31S-258. 18 Feby 1823.

DAVID LINDSEY states that he is 64 years old and served in the wars under King Charles the second; also full term of four years in this country with Thomas Gregg. Staff. cty, Va. i-121. 10 Dec 1690.

JOHN DAY, now in the Continental service, desired that his two sons John, two years and ten months old, and Archibald, four years old the 1st April last, be apprenticed to Michael Kernhart. The Court so orders. Fredk cty, Md. Minute Book of the O. C. 24 Apr 1778.

JOHN SNIDER, wounded and lost his leg in the Flying Camp, and acted as Corporal in Capt. Adam Grosh's company, as appears from the Testimony of Major Peter Mantz; Ordered that the Lieut. of this county be requested to pay said JOHN SNIDER from 1 Dec 1776 to 1 May 1778, being 17 months' pay. Fredk cty, same record. 24 Apr 1778.

SAMUEL HENNYS[?] who was wounded, to receive half-pay for a year. Same record. 13 Oct 1778.

WILLIAM HAYS; David Robinson certifies that WILLIAM HAYS served in his Company 112 days. Now discharged. [Where?] Draper 2QQ-60. 27 Dec 1764—7 June 1765.

ROBERT EDMANDSON; James Keys testifies to his services in Rev. War. Draper 3ZZ-43. [About 1777]

Common Abbreviations

used in old books and MSS.

- ꝰ ↄ *is for* er, ov̓=*over*
- — over or through a letter means *m* or *n* omitted following such letter, ā=an *or* am.
- ~ means omission of a single letter, not *m* or *n*, or more than one letter before or after; dñs=dominus
- ã ac, aut, autem, apud, &c., ãs=alias
- ƀ bet
- ƀ beatus, baptistus, bis, bit, ber; liƀ=liber
- ƀƀ a common form of final *bb*
- ʼ used 12th. cent. and before for *er*
- C̄ 100,000
- c̃ ceteris, caput, cum, &c.
- c̓ cer, cre
- đ den
- đ d̃ datum, de, dicit; viđ=vidua
- ē enim, est
- ẽ ecclesia, erit, est
- ę =æ
- f̓ fer
- f foresta, fugitivus
- g̃ gratia, genera, genus
- g̓ ger
- ħ habent, habet, hoc, heres, &c. Joħes=Johannes
- ī ibi, id est, &c.
- ĩ ibi, id est, igitur
- k car
- ƚƚ a common form of *ll*, also marks an omission. William may be Wiƚƚiam, Wiƚƚm or Wiƚƚm̃s
- ƚ le
- ƚƚ libra, librata
- m̄ -men, -man
- m̃ mem, mer, &c.
- m̓ mer
- n̄ nat
- ñ natus, nec, nisi, &c.
- ō om
- õ omn; õa=omnia
- ꝑ par, per, pro; ꝑish=parish
- ꝓ pro
- p̃ post, potest
- p̓ præ, prætium
- ꝗ quod, quæ, quam, qui, que
- q -que, (et), e.g. populusq
- qq queque
- r̃ reddit, rei, responsum
- ꝭ ser, ꝭvant=servant
- t̄ ter
- t̃ talia, tam, 160,000
- ꝉ et
- ꝉ ꝉ ter, terra, tertiam
- þ Saxon form of *th*; þˢ =this, þᵉ =the
- ū un
- ũ verbi
- v̓ ver
- ꝉ & etiam
- x̃ decem, decimus
- x̓ xer, xor; ux̓=uxor
- X̄ 10,000
- ẏ old form of *y*
- Ð De, Deum
- 7 ʒ et, que, us
- ꝝ -rum ꝝ es
- ꝭ es, is
- ꝰ us
- , all kinds of pauses
- ✝ est
- ʒ et, que, us qʒ quia
- ; period. ! comma
- ʒ Saxon *g*
- ꝺ qꝺ=quod

—Contributed by Edward Dwelly, H. S. A. Scot., H. S. G.

THE AGES OF SOME FREDERICK COUNTY (MARYLAND) ORPHANS

(Continued from May number)

CHRIS'R STANLEY, of age 7 May 1779.
GARRET STANLEY, of age 17 May 1774.
THOMAS STANLEY, of age 6 Aug 1781.
ALCHEA [ALTHEA?] STANLEY, of age 22 Feby 1779.
MARY THATCHER, of age in 1751.
ELISABETH THOMAS, of age in 1759.
MARY TOMLINSON, of age in Apr 1762.
JACOB THOMPSON, of age in June 1778.
SHADRICK TURNER, of age in May 1777.
ROBERT TUNE, of age in June 1777.
JOHN TOON, of age in Mch 1776.
CATHERINE TOON, of age in Mch 1776.
SAM'L TOON, of age in Mch 1783.
THOMAS TOMLINSON, of age 11 Apr 1775.
GEORGE LEWIS TENELLY, of age 19 Feby 1777.
JAMES TURNER[?] of age 10 Mch 1779.
DAVID TURNER[?] of age in 1780.
SARAH WARD, of age in 1761.
THOMAS WALES, Jr., of age in 1760.
MARTHA WEAVER, of age in 1761. [?]
JOSEPH WEATHERLOW, of age in June 1774.
DAVID WHITE, of age in Dec 1768.
ROBERT WALLACE, of age in Jany 1768.
WILLIAM WALLACE, of age in Feby 1772.
GUY WALLACE, of age in Feby 1774.
CHRISTOPHER WHITE, of age in Aug 1775.
ANDREW WOLF, of age in Nov 1773.
ANDREW WILLIAMS, of age in 1762.

Heretofore omitted:

JOHN STEWARD KENNEDY, of age Sept 1769.
RICHARD KEENE, of age 17 Oct 1771.
THOMAS JONES, of age Aug 1775.
JAMES McGILL, of age Jany 1775.

NOTES FROM KENTUCKY RECORDS

(*Contributed by Miss Hattie M. Scott, of Frankfort, Kentucky*)

CATHERINE SAMUEL, married; "husband a gentleman;" b. Botetourt county, Va., dau. of Francis Graham; d. 30 Sept 1855, aged 70.

THOMAS W. SHEPHERD, b. Penna., son of Benj. and Margaret Shepherd; d. 12 Oct 1856, aged 71.

WILLIAM SANDERS, b. Virginia; son of Henry and Rhoda Sanders; d. 23 June 185— [?], aged 67.

CATHERINE STOUGHTON, b. Schenectady, N. Y. dau. of James and Catherine Stoughton; d. 17 Mch 1859, aged 66.

L. B. STOUGHTON, bridge-builder; b. Montfort, Conn., son of Augustine and Sebina Stoughton; d. 18 July 1859, aged 75.

JOHN TRACY, b. Culpeper cty, Va.; son of Sample and Mary Tracy; d. 28 Feby 1855, aged 80.

MARY TAYLOR, b. Frederick cty, Va., dau. of Sarah and Edmund Taylor; d. 9 Dec 1856, aged 76.

SAMUEL TODD, b. Virginia; d. 7 Mch 1859, aged 81.

MONARCHA TODD, "female;" b. Maryland; d. 7 May 1859, aged 78.

MARY WARREN, b. Brownsville, Penna.; dau. of Robert and Keziah Taylor; d. July 1855, aged 62.

VACHEL WARFIELD, b. Maryland; son of Giles and Polly Warfield; d. 8 Dec 1857, aged 77.

JAMES WALSTON, b. North Carolina; d. 7 Nov 1869, aged 66.

WILLIAM WEST, b. King William cty, Va.; d. 11 Jany 1854, aged 60.

SNELLING WILKERSON, b. Charlotte cty, Va.; son of Daniel and Molly Wilkerson; d. 1 Apr 1855, aged 77.

DAVID WILLIAMS, b. Virginia; d. 24 Jany 1859, aged 65.

SOLOMON WINEBRENER, b. Maryland; son of Catherine Winebrener; d. 2 Apr 1859, aged 50.

Omitted:

MARY McDANIEL, b. Culpeper cty, Va.; dau. of Samuel and Catherine Wise; d. 10 Oct 1857, aged 69.

(*End of this section of Kentucky Notes.*)

A MARRIAGE RECORD from the U. S. CONSULATE at HAVRE, France.

American Consulate, Havre. June 11th 1835.
No. 5.

I Reuben G. Beasley, Consul of the United States for the port and district of Havre, do hereby certify that the Rev'd David DeForest Ely, resident American minister at this port, born at Lebanon in the State of Connecticut, son of the Rev'd Zebulon Ely and of Sarah Ely of Lebanon aforesaid in the United States of Am[erica] Was, on the eleventh day of June 1835, married in this Consulate by the Rev'd Edward Blanchard, resident Swiss Protestant Minister at this port, to JANE CHANCELLOR of Havre de Grâce, aged 18 years, Daughter of Samuel and of Sarah Chancellor. formerly of Kensington in the County of Middlesex, in the Kingdom of Great Britain, in my presence and that of Samuel Chancellor aforesaid, of Louisa Maria Castle, Carlisle Norwood, Sarah and Elizabeth Chancellor and of Thomas Taylor, Chancellor of this Consulate. In testimony whereof the said parties have hereunto subscribed their names, Samuel Chancellor, Sarah Chancellor, Elizabeth Chancellor, Carlisle Norwood, Ed. Blanchard, *Min. du St. Evangile,* Thos. Taylor. (Sig.) R. G. Beasley.

RECENT MAGAZINES

The VIRGINIA MAGAZINE for July contains 76 pages of material useful to the biographer and historian: an article on the Virginia clergy, with Gov. Gooch's letters to the Bishop of London (27pp.); the Virginia Council Journals (23pp.); the Kennon Letters written in 1810 (26pp.); several interesting English wills; the very valuable Gloucester Rent Rolls of 1704; and 17 pages of Notes and Queries and other genealogical material.

The MARYLAND HISTORICAL MAGAZINE for June contains 212 pp. The Extinct River Towns of the Chesapeake Bay Region, containing many extracts from Maryland legislation, covers 17 pp. The Life of Thomas Johnson and the biography of James Alfred Pearce, cover 37 pp. and the Account and Letter-Books of Dr. Charles Carroll, 14 pp. Proceedings of the Maryland Historical Society, 9 pp. Mr. Francis B. Culver gives a brief and good article on the Ancestry of Rev. Hatch Dent. No matter what or whom Mr. Culver writes about it is always interesting from the clearness and precision of his style, and the absolute accuracy of his facts. Mrs. Hodges contributes an interesting note from the records, and the small amount of genealogical matter in the number is enhanced by the list of inscriptions from Ellicott City Tombstones, though they are rather modern, there being only two previous to 1820.

VALUABLE PUBLICATION: A List of the Marriage License Bonds of Richmond County, Virginia, from 1740, is about to be published by Mr. E. Carter Delano, of Warsaw, Virginia.

The Society for the Preservation of New England Antiquities announces that the Shaker House, now moved to Prospect Hill, Harvard, Mass., and situated close to "Fruitlands," is open to the public Tuesdays, Thursdays, and Saturdays (holidays included) from June 3rd to end of September, from 12 m. to 6 p. m. Admission, 10 cents.

GENERAL INFORMATION

Searchers or tourists going by way of the state road from Fredericksburg to Warsaw, Virginia, a distance of sixty miles, either by private car or autobus, will find very satisfactory accommodation at Mrs. Mason's, King George Court House, also at Mrs. Walker's, at Montross. Both these ladies set excellent tables and are kindly hostesses.

The Rural Hill Tea Room in Accomac is now next door to the drug store at the corner of the state road.

GENEALOGISTS AND OTHERS INTERESTED IN RESEARCH WORK

FIFTY DOLLARS REWARD!
FIFTY DOLLARS REWARD!
See page 21

PUBLICATIONS, ETC., OF VALUE TO HISTORIANS AND GENEALOGISTS

Reasonable price will be paid for numbers 1, 2, 3, and 5, COUNTY COURT NOTE-BOOK, 1921-1922. Address Editor.

COLUMBIAN PRINTING CO., INC., WASHINGTON, D. C.

The
County Court Note-Book

A Little Bulletin of History and Genealogy

Vol. III, September, 1924 No. 5

FORENAMES OF COLONIAL USAGE

It seems a pity that a name like Bridget, once so common, and with its associations with the Saint, should have so dropped into disuse. Certainly the form Brigitta is very pretty.

BRIDGET BERRY m. Samuel Mitchel. Overwharton Psh Reg. 30 Jany 1749.

BRIDGET BOSMAN, dau. of William. N-n, Va. ix-22. 1 Sept 1658.

BRIDGETT BALLIOTT, wid. of John, m. —— Vines. N-n, Va. viii-20. Before 28 June 1658.

BRIDGET BRADFORD, was dau. of Phillip Fisher. N-n, Va. xviii- 1701.

BRIDGET BAGALE. Acco., Va. ix-65. 12 May 1685.

BRIDGETT BOSSMAN, was dau, of John and Blandina Bossman. Som., Md. D. B. I. K. L., 13. She was born 12 Sept 1687.

BRIDGET COOPER m. John Sylva. Overwh. Psh Reg. 1 July 1750.

BRIDGETT CHARLTON. N-n, Va. viii-108. 28 Oct 1661.

BRIDGET CRAFT, svt of Mr. John Wilkins. N-n, Va. i-55. 8 Aug 1636.

BRIDGET CUSTIS, wf of Col. Wm. Custis. Also BRIDGET CUSTIS, his dau. Acco., Va. xvi-262. 1725-1726. The wf. releases dower, xviii-4. 1 Sept 1719.

BRIDGET DAVIS, legatee under Mrs. Jane Hartsee's will. N-n, Va., ix-242. 11 Mch 1665.

BRIDGETT FISHER, was the god-dau. of Robt Clarke. N-n, Va. xvii-523. 1698.

BRIDGETT FOSTER, wf of John. N-n, Va., ii-194. 3 Jany 1642. See also i-145, 23 Sept 1639.

BRIDGETT FOSTER, dau. of Robert. N-n, Va. xvii-154. 1691.

BRIDGET FLOWERS, a head right under John Foster. N-n, Va. ii-45. 11 Jany 1640.

BRIDGET GASCOIGNE m. William Harmanson. N-n, Va., xviii-417. About Aug 1688.

BRIDGET HARMANSON was dau. of George. N-n, Va. xxviR-123. 18 Apr 1734.

BRIDGET HARWOOD. Acco, Va. iv-122. 10 May 1660.

BRIDGET HARMANSON and Littleton Eyre. N-n, Va. M. L. B. 1734.

BRIDGETT JOHNSON, was gr-dau. of Thomas Savage. Savage's wife was also BRIDGETT. N-n, Va. xxiiiR-141. 1721.

BRIDGET MARCEY. Acco, Va. xviii-40. 6 Mch 1722.

BRIDGET MIDDLETON, age about 22. Acco, Va. ix-2 19 Feby 1682.

BRIDGET MICHEL was wf of Samuel. Overwh. Psh Reg. 1752.

BRIDGETT MURPHY, was wf of John, and they had a dau. BRIDGETT. She was born 28 Jany 1682. Som, Md, records.

BRIDGETT WINDER, wf of John. 1679. Som, Md, records.

BRIDGET MIDDLETON was wf of George, of Hunting Creek. Acco, Va. vi-40. 31 Aug 1685.

BRIDGET RATLIFF, was dau of Bridget and Charles. N-n, Va. ix-113. Bap. 5 May 1661.

BRIDGETT SEAVERNE, wf of John. N-n, Va. ii-159. 29 Aug 1642.

BRIDGET SACKER, was dau of Frances, a widow. Acco, Va. vi-102. 3 May 1672.

BRIDGET SILVERTHORNE m. George Middleton. Acco, Va. ix-155. Before 19 Mch 1688.

BRIDGET TAYLOR asks admn on her husband, William Taylor's est. Acco, Va. x-199. 15 Sept 1696. She petns the Court as admx of her husband. Acco, Va. x-212. 6 Jany 1696.

BRIDGET WITHERS m. William Allen. Overwh. Psh Reg. 15 Feby 1743.

BRIDGET WHITECOTTON, wf of George. Overwh. Psh Reg. 1739.

BRIDGET WALE, dau of Edward and Elizabeth. Som., Md. records, D. B. I. K. L. She was born 8 Oct 1681.

MARRIAGES BY INFERENCE*

The first eight references are from the records of Accomack cty, Virginia. The following twenty-six are from Northampton cty, Virginia. See NOTE-BOOK for April and June, 1923.

PETER COLLIER and ANN KENDALL, extx of Capt. William Kendall, late Shff N-n co. Before 7 Apr 1698. xii-26.

EDWARD x CHAPMAN and MARY x HARRIS, dau. of Richard, late of the county of Albemarle in the Precinct of "Couratuck" in North Carolina. Before or about 7 July 1713. xi-603.

THOMAS CHAPPELL and MARY EBORNE, wid. of William. Before 18 Dec 1677. vii-88.

PETER COLLIER and ELIZABETH WATTS, dau. of Pricilla. See xx-53. (1730.)

GEORGE CUTLER and ARCADIA WELBOURNE, dau. of Thomas and Arcadia. Before 3 Apr 1716. xv-18.

GEORGE DOUGLAS and TABITHA DRUMMOND, dau. of Hill Drummond, Before 6 Mch 1732. xx-131.

THOMAS DUNTON and SUSANNA BELL, dau. of Robert. Before 1791. L. C.

MICHAEL DUNTON and SARAH BELL, wid. of Thomas, who d. 1791. L. C. 9.

JOHN MOOR and ELIZABETH SATCHELL, prob. wid. of Absalom. (Old loose papers.) About 1721.

JOHN MURPHEE and BRIDGET HARMANSON, wid. of William. 29 Nov 1709. xix-106.

WILLIAM PETTIT, Jr., and MARY CUSTIS, widow. Before 8 Apr 1755. xxixR-28.

—— POWELL and FRANCES SAVAGE, dau. of John, Gent. Before 11 Nov 1747. xviii-368.

SAMUEL POWELL and FRANCES ——; a kinswoman of John Robins, Sr. Before 1707. xix-23.

WILLIAM RAISIN [sic] and SARAH SAVAGE., dau. of Thomas, Gent., and wf Esther. Before 10 Aug 1756. xix-327.

THOMAS RESPESS and ESTHER HARMANSON, dau of Thomas and Elizabeth Harmanson. Before 14 Aug 1750. xix-13.

JOHN SAVAGE and a dau. of Berry Floyd. Before 26 May 1749. xxviiR-529.

Mr. WILLIAM WATERS and MARGARET CLARKE, widow of Mr. George Clarke. Before 28 Oct 1650. iii- (See also iv-70, "George Clarke, chirurgeon.")

DERICK VANHAMELL and SOPHIA VANWEKER [VANWEKES?] See record 8 Sept 1679. xiii-59.

CHARLES WRESSELL and MARY LOUGHLAND, widow of Dorman. About 1688. xiv-242.

WILLIAM WATERS and ISABELL HARMANSON, dau. of Thomas, Sr. Before 26 Mch 1696. xviii-112.

JOHN WRAY and SARAH HOW, widow of George. Before 28 Mch 1700. xviii-61.

THOMAS WARD and JANE NOTTINGHAM, widow of Robert. About or before 28 Apr 1703. xviii-139.

JOHN WESTCOTT and ELIZABETH CLARKE, widow of George. Before 29 July 1690. xvii-56.

JAMES WARREN and FRANCES WARREN, (Ctf of John Heroett??) Before 7 Nov 1693. xvii-263. (JAMES WARREN and widow WARREN produce ctf of marriage. Court 29 Jany 1693. xvii-257).

MORGAN WILLIAMS and FRANCES STOTT, dau of Henry Stott, 28 Dec 1692. xvii-208.

ARGOLL WARREN and URSULA PATRICK. After 1674-5. Land Causes (no page.)

JOHN WARREN, the Elder, and ELIZABETH PATRICK. Before 1725 (when Warren died). Land Causes (no page). (See also xiv-78... before 7 Nov 1683).

WILLIAM WARD and ANN S—— [name uncertain]. Widow of Edward ——. Before 28 Apr 1653. iv-179.

FRANCIS WAINHOUSE and PATIENCE FISHER, widow of Thomas. About 28 July 1709. xviii-533. (See also xviii-488).

LEWIS WHITE and KATHRYNE DEWIN, the relict of Thomas. Before Mch 1645, iii-37. (See also iii-244).

JOHN WILLIAMS and ELIZABETH COOPER. About 1647. vii-10.

ALEXANDER WILLIAMS [WILLIAMSON?] and ANNE WYATT, widow of Thomas. Probably between Apr and Aug 1642. ii-165, 189.

HENRY WARREN and SUSANNAH KENDALL, widow of John, Aug or Sept 1680. xi-241. (See also xiv-248).

JAMES WILLIAMS and ELIZABETH TODD, admx of William Todd. Before 28 Nov 1695. xvii-333-4.

(To be continued)

WILLS PROBATED AND ADMINISTRATIONS GRANTED IN PRINCE WILLIAM COUNTY, VIRGINIA, 1761-1763

(From the fourth remaining Order Book)

(See December, 1923, and previous issues of the NOTE-BOOK.)

JOHN WHITLEDGE; admn his estate granted to Elizabeth Whitledge, his widow. John Graham and Thomas Dagg, sec. Ct 26 Oct 1761. p. 32.

RICHARD HAZILRIGG; his will presented by William Hazilrigg, James Hazillrigg and Abell Hazilrigg, extrs. Proved by oaths of John Summers and Elizabeth Viccars. Ct 22 Feby 1762. p. 55.

JOHN McMILLION; his will presented by John McMillion the extr. Proved by Margaret Glascock and Edward Gwatkin, wit. Ct 22 Feby 1762. p. 56. SETH McMILLION prays that the provisions of her husbands will be set aside so far as she is concerned. Ct 22 Mch 1762. p. 85.

RICHARD CRUPPER; his will presented by George Calvert, Jr., and Jacob Calvert, extrs. Proved by Thomas Machen, John Calvert and Nathaniel Overall. Ct 22 Feby 1762. p. 58.

ELIAS WICKLIFF; admn his estate granted to Robert Wickliff; Isaac Davis, sec. Ct 23 Feby 1762. p. 65.

EWELL JONES; admn his est granted to William Watkins. William Whitesides and Edward Cornwall, sec. Ct 22 Mch 1762. p. 84.

WILLIAM MELTON; admn of his estate granted to Sarah Melton, his widow. William Bird and George Reeve, sec. Ct 4 Mch 1762. p. 109.

JOHN BLAND; his will presented by Patience Bland, extx. Proved by Benjamin Bland and David Stewart, two of the wit. Ct 7 June 1762. p. 157.

JAMES CULLINS; his will presented by James Cullins, the extr. Proved by wit. [names not given.] Ct 7 June 1762. p. 157.

JOHN FOLEY; admn on his estate granted to James Foley. William Ellzey, sec. Ct 7 June 1762. p. 163.

ROBERT NEAVILL; admn on his estate granted to John Baylis, Gent. William Baylis, sec. Ct 6 Aug 1762. p. 285.

SARAH MOSS; admn on her estate granted to Thomas Moss. Daniel Kincheloe, sec. Ct 8 Feby 1763. p. 395.

THOMAS MOLLOHON; admn on his estate granted to Ann Mollohon, widow. George Johnston, sec. Ct 8 Apr 1763. p. 474.

GRIFFIN MATTHEW; his will presented by Newman Matthews, extr, Ct 2 May 1763. p. 499.

THOMAS HART; his will presented by Leonard Hart, extr. Proved by James Bridges, John Peyton and John Lumsdell. Ct 6 June 1763. p. 521.

WILLIAM MELTON; admn of the estate of William Melton unadministered by Sarah Melton, dec'd, his late admx, granted to Richard Melton. Ct 4 July 1763. p. 544.

(End of this volume of Orders)

VIRGINIA COLONISTS

(Head rights from Old Volume 5, State Land Office, Richmond. Continued from JULY issue. Those starred are reprinted from MAY issue.)

To avoid confusion, there being already two publications concerning Virginia Immigrants, it has seemed advisable to change the title of the lists now being published in the NOTE-BOOK to VIRGINIA COLONISTS.

Fac-similes of some of the entries will be found on page 6.

WILLIAM BIRD [county not mentioned], 1656;

Head rights: Ann Turk, Edw. Clanterne, Jno. Kite, Jno. Chapman, Wm. Munteth, Margaret Sweetman.

Mr. HUMPHREY BOOTH, Rappahannock county, 1656.

Head right: David Jones.

Mr. ROBERT BOTT, Lower Norfolk county, 1656.

Head rights: Andrew Sheetes, Bartho: Ball, Marg: Allen, Tho: Encrid [Enerid?], Bridgett Ellunor[?]

THOMAS BROUGHTON, "in Patomeck Freshes", 1657.

Head rights: Mary Dibbin, Jno. Margaretts, Joseph Bennett, Margarett Tucker, Ann Shepard, Mary Midleton, Tho. Meddars, Jno. Rose, Jno. Badworth, Eliz. Phillips.

THOMAS BELL, New Kent county, 1657.

Head rights: Hannah Howard, Edward Huntstone, Rich. Davis, Humphry ——, Jno. Hunter.

Major EDWARD BRUMFIELD & Mr. JOHN SNELLINGE, "on the West side of Hoccadies Creeke in Peanketank River," 1657.

Head rights: John Snellinge, EDWARD BROMFEILD, Wm Simpson, Wm. Feild, Jno. Mutton, Jno. Williams, Hen. Coniers, Georg Harber, Sarah Masly [Mosly?], Nath. Ruford, Nath. Pincon, Jno. Abbott, Ann Delne [Delue?], Rob. Hollaway, Jno. Cranfeild, Xpher. Hare, Winifred James, Rob. Fletcher, Tho. "a Scott," Thom. "a Boy," a maid servant, James Hunt's wife.

FRANCIS BURNELL, Gent., "on the South West side of York River," 1657.

Head rights: Margarett Boaton, Jno. Needham, Tho. Cappinge, Robert Crost, Jno. Clerke, Eliz. Bailinge.

FRANCIS BURNELL, New Kent county, 1657.

Head rights: Wilmott Allinge [Allings?], Elizabeth Holt, Rich Needham, Kath. Bridge, Mary Holmsly, Mary Blunder [Blundon?], Mary Manes, Philip Russell, Jno. Hoemane[?]

ROBERT BRADSHEW & JAMES CLOUGHTON, "above Puscatoway in Petomeck freshes," 1657.

Head rights: Tho: Mannor, Tho. Webster, Eliz. Phillips, Mary John & Mary, Eliz. Hartford, John Butcher, Tho. Rogers, Tho. Dixon, James Lessell, Wm. Collings.

THOMAS BELL, Northampton county, 1657.

Head rights: Elinor Lathberry [Leatherbury?], Howell Gladinge, Wm. Mitchell, Mary Batchelor.

WM. BACON, Gent., Northumberland county, 1657.

Head rights: John Fluncher, Robert Joggins, [Only two names.]

THOMAS BELL, Northampton county, 1657.

Head rights: Ellinor Lashberry, Hoell Gladeinge, Wm. Mitchell, Mary Batchellor & Elizabeth Rosser.

THOMAS BRERETON, "being in Patomek river," 1657.

Head rights: Mr. Thomas Manninge, twice; Mr. Henry Bastard, Mr. Wm. Bastard, Jno. Abrams, Tamicke Bastian, Arryanka Ariays [??], Peter Franke, Wm. Middleton, James Cunningham, Robert Raddocke, Henry Alexander, Wm. Millett, Robert Stedman, Tho: Wilson, Mr. Daniell. Mary Callaway, Susan Bennett, William ——, Mary Hamon.

ALPHONSO BALL, Northampton county, 1658.

Head rights: Ellinor Collins, Ann Cooke, Wm. Scott, Sam Younge, Rich. Nuttingham, Eliz. Nuttingham, Step: Yeo.

Capt. John Blake, "Beinge at the head of Parkers Creek," 1658.

Head rights: Francis Deplaie, Jno. Carpenter, one negro.

Capt. JOHN BLAKE, "Being in a Creeke called Mathewes his Creeke," 1658.

Head rights: Susan Ashly, Wm. Jones, Tho. Peterson, Mary Corbett, Wm. Daniel, Andrew Ston, Tymothy Jones, Wm. Norcott.

SILVESTER BAKER, at the head of Parker's Creeke, 1658.

Head rights: James Mote, Alexander Jemmison, Bryan Farrell, Margarett Farrell, Wm. Lowder.

THOMAS BRERETON, land "Lieing within the mouth of Mathotick river," 1658.

Head rights: Mary Broder, Jno. Multis, James Felton, George, a Scotchman; Frances ——, Symon Richardson, Jno Slattor, Jno. Fornor, Jno. Gibbins, and Mollettoe [mulatto?]

THOMAS BREWER, Northumberland county, 1658.

Head rights: Tho. Pindleton, Geo. Pindleton, Wm. Harbutt, Eliz. Reinolls, 3 negroes.

Major MILES CAREY, Warwick county, 1655.*

Head rights: Tho. Wilkinson, John Thomas, Margaret May, John Tistull [Tisdall?]

(To be continued)

The County Court Note-Book

An every-other-monthly devoted to abstracts from County Court and other records, prior to 1800, and with a department of notes and queries.

MILNOR LJUNGSTEDT, Editor and Publisher. Bethesda, Route 1, Maryland.

Published six times a year. Subscription, two dollars a year, in advance; must begin with the year. Advertising rates moderate.

VOL. III SEPTEMBER, 1924 No. 5

MORE ABOUT COUNTY COURTS

Some time ago the Editor began a running series of comments on conditions as she has found them in various offices of Recorders, Registers, Clerks and Prothonotaries. So many interesting matters have turned up, and the Editor has gossiped so much by the way, that she rather hesitates to try to pick up the thread of her subject again. Especially as she finds to her dismay that what should have been the prologue has been pushed aside for the chapters... reminding her of the timeworn advice to young writers, to cut off both ends and throw away the middle.

Yet, by constantly talking about a matter, it is curious how it will, in the end, catch the attention. Note, for example, the National Game. The Editor has never taken any interest in it since she discovered it was professional... a business, so to speak, and that the Bostons were not, in fact, Bostonese! But under the psychological influence (it must have been that) of the state of mind of collected Washington during the last ten days, the Editor finds herself asking at night, *"Well, who won?"*

But, as for County Courts: the Editor has personally visited and examined the records of over one hundred and fifty offices. Some of these offices have already been written about. Perhaps if the Editor headed this article "How to Run a County Court," it might sound a bit bumptious, but would convey what she has in mind. If she began *"County Courts should be divorced from politics,"* her readers would certainly put her down as belonging to that large and aggressive army of what was once the gentle sex, who are now engaged in an endeavor to improve everything in general... in the outside world. But the Editor is a weak-minded person, who holds to the views of most of her ancestresses (she has her private doubts as to one) that women have their hands full already, and more than full.

Still, to come back to County Courts, they ought to be out of politics. The Editor is sure she doesn't know how Clerks, Recorders, and Registers would or should be selected, but personally thinks that the good old Virginia way of keeping the office in the family was very satisfactory... except when, as in a large Register's office in a Maryland county, a young cub of 21 is made Register out of love and affection for his deceased father, the said young person having no other quality whatever to fit him for the place. But when, speaking generally, a Clerk is elected or appointed, who had a Clerk for a father, and a Clerk for a grandfather, and maybe a Clerk for a great-grandfather, a sort of pride and affectionate interest go with the descent. Such a Clerk may be far from modern in his methods of keeping the records, but he has the first requisites, interest and pride.

The Clerk of the Court in many communities, especially in those where he is, in himself, the several officers of the Court, becomes the guide, counsellor and friend of the community. The Editor personally knows two Clerks, perhaps more, whose election was unanimous, or practically so... and one belongs to the party commonly in opposition. She also knows a County Judge on whom all three parties agreed, though the law required him to select among them.

In the greater number of offices visited by the Editor she has found courtesy, and sometimes friendly courtesy. Pleasant pictures are in her mind of open fires, gossiping constituents and helpful hands. Had the Editor the pen and pencil of a Porte Crayon, she would be the historian of the Courts.

Very different pictures sometimes recur... these exceptions, as a rule, are in the large city offices where the dollar and the attorney are in control... yet, strange to relate... more friendly help was found in Pittsburgh than in Portsmouth, Virginia, or Charleston, West Virginia! The exception must also include a few of the older courts where, occasionally, a young man, new to the dignity, and overfull of importance struts about, very much reminding the Editor of a young rooster whose next-door enemy can't get at him because of the fence. Among the undesirables are some particularly bad cases, as to which others than the Editor quite agree... (in private); five of these are in Virginia, and one in Maryland. As the Editor cannot mention by name or office the charming and kindly gentlemen of the old school who have done the honors of their office, so she cannot mention those who have not. She can only hope they will not be re-elected, even if it throw the whole county machine out of gear.

Will the subscriber who asks the Editor for certain information as to the LINCOLN-HANKS families kindly write again? The Editor regrets that she has forgotten the name of the writer. She wishes to send him the desired information.

It is with honest regret that the Editor is compelled to raise the price of the NOTE-BOOK to $2.50 a year; $2.00 renewal. But the Editor does not feel warranted in any longer meeting the discrepancy between her subscription list and the expense of printing and postage out of her, that is to say, the family pocket. Moreover, the very serious loss of her southern notes sent by express, and the refusal of the company to make any equitable arrangement, places upon the Editor the burden of a return visit, since the trip was taken in behalf of others. This cripples the Editor's means very seriously.

The expense of satisfactory printing is, as every one knows, very high. Postage is considerable... so many of the NOTE-BOOKS were lost in the regular newspaper mail that nearly all the copies are now sent in sealed envelopes, first-class. The Editor is constantly reminded of MARK TWAIN who tells in one of his stories how he started out to right all the minor wrongs and injustices. I believe that in the end he was beaten. Possibly he also tried the post office, as well as the express.

FIFTY DOLLARS REWARD and no questions asked, will be paid for the contents of a khaki-covered mailing case, mislaid, lost, or stolen, between Trenton and Columbia, S. C., or in Columbia, while in transit to Abbeville, S. C., via the Southern Railroad, in care of the Southeastern Express Company. EDITOR.

OCCASIONAL

The Intricacies of the Law. From a PRINCE WILLIAM, Va., deed:

R... and B... W... convey our rights & title to a negroe Girl named Rose left by the last will of our Father to the children of O... R... which negro if they died without Heir was to Return to us.... [which negro they now sell] [but] as our brother W... W... is deceased & it is not known whether [there are] three or four parts in the said negro if only three the said E——[grantee] is to make up our proportion over and above the half... U-460. 1783.

In the Clerk's Office: County Clerk, who is the recipient of five hawks' heads and is laying the claim of the sender before the County Supervisors, and admits he doesn't know one hawk from another... code open before him: "The law says that you must say just how many Cooper's hawks and how many sharp-shinned hawks. Do any of you gentlemen know one from the other?" Apparently nobody does. One supervisor makes a suggestion: "Why not say three Cooper's hawks and two sharp-shinned?" Bothered but conscientious Clerk: "The law says you must say just how many of each kind, and you've got to know 'em." Somebody comes in. "Smith, do you know a Cooper's hawk when you see 'em?" "Not I... send for Jones, he knows them." Late in the afternoon, a keen, spare gentleman appears, something like a hawk himself. The Board turns hopefully toward him... "Jones, they say you know all about hawks." "I reckon I do." He steps up to the table where the hot, tired, but patient Board sits, tips up a brown paper bag... "Two Cooper's hawks, three sharp-shinned." A sigh of relief goes over the Board. The Clerk sets down the account: "To two Cooper's hawks, three sharp-shinned hawks." *In Virginia.*

COLONIAL AND REVOLUTIONARY AND OTHER MILITARY NOTES

From the Minute Book of the Orphans' Court, Frederick county, Maryland.

MARY PARSONS, widow of WILLIAM PARSONS, who marched with the militia for the State under Captain William Duvall & was taken prisoner 4 Oct 1777 at the battle of Germantown & died in Philadelphia. ORDERED that thirty pounds be paid said Mary Parsons being a private's full pay, from 4 Oct 1777 to 4 Oct 1778. Ct 13 Oct 1778.

SARAH BRIGHT, widow of WILLIAM BRIGHT, who marched with the militia from this State, under Capt. James Maikall [?] & died 4 Feby 1778, While in actual service as appears by ctf of William Luckett, Junior, Lt. Col., leaving four small children; ORDERED that sd Sarah Bright be paid thirty-six pounds, a serjeant's full pay from 4 Feby 1778 to 4 Feby 1779. Ct 9 Feby 1779.

SPERA McGEA[?] petitions that her husband, while in the Continental service was crippled & is unable to support his family. ORDERED that the petitioner apply to the Colonel of the Regiment for a certificate. 13 Apr 1779.

JOHN SNIDER, acted as Corporal in the Flying Camp; lost a leg. Half-pay ordered from 1 May 1781 to 1 May 1782. Ct 13 Aug 1782.

SARAH BRIGHT [see above], widow of WILLIAM BRIGHT... who died in actual service, as per sundry certificates, also by a certificate now produced signed by James Burgess and Johonnes Thomas. to be paid a serjeant's full pay from 4 Feby 1779 to 4 Feby 1780. Ct 15 Aug 1780.

CHARLES WILLIAMS, died in the Service of the United States as per certificate signed by Lodowick Kemp. Payment ordered to his widow, Elizabeth. Ct 21 Mch 1783.

List of wounded soldiers to whom half-pay was allowed, 14 April 1784.

JOHN BROWN, Sjt, of Washington cty; battle of Camden;

JOHN NEECH, private, of Frederick cty; at Guilford C. H.

PHILIP FISHER, private, of Frederick cty; at Guilford C. H.

HENRY CROOK, private, of Frederick cty; at Guilford C. H.

JAMES SPEAR, of Frederick cty; at Monmouth.

DAVID CONNER, of Frederick cty; sickness.

CHARLES BURKLIFF, of Frederick cty; at Eutaw Springs.

THOS. BISHOP, of Frederick cty; at Guilford.

JOHN OBER[?], Sjt, of Frederick cty; at Eutaw Springs.

JAMES SMITH, private, of Frederick cty; at Camden.

JOHN ALTHROP, of Frederick cty; "in the Barges;"

ROBERT KERNS, Sjt, of Frederick cty; at York.

JAMES BUCK, private, of Frederick cty; at Cowpens.

AS THEY ARE WRITTEN

See Virginia Colonists

(Kindly contributed by Mr. Archibald P. Hodnett, of the Virginia Land Office)

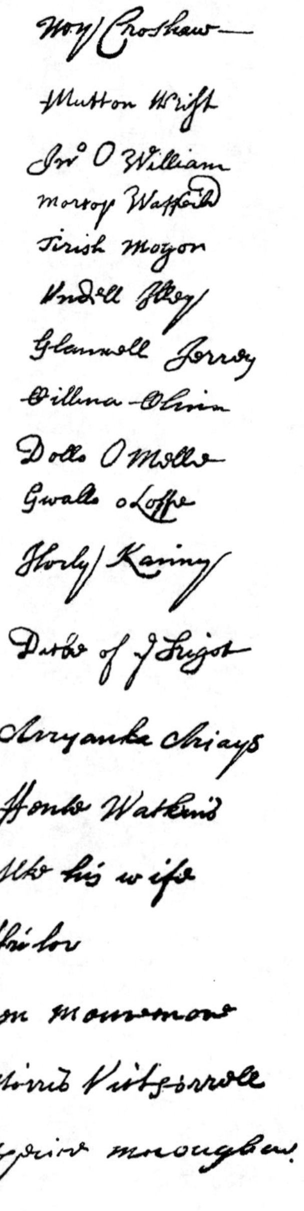

A LIST OF ORPHANS FROM THE RECORDS OF ANNE ARUNDEL COUNTY MARYLAND (Liber T. B. 1.)

(Contributed by Mrs. Geo. W. Hodges)

June Court, 1706. Orphans in Middle Neck hundred, West River hundred, Herring Creek hundred, South River hundred, Town Neck hundred, and Broad Neck hundred:

RICHARD ACTON, with Mr. John Marriot.
"One of JOHN ATTKINSES," with Jno. Gaile.
ISAAC ABRAHAM, with Thomas Larkins.
MATHE [Martha?] AIERS, dau. of Thomas, with Edward Peak.
MARY ARICE[?], orphan of the Court, with Edw'd Talbutt.

JOHN and RACHELL BEARD, at Mrs. Susanna Beard's.
ELIZA: BAYLY, with Christopher Smithers.
"One of ANDREW BEARD'S", with Rich'd Jones, Jun'r.
MARY and ELIZA: BENIT, orph'ts of Jno. Bennitt, with Alex'r Garner.
JOHN BAKER, orphant of Morrice, with Morrice[?] Baker.

JOHN, JAMES and WILLIAM CULLINS, with Mr. Thomas Bruff.
WM. COOLY, with Christopher Smithers.
"One of the Wdow Crouches now living," with John Mettcalfe.
"One of CHR. CHOATES", with Edward Parish.
HERMAN CHURCHYARD, with George Bradley.
JAMES COPLEY, at John Stool's.
EDWARD CHRISTIN, with John Ratford.
ANN, SARAH, JOHN and WILLIAM COTTER, with James Sanders and estates in his hands.
JOSEPH, BENJA., ANN, SAM'LL, HANNAH and SUSANA CHENY, with the widow CHENY; estate left to her[?].
THOMAS CLARKE, with the widow James, and estate in her hands.
THO: GASSAWAYS at John Bradley's.
ELIZA: and ELLINER CROUCH, orphts of James Crouch, with Phillip Jones.
SARAH CHAPPELL, dau. of Henry Chappell, with Mr. Thomas Homewood.
MARY CHAPPELL, dau. of Henry Chappell, with Joshua Merekin.
JOHN, EDWARD and JOSHUA COCKEY, sons of Wm. COCKEY, with Thomas Cockey.
ELIZA: CODREY, with Wm. Rigley.

"One of JACOB DEHATTAWAYE'S" with Jno. Gaile.
"Two of THOMAS DAY'S" with Jno. Blackmoore.
FRANCES DAY, with James Lewis, and estate left in his hands.
JNO. DAVIS, with Jno. Edwards.
KATH. DUARNE, orfan of Menass Deuourne [sic], with Seb. Oley.
ELIZA:, MARY and ANN DAVICE, orphans of Jno. Davis, with Wm. Anderson.

(To be continued)

NOTES AND QUERIES

MICHAEL DARLEY; settled in Alexandria, Va., about 1780. WANTED: his previous residence; also family name of his wife, Caroline. E. S. C.

JAMES BRIDGER; born Richmond, Va.; was in Missouri, 1820; Names of his parents wanted. M. M. H. V.

WADE: Twenty-five dollars will be paid for definite information as to Capt. JOHN WADE, of Chester or Marcus Hook, Penna. He was living in 1754. Was he in the "Pennsylvania Navy?" Was he the father of the several WADE brothers who died in the Revolutionary service? Proportionate payment for part information. Mrs. C. A. D. I.

UNDERWOOD-POUND; Wanted, the ancestors of Fannie Underwood who married WILLIAM POUND; said to be the granddaughter of WILLIAM UNDERWOOD, of Virginia, a member of the House of Burgesses in 1652. M. B. C. W.

WANTED: Names of wives of JOSEPH STOCKLEY and ALEXANDER STOCKLEY, both of Accomack, Va. Joseph died about 1736; Alexander, about 1763. M. B. C. W.

THADDEUS BARNARD and his wife HANNAH were married in Oneida cty, New York, in 1805. Hannah was the sister of Dr. Levi GOLDSBOROUGH. She was born in Newcastle cty, Delaware in 1789. Information as to her parentage is greatly desired. Mrs. T. W. C. A.

WANTED: The parentage of ISAAC MILNOR (or MILNER) of Bristol, Bucks cty, Penna., who died early in the 1700's, is unknown. Can any one supply his father's name? He is said to have been the son of DANIEL, the immigrant, but this is a mistake. M. L. M.

FIVE DOLLARS will be paid for the names of the parents of THOMAS BAYLEY RUSSUM, born in Maryland, in one of the Eastern Shore counties, 1 June 1811. He was, perhaps, a grandson of Thomas Bayley of Accomack cty, Virginia. L. P. W. M.

Answering an inquiry by L. J. H., a Washington correspondent suggests that the wife of Henry Pope was probably Tabitha Burwell.

RECENT MAGAZINES

The third number of volume eight of the Publications of the Pennsylvania Genealogical Society, has recently been received. It is, as usual, a little library in itself of most interesting and valuable material, for the historian as well as the genealogist, as also for the reader of general culture and broad interests. It contains an interesting essay on Given Names Formerly in Common Use; Abstracts of New Jersey Commissions, from 1726 on; the Marriage Licenses of Dorchester, Maryland, contributed by Archdeacon Turner; the very valuable abstracts of the minutes of the Philadelphia Monthly Meeting of Friends; the conclusion of the marriage list from the Fairfield County Record, Book, Connecticut; fifteen pages of Bible records; Notes, Queries, Corrections and Reviews. The issue could not be better.

The Maryland Historical Magazine for September contains an article on Gen. John Spear Smith; the Memoirs of the Rev. James Jones Wilmer (26 pp.); the Life of Thomas Johnson (14 pp.); an unusually interesting and valuable collection of depositions from the records, made by Mr. William B. Marye, and covering 22 pages, the sort of thing that many more searchers might bring to light; extracts from Dr. Charles Carroll's voluminous account and letter-books (20 pp); and an article on Gen. William Smallwood, by Dr. A. L. Keith, correcting errors in print. Two local publications are reviewed.

The Legislature of Maryland has authorized the acquisition by the State of ten thousand more of Mrs. Hodges' Marriage References. These have been card indexed and will be available for examination by November first. It is difficult to describe the value of these references... those who are familiar with them know their importance and appreciate Mrs. Hodges' untiring work.

Mr. Charles Shepard, 2153 California street, Washington, D. C., calls attention to the fact that the MEMBERSHIP and VITAL RECORDS of the SECOND CONGREGATIONAL CHURCH of ATTLEBORO, MASSACHUSETTS, copied from the original records by Marion Williams Pierce Carter, is now ready for delivery. As the vital records of Attleboro have never been published, this is the first available genealogical source material relating to this town. The publication contains an historical introduction and an index. Bound in cloth, $4.85, net.

Mr. Shepard has also gotten out a new chart of the Plantagenets. For information and descriptive circulars address as above.

From England the Editor has received the thirteenth volume of Mr. Dwelly's PARISH RECORDS containing further North Peterton Registers (Somerset county, England), annotated with the "Bishop's Transcripts" of the same records. These Bishop's Transcripts are at Wells, and in an early number of the NOTE-BOOK will be found an explanation of their value and their relation to the parish registers. Attention is invited to the very interesting statement in the preface to the recent volume that a number of ancient documents have been recently discovered at Wells, including many Bishop's Transcripts hitherto supposed to have been lost. Vol. 14 of the Registers will contain all of these recently discovered Transcripts that belong to parishes already published.

Mr. Dwelly comments upon the fact that his American subscribers are his chief support in his work of publication of these ancient and most valuable records.

See page 37

COLUMBIAN PRINTING CO., INC., WASHINGTON, D. C.

The

County Court Note-Book

A Little Bulletin of History and Genealogy

Vol. III, November, 1924 No. 6

NEW ENGLANDERS AND SOME OTHERS IN EARLY VIRGINIA AND OTHER SOUTHERN RECORDS

(Eighth instalment)

THOMAS BARBER, of Boston, N. E., cty of Suffolk, mariner; power to Robert Pitts of Virginia. Acco, Va. xx-65. 10 Mch 1730-1.

Mr. WILLIAM BRENTON, of N. E., Mcht. N-n cty, Va. v-135. 1 May 1655.

JOHN BUTTERWORTH, Victualer in the Town of York, York-Hampton Psh, Va., gives power to Mr. John Snead, Gent. Acco, Va. xx-119. 7 Nov 1732.

ROBERT BRINSTON & JOHN INDICOT of Boston; power to Wm. Whittington. Acco vi-418. 19 Jany 1685.

THOMAS COX, an Englishman, takes oath of allegiance; testifies that on his voyage from Great Britain he landed in Charleston, S. C., 17 Sept 1796; lived some time there and removed to Georgia; residing in Louisville [Ga.] from 3 Feby 1797. Jeff'n cty, Ga., Minutes Superior Ct. 13 Apr 1799.

JOHN COLLUME [Columes, Çollome], late of Plymouth in England, dec'd intest. Peter Baker asks l. a. Staff. Va. i-13. 10 Mch 1689-90.

JOHN CALDWELL; *"LATE AT NIGHT,"* a tract of 60 acres surveyed for him, belongs to Wm. Burton in "Carrolina." Wor. cty Rent Roll, Md. 1744. Also *"PINEY NECK."* [Same record.]

WILLIAM CASE, of Boston, in N. E., mariner. Power to John Simpson. Acco, Va. xx-18. 12 Apr 1729.

SIMON EDGILL of the City of Philadelphia, Mcht. Power to Isaac Morris, of Som. cty, Md. Acco, xx-270. 3 Feby 1736.

URSULA FOWLER, in Pennsilvania, owened 50 acres of *"BRADSHAW'S PURCHASE."* Wor. cty, Md. Rent Roll. 1744.

WILLIAM FOXE, late of N. E.; THOMAS BAXTER, sometime an inhabitant of N. E. N-n, Va. v-150. 2 Nov 1654.

JOHN FRAZIER; record of his naturalization; was a citizen or subject of Great Britain. Jeff'n cty, Ga. Minutes Superior Ct. 11 Apr 1799.

CHARLES GACHETT; formerly a native of France; now a resident of Louisville in the cty of Jefferson, solemnly swears that he has resided four years within the United States, and during the whole of that term within the State of Georgia. (Takes oath of allegiance.) Jeff'n cty, Ga. Minutes Superior Ct. 11 Oct 1798.

Messrs. HILL and LAMAR, Mchts in Madeira. Dor. cty, Md. (Old Ledger. 1749-50.)

Dr. JOHN HARMAN; depn of the minister that he was alive in July, 1672. Dr. Harman was formerly Greek reader of the University of "Oxon." Acco, Va. viii-40. Ct 11 Nov 1678.

A LIST OF QUAKERS BANISHED FROM ENGLAND BETWEEN 1660 AND 1666

(From Joseph Besse's Sufferings of the Quakers)

WILLIAM ADAMS, from Hartfordshire.
JOHN APTHORP, from Bedfordshire.
GEORGE ADAMSON, from Berkshire.

ROBERT ALLEN,
ROSE ATKINS,
EDWARD BRUSH,
ANNE BLOW,
EDWARD BOYCOTT,
WILLIAM BREND,
THOMAS BURBAND,
} from London or Middlesex.

CANANIEL BRITTON, from Bristol.
MATTHEW BREMWELL, from Cumberland.

JOHN BLINDELL,
JOHN BRESBON,
WILLIAM BROWN,
THOMAS BURR,
WILLIAM BURR,
} from Hartfordshire.

SARAH BAKER,
MARY BOTHAM,
ELIZABETH BRUCE,
} from Bedfordshire.

BARTHOLOM. CROCKER, from Bristol.
NICHOLAS COMPLIN, from Hampshire.

THOMAS CRAWLEY,
ROBERT CROOK,
} from Hartfordshire.

ANNE COX, from Bedfordshire.

JOSEPH COLE,
LEONARD COLE,
THOMAS CURTIS,
ANNE CURTIS, wf of THOMAS,
} from Berkshire.

MARY CALLOW,
WILLIAM CALLOW,
EVAN CHRISTIAN
JANE CHRISTIAN,
} from Isle of Man.

KATHARINE CHARLES,
HANNAH CAMMACK,
JAMES CARTER,
WM. CAUDERWOOD,
JOHN CLAUS,
ELIZABETH COLLIN,
HENRY COMINGS,
THOMAS COX,
} from London or Middlesex.

(To be continued)

MARRIAGES BY INFERENCE*

(Continued from September number)

JOSEPH AUSTIN, of Libty cty, Ga., and SARAH ANN HINSON, of the same. Mar. contr. 15 Oct 1795. Libty cty, DD-68.

ARTEMAS BAKER and EUPHEMIA DARLING, dau. of the late Andrew Darling, Esq., of Sunbury, Ga. Mar. contr. 25 Sept 1787. Libty cty, B-139.

WILLIAM BAKER and SUSANNAH HORNBY, widow and relict of "Pilip" Hornby, dec'd. Mar. contr. 18 July 1793. Libty cty, Ga. C-75.

JOHN BAKER, Esq., of Sunbury, Libty cty, Ga., pltr, and MARY BLACKSELL, dau. of Thomas, of Chatham cty, pltr, Spr. Mar. contr. Nov. 1793. Libty cty, C-102.

JAMES BELCHER, of Savannah, Gent., and GRACE CARR, of Libty cty, widow. Mar. contr. 28 June 1787. Libty cty, B-49.

JOHN COUPER, of Libty cty, Ga., Mcht, and REBECCA MAXWELL, same, dau. of James, dec'd. Mar. contr. 14 May 1792. Libty cty, C-92.

ARON CROSBY m. ELIZABETH, dau. of Sarah x FRIARMOND, before 16 Oct 1792. See Effm cty, Ga., B-23.

ANDREW DARLING, St. John's Psh, Ga., Mcht, and JEAN BAILLIE, "Sempstress," dau. of Kenneth Baillie. Mar. contr. 10 Sept 1764. Libty cty, B-134.

JOHN DEWS and MARY PATTERSON, widow. Mar. contr. 17 Jany 1799. Chatham cty, Ga. W-125.

PETER DUNWORTH, Mcht, of Sunbury, and Mrs. MARY ANDERSON, widow of Capt. David Anderson. Mar. contr. 18 Oct 1785. Libty cty, Ga., B-75.

JAMES GREENHOW, Jr., Gent., of Effingham cty, Ga., and ANN ABIGAIL SCRUGGS, same, spinster. Mar. contr. 12 Mch 1794. Chatham cty, N-8.

Mr. GREEN HILL, of Scriven cty, Ga., m. Miss Chrisy Bridget. 2 Oct 1799. Effm cty. B-106.

JOHN IRVINE and ANN ELIZABETH BAILLIE, "Sempstress," dau. of Kenneth Baillie. Mar. contr. 5 Sept 1765. Libty cty, Ga. B-135.

CHARLES IRVINE and ELIZABETH DARLING, dau. of the late Andrew Darling, Esq., of Sunbury. Mar. contr. 13 Sept 1787. Libty cty, Ga. B-137.

JAMES JAMES and KERENHAPPUCK POWELL. Mar. contr. 14 May 1793, Libty cty, Ga. C-32.

PHILIP LOW, of Chatham cty, Ga., and MARY JONES, widow, of same, Mar. contr. 28 May 1783. Libty cty, B-348.

DAVID LYNAM, Jeffn cty, Ky, m. ELIZABETH DANIEL, dau. of Thomas. Before 26 Sept 1797. Jeffn cty, Ky. iv-529.

ABSALOM MADDOX, of Shelby cty, Ky, m. NANCY DANIEL, dau. of Thomas [Sr.], of Jeffn cty. Before 26 Sept 1797. Jeffn cty, iv-529.

HENRY MYERS, of Libty cty, Ga., and MARY TIMMONS, spr., of same, dau. of Richard Timmons, and granddaughter of Susannah Mahan. Mar. contr. 10 Mch 1794. Libty cty, C-134.

MATTHEW RAHN, of Effm cty, Ga., wheelwright, and Miss HANNAH ELIZABETH DOLWICK, of same, "spinstress," Mar. contr. 23 Jany 1802. Effm cty, B-155. [This volume is also marked "1"]

DANIEL ROBERTS, late of Wales, but now of St. John's Psh, Gent., and AMARANTHA ELLIOTT. Mar. contr. 12 May 1774. Libty cty, Ga. A-128.

MARYLAND'S NEXT OF KIN *

(Continued from July number)

Mrs. ANNE BICKERDICKE; inv. Richard Bickerdike of A. A. cty. 23 Sept 1719. iii-152.

GEORGE SMITH; inv. Richard Moore of Q. A. cty. 11 Apr 1719. iii-156.

TRUSTRUM THOMAS and SARAH KING; inv. Mrs. Julian King of Q. A. cty. 25 Mch 1719. iii-160.

MATHEW & JOHN EARRICKSON; inv. Charles Earrickson of Kent Island, Q. A. cty. 1 June 1719. iii-162.

ANN BUTLER, RACHEL CLAYTON; inv. Renatus Smith of Q. A. cty, 4 Aug 1719. iii-163.

WILLIAM THOMAS, SIMON THOMAS; inv. Thomas Woodward of Dorchester cty. 29 July 1719. iii-171.

JOSEPH FEDDEMAN, MARY ANDREW; inv. Walter Reed of Somerset cty. 6 Sept 1719. iii-173.

CHRISTOPHER and JOHN TILLOTTSON; inv. Thomas Tillottson of Q. A. cty, 12 Feby 1718. iii-174.

FRANCIS HAMERSLEY, MARY LATTIMER; inv. Jacob Brandt of Charles Cty. 29 Oct 1719. iii-175.

WILLIAM MAONCHIR(?), JOHN HANSON; inv. Benj. Hanson of Charles cty. 3 Aug 1719 iii-177.

JOHN and HENRY GILBERT; inv. Ralph Distance of Q. A. cty. 9 Mch 1717. iii-179.

THOMAS LOYDE; inv. James Gardner of Pr. Geo's. cty. 16 Oct 1719. iii-180.

DIANA LANGFORD; inv. Vincint Langford of Som. cty. 29 Nov 1718. iii-182.

WILLIAM HOLLAND; inv. William Holland, of St. Mary's cty. 30 Nov 1719. iii-183.

RICHARD LINWED(?) and THOMAS MEDFORD; inv. Thos. Medford of Kent cty. 16 Aug 1719. iii-185.

JOSEPH RYE, "being the eldest son;" inv. John Hancock of Cecill cty. 18 Aug 1718. iii-187.

WILLIAM and CHARLES STEVENS; inv. John Stevens of A. A. cty. 6 Dec 1719. iii-188.

SARAH YOPP. SUSANNAH MATHEWS; inv. Roger Yopp of Charles cty. 6 Dec 1719. iii-190.

WILLIAM KEY, JOBE KEY; inv. John Barron of Charles cty. 31 Aug 1719. iii-191.

SARAH SPENSOR, "als Dyson;" inv. Daniel Spensor of Calvert cty; 29 July 1719. iii-192.

RICHARD RANSOM, "brother to the deceased;" inv. William Ransom, of Balto. cty, 19 Nov 1719. iii-196.

DAVID MACALL, HANNAH BARNEY; inv. Mathew Barney of Dorchester cty, 20 Aug 1719. iii-196.

GAROTT GARETSON, RICHARD BURROUGH; inv. William Lowe of Balto. cty. 23 June 1719. iii-198.

BARTON HUNGERFORD, BARTON SMOOT; inv. Thomas Smoot of Charles cty. 20 Nov 1719. iii-199.

MARY HAMILTON; inv. Andrew Hamilton of Pr. Geo's cty. 22 Aug 1719. iii-202.

WILLIAM ARSUTON [AUSTIN?]; inv. Prudence Woolman of Talbot cty. 17 Oct 1716. iii-208.

WILLIAM BECKETT, THOMAS MEARTIN; inv. Thomas Meartin, Jr. of Talbot cty. 3 Feby 1719. iii-209.

(To be continued)

VIRGINIA COLONISTS

(Head rights from Old Volume 5, State Land Office, Richmond. Continued from SEPTEMBER issue. Those starred are reprinted from MAY issue.)

ROBERT CASTLE, James City county, 1655.*
Head rights: John Nayler, Wm. Franklin, Kath. Browninge, Mary Cobb, Rob. Whitefare, John Hayall.

PHILIP CHARLES [county not given], 1656.*
Head rights: Thos. Beggon, Eliz. Marin, Hugh H.... [?]

HENRY CHICHLEY, Knt, "North side of Rappahannock River," 1656.
Head rights: Rich. Scarbrow, Tho: Thomas, James Howard, Antho. Candell [Kendall?], Tho. Beardwell, Rob Hane (x), Jno. White, Jno. Ray, Henry Rice, Arthur Chandler, Wm. Byler, Wm. Chelmedge, Rich. Arrundell, Tho. Mason, Georg Haynes, Sam. Parry, Tho Pones, Peter Mason, Wm. Hurt, Tho. Howell, Samll. Goodwin, Tho. Harris, Rob. Taylor, Tho. Richd, Jones Alpatt or Alpott, Jno. Woodson. Edw. Buckingham, Edward Freeman, Henry Lambert, *Jest* Wms., Tho. Wearington [Warrington?]

Capt. WILLIAM CANFILL, Surry cty, 1656.
Head rights: Walter Taylor, Joane Gurney, Fran: Butler, Hugh Kennicke, Gillien Corners, *Onory* Sullivan, *Onory* Linsey [these forenames are perhaps *Honora*], Joane Davis, Mary Hall, James Filline, Timothy Issall.

WILLIAM CRUMP and Mr. HUMPHRY VAULX, James City Cty, 1656.
Head rights: Thomas *Prescon* [Preston?] Jno. Steevens, Jno. Lyon, Jno. Childecock, Rebecca Molson, Tho. Ballister, Jane Goss, John Short, John Fort, Elinr, Flettcher, John Taylor, Anne Phippa, and eight negroes; all [of] wch are assigned by Majr. Chroshaw.

Major THOMAS CURTIS, "North side of Ware River in Mock Jack bay," 1656.
Head rights: Elizabeth Boston, Hannah Blackwell.

JOHN CURTIS, "in North River, in Mock Jack Bay," 1656.
Head rights: Silvanus Wood, John Snell, five negroes.

Lt. WILLIAM COCKERAM, Surry cty, 1656.
Head rights: Henry Armestrong, John Pinder, Robert Jenckinson.

Mr. JOHN CHANDLER, Northumberland cty, 1656.
Head rights: Jno. Brigges, Anth: Taylor, Ja. Francis, Anne Stannenite[?] Jane Catesby, Roger Stillwell, Hump: Smith, Wm. Morrice, Marg: Morfrey, Nich: Prichard, Est: Fenton, Charles Thompson, Hen: Copley, Roger Moore, Alice May, Nich: Spront, Zach: Foster, Samuell Dobson, Jno: Stubb, Tho: Woodham, Nich: Thomas, Jno. Tucker, Jno: Lea, Henry Stanley, Marg. Long, Nich: Mason, Wm. Robinson, Marg: Franklin, Jere: Cottrell, Wm. Mace.

Mr. JNO: CHANDLER, Northumberland cty, 1656.
Head rights: David Watson, Dunken Ryd, Jno: Blacke, Thomas Kamp, Robrt. Parry, Lewis Sheapard. Jno: Chickett (or Checkitt).

Capt: WM. CANFILL, Surry cty, 1656.
Head rights: Margery Webber, James Wilson, Thomas Bayly.

Major THOMAS CURTIS, "North side of Ware River in Mockjack bay," 1657.
Head rights: Wm: Browne, Jno. Dowdy, Wm. Harman and his wife Alice.

Capt. LEONARD CHAMBERLINE, New Kent cty, 1657.
Head rights: Mary Woodered, Jno. Lee, Jno. Martin, Jno. Hooke, Rich. White, John Hogg, Tho. Maple.

Capt. LEONARD CHAMBERLINE, New Kent cty, 1657.
Head rights: Jno. Woodington, Charles Woodington.

HENRY COLLIER, New Kent cty, 1657.
Head right: John Rosly.

ZACHERY CRIPPS, "in Warenecke," 1657.
Head rights: Charles Grimes, Ralph Danby, Rich. Stone, Tho. Faulkner, Jno. Woodgeare, Jno. Willoughby, Ann Hegnone[?] Jno. Workeman, Jno. Elcock [Alcock?] and one negro.

WM. CLAPHAM, Junior, Lancaster cty, 1657.
Head rights: Clemt. Corbell, Angell his wife, Gabriel Corbell, Jno. Corbell, Rich. Mocfell [McFell?] [and] his wife; George Stubbs, Samll. Percy, Jno. Andrewes, Hannah Rogers, Jno. Heath.

ROBERT CASTLETON, "in Petomeck Freshes on the North East side of a Creeke below Puscatoway, but on the *oposite* side of the River of Petomeck," 1657.
Head rights: Wm. Gill, Rich. Heath, Eliz. Arnold, Reb: Stone, Jane Hunt, Anis Browne, Ales Tiller, Geo. Ray, Fra. Covey, Anth. Barwick, Walter Pratt, Jasper Grey, Arth: Newsombe [Newcombe?] Tho. Harrington, Prudence Greene, Wm. Corey, James Slaner, Isabell Meldron, Jane Mountford, Willm. Holeman.

(To be continued)

The County Court Note-Book

An every-other-monthly devoted to abstracts from County Court and other records, prior to 1800, and with a department of notes and queries.

MILNOR LJUNGSTEDT, Editor and Publisher. Bethesda, Route 1, Maryland.

Published six times a year. **Subscription, two dollars and fifty cents a year,** in advance; must begin with the year. **Renewals, two dollars.** Advertising rates moderate.

VOL. III NOVEMBER, 1924 No. 6

EXPLANATORY AND OTHERWISE

The Editor of the NOTE-BOOK faces the coming year with some small confidence. The thing that she is most afraid of as she goes over in her mind the list of distinguished libraries and equally distinguished individuals who are encouraging the NOTE-BOOK by their subscriptions, is that, like the toad, she will be led to imagine that the NOTE-BOOK has a sizable standing. "Pride goeth before destruction and an haughty spirit before a fall." The teachings of her home land recur to her... when she was always first or second in her class... but never made any great mark in the world after all.

It does seem sometimes as if everything that ever happens is a mere accident. The NOTE-BOOK came into existence in the most inconsequential fashion but seems intent on remaining. The Editor asks your kindly aid towards its continuance.

Among the Libraries, the past few months have brought the Newberry Library of Chicago; the Houston Library of Texas; the Carnegie Library of Atlanta. And the Raleigh State Library took a second look and also signed up. The Athenaeum Library of Boston—or, rather, the Library of the Boston Athenaeum—is an acquisition very dear to the Editor's heart. It was quite a shock to meet lately a gentleman of considerable reading who said he had never heard of it. It is perhape good for us of Boston to occasionally get a cold douche of this kind.

Individual subscribers of just as much note in their special lines as the libraries, have signified their approval. On the whole, while in the financial doldrums, the COUNTY COURT NOTE-BOOK is really an otherwise success.

It seems advisable to repeat the explanation heretofore given, that the abstracts of probates and administrations from the ORDER BOOKS of PRINCE WILLIAM and KING GEORGE counties, Virginia, are given because they are the only records (with some exceptions too long to go into here) of the wills and administration proceedings of certain decades, the record volumes proper having been lost or destroyed. No copies are known to exist of the wills mentioned in the probates... though occasionally such copies appear in later suits before district or other higher courts.

The Editor is much pleased to say that she has made arrangements with the Deputy in Richmond county for abstracts of the probates and administration for the period covered by the first non-existent will book. These will begin in FEBRUARY or APRIL.

The abstracts from PRINCE WILLIAM and KING GEORGE will be brought up to the date of the will records, or as far as the ORDER BOOKS go, and the Editor hopes to give similar material from FAIRFAX and perhaps other counties.

The notes from the ORDER BOOKS of MONONGALIA county, West Virginia, appearing in this issue, are kindly furnished by Mr. THOMAS RAY DILLE, Secretary of the State Society of the S. A. R., Morgantown, West Virginia.

The list of land-owners from the tax-lists or "land books" of OHIO county, West Virginia (then Virginia), which was given in the NOTE-BOOK, has been found to cover only one district.

The list of taxables from the personal property tax-list for the other district will be published before long. These two will probably give the names of the greater proportion of the residents of the county at the time.

Some interesting and absolutely accurate information as to South Carolina Districts and Counties will be published in the next issue.

News item from Washington, D. C., POST.

> Upper Marlboro, Md.: Prince Georges county commissioners have approved plans for enlargement of the county courthouse. The work will cost about $80,000, the necessary bonds having already been sold. C. M. Lightbrown is the architect. Plans call for two wings on the rear of the present building, each approximately 40x45 feet. These wings will be two stories, and practically fireproof construction. It is expected the addition will be ready for occupancy early next spring. Most of the addition will be used for housing records.

This is really too good to be true. This county has been on the black list of every searcher who ever had the temerity to visit its courthouse.

The LIST OF QUAKERS, banished from their homes in England, between 1660 and 1666, mostly to the West Indies, from whence a number unquestionably came to the American colonies, is taken from Besse's Sufferings of the Quakers, edition of 1733-1738. These volumes, as well as the next edition, contain a very long list of Quakers who suffered in many ways for their belief. The names of those banished have been picked out by the Editor. Their names and their English counties may help to solve some genealogical problems.

COLONIAL AND REVOLUTIONARY AND OTHER MILITARY NOTES

From the records of the COUNTY COURT OF MONONGALIA COUNTY, VIRGINIA.

(Order Book 4 1810. Pages 241 and 243.)

At a court held for Monongalia County on Wednesday the 13th day of November, 1811, present James Scott, John Evans Jr. John S. Roberts and Charles Byrn Gentlemen.

Peter Haught personally appeared in Court and made oath that Richard Tennant Served in McIntoshes Campaign as a Drummer, and that he also Served in Dunmores War as a Drummer, which is ordered to be Certif'd.

Richard Tennant personally appeared in Court and made Oath that Peter Haught Served as a private Soldier in McIntoshes Campaign, and that he also Served as a Private Soldier in Dunmores War, which is ordered to be Certified.

Peter Haught personally appeared in Court and made oath that James Snodgrass Served as a private Soldier in McIntoshes Campaign which is ordered to be Certified.

John Evans Jr personally appeared in Court and made Oath that Joseph Snodgrass and Elisha Snodgrass are the reputed heirs of James Snodgrass deceased, which is ordered to be Certified.

At a Court held for Monongalia County on Friday the 15th of November 1811, present William John, Boz Burrows, William N. Jarrett and Rawley Scott, Gentlemen.

David Scott personally appeared in Court and Made Oath that John Evans Senior now of Monongalia County Served in McIntoshes Campaign as a Lieutenant Colonel in the year 1778, that he also served as a Lieutenant in Dunmores Campaign in the year 1774, which is ordered to be Certified.

John Evans Senior personally appeared in Court and made Oath that David Scott Senior Served as a Captain in Dunmores War in the year 1774, which is ordered to be Certified.

John Evans Senior personally appeared in Court and made Oath that James Daugherty served as a Captain under him in the year 1778 during McIntoshes Campaign, which is ordered to be Certjfied, and it is further ordered to be certified that Enos Daugherty is the Sole devisee of the said James Daugherty deceased as appears to the Court from the Will of the said James Daugherty.

SEVENTY-FIVE DOLLARS REWARD, and no questions asked, will be paid for the contents of a khaki-covered mailing case, mislaid, lost, or stolen, between Trenton and Columbia, S. C., or in Columbia, while in transit to Abbeville, S. C., via the Southern Railroad, in care of the Southeastern Express Company. Editor.

NEW HERALDIC DICTIONARY IN PREPARATION.—Mr. Charles K. Bolton, 10½ Beacon Street, Boston, Mass., is preparing to publish a dictionary describing coats-of-arms that have been used in this country on book-plates, old silver, gravestones, seal rings, etc. He would like to correspond with persons interested.

A LIST OF ORPHANS FROM THE RECORDS OF ANNE ARUNDEL COUNTY MARYLAND (Liber T. B. 1.)

(*Contributed by Mrs. Geo. W. Hodges*)

GEORGE ELLVIDGE, with Mr. Jones, baker.

KATHERINE ELVEGS(?), with James Lewis.

JOHN ELDER, with Lewis Duvall.

JOB EVANS, SAMUELL EVANS and JOHN EVANS, with John Enser.

ELIZA: FREBORNE, with Roger Roberts.

THOS: RICHARD and NATHANIELL FARBROTHER, orphans, with the Widow FARBROTHER, and estate left in her hands.

BENJ. FREEMAN, at Thos: Gassaway's.

ELIZABETH FRANCIS, dau. of Henry Francis, with Widow Ryder.

DARCAS FRANCIS [sic] dau. of Henry Frances, with Joshua Jones.

MARY, SARAH, ELIZA: and DEBORAH FULLER, orphts of Edward Fuller, with Thos. Dauson.

CHRIS: GREEN son of Christopher Green, with Widow Ryder.

WILLIAM GROVES(?), with John Beacher.

GEORGE GROVES, with James Wood.

ROBERT, MARGARETT and ELIZA: GOTT, with Wm. Smith.

SARAH GOLESBURY, with Wm. Smith.

EDWARD, RACHELL, MARY, REBECCA, and SUSANA GAITHER, orphans, with Fra[n]ces Harden and estate in his hands.

MARY GROSS, with John Bradley.

OLANDER, SOPHIAH, WM. and CHARLES GREFETH, with Mr. Thomas Reynolds.

One of JNO. GASSOWAY'S orphans with Richd Galloway.

(*To be continued*)

A LIST OF PERSONS NATURALIZED BY PARTICULAR ACTS

From Bacon's Laws of Maryland *

(*Contributed by Mrs. George W. Hodges. Continued from July number.*)

PETER SAUNDERS, of Talbot cty, Pltr, and his children. 3 Nov 1711. 20.

PETER SCAMPER, of Prince George's cty. 17 May 1701. 6.

HERMANS SCHEE, Gent., of Cecil cty. 25 Mch 1702. 6.

JACOB SETH. 26 Sept 1684. 9.

* Figures other than dates refer to chapters.

PETER CLAYTER. 26 Sept 1684. 8.
GEORGE SLECOMBE, a German. 11 June 1697. 9.
HENDRICK SLUYTER, and JACOB SLUYTER, Jr. 18 Oct 1694. 14.
CHRISTOPHER SMITHERS, taylor, of the Port of Annapolis. 3 May 1704. 2.
JOHN HANS STEELMAN, and his son JOHN STEELMAN, of Cecil cty. 19 Oct 1695. 25.
AXELL STILLE. 6 June 1674. 12.
JOHN SWINEYARD, of Balto. cty., pltr. 4 Nov 1724. 8.
CHRISTIAN SWORMSTEAD, of Calvert cty., chirurgeon. 4 Nov 1710. 16.
MARCUS SYFERSON. 6 June 1674. 12.
JOHN TAWERT, of Cecil cty, gentleman. 3 May 1704. 2.
WILLIAM TICK. 6 June 1674. 12.
ANDREW TOULSON, of Balto. cty. 19 Apr 1681. 10.
THOMAS TURNER, of A. A. cty. 19 Apr 1671. 10.
JOHN BAYTIST TYLER, of Pr. Geo's cty, pltr. 19 Apr 1706. 12.
MICHAEL URY, a Greek, of Pr. Geo's cty, 6 Nov 1725. 16.
JOHN de VAGHA, 18 Oct 1694. 4.
ISAAC VANBIBBER, Gent. Cecil cty. 25 Mch 1701. 6.
JOHN VANBEECK, 8 May 1669. 4.

(*To be concluded*)

KING GEORGE COUNTY, VIRGINIA, PROBATES AND ADMINISTRATIONS

(*Continued from July number*)

JOHN PARSONS; L. a. to Jeremiah Murdock, Esq., greatest creditor; Harry Turner, sec. 3 June 1743. ii-334.
JOHN BELL; L. a. to Margaret Bell, widow; John Fooley(?) sec. 3 June 1743. ii-335.
GERRARD SMITH; his will presented by Precilla Smith, his extx; proved by John and Margaret Smith. John Simpson, John Patterson, sec. 1 July 1743. ii-347.
WILLIAM DUFF, Jr.; L. a. to MATHEW TOOLE; Robert Green, Gent., James Jones, sec. (ANN DUFF chooses Matthew Toole for gdn.) 4 Nov 1743. ii-367.
NEAL McCORMACK; his will presented by Stephen McCormack his extr; proved by Isaac Arnold and Edmund Donohoe. 2 Dec 1743. ii-377.
JOHN EDWARDS; L. a. to Richard Tutt, Ann Edwards, the widow, having relinquished her right to admr. John Fox and Abraham Kenyon, sec. 2 Dec 1743. ii-378.
WILLIAM CARTER; will presented by Richard Drake, extr. 2 Dec 1743. ii-378.
THOMAS MUSTIN; L. a. on his estate granted to James Dishman; John Butler, sec. 6 Jany 1743. ii-380.
NICHOLAS SMITH; L. a. on his estate to Harry Turner. John Champe, Gent., sec. 3 Feby 1743. i-381.
WILLIAM THORNTON; his will presented by Francis Thornton, his extr. Proved by Ignatius West and Elizabeth Winton. John Champe, sec. 2 Mch 1743. ii-383.
ROBERT DONIPHAN; his will presented by James Hackley and Ellen Doniphan, extrs. John Fox, sec. 2 Mch 1743. ii-383.
WILLIAM SUMMERTON; his will presented by Rebecca Summerton, his extr. Proved by Richard Owens and Nathaniel Elkins. 2 Mch 1743. ii-384.
MARGARET PALMER; L. a. on her estate to John Glendening. John Champe, Gent., sec. Simon White, heir-at-law, relinquishes right to admr. 5 Jany 1744. ii-
DANIEL HARPER; L. a. on his estate to Thos. Harper; John Fox, sec. 2 Mch 1743. ii-384.
JAMES JONES; will presented by Hester Jones, his extx. Proved by Frances Benson, William Hill, and Henry Machen. 1 June 1744. ii-396. (*To be continued*)

WILLS PROBATED AND ADMINISTRATIONS GRANTED IN PRINCE WILLIAM COUNTY, VIRGINIA

From the first remaining Order Book (see APRIL, 1923). The list which follows, and which completes that volume, has been accidentally overlooked.

WILLIAM PATTISON; will presented by Francis Burgess, extr. Proved by Bailey Johnson, Alexander Parker and James Stack. 26 Feby 1753. p. 96.
ALICE ASHWORTH; will presented by Elias Edmonds, extr. Proved by oaths of William Wright and Simon Morgan, two of the wit. 26 Feby 1753. p. 97.
NATHANIEL TRIPLET; admn of his estate granted to John Triplet. James Turner, sec. 26 Feby 1753. p. 98.
THOMAS YOUNG; will presented by Margaret Young and Foushee Tebbs, extrs. Proved by oaths of Thomas Machen and Joseph Butler. 25 June 1753. p. 160.
PHILEMON WATERS; will presented by Catherine Waters, extx, and proved by Sarah Tacket, John Metcalfe and William Tacket. 25 June 1753. p. 160.
DANIELL MARR; will presented by Ann Marr, extx, and proved by George Wheatley and John Jordan. 25 June 1753. p. 160.
JAMES KEITH, Clerk; will presented by Mary Isham Keith, and Charles Green, Clerk, two of the extrs. 25 June 1753. p. 163.
JOSEPH ARNISHEE, admn on his estate asked by Elias Edmond. Denied. 26 June 1753. p. 168.
MICALL OWINS; admn on his estate granted Joshua *Owin.* Isaac Foster, and Henry Watkins, sec. 24 July 1753. p. 191.
THOMAS DAVIES; will presented by Judith *Davis,* one of the extrs. 27 Aug. 1753. p. 219.
PEMBROKE ODEN; will proved by Lewis Oden and Joseph Willis, two of the wit. Admn granted to Mary Oden; William Rookard and Thomas Boggess, sec. 27 Sept 1753. p. 290.
JACOB SMITH; admn on his estate granted to Harmon Button and wf Catherine. 27 Sept 1753. p. 291. (*End of this volume*)

NAMES OF INHABITANTS NEAR RED STONE [now in Pennsylvania] 1768.

From the Colonial Record of Penna. v. ix-508.

John Wiseman, William Linn, John Vervalson, Thomas Brown, John Delong, Geo. Martin, Henry Prisser, William Colvin, Abraham Tygard, Richard Rodgers, Peter Young, Thos. Down;

Andrew Gudgeon, James Crawford, Henry Swats, Jesse Martin, John Verval, Jr., Thos. Douter, Michael Hooter, Gabriel Conn, Hans Cack(?). Josias Crawford, Phil. Sute;

John Peters, Jos. McCleon, Adam Hatton, James Waller, Capt. Coburn, Andrew Linn, John Martin, Dan'l McCay, ... Provence?

NOTES AND QUERIES

THADDEUS BARNARD'S wife was HANNAH. They were married in Oneida county, New York, it is stated, in 1805. Hannah Barnard was the sister of Dr. Levi Goldsborough. She was born in Newcastle county, Delaware, in 1789. Definite information as to her family is greatly desired.
Mrs. T. W. C. A.

WADE: Twenty-five dollars will be paid for information as to the parentage of Capt. JOHN WADE, who was living in Chester county Penna. in 1754; for date of birth and death; place of death; names of his children, &c. His wife appears to have been Martha Robinson. She may have been a widow when they married. It is probable Capt. Wade died in or during the Revolution. Did he die on the prison ship Jersey?
M. L. M.

WANTED: The wife of JOSEPH STOCKLEY, son of JOHN, of Accomack cty, Va., and the wife of ALEXANDER STOCKLEY, his son, also of Accomack. JOSEPH died about 1736; Alexander about 1763.
M. B. C. W.

WANTED: The parentage of ISAAC MILNOR, of Bucks county, Penna, who was of Bristol tshp, and died early in the 1700's.
M. L. M.

WITHERS - ROBINSON. Who was the father of NANCY ROBINSON who married BENJAMIN WITHERS in Fauquier cty, Va., in 1783. Her mother's name was Martha.

McMAHON. Did John McMahon, who married Rosannah Hardin, dau. of Martin Hardin of Fauquier cty, Va., have Revolutionary service?
C. M. I.

WANTED: The record of the marriage of WILLIAM FLOYD, of Amherst cty, Va., and ABADIAH DAVIS. This marriage was some time prior to 1750. Said to have taken place about 1747. What is the authority?
M. L. M.

MATTHEW STEWART CLAN. Formed 15 August 1924. Will meet on the third Thursday of August every year. All who are direct descendants of MATTHEW STEWART are invited to attend. Mrs. ELIZABETH STEWART BUNDY, of Monroe, N. C., can give further information and will be glad to correspond with any one who can give definite information concerning the parentage of Matthew Stewart aforesaid.

The very valuable lists of marriages and marriage licenses contributed by Mr. E. CARTER DELANO, of Warsaw, Richmond cty, Virginia, to the D. A. R. magazines of November, 1923, and October, 1924, are a trifle misleading in the headings, as printed.

The first list, in 1923, is a list of marriage licenses, considered by expert genelaogists not as marriage records but as very safe proof in nearly all cases that a marriage took place.

Mr. Delano's second list should read, *Marriages in Farnham Parish,* rather than Farnham. The name Farnham by itself, carries to a New Englander or a westerner the idea of a township or a town ... though, of course, most searchers are familiar with the parish as a political division of Virginia and some other colonies.

A limited number of the KEENE FAMILY HISTORY is for sale at the HAYES BOOK ROOM, 3526 Roland avenue, Baltimore, Maryland. It contains 342 pp., 29 halftone portraits, is well printed, and carefully and handsomely bound. The American KEENES are traced from their arrival, and a chapter is given to the English ancestral record. Price $6.50.

The voluminous record of marriage licenses at the Baltimore County Courthouse has been indexed. This will be a tremendous help to searchers. It was while reading through these interminable lists that the Editor's attention was called, by the gifted and exact Mr. Story, now dead, to the fact that marriage licenses are not marriages.

Since the previous issue of the NOTE-BOOK the Editor has learned that by writing to Mrs. Marks, at Warsaw, Richmond county, Virginia, arrangements can be made for a most comfortable and pleasant room, and perhaps for breakfast. Excellent meals, breakfast, dinner, and supper, can be had at Settle's Hotel nearby. The Editor writes from actual experience.

The ancient hotel at Heathsville, Va., kept by Mrs. Rice, is a most attractive place, and Mrs. Rice sets another excellent table. Heathsville has a great many records from 1750 on.

There is a very pretty modern hotel at Irvington, Lancaster county, Va., but there is no satisfactory hotel at the courthouse town.

Every one who has been to Tappahannock, Va., knows the Misses Gresham and their homelike and comfortable house. The table is excellent, and the house is directly opposite the courthouse.

See page 45

COLUMBIAN PRINTING CO., INC., WASHINGTON, D. C.

Volume II

Abbey, 46.
Abbot, 17, 18.
Abdill, 17.
Able, 10.
Aboghell, 35.
Achillis, 1.
Adason, 17.
Adams, 22, 26, 38, 46.
Adkins, 18.
Adlington, 1.
Adolph, 10, 43.
Aiking, 21.
Aldick, 26.
Aldriss, 18.
Alexander, 13, *25.
Alkire, 13.
Allen, *10, 13, 17, 20, 27, 38, 46.
Allison, 13, 38, *41.
Almery, 17.
Alsup, 5.
Alward, 1.
Ambrose, 1.
Anderson, 1, 10, 13, *22, 44.
Andrews, 9, 10, 13, 14, 17, 21, 30, 41.
Anleton, 1.
Ansell, 10.
Appleton, 17.
Applewhaite, 2.
Ardery, 7, 8.
Arenson, 1.
Armitrading, 10, *17.
Armstrong, 13.
Arnell, 10.
Arnold, 14, 35, 38.
Ashcom, 2.
Ashley, 1.
Ashmore, 38.
Atkinson, 10.
Atkison, 21.
Atton, 18.
Atwell, 46.
Averill (?), 25.
Aylett, 26.
Ayres (see also Eires and Eyres), 3, 10.

Baggs, 3.
Bagnal, 2.
Bagwell, 1, 10, 18.
Bailey, Bayley, Baylie, 1, 14, 18, 34.
Bailis, 22, 30.
Baker, 9, 17, 26, 33, 45.
Ball, 20.
Ballantine, 33.
Ballard, 17.
Banger, 19.
Bannister, 11.
Barker, 17, 33.
Barlowe, 41.
Barnes, 18, *46.
Barnet, 22.
Barnhart, 34.
Barr, 30.
Barrett, Barratt, 21, 46.
Barrette, de, 1.
Barringer, 38.
Barron, 18.
Barteaud, 1.
Bartlett, 5, 45.
Barton, 14, 21.
Baseman, 13.
Battell, 2, 42.
Baxter, 30.
Baylis, 22, 30, 38.
Beale, 27, 33.
Beard, 21.
Beck, 21.
Bedder, 27.
Beek, 21.
Been, 21.
Beenson, 1.
Belfare, 38.
Bell, 10, 13.
Bellamy, 17.
Bellicame, 1.
Bellote, 18.
Belsher, 21, 46.
Benger, 10.
Bennett, 27, 38, 46.
Benthall, 9, *10.
Bently, 43.
Berry, 1, 31.
Berte, 1.
Bevins, 13.
Bickley, 26.
Biggs, 21.
Billington, 9.
Biscoe, 18.
Black, 13.
Blackenstein, 1.
Blackiston, 2.
Blackwell, 3, *14, 45.
Blades, 19.
Blair, 38.
Blake, 19.
Blanck, 25.
Bland, 37, 38.
Blaney, 1.
Blindell, 37.
Blunt, 2.
Boddington, 5.
Bodien, 1.
Bolton, 30, 39.
Bonner, 21.
Booler, 27.
Booth, 7, 14, 37.
Boquet, 2.
Boreing, 42.
Bosley, 47.
Boswell, 10.
Boteler, 11.
Bowdoin, 1, 6, 17, 23.
Bowes, 3.
Bowing, Bowen, 43.
Bowles, 27, 42.
Boyd, 13.
Boyer, 44.
Boyle, 5, 37.
Boys, 2 ,17.
Bozman, 42.
Bracewell, 35.
Bracket, 1.
Bradcutt, 38.
Braddock, 38.
Bradford, 17.
Branch, 2.
Brawner, 38.
Bray, 43.
Brent, 37, 38.
Brenton, 1.
Bressie, 2.
Brewer, 10, 18.
Brickhouse, 10.
Bridger, 2, 14, 23.
Bridges, *30.
Briggs, 43.
Brispoe, 2.
Bronagh, 5.
Bronsden, 1.
Brooke, 11, 26.
Broord, 2.
Brown, *2, 5, 10, 11, 13, *14, 17, *18, 21, *27, 30, *38, 45, *46.
Bruce, 21.
Brune, 2.
Brush, 13.
Bull, 2.
Bullen, 38.
Burcham, 38.
Burchanel, 34.
Burdette, Burdit, 10, 44.
Burford, 31.
Burgess, 26.
Burkele, 2.
Burns, 13.
Burr, 46.
Burroughs, 1, 26.
Burt (?), 1, 42.
Burtney, 34.
Burton, 13, 17.
Butler, 1, 5, 14, 21.
Butts, 38.
Byard, 1.
Bynam, 43.

Cain, 7.
Cale, 3.
Callander, 21.
Calvert, *22, *30, 34.
Cammil, 46.
Campbell, 17.
Camperson, 2.
Campion, 43.
Canterbury, 30.
Carey, 11.
Carny, 21.
Carlisle, 45.
Carr, 30, *38.
Cartwright, 2.
Carver, 2.
Carvich, 3.
Case, 46.
Castle, 10.
Cathey, 7.
Catton, 18.
Cavey (?), 26.
Chaires, 3.
Chambers, 21.
Chamblin, 22.
Champ, 13.
Chancy, 18.
Chandler, *17, 44.
Channell, 2.
Chap, 46.
Chaplin, 21.
Chapman, 30, 39, 42.
Chappell, 9.
Chavalier, 44.
Chenault, 17.
Chenoweth, 30.
Chesyldine, 3.
Chew, 18, 46.
Chinn, 38.
Christian, 2, 17, 42.
Church, 25.
Churchill, 38.
Churchman, 45.

Clark, *1, 11, *13, 15, 41.
Clarkson, 13.
Clements, 2.
Clifford, 13.
Coachman, 1.
Cochin, 2.
Cocks, 21.
Codin, 2.
Cody, 2.
Coffin, 46.
Cogswell, 13.
Coker, 46.
Cole, 1, 17.
Coleman, 2, 26, 46.
Colieman, 2.
Colke, 2.
Collier, 17.
Collins, 2, 13.
Comegys, 2.
Compton, 27.
Congleton, 13.
Connal, 21.
Connar, 22.
Conrod, 46.
Constant, 13.
Conway, 22.
Conyers, *30, 38.
Coode, 2, 3.
Cook, 2, 13, 23, 30, 46.
Cookson, 33.
Cooper, 2, 25, 30.
Copeland, 46.
Copes, 25.
Corbin, *22.
Cordea, 18.
Cornelius, 17.
Cornwell, 42.
Costa, de, 18.
Coston, 19.
Couchman, 13.
Councellinge, 2.
Coursey, 3, 42.
Covey, 26.
Cox, 1.
Craig, 13.
Craugh, 18.
Crawford, 41.
Craycroft, 2.
Creagh, 18.
Creele, 45.
Cresap, 39.
Creswell, 6.
Crew, 17.
Cripps, 2.
Crismand, 18.
Crockett, 11.
Crooke, 47.
Croshaw, 10.
Crossle, Crosley, 10.
Croswell, 46.
Crump, 14.
Crupper, 30, 45.
Cudworth, 1.
Cumming, 46.
Cundiff, 14.
Cunningham, 31.
Curle, 17.
Curry, 13.
Curtice, 21.
Curtis, 18, 21.
Cusenberry, 13.
Cussen, 3.
Custis, 9, 19.

Dabney, 26.
Daffour, 18.
Daines, 25.
Daisy, 13.
Dallas, *38.
Daly, 21.
Dangerman, 18.
Daniel, *6.
Daning, 43.
Danison, 18.
Darnall, Darnel, 27, 38, 41.
Darrell, 5.
Dash, 2.
Dashiell, Dashell, 42, 43.
Dauntress, 18.
Davenport, 15.
Davis, *3, 11, *13, 17, 18, *27, 30, 31, 38, *42, *43, 46.
Davison, 35, 46.
Dawes, 46.
Dawkins, 14.
Dawson, 23.
Day, 10, 44.
Debruter, 18.
DeCosta, 18.
Dehaven, 34.
Delamaire, 18.
Delastatius, 1.
Dellohunt, 27.
Demonderer, 18.
Dennis, 13.
Denny, 3.
Desjardins, 18.
Dhyniossa, *18.
Dick, 14.
Dicks, 19.
Dickason, 5.
Diggs, 27.
Dillon, 27.
Diskin, 13.
Dixon, 10, 45.
Dodson, 14, 38.
Doe, *35.
Donald, 13.
Doolittle, 45.
Doss, 5.
Dougherty, 41.
Douglas, 13, 26.
Dowdee, 18.
Dowden, 13.
Downing, 45, 46.
Doxcey, 2.
Drake, 2.
Drummond, 9, 17, 42.
Dubruter, 18.
Duckett, 18.
Dudley, 3, 13.
Duffield, 13.
Dugan, 34.
Dugar, 26.
Duke, 21.
Duncan, 13, 38.
Dunlap, 13, 21.
Dunn, 9, 10, 46.
Duparkes, 9, 41.
Dupra, 2.
Durant, Durrant, 1, 27.
Dutitree, 18.
Dyer, 21.
Dyhattoway, Duhaddaway, 18.

Eagen, 21.
Earle, *3.
Eason, 42.
Eastham, 46.
Edgar, 18.
Edgill, 17.
Edmiston, 13.
Edson, 15.
Edwards, 5, 13, 15, 17, 33, *45.
Eldridge, 17.
Elexon, 18.
Elgar, 46.
Elkenton, 9.
Elkins, 5.
Ellett, 26, 27.
Elligood, 6, 9, 14, 23, 25.
Elliott, 13, 19.
Elm, 43.
Elzey, Elzye, 1, *17, 45.
Emperor, 25.
England, 2.
English, 15, 47.
Enloes, 18.
Ennalls, 3, 42.
Erford, 34.
Erickson, 19.
Erskine, 34.
Ervaine, 18.
Erwin, 45.
Esham, 18.
Esterbrook, 9.
Etchison, 44.
Evans, Evens, 13, 18, 46.
Everett, 35.
Ewell, 38, 45.
Eyers (see also Ayres and Eires), 17.

Fairfax, 26.
Falkiner, Falkner, 3, 30.
Fants, 21.
Farrow, 7, *22, 30, 38.
Faulkner, 13.
Faulkum, 3.
Fearn, 13.
Fearnsley, 45.
February, 1.
Feddeman, 43.
Fencher, 13.
Fendryear, 1.
Fenn, 43.
Ferdinands, 19.
Field, 26.
Fight, 13.
Finckes, 27.
Findley, 21.
Finley, *6, 34.
Fitzsumons, 41.
Fleet, 26.
Fleming, 6.
Florence, 13.
Flowers, 19.
Floyd, 19, 31.
Foard, 27.
Folker, 13.
Fonderace, 34.
Fookes, 6, 7, 14, 23, 30.
Forbas, 19.
Forsyth, 35.
Foster, 3, 13, *26, 27, 33.
Fountain, 19.
Fowcate, 19.
Fowke, 6, 7, 14, 23, 30.
Fowler, 41.
Fowset, Fawcett, 35.
Fox, 45.
Francis, 19.
Frank, 9, 34.
Franklin, Frankling, 13, 18.
Frazer, *26.

Freeman, 33.
French, 5.
Freshwater, 9.
Fryer, 6.
Furnace, 13.

Gallahue, 22, 38.
Gallop, 9.
Galloway, 13.
Garner, 14, 38.
Garnett, 26.
Garrets, 33.
Garrett, 27.
Gascoigne, 10.
Gatewood, 26.
Geift, 33.
Gellaraid, 21.
Gendron, 3.
Gerdine, 6, 14.
Gething, 27.
Gibson, 5, 6, 7, 10, 17, 33, 45.
Gilberts, 13.
Gill, 5.
Gilledon, 13.
Gillespie, 13.
Gillis, 45.
Giradin, 6, 14.
Gissedge, *26.
Gist, 13.
Glasgow, 13.
Glass, 21.
Gledhill, 3.
Glendall, 33.
Glover, 11.
Goar, 22.
Godman, 13.
Godwin, 2, 3, 9, 19.
Goldthwait, 33.
Gollathan, 5.
Golley, 33.
Golorth (?), 42.
Gore, 17.
Gorham, 33.
Gorral, 21.
Gough, 5.
Gouttee, 33.
Graham, 21, 22.
Grande, de la, 33.
Granger, 10.
Grant, 5.
Grantham, 25, 39.
Gravenrate, 39.
Gray, 14, 17, 34, 38, *43.
Grapham, 21.
Green, 2, 13, 27, 33, 35, 38.
Greening, 34.
Gregory, 2.
Grier, 31.
Griffith, 13.
Grigsby, 38.
Grimes, *13.
Grimsley, 5.
Gromarrin, 2, 10.
Guibert, 11, 34.
Guichard, 34.
Gurney, 13.
Gwathmey, 26.
Gwatkin, 38.

Hack, 34, 37.
Hackley, 14.
Hagall, 27.
Hains, 37.
Haldiman, 34.
Hall, 7, 14, 27, 30, 42, 46.
Hamil, 34.
Hamilton, 6, 13.
Hamon, 3.
Hammon, 39, 47.
Hammond, 13, 21, 45.
Hammott, 42.
Hamrick, 38, 45.
Hanby, 42.
Handley, 34.
Handon, 3.
Hardfield, 21.
Hardy, 14.
Harman, 34.
Harmanson, *9, 41.
Harper, 33.
Harratt, 47.
Harriot, 39.
Harris, 2, 21.
Harrison, 5, 22, 27.
Hart, *7.
Harvard (?), 25.
Harvey, 34.
Hatton, 3.
Haven, 34, 46.
Haward (?), 25.
Hawker, 13.
Hawkins, 3, 23, 45.
Hayden, 13.
Hayes, 2, *34.
Head, 5.
Heath, 3.
Hedges, *21.
Hellen, 11.
Helm, 38.
Hemlocke, 33.
Henderson, 13, 34.
Hendricks, 13.
Hendrickson, 18, 34.
Henry, 34.
Henson, 34.
Herriott, 39.
Hesselius, 34.
Hewlett, 46.
Hews, 19.
Hicks, 14.
Higgason, 26.
Higgins, 13.
Highway, 27.
Hill, 10, 11, 17, 26, 34, 38, *43.
Hinkson, 13.
Hitt, 13.
Hoagland, 21.
Hodges, 43.
Hodgson, Hodson, 3, 33.
Hogan, 22.
Holdbrook, 5.
Holden, 17.
Holland, 11, 34.
Holmes, 21.
Holsteen, 18.
Holtzclaw, 13, 30.
Homans, 13.
Hood, 42.
Hooe, 13, 30, 44.
Hook, 47.
Hopewell, 42.
Hopkins, 7, 33, 44, 46.
Hopper, 30.
Hornback, 13.
Horne, 18, 42.
Hoskins, 2, 3.
Howell, 25.
Hoye, 46.
Huckins, 42.
Hudson, 5, 25.
Huffstetter, 13.
Hughes, 13, 44.
Hughland, 13.
Humble, 13.
Humphries, 21.
Hunkins, 25.
Hunnicutt, 46.
Hunt, 9, 10, 42, 43.
Hutchinson, 34.
Hute, 1.
Hutt, 1.
Hutsell, 13.
Hyatt, 21, 33.

Illingsworth, 5.
Ingle, 25.
Inglish (see English), 15.
Irvin (?), 18.
Irwin (?), 45.

Jack, 34.
Jackson, 13, 21, 30.
Jacob, 9, 10, 13.
Jacobs, 13, 18.
Jacobson, 34.
Jacoby, 13.
James, 30.
Jameson, 13, 34.
Jarbo, 34.
Jarrell, 2.
Jefferies, Jeffereys, 2, 25.
Jemmison, 34.
Jenifee, 13.
Jenkinson, 22.
Jennings, 43.
Jessup, *27.
Jeter, 30, 39, 47.
Jobson, 18.
Johns, 25, 26, 27.
Johnson, 2, 22, 35, 41, *42.
Johnston, 10, 14.
Jolly, 13.
Jones, *2, 5, 11, 12, 13, *26, 35, 38, 47.
Jordan, 2, 34, 42, 46.
Joyne, 43.
Jump, 18.

Kae, 43.
Kannebrook, 13.
Keely, 30.
Keene, 23, 31.
Keener, 14.
Keer, 5.
Keith, 34, 39.
Kellam, 17.
Kellar, Keller, 13, 21.
Kelly, 45, 46.
Kemp, 44.
Kendall, 10, 33, 42.
Kennedy, 6, 7, 13.
Kenner, 22.
Kennerly, 19.
Kenny, 13, 25.
Kerwan, 11.
Kid, 21.
Killam, 42.
King, 19, 27, *42.
Kincheloe, 13.
Kinkead, 13.
Kinsell, 26.
Kirkpatrick, 13, 34.
Kitson, 35.
Knight, 44.
Kunneloe (?), 21.
Kuykendall, 13.

Lail, 21.
Lair, 21.
Lamey, 21.
Lamme, 21.
Lampton, 5.
Lane, 9.
Langhurst, 11.
Laughland, 41.
Laughlin, 21.
Laughton, 27.
Lawrence, 2, 3, 42.
Lawson, 39, 47.
Lawton, 27.
Lee, 1, 33.
Leer, 21.
Levell, 43.
Levy, 38.
Lewis, 2, 14, *19, 26, 38, 43, *46, 21 (?).
Ligon, 30, 39, 47.
Lin, 21.
Lindsey, 25.
Lingo, 20.
Linton, 22.
Lipscombe, 12, *26, 39.
Little, 2, 34.
Lockwood, 21.
Loftis, 3.
Logan, *21.
Long, 9.
Longo, *13.
Lord, 18.
Louge, 21.
Love, 34.
Lowder, 3.
Lowe, 2, 23, 27.
Lowther, 9.
Lucas (?), 21, 43.
Luies, 21.
Lund, 1.
Lurry, 21.
Lutterall, 22.
Lutterell, *22.
Lynaugh, 38.
Lyne, 21.

McAllister, 37.
McCann, 21.
McCarty, 5, *47.
McCaul, 45.
McClannahan, 21.
McClelland, 21.
McClintock, 21.
McCloud, 35.
McClure, 21, 22.
McColloh, *22.
McConnell, 21.
Macrae, 38, 45.
McCullough, 21, *22.
McCutchen, 21.
McDaniel, 21.
McDonald, 5, 26.
McGuire, 10.
McMahan, 22.
McMillan, 21.
McMullen, 21.
McMurphy, 10.
McNab, 22.
McNay, 21.
McNickle, 21.
McShain, 21.
McVeagh, 10.
McWilliams, 10.
Machen, 14, 38, 45.
Macon, 10, 26.
Madden, 22.
Madison, *26, 46.
Maider, 43.
Maisey, 43.
Makings, 11.
Mallery, 46.
Mallory, 10.
Malsby, 45.
Manatear, 46.
Marcey, Massey, Mercy, 43.
Marney, 21.
Marriott, 42.
Marsh, 17.
Marshall, 2, 22, 45.
Martin, 21, 34, 41, 42, 43.
Masman, 42.
Mason, 7, 14, 21, 33, 35, 38.
Masquerier, 21.
Matheney, 21.
Mathews, Matthews, 2, 10, 34, 45, 46.
Matthiason, 33.
Mauck, 21.
Maxwell, 21.
Mayor, 2.
Meakings, 11.
Meares, 3.
Meredith, Meriday, 12, 18.
Metcalfe, 22, *38.
Metheny, 21.
Michell, 1.
Miles, 19.
Miller, 21, *22, 23, 34, 42, 45.
Mills, 10, *22.
Mitchell, 21, 22, 26, *38.
Mitts, 21.
Mohr, 34.
Monroe, 3, 21 (?).
Monroy, 21.
Moody, 26.
Moore, 2, 3, 5, 21.
Mordick, 27.
More, 22.
Morgan, *22.
Morin, 21.
Morris, 17.
Morrison, 21.
Morrogh, 19.
Moss, 21, 38, 45.
Mounteine, 18.
Moxley, 45.
Moy, 5.
Mullinix, 45.
Mumford, 5.
Munday, 18.
Murdick, 27.
Murray, 41.
Musgrave, *10.
Musgrove, 10.

Naylor, 5.
Neale, 14, 21, *45.
Neavill, Nevill, *22, 30.
Neech, 34, 35.
Nelson, 5, 9, 21.
Nesbitt, 21.
Newell, 21.
Newsum, 10.
Nichols, 26.
Nicholson, 3, 18, 42.
Nickless, 33.
Nicolet, 37.
Nicoll, 10.
Nisbitt, 21.
Noell, 11, 26.
Nolan, 33.
Noland, 13.
Norgrave, 5.
Norman, 46.
Norris, 21.
Norwood, 44.
Nottingham, 15.
Nugent, 10.

Oakly, 30.
O'Deare, 35.
Ogle, 21, 41.
O'Neil, 41.
Orgain, 22.
Osborne, 10.
Overall, 22.
Owen, 21, 25, 35.
Owens, 13.

Page, 26.
Palmer, 6, 14, 21, 23, 39.
Panewell, 10.
Parish, 11.
Park, 41.
Parker, 1, 2, 10, 17, 20, *33, 37.
Parks, 6, 21.
Parkwood, 42.
Parramore, 9, 17.
Parrot, 3.
Patishall, 5.
Patton, 21.
Paul, 34, 42.
Pawley, 34.
Payne, 21, 33.
Paxson, 35.
Peale, 1.
Peele, 42.
Penington, 21.
Penivell, 41.
Penwell, 41.
Pennybaker, 26.
Perkins, 10, 15.
Perry, 2, 21, 46.
Peters, 46.
Pettypool, 10.
Peyton, 21, 22, *38.
Phillips, 21.
Pickett, 22.
Pirkins, 15.
Pitt, *9, 25.
Pitts, 17.
Pleasants, 46.
Polhouse, 38.
Pollard, 10, 11.
Pope, 10, 11, *14, 38.
Porter, 11.
Porterfield, 25.
Portress, 14.
Potter, 41.
Potts, 46.
Poulson, 22.
Pound, 47.
Powell, 5, 19, 46.
Powers, 27.
Price, 5, 10, *11, 21.
Prigg, 27.
Prince, 19.
Pritchett, 5, 10.
Pullams, 43.
Pulliam, 43.
Purcell, 13.
Purchas, 33.
Pynes, 26, 27.

Quiett, 21.
Quillian, 3.

Ragon, 18.
Raimey, 45.
Randle, 27, 41.
Ratcliff, 2.
Rawlings, 21.
Read, 13.
Reading, 21.
Redman, Redmon, Readman, 21, 43.
Reasoner, 25.
Reed, 11.
Reeves, 3, 22.
Reids, 5.
Reigel, 34.
Reno, 30.
Renshaw, 19.
Reverdy, *9.
Reynolds, 21.
Richards, 18.
Richardson, 46.
Rickards, Ricketts, 42, *43.
Rickey, 21.
Rigby, 43.
Ringold, 42.
Rippey, *34.
Ritchey, 21.
Roberts, 14, 19.
Robertson (see also Robinson), 7, 47.
Robin, 10.
Robinson (see also Robertson), *1, 6, *7, 11, 14, 20, 21, 23, *25, 30, 35, 39, 46.
Rogers, 35.
Rolfe, 33.
Rookard, 22.
Roper, 2, 42.
Rose, *15.
Ross, 21.
Rosser, 5.
Rowe, 9, 18.
Rowland, *13.
Ruddells, 21.
Ruddle, 21.
Ruder, 21.
Ruffin, 43.
Rungy (?), 43.
Rupley, *34.
Russell, 9.
Ruston, 34.
Rymer, 5.

Sacker, 18.
Sample, 34.
Sampson, 29.
Sands, 43.
Sargeant, 46.
Saule, 6, *14, 23, 30.
Savage, Savedge, 1, 6, 9, *14, 41.
Scarburgh, Scarborough, Scarbragh, 11, *18, 34, *41.
Scarlet, 25.
Scott, 23, 29, 30, 35, *42.
Scholfield, 27.
Schute, 3.
Sconce, 29.
Sears, Seers, *20.
Sebastian, 38.
Selby, 42.
Senior, 25, 42.
Sevell (?), 43.
Severne, 42.
Seymour, 42.
Shanks, 29.
Shawhan, 29.
Shelton, 26.
Shepard, Shepheard, 10, 42.
Sheredin, 42.
Sherwood, 43.
Shield, 27.
Shirley, 45.
Shore, 19.
Short, 21.
Shreve, 46.
Shute, 30.
Sias, 38.
Simmons, 5.
Simons, 10, 33.
Simms, Sims, 13, 22.
Sinclair, 30.
Skinner, 27.
Slater, 29.
Slaughter, 14.
Slye, 1, 3.
Small, 42.
Smallwood, 47.
Smart, 41.
Smelzer, 29.
Smith, 5, 11, 13, 21, 22, 26, 29, 33, *41, *42, 45, 46.
Smithers, 42.
Smothers, 10.
Smythe, 41, *42.
Snails, 30.
Snowden, 10.
Somerville, 42.
Southland, 18.
Spady, 41.
Spenny, 23.
Spiller, *38.
Spink, 42.
Sprigg, 42.
Sprignell, 18.
Stamps, 14, 38.
Stanbridge, 26.
Starr, 45.
Stayton, 42.
Steele, *34, *38.
Stephenson, 29.
Stevens, 19.
Stewart, Steward, 2, 15, 23, *31, 46. (See Stuart.)
Stockman, 45.
Stoddart, 46.
Stokes, 29, 42.
Stone, 3, *23, 30, *38, 45.
Stow, 43.
Streater, 42.
Stribling, 5, *30.
Stringer, 5, 9.
Strother, 5, 29.
Stuart (see Stewart), 18, 29.
Sullivant, 5.
Summers, 22, 29, 38.
Susong, 25.
Suttle, 14.
Suttwell, 17.
Swale, 18.
Swift, 15.
Symons, 10.

Taberer, *35, 43.
Tackett, 38.
Talbott, 29.
Taliaferro, 5.
Tarr, 29.
Tate, 29.
Tayler, 43.
Taylor, 29, 42.
Teackle, 37.
Teale, 30.
Tebbs, 45.
Temble, 3.
Terrell, 46.
Thatcher, 5.
Thixton, 15.
Thomas, 9, 11, 29.
Thompson, 29, 30, 43, 45.
Thorne, 9, 22.
Thornhill, 29.
Thornton, 30.
Thurman, 29.
Till, 13
Tiller, 5.
Tilton, 46.
Tinnix (?), 45.
Tipshott, 10.
Todd, 29, 42.
Tootall, 18.
Towers, 35, 38.
Towles, 15.
Townsend, 1, 10, 35.
Trafford, 25.
Traveller, 9, 10.
Trammel, 45.
Trap, 46.
Trimble, 29.
Trimmer, 10.
Trombell, 9.
Trueblood, 21.
Truitt, 18.
Trundle, 29.
Tucker, 5, 29.
Tull, 3.
Tullos, 14.
Turberville, 5.
Turbutt, 27.
Turner, 5, 23, 29.
Tyler, Tylor, 5, *46.

Underwood, 29, 47.

Vansweringen, 1.
Vanweker, 10.
Vaughan, 18.
Vaulx, 9.
Very, *1.

Wade, 9, 41, 47.
Waldron, 33.
Wale, 27.
Walker, 19, 41.
Wall, 11.
Wallace, 18, 29.
Waller, 29, 46.
Wallop, 37.
Walter, 46.
Ward, 3, 17, 29, 42.
Warfield, 3, 11, 42.
Warson, 29.
Washington, 20.
Waterland, 25.
Watkins, 22.
Watts, 9, *22.
Weakland (?), 29.
Weaklin, 29.
Weath, 3.
Webb, 3, 7, 11, 15, 19, 27, 29, 34, *42.
Webster, 42.
Welch, Welsh, 14, 29.
Wells, 42.
West, 10, 25, 26, 29, 34, *35.
Westoll, 18.
Whaley, 29.

Wharton, 5.
Wheeland, 14.
Wheeler, 19, 27, 46.
White, 3, 10, 15, 18, 21, 42.
Whitehouse, 43.
Whitledge, 29.
Wickersham, 29.
Wilcox, 7, 15.
Wilds, 2.
Wildey, 11.
Wilkins, 34.
Wilkinson, 2.
Williams, 20, 21, 29, 46.
Williamson, 10.
Willinson, 27.
Willis, 5.
Willison, 27.
Wills, 29.
Wilson, *6, 7, 14, 21, 29, 45, 46.
Winder, 21.
Wineter (?), 43.
Wing, 5.
Winn, 29.
Wise, 33.
Witherington, 43.
Wood, 29, 34.
Woodward, 26.
Woodyard, 22.
Woolford, 42.
Worrell, 29.
Wray, 19.
Wright, Write, 14, *21, *27.

Yardley, 17.
Young, *3, *14, 29, 45.

Zimmerman, 38.

Volume III

Abbott, Abbot, 9, 19, 25, *27, 35.
Abington, 10.
Abraham, 38.
Abrall, 27.
Abram, 35.
Acton, 38.
Adams, 27, 41.
Adamson, 41.
Adiggin, 27.
Adwicke, 17.
Aggor, 17.
Aiers (see Ayres, Eires, Eyres), 38.
Aisquith, 10.
Alcock (?), 42.
Aldred, 10.
Alexander, 35.
Allen, Allan, *10, 17, 19, 25, 27, 29, 35, 41.
Allerton, 9.
Allinge, 35.
Allings (?), 35.
Allvit, 17.
Allyson, *27.
Alpatt, 43.
Althrop, 37.
Aman, 27.
Ammon, 27.
Amolochan, 17.
Ancell, 18.
Anderson, 11, 38, 42.
Andrew, 10, 42.
Andrews, 9, 25, 43.
Angell, 18.
Apthorp, 41.
Archer, (?), 29.
Ariays, 35.
Arice (?), 38.
Arlenton, 25.
Armstrong, *1, 43.
Arnell, 27.
Arnishee, 46.
Arnold, 10, 43, 46.
Arrundel, 43.
Arsuton, 43.
Ashley, 27, 35.
Ashworth, 46.
Athey, 19.
Athworth, 10.
Atkins, 9, 10, 38, 41.
Atwood, 26.
Aubrey, 10.
Austin, 10, 19, 42, 43.

Backer, 18.
Bacon, 35.
Badworth, 35.
Baggale, Bagale, 26, 33.
Baid, 10.
Bailey, Baillie (see also Bayley and Bayly), 3, *26, *42.
Bailinge, *35.
Baker, 17, 18, 27, 35, 38, *41, *42.
Balsone, 27.
Baldwin, 26.
Ball, 14, 35.
Ballard, *27.
Balliott, 33.
Ballister, 43.
Bancks, 26.
Barber, 26, 41.
Barker, 25, 27.
Barnaby, 18.
Barnard, 18, 39, 47.
Barnehouse, 27.
Barnes, 10, 25, *26.
Barney, 43.
Barwell, 14.
Barraclough, 18.
Barrow, 42.
Barwick, 43.
Bastard, 35.
Bastian, *35.
Batchelor, Batchellor, *35.
Baxter, 41.
Bayley, 10, 39, 43.
Baylis, 34.
Bayly, 25, 26, *27, 38.
Beacher, 45.
Beale, 19.
Bean, 2.
Beard, 38.
Beardwell, 43.
Beasley, 31.
Beck, 18.
Beckett, 43.
Beckley, 6.
Beggon, 17, 43.
Belcher, 42.
Belding, 2.
Bell, 10, 18, 26, 27, 34, *35, 46.
Benbow (?), 27.
Benhowe, 27.
Bennard, 26.
Bennett, *1, 17, 26, 35, 38.
Benson, Benston, 10, 18, 26, 46.
Berry, 7, 27, 33.
Beswick, 26.
Bickerdike, 42.
Biggs, 10.
Billiot, 27.
Binns, 27.
Bird, 34, 35.
Bishop, 37.
Blacke, 43.
Blackey, 27.
Blacklock, 17.
Blackmore, 38.
Blacksell, 42.
Blackwell, 43.
Bladen, 17.
Blair, 25.
Blake, 10, 25, 35.
Bland, 34.
Blevins, 29.
Blindell, 41.
Block, 15.
Blockson, Bloxson, *26.
Blow, 41.
Blunder, 35.
Boaton, 35.
Boggess, 46.
Bond, 17.
Boot, 26.
Booth, 35.
Bosman, Bossman, 23, 33.
Boston, 43.
Botham, 41.
Bott, 35.
Boulton, 26.
Boums (?), 14.
Bounds, 10.
Bowdoin, 9.
Bowen, Bowinge, 18, 26, *27.
Bowyer, 23.
Boycott, 41.
Boys, 9.
Bradford, *25, 26, 33.
Bradie, 10.
Bradley, *38, 45.
Bradshaw, 27, 35.
Brandt, 42.
Brattan, 10.
Breeding, 26.
Brend, 41.
Brenton, 41.
Brereton, *35.
Bresbon, 41.
Brewer, 35.
Bridge, 35.
Bridger, 23, 39.
Bridges, 14, 19, 35.
Bridget, 42.
Briggs, 43.
Bright, 27, *37.
Brinston, 41.
Britton, 41.
Brock, 1.
Brockhum, 27.
Broder, 37.
Bromfield, 27, 35.
Brooke, Brookes, 10, 18.
Broughton, 35.

Brown, 1, 10, 23, 26, 29, 37, 41, *43, 47.
Browning, 17, 43.
Bruce, 41.
Bruff, 26, 38.
Brumfield, 35.
Brusbank, 18.
Brush, 41.
Bryan, 10.
Bryne, 18.
Budd, *26.
Budworll, 27.
Buck, 37.
Buckingham, 43.
Buckner, 13.
Buffield, 17.
Bullifant, 27.
Burbank, 41.
Burdette, 19.
Burgess, 37, 46.
Burkliffe, 37.
Burnell, 35.
Burr, 41.
Burrough, 43.
Burrowes, 27, 45.
Burton, 10, 41.
Burwell, 39.
Busbie, 27.
Busey, 2.
Butcher, 17, 35.
Butter, 1, 14, 42, 43, 46.
Butt, 1.
Button, 46.
Byler, 43.
Byrn, 45.

Cack (?), 47.
Cain, 1.
Calcoat, 25.
Caldwell, 41.
Callaway, 35.
Callow, 41.
Calvert (see Colvert), 34.
Cammack, 41.
Campbell, 5, 15, 23.
Candell, 43.
Canfill, *43.
Cannon, 10.
Cappinge, 35.
Carberry, 10.
Carey, 10, 17, 35.
Carpenter, 5, 35.
Carr, 42.
Carroll, 3.
Carrott, 27.
Carter, 1, 2, 15, 29, 41, 46.
Case, 41.
Castle, 17, 43.
Castleton, 43.
Catesby, 43.
Cauderwood, 41.
Cawood, 7.
Chamberline, *43.
Chambers, 1, 27.
Champe, *46.
Chancellor, 1, 15, 31.
Chandler, 25, *43.
Chapman, 33, 35.
Chappell, 33, *38.
Charles, 17, 41, 43.
Charlton, 33.
Chattem, 5.
Checkitt, 43.
Chelmedge, 43.
Cheny, 38.
Cherrieholm, 9.
Cheseldine, 15.
Cheshire, 3.
Chickley, 43.
Chichester, 25.
Childecock, 43.
Chisholm, 1, 23.
Chism, 1.
Choate, 38.
Christian, 23, 38, 41.
Chroshaw, 43.
Churchyard, 38.
Clanterne, 35.
Chapham, 43.
Clarke, *1, 2, 11, *18, 27, *34, 38.
Claus, 41.
Clayter, 46.
Clayton, 26, 42.
Clem, 7.
Clerke (see also Clarke), 17, 35.
Cloughton, 35.
Cobb, 17, 43.
Coburne, 47.
Cockeram, 43.
Cockney, 27, 38.
Cocney (?), 27.
Codrey, 38.
Coe, 17, 21.
Colbert, 27.
Cole, 1, 17, *41.
Colhoun, 1.
Collier, 33, 43.
Collin, 41.
Collins, Collings, 1, *35.
Collome, 9.
Collume, 41.
Colvert (see Calvert), 14.
Colvin, 47.
Cometon (?), 26.
Comings, 41.
Complin, 41.
Compton, 9.
Coniers, 35.
Conn, 47.
Connor, Conner, 17, 37.
Conover, 1.
Cooke, 3, 18, 27, 35.
Cooly, 38.
Cooper, Couper, 15, 33, 34, 42.
Copley, 38, 43.
Coppock, 15.
Corbell, *43.
Corbett, 14, 35.
Corbin, 26.
Corey, 43.
Cornelius, 17.
Corners, 43.
Cornwall, 34.
Corprew, 1.
Corson, 17.
Cotter, 38.
Cotton, 19.
Cottrell, 43.
Councell, 10.
Covey, 43.
Cowgill, 3.
Cox, 1, 18, *27, *41.
Craft, 33.
Cranfield, 35.
Crawford, *47.
Crawley, 41.
Creede (?), 10.
Cretchett, 17.
Cripps, 43.
Crisp, 1.
Crocker, 41.
Crockett, 15.
Croffe, 27.
Crook, 41.
Crosby, 42.
Crosle, Crosley, 9.
Crost, 35.
Crouch, 27, 38.
Crumbaugh, 1.
Crump, 43.
Crupper, 34.
Crutcher, *1.
Cullins, 34, 38.
Cummins, 23.
Cunningham, 35.
Curtis, *41, *43.
Custis, 11, 18, 22, 33, 34.
Cutler, 34.

Dagge, 34.
Dalton, 17.
Danby, 43.
Danford, 2.
Daniel, Daniell, 1, 9, 27, *35, 42.
Dare, 26.
Darley, 39.
Darling, *42.
Darnall (?), 26.
Daugherty, 1, 45.
Dauson, 45.
Davies, 46.
Davis, 9, 14, 17, 23, 34, *35, *38, 43, 46, 47.
Davison, 9.
Daw, 17.
Dawson, 10, 18, 45.
Day, 29, *38.
Deane, 27.
Dear, 15.
Dearsley, 19.
Dehattaway, 38.
De Jernatt, 14.
Delne (?), 35.
Delong, 47.
Denegoe, 18.
Dent, 26.
Denwood, 9.
Deplaie, 35.
Derrickson, 25.
Devagha, 46.
Dewin, 34.
Dews, 42.
Dibbin, 27, 35.
Dick, 17.
Dickinson, 18.
Diggens, 3.
Dishman, 46.
Dissey, 27.
Distance, 42.
Divard (?), 18.
Divier, 18.
Divines, 29.
Divyor, 18.
Dixon, 2, 35.
Dobson, 2, 26, 43.
Dolwick, 42.
Donahoe, 46.
Doniphan, 46.
Donoh, 17.
Dorman, 17.
Dornell (?), 26.
Douglas, 17, 18, 34.
Douter, 47.
Dowde, 27.
Dowdridge, 27.

Dowdy, 43.
Down, 47.
Drake, *27, 46.
Dringe, 27.
Drummond, 2, 21, 26, 34.
Dryden, 26.
Duarne, 38.
Duff, 46.
Dunton, 18, 34.
Dunworth, 42.
Duparks, 18.
Durant, 1.
Duvall, 1, 37, 45.
Dwiggens, 3.
Dyer, 17.
Dyson, 43.

Earrickson, 42.
Earle, 25.
Easterfield, 27.
Eborne, 33.
Edgill, 41.
Edmandson, 29.
Edmond, 46.
Edmunds, Edmonds, 17, 46.
Edwards, 1, 38, 46.
Elcock, 43.
Elder, 45.
Elderington, 26.
Elkins, 27, 46.
Ellegood, 18.
Elliott, 42.
Ellis, 7.
Ellunor (?), 35.
Ellvidge, 45.
Ellzey, 34.
Elvegs (?), 45.
Ely, 31.
Encrid (?), 35.
Endicott, 41.
English, 14.
Enser, 45.
Evans, 3, 27, *45.
Everhart, 7.
Ewing, 23.
Eyre (see Ayres, Aires), 18, 33.

Farbrother, 45.
Farmer,18.
Farrell, 7, 35.
Faulkner, Falkner, *9, *43.
Fawne, 27.
Feddeman, 2, 42.
Feild, 35.
Felton, 35.
Fenton, 43.
Fenwick, 1.
Fielder, 2.
Filline, 43.
Finch, 17.
Finney, 26.
Fisher, 7, 27, *33, 34, 37.
Fitchett, 11, 18.
Fitzgerald, 23.
Fleeharty, 7.
Fleetwood, 17.
Fleming, Flaminge, *17, 23.
Flenniken, 14.
Fletcher, 35, 43.
Flood, 10.
Flourney, 1.
Flowers, 33.
Floyd, 34, 47.
Fluncher, 35.
Foley, 34, 46 (?).
Fooks, 26.
Fooley (?), 46.
Ford, 15.
Fornor, 35.
Fort, 43.
Fosdick, 9.
Fossett, 7.
Foster, 18, 33, 43, 46.
Fout, 7.
Fowke, 9.
Fowler, 7, 41.
Fox, 7, 25, 41, *46.
Frame, 10.
Francis, 7, 43, 45.
Franke, 35.
Franklin, 17, 43.
Frazier, 41.
Freborne, 45.
Freeborne, 26.
Freeman, 43, 45.
French, 14, 15, 27.
Freshwater, 17.
Friarmond, 42.
Frith, 2.
Fry, 25.
Fryer, 9.
Fuller, 45.

Gachett, 41.
Gaile, *38.
Gaines, 15.
Gaither, 45.
Galloway, 45.
Gambol, 7.
Garber, 3.
Gardner, 17, 42.
Garetson, 43.
Garey, 7.
Gascoigne, 33.
Gassaway, 38, *45.
Gates, 7.
Gayle, 15.
Gelfard, 18.
George, 19.
Gibbons, Gibbins, 9, 35.
Gibson, 2, 7, 15.
Gifferd, 26.
Gilbert, 42.
Gill, 43.
Gillentine, 23.
Gillington, 23.
Gittens, 27.
Gladinge, *35.
Glascock, 34.
Glaster, 7.
Glendenning, 46.
Glover, 17.
Goar, 15.
Godwin, 17.
Goldsborough, 39, 47.
Golesbury, 45.
Good, 1, 15.
Goodman, 17.
Goodson, 27.
Goodwin, 43.
Gore, 15, 25.
Goss, 43.
Gott, 45.
Gough, 7, 19.
Gould, 26.
Gowers, 17.
Graham, 7, 15, 23, 31, 34.
Granger, 2.
Grant, 7, 26, *27.
Gratten, 23.
Graves, 3.
Gray, 27.
Greene, 7, 9, 18, 27, *43, *46.
Greenhill, 42.
Greenstreet, 27.
Greenwood, 17.
Gregg, 29.
Grey, 43.
Griffin, *10.
Griffith, 18, 45.
Griffton, 27.
Grilfin, 10.
Grimes, 43.
Groos, 9.
Gross, 7, 45.
Groves, 45.
Gudgeon, 47.
Guibert, 10.
Gullam, 17.
Gurney, 43.
Gwatkin, 34.
Gyles, 7.

Hack, 26.
Hackley, 46.
Haddaway, 2.
Hadder, 10.
Hadger (?), 17.
Halbrooke, 10.
Hale, 7, *15.
Hall, 15, 17, 18, 28, 29, 43.
Hallowes, 10.
Hamby, 9.
Hamersley, 42.
Hamilton, 43.
Hamlin, 27.
Hammett, 17.
Hammon, 7.
Hammond, 7.
Hamon, 35.
Hanby, 2.
Hancock, 42.
Hane, 43.
Hankins, 23.
Hanson, 29, 42.
Harber, 35.
Harbert, Harbutt, 26, 35.
Harden, Hardin, 7, 19, 26, 45, 47.
Harding, *19, 26.
Hare, *7, 35.
Harkelford, 29.
Harlan, 3.
Harman, Harmon, 1, *29, 41, 43.
Harmanson, 2, *18, 19, 33, *34.
Harper, 14, 46.
Harrington, 43.
Harris, 10, 33, 43.
Harrison, 2, 14, 15, 25.
Harrod, 15.
Hart, 35.
Hartford, 35.
Hartline, 7.
Hartse, 33.
Harwood, 33.
Haseler, 17.
Hatley, 17.
Hatton, 47.
Haught, *45.
Hawkins, 15, 17.
Hayall, 17, 43.
Haynes, 43.
Hays, Haies, *17, 29.
Hazilrigg, 34.
Head, 18.

Heath, 2, *43.
Hebb, 2.
Hegnone (?), 43.
Hemsley, 9.
Hendel, 13.
Henn, 7.
Hennys (?), 29.
Henry, 26.
Herbert, 18.
Heroett (?), 34.
Hickman, 17, 29.
Higginbotham, 13.
Higgins, 18.
Highfield, 23.
Hill, 14, 19, 23, 41, 42, 46.
Hilton, 27.
Hillyer, 17.
Hinson, 42.
Hobby (?), 27.
Hobs, 17.
Hodges, 2.
Hogg, 17, 43.
Hogill, 18.
Hoemane (?), 35.
Hohne, 27.
Holder, 15.
Holeman, 43.
Holland, 2, 42.
Holliday, 17.
Hollins, 18.
Holloway, 35.
Holmsley, 35.
Holson, 3.
Holt, 35.
Homewood, 38.
Hook, 7, 15, 23, 39, 43.
Hooper, 2.
Hooter, 47.
Hopewell, 17.
Hopkins, 26.
Hore, 1.
Hornby, 42.
Houston, 23.
How, 34.
Howard, 7, 35, 43.
Howell, 43.
Hubbard, 11.
Huddy, 14.
Hughs, 7.
Hulbert, 27.
Humbleton, 18.
Humphreys, 27.
Hungerford, 43.
Hunt, 7, 9, 18, 29, 35, 43.
Hunter, 25, 35.
Huntley, 17.
Huntstone, 35.
Hurt, 43.
Husband, 25.
Hutchins, 17, 18.
Hutt, 21.

Imbert, 6.
Indicott, 41.
Ingan, 27.
Ingle, 11.
Innis, 19.
Insley, 10.
Irvine, *42.
Irwin, 23.
Isham, 40.
Issall, 43.

Jacksall, 17.
Jackson, 3, 15, *17, 27.
Jacob, 2.
James, 3, 18, 35, 38, 42.
Jarrett, 45.
Jemmison, 35.
Jenckinson, 43.
Jenifer, 9, 25.
Jenkins, *14, 26, *27.
Jernatt, de, 14.
Jett, 15.
Joggins, 35.
John, 35, 45.
Johns, 10, 17.
Johnson, *6, *11, 15, 17, 21, 25, 39, 46.
Jones, *10, *11, 17, 26, *27, 30, 34, *35, *38, *42, *45, *46.
Jordan, 46.
Jourdain, 6.
Judge, 19.
Justice, 29.

Kae, 2.
Kamp, 43.
Kemp, 37.
Keene, 30, 47.
Keevey, 27.
Keith, 10, 15, 46.
Keizer, 11.
Keley, 3.
Kellor, 11.
Kendall, 11, *18, 19, 22, 33, 34, *43.
Kennedy, 11, 30.
Kennicke, 43.
Kenyon, 27, 46.
Kern, 11.
Kernhart, 29.
Kerns, 37.
Key, 42.
Keys, 29.
Kicherley, 27.
Kimbrough, 14.
Kinchelo, 35.
King, 1, 2, 10, 17, 26, 42.
Kinkel, 6.
Kirby, 27.
Kirkland, 15.
Kitchen, 6.
Kite, 35.
Knite, 18.
Knowles, 27.

Lace, 27.
Lacey (?), 27.
Lamar, 41.
Lambert, 43.
Lamee, 6.
Lane, 11.
Langford, 42.
Lanyott, 17.
Larkin, 11.
Larkins, 38.
Larrington, 18.
Lashberry, 35.
Lathberry, 35.
Lattimer, 42.
Laviele, 6.
Lavington, 27.
Laurence, 17, 19.
Lazear, 6.
Lea, 43.
Leasure, 27.
Leatherburgh, 26.
Lecompt, 6.
Lecount, 6.
Lederer, 6.
Lee, 18, 28, 43.
Leman, 9.
Lennington, 5.
Lessell, 35.
Leward, 17.
Lewis, *17, 19, *23, *27, 38, 45.
Liefford, 27.
Lindsay, 29, 43.
Linn, *47.
Linsey, 43.
Linwed, 42.
Littleton, 17, 18.
Livers, 6.
Lloyd, Loyd, *17, 18, 42.
Lock, 2.
Locken, 6.
Lockerman, 6.
Loflin, 11.
Long, 17, 19, 29, 43.
Looten, 6.
Loughland, 34.
Love, 9.
Lovett, 27.
Lowder, 35.
Lowe, 42, 43.
Lowell, 27.
Lowther, 6.
Lucas, 17.
Luckett, 37.
Ludlow, 19.
Lukens (?), 9.
Luker, 9.
Lumsdell, 35.
Lyle, 23.
Lynam, 42.
Lyon, 7, 43.

McCall (?), 37, 43.
McCay, 47.
MackClayne, 17.
McCleon, 47.
McClure, 6.
McCollah, *6.
McCormack, 6.
McCulloch, 11.
McCune (?), 27.
McDaniel, 19, 31.
McDeed, 6.
McDowell, 23.
McFell (?), 43.
McGee (?), 37.
McGill, 30.
Machoone, 27.
Mackall (?), 37.
Mackay, 27, 47.
McLean, 17.
McKee, 23.
McKenzie, McKinzie, 11, 25.
McMahon, 47.
MackMillian, 17.
McMillion, *34.
McMurphy, 9.
McNab, 6.
McPheeters, 23.
McWilliams, 5.
Mace, 43.
Machen, 34, 40.
Machin, 27.
Macy, 19.
Maddox, 18, 42.
Maden, 26.
Maffett, 23.
Mahan, 42.
Maikall (?), 37.

Maize, 10.
Mallett, 27.
Malloy (?), Maloye, *26
Mannadoe, 6.
Manes, 35.
Manning, 35.
Mannor, 35.
Mantz, 29.
Maonchir, 42.
Maple, 43.
Marcey, 33.
Margaretts, 35.
Marin, 17, 43.
Marr, 46.
Marrett, Marriot, 9, 38.
Martin, 14, 43, 47.
Masley (?), 35.
Mason, 19, 25, *43.
Mathas, 2.
Matthews, Mathews, Matthew, 10, 11, 23, 35, 42.
Matthiason, 10.
Matson, 10.
Mattocks, *5.
Maugridge, 11.
Maus, 6.
Max, 17.
Maxfield, 18.
Maxwell, 42.
May, 17, 35, 43.
Maynadier, 10.
Meadcalf, 2.
Mears, 26.
Meartin, 43.
Medcalf, 2, 11.
Meddars, 35.
Medford, 42.
Meldson, 43.
Melton, 14, 34, 35.
Menfinger, 11.
Mercy, 26.
Merebell, 17.
Merekin, 38.
Merrel, 14.
Metcalfe, 38, 46.
Mettor, 14.
Meyricke, 11.
Michel, 33.
Middleton, 26, 27, *33, 35.
Miles, 2, 27.
Milhouse, 11.
Miller, 6, 11.
Millett, 35.
Mills, 6, 10, 11.
Milnor, 39, 47.
Minton, 27.
Misomer, 17.
Mitchell, 6, 14, 35.
Mocfell, 43.
Mockbee, 11.
Modekann (?), 27.
Moffett (?), 23.
Moigne, de, 10.
Molletoe (?), 35.
Mollophon, 35.
Molson, 43.
Montagne, de la, 10.
Moor, 2, 3, 19, 25, 27, 34, 42, 43.
More, 6, 27.
Moredock, 23.
Morehead, 17.
Morfrey, 43.
Morgan, *6, 17, 46.
Morn, 22.
Morris, Morrice, 11, 19, 41, 43.
Moss, *27, 35.
Mote, 35.
Mounseer, 26.
Mountford, 43.
Mounts, 10.
Mowers, 11.
Mugenbourg, 11.
Mulliken, 18.
Mullock, 11, 29.
Multis, 35.
Munday, 17.
Munger, 2.
Munk, 26.
Munkester, 2.
Munteth, 35.
Murdock, 46.
Murfee, 34.
Murhead, 17.
Murley, 27.
Murphy, 33, 34.
Murray, 17, 27.
Mustin, 46.
Mutton, 35.
Myers, 23, 42.
Mynskie, *11.

Nash, 22.
Nayler, 17, 43.
Neale, 2, 11, 26.
Neat, 19.
Neavil, 34.
Neech, 37.
Needham, *35.
Neilson, 3.
Nelson, 10, 11.
Newes, 27.
Newcombe (?), 43.
Newman, 2.
Newson, 43.
Newton, 17.
Niblet, 26.
Nicholson, 14.
Nicles, 18.
Nimcahoe, 27.
Noel, 19.
Noland, 19.
Norcott, 35.
Norns (?), 22.
Norris, 22.
Nottingham, Nuttingham, 34, 35.

Ober, 37.
O'Bryan, 6.
Oden, 46.
Oeth, 11.
Oger, 17.
Ogle, *6.
Ogley, 3.
O'Kelly, 27.
Oldson, 11.
Oley, 11, 38.
Omarwrare (?), 17.
O'Mulligan, 17.
Othoson, 29.
Otley, 27.
Ougbourne, 2.
Overall, 34.
Overton, 17.
Owen, *17.
Owens, 46.
Owerard, 29.
Owin, 46.
Owins, 46.

Packet, 29.
Pacquet, 29.
Paddison, 27.
Page, 19.
Paget, *29.
Paine, 9, *27.
Palmer, 7, 15, 27, 46.
Palmeter, 14.
Parandier, 29.
Parish, 38.
Parke, 9.
Parker, 9, 17, 19, 25, 26, 27, 46.
Parks, *18, 22.
Parremore, 25.
Parry, *43.
Parsons, 37, 46.
Passemer, 9.
Patrick, *34.
Patter, 27.
Patterson, Pattison, 6, 42, *46.
Payne, 9, 15.
Peake, 38.
Peane, 29.
Pearce, 6, 18, 22.
Pearson, 25.
Pelloone, 17.
Pendleton, 1, 15, 35.
Penn, 19.
Percy, 43.
Perg (?), 9.
Perry, 9, 19, *27.
Person, 25.
Persons, 6.
Pery (?), 9.
Peters, 29, 47.
Peterson, *29, 35.
Pett, 22.
Pettit, 34.
Peyton, 35.
Phillips, *35.
Philpott, 2.
Phippa, 2.
Pickering, 17.
Pincon, 35.
Pinder, 43.
Pinders, 26.
Pindleton, 35.
Pinner, 10.
Pippinge, 17.
Pitts, 21, 41.
Ploomer, 26.
Plumer (?), 26.
Pones, 43.
Pope, 39.
Porter, 9, 27.
Posey, 14.
Posford, 25.
Poulson, 29.
Pound, 7, 39.
Powell, 2, 10, 11, 14, 17, *18, 19, 34, 42.
Power, 17.
Prather, 9.
Pratt, 43.
Preeson, 9.
Prescon, 43.
Preston, 22, 23, 43.
Prewitt, 1.
Price, 22.
Prichard, 43.
Prisser, 47.
Proctor, 9, 23.
Prother, 27.
Proude, 27.

Prouting, 14.
Provence (?), 47.
Pryde, 27.
Pryer, 17.
Pumpry, 6.
Pyatt, 6.
Pye, 17.

Quin, 19.
Quisenberry, 1.

Raddock, 35.
Radlace, 9.
Raffey, 27.
Rafhoone, 29.
Rahn, 42.
Raisin, 34.
Randolph, 9.
Ransom, 43.
Rassey, 27.
Ratcliffe, 10.
Ratford, 38.
Ratliff, 33.
Ray, *43.
Rayman, 29.
Razolini, 29.
Reade, 9.
Ready, 1.
Reed, 6, 45.
Reesling, 22.
Reeve, 34.
Reeves, 17.
Reid, 27.
Reinolls, 35.
Remington, 14.
Respess, 34.
Reynolds, 45.
Rhoddy, 22.
Rice, 43.
Rich, 27, 29.
Richard, 29, 43, 45.
Richards, 10, 28.
Riddle, 22.
Ridley, 9.
Rigley, 38.
Ring, 29.
Ritch, 27.
Roach, 29.
Robb, 19.
Robenett, 3.
Robert, 22, 29.
Roberts, 22, 29, 42, *45.
Robertson (see also Robison and Robinson), 23.
Robins, 1, 18, 34.
Robinson (see also Robertson and Robison), 7, 10, 19, 23, 27, 43, *47.
Robison, 6.
Roche, de la, 29.
Rodes, 27.
Rodgers, Rogers, 6, 19, 35, 43, 47.
Roe, 15.
Roelands, 29.
Rogges, 6.
Rookard, 46.
Roper, 27.
Rose, 22, 25, 35.
Rosly, 43.
Ross, 3.
Rosser, 35.
Rosson, 14.
Rotch, 9.
Rowles, 26.
Rowley, 17.
Rowse, 9.
Rue, 22.
Ruford, 35.
Rumbly, 10.
Russell, 35.
Russum, 39.
Ryan, 19, 22.
Ryd, 43.
Ryder, 14, 45.
Ryding, 9.
Rye, 42.

St. Clair, 27.
Sacker, 33.
Samuel, 15, 31.
Sanford, 17.
Sansome, 27.
Satchell, 34.
Saunders, Sanders, 7, 15, 19, 31, 38, 45.
Savage, 1, 11, 18, 26, 33, *34.
Scag, 23.
Scaggs, 22, 23.
Scamper, 45.
Scarburgh, Scarborough, Scarborow, Scarbrow, *25, 26, 43.
Schee, 45.
Scott, 2, 14, *35, *45.
Scoolfield, 10.
Scruggs, 42.
Seaman, 6.
Seaverne, Severne, 33.
Segrave, 11, 19.
Selby, 10.
Sellick, 2.
Seth, 45.
Seward, 19.
Shaffer, 29.
Shaffers, 29.
Shanks, 2.
Sharmahan, 9.
Sharp, 27.
Shaver, 22.
Sheeter, 35.
Shepard, 14, 18, 35, 43.
Shepheard, 14, 25.
Shepherd, 31.
Sherwood, 18.
Shingers, 27.
Shipman, 15.
Shoare, 27.
Shoat, 22.
Shoemaker, 22.
Short, 1, 43.
Sill, 27.
Silverthorne, 33.
Simpson, 26, 35, 41, 46.
Sinckler, 17, *27.
Sincler, 22.
Sincoe, 11, 18, 19.
Skaggs, 33.
Skinner, 17
Slaner, 43
Slater (?), 35.
Slattor, 35.
Slaughter, 17.
Slecombe, 46.
Sloane, 14.
Sluyter, 46.
Smallwood, 7, 39.
Smart, 2.
Smith, 1, 2, 6, 14, *17, 18, *22, *25, *26, *27, 37, 39, *42, 43, 45, *46.
Smithers, *3, 46.
Smithson, 26.
Smoot, 43.
Snead, 10, 41.
Snell, 43.
Snelling, *35.
Snider, 29, 37.
Snodgrass, *45.
Somervell, 27.
Span, 6.
Spear, 37.
Speck, 22.
Spencer, 27, 43.
Spicer, 27.
Spinks, 2.
Splatt, 19.
Sprigg, 6, 23.
Sprout, 43.
Squire, 27.
Stack, 46.
Stackhouse, 6.
Stacy, 27.
Stanley, 30, 43.
Stannenite (?), 43.
Starke, 19.
Start, 2.
Stedman, 35.
Steele, 14.
Steelman, 46.
Steevens, 43.
Stephens, 14.
Stevens, 9, 43.
Stevenson, 6.
Stewart (see also Stuart), *14, *23, 34, 47.
Stille, 46.
Stillwell, 43.
Stockley, 14, 23, 39, 47.
Stokes, 27.
Stool, 38.
Stone, 35, 43.
Stott, 2, 34.
Stoughton, 31.
Stowell, 27.
Stratton, 9.
Stringer, 2
Strother, *27.
Stroup, 22.
Stuart (see also Stewart), 14.
Stubb, 43.
Stubbs, 29, 43.
Stull, 22.
Sturgis, 29.
Sullinger, 19.
Sullivan, 19, 43.
Summers, 34.
Summerton, 46.
Suppert (?), 23.
Sute, 47.
Swan, 17.
Swats, 47.
Sweatman, 46.
Sweetman, 35.
Swerengen, 18.
Swetnam, 15.
Swineyard, 46.
Swormstead, 46.
Sydenham, 27.
Syferson, 46.
Sylva, 30.
Symons, 17.

Tacket, 46.
Tagert, 5.
Talbutt, 38.
Taney, 14.

Tankred, 2.
Tard, 27.
Tawert, 46.
Taylard, 18.
Taylor, 2, 14, 23, *27, *31, 33, 43.
Teacle, *5.
Tebbs, 46.
Tegh, 17.
Teigue, 2.
Tenelly, 30.
Tennant, 45.
Terrill, 14.
Thacher, 27.
Thacker, 27.
Thatcher, 30.
Theed, 27.
Thomas, 2, 17, 26, 30, 37, 42, 43.
Thompkins, 22.
Thompson, 14, 26, *27, 30, 43.
Thomson, 10.
Thornton, 26, *27, 46.
Tick, 46.
Tilfaite, 19.
Tiller, 43.
Tillghman, 2.
Tillotson, 42.
Tilney, 2.
Tilton, 6.
Timmons, 42.
Tisdall (?), 17, 35.
Tistull, 17, 35.
Todd, 10, 31, 34.
Tollett, 29.
Tomlinson, *30.
Tompkins, 11.
Tompson, 2.
Toole, 17, 46.
Toon, 30.
Toulson, 46.
Towles, 23.
Townsend, 1, 2, 9.
Tox, 27.
Tracy, 31.
Tray (?), 6.
Trenis, *27.
Triplet, 46.
Truett, 17.
Trunhitt, 9.
Tucker, 14, 27, 35, 43.
Tull, 3.
Tully, 25.
Tune, 30.
Turk, 35.
Turner, 2, 10, 14, 26, *27, 30, 46.
Tutt, 46.
Twoale, 27.
Twyman, 23.
Tygard, 47.
Tyler, 27, 46.
Tyson, 2.

Underwood, 36.
Ury, 46.

Vagha, de, 46.
Vanbeeck, 46.
Vanbibber, 46.
Vanbuskirk, *6.
Vanhamell, 2, 34.
Vanmatre, *6.
Van Swaringen, Vanswerin-gen, 6, 17.
Vanwecker, 34.
Vanwekes (?), 34.
Vaughop, 18.
Vaultier, 27.
Vere, 27.
Verval, 47.
Vervalson, 47.
Viccars, 34.
Vincent, 18.
Vines, 33.

Waddell, 23.
Wade, *1, 7, 15, 23, 27, 39, 47.
Wainhouse, 34.
Wale, 33.
Wales, 30.
Wallace, *30.
Waller, 47.
Wallis, 3.
Walston, 31.
Warburton, 27.
Ward, 23, 26, 30, *34.
Wardell, 17.
Ware, 27.
Warfield, 2, 31.
Warner, 25.
Warpinbay, 6.
Warren, 14, 31, *34.
Warrington, 10, 43.
Washington, 27.
Wassell, 27.
Wasson, 14.
Waters, *34, 46.
Watkins, 34, 46.
Watson, 9, 17, 26, 43.
Watts, 14, 18, 33.
Wayfield, 27.
Wearington, 43.
Weatherlow, 30.
Weaver, 2, 30.
Webb, 2, 10, 26.
Webber, 43.
Webster, 35.
Welbourne, 34.
Wellman, 17.
Wells, *6, 18.
West, 14, *27, 31, 46.
Westcott, 34.
Wheatley, 2, 46.
Whitby, 19.
White, 10, 17, 25, *27, *30, 34, 43, 46.
Whitecotton, 33.
Whitefare, 17, 43.
Whitesides, 34.
Whitledge, 34.
Whitley, 23.
Whitsorrell, 27.
Whittington, 41.
Wickliffe, 34.
Widgeon, 18.
Wiggens, 14.
Wiggenton, 23.
Wilcock, 7.
Wilkerson, 31.
Wilkins, 18, 33.
Wilkinson, 17, 27, 35.
Williams, 19, 27, 30, 31, *34, 35, 37, 43.
Williamson, 6, 29, 34.
Willis, 46.
Willoughby, 43.
Willy, 10.
Wilmer, 39.
Wilson, 1, 3, *6, 17, 26, 27, 35, 43.
Winebrener, 31.
Winder, 33.
Winn, *27.
Winscombe, 14.
Winser, 10.
Winton, 46.
Wintworth, 25.
Wise, Wyse, *17, 19, 31.
Wiseman, 2, 47.
Withers, 19.
Wolf, 30.
Wood, 6, 43, 45.
Woodby, 27.
Woodered, 43.
Woodgeare, 43.
Woodham, 43.
Woodington, *43.
Woodman, 14.
Woods, 6.
Woodson, 43.
Woodward, 42.
Woolman, 43.
Workman, 43.
Wouldhave, 10.
Wraxhall, 25.
Wray, 34.
Wressell, 34.
Wright, 17, 23, 26, 46.
Wyatt, 34.

Yearkey, 27.
Yeo, 35.
Yopp, 18, 42.
Young, 3, 9, 10, 17, 35, 46, 47.

The

County Court Note-Book

A Little Bulletin of History and Genealogy

February, 1925. Vol. IV, No. 1

SHIPS IN PORT

Pincke called the *John & Sarah,* of Boston; Wm. Gard, master. N-n, Va. x-187. 28 Apr 1673.

Ship *John & Sarah;* Hockenhull Short, master. Acco., Va. xix-107. 5 June 1728.

Ship *John & William;* Mr. Daniell Penfax, master. Acco., Va. v-119. 17 Mch 1673. Also 1671.

Shipp *Joseph;* Ralph Wim . . . ? commdr. Acco, Va. ix-39. 26 Mch 1684.

Shipp *Jonghopfull;* a letter was written aboard this vessel by Barnes Johnson. N-n, Va. iv-165. 1653.

Ship *Katherine,* of Milford, Wales; John Gundry, master, was at the house of Mr. Nehemiah Storke on the River of Upper Machohick. Staff., Va. Orders I, 2d part. p. 254. 11 May 1692.

Ship *Katherine,* of London; John Blake, master; Acco, Va. ix-60. 14 Feby 1684. Also vi-403. 1684. John Lake [?], Master.

Ship *Katherine;* John Harrison, Commdr. Acco, Va. 17 May 1687. vi-461.

Ship *Littleton;* "For this present voyage, Edward Tomlin, master." Lanc, Va. ix-253. 17 Sept 1703.

The *Leopoldus,* a Shipp. L. Norf, Va. C-52. 1653.

Schooner *Lively;* Michael Parker, master. Acco, Va. Naval Officer's Book. 7 Aug 1781.

London Shipp; Mr. Tunnell [?] and Mr. Reade, masters. L. Norf., Va. C-52. 15 Aug 1653.

Ship *London;* Mr. Gingey, master; Mr. Clifton, mate. Acco, Va. 4 Mch 1672. iv-179.

The *Love,* a Pinck; Franc: Wells, master. P. R. O. (Eng.) 33-xix. 1703.

Ship *Loyaltie,* of London; N-n, Va. i-159. 11 Dec 1634.

Sloop *Lucy;* John Robertson, of Catt Island, part owner. Norf. Corp. Ct, Va. 1785.

Barke *Martha and Mary;* Hugh Perring, master. Acco, Va. ix-9. 17 May 1682.

Sloop *Martha and Miriam;* John Waide, of Marcus Hook, master and half owner. Geo. Warner, of Philada., one-half owner. 10 tons. Built at Marcus Hook. Ship Registers. Pa. Mags. vol. xxv, p. 276. 6 July 1752.

The *Mary,* lately arrived from the Barbadoes; Mr. Fortesque Howse, "maister." Surry, Va. i-203. 13 Oct 1662.

Ship *Mary;* inventory, of Capt. Robt Pitt. Acco, Va. iv-170. 16 Dec 1672.

Sloop *Mary;* Nathaniell Maclenahan, part owner, Pr. Anne, Va. i-117. About 1697.

Brigantine *Mary and Dorothy;* Edmund Feberyear, master; Mr. Samuel Bucker, supercargo (then deceased). I. W., Va. iv-55. 9 Feby 1692-3.

Ship *Mary and Ellery;* of Jopson. 100 tons. Thomas Carpenter, commdr, from New found Land. Va. St. Pa. i-48. 8 Jany 1693-4.

Ship *Mary Gold* (Marygold) of London; Acco, Va. viii-147. 16 Dec 1679. Also iii-45. 23 Apr 1667.

Sloop *May Flower;* John Robinson, master; owned by Robt Parsons of Cape May, N. J., David Welldon and Ezekiel Eldredge. Built at Cape May. 25 tons. Ship registers. Penna Mags, xxv-129. 6 May 1750-1.

The *barke Mayeflower* is excepted from an agreement made by Edm. Scarburgh [Lt. Col.] N-n, Va. iv-135. 6 Aug 1651.

Bark *Mayflower;* Edm. Scarburgh conveys to Wm. Brentton of Boston in Massachusetts, all the goods underwritten . . . a pltn at Occahannocke, cattle, &c., &c., and the Bark *May Flower;* a Galliott, the *King David,* and a Shallopp. N-n, Va. iv-153. 31 Jany 1652.

Schooner *Mayflower;* Thomas Robinson, master. Pa. Arch. (2) i-548. Registered 5 July 1764.

Schooner *Mayflower;* Woolsey Hathaway, master. Ship Registers. Pa. Arch (2) i-569. 21 June 1773.

STARTING THE MACHINERY OF A COUNTY COURT

From the first Order Book of Ohio county, now in West Virginia.

Black's Cabin Ohio County Jany 6th 1777.

In pursuance of an order of the General Assembly of this Commonwealth [Virginia] for the division of the district of WEST AUGUSTA into three distinct Counties, whereof the County of Ohio is one distinct & seperate County, Agreable to its Circumscribing Boundaries—In Compliance with which & Certain other Instructions directed to John McCullock Esqr directing him the sd McCulloch to summon the several landholders within sd County to meet at the house of Ezekiel Dewits on Buffelloe Creek on the 27th of Decembr last as well for the purpose of Electing & Consulting Constituting a Courte in & for the sd County, as for the makeing Choise of the seat for County Coarts to be held at in future. within sd County which was done accordingly & a Majority determin'd in favour of a place known by the name of Blacke Cabbin on the waters of Short Creek to be the place of holding Coarts in future,— Accord[ing]ly & in Complyance with a Certain Writ... directed to Willm Scott& James McMichen[?] & David Rodgers Impowering eighter of them to admr unto Mesrs David Shupherd Silus Hedge Willm Scott & James Caldwell & oth[ers]... the oath of Justice of the Peace... therefore the Commn being red at Black Cabbin aforesd... James McMichen there did on Monday the sixth of this Instant, admr unto Sh[...] Hedge Scott Caldwel the oath of Justice of the Peace who being duly Qualifyed the aforesd did administer unto Mesrs Zachariah Sprigg Thomas Waller & Dan[iel] McClain the sd oath... who took their seats on the Bentch accordingly...

John McColloch Esq. as high sheriff offered security & his bond was executed & he took the oath, He also gave bond as collector. James McMechen took the oath as Clark "and took his seat at the Clark's table"...

The first business was the passing of a recommendation that David Shepherd, Esq., be County Lieutenant. Silas Hedges, Esq. be Colonel, & Mr. David McClure be Lieut. Colonel, & Mr. Saml McCollach be Major of Militia.

MARRIAGES BY INFERENCE*

Mr. JOS. BAYLEY and ANNE BUTLER. Before 16 Feby 1708-9. Wmld, Va. iv- (See will of Caleb Butler.)

HENRY BERRY, of Pr. Wm cty, Psh Hanover, and WINEFRED HAYNIE, of Nthd cty, Psh St. Stephen. Mar. contract. 20 Mch 1756. Nthd, Va. iv-7.

HUGH BRENT, Lanc. cty, Psh Christ Church, and JUDITH KENNER, relict and widow of Brereton[?] Kenner, Nthd cty, Psh St. Stephens. Mar. contract. 13 Jany 1766. Nthd, Va. vi-717.

HUGH BRENT and EASTER SHEARMAN, dau. of Martin Shearman. Mar. contr. Lanc., Va. 26 Oct 1761. xviii-25.

GEORGE BLUFORD and MARY KENNEDY, one of the daus. of John Kennedy. Before 25 Aug 1704. Rchmd, Va. iii-149.

CALEB BUTLER and Mrs. MARY DUDDLESTON, *extx of Mr. Alex'r Gorge.* Before 25 Mch 1692. Wmld, Va. [3] 55.

BENJAMIN BLANCHFLOWER, and TEMPERANCE CRABB, wid. of John Crabb. Before 29 Nov 1694. Wmld, Va. [3] 159.

[THOMAS?] CORNELIOUS and TEMPERANCE WEST, dau. of Thomas. Before 14 Sept 1747. Nthd, Va. i-57.

RICHARD CHEEK and ELIZABETH RYLAND. Mar. agreement. Oct. Ct. 1779. Essex, Va. xxiv-452.

ALEXANDER DONIPHAN, Gent., of St. Mary's Psh, Rappa. cty, and MARGARET MOTTS. Before 2 Nov 1691. Rchmd, Va. i-8.

JOHN EUSTACE and SARAH JAUNCEY, dau. of William. Before 10 June 1678. Lanc, Va. viii-63.

EDWARD GEORGE and MARGARET BERRY, dau. of Edward and Catherine Berry. Before 4 Sept 1685. Rappa., Va. Orders—p. 171.

Mr. RICHARD GARDER, of Maryland, and the only sister of John WEIRE. [She was dau. of Mrs. Honoria Jones.] Before 6 May 1685. Essex, Va. Orders—p. 117.

WILLIAM HEABEARD and ELIZABETH BALDRIDGE, wid. Before 21 July 1665. Wmld, Va. i-280.

RICHARD HEABEARD and MARY BALDRIDGE, dau. of Maj. Tho. Baldridge, dec'd. Contract of mar. 15 June 1657. Wmld, Va. Orders i-83.

MANUS MacGLATHLIN and ELIZABETH WOODBRIDGE, dau. of Paul. Before or about 3 Jany 1693. Rchmd, Va. Orders.

JOSEPH MOORE and SUSANNA SWANSON, "Widow or Relict" of Aaron Swanson. Mar. contract. 7 Oct 1769. Nthd, Va. vii-422.

JOHN PEIRCE and Mrs. EASTER TOMLIN, admx of Robt Tomlin, Jr. Before or about 3 Aug 1692. Rchmd, Va. Orders.

MARYLAND'S NEXT OF KIN*

ABIGALE WISE, "my mother;" inv. Anthony Wise of Talbot cty. 19 June 1718. iii-210.

WILLIAM TURNER; inv. Edward Turner, of Talbot cty, 19 June 1719. iii-213.

KATHERINE DODD; inv. Edmond *Dods,* of Talbot cty. 11 Nov 1719. iii-213.

JOHN WILLIAM BOND and STEPHEN GILL; inv. Peter Bond, of Balto. cty. 17 May 1718. iii-216.

KATHERINE SCHURLOOK, "my wife;" inv. Richard Schurlook, of St. Mary's cty. 3 Mch 1720. iii-219.

MARY HARRARD; inv. William Harrard, of St. Mary's cty. 17 Mch 1720. iii-219.

JOHN CLARK, Jr.; inv. Thomas Clark, of St. Mary's cty. 12 Feby 1720. iii-221.

JAMES BAKER and "PRISCILLA his wife the admx;" inv. William Hebb of St. Mary's cty. 19 Mch 1720. iii-221.

EDWARD MILLER; inv. Edward Miller, Jr., of St. Mary's cty. 9 Dec 1719. iii-222.

SARAH and THOMAS BENECRAFT; inv. James Herdman of St. Mary's cty. 3 Feby 1719. iii-222.

MARY BURCH; inv. Mary Rose, of St. Mary's cty. 29 Jany 1711. iii-223.

WILLIAM TOMSON and "ELLINOR THOMSON allias HERBERT;" the admx; inv. William Herbert of St. Mary's cty; 20 Feby 1720. iii-225.

GILES and GRACE JONES, "children of dec."; inv John Jones of Som. cty. 28 Apr 1719. iii-225.

RICHARD LOOGWOD, THOMAS DEATHSELL[sic]; inv. Charles Shewell of Som. cty. 26 Aug 1719. iii-226.

VIRGINIA COLONISTS

(*From "Old Volume 5," S. L. O., Richmond*)

JOHN CUSTIS, Junr., "In old plantacon Creeke" [now Northampton cty], 1657.

Head rights: Wm. St. John, Wm. Marshall, Georg Welfe, JOSEPH CURTIS [CUSTIS].

WILLIAM CORNIX, Lower Norfolk cty, 1657.

Head rights: Daniel Hoser, Rich: Midleton, Fran: Gray, Henry Smith, Symon Cooke, Dorathy Mason, Jno. Andersly, Wm. Blacke, David Anderson, Wm. Shawe.

Mr. HENRY CORBYN, Lancaster cty, 1658.

Head rights: Edmond Benson, Penelope Staples, Gillam Parrett, Stephen Webb, Jo. Rickings, Mary Molden, Richard White, Diana Perkins, Martha Ludgford, Susan Burham, Jno. Freeman, Thomas White, and two negroes. [Sixteen persons called for but only fourteen mentioned.]

Mrs. JANE CLAIBORNE; Northumberland cty, 1657.

Head rights: Tho. Mow, Rich. Dobbins, Wm. Ringly, John Edgcome, Wm. Angell, Abra. Paternoster, Henry Bellamy, Walter Rich, Robert Norton, Kath: Silvester, Andrew Felton, Edward Barnett. Rich. Albert, Tho. Minstrell.

Mr. EDWIN CONNAWAY and Mrs. Hannah MOUNTNEY, Lancaster cty, 1657.

Head rights: Henry Patten, Thomas Roffe, Griffin Thomas, Paul Harwood, Robert Wilson, Thomas Parrish, Robert Watts, Fortune Greene, Georg Hawkins, ALEX. MOUNTNEY, THOMAS MOUNTNEY, JNO. MOUNTNEY, LEONARD MOUNTNEY, Edward Jnoson [sic], Bryan Harris, ROGER MOUNTNEY, Rich. Rostall, Georg Hewes, Nicholas Battinge, Nicholas Paryne, Wm. Berryman, Tho. Howell, Mary Linsey, Mary Hall, Henry Paulle, Wm. Edwinn, Roger Winter, Geo. Shalin, Wm. Duce, Edwd. Goodwinn, Ann Boyle, Ann Lightfoote, Rich. Ashworth.

WILLIAM CUSTIS, Accomack cty, 1657.

Head rights: WM. CUSTIS, Wm. Hanwell, Elizabeth Bankes, Rich, Jones.

Major JOSEPH CHROSHAW, New Kent cty, 1659.

Head rights: Tho. Wharton, Jno. Tayler, Jno. Fourth, Wm. Brown, CUTHBERT CHROSHAW, [MARY?] CROSHAW, Geo. Tomlin, Eliz. Broadert, Rob. Wigg, Timothy Wigg.

THOMAS DAVIS,* Warwick cty, 1655.

Head rights: Thomas Morgan, Mary Goodman, Jno. Gullam, Phillip Baker, Phillip Parker, Rob. Reeves.

JOHN DORMAN,* Northampton cty, 1655.

Head rights: SARAH DORMAN, Wm. Hickman, Mary Overton, Ellenor Higgenson, James Murhead, Wm. Jones, Giles Pickfrizell, Job Edmunds, Eliz. Holliday, Anne Haies, Rog: Amolachan [O'Mulligan?] Elizabeth Haies, Tho. Younge, Marg: Cornelius, John Toole, James Adwick, Grace Adwick.

JOHN DYER,* Lower Norfolk cty, 1655.

Head rights: James Cole, Wm. Jackson.

GRIFFITH DICKINSON, James City cty, 1656.

Head rights: "Himself, twice;" ELIZ: DICKENSON, Wm. Jones, Susan Croch or Croth.

RALPH DUNSTON, Surry cty, 1656.

RALPH DUNSTON, Robt: Wells, Johanna Mathews; Ester Clarke, Grace Harly, Ester Clarke [repeated], Tho: Busy [or Burby.]

Mr. GERVASE DODSON, Lancaster cty, 1656.

Head rights: Jno. Glandfield, Jno. Newman, Tho. Blackborne, Walter Spurr, Wm. Greenhoure, Wm. Watts, Wm. Smoocker, Eliz: Hopkins, Abra: Watson, Tho. Priors, Jno. Bunch, Tho. Hake.

WM. DUDLEY, Lancaster cty, 1657.

Head rights: Alice Smith, John Russell, Abraham Jones, Tho. Hooper. Wm. Onery, Jno. Norman, John Browne, John Danse, John Fletcher, Margaret Welton, Eliz. Forrest, Tho. Floid, Jno. Stoke, Edwd. More. Joseph Wellman, Jacob *Jnoson,* Wm. Jones, Tho. Machir [?] Tho. Farthinge, Tho. Clerke, John Wilson, Henry Forrest & his wife, Eliz: Hunt, Mary Horner, Edwd. Fox, Wm. Jones, Rich. West, Sarah Newell, Edward Wilson, Ann Kinge, Mary Barnham.

MILES DIXON, Northumberland cty, 1656.

Head rights: Anthony Alford, James Whittle, Richd. Goade, Tho. Lawson, Rob. Lipp, Geo. Shelly, Wm. Wilson, Geo. Everett, Edwd, Flowers. Jno. Dule [Dooley?] (Last six persons by assignment from Coll. Richd Lee.)

Lieut: Coll: EDWARD DOUGLAS; Northampton cty, 1657.

Head rights: Wm. Milles, Wm. Prichard, Robrt: Rowlson, Wm. Barrett, Alice Staples, Alice Alsop, Jno. Powell, Gilb. Couling. Hugh Eglestone. Charles Hollingsworth, Marion Cole, Thomas Poynter.

THOMAS DREW, Gent., Charles City cty, 1657.

Head rights: Robert Bourne, Wm. Gabell [Cabell?], Wm. Peck, Arthur Perce, Archebald Sinclur [St. Clair], Hugh Coeman, Jno. Moore, Hen Mouremore[?], Edward Lay, Rich. Maypin [Maupin?]

WILLIAM DAVIS, "Bounding Easterly upon the River of Petomeck in the Freshes above Puscatoway," 1657.

Head rights: Hen. Thornton, James May, James Jolly, Rob: Brooke, James Battin, John Conell, Edd. Mason, Sil: Baker, Edd. Snape, Mathew Shorte.

WM. DENSON, Gent., Nansemond cty, 1657.

Head rights: Peter Dunkey, Jno. Bevington, Elizabeth Ireland, Richard Wilden, Jno. Groome, Elizabeth White, Thomas Kinder, Francis Kinder, Robert Arnolld. [Note: *Francis* Kinder may have been meant for *Frances.*]

WILLIAM DREWE, Lancaster cty, 1657.

Head rights: Fenld.[?] Watkins, Tho. Udall, Rich. Smith, Stafford Billson, Katherine Capman. [List should be for ten persons, but only five names given.]

The County Court Note-Book

An every-other-monthly devoted to abstracts from County Court and other records, prior to 1800, and with a department of notes and queries.

MILNOR LJUNGSTEDT, Editor and Publisher. Bethesda, Route 1, Maryland.

Published six times a year. **Subscription, two dollars and fifty cents,** in advance; must begin with the year. **Renewals, two dollars.** Advertising rates moderate.

FEBRUARY, 1925 VOL. IV, No. 1

THE EDITOR'S CHANCE

IT IS bad to begin the year with excuses. Moreover, a friend of the Editor quotes to her, "Never try to explain; unnecessary with your friends and useless with your enemies." The Editor feels sure she is paraphrasing, but like the man with the framed prayer, the sentiment is the same.

But the Editor would like to say that she has had a hard year. The loss of her southern notes and her subscription list has been very trying. There is only this mitigation, if she has to go to southeast Georgia again, she will have another and last look at St. Augustine and will be compelled to revisit that very delightful St. Mary's, the county seat, as it was, of Camden county.

Something might also be said about the mail. But what is the use? A check was received the other day from a middle west library. That check was mailed last March. It travelled to Georgia and stayed there a while, quite some while; then it went back to the sender. In course of time it reached the Editor. Meanwhile the Editor did not know that the subscription had not been paid, and presumably the library did not know where the Editor was prospecting. Possibly there are other similar cases and this may be in part the reason why the Editor is so tied up she can't afford a title-page.

But the Editor is doing the best she can and the cordiality with which very big libraries, and very big people, and middle-sized libraries and people, send in their subscription at the advanced rates warms the cockles of the COUNTY COURT NOTE-BOOK'S heart. (Sometime the Editor means to find out what "cockles" and a lot of other things are. Today she is feeling unusually humble having just been corrected for calling a brass memorial tablet a *"brass."*)

On the second of the first month the Editor leaves for ancient counties, where she will explore the records for the next three months. Because of reasons heretofore given, and for the psychological effect of FEBRUARY sounding much nearer to APRIL than it really will be, this first issue of 1925 is as of FEBRUARY. The next will be some time off and will be called APRIL.

The issues for 1925 will contain the inferential marriages; the Maryland kin; more naturalizations; the remainder of the Anne Arundel orphans; military material, colonial and revolutionary, wherever it can be found; shipping news and the names of those wandering in countries, colonies and counties other than their own; and the very important testamentary and administrative proceedings of those Northern Neck counties which have lost the full record of this material.

The Editor thinks it may not be amiss to balance the woes of her first paragraph by a slight appreciation of her printers, of their skill, courtesy and ready helpfulness. In the strictest confidence it may be stated that they are the deserving possessors of two "blue ribbons."

OCCASIONAL

One hundred acres of Ryon's Chance survey'd for JOHN CALDWELL..."By mistake Lyeth in Pocomoke River." Wor. Cty Rent Roll. 1744.

NEW KENT CTY, VA. St. Peter's psh. The *office* and Prison Burnt the night of the 15th of July 1787. Further record shows that the fire was incendiary & "Executed by a former Magistrate & person of standing." See Register of St. Peter's Psh.

FRANCIS CREAH [CREAHO?] was a soldier in Tangier 18 years after the disbanding of the Army by the late King James, and came as a servant to this country. Staff. cty, Va. Orders i-163. 6 Oct 1691.

From the Diary of Joshua Hempstead, 1749. p. 524. "I went to the house of Mr. Bellamie and delivered a letter to his wife which I brought from Horse Neck in Connecticut from her father Justice Lockwood." [This Bellamy house was near Northeast, Maryland.]

ERRATA: The following corrections should be made in the lists of NEXT OF KIN, published in May and July 1924.

THOMAS BRUKE, Jr., and JOSEPH STICOY; inv. of Rivhard Brook of St. Mary's cty. 6 Aug. 1719. iii-54. ("Uncle Leonard Brooke, admr.")

WILLIAM HARRISON and JAMES DECKINSON; inv. William Dickinson of Talbot cty. 29 June 1719. iii-64.

DAVID HUGHES and WILLIAM BROWNE; inv. Edward Pinders of Talbot cty. 11 Feby 1718. iii-69. (Omitted.)

R. GRUNDY; inv. of Thos. BESWICK, of Talbot cty. 10 Jany 1718, iii-74. (Omitted.)

JOHN THOMPSON and RICHARD THOMPSON, of Cecil cty. 25 July 1719. iii-123.

WILLIAM RESWICK; inv. Thos. Reswick, of St. Mary's cty. 26 Mch 1719. iii-130. (This was printed *Beswick.*)

CONTINUED articles COUNTY COURT NOTE-BOOK, and the dates on which they first appeared. For the sake of neatness and to avoid unnecessary printing, the usual headings and tail-notes attached to these articles will be discontinued, and this paragraph will take their place.

MARRIAGES BY INFERENCE. Began with May, 1922.

MARYLAND'S NEXT OF KIN. Began with July, 1922.

VIRGINIA COLONISTS. This alphabetized list began with July, 1924.

ANNE ARUNDEL ORPHANS. Began with September, 1924.

MARYLAND NATURALIZATIONS. Began with February, 1923.

KING GEORGE PROBATES, &c. Began with July, 1924.

PRINCE WILLIAM PROBATES, &c. Began with April, 1923.

The LIST of BANISHED QUAKERS. Began with November, 1924.

MILITARY NOTES, both COLONIAL and REVOLUTIONARY, and some later MILITIA NOTES, will appear in every issue, if possible.

SHIPS IN PORT, NEW ENGLANDERS AND OTHERS and COLONIAL FORENAMES, will appear in alternate issues, or as space can be found for them.

QUAKER REGISTERS IN ENGLAND

(*Contributed by Mr. Edward Dwelly*)

Non-conformist registers in England, that is, all those not kept by the Church of England, are known as "Non-parochial Registers." They were all called in and deposited at Somerset House, London, under the Registration Act of 1837, as Civil Registration as now carried out was definitely established on the 1 July in that year. The Registers kept by the Society of Friends, by far the most important of all non-conformist registers, are an example of the thoroughness with which such records should be kept everywhere, and with the transcripts made each year by order of George Fox in 1668 to correspond with the Bishops' Transcripts of the Church of England show what an immense treasure has been lost by the latter church through neglect to conform to the Order in Council of Queen Elizabeth! **Consequently there is at Devonshire House, London, the headquarters of the Society of Friends, a complete alphabetical list of every birth, marriage and death of which any record is preserved from about 1650 to the present time.**

When the Registers were called in under the act of 1837, a total of 1622 separate registers were deposited.

It should be borne in mind that Quakers did not belong exclusively to any one class of the community, but were drawn from all classes. It would probably be difficult to find a single member of the House of Commons who had no Quaker ancestor. In George Fox's time they numbered over 60,000, and thousands came of the best County families, hundreds being able to prove a Royal Descent. As an example of the value of Quaker Registers, a marriage entry of 1712 records the signatures of the wedded pair as well as those of thirty-one of their friends present at the ceremony.

Note: Referring to a previous article on Parish Registers, Mr. Dwelly adds that when the ceremonies of baptism, marriage or burial were celebrated in Chapels-of-ease, or subsidiary chapels, the facts were entered in the Register kept at the Mother Church of the parish, and certificates of all such entries, it should be borne in mind, are not valid unless the signature of the Vicar or Rector in charge of the parish is followed by "Vicar (or rector) of the aforesaid parish of..." so-and-so, as he is the legal custodian, and one signed by a church warden or parish clerk is of no value. A certificate from a Civil Register should be signed by the Registrar of the Parish, and one from the Bishops Transcripts by the Bishop's Registrar.

QUAKERS BANISHED FROM ENGLAND BETWEEN 1660 AND 1666

THOMAS CHAPMAN
ANNE CHILD
JOH. CHILD
THOMAS CHITHAM
JOHN CHOPPIN
JOHN CLAYDON
MARY COOKE
ELIZABETH COURT
STEPHEN CRISP
JOHN CROSIER
EDMUND CROSSE
} from Essex.

RICHARD CANTON, from Derbyshire.

GEORGE CLARKE
HENRY CLIFTON
ANNE COCKS
CLEMENT CRABB
WALTER CRANE
JOHN CRANFORD
} from Cambridgeshire and the Isle of Ely.

JOHN CATER
ELIZABETH CATLAND
JOSEPH COLE
PRISCILLA COTTON
ROBERT CRABB
THOMAS CURTIS
} from Devonshire.

ANNE COLBURNE
JOSEPH COLE
JOSIAH COLE
ROGER COWARD
WILLIAM COWARD
SAMUEL CURTIS
} from Dorsetshire.

TRISTRAM CLARKE
JOSEPH COALE
} from Cornwall

JOSEPH COLE
LEONARD COLE
THOMAS CURTIS
ANNE CURTIS
GEORGE ADAMSON COLE
} from Berkshire.

A LIST OF ORPHANS, ANNE ARUNDEL COUNTY, MARYLAND (Liber T. B. 1.)

(*Contributed by Mrs. Geo. W. Hodges*)

JOHN and WILLIAM HEMPTON, with Mr. John Baldwin.

SAMUEL, JAMES, RACHELL, PHILLIP, and PRESILLA HOWARD, with Mr. Henry Pinkney.

BENJA: HOWARD, with Mr. Rich'd Warfeild.

JAMES HOSKINS, with Mrs. Ruth Howard.

THOMAS HEMPTON, with Henry Carter.

"Two of ANTHONY HOLLAND'S" with Mordecay Price.

"One of CHARLES HALL'S", with Tho: Harris.

"One of MATHEW HAWKIN'S with Edward Parish.

EDWARD HAREY, with William Harey.

RICHARD HAREY, with Josias Toogood.

JACOB HIGHT, at Samuel Gushard's[?]

THOMAS, JACOB, and ABRAHAM HOLLAND, with Benja: Capell.

JOHN HUGGINS, with Joseph Sanders.

JAMES HOPER, orphan, and estate in his mother's hand.

THOS: HALBYATT[?] with Lewis Duvall.

JOHN, ELIZA:, OTHO, MEHITABLE, THOMAS and JANE HOLLAND, with Jno. Parpint[?]

KATH: HOWARD, orphan of John Howard, with Maj'r Greenberry.

JAMES HALL, son of Wm., with William Lewis.

THO: and SARAH HOMWOOD, son and dau. of James Homwood, with Mrs. Mary Homewood.

JAMES HOMWOOD, son of James, with Mr. Thomas Homewood.

ABRAHAM HOWARD, son of Isaac, with Edward Peak.

ALICE HOW, dau of William, with Edward Peak.

MATTHEW, JOHN, GIDION, LEMUEL, HENRY, ABNER, orphts of John Howard, with Wm. Crouch.

MARY ADOSIA HARRINGTON, an orphan, placed by the Court with John Clark.

KING GEORGE COUNTY, VIRGINIA, PROBATES AND ADMINISTRATIONS

MARGARET HARPER; her will presented by Thomas Harper, Samuel Harper, and George Harper, her extrs. Proved by Charles Ewell and Joshua Farguson. 3 Aug 1744. ii-405.

THOMAS MINTON; l. a. on his est. to George Deavenport; Henry Drake, sec. 2 Nov 1744. ii-411.

MARGARET PALMER; l. a. to John Glendening; John Campe, Gent., sec. 5 July 1744. ii-417.

CYPRIAN ANDERSON; l. a. to Susannah Anderson, his widow; Edward Hoyle, sec. 1 Feby 1744. ii-424.

MARY BROCK; her will presented by William Deaner[?], extr. Proved by Thomas Vivion and John Jones; Charles Deane sec. 1 Feby 1744. ii-425.

JOHN SIMPSON; will presnted by William Simpson, his extr. Proved by Burton Milligan and Samuel Angel. Mary Simpson, widow and relict, refuses to stand by will. 1 Mch 1744. ii-428.

FRANCES THORNTON; will presnted by FRANCES THORNTON her extr. Proved by wit. Samuel Donne, sec. 5 Apr 1745. ii-433.

MARY BUTLER; l. a. to Elias Powell; James Hackley and Samuel Reid, sec. 5 Apr 1745. ii-441.

SARAH STANTON; will presented by William Scott, her extr. Proved by James Jones; James Jones, sec. 3 May 1745. ii-440.

MAXFIELD BROWN; will presented by Newman Brown and George Brown his extrs. 7 June 1745. ii-445.

WILLIAM DUFF; will presented. Proved by Benjamin Strother and William Maiders; Maj. John Champe, sec. Elizabeth Duff refuses to stand to her husband's will. 2 Aug 1745. ii-449.

GEORGE PAYNE; will presented by William Jett and Martha Payne, extrs, and proved by Richard Golding and Thomas Greenstreet. Harry Turner, sec. (John Payne is one of the appraisers appointed.) 4 Oct 1745. ii-454.

ANN EDMONDS; will presented by George Davenport, extr. Proved by Thomas Pratt and Charles Deane. 1 Nov 1745. ii-456.

JAMES MICOU; will presnted by William Fauntleroy and Elizabeth Micou, his extrs. 6 Dec 1745. ii-464.

ELIAS SHARP; l. a. to Margaret Sharp his widow. Richard Elkin and John Booth, sec. 6 Dec 1745. ii-465.

WILLIAM MUMFORD, Sr. L. a. on his est. to Wm. Mumford, his son. William Marshall and Joel Berry, sec. 7 Dec 1745. ii-471.

GILES CARTER; will presented by John and Mary Carter, his extrs. Robert Spence, sec. 7 Feby 1745. ii-473.

WILLIAM STRINGFELLOW; l. a. on his est, to Sarah Stringfellow; Richard Elkin, sec. 2 May 1746. ii-478.

THOMAS MONROE; will presented by William Monroe, his extr. Proved by Charles Deane and William Monroe. Thomas Monroe, one of the extrs, relinquishes. Charles Deane and John White, sec. 3 Oct 1746. ii-494.

WM. MARSHALL; will presented by Ann Marshall, one of his extrs. Proved by Sarah Dixon, late Sarah Turner. 3 Feby 1748. ii-[page not given.]

(The foregoing notes are from ORDERS 1735-1751.)

A LIST OF PERSONS NATURALIZED BY PARTICULAR ACTS

From Bacon's Laws of Maryland *

ANDREW TOULSON, of Balto. cty. 19 Apr 1671. 10.

THOMAS TURNER, of A. A. cty. 19 Apr 1671. 10.

JOHN BAPTIST TYLER, of Pr. Geo's. cty, pltr. 19 Apr 1706. 12.

MICHAELL URY, a Greek, of Pr. Geo's cty. 6 Nov 1725. 16.

JOHN DE VAGHA, 18 Oct 1694. 4.

* Figures other than dates refer to chapters.

ISAAC VANBIBBER, Gent., of Cecil cty. 25 Mch 1701. 6.

MATTHIAS VANBIBBER, Mcht, of Cecil cty. 25 Mch 1701. 6.

JOHN VANBEECK, 8 May 1669. 4.

GARRET VANSWERINGEN and his wife BARBARA DE BARRETTE VANSWERINGEN; his dau. ELIZABETH, and son ZECHARIAS. 8 May 1669. 4.

NICHOLAS VERBRACK, 26 Sept 1684. 7.

FREDERICK VICTOR. 24 Apr 1762. 29.

GERARDUS WEESELS, and son JAMES, 18 Oct 1694. 4.

JOHN WOOLF, shoemaker, of the City of Annapolis; also his wife, HANNAH, his son PETER, and his daus. ANNELEFFE and HANNAH. 30 Oct 1727. 17.

MAUDLIN WOOLF, spinster, of the City of Annapolis. 30 Oct 1727.

GARRETT WOOLF, of the City of Annapolis, shoemaker, 30 Oct 1767. 17.

JACOB CLAUS DE YOUNG, of Balto. cty. 19 Apr 1671. 10.

JOHN PELER(?) ZENGER, of Kent cty, and his children. 27 Oct 1720. 18. (*End of Vol. I.*)

PROBATES AND ADMINISTRATIONS GRANTED IN PRINCE WILLIAM COUNTY, VIRGINIA

From the fifth remaining Order Book.

JECHONIAS COOPER; l. a. to Robert Brent. 6 Oct 1766. v-16.

JUDITH BARR; her will probated by William Barr, Jr.[?] 8 Oct 1766. v-18.

GEORGE HARPER; his will presented by Betty Harper, one of the extrs. 1 Dec 1766. v-22.

ALLAN MACRAE: will presented by Thomas Lawson and John Lee, Gent., Proved by William Dobbie and William Savage. 1 Dec 1766. v-22.

JAMES DOUGLASS, Gent. Will presented by Alexr Henderson and John Riddle and William Carr. Proved by Cuthbert Bullett, William Grayson, and Robert Brent. 1 Dec 1766. v-22.

THOMAS STEWART; admn of his est. granted to Rich'd Stewart. John Graham, sec. 6 Apr 1767, v-33.

THOMAS DAVIS; admn his est., with will annexed, granted to William Barr, the extrs refusing extrship. 2 June 1767. v-45. (Isaac Davis refused. 1766—v-4.)

THOMAS THORNTON; will presented by Lettice Thornton, the extx; proved by Henry Peyton, John Peyton and John Matthews. Codicil proved by Jno. Matthews and Chichester Curtis. 7 Dec 1767. v-8.

WILLIAM FOSTER; will presented by William Foster, extr. Proved by James Bridges, Alexander Davis, and William Wyat. 7 Dec 1767. ii-65.

RICH'D WRIGHT; will presented by Mary Anne Wright, Wm. and Joseph Wright, the extrs. Proved by Jacob Garroon Pearce and Wm. Estebe. 7 Dec 1767. v-65.

Mr. CHARLES SHEPARD II, of Washington, D. C., who, owing to his extensive work in the Library of Congress and elsewhere, is very familiar with published records, has called the Editor's attention to the fact that some fifty per cent or more of the names in the lists now appearing under the caption "Virginia Colonists," in the NOTE-BOOK, are in Greer's "Early Virginia Immigrants," published in 1912. The Editor does not question this statement, but has found that authorities of the highest standing have very seriously questioned the completeness of Greer's work. (See Virginia Magazine of History and Biography, 1912, v. 20, p. 445.) It has also been stated to the Editor at the Virginia State Land Office that Greer examined but a part of the volumes containing these names. It seems to the Editor, therefore, that a bona fide page-to-page list of this very important "Old Five" ... the volume being used ... is quite worth publication. There will doubtless be some difference of opinion as to the correct form of many of the names. This difference may lead to exact identification. The Editor would appreciate any suggestion, except as to the form of publication. The latter has been settled upon as the most useful and as taking the least space. At some later time the full list will be published in pamphlet form.

NOTES AND QUERIES

THADDEUS BARNARD'S wife was HANNAH. They were married in Oneida county, New York, it is stated, in 1805. Hannah Barnard was the sister of Dr. Levi Goldsborough. She was born in Newcastle county, Delaware, in 1789. Definite information as to her family is greatly desired.
Mrs. T. W. C. A.

WADE: Twenty-five dollars will be paid for information as to the parentage of Capt. JOHN WADE, who was living in Chester county Penna. in 1754; for date of birth and death; place of death; names of his children, &c. His wife appears to have been Martha Robinson. She may have been a widow when they married. It is probable Capt. Wade died in or during the Revolution. Did he die on the prison ship Jersey?
M. L. M.

WANTED: The wife of JOSEPH STOCKLEY, son of JOHN, of Accomack cty, Va., and the wife of ALEXANDER STOCKLEY, his son, also of Accomack. JOSEPH died about 1736; Alexander about 1763.
M. B. C. W.

WANTED: The parentage of ISAAC MILNOR, of Bucks county, Penna, who was of Bristol tshp, and died early in the 1700's.
M. L. M.

COLUMBIAN PRINTING CO., INC., WASHINGTON, D. C.

The
County Court Note-Book

A Little Bulletin of History and Genealogy

April, 1925. Vol. IV, No 2.

SOUTH CAROLINA; ITS DISTRICTS AND COUNTIES

Courtesy of Mr. A. S. Salley, Jr., Secretary of the Historical Commission

In 1683 three *counties* were laid off in South Carolina: COLLETON, BERKELEY and CRAVEN. A few years later CARTARET was added and its name was shortly changed to GRANVILLE.

These *counties* were legislative, judicial and militia units. There were no seats, no local government, and *no records* were kept in the counties. Their boundaries were indefinite.

In 1706, the *counties* were supplanted by *parishes* as legislative units, and the *county courts* (that is, the courts of General Sessions and Common Pleas) were abolished when the proprietary government was overthrown in 1719.

In 1768, the province was divided into seven *judicial districts:* CHARLES TOWN, BEAUFORT, GEORGE TOWN, CHERAWS, CAMDEN, ORANGEBURGH, and NINETY SIX. Courthouses and jails were erected at the seat of each district, which bore the same name as the district, the districts having been named for existing towns which were made the seats thereof. No records were kept in these districts save the records of the courts of General Sessions and Common Pleas. All other classes of records were kept at CHARLES TOWN, the provincial seat of government, until 1785, when the recording of wills, deeds, &c., at the district seats, was authorized.

In 1793, PINCKNEY and WASHINGTON districts were added. In 1798, these nine districts were carved up into twenty-four: LANCASTER, CHESTER, FAIRFIELD, KERSHAW, SUMTER and YORK from CAMDEN; ABBEVILLE, EDGEFIELD, NEWBERRY, PENDLETON, GREENVILLE, LAURENS, SPARTANBURG and UNION, from NINETY SIX; CHESTERFIELD, MARLBOROUGH and DARLINGTON from CHERAWS; MARION AND GEORGE TOWN from GEORGE TOWN; CHARLESTON and COLLETON from CHARLES TOWN; BARNWELL and ORANGEBURGH from ORANGEBURGH; and BEAUFORT, without change.

In 1800, RICHLAND was erected from KERSHAW, and WILLIAMSBURG from GEORGETOWN; in 1802, HORRY was erected from GEORGETOWN; and in 1804, LEXINGTON from ORANGEBURGH. In 1825, PENDLETON was divided into ANDERSON and PICKENS. In 1858, CLARENDON was taken from SUMTER.

In 1868, under the "Reconstruction" Constitution, the name *district* was changed to *county*. There were then thirty *counties*, and since that date there have been added fifteen others: AIKEN, HAMPTON, BERKELEY, FLORENCE, SALUDA, BAMBERG, DORCHESTER, CHEROKEE, GREENWOOD, LEE, CALHOUN, DILLON, JASPER, McCORMICK and ALLENDALE.

MARRIAGES BY INFERENCE*

AMORY BUTLER, Clerk, and Mrs. ELIZABETH CATLETT, wid. of Col. John Catlett. She appears to have been also the widow of William Underwood. Mar. contr. Rappa. cty, Va. vol. 1664-1673. 29 Apr 1672.

ABRAHAM BLAGG and MARGARET JONES, dau. of Honoria Jones. Rappa. cty, Va. Before or about 1685. vol. 1677-1682. p. 84.

ALEXANDER BAGWELL and ELIZABETH STERLING, wid of William, N-n cty, Va. before 1738. Court record.

JOHN BOYD prob. m. MARY MERRITT, sister of Benjamin Merritt. Granv. cty, N. C. Before Feby 1777. i-205.

RICHARD CARTER and MARY HAILE, dau. of Thomas Haile. Mecklb. cty, Va. Before 24 Oct 1916. Will book VIII.

THOMAS CLARK and MARGARET James, widow of Philip James. N-n cty, Va. Before Nov 1738. Court record.

THOMAS CONNARLY and MARTHA ADDISON, wid of John Addison. N-n cty, Va. Before 8 Apr 1740. Court record.

JOSIAH DOWTY and ELISHA BELOTE, dau of John Belote. N-n cty, Va. Before Jany 1754. Court record.

STEPHEN DUNTON and ELIZABETH SENEOR, dau. of Jno. Seneor. N-n cty, Va. Before Dec 1739. Court record.

PETER FOXSON and MARY BARROW, eldest dau. of John x Barrow (wf Mary.) Rappa. cty, Va. Mar. agreem't. 27 Apr 1677. 1677-1682, p. 127.

NEHEMIAH FITCHETT and MARY WILLET. N-n cty, Va. Before 22 Dec 1740. Court record. [See also xviii-368, for his m. to Mary Powell.]

REED FLETCHER and the widow of Solomon[?] Walter. N-n cty, Va. About or before 1742. Court record.

FRANCIS GOWER and ANN CLARKE. Rappa. cty, Va. Before 8 Mch 1682. 1677-1682. p. 5.

MOSES GRIFITH and BETTY CLAY, dau. of Elizabeth. [Betty (Clay) Grifith first m. William Whitehead.] N-n cty, Va. Before 8 Apr 1755. Court record.

ELEAZAR JOHNSON and ISABELL ROBARTS, dau. of Arthur Robarts. N-n cty, Va. Before 10 Jany 1753. Court record.

GEORGE JONES and HONORIA WEIRE, wid. of Maj. John Weire. Rappa. cty, Va. Before 5 May 1676. 1677-1682. p. 119.

JOHN JONES and ELIZABETH CLAY, wid. of John Clay, [See above.] N-n cty, Va., Before 12 May 1741. Court record.

ALEXANDER KEMP and COMFORT SATCHEL, dau. of William Satchel. N-n cty, Va., before 1753. Court record.

JOHN KINCAID and MARGARET PREESON, wid. of Zerubbable Preeson, Gent. N-n cty, Va. Before 8 Oct 1732. Court record.

DANIEL LUCAS and TABITHA BENTHALL, dau. of Daniel Benthall. N-n cty, Va. Before 9 Sept 1740. Court record.

WILLIAM MILLS and ANN BULL, dau. of Richard Bull. N-n cty, Va. Before Jany 1733. Court record.

TEIGUE O'DEAR and ESTHER COSTEN, dau. of Stephen Costen, Sr. N-n cty, Va. Before 22 June 1685. Court record.

PETER PRESTLY, of Northbld cty, Va. and ELIZABETH THOMPSON. Va. S. L. O. Before 4 Oct. 1664. v-452.

ANDREW PEDIGREW, Northbld cty, and ISSABELLA DODSON, wid. of GERVAS DODSON. Before 10 Jany 1704. Va., S. L. O. iii-72.

JOHN PEARCE and ESTHER WALKER, dau. of Col. John Walker of Richmond cty. Before 25 Jany 1705. Va. S. L. O. iii-123.

ZERUBBABELL ROBERTS and ESTHER ROBERTS, extx of Jacob Roberts. N-n cty, Va. Before 11 Apr 1733. Court record.

EZEKIELL ROBERTS and ... BELOTE, widow of John Belote. N-n cty, Va. Before Jany 1754. Court record.

JOHN ROBARTS and MARY BAKER, widow of William, dec'd. Mar. contr. Libty cty, Ga. 28 July 1791. C-212.

AURDLY SANDERFORD, Libty cty, Ga., and JEMIMA TAYLOR, of same. Mar. contr. (Sig. is Audly Sandiford.) 29 June 1793. Libty cty, B-520.

HENRY DASSEX STONE, Gent., infant under 21, son of Thos. Stone of Chatham cty, and SUSANNAH McCLELAND, sp., infant under 21, dau. of Mary Dunworth, of Libty cty. [1787] Libty cty, B-148.

HENRY D. STONE, of Libty cty, Ga., and ANN OSWALD, dau. of Thomas Maxwell, Esq., dec'd. 15 Sept 1791. Libty cty B-494.

JOEL WALKER, Libty cty, and MARY JONES, Libty cty. Mar. contr. 30 Jany 1788. Libty cty, DD-58.

JAMES WILKINSON prob. m. a dau. of Joseph OSWALD. Before or about 17 Feby 1794. See Libty cty. Ga. DD-101.

MARYLAND'S NEXT OF KIN *

"MARY, wife of John CARROLL, lately called MARY FORREST, admx."; inv. Peter Forrest, of A. A. cty. 13 Mch 1719. iii-227.

BARBERY JACKSON; inv. Ralph Arnold of Q. A. cty. 13 Mch 1718. iii-228.

MANUEL and SILVANUS MARRIOTT; inv. John Marriott of A. A. cty 18 Oct 1719. iii-229.

JOHN WILLMOTT; inv. John Willmott Sr., of Balto. cty. 18 Oct 1719. iii-231.

JOHN GWINN, THOMAS BAYLEY; inv. Thomas Dixon of Chas. cty. 4 Dec 1719. iii-237.

THOMAS WALTER, MARY STELL; inv. Thomas Watterman of Chas. cty.... 1719. iii-238.

ANTHONY DREW and MARGARET his wife the nearest of Kin"; inv. John Brown of Balto. cty. 25 Feby 1719. iii-241.

THOMAS BUCKMAN, KATHERINE BUCKMAN and HENRY PARRATT; inv. Izaiah[?] Parratt of Talbot cty. 27 June 1717. iii-244.

NATHANIEL HORSEY, CHARLES POTTINGHAM; inv. William Wheatley of Som. cty. 16 Mch 1719-20. iii-246.

DAVID JOHNSON; inv. Emanuel Johnson of Som. cty. 17 Mch 1719-20. iii-247.

JAMES and JOSEPH POLCK; inv. Ephraim Pole of Som. cty. 30 July 1719. iii-247.

ISRAEL BOSTON; inv. Esau Boston of Somerset cty. 17 Mch 1719-20. iii-248.

EDWARD ROUND; inv. Capt. William Round of Som. cty. 22 May 1719. iii-249.

ROGER LEE; inv. Winefred Lee, of Charles cty. 4 Jan 1719. iii-251.

JANE EVANS; "natural mother of dec.", THOMAS HARRISON, "Brother to ye dec.", and RICHARD HARRISON, "*nearstt* Relation to ye dec."; inv. Elizabeth Hague of Charles cty. 19 May 1718. iii-252.

JOHN TAYLOR; inv. Jane Boy of Charles cty. 17 Feby 1719. iii-254.

MARY GRAY, GEORGE BRETT; inv. Henry Brett of Charles cty. 22 Jany 1717-21. iii-255.

JANE EVANS, "ye Natural Mother," THOMAS HARRISON, "brother of ye whole blood;" inv. Richard Harrison of Charles cty. 15 Feby 1719. iii-256.

HANNAH JONES, HANNAH RATTENBURY; inv. John Rattenbury, Baltimore cty. 6 Apr 1720. iii-257.

WILLIAM MEDLEY; inv. James Jubbs of St. Mary's cty. 6 June 1720. iii-261.

JOHN and THOMAS JONES; inv. Jonathan Jones of A. A. cty, 23 Apr 1719. iii-265.

JAMES and ISACK ANDERSON; inv. Hennery Conyers of Dorchester cty. 23 Jany 1719. iii-266.

ELIZABETH GRAVES, MARTHA TREW; inv. William Pope of Kent cty. 25 May 1720. iii-270.

JOHN WATT, "brother-in-law;" inv. Joseph More, of Kent cty. 25 May 1720. iii-270

CHRISTOPHER THOMPSON, "Unkle;" inv. James Shaw of Pr. Geo's cty. 13 Sept 1719. iii-270.

JOHN and SARAH BAWYLLS[?]; inv. William Downs of Pr. Geo's cty. 2 Apr 1720. iii-271.

THOMAS and JOHN COMERFORD and HERCULES COOKE; inv. Norton Knatchbull of Q. A. cty. 7 May 1720. iii-271.

VIRGINIA COLONISTS

(From "Old Volume 5," S. L. O., Richmond)

JOHN EVANS, Northampton cty, 1655.
Head rights: Kath. Gardner, Eliz: Johnson, John Knight, Rob. Wright, Miles Grey, Jane Wms, Lydia Easterfeild, Eliz: Vincent.

CHARLES EDMONDS, New Kent cty, 1657.
Head rights: Jno. Clerke, Tho. Maddin, Nicho. Dewes, Rebecca Clerke, Tho. Burton, Ra. Wms, Ann Clerke, An Savage, Mary Savage, Ann Mitchell, Wm. Bartlett, Robert Tuck. Paul Ceser; Tho. Wms, Wm. Tuck.

WILLIAM EDWARDS, Surry cty, 1657.
Head rights: Wm. Avery, Mary Gonn, Jno. Hoskins, Eliz. Johnson, Marg: Maddison, Wethers Cocken.

WILLIAM EDWARDS, Surry cty, 1657.
Head rights: Mrs. Sarah Newton, Barnaby Goffe, Francis Warne, Teige Oswillan, Waltr. Rouse, Walter Lashley, Dorathy Moule, Elizabeth Bashwell, Geo. Harrison, Thomas Benson, Jane Wattkins, Antho: Evans, Robert Willson, one negro.

CHARLES EDMONDS and WILLIAM PULLAM, New Kent cty, 1658.
Head rights: Jane Blinde, Tho. Rewells, Wm. Webb (for transportation of 17 persons; only 3 mentioned.)

ROGER FOUNTEINE, Lower Norfolk cty, [date not given]. [About 1655.]
Head rights: James Flaharty, Garret Burry, Sarah Tompson, John Kirke, Job Chandler, Alex. Simpcock, Dan: Gerdan [Jordan?], Rose Springe, Gab: Johnson, Archibald Wahoope [Waughop], Hum. Twillye, Archiball Hunter.

Capt. HENRY FLEETE, cty not given, 1656.
Head rights: Darby Howranley, Katherine Cullin, Wm. Tall, Daniel Morrell, Jno. Bryant, Tho. Hinde, James Ludwell, Tho. Harris, Joane Wood, Tho. Boase [perhaps Boyce?] Bridges Lee.

DOMINICK FERRIATT, "of Corotoman," Lancaster cty, 1657.
Head rights: Wm. Ball, 4 times; Hugh Davis, Rich. Ball, Wm. Butler and Joane his wife; 2 maid servants, Wm. Perkins, John Jones, Sarah Lee, Ann Whord, Patience Martin, Nicho. Jackson, Francis Jackson, Wm. Sparrow, Rich. Franklin, "& Francis," Tho. Coote, Eliz: Bloy, Judith Sewell. [32 head rights called for, but only 23 names.]

Mr. RICHARD FLINTE, Northampton cty, 1657.
Head rights: Elizabeth James, Margaret Davis, Joane Pawly.

Capt. THOMAS GODWIN,* Nansemond cty, 1655.
Head rights: Dorothy Loyd. [Four head rights, but only one mentioned by name.]

WILLIAM GOWERS,* Northampton cty, 1656.
Head rights: Six negroes assigned by Col. Scarburgh.

RICHARD GIBLE, Northumberland cty, 1656.
Head rights: Robert Newman, Wm: Winterton, Mary Robinson, Ann Pettite, John Dunnidge, John Wilkinson, Anne Wilkinson, Vincent Standford, Wm. Chapman, John Branch, Mary Branch, Mary Branch, Jnr., Edward Toogood. David Griffin, John Willis, Wm: Wade.

ROBERT GRYMES, on a branch of the Western Branch of Elizabeth River, 1656.
Head right: Arthur Dennis.

THOMAS GRAVES, Westmoreland cty, 1656.
Head rights: Moore Lyon, Garrett Hamon, George Streaton, Jno. Canadie [Kennedy], Tho: Derricke, John Davis.

PEETER GREENE, Surry cty, 1656.
Head rights: John Wms., Rich. Henson, Thomas Sarson, Eliz: Sawer.

Major THOMAS GOODRICH, "south side Rappahannock river," 1657.
Head rights: John Gouldinge, Edmond Reeves.

WILLIAM GAPEINGE, Surry cty, 1657.
Head right: Mary Willsford.

THOMAS GRAVES, Gloucester cty, 1657.
Head rights: Phillipp Stephens, Thomas Feard [Foard?]

THOMAS GRAVES, Gloucester cty, 1657.
Head rights: Edward Lashly, Sam Claton, Phillip Soloman, Judith Haselwood.

FRANCIS HUTCHINS,* Nansemond cty, 1656.
Head rights: Elizabeth Pye, Daniell Murray, Mary Misomer[?], Armagall Greenwood.

REES HUGHES, New Kent cty, 1656.
Head rights: John Morely, Eliz: Harwood, Griffith Jones, Joane Urlin, Martin Weele, "Margaret & Jno. &c."

JOHN HAYLES, upon Petomeck river above Anacosta island, 1657.
Head rights: Tho. Fourty, James Wilkinson.

THOMAS HILL, "Aquaconde river" [Occoquan?] 1657.
Head rights: Capt. Thomas Hill, 3 times; Mary Bushrode, twice; Jno. Hill, Georg Hill, Mary Hill, Francis Hill.

RICHARD HEABERD, Westmoreland cty, 1658.
Head rights: Gerrett Bicker, Alke, his wife; John, Frilor[?] and Katherine, his chn.

Mr. CHRISTOPHER HARRIS, James City cty, 1658.
Head rights: Clemt. Harris (twice), Peeter Arbo, Hen. Richman, Alex. Rashbrooke, Wm. Alden, Eliz: Burnet, Jane Fowke, Hanah Church.

---

*Previously listed.

The County Court Note-Book

An every-other-monthly devoted to abstracts from County Court and other records, prior to 1800, and with a department of notes and queries.

MILNOR LJUNGSTEDT, Editor and Publisher. Bethesda, Route 1, Maryland.

Published six times a year. **Subscription, two dollars and fifty cents,** in advance; must begin with the year. **Renewals, two dollars.** Advertising rates moderate.

APRIL, 1924
Vol. IV., No. 2

The Editor intended to devote this number and the one which will follow, largely to the Carolinas and Georgia. Her long absence, however, has so delayed publication that it has seemed better to use material already in shape, and not even to indulge in any comment on conditions as found in these three very interesting States. If possible, the many marriage records and other material from their courts, will be published, at least in part, in the JUNE and AUGUST issues. The Editor wishes that her means permitted the reproduction of photographs, and that her typewriter had the wings of genius or at least of an airplane, so that her readers might see all that she saw . . . nine-tenths of which is off the route of the railroad and the touring auto.

The Editor is gratified to say that the express company in whose care her lost notes and subscription list were, has made a settlement on a very fair basis. The payment made, however, could not replace the work, and so it had to be done over. Fortunately the Editor has as a rule, kept her indices separate from her notes, and these indices were not lost, except in one case. Their use saved some wearisome search. It is sad to relate, however, that one county seat had been changed and it was impossible to say what dilapidated folios had been left behind. A friend of the Editor has promised to "check up."

While in search of SOUTH CAROLINA material a year ago, the Editor, having previously made a fruitless appeal to the Secretary of that State, wrote to Mr. A. S. Salley, Jr., the Secretary of the Historical Commission for South Carolina, and received from him the information given on the first page of this issue, but in a more skeletonized form. Afterwards, the Editor had the pleasure of meeting Mr. Salley and of receiving from him a somewhat enlarged statement but still suitable for the limitations of the NOTE-BOOK, and this memorandum Mr. Salley kindly permits the Editor to publish. The Editor understands that a full account of these puzzling district-counties, their erection and their powers, will shortly appear in the official South Carolina publication. What appears in this issue of the NOTE-BOOK is sufficient to guide the searcher to the material in the counties. It should be added, however, that some of the colonial records are in Columbia, and some have been destroyed.

The Editor, at the risk of being too personal, must say that Mr. Salley is in himself a perfect mine of information, with a most marvelous memory, the envy of those who are devoted to exact research. And what especially appeals to this Editor, the information he gives is direct and to the point, devoid of either frills or hesitancy. The publications of the Commission, issued under his supervision, are most interesting and valuable. A list can be had upon application to the Historical Commission of South Carolina. And the Editor advises, as the result of experience, that before making any personal search in Columbia, the published records be thoroughly examined.

The Editor has been for some time collecting unusual names. It would seem that the people who gave the following forenames must really have done it "a-purpose." They are found in southeast Virginia, and in North Carolina.

OLIVE BRANCH, SION HILL, GREEN HILL, RIVER JORDAN, SCARLET REDD, and in Georgia, BROWN DYE.

ENGLISH QUAKERS BANISHED BETWEEN 1660 AND 1666

ANTHONY CASE SAMUEL CLIFT JOHN COX	from Gloucestershire.
JOHN CANNON, from Hampshire.	
JOHN CRANWELL JOHN CROOK RICHARD CHATTERIS	from Huntingtonshire.
JOHN CHRISTEN PETER COSNOCK	from the Isle of Man.
HENRY CLARKE WILLIAM CATON	from Kent.
ANNE CLAYTON MARY CLAYTON GEORGE COWSON RICHARD CUBHAM THOMAS CURWEN	from Lancaster.
JOHN CARR THOMAS CAVE	from Leicestershire.
HEZEKIAH CROFT JOHN CAPES	from Lincolnshire.
WILLIAM CLATER JAMES CORNEY	from London or Middlesex.
THOMAS COCKETT ANNE CORBEY JOHN CROOKE ROBERT CURTIS	from Northamptonshire.
WILLIAM CLAYTOR, from Nottinghamshire.	
RALPH CHARLES MICHAEL DAY JEREMY DEANE	from Hartfordshire.
JOHN DAY RICHARD DEANE	from Hampshire.

CONTINUED articles COUNTY COURT NOTE-BOOK, and the dates on which they first appeared. For the sake of neatness and to avoid unnecessary printing, the usual headings and tail-notes attached to these articles will be discontinued, and this paragraph will take their place.

MARRIAGES BY INFERENCE. Began with May, 1922.

MARYLAND'S NEXT OF KIN. Began with July, 1922.

VIRGINIA COLONISTS. This alphabetized list began with July, 1924.

ANNE ARUNDEL ORPHANS. Began with September, 1924.

MARYLAND NATURALIZATIONS. Began with February, 1923.

KING GEORGE PROBATES, &c. Began with July, 1924.

PRINCE WILLIAM PROBATES, &c. Began with April, 1923.

The LIST of BANISHED QUAKERS. Began with November, 1924.

MILITARY NOTES, both COLONIAL and REVOLUTIONARY, and some later MILITIA NOTES, will appear in every issue, if possible.

SHIPS IN PORT, NEW ENGLANDERS AND OTHERS and COLONIAL FORENAMES, will appear in alternate issues, or as space can be found for them.

NOTES FROM ACCOMACK COUNTY, VIRGINIA

The following appears in the form of a footnote, Virginia Magazine, vol. xviii, p. 22, with references to the N. E. H.-G. Magazine, and the William and Mary Quarterly.

"...SOUTHEY LITTLETON [son of Col. Southey Littleton] married Mary, daughter of Thomas Brown [of Northampton cty]. She married (2) HANCOCK CUSTIS, and had a son SOUTHEY, who *d. s. p.*, and a dau. LEAH, who married Col. JOHN GALE."

The records of Accomack cty, Virginia, read as follows:

Will of HANCOCK CUSTIS: v. xx, fo. 5, 30 Aug. 1725-7 May 1728-3 June 1729. "Son and daughter-in-law, LEVIN and LEAH GALE, each thirty shillings with a Ring, in remembrance of Hancock Custis and Mary his wife..." [It would appear this should read: *for* a ring.]

Vol. xx, p. 70. EDWARD MIFFLIN, of Northampton cty, Va., Gent, & Mary his wife, to LEVIN GALE of Somersett cty, Md., Gent., and wf LEAH... parcel of land & Marsh lying on the north side of Nandua Creek in Acco. cty, now in the possession of sd LEVIN GALE & wf LEAH "which Coll'll SOUTHEY LITTLETON of the said County... by his last will devised unto his Son SOUTHY LITTLETON Father to the said LEAH GALE." 1 June 1731.

Vol. xx, p. 212. Will of LEVIN CUSTIS 7 Mch 1733-4. "...All my estate... unto my Sister LEAH GALE and her three children, Betty Gale, Sarah Gale and Leah Gale ...and I do appoint my brother-in-law LEVIN GALE and my Sister LEAH GALE extrs of this my last will &c."

Vol. xvi-244. LEAH GALE mentioned as the wife of LEVIN of Maryland, and a legatee of SARAH MICHAEL, wife of Adam. 2 Feby 1725.

Vol. xvi, p. 244. HANCOCK CUSTIS, Gent., to LEVIN GALE and wife LEAH, negroes which belonged to said LEAH'S father and brother SOUTHEY LITTLETON, both dec'd, 24 Aug 1725. Also receipt by LEVIN and LEAH GALE, of Somerset cty, Maryland, to HANCOCK CUSTIS of Acco. cty, Gent. and wf MARY, admrs of Southey Littleton.

REVOLUTIONARY SOLDIERS AND PENSIONERS

The folowing notes are kindly furnished by Mr. Dille, Secretary of the S. A. R., from the Order Books of Monongalia county, West Virginia.

PETER MILLER, aged 72, makes oath that he was a Revolutionary soldier. The Court declare their opinion that he served as stated in his declaration. 24 July 1832. x-293.

JACOB HOLLAND, aged 79, makes a similar declaration, which is accepted and approved by the Court. 24 July 1832. x-294.

ZACKQUILLE MORGAN, JAMES SCOTT, JOHN DENT, EVAN MORGAN, CALEB FURBEE, JACOB VANGILDER, JOHN BURDIN, PETER HAMMER, AMOS MORRIS, THOMAS McELROY, GEORGE WADE, SAMUEL DUDLEY and JAMES TROY, severally make oath that they served as Revolutionary soldiers, and the Court accepts their declarations. 28 Aug 1832. x-300.

PETER HAUGHT, ZACHARIAH PILES and HENRY YOHO, make similar affidavits which are accepted and certified. 25 Sept 1832. x-309.

PURNELL HOUSTON, RICHARD CHEW, JOHN WELLS, WILLIAM HALL and NICHOLAS MADERA, make similar declarations and are certified by the Court. 22 Oct 1832. x-316.

ISAAC REED also makes declaration and is certified. 19 Nov 1832. x-318.

HENRY DORTON makes declaration under oath, and his claim is certified. 21 Nov 1832. x-324.

WILLIAM FORD, JAMES DEVERS, RICHARD PRICE, and GEORGE KELLER, made declaration and the Court orders that they be certified. 28 Jany 1833. xi-344.

SAMUEL DAVERS and JOHN McFARLAND produce their declarations which are ordered certified. 25 Feby 1833. xi-349.

SAMUEL HANWAY makes declaration and certificate is ordered. 26 Aug. 1833. xi-447.

JAMES COLLINS and NOAH RIDGWAY make oath to their declarations and are ordered certified. 26 Aug 1833. xi-447.

JOHN VERDIN makes oath to declaration and is ordered certified to the War Department. 26 Aug 1833. xi-460.

NEW HERALDIC DICTIONARY IN PREPARATION.—Mr. Charles K. Bolton, 10½ Beacon Street, Boston, Mass., is preparing to publish a dictionary describing coats-of-arms that have been used in this country on book-plates, old silver, gravestones, seal rings, etc. He would like to correspond with persons interested.

PROBATES AND ADMINISTRATIONS RICHMOND COUNTY, VIRGINIA

When "Old Rappahannock" County was extinguished in 1692, Richmond and Essex counties were formed from it. The first volume of wills for Richmond county is not in the Clerk's Office at Warsaw. The Order Books are complete, however, for the period covered by the missing will book, and the following abstracts are made from those volumes. This valuable material is kindly contributed by Mr. E. Carter Delano, of Warsaw.

GILES WEBB; will presented by Mrs. Margaret Webb, extx. Proved by John Taverner and John Parker, witnesses, and probate granted to extx. 3 Aug 1692. i-35.

ELIZABETH LLOYD; will presented by Mrs. Elizabeth Carter, extx. Proved by John Taverner and Margaret Leggins, wit. 1 Feby 1692. 1-84.

ELIAS YATES; will presented by Mary Yates, extx. Proved by Mr. Thomas Lloyd and Wm. Smith. Probate granted extx. 1 Feby 1692. 1-85.

ROBERT BAYLIS, Sr.; will presented by Thomas and John Baylis, extrs. Proved by Samuel Sanford and John Taverner, wit. Probate granted his sons, the extrs, and Wm. Baylis, a grandson. 5 April 1693. i-87.

ROGER RICHARDSON; will presented by widow Elizabeth, extx. Proved by Nebuch'r Jones, Mary Hews and Elizabeth Packford. Probate to extx. 5 Apr 1693. i-88.

HENRY THACKER; will presented by Matilda Thacker, extx. Proved by Joshua Davis, wit. Probate to extx. 2 Aug 1693. i-182.

JOHN PITMAN; will presented by Rebecca Pitman, extx. Proved by Jos. Hennings (who wrote the will) and Henry Arkhill, wit. Probate to widow, the extx. 4 Oct 1693. i-140.

JOHN RICE; will presented by Capt. Samuel Travers, one of the extrs. Proved by John Pond, Walter Pavey, Wm. Witt and Cornelius Kinselloe, wit. Probate to Col. John Stone and Capt. Samuel Travers, extrs. 6 Dec 1693. i-145.

DAVID PURSELL; will presented by Bellinda Pursell, extx. Proved by Daniel Jackson, Thomas Newman and Evan Thomas, wit. Probate to extx. 3 Jany 1693. i-155.

JOHN MORRIS; will presented by Elizabeth Morris, extx. Proved by Isaac Wright and John Hartford. Probate to extx. 7 Mch 1693. 1-165.

MATTHEW BOWEN; will proved by Allen Mountjoy, Rebecca Hunseman and David Coleburne, wit. Probate to extrs. 7 Mch 1693. i-65.

WILLIAM HASLE; will presented by Ann Hasle, extx. Proved by William Sisson and Thomas Walker, wit. Probate to extx. 7 Mch 1693. i-169.

BRIDGET EALE; will proved by Thomas Deadman and William Cleaton, wit. Probate to George and William Eale, extrs. 7 Mch 1693. 1-169.

JAMES SCOTT; admn his est. to Mary Scott, his widow. 6 June 1694. 1-186.

RICHARD WINTER; will presented by Capt. Alexander Swan, surviving extr. Proved by Henry How and Lawrence Prescott, wit. Probate to extr. 6 June 1694. i-186.

ISAAC WEBB; will presented by John Webb; extr. Proved by Samuel Peachey and John Suggett. Probate to extr. 5 Dec 1694. ii-16.

EVAN WILLIAMS; will presented by extr. Proved by George Lodge and Stephen Fenell. Probate to extr. 6 Feby 1695. ii-27.

HENRY BURDETT; will presented by Thomas Newman, extr. Proved by Elizabeth Burgess, Mary Morrell and Thomas Rose, wit. Probate to extr. 5 June 1695. ii-55.

THOMAS REYLY; will presented by Elizabeth Reyly, extx. Proved by John Baptist and Richard Wood. Probate to extx. 5 June 1695. ii-56.

KING GEORGE COUNTY, VIRGINIA

WILLIAM BERRY; will presented by Joseph Berry, extr. Proved by William Mumford and Thomas Apperson. 2 June 1721. Orders 1721-1734, p. 2.

FRANCIS JAMES; will presented by Margaret James, extx. Proved by Peter Jett and Mary Hasell. Peter Jett, sec for widow. 7 July 1721. p. 6.

ROBERT HAIRN [or KAIRN?] L. a. on his est to John Dinwiddie. Edward Price, sec. 7 July 1721. p. 8.

JOHN MORRIS; l. a. on his est. to John Dinwiddie. 7 July 1721. p. 9.

JOSEPH LITTLEFIELD; l. a. his est. to John Plunket. Isaac Arnold sec. 3 Nov 1721. p. 20.

LEWIS JONES; l. a. on his est. to Elizabeth Jones, widow. Samuel Wharton and John Grimsly, sec. 1 Dec 1721. p. 24.

PETER FURLONG; l. a. his est to widow Elizabeth Furlong, William Pullen, sec. 1 Dec 1721. p. 25.

JOHN ANDERSON; will presented by William Brown, extr, and proved by Isaac Arnold, William Pullen and William Harvey. Isaac Arnold sec. for Wm. Brown. 1 Dec 1721. p. 26.

HENRY WOOD; Rush Hutson and wf Sarah get l. a. on est. of Henry Wood. 6 July 1722. p. 52. Hutson ackn. bond for admn of the est. p. 52.

THOMAS PRICHARD; l. a. on his est. to William Smith, Edward Price and Henry Woodcock, sec. 7 Sept 1722. p. 64.

THOMAS BROOK; will presented by Mary Brook, extx. Proved by Joseph Wing, Cornelius Edmonds, John Branam. Cornelius Edmonds sec. 5 Oct 1722. p. 65.

FRANCES WHITE; William Lampton gets l. a. on her est. William Rowles and Edward Price, sec. 2 Nov 1722. p. 68.

CORNELIUS EDMONDS; will presented by Ann Edmonds, wid. and extx. (John Gilbert refusing.) Proved by George White,

Alexr Carron[?] and Wm. Shaw. 7 Dec 1722. p. 72. John Pratt, sec. p. 73.

JAMES SCOT; will presented by Hugh French, extr. Proved by Richard Bellew, John Raffle. John Prat sec. for French. 4 Jany 1722. p. 77.

WILLIAM LAMPTON; will presented by Hester Lampton, his widow and extx. Proved by Joshua Davis, James Butler, and John Stone. John Dinwiddie and William Skrine, sec. for extx. 1 Feby 1722. p. 90.

WILLIAM BROWN; nun-cup. will presented by Margaret White and further proved by Leonard Young and Dorothy Kerchwall. L. a. to Margaret White. 1 Feby 1722. p. 90.

ROBERT McKEE; will presented by Ann Edmonds, widow, his extx. Proved by George White, John Farnam, Alexander Carson. 1 Feby 1722. p. 93.

PRINCE WILLIAM COUNTY, VIRGINIA

SARAH CASTOR; admn with will annexed to Isabella Castor. 7 Dec 1767. v-65.

ANN FARROW; admn her est. and of WILLIAM FARROW dec'd (ANN FARROW having been his extx) granted to William Farrow. 8 Dec 1767. v-12.

EDWARD GWATKINS; will presented by extrs, Charles Gwatkins, heir-at-law (son of Edward) agreeing. Ctf granted JOHN and James Gwatkins for probate. 8 Dec 1767. v-67.

BENJAMIN DRUMMOND; will presented by Aaron Drummond, his extr, who refuses extrship. Proved by Sarah Drummond and John Bryan. L. a. to Norman Drummond. 1 Feby 1768. v-69.

JOSHUA DOING; admn on his est. to Violetta Doing, his widow. Wm. Carr, Gent., sec. 8 Mch 1768. v-83.

JOHN RENO; will proved by Will'm Wilson and Thos. Reno, Jr. Eleanor and Lewis Reno, extrs, give bond. 10 Mch 1768. v-88.

SARAH ENGLISH; admn her est. granted to Robert English. Robert and John English. Thos. Carter sec. 4 Apr 1768. v-95.

MARY WELLS; will proved by William Martin and James McIntosh. 5 Apr 1768. v-95.

ROBERT FOSTER; will presented by Sarah Foster. Proved by Thomas Moss and Thomas Ramey. 2 May 1768. v-97.

WILLIAM TRIPLETT; will and codicil. Proved so far as relates to the execution of the will by Geo. Graham, John Hodges and Evan Williams, and as to codicil, by John and Robert Hodges. 2 Aug 1768. v-128.

MARY WELLS; William Carr gets l. a. on her est. 3 Aug 1768. v-133.

WILLIAM WHITE; will produced by Ann White. Proved by Wm. Garrard and *Joseiah* Bonham. 3 Oct 1768. v-148.

CUTH: HARRISON, Gent. L. a. on his est. to Cuth: Harrison his son, the widow releasing. 3 Oct 1768. v-148.

JOSEPH KELLEY; will exhibited by extx and proved by John Matterson and Mary Hooper. 3 Oct 1768. v-148.

JNO. DALTON; will exhibited by Rachel and James Dalton, two of the extrs. Proved by Wm. Carr, Thos. Johnson and John Jennens. 7 Nov 1768. v-155.

THOS. HARRINGTON; Peggy *Arrington* exhibits his will; further proved by James Johnson and Thos. Ryley. [In the next paragraph the name is given as Arrington.] 6 Mch 1769. v-164.

WILLIAM CROUCH; will proved by Hannah Jones and William Jones. Admn with will annexed to Jacob Crouch, heir-at-law. 1 May 1769. v-170.

WILLIAM GLOVER; admn his est to Martha Glover. William Askins and Jesse Moor, sec. 1 May 1769. v-172.

WILLIAM HORTON; admn his est. to Mary Horton, Geo. Calvert, sec. 6 June 1769. v-194.

SAMUEL STONE; Sarah Stone, extx, exhibits its will. Proved by John Reeve and Ann Reeve. 3 July 1769. v-203.

(End of volume 5 of Orders.)

A LIST OF ORPHANS, ANNE ARUNDEL COUNTY, MARYLAND (Liber T. B. 1.)

(Contributed by Mrs. Geo. W. Hodges)

RACHELL HOWARD, with Mr. Caleb Dorsey.

MOSES HURDOCK, with John Botie.

THOMAS MORLOW, with Robert Smith.

THOMAS MORE, with Walter Emerton.

SARAH MANSFIELD, with Solomon Birkhead.

GRIFIN MORLOW, CATRIAN MORLOW, with Robert Woods.

ROBERT MARTIN, orphan of Robert, with Wm. Pennington.

THOMAS MOSS, son of Ralph, with Mr. Thomas Homewood.

SARAH MOSS, dau. of Richard, with Mary Eagle.

JOSHUA MEREKEN, ANN MEREKEN, son and dau. of Hugh, with Joshua Mereken.

JAMES and RICHARD MOSS, sons of Richard, with Robert Boon.

RALPH, EDMAND and MOSES MOSS, sons of Ralph, at Henry Brown's.

ROSE and REBECCA MURPHEY, daus. of Patrick, with Mr. John Peasley.

ROBERT MOSS, son of Ralph, with Mrs. Mary Homewood.

HESTER MATTUX, orphan of Edward, with Richard Hampton Edward[?].

JNO. MACOMUS, ALEXANDER MACOMUS and DANLL MACOMUS, with Stephen Gill.

ELLINOR MACOMUS, with Wm. Stephens.

WILLIAM MACKOMUS, with Mr. John Warfeild.

JOHN MOONSHOT, DAVID MOONSHOT, MARY MOONSHOT, with Garret Tapping.

NOTES AND QUERIES, as well as some other important matter, omitted from this issue, will appear in the June NOTE-BOOK.

COLUMBIAN PRINTING CO., INC., WASHINGTON, D. C.

The

County Court Note-Book

A Little Bulletin of History and Genealogy

June, 1925.

Vol. IV, No 3.

SHIPS IN PORT

Ship *Merchant's Adventure;* Capt. Peter Wallis, master. Va. St. Pa. i-92. 2 June 1705.

Ship *Mermaid,* of Liverpool. Enoch Robertson, master. Va. St. Pa. i-184. 1715.

Ship *Morning Starr,* of Liverpool; James Horneby, commander. Acco, Va. ix-235. 29 Jany 1691.

The *Peace;* Thos. Nelson, master. P. R. O. (England). 30-xii. 1703.

Ketch *Neptune;* sold by Alice Leyster, wf of Jacob, of the City of New Yorke, under power of atty to Capt. Wm. Dyre. N-n, Va., xi-115. 14 Dec 1675.

Brigantine *Northampton* (bound for England); Mr. John Bowdoine, commandr. N-n, Va. xviii-395. 29 Dec 1707.

Brig *Olive Branch;* Capt. John Robertson. Cleared from Philada., for Salem, N. J. Arch. 1762.

Ship *Pearle,* of Liverpool; Wm. Trenow, master. Va. St. Pa. i-30. 28 Oct 1691.

Sloop *Peggy;* Thomas Robinson [master]; owned by Joseph Forman and Thos. Robinson, N. Y. City. 15 tons. Blt. N. J. Ship registers. Penna. Mags. vol. xxv. 21 May 1752.

Shipp *Peter and John;* Mr. Nathll Cooke, master. N-n, Va. iv-202. 28 Sept 1653.

Barke *Phenix;* built by James Fooks at Matchatank, Acco. cty, Va. Measured, Acco, Va. vi-43. 1685.

Ship *Philadelphia,* from Sweden; Capt. Spencer. Records Holy Trinity, Wmton, Dela. p. 147. Oct. 1712.

Ship *Planter,* of Bristol; Wm. Randolph, master. Norf. Corp. Ct. Va. 7 Mch 1761.

Sloop *Polly;* James Craven, of Acco, conveys to Wm. Andrews one-half of sd sloop, now bound on a voyage to New York. Acco, Va. Deeds, iii-392. 1765.

Schooner *Polly;* owned in part by Jesper Aydelott. See his will. Sussex, Dela. 1783.

The *Portsmouth Pincke;* N-n, Va. xv-191. 30 Jany 1685.

Ship *Prince Eugene;* 180 tons, 8 guns and 18 men; William Bastin, commdr. Va. St. Pa. i-111. 14 Mch 1706-7.

Ship or "flyboat" the *Prosperous,* of Hull; Wm. Marr of Kingston upon Hull, master. Acco, Va. viii-73. 1678.

The Ketch *Providence,* of Boston; Timothy Prout, Jr., master. This ketch is also called the *Virginia Merchant* in the Accomack records of 1668. She was "cast away" some time in December, 1672, on Wreck [?] island, on the seaboard side of Northampton cty. There are numerous references to her and to the salvage of her rigging and other fittings, in the records of the county. See N-n, Va., x-163, 167, 170. 1672.

The *Virginia Ship;* Capt. John Stone, Stephen Charlton and Primstone Foster were joint owners, N-n, Va. i-22. 15 Sept 1634.

MARRIAGES BY INFERENCE*

GEORGE BARNET and ANN LOUGHTON, wid. David, Charleston, S. C. About 1713-1714. T-602. [She m. (3) DAVID HEXT.]

WILLIAM BELL and Miss SARAH MAGEE, Sumter cty, S. C. 16 Aug 1816. Mar. Li.

SAMUEL BIGHAM and Miss MARY MULDROW. Darlington cty, S. C. 13 Mch 1813. Mar. 1 April 1813. M. L. B. "36"—527.

JAQUES BISHOP and PENELOPE BROCKINGTON. Darlington cty, S. C. 29 Nov 1803. M. L. B.

WILLIAM BISSETT and CATHERINE LOYER, wid., of Charles Town. Mar. agreement. Charleston, S. C. 29 Oct 1755. 1754-1758, p. 444.

JOHN BOWEN and ELIZABETH MAY, Charleston, S. C. Mar. 13 Feby 1788. 1787-1791, p. 82.

PETER BRACOT and HANNAH MASON. Darlington cty, S. C. 30 May 1804, 6 June 1804. Mar. Li. and Mar. Return.

JOHN BRADLEY, of Salem, and Miss SARAH MARGARET MURRAN, now of Kershaw District. Sumter cty, S. C. 6 Jany 1817. Mar. Li. A-34.

ROBERT BRAILSFORD, factor, of Charleston, S. C., and ELIZABETH JAMES, of St. Mark's psh, Claremont cty, sp. (Dau. of John James, dec'd.) Mar. settlement. Sumter cty, S. C. 14 Apr 1803. A-250.

ANDREW BROUGHTON, Gent., of Berkley cty, and ANNE SINGLETON, same, sp. Mar. settlement. Charleston, S. C. 19 Nov 1750. HH-99.

JOHN CALVERT and JANE ELIZABETH HOLMES, wid., both of Charlestown. Mar. agreement. Charleston, S. C. 29 Jany 1781. TT-7.

Mr. HUGH E. CANNON and Miss ANN MULDROW. Darlington cty, S. C. 1 Oct 1809. "36"—480. Mar. Li. and Mar. Return.

WILLIAM HENRY CANNON and Miss SARAH McTIER. Darlington cty, S. C. 12 May 1804. Mar. Li.

CHARLES P. CHANDLER and Miss ... CHANDLER. Sumter cty, S. C. 10 Mch 1817. Mar. Li.

THOMAS COOPER, Gent., and ELEANA WRIGHT. Charleston, S. C. 7 Feby 1728. 1729-1731, p. 15. [See her will.]

TIMOTHY CROSBY, bricklayer, and MARGARET VANDERHORST, of Berkley cty, wid. of William. Mar. settlement. Charleston, S. C. Jany, 1768. TT-339.

RANDOLPH EVANS and SARAH NORTON, dau. of John. Charleston, S. C. Before 12 Jany 1735. T-522.

SKILES FOSTER and SARAH THOMSON, Sumter dist. Sumter cty, S. C. 18 Apr 1817. Mar. Li.

SAMUEL FREDERICK, pltr, and SARAH BRADWELL, sp., of St. George's psh, Dorchester; dau. of Isaac. Mar. settlement. Charleston, S. C. 4 Apr 1777. TT-781.

JOHN GIBBES, Esq., and MARY SMITH, of Charleston, Sp., dau. of Benj. Smith, Esq. Mar. settlement. Charleston, S. C. 27 Nov 1787. Y5-258.

DANIEL HALL, Mcht, of Charles Town, and SUSANNA MATTHEWS, dau. of William. Mar. agreement. Charleston, S. C. 23 Feby 1775. TT-498.

VALENTINE HARDMAN and MARY PICKING. (Copy from register St. George's psh.) Charleston, S. C. 1754-1758. 11 Dec 1730.

LEWIS HARRELL, Jr., and Miss ELIZA HOLLAWAY. Darlington cty, S. C. 24 Dec 1813, 18 Jany 1814. Mar. Li. and Mar. Ret. "36"—528.

DAVID HEXT, Gent., and ANN BARNET, wid. of George [She was also wid. of David Loughton.] Charleston, S. C. Before 3 May 1740. T-602.

DANIEL HUGER [HUGES?] and BINKEY ELLIOTT, dau. of William, Esq. Charleston, S. C. Before 4 July 1783. TT-318.

THOMAS HUNTER and MARGARET WRIGHT. Darlington cty, S. C. 17 Aug 1803. Mar. Li.

JAMES LANE, of Pr. Frederick psh, Craven cty, and URSULA HENNING, Sp., of Pr. Geo. psh, same cty. Mar. settlement. Charleston, S. C. 29 Dec 1756. 1754-1758, p. 747.

GEORGE LOGAN, Sr., and MARTHA DANIELL, Sr., wid. of Hon. Col. Robert Daniell, late Depty Govr of South Carolina, dec'd. Mar. contract. No date, but prob. 11 Mch 1720-1... or before that date. Charleston, S. C. A-236.

DUNCAN McLAUGHLAN and MARGARET MULDROW, Darlington cty, S. C. 24 Sept 1804. Mar. Li. B.

WILLIAM MATHEWS and MARY LOUGHTON [prob. dau. David.] Charleston, S. C. Before 3 May 1740. T-602.

LEWIS MORRIS and ANN ELLIOTT, dau. of William, Esq. Charleston, S. C. Before 4 July 1783. TT-318.

GEORGE PAWLEY [?] Esq., of George Town, Craven cty, and MARY MILLER, psh St. Thomas and St. David [?], Berkley cty, wid. Mar. settlement. Charleston, S. C. 21 May 1755. 1754-1758, p. 546.

GABRIEL PLOWDEN and JANE MONTGOMERY. Sumter cty, S. C. 23 Nov. 1816. Mar. Li.

MARYLAND'S NEXT OF KIN *

JAMES PEACOCK; inv. William Peacock of Calvert cty. 19 Mch 1719. iii-281.

SAMUEL CHEW; inv. Richard Bond of Calvert cty. 24 Nov 1719. iii-282.

THOMAS REEVES; inv. Thomas Reeves, sen., of Buckford Manor, St. Mary's cty. 6 Apr 1720. iii-288.

MARY ALEXANDER, "grandmother to children"; inv. George Polly of New Munster, Cecil cty, 2 Dec 1719. iii-292.

MORRIS RAWLEY, WILLIAM RAWLEY; inv. Samuel Rawley of Dorchester cty. 3 Feby 1719. iii-297.

DAVID MACKALL, WILLIAM PHILLIPS; inv. Godfell Modlig (?) of Dor. cty. 3 Feby 1719. iii-299.

THOMAS WILMOTT, ANNE LEWIS; inv. James Willmott of Calvert cty. 20 Jany 1719. iii-315.

RACHEL FREEBORN, HESTER WORMAN; inv. John Beard, of Annapolis. 4 Mch 1719. iii-316.

JOHN PRISE; inv. John Holland of Q. A. cty. 14 May 1720. iii-319.

RICHARD KEEN; BENJAMIN BERRY; inv. Benjamin Berry, sen., of Pr. Geo's cty. 28 Apr 1720. iii-323.

MARY COLE, widow of dec'd; inv. John Cole of A. A. cty. 4 Mch 1719. iii-330.

THOMAS COCKEY; inv. William Cockey, Baltimore cty. 12 Mch 1720. iii-333.

ANN GARSH, "alias Farthing"; inv. Samuel Garsh of St. Mary's cty. 4 Aug 1720. iii-343.

JOHN HORN; ELIZABETH AISQUETH; inv. Henry Horn of St. Mary's cty. 26 June 1720. iii-344.

JOHN WARD, Jr.; inv. William Ward of Cecil cty. 7 May 1720. iii-345.

JEAN MARRIT; inv. Thomas Merritt of Cecil cty. 7 May 1720. iii-349.

WILLIAM HARCUM of Kent cty. "No kindred in this Province." 6 July 1720. iv-1.

PEREGRINE and WILLIAM FRISBY; inv. Capt. James Frisby of Cecil cty. 30 Mch 1720. iv-p...

ROBERT EYRE, "sister's sone"; inv. Francis Smith of Elke river, Cecil cty. 14 Apr 1720. iv-6.

JOHN COX; inv. Guisebird Cock of Cecil cty. 15 Feby 1719-20. iv-7.

NICHOLAS GEORGE; inv. Nicholas Hilliard of Cecil cty. 9 Sept 1719. iv-8.

Madam MARTHA SMITH, extx of Col. Thos. Smith of Kent cty. "Nearest of kin neglected to be sent." 9 Sept 1719. iv-11.

JAMES CROSE, HANNAH CROSE; inv. James Crose of Kent cty. 6 May 1720. iv-21.

BENJ. ELLIS, "sone of ye Dec." Inv. John Ellis of Kent cty. 15 Apr. 1720. iv-24.

VIRGINIA COLONISTS

(From "Old Volume 5," S. L. O., Richmond)

WM. JUSTICE, Charles City cty, 1656.
Head rights: Mary Sherwood, Mathew Baile, Rich. Lee, Jno. Barber, Edmond Joyner, Wm. Phillips, Tho. Whitter, Wm. Coleman, Joseph Errence [?], Tho. Haistwood, Alice

Michell, Rebecca France, Fra. Nelson, Wm. Price, Wm. Lawrence, Mary Lawrence (twice), Anne, Arthur and Sarah Lawrence, Wm. Ballance, John Hally, Eliz. Heath, Peter Plumer.

DANIELL JAINES, and JOHN JENNINGES, "South side Rappahannock River" [1656].

Head rights: Charles Leech, Robert Fillkin, Peeter Leech, Peter Garland, Robert Thompson, Robert Smith, Tho. Henson, John South.

WILLIAM JOHNSON, "Northwest side of Pasckatequon alias Coxes Creek," 1656.

Head rights: Mr. Thomas Prittyman, Richard Redding, Francis Coulston, Elizabeth Howman.

JOHN JENKINS, Northampton cty, 1655.

Head rights: Rich'd Browne, Jno. Harrold, Wm. Farr, Jeffrey Hughes, Toby Calgey, Anne Jordan, Marg: Willmade [Wilmott?], Wm. Lemon.

RICHARD JOANES, "being in the Western branch of Elizabeth River," 1655.

Charles Hodges, Geo. Wahab [Waughop?], Jno. Makefashion[?].

WM. JENNINGS, Surry cty [1657].

Head rights: Mercy Briggs, Wm. Lewes, Abraham Land, Ann Woshe [?].

RICHARD JAMES, James City *Island,* 1657.

Head rights: Rich. James (twice), Phillip Minton.

JOHN JOHNSON, Jr., Northampton cty, 1658.

Head rights: John Garnell, Walter Hawes, Tho. Willson. (8 rights only three names given.)

WM. JORDEN, Northampton cty, 1658.

Head rights: Alexander and Thomas Mountney; Roger, ..., Jno. and Leonard Mountny.

LEONARD JOANES, Rappahannock cty, 1657.

Head rights: John Smith, Elizabeth, his wife; Thomas Williams.

NICHOLAS JERNEW, "Petomeck freshes beyond doegs Island," 1657.

Head rights: Peter Lefebur, Margaret Lefebur, Abm, Isaack, and Jacob Lefebur; Tho: Williams, Gilbert Cray [Gray?], Anne Burton, Patrick Crispe, John Woodington heire [?], Hen. Hawkins, Jno. Reade, Phillys Wadden, Jno. Giles.

Mr. PETER KNIGHT, "in Petowmack River," 1656.

Head rights: John Waddington, Andrew Cockerin, Wm. Ballingall, Edwd Meeres, Wm. Mundy, Rich. Wall and one Svrnt named Thomas; James Hawly, Ann, his wife, and three children; Jno. Foster, Ruth Darlinge, James Hill, James Logd [?], Jno. Seaman, Gilberd Seaman.

Mr. PEETER KNIGHT, Northumberland cty, 1657.

Head rights: Robert Burwell, his wife and three chn; Wm. Bradley, Deborah Come [?], James Jones, Jno. Gerrell, Wm. Shinton.

Mr. GEORG KEMPE, L. Norf. cty, 1657.

Head rights: Robert Buckler, Tho. Willmott, James Macoy, Phillip Browne.

MARY LEWIS; Northampton cty, 1656.

Head rights: Kath. Merifell, Anne Jones, Mary Allvit, Jno. Macknilliam, and four negroes, two of them assigned by Col. Scarburgh.

Coll. RICHARD LEE, Gloucester cty, 1656.

Head right: Morris Plummor.

WILLIAM and HANCOCK LEE (sons of Coll. Richd Lee), Gloucester cty, 1656.

Head rights: Roger Sheely, Jno. O'Leally, Patrick O'Crahan, John Mathew, David Mahoone, Douny Carby, Richd Joy, Dermort O'Farne. [The apostrophes have been supplied, the names being written as given but without the symbol.]

JOHN LEAR, Westmoreland cty, 1656.

Head rights: John Lear, Xphian Winkle.

MOSES LYNTON; L. Norf. cty, [no date].

Head rights: John Townshend, Charles Blanchernell, John Scot, Eliz. Church.

Major WM. LEWIS, "S. W. side freshes of York river," 1656.

Head rights: John Smith, Junior. Tho: Holliday, Joseph Peasly, Isack Franklin, Xpr. Meadcroft, John Smith, Senior, Daniell Odaley, Abigall Millis [Willis?], Mary Cuffin, Margaret Isom, Francis Burwell, John Holley, John Brocas, Sarah Constable, Mary Bartlett, Tho: Younge, Georg Maurice. Assigned to Major Lewis by Mr. Jerom Ham.

Mr. RICHARD LAWSON; "South side of Occapason Creeke," 1656.

Head rights: Rich: Cooper, Jno. Cornelis, Hen: Clay, Jane Bedicant[?], Eliza: Warner, Wm. Crispe, Jno. Browne, Ribb: [perhaps Broadbank?] Francis Atkins, Jno: Dixon, Kath: Jones.

WILLIAM LACY, New Kent cty, 1656.

Head rights: Mary Reede, Thomas Jones.

Coll. RICHARD LEE, Northumberland cty, 1656.

Head rights: Coll, Richd Lee's 3d adventure; Mrs. Anne Lee's 2d adventure; John Roper, Nich. Britton, Owen Kelly, Richd Porke, Walter English, Coniers Murally, Anne Firsh, Morris Roch, Doctar Goodiand, Alice Parker.

Mr. HUGH LEE, "in Petomeck freshes above Puscatoway on the Westward side of the River," 1657.

Head rights: Jonathan Marrow, Mary Marrow, Dorithy Marrow, Wm. Browne, Wm. Hanniver, Geo. Wilson, Hannah Lee, Mr. David Linsey, Anne Murrall, Josua Esto [?], Anne Moore, Sr. and Jr., Dan Lile, Jno. Carr, Eliz: Parry, Mary Harris, Eliz: Hardinge, Mary Barkinton, Anne Murrall, Joshua Estoe, Wm. May, Rob. Smart.

Capt. GEORG LYDDALL, New Kent cty, 1657.

Head rights: Wm. Hill, Robert Harman, Francis Smith, Thomas Smith, Jno. Makepeace, Thomas Masque, Charles Havennest, Penelope Best, Michaell Tucker, Roger Parker, Daniell Welch, John Davis, Tho. Jones.

The County Court Note-Book

An every-other-monthly devoted to abstracts from County Court and other records, prior to 1800, and with a department of notes and queries.

MILNOR LJUNGSTEDT, Editor and Publisher. Bethesda, Route 10, Maryland.

Published six times a year. **Subscription, two dollars and fifty cents,** in advance; must begin with the year. **Renewals, two dollars.** Advertising rates moderate.

JUNE, 1925
Vol. IV., No. 3

Again the Editor must express regret for delay in publication, caused by overwork and some illness. And again it has seemed best to take up material already arranged rather than devote an issue to the very interesting colonial States south of Virginia, including in this number, however, a list of SOUTH CAROLINA marriages indexed some time ago. The Editor is "up against it" on some of these marriages. It will be noted that a number of them are from the records of licenses issued in South Carolina. Now, everybody says there weren't any licenses in South Carolina. Even the very helpful and charming young lady who assisted the Editor to some of these said there weren't any. Well, anyhow, she said, after they were found [apparently found], "nobody in that courthouse knew they were there!" A very high authority says they were perhaps licenses to the minister to marry. The Editor thinks that one of them was, because the bond was for some ten thousand dollars. [Like the ten thousand cats on the back fence ... it may have been one thousand dollars, but the Editor truly thinks it was ten thousand.] As for the others, no explanation is offered. There isn't any particular use in the Editor's looking up the statutes, because the people who say there weren't any licenses know a great deal more about the statutes than the Editor does or ever will ... life being of a shortness so abominable.

Attention is again invited to the value of the lists of probates and administrations from several Northern Neck counties of Virginia. Mr. Delano has sent additional lists from Richmond county, and will continue until the date of the recorded wills. The Editor cannot but think that these missing Richmond will records may be in another county. The petitions in the old Richmond records as to the location of the county-seat, the places where courts were held, &c., suggest in a vague way the possibility of the wills having been probated elsewhere, or at least carried elsewhere for record.

The movable court reminds the Editor of ONSLOW COUNTY, NORTH CAROLINA. The Clerk's Office (probably in the Courthouse) was taken up by a tornado many, many years ago, and carried across the river ... a small one on which the town is located. Incidentally the records were also carried away but spread themselves in flight upon the surface of the water. They were gathered up, dried, and the pile of loose leaves and signatures still in existence tells the tale. In this pile, perhaps three feet high, the Editor found one leaf, the first or second, of the first ORDER BOOK. Why only one leaf? Some one else may discover the remainder of the volume ... unless it was so heavy it went to the bottom of the river. Anyhow it is hoped that the North Carolina Historical Commission, which is doing such excellent work, will gather up that one leaf and all the other forlorn fragments.

Index to the Note-Book. One of the Editor's friendly subscribers has prepared an index of every surname in vols. I, II, III. This will be printed if sufficient subscriptions are received to cover the cost. It will be a stitched pamphlet of about twenty pages, and the price will be three dollars. Early notification of subscription is requested.

OCCASIONAL

A deed as late as Feby, 1699 (Acco cty, Va. xi-241), conveys land in "this His Majesties most Antient Colony and great Dominion of Virginia."

DANIEL WEBSTER was a member of a coroner's jury in Surry, Va. 1660. i-151.

JACOB REMY, a natural born subject of the French King, takes the oath of allegiance. Wmld, Va. iii-93. 8 Oct 1702.

MABLE ROBINSON; to be fined according to Rule of Court for Smoaking in the Court. John Fisher appear'd and assum'd to pay her fine. Som. cty, Md. GI-59. 13 of 7th, 1703.

A MATTER OF OPINION: The Deposicon of Henrick Abell, aged 34 yeares or thereabouts Saith ... That ... Mr. Tilney ... said that the said M ... was very hard with him for keeping his [Tilney's] youngest Daughter Margaret for hee would halve foure pounds of Soape a yeare for her Washinge & that the sd Tilney replyed hee never use to give but three when he was a Single Man. N-n, Va. xii-284.

THE LAW'S PRECISION: Philip Jacob petitions for administration on the estate of his "son-in-law" Jacob Warren, lately deceased, under age. That the petitioner's son, brother by his mother to the said Jacob Warren (as yr Petr is advised) Hath a Right to administer the Goods and Chattels but is under age, &c., &c. N-n, Va. Ct. record.

CONTINUED articles COUNTY COURT NOTE-BOOK, and the dates on which they first appeared. For the sake of neatness and to avoid unnecessary printing, the usual headings and tail-notes attached to these articles will be discontinued, and this paragraph will take their place.

MARRIAGES BY INFERENCE. Began with May, 1922.

MARYLAND'S NEXT OF KIN. Began with July, 1922.

VIRGINIA COLONISTS. This alphabetized list began with July, 1924.

ANNE ARUNDEL ORPHANS. Began with September, 1924.

MARYLAND NATURALIZATIONS. Began with February, 1923.

KING GEORGE PROBATES, &c. Began with July, 1924.

PRINCE WILLIAM PROBATES, &c. Began with April, 1923.

The LIST of BANISHED QUAKERS. Began with November, 1924.

MILITARY NOTES, both COLONIAL and REVOLUTIONARY, and some later MILITIA NOTES, will appear in every issue, if possible.

SHIPS IN PORT, NEW ENGLANDERS AND OTHERS and COLONIAL FORENAMES, will appear in alternate issues or as space can be found for them.

ENGLISH QUAKERS BANISHED BETWEEN 1660 AND 1666

MARY DALE, from London or Middlesex.
ELIZ: DOUBLEDAY, from Leicestershire
ANNE DANCE, BRIDGET DIXON, WILLIAM EBURNE, ELEANOR EDMONDS — from London or Middlesex
WILLIAM EDMONDS, from Bedfordshire
JOHN EVANS, from Berkshire
ROB. FAIRMAN, HENRY FEAST — from Hartfordshire
EDWARD FRANKLIN, GEORGE FRANKLIN — from Bedfordshire
HENRY FAWCETT, RICHARD FAWCETT — from Cumberland
ELIZABETH FISHER, CHRISTIAN FORD, LAWRENCE FULLOVE — from London or Middlesex
WILLIAM FORD, from Bristol
JOHN GRANE, from London or Middlesex
FRANCIS HADDON, THOMAS HARRIS, ROBERT HART, JEREMIAH HERNE — from Hartfordshire
EDWARD HIDE, ROBERT HODGSON — from Berkshire
ISABEL HACKER, ANNE HALEY, ELIZ: HARDING, JOHN HARDING, SARAH HAWES, THOMAS HEMSIE, BATHOL. HERNE, ANNE HORNIBLOW, SUSANNA HORNE, ISAAC HOW — from London or Middlesex

[Note: The foregoing is a first alphabet only. A second alphabet will include those omitted on account of the lists being given by counties and in two separate volumes.]

A LIST OF ORPHANS, ANNE ARUNDEL COUNTY, MARYLAND (Liber T. B. 1.)

(Contributed by Mrs. Geo. W. Hodges)

THO: MARSHALL, at John Watts.
ANDREW, ANN, RUTH and HANNAH NORWOOD, with Mr. Andrew Wellsley.
WILLIAM and SUSA NUTHEAD, orphans of William, with Seb [Teb?] Oley.
GEORGE NORMAN, orphan, of George with Moris Baker.
WILLIAM NORMAN, orphan of George, with John Gadsbery.
JOHN NEAL, son of Jonathan, at Robert Gibbs'.
ELIZA: and SARAH OGEGER[?] daus. of Nicholas, with Edward Chapman.
GILBERT and ELIZA: PATTERSON, with Chas. Cheney, and estate in his hands.
JAMES POWELL at Richard Liston's.
THOMAS and JOHN PETTEBON, sons of John, with William Lewis.
SARAH RAWLINGS with John Turner.
ANN and ELIZA: RIDGLEY, with Maj. Greenberry.
JAMES RYLEY, with John Gaterill.
One of John RIGBYE'S with Rich'd Galloway.
One of James RIGBYE'S with Tho: Tench, Esq.
JOHN ROBINSON, son of George, at Mrs. Mary Homewood's.
BENJA. STEVENS, SAM'LL, ELIZABETH and SARAH STEVENS, at Thomas Brown's.
EDWARD SAUNDERS, with Mrs. Jabez Pierpoint.
EDWARD SELBY at Mr. Graham's.
ANN SMITHALL, at Thomas Larkins'.
MARTHA SMITH with Kath: Gitting.
ELIZABETH SILLIA[?] with Benj. Capell.
JOHN, JAMES and MARY SMITH, orphans of John Smith, Irish, with Wm. Jones.
ALICE and JANE SCIDMORE, daus. of Samuell, with John Ching.
JOHN SHAW, son of JANE SHAW, at Robert Boone's.

PROBATES AND ADMINISTRATIONS RICHMOND COUNTY, VIRGINIA

WILLIAM STARKE, his will presented by Frances Starke, extx and wid. Proved by oaths of Thomas Parker, Thomas Philpin and Richard Grubbs, wit. Probate to extx 5 June 1695, ii-56.

JOSEPH DAVIS; will presented by Catherine Davis, extx. Proved by Edward Jones and Thomas Gladman. 5 June 1695. ii-56.

JOHN BAPTIST; will presented by Anne Baptist, extx. Proved by Thomas Newman and Elizabeth Burgess. Probate to extx. 7 Aug 1695. ii-64.

EDWARD PRICE; will presented by Anne Price, extx and wid. Proved by Andrew Bourne and John Bourne, wit, who make oath. Probate to extx 2 Oct 1695. ii-85.

MAXMILIAN ROBINSON; will presented by Henindge Robinson, one of the extrs. by his attorney, Mr. Arthur Spicer, presenting an authentic copy of sd will to the Court, which sd will appearing to be duly proved in the ecclesiastical Court of the Diocese of London, the Court do allow sd will and do grant probate to sd Henindge Robinson. 7 Oct 1696. ii-164.

HENRY BERRY; will presented by Sarah Berry, extx. Proved by Alexander Spence and James Wofendall. Probate to extx 7 Oct 1696. ii-165.

JOHN DALE; admn his est. to Mary Dale, his widow. 7 Oct 1696. ii-167.

ISAAC WRIGHT; admn his est, to John Taverner; Samuel Peachey and Samuel Bayley, sec. 2 Dec 1696. ii-197.

LEONARD ROBINSON; his will presented by Joseph Dike, extr. Proved by Thomas Lewis and John Wakeman. Probate to extr. 2 Dec 1696. ii-197.

JOHN OAKLEY; will presented by Thomas Glascock. Proved by Richard White and Dr. Henry Clarke, wit. 2 Mch 1697-8. ii-274.

JOHN WEBB; will presented by Giles Webb, extr. Proved by Samuel Samford and Thomas White. Codicil thereto, proved by John Baker. Probate to extr. 2 Mch 1697. ii-274.

FRANCIS ELMORE; will presented by Thomas Newtown, extr, who relinquishes extrship. Proved by John Hinds and Richard Knowles. Admn to John Tarpley for and on behalf of the orphans of sd Elmore. 2 Mch 1697-8. ii-275.

WILLIAM DAVIS; will preented by Nathaniel Thrift, extr. Proved by Elias Hughs and Thomas Lewis. Probate to extr. 2 Dec 1697-8. ii-275.

RALPH WHITING; will presnted by extrs. Proved by John Silvester and John Hardey. Probate to extrs. [Names not given.] 2 Mch 1697-8. ii-275.

THOMAS SWINBURNE; will presented by Martha, one of the chn of sd Thomas. Proved by Paul Micou and Stephen Mannering. Probate to sd Martha, as surviving extx. 2 Mch 1697-8. ii-276.

WILLIAM DOWGAN; admn his est. to Hugh French. 2 Mch 1697-8. ii-276.

JOHN ALEXANDER; will presented by extrs [not named in Court record.] Proved by William Miller. Probate to extrs. 2 Mch 1697-8. ii-277.

SAMUEL DAWS; admn his est. to Grace Bryant, of Essex county, wid. (she being nearest of kin.) Wm. Yates, sec. 1 June 1698. ii-294.

WILLIAM SLOUGHTER; admn his est. to Mrs. Phebe Sloughter; Samuel Peachey and Thomas Glascock, sec. 1 June 1698. ii-295.

JOHN PEIRCE, Gent.; will presented by Col. William Peirce, extr. Proved by George Gibbs and Ralph Berkley. 1 June 1698. ii-295.

MATTHEWS BURROWS; admn his est., with will annexed, to Patience Burrows, his wid. 1 June 1698. ii-295.

KING GEORGE COUNTY, VIRGINIA

SAMUEL KERCHIVAL; l. a. to Dorothy Kerchivall. John Dinwiddie, Gent., sec. 1 Mch 1722. Orders 1721-1734. p. 103.

JOHN UNDERWOOD; his will presented by Elizabeth Underwood, his widow and extx. William Underwood, another extr, refuses. Proved by William Pullen and Samuel Wood. William Underwood and Francis Jet, sec. 5 Apr 1723. p. 109.

HENRY DRAKE; will presented by Mary Drake, widow and extx. Proved by William Woffendall and Ann Drake. 5 Apr 1723. p. 109.

WALTER ANDERSON; l. a. on his est, to Jonas Allen [and Walter Anderson?]. Isaac Arnold, sec. 5 Apr 1723. p. 110.

HUMPHRY QUISENBERRY; his will presented by Mary Quisenberry, his widow. Proved by John Deane and William Humphrys. 7 June 1723. p. 123.

OWEN DERMOT; l. a. on his estate to Margaret Dermot. 7 June 1723. p. 123.

RICHARD WHITE; Margaret White, widow, gets l. a. on his estate. John Glendening, sec. 2 Aug 1723. p. 126.

WILLIAM WOFENDALL; will presented and proved by William Stone and John Price. Orders 1735-1751. 6 Feby 1746. p. 498.

THOMAS MONTEITH; will presented and proved by Richard Bryan and William Rowley, Phillis Monteith, relict and extx declared her "Descent" to Stand to her Husband's will, Whereupon admn was granted to her. Richard Bryan and William Rowley, sec. 6 Mch 1746. p. 502.

ISAAC PITMAN; will presented by Moses Pitman and George Riding. Proved by wit. Joseph Tutt and Thomas Underwood sec. for extrs. 6 Mch 1746. p. 502.

WILLIAM WOFENDALL; admn his est. granted to Tabitha Wofendall. Bowen Price and Joseph Strother, sec. 6 Mch 1746. p. 502.

BENJAMIN GRAVES; l. a. on his estate to Sarah Graves, his widow. Joel Berry and George Wringlesby sec. 1 May 1747. p. 504.

WILLIAM DEAN; will presented by John Deane, one of his extrs, and proved by Daniel White, Jr., and John Nunn. Charles Deane and Bowen Price, sec. 3 July 1747. p. 514.

WILLIAM ROSSER; will presented by James Rosser, his extr, and proved by James Glendining and John Hobby. John Grant gives bond for extr. 7 Aug 1747. p. 525.

GEORGE MOTHERSHEAD; will presented by Mary Mothershead his widow and extx. Proved by John Quisenberry and Christopher Collins, and admitted to record. 7 Aug 1747. p. 527.

MARGARET GILL; will presented by James Jones, her extr. Proved by Evan Jones and Joseph Morris.

WILLIAM SHIRLEY; admn with will annexed to Joseph Morton, Gent. George Morton, Gent., sec. 4 Sept 1747. p. 535.

MOSES MANNING; admn with will annexed to Anne Manning. Proved by wit. Henry Drake, sec. 4 Sept 1747. p. 542.

WILLIAM BRUCE; will presented by Hensfield Bruce, his extr, and proved by wit., George Morton, Gent. 3 Feby 1748. p. 599.

DANIEL WHITE; will presented by Daniel White and Thomas White, his extrs. Proved by wit. Joseph Morton and Rowland Thornton, sec. 3 Feby 1748. p. 599.

SAMUEL BEAR; admn granted to Margaret Bear; Charles Carter, Gent. sec. 3 Feby 1748.

JOSEPH ARMSTRONG; admn his estate to William Rowley. William Bruce, sec. 3 Feby 1748. p. 599.

WILLIAM MARSHALL; will presented by Ann Marshall, one of the extrs, and proved by Sarah Dixon (late Sarah Turner). 3 Feby 1748. p. 600.

COLONIAL AND REVOLUTIONARY SERVICE

CHARLES SIMPKINS, HENRY STONE, and JOHN EVANS, applicants for pensions, filed declarations of service and are ordered certified. Monon. cty, W. Va. 27 Mch 1833. ll-357.*

JOSEPH DUNLAP, makes oath as to his declaration, and is ordered certified. 23 Apr 1833. ii-367. Monon. cty, W. Va.*

WILLIAM WILSON and GEORGE WHETSEL, make oath to declarations, and are certified. Monon. cty, W. Va. 22 July 1833. ii-398.*

* Contributed by Mr. Dille, of Morgantown, W. Va.

PHILIP SMELL, makes oak to his declaration, and is certified. Monon. cty, W. Va. 26 Aug. 1833. ii-405.*

MATTHEW FOWLER, proves that he served as a Corporal in the Old Virginia Regiment, before 1763. Ohio cty, W. Va. Ct. 6 Mch 1780.

JOHN CARPENTER proved that he served as a soldier in the same Regiment, before 1763. Same ct.

JOHN MARTIN, proves his service as an Ensign in Virginia, in 1758. Same ct.

JESSE MARTIN, proved his service as an Artificer in the Virginia service in 1760. Same ct.

JAMES PARKS, proved that he served as an Artificer, Virginia service, in 1760. Same ct.

JOHN CASEY'S certificate as a pensioner proved. Hampshire cty, W. Va. Ct 10 Jany 1788.

ORDERED that it be certified that JEMIMA HOWELL, widow of GEORGE HOWELL, who was a soldier in the service of the United States, and was killed at Buford's Defeat, is still a widow with six children, four of which are under her care ... one of the two youngest being nine years old, and the other eight, and blind. She makes it appear that she is the person mentioned in the pension list for the year 1787, and the sheriff is ordered to pay her ten pounds. Ct 10 July 1788.

MARY LYON, widow of WILLIAM LYON, deceased, who was a soldier and killed in the Continental Service, proves that she is in indigent circumstances and has six children to maintain, the oldest being only twelve years of age. Ct. 16 Oct 1788.

Omitted from PRINCE WILLIAM PROBATES and ADMINISTRATIONS.

JOHN HARTSHORN; admn his est, to John Hartshorn, Alex'r Henderson, sec. 7 Mch 1768. [5] 81.

NOTES AND QUERIES

RIDGELEY: Wanted, the parentage of Susannah Ridgeley, born in Maryland about 1796, who married ... Penn before 1815. Also wanted, the PENN family. Would like to correspond with members of either family. C. S. P. N.

SEVENTY-FIVE DOLLARS will be paid for the ancestry of CHILLIAM and MARTIN PALMER, both of Charlotte cty, Va., back to the immigrant into this country from England. Facts from civil and church records desired, with exact references. Address W. B. P. A., care of the Editor.

ROBINSON-WITHERS: Who was the father of Nancy Robinson who married Benjamin Withers in Fauquier cty, Va., in 1783. Her mother's name was Martha.

McMAHON: Did John McMahon who married Rosannah Hardin, dau. of Martin Hardin, of Fauquier cty, give Revolutionary service? C. M. I.

COLE: Particulars wanted of birth and marriage of JOHN COLE in Maryland; he emigrated to Kentucky shortly before 1790. Probably son of George Cole who married, 1778, Priscilla Hooker in Prince Georges cty, Maryland. C. B. A. C.

JAMES BRIDGER: Explorer and prominent in early western life. Who were his parents? He was born in Richmond, Va., 1804. M. M. H. V.

JOHN WADE: Twenty-five dollars will be paid for full information as to Capt. John Wade, of Chester and Marcus Hook, Penna., who died during the Revolution. He was living in 1754 in Chester, and was the master and owner or part owner of the *Martha and Miriam*, a coasting sloop or pilot boat. M. L.

NEW HERALDIC DICTIONARY IN PREPARATION.—Mr. Charles K. Bolton, 10½ Beacon Street, Boston, Mass., is preparing to publish a dictionary describing coats-of-arms that have been used in this country on book-plates, old silver, gravestones, seal rings, etc. He would like to correspond with persons interested.

OF IMPORTANCE TO OWNERS OF OLD MANUSCRIPTS

It is quite often the case that little is known about the modern methods of restoration of ancient documents and this applies not only to court officials but to those individuals who are fortunate enough to have in their possession, valuable letters, or papers, or early manuscript of any form which has become damaged in any way by careless handling or having been exposed to damp.

As an example of what can be done, a Virginia patent two hundred and seventy years old, was recently discovered by a lady who knew of the work of the EMERY RECORD PRESERVING COMPANY, of Taunton, Massachusetts, and was sent to that company for restoration. The patent (which was an "exhibit" in an ancient equity case) has now been framed and is hanging in a Virginia Clerk's Office as one of its most treasured possessions. Photostats of the paper, which could not even be handled as it was found, were included in the work of the Company.

[See the advertisement of this Company on page 24.]

The WILLIAM AND MARY QUARTERLY—The Editor of this magazine is advertising for early numbers of the first series. The magazine has begun the publication of contributed genealogical material which reads as if compiled by serious and careful searchers. It will add to the value of the serial and enhance its popularity.

The MARYLAND HISTORICAL MAGAZINE continues the Life of THOMAS JOHNSON and the ACCOUNT BOOKS of Dr. CARROLL, but adds an excellent rendition of the early RENT ROLLS of the province. These will be of value to many readers who are not specially interested in Maryland biographies.

Volume I, of ULSTER COUNTY, N. Y., GRAVESTONE INSCRIPTIONS. By Lila James Ronery. 1924. A most praiseworthy effort to preserve the names of those who lived and died in this county.

Columbian Printing Co., Inc., Washington, D. C

The

County Court Note-Book

Supplement for June, 1925

FAMILIES OF THE EASTERN SHORE

CUSTIS OF VIRGINIA

The following is by way of a preamble to a considerable amount of early CUSTIS data which the Editor has gathered from those original records which are technically classified as *source* material, and which she hopes to publish from time to time as a supplement to the NOTE-BOOK.

BISHOP MEADE, page 262, of vol. i, Old Churches and Families of Virginia, says:-

"A friend on the Eastern Shore, whose de- "light is in searching its ancient records, has "sent me a full account of the Custis family, "which so abounds in that part of the State. "Its name and blood are intermingled with "those of most of the families of Northamp- "ton and Accomack, whether rich or poor. I "give a brief statement of it. The name of "JOHN CUSTIS first appears on the record "in 1640. It is probable that he was the person "of whom Colonel Norwood speaks, in his "account of his voyage to America and ship- "wreck on the Eastern Shore in 1649, as hav- "ing been a hotel keeper in Rotterdam and a "great favorite with English travellers. He "had six sons and one daughter. The daugh- "ter married Colonel Argal Yeardley, son of "Governor Yeardley, of Virginia. His sons "were JOHN, WILLIAM, JOSEPH, who "were in Virginia; THOMAS, who was in "Baltimore, Ireland; ROBERT, who resided "in Rotterdam; and EDMUND, who lived "in London. The family is of Irish descent."

Bishop Meade further quotes his correspondent as saying that JOHN CUSTIS received Arlington by his first wife. Of this more anon. And that his second wife was daughter of Colonel Edmund Scarborough. This is an error, as she was his third, and last, wife, having outlived him and taken a fourth husband.

From the records:

JOHN CURTIS; his certificate for 150 acres; head rights: John Smith, Joane Palmer, John Tully. N-n, Va., ii-35. 1640.

ELIAS HARTREE, deposition. This deposition is called forth by a case between two women concerning a cow. The wife of JOHN CURTIS is mentioned, called "Goody Curtis." The other party to the "difference" is the Widow Taylor, and she is ordered to pay JOHN CURTIS or any other, for his use, a pint of milk a day. JOHN CURTIS' plantation is referred to. N-n, Va. ii-86. 2 Aug 1641.

At this time, 1640-1641, JOHN CUSTIS, the head of the American family, was, perhaps, fourteen years old. There is no reason to suppose that his father, JOHN CUSTIS, of Rotterdam, who was known to be established in an important business over there, was in America. Certainly if he had come over at that date, and brought with him his son, his certificate would have included lands for himself and son, and there would have been some record concerning him in the old Accomack court proceedings, or in Lower Norfolk, where the son JOHN CUSTIS first appears.

It does appear from a record in 1655 (fourteen or fifteen years afterward) that two JOHN CUSTISES were temporarily in Northampton county; that is, JOHN, Senior, and JOHN, Junior, appear as members of a petit jury (not a grand jury). It seems possible that the elder JOHN was on this side of the water merely on a visit, probably on business... taking up land or "merchandizing."

Concerning this question of CUSTIS or CURTIS, the Editor has not only examined the original record herself, but has also used the very fine copy made by the late Mr. Upshur. There is probably no one now living, with perhaps one exception, who is as familiar with the early writing of the Eastern Shore records as was Mr. Upshur. Mr. Upshur makes the name CURTIS, as does the Editor. The Editor has also consulted two gentlemen who have made numberless examinations of these particular records, and both are willing to endorse the reading as CURTIS. Bishop Meade did what so many do, relied on some one else, who was unfamiliar with the meticulous exactness of the old scribes, especially of those of the very earliest days.

There is no record in Northampton county of any CUSTIS in the 1640's.

The

County Court Note-Book

A Little Bulletin of History and Genealogy

August, 1925.

Vol. IV, No 4

INTERCOUNTY AND INTERCOLONIAL

PATRICK McDOWELL, Edgecomb county, N. C.; power to Levin Parker of Accomack, Va. 20 Oct 1766. Acco Diii-446.

JESSEY HUNT, late of New York, marriner, to Luke Luker, pltr; land on Cedar Island. 26 May 1767. Acco, Va. Diii-476.

DANIEL READ, of Gloucester county, Va., conveys a negro to James Twiford of Accomack. Acco, Va. Diii-379. 29 May 1765.

DANIEL MAXWELL, late of Accomack, now of North Carolina, and wf Patience; and Ann Wainhouse, wid. of Francis, late of sd cty, and Elizabeth and Sarah, daus. and co-heirs of sd Francis, dec'd. 28 Aug 1765. Acco Diii-390.

WM. CHOAT, marriner, of New England; power to John Hutchenson. 27 Feby 1765. Acco, Va. Diii-377.

OBEDIAH COOKSON, county of Suffolk and province of *the* Massachusetts Bay in New England, mcht; power to John Wise of Accomack. Acco., Va. 27 Jany 1731. xx-95.

SIMON EDGILL, of Philada., Mcht; power to Isaac Morris of Sommersett cty, Md. 1736. Acco, Va. ix-270.

PEDIGREENE [*sic*] WHITE, of New England. See N-n, Va. 29 May 1656. v-97.

HANNAH HENDERSON, of the City of Philadelphia, was the beloved friend of John Murray, of Somerset cty, Maryland, and receivedd £50. Will dated 19 Sept 1736. Acco, Va. xx-256.

THOMAS JERVICE, signs a ctf as church warden, Hearne psh, Kent cty, concerning ages of two Toulsons. 30 Sept 1638. N-n, Va. ix-111.

WALTER LANE, for whom Friend's Discovery was surveyed, was in "Carrolina" in 1744. Wor. cty, Md. Rent Roll.

WILLIAM LANE, of Norfolk cty, Virginia, Gent., was the eldest son and heir of William Lane, late of Worcester cty, Md. Wor. cty. 19 Feby 1753. B-509.

[Mr.] RICHARD LORD, of Hartford on the River of *Conectecatt,* in New England, Mcht; power to well-beloved brother John Lord of the same Towne. Wmld, Va. 21 Dec 1657. Orders i-91.

WILLIAM MANOAR[?] of Onslow cty, N. C.; bond to John Nelson. Acco, Va. Dii-122. 8 June 1748.

WILLIAM MARSHALL, mariner, of Whithaven, cty of Cumberland, England, m. Mary, dau. of Elianer Atkinson, who was sister of Joseph Troughear, late of Essex cty, Va. K. Geo., Va. 26 Oct 1727. i-503.

JAMES MILLS, of New Haven, in New England; ackn. he is truly indebted to Mr. John Hawkins, of Boston, in N. E. Wmld, Va. 20 Apr 1661. ii-42.

JOSEPH WADE, of Randolph cty, and ELIZABETH WADE, of Montgomery cty, N. C., give power to James Claxton of Granville cty, N. C. to receive from William Roberson of Mecklinburg cty, Va., extr of the will of Andrew Wade, late of Halifax cty, Va., all negro slaves, and other property "to which we are entitled to lately of Andrew Wade's estate." Sig. Jos. Wade, Elizabeth Wade, Andrew Wade. Granville cty, N. C. 14 Aug 1794. ii-165.

JOHN LANGLEY, of Newport, R. I., from Thomas Norris, of St. Mary's, Camden cty, Ga., lot in St. Mary's. Camden cty, Ga. 17 June 1795. B&C. p.32.

CLAUD BOREL, late of Saint Domingo, now of Camden cty, Ga., pltr. Camden cty, Ga. 29 Jany 1796. B&C. p.235.

THEODORE, CHARLES and THOMAS HOPKINS; STEPHEN AUSTIN and wf HULDAH; ASHBELL WELLS and wf MARY, of Connecticut; ELISHA BUCKINGHAM HOPKINS and wf SARAH; and PETER WALLACE GALLAUDETT and wf JANE, of Pennsylvania; to Robert Watts of Georgia; WHEREAS Jason Hopkins died seized of the premises hereinafter mentioned, in trust nevertheless for the sole use of afsd Sarah Hopkins as her separate estate, Now . . consideration $1.00 . . . . . all that tract called Cabbage Bluff on Turtle River, near Brunswick, Ga., containing 1100 acres . . . in trust for the benefit of sd Sarah. Glynn cty, Ga. 8 Mch 1800. AB-EF p.312.

MARRIAGES BY INFERENCE*

The following marriages are from the Minutes of the Orphans' Court, York cty, Penna.

HUMPHREY ANDREWS and AGNES ANDERSON, dau. of Allen. Before 24 Mch 1785. E-261.

THOMAS ARMSTRONG and MARY McCLEARY, wid. of John. Before 3 June 1784. E-166.

WILLIAM BOYD and ELIZABETH EMMACH, wid. of Andrew. About 2 Sept 1761. A-196.

JAMES BOYD and MARGARET McDONAUGH, wid. of Henry. About or before 26 May 1761. A-173.

MATHIAS BRINDLEY and BARBARA BRINDLEY, dau. Jacob. Before 4 Jany 1786. E-349.

SAMUEL BROWN and MARY GIBSON, dau. William. Before 24 Mch 1785. E-256.

HENRY CONRAD and CATHARINE ALT, wid Valentine Alt, yeoman. About or before 28 Nov 1759. A-129.

JAMES CARLYLE and JEAN WILSON, dau. William. Before 31 May 1770. B-251.

WILLIAM CARSON and CATHARINE SCOGGIN, dau. John. Before 23 Mch 1784. E-249.

JOHN DORRAUGH and JANE McCORD, dau. Richard. Before 4 Feby 1786. E-355.

JOSEPH DYSART and MARY SCOGGIN, dau. John. Before 23 Mch 1784. E-249.

JOHN GASTIN and SUSANNA FERGUSON, Before 30 Oct 1784. E-195.

HENRY GERLACH and MARIA MAGDALENA FRENCH, wid. Philip. Before 24 Nov 1761. A-207.

JOHN GIBSON and MARGARET RHEA, wid. Joseph. About or before 28 Nov 1759. A-196.

FREDERICK HERMAN and MAGDALENA BRINDLEY, dau. Jacob. Before 4 Jany 1786. E-349.

EBENEZER HORSEMAN and CATHARINE BRINDLEY, dau. Jacob. Before 4 Jany 1786. E-349.

WILLIAM HANNAH and GRACE VANCE, wid. John. Before 24 Mch 1785. E-258.

JOSEPH HOPSON and ANN SCOGGIN, dau. John. Before 23 Mch 1784. E-249.

WILLIAM HUTCHISON and MARY ANN ANDERSON, dau. Allen. Before 24 Mch 1785. E-261.

ROBERT IRWIN and ROSANNA McCARTER, dau. Alexander. Before 24 Mch 1785. E-269.

JAMES M'CLEAN and JANE HART, dau. Andrew. Before 27 Mch 1781. D-204.

JACOB MYER and SARAH GIBSON, dau. John. Before 26 Nov 1766. B-133.

ROBERT MAXWELL and EMELIA SCOGGIN, dau. John. Before 23 Mch 1784. E-249.

WILLIAM MALSBY and ANNE DAVIS, dau. David. Before 30 May 1787. F-103.

SAMUEL McKINNEY and ELIZABETH FERGUSON. Before 27 Oct 1784. E-194.

Capt. JOHN McDONALD and ANNA MARIA FISSELL, wid. Frederick. Before 22 Mch 1785. E-243.

JOHN MILLER and AGATHA SITES, wid. Casper. Before 24 Mch 1785. E-259.

BALTZER PFAUST and EVA FISSELL, dau. Frederick. Before 22 Mch 1785. E-243.

DANIEL RIDER and MARGARET FISSELL, dau. Frederick. Before 22 Mch 1785. E-243.

HANS NICHOLAS RISINGER and the widow of Laurence SMALL. Before 26 Mch 1753. A-31.

JACOB SINN and HANNAH HOFFMAN, dau. Nicholas. Before 30 Oct 1784. E-199.

HENRY STEINHEIFFER and ELIZABETH HOFFHEINS, eldest dau. of Adam. Before 22 Mch 1785. E-242.

THOMAS SILLIKS and RACHEL SCOGGIN, dau. John. Before 23 Mch 1784. E-249

MARYLAND'S NEXT OF KIN *

DENNIS SULLAVAN, of Kent cty. "There is noe Kine . . . as is known." 12 Apr 1720. iv-27.

VINCENT and BENJAMIN BLACKISTONE, brothers; inv. John Blackistone, Jr. 5 Aug 1720. iv-29.

NOAH LAWRENCE, of Kent cty. "There is no Kin in this Prov. as is known." 12 Feby 1719. iv-30.

ABRA: BIRCKHEAD, ABRA'M BIRCKHEAD, Jr; inv. Nehemiah Birckhead of A. A. cty. 20 July 1720. iv-31.

MARY and ANN HEMSLEY; inv. Philemon Hemsley. of A. A. cty. 6 July 1720. iv-33,38.

EVAN HOWELL, of St.Mary's cty; "Noe kindred appears." 2 Oct 1719. iv-40.

ELIZABETH SCOTT, ELIZABETH RULSTAN; inv. Benjamin Reeder of St. Mary's cty. 25 July 1720. iv-41.

ANN HEAD, CUTHBERT SEWELL; inv. John Fenwick, of St. Mary's cty. 23 May 1720. iv-43.

RODGER MATTHEWS and JOHN THOMAS; inv. Samuel Jackson, Balto. cty. 12 Apr 1720. iv-46.

SAMUEL and ROBERT POTTENGER; inv. John Pottinger, Jr. of Pr. Geo's cty. 12 Apr 1720. iv-

ANTONY RAWLLINGS, THOMAS PEARSON; inv. John Pearson of Dor. cty. 15 July 1720. iv-53.

RICHARD WOODLAND, MORGAN ADAMS; inv. Joseph Stanaway of Dor. cty. 16 Apr 1720. iv-54.

ISAAC JONES, of Dor. cty. "No Kinn but Infants." 3 June 1720. iv-56.

EDWARD COLE, ROBERT FORD, Jr.; inv. Robert Cole, of St. Mary's cty. 26 Apr 1720. iv-26.

V . . . . . .[?] and FRANCIS HARBERT; inv. William Herbert, of St. Mary's cty, 27 June 1720. iv-58.

VIRGINIA COLONISTS

(From "Old Volume 5," S. L. O., Richmond)

SOUTHEY LITTLETON, Northampton cty, 1656.†

Head rights: Rich'd Smith, Geo. Daw, Sam. Lucas, Tho. Buffeild, Rob. Max, Dick of the Frigate, Elinr Glover, Dorothy Slaughter, Fra. Rowles, Geo. Butcher, Phillip Gardner, Jno. Jackson, Richd Johns, Margaret Alen, Eliz. Bond, Tho. Newton, Geo. Freshwater, Tho. Blacklock, his wife and child; Gabriel Powell, Mathew Pippinge, Step. Corson, Richd Pickeringe, Sanders Wilson, Thomas Hogg, Mathew Wardell, Xpher Donoh, Richd Conner and Daniel, Irishmen; Jno. Pryer, Dan. Baker Will Fisher, John Wyse, Mary Fleetwood, Wm. Smith, Geo. Smith, Mathy Bennet, Wm. Clerke, Richd Smith, Jno. Symons, Jno. Munday, Tho. Fowler, Richd Skinner, John Johnson.

Mr. GEORG MARSH, Northampton cty, 1657.

Head rights: David Miles, Andrew Scott, Hugh Perry[?] Jno. Allen, Rich. Grimes, Robert Peck, Tho. Powell, Tho. Hatton, Ncla

†Previously printed.

Enorahoo[?] Gen Hickson, Joseph Chizell, Tho. Cooke, Ralph Brickes, Jno. Parker, Daniell Cooper, Wm. Call, Edward Foster, Jno. Walker.

JOHN MARSHALL; L. Norf. cty. [No date.]
Head rights: Timothy Ives and wf Margaret.

WM. MELLINGE, Northampton cty, 1655.
Head rights: Fra. Cutt, Roger Barr, Wm. Sterlinge, Timothy Tralley, Alex. Wignall, Tho. Wignall, Wm. Smarth [Smart?] Henry Mitchell, Grace Lewis.

JOHN MOTTRON, Northumberland cty, 1655.
Head rights: Lidia Sawyer, Edwd Gower, Tho. Glover, Lyonell Britten, Tho. Jones.

JOHN MOTTERON, [The spelling of this name varies in the patent from "Matron" to "Motteron."]

EDWARD MOORE, Northampton cty, 1656.
Head rights: Edward Moore, Sr., Mary MOORE, EDWARD MOORE, Jr., RICH. MOORE.

THOMAS MEREDITH, New Kent, 1656.
Head rights: Wm. Parkes, Francis Webb, Margarett [illegible], Isaack Watson.

NICHOLAS MERRIWETHER, and JOHN LEACH, James City cty, 1656.
Head rights: Eliz. Heines, Jno. Bradbury, Tho. Abreshall, Tho. Allen.

MARGARET MYLES, Westmoreland cty, 1656.
Head rights: MARGARETT MILES, Francis Roland, Sarah Smith, Katherine Russell, Jane Leech, Abraham Foiles, John Tushan, Walter Morgan, Thomas Powell, Georg. Watts and his wife; Xpian Looker, Mundeff[?] Kerby.

NICHOLAS MERIWETHER, James City cty, 1656.
Head rights: Wm. Corker [twice], Lewis De Courtier, Jno. Mackery [Mackoy?] Jno. Giles, Jno. MacKenny.

JOHN MADDISON, New Kent cty, 1657.
Head rights: Jno. Reynolds, Timothy Pell, Wm. Hardin, Tho. Antell [Ansell?] Robert Titterson, Rob. Dale, Wm. Clerke, Lawrence Baker, Rob. Seale, Tho. Lee, Rob. Dart, Tho. Watkins, Nich. Parsins, Joseph Ridge, Rob. Wheelden.

THOMAS MOLTEN, "North east upon a branch of Petomeck freshes," 1657.
Head rights: Thomas Hartly, Jno. Greene, Wm. Moore, Alex. Herringe, Jno. Barber, Richd. Packer, Jno. Chadwick, Jno. Huckle, Eliz. Williams, Edwd Gibbs.

SAMUELL MATHEWES; "East on Patomeck river, north on Quantecot River or Creeke," 1657.
Head rights: Henry Peckett, Henry Lawrence, Edmond Potter, John Mather, Arthur Coventon, Lewis Beckwith, Richard Hand, Rich. Tiller, James Harris, Tho. Harris, Marmaduke Ladd, Jerem. Burditt, Wm. Richardson, Jane Bell, Rebecka Goldinge, Mary Killingall, Eliz: Bowyer, Mary Ramsey, Morris Victsorrell [Fitzgerald], John Farner, Rich. Kent, Richard Walton, Jone Welson [Nelson? or Wilson?] Andrew Keateley, Ambrose Parkes, James Wyner, James Hunt, Olliver Jewitt, Nich: Lawrence, Edward Arney, Sameuel Jeffers, Richard Lacy, Anth. Barrwell, Robert Moores, Hugh Jones, Robert Whitehige[?] Bartho: Croste, Peter Heath, John Smallwood, John Hancock, John Cornehouson, John Gibbins, Timothy Gunter, Joane Palmer, Martha Fryer, Fran. Rolls, Katherine Hart, Paul Cartwright, Benjamin Chandler, Robert Biggs, Lawrence Achpoole[?], John Cornelius, Mary Cornelius, Adolph Johnson, Sarah Greene, Mary Leftford, Jone Heors[?], Ann Benbowe, Robert Mesctaken[?]. Fran. Gurman, Adrian Adrianson[?], Tho. Tawtam, [Tatham?], John Slattor, Robert Higginson, Daniel Ingoll. (105 rights but only 65 names given.)

EDMOND MOORE; Lower Norfolk cty, 1657.
Head rights: Black Jacks [prob. negro?], Hendrick Hinderson.

WILLIAM NEWMAN; Gloucester cty, 1657.
Head rights: Robert Davis, Wm. Jenkins, Jno. Foster, Daniell [no surname], Tho: Jones, Adam Church, Jno. Turbey, James Fisher.

HESTER OAKHAM; James City cty, 1656.
Head rights: Margarett Delton, Sarah Core, Mary Hull.

LEWIS PERRY; on a "branch of Nansemond river," 1656.
Head rights: John Marshall, James Yeoman, Eliz: Stiles, Mary Nicholls.

JOHN PAINE; "north side Rapahanocke river," 1656.
Head rights: JNO: PAINE, Jr., MARGA: PAINE, Wm. Emason, Morris Williams, Elizabeth Pusie[?]Jno: Capell, Raughley Travers, Rich. Peacock, Mary Smith, Lau: Thompson, Wm. Walker, Tho: Jelly.

WILLIAM PULLAM; New Kent cty, 1656.
Head rights: Jno. Jenninges, Wm. Walker, Wm. Richards, Tho. Tuffes, Anne Parker, Robert Morris, William Jackson.

NATHANIELL POPE; Westmoreland cty, 1656.
Head rights: Jacob Curteanceau [Coutanceau?], Anne, his wife, John Jacob and Willm his sonnes; Rob. Dawes, Edmond Singlar, Rob. Sicoh[?] Maudlin Hoskins, Susan Hart.

WILLIAM POPE; Nansemond cty, 1656.
Head rights: Obedience Perkins, John Godwin, Rob. Beadle.

JAMES PRICE; Northampton cty, 1656.
Head rights: Wm. Haminack, Elder Adkin, Ann Smith, Barbara Mathewes, Eliz: Eaton, Wm. Barker.

Mr. WILLIAM PRESLY, "in Petomeck freshes," 1657.
Head rights: Roger Bell, James Arden, Corl. May, Ro. Rodes, Tim: Lawrence, Bernard Nash; Jno. Varnell, Edd. Cooper, Law: Seines, Dan: Armstrong, Hugh Davis, Tho. Madrin, Nich. Peake, Rand: Jackson, Tho. Beale, Peete Hughes, Mary James, Martha Hiller, Judith Croshaw, Wm. Batty.

JOHN PARKER, Jr., Surry cty, 1657.
Head rights: Edmond Janeck, Tho. Wakefeild, Jno. Fairepoint, Anna de Wilde, Roger WmSon, Wm. Foster, Petronella Jackson, Tho. Good, Rich. Bidalph, Arthur Patience, Jno. Staples, Fran. Lattur.

The County Court Note-Book

An every-other-monthly devoted to abstracts from County Court and other records, prior to 1800, and with a department of notes and queries.

MILNOR LJUNGSTEDT, Editor and Publisher. Bethesda, Route 10, Maryland.

Published six times a year. **Subscription, two dollars and fifty cents,** in advance; must begin with the year. **Renewals, two dollars.** Advertising rates moderate.

AUGUST, 1925

Vol. IV., No. 4

METHODS OF WORK

Every now and then the Editor is impressed with the tremendous amount of waste in so-called "research work." And the Editor has very recently had an extraordinary proof of the possibilities that lie in all-over, warp-and-woof, piecemeal search in a limited locale. These comments, please understand, apply only to the first one hundred and twenty-five or one hundred and fifty years of our colon records. After that new families moved in .... and, anyhow, they aren't interesting. Of course, the Editor doesn't mean to say that the Revolution isn't interesting, but not nearly so much as the working out of the people who fought it ... how they came to be there, in the town-halls and behind the stone walls, and where they got the protesting and the fighting *timbre*. And, of course, in this specious generalizing, the Editor nearly cuts out the numbers of Scotch and Irish who came not so very long before our first fight of protest, and fell into the ranks with no uncertain promptness. At least this is what the Editor understands, but doesn't mind being corrected. The Revolution is not her strong point. She once knew just about as much about the invasion of the Danes, the Normans, and the Wars of the Roses .... and George Washington and the cherry-tree was certainly not more than even in her affections with Alfred and his pancakes. (George Washington has grown somewhat more impressive, considerably more so, and Alfred a fainter figure.

But and anyhow ... as the old petitions more quaintly say ... "*But so it is*" ... It took four generations to make the American who broke loose, and the records of three of those generations are a very fascinating study. The necessity of allowing (in certain sections) for the awful percentage of death; the confusing "intermixing by marriage and remarriage; the similarity of names .... all this makes such a search as the Editor refers to above of an absolute necessity. The Editor has in mind a certain genealogist in Baltimore of many years experience; this gentleman *abstracted every testamentary proceeding* of one Maryland county. It took only one month ... the result is invaluable. He had the means and the time to go to Annapolis and stay there. Compare this patient, detailed work with the demands of the would-be eligibles of more than one society ... ladies of independent incomes, who do not understand how results can be achieved, and who have, apparently, an idea that everything can be found by ... looking under "S" for Smith!

The Editor calls attention to the fact that these remarks apply only to sections with which she is familiar .... those where the County Court kept not only a measure of the "vital statistics," the hereditary rights and such matters, but the religious belief and the morals of the community, more or less in charge, and so, of record. The interminable chancery cases and "Land Causes" may be of record much later, but contain the same desired minutiae of previous generations ... and take even more time to decipher and digest on account of their verbosity ... the verbosity of the law. The fiction of "JOHN NOTITLE vs. JAMES GOODTITLE" is far more wearisome than the involved English of the earlier local Dogberrys .... and just as hard to distill into a clarified abstract.

But what the Editor really minds and is making a sort of round-about appeal concerning, are the lost opportunities for the weaving together of *all* the threads of local history. The charting out of what might be called "Cross-Country Genealogy, or True Relations," of every family in any one early locality, for no family is so unimportant or so poor that it will not sooner or later be found to bind an eligible daughter into the circle of the greater family .... and, considering the ups and downs of royalty and nobility in our dear motherland ... it is rather strange that Americans draw the line so closely as to their own American ancestry.

The notes heretofore printed under the caption NEW ENGLANDERS AND SOME OTHERS IN EARLY VIRGINIA RECORDS, &c, will be continued under the heading INTERCOUNTY AND INTERCOLONIAL. While commerce, and even friendly intercourse is oftener of record with New England, there are many interesting notes showing migration between counties of the same colony, between Virginia and North Carolina, and between the more southern colonies and the West Indies. The title is to be considered flexible.

OCCASIONAL

MARY MORRILL appointed to be keeper of the State house. 3 May 1782. (Charleston, S. C. TT-145.

LEWIS SEEGER, Gentl., late a subject of the Duke of "Wirteenbergh," becomes a citizen, having taken the oath. 10 Apr 1788. (Charleston, S. C. (Vol. 1787-1791. p.238).

WILLIAM BROWN, son to JOHN BROWN and RUTH, his wife, was Born August the 16th day, 1778. BETSEY BROWN, Daughter of JOHN BROWN and RUTH his wife, was Born January the 20th day 1780. (Record found in Onslow cty, N. C.)

CONTINUED articles COUNTY COURT NOTE-BOOK, and the dates on which they first appeared. For the sake of neatness and to avoid unnecessary printing, the usual headings and tail-notes attached to these articles will be discontinued, and this paragraph will take their place.

MARRIAGES BY INFERENCE. Began with May, 1922.

MARYLAND'S NEXT OF KIN. Began with July, 1922.

VIRGINIA COLONISTS. This alphabetized list began with July, 1924.

ANNE ARUNDEL ORPHANS. Began with September, 1924.

MARYLAND NATURALIZATIONS. Began with February, 1923.

KING GEORGE PROBATES, &c. Began with July, 1924.

The LIST of BANISHED QUAKERS. Began with November, 1924.

MILITARY NOTES, both COLONIAL and REVOLUTIONARY, and some later MILITIA NOTES, will appear in every issue, if possible.

SHIPS IN PORT, NEW ENGLANDERS AND OTHERS, INTERCOUNTY and INTERCOLONIAL and COLONIAL FORENAMES, will appear in alternate issues or as space can be found for them.

The STATE LIBRARY of VIRGINIA has been enabled by the use of the photostat machine, a gift from the Colonial Dames of America, to copy the following parish records, vestry books and registers . . . unfortunately, vestry books are more plentiful than registers. Lexington parish, Frederick parish, St. Paul's parish, Lynnhaven parish, Christ Church parish, Cumberland parish, Shelburne parish, Kingston parish, St. Peter's parish, Blissland parish, Wicomico parish, Dettingen parish, Albermarle parish, Lunenburg parish, and Charles City parish. A more detailed statement is in the Librarian's recent report. The NOTE-BOOK has not space to say more than this: of this list only Frederick parish is in the county of the same name. Cumberland parish is not in Cumberland county, nor is Lunenburg parish in Lunenburg county. And Hanover parish, not in this list, is not in Hanover county. This lack of agreement as to county and parish names has probably been a stumbling-block to more than one searcher.

The Colonial Dames have a great deal of money by and large, and if more of them would supply photostat machines, and the moral suasion to get the things to be photostated, many of us would be inclined to crown them with blessings!

THE DISTRICT OF WEST AUGUSTA, VIRGINIA

Those who have, like the Editor, "chased after" the records of this judicial (and legislative) district, which comprised the later counties of Monongalia, Ohio, and Yogohania, will, it is thought, be glad to know that these records have been copied and published in the ANNALS of the CARNEGIE MUSEUM at PITTSBURGH. This note is, of course, written for those who do not know that the records have been thus published, and who naturally would not look for such matters sandwiched between post-glacial records, prehistoric skeletons and the like.

The list of records follows:

Minute Book of the Virginia Court held at Ft. Dunmore [Pittsburg] for the District of West Augusta, 1775-1776. Annals, vol. i, p. 525 to p.569.

Minute Book of the Virginia Court held for Yohogania County, first at Augusta Town (now Washington, Pa.) and afterwards . . . near West Elizabeth; 1776-1780. Annals, vol. ii, pp. 71,205.

Minute (or Order) Book of the Virginia Court held for Ohio county, Virginia, at Black's Cabin [see COUNTY COURT NOTE-BOOK, vol. iv. No. 1] (now West Liberty, West Virginia) from January 6, 1777, until September 4, 1780 . . . . . . Annals, vol. iii, p.5.

The records of deeds for the district of West Augusta, Virginia, for the court held at Fort Dunmore [Pittsburgh, Penna.] 1775-1776. Annals iii, p. 237. [Followed by abstracts of some Old Virginia Wills.]

The publication of these valuable records is due to Mr. Boyd Crumrine, of Washington, Penna., of the Historical Society of that county.

ENGLISH QUAKERS BANISHED BETWEEN 1660 AND 1666

JAMES HARDING THOMAS HODGE THO. HUBBARD MANASSEH HOWARD JOHN JOHNSON MARGARET JACKSON EVAN JONES ELIZABETH IVERS THOMAS KENT JAMES KENDALL JAMES KIRTON ANNE MERCER EDWARD MALETRAT FRANCIS MARLOE DEGORY MARSHAL JOHN MASON MARY MIDDLETON ELIZABETH MORTIMER KATHARINE MUNDAY	from London or Middlesex
LEWIS LAUNDY NICH. LUCAS HEN. MARSHALL THO. MOSSE	from Hartfordshire

Note: Owing to a misunderstanding of symbols (in reality to a different use of the same symbol in the two volumes of the Sufferings) the following Quakers were listed as banished. A later reading shows that they suffered imprisonment. George Adamson, John Apthorp, Sarah Baker, Mary Botham, Elizabeth Bruce, Joseph Cole, Leonard Cole, Thomas Curtis, Anne Curtis, Anne Cox, Richard Cubham, John Cannon, Ralph Charles, Richard Chatteris, John Cranwell, John [or Jane?] Christen, Peter Cosnock, William Caton, Henry Clarke, Anne Clayton, Mary Clayton, George Cowson, Thomas Curwen, John Carr, Thomas Cave, John Capes, Hezekiah Croft, William Clater, James Corney, Thomas Cockett, Ann Corbey, John Crooke, Robert Curtis, William Clayton, John Day, Richard Deane, William Edmonds, John Evans, Edward Franklin, George Franklin, William Ford, Edward Hide, Robert Hodgson.

SERVICE AND SUPPLIES; COLONIAL, REVOLUTIONARY AND MILITIA

ARTHUR TEACKLE allowed one pound eight shillings "for service performed for the State & forty-five pounds for the Continent." 26 Nov 1783. Acco xxxvii0-166.

CLEMENT PARKER'S est. allowed for supplies impressed for the use of the State. 30 Oct 1783. xxxvii0-147.

WILLIAM SNEAD, allowed for the Barge *Ranter,* impressed, five pounds, seventeen shillings & sixpence. (Same Court, same refs.)

SACKER PARKER allowed twenty-four pounds, eighteen shillings. 30 Sept 1783. Acco. xxxvii0-109.

SOUTHY SIMPSON'S est. allowed an acct to the amount of twenty-four shillings paid for an express going to Philadelphia for the service of the State. 30 Sept 1783. Acco. xxxvii0-103.

JOHN BURTON'S property taken off by the enemy is ordered entered of record, to wit: Daniel aged twenty-one years taken off at Whitsuntide, 1781; and Wallace, aged twenty years, taken off September 1782; each valued at one hundred pounds. 28 Aug 1783. xxxvii0-86.

SHUBALD PRATT makes oath that he had served fifteen months as a junior surgeon in the hospital at Alexandria, being a Continental Hospital, and that on the first day of June 1780, he had received five hundred and thirteen pounds. 27 Aug 1783. xxxvii0-79.

JOHN UPSHUR is allowed for fifty gallons of Rum and fifty gallons of wine, "impressed for the use of the Continent." "Mem'r. This allowed before." 26 Aug 1783. Acco. xxxvii0-71.

Lieut. JOSEPH MATHEWS allowed his acct for keeping guard. Acco. xxxvii0-48. 29 July 1783.

BOWDOIN ROBINS, allowed for provisions. (Same refs. and date.)

JOSEPH MATHEWS for carting. (Same refs. and date.)

ZOROBABLE GROTEN, for provisions, &c. (Same refs. and date.)

JOHN KELLY, allowed for Transporting "Artiliry" and Stores for the Militia. 29 May 1783. Acco. xxxvii0-2.

ESTHER BUNTING, wife of RICHIE BUNTING, a soldier now in the service of the Continental States, to be allowed twelve shillings six pence per month, from the first day of June last, to this time, for her support and maintenance. 26 Nov 1777. Acco. xxxv0-41.

COMFORT BLOXOM (widow of Charles Bloxom) to be allowed twelve shillings six pence per month from the middle of June last to the middle of September. for the support of herself and child. Acco. 26 Nov 1777. xxxv0-41.

AGNES HOGSHIRE (wf of ROBRT HOGSHIRE a soldier now in service) to be allowed thirty shillings per month from the 5th day of May last to this time for the support of herself and her three children. 26 Nov 1777. Acco xxxv0-41.

EDMUND CUSTIS makes oath to an acct amounting to two thousand nine hundred and twenty-three pounds, two shillings and six pence, paper money, for bread and flour impressed the 30 May 1779. Acco. 25 May 1784. xxxvii0-317.

A LIST OF ORPHANS. ANNE ARUNDEL COUNTY, MARYLAND (Liber T. B. 1.)

(*Contributed by Mrs. Geo. W. Hodges*)

JOHN ROWLES, with Mr. John Warfeild.

JOHN ROWLS, orphan of John Roles, with Phillip Jones.

CHARLES SAUNDERS, with Mr. John Freeman.

ROBERT SYMES, orphan of Robert, with John Sumberland.

MARY TEMPLE, at Richard Duckett's.

NATHANIEL THERALD, at Thomas Larkins'.

THOMAS TAYLOR, with Samuel Dryer.

One of old TINDALL'S, with Benja. Lawrence.

THOMAS TOSIOR, with Mr. Wm. Gibbons.

SARAH THORNBERRY, at John Thornberry's.

JOHN TRONDLE, at Jeremiah Larkins'.

ELIZA: TAYLOR, dau. of Robert, at Mrs. Mary Homewood's.

JOHN WRIGHT, orphan of Robert, with Wm. Pennington.

MARG'TT WOOTON, dau. of Simon, at Robert Gubb's.

ELIZA: WHELOCK, dau. of Edward, at Henry Waters.

RUTH WOMSLEY, dau. of Thomas, at Richard Womsley's.

THO: WOMSLEY, son of Thomas, at Richard Womsley's.

ESTHER WHITE, at Walter Emerton's.

RICHARD, GEORGE, JOHN, ALLS [ALICE?], and RACHEL WESTERELL, all orphans, with Joseph Button and estate in his hands.

JOHN WORTHINGTON, THOMAS, WM*, SARAH and CHAS. WORTHINGTON, orphans of Capt. John Worthington, with John Brice.

WM. WRIGHT, with Mary Barnett.

JANE WELLS, with Mr. Edward Rumney.

JOSEPH and DINAH WHITE, with Samuel White.

WILLIAM and HENRY WHITEHEAD, with John Shivers.

CHARLES, JOHN and JOSEPH WHITEHEAD, with John Shivers.

Heretofore omitted:

WILLIAM INGLE, with Mrs. Susanna Beard.

THOMAS CLARKE, and GEORGE JAMES, with the widow James, and estate in her hands. [It is uncertain whether this is THOMAS CLARKE and GEORGE JAMES, or that they are all JAMES orphans.]

NICO: KELE, at Henry Mereday's.

ELIZABETH KILBURNE, with Mr. John Freeman.

WM. KILBURNE, with Matthew Middiat.

FRANCIS LEE, with Mr. Richard Warfeild.

WM. LEWIS, at Henry Carter's.

(*End of the list.*)

PROBATES AND ADMINISTRATIONS PRINCE WILLIAM AND OTHER COUNTIES OF VIRGINIA.

The five Order Books of Prince William county, Virginia, coming between the will records of 1744 and 1778, have been examined. Unless some new record has been discovered within the last year, no other data concerning testamentary and administration proceedings of this period, is known to exist, excepting bonds heretofore published.

The Editor regrets that further notes from RICHMOND county have not been received in time for this issue of the NOTE-BOOK.

KING GEORGE COUNTY, VIRGINIA

CHARLES DEANE; will presented by Charles Deane, Jr., his extr, and proved by William Deane and William Monroe. William Deane, sec. Orders 1735-1751. p.552.

ROBERT RANKINS; will presented by Thos. Turner, Gent., and proved by Charles Holdsworth, wit. Extrs resign and l. a. granted to Thomas Turner. Harry Turner, sec. 1735-1751. p.555. 4 Mch 1747.

RICHARD BRYAN, Gent.; will presented by Richard Bryan, his extr, and proved by James Sommervile and Richard Elkins. p.567. 1 Apr 1748.

WILLIAM BUTLER; admn to Elias Powell; George Morton, Gent., sec. p.567. 1 Apr 1748.

JAMES HACKLEY; will presented by Elizabeth Hackley and John and Joseph Hackley, his extrs. Proved by Samuel Reids and John Carter. 6 May 1748. p.573.

JOHN GLENDENNING; will presented by James Glendenning, his extr. Proved by Thomas Armstrong and Charles Bruce. 6 May 1748. p.574.

JOHN TAYLOR; admn his est. to Rowland Thornton, John Grant, sec. 3 June 1784. p.577.

SAMUEL MOONE; admn his est. to Behethland Moon; John Taliaferro, Gent., sec. 1 July 1748. p.582.

THOMAS BARTLETT; will presented by extrs; proved by John Thornley and Edward Marshall. 7 Oct 1748. p.591.

MARY JENNINGS; will presented by Frederick Coghill, the Elder, one of her extrs. Proved by John McCormick and Sarah McDonold, late Sarah Dickenson. Benjamin Strother, sec. 7 Oct 1748. p.591.

GEORGE BLAIR; admn his est. to Andrew Monroe, Gent. Thomas Turner and Samuel Donne, Gent., sec. 7 Oct 1748. p.590. Note: Blair not being a resident in this Colony, admn is granted in this Court to secure merchants in Gt. Britain.

MARGARET RICHARDS; will presented by William Bunbury, her extr, and proved by wit. Enoch Berry, sec. 6 Jany 1748. p.596.

EDM'D DONOHOE; will presented by Francis Thornton and John McCormick, extrs. Proved by wit. Josiah Ferguson, sec. 6 Jany 1748. p.596.

DAVID WILLIAMS; admn his est. to Francis Balthrop; Benjamin Edwards, sec. 6 Jany 1748. p.597.

MARY FISHPOOLE; admn her est. to William Brockenbrough. John Champe, Gent., sec. 3 Feby 1748. p.598.

JOHN CAMPBELL; admn his estate to Clapham Richardson. John Johnston, sec 4 Feby 1748. p.602.

ARTHUR SPICER; will presented by William Brockenbrough, extr. Proved by William Daggs, John Beale and Richard Neale. John Champe, sec. 3 Mch 1648. p.609.

FRANCIS STONE; admn with will annexed to Harry Turner, Sarah Stone, the extx, releasing her right, and the other extr under age. Proved by John Nichols. Thomas Turner, gent. sec. 3 Mch 1748. p.609.

WILLIAM LONGMIRE; Susanna Longmire presents his non-cup. will. Admn granted to her. Proved by Martha Knighting[?] 3 Mch 1748. p.610.

NOTES AND QUERIES

WANTED: The ancestry of JAMES TAYLOR and wife FRANCES (died 1680) of Virginia. They had sons James (b. 1674) and Edmund and John. A MADISON chart shows a JAMES TAYLOR earlier than JAMES, husband of FRANCES. Who was he? Mrs. E. W. D.

RIDGELEY: Wanted, the parentage of Susannah Ridgeley, b. Maryland about 1796, who m. . . . . . Penn before 1815. Also wanted, the PENN family, Would like to correspond with members of either family. C. S. P. N.

SEVENTY-FIVE DOLLARS will be paid for the ancestry of CHILLIAM and MARTIN PALMER, both of Charlotte cty, Va. Facts from civil and church records desired, with exact reference, Address W. P. N. A. care of the Editor.

COLE: Particulars wanted of birth and Marriage of JOHN COLE, in Maryland; he emigrated to Kentucky. Probably son of George Cole who m. Priscilla Hooker. C. B. A. C.

THE COURT RECORDS OF NEW YORK STATE: A series of Indexes to Wills, administrations and Guardianships, of the counties of New York, from the earliest records down to 1850, will soon be published by Mr. Charles Shepard, II, 2153 California street, Washington, D. C. There will be one volume for each county, clothbound. Publication cannot, however, be undertaken, until sufficient subscriptions are received to cover the cost. The price will be between $4 and $5 for each volume. Those interested either in a single county, or in the whole series, should communicate with Mr. Shepard at once, so that he may be informed whether there is sufficient response to justify the undertaking. The first volume which will be issued will probably be that for Richmond county (Staten Island).

[The Editor of the NOTE-BOOK is sufficiently familiar with the New York records to strongly commend Mr. Shepard's purpose to publish these indices.]

COLUMBIAN PRINTING CO., INC., WASHINGTON, D. C.

Supplement for August, 1925

FAMILIES OF THE EASTERN SHORE*

CUSTIS OF VIRGINIA

JOHN CUSTIS first appears in the records of Northampton county, Virginia, on the 28 Apr 1650 (v-34): JOHN CUSTIS' land surveyed. On the 28 Feby 1650-51, Mr. JOHN CUSTICE'S certificate for 600 acres is recorded, being an assignment of right from Argoll Yardley; head rights: Mrs. Ann Yardley, JNO. CUSTIS, Dan'll Jackson, James Stanfast, Mary Stanfast, Foulkerd Obbine, Edw: Sacker, Abrh. Smith, Wm. Smith, Elizabeth Roberts, Elizabeth Mount[?] George Greene. (N-n, Va. iv-8) He is a witness in 1650 [date uncertain] (N-n, Va. iv-173.) Takes the oath to the Commonwealth, 30 Mch 1651. (N-n iv-188)

JOHN CUSTIS m. (1) ELIZABETH EYRE. "John Custis who intermarried with ELIZABETH, the relict of Robt Eyre, is to make a payment out of the estate." (L. Norf. Va., court following 16 June 1651. B-184.) [The record is very difficult and in places illegible or damaged.]

There has been found no direct statement that ELIZABETH EYRE, widow, was born ROBINSON. However, the will of ELIZABETH ROBINSON, later presented by JOHN and ALICIA CUSTIS, mentions her grandson JOHN CUSTIS, and it is fairly well established that he was not the son of the second wife, ALICIA. In a much later patent, however, JOHN CUSTIS claims rights for ELIZABETH EYRE, MARY ROBINSON, and JOHN CUSTIS, Jr. So far as the Editor knows, the baptismal name of the father of ELIZABETH CUSTIS (the widow of EYRE) has not been established. A forthcoming volume, however, will give some data which may identify the family.

CUSTIS must very shortly have removed to Northampton as a permanent residence, as he is again a witness on the 12 Jany 1651-2. (Ct 1 July 1652, iv-93). But on the 15 Apr 1652, he presents in the Lower Norfolk court, an account of the estate of Robert Eyre, dated the 11 Apr 1652. At the same court CUSTIS "who intermarried with the relict and administratrix of Robert Eyer deceased, and Simon Overzee, marchant" . . . . give security to satisfy orders against the estate of Robert Eyer, Gent., dec'd , , , , (L. Norf. C-4.)

In May, 1652, Mr. JOHN CUSTICE appears in a Northampton court case, as assignee of "Antient" Lambert, (N-n iv-85.) And in the same month as a witness to the signature of Henry Field. And again to a deed by Ward and wife to Cornelius. This time the name is CUSTIS . . . but the signature again as a witness (N-n iv-111) appears to be JOHN CUSTISE. He is a juror as JOHN CUSTICE, 7 Aug 1652. (N-n iv-96). And as Mr. JOHN CUSTICE he receives a power from John Holland, Mcht, of Dorchester, N. E. 29 Sept 1652. (N-n iv-107). Other appearances of JOHN CUSTIS in court, are not necessary for identification . . . they merely prove continued residence.

The entry under JOHN ROBINSON, Jr., 12 Oct 1652 (S. L. O. iii-123) is JOHN CURTIS, not CUSTIS.

On the 25 August, 1653, JOHN CUSTIS buys a bay mare from Argoll Yardley, and on the 13 September, two cows. On the 25 August, he buys a negro, called Doll. and on the 13 September, buys lambs. And in December he buys a cow from Thomas Savidge. (See vol. iv, N-n records.) It seems probable that about this time JOHN CUSTIS, the son, was born, and that about this time the wife died. She never appears in the records after her marriage.

15 October 1653, Mr. JOHN CUSTIS, Mcht, obtains a patent for 100 acres in Northampton county, in the middle parish, on the south side of Naswattoxe's Creek, by the Fishing Hawk branch . . . . adj. Mt. Charlton's land. The head rights are Negro Doll and George Sutch. The patent is assigned by Col. Yardley. (S. L. O. iii-57.)

The 23 November, JOHN CUSTIS, Mcht, farm-leases from Argill Yardley, Esq., land called the Old Town, with part of a neck of land beginning at the first branch that goeth from Luke Billington's to John Johnson's . . . including the leased land of Richard Hudson. (N-n, ix-233.)

A deposition made by Mr. JOHN CUSTIS, 5 Mch 1654, states that in 1652, about the last of August, Capt. Jno. Dollinge, came to his, CUSTIS', house. (N-n vii-13) So that he, CUSTIS, had a house at that date.

In 1654, 21 Apr, CUSTIS gets another patent, this time for 1400 acres. The head rights are Richard Phillips, Jno. Davis, Jno. Ball and others. (N-n v-5).

In 1654, JOHN and WILLIAM CUSTIS are witnesses to a Yardley deed to Billington.

He appears in various matters before the court for several years.

5 Dec 1654, JOHN CUSTIS, of Northampton cty, from Col. Francis Yardley, one neck of land, north side Nuswattock Creek, between two branches, commonly called Davis' Necke. (N-n vii-26).

JOHN CUSTIS, ctf for 200 acres, for the transportation of Davy Tompson and Geo. Such. L. Norf. 16 May 1655. C-46. As no "Senior" or "Junior" is mentioned, and if this be CUSTIS and not CURTIS . . . it will be seen that CUSTIS also had land in Lower Norfolk as late as 1655.

On the 22 November, 1655, JOHN CUSTIS, Senr, and JOHN CUSTIS, Jr., appear as members of a jury in a civil case. (N-n vi-16.) This item and the following, and a later reference to a JOHN CUSTIS, Jr., are the only records which would seem to show that JOHN CUSTIS of Rotterdam, was actually, for a time, in Northampton county, Virginia.

The second reference is to an assignment of a land right by Wm. Waters to Robert Tompson to which "JOHN CUSTIS, Senior," is a wit. (N-n v-106.)

On the 5 Feby 1655-6, JNO. CUSTIS appears as one of the appraisers of the estate of Maj. PETER WALKER. (N-n v-111.)

---

*See June, 1925.

The
County Court Note-Book

A Little Bulletin of History and Genealogy

October, 1925. **Vol. IV, No 5**

SHIPS IN PORT

Brig. *Margaret,* wrecked on the sand bar off Cumberland Island, Georgia. Camden, Ga. 28 Oct 1796, B-C-311.

Sloop *Peggy,* Capt. Williams, master. Camden, Ga. Mch 1801. E-216.

Barke *Phenix,* measured; built by James Fooks. Acco, Va. 1685. vi-413.

Ship *Peter;* John Younge, master. N.E.H-G. xxxix-72. 1652.

Ship or "flyboat," the *Prosperous,* of Hull. Wm. Marr of Kingston upon Hull, master. Acco, Va. 18 Mch 1678. viii-73.

Ship *Planter,* of London; Capt. Wm. Odinn[?]. L. Norf, Va. 1661.

"Scooner," the *Porpos*; Lying at Arlington in Old Plantation Creek. William Bentsol[?] agrees to hire her for one pistole to sail to Rappahannock River, and return her safely. N-n, Va. Ct. Records. 30 Dec 1754.

Ship the *Portsmouth Pink;* John Fletcher, master. Acco, Va. 1684. vi-404.

Ship *Rainbow,* of Lancaster; N-n, Va. Sept 1702. xviii-117.

Ship *Rainebowe;* Mr. Lewis Road[?] master. L. Norf, Va. 25 Nov 1657. D-113.

Sloop *Ranger;* Capt. John Martin. Va. St. Pa. 1 Mch 1720. i-198.

The *Ranger,* Capt. Benj. Hornego appears to have been a private vessel. Cal. Va. St. Pa. 1718. i-194.

Shipp *Reformacon;* Mr. Richard Ingle, master. (Also spelled Engle.) N-n, Va. 28 Apr 1643. Also 6 Jany 1645. ii-230 and iii-1. [This is the vessel and captain of which a very interesting account will be found in histories of the Eastern Shore of Virginia.]

Schooner *Reformation;* John Custis, master. [In spite of its name, this vessel carried a cargo of rum.] Acco, Va. Naval Officer's records, E & C. 28 Aug. 1782.

The *Recovery,* formerly called the *Reformacon;* Richard Ingle, master. N-n, Va. 10 Feby 1643. ii-281.

Ship *Resolution;* Mr. Richard Kelsick, commdr. Essex, Va. 1693.

Sloop *Retrieve;* Capt. Robinson, Allentown, N. J. 1778-1779. N. J. Arch.

The *Returne,* a bark; sold by Mrs. Sellick. John Lambert, master. N-n, Va. 1 May 1655. vii-17.

Ship *Richard and James;* N-n, Va. 6 Nov 1674. Also The *Richard and James;* Acco, Va. 14 Apr 1675. v-276.

Frigate *Richard Poopely.* N-n, Va. 19 Feby 1633. i-13.

Ship *Robert.* N-n, Va. 1 Feby 1635. i-47.

Sloop *Rosanna,* lying in "Acquier's" Creek, Patomoke river, Va. See will of Tho. Rose, Acco, Va. 2 Nov. 1722. xvi-172.

Shipp *The Royall Oake;* John Mellish, master; John Shepheard probably supercargo. Her harbor was Cheristone. See N-n, Va. 1661 and 1663, viii-112, and Acco, Va. 1663 and 1664; i-46. &c.

MARRIAGES BY INFERENCE*
GEORGIA RECORDS

JOHN COURSON and LIDEA SHARP. Mar. Li. Bullock cty. 2 Nov 1797.

PEIRCE CROSLEY and SUSANNAH McCOWAN. Mar. Li. Warren cty. 2 Nov 1800.

Mr. JAMES DESVERGERS and Miss MARTHA DE LA RUE, both refugees from the Island of St. Domingo, were legally m. by Walter Monteath, pastor of the Presbyterian Church in Savannah. Chatham cty. See 21 July 1797. R-113.

CHARLES HENRY DUBIGNON, of the psh of Planguenoue[?] [Dept.] of St. Brieux in Brittany, France, and ANN AMELIA NICOLAU, of Bordeaux, France, both now residing in Glynn cty. (Charles Henry a minor under gdnship of his father, Christopher Poulain Dubignon, and the sd Ann Amelia under the gdnship of Bernard Nicolau.) Glynn cty. 30 Apr 1807. R-530.

JOHN DILWORTH, Gent., and ARMARTHA [ARAMINTA] SOWERBY, widow of Henry Sowerby. Mar. contr. Camden cty. 8 June 1787. D-70.

THOMAS GRUBBS and ANN DYASS, dau. Moses. Richmond cty. Before 20 Apr 1767. A-1.

ABNER HAMMOND and NANCY JONES. Camden cty. Before 26 Mch 1797. B & C-359.

JOEL HILL and ANNY WATSON, sp. Richmond cty. Mar. Li. 11 Oct 1791.

MILES HILL and TABITHA POPE. Mar. Li. Oglethorpe cty, 26 Jany 1795.

NOAH HILL and NANCY POPE. Mar. Li. Oglethorpe cty. 28 Sept 1796.

ABRAHAM JACKSON, of Savannah, Atty-at-law, and ANN AGNESS YONGE, sp., Savannah. Mar. settlement. Chatham cty. 26 Jany 1788. R-144.

ROBERT JORDAN and SARAH MILLS. Chatham cty. Before 4 Nov 1797. R-24.

JOHN LYNN and VINCY IRBY. Mar. Li. Warren cty. 28 Oct 1805.

JOHN McINTOSH, Esq., of Glynn cty, and AGNES STEVENS, widow, of Liberty cty. Mar. contr. Glynn cty. 26 Sept 1799. C & D-333.

PLEASANT MORIMAN and NANCY BEALL. Mar. Li. Warren cty. 15 Jany 1801.

Dr. J. L. E. W. SHECUT (or Shecat) and SARAH CANNON, dau. of John and Sarah Cannon. Glynn cty. Before 13 June 1797. C & D -338.

THOMAS STONE, Esq., of Brunswick, Ga., and ELIZABETH CLUBB, widow of Thomas, of Saint Simon's Island. Mar. agreement. Glynn cty. 19 May 1799. C & D-350.

JAMES SPALDING, of Frederica, psh St. James, Mcht, and MARGERY McINTOSH, sp. Mar. contr. (The trustees were William McIntosh, Sir Patrick Houstoun, Bart., and Roger Kelsall, Esq.) Glynn cty. 5 Nov. 1772. Vol. (?) p.12.

PEYTON SKIPWITH, Jr., and CORNELIA LOTT GREENE, formerly of Newport, R. I., both of Camden cty. Mar. contr. Camden cty. 22 Apr 1802. G-83.

SAMUEL SCARBOROUGH and ELIZABETH BENNET. Bulloch cty. Mar. Li. 5 Oct 1796.

JOHN SELLERS and JANE EASTER. Bulloch cty. Mar. Li. 28 July 1798.

OBADEAH M. SALLEY and RACHEL HAMNER. Oglethorpe cty, Ga. 18 June 1805. Mar. Li.

JAMES THOMPSON and SARAH JERNIGAN, dau. of James. Bulloch cty. Before 15 Sept 1800. Misc. vol. p.32.

CHARLES WOLF and ELIZABETH MEZEL. Mar. Li. Bulloch cty. 27 Mch 1798.

ZACHARIAH YERKINS and SARAH BAILEY. Mar. Li. Bulloch cty. 16 May 1797.

MARYLAND'S NEXT OF KIN *

KENSEY JOHNS; inv. Richard Johns, Jr., of Calvert cty. 14 Dec 1719. iv-60.

JOHN and EBENEZER FRANKLIN; inv. John Evans, of Som. cty. 18 June 1720. iv-66.

SARAH NICKESSON, ELIZABETH MURRY and MARGARET KELLAM; inv. John Kelam of Som cty. 16 June 1720. iv-68.

THOMAS and JOHN NEWBOLD; inv. William Newbold of Som cty. 5 May 1720. iv-69.

ROLAND and JOHN JONES; inv. Sam'l Jones of Som cty. 8 Mch 1719-20. iv-69.

WILLIAM and THOMAS DIXON; inv. Capt. Thomas Dixon of Som cty. 9 June 1720. iv-71.

NICH: and MARY NICHOLSON, inv. John Erving of Som cty. 5 May 1720. iv-73.

FANTOLENA PENN and MARY JENKINSON; inv. Thomas Clarke of Charles cty. 26 June 1720. iv-81.

EDWARD MILES and JAMES HAGAN; inv. Henry Miles of Chas. cty. 9 May 1720. iv-82.

RALPH CRABB, "Brother to the Deceas'd, and WILLIAM WILKINSON, as being married to the Dau. of the Deces'd," Inv. of Coll Thomas Crabb, of Charles cty. 30 June 1720. iv-83.

BENJAMIN BULLOCK, Brother to the Deces'd and JOHN BULLOCK, son of the Dec. Inv. Joseph Bullock, of Talbott cty. 5 Apr 1720. iv-88.

JOHN WILSON and RICHARD DUDLEY; inv. Elizabeth Stoot of Talbot cty. 11 May 1720. iv-91.

REBECCA WEBB and ABRAHAM MORGAN; inv. John Parrat of Talbot cty. 29 Apr 1720. iv-94.

JAMES MACNEMARRA; inv. Thomas Macnemarra of Balto. cty. 24 Aug 1720. iv-99.

Inv. WM. NORRIS; "There is neither Creditor nor any Reladed to the Dec. but the wife of the Admx., and one Child under age." Balto cty. 17 Aug 1720. iv-103.

ELIZABETH STONE, widow, and three children; inv. Thomas Stone of Balto. cty. 7 Sept 1720. iv-105.

FRANCES SPRY and CALEB ESGATE; inv. James Bennett of Q. A. cty. 8 Dec 1719. iv-112.

NOTHA MACLANAHAN and CHARLES CAVENEAR; inv. Elizabeth Cavenear of Q. A. cty, 26 Oct 1719. iv-113.

LEWIS and JACOB BLANGEY; inv. Jacob Blangey of Q. A. cty. 5 Apr. 1720. iv-116.

VIN. HELMSLEY and TRUSTRAM THOMAS; inv. Philemon Hemsley of Q. A. cty. 30 May 1720. iv-119.

RICHARD POWELL and NATHANIEL WRIGHTE; inv. Nathaniel Tucker of Q. A. cty. 27 May 1720. iv-123.

MICHAEL ROACH and SUSANNA PERKINS; inv. John Perkins of Som. cty. 17 Aug 1720. iv-127.

WILLIAM BOWEN, Jr.; inv. Edward Bowen of Dor. cty. 22 July 1720. iv-135.

HILL DRUMMON; inv. Dracke Drummon of Som cty. 26 Aug 1720. iv-136.

JOHN and ANN VINSON; inv Petegrew Salsbury of Dor. cty. 20 Mch 1719. iv-140.

VIRGINIA COLONISTS

WILLIAM PULLAM, New Kent cty, 1657.

Head rights: George Morris, Ellinor Morry, Jno. Braine, Katherine Baker, Robert Tucke, Elias Williams, Humphrey Jones, Rowland Powell, Mary Clerke, Ann Clerke, Eliz: PULLUM, Tho: Blake, Judith Rowlett, Fran Falkner, James Hulett, Stephen Rogers, Vallentine Morgan, Wm. Sackwell, [Stackwell Shackwell?], Rebecca Cole, Henry Clavill.

EDWD. ROBINSON and THOMAS HALL, Lower Norfolk cty, 1656*.

Head rights: Thomas Browne and wf Ann, David Tompson, George Such.

THOMAS ROLFE, gent., James City cty, 1656*.

Head rights: Richd Gummy, John Huson, Wm. Hollyman, Katherine Hockwell, Wm. Morley, Geo. Marler.

SAMPSON ROBINS, Northampton cty, 1655.

Head rights: John Hill, Dan'll Denwood, Brian Teagle, Dun Ogle[?], C . . . Hoe [Hue?], Annis Clarke, Joane Hewis.

SAMUELL RUTLAND, Lower Norfolk cty, [date not given] [About 1655]

Head rights: Penelope Gilbert, John Bradshaw, Dorothy Bright, Aug. Addison.

JNO: ROSIER, Clerke, Westmoreland cty, 1656.

Head rights: Tho. Ardington, Georg Spell, Wm. Cowdery, John Lawrence, Andrew Rayne.

Mr. RICHARD RICE, Northumberland cty, 1656.

Head rights: Morgan Rossers, Maudlin Allen, Ann Cooper, Sarah Bride, Robert Parkes, Giles Wilson, John Drunkin [?], Tho: Davis.

FRANCIS ROBERTS, " . . . beyond the doegs Island," 1657.

Head rights: James MacDonnell, Hugh Carty, Tho. Holder, Ro: Barnes, Rob. Huett, Edmond Taylor, Richd. Johnson, Peeter Edwards, Rob. Jones, Jane Bently.

JOHN RAVEN, "on Westward side of Petomeck river above Puscatoway," 1657.

Head rights: Lancelott Heines, Peeter Greene, Patrick Davision, Eliz: Norton, Prudence Neale, *Iruna* Johnson, Margaret Bell, Jane Denny, Paule Hinson, Roger Andrews.

THOMAS ROWE, Petomeck freshes, 1657.

Head rights: Hen. Crockett, Wm. Rose, Tho. Hart, Joane Wright, Peeter White, Edwd. Whitinge, John How, Edmond Williams, Wm. Clerke, Jeffry Moore.

WILLIAM ROBERTS, Northampton cty, 1657.

Head rights: Richd. Richard, Kath. Florra, Owen Adwin, Donnath Dennis, Law. Stegg.

MAURICE ROSE, Charles City cty, 1657.

Head rights: Herbert Greene, Elizabeth Tanner, Marg. Hally, Robert Bovy, David Humphryes, John Elliott, Elinor Fowler, Alice Towardy[?], Bryan Watts, Wm. Whittingham, Tho. Beale, Robert Kerby, Antho. Royes, James Preston, Humphry Paine, Edward Carrington, Robert Smith, Fran. Hull, Wm. Wells, Arth. Arnold, Archebell Mac:Craw, John Comings, Hugh Morris, Sarah Lacie, Jane Mabbett, Henry Wrench, Tho. Wood.

WILLIAM ROBERTS, Northampton cty, 1657.

Head rights: Richard Richards, Katherine Florra, Owen Adroune, Donath Dennis, Lawrence Hogge, Jno. Williams, Elizabeth Hobson, Robert Atkins, Tho. Broadwaye, Alexander [*no surname given*], DAVID Connawin, Jno. Devrowe.

Capt. JOHN ROGERS, Northumberland cty, 1657.

Head rights: Abraham Joyce, Jno. Roe, Roro Molletta [*a mulatto*?] Rich. Smith.

RICHARD RUSSELL, Northumberland cty, 1657.

Head rights: Rich'd Eaton, Tho Arnoll, Jno. Cross, Tho. Dakin, Wm. Cutts, Charles Addams, John Varny, Stephen Trapp, Hen. Bosworth, Jane Kinge, Wm. Wilson, Su: Wilson, Giles Abbot, Joane Emmett, Abagile Hare, Wm. Pot, Sarah Pott, and three negroes.

Lt. Coll. THOMAS SWAN,* Surry cty, 1655.

Head rights: Margaret Delton, Sarah Coe, Susanna Coe, Thomas Smith, Rich. Jacksall, Jno. Sinckler, Jane Sinckler [St. Clair] Jno. Douglas, Mary Hawkins, Tegh, an Irish boy, James Leward, Michaell White, Jno. Long, Jno. Lewis, Jno. Pelloone, James Pelloone, Wm. Sanford, an Irish woman.

JOHN SYMONS,* western branch of Nansemond river, 1656.

Head rights: John Aggor [Hadger?], John Morehead, Elizabeth Hatley [Atley?] Mary Finch.

*Previously printed.

TABITHA and MATILDA SCARBURGH, Northampton cty, 1656.*

Head rights: Mackwilliam, A . . . Thomas, Jane O'Tire, Trorell[?] Ogley, Murell Jones, Horley Kanny [Hawley Kenny?], Orsell Derry, Nell O'Lanny, Morris Kiffe, Jno. Ockmond, Wm. Mory, Wm. Gowny, Jonny Wallon, Donio[?] John, Fra. Smalewell, C . . . Moore, Morley Morry, Hareo Kennell [Harry O'Kennell?] Mutton Wrist, Jno. O'William, Morcop [?] Waffeild, Henry Carey, Tirish [Irish?] Morgon. U . . . [Key?] Glannel Jerrey [probably Jerry Glannell], Cillina [Selina] Clinn, Doll O'Melle [O'Malley?] Gwallo O'Loffe [Oliff or Aliff?] Regnior Wicke, and 41 negroes.

NICHOLAS SMITH, Isle of Wight cty, 1655.

Head rights: NICHOLAS SMITH and wife SARAH.

VINCENT STANFORD, "North side of Rappahannocke," 1656.

Head rights: Rich. Colt (twice), Thomas Flood, Georg Stanley, Grace Dains or Davis, Robert Newley (twice).

PEETER STACKLEY, "in the New Pocoson, commonly called Oxford," 1655.

Head rights: Tho. Sutton, Nich. Press.

VINCENT STANFORD, north side of Rappahannock river, 1656.

Head rights: Robert Newly (twice), Antho. Barls, Tho. Walgrow, Wm. Kinge, Richard Robison, Tho. Knowles, Jno. Allen, Constant Winshew, Giles Robison, Margaret Gudloe, Mary Savary, Jone Burby, Margarett Arnoll.

THOMAS SALSBURY, Northampton cty, 1656.

Head rights: Francis Gray, his wf Alice, Mary Gray, Josua Gray, Ann Gray, Wm. Butler.

HERBERT SMITH, Gent., Westmoreland cty, 1656.

Head rights: John Ingram, John Varnham, John Simmes, Edward Stephens, Math. Skipp.

Mr. HENRY SOANES, New Kent cty, 1656.

Head rights: Robert Ellyson, Jno. Walton, Wm. Morgan, Daniell Whitby, John Lirgson, Wm. Appellton, Jno. Hathrone, Wm. Sewins, Joane Cole, Henry Pate, Ann Hardin, Ann Mattocks, Tho. Torrowgood [Thoroughgood], Abraham Harris, Wm. Stephenson, Julian Allerneck, Robert Jernis, Eliz: Pate, Susan Knott, Katherine Pate, Thomas Peckin, Jno. Whitty, Dorathy Miller, Jno. Hamellton, Denni . . . Callim[?] Robert Trueman, Wm. Jolly, Robert Cock, Jno. Hopkins, and three negroes.

JOHN SHARPE, Lancaster cty, 1655.

Head rights: Tho: Maws, Charles Thorowgood, Tobias Maynard, Jno. Macklayer, Jno. Rampe, James Rusby.

CHARLES SNEADE, Rappahannock cty, 1657.

Head rights: Geo. West, Rich: Rice, Rich: Jones, Jno: Price, Step: Hall, Anne Hall, Jno: Moore, Eliz: Moore, Giles Cooke, Gilb: May, Hannah Price, Ja: Toogood, Tho: Bird, Joane Griffith, Mary Jnoson, Peeter Wild, Geo: Bucke, Edmd: Herbert, David Jones, ("the last Right for 50 Acres for Humphrey Booth's pattent.")

The County Court Note-Book

An every-other-monthly devoted to abstracts from County Court and other records, prior to 1800, and with a department of notes and queries.

MILNOR LJUNGSTEDT, Editor and Publisher. Bethesda, Route 10, Maryland.

Published six times a year. **Subscription, two dollars and fifty cents,** in advance; must begin with the year. **Renewals, two dollars.** Advertising rates moderate.

OCTOBER, 1925
Vol. IV., No. 5

Perhaps no better example can be found of the manner in which a family history can be constructed solely upon the basis of the old Virginia County Court records, than the CUSTIS data now appearing as a Supplement to the NOTE-BOOK. The Editor has never seen or heard of any contemporary CUSTIS Bible record. There is no register of any parish of the Eastern Shore of Virginia in existence, or, if there be, no one will admit ever having seen such. Nor is there any explanation of what became of these registers. Two lists of marriages, births and burials are to be found in Northampton in a court record, but they cover two years only.

Of course, no perfect family register can be constructed without church records. They parallel and fill out the civil record The parish register recorded the birth or at least the baptism of the first-born son who bore the grandfather's name, but if the child did not live long enough to receive a cow or a cow calf and have his "mark" recorded, the civil record knows him not. So far as that record goes, he never existed. The parish register gave, not only the birth or baptism of the daughters, but their marriages. But if they died in early married life before their father, and if the father did not give them a cow or a slave or a piece of land at marriage, for all the civil records show they passed into eternity and left not a ripple in the life about them. Many of these early first wives will never be known. Occasionally a grandfather remembers them in his will, or their fathers mention their children . . . but too often merely as "the children of my daughter," or the children of "my deceased daughter."

Sentiment is not the distinguishing characteristic of the times. Having died, the dead seem to have been soon forgotten. It was a most unusual father in the old county of Surry who provided (at least he meant to) for services on the anniversary of his beloved daughter's death . . . "even if it be a thousand generations hence." And a most unusual husband (John Michaell, of Northampton,) who desired to be buried in the grave of his first wife.

But the church buried these forgotten daughters, and married their successors, and baptised the children, and could help a man to remember whether he had ten or eleven children, and whether Jonathan was John, or John, Jonathan. Could those church records be found, possibly more than a few carefully constructed families would find themselves upon most uncertain foundations . . . uncertain because of records diametrically opposed to their favored theories.

ERRATA: In the August Supplement, "Mt. Charlton," should be Mr. Charlton.

The abstracts of King George county, Virginia, probates and administrations are omitted from this issue as the Editor could not go to King George Courthouse in time to get the material. The abstracts will be continued in the DECEMBER NOTE-BOOK.

OCCASIONAL

"April 11th 1838. Maj'r P. Harralson Sir "You will please let Mr. I. Stephens have some "kind of paper that will Keep him from run-"ning about for which I Will pay you at our "next Court. Wm. Harrison"—*From the Caswell cty, N. C. marriage license bonds.*

"ABRAHAM BELUE, An Inventory of the "Estate of Abraham Belue Killed A Tory To "Wit . . . Anson County July Court 1782. OR-"DERED that the Sheriff sell the above Killed "Mans estate & return a true acc't of sales to "October Court."

ANDREW and JOHN BOURNE, late of Plymo., Devon., Eng., contracted to serve George Luke, four years from 14 April after the preceding 14 October, "in consideration of paying their passage with their mother and one child more." Staff., Va. i-16, Ct 10 Mch 1689-90.

YORK COUNTY, Charles River Parish Register. Copy at Library of Congress. "Two years registering of deaths was lost by James Shelton Clerk of this Parish." [From the context these years appear to have been parts of 1714 and 1716, and all 1715.]

THE LAST RECORD in Volume A, in the office of the Clerk of the Superior Court [this office corresponding in a general way with the Clerk of the Court in Maryland, or that part of the Clerk's duties in Virginia which does not relate to testamentary affairs] for the county of SCREVEN, GEORGIA, is this. Although the date is later than the usual limits of the NOTE-BOOK material the copyist's remarks are too apropos to pass over.

To the Justices of the Inferior Court,

Gentlemen. I have the satisfaction of informing you that I have completed the transcript of the old records and have Extra out of my Contract completely Indexed them for which Index I consider Fifty-five dollars a very moderate compensation, which will make only one hundred and Fifty dollars for work worth Four Hundred dollars—And let this remain a Monument of the Folly of ambition,

Yours most Respectfully,

Mulford Marsh. *Feby* 20, 1830 [1835?]

FROM THE FIRST BOUND RECORD OF THE COURT THAT THE EDITOR COULD FIND IN THE OFFICE OF THE CLERK OF THE COURT, AT SNOW HILL, WORCESTER COUNTY, MARYLAND.

This first record reads: June Court, 1769.

It is to be observed that part of the Proceedings of June Court in the year of our

Lord one thousand Seven hundred and Sixty-nine are Entered in Liber [blank] and there not being Sufficient Room for the Courts Proceedings the Residue are entered in this Book and to save the Trouble of turning to Liber [blank] for the Stile of the Court in that Book for anything Entered in this the Stile of the Court is also entered here as follows viz.

Worcester County SS Att a Court------ held at Snow Hill Town------Sixth day of the same Month [June]------one thousand seven hundred and Sixty-nine------Present: The Worshipful Joshua Mitchell, John Selby, Adam Spence, Cornelius Collick, Ebenezar Campbell, Milby Arkinson, Jonathan Vaughan, Nehemiah Holland, George Farrington, Esquires, his Lordships Justices. Henry Johnson Clk, Samuel Handy Shff.

[What became of Liber blank?]

CONTINUED articles COUNTY COURT NOTE-BOOK, and the dates on which they first appeared.
MARRIAGES BY INFERENCE. Began with May, 1922.
MARYLAND'S NEXT OF KIN. Began with July, 1922.
VIRGINIA COLONISTS. This alphabetized list began with July, 1924.
MARYLAND NATURALIZATIONS. Began with February, 1923.
KING GEORGE PROBATES, &c. Began with July, 1924.
The LIST of BANISHED QUAKERS. Began with November, 1924.
MILITARY NOTES, both COLONIAL and REVOLUTIONARY, and some later MILITIA NOTES, will appear in every issue, if possible.
SHIPS IN PORT, NEW ENGLANDERS AND OTHERS, INTERCOUNTY and INTERCOLONIAL, and COLONIAL FORENAMES, will appear in alternate issues or as space can be found for them.
EASTERN SHORE FAMILIES, in the form of a one-page supplement, began with June, 1925.

NOTES AND QUERIES

GRAVENRAEDT-BROWER: Margaret Brower, dau. of Adam and Deborah Brower of New Jersey, born 1724, is said to have been the wife of Andrew Gravenraedt. Gravenraedt and wife Margaret were married in 1738. Would like authority for claim that this Margaret was Margaret Brower. T. (D. C.)

CHILLIAN and MARTIN PALMER, Charlotte cty, Va. Seventy-five dollars will be paid for their ancestry. Must be proved by civil and church records. W. B. P. A.

LOWE-BARTLETT: Information wanted as to the ancestors of the JOHN LOWE, who m. 1 Feby 1700. MARY BARTLETT, dau. of Thomas Bartlett and Mary Goodchild. John Lowe was living in Bayside, Talbot County, Maryland, at the time of his death, 1726. C. F. H. S.

NAMES FROM THE EARLY RECORDS

In the records of Surry county, North Carolina, are, perhaps, the most unusual set of names yet found. They are sent to the Editor by Mr. Alfred L. Holman, Chicago, well-known for his exhaustive searches. In the deeds of this county he found the name, ICE AND SNOW, also FROST AND SNOW; both are names of individuals. A descendant of these men is now living in the county. . . . his name is FROST SNOW. In the tax-lists of one of the counties of Virginia, bordering on North Carolina, Mr. Holman found a man named HAIL SNOW, evidently of the same family.

Some time ago the Editor gave a list of odd names including GREEN HILL; another name of the same class in GREEN FEILDS [*sic*], also found in the records of the same section.

Part of the name HATHAN FETTAPACE CHANLER . . . the first two names sometimes written together . . . has turned out to be a real name and to have a recorded background. GILES FETTIPLACE and MARY PURNELL appear in the list of marriage licenses issued by the Faculty Office in London, in 1661.

Concerning the odd name, RIVER JORDAN, one of the editor's subscribers sends this explanation. "Sir William Deandon, of Devon, England, was a banner bearer in the Crusades and distinguished himself in many battles, but particularly in one upon the banks of the Jordan. In this conflict he was felled to the ground three times, but owing to his great size and strength, and to his valor, he succeeding in escaping death by the Saracens, and in keeping erect the banner of the Cross. On account of this his name was changed to JORDAN, and the motto of his house was also changed . . . the Latin reading, in translation: 'Though I fall, I rise.' . . . Following this, for generations the fore-name 'RIVER' appears in the JORDAN family in memory of this ancestor." (*Contributed by Mrs. Edwin S. Moss, who gives Prof. David Starr Jordan as authority.*)

Among the names which the Eastern Shoreites were fond of are many which are pleasant to the ear and perhaps are still made use of.

ZEPORAH MEARS had a marriage license in Accomack, 1796.

ZIPPORAH PARKER was a wit, to a will recorded in Annapolis. 1773.

ZIPPORAH PURNELL was in Worcester cty, Md. 1755.

ZIPPORAH TEAGUE in the same county. 1822.

ZEPORAH RATCLIFF, was wife of John, of Worcester cty. 1749.

ZIPPORAH BRUFF was the extx of James Bruff. Somerset cty, Md. 1787.

ZIPPORAH DAVIS was born in Worcester cty, Md., 1753.

ZIPPORAH ROBINSON m. John Webb, Jr. in 1772... this was in Connecticut.

ZIPPORAH HILL m. Hillary Potts (his third wife) in Worcester cty, Md. 1788.

ZIPPORAH CAIN was the dau. of John... this was in Edgecombe cty, N. C. His will 1755-1757.

ZIPPORAH (SEPPORAH) MASSEY, was youngest dau. of . . . Massey, Annap. Records. xxxvi-621. 1768.

Among the names which, perhaps, had some other form originally, are:

DIRECTOR LAYLOR, dau. of Arthur. Acco., Va. 1720-1.

DIRECTOR SMITH, dau. of Mr. John Smith. Also Acco. cty, 1699.

DIRECTOR ROBERTS mentioned in the will of Joane x Brooks, N-n cty, Va. 1708-9.

DIRECTOR WATSON, of N-n cty, Va. See L.C. Acco, Va. 1806-1829. p. 134.

FILLOCLEAR CHAMBERS, dau. of Francis, certainly had some other spelling. This is in Acco. cty, Va. 1746.

Another dau. of Francis Chambers was ANNABELAH, which was more common in another section, with a restricted spelling.

ANNADANEELAH BUDD, wf of Thomas, 1721, Acco. cty, was a puzzle for a long time with its various spellings, but finally resolved itself into ANNA DANELLA. However, as the "lawful wife" of Thomas, in 1718, she spells herself ANNADENALAH.

MEMORABLE WALKER was a son of Jeremiah. Elbert cty, Ga. 1792.

LEANNA MARTIN was the admx of Hezekiah. Prince William cty, Va. 1830.

LEANNA WILDY, dau. of William. Nthld cty, Va. 11 Apr 1742. 1738-1743, fo.196. This rather pretty name is found several times in the records.

But the only note the Editor has of CITIZEN BEALL, son of Basil, is from Ohio cty, West Va. 1818.

TAX LISTS OF OHIO COUNTY, WEST VIRGINIA. PERSONAL PROPERTY. 1788.

(Charles Wells' list)

(*See NOTE-BOOK for June*, 1923, *and January and November*, 1924)

Edward Armstrong, Jonas Armspoker[?] Joseph Alexander, James Anderson, John Alexander, Robert Andrews.

John Bowman, William Baxter, Edmond Baxter, Charles Bilderback, [the next name illegible], Bethell Baxter, Elizabeth Baxter, widow; Richard Brown, Philip Beal, Thomas Burton, James Browne, David Brude;

Abram Cupps, George Cox, and Nathaniel Glaze), Robert Caincaid [Kincaid], John Camell, Dennis Cahall, William Capes, (and John Hamlington), James Campbell (and James Campbell, Jr.), James Canady, Jacob Cumton, Cornelis Crawley, Abram Croxton(?), Jacob Clark, John Cowing, William Cowing, Hugh Cowing, Jacob Coughran, William Carpenter;

Sam'l Dunlap, Nicholas Davis, Thomas Davour, Nicholas Dossen;

William Engle, George Edgington, Jr., John Edgington, Isaac Edgington, Richard Ellson, Thomas Ellson, George Edgington, (and Asa[?] Edgington, and Daniel Kenny); Henry Emmons, Alexander Edy;

Reuben Freshwater, Nathaniel Fleming, John Fleming;

John Grayham, William Greathouse, (and Mikel Cain); Harmon Greathouse, Jr., Isaac Greathouse, Harman Greathouse, Jonathan Greathouse, William Gibbs, William Griffith (and John Blair and Mikel Gragon), Thomas George, Andrew Garrard, Samuel Garrard, John Godard, Joseph Godard;

William Harper, John Henderson, William Hogeling, John Hays, William Homes, Andrew Huston, James Hamlington, John Harmon, Samuel Hull, Adam Hattfield, William Hibbitt, Charles Hyle.

ENGLISH QUAKERS BANISHED BETWEEN 1660 AND 1666

(*From Besse's Sufferings of the Quakers*)

ANNE MERCER,
EDWARD MALETRAT,
FRANCIS MARLOE,
DEGORY MARSHALL,
JOHN MASON,
MARY MIDDLETON,
ELIZABETH MORTIMER,
KATHARINE MUNDAY,
EDMUND OVERED,
JOHN OTTER,
} from London or Middlesex.

FRANCIS PRIOR, from Hartfordshire.

ROBERT PATE,
THOMAS PARKER,
WILLIAM PARKER,
EDWARD PATTESON,
JOHN PEACHEL,
JAMES PEARCE,
JAMES PERNE,
JOHN PIERCE,
RICHARD POULTON,
JOHN PRICHETT,
ANNE PRIEST,
} from London or Middlesex.

LEWIS ROGERS, from Bristol.

JOHN REYNOLDS, from Hartfordshire.

ROGER ROBERTS,
JOHN RANCE,
ALICE RICHARDSON,
WIL. ROBERTS,
THOMAS ROBINS,
CHARLES ROGERS,
JOHN ROSIER,
THOMAS ROSE,
} from London or Middlesex.

JUDITH SMITH, from Berkshire.

HENRY STOUT,
HENRY SWEETING,
} from Hartfordshire.

SERVICE AND SUPPLIES COLONIAL, REVOLUTIONARY AND MILITIA

HARRISON MANLEY, Gent., presents comm'n as Ensign of militia and takes oath. Ffx cty, Va. Orders 1770-1772. p.2. 16 Apr 1770.

JAMES WREN, Gent. Takes oath as Lieut. militia. Same ct, same date. p.3.

THOMAS GUNNELL; takes oath as Lieut. militia. Ffx cty. Orders 1770-1772. 31 May 1770. p.20.

MAJ'R JOHN CARLYLE; comm'n as Commissary for provisions and stores for an expedition intended to the river Ohio. Takes oaths. Ffx cty. Orders 1754-1756. 19 Mch 1754. p.58.

Lt. Colo. GEORGE WASHINGTON, Lt. JOHN WEST, Jr., and JAMES TOWERS, take oaths pursuant to their military commissions. Ffx cty. Orders 1754-1756. 19 Mch 1754. p.58.

Ensign WILLIAM De PARAENY takes oath. Ffx cty. Orders 1754-1756. 19 Apr 1754. p.84.

THOMAS BULLETT, Gent. Takes oaths pursuant to his military comm'n. Ffx cty. Orders 1754-1756. p.82. 19 Sept 1754.

WILLIAM PEAKE was a pensioner . . . payment of pension ordered. John Wise, his att'y. Ffx cty. Orders 1788-1792. 19 Jany 1789. p.82.

THOMAS CLARKE, presents duplicate ctf that he is a pensioner. Ordered paid. Ffx cty. Orders 1783-1788. 19 May 1788. p.-506.

Ensign JOHN DEAN takes oath. Ffx cty. Orders 1754-1756. 20 Jany 1756. p.444.

Col. CATESBY COCKE takes oath. Same ct and same date.

Capt. WILLIAM RAMSAY takes oath. Ffx cty. Orders 1754-1756. 21 Jany 1756. p.448.

JABEZ PITT makes oath to an account "agt the States" amounting to one hundred and sixty-two pounds, twelve shillings and six pence, for serving as a Surgeon's Mate in the years 1778, and 1779, in the General Hospital for the middle department. Acco. 26 Feby 1784. xxxvii0-210.

RICHARD DRUMMOND, junr, is allowed for finding himself rations for two months on duty in the militia light horse, which is ordered to be certified to the Auditors. Acco. 26 Nov 1783. xxxvii0-166.

GARRET TOPPING allowed three pounds, thirteen shillings for services performed in the militia. (Same date and refs.)

WILLIAM POLK, allowed for repairing arms for the Militia, thirteen shillings. (Same date and refs.)

CHARLES SNEAD of this county, who had served as a Captain in the Continental Army, makes oath that he lost his ctf for his arrears of pay and depreciation, and entered into recognizance with Major SMITH SNEAD his security . . . . . under condition to indemnify the United States from the consequences of any person receiving any benefit from said ctf. 29 Apr 1784. Acco. xxxvii0-295.

PROBATES AND ADMINISTRATIONS RICHMOND COUNTY, VIRGINIA

WILLIAM WHELER; will presented by Nathaniel Pope, wit. 1 June, 1698. ii-296.

DECEMIA DALTON; adm. her est. to Samuel Samford. 1 June, 1698. ii-296.

EDWARD LEWIS, adm. his est. to Martha Hammond and Mary his wife (as nearest of kin). 1 June, 1698. ii-297.

JOHN ALLIN; will presented by Cornelius McCarty, wit. 1 June, 1698. ii-298.

JOHN CARRELL; will proved by John Hardy & Edward Russell. Probate to John Size, Extr. 1 June, 1698. ii-298.

RICHARD DUDLEY; will presented by Richard Jesper Sr., & Thomas Jesper, Extrs. Proved by George Madox & Henry Heyes, wit. 1 June, 1698. ii-298.

JOHN JENNINGS; adm. his est. to Ann Jennings, Widow Relict of sd. John. George Payne & Neb: Jones, sec. 1 June, 1698. ii-299.

Capt. ALEXANDER NEWMAN; will presented by Mrs. Elizabeth Newman, extx. Proved by Wm. Woodbridge & Geo. Woodbridge. Probate to extx. 1 June, 1698. ii-299.

RICHARD SHIPPIE; will presented by James Shippie, extr. Proved by Luke, William Simmes & George Barnett. 1 June, 1698. ii-299.

PHILLIP COUZENS; will presented by James Trent, extr. Proved by Francis Stone & Richard Hayden. 1 June, 1698. ii-299.

KITT a Christian Indian; will presented in Ct., was proved by William Hutson & Thomas Davis. Probate to John Jones, extr. 1 June, 1698. ii-300.

JOHN KERBY; adm. his est. to Elizabeth Kerby, widow. George Gibbs & Thos. Tayler, sec. 1 June, 1698. ii-300.

WILLIAM JEFFERYES; adm. his est. to Thomas Tayler. 1 June, 1698. ii-300.

DAVID ROSER; adm. his est. to Margarett Roser, wife. Francis Stone & Francis Triplett, sec. 1 June, 1698. ii-300.

FRANCIS TAYLOR; will presented by Charles Snead, extr. Proved by John Bernard. 1 June, 1698. ii-306.

THOMAS TRIPLETT; will presented by Margritt, extx. Proved by Peter Rawlls. 6 July, 1698. ii-311.

JOHN TAVENER; will presented by his dau. Sarah & his son James Tavener, extr, & Samuel Peachey & John Baker. 6 July, 1698. ii-311.

ROBERT SISSON; will presented by Ralph Berkley, William Lawson & Thomas Lewis. 6 July, 1698. ii-311.

JOHN LANDMAN; will presented by extr. Proved by Abigall Sisson. 6 July, 1698. ii-311.

HENRY LEWIS; will presented by Mary, his Relict & extx. Proved by William Smith. 6 July, 1698. ii-312.

WILLIAM WHELER; will presented by Lewis Markham, extr. Proved by Nathaniel Pope & Walther Anderson. 6 July, 1698. ii-313.

WILLIAM POWELL; admn. his est. to Joseph Dike. 6 July, 1698. ii-326.

JAMES KEY; admn. his est. to Mrs. Mary Key, widow. 6 July, 1698. ii-330.

WILLIAM JETT; will presented by Elizabeth his wife, extx. Proved by William Underwood & George Green. 6 July, 1698. ii-331.

RICHARD WHARTON; will presented by Neb: Jones & James Scott, extrs. Proved by John Tillett & Thomas Smyth. 6 July, 1698. ii-331.

COLUMBIAN PRINTING CO., INC., WASHINGTON, D. C.

Supplement for October, 1925

FAMILIES OF THE EASTERN SHORE*

CUSTIS OF VIRGINIA

JOHN CUSTIS m. (2) ALICIA WALKER, widow of Maj. PETER WALKER. The date of this marriage was before 26 June 1656. On that date he presents a true list of the cattle in his hands belonging to "orphants." and an account. The "orphants" are George Traveller, Francis Walker, Elizabeth Walker, Argoll Yardley. (N-n vii-34.) On the 27 June, 1656, JNO. CUSTIS, "who married the administratrix and relict of Maj. Peter Walker" . . . receives a bond from Jno. Michaell. (N-n vii-35.) On the 8 August 1656, Mrs. ALICIA WALKER, "now the wife of Mr. JOHN CUSTIS, did present the inventory of the estate of her late husband, Major Peter Walker, deceased." (N-n v-111.)

ALICIA [there seems reason to believe that she was also called ELISHEBA] WALKER was born about 1616. (N-n viii-151.) Her maiden name is unknown. Her first husband was George Traveller (see N-n xi-135.) After his death she married William Burdette, who died before the 31 August, 1643 (N-n ii-253), and she then married Maj. Peter Walker. A quaint record of a suit for slander shows that she had at one time lived on the "Western Shore." There is no record of any CUSTIS children by ALICIA (——) (TRAVELLER) (BURDETTE) (WALKER) CUSTIS.

ALICIA CUSTIS appears in the records many times, as ALICIA TRAVELLER, ALICIA BURDETTE, and ALICIA WALKER, and signs by "mark" as late as 1655. GEORGE TRAVELLER, her first husband, was in Northampton county (then Accomack) as early as 1633, perhaps before that. (N-n, i-5.) He bought land of Roger Sanders in 1634, and he and Capt. Roper were admrs of an estate in 1636. He was a coroner's juror in 1640, and the 3d of August that year, claims a ctf. for 150 acres. (N-n ii-22.) On the same date he is referred to as "Goodman Traveller," which would seem to show that he was, at least, not a young man. There is a very interesting record concerning his land, the 1 Feby. 1640 (N-n ii-53). His will is dated 10 Feby. 1642; in that he mentions his son George and daughter Elizabeth, who is to be of age at fifteen or at marriage. Makes wife, "Alice," extx. He died that month. (N-n ii-209.) The widow, ALICE or ALICIA TRAVELLER, married WILLIAM BURDETTE about the 28 Apr. 1643. (N-n ii-231.) [These dates are all Old Style.]

Mr. WILLIAM BURDETTE was also on the Eastern Shore at an early date. That he had a wife before the widow TRAVELLER, is shown by the records. (See N-n i-12. 19 Feby. 1642.) That he was a widower in 1633 is shown by a very quaint record in which a certain Scovell makes a wager that "Mr. Burdette should never have the widow Sanders." (N-n i-12.)

Mrs. ALICE [ALICIA] BURDETTE was still a widow the 31 Aug. 1643, as Capt. William Roper denies before the Court that there was a health drunk at the house of Mrs. Burdett "to the damnation of * * * [illegible] and the confusion of Parliament." (N-n ii-253.) On the 10 Feb. same year, she was still a widow. (N-n ii-298.)

PETER WALKER, who was the next husband of ALICIA, was born about 1617 (N-n i-154), and gets ctf. for plantation at "Maggeti Baye" in 1640. (N-n i-162.) In 1644 he was the guardian of Edmund Bibbye. It is not improbable that he had a first wife who was related to the Bibbys. A record of 20 Sept. 1644 mentions PETER WALKER, of Virginia, planter, son of Andrew Walker, citizen and Tallow Chandler of London. (N-n ii-340.) PETER WALKER [Jr.] who is mentioned in 1645 as the godson of the elder PETER and his wife ALICIA, was the son of Henry Walker. He had a sister Elizabeth, and another sister Bethewell Walker. (See N-n iii-89 and 94.) WALKER had 150 acres on Old Plantation Creek (S. L. O. ii-44), but in 1641 conveys half his plantation called "Maggetye Baye" to William Fisher. (N-n ii-127.)

He married the widow BURDETTE before 28 Jany 1645-6. (N-n iii-12) WALKER is mentioned as a Justice in 1654-5, and died about the 29 Jany 1655-6. (N-n v-111.) The widow WALKER married JOHN CUSTIS on or before the 26 June 1656. Probably about that date. [See preceding note.]

ALICIA CUSTIS continues to appear in the records, sometimes as acting for her husband in his absence, as when she petitions concerning the "spoyle" done to the orchards of Argoll Yardley, orpht. (29 Apr 1661, N-n viii-94.) "ALISHA" CUSTIS is the foreman of a jury of women, 28 Jany 1661. (N-n viii-124.) In a quaint deposition 29 Dec 1662, she states that she is about 46 years old. (N-n viii-151) so that she was born about 1616, and was considerably older than her CUSTIS husband. She gives notice, 31 Oct 1672, of rope, sail, &c. taken up on Smith's Island, Capt. CUSTIS' land. (N-n x-163.) As the wife of Maj.-Gen'l JOHN CUSTIS, she quit-claims her interest in land which was granted "to her first husband, GEORGE TRAVELLER," to her granddaughter and her granddaughter's husband, Elisheba and Peter Reverdy. (29 Jany 1676-7. N-n xi-135) (It is to be noted that Elisheba's husband calls himself "Peter Reverdy als Greene, Gent." in a conveyance of land in 1676-7. N-n xi-136.) No record of the death of ALICIA CUSTIS is found.

On the 19 July 1676 (Acco. vii-14), Col. JOHN CUSTIS appears as an appraiser of the estate of Mr. "Devorax" Browne. He is a witness to a letter by TABITHA BROWNE [widow] to her attorney, Holden, 1 Aug. 1677, (N-n xii-234) and appears in Court concerning a servant "of Mrs. TABITHA BROWNE now CUSTIS' servant" 16 Mch. 1679-80. (Acco. viii-156.) and again on the 16th Aug. 1681, "as marrying TABITHA BROWN, admx in the behalf of Devorax Browne on the estate of Robert Pitt." (Acco. viii-249.)

JOHN CUSTIS m. (3) TABITHA (SCARBURGH) (SMART) Browne, the dau. of Lt. Col. Edmund Scarburgh and his wife MARY (......) and the widow of John Smart and Devereux Browne.

[Note: The SCARBURGH family has been so often written up (and so often argued over), and Mme. TABITHA HILL as she is usually called * * * she having survived Maj.-Gen'l JOHN CUSTIS and m. (4) Col. Edmund Hill * * * appearing so often in every published account of these families and history of this section, the Editor omits her numerous Scarburgh notes for the time being, merely adding that TABITHA SCARBURGH was born about 1640. (N-n xvii-235.) and m. her first husband, Smart, about 1653. The records show that she had a daughter Tabitha Smart and a son Edmund Browne. She died between August and January, 1717. (Acco. xvi-37.)]

*See June, 1925.

The
County Court Note-Book

A Little Bulletin of History and Genealogy

December, 1925. **Vol. IV, No 6**

THE COUNTIES OF VIRGINIA FORMED BEFORE 1800*

(Arranged in related groups)

NORTHAMPTON, 1634; Accomack, 1663.

CHARLES CITY, 1634; Prince George, 1703; Brunswick, 1732; Lunenburg, 1746; Halifax, 1752; Pittsylvania, 1767; Henry, 1777; Patrick, 1791.

(*Lunenburg*) Bedford, 1754; Campbell, 1782.
(*Bedford*) Franklin, 1786.
(*Lunenburg*) Charlotte, 1765.
(*Lunenburg*) Mecklenburg, 1765.
(*Brunswick*) Greensville, 1781.
(*Prince George*) Amelia, 1735; Prince Edward, 1754.
(*Amelia*) Nottoway, 1789.
(*Prince George*) Dinwiddie, 1752.

YORK, 1634; Gloucester, 1651; Mathews 1791.
(*York*) New Kent? 1654; King and Queen, 1791; King William, 1702.
(*New Kent*) Hanover, 1721; Louisa, 1742.

ELIZABETH CITY, 1634; Norfolk, 1636.
(*Norfolk*) Princess Anne, 1691.
(*Norfolk*) Nansemond, 1642.

HENRICO, 1634; Goochland, 1728; Albemarle, 1744; Amherst, 1761.
(*Albemarle*) Buckingham 1761.
(*Albermarle*) Fluvanna, 1777.
(*Goochland*) Cumberland, 1749; Powhatan, 1777.
(*Henrico*) Chesterfield, 1749.

JAMES CITY, 1634; Surry, 1652; Sussex, 1754.

ISLE OF WIGHT, 1634; Southampton, 1749.

WARWICK, 1634.

NORTHUMBERLAND, 1648; Lancaster, 1651; Essex, 1692; Caroline, 1728.
(*Essex*) Spotsylvania, 1721; Orange, 1734; Frederick, 1743; Shenandoah, 1778.
(*Lancaster*) Richmond, 1692; King George, 1721.
(*Orange*) Augusta, 1745; Botetourt, 1770; Montgomery, 1777; Wythe, 1790; Grayson, 1793.
(*Botetourt*) Washington, 1777; Russell, 1786; Lee, 1793.
(*Augusta*) Rockbridge, 1778.
(*Augusta*) Rockingham, 1778.
(*Augusta*) Bath, 1791.
(*Orange*) Culpeper, 1749; Madison, 1793.
(*Lancaster*) Middlesex, 1673.
(*Northumberland*) Westmoreland, 1653; Stafford, 1664; Prince William, 1731; Fairfax, 1742; Loudoun, 1757.
(*Prince William*) Fauquier, 1759.

---

*See note on page 45.

INTERCOUNTY AND INTERCOLONIAL

JOHN S. ADAMS, in his will, mentions his interest in a certain freehold in the village of Randalstown, in the county of Antrim, Ireland, bequeathed to him by his father. Charleston, S. C. 3 May 1809. E-294.

THOMAS COE, of Kent cty upon Delaware; deed to John Riley of Acco. Acco., Va. 4 Dec 1734. xx-185.

ADAM CHRYSTIE, of the province of West Florida, Esq., bond. Charleston, S. C. 20 Oct 1784. TT-10.

ELIZABETH HEWS, formerly wife of Dorman Sullivant, of Acco., now wf of William Hews, of Stafford cty, Va. Power to John Watson to release her dower in land sold by her son. Acco., Va. 30 Aug 1708. xi-456.

THOMAS JOHNSON and wf Elizabeth, of Cecill cty, Md., to Josias Macey, Dor. cty, Md., tract called Browne's Rest. Dor., Md. 10 May 1705. vi-64.

JOHN KERR, Rowan cty, N. C., yeoman, extr of Wm. McKnight, late of sd cty, to James Wilson, West Namtmel, Chester cty, Penna., yeoman, and Francis Alexander, same. Chester cty, Pa. 20 May 1761 M2-7

GEORGE LUCAS, Esq., late of the Island of Antigua, now of South Carolina; bond to Richard Boddicott of London. Charleston, S C. 3 Nov 1739. T-614.

LUKE MANLOVE [sig.] and wf Anne, of the Territories of Pensilvania in the county of Kent, farmer, to John Rider, of the county of Dorchester, all that tract called Penninepoint, south side of Ireland Creeke . . . 100 acres. Dor. cty, Md. 5 Nov 1707. vi-104.

MORRIS MATHEWS, of Great Chontank, Dor. cty, Md. Power to Mr. Devereux Browne to ackn. sale of land at Nandua. Acco. cty, Va. 19 July 1671. iv-7.

DENNIS MORRIS, being charged with concealing tithes in 1696, pleads that he was living in the Govt of *Penna.* from April to July, and John Morris makes himself security. Acco. cty, Va. 4 Feby 1696. x-221.

WILLIAM MERIWETHER, of the psh of St. Paul, New Kent, Va., to John Spratley, two tracts on Blackwater (1280 a.) formerly granted to Nicholas Meriwether, Gent. late of Surry, who was grandfather to the sd William. Surry cty, Va. 16 July 1711. iii-66.

THOMAS MARSH, of Providence, Md., Gent., and wf Sarah. L. Norf. cty, Va. 1658. D-154.

FRANCIS MARTIN'S wife came from New England. N-n cty, Va. 12 Nov 1642. ii-199.

MARRIAGES BY INFERENCE*

VIRGINIA RECORDS

JOHN ARRIS [*sic*] and Frances SPENCER, dau. of John, Gent., late of Cople psh. Before 28 Mch 1726. Wmld, viii(1)-279.

THOMAS ALLEN and ELIZABETH BANKS, dau. James, Sr. Before 18 May 1785. Essex, xii-502.

JOHN ANDERSON and the widow of Mr. Joseph Wildy. Before 10 May 1779. Nthd, x-455.

WILLIAM BLACKERBY, psh Wico., and ELISABETH HILL, same. Mar. contr. 30 Oct 1765. Nthd, vi-660.

THOMAS BACON and ELIZA: HAGGETT, [This is doubtful. ELIZA: BACON wid., may have m. HAGGETT . . . perhaps HUMPHREY.] Before 21 Dec 1657. Wmld, i-89.

Mr. WILLIAM BANKS and ELIZABETH ROBINSON [dau. of Henry?] Before 28 Jany 1765. Essex, xii-296.

WILLIAM BROOKIN [?] SALE and NANCY DAVIS. Before 20 Feby 1804. Essex, xvi-267.

LAWRENCE BARKER and the Relict of Mathew KELLEY. Before 3 Jany 1693. Richmd, Orders.

THOMAS CHILTON and SARAH CHINN, dau. John, Sr. Before 15 Dec 1691. Lanc., viii-34.

Sir HEN: CHICHELEY, of Rappahannock in the cty of Lancaster, Knt, and Dame AGATHA WORMLEY, late widow of Coll. Ralph Wormley. Before 18 Apr 1654. Lanc, i-129.

Maj. . . . . CARTER and the relict of Capt. Will. BROCAS. Before 26 July 1656. Lanc, ii-120.

WILLIAM COLES and SARAH WILDY, dau. Joseph. Before 10 May 1779. Nthd, x-455.

WILLIAM COOPER and ELIZABETH, dau. of Mary Billington. [At this date Elizabeth was deceased.] See 23 July 1727. Essex, iv-248.

JAMES COWARD and MARY COLLIDGE, wid. *Hezechia*. Before 3 Jany 1693. Richmd, Orders.

WILLIAM COOPER, Jr., Planter, of Brunswick cty, and WINIFRED FORREST, dau. Benjamin. Before 16 Oct 1764. Nthld, vi-522.

JOHN COLLINS, of Rappa. and dau. of Mr. Abraham WEEKES, of Middx. [Collins was dec'd at the date of this refs.] Before 7 July 1686. Essex, Orders, 232.

WILLIAM COLSTON and Mrs. ANN HULL. Before or about 19 May 1686. Rappa, Orders, 231.

DENNIS COMERON and JANE WELSH, wid. Walter. Before 4 Oct 1693. Richmd, Orders,

JOHN CRASK and ELIZABETH MOSS, youngest dau. Wm. Moss, Sr. Before 7 Dec 1693. Richmd, Orders.

ELISHA EDWARDS and dau, of George BERRY. Before 24 Jany 1758. Nthd, iv-190.

GEORGE FINCH prob. m. ANN, the dau, of Frances Pritchard. Before 2 Oct 1679. Lanc., v-67.

*Copyright, 1925, Pauline Stewart Crosley.

Capt. DAVID FOX and HANNAH, the dau. of Hannah Ball, who was the widow of Col. William Ball. Before 5 Dec 1694. Lanc., viii-51. [See also 9 Oct 1695.]

GABRIEL JONES and MARY EDMUNDSON, wid. John. Before 18 Nov 1735. Essex, v-45.

RODERICK JONES and MARY, late svt to Robt Henly. Before 3 Sept 1685. Rappa., Orders, 163.

MARYLAND'S NEXT OF KIN*

HENRY GUNALL and ANNE HOOPER; inv. Richard Hooper, Dor. cty. 25 July, 1720. iv-142.

DAVID CORSON and JOHN CORSON; inv. David Corson, Dor. cty. 30 July 1720. iv-143.

EDWARD TAYLOR and WILLIAM PHILPOT; inv. Stephen Ross, Dor. cty. 10 Aug 1720. iv-144.

"The Kin refuseth to signe;" inv. Stephen Warner, Dor. cty. 29 Sept 1718. iv-146.

WILLIAM ARENTON; inv. Prudence Woolman, Talbott cty. 1 Sept 1720. iv-150.

THOMAS BERRY and THOMAS PEALL; inv. John Berry, Talbott cty. 11 May 1720. iv-150.

JAMES HURLOCK and AMBROSE FORD; inv. Ambrose Ford, Talbott cty. 31 May 1720. iv-160.

JOHN and PHILEMON EMERSON; inv. Maj. Thomas Emerson, Talbott cty. 30 July 1720. iv-165.

MORRICE and ANDREW OROM; inv. Arthur Rigby, Talbot cty. 26 Sept 1720. iv-174.

THOMAS, CHARLES and ELIZABETH GORSUCH; inv. Robert Gorsuch, Balto. cty. 12 Sept 1720. iv-177.

BENJAMIN and THOMAS OSBURN; inv. Wm. Loney, Balto. cty. 13 Sept 1720. iv-182.

LAUGHLIN and EDWARD MacDANIELL; inv. Laughlin MacDaniell. Talbot cty. 22 Apr 1720. iv-189.

JOSEPH and WINIFURT WHEATLEY; inv. James Wheatly, St. Mary's cty. 15 Dec 1720. iv-195.

ELIZABETH and REBECCA ASKIN; inv. Wm. Askin, St. Mary's cty. 10 Jany 1720. iv-195.

EDWARD BAXTER; inv. Richard Baxter, St. Mary's cty. 1 Dec 1720. iv-196.

NICHOLAS LOWE and JAMES BOWLES; inv. Henry Lowe. Eastern Shore. 19 Apr 1720. iv-207.

ABRAHAM and ISAAC SIMMONS; inv. Geo. Simmons, A. A. cty. 3 Oct 1720. iv-207.

JOHN RAWLINGS and NICHOLAS REDGLEY; inv. Richard Rawlings, A. A. cty. 28 June 1719. iv-208.

THOMAS JONES; inv. Wm. Jones, Kent cty. 15 Aug 1720. iv-213.

ROSE and PHILLIP HISSETT; inv. Phillip Hissett, Kent cty. 29 Aug 1720. iv-214.

JEAN CLEMANS and JOHN PHILIPS; inv. John Cleamons. Q. A. cty. 23 Aug 1720. iv-218.

JOHN and JAMES CHAIRES; inv. Robert Walker, Q. A. cty. 16 June 1720. iv-219.

*Copyright, Mrs. Geo. W. Hodges, 1925.

MARK BENTON; inv. Francis Benton, Q. A. cty. 16 June 1720. iv-221.
JAMES and JOHN WILLIAMS; inv. James Williams, Senr, Q. A. cty. 9 Apr 1720. iv-222.
JOHN and WILLIAM HARPER; inv. William Harper, Dor. cty. 3 Sept 1720. iv-224.
JOHN MENIES [MENICS?] and ENOCK BARLLINTON, Jr.; inv. Enoch Barllinton, Dor. cty. 6 Aug 1720. iv-225.
WILLIAM DOXEY; inv. James Doxey, St. Mary's cty. 10 Oct 1720. iv-227.
T. T. GREENFIELD [Thomas Truman Grenfield]; inv. Peregrine [Jowles?], St. Mary's cty, 24 Aug 1720. iv-228.

VIRGINIA COLONISTS

(From Old Volume, 5, S. L. O.)

WILLIAM STEPHENS "on Black Swamp" (partly in Warwick cty), 1657.
Head rights: James [?] Colles, Rich. Partlett, Math. Perry, May Purgrave, Edmund Ivory, and a negro.
RICHARD SPANN, Northumberland cty, 1657.
Head rights: Mary Alcock.
TOBY SMITH, Gent., Rappahannock cty, 1657.
Head rights: Abigall Ridge, Thomas Crowder[?], Seth. Edwards, Tho. Bumbridge, Wm. Swann, Wm. Talbott, Jno. Warner, Jno. Clouen, Katherine . . . . . . [?]
HENRY SAYNE, "at the head of the upright branch of the Estermost River," 1657.
Head rights: Wm. Miller.
GEORG SMITH, New Kent cty, 1657.
Head rights: James Davis, Tho. Redinge, Roger Gibbs, Edward Darry, Mary Crusty[?] Eliz: Smith, Mary Codin, Jone Walter.
PEETER SMITH, Petomeck freshes, 1657.
Head rights: Rob: Clerke, Rob. Holmes, Math. Wardle, Anne Hamond, Tho. Dorwood, Anne Forty, John Ayres, Francis Ayres, Richd. Hardman, Tho. Webster.
Capt. JOHN SMITH, Gloucester cty, 1657.
Head rights: Thomas Lucy, Georg Lucy, Jno. Drewe, Tho. Berry, Richard Langley, Wm. Pritchett, Katherine Rock, Margarett Watten, Jane Hutchison, Jno. Readman.
GEORG SEATON, Westmoreland cty, 1657.
Head rights: Ann Kinge, Cary Fitts, Jno. Burton, Daniell Mokay, John Hill, Hutton Tritter[?].
WM. SHORTE and WM. LIPPEATE, Lancaster cty, 1657.
Head rights: Teage Flide [Floyd] and Eliz: his wife; Robert Milliscent, Jno. Braddie, Alice Jaxon, Constant Harrwood, Henry Barten, Giles Kinge.
THOMAS STRATTON, Northampton cty, 1657.
Head rights: Ann Cley, Wm. Collum, John Dency, Darman Nehuelian, Mary Turrough, Margaret Irish [Irish woman?]
JOHN SMITH and WILLIAM SMITH, Western branch of Patomeck freshes, 1657.
Head rights: Mathew Hill, Ann Smith, Sarah Smith, Rose Gilbert, Jno. Clare, Wm. Stratford, Mary Stratford, Alice Rogers, Ralph Lee, Su: Loe [Lee?]
Capt. EDWARD STREATER, Westmoreland cty, 1657.
Head rights: Miles Atkinson, Wm. Brickwell, Rich. Hogson, Thompson Symons, Wm. Massinborne, Eliz: Hooper, Jno. Ware, Jno. Debarr, Mary Benfor, Rob. Niccolls, Rich. Goodman, Jno. Throught, Wm. Higginbottom, Jno. Morgan, Bryan Harkin, Rich. Stanton, Donaughe [Donnack, Donath] Bryan, Wm. Stephens, Wm. Sharpe, Eliz: Brooke, Dennis Shollman [perhaps Sullivan?], Edwd. Jones, Edwd. Tanner, Roger Preston, Tho. Beedles, Robert Mason, Wm. Wildy, Andrew Bonny, Eliz: Ackers, Rob.Brenore, Wm. Mundy, Rowland Trevers, Edmond Methoe, Wm. Hurden, Clemence Herbert, Dan'l Waller, Garrett Sennett, Edwd Legge, Wm. Clemence, Wm. Paine, Roger Wilkins, Margaret Davis, Mary Seamore, Jno. Clerke, Jno. Henland, Geo. Merritt, Rich. Browne, Rob. Younge, Tho. Ringe, Wm. Webb, Jno. Tunstead, Jno. Hackev, Fran: Stephens, Sam. Yates, Nath. Palley [Talley?], Jno. Penry, Wm. Breeham, Wm. Greens, Richard Nelmes, Wm. Rayle.
GEORGE TRUETT, Northampton cty, 1655.*
Head rights: Alice Watson, John Omarwrare, MackWm. Owen, John Huntley, James Oger, Thomas Jones.
HUMPHRY TAB, Elizabeth City cty, 1656.
Head rights: Rich: Lowe, Wm. Allen, Thomas Tompson, Andrew Blarke [Blacke?]
WILLIAM TAYLOR, Northampton cty, 1655.
Head rights: Barth: Meares, Oneale Bulker [Balker?].
Mr. RICHMOND TERRILL, New Kent cty, 1656.
Head rights: RICHMOND TERRELL, Thomas Elsford, Nicholas Jarsey [?], Wm. Spillamore [?], Thomas Knight, Marth: Kirke, Israell Hardeman, Dorothy Gibson, Francis Cole, David Causey, "The Transportacon of ROBERT TERRELL Sevrll Tymes."
WILLIAM THOMAS, Westmoreland cty, 1657.
Head rights: Fra. Low, Xph. Dansfield, Wm. Hutchins, Rob. Baymond, Wm. Salter, Wm. Smith, Barnaby French, Sam Smith, "Six hundred acres . . . to Geo. Lob . . . assigned to Jno. Wood . . . by Wood assigned to Thomas the Names beinge omitted to bee inserted in the Certificate."
JOHN TINGY, Upon Petomeck river in the freshes, 1657.
Head rights: Isaack Hart, Wm. Hatly, Mary Meredith, Kath. Hermy, Ales Foy, Jeffry Munson, Tho. Dallison, Jno. Hall, Dan Ross, Marmaduk Clanton.
THOMAS TANNER, Charles City cty, 1657.
Head rights: Richard Hughes, Edward Willson, Arthur Downes, Robert Wyes, John Price, Ann Tinker.
Mr. THOMAS TEAGLE, Minister, Northampton cty, 1658.
Head rights: Andrew Abernath, Artr. Gillett, Patrick Comball, Thomas Davis.
GEORGE THOMPSON, Lancaster cty, 1657.
Head rights: Robert Franke, Elizabeth Woolbridge, Giles Sallett, Jno. Patriarch, Gloys Blaze, Jno. Guy, Tho. Peteete, James Fisher.
JOHN TEAGE and EDWARD MORGAN, North side Horne Harbor Creeke, 1657.
Head rights: Jno. Peade, Richard Cheny, Wm. South.

The County Court Note-Book

An every-other-monthly devoted to abstracts from County Court and other records, prior to 1800, and with a department of notes and queries.

MILNOR LJUNGSTEDT, Editor and Publisher. Bethesda, Route 10, Maryland.

Published six times a year. Subscription, two dollars, in advance; must begin with the year. Advertising rates moderate.

DECEMBER, 1925
Vol. IV., No. 6

THE ODDITIES OF FINDINGS

There is a record book in the Court of Ordinary, in Elbert county, Georgia, which was printed and sold by John Grigg, No. 9, N. Fourth street, Philadelphia. It contains the minutes of the Court and begins in 1830. The cover of the volume bears the eagle, with olive branch, arrows, Mercury's caduceus, stars, and *E pluribus unum.* Underneath the eagle is *"The Eagle suffers little Birds to sing."* Beneath this motto is a wood cut of cavalry, and guns, the soldiers with swords erect and stiff plumes in their hats . . . some Napoleonic style and some more like helmets . . . and beneath this war-like print the following verses:

"The Gallant soldier in his country's cause
Moves bravely on and gains a just applause.
And those who forward in their studies press,
Shall from their friends and country gain no less."

The back cover of the volume is given over to advertisements. One of these follows: it is headed New School Books. John Grigg, No. 9, N. Fourth St. Philadelphia.

A PLEASING COMPANION FOR LITTLE GIRLS AND BOYS, blending instruction with Amusement; being a selection of interesting Stories, Dialogues, Fables and Poetry. Designed for the use of Primary Schools and Domestic Nurseries. By Jesse Torrey, Jun. Preferred generally to Murray's Introduction, and works of that class.

Report of the Committee of the Philadelphia Academy of Teachers: adopted . . . The Committee to whom was referred Mr. Jesse Torrey's "Pleasing Companion for Little Girls and Boys" beg to report, That they have perused the "Pleasing Companion," and have much pleasure in pronouncing as their opinion, that it is a compilation much better calculated for the exercise and improvement of small children in the art of reading, and especially in the more rare art of understanding what they read, than the books in general use. All of which is respectfully submitted, I. I. Hitchcock, Pardon Davis, Charles Mean, Committee.

Curiosity led the Editor to the Library of Congress, where a little research developed the following. The Pleasing Companion, first published in 1824, reached its twenty-fifth edition in 1825, and was still being published as late as 1844. The Elm Tree Press, of Woodstock, Vermont, has brought out in the "Librarians Series," a very interesting account of Jesse Torrey, Jr., with reprints. Torrey was an anti-slavery agitator, an advocate of popular education, a total abstinence pioneer, and the projector of free libraries. The oddity of finding the advertisement of his "Pleasing Companion" in a Georgia county Probate Court strikes the Editor as worthy of note . . . and for his project of free libraries, he deserves at least a tablet.

The Editor desires to express her thanks for the courtesy of the young lady deputy who copied the "ad." for her, whose very pretty name was *Eulalia.*

AND HAPPY ACCIDENTS

The Editor is quite unable to say how long she mulled over that curious name, hitherto mentioned in the NOTE-BOOK, HATHAN FETTAPACE CHANLER. Back and forth through the records she searched, and the records varied mightily. No one knew anything more about it than the Editor. Suggestions included "Nathan Set-a-place." That there was such a name as Fettapace or Fettaplace, the English records finally showed and now the following turns up, and this, it is at once perceived, is of ancestral value.

MICHAEL PHETTIPLACE, WILLIAM PHETTIPLACE, and RICHARD WIFFING, Gentlemen, and Souldiers under Captain Smiths Command: In his deserved honor for his Worke, and worth.*

WHy may not we in this Worke have our Mite,
That had our share in each black day and night,
When thou Virginia soild'st, yet Kept'st unstained;
And held'st the King of Paspeheh enchained.
Thou all alone in Salvage sterne didst take.
Pamunkes king wee saw thee captive make
Among seven hundred of his stoutest men,
To murther thee and us resolved; when
Fast by the hand thou ledst this Salvage grim,
Thy Pistoll at his breast to governe him:
Which did infuse such awe in all the rest
(Sith their drad Sovereraigne thou had'st so distrest)
That thou and wee (poore sixteene) safe retir'd
Unto our helpless ships. Thou (thus admir'd)
Didst make proud Powhatan, his subjects send
To James his Towne, thy censure to attend:
And all Virginia's Lords, and pettie Kings,
Aw'd by thy vertue, crouch, and Presents brings,
To gaine thy grace; so dreaded thou hast beene:
And yet a heart more milde is seldom scene,
* * * * * * * * * * * *
And for this paines of thine wee praise thee rather,
That future times may know who was the father
Of this rare Worke (*New England*) which may bring
Praise to thy God, and profit to thy King.

The omitted verses do not recount any more of Capt John Smith's strong-arm methods with the unfortunate Indians, but are merely an interesting study of the preciosity of the rhymed composition of the age.

It would seem that a descendent, one or

*See Peter Force's Tracts. Vol ii, Tract 1.

more, of the gallant *Phettiplaces* must have lived in the Eastern Shore counties of Virginia.

Note: The information upon which the list of Virginia Counties is based, is drawn from a very valuable bulletin compiled by the Archivist of Virginia, Mr. Morgan P. Robinson, and issued by the State Library. (If not out of print, copies can be had for $1.00 each. Requests should be addressed to the State Librarian, Dr. H. R. McIlwaine, Richmond, Va.) It is not possible in a limited space to explain more fully the descent of the present counties from the eight original shires and from the county of Northumberland. The reader is referred to the bulletin mentioned above. In the list here given only the modern name of the county has been used; several counties have had changes of name, and in two instances counties now extinct are not mentioned in the genealogical sequence. The county name in capitals is that of the parent county of the line. The italicized names in parentheses are those of the immediate and principal ancestor of branch lines.

CONTINUED articles COUNTY COURT NOTE-BOOK, and the dates on which they first appeared.
MARRIAGES BY INFERENCE. Began with May, 1922.
MARYLAND'S NEXT OF KIN. Began with July, 1922.
VIRGINIA COLONISTS. This alphabetized list began with July, 1924.
KING GEORGE and other VIRGINIA COUNTY PROBATES, &c. Began with July, 1924.
The LIST of BANISHED QUAKERS. Began with November, 1924.
MILITARY NOTES. both COLONIAL and REVOLUTIONARY, and some later MILITIA NOTES, will appear in every issue, if possible.
SHIPS IN PORT, INTERCOUNTY and INTERCOLONIAL, and COLONIAL FORENAMES, will appear in alternate issues or as space can be found for them.
EASTERN SHORE FAMILIES, in the form of a one-page supplement, began with June, 1925.

With this number the list of Richmond county, Va., probates and administrations from the Order Books antedating the first will record, comes to an end. Mr. E. CARTER DELANO, who has kindly furnished this list, states that the last Court in the Order Book No. 2, is of 2nd day of Nov., ano. 1699.

The first will of record was probated before the Court of 1st 8 ber Ano. Dom. 1699, and is recorded in Will Book No. 2, p. 1. From thence on, the records are complete.

The INDEX for the first three volumes of the COUNTY COURT NOTE-BOOK has been printed and is ready for distribution. It is a pamphlet of eighteen pages and contains about 3,500 names. Price $3.00.

CHURCH OR CHAPEL ON OLD PLANTATION CREEK, at the Gates of Arlington (on a neck of land.)

Hon. Thos. B. Robertson writes in William and Mary, vol. xxi-67, concerning the old church which stood at Arlington gates, and gives a deed from Willett to Baker [N-n cty records] in which it is mentioned. Judge Robertson says that in 1826 the bricks were sold at auction and the money used toward the building of Christ Church, Eastville, [now the church of that neighborhood and one of the two churches of Hungar's Parish.] The graveyard of the earliest church was the burial place of all the people of the lower part of the county.

OCCASIONAL

CHARLES SPOO, a natural borne subject of the French King having settled & Inhabited for severall yeares in the county of Richmond in this Colony . . . & having taken the Oathes prescribed by Law & Subscribed the Test . . . is declared to be fully & compleatly Naturalized. Richm'd cty, Va. 23 Oct 1705. vi-53.

At a Court holden in the Town of Sunbury in the Parish of St. John, Tuesday 17th April 1778: Deposition of Benjamin Baker... That JOHN LUPTON now deceased, settled with his family in the Parish of St. John in 1755. Baker was also well acquainted with SAMUEL WAY, formerly of the same Parish, with REBECCA the wife and afterwards Relict, with ELIZABETH WAY his Sister and WILLIAM WAY his Brother by the Father's side . . . Liberty cty, Ga. A-62. [PARMENAS WAY was a Justice of the Peace in 1774, same cty. A-78.]

MARY McDANIEL being offered as an evidence [*witness*] . . . objection was made to her being a Witness as she was a Roman Catholic and it was ordered by the Court that the Oath of Allegiance should be tendered to her or not admitted as an evidence. To which order Cuth Bullett of Council for the King objected that it could not be made till she had been legally convicted of Recusancy & cont'g in the same Opinion prayed an appeal which is granted. Pr. Wm. cty, Va. Orders [5], p.81. 7 Mch 1768.

The will of WILLIAM DUFF, psh Hanover, King George cty, Va., includes the following . . . "To the friends of the monthly "meeting at West River in Maryland, called "Quaker, in trust . . . for the use of such "travelling friends as shall come to visit us "and have a meeting among the people here "being recommended by the meeting to which "they belong as such who are in unity with "them and likewise for to produce a *guide "to conduct them either to Chesterfield or else "to the Cliffs in Maryland and over the Patux-"ent River and to pay their ferriages* & to "keep the meeting house in repair . . ." further provides that if the visiting friends should be neglected the whole trust to be in the monthly meeting aforesaid. Pr. Wm. Land Causes, 1790-1793. p. 526.

FROM THE MARRIAGE RECORD OF FREDERICK COUNTY MARYLAND

EVE BEARINGER and Abraham BOYES. 20 June, 1786.

EVE BIDDLE and PETER SHRIVER, 1789.

EVE-MARGARET BARE and STALEY MELCHOIR. 1790.

EVE BAKER and ABRAHAM CRUMPACKER. 1803.

EVE ALBAUGH and PETER CREAGER. 1799.

EVE CRONICE and MICHAEL ZIMMERMAN. 1788.

EVE CRISE and NATHAN VICKROY. 1796.

EVE DERR and CONRAD HOLTZMAN. 1795.
EVE GROVE and JACOB WILYARD. 1791.
EVE GRABLE [GRABILL?] and JOSHUA CUMSTON. 1798.
EVE HERSHALBERGER and MICHAEL RUNNER, Jr. 1799.
EVE JACOBS and ISAAC LINN. 1799.
EVE KEMP and JOHN CRONISE, Jr. 1797.
EVE LIVINGSTON and RICHARD CREALE. 1778.

EVE LAMON and ADAM SWAIDNER, 1797. EVE LEMMON and ADAM SWEADNER, 1797.	[Evidently the same.]

EVE MYERS and DAVID SHULTZ. 1782.
EVE MOON and JACOB BIGGS, 1785.
EVE MILLER and WILLIAM KULP. 1797.
EVE RUNNER and RICHARD TEMPLIN. 1795.
EVE SHIVELEY and GUDLIP SIDLE. 1778.
EVE SHITEARE and HARRY ROWSER. 1782.
EVE SABINE and JACOB WEAST. 1780.
EVE SMITH and ROBERT EVANS. 1794.
EVE SMITH and JACOB EAGGONER. 1799.
EVE WALTZ and DAVID NUSBAUM. 1792.
EVE WADDLE and CALEB EVANS. 1787.

ENGLISH QUAKERS BANISHED BETWEEN 1660 AND 1666

ELIZABETH TUDWAY, from Berkshire.

RICHARD THOMAS JOHN THURGOOD SAMUEL TRAHERN	from Hartfordshire.
DOUGLAS TEMPLER JOHN TYSOE FRANCIS TARCY THOMAS TAYLOR JOHN TERRY ROBERT THOMAS JOHN TILBY WILLIAM TILBY WILLIAM TILLETT CHRISTOPHER TODD ISABEL TREVILIAN JOHN FRANCIS TRIPONET REBECCA TRUMP GEORGE TURKINGTON MARGARET USHER	from London or Middlesex.

JOHN USHAW, from Durham.

THOMAS VOSSE AMY WALKER	from London or Middlesex.

MARY WINTER, from Berkshire.

JOHN WITHAM JOHN WINCHESTER SAM. WOOLASTON MARGARET WALSBY ISAAC WARNER MABELL WHEELER PATIENCE WILSON ROBERT WITHAM HENRY WOODING	from Hartfordshire.

ELIZABETH PRUDAY, from London or Middlesex.

SERVICE AND SUPPLIES COLONIAL, REVOLUTIONARY AND MILITIA

Upon the application of Mr. PETER GROSH, in behalf of CHRISTIANA GROSH widow of MICHAEL GROSH who lost his life in the military service of the State, as appears by a certificate of Lieutenant Christian Weaver, setting forth that the said MICHAEL GROSH was a second Lieutenant under the command of Colonel Baker Johnson and met with his death in the engagement at Germantown. Mr. John Beatty and Mr. Peter Mantz testified that the said CHRISTIANA GROSH is a resident of Frederick Town and has two young children one 6 years and one 3 years old and they have sustained a very heavy loss by the death of the said MICHAEL GROSH, though not left in indigent circumstances, but that it is just and necessary that an allowance for their support should be made. ORDERED That the Lieutenant of the County be requested to pay unto the said CHRISTIANA GROSH from the 18 October 1772 to 18th October 1778, at the rate of 5 lbs per month, amounting to 60 lbs . . . agreeable to the act of Assembly for regulation of the militia. Minute Book, O. C. Fredk cty, Md. 12 Aug 1778.

(*Contributed by Mrs. Francis Markell.*)

THOMAS STRIBLING, takes oath as Lieutenant. Pr. Wm, Va. 27 Feby 1762. Orders [4] p. 57.
ROBERT FOSTER, takes oath as Ensign. 4 May 1762. Pr. Wm, Va. Orders [4] p. 102.
JOHN TYLER, Jr., oath as Lieut., Capt. Tibbs' Co. 5 May 1762. Pr. Wm, Va. Orders [4] p. 120.
THOMAS BLACKBURN, Esq., oath as Captain. 6 July 1762. Pr. Wm, Va. Orders [4] p. 173.
JOHN HANCOCK, subscribed Test as Lieut., Capt. Thos. Blackburn's Co. Pr. Wm, Va. 9 Apr 1763. Orders [4] p. 497.
JOHN SIMMS, sworn Lieut. Lewis Reno, Gent's Co. 6 June 1763. Pr. Wm, Va. Orders [4] p. 522.
JOHN MACMILLION, sworn Ensign in Lewis Reno's Co. 4 July 1763. Pr. Wm, Va. Orders [4] p. 544.
GEORGE CALVERT, the younger, makes oath to service for his Majesty. Ordered certified. Pr. Wm., Va. 17 Mch 1756. Orders [3] p. 46.
JOHN FROGG, Gent. Oath as military officer. Pr. Wm, Va. 26 Apr 1756. Orders [3] p. 65.
JOHN BELL, Gent., takes oath as Major of Horse of the county, Pr. Wm, Va. 28 June 1756. Orders [3] p. 117.
JOHN BAILISS, Gent., takes oath as Major of Foot. Pr. Wm, Va. 28 June 1756. Orders [3] p. 117.
FOUSHEE TEBB, Gent., oath as Captain of a troop of Horse. Pr. Wm, Va. 25 Aug 1756. Orders [3] p. 211.
JOHN BAYLIS, Gent., produces receipt for money expended by Capt. William Baylis for use of the militia Commanded by him on the Frontiers, Pr. Wm, Va. 17 Mch 1756. Orders [3] p. 46.

THOMAS McCLANAHAN, sworn captain. Pr. Wm, Va. 27 May 1757. Orders [3] p. 308.

HENRY O'KELLY, alias HENRY KELLY, states that he served in Col. Henry Lee's Partizan Legion and has never received any pay since 1 Apr 1780. Power to Thomas Wells to claim pay that is due him. Kent cty, Dela. 1 Mch 1791. B2-232.

ELIZABETH DICKEY, widow of Lt. JOHN McCLELLAN, who died in the service of the U. S. A., prays that she may be granted half-pay for four years and seven months, when she m. James Dickey. Produces proof of service. Cumb. cty, Pa. 21 Nov 1787. O. C. iii-37.

The following notes are from the Draper Mss. Wisconsin State Library.

PHILLIP HAMMON, Capt. Lewis' Co., Botetourt and Fincastle cty, Va. troops. 2ZZ-27, 1774.

ISRAEL HARMAN, receipts for pay of JACOB HARMON, Sr., and JACOB HARMON, Jr., and JO. HARMON'S pay as soldiers in Capt. Thos. Martin's company of militia. 23 May 1777. 5ZZ-72.

VALENTINE HARMAN [Aug. cty] killed at New River. Feby 1756.1QQ-83. JACOB HARMON and one son, also killed same place. (Same reference.)

PROBATES AND ADMINISTRATIONS RICHMOND COUNTY, VIRGINIA

EDWIN CONWAY; will presented by Elizabeth, his wife, extx. Proved by Alexander Spence & John Size. 6 July, 1698. ii-331.

PETER BUTLER; admn. his est. to Rebecca Butler. 6 July, 1698. ii-332.

RICHARD TOMPKINS; will presented by Rowland Thornton, extr. Proved by Nathaniel Hall. 8 Sept., 1698. ii-335.

THOMAS HARVEY; nuncupative will presented by Alexander Spence & George Green, extrs. Proved by John Hauksford & John Bennett. 8 Sept., 1698. ii-338.

WILLIAM TAYLOR; admn. his est. to Margarett Taylor, his wife. 8 Sept., 1698. ii-343.

JOHN PARTRIDGE; will presented by Frances Partridge, extrx. Proved by John Peck & Mary Wollard. 8 Sept., 1698. ii-344.

ANGELL JACOBUS; will proved and recorded in this cty. 8 Sept., 1698. ii-345.

HENRY TILLERY; will presented by Mary Tillery, extrx. Proved by John Peck. 3 Nov., 1698. ii-348.

Col. JOHN STONE; will presented by Mrs. Ann Metcalfe. Proved by Elias Wilson & Thomas Lawson. 3 Nov., 1698. ii-405.

RICHARD METCALFE; admn. his est. to Mrs. Ann Metcalfe, his wife. 3 Nov., 1698. ii-405.

WILLIAM BROWN; will presented & proved by Alexander Spence & John Crask. Probate to Francis Brown, extr. 3 Nov., 1698. ii-409.

MARY ANDERSON; admn. her est. to Charles Barber. 2 Aug., 1699. ii-430.

JOHN WOOLARD; admn. his est. to Rawleigh Travers. 2 Aug., 1699. ii-432.

JOHN BURNETT; (Minister of Gospel) admn. his est. to Samuel Peachey. 1 Nov., 1699. ii-490.

BOOK NOTES

Two interesting and valuable volumes recently out are Mr. Walter B. Norris' ANNAPOLIS, ITS COLONIAL AND NAVAL STORY, and the REVISED HISTORY OF DORCHESTER COUNTY, MARYLAND, by Elias James. Both of these volumes are extremely noteworthy as additions to local American history. Annapolis is more than interesting; coming from Washington, one is thankful for its quaintness, its "atmosphere," which Washington so entirely lacks, and a Bostonian will greet with delight its Capitol, its diverging streets, and above all its passage-ways, which, not streets and not quite alleys, are reminiscent of similar breaks in the crowded squares of old Boston.

The Clerk's Office of Dorchester county, its *records,* point to an historic background of great interest. Dr. Jones' book is highly spoken of and will perhaps lead to other "revised" county histories that will be something more than "Portrait and Biographical Sketches."

One should be very grateful for the "copy" now coming out in the MARYLAND HISTORICAL MAGAZINE, the Rent Rolls of Baltimore county. It is suggested, however, that the collated material, while a very excellent thing to have, has the air in the manner of its printing, of being the beginning rather than the end of each paragraph. A better use of italics and capitals could have been made.

But what can be said of the PENNSYLVANIA GENEALOGICAL SOCIETY'S "PUBLICATION?" Nothing that doesn't sound too extravagant. The numbers are simply *mines,* mines of richness. There is an air of generous and friendly sharing about the publication of so much material that should certainly bring members to the fold.

Attention is invited to the address by Mr. Edwin Jaquett Sellers, most helpful to the amateur searcher in its notes of guides to genealogists and of valuable records abroad. A comment made by Mr. Sellers on complete genealogies is well worth repeating here. Mr. Sellers says: "The compiler [of a complete "family genealogy] often gives the best at-"tention to his own branch and is apt to ac-"cept information given him of the collateral "branches as correct, without personal verifi-"cation, the consequence being that errors are "often found in these branches and the repu-"tation of the author suffers accordingly."

The Editor has just received a booklet advertising a new and very valuable work, THE EARLY FRIENDS' FAMILIES OF UPPER BUCKS, Bucks county, Pennsylvania, being one of the three early counties of that State. The volume is compiled by Clarence V. Roberts, with the assistance of Warren S. Ely, the well-known Secretary of the Bucks County Historical Society. It contains 680 pages, so that there is space for a very respectable number of families, four maps and sixty-three illustrations. The index contains 22,-000 references.

Columbian Printing Co., Inc., Washington, D. C.

Supplement for December, 1925

FAMILIES OF THE EASTERN SHORE*

CUSTIS OF VIRGINIA

JOHN CUSTIS, as a merchant and large landowner, as guardian of children and of their estates, &c., appears constantly in the records up to a few years before his death. There are, perhaps, five hundred references to him, between 1650 and 1696...including his appearances as an official of the court or county. References to his political offices are omitted in these published notes for two reasons. The first reason is that the Editor has not the exact references, without which she does not care to publish, for CUSTIS' appointments, qualifications, and appearances on the bench, officially before the court, or at Jamestown.

The second reason is that the offices held by JOHN CUSTIS and others of his standing have been pretty thoroughly listed and will be found recorded in the official history of the colony. They are easy to find. The record here published, combines "vital statistics," with as much of the daily life of the family concerned as came before the court and can be crowded into brief abstracts.

JOHN CUSTIS; patent for 500 acres, south side of "Potomack" Creek. Ten head rights, names not given. [These names are probably in "Old Volume 5, S. L. O.] Mr. JOHN CUSTIS; an attachment is granted against his estate and returned executed by the sheriff on a negro, who is bailed out by a Mr. Overzee and afterwards carried by Overzee or at his instigation, [to Accomack.] The Court grants an order against Overzee for the payment of 800 lbs, of tobacco, 200 lbs for a voyage to "Accawmacke" with a boat and three hands, (L. Norf., Va. D-, 4. 17 Nov 1656.)

CUSTIS signs a petition in favor of Rev. Thos. Teackle [this is subsequent to Teackle's troubles with Scarburgh.] (N-n v-105, 28 July 1657.) CUSTIS gives a cow to Ursula Kennett, dau-in-law to Walter Price, also a heifer to Ann Price. (N-n, ix-39. 14 Sept 1657.) [We do not know anything about possible sisters of the CUSTIS brothers. Some of these gifts may be to "cousins."]

JOHN CUSTIS, SENR., patent for 200 acres, Accomack cty, on the seaboard side, Four head rights, no names given. (S. L. O. Old Vol. V, p. 96. 1657.) JOHN CUSTIS, Jr., patent for 250 acres, Old Plantation Creek. Five head rights, no names, (S. L. O. 5 Oct 1657. iv-181.) [The names are given in Old Vol. 5; JOSEPH CUSTIS, Wm. St. John, Wm. Marshall, Geo. Welfe.]

Note by the Editor: There are two explanations of the above, one is that JOHN CUSTIS, being now the father of a son, JOHN CUSTIS calls himself "Senior," and also takes occasion to enter lands for his son. This was done. The other explanation is that JOHN CUSTIS of Rotterdam was again temporarily in the Colony.

JOHN CUSTIS; patent for 2000 acres, in the freshes of the Petomack, above Anacostia, joining Sharles' land, Forty head rights, no names given. (S. L. O. 3 Dec 1657. iv-281.) JOHN CUSTIS discharges Luke Billington from all Debts, Dues & Demands . . . Myself and JOSEPH and JOHN CUSTIS, Junr, from the beginning of the world untill this . . . 3d January 1657. (Rappa. cty, Va. i-31. 1657.) [This is probably JOHN CUSTIS of Rotterdam.] In 1657, Thomas Burdit assigns a patent for 500 acres to JOHN CUSTIS, (N-n viii-4.) JOHN CUSTIS, Mcht, east side Plantation Creek, The 200 acres patented above to JOHN CUSTIS, Senr, are conveyed by JOHN CUSTIS to James Bonewell. This was formerly land of George Traveller, "which being deserted was patented to Custis." (N-n viii-7. 28 Jany 1657.)

JOHN and WILLIAM CUSTIS, being by descent tho not by birth, natural Englishmen . . . take the oath and are naturalized. (7 Apr 1658. N-n ix-6.) JOHN CUSTIS, Mcht, and John Wilcox, lease an orchard which was Esq. Yardley's, but of which two-thirds now belong to CUSTIS as gdn of the heir of Yardley, and one-third to Wilcox in right of his wife. (4 June 1658, N-n ix-16.)

Thomas Taylor, son of Philip, chooses Mr. JOHN CUSTIS as gdn. (30 Apr 1660. N-n viii-66.) CUSTIS appears in a list of sheep owners as having 110. (28 June 1660. N-n viii-89.) CUSTIS and Mr. John Michael get a legacy from Thomas Granger (a mariner?) . . . "Silk Stockings and a half shirt." (4 Nov 1661. N-n ix-100.) JOHN CUSTIS, a witness to the pre-nuptial marriage contract of John Parramore and Mary Robinson, widow. (29 Apr 1662, N-n ix-114.) JOHN CUSTIS from John Vines, 350 acres. (1662, N-n ix-119.) And a ctf. for 550 acres, the 28 June; head rights, six negroes and John Steward. (N-n viii-160.) In 1664, JOHN CUSTIS "presents" the wife of Jeremy Robinson for "backbiting." (N-n viii-189.) On the 28 June, 1664. he is to be paid for Cider "prest" for the county's use. N-n viii-192.) In 1664 he receives a patent for 400 acres at the Bayside, south side Boloman's Branch. (S. L. O. iv-620.) In 1664 he had eleven whites and six negroes as tenants and servants. (N-n viii-196.) The same year he assigns to William Brooke, a patent for 500 acres in Lower Norfolk. The names of the ten head rights are given. (L. Norf. D-409.) He assigns another patent in Lower Norfolk to Peter Malbone, this for 250 acres. (L. Norf. D-409.)

A payment to Capt. CUSTIS and his brother Mr. WILLIAM CUSTIS appears in the Northampton cty accounts in 1664. (N-n x-2.) As High Sheriff, CUSTIS petitions for a suitable prison. (N-n, 3 Apr 1665. x-4.) On the 15 May, 1666, (N-n vii-2) he was gdn to Mary Dorman.

In 1668, Capt. JOHN CUSTIS and Mr. Peter Reverdy sign an agreement . . . CUSTIS is to deliver land on the island of Mockon. (N-n vii-23.) The same year, 29 June, JOHN and ELISHA or ALISHE[?] CUSTIS make an affadavit in connection with the legacy left by will of ELIZABETH ROBINSON to the wife of her son WILLIAM. On the same date they prove the will [although they are not witnesses.] (N-n vii-26.) Patent is issued to Capt. JOHN CUSTIS, for 200 acres, near the head of Pimmenoe[?] branch. (S. L. O. 7 Feby 1669. v-273.) Another ctf. for 250 acres, the 28 Mch 1670. The head rights are Jane Edwards, Sarah Olive, Geo. Williams, a negro and an Indian. (N-n x-82.) The 18 Nov 1671, Capt. JOHN CUSTIS assigns a ctf. for 1000 acres to Miles Gray. There are twenty head rights, of these eight

*See June, 1925.

(over)

are for CUSTIS himself, "for transporting himself eight times." The others are Dorothy Booth, Mary Humphreyes, Chas. Crosse, Rich'd Aldridsge, Bartholemew Herron, Hiscott Trissell, Chas, Trissell, and four negroes. (Acco. iv-22.)

The 19 Jany 1671, Capt. JOHN CUSTIS gets 600 acres, the head rights are: JOHN CUSTIS, Jr., MARY ROBINSON, ELIZABETH EYRES, Gabriell Jacob, Richard Walpoole, Tiague O'Deare, George Such, Jno. Alford, John Marshall, two Indians and a negro. (Acco. iv-55.)

About 1671, JOHN CUSTIS, Jr., begins to appear in the records, and the 7 Nov 1673, his father, then Coroner, makes his son a deputy. (N-n xii-86.) In 1673, CUSTIS gets a ctf. for 400 acres, the head rights are given as Mary Sowton[?], Jane *Broadhurst,* John Tillery, Sam, Herringe, Owen Hughes, John Brewer, Mathew Wilson and William Wilson. (N-n x-223.) In 1675, CUSTIS is ordered by the court to take care of William and Frances, orphans of Edward Parke. In 1676 he claims admn of Mr. Edmond Yardley's estate [who died about July 1675.] as nearest of kin. (N-n xii-129.) In 1676 Wm. Whittington conveys to Col. JOHN CUSTIS 1500 acres upon Hungar's Creek . . . part of 1800 granted Capt. Wm. Stone, (N-n xi-131.) This land he conveys to son JOHN CUSTIS, Jr. (N-n 15 May 1677. xi-179.) In 1680, 20 April, Maj.-Gen'l JOHN CUSTIS receives a patent for an island in Pocomoke River, 100 acres, formerly called Cobham's Island, Head rights: EDWD CUSTIS and Walt'r Young. (S. L. O. xi-179.)

An interesting letter is recorded in Northampton, dated the 29 Dec 1680. It is written by Maj.-Gen'l CUSTIS at Arlington, and begins, "Gods hand haveinge a long time layne heavy on me . . . " N-n xiii-126.) He appears in Court, however, in March, 1681, and probably before that, He certified in Feby, 1682, that about three years before that date, Dr. James Watts came into the country in a ship with him. (N-n xiii-278.)

A record about Jany, 1683, but dated London, 5 Jany 1675 is an acknowledgment by JOHN CUSTIS or receiving full satisfaction (in the sum of £50) and that he resigns his whole interest in the repayment of duties of Customs paid on the lading of the *Carolus Secundus* (which had been cast away). Reference is made to his brother, ROBERT CUSTIS, of Rotterdam, and Mr. Richard Banks, Mcht, of London. The witnesses are Isaac Key and Oliver Hering. In 1684 (the Northampton record is about April, 1684) JOHN CUSTIS (an inhabitant of Rotterdam) gets a license to come from Holland and to enter the Port of London or any other port within the Kingdom of England. This safe-conduct is endorsed "License for JOHN CUSTIS to come from Holland." (N-n xiv-94.)

JOHN CUSTIS, Senr, of Northampton Mcht, and wife TABITHA, give to kinsman (consideration, "love and affection,") 500 acres out of the fourth part of a dividend of 6,000, which belongeth to said JOHN CUSTIS, Sr., and TABITHA, in Accomack, upon the branches of Metomkin. (N-n, 21 May 1684. vi-387.)

JOHN CUSTIS, Sen'r, does not often appear in the records at this time, but the 3 Oct 1690 (Acco. vi-532), he gives to his "well-"beloved nephew ERMUND CUSTIS, of Ac-"comack, son to my deare brother THOMAS "CUSTIS, formerly resident at Baltamore in "Ireland, from whom I brought my sd kins-"man in his minority, with promise . . . and "for that he hath intermarried with the grand-"daughter of my present wife" . . . a negro, Mary, and a boy child called Ned; also a man, Ned Tucker (negro) for four years and an Irish woman named Ellenor Cartee; also cattle, tools, &c., at the plantation EDMUND CUSTIS now lives on, at Deep Creek. EDMUND'S wife, TABITHA, is referred to. About this time CUSTIS and wife, TABITHA, convey to John Drummond, 300 acres given by the will of George Watson to TABITHA CUSTIS, when she was the widow of "Devorax" Browne, Mcht. (18 Nov 1690. Acco. vi-533.)

In the Library of Congress is a patent to JOHN CUSTIS, Esq., for all of Smith's Island, Northampton cty, containing 1600 acres. Fifty-two head rights, names not given on the patent. (28 Apr 1691. L. C. 2006.)

The Order of Council granting the petition of Col. CUSTIS that he be discharged from his office, is recorded 15 Apr 1692. (N-n xvii-177, 178.) The 19 Apr 1693, CUSTIS gives to his "nephew or kinsman" John Bradhurst of Accomack, Mcht, 500 acres, part of Jolly's neck. (Acco xi-12.) No further record of interest is found until his will is proved.

JOHN CUSTIS died about the 10 Feby 1695, probably just before that date. Madam TABITHA CUSTIS, the widow ["of the Hon'ble Coll: JOHN CUSTIS"] presents his will on that day. (N-n xvii-344.) The will is dated 18 Mch 1691, and is to be found on p. 356 of the same volume. A brief abstract, only, can be given.

To his kinsman, John Bradhurst, 500 acres... "according to my free deed of gift." Also directs that Bradhurst shall buy a servant for whom the extrs are to pay. Kinsman EDMOND CUSTIS, son of my brother, THOMAS CUSTIS, 800 a. at Deepe Creeke..."noe part of 1750 acres given by me to my wife TABITHA CUSTIS, but abutteth upon the same and that 1000 acres patented and belonging to Tabitha Smart, deceased and her heirs." Quit-claims to Smart Whittington, son of William, any right he (CUSTIS) may have to the said 1000 acres. To wife, 1750 acres at Deepe Creeke, one-half of 3500 acres patented in her and her sister Matilda's name. Also gives her negroes and an Indian, Arlington house and plantation, and the island of Mockon, with reversion to grandson JOHN CUSTIS. Negroes to grandson and Smith's Island. Remainder of lands, &c., to son JOHN CUSTIS, Cattle, &c., in equal thirds to wife, son and grandson. Provides for education of grandson in England.

CUSTIS is usually said to have been born in 1630, this statement based, probably, upon the inscription on his tombstone. His own affidavits show that he was born in 1628 or 1629 (Old Style.) He is buried not far from the probable site of the house at Arlington, on Old Plantation Creek, somewhat to the southward of the frame shack now standing there.

INDEX TO COUNTY COURT NOTE-BOOK. VOLUME IV.

Abbott 35
Abell 20
Abernath 43
Abreshall 27
Achpoole ? 27
Ackers 43
Adair ? 10
Adams 26,35,41
Adamson 29
Addison 9,34
Adkin 27
Adoune 35
Adrianson 27
Adwick 3
Adwin 35
Aggor ? 35
Albert 3
Albough 45
Alcock 43
Alden 11
Alexander 18,22,38,41
Alford 3
Allen 22, 26,27,35,39, 42,43
Allerneck 35
Allvit 19
Alsop 3
Alt 26
Amolichan 3
Andersley 3
Anderson 3,6,10,14,22 25,38,39,42,47
Andrews 17,25,35,38
Angell 3,6
Antell 27
Apperson 14
Appleton 35
Apthorp 29
Arbo 11
Arden 27
Ardington 34
Arenton 42
Arkhill 14
Arkinson 37
Armspoker ? 38
Armstrong 22,25,27,31,38
Arney 27
Arnold 3,10,14,22,35
Avington 15
Ashworth 3
Askin,Askins 15,42
Asquith 15
Atkins 19,33
Atkinson 25,37,43
Austin 25
Avery 11
Aydelotte 17
Ayres 43
(See also Eyres)
Bacon 42
Bagwell 9
Baker 2,3,10,21,26,27, 29,34,39,45
Baldridge 2
Baldwin 5
Balker ? 43
Ball 11,42,sup.2
Ballance 19
Ballingall 19
Balthrop 31
Bankes 3,42
Baptist 14,21
Barber 18,27,47
Bare 45
Barker 27,42
Barkinton 19
Barls 35
Barlinton 43
Barnard 7
Barnes 35
Barnett 3,17,18,30,39
Barnham 3
Barr 7, 27
Barrett 3
Barrow 9
Bartlett 11,19,31,37
Barton 43
Barwell 27
Baskwell 11
Bastin 17
Batten 3
Batting 3
Batty 27
Bawyells? 11
Baxter 38,42
Bayley,Bailey 2,10, 18,21,34
Baylis 14,46
Baymond 43
Beadle 27
Beale 27,31,33,36,38
Bear 22
Beard 18,30
Bearinger 45
Beatty 46
Beckwith 27
Bedicant(?) 19
Beedles 43
Bell 17,27,35,46
Bellamy 3,4
Bellew,Bellue 15,36
Belote 9,10
Benbow 27
Benecraft 2
Benfor 43
Bennett 26,34,47
Benthall 10
Benson 11
Bentley 35
Benton 43
Bentsoll 33,43
Berkeley 22,39
Bernard 39
Berry,Bury 2,6,11,14 18,21,22,31,42,43
Berryman 3
Best 19
Beswick 4
Bevington 3
Bibby sup.3
Bicker 11
Bidalph 27
Biddle 45
Biggs 27,46
Bigham 17
Bilderback 38
Billington 42,sup.2,4
Billson 3

INDEX TO COUNTY COURT NOTE-BOOK. VOLUME IV.

Bird 35
Birkhead 15,26
Bishop 17
Bissett 17
Black 3,43
Blackburn 3,46
Blackerby 42
Blackistone 26
Blacklock 26
Blagge 9
Blair 31,38
Blake 1,34
Blancherwell 19
Blanckflower 2
Blangey 34
Blaze 43
Blinde 11
Bloxom 30
Bloye 11
Bluford 2
Boase 11
Boddicott 41
Bond 2,18,26
Boneham 15
Bonewell sup.4
Bonny 43
Boon 15,21
Booth 6,35
Borel 25
Boston 10
Bosworth 35
Botham 29
Botie 15
Bowrne 3,21,36
Bovey 35
Bowdoin 17
Bowen 14,17,34
Bowles 42
Bowman 38
Bowyer 27
Boy,Boys 10,45
Boyd 9,25
Boyle 3
Bracot 17
Bradbury 27
Braddie 43
Bradley 17,19
Bradshaw 34
Bradwell 18
Brailsford 17
Braine 34
Branam 14
Branch 11,12
Breeham 43
Brenore 43
Brent 2,7
Brenton 1
Brereton 2
Brett 10
Brice 30
Brickes 27
Brickwell 43
Bride 35
Bridger 23
Bridges 7
Briggs 19
Bright 34
Brindley 25,26
Britten,Britton 19.27
Broadbrank 19
Broadert 3
Broadway 35
Brocas 19,42
Brock 6
Brockenbrough 31
Brockington 17
Brooke 3,4,14,35,43 sup.4
Brookin (?) 42
Broughton 17
Brower 37
Brown 3,4,6,10,13,14, 15,19,21,26,28,34,38, 41,43,47,sup.3
Bruce 22,29,31
Brude 38
Bruff 37
Bryan 15,22,43
Bryant 11,22
Buck 35
Bucker 1
Buckingham 25
Buckler 19
Buckman 10
Budd 37
Buffield 26
Bulker 43
Bull 10
Bullet 7,39,45
Bullock 34
Bumbridge 43
Bumbury 31
Bunch 3
Bunting 30
Burby 3,35
Burch 2
Burdette 14,27,sup.3, 4
Burdin 13
Burgess 14,21
Burham 3
Burnett 11,47
Burrows 22
Burton 11,30,38,43
Burwell 19
Bushrod 11
Busy 3
Butcher 26
Butler 15,31,35,47
Button 30
Cabell 3
Cahall 38
Cain 37,38
Caldwell 2,4
Cale 27
Calgey 19
Callum(?) 35
Calvert 15,17,46
Cameron,Comeron(?) 42
Campbell 31,37,38,43
Campe 6
Canadie(y) 11,38
(See also Kennedy)
Cannon 12,17,29,34
Canton 5
Capell 6,21,27
Capman 3
Capes 12,29,38

INDEX TO COUNTY COURT NOTE-BOOK. VOLUME IV.

Carby 19
Carey 35
Carlyle 26,39
Carpenter 1,23,38
Carr 7,12,15,19,29
Carrington 35
Carroll 10,23,39
Carron 15
Carson 15,26
Carter 5,6,9,14,15,22, 30,31,42
Cartwright 27
Carty 35
Case 12
Casey 23
Castor 15
Cater 5
Catland 5
Catlett 9
Caton 12,29
Causey 43
Cavanear 34
Cave 12,29
Ceser 11
Chadwick 27
Chaires 42
Chamber 38
Champe 6,31
Chandler, Chanler 11,18, 27,37,44
Chapman 5,11,21
Charles 12,29
Charlton 17,36,sup.2
Chatteris 12,29
Cheek 2
Cheney 21,43
Chew 13,18
Chicheley 42
Child 5
Chilton 42
Ching, Chinn 21,42
Chitham 5
Chizell 27
Choate 25
Choppin 5
Christen 12,29
Chrystie 41
Church 11,19,27
Claiborne 3
Clanton 43
Clarie 43
Clark, Clerk 2,3,5,6,9,11, 12,21,27,29,30,34,35, 38,39,43
Clater, Clator 12,29
Clay, Cley 10,19,43
Claydon, Clayton,
Cleaton, 5,11,12,14,29
Clavill 34
Claxton 25
Clemans, Clemence 42,43
Clift 12
Clifton 1,5
Clinn 35
Clonen 43
Clubb 34
Cocken 11
Cockett 12,29
Cockey 18
Codin 43
Coe 35,41
Coeman 3
Coghill 31
Colburne 5,14
Cole, Coale, Coles 3,5,18 23,26,29,31,34,35,42,43
Coleman 18
Collick 37
Collidge 42
Collins 13,22,42
Collum 43
Colston, Coulston 19,42
Coet 35
Come 19
Comerford 11
Comings 35
Conell 3
Connarly 9
Connawin 35
Conner 26
Conrad 26
Coutanceau 27
Constable 19
Conway, Connaway 3,47
Conyers 10
Cooke 3,5,11,17,27,35
Cookson 25
Cooper 7,18,19,27,35,42
Coote 11
Corby 12,29
Corbyn 3
Core 27
Corker 27
Corkering 19
Cornehousen 27
Cornelis, Cornelius 2,3, 19,27
Corney 12,29
Cornex 3
Corson, Courson 26,33,42
Cosnock 12,29
Costen 10
Cotton 5
Coughran 38
Couling 3
Court 5
Couson, Cowson 12,29
Couzens 39
Coventon 27
Coward 5,42
Cowdery 34
Cowing 38
Cox, Cock, Cocks, 5,11,18, 29,35,38,39
Crabb 2,5,34
Crane 5
Cranford 5
Cranwell 12,29
Crask 42,47
Craven 17
Crawley 38
Cray 19
Creager 45
Creah, Creaho 4
Creale 46
Crise 45
Crispe 5,19
Crockett 35

Croft 12,29
Cronice,Cronise 45,46
Crooke 12,29
Crosby 18
Croshaw 27
Crosley 33
Crosier(Crozier) 5
Crose,Crosse 5,18,35
Croste 27
Croth 3
Crouch,Croch 3,6,15
Crowder 43
Croxton(?) 38
Crumpacker 35
Crusty(?) 43
Cubham 12,29
Cuffin 19
Cullin 11
Cumberland 30
Cumton,Cumston 38,45
Cupps 38
Curtis 5,7,12,29,sup.1, 2,3
Curwen 12,29
Custis 3,13,30,33, sup.1,2,3,4,
Cutt,Cutts 27,35
Daggs 31
Dains 35
Dakin 35
Dale 21,27
Dallison 43
Calton 15,39
Dance,Danse 3,21
Daniell 18
Dansfield 43
Darling 19
Darry 43
Dart 27
Davenport 6
Davers,Devers 13
Davis 3,7,11,14,15,19, 21,22,26,27,35,37, 38,39,42,43,sup.2
Davison 35
Davour 38
Daw,Dawes 22,26,27
Day 12,29
Deadman 14
Deane 6,12,22,29,31,39
Deandon 37
Deaner ? 6
Deathsell 2
Debarr 43
DeCourtier 27
De la Rue 33
Dalton 27,35
Dency 43
Dennis 11,35
Denny 35
Denson 3
Dent 13
Denwood 34
DeParaeny 39
Dermot 22
Derr 46
Derricke 11
Derry 35
Desnergers 33
Devagha 6
Devrowe 35
Dewes 11
Dewit 1
DeYoung 7
Dickenson 3,4,31
Dickey 47
Dike 21,39
Dilworth 33
Dinwiddie 14,15,22
Dixon 3,6,10,19,21,22, 24
Dobbie 7
Dobbins 3
Dod,Dodds 2
Dodson 3,10
Doing 15
Dolling,sup.2
Doniphan 2
Donne 6,31
Donoh,Donohoe 26,31
Dooley,Dule 3
Dorman 3,sup.4
Dorraugh 26
Dorsey 15
Dorton 13
Dorwood 43
Dossen 38
Doubleday 21
Douglas 3,7,35
Dowgan 22
Downs 11,43
Dowty 9
Doxey 43
Drake 6,22
Drew 3,10,43
Drummond 15,34,39
Drunkin(?) 35
Dryer 30
Dubignon 33
Duce 3
Duckett 30
Dudlestone 2
Dudley 3,13,34,39
Duff 6,45
Dunkey 3
Dunlap 22,38
Dunnidge 11
Dunston,Dunton 3,9
Dunworth 10
Duvall 6
Dyass 33
Dye 12
Dyer 3,17
Dysart 26
Eaggoner 46
Eagle 15
Eale 14
Easter 34
Easterfield 11
Eaton 27,35
Eburne 21
Edgcome 3
Edgill 25
Edinton 38
Edmonds,Edmunds 3,6,11, 14,15,21,29
Edmundson 42

INDEX TO COUNTY COURT NOTE-BOOK. VOLUME IV.

Edwards 11,31,35,43,43, sup.4
Edwinn 3
Edy 38
Eglestone 3
Eldrege 1
Elkin,Elkins 6,31
Elliott 18,35
Ellis 18
Ellyson 35,38
Elmore 22
Elsford 43
Emerson,Emason 27,42
Emmerton 15,30
Emmett,Emmack 25,35
Emmons 38
Engle 33,38
English 15,19
Enorahoo(?) 27
Errance(?) 18
Erving 34
Esgate 34
Estebe 7
Esto 19
Eustace 2
Evans 10,11,18,21,22,29 34,46
Ewell 6
Eyre,Eyer 18,sup.2 (See also Ayres)
Fairepoint 27
Fairman 21
Falkner 34
Farnam 15
Farner 27
Farr 19
Farrington 37
Farrow 15
Farthing 3,18
Fauntleroy 6
Fawcett 21
Feard 11
Feast 21
Feberyear 1
Felton 3
Fennell
Ferguson 6,26,31
Ferriatt 11
Fettislace 37,44 (See Phettiplace)
Field,sup.2
Filkin 19
Finch 35,42
Firsh 19
Fisher 20,21,26,27,43, sup.3
Fishpoole 31
Fissell 26
Fitchett 9
Fitts 43
Fitzgerald(?) 27
Flaharty 11
Fleet 11
Fleetwood 26
Fleming 38
Fletcher 3,9,33
Flinte 11
Flood 35
Florra 35
Flowers 3
Floyd,Floid3,43
Foiles 27
Fooks 17,33
Ford, Foard 11,13,21,26 29,42
Forman 17
Forrest 3,10,42
Forth,Fourth 3
Forty 11,43
Foster 7,15,17,18,19,27 46
Fountain 11
Fowke 11
Fowler 23,26,35
Fox 3,42
Foxson 9
Franke,France 19,43
Franklin 11,19,21,29,34
Frederick 18
Freeborn 18
Freeman 3,30
French 15,22,26,43
Freshwater 26,38
Frilor(?) 11
Frisby 18
Frogg 46
Frost 37
Fryer 27
Gabell 21
Gadsberry 3,11
Gale 13
Gallandet 25
Galloway 21
Gapeing 11
Gard 1
Garder 2
Gardner 11,26
Garland 19
Garnell 19
Garrard 15,38
Garsh 18
Gastin 26
Gaterill 21
George,Gorge 1,2,18,38
Gerdan(Jordan?) 11
Gerlask 26
Gerrell 19
Gibbons,Gibbins 27,30
Gibbs 18,21,22,27,38, 39,43
Gible 11
Gibson 26,43
Gilbert 14,34,43
Giles 19,27
Gill 2,15,22
Gillett 43
Gingey 1
Gitting 21
Gladman 21
Glandfield 3
Glannell(?) 38
Glascock 21,22
Glaze 38
Glendenning 6,22,31
Glover 15,26,27
Goade 3
Godard 38
Goffe 11

INDEX TO COUNTY COURT NOTE-BOOK. VOLUME IV.

Golding 6,11,27
Goldsborough 7
Gonn 11
Good 27
Goodiand 19
Goodman 3,43
Goodriche 11
Goodwin,Goodwin 3,11,27
Gorsuch 42
Gower,Gowers 9,11,27
Gowny 35
Grabill? 46
Gragon 38
Graham 7,15,21,38
Grane 21
Granger,sup.4
Grant 22, 31
Gravenraedt 37
Graves 10,11,22
Gray 3,10,11,19,35,sup.4
Grayson 7
Greathouse 38
Greene 3,11,27,34,35,39, 43,47
Greenberry 6,21
Greenfield 43
Greenhoure 3
Greenstreet 6
Greenwood 11
Griffin 3,11
Griffith 10,35,38
Grigg 44
Grimes 26
Grimsley 14
Groome 3
Grosh 46
Groten 30
Grove 46
Grubbs 21,33
Grundy 4
Grymes 11
Gubb 30
Gudloe 35
Gullam 3
Gummy 34
Gundry 1
Gunnall,Gunnell 38,42
Gunter 27
Gurman 27
Gushard 6
Guy 43
Gwatkins 15
Gwin 10
Hacker 21
Hackey,Hackley 6,31,43
Hadger(?) 35
Haddon
Hagan
Haggett
Haigh,Hague
Hairn
Haistwood
Hake
Halbyatt(?) 6
Hale,Hales,Haile 9,11
Hall 3,6,13,18,34,35, 43,47
Hally,Haley 19,21,35
Ham 19
Hamilton 35,38
Hamenack 21
Hammer,Hamner 13,34
Hamon,Hamond 11,33,39, 43,47
Hampton 15
Hancock 27,46
Hand 27
Handy 37
Hannah 26
Hanway 13
Hanwell 3
Harcum 18
Harding,Hardin 19,21,23 27,29,35
Hardman 18,43
Hardy 22,39
Hare 35
Harey 6
Harkin 43
Harly 3
Harman,Harmon 19,38,47
Harper 6,7,38,43
Harralson 36
Harrard 2
Harrell 18
Harrington 6,42
Harris 3,6,11,19,21, 27,35,43
Harrison 1,4,10,11, 15,36
Harrold 19
Hart 21,26,27,35,43
Hartford 14
Hartley 27
Hartree,sup.1
Hartshorn 23
Harvey 14,47
Harwood 3,11,43
Hasel,Hasle 14
Haselwood 11
Hatfield 38
Hathaway 1
Hathrone 35
Hatley 35,43
Hatton 26
Haught 13
Hauksford 47
Havennest 19
Hawes 19,21
Hawkins 3,6,19,25,35
Hawly 19
Hayden 39
Hayes,Heys,Haies 3, 38,39
Haynie 2
Heaberd 2,11
Head 26
Heath 19,27
Hebb 2
Hedge,Hedges 2
Heines 27,35
Helmsley,Hemsley, Hemsie 21,26,34
Hempstead 4
Hempton 5
Henderson,Henson 7,11 19,23,25,27,38
Henland 42

Henly 43
Hennings 14,18
Heors (?) 27
Herbert,Harbert 2,26,35, 43
Herdman 2
Herman,Hermy 26
Hermy 43
Herne 21
Herring 27
Hershalberger 46
Hestwood(?) 18
Hewes,Hews,Hewis 3,14,34, 41
Hext 18
Hibbitt 38
Hickman 3
Hickson 27
Hide 21,29
Higginbottam 43
Higginson 3,27
Hight 6
Hill 11,12,19,33,34,37,42 43,sup.3
Hiller 27
Hilliard 18
Hinde,Hindes 11,22
Hinson 35
Hissett 42
Hobson 35
Hockwell 34
Hodge 29
Hodgers 15
Hodgson 21,29
Hoe 34
Hoffheims 26
Hoffman 26
Hogeling 38
Hogg 26,35
Hogshire 30
Hogson 43
Holder 35
Holdsworth 31
Holland 6,13,18,37,sup.2
Hollaway 18
Holliday 3,19
Hollingsworth 3
Holly 19
Hollyman 34
Holmes,Homes 17,38, 43
Holtzman 46
Homewood 6,15,21,30
Hool 1,23
Hooker 23,31
Hooper 3,6,15,42,43
Hopkins 3,25,35
Hopson 26
Horn 18,21
Hornblow 21
Hornby 17
Hornego 33
Horner 3
Horseman 26
Horton 15
Hoser 3
Hoskins 5,11,27
House 1
Houston,Huston 13,34 38
How 6,14,21,35
Howard 5,15,29
Howell 3,23,26
Howman 19
Howranley 11
Hoyle 6
Hubbard 29
Huckle 27
Hudson, sup.2
Hue 34
Huett 35
Huger 18
Huggins 6
Hughes 4,11,18,19,22 27,43
Hulett 34
Hull 27,35,38,42
Humphreys 22,35
Hunseman 14
Hunt 3,25,27
Hunter 11,18
Huntley 43
Hurden 43
Hurlock 15,42
Huson 34
Hutchins 11,43
Hutchison,Hutchinson 25,26,43
Hutson 14,39
Hyle 38
Ingall,Ingle 27,33
Ingram 35
Inman 30
Irby 33
Ireland 3
Irish 43
Irwin,Irving,Erving 26,34
Isaack 19
Isom 19
Ivers,Ives 27,29
Ivory 43
Jackson 3,10,11,14,26 27,29,33,43,sup.2
Jacob,Jacobs 20,40
Jacobus 47
Jacksall 35
Jaines 19
James 9,11,14,17,19, 27,30
Janeck 27
Jarsey(?) 43
Jauncey 2
Jeffers 27
Jefferys 39
Jelly 27
Jenkins 19,27
Jenkinson 34
Jennings,Jennens 15, 19,27,31,39
Jernew 19
Jernigan 34
Jernice,Jervies 25,35
Jesper 39
Jett 14,22,39
Jewitt 27
Jnoson 3,35
Johns 26,34,35

INDEX TO COUNTY COURT NOTE-BOOK. VOLUME IV.

Johnson,Johnston 1,3, 10,11,15,19,23,26, 27,29,31,35,37,41, sup.2
Jolly 3,35
Jones 2,3,6,9,10,11,14 15,19,21,22,26,27,29 30,33,34,35,39,42,43
Jordan 11,12,19,33,37
Jowles ? 43
Joy,Joyce 19,35
Joyner 18
Jubbs 10
Justice 18
Kairn 14
Keateley 27
Keen 18
Kellam 34
Keller 13
Kelly,Kele 15,19,30,42 47
Kelsall 34
Kelsick 33
Kemp 10,19,46
Kendall,Kennell 29,35
Kennedy 2,11,38 (See also Cannida)
Kenner 2
Kennett,sup.4
Kenny 35,38
Kent 27,29
Kerby 27,35,39
Kerchivall 15,22
Kerr 41
Key 39
Kiffe 35
Kilburne 30
Killingall 27
Kincaid 10,38
Kinder 3
King 3,35,43
Kinseloe 14
Kirke 11,43
Kirton 29
Knatckbull 11
Knight 11,19,43
Knighting(?) 31
Knott 35
Knowles 22,35
Kulp(Culp?) 46
Lacie,Lacy 19,27,35
Ladd 27
Lake 1
Lambert 33,sup.2
Lampton 14,15
Land 19
Landman 39
Lane 18,25
Langley 25,43
Larkin 21,30
Lashley 11
Lattur 27
Laundy 29
Lawrence 19,26,27,30,34
Lawson 3,19,39,47
Lay 3
Laylor 38
Leach,Leech 19,27
Lear 19
Lee 3,7,10,11,18,19, 27,30,43
Lefebur 19
Leftford 27
Legge 43
Leggins 14
Lemon,Lamon 19,46
Leward 35
Lewis 6,18,19,21,22,27 30,35,39
Leyster 17
Lightfoot 3
Lile 19
Lindsay,Linsey 3,19
Linn 46
Lipp 3
Lippeate 43
Lirgson 35
Liston 21
Littlefield 14
Littleton 13,26
Livingston 46
Lloyd,Loyd 11,14
Lob, 43
Lockwood,Loogwood 2,4
Lodge 14
Logan 18
Loney 42
Long 35
Longmire 31
Maclanahan,Maclenahan 1,34,47
McLaughlan 18
Macklayer 35
McMahon 23
McMichen 2
Mackmillion,Macknillian 19,46
Macnamarra 34
McTier 17
Mackwilliam 35
Mabbett 35
Macey 41
Madera 13
Madison 11,27,31
Madox 39
Madrin 27
Magee 17
Mahoone 17
Maiders 6
Makefashion(?) 19
Makepeace 19
Malbone,sup.4
Malsby 26
Maltrat 29,38
Manering 22
Manley 38
Manlove 41
Manning 22
Manoar(?) 25
Mansfield 15
Mantz 46
Markham 39
Marler 34
Marloe 29,38
Marr 17,33
Marriott 10,18
Marrow 19
Marsk 26,41

INDEX TO COUNTY COURT NOTE-BOOK. VOLUME IV.

Marshall 3,6,21,22,25,27
29,31,38,sup.4
Martin 11,15,23,33,38,41
Mason 3,17,29,38,43
Masque 19
Massey 38
Massinborne 43
Mather
Mathew,Mathews 3,7,18
19,26,27,30,41
Matson 27
Matterson 15
Mattocks,Mattux 15,35
Maupin,Maypin 3
Maurice 19
Maws 35
Max 26
Maxwell 10,25,26
May 3,17,19,27,35
Maynard 35
Meadcroft 19
Mears,Meeres 19,43
Medley 10
Melchoir 45
Melling 27
Mellish 33
Menies(?) 43
Mercer 29,38
Mereday 30
Meredith 27,43
Mereken 15
Merifell 19
Merivether 27,41
Merritt 9,18,43
Mesctaken(?) 27
Metcalf 47
Methoe 43
Mezel 34
Micahel 13,36,sup.3,4
Micon 6,22
Middiat 30
Middleton 3,29,38
Miflin 13
Miles 26,27,34
Miller 2,13,18,22,26,35
43,46
Milligan 6
Milliscent 43
Milnor 7
Mills 3,10,19,25,33
Minstrell 3
Minton 6,19
Misnomer(?) 11
Mitchell 11,19,27,37
Modeig(?) 18
Molden,Molten 3,27
Molletta 35
Monroe 6,31
Monteith 22,33
Montgomery 18
Moone 31,46
Moonshot 15
Moore,More 2,3,10,15
19,27,35
Morehead 3,35
Morgan 3,13,27,34,35
43
Moriman 33
Morley,Morlow 11,15,
34
Morrell,Morrill 11,
14,19,28
Morris 13,14,18,22
25,27,34,35,41
Morry 34,35
Mortimer 29,38
Morton 22,31
Moss 15,29,42
Mothershead 22
Motteron 27
Motts 2
Moule 11
Mount(?) sup.2
Mountjoy 14
Mountney 3,19
Mouremore 3
Mow 3
Muldraw 17,18
Mumford 6,14
Mundy 19,29,38,43
Munson 43
Murally 19
Murphy 15
Murran 17
Murray 11,25,34
Myer,Myers 26,46
Myles 27
Nash 27
Neale 21,31,35
Neheulian 43
Nelmes 43
Nelson 17,19,25,27
Newbold 34
Newell 3
Newley 35
Newman 3,11,14,21,27,39
Newton 11,22,26
Nicholls,Nicols 27,31,43
Nicholson 34
Nickesson 34
Nicolan 33
Norman 3,21
Norris 25,34
Norton 3,18,35
Norwood 21,sup.1
Nunn 22
Nusbaum 46
Nuthead 21
Oakham 27
Oakley 2
Obbine,sup.2
Ockmond 35
O'Crahan 19
O'Daley 19
O'Dear 10
Odium(?) 33
O'Farne 19
Ogeger(?) 21
Oger 43
Ogle,Ogley 34,35
O'Kelly 47
O'Kennell 35
O'Lanny 35
O'Leally 19
Oley 21
Oliffe,Olive 35,sup.4
O'Malley(?) 35
Omararare 43

INDEX TO COUNTY COURT NOTE-BOOK. VOLUME IV.

O'Mulligan 3
Onery 3
Orom 42
Osburn 42
Oswald 10
Oswillan 11
O'Tire 35
Otter 38
Overed 38
Overton 3
Overzee, sup.2,4
Owen 43
O'William 35
Packer 27
Packford 14
Paine, Payne 6,27,35,39
43
Palley 43
Palmer 6,23,27,31,37,
sup.1
Paraeny de 39
Parish 3,6
Parker 1,3,14,19,21,25,
27,30,37,38
Parks 23,27,35
Parpint(?) 6
Parramore, sup.4
Parrett, Parratt 3,10,34
Parry 19
Parsons 1,27
Partlett 43
Partridge 47
Paryne(Perrine?) 3
Pate 35,38
Paternoster 3
Patience 27
Patriarch 43
Patten 3
Patteson, Patterson 21,38
Paulle 3
Pavey 14
Pawley 11,18
Peachell 38
Peachey 14,21,22,39,47
Peacock 18,27
Peade 43
Peak 6,27,39
Peall 42
Pearce, Perce, Pierce 2,
3,7,10,22,38
Pearson 26
Peasly 15,19
Peack 3,26,47
Peckett 27
Peckin 35
Pedigrew 10
Pell 27
Pelloone 35
Penfax 1
Penn 23,31,34
Pennington 15,30
Penry 43
Perkins 3,11,27,34
Perne 38
Perring, Paryne 1,3
Perry 26,27,43
Pettebon 21
Pettite 11,43
Peyton 7
Plaust 26
Phetteplace 44
(Fettiplace)
Phillips 18,42, sup.2
Philpin 21
Philpot 42
Pickering, Picking 18,
26
Pickfrizell 3
Pierpoint 21
Piles 13
Pinders 4
Pinkney 5
Pippinge 26
Pitman 14,22
Pitt 1,39, sup.3
Plowden 18
Plumer 19
Plunket 14
Pole 10
Polk, Polck 10,39
Polly 18
Pond 14
Pope 10,27,33,39
Pork 19
Pott, Potts 35,37
Potter 27
Pottinger 26
Pottingham 10
Poneton 38
Powell 3,6,9,21,26
27,31,34,39
Poynter 3
Pratt 6,15,30
Preeson 10
Prescott 14
Press 35
Presley, Prestley 10,27
Preston 35,43
Price 18,19,21,22,27
35,43, sup.4
Priest 38
Prill 6,13,14
Prior, Priors, Pryer 3
26,38
Pritchard, Prichard 3
14,42
Pritchett 38,43
Prittyman 19
Prout
Pudsey
Pullen, Pullam 11,14
22,27,34
Purgrave 43
Purnell 37
Pursell 14
Pusie(?) 27
Pye 11
Quisenberry 22
Raffle 15
Ramey 15
Rampe 35
Ramsay 27,39
Rance 38
Randolph 17
Rankins 31
Rashbrooke 11
Ratcliffe 37
Rattenbury 10

INDEX TO COUNTY COURT NOTE-BOOK. VOLUME IV.

Raven 35
Rawley 18
Rawlings 21,26,42
Rawlls 39
Rayle 43
Rayne 34
Read,Reed,Reid 1,6,13, 19,25,31
Readman 43
Redd 12
Redding 19,43
Reeder 26
Reeve,Reeves 3,11,15,18
Remy 20
Reno 15,46
Reswick 4
Reverdy,sup.3,4
Rewells 11
Reynolds 27,38
Rhea 26
Rice 14,35
Rich 3
Richard,Richards 27,31, 35
Richardson 14,27,31,38
Richman 11
Rickings 3
Riddle 7
Rider 26,41
Riding 22
Ridge 27,43
Ridgley,Redgley 21,23 31,42
Ridgway 13
Rigby 21,42
Riley 41
Ring 43
Ringly 3
Risinger 26
Roach,Roch 19,34,43
Road 3
Roberts 10,35,38,sup.2
Robertson,Roberson 1,17 25(See also Robinson)
Robins 30,34,38
Robinson 1,7,11,17,20, 21,23,33,34,35,37,42 sup.2,4 (See also Robertson)
Rock,Roch 19,43
Rodes 27
Roe,Rowe 35
Rogers,Rodger 2,34,35, 38,43
Roland 27
Rolfe,Roffe 3,34
Rolls 27
Rolston,Rulstan 26
Roper 19,sup.3
Rose 2,33,35,38
Rosier,Roser 34,38,39
Ross 42,43
Rosser,Rossers 22,35
Rostall 3
Round 10
Rouse 11
Rowles,Rolls,Rawls 14 26,27,30,39
Rowlett 34
Rowley 22
Rowlson 3
Rowser 46
Royes 35
Rumney 30
Runner 46
Rusby 35
Russell 3,27,35,39
Rutland 34
Ryland 2
Ryley,Reyly 14,15,21
St.Clair 3,27,35
St.John 3,sup.4
Sabine 46
Sacker,sup.2
Sackwell 34
Sale 42
Salisbury 34,35
Sallett 43
Salley 34
Salter 43
Sanders,Saunders 6,30, sup.3
Sanford,Sandiford, Samford 10,14,21,35
Sarson 11
Satchel 10
Savage 7,11,sup.2
Savery 35
Sawyer,Sawer,11,27
Sayne 43
Scarborough,Scarburgh 1,11,34,35,sup.1,3
Schurlook 2
Scidmore 21
Scoggin 26
Scott 2,6,14,19,26,39
Scovell,sup.3
Seale 27
Seaman 19
Seamore 43
Seaton 43
Seeger 28
Saines 27
Selby 21,37
Sellers 34
Sellick 33
Seneor 9
Sennett 43
Sewell 11,26
Sewins 35
Shalin 3
Sharles,sup.4
Sharp 6,33,35,43
Shaw 3,11,15,21
Shearman 2
Shecut 34
Shelly,Shealy 3,19
Shelton 36
Shepherd,Shepheard 2,23
Sherwood 18
Shewell 2
Shinton 19
Shippie 39
Shirley 22

Shiteare 46
Shiveley 46
Shivers 30
Shollman 43
Short 1,3,43
Shriver 45
Shultz 46
Sicoh(?) 27
Sidle 46
Sillia(?) 21
Silliks 26
Silvester 3,22
Simcock 11
Simmons 42
Simms 35,39,46
Simpkins 22
Simpson 6,30
Singlar [illegible]
(Sinclair) 27
Singleton 17
Sinn 26
Sisson 14,29
Sites 26
Size 39,47
Skinner 26
Skipp 35
Skipwith 34
Skrine 15
Slattor 27
Slaughter 22,26
Smalewell 35
Small 26
Smallwood 27
Smart 19,27,sup.3
Smell 23
Smith 3,14,15,18,19,21,
26,27,35,38,39,43,46
sup.1,2
Smithall 21
Smoocker 3
Smythe 39
Snape 3
Snead 30,35,39
Snow 37
Soanes 35
Solomon 11
Somerville 37
South 19,43
Sowerby 33
Spalding 34
Spann 43
Sparrow 11
Spell 34
Spence 6,21,37,47
Spencer 17,42
Spicer 21,31
Spillamore 43
Spoo 45
Spratley 41
Sprigg 2
Spring 11
Spry 34
Spurr 3
Stackley 35
Stanaway 26
Stanfast,sup.2
Stanford,Standford 11
35
Stanley 35
Stanton 6,43
Staples 3,27
Starke 21
Stegg 35
Steinheffer 26
Stell 10
Stephenson 35
Sterling 9,27
Stevens,Stephens 11,15
21,33,35,36,43
Stewart,Steward 7,sup.4
Sticoy 4
Stiles 27
Stockley 7
Stoke 3
Stone 10,14,15,17,22,
31,34,39,47
Storke 1
Stout,Stoot 34,38
Startford 43
Stratton,Streaton 11,
43
Streater 43
Stribling 46
Stringfellow 6
Strother 6,22,31
Such,Sutch,34,sup.2
Suggett 14
Sullivan 26,41,43(?)
Sutton 35
Swaidner,Sweadner 46
Swan 14,35,43
Swanson 2
Sweeting 38
Swinburne 22
Symes 30
Symons 26,35,43
Tab 43
Talbott 43
Taliaferro 31
Tall 11
Talley(?) 43
Tanner 35,43
Tapping 15
Tarcy 46
Tarpley 22
Taverner 14,21,39
Tawtam(?)27
Taylor,Tayler 3,10
30,31,35,39,42,43
46,47
Teage,Teague 35(?)
37,43
Teagle,Teackle 30,34
43,sup.4
Tebb,Tab 43,46
Temple 30
Templer 46
Templin 46
Tench 21
Terrell 43
Terry 46
Thacker 14
Therald 30
Thomas 14,26,34,35,
43,46
Thomson,Thompson,
Tomson 2,4,10,11,18
19,27,34,43,sup.2

Thornberry 30
Thornley 31
Thornton 3,6,7,22,31,47
Thorowgood 35
Thrfit 22
Throught 43
Thurgood 46
Tibbs 46
Tilbey 46
Tiller 27
Tillery 47
Tillett 39,46
Tilney 20
Tindall 30
Tingy 43
Tinker 43
Titterson 27
Todd 46
Tomlin 1,2,3
Tompkins 47
Toogood 35
Toole 3
Topping 39
Torrey 44
Tosier 30
Toulson 6,25
Towardy(?) 35
Towers 39
Townshend 19
Traherne 46
Tralley 27
Trapp 35
Traveller,sup.3,4
Travers,Trevers 14,27,43
47
Trenow 17
Trent 39
Trevilian 46
Trew 10
Triplett 15,39
Triponet 46
Tritter(?) 43
Trondle 30
Trorell 35
Troughear 35
Troy 13
Trueman 35
Truett 43
Trump 46
Tuck 11,34
Tucker 19
Tudway 46
Tuffes 27
Tully,sup.1
Tunnell(?) 1
Tunstead 43
Turby 27
Turkinton 46
Turner 2,6,21,22,31
Turrough 43
Tushan 27
Tutt 22
Twiford 25
Twillye 11
Tyler 6,46
Tysoe 46
Udall 3
Upshur 30
Underwood 9,22,39
Urlin 11
Ury 6
Usher,Ushaw 46
Vagha de 6
Vanbeeck 7
Vanbibber 7
Vance 26
Vanderhorst 18
Vangilder 13
Vansweringen 7
Varnell 27
Varney 35
Varnham 35
Vaughan 37
Verbrack 7
Verdin 13
Vickroy 45
Victor 7
Victsorrell(Fitzgerald)
27
Vincent 11
Vines,sup.4
Vinson 34
Vivion 6
Vosse 46
Wadden 19
Waddington 19
Waddle 46
Wade,Waide 1,7,11,13
23,25
Wainhouse 25
Wakefield 27
Wakeman 21
Walgrow 35
Walker 10,14,27,38,42,
46,sup.2,3
Wall 19
Waller 43
Wallis 17
Wallon 35
Walsby 46
Walter 10,43
Walton 27,35
Waltz 46
Ward 18,sup.2
Wardell 26
Ware 43
Warfield,Waffield 5,
15,30,35
Warne 11
Warner 1,19,42,43,46
Warren 20
Washington 39
Waterman 10
Waters 30,sup.2
Watkins 3,11,27
Watson 3,27,33,38,41,43
Watt,Watts 3,10,21,25,
27,35
Watten 43
Waughop 11,19
Way 45
Weaver 46
Webb 3,11,14,21,27,34
37,43
Webster 20,43
Weekes 42
Weele 11
Weesels 7

INDEX TO COUNTY COURT NOTE-BOOK. VOLUME IV.

Weire 2,10
Weldon 1
Welfe 3,sup.4
Wellman 3
Wells 1,3,13,15,25,30, 35,47
Welsh,Welch 19,42
Wellsley 21
Welton 3
West, Weast 2,3,35,39, 46
Westerell 30
Wharton 3,14,39
Wheatley 10,42
Wheeldon 27
Wheeler 39,46
Whelock 30
Whetsel 22
Whitby 35
White 3,6,14,15,21,22 30,35
Whitehead 10,30
Whitehege(?) 27
Whiting 22,35
Whitter 18
Whittingham 35
Whittle 3
Whitty 35
Whord 11
Wicke 35
Wiffing 44
Wigg 3
Wignall 27
Wilcox,sup.4
Wilde 35
Wilden 3
Wildy 38,42,43
Wilkins 43
Wilkinson 10,11,34
Williams 11,14,15,19,27 31,33,34,35,43,sup.4
Williamson 27
Willis 11,19
Willmot 10,18,19
Willsford 11
Wilson 3,11,19,22,26 27,34,35,41,43,46 47
Wilyard 46
Wim (?) 1
Winchester 46
Wing 14
Winkle 19
Winshew 35
Winter 3,14,46
Winterton 11
Wise,Wyes,Wyse 2,25 26,39,43
Witham 46
Withers 23
Witt 14
Wolfendall 21,22
Wolf,Woolf 7,34
Womsley 30
Wood 11,14,15,22,35 43
Woodbridge,Woolbridge 2,39,43
Woodcock 14
Wooding 46
Woodington 19
Woodland 26
Woolard 47
Woolaston 46
Woolman 42
Wooton 30
Wormly 42
Worman 18
Worthington 30
Woshe (?) 19
Wren 38
Wrench 35
Wright 7,11,14,18,21 30,34,35
Wringlesby 22
Wrist 35
Wyat 7
Wymer 27
Wyse,(see Wise)
Yardley,Yeardley,sup.1 2,3,4
Yates 14,22,43
Yeoman 27
Yerkins 34
Yoho 13
Young,Yonge 3,15,17 19,33,43
Zenger 7
Zimmerman 45

More than one entry on the same page is indicated by underscoring.

The

County Court Note-Book

A Little Bulletin of History and Genealogy

February, 1926. **Vol. V, No. 1**

SHIPS IN PORT

Ship *Russell Galley;* of London, "sayleing from the Island of Jamaica." Robert Robertson (Robinson) commdr. Thomas Tackerbury, mate, and Adolph Vanderville[?] Bo's'n. A "protest." E. C. cty, Va. 7 Aug 1696. 1684-1699, p. 209. Capt. Robt Bickford, Pylott for the Windward Passage.

St. John of Amsterdam, a Dutch ship. N-n Va. 28 Apr 1653. iv-182.

Ship *St. Laurence;* Capt. Tho. Turnifall. Acco. Va. 1675.

Ship *St. Nicholas,* of Galloway, Ireland. Acco. Va. 1672. iv-188.

Ship *Symon and Frances;* Capt. Daniel Penfax, commdr. N-n, Va. 1674. x-270.

Sloop *Sachem;* Isaiah Robinson, Captain. Philada, Penna. 1777-1781. Penna. Arch.

Ketch *Salem,* from Boston to Virginia. L. Norf, Va. 1656.

Ketch *Salisbury;* N-n, Va. 29 Aug 1673. x-209.

Sloop *Salley;* James Jordan, of Camden cty, and Joseph Gardner, of Boston, agree to charter. Camden cty, Ga. 1796. E—

The *Sarah;* Henry True, Master. N-n, Va. 21 May 1655. v-43.

Shipp *Santa Maria;* N-n, Va. 3 Apr 1643. ii-253. Aries Top, merchant, of the Ship *Sancta Maria, Amerstand.* N-n, Va. 2 Sept 1643. ii-274.

Shipp *Sarah and Elizabeth,* of Bristoll; Rich'd White, master. Dor. cty, Md. 20 Apr 1680. iv-

Ship *Sarah and Susan;* Mr. John Chapman, commdr. Essex cty, Va. 1693.

Ketch *Speedwell,* of Boston; Thos. Berry, commdr. N-n, Va. 10 Mch 1669. xi-13. In 1654, the *Speedwell,* of N. E. belonged to Mr. Jno. Holland. N-n, Va. 1 Dec 1654. v-73.

Ship the *Speedwell:* Mr. James Harris, master. L. Norf, Va. 1661.

The *Seaflower;* Capt. Robert Wilkinson, commdr. I. W. cty. 2 May 1664. iii-8.

Ship *Seville Merchant;* John Jewitt, commdr. L. Norf, Va. 1645.

Ship *Sheppard;* John Michael and Col. Wm. Kendall part owners. N-n, Va. 1660. ix-81.

The good Ship *Society* of Liverpoole, Lancaster cty, England; Jonathan Liveseley [?], marriner, master. [An Instrument of Protest.] Acco., Va. 15 Dec 1691. ix-231.

Ship *Society,* of Bristol; wrecked on the Eastern Shore of Virginia. John Skeetch, master. Va. Cal. St. Pa. 7 Aug 1787. i-30.

Ship *Spencer,* of London; Nicho's Goodridge, mariner, master. Staff. Va., Orders, 12 Mch 1690. i-131.

The *Spred Egle,* of Bristoll; Mr. Wm. Carver [master?] L. Norf., Va. 1657. D-127. Capt. John Whittey, Commdr. 4 Apr 1661. D-299.

The good ship *Spred Egle,* Capt. John Whittey, commdr. Cast away at the "Bermodus." L. Norf., Va. D-299. (James City Quarter Court, 4 Apr 1661.)

Ship *Starr frigott;* Abraham Le Messurier, commdr. Va. St. Pa. 1710. i-139. Also 4 May 1710. Acco., Va. xiv-1.

Ship *Stephen and Edward;* Thos. Saywell, commdr. Essex, Va. 1693. i-153.

Ship called the *Surratt or Sarratt Marcht.* N-n, Va. 1679. xiii-75.

Brigantine *Sidney;* Capt. Richard Moseley, master. Norf., Va. About 1723. F-153.

Barke *Supply;* James Mills conveys all his interest in her to Ellis Else [*sic*] and it is also agreed that Else shall sayle with the sd Barke to New Haven, and there require a bill of sale for said barke from Mrs. Johanna Allerton. Surry, Va. 4 July 1662. i-192.

MARRIAGES BY INFERENCE* WESTMORELAND COUNTY VIRGINIA†

WILLIAM ARMIGER and SUSANNA FISHER, probably a widow. Before 25 May 1681. Orders 1676-88, pp.205, 221.

ABRAHAM BLAGG and MARGARET WATTS, widow of John. Before 8 Oct 1679. Orders, 1676-88, pp. 164, 329.

Capt. ANTHONY BRIDGES and ELIZABETH ROSIER, widow of Mr. John Rosier, Clerke. Before 27 Apr 1664. Orders, 1662-64, f.26. Also 1676-88, p.223.

Mr. ANTHONY BRIDGES and Mrs. ELIZABETH SOLLEY [wid. Mr. Thomas Solley]. Before 27 Apr 1664. Orders, 1662-64.

ANTHONY BRIDGES and ELIZABETH HYLLYARD, heiress of John Hyllyard. Before 29 Nov 1671. Orders, 1668-77, f. 98.

THOMAS BUTLER and the widow of Capt. Alex'r BAYNHAM, Before 27 Apr 1664. Orders, 1662-64, f. 25.

Mr. WILLIAM BUTLER, Minister, and JANE, the widow of Dan'll LISSUMM[?] Before 5 Nov 1679. Orders, 1676-88, p.168 and p. 197.

WILLIAM BUTLER and JOANNA WARD, the Relict and extx of John Ward. Before 27 May 1685. Orders, 1676-88, p.409.

JAMES BROWSFORD and JANE BUTLER, widow of Daniel Lysson and also

†See note on p. 4.

of [William] Butler. Before 26 Mch 1684. Orders, 1676-88, p.325.

JOHN BOLTON, Clerk, and FRANCES SPENCER, widow. Before . . . Nov 1693. Orders [5], p.219.

Mr. JOHN BERRYMAN and the Relict of Tho: BUTLER. Before 28 July 1680. Orders, 1676-88, p.183.

Mr. RICHARD BLACKBURN and MARY ASHTON, widow of Col. Henry Ashton, Before 31 Aug 1742. Fid. Accts, i-272.

ORIGINELL BROWNE and . . . BROOKS, dau. Henry, Before 11 Jany 1682. Orders 1676-88, p.275.

JOHN BEERE and the relict of John MASON, About 25 June 1684. Orders, 1676-88, p.341.

THOMAS BURKLEY[?] and SUSANNA CARIER[??] widow of John. Burkley now dec'd; the widow m. Rich. Sutton, "who also is dead, and now [married] to "Joseph Hardwick who may be supposed to "be in the actuall 'possession' of the 'or-"phant's'" estate, [Burkleley was probably the "orphant's" father.] Before 24 Sept 1684. Orders, 1676-88, p.351.

Mr. WILLIAM CLEMENTS and FRANCES POWELL, wid. Mar. contr. 26 July 1670. Orders, 1668-77, f. 64.

JOHN CARPENDER and the widow of . . . SAUNDERS. Before or about 17 Apr 1678. Orders, 1676-88, p.117.

JOHN DINELY [?] of Nomynie, Wmld, and KATHERINE BRENT, dau. of Mr. Edward Brent. Before 7 Apr 1769. Orders, 1668-77, f.48.

DARBY DRISCO[?] and MARY HODSON, dau. of Marmaduke. Before 29 Nov 1682. Orders, 1676-88, p.267.

ABRAHAM FEILD and MARY BELL, Before 27 July 1670. Orders, 1668-77, f. 74.

MARYLAND'S NEXT OF KIN *

EDWARD and MARGARET PHILLPOTT; inv. John Bryfield of Charles cty. 27 July 1720. iv-239.

THOMAS BILLINGSLEY and REBECCA YOUNG; inv. Elizabeth Bourne of Calvert cty. 16 June 1720. iv-248.

CLARK SMITH; inv. John Smith, of Pr. Geo's cty. 24 Oct 1720 iv-250.

JOHN and LEWIS WILLCOXON: inv William Jervis, of Pr. Geo's cty. 8 June 1720. iv-251.

MARY ELLITT, his mother, and JOHN BRONER, his brother; inv. William Broner, of Pr. Geo's cty. 25 Feby 1720. iv-253.

ABRAHAM TAYLOR and WILLIAM DAWTERIDGE; inv. Abraham Taylor of Q. A. cty. 27 Aug 1719. iv-254.

JOSHUA JONES; inv. Joshua Jones, of A. A. cty. 1 Aug 1720. iv-256.

HENRY SMITH, "only Relation in this Province"; inv. Capt. George Brown of A. A. cty. 13 Sept 1720. iv-258.

SAM'L WARD and EDWARD WARD; inv. Robert Ward of A. A. cty. 15 Aug 1720. iv-262.

MARK HERBERT and FRANK HERBERT; inv. Wm. Herbert of St. Mary's cty. 2 Feby 1720. iv-269.

THOMAS TANEY; inv. John Taney of St. Mary's cty. 19 June 1720. iv-270.

THOMAS HOOPER, son of the dec., RODGER HOOPER, brother; inv. Henry Hooper of Dor. cty. 17 Nov 1720. iv-273.

JOHN BEALL and J. NICHOLSON; inv. William Nicholson of Pr. Geo's cty. 19 Dec 1720. iv-280.

JOHN and HANNAH ORRICK, and MARY EAGLE; inv. Wm. Orrick of Balto, cty. 2 Nov 1720. iv-288.

MARGARET YOUNG; inv. Edward Brian of A. A. cty. 2 May 1720. iv-290.

BRACH'LL[?] PINNER and MARTHA PIPER; inv. William Glanvill, Sr. of Kent cty. 21 Nov 1719. iv-293.

GEORGE DREW, the extr, and SARAH DREW; inv. Anthony Drew of Balto cty. 14 Jany 1720. iv-302.

BENJAMIN CHEW and MARGARET BRANN; inv. Wm. Chew of Balto cty. 14 Jany 1720. iv-309.

JOHN, PETTER, JOSEPH and RICHARD GALLOWAY, sons; inv. Samuel Galloway of A. A. cty. 22 Apr 1721. iv-313.

THEODORE MATT and RICHARD HILL; inv. Stephen Ross of Dor. cty. 16 Mch 1720. iv-319.

JOSEPH and EDWARD ALFORD; inv. Elizabeth Helpin of Dor. cty. 23 Aug 1720. iv-319.

NATHANIEL HYNSON; inv. John Hynson of Kent cty. 18 June 1720. iv-323.

JOHN SANDERS, brother of deceased; inv. Edward Sanders of Charles cty. 6 Oct 1720. iv-327.

PHILLIP and THOMAS GITTINGS; inv. Phillip Gittings, Sen., of Pr. Geo's cty. 27 Feby 1721. iv-331.

JOSEPH HOUSTON and ROBERT MILLS; inv. Robt. Huston, of Dor cty. 18 Nov 1720. iv-335.

RICHARD COLEGATE and WILLIAM RODGERS; inv. Nicholas Rodgers, of Balto cty, 3 Jany 1720. iv-336.

STEPHEN BALEY; inv. John Parsons of Som. cty. 26 Sept 1720. iv-348.

BARNETT RAMSEY, Sen., and CHARLES RAMSEY; inv. Barnett Ramsey, Jr., of Som cty. 27 Oct 1720. iv-350.

JAMES BOUND and THOMAS BENSON; inv. James Bounds of Som. cty. 14 Oct 1720. iv-351.

CHRY'E[?] NUTTER and WILLIAM YEER[?]; inv. Matthew Nutter, of Som. cty. 17 Nov 1720. iv-355.

ROBERT BLADES and JOHN PAINE; inv. John Upshutt of Som. cty. 15 Nov 1720. iv-356.

VIRGINIA COLONISTS

(From Old Volume, 5, S. L. O.)

WILLIAM WRIGHT, (at the head of Parker's Creek). 1655.

Head rights: WM. WRIGHT, Dorothy Hall, Alexander Flaminge, Marie Owen.

JOHN WYSE, North'ton cty, 1655.

Head rights: Nohab Hobs, Lawrence Hillyer, HANNAH WISE, Wently[?] Macklayne.

ROGER WOLMSLY & RICHD. INGRAM, James City cty, 1656.
Head rights; Herbert Margerom, John Eells, Rob. Bryer, David Roberts.

JOHN WILLIAMS, L. Norf. cty, 1655.
Head rights: Jno. Grey, Sarah Miller.

JOHN WOOD, South side Patewmacke River, 1656.
Head rights: Phillip Chetter, Peter Browne, Robert Walker, Alexander Farrell, James Williams, Andrew Berry, Jane Griffith, Tho. Senior, Tho. Pond [Pound??] Jane Abbott, James Joyner, Fran. Gregory, James Kirke, Michaell Long, James Mackiney, Edward Allen, Ellis Benison, Wm. Seale, Joseph Kent, John Moyses.

HENRY WESGATE, L. Norf. cty. [Date not given, but probably 1655.]
Head rights: John Browne, Morgan Jones, Mathew Henderson, ELLEN WESGATE, Tho. Woolner.

NICHOLAS WADDISON [WATERSON?? perhaps WADDILOW??] North'ton cty, 1656.
Head rights: George Johnson, Wm. Smithson, Wm. Willson, Cornelius Clinton, Derrick Aryson[?], Derrick Arbson[?], John Willy.

JOHN WILLIAMS, North'ton cty, 1655.
Head rights: JNO. WILLIAMS, Eliz: Hobson, Rob. Atkins, Tho: Broadway, Alexander [no surname].

RICHARD WHEELER, L. Norf. cty, 1656.
Head rights: Mary Boggis, Rob. Boggis, Jno. Boggis, Geo. Sheeves, Eliz: Bowe, Jno. Harris.

NICHOLAS WADDELOW, North'ton cty, 1656.
Head rights: Alexander Coote, Dorman Usshullevan, Daniell Usshullevan [probably O'Sullivan], Teague Longe, Nath. B . . . [?] Tho. Southerne, Elizabeth Tarry [Terry].

ROBERT WILSON, Nthd cty, 1656.
Head rights: Jno. Ball. [Eight rights but only one name given.]

Capt. HUGH WILSON, Nthd cty, 1656.
Head rights: Wm. Thorpe, Tho. Robinson, Nicholas Allen, Gowen Canada [Kennedy], Richd Lilborne, Wm. Barefott, [Burfoot, Barefoot, and perhaps Burford], Lawrence Stockwell, Richd. Lee, Annie Lee, Florentine Paine. [These rights are assigned by Col. Lee.]

JOHN WOOD, "of Wicocomocoe," "easterly upon Petomeck river," 1657.
Head rights: Susan Bury, Jane Bluney, Reb: Jackson, Wm. Huntly, Roger Harlston, Judith Page, Eliz: Weaver, Eliz: Maior [Major], Mary Smith, Hannah Dixon.

JOHN WOOD, "Bounding northeasterly upon Yocococomoco Creeke in Petomeck freshes." 1657.
Head rights: Grace Harrison, Geo. Burton, James Davis, Nich. Coaleman, Hen. Rowse, Mary Linton.

The same.
Head rights: Mary Jones, James Coxe, Edwd Burly, Richd. Atkins, Richd. Alcock, Mich. Waller.

JOHN WOOD, Westmoreland cty, 1657.
Head rights: Walter Bird, Wm. Lacy, Wm. Lee, Jeremy Lawes, James Lewis, Rob. Haines, John Fryer, Ellner. Read, Joane Sands, Jane Williams.

JOHN WOOD, "Bounding North Easterly upon a Creeke in Petomeck freshes," 1657.
Head rights: Edd. Spicer, Nch. Titbury, Mich. Waterford, Hugh Jeffers, Bar: Stilt, Jeffrey Speed, Rob. Fostly[?], Tho. Tiller, Jno. MackoMack, Marg: Merrick.

ROGER WALTERS, s. w. side "Aquaconde" River, 1657.
Head rights: Joice Coventon, Andrew Moss, Hen. Walker, James Bowles, Richd. Perrin, Charles Howard.

WILLIAM WALTHALL, Henrico cty, 1657.
Head rights: WM. WALTHALL, Anne Hughs, Joane Watts, Rob. Plaine, Geo. Dice, Ed. Markham, Jam: Ekin, Gab: Bolton, Edwd. Crawford, Richd. Parsons, Marg. Heines, Eliz: Thomas, Hamond Woodhouse, Edwd. Atkins, Alice and Willm, Irish persons.

ROBERT WARREN, North'ton cty, 1657.
Head rights: Susana Spratlin, Wm. Rodolphus, Kath. Rodulphus.

The same. [Probably re-recorded.]

WM. WILDY, Hopkins Creeke in Patomeck freshes, 1657.
Head rights: Tho: Radly, Thomas Chester, Jno. Withers, Dorathy Jones, Eliz: Cooke, Tho. Hopkins, John Hopkins, Richard Walter, Isaack Hill, Eliz: Briggs, Jno. Morgan, Jno. Tally, Robert Digby, Mary Sadler, Elizabeth James, Katherine Chester, Roger Payton, David Lewellin, Richard Luckett, Jno. Adlome.

EDWARD WILLIAMS, in Petomeck freshes, 1658.
Head rights: Tho. Young, James Gainsbrooke, Abigall Wills, Eliz: Dowesby, Tho. Shelton, Charles Blackmore, John Greensell, Ro: Huffe, Elizabeth Sharpe.

ARTHUR UPSHOTT, North'ton cty, 1655.
Head rights: Mary Risden, James Risden, Land . . . [?] Riden, Arth. Carpenter, Phillip Soccohack[?], John Alber.

Mr. ROBERT VAULX, York cty, 1657.
Head rights: Mr. Charles Woodington, Ann Michell, Jno. Clarke.

HENRY VINCENT, in Petomeck freshes, 1657.
Head rights: Ann Leeson, Ellinor an Irish Mayd, James Wmson, Tho. Lynard, Tho. Hackett, Rob. Hogg, Jno. Lucas, Eliz. Edom, Eliz. Pettus, Jno. Rookes.

HENRY VINCENT, in freshes of Patomeck River, 1657.
Head rights: Jno. Watson, Moses Hill, Rob. Bryan, Arthur Kinge, Tho: Morrice, James Boswell, Jno. Berry, Mary Berry, Ruth Mason, James Jnoson.

WILLIAM YARRET, Isle of Wight cty, 1657.
Head rights: Francis Short, Anne Morris, Edward Tyson.

RICHARD YOUELL, "orphant sonne of Mr. Tho. Youell, dec'd," Bounding Easterly upon Petomeck river in the freshes, 1657.
Head rights: Edmond Ayres, Richd. Ayres, Eliz: Swansy, Tho. Pope, Henry Poise, Anne Williams, Mary Ellice, Andrew Burchell, James Staple, Martha Wright.

(*End of first alphabet, Old Volume* 5.)

The County Court Note-Book

An every-other-monthly devoted mainly to abstracts from County Court records, prior to 1800.

MILNOR LJUNGSTEDT, Editor and Publisher. Bethesda, Route 10, Maryland.

Published six times a year. Subscription, two dollars, in advance; must begin with the year. Advertising rates moderate.

FEBRUARY, 1926

Vol. V., No. 1

DO IT NOW

Were you born a putter-off? Did it always seem to you that anything could be done any time, until all of a sudden you awoke to the fact that the thing that is not done on the spot is too often never done? That "putting off an easy thing makes it hard; putting off a hard thing makes it impossible."

This small sermon is about family records, those tiresome statistics which optimistic ladies skip over with the lightness of fairies, and with the same indifference to detail which we may imagine those fanciful creatures to possess. We might recall, nevertheless, that however little *Iolanthe,* the immortal, was troubled with Burke and DeBrett, the son of Iolanthe was very much concerned over his half-fairy heredity, he could get but part way through a key-hole!

Concerning this question of deferring, have you not said to yourself or your family, "I'll go and register to-morrow," or "I'll write that down just as soon as I go upstairs," and then you didn't, for some perfectly good reason, perhaps, and by-and-bye neither you nor the family could be certain of the exact date or the exact figure. Or, maybe, there was an old aunt living. You promised yourself (and the family) that some day you would see that old aunt and ask her whether she remembered the name of your great-grandfather's second wife. Some day and any day passed, and the old aunt died, and with her the information you desired.

It would seem impossible that a man should forget the dates of the birth of his children, but he does and did. No less than two records have been copied by the Editor in which men of considerable prominence in colonial days, failed to keep the list of their "tithables" straight, because, apparently, they forgot to record a birth and then forgot the birth!

Do it now! Write or call in person on the distant relative or family friend who knows, and ask questions, even if you do have to invite them to the next family gathering. A long time ago when the Editor began to explore she was cordially received and asked to spend the night at a great uncle's. She did, in a fat feather-bed with a very old great-aunt by marriage. The next day, however, she was rewarded with three pieces of the real blue china, with gilt edges, made that way per order of an old sea-captain, for whom the plain Canton or Nankin was not good enough. Possibly had she spent a week, she would have also received from those friendly old folk some of the goblets, with initials cut in, that graced the captain's table. These kindly folk recognized that the Editor, being a descendant, had a sort of right to share in the heir-looms. That recognition was also part of their inheritance.

But don't take your relatives literally, unless you have means of checking up. The Editor has hitherto called attention to the fact that a lady who was a widow in 1759, with already four children, and who married a second time in 1760, was hardly alive and visited by another lady who is now only some seventy-three years old. Yet the lady who is seventy-three, or at most, seventy-four, believes that she did so visit and has mentioned it in a book she published. This is that common case of two or more members of a family, belonging to different generations, bearing the same name.

Some of us, like the Editor, may have started life with quite a normal family as to numbers, but within the span of two or three decades, have found ourselves at the end of a branch, a fluttering leaf of a tree from which all other leaves have fallen; a tree in which there is no more gay or gentle whispering among its company, and none to tell how it germinated or who planted the seed on this side of the great water.

There is nothing ridiculous in wishing to know one's ancestry. Many a peasant in the older lands can no doubt recount his forbears for generations back. He reads his own book. Why should we not read ours?

ERRATA: The name TILFAITE, NOTE-BOOK for May, 1924, COLONIAL FORE-NAMES, should be TILFAIRE, (WILMOT TILFAIRE).

The following marriages by inference in January, 1924, of the NOTE-BOOK, gave no county. They are all from NORTHAMPTON COUNTY, VIRGINIA.

JOHN SAVAGE, Gent., and MARY ROBBINS, Sp. Mar. contract. 16 Dec 1667. vii-24.

JACOB STRINGER and ELESHA HARMANSON, dau. of Thomas. Before 10 Mch 1724. xxiiiR-206.

JONATHAN STOTT [SCOTT?] and AMYAH[?] JACOB. Before 10 Sept 1702. xviii-172.

SIMON THOMAS and REBECCA HANBY, dau. of Richard. Before 22 Aug 1682. xiii-

LAWRENCE TEIGUE [?] and MARY KATHERINE VAN HAMELL, dau. of Derrick and Sophia. See entry 8 Sept 1679. xiii-59.

JOHN TANKRED and SARAH SMART, dau. of William. Before 26 July 1708. xviii-437.

Mr. ROBERT TILLGHMAN and Mrs. SUSANNA SELLUCK, widow of Daniel Sellick, Mcht. Before 1 May 1655. v-134.

The marriages listed in this number of the NOTE-BOOK are from the records of Westmoreland county. Westmoreland was formed from Northumberland county in 1653. To understand its present extent it is advisable to consult the County Bulletin published by the State Library of Virginia, as boundaries were changed and the later formation of King George, sandwiched between Stafford and the older county, is at times confusing.

When the Editor left Westmoreland on her last visit, the Clerk of the Court said to her apropos of these marriages, *"You are going to make me a lot of trouble!"* The Editor promptly answered that she was quite aware of it, but that she would do her level best in the way of explanation, so that he would not be called upon for copies of marriage records which do not exist *as such* in the office of the Clerk of Westmoreland county.

There are no marriage records either as licenses, bonds or marriage returns in Westmoreland civil records, prior to 1786. The list in this issue of the NOTE-BOOK and the lists which will follow (the Editor has notes of over one hundred references) are made up from inferential statements in wills, deeds, settlements of estates, depositions, &c. The Clerk will not, of course, furnish a certified copy of any such abstract, but probably in a case of importance he would furnish a certified copy of the entire record. He would hardly have time, however, to search through the body of such a record in order to identify the marriage item. The Editor makes this statement merely as a matter of fairness to the Clerk, and in appreciation of his courtesy.

An Unusual and Valuable Deposition.

Richard Edelen, Sen., aged eighty-three years and upwards being Duly Sworn on the holy Evangelists of Almighty God Declares that he very well Remembers and was acquainted with MARMADUKE SIMMES About Seventy years ago and that the said MARMADUKE SIMMES has been dead above Sixty years and his Eldest son was Named ANTHONY with whom Deponent was very Intimate and the said Anthony Simmes eldest son was named MARMADUKE and with whom he this Deponent was also very well Acquainted and the said Marmaduke Simms his eldest son is named ANTHONY now alive and further saith not. Charles cty, Md. Deeds, A3, pt 1, p.366. 10 May 1775.

WILLIAMS NOTES MARYLAND-VIRGINIA SECTION

ABRAHAM WILLIAMS, JOHN WILLIAMS and wife MARGARET ("Peggy"), of Shenandoah cty, Va. to John Cullers, same; part of six acres on west side of Hawksbill crk, conveyed to ABRAHAM and JOHN WILLIAMS, in 1815, by Kizer and wf. Shenan, Va. 10 June 1819. Z-309.

ABRAHAM WILLIAMS and JOHN WILLIAMS: deed from Andrew Kiser and wf Sarah. Shenan., Va. 19 Aug 1815. W-101.

AGNES WILLIAMS, age 24. N-n, Va. 19 May 1634. i-16.

ALFORD WILLIAMS in Fred'k cty, Va. Tax-list. 1782.

ANDREW WILLIAMS had wf Anne. Pr. Wm, Va. Orders. Ct July 1762.

ANN WILLIAMS m. JOSIA JENKINS. Shenan, Va. Mar. ret. 11 Jany 1798.

BARNETT WILLIAMS, ALFORD WILLIAMS, HAZIL WILLIAMS, ELISHA WILLIAMS. Fred'k, Va. Land Book. 1782.

BETSY WILLIAMS m. JOHN COFFETT. Shenan, Va. Mar. ret. 14 Dec 1794.

BENJAMIN and ROBERT WILLIAMS. Voters. Staff, Va. P-181. 24 July 1758.

BENJAMIN WILLIAMS; admn on his est. to JOSEPH WILLIAMS, widow having renounced. Shenan, Va. Minutes, Ct 25 Mch 1777.

BARUCH WILLIAMS, est. Jeremiah Crabb, one of extrs, LUCY WILLIAMS another. Pr. Geo's, Md. 24 Feby 1756. DD6-128.

BARRUGH [BARUCH] WILLIAMS; 200 acres of the Three Sisters possessed by his orphans. Pr. Geo's Rent Roll, Md. 1723.

BENJAMIN WILLIAMS; est. appraised. See also JOSEPH WILLIAMS, admr. Shenan, Va. A-437. 29 Aug 1782.

CHARLES WILLIAMS, Fauquier cty, Va., from NATHANIELL WILLIAMS of Stafford. GEO. WILLIAMS one of wit. Fauq, Va. 16 Apr 1777. vi-400.

CHARLES WILLIAMS, Fauq. cty, Va., wf Nancy, to Wm. Allason. Fauq., Va. vii-228. 1779.

DANIEL WILLIAMS; suit. Pr. Wm, Va., Orders, 323, Ct 10 Sept 1762.

DAVID WILLIAMS, 200 acres. Aug. cty, Va. Land Book. 1782.

DAVID WILLIAMS and wf Sarah, to William Wilson, tract on Lost River of Great Cape Capon [*sic*]. Hamp, Va .iii-6. 7 Aug 1771.

DAVID WILLIAMS and wf Elizabeth, Fauquier cty, Va., to John Knox of K. Geo., Mcht, 77 acres on branch of the Elkmarsh. Lease and release, 10 June 1764. ii-150.

DAVID WILLIAMS; inv. his estate. Pr. Wm, Va. 27 June 1743. C-421.

EDWARD WILLIAMS; Rockingham Land Entries, Va. p.4. 1782.

ELIJAH WILLIAMS' estate; REBEKAH WILLIAMS, admx. Fauq. cty, Va. 25 Oct 1815. vi-162.

ELISHA WILLIAMS; Fred'k cty, Va., land tax list. 160 a., 112 a., "Do for Alnut", 400 a. 1782.

ELIZABETH WILLIAMS and James Knight, Jr. Fred'k cty, Va. Mar. Ret. 23 Oct 1783.

ELIZABETH WILLIAMS and Jno. Ross. Shenan. cty, Va. Mar. Record. 15 Apr 1795.

ELIZABETH WILLIAMS; Ldn cty, Va. land tax list. 136 a. 20 years' purchase. 1784. (Also listed 1782.)

ELLENDER WILLIAMS and Bennet Woodard. Shenan. cty, Va. Mar. Record. 4 Mch 1798.

FRANCES WILLIAMS, wf of John. See his will. Acco. cty, Va. 14 Feby 1666. ii-68.

FRANCES WILLIAMS, dau. of CHARLES and MARY WILLIAMS, Bap. 22 Oct 1792. St. Paul's Church, Balto. Md.

FANNY WILLIAMS and Loughland McIntosh. Shenan. cty Va. Mar. Record. 16 Mch 1790.

INTERCOUNTY AND INTERCOLONIAL

Mr. LUTHER HAYMOND, Clarksburg, W. Va. in a letter written in 1842, states that his father removed to West Virginia "from Montgomery County Court House, within three miles of Rockville." That he was a wagon-maker by trade. The writer of the letter was born in Maryland in 1771. Understands his father commanded a company at Fort Duquesne. Transallegheny Mgs. Vols. 1-2. p.279.

JOHN MORRAH'S nun-cup. will mentions godson Thomas Wardon of Barbadoes, to whom he gives 1000 lbs. of *Muscovada* sugar, in the hands of Joseph Warden of Barbadoes, father of sd Thomas. Old Rappa., Va. 14 Sept 1682. 1677- p.17.

DOUGLAS NEWPORT, the widow of Richard, writes from "Redriffe." N-n, Va. 11 Sept 1643. ii-328.

JOHN O'DEAR, in "Carrolina," was the possessor of 160 acres of Emmett's Discovery. Wor. cty, Md, Rent Roll, 1744.

NATHANIEL OLDIS, Gent., and Wm. Parry, both of Kicoughtan [Va.] N-n, Va. 10 Feby 1643. ii-281.

THEOPHILUS PUGH, Mcht, and wf Mary, of Nansemond, Va. Power to Stratton Burton, Acco., Va. 19 Mch 1723. xvi-200.

STEPHEN RANDALL, mariner, living in New England; power to William Young, Jr., of Acco., Va. Acco., 1 Apr 1735. xx-203.

DOMINICK RICE, in his will orders his son Stephen to be sent to Ireland "to my father, when he is five years old." Reversion of son's legacy to eldest son of eldest sister in Ireland. He also gives to son Stephen, 500 acres in Choptank, Md; also lands near Farnham Creek. Old Rappa. cty, Va. 28 Oct 1683-4 Mch 1684-5.

JOHN STERRITT, county of Scott, State of Kentucky, by atty conveys land in Shenandoah county, Va. Shenan. K-413; 3 Mch 1797.

Mr. JOSEPH SENIOR was a Mcht of Barbadoes. I. W. iv-19; about 1689.

JOHN SOLWAY, of Surry, Va., pltr, from John Dunston, of Maryland, pltr, and James Redick, pltr, and wf Mary, of Surry; land head of Lownes Creek. west side. Surry 1-394; 30 Oct 1671.

JANE SMYTH, of the Isle of Kent, *Gent.* [probably abbreviation of *Gentlewoman;*] two deeds. N-n ii-281; 10 Feby 1643.

DANIEL STONE, of Loudoun cty, Va., son of Thomas Stone and wf Jamimah, dec'd, of Westmoreland cty, Va., married Sarah Hough, of Loudoun cty, dau. of William and Elinor. Friends' Records, Ffx Mtg. 30-5-1798. p.125.

ELIAS TAYLOR, [removed to] "East Jersey Co., Penna." Acco. xx-16; Record 1 Aug 1729.

JOHN VIRGIN, of Pensilvania; power to Thomas Davis, concerning a land warrant. 29 Sept 1786. Bourborn cty, Ky. A-62.

THOMAS WILLOUGHBY, of the Barbadoes, Marriner; power to Thomas Willoughby, Gent., of Va. L. Norf. D-285; 28 Feby 1660.

HENDERICK WAGOMAN, carpenter, a Dutchman, of the City of Amsterdam. N-n, Va. 9 May 1660. ix-70.

ISAAC WATERHOUSE, of Halifax, dyer; kinsman of Isaac Foxcroft. N-n Va. 29 Mch 1704. xviii-188.

TIMO. WILLIAMSON, of Hartford, *Coniticute,* N. E., mariner. Acco., Va. 1718. xvi-53.

JAMES WATTS, will. Two sons, John and Spencer Watts, 300 acres on the Eastern Shore. Wf Elizabeth, extx. Wmld, Va. 31 June 1699-30 Aug 1699. i-189.

WILLIAM WILTON, of Philada., going to live in Newbern, N. C., gives power to Ann Musgrove and Thos. Canby, of Philada., Mchts, N. C. cty, Dela. 18 Aug 1764. Z1-161.

TAX LISTS OF OHIO COUNTY, WEST VIRGINIA. PERSONAL PROPERTY. 1788.

Abel Johnson, John Johnson, William Johnson, Stephen Johnson, David Johnson, Thomas Johnson, Ruben Juitt;

William Leadom, James Leaper, William Ladely, John Littleton;

John McCoy, John Miller, Robert Murtling, John McKnight, James McEllroy, James McGuire, Thomas Maden, Alexander Mountgomary. Robert Meek, Samuel Meek, William McDonald, Cornelius McIntire, Malcolm Madcalf; John McConel, John McMillion, Daniel McCloud, Anguish McCoy, William McClain;

Benjamin Nailor, William Norris. James Nailor, Samuel Nailor, William Nailor, Jacob Neasley;

Moses Oron [?] Samuel Osbrin, John Otter.

Daniel Preston, Jesse Pamer, Sen'r, (and Benjamin Pamer); Jesse Pamer, Jr., Peter Peterson, Conrod Peterson, Thomas Peterson, Christephor Price (and Edward Hatfield);

John Quick;

Saml Robinson, John Ramage, Samuel Ramsey, William Roberts, Benjamin Reed, Elijah Rittenhouse, Joseph Ralston, Samuel Ralston, Hugh Ralston, John Rogers, Daniel Ross, Forges [*sic*] Smith, James Stean, William Strain, William Stewart, William Sutherland, James Stevenson, Isaac Swin, Richard Spear;

Stephen Treakle (and Thomas Treakle), John Towling, John Totton;

William Wells, Thomas Walling, Richard Williams, Mathew Williams, James Williams, John Williams, Edward Wiggins, Thomas Wiggins, Graybaird Richard Wells, Jacob Walker, Samuel Wright, Thomas Wilson on Indian Creek; Thomas Wilson on Harmon Creek; Jacob Wilde, Joseph Woods, David Work, Charles Wells, James Young.

Note: The foregoing list (see also October, 1925,) was returned by Charles Wells, Commissioner. At present the Editor is unable to say whether it is a complete list, but judging by other counties, it is not. Comparison with the Land Tax Book previously published in the NOTE-BOOK may assist in supplying a full list of taxables in the county.

SERVICE AND SUPPLIES COLONIAL, REVOLUTIONARY AND MILITIA

SCARBROUGH CLERK, widow of GEORGE CLERK, a poor soldier who died in the service of the States, is to be allowed three pounds per month from the first day of January, 1779, to this date for her support and maintenance. Acco. Va. 27 Apr 1779. xxxv0-332.

GEORGE ARBUCKLE makes oath to an acct against the State for twenty pounds, three shillings and three pence, for his pay and rations as "Commissary of Issues" under Major John Poulson, 1 Jany 1781, until the last of April following, Ordered certified Acco. 28, July 1784. xxxvii0-379.

JOHN BOWLES; Rebecca Baker, gdn of Joseph and Clara Bowles ctfies that they are orphans of John, late a private, Continental Army, who d. in service of U. S. (Ctf of Gov'r of Virginia.) York cty, Va. 6 Aug 1791.

BENJAMIN NELSON, repr. of Wm. Nelson, dec'd his warrant for 2666 2-3 acres due sd *Benj.* [*William?*] Nelson for service as a Lieutenant of the Continental Line. Assigned by Eliz: Nelson, widow. L. O. Mil. War. 4784. (L. C.) 1 Mch 1797.

LEIGHTON WHITE came into Court and proved by wit. that he served in Col. Clark's Reg't as a soldier from July 1779, till July 1780 . . . and that he came down the River Ohio with Col. Clark in May 1778 and served . . . until the reduction of the several posts at the Illinois . . . Draper Mss. Extracts. Ct 3 Apr 1781, Jeff'n cty, Ky.

Lt. Col. JAMES MURRAY and BENJAMIN ALLISON, surgeon, certify that HENRY DOUGHERTY, a private, was so badly wounded at Piscataquay, N. J., as to render him incapable of labour. His service ended 28 Mch 1777. Pension ordered. North'd, Penna. Ct Sept 1778. O. C. Docket 1-11.

TIMOTHY LENONTON, of Tyrone tshp, age 38; late a serjeant 4th Batt'n Mil., having received sixteen wounds at the Gulf Mills, 11 Dec 1777, is granted a pension. Cumb. cty, Penna. 18 Nov 1785. O. C. ii-380. (See Jany. 1924.)

SARAH BRADLEY, widow of EDWARD, a pensioner, who d. 7 Feby 1785, aged 28, having been a serjeant in Gen. Hezen's Regt, and wounded at Germantown. Cumb. cty, Penna. Ct 18 Nov 1785. O. C. ii-380.

JAMES GALBRAITH, Washington tshp. 56 years old. Was a private 4th Penna. Regt and wounded at Green Springs, Va. Pension granted. Cumb. cty, Penna. Ct 18 Nov 1785. O. C. ii-380.

SIMON COCHRAN, was a soldier in Capt. Berry's company. Discharge given by Jno. Gibson, Col. 9th Va. Regt, at Fort Pitt, 28 Oct 1780. Presented in Court and ordered recorded. Hamp. cty, W. Va. 13 Mch 1781. Deeds, vol. v, (at back of book.)

WILLIAM LYON; ctf signed "P. Henry," to MARY LYON, relict of William, private 7th Va. and killed "in the service of the Continent." Hamp. cty. W. Va. 1786. vii-148. (See also June, 1925.)

DAVID ZABETRENE, dragoon. Entered in the U. S. service in 1778, 20 July, in the troop under Barth'w Von Heer, Captain. Served three years; has behaved as a good and faithful soldier. Alleg. cty, W. V. 11 Aug 1787. ii-214.

BROOKE FAMILY CHART AMENDED

Genealogists and other investigators are familiar with a certain generally accepted chart which purports to be the "Pedigree Chart of ROBERT BROOKE, who arrived in Maryland 30 June 1650, and MARY BAKER, his first wife, who died in England in 1634."

Mr. Francis B. Culver, of Baltimore, several months ago contributed to the Maryland Historical Magazine, a number of very interesting comments upon this chart, in which he corrected certain typographical and other errors. Mr. Culver writes that "those who are "seeking genealogical information frequently "have recourse to this chart as an authoritative "work, and in several instances it has been "copied in its entirety." He directs attention to such errors as the setting down of William the Conqueror, and Matilda, his wife, as the parents of Gundred (1053-1085), who became the wife of William de Warren, the first Earl of Surrey. Gundred was the daughter of Matilda, but not of William the Conqueror. Other errors of a more serious nature are noted, and Mr Culver states that "A proper revision "of the chart *will do away with over one-half "of the lineages,* as published; but that the "descent from Charlemagne will stand, be-"ing established through another line, that "of Margaret de Beaumont, wife of Saher de "Quincy." (See M. H. Mags. xix-4.)

In a note to the Editor, Mr. Culver makes a change in the fourth paragraph of his published article, writing that "Roger de Quincy, *second Earl of Saher and Winchester,*" should read *second Earl of Winchester.* This second Earl of Winchester was son of Saher de Quincy, a surety of the Magna Charta.

In the AUGUST NOTE-BOOK it was stated that the indices of New York wills, administrations and guardianships, to be brought out by Mr. Charles Shepard, II, of Washington, D. C., would probably begin with the records of Staten Island (Richmond county.) It has been decided to publish Kings county first, this including Brooklyn, as the editor says, "A very populous place." The price of the volume has not yet been determined.

Columbian Printing Co., Inc., Washington, D. C.

The

County Court Note-Book

A Little Bulletin of History and Genealogy

April, 1926.

Vol. V, No. 2

THE COUNTIES OF TENNESSEE FORMED BEFORE 1850*

ANDERSON, 1801. (East).
BLEDSOE, 1807. (East).
BLOUNT, 1795. (East).
BRADLEY, 1835. (East).
BEDFORD, 1808. (Middle).
BENTON, 1835. (West).
CAMPBELL, 1806. (East).
CARTER, 1796. (East).
CLAIBORNE, 1801. (East).
COCKE, 1797. (East).
CANNON, 1835. (Middle).
COFFEE, 1846. (Middle).
CARROLL, 1818. (West).
CROCKETT, 1845. (West).
DAVIDSON, 1783. (Middle).
DeKALB, 1837. (Middle).
DICKSON, 1803. (Middle).
DECATUR, 1845. (West).
DYER, 1823. (West).
FENTRESS, 1823. (Middle).
FRANKLIN, 1807. (Middle).
FAYETTE, 1824. (West).
GRAINGER, 1796. (East).
GREENE, 1783. (East).
GILES, 1809. (Middle).
GRUNDY, 1844. (Middle).
GIBSON, 1823. (West).
HAMILTON, 1819. (East).
HANCOCK, 1844. (East).
HICKMAN, 1807. (Middle).
HUMPHREYS, 1809. (Middle).
HARDEMAN, 1823. (West).
HARDIN, 1819. (West).
HAYWOOD, 1823. (West).
HENDERSON, 1821. (West).
HENRY, 1821. (West).
JEFFERSON, 1792. (East).
JOHNSON, 1836. (East).
JACKSON, 1801. (Middle).
KNOX, 1792. (East).
LAWRENCE, 1817. (Middle).
LEWIS, 1843. (Middle).
LINCOLN, 1809. (Middle).
LAUDERDALE, 1835. (West).
McMINN, 1819. (East).
MARION, 1817. (East).
MEIGS, 1836. (East).
MONROE, 1819. (East).
MORGAN, 1817. (East).
MACON, 1842. (Middle).
MARSHALL, 1836. (Middle).
MAURY, 1807. (Middle).
MONTGOMERY, 1796. (Middle).
MADISON, 1821. (West).
McNAIRY, 1823. (West).
OVERTON, 1806. (Middle).
OBION, 1823. (West).
POLK, 1839. (East).
PERRY, 1821. (Middle).
PUTNAM, 1842. (Middle).
RHEA, 1807. (East).
ROANE, 1801. (East).
ROBERTSON, 1796. (Middle).
RUTHERFORD, 1803. (Middle).
SCOTT, 1849. (East).
SEVIER, 1794. (East).
SULLIVAN, 1799. (East).
SMITH, 1799. (Middle).
STEWART, 1803. (Middle).
SUMNER, 1786. (Middle).
SHELBY, 1819. (West).
TIPTON, 1823. (West).
WASHINGTON, 1777. (East).
VAN BUREN, 1840. (Middle).
WARREN, 1807. (Middle).
WAYNE, 1817. (Middle).
WHITE, 1806. (Middle).
WILLIAMSON, 1799. (Middle).
WILSON, 1799. (Middle).
WEAKLEY, 1823. (West).

*See note on page 12.

MARRIAGES BY INFERENCE* WESTMORELAND COUNTY VIRGINIA†

JOHN FRODESHAM and REBECCA STURMAN, widow of Mr. Rich: Sturman. Mar. contr. 25 May 1670. Orders, 1668-77, f. 56. See also ffo. 150, 154.

Mr. EDWARD FRANKLIN and the widow of . . . REDMAN. Before 24 June 1685. Orders, 1676-88, p.425.

RICHARD FRY and the Relict of Spence MUNROE. Before 28 Nov 1738. Fid. Accts, i-205.

Mr. THO: GARRARD and Mrs. ROSE TUCKER, widow of Mr. John Tucker. Before 28 Jany 1672. Orders, 1668-77, f. 144.

WILLIAM HARDIDGE and the admx of Capt. JOHN APPLETON, Before 31 Mch 1680. Orders, 1676-88, p.180.

JO. HARVEY and the relict of THOMAS BUTLER, Before 26 Oct 1681. Orders, 1676-88, p.231.

JOHN HARDIE and CHARITIE ODGER[?] dau. Gabriel Odger, Before 4 Oct 1672. Orders, 1668-77, f. 123.

JOHN HATTON and JANE BOAZE, widow of Christopher, Before 24 June 1663. Orders, 1662-64, p.15.

GEO: HORNER and [ELIZABETH] MONROE, wid. Andrew. Before 30 July 1679. Orders, 1676-88. p.158.

THADDEUS JACKSON and ELIZA: FLEMMING, dau. William. Before 7 Jany 1767. xiv-445.

†See note on page 4, February NOTE-BOOK.

JAMES JOHNSON and ELIZABETH GERRARD, widow of John. Before 25 May 1681. Orders, 1676-88, p. 218.

THOMAS KITCHIN and SARAH GREY, relict of Francis, Before 23 Feby 1686-7. Orders, 1676-88, p.549.

WILLIAM KIMBAR[?] and . . . BROOKS, dau. Henry. Before 11 Jany 1682, Orders, 1676-88, p.275.

Mr. RICHARD KIRTON and ANNA COLE, wid. Mr. Richard COLE. Before May, 1676. Orders, 1676-88, p.62.

Mr. JAMES KAY and the wid. of Capt. Jno. ASHTON [Mrs. GRACE ASHTON. She was probably also the wid. of . . . Lewis.] Before 11 Dec 1678. Orders, 1676-88, pp. 135, 136.

ROBERT KING, Gent., and ELIZABETH BARNES, dau. Thomas Barnes, Gent. Before 23 Feby 1741. Fid. Accts i-265.

JOHN MILES and MARGARET WATKINS, wid. Nicholas. Before 29 Sept 1670. Orders, 1668-77, f. 61.

EDWARD MOUNTJOY and ELIZABETH HORNER, relict of George. [She was also the wid. of Andrew Monroe.] Before 23 Feby 1686-7. Orders, 1676-88, p.50.

JOHN MANLY and RESTITUTE[?] STEELE, widow of Matthew. Before 28 July 1680. Orders, 1676-88. pp.183, 220.

JOHN NEWTON, the younger, and SARAH . . . a widow. Ordered . . . that John Newton the younger have liberty to remove what Estate belonged to the orphants of Price one of her [Sarah's] former husbands now being or remayning in any place or in the hands of any Pson within this County unto the County of Stafford . . . Ct 6 Jany 1685. Orders 1676-88, p.480.

RHODAM PRITCHETT and PEGGY FLEMMING, dau. William. Before 28 Apr 1767. xiv-445.

NATH: PYECROFT and the relict and extx of Robt EDWARDS. Before 28 May 1685. Orders, 1676-88. p.429.

JOHN PRATT and MARY SHARP, widow and extx of Thomas. Before 24 June 1685. Orders, 1676-88, p.429.

Mr. JOHN RICE and the relict of Mr. Wm. GRAVES [?] Before 24 Nov 1680. Orders, 1676-88. p.193.

JOHN RICE and REBECCA TRAVERS, late wife of William Travers, Before 25 May 1681. Orders, 1676-88. p.206.

JOHN REMEY and MARY SANFORD, widow of Robert, Jr. Before 14 May 1740. Fid. Accts, i-232.

BUNCH ROE and ELIZ: MONROE, dau. Andrew. Before 30 July 1679. Orders, 1676-88, p.158.

GEORGE RICHMAN and ELIZABETH WATKINS, dau. and heir of Nicholas Watkins. Before 29 Sept 1670. Orders, 1668-77, f. 61.

JOHN ROSYER and MARY WILLIAMSON. Before 29 Nov 1671. Orders, 1668-77, f. 98.

Mr. THOMAS SOLLEY and the extx of Mr. John ROSIER. Before 29 Apr 1663. Orders, 1662-1664, p.[17]

THOMAS STALY and the Relict of Henry DURANT. Before 25 June 1684. Orders, 1676-88, p.342.

MARYLAND'S NEXT OF KIN *

JOHN DINNING and GEORGE DINNING; inv.˙ Stephen Duning of Kent cty, 1 July 1720. v-6.

JAMES HAITT; inv, James Hyatt of Q. A. cty. 6 Sept 1720. v-13.

JOHN BROWN, son of dec'd; inv. John Brown of Q. A. cty. 6 Sept 1720. v-16.

JOHN and NATHAN HINES; inv. Thomas Hines of Q. A. cty. 21 Sept 1720. v-17.

THOMAS HYNSON WRIGHT and JOHN WRIGHT; inv, Charles Wright of Q. A. cty. 3 Aug 1720. v-20.

MARY HEMSLEY; inv. Phillemon Hemsley of Q. A. cty. 3 Apr 1721. v-28.

EZEKIEL GILLISS; inv. John Gillis of Som. cty. 8 Jany 1720. v-29.

THOMAS BANNISTER; inv. William Bannister, Som. cty. 27 Aug. 1720. v-32.

ELIZABETH NELSON; inv. Thomas Shiellds of Som. cty. 19 Oct 1719. v-33.

WILLIAM MEADS, THOMAS HARDESTY, JOHN PHILLIPS; inv. William Meads of Calvert cty. 6 Jany 1720. v-35.

WILLIAM SMITH, ROBERT CLARK; inv. David Thomas of Balto. cty. 30 May 1720. v-39.

JOHN and WILLIAM TEAL, brothers of dec'd; inv. Edward Teal of Balto. cty. 27 Jany 1720. v-42.

THOMAS LONG; inv. John Henderson of Balto. cty. 18 Feby 1720. v-44.

EDMOND STANDFORD and MARGARET STANDFORD; inv. John Standford of Balto. cty. 12 Feby 1720. v-46.

MARY CRUCKSON and JAMES CRACKSON; inv. Daniel Smith of St. Mary's cty. 8 Mch 1720. v-50.

LUKE DILLION[?] inv. Thos. Dillon of St. Mary's cty. 13 Mch 1720. v-54.

JOHN DILLICOATE; inv. Thos. Dillicoate of St. Mary's cty. 8 June 1721. v-55.

JOHN POLSON; inv. Thomas Polson of Prince Geo's cty. 28 Oct 1720. v-56.

WILLIAM and UNIS BESWICK, chn of dec'd; inv. Thomas Beswick of Talbot cty. 31 Mch 1720. v-58.

CHARLES STRABURY; inv. William Strabury of Calvert cty. 15 Apr 1721. v-66.

PHILIP and SUSANNAH BRISCOE; inv. George Briscoe of St. Mary's cty. 9 Mch 1720. v-71.

JEAN BOOMER; inv. John Bumer of St. Mary's cty. 18 Feby 1720. v-71.

MARY CARROLL; inv. John Carroll of A. A. cty. 3 July 1720. v-72.

HENRY ATTWOOD and JOSEPH PRATT; inv. Jane Pratt of A. A. cty. 24 Mch 1721. v-73.

WILLIAM PHILLIPS and WILLIAM WEBSTER; inv. David Mackall of Dor. cty. 20 May 1720. v-74.

HENRY and JOSEPH SCHOOLFIELD; inv. Benjamin Schoolfield of Som. cty.. 30 Nov 1720. v-75.

KATHRIN WARWICK; inv. William Warwick of Som. cty. 29 Mch 1721. v-80.

THOMAS and BENJAMIN SERMAN; inv. Edward Serman of Som. cty. 17 Sept 1720. v-81.

VIRGINIA COLONISTS

(From "Old Volume 5," S. L. O., Richmond.)

CHRISTOPHER ABBOT, Gloster cty, 1657.
Seven head rights: "Certificate of Gloster court so torn it could not be read."

Lt. Coll. ROBERT ABRALL and JOHN PIGG, New Kent, 1658.
Head rights: Jno. Larrat, Randall Burne, Jno. Roberts, Anne Davenport, Edwd Husdon, James Scot, James Patterson, Rose Allin, Geo. Renison, John Wenn, Hen. Ekins, Edwd Byard, Tho. Blancher, Robt. Joanes, Mary Andersin[?] Sarah Williams, Richd Branch, Robt Harmon, Edward Roberts, Hen. Bretherton, Tho. Cockerell, John Barchard, Geo. Lee, Tho. Pratt, Nicholas Moore, Wm. Norcot.

Lt. Coll. ROBERT ABRALL and JOHN PIGG, New Kent, 1658.
Head rights: Fra. Miller, Richd Preston, John Mottrom, Jane Bolt, John Masters, John Patterson, Hen. Copeland, John Bose [Base?] John Sparke, Esebius Willard, Daniell Peirce.

JAMES ALLEN, Northumberland cty, 1657.
Three head rights, no names given.

JOHN AXELL and ANTHO. HAYNES, New Kent, 1658.
Head rights: James Vanner, Tho. Jones, Symon Perry, Bellinda Hayes, Edward Terrell, Georg Goddinge, Eliz. Penfack[?] Elizabeth Streete, Tho. Hinde, Rich. Hill, Jno. Rose, Jno. Latham.

Mr. CHARLES ASHTON, Northumberland, 1658.
Head rights: John Jenny, Wm. Longman.

JOHN ADKESON, New Kent, 1658.
Head rights: Margarett Mathews, Margaret Aprickett[?]

WILLIAM BASNETT, Lower Norfolk, 1658.
Head rights: Rob: Persephers and his sonne; Jno. Hasnet [perhaps Basnet?] Tho. Dickson, Martin Coale, Amy Morris, Eliz. Bonden, Gilbert Fouch, Richard Satton, Jone Cornix, Martha Cornix, Wm. Cornix, Tho. Cornix, Jane Tymouth[?]

THOMAS BURDITT. Northampton cty. 1658.
Head rights not given. "By virtue of a patent formerly granted to his father William Burditt."

THOMAS BROUGHTON, above the Doeg's Island in Petomeck freshes, 1657.
Head rights: Jno. Rodman, Anne Pomfrett, Mary Jess, Tho. Darley, Edward Hull, four Irish servants, Roger Fishpoole, James Poppey, Wm. Clements, James Vazey [Veazey?] Wm. Daniell, Edward Cooke, Tho. Haydin, Mary Rutland, Ed. Arrundell, Tho. Adames, Pressilla Parker [Parkes?]

THOMAS BROUGHTON, Northumberland cty, 1657.
Head rights: William O'Kelly, Mary Smith, Rich Symons, one Irishman, Edward Darby. [Note: in these early lists the apostrophe is not given after the "O" in the Irish names. It is inserted here by the copyist.]

THO. BROUGHTON, Northumberland cty, 1657.
Head rights: Tho. Davis, Wm. Richards, Mary Edwards, Kat Chester, Edward Conny, Rebecca Haines.

THO. BROUGHTON, Northumberland cty, 1657.
Head rights: Richard Caidy, Humphrey Pester.

THOMAS BROUGHTON, Northumberland cty, 1657.
Head rights: Roger Large, John Tanner.

JOHN BENNETT, "upon Petomeck River in freshes above Anacosta," 1657.
Ten head rights, no names given.

JAMES BAUGHAN, Rappahannock cty, 1658.
Five head rights, no names given.

FRANCIS BROWNE, Rappahannock cty, 1658.
Six head rights, no names given.

JOHN BENNETT, Westmoreland cty, 1658.
Head rights: Stephen Banbury, Sam. Gollings, Robert Warner, "and Mable."

JOHN BISHOPP, son and heir of JOHN BISHOPP, dec'd, James City cty, 1658.
Head rights: Wm. Marriott, George Duell, Wm. Roberts, Joane Hill, Thomas Jarrell, Abigall Adcocke, Martin Johnson, Margery Longman.

GEORGE BRYER, Rappahannock cty, 1657.
Head rights: Wm. Denister, Sam. Newman, Jno. Craig, Anne Willis, Tho. Gregory, Tho. Grey, John Fisher, Jno. Atheser [Achesen?]

FRANCIS BROWNE, Rappahannock cty, 1657.
Head rights: James Hughes, Tho. Juniper, Mary Evelin, Wm. Brookes, Jno. Newburne, Fra. Cooke, Kath Greene.

JOHN BOSBY, New Kent, 1657.
Head right: Edward Taylor.

WM. BUTCHER, Lancaster cty, 1658.
Head rights: Ann Forrest, Elizabeth Forrest, Jno. Forrest.

WM. BROOKE, Lower Norfolk cty, 1658.
Head rights: Arthur Ball, Rich Williams, Nicho. Williams, Sarah Edricke, Wm. BROOKE and his wife and one child.

NATHANIEL BRADFORD, Northampton cty, 1658.
Head rights: James Browne, Mary Chandler, Lidia Easterfeild, Roady Patriarke, Robert Hopkins, Mary Earle, Rich. Perry, Wm. Treunis.

Mr. THO. BALLARD, New Kent, 1658.
Head rights: Wm. Reynolds, Hannah Reynolds, Abygall Reynolds, Jno. Reynolds, James Glower, Cuthbert Jackson, James Smith, Hannah Reynolds, Deborah Reynolds, James Cooke, Robt Fisher, Tho. Pratt, James Cooper, Sarah Talbott, Tho. Crumpe, Wm. Jnoson, Wm. Cunningham, Eliz. MacFerson, Toby Forrester, Wm. Smith, Grace Farloe, Tho. Pritchard, Grace Fisher, Anna Sympson, Richard Proby, Francis Croyer.

ROBERT BOURNE and DANIEL PARKE, Gent., York cty, 1658.
Twelve head rights, no names given.

Capt. RICH. BARNHOUSE, James City cty, 1658.
Head rights: Wm. Halliard, Tho. Warder, Martin White, Mary Wild, Tho. Jones, Rog. Walke, Fran. Fulker, Edward Richards, Wm. Clarke, Rich Adams, Mary Farlinge.

Mr. WM. BLACKEY, New Kent, 1658.
Head rights: Symon Butler, John Cocke [or Cooke], Jone Wheeler, James Carter, Jno. Lousell, Jno. Rigbee, Jone Goldfing[?] James Harvey.

THO. BOSWELL, "upon Patomeck River in the freshes above Anacosta Island," 1658.
Head rights: Wm. Sanders, John Angell, Ellinor Fishbrooke, John Perry, George Ball, Tho. Dauncy, Wm. Wilson, Georg Grey, Sarah Johnson, John Wotton.

The County Court Note-Book

An every-other-monthly devoted mainly to abstracts from County Court records, prior to 1800.

MILNOR LJUNGSTEDT, Editor and Publisher. Bethesda, Route 10, Maryland.

Published six times a year. Subscription, two dollars, in advance; must begin with the year. Advertising rates moderate.

APRIL, 1926

Vol. V., No. 2

APOLOGY AND APPRECIATION

The Editor is very sorry that this number of the NOTE-BOOK is so late in coming out. The Editor was unfortunate enough to have a severe case of "flu" in Virginia and had not fully recovered even at the time of her return home, which was several weeks later than it should have been. After that, illness in the family made further calls upon the Editor's somewhat dilapidated energy so that the work of getting material in shape for the printer has been delayed until now. The JUNE issue will follow as soon as possible to make up in part for this present unpunctuality.

The Editor would like to make this column just a running account of her adventures by coach and rail through Virginia, across Kentucky and Tennessee, and home by that always wide-awake, friendly and interesting North Carolina. But she feels sure that many of her subscribers would say: *"This is no place for personal reminiscences, unless they concern ancestors."*

But the Editor simply must touch upon the high lights; the friendly hospitality and fine courtesy of Frankfort and of Nashville (she has previously paid her compliments to North Carolina . . . its State Historical Commission) . . . the high archival courts where one sits in beautiful rooms, at real desks, on comfortable chairs, in pleasant lights, and, above all, in the company of friendly folk, the value of whose work does not seem to require chill formality, or the constant unwinding of official red tape. These are not the only two places where one is received as a welcome guest . . . there are others . . . but circumstance made the Editor especially appreciative just at that time.

Between Frankfort, with its Historical Society housed in the beautiful old Capitol; and Nashville, with its State Library in the Capitol itself, with beautiful things all about one, and a circular stair (made in Philadelphia) that is an utter delight, the Editor just had to drop into Mammoth Cave, and can excuse the mention of it here because one of the heirs is a Maryland lady of the Blair family. The old family servant who told the Editor this also told her that the lady in question (Mrs. J---------) once took him to Washington, where he stayed with the family in a house just across from the White House . . . of which he was very proud. However, he put up with Washington for just one week, and then he came back to Kentucky.

Should the reader go to the Cave, he should choose the "old entrance," going by way of Glasgow Junction, for this is the cave we have read about as children, and whose surroundings Porte Crayon may have sketched. No poor words of the Editor can give any idea of this vast and wonderful place. As awe-inspiring as Niagara, and as far beyond all previous imaginings.

In Nashville, the Memorial Building (the Great War Memorial) its peristyle, the plaza in front, the latter still unfinished when the Editor was there, are witnesses to the honor which Tennessee gives its own. The Tennessee Capitol is rather a remarkable building, though somewhat grandiose in style, its splendid situation upon a high bluff, with tremendously steep approaches, and what one might almost call its naive belief in itself, leave an impression of dignity if not simplicity. The view from its upper terrace is not easily forgotten . . . in an older country that terrace would have dominated the town, not only in height but in beauty. As it is, a smoky sunset seen from its parapet lends something of mystery and charm to unstudied architecture and railroads unadorned.

After Nashville, Knoxville is just a metropolis, but even there one does not find oneself entirely out of place in the county offices.

Old Jonesboro, so closely connected with the earliest frontier history, and a bit later with Andrew Jackson, is quaint and interesting. The hotel man sent the Editor on a wonderful drive along the edges of quite respectable precipices above an unspellable river.

From Tennessee to North Carolina the trail lies over the Great Smokies, and one should always take the route by way of Lonesome, unless travelling in one's own machine, when one might have to stay at the top of one of the divides if afraid to descend in a rainstorm. (This did happen to some belated tourists.) The coach which goes over Lonesome, starts from Johnson City, and the route lies through Erwin and Marshall to Asheville. The Editor spent five-and-a-half hours in complete confidence that the coach could not skid having double wheels in the rear, because the man behind her said it had. Inspection at Marshall, after the most exciting part of the trip was over, revealed the usual one pair of wheels and no more. The Editor is still wondering why the man behind her said there were two pair.

From Buncombe county (Asheville) N. C., one can go almost anywhere by coach. The route to Danville, Virginia, takes one through or near several interesting county seats. At Danville, one is on the main line to everything.

The list of TENNESSEE counties formed before 1850, is taken from a book of 124 pages, prepared by the Assistant State Librarian and Archivist, Mr. Austin P. Foster, one of the State officers the Editor had the good fortune to meet. The little volume is called The Counties of Tennessee. It has a lot of history in it, and is very good reading. It costs only fifty cents and is recommended to searchers.

Tennesseans usually refer to their State as being in three divisions, the eastern, middle, and western. The counties in Mr. Foster's book are, therefore, classified in this way.

This division is, in a measure, historical, so the Editor has given the section in which the county lies, with its name and date of erection.

The second alphabet of VIRGINIA COLONISTS begins with this number. The State Land Office, where these records are kept, is made a pleasant place to visit, by the intelligence, courtesy and tact of the lady who is in charge. I hope she will forgive the Editor for mentioning this, and also for saying that the Land Office is worthy of a more commodious and dignified housing . . . not to mention better lighting and a modern system of ventilation.

The KENTUCKY notes in this issue are contributed by Miss HATTIE M. SCOTT, of Frankfort, who is doing some most excellent work in the way of examination of certain records which were, for no very clear reason, deposited in Frankfort. Miss Scott is indexing this material.

Mr. STRATTON NOTTINGHAM, whose card appears on page 16, is more familiar with the early records of the two old counties of Northampton and Accomack (the Eastern Shore of Virginia) than any one the Editor knows. He is an expert in reading the old writing, and has done a great deal of excellent work in the compilation of marriage records, indices of wills and conveyances, and in preparing sketch charts of the early families.

The deposition of RICHARD EDELIN, Sen., in the February NOTE-BOOK, was contributed by MRS. FRANCIS H. MARKELL, of Frederick, who also sends the following quaint record. The Editor understands from Mrs. Markell that she is making a systematic examination of the early Minute Books.

ELIZA BRIM aged 12 yrs, 10 Jany 1793. whose father hath left the State without making any provision for her maintenance with the approbation of her mother, Dorothy Brin, present in Court, is bound unto Michael Culp, Jr., until she arrives to the age of 16 years, during which term the master is to send her three months to the Dutch & three months to an English School, to learn or cause her to be taught Housewifery, to find her in sufficient Diet, apparel, lodging & washing, & when free to give her a new Spinning Wheel & Chest, and a suit of clothing of the value of five pounds or that sum in cash at her option. Fred'k cty, Md. November Court, 1792.

QUERY: Parentage wanted of AMON WOODWARD, born in Prince George's county, Maryland, in 1793, and died in 1874 (about March 10.) Was an officer in Colo. Carberry's Regt, 36th U. S. Infantry, in the War of 1812-14. Married (1) in 1817, SARAH MARTIN (1797-1837) and had issue; married (2) in 1845, BARBARA LOWE (no issue). F. B. C.

The INDEX for the first three volumes of the COUNTY COURT NOTE-BOOK has been printed and is ready for distribution. It is a pamphlet of eighteen pages and contains about 3,500 names. Price $3.00.

CONTINUED articles COUNTY COURT NOTE-BOOK, and the dates on which they first appeared.

MARRIAGES BY INFERENCE. Began with May, 1922.

MARYLAND'S NEXT OF KIN. Began with July, 1922.

VIRGINIA COLONISTS. This alphabetized list began with July, 1924.

KING GEORGE and other VIRGINIA COUNTY PROBATES, &c. Began with July, 1924.

MILITARY NOTES, both COLONIAL and REVOLUTIONARY, and some later MILITIA NOTES, will appear in every issue, if possible.

SHIPS IN PORT, INTERCOUNTY and INTERCOLONIAL, and COLONIAL FORENAMES, will appear in alternate issues or as space can be found for them.

EASTERN SHORE FAMILIES, in the form of a one-page supplement, began with June, 1925. This will be continued later.

VIRGINIANS AND OTHERS IN CONVEYANCES AND POWERS KENTUCKY COURT OF APPEALS

RICHARD ADAMS, of Henrico cty, Va. 6 Dec 1785.

CHAPMAN AUSTIN, of Hanover cty, Va., from MARTIN HAWKINS of Richmond, Va. Land in Nelson cty, Ky, 1786. WM. AUSTIN, of Henrico cty, a wit.

JAMES BARBOUR, of Culpepper cty, Va., to James Speed, of Lincoln cty, Ky; one-third of 1400 a. 24 May 1785.

HARRY BARTLETT, of Spotsylvania cty, Va., from PRITTYMAN MERRY and wf, of Orange cty, Va. 1786.

TAVENER BEALL, of Sanandoe [Shenandoah] cty, Va., mentioned. No date.

WALTER BEALL, [of Montgomery cty, Md.], then of Nelson cty, Ky, from Myers. 20 Mch 1787.

AARON BLEDSOE, of Orange cty, Va., and wf Mary, to John Quisenberry, same. 1788.

JACOB BOWMAN, of District 96, S. C., heir-at-law to JOSEPH BOWMAN, dec'd, 1788. (John, Abraham, Joseph Bowman, *et al*, mentioned.)

JAMES BRIDGES, of South Carolina, to WILLIAM LIPSCOMB, formerly of Louisa cty, Va., now of South Carolina. 400 a., Lincoln cty, Ky. 14 Nov 1786.

HENRY BROTHERS, of Maryland, mentioned. 1787.

THOMAS BUCK, of Frederick cty, Md, from Rector. 1788.

MICAJAH BULLOCK, of North Carolina. 1786.

ROBERT BURTON, of Granville cty, N. C., power to Thomas Allin to sell land in Fayette cty, Ky. 7 Nov 1786.

JAMES CALLOWAY, of Amherst cty, Va., from William Hays, of Fayette, 1000 a., Madison cty, Ky. 1788.

JAMES CAMPBELL, of Botetourt cty, Va., to [?] Thomas Underwood. 8 Sept 1786.

SAMUEL CHASE, of Maryland, buys of J. Myers, Nelson cty, Ky. 27 Mch 1786.

CHARLES CHILTON, of Fauquier cty, Va., power to Thomas Marshall, Jr., of Fayette cty, Ky. 14 June 1788.

WILLIAM CHRISTIAN and wf ANN, of Montgomery cty, Va., to John Shelby, Jr. 19 Sept 1783. (*Court at John Crow's Station.*)

ROBERT CLARKE, Jr., and wf ELIZABETH, of Bedford cty, Va., to Myers. Land in Madison cty, Ky.

JAMES COATS, of Caroline cty, Va., a wit. 1786.

JOHN CRAWFORD and wf MARY, of Amherst cty, Va., to Thomas LUCAS of same. 400 a., Nelson cty, Ky. Nov, 1787

ROBERT CRAWFORD, of Balto. cty, Md, buys land of Crosland. 9 June 1788.

FORE-NAMES OF COLONIAL USAGE

TABITHA, wf of Francis Ayres. Acco, Va. 3 May 1726. xix-52.

TABITHA, dau of Edmund Ayres. Acco, Va. 1736. See xx-246. See also xvi-84.

TABITHA, dau Capt. John Allen, seaman. Acco, Va. L. C. p.355.

TABITHA-SCARBURGH, wf of James Arbuckle. Acco, Va. 1765. Diii-408

TABITHA, wf of John Bagwell. Acco, Va. 4 Nov 1719. xviii-11.

TABITHA, dau Henry Bagwell, See Acco, Va. 1734. xx-179.

TABITHA BAGWELL, dau of Elizabeth Scarburgh. Acco, Va. V-9. xvi-83.

TABITHA BAGWELL, dau Sharles Scarburgh. Acco, Va. 6 July 1713. xi-633.

TABITHA, dau Edmund Bayley. Acco, Va. 6 Feby 1717. xvi-43.

TABITHA BAYLEY. See Acco, Va. 10 Feby 1756. Dii-654.

TABITHA BELL, born Scarburgh. See Acco, Va. 1713. xi-615.

TABITHA, wf and afterwards wid. of Robert Bell. N-n, Va. 1709-1710. xix-124, and xviii-510.

TABITHA, dau of Nathaniel and Mary Bell, was gr. dau. of Robert Bell. Acco, Va. 1724. xvi-221.

TABITHA, dau. of Ambrose and Rebecca Benston, m. Massey *Benson.* Acco, Va. See 14 May 1733. xx-145[?] 1737. xx-282. 22 Jany 1763. iii-216.

TABITHA, dau. Thomas Custis. See will, 1719-1720. xvi-136.

TABITHA-SCARBURGH and MARGARET, were daus. and co-heirs of Henry Custis. See Acco, Va. 26 Apr 1760. L. C. p.231.

TABITHA COOPER, one of the heirs of Garrison Milby. Aco, Va. 14 Dec 1737. xx-295.

TABITHA CARY, dau. of John Melson. Acco, Va. 30 Dec 1736. xx-287.

TABITHA CANADA [Kennedy?], was wf of James. 1727. H. T. records, Wmton, Dela. p.300.

TABITHA, third dau. of Hill Drummond, Acco. 1730, xx-44.

TABITHA DOUGLAS was wf of Tully Robinson Wise. See Acco, Va. 13 Dec 1760. Diii-130.

TABITHA DOUGLAS was wf of George. Acco, Va. 28 Nov 1749. ii-234.

TABITHA EWELL, wf of Mark Ewell. Acco., Va. 1754. ii-481.

TABITHA FENTON, dau. of Moses and Margaret Fenton. Som. Cty Md. D. B. I. K. L. 11 June 1686.

TABITHA HARMANSON, dau. of Henry. N-n, Va. 15 Apr 1709. xix-59. (Henry Harmanson's will.)

TABITHA HUNT, wf of William, of Charles City cty, Va. Surry, Va. 21 Apr 1714. iii-199.

TABITHA HUFFINGTON, was extr with husband John Huffington, of John Milby. Acco., Va. 6 Jany 1730. xx-67.

TABITHA HARRISON, dau. of Richard and Jone Harrison of "Nanjemy." Chas. cty, Md. Record of births, &c. Born 23 June 1693.

TABITHA JOHNSON, wf of William. Overwh. Va., Psh Reg. 1755.

TABITHA LOWRY, wf of William. Same register, 1742.

TABITHA LITCHFIELD, wf of William. Acco., Va. Deeds iii-230. 1763. Also TABYTHA LITCHFIELD, dau. of William. Acco. Va., xvi. Will, 1718.

TABITHA LAWRENCE, wf of Joseph. Acco., Va. 1752. ii-395.

TABITHA MERCY, wf of William Mercy, of Somerset, Md. Acco., Va. 7 Jany 1734. xx-191.

TABITHA MERIKEN, dau. of John and Mary Meriken. Born 5 June 1715. Westmld, Va., Psh Reg.

TABITHA MELSON, wf of John. [She was dau, of Edmund Ayres.] See Acco., Va. 1731. Also 1736. xx-287.

TABITHA MILBY was dau. of John Milby Acco., Va. 1730. xx-67. She was granddau. of John Milby, Sr. 1727. xvi-318.

TABITHA MILBY m. Isaac Cooper, See Stepney Psh, Som. cty, Md. p. 37. 22 Feby 1731. She d. 29 Oct 1737.

TABITHA NELSON [MELSON??], wf of John, was perhaps a dau. of Thomas and Tabitha Onions. Acco., Va. 1728. xvi-321.

TABITHA NICHOLSON was wf of John Nicholson, of Som. cty. Md. Som. cty, Md. 14 Feby 1734. AZ-203.

TABITHA ONIONS was dau. of Edmund Ayres. Acco. Va., xvi-84. 10 Dec 1718. Also xvi-214.

WILLIAMS NOTES MARYLAND-VIRGINIA SECTION

FRANCES x WILLIAMS, a wit., with Jno. x Bowling, Ger. Banks and Wm. Rowley to deed by Frans. Strother, K. Geo. cty, Va. 1757. i-295.

FRANCIS WILLIAMS, of Sussex cty, Territories of Penna., pltr, to James Walker, Acco. cty, Va. Land sold by Thomas Hunt, N-n cty, dec'd, to HENRY and FRANCIS WILLIAMS. Acco. cty, Va. 20 June 1693. xi-14.

Mrs. FRANCES WILLIAMS was admx of Mr. ROBERT WILLIAMS (Lt. Col.) 30 Aug 1665. Staff. cty, Va. Orders i-22.

FRANCES WILLIAMS. Pr. Wm, Va. 9 Sept 1762. Orders, 304.

FRANCES WILLIAMS, dau. of William and Hannah. B. 23 May 1749. York-Hampton Psh, Va.

FRANCES WILLIAMS, to recover agt John Cooper, [for false charges]. Pr. Wm, Va. Ct 6 Apr 1763. Orders, p.445.

GEORGE WILLIAMS; had sons John Pope, Jesse, Charles, of Stafford. See Fauquier, Va. 1767. iii-7. His wf was Alice. Fauq., i-275.

GEORGE WILLIAMS, Hamilton psh, Fauq., and ANNE x SHARP, wid.; marriage contract. John Blackwell, James Freeman, sec. Fauq., Va. 29 Oct 1782. vii-468.

GEORGE WILLIAMS, Jr., and RICHARD WILLIAMS, had a patent for land in 1730. See Fauq., 1779. vii-288. Nathaniel, Jesse, John Pope, and Charles "being the brothers and sons of GEORGE WILLIAMS, dec'd, formerly of Stafford cty."

GEORGE WILLIAMS, of Pr. Wm. See S. L. O. E-443. 1742.

GEORGE WILLIAMS, Sr., left land by will to Jesse, Charles and John Pope Williams. See Fauq., Va. 1780. vii-294.

GEORGE WILLIAMS, will. Fauq., 1786. ii-112. [Not abstracted.]

GEORGE WILLIAMS, [Sr.], estate appraised. Fauq., Va. 26 Feby 1787. ii-115.

GEORGE WILLIAMS, Stafford cty, Va. "Founder." Will. Son Nathaniel; wf Jane; son Benjamin; son George; dau. Margaret Ralls, land in Pr. Wm. Three sons, John Pope, Jesse, Charles, remdr Pr. Wm. lands. Five youngest sons, Benjamin, George, John Pope, Jesse, Charles (minors). Gr. dau. Lydia Beck Ralls; son John who is resident in some part of England, 1 sh. Son-in-law, John Ralls. Mentions *Accotink Iron Mine Co.* Watch to friend George Waller. Wf, son Nathaniel and Mr. Nathaniel Chapman, Maj. Peter Hedgman and George Waller, extrs. Wit: Allen, Honey, Randall, Holbrook. Stafford, Va. 31 Jany 1749-50 — 10 Apr 1750. O-89.

GEORGE WILLIAMS m. CATHARINE HORE, before 1811. Fauq., Va., xviii-238.

GRACE WILLIAMS, wid. of James, m. (a) James Rowland; also (b) Christopher Thompson. Annap., Md. Inv. and Accts, 1695. xiiib.-26.

GEORGE WILLIAMS, WILLIAM WILLIAMS, ELIJAH WILLIAMS, Hamilton psh, Fauq., Va., to James Freeman, Sen'r, same. Recites that George Williams, Sr., late of Fauquier, died leaving land on Hedgman River; George and William Williams, as extrs in trust, and Elijah Williams (being particularly interested), convey 90 acres, half of the land in Elijah's possession, Fauq., Va., 16 Sept 1788. x-69.

GEORGE x WILLIAMS, Sr., Fauquier cty, Va. Will. Wf Ann, son Elijah; son George; son William; son John; two sons Richard and George; dau. Elizabeth Butler; dau. Ann Butler; gr. son Benj. Butler, Jr., his younger bro. mentioned; gr. son George Butler, son to John Butler; thirty pounds to son William for support of Catharine Williams; contract with wife mentioned; dau. Margaret Freeman; three grandchn: James, George. and Anne Collins; the heirs of my dec dau. Mary Collins; Sons William, and George extrs, Wit: James Routt, Augustine Jennings, Joseph Selman. Fauq., 13 Nov 1780-25 Dec 1786. ii-112.

GEORGE x WILLIAMS, will. dau. Peggy, Nancy, Elizabeth. Son John; blacksmith shop mentioned. Fauq., Va. 1819. vii-293.

SERVICE AND SUPPLIES COLONIAL, REVOLUTIONARY AND MILITIA

JOHN BRICKELL (of Wilkes cty), was Inspector of Invalids, Chthm cty, Ga. about 1790. R-30.

JOHN BOWLES, a private in the Continental army, died in service, Rebecca Baker, gdn of Joseph and Clara Bowles, ctfies that they are Bowles' orphans. Ctf also, of Lt. Gov. of Virginia. York cty, Va. 6 Aug 1791. (Va. S. L.)

JOHN BLACK and RICHARD LANIER, produce commissions as Lieutenants, Lunenb, Va. Oct. Ct 1748. Orders iii-452.

HEZEKIAH CLARK, killed in service, Widow, Sarah. Ohio cty, W. V. Orders i. 1778. [See Annals Carnegie Museum.]

DANIEL CONNOR, Lieut. Militia, residing in Georgia, about 47 years of age, had his knee disabled in battle, while acting in the service of the U. S. in the last war. Chthm cty, Ga. Ctf 20 Aug 1790. R-30. Elijah Clarke, of Wilkes cty, Brig.-Gen'l, also ctfies that Connor was a Lieut. in Capt, Micajah Williams' company, in the regt of militia under his command, and was wounded in Augusta, 14 Sept 1780. Chthm cty, Ga. 29 Dec 1791. R-30.

JOHN CROPPER, of Acco., Va., commissioned a Captain, 9th Regt Regular forces; commissioned Major, 7th Va. Regt; appointed Lt. Col. 7th Va. Cont. Line. Va. St. Pa. i-271 and 317. Feby 1776, and Jany and Oct 1777.

SIMON COCHRAN was a soldier in Capt. Berry's company, Discharge given by Jno. Gibson, Col. 9th Va. Regt, at Fort Pitt, 28 Oct 1780. Presented in Court and ordered recorded. Hamp cty, W. V., 13 Mch 1781. Deeds, vol. v.

ANN FLEMMING; her husband was in the service. Ohio cty, W. Va. Orders i-1778. [See A. C. M.*]

JONATHAN GRYMES was a soldier at Port Royall, for the county of Northampton, Va. He seems to have died before his year of service was up. N-n, Va. iii-21. Ct 25 Feby 1645.

JAMES IRVINE, of Philada., hatter, was Captain in the Penna. Regt. Nthld, Penna. See i-320. 30 Nov 1774.

RICHARD JAINES, a poor soldier in the Continental service; wife to be furnished with four pounds a month for the support of herself and three chn. Yohog. cty, Va. i-39. 27 Oct 1777. [See A. C. M.*]

Mrs. KNOX, wife of . . . KNOX, a poor soldier in the Continental service for Virginia; allowed three pounds a month for herself and three chn. Yohog. cty, Va. i-39. 27 Oct 1777. [See A. C. M.*]

MARY KNOW [perhaps Knox?] widow of a Revolutionary soldier. Ohio cty, W. Va. Orders i-37. 2 Mch 1779. [See A. C. M.*]

PATRICK LAFFERTY, Ensign, militia. Yohog. cty, Va. About 1778. i-42. [See A. C. M.*]

EDWARD McCAWLEY; provision to be made for his chn and the funeral charges for one of the chn. [He was a Revolutionary soldier.] Yohog. cty, Va. i-36. 3 Sept 1777. [See A. C. M.*]

*Annals Carnegie Museum.

Mr. FRANCIS B. CULVER

3204 Guilford Avenue, Baltimore, Md.

Member of Committee on Genealogy and Heraldry of the Maryland Historical Society; Genealogical Editor of "THE MINUTE MAN" magazine. Researches in genealogy and heraldry for American and English lineages. Historical biographies compiled and coats of arms investigated and supplied.

Mr. ALFRED L. HOLMAN

Genealogist
2036 Indiana Avenue
Chicago, Ill.

Refers by special permission to Mr. George B. Utley, Librarian Newberry Library.

CHARLES SHEPARD, II

Genealogist and Antiquarian.
2153 California Street, Washington, D. C.

Author of works on Bowen, Coward, Dole, Martin, Rochester, Shepard, and Wildes families; Rensselaer Co., N. Y., wills, tombstone inscriptions, etc. Agents throughout New England and other states.

"Problems of More Than Ordinary Difficulty"

Mr. STRATTON NOTTINGHAM

Genealogist
Onancock, Virginia

Researches in Northampton, Accomack, and nearby early counties of Virginia. Mss. indices and notes of many early families available.

EDWARD DWELLY, F. S. A. Scot., F. S. G.

Record Searcher and Genealogist.
36 Pemberton Road, East Molesey, Surrey, England.

Searches at Somerset House, British Museum and Public Record Office, London. A few sets of "Dwelly's Parish Records" still in stock. Indices containing over 3 million names.

UNITED STATES CENSUS AND PENSION OFFICE RECORDS

Searches at moderate rates will be made of early original Census schedules or of Revolutionary pension claims, in the Census and Pension offices at Washington, D. C.

For further information, address the Editor, County Court Note-Book, after April **first.**

Mrs. GEORGE W. HODGES

Gloucester Apartments,
Annapolis, Maryland.

Special facilities for genealogical and historical research. (Compiler of the Marriage References of Maryland.)

Mrs. LETITIA P. WILSON

3905 Gwynn Oak Avenue,
Baltimore, Maryland.

Special facilities for genealogical and historical research.

Mrs. FRANCIS H. MARKELL

Frederick, Maryland.
Genealogical research

Refers by permission to Mr. Frank E. Norwood, president Frederick County Historical Society, Frederick, Maryland.

Mrs. WILLIAM HYDE TALBOTT

Rockville, Maryland,

Genealogical and historical research. Special facilities for all western and southern **Maryland.**

EMERY RECORD PRESERVING COMPANY

Taunton, Mass.

Bookbinding Specialists in Restoring and Preserving Records and Documents

Emery Silk Process Patent Mount

Records Kept in Fireproof Vaults

PUBLICATIONS OF THE CARTER BRAXTON CHAPTER, D. A. R.

Baltimore, Maryland

Marriage licenses of Talbot county, Md., beginning 1794. One thousand licenses; two thousand names. $5.50 post paid.

Index of wills, St. Mary's county, Md. Index of wills, Anne Arundel county, Md. Price $12.50 each volume.

Address Mrs. Letitia P. Wilson, Regent,
3905 Gwynn Oak Avenue
Baltimore, Md.

Reasonable price or two years' subscription will be given for numbers 1, 2, 3, 4, 6, and 7, COUNTY COURT NOTE-BOOK, 1921-1922. Address Editor.

COLUMBIAN PRINTING CO., INC., WASHINGTON, D. C.

The

County Court Note-Book

A Little Bulletin of History and Genealogy

June, 1926. Vol. V, No. 3

THE COUNTIES OF NORTH CAROLINA FORMED BEFORE 1800*

(Arranged in related groups)

ALBEMARLE (the first county) 1663; formally erected, 1665.* Chowan, 1672; Currituck, 1672; Pasquotank, 1672; Perquimans, 1672; Bertie, 1722; Tyrrell, 1729.

(*Chowan*) Gates, 1778.**

(*Pasquotank*) Camden, 1777.

(*Bertie*) Northampton, 1741; Hertford, 1759;** Edgecombe, 1735;**

(*Tyrrell*) Washington, 1799.

(*Edgecombe*) Granville, 1746; Halifax, 1758; Nash, 1777.

(*Granville*) Bute, 1764. (*Extinct.*)

(*Bute, extinct*) Franklin, 1779; Warren, 1779.

(*Halifax*) Martin, 1774.**

BATH, *extinct;* Beaufort, 1705; Hyde, 1705; Craven, 1712; Carteret, 1722; New Hanover, 1729;* Bladen, 1734;* Onslow, 1734;* Brunswick, 1764.**

(*Beaufort*) Pitt, 1760.

(*Craven*) Johnston, 1746;** Jones, 1778.

(*Johnston*) Wake, 1770;** Dobbs (*extinct*) 1758.

(*Dobbs, extinct*) Wayne, 1779;** Lenoir, 1791;** Glasgow, 1791, (*extinct.*)

(*Glasgow, extinct*) Greene, 1799.*

(*New Hanover*) Duplin, 1749.

(*Duplin*) Sampson, 1784

(*Bladen*) Anson, 1748; Orange, 1753;** Cumberland, 1754; Robeson, 1786.

(*Anson*) Mecklenburg, 1762; Montgomery, 1778; Richmond, 1779; Rowan, 1753; Tryon, 1762 (*extinct*).

(*Mecklenburg*) Cabarrus, 1792.

(*Rowan*) Surry, 1770; Iredell, 1788; Guilford, 1770;** Burke, 1777.

(*Surry*) Wilkes, 1779 ** Stokes, 1798.

(*Wilkes*) Ashe, 1799.

(*Guilford*) Randolph, 1779; Rockingham, 1785.

(*Burke*) Buncombe, 1791.

(*Tryon, extinct*) Rutherford, 1779;** Lincoln, 1779.

(*Orange*) Caswell, 1777; Chatham, 1770.

(*Caswell*) Person, 1791.

(*Cumberland*) Moore, 1784.

CLARENDON, an original county, *extinct.*

CRAVEN, 1665. (*This original county appears to be extinct, although a county of that name was erected later.* See BATH.)

*See note on p. 20.
**Formed from more than one county.

MARRIAGES BY INFERENCE* WESTMORELAND COUNTY VIRGINIA**

RICH: SUTTON and SUSANNA BURKLEY, widow of Thomas. Before 24 Sept 1684. [Sutton then deceased.] Orders, 1676-88, p. 351.

JOHN STURMAN and ELIZABETH JORDAN[?] eldest dau. of Dorcas Jordan. Before 1708, Wmld Wills. Crozier, p. 31.

GEORGE SOUTH and ANN SHEPHERD, widow of Isaac. Before 1719. Wmld Wills, Crozier, p. 29.

ROBERT SANFORD and MARY MUSE, dau. John. Before 14 June 1725. Wmld Wills. Crozier. p. 34.

------ SPENCER and ANN AUCHRAM. [She had also been the wife of Richard Chapman. The order of her marriages is uncertain. See her will.] Before 29 Aug 1695. ii-77.

JOHN TAYLOR and ELIZA: BROWNE, widow of John. Before or about the 30 July 1679. Orders 1676-88, p. 15.

HENRY TYLLERY [TILLORY] and MARY WESTCOATE, dau. William, dec'd. Before 20 Dec 1682. Orders, 1676-88, p. 269. Prob. before 4 June 1673. See p. 288.

WILLIAM TEBBS and MARY POPE, widow of Thomas, About 1741-2, i-317.

EDWARD THOMSON and -------------- BUTLER, a widow. Prob. about 15 Apr 1657. Orders, i-79.

GEORGE TURBERVILLE and MARTHA CORBIN, dau. of Gawin. Before 1790. xviii-278.

GEORGE TURBERVILLE, of Hiccory Hall, Cople psh, Wmld, Gent., and FRANCES ASHTON, dau. of Col. Henry Ashton. Before 16 Oct 1740. ix-200.

JOHN VICCARS and JOANE WEBB, dau. Elias and Katherine Webb. Before 13 Jany 1673. Orders, 1668-77, f. 140.

JOHN WHISTON and JUDITH JONES, widow and extx of Nathaniel Jones. [She was also extx of Abraham JENMAN [JERMAN?] Before 27 Apr 1664. Orders 1662-64, f. 26.

Lt. Coll. JOHN WASHINGTON and Mrs. ANN BRETT, relict and admx of Henry Brett, Mcht., of Plimouth, Eng. Orders 1668-77, f. 73.

Coll. JOHN WASHINGTON and [FRANCES] the relict of Capt. Jno APPLETON. [She appears to have been also the widow of ----------- Payton. See p. 123.] Before 26 Sept 1677. Orders, 1676-88 p. 90.

*Copyright, 1926, Pauline Stewart Crosley.
**See note on p. 4, February NOTE-BOOK.

Mr. FRANCIS WRIGHT and Mrs. ANN WASHINGTON, Before 20 Dec 1682. Orders 1676-88, p. 269.

WILLIAM WALKER and MARY JEPHS[?] sister of William Jephs (who removed to Maryland, 1658 or 1659.) See record 24 Sept 1707. iv-40.

RICHARD WRIGHT, of Chickasone, Northumberland, and ANN MATTROM, dau. Col. John Mattrom. About 15 Aug 1652. ii(B)-21. [ANN WRIGHT calls Mr. Nicholas Spencer, brother.]

THOMAS WILSFORD and MARGARET BROWNE, widow. About or before 20 June 1656. i-113, and Orders, i.

WILLIAM WEBB, sergt[?] and the relict of Geo. CAMPION, Before 17 Dec 1679. Orders, 1676-88, p. 172.

THOMAS YOWELL and ANNE LEE, dau. Col. Richard Lee, late of Stratford Laughton, cty of Essex, England. Before 23 June 1673. Orders, 1668-77, f. 149.

JOHN YOUNG and CHRISTIAN BRUCE. Before 27 Jany 1741-2. Wmld Wills, Crozier, p. 47.

Additional list:

WILLIAM BALL, of Lancaster, Gent., and LETTICE LEE, dau. of Henry. Before 28 Aug 1747. Wmld Wills, Crozier. p. 50.

GEORGE BROWNE, Taylor, and FRANCES ROWLAND, dau.-in-law of William Onered[?] About 12 July 1662. ii(B)-16.

JOHN BUTLER prob, m. the widow of ---- BURRELL. Before or about 26 June 1661. ii-42.

GAWIN CORBIN and HANNAH LEE, dau. of Thomas. Before 1749-50. Wmld Wills, Crozier. p. 53.

JOSEPH HARDWICK and SUSANNA SUTTON, widow of Richard. [She had also m. (1) ——— Burkley.] Before 24 Sept 1684. Orders, 1676-88, pp. 351-390.

GEORGE HORNER and [ELIZABETH] MONROE, widow of Andrew. Before 30 July 1679. Orders, 1676-88, p. 158.

JOHN JORDAN and the Relict of Patrick SPENCE, Before 24 Aug 1685. Orders, 1676-88. p. 447.

-------- JORDAN and MARY MARTIN, Before 12 Dec 1670. Orders, 1668-77, p. --.

JAMES NEALE and ELIZA: CALVERT, dau. William, Before 27 Nov 1707. iv-96.

-------- SILVESTER and SARAH KIRK, widow of Randolph. Before 26 Nov 1684. Orders, 1676-88, p. 367.

MARYLAND'S NEXT OF KIN *

MARY DONOCK; inv. Patrick Donock of Som. cty. 21 May 1720. v-82. [This name appears in the Virginia records in two or more spellings, one of which is *Donath*. Editor.]

RICHARD REEALY[?]; inv. John Daine of St. Mary's cty. 16 Jany 1720. v-92.

THOMAS and WILLIAM BOND, brothers inv. Benjamin Schoolfield of Som. cty 30 Aug 1720. v-95.

SARAH and WILLIAM JENKINS; inv. William Jenkins, Sen., of Balto. cty. 14 Jany 1700. v-100.

BENEDICT and FRANCIS IGNATIUS BOARMAN; inv. Wm. Boarman of Chas. cty. 24 June 1720. v-101.

D. VANSWERINGEN; inv. Joseph Vansweringen of St. Mary's cty. 15 Mch 1721. v-105.

THOMAS SMITH; inv. Daniell Smith of Talbott city. 20 Feby 1719-20. v-133.

WM. and EDWD TURNER; inv. John Turner of Talbot cty. 18 June 1720. v-134.

HANNAH KEMP and REBECCA CLARK; inv. Elizabeth Meers of Talbot cty. 8 Mch 1720. v-136.

DANIELL POWELL; inv. Wm. Harrison of Talbot cty. 8 Feby 1719. v-137.

MICHAELL TODEL and WM. ROBINSON; inv. James Foxon of Dorchester cty. Apr, 1721.

EDWARD and FRANCIS POOLE; inv. Edward Poole of Dorchester cty. 17 Apr 1721. v-146.

WILLIAM and HENRY DEAN; inv. Robert Johnson of Dorchester cty. 15 May 1720. v-147.

NICHOLAS PARRISH; inv. Richard Parrish of Dorchester cty. 24 Mch 1719. v-148.

THOMAS CAMBLE and JOHN SQUIRES; inv. James Green of St. Mary's cty. 10 June 1721. v-148.

JOHN and WILLIAM SANDERS; inv. Matthew Sanders of Charles cty. 11 May 1721. v-151.

JOSEPH and MARY ALLEN; inv. Joseph Wilson of Chas. cty. 1 May 1721. v-151.

FRANCIS and THOMAS SPRY; inv. John Spry of Q. A. cty. 10 June 1721.

WILLIAM MACKDONELL and MARGARET BURDIN; inv. John Burdin of Q. A. cty, 13 May 1721. v-155.

VIRGINIA, COLONISTS

(From "Old Volume 5," S. L. O., Richmond.)

THOMAS BELL, New Kent cty, 1658.
Head rights: ten persons, no names given.

Coll. WM. BERNARD, Esq., Lanc. cty, 1657.
Head rights: Sixteen persons, no names given.

JOHN BENNETT, "Westmoreland or Northumberland cty," 1658.
Head rights: three persons, no names given.

GEORGE BROWNE, New Kent, 1659.
Head rights: John Haynes, Sr., John Heines, Sr. [*sic.*] Evan Johannes, Robert Scottell.

Mr. FRANCIS BURNELL, New Kent, 1659.
Head rights: Marg. Boater, Robert Crup[?] Jno. Needham, Robert Allen, Tho. Copinn, Jno. Clarkey [Claskey?] Eliz: Baileinge[?] Jno. Darker [or Darken] James Johnson, Robert Miller, Robert Jinkins, James Tanner, Wm. Hazard, Richd Smyth, Mary Barnes, Geo. West, two negroes.

WILLIAM BROCK, Lower Norfolk, 1664.
Head rights: Dennis Cragh, John Berwick, John Keene, Owen Kene, Darby Kenland, John Covall, Wm. Edwards, Denis Deuly, Edm. Power.

WILLIAM BROCK, L. Norfolk, 1664.
Head rights: Dennis Murragh, Alice Morton. 1664.

Mr. WILLIAM BASNETT, L. Norfolk, 1664.
Head rights: Robert Powes, Sr., John Powes, Jr., Mary Tudman[?] Richard Hopham, Wm. Jeremie, John Warton, Martha Fennell, Penelope Burt [Burk?] WILLIAM BASNETT'S wife [or William Basnett and wife] James Miller, William Griffin.

HUGH BRENT, n. s. Rappahannock River, 1663.
Head rights: Wm. Lumpton, Thomas Bromstead.

GEORGE CHAPMAN, New Kent, 1658.
Head rights: Walter Price, James Kinge, Tho. Tallott, John Fry, Nich. Richinge, Robert Munday, Marg: Hawkins, Alice Hobbs, John Williams, Wm. Sidney, John Padey, Antho. Moore, John Peane, Tho. Hadway, Joseph Lucas, Rich. Keyes, Mary Guny [Gunn?] Tho. Reekes, Wm. Mills, Tho. Shore.

THOMAS CHRISTIAN, James City cty, 1657.
Head rights: THO. CHRISTIAN, John Wilkinson.

EDWIN CONAWAY, Lancaster cty. [1657.]
Head rights: twenty-five persons, no names given.

ROBERT CHOWNINGE, Lancaster cty, 1657.
Head rights: John Connolam, Gill Hargessey, Will Sawyer, Math. Parry.

PHILLIP CARPENTER, Northumberland cty, 1657.
Head rights: Wm. Hall, John Harris, Nicholas Walter, George Browne, Moses Turner, Marmaduke Allen, Prudence Lowe.

Mr. JOHN CUSTIS, Accomack, 1664.
Head rights: Mary Knight, Jno. Norgood, Jno. Abram, William Briggs, Tho. Somersett, Jno. Watts, Tho. Coleman.

JOHN CANNIDA, Rappa. cty, 1663.
Jno. Golding, Ed. Reeves, Ann Blandon, Wm. Griffin.

WILLIAM COOKE, Lancaster cty, 1663.
Head rights: John Potter, Edward King, Samuell Gough.

JOHN CHINN, Lancaster cty, 1664.
Head rights: James Potter, Thomas Coate.

ROB. CLERKE, upon a Creeke which issueth out of Petomeck freshes above the narrows at Puscatoway, 1657.
Head rights: forty persons, no names given.

VINCENT COCKE, upon Petomeck River, in the freshes above Anacosta, 1657.
Head rights: ten persons, no names given.

GEORGE CHAPMAN, New Kent cty. 1658. (North side Mattopany River.)
Head rights: Mary Hewes, Charles Winterne, Mary Bateman, John Bateman, Mabell Jones, John Knight, Wm. Hanwell, Robert Wright, Miles Grey, Fran. Aston, Tho. Winn, Thomas Willett, Richard Perry, Roger Shepherd, Robert Wilson, Tho. Hawkings, Mary Griggs, James Harvey[?] Rich. Williams, Robert Brome, Tho. Franke, Mary Woodbridge, Robert Sallitt, John Fisher, Wm. Norton, Tho. Telton[Tilton] Wm. Port, Walter Rigson, Symon Heale, Tho. Edgcome.

JOHN CURTIS, freshes of Potomeck River, 1657.
Head rights: forty persons, no names given.

JOHN CURTIS, Lancaster cty. 1657.
Head rights: twenty-four persons, no names given.

Capt. WM. CLAIBORNE, New Kent cty. 1658.
Head rights: twenty persons, no names given.

Mr. ROBERT COLLINS, Northumberland cty. 1658.
Head rights: ROBERT COLLINS, twice; MARY COLLINS, Edward Hales, Wm. Stone. Mary Davis, ANN COLLINS, REBECCA COLLINS, Francis Parker, Samuel Morris, Hugh Coates, ROBT. COLLINS, Jr., Tho. Duns[?] Susan Parker, Wm. Molton, Wm. Barrett, Ralph Lowe, Sarah Holdin, Edward Davis, Ann Barrett.

THOMAS CARTER, Nansemond cty. 1658.
Head rights: THOMAS CARTER and wife, Wm. [perhaps Mrs. or Mme] Read, Wm. Smith.

Mr. HENRY CORBYN[CORBYM] and Mr. GERRARD FOWKE, Patomecke Freshes, branch toward Herne Islands. 1658.
Head rights: Andrew Bellarke, Wm. Allen, Jno. Powell, Bridgett Gardner, Rich. Huskly, Patrick Purser, Shadrack Wallimur [Walliver?] Rich. Lowe, Wm. Allen, Tho. Thompson, Andrew Blacke, Wm. Baily, Rich. Price, Rich. Page, Elinor Abbott, Jno. Cahowne, Alex. Nicholson, Jno. Makinney, Wm. Bourne, Wm. Corman, Dunkin Makeny, Alex, Mackenny, Tho. Jelliby, Daniel Mathewe, Fran: Lyelle, Susan Michell, Samuel Alexander, Margaret Rookesby, Christian Dennis, Geo. Dau, Jno. Moses, Robert Reyman, Dorcas Jones, Mr. Horsmandine (?) (twice), Susanna Horsmandine, John Stith[?] Jane Sumer, Wm. Jane, Thomas ________, Rich. Curd, Nich. Jenkins, Jno. Turner[?] Ro: Brisley, Christian ______, Anne ______, Hen Wenne, Clemt Mallin, Jno. Codier, Robt. Jones, Jno. Lock, Margt Raymond, Mary Rolfe, Mary Bingley, Eliz. Hayes, Ann Jenkins, Geo. Walke.

JOHN COSSENS and THOMAS STEED, Northumberland cty. 1658.
Head rights: Robert Davis, Miles Allen, Wm. Greene, Henry Clarke, John Allen, Tho. Dunn, Antho. Jones, Perry Evans, Arthur Longe, Francis Loe, Thomas ________, Anthony Roe.

WM. CORDEROY, west side main swampe upon the head of Crany Creeke. 1657.
Head rights: three persons, no names given.

GEORGE CHAPMAN, New Kent cty, 1658.
Head rights: Georg Morse, David Briggs, Richard Button, Andrew Morgan, Tho: Washbrow, Thomas Dooding, Wm. Haines, Wm. Hutton, Ro. Stoute, Adrew Scellson[?] Jone Forrest[?] Mary Wasbrough, Edmond Rutland, James Harris, Nicholas Fishpoole, Jr., Wm. (Dobson?) Whittson [both names given] Thomas Jones, Peter Redman, Tho. Parke, Tho. Payton, Ann Gibbs, Charles Meredith, James Martin, Andrew Rayne, Wm. Cowdery, Mary Cope, Tho. Cawlins, Tho. Moody.

HENRY CORBIN, Gentleman, n. e. side Mattapony River. 1658.
Timothy Donis[?] Elizabeth Pickett, Henry James, Owen Davis, Richard Tatsall [Hatsall?] David Watkins, Jno. Henley, Francis Brooke, John Birke, Tho. Brookes, Jane Hornshey[?] Jno. Steadman, Jno. Lewis, Jno. Hagg.

The County Court Note-Book

An every-other-monthly devoted mainly to abstracts from County Court records, prior to 1800.

MILNOR LJUNGSTEDT, Editor and Publisher. Bethesda, Route 10, Maryland.

Published six times a year. Subscription, two dollars, in advance; must begin with the year. Advertising rates moderate.

JUNE, 1926

Vol. V., No. 3

The JUNE and AUGUST NOTE-BOOKS, the latter issued at the same time as the former, are very late. The Editor has not only been in ill health for several months, but has been met with a sudden and unexpected increase in the cost of publication, so much of an increase than unless better arrangements can be made the NOTE-BOOK cannot continue beyond the present year at the present price.

TELEPATHY, ANCESTRAL DUPLICATION AND SUCH

The Editor would probably be considered an opinionated person. Opinions will come and what are you going to do with them? One of the opinions of the Editor has been that the NOTE-BOOK would speak for itself as an absolutely reliable collection of facts, merely that and nothing more, put out without any expressed opinion whatever, except in the case of the Marriages by Inference, and they have been explained in an early issue. They are logical deductions . . . probably a deduction is an opinion.

But a short time ago a former correspondent wrote the Editor as follows: "I would "like to correct an article published July, 1922, "page 5 of the County Court Note-Book, "where you speak of 'Captain George Nich-"olas Hack omitting his son Spencer on his "list of Tithables.' Spencer was not the son "of Captain George Nicholas Hack of Acco-"mack, but a descendant of Peter Hack who "was Ranger General of Northumberland "County, and brother to said Captain George "Nicholas Hack."

The Editor was "stumped." The note in question was made in 1921, from the records of Accomack county, Virginia, at a time when the Editor had never heard of a Spencer Hack (except the one omitted from the list of tithables) and on its face it appeared to be a reliable abstract. As the Editor had never heard of Spencer Hack, how could she have supplied him? Could it be possible that she had been in telepathic communication, unrealized by herself, with some person who did know that there was another Spencer Hack elsewhere? All that the Editor knew of the family was that there was a certain George Nicholas Hack of a certain prominence, who was sometimes recorded as a Dutchman, sometimes as an High German. Could this telepathic communication have come from the family tomb? Not the Editor's family tomb, but a tomb somewhere in Accomack county. The Editor's faith in her clarity of mind began to be shaken . . . how could she account for this uncalled for Spencer?

A correspondent on the Eastern Shore* helped to solve the mystery. He sent the Editor an extract from some parish record which gave the birth of Spencer Hack of the Western Shore, son of George Nicholas Hack, in 1700. The Eastern Shore Spencer Hack was of tithable age in January, 1696.

All descendants of George Nicholas Hack, will please take notice that two Spencer Hacks are sons of two George Nicholas Hacks, and that one is recorded on one side of Chesapeake Bay, and one on the other.

Not very important, but an excellent illustration of several things. And the Editor's faith in the bald truthfulness of the NOTE-BOOK is restored (for the time being).

The arrangement of the counties of NORTH CAROLINA in a convenient tabulated form proved to be a somewhat difficult matter. The Editor intended to follow the dates of formation as given in Col. Fred. S. Olds' "Story of the Counties," and to use the chart prepared by the Secretary of State as a help to the tabulation. That chart, however, does not agree in all points with Col. Olds' bulletin, and it has seemed advisable to follow the latter authority rather than to try to fit the two together.

Additional trouble and some doubt as to the correctness of the table arises from the lack of definite dates of formation of the three earliest counties. ALBEMARLE was in existence and was called a "county" in 1663. But whether that or the date next given, 1665, is the official date, is not quite clear. The official date of CRAVEN county is also not clear. For further information, the reader is referred to Col. Olds' very interesting publication.

A number of county names have been changed, and in some cases, the counties became extinct by division. This also added to the difficulty. In fact, the North Carolina counties, while not as puzzling in their history as those of South Carolina, appear to have enjoyed a sort of trial system of nomenclature, much upset by later Revolutionary sentiment, reminding one of the danger of naming any one or anything after prominent personages, until those personages have safely passed into political history.

As in the Virginia table, the immediate ancestor of a county appears in italics in parenthesis. Where two or more ancestors should be given, the name of the one first mentioned in the bulletin is that selected. As such county was perhaps not the most important parent, it is advisable to consult the bulletin for more complete detail.

IT is gratifying to note that the Magazine of the Maryland Historical Society has taken up again the publication of the Maryland Rent Rolls.

Attention is invited to the foot-note on page 272, of the issue for September, 1926, which states that Liber A, of Charles County, Maryland, has recently been found in the vault of the Historical Society, *where it had lain for forty years.* The volume, it is interesting to know, has been repaired and rebound, "and as soon as a transcript has been

*Mr. Stratton Nottingham.

made, will be restored to its proper place in the Charles County Court House." The Editor has a dim recollection of having been told of this volume while in Charles County some years ago, but has never heard it mentioned elsewhere by any one. It seems possible that a few other "lost" county records may from time to time be found in the vaults of historical societies or of state archives.

Errata:

The Westmoreland marriage, KIRTON-COLE in the APRIL NOTE-BOOK, should read:

Mr. THOMAS KIRTON and ANNA COLE, widow of Mr. Richard COLE. Before May, 1676. Orders, 1676-88, p. 62. (See also [iii]-68.) The name given, Richard Kirton, is incorrect.

-------- PAYTON and Mrs. FRANCES SPEKE, widow of Col. SPEKE. (See his inventory.) Before 7 Aug 1661. ii-48.

NOTES FROM NORTHAMPTON COUNTY, VIRGINIA, COURT RECORDS

Deposition of ANN WARDE, wife of William; "Upon the same day the house of ARGOLL YARDLEY was burned Robert Berry, his wife, and father in Lawe (Daniel Wheatley) came to the Deponent's house . . ." N-n, Va. iv-18, 28 Apr 1651.

LITT. TAZWELL, writing from Brunswick cty, 28 Nov 1753, says: "I am informed that my deceased mother Mrs. SOPHIA TAZEWELL late of your county . . . made her will . . . and appointed me whole and sole executor . . ." He asks stay of probation as his attendance at court in Brunswick is absolutely necessary.

The petition of LITTLETON TAZEWELL and GERTRUDE TAZEWELL, the former of Brunswick cty, and the latter of Northampton cty, states that GERTRUDE HARMANSON, late of Northampton, a widow, by will 11 Sept 1732, appointed Henry Harman and William Tazewell late of Northampton, extrs; that by her will she lent to sd William and to her dau. Sophia Tazewell, the father and mother of the petitioners, during life the use of certain slaves, and after the decease of William and Sophia, she gave the slaves to their children. William and Sophia are deceased, leaving issue only the petitioners and one other son and daughter, namely, John and Anne, both under 21. [About 1753. N-n, Va. Court records.]

FOR SUNDRY ARTICLES & Expenses provided for a Supper on His Majesty's Birth night, to yr Order, £5. To 19 Bottles of Wine, 19 Bowls punch, £5-14. To Negroe hire & diet for the Burn fire [*sic*] £2-5-4 1-2. To Carpenter's work in fixing Lights, 2-6. To Coffee after Supper [and] 6 Quarts Rum, 19-6. To Limes & Sugar [and] 4 Glasses (broke) 5-6. To Carting Swivels to & from Cherryton's, 10 [sh.] To Punch at the Burn fire, £1. By Cash in part, 5-1-0. [Bal.] 10-15--10 1-2. [A suit for this bill for "ball & entertainment" was brought by William Galt against Mr. John Manby, 16 July 1761. N-n cty, Va. Court records. The date of the entertainment was 10 Nov. 1758.]

JOHN GOFFINGON humbly complains that he is advised that on or about the year of our Lord MDCCLX a Letter or Letters was received at some Port in Virginia from England informing him that a considerable estate both Real and Personal had lately descended to him as Heir to THOMAS GOFFIGON the Elder one of his Ancestors in or near the City of London . . . and that William Ronald and James Parker have in their Possession the said Letter or Letters & refuse to deliver them. Petition filed 11 June 1771. [N-n cty, Va. records.]

CONTINUED articles COUNTY COURT NOTE-BOOK, and the dates on which they first appeared.

MARRIAGES BY INFERENCE. Began with May, 1922.

MARYLAND'S NEXT OF KIN. Began with July, 1922.

VIRGINIA COLONISTS. This alphabetized list began with July, 1924.

MILITARY NOTES, both COLONIAL and REVOLUTIONARY, and some later MILITIA NOTES, will appear in every issue, if possible.

SHIPS IN PORT, INTERCOUNTY and INTERCOLONIAL and COLONIAL FORENAMES, will appear in alternate issues or as space can be found for them.

EASTERN SHORE FAMILIES, in the form of a one-page supplement, began with June, 1925. This will be continued later.

WILLIAMS NOTES
MARYLAND-VIRGINIA SECTION

GEORGE WILLIAMS. His admr d. b. n. was William C. Freeman. Fauq., Va. 1824. xxvii-412.

HANNAH WILLIAMS, Pr. Wm, Va. 1762. Orders—95.

HUGH WILLIAMS m. a dau. of . . . Johnson. Before 1696. Annap, Md. Inv. and Accts. xiv-57.

HENRY WILLIAMS to be surveyor of the highway in place of Mr. Henry Custis. Acco, Va. 25 Oct 1689. ix-84.

HENRY WILLIAMS, MARY and JANE WILLIAMS, were devisees under the will of Nicholas Hall. N-n, Va. 28 July 1646. iii-41.

HENRY WILLIAMS, late deceased. Acco, Va. 16 Mch 1691. x-63.

HENSON WILLIAMS was a legatee of Wm. Hardin. He was paid a legacy left John Williams by Hardin [Harden]. He was also paid for his part Alexander Williams' estate, and John Williams, do. Henson Williams lived with Charles Hardin, extr of William Hardin, 1791-1793. Estate acct of Charles Hardin. Ldn, Va. 1801. H-290.

HONOR WILLIAMS, in suit. Pr. Wm. Va. 6 Aug 1762. Orders-283.

JACOB S. WILLIAMS; estate. Fauq., Va. 1819. vol. vii.

JAMES WILLIAMS, *Something,* 200 a., surveyed for him. Patent to John Demall. Pr. Geo. R. R., Md. (1723.) 16 Dec 1672.

JAMES WILLIAMS, late of Charles cty, Md. Gilbertus Simpson and wf Elizabeth are his heirs, and convey their interest in St. Thomas. Sig. Thomas Sympson, Jr. Semmes Mss. 6 Apr 1730.

JAMES WILLIAMS, of Orange cty, Va. Kennedy and wf convey land to him. Shenan. cty, Va. 1796. K-200.

JAMES WILLIAMS, of Orange cty, Va., was an agent with Jonathan Clark to sell certain lands. Shenan. cty, Va. 8 Apr 148. K-148.

JAMES WILLIAMS, of Annapolis, bought land in Fauquier, Va. Fauq. cty, Va., 1795. xiii-433.

JAMES WILLIAMS, of Annapolis, A. A. cty, Md, to John Guyer, same, land in Fauquier. Refers to a conveyance by John Clark and wf Sarah, in 1795. Fauq. cty, Va. 27 Jany 1802. xv-155.

JAMES WILLIAMS, I, m. Grace Fleming; had chn: Nancy, John, James II. (Others?) JOHN resided Poplar Grove, near Pocomoke City, Nassawadox neighborhood. Had two sons, and daughters. Sons were Dr. John Fleming Williams, James W. Williams. James W. resided in Hartford cty, Md. and d. 1842. A descent from Pocohontas indicated. Stevenson Sketch at Md. Hist. Soc. p. 13.

JAMES WILLIAMS. Fredk cty, Va. Tax-list. 1782.

JANE WILLIAMS m. John Able. Shenan. cty, Va. Mar ret. 1788.

JARED WILLIAMS m. Martha Carson, dau. of Simon Carson, Jr. Shenan cty, Va. M. L. B. 8 May 1790.

JENNETT WILLIAMS; inventory. Ret. 9 Nov 1755. Staff., Va. O-314.

JESSE WILLIAMS, Fauquier. See deed to him by NATHANIEL WILLIAMS. Fauq. cty, Va. 1777. vi-401.

JESSE WILLIAMS, and wf Mary, Fauquier, convey to George Calvert of Culpeper cty, Va., 161 1-2 a. (See deed of Nathaniel to Jesse.) They also convey land to Samuel Porter. Fauq. cty, Va. 25 Aug 1777. vi-393. Also 26 Mch 1780. vii-258. (In this second deed Charles Williams' corner is mentioned.)

JOEL WILLIAMS, of Shenandoah cty, Va., from Isaac Ruffner and wf Molly. A lot in Luray. Shenan., 9 May 1818. Y-302.

JOHN WILLIAMS, trustee of estate of John Porter of this cty, who was "casually found dead upon the King's Road." Staff., Va. 12 Nov 1690. i-105.

INTER-COUNTY AND INTER-COLONY

SAMUEL JACKSON, of Georgetown, in Montgomery cty, Maryland, conveys to Jacob Formawall[?] of Knox cty, Tenn., a lot in Knoxville, conveyed by John B. Evans to Samuel Jackson, 28 Apr 1800. 10 July 1800. Knox cty, Tenn. B2-278.

ROBERT MOORE, of Rockbr. cty, Va., from Michael Fraker, Sr., Washington cty, Tenn., tract of land. Washington cty, Tenn. 8 Dec 1797. H-231.

JOHN ROBERTSON, Pendleton cty, S. C., to John Wearen of Washington cty, N. C., land on the waters of Big Limestone crk, called the West Fork. 53 a. Washington cty, Tenn. 25 July 1789. iv-215.

PETER RUBLE, of Frederick cty, blacksmith, from John Hunter, of Wash'n cty, Territory South of the Ohio; 57 a. on Cherokee creek. Wash'n cty, Tenn. 1 Aug 1792. v-119.

JOSIAH WATSON, of Alexandria, Va., to John Caffrey and George M. Deaderich, of Davidson cty, Tenn., 640 a. granted Willoughby Williams of North Carolina, in 1790. Davidson cty, Tenn. 25 Oct 1797. D-374.

THOMAS CHURCHMAN, of Cumb. cty, Va., from Isaac Butler, Davidson cty., a mortgage in order to secure the payment of £300, and interest from Jany, 1804, to Samuel Butler of Surry cty, Va. Davidson cty, Tenn., 10 May 1810. I-22.

THOMAS BRALY, d. December, 1764. His eldest bro. William, expected from Ireland. Rowan cty, N. C. A-5.

JOHN HALE; of *Strabaun* tshp, York cty, Penna. Will. Mentions uncle Henry Thomson and William Simpson, extrs. Two sisters, Anne and Arminta Hale. Cousin Alexander Thomson. Probated Oct 1766. Rowan cty, N. C. A-68.

PETER FREY, lately of Heidelberg tshp, Berks cty, Penna., now living in Rowan cty, N. C. Will. Wf Ann Barbara Frey. "Vide the Original in Dutch." Rowan cty, 1765-1767. A-53.

ALEXANDER GIBSON, late of the cty of Chester, Penna., now of the Psh of St. Luke, Rowan cty, N. C. Will. Mother [and father?]; bro. Dr. Isaac Gibson; nephew Alexander Gibson, son of James. Sister's son Alex'r Fleming. "Every niece I have;" Three bros. John, James, Samuel. Bros-in-law William Dijart[?], James Fleming, Andrew Newbry. Bro. James and Andrew Newbry, extrs. Wit: James Morrison, Thomas Morrison, Joseph Steel. Rowan cty, 1773-1775. A-200.

WILLIAM TEMPLE COLES, will. Born in Angier street, Dublin, nearly opposite to the new [now?] playhouse, now of Salisbury, Rowan cty, N. C. . . . Directs that he be "buried under the care of the friendly Brethren of the Society of Free Masons" Leaves land for a Burying ground, one half for the inhabitants of the town of Salisbury and "the moiety to the Society of Free Masons and to Strangers." "Gives the Lott where the Gallows now stands to the district of Salisbury to be and remain as a place for the execution of Felons, forever." [Date about 1775.] Rowan cty. A-221.

ROBERT LATTA, lately of the cty of Tyrone in the Kingdom of Ireland, gives bond in connection with the estate of William Latta, deceased. He is atty for the heirs. Rowan cty, N. C. Minute Book, August, Sept 1775.

MOSES ANDREWS, of Cecil cty, Md., and wf Letice, to David Criswell, of same cty, WHEREAS a certain John McConnel of Rowan cty, obtained a patent to land in St. Luke's psh, on both side of Davis' Creek, 5 Nov 1757 . . . and did convey to Moses Andrews, 16 Jany 1759, Now, &c., &c. Rowan cty, N. C., 16 May 1763. vi-27.

VIRGINIANS AND OTHERS IN CONVEYANCES AND POWERS KENTUCKY COURT OF APPEALS

THOMAS DANIEL, of Caroline cty, Va. Witness. 1786.

ROBERT DANIEL, heir-at-law to Walker Daniel, to William Fleming of Botetourt cty, Va. (Martin Daniel's name appears.) 9 Mch 1785.

JOSEPH ELAM, Henrico, Va. Witness. 1786.

WILLIAM FOUSHEE, of Henrico cty, Va. 1785.

FREDERICK FRY, Massachusetts, Witness, 1787.

WILLIAM GIBSON, Baltimore, Md. Witness, 1787.

ANN GREEN, of Lincoln cty, Ky., power to Hon. Geo. Muter to receive from Wm. Lightfoot, Esq., of Charles City, Va., extr of the will of Mildred Lightfoot, a legacy devised to her. 24 Sept 1785.

JOHN PEYTON HARRISON and wf Frances, of Fauquier cty, Va., conveyance to Chinn's extrs. 1787.

MARTIN HAWKINS and wf Elizabeth, of Richmond, Va., to Chapman Austin, of Hanover, Va. 24 Sept 1786.

WILLIAM HAYS and wf Susannah, of Fayette, to James Calloway of Amherst, Va. 1000 acres in Madison cty, Ky. 6 Mch 1788.

ISAAC HITE, of Jefferson cty, Ky., appoints Abraham Hite of Hardy cty, Va., attorney to convey lots in Moorefield, Va. 13 Nov 1786.

WILLIAM HOLT, of Williamsburg [Va.], agreement with William Pope. Jefferson cty, Ky. Oct 1783.

ZEB. HOLLINGSWORTH, witness. Baltimore, Md. 1787.

JOHN HORD, Caroline cty, Va. Witness. 1786.

JOSHUA HUMPHRIES, of Richmond, Va., and wife ANN, to Benj. Logan, land in Fayette cty, Ky. 6 Dec 1785.

GILBERT IMLAY, of Virginia, and wf. Elizabeth, of Mercer cty, Ky. 1788.

EDWARD IRELAND, of Baltimore, Md., Merchant, to Benj. Fuller of Philadelphia, Penna. 21 Feby 1787.

GEORGE JAMES, of Culpeper cty, Va, to James Nourse, of Nelson cty, Ky, Agreement. (Eliza Field's name appears.) 13 Sept 1785.

THOMAS JOHNSON, late of Louisa cty, Va., now of Fayette. 23 Sept 1786.

SERVICE AND SUPPLIES COLONIAL, REVOLUTIONARY AND MILITIA

JAMES McGOWAN, a soldier in the Corps of Invalids, is found unfit for further duty. Ctf of Walter Stewart, Col. Inspector, North'n Army. Charleston, S. C., 15 Sept 1782. TT-215. Record of his discharge follows . . . "By his Excellency [George Washington's] Command, Jona. Trumbull, Jr., Secretary."

JAMES MUSGROVE, a private in the Continental Army, died in the service of the U. S. Pinkethman Musgrove, gdn of William Musgrove, ctfies that William is the orphan of James. Also ctf of James Wood, York cty, Va. 6 Aug 1791.

MATTHEW MARKLAND, Ensign of militia. Ohio cty, W. Va. Orders i-68. 5 June 1781. [See A. C. M.*]

JACOB OGLE, killed in service, Wife, Mary. Ohio cty, W. Va. Orders i-1778. [See A. C. M.*]

JOHN PETERSON, THOMAS TWITTY and BATTE[?] PETERSON, produce comm'ns as Captains of militia. Lunenb. cty, Va. Oct Ct 1748. Orders iii-452.

JOHN PREWITT; age 72; was a Revolutionary soldier; was in Capt. Michael Dougherty's company. Declaration for pension, 20 Nov 1832. John McLaughlin testifies to his services as a Rev. soldier, as well as to his own service. 25 Nov 1832. See Histy Tazewell cty, Va. pp. 229, 232.

JAMES PARK was in the regular service; ctf ordered, Ohio cty, W. Va. Orders i-59. Ct 3 Apr 1780. [See A. C. M.*]

DAVID RANDLE; killed on the field of battle; served as Lieut. in the regular service in 1763. Bethsheba Randle, heiress-at-law; ctf ordered. Ohio cty, W. Va. Orders i-59. Ct 3 Apr 1780. [See A. C. M.*]

SIMON ROBINSON; in consideration of services rendered as a Private in the late Army of the U. S., is granted 200 a, in Wmld cty, Penna. Harrisb'g, Penna. S. L. O. P13-313.

CATHERINE SMITH was the widow of . . . SMITH, killed in service. Ohio cty, W. Va. Orders i- . 1778. [See A. C. M.*]

ALEXANDER SAYERS is ctfied as a Revolutionary soldier. 20 Nov 1832. See Hist Tazewell cty, Va, p.237.

THOMAS SMITH makes oath to his declaration and the Court declares their opinion that he was a Revolutionary soldier. Mad. cty, Va. Orders, viii. 23 Aug 1832.

JOHN SPOLDIN, same. Same record and date.

WILLIAM SHEPHERD; order made in his favor, in Mch 1791, concerning his pension, is amended. Orders, ii-307. 28 Feby 1792. Mad. cty, Va.

JAMES TEBBS; oath as Captain, Pr. Wm cty, Va. 27 Feby 1762. Orders, [4], p. 57.

HARRY TURNER, Gent., presents Major's commission and takes the oaths. G. Geo. cty, Va. 1 Sept 1749. Orders 1735-1751, p. 625.

JOHN THORNLEY, presents Lieutenant's commission and takes oaths, K. Geo. cty, Va. 1 Sept 1749. Orders, 1735-1751, p. 625.

Reasonable price or two years' subscription will be given for numbers 1, 2, 3, 4, 6, and 7, COUNTY COURT NOTE-BOOK, 1921-1922. Address Editor.

Columbian Printing Co., Inc., Washington, D. C.

The

County Court Note-Book

A Little Bulletin of History and Genealogy

August, 1926. Vol. V, No. 4

SHIPS IN PORT

Ship *St. Tamany*. About 1800. Ptsburg. 1-301.

Shipp *Swallowe*, of "Neershanen" in N. E. Wm. Westerhouse of N. E. sells one-eighth to John Stringer[?] 9 Apr 1650. N-n, Va. iii-214.

The Ship *Speedwell*, of London, John Julian, master; Wm. Stanley sets forth that he "shipped on Board the above Shipp. with provisions and Liquors for himselfe, family and servts' subsistence att Sea & Shore from Galloway in Ireld to Virginia and Pensilvania to the vallue of three Hundred pds. sterl." He charges thefts on board. Wmld, Va. Ct 25 Mch 1685. Orders, 1676-88. p. 387.

Ship *Tayloe;* Capt. John Heard, murdered. Va. Sta. Pa. 1726. 1-209.

Bark *Tryall*. N-n, Va. 1669.

Pink called the *Triall of Galloway,* in Ireland; Capt. Thos. Smith, Commdr, Acco., Va. 1688. vi-513.

Schooner *Tryal;* belonging to Edward Lloyd, Province of Maryland; Zabdiel Potter, master; Nathaniel Potter, mate; Robert Donavin and Daniel Ryan, sailors; make oath that they sailed from the Island of Barbadoes the fifth Day of February Last past bound to Wye River in Maryland under the Convoy of His Majesty's Ship *Anson* with Severall other Men of Warr, [The *Tryal* was wrecked at the mouth of Onancock creek, Virginia.] Acco. cty, Va. 8 Mch 1751. Deeds iii-1.

Ship *True Love*. 28 July 1644. N-n, Va. ii-316.

Schooner *Two Brothers;* Robinson Custis, master; [bound for] Charlestown. Acco., Va. Naval E. and C. 6 June 1785.

Ketch *Unity;* James Rany [Ranny] mariner, master and part owner. Acco., Va. 13 May 1680. vi-210. Also viii-112. 4 Sept 1679.

Ship *Vincent;* Mr. Nathaniel Coledick, master; Richard Cobb, Bo's'n. N-n, Va. 28 June 1662. viii-154. Also 2 Mch 1662. viii-160.

Ship *The Vine;* Mr. Wm. Preason, owner. Acco., Va. 22 Dec 1685. ix-79. Also 3 Feby 1685. ix-79.

Catch *Virginia Merchant;* Robert Risdon, master. Acco., Va. 1663.

Catch *Virginia Merchant, als Providence,* of "Garnsey." Acco., Va. 26 June 1666. i-122. Old vol. V Va. S. L. O., p. 439, 1665. mentions the *Virginia Merchant* as "cast away."

The *Warren Brigantine;* Joseph Palmer, Captain; 1706. Records of Holy Trinity, Wmton, Dela. p. 117.

The *Water Duck,* of Rotterdam; Peter Simms, master. N-n, Va. 26 Mch 1645. ii-365. [His signature is Peter Sims.]

Ship the *White Horse;* 13 Nov 1656. N-n, Va. vii-53.

The *White Swanne,* a shipp. L. Norf., Va. 1653. C-52.

The *William and Elizabeth,* of London; Mr. Geo. Broad, master. Acco. Va. 1672.

The *William and George,* of London. Mr. Thomas Babb, of London, master. N-n, Va. 1645. iii-24.

Shipp *William and Mary;* Thomas Meech, master. 1698. N-n, Va. xvii-532.

The *William and Ann*. Acco., Va. 1677.

Shipp *William,* of London; Capt. Wm. Barker, commdr. Deposition of Rich Wright, Wm. Barker, and Francis Clay. [A "protest."] Rappa., Va. 20 May 1656. i-84. See also Acco. records, 1675.

Ship *William and John*. Acco., Va. 1675. vii-17.

Schooner *William Robinson;* Johannes Watson, master. 40 tons, no guns, Virginia built; [bound for] St. Eustatius. Acco., Va. Naval E. and C. 24 June 1782. Also 19 Aug 1782. [This vessel appears in these records until 1783, for and from various West Indian ports.]

Ship *Willing-Minde;* Wm. Gingel, commdr. Dec 1672.

H. M. *"Hired Ship" Wolfe;* Capt. Robt Willmott, master. Va. St. Pa. i-43. 21 Oct 1692.

Schooner, *Young Mans Endeavor;* Jonathan Robinson, master. Owners, Jonathan Robinson and John Hodson, both of Kent cty, Dela. Built Kent cty on Delaware; 8 tons. Ship Registers, 17 Sept 1756. Pa. Mags, xxv-571.

MARRIAGES BY INFERENCE*

(The following marriages are deduced, in the main, from South Carolina and Georgia court records.)

Rev. THOMAS ADAMS and DINAH WYLY, dau. of William, late of Camden, S. C. Kershaw cty, S. C. Before 21 Aug 1795. B-498.

JOHN BARRON and ELLIONAR MILLER, widow of Alexander. Greene cty, Ga. About Sept 1789.

LEWIS BENTLY and ELIZABETH GARTRELL, dau. of Francis. Lincoln cty, Ga. Before 1825. ii-198.

STEPHEN BOSTICK and ANNE RICHARDSON, widow of William. Abbeville cty, S. C. About 14 Sept 1798. i-224.

JAMES COOK and PEGGY HAWTHORNE, apparently dau. of Nathaniel Hawthorne. [See record.] Liberty cty, Ga. Before 14 Oct 1782. A-129.

JOHN DEAN and REBEKAH FINLEY, dau. of John. [See his will.] Before 22 June 1801. Greene cty, Ga.

JOHN GERRARD and MARGARET ROGERS, About or before 10 Mch 1637. Va. S. L. O. i-539.

ANDREW GREER and RUTH KINCAID, dau. of Joseph. (Married in Albemarle cty, Va.) About 1751. He m. (2) Mary Vance. See Tenn. Hist. Mags. Vol. vii.

Capt. ------ JACKSON and ELIZ: CUTTS. (She was perhaps widow of Baker Cutts.) Stafford cty, Va. Before or about 1653. Va. S. L. O. v-217.

WILLIAM JETER and MARGARET GATRELL, dau. of Francis, Lincoln cty, Ga. Before 1825. ii-198.

ISAAC JOHNSON and SUSANNAH EMBREY, dau. of William. Oglethorpe cty, Ga. Before 24 July 1829. C-78.

JORDAN KENNEBREW and MARY GATRELL, dau. of Francis. Lincoln cty, Ga. Before 1825. ii-198.

WILLIAM LANCASTER and SUSAN TURMON, dau. of Geo. Turmon, Sr. Lincoln cty, Ga. Before 30 Jany 1818. ii-76.

DANIEL McELDUFF[?] and RUTH LEWALLER[?] Newberry cty, S. C. Before 24 Feby 1790. A-1029.

EDWARD MANNING and OBEDIENCE BOHANNON, dau. of Dunkan. Lincoln cty, Ga. Before 24 Mch [1811?] ii-17.

WILLIAM MOORE and MASSEY BOHANNON, dau. of Dunkan. Lincoln cty, Ga. Before 24 Mch [1811?] ii-17.

ALEXANDER MOSS and PRUDENCE BOHANNON, dau. of Dunkan. Lincoln cty, Ga. Before 24 Mch [1811?] ii-17

CHRISTOPHER NICHOLSON and ANN ATWOOD, Quaker record of Perquimans, N. C. 1682. See vol. vii, p. 278, N. C. Booklet.

JOHN PEARCE [Richmond cty] and ESTHER WALKER, dau. of Col. John, Va. S. L. O. N. N. iii-123. Before 1691.

DAVID SEARS and CHARITY ROBINS. Before 7 Apr 1779. Edgecomb Records, N. C. N. C. Booklet, xvi-97.

JAMES SMITH and HANNAH CLOSE, widow of Henrv. Before 1775. Ga. Arch. xi-148.

JOHN SIMPSON and ANNA MACKENZIE, dau. of William, Before 16 Apr 1773. Ga. Arch. B-35.

Dr. ANDREW SMITH and MATILDA SHAW, at the house of William Shaw, Esq. Abbeville cty, S. C. Sunday, 1 Jany 1792. i-79.

JOHN TULLY, Lancaster cty, Va., and the half-sister of William Rankin, of Northumberland cty. Before 27 Nov 1739. Va. S. L. O. E-111.

THEODOCIA TURK [*sic*]and LIND FINLEY, dau. of John. (See his will.) Green cty, Ga. Before 22 June 1801.

CHARLES WATSON and SARAH DUDLEY. 8 Nov 1770. Ga. Arch. AA-362.

JOHNSTON WELBORN and RACHEL GATRELL, dau. of Francis. Before 1825. Lincoln cty, Ga. ii-198.

NATHAN WHITMON and PIETY BOHANNON, dau. of Dunkan. Before 24 Mch [1811]. Lincoln cty, Ga. ii-17.

WILLIAM WILSON and ABIGALL GREENHOW, widow of James Greenhow, Jr. About or before 1801. Chatham cty, Ga. W-251.

THOMAS WILLIAMS and ELIZABETH ROBBINS. Before 7 Apr 1779. Edgecomb, N. C. Records. N. C. Booklet xvi-97.

INTERCOUNTY AND INTERCOLONY

Letter of Mr. Samuell Maverick of N. E. Letter, 1633. N-n, Va. 1645 iii-24.

Mr. JONATHAN MATHEWS, WILLIAM JONES, of London, Mcht; WILLIAM WILLSON, of London, Gent., and JAMES WAGSTAFF, of London, Ironmonger; action of debt agt Mr. Valentine Mathews. Acco, Va. 13 Sept 1688. ix-138.

NICHOLAS MOORE, Esq., "President of Pensilvania." Acco, Va. Ct. 3 July 1683. ix-15.

Mr. MOORE, a Minister in N. E. L. Norf. Va. D-28. 17 Nov 1656.

JOHN MARTIALL, was of Boston. See power to John Bowdoin, N-n cty, Va. 1711.

JOHN MARTIN, of Plymouth, Eng. Mariner. Staff., Va. Orders i-143. Ct 8 Apr 1690-1.

THOMAS OLCOTT in N. E. referred to. Wmld, Va. 20 Oct 1657. O. i-87.

JOSEPH RUSSELL, EPRIAM [*sic*] and SAMUELL RUSSELL, Sussex cty, yeomen, and Jacob Thomas, of Chester cty, yeoman, wf Sarah, to Parker Robinson. Sussex, Dela. 7 Jany 1755. i-89.

JOHN SIMPSON owes a debt in Holland. N-n, Va. 2 Mch 1662. viii-165.

WILLIAM SMYTHSON, late of N. E. N-n, Va. 12 Dec 1643. ii-333.

ROBERT SNEAD'S will: . . . To my dau. Francis Snead who is now in England, who I understand is married to one Mr. [blank] Ossester, who was sometimes Marchent to Virginia but now keeps a great Stillhouse neare Hatton Garden in Holbourne . . . I give my dau. Frances Tenn pounds Sterling to buy her a Silver Tankard and I doe desire that my Coat of Armes be put upon it . . . Acco, Va. 27 Aug 1711. xi-595.

PETER SEVERNE of Patuxent river, Calvert cty, Md. Will: Acco., Va. 13 Jany 1667. ii-108.

Mr. SAMLL SHRIMPTON in New England, buys 2230 lbs. tobacco from Mr. Ro: West. Surry, Va. Joshua Barker's passage to N. E. mentioned. Surry, Va. 16 Mch 1674. i(2).

HENRY SMITH, Gent., Somerset cty, Md. Sells Oake Hall in Acco. Acco, Va. 19 July 1671. iv-1.

WILLIAM SMITH, dec'd, late of Somerset cty, Md. Lt. Col. John West, extr. Acco., Va. 20 Feby 1688. ix-15.

JOSEPH TOWNSEND, of Boston, Mcht. Bond to John Daniell. N-n, Va. 16 May 1679. xi-206.

MICHAEL TANTOR, of Branford in New England, marener. Power to Mr. Isaac Allerton, of New Haven, Mcht. Wmld, Va. 15 Oct 1655. O. i-103.

JACOB THOMAS, Newton Tshp, Chester cty, Penna., and wf Sarah, to Parker Robinson. Sus., Dela. 18 Nov 1757. i-166.

DANIEL TUCKER, Psh Bristol, Pr. George cty, Va. Surry, 1738. iii---

Mrs. TRAUGHTON of St. Mary's, Md. N-n, Va. 24 Feby 1642. ii-224.

ROBERT VAULX of Dor. cty, Md. Power to William Coman, of York cty. N-n, Va. 7 Sept 1704. xix-91.

OBADIAH WALKER, late of N. E., bro. to Capt. Nathaniel Walker, left a widow who m. Mr. Ephriam Savage. N-n Va. Before 27 Apr 1683. xv-26.

FAMILIES OF THE EASTERN SHORE CUSTIS OF VIRGINIA

(Continued from the Supplement to the NOTE-BOOK for December, 1925.)

JOHN CUSTIS, II, of Virginia, so far as the records show, the only child of JOHN CUSTIS, I, of Arlington, was born about 1653. (Dep'ns, 29 Dec 1681, N-n xiii-206; 6 Feby 1682, xiii-272; 28 Nov 1701, xviii-84. There is no reason to doubt that his mother was a daughter of ELIZABETH ROBINSON, and it seems probable that she was the widow ELIZABETH EYRES who m. JOHN CUSTIS, I, as shown in previous notes. JOHN CUSTIS, II, is usually called of Wilsonia, the place where he lived. [The house is now burned down, and the tomb of CUSTIS and his wife is shamefully neglected. This is the burial plot which is bordered by a hog-pen.]

JOHN CUSTIS, II, of Wilsonia, begins to appear in the records about 1671, he is then a witness to an assignment by his father. He is found in various matters before the Court, usually suits and the like, as well as appearances in his various official capacities. [Note: for the same reasons as given before, no full list is included in these notes of his civil and military offices.] One of the entries connected with this JOHN CUSTIS has rather a modern sound. Richard Watkins having carelessly fired the fence of Mr. JOHN CUSTIS, Jr., is ordered by the Court to replace it. (N-n, xii-195. 12 Nov 1677.) He has a difference with his uncle, BENJAMIN ROBINSON, in 1678. (N-n, xii-277.) ROBINSON went to live with his nephew and claims he was to have a salary, probably as overseer of the plantation, but CUSTIS denies that anything more was agreed to than a share of the crop. He has another difference with Mr. JOHN BELLAMY. [This BELLAMY was probably a connection, through the ROBINSONS. Ed.] JOHN ROBINSON [another uncle of CUSTIS] dies, and CUSTIS goes on the bond of BENJAMIN ROBINSON, the admr. (N-n, 29 Jany 1678. xii-352.) Mr. JOHN CUSTIS, Jr., was joint gdn of Adam Michael, son of John Michael, Sr. (N-n, 3 June 1679. xiii-20.) In a suit which BENJAMIN ROBINSON brings against Charles Holden, in connection with the estate of JOHN ROBINSON, CUSTIS appears as a witness for ROBINSON. (N-n, 28 Sept 1680. xiii-91.)

In 1681, JOHN CUSTIS, Gent., and Argoll Yardley, convey to John Cutlin(or Cuttin) 250 acres on Nuswaddocke Creek, part of the grant to Col. Francis Yardley. (N-n xiv-39, 29 Nov 1681.) He is sworn High Sheriff, 30 May 1682 (N-n, xiii-221.), and later, petitions for a prison. The Court answers that there is one. (N-n, xiii-291. 29 Mch 1683.) 31 Mch 1683, Mr. JOHN CUSTIS, Jr., is discharged from being any longer High Sheriff. (N-n, xiv-46.) [Note: This term "discharged," is not used in our modern sense, it rather conveys that the holder of the office is released from further responsibility at the end of his term, or at his own request.] On the 29 Mch 1683, he was allowed for prisoners in jail, &c. (N-n, xiii-291.) In 1683 he was witness to a deed of gift by RICHARD ROBINSON, who, later records show was his "kinsman." He appears in several suits before the Court. In 1684, he gets a power of attorney from his father, JOHN CUSTIS, Sr. The 28 Jany 1684, he complains that members of his troop did not appear at the last General Muster. (N-n, xv-108.) Capt. JOHN CUSTIS is given liberty to build a pound for unruly horses at Hungars, where he lives. (N-n, xv-129. 31 Mch 1685.) Gets ctf for 450 acres, 28 July, 1685. Head rights: Frans. Armitage, David Englishman [an Englishman?] George Greene, Eliz: Reade, Eliz: Knott, and negroes. (N-n, xv-144.) Robert Peale, mariner, and wf Rose, convey to CUSTIS their interest in 700 acres called Occocomson, during wife's [Rose Peale's] life. The land had belonged to Thomas Riding. (Acco. vi-430. 20 Mch 1685.)

In the will of Dr. James Watt he mentions his "brothers Capt. JOHN CUSTIS and Mr. Adam Michael." (N-n xii-209. 28 May 1686.) In 1686, Adam Michael conveys to CUSTIS 500 acres in Accomack. (Acco. vi-425.) On the 8 June 1686 (the day after this conveyance) JOHN CUSTIS, Jr., gets a release from his ward, Adam Michael. (N-n, xiv-129.) The 8 Sept 1686, JOHN CUSTIS, of N-n, Esq., conveys to John Baily, 700 acres in Jolly's Neck, Acco. Part of Scarburgh's patent for 2,000 acres (Acco. vi-431.), and William Kendall, of N-n, conveys to JOHN CUSTIS "the younger," 400 acres on Jencoteague Island. (Acco. vi-445. 2 Feby 1686.)

31 Jany 1687, Capt. JOHN CUSTIS, on behalfe of the Hon. Coll. JOHN CUSTIS and himself. appears in the records concerning arms for the militia. (N-n xv-329.) He is an agent with John West, to settle the county line. (Acco. vi-484. 22 Mch 1687-8.) As Sheriff again in 1688 (appointed 28 May of that year) he petitions for a jail. The Court decides that he provide and find one. (N-n xv-355 and 357.) In 1690 he appears in the Accomack tax-list, in Mr. Tho: Welburne's precinct, as having 8 tithes. [This was presumably his Accomack estate and not where he resided.] (Acco. ix-190.) He was sworn High Sheriff again in 1690. (N-n xvii-33.)

In 1690, Robert Peale and wf Rose convey to JOHN CUSTIS, Jr., land on Nuswaddox crk, late the land Mr. Thos. Rydinge formerly lived on; afterwards conveyed to Rose Rydeinge, widow of sd Thomas, and now the wife of the sd Robert Peale [spelled Peele], by Mr. Argoll Yardley, gentleman. (N-n, xiv-269.)

(To be continued)

The County Court Note-Book

An every-other-monthly devoted mainly to abstracts from County Court records, prior to 1800.

MILNOR LJUNGSTEDT, Editor and Publisher. Bethesda, Route 10, Maryland.

Published six times a year. Subscription, two dollars, in advance; must begin with the year. Advertising rates moderate.

AUGUST, 1926
Vol. V., No. 3

CONDITIONS NOW AND THEN

Two or three years ago, when the NOTE-BOOK was younger (it is still very young!) the Editor had in mind a series of articles on conditions in the County Courts. So many other things got into her mind, and maybe the first shock of *some* conditions wore off, and so and so . . . the articles were never finished. But this last season the Editor revisited several counties. One of these was Bedford county, Virginia. It is visualized in the Editor's memory by a group of unrelated circumstances. One of them is that she, one morning, built a fire in the very damp and decidedly chilly "fire-proof," none of the attorneys present offering any objection. Another is that the Episcopal church had four quaint *spikes,* one at each corner of the tower, resembling nothing in the world, but evidently to be dedicated to Matthew, Mark, Luke and John! (Alas, the spikes have gone!)

Still a third memory is of the very wonderful growth of gorse along the otherwise ugly banks, which Virginians of the locality insist was planted by Thomas Jefferson. As the same beautiful plant is thick in Prince George's county Maryland, Thomas Jefferson must have had a "growing hand," and a spreading one.

A fourth recollection is that the marriage bonds under "O" or "P" or "R," or some other letter or letters were missing. It was very trying. It is pleasant to state that the Deputy Clerk, a lady of fine intelligence, is at work on the bonds, and the Editor understands will make a list for publication. It is not clear to the Editor, however, the bonds having been partially re-arranged for listing, whether the missing packages were found after her visit or not. Sometimes things have come to light during the Editor's visits.

But the strongest memory of all is the hotel. And the hotel is still there and no one appears to consider it has improved. Meeting up with a dear and gallant old member of the Court in another county, he at once said when the Editor recited her experience, *"That ain't no place for a lady!"* And it wasn't. It was, however, and is, the only hotel in the place and the owner is of the sex noted for its patient endurance, namely, "the female of the species." The Editor was given the (apparently) best room, and then the thoughtful manager gave her for company in the room directly in the rear, three gentlemen bent on "hitting it up" in the line of cards and drinks. This they did so successfully until seven o'clock the next morning, when they were evidently too drunk and too sleepy to continue, that the Editor was able to keep check on the long hours of the night. (This is one of the incidents of searching.)

The Editor was so mad, so very and intensely mad, that if there had just been two of her, to meet the requirements of the law, she would then and there have filed a complaint to be placed before the next grand jury, and would have appeared as a witness. For, although this was before the Amendment, at that time the Virginia prohibition act was supposedly enforced. Complaints of other kinds have been made of this hotel, but the Editor had enough on her mind not to notice anything but her neighbors.

Conditions in the Clerk's Office have very much changed and somewhat improved. There is an heating system for the "fire-proof," but the Editor was about as comfortable with the fire in the little stove. But there is more room, and the records of the two former courts are now together. There has long been in the Bedford office somebody interested in its records, a very fortunate thing.

It is to be regretted that the office of the Clerk is one of those built on the ground floor of the Courthouse. This type of office, and in this case, the type of building, is particularly appealing to the Editor . . . the crowded pigeon-holes, the often makeshift apparatus, and so often a certain type of old Clerk, somehow fit together and make a picturesque, if not up-to-date picture. But . . . sooner or later the Courthouse burns . . . and when it does, so does the Clerk's Office. This office is an especially bad risk . . . even if, as is probable, the "vault" is of concrete and iron.

For the benefit of other searchers it may be added that one can secure a very good room in a nearby house, but the Editor knows of no satisfactory place for meals . . . at least within convenient distance.

CONTINUED articles COUNTY COURT NOTE-BOOK, and the dates on which they first appeared.
MARRIAGES BY INFERENCE. Began with May, 1922.
MARYLAND'S NEXT OF KIN. Began with July, 1922.
VIRGINIA COLONISTS. This alphabetized list began with July, 1924.
MILITARY NOTES. both COLONIAL and REVOLUTIONARY, and some later MILITIA NOTES, will appear in every issue, if possible.
SHIPS IN PORT, INTERCOUNTY and INTERCOLONIAL and COLONIAL FORENAMES, will appear in alternate issues or as space can be found for them.
EASTERN SHORE FAMILIES, in the form of a one-page supplement, began with June, 1925.

The NEXT OF MARYLAND KIN, and the VIRGINIA COLONISTS are omitted from this issue, copy not being at hand. They will be continued later. A fifth installment of the CUSTIS family (see supplements for June, August, October and December, 1925) is substituted.

WANTED: the parentage of ISAAC MILNOR, of Bristol, Bucks county, Penna. Ten dollars will be paid for definite information of his ancestry, with references. ISAAC was not the son of either DANIEL or JOSEPH MILNOR, the immigrants, but was very probably of the same family. He died in the early part of the 1700's. Address Editor.

CHILLIAN and MARTIN PALMER, Charlotte cty, Va. Seventy-five dollars will be paid for their ancestry. Must be proved by civil and church records. W. B. P. A.

OCCASIONAL

A conveyance of 9 Apr 1741, refers to the "late Dreadful Fire," Charleston, S. C. v-295.

From an Order of the Northampton, Virginia, Court, 28 Sept 1655. (viii-191). Concerning smoking at the Court table, which is prohibited . . . "and if any officer of the Court . . . shall smoke tobacco in the Court House . . . when the Court is setting . . . [he] is to be fined." (In the same Order the Court also objects to the wearing of hats in the Court room.)

We the Grand Inquest for the Body of Frederick Co., do present Hugh Donehough for cursing and damming our Sovereign King George of England, and Contrary to an act of Assembly in that case made and provided by the information of Samuel Hull and John Beard. Basil Beall, Foreman. Minutes of the Court, Aug 24th 1771. Frederick, Md.*

At the request of DANIEL McCRORY, the following discharge was recorded the second day of July in the year of our Lord one thousand seven hundred and fifty-seven, to and by Captain John Dagworthy, Commander of one of the Maryland Company's of foot, These are to certify that the bearer hereof, DANIEL McCRORY, hath served honestly and faithfully in my Company upwards of six months, and the time of his enlistment being expired is hereby discharged agreeable to act of Assembly, having just received a full and true account of all his pay, cloathing, and all other demands. Given under my hand and seal at Fort Frederick in Maryland this 10th day of February, 1757. Jno. Dagworthy . . . Frederick cty, Md. F-275.*

*Contributed by Mrs. Francis H. Markell, Frederick, Md.

FORE-NAMES OF COLONIAL USAGE

The name Tabitha continued.

TABITHA READ, a dau. of Henry Read. Acco. Va., 1724-5. xx-172. See his will.
TABITHY RENNY, Bap. 8 Mch 1745. Overwh. Psh Reg., Va.
TABITHA RUSSELL, dau. of William, of Sussex cty, Dela. Sussex, Dela. 1770-B2-385.
TABITHA ROGERS, dau. of Peter. Acco., Va. His will, 1717. xvi-178.
TABITHA ROWLES, Acco., Va. 1756. ii-632.
TABITHA SCARBURGH, wf of John. Also their dau. Tabitha. Acco., Va. 26 Dec 1749. ii-236-7.
TABITHA STROTHER, wf of George. K. Geo., Va. 1761. i-135.
TABITHA SCOTT, wf of George, Sr. Acco., Va. 1755. ii-560.
TABITHA TATHAM, wf of Thomas. Acco, Va. 1752. ii-429.
TABITHA TAYLOR, dau. Mr. William Taylor, of age 26 Aug 1708. Acco., Va. xi-649.
TABITHA TATHAM, dau. of Edmond. His will 1720. Acco., Va. xvi-192.
TABITHA THORNTON, wf of Edward. 1750. Acco., Va. ii-295.
TABITHA WISE, wife of Tully Robinson Wise, was dau. of George Douglas, Gent. 26 Dec 1763. Acco., Va. Deeds iii-262.
TABITHA WHITE, was dau. of Henry. Will 1708. N-n, Va. xix-81.
TABITHA WHITE, dau. of Richard Grinalls. 1715. Acco., Va. xvi-2.
TABITHA WOOD, wf of Archibald. 1741. Overwh. Psh Reg., Va.
TABITHA WATTS, dau. of John. Mar. John Tarry or Cary, before 29 Apr 1680. Acco., Va. vi-381.
TABITHA YOUNG, dau, of Francis. See Acco., Va. xx-174. 8 Aug 1734.
TABITHA GARRETSON, head right under Derricke Garretson. N-n, Va. iv-93. Ct 1 July 1652.

A QUAKER CERTIFICATE OF CHARACTER AND CELIBACY

Dear Friends

To our Friends and Brethren of the Falls Monthly Meeting in the County of Bucks, Greeting,

These with our salutation of our tenderest Love to our blessed Lord and Saviour, Jesus Christ, desiring your prosperity with our own in Him. And may let you know that our friend JOHN SAUL signified to us his intention of settling for some time within the verge of your Meeting and requesteth our Certificate to you on his behalf. NOW THIS MAY CERTIFY all whom it may concern that according to the good order used among us, due inquiry hath been made concerning him, and we do not find but that his conversation has been orderly and agreeable to our Holy profession, and clear from all here in relation to marriage. The like was also signified to us by Friends of Dublin Monthly Meeting in Ireland. He sometimes appears in public testimony, which was well received among us. So we recommend him unto your brotherly care, desiring his growth and prosperity in the Truth, and remain your friends in the Gospel of peace.

Signed by order and in behalf of our Monthly Meeting held at Providence, the 30th. of 4th. Mo. 1716.

Caleb Pusey	Randle Vernon
John Salikild	Jacob Simcock
Thomas Dell	Samuel Jaull, [?]
Henry Miller	William Lewis
Ellis Davis	Thomas Simley
Lewis Lewis	William Codince
Jonatham Wright	David Lloyd
Nicholas Fairlamb	Thomas Marshall
Ephriam Jackson	Joseph Selby
Edward Ward	Caleb Coopland
Jacob Howell	Thomas Vernon
Jacob Howell	Jacob Taylor
Joseph Baker	Robert Parnell
John Martin	Thomas Lancaster
John Sharpless	Jacob Edge
Thomas Winn	Evan Lewis
Henry Warley	William Traford
David Gibbonson	Joseph Coburn

From "A record of Certificates of Friends removal commencing in the year 1682." Copied from the original in 1889.

QUERY: Does any one descend from this JOHN SAUL, or know where he went? If so, some interesting information will be given in exchange. Editor.

WILLIAMS NOTES MARYLAND-VIRGINIA SECTION

JOHN WILLIAMS; had patent in Nthd cty, Va. 1654, S. L. O. iii-329.

————————; testifies he heard Edward Southerne say that "God was old and growne Ignorant and childish." N-n cty, Va. 29 June 1658. viii-24.

————————; was of Rappahannock cty. Acco. cty, Va. 4 Feby 1664-5. ii-8.

————————; a tithable. N-n cty, Va. 1664. viii-196.

————————; constable at Pocomoke. Acco. cty, Va. 15 July 1667. iii-28.

————————; of Maryland, carpenter, wf Elizabeth; sells to Geo. Parker of Acco. 350 acres on Anancock crk, "& by patent 500 acres." Acco. cty, Va. 17 May 1669. ii-114.

————————; of Westmoreland, Va. S. L. O. 1698. ii-287.

————————; had patent for land in the forest of Yeocommocoe, Westmoreland. S. L. O. 1715. v-117.

————————; wit. to will of Geo. Robinson, N-n cty, Va. 1719-1729.

————————; John Lawrence, admr Dianah Williams [sig. given as Daniel] is referred to as only "creditor or other relation." Pr. Geo's cty, Md. 25 June 1746. DD1-419.

————————; married Mary ———— Was a farmer, Fred'k cty, Md. 21 July 1756 - 10 Sept 1756. Fred'k cty, A1-93.

————————; Fred'k cty, Md. Will. Had wf, son John (under 14). 5 chn mentioned. Bro. William Williams. Friend John Chriessman[?] Fred'k cty. 16 Mch 1764-7 Apr 1764. A1-211.

————————; married Esther Taylor, dau. of Elias. Before 1 Oct 1764. Acco. cty, Va. Diii-350.

————————; 150 acres and 327 acres. Aug. cty, Va. Land Book. 1782. Also in tax-list 1783.

————————; 400 acres. Fred'k cty, Va. Land Book. 1782. Also 300 acres, and 344 acres. Same record.

————————; 200 acres and 136 acres. Loudoun cty, Va. 1782. Land Book. Also in Land Book, 1784.

————————; of Shenan. cty, Va., from William Strother and wf Hannah (widow of Davis), life interest in 61 acres on North River of Shenandoah. 12 Nov 1787. F-531. Shenan. cty. Va.

————————; of Woodstock, Shen., to William Clavton Williams. Shenan. cty, Va. 30 Aug 1788. i-309.

————————; and wf Martha, of Loudoun cty, Va. to Stacy Bevan. Hamp. cty, Va. 1 Oct 1794. 11-189.

————————; eldest son and heir-at-law of Richard Williams. Hamp. cty, Va. 10 Oct 1796. 11-518.

————————; Stephens Neck, Berkeley cty, Bkly cty, Va. Tax List, 1800.

JOSEPH WILLIAMS, Fauquier, and wf Elizabeth, to Joseph Blackwell and Richard Lewis; 140 acres. Fauq. cty, Va. 27 Oct 1763. iii-95.

JOHN POPE WILLIAMS, JESSE WILLIAMS, CHARLES WILLIAMS, of Stafford, to Henry Mauzy, of Fauquier; tract in Hamilton psh, being one-third of a larger tract devised by George Williams (their father) to them. Fauq. cty, Va. 15 Sept 1767. iii-7.

JOHN POPE WILLIAMS; see deed from Nathaniel Williams of Stafford.

JOHN POPE WILLIAMS and wf Hannah, to William Freeman and wf Sally. Fauq. cty, Va. 24 Oct 1791. x-395.

JOHN POPE WILLIAMS and wf Hannah, Fauquier cty, to Martin Pickett; part of a tract taken up by George Williams, Sr., where sd Williams now lives. Fauq., cty, Va. 29 Sept 1779. vii-256.

JOHN POPE WILLIAMS and wf Hannah, Fauquier, to Samuel Porter. Fauq. cty, Va. 13 June 1787. ix-398.

JONAS WILLIAMS, a voter. Fauq. cty, Va. xi-107.

JONAS WILLIAMS, Jr. Pr. Wm. Will. Sons David, Jonas, James; wf Ann and friend John Wright, Gent., extrs. Wit: Vincent Garner, John Lloy'd, Elizabeth Sinclair. Pr. Wm cty, Va. 30 Jany 1743-4 - 23 Apr 1744. C-473.

JONAS WILLIAMS, Jr., to Samuel Gray, Sr. Fauq. cty, Va. 1798. xiv-243.

JONAS WILLIAMS and wf Mary, to Jonas Williams, Jr., their son. Fauq. cty, Va. 18 Apr 1827. xxix-310.

JOSEPH WILLIAMS, Sr. Will. Wf Catherine; chn: Joseph, John, Wm, Sarah, Mary. Grandson Joseph Williams. Wit: Stoddert, Vermillion, Owen. Pr. Geo's cty. Md. 26 Nov 1746 - 13 Feby 1746-7. i-378.

JOSEPH WILLIAMS; Mrs. Catherine Williams, extx. Pr. Geo's, Md. Oath 9 Aug 1748. DD6-14.

JOSEPH WILLIAMS, of Fauquier, from Fairfax. 200 acres, Hedgman's River, during the life of Mary Williams, his dau., and Joseph Robinson, his grandson. [A "lease for lives."] Fauq. cty, Va. 24 Sept 1759. i-41.

VIRGINIANS AND OTHERS IN CONVEYANCES AND POWERS KENTUCKY COURT OF APPEALS

JAMES JOHNSTON, of Monongalia cty, Va. Buys land in Nelson cty. Ky. 1787.

JOSEPH JONES, of Dinwiddie cty, Va. Power to John May. 1786.

JOSEPH JONES, of Pr. Geo's cty, Md. Power to Walter Beall, of Montg. cty, Md. (Land in Nelson cty, Ky.) 1787.

WILLIAM LIPSCOMB, formerly of Louisa cty, Va., now of South Carolina. 1786.

THOMAS LUCAS, of Amherst cty, Va. Buys 400 acres in Nelson cty, Ky. Nov. 1787.

GEORGE McCULLY, of Ft. Pitt, Penna. Power to Percival Butler, of Lexington, Ky. 9 Nov 1785.

PETER McDANIEL, of Caroline cty, Va. Witness. 1786.

SAMUEL McDOWELL, of Lincoln cty, Ky; power to son JOHN McDOWELL, of Rockbridge cty, Va., to dispose of lands in Cumberland Mts. Dated at John Crow's Station, Lincoln cty. 4 Nov. 1783.

PRUDENCE and JOSEPH McFAWL, of Lincoln cty, Ky, widow and son of MALCHAM McFAWL, of Bedford cty, Penna., power to DAVID McFAWL to sell 300 acres in Bedford, 7 June 1785.

DANIEL McNEIL, of Hardy cty, Va., to Abram Hite of same. Convey land. 2 Apr 1787.

JOHN MAY, of Dinwiddie cty, Va., now of Lincoln cty, Ky, to Jesse Hollingsworth, of Baltimore, Md. 1780.

FRANCIS MERRIWETHER, of Spots. cty, Va., power to Jas. Overton, Jr.

PRITTYMAN MERRY and wf Catherine, of Orange cty, Va., to Harry Bartlett, of Spots. cty, Va. 500 acres in Fayette cty, Ky. 28 Sept 1786.

RICHARD MORRIS, of Louisa cty, Va., power to Gen. Chas. Scott and others, to sell "Oxmoor." 17 Nov 1787.

NICHOLAS MERIWETHER, Jeff'n cty, Ky, to son and dau. Richard and Patty (minors), 1000 acres in Illinois. Also lands bought of Robt Daniel on Bear Grass Crk, Ky, and furniture in the house of David Wood Meriwether. 24 Feby 1786.

WILLIAM NELSON, clerk, Caroline cty, Va. 1786.

SERVICE AND SUPPLIES COLONIAL, REVOLUTIONARY AND MILITIA

JOHN GIRAULT, Captain in the Illinois Regt, about to embark for the settlement of the Natchez . . . gives power to friend William Clark, Lieut. in sd Regt. Jeff'n cty, Ky. 13 Apr 1782. A-36.

WILLIAM HELMS: satisfactory proof is made to the Court that James Helms is the true and lawful heir of his brother, William, dec'd, who died in the service. Ordered Certified. Jeff'n cty, Ky. 8 Apr 1784. A-14.

EDWARD MURRAY; ctf by Col. G. R. Clark commdr, that he served as a soldier in the Illinois Detatchment, Jeff'n cty, Ky. 22 Nov 1779. A-44.

JOHN McCULLOM proves that he was prevented from laying his claim before the Commissioners on account of his being in the Continental Service . . . and is entitled to the preemption of 1000 acres on the . . . run of the south fork of Simpson's Creek, including the foundation of a cabbin about ten foot square . . . made 20 May 1776. Jeff'n cty, Ky. 4 Dec 1781. A-16.

HENRY PREATA [?]; ctf of G. R. Clark, commdr, that Preata served as a soldier in the Illinois Detatchment. Jeff'n cty, Ky. 22 Nov 1779. A-44.

BENJAMIN RUSSEL; satisfactory proof is made that William Russel is the heir of his father, BENJAMIN, who died in the service. Certificate ordered. Jeff'n cty, Ky. 8 Apr 1784. A-14.

GARRETT PENDERGRASS; Margaret Pendergrass, widow of Jesse, testifies that Garrett Pendergrass, acted under a warrant or "Brevet" as the second in command of a company of guides to the armies commanded by General Forbes in the year 1758, and by General Stanwik in the year 1759 . . . that he was engaged in the sd service by. Col. Adam Steven and continued therein until he was regularly discharged; that he received Lieutenant's pay and that he, the sd Garrett, never in his lifetime, nor the sd Jesse, since his death, to the knowledge of the sd Margaret, ever before made proof, &c., &c, Jeff'n cty, Ky. Ct 7 Mch 1781. A-3.

ABRAHAM TAYLOR; "At a Court held for Lincoln cty;" ctf granted that Taylor proved that he was entitled to a preemption settlement in Kentucky District, on account of his having been in the Regular service in Col. George Rogers Clark's Regt. Jeff'n cty, Ky. 15 May 1781. A-25.

MARY ROEBUCK, widow of WILLIAM ROEBUCK, who was a private in the militia of Culpeper and died in the service of the Commonwealth, produced a pension warrant which is ordered to be recorded. Mad. cty, Va. Ct 27 Feby 1794. Orders, i.

NATHANIEL WELCH: On the motion of Oliver Welch and Nathaniel I. Welch, extrs, ordered ctf'd that Nathaniel Welch departed this life on the 20 Nov 1815, and that he was the same Capt. Nathaniel Welch who held a command in the 2d Va. State Reg't, War of the Revolution, commanded by Col. Wm. Brent and Lt. Col. Chas. Dabney, and that he was entitled to half-pay for life from the State of Virginia (Act of Assembly 1779); further ordered certified that sd Oliver and Nathaniel are his legal representatives. Mad. cty, Va. 26 July 1832. Orders, viii.

JOHN HARRISON makes oath to his declaration [of service], and the Court declare their opinion that he was a Revolutionary soldier. Mad. cty, Va. 23 Aug 1832. Orders, viii.

The following make declaration at same Court, same date:

JOHN JONES;
TAVERNER JONES;
JAMES CLATTERBUCK;
AMBROSE RICHARDS;
HUMPHREY MAJOR;
BENJAMIN POWELL.

JOHN TALIFERO, Gent., presents commission to be Captain, upper troop of county, K. Geo. cty, Va. 1 Apr 1748. Orders 1745-51, p. 566.

WILLIAM TAYLOR, makes oath to his declaration and the Court declare their opinion that he was a Revolutionary soldier. Mad. cty, Va. 23 Aug 1832. Orders, viii.

WILLIAM TWYMAN, same. Same record and date.

ABRAHAM TANNER, same. Same record and date.

JOSEPH VANMETRE; Court orders ctf of regular service in 1763. [Killed?] Ohio cty, W. Va. Ct. 3 Apr 1780. Orders, i-59. [See Annals Carnegie Museum.]

Reasonable price or two years' subscription will be given for numbers 1, 2, 3, 4, 6, and 7, COUNTY COURT NOTE-BOOK, 1921-1922. Address Editor.

COLUMBIAN PRINTING CO., INC., WASHINGTON, D. C.

The

County Court Note-Book

A Little Bulletin of History and Genealogy

October, 1926. **Vol. V, No. 5**

AN ADAPTED PIRATE

The Right Honble. Robt. Johnson—

Esquire Governor Cap: General Admirall and Commander In Cheife In the province of South Carolina.

Whereas his majesty by his royall Proclamation bearing date the fifth of September anno Domini 1717 hath been pleased to extend his Gracious Pardon to all such persons that having committed piracy shall surrender themselves to the Governor In any of his Majestyes Plantacons In America as is fully set forth in the said Proclamacon

These are to certify to all whome it doth Concern that Othniel Davis Late Quartermas'r of ye Sloop *Egale* Thomas Reynolds, marmaduke Ge[?] Samuell Richardson Thos. Reynolds James Gartrich. Robert Hawkes Benjamin Turner Samuel Boyce—hath surrendered themselves to me and Claimed the Benefit of his Majesties Gracious Pardon according to the Said Proclamation which I doe hereby grant them.

In Testimony whereof I the aforesaid Governor have hereunto set my hand and Caused the Publick Seale of the Province to be affixed this Thirtyeth Day of June in the fourth year of the Reign of our Sovereign Lord George by the Grace of God of Great Brittain, France and Ireland King Defender of the Faith &c An: Dom: 1718. Robt. Johnson

Recorded ye 2d. July 1718.
Charles Hart Secty.

SOUTH CAROLINA

To All to whom these Presents Shall Come Othniell Davis and Thomas Porter of the Island of Providence marriners now residing in the Province of South Carolina Send Greeting Whereas the said Othniell Davis is purposed to proceed a Voyage beyond the Seas in the Sloop *Mexico Cruiser* and hath obtayned a Commission from the honble. Robert Johnson Esq. Govern. of the Province aforesd. to Seize take Sink burn and Destroy the Subjects of the King of Spain their Vessels and Effects and Whereas by Virtue of a Commission from his Excellency Woodes Rogers Esq. Govern. of the Bahama Islands the Said Othniell Davis and his Marriners have heretofore taken and Seized a Ship Called *Nuestra Senora De La Assumption* Layden with Cocoa late belonging to the Subjects of the King of Spain in and with a Certain Sloop Called the *Movill Trader* which Said Ship is yett at Sea or Sailed into Some Port to the Said Othniell Davis unknown, and whereas the said Thomas Porter is Entitled to an Equal number of Shares with the Said Davis in the Said Ship NOW KNOW YEE that the Said Othniell Davis and Thomas for Divers Good Causes & Considerations them thereunto moving have made ordain'd Constituted and appointed and by these Presents do make ordain Constitute and Appoint and in their Stead and Place Put William Gibbon and Andrew Allen of the Province of So. Carolina Merchts. their True and Lawful Attorneys * * * to Proceed against the Said Ship Called *Nuestra Senora De La Assumption* and against all other Ships & Vessells belonging to the King of Spain or his Subjects which Shall Hereafter be taken or Seized by the Said Othniell Davis or Thomas Porter and their Marriners by Virtue of the Comission aforesd. and when any such Ship or Vessell Shall be Condemned to Expose to Sayle and for their use to receive their Share or Shares of the Moneys Arising from the Sale thereof Giving and by these Presents Granting unto their said Attorneys * * * all their full Powers and Authority and [to] Commence and Prosecute in their Names and Lawfull action or actions suit or suits in any Court or Courts for the recovery of all or any part of the Premises * * * by Virtue hereof. IN WITNESS whereof the Sd. Othniell Davis and Thomas Porter have hereunto Sett there hands and Seals the [----] day of September In the Sixth year of Ye. Reign of our Sovereign Lord George by the Grace of God and of Great Britain France and Ireland King Defender of the Faith Anno Dom 1719

Othniell Davis (Seal)
Thomas Porter (Seal)

Sealed & Delivered in the presence of John Sheppard Josuah Lankester

MARRIAGES BY INFERENCE*

Some Smiths of Virginia

CHARLTON SMITH and ELIZABETH WATSON, gr. dau. of Mr. John Shepard, Before 5 Dec 1715. Acco, xvi-5.

EDWARD SMITH and ANN JOHNSON, widow of John. Before or about 29 Apr 1658. N-n, viii-13.**

Mr. GEORGE SMITH m. ELIZABETH ROBINSON, dau. of William. Pr. A. Before 16 Apr 1695. 1-118.

GEORGE SMITH, Sr., and LUCRETIA COSTIN. Before 1826. N-n, L. C. 1815-1834, p. 274.

GEORGE SMYTH and the widow of Thos. WARD. Before 28 Apr 1653. N-n, iv-175.**

**Reprinted from former lists.

GEORGE SMITH and MARY LAUGHLAND, dau. of Dorman, Before 20 Mch 1715. N-n, xix-322.**
GEORGE SMITH of Curratock creek, and MARY HEWETT, dau. of Robert. See record 2 Mch 1702-3 [Smith then deceased.] Acco, xi-303.
HENRY SMITH and JOANNA MATRUM, wid. of Joseph. [She had also been Joane Mickell.] Before Dec 1668. Acco, iii-74.
JAMES SMITH and ELIZABETH PANNILL. Before 1805. K. Wm. "ix"-89.
JOHN SMYTH and REBECCA, the widow of Thos. SAVAGE. About or before 1 Mch 1656. N-n, v-142.**
JOHN SMITH and ELIZABETH WEST. [Long] before 29 May 1753. Acco, "ii"-437.
JOHN SMITH, son of James, and ESTHER AYRES, dau. of Richard-Hill Ayres. Before 7 Oct 1735. Acco, xx-216.
JOHN SMITH and the relict of Luke MEZELL[?] About 29 Sept 1672. Surry, Orders i-15.
JOSEPH SMITH and FRANCES EASTHAM, dau. of Robert. Halifax. Before 2 Dec 1803. xx-234.
Capt. LAWRENCE SMITH and MILDRED [GOODWIN, widow of James, of York? He died Sept 1719.] N-n, Va. (Old papers . . . not an official record.)
RICHARD SMITH and ELLINOR MARKS, widow. Before 15 Apr 1672. L. Norf. E-110.
RICHARD SMITH and BETTY WELBURN, dau. of Samuel. Before 26 Nov 1751. Acco, Deeds ii; p. 354.
RICHARD SMITH and the widow of George BLOW, Before 2 Sept 1675. Surry, Orders i-106.
SIMON SMITH and GRACE EVINS, dau. of John. About 18 Sept 1693. Acco, xi-37.
WILLIAM SMITH and SARAH BROWNE, dau. of John. Before 29 Oct 1662. N-n, viii-143.
WILLIAM SMITH, carpenter, and EVE WILLIAMS, relict of John of Morattico Creek. [Pre-nuptial gift to children.] 9 Mch 1680. Rappa. 1677-1682, p. 369.

MARYLAND'S NEXT OF KIN*

ABRAHAM VISEN, RACHEL VISEN and MARTHA MEERS; inv. Frances VISEN, A. A. cty, 28 Apr 1721. vi-7.
EDMOND WAYMAN; inv. Leonard Wayman, A. A. cty, 25 June 1721. vi-8.
JANE THOMAS; inv. Robt. Thomas, A. A. cty, Apr 1720. vi-13.
JOSEPH and WILLIAM ANNIS; inv. Thomas Annis, Chas. cty, 25 Mch 1720. vi-17.
MARY THOMPKINS; inv. Giles Thompkins, Charles cty. 26 June 1721. vi-18.
THOMAS and MARY NEVELLS; inv. William Golding, Cecil cty. vi-25.
WILLIAM PRICE, Jr.; inv. Wm. Price, Sen., Cecil cty. 5 May 1721. vi-27.
PHILAMON and JOHN EMORSON; inv. Joseph Gregory, Talbot cty. 18 July 1721. vi-40.

JAMES, HERBERT and MARGARET THOMAS; inv. Robert Thomas, St. Mary's cty. 23 May 1721. vi-43.
JOHN WRIGHT and THOMAS HINSON WRIGHT; inv. Charles Wright, Jr. Queen Anne's cty. 26 May 1721. vi-45.
CHARLES SEK and GEORGE JACKSON; inv. Barbara Jackson, Q. A. cty. 2 Feby 1719. vi-46.
HENRY ALER, Jr., and ANN OLDSON; inv. Henry Aler, Q. A. cty. 14 Dec 1720. vi-55.
HENRY and ANDREW OLDSON; inv. Abraham Oulson, Q. A. cty. 11 May 1721. vi-58.
JOSEPH ENGLAND; inv. Isaac England. 4 Jany 1720. vi-60.
JOHN and RICHARD DAVIS, brothers; inv. Robert Carey, Kent cty. 24 Apr 1721. vi-63.
CHARLES MERRYMAN and SUSANNAH LONG; inv. Thomas Long, Balto. cty, 19 Aug 1721. vi-70.
WILLIAM OSBORN and BENJAMIN HANSON, brothers-in-law; inv. Clark Hollis, Balto. cty. 7 June 1721. vi-73.
EBENEZER and NATHAN PUMPHREY; inv. Walter Pumphrey, Balto cty. 12 May 1721. vi-75.
CHARLES PEIRPOINT; inv. Jabez Peirpoint, Balto. cty. 20 July 1721. vi-77.
JOHN, ISAAC and MARY WEBSTER; inv. John Webster, Jr., Balto. cty. 28 June 1721. vi-81.
HEUGH JOHNS, JOHN BUTRUM; inv. Henry Sheles, Balto. cty. 17 June 1721. vi-85.
JOHN POPE; inv. Job Pope, Som. cty. 7 June 1721. vi-87.
WILLIAM PRISSEY and JOSEPH LANGFORT; inv. Wm. Prissey, Som. cty. 9 Apr 1721. vi-93.
WILLIAM and JOHN JONES; inv. Danville Jones, Som. cty. 20 May 1720. vi-94.
RACHEL POYNTER and CHARLES RATTLIFFE; inv. Wm. Rattliffe, Som. cty. 14 Apr 1721. vi-96.
BETTY GALE and ESTHER DENWOOD; inv. Richard Waters, Som. cty. 20 Aug 1720. vi-97.
WILLIAM KENNETT, Jr., MARTIN KENNETT; inv. Margaret Towers, Som. cty. 22 Apr 1721. vi-105.
GAEBRILL POWELL; inv. Samuel Powell, Som. cty. 1 June 1721. vi-106.
JOHN, MICHAEL and WILLIAM ROACH; inv. Nathan Roach, Som. cty. 6 May 1721. vi-107.
GABRILL POWELL; inv. William Powell, Som. cty. 1 June 1721. vi-109.
JOHN BROTON; inv. John Broughton, Som. cty. 21 June 1721. vi-111.
ABRAHAM and JACOB BROMWELL; inv. Rebeckah Brumwell, Talbot cty. 15 Aug 1721. vi-112.
ROGER and JOHN CLAYLAND; inv. John Ross, Talbot cty. 15 July 1721. vi-115.
CHARLES BRADEY and PATTRICK BRADEY; inv. Elizabeth Bradey, St. Mary's cty. 21 Aug 1721. vi-127.
CHARLES KIRKLEY and REBECAH KIRKLEY; inv. Mrs. Elizabeth Burrell, St. Mary's cty, 13 May 1721. vi-128.

FAMILIES OF THE EASTERN SHORE

CUSTIS OF VIRGINIA

(*Continued from August Number*)

Capt. JOHN CUSTIS, his brother-in-law, is chosen as gdn by Yardley Michael, fourteen years old and upwards. (N-n, xvii-123. 28 July 1691.) Further records as to this guardianship (N-n xvii-126 and 127.) Elected vestryman. 11 June 1691. (N-n, xvii-117.) Appointed a Justice 20 May 1691. (N-n, xvii-98.) Michael estate divided between Capt. JOHN CUSTIS and Yardley Michael. (N-n, xvii-129, 29 Aug 1691.) In 1691 the Acco. tax-lists give him nine tithes at Jolley's Neck. (ix-227.)

JOHN CUSTIS, Jr., and wf SARAH CUSTIS . . . love and affection to Richard Waters and wf Elizabeth . . . land near Pungoteague. being part of a greater quantity belonging to Col. Southy Littleton and by his will given to his daughters [of whom SARAH CUSTIS was one.] (Acco., ix-222. 17 Nov 1691.) CUSTIS is chosen gdn by Southey Littleton, youngest son of Col. Southey Littleton, being arrived at lawful age [fourteen.] (Acco. x-102. 20 June 1693.) JOHN CUSTIS, Jr. apprentices Yardley Michael to John Northam, "cordwinder." (N-n, xvii-250. 26 Sept 1693.) John Stringer chooses Maj. JOHN CUSTIS as gdn. (N-n, xvii-403. 28 Jany 1696.)

Maj. JOHN CUSTIS, "Senr," sends negro children to have age adjudged. (N-n xvii-447. 28 Sept 1697.) [JOHN CUSTIS, I, having died in 1695, his son now becomes "Senior," JOHN CUSTIS, III, having long been of age.] CUSTIS is appointed Justice, 1 July 1699. (N-n, xviii-11.) Maj. JOHN CUSTIS (in a suit v. Mr. John West) is lame and not able to come to Court. (N-n, xviii-i. 28 Feby 1698.) Col. JOHN CUSTIS is appointed admr of Henry Gascoigne, deceased. (N-n, xviii-26. 29 Nov 1699.)

JOHN CUSTIS, of N-n, Gent., and wife SARAH, to our brother Southey Littleton, 600 acres at Pocomoke, formerly granted to Adam Michael, of N-n, Gent., former husband to the aforesaid SARAH [CUSTIS], by patent in 1685. (Acco., xi-238. 6 Feby 1699.) Col. JOHN CUSTIS, and wf SARAH, ackn. a gift to son HENRY [CUSTIS.] (Acco, xii-82. 6 Feby 1699.)

Col. JOHN CUSTIS, Esq., his ctf for lands, 900 acres. Head rights: Jno. Tompson, Eliz: Nihil, Eliz: Wood, Margt Shear, and 14 negroes. (N-n xviii-51. 30 Sept 1700.) CUSTIS is gdn of John Andrews (N-n, xviii-54. 30 Sept 1700.) Andrew Andrews, son of Mr. Andrew Andrews, chooses Col. CUSTIS as gdn. (N-n, xviii-57. 28 Jany 1700.) Bethia Taylor is to be whipped for "scandalizing" Col. JOHN CUSTIS, but makes submission on her knees and the Court remits the whipping. (N-n, xviii-51. 30 Sept 1700.) During the years 1700-1704, CUSTIS is made the guardian of Ann Baynum (who choses him); William Brookes (also chooses); also John Powell and John Hall. (See N-n, xviii-57, 97, 226.) CUSTIS has a difference with Benj. Robinson. (N-n, xviii-49. 29 July 1700.)

Matthew Moore and Neech Eyre certify that they have hunted over Smith's Island for Mr. CUSTIS' cattle, but can find only two old bulls. (N-n, xvii-79. 29 Sept 1701.) Col. CUSTIS complains of Gethinge Hawkins for ranging and shooting on Mockon Island, and Hawkins is fined. (N-n, 28 Jany 1701. xviii-90.) His slave is tried for burning a barn. (N-n, xviii-244. 7 June 1705.)

JOHN and SARAH CUSTIS are witnesses to the marriage license bond of Benjamin Dolby to marry Ann Rot [Pot?] [The seal apparently shows the impress of a thimble.] (N-n, 14 Feby 1705-6.) JOHN CUSTIS, Esq., and SARAH CUSTIS, wife of said JOHN . . . convey to John Granger and John Douglas, of N-n cty, 200 acres sold to Mr. John Michael, Sr., by Mr. Argoll Yardley, and given to his son Simon Michall, and descended to Mr. Adam Michael as heir-at-law to Simon . . . and Adam Michael gave it to Mrs. Sarah Michael, now wife of the said JOHN CUSTIS. Wit: John Custis, Jr., and Henry Custis. [Note: the John Custis, Jr, is John Custis, III, usually called of Williamsburg.] (N-n, xvi-447. 18 Jany 1706.) JOHN CUSTIS, Esq., acknowledges sale of land to Henry Towles. Mme. SARAH CUSTIS, releases dower. (Acco, 6 June 1710. xiv-6.) JOHN CUSTIS, of N-n, to Elias Taylor; 500 acres at Accocomson, Acco. cty, patented to John Michael, Sr., dec., and devised by will to son John Michael, Jr., and John Michael, Jr., died in his minority without issue, so that the land came to Adam Michael, eldest son and heir, who conveyed said 500 acres to said JOHN CUSTIS, 1686. SARAH CUSTIS, wife of JOHN, releases dower. (Acco, 5 Sept 1710. xi-532.)

Col. JOHN CUSTIS, Esq., cattle-mark. (N-n, 12 Jany 1710-11. vol. v) CUSTIS presents deed of sale of land to son Henry. (Acco, xiii-112. 3 Mch 1707.) Col. CUSTIS' slave, Old King, made tax free on account of age. (Acco, 18 Jany 1712-13. xiv-54.)

JOHN CUSTIS, II, of Wilsonia, was b. about 1654. (See dep'n N-n, xvii-306; also xviii-84; also xiii-206.) He died about 1713.

He m. (1) MARGARET MICHAEL, dau. of John Michael, a native of Holland. (2) Mrs. SARAH (LITTLETON) MICHAEL, the widow of his brother-in-law, Adam Michael. This marriage was before 21 Feby 1692. (See Acco, x-95; also xii-82.)

The children of JOHN CUSTIS of Wilsonia are shown by various records. They were:

JOHN, III, (of Williamsburg);
ELIZABETH,
HANCOCK,
HENRY,
SORROWFUL MARGARET. [Her signature was S. Margaret.]

The County Court Note-Book

An every-other-monthly devoted mainly to abstracts from County Court records, prior to 1800.

MILNOR LJUNGSTEDT, Editor and Publisher. Bethesda, Route 10, Maryland.

Published six times a year. Subscription, two dollars, in advance; must begin with the year. Advertising rates moderate.

OCTOBER, 1926

Vol. V., No. 5*

SCRAMBLED FAMILIES

In William and Mary Quarterly (first series), vol. vii, p. 108, certain genealogical material is given. The following extract covers it:

"Lieut.-Col. Edmund Scarbrough had issue: Tabitha Scarbrough married Col. "William Smart, who had issue: Tabitha "Scarbrough Smart Married Richard Hill "of Hill's Farm, who had issue: Patience "Hill . . . Tabitha Scarbrough, widow of "Coll. William Smart afterwards married "Col. Edward Hill, of Shirley."

From the records of Northampton and Accomack counties, Virginia, the following information is gathered:

TABITHA SCARBURGH, dau. of Lieut. Col. Edmund Scarburgh (son of Capt. Edmund Scarburgh) was born about 1639. (See dep'n N-n, xvii-342. Also xvii-233.) TABITHA SCARBURGH m. JOHN SMART [he had a brother William] about 12 July 1653. (N-n iv-152.) The date of JOHN SMART'S death is unknown. TABITHA (SCARBURGH) SMART, his widow, m. (2) DEVEREUX BROWNE, probably before or about 1672. BROWNE died before 4 Nov 1674. (See Acco, Va. v-242.)

TABITHA (SCARBURGH) (SMART) BROWNE m. (3) Lieut. Col. JOHN CUSTIS, about 1681. (Acco, viii-249.) CUSTIS died in 1695, and about 30 Aug 1696, his widow m. Col. EDWARD HILL. (See N-n, xv-96.) Mme. HILL, as she was called, died about Jany, 1717. Her will was probated on the 7th of that month. (Acco, xvi-37.)

By the records TABITHA SCARBURGH is shown to have had only two children: a daughter, by JOHN SMART, and a son, EDMUND, by DEVEREUX BROWNE. The son EDMUND m. Martha . . . and died quite young, in a Turkish prison. No record is found of any child of his.

TABITHA SCARBURGH'S daughter, by her husband, JOHN SMART, married WILLIAM WHITTINGTON, WILLIAM WHITTINGTON had a son SMART and a daughter TABITHA. TABITHA WHITTINGTON married EDMUND CUSTIS, and one of their children was TABITHA-SCARBURGH CUSTIS, whose marriages will be given in the CUSTIS family notes.

*The August number was incorrectly marked 3.

References:

(1) EDM. SCARBURGH, mcht, in part of a portion for my daughter TIBITHA (nowe wife unto Jno. Smart) all that tract . . . at Maggottey Baye . . . also cattle. (N-n, 12 July 1653. iv-152.)

(2) TABITHA SMART, 1000 acres in Accomack cty, at Deep Creek . . . bounded by the termination of the one-half of a former divident of 3,000 acres granted to Mrs. Tabitha and Matilda Scarburgh . . . (S. L. O. 10 July 1664.)

(3) WILLIAM SMART being bound for England and his late wife now deceased, which wife having some children by her former husband, Lt. Col. Wm. Andrews . . . (N-n, ix-68. 19 Feby 1659.)

(4) GEO. WATSON, will . . . To TABITHA WHITTINGTON, daughter of WILLIAM WHITTINGTON and wife TABITHA a . . . colt bought of Mrs. TABITHA BROWNE. Also mourning rings . . . to TABITHA, wife of William, and one for William and one for Mr. Edm. Browne, Mrs. TABITHA BROWNE, relic of Mr. Devereux Browne to be extx . . . (Acco, v-242, 4 Nov 1674.) [Note: the spelling of Devereux varies . . . for simplicity the correct form has been adopted.]

(5) SARAH SMART, daughter of William, of Gloucester cty, m. John Tankred. Before 28 Mch 1687. (N-n, xiv-152.)

(6) EDMUND CUSTIS, Jr., and wife TABITHA, to receive certain three acres by will of Charles Holden, if wife of Holden die without heirs. (N-n, xvii-30. 29 Mch 1690.)

(7) Will of JOHN CUSTIS, I: . . . Quitclaims to SMART WHITTINGTON, son of WILLIAM WHITTINGTON, any right to 1000 acres patented and belonging to TABITHA SMART, deceased . . . to wife [TABITHA] 1750 acres at Deepe Creeke one-half of 3500 acres patented to her and her sister Matilda . . . (N-n, xvii-356. 18 Mch 1691-10 Feby 1695.)

(8) Will of EDMUND CUSTIS: . . . dau. TABITHA SCARBURGH CUSTIS, 850 acres given me by my honored unkle Col. John Custis, Esq., of Arlington, deceased, near Deep Creek, bounding on the 1750 acres given by him in his will to his wife TABITHA CUSTIS, and on 1000 acres patented and belonging to TABITHA SMART, deceased. Gives his daughter . . . all my deceased wife her mother, her wearing apparel . . . To Francis Makemi his sloop called TABITHA. (Acco, xi-262. 12 Aug-1700-4 Feby 1700.)

(9) Mr. FRANCIS MAKEMIE and wife Naomi, extrs in trust of the will of Mr. EDMUND CUSTIS, as also Mme. TABITHA HILL, great-grandmother to THOMAS and TABITHA [SCARBURGH] CUSTIS, minor children of said EDMUND, are to give an inventory, &c., &c. (Acco, 3 Dec 1701. xii-124. See also xii-116.)

(10) TABITHA CUSTIS, widow and co-extr of JOHN CUSTIS; deed of gift to her *great*-grandchildren, THOMAS and TABITHA-SCARBURGH CUSTIS, son and daughter of EDMUND CUSTIS and TABITHA his late wife, her granddaughter. (N-n, xvi-98. 5 Sept 1696.)

(11) On p. 136 of Land Causes, Acco., 1727-1773, will be found a reference to a deed which mentions "SMART WHITTINGTON, son of WILLIAM WHITTINGTON, Gent., and brother of TABITHA CUSTIS wife of EDMUND." This deed the Editor did not find; it is possible it was recorded a number of years after it was made.

[Note: From abstracts 6 and 8, it appears that TABITHA CUSTIS, wife of EDMUND, died between Mch, 1690, and 12 Aug, 1700.]

For TABITHA SCARBURGH'S CUSTIS and HILL marriages, see also Acco, viii-249; N-n, xiv-40; and N-n, iv [a record of cattlemarks.]

Another statement concerning the marriage of the daughter of TABITHA SCARBURGH, appears in Virginia Heraldica (Crozier.) Whether the statement in William and Mary was taken from Crozier, or whether Crozier took his from William and Mary, the Editor does not know. The course of a published statement is long and devious. The Crozier article says that:

TABITHA SCARBURGH SMART, dau. of Mme. TABITHA, married RICHARD HILL, of Accomack. That TABITHA SCARBURGH (SMART) HILL, had a dau. TABITHA, who married EDMUND CUSTIS, of Deep Creek, Accomack. Proof of these statements has not been found. The only known wife of the RICHARD HILL referred to was named MARY. Her family name was *not* SMART. The marriages of Richard Hill's daughters are easily proved, and well-known to searchers. Neither one married a Custis.

The piratical pardon and privateering power of attorney on page 33 of this issue, are in one case copied, and in the other abstracted from records in South Carolina. One, if not both, are in the old Court of Ordinary (Probate Court) at Charleston. The Editor failed to note that the official copyist omitted volume and page.

Attention is especially directed to the lists of Maryland Marriages (see p. 40) dug out (there is no better word) from the court records now preserved in the Maryland State Land Office. This is the same sort of material that the Editor is gathering in Delaware, Pennsylvania, Virginia, West Virginia, the Carolinas, Georgia, Kentucky and Tennessee. But while the Editor can only cover a certain number of years at each visit, the Maryland notes, it will be seen, are taken from a complete set of 104 volumes.

The recognition of a marriage before a court, as shown in so many incidental ways in the official minutes of the court, is, like possession, certainly nine-tenths of the law of evidence, if not the even ten. Exact dates are usually missing.

The list of Virginians and others appearing in certain volumes of powers and land conveyances, now in the Court of Appeals at Frankfort, Kentucky, is the work of Miss Hattie M. Scott of Frankfort, who has most kindly allowed the Editor to use them for the NOTE-BOOK. A recent index mentioned elsewhere, will also contain these names, but possibly without mention of the county or State, although the index covers a very great amount of other material.

IMPORTANT.—A subscriber to the NOTE-BOOK, and correspondent of the Editor, will pay TWENTY-FIVE dollars for full information as to the ancestry of ISAAC MILNOR, of Bristol, Bucks county, Penna. ISAAC MILNOR came into Bucks county from Burlington county, New Jersey, *circa* 1700 or 1710. He married at Friends' Meeting SARAH WILSON, a prominent minister among Friends. He is not son of JOSEPH MILNOR, a member of the Assembly from Bucks in 1696, nor of DANIEL, brother to JOSEPH. DANIEL MILNOR died soon after his arrival, and JOHN MILNOR, son of JOSEPH, was heir to both DANIEL and JOSEPH.

CHILLIAN and MARTIN PALMER, Charlotte cty, Va. Seventy-five dollars will be paid for their ancestry. Must be proved by civil and church records.
W. B. P. A.

TWENTY-FIVE dollars will be paid for full information as to Capt. JOHN WADE of Chester and Marcus Hook, Chester, now Delaware county, Penna. This is not JOHN WADE who inherited and bought the lands of Essex House, but a cousin. It seems to be proved that he married MARTHA ROBINSON. He had a daughter, MIRIAM, and probably a son THOMAS and perhaps JOSEPH. Address Editor.

Errata: The reference for the marriage of THOMAS BLAIR, in July, 1924, issue, should be Acco., Va. xvi-287, not xiv-287.

OCCASIONAL

JOHN CHRISTOPHER was a "Lutherian." K. Geo., Va. Orders, 1721-1734, p. 123. 7 June 1723.

"MARGARET MADREGAR was sister of "JOHN PATTERSON'S mother by mother's "side. No other person known to be kin to "sd JOHN PATTERSON in this Country." Acco., Va. 7 June 1709. xiii-143.

RUSH HUTSON [HUDSON] presented for not going to Church; alleges that he belongs to the Quaker communion, [Rush Hudson and his wife Sarah, afterwards removed to Orange cty, Psh St. Mark, about 1746. He was son and heir-at-law of Rush Hudson, Sr., who died intest. 1735.] K. Geo., Va. Orders, 1731-1734, -. 123. 7 June 1723.

GEORGE JORDAN, in his will directs that the 15th day of every October there shall be a sermon of Mortality preached at his house . . . "it being the day that my daughter FORTUNE HUNT dyed . . . although it be a Thousand Generations hence . . . this Sermon and prayer is to be given." Surry, Va. ii-fo. 191. 25 Feby 1677-8. Codicil 28 May 1678. (One of the heirs is a River Jordan.)

From a deposition: Mr. MICHAELL POWELL, a Mcht (of Monmouthshire, but then of Westmoreland, Va.) said at first that he could not then Resolve whether MARY POWELL (a servant in Westmoreland) was related to him, but afterwards owned her for his Kinswoman & "saluted her very Kindly with a Kysse & told her that he would give her something towards housekeeping." Wmld, Va. Orders, 1668-1677, f. 108. Ct 14 Dec 1670.

CONTINUED articles COUNTY COURT NOTE-BOOK, and the dates on which they first appeared.
MARRIAGES BY INFERENCE. Began with May, 1922.
MARYLAND'S NEXT OF KIN. Began with July, 1922.
VIRGINIA COLONISTS. This alphabetized list began with July, 1924.
MILITARY NOTES. both COLONIAL and REVOLUTIONARY, and some later MILITIA NOTES, will appear in every issue, if possible.
SHIPS IN PORT, INTERCOUNTY and INTERCOLONIAL and COLONIAL FORENAMES, will appear in alternate issues or as space can be found for them.
EASTERN SHORE FAMILIES, in the form of a one-page supplement, began with June, 1925.

VIRGINIANS AND OTHERS IN CONVEYANCES AND POWERS KENTUCKY COURT OF APPEALS

BENJAMIN NETHERLAND, power to John Jones and John May, in a dispute with Hugh Shiell and Daniel Brodhead, Jr. in Powhatan cty, Va. 9 July 1785.
Rev'd Mr. HENRY OGILVIE, dec'd. of Scotland. 1785.
BENJAMIN OLIVER, of Hanover cty, Va. 1786.
JOHN COCKEY OWINGS, of Baltimore, Md.; bond. 1786. (He buys land in Lincoln cty, Ky.)
J. OVERTON, Jr., wit. Atty for FRANCES MERRIWETHER, Spots. cty. Va. 1785.
THOMAS PERKINS, mar. MARY PRATT, at Plymouth. 5 Apr 1748. Their issue.
ENOCH PERKINS, of Bridgewater cty, Plymouth, Mass., mentions "late brother THOS. PERKINS of Danville." 24 Aug 1788. (Power to Geo. Neuter?)
AMY POTTS, power to John May to recover property devised to her by her mother, whose maiden name was Sarah Price; (lands in Kent cty, Delaware.) David Potts, wit. nov 1786.
BASIL PRATHER, of Monongalia cty, Va., to John Brown Mercer. 1787.
SAMUEL and ROBT PURVIANCE, of Baltimore, buy 1000 acres in Fayette cty, Ky. 25 Jany 1787.
JOHN QUISENBERRY, of Orange cty, Va., buys lands in Fayette. 1788.
CHARLES RECTOR, wife Peggy Ann, to Thos. Buck, land in Bourbon cty, 1788. Both of Frederick cty, Va.
CHARLES RIDGELY, of Baltimore, Md., buys 800 a. in Nelson cty. 23 June 1786.
TURNER SOUTHALL, of Henrico cty, 1785.
ALEX. St. CLAIR, of Augusta cty, Va. Power to James Knox.
DAVID SIMPSON, Amherst cty, Va., to Thomas Kennedy of Madison cty Ky. 1788.
JOHN SMITH, Sr., and Jr., of Botetourt cty, Va. mch 1788.
GEORGE SMITH, of Powhatan cty, Va. Power to John Bryant. 1788.
THOMAS SPILMAN, of Culpeper cty, Va., Power from Nathaniel Spillman of Lincoln cty, Ky. 1789.
WILLIAM SYMMS, Jr., of Andover, Essex cty, Massachusetts; power to Geo. Muter. 1787.
JOHN TENNANT, of Port Royal, Caroline cty, Va., to Hubbard Taylor, of Orange cty, Va. Conveys land. Oct, 1786.
ROBERT WARE, Caroline cty, Va., to Rich. Taylor, same. 1000 acres in Nelson cty, Ky. 19 Jany 1786.
JOHN WATKINS, Caroline cty, Va., to Jas. Hord, of Lincoln cty. 18 Apr 1786.
JOHN WILLIAMS, of Shenandoah cty, Va., power to John Machir. 1786.
BENJ. WYNKOOP, of Philadelphia, to Fuller. 1787.
JOHN WILKINS, of Caroline cty, Va., to James Hoard. 1786.

(*End of these notes. See p. 37.*)

WILLIAMS NOTES MARYLAND-VIRGINIA SECTION

JOSEPH WILLIAMS, Fauq, cty, Va., from Col. Richard Henry Lee; 50 acres, during the lives of Elizabeth and Frances Williams. [A lease for lives.] Wit: Blackwell, Picket, Winn, Winn. Fauq., 28 Oct 1765. ii-493.
JOSEPH WILLIAMS, of Deep Run, Fauq. cty, Va., is discharged from payment of levy. [Probably on account of great age.] Fauq., Va., Minute Book. 1768-1772. p. 14. Apr. Ct 1769.
JOSEPH WILLIAMS; Catherine Williams, extx, John and Joseph Williams, "relations." Pr. Geo's, Md. 5 Apr 1747. DDi-446.
JOSEPH x WILLIAMS, Fauq., Va. from Thomas James, same, who farmlets during lives of sd Joseph, his wf Mary, and Joseph Williams, his son, the younger, plntn Williams now lives on, incl. 100 acres on Deep Run. [A lease for lives.] Fauq., 19 Aug 1769. iii-484.
JOSEPH WILLIAMS' bond as admr of Benjamin Williams. Edwin Young and John Newman, sec. Shenan., Va. 25 Mch 1777. A-113.
JOSEPH WILLIAMS, 150 acres Ldn cty, Va. Land Book.
JOSEPH WILLIAMS is granted admn on the est of Benjamin Williams, the widow renouncing. Shenan. Va. Ct. 25 Mch 1777. Minute Book.
JOSEPH WILLIAMS, claim for pasturage and pork. Shenan. cty Minutes. Ct 1782. [Supplies to Army.]
JOSEPH WILLIAMS, Ldn cty, Va. Land Book. 1784.

JOSEPH WILLIAMS and wf Elizabeth, of Wash'n cty, Md. to John Kent of Hamp. cty, Va. Wit. Burnit Williams, Nathaniel Williams, Mary Wick[?] Hamp. cty, Va. 9 Aug 1783. vi-86. Another deed from the same, of Hamp. cty, to MOSES WILLIAMS, same. 1784. vi-166,167.

JOSEPH WILLIAMS, of Washington cty, Md. buys land. Hamp., Va. 1783. vi-117.

LILBURN WILLIAMS, of Pr. Wm cty, Va. See Fauq. cty, 1796. xiii-152.

MARIENE [*sic*] x WILLIAMS, a witness. N-n, Va. 1658. ix-210.

MARY WILLIAMS and JOHN STOTTS; mar. return. Wythe cty, Va. 13 Feby 1798.

MARY WILLIAMS and JOHN McDANELD. Mar. return. Montg. cty, Va. 17 [?] Oct 1785.

MARY WILLIAMS, a head right. See Col. Edmund Scarburgh. 1664.

MARY WILLIAMS, final account, John and Richd Williams, extrs. Distributions to Charity Williams, Anne Isaac, William Williams, residue between deceased's five chn. Pr. Geo's, Md. 13 Mch 1788. STi-335.

MOSES WILLIAMS, 300 acres. Aug. Land Book. Va. 1782.

NATHANIEL WILLIAMS, Blksmth, Stafford cty, Va. to JOHN POPE WILLIAMS, Fauq. cty. 199 acres on branch Great Run, Cor. Charles Williams, Jesse Williams, William Jennings. Wit: Jesse, Charles, Lewis, George Williams. Fauq., Va. 15 Apr 1777. vi-398. His bond to convey land, 7 Feby 1777. vi-534.

SERVICE AND SUPPLIES COLONIAL, REVOLUTIONARY AND MILITIA

JACOB ALFORD produces ctf from the Gov'r of Virginia, from which it appears that he was entitled to a pension of eight pounds yearly, to commence 1 Jany 1786. Jeff'n cty, Ky. 27 Oct 1789. Orders, i-408. 28 Feby 1782, ALFORD exhibits a ctf from Gov'r Randolph that he served as private in the 7th Virginia Reg't, and appears to have been disabled in the service of the U. S. . . . Having made oath is certified. Orders, i-307.

JAMES BURK, a private 2d Reg't, wounded at Cowpens [to receive] ten pounds current money being half pay up to the 10th December. Fred'k cty, Md. Orphans' Ct. 14 Dec 1784.

WILLIAM BENNETT, oath as Captain, Pr. Wm cty, Va. 27 Feby 1762. Orders [4], p. 57.

PETER DICKERSON, to be 2d Lieut., Capt. John Mapp's Co. N-n, Va. 12 Aug 1777. xxxv0-11.

THOMAS EVANS, to be 2d Lieut, Capt. Richard Dunton's Co., N-n Va. 12 Aug 1777. xxxv0-11.

JAMES HOPKINS, recommended to be Lieut. of Militia. Yohog. cty, Va. About 26 Mch 1778.

JOHN HOPKINS, Ensign in Baxter's Co., Aug. cty, Va. 1783. ii-370.

WILLIAM HUGHES, Sgt in Capt. Wm. Phillips' vol. Co. of Rangers in 1763, then legally discharged. Louisa cty, 14 Feby 1780. i-21.

JOHN HUGHES, soldier, Capt. Obadiah Woodson's Co. of Rangers, in 1755, then legally discharged. Since dec'd. Proved by oath of Capt. Robt Anderson, Wm. Hughes, hr-at-law. Louisa cty 14 Feby 1780. i-21.

BOWDOIN KENDALL, to be 2d Lieut., Capt. Person's Co., N-n, Va. 12 Aug 1777. xxxv0-11.

HEARTS OF HICKORY. This book by John Trotwood Moore, which came from the press very early last spring, while written mainly for young readers, is a very interesting volume, and carries one along at times with somewhat of the fiery impetus of Andrew Jackson, himself. The Editor did not know very much about Andrew Jackson, except that he had been President, had fought the battle of New Orleans, was the husband of the sister of an ancestress of a friend of the Editor (which sounds like the oft-quoted Ollendorf), and that he was a very earnest partisan in any cause he championed. So when she arrived in Tennessee and had this house and that pointed out, and saw the portrait of Rachel Jackson as she hangs placidly . . . the storm and stress all gone by . . . above Mr. Moore's desk; handled the very manuscript arithmethic out of which the little Donelsons learned to cipher, Andrew Jackson slipped out of the Battle of New Orleans and the White House back to Tennessee and his home town. And "Hearts of Hickory" opened the pages of much frontier history. Such books, written after much study, lead to study, and, moreover, it *is* a very readable volume.

The Editor received some time ago, through the courtesy of the Registrar-General, Mr. Francis B. Culver, a copy of the Official Bulletin of the National Society of the Sons of American Revolution. The pamphlet was accidentally misplaced and it is now rather late to set down what the Editor has had in mind. However, perhaps there are others, who, like the Editor, have not had an opportunity heretofore to examine this very carefully edited, valuable and interesting publication. There is so much in it! And the records covering the claims of 504 new members and 132 supplemental lines, which begin on page 122, are full of most valuable information for every one who has the slightest interest in Revolutionary service. The Editor cannot but comment on the generous common sense of so publishing this material, so that he or she who goes to a library may read and make use of it.

The annual address of the President-General is of great personal interest to the Editor because of his views on a burning subject, and his use of one of her favorite texts . . . "If meat maketh my brother to offend I will eat no flesh while the world standeth."

Reasonable price or two years' subscription will be given for numbers 1, 2, 3, 4, 6, and 7, COUNTY COURT NOTE-BOOK, 1921-1922. Address Editor.

COLUMBIAN PRINTING CO., INC., WASHINGTON, D. C.

The County Court Note-Book

A Little Bulletin of History and Genealogy

December, 1926. **Vol. V, No. 6**

MARYLAND COUNTIES*

(Compiled from Mr. Edward B. Mathews' Bulletin. Arranged in related groups)

ST. MARY'S, 1637; temporarily called *Potomac,* 1654-1658.

Old Charles, 1650; changed to Calvert. (See below.)

Anne Arundel, 1650; first called *Providence,* and again in 1654-1656; Baltimore, 1659.

(*Baltimore*) Cecil, 1674;** Harford, 1773;

Charles, 1658;** Prince George's, 1695.

(*Prince George's*) Frederick, 1748;

(*Frederick*) Montgomery, 1776; Washington, 1776.

(*Washington*) Allegany, 1789.

Calvert, 1654;** temporarily called *Patuxent,* 1654-1658; (originally "Old" Charles county.)

Patuxent . . see Calvert.

Potomac, . . see St. Mary's.

Providence, . . see Anne Arundel.

SOMERSET, 1666; Worcester, 1742.

TALBOT, about 1661.** (According to chart covers part of Kent.) Queen Anne's (in part) 1706.**

DORCHESTER, 1668; Caroline, 1773.**

DURHAM, 1669. Never fully organized. Intended to include the northern part of what is now the State of Delaware.

WORCESTER (old) 1669 and 1672. Never fully organized. The county of 1672 apparently included the former projected county of Durham as well as the southern part of what is now the State of Delaware.

Four counties have been formed since 1800. Carroll, 1836, from Frederick and Baltimore; Garrett, 1872, from Allegany; Howard, 1850, from Anne Arundel; and Wicomico, 1867, from Somerset and Worcester.

---

*See notes on page 44.

**Formed from two or more counties.

MARRIAGES BY INFERENCE†

RICHARD BUCKNER and JUDITH EDWARDS. Ffx, Va. M. L. B. 27 Feby 1772.

WILLIAM BLACKEY and MARGARET GYBSON. Before 28 Mch 1652. York cty, Va. i-37.

JOHN BEST and MARTHA HAVILD [?] (She d. about 1693.) I. W. cty. See. iv-148. 1693. Martha was dau. of Silvestra Hill.

W. BLUNT and ANN NICHOLSON. Sussex, Va. M. L. B. 1756.

. . . BOWLING and MARY BROWNE, dau. David. Wmld, Va. Before 8 July 1727. viii(1)-418.

DANIEL BENTHALL and ELIZABETH GASCOIGNE, wid. of Henry. About 30 May 1692. N-n, Va. xvii-169.

NICHOLAS BARNES and SARA SARRELL. 14 Dec 1661. N-n, Va. ix-115.

JAMES BARNES and SALLY PECK or PAKE, dau. of Elizabeth. N-n, Va. M. L. B. 25 Aug 1790.

THOMAS BURDIT and VERLIND[A] COTTON, marriage contract. She was the dau. of Ann, wife of Francis Doughty. N-n, Va. 1 Sept 1658. ix-19.

Mr. WILLIAM BURDETTE and ALICE TRAVELLER, wid. of George. About 28 Apr 1643. N-n, Va. ii-231.

Lt. Coll. SAM'LL BRIDGER and ELIZABETH WOORY, widow of Mr. Joseph Woory. Before 9 Oct 1693. I. W., Va. iv-4. See also ii-341.

WILL CHURCHILL and ELIZABETH EDWARDS. 23 Sept 1762. Lanc, Va. M. L. B. W. and M. xii-177.

JOHN CROOKSHANK and MARY CLOVERFIELD. Before 17 Sept 1799. Rock'm, Va. oo-363.

CHARLES CARPENTER and BRIDGET MATTHEWS. 8 Nov 1768. N-n, Va. M. L. B.

WILLIAM A. CARUTHERS, M. D. and LOUISA CATHERINE GIBSON of Savannah, dau. of Robert S. Gibson. Contract of marriage. 3 July 1823. Rockbr., Va. Q-333.

CHARLES CARROL and AGNES GIBSON. 22 Dec 1786. Wash'n cty, Va. Mar. Ret.

JAMES CARSON and ISABELLA GIBSON. 27 Jany 1789. Rockbr. cty, Va.

MAXMILIAN CALVERT and Mrs. MARY SAVAGE. Cornelius Calvert, sec. 28 July 1744. L. Norf, Va. M. L. B.

DANIEL CUGLEY and HANNAH SAVAGE, wid. Ensign Thomas Savage. Before 17 May 1741. (She died about that date.) N-n, Va. ii-11.

JOHN CLEGG and JOAN LANGE, dau. of Peter. Before 2 Dec 1684. N-n, Va. xv-95.

ISAAC FOXCROFT and BRIDGET CHARLTON, dau. Stephen. N-n, Va. Before 1662. viii-8.

WILLIAM FULLEN and MARY GIBSON. Wash'n cty, Va. Mar. Ret. 7 Mch 1796.

HENRY GIBSON and SARAH HESTER GILBERT. Rock'm, Va. M. L. B. 2 Dec 1782.

JOHN GIBSON and HANNAH FITZGERRALL. Henry, Va. Mar. Ret. 3 Dec 1789. [This date is given in another place as 8 Dec 1788.]

WILLIAM GIBSON and MARY SHARD. Henry, Va. Mar. Ret. 6 July 1788.

WILLIAM GIBSON and ELIZABETH McCORMECK. Rockbr., Va. 29 Apr 1794.

JOHN GIBSON and ISABELLA ROBINSON. Campbell, Va. 8 Jany 1793.

TIMOTHY GREEN and EPHIA ROBINSON. She was probably widow of Thomas. Lanc., Pa. St. James Psh, also O. C. records. 11 Apr 1760.

JOHN GUY and SUSANAH BURTIN, dau. of John, Gent. She was kinswoman of John Kendall. N-n, Va. M. L. B. 27 Sept 1760.

JOHN GITTING and ELIZABETH CHARLTON. N-n, Va. About 1661. viii-111.

THOMAS GREGG and NAOMIA WHITACRE[?] Ldn, Va. (About) 26 Aug 1803.

GEORGE GREGG and ELIZABETH WILSON. Ldn, Va. Mar. Li. 8 Nov 1800.

AARON GREGG and MARY HIXON. Ldn, Va. About 7 Jany 1804.

SAMUEL GREGG and SARAH RATTICAN. Ldn, Va. About 6 Dec 1802.

STEPHEN GREGG and SUSANNAH DIXOB, at Centre Mtg, Newark Friends' Records. 1768.

WILLIAM GIBSON and SALLY WINN. Fauq., Va. M. L. B. 17 Dec 1791.

JONATHAN GIBSON and LUCY SHUMATE. Fauq., Va. M. L. B. 12 Sept 1797.

JOHN GIBSON and POLLY PEACH. Fauq., Va. M. L. B. 26 Sept 1796.

MOSES GIBSON and BETTY WINN. Fauq., Va. M. L. B. 30 Mch 1795.

WILLIAM GRIGSBY, Overwh. Psh, Stafford, and URSLEY [URSULA] MANN, dau. James. Pr. Wm, Va. Before 16 Dec 1640. E-265.

EDWARD GUPHELL and ELIZABETH FORMAN, wid, of Benj. Hamp., Va. 22 June 1769. ii-156. (Guphell and wife are of Craven cty, S. C.)

THOMAS HODGE, of Wmld cty, Va., and MARY ROSE, King Wm., Va. Before 27 Feby 1797. "11"-328. (Hodge was deceased at this date.)

WILLIAM HAINEY and ANN EDWARDS, *widow,* dau. of T. Edwards. Lanc., Va. M. L. B. 16 Oct 1747. (Wm and Mary. xii-101.)

GARRET HADEN and ELEANOR WOOD. Alex. cty, Va. M. L. B. 15 Apr 1803.

HENRY HEWBANCK and MARY BONEWELL, wid. James. Acco, Va. About 6 Oct 1702. Acco, xii-132.

WILLIAM HOPKINS and PATSEY PATTON, Rockbr., Va. 3 Jany 1805.

JOHN HALL and RACHEL HOPKINS. Rockbr., Va. 28 May 1795.

RICHARD HALL and ELIZABETH STONE. Wythe, Va. Mar. Ret. 10 Nov 1791.

JOSIAS HALL and MARY NIXON. Ldn, Va. 13 Mch 1793.

JONATHAN HALL and FRANCINIA FRANCIS. Ldn, Va. 19 Nov 1790.

DAVID HARPER and WILSON BUTT. Norf., Va. M. L. B. 14 Apr 1784.

HOLEMAN HUMPHREY and POLLY PADGETT. Shenan., Va. Before 10 Jany 1814. v-188.

NICOL. HARDING and ANN PAGET. Shenan., Va. Mar. Ret. Before 19 Apr 1773.

Mr. JAMES KEMP and NAOMI MAKEMIE, wid, Mr. Francis Makemie. Acco, Va. Before 3 Aug 1710. xiv-9.

CUSTIS KENDALL and ELIZABETH BOWDOIN, dau. Peter. See N-n, Va. 14 Aug 1753. xxviiiR-453.

RICHARD LEE and MARY DAVENPORT. Wash'n cty, Va. Mar. Ret. 30 Sept 1795.

QUAKER RECORDS

From the records of Marriages, Births and Burials, Society of Friends, Bush River Meeting, S. C. (At Guilford College, N. C.)

MARTHA COPPOCK, dau. of Moses and Martha Coppock, m. William, son of Josiah Tomlinson, of Fred'sburg Tshp. 30-12 mo. 1771. At Back River.

JOHN COPPOCK'S children:

Aaron, son of John and Abigail. B. 20-9 mo 1762.
John, son of same. B. 20-8 mo. 1766.
Susannah, dau. of same. B. 14-11 mo. 1769.
Marget, dau. of same. B. 20-12 mo. 1771.
Abigail, dau. of same. B. 28-2 mo. 1774.
Mary, dau. of same. B. 16-6 mo. 1776.
Isaac, son of same. B. 2-12 mo. 1779.
Ann, dau. of same. B. 18-3 mo. 1781.
Samuel, son of same. B. 1-11 mo. 1783.

Children of JOSEPH and JANE COPPOCK:

John, b. 12-2 mo. 1770.
Thomas, b. 20-2 mo. 1771.
Benjamin, b. 30-10 mo. 1772.
Joseph, b. 28-9 mo. 1774.
Elisabeth, b. 9-11 mo. 1776.
William, b. 29-3 mo. 1779.
Margaret, b. 10-5 mo. 1781.

FAMILIES OF THE EASTERN SHORE CUSTIS OF VIRGINIA

(Continued from October number)

JOHN CUSTIS, III, who, though he inherited Arlington (see will of JOHN CUSTIS, I.) is usually called of Williamsburgh, and who comes next in line of descent, was the ancestor of Gen. Washington's step-children. He does not appear as do the earlier Johns so frequently in the daily life of the Eastern Shore as we find it recorded by the courts, but he is buried in Northampton county under a tomb near that of his grandfather, with an inscription above him, often quoted, and which is calculated to make the world think that he had a very unamiable wife. She was FRANCES PARKE, daughter of that DANIEL PARKE whose tragic end is told in the records of the British West Indies. Before his marriage with FRANCES PARKE, however, JOHN CUSTIS, III, had married about the latter part of 1696, BRIDGET TAYLOR, the widow of William Taylor. BRIDGET died about 8 Dec 1697, leaving six Taylor children. CUSTIS obtained letters of administration on the Taylor estate in the same month in which she died. Her brother-in-law, Elias Taylor, intervened, and then followed a long and tedious controversy before the court. (See Acco, xii-7, 9 Dec 1697; xii-29, 7 June 1698; xii-77, 8 Nov 1699; xii-21, 5 Apr 1698; xii-87, 6 Mch 1699; xii-119, 7 Oct 1701.)

In the Library of Congress is the Act enabling JOHN CUSTIS and his wife FRANCES, "eldest daughter of DANIELL PARKE," to break the entail on the Parke lands. The date is 7 Nov 1711. The date of his marriage is not found in the Eastern Shore records or in any original record the Editor has examined.

There are, no doubt, many descendants of the five children of JOHN CUSTIS, of Wilsonia, grandson of JOHN of Rotterdam, but the Editor believes that far more of the present day families who claim CUSTIS blood, are descended from EDMUND CUSTIS, nephew of JOHN, I, and from WILLIAM CUSTIS, his brother. It is interesting to note that the descendants of JOHN, I, of Arlington, have Dutch blood, while the descendants of WILLIAM are of English descent, excepting, of course, the Scotch, Irish, and other occasional intermingled nationalities of the Eastern Shore. Some of the descendants of EDMUND, through the marriage of his son and his daughter with their cousins, are also descended from JOHN MICHAEL, of Graft, Holland.

WILLIAM CUSTIS, the younger brother of JOHN CUSTIS, I, first appears in the records of Northampton county, when he takes the oath of allegiance to the Commonwealth. (30 Mch 1651. N-n, iv-188.) He appears as a witness in 1652, and again in 1654; in the latter case to a deed from Yardley to his brother JOHN CUSTIS. In the same year he is a witness with his brother to Yardley's deed to John Robinson, Sr. (N-n, v-51. 10 Dec.) He appears several times as witness to deeds by Yardley (Col. Francis) and by his brother JOHN CUSTIS. He and Geo. Traveller are wit. to a power from Augustine Harman to JOHN CUSTIS, 27 June 1656. (N-n, vii-45.) The 22 Mch 1657, WILLIAM CUSTIS is granted a patent for 200 acres in *Accomack;* the land of Francis Stockley mentioned, now in possession of William Custis; the line of Lt. Col. Douglas, and of Thomas Hunt. Four head rights, but names are not given. (S. L. O. iv-224.) The names, however, are given in "Old vol. V," p. 151, as follows: William Custis, William H-[illegible], Elizabeth Bacles [?], Richard Jones.

WILLIAM CUSTIS' house is mentioned. (N-n, 28 July 1658. viii-27.) He buys a mare from William Kendall. (N-n, ix-46. 1659.) Sarah Bonwell, the mother of John Darmon, leaves him her son "to learn his trade." [She gives her eldest daughter Mary Darmon to Mrs. Alicia(?) Custis. N-n, ix-48. 19 May 1659.] CUSTIS appears as wit. to deeds, and also as witness to the will of Katherine x Pennell. (22 Nov 1660. ix-78.) In 1660, 28 June, he is listed as having twenty-five sheep. (N-n, viii-89.) Mr. WILLIAM CUSTIS appears in behalf of JOHN DORMAN, "orphant," 28 Jany 1661. (N-n, viii-122.) He appears in the court records a number of times, the 2 Mch 1662, as a juror. (N-n, viii-161.) In 1665, 16 June, he is listed on the Accomack tax-list as having 4 tithes. (Acco. i-102. On the 16 Sept 1665, Col. Edm. Scarborough conveys to him 1200 acres on the seaside . . one boundary is Nuswattox creek. (Acco, ii-18.) He is a witness to an assignment by Stephen and Mary Barnes. (Acco, ii-20. 16 Nov 1665.) In 1665 he has three tithes. This is in Northampton. (N-n, x-14.) Foreman of the grand-jury 16 Feby 1665. (Acco, i-116.) He is ordered to give an official notice "from his house upward on the seaside." (Acco, i-123. 16 July 1666.) He is an appr'r of John Dye's estate. (Acco, i-125. 18 Sept 1666.) And that year he has four tithes. (Acco, ii-35.) Foreman of the jury in 1667. (Acco, iii-21.) Three tithes in 1667. (Acco, iii-60.) He brings an Indian girl, *Anne Custis,* to court to have her age adjudged. (Acco. 1667.) He is an appr'r of Alphonso Ball's estate. (Acco, ii-56. 11 June 1667.) Foreman of the jury in 1667. A "delinquent of Horse," with many others. (Acco, iii-35. 16 Aug 1667.)

The 24 Oct 1667 (Acco, iii-36) he is foreman of the jury and is dismissed for pleading in behalf of the prisoner, William Benston. [Note: the Editor thinks it possible Benston was a Quaker.] (As a sample of the personal and quaint matters that get into the early courts, an order is recorded that a black walnut should be sawed for Mr. WILLIAM CUSTIS, for table lumber. Acco, iii-29. 25 Oct 1667.) CUSTIS brings an Indian boy, seven years old, who is given the name of *George Custis*. He is to serve until twenty-four. (Acco, 25 Oct 1667. iii-39.) The girl mentioned above was twelve years old and was also to serve until twenty-four.

In 1668, CUSTIS had three tithes. (Acco, ii-80.) He was appointed surveyor of the highways, on the Bayside from Deepe Creek to Pungoteague, and on the Seaside from Great Matomkin to Nath'l Bradford's. (Acco. iii-119. 17 May 1669.) He has three tithes, 1669 and 1670. The 17 Nov 1771, he is added to the Commission for *Northampton* county. (N-n, iv-25.) [For a short time the two counties were thrown together again under the name of Northampton. For a copy of the record concerning this, see William and Mary Quarterly, Second Series.]

WILLIAM CUSTIS, of Accomack, gives to the dau. of Ann Johnson, a feather-bed, four "Kowes," &c. (Acco. x-229. 15 Dec 1691.)

The County Court Note-Book

An every-other-monthly devoted mainly to abstracts from County Court records, prior to 1800.

MILNOR LJUNGSTEDT, Editor and Publisher. Bethesda, Route 10, Maryland.

Published six times a year. Subscription, two dollars, in advance; must begin with the year. Advertising rates moderate.

DECEMBER, 1926 Whole
Vol. V., No. 6 No. 31

IF YOU PLEASE!

A friend of the Editor, who would not wish his name blazoned forth, but lives in a southern city and is well known as a scholarly lawyer and genealogist, has secured for the Editor no less than four new subscribers, merely by sending copies of the NOTE-BOOK to correspondents of his own . . . and asking. This is a very great help and the Editor wishes that a few other friendly folk would be moved to do the same. It is not the Editor's fault that the printers swallow the NOTE-BOOK much as the whale is supposed to have swallowed Jonah. Like Jonah, the NOTE-BOOK comes back, but poor as Job.

A friend, the Librarian of a very large association, suggests a sort of pro rata charge. This the Editor does not fancy . . . it is too much like newspaper "opportunities." It may be remarked that when the Index was published on this plan, the Librarian of one important State Library (only one) suggested that the price was too high, and intimated that probably others thought so, too, but didn't say it. Anyhow, no one else did say so and they all seemed glad to get the Index and help pay for it . . . excepting the exception.

But, if you please, returning to subscriptions, kindly reader, twenty-five more subscribers will "fill the bill," . . . and fifty subscribers will allow for some occasional research in forgotten pigeon-holes.

The tabulation of the counties of Maryland in such form that they may be useful to persons engaged in research has been no easy task, and except for the fascination of working out a puzzle, the Editor would wish for some one like Mr. Salley, of South Carolina, to arrange these matters historical for her. What the Editor gives is extracted from the valuable bulletin brought out by Mr. Edward B. Mathews, as a publication of the Johns Hopkins Press, in 1907. It is part of the sixth volume of the Maryland Geological Survey.

The reasons why the Maryland counties are a "hard proposition" is, first, that several of them have no contemporary record of their formation. Is this surprising in a State where an original county record is "lost" for forty years in an historical society? Second, they changed their names; and, third, four or five of them, instead of following dutifully in the trail of some parent, had no family at all, but were created (with very uncertain boundaries) out of the marshland homes of the muskrats; the blue inlets; the fertile, sandy fields, and the forests of that delightful section, the Eastern Shore.

All our coasts and coastal lands are delightful in various ways, from the red and gray rocks of Maine topped with their pointed firs; the dunes of Long Island with moors of pink and bays of peacock blue; the wide sands of Cape May; the mountainous sand-hills of Cape Henry and the lower Chesapeake; the black-green of the live oaks and the wind-stressed cedars of St. Simon's, to the dazzling beaches of Florida . . . but no special section is more beautiful than the broad levels of the Eastern Shore, cut as they are by innumerable winding water-ways of Heaven's own color, and belted with the marching pines that still remain . . . seedlings of its early forests.

One might, it is true, grow to long for the dash of the waves at Nahant or Newport, or the line of the Presidential Range, but for paintability there is nothing beyond certain "rivers" which wander about on this Eastern Shore peninsula, and no sunset can be finer than a perfect one across the Chesapeake, except one, and that is one of the "scenic properties" of Eggemoggin Reach, Maine.

And yet there are those who would give it all to be sloshing down Beacon Hill on a misty, moisty February day.

For further details as to the Maryland counties, the reader is referred to Mr. Mathews' volume. It is not possible to go into them here.

As in former lists, the immediate parent of a county is given in parenthesis.

OCCASIONAL

BEERE is to be made of English grayne & nott Molasses. L. Norf., Va. 15 July 1671. E-67.

JOHN EYRE, Gent., not being satisfied in his conscience of the lawfulness of an oath . . . would not take it as Justice. N-n, Va., 30 Dec 1692. xvii-220.

STEPHEN FLETCHER complains of Nathaniel Isdall . . . a plea of trespass . . . that sd Nathaniel on the first Day of August in the year of our Lord one thousand seven hundred and sixty-eight with Force and Arms entered the Close of him the said Stephen at Hog Island in the Parish of Hungar's in the County aforesaid [Northampton] and then and there plucked, gathered and carried away one hundred bushels mrytle Berries [the bayberry of New England] of him the said Stephen then and there growing to the Value of twenty pounds. N-n, Va. Records.

UNUSUAL CASE: S. B. by his nun-cup will leaves to servant A. W. and her children, the greater part of his estate. She asks administration and it is granted to her. Further record shows that S .B. had a wife in England, and the Court orders that the servant, A. W., should pay the wife 200 lbs of tobacco yearly. 28 July 1685. N-n cty, Va. [A. W. was possibly a preferred creditor!]

Upon the information of Zacheriah Connell, Gentleman, That James Johnston did this day swear two profane oaths and two profane Cusses . . . ordered that the said James Johnston be fined Twenty Shillings . . . Yohog. cty, Va. Minute Book i-17. 25 June 1777.

The Editor is sure that many of her readers will be glad to know that Mr. Stratton Nottingham, of Onancock, Va., has in preparation and will shortly publish a list of the marriage license bonds of Accomack county, Va. The volume will contain over 1,000 bonds alphabetically arranged as to men's names, with an index of women's names. The price will be moderate. Further information may be had from the Editor and subscriptions will be received at any time. Mr. Nottingham intends to follow this work with the wills and administrations of the same county.

The Next of Kin is omitted from this number on account of the serious illness of Mrs. Hodges. And the Editor has been compelled to temporarily discontinue her Virginia Colonists until she can return to Richmond for further material.

The following Quakers are found to have been banished from England, and should be added to the list formerly given. See NOTE-BOOK for October, 1925.

RICHARD SMITH, ANNE STANDRIDGE, WILLIAM STEVENSON, THOMAS STOKES. All from London or Middlesex. (See Besse's Sufferings of the Quakers.)

CONTINUED articles COUNTY COURT NOTE-BOOK and the dates on which they first appeared.
MARRIAGES BY INFERENCE. Began with May, 1922.
MARYLAND'S NEXT OF KIN. Began with July, 1922.
VIRGINIA COLONISTS. The alphabetized list began with July, 1924.
MILITARY NOTES, both COLONIAL and REVOLUTIONARY, and some later MILITIA NOTES, will appear in every issue, if possible.
SHIPS IN PORT, INTERCOUNTY and INTERCOLONIAL and COLONIAL FORENAMES, will appear in alternate issues or as space can be found for them.
EASTERN SHORE FAMILIES, in the form of a one-page supplement, began with June, 1925.

In the article entitled SCRAMBLED FAMILIES, the Editor omitted a deed of 1693. It is as follows [abstract]:

JOHN CUSTIS, Sr., of Northampton, Va., Esq., and wife TABITHA, to their nephew and grandson, EDMUND CUSTIS of Accomack county, and TABITHA, his now wife, our granddaughter . . . all that tract whereon the said EDMUND CUSTIS and wife TABITHA now live, . . . at Deep Creek, Accomack county, containing 1,750 acres . . . being one-half of 3500 acres granted by patent to the said TABITHA, now the wife of JOHN CUSTIS, Sr., and her sister, MATILDA SCARBURGH, now the wife of Col. JOHN WEST, both the daughters of Col. EDMUND SCARBURGH, which patent was dated 29 Mch 1656 . . . and after their decease to their son THOMAS CUSTIS, and his heirs, but should there be no heirs . . . to the next heir of EDMUND and TABITHA, and in failure of them to our grandson SMART WHITTINGTON, son of WILLIAM WHITTINGTON, Gentleman, and brother of the said TABITHA CUSTIS, wife of EDMUND, for life, and then to his heirs and for want of such heirs to our grandson JOHN CUSTIS, the son of JOHN CUSTIS, Jr., of Northampton, and for want of heirs to the heirs at common law of the said JOHN CUSTIS, Sr. 15 June 1693. vol. xi-10.

(*Courtesy of Mr. Stratton Nottingham.*)

IMPORTANT.—A subscriber to the NOTE-BOOK, and correspondent of the Editor, will pay TWENTY-FIVE dollars for full information as to the ancestry of ISAAC MILNOR, of Bristol, Bucks county, Penna. ISAAC MILNOR came into Bucks county from Burlington county, New Jersey, *circa* 1700 or 1710. He married at Friends' Meeting SARAH WILSON, a prominent minister among Friends. He is not son of JOSEPH MILNOR, a member of the Assembly from Bucks in 1696, nor of DANIEL, brother to JOSEPH. DANIEL MILNOR died soon after his arrival, and JOHN MILNOR, son of JOSEPH, was heir to both DANIEL and JOSEPH.

CHILLIAN and MARTIN PALMER, Charlotte cty, Va. Seventy-five dollars will be paid for their ancestry. Must be proved by civil and church records.
W. B. P. A.

TWENTY-FIVE dollars will be paid for full information as to Capt. JOHN WADE of Chester and Marcus Hook, Chester, now Delaware county, Penna. This is not JOHN WADE who inherited and bought the lands of Essex House, but a cousin. It seems to be proved that he married MARTHA ROBINSON. He had a daughter, MIRIAM, and probably a son THOMAS and perhaps JOSEPH. Address Editor.

INTER-COUNTY AND INTER-COLONY

MARY x CHAPMAN, wf of EDWARD CHAPMAN of Acco. cty, Va., was the dau. and heir of RICHARD HARRIS, of Albemarle cty, N. C. She gives power to John Evans to sell Albemarle land. Acco, 7 July 1713, 603.

CHARLES CALVERT, of Stafford cty, Va., Gent., to James Neale, of Charles cty, Md., Gent., Conveys 600 acres in Charles cty, part of a grant to William Calvert, Esq., father to said Charles. The sd 600 acres was intended to be given in marriage with Elizabeth Calvert to said James Neale. (Charles Calvert releases his right.) Wmld, Va. 27 Nov 1707. iv-96.

THOMAS DENIS transports his cattle to Maryland. Acco, Va. 15 May, 1666.

JOSEPH DOHERTY, of Fayette cty, District of Kentucky; power to Sam'l Barton, of Davidson cty, N. C. Davidson cty, Tenn. i-202. 8 June 1790.

BARTHOLOMEW GREENE, of Charlestowne, in N. E., marriner; power to Maj. Thomas Tabirer [*sic*] of I. W. cty, Va. Wit: Ja. Daye, John Pitt.

EDWARD HASSARD, now at Wiccocomico. Acco, Va. 16 Dec 1664. ii-4.

AUGUSTINE HARMAN, power to Mr. John Custis to demand of Dr. Geo. Hacke, &c., &c. N-n, Va. 27 Apr 1657. vii-48.

ROBERT HAMBLETON had land in Sussex cty. [Dela. or Va.?] N-n, Va. 28 Mch 1688. xv-347.

JOHN HUDSON, of Nansimon cty, Va. Power to John Badham. N-n, Va. 29 Dec 1655. vii-49.

[Mr.] JOHN HAWKINS, mariner [of Boston.] N-n, Va. 27 Apr 1657. vii-46. Also 13 Nov 1656. vii-53.

JOSEPH HADFIELD, late of Manchester, Great Britain, but now of Baltimore. Fred'sburg, Va., District Court. 30 Apr 1789. A-6.

WILLIAM HARPER; moved to Somersett cty, Md. N-n, Va. About 1675. xi-112.

WILLIAM HOLLINGSWORTH, of Salem, in New England, Marriner; power to Major Isaac Allerton of Lower Machotick. Wmld, Va. 22 May 1671. Orders, 1668-1677, f. 112.

JOHN HUGBIN [or HUGHBEY] of Northampton cty, Va., planter, left by will to SUSANNA CARPENTER, 100 acres, known by the name of Forked Neck; Susannah then an infant of about seven years and soon after was removed to Cecil cty, Md, where she married CORNELIUS ELIASON; both departed this life without coming into Virginia. (Susanna settled in Bohemia Manor in Cecil Cty, in Maryland, "beyond seas as aforesaid.") Elias Eliason was the eldest son and heir-at-law of said Cornelius and Susanna. Deposition of Richard Thompson, Sr., Gent., aged about 88 years: That about 40 years ago he put into Occohannock Creek and was asked about a certain Obedience Oben and wife and daughter-in-law, Susanna, who then lived at the head of said bay; that the daughter-in-law Susanna, married Cornelius Aliason and had eldest son Elias. William Crow deposes that the daughter-in-law [step-daughter] of Obedience Oben was called Susanna Carpenter. The date of this suit is about 1767 or 1768, and the record is to be found among chancery matters, N-n cty, Va.

WILLIAMS NOTES

MARYLAND-VIRGINIA SECTION

NATHANIEL WILLIAMS, Stafford cty, Blksmth, to JOHN POPE WILLIAMS, Fauq. cty; 199 acres on branch of Great Run. cor Chas. Williams; JESSE WILLIAMS line mentioned, also Wm. Jennings. Wit: are Jesse, Charles, Lewis, and George Williams. Fauq., Va. 15 Apr 1777. vi-398.

NATHANIEL WILLIAMS, wf Elizabeth, Stafford cty, to Martin Pickett, part of a tract divided bet. Nath'l, Charles, Jesse, and "Pope" Williams. Fauq., Va. 1778. vii-68.

OTHO HOLLAND WILLIAMS, of Balto., Md. Will. Shows that he had bro. Elie Williams; sisters, Cassandra (minor); Teresa Davis wf of Amos; Priscilla Israel; Mercy Stull [Hull?] His wife was Mary, dau. of Wm. Smith. Minor chn mentioned, Wm. Elie Williams, Edward Greene Williams, Henry Lee Williams, Otho Holland Williams. Fred'k cty, Md., 1794. GM3-38.

OWEN WILLIAMS, charged in the list of tithables, 1785. Rock'm cty, Va. Minutes, i. Ct 24 Apr 1787.

PAUL WILLIAMS m. the widow of James Fox. See Fauq., Va. iii-293-294. and Minute Book, Aug. Ct 1768. Married about August, 1768.

PAUL WILLIAMS and Sarah x Wheatley; mar. contract. James Craig and Daniel Marr, wit. Fauq., Va. 28 June 1786. ix-258.

PETER WILLIAMS and wf Catherine x, of Rock'm cty, Va. to THOMAS WILLIAMS, same. Half-acre in town called. George Town, Shenan. cty. Shenan., 10 June 1811. S-199.

PHOEBE WILLIAMS; mentioned in the will of Elizab. Plummer, Pr. Geo's cty, Md. 1736.

PHILIP WILLIAMS, Woodstock; from Abraham Brewbaker, Jr., of same. Lot in Woodstock. Shenan, Va. 29 July 1790. G-510.

PHILIP WILLIAMS married Sarah Croudson. Shenan., Va. Mar. Ret. 18 Oct 1791. She was dau. of John. See also M. L. B. 15 Oct 1791.

PHILIP WILLIAMS buys lot 16, Woodstock. Shenan., Va. 24 Feby 1791. H-67. Also another lot. p. 124.

PHILIP WILLIAMS, Clerk of the Court. Shenan., Va. 1792 et seq.

RICHARD WILLIAMS m. Sarah Ward, dau. of Alex. Moore. Annap. records. Inv. and Accts. xiiia-216. 1694.

REBECCA WILLIAMS and Nathan Hudlen. Shenan. Mar. Ret. 19 June 1795.

REBECKAH WILLIAMS and David Harper. Wm. Pritchard, sec. Norf., Va. M. L. B. 23 Aug 1799.

RICHARD WILLIAMS, Gent., and Elizabeth Robinson, dau. of John, of London, mariner. London Mar. Li. 23 Mch 1630.

RICE WILLIAMS, Westmoreland, Va. Patent for 107 acres. S. L. O. 1691. i-144.

RICHARD WILLIAMS, Ldn, Va., Land Book. 1784.

RICHARD WILLIAMS, Hamp. cty, Va. Will. Mentions father (John) brothers and sisters. Bro-in-law, Ezekiel Whitman. Wit: Loan, Kimberlin, Stafford. 30 Mch 1788-12 June 1788. ii-186.

RICHARD WILLIAMS, 120 a. Land Book, Aug. cty, Va. 1782.

RICHARD WILLIAMS, Ldn cty, Va. Land Book. 1782.

RICHARD WILLIAMS mentioned in Davis will. Wythe, Va. 29 Dec 1813- 12 Nov 1816. i-172.

ROBERT WILLIAMS and wf Margaret. Ackn. deed of B. and S. Rock'm, Va. Minute Book. Ct 26 May 1778.

ROBERT WILLIAMS, on Smith's Creek. Rock'm Entries. p. 27. 1790. Again 28 June 1786. p. 22.

ROWLAND WILLIAMS, svt to Mr. John Michael. N-n, Va. 28 Apr 1664. viii-189.

SERVICE AND SUPPLIES COLONIAL, REVOLUTIONARY AND MILITIA

LARNER WATSON makes oath to declaration and Court declare opinion he was a Revolutionary soldier. Mad. cty, Va. 23 Aug 1832. Orders, viii.

LEIGHTON WHITE proves that he served in Col. Clark's Regt, as a soldier, from July 1779, to July, 1780; that he came down the Ohio with Col. Clark in May, 1778, and served as a soldier until the reduction of its several posts at the Illinois, after which he returned to the then county of Kentucky, and in Feby, *1779,* built a cabin on a branch of Green River . . . about four miles from Hardin's settlement. Court gives opinion that he is entitled and grants ctf. Jeff'n cty, Ky. 3 Apr 1781. A-28. [See also extract from Draper Mss. Feby Note-Book.]

WILLIAM YOWELL makes oath to his declaration, and the Court declare their opinion that he was a Revolutionary soldier. Mad. cty, Va. 23 Aug 1832. Orders, viii.

JOHN YAGER; Ordered ctf'd to the Register of the Land Office that John Yager, late of this county died intestate, and that letters of adm'n were granted to Thomas Yager, and that he left as heirs and legal representatives, now living in Maryland, his widow, Hannah; and chn: Thomas, Elizabeth, John H., and Lucinda. Mad. cty, Va. Ct. 25 Oct 1832. Orders, viii.

The following are shown by the records of Northumberland cty, Penna. (2d vol. O. C. Docket) to have performed military service, or to have been widows of soldiers.

ADAM CHRIST, Sjt.

PATRICK CALLAHAN (age about 39 in 1786).

CHARLES CLARK, an officer.

HENRY DOUGHERTY (mentioned twice).

CHRISTOPHER GETTIG[?]

DAVID HAMMOND, an officer.

MARY KEMPLIN, widow of Capt. Thomas Kemplin. (Kemplin and his eldest son were killed by Indians.)

MARY ANNE LEPLEY, widow of Michael. (Christian Hetlig's orphans mentioned).

REBECCA LEWIS, widow of Lemuel, an officer.

MARY McCRACKEN, widow of Henry.

JOHN McPHERSON, late a midshipman on the *Randolph* Frigate.

GEORGE MARTIN.

JANE MARTIN, late Jane McClung, widow of William.

MARY NEESE, widow of Peter.

JOHN NORCROSS.

ANN WATT, widow of James Watt, the elder. (Watt, previous to his enrollment in the service of the State, "Commorant" within the county.)

A NEW BOOK OF KENTUCKY RECORDS. Dr. Willard Rouse Jillson has recently compiled a very valuable index of Land Entries in Kentucky. The volume also includes a complete index to a large number of deeds which are recorded in an office of the State Capitol at Frankfort; an index to the wills also filed there, and to the military grants. Next in value to direct examination of original records, is a reliable index. When all the early States have made a "show-down" of what they have in their various offices, we shall know somewhat more than we do now, and much valuable information will be open to everybody, rather than confined to the knowledge of specially favored individuals. Moreover, such an index as this is a great saving of time. At present there are many depositories where it is only possible to get at the knowledge of their material by long stay, and persistent questioning. This new Kentucky book is immensely valuable. The extracts from Kentucky records which the Editor has been publishing are taken from some of the material which is indexed in this volume.

The ROBINSON GENEALOGICAL SOCIETY has recently published volume I, of the data compiled by the late Charles Edson Robinson. It contains the names of nearly 4,000 descendants of the Rev'd JOHN ROBINSON, pastor of the Pilgrims. The book has 375 pages, and a number of fine illustrations, including one of the prison where some of the Pilgrims were confined before they went to Holland. Copies of the wills of JOHN ROBINSON'S parents, and of his widow, with a brief account of the early life of this distinguished teacher, together with a little of the *Mayflower* history and a list of the "compact signers," make it a valuable book for those interested in genealogical matters, and especially those who claim kinship to the family of the "wise and tolerant" scholar, preacher and leader.

A limited number of copies are for sale by the Treasurer of the Society, FREDERICK W. ROBINSON, 950 Park Square Building, Boston, Mass., to whom inquiries should be addressed.

(This is an unusually valuable book . . . one of the very few which unquestionably connect a family with its old English home. Its pages carry conviction with them, and are a testimonial to the many years of painstaking care its compiler gave to its preparation. Editor.)

Reasonable price or two years' subscription will be given for numbers 1, 2, 3, 4, 6, and 7, COUNTY COURT NOTE-BOOK, 1921-1922. Address Editor.

COLUMBIAN PRINTING CO., INC., WASHINGTON, D. C.

INDEX TO COUNTY COURT NOTE-BOOK. VOLUME V.

Abbott 3, 11, 19
Able 22
Abrall 14
Abram 19
Acheson 11
Adams 11, 13, 25
Adcocke 11
Adkeson 11
Adlome 3
Alber 3
Alcock 3
Aler 34
Aleander 19
Alford 2,39
Allen 3,11,13,14,15
18,19,33
Allerton 1,26,46
Allison,Allason 5,6,46
Anderson 11,39
Andrews 23,35,36
Angell 11
Annis 34
Appleton 9,17
Aprickett 11
Arbson 3
Arbuckle 7,14
Armiger 1
Armitage 27
Arundell 11
Aryson 3
Ashton,Aston,2,10,11,
17,19
Atheser 11
Atkins 3
Attwood 10,26
Auchran 17
Austin 13,23
Axell 11
Ayres 3,14,34
(see also Eyres)
Babb 25
Bacles 43
Badham 46
Bagwell 14
Baileinge(?) 18
Bailey,Baley 2,19
Baker 7,29
Ball 3,11,18,43
Ballard 11
Banbury 11
Bannister 10
Barbour 13
Barchard 11
Barefott 3
Barker 25,26
Barnes 10,18,41,43
Barnhouse 11
Baron 25
Barret 19
Bartlett 13,31
Barton 45
Base 11
Basnett 11,19
Bateman 19
Baughan 11
Baxter 39
Bayley 14
Baynham,Baynum 1,35
Beall 2,13,29,30
Beard 29
Beere 2
Bell 2,14,18
Bellamy 27
Bellarke 19
Bennett 11,18,39
Benson,Benston,Benison,
3,14,43
Benthall 44
Bentley 25
Berkeley,Burkley,2,17
18
Bernard 18
Berry 1,3,21
Berryman 2
Berwick 18
Best 41
Beswick 10
Bevan 30
Bickford 1
Billingsly 2
Bingley 19
Bird 3
Bishopp 11
Black 15,17
Blackburn 2
Blackey 11,41
Blackmore 3
Blackwell 15,30,38
Blagg 1
Blair 37
Blancher 11
Blandon 19
Blaydes 2
Bledave 13
Blow 34
Bluney 3
Blunt 41
Boarman 18
Boater 18
Boaze 9
Boggis(Boggess) 3
Bohannon 26
Bolt 11
Bolton 2,3
Bond 18
Bonden 11
Bonwell,Bonewell 24,43
Boomer,Bumer 10
Bose 11
Bostick 25
Boswell 3,11
Bound 2
Bourne 2,11,19
Bowdoin 26,27
Bowe 3
Bowles 3,15,17
Bowling 41
Bowman 13
Boyce 33
Bradford 11,43
Bradley 7
Brady,Bradey 34
Braby 22
Branch 11
Brann 2
Brent 2,17
Bretherton 11
Brett 17

INDEX TO COUNTY COURT NOTE-BOOK. VOLUME V.

Brewbaker 46
Brian 2
Brickell 15
Bridger 41
Bridges 1,13
Briggs 3,19
Brim 13
Brin 13
Briscoe (?) 2,10
Brisley 19
Broad 25
Broadway 3
Brock 18
Brodhead 38
Brome 19
Bromstead 19
Bromwell 34
Broner 2
Brook, Brooks 2,7,10, 11,19,35
Broughton 11,34
Browne 2,3,10,11,17, 18,19,34,36,38,41
Browsford 1
Bruce 18
Brumwell 34
Bryan 3
Bryant 38
Bryer 3,11
Bryfield 2
Buck 13,38
Buckner 41
Bullock 13
Bumer 10
Burchell 3
Burdett, Burditt 11,41
Burdin 18
Burke, Birke 19,39
Burly 3
Burne 11
Burnell 18
Burrell 18,34
Burt 19
Burtin, Burton 3,6,13,42
Butrum 34
Bury 3
Butcher 11
Butler 1,2,9,11,15,17, 18,22,30
Butt 42
Byerd 11
Caffrey 22
Cahoune 19
Caidy 11
Callahan 47
Calloway 13,23
Calvert 18,22,41,45
Camble, Campbell 13,18
Campion 18
Canada, Cannida 3,14,19 (see also Kennedy.)
Canby 6
Carier 2
Carpenter 2,3,19,41,46
Carroll 10,41
Carson 22,41
Carter 11,19
Caruthers 41
Carver 1
Cary 14,29,34
Cawlins 19
Chandler 11
Chase 13
Chapman 1,15,17,19,45
Charlton 42
Chester 3,11
Chetter 3
Chew 2
Chilton 13
Chinn 19
Chowninge 19
Chriesman 30
Christ 47
Christopher 37
Christian 13,19
Churchill 41
Churchman 22
Claiborne 19
Clarke 3,10,11,13,15, 18,19,22,31,47
Clarkey 18
Clarkey (?) 18
Clatterbuck 31
Clay 25
Clayland 34
Clegg 42
Clements 2,11
Clerke 7,19
Clinton 3
Close 26
Cloverfield 41
Coaleman 3
Coate, Coates 13,19
Cobb 25
Coburn 29
Cochran 7,15
Cooke 11,19
Cockerel 11
Codier 19
Codince 29
Coffett 5
Cole, Coale, Coles 10, 11,21,22
Coledick 25
Colegate 2
Coleman 3,19
Collins 15,19
Coman 27
Conaway 19
Connell 45
Connolam 19
Conny 11
Cooke 3,11,19,25
Cooper 11,14
Coopkand 29
Coote 3
Cope 19
Copland 11
Coppin 18
Coppock 42
Corbin, Corbyn 17,18,19
Corderoy 19
Corman 19
Cornix 11
Cossens 19
Costin 33
Cotton 41
Covall 18

INDEX TO COUNTY COURT NOTE-BOOK. VOLUME V.

Coventon 3
Cowdery 19
Cox 3
Crabb 5
Crackson 10
Cragh, Craig 11,18,46
Crawford 3,14
Criswell 23
Crookshank 41
Cropper 15
Croudson 46
Crow 46
Croyer 11
Cruckson 10
Crump 11
Crup 18
Cuglay 42
Cullers 5
Culp 13
Cunningham 11
Curd 19
Curtis 19
Custis 14,19,21,25,27, 28,35,36,37,42,43, 45,46
Cutlin 27
Cuttin 27
Cutts 26
Dagworthy 29
Daine 18
Daniel, Daniell 11,23,26, 30
Darby 11
Darken 18
Darker 18
Darley 11
Darmion 43
Dau 19
Dauncy 11
Davenport 11,42
Davis 3,6,11,19,29,30,33, 34,46
Dawteridge 2
Daye 45
Deaderick 22
Dean 18,26
Dell 29
Demall 22
Denister 11
Dennis 19,45
Denwood 34
Denly 18
Dice 3
Dickerson 39
Dickson 11
Digby 3
Dijart (?) 22
Dillicoate 10
Dillon 10
Dinely 2
Dinning 10
Dixon, 3,42
Dobson (?) 19
Doherty 45
Dolby 35
Donahough 29
Donath 18
Donavin 25
Donelson 39
Donis (?) 19
Donoch 18
Dooding 19
Dorman 43
Dougherty 7,23,47
Doughty 41
Douglas 14,29,35,43
Dowesby 3
Drew 2
Drisco (?) 2
Dudley 26
Duell 11
Duning 10
Dunn 19
Dunston 6
Dunton 39
Durant 10
Drummond 14
Dye 43
Eagle 2
Earle 11
Easterfield 11
Eastham 34
Edelen 5
Edgecombe 19
Edge 29
Edom 3
Edriche 11
Edwards 10,11,18,41,42
Eels 3
Ekin 3,11
Elam 23
Eliason 46
Ellis, Ellice 1,3
Ellit 2
Elce 1
Embrey 26
Emorson 34
England 34
Englishman 27
Eubanks
(see Hewbanck)
Evans, Evins 19,22,34, 39,45
Eveten 11
Ewell 14
Eyre, Eyres, 27,35,44
(see also Ayres)
Fairlamb 29
Farling 11
Farloe 11
Farrell 3
Fennell 19
Fenton 14
Field, Feild 2,23
Finley 26
Fishbrooke 11
Fisher 1,11,19
Fishpoole 11,19
Fitzgerrall 42
Fleming, Flaming 2,9, 15,22,23
Fletcher 44
Forbes 31
Forman 42
Forrest 11,19
Forrester 11
Fostley 3
Fouch 11

INDEX TO COUNTY COURT NOTE-BOOK. VOLUME V.

Foushee 23
Fowke 19
Fox 46
Foxcroft 6,42
Foxon 18
Fraker 22
Francis 42
Franke 19
Franklin 9
Freeman 15,21,30
Frodsham 9
Fry, Frey 9,19,23
Fryer 3
Fullen 42
Fuller, Fulher 14,23
Gainsbrooke 3
Galbraith 7
Gale 34
Galloway 2
Galt 21
Gamble (?) 18
Gardner 1,19
Garner 30
Garretson 29
Gartrell, Gattrell, 25,26
Gartrick 33
Gascoigne 35,41
Gettig (?) 47
Gerrard, Garrard 9,10,26
Gibbon 33
Gibbonson 29
Gibbs 19
Gibson, Gybson 15,22,23, 41,42
Gilbert 42
Gillis 10
Gingel 25
Giranet 31
Gitting, Gittings 2,42
Glanville 2
Glower 11
Goddinge 11
Goffinger 21
Golding, Goldfing 11,19, 34
Gollinges 11
Goodridge 1
Goodwin 34
Gongle 19
Granger 35
Graves 10
Gray, Grey 3,10,11,19, 30
Greene 11,18,19,23, 27,42,45
Greenhow 26
Greensell 3
Greer 26
Gregg 42
Gregory 3,11,34
Grigsby 42
Griffin 19
Griffiths 3
Griggs 19
Grinalls 29
Grymes 15
Gunn 19
Guphell 42
Guy 42
Guyer 42
Hacke 20,46
Hackett 3
Haden 42
Hadfield 46
Hadway 19
Hagg 19
Haines 3,11,19
Hainey 42
Haitt 10
Hale, Hales 19,22
Hall 2,19,21,35,42
Halliard 11
Hambleton 46
Hammond 47
Hamp 42
Hanby 4
Hanson 34
Hanwell 19
Harden, Hardin, Harding 22,42
Hardidge 9
Hardie 9
Hardisty 10
Hardwick 2,18
Hargesy 19
Harlston 3
Harman, Harmon 11,46
Harmanson 4,14,21
Harper 42,46
Harris 1,19,45
Harrison 3,14,18,23,31
Hart 33
Harvey 9,11,19
Hasnet 11
Hassard 46
Hatfield 6
Hatsall (?) 19
Hatton 9
Havild (?) 41
Hawkes 33
Hawkins, Hawking 13, 19,23,35,46
Hawthorne 25
Hayden, Haydin 11
Hayes, Hays 11,13,19,23
Haymond 6
Haynes 11,18
Hazard 18
Heale 19
Heard 2
Hedgeman 15
Helmes 31
Helpin 2
Helmsby 10
Henderson 3,10
Henley 10
Henry 13
Herbert 2
Hetlig 47
Hewbanck 42 (Eubanks?)
Hewes 19
Hewitt 34
Hill 2,3,11,35,36,37, 41
Hilliard 1
Hillyer 2
Hinde 11
Hines, Heines 3,10,18

INDEX TO COUNTY COURT NOTE-BOOK. VOLUME V.

Hite 23,31
Hixon 42
Hobbs 2,19
Hobson 3
Hodge 42
Hodson 2,25
Hogg 3
Holbrook 15
Holden 19,36
Holland 1
Hollingsworth 23,30,46
Hollis 34
Holt 23
Hook 37
Hooper 2
Hopham 19
Hopkins 3,11,39,42
Hord,Hoard 23,38
Hore 15
Horner 9,10,18
Hornsher (?) 19
Horsmandine 19
Hough 6
Houston 2
Howell 29
Hudlen 46
Hudson 37,46
Huffe 3
Huffington 14
Hugbin 46
Hughbey 46
Hughes 3,11,39
Hull 11,29,46
Humphrey,Humphries,23,42
Hunt 14,38,43
Hunter 22
Huntly 3
Husdon 11
Huskly 19
Huston 37
Hutton 19
Hyatt 10
Hynson 2
Imlay 23
Ingram 3
Ireland 23
Irvine 15
Isaac 39
Isdall 44
Jackson 3,9,10,11,22,26,29,34,39
Jaines 15
James 3,19,23
Jane 19
Jarrell 11
Jaull(?) 29
Jeffers 3
Jelliby 19
Jenkins 5,18,19
Jenman 17
Jennings 15,46
Jenny 11
Jephs 18
Jeremie 19
Jerman 17
Jervis 2
Jess 11
Jewitt,Juitt 1,6
Jillson 47
Johannes 18
Johns 34
Jonson,Johnson 3,6,11,14,18,21,23,26,33,43
Johnston 30,45
Jones,Joanes 2,3,11,17,19,26,30,31,34,38,43
Jordan 1,17,18,38
Joyner 3
Juniper 11
Keene,Kene 18
Kemp 42
Kemplin 47
Kendall 1,27,39,42,43
Kenland 18
Kennebrew 26
Kennedy 3,14,22,38 (see Cannada)
Kennett 34
Kent 3,39
Keyes 19
Kimbar (?) 10
Kimberlin 46
Kincaid 26
King 3,10,19
Kirke 3,18
Kirkley 34
Kirton 10,21
Kiser 5
Kitchen 10
Knight 5,19
Knott 27
Know 15
Knox 5,15,38
Lacy 3
Ladely 6
Lafferty 15
Lancaster 26,29,33
Lang 42
Langfort 34
Lanier 15
Large 11
Larratt 11
Latham 11
Latta 23
Laughland 34
Lawes 3
Lawrence 14,30
Leadom 6
Leaper 6
Lee 3,11,18,38,42
Leeson 3
Lenonton 7
Lepley 47
Lewellin 3
Lewis 3,10,19,29,30,39,46,47
Lightfoot 23
Lilborne 3
Linton 3
Lipscomb 13,30
Lissum 1
Litchfield 14
Littleton 6,35
Lively 1

INDEX TO COUNTY COURT NOTE-BOOK. VOLUME V.

Loan 46
Lloyd 25,29,30
Lock 19
Logan 23
Long 3,14,19,34
Longman 11
Lousell 11
Lowe,Loe,13,19
Lowry 14
Lucas 3,14,19,30
Luckett 3
Lumpton 19
Lyelle 19
Lynard 3
Lyon 7
Lysson 1
McCauley 15
McClain,McClayne 2,6
McCloud 6
McClung 47
McConnell 6,23
McCormick 42
McCoy 6
McCracken 47
McCrory 29
McCullum 31
McCully 30
McDaniell 30
McDonald,McDaneld,6,39
Macdonnell 18
McDowell 30
McElduff 26
McElroy 6
McFawl 3
MacFerson 11
McGowan 23
McGuire 6
McIntire 6
McIntosh 5
Mackall
Mackenzie
Mackiney,Makenny 3,19
McKnight 6
Mackomack 3
McLaughlin 23
McMilliom 6
McNeil 31
McPherson 47
Machir 38
Maden 6
Madregar 37
Major 3,31
Makenie 36,42
Mallin 19
Manby 21
Manly 10
Mann 42
Manning 26
Mapp 39
Margerom 3
Markham 3
Markland 23
Marks 34
Marr 46
Marriott 11
Marshall 13,29
Martial 26
Martin 13,18,19,26,29, 47
Mason 2,3
Masters 11
Matt 2
Matthew,Mathews,18,33
Mauzy
Maverick
May
Meads
Mears,Meers,18,34
Meech 25
Meek 6
Melson 14
Mercer 38
Mercy 14
Meridith 19
Meriker 14
Merrick 3
Merriwether 31,38
Merry 13,31
Merryman 34
Messurier le 1
Metcalf,Madcalf 6
Mezell (?) 34
Michael 1,27,35,43,46
Michell,Mickell 3,11,34
Milby 14
Miles 10
Miller 3,6,11,18,19,25, 29
Mills 1,2,19
Milnor 28,37,45
Molton 19
Monroe,Munroe 9,10,18
Montgomery 6
Moody 19
Moore 11,19,22,26,35,46
Morgan 3,19
Morrah (see Murragh)
Morris,Morrice 3,11,19, 31
Morrison 22
Morse 19
Morton 18
Mosely 1
Moses 19
Moss 3,26
Moltram 11
Mountjoy 10
Moyses 3
Munday 19
Munroe,(see Monroe)
Murragh,Morrah 6,18
Murray 7,31
Murtling 6
Muse 17
Musgrove 6,23
Muter 23,38
Myers 13
Nailor 6
Neale 18,45
Neasley 6
Needham 18
Neese 47
Nelson 7,10,14,31
Netherland 38
Neuter (?) 38
Nevell 34
Newbry 22
Newburne 11

INDEX TO COUNTY COURT NOTE-BOOK. VOLUME V.

Newman 11,38
Newport 6
Newton 10
Nicholson 2,14,19,26,41
Nihil 35
Nixon 42
Norcot 11
Norcross 47
Norgood 19
Norris 6
Northam 35
Norton 19
Nourse,Norse 23
Nutter 2
Oben 46
O'Dear 6
Odger 9
Ogilvie 38
Ogle 23
O'Kelly 11
Olcott 26
Oldis 6
Oldson 34
Oliver 38
Onered (?) 18
Onions 14
Oron 6
Orrick 2
Osborne,Osbrin 6,34
Ossester 26
O'Sullivan 3
Otter 6
Oulson 34
Overton 31,38
Owen 2,30
Owings 38
Padey 19
Padgett 42
Page 3,19
Paget 42
Paine 2,3
Pake 41
Palmer 25,28,37,45
Pamer 6
Pannill 34
Parke,Parkes 11,19,23,43
Parker 11,19,21,30
Parnell 29
Parrish 18
Parry 6,19
Parsons 2,3
Patriarke 11
Patterson 11,37
Patton 42
Payton 3,17,19,21
Peach 42
Peale,Peele 27
Peane 19
Pearce,Peirce 11,26
Peck 41
Pendergrass 31
Penfax,Penfack 1,11
Pennell 43
Perkins 38
Perrin 3
Perry 11,19
Persephers 11
Person 39
Peter 11
Peterson 6,23
Pettris 3
Phillips 10,39
Phillpot 2
Pickett 19,30,38,46
Pierpoint 34
Pigg 11
Pinner 2
Piper 2
Pitt 45
Plaine 3
Plummer 46
Poise 3
Polson 10
Pomfrett 11
Pond 3
Poole 16
Pope 3,17,23,34,39
Poppey 11
Port 19
Porter 22,30,33
Potter 19,25
Potts 38
Poulson 7
Powell 2,18,19,31,
34,35,38
Power 18
Powes 19
Poynter 34
Prather 38
Pratt 10,11,38
Preason 25
Preata(?) 31
Preston 6,11
Prewitt 23
Price 6,10,19,34,38
Prickett (?) 11
Prissey 34
Pritchard 11,46
Pritchett 10
Proby 11
Pugh 6
Pumphrey 34
Purser 19
Purviance 38
Pusey 29
Pyecroft 10
Quick 6
Quisenberry 13,38
Radly 3
Ralls 15
Ralston 6
Ramage 6
Ramsey 2,6
Randall,Randle 6,15,23
Rankin 26
Ranny 25
Ratcliffe 34
Rattican 42
Raymond 19
Rayne 19
Read,Reed 6,19,27,29
Really (?) 18
Rector 38
Redick 6
Redman 9,19
Reekes 19
Reeves 19
Remey 10

INDEX TO COUNTY COURT NOTE-BOOK. VOLUME V.

Renison 11
Renny 29
Reyman 19
Reynolds 11,33
Rice 6,10
Richards 11,31
Richardson 25,33
Riching 19
Richman 10
Riden 3
Ridgely 38
Rigbee 11
Rigson 19
Risdon,Risden 3,25
Rittenhouse 6
Roach 34
Roberts 3,6,11
Robertson 1,22
(see Robinson)
Robins,Robbins 4,26
Robinson 1,3,6,18,23,25,
26,27,29,30,33,35,42
(see Robertson)
Rodman 11
Rodolphus 3
Roe 10,19
Roebuck 31
Rogers,Rodger 2,6,26,29
Rolfe 19
Rookes 3
Rookesby 19
Rose 11,42
Rosier,Rosyer 1,10
Ross,2,5,6,34
Routt 15
Rowland 15,18
Rowley 14
Rowles 29
Rowse 3
Ruble 22
Ruffner 22
Russell 26,29
Rutland 11,19
Ryan 25
Ryding 27
St.Claire 38
Sadler 3
Salikeld(Salkeld?)29
Sallitt 19
Sanders 11,18
Sands 3
Sanford 10,17
Sarrell 41
Satton 11
Saul 29
Saunders 2
Savage 4,27,34,41,42
Sawyer 19
Sayers 23
Saywell 1
Scarborough,Scarburgh
14,29,36,39,43,45
Scellson(?) 19
Schoolfield 10,15
Scott 4,11,29,31
Scottell 18
Seale 3
Sears 26
Sek 34
Selby 29
Sellick 4
Selman16
Senior 3,6
Serman 10
Severne 26
Shard 42
Sharpe 3,10,15
Sharpless 29
Shaw 26
Shear 26
Sheeves 3
Shelby 13
Shelton 3
Shepherd 17,19,23
Shepard,Sheppard 33
Shields,Shiell,
Sheles 10,34,38
Shore 19
Short 3
Shrimpton 26
Shumate 42
Sidney 19
Simcock 29
Simmes,Simnes,5,26
Simpson,Sympson 2,3,6,
10,11,18,19,23,25,26,
33,34,38,45,46
Smithson,Smythson 3,26
Smythe 6,18,33,34
Snead 26
Soccohack (?) 3
Solly 1,10
Solway 6
Somerset 19
South 17
Southall 38
Southerne 3,29
Sparke 11
Spear 6
Speed 3,13
Spike 21
Spence 18
Spencer 2,17,18
Spicer 3
Spilman 38
Spoldin 23
Sprathin 3
Spry 18
Squires 18
Stafford 46
Staly 10
Staple 3
Standford 10
Standridge 45
Stanley 25
Stanwick 31
Staple 3
Steadman 19
Stean 6
Steed 19
Steele 10,22
Sterritt 6
Steven 31
Stevenson 6,45
Stewart 6,23
Stilt 3
Stith 19
Stockley 43

INDEX TO COUNTY COURT NOTE-BOOK. VOLUME V.

Stockwell 3
Stoddert 30
Stokes 45
Stone 6,19,42
Stott,Stotts 4,39
Stonte 19
Strabury 10
Strain 6
Street 11
Stringer 4,25,35
Strother 16,29,30
Strill 46
Sturman 9,17
Sutherland 6
Sutton 2,17,18
Swansy 3
Swin 6
Sylvester 18
Symms 38
Symons 11
Tabirer 45
Tackerbury 1
Talbot 11
Talisfers(?)31
Tallott 19
Tally 3
Taney 2
Tankred 4,36
Tanner 11,18,31
Tantor 26
Tarry 3,29
Tatham 29
Tatsall 19
Taylor 2,6,11,17,29,30, 31,35,38,43
Tazewell 21
Teal 10.
Tebbs 17,23
Teigue 4
Tennant 38
Terrell 11
Terry 3
Thomas 3,4,10,26,27,34
Thompkins 34
Thompson,Thomson 15,17, 19,22,46
Thornley 23
Thornton 29
Thorpe 3
Tilbury 3
Tilfaire 4
Tiller 3
Tillghman 4
Tillory 17
Tilton 19
Todel 18
Tomlinson 42
Tompson 35
Top 1
Totton 6
Towers 34
Towles 35
Towling 6
Townsend 26
Traford 29
Traughton 27
Traveller 41
Travers 10
Treakle 6
Trennis 11
True 1
Trumbell 23
Tucker 9,27
Tudman 19
Tully 26
Turverville 17
Turk 26
Turmon 26
Turner 18,19,23,33
Turnifall 1
Twitty 23
Tuyman 31
Tymouth 11
Tyson 3
Upshott,Upshutt 2,3
Underwood 13
Vance 26
Vanderville 1
Van Hamell 4
Vanmetre 31
Vanner 11
Vanswerigen 18
Vaulx 3,27
Vazey 11
Veazy 11
Vermillion 30
Vernon 29
Viccars 17
Vincent 3
Virgin 6
Visen 34
Von Heer 7
Waddilow 3
Waddison 3
Wade 37,45
Wagoman 6
Wagstaff 26
Walke 11,19
Walker 3,6,18,26,27
Waller 3,15,26
Walling 6
Walliver 19
Walter,Walters 3,19
Walthall 3
Ward 1,21,29,33,46
Warden 6
Warder 11
Ware 38
Warley 29
Warner 11
Warren 3
Warton 19
Warwick 10
Washbrow 19
Washington 17,18
Waterford 3
Waterhouse 6
Waters 34,35
Waterson (?) 3
Watkins 10,19,38
Watt,Watts 1,3,6,19,29,47
Watson 3,22,25,26,33,36,47
Wayman 34
Wearen 22
Weaver 3
Webb 17,18
Webster 10,34
Welborn,Welburn 26,27,34

INDEX TO COUNTY COURT NOTE-BOOK. VOLUME V.

Welch 31
Wells 6
Wenn,Wenne 11,19
Wesgate 3
West 18,26,27,34,45
Westcoat 17
Westerhouse 25
Wheatley 21,46
Wheeler 3,11
Whiston 17
Whitacre (?) 42
Whitman,Whitmon 26,46
Whitson 19
Whittey 1
Whittington 36,37,45
Wick (?) 39
Wiggins 6
Wilcoxon 2
Wild 6,11
Wildy 3
Wilkins 38
Wilkinson 1,19
Willard 11
Willet 19
Williams 3,5,6,11,14,
15,19,21,22,26,30,
34,38,39,46
Williamson 3,6,10
Willis 11
Willmott 25
Willoughby 6
Wills 3
Willy, Wylly 3,25
Wilsford 18
Wilson 3,5,6,11,19,26,
37,42,45
Wilton 6
Winn 19,29,38,42
Winterne 19
Wise,Wyse 2,14,29
Withers 3
Wolmsley 3
Wood,Woods 3,6,29,35,42
Woodbridge 19
Woodhouse 3
Woodington 3
Woodson 39
Woodard,Woodward 5,13
Woolner 3
Woory 41
Work 6
Wotton 11
Wright 2,3,6,10,18,19,
25,29,34
Wynkoop 38
Yager 47
Yardley 21,27,35
Yarrett 3
Yeer 2
Young 2,3,6,18,29,38
Yowell 3,18,47
Zabetrene 7

More than one entry on the same page is indicated by underscoring.

The

County Court Note-Book

A Little Bulletin of History and Genealogy

February, 1927.

Vol. VI, No. 1

THE ANCESTRY OF COL. JOHN DONELSON OF TENNESSEE, EXPLORER AND PIONEER*

The limited space of the NOTE-BOOK will not permit even a brief sketch of the life of Col. JOHN DONELSON, but only the presentation of such facts as are found in the county records, identifying his family and that of his wife, establishing their origin in Maryland and Virginia, and their standing as persons of education and property, and even of historical importance. Col. DONELSON'S grandfather, as a member of the first presbytery in America, appears in Presbyterian archives, and his name is recorded upon a memorial tablet in Philadelphia, as one of the seven ministers comprising that presbytery. One of DONELSON'S aunts was the wife of the Rev. William Stewart, of Somerset county, Maryland, the most prominent of his denomination in the section which is now Somerset county, while through his wife and the wife of his uncle, Samuel Davis (a Justice of the Sussex, Delaware, court) there was a connection with the Rev. Francis Makemie . . . a complicated connection difficult to show, except by chart, and probably the basis for one of the numerous misstatements as to the family of DONELSON'S wife.

The offices held by Col. DONELSON in the Virginia counties of Halifax and Pittsylvania, will be touched upon by reference to court entries. The account of his remarkable journey to the present city of Nashville, Tennessee, by way of the Holston, Tennessee, Ohio and Cumberland rivers, will be found in his Journal, published in Ramsey's Annals of Tennessee. The original manuscript is in the possession of the Tennessee Historical Society. Histories of Virginia and of the southwest frontier will give the details of the Donelson Line, which he ran between Virginia territory and the Indian country.

Col. JOHN DONELSON was the son of Capt. JOHN DONELSON, who was son of PATRICK DONELSON, both of Somerset county, Maryland. PATRICK DONELSON'S wife was JEAN, her family name unknown. Capt. JOHN DONELSON'S wife was CATHERINE DAVIS, the daughter of Rev. SAMUEL DAVIS, of Snow Hill, Maryland, one of "Makemie's young men," and pastor of one of Makemie's five churches. He was, as mentioned above, one of the seven members of the first presbytery. Rev. SAMUEL DAVIS was also a "chirurgeon."

The following references identify the DONELSON and the DAVIS families, and will be followed by the identification of the family of RACHEL STOCKLEY, Col. DONELSON'S wife. These references give substantially all that the civil records show. Three sets of church records are lacking; two destroyed by fire, the fate of the third, unknown.

PATRICK DONNELSON, of Som. cty, from James Caldwell, Jr., 50 acres of Pharsalia ("Pharsila") on the south side of Kowastico[?] Branch. Consideration 1750 lbs. tobacco. 12 July 1721. Som., Md. IK-196.

PATRICK DONELSON, of Som. cty, Md., from Robert Givan and wife Mary, same. 165 acres called Flowerfield. Consideration 4,400 lbs. tobacco. 30 June 1721. Som. cty. IK-197.

PATRICK DONOLDSON (Donaldson) of Stepney Psh, Som. cty, Md. Will. (Signed.)
Son JOHN, large Bible and silver signet; two grandchildren, George and Patrick Mckean, estate left to them by their father and mother; son-in-law Mr. William Stewart and wife Catherine, an equal part of personal estate until they have as much as my dau. Jane McKean dec'd hath had; care of grandchildren to wife, JEAN, and Mr. William Stewart and his wife Catherine. Wife, JEAN. Mr. William Stewart, extr. Wit. Mary x Greer, George x Greer, Robert Givan. Annap. Wills, xviii-455. 29 Sept 1725-2 Nov 1725.

Mr. PATRICK DONELSON, Inventory. *Kindred, JEAN* DONELSON and Kathrin Steward. Jean Donelson makes oath. Annap. Inv. xi-385. 5 Feby 1725. [Note: It is probable, unless this was intended for JOHN DONELSON, that the latter was out of the country, and that Jean Donelson the widow, is set down as one of "kindred."]

JANE (Jean) DONALDSON, extx of PATRICK DONALDSON, late of Somerset. [No information.] Annap. Accts, vii-418. 20 June 1726. Also vii-49. 4 June 1726. (Patrick "being the extr of Jean McKean, both late of Somerset.")

That PATRICK DONELSON had also a son PATRICK is shown by the will of JEAN McKEAN, daughter of PATRICK, Sr., who pre-deceased her father.

JEAN McKEAN, of Greenhill, Somerset cty, Md. Will.
Two sons, George and Patrick; extrs, father, PATRICK DONELSON and bro. PATRICK DONELSON. Wit: J. Donelson, Katherine Donelson. Annap. Wills, xviii-332. 22 Mch 1723-25 Nov 1724.

There appears to have been some close connection, probably relationship, between the DONELSONS and the GIVENS. So far, no explanation has been found. It seems likely that they were intermarried in Ireland. In 1723 (Md. Wills v-164) PATRICK DONELSON, Sr., was one of the overseers and wit. to the will of JAMES GIVAN. JANE McKEAN and KATHERINE STEWARD (Stewart) were also witnesses. ROBERT GIVAN, as shown above, was one of the witnesses to PATRICK DONELSON'S will.

(*To be continued.*)

MARRIAGES BY INFERENCE*

(From the records of Georgia and the Carolinas)

Maj. SAMUEL ASHE and SARAH MERRICK. Before 22 Mch 1787. N. Han. N. C. H-470.

WILLIAM BRUMMETT and JANE BURRIS, dau. of Mrs. Kitty Burriss. Before 21 July 1790. Anderson, S. C. A-175.

ARNOLD JOHN BASSET and ZILPHA PARKER, dau. of Thomas. Before 19 Nov 1757. Onslow, N. C. (Loose leaf of deed book.)

MARTIN BOWLES and SALLY EMBRY, dau. of John. See record of 11 Dec 1843. Madison, Ga. B-10.

WILLIAM BRIERLY and RUTH JONES[?] dau. of Margaret Jones, of Bath cty, N. C. Before 13 Mch 1744. Beaufort, N. C. ii-433.

THOMAS BLOUNT and the widow of Joseph SCOTT. About 5 Feby 1686. N. C. H-G. i-139.

JOSEPH BLOUNT and SARAH DURANT. Before 3 Aug 1745. N. C. H. G. i-118.

AARON BROWN, of Jefferson cty, Ohio, and ANN STANTON, dau. of Benjamin. Before 31st 3d mo 1803. Carteret, N. C. O-366.

WILLIAM COOK and ELIZA BARRINGTON [ELIZA:? i.e. ELIZABETH?] eldest dau. of Sally Barrington, Marriage contract. 17 Nov 1793. [It is uncertain whether this date is 1791 or 1793.] Glynn, Ga. R-434.

WILLIAM W. CLARKE and SARAH BAILEY, wid. of Richard, of West Florida, dec'd. Before 22 Oct 1804. Richmond, Ga. K-4.

JOSEPH SCOT CRAY and FRANCES . . . [?] Marriage contract. Date not found. Onslow, N. C.

CHARLES W. CHRISTIAN and NANCY RUFF. 6 June 1807. Elbert, Ga. Vol. ix, wills, &c.

JESSE CANNON and FANNY HARDESTY, dau. of Joseph. Before 1 Apr 1795. Carteret, N. C. N-101.

ISHMAEL DUNN and LUCY G. TALLAFERRO [*sic*] dau. of Warren. Before Nov, 1825. Oglethorpe, Ga. Minutes Probate Ct.

ROBERT "TOWN'D" DADE, of K. Geo. cty, Va. and ELIZABETH PARKER, of Carteret cty, N. C. Marriage contract. 15 June 1773. Carteret, N. C. H1-44.

JOHN EVANS and JEAN BURRIS, dau. of Mrs. Kitty Burriss. Before 21 July 1790. Anderson, S. C. A-175.

JACOB FOUNTAIN probably m. MARY JAMES, one of the daus. of Mathew James. Before Aug 1765. Onslow, N. C. vol. D, p . . .

SOLOMON GROVER and Miss HANNAH ELIZABETH POULIDGE, both of Effingham cty. Mar. Li. 7 Oct 1791. Eff., Ga.

JOHN GROVENSTINE and Miss SARAH SEIGLER. Mar. Li. 30 Apr 1793. Eff., Ga.

JAMES GREEN and ROSE WILLIAMSON, the wid. of John. Before 7 Jany 1734. Onslow, N. C.

. . . GLENN and JEAN EVANS, wid. of John. She was the dau. of Mrs. Kitty Burris. Before 21 July 1790. Anderson, S. C. A-175.

JOHN GLENN and CHARLOTTE EMBRY, dau. of John. See record 11 Dec 1843. Madison, Ga. B-10.

JACOB GARRETT and PATSEY HARDEN, dau. of Mark. Before 7 Sept 1818. Warren, Ga. Minutes Ct of Ordinary.

JOHN HORNBUCKLE and the extx of Jesse Carter. Before 18 Mch 1805. Greenville, S. C. Ct Minutes.

THOMAS RASBERRY CLARK HAMILTON, of Savannah, Chatham cty, Mcht, and MARY DAVIS, Sp., dau, of John. Marriage settlement. 1 Apr 1797. Chatham, Ga. R-259. See also p. 408 . . . HAMILTON m. ANN RASBERRY, dau. of Thomas and Ann, of Savannah. They had a son, Thomas, who m. Mary . . .

JAMES MILLIKINS, late of Edgecomb Precinct, Esq., and ELIZABETH JOYNER, dau. of Joseph. Before Feby Ct, 1737. Halifax, N. C. Court Minutes.

RICHARD PITTS and MARY GRANT, dau. of Alexander. [Alexander died about 1738.] Before 12 July 1763. Onslow, N. C.

MARYLAND'S NEXT OF KIN**

CHRISTOPHER COMBES and MARY COMBES; inv. Thomas Comes, St. Mary's cty, 26 Oct 1721. vi-131.

JOHN THOMPSON and ELIZABETH GRIGGS; inv. James Thompson, St. Mary's cty, 25 Sept 1721. vi-134.

PHILIP CONER and JOHN CONER[?] Inv. Moses Owen of Som. cty. 20 May 1721. vi-135.

ISAAC WILLIAMS and MARY PATRICK; inv. of Jane Rich, Som. cty. 1 July 1721. vi-136.

MARY POPE; inv. Thomas Oxford of Som. cty. 15 July 1721. vi-138.

NATHANIEL WALLER and TABITHA SMITH; inv. Nathaniel Ratcliffe, Sr., of Som. cty. 18 May 1721. vi-139.

THOMAS HEPBOURN[?] inv. John Kersly of Kent cty. [No date.] vi-141.

[SARAH WYAT, "one of the greatest creditors." No kin?] inv. John Butler of Kent cty. 2 Aug 1721. vi-142.

JAMES WILLIAMSON and JAMES HARRIS; inv. Mr. James Rae, of Kent cty. 5 June 1721. vi-144.

JAMES BREWARD, PETER NORTHCUTT, HUGH MATTHEWS. [It is uncertain whether Breward and Matthews are kin.] Inv. Ann Heading, of Kent cty, 11 Aug 1721. vi-151.

THOMAS MUMFORD, JNO. JARMON, HENRY JARMON and THOMAS MAREY, "nearest of kin and greatest creditors," Inv. Truitt Jarman, of Som. cty. 5 Oct 1721. vi-154.

D. PEARCE and GID'N PEARCE Creditors. "As nearest of Kin considering the Estate is Left to our Mother we are Content with the . . . appraisers." Inv. William Pearce, of Kent cty. 29 June 1721. vi-155.

JAMES SMITH and CHARLES SMITH; inv. Sarah Juers[?] of Kent cty. vi-162.

ANNE POPE, wf of John, admx. No kindred. Inv. Francis Joyce, of Som. cty. 13 Aug 1721. vi-167.

WM. TURPIN, JNO. WILLIAMS, CHARLES REVELL, ESTHER CURTIS, approve; inv. James Curtis, of Som. cty. 13 May 1721. vi-169.

JOHN POPE; inv. of John Pope of Som. cty. 20 July 1721. vi-172.

SAM'LL MILES and WILLIAM PLANNER; inv. Alice Miles, Som. cty. 24 June 1721. vi-174.

RICHARD SMITH and THOMAS HARVEY; inv. Henry Johnson, of Calv. cty. 27 July 1721. vi-186 or 187.

ELIZABETH WILLIAMS makes oath, no kin given; inv. Hugh Williams of Calv. cty. 6 June 1721. vi-186 or 187.
WILLIAM FASSITT; inv. John Fawsett, Sr., Som. cty. 4 Aug 1721. vi-188.
MATTHEW DUTTON; inv. Ledia Oeane [probably Owen?] 18 May 1721. vi-191.
ELIZABETH REED, admx. No kin given. Inv. Pearce Reed, of Som. cty. 29 Apr 1721. vi-191.
NATHL WALE and TABITHA SMITH approve. Inv. Nathaniel Rackliffs, Jr., Som. cty. 13 June 1721. vi-193.

FAMILIES OF THE EASTERN SHORE CUSTIS OF VIRGINIA

(*Continued from December*)

WILLIAM CUSTIS, continued:

A deed of WILLIAM CUSTIS, conveying 300 acres in Northampton, mentions Edward Sacker, the late father of William and Francis Sacker. (Acco, 16 May 1672. iv-109.) [See note on page 4.] CUSTIS is a vestryman, 4 Mch 1672. (Acco, iv-193.) He is a witness to John Stokely's will. (Probated Acco, 18 Aug 1673. iv-222.) Mr. WILLIAM CUSTIS is commissioned Justice. (Acco, 7 Nov 1673. v-18.) Capt. WILLIAM CUSTIS' list of tithes. (Acco, 1674. v-193.) Power to Tabitha Browne [whom his brother married] (Acco, 26 Apr 1675. v-288.)

Capt. WILLIAM CUSTIS and Mr. EDWARD REVELL petition in behalf of the "orphants" of John Stokely, dec'd, agt John Stratton; Stratton being, it is alleged, about to depart; he is ordered to give bond. (Acco, 16 Nov 1675. v-329.) Capt. WILLIAM CUSTIS is att'y for Mrs. Tabitha Browne. (Acco, 16 Nov 1675. v-329.) As coextrs of John Stokely. dec'd, CUSTIS and Mr. Edward Revell file a petition. Stratton [who m. the widow of Stokely] is ordered to give security. (Acco, 17 Jany 1675. v-360.)

Capt. WILLIAM CUSTIS is to take tithes, Hungars Parish. (Acco, 20 Apr 1676. vii-6.) WILLIAM "CUSTUS" gives a cow and a calf to the two sons of Richard Franklin, Thomas and Richard. (Acco, 12 Aug 1678. vi-113.) He is Coroner, 2 Sept 1678. (Acco, vi-14.) WILLIAM CUSTIS, from Charles Leatherbury, of Onancock, a messuage in Onancock called the Schoolhouse. Ben. Eyre and Ambrose White, wit. (Acco, 18 Mch 1678. vi-149.) Power from John Tilney. Wit. John Custis, Jr., and Charles Holden. (Acco, 15 Dec 1679. vi-180.) He was still Coroner in 1679. (Acco, viii-161.) He appears on the Rent Roll of 1680 as owning 900 acres. (L. C. 1391.) A Justice, 6 July 1680. (Acco, vi-221.) Had six tithes same year. (Acco, vi-210.)

Capt. WILLIAM CUSTIS enters himself as security for his son, Mr. HENRY CUSTIS, in a case before the court. (Acco, 17 Dec 1681. viii-278.) Gets ctf for 700 acres; head rights: Barker, Edrington, Jarmain, Senior, Malloney, Norman, Sisson, Sluse[?] Crippin, Elizabeth Lange, Chambers, Elizabeth Boorne [?] and three negroes. (Acco, 17 Feby 1681. viii-285.) He is guardian for the orphans of Edward Sacker. (Acco, 3 Jany 1682. viii-327. See also 19 Feby 1682. ix-2.) See also 17 Oct 1682, where he appears as gdn of William Sacker, son of Frances Sacker. (Acco, viii-319.) [See note on page 4.]

WILLIAM CUSTIS, Gent., of Accomack, gets power from JOHN CUSTIS, Sr., of Northampton cty, Mcht. (William Waters associated.) (N-n, 20 May 1684. xiv-95.) CUSTIS gets ctf for 250 acres. Head rights: James Burrell, Peter Burnly, Ann Johnson. (Acco, 16 Mch 1686. ix-111.) Brings Indian boy to have age adjudged. (Acco, 11 May 1686. ix-86.) CUSTIS has five tithables, 1691. (Acco, ix-227.) In 1692 has six tithables. Capt. WILLIAM CUSTIS' wife was JOAN, the 19 Sept 1693. (Acco, x-107.) He was a church warden 1695. (Acco, x-152.) In 1714, WILLIAM CUSTIS' wife was BRIDGETT. (See Acco, xiv-82, also xv-2.) [There is a gap in the Editor's notes of WILLIAM CUSTIS, between 1695 and 1714, and there is no record of the death of JOAN CUSTIS or the marriage of BRIDGETT CUSTIS. It may be possible to fill the break in the dates later, and some will may give the family name of the second wife.]

In 1719, WILLIAM CUSTIS, Gent., conveys to William Black, 200 acres on the seaboard. Witnesses are THOMAS CUSTIS and Tabitha Bagwell. In 1718, 4 Nov., CUSTIS' wife BRIDGETT, appears as his attorney. (Acco, xvii-24.) Col. WILLIAM CUSTIS receives a bond from William Hope: "WHEREAS the above named Collonel WILLIAM CUSTIS upon the Espousals had & Celebrated between the above bound William Hope & JOANNA MARY, the dau. of the sd Collonell WILLIAM CUSTIS, who is now lately deceased" .. &c., &c. The daughter of JOANNA-MARY HOPE is mentioned and called JOANNA-CUSTIS HOPE. [Hyphenating by Editor.] (Acco, 6 Aug 1718. xv-55.) BRIDGETT CUSTIS, wife of WILLIAM, releases dower in land. (Acco, 1 Sept 1719, xvi-86.) WILLIAM CUSTIS, of Accomack cty, power to Capt. Mitchell Scarburgh to make over all the lands, &c., that he, WILLIAM CUSTIS, "hath given to his dau. BRIDGET CUSTIS." (Acco, 6 Aug 1724. xvi-214.) This is followed by a deed of gift, with reversion to JOANNA-CUSTIS HOPE, and then to wife BRIDGET. Action is brought by Frances Norton against CUSTIS and wife BRIDGET. (Acco, 9 Dec 1725. xix- . . .)

The will of WILLIAM CUSTIS, aged and weak. Wf Bridgett, slaves and 200 acres; dau. Bridget all lands except what he gives wife; granddaughter Joanna Custis Hope (under 18) two of the slaves should wife die, and 200 acres; also the slaves which he lent Joanna Mary Hope. Dau. Bridget, extx. Wit. Robt Coleburne, Wm. Burton, Charles McClester, Will: Wood. 27 Nov 1725. Presented by Mrs. Bridgett Custis, 6 Apr 1726; Probate July, 1726. (See Acco, xvi-262, and xix-52.) The inventory returned and ordered recorded 4 Sept 1728. (Acco, xvi-338.) [Note: the record states that Mrs. BRIDGETT CUSTIS and BRIDGETT CUSTIS, Jr., extrs, present the will 5 July 1726, the heir-at-law being present.]

WILLIAM CUSTIS was born about 1633. (See dep'ns 16 Feby 1686, and 17 Dec 1681. Acco., ix-110 and viii-278.)

He m. (1) or (2) JOAN . . .
He m. (2) or (3) BRIDGETT . . . . [See note on p. 4.] BRIDGET, who survived him, m. (2) William Arbuckle, ab. 27 May 1729.

His children, as shown by the records, were:
- EDWARD;
- HENRY, b. ab. 1657; d. 1698-1708; m. Rachel Revell. who d. 1719;
- BRIDGET, died unm. 1727;
- JOANNA-MARY, who m. before 1718, William Hope.

The County Court Note-Book

An every-other-monthly devoted mainly to abstracts from County Court records, prior to 1800.

MILNOR LJUNGSTEDT, Editor and Publisher.
Bethesda, Route 10, Maryland.

Published six times a year. Subscription, two dollars, in advance; must begin with the year.

FEBRUARY, 1927 **Whole**
Vol. VI., No. 1 **No. 32**

TO CARCASSONNE

The Editor has adopted a motto. It might well have been "Hitch your wagon to a star," or the similar "*Ad astra,*" but the Editor feels no particular drawing to the chilly spaces of the universe, preferring the comfortable medieval or even mid-Victorian. For those who have not read or have forgotten the poem, the Editor will explain that there was a man who lived ten leagues (or ten miles) from Carcassonne. All his life he had dreamed of Carcassonne, the wonderful; all his life had dreamed of going there, yet never went. So the Editor has set the towers of Carcassonne just beyond the NOTE-BOOK . . . and other things.

The Editor has discovered that she comes in touch with a number of her subscribers through the Editorial page. This is very comforting, in spite of a clear inner consciousness that another number think it a great waste of time and space. The Editor can hear them now, with her mind's ear, and they are perfectly right. But you understand, those who do read the "Editorial column," that while the Editor never really tires of 1660 or 1680 doings, the marriages and the migrations, yet they are mere facts, and the state of mind they induce, the philosophy and far-reaching thought has to find expression somehow. There were so many of those folk who came into court and went out of court; went on their little journeys and never returned; went home to their beds and never got up . . . so many of them . . . and they have been a long time dead. The shades of the forgotten wives and the little children ("d. y." and "d. s. p.") hang about one. "*What was my name, my family?*" asks the eighteen-year old bride, who died 300 years ago. No one knows. Yet through perhaps half of such swept the eternal life that goes on all about us of to-day. Races, tribes, groups, are fundamentally interesting, but the individual and not the aggregate was the link.

The worship of one's ancestry is so old a thing, it must be part of us. The bragging about one's ancestry is as natural as breathing. Evidently, only fine cultivation and the losing oneself in vaster matters has enabled some here and there to appear calmly indifferent. The Editor doesn't think that any one really is indifferent.

This reaching back is at times very pathetic. Who and what was I a thousand years ago?

In a recent Saturday Evening Post is a story called The Viking's Daughter . . . not a very good title. It is a clever story and is recommended for its basis of truth. The Editor is pretty sure she has been on that island which the author calls "Mud Island," . . . and she has met those people up there. They are remarkable for their simplicity and candor. It is quite true about the education. The waitress, whom we called Miss X . . ., was a school teacher, graduate of some fine normal school, and in addition to her table duties, either she or her co-worker, who maintained the establishment, had coached the young son of one of the boarders in the Latin in which he was deficient. What particularly impressed the Editor was the democracy and the dignity of the coastal people, and the quaint and precise English of the children. The independence of this or that village in everyday matters is amusingly shown by one fish factory community. When the Editor was there it kept *three* "times." It kept standard time; true time, and "fish" time. This was long before "daylight saving" . . . but in the summer, when the fish are "running" and the factories open, the factory whistle blows twenty-five minutes before standard time. The population will not change its hour of rising, so the factory changes the time.

Such nice, friendly letters! A bit of praise, a little flattery now and then . . . helpful to the best of men. The Editor forgets that she was born a pessimist (was she? Or was she an early crushed optimist?) and that she believed herself turning into a hard-boiled cynic. This is just a word of appreciation to the writers. They do help!

Errata:

The NOTE-BOOK for December has a serious omission in the list of MARYLAND COUNTIES. The list will possibly be reprinted, meanwhile the county of KENT should be inserted. There is a difference of opinion as to the date of its erection. The date usually accepted is 1642. The first four lines of the list should read:

ST. MARY'S, 1637; temporarily called *Potomac*, 1654-1658; Kent, 1640 [1642?] Note: as a hundred of St. Mary's there had been a sheriff for the Isle of Kent since 1637.
(*Kent*) See Queen Anne's and Talbot.

The name "DIXOB" on lines 43 and 44, page 42, DECEMBER NOTE-BOOK, should be DIXON.

The following are additional to a list of Frederick cty, Md. orphans, published in 1923 and 1924.
SARAH HUNT, of age Nov 1769.
MICH'L HATCHETORN, of age Feby 1775.
JAMES HARE, of age Mch 1776.
JONATHAN HACKETT, of age Aug 1782.
OWEN HAYMOND, of age May 1779.
EMANUEL HUNT, of age 16 Feby 1777.

CONTINUED articles COUNTY COURT NOTE-BOOK, and the dates on which they first appeared.
MARRIAGES BY INFERENCE. Began with May, 1922.
MARYLAND'S NEXT OF KIN. Began with July, 1922.
VIRGINIA COLONISTS. This alphabetized list began with July, 1924.
MILITARY NOTES. Both COLONIAL and REVOLUTIONARY, and some later MILITIA NOTES, will appear in every issue, if possible.
SHIPS IN PORT, INTERCOUNTY and INTERCOLONIAL and COLONIAL FORENAMES, will appear in alternate issues or as space can be found for them.
EASTERN SHORE FAMILIES, in the form of a one-page supplement, began with June, 1925. This will be continued later.

Note to CUSTIS FAMILY:

Mr. Stratton Nottingham believes that WILLIAM CUSTIS had a first wife, prior to JOANNA, and that by this wife he had a daughter FRANCES, who married a SACKER. The Editor is not convinced of this, although it is possible.

ADDITIONAL NOTES
LEVIN AND LEAH GALE

(*See April, 1925.*)

LEVIN and LEAH GALE mentioned; are of Somerset cty, Md. (Acco, xix-114. 6 Aug 1728.)

LEAH GALE, wife of LEVIN GALE, joins in conveying 600 acres near Pocomoke . . . which Sarah, wife of Adam Michael, bequeathed to the aforesaid LEAH GALE . . . it having been devised by "Machael" to his wife, Sarah, in fee simple. (Acco, Va. 2 Feby 1725-24 Aug 1725. xvi-224.) LEVIN and wife, as above, same reference, acknowledge receipt from Hancock Custis, admr of Southy Littleton, brother of sd LEAH, and discharge sd Hancock and wife Mary in relation to the estate of Southy Littleton, or her brother, Southy Littleton.

THOMAS SAVAGE, of N-n, Va., Gent., and wife Esther. to LEAH GALE, wife of LEVIN GALE of Som. cty, Md.; consideration 5 sh., tract at Andua which Col. Southey Littleton bequeathed to son Southey for 2,220 acres. (Acco, xv-326, 3 July 1728.)

Attention is again invited to the advertisement on page 8, of the Maryland Marriages. This is not a publication as some readers have taken it to be, it is a collection of marriage references. These marriages are shown, as are the Marriages by Inference, by the various records of the court, perhaps authenticated would be the better word. One dollar is the very moderate charge for a search. For a full copy of the record in which the marriage is mentioned, or is logically inferred, the charge is five dollars. Considering the time and intelligence which this sort of research requires, this is a not unreasonable charge.

It is hoped that Mr. Nottingham's Accomack Marriage Bonds will be out before long. They will appear in a mimeographed pamphlet, on good quality of paper, of a convenient size for shelving, and will be securely bound in a heavy paper cover. See advertisement on p. 8.

The work of the Emery Record Preserving Company is so very well known in libraries and courthouses that it seems unnecessary to do more than mention it. There is a side to this work, however, which the Editor desires to impress upon her readers. Some of these readers have valuable family papers which through age and frequent handling, are gradually, one might say, being *dissolved*. These can be perfectly and safely restored; can be made suitable for framing, either with a backing or between glass; or can be mounted in portfolios . . . or simply bound, with covers. The Editor has seen this work and knows what can be done.

CHILLIAN and MARTIN PALMER, Charlotte cty, Va. Seventy-five dollars will be paid for their ancestry. Must be proved by civil and church records.

W. B. P. A.

TWENTY-FIVE dollars will be paid for full information as to Capt. JOHN WADE of Chester and Marcus Hook, Chester, now Delaware county, Penna. This is not JOHN WADE who inherited and bought the lands of Essex House, but a cousin. It seems to be proved that he married MARTHA ROBINSON. He had a daughter, MIRIAM, and probably a son THOMAS and perhaps JOSEPH.

Address Editor.

OCCASIONAL

ANGUISS McDONALD: this curious spelling and the form ANGUISH sometimes appear to be the equivalent of AGNES, sometimes of AGNUS. See Pr. Wm. Va., Orders [3] p. 40. 24 Feby 1756.

Mr. WILLIAM BURTON, church warden, presents persons for not abiding in the church during the time of Common prayer and preaching. Acco, Va. 5 Aug 1712. xiv-45.

WHEREAS RICHARD TIDWELL brought into Co't James, an Indian, to bee adjudged The Co'rt adjudge him a tithable by Act of Assembly and Order that hee bee listed in the list of tithables for this County. Wmld, Va. Orders, 1676-1688, p. 103.

[One of the few.] HENRY TALBOTT, Wmld cty, Va. Nun-cup. will . . . said "that JOHN RICE was a poore man & had many small children and I will give him what I have . . . " Wmld, Va. Orders, 1668-1677, f. 118. 28 Feby 1671.

"HENRY CECILL borne on his Lordships Mannor of Patuxent the 4th Nov, being Wednesday about half an hour after two o'clock in the morning A. D. 1696 and his brother twinn named ISAAC CECELL was borne half an hour after being one o'clock the same morning and they were Christened the same morning about 11 O'clock by Mr. Jones Minister of the Home Church belonging to Christ Church Parish in Calvert Co." Deeds, A, 318, Pr. Geo's cty, Md. (*Contributed.*)

[It is probable that instead of "two" the record should read twelve.]

M . . . H . . . petitions that T . . . P . . . deliver to him the indenture of A . . . D . . . formerly servant of P . . . whom H . . . bought and married, and *who is now dead.* So ordered. N-n, Va. ii-3. 6 July 1640.

INTERCOLONY and INTERCOUNTY

JAMES ANDERSON, of Halifax cty, Va.; power to son John Anderson, of Augusta cty, Va., to demand and receive rents, &c. in Somerset, Md. 24 Feby 1758. B-204.

WILLIAM BELL, Sussex cty, Penna., and wf Sarah, to Nathaniel Bell, of Accomack, land on the Matchepungo river; 250 acres, part of Nevel's [Revell's?] Neck. Acco, Va. 12 Nov 1768. Diii-603.

EDWARD HASARD, bound for England. Acco, Va. 18 May 1674. v-148.

Mr. AUGUSTINE HARMAN, Merchant of Manhattan. N-n, Va. ix-51. 1659.

ELIZABETH, JAMES and THOMAS HILL, of Montgomery cty, Ky., and WILLIAM HILL, of Clark cty, Ky. to William and Peter Deckert, Wash'n cty, Va. 10 Apr 1801. ii-396.

JOHN JOHNSON, of Kingsale, in the Kingdom of Ireland, mariner; power. Wmld cty, Va. 27 Apr 1670. Orders, 1668-1677, f. 109.

THOMAS JACOB, of Rochester, Kent cty, England. Gives negro Susan to Mrs. Bridget Seaverne and her little son, John. N-n, Va. 29 July 1642. ii-276.

NEHEMIAH JONES, of the Kingdom of England, buys land at Onancock [Acco cty, Va.] Acco, Va. 1 June 1703. xi-309.

JAMES JENKINS' letter,' from Graves End, in which he says "I gave an account of it by Capt. Tulley." Surry, Va. 10 Jany 1653. i-82.

NICHOLAS JACKSON, citizen and mercer, of London, Acco, Va. 13 May 1659. ix-43.

GEORGE KNIGHT, a shoemaker: Thomas Richards, master of a brigantine arrived from New England, in Pongoteague river or creek, Accomack, about thirty-two years before, brought Knight with him. Acco, Va. 1748. iiD-128.

FRANCIS LEE, of London; power to wife Annabella. Acco, Va. 25 Oct 1689. ix-184.

JAMES LINDALL, of Salem, Essex cty, N. E., mcht. Power to Capt. Benjamin Pickman, same town, and John Harmanson, Esq., and Mr. John Bowdoin, of Accomack, in Virginia, or either of them. Wit: Bejamin Rush, Henry Elkins. N-n cty, Va. 6 Nov 1713. xxiR-58.

RICHARD MOORE, mariner, of Salem, in New England. gdn of William Henfield, of same place, son and heir of Capt. Robt Henfield, dec'd, gives power to Col. Nicholas Spencer. Wmld, Va. 23 Nov 1668. Orders, 1668-1677, fo. 39.

RICHARD PAGE died on the seas in a voyage from Barbadoes to Virginia. Wmld, Va. Orders, 1676-1688, p. 380. Ct 25 Feby 1684.

WILLIAM ROWAN, of Maryland; power to Daniel Rowan, of Davidson cty, N. C. Davidson cty, Tenn. 23 Aug 1790. i-177.

JOHN TODD went to Bath cty, N. C. Pr. Wm, Va. Before 2 June 1738. L. C. p. 175.

THOMAS TAYLOR (a son of Capt. Philip Taylor and wife Frances, of Potuxen, Md.) power to John Custis. N-n, Va., ix-193. 1664.

Capt. NATHANIEL WALKER (from N. E. as shown by his will) gives to his bro-in-law, Capt. Wm. Dyre, "all my lands in the Gov't of Penna., at the place formerly called the Whorekill, since New Deal. and now called Lewis." N-n, Va. 27 Apr 1683-29 Oct 1683. xv-26.

JAMES WALKER, of Sussex cty, Territories of Penna., to Elizabeth Tilney. Acco, Va. 10 Dec 1698. xi-222.

JOHN WALKER, of Gloucester cty, Va., power to Capt. James Neale, of Md. Wmld, Va. 28 Oct 1661, ii(2)-5.

PETER WALKER was son of Andrew Walker, citizen and tallow-chandler of London, N-n, Va. 9 Oct 1644. ii-340.

PETER WALKER, of London, mcht, had pltn called Maggetye Bay, conveyed to him by Will Holmes. N-n, Va. 7 Jany 1638. i-125.

WILLIAMS NOTES
MARYLAND-VIRGINIA SECTION

ROBERT C. WILLIAMS; inventory. Campbell cty, Va. 1 Nov 1819. v-248.

SAMUEL WILLIAMS and wf SUSANNA, convey land. Fauq., Va. 20 May 1817. xxii-54. Also 11 Oct 1817. See xxii-214.

SAMUEL WILLIAMS m. ELIZABETH CRUMP. Shenan., Va. Mar. Ret. 21 Sept 1790.

SAMUEL WILLIAMS, York-Hampton Psh, Va. Died 22 Aug 1703.

SARAH WILLIAMS m. GEORGE JONES. Shenan., Va. Mar. Ret. 1783 or 1784.

SARAH WILLIAMS m. HENRY PAINTER. Shenan., Va. Mar. Ret. 20 July 1794.

SHADRACH WILLIAMS m. HANNAH JONES. Shenan., Va. Mar. Ret. 27 June 1786.

SAMUEL WILLIAMS. In Madison cty, Ill. Census, 1820.

THOMAS WILLIAMS in White cty, Ill. Census, 1820.

TERRY WILLIAMS in Gallatin cty, Ill. Census, 1820.

THOMAS WILLIAMS. Account of CAVE WILLIAMS and THOMAS WILLIAMS, his admrs. Pr. Geo's, Md. 14 Mch 1774. S. T. 1, p. 423.

THOMAS WILLIAMS; had wf Frances who was an heir of (presumably dau. of) Edward Nugent. Fauq., Va. Chancery records. 22 Feby 1795. ii-400.

THOMAS WILLIAMS; Mrs. ELINOR WILLIAMS, widow and extx. Disbursements to BARUCH WILLIAMS, WALTER WILLIAMS, and William Head. Pr. Geo's, Md. 25 Mch 1752. D. D. 6-83. Further acc't, 12 July 1753. p. 128.

THOMAS WILLIAMS; taxed for 248 acres. Ldn, Va. Land Book, 1782. See also Land Book for 1783.

THOMAS WILLIAMS, Sr. Final acc't of CAVE WILLIAMS, surviving admr. Nine chn are mentioned: Eleanor, Elizabeth, Thomas, Basil, Baruch, Lilburn, Elisha, Osburn, Cave. Pr. Geo's, Md. 3 June 1790. S. T. i-431.

THOMAS WILLIAMS; Rock'm, Va. 1786. Entries, p. 26.

THOMAS WILLIAMS' orphans, Elisha and Thomas. William Blunt's bond as gdn. Shenan., Va. 9 Sept 1794. D-360.

TABITHA WILLIAMS returns inv. of JOHN WILLIAMS, of Queen Anne's, Md. Annap. Inv. 19 May 1742. xxvii-194.

Dr. THOMAS WILLIAMS, of Queene Anne's, Md. Annap. Inv. 17 Apr 1721. vii-16.

THOM'S WILLIAMS; kin: JOHN and ISAAC WILLIAMS. Annap. Inv. 7 May 1720. iv-77.

THOMAS WILLIAMS, Pr. Geo's, Md. ELEANOR WILLIAMS, extx. Annap. Balance Book. 25 Mch 1752. i-37.

THOMAS WILLIAMS' wife was RHODA. Pr. Wm, Va., Orders, Ct 1762.

VIOLETTA WILLIAMS, dau. of John and Mary. Reg. Westminster Psh, Md. Born 2 Sept 1729.

VINCENT WILLIAMS; kin: Antoney x Williams and Gy [*sic*] Williams. Sarah Parlitt. William Guy, *alias* Williams, admr. Annap. Inv. 7 May 1751. xxx xlvii-302.

WILLIAM WILLIAMS, among the list of convicts transported to Maryland. Annap. Records. P. L. 5-247. Jany 1720.

WILLIAM WILLIAMS, of Chas. cty, Md. Will. Wf; son Thomas, Williams' Chance, 72 acres; son William, Frankum, 350 acres, also 28 acres called Williams' Addition. Chn: William, Thomas, Lewcresea, Mary; legacy to Elizabeth Annis. Wf Ann, extx. Wit: Thomas x Wright, John Wright, Jonathan x Williams. Annap. Wills, 19 Nov 1735-5 May 1736. xxi-548.

WILLIAM WILLIAMS, dep'n. Age about 47. Annap. Wills, 3 Nov 1732. xx-462.

WILLIAM WILLIAMS, dep'n. Of Charles cty, Md. Age about 48. Testifies to nun-cup. will of Joseph Chambers. Ann. 1 Oct 1733. xx-839.

WILLIAM WILLIAMS, of Calvert cty, Md. Will. Son Francis and wf Susan, extrs. Wit: William x Griffen, Henry x Bussey, Anne x Evans. Annap. Wills. 12 Jany 1713-13 Mch 1720. xvi-403.

WILLIAM WILLIAMS, of Fred'k cty, Md., Gent. Had dau. Ahalamah(?) Chapline wf of Joseph; dau. Sarah Price, who had a son William Price;

a dau. Jane Chambers, wf of Benjamin. See Frd'k cty, 23 Sept 1759- 5 Oct 1759. Al-130.

WILLIAM WILLIAMS, of Fred'k, Md., son of THOMAS, had wf Barbara. Had son Thomas-Owen, dau. Elizabeth-Owen, son Elisha-Owen, son William-Prather, dau. Elinor-Hillary, dau. Martha, son Edward-Owen, dau. Barbara. See Fred'k, Md, 27 Apr 1767- 22 Mch 1769. Al-330. [It is uncertain whether the name is Owen or Owens as written.]

SERVICE AND SUPPLIES COLONIAL, REVOLUTIONARY AND MILITIA

ADLER ARRINGTON, makes declaration of service as a soldier in the Revolutionary War. Court orders ctf. Camp. cty, Va. Orders, 1831-1833. p.189. Court, Aug 1832.

NELSON BROOKS, same. p.186.

JAMES BROOKS, same. p. 187.

HENRY BLANKENSHIP, same. Aug Court, 1832. p.190.

JOSEPH H. BOULDEN; ctf of qualification to his comm'n as "Coronet of Cavalry" returned and ordered recorded. Henry cty, Va. Ct of Quarterly Sessions. 11 June 1833.

WILLIAM BOLLING; Elizabeth Cooper makes oath that John Bolling is the lawful heir of William Bolling, dec'd, who went from Henry cty into the Continental service and there died. Ordered certified. Henry cty, Va. Court 22 Sept 1778.

ROBERT CARDWELL, makes declaration of Revolutionary service. Ctf ordered. Camp. cty, Va. Orders, 1831-1833. p. 202. Sept. Court.

WILLIAM CANDLER, same. Oct Court. p.211.

WILLIAM CAMPBELL, a soldier of the Revolutionary War, makes declaration and is ordered certified. Franklin cty, Va. Court Sept 1832.

ROBERT CHILDRESS, same. Court Oct 1832.

GEORGE DINGUID[?] makes declaration of service, Revolutionary War, and is ordered certified. Camp. cty, Va. Sept Court, 1832. p.199.

RICHARD DANIEL, same. p.184.

WILLIAM DESHAZO, a Revolutionary soldier. Declaration ordered certified. Henry cty, Va. Min. Ct of Quar. Sess. 14 Aug 1832.

SAMPSON EVANS, makes declaration. Camp. cty, Va. Orders, 1831-1833. p. 182. Sept Court, 1832.

WILLIAM FRAZIER, same. p.207.

THOMAS FRANKLIN, same.

EDWARD GIBBS, makes declaration of Revolutionary service and Court orders ctf, Camp. Cty Va. Orders 1831-1833, p.182. Sept Court 1832.

CHARLES GLASS, same. p.188.

RICHARD GILLEY, makes declaration and is ordered certified. Henry cty, Va. 12 Mch, 1833. See also 8 July 1833.

PETER HARRIS, produces comm'n as Ensign, and takes oath. Henry cty, Va. 25 Mch 1779.

SWINFIELD HILL, appointed Captain of Militia, in the room of Ed. Short, "who hath resigned to the said Hill." Henry cty, Va. 25 Mch 1779.

THOMAS HAILE, appointed Captain of the Militia in the room of Peter Vardeman. Henry cty, Va. Court 22 Apr 1779.

BENJAMIN HINSLEY, served as Lieutenant in the Virginia Battalion in the year 1760. Ordered certified to the Clerk of the Register of the Land Office. Henry cty, Va. Court 26 Aug 1779.

BENJAMIN HUGHES, makes declaration of Revolutionary service. Camp. cty, Va. Sept Court, 1832. p.198.

THOMAS HARVEY, same. p.183.

WILLIAM KING, same. p.194.

WILLIAM LECKIE or LUCKIE, same. p.200.

ARTHUR LITCHFORD, same. p.201.

Gen'l JOEL LEFTWICH, same. Oct Court, 1832. p. 218. Also Aug Court, p.175.

SAMUEL MATHEWS, same. Orders 1831-1833. p. 184.

JAMES PETTIT, same. p. 187.

JOHN PRIBBLE, same. Aug Court, 1832. p.189.

WILLIAM ROSSER, same. p. 186.

JOHN REDD, declaration, applicant for pension. Ordered certified. Henry cty, Va. Court 8 Oct 1832. See also Court of 11 Feby 1833, and 14 Oct 1833. (Ctf ordered in each court.)

BENJAMIN STRATTON, declaration of service ordered certified. Henry cty, Va. Court 14 Oct 1833.

BOOK NOTES:

An "Index to the wills, administrations, and guardianships of Kings County, New York, 1650 to 1850", compiled by Milton Halsey Thomas, has just been published by Mr. Charles Shepard II, 2153 California St., Washington, D. C. The volume contains approximately four thousand entries arranged alphabetically, with variant spellings of the same surname grouped together for ease of reference. Kings County contains Brooklyn and other densely populated areas, and is, therefore, one of the most important counties in the state, from a genealogical point of view. The book is printed on a high grade of bond paper, and is substantially bound in buckram, with gilt lettering. It is issued in a limited edition of 100 numbered copies, price $10.

THE ROBINSON GENEALOGY, volume one. Now in print. For sale by Mr. Frederick W. Robinson, 950 Park Square Building, Boston, Mass.

UNITED STATES CENSUS AND PENSION OFFICE RECORD

Searches at moderate rates will be made of early original Census schedules or of Revolutionary pension claims, in the Census and Pension offices at Washington, D. C.

For further information, address the Editor, County Court Note-Book.

Mr. FRANCIS B. CULVER
3204 Guilford Avenue, Baltimore, Md.

Member of Committee on Genealogy and Heraldry of the Maryland Historical Society; Genealogical Editor of "THE MINUTE MAN" magazine. Researches in genealogy and heraldry for American and English lineages. Historical biographies compiled and coats of arms investigated and supplied.

Mr. ALFRED L. HOLMAN
Genealogist
2036 Indiana Avenue
Chicago, Ill.

Refers by special permission to Mr. George B. Utley, Librarian Newberry Library.

Mr. CHARLES SHEPARD, II
19 West Main Street
Rochester, New York
Genealogist and Antiquarian.
Consulting service and original research.

Mr. STRATTON NOTTINGHAM
Genealogist
Onancock, Virginia

Researches in Northampton, Accomack, and nearby early counties of Virginia. Mss. indices and notes of many early families available.

Marriage License Bonds of Accomack county, Va. 1774 to 1806. $3.50.

Index of wills and administrations in preparation.

Mrs. GEORGE W. HODGES
Gloucester Apartments,
Annapolis, Maryland.

Special facilities for genealogical and historical research. (Compiler of the Marriage References of Maryland.)

Mrs. FRANCIS H. MARKELL
Frederick, Maryland
Genealogical research

Refers by permission to Mr. Frank E. Norwood, president Frederick County Historical Society, Frederick, Maryland.

Mrs. WILLIAM HYDE TALBOTT
Rockville, Maryland

Genealogical and historical research. Special facilities for all western and southern Maryland.

Mrs. LETITIA P. WILSON
3905 Gwynn Oak Avenue,
Baltimore, Maryland.
Genealogical and historical research.

EDWARD DWELLY, F. S. A. Scot., F. S. G.
Record Searcher and Genealogist.

Publisher of Dwelly's Parish Records. Indices containing over 3,000,000 names.

36 Pemberton Road, East Molesey, Surrey, England.

EMERY RECORD PRESERVING COMPANY
Taunton, Mass.

Bookbinding Specialists in Restoring and Preserving Records and Documents
Emery Silk Process Patent Mount
Records Kept in Fireproof Vaults

TYPEWRITING and MIMEOGRAPHING of RECORDS and MANUSCRIPTS

Accurate and legible work in attractive style. Printed title covers and binding if required. Prompt service guaranteed.

Batt, Bates & Co., Inc.
914 Fourteenth St., N. W.
Washington, D. C.

MARYLAND MARRIAGES from COURT RECORDS

4,000 marriage references from 104 volumes of "Judgment Records," Maryland State Land Office. 1679 to 1807. Fee for search, one dollar. Full copy of record proving marriage, five dollars.

MISS LOUISE MAGRUDER,
Hockley Hall, Annapolis, Md.

PUBLICATIONS OF THE CARTER BRAXTON CHAPTER, D. A. R.
Baltimore, Maryland.

Marriage licenses of Talbot county, Md., beginning 1794. One thousand licenses; two thousand names. $5.50 post paid.

Index of wills, St. Mary's county, Md. Index of wills, Anne Arundel county, Md. Price $12.50 each volume.

Address Mrs. Letitia P. Wilson, Regent,
3905 Gwynn Oak Avenue,
Baltimore, Md.

Reasonable price or two years' subscription will be given for numbers 1, 2, 3, 4, 6, and 7, COUNTY COURT NOTE-BOOK, 1921-1922.
Address Editor.

The

County Court Note-Book

A Little Bulletin of History and Genealogy

April 1927. Vol. VI, No. 2

THE ANCESTRY OF COL. JOHN DONELSON OF TENNESSEE, EXPLORER AND PIONEER*

The first appearance of Capt. JOHN DONELSON, son of PATRICK (except as he appears as a witness to his sister's will), is in a suit which he brings against one Roger Nicholson, Jr., for slander. (Som. cty, Jud. Rec. S. C. No. B. fo. 4, 16 Mch 1724.) The very quaint wording of this suit shows that "the aforesaid JOHN was married and had Long Before and Ever Since had a wife residing and Inhabiting in the County aforesaid" . . . and that the said Roger "did rehearse Pronounce and with a high Voice publish false feigned and Scandalous & Malitious and Aprobious words and Lyes". The jury convicted Nicholson and awarded damages to the outraged and fiery Capt. JOHN [Mariner.]

JOHN DONELSON was the admr of Samuel Cox, of St. Michael's Parish, Barbadoes, 10 Apr 1724-5 Feby 1724. (Md. Wills, v-65.)

An entry in the Testamentary Proceedings, Annapolis Records, (vol. xxvi-14; 14 Nov 1724) mentions JOHN DONALDSON, mariner, as petitioning concerning the Cox estate. He returns the add'l account of Samuel Cox, Esq., of Somerset, 1 Oct 1728. (See Annap. Records ix-301.) And at the same court as attorney in fact for Phillip Russell [at one time member of the Delaware Court, and the husband of DONELSON'S sister-in-law] who was the admr of Doctor SAMUELL DAVIES, late of Som. cty. returns account. (ix-303.)

Several records are found in the records of Snow Hill, Worcester county, which are of date prior to the erection of that county. In one of these JOHN DONALDSON (James Round, security) gives bond as admr of John Patrick. The wit. are David and Betty Wilson. (Bonds, 266, 11 Mch 1727.)

In 1727, DONELSON was a wit. to Robert Hudson's will, Som. cty. And a wit. to the will of Benjamin Burton, of Som. cty, 17 Mch 1728. Probate 21 Aug 1728. (Md Wills, v-75.) DONELSON and John Dennis were security for Margarett Hudson, the widow of Hudson, and DONELSON was also security with Edward Franklyn for Elizabeth Burton, extx of Burton. JOHN DONALSON, of Som. cty, Md., Mcht, from Rebecca Clark, dau. and heir of William Clark, Jr., late of Sussex upon Delaware, Mcht, consideration sixty pounds, tract fronting Lewes Creek, between Wiltbanck and Hall . . . Pagan creek mentioned . . . 50 acres. Wit: Richardson, Hepburn, Anderson. Proved by wit. (Sus. cty, Dela. 12 May 1728. F6-312.)

The 14 Jany 1734, JOHN DONELSON was security (with Robert Hodge) for Katherine Steward [Stewart], admx [or extx?] of William Steward. (Som cty, IW 14-372.) And the Annapolis "Debt Books" (xliii-158), for the year 1735, Somerset county, show that JOHN DONALDSON was in possession of "Beyond Expectation," 220 acres; "Chance," 100 acres, and lot No. 6, Snow Hill, Worcester cty. [These so-called "Debt Books," are merely lists of Lord Baltimore's rentals.]

The next entry shows that sometime in or before Nov. 1736 (Old Style) Capt. DONELSON returned to port no more, leaving, as later records show, a minor son JOHN and a daughter MARY.

KATHERINE DONELSON gives bond as admx of JOHN DONELSON; James Martin and Adam Bell, of Somerset cty, her security. Amount of bond, £100 sterling, 18 Nov 1736. (Annap. T. P. xxx-256.) The inventory of Capt. DONELSON'S personal property amounted to £42-19-11.

CATHERINE DONNELSON, Gentlewoman, now *femme sole*, buys from Abraham Smith, Som., Md., pltr, consideration £50, a lot in Snow Hill, adjoining Pocomoke River, called Deep Landing Lott. Wit: John Scott and Wm. Lane. (Som. E. I. 143. 17 Mch 1736.) She petitions before the November Court that she hath an old negro called Cudjoe, so infirm, &c., &c., and prays that he may be levy free. So ordered. (Som. cty Minutes. Nov. 1737.)

The 25 May 1739, CATHERINE DONALSON, Relict of JOHN DONALSON, late of Som. cty, conveys to MARY DONALSON and JOHN DONALSON, son and dau. of Catherine, consideration, love and affection, a certain lot called Deep Landing Lott, in Snow Hill Town, "in such manner" that MARY DONALSON shall have the Largest House in sd Lott, with two-thirds of the said Lott, and the lesser house and remaining one-third to JOHN DONALSON, which sd Lott was conveyed to CATHERINE DONALSON by Abraham Smith of sd county. (Som. Md. M. F. P. 68.) Sig. Kat'e DONELSON. Wit: William Turpin, Ephm Waggaman. Ackn. in person. Consid'n 1 penny sterling.

THE DAVIS LINE

CATHERINE DONELSON, the wife and widow of Capt. JOHN DONELSON, was the daughter of Rev. SAMUEL DAVIS, a Presbyterian minister of Snow Hill, Somerset (now Worcester) county, Maryland. Mr. DAVIS was also a physician. Her mother was perhaps MARY, who was the widow of Robert Simpson, before she married Mr. DAVIS. These facts will be shown by the following references.

Note: The Presbyterian Historical Society Journal, in an article by its able Secretary, Rev. Joseph B. Turner, states that Rev. SAMUEL DAVIS was the first pastor of Makemie Memorial Presbyterian Church at Snow Hill, Maryland; that no record can be found of Mr. Davis in Maryland before 1684, but that he was at Snow Hill from 1684 to 1697. Mr. Turner also states that Mr. DAVIS was a member of the first Presbytery in America, and his name, with other members of that presbytery, is recorded on a memorial tablet in the

First Presbyterian Church of Philadelphia. (See vols. iv, vi and vii, of the Journal.)

The first reference in the civil records of Somerset county is that on p. 16, of the vol. D. B. I. K. L., where Rev. SAMUEL DAVIS is mentioned as a minister. On the 18 Sept 1684, he receives a patent for 500 acres called "Inch." (Som. R. R. of the approximate date of 1724.) The name is here given as DAVIES. At the date of the Rent Roll the land was in possession of John Fawcett, of Poquadenorton hundred.

The 10 June 1687. SAMUEL DAVIS, of Somerset, Minister, buys of William Round, of Somerset, Mcht, and wf Martha, 167 acres, part of an original patent called "Mulberry Grove," for 3500 lbs tobacco, the tract now being called "Grove." Wit: Elizabeth Stevens, Edmund Howard. (Som. cty, MA-853. 10 June 1687.) In 1695, Rev. SAMUEL DAVIS received by the will of James Durkan, his personal estate. Durkan has a cousin Morgan Paton and a wife Elizabeth. The wit. to the will are Sam'l Davis, Wm. Shankland, Henry Read. (Som. cty, Md., Wills. ii-116. 1695-1696.) In 1700, SAMUEL DAVIS was the extr and residuary legatee of Robert Simson of Som. cty. (Md. Wills, ii-222.) The 17 Nov 1702, SAMLL DAVIS conveys to Mr. Ephraim Heather, his "stock of Hoggs, marked left ear with a swallow fork; right ear hole," belonging to the plantation called "Grove." Wit: Boggs and Reed. (Som. cty, P-200. 17 Nov 1702.)

The Sussex, Del., records show that SAMUEL DAVIS, Gent., bought of Nathaniell Hall, Marriner, both of Sussex, 1 3-8 acres on the south side of the Town of Lewes. (A-98. Before 1702.) This is explained by the following deed showing that Mr. or Dr. Davis had removed to Sussex. Mr. SAMUELL DAVIS, formerly of Somerset, Md., Minister, alias Doctor, now of Lewis Town, in the Territories of Penna., and MARY, his now wife, extrs of Robert Sympson, lately deceased, to Robert Ironshire, of Somerset, pltr, consideration 5,500 lbs tobacco, 150 acres called "Carpenter's Enjoyment," which John Browne and wf Elizabeth conveyed to Thomas Durkin, and 100 acres called "Bettie's Rest," both sold by Durkin to Sympson. Wit: Cornish, Cropper. Sig. SAML DAVIS. (Som. cty, Md. Gl-83. 8 June 1703.)

(*To be continued.*)

AUTHENTIC REFERENCES FOR INFERRED MARRIAGES*

JOHN ARCHBELL and FRANCES CLIFFORD, relict of Robert. Before or about 18 Mch 1713. Nthld cty, Va., 1713-1719, p. 24.

JOHN ARCHER and . . . SHIPPEY, dau. Thomas. Before 22 Sept 1698. Hen. cty, Va., 1677-1739, p. 40.

JACOB BLITHE, of Hanover, St. Paul's Psh, and MARY ANN PARKER, widow, same. Marriage contract, "in solemn confirmation." 8 May 1787. Han. cty, Va., [ii]-21.

ELIAS P. BURNETT and MARY A. H. ELLIS. Before 16 July 1832. Gchld, Va., Orders, p. 129.

. . . BUTLER, of Wmld cty, and DOROTHY BROOKES, wid.[?] of Henry. Before 23 Mch 1664. S. L. O., Va., v-55.

THOMAS BONUM and REBECCA THOMAS, dau. and sole heir of William. Before 16 Sept 1712. Nthld, Va., 1710-1713, p. 227.

NATHANIEL BRADFORD, of Acco, and JOAN FRANKLING, sister of Henry Frankling. Before 17 Aug 1713. Nthld, Va., 1710-1713, p. 335.

. . . BALL and GRACE HAYNIE, dau. of Sarah Haynie, and grand-dau. of John Harris. Before 23 Feby 1709. Nthld, Va., 1710-1713, p. 318.

CHARLES BROWNE and SUSANNAH BERRY, only dau. and heir of Edward Berry. Before 22 Sept 1798. Essex, Va., 1695-1699, p. 66.

PETER COTTOM[?] and MARTHA-DANDRIDGE FLEMING, dau. of Thomas M. Fleming. Before 9 Nov 1831. Gchld, Va., xxix-190.

PITTS CURTIS and the relict of David FLUKES [FLUKER?] Before 22 Oct 1712. Nthld, Va., 1710-1713, p. 259.

JOHN CORDEROY, son and heir of Edward Corderoy, of Gloucester cty, and HANNAH JONES. Mar. contract. 20 Oct 1682. S. L. O., Va., viii-. [She seems to have m. (2) Samuel Worrington, prior to 28 Apr 1691.]

JOHN CHILDERS and LUCRETIA JONES. About or before 31 Aug 1710. Hen., Va., 1677-1739, p. 51.

JAMES DAVIS and MARY PRICE, dau. of Calem[?] Price. Before 23 June 1777. S. L. O., Va., Q-153.

RICHARD DAY and MARY BUNBERY, dau. of Robert. Before 10 Nov 1698. Essex, Va., 1695-1699, p. 126.

. . . EMPEROUR probably m. ANNE HARDING, of L. Norf, wid. of Thomas. [This is obscure.] Before 20 Apr 1682. S. L. O., Va., vii-145.

PRICE FRAYZER and SARAH ANN WOOD. Before 17 Dec 1832. Gchld, Va. Orders, p. 177.

DANIEL FORE and ELIZABETH HUDSON, wid. of William. About or before 31 Aug 1710. Hen., Va., 1677-1739, p. 31.

GILL FUEQUE [FUQUA] and JANE EYRES, dau. of Joseph, and gr-dau. of William Humphreys. Before 20 Aug 1692. Hen., Va., 1677-1739, p. 32.

JOHN GRAVES, Jr., and LUCY ADAMS, dau. of Robert. Before 18 Oct 1743. Gchld, Va., iv-248.

ROBERT GRIGG and TABITHA GOWER, orphan of Mr. Abell Gower. Before or about 20 Aug 1700. Hen., Va., 1677-1739, p. 43.

. . . HALE and SARAH RICHARDS, a wid. [Afterwards of Henrico.] Before 24 Apr 1806. Gchld, Va., xix-538.

MARYLAND'S NEXT OF KIN*

JOHN PORTER and JAMES NOBLE; inv. Jonathan Noble, Som. cty. 22 Aug 1721. vi-194.

MARY BURSE, ANN PAIN and ROBT PAIN; inv. Francis Colyer; 20 July 1721. vi-196.

ELIZA: HOLLAND, admx. Inv. Nehemiah Holland of Somerset cty, 4 Aug 1721. vi-175.

JOHN HARRIS and FRAN: MARTIN "approve." Inv. Thomas Moor of Somerset cty, 8 July 1721. vi-177.

JOHN TROUTT, Sr. Inv. Jeremiah Poynter, of Somerset cty, 23 Aug 1721. vi-178.

JOHN FRANKLIN, WM. WALTON and ELIZA: MAUKLIN[?] Inv. William Collins of Somerset, 16 June 1721. vi-180.

No kin given; inv. of EDWARD MARTIN, of Som., who deceast 25 Dec 1720.

. . . HINCHINS or HUTCHINS and SAM'LL BUALL [BEALL?]. Inv. Nathaniel Waite of Somerset, 2 Sept 1721. vi-182.

JAMES HOGG. Inv. Richard Woodcraft of Somerset, 3 Aug 1721. vi-183.

JNO. RICKARDS and THO: ROBINSON. Inv. Leonard Johnson of Somerset, 21 July 1721. vi-184. [Joyce Johnson and Peter Johnson were admrs.]

NICHOLAS GASSAWAY and JOHN DORSEY, Jr. "Related." Inv. Benjamin Lawrence of Balto. cty, 26 Aug 1721. vi-197.

No kin given: Inv. Mrs. ELIZA: MAULDIN of Calvert cty, 16 May 1721. vi-199.

SARAH HUNT, a sister; THOMAS DAY, a brother. Inv. Robt Day of Calvert cty, 17 July 1721. vi-201.

P. . . MAKGILL, JOHN HUES. [Creditors or kin?] Inv. Thomas Gilley, Calvert cty. vi-205. [Date not found.]

MARY NEWSOME, "Mother of the Heirs." Inv. Thomas Newsome, of Balto. cty, 6 Sept 1721. vi-207.

WILLIAM RATCLIFF, JOHN FALLOW, JOHN KENEDY; "Creditors and Kin." Inv. Richard Ratliff, of Talbott cty, 17 July 1721. vi-210.

THOS. CUTTIN and WM. JENKINS. Inv. Wm. Jenkins of Balto. cty, 21 July 1721. vi-212.

JNO. LECOMPTE and NEHEMIAH BICKWITH. Inv. of Moses Lecompte of Dorchester cty, 27 Mch 1721. vi-214.

RANDALL PHIDEN[?] and WM. PALE. Inv. Thomas Bradshaw, of Dorchester cty, 21 June 1721. vi-216.

EDWARD GRANGER and SARAH LOWE. Inv. Thomas Heather of Dorchester cty, 26 Aug 1721. vi-289.

"No kindred on this Side of the Bay to sign." Inv. Mrs. AUDRY TAYLORD, of St. Mary's, 1 Jany 1721. vi-220.

THOMAS JAMESON, Jr., and FRANCIS JAMESON. Inv. Mrs. Margaret Butler, of St. Mary's, 9 Oct 1721. vi-223.

"Wee the Subscribers being the Father in Law and Naturall [*sic*] of the Dec, "THOMAS MARTIN and JOANE MARTIN. Inv. of Wm. Elliott, of Charles cty, 16 Aug 1721. vi-225.

"No relations save minor children." ELIAZBETH PETIT makes oath. Inv. John Pettitt of Balto. cty, 7 Nov 1721. vi-227.

"No relations save minor children," SARAH TAYLOR, widow and admx. Inv. Martin Taylor of Balto. cty, 17 June 1721. vi-230.

"Wittnesses," JONA. MASSON and EDWARD JACKSON. Inv. Robert Jackson of Balto. cty, 9 Aug 1721. vi-232.

VIRGINIA COLONISTS

(From Old Volume, 5, S. L. O.)

GILES DRIVER, I. W. cty, 1657.
Head rights: Elizabeth Williams, Elizabeth Reynolds, Jno. Goodale, James Crow.

GILES DRIVER, I. W. cty, 1657.
Head rights: Anne Jones, Thomas Butcher.

GERVASE DODSON, Patomeck Freshes, 1658.
Head right: Ann Starr. Assigned to Mr. Henry Corbyn, and by him made over to his daughter Alice Corby. 19 Oct 1660.

GERVASE DODSON, Westmoreland, 1657.
Head rights: Jno. Ball, Wm. Hoble, Wm. Bassett, Alexander Cooper, Wm. Langle, Jno. Butler, Daniell Dunn[?] David Norrey, Wm. Pott, Walter Blade, Easter Jury[perhaps Ivry?] Mary Beachampe [*sic*] Roger . . . [?] Tabitha, Susan, Tho. Pritchett and his wife, Tho. Oliver, Wilkes Mander, James Willson, Anthye Watts, Nich Hewes, Tho: Wasdall, Francis Pether, Robert Rigge, John Neale.

GERVASE DODSON, on a Creek issuing out of the Bay ("Corrotman" Creek mentioned), 1658.
Head rights: Mary Parrott, Jno. Mason, Eliz. Attkeson, Edward Harris, Barnaby Lowe, Ann Evans, Leonard Singlton, James Garrett, Thomas Morris, Peter Hughes.

GERVASE DODSON, Westmoreland cty, 1658.
Head rights: Simon Pratt, Elinor Wheeler, Edward Merriman, Jno. Mocoy [McCoy?] Francis Wheeler, Francis Hall.

THOMAS DODSON, Northumberland, 1658.
Head rights: THO. DODSON, Jno. Palmer, Davis Jenkin, Mary Linton, Thomas Henly, Edward Dennis, Rich. Person, Abigall How, Wm. Gosnell, Tho. Arthur, Abreall[?] Harvey, Ann Parker, Rice Jones [Rees], Richard Nealmes[?], Susan Roe, Tho. Addams, Richard Golbourne [Colbourne?], Jno. Farmer, Wm. Weekes, Luke Morris, Mathew Morris, Tabitha Hart, Jno. Addams, Bridgett Freman.

JOHN DORRANT, New Kent, 1658.
Head rights: Jno. Hollman, Wm. Thomas, Henry Foard.

THOMAS DYER, L. Norfolk, 1658.
Head rights: Ann Sedger, Wm. Shreive, Rich. Skegs, Rich Reynolds, Wm. Merriday, Ann Crafore [Craford?]

Capt. JOHN ENGLISH, Northumberland, 1657.
Head rights: Wm. Harris, Jno. Greene, Michaell Sparks, Mary Hatton, Barnaby Sprigge, Tho. Spier, Robert Watts, Oliver Kinge, Rice [Rees] Jones, Jone Thorp, Dan: Wells, Wm. Alcock, Ann Hughes, Tabitha Collins.

JOHN EDWARDS, Lancaster county, 1657.
Head rights: JOHN EDWARDS, MARY EDWARDS, Leonard Cassott or Casson.

JOHN EARLE, Northumberland county, 1658.
Head rights: Mary Pitt, Roger Walke.

Mr. JOHN ELLIS, Westmoreland county, 1658.
Head rights: JNO. ELLIS, Henry Cooke, James Hill, Aron Hughes, Charles Loyder, Everad Roberts Robert Greene, Wm. Leeke, Mary Thompson, Alex. Ellcock, Jane Harris, Jno. Moore, Tho. Atkins, Wm. Waters, Daniell Cole, Xphr Granger, Rich. Kibbourne, Jno. Dorsey, Wm. Charlton, Robt Harwell, Walter Stoake, Hugh Lee.

JOHN EVANS, Westmoreland, 1658.
Head rights: JNO. EVANS, JOHN EVANS, Junior, Timothy Hill, Robt Lowe, MARY EVANS, Step. Allen, Tho. Sharpe, Abigall Parker, James Allen, Barnaby Little, Rice Jones, Peter Lowe, Tho. Alstone, James Morrison, Leonard Stronge, John Batt, Edward Hill, John Moyses, John Clarke, Henry Kinge, Charles Hill, John Stoile[?] Arthur Sheare, Mary Lord, John Thorpe, Eliz. Lord, Sarah Vaux, Tabitha Hare, Ann Thompson, Ann Dakins, Elinor Thompson, Edward Person, Rich: Allen.

The County Court Note-Book

An every-other-monthly devoted mainly to abstracts from County Court records, prior to 1800.

MILNOR LJUNGSTEDT, Editor and Publisher.
Bethesda, Route 10, Maryland.

Published six times a year. Subscription, two dollars, in advance; must begin with the year.

APRIL, 1927 **Whole**
Vol. VI., No. 2 **No. 33**

SOME CONDITIONS SOME EXPERIENCES

It has been more than a decade since the Editor began her explorations, and numerous changes have taken place in the courthouses, clerks' offices, and, praise be! the hotels. But, as a rule, the same Clerk holds office, and it is pleasant, indeed, to return and find the familiar face, the courteous reception, of an official acquaintance, a friendly acquaintance. Death has cancelled the popular vote in several counties . . . the Editor is, perhaps, more conscious of the loss than some of those who remain in the community, the daily routine of whose steps across the well-worn doorsill has somewhat dulled the keenness of their feeling.

Among the amusing experiences which are more cheerful in the backward look than at the time they occurred, is a visit to a county near the middle of the State of Virginia. As the Editor's experiences were purely personal, names will not be mentioned. They began with the departure from Richmond. The particular county the Editor was intending for, is or was reached by boat and by automobile . . . the courthouse being some miles from the river landing.

The advertisement of the steamboat company stated that passengers who desired to do so could secure staterooms the evening before, for the morning boat, and remain on board. This attracted the Editor, who would rather sleep in any ship's cabin than any hotel room. Inquiry of the local agent brought the assurance that it would be perfectly all right for her to stay on board, proper and safe and everything. So, early in the evening of a certain Sunday, but well after dark, the Editor betook herself to the riverside. The wharf was in midnight blackness, so was the boat. A watchman appeared, however, with a lantern and the smallest of small dogs. The watchman knew nothing about the Editor's cabin, and there was no officer of the boat aboard. The purser lived up town, and spent the night there; the Captain wouldn't be back until late; the stewardess was off duty. But the Editor knew she had a cabin there and meant to stay, and the watchman was equal to the occasion . . . he found a cabin (not the one reserved for the Editor) and having settled her there, he betook himself, lantern and dog back to the dock.

The Editor looked about and took stock. An empty pitcher . . . how to get water, With the pitcher she started to find the watchman. Two great, hulking roustabouts flanked the gangway, but did not wake. The watchman, the lantern and the dog were found, and, thus escorted, the Editor got some water from a hydrant and so back to her cabin.

Well, nothing happened . . . except that a gang of mechanics repaired the engines most of the night. The Captain returned between ten and twelve or "thereabouts," and, presumably, officially chaperoned the Editor. The night was dark, mysterious, fine. And the morning! Any morning on any river is beautiful . . . this was a dream of delight.

The passage down the river was very pleasant, and would have been every way satisfactory if there had been some one to point out the historic spots. As it was, some interested and equally uninformed Ohio people, who had come on board, foregathered with the Editor and we tried to imagine we knew where we were.

Just after breakfast the landing was reached. The Editor walked up to the usual store and the first thing she noticed was that the door had a real pioneer latch, and the string was out. After the storekeeper had waited on his early morning customers he got out his machine and drove the Editor to the courthouse, some three miles away.

The hotel man of the courthouse town was in the general store of the courthouse village. He did not welcome the Editor with any effusion . . . this explained itself later . . . but he admitted he could take care of her over night and departed to have a room made ready. There was also in the store a rather jolly old gentleman, who it turned out was uncle or some other kin to the young hotelkeeper. He said, "You know Mrs. . . . died a short time ago and we are sort of keeping bachelors' hall here." The Editor realized at once that visitors of the female sex and all alone by themselves were an embarrassment. But presently the Editor was shown a large and comfortable room, a wing of the house proper, where a friendly maid was making a fire and doing everything to take the place of the hostess who had gone beyond. In spite of the depressing consciousness that this was the room of the vanished mistress, the Editor determined to stick it out.

In the Clerk's office, which is seldom visited by outsiders, and in which there was little business, the Clerk usually "quit" about two o'clock. This one most kindly said he would stay until the Editor got ready to go, and he did stay until about five. At that hour the Editor had found about all that was findable . . . the records had been lost during the war . . . so she returned to the store. "Mr. X," she said, "I find I won't have to stay over night after all. If you will drive me to the nearest railroad station [about eight miles] you can do so before or after supper, whichever suits you best."

The Editor still seems to feel the immense air of relief which swept the apple barrels and the tomato cans; the bushel baskets and the rubber boots. "*I'll take you over before supper, just as soon as I can get away from here.*" Never did an unwished-for guest depart more speedily and with more good feeling on both sides. We talked automobile and the Editor learned a lot . . . finding out that if you used a certain make of tire for unnumbered miles and had any of it left you could turn it in and get a new one! Which was very interesting.

So that was that.

In Mr. Wise's book about the descendants of JOHN WISE, of Virginia, he makes the statement that the ROBINSON family to which the wife of JOHN CUSTIS belonged [ELIZABETH (ROBINSON) (EYRES) CUSTIS], lived upon a tract or estate called "Craney Island," after the island of that name near Portsmouth, Va.

An old tax list of NORFOLK COUNTY, under the head of directions for the Sheriff of Norfolk County, gives the bounds of the various taxing districts and among them this:

"Those that has (E) marked against their names is in the district of Ensign Willis Eastwood, *Crany Island*, in Portsmouth Parish, bounded on the North by James River, on the East by Elizabeth River, on the South by the Western Branch & on the West by the line that divides this Company from Capt. John Bower's Company of Militia."

As the brother of ELIZABETH (Robinson) (Eyre) CUSTIS and his sons and daughters, &c., &c., lived in what is now Princess Anne, on or near Lynhaven Bay, and as the name of Craney Island is not mentioned in any of the records touching them, Mr. Wise's statement is extremely puzzling.

The awakening of those States east of the Mississippi, which used to be the "West," to the value of their local records, to the day-by-day details of their pioneer history, is most remarkable and most interesting. In the Register of the KENTUCKY STATE HISTORICAL SOCIETY for September, 1926, is an editorial comment on the meetings of the Harrodsburg Pioneer Memorial Association, and on the most noteworthy gift of Old Fort Harrod and the grounds about it to the State Park Commission. Old Fort Harrod, as the Editor saw it on a wintry evening was a most desolate and lonely spot, but one filled with great interest to those of us who are more taken up with visions of the past than with the bread-and-butter existence of the day. Harrodsburg is to be congratulated on the gift, and the Park Commission upon its acceptance.

In this same number Miss Martha Stephenson gives a very logical explanation of Harrodsburg's title . . . "The Mother Town." It is noted, however, that she gives, as authority, Collins the historian. It would seem from the McAfee papers published in January, 1927, in the Register, that one of the McAfees is the real authority.

Mr. E. Dwelly, of East Molesey, England, sends the following explanation of the appearance of Volume XV, of his Parish Records, before Volume XIV. A very interesting article from Mr. Dwelly as to English wills, will appear in the June NOTE-BOOK.

Volume XIV, "Dwelly's Parish Records," has not yet appeared, for when Volume XV was commenced it was intended to be reserved for the transcripts recently found at Wells for those parishes already published; but when they had been sorted and copied, it was found possible to include them in Vol. XV. It is hoped that Vol. XIV will be commenced very shortly, and an attempt will be made to make a start with some *Bristol Registers* which are of great value to so many *Somerset* families, and have hitherto been entirely neglected.

Miss M. E. STATHAM, 1190, Oak Knoll Avenue, Pasadena, California, will be glad to hear from any one who is interested in the DAVIS family of Virginia.

In the mention in the February NOTE-BOOK of Mr. Shepard's Index to Kings County, N. Y., Wills, &c., the address was wrongly given as in Washington, D. C. Mr. Shepard's present address is 19 West Main Street, Rochester, New York. Mr. Shepard has done a great deal of valuable work of this kind, and it is to be hoped that he will continue. A good index is like a modern A. A. A. signboard.

CONTINUED articles COUNTY COURT NOTE-BOOK, and the dates on which they first appeared.

THE ANCESTRY OF COL. JOHN DONELSON, Began with February, 1927.

MARRIAGES BY INFERENCE. Began with May, 1922.

MARYLAND'S NEXT OF KIN. Began with July, 1922.

VIRGINIA COLONISTS. This alphabetized list began with July, 1924.

MILITARY NOTES. both COLONIAL and REVOLUTIONARY, and some later MILITIA NOTES, will appear in every issue, if possible.

SHIPS IN PORT, INTERCOUNTY and INTERCOLONIAL and COLONIAL FORENAMES, will appear in alternate issues or as space can be found for them.

EASTERN SHORE FAMILIES. in the form of a one-page supplement, began with June, 1925. This will be continued later.

The CUSTIS material which has been running in the NOTE-BOOK will be continued later.

OCCASIONAL

The trade of the Susquehanna and for the Isle of Kent is mentioned. N-n cty, Va. 29 June 1647. iii-103.

Sr. GRAY SKIPWITH, Barronett, makes a gift to his daughter-in-law, Eliz: Kempe. Lanc. cty, Va. 10 July 1651. ii-216.

Capt. JOHN HOWE was buried in the chancel [of the church in Northampton cty, Va., then Accomack.] See N-n, 12 Feby 1637. i-96.

The "ENGLISH VIRGINIA," a term used in a letter from Holland. N-n, Va. 16 Apr 1657. vii-65.

WILLIAM WALKER, the Elder, is mentioned as "now having a younger Brother Called Alsoe by the said Name, WILLIAM WALKER, Junior," but is the sonn of another wife. This wife married Stephen Bayley, planter. Wmld, Va. Orders, 1668-77, fo. 122. 12 July 1672.

RULES for regulating the proceedings & practices of the Superior Court to be held in the Counties of this State: . . . For the Sake of Decent Conformity to Ancient Custom In the Profession the Attorneys Ought to be heard in a Black Robe Especially In Criminal Cases but this is not to be Insisted on With those who have not provided themselves With Such Habits untill the Second Term. . . . See the Court of 1 Apr 1797. Oglethorpe cty, Georgia.

An index of Volumes IV and V of the NOTE-BOOK has been prepared. It will be published shortly in mimeograph form, of the same size and shape as the printed index of Volumes I, II and III. Each index will be separate. The Editor regrets that she cannot afford to print. Each index will contain about sixteen pages. The price of the two will be $1.60. The price of one will be one dollar. The printed index of Volumes I, II and III, and these two, may be had at the special price of four dollars. The Editor will be glad of prompt subscriptions. Money can be sent later. *Good, clear print is guaranteed.*

CHILLIAN and MARTIN PALMER, Charlotte cty, Va. Seventy-five dollars will be paid for their ancestry. Must be proved by civil and church records.

W. B. P. A.

INTERCOLONY AND INTERCOUNTY

JOHN WALLEY was a Mcht of Boston, N. E. Also ANTHONY CHICHLEY. 28 Apr 1673. N-n, Va. x-187.

WILLIAM WEBB, of Tewkesbury, Gloucester, England; power of attorney. Surry cty, Va. 4 Oct 1667. 1-327.

RICHARD WEST, of Boston, N. E. Surry, Va. 1676. Vol. ii.

JOHN WASHINGTON was atty for Capt. Francis Emperour, Rappahannock, Va. 1652.

Mr. JOHN HORTON, of New England. Mentioned in an action for debt against Mr. Joseph Robinson. Acco, Va. 7 Sept 1685. ix-89.

JAMES WALKER, of Sussex cty, Territories of Penna., to Elizabeth Tilney, Acco, Va. 10 Dec 1698. xi-222.

RANDOLPH HEWITT, of Cape May, in "New West Jersey," and wf MARGRITT; power to John Washbourne and Southey Littleton, to ackn. a deed. [Margaret was granddau. of Susanna, dau. of Lt. Col. Wm. Andrews.] Acco, Va. 30 Mch 1698. xi-203. (See also xi-259.)

SAMUEL HANSON (of Barbadoes), bro. of John Hanson, dec'd. Acco, Va. 8 Nov 1679. viii-131. (See also viii-237. 12 July 1681.)

CORNELIUS KOLLOCK, of Boston, Mcht; power to Geo. Douglas. Acco, Va. 1729. ix-28.

ZACHARIAH THOMPSON, of Wilks cty, N. C., pltr, to Robert Owen, of Montgomery cty, Md., Innholder, a negro boy. 13 Feby 1781. Montg. cty, A-607.

PETER SPYKER, of Penna., to Robert Peter, Montgomery cty, Md., a lot in Georgetown. 13 Oct 1780. Montg. cty, A-610.

SAMUEL CARY, eldest son and hr-at-law, of John Cary, late of Sussex upon Delaware, in Penna., dec'd, and Stephen Hobbs, grandson and hr-at-law of Joy Hobbs, late of Somerset cty, Md., dec'd, and Robert Austen, hr-at-law of Joseph Austen, dec'd, to Henry Waggaman, of Somerset cty, Gent. (A conveyance.) Som., Md. 11 Mch 1750.

GEORGE and MARY TUCKER, of the Island of Barmudos, power to Capt. Isaac Handy, to ackn. deed to Samuel Handy, Som. cty, for 514 acres. The deed which follows shows that Samuel Handy, the Elder, died and left the land to two of his sons, Samuel and Thomas; Thomas died, leaving only one daughter, who m. George Tucker, the grantor. Som. cty, Md. 26 Oct 1747. xxi-299.

WILLIAMS NOTES MARYLAND-VIRGINIA SECTION

WILLIAM WILLIAMS m. PRISCILLA WALKER. Som. cty, Md. 15 June 1797. (Dr. C. H. B. Turner's notes.)

WILLIAM WILLIAMS, Sr. Patentee of *Chance*. Surveyed 1702. Calv. cty Rent Roll, Md. 1707.

WILLIAM WILLIAMS, Jr. Patentee of *Security*. 87 acres. Surveyed about 1702. Same reference. Also patentee of *Williams Purchase*. 206 acres. Same reference.

WILLIAM WILLIAMS, head of family. Ldn cty, Va. Tax list. 1782.

WILLIAM, BARUCH and BENNET WILLIAMS were evidently minors. William was son of John, Bennett son of William. Records of Harford cty Md. 1799.

WILLIAM WILLIAMS, Sleepy Creek, Berkeley cty, Va. Tax list. 1801.

WILLIAM WILLIAMS m. JINNY JOHNSON dau. Andrew and Mary Ann Johnson, 2 Mch 1790. Shenan., Va. M. L. B.

WILLIAM WILLIAMS, St. Mary's cty, Md. Will. Wf Frances, dw. pltn called *Roberts Neck*, during life, &c. Sons, James, Joseph, all my other lands and tenements, Gr.dau. Nancy Williams; Eleanor Ray; chn: Monica Williams, James, Joseph, Nancy James. Wf Frances and son James extrs. 21 Nov 1775-12 Mch 1776. Annap. Wills, xxx-643.

WILLOUGHBY WILLIAMS, of N. C. Grant of 640 acres in 1790. See Davidson cty, Tenn. 25 Oct 1797. D-374.

WILEY WILLIAMS, also LEONARD, WILLIAM, NATHANIEL and CHARLES WILLIAMS; also JOHN, HENRY and ROBERT WILLIAMS. In Granv. cty, N. C. Census. 1810.

WILLIAM and FRANCES WILLIAMS had dau. ELIZABETH, born 2 Feby 1752. Reg. St. John's (Piscataway) Psh, Md.

WILLIAM and ELIZABETH WILLIAMS had son JOSIAS, born 6 Jany 1775. Same reference.

WILLIAM WILLIAMS signs pet'n of civil and mil. officers, Staff cty, Va. Cal. St. Pa. i-70. 10 July 1700. Also p. 60, 1698.

WILLIAM WILLIAMS m. PHILLIS, the widow of Thomas EASTMEAD. Between 30 Oct 1683 and 29 Sept 1684. N-n, Va. xv-155. (Chanc'y and other records.)

WILLIAM WILLIAMS, Fauq., Va., sells horse, cow, &c., to Jeremiah Dearing. 1792. Fauq., Va. xi-170.

WILLIAM WILLIAMS m. JEAN JUDKINS, widow and relict of Charles. About or before 12 Sept 1711. Surry, Va. iii-80.

WILLIAM WILLIAMS m. MARY ROBERTS, widow, N-n, Va. Chanc'y and other records. (Date missing.)

WILLIAM WILLIAMS, of Dorchester, Md. Inventory. John Sexton his admr. Inv. returned 13 Apr 1730. Annap. Inv. xv-432.

WILLIAM and FRANCES WILLIAMS [see preceding record] had a second dau. ELIZABETH, Bap. 10 Oct 1754. And a son, BENJAMIN, Bap. 26 Feby 1764. St. John's (Piscataway) Reg. Md.

WILLIAM C. WILLIAMS and ALICE GRYMES, his wife, to John Croudson, house and lot which WILLIAMS purchased of JOHN WILLIAMS, 15 Feby 1797. Shenan. cty, Va. K-510.

WILLIAM C. WILLIAMS, of Shenan. cty, Va., from Martin Shaner and wf Catherine, of Hawkins cty, "Territory South of the Ohio"; two lots in Woodstock, Shenan. cty. Wit: Allen, Lee, F. Williams. 28 Apr 1792. Shenan., Va. H-371.

WILLIAM CLAYTON WILLIAMS, of Culpeper cty, Va., from John Sterritt, cty of Scott, Ky.

Conveyance. 13 Mch 1797. Shenan., Va. K-413.

WILLIAM C. WILLIAMS and wf ALICE G. and WILLIAM JENNINGS, Jr., to Thomas Allen. 136 acres on Drains of Cabbin Run (Fort Mountain mentioned). 1788. Shenan. cty, Va. I-315.

"*WILLIAMS VENTURE.*" See will of WILLIAM WILLIAMS, Fredk, Md. 1767-1769.

WALTER WILLYAMS to John Custis, 8 Oct 1652. N-n, Va. iv-423.

ZOPHER WILLIAMS, Census. 1820. Monroe cty, Ill.

Note: This list will be followed by an additional one as soon as space can be found.

SERVICE AND SUPPLIES COLONIAL, REVOLUTIONARY AND MILITIA

(From the Order Book of Hanover county, Va., 1831-1835.)

RICHARD BURNETT, a Revolutionary soldier, his declaration ordered certified. p. 56. 28 Nov 1832.

Capt. AARON CAMFIELD: On the motion of Richard Camfield, of Shelby cty, Tenn. whose dep'n taken before Judge of the Court of Marion cty, Alabama, on the 3 Feby 1834 is produced in court, ORDERED certified to the Register of the State Land Office of Virginia that the Court is satisfied that the late Capt AARON CAMFIELD, an officer in the Continental line of Virginia, shortly after the war of the Revolution removed from Virginia to Hancock county, Ga., and married, that he died two or three years after his marriage, leaving a widow and only son; that his widow survived him but a short time, and both died intest., and that the afsd Richard Camfield is the son and only surviving heir-at-law of sd Capt. Aaron Campfield, p. 158. Ct 28 Nov 1832.

Ensign ROBERT WATKINS: On the motion of James Watkins of Dallas cty in Alabama, and upon the testimony of John Nails, Richard K. Meade, and George W. Watkins, whose dep'ns before the Court of Colbert cty in Mississippi, 7 Jany 1834, are here produced, ORDERED certified to the Register of the Land Office of Virginia, that the Court is satisfied that the late Ensign Robert Watkins, an officer of the Continental Line of Virginia, died intest. in the service as Ensign during the War of the Revolution and left a widow and two children, Ann and James, that Ann died young, and her mother, the widow of Robert, died soon afterward, intest. leaving sd James, and that he is the son and only surviving heir-at-law of said Ensign Robert Watkins. p. 158. Ct 28 Nov 1832.

Lieut. JOHN GOGGIN: On the motion of Richard Goggin of Monroe cty, Miss., his testimony, and upon consideration of the testimony of John Nails, Richard K. Meade, and George W. Watkins, whose dep'ns before the Judge of Colbert cty, Miss., are here produced, 7 Jany 1834, ORDERED certified to the Register of the Land Office, that this Court is satisfied that the late Lieut. John Goggin, an officer of the Continental Line of Virginia, d. intest. in the service as Lieut. during the War of the Revolution, and that he left a widow and only son, and that his widow subsequently died intest. leaving no other child, and that Richard Goggin aforesaid is the son and only surviving heir-at-law of said Lieut. John Goggin.

Col. HENRY AIMS [*sic*]: In similar form Samuel Aimes and Fisher Aimes of Sumpter cty, Alabama, bring before the Court the claim of the heirs of Col. Aimes, and furnish the testimony of Richard K. Meade, and Cornelius Dabney. whose depositions were taken before the Court of Marion, Marion cty, Alabama, 3 Feby 1834; and the Court orders the usual certificate to the effect that Col. Aimes was an officer in the Continental Line of Virginia, and shortly after the close of the war removed to Georgia where his wife died and all his chn while infants, but two, and that he afterwards died intest. leaving two sons, Samuel and Fisher, and that the aforesaid Samuel and Fisher Aimes are his sons and the only surviving heirs-at-law of the said Col. Henry Aimes. 28 Nov 1832.

JAMES HAZELGROVE, a Revolutionary soldier, presents his declaration, with the affidavit of Charles Talley and Parke Street, and is ordered certified. 30 Nov 1832. p. 63.

JAMES MEREDITH, a Revolutionary soldier, presents his declaration, with the affidavits of William Wood and Parke Street. Ordered certified. 27 Apr 1833. p. 87.

JOHN WILLIAMS, a Revolutionary soldier, presents declaration and affidavits of George Smith, John Cook and Thomas Doswell. Ordered certified. 1 Dec. 1832. p. 64.

GEORGE SMITH, a Revolutionary soldier, makes declaration, with affidavits of John Williams, John Cooke and Thomas Doswell. Ordered certified. 1 Dec. 1832. p. 64.

BILLEY TALLEY, a Revolutionary soldier, presents declaration for pension. Affidavits of Charles Talley and Parke Street. 4 Dec 1832. p. 70.

RICHARD BURNETT: George Burnett, of Hanover cty, aged 70, appears in open Court and deposes that he recollects that a short time before the siege of York Town in Virginia . . . his brother Richard Burnett, late of Hanover cty, was drafted as a private soldier of the militia to serve a tour of six months . . . that he was under the command of a Capt. Scott, was stationed near the City of Richmond for some time then moved to a place called Westham. The affiant went to see said Richard when in service. Richard died in the summer of 1833 without ever having had any children; was survived by Margaret his wife, who died about twelve months after her husband. 29 Apr 1835. p. 235.

REUBEN TRIPLETT: Ordered certified that Midshipman Reuben Triplett died in Loudoun cty, intest. and left eleven chn, his only heirs at law, viz: five sons, Felix, Willis, Rodricks, Reuben and John; and six daughters, Fanny, who m. Thornton Walker; Harriet, who m. John Keen; Malinda, who m. John Anderson; Kitty Rossel; Elizabeth, who m. Joseph Edson, and Delilah Church, who died and left two chn., Kitty and Sarah Church, her only heirs-at-law. p. 150. 26 Apr 1834.

The

County Court Note-Book

A Little Bulletin of History and Genealogy

June 1927.

Vol. VI, No. 3

THE ANCESTRY OF COL. JOHN DONELSON OF TENNESSEE, EXPLORER AND PIONEER*

(Continuation of the identification of Rev. SAMUEL DAVIS, grandfather of Col. DONELSON, by means of the records of Delaware and Maryland.)

Before the deed mentioned in the last instalment of this Ancestry, James Round, of Somerset cty, Md., by his will, 5 Apr 1700, probate 26 May 1700, leaves a legacy to the Rev. SAMUEL DAVIS. Round's wife was Mary. (See Md. Wills, ii-221.)

Mr. DAVIS, the 5 Feby 1704, calling himself Gent., of Sussex county, buys from Elizabeth Stuart, 474 acres on the south side of a creek called "Rehobat's" or Love's Creek. It is noticeable that this deed locates the land on the "west side of Delaware Bay." (Sus., Dela. A1-313.)

The 5 Sept 1704, a record in Som. cty, Md. (G1-85), shows that the wife of Rev. SAMUEL DAVIS was MARY. The 30 May 1705 (G1-141) ELIZABETH was his "now wife." On that date he is called "Doctor" and sells to Ephraim Heather, Som. cty, Joyner, all that land called Mulberry, on the south side of Pocomoke River, near its head . . . part of Mulberry Grove. In this deed Dr. DAVIS is described as of Lewis Town. The 4 June 1705, SAMUEL DAVIS, of Sussex cty, Dela., and wf ELIZABETH, convey to John Fassett of Somerset cty, Carpenter, all of Overton's Lott, on the Seaboard side, up a branch of St. Martin's Creek, formerly surveyed for Samuel Shewell (grant to Overton, 1689). Consideration, 20,000 lbs tobacco. Wit: Francklin, Edgar, Morris[?] Ackn. in person. (Som. cty, Md. G1-113.)

The 24 Mch 1706, SAMUEL DAVIS, Sussex, Gent., buys of [Mr.] John Huling, mariner, of Rhode Island in America, a lot on the Second street of Lewis, Sussex. Consideration £40. Wit: Fisher, Russell, Parker. (Sus., Dela. C-303.)

In the Presbt'n Hist. Soc. Journal (x-42) is a reference in a deed of land to the Presbyterian Church at Lewes, of the land belonging to Mr. SAMUEL DAVIS; and in Mr. Sellers' Allied Families of Delaware, Rev. SAMUEL DAVIS is shown by the will of Thomas Fenwick to have been one of his executors.

No further record appears until 1714. On the 4 May of that year, SAMUEL DAVIS, Esq., of Sussex, receives from John Hepburn, Gent., of Sussex, an acknowledgment of a deed to land near the south or southeast end of Lewes Town. (Sus., Dela. A1-297.) [This conveyance is noticeable for its description of the land . . . *12,600 feet.*] Sussex, Dela., warrants show that Rev. SAMUEL DAVIS was granted a piece of marsh, the 10th 7th 1717. And on the 6 Aug same year, SAMUEL DAVIS, of Sussex, Gent., buys from Nethaniel Hall, of Sussex, mariner, 1 and 3-8 acres, south side town of Lewes. (Sus., Dela. A1-98.)

Mr. DAVIS brings a negro to have his age adjudged. (Som. cty, Md. C. H.-2. 17 Mch 1718.) And he petitions the Somerset court to ascertain the bounds of Beyond Expectation. Petition granted. (Som., Md. Minutes. A-132. 13 Dec 1720.) The 6 July 1722, SAMUEL DAVIS, of "Summersett" cty, Md., Gent., sells to William Becket of Lewes, for £68, one lot in the second street of Lewes, binding on a lot now William Godwin's. Wit: Brooke, Till, Russel. (Sus., Dela. F6-6.) DAVIS acknowledges conveyance to Philip Russell, Esq., of the land on the south side of the town of Lewes, where Russell now dwells, as also 1 7-8 acres "savanah" land near thereunto. (Sus., Dela. A1-251. 4 Feby 1723. Date of deed.)

[It has been extremely difficult to follow the identification of Rev. Mr. DAVIS through the records of two different colonies, and it has only been possible to do it by the various deeds of conveyance. They are, therefore, given in some detail in this article. The following record shows that Mr. DAVIS in 1724 had, apparently, resumed his profession as a minister.]

SAMUEL DAVIS, Minister of the Gospel in Somersett cty, and ELIZABETH his Spouse, give bond to Samuell Hopkins, Sr., and Adam Spence, Sr. of sd cty, Gentlemen, in the sum of £400, to deliver at or before the death of ELIZABETH, three negro boys, Simon, Will and Sam; also everything that shall remain of the personal estate of the sd ELIZABETH that she had at the time of her intermarriage with sd SAMUEL. Wit: Robt Martin, James Martin. (Som. cty, Md. GH-189. 11 Nov 1724.)

The Rent Roll of Somerset cty, Md., of which the date is supposed to be 1723 or 1724, p. 251, shows that Beyond Expectation, on the seaboard side, on Newport Neck, was surveyed for SAM'LL DAVIS. (A later rent roll of Worcester cty, 1744, shows that the property was resurveyed for DAVIS and contained 220 acres.)

The 30 Mch 1725, Philip Russell gives bond as administrator of SAMUEL DAVIS, with JOHN DONELSON and Capell King as security. (Annap. T. P. 27-168.) The inventory of the Rev'd Mr. SAM'LL DAVIS, late of Som'sett, Md., was taken the 3 Apr 1725. The total amount (personal property) is shown to have been £108-8-5. And the nearest of kin, J. DONELSON, KATH: DONELSON. (Annap. Inv. xi-59.)

Rev. SAMUEL DAVIS had one son and two daughters. The son, SAMUEL, was also a chirurgeon. The following references are given merely to make entirely clear the distinction between father and son and the marriages of the daughters. SAMUEL DAVIS, the son, was Coroner and member of the Commission in Sussex, Dela. As early as 1708, Philip Russell, who married one of the daughters, was one of "three gentlemen commissioned for the probate of wills, &c." He was later a member of the regular Court.

SAM'L DAVIS, of Acco. [Va.], chirurgeon, and wife Naomy, to Hugh Stevenson, Somerset, "Clark," consideration £150, land called Grove, taken out of Mulberry Grove, south side Pocomoke river, near head, which land was sold by Mr. William Round and wf Martha, to Mr. SAMUEL DAVIS, deceased, father of sd SAMUEL. (Som. cty, Md. AZ-133. 21 Jany 1733.)

SAM'L DAVIS, Acco., Va., Pract'cer of Physick, and wf Naomy, and JOHN DONNELSON, of Som. cty, Mariner. . . . WHEREAS SAM'L DAVIS, Clerk, father of the afsd SAM'L DAVIS, had patent to 500 acres called Beyond Expectation, originally belonging to Elizabeth Duncan, who died without heirs, so that the land escheated, and a resurvey showing the tract to contain 220 acres only, chiefly marsh, the sd land lying in a Neck called Newport, on the n.w. side of Assateague river, near Benj. Burton's pltn; and WHEREAS SAM'L DAVIS, party to this being the only son and lawful heir to SAM'L DAVIS, deceased, who died intestate . . . he and wf NAOMY convey to JOHN DONNELSON all the sd tract. Both sign. Ackn. in person. Wit: Scarbrough, Brown. (Som. cty, 21 Jany 1733. AZ-125.)

SAMUEL DAVIS, Esq., of Sussex cty, and wf NAOMI; JOHN DONNELSON of Somerset cty, yeoman, and wf CATHERINE; and PHIL. RUSSEL, of Sussex cty, and wf MARY, to William Becket of Sussex, Clerk; consideration £270, tract on the so. side of Love's Creek, a white oak mentioned, edge of the marshes . . . 400 acres. Wit: Wm. Till, Robert Smith, Sim: Kollock. Followed by a statement of Philip Russell that he was indisposed, &c., but is willing to make over his right as intermarrying with one of the daughters of SAM'L DAVIS, Sen'r, dec'd. Wit: Joseph Downing, Daniel Nunez, Susan Pemberton. (Sus., Dela. G7-153. 28 Mch 1733, and 4 May 1736.)

It is now necessary to take up the Rent Roll of Worcester county, Md. The date of this roll is 1744, but two of the properties of the family are still listed under the name of SAMUEL DAVIS.

Beyond Expectation, 200 acres. Resurveyed for SAM'L DAVIS. Belongs to the heir of JNO. DONNELSON, a minor.

Inch, 500 acres; surveyed for SAM'L DAVIS. In possession of Pirkins, Fausitt, &c.

Partnership, 200 acres. Surveyed for Capt. JOHN DONALDSON; belongs to his heir, a minor.

John's Purchase, 50 acres, surveyed for Capt. JOHN DONALDSON, and belonging to his heir, a minor.

Also Chance, 100 acres, surveyed for Christopher Glass. Belongs to the heir of JNO. DONNELSON, a minor.

(*To be continued.*)

MARRIAGES BY INFERENCE* WESTMORELAND COUNTY VIRGINIA**

LAWRENCE ABBINGTON and DOROTHY FINCH, widow of Richard. Before 23 Feby 1686. Orders 1676-88, p. 549.

PHILIP AHERNE and ALICE JEFFERIS, "reputed wife of Robert." Before 11 Jany 1687. Orders, 1676-88, p. 263.

HENRY BELL and ELIZABETH SANDERS [widow of Thomas]. Before 26 Jany 1686. Orders 1676-88, p. 543.

WILLIAM BOOTH and . . . BLAGDEN, dau. of John. Before 26 July 1688. Orders, 1676-88, p. 673.

Doctor JOHN COOPER and HANNAH ALLERTON, widow of Col. Willoughby Allerton. Before 28 June 1727. Fid. Accts, i-65.

ZIPORUS DEGGE and SUSANNAH PERRY, relict of John. Before 28 Aug 1744. Fid. Accts, i-300.

DAVID DISHMAN and SARAH WEEDON, dau. of John. Before 18 Mch 1740. Fid. Accts i-244.

JAMES DISHMAN and MARY WEEDON, dau. of John. Before 18 Mch 1740. Fid. Accts i-244.

EDWARD DUDDLESTON and MARY VAULX, extx of Robert. Before 31 May 1688. Orders, 1676-88, p. 650, 663.

RICHARD EOUELL[?] and ELIZABETH POPE. Before 27 July 1687. Orders, 1676-88. [This name is probably Ewell.]

WILLIAM FITZHUGH, of Stafford, Gent., and LETTICE TURBERVILE, dau. Maj. George and Martha Turbervile. Mar. settlement. 7 Mch 1743. Fid. Accts i-293.

RICHARD FRY and CHRISTIAN MONROE, relict and admx of Andrew. Before 27 July 1744. Fid. Accts, i-299.

ALEXANDER GORGES and MARY VAULX, widow of Robert. [She was also widow of Edw Duddleston and m. Caleb Butler.] Before 24 Nov 1686. Orders, 1676-88, p. 525.

RICHARD HENWODD[?] and the dau. of Richard CHAPMAN. Before 26 July 1688. Orders, 1676-88, p. 674.

JAMES JOHNSON and ELIZABETH GERRARD, widow of John. 27 July 1687. Orders, 1676-88, p. 594.

THOMAS JOHNSON, Gent., and ELIZABETH ASHTON, dau. Col. Henry Ashton. Before 31 Aug 1742. Fid. Accts, i-272.

JOHN MORRIS and ELIZABETH MARTIN, widow of John. Before 27 July 1687. Orders, 1676-88, p. 592.

JACOB MARTIN and SARAH SCOTT, widow of John. [She was also the widow of George Cross.] Before 5 June 1736. Fid. Accts, i-167.

JAMES MAXWELL and RACHELL POPHAM, widow of John. Before 31 July 1739. Fid. Accts, i-214, 302.

JOHN McCAVE and the widow of Mr. Thomas SMITH. Before 28 May 1740. Fid. Accts, i-236.

JOHN NEWTON and ROSE GERRARD, widow Thomas. Before 27 July 1687. Orders, 1676-88, p. 594.

JOHN PARVIN probably m. ANN [POUNCEBEE??] a widow. [Uncertain.] Before 27 July 1687. Orders, 1676-88, p. 592.

THOMAS PARRY and JANE WHITE, relict of Thomas. Before 1 Sept 1687. Orders, 1676-88, p. 598.

THOMAS PEACH and MARY SMITH, relict and extx of John Smith. Before 2 May 1743. Fid. Accts, i-291.

JOSEPH READ and HENRYETTA HARDWICK, one of the extrs of James Hardwick. Before 31 Aug 1742. Fid. Accts, i-269.

WILLIAM RUSH and DOROTHY THOMAS, widow of Christopher. Before 25 Aug 1686. Orders, 1676-88, p. 516.

**See December, 1925.

WILLIAM SAMPLE and the relict of Thomas TRAYMAN. Before 11 Jany 1687. Orders, 1676-88, p. 626.
WILLIAM SAMPLE and the widow of . . . MASON. Before 28 Mch 1688. Orders, 1676-88, p. 642.
JOSEPH SANFORD and ANNA-BARBARY MUSE, dau. William. About 29 May 1744. Fid. Accts, i-295.
JOHN SCOTT and SARAH CROSS, widow of George. Before 5 June 1736. Fid. Accts, i-167.
THOMAS SPENCE and MARY MURPHY, widow of John. About 30 Oct 1744. Fid. Accts, i-302.
WILLIAM TEBBS and MARY POPE, relict and admx of Mr. Thomas Pope. Before 27 Aug 1745. Fid. Accts, i-317, 326.
RICE WILLIAMS and the relict of Jo. HADNUTS. Before 27 Jany 1685. Orders 1676-88, p. 483.
ROBERT KING, Gent., and ELIZABETH BARNES, dau. Thomas Barnes, Gent. Before 23 Feby 1741. Fid. Accts, i-265.
SIMON LUTTERELL prob. m. ELIZA: CANFIELD, widow of Richard. Before 10 Mch 1723. Fid. Accts, i-fo. 4.
MATTHEW MASON, of St. Mary's cty, Md., Gent., and ELIZABETH SPENCE, dau. Capt. Alexander Spence of Wmld, Va. Before 4 May 1724. (She was then dec'd.) Wmld, viii-33. See also v-537. 30 May 1716. The marriage was before that date.

(THE FOLLOWING MARRIAGES ARE FROM THE RECORDS OF NORTHAMPTON COUNTY, VA.)

JAMES ANSELL and SARAH PANEWELL, extx of John Panewell and dau. of Henry Mathews. Before 28 Feby 1694. xvii-304.
JAMES ANCELL and ANN SHEPHARD, extx of Thomas. Before 29 Sept 1710. xix-211.
RALPH ARNELL and MARY TIPSHOTT, widow of William. Before 30 Mch 1685. xv-125.
WILLIAM ANDREWS and DOROTHY EVELIN, widow. Before 24 July 1673. x-211.
HENRICH ABLE and SOPHIA VANWEKER, dau. of Henrick Vanweker of Ulrick in the Netherlands. Before 3 Mch 1679. xiii-75.
JOHN ADOLPH and MILLICENT DIXON, widow of Christopher. Before 29 July 1675.
EDMUND ALLEN and ANNE BAGWELL, widow of John. Before 29 Dec 1687. xv-324.
HENRY ALLEN and ELIZABETH ATKINSON, widow of James. Before 28 Mch 1700. See xviii-60; see Acco. xii-94.
GARRETT ANDERSON and AMY PRITCHETT [widow]. Before 1647. iii-147.
ROBERT ANDREWS and ELIZABETH SHEPHEARD, dau. John and Elizabeth. Before 27 July 1696. See also Acco. xi-126.
WILLIAM ANDREWS, mar. contract with ELIZABETH TRAVELLER, 17 Jany 1651. v-47. [Probably dau. of George Traveller, first husband of Alicia Custis.]
JOHN AYRES, mariner, and MARY HILL, dau. of Richard. Before 28 Sept 1688. xiv-184.
PETER BOWDOINE and ADAH HARMANSON, one of the daus. of Susannah Harmanson. See pet'n filed Mch Ct 1724.
MARK BECKET and MARGARET DRIGHOUSE, widow Azaricum. Before 13 July 1743. Ct records.
JAMES BONWELL and SARAH DORMAN, widow. Before 1662. viii-146.
ROBERT BOLLING, Jr., and MARY BURTON, dau. of William. M. L. B. 3 June 1763.
NICHOLAS BOOTY and BRIDGET JARVIS. Before 11 Apr 1726. Ct records.
LUKE BATSON and SARAH WARREN, dau. John. Before 1751. L. C. (no page.)
JONAS BATSON and TABITHA KENDALL, widow of William. [Before?] 13 Sept 1722. Ct records.
WILLIAM BLOXSON and MARY JOHNSON, wid. of Robinson Johnson. 3 Aug 1790. M.L.B.
ISAC BALY [BAILEY] and ELISHA SAVAGE, dau. of Elkington, the Elder. Before 14 Mch 1731. xviii-251.
JOHN BOWERING and ELLENOR DOLTON. About 15 Apr 1660. D-255.
JOHN BALDWIN and MARY WILKINS, dau. of John. Before Feby 1650. iv-10.
THOMAS BAGLY and the widow of Henry Field. Before 26 June 1665. x-70[?]
FRANCIS BATSON and ANNE ALLEGOOD, widow of John [ELLIGOOD]. Before 1735-6. Ct records.
JOHN BAZEY[?] and the widow of Thomas CHURCH, Jr. Before 28 Jany 1677. xii-225.
CHRISTOPHER BARRATT probably m. ESTHER EASTMEAD. Before 26 Oct 1685. xv-162.
THOMAS BELL and BARBARY ROBINS, extx of Capt. Arthur Robins. Before 28 May 1695. xvii-343. See also xvii-246.
JOHN BISHOP and GRACE SMITH, sister of Littleton Smith. Before 9 Sept 1760. L. C. 1754-1771.
ABRAHAM BOOKER and MARY BRICKHOUSE, widow of George. Before 10 July 1728.
HENRY x BROOKS and ANNE RANIER, dau. of John and Frances. Contract of marriage. 20 Nov 1677. xi-153.
WILLIAM BROOKES and JANE DARLING, widow of Francis Darling. [Perhaps widow of Capt. William Whittington?] Before 23 July 1690. xvii-51.
WILLIAM BURDITT, Gent., probably m. FRANCES SAUNDERS, widow. About 16 Sept 1633. ii-106.
WILLIAM BURTON, Jr., and ELIZABETH EYRE. 25 Dec 1721. M. L. B.
WILLIAM BURTON, Gent., and Mrs. MARGARET WATERS, admx of Maj'r William Waters. Before 12 Dec 1732. Court records. See also 11 July 1732 [the marriage before that date]. ix-19.
THOMAS BULLOCK and SARAH WATERSON, dau. of William. Before 15 May 1728. Ct. records.
JOHN BURTON and BRIDGET DALBY. 21 Jany . . .? M. L. B.
STRATTON CAPELL and ABIGAIL SCOT, widow of John. Before Oct 1730. Ct records.
JOHN CARPENTER and MARY [ROBERTS?], sister of Moses Roberts. Before 13 Nov 1754. Court records.
THOMAS CHRECKLY [*sic*] and MARGARET BALDING, dau. of John, Sr. Before 28 Apr 1671. xi-22.
MICHAEL CHRISTIAN and a dau. of John and Sarah Powell. Before 13 Feby 1722.

See Page 22.

The County Court Note-Book

An every-other-monthly devoted mainly to abstracts from County Court records, prior to 1800.

$ $ $

MILNOR LJUNGSTEDT, Editor and Publisher.
Bethesda, Route 10, Maryland.

$ $ $

Published six times a year. Subscription, two dollars, in advance; must begin with the year.

JUNE, 1927 Whole
Vol. VI., No. 3 No. 34

PICTURESQUE MEMORIES

Not so many of the Editor's experiences as an explorer have been difficult or unpleasant, some of those that were are in process of being forgotten, if not forgiven; others, like the showy little hotel where the stylish hostess changed but one sheet; the two or three where sleep was impossible on account of noise; the one far south where a fire was "extra" even in bitter cold weather (the only case of this kind); the kennel provided by another stylish hostess with the most obvious of pretty shoes and silken stockings and a small car of her own; these will always be somewhat indignantly remembered; also the "hotel" where the mistress went off to church and left her two guests, one of them a wet and miserable young travelling man, to rummage for firewood. (The Editor has the solid satisfaction of recalling that she burned up quite a variety of material.) Against all these, however, are many pleasant memories, and one of the most delightful is that of an old, old, rambling inn near the top of the steepest kind of a hill, with the small courthouse perched above it apparently a-top of an Alpine peak. I hope if any one recognizes this locality that reader will be of the same type as the Editor, responsive to kindly hospitality and indifferent to sagging doors and paper-off-the-walls, and not in the least minding misfit bowls and pitchers and variety in towels.

This courthouse town was reached at that time by one of those hybrid trains, called, the Editor believes, "mixed." It had two ramshackle coaches, and the rest was freight without discrimination. It travelled at the rate of about fifteen miles an hour, and if it happened to be loaded up with school-teachers on some semi-professional jaunt, the teachers had time at any stop to go up to the drug-store for chewing-gum and post cards, and the Editor had time to photograph them.

After two or three or more hours we arrived in a rainstorm and in the dark at the station of the courthouse town. It then developed that there was no hotel bus, no taxi. Fortunately some young gentlemen with a car took the Editor in, and up the steepest street, if it can be called a street, that the Editor recollects in this country, excepting Lynchburg and the far side of Beacon Hill. It probably was not possible to go up that hill except by twisting around it. When the Editor walked down the next day, for there was no auto to be had, it actually made her feet ache.

At the hotel the Editor was met by the most friendly and hospitable of Clerks. Being taken to her room she discovered that she had struck one of the old-time galleried inns of Virginia. First you went out, and then you went in, and then you went up, and then you went out again, and there was your room on a mysterious dark gallery, with the street almost under your feet, doors that didn't fit, all kinds of curtains, and an immense "air-tight" and the usual two beds. The clerk had a great armful of narrow pine strips . . . he made the fire, lighted it and then looked at his watch. . . . "I'm coming back in ten minutes to see if that fire burns." And he did.

In the morning a negro came up to start the fire again, but the Editor had long become a master hand at "air-tights," and did not need him. A view from the gallery showed that she was in a quaint hill-town, only part of the way up. It took some searching to find the dining-room. Long will the Editor remember that breakfast and the waiter. Not only for his garb of office, which was a snow-white sheet or tablecloth tied about his neck and reaching nearly to his feet, but for the friendly and personal way in which he urged the excellent food upon the Editor. The good soul was one of the left-overs. Where is he now?

About at the top of the hill were the church and the courthouse. The Clerk's office was so small that there was just room for two tables, the Clerk, his deputy, the Board of Supervisors and the Editor. It was very cold . . . so the Board, being three gallant elderly gentlemen, and the Clerk equally gallant, moved away from the tiny open fire and gave the warmest place to the Editor.

The Editor has attended several Supervisors' meetings, mainly because she happened to be there and they happened to be there, and nobody had the heart to turn her out (this in Virginia by-and large, and not in metropolitan Virginia) but that special meeting was the most delightful. For the Board was giving most thoughtful consideration to the subject of a pension for two impoverished maiden ladies, and there was some question upon the part of one or two of the Board as to just how and when the monthly allowance of ten dollars should be paid.

When the Editor left for the near-by city of Danville, she told the clerk at the hotel that she was happy to have found that one, at least, of the old "have-some-more-fried-chicken" inns was still in existence, and she sincerely congratulated him. The memory of that town has softened many less friendly experiences. The Editor would like to go back, but, alas, the march of improvement may have struck the little hill village, and even the Clerk's office may have steam heat . . . and modern bad manners. But, in her heart, the Editor doesn't believe they have changed that much.

OCCASIONAL

In the lives of our ancestors, we become parties concerned. Hewitt. S. G. & G. Vol. i-2.

The following calls attention to the uncertain lines of early counties:

A deed from Taylor and wife; Jesper and wife; and Pridham and wife; to Deeke and Lynton, makes reference to a patent to Thomas Lewis, Edward Morgan and Edward Lewis, of a tract of land, part in Rappahannock, Virginia, and part "supposed to be" in Northumberland; and another patent to Thomas and Edward Lewis, part in Northumberland and part in Rappahannock. Richmond cty, Va. iii-178. [About 1704.]

PETER MASSOT receives a certificate from the county court for 350 acres for the importation of seven persons: Peter Massot and Frances his first wife; Elizabeth, his second wife; John Lozanne, her first husband; Elizabeth Lozanne his daughter; James Chevair, her second husband, and Elizabeth Chevair, his first wife. Henrico Orders, p. 24. Ct 1 May 1708. (Practical thrift.)

Collected:

SHARP to RAZOR (backing on a marriage license bond in Albemarle county, Va.) JACOB RASON and ELIZABETH SHARP. About 1791.

HENRY SPRING and ELIZABETH FROG. Marriage license bond, Albemarle county, Va., 1792.

JOHN VICE and LOUISA MILDEW. Balto. county, Md. Married 16 May 1820.

ADAM VIRTUE and MARGARET MUNGAN. Same. 6 Nov 1820.

The following is from the fly-leaf of "Liber K, 1681–95," Kent cty, Maryland,

ROBERT ROGERS, sonn of EDWARD and ANN ROGERS, Born 14 Aug 1681.

MARY TILDEN, dau. of CHARLES and MARY TILDEN, born 21 July 1681.

ARTHUR, son of MICHAEL and ANN MILLER, born 1 Sept 1681.

JOSEPH, son of FRANCIS and MARY ASHBURY, born 27 Mch 1681.

ELIZABETH, dau. of THOMAS and . . . DAVIES, born 28 Aug 1681.

ANN, dau. of EDWARD and ELIZABETH FRY, born . . . 1681.

JANE, dau. of WALTER and JANE KIRBY, born 14 Mch 1682.

JANE KIRBY, wife of WALTER KERBY, died 25 Mch 1682.

And so the record ends.

The mimeographed index of Volumes IV and V, COUNTY COURT NOTE-BOOK, is ready. It contains 24 pages. The impression is excellent. Same size as printed index to Volumes I, II and III. Price $1.60 for the indices for IV and V, or one dollar each. The full set may be had at a special price of four dollars.

CONTINUED articles COUNTY COURT NOTE-BOOK, and the dates on which they first appeared.

THE ANCESTRY OF COL. JOHN DONELSON, Began with February, 1927.

AUTHENTIC REFERENCES for INFERRED MARRIAGES (formerly called MARRIAGES BY INFERENCE). Began with May, 1922.

MARYLAND'S NEXT OF KIN. Began with July, 1922.

VIRGINIA COLONISTS. Alphabetized lists began with July, 1924.

MILITARY NOTES. both COLONIAL and REVOLUTIONARY, and later MILITIA NOTES. Began December, 1923.

INTERCOUNTY and INTERCOLONY (formerly called New Englanders and Others, &c., &c.). Began with March, 1922.

EASTERN SHORE FAMILIES. in the form of a one-page supplement, began with June, 1925. This will be continued later.

SHIPS IN PORT and COLONIAL FORENAMES, will appear in alternate issues or as space can be found for them.

Errata:

In the WILLIAMS notes for February, 1927, family of WILLIAM WILLIAMS, of Frederick, Md., the dau., given as Elinor-Hillary, should be Elinor Hillary, without hyphen.

In the April issue the name of ELIZABETH ROBINSON'S first husband is once given EYRES and once EYRE. It should be EYRE . . . although sometimes one spelling is used, sometimes the other. The little flourish at the end of a word, in which the early scribe so often indulged, is no doubt responsible for many added "s's."

In December, 1926, the marriage of Daniel Cugley at the top of page 42 should, of course, read "*Before 17 May 1641.*"

IMPORTANT

The NOTE-BOOK is now printed at some distance from Washington, and the Editor finds it difficult to properly allocate space for the various subjects. For that reason, at least for the present, each issue of the NOTE-BOOK will contain but three or four subjects, the material being alternated between issues. The present number contains the Donelson Ancestry, a good proportion of marriages indexed, but not heretofore published, and notes as to Revolutionary service. The remainder of the NORTHAMPTON marriages will appear in October, to be followed as soon as possible by marriage references from the neighboring county of ACCOMACK.

The Virginia Soldiers of 1776, two volumes of which have recently been published by Mr. Louis A. Burgess, of Richmond, Virginia, is a very valuable publication. The source material therein contained is drawn directly from the files of the State Land Office and has probably been known to and used by local searchers, but why these papers have not been copied and edited before is a mystery. They are invaluable, containing as they do, not only the statements of the applicants under oath, but copies of or even original wills and other papers filed with the application for bounty land in order to substantiate the applicants' rights.

It is almost a pity that, in order to enhance the value of his book, Mr. Burgess has included contributed material. This, in the Editor's view, was entirely unnecessary, the Land Office files being a gold-mine in themselves; and inexperienced readers will fail to mark the sharp line of demarcation between the two classes of information.

All historians and genealogists should have the volumes, as well as every library.

Mr. Stratton Nottingham is at work on the LANCASTER COUNTY MARRIAGE LICENSE BONDS, of which there is a very large number. The volume will be brought out shortly in mimeographed form, bound. Price $4.00. Subscriptions may be sent to Mr. Nottingham, at Onancock, Virginia.

QUERIES

CHILLIAN and MARTIN PALMER, Charlotte cty, Va. Ancestry wanted. Seventy-five dollars will be paid for accurate information accompanied by proof from civil and church records. W. B. P. A.

SAPIENS HARRIS; of Newcastle county, Dela. Five dollars will be paid for information concerning him. Will 1750. T.

ISAAC CAULK died in Cecil county, Maryland, 1748. Wife TEMPERANCE. Wanted: the parents of both.

MARRIAGES, *see page 19.*

Sir HENRY CHISLEY and the widow of Capt. Ralph WORMELEY. Before 28 Apr 1653. iv-178. [Note: records of Lancaster cty, Va., i-129, show that Sir Hen: Chicheley, of Rappahannock in Lancaster cty, Knt., m. Dame Agatha Wormley, late widow of Coll. Ralph Wormeley. Before 18 Apr 1654. The variation in the spelling of the name makes these references interesting.]

SAMUEL COBB and MARY COPES, dau. of Giles. Before 23 July 1696. xvii-412.

RICHARD COX and ELIZABETH WATTS, admx of John. About 1 Dec 1696. xvii-398.

HENRY CLEGG and ELIZABETH [LANGE] co-heir of Peter Lange. Before 28 July 1692. xvii-180.

THOMAS CLAY and MARGARET GRIMBALSON, dau. of Robert and Margaret (Harmanson) Grimbalson. Before 28 May 1694. xvi-28.

THOMAS CLAY and JANE DUPARKS, widow of John. About 1687. xv-337.

JOHN COOPER and ELIZ: COOPER [widow?]. About or before 12 Apr 1644. ii-366.

THOMAS COFFIN and ISABELL HAYES. Before 9 Nov 1683. xiv-85.

FRANCIS DOUGHTY, minister, and ANN EATON. Marriage contract. 8 June 1657. vii-48 [Reference to ix-19, 1 Sept 1658, seems to show than ANN EATON had been the widow COTTON.]

RICHARD DRUMMOND and ANN TILNEY, dau. of John Gent. Before 6 Apr 1700. xviii-68.

THOMAS DOWNS and RACHEL WILKINS, widow of Nathaniel, son of John. Before 10 Dec 1734. Ct Records.

JOHN DYNES and BRIDGETT BELLYERTE [BELLIOTE]. Before 25 June 1656. vii-28.

THOMAS DIMES [*sic*] and MARY RUTTER. Before 29 May 1658. viii-17.

JOHN DARCH and MARY, the extx of Conogh MacALEB. Before 28 July 1696. From xvii-45, the marriage seems to have taken place about 30 Nov 1691.

AMBROSE DIXON and the relict and admx of Henry PEDDENTON. Before 28 Oct 1647. iii-121.

WILLIAM DYNHAM and the widow of William BURWELL. About Nov 1648. iii-158.

ISAAC DOLBY and PEGGY MATTHEWS, dau. John Custis Matthews. 1759. M. L. B.

ISAIAH DRIGHOUSE and SARAH . . . [DRIGHOUSE?]. Before 13 July 1743. Ct records.

THOMAS DOLBY and ANN JACOB. Before 10 Sept 1702. xviii-172.

THOMAS DOLBY, Jr., and MARGARET HAZE, orphan of John. 14 Aug 1772. M. L. B.

JOHN DALBY and SUSANNA JACOB. 25 Feby 1769. M. L. B.

JOHN DOLBY and KEZIAH WESTERHOUSE[?] 1769. M. L. B.

BENJAMIN DOLBY and ANNE ROT . . . [?]. 14 Feby 1705. M. L. B.

JOSEPH DOLBY and JANE LUKE, widow. 19 May 1764. M. L. B.

ARTHUR DENWOOD and ESTHER ROBINS, dau. of John, Sr. Before 1707. xix 23.

SIMON ELLETT and a sister of Littleton WESCOTT. Before 12 Mch 1728. Court records.

THOMAS EDMUNDS and SARAH FISHER. Before Nov 1743.

CORNELIUS ELIASON, and SUSANNA CARPENTER. [She was born about 1684.] Before 1725. L. C. 1754-71.

JOHN ELLISON and ESTHER SHAPHARD, widow of John. Before 28 Nov 1705. xviii-266.

THOMAS EARLY and MARY SPRINGUISH[?], widow of Arthur. Before 29 Nov 1683. xv-30.

WILLIAM ENCH and ELIZABETH WALTER, extx of Ben: Walter. Before 28 Mch 1704. xviii-230.

JOHN ELLIGOOD and SUSANNAH WILKINS, widow of Jonathan. Before 15 May 1754. Ct records.

. . . EDWARDS, late citizen and freeman of London, and KATHRYNE HEMLOCKE, widow of Mr. Edw. Hemlocke. Before 30 Apr 1655. viii-18.

MOUNTJOY EVELING and DOROTHY ROBINS, dau. of Obedience. Before 29 Nov 1653. iv-174.

THOMAS EYRE and JANE SEVERNE, dau. of Mr. John Severne. Before 28 Oct 1678. xi-177. See also xvi-14. [She was also the only heir and granddau. of Mathew Gethinge. See xiv-152.]

WILLIAM FOSTER and MARGARET NEALE, dau. and heir of John Neale. Before 9 July 1668. xi-1.

WILLIAM FOSTER and the widow of Daniel PAINE. About 28 Mch 1710. xviii-527.

WILLIAM FINNEY and SARAH BRICKHOUSE, dau. of George. Before 29 Nov 1700. xvi-266.

ALEXANDER FLEMING and JOYCE HOPKINS, widow of Mr. Anthony Hopkins. Marriage contract. About 15 May 1666. vii-1.

ROBERT FLETCHER and MARY PRICE, widow and extx of Charles. Before 29 Mch 1692. xvii-163. [See also xvii-416.]

MARK FRESHWATER and ELISHE NELSON, widow. About or before 1753.

JOHN FURRS[?] and MARY NEVELL, widow of Richard. Before 28 Jany 1696. xvii-407.

JOHN FATHREY and . . . HALL, dau. of Emanuel and Ann HALL. Before 29 July 1690. xvii-56.

JOHN FISHER and the extx of Luke MASMAN. Before 30 Nov 1692. xvii-42.

STEPHEN FISHER, pltr, and ROBERTA ANDREWS, widow. 20 April 1657. [Possibly before that date.] vii-48.

ANDREW JOHN FABIAN and SUSANNA BATSON, widow of Thomas. Before 10 Sept 1734. Ct records.

PAULE FABIAN and MARY TULLOCK, widow of Richard. Before 2 Sept 1684. xv-79.

SERVICE AND SUPPLIES COLONIAL, REVOLUTIONARY AND MILITIA

JOHN ALLDAY; a soldier in the U. S. service. His wife, Mary, furnished provisions. Charl. cty, Va. Orders, iv-212. Ct Mch 1780.

ZACHARIAH ALVIS; makes declaration of Revolutionary service and Court approves. Gchld cty, Va. Orders. 22 Aug 1832.

JOSEPH ATKINSON makes oath that he enlisted in one of the Virginia Reg'ts raised for the "defense of this State" in the war between the King of Great Britain and the French King. Ordered certified to the Register of the Land

Office. Essex cty, Va. Orders, xxix-464. Feby Ct, 1780.

WILLIAM BARTON also makes oath. Same; same.

RICHARD BURNETT: George Burnett, of Hanover cty, aged 70, appears in open Court and deposes that he recollects that a short time before the siege of York Town in Virginia . . . his brother Richard Burnett, late of Hanover cty, was drafted as a private soldier of the militia to serve a tour of six months . . . that he was under the command of a Capt. Scott, was stationed near the City of Richmond for some time then moved to a place called Westham. The affiant went to see said Richard when in service. Richard died in the summer of 1833 without ever having had any children; was survived by Margaret his wife, who died about twelve months after her husband. 29 Apr 1835. p. 235.

WILLIAM BAREFOOT makes oath as to service. Certificate ordered. Essex cty, Va. Orders, xxix-463. Feby Ct, 1780.

THOMAS BROOKS, a resident of Gchland cty, Va., age about 88; enlisted in the army of the U. S. for three years, and served in Gen'l Stephens' company on the Continental Establishment. Enlisted in Spots. cty and was discharged in Fredericksburg. Was in no battles. Court declares opinion that he was a Revolutionary soldier. Gchld, Va. Orders, p. 135. Ct 20 Aug 1832.

WILLIAM BUSBY swears to declaration of Revolutionary service and Court declares, &c., &c. Same, p. 139. 20 Aug 1832.

JACOB BANKS; same; same. p. 152. 22 Aug 1832.

JOHN BRAFFORD; Court orders ctf that he died in the service of the U. S. at the northward. Widow, Elizabeth Brafford. Charl. cty, Va. Orders, iv-218. Mch Ct, 1780. A previous entry as to BRAFFORD states that he is a soldier in the Continental service; his wife Elizabeth is very poor and much in need of provision for support of herself and family. Charl. cty, Va. Orders, iv-94. May Ct, 1777.

BUTLER BUCKLEY makes oath; served as private Capt. Thomas Fleming's company, 1st Va. Regt, last war bet. Great Britain and France. Ctf ordered. Charl. cty, Orders, iv-209. Feby Ct, 1780.

RICHARD BUCK, heir-at-law to brother THOMAS, makes oath as to his service. Essex cty, Va. Orders, xxix-462. Feby Ct, 1780.

JOHN BOUGHAN, heir-at-law to brother JAMES. Same; same. Feby Ct, 1780.

JOHN BULLARD; same; same. Feby Ct, 1780.

MORDECAI BUCKNER makes oath that he served as Captain until disbanded, in one of the Va. Regts commanded by Col. Adam Stevens. Certified. Same; same. Mch Ct, 1780. In another declaration makes oath that he served as Quartermaster until disbanded under Col. Adam Stevens. Same reference.

ANNE BOULWARE, wife of ELIAS BOULWARE, a soldier in the Continental service, is allowed three barrels of corn and 150 pounds meat for the support of herself and three children. Essex cty, Va. Orders, xxix-476. May Ct, 1780.

A ctf of WILLIAM BOUGHTON from under the hand of General William Woodford was sworn to by the said Boughton and was ordered to be recorded. Same; same. Aug Ct, 1780.

BENJAMIN CHILDRESS; ctf ordered that he was a serjeant, 2d Batt. Ga. Continental troops, and died in that service, and that SUSANNA CHILDRESS is his widow. Charl. cty, Va. Orders iv-218. June Ct, 1780.

STEPHEN CRUTCHFIELD, age 73. Makes declaration 20 Sept 1831. Enlisted in the army of the U. S. in 1777, for three years, with Lt. Geo. Holland, a recruiting officer, and served in the 14th Regt Continental Line under Col. Charles Lewis and a number of others. Left the service Mch. 1780, and afterwards enlisted in the cty of Goochland in which he resided. Was in the battle of Germantown, &c., &c. Court declares opinion that he was a Revolutionary soldier. Gchld cty, Va. Orders p. 134. 20 Aug 1832.

JOHN CLEMENTS; makes declaration of Revolutionary service, and Court declares, &c., &c. Same; same. p. 152. Ct, 22 Aug 1832.

LEWIS CHAUDOIN; same; same. p. 146. Ct 21 Aug 1832.

JAMES COOPER; heir-at-law to his two brothers THOMAS and WILLIAM COOPER, who served under Col. William Bird. Assigns claim to John O'Neal. Essex cty, Va. Orders xxix-462. Feby Ct, 1780.

ROBERT CHILDRESS, makes oath as to service and ctf is granted. Franklin cty, Va. Ct Sept 1832.

WILLIAM CAMPBELL, a soldier of the Revolutionary War, makes oath to declaration and is ordered certified. Franklin cty, Va. Ct Sept 1832.

The following file declarations and make oath:

ANTHONY CAMPBELL, Nov. Ct 1832; Also in Jany 1833; ISAAC CUNDIFF, Jany Ct 1833; both of Bedford cty, Va. See Court Orders of that county.

Also: WILLIAM DEVENPORT, Sept Ct 1832.

JOHN DALLEY, makes oath that he is heir-at-law to his brother THOMAS DALLEY, Drummer, who enlisted and served until disbanded, Assigned to THOMAS DALLEY. Essex cty. Va. Orders xxix-466. Mch Ct 1780.

AMOS EVANS; makes oath that he served as a soldier under Capt. James Gunns in Col. Byrd's Regt in the year 1760, and that he has not received his bounty of Land agreeable to the King of England's proclamation in the year 1763. Henry cty, Va. Ct 25 May 1780.

GEORGE ELLIOTT is allowed for two horses, wagon gears and jackscrew (lost); 107 days' service of wagon and team, twenty days for another, and three casks. Henry cty, Va. Ct 29 Mch 1782.

RICHARD EVANS; ELIZABETH EVANS, the widow, testifies that the sd Richard served as a soldier in a corps raised for the defense of Virginia, and that he died without any children or blood relations within the United States. Ordered certified to the Register of the Land Office. Essex cty, Va. Orders xxix-464. Feby Ct 1780.

THOMAS FANDRUE or FANDREE, makes declaration and Court declares, &c., &c. Gchland cty, Va. Orders, p. 162. Ct 4 Oct 1832.

LEWIS FRANKLIN; makes declaration for a pension. Ordered certified. Henry cty, Va. Ct 13 Nov 1832.

JOHN FONTAINE, Esq., Captain of militia, resigns. Henry cty, Va. Ct 6 May 1782.

Mrs. George W. Hodges, a personal friend of the Editor; a conscientious and enthusiastic and hard worker in the old records, and a very brave woman, fighting an incurable disease, died the 14th of May, 1927.

The

County Court Note-Book

A Little Bulletin of History and Genealogy

August 1927. Vol. VI, No. 4

THE ANCESTRY OF COL. JOHN DONELSON OF TENNESSEE, EXPLORER AND PIONEER*

There is little in the records of Somerset and Accomack counties concerning the younger JOHN DONELSON, who afterwards made history on our western frontier; there is no record of his birth, of his marriage, or of his removal to the "continent" of Virginia. His birth would have been recorded in the Snow Hill church records, but these were burned years ago. The record of his marriage would have been in the old Presbyterian church in Accomack, or in the established church of the parish. All these records are gone. Possibly his wife, RACHEL STOCKLEY, had Quaker leanings at the time. Some of the STOCKLEYS were Quakers or intimately associated with Quakers. But the records of the local meetings have also disappeared.

JOHN DONELSON, II, son of Capt. JOHN DONELSON and his wife CATHERINE DAVIS, was born about 1718. The first conveyance of land by him is dated about 1747. However, his mother, CATHERINE DONELSON, conveys property to him and to his sister in 1739, and the following deed of 1747 mentions a patent to him in 1741. The references follow:

JOHN DONALSON, Gent., Wor. cty, Md., to Thomas Purnell, same; consideration £50, all that part or parcel called "Partnership," Worcester cty, near the Seaboard . . . side of Buck Ridge . . . south side of a Great Swamp, near to Patrick's Hill; 200 acres, granted to said DONALSON, 10 Nov 1741. Signed JOHN DONELSON. Ackn. in person. No wife appears. Wit: Hopkins, Purnell. Wor., Md, about 1747. B-126.

JOHN DONNOLDSON conveys "Partnership," 200 acres, to Thos. Purnell. Wor. cty "Alienations." Returned 1748.

In 1754, 29 Jany, JOHN DONNALDSON was in Accomack, Va., and with two others appraised the estate of Nathaniel Shae, dec'd. (Acco., 29 Jany 1754. xxv-24.) On the 5 Nov that year, calling himself of Accomack cty, he conveys to James Round, of Worcester (reciting a grant to SAMUEL DAVIS, "Clark," 20 Feby 1724) all that tract in Somerset, but now Worcester, in a neck called Newport, called "Beyond Expectation;" said tract bounded on the east side by a tract called "Newport," and by the line of Benjamin Burton, and near the pltn where Capt. Edmund Hammond formerly lived, and near the marsh side; 220 acres. "Whereas the afsd Tract by sundry mean conveyances and Mutations of Possession is now become the right of the afsd JOHN DONELSON"; consideration £100. Sig. JNO. DONELSON. Wit: John Scarborough, John Evans. Ackn. in person. Wife RACHEL, releases dower.

In 1754, the records show that DONELSON had a house in Accomack. (Acco., 31 Dec 1754. xxvO-72.)

The 1 July 1756, JOHN DONELSON, of Accomack, conveys to Stephen Sturgis, of Worcester, 100 acres near Corker's Creek. Consideration, £20. Proved by witnesses. No wife appears. (Wor., Md. 1 July 1756. D-70.) And on the 21 July, same year, still of Accomack, he conveys 50 acres, on a creek "issuing out of" Pocomoke river. Proved by witnesses. No wife mentioned. (Wor., Md. 21 July 1756. D-68.) This is the last record that the Editor has of Col. DONELSON on the Eastern Shore.

Col. JOHN DONELSON married RACHEL STOCKLEY, dau. of ALEXANDER STOCKLEY, of Accomack cty, Virginia.

THE STOCKLEY LINE

The STOCKLEY line goes very far back in the history of the Maryland-Delaware-Virginia peninsula and is a very difficult line to trace with exactness. This is largely because of the confusion between the senior and the cadet line, and the interchange of names between these lines. The two brothers who first appear in the records of Northampton county, Virginia, were FRANCIS and JOHN. There was also a WOODMAN STOCKLEY. It is probable that he was the WOODMAN STOCKLEY who a few years later occupied an important position in the Maryland government, but no proof has been found that these two were the same person. It is also probable that he was a brother of FRANCIS and JOHN, and if one were inclined to "guess," it may be supposed that WOODMAN, FRANCIS and JOHN were sons of JOHN, and that their mother was a WOODMAN. So far no actual proof has been found, nor of any connection with JOHN STOCKLEY of the Virginia Company. (See Hening, i-86. JOHN STOCKLEY, Mcht Taylor, member of the Va. Co. 23 May 1609.) The English wills, while they do not at all clear the matter up, seem to point to this conclusion.

FRANCIS STOCKLEY, the elder brother, had a son JOHN; who remained in Northampton; JOHN, brother of FRANCIS, had a son FRANCIS. JOHN, the brother of the first FRANCIS, was the owner of lands in Accomack, and shortly before his death he was elected to the House of Burgesses. Part of the confusion which has existed as to the brothers has been due to the erroneous setting down of FRANCIS' daughter FRANCES, as a son. So far as we have definite data, JOHN STOCKLEY, the younger brother of FRANCIS, is the head of

*Including the family of Rachel Stockley, his wife.

the STOCKLEY line of Accomack county, the cadet line.

FRANCIS STOCKLEY was in Northampton, then called Accomack, as early as 1633, as shown by a reference. (N-n, i-25. 10 Jany 1633. See also i-111, 13 Aug 1638, mentioning STOCKLEY as having been there four years before.) He appears in a suit before the court in Jany and Feby, 1635. (N-n, i-47.) In July, 1637, the Court admonished him that he must not work on Sundays. (N-n, i-75, 3 July 1637.) The 22 Dec 1636, STOCKLEY gets a grant of 50 acres on Old Plantation Creek, Accomack cty. for the transportation of Francis Jarvis. The line of Henry Williams is mentioned. (S. L. O. i-406.) The 6 July 1640, he petitions concerning the hire of his brother JOHN STOCKLEY by a Mr. John Angood. (N-n, ii-6.) He files a deposition as to his brother's transportation by himself [FRANCIS], and claims that his brother was bound to him for three years. The Court decides that FRANCIS shall have his brother's services. (N-n, ii-54. 1 Feby 1640.)

STOCKLEY was a juror in 1643, and in the same year FRANCIS STOCKLEY and DANN KNIFFIN assign a ctf for 200 acres to Henry Armitrading. [This name later became Trader.] The head rights were: FRANCIS STOCKLEY, Katherine Abbott, JOHN STOCKLEY, Christian Folly [Solly? Tolly?]. (N-n, 12 Dec 1643. ii-338.) STOCKLEY appears a number of times in the records of the court, in one of these in a suit concerning a looking-glass which was sent from England by the mother of his wife, but not delivered. It appears from this record that his wife was Joane. The looking-glass was valued at £4-6d. sterling, and John Johnson, whose wife Anne "detained" it, is ordered to satisfy FRANCIS. (N-n, 6 Feby 1645. iii-6.) STOCKLEY appears in different suits, and as a juror, and one matter before the court shows that his house was at or near the seaboard. Jno. Stringer in a petition says: "Having occasion . . . to ride unto the Seaboard side . . . was directed to Jno. Little to inquire his waye unto Francis Stockley's house." (N-n, 20 Feby 1652. iv-141.) He continues to appear in matters before the court until 1655. He died in that year.

FRANCIS STOCKLEY. Will.

Wife; dau. Ann Stockley; son John; dau. Frances Stockley, godson Francis Willyams; brother JOHN STOCKLEY'S son William; debt of Richard Wootten, dec'd, when paid, to be divided between John Stockley and his sister Francis [*sic*] Stockley. Wit: William Geldinge, William Ennis, JOHN STOCKLEY. 12 Dec 1655-1 Jany 1655. (N-n, v-113.) The will was proved by the oaths of Geldinge, Ennis and Stockley. (See vi-25.)

The will of RICHARD x WOOTON was proved 1 Jany 1655; after other legacies he gives "the rest of my estate unto FRANCIS STOCKLEY and JNO: his Brother." The date of the will is 29 Nov 1655. (v-83.) English wills seem to point to a relationship between the STOCKLEYS and WOOTONS but the matter is not as yet cleared up.

As intimated before, the two branches of the STOCKLEY family in Northampton and Accomack have been confused, some insisting that the daughter of FRANCIS was a son, and others transposing JOHN of the first generation, brother fo FRANCIS, with JOHN of the second generation, son of FRANCIS. For this reason the line of FRANCIS is touched upon, as having some general interest. His son JOHN remained in Northampton county, patented a quantity of land, and died there in 1712. Various depositions show that he was born about 1652.

(*To be continued*)

MARYLAND'S NEXT OF KIN*

(See Notebook for April, 1927.)

MARY MORGAN, MARY SIMMS; inv. Mr. Cornelius Manning of St. Mary's cty. 14 Oct 1721. vi-238.

CATHERINE SINNOTT, STEPHEN MACKEY; inv. John Sinnot of St. Mary's cty. 23 Oct 1721. vi-243.

ALEX'R x OGSTON, FRANCIS BARNES and THOMAS GODMAN sign; inv. John Barnes of Q. A. cty. 13 June 1719. vii-1.

RICH'D x PARISH, JOS'PH x PARVISH [evidently meant for PARRISH]; inv. Robert Parvish [Parrish] of Q. A. cty. [No date.] vii-3.

WILLIAM GOULT, GEORGE GOULT; inv. George Goult of Q. A. cty. 10 Sept 1721. vii-3.

EDWARD x HOULDMAN, GEORGE x SANDERS; inv. William Johnson of Kent cty. 12 Aug 1721. vii-6.

WM. x WINN, ESTHER x RIGHT, JOSEPH x RIGHT; inv. Thomas Winn of Kent cty. 29 Jany 1722. vii-7.

JOHN COALE, Sen'r, JOHN x COALE, Jr.; inv. Joseph Cole of Balto. cty. 18 Mch 1721. vii-10.

DAN'L x TOWNSEND; inv. James Townshend of Som. cty. 4 Jany 1721. vii-14.

ELIZABETH NELSON, RICHARD CROCKETT; inv. Mrs. Jane Elzey of Som. cty. 30 Oct 1721. vii-14.

JOHN x PORTER, CLINTUCK PORTER; inv. Hugh Porter of Som. cty. 12 June 1721. vii-15.

JOHN PAYNTER "nearest kinn;" Thomas Paynter, county not given. 28 Nov 1721. vii-16.

JO. EARLE, WILL. CLAYTON, JNO. SILDEN[?] [perhaps creditors?]; inv. Doctor Thomas Williams of Q. A. cty. 17 Apr 1721. vii-17.

THOS. x THOMAS, TRISTRAM THOMAS [Kin?]; inv. Elizabeth Williams of Q. A. cty. 4 Jany 1720. vii-18.

DANIEL x LAUGHLAN, ELIZ: LAUGHLAN; inv. John Laughlan of Calv. cty. 25 Nov 1721. vii-21.

GRACE x BAKER, SARAH x MANNYNG; inv. Grigory Mannyng of Calv. cty. 6 Feby 1721. vii-23.

FRANCES BEACH, FRANC'S x HORN[?]; inv. Frances Merritt of St. Mary's cty. 6 Jany 1721. vii-24.

"No kindred;" inv. John Brin of St. Mary's cty. 8 Feby 1721. vii-27.

WM. BANISTER; inv. Hector Macclain of St. Mary's cty. 15 Nov 1721. vii-30.

JOHN POWELL, REBECCA POWELL; inv. Frances Harrison, of Talbot cty. 12 Dec 1720. vii-32. [Daniel Powell, extr, was a Quaker and affirms.]

JOHN . . .[?], JOHN x NEIGHBOURS; inv. Robert Morton of Talbot cty. 20 Feby 1721. vii-35.

N. GOULSBOROUGH & ux, SAM'LL CHAM-

BERLAIN, ISAAC KITTSON [Kin?]; inv. Foster Turbutt of Talbot cty. 27 Apr 1721. vii-40.

RICHARD x BREAWER[?] inv. Benjamin Burch of St. Mary's cty. 30 June 1721. vii-52.

SARAH HICKY, admx. "Kindred there are not any." Inv. Cornelius Dyer of Calvert cty. 7 Dec 1721. vii-54.

"Kindred refused to be there." Inv. John Chittam of Calvert cty. 20 Dec 1721. vii-55.

JANE x MEAD, ANNE x HARDESTY; inv. William Meade of Calvert cty. 23 Dec 1721. vii-56.

MARY x HUTTON; inv. James Beacham of Calv. cty. 11 Sept 1721. vii-57.

RICH'D TUCKER; inv. John Tucker of Calv. cty, 22 Aug 1721.

SARAH x MURRAIN, THOMAS MURRAIN; inv. James Murrain of Calv. cty. 14 Mch 1722. vii-59.

JOHN DAWSON, OBADIAH DAWSON; inv. Richard Dawson of Dor. cty. 31 Jany 1721. vii-61.

WM. x CLIFTON, JNO. x BOUND; inv. Jno. Bound. Aug. 1721. vii-62.

GRIFFITH x REES, JOHN PARRY; inv. Evan Reed of Cecill cty. 17 Aug 1721. vii-64.

JAMES WILSON, SARAH x LINEGER[?]; inv. George Wilson of Kent cty. [No date.] vii-67.

JAMES WILSON, SARAH x LINGER; inv. James Wilson of Kent cty. [No date.] vii-67.

FRAN: THOMAS; inv. Thomas Pryor of Kent cty. 1722. vii-68.

MARTHA DANSEY; inv. John Ashcom, Gent., of St. Mary's cty. 8 Dec 1721. vii-69.

RICH'D HALL, HENRY DARNELL; inv. Benja. Hall of Pr. Geo's, Gent. [No date.] vii-74.

NATH'L HYNSON, GEORGE HANSON; inv. Col. Nathaniel Hynson of Kent cty. 6 Mch 1722. vii-93.

CORNELIUS ENNIS, WM. POYNTER; inv. Nathaniel Ennis. [County not given.] 7 Aug 1721. vii-121.

JNO. HOLLAND, RICH'D HOLLAND; inv. Elisha Coalton. 2 June 1720. vii-122.

RICH'D ACWORTH, JOHN ACWORTH; inv. Sarah Ackworth. 23 Mch 1721. vii-125.

RICH'D ACKWORTH, CHAS. ACKWORTH; inv. Joseph Haines of Som. cty. 20 Jany 1721. vii-127.

JOHN WILL, THOMAS INGLOSED[?]; inv. Robert Hill, of Som. cty. 31 Jany 1721. vii-128.

ESTHER KING, JOHN DENWOOD, BETTY DENWOOD; inv. Mr. Arthur Denwood of Som. cty. 9 Aug 1720. vii-129.

"No Kin." Inv. Thomas Warrington of Pokeamoke in Som. cty. 7 Oct 1721. vii-131.

ROBERT MILLS, JOHN MILLS; inv. William Smith of Som. cty; 13 Feby 1722. vii-133.

AFFRADOSI JOHNSON, JOHN TRUITT; inv. George Truitt of Som. cty. 17 Jany 1721. vii-133.

JOHN DREDAN, JAMES STEVENSON; inv. Robert Woods. [County not given.] [Date not given.] vii-134.

LEONARD x JOHNSON, JOYCE x JOHNSON; inv. Peter Johnson of Som. cty. [No date.] vii-136.

SAMUEL BRATTEN, JAMES BRATTEN; inv. James Bratten, of Som. cty. 20 Aug 1720. vii-137.

"Allowed by me widow of Samuel Ball." MARY x BALL. Inv. SAMUEL BALL. [County not given.] 25 Dec 1721. vii-137.

WILLIAM x PEPPER; inv. Tobias Pepper, of Som. cty. 11 Mch 1720. vii-138.

"Approved off by WILL'M SELBY, PARKER SELBY; There is No Orphans nor Legatees & few or No Debts. . . ." Inv. Daniel Selby of Som. cty. 1 Nov 1721. vii-139.

MARY KENNELLY makes oath that her Husband had no Kindred in the Land but her Self & 4 Children minors. Inv. of Darby Kennelly of Som. cty. 29 June 1721. vii-141.

JOHN x HUDSON, ROBERT MARTIN, JOSEPH HOLFIELD[?] Sen'r; inv. Jonathan Hudson of Som. cty. [No date.] vii-143.

ROGER x PATRICK, MATHEW x PATRICK; inv. Daniel Patrick of Som. cty. 9 Oct 1721. vii-144.

THOMAS x COOK, ROBERT x TUNNELL; inv. Robert Mossley of St. Mary's cty. 23 Feby 1721. vii-148.

MATHEW x KINDRICK, MARY x CRUCHSON; inv. Edward Kindrick of St. Mary's cty. 5 Mch 1721. vii-149.

JOHN J. HOWELL; inv. Francis Clarvo of Pr. Geo's cty. 27 Jany 1721. vii-153.

GEO. x ERBANK, EDWARD ERBANK [perhaps EIBANK? Meant for EUBANK?]; inv. Richard Eubanks of Kent cty. 5 Jany 1718. vii-157.

LEMMON[?] JOHN CATROP[?], JAMES x BARNSELE; inv. Sarah Evins of Talbot cty. 10 Apr 1722. vii—

JOHN SHERWOOD, JAMES BERRY; inv. Absalom Thrift of Talbot cty. 9 Feby 1721. vii-171.

FRANCIS BARNEY, ELIZABETH x ATTWIX, JOSEPH BARNEY; inv. Francis Barney, Sen'r, of Kent cty. [No date.] vii-177.

JAS. SMITH, PHILIP DAVIS; inv. Wm. Smith, of Kent cty. 17 Apr 1722. vii-181.

"No Kindred." Inv. George Worsley, of Kent cty. 9 Feby 1721. vii-184.

"No Kin to be found;" inv. William Nicholls of Kent cty. 27 Apr 1722. vii-185.

RICHARD x HOLMES, JAMES MULLIKIN; inv. Rich'd Holmes of Talbot cty. 14 Mch 1721. vii-190.

ABRAHAM CORD, THOMAS CORD, "two of the sons;" inv. Thos. Cord. 21 June 1721. vii-195.

SILVIA DARE, MARY THOMPSON; inv. Mr. William Dare of Cecill cty. [No date.] vii-202.

WILL SCOTT[?], MARY SCOTT, CHARLES LUCAS; inv. Thomas Lucas of Pr. Geo's cty. 26 Mch 1722. vii-208.

JOHN PITT, MARY FISHER[?]; inv. Thos. Pitt, Dor. [No date.] vii-212.

AMBROSE ARON[?]; inv. Magnus Creage of "Dorset" cty. 20 Feby 1721. vii-213.

WILLM x ROBINSON, WM. x POLLARD; inv. Wm. Green, Sen'r, of Dor. cty. 28 Mch 1722. vii-216.

SIMON THOMAS, JAS. DELAHAH; inv. Simon Richeson. 12 June 1722. vii-218.

THOMAS x JONES, JOHN ECCLESTON, RICH'D x GOOSTIN. [Uncertain whether these are kin or creditors.] Inv. Redmond Fallin of Dor. cty. 2 Apr 1722. vii-219.

WILLIAM x MORGAINE; inv. William Morgaine of St. Mary's cty. 27 Apr 1722. vii-221.

The County Court Note-Book

An every-other-monthly devoted mainly to abstracts from County Court records, prior to 1800.

MILNOR LJUNGSTEDT, Editor and Publisher. Bethesda, Route 10, Maryland.

Published six times a year. Subscription, two dollars, in advance; must begin with the year.

August, 1927 **Whole**
Vol. VI., No. 4 **No. 35**

JUST NOTHING AT ALL

The Editor is tired, tired physically and mentally . . . morally, also, perhaps. It is so absurdly hard to keep a nice little paper like this NOTE-BOOK going, without so much fuss about dollars and cents . . . especially dollars. The Editor begins to think she would like to be subsidized just like more important people.

It isn't the work on the NOTE-BOOK, not even trying to keep an independent typewriter tractable, a typewriter that persists in spite of the strong will and vigorous fingers of the Editor in *always* printing "m's" for commas and asterisks for periods. Now that last is worth a bit of study. The Editor once had an ancient Remington. She bought it of a Virginia County Clerk for twenty-five dollars, and the County Clerk, so the Deputy said, got it for cigarette papers. Meanwhile, the janitor, a tremendous and very black negro, used to write his Society announcements upon it, so that when the Editor sealed the bargain, she tied the machine up with much red tape, and left it in silence for a while. But that old Remington was a good one. It had its faults, it is true, but it behaved better about the asterisk. It didn't have any, to the best of the Editor's remembrance. However, the Editor wanted an asterisk and a pair of brackets, and a pound mark. So when she bought the Underwood she swapped a few extras and got the asterisk and the brackets, but not the pound mark. And the asterisk is where the period used to be. The period is downstairs, while the asterisk is up. But, in spite of the greater ease in striking a lower case key, the Editor's third finger on the right hand cannot forget the ways that left them twain . . . it will strike the asterisk. The reason of that is that it follows caps. Maybe now that the Editor has written it all out and thought severely about it, the combination will adjust itself. Such things do happen.

(N. B. Since writing the above, some time ago, the asterisk and the period and the comma have come to terms, and the Editor has very little trouble with them. This is without doubt a clear case of the triumph of mind over matter.)

The financial stringency, however, is uncontrolled.

There is an excellent young periodical coming out in a neighboring state, It has a higher and better flavor than several of its contemporaries. Its Editor is not only one of the intelligentsia but he has a delightful sense of humor. He is also truthful. He remarked to the Editor that it would take five hundred subscribers just to pay for the publication of his quarterly. The Editor wonders if he will keep on. Personally she has a very favorable opinion of that Editor, not only on account of his ability and his wit and humor. He exchanges with this Editor, and he said, he truly did, that he neglected some extremely important work in order to read the back numbers of the NOTE-BOOK. There is a man of taste and intelligence. All the same, he has the Editor's sympathy.

Mr. CHARLES KNOWLES BOLTON has brought out his valuable and interesting volume, listing arms which have been and are in use in this country, in the form of book-plates, engraved on silver, or cut on tombstones. Mr. Bolton is a charming and easy writer and the book is not only valuable for its information, but the explanatory preface is good reading. The preface also contains a condensed heraldic grammar. Commenting with an official of one of our four great libraries, this official expressed the greatest interest in Mr. Bolton's work, saying, to the Editor's surprise, that no such list of arms in use in America had ever been brought out.

The Editor regrets that the volume has been lent to a dear old "shut-in" friend, and she cannot remember the exact title. By addressing Mr. Bolton at the Athenæum, Boston, Massachusetts, full information may be had.

Mr. FREDERICK W. ROBINSON writes the Editor that there has been so gratifying a demand for the ROBINSON GENEALOGY, that the stock of remaining volumes has been brought quite low. As is the case with all such works the price of copies of out-of-print publications in the hands of dealers is usually greatly advanced. Those who wish to own this excellent genealogy should order now.

Mr. BURGESS also tells the Editor that the bound edition of VIRGINIA SOLDIERS OF 1776 has been in great demand, so that the remaining stock is gratifyingly small. It will probably be necessary to bring out a new edition of bound copies. In the June NOTE-BOOK the Editor commented on the great value of this publication, based, as it is, so very largely on "source" material.

OCCASIONAL

PETER LOVE and MARY EDEN. Mar. Li. Balto. cty, Md. 17 Apr 1802.

JOHN LOVEALL and MARY APPOLD. Mar. Li. Balto. cty, Md. 5 Apr 1804.

DECIMUS FILIUS AMBLER, of Stafford cty, Va. S. L. O. iv-27. 1710.

NICHO: COCK, his Denizacon. WHEREAS Nicholas Cocke an Alien having long lived in this country & truely & honestly behaved himselfe . . . & having full resolution to make his constant abode in this Country . . . [he] is made a free Denizen of this country of Vir'ga. . . . Nthld, Va. 1666-1672, p. 51. 20 Sept 1664.

RICHARD COLEMAN of Rappa. cty, by bill of sale bearing date of June, 1655, "sells unto WILLIAM VEAL & JOHN VAUX & their assignes a tract of Land containing six hundred acres." Rappa., Va. 7 Oct 1663. 1656-1664, p. 309.

THOMAS BUSHROD, of Essex Lodge, York parish and county . . . desires "to be buried in my old Garden by the side of my wife Mary, without 'cornor'[?] prayers or other Customes used at funeralls."

THE Court was by Proclamation adjourned to be held at the French "ordonary" the 24th Day of Feby next. . . . York, Va. vi-182. 26 Jany 1679-80.

CONTRACT BUILDING. In pursuance of a former order relative to the building of a prison "The Court are of opinion that the said Prison shall not be built by the person who shall offer to build it for the least money but at the laying the county levy they will agree with such person to build the same as *they shall judge most capable to perform the work.*" Henrico cty, Ct of Oct. 1724.

To Have and To Hold: WHEREAS the sd ANNE GAYLORD informed this Cort that the Cort had bound unto her Rebecca Dunkin for three years and that she was abt to marry and had scarce clothes to her back and that shee could not provide any till shee had the Corts opinion whether shee should serve out her time The Cort ord'd that she doe serve till the sd three years been expired. Wmld, Va. Ct 25 Mch 1685. 1676-1688, p. 391.

QUERIES

CHILLIAN and MARTIN PALMER, Charlotte cty, Va. Ancestry wanted. Seventy-five dollars will be paid for accurate information accompanied by proof from civil and church records.
W. B. P. A.

SAPIENS HARRIS; of Newcastle county, Dela. Five dollars will be paid for information concerning him. Will 1750. T.

ISAAC CAULK died in Cecil county, Maryland, 1748. Wife TEMPERANCE. Wanted: the parents of both. T.

JOSEPH HARRIS, of New Castle county, Dela., living 1764, had wife ELIZABETH. Who were her parents? T.

WILLIAM HOLLIDAY, of New Castle county, Dela. Wanted: his parents and grandparents. Holiday died 1754-1755. Wife was Ann. Had chn William, John, Joseph, Benjamin, Ann, Rachel. Five dollars will be paid for desired information. T.

TWENTY-FIVE dollars will be paid for full information as to Capt. JOHN WADE of Chester and Marcus Hook, Chester, now Delaware county, Penna. This is not JOHN WADE who inherited and bought the lands of Essex House, but a cousin. It seems to be proved that he married MARTHA ROBINSON. He had a daughter, MIRIAM, and probably a son THOMAS and perhaps JOSEPH.
Address Editor.

FORE-NAMES OF COLONIAL USAGE

VIRLINDA ADDISON, dau. of John and Mary Addison, K. Geo. cty, Va. St. Paul's psh Reg. Born 8 Oct 1764.
VIRLINDER BALTHROPE (mentioned in will of Daniel White), 14 July 1770. K. Geo. 1-308.
VERLINDA BERRYMAN was gr. dau. of Dorothy Spiller. Wmld wills (Crozier). 1722.
VIRLENDER BEALL, was extx of John Beall. Josiah Beall was extx of Vurlenda. Pr. Geo's cty, Md. Ct Minutes, 1758-1760, p. 676.
VIRLINDA DADE was wife of Baldwin Dade, K. Geo. cty, Va. St. Paul's psh Reg, 1760 and 1763. See also K. Geo. ii-221. 7 Mch 1798.
VIRLINDA DUNAHOO m. John Taylor. St. Paul's psh Reg., K. Geo. cty, Va. 13 Dec 1776.
VERLINDA GOUGH, was wife of Francis, Staff. cty, Va, 10 Feby 1785. S-179.
VERLINDA GREENE, dau. Francis and Elizabeth. Born 16 Aug 1692. Chas. cty, Md. Record of Births, &c.
VERLINDA GRIGSBY, was dau. of James White, Wmld Wills (Crozier), p. 64. See White's will, 1762-1763.
VIOLINDA HARRISON, dau. of Rice and Tabitha Hooe, K. Geo. cty, Va. St. Paul's psh Reg. Born 28 Feby 1762.
VERLINDER, dau. Elizabeth and Robert Clark Hall. St. John's (Piscataway) Md. Reg. Bap. 12 Dec 1762.
VIROLINDA LITTLE m. Joel Ancrom. 12 Sept 1745. K. Geo. cty, Va. St. Paul's psh Reg.
VIRLINDA LANHAM and John Allen. Pr. Geo's cty, Md. 30 Oct 1781. (See Md. Marriages.)
FELINDOR[?] SANDERS, a witness. Acco., Va. 11 Oct 1713. xi-612.
VIRLINDA SANDERS was wife of Richard. N-n, Va. 13 July 1661. Psh record.
VIOLINDA STAMINET, dau. of Daniel and Elizabeth, Born 28 July 1739. K. Geo., Va. St. Paul's psh Reg.
VIROLINDA THOMAS, dau. of William. Born 20 Apr 1728. K. Geo., Va., St. Paul's psh Reg.
VALINDA WADE, wife of Zephaniah Wade, of Pr. Wm., Va., Gent. Pr. Wm., 1740. E-37.
VIRLINDA WILLIAMS, a wit. to deed of Isaac Williams. Wilkes cty, Ga. 17 Aug 1787. DD-205.
VERLAND WILSON, aged 80. N. W. Hd, Fredk cty, Md. Census 1776.
WILLIAM VERLANDA; wf was Mary Ellen, prob. dau. of Joseph L. Brown. K. Wm., Va. 1849. "7"-500.

ARCHILUS AUSTIN, land owner. Survey for him, 366 acres, 29 Apr 1783. Buck'm cty, Va. Surveys, p. 57.
ARCHALOUS GOALDIN prob. m. Allah[?] Hardin, widow. Alb., Va. M. L. B. 21 Dec 1785.
ARCHELAUS HARRIS; deed to John Talbot. Wilkes cty, Ga. 3 July 1788. DD-196.
ARCHELAUS HUGHES mentioned. St. Paul's, Hanover cty, Va. 1767.
ARCHILUS JARRATT, returns est. of Thomas Andrew. Elbert cty, Ga. 1804-1809, p. 172.
ARGELUS MERRIL was eldest son and heir-at-law of Thomas. [He d. s. p. leaving a bro. William, who d. s. p. also, and the land of both

descended to Martha Robins, wife of William Robins, and only surviving sister of the whole blood of William Merril.] Acco., Va. 26 Sept 1752. ii-390. See also NOTE-BOOK for Mch, 1924.

ARCHELAUS MITCHELL, wife Ann. Dau. Lucy born 18 July 1736. New Kent, Va. St. Peter's psh.

ARCHLUS PAIN; land warrant. Liberty cty, Ga. 2 Mch 1801.

ARCHELUS PRIER; Elbert cty, Ga. Feby 1805.

ARCHELIUS RECORDS[?] Som. cty, Md. Rev. militia. M10(B)-15.

ARCHELAUS WATKINS was a justice. Kershaw cty, S. C. 9 Apr 1808. E-486.

HARCKLAS WILSON'S land mentioned. Aug., Va. Chron. 1754. iii-32.

HERCULES x HAYLES, pltr. Suit. Chas. cty, Md. 28 Jany 1661. i-182.

HERCULES DANIEL BIZE. late of the Island of St. Eustatius. Cha'ston, S. C. 22 May 1784. 1787-1791, p. 120.

HERCULES COATS, Sheriff of Kent cty, Md. Annap. Adm'n Accts, lxiv-110. 22 June 1770.

HERCULES COMPTON, was the svt of one Mannering. Wmld cty, Va. 27 Apr 1687. 1676-1688, p. 561.

HERCULES COURTNEY, Capt. Lt., 2d Co. Penna. Artillery. Penna. Col. Records. 1 Nov 1776. x-775.

HERCULES COUTTS, born in Montrose, Gt. Brit. D. 30 Sept 1707. Imm. Ch., Newcastle, Dela., Tombstones.

HERCULES COYTE, of St. Thomas psh, S. C. Cha'ston, S. C. 1745. HH-115.

HARKLUS was a negro slave belonging to John Musgrove. Cha'ston, S. C. 28 Apr 1724. 1722-1724, p. 281.

HERCULES RONEY, Ohio cty. W. Va. 2 Mch 1779. Minutes i-37.

HERCULAS SHEPARD; warrant for 1200 acres. Sussex, Dela. 16 Mch 1681-2. A1-8.

HERCULES SHEPHEARD (his sig.) goes to "New Deale." Acco., Va. 18 Oct 1682. vi-321.

(Note: For the possibility of a confusion between the names Archelaus and Hercules, see the N. E. H.-G. xxxix-62.)

WILLIAMS NOTES
MARYLAND-VIRGINIA SECTION

AARON WILLIAMS; Little Field and part of William's Hardship. Calv. cty Rent Roll. Md. 1759.

ABRAHAM WILLIAMS; census. Madison cty, Ill. 1820.

ABRAHAM WILLIAMS, Q. A. cty, Md. REBECCA WILLIAMS, admx. Annap. Bal. Book. i-23. 31 Jany 1752.

ALEXANDER WILLIAMS [WILLIAMSON?] m. Anne Wyatt, widow of Thomas. Prob. bet. Apr and Aug 1642. N-n, Va. ii-165.

ANDREW WILLIAMS; census. Madison cty, Ill. 1820.

AARON WILLIAMS; census. White cty, Ill. 1820.

ARTHUR WILLIAMS; same.

ARGULUS WILLIAMS, Jr., buys land. Wor. cty, Md. 31 July 1756. D-71.

ATCHESON WILLIAMS, Sr. 2 tithes. Tax-list, Hardy cty, W. Va. 1786.

ATCHESON WILLIAMS, Jr. 1 tithe. Same.

BARUCH WILLIAMS, Pr. Geo's cty, Md. Pltr. Kindred: THO: WILLIAMS, Benja. Berry. ELEANOR WILLIAMS, extx. Annap. Inv. 15 Mch 1724. x-89.

BRAZURE WILLIAMS; pat. for 360 acres, mouth of Wickware Run, Chas. City cty, Va. 20 Oct 1792. Va. S. L. O. xxviii-88.

[Note: So far as possible the spelling of the names is given as written.]

BENJ: WILLIAMS m. Susan Clark, dau. of Richard. Balto cty, Md. Before 2 Apr 1813. ix-315.

CHARLES WILLIAMS, Jr.; 197 acres surveyed for him. Surv. Book, Pr. Geo. cty, Va. 22 Jany 1714.

CHARLES WILLIAMS m. Margaret, extx of Richard Tule [probably Tull]. Before May Court, 1719. Annap. T. P. xxiii-381.

CHARLES WILLIAMS; census, Madison cty, Ill. 1820.

CHARLES WILLIAMS; census. White cty, Ill. 1820.

CHARLES WILLIAMS, son of John and Elizabeth. Born 4 Sept 1736. Som. Psh Reg., Md. (Dr. Turner's notes.)

CASSADA B. WILLIAMS; census. White cty, Ill. 1820.

CUTHBERT WILLIAMS; Pr. Geo., Va. 364 acres surveyed for him and John Hill. 6 Dec 1718. Surv. Book, Pr. Geo., Va. 85 acres surveyed 15 Nov 1719.

DIANAH[?] WILLIAMS; only "creditor or other relation" of JOHN WILLIAMS. Pr. Geo's cty, Md. 25 June 1746. DDi-419.

DOROTHY WILLIAMS, widow of WALTER, m. . . . Watts. N-n, Va. Before 4 Apr 1659. N-n, Va. viii-46.

EDWARD WILLIAMS, Rappa. cty, Va. Power to John Rotheram. 22 Oct 1668. Nthld, Va. 1666-1672, p. 41.

EDWARD WILLIAMS; 1 tithe; tax-list. Hamp. cty, W. Va. 1783.

ELIZABETH WILLIAMS, Q. A. cty, Md. The "kin" are either Tho. x Thomas and Tristram Thomas, or John Emory and Wm. Greenwood. Annap. Inv. 4 Jany 1720. vii-18.

EVAN WILLIAMS m. the widow of Richard Whithurst before 15 June 1663. L. Norf., Va. D-373.

EVAN WILLIAMS m. Marg't Richard. About or before 1703. Pa. Arch. xix, 2d ser. p. 409.

FRANCES WILLIAMS and Abraham Davenport. Md. Mar. Montg. cty. 21 Jany 1779. [Note: information as to the parents of Frances is very much desired.]

FRANCES WILLIAMS and Samuel McCubbin. Frances was of Balto. cty, Md., but the marriage was in A. A. cty, Md. Mar. 16 Nov 1797.

FRANCIS WILLIAMS and . . . Sweeny. St. Paul's psh, K. Geo. cty, Va. 24 Dec 1728.

GEORGE WILLIAMS; 2 tithes; tax-list. Hamp. cty, W. Va. 1783.

GILES x WILLIAMS, of Bedford, to JOHN and GILES WILLIAMS, Jr., of same. 280 acres. Consideration 5 sh. Bedford, Va. 20 Mch 1761, A-356.

GEORGE WILLIAMS m. Alce Fowler, of Brunswick psh. 3 Dec 1734. St. Paul's psh, K. Geo., Va.

HENRY WILLIAMS; bound by his mother Joyce x Smith. He was 11 years old 12 Jany 1725. K. Geo., Va. 6 Nov 1725. i-539.

HELENA WILLIAMS. Died 6 Oct 1728[?]. St. Paul's psh Reg., K. Geo. cty, Va.

HEN: WILLIAMS was an "ancient planter in the time of Sir Thomas Dale." Receives 150 acres, 6 Sept 1636. N-n, Va. See court Feby 1642. 1-216.

HENRY WILLIAMS, pltr, m. Sarah Black, dau. of William. Before 31 Jany 1681. Rappa. cty, Va. 1677-1682, p. 339.

ISAAC WILLIAMS; census; Union cty, Ill. 1820.

JACOB WILLIAMS and Elizabeth Miller. St. Paul's psh Reg. K. Geo. Va. 3 Dec 1747.

JACOB WILLIAMS; born 5 May 1722. St. Paul's psh Reg. K. Geo. cty, Va.

JAMES WILLIAMS; census. Pope cty, Ill. 1820.

JAMES WILLIAMS; son of JAMES and ELIZABETH. Born 11 Jany 1774. St. Paul's psh Reg. K. Geo. cty, Va.

JAMES WILLIAMS m. Elizabeth Todd, admx of William Todd, dec. Before 28 Nov 1695. N-n, Va. xvii-333, 334.

JAMES WILLIAMS and Molly Price. 24 Apr 1782. St. Paul's psh Reg. K. Geo., Va.

JAMES WILLIAMS, Q. A. cty, Md. Kin: JAMES and JOHN WILLIAMS. Annap. Inv. 1720. iv-222.

JAMES, CHARLES and JOHN WILLIAMS, sons of JOHN WILLIAMS, dec'd, grant of land in the psh of Bristol south side Gravely Run. [Chas. City cty?] 25 Apr 1702. Va. S. L. O. ix-451.

JAMES WILLIAMS m. Elizabeth Buckner, dau. of John Buckner of Gloucester cty, Va., and Deborah Ferrers. W. and M. Mags. Ser. 2, vi-173. Before 1680[?].

JACOB WILLIAMS m. Elizabeth Miller. St. Paul's psh Reg. K. Geo., Va. 3 Dec 1747.

JEROME WILLIAMS; tax-list. Hamp. cty, W. Va. 1783.

JESSE WILLIAMS; census. Gallatin cty, Ill. 1820.

JOB WILLIAMS, late of London, now of York river, Va., Mcht. 24 June 1702. York, Va. xii-594.

JOEL WILLIAMS (2); census. Pope cty, Ill. 1820.

JOHN WILLIAMS; census. Granv. cty, N. C. 1810.

JOHN WILLIAMS; census. Pope cty, Ill. 1820.

JOHN WILLIAMS m. Elizabeth Cooper, about 1647. N-n, Va. vii-10.

JOHN WILLIAMS; had bro. CHARLES and sister, ELIZABETH HARDING. Mrs. LUCY WILLIAMS makes oath. Pr. Geo's, Md. P[?]-339. 1 Oct 1729.

JOHN WILLIAMS, Pr. Geo's, Md. Died about 1740. Mrs. DIANAH WILLIAMS, admx. Kin: Elizabeth x Mason, Belinda x Busey. Annap. inv. xxv-180.

JOHN WILLIAMS and PHILIP WILLIAMS, wit. to deed by William Strother. Shen., Va. 14 Nov 1780. F-531.

JOHN WILLIAMS, son of ALEXANDER and ANNE. Born 19 Feby 1746. St. Paul's psh Reg. K. Geo., Va.

JOHN WILLIAMS; tract called Hay Marsh, east side Patuxen river; in possession of Edward Dorren for WILLIAMS' orphans. Surv. 25 Feby 1685. Calv. cty, Md. Rent Roll. 1707.

JOHN WILLIAMS, Pr. Geo's cty, Md. Inv. CHARLES WILLIAMS signs as brother, and ELIZABETH x Harding, a sister. 22 Jany 1728. Annap. Inv. xv-83. [See above.]

JOHN WILLIAMS, county not given; no kin given. See JOHN WILLIAMS, Kent cty, Md. JOHN WILLIAMS and William Trulock, nearest "kinn." 16 May 1723. Annap. Inv. viii-344.

JOHN WILLIAMS, Som. cty, Md. Power to Capt. Henry Lewes et al. 18 June 1750. Som, Md. xxii-159.

JOHN WILLIAMS, of Somerset, Md., m. Esther [White] admx of William White. Before 8 Aug 1737. Annap. T. P. xxx-300.

JOHN WILLIAMS of Somerset, Md. ELIZABETH WILLIAMS [prob. wid.,] CHARLES WILLIAMS, only child. Annap. Bal. Book. 9 Jany 1751. i-27.

Mr. JOHN WILLIAMS, of Fred'k cty, Md. THOMAS WILLIAMS, MARTHA WILLIAMS, next of kin. William Thielos[?] and William Blair, extrs. Inv. returned 16 Mch 1757. (Inv. taken 9 Oct 1756.) Annap. Inv. lxiii-16.

JOHN WILLIAMS, JOHN WILLIAMS, Jr., THOMAS WILLIAMS. List of tithables. 1744. N-n, Va.

JOHN WILLIAMS m. Hannah Henry. 18 Nov 1785. Shen. cty, Va. Mar. Retns. p. 17.

JOHN WILLIAMS; census. Gallatin cty, Ill. 1820.

JONAS WILLIAMS; tax-list. Fauq. cty, Va. 1782.

JONATHAN WILLIAMS; census. White cty, Ill. 1820.

JOSEPH WILLIAMS, A. A. cty, Md. Kin JOSEPH WILLIAMS, Jr., ZACHERIAH WILLIAMS. PHEBE WILLIAMS, admx. (Quaker.) Inv. 4 Nov 1740. Ret'd 9 Dec 1740. Annap. Inv. xxv-316.

JOSEPH WILLIAMS; tract called "Wooten," 100 a., side of Patuxen river. Surveyed 14 Mch 1676. "Catch," 50 a., surveyed 9 May 1681. "Puddington," 50 acres. Surveyed 29 Apr 1671, for Francis Fawks, west side main branch of Iseland creek. Calv. cty, Md. Rent Roll. 1707.

JOSEPH WILLIAMS, Fauq. cty, Va., and wife ELIZABETH, to Joseph Blackwell and Richard Lewis; 140 acres, Fauq., Va. 27 Oct 1763. iii-95.

JOSEPH T. WILLIAMS; census. Gallatin cty, Ill. 1820.

LEVI WILLIAMS; census. White cty, Ill. 1820.

LEWIS B. WILLIAMS m. Mary W. Catlett. Feby 1828. St. Mark's psh, Culp. cty, Va.

LUCY WILLIAMS, widow of JACOB, m. Benjamin Farrow. About 1794. Fredsbg, Va., Chancery court.

MARGARET WILLIAMS m. Peter Ryan. Balto. Mar. Li. 17 Nov 1812.

MARY WILLIAMS; census. Pope cty, Ill. 1820.

MARY WILLIAMS m. William Webb. About 4 June 1685. Rappa., Va.

MORGAN WILLIAMS m. Frances Scott [dau. of Henry]. Before [?] 29 Dec 1692. N-n, Va. xvii-208.

MORRIS WILLIAMS' widow; in possession of "Readby" also of "Perry Neck." Calv. cty, Md. Rent Roll. 1707.

MOSES WILLIAMS; census. Clark cty, Ill. 1820.

PAUL WILLIAMS; tax-list. Fauq. cty, Va. 1782.

The

County Court Note-Book

A Little Bulletin of History and Genealogy

October, 1927. Vol. VI, No. 5

THE ANCESTRY OF COL. JOHN DONELSON OF TENNESSEE, EXPLORER AND PIONEER*

JOHN STOCKLEY first appears in Northampton (then Accomack) county, in 1640, when he makes a deposition. (N-n, ii-1.) In another deposition (N-n, i-54, 1 Feby 1640) he states that he was transported by his brother FRANCIS. In 1645 he is before the court in connection with the estate of Luke Stubbin, William Ennis and JOHN STOCKLEY being security. This is valuable as showing some probable connection or relationship with Stubbin. (N-n, ii-386. 24 Sept 1645.) In 1647 he is set down as an head right under Capt. Sam'll Lucas. (N-n, ii-112, 30 Aug 1647.) As his brother FRANCIS had already proved his rights, including JOHN, this cannot be explained unless JOHN had meanwhile returned to England. It is probable that he did, as a later record mentions. He appears in the records in a number of small matters until 1651. In that year (15 Jany, N-n, iv-73) a dep'n of one Mary Little shows that he had a wife and a house the year before. Mary Little deposes in connection with some trouble between neighbors, that she went there and asked STOCKLEY'S wife for some Rosemary. (N-n, 15 Jany 1651. iv-73.)

JOHN STOCKLEY gets a ctf for 350 acres in 1653. Head rights: Archibald Alleyn, Reignold the Frenchman, Robert Trilley, Tho: West, ELIZ: STOCKLEY, JNO. STOCKLEY, Margaret Carrell[?]. In 1654 John Daniell's wife is fined for "scandalizing" him. (v-20.) JOHN STOCKLEY of N-n buys from William Whittington of N-n, 400 acres. on the seaboard side, bounded on the north by Mountneye Creek, east by the sea . . . Henry Fields old house mentioned. Consideration 4,000 lbs. tobacco. Wit: William Waters. (N-n, 30 July 1655. v-84.)

JNO. STOCKLEY, of Northampton, planter, to Simon Flye, same. Conveys 200 acres, part of 400 acres belonging to William Ennis, by patent, and sold to William Johnson, 1648, and "now becoming due to me by the free Gift and Donation of *the said* Philip [Watkins] upon his deathbed." (N-n, 29 Oct 1651. ix-147.) [No will of Philip Watkins could be found.]

John Park, a servant, complains against STOCKLEY concerning his freedom. The Court decides that he is to remain in the custody of STOCKLEY "(unto whom the estate is by will of Wootton bequeathed and the ex's of FRANC. STOCKLEY.)" (N-n, 2 Jany 1655. vi-26.)

John Daniell is directed to ask forgiveness of JOHN STOCKLEY'S wife. (N-n, 28 July 1658, vii-24.) However, the trouble still continues, and STOCKLEY gets a verdict against Daniell in 1658, but a new hearing is granted. And ELIZABETH STOCKLEY, his wife, is attorney for him. (N-n, 28 May 1658. viii-18.) The case, however, crops up again, STOCKLEY this time suing Daniell for trespass. (N-n, 28 Dec 1658. viii-38.) Mention in one of these records of STOCKLEY'S arrival in Virginia, from some trip abroad, "which was the day prefixed or upon the last of June, 1658." (N-n, viii-18.)

STOCKLEY appears before the court as appraiser, as juror, and in cases of debt. His servant accidentally kills a heiffer, and the Court orders that STOCKLEY give a heiffer in exchange. (N-n, 25 June 1662. viii-135.) In 1662, STOCKLEY, still of Northampton, has three tithes. In 1663 he has some trouble with the vestry of Hungar's and Nuswattock parish. Perhaps over tithes. [This entry is interesting as showing that the two parishes were together.] (N-n, 28 Apr 1663. viii-166.) In June of that year he brings an Indian boy to have his age adjudged. [Six years old.] (N-n, 25 June 1663. viii-169.) JOHN STOCKLEY, pays an heiffer to Richard Burkham for the use of John Coulston's children. (Acco., i-36. 10 Nov 1663.) [In this year the county of Accomack was erected.]

STOCKLEY gets a ctf for 400 acres. Head rights: JOHN STOCKLEY, ELIZA: STOCKLEY, Abraham Heath, Benj. Hickman, John Bowin, James Owin, John Moore, Eliza: Ashdon. (Acco., 19 July 1664. i-69.) He is a tithable in 1664. He gets another ctf for 800 acres. Head rights: Court, Smith, Morgan, Martha Ellford, Owin, Rebecca Walbrooke, Hopkins, Wellington, Hill, Lewis, Wood, Thornbush, Price, Anne Delfe, Price, Florance Allgood. (Acco., 16 Aug 1664. i-71.)

The records of the State Land Office, Richmond, Va. (old vol. v, p. 187), show that JOHN STOCKLEY, 2 Sept 1664, received a patent for 600 acres in Accomack, on the Seaboard side, on Corrattawaman and Stokeley's Creek, for fifty-two head rights. Among these were JOHN STOCKLEY, ELIZ: STOCKLEY, and ELIZ: and JOHN STOCKLEY again. [This also appears in v-71, head rights not given, land placed at 2600 acres.] STOCKLEY receives another ctf in the same year, 17 Nov. for 1050 acres. The head rights given are: Lewkner, Smith, Heyman, Brewer, Pett, Rye, Bane, Radley, Leigh, Carns, Cane, Orton, Bent, Hunt, Hitley[?] Newton, John Palmer, Easter Bayley, Thorey, Bishopp and John Boyes.

JOHN STOCKLEY is foreman of the grand jury 6 Nov 1665. (N-n, x-17.) He is a tithe in *Northampton* in 1665. Foreman of jury again in 1666. (N-n, x-29.) He is charged with not clearing the highway. He "declares some reasons" wherefore he could not send his man to work the highways and is discharged from his summons. (N-n, 28 Oct 1667. x-43.) In 1667 he is in Accomack again and from 1669 on appears to have made his residence in that county. Gets a ctf for 200 acres; head rights: Givin, Morris, Powell, Michaell Leigare[?]. (Acco., 16 Mch 1668. iii-119.) In

*Including the family of Rachel Stockley, his wife.

1668, he and his oldest son, William, are listed as tithes in Northampton. He assigns his ctf for 200 acres near the Seaboard side to Thomas East. (N-n, 30 Oct 1669. xi-15.) In 1669 he has some association with Alexander Addison. And that year he has two tithes in Accomack.

In 1672, "The names of the Vestry-men lately Elected and confirmed for the Upper Parish" were John Smith, Jonah Jackson, Rich: Bayly, Southy Littleton, Wm. Custis, Wm. Burton, Roger Mikeell, Jno. Drumond, Timothy Coe, Geo. Johnson, JOHN STOKELEY, Griffin Savage. "For the Upper part of North'ton County the 4th day of March Adom. 1672." (Acco., 1672. iv-193.) [At this date the two counties had been temporarily thrown together under the name of Northampton. See the Editor's contribution to W. and M., New Series.]

STOCKLEY is foreman of the Jury (N-n-Acco.) and on the 3 Oct that year, 1671, he gets a grant of 200 acres on the Seaboard side, between a former divident of his and the lines of Billiott[?], Hudson and others. (S. L. O. 3 Oct 1671. vi-377.) In 1671 he has four tithes. The 28 Apr 1671, he conveys to Christopher Stanly (describing himself as Gent., of Northampton *als* Accomacke) 200 acres, a neck belonging to the said JOHN STOKELY his grant patent, bounded by Poplar Neck, the maine branch of Assawoman Creek, &c. Wife ELIZABETH releases dower. (N-n, 28 Apr 1671. xi-22.) He appears before the Court in the usual matters, and the 8 Feby 1672 is described as JOHN STOKELEY, Sen'r. On that date he is chosen, by vote, one of the nine Representatives for the county to the Virginia Assembly. (Acco., iv-165.)

The 15 Aug 1673 (Acco., iv-231) ELIZABETH STOKELY asks probate of her husband's will. John Stratton appearing as witness.

JOHN STOKELY, N-n cty, pltr. Will.
- Pltn at Assawoman, 2700 acres, to all his surviving sons, each to take his share at eighteen, provided wife is also deceased. If wife survive, not to have shares until twenty-one.
- Wf ELIZABETH to keep plntn they are seated upon during widowhood, reversion to son Thomas;
- Three daus., Jene (or Jane), Hanna, Anne (under mar. age); has provided for dau. Elizabeth;
- Sons William, Woodman, and John have had their share of cattle, &c.
- William Custis, Thomas Bagwell, wit. 3 Feby 1670-18 Aug 1673. (Acco., iv-231.)

JOHN STOCKLEY was born about 1621. (See Acco., iv-60.) ELIZABETH his wife was born about 1633. (See Acco., v-39.) She m. (2) John Stratton, before the 16 Apr 1675. (See Acco., v-262.) She died in 1706.

ELIZABETH STRATTON. Will. "Weak in body."
Mentions her dau. Ann Atkins' son, Joseph Atkins; Matilda Atkins, John Atkins, grandson Woodman Stockley, Henry Toles, Jr., Stockley Toles, Thomas and Job Toles, Kendall Toles; John, Frances, Thomas, JOSEPH, and Charles Stockley; Hannah Bally all my cattell; Hannah Ballye and the rest of her brothers and sisters to have two shares, that is to say as much again as one of my sonns. Woodman and Thomas Stockley, extrs. ELIZABETH x STRATTON. 17 June 1697-6 Aug 1707. Wit: John Bradford, Henry Hemson, Mary Sampell. (Acco. xi-422.) [ELIZABETH STRATTON became blind before she died.]

It has been rather difficult, even with the two wills of JOHN and ELIZABETH STOCKLEY, to make a correct list of their children, and impossible to place all of them in their proper order. It is shown that WILLIAM STOCKLEY was the eldest son and heir apparent (see N-n, 28 Nov 1673. xi-65.), ELIZABETH STOKELY, widow and relict of JOHN STOKELEY, Sr., pltr, of the upper part of the county of Northampton *als* Accomack, and WILLIAM x STOKELY, the eldest son and heire apparent . . . deed to Emanuel Hall. A deposition by William Stockley shows that he was born about 1648. Another deposition makes it 1649, which is more likely, as his mother was born about 1633. Depositions by Woodman Stockley show that he was born about 1654.

After the death of William Stockley, Woodman, John and Thomas join in conveying to JOSEPH STOCKLEY, the land which came to them as heirs of William. (See Acco., 21 June 1687.) The three elder sons appear to have been William, Woodman and John. The order of the others is uncertain, except that Charles seems to have been the youngest.

The children of JOHN and ELIZABETH STOCKLEY, as shown by these various records are: William, b. ab. 1649; m. Mary . . . Died 1686. Elizabeth; Jane; Woodman, b. about 1654; m. Jane . . . Died bet. 1710 and 1713. Hannah, m. Bailey. John, b. about 1657; m. Mary Smith, wid. of Edward. Thomas, d. 1719? 1726? m. Hannah . . . Francis, m. Sarah . . . and died ab. Aug. 1698. Anne [dau. of STOCKLEY?] m. Atkins. Charles, d. 1728. Prob. m. Mary Tunnell, a widow, and JOSEPH. b. ab. 1659, m. Rachell Benston, before 20 Sept 1693, who died without issue. It is probable that he also m. Mary Massey, before 1696. It has been impossible so far to prove who was the mother of his children, as the second wife also died early. With the exception of Joseph, the above list is in a sort of approximate order.

JOSEPH STOCKLEY, b. about 1659, first appears in the records in 1680, when he is in the list of Accomack tithables. (vi-210.) In 1686 he was extr with Mary, the wife of William, of William Stockley's will. (Acco., 17 Feby 1690. ix-194.) And in the same year he was on the list of tithables with two tithes. JOSEPH STOCKLEY and JOHN, his brother, exchange properties in 1691 and 1692 . . . each one having 264 acres at Assawoman. (See Acco., 17 Nov 1691 and 21 June 1692. ix-218 and 239.) Woodman, John and Thomas Stockley, of Accomack, brothers and pltrs, to JOSEPH STOCKLEY, a tract of land which was their brother William's, said land left by their father, Mr. John Stockley, on Assawoman Creek. Wit: Francis x Benston, Edmund x Baley. (Acco., 21 June 1687. vi-448.) In 1696, JOSEPH STOCKLEY also buys land from Charles Stockley. (Acco., xi-116.) He ackn. a deed to Charles the 7 Mch 1710. (Acco., xiv-16.)

JOSEPH STOCKLEY, Sr., is to have all remaining part of swamp land bet. Joseph Staton and

Ralph Justice, for value of 2,000 lbs. tobacco. Will of John Morris, yeoman. (Md. Wills. 17 Sept 1719-10 Sept 1721. v-69.) JOSEPH STOAKLEY and Jacob Stockley give bond to Francis Stoakly as to land bought by JOSEPH of Jacob, excepting the right of Joseph, the son of Charles, to timber. Mary Stockley a wit. (Acco., 12 July 1722. xvi-181.) JOSEPH STOCKLY and Joseph Stockly, Jr., sign the inventory of Joseph Staton. (Acco. 7 June 1725. xvi-236.)

JOSEPH STOCKLEY, Sen'r, yeoman. Will.
Son Joseph, 300 acres, where he lives;
Sons ALEXANDER and Elias. plntn where I live, called Assawaman, the north part to ALEXANDER;
Grandson Joseph;
Granddau. Comfort Stockley.
Sons ALEXANDER and Elias, extrs. Wit: Kennet Scarburgh, Samuel Rain, John Stockley. 27 Dec 1731-3 May 1737. (Acco., xx-274.)

As stated before, JOSEPH STOCKLEY married RACHEL BENSTON, and perhaps MARY MASSEY, and perhaps a third time. He had no wife when he died, and careful search cannot at present prove who was the mother of his children, especially of ALEXANDER, who was the father of RACHEL DONELSON.

ALEXANDER STOCKLEY, son of JOSEPH, son of JOHN, was of age in or before 1726, when he bought or exchanged land. (Acco., 1726. xvi-281.) In 1745 he appears in the records of Accomack when he sells to the Rev'd Arthur Emmerson, for 1200 lbs. tobacco, levyed for his use by the Vestry, all that Parcel of Land whereon Assawaman Church now stands . . . one acre . . . for the use of the Parishioners of Accomack Parish for a Church and Churchyard. Ackn. in person. (Acco. 27 May 1745. Deeds i-502.) The 16 Apr 1751, he conveys to Elias Stockley for £100 the tract on the west side of Assawoman Creek, 100 a. (Acco. 16 Apr 1751. ii-325.) Conveys to Thomas Stockley, £100, 335 acres on the west side of Assawaman Creek and Branch. Ackn. in person. (Acco. 24 Aug 1752. ii-362.) He further conveys to Elias Stockley 150 acres on the west side of Assawaman Creek. Consideration £100. No wife appears in any of these deeds, and must have died early. (Acco. 24 Aug 1752. Deeds ii-381.) In 1752 he also conveys to Thomas Stockley for £100, a tract on the west side of Assawaman Creek. His milldam mentioned, and the line between himself and the land Thomas conveyed to him in 1750. No wife appears. (Acco., Deeds ii-382.)

ALEXANDER STOCKLEY, born *circa* 1700. No clue as to whom he married has been found. His will follows:
Dau. RACHEL DONELSON, wife of JOHN DONELSON, all the negroes in their possession.
Grandau. Comfort Stockley Nock, a minor;
Grandson William Nock;
Remainder estate to son Alexander Stockley. Grandson ALEXANDER DONELSON and son Alexander, extrs. Wit: Charles Stockley, Mary Walker, Joseph Stockley. 23 July 1763-27 Sept 1763. (Acco. xxvii W-206.)

AUTHENTIC REFERENCES FOR INFERRED MARRIAGES*

(Northampton County, Va.)

THOMAS BANKS and a dau. of Robert HARRISON. Before 1697. iv-243. (Before 25 Aug 1683. See xiv-76.)
THOMAS BARLOW, of Hungar's psh, Gent., and ANNE STOTT, dau. of Jonathan. About 10 May 1775. Chancy records.
NICHOLAS BARNES and SARA SARRELL. 1661.
THOMAS BELL and TAMAR SMITH, dau. of William. Before June 1769. Chancy records.
THOMAS BELL and SARAH GASCOYNE, dau. of Henry. Before 1784. Chancy records.
EDWARD BELOTE and MARY NOTTINGHAM. [Probably.] Before May, 1763. Chancy records.
JOHN BILLIARD and BRIDGETT FOSTER, wid. of John. Before or about 1 Nov 1650. iv-22.
EDMOND BIBBY and FRANCES HUNT, dau. Lt. Thomas HUNT [and wf Joane.] Before 22 May 1655. v-90.
JACOB BISHOP and SUSANNAH GOFFIGON, dau. of James. Before 10 Mch 1762. Chancy records.
JOHN BIGGS and TABITHA GOFFIGON, dau. of Peter. Before April, 1774. Chancy records.
NATHANIEL BURGESS and ANNE GOFFIGON, dau. of Peter. Before April 1774. Chancy records.
. . . BASNETT and FRANCES PRICE, dau. of Walter. Before 11 Jany 1680. xiii-262.
MATTHEW BUSQUETT and POLLY HARRISON. Before 1783. Chancy records.
. . . BENTHALL and FRANCES HUNT, dau. of Thomas. Before 15 Jany 1700. xviii-71.
. . . BEEDLE and . . . SATCHEL, a widow. Before 29 Jany 1667. ix-171.
PETER BOWDOIN and SUSANNA PREESON [a Quaker], dau. of Thomas and Elizabeth. [Elizabeth d. 1 Apr 1733. Thomas d. 5 Apr 1733.] See chancy record 10 July 1759. (Land Causes, p. 49.)
JOHN BOWDOIN and GRACE STRINGER. M. L. B. 10 Jany 1754.
THOMAS CABLE and SORROWFUL MARGARET KENDALL. M. L. B. 25 May 1723. [She was extx of William.]
[STEPHEN] CHARLTON and BRIDGET SEVERN, wid. of John. Before 28 Aug 1648. iii-151.
. . . CLARK prob. m. MARY BENTHALL, dau. of Joseph, Sr. Before 1703. xix-105.
MICHAEL CORMICK and FRANCES MULLS, dau. of John. Before 11 Dec 1697. xvii-437. (Before 12 Jany 1668. See chancy records.)
THOMAS COWDREY and ALICE SATCHELL, extx of John. Before 30 May 1698. xvii-477.
WILLIAM COWDREY and MARY ROBINS, dau. of Col. Obedience and Grace ROBINS. Before 2 Mch 1683. xiii-285.
Mr. GEORGE CORBIN and GRACE SAVAGE. Before 3 Jany 1688. xv-399. [This reference is a little uncertain.]
GEORGE DEWEY and ANNE RODOLPHUS. Before 1780. Chancy records.

See page 37.

The County Court Note-Book

An every-other-monthly devoted mainly to abstracts from County Court records, prior to 1800.

MILNOR LJUNGSTEDT, Editor and Publisher.
Bethesda, Route 10, Maryland.

Published six times a year. Subscription, two dollars, in advance; must begin with the year.

October, 1927 **Whole**
Vol. VI., No. 5 **No. 36**

When Defoe wrote the lines which head the OCCASIONALS it is not likely that he had been making a search for anybody's ancestry, but he might well have been trying to prove the beginnings of one of our colonial families and, in exasperation, after honest endeavor to carry Peter Jones, or John Smith, or Samuel Davis back through the records, have expressed himself as he did . . . for the scandalous loss of parish registers, of contemporary Bibles, and the careless handling of civil records is an old and familiar story.

And, even at this day, like other tiresome things, such as the newspaper picture strips, this indifferent carelessness seems to "continue on." The Editor had occasion recently to visit a county. She does not mention it by name because the Clerk, after he found out that the Editor was harmless, even if intelligent, was inclined to be helpful and was very nice to her. The Editor thinks he even asked her to come again! There is one pleasant side to this, Clerks are, as a rule, independently honest. They may not care a picayune what you think about their system of un-system, but they don't ask you to come again unless they mean it. Truth is better than flattery, even if it is often pleasant to be beguiled into thinking that flattery is truth. Clerks don't "enthuse" and say nice things which they don't mean; at the most they are courteous and helpful, and when they have a hobby of their own, they are very interesting. To this must be excepted the radio. But that would be quite another story.

This county, which the Editor started to comment upon in the middle of the last paragraph, is not fifty miles away. It is an old county, and its fine old Minutes, considered to be complete, were heaped, as the Editor saw them, upon the floor of a dark and dirty room. All the volumes were damp (there is no cellar under this room) and one volume was decidedly wet.

Somebody says, "Why not write the Governor?" What's the use? A people have been said to have just as good a government as they deserve. If a county has no historical pride, why bother with it?

Every now and then some one asks the actual date of the Virginia State Land Office records, that is, the date of their transcription. On the inside of the original cover of volume one, Royal or Colonial Grants (this volume had in the neighborhood of 1,000 pages. but has been cut in two), is written "This Booke was Transcribed [by] EDWARD HARRISON in the yeare 1683." Under the patent recorded on page 944, the transcriber frankly writes "The Severall Names I Cannot reade they are soe defaced." The date of the "soe defaced" paper is 28 Sept 1643. It may well be that some of the extraordinary names listed in the "Virginia Colonists" of the NOTE-BOOK were the best that the transcriber could do with other damaged papers. This 1683 handwriting, by the way, has been identified by an authority as of some ten or twenty years earlier. It is very natural to suppose that the colonial fashions were somewhat behind the very latest schools in England.

Dr. Stewart, in the RESEARCHER, is giving abstracts of the earliest grants, and so far, the most ancient one found is of 1621.

OCCASIONAL

"Great families of yesterday we show,
And lords, whose parents were the Lord knows who." Defoe.

"TAKEN up on the Roade within six dayes a Gold Ringe if any person can tell the posey they shall receive the same payinge some reasonable charges to Teigue Harman." 30 and 31 Jany 1681. N-n, Va. xiii-214.

MR. ROWLAND JONES, Minister; Information against him for illegally marrying Capt. James Archer and Miss Elizabeth Huburd without license. "Referred for better proof." York, Va. 10 Dec 1677-8. vi-30. [The ministers sometimes found that their charges were not "chapels of ease."]

NICHOLAS CASTIGAN, Sarv't to James Westcomb, and wife Margaret, late Margaret Maddison, likewise svt to sd Westcomb, agrees to serve nine calendar months after the expiration of his [Castigan's] term of service, and James Westcomb promises to release Margarett Madison als Castigan from all further service. Wmld, Va. Recorded 25 Feby 1707. iv-95. [In these days of general revision, the Editor thinks this is rather beautiful.]

THE Jury that was Impanneld & Sworne concerning a Horserace was called, and all of them did appear, & the foreman Michael Wellington did declare that they neither had nor could prepare a verdict. The Court therefore Order, that the Sheriffe take the jurors into his Custody and keep them without meat drinke fire or candle, until they have concluded on a full & perfect verdict, and the Court further Order Collo Wm Peirce to receave this Verdict when it may be tendered him by the said Jury.

QUERIES

CHILLIAN and MARTIN PALMER, Charlotte cty, Va. Ancestry wanted. Seventy-five dollars will be paid for accurate information accompanied by proof from civil and church records. W. B. P. A.

SAPIENS HARRIS; of Newcastle county, Dela. Five dollars will be paid for information concerning him. Will 1750. T.

ISAAC CAULK died in Cecil county, Maryland, 1748. Wife TEMPERANCE. Wanted: the parents of both.

JOSEPH HARRIS, of New Castle county, Dela., living 1764, had wife ELIZABETH. Who were her parents? T.

ANDREW LEE; Who were his parents? He was born in New Jersey about 1745, and died in Edgefield county, S. C., 1796. Revolutionary soldier. Mrs. D.

RUSSELL WILSON; Wanted the maiden name of his wife. Wilson was a Revolutionary soldier; moved from Virginia to Edgefield county, S. C. Mrs. D.

JOSEPH A. BYERS m. REBECCA ROWAN, in York or Chester county, S. C. When? Byers was a Revolutionary soldier. Mrs. D.

TWENTY-FIVE dollars will be paid for full information as to Capt. JOHN WADE of Chester and Marcus Hook, Chester, now Delaware county, Penna. This is not JOHN WADE who inherited and bought the lands of Essex House, but a cousin. It seems to be proved that he married MARTHA ROBINSON. He had a daughter, MIRIAM, and probably a son THOMAS and perhaps JOSEPH. Address Editor.

The mimeographed index of Volumes IV and V, COUNTY COURT NOTE-BOOK, is ready. It contains 24 pages. The impression is excellent. Same size as printed index to Volumes I, II and III. Price $1.60 for the indices for IV and V, or one dollar each. The full set may be had at a special price of four dollars.

CONTINUED articles COUNTY COURT NOTE-BOOK, and the dates on which they first appeared.
THE ANCESTRY OF COL. JOHN DONELSON. Began with February, 1927.
AUTHENTIC REFERENCES for INFERRED MARRIAGES (formerly called MARRIAGES BY INFERENCE). Began with May, 1922.
MARYLAND'S NEXT OF KIN. Began with July, 1922.
VIRGINIA COLONISTS. Alphabetized lists began with July, 1924.
MILITARY NOTES. both COLONIAL and REVOLUTIONARY, and later MILITIA NOTES. Began December, 1923.
INTERCOUNTY and INTERCOLONY (formerly called New Englanders and Others, &c., &c.). Began with March, 1922.
EASTERN SHORE FAMILIES. In the form of a one-page supplement, began with June, 1925. This will be continued later.
SHIPS IN PORT and COLONIAL FORENAMES, will appear in alternate issues or as space can be found for them.

MARRIAGES, *see page 35.*

ISAAC DUNTON and the widow of William SCARBURGH. About 13 Apr 1758. Chancy records.
SIMON ELLETT and a sister of Littleton WESCOTT. Before 12 Mch 1728. Chancy records.
. . . ELLIOTT and MARY FITCHETT, dau. of Nehemiah. Before 1774. Chancy records.
GUSTAVUS EWING and the widow of Robert JAMES. About 1759. Chancy records.
THOMAS EDMUNDS and SARAH FISHER, widow of Thomas. Before Nov 1743. Chancy records. She had also m. JOHN BENSTON, who d. ab. 1739.
. . . FINNEY and JOANNA STOTT. Before 7 Jany 1768. Chancy records.
THOMAS FISHER and SARAH SMITH, dau. of William. Before June 1769. Chancy records.
NEHEMIAH FITCHETT and RACHEL STRINGER. Before May 1766. Chancy records. (The marriage was on the 25 July 1762. Fitchett died 1764. Rachel was the widow of John, who died about 26 July 1761. See further records.)
THOMAS FOX and . . . JOHNSON, wid. of John. Before or about 8 Mch 1724. Chancy records.
MARK FRESHWATER and the widow of John WATERSON. Before or about 1744. Chancy records.
PAUL FABIAN and SARAH MULLS, dau. of John. Before 11 Dec 1697. xvii-457.
ISAAC FOXCROFT and BRIDGET CHARLTON, dau. of Stephen. Before 28 June 1662. viii-8.
THOMAS FOX and the widow and extx of John JOHNSON. Before or about 8 Mch 1724-5. Ct records.
MATHEW FRESHWATER and HANNAH BAKER, dau. of John. Before 8 Sept 1724. Ct records.
ALEXANDER FLEMING and URSULA BROWN, widow of John. Before 5 July 1658. ix-18.
THOMAS FROST and ANNE BANKS, dau. of Thomas. Before 25 Aug 1697. iv-243.
JOHN FORSITH and JANE WILLIS, dau. of George. Before 2 Mch 1673. xi-68. See also xi-177. [She m. (2) Thomas Hogg.]
ROBERT FLETCHER and FRANCES KELLEY, wid. of Edmund. [It appears probable that she was a widow Johnson before she m. Kelley.] See 8 Aug and 29 Sept 1684. xiv-104, 106.
HAMONDxFIRKETTLE and SUSANNA KENDALL, widow of John, her "first husband." Before 28 July 1692, xvii-180. See also xvi-47 and xvii-418. [She was also the extx of Henry Warren, and admx of Sam'll Powell. See xvii-431. Other records show that SUSANNA was born SAVAGE, and was the dau. of John. See xvi-47 as above.]
SIMON FOSHUTT [FAWCETT?] m. ELIZABETH, dau. of Ann JORDAN. See 1653. iv-203.
THOMAS GOHOGAN and a dau. of Thomas DUPARKES, Before [?] 1702. [Judge Robertson kindly supplies the name ELIZABETH DUPARKS and another form of the name: GOFFIGON.]
JOHN GITTING and ELIZABETH CHARLTON. About 1661. viii-111.
Mr. JOHN GUY and SUSANAH BURTIN, dau. of John, Gent., dec. John Kendall gives consent . . . "my kinswoman." 27 Sept 1750. M. L. B.
THOMAS GIDDENS and ELIZABETH BELL, dau. of Thomas. Before 12 Dec 1678. xii-314. (About 10 Sept 1674. See v-191.)
JOHN GARRIS and MARY FLOYD, dau. of James. Before Dec 1770. Chancy records.
HENRY GASCOYNE prob. m. SARAH UPSHUR, widow of Thomas. (Will 1751.) About 1753. Chancy records.
CANTWELL GARRISON and the widow of Hillary HUNT. Before 12 Oct 1743. Chancy records.
JAMES GIBSON and SARAH PREESON, dau. of Thomas and Elizabeth. Before 2 June 1736. Land Causes.
CHARLES GELDINGE and ABIGALL DIXON, dau. of Christopher. Before 29 July 1675. xii-64.
DEVERIX GODING and ANN POWELL, dau. of Nathaniel. Before 1756. Court records.
DEVORAUX GODWIN and SUSANNA KENDALL, dau. of Capt. William. About 28 Feby 1701. xviii-91.
LAMBERT GROTON and MARY CABLE, widow of Edward. About 28 July 1680. xiii-84.
PETER GOFFIGON and TABITHA NOTTINGHAM, extx of Michael. Before 2 Dec 1766. Chancy records.

BENJAMIN GRIFFITH prob. m. the widow of William BAKER. Before 27 Jany 1700. xviii-209.

JEROM GRIFFITH and ELIZABETH, dau. of Elizabeth GELDING. Before latter part of 1698. xvii-526.

DANIEL GRIFFITH and ANN HUNT, widow of Azariah. Before July 1761. Chancy records.

THOMAS GREEN and SARAH SMITH, sister of Littleton. Before 9 Sept 1766. Land Causes.

JOHN GREENE and ALICE COBB, dau. of John. Before 23 June 1688. xv-392.

HENRY GREEN and MARGARET FATHERY, widow of John. Before Sept 1767. Chancy records.

JAMES GOODWIN, of York, and MILDRED . . . who later m. Capt. LAW. SMITH. GOODWIN d. about Sept 1719. Misc. loose papers. [This is evidently not a Northampton County record.]

JOHN GRAINGER and MARGARET DALBY, dau. of Edward. Before 31 Oct 1683. xiv-88.

NICHOLAS GRAINGER and DOROTHY DALBY, widow of Edward. Before 28 Nov 1677. xii-209.

NICHOLAS GRAINGER and ANNE DALBY, dau. of Edward. Before 28 Nov 1683. xiv-87. [Perhaps son of Nicholas above?]

PETER GRICE and MARY STOTTS, dau. of Henry. Before 29 Dec 1692. xvii-208.

JEREMIAH GRIFFIN and the widow of Charles WEBB. Before 14 Mch 1737. Chancy records.

ROBERT GRIFFIN and JANE YOUNG, widow of Gower[?]. Before 1728. Chancy records.

. . . GRIFFIN and ELIZABETH GELDING, dau. of William. Before 11 Nov 1684. xv-349.

ROBERT GRIMBALSON and MARGARET HARMANSON, dau. of Thomas, Sr. Before [?] 28 May 1694. xvi-28.

JOHN GROVES and MARGARET ESDALL. Before Sept. Ct 1724. Chancy records.

DANIEL GUY and the widow of Lazarus JACOB. Before 11 Mch 1739. Chancy records.

JOHN HUDSON and . . . SENIOR, widow. Before 4 Mch 1684. xv-115.

WILLIAM HEATH and the widow of John CARPENTER. Before Sept 1769. Chancy records.

PATRICK HARMANSON and ELISHE KENDALL, extx of George KENDALL. Before Dec 1770. Chancy records.

. . . HAGGOMAN prob. m. MARGARET MICHAEL, widow of Joachim. Before Jany 1767. Chancy records.

THOMAS HUNT and ANNE WILKINS, dau. of John. About 1 Aug 1666. Chancy records.

OBADIAH HUNT and ROSE GOFFIGON, dau. of James. Before 10 Mch 1762. Chancy records.

JOHN HUTCHINSON and ANNA TAYLOR, widow of Elias. Before 20 Sept 1641. i-100.

MARKE HAMMOND and ANNE DENNIS, svt of Thomas Powell. Before 16 July 1640. i-3.

SERVICE AND SUPPLIES COLONIAL, REVOLUTIONARY AND MILITIA

JOHN ANDERSON, private, 7th Maryland; wounded at the Battle of "Katen Island," 22 Aug 1777. To be paid £3, 15s. for three months' half-pay. Balto. cty, Md. Proc. ii-93. 9 Dec 1788.

WILLIAM ARCHER, a poor militia man; wife Anne to be supplied with necessaries during her husband's absence in the service in Georgia. Meckl., Va. 14 June 1779. iv-476.

The following persons make declaration before the Court that they served in the Revolution, and the Court declare their opinion that they did.

REUBEN BIZENDINE[?], DAVID BARTEE, ELIJAH CLARK, WILTSHIRE CARDWELL, Sr., DANIEL HENDRICK, ALEXANDER HUNTER, NAUN JOHNSON, THOMAS McDEARMAN, JAMES MULLINS. Charl., Va. 3 Sept 1832. Orders xxix-2.

JOHN BRUNET, a private, 2d Md. Regt, wounded at Camden, 16 Aug 1780. To be paid £7, 10s. "One-half pay." Balto. cty, Md. Proc. 14 Feby 1787. ii-2.

JACOB BARNITZ was wounded in the Revolution and lost the use of one of his legs. See will of Ann Elizabeth Hartway, wid. Balto. cty, Md. Wills. 18 June 1785. iv-41.

WILLIAM BROOKS makes declaration of service. Court declare opinion that he was a Revolutionary soldier. Charl., Va. Orders. 3 Dec 1832 xxix-16.

MILLINER BRYANT, wife of John, a poor soldier in the service of this county. Supplies ordered. Charl., Va. Jany Ct 1778. Orders iv-122.

DANIELL BROWN was imprest in the country's service, himself and horse, to bring down the corn and lumber belonging to the Rappa. Indians, Referred to the Honorable Assembly. Ct. 2 Apr 1684. Rappa., Va. Orders.

ABRAHAM BROWN was Imprest into the service, himself and horse, to bring down corn and lumber belonging to the Rappahannock Indians from their fort to the river side; in which service he was Imployed nine days and for Satisfaction is Refered to the Hon'rable Assembly. Rappa. cty, Va. Orders. Ct 2 Apr 1684.

ROGER COCK BAILEY, served as corporal, Capt. James Greene's Co., Va. Regt. War between the King of Great Britain and the King of France. Ordered certified. Charl., Va. Ct Mch 1780. Orders iv-209.

ROBERT BLAKE, a poor militia man; Ann Blake, his wife, to be supplied with necessaries during her husband's absence in the Service in Georgia. Meckl. cty, Va. Ct 11 May 1779. iv-474.

CHARLES CLARK makes oath that he served in a Va. Regt in the War between the King of England and the King of France. Essex, Va. Feby Ct 1780. xxix-463.

ROBINSON CUSTIS, recommended for commission as Lieut. in the militia. Acco., 30 July 1777. xxxvO-17.

SOUTHY COPES, recommended for Lieut. militia. Acco., Va. 30 July 1777. xxxvO-17.

THOMAS COPES, to be 2d Lieut., militia. Acco., Va. 29 July 1777. xxxvO-12.

JAMES COLLINS, a sjt, 1st Maryland Regt, wounded at siege of York, Va. Allowed £11, 5s. (six months' half-pay.) Balto. cty, Md. 14 Feby 1787. Proc. ii-2.

BENJ. CAGE proves by his own oath and that of John Tredway, that he served in the last war [French and Indian] as private in Capt. Richard Dogget's Co., in a Virginia Regt. Ctf ordered. Charl., Va. Mch 1780. Orders iv-209.

GEORGE CARTER recommended for Lieutenant, county militia. Pittsyl., Va. June Ct, 1777. iv-12.

URIAH CAMMERON makes oath that he served as a soldier under Capt. John Powsey agt the Indians in 1760. Is a native of Virginia. Pittsyl., Va. June Ct 1780. iv-32.

WILLIAM DEAVER, private 3d Md. Regt, having lost a limb in the Battle of Camden, 16 Aug 1780, is to receive £15 for 12 months' half-pay, due 15 June 1787. Balto. cty, Md. 13 June 1787. Proc. ii-21.

FREDERICK FITZGERALD; makes oath that he served as a soldier under Capt. William Preston, in his company of Rangers, in 1762, and has not received his bounty. Henry cty, Va. Ct 25 May 1780.

JOHN FOSTER makes declaration of Revolutionary service and Court declare opinion that he was a Revolutionary soldier. Charl., Va. 1 Oct 1832. Orders xxix-5.

NICHOLAS GENTRY was a soldier at Mattapony Garrison; "ordered that [there] be paid to Nicholas Sabrell by the forty wch Gentry serves for, And that Sabrell pay Gentry what wages is due him." York, Va. 24 Nov 1680. vi-268.

ROBERT HANNA; Jeane Hanna, his wife, to receive supplies. Charl., Va. Ct Oct 1778. Orders iv-153.

JANE HANNA, a poor woman, who has a son, a soldier in the service of the United States to be supplied with corn and pork or bacon. Charl., Va. Mch ct 1780. Orders iv-211.

GEORGE HUDLEY, a soldier in the country's service; wife allowed £1, 11s. Pittsyl., Va. Feby Ct, 1778. iv-62. See also June Ct, 1777.

JOHN HUDSON; brother William Hudson makes oath that he is heir-at-law to John, who enlisted in a Va. Regt, in the war bet. the King of Great Britain and the French King, and served until disbanded. Essex, Va. xxix-463.

JAMES IRBY; Thomas Faris makes oath that Irby served as sjt in the "Expedition of the taking of the Illinois" until he departed this life in Capt. John Montgomery's company under Col. George Rogers Clark. Pittsyl., Va. Jany Ct 1781. iv-356.

DAVID IRBY makes oath that he was a private soldier in the expedition of the taking of the Illinois in Capt. John McGomery's [*sic*] company, under Col. George Rogers Clark; at the time of his enlistment was a native of Virginia [*sic*] Pittsyl., Va. June Ct 1780. iv-329.

GEORGE JUSTICE, recommended for Lieutenant of militia. Acco., Va. 30 July 1777. xxxvO-17.

PHILIP JOHNSTON, a soldier in the Continental service; statement relative to the service of the father of Joseph Gatewood, in 1754, when said Johnston also served. Essex, Va. June Ct 1780. xxix-478.

WILLIAM JOHNSON, dec'd; Philip Johnson, now a soldier in Col Harrison's Regt of Artillery, makes oath that he is heir-at-law to William Johnson, dec'd, formerly a soldier in the 1st Va. Regt, commanded by Col. George Washington, and that he has reason to believe that his said father continued in the said Regt during the time for which he enlisted, Signed before Edward Hill, of K. and Q. cty, and admitted to record. Essex cty, Va. 19 June 1780. xxix-497. See Ct 15 Jany 1781.

JOSEPH KELLY, recommended for 2d Lieutenant. Acco., Va. 30 July 1777. xxxvO-17.

JOHN KITCHEN [or Kitcher]; Lucy Morton, who was his widow, makes oath that said John served in a corps commanded by Col. George Washington, in the war bet. the King of Great Britain and the French King. He had no children or blood relations in the U.S. Ordered ctf'd. The said Moreton ackn. an assignment of claim to Olive Noell. Essex, Va. Ct Feby 1780. xxix-464.

THOMAS LILLISTON, recommended for Ensign of militia. Acco., Va. 30 July 1777. xxxvO-17.

DAYLEY LONGEST; brother Timothy makes oath that he is heir-at-law to brother Dayley, who enlisted in a Virginia Regt in the war between the King of Great Britain and the French King, and served until the same was disbanded. Essex, Va. Ct Feby 1780. xxix-464.

RICHARD LONGEST; Timothy Longest makes oath that he is heir-at-law to Richard Longest, who served in the war between the King of Great Britain and the French King. Essex, Va. Feby Ct 1780. xxix-463.

ZACHARIAH LEWIS proves his service in the 10th Va. Regt for three years as a sjt. Has lost his discharge. Certified to the Register of the Land Office. Pittsyl., Va. June Ct. 1781. iv-371. At the Apr Ct, 1782 (iv-396), he proves that he served under Capt. Nathan Reid and Col. William Davis. Again ordered certified.

JOHN MANTLO: Ordered certified as a Revolutionary soldier. Affidavits of Charles Talley and Parke Street presented. Hanover, Va. 28 Nov 1833.

STEPHEN MARSHALL, recommended for Ensign of militia. Acco., Va. Ct 30 July 1777. xxxvO-17.

CHARLES MARSHALL recommended for Captain of militia. Acco., Va. Ct 30 July 1777. xxxvO-17.

GEORGE MARSHALL to be 2d Lieutenant of militia. Acco., Va. Ct 29 July 1777. xxxvO-12.

JOSEPH MATTHEWS to be 1st Lieutenant of militia. Acco., Va. Ct 29 July 1777. xxxvO-12.

ISAIAH MOODY; Mary Moody, his wife; supplies ordered for herself and children. (Moody is a soldier for the county.) Charl., Va. Oct Ct 1777. Orders iv-109.

Mrs. MALONE and MARGARET MILAM (the latter the wife of William Milam) wives of poor soldiers, are to receive supplies. Charl., Va. 1777. Orders iv-111 and 145.

WILLIAM PARKER, recommended to be Captain of militia. Acco., Va. 30 July 1777. xxxvO-17.

AUGUSTINE RAMSAY; Mary, Margaret, Milly and Anne, make oath that they are heirs-at-law to their brother Augustine, who enlisted in a Virginia Regt in the war between the King of Great Britain and the French King, and served until disbanded. Certified. Essex, Va. Feby Ct 1780. xxix-464.

The

County Court Note-Book

A Little Bulletin of History and Genealogy

December, 1927.

Vol. VI, No. 6

THE ANCESTRY OF COL. JOHN DONELSON OF TENNESSEE, EXPLORER AND PIONEER*

This account of the DONELSONS, DAVISES and STOCKLEYS might very properly close with the identification of Col. DONELSON and his wife, RACHEL STOCKLEY, and their departure from the Eastern Shore of Virginia for the so-called "continent" of the Old Dominion. The compiler has, however, briefly followed the public career of Col. DONELSON in Virginia, and the appearance of himself and wife in the county records, until Davidson County, Tennessee, records the settlement of his earthly estate. The record of Col. Donelson's activities seems never to have been put in any definite shape, and the notes here set down may assist some descendant or other interested person to go into the matter further and discover those details which this compiler admits are missing.

In February, 1763 [the date of the conveyance is destroyed], JOHN DONELSON, of Halifax county, Virginia, buys of Thomas Gray, 400 acres on both sides Banister river; one tract on the north side called the "town land," and other part on the south side. Hal., Va. iv-169. The 23 June 1764, Donelson files his bond as county surveyor. Securities, Clem. Reade, Jr., P. Carrington. Hal., Va. v-130.

At the April court of Halifax county, JOHN DONELSON takes the oath as Justice (Orders, p. 35), and on the 18 June 1767, he appears as a member of the Commission (of Justices). (Orders, p. 439.)

Upon the erection of Pittsylvania county, DONELSON became, automatically, a resident of that county.

The first volume of the Orders of the Court of Pittsylvania county, Virginia, contains some interesting matter concerning Col. Donelson, which is also historical in its nature. At the November Court, 1767 (i-21), JOHN DONELSON, Gent., produces a commission from the President and Masters of William and Mary "Colledge" [the usual proceeding] and took the usual oaths as Surveyor of the county. His securities were Benjamin Lankford, Gent., and Theophilus Lacy. Further record (p. 53) states that JOHN DONELSON, Gent., Surveyor of the County, comes into Court and gives the Court to understand and be informed that the Court of Halifax hath made an Order for him to deliver up to the Surveyor of that county, the Record and Entry Books in his possession before the division of the county. The Court [of Pittsylvania] is of opinion that said books ought to remain in his possession as the greatest number of the Entrys are in Pittsylvania county, and as to those Entrys which lie in the said county of Halifax, the said JOHN DONELSON "here in Court" agrees to give Copies thereof without fee or reward.

At the July Court, 1770, DONELSON takes the oath as a member of the commission, and also takes the oath as a Justice of Oyer and Terminer, which places him in what might be called the "upper chamber" of the justices of the County Court. (See Orders i-212.)

At the March Court, 1773, JOHN DONELSON, Jr., produces his commission as assistant surveyor to his father, JOHN DONELSON, then again Surveyor of the County, and takes the usual oath. (Pitts. ii-111.)

In July of the same year, JOHN DONELSON and Crispin Shelton, Gent, are ordered to let the building of a bridge. (Pitts. ii-225.) The 22 July 1773, DONELSON places a mortgage on his land (1019 acres) and slaves for £1000. (iii-359.) In 1775 he buys of Francis Bird, both described as of Pittsylvania, for £125, 200 acres on the north side of Pigg river. (Pitts. iv-154. 20 June 1775.) The 27 Sept 1775, JOHN DONELSON, Esq., is nominated for County Lieutenant. (Pitts. iv-293.)

At the November Court, 1776, JOHN DONELSON, Gent., Surveyor of the County is appointed to run the dividing line between Pittsylvania and Henry counties. (iii-25.) At the March Court, 1777, it is directed that this line is to run "from the line of Halifax county at the mouth of Straight Stone Creek to where the line between this county and Henry county intersects the county line. and that the center of that line be the place for holding Court." (iii-40.) At the November Court, 1776, DONELSON again takes oath as Justice. And at this same Court the junior DONELSON takes oath as deputy-surveyor. At the January Court, 1777, DONELSON is again recommended for Justice. (iii-29.) And at the February Court he and Crispin Shelton (who is also a member of the new commission of the peace and of Oyer and Terminer) administer the oath to the other Justices, and then, in like manner, Justice Dillard administers the oath to DONELSON. (iii-83.)

DONELSON buys from John Brent and wife Margaret, of Charlotte county, for £200, 354 acres on the south side of Banister river. Stockley Donelson is one of the witnesses. (5 Mch 1777. iv-339.) And from William Dandridge Claiborne, of King William county, for £87, 10sh. other land in the same locality. (20 May 1777. iv-385.)

In September, 1777, JOHN DONELSON, Jr., gives bond as Surveyor of the county. (iv-412.)

In the February Court, 1778, JOHN DONELSON, Gent., County Lieutenant of Militia, resigns his commission. (Pitts. iv-62.) And the same year he conveys to John Markham, of Chesterfield county, consideration £2800, all the four tracts containing 320 acres, conveyed to him by Claiborne, at the mouth of White Thorne Creek, up Banister river, and 281 acres patented to himself, and 400 acres patented to William Caldwell. The February Court of 1779 issues a commission to take the

*Including the family of Rachel Stockley, his wife.

release of dower of RACHEL DONELSON, and the commission returns report. (iv-191.)

The 17 June 1779, JOHN DONELSON and wife RACHEL, of *Washington county, Virginia*, convey to James Callaway and Jeremiah Earley of Bedford county, consideration £4000, two tracts in Henry county, one on both sides a branch of Pigg river, called Iron Mine branch (400 acres), Robert Hill's line mentioned . . . the other is the tract conveyed by Byrd to DONELSON, lying on Pigg river. (Henry cty, Va. i-300.) A commission is ordered to take the release of RACHEL DONELSON (i-303) and the examination is held in Washington county. the 21 Aug 1779. The witnesses to this deed are Jas. Thompson, Harry Innes, Alexander Donelson, H. Henry, Jr., Caleb Tate, Swinfield Hill and Mordecai Moley.

In the same year, 17 August, a marriage license bond is filed by JOHN DONELSON [Jr.] for his marriage with MARY PURNELL. Mary Purnell, Sr., gives consent. William Purnell, one of the witnesses to the consent, and James Akin, security for DONELSON. (See Pitts. cty, M. L. B.) The 23 Sept 1779, JOHN DONELSON, late of Pittsylvania, conveys to John Dotson [Dodson] of the same cty, 300 acres . . . on or near Cascade creek. (vi-242.) This is proved by witnesses, as also another deed to Daniel Dodson, proved at the Mch Court, 1780. (iv-295.)

At the April Court, 1780, justices are recommended in the room of Robert Payne, George Carter and JOHN DONELSON, Gent., they being removed out of the county. (Pitts. iv-317.)

Col. DONELSON'S journal of his most remarkable voyage from the settlement or camp at Fort Patrick Henry on the Holston, approximately the site of the present Kingsport [the Editor cannot find a definite statement], by way of the beautiful Holston, the Tennessee, the Ohio and the Cumberland rivers, to the landing below the bluff on which Nashville, Tennessee, erected itself, may be found in Ramsey's Annals of Tennessee (p. 197). The original journal, as previously mentioned, is in the possession of the Tennessee Historical Society. It begins, it may be stated, the 22 December 1779.

The Journals of the Virginia House of Burgesses show that Col. DONELSON was a Burgess from Pittsylvania (with Hugh Innes) in 1770, 1771, 1772, 1773 and 1774, and Meade, in his Old Churches and Families, states that DONELSON was a vestryman of Camden parish, Pittsylvania. This was about 1773. (See p. 14.)

The Editor finds no other record in her notes until this: JOHN DONELSON; the inventory of his estate returned by William Donelson, admr. Davidson cty, Tenn. July 1789. (i-109.)

An additional inventory was returned in October, 1790. (i-176.)

The 21 Jany 1789, STOCKLEY DONELSON, of Hawkins county, N. C., ". . . for the real affection I bear to RACHEL DONELSON as well for the consideration of £300, [conveys to her] all my right, title and interest to the personal estate of my father, JOHN DONELSON, dec'd." Ackn. in person. Wit: Andrew Jackson. (Davidson cty, Tenn. i-91.)

An account of Col. DONELSON'S estate returned in July, 1790, (D-n cty, Tenn. i-166), WILLIAM DONALDSON, admr. shows payments to Rachel Donelson, Sam'l Donelson, Robert Hays, Wm. Donelson, Major Tatum, John Donaldson, Mary Caffrey, Samuel Donaldson.

An inventory of the personal estate of Col. DONELSON was made in Jany 1791, and a division of the property in April of that year. (See i-196.) The inventory was made by Henry Bradford, Robert Cartwright and John Overton. The Court order of October, 1790 and extended order of Jany, 1791, are extended to April, 1791. The inventory includes 28 negroes, one named *Somerset*, one named *Willoughby;* 19 horses, &c., &c. The estate is divided among the widow and eleven children, who are listed as follows: Mrs. Donelson, widow; Alexander Donelson, Catherine Hutchings, John Donelson, Mary Caffrey, William Donelson, Stockley Donelson, Jane Hays, Rachel Jackson, Samuel Donelson, Severn Donelson, Levin Donelson. Rachel was the wife of ANDREW JACKSON.

Merritt's History of Tennessee states that *Somerset* was the name of Col. Donelson's body servant. No doubt he got his name in or from Somerset county, Maryland.

A settlement of the estate was had in 1805, and a supplementary return of the division was filed the 12 Nov of that year. (D-n cty. iii-82.) The lists mention the "representatives" of the widow; the "representatives" of Samuel Donelson, and of Stockley Donelson. The other heirs are living.

Although the Editor has undertaken so far to give only the data found in the records of the County courts, with such exceptions as the Maryland Rent Rolls, and the just mentioned Virginia Journals and Bishop Meade, there are two groups of events in Col. DONELSON'S career that are too important to omit. One of these is his connection with the Cherokee treaty of 1770, in which he represented the Virginia Colony, in association with Capt. JOHN STUART, the Indian Commissioner for the home government. Subsequent to this treaty DONELSON ran two lines across what is now the state of Kentucky . . . these lines coincided part of the way and this, the southern part, began somewhat south of the [now] Kentucky boundary. Which of these lines is the commonly referred to "Donelson Line," after search in many publications, the Editor is unable to say. In the Draper Mss. (10NN, p. 110), a certain John Redd writes: "In 1771, Col. DONELSON was employed . . . to run a line . . . to the head of Kentucky river or the Louisa branch of Sandy . . . I am not certain which, but this line must have crossed Powell's Valley in quite a different direction from the line you mention."

This uncertainty runs through nearly every reference, though not so frankly admitted. The official references, necessarily made very brief, follow.

Letter of William Nelson, President of the Virginia Council, 15 Dec 1770. (L. C. 290. 1349, p. 33. British Transcripts.) "My Lord, Colonel "DONELSON the Gentleman whom Lord Botetourt appointed to attend the Superintendent "[John Stuart] at the treaty with the Cherokee "Indians at Lochaber [S. C.] having brought me "the Deed of Cession for [their] Lands . . . I now "transmit a copy. . . . I have by the advice of "the Council appointed Colonel DONELSON . . . "to execute the running of the Line in May next; "as I think he may be confided in. . . . "

John Stuart, writing to Lord Botetourt, 25 Oct 1770 ; . . "I arrived here [Lochaber] the 15th, "where I found all the Cherokee Chiefs with their "followers . . . about a thousand in number. . . . "I had also the pleasure of finding Col. DONEL-"SON here; he was exactly punctual to the time "appointed. [Stuart was two days late.] . . . I "beg leave to return your Lordship my most sincere "thanks for having sent a Gentleman of Col. "DONELSON'S Discernment and Probity to assist "me. . . . I beg leave to refer your Lordship to "him for every Particular. . . ."

From the Council Proceedings [Virginia] 12 Dec 1770.

"Col. JOHN DONELSON, who was appointed "by his late Excellency the Commissioner on the "Part of this Colony to treat, jointly with John "Stuart, Esq., . . . for the Cession of some Part "of their Lands . . ." [reference to the treaty of 18 Oct 1770 follows.] ". . . . Col. DONELSON "being introduced into the Council Chamber" commends Stuart for his conduct of the treaty, and, concerning the line, agrees with the Council to run it and upon the terms.

In March, 1772, the Earl of Dunmore writes to the Earl of Hillsborough, "The Boundary line be-"tween this Colony and the hunting Grounds of "the Cherokee Indians hath been run . . . by a "Mr. DONELSON and others. . . . Your Lord-"ship will observe that this Line is not exactly "run according to the Instructions formerly sent ". . . but that it takes in a larger tract of Coun-"try. . . ." Dunmore then strongly urges this line. No approval by the home government can be found. [The explanation of the differing line, to be found in several publications, is in every way creditable to Col. D.—Ed.]

The other occurrence of outstanding importance in Col. DONELSON'S career is his connection with the signing of the two "Associations" of Virginia legislators and merchants, copies of which may be found in the Library of Congress. These "Associations" were in the nature of protests following upon the events in Boston and elsewhere. They are signed by Washington, Jefferson, Richard Henry Lee, Benjamin Harrison, Patrick Henry, Jr., in one case by 25 members and in the other by 89. These papers, catalogued as "Broadsides," are fully described in histories of what one might call the Revolutionary preamble. DONELSON signed both instruments.

AUTHENTIC REFERENCES FOR INFERRED MARRIAGES*

(Northampton County, Va.)

MARKE HAMMOND and MARY CLARKE. Before[?] 13 Dec 1641. ii-97.

RICHARD HANBY, shoemaker, and MARIA CHILCOTT, single woman. Marriage contract. 20 Aug 1656. vii-8.

THOMAS HIGHBY and Mrs. ANN WILKINS, widow of Mr. JOHN WILKINS. Before Feby 1650. iv-10.

THOMAS HOGG and the widow of John FORSITH. Before 28 Oct 1678. xi-177.

STEWART HOLT and ANN JOHNSON, dau. of Benjamin. Before 1773. Chancy records.

ROBERT HOWSON and SARAH PALMER, widow. About 30 May 1710. xviii-535.

JOHN HUDSON and the widow of William SENIOR. Before 30 July 1677. xii-181.

WILLIAM HARMANSON and MARGARET MAPP, dau. of Robins Mapp. Before 1774. Chancy records.

THOMAS HUNT and ANN HUNT, widow of Azariah. Before or about Mch 1736. Chancy records.

JOHN HAGGOMAN and SARAH POWELL, See p. 347, Amer. Mags. vol. i. (Upshur.)

JOHN ISAAC and AMY COSTIN, dau. of Stephen, Sr. Before 22 Jany 1685. xv-211. See also 29 Dec 1680. xiii-119. Marriage before that date.

ISAAC JACOB and ANNE SAVAGE [widow of John?] Before 12 Feby 1752. Chancy records.

RICHARD JACOB and ELIZABETH CLARKE, dau. of Robert. Before 1 Mch 1702. xviii-127.

ANDREW JACOB and the widow of Richard WILSON. Before or about 3 Aug 1640. ii-34.

RALPH JUSTICE and SARAH MARSHALL, dau. of Thomas. 13 Mch 1738. M. L. B.

GEORGE JORDAN and SUSANNAH CAUL. Before 8 Apr 1766. L. C. 1754-1771, fo. 106.

ROBERT JACOB and ANNE JACOB, admx of Isaac. Before 1765. Chancy records.

SAMUEL JOHNSON and JOS[EPHA] MARIA WEST, wid. of John. Before 10 Feby 1730. Chancy records.

SAMUEL JOHNSON and AGATHA GELDING, sister of Charles, Before 9 Jany 1727. Chancy records.

SPENCER JOHNSON and SARAH JAMES, widow. Before 13 Oct 1730. Chancy records.

SPENCER JOHNSON and . . . SAVAGE, widow of Nathaniel. Before 12 Oct 1737. Chancy records.

THOMAS JOHNSON and SALLY FLETCHER. 31 Aug 1795. M. L. B.

GEORGE JOHNSON prob. m. ELLYNOR MERRIDAY, widow. About Dec 1656. vii-21 (1st part).

CORNELIUS JOHNSON and ALICE BAILY. About 1652. iv-161.

ADOLPH JOHNSON and JUDITH PATRICK, widow of Mathew. Before 30 May 1681. xiv-16.

OBEDIENCE JOHNSON and ELISHE GODWIN. 8 Feby 1772. Chancy records.

MOSES JOHNSON and SARAH POWELL. 1770. M. L. B.

WILLIAM JOHNSON and ALICE FLYE, a widow. Before 29 May 1654. v-8.

JOHN JOHNSON prob. m. the widow of Walter IRBY. Before 19 Nov 1655. vi-13.

BENJAMIN JOHNSON and ROSE HUNT, widow Abadiah. [His second marriage.] Before 1763. Chancy records.

WILLIAM JERVIS and ANN GOFFIGON, dau. of James. Before 10 Mch 1762. Chancy records.

PHILIP JACOBS and ANNE JANES, dau. of Thomas. Before 11 July 1737. Chancy records.

ESAU JACOB and BETTY HAGGOMAN, dau. John. Before 12 Jany 1764. Chancy records.

THOMAS JAMES and the widow of Levin SMITH. Before 13 June 1736. Chancy records.

WILLIAM JARVIS and SARAH HUNT, widow of Azariah. Before 1784. Chancy records.

ROBERT CLARK JACOB prob. m. ANNE SAVAGE widow of John. Before 1778. Chancy records. [See previous marriage of ISAAC JACOB. Explanation at present lacking.]

GEORGE JOURDAN and SUSANNAH CAUL, dau. of Daniel. Before 8 Apr 1766. L. C. 1754-1771, fo. 106.

JOHN JAMES and a dau. of Emanuell HALL. Before 1695-6. xvii-384[?]

The County Court Note-Book

An every-other-monthly devoted mainly to abstracts from County Court records, prior to 1800.

MILNOR LJUNGSTEDT, Editor and Publisher.
Bethesda, Route 10, Maryland.

Published six times a year. Subscription, two dollars, in advance; must begin with the year.

December, 1927 **Whole**
Vol. VI., No. 6 **No. 37**

The Editor's intelligence is in a low state at this time of year. It may be the remembrance of old Thanksgivings when nobody was unhappy unless it were the children, unable to eat pumpkin pie, mince pie, nuts, raisins, figs, oranges and apples in sufficiency after turkey legs, stuffing, gravy (made in the pan), mashed potatoes, ham, mashed turnips, cranberry jelly and celery; very like it is the result of having to read proof, which is a deadly thing; but more likely it is the hunting,—they did not shoot rabbits and querulous little quail in the streets of Boston. Boston always was a civilized place.

So in place of an Editorial she will borrow from a helpful friend, Mr. Gilbert Cope, the Quaker genealogist, and republish with his supposed permission part of a very clear article upon the calendar, which he gave to the Editor long ago. Those who know all about dates can skip it, but some have forgotten things learned at school, and others have not had their attention called to the variations in which our years have indulged.

Apropos of this, the Editor always uses Old Style, without change, when it is Old Style. But she will have to confess that she doesn't really know when George Washington was born, so many rectifications have been made.

OUR CALENDAR

We are so accustomed to accepting things as they are that we seldom stop to think of their origin or how we should get along without them. The keeping of exact dates is a very important matter in all civilized countries, but a date suggests a starting point from which to count time. In this, as in all Christian countries, we are supposed to begin with the birth of Christ, though this method of computing time was not adopted until long after that event and the exact date is unknown. As the Christians came into power and influence under the Roman government they made use of the Roman calendar, simply changing the starting point from the building of the city of Rome to the birth of Christ, in stating the number of the year. The calendar of the Romans had, however, been subject to the caprice of the rulers, who added or subtracted days and months at will until the time of Julius Cæsar, who, with the aid of a famous Egyptian mathematician, revised the calendar, which was thereafter known as the Julian calendar, and continued in use for over 1600 years.

This calendar did not agree with the solar year, on which it was based, by about one day in 131 years, so that in 1582, when the year was about ten days wrong Pope Gregory XIII, with the aid of a learned astronomer and physician of Naples, gave us what is known as the Gregorian Calendar, dropping ten days from October in the year 1582, and making the 5th the 15th of the month. This calendar, originating with the Roman Church, was not at once accepted by Protestants, and in England, the change was not made until *1752*, by which time the error had amounted to eleven days.

The accepted commencement of the year, according to the Julian calendar (45 B. C.), was December 25th, and the selection of that day in after years as the anniversary of the birth of Christ, is believed by some to have had its origin in a very remote antiquity, and among the worshippers of the sun. However, as a matter of fact, from the 7th to the 12th century, in England, the year began on the *25th of December;* but in the latter century the Anglican Church decreed that the year should begin on the 25th of March, Annunciation, or Lady Day (the Vernal Equinox—another important point with reference to the sun), which rule was adhered to until 1752.

The year thus beginning on the 25th of March was known as the Ecclesiastical, Legal, or Civil year.

. . . . .

In remote times, before the advent of Quakerism, the months were known by numbers, and some of them which bear Latin numerals, as September, October, November and December, are simply survivals of the old forms, though now incorrect since the change of the beginning of the year from March to January.

. . . . .

The Friends, or Quakers, arose (about 1650) in an age of much superstition and corruption in church and state, and in their reaction from these they felt it necessary to draw the line at everything that savored of paganism. Accordingly they declined to use those names of months and days, which had been bestowed in honor of pagans or their idols. Here, in Pennsylvania, a colony founded by William Penn, in 1682, where the society controlled the legislation for many years, the numerical form of dating was not only largely used, but sanctioned by law. In "The great law or the body of laws of the Province of Pennsylvania and territories thereunto belonging, past at an assembly held at Chester (alias Upland), the 7th day of the 10th month, called December, 1682," we find the following section:

"35. And Be it further enacted by the authority aforesaid that the dayes of the Week and the months of the year shall be called as in Scripture, & not by Heathen names (as are vulgarly used) as the first second and third days of the Week and first second and third months of the year, and beginning with the Day called Sunday and the Month called March."

This was somewhat crude, though well meaning, legislation, and after a few years became obsolete. It was only expected to be effective so far as public records were concerned. As a quaint and rather extreme example of adherence to this enactment I quote from our Court records: "Att a Court held att Chester for the County of Chester the 3d day of the 1st Week of the 8th moneth 1688." The voluminous records of the Society of Friends, as well as their private family records, are, of course, in the numerical style. Their descendants of other denominations, and genealogists, now, in copying the old dates, change the numbers to names; and for those prior to 1752, almost universally make errors. Others find, for example, that some person's will was made in August and probated in January of the same year, and at once conclude the record is erroneous. Again in arranging a number of documents bearing on a certain subject, those dated in January and February will be supposed to precede those of the other months in the same year. In the "Memorials of Bartram and Marshall," edited by Dr. William Darlington, the dates prior to 1752, when changed from the style of Friends, are all wrong, and in some cases the error amounts to ten months. Some historians are aware that March was formerly the first month, but forget that March 25th was New Year's Day.

An Act of Parliament was passed in 1751, prescribing the adoption of the Gregorian Calendar throughout Great Britain and her colonies; making the succeeding year begin with the first of January and dropping eleven nominal days (3-13) from the month of September, 1752, so that what would have been the 3d of the month was called the 14th. The yearly meeting of Friends in London followed by that of Philadelphia, directed its members to recognize the change of style, and that thereafter the months should be numbered, beginning with January, "all other methods of computing or calling the months unavoidably leading into contradiction."

OCCASIONAL

Man is but the sum of his Ancestors.
Emerson.

JOHN THE GREATE [John Le Grande]. He had a "brother" James Stephens, son of George Stephens. Surry, Va. 1667. i-284.

PETER GRUGER and a reformed Widow. [Married.] St. Michael's and Zion Church, Phila., Pa. Arch. ix, p. 287. "2d East day," 1745.

THOMAS JONES; gets ctf for 150 acres for himself, Elizabeth his first wyfe, Katherine his last wyfe. N-n, Va. Sept 1641. i-98.

"JAMES MASHIELL, otherwise James Dashiell," of Somerset cty, Gent. Som. cty, Md. 12 June 1677. v-166.

The ACT OF PARLIAMENT naturalizing William Lawrence, Martha Lawrence, Theodora Lawrence and others, including two Silvesters, will be found recorded in Northampton cty, Va. 17 Sept 1656. vii-52. The record shows that William Lawrence was born at Arnhan [*sic*], province of Gelderland, the Netherlands; Martin Lawrence was born at Viana in the Netherlands; Theodora was born at Delph in Holland; all sons and daughters of Henry Lawrence (Lord President of his Highness' Council), and of Amey, his wife.

A LIGHT UPON CONDITIONS: Dorothy Thorne is to serve Charles Barham and his wife, six years, and they are to find her sufficient lodging and victuals, and "*not to put her into the ground and the Mortar,*" but to teach her to reed and sow and to give her a cotton suite and a [illegible] suite and other things belonging to them, and a heifer at the expiration of her time and three bbls Indian corn. Dorothy x Thorne, Charles Barnham, Elizabeth x Barnham. Surry, Va, 2 Feby 1666. i-342.

Errata:

The BURDITT-SAUNDERS marriage note in June, 1927, should omit "probably." The date given, 16 Sept 1633, is that of their marriage agreement. The marriage usually followed the same day or the next.

The note in the October NOTE-BOOK concerning the horse-race jury should have this reference: Wmld cty, Va. Vol. 1676-1688, p. 640.

CONTINUED articles COUNTY COURT NOTE-BOOK, and the dates on which they first appeared.

THE ANCESTRY OF COL. JOHN DONELSON. Began with February, 1927.

AUTHENTIC REFERENCES for INFERRED MARRIAGES (formerly called MARRIAGES BY INFERENCE). Began with May, 1922.

MARYLAND'S NEXT OF KIN. Began with July, 1922.

VIRGINIA COLONISTS. Alphabetized lists began with July, 1924.

MILITARY NOTES, both COLONIAL and REVOLUTIONARY, and later MILITIA NOTES. Began December, 1923.

INTERCOUNTY and INTERCOLONY (formerly called New Englanders and Others, &c., &c.). Began with March, 1922.

EASTERN SHORE FAMILIES. In the form of a one-page supplement, began with June, 1925. This will be continued later.

SHIPS IN PORT and COLONIAL FORENAMES, will appear in alternate issues or as space can be found for them.

MR. STRATTON NOTTINGHAM is at work on the Revolutionary records of Accomack county, Virginia, and intends to bring the volume out before long, to be followed by similar records of Northampton county. These records are of the same class as those published by the NOTE-BOOK from various Virginia counties, but will be far more complete. Mr. Nottingham's volume will contain full copies; the NOTE-BOOK is restricted to brief abstracts. These county records give the local or court side of such material as is used by Mr. LOUIS A. BURGESS in his VIRGINIA SOLDIERS OF 1776, and sometimes supply data which are missing in the Richmond Land Office. Any one interested in Revolutionary matters should have both publications.

THE Editor's friend has returned BOLTON'S AMERICAN ARMORY. The delightfully written preface includes a quotation from an English authority which Mr. Bolton takes as his legend: "We have been content to record the arms which have been in use by the families whose names are attached to them," omitting any comment or argument as to inherent right. The five pages of heraldic terms and accompanying four plates are simple and good, and cover the ground as well as the shield. The volume has a heraldic index and index of mottoes. The Editor suggests it is just the kind of book everybody wants, especially those who are listed within it. It is No. 33 of Useful Reference Series.

CHILLIAN and MARTIN PALMER, Charlotte cty, Va. Seventy-five dollars will be paid for their ancestry. Must be proved by civil and church records. W. B. P. A.

INTERCOUNTY AND INTERCOLONY

Mr. JAMES AUSTEN left land in Somerset cty, Md., to his grandson Thomas Webb, son of Thomas Webb. See the latter's will. (Formerly John Bowler's land.) Nthld, Va. 1702. Vol. 1706-1720, p. 3.

WILLIAM BELL, Sussex cty, Penna., and wf Sarah; convey to Nathaniel Bell, of Acco., Va., land on the Matchepungo river, 250 acres, part of Nevel's[?] Neck. 12 Nov 1768. Acco., Diii-603.

EDWARD BLAGG, of Plymouth, mariner, was master (under God) of the Good Shipp *Industrie* of Plimouth . . . shortly bound forth on a voyage into Virginia; Thomas Hunt mentioned as of Plimouth, and Samuel Brett as owner of the *Industrie*. Wmld, Va. 31 May 1671. Orders, 1662-1664, fo. 100.

EDWARD BAKER, late of London. Will. The "Sealed Gold Ring that I now were to son Edward Baker." Bro-in-law, Lt. Col. William Kendall, a gold ring. Capt. Robert Pitt, a gold ring. Lt. Col. William Kendall and Capt. Robert Pitt "my executors in trust of all goods and chattels that I have now with mee in the Shipp *Mary* of London upon her voioage."

JOHN BEALE had a son Richard in Essex cty, Va. 1733. Annap. Md. Wills, xxviii-74.

OWEN BRADY, and wf Hanover, of St. Mary's cty, Md. Deed to John Carlyle of Fairfax cty, Va. 2 May 1763. Pr. Wm., Va. L. C. p. 165.

THOMAS BARD, of St. Maries in the Province of Maryland, pltr, to William Lambard, of Westmoreland in Virginia, Taylor. 16 May 1668. Wmld, Va. vol. 1668-1677, fo. 49.

JOHN S. BAISDEN and wf Rhoda, of Wythe cty, Va., to Samuel Pain of the City of Richmond; land in Franklin (formerly Pittsylvania) county. Franklin cty, Va. 26 June 1795. iii-328.

Mr. THOS: BROUGHTON, of Virginia, conveys his right to 200 acres to John Saffin, of Boston, and gives power to Mr. James Gaylard. 3 Oct 1664. Nthld, Va. Vol. 1658-1666, fo. 137. See also fo. 24, same vol.

ELIZABETH BYRD, late of Edmonton, cty of Middlesex, England. Will dated on board ship *Hopewell*, bound for Virginia. Henrico, Va. 24 Nov 1678. i-72.

JOHN COGAN[?] of New England, Mcht. See N-n, Va. iii-1. 1645.

Mr. CHARLES DE SALLY and Mr. DAVID MINITREE, entered into recog. 1 Feby 1702, with Mr. ABRAHAM SALLE, extr of Mr. Sollomon Delalue . . . . and Whereas Mr. CHARLES DE SALLY being since gone for England and Mr. MINITREE has removed into some remote part of Government . . . new security is ordered. Hen., Va. Aug. 1706. vol. 1677-1737, p. 48.

JOHN DICKENSON; At the request of his admr, Josiah Woods, his estate was allotted as follows: "To John Clay and wife, 66 acres on the Bush Fork of Stuart's Creek in Patrick county (patent 10 Sept 1780), and also all the lands to which John Dickinson, Sen'r, would have been entitled as being heir-at-law to the land of his father in Hanover county, for the purpose that said Clay may make sale of the same and render to the admr the whole proceeds of such sale." Franklin cty, Va. Wills i-286. 2 Oct 1806.

JOSEPH DOHERTY, of Fayette county, District of Kentucky, power to Sam'l Barton, of Davidson cty, N. C. Davids. cty, Tenn. 8 June 1790. i-202.

Mrs. ANN EATON; Ordered that ctf be granted unto her, to the Mayor and Aldermen of the Citty of Exeter, according to her petition. N-n, Va. 29 Jany 1649. iii-201.

SAMUEL EDWARDS, of London, mariner; power to Mr. Richard Boshen[?] of Gloucester county upon Yorke river. York, Va. 1 Aug 1672. V-40.

DANIEL FOXCROFT removed to Elizabeth City county. Acco, Va. 17 Mch 1673. v-126.

JOHN x GALE, of North Carolina, near Old Corotuck Inlett; will. Son John, living in Kent cty in "Mereland"; mentions son *George Lewis*, and son *Evan Jones*, as well as other chn. Hen., Va. Vol. 1725-1737, p. 426. 2 Oct 1733.

TACITUS GILLARD, Esq.; late an inhabitant of the State of South "Carolinia," being on his way to Florida or some of the countries or places on this side thereof, or adjacent thereto . . . (presents a passport from the Board of War). Yohog. cty, Va. Minutes ii-21. 26 May 1778.

EDWARD GUPHELL and wf Elizabeth, who formerly was wife of Benj. Forman the younger, of Frederick cty, now dec'd, and John Forman, eldest son and heir-at-law of said Benjamin . . . all of Craven county, S. C., to William Forman of Hampshire county, Va. . . . convey tract No. 26. John Forman one of the wit. Hamp., W. Va. ii-156. 22 June 1769.

ONSLOW COUNTY, N. C. Deposition of JANE GRANT, aged about 53; sayeth that her maiden name was JANE STARAIT[?] and that she married Francis Binney[?] after whose death a certain Alexander Grant, whose widow she is, living in Somerset somewhere nigh where a certain Thomas Houston then lived, and with his eldest son William; and about 20 years ago this deponent and the said Thomas Houston removed to North Carolina. That Thomas Houston died about 11 years ago and left William Houston his eldest son, &c., &c., Wor. cty, Md. 28 Aug 1742. A-30.

WILLIAM HOLLINGWORTH, mariner, of the Towne of Salem, in New England; power to Nicholas Owen, pltr, of Cherry-Neck in Nthld, Va. [Appears to have been associated with Mr. Wm. Browne.] Nthld, Va. Vol. 1658-1666, fo. 32. 23 Feby 1658.

ANNE HOYER, of Barkin in the county of Essex, widow; power to Gawen Kanady, of Virginia, Mcht. Nthld, Va. Vol. 1658-1666, fo. 70. 21 Jany 1661.

Mr. PETER HACK, of the Western Shore, Virginia; in possession of 470 acres in Cecil county, Md., at the date of the Rent Roll. Resurveyed, 8 Sept 1683. Cecil cty R. R. p. 128.

JOHN HILL, mariner, of Essex cty, Eng., was son of Nathaniel Hill, late of Henrico, Va. Hen., Va. Orders p. 132. 1 Apr 1709. See also 8 Feby 1707, p. 97. He was son of Nathaniel and Jane Hill, "Burmonda" Hundred. Frances Smith was his aunt.

WILLIAM HOUSTON, of N. C., eldest son and heir of Thomas Houston, pltr, late of Somerset, Md. who was one of the sons of Robert Houston of Somerset, lately dec'd, and Dixon Quinton, of Worcester cty, Md., and Collins Adams, of Somerset. This is a tripartite agreement as to a tract called Second Choice. Consideration, 5 sh. Som., Md. 28 Feby 1742. A-27.

HENRY HICKS, Gent., late of Dorchester, Md., now of Carolina, to John Beerd, of Dorchester, pltr; conveys Luck by Chance. [Line of descent of property given.] Dor., Md. 23 Oct 1754. xv-139.

WILLIAM HANDY had an aunt Esther Raynet, in "Bermudas"; leaves her "forty shillings current money of Maryland to be Laid out by my Executors in such Specie as may be by them supposed to be to her Advantage and by them sent to her to Bermudas at her own proper Risque. . . ." Wor., Md. JWii-81. 19 May 1751.

WILLIAMS NOTES
MARYLAND-VIRGINIA SECTION

PAUL WILLIAMS and Sarah x Wheatley; marriage contract. James Craig and Daniel Marr, wit. Fauq., Va. 28 June 1786. ix-258.

PAUL WILLIAMS m. the widow of James Fox. About August, 1768. See Fauq., iii-293, 294. Also Minute Book. Aug. Ct 1768.

PHILIP WILLIAMS and Sarah Croudson, dau. of John. Shenan., Va. M. L. B. 15 Oct 1791.

PHEEBE WILLIAMS was the youngest daughter of Elizabeth Plummer. Pr. Geo., Md. 1736. i-260.

POWELL WILLIAMS and Lucy Woodward. Gchld, Va. M. L. B. 17 Oct 1796.

PROVIDENCE WILLIAMS, admr with ANN WILLIAMS on estate of JOHN WILLIAMS. Newberry cty, S. C. 17 May 1796. B-16.

REBECCA WILLIAMS and Nathan Hudlen. Shenan., Va. Mar. Ret. 19 June 1795.

REMEMBRANCE WILLIAMS. On tax-list, one tithe. Hamp. cty, W. Va. 1783.

RICE WILLIAMS and the relict of Jo: Hadnuts. Married. Before 27 Jany 1685. Wmld, Va. Orders, p. 483.

RICHARD WILLIAMS m. Sarah Stanton, dau. of Benjamin. Before 31 of 3d mo., 1803. Carteret, N. C. O-366.

ROBERT WILLIAMS (in Kent cty, Md.) of Long Island, "near of the bay in the north side of New York Shire in America"; now lying Sick and Weak of body. . . . Will. Wf Sarah; son John; young son Robert. son Hope; Daughters, wife and Samuel Spicar[?] and John Bonn overseers. [This name is very probably Bowne.] "And if any of my Sons and Daughters doth walk disorderly according to the truth then they shall have no part or parcell in this will." Wit: Isaac Winchester, Raynold Haws. Annap. Wills, ii-166. 2 Dec 1680-13 Dec 1681.

ROGER WILLIAMS, cooper; conveys to John Watkins, 200 acres on Pidgeon Swamp. Surry, Va. 5 June 1680. i(2)-298.

ROBERT C. WILLIAMS; inventory. Campbell cty, Va. 1 Nov 1819. v-248.

ROGER x WILLIAMS: will. Sons Roger, Shedrach; wf Jane; elder dau. Betty Williams. Wit: Greenwood, Sisson. Rappa., Va. 26 Feby 1675-2 May 1677. Vol. 1677-1682. p. 8.

ROLY[?] WILLIAMS. White cty, Ill. Census 1820.

ROGER WILLIAMS and Cassean[?] Blair, dau. of William. Amherst, Va. M. L. B. 22 Feby 1775.

RICE WILLIAMS, Dor. cty, Md. Kin: John Robson, Isaac Meekins. Mary Williams, admx. Annap. Inv. Returned 29 Aug 1724. x-119.

RICHARD WILLIAMS, Sr. Tax-list. One tithe. Hamp. cty, W. Va. 1783.

ROWLAND WILLIAMS; cattle-mark. N-n, Va. 15 May 1677. iv-235.

SAMPSON WILLIAMS m. the widow of John Inglies. Before Aug. 1765. Cumb. cty.

SAMUEL WILLIAMS, Montg. cty, Md., to Stacey Pancoast, same; Consideration £58, conveys all the time of servitude of a negro man named Neale, supposed to be [that is, the time] seven years, nine and one-half months from the date hereof. whom I purchased as a Slave and manumitted in October, 1792 . . . his freedom to commence from a certain day therein named. Following the above . . . Samuel Brayfield makes over all his right to James Higdon, 20 Oct 1797. . . . Whereas the negro Neale became the property of Samuel Brayfield by his marriage with Jane Pancoast, widow of Stacy Pancost . . . Higdon then manumits Neale for the time unexpired. Ackn. in 1800. Montg., Md. I-283. 18 Apr 1794.

SAMUEL WILLIAMS and Sukey Dixon. N-n, Va., Mar. record. Bet. Feby 1799 and 1800.

SAMUEL WILLIAMS; census, Madison cty, Ill. 1820.

SARAH WILLIAMS and Thomas Lewis. N-n, Va. Mar. record. Bet. Feby 1799 and 1800.

SARAH WILLIAMS, wife of Thomas. Died 22 Apr 1718. St. Paul's Psh. Reg. K. Geo., Va.

THOMAS WILLIAMS and Helen Morphew. Married. 4 Sept 1723. St. Paul's Psh. Reg. K. Geo. cty, Va.

THOMAS WILLIAMS; tax-list. One tithe. Hamp. cty., W. Va. 1783.

THOMAS OWEN WILLIAMS, Fred'k cty, Md., from Sam'l Hardy, same. All Moore's lott, Horsepen Branch leading into Potomack river. Fred'k, Md. O-573. 1771.

THOMAS x WILLIAMS m. Susanna Davis, widow of Thomas. Before 5 Mch 1726. I. W., Va. vii-38.

THOMAS WILLIAMS and Jannet Johnson. 13 Nov 1744. St. Paul's Psh Reg. K. Geo. cty, Va.

THOMAS WILLIAMS, son of THOMAS and Sarah, dec'd. Baptized 15 Feby 1717. St. Paul's psh Reg. K. Geo. cty, Va.

THOMAS x WILLIAMS, of Gt. Wickocomico psh, Nthld cty, Va., deed to children: Son Thomas; intended wf Margery Herald; dau. Ann Williams; friends Capt. Edmund Lyster and Mr. Robert Jones, overseers of this deed of gift. Wit: Rand'l Catherall, Jno. Barber. Nthld, Va. 24 Jany 1670. 1666-1672, fo. 100.

THOMAS WILLIAMS; nun-cup will. Proved by Alexander Douglass and John Smith and Francis Mills. Williams d. 11 Nov 1753. Legacies to friends; sister Sarah Douglas' children; sister Ann Limit's children; negro to Alexander Douglass and John Limit; godson Johnson. Jane x Williams, widow, being in a low state of health assigns her right to administer to Alexander Douglass. Frances x Mills Wit. Staff., Va. O-265.

THOMAS WILLIAMS, Jr. Wife Mary. Conveyance. Rappa. 1 Sept 1673. Rappa. 1671-1676.

VINCENT WILLIAMS, Gent. Tax-list. One tithe. Hamp. cty, W. Va. 1783. In 1786 was in Hardy cty, with two tithes.

WILLIAM and BARBARA WILLIAMS, of Prince George's Psh, Maryland [this parish included families in both Prince George's and Frederick counties], had the following children:
Thomas-Owen Williams, b. 21 Feby 1747;
Elizabeth, b. 30 Oct 1749;
Elisha, b. 9 May 1752;
Ellinor-Hilleary, b. 5 Apr 1757;
Martha, b. 22 Dec 1759;
Edward-Owen, b. 18 Apr 1761. From the Reg. of Pr. Geo's Psh.

INDEX TO COUNTY COURT NOTE-BOOK. VOLUME VI.

Abbington 18
Abbott 26
Able 19
Acworth 27
Adams,Addams 10,11. 46
Addison 29,34
Adolph 19
Aherne 18
Akin 42
Alcock 11
Allday 22
Allen 11,14,19,29
Allerton 18
Alleyne 33
Allgood 33
Alstone 11
Alvis 22
Ambler 28
Ames,Aimes 15
Ancrom 29
Anderson 5,9,15,19, 38
Andrew,Andrews 14, 19,22,29
Angood 26
Annis 6
Ansell,Ancell 19
Appold 28
Arbuckle 3
Archer,10,36,38
Armitrading 26
Arnall 19
Aron (?) 27
Arrington 7
Arthur 11
Ashbury 21
Ashcom 27
Ashdon 33
Ashe 2
Ashton 18
Atkins 11,34
Atkinson,Ankinson, 11,19,22
Attwis 27
Aukeson 11,19,22
Austen,Austin 14,29, 45
Ayres 19
(See also Eyres)
Bagle 19
Bagwell 19,34
Bailey,Baily 2,19,34, 38,43
Baisden 46
Baker 26,37,38,46
Baldwin,Balding 19
Ball 10,11,27
Balthrope 29
Bane 33
Banks 23,35,37
Bannister 26
Barber 47
Bard 46
Barefoot 23
Barham 45
Barker 3
Barlow 35
Barnes 19,26,35
Barney 27
Barnitz 38
Barnsele 27
Barratt 19
Barrington 2
Bartee 38
Barton 23,46
Bartram 23,46
Baruch 14
Basnett 35
Bassett 2,11
Batson 19,22
Batt 11
Bayley 11,33,34
Bazey 19
Beach 26
Beacham,Beachampe 11, 27
Beall 11,29,46
Beard 46
Becket 17,18,19
Beedle 35
Bell,5,9,18,19,35, 37,45
Belote,Belliote 22,35
Benston 34,35,37
Bent 33
Benthall 35
Berry 10,27,30
Berryman 29
Bibby 35
Bickwith 11
Biggs 35
Billiard 35
Binney (?) 46
Bird 23,41
Bishop 19,33,35
Bize 30
Bizendine 38
Black 3,31
Blackwell 31
Blade 11
Blagden 18
Blagg 46
Blair 31,47
Blake 38
Blankenship 7
Blithe 10
Blount 2
Bloxam 19
Blunt 6
Boggs 10
Bolling 7,19
Bonn 47
Bonum 10
Bonwell 19
Booker 19
Boorne (?) 3
Booth 18
Booty 19
Boshen (?) 46
Botetourt,Lord 42
Boughan 23
Boughton 23
Bouldin 7
Boulware 23
Bound 27
Bowdoin 6,19,35
Bowin 33
Bowler 45

Bowles 2
Bowne 47
Boyes 33
Bradford 10,34,42
Bradshaw 11
Brady 46
Brafford 23
Bratton 27
Brayfield 47
Brent 41
Brett 46
Breward 2
Brewer,Breawer 27, 33
Brickhouse 19,22
Brierly 2
Brin 26
Brooke,Brooks 7,10, 17,19,23,28
Broughton 46
Brown 2,3,10,18,29, 37,38,46
Brummett 2
Brunet 38
Bryant 38
Buck 23
Buckley 23
Buckner 23,31
Bull 11
Bullard 23
Bullock 19
Bunbury 10
Burch 27
Burditt 19
Burgess 35
Burkham 33
Burnett 10,15,23
Burnly 3
Burrell 3
Burris,Burriss 2
Burse 10
Burton,Burtin 3,5,9, 18,19,25,34,37
Burwell 22
Busby 23
Bushrod 29
Bussey,Busey 6,31
Butcher 11
Butler 2,10,11,18
Byers 30,37
Byrd 42,46
Byze

Cable 35,37
Caffrey 42
Cage 39
Caldwell 1,41
Callaway 42
Cameron 39
Campbell 7,23
Candler 7,23
Cane 33
Cannon 2
Canfield,Campfield 15,19
Capell 19
Cardwell 7,38
Carlyle 46
Carns 33
Carpenter 19,22,38
Carrell (?) 33
Carrington 41
Carter 2,39,42
Cartwright 42
Cary 14
Casson 11
Cassott 11
Castigan 36
Catherall 47
Catlett 31
Catrop (?) 27
Caul 43
Caulk 21,29,36
Cecill 5
Chamberlain 26
Chambers 3,6,7
Chapline 6
Chapman 18
Charlton 11,35,37
Chaudoin 23
Checkly 19
Chevair 21
Chicheley,Chisley 14,22
Chilcott 43
Childers,Childress 7, 10,23
Chisley 22
Chittam 27
Christian 2,19
Church 15,19
Claiborne 41
Clark 2,9,11,30,35, 38 39,43
Clarvo 27
Clay 22,46
Clayton 26
Clegg 22
Clements 23
Clifford 10
Clifton 27
Coale 26
Coats 30
Cobb 22
Cock 28
Coe 34
Coffin 22
Cogan 46
Colbourne,Colburn 3, 11
Cole 11
Coleman 29
Collins 10,11,38
Colton,Coalton 27
Colyer 10
Combes 2
Compton 30
Coner (?) 2
Cook 2,11,15,27
Cooper 7,11,18,22, 23,31
Copes,22,38
Corbin,Corbyn 11,35
Corby 11
Cord 27
Corderoy 10
Cornick 35
Cornish 10
Costin 43
Cottom(?) 10,22
Coulston 33

Court 33
Courtney 30
Coutts 30
Cowdray 35
Cox 9,22
Coyte 30
Crafore 11
Craig 47
Cray 2
Creage 27
Crippin 3
Crockett 26
Croudson 14,47
Cropper 10
Cross 18,19
Crow 11
Cruchson 27
Crump 6
Crutchfield 23
Cugley 21
Cundiff 23
Curtis 2,10
Custis 3,4,5,6,12,
13,15,34 38
Cuttin 11

Dabney 15
Dade 2,29
Dakins 11
Dalby,Dolby 19,22
28
Dalley 23
Daniel,Daniell 7,33
Dansey 27
Darch 22
Dare 27
Darling 19
Darwell 27
Dashiell 45
Davies 9,10,21
Davis 1,2,9,10,13,17,
18,25,27,39,47
Dawson 27
Day 10,11
Dearing 14
Deaver 39
Deckert 5
Deeke 20
Degge 18
Delahah 47
Delalue 46
Delfe 33
Dennis 9,11,38
Denwood 22,27
De Sally 46
Deshazo 7
Devenport 23,30
Dewey 35
Dickinson 46
Dillard 41
Dimes 22
Dinguid (?) 7
Dishman 18
Dixon 4,19,22,37,47
Dodson 11,42
Doggett 39
Doherty 46
Dolby,Dalby 19,22,28
Dolton,19
Donaldson,Doneison 1,
9,17,18,21,25,33,
35,41,42
Dorman 19
Dorren 31
Dorsey 11
Doswell 15
Dotson 42
Doughty 22
Douglas 14,47
Downing 18
Downs 22
Dredan 27
Drighouse 19,22
Driver 11
Drummmond 22,34
Duddleston 18
Dunahoo 29
Duncan,Dunkin 18,28
Dunmore,Earl of 43
Dunn 2,11
Dunton 37
Duparks 22,37
Durant,Dorrant 2,11
Durkin,Durkan 10
Dutton 3
Dyer,Dyre 6,11,27
Dynes 22
Dynham 22

Earle 11,26
Early 22,42
East 34
Eastmead 14,19
Eastwood 13
Eaton 22,46
Eccleston 27
Eden 28
Edgar 17
Edmunds 22,37
Edrington 3
Edson 15
Edwards 11,22,46
Elford,Ellford 33
Eliason 22
Elkins 6
Ellcock 11
Ellet 22,37
Elligood 19,22
Elliott 11,23,37
Ellis 10,11
Ellison,Eliason 22
Elzey 26
Embrey 2
Emmerson 35
Emory 30
Emperour 10,14
Rnch 22
English 11
Ennis 26,27,33
Esdall 38
Eubanks 27
Evans 2,6,7,11,23,
27
Eveling,Evelin 19,22
Ewell,Eouell 18
Ewing 37
Eyre,Eyres 3,10,19,
21,22
(See also Ayres)

Fabian 22,37

Fallin 27
Fallow 11
Fandrue,Fandree 23
Faris 39
Farmer 11
Farrow 31
Fassett, see Fawcwtt
Fathrey,Fatherey 22, 38
Fawcett,Fausitt 3,10, 17,18,37
Fawks 31
Fenwick 17
Ferrers 31
Field 19,33
Finch 18
Finney 22,37
Firkettle 37
Fisher 17,22,27,37
Fitchett 37
Fitzgerald 39
Fitzhugh 18
Fleming 10,22,23,37
Fletcher 22,37,43
Floyd 37
Fluker,Flukes 10
Flye 33,43
Foard 11
Fontaine 23
Fore 10
Forman 46
Forrith 37
Forsith 43
Foster 22,35,39
Fountaine 2
Fowler 30
Fox 37,47
Foxcroft 37,46
Franklin 3,7,9,10, 17,23
Frazier,Frayzer,7,10
Freeman 11
Freshwater 22,37
Frog 21
Frost 37
Frey 18,21
Fuqua 10
Furrs (?) 22

Gale 5,46
Garrett 2,11
Garris 37
Garrison 37
Gascoyne 35,37
Gassaway 11
Gatewood 39
Gaylard,Gaylord 29, 46
Gelding 26,37,38,43
Gent 22
Gentry 39
Gerrard 18
Gethinge 22
(See Gitting)
Gibbs 7
Gibson 37
Giddens 46
Gilley 7,11
Gitting 37
(See Gethinge)
Givan,Givin 1,33
Glass 7,18
Glenn 2
Goaldin 29
Goding 37
Godman 26
Godwin (Goodwin) 17, 37,38,43
Goffigon 35,37,38,43
Goggin 15
Gohogan 37
Golbourne 11
Goodale 11
Goostin 27
Gorges 18
Gosnell 11
Gough 29
Goulsborough 26
Goult 26
Gower 10,38
Granger,Grainger 11, 38
Grant 2,46
Graves 10
Gray 41
Green 2,11,27,29,38,
Greenwood 30,47
Greer 1
Grice 38
Griffin,Griffen 6,38
Griffith 38
Grigg,Griggs 2,10
Grigsby 29
Grimbalson 22,38
Groton 37
Grovenstine 2
Grover 2
Groves 38
Gruger 45
Grymes 14
Gunns 23
Guphell 46
Guy 6,37,38

Hack 46
Hackett 4
Hadnuts 19,47
Haggoman 38,43
Haines 27
Hale,Haile 7,10
Hall 10,11,17,22,27 29,43
Hamilton 2
Hammond,Haymond 4, 25,38,43
Hanby 43
Handy 14,46
Hanna 39
Hanson 14,27
Hardesty 2,27
Harding,Harden 2,10, 29,31
Hardwick 18
Hardy 47
Hare 4,11
Harman 5,36
Harmanson 6,19,22, 38,43
Harris 2,7,10,11,21, 29,36

Harrison 26,29,35, 39
Hart 11
Hartway 38
Harvey 2,7,11
Harwell 11
Hasard 5
Hatchetorn 4
Hatton 11
Haus 47
Hayes,Hayes,Haze 22,42
Hayles 30
Haymond 4
Haynie 10
Hazelgrove 15
Head 6
Heading 2
Heath 33,38
Heather 10,11,17
Hemlock 22
Hemson 34
Hendrick 38
Henfield 6
Henly 11
Henry 31,42
Henwodd 18
Hepburn,Hepbourne 2,9,17
Herald 47
Hewes 11
Hewitt 14
Heyman 33
Hickman 33
Hicks 46
Hicky 27
Higby 43
Higdon 47
Hill 5,7,11,19,27, 30,33,39,42,46
Hillary 7,21
Hinchens 11
Hinsley 7
Hitley (?) 33
Hobbs 14
Hoble 11
Hodge 9
Hogg 11,43
Holden 3
Holfield (?) 27
Holland 10,23,37
Holliday 29
Hollingworth 46
Holman 1
Holmes 6,27
Holt 43
Hooe 29
Hook 29,37
Hope 3
Hopkins 17,22,25,33
Horn 26
Hornbuckle 2
Horton 14
Houldman 26
Houston 46
How,Howe 11,13
Howard 10
Howell 27
Howson 43
Hoyer 46
Huburd 36
Hudlen 47
Hudley 39
Hudson 9,10,27,34, 38,39,43
Hughes,Hues 7,11,29
Huling 17
Humphreys 10
Hunt 4,11,33,35,37, 38,43,46
Hunter 38
Hutchins 42
Hutton 27
Hynson 27

Inglies 47
Inglosed (?) 27
Innes 42
Irby 39,43
Ironshire 10
Isaack 43
Ivry (?) 11

Jackson 6,11,34,42
Jacob,Jacobs 5,22,38, 43
James 2,14,43
Jameson 11
Janes 43
Jarman,Jarmain,Jarmon 2,3
Jarratt 29
Jarvis 19,43
Jefferis 18
Jenkin,Jenkins 6,11
Jennings 15
Jervis 43
Jesper 20
Johnson 2,3,5,11,14, 18,19,26,27,33,34, 37,38,39,43,47
Johnston 39
Jones 2,5,6,10,11,27, 36,45,46,47
Jordan,Jourdan 37,43
Joyce 2
Joyner 2
Judkins 14
Juers (?) 2
Jury 11
Justice 35,39,43

Kanady 46
Keen 15
Kelly 37,39
Kempe 13
Kendall 19,35,37,38, 46
Kendrick 27
Kennedy,Kennady 11,46
Kennelly 27
Kersly 2
Kibbourne 11
King 7,11,17,19,27
Kirby,Kerby 21
Kitchen 39
Kitson (?) 27
Kniffin 26
Knight 6
Kollock 14,18

INDEX TO COUNTY COURT NOTE-BOOK. VOLUME V1.

Lacy 41
Lambard 46
Lane 9
Lange 3,22
Langle 11
Langford,Lankford 41
Lanham 29
Laughlan 26
Lawrence 11,45
Leatherbury 3
Leckie,Luckie 7
Lecompte 11
Lee 6,11,14,36
Leeke 11
Leftwich 7
Le Grande 45
Leigare (?) 33
Leigh 33
Lemmon (?) 27
Lewis,Lewes 20,21,31, 33,39,46,47
Lewkner 33
Lilliston 39
Limit 47
Lindall 6
Linger 27
Linton 11
Litchford 7
Little 11,26,29,33
Littleton 5,14,34
Longest 39
Lord 11
Love 28
Loveall 28
Lowe 11
Loyder 11
Lozanne 21
Lucas 27,33
Luckie,Leckie 7
Luke 22
Lutterell 19
Lynton 20
Lyster 47

McAleb 22
McCave 18
McClester 3
McCoy (?) 11
McCubbin 30
McDearman 38
McDonald 5
McGill,Makgill 11
McGomery 39
McKean 1
Mackey 26
McLean,Macclain 26
Maddison 36
Mags 31
Malone 39
Malloney 3
Mander 11
Mannering 30
Manning,Mannyng 26
Mantlo 39
Mapp 43
Marey 2
Markham 41
Marr 47
Marshall 39,43,45
Martin 9,10,11,17, 18,27
Mashiell 45
Masman 22
Mason 11,18,19,31
Massey 34,35
Masson 11
Massot 21
Mathews,Matthews 2, 7,22,39
Mauldin 11
Mauklin (?) 10
Maxwell 18
Meade 15,27
Meekins 47
Meredith 15
Merrick 2
Merriday 11,43
Merril 29,30
Merriman 11
Merritt 26
Michael,Mikeel 5, 33,38
Milam 39
Mildew 21
Miles 2,27
Miller 21,31
Millikens 2
Mills 47
Minitree 46
Mitchell 30
Moley 42
Monroe 18
Moody 39
Moore,Moor 6,10,11, 33
Morgan,Morgaine 20, 26,27,33
Morphew 47
Morris 11,17,18,33
Morrison 11
Morton,Moreton,26,29
Moseley 27
Moyses 11
Mullikin 27
Mullins 38
Mulls 35
Mumford 2
Mungan 21
Murphy 19
Murrain 27
Muse 19
Musgrove 30

Nails 15
Neale 6,11,22
Nealmes 11
Neighbours 26
Nelson 22,26,42
Nevell 22
Newsome 11
Newton 18,33
Nicholls 27
Nicholson 9
Noble 10
Nock 35
Noell 37,39
Norman 3
Norrey 11
Northcutt 2
Nottingham 35
Nugent 6

INDEX TO COUNTY COURT NOTE-BOOK. VOLUME V1.

Nunez 18

Ocane 3
Ogston 26
Oliver 11
O'Neale 23
Orton 33
Overton 42
Owen,Owens 2,3,7,14,33,46
Oxford 2

Paige 6
Paine 10,22,30,46
Pale 11
Palmer 11,13,21,29,33,36,43,45
Pancoast 47
Panewell 19
Park 33
Parker 2,10,11,17,39
Parlitt 6
Parrish 26
Parrott 11
Parry 18,27
Parvin 18
Paton 10
Patrick 2,9,27,43
Payne 42
Paynter 6,26
Peach 18
Pearce 2
Peddenton 22
Peirce 36
Pemberton 18
Pepper 27
Perkins,Pirkins 18
Perry 18
Person 11
Peter 14
Pether 11
Pett 33
Pettit 7,11
Phiden (?) 11
Pickman 6
Pirkins 18
Pitt,Pitts 2,11,27,46
Planner 2
Plummer 47
Pollard 27
Pope 2,18,19
Popham 18
Porter 10,26
Pott 11
Poulidge 2
Pouncebee 18
Powell 19,26,33,37,43
Powsey 39
Poynter 10,27
Prather 7
Pratt 11
Preeson 35,37
Preston 39
Pribble 7
Price 6,10,22,31,33,35
Pridham 20
Prior,Prier 27,30
Pritchett 11,19
Purnell 25,42

Quinton 46

Radley 23
Rae,Ray 2,14
Rain 35
Ramsay 39
Ranier 19
Rasberry 2
Rason 21
Ratcliffe,Rackliffe 2,3,11
Ray,Rae 2,14
Raynet 46
Read,Reed 3,10,18,41
Records (?) 30
Redd 7,42
Rees 27
Reid 39
Revell 2,3
Reynolds 11
Rice 5
Rich 2
Richards 6,10
Richardson 9
Richeson 27
Rickards 11
Rigge 11
Right 26
Roberts 11,14,19
Robins 19,22,30,35
Robinson 11,12,13,14,21,27,28,29,37
Robson 47
Rodolphus 35
Roe 11
Rogers 23
Roney 30
Rosser 7
Rot 22
Rotheram 30
Round 9,10,17,18,25
Rowan 6,37
Ruff 2
Rush 6,18
Russell,Rossell 9,15,17,18
Rutter 22
Ryan 31
Rye 33

Sabrell 39
Sacker 3, 4
Saffin 46
Salle 46
Sample,Sampell 19,34
Sanders 18,26,29
Sanford 19
Sarrell 35
Satchell 35
Saunders 19
Savage 5,19,34,35,37,43
Scarburgh,Scarbrough 3,18,35,37
Scott,scot 2,9,18,19,27,31
Sedger 11
Seigler 2
Selby 27
Senior 3,43

Severne, Seaverne 5, 22,35
Sexton 14
Shae 25
Shaner 14
Shankland 10
Sharp 11,21
Sheare 11
Shelton 41
Sheppard, Shepheard 19,22,30
Sherwood 27
Shewell 17
Shreive 11
Shippey 10
Short 7
Silden 26
Silvester 95
Simpson, Sympson 9,10
Sims 26
Simson 10
Singleton 11
Sinnott 26
Sisson 3,47
Skegs 11
Skipwith 13
Sluse (?) 3
Smith 2,3,9,15,18,19, 27,30,33,34,35,37, 38,43,46,47
Sparks 11
Spence 19
Spencer 6
Spicar 47
Spier 11
Spiller 29
Sprigge 11
Spring 21
Springuish 22
Spyker 14
Staminet 29
Stanly 34
Stanton 2,47
Starait (?) 46
Starr 11
Staton 34,35
Stephens 45
Sterritt, Starait 14,46
Stevens 10,23
Stevenson 18,27
Steward 1,9
(See also Stuart)
Stoake 11
Stockley 1,3,25,26,33, 34,41
Stoile (?) 11
Stott, Stotts 35,37,38
Stratton 7,34
Street 15,39
Stringer 26,35,37
Strong 11
Strother 31
Stuart 17,42,43
(See also Steward)
Stubbin 33
Sturgis 25
Sweeny 30

Talbot 5,29
Tallaferro 2
Talley 15,39
Tate 42
Tatum 42
Taylor, Taylord 6,11, 20,29,38
Tebbs 19
Thielos (?) 31
Thomas 10,11,18,26,27, 29,30
Thompson 2,11,14,27,42
Thorey 33
Thorne 45
Thornbush 33
Thorp 11
Thrift 27
Tidwell 5
Tilden 21
Till 17,18
Tilney 3,14,22
Tipshott 19
Todd 6,31
Toles 34
Townshend 26
Townsend 26
Trader 26
Travellor 19
Trayman 19
Trilley 33
Triplett 15
Troutt 10
Truitt 27
Trulock 31
Tucker 14,27
Tule 30
Tulley 6
Tullock 22
Tunnell 27,34
Turberville 18
Turbutt 27
Turner 9
Turpin 2,9

Upshur 37

Vanweker 19
Vardeman 7
Vaux, Vaulx 11,18,29
Veal 29
Verlande 29
Vice 21
Virtue 21

Wade 5,29,37
Waggaman 9,14
Waite 11
Walbrooke 33
Wale 3
Walk 11
Walker 6,13,14,15, 35
Waller 2
Walley 14
Walter 22
Walton 10
Warren 14,37
Wasdall 11
Washbourne 14
Washington 14
Waters 3,19,33
Waterson 19,37
Watkins 15,30,33,47

Watts 11,22,30
Webb 14,31,38,45
Weedon 18
Weekes 11
Wellington 33,36
Wells 11
Wescott,Westcott 22,
37
West 14,33,43
Westcombe 36
Westerhouse 22
Wheatley 47
Wheeler 11
White 3,18,29,31
Whithurst 30
Whittington 19,33
Wilkins 19,22,38,43
Will 27
Williams 2,3,6,7,11,
14,15,19,21,26,29,
30,31,47
Williamson 2,30
Willis 37
Wilson 9,11,27,29,30,
37,43
Winchester 47
Winn 26
Wise 12
Wood,Woods 3,7,10,15,
27,33,46
Woodcraft 11
Woodford 23
Woodman 25
Woodward 47
Wooton 26,33
Wormley,Wormeley 22
Worsley 27
Wright 6
Wyat,Wyett 2,30

Young 38

More than one entry on the same page is indicated by underscoring.

The

County Court Note-Book

A Little Bulletin of History and Genealogy

February, 1928. **Vol. VII, No. 1.**

SHIPS IN PORT

The *Good Ship Augustine*; Zachary Taylor, of Wapping, mariner, county of Middlesex, master; now bound on a voyage to Virginia. York, Va. 5 Oct 1680. vi-296. See also vi-183; vi-35; vi-178.

The *Barnaby*; Capt. Mathew Rider, Comdr. York, Va. 24 Feby 1681-2. vi-374.

Ship Brimptone [?]; Capt. Giles Russell, commander; makes oath to indentures of John Gray, Edwd Welch, Mary Mahoones and Ellenor Ring, for seven years. Nthld, Va. [5]-346. 8 Nov 1719.

The *Charles* of London; Capt. Robt Munden in command; rioters sent to Virginia. [The "Ryott" was on an island, the name of which is illegible.] Nthld, Va. 19 July 1664.

The *Concord*; Capt. Thomas G[r]antham, Commdr. York, Va. 19 July 1664.

The *Good Shipp Concord*, of London. Capt. Thos: Grantham, Commdr. York, Va. 9 Feby 1679. vi-214.

The *Constant Mary*; Capt. Edwd Rhodes, Commdr. York, Va. 2 Dec 1681. vi-360.

Sloope called the *Crowne*; sold by M..... Dordes [?] of Virginia, mariner, to Wm. Chappell, also of Virginia, mariner. Nthld, Va. 1658-1666, fo. 148. 1664.

The *Diamond*; Capt. Jno. Badwin [? perhaps Bowdoine?] Commdr. York, Va. 5 Jany 1681-2. vi-366.

Ship *Endeavor*; Henry Edgate, Commdr. John Brunskin, mate. York Va. 26 Jany 1679. vi-191.

The *Ketch Eunice*; of New England. York, Va. 24 Oct 1682. vi-432.

The *George*; Capt. Thomas Grantham, Commdr. York, Va. 25 Jany 1674.

The *Golden Fortune*; Capt. William Jefferys, Commdr. York, Va. 24 Apr 1678. vi-35.

The *Humphry and Elizabeth*; Capt. John Martyn. York, Va. 25 June 1683. vi-506.

Shipp Industry; Mr. Phineas Hide, Commdr; Capt. Hide makes claim to a sloop belonging to the sd Shipp which was burnt; case referred to England, being their owne desire. York, Va. 3 Apr 1672. v-23.

The *Jonathan*, of Topsham; Mr. John Frisco, master, dec'd, about or before 13 Feby 1679. Mr. Wm. Richards, late mate, now master. York, Va. v-191.

The *Judith*; Capt. Mathew Trim, Commdr. 26 May 1684. York, Va. vi-579.

Sloop called the *Good Luck*; belonged to John Le Breton. Nthld, Va. 19 Mch 1664. (Record.) 1658-1666, f. 146.

Sloop Lively; of Westmoreland, 15 tons; built in Maryland, 1771. Registered South Potomack [?] 9 July 1777. John Turberville, Esq.,owner; Thomas Lacock, [master.] Naval Officers' Returns. Va. S. L.

Ketch Love's Increase, of Va. Mr. John Palmer, Commdr. Rappa., Va. 12 Nov 1696. 1677-1682, p. 100.

The *Good Ship Mary*, of Salem, in New England; Shipped by the grace of God in good order & well conditioned by me, Thomas Thoresby, in and upon . . . . whereof is Master under God for this present voyage, Capt. Edward Fevery, and now riding at anchor in James River, and by Gods grace bound for Barbadoes. . . . . God send the Good Ship to her desired port in safety. Amen. Signed Edmond Feveryeare. York, Va. 15 Feby 1678. vi-431.

The *Planter's Adventure*; Mr. Laman [?], Commdr. York, Va. 16 Aug 1682. vi-579.

The *Richard and Jane*; Capt. Thomas Arnall [or Arnold] Commdr. York, Va. 25 Jany 1674.

The good Ship called the *Recovery*, of Bristol, lying in Wicomoko river; Joseph Hines was boatswain. Nthld, Va. 14 Nov 1660. 1658-1666, fo. 47.

Brigantine Reformation, 60 tunns burden; William Whittington, of Calvert cty, Md., house carpenter, owner. Now lying in Bohemia River. Annap. Records. P. L. vi-181. 23 Apr 1726.

Ship Sarah; Mr. Joseph Jeffreys was brother and extr to nun-cup. will of Capt. William Jeffreys, late Commdr, deceased. York, Va. 24 Mch 1696. xi-368. See also p. 390.

Shipp Speedwell; of London; John Julian, master; now riding at Anchor in the port of Nominy, which was seized together with her goods & merchandize by Capt. Thomas Allen, Comandr of his Majti's Ketch the *Quaker*, for that the said Julyan had no "coquetts" whereby it might appeare that the goods and Merchandizes loaden and shipped on board his said Shipp were entered within any port of the Kingdome of Engl'd principallity of Wales or Towne of Berwick upon Tweed. . . . . Wmld, Va. Ct 4 Feby 1684. 1676-1678, p. 373.

Shipp Speedwell, of London; Wm. Stanley sets forth that shipped on Board her, John Julian, master, with provisions and Liquots for himselfe, family and servts' subsistence att Sea and shore from Galloway in Ireld to Virginia and Pennsylvania to the value of Three Hundred pds sterl. [Stanly charges theft on board.] Wmld, Va. Ct 25 Mch 1685. 1676-1678, p. 387.

Ship the *Susan*; also the *Elizabeth and Mary*; the master of the latter appears to have been Capt. Whitly. Nthld, Va. 1661. 1658-1666, fo. 141.

The *Thomas and Ann*; Capt. John Fox, formerly commander. Rappa., Va. 1656-1664, p. 98. 1659.

Ship William and Mary; Capt. Sam: Groome; Dep'n of John Gustinge of Gloucester cty that Tho: Colley m. Sarah Ropier [Rapier?] who came into this country about one and one-half years before in the *William and Mary*. Similar dep'n by Edw: White. Nthld, Va. 20 Jany 1664. 1658-1666, fo. 149.

AUTHENTIC REFERENCES FOR INFERRED MARRIAGES*

(Northampton County, Va.)

JOHN LALOR [LAWLER] and the admx of Cornelius JOHNSON. Before 30 Mch 1696. xvii-369.

HANCOCK LEE and MARY KENDALL, dau. of William. Before 29 Oct 1685. xv-225.

JAMES LIPSEY and a dau. of Arthur RASCO [RASKO]. Before 24 Nov 1724. Chancy records.

Mr. EDWARD LITTLETON and FRANCES ...... she m. (2) Mr. Francis Pigott. See x-95. Before 15 May 1677. See xi-145.

Mr. EDWARD LITTLETON was to marry SARA DOUGLAS... see her father's will. 15 Oct 1657. vii-76.

JOHN MAJOR and WINIFRED FLETCHER, wid. of Robert [?] Before 1730 or 1731. Chancy records.

JOHN MILBY and LEAH COWARD, widow of Samuel. Before Feby 1757. Chancy records.

Mr. THOMAS MADDUX and SARAH YARDLEY, widow of Argoll Yardley, Gent. (Her will, 1694-1697.) Before the 20 Mch 1694. xvii-419. [She had been the widow of Dr. James Watt.]

ALEXANDER MOUNTNEY and the widow of Thomas SPILLMAN and Edward HILL, (both deceased. Both belonged to Eliz. City cty.) Before 28 Oct 1642. ii-178.

JOHN MECHAELL [MICHAEL] and HELLEN CORNAH. 24 Mch 1660. ix-92. Mar. record.

JOHN MICHAELL, Gent., and ANNE JONES, widow of Capt William JONES. Before 26 Aug 1671. xi-21.

LITTLETON MILLS and ANNE MOORE, dau. of Matthew. Before 1758. Chancy records.

ALEXANDER MILLS and JOAN HEWETT[?] widow. Before 28 Dec 1671. xi-29.

THOMAS MILLS and MARY COWELL. widow of Benjamin. Before or about 2 Mch 1702. xviii-129, 140.

DANIEL MACKENNY and ELIZABETH BROOKS, admx of Humphry. Before 29 Mch 1697. xvii-416. See also xvii-526 and xviii-28.

EDWARD MILLS and SUSANNA FITCHETT, dau. of Nehemiah. Before 1774. Chancy records.

JOHN MAJOR and ANNE JOHNSON, dau. of Obedience, dec'd. 11 Oct 1791. M. L. B.

JOHN MAJOR and the widow of Elkinton SAVAGE. Before 14 Mch 1731. Chancy records.

ARTER MOUNTENEY and the relict of Tho: SPILLMAN, and also of Edward HILL. Before 28 Oct 1642. i-178. [She had in her possession 115 acres of land in Eliz. City cty, belonging to the orphans of sd Hill and Spillman. This is probably the same Mounteney marriage as that referred to above.]

THOMAS MASLIN and ELIZABETH PIGOT, widow of John. 1772.

THOMAS MOORE and ELLENOR, dau. of Elizabeth GELDING. Before latter part of 1698. xvii-526.

GILBERT MOORE and KATHERINE, dau. of Elizabeth GELDING. Before latter part of 1698. xvii-526.

JOHN MOORE and MARGARET TILNEY, dau. of John, Gent. Before 6 Apr 1700. (See xvi-242. Before 26 Sept 1699. See also L. C. 1754-1771. fo. 147.)

THOMAS MOOR and ELIZABETH MOOR, widow of Matthew. Before 14 July 1725. Chancy records.

WILLIAM MELLING and ANNE SCOTT, sister of William. Before 30 May 1681. xiv-19.

JOHN MICHAEL, Jr., and ROSE WAINHOUSE. 23 Jany 1771. M. L. B.

THOMAS MADDOX and the widow of William SMITH. Before 11 Dec 1678. xii-308.

ABRAHAM MORGAN and ANNE SHAWE. Before 2 Nov 1654. v-55. See also vii-21.

Mr. EDW. MOSELY and FRANCES TAYLOR, widow of Mr. Bartlett TAYLOR, and dau. of John STRINGER. About [?] 29 July 1685. xv-147, also xvii-7.

MARK MANLOVE and ELIZABETH WILLIAMS. About or before 26 July 1682. ix-129.

WALTER MANNINGTON and MARY the admx of Charles WRESSELL. Before 30 May 1693. xvii-232. She was also the widow of Dorman Loughland. See xvi.-224. Her marriage to MANNINGTON was before 2 Mch 1692.

PAUL MARSH and ELIZABETH MEREDITH, eldest daughter of Philip. Before 9 Oct 1672. Va. S. L. O. vi-430.

THOMAS MIDDLETON [?] and ELLENOR SATCHELL, daughter of William. Before 28 Feby 1680. xiii-141.

JOHN MILES and MARTHA UNDERHILL, widow of Michael. Before 28 Mch 1704. xviii-229.

JOSEPH MASON and ROSE VAN SOLDT, daughter of Abraham. Before 28 Mch 1679. xiii-4.

DANIELL NEECH and MARGARETT SAUNDERS, widow of Eustace. Before 30 Nov 1674. xi-87.

CHRISTOPHER NUTTER and MARY DORMAN. About[?] 1662. viii-141.

ADDESON NOTTINGHAM and ANN EVANS, dau. of John, Sr. [and wife Leah?] Before 1754. Chancy records.

ROBERT NOTTINGHAM and JANE JOHNSON, admx of Harman. Before 28 Feby 1692. xvii-222.

WILLIAM NICHOLSON and BARBARA BELL, widow of Thomas, Jr. Before [?] 31 May 1698. xvii-480. See also xviii-91.

WILLIAM NICHOLSON probably m. BARBARA ROBINS, extx of Capt. Arthur Robins. About 1701. xviii-91. See also xvii-480.

PROVIS NELSON and ANNE TOMPSON, widow of Robert. Before or about 26 June 1668. vii-28.

JOHN NELSON and the extx of Paule TANNER [also extx of WATERSON?] Before 29 Nov 1709. xviii-5o5.

JOHN NORTHAM and the extx of John Marriott. Before 22 Aug 1684. xv-75.

JOHN NELSON and ADAH CARPENTER. William Carpenter, sec. 6 July 1770. M. L. B.

JOHN NOTTINGHAM and SARAH TATUM, widow of Thomas. Before 1 Mch 1702. xviii-126. See also xviii-161.

ADDISON NOTTINGHAM probably m. BARBARY POWELL. About 1764. Chancy records.

RICHARD NOTTINGHAM and ANN JOHNSON, widow of Harman. Before 22 June 1747. Chancy records.

SEVERN NOTTINGHAM and ELIZABETH EVANS, daughter of Arthur. Before Nov 1770. Chancy records.

ISAAC NOTTINGHAM and Mrs. MARY KENDALL. [Widow?] Bet. Apr 1761 and Nov 1764. Chancy records.

OBEDIENCE OBEN and . . . . CARPENTER, a widow. About 1740-1745. Chancy records.

TEAGUE ODEERE and the widow of John STEVENS. Before 28 Jany 1667. x-46. See also xv-211 for his marriage to ESTHER COSTIN, widow. [Previously published.]

WILLIAM ORTON and a daughter of George ISDELL. Before 8 Oct 1687. xv-315.

OBEDIENCE PARRAMORE and ALICE BRYANT, daughter of John. Before 7 Oct. 1728. Chancy records.

THOMAS PITTS and TABITHA WILLS, daughter of Thomas. Before 12 Sept 1732. Chancy records.

ANDREW PITTS and the widow of John GREEN. Before 1724. Chancy records.

EZRA PARRAMORE and Elizabeth STURGIS, daughter of Jacob. Before August, 1769. Chancy records.

JOHN PARRAMORE and JANE DRAKE. Record 6 July 1640. ii—

OBEDIENCE PARRAMORE and ELIZABETH KNIGHT, widow of George. Before 1729. Chancy records.

ARNALL PARRAMORE and BRIDGETT ROBINSON, daughter of John and Mary. Before 30 Nov 1695. xvii-338.

WILLIAM PARRAMORE, Gent., son of Thomas, of Accomack, and SARAH SEYMOUR, daughter of Digby. 22 Oct 1763. M. L. B.

JOHN PARSONS and ESTHER EVANS, daughter of Arthur. Before Nov 1770. Chancy records.

JOHN PARSONS and ALICE CASTLE, widow of Robert. Before 7 Nov 1764. xii-5.

EUSTACE PARSONS and ANN HALL, widow. She died before 29 July 1690. xvii-56.

WILLIAM PARSONS and SARAH CABLE, daughter of Sorrowful Margaret CABLE. Before 24 Oct 1750. Chancy records.

THOMAS PREESON and ELIZABETH BROWN, daughter of Thomas. See 28 Aug 1706. xvi-439. Preeson died 5 Apr 1723; wife died 1 Apr 1733. See L. C. fo. 43.

JOHN PANEWELL probably m. a daughter of Henry MATTHEWS. Before 3 Oct 1690. xvii-79.

JOHN PALMER and Mrs. SARAH KENDALL. (She also married Matthews.) See 29 Sept 1692. xiv-332.

THOMAS PEELE and MARY STUDSON. Before 30 Nov 1695. xvii-338. [This Mary Studson was the dau. or granddau. of Mary Parramore, whose last husband was John Parramore.]

THE DEPUTY COMMISSARY'S GUIDE WITHIN THE PROVINCE OF MARYLAND

Written principally with the view of introducing a general uniformity in the proceedings of deputy commissaries, and of assisting executors and administrators in the performance of their duties . . . . submitted to the candour of the public. Elie Vallette.

Concerning intestates, administrators, &c.

By the Statute of 13th Edward, 1st, Cap. 19, it was enacted, "where a man dies intestate, and "in debt, ... the ordinary shall satisfy the "debts, so far as the goods extend in such sort, "as the executors of such persons should have "done, in case he had made a will." Before this Statute there was no direct law compelling the ordinary [now the Register of Wills, the Clerk of the Court, the Judge of Probate or of Ordinary] to pay the debts of intestates. Then the 31st Edward 3d, Cap. 11, directed that "where a man "dieth intestate, the ordinary shall depute the "next, and most lawful friends of the deceased, to administer his goods." By this statute the name *administrator* was first introduced.

By the statute of 21st Henry 8th, Cap. 5, the ordinary was empowered and directed "in case any person died intestate, or the "executors "named in any testament refuse to prove said "testament . . . . . to grant administration to "the widow, or to the next of his kin, or to "both." . . . . "When divers persons claim the "administration as next of kin, which be equal "in degree of kindred to the testator or person "deceased; . . . . . the ordinary to be at his elec-"tion and liberty, to accept any one or more "making request [for "administration.]"; but when they are not "all in equality of degree" [of relationship] "then the ordinary to admit the widow, and him "or them only making request or any one of them at his pleasure."

[The above was the English law as applied in all English colonies.]

In Maryland, the Assembly of 1715 provided that the commissary-general or the judge or judges in testamentary causes, should appoint some able and sufficient person "of good repute and a freeholder," in every county to take the probate of any last will, "even though the same be concerning titles of land," and to grant in the respective county or counties, where each person or persons so appointed shall reside and inhabit, and authorizes such person to grant letters testamentary or administration. But if any contest shall arise, it is to be decided by the commissary-general, or judge in testamentary causes, and not by persons appointed by the county as aforesaid.

The deputy commissaries are further empowered to audit and allow accounts, relating to dead men's estates, not exceeding fifty pounds in money, provided there be no controversy thereon.

(*To be continued.*)

The County Court Note-Book

An every-other-monthly devoted mainly to abstracts from County Court Records, prior to 1800.

MILNOR LJUNGSTEDT, Editor and Publisher.
Bethesda, Route 10, Maryland.

Published six times a year. Subscription, two dollars, in advance; must begin with the year.

February, 1928 **Whole**
Vol. VII., No. 1 **No. 38**

ELIE VALLETT'S DEPUTY COMMISSARY'S GUIDE. The Editor understands that when one plays golf one must do it in a very set and proper way, following fixed rules and not depending on any sudden illumination of genius. When the Editor began on the never-ending task of digesting colonial records, questions came thick and fast into her mind. Why did they do this that way? How long did a person have to be dead before his estate was administered? Who inherited? Why did they make such a to-do over paying the debts of a person deceased? Nobody could answer her questions. Of course, *somebody* knew, but the local court was more concerned in the last election or the next one, or in hunting licenses or dog taxes, and now it is the radio. "I just almost got San Francisco last night," says one gentleman. "Pshaw!" says the other, "I get Honolulu every night." [If it were not Honolulu it was "equally as."]

One happy day in some old Maryland office the Editor spied a small book . . . the *Deputy Commissionary's Guide.* She has never ceased to wish to own that book . . . it was only seven dollars then . . . it is now twelve and over. The great Baltimore fire burned up a lot of them. Application at the Library of Congress through the kindly interest of an able assistant brought to light two copies of this little volume, not valued for its digest of old English law, but because it is an early American imprint!

The Editor wants to share the information she gobbled . . . there is no other word . . . out of the yellowing pages . . . wants to share it with perhaps the very few who also "want to know," and are not read in Edwards and Henrys, and Elizabeths of "blessed memory."

It is hardly necessary to say that these laws applied to all the English colonies . . . the Editor has the word of the very helpful chief of the Law Library for that . . . so that it makes no difference whether Maryland titled her officers in one way and South Carolina in another . . . the road to settlement was the same.

So ELIE VALLETTE, with his crest on the title-page, will still continue to serve his readers, that is, those who will take him as abstracted for this NOTE-BOOK.

FIFTY CENTS each will be paid for a few copies of the February NOTE-BOOK for 1927.
EDITOR.

SUNDRY ABSTRACTS

BERKELEY COUNTY, SS. May Court, 1810.
SAMUEL ROBERTS against
William Burns, John Burns, George Burns; Abraham Van Metre, senr, and wife Elizabeth (Burns); Abraham Van Metre, Jr., and wife Hannah (Burns); Henry Whiteneck and wife Margaret (Burns); William Van Metre and wife Rebecca (Burns); James McDonald and wife Isabella (Burns); William Van Metre; James Ramsey and wife Ruth (Van Metre); . . . . . . Lancaster and wife Joane (Van Metre); . . . . . Polk and wife Axa (Van Metre) ; . . . . Whitaker and wife Milca (Van Metre); Abigail Van Metre, Amasa Van Metre, Rebecca Van Metre, children and heirs of Mary Van Metre late Mary Burns, and late wife of Isaac Van Metre, deceased; . . . . . Ford and wife Susanna (Colgan); Daniel Colgan, Mary Colgan, Robert Colgan and Harvey Colgan, children of Ruth Colgan, deceased, late Ruth Burns . . . . . heirs and representatives of WILLIAM BURNS, deceased. (From the Martinsburg, W. Va., Gazette, 8 June 1810.)

Mr. WILLIAM WEAVER, in right of his wife Mary, impleading Mrs. Elizabeth Diggs, extx of Edward Diggs, Esq., for some money given her (Mary) by the last will of John Githings, dec'd, being in possession of said Edward Diggs as also for his wife's fredome corn and clothes having served her full time. An appeal is taken to next taken to next General Court. 24 Jany 1675-6. York, Va. v-293.

Estate of WILLIAM TOMBS: By consent of William Toombs, Gabriel Toombs, William Traynum the husband of Ann Toom[b]s; William Toombs in behalf of Thomas Toombs; also on behalf of John Toombs, and Reuben Traynum on behalf of John Worsham, the husband of Mary Toombs; being properly authorized for the purpose, we have proceeded to allot off and divide the estate of said William Toombs, dec. Charl. cty, Va. 25 Mch 1783. i-329.

A GEORGIA RECORD: A certificate from Chesterfield county, Virginia, states that JUDITH BRANCH, the widow of WILLIAM BRANCH, deceased, and mother of WILLIAM BRANCH, Jr., departed this life the fourth September, 1820. This follows a copy of the will of THOMAS BRANCH, Jr.

PETITION OF NOAH BOWEN: That since 14 Feby 1821, Isaac Bowen, his father, has died, leaving the following children and grandchildren, his heirs-at-law: Noah, Stephen, Joshua, Zaccheus, Moses, Amelia, wife of Joseph Richardson; and James, Augusta and Levicey H. Bowen, minors; also children of his daughter, Arra, who married Schoolfield Lamberson and died in the lifetime of her father: Julian, Annah-Mariah, Jane-Jenkins, and Mary-Arralanta Lamberson, also minors. Petition for division of lands granted. Som. cty, Md. Ct. Proceedings. vol. iv. Nov. Term, 1833.

ERRATA:

In the Supplement to the NOTE-BOOK for December, 1925, Eastern Shore Families, the fifth line from the bottom of the first column should read: "[John Custis,] Mcht, and wife Tabitha, give to kinsman Joseph Webb. . . .

In an early number of the NOTE-BOOK (July, 1922, p. 3) the marriage of William Richardson and Ann Abbott is given. This should be Cobbett, not Abbott.

In September of the same year (p. 3) "Jemina Odell and Job," should read: "she was the dau. of James Job."

QUERIES

CHILLIAN and MARTIN PALMER, Charlotte cty, Va. Ancestry wanted. Seventy-five dollars will be paid for accurate information accompanied by proof from civil and church records. W. B. P. A.

ANDREW LEE; Who were his parents? He was born in New Jersey about 1745, and died in Edgefield county, S. C., 1796. Soldier War of 1812. Mrs. D.

RUSSELL WILSON; Wanted the maiden name of his wife. Wilson was a Revolutionary soldier; moved from Virginia to Edgefield county, S. C. Mrs. D.

JOSEPH A. BYERS m. REBECCA ROWAN, in York or Chester county, S. C. When? Byers was a Revolutionary soldier. Mrs. D.

CONTINUED articles COUNTY COURT NOTE-BOOK, and the dates on which they first appeared.

THE ANCESTRY OF COL. JOHN DONELSON. Began with February, 1927.

AUTHENTIC REFERENCES for INFERRED MARRIAGES (formerly called MARRIAGES BY INFERENCE). Began with May, 1922.

MARYLAND'S NEXT OF KIN. Began with July, 1922.

VIRGINIA COLONISTS. Alphabetized lists began with July, 1924.

MILITARY NOTES, both COLONIAL and REVOLUTIONARY, and later MILITIA NOTES. Began December, 1923.

INTERCOUNTY and INTERCOLONY (formerly called New Englanders and Others, &c., &c,). Began with March, 1922.

EASTERN SHORE FAMILIES. In the form of a one-page supplement, began with June, 1925. This will be continued later.

SHIPS IN PORT and COLONIAL FORENAMES, will appear in alternate issues or as space can be found for them.

MARYLAND'S NEXT OF KIN

FRANCIS HOPEWELL, JOHN COLE; inv. Alexander [Lickey?] of St. Mary's county. [No date.] vii-223.

THOMAS PETERS, EDW'D STONE; inv. Joseph Peters of St. Mary's cty. 20 Nov 1721. vii-224.

ELINOR EGAN signs inv. of Dr. Charles Egan, of Pr. Geo's cty. 23 Apr 1723. vii-226.

"No Relations." Inv. Mr. Rich'd Llewellin of Chas. cty. 7 May 1722. vii-227.

JOHN LOW, THOMAS x LOW; inv. Gallent Lane of Q. A. cty. 17 Feby 1721. vii-231.

ALEX'R x BRILSON, son [? meant for senior?] BARBARA CANNON, dau. Inv. John Fitz Redmond of Balto. cty. 16 Dec 1721. vii-236.

"No Kindred." Inv. Michael Dean of Dor. cty. 12 June 1722. vii-237.

GEORGE COOPER, JANE FOURD "Creditor;" inv. William Fourd of Talbot cty. 2 June 1722. vii-238.

ANN x GILBERT, MARGT x GILBERT; inv. Edward Gilbert of Talbot cty. 9 July 1722. vii-241.

ELIZABETH CURSITOR, extx, makes oath that she knows not of any Relations the said Alex'r hath in this province. Inv. Alex'r Cursitor of Talbot cty. 9 July 1722. vii-242.

SARAH x SONGO, SOLOMON x SONGO; inv. William Songo of Talbot cty. 5 June 1722. vii-244. [It would see that this must have been meant for the name LONGO, which is found in a nearby section, but the initial letter of the record is very plainly "S".]

GEORGE HADDAWAY, THOS. HADDAWAY; inv. George Hadaway of Talbot cty. 13 June 1722. vii-245.

THOMAS x CARWARDING, JOHN x CARWARDING, "Kin and Creditor;" inv. Thomas Carwarding, of Kent cty. 10 July 1722. vii-249.

"No Kindred;" inv. Philip Bradish of Kent cty. 5 May 1722. vii-250.

WILLAM GILHAGE, "near Kinsman;" inv. of William Gilhage of Kent cty. 4 May 1722. vii-251.

"No Debtors or Kindred to be heard of;" inv. Darby Cafte of Kent cty. 23 Apr 1722. vii-251.

MARY HEMSLEY [Kin.?]; inv. Thomas Britts, of Annapolis. 29 Mch 1721. vii-254.

JOHN x ROCKHOLD, THOMAS COCKEY; "Nearest of Kinn and greatest Creditor." inv. Thomas Rockhold of A. A. cty. No date. vii-255.

FRANCIS x GARTERELL, JOHN x GARTERELE; "Relations;" inv. John Garterell of A. A. cty. 7 May and 13 June 1722. vii-256.

JOHN WOODING, ELEZ. WOODING; inv. Sparrow Carteris[?] of A. A. cty. 21 Apr 1722. vii-257.

WILLIAM WORTHINGTON, SARAH BRICE [Kin]; inv. DARBY DOWNS of A. A. cty. No date. vii-258.

THOMAS WHITEHEAD, Samuel Whitehead; inv. Richard Whitehead of A. A. cty. 2 June 1722. vii-259.

RICHARD HAMTON, MARY x RIGHT, [Kin?] inv. John Smith of A. A. cty. (Westminster psh.) 3 Mch 1722. vii-261.

ANN HUTTON, RICHARD EVANS [Kin?] inv. William Chaloner of Annapolis. 8 May 1722. vii-263.

WILLIAM JONES, SAMUEL x JACOBS, apparently sign as kin; inv. Joshua Mayo of A. A. cty. 29 Dec 1721. vii-265.

BENJ. TASKER [Kin? uncertain.] inv. John Slatter[?] of Annapolis. 14 Aug 1721. vii-268.

THOMAS x DISNEY, JAMES DISNEY; inv. William Disney of A. A. cty. No date. vii-270.

JOHN WARD, SAM'L x WARD; inv. Henry Leeke of A. A. cty. 19 July 1721. vii-271.

WILLIAM x CHICK; inv. John Evitt. 9 Apr 1722. vii-275.

No kin given, but the appraisers were EPHRA. AUG'T HERMAN and HARMAN BURKELOE; inv. Samuel Byard of Cecill cty, Gent. 10 June 1722. vii-276.

MARY x SHAW, JOHN x CONNOWAY [Kin?] inv. John Shaw of Balto, cty. 9 May 1722. vii-281.

A. N. PRICE, WILL PRICE; inv. Thomas Price of Q. A. cty. 15 June 1722. vii-282.

STEPHEN HOLLINGSWORTH, THO. JACOBS: inv. Henry Hollingsworth of Cecill cty. 20 Mch 1721-2. vii-288.

SIMON x NICHOLLS, Sr., MATTHEW MOGBEE; inv. Wm. Nickolas of A. A. cty. 5 May 1722. vii-296.

SAMUEL MAGRUDER, WILLIAM BENNES ELIS x BOWEN, THOMAS x WINTER; sign inv. Mrs. ANN DORSETT of P. G. cty. [It is not clear which are kin and which are creditors.] 27 Nov 1721. vii-297.

LEONARD BROOKE, "Relation;" inv. Mr. John Craycroft of Pr. Geo's cty. No date. vii-299.

HENRY HILL; inv. HENRY HILL, Jr. of A. A. cty. 8 June 1722. vii-309.

CUTHBERT x FENWICK, ENOCH x FENWICK; inv. Mr. Richard Fenwick of St. Marie's cty. 20 July 1722. vii-315.

JACOB x CROUCH, RICHARD PHILLIPS; inv. Robert Crouch. County not given. 8 Nov. 1721. vii-318.

GEORGE x BAYLE, JOHN x PARSONS; inv. Graves Jarrett. 1 June 1722. vii-320.

ISAAC NOBLES, THOMAS HOBS, J. LEATHERBARY, ESTHER DENWOOD sign. [Probably these are kin and creditors together.] Inv. John Noble of Som. cty. 6 May 1722. vii-322.

ROBERT MELVIN, THOMAS DUCKET, ELIONER x STEVENS inv. Mary Stevens of Som. cty. 2 May 1721. vii-333.

"No near relations" appeared; inv. Parthenia Morris of Som. cty. Signed by Eliz'th x Window, Henry Smock, "Nearest of kind." [*Sic.*] No date. vii-336.

JOHN x RIGGEN, SAM'L x RIGGEN; inv. Teague Regen of Som. cty. 9 Apr 1722. vii-337.

THOS. x GLENDON; inv. James Mills of Som. cty. 6 May 1721. vii-340.

RANDELL HORSEY [kin?]; inv. Nath'l Horsey of Som. cty. 6 June 1722. vii-341.

JNO. ATKINSON, ISAAC ATKINSON; inv. James Atkinson. County not given. 26 Mch 1722. vii-342.

JACOB MORRIS, THOM'S ROBINSON; inv. John Morris. County not given. 30 Nov 1721. vii-344.

ELIZA: HUDSON, DAN'L HUDSON; inv. Henry Hudson. No county given. vii-345.

CHAS. COLLINS, RICH'D BEADARD; inv. Thos. Collings. County not given. No date. vii-345.

EDWARD ELLIOTT, THO'S ASHCROFT; inv. Mr. James Auld of Talbot cty. 15 May 1722. vii-346.

(NOTE: For a space of some years these entries are so carelessly made in the records of the prerogative court, that it is frequently very difficult to ascertain which signatures are those of kin, and which of creditors. See Dep'ty Comm'y's Guide for requirements.)

SERVICE AND SUPPLIES COLONIAL, REVOLUTIONARY AND MILITIA

BENJAMIN ARTHUR proved that he furnished Ezekiel Offut with 143 bundles of fodder for use of the Continental troops under Captain Gammell. Order certified. Camp. cty, Va. 7 Mch. 1782. 1-9.

BENJAMIN ARTHUR, JAMES GREER and JOHN WEBSTER GILBERT proved that they worked 168 days as Gunsmiths and found their own tools and provisions in repairing 170 Continental guns. Camp. cty, Va. 7 Mch 1782. i-9.

THOMAS BROWN, files declaration of service and Court is of opinion he was a Revolutionary soldier. Bedford, Va. Aug. Ct. 1832.

HENRY BROWN, same. Oct. Court. 1832.

PHILIP BAILEY, same. Nov. Court. 1832.

JOHN BRICKELL (of Wilkes cty), Inspector of Invalids. Chatham cty. Ga. About 1790. R-30.

JAMES BARNETT was a sergeant in Capt. Christian's Company of Regulars and served until the Regiment disbanded. Bot., Va. Orders. 13 Apr 1780.

THOMAS CARTWRIGHT, a trooper. Fairfax militia. Mch 1756. Hening, vii-24.

CHARLES CORNELIUS, makes declaration of service, and Court approves. (Revolutionary.) Gchld, Va. 20 Aug 1832. Orders, p. 139.

ZOPHER CARPENTER; Ordered that it be added to the Order made at Nov'r Court granting Land to Carpenter for Military services perf'd as a Drummer; the proof was made that he served til He was Legally disch'd & the Company disbanded & that he is an Inhabitant & Land owner of this State. Bot. Orders. 13 Apr 1780.

JESSEE DONELSON, a private, is granted 640 acres for his "signal bravery & persevering zeal;" assigned to Stockley Donelson. Land lies in Davidson cty, on waters of Stone's river. D-n cty, Tenn. 20 July 1796. G-639.

JONATHAN GROOME files declaration of service, and the Court is of opinion that he was a Revolutionary soldier. Bedford, Va. Aug. 1832. Court Orders.

WILLIAM GRINSTEAD, makes declaration of Revolutionary service, and Court declares opinion that he was a Revolutionary soldier. Gchld, Va. Orders, p. 47. 21 Aug 1732.

HENRY HUDSON makes oath that his son, FORREST, who was "draughted" was only 16 the 19 Jany 1778. Ordered certified to the commanding officer of the Continental troops at Wmsbg. Va. Mecklinb., Va. Court 9 Mch 1778. iv-395.

JOHN HAMILTON, a poor soldier; His wife, Judith, to be supplied with necessaries for herself and children. Mecklinb., Va. 8 Sept 1777. iv-370.

JOHN HOPKINS; oath as Captain of Militia. 22 June 1778. Rock'm, Va. Minute Book.

WILLIAM HUTCHESON made proof of service in Capt. Preston's Company of Rangers, in the last war and on the frontiers, until disbanded in 1759. Bot. cty, Va. 13 Apr 1780. Orders.

JAMES HUGHES makes declaration of Revolutionary service. Court declares opinion that he was a Revolutionary soldier. Gchld, Va. Court 22 August 1832.

AUSTIN HUNTER makes declaration of Revolutionary service and Court declares opinion he was a Revolutionary soldier. Gchld, Va. 22 Aug 1832.

HENRY ISBELL makes declaration of service and Court declares opinion he was a Revolutionary soldier. Gchld, Va. 22 Aug 1832.

WILLIAM JOHNSON; application is made in behalf of William Johnson and the Court is satisfied from affidavits that Johnson is unable to appear, and mentally incapable of making declaration, but he, having made a Declaration of his enlistment and services on the 15 Dec 1828, before this Court, the Court declares opinion that he was a Revolutionary soldier. 30 Aug 1832. Gchld, Va.

CHARLES JOHNSON, age 83, 24 Apr. last. Declares that he enlisted 1776 and served in the 5th Virginia. Court declares opinion that he was a Revolutionary soldier. 20 Aug 1832. Gchld, Va.

PETER LOONEY, de'cd. Peter Looney, heir-at-law, proved that sd Looney, de'd, served in Capt. Smith's Company of Rangers, last war, as a serjeant, until he was taken prisoner by the French and Indians in 1756. and that he did not return from them for nearly two years. Bot., Va. 13 Apr 1780. Orders.

CHARLES LYNCH, Gent., furnished the militia at the Lead mines with three pounds of powder. Camp. cty, Va. 7 Mch 1782. i-8.

ANTHONY LANE, makes declaration of service and Court declares opinion that he was a Revolutionary soldier. Gchld, Va.: 22 Aug 1832.

JOHN H. LONG, the same. Gchld, Va. 22 Aug. 1832.

SCARLET MADDEN, sworn Captain. Pr. Wm. cty, Va. 25 Jany 1762. Orders [4], 54.

WILLIAMS NOTES
MARYLAND-VIRGINIA SECTION

WILLIAM WILLIAMS sells a horse. Fauq, Va. 27 Nov 1792. xi-170.

WILLIAM WILLIAMS, of Pr. Geo cty, and MARTHA REESE, Mar. 5 Jany 1788. Bristol Psh, Va. Reg.

WILLIAM and ELIZABETH WILLIAMS; son JOSIAS, born 6 Jany 1775. St. John's (Piscataway) Register, Md.

WILLIAM WILLIAMS and BETTY ANDERSON, of Pr. Geo. Mar. Bristol Psh Reg. Va. 10 Sept 1789.

WILLIAM WILLIAMS; on tax-list. Two tithes. Hamp. cty, Va. 1783. [Now W. Va.]

WILLIAM WILLIAMS; will. Mentions Molly Williams, dau. of Thomas; Mathew, son of Thomas; supposed son Luke White, Thomas Williams, exrt. Wit: Watkins, Barnes, Francis. Charl., Va. 7 Oct 1775-6 Jany 1777. i-144.

WILLIAM WILLIAMS and JUDITH SAUNDERS 1785. Cumb. cty, Va. 1785. M. L. B.

WILLIAM LIGON WILLIAMS and MARY GANAWAY. 1785. Cumb. cty, Va. M. L. B.

WILLIAM WILLIAMS m. BARBARA . . . . . Chn: Thomas-Owen, b. 21 Feby 1747; Elizabeth, b. 30 Oct 1749; Elisha, b. 9 May 1752; Ellinor-Hilleary, b. 5 Apr 1757; Martha, b. 22 Dec 1759; Edward-Owen, b. 18 Apr 1761. Pr. Geo's Psh Reg., Md.

WILLIAM WILLIAMS and MARY ROBERTS, widow. Before May Ct, 1770. Chancy records.

WILLIAMS' LOTT; 50 acres; surveyed 1721 for Daniel Newman. In 1760 in possession of Joseph Elliott's heirs and Solomon Newman. Queen Anne's cty, Md. Rent Roll. 1760.

(Additional alphabet will be published at some later date.)

Printed at the Industrial School for Crippled and Deformed Children, 241 St. Botolph St., Boston, Mass.

The County Court Note-Book

A Little Bulletin of History and Genealogy

April, 1928. **Vol. VII, No. 2.**

UNPUBLISHED NORTH CAROLINA WILLS

The following wills, of which abstracts are here given, were found in an old volume of records in Hyde county, North Carolina. The volume is lettered " A," and such pages as are set down are pages of that volume. For want of time the wills are given in chronological order as they were copied.

WILLIAM x FORTESCUE, of Hyde county. Will. Son John; son Samuel; son William; dau. Lurana Jasper; dau. Racheal Fortescue; four daus. Jane, Philanda, Casandra, Winifred; wife Hannah. Wit: Tho: Smith, Step'n Denning, Sam'l Smith. 17 Sept 1759. Ct Sept 1760.

LITTLETON EBERNE, HYDE cty. Will. Son Elisha; son Henry; son William; dau. Rebekah Ebern; Wife Ann; legacy to Ann McSwain; Wife, James Eberne, and Edward McSwain [extrs]. Wit: Joseph Gurganus, William Gurganus, Stephen x Langley. 5 Oct 1759. Sept 1760.
[Codicil.] Elias Gurganus to have one-fourth what catel he raised while he has been on a plntn he gives son Henry.

ARNELL BAYLEY, Hyde cty, planter. Will. To Joseph Foreman his land and possessions and makes him exector. "ARNIAL x BALEY." Wit: John Thorowgood, Webster, Thomas Jordan, Ezekiel Chambers. 18 Dec 1759. Proved Sept 1760.

FRANCES x ELLETT, Hyde cty, widow. Will. Dau. Siana [Sinia?] Harvey; dau's son Nathan Harvey; dau. Cezia [Keziah?] Conner; dau. Elizabeth Mandowell; friend and son-in-law Lamuel [Lemuel] Harvey, extr. Wit: Elizabeth x Linquist, Elizabeth x Harvey, Fran: Kipps. 29 Apr 1758.

OLIVER x SMITH; will. Son John, 1sh. 6d. wf Ann; dau. Sarah Farr and grandson John Farr extrs. Wit: Samuel Ethredge, Benjamin Williams. 5 Oct 1758. June 1761.

THOMAS x GOODWIN, Hyde county. Will. Son Goodwin land lying below Thomas Goodwin, Jr., containing 300 acres; dau. Kessia Wollis [*sic*]; son Thomas extr. Wit: Anthony Tuley, Jacob Tuley, Thomas Tuley. . . . Aug 1758. p. 36.

THOMAS BARROWS, Hyde cty. Will. Son Enoch; son George; wife Tamor; daus. Barbra, Bathsheba. Chn: Enoch, George, Barbara Barrows, Bethsheba Barrows (both under 15). Leaves dau. Barbara to her aunt Rebacah Odon. Friend Roger Ormond, Thomas Smith "Shiprate," bro. Zachariah Barrows, extrs. 31 July 1762. Sept Ct 1762. Proved by Thomas Jordan, Charles Read and Stephen Denning. [Apparently no witnesses.]

JOHN SPRING, Hyde cty. Will. Wife Rebekah; daù. Lucy Spring; dau. Dorcas Spring; dau. Elizabeth Spring; son Zachariah; wife's brother William Adams. Son Zacheriah Spring, wife Rebekah, John Winfield and Francis Gallowell, extrs. Wit: Abs'lm Price, Abbet Beloat. 15 July 1762. Mch Ct 1763. p. 55.

JOHN SLADE, Hyde cty. Will. Son Jeremiah Slade; wife Elizabeth; dau. Jemima Slade; dau. Dorcas Slade, both minors. Son Jeremiah and wife extrs. Wit: Thomas Smith, Daniel Willis, Timothy Green. 12 Oct 1758. p. 56.

[The following note here appears "Carried to page 57 as you may see right opposite."]

NATHANIEL DAVIS, Hyde cty. Will. [A full abstract of this will is reserved for future publication in the FLOYD, STEWART, DAVIS and DANIEL CATALOGUE.]

HENRY GIBBS, Sen'r, Hyde cty. Will. Son Henry, tract on which he lives; sons Henry and Joseph mentioned as the eldest; son William; son Robert; son Thomas; son Benjamin; dau. Mary; dau. Sarah; gr. dau. Sarah Lockhart; dau. Rebecah; dau. Priscilla; gr. son Henry Gibbs; wf Ann Gibbs; sons Henry and Joseph extrs [?] Wit: James Davis, Caleb Swindall. 8 Dec 1759. Sept Ct 1763. p. 74.

ISRAEL WINDLY, Hyde cty. Will. Wife Elizabeth; son John; son Aaron; son Moses; son Isaack; son Israel; dau. Tamer Barrow; dau. Elizabeth Eborne. Six chn: John, Aaron, Moses, Israel, Tamer, Elizabeth. Sons Aaron and Moses, extrs. ISRAEL x WINDLEY. Wit: John Windley, Israel Windley, Isaac x Murphy. 9 Aug 1763. Sept Ct 1763. p. 78.

ABRAHAMxWILKINSON, Hyde cty. Will. Son Abraham; son Israel; dau. Ann Banks; son Richard; son-in-law Abraham Sattathwaite 1 sh. having given him already as much as I think proper. Wife Elizabeth, Edward McSwain and William Cambell to divide the rest of the estate bet. chn: James, Israel and Richard, Abraham and William and Thomas Jordan my son-in-law and Ann Banks. Appoints James Wilkinson, Israel Wilkinson and Thomas Jordan extrs. Wit: William Davis, Abraham x Wilkinson, Thomas Jordan, Israel Wilkinson. 14 Oct 1763. p. 79.

Note: The inventories in this volume will be listed later.

VIRGINIA COLONISTS

(*From "Old Volume 5," S. L. O., Richmond. Continued from April, 1927.*)

PETER FFOARD or HOARD and EDWARD R. . . . . . ? New Kent cty. 1658.
Head rights: Thomas Baile, Richard Drewe, Mary Willis, Benjamin Houlsworth, Margery Partworthy, Edward Howe, Jane Heire, Wm. Graves, Ann Graves, Wm. Trencher, Jno. Gilles, Tho. Bannister, Elinor Rohocke [?]

ALEXANDER FLEMMINGE, North side Rappa. River. 1658.
Head rights: Jno. Wright, Margaret Edderman, Finniell Donok, Jno. Mill, Phillip Pascall.

MARKE FOSTER, Mockjack Bay. 1658.
Head rights: Grace Farrwell, Eliz: Sternell, Robert Read, Jno. Correld. Robert ———, Silvester Wells, Jno. Mack Daniell, Geo. Burt, John Ham, Wm. Ableck.

JOHN FLEMING, New Kent. 1661 or 1662.
Head rights: Jno. Jones, Wm. Jacobs, Henry Linny, Denis Corbell, Doro. Farmer, Wm. Farmer, Jno. Shaw, Mary Spratt, Wm. Ward, Tho: Claughton.

JOHN FRUMPTON, Rappa. cty. 1662.
Head rights: Jane Robinson, Eliz: Vaughan, Tho: Micholls, Ann Burny, Henry Caple, James Pyett, Noble Martin, Rich: Arther, Walter Brookes, Abra: Law, Elizabeth Morter [?] Tho: Jarvis, Mary Young, Tho: Boote, James Hirton [?] Jno. Ingleton.

Maj. JAMES GOODWIN, "Petomeck Freshes." 1658.
Head rights: JAMES GOODWIN, 4 times; John Waler, Henry Molson, Nath Smith, Eliz: May, Eliz: Blackburne, Henry Edge, Henry Baxter, Eliz: Adams and a negro.

Maj. JAMES GOODWIN, Westmoreland cty. 1657.
Head rights: Eliz: Turner, Eliz: Sparrow, Daniell ———, Lewis or Levy Angulliott [?] Tho: Vinsent, John Faire, Mary Hudson, Jno. Bartley, Jno. Greene, Jno. Hewett, Dennis Hoger [?] James Shane, Darby Hoccaday, ——— Heughes, Teague Grim [Gruin?] Henry Hammond, Sarah Rose, Jno. Clotheire, Tho: Hardy, Abigall Cherrey.

CHRISTOPHER GARLINGTON, Northumberland cty. 1658.
Head rights: Thomas Harris, twice; Mary Harris, Amy Hoskins, Mathew Harris, Wm. Allen, Dorothy Parke, Hugh Wattson.

RALPH GREENE, Gloucester cty. 1658.
Head rights: Wm. Turner, Geo. Froster or Foster; John Logg, Henry Jones, Jane Young, Andrew Pight, Wm. Stiples, John Haies, Robert Bellfinn, Richard Foster, Edward Pinton, Roger Collins, James GREENE.

ROBERT GRAY, Elizabeth City cty. 1658.
Head rights: John Farrast [Forrest?]

JOHN GORE, Lancaster cty. 1658.
Head rights: Henry Chickley, Rich: Chamley, Jno. Layward.

ANDREW GILSON, county not given. 1661.
Head rights: 14 negroes.

SAMUEL GRIFFIN, Mcht. Rappa cty. 1662.
Head rights: David GRIFFIN, Bagnell Vincent, Wm. Benden, Edw. Wetherhorne, Ambrose Clare, Wm. Gunter, Thomas Bell, Lewis Butler, Wm. Feild, Henry Margrett, Alice Arsly, Ellin Meredeth, Jno. Back, Robt Sanders, Roger Barbar, Rich'd Hartley, Emanuell Consues [?] Tho: Symmons, Richard Appleby, Richard Collins, Edward Franklin, Rice Cookman, Tho: a negro; twelve more negroes; Nathaniell Medly, Henry Turner, Richard Williams, William Conaway, Jno. Bayle, Mary Burd, Nicholas White, Francis Cossens, Christopher Walker.

Lt. Coll. Tho: GOODRICH, south side Rappa. river. 1661.
Head rights: Abigall Rige, Tho: Clowel, Seath Edward, Tho: Bunbridge, Wm. Suran, Wm. Talbott, Jno. Warner, Jno. Clower, Kath: Moreaghen, Nich: Stelman.

ROBERT GRIGG and Mr. EDWARD WYATT, Gloster cty. 1662.
Head rights: Mary Jones, Wm. White, Jno. Tappin, Andrew Maybe [?] Jane Carter, Stephen Godlad, Wm: Hankin, Antho: Grigson.

CHRISTOPHER HARRIS, Westmoreland. 1658.
Head rights: Jno. Snellings, Edward Bromfeild, Wm. Symson, Wm. Feild, John Mutton, Jno. Williams, Henry Coniers, Georg Harper, Sarah Mathy, Nath: Ruferd, Nath: Pinson, John Abbott, Ann Delue, Robert Hollaway, Jno. Crawfield, "assigned by Mr. Jno. Lewellinge;" Margarett Munday, Georg Covell [?] Jane Dawson, Mary James, Wm. Newsome, [or Newcombe], Roger Sloe [or Hoe?] Edmond Lucas, Matthew Batts, James Mahue, Thos: Clements, Hugh Thomas, Joseph Fairpointe, Wm. Nicholls, Jno: Prevett or Trevett; Symon Hall, Wm. West, Nath: Crosby, Ja: Hollis [?] James Male, Charles Davison, John Markhamson [?]

WM. HEABERD and JOHN HEABERD, Westmoreland cty. 1658.
Head rights: Anne Browne, Rachel Willis, Thomas Jones, Lafaland Foland [Holand?] Jno. Haies.

THOMAS HAMPTON, Clerke. On the east side of Chickahominy river. 1658.
Head rights: Dorman Kygan, Cornelius Nehon, Wm. Dolly.

Mr. JOHN HANSFORD, Yorke cty. 1658.
Head rights: Rowland Thomas, Charles Dunn, Tho: Symmons [uncertain.]

THOMAS HARRIS, Isle of Wight. 1658.
Head rights: Jno. Hardy, Eliz: Jones, Fran: Anderson, Weltin Harris, Thomas Fier, Alexander Vaughan, Mary Wood, Jno. Pew, Anth: Arnold, Thomson Butt, Ann Lees, Jno. Davis, Ann Greene, Sam'l Trobury, James Rogers, Wm. Todd, Jno. Griffin, Eliz: Ensome or Eusome; Alexander Canill, Geo. West.

Mr. THOMAS HAMPTON, James City cty. 1658.
Head rights: Eliz: Sanders, Elizabeth Dollinge, Tho: Gibson, Mary Loyd, Susan Duffell, John Raslin, Wm. Skame, Jaine Cooke.

CHARLES HILL, no county mentioned. 1658.
Head rights: Roger Smith, Tho: Allen, Wm. Jordan.

AUTHENTIC REFERENCES FOR INFERRED MARRIAGES

(North Carolina. The place names are those of counties.)

ANTHONY ALEXANDER and KEZIAH SPRUILL, dau. of John Spruill, Sr. Tyrrell cty. Before 5 May 1790. i-231.

JOHN ALLEN and ANNE FARRELL, dau. of John. Franklin, N. C. Before 14 Apr 1779. i-38.

JOSEPH BURNHAM and SALLY ROBERTSON. Camden. Before 29 Sept 1841. N-169.

THOMAS BELL and ELIZABETH GRANDY, dau. of Ammon Grandy. Camden. Before 27 Mch 1798. H-150.

BENJ. BALANCE and SARAH DAVIS. Pasquotank. Before 20 Sept 1769. D & E-479.

.... BARCLIFT and ANNE PARRISH, dau. of John. Perquim. Before 18 Mch 1734. C-162.

JOHN BUCKHOUSE [perhaps BRICKHOUSE?] and a dau. of Samuel CASWELL. Tyrrell. Before 11 May 1808. ii-55.

WILLIAM BOYD and ELIZABETH [EBERN]; prob. dau. of Mrs. Rebecah EBERN. Hyde. Before Dec 1758.

JACOB BLOUNT and JOANNA SPRUILL, dau. of Samuel, Sr. Tyrrell. Before 19 Aug 1760. i-8.

YOUNGER BURT and MASON BATTLE, dau. of James. Cumberl'd. Before 22 Apr 1812. A-184.

THOMAS BROWN and SARAH BARTRAM, dau. of William Bartram, late of Bladen. Bladen. Before 8 Feby 1776. i-38.

.... CHANDLER and ELIZABETH CATCHMAID. dau. of Edward, who was eldest son and heir of Thomas, who was bro. of George CATCHMAID, formerly of "Nancemen, in Carolina." (Elizabeth Chandler was of the psh of St. George, Bloomsbury, Middx, England.) Perquim. Before 25 Mch 1735. C-221.

AARON COX and SARAH WEEKS, dau. of Ezekiel and Deliverance (Shaw) WEEKS. Hyde. Before 14 Nov 1759.

JOAB CHAMPION and MARTHA LONG, wid. of Joshua. Perquim. Before 5 June 1794. L-40.

JOSEPH COCKE and WINNIFRED HILL, wid. of Henry. Franklin. Before 24 Nov 1782. iv-100.

.... COUSSINS and MARGRET ARMSTRONG, wid. of David. Tyrrell. Before 14 Oct 1742. A-156. (Margret Coussins was of Abington Psh, Gloucester cty, Va.)

EVAN DAUGE and NANCY GRANDY, dau. of Ammon Grandy. Camden. Before 27 Mch 1798. H-150.

FRANCIS EARL and SARAH JONES, one of the heirs of Evan JONES. Camden. Registered 27 Aug 1794. F-257.

SANFORD EDWARDS [then dec'd] and the widow of William PERRY. Perquim. Before 9 Feby 1802. N-76.

TOWNSEND ELLIOTT prob. m. SARAH SIMONS. She m. (2) Davis. Chowan. Long before 10 Dec 1819. C-79.

JONATHAN FELLOWS, of Newburn Town, Craven cty, Blacksmith, and ELIZABETH PUGH, wid. of Hugh, Jr., Pitt cty. Mar. contract. Pitt. 22 Apr 1801. F-562.

.... GASKINS and ANN JONES, dau. of Abraham. Hyde. Before 18 May 1787. i-495.

.........GIBBS and SARAH JONES, dau. of Abraham. Hyde. Before 18 May 1787. i-495.

MARK HARDIN and ELIZABETH BECTON [?] wid. of Richard, of Beaufort cty, N. C. Pitt. Before 1 Sept 1762. B-447.

WILLIS JONES and MARY DAVIS. Perquim. Before 18 Aug 1764. G-164.

JOHN JACKSON and SARAH HENDRICK, dau. of Solomon. Perquim. Before 13 Oct 1750. F-14.

ROBERT JORDON, of Nancemond, Va., and SARAH SKINNER, relict of John. Marriage contract. Perquim. 3 Mch 1777. I-584.

JEAN BAPTISTE ANDRE LE DAUX, aged about 38 years, an inhabitant of the *Cul de Sac* in the parish . . . *de La Croix des borequets* [*sic*] *quartier du Port au Prince in the* Island of St. Domingo, lawful son of Jean Baptiste LE DAUX and of Dame Maria Louisa Pere his wife, both inhabitants of the *Cul de Sac* in the same Parish, &c., and FRANCES MAGDALIN JURE aged about 26 years [an inhabitant of the same place] dau. of Rene JURE and Dame Rose Margaret Boissanniere his wife, her Father and Mother being Both Inhabitants of the *Cul de Sac* [in the same Parish, &c.] . . . followed by marriage settlement. Both sign. Wit: John Louis Taylor, P. A. Tarbé. Cumberl'd. 21 Oct 1793. M-348.

THEOPHILUS LEONARD and ANN SYMONS, dau. of Benjamin. Pasquo. Before 12 Oct 1763. D & E 207.

RICHARD LEIGH and ROSIAN SPRUILL, dau. of Hezekiah. Tyrrell. Before 20 May 1802. ii-87.

EMANEULL LOW and ANNE ARCHDALE, dau. of John. Pasquo. Before 2 Feby 1712. A-112.

BENJ: MANNING and SARAH HILL, prob. dau. of Robert HILL. Tyrrell. Before 18 Mch 1758. i-413.

WILLIAM MAGORINE [?] and FRANCES HENDRICK, dau. of Solomon. Before 13 Oct 1750. F-14.

JOHN MILLER and SUSAN HUMPHRIES. Perquim. Before 1822. Ct Minutes.

.... MILLER and WINNEFORD WHITFIELD, dau. of Constantine. Duplin. Before 25 Mch 1795. i-53.

EDWARD POPE and SARAH DAVIS. Pasquo. Before 1700. A-329.

PETER POYNER [?] and SOPHIA TAYLOR, dau. of Thomas. Currit'k. Before 14 Apr 1719. ii-—

ROBERT ROWAN and [SUSANNA] GROVE, widow. Cumberl'd. Before 8 Oct 1798. A-19.

MILES SKINNER and RACHEL FLOYD, dau. of Halsy. Perquim. Before 28 Dec 1828. F-200.

.... SAULS and ELIZABETH THOMPSON, dau. of John. Wayne. before 13 May 1825. v-192.

THOMAS H. STACY and MARTHA MILLER, dau. of John. Perquim. Before 1822. Ct Minutes.

.... SPENCE and ELIZABETH SELBY, dau. of Samuel, Sr. Hyde. Before 27 May 1761. A-41.

EBENEZER SPRUILL and .... LONG, dau. of John LONG, Sr. Tyrrell. Before 5 May 1790. i-231.

WILLIAM THROOP prob. m. MARY ANN MARTIN, dau. of Benjamin. Hyde. Before 1 Oct 1780. I-112.

WILSON TAYLOR and SARAH MOORE, dau. of "Little" Edward MOORE. Nash. Before 8 Nov 1790. Ct Minutes.

WILL WILSON and SARAH GARRET. Tyrrell. 20 Aug 1735. Ctf. W-352. (They had two daus. Mary and Sarah.)

WILLIAM WARD and CLARISEY or CLAUSY [?] FLOYD, dau. of Halsy. Perquim. Before 28 Dec 1828. F-200.

EZEKIEL WEEKS and DELIVERANCE SHAW. Rebecca Sattathwaite and Ann Nixon testify that they saw the marriage, which was by Thomas Smith, Esq., a Justice, and that there were two chn of the marriage, Ezekiel, now dead, and Sarah. Hyde. Before 14 Nov 1759.

JOSEPH WILLIAMS and a dau. of William PORTER. Hyde. Before 10 June 1794. ii-255.

(Northampton county, Virginia. Continued from February, 1928.)

SAMUEL POWELL and FRANCES SAVAGE, dau. of John, Sr. [His will 1670.] Long before 15 July 1752. xxxixO-65. (She m. (2) John Jones. Before 1748.

ROBERT PETERS and PATIENCE MASMAN, dau. of Henry, Sr. Before 28 Feby 1697. xvii-470.

Capt. FRANCIS PIGOT and MARY MICHAEL, wid. of John, Sr. About [?] 3 June 1679. xiii-54. See also xiii-43.

Mr. FRANCIS PIGOTT and FRANCES LITTLETON widow of Mr. Edward Littleton. Before 30 Jany 16 70. See x-95. See xi-145.

.........PIGOT m. ANN HUNT, dau. of Thomas. Before 15 Jany 1700. xviii-71.

Capt. RALPH PIGOT prob. m. FRANCES BENTHALL, widow of Daniel. Before 11 July 1726. Chancy records.

JOHN POWELL, of N-n, Gent. and SARAH YARDLEY, dau. of Argoll and Sarah (Michael) YARDLEY. See 28 Jany 1701. xvi-295.

ABELL POWELL and BARBARY BATSON, dau. Anne and Francis. Before 1735 [?] Chancy Records.

WILLIAM PARSONS prob. m. SARAH CABLE, dau. of Sorrowful Margaret Cable. Before 24 Oct. 1751. Chancy records.

ZADOCK PURNEL, Gent. and SARAH MARSHALL, wid. of Thomas. Before 9 Dec 1754. Chancy records.

JOHN POWELL and FRANCES WILKINS, dau. of Nathan'l. Before 7 Feby 1697. xvi-214.

BARTHOLOMEW PETTIT and LEAH PITTS. Before 10 Dec 1768. Chancy records.

.........POWELL and SUSANNAH GODWIN, wid. of Devoreux. Before 1741. ix-45.

MORGAN POULDEN and the wid. of Peter LANGE. Before 1 July 1684. xv-62.

CHARLES RUSSELL and MARY x HICKMAN. About 14 May 1643. ii-313.

JOHN ROBERTS and ELIZABETH WALTOM, wid. of John. Before "vicesimo Jany" 1651. iv-75.

JOHN ROBERTS and BRIDGET NOTTINGHAM, wid. of Joseph. Before 10 Nov 1747.

ARTHUR ROBERTS and MARGARET BAGWELL, dau. of Alexander. Before 14 June 1726. Chancy records.

WIL: ROBERTS and HESTER SEADY [?]. Before 14 Nov 1722. Chancy records.

ARTHUR ROBINS prob, m. BARBARA WISE [?] sister of John WISE [?] Before 1692 xvii-246.

JOHN ROBINS, Jr. and SARAH HARMANSON, dau. of Susanna. M. L. B. 8 Oct 1729.

Mr. LITTLETON ROBINS and MARGARET STRINGER, wid. of John. Before 31 Jany 1698. xvii-516.

.........ROBINS and Mrs. GRACE WATERS, widow. Before 28 Feby 1650. iv-8.

ANTHONY x RABOONE and JOANE x WARREN, wid. of Richard. About 22 Aug 1650. iii-216.

WILLIAM RABYSHAW and GRACE HARMANSON. M. L. B. 19 Mch 1709.

WILLIAM RABYSHAW and MARY, extx of Robert FLETCHER. (She had been the relict of Chas. Price.) Before 30 Mch 1696. xvii-369. See also xvii-416; xix-256.

ROBERT RICHARDSON and SUSAN SMITH, dau. of Richard. Before [?] 28 Mch 1667. vii-10. 2d part.

DAVID RICE prob. m. .... WICKS, widow, as he is the "father-in-law" of Melchesedec Wicks age ten, and Mathew Wicks age eight. Before 28 Sept 1692. xvii-190. (Also xvii-189.)

MICHAELL RICKARDS and ANN JONES, dau. of Capt. Wm. JONES. Before 4 May 1674. xii-33.

THOMAS RICHARDS and LETTICE ASHBY, wid. of Mr. Edward ASHBY. Before 8 Oct 1694. xvii-286.

ROBERT RICHARDSON and SUSAN SMITH, dau. of Richard. Before 28 Mch 1667. vii-10.

WILLIAM RONALD and ELIZABETH KENDALL, dau. of George. Before Dec 1770. Chancy records.

JOHN SAMPSON and ANNE HOLT, admx of George. Before 13 May 1760. Chancy records.

JOHN SATCHELL and the wid. and extx of Thomas Ward ELLEGOOD. Before 1738 or 1739. Chancy records.

.... SAUNDERS prob. m. FRANCES LAKE, who afterwards m. WILLIAM BURDETT. See her will 23 Mch 1641.

THOMAS SIMES prob. m. SARAH JOHNSON, widow. Before 28 Nov 1695. xvii-363.

WILL: SMITH and ELIZABETH MARRIOTT, widow. Mar. agreement. 17 July 1666. vii-3.

THOMAS SPADY and SARAH JONES, dau. of John Jones, pltr, and wife Francis. Before 1748. Chancy records.

WILLIAM SCARBURGH probably m. NANCY MEREDITH. dau. of Mr. Wm. Meredith. Before 1772. (Scarburgh died 1756.) [She m. (2) Isaac Dunton.] Chancy records.

ZEROBABELL SCOTT and MARY BELL. Before 1783. Chancy records.

LITTLETON SAVAGE and MARGARET BURTON, dau. of William. M. L. B. 14 Jany 1768.

THOMAS SPADY and SARAH POWELL, dau. of Samuel. Before 15 July 1752. Chancy records.

Mr. WILLIAM SPENCER and ELIZABETH WHITTINGTON, wid. of Capt. William WHITTINGTON. Before 28 June 1664. ix-197. M. 14 June 1660. See ix-92.

.... STRINGER and SUSANNA ANDERSON, dau. of William. Before 20 Feby 1654. iv-85.

WILLIAM SMART and Mrs. MARY ANDREWS, widow of Lt. Col. William ANDREWS. Before 30 Jany 1659. ix-57. (She died before 20 Feby 1659. See ix-68.)

NATHANIEL SAVAGE and SARAH BOLD, relict of Henry. Before 1728. Chancy records.

JOHN SMARTE and TABITHA SCARBURGH, dau. of Edmund. Before or about 12 July, 1653. iv-152.

UNRECORDED WILLS SAMPSON COUNTY, N. C.

(It is probable that some of these wills were probated and recorded.)

Thomas Ammons, 1792; Mary Adams, 1808; Drury Aughtry, 1808;

Robert Bell, 1816; Robert Butler, 1802. Gabriel Butler, 1823; Ann Bryan, 1817; William Boykin, 1803; Charles Butler, Sr., 1811; Stephen Butler, 1824; William Blackburne, 1822; Col. William Blackman, 1818; Joseph Boykin, 1806; Jesse Bradshaw, 1821; Nun-cup. will of Jeremiah Butler, 1792; Isabel Barfoot, 1797; John Bradshaw, 1827; Andre Bass, 1786; David Bunting, 1828; Michael Bel[l], 1831; Samuel Buchanan, 1791; William Bass, 1802; Joseph Barks [?] 1807; Byus [Tobias] Boykin, 1812;

Fleet Cooper, 1795; Patrick Cannady, 1811; Patience Carr, 1818; Jacob Crumpler, 1817; Jesse Carrel, Sr., 1802; Naaman Carter, 1814 [?] Thomas Coggin, 1797; John Carell, 1814; Elizabeth Caraway, 1816; Fleet Cooper, 1816; Driver Chestnutt, 1830; David Chestnutt, 1831; William Cole, 1807; Charity Cason, 1808; Alexander Carrell, 1827; James Cook, 1786; "Proved in open Court and ordered to be registered;" Jacob Chestnutt, 1826; Thomas Carr, 1798; John Crumpler, 1782; marked "Copy of John Crumpler's will;" John Crumpler, Duplin cty, "Copy of will & letters, 1782;" Patrick Carr, 1825;

George Devans, 1810; Betty Darden, 1818; Magdalena Duack, 1785; Aley Drew, 1825; Lydda Daughtry, 1813; Levi Dudley, 1808; Jonathan Daniel, 1811;

Samuel Faircloth, 1807; Jacob Freyer, 1785; James Faison, Sr:, 1810; James Frederick, 1819; Henry Faison, 1826; James Faison, 1782; Elisha Faison, 1814.

Lott Gregory, 1811; Nathan Godwin, 1821; Samuel Gavin, 1807; Bartholomey Gainey, 1818; Edmund Ganey, 1791; Thomas Ginkins, 1809;

Jacob Herring, no date; Joshua Herring, 1811; Uzzill Herring, 1803; Hardy Holmes, 1825; Thomas Holland, 1819; Armiger Hall, 1811; Stephen B. Herring, 1817; Abraham Herring, 1790; John Hair, Sen'r, 1809; William Hair, 1825; Sarah Haney, 1814; George Holder, 1799; William Hair (incomplete) 1825; Abner Hopton, 1803; [in this will the testator leaves estate to the four chn of his bro. Enoch Hopton: Abner, John-Rose, Stephen and Hetty Hopton, "now living on Eluthara Rack Sound one of the Bahama Islands."] William Hudson, 1829; Charles Hay, 1784; Arthur Hargroves, 1815; Henry Hollingsworth, 1795.

William Johnson, no date; Ephraim Johnson, 1818; James Jackson, 1825; John Jones, 1824; Abraham Jacobs, 1807; Thomas Ivey, 1813; Richard Jackson, 1822; Jenny Joyner, 1805; Shadrick Jones, 1802; Solomon Johnson, 1830; John Johnston, 1814; "Soasbe" Johnson, 1822;

William King, Sr., 1816; John Keen, Sr., 1803; David Kornegay, 1821; Amy King, 1818;

Unity Merritt, 1819; John McIlwiner [?] 1792; Gabriel Merritt, 1820; Northial [?] Merritt, 1819; Bigars Moblay, 1802; Jane Morisey, 1807; Joel Mathis, 1821; Frances Marley, 1824; Ann Moore, widow, 1804; Richard Martin, 1810; Neill McLeod, Sr., 1818; Zaceaus Matthis, 1837; Lewis McLendon, 1778; [damaged, apparently Craven county.] West Mackelmore, 1814; Bethany Millard, 1823;

Sarah Odom, 1787; Jethro Oates, 1821; Mary Ann Oates, 1821; Stephen Oates, 1816;

John Treadwell, 1819.

The County Court Note-Book

An every-other-monthly devoted mainly to abstracts from County Court Records, prior to 1800.

MILNOR LJUNGSTEDT, Editor and Publisher.
Bethesda, Route 10, Maryland.

Published six times a year. Subscription, two dollars, in advance; must begin with the year.

April, 1928 **Whole**
Vol. VII., No. 2 **No. 39**

The Editor regrets the usual delay in bringing out the APRIL issue. Almost four months "in the field," that is, from the middle of January to the 4th of May, has meant the accumulation of a great deal of material, and a great deal of correspondence. To make up in part, and because of the really immense amount of North Carolina notes and their undoubted value, this APRIL issue will contain twelve pages, and it will be mostly North Carolina.

A short stay in Richmond, Virginia, enabled the Editor to continue her list of head rights from the old original of the present volumes 4 and 5, and it also enabled the Editor to work out a scheme by which a copy in 4 or 5 can be traced in "Old Five." Hitherto this has been impossible, though it isn't the first time the Editor has endeavored at it. The Editor has confided this information to Mrs. Nell Marion Nugent, now in charge of the Land Office records under the Secretary of the Commonwealth, and has no doubt but that Mrs. Nugent will make use of it in her forthcoming immensely valuable Calendar of Patents . . . for more detailed mention of this see page 19.

After the "lost provinces" of North Carolina, and a few from the central part of the State, the Editor made a brief but satisfactory trip to Atlanta. The progress made by the Historical Department under the able hand of Miss Ruth Blair, since the Editor's previous visit, is most remarkable. The Archives are now housed in well-lighted and comfortable quarters; the indexing is going forward beautifully, and the records are accessible with the least possible red tape . . . something all of us know how to appreciate. If you happen to be a scientist in search of a six-legged water creature with a leg extra or a leg short, everything is open to you, and you are treated as if you were honest, at least, if peculiar. If you are bent on the identification of a "mixed" iris, if any one knows any more than you do you can soon find it out. But if you are "chasing" after a generation of your own kind who appear to have spent their time "moverin' along" from sea and sound to plateaus or hidden valleys . . . it is sometimes quite a different story. Influence or ability will give you the privilege of a library stack . . . but not so with an up-to-date Archives . . . in some places. Influence might, but not ability.

North Carolina.

Pretty nearly every one knows by now of the fine work North Carolina is doing in every way, and it is especially marked in her collective historical work, and the spirit of that work has reached out into the counties. New and convenient courthouses are everywhere; records are being classified and placed in order. Many are sent to Raleigh. The Editor has one serious quarrel with this movement . . . the copies of the volumes found in the counties are, as is almost universally the case everywhere, made by inexperienced persons. The result is at times trying. Yet, on the other hand, many of these copies the Editor thinks were made some time ago and show that the counties themselves made an effort to preserve their history. How vastly different from a county in another State where money has been plentiful but local pride lacking. Pride is there, but it rests content with tradition.

Carolina is truly a friendly place. Perhaps the Editor sensed something of her Quaker forbears in the "lost provinces," perhaps of New England, but certainly of the sea, which modifies the climate and enlarges the understanding as to the world outside.

As to the list of unrecorded wills begun in this issue of the NOTE-BOOK, as found in SAMPSON COUNTY, North Carolina, it is well to say that the Editor is by no means certain that *all* these wills were unrecorded. For one thing, among them will be found copies, and in the same file box were some recent wills possibly out of place. Conditions were such in this particular office of the Clerk of the Court that comparison could not be made. The Editor had to take her choice between sitting with her back to a hot stove at a small table, under which there was no space for one's very necessary knees, standing up in the fireless fire-proof, or using as a table a large plat-book supported by a heavy record volume projecting from a shelf.

However, the authorities in authority stated that these wills were unrecorded. It will be noted that the alphabet is not very evenly distributed.

It is pleasant to add that matters were different in the Register's office.

Searchers who wish to visit Currituck and Camden are advised that the offices in these two counties are open only on Saturdays and Mondays. The Editor desires to express her appreciation of the helpful courtesy of a County Attorney who "saved her life" at Currituck by building fires and presiding over the records. At Camden, being forewarned, the Editor struck an open day, and also had the pleasure of being picked up by the Judge and the Register of Deeds at the somewhat damp cross-roads where the bus left her. The simple friendliness of these out-of-the-way counties can best be appreciated by those who have been . . . . . elsewhere.

But to give the list of the offices of the Clerks of the Superior Court and the Registers of Deeds in North Carolina who received the Editor as a welcome guest and not as a boresome searcher, *and who are interested in their own records,* would cover almost the entire list of 43 counties explored. The Editor can only express her appreciation of the general kindliness and repeat, as many times before, "*I like North Carolina!*"

In several counties the Editor had the assistance of well-informed gentlemen who might also be called experts. Due to a young lawyer in one county, a very unusual Revolutionary record was found. Windsor will also be remembered for the most interesting and helpful local historian, Judge Winston, whose fund of knowledge and clever anecdote is inexhaustible. One of Judge Winston's best stories is that in which he describes how he assisted a negro applicant for a pension to convince the authorities that his name "Tony Vincent," as set down by a Northern "cub-lieutenant," was really "Anthony Winston" . . . apropos of an explanation to the Editor of the local, illiterate "W."

The Editor cannot mention the Clerk at Windsor without mentioning a lot of others, moreover, she is sure that if she said too much about him, and about the Register at nearby Hertford, and the clerk at Edenton, she would bring an avalanche of searchers upon these well-remembered gentlemen. And there is the Clerk at Swan Quarter, and the Deputy at Kenansville, and the postmistress there . . . . and so many others.

The Editor had hoped to add in this number some further information as to the DONELSON Line, but it will be given later. There is an error in the DONELSON material to which the Editor wishes to call attention. The date of Col. DONELSON'S birth should be placed in all probability in 1724 or 1725 rather than 1718. It is true that 1725 does not agree with statements made in personal letters by DONELSON'S grandson, but that must be overlooked.

CONTINUED articles COUNTY COURT NOTE-BOOK, and the dates on which they first appeared.

THE ANCESTRY OF COL. JOHN DONELSON. Began with February, 1927.

AUTHENTIC REFERENCES for INFERRED MARRIAGES (formerly called MARRIAGES BY INFERENCE). Began with May, 1922.

MARYLAND'S NEXT OF KIN. Began with July, 1922.

VIRGINIA COLONISTS. Alphabetized lists began with July, 1924.

MILITARY NOTES, both COLONIAL and REVOLUTIONARY, and later MILITIA NOTES. Began December, 1923.

INTERCOUNTY and INTERCOLONY (formerly called New Englanders and Others, &c., &c,). Began with March, 1922.

EASTERN SHORE FAMILIES. In the form of a one-page supplement, began with June, 1925. This will be continued later.

SHIPS IN PORT and COLONIAL FORENAMES, will appear in alternate issues or as space can be found for them.

SAUL, SAULE, SAULS [Irish]

The Editor will be glad to receive any information from any branch of the Saul, Saule or Sauls family, of Irish extraction, especially those of North or South Carolina, or those who know anything of the immigrant Saul of Delaware or Pennsylvania or New York. An Irish Quaker came over to Pennsylvania, named JOHN SAUL or SAULS, between 1712 and 1720. He was unmarried. Did he marry a ROBINSON?

NOTES HERE AND THERE IN NORTH CAROLINA

From a fly-leaf:
Have communion with few,
Be familiar with one,
Deal Just[ly] with all
And Speak Evil of none.
D'd Ricks 27th May 1811.

A preamble which sounds odd in the U. S. A. "His Excellency the most Noble Henry Duke " of Beaufort Pallatine and the Rest of the Lords " and Proprietors of Carolina. . . ." Perquimans. DeedBook record 310. 1 July 1713.

I SOLOMON ALCOCK Shr. of [Currituck] county, by virtue of an order of Court . . . commanding me to sell at Publick auction two thirds of a Negro Man called Gidion the property of Thos. Simmons orphan of Limuel Simmons Deceased . . . did offer the said Negro Gidion at Publick Vendue on the first Day of January in the year of our Lord one thousand Eight hundred and two and Jonathan Lindsey Esq'r appeared and bid one hundred and Nineteen pouns thirteen shilling and four pence which was the highest bid for the two thirds of the said Negro Man. I do therefore Make over & convey & confirm forever the right Title and property . . . . to the whole and sole Benefit and use of him the said Jonathan Lindsey and his heirs . . . ." Currituck cty, Feby 1802. iii-217.

ANDREW JACKSON, Esquire, Produced a license from the Honorable the Judges of the Superior Courts of Law & Equity Authorizing him to practice as an Attorney in the Several County Courts. Took the Oath prescribed and proceeded to practice in Said Courte. Randolph cty. Tuesday morning. 11 Dec 1787. Ct Minutes. p. [16].

The Will of DONALD McINNISH, of the Town of Fayetteville, Cumberland cty, directs that a brick wall be erected round his grave covered with common marble stone with these words "here lies the Remains of Donald McInnish Native of Scotland Born the 16th August 1772 Departed this life .... Days of ...... aged ...... years ...... months and ...... Days Landed in Wilmington North Carolina October 2d 1772." McInnish gives to Mr. Lauchton McLeran of Fayetteville "*Admiral Nelson's Plate* also the Ship Mars and a Ladies Picture." Mentions his mother Margaretta MacInnish. Signed Donald MacInnish. 4 June 1810. A codicil is dated 28 Jany 1811. Probate Dec Term 1811. Cumberl'd cty. A-184.

MONET, MONNET, MONNETT (sometimes spelled Money or Monay.)

SOME BERTIE COUNTY, NORTH CAROLINA, RECORDS

A small parchment covered volume, containing inventories, &c., from 1728 to 1744, inclusive, unindexed, is in the office of the Clerk of the Superior Court of Bertie county. The items are briefly listed herewith. The name first given is that of the decedent.

THOMAS FOXHALL'S estate; signed by Johanna x Fox [hall] [Admx.] [1728.]

. . . . . . SCOTT; [Capt.] Sam'l Else [Elson?] signs. 13 Aug. 1728.

ROBERT SCOTT; proved by affirmation of admr.

ROB'T DIXSON; John Low signs. 29 Dec 1727.

JOHN MAYNER, sen'r, sales; admr's name not found, or date.

HENRY WHEELER; Anna Wheeler, extx. [173-?]

JAMES NAVILL; Eliz. Norvill, admx. 22 Sept 1732 [?]

JOSEPH REGAN: Elizabeth x Regan signs. About 1732.

ROBERT SLATER; Mary Slater, admx.

JOHN GRIFFITH; Jemima x Griffith signs.

SAMUEL CANNADY; notice of sale of estate.

. . . . HILL, inv. [In margin.]

There was thirty Barrills of pitch sent to New England by Capt. Cudworth which I have account of and 50 Bushells of wheat was sent by Capt. Dogit to Boston which I have a Count of But Never Received one penny for them. [No sig. no date.]

DANIEL MAGEY; Wm. x Patchitt, Aaron Oliver, Charles Sowell [Appraisers?] p. 14.

JOHN BROWN, Jr's estate sold 2 Feby 1727. Signed John x Warren; Robert Warren in list of buyers. p. 14.

ROBERT EVANS estate sales. 4 May 1727. Ann Evans, admx. Also account of estate and additional inventory, p. 15.

DAN'L MAGEE'S Estate. No date. p. 17.

THOMAS WATERS, "praised by we the Subscribers," 6 Mch 1727. Richard Pall, Henry x Jones, John Lennard. p. 18.

JOHN BROWN, Jr. Admr's name not given. p. 19.

WILLIAM DAWS; Elijah x Daws, admr. 8 Feby 1727. p. 20.

JAMES BARNES; sales. William Baldwin [admr?] James Barnes and wife in account. 16 Sept 1728. p. 21. Followed by inventory; W. Baldwin, admr. p. 22.

JOHN BROWN, Sr. John Warren, admr. No date. p. 23.

. . . . . . WARREN; sale of estate at John Warren's house. 18 Oct 1728. p. 23.

JOHN CHERRYHOLM'S estate sold. 20 Oct 1729. p. 24.

JOHN MAINARD; Thos. Banks signs. No date. p. 25.

Order: Moore Carter, Francis Parker, James Bryant and John Dickenson, to divide the estate of JOSEPH CARTER bet. the widow and chn. Followed by division. Matthew Carter's part; Jos. Carter's part; Rachel Carter's part. Signed Moor x Carter, Frans Parker, John Dickenson. 6 Feby 1730. p. 26.

MICAEL MACKINNE; admr's name not given. May Ct 1731. p. 28.

JOHN Mac MILLS, sales; returned by admr. 17 Aug 1731. p. 29.

JOHN COTTEN; completing division his estate [. . . . .] met at house of Mrs. Martha Green and delivered into the hands of Capt. Thos. Bryant and Mrs. William Bennet . . . . for the use of the four small children. 5 June 1732. p. 30.

THOS. BOON; Nicholas Boon signs. No date. p. 31.

Dr. JAMES SPEIR; inv. returned by Anne Speir his extx. "To 20,000 bricks on the plantation not as yet paid for the making." 6 May 1732. p. 31.

RICHARD MELTON; Jonathan Melton, admr. 23 June 1732. p. 33.

JOHN COTTEN; Pursuant to order of Court appointing James Moor Titus Moor, John Jones, Sr., and Samuel Williams to divide his estate according to the express words of his will . . . met at the dwelling-house of Martha Green, 21 Nov 1731, and being qualified by John Edwards one of his Majestie's Justices . . proceeded to divide the estate.

For Priscilla Cotten (Mr. Thomas Bryant and Mr. William Bennet, trustees): for Thomas Cotten; for Martha Cotten; for James Cotten; four small chn Arthur, Priscila, James and Thomas; to Martha Green one-fifth, and the residue for the use of the four small children (to the trustees.) p. 34.

ISAAC HILL; Inv. returned by Nath'll Hill. 21 Jany 1733. p. 38.

Capt. SIMON JEFFREYS; Capt. Thos. Bryant, John Edwards, William Bennettt met at the dwelling-house of Elizabeth Jeffreys, widow, in order to complete the division of the estate between the widow and two children: Mrs. Eliza: Jeffreys, Osberre [Asbury?] Jeffreys, Bettey Jeffreys. 7 Dec 1734. p. 40.

BRYAN O'QUIN; Fran's O'Quin petitions that she have admn on the estate of her late husband. p. 41.

R'D MALPUS; William Williamson, admr, returns acct. p. 41.

ROBERT SMITH; John Spann signs. 24 Jany 1727. p. 42.

Capt. SIMON JEFFREYS, inventory. p. 46. [Jany 1727?]

DANIEL RIGGAN; Sarah x Regan signs. p. 51. [Jany 1727?]

GEORGE WILLIAMS, Jr. G. Williams and R'd Williams extrs. p. 51. [Jany 1727?].

HEZEKIAH MASEY; John x Massey signs. 20 Jany 1727. p. 52.

JOHN PACE, sen'r; John x Pace signs. 1 Feby 1727. p53.

JOHN CHERRYHOLME; Jane x Cherryholme signs. p. 54.

JOHN COTTEN; In obedience to order of Febry, 1728, we the subscribers did meet at the house of JOHN COTTEN, dec'd, 12 Mch 1728, and divided his estate pursuant to his will. To William Cotten; to Samuel Cotten; to Elexander Cotten; to John Cotten, gdn of Susanah; to Martha Bentne [?] widow; to the four small children of sd John......we could not divide their estate according to will because there was no person to represent them. John Dew, Simon Jeffrey, James Moor, R'd Brasswell. p. 55.

HENRY BARFIELD; Wm x Hales signs. 26 Dec 1728. p. 56.

R'D BARFIELD. signed by Wm Moor and R'd Barfield. 11 July, 1729. p. 57.

JOHN NELSON; acc't sales. James Nelson signs. Present, John Dew. 17 Dec 1729. p. 59.

JAMES PEEKE; pltr; Rich'd Oldner and Thos. Banks, extrs. 13 Nov 1729. p. 60.

ROBERT HART; Martha Hart, wife of Robert Hart dec. have condersended That William Hart should administer in my Behalf Upon The sd Estate. Martha x Hart. Jno. Simpson, wit. 5 Nov 1729. p. 62.

RICHARD SUMNER; remaining parts of his estate [division.] His son Richard Sumner's filial part and portion accoring to the Dec'd last will and testament. John McDaniel signs. 20 July 1731. p. 66.

THO: PARNELL, est. James Millikin, admr. 20 July 1731. p. 66.

WILLIAM BOON; Thos x Boon admr. Mention of a gift to Eliza: Boon in his life-time. 8 Feby 1731. p. 67.

THOMAS CRAGHILL; Mary Craghill, admx. William Smith, admr. 8 May 1731. p. 68.

THOS. WIMBERLY; George and Joseph Wimberly, extrs, &c. Signed by George Wimberly. 6 July 1732. p. 71.

WILLIAM BOON; acct sales. 1 May 1732. p. 72.

MARY COULSON; Thos. Whitmill signs. Inventory excepts "her wearing clothes which her daughter had." 11 Nov 1734. p. 73.

JOHN GAVIN; returned by Charles Gavin, admr. 7 Nov 1734. p. 74. Acct sales see p. 76.

J. MALPUS; William x Williamson signs. 3 Dec 1734. p. 74.

MATTHEW EDWARDS; inv. signed by John Bazemore. 6 Nov 1734. –. 75.

THOS. WILLIAMSON; acct sales. Thomas Asheley, admr. 27 Sept 1734. p. 76.

............MANN; John Mann returns inventory. p. 77.

JONATHAN AND MARY JACOCKS; inv. signed by J. Blount. 6 Feby 1735. p. 78.

Capt. DAVID HENDERSON;......Henderson, extr. p. 82.

THOS. WHITMELL; Thos. Whitmell signs. 10 May 1736. p. 85.

CLEMENT HAMMOND; Thos. Jackson signs "in Right of my wife Esther Jackson." p. 86.

WILLIAM HINTON, late of Chowan, dec'd; inv. taken by Eliza: x Hinton, widow and admx. Oath taken before Aaron Blanshard. 2 July 1736. p. 89.

BRYAN O'QUIN [Sen'r]; John Rose, adm'r, petitions that the estate be sold to pay the debts and pay off the orphans. p. 90.
Acc't sales returned by John Rose and wf Francis, relict of O'Quin. 10 June [1736?] p. 91.

RICHARD BROWN, late of Bertie Precinct, dec'd. Inv. returned by Edward Tidman. 6 Aug 1736. p. 94.

WILLIAM HINTON; division his estate bet. widow and orphans. Names not given. 16 Aug 1736. p. 95.

JOHN BASS; division his est. John Bass, extr. Nov Ct 1736. p. 96.

JOHN JONES; John Jones, extr. Inv. taken 15 May 1736. p. 97.

WILLIAM JONES; Francis Hobson signs. Nov. Ct 1736. p. 100.

SERVICE AND SUPPLIES COLONIAL, REVOLUTIONARY AND MILITIA

TALLY x GODFREY, of Perquimans cty, N. C., aged 68, says that he was well acquainted with JOHN MILLER late of same county; that sd MILLER came from Virginia when about 18 years of age and continue to reside in Perquimans to the time of his death, which was in the year A. D. 1822; that said JOHN intermarried with SUSAN HUMPHRIES by whom he left children James and Martha, both living. Martha m. Thomas H. Stacy, now also alive. Said JAMES MILLER, Martha Stacy and her husband Thomas S. [?] are residents of Perquimans. Frequently informed by JOHN MILLER that he had two brothers, JAMES and THOMAS MILLER, both of whom were engaged in the Revolutionary War between Great Britain and the United States [*sic*] and that they served during the said War or part thereof in the Virginia Continental line. Further states that he has frequently been informed by said JOHN that his two brothers died without issue, and he never heard said JOHN speak of any other brothers nor of having any sisters. Perq., N. C. Fall Term 1833.

BENJAMIN ASHBY, an officer in the Virginia line, in Continental service, claims pre-emption of 1000 a. on a branch of the north fork of Elkhorn, improvements made in 1775, Warrant for 1000 acres. Ct. Held for Kentucky cty, 8 Feby 1781. S. L. O. iii-48.

JOHN SCARF, a private. Grant of 297 acres in our County of Tennessee, n. side of Cumberland river, on Macador creek, pursuant to an act of the General Assembly for the relief of officers and soldiers in the Continental line and in consideration of his signal bravery and personal zeal. Camden, N. C. 20 May 1793. H-204.

JAMES WININGHAM, aged 76, makes declaration of Revolutionary service. States that he entered under the following named officers and served as stated. Entered in Granville cty, N. C. as a Substitute for one Stovall or Stobal, for three months, under Capt. Andrew Potter, Col. Gill and Gen. Butler . . . believes about a year before the battle of Guilford; was honorably discharged by his Captain, Abraham Potter; was mostly employed in pursuit of the Tories in the counties of Chatham, Randolph, Guilford and Rowan, N. C. Was not in any battle. Was then drafted to enter the foot service for three months shortly before the battle of Guilford, but was permitted by sending his own horse to enter a company of Light Horse commanded by Capt. John Henderson. That Pleasant Henderson was his Major, and a Frenchman, whose name he thinks was Malbury was his Colonel, and Butler his General. At the time of the battle of Guilford was on furlough. Was afterwards in Cumberland county, N. C. (Gives route of march as he remembers it.) Was honorably discharged in Granville by Capt, John Henderson. No documentary proof; those who know of his service are dead or in distant parts. Signed JAMES WININGHAM.

The Court declares opinion that he was a Revolutionary soldier. Randolph cty, N. C. Minute Docket, 11 Aug 1832.

HUGH MOORE, Gent., produces commission as Captain of a foot company and takes the oath. Hal. cty, Va. 26 May 1753. 1st "Pleas."

WILLIAM McCULLAM, proved that he improved land in Kentucky cty, 10 Apr 1776, but was prevented from "laying his claim on account of being in the regular service." Court is of opinion that he is entitled to pre-emption of 1,000 acres. Jeff'n cty, Ky. Court Mch, 1782. A-20.

EDWARD McDONALD; frontier soldier, Augusta county. Hening, vii-192, 1758.

BRYAN McDONELL, assignee of Joshua M Cormack; paid for horse and mare lost in Shawnese expedition. Aug. cty, Va. Sept 1758. Hening vii-187.

INTERCOUNTY AND INTERCOLONY

Drawn mainly from North Carolina records.

STEPHEN WELLS of Edgecomb cty, N. C., from Redmund [Redmon] Wells of Craven cty, S. C. Tract in Edgecomb cty, n. side Tar river 100 acres. [This deed recites a patent to Stephen Wells, Sr.] Nash cty, [1778.] i-76.

JAMES DRAKE, late of Nash cty, died in Richmond, Va., having made his will there. Depositions of witnesses to be annexed to the will. 8 Aug, 1791. Minutes of Nash Ct. No page.

ZACHARIAH MARTIN, of Craven cty, S. C., conveys to Rachel Martin of Bute cty, N.C., consideration love and affection and £20 proclamation money, all my portion of John Martin's estate, late of Granville cty, dec'd. Martin Friday, one of wit. 11 Aug. 1766. Warren cty, N. C. A-16.

ZACHARIAH MARTIN, late of Orange cty, N. C., now of Craven cty, S. C., revokes power to friend Thomas Bell of Granville cty, to convey land n. side Sandy Creek. 18 Nov 1766. Warren cty, N. C. A-16.

WILLIAM x KING, of Lunenburg cty, Va. to Hennery King, Jr., of Bute cty, N. C., 100 acres. Wit: George x King, Sr., Robert x King, George King. 1 Oct. 1765. Warren cty, N. C. 1-117.

ROBERT WILLIAMS and wife Anne, of Granville cty, N. C., to Blanchflower Dunkin.— Feby 1766. Warren cty, N. C. 1-147.

JAMES LOCKETT, of Amelia cty, Va., from Thomas Byrd, of Bute cty, N. C. (Wf Martha.) 250 acres n. side Tarr river. 29 Oct 1766. Warren cty, N. C. 1-187.

SOLOMON ALSTON, the younger, Gent., and wf Sarah, of Bute cty, to Willie Jones of Northampton cty, N. C., Gent. 27 Oct 1766. Warren cty, N. C. 1-193.

GEORGE KING of Mecklenburg cty, Va., to Richard Fox of the same. Deed. 20 Aug 1766. Warren cty, N. 1-228.

NICOLAS ROBERSON, of Bute cty, N. C., to Robert Alexander, of "Lunengburg" cty, Va., 100 acres on the bank of Reedy Branch. Warren cty. N. C. 10 Sept 1764. 1-268.

COLIN CAMPBELL provides for payment of expenses in case "of my death in this country." Had sister Mrs. Mumford. His extrs Dr. Colin Dallas and David Boyd, Esq., in St. Vincent's, are mentioned. Cumberland, N. C. Will dated 24 Mch 1804. Admitted to record June, 1804. A-67.

NATHANIEL ALLEN, of Edenton, N. C. Will. Dau. Mary Allen; sister Hannah Gill, of Philada., Penna. Sister Mary Davis, of Alexandria, Va.........John Granbery, Norfolk Borough, Va., John Roulhac, of Martin cty, Va., and Samuel Tredwell, of Edenton, Esq., extrs. Chowan cty, N. C. B-253. 11 Nov 1805. [The abstract of this will is not given in full.]

SIMON DANIELL of Edgecombe cty, N. C., to Henry Goodman, of Chowan cty, N. C. Conveys land on Peters swamp. Tyrrell cty, N. C. A-242. 25 Oct 1743.

DANIEL GORDON, of Hertford, Perquimans cty, N. C., will. He gives to his two sons James Gordon (*als* James Blades) and Nicholas Gordon (*als* Nicholas Blades) the reversion of a certain lot in Manchester, Chesterfield cty, Virginia. To Col. Mathew Cheatham the reversion of a tract in "Bottertourt" in trust for his, Gordon's daughter. . . . "Believing that . . . Having finished these days of Misery and Mortality, I shall Inherit everlasting Quiet." Dated 5 Dec 1812. Perq., N. C. E-373.

ROBERT ADAMS, appoints friend and cousin, William Parker, Esq., son of John Parker, Esq., of Kilmarnock in Scotland, one of his extrs. 2 May 1801. Cumb. cty N. C. A-42.

The will of JOHN INGRAM, 16 Mch 1794, begins: "There is an old woman in Maryland, in Hartford [*sic*] County, whose name is Esther Northington, to whom I leave fifty silver dollars per year . . . . I am under great obligations to her for her kind and friendly attentions to my mother, many years . . . besides she is old and infirm. To my niece Sally Sinclair wife to a Moses Sinclair, Junr (if there are two) of Baltimore County, Maryland, I leave £100 per year to be paid herself not to her husband. To my friend and benefactor Doctor Robert Harris of the City of Philadelphia, or to his wife . . . . $100 per year. Desires his mulatto slave, Sally. set free, and leaves her $30 silver a year for four years; the house opposite to Murchison the Taylor is her own property. Executors directed to account with her for its rental. Desires remainder of estate reserved as a fund for Educating the Children of niece Sally Sinclair and James Cole, son of Ann Cole, wife of Mark Cole, with final division among their children. Provides for final division of estate, failing these children. Wit: John x Eccles, David Anderson. Probate Oct. Term, 1797. Cumb. cty, N. C. A-5.

THOMAS DAILY, Marriner, late of the City of London. Will: Wf Eliz:, son Samuel, dau. Jane, son John and his son Thomas; son Thomas, son William. Son Samuel and wf Elia: extrs. Wit: Ormand Elsbee, John Webster. 31 Aug 1788—Feby 1791. Hyde cty, N. C. i-598.

WILLIAM MASSURY, of Salem, Province of Massachusetts. Account sales his estate. 9 June 1762. Hyde cty, N. C. Old vol. marked "A". p. 57 [?]

ABRAHAM DUNCAN, of Beaufort cty, N. C., Mcht, extr of Walter Davey, formerly of Dublin, Kingdom of Ireland, but late of Beaufort cty, dec'd, to John Smith of Hyde cty, Shipwright. Refs to Davey's will, 22 June 1743. Hyde cty, N. C. 15 Dec 1743. A-161.

SAMUEL MASON, of Hyde cty, N. C., to Henry Roberson, a parcel of land in Curratuc, 8 acres; refers to patent to father Thomas Mason. 2 Oct 1773. B-505.

SOLOMON CARTER, wf Elizabeth, conveys 75 acres in "New Currituck", which Roger Mason left in his will to his dau. Dorcas Mason. 30 Sept 1773. Hyde cty, N. C. B-506.

VALUABLE PUBLICATIONS

Mrs. NELL MARION NUGENT, Clerk of the Virginia Land Office, at Richmond, is about to bring out one of the most important publications ever undertaken for the benefit of historians and genealogists. It will be the CALENDAR OF VIRGINIA LAND PATENTS, 1623 to 1800. Mrs. Nugent has decided to publish this in bulletin form, twelve issues a year, at $1.50 a month, $14.00 per year. This Calendar will include the names of all head rights (when given), including those now published in the NOTE-BOOK, but will give details which the Editor of the NOTE-BOOK has been obliged to omit, such as the exact location of the patent, the number of acres, &c., &c. The Calendar will also include the list of grants made by virtue of the pre-emption warrants, for services in the Colonial Wars, and in the Revolutionary War, as they appear of record in the Land Office. More complete information than the Editor has space to give, may be had upon application to Mrs. Nugent, whose address will be found on the advertising page.

Mr. LOUIS A. BURGESS, of Richmond, Virginia (212, West Broad street), advises the Editor that his third volume of the VIRGINIA SOLDIERS of 1776, is now in press and will very shortly be ready to distribute. Those who have had the benefit of the first two volumes brought out by Mr. Burgess do not need to be assured of the very great value of the "source" material Mr. Burgess has compiled. Mr. Burgess is now at work upon a fourth volume which will contain Chancery Court reports of the settlement of estates; marriages and obituary notices, and records of the War of 1812 . . . all of Virginia. Concerning this new publication the Editor will say that the chancery records of the courts stand among the very most important sources of genealogical information. Too many have been lost or destroyed, but a great number are still upon the shelves or in the pigeon-holes of the old Clerks' offices, little known except to experts.

Mr. STRATTON NOTTINGHAM, Onancock, Virginia, has now ready for delivery still another volume of marriage license bonds, those of WESTMORELAND COUNTY, VIRGINIA, the home of a lot of ancestors, including the Washingtons, the Lees, Monroes, *et al.* The N. Y. Genealogical and Biographical Record "heartily recommends to all genealogical libraries" Mr. Nottingham's previous publications, and this is even more valuable. Mr. Nottingham is doing work which should have been done in this complete and thorough way years ago, before he entered the field, and the information now made available is of the most important. Not only that, but future fires will be less hopelessly destructive, and searchers will not stand helplessly before them and poke from the ashes a scorched leaf here and there, realizing that all documentary proof has vanished in the upper "ceiling."

Previously published in this series are the bonds of Lancaster county, of Accomack, and the Revolutionary Soldiers and Sailors of Accomack.

The index to Volume VI has been prepared and will soon be published. Price $1.00.

The mimeographed index of Volumes IV and V, COUNTY COURT NOTE-BOOK, is ready. It contains 24 pages. The impression is excellent. Same size as printed index to Volumes I, II and III. Price $1.60 for the indices for IV and V, or one dollar each. The full set may be had at a special price of four dollars.

Reasonable price or two years' subscription will be given for numbers 1, 2, 3, 4, 6, and 7, COUNTY COURT NOTE-BOOK, 1921-1922. Address Editor.

Fifty cents will be paid for a copy of February 1927.

Printed at the Industrial School for Crippled and Deformed Children, 241 St. Botolph St., Boston, Mass.

The

County Court Note-Book

A Little Bulletin of History and Genealogy

June, 1928. **Vol. VII, No. 3.**

MARYLAND'S NEXT OF KIN

WILLIAM x CHICK; inv. John Evitt. 9 Apr 1722. vii-275. [This name Evitt, perhaps Euitt.]

No kin given, but the appraisers were EPHRA. AUG'T HERMAN and HARMAN BURKELOE; inv. Samuel Byard of Cecill cty, Gent. 10 June 1722. vii-276.

MARY x SHAW, JOHN x CONNOWAY [kin?] Inv. John Shaw of Balto. cty, 9 May 1722. vii-281.

A. N. PRICE, WILL PRICE; inv. Thomas Price of Q. A. cty. 15 June 1722. vii-282.

STEPHEN HOLLINGSWORTH, THO. JACOBS; inv. Henry Hollingsworth of Cecill cty. 20 Mch 1721-2. vii-288.

SIMON x NICHOLLS, Sr., MATTHEW MOGBEE; inv. Wm. Nicholas of A. A. cty. 5 May 1722. vii-296.

SAMUEL MAGRUDER, WILLIAM BURNES, ELIS x BOWEN, THOMAS x WINTER; sign inv. Mrs. Ann Dorsett of Pr. Geo's cty. 27 Nov 1721. vii-297.
[It is not clear which are kin and which are creditors.]

LEONARD BROOKE, "Relation;" inv. Mr. John Craycroft. No date. vii-299.

HENRY HILL; inv. Henry Hill, Jr., of A. A. cty. 8 June 1722. vii-311.

CUTHBERT x FENWICK, ENOCH x FENWICK; inv. Mr. Richard Fenwick of St. Marie's cty. 20 July 1722. vii-315.

JACOB CROUCH, RICHARD PHILLIPS; inv. Robert Crouch. County not given. 8 Nov 1721. vii-318.

GEORGE x BAYLE, JOHN x PARSONS; inv. Graves Jarrett. 1 June 1722. vii-320.

ISAAC NOBLES, THOMAS HOBBS, J. LEATHERBARY, ESTHER DENWOOD sign. Inv. John Noble of Som. cty. 6 May 1721. vii-322. [Probably these are kin and creditors together.]

ROBERT MELVIN, THOMAS DUCKET ELIONER x STEVENS; inv. Mary Stevens of Som. cty. 2 May 1721. vii-333.

"No near relations" appeared; . inv. Parthenia Morris of Som. cty. Signed by ELIZ'TH x WINDOW, HENRY SMOCK, "Nearest of kind." No date. vii-336.

JOHN x RIGGEN, SAM'L RIGGEN; inv. Teague Regen of Som. cty. 9 Apr 1722. vii-337.

THOS. x GLENDON; inv. James Mills of Som. cty. 6 May 1721. vii-340.

RANDELL HORSEY; inv. Nath'l Horsey of Som. cty, 6 June 1722. vii-341.

JNO. ATKINSON, ISAAC ATKINSON; inv. James Atkinson. County not given. 26 Mch 1722. vii-342.

JACOB MORRIS, THOM'S ROBINSON: inv. John Morris. County not given. 30 Nov 1721. vii-344.

ELIZA: HUDSON, DAN'L HUDSON; inv. Henry Hudson. No county given. vii-345.

CHAS. COLLINS, RICH'D BEADARD; inv. Thos. Collings. County not given. No date. vii-345.

EDWARD ELLIOTT, THO'S ASHCROFT; inv. Mr. James Auld of Talbot cty. 15 May 1722. vii-346.

[Note: for a space of some years these entries are so carelessly made in the records of the prerogative court, that it is frequently very difficult to ascertain which signatures are those of kin, and which are of creditors. See Dep'ty Comm'y's Guide for requirements.]

WILLIAM x FOREMAN, JOHN x WHITE, MATHEW x HAWKINS; inv. William Hawkins, Balto. cty. 24 Apr 1722. vii-349.

MARTHA LINGAN, ELIZABETH COCKSHUTT; inv. Mr. Thomas Cockshutt of Calv. cty. 16 Nov 1722. vii-353.

THOMAS RUTLAND, JOHN SAPPINTON; inv. Thos. Sappinton of A. A. cty. 24 Sept 1722. viii-1. [Two pair of "Quern stones" mentioned.]

LIVIN HICKS, THOMAS HICKS; inv. Mr. Thomas Hicks of Dor. cty. 7 Dec 1722. viii-2.

JOHANNA McDANNIELL signs as extx, no kin given; inv. James Barlow, Den'r, of Balto. cty. 6 June 1721. viii-5.

AUTHENTIC REFERENCES FOR INFERRED MARRIAGES

(Northampton county, Virginia. Continued from April, 1928.)

BENJAMIN SCOTT and ESTHER SANDERS, dau. of Richard. Before 9 Nov 1725. Chancy records.

THOMAS SCOT and MARY HARDING, widow of Samuel. About 9 Oct 1728. Chancy records.

JONATHAN STEVENS and ARIDA BENTHALL, dau. of Daniell and Frances. Before 11 July 1726. Chancy records.

JOHN STRINGER and FLAVEY SAVAGE, dau. of " Elkerton." Before September Ct 1730. Chancy records.

MR THOMAS SAVAGE and ELITIA HARMANSON, dau. of Thomas, Sr. Before Sept 1702. xviii-112.

JOHN SAVAGE and ELIZABETH GASCOIGNE, dau. of Henry. Before 28 May 1697. xvii-428,

JOHN SAVAGE and DOROTHY JORDAN. 18 Nov 1660. ix-92.

JOHN SMITH and REBECCA SAVAGE, widow of Thomas. Before 16 June 1655. v-142.

CHRISTOPHER SEGAR and ANN HUNT, dau. of Thomas. Before 10 Mch 1728. Chancy records.

DIGBY SEYMOUR and ROSE CHRISTIAN, widow. Before 12 Apr 1737. xviii-98.

HILLARY STRINGER and GRACE ROBINS, dau. of John, Sr. Before 1707. xix-23.

JOHN SMITH and JEAN MARSHALL, dau. of John. About 28 May 1707. xviii-34.

WILLIAM SMITH and BRIDGET JAMES, widow of Thomas. Before 11 July 1737. Chancy records.

JONATHAN STOTT and the widow of Ralph BATSON. Before 7 Sept 1735. Chancy records.

...... SMOTHERS and ELIZABETH DUNTON, dau. of Thomas. Before [?] 15 Aug 1689. xiv-227.

HENRY SPEAKMAN and the widow of David DALBE. Before 13 Jany 1735. Chancy records.

FRANCIS STOKELY and ROSE WILLETT, extx of William. Before 22 Dec 1740. Chancy records.

ABEL STOTT and PATIENCE PITTS, dau, of Jacob. Before Aug 1769. Chancy records.

JONATHAN STOTT and ABBIGALL TEAGUE. Before 10 Apr 1741. Chancy records.

LEVIN SMITH and ELIZABETH SCOTT, widow of Baily SCOTT. Before June 1770. Chancy records.

LEVIN SMITH and ELISHE FRESHWATER, dau. of Matthew. Before 1783. Chancy records.

LUKE SMAW and ABIGAL WATERSON, dau. of John. Before 10 Dec 1742. Chancy records.

ISAAC SMITH and SARAH WEST. Before 12 Feby 1724. Chancy records.

JOHN SMITH and SARAH JOHNSON dau. of Benjamin. Before 1773. Chancy records.

.... STEER and AGNES PATRICK, dau. of Richard. Some time after 16 Feby 1674. Chancy records.

GRIFFIN STITH, Jr., and ANNE STRATTON, dau. of John. 25 June 1778. Chancy records.

THOMAS STAYTON and ELIZABETH DRUMMOND, dau. of Hill DRUMMOND. Before 2 June 1736. Chancy records.

AZARIAH TANKRED and RACHEL PETTIT, dau. of William. Before or about 1767. Chancy records.

JOHN TOMPKINS, Gent. and ANN CUSTIS, widow of John. Before 13 May 1760. Chancy records. [ANN CUSTIS was ANN KENDALL. She m. TOMPKINS before 25 Feby 1747. See xviii-372.]

THOMAS TEACKLE and ISABELLA DOUGLAS, widow. Before 30 Jany 1670. x-105

JOHN TAYLOR and MARY WEBSTER, dau. of Sampson and Mary. 5 Jany 1709. xiv-126.

GEORGE THOMAS and ELIZ: GASCOIN, dau. of William. Before 1725. Chancy records.

GEORGE TREWET and ELIANOR MEREDITH, third dau. of Phillip. Before 9 Oct 1672. Va. S. L. O. vi-430. (N-n cty.)

JOHN TANKRED and SARAH SMART, dau. of William of Gloucester cty. Before 28 Mch 1687. xiv-152.

JOHN THOROUGHGOOD prob. m. ANN STRINGER. Before 21 Dec 1689. xvii-7.

WILLIAM TAZEWELL and SOPHIA HARMANSON, dau. of Gertrude. Before 15 July 1752. xxxix0-136.

BARTHOLOMEW TWYFORD [TWIFORD] and SARAH SAVAGE, dau. of Benjamin. Before 1770. Chancy records. "A man very illiterate who never could be persuaded to ride to Northampton to search the Records........." [Part of the testimony.]

THOMAS UNDERHILL and SUSANNA EVANS, dau. of Arthur. Before Nov 1770. Chancy records.

DERICK VANHAMELL and SOPHIA VANWEKER. See record 8 Sept 1679. xiii-59.

JACOBUS VAN NORCOWE [?] Mcht of Amsterdam, and ADRIANTIA CORNELIS VAN AGTHOVE [?] Before 15 Apr 1657. vii-65. [This was almost illegible.]

.........VOSSE and ANNE WILKINS. [Note: ANNE VOSSE was mother of NATH'L WILKINS, also of ANNE HUNT, also of LYDIA JACKSON.] Before 4 Nov 1680. xi-225. See also xi-16.

JOHN VYNES and BRIDGETT BILLYEATE Before [?] 25 June 1656. vii-28. [This name probably Balliott.]

JOHN WARREN and the widow of George ROBERSON. Before 11 Jany 1739. Chancy papers.

.... WARREN and ELIZABETH PATRICK, dau. of Richard. Some time after [?] 16 Feby 1674. Chancy records.

HENRY WARREN and URSLY PATRICK, dau. of Richard. Same refs.

BENONI WARD prob. m. SARAH HEWETT, a widow. Before 10 July 1694. iv-241. [Was she also a widow Elligood?]

ELIJAH WATSON and RUHAMAH SMITH. Before July 1767. Chancy records.

Dr. JAMES WATT and SARAH, the extx of Mr. Argoll YARDLEY. About 1683. xv-40. See also xv-85.

Mr. JOHN WILLETT, Mcht, and Mrs. ELIZABETH DOUGLAS. See 5 May 1670, and 24 Nov 1669. x-86 and xi-9.

CORNELIUS WATKINSON and SUSANNA SAVAGE, widow of Benjamin. Before 1770. Chancy records.

VIRGINIA COLONISTS

(*From "Old Volume 5," S. L. O., Richmond.*)

CHARLES HILL, no county mentioned, 1655 and 1658.
Head rights: James Hill, William Rogers, Mary Jones.

JOHN HUGHLETT and THOMAS SALISBURY, Northumberland cty, 1661.
Head rights: Edward Sanders, Joseph Hary, Nich: Smith, Wm. Henwell, Robert Wright, Myles Cray, Jno. Knight, Francis Acton.

JOHN HUGHLETT, Northumberland cty, 1662.
Head rights: Wm. Sandiford, Manell [?] Jones, Jno. Bateman, Mary Bateman, Charles Winter, Mary Hewes, Thos: Hewes, Tho: Efford, Sarah Bradford.

JOHN HARRIS, Lancaster cty, 1661.
Head rights: An Harris, Margtt Tompson, Jno. Cole, Stephen Norman, Wm. Stephens, Hannah Mills, Jno. Hunt, Marye Tye, Henry Nicholls, Thomas Norton.

Capt. THOMAS HAWKINS, 1661
Head rights: Maudlin Davis, Rice Harvy, Edwd Porter, Giles Tonning, Mary Howard, Hugh Weekes, Edwd James, Elianor Parry.

JAMES HILL, Northumberland cty, 1661.
Head rights: Susan Hunt, Timothy Cole, Wm. Seward, Mary Godale, Andrew Stevens, Henry Creighton, Walter Ashdarne [?]

(Third alphabet.)

JAMES ALLEN, Northumberland cty, 1661.
Head rights: Xtopher Wright, Nich: Spencer, Jno. Motrom.

JAMES AUSTIN, Northumberland cty, 1661.
Head rights: Seven negroes, Ann Young and Mary Tompson.

JOHN ASHLEY, Lancaster cty, 1662.
Head rights: Jno. Cone, John Bolton, Jno. Pritchett, Eliz: Poore, and a negro.

ISAAC K. ALLERTON, Westmoreland cty, 1662.
Head rights: Anthony Harris, Stephen Harris, Peter Mackes or Markes, Wm. Andrewes.

JOHN ADKESON, New Kent, 1658. Head rights: Margaret Mathew or Mathers, Margaret Apriskett.

THO: BOSWELL, "in the Freshes above Anacosta Island," 1658.
Head rights: Wm. Sanders, John Angell, Elliner Fishbrooke, John Perry, George Ball, Tho. Dainsy [?] Wm. Wilson, Georg Grey, Sarah Johnson, John Wotton.

AUGUSTINE BLITHENBORGE, county not given, 1658.
Head rights: James Jones.

GEORG BROWNE, New Kent cty, 1659.
Head rights: John Heynes, Sr., John Haines, [Jr.?] Evan Johannes, Robert Scottell.

Mr. FRANCIS BURNELL, New Kent cty, 1659.
Head rights: Marg. Boaten, Robert Cruft, Jno. Needham, Robert Allen, Tho. Copinn, Jno. Clarkey, Eliz: Baileinge, Jno. Darken, James Johnson, Robert Miller, Robert Jinkins, James Tanner, Wm. Hazard, Rich. Smith, Mary Barnes, Geo. West, two negroes.

JOHN BARROW, Rappahannock cty, 1658.
Head rights: Tho. Southrene, Daniell O Sulevan [?], Tony Long, Derrick Arseson [perhaps Aryson.]

JNO. BARROW, 1658.
Head rights: Geo. Johnson, Wm. Smithson, Wm. Wilson, Cornelius Clinton, Eliz: Parry, Derrick Aryson, Alex. Coute, Derman, John Witty, Dorman "v. Sulanam" [possibly O'Sulavan?]

WM. BODY, I. W. cty, [1661 or 1662.]
Head rights: Wm. Young, Jno. Sharpe, Mary Stephens, Edward Wise, Edw. Marlow, Tho: Cawsey, James Hall, Tho: Turner, Ben. Jones, Tho: Smart, Alice Parr.

JOHN BARROW, county not given, 1660.
Head rights: Alexander Coote, Dorman Ossulevan, Derrick Arleson, Daniell OSulevan, Teague Longoe.

WM. BALLINGALL, Northumberland, 1661.
Head rights: Thomas Winn, Jno. Moore, Robt Burley, Robert Hampton, Thomas Gay, Wm. Petres, Jno. Aeshwin [?] Henry Mayne.

ABYA BONYSON, Lancaster cty, 1661.
Head rights: Margtt Grimes, Jno. Jones, Phill Norton, Stephen William, Ann Harte, Mary Sharpe, Susan Jones.

ROBT BAYLY, Rappahannock cty, 1661.
Head rights: Sarah Bunny, Jno. Smith, Rich, Reckes, Henry Michaell, Ann Mills, James Nailor.

Capt. HUMPHRY BOOTH, Rappahannock cty, 1661.
Head rights: And. Davis, Mary Wild, Tho. Webb, Joane Webb, Wm. Jones, Giles Hope, Peter White, Jno. Gray, Geo. Wood, Jasper White, Wm. Cooke, Tho. Sherman, Wm. Gower, James Stevens, Walter Hues, Xtop Wilson, Rog'r Evans, Tho. Williams, Jane Welch, Machaell Grant.

Capt. GYLES BRENT, county not given, 1662.
Head rights: Wm. Harris, Tho. Martin, Mary Wood, Edw. Jones, Sam'll Clay, Fra: Faire.

The County Court Note-Book

An every-other-monthly devoted mainly to abstracts from County Court Records, prior to 1800.

MILNOR LJUNGSTEDT, Editor and Publisher. Bethesda, Route 10, Maryland.

Published six times a year. Subscription, two dollars, in advance; must begin with the year.

June, 1928 **Whole**
Vol. VII., No. 3 **No. 40**

ENGLISH WILLS

Some time ago Mr. EDWARD DWELLY, a very reliable and experienced antiquarian in England, whose Gaelic Dictionary alone is a monument to his knowledge and his patience, wrote for the Editor an interesting article concerning the disposition of early English wills, and commenting on some of the difficulties of search, he explains that before 1858 there were 325 Probate Courts in England where wills could be proved, yet cases often occurred where the only copy extant of a will had been found written on a Manor Roll or other unlikely document. In the year 1853 the records of all these minor depositories were transferred, or supposed to be, to the Probate Courts. These courts consist of, first, the Principal Registry at Somerset House, London, which contains by far the greatest bulk of them. It is thought that there are very few family names that do not appear at all in the official calendars of this Registry.

During the Commonwealth all wills from every part of England were proved and registered at Somerset House, but before and after that period, if all a man's estate was within the jurisdiction of a Provincial Court the will was proved at that Court and a copy sent to Somerset house; if the estate came within the jurisdiction of more than one Provincial Court, the will was proved in London.

Mr. Dwelly writes further that there are now about 40 Provincial Courts, mostly in county towns such as Exeter, Taunton, Bodmin, Norwich, &c., but that the boundaries of the various jurisdictions of these 40 odd courts are rather confusing. He recommends MARSHALLS HANDBOOK TO THE ANCIENT COURTS OF PROBATE as a full and reliable guide, but adds that, in the matter of wills which have been scattered far and wide for centuries, it is almost impossible to trace out the depositories of all. As an example, he states that wills from the Peculiar Court of Selgley, Staffordshire, were in boxes in the garrets of Lord Dudley's house at Himley.

Further, numbers of wills are also contained in the Bishop's Books of most Dioceses, and there is no means of ascertaining anything about these except by personal search. A Bishop's Consistory Court had jurisdiction over a whole diocese, an Archdeaconry Court over the Archdeaconry only, and a Peculiar Court over the Peculiar only.

THE DEPUTY COMMISSARY'S GUIDE WITHIN THE PROVINCE OF MARYLAND

(*Continued from February, 1928*)

Every deputy Commissary then, appointed & qualified & given bond [see previous extracts], is to proceed to execute his office in the following manner & form.

Within a convenient time after the death of any person dying intest., it is his duty to call upon the next, most lawful friends of the deceased, to take out letters of administration. If none such, or if they refuse, letters may be granted to a creditor or other person.

Administration on the estate of intestates, is to be granted in the following order: If the intestate be a married woman, the administration belongs to her husband; And if the Husband die before administration is granted to him, his executors & administrators and not the wife's next of kin, shall be entitled. But if the wife was the executrix or administratrix of another, then as to the goods she had in such capacity, administration must be granted to the next of kin of the person on whose estate she administered.

If the intestate be a married man, administration is to be granted to the widow, or to the next of kin, or to both as the Commissary shall think fit. And he may grant several administrations of several parts of the goods of the intestate.

Administration is to be granted to the father of an intestate leaving no issue or widow; if leaving a widow, to her or to the father or to both.

Brothers and sisters, whether of the whole or half blood are to be preferred before uncles and aunts, "because the former have the immediate blood of the parent."

In a dispute between the grandfather or grandmother and an uncle or aunt, the grandfather or grandmother are nearer of kin. "The relation is thus traced; from the intestate to his or her father or mother to the brothers and sisters"...... "from the intestate to his or her father and mother to his or her grandfather or grandmother, and then to the said grandfather's or grandmother's child, who will be the aunt or uncle of the intestate." ... "The grandfather or grandmother is the root of the kindred, and the uncle and aunt only a branch."

If the intestate have "any descendant of either sex or of whatsoever degree," such descendant is to be preferred before all *ascendants* & collaterals.

The half blood is esteemed as near as the whole; but if there be a brother & sister of the half blood, and the sister be married, the administration belongs to the brother & not to her & her husband, "because in effect it makes the sister's husband administrator, who is not of kin to the intestate."

There is an exception to the rule about next of kin where there is a will & the executor refuses or dies intestate, a residuary legatee then has the best title to administration.

(*To be continued*)

NOTES HERE AND THERE

JOHN BEALL, Jr., petitions that his father James Beall, dying some time ago, left three sons, brothers to the petitioner, vizt: Robert Beall, now 10; Joseph Beall, about 7, and Zephaniah Beall, about 5. Sarah, the relict of James Beall, m. Dr. John Haswell. Petitioner asks that children may have proper maintenance or be placed in his care. Pr. Geo's cty, Md. Vol. M, Nov ct 1726.

ROGER THOMAS (will) desires to be buried in the churchyard at St. Martin's. Wor. cty, Md. M. H. iii-51. 26 June 1703.

JOHN WHITE, of Pocomoke, Gent. Leaves remainder his estate (after legacies) to be "divided amongst my twins; TABITHA and PRISCILLA; SARAH and JOHN WHITE." Wor., Md. M. H. iii-10. 1 June 1685.

Mr. NATHAN'LL HILL, Schoolmaster; petitions that he be for his encouragement in that employment exempted from levy; referred [by Court] until he qualify for license. Hen., Va. 2 Aug 1686. Another petition (1 Dec 1686) shows that he removed out of "Glouster" cty and settled in Henrico. Petitions that he be free of levy.

MARY SMITH had a daughter whose name was MARY, which Daughter married a BOTSON and had a Daughter by the name of ELIZABETH to whom the negro Betsey was given by the will of her Grandmother MARY SMITH. At the August Term, 1785, William Russell, Esq., was appointed Guardian to ELIZABETH BOTSON. At the previous May Term a commission was issued to Seth Harvey or some other Justice. . . . to take the deposition on oath of Samuel Davis in Behalf of T. S. Babtest Moygnard in a suit against this William Russell, Esq., executor of MARY BATSON [*sic*] "Diseased" August, 1785. The suit of a James Jasper is quoted, and of Elizabeth Jasper, executor and executrix of MARY SMITH, vs. T. L. B. Moygnard. (On a loose paper found in vol. iv, Hyde county, N. C.)

JOHN BENSTON and RACHEL MOODY; Bans of matrimony.

"*But John Walker Freeman in the behalfe of Rachill Moody underwrites in these words Rachell Moody hath nothing to Say to John Walker in the way of Matrimony therefore is of no effect.*"

Som. cty, Md. Ct. Record. 3 Feby 1668.

HUNGARS CREEK CHURCH, Northampton county, Va. THOMAS PREESON, in his will, conveys one acre where the *new church* now stands. N-n, Va. Land Causes, 1756.

From the will of MARY ANN HARRISON: "I have lately purchased a lottery ticket in case the same should draw a prize I desire that my Executor will dispose of the proceeds among my two daughters. . ." Pr. Wm, Va. I-8. 4 Nov 1803.

Errata:

In the supplement to the NOTE-BOOK for December, 1925, Eastern Shore Families, the fifth line from the bottom of the first column should read: [John Custis,] Mcht, and wife Tabitha, give to kinsman Joseph Webb. . . .

In an early number of the NOTE-BOOK (July, 1922, p. 3) the marriage of William Richardson and Ann Abbett is given. This should be Cobbett, not Abbett.

In September of the same year (p. 3) "Jemima Odell and Job," should read: "she was the dau. of James Job."

CONTINUED articles COUNTY COURT NOTE-BOOK, and the dates on which they first appeared.

THE ANCESTRY OF COL. JOHN DONELSON. Began with February, 1927.

AUTHENTIC REFERENCES for INFERRED MARRIAGES (formerly called MARRIAGES BY INFERENCE). Began with May, 1922.

MARYLAND'S NEXT OF KIN. Began with July, 1922.

VIRGINIA COLONISTS. Alphabetized lists began with July, 1924.

MILITARY NOTES, both COLONIAL and REVOLUTIONARY, and later MILITIA NOTES. Began December, 1923.

INTERCOUNTY and INTERCOLONY (formerly called New Englanders and Others, &c., &c,). Began with March, 1922.

EASTERN SHORE FAMILIES. In the form of a one-page supplement, began with June, 1925. This will be continued later.

SHIPS IN PORT and COLONIAL FORENAMES, will appear in alternate issues or as space can be found for them.

A mimeographed INDEX to Volume VI, of the NOTE-BOOK is now ready. It contains nine pages, about 1200 names, and is an unusually good impression. Price 65 cents. To save the trouble of sending part of a dollar, checks for one dollar will be received, and the balance of 35 cents will be allowed on the next subscription. Or a reasonable amount of two cent stamps will be acceptable.

A FEW ADDITIONAL WILLIAMS NOTES

WILLIAM and BARBARA WILLIAMS* of Prince George's Psh, Maryland [this parish included families in both Prince George's and Frederick counties], had the following children:
Thomas-Owen Williams, b. 21 Feby 1747;
Elizabeth, b. 30 Oct 1749;
Elisha, b. 9 May 1752;
Ellinor-Hilleary, b. 5 Apr 1757;
Martha, b. 22 Dec 1759;
Edward-Owen, b. 18 Apr 1761. From the Reg. of Pr. Geo.'s Psh.

[Note: this copy of the Register, which is in Washington, D. C., ends about 1765.]

WILLIAM WILLIAMS and Mildred Duncomb, Mar. 8 Dec 1743. St. Paul's psh Reg. K. Geo. cty, Va.

WALTERxWILLIAMS; will. Mentions Elizabeth Thatcher, John Cammock, Warwick Cammock. Makes the latter extr. Wit: Dunnincan [?], Samuel Johnson. Rappa., Va. Vol. 1664-1673, p. 59. 8 May 1672-3 July 1672.

WILLIAM WILLIAMS m. the widow of Thomas Eastmead. N-n, Va. Before 28 July 1685. xv-155. [Her name was Phillis, and the marriage was bet. 30 Oct 1683 and 29 Sept 1684. See Chancy records.]

WILLIAM WILLIAMS m. Mary Roberts, widow. N-n, Va.Chancy records.

*Re-printed.

WILLIAM WILLIAMS; will. Wife Mical; son John; son William; dau. Elizabeth Williams; dau. Ann Williams; son Pugh; youngest daus. Elizabeth, Tabby and Sally Williams; Pugh Price, William Morton, Mical Williams, extrs. Wit: Watkin, Boulden; Mary Carington, Elizabeth Townes. Charl, Va. 23 Mch 1775-4 Sept 1775. 1-125.

INTERCOUNTY AND INTERCOLONY

GEORGE HARDINGE, citizen and grocer of London, and wife Mary, dau. of Thomas Orley, of London, and wife Anne, dec'd, and sister of . . . Orley, late of Cherry Poyntt in Potemeck, pltr, dec'd. Power. [see marriage reference Jallens-Orley.] Mary Orley, dau. of Thomas and Anne, was Baptized in the parish "churge" of St. Mary White Chappell, 25 Apr 1622. John Johnson, D.D., White Chappell, Rector. Nthld, Va. Vol. 1658-1666. fo. 144, 145. 22 Sept 1664.

HENRY HURD; Arthur Spicer pet'ns to have the trust of Henry Hurd's estate, so that he may returne the effects to the relacons in England. Wmld, Va. 29 Feby 1687. Vol. 1676-1688, p. 632.

HENRY ISHAM, son of Katherine, had some estate in England. Had also pltn in Charles City cty, called Doggans. Hen., Va. 1678. 1-72. See also 1-78. 31 Dcc. 1678. Henry Isham, of London, Mcht, only son and extr of Henry Isham of Virginia, Gent.

JOHN JOHNSON, of Kingsale, in the Kingdom of Ireland, mariner; power to James Claughton. Wmld, Va. 1668-1677, fo. 109. 27 Apr 1670

DAVID JAMESON, Jr., and wife Sarah, of Caroline cty, Va., to Reuben Garnett of Essex cty; consideration $1000; convey 1480 acres in Franklin cty, on Chesnut and Town Creek waters. Wit: John x Gatewood. Carter Wood, Lewis x Tarrant. Frank. cty, Va. 4 Oct 1799. iii-717.

SAMUEL JAQUESS, of Rayway, Middx cty, N. J., blacksmith; power to Obediah Wells, of Eliza-beth Town, Essex cty, N. J. Som., Md. 5 Jany 1739. xx-143.

WILLIAM "JAMERSON" and Floreana "Jamison," his wife, being seized in fee of part of a lot in the town of Charlestown in the State of Maryland, containing one acre; also a parcel of land in sd State county of "cesiel," where Joseph Thompson formerly lived; and Whereas the sd Thompson died intest., the sd lot and other parcel of land descended to Jean Arskins and the sd Floreana Jamison, daus, of the sd. Joseph Thompson as coheiresses of their sd father; therefore, Jamison and wife give power to Henry Arsken of Maryland, to lease and demise the sd. land. Wit: Edwards Randolph. Henry cty, Va. ii-275. 27 Nov 1782.

THOMAS JEFFRESS, one of the "legal Legatees" of Nathaniel Jeffress, Jr., dec'd, of Abbeville cty. S. C., promises to pay to Samuel Thompson of Franklin cty, Va. . . . £24. (This record begins: "To the Commissioners that may be appointed to divide or lot out different parts of the legatees of Nathaniel Jeffress dec'd of Buckingham county. . . . ") Frank cty, Va. 8 Mch 1810. vii-72.

JAMES KELLY, Mcht, of Eden Town, N. C., to Robert Jenckins Henry, of Somerset, Gent. For £30 conveys parcel of land now called Eden Town being part of a tract called Landing, being on the southermost side of Pocomoke river. Som., Md. 9 July 1741. xx-239.

HANNAH x Lee, admx of Hugh. late of St. Marie's dec'd. Power to James Claughton. Nthld, Va. 1 Jany 1661. 1658-1666, fo. 91.

JACQUES LEGRAND, late of La Haye in Holland. Hen., Va. 1716.

Col. RICH. LEE, Esq., late of Stratford Laughthon, in cty. Essex, England. Wmld, Orders. 1668-1677. Died before 23 June 1673.

MUNGO MUSCHET, of Charles county, had a bro. John Muschet in Virginia. Annap. Wills. 13 Nov 1768. xxxvi-684.

HAIL MAXEY, of Oglethorpe cty, Ga. Power to James L. Hail, of Franklin cty, Va., to demand, &c., &c., for a certain tract on the big branch of Black Water. Fran. cty, Va. 10 Jany 1825. vii-243.

CHARLES MORGAN, Citty of Bristoll, mariner; atty for Edward Feilding. Rappa., Va. 28 Feby 1678. 1677-1682, p. 204. Mr. Edward Feilding of Bristol [Eng]., Soap Boyler, was admr of Mr. Ambrose Feilding, late of Rappa., Mcht. See p. 25, same vol.

JOHN MADDISON, Sr., Psh St. Stephen's New Kent, Va., from John Pigg, all interest in 280 acres in Rappa. cty. The land was formerly Madison's but his right was allowed to lapse, and afterwards patented to Edward Hudson who deserted it. Rappa., Va. 1677-1682, p. 228. 10 June 1673.

JOHN McCAMEY (wf Margaret also signs); mentions in his will his plntn in Sugar Creek Settlement, N. C., which he leaves to his dau. Margaret Alexander. Cumb., Penna. 1765. A-143.

RICHARD MOORE, mariner, of Salem in New England, gdn of William Henfield of same place, son and heir of Capt. Robert Henfield, dec'd; power to Col. Nikolas Spencer. Wmld, Va. 23 Nov 1668. 1668-1677, fo. 39.

HENRY NELSON, county of Washington and Territory of the United States south of Ohio, conveys land in Shenandoah county, corner to William Nelson. Shenan., Va. i-529. 8 Sept 1794.

JOHN PATTON, Mcht. now residing in the Province of Maryland, by virtue of a letter of attorney from Mr. William Bushie of Barbadoes, received of Mr. John Dinely, 1000 lbs tobacco. Wmld, Va. Vol. 1668-1677, p. 48. 7 Apr 1669.

SERVICE AND SUPPLIES COLONIAL, REVOLUTIONARY AND MILITIA

Note: The reference "J. H. B. Va." is to the published journals of the Virginia House of Burgesses. The names have, no doubt, been listed in the Virginia State Bulletins. The additional detail given here may be found helpful.

JAMES BRADLEY, private; served 15 days. Claim favorably reported. J. H. B. Va. 26 June 1777.

FRANCIS BERRY; soldier in Capt. JOHN FLOYD'S company on the Shawanese expedition. Served 105 days. J. H. B. Va. 26 June 1777.

JOHN BROWN; soldier in the "Minute Service" of Virginia; to be reimbursed for expenses of physician and medicines. J. H. B. Va. 26 May 1777.

WILLIAM BRISTOW petitions; was private in Capt. Nicholas' company in 1775. J. H. B. Va. 6 Nov. 1777.

JAMES BEETS; soldier; served 93 days, claim favorably recommended. J. H. B. Va. 26 June 1777.

GEORGE COON; soldier; served 93 days. Claim favorably recommended. J. H. B. Va. 26 June 1777.

ROBERT CAMPBELL petitions; enlisted in Capt. Thompson's company against Indians, year 1774, and was accidentally wounded. J. H. B. Va. 3 Nov. 1777.

JACOB COGAR; petitions; was out under Capt. Dan'l Smith in the expedition against the Indians. Had rec'd no pay. J. H. B. Va. 8 Nov 1777.

ALEXANDER CAMERON, of Mifflin cty, Penna. Declaration for pension. Service began Sept 1777, under Capt. Wm. Wilson. [Probably Cumberland cty.] Draper Mss. 6ZZ-15.

BENJAMIN CLEMENTS; served as private in Capt. Wm. Temple's company, 1st Va. War bet. Great Britain and France. Ordered certified. Charl. Va. Orders iv-209. Ct Feby 1780.

THOMAS COOPER; David Lanier is appointed to furnish Elizabeth Cooper, wife of Thomas, who is in the Continental service, with £40 worth of provisions. Henry cty, Va. Ct 27 May 1779.

JOHN CRANE; soldier; served 59 days. Claim favorably reported. J. H. B. Va. 26 June 1777.

LEWIS CRANE; soldier. Same. J. H. B. Va. 26 June 1777.

ONSBY CARNEY; soldier; served 59 days in Revolution. Claim favorably reported. J. H. B. Va. 26 June 1777.

JOHN DOSS was a soldier in the Continental service; had wife Judith and one child. Cumb. cty, Va. 24 Nov 1777.

BENJAMIN DRAKE; soldier; served 93 days. Claim favorably reported. J. H. B. Va. 26 June 1777.

DAVID DALTON; wounded soldier; Capt. Nicholas Lewis' company of minute men. Expense of doctor to be reimbursed. J. H. B. Va. 26 June 1777.

NICHOLAS EDWARDS; soldier; served 93 days. Claim favorably reported. J. H. B. Va. 26 June 1777.

THOMAS FOWLER; soldier; served 93 days. Claim favorably reported. J. H. B. Va. 26 June 1777.

HAMNER FEAR; accidentally wounded in the Continental service, is allowed £20 for his personal relief. J. H. B. Va. 26 May 1777.

LEWIS x FRANKLIN of Henry cty, Va. Testifies to his service in 1780. Draper Mss. x-NN.

JAMES GRIFFIN; further allowance of 11 days' pay as private in Capt. Moffett's company. J. H. B. Va. 26 June 1777.

PUBLICATIONS

The Editor has received from Mr. J. Adger Stewart, 4780, Crittenden Drive, Louisville, an interesting and somewhat unusual pamphlet. It is entitled the STEWARTS OF BALLINTOY, with Notices of Other Families . . . in the Seventeenth Century, and was compiled in 1865 by the Rev. George Hill. It was published, however, many years later in the *Ulster Journal of Archeology*, and then revised by the author who was still living,.

The Editor has a fancy for quotations, especially good ones, and so copies here two lines which head the compilation, taken from Bacon's Advancement of Learning. "Out of monuments, traditions, private recordes, fragments of stories, passages of bookes, and the like, we doe save and recovere somewhat from the deluge of time." [This would be more beautifully impressive if one had never adventured the "private recordes, fragments of stories," of certain genealogies.]

But Mr. Stewart has recovered for us by means of this pamphlet, "somewhat from the deluge of time," and it is very readable and valuable. There is much history and genealogy in it and copies of important records, also copies of gravestone inscriptions. An early stone bears this: "*Under this stone Bernardo Stewart doth ly who pangfull Death overcame victoriously. 1663.*"

Some years ago Mr. Stewart published a Stewart chart, which the Editor regrets not having heretofore mentioned.

The following important publications may be had from Mr. Charles Shepard II, whose address will be found on p. 28. Mr. Shepard's excellent work is well-known.

Index to the wills, administrations, and guardianships of Kings county, New York, 1650 to 1850, by Milton H. Thomas. 1926. Bound in buckram, gilt lettering. Limited edition of 100 numbered copies, of which many are already disposed of. Price $10.00.

Membership and vital records of the Second Congregational Church of Attleboro, Mass., by M. W. P. Carter. 1924. Includes baptisms, marriages, deaths, and church membership rolls. Bound in cloth. Price $4.85.

Some Rensselaer County (New York) Gravestone Inscriptions, by Shepard and Thomas. 1923. Contains about 500 tombstone records, heretofore unpublished. Bound in cloth. Price on application.

Reasonable price or two years' subscription will be given for numbers 1, 2, 3, 4, 6, and 7, COUNTY COURT NOTE-BOOK, 1921-1922. Address Editor.

Fifty cents will be paid for a copy of February 1927.

Printed at the Industrial School for Crippled and Deformed Children, 241 St. Botolph St., Boston, Mass.

The

County Court Note-Book

A Little Bulletin of History and Genealogy

August, 1928. Vol. VII, No. 4.

SHIPS IN PORT

Ship *Avarelia* [*Avarilla, Aurelia?*] See will of Maximilian Robinson. 28 Oct 1694. Va. Mags. xxii-22.

The Shipp *Ann Cleare*; Capt. Zacharias Browne, Commdr. Lt. Col. Edmund Scarburgh complains that his cloathing was sold during his illness by a servant to the Boatswayne and other seamen. 28 Aug 1654. N-n, Va. iv-22.

The *Amity*; Peter Nowell, "Maister." 15 Dec 1663. L. Norf, Va. D-392.

Good Ship *Amity*, of New Castill in England; Jirimiah Sympson, mariner and part Owner. 18 June 1683. Wmld cty, Va.

The Pink called the *Amitie*, now or lately Riding in Potomack River; John Foxall of Poe's Creek, Mcht, owner . . . "or one of the owners;" Jonathan Parker Entertained, Imployed and Shipped as Master from 12 Jany 1683-4 to 5 Mch 1684-5. Essex, Va. Orders, p. 205.

Ship *Arundel*; Capt. Wm. Mainwaring. 15 Apr 1762. Va. St. Pa. i-258.

The *Ann and Mary*; Richard Tibbott, Commdr. 1694. I. W. cty, Va. ii-339.

Sloop *Arcadia*; Thos. Derrick, master; David Derrick of Marcus Hook, owner. Built at Marcus Hook, 1756. Penna. Mags. Ship Registers.

Ship *Brittania*; Capt. Robeson gets letters of marque. Pa. Arch. 2d Series. i-541.

Ship called *The Brothers*, now riding at anchor in Wickacomoco river, taketh freight tobacco on Board, consigned to Mr. Neal Buckhannon, Merchant in London. Ctf of William Camplin [?] Master. 21 June 1739. Som. cty, Md. xx-71.

Sloop *Betsey*; one half "as she came from Sea", devised by will of Joseph Wade. 25 May 1786. Philada. Inventories.

The Betty Galley; had 16 guns and 30 men. (Capt. Brookes?) 1708. Va. St. Pa. i-126.

The *Blessing*, a barque. 1654. N-n cty, Va. v-127.

Ship *Blessing*; Quakers met on board of her; James Gilbert, master. (See case in Court.) 1663. L. Norf, Va. D-392.

Brigantine *Bon Adventure*; Brinoldus de Haes, Master. 8 Mch 1708. Va. St. Pa. i-128.

The Brothers Adventure, of London; Jenifer Plover, Commdr, gives power to Allex. Fleming, of Rappa., Gent. 2 Feby 1662. Rappa. cty, Va. 1656-1664, p. 406. Plover was of Lower Shadwell, psh Stepney, Middx cty, England. See p. 203, vol. 1662-1668. 20 June 1665.

Ship *Barbadoes Merchant*, of Bristol; Nathaniel Hallett, Master. 17 Mch 1674. Acco. cty, Va. v-255.

Sloop *Benjamin*; John Lewis commander. 5 Jany 1721. N-n cty, Va. Chancy records.

Sloop *Comfort and Mary*; mentioned in the will of Solomon Davis. 30 Aug 1734. Acco. cty, Va. xx-180.

Shipp *Daniel*; Jno; Lacock, Master. 18 Sept 1666. Acco. cty, Va. 1-123.

Sloop *Dolphin*; one-half "as she came from Sea" devised by will of Joseph Wade. 25 May 1786. Philada. Inventories.

The Shipp *Endeavour*; of Weymouth in England. Richard White, Master. The Master's Merchant was Mr. Phillip Lynes. 4 Feby 1684. Wmld cty, Va. 1676-1688, p. 374.

Sloop *Comfort and Mary*; belonged to [Col.] Solomon Ewell, see his will. 1734. Acco. cty, Va. xx-181.

Ship *Catherine*; John Crussey [?] Captain. He d. 2 June 1691. York-Hampton Psh Reg. Va.

Ship *Crown Ffrigot* Cornelius Serjeant & Co., of Bristol, Mchts, owners. 7 June 1723. K. Geo. cty, Va. i-120.

Ship *Curryoman* [*Corioman*] was included in the inv. of John Chilton. 22 Feby 1726. Wmld cty, Va. Fid. Accts. i-47.

Ship *Caesar*, of London; William Loney, Commander. Bartholomew Harnett, a native of Ireland came in this ship as a svt, the 20 Feby 1733. He was an "under clerk or writer." 27 Aug 1745. Wmld, Va.

AUTHENTIC REFERENCES FOR INFERRED MARRIAGES

(*The following marriages are from Maryland records. See note on page 32.*)

WILLIAM ADAIR and ELISABETH GRAHAM, 17 June 1779. Wash'n cty. Md. Marriages.

...... ADKINS and ELESEBETH HIGHWAY. Before 29 Mch 1717. Wor. cty. M. H. iii-138.

STEPHEN ADAMS and ANDASIA HUDSON, dau. of Dennis. Before 18 Feby 1813. Wor. cty. A. D.-77.

JOSHUA ATKINSON and ELIZABETH SCOTT, dau. of William. Before 1746. Som cty. xix-172.

FOUNTAIN BEAUCHAMP and RHODA ADDAMS, dau. of Phillip. See Som. cty, 1747-8. xxi-292.

JOHN BOWEN and ELIZABETH, admx of Wm. Merrell. Before 6 Dec 1712. Wor cty. J. W. xv-330.

GEORGE BLIZARD and SARAH IDOLET, dau. of Benjamin, Sr. Wor. cty. Before 16 June 1703. M. H. iii-54.

JOHN BLIZARD and MARY IDOLEL, dau. of Benjamin, Sr. Wor. cty. Before 16 June 1703. M. H. iii-61.

WILLIAM BEVANS and MARY LANE, dau. of Walter. Before 20 Dec. 1715. Wor. cty. M. H. iii-132.

.... BOWEN and MARY HAMMON, dau. of Edward. Before 17 July 1718. Wor. cty. M. H. iii-145.

BARNETT BAXTER and RUTH HAILE. 18 Sept. 1783. Balto. cty. Md. Marriages.

HENRY COSTON and ANN RIGGEN, dau. of Teague Riggen. 6 Jany 1807. Som. Md. R-111.

JOHN COTTINGHAM and MARY CONNER, dau. of Philip, Sr. Before 21 Feby 1702. Wor. cty. M. H. iii-49.

JOHN CHRISTOPHER and ANNE DAVIS. Before 23 May 1793. Wor. cty. P-13.

DEVORIX DREGORS and SARAH BISHOP, widow of Henry. Before 22 Mch 1707. Wor. cty. J. W. xv-307.

.... DUNNAHOW and ARCADIA TURVILL. Before 27 Feby 1691. Wor. cty. M. H. iii-36.

THOMAS DASHIELL and ANN PORTER, admx. of William. Before 18 May 1803. Som. cty. E. B. xxiv-226. [Was she also widow of Elijah Johnson?]

EZEKIEL EVANS and ELEANOR WRIGHT. extx of John. Before 8 Apr 1783. Fred'k cty. O. C. Docket.

NICHOLAS EVANS and SUSANNA WALKER. Long before 31 Jany 1751. Som. cty. xxii-157.

.... FRANKLIN and BRIDGET WALE, dau. of Edward. Before 21 Apr 1718. Wor. cty. M. H. iii-143.

Col. GERRARD FOWKE or FOUKE and the widow of Mr. JOB CHANDLER of Wmld cty, Va., Gent. About Feby 1661. Chas. cty, i-216.

WILLIAW FREEMAN and ELIZABETH WEST, extx of Thomas. Before 28 Sept 1709. Wor. cty, J. W. xv-53.

DAVID GOGEN[?] prob. m. SARAH BROTON, dau. of John. Before 14 Sept 1720. Wor. cty. M. H. iii-159.

JOHN GERMAN and ANNE BISHOP, only dau. of Henry Bishop, Jr., and wife Sarah. Before 23 June 1713. Som. cty, x-890.

EDMOND HOUGH and HANNAH WHITTINGTON. Before 3 Oct 1752. See Wor. cty. B-509. [This marriage occurred long before the date given as reference.]

JOHN JARMIN and ANN BISHOP, dau. of Henry, Jr. Before 7 Aug 1726. Som. cty. xvi-39. [This is the same marriage as that above under GERMAN.]

WILLIAM HANDY and MARY WHITTINGTON, extx of William. Before 24 Feby 1781. Wor. Md. Inv. 1762–1783, p. 359.

WILLIAM HOLLAND and MARGRET admx of Henry SCHOOLFIELD. Before 1 July 1718. Wor. cty. J. W. xv.

NEHEMIAH HOLLAND prob. m. the dau. of Benjamin IDOLET, Sr. Before 16 June 1703. Wor. cty. M. H. iii-54.

EPHRAIM HEATHER m. "Wm", admx of Daniel SELBY. Before 18 Aug 1708. Wor. cty, J. W. xv-236. This appears again as " Mr. EPH'M HEATHER and ANN SELBY, relict of Daniel, and is probably correct. p. 236 of same vol.

.... ISRAEL and PRISCILLA WILLIAMS, sister of Otho-Holland WILLIAMS. Before 5 June 1794. Fred'k cty, G. M. iii-38.

DAVID FITZPATRICK and JANE GIVANS. Before 9 Apr 1753. Som. cty, xxii-272.

WILLIAM KENNETT, Sr. and MARGRATT TOWERS, dau. of Jonathan and Margarett. Before 12 Oct 1719. Wor. cty, M. H. iii-163.

.... KELLAM and TABITHA TRUETT, dau. of James, Sr. Before 28 Mch 1715. M. H. iii-142.

VIRGINIA COLONISTS

(*From "Old Volume 5, S. L. O., Richmond.*)

THOMAS BELL, New Kent, 1662.
Head rights: Rebecca Newell, Fra: Drinkwater, Wm. Maior, Mary Bennett, Charles Nicholls, Jno. Tegnall, Mary Neckolls, Mary Browning, Robt Horsington, Edward Thompson, Wm. Ines or Ives, Isabell Taylor.

RICHARD BROWNE, Westmoreland, 1661.
Head rights: Mary Phillips, Susan Jones.

THOMAS BELL, New Kent, 1662.
Head rights: THO. BELL, twice; ANDREW BELL, SUSAN BELL, Mary Jones. George Austin, Jno. Williams, Wm. Pope, Thomas Stephens, Wm. Lewis, Wm. Caps, Roger Sheely, Jno. Mathews, Rich. Joy, eight negroes.

ALPHONSO BALL, Northampton cty, 1658.
Head rights: Ellinor Collins, Ann Cooke, Wm. Scott, Samuel Younge, Rich. Nottingham, Eliz. Nottingham, Step: Yeo.

Capt. JOHN BLAKE, county not give, 1658.
Head rights: Francisco, a negro; Francis Deplaie [?] Jno. Carpenter.

SILVESTER BAKER, 1658. County not given.
Head rights: James Mote, Alexander Jemmisson [?] Bryan Farrell, Margaret Farrell, Wm. Lowder.

THOMAS BRERETON, county not given, 1658.
Head rights: Mary Broder, John Multis, James Felton, George, a Scotchman; Francis ...., Symon Richardson, Jno Slattor, Jno Fornor [?] John Gibbine, and a mollettoe. [It is uncertain whether one of these, Symon Richardson, is the mulatto, or not.]

THO: CHETWOOD, Lancaster cty, 1662.
Head rights: Tho: Reynolds, Hen: Reynolds, Henry Parker, Jno. Aires, Joseph Baker.

JOHN COX, Lancaster cty, 1653, 1652.
Head rights: Judeth Holman, Eliz: Rensom [?]

VINCENT COX, Northumberland cty, 1661.
Head rights: William Jones, Thomas Cooper, Mary Coop[er], Wm. Peterson, Peter Stewart, Wm. Stephens, Wm. Stone.

RICHARD COLE, Northumberland, 1661.
Head rights: Jno. Edwards, Jno. Williams, Susan Edwards, Edwd James, Peter Story, Hanah Dew.

Mr. RICHARD DUDLEY, "Glocester" cty, 1659.
Head rights: John Everilla, Tho. Kinge, John Bolton, John Cooper, Tho. Reyland, Edward Smith.

RICHARD DAVIS, New Kent cty, 1660.
Head rights: Tho. Johnson, MARY DAVIS, Wm. Rider, James Jones, Rich. Smith, Jenkin Jones, Wm. Hickes, Roger Marley, Ed. Tressum, Wm. Jones, Tho. Rosser, Ed. Tyler.

THOMAS DORROW, Northumberland cty, 1661.
Head right: James Henryfold.

RICHARD DAVIS, Lancaster cty, 1662.
Head rights : Tho: Joyner, Wm. Ward, Mary Farmer, Tho: Cartwright, Wm. Gulin [? perhaps Gul'm.] Tho: Wood, Jane Sherly, Kath: Woold, James Coffer.

Mr. WM. DRUMMOND, James City cty, 1662.
Head rights: John Jarvy, Peter Gillard, Eliazur ....

THOMAS DYER, county not given, 1662.
Head rights: Ann Loveing, Andrew Jones, Wm. Holmes, Peter Sutor, Mary Nitter, Tho. Mines.

WILL DRUMMOND, Gent., Westmoreland cty, 1661.
Head rights: Sam'll Howard, Jno. Thomson, Wm. Cooke, Eliz: Smith, Jno. Warren, Fran James, Rich'd Harma, Jno. Cotton, An Dunbar, Wm. Worden, Mary Rawlins, Geo. Howkett [?] Sam'll Harford, Robt Floring, Jno. Greene,
Tho. Wood, Rich. Parker, Fran. Willis, Henry Mills, Alice Porter, Mary Hunt, Daniel Williams, Dennis Thorpe [Sharpe ?] James Adkins, Jno. Poore. James Man, Erasmus Perry, Mary Smith, Wm. Cooke, Laurence Hooker, Sam'l Welch;
Dennis Watkins, Dan'll Dickins, Michaell Wadloe, Nich. Spruce, Mary Spruce, Henrick Vandulett, Robt Surlin [?] Elinor Woodbridge, James Bruce, Henry Sanders, Silvert [?] Thacker, Dorothy Thacker, Jno. Deane, Wm. Hope,
Francis Jones, Jno. Woılock, Nath. Spensor, Rich. Spicor [?] Mathew Harris, Wm. Thomson, Jane Salter, Mary Wood, Daniell Parker, Walter Williams, Gartred Sparker [?] Francis Spie, Martin Woodliffe, Robt. Savin, Rich. Palmer.
Sam'l Prince, Nich. Wells, Wm. Johnson, Isaac Rose, Patrick Wicks, Jno. Hobbs, Mary Hart, Sam'll Davis, Tho. Postman [?] Nich. Smart, Dan'll Wills, Rich. Fosset, Jno. Roah [?] Jane Wallis, Tim Salter, Robt Datsill;
Phil Woodford, Wm. Garrett; Tho. Johnson, Ralph Mathew, Henry Betts, Mary Bateman, Robt Serly, Davy Darling, Roger Armor, Jno. Hugh, Tho. Kerton, eight negroes.

CHARLES EDMONDS, "New York," 1658.
Head rights; Adam Walker, Peter Mackereel, Margeret Ibsam (assigned by John Davis.)

CHARLES EDMONDS, New Kent, 1658.
Head rights: Tho Holliday, Robert Watts, Fran. Faulkner, Rich Joy, Mary Wilson, Willy Volly [?] Howell [this looks as much like Hilly Vally], Eliz: Rohoke [?] Wm. Walker, Jno, Leeper, John Parke, Jude Bryatt, Joseph Peate. Thomas Tilsby, Tho. Parton,

Jude Rollett, Eliz. Panton, Peter Gill, Wm. Richards, Cone Cowe [?] Mary Batchelor, Tho. Townell, R......... Norman, Jno Smith, Abigail Willes, Fran. Warren, Jones Howes, Geo. Wood, Mary Gill, Ann Parker. Tho. Tuffes [?]
George Carter, Mary Coulter, Frances Grigges, and 4 negroes ; Henry Bennett, Isaack Franklin, Tho. Blacke. Edward Terrell, Eliz: Peake. Phillip Gill, Jno. Jennings, Jno. Blossee, Richard Bayley, Rich. Terrell, Jno Williams, Jane Bradman, Mary Sue [?]

WALTER ENGLISH, Northumberland cty, 1661.
Head rights: MARY ENGLISH, Peter Mills, Andrew Stone, Stephen Norman, JNO. ENGLISH, Tho. White, Roger Norton, and a negro.

RALPH ELKINS, York cty, 1661.
Head right: Peter Nicholls.

HENRY FORREST, Gloucester cty, 1658.
Head rights: Alexander Hall, John Cavelery, HENRY FORREST and his wife; Richard Bachelor, EDWARD FORREST, John Bachelor, Rice Aldock, ELIZABETH FORREST.

Maj. JAMES GOODWIN, county not given, 1658.
Head rights: JAMES GOODWIN, four times; Jno. Waler, Henry Molson, Nath. Smith, Eliz-May, Eliz: Blackburne, Henry Edge, Henry Baxter, Eliz: Adams; a negro.

RICE JONES and ANTHONY JACKMAN, Rappahannock cty, 1658.
Head rights: Edward Howgrave, John Anderton, James Payne, Christian Gorein, James Fossett, Tho. Bowman, Pressilla Halloway, Alice Kinge, Mary Floyd, Mary ...., Eliz: Farme, Edward Allen, Tho. Gill, Robert Doore, John Cox, Fran: Overton, Susanna Nurse, Wm. Mathewes, Fran. Morgans, D......... Williams, Adam Higgison.

The County Court Note-Book

An every-other-monthly devoted mainly to abstracts from County Court Records, prior to 1800.

MILNOR LJUNGSTEDT, Editor and Publisher.
Bethesda, Route 10, Maryland.

Published six times a year. Subscription, two dollars, in advance; must begin with the year.

August, 1928 **Whole**
Vol. VII., No. 4 **No. 41**

QUEEN VICTORIA'S DESCENT FROM ADAM

The Editor, with an aspiring thermometer running from eighties to nineties, feels decidedly lazy and inclined to take what comes handy. However, perhaps she has earned a respite (kind subscribers please notice that she is a "Missus") as two NOTE-BOOKS are almost in the press. Be that as it may, anyhow and whatever, here is the Queen's Royal Descent from King David the Psalmist, prepared by the Rev. A. B. Grimaldi, M. A., years ago... the Editor doesn't know when. The Rev, Mr. Grimaldi writes that he ("WE") issues this Leaflet to supply a necessary link in proving the Identity of the British Nation with the Lost Ten Tribes of Israel. Now the Editor hesitates at this. She is an Anglo-maniac and always was, having reached the mature age of fifteen on Dickens's Child's History of England, Scott, and Abbott's Life of Napoleon. Also Porte Crayon's Sketches of Virginia, though that had nothing to do with the case. And to claim that the English are of Hebrew descent will please the ultra-American particularly for he will forget all about his own ancestry. But the Editor admits to a certain fascination in this claim to the Lost Tribes; she is sure that somebody says they got to Wales and Ireland, and she believes it.

Rev. Mr. Grimaldi says that, in "England, the Remnant of Judah" (London, 1861, Rev. F. R. A. Glover, M. A.), this descent of the late revered Majesty was first entered upon, but he gives a number of references for his work, which begins, very naturally with ADAM. And EVE. And he places them B. C. 4000 to 3070. The Editor rather thought they lived longer. Perhaps they had enough of it.

For this first section it is only necessary to say that he continues with SETH, "B. C. 3070," through thirty-one generations to JESSE (no date). The thirty-second generation is that of King DAVID (B. C. 1085–1015), and BATHSHEBA, to King ZEDEKIAH of the forty-ninth generation (B. C. 578–599).

Although the compiler says, himself, that perfect accuracy is hardly to be expected, the fiftieth generation is a stumbling-block to the Editor, for it begins with the Kings of Ireland, the first on this list being King HEREMON (flourished B. C. 580) and his Queen TEA TEPHI, *daughter of Zedekiah.* In the Editor's ignorance comment on this wandering Princess would be out of place. But how did she get to Ireland? The next fifty-two kings the Editor skips, the type-writer lacks Gaelic experience. It is true they are not quite so difficult as the names of the Welsh ladies who are responsible for the Editor but a sample will suffice: the ninety-ninth king was "Eochaidh Moigmeodhin"... he reigned only seven years . . . perhaps he got tired of signing his name.

Then come the Kings of Argyleshire; as they begin in A. D. 487, they seem rather reasonable, though a note made by the Editor some years ago says that Feargus More, the first of the line and the 104th from ADAM, was "supposed to be the son of Earca, the last of the Irish list, or of the same line." Supposed to be does not carry weight. Down through Argyleshire and Scotland proper we come through familiar names to Queen MARY and Lord HENRY DARNLEY, and so to JAMES VI, and ANN of Denmark; Princess ELIZABETH and FREDERICK of Bohemia; Princess SOPHIA and EARNEST of Brunswick; GEORGES I and II; Prince FREDERICK of Wales; GEORGE III, and the Duke of Kent to Queen VICTORIA herself.

It was a mistake to mention GEORGE III; our finest societies are still at war with him.

It will not do to dismiss this without noticing a statement in the preamble. Mr. Grimaldi says: "The descent of our Royal Family from the royal line of Judah is . . . no new discovery. The Saxon kings traced themselves back to Odin, who was traced back to his descent from David, as may be seen in a very ancient Mss. in the Herald's College . . ." The Editor is well acquainted with a descendant of the Vikings (who were no better than pirates, he says) and she must ask him what he thinks about this mix-up of Odin and David.

* * *

Attention is invited to the somewhat depressing statements on page 35 that these unfortunate immigrants, listed on that page, had never been members of *any order of Nobility.* The Editor must look up the Statute current at the time and see what would have happened to an immigrant who was of the nobility. It is quite a blow to admit that there were immigrants who were not younger sons, but just plain, ordinary folk. *Perhaps* they were not telling the truth!

The list of decedents, orphans, &c., from Hyde county, North Carolina, is made, as were the wills in the APRIL NOTE-BOOK, from the reverse of what was very evidently the first record of the Orphans' Court, the reverse of an old, parchment covered volume which had been overlooked for years. It was very difficult to read, paging either lacking or uncertain; courts ditto and this is the excuse for the rather unsatisfactory form of the notes.

A note of explanation as to the MARYLAND MARRIAGES in this issue is desirable. While the late Mrs. Geo. W. Hodges was alive, the Editor refrained from publishing any but very incidental Maryland marriages, as Mrs. Hodges was collecting these in large quantity, mainly from the records in Annapolis, and the State from time to time was acquiring these lists. Since Mrs. Hodges' death the Editor is constrained to believe that her own collection, made from records not always easily accessible to Mrs. Hodges, will be valuable to her readers. In some cases these notes may add a verification to the others; some times they may differ.

The list of BEHETHLANDS (Colonial Fore-Names) in this NOTE-BOOK is made in the main, as is shown, from the Parish Register of St. Paul's, King George's county, Virginia. This register was copied by some one some years ago, and the copy is in the Virginia State Archives. It was then photostated. This list is made from both, and both were of an equal difficulty to read. The Editor would like to say "Errors excepted." The Editor never did know just what this phrase at the end of an estate account means . . . whether the estate, or the executor or administrator was to be given credit.

Will every one who is interested please write the nearest big library and ask when the library will have a copy of the "Servants to America?" found in Bristol, England.

OCCASIONAL

ANCESTRAL RECORDS?

WILLIAM ROBISON, of age, the Court find *"by probable proofs."* Wmld, Va. 11 Jany 1687. To those who have used Virginia genealogies "as is," there is something familiar about this.

Capt. GEO. WATKINS was buried in the Chancel of Lawnes Creek Parish Church. Surry, Va. Court 3 Sept 1675. Oi-109.

HENRY CLAY, son of HENRY CLAY, v. HENRY CLAY, an Infant, son of CHARLES CLAY, and the said CHARLES CLAY. Cumb., Va. Chancery suit. 23 June 1761.

Upon the oath of Mr. Darril that THO: HILL gave his estate by will to Fra. Grey, his wife and children, probate of the said estate is granted, the former will "being cassually lost." Wmld, Va. 1676-1688. 28 Aug. 1678.

"THE DIGNITY OF DEBTS." "Upon the " motion of Mr. Jno. Mickell, Senior, that the " Court would give their opinion concerning the " dignity of debts due from the estate of Mr. Jno. " Culpeper, dec'd, the Court accordingly gives " their judgment — next to the Honorable Gov- " ern'r — Funerall Charges to have Priority then " Publique dets & then judgments in his life- " time, then sealed Bonds, then Bills, then Noates " & accts signed under his hand." Acco., Va. 17 Oct 1665. v. 330.

CHRIST'R DE GRAFFENREID [a foreign Protestant], delivered a certificate of his Taken the Sacriment of the Lord's Supper according to the directions of sd Acts and made due proof, &c. &c . . . . & subscribed the Oaths . . . . & the Declaration, &c. [Is naturalized.] Annap. Md. records. 3 Oct. 1720. P. L. v-123.

ZACAHARY TAYLOR'S ctf for 200 acres for serving in the last war. Desirous to locate in Fincastle. Signed by Dunmore. Draper Mss. QQ-7. 12 Feby 1774.

MARGERT X BRENT, age about twenty, sayeth that she heard Mr. Parkes say to her master, William Marshal: "Shall I make a bill for the cattel?" Her master Replied "Noe" . . . . About 12 May 1659. Charles cty, Md. Records, vol. i.

A MATTER OF IMPORTANCE

The Editor of the NOTE-BOOK will pay ten dollars ($10) for a copy of the WILL of WILLIAM FLOYD, or a copy (in full) of the administration of his estate.

WILLIAM FLOYD was living in 1783; had wife ABADIAH, and probably living sons ROBERT CHARLES and NATHANIEL. He was also the father of Col. JOHN FLOYD. WILLIAM FLOYD may have died in one of the frontier counties of Virginia, in Kentucky, or in one of the Territories northwest of the Ohio. He was about 56 years old in 1783 and owned land in the upper Valley of Virginia. He had removed to the frontier but was driven back by the uprising among the Indians. Where he then settled is unknown.

A little while ago the Editor received from Mr. Herbert C. FOOKS, of Baltimore, the author of Forms of Wills, Prisoners of War, and other valuable publications, a pamphlet entitled the FOWKE (FOOKS) FAMILY. It contains 47 pages, eight of which are devoted to the English family and the rest to the descendants of JAMES FOWKE, of ACCOMACK county, Virginia. The publication shows much painstaking work in the way of research and gives an unusual number of full copies of wills and conveyances touching the family. Too much commendation cannot be given to every bit of sincere work of this kind. What is needed now is a sort of clearing-house where cousins by publication can get together and study their likes and their differences.

CONTINUED articles COUNTY COURT NOTE-BOOK, and the dates on which they first appeared.

THE ANCESTRY OF COL. JOHN DONELSON. Began with February, 1927.

AUTHENTIC REFERENCES for INFERRED MARRIAGES (formerly called MARRIAGES BY INFERENCE). Began with May, 1922.

MARYLAND'S NEXT OF KIN. Began with July, 1922.

VIRGINIA COLONISTS. Alphabetized lists began with July, 1924.

MILITARY NOTES, both COLONIAL and REVOLUTIONARY, and later MILITIA NOTES. Began December, 1923.

INTERCOUNTY and INTERCOLONY (formerly called New Englanders and Others, &c., &c.). Began with March, 1922.

EASTERN SHORE FAMILIES. In the form of a one-page supplement, began with June, 1925. This will be continued later.

SHIPS IN PORT and COLONIAL FORENAMES will appear in alternate issues or as space can be found for them.

FORE-NAMES OF COLONIAL USAGE

ROBERT BEHEATHLAND, one of the signers of a petition for the appointment of a nobleman as Governor. 1621. Virginia Vetusta, p. 118.

Behethland Beach and James Scribner. Married. 7 Nov 1773. St. Paul's Psh Reg. K. Geo. cty, Va.

BEHETHLAND BENNET and Hezekiah Thirk [?] [Note, this is from a copy of the Register.] Married 10 Feby 1778. St. Paul's Psh Reg., K. Geo. cty, Va.

BEHETHLEM BENNET, dau. James and Elizabeth. B. 15 Feby 1746. Same refs.

BEHETHLAN BERRYMAN, dau. of Giles and Hannah. B. 23 Mch 1743. Same refs.

BEHETHLEM BERRYMAN m. Thomas Booth. 10 Oct 1727. Same refs.

BEHETHLAND BOOTH, died 9 Oct 1727. [This date is evidently wrongly copied by the copyist of the Register or the Editor.] Same refs.

BEHETHLEM BOWLING, m. John Dey. 23 Feby 1748. Same refs.

BEHETHLAND BUNBURY, wife of Thomas. 1755. Same refs.

BEHETHLAND CHANDLER, wife of John. 1768. Same refs.

BEHETHLAND DADE. Died 29 Jany 1726. Same refs.

BEHETHLAND DADE m. Justinian Birch. 30 June 1777. Same refs.

BEHETHLEHAM-ALEXANDER DADE, dau. of Robert and Elizabeth. B. 23 Dec 1745. Same refs.

BEHETHLEM DERRICK, dau. of Benjamin and Katherine. B. [Baptized] 6 Sept 1739. Same refs.

BEHETHLAND-GILSON BERRYMAN m. John Thornton. 13 Dec 1761.

BEHETHLAND GRAVAT, wife of John. Dau. Ursula. B. 10 June 1751. Same refs.

BEHETHLAND GRAVAT m. Alexander Jordan. 30 Oct. 1750. Same refs.

BEHETHLAND HURLEY, wife of John. 1766. Crozier, Wmld Wills, Va.

BEHETHLAND JONES was wife of Rev. Walter Jones. 1727. Crozier, Wmld Wills, Va.

BEHETHLEM JONES, dau. of John and "Heliner" Jones. B. 14 July 1748. St. Paul's Psh Reg. K. Geo. cty, Va.

BEHETHLEM KELLY, was the wife of Samuel. 15 Sept 1748. Same refs.

BEHETHLAND KELLY m. John Gravat. 27 Dec. 1751. Same refs.

BEHETHLAND KENNEDY m. Luke Hughes. 10 July 1779. Same refs.

BEHETHLAND JOHNSTON m. William Mitchell. 4 Sept 1787. Same refs.

BEHETHLAND JONES, m. John Peed. 14 Feby 1770. Same refs.

BEHETHLAND MASSEY; owner of negro boy Brooks. 1751. Same refs.

BEHETHLAN PATERSON, dau. of Mary. Born 17 Apr 1750. Overwharton Psh Reg. Va.

BEHETHLAND PEED "?" wife of John. 1772. St. Paul's Psh Reg. K. Geo. Va.

BEHETHLEM POLLY, dau. of John and Mary, B. 30 Mch. 1728. Same refs.

BEHETHLAND REDDISH, dau. of Joseph and Sarah. B. 22 Aug 1751 Same refs.

BEHETHLAND ROGERS m. John Chandler. 17 Sept 1767. Same refs.

BEHETHLAND SMITH, dau. of George and BEHETHLAND. B. 16 Apr. 1772. Same refs.

BEHETHLAM STORKE m. Anthony Strother. 25 Aug. 1733. Same refs.

BEHETHLEM WHITE m. Samuel Kelly. 25 Aug 1741. Same refs.

DECEDENTS IN HYDE COUNTY, N.C. SHOWN BY INVENTORIES, &c. 1756-1761.

RICHARD LIERMONT, Esq. Estate account, begun 1752. Last item dated 1755. This is followed by Margaret Leirmont's estate, evidently an orphan. Thomas Smith, her guardian. Account includes payment to dancing-master.

JOHN SMITH; William and Dinah Cording, adm'rs.

(The heading before the next entry is "At a Court at Woodstock, June 1758.")

SAMUEL MANDUELL,S estate; Thomas Windly, Gdn. This is the inventory of an orphan's estate. It includes " one homespun pattolier."

MARY DAVIS, dec'd; estate. John Winfield (Gdn ?) 19 Apr 1758.

THOS. BLEY, dec'd; estate. James Batchelor, adm'r. Sept Ct, 1758.

JOSEPH TART, Esq. Philip Folley, extr.

RUTH MANDOWEL, estate; Lamuel Harvey signs (by mark.) 1757.

JOSEPH TART, son of Joseph, dec'd. Richard Newman returns account. 1758, &c.

JOHN MANDOWELL, estate; Littleton Jarman, extr. 1757.

JOSHUA WALLS, estate; Anthony Tuley signs. 5 Sept 1758.

HEZEKIAH SLAD, estate; Jane Hamilton signs. 1758.

BATHAL [perhaps BACHEL* ?] BALEY; Mary "Bachlder" brings account. 1758.

SEBASTION SILVERTHORN; John Rew's account his estate. 1757.

ABRAHAM EASTER; Tho. Easter, extr, renders account. 1758. (Amount is £9,469-10 1-2 " Old Tennor.")

WILLIAM MARTIN; administration account by Sarah Martin, admx.

Mrs. REBECAH EBERN, estate; William Eborn, extr of Littleton Eborne's estate, brings this account [The record is not at all clear.] Division follows; dau. Eliz'h Boyd; wife of William Boyd . . "his right by his wife." Division seems to have been made at the request of William Eborne, Jr., and William Boyd, who met at the house of Mr. Littleton Eborne, dec'd, 13 Mch 1759, and the estate was then valued. This record is of the Court of December, 1758.

WILLIAM McNORVEL, Jr. Henry Eborne, gdn, presents account. 1758.

JOHN TIDINGS, estate; Marg't Foreman, extx. Presents account. Sept 1759;

FREDERICK BARROW, estate; Thos. Barrow, admr.

JOSEPH TART; additional estate. Signed by Richard Newman. Sept Court, 1758.

TIDINGS FOREMAN; sale of his estate. 4 May 1759.

FOSTER JARVIS; inventory his estate; Josiah Jarvis, extr. 1 Sept 1759.

WILLIAM SILVESTER; inventory his estate; Joseph Weston, admr. 1 Sept 1760.

JOHN HARVEY, account sales his estate. Order of 14 Dec 1759.

WILLIAM FORTESCUE; John Fortescue and Hannah Fortescue, extrs. Returned Dec 1761.

LITTLETON EBORNE; inventory signed by Jas. Eborne and Ann Eborne. Taken 22 May 1760.

ANTHONY TULEY; division his estate. 5 Aug 1757.

MORRIS JONES; division his estate. 29 Aug 1758.

WILLIAM McNORVAL; his estate; Henry Eborne, guardian. Ct Mch 1761.

LITTLETON EBORNE, estate; James Eborne, extr. Returns acct Mch 1761.

FREDERICK BARROW, estate; George Barrow, Gdn, returns account. 5 June 1759.

JAMES BACHELOR, inventory his estate; James Bachelor, admr.

JOSEPH TART, estate; Richard Newman, extr. 1759–1760.

LITTLETON EBORNE; division his estate. 2 June 1761.

JAMES BACHELOR, account sales. 4 and 13 Mch 1761.

WILLIAM SILVESTER; account sales his estate. Returned 2 June, 1761.

WILLIAM and REBECA EBORNE; account sales their estate. They were children of Littleton Eborne. [About 1761?]

RUTH MANDUELL, orphan; Lamuel Harvey, gdn, returns account. 15 Oct 1759.

FOSTER JARVIS, partial inventory his estate. 16 May 1761.

RENUNCIATION OF FOREIGN ALLEGIANCE

JAMES-SIMON DRINAN or DRINAU; JAMES GREGORIE, JOHN PIKE, JOHN WATSON, all renounce allegiance other than to the United States and take prescribed oath. *Have not been of any order of nobility.* 24 May 1799. Pr. Wm cty, Va. Superior Ct at Dumfries.

JAMES DAVENPORT, a native of Ireland, age 54, a farmer; has resided in the U. S. ever since October, 1796, and MICHAEL CLAREY, a native of Ireland, age 25, Merchant; has resided in the U. S. ever since July, 1795; both now residing in Alexandria, Va. Make usual declaration and are admitted to citizenship. 22 May 1799. Pr. Wm cty, Va. Superior Ct at Dumfries.

ROBERT FERGUSON, Jr., LUKE-JOHN ROBINS, and THOMAS HUGHES, all renounce allegiance to the King of Great Britain; *have not been of any order of nobility*; are admitted to citizenship. 21 May 1799. Same Court.

WILLIAM HALL, JESSE TAYLOR, Jr., JOHN GADSBY, EDWARD KEATING, THOMAS TOWERS, and SAMUEL LOWDEN [?] make oath of residence and renounce Great Britain. *Have not been of any order of nobility.* 24 May 1799. Same Court.

THEOPHILUS HARRIS, WILLIAM EMOCK, JONATHAN MANDEVILL, JOHN HUBBELL, JAMES MITCHELL, JAMES KEMP; make oath that they have been residents of the U. S. previous to the 29 Jany 1795; will support the Constitution, &c., &c., and the Court finding that they are of good moral character and *have not been of any order of Nobility*, are admitted to citizenship. 20 May 1799. Same Court.

EMANUEL-JOSEPH HUBER, has resided in the U. S. A. previous to 29 Jany 1795, renounces allegiance to the Sovereignty of Wirtenberg, Empire of Germany . . . *has not been of any order of Nobility.* Is admitted to citizenship. 22 May 1799. Same Court.

RICHARD LIBBY, a native of England, of the age of 34; resided in the U. S. ever since October, 1795; also JOHN LUMSDON, a native of England, 30 years of age, a painter and glazier, resident since June, 1795, and DANIEL MACLEOD, native of Scotland, age 35, painter and glazier, resident since June 1795, all now residing in Alexandria, Va.; renounce Great Britain. 26 Oct 1798. Pr. Wm cty, Va. District Court.

JOHN LEMOINE, makes oath as to residence, renounces allegiance to the French Republic; *is not of any order of nobility.* 24 May 1799. Pr. Wm cty, Va. Superior Court at Dumfries.

CHARLES MAXWELL makes oath that he *has not been of any order of nobility.* 28 May 1799. Same Court.

JOHN O'NEIL, native of Ireland, age 24, "Victular;" resided in the U. S. A. ever since July, 1796. Resident of Alexandria. Renounces Great Britain. 27 May 1799. Same Court.

Reasonable price or two years' subscription will be given for numbers 1, 2, 3, 4, 6, and 7, COUNTY COURT NOTE-BOOK, 1921-1922. Address Editor.

Fifty cents will be paid for a copy of February 1927.

Printed at the Industrial School for Crippled and Deformed Children, 241 St. Botolph St., Boston, Mass.

The County Court Note-Book

A Little Bulletin of History and Genealogy

October, 1928. Vol. VII, No. 5.

THE TITHABLES OF NORTHAMPTON COUNTY, VIRGINIA, in 1744

(*From original lists*)

Benjamin Johnson, Walter Carter;
Marke Freshwater, Robert Tompson;
Stratton Caple, Waterson Caple;
Thomas Scott, "cunstable;" John Bullock;
Mr. Benjamin Stratton, Henery Wilkins;
John Satchel, Thomas Ward Elligood;
John Sheppard;
Woodman Stockley, Thomas Thornman, John Wilson;
William Talor;
John Stripe, Jr.;
John Stripe, Sr., Joseph Stripe;
John Williams, Sr., Thomas Williams, John Williams, Jr.;
Thomas Hunt, William Joynes;
James Biggs;
Mr. John Stratton, Thomas Stratton;
Jonathan Wilkins;
John Richards;
Thomas Downes;
William Benthall;
Daniel Benthall, Richard Hearitage;
Thomas Garrat;
Jonas Dixon;
Jonathan Roberts, William Hollon;
Henery Tolmon;
Richard Hanby;
John Nelson;
William Mills;
At Briggit Pigot's, John Pigot;
William Wilson;
Henry Smaw;
John Wats;
Marrat Persons;
Mr. Edward Robins;
At Madom Robins (list of negroes);
John Robins "Olphin";
Stockly Wilkins;
Matthew Welch;
Thomas Speakman.
Robert Tompson;
William Brumfield;
M. . . . . . [?] Bushop, William Carter;
Richard Respus, "pattroler;"
John Knight, Dixon Knight;
William Scott, Abell Scott;
John Chees;
Josiah Willis;
Charles Webb;

(*To be continued*)

AUTHENTIC REFERENCES FOR INFERRED MARRIAGES

(Northampton county, Virginia)

JOHN WATERFIELD, Jr., prob. m. MARY DUNTON. Before October, 1768. Chancy records.

DANIEL WELBURN and BARBARA DRUMMOND, dau. Hill DRUMMOND. Before [?] 2 June 1736. L. C.

.... WESTERHOUSE and ANNE ANDREWS, widow of William. After 12 Nov 1760. (Before 1770.) Chancy records.

.... WESTERHOUSE prob. m. LEAH MAPP, widow of Howson MAPP. Before Aug 1765. Chancy records.

ROBERT WEST and MARY RAYNE, relict of Rowland RAYNE. Before 28 Nov 1642. i-184.

WILLIAM WESTERHOUSE prob. m. ANN JACOB, dau. of Abraham. Before Oct 1768. Chancy records.

LEWIS WHITE and the relict of Tho: DEWIN [DOWIN?] Before 29 June 1640. iii-36.

EDWARD WEB and ELIZABETH SATCHEL, dau. of William. Before 11 July 1738. Chancy records.

Mr. PETER WALKER and ALICIA BURDETT, widow of Mr. William BURDETT. Before 28 Jany 1645. iii-16. [She had been the widow of George Traveller.]

BENONI WARD and SARAH HEWETT. Before 10 July 1694. iv.

THOMAS WATTS and FRANCES WILKINS, dau. of John. Before 12 Sept 1719. ix-62.

PETER WATSON of Acco. and ANN SHEPHEARD eldest dau. of John and Elizabeth. Before 27 July 1696. xvi-39.

ARGOL WARREN and URSULA PATRICK. Before 1725. L. C. 1754–1771.

JOHN WARREN [Jr.] and BETTY WILSON, dau. of James and Mary. Before 11 Feby 1724. Chancy records.

Mr. JOHN WESTCOTT and ELIZABETH CLARKE, widow of George CLARKE, Gent. Bet. 1690 and 1700. Chancy records.

STEPHEN WESTCOTE and RACHEL ASHBY, dau. of Francis. Before or about 10 Nov 1747. Chancy records.

SAMPSON WEBSTER and MARY SAVAGE, dau. of Capt. John SAVAGE. Before 28 July 1690. xiv-261.

JOHN WATERSON, tailor, and FRANCES WILKINS, dau. of Mrs. Ann Vos. About or before 1658. ix-33.

JOHN WATERSON and KEZIAH GELDING. Before 9 Jany 1727. Chancy records.

JOHN WISE and ELIZABETH CABLE, dau. of Sorrowful Margaret Cable. Prob. before 24 Oct 1750. Chancy records.

JOHN WILLETT and Mrs. ELIZABETH DOUGLAS, dau. of Lt. Col. Edward DOUGLAS. Mar. contract. 24 Nov 1669. xi-9. See also x-86 and xv-198.

GEORGE WEST and SUSANNA DUPARKES, widow of Peter. Before 28 Mch 1688. xv-345.

JOHN WEST, Jr., Gent., and FRANCES YARDLEY, dau. of Argoll YARDLEY, Gent., and wife Sarah. See record 28 May 1702. xvi-296.

RALPH WORMLEY of Psh and cty of York, Gent., and AGATHA STUBBINGS, widow of Luke, of N-n, Gent. Mar. contract. 2 July 1645. ii-364.

WILLIAM WARE and BARBRA BATSON, widow of Jacob. Before 9 Apr 1723. Chancy records.

.... WEST and Mrs. ANN BARLOWE, widow of Ralph. Before 28 Sept 1653. iv-202.

JOHN WILKINS, Jr., and KATHERINE CUSTIS, extx of Edmund Custis, Before 11 Sept 1751. xxxix 0-9.

Lt. WILLIAM WATERS and .... CLARKE, widow of Mr. George CLARKE. Before 31 Jany 1652. iv-155.

JOHN WILLYAMS; "ELIZABETH COOPER was marryed to him & lived with him [as] his wife one yeare & a halfe; then dyed in the yeare 1649 And lyeth buried in North'ton county. Teste Edm. Mathews Cler. Cur." Court 7 Mch 1654. iv-226.

JOHN WILKINS and AGNES JOHNSON. Before 1773. Chancy records.

.... WINDLEY and JOANE YOUNG, widow of Richard. Before 18 July 1642. ii-154.

THOMAS WILSON and MARY TURNER, widow of Christopher. About 9 Sept 1670. x-90.

WILLIAM WIDGEON and RACHEL PITTS, widow of Jacob. Before Aug 1769. Chancy records.

.... WRESSELL and MARY LOUGHLAND, widow of Dorman. Before 21 Apr 1692. iv-240.

CHARLES WEBB and SARAH LAUGHLAND. Before 1715. xix-322.

SAMUEL WILSON, Som. cty, Md., Gent., and PEGGY CUSTIS, dau of John CUSTIS, Gent. Before 13 May, 1760. Chancy records.

ALEX'R WILLIAMSON and ANNE WYATT. Before 28 Nov 1642. ii-189.

HENDRICK WAGOMAN, carpenter, a Dutchman, of the City of Amsterdam, and Mrs. WINIFRED SCHIN [SCKIN] dau. of Margaret Westerhouse. Mar. contract. 9 May 1660. ix-70.

.... WHITMARSH and ELIZABETH WALTHOM, widow of John. Before 28 Feby 1664. x-1.

NATHANIEL WILKINS and FRANCES BIBBY, widow of Edmund. Before 31 Jany 1661. See ix-113, 193. See also ix-209. [She seems to have been FRANCES HUNT. See xi-4.]

ARGOLL YARDLEY, Gent., and SARAH MICHAEL, dau. of John, Sr. Before 29 Aug 1678. xi-167.

Omitted from the foregoing alphabet:

THOMAS HUNT and the widow of Robert DRAKE. Before or about 29 Mch 1641. i-60.

Mr. THOMAS HARMANSON, Sr., and [ELIZABETH] DANIEL, widow of John. Before 29 Sept 1692. xvii-191.

GEORGE HARMANSON and ELIZABETH, dau. of Sarah ( ) (Yardley) Maddux. Before 20 Mch 1694. xvii-419.

WILLIAM HARPER, about to marry ELIZABETH HARPER, relict and extx of Francis HARPER. 22 July 1673. xi-85.

...... HAYES and DORATHY GRIFFETH, dau. of Jerome. Before 1707-8. xviii-420.

THOMAS JARVIS and a dau. of Thomas DUPARKES. Before 1702. xviii-135.

JOHN JONES and the widow [FRANCES?] of John CLAY, Sr. Before 14 Feby 1737. Chancy records.

WILLIAM KENDALL, Sr. and SARAH x MATHEWS; marriage contract. She was a widow. 6 June 1684. xiv-109.

THOMAS KELLUM and MARY BOLD [widow]. Before 10 July 1723. Chancy records.

JOHN KNIGHT and LICIA WILLIS. Before 13 Oct 1729. Chancy records.

DIXON KNIGHT and ELLEN TOMSON, relict of George. Before 1729. Chancy records.

ROBERT KING and ELIZABETH, sister of Peter WALKER. Before 2 Jany 1659. ix-86.

JOHN LINCH and BETHIA KENNINGHAM [CUNNINGHAM?] About 1 May 1693. xvii-250.

DORMAN LOUGHLAND prob. m. MARY WRESSELL, widow of Charles. She married (3) Walter Mannington. The latter marriage before 2 Mch 1692. xvii-232.

RICHARD LESTER and ISBELL PETTI-JOHN, dau. James. Before 11 Dec 1678. xii-307.

Mr. RICH. LEMON and JANE JACKSON, widow. Long before 28 Jany 1645. iii-12.

WILLIAM LAWRENCE and SARAH BASNET, dau. of Charles. Before 1730. Chancy records.

ELIZ'TH x BURROUGH [kin?] "Children minors." Inv. Jno Brown, of Balto. cty. 6 Dec 1722. viii-8.

"Relation none Nor Creditors none." Inv. John People of Dor. cty. 19 Jany 1722-3. viii-9.

WALTER x NEWMAN; inv. John Newman. County not given, 17 Sept 1722. viii-12.

ROBERT SCOTT, SARAH HANDY; inv. Sam'll Prior. County not given. 19 Jany 1722. viii-13.

ELIZTH x BURROUGH [kin? "Children minors." Inv. Jno. Brown, of Balto. cty. 6 Dec 1722. viii-8.

"Relation none Nor Creditors none." Inv. John People of Dor. cty. 19 Jany 1722-23. viii-9.

WALTER x NEWMAN; inv. John Newman. County not given. 17 Sept 1722. viii-12.

ROBERT SCOTT, SARAH HANDY; inv. Sam'll Prior. County not given. 19 Jany 1722. viii-13.

DOROTHY EASON, lately called DOROTHY HARRISON, extx; WILLIAM HARRISON, sign. Inv. Francis Harrison of Talbot cty. No date. viii-14.

CHARLES x TUCKER, JOHN x TUCKER; WILLIAM BULLEN [kin?] Inv. James Tucker of Talbott cty. 9 June 1722. viii-15.

WILL MATTHEWS, ELIZ: MATHEWS. Inv. William Mathews. County not given. 15 Mch 1721. viii-16.

ELIZA: TONNART [?] EDW'D NEEDLES. Inv. Joseph Turner, Carpinter, St. Peter's psh [county?] 2 Aug 1722. viii-19.

ROBT. GOLDSBOROUGH, R [?] GOLDSBOROUGH. Inv. Thomas Robins, Gent., of Talbot cty. 30 Jany 1721. viii-19.

Inventory of Robt Creaston of St. Mary's cty, "noe" kindred." viii-30.

THOS. COCKAYNE, Sam'l COCKAYNE. Inv; Mr. Wm. Cockayne of Talbot cty. 3 Feby 1721. viii-31.

JOHN x NEALL, THOMAS KIRKE.Inv. Dennis Roch, of Talbot. [Rock?] 14 May 1722. viii-34.

THOS. MARTIN, HANNAH MAYNIADIER· Inv. Wm. Martin, Talbot cty. 5 Oct 1722. viii-35.

VIRGINIA COLONISTS

(From "Old Volume 5," S. L. O., Richmond.)

THOMAS KIRKE, James City cty, 1658.
Head rights: THOMAS KIRKE, Thomas Herman, Ellinor Woodstock.

JAMES KYNNYGAM [a form of Cunningham?] and JAMES FULLERTON, Rappa. cty, 1658.
Head rights: Thomas Parsons, Henry Jenings, Nicho. Andrews, James Bridgman, Ann Worth, Peter Holden, Henry Benson, Rich Wallis, Mary Hamsin.

THOMAS KEDBY, Northumberland cty, 1658.
Head rights: Robert Tomkins, Jno. Martin, John Trevin [?] Wm. Surtur [?]

WILLIAM KILLMAN, 1661.
Head rights: Mary Phillips, James Young, Wm. Wright, Wm. Long.

DANIEL LISTON, Westmoreland cty, 1658.
Head rights: Martha Jackson, Sarah Southerne, Judith Southerne, Paul Simpson.

THOMAS LULLAMAN, "in Patomeck Freshes upon a Creeke by some called Yocococoemocoe Creeke being a faire navigable creeke & the Second Creek above Chapawansick or the next Creeke above Quanticott," 1658.

Head rights: Wm. Leprask, Jno. Parkes, Wm. Rider, Nicho. Parr, Mary Atkins, Symun Shelton, Tho. Barker, Fran: Harrington.

ROBERT LINNEE [?], no county given, 1658.
Head rights: Antho. Stephens, four times.

RICHARD LEWIS, Lancaster cty, 1658.
Head rights: Adry White, Tho. White, Tho. Surpleete, Jno. Castle.

Mr. LOCKEY, 1658.
Head rights: John Emerson, Abraham Canby, Jno. Walker, RICHARD LUCKE, Rich Cleaton, Edward West, Thomas Will, Richard Lendall, John Cole, Tho. Treverstone, Jno. Townsend, Xpher Edy, Tho. Evans, Richd Bennett, Edmund Gosse, Robt Montgomery, Wm. Campion, Jno. Lobdenne [?] Cle......... [?] Smith, Richard Jones;
Edmond Richeson, Jno. White, James Morfrey, M......... Mells, Wm. Lawrence, Abra. Person, Georg Fendall, Wm. James, Wm. Shepard, Wm. Hall, Peter Fisher, John Cliford.

Col. RICHARD LEE, no county given, 1658.
Head rights: Jno. Slattor, Jno. Wornor, Jno. Gibbinne [?] Robert Higginson, Rich. Kent, Timothy Gunter, Daniell Gugoll, Rich. Watton, Wm. Ruyleton [Rugleton?] Tho. Dollings, Jone Palmer, Mary ...., Sarah Hickman, Eliza: Percey, Eliz: Holladay, Susanna Roberts, Jno. Pashe, Peter Walker [?] Tho. Cooke, Peter Wade;
Tho. Wade, Tho. Mase, Wm. Angell, Rob't, Norton, Edward Barnett, Rich. Dobbins, Abraham Patermacke, Kath. Silverton, Rich. Abbert, Robert Girringe, Wm. Bingly, John Bellamy, Andrew Felton, Tho. Minstrell [?] Jno. Edgcombe, Walter Rich, Elias Port, Hugh Gouch, Taunton Heale, Walter Rickson [?]

GEORGE LIGHT and THOMAS SPENCER New Kent cty, 1661.
Head rights: Wm. Maris, Mary Stephens, Ann Brodhurst, Jane Bandon, Wm. Sewell, Mary Jones, Jane Godlad, and 16 negroes.

Note: In copying a copy of the list under Mr. Wm. Drummond (see August NOTE-BOOK), the Editor accidentally omitted a number of names of head rights. The full list is given herewith.

Mr. WM. DRUMMOND, James City cty, 1662.

Head rights: John Jarvy, Peter Gillard, Eliazue . . . ., Jno. Ingram, Machuett [?] Hammond, Abram Vodin, Marice Vodin [Vadin?], Jno. Vodin, Isaak Vodin, Rich. Stanford, Abram Hill, Wm. Grum, Wm. Davye [uncertain], Susanna Child, Susanna Catts, Susana Garment, Wm. Hearny, Jno. James, Wm. Wells, Susan Carter, Edw'd Wells, Jno Turner and two negroes.

The County Court Note-Book

An every-other-monthly devoted mainly to abstracts from County Court Records, prior to 1800.

MILNOR LJUNGSTEDT, Editor and Publisher. Bethesda, Route 10, Maryland.

Published six times a year. Subscription, two dollars, in advance; must begin with the year.

October, 1928 **Whole**
Vol. VII., No. 5 **No. 42**

CONCERNING THE DONELSON MATERIAL OF LAST YEAR

The Editor being about to attack another Eastern Shore line......that of the WHITTINGTON-LITTLETON-SOUTHY-BOWMAN link-up, feels that it will not be out of place to offer some sort of an apology for her shortcomings.

The Editor is not a historian, never had any training in historical research, is not a college-bred person and so knows nothing about heads of thesises and the science of argumentation, and a good many of her comments have a rather hit or miss sound as she runs them over. The Editor has, however, a critical turn of mind. That belongs to most of us born on the frigid side of the line.

The Ancestry of Col. John Donelson, finished some time ago, should not, of course, include Col. Donelson's career, and the statements at its outset, that is, of the Ancestry, don't fit in with the statements at the end. This is partly the result of a time to time method of writing and a bad habit of doing things in a hurry.

At least if the Ancestry lacks the unities, it does present facts. And facts hard to get at. Wandering into Col. Donelson's political and official career, the Editor feels that she should have gone further......but that not having been her original intention she let the matter go with the little she really knew.

As for the remonstrative "*Associations*"...... who would believe that so little is known about them? Had it not been for the helpful courtesy of the gentleman acting as the head of the Manuscript Division of the Library of Congress, this Editor would never have known that there were two of the things, quite different from each other, nor would she have known that they were quite outside of the regular proceedings of the Virginia House of Burgesses.

And the "*Line.*" Which one of the two bounded the "Path Treaty"...so important in Virginia history?

In the forthcoming LITTLETON notes the Editor will make no deliberate effort to gather all the political and official side of Col. WHITTINGTON'S career, but will give such facts as the local county records and the published Archives offer. At any rate they will not be personal opinions of this or that "collateral descendant."

......A word more as to the Donelson Line. The following is from Hanson's Journal, now in the University of Chicago (see also Mr. Thwaites' and Miss Kellog's Dunmore's War, p. 122). Under date of the 15th of May, Hanson writes, "*We lay here in hopes of somebody's coming down to let us know where the line came down the Ohio (i. e. the line Col. Donalson run between us and the Cherokees, which line is said to be the Kentucky River itself.)*"

THE DEPUTY COMMISSARY'S GUIDE WITHIN THE PROVINCE OF MARYLAND

(*Continued from June, 1928.*)

The bond for the administrator was generally double the sum of the supposed value of the whole personal estate; inventory was to be returned within three months, and final account within twelve months after the date of letters of administration.

A following paragraph refers to the fact that Administrators did not deal with *real estate*; security was to cover the whole personality, but an executor authorized by will to sell real estate was required to give security to cover both.

Warrants for appraisement were next to be made out......to two persons *perfectly disinterested*: [this does not seem to fit in with many appraisements as they were actually made. ;Editor.] and the text goes on to say that "great caution and circumspection ought to be used in the choice of appraisers; such only should be appointed, as are skilful, honest and impartial, entirely free from entertaining either favour or prejudice, or having any interest in over-rating or under-valuing, the effects."

Concerning inventories: The appraisers must give notice of time and place to *two of the next of kin*, and also to *two of the creditors*, and in their presence, proceed to the valuation of all goods, chattels, wares and merchandises, such as ready money, household furniture, cloathing, negroes, cattle, corn, crop in hand, and every sort of property in and about the house, *not being a freehold, or parcel of it, or fixed to it*; "the convenient apparel of the widow, according to her degree excepted," as also of all leases for years, how long soever the term may be, and likewise "continuing freeholds, not descendible; but care to be taken not to confound a descendible freehold, which belongs to the heir, with one that is not so;"...... "A freehold descendible is where land is granted to the deceased and his heirs during the life of another, such lease is not to be inventoried." But if the lease be generally limited to the grantee, or to the grantee, his executors and administrators, "the same is legal assets," and therefore accountable for in course of administration. [Reference given to a difficult statute, *pur auter vie.*]

What is deemed parcel of the freehold and what is not: "What may be taken away without prejudice to the fabrick of the house, are to be considered as chattels and not as parcel of the freehold; as tables, though fastened to the floor; *furnaces*, if not made part of the wall; grates, iron ovens, jacks, clock cases, and such like, tho' fixed to the freehold by nails or otherwise." The compiler notes that the law "*seems not to be held so strict as formerly.*"

The inventory must be signed by the two sworn appraisers, as also by the two next of kin, and the two creditors who were present at the appraisement.

Should there be but one creditor, or none at all, or only one relation, or none in the province ......the inventory may be accepted, the executor or administrator making oath to that purpose.

A paragraph as to valuation, directs that the valuation is to be made at the rate of six shillings per dollar; but comments that the greater part return inventories calculated in dollars at seven shillings six pence, and states that the Administrator in this way loses eighteen pence in every dollar.

(To be continued)

Note: The list on page 38 finishes this alphabet of Northampton county marriages. Previous alphabets will be found by reference to earlier issues of the NOTE-BOOK. The next number of the NOTEBOOK will contain Maryland marriages, and the other one after that, a list of marriages from York county, Va. Marriages from Accomack county, Va., will appear in the early part of next year.

CONTINUED articles COUNTY COURT NOTE-BOOK, and the dates on which they first appeared.

THE ANCESTRY OF COL. JOHN DONELSON. Began with February, 1927.

AUTHENTIC REFERENCES for INFERRED MARRIAGES (formerly called MARRIAGES BY INFERENCE). Began with May, 1922.

MARYLAND'S NEXT OF KIN. Began with July, 1922.

VIRGINIA COLONISTS. Alphabetized lists began with July, 1924.

MILITARY NOTES, both COLONIAL and REVOLUTIONARY, and later MILITIA NOTES. Began December, 1923.

INTERCOUNTY and INTERCOLONY (formerly called New Englanders and Others, &c., &c.). Began with March, 1922.

EASTERN SHORE FAMILIES. In the form of a one-page supplement, began with June, 1925. This will be continued later.

SHIPS IN PORT and COLONIAL FORENAMES will appear in alternate issues or as space can be found for them.

OCCASIONAL

The Glory of children are their fathers. Prov. xvii-6.

TRULOVE BAILY was the daughter of Bethuell Baily. Hyde cty, N. C. 1790. i-199.

SUGAR CAIN; patent for land on the waters of Crooked Creek. 25 June 1812. S. L. O. lxiii-491.

SAMUELL COLLINS brings suit against Jno. Robbins and wife, for accusing Collins' wife of being a witch, "*whereby the pltff's wife's life may be endangered.*" Defendant fined, &c. Som. Md. 11 Sept 1668. Vol. 1690-1692, p. 77.

MISS JANE BARBOUR, who is to marry John R. Drexel, Jr., descends from James Taylor, who came to St. Stephen's Parish, New Kent county, [Va.] in 1600, and of Zachary Tayler, President. N. Y. Times, 14 Dec, 1924.

STEPHEN CHARLTON directs his wife to "bee his *relict* and executrix." N-n cty, Va. 28 Oct 1654. v-56.

WILLIAM GRAY, 14 years old, as punishment for crime, is to be hangman for the next [present] execution. N-n cty, Va. 26 July 1653. iv-181.

CHURCH OR CHAPEL at "Diffical," Fairfax cty, Va. In 1778 there was a Welsh Baptist church at this place, see Records of the Welah Tract. Delaware. p. 60.

CHARLES CITY COUNTY, Va. The markets of this County to be held and kept at Weston and Floriday hundreds. C. C. cty, Va. 1 Jany 1655. Records 1655-1665. p. 1.

DINAH x BURNETT, Sampson cty, N. C., indentures herself to Charles Hays, of the same cty, for twenty-five pounds, for the term of ninety and nine years. Davidson cty, Tenn. 20 Sept 1797. ii-110.

INTERCOUNTY AND INTERCOLONY

Mr. SAMUEL ANDREWS, of N. E., deceased. See N-n, Va. 29 Dec 1659. viii-59.

ALEXANDER BRECKINRIDGE, of "Burbon" cty, Ky, gives power to John Davis, of Davidson cty, Tenn., to sell his part of a tract granted to Capt. John Eburn, lying between the West Fork of Stone's river and Overalls Creek. D-n cty, Tenn. 11 Oct 1796. ii-55.

EDWARD BURTON, of Kederminster, Wor. cty, Gent., was uncle of William Underwood, son of William Underwood, Sr., who was also a nephew of William Moseley, See power to Moseley. Rappa. cty, Va. 1656-1664. 20 July 1663.

JOHN COGHAN of N. E., Mcht, See N-n, Va. 28 Dec 1652. iv-124.

JOHN DARR of Davidson cty, Tenn., was son of John Darr of Orange cty, Va., and had bro. Rubin, then dec'd. D-n cty, Tenn. 20 Aug 1804. ii-388.

JOHN DONALDSON, one of their Matie's Justices for the County of New Castle, being sworn upon the holy Evangelist declares that Some time in October, 1691, in the Citty of New Yorke, he saw Robert Darby who was well in health and affirmed himself to be the Brother of John Darby & that he lived in the Collony of Connecticut in New England and further saith not. Taken before me this 25th May 1693. One of their Matie's Counsel for the T[hree Lower Counties] of PennSilvania, &c. Jno. Cann [Sig]......Came JOHN DARBY ......& Declares to his Certain Knowledge not above four months past ROBERT DARBY his Brother was alive and in health resyding in New England, and about five years since he went hence to the County of Sussex and from thence to Maryland & Virginia where he gott a passage to New England, but went away Privately being in debt......Edw. Blake [Sig] [one of the Justices in New Castle, aferwards Delaware] 5 May 1693. Somerset cty, Md. records.

DAVID HAY, Davidson cty, Mero Dist., Tenn. Power to Maj. John Hays, John Caruthers and James Caruthers, of Rockbridge cty, Va., to convey land in Lexington, Rockbr. cty, to Andrew Reid. D-n cty. Tenn. 16 Apr. 1791. i-203.

JAMES HUNT [HUNTER?], ADAM HUNTER, heir-at-law and devisee of JAMES HUNTER, ABNER VERNON, and PATRICK HORNE of Virginia, extrs of JAMES HUNTER, late of Virginia, dec'd, convey to Zachariah Clagett, Frederick cty, Md., all that part of Fieldena [?] in Frederick cty, containing 88 acres. Fred'k Cty, Md. 28 June 1792. Page 1072 of an early volume of *abstracts.*

WILLIAM PAYNE of Ipswich, in N. E., Mcht. Power to Willm. Strangwidge of Va. N-n iv-191 1652.

WILLIAM PETTY is granted "letters & Testimony" on the Estate of John Petty, late of Anne Arundel county and State of Maryland. Richmond cty, Ga. 17 Apr 1794. A-40.

JOHN PLEASANTS, will. Mentions brothers and sisters in England, and gives land to Quakers; (His children also mentioned.) Hen. Va. 1690-1698. i-80.

WILLIAM ROWAN, of Maryland; power to Daniel Rowan, of Davidson cty, N. C. D-n cty, Tenn. 23 Aug 1790. i-177.

ISAAC RALSTON gives power to ROBERT HAYS; Ralston was late a captain on the Continental line; Hays is to demand pay, rations, or land due from the State of North Carolina. Assigns right to land or monies due, to Robert Hays. D-n cty, Tenn. 14 May, 1793. ii-26.

DANIEL SULLIVANT, of Stafford cty, Va., pltr, conveys land which belonged to his father, Dorman Sullivant ". . . all that part or parcell of Land . . . in the county of Accomack . . . att Occahannock Creek, containing one hundred and twenty-five acres . . .being the one half or *mojety* of two hundred acres which Dorman Sullivant Father to me . . . died seized of. . . ." Acco., Va. 5 Oct 1708. xi-455.

WILLIAM POUNDS, of Granville cty, N. C., to Elijah Thomas, Halifax cty, Va., 110 acres on the waters of "Steaur'ts Creek." Hal., Va. 26 Mch 1804. Deeds xx-505.

WILLIAM ROWAN, of Maryland; power to Daniel Rowan, of Davidson cty, N. C. Davids. cty, Tenn. 23 Aug 1790. i-177.

GEORGE RANDALL, Sen'r, was of "Corne Abbass" in Dorsett cty, Gt. Britain. Wmld, Va. 1723. Fid. Accts i-5.

DAVID REID, of Lancaster cty. Penna., buys land on Rockfish river, Alb., Va. 9 Aug 1760. ii-299.

JOHN SAFFIN, of Boston in New England Mcht; power to Mr. William Presley of Chicacoan in Virginia. Nthld, Va. 1658-1666, fo. 24. 20 May 1659.

DAVID SCOTT, of Monongalia city, Va. Power to Thomas Harrison, of Davidson cty, Tenn., to convey land on Richland and Hurricane Creeks. D-n cty, Tenn. 14 Mch 1797. ii-94.

ALEX x WILLIAMS, age 65, previous July, says his father moved his family from Maryland to Clifton's Neck, about forty-four years ago. Pr. Wm. cty, Va. 24 Aug 1785. L. C. p. 316.

SERVICE AND SUPPLIES COLONIAL, REVOLUTIONARY AND MILITIA

WILLIAM GRIFFIN makes oath that he served in the last war bet. Great Britain and France as a private in Capt. Robert Munford's company, 1st Va. Regt. Ctf. ordered. Charl cty, Va. Orders iv-209. Mch Ct 1780.

JOHN GUTTERY; claim rejected, being for Continental service. J. H. B. Va. 26 May 1777.

JOHN GILMORE; petition favorably reported; served in 1774 in the expedition agt the Shawanees. [*sic.*] J. H. B. Va. 31 May 1777.

CHARLES HAY; soldier Revolutionary service; claim allowed. J. H. B. Va. 26 May 1777.

JAMES HAMILTON; files declaration and Court is of opinion that he was a Revolutionary soldier. Bedford cty, Va. Ct of Jany 1833.

JOHN HOLLEY; same as above.

JOHN HARRIS; soldier; served 59 days. Claim favorably reported. J. H. B. Va. 26 June 1777.

JAMES HARRIS; same.

AMOS HEATON; pay as Lieut. for 93 days allowed. J. H. B. Va. 26 June 1777.

MORDECAI HOARD was wagon-master with Braddock, 1755. See letter of John Redd. Draper Mss. 10NN-99.

DAVID HUNTER, soldier: served 53 days. Claim favorably reported. J. H. B. Va. 26 June 1777.

JOHN Harris, Jr. Soldier; served 93 days. Claim favorably reported. J. H. B. Va. 26 June 1777.

JAMES HAMILTON, soldier; served 93 days. Claim favorably reported. J. H. B. Va. 26 June 1777.

ROBERT HORSLEY; soldier, Revolutionary service. Claim allowed. J. H. B. Va. 26 May 1777.

JESSE HENSON; served 49 days. Claim favorably reported. J. H. B. Va. 26 June 1777.

WILLIAM HENSON; served 49 days. Favorably reported. J. H. B. Va. 26 June 1777.

JOHN HODGES; entered the "minute service," was taken ill and died, Martha Hodges, his widow, petitions. J. H. B. Va. 8 Nov. 1777.

DAVID IRWIN; soldier; served 93 days. J. H. B. Va. 26 June 1777.

JAMES JONES; in Revolutionary service. See will of Watkins. Charl. Va. 2 Apr. 1781. i-365.

WILLIAM JAMESON, Gent. Takes oath as Lieut. of militia. Charl. cty. Va. Jany ct 1778. iv-121.

DAVID JEANE, a soldier for this county; Betty Jeane, his wife, to be supplied. Charl. cty, Va. May Ct 1777. Orders iv-95.

ANDREW KING, a poor soldier; Mary Hammond King, his wife, to receive supplies. Charl. cty, Va. May Ct 1778. iv.-134.

HUMPHREY LUCAS, a soldier in the service of the U. S. Wife, Elizabeth, gets provisions. Charl. cty, Va. Mch Ct 1780. iv-218. See also iv-153 and iv-109. 1777 and 1778.

SARAH LUNDERMAN, a poor person who has two sons in the Continental service for this county, to be furnished with half a bushel of salt for the support of her family. Charl, cty, Va. Ct Dec 1778. iv. 118.

RICHARD LIPSCOMB makes declaration for pension. Court declare opinion that he was a Revolutionary soldier. Charl. cty. Va. 3 Dec 1832. Orders xxix-16.

PHILIP MALONE, a poor soldier in the service of the U. S. Mary Malone, his wife, furnished with provisions. Charl. cty, Va. Ct. Mch 1780. iv.-212.

BENJAMIN MARSHALL makes declaration of service. Court declares opinion that he was a Revolutionary soldier. Charl., Va. 3 Dec. 1832. Orders xxix-16.

MICHAEL MURPHY, Loudoun cty, Va., foot soldier; enlisted by and under Lieut. Abraham Warford of the Continental Establishment, being entitled to 100 acres of land, &c., &c. Ldn, Va. 1785. C-128.

HUGH MOORE, Gent., produces commission as Captain of a foot company and takes the oath. Hal. cty, Va. 26 May 1753. 1st "Pleas."

WILLIAM McCULLAM; proved that he improved land in Kentucky cty, 10 April 1776, but was prevented from "laying his claim on account of being in the Regular service." Court is of opinion that he is entitled to preemption of 1,000 acres. Jeff'n cty, Ky. Court Mch, 1782. A-20.

EDWARD McDONALD; frontier soldier, Augusta cty, Hening, vii-192. 1758.

BRYAN McDONELL, assignee of Joshua McCormack; paid for horse and mare lost in Shawnese expedition. Aug. cty, Va. Sept 1758. Hening, vii-187.

BENJAMIN MARSHALL makes declaration of service. Court declares opinion that he was a Revolutionary soldier. Charl. , Va. 3 Dec 1832. Orders, xxix-16.

MICHAEL MURPHY, Loudon cty, Va., foot soldier; enlisted by and under Lieut. Abraham Warford of the Continental Establishment, being entitled to 100 acres of land, &., &., Ldn, Va. 1785. C-128.

JACKSON MILLS, makes declaration of service, and Court declare opinion that he was a Revolutionary soldier. Ct 21 Aug 1832. Gchld cty. xix-147.

AMOS L. MOORE, same, same. 22 Aug 1832. xx-152.

JAMES MEALY. same, same. 22 Aug 1832 Gchld cty, xxi-152.

THOMAS McCLANAHAN, sworn captain. 27 May 1757. Pr. Wm cty, Va. Orders [3], p. 308.

SAMUEL MITCHELL; files declaration and Court is of opinion that he was a Revolutionary soldier. Bedford cty, Va. Ct Jany, 1833.

JOHN McCORMAHA; same, same.

JOHN MITCHELL; same, same

BENJAMIN MEADOR; same, same.

BENJAMIN MEADOWS; files declaration and Court is of opinion that he was a Revolutionary soldier. Bedford, Va. Ct Aug. 1832. [This probably the some man as the preceding.]

JOHN McCONNEHAY; same, same.

JOHN MITCHELL; same, same.

JAMES MITCHELL; same, same.

THOMAS McDEARMAN; amends his declaration for pension. Charl., Va. 3 Dec 1832. Orders xxix-40.

THOMAS MILBURN, a soldier in the Country's service, allowed £4-10sh. Pittsyl.,Va. Feby Ct 1778. iv-62.

CHARLES NICHOLS makes oath that he served as a soldier in the 1st Va. Reg't, three years and ten months. Ordered certified to Land Office. Pittsyl., Va. Sept Ct 1779. iv-259.

Reasonable price or two years' subscription will be given for numbers 1, 2, 3, 4, 6, and 7, COUNTY COURT NOTE-BOOK, 1921-1922. Address Editor.

Fifty cents will be paid for a copy of February 1927.

Printed at the Industrial School for Crippled and Deformed Children, 241 St. Botolph St., Boston, Mass.

The

County Court Note-Book

A Little Bulletin of History and Genealogy

December, 1928. Vol. VII, No. 6

FAMILIES OF THE EASTERN SHORE THE WHITTINGTONS

Collated notes from provincial and county records touching Capt. WILLIAM WHITTINGTON, of Northampton county, Virginia; his son Col. WILLIAM WHITTINGTON, of Virginia and Maryland, and the sons of the latter, WILLIAM and SOUTHY WHITTINGTON, of Maryland and Virginia, with some record of the daughters, and of the allied families.

WILLIAM WHITTINGTON first appears in the records of Northampton county, Virginia, when he makes a deposition in some matter before the Court, the 20 Jany 1640. (vol. ii, p. 51.) The 6 July 1641, he makes another deposition, in which he says that he was at the house of Elias Taylor, dec'd . . . where some one used language . . . "words not fitting to be uttered nor at present by me [Whittington] remembered." (ii-77.)

In another deposition (28 Apr 1643) he makes statements wnich appear to show that he was in Maryland with Mr. Richard Ingle [see the matter of the Ship *Reformation.*] (N-n, ii-230.)

WILLIAM WHITTINGTON obtains a patent for 450 acres in Northampton, at Naswattocke Creek, between Davis Neck and Major Neck; nine head rights: WILLIAM WHITTINGTON; SUSAN, his wife, and seven others. (Va. S. L. O. 13 July 1647. ii-109) Nothing further is known about this wife, SUSAN. The will of THOMAS SHEPHARD shows that WHITTINGTON had married ELIZABETH WESTON before 29 Sept 1648. (N-n, iii-164.) It is probable that in this case as in others the patent included the right of a wife who was then dead.

The 10 Jany 1650, WILLIAM WHITTINGTON, of Northampton, planter, appears as attorney for Capt. William Stone, who was the admr of one Burditt. (N-n, iv-31.) At the same Court, Richard Smyth, of Northampton, planter, agrees to serve WHITTINGTON until Christmas, 1652. (iv-30.) WHITTINGTON again appears for Capt. William Stone (of Maryland), 8 Dec 1651. (iv-149.)

Lieut. WHITTINGTON voluntarily gives to the widow of John Charles, 606 lbs. tobacco, which seems to have been adjudged due to Whittington by the court. 29 Dec. 1651. (iv-71.) Lieut. WHITTINGTON is on the bench as one of the justices, 28 Sept 1652. (iv-99.)

Capt. WILLIAM WHITTINGTON presents to the Court a bill of sale for all the cattle belonging to Capt. William Stone, Esq., Governor of Maryland, in Northampton county; also the cattle "appertaining to said Capt. Stone his sonne Richard Stone in Northampton," 4 Oct 1653. (iv-207.)

Jaffrey Minshall is charged with scandalously defaming "Capt. Lieut." WHITTINGTON. Public acknowldgement by Minshall accepted. (iv-143.)

Certificate granted Mr. WILLIAM WHITTINGTON for 700 acres, assigned by Hon'ble Capt. William Stone, Esq., Gov'r, &c. Fourteen head rights. 3 Feby 1653. (v-4) [This appears to be recorded twice, previously in vol. iv.]

Patent to Capt. WILLIAM WHITTINGTON for 800 acres in Northampton county; beginning at the northern end of a "divident" bought by the said Capt. WHITTINGTON from Capt. William Stone . . , at the head of Mattawamps [?] Main Branch . . . towards another tract bought by the said Capt. WHITTINGTON of the said Capt. Stone . . being at the seaboard side. . . 16 head rights. The list includes "WILLIAM WHITTINGTON; MARY, his wife." 11 Mch 1653. (Va. S. L. O. iii-286.)

[No explanation has been found anywhere of this wife, MARY. It will be shown that WHITTINGTON'S wife, ELIZABETH, did not die until after this date. It can only be supposed that this MARY was also a former wife for whom land was claimed. As said before this was not uncommon.]

In 1654, 24 Nov, Capt. WILLIAM WHITTINGTON assigns 200 acres to John Curtis. (Va. S. L. O. iii-295.)

The 28 Aug 1654, Mr. WILLIAM WHITTINGTON is made trustee (or guardian) of the estate of Charles Scarburgh (the son of Lt. Col. Edmund Scarburgh), at the request of Lt. Col. Scarburgh, during the latter's absence. Charles Scarburgh evidently a minor. [His depositions show that he was born about 1643.] (v-23.)

WHITTINGTON was also the guardian of Phillipp Taylor, an "orphant," appearing in the matter of an attachment against the estate of Taylor's step-father, Mr. William Eltonhead, of Maryland. 28 Aug 1654. (v-27.)

Capt. WILLIAM WHITTINGTON buys a "Barke" called the *Return* from a Mrs. Sellick. 1 May 1655. (vii-17.) [See *Ships in Port*, in early NOTE-BOOK.] WILLIAM WHITTINGTON, Gent., conveys to John Stockley, pltr, 400 acres. 30 July 1655. He is a Justice of the Court. 1656. (vii-22.)

WILLIAM WHITTINGTON, one of the feofees in trust for the orphans of Capt. Stephen Charlton, is about to take a voyage out of Virginia, and asks to be freed of the charge, and that his account may be perused. He is discharged as requested and his account is evidently satisfactory. 27 Feby 1656, and Mch and June, 1656. (vii-37.)

WILLIAM WHITTINGTON, Gent., conveys tract on Hungar's Creek (the patent sold to WHITTINGTON by Capt. Wm. Stone.) 18 Apr 1657. (ix-35.)

Capt. WILLIAM WHITTINGTON, of Northampton, Gent., conveys to William Satchel, pltr.,

100 acres on the seaboard side . . . running by his *now dwelling-house.* 30 Apr 1657. Wit: Samuell Luddington, Cornelius Berry. ELIZABETH SPENCER, former wife of Capt. WILLIAM WHITTINGTON, releases dower. 31 Dec 1660. (ix-81.)

[The Editor ventures to call attention to this, on the face, somewhat puzzling record. It is explained later by the death of WHITTINGTON. In a very similar case, where another widow had re-married and had after that re-marriage released her dower rights in certain property of her former husband, the comment was made by a supposedly high authority "*Looks like a divorce!*"]

WILLIAM WHITTINGTON makes a deed of gift to his daughter URSULA WHITTINGTON and to Hannah Pennuell, dau. of John Pennuell . . a mare foal and ewe lambs "and a ram of next year's yeaning" . . . . and to Katherine wife of John Pennuell, an ewe lamb; John Pennuell to be "feofy in trust." 20 Apr 1659. (ix.56.)

Capt. WILLIAM WHITTINGTON, of Northampton, Virginia. His will:

"Am intended by God's Assistance to take "a voyage very Shortly for Holland & not "Knowing how it Shall please God to dispose "of me" . . . . gives all his lands in Virginia to son WILLIAM WHITTINGTON, excepting 300 acres . . upon the branch lying where Mr. Edw. Gunter liveeth & Richard Clark (reference to patent) & all the land that I have lying in Maryland to expected child . . . . "be it Boy or Girl." The 300 acres excepted from Virginia land to dau. URSELEE WHITTINGTON; to James Beaman, my servant, cows and sheep; to Argoll Yardley, a mare foal to be delivered within four months next after my Death; also gives *to the use of a free school if it go forward in Northampton county 2,000 lbs. tobacco.* Remainder estate to wife ELIZABETH WHITTINGTON, and son WILLIAM WHITTINGTON, and dau. URSELIE WHITTINGTON and expected child. Division to be made immediately after his death; if widow marry, appoints friends William Waters and Mr. John Pennuell to take care of children's parts. Wife to have use of all his land until son WILLIAM attain the age of 18, provided she remain a widow, but should she marry she is not to have the benefit of any part of his land "save only that which I bought of William Taylor which she now dwelleth upon." Wife, sole executor. Should she marry before children are of age, then appoints son, WILLIAM, executor. Entreats friends mentioned to assist wife and children. Gives friends mentioned "£10 between them to buy each of them two rings a piece for themselves and wives to wear in remembrance of their Friend." . . . . Estate not to be appraised but equal division made. WM.;WHITTINGTON. [Signed.] Wit: Will: Melling, John x Turner, Margaret Neale. 4 May 1659. Recorded 4 Feby 1659. (ix-56.) The will was proved by John Turner and Margitt Neale. 30 Jany 1659. (viii-60.)

ELIZABETH WHITTINGTON, the lawful attorney of her husband, Capt. WILLIAM WHITTINGTON, gets a judgment for 6,440 lbs. tobacco. 28 Feby 1659. (viii-58.)

List of "Particulars" to be delivered to the several children of Capt. WILLIAM WHITTINGTON, by name: WILLIAM, URSLIE, and ELIZABETH WHITTINGTON . . . . each of them to be paid by their father-in-law, Mr. William Spencer, at the time they attain to lawful age . . . and Spencer is to bring them up to Learning to the best of his Capacity. This list of "Particulars" is in full of the said Children's Portions left them by their dec'd Father. signed Willm Spencer. Wit: John Ferebe, Charles Holden. 28 June 1664. ix-197.

Capt. WILLIAM WHITTINGTON, of Northampton county, Virginia, was born about 1616. See his deposition, 14 May 1653. Nthld cty, Va. (i-145.) [So far no actual proof has been found that this is Capt. WILLIAM WHITTINGTON of Northampton county. But there is every reason to believe that it is the same man.] He died between the 4 May 1659 and the 30 Jany 1659. (O. S.)

Capt. WHITTINGTON m. (1) [probably] MARY ....

He m. (2) SUSAN ....

He m. (3) ELIZABETH WESTON, who was a "cousin" of Thomas Shephard. [Will of Tho: Shephard. 29 Sept 1648. Recorded 10 Jany 1648. Makes and appoints his cousin WILLIAM WHITTINGTON "(by marriage of my cousin Elizabeth Weston)" extr for his estate in Virginia............For his estate in England, freely gives it to his uncle Weston. N-n, Va. iii-164.] Elizabeth (Weston) Whittington m. (2) Mr. William Spencer. 14 June 1660. (ix-92.) (See also x-51 and iii-164.)

The children of Capt. WILLIAM WHITTINGTON were:

URSULA, probably m. Col. Edmund Scarburgh

WILLIAM, born 1649-1650, m. (1) Tabitha Smart; (2) Hester Littleton; (3) Attalanta (Toft) Osborne; (4) Hannah [Hopkins?] (5) Elizabeth .... (who m. 2. Rev. Samuel Davis.)

ELIZABETH, baptized 16 May 1660, aged 8 months. (See vol. ix, N-n, Va. records.)

(To be continued)

AUTHENTIC REFERENCES FOR INFERRED MARRIAGES

(From Maryland records.)

DAVID KIRKPATRICK and JANE, admx of Robert GIVAN. Som. cty. E. B. 12-20. (The Givan children were Eliza:, age about 13; Mary, about 5; William, about 4.)

THOMAS LARRAMORE and the extx of Robert HOPKINS, Sr. Before 14 July 1710, Som. cty. E. B. 13-43.

GEORGE LANE and TEMPERANCE POPE. Banns of matrimony published." August the 6th Ano. 1720, Georg Lane made return of his Certificate to which I gave the County Seal. George Lane. Temperance Pope." [This note probably made by the Clerk.] Som. cty. 8 July 1720. I. K.-29.

.... LANKFORD and HARRIET STERLING, dau. of Aaron. Som. cty. Before 1749. J. P. 5-156.

HENRY LANGSDALE and ELIZABETH PORTER, admx of Joshua. Before 11 May 1803. Som. cty. E. B. 24-

JAMES LYON and ANNA SPENCER. Balto., Md. 16 July 1797. 1st Presbytr Ch. Reg.

NATHAN LANHAM and CATHERINE TUCKER, gr. dau. of Isaac Stallings. Fred'k cty. Before 27 Oct 1788. T-102.

THOMAS MANLOVE and JANE DELAMAR. Som. Md, About Sept 1668. B (1)-134.

HENRY MILES and MARY BARNEBE, widow. "Bonds of matrimony." Som. Md. 28 Jany 1667. B (1)-107.

GEORGE MITCHELL and IZABELL HIGGENS. "Bonds." Som. Md. 29 Sept. 1668. B (1)-136.

THOMAS MANLOVE and JANE DE LAMAR. [This is the same marriage as that indicated above. The "De" is inserted later by another hand and in different ink.] B (1)-79. 30 July 1667.

JOHN MACKETTRICK and MARY ALLEN, wid. "Bonds." Som. cty, 28 May 1667. B (1)-68.

JOHN MARLETT and HANNAH MANLOVE. "Bonds." Som. cty. 28 May 1667. B (1)-68.

.... MACLANEY; .... PURNELL; .... HAMMOND; .... NICHOLSON; all these seem to have been the husbands of ELIZABETH NICHOLSON, see her will. She also had a dau. Eleanor Jones. Som. cty. 12 Sept 1730. E. B. 9-148.

RICHARD MITCHELL and MARY, "Joint Administrator and Trix of Owen O'DAY's estate." Som. cty. Before 12 June 1736. E. B. 12-147.

JOHN McCLESTER and ELIZABETH WHITTINGTON, widow of Andrew. Som. cty. Before 9 Nov 1697. D. D. 17-269.

THOMAS MORRIS prob. m. the widow of Sam'll INNIS. She was evidently the dau. of Edward SMITH. See Smith's will. Som. cty. Before 10 Nov 1691. B. W. Z.-121

MARTIN MOORE and MARGARET CORNELIUS. Banns. 30 July 1667. Som. cty. B (1)-62.

ROBERT MORRISON and SARAH DENSTON, only dau. and hr-at-law of John. Wor. cty. Before 7 Dec 1759. D-498.

JEFFREY MITCHELL and ELEENOR CONNER, dau. of Philip. Sr. Wor. cty Before 21 Feby 1702. M. H. iii-49.

.... MORRIS and CATHERINE BURTON. dau. of William. Wor. cty. J. W. ii-30. 1744.

JEREMIAH MORRIS and ELNOR DENNIS, dau. of Donnack. Wor. cty. Before 16 Feby 1716. M. H. iii-123.

JOHN MUMFORD and NEOMI AYDELOTT, dau. of BENJAMIN. Wor. cty. Before 24 Mch 1775. i-590.

RALPH MILBOURN and MARY HALL, dau. of Henry. Before 27 Oct 1708. Wor. cty. M. H. iii-72.

Mr. JOHN MINOR and CASSANDRA WILLIAMS, sister of Otho-Holland WILLIAMS. Fred'k cty. Before 5 June 1794. G. M. iii-38.

NATHAN MAGRUDER and REBECCA BEALL, dau. of John. Before 7 Apr 1742. Pr. Geo's cty. i-340.

THO: MACHELL and .... POWELL, widow of Charles and dau. of Stephen GERY. Chas. cty. Before 1723. i-250.

WILFORD MELTON and FRANCES DAVIS. Montg. cty, Before 13 Aug 1800. D-420.

.... NOBLE and ELIZABETH PORTER, widow of William. Som. cty. Before 18 June 1718. E. F. -167. (After 6 Dec 1695.)

JOHN NOBLE and MARGARET, admx of Peter BOOTH. Som. cty. Before 30 Aug 1715. A. C. (12)-257.

BENJAMIN NESHAM and ELIZABETH JAMISON, dau. of Alexander. Long before 17 Nov 1721. I. K. -174. Som. cty.

HUETT NUTTER and ELIZABETH WHITTINGTON, admx of Joshua. Som. cty. Before or about 12 Nov 1767. E. B. x-38.

.... NUTTER and ELIZABETH PURNELL, dau. of Thomas. Before 5 Mch 1693. Wor. cty. M. H. iii-34.

.... NOBLE prob. married MARGRIT LAYFIELD, Wor. cty. Before 25 May 1709. M. H. iii-76.

JAMES ODEL and MARTHA PRATHER, sister of Jeremiah. She m. (2) .... LAZENBY. Montg. cty. Before 15 May 1779. A-195.

JOHN OBER [hardly legible] and MARY VINCENT, both of Manoakin. Banns. Som. cty. 1 Sept 1666. B (1)-29.

HUGH PORTER and ELIZABETH WALLACE, dau. of John. Som. cty. Before 7 Sept 1764. C-234.

WRIXAM L. PORTER and PRISSELLA RIGGEN, dau. of Teague. Som. cty. Before 6 Jany 1807. R-111.

.... PATRICK and AGNES DAVIS, dau. of Edward. Before 3 Oct 1709. M. H. iii-89.

CHARLES POWELL and a dau. of Stephen GERY. Chas. cty. Before 1723. i-250a.

STEPHEN PAGE and BRIDGET PARRAMORE, admx of Arnold. Som. cty. Before 11 Nov 1691. B. W. Z.-131.

JOHN PURNELL and TABITHA, admx of Parker SELBY. Wor. cty. Before 11 Aug 1708. J. W. xv-324.

THOMAS POINTER and MARY, admx of Andrew DIRREC[K]SON. Wor. cty. Before 5 Aug. 1718. J. W. xv-311.

THOMAS PORTER and JANE HARRIS, sister of David. Before 28 Nov 1693. Som. cty. L-217.

JOHN PARREMORE, Jr. and ABIAH MANLOVE. Som cty. Before 8 Aug 1671. S. C. (3)-1.

ROGER PHILLIPS and DOROTHY VANCE, dau. of Alexander, Taylor. Som. cty. Before 16 Nov 1715. Vol. 1715-1716-10.

.... PITT and JANNET NEARN, widow. Wor. Md. Before 18 Apr 1767. G-72.

VIRGINIA COLONISTS

(From "Old Volume 5, S. L. O., Richmond.)

RALPH GREENE, "Glosester" cty, 1658.

Head rights: Wm. Turner, Geo. Foster, John Logg, Henry Jones, Jane Young, Andrew Pight, William Shipley [? perhaps Stipley], John Haies, Robert Bellfinn, Rich. Foster, Edward Pinton, Roger Collins, James Greene. [The name Pight is possibly cockney for *Pate.*]

ROBERT GRAY, Elizabeth City cty, 1658.
Head right: John Farrast [probably Forrest.]

MICHAEL GRAFTON, 1658.
Head rights: Henry Furr, Tho. Lucas, John Stevens.

JOHN GORE, Lancaster cty, 1658.
Head rights: S'r Henry Chickley, Rich. Chambey, Jno. Layward.

PHILIP HIMLY, Mockiack [Mockjack] Bay, 1658.
Head rights: Sanders Blacke, Sanders Mackdowell, Wm. Mack Loyd, Wm. Morrison, Mackin Mackloyd, Andrew Trumbell.

ANTHONY HAYNES, New Kent cty, 1658.
Head rights: (13 persons, names of five only given), David Steed, Fortune Perkins, Thomas Coates, Richard Lendy. Balt [?] Ingerbanke.

ANTHONY HAYNES, Rappa. cty, 1658.
Head rights: Mary Willis, Thomas Boyes, Margery Puttinge [Pullinge?] Ben Hurstwell, Tho. Bell, Rich. Damsies [?] Rich. Joy, Mary Joy, Jaine Irish, Georg Devarr, Georg Poole, Thomas Porter, Wm. Bodd [?] Lawrence Yorke, thrice; Martha Pane, Richard Smith, Richard Steale, A...... Tulmarsh, Charles Quarles.

WM. HAY, Gent., Yorke cty, 1658.
Head rights: Thomas Stephens, Wm. Roberts, Edward Braybrooke, Charles Perry, Richard Willson.

REES HUGHES, New Kent cty, 1657.
Head rights: Adam Denny, Robert Gray, Jno. Wilkins, David Morgan, Mary Marshe [?] Ann Leiry [Lorry?] Robert Kiggs, Wm. Tillen.

CHRISTOPHER HARRIS, Westmoreland cty, 1658.
Head rights: Jno. Snellinge, Nath. Pinson, Georg Covell [?] [this is possibly Canill] James Mahue, Wm. West, Edward Bromfield, John Abbott, Jane Davison, Thos. Clemente, Nath. Crosby, Wm. Symson, Ann Delue, Mary James. Ja: Hollcrofte [?] Wm. Feild, John Mutton, Jno. Williams, Henry Coniers, Georg Harper, Sarah Massy [?] Nath. Ruferd, Robert Hollaway, Jno. Cranfeild, Margaret Munday, Wm. Newsome, Roger Sloe, Edmond Lucas, Mathew Batts, Hugh Thomas, Joseph Fairepointe, Wm. Nicholls, Jno. Prevett, Symon Holl, Jacords Male [?] Charles Davison, John Mackhannin. 40 persons, only 38 listed.

Mr. THOMAS HAMPTON, Clerke; "on the east side of Chickahominy River, 1658.
Head rights: Doman [Dorman] Kygan, Cornelius Niken [Nehon?] Wm. Dolly.

Mr. JOHN HANSFORD, 1658.
Head rights: Rowland Thomas, Charles Dunne, Tho. Symmons.

THO. HARRIS, Isle of Wight cty, 1658.
Head rights: Jno. Hardy, Eliz: Jones, Fran: Anderson, WELTIN HARRIS, Thomas Tier, Alexander Vaughan, Mary Wood, Jno. Pen, Anth. Arnold, Thomson Butt, Ann Lees [or Loos], Jno. Davis, Ann Greene, Samuel Trobury, James Rogers, Wm. Todd, Jno. Griskin [?] Eliz: Ensome [?] Alex. Canill, Geo. West.

Errata in previous lists:

In June, 1925, NICHOLAS JERNEW it is thought should be JERMAN or JERNAN.

In October, 1928, under LULLAMAN, the name RIDER is uncertain. It may be RICTER. In the same issue under LEWIS, SURPLEETE should be SURFLEETE.

THE TITHABLES OF NORTHAMPTON COUNTY, VIRGINIA, IN 1742

(From original lists)

Alderton Gilding, Marke Short;
John Millard;
Henery Spakeman, John Spakeman;
Samuell Floyd;
Wattkins Wilkins;
John Johnson;
John Warren;
William Wilkins, Jr.;
William Wilkins, Sr., Nathaniell Wilkins;
Major Guy; Thomas Respes;
John Wilkins;
Mr. William Burton, Wimbleton Daniell [?] Peter Elliot?
Robert Warren, Sr.;
Joseph Cob;
Robert Banks;
James Floyd;
George Powell;
John Elligood, "Cunstable;" John Elligood, Jr., John Smay;
Solomon Warren, "Pattroler;"
Joseph Ash, "Pattroler";
Benjamin Jenkins;
Marke Beckit, Margrat Beckit [*sic*], Sarah Drighouse [*sic*];
Edward Wite;
Mr. Edmond Custis;
Jacob Harnage;
Ralph Pigot, Sr., Ralph Pigot, Jr., John Harding;
John Respus;
Isaac Sheppard;
Moses Stripe;
Joseph Benthall.

(Another District.)

Thos. Preeson, Jacob Pitts;
Rev. Mr. Holbrook, Edw'd Holbrook, Peter Roscoe, Jr.;
Major Brickhouse, John Brickhouse. George Brickhouse;
John Reynalds;
David Stott;
Wm. Smith, Sr.;
Sam'll Grafton, Will. Natts;
William Pettit, John and Henry Pettit;
Edward Isdall, Sr., Edw'd Isdell, Jr.;
John Pettit;
Rich'd Sturges;
Jacob Sturges;
Dan'l Godwin;
Geo. Beloat;
Thos. Willson;
Littleton Beloat, John Jacob;
Alexander Melvin;
William Stott, Abr'm Westerhouse;
Joachim Michael, Tylney Michael, Thomas Michael; Sarah Morris [*sic*] Beck Becket [*sic*];
John Walter, Sr., John Walter, Jr.
John Dolby, Thos. Dolby, Eliz'th Dixon [*sic*], Jacob Fox.

Capt. Thos. Marshall, Isme Marshall, Thos. Marshall, Jr., Bartholemew Larrance, Hug [*sic*] Keeve, Edwd Forman;
Solomon Wilson;
Dan'l Teague;
Wm. Smith (Leeds?)
Isaac Smith, Jr.;
Dan'l Rascoe;
Henry Gascoine, Jacob Andrews;
Jonathan Edmonds;
Thos. Upshur;
John Luke, Dan'l Luke;
Jonathan Bell;
Edm'd Johnson;
James Heath, Bartholomew Heath, Wm. Heath;
Stephen Carpenter, John Carpenter;
Geo. Thomas, Jonathan Moore;
William Parsons;
Abel Beloat;
Edwd White;
Dan'l Lucas;
Jeptha Douty;
John Smith;
Howland Douty, Sarah Becket;
George Green, Mark Isdell;
James McManus;
Major Hitchens, [It is hardly necessary to remark that this name "Major" was a family name used as a forename]; Tamer Hitchens, Ann Hitchens;
Florence Dunfee;
Sylv's Haggoman, Caleb Benthall;
John Lucas, Sr., John Lucas, Jr.,;
Geo. Letyn [?]
Abel Upshur, Jacob Morris;
Rich'd Parramore, const., Peter Rascoe, Sr.;
Charles Carpenter;
Abel Nottingham; Littleton Abdel;
Jno. Custis Matthews, Wm. Andrews, Henry Clegg;
John *Merry*;
Tho's Westerhouse;
Jonathan Smith;
John Rascoe, Th's Rascoe;
Joseph Dolby, Esau Dolby;
Will'm Westerhouse;
Upshur Dolby;
Nath'l Bell;
Jonathan Stott, Ralph Batson;
Jno. Addison;
John Abdel;
Ezekiel Bell;
George Bell;
Wm. Tankred;

(*To be continued*)

FORE-NAMES FROM COLONIAL RECORDS

ANJELLATA GAULT. Wor. cty, Md. About 1774. IW-7.

ANGILLICA NOELL [NOVELL?] Court orders all her clothes to be delivered by Esther Fitchett to Capt. Francis Costing. N-n, Va. 1711. xv-155.

APPHYA MILLER and Francis Ridgers, E. C. City. Va. Mar. Li. 15 Oct 1698.

APPHIA YARBROUGH. wf of John. Caroline cty, Va. 10 Feby 1745. Orders, p. 563.

APPHIA DANGERFIELD, sister of Hannah Robinson. Wmld Wills, Crozier, p. 72. 1778

ARRABELLA EVANS, wf of John, of Somerset, Md. Acco., Va. 1 May 1731. xx-72. Also xix-240.

ARRABELLOW CHAMBERS, dau. of Mrs. Frances Chambers, Acco., Va. 16 July 1682. vi-327.

ARRALANTOR [?] ROBINS, dau. of John Purnell. Wor, cty. Md. 8 Jany 1755. i-147.

ARCADIA NICHOLSON; mar. contact [probably] with Jacob Broadwater. Acco., Va. 5 Dec 1764. Deeds iii-377.

ARCADIA WELBURNE, widow of Thomas, She had son Daniel, also sons Francis, Benjamin and Samuel, Acco., Va., 4 May 1710. xi-52. Also xi-529, 530.

ARCADIA NICHOLSON, wf.of William, Acco., Va. 1757. iii-63.

ARCADIA CUTLER had bro. Samuel Cutler, Acco., Va.

ARCADAH DIRICKSON, was wf. of William. of Wor. cty, Md. See Sussex city, Dela. IW2-188. 1758.

ARCADA HAZZARD, was wf. of John, Wor, cty, Md. IW13-109. 1752. ARCADA was also a dau. of William Hazzard. See Sussex, Dela. 1782. ARCADA ROBINSON was daughter of Rachel Hazzard.

ATTALANTA OSBORNE was wf of Capt. John Osborne. See his willm Acco., Va. 1686. xi-3.

ATTALANTA TOWNSEND was wf. of Caleb, Acco., Va. 28 Oct 1783. xxxviW-411.

Mrs. ATTALANTA WHITTINGTON, Acco.. Va. 20 Feby 1888. ix-152.

NOTE: So far as the Editor knows the names Arcadia and Attalanta began in this section of Va-Md with the daughters of Ann Toft. It is not as certain about Arrabella . . . who was a third daughter of the same mother.

Attention is invited to the following important offers. Information should be sent to

Mr. Orra E. Monnette,
350, South Oxford avenue,
Los Angeles, California.

ROBERTSON.—Ten Dollars for original information concerning JOHN ROBERTSON (possibly William or Nathaniel) born Baltimore 1795, son of George Robertson, Revolutionary Patriot, whose family removed to New Brunswick, Canada, before 1800. Married (1) Mary Matthews; (2)1820 [?] nnknown, leaving descendents in Baltimore.

MERCER.—Ten Dollars for original information concerning JOSEPH MERCER, Loyalist, Revolution, leaving America for New Brunswick, Canada, 1783. (See Sabine). He was born about 1745 in Virginia; lived in Bladen County, North Carolina, 1773, was ensign in. British Army; wife, Sarah Baxter, born 1747, Said to have been son of Gen. Hugh Mercer Revolutionarv Patriot.

The County Court Note-Book

An every-other-monthly devoted mainly to abstracts from County Court Records, prior to 1800.

MILNOR LJUNGSTEDT, Editor and Publisher. Bethesda, Route 10, Maryland.

Published six times a year. Subscription, two dollars, in advance; must begin with the year.

December, 1928 **Whole**
Vol. VII., No. 6 **No. 43**

THE OLD STREET

The records of the City say that this part of the street was opened through the garden (perhaps the farmyard?) of quite a large property . . . perhaps the old house across the way, with the brass plate on the tall, close boarded gate, and the Lombardy poplars screening the new wing, perhaps that was what some might call the "Great House", . . . perhaps the lilies of the valley that grew so thick and heavenly scented in the corner of the garden squeezed in by the backyards of the houses on the street around the corner, and cut off from the Street by the high board fence, perhaps they were the great-great-great-grandchildren of the lilies of the valley cherished through many generations of colonial times . . . who knows, and perhaps they were brought up from Plymouth town to the metropolis . . . who knows?

I am sure that when the Little Street, then a new street, was cut through, that the ladies of the house that faced on it could not abide the publicity, and so had those Lombardy poplars planted. It must have seemed to those gentlefolk like getting up in the morning and finding that the shades had fallen . . . moths or mice having severed the cords that held the counter-weights, all nicely dressed up in fuzzy stuff and green tassels. Those weights made very fair *pretended* dolls, the little girl who lived on the new side of the street thought, for above their dangling fringes was there not a sort of a plump body and a waist . . . but, my! their leaden hearts were heavy!

And the poplars grew and flourished, and kept their heads high and looked over the smaller houses that set themselves up to face the big house, as if they never even saw across the street. And people came and went, and ladies in the big house lived behind the poplars and left the brass knocker, which was then quite out of style, on the second door, to the great delight of the little girl on the new side of the street, who went over occasionally, to eat cookies and look at picture-books in the big house.

Her own house was a very respectable house, indeed, though it was young in comparison with the big house. It also was of brick. It had its inset door, with windows each side, and a vestibule; the plate and the numbers on the door were of siiver; and an iron balcony projected from the second story so that when one was out on it, it did seem that one might suddenly come down on top of the passersby. It was the nicest house between the two corners and it was shaded as was all that part of the street just west of the poplars by the great sycamores . . . "button-ball trees" . . . that also grew in the yard of the older house across the way.

On account of two streets coming together as they did, at an acute angle, and squeezing the lilies of the valley and their corner of the garden, the service entrances to a few of the houses backing in this awkward way on everybody's view, were on the west of the yard of the big house, directly on the Street. One of them had a long covered way to the kitchen, and a doorway of stone. In this doorway the maid used to stand. She was Irish and *very* red-headed with a natural marcel that was waterproof. Just like the waves that the dark-eyed heroines of the "Annuals" wore, rippling down their white muslin backs. It was impressed upon the little girl's mind that all red-headed people had bad tempers and she was sure that this maid-of-all-work was a person to be considered seriously on that account. (But how does it happen that the stone doorway explained the "lintels" of the Bible and the Passover?)

Alack! The red-headed girl with the theoretical bad temper must have died these many years ago. Did she marry the ice-man and have childern with naturally marcelled heads?

And where is the fat and good-natured policeman who belonged on the corner and early in life gave the Editor a friendliness for all policemen. He could not have spent all his life on corners, yet memory puts him no where else.

Corners: at the left corner just across another street......the street that pushed back on the old garden and the lilies...... was a livery stable. How did that livery stable happen to be there? Had it crept up through the interest of some City Father from a less respectable quarter, or just suddenly bounced in? It had a ramp to the second story......and a ramp is a delightful structure to a child with small chance to indulge in any sort of activity. Of course, thelivery stable was forbidden, but a ramp and horses, who could resist them? Morever, if you were fearless and friendly and they had grown used to your taffy-colored locks and rosy cheecks you could be permitted to ride on top of the "hack" with the coachman when sent to school, supposedly inside. How many of my readers have known the transcendental bliss of riding down Washington street *on top* of a hack?

The other corner held no great interest. Before it became a corner grocery (as the Street descended socially, so did the corners), it had been a modest dwelling, wherein, on the second floor, was the abode of the dressmaker. She was a very genteel old lady, and her name was Miss McKenna. She inflicted tortures, at intervals, on the little girl who lived on the Street, by means of linings, and pins and scissors. The little girl wriggled, and wriggled, and just did behave, and that's all. Can you compare those hours with others spent on the ramp?

The Little old Street......you would not know it now. There is no great house, no garden, no trees. Even the Court beside the next best house is gone. The street is a bit wider......it looks as if part of the pavement lies where the dining-room windows used to be, and where the head of the family sat to read the morning Post, perhaps catching a ray from the early sun......the hustling generation of to-day surges east and west......but houses and households are gone.

Is it better?

NOTES HERE AND THERE IN MARYLAND

The CLERK being about to remove his lodging from Capt. G. West to Madam Mary King's house Humbly prayes the Wor'll Court that the Records of Somerset County may be lodged att the sd Ma'am Mary Kings Which was Granted by the Court. 16 Nov 1706. A. B. (9)-229.

WILL of THOMAS LARIMER, SEN'R, planter. "Item I give and bequeath unto the Boy John Larimur which my Eldest Son John Larimur got from the Indians and thinks it to be his Son which was Lost seventy five acres of land.........a tract called Turnstil.........in case the said Boy will come and live with me during my natural life but in case he will not come and dwell with me I give.........the aforesaid Seventy-five acres unto William Larimore." Som. cty. 7 Feby 1732-4 Apr 1732. E. B. ix-140.

A LIST OF CONSTABLES chosen for the year, 1723.

Jno. White, Constable of Monigh Hund'd; Chris: Glass of Mattapony, *ut supra*; Wm. Porter, of Pocomoke, *ut supra*; Mich'l Holland, Jr. of Annamessix; Jas. Bounds for Nanticoke; Jno. Richards for Wiccocomico; Wm. Eskridge, for Monokin; Jno. Truet, son of George Truet, for Bogettinorton; Edmond Crapper, for Baltimore; Som. cty. G. H. -2.

Mrs. Sarah Acword, widow of Mr. Henry Ackword, died 13 Mch 1720. See Ct 20 Nov 1722. G. H. (Reverse) p. 3.

The PETITION of Sarah Driggers and the rest all negroes desiring that they might be putt out of the list of Tythables being free borne Negroes ....Ordered that the four women be exempted and that the men pay Taxes for this year and that they bring a certificate under the Minister's hands Where they formerly did live or were borne that they are free Negroes and baptized. Som. cty 14 Aug 1688. Vol. 1690-1691-p. 58.

THO. HOLLIDAY Came into Court and the usuall Oaths administered in Order to teaching of School. Som. cty. Ct Aug 1719. A. C. (12) p. 416.

ELIZABETH SMITH, born 4 April 1676, as appears writt in a Bibble. She chooses Samuel Shewel for her guardian. Som. cty. 9 June 1690. E. F. G. -p. 111.

ROBERT POLLOCK of this county, otherwise called *Robert Polke* appears in a suit. Som. cty. Ct 14 Mch 1693. L. D. p. 87.

From the will of ANN x SMITH, of Somerset cty, Md; wife of EDWARD SMITH: "I bequeath to the sd RICHARD HILL [her son] ....upon condition that he give to SAMUEL DAVIS min[ister] a mare. Brother SAMUELL SHEWELL.........dau. MARTHA HILL.........my bible or small Sermen booke writt by Increase Mather of Boston." Wit: Samuel Davis, John Johnson. An additional memorandum mentions sons-in-law, "Dr. John Vigerous, Samuel Ennis, Richard Hill and dau. Elizabeth." 13 and 21 Aug 1688. M. H. iii-22. This will is recorded in Worcester cty, although in 1688 it was Somerset. An explanation of this will be found in an earlier NOTE-BOOK

ANOTHER VALUABLE VOLUME has been put out by the indefatigable "Daughters." The CAPTAIN JEREMIAH BAKER CHAPTER of the D. A. R., of Cecil County, Maryland, have copied the earliest record of Marriage Licenses in Cecil County, dating from July, 1777, to 1840, and had them printed and well bound. They offer the book for sale at $5.25 post paid. The work is indexed. Address either Mrs. Harry T. Alexander, East High street, Elkton, Maryland, or Miss Mollie Howard Ash, same post office.

This is excellent work to do......the publication, and so the preservation, of the records of the county court. These earnest and sincere ladies are to be complimented and encouraged.

CONTINUED articles COUNTY COURT NOTE-BOOK, and the dates on which they first appeared.

THE ANCESTRY OF COL. JOHN DONELSON. Began with February, 1927.

AUTHENTIC REFERENCES for INFERRED MARRIAGES (formerly called MARRIAGES BY INFERENCE). Began with May, 1922.

MARYLAND'S NEXT OF KIN. Began with July, 1922.

VIRGINIA COLONISTS. Alphabetized lists began with July, 1924.

MILITARY NOTES, both COLONIAL and REVOLUTIONARY, and later MILITIA NOTES. Began December, 1923.

INTERCOUNTY and INTERCOLONY (formerly called New Englanders and Others, &c., &c.). Began with March, 1922.

EASTERN SHORE FAMILIES. In the form of a one-page supplement, began with June, 1925.

SHIPS IN PORT and COLONIAL FORENAMES will appear in alternate issues or as space can be found for them.

THE DEPUTY COMMISSARY'S GUIDE WITHIN THE PROVINCE OF MARYLAND

(Continued from June issue.)

Under the heading of ACCOUNTS:........ "Every account.........in order to pass the commissary, must consist of enumerated articles without the least ambiguity; lumped balances of a former account, without the particulars, sums of money paid on *orders*, without producing such orders, nor any other charge not clearly specified, for what the same became due, or was paid, must be no part of such account. The truth of the account must be proved within twelve months after the first article therein charged becomes due, in this manner, if the account contains dealings only for one year.........then the account must appear to have been proved before a Magistrate within a twelve month" [from the date of the first article charged.]

If the creditor whose account is in question be dead, then the executor or administrator must make oath in form as required to the account.

"As to funeral expenses, the allowance ought not to exceed three or four pounds currency, except where the rank or opulence of the deceased may require a larger allowance.........but for small estates, such part only should be allowed as will merely defray the costs arising from the coffin and interment of the deceased, without any allowance for vain pomp and ostentation. When a testator directs an expensive funeral, if the claims of creditors should not be affected by the performance, the direction ought to be pursued; but the allowance will be made as in case of a legacy paid by an executor.".........

"In case where there are no known relations of the intestate, or representatives legally entitled to the residue, the administrator is directed........ to pay the balance into the hands of the visitors of the publick school of that county, wherein deceased resided........."

"The account [being] so finished, being returned to the prerogative office, is there recorded, and the balance thereof (if any) is from thence transmitted to the county court, with a distribution of ......[the] surplusage among the several representatives of the deceased; the performance of which is enforced by process out of the said court."

[It will be noted what powers and authority are left to the County Court.]

The Commissary-General is directed to transmit the balance of all intestates' estates, within three months, to the respective county courts.

....

"As proper in this place" the compiler subjoins a table "of the reduction of coins" together with their practical way of calculation.

TABLE

£100 sterling money is equal to £133 1-3 current money, or £166-2-3 common currency.

£100 current money is equal to £75 sterling money; or £125 common currency.

£100 common currency is equal to £60 sterling money; or £80 current money.

SERVICE AND SUPPLIES COLONIAL, REVOLUTIONARY AND MILITIA

WILLIAM NICHOL;S, a poor soldier who diep in the U. S. service; widow Elizabeth to receive supplies. Charl. cty, Va. Nov Ct 1778. Orders iv-161. Enlisted in Medford cty. See Ct Oct 1777. iv-109.

THOMAS NORTH; makes declaration of service, Court declare opinion that he was a Revolutionary soldier. Charl. cty, Va. Ct 1 Oct 1832. Orders xxix-5.

ELIZABETH NUNELLY, wife of ALEXANDER, a poor soldier, to receive supplies. Charl. cty, Va. Sept Ct 1780. Orders iv-145.

CLAIRBORNE OSBORNE; makes declaration for pension. Court declare opinion he was Revolutionary soldier. Charl. cty, Va. 7 Jany 1833. Orders xxix-18.

JOHN O'BRYAN, a poor soldier in the U. S. service. Wife Mildred to receive supplies. Charl. cty, Va. Ct Oct 1778. Orders iv-153.

JOHN PARROTT was a continental soldier. and died. Admn granted to Joseph Parrott. Nash cty. N. C. Ct 13 Feby 1792. Ct Minutes,

ABRAHAM PENN, Esq.; produces comm'n as Lieut. Col. of militia and takes oath. He is appointed Lieut. Col. in the room of Edmund Lyne, Esq., who has resigned. (See Ct 20 Oct 1778.) Henry cty, Va. Ct 15 Feby 1779.

JOHN PRYOR made due proof that he served in Capt. Preston's Company of Rangers in 1757, 1758 and 1759, till the company was disbanded. Bot. cty, Va. 13 Apr 1780. Orders.

ROBERT PACE; makes declaration and Court declare opinionhe was a Revolutionary soldier. Gchld, Va. 22 Aug. 1832.

ROBERT PLEASANTS, Same. Same county and date.

HEZEKIAH PITTS; recommended to the 2d Lieut., Capt. Thomas Fisher's Company. N-n, Va. 12 Aug 1777. xxxvO-11.

JOHN RIDDLE; makes declaration and Court declare opinion that he was a Revolutionary soldier. Gchld cty, Va. 4 Oct 1832.

JOHN RIDDLE, "Upper end of the county." Same. 4 Oct 1832.

JOHN RICHARDS. Same. 22 Aug 1732.

FINCH RAGLAND. Same. 21 Aug 1832.

MARY MAGDLENE ROW, widow of GEORGE ROW Rev. soldier, of Penns Tshp. Northumberland cty, Penn.

EDWARD ROSE, a private who had marched with the militia in the service of the U. S., and was wounded in the hand in Jersey and thereby rendered incapable of getting a livelihood......(to receive) three pounds, fifteen shillings in part private's pay from 24 Oct 1787 to 24 April 1788. Orphan's Court, Fred'k cty, Md. 10 June 1788. The following is pasted on the Minutes of 12 Dec 1786. "Fredericktown, Sept 26, 1786. I certify that EDWARD ROSE was wounded in the hand in an engagement in Jersey whilst the Maryland militia was on duty.........B. Johnson."

EDWARD ROADS, soldier in the U. S. service; wife Prudence receives provisions. Charl. cty, Va. Mch Ct 1780. Orders iv-218. Also Dec Ct 1779. iv-236.

JESSE REED was a Captain in the Continental line; Guilford Dudley Reed, his heir gets 3840 acres in Davidson cty, Tenn. D-n cty, Tenn. 1790.

ROBERT REDDING, a wounded soldier, entitled to pension. Pr. Edw. cty, Va. Ct 6 June 1783. Orders.

JOHN REDD, resident of Henry cty, Va., age 78. Declaration of service. Born Orange cty, Va., October 1755; removed to Henry cty, then Pittsylvania, Mch 1774, and under Capt, Joseph Martin, marched July, 1776, from Henry (then Pittsylvania) as Orderly Serjeant. Col. William Christian was in command on the Long Island of Holston. Re-enlisted 1 Dec 1776. In 1777, commissioned Ensign of Militia in Capt. Brice Martin's Company. Served one month in 1780. In 1781 was a Lieutenant. Afterwards a wagonmaster, then a Lieutenant again at Yorktown. Draper Mss. 10-NN.

JOSEPH ROSS, a soldier in the Continental service; wife Rosanna is allowed three barrels of corn and 150 lbs. of meat for support of herself and three children. Essex cty, Va. May Ct, 1780. xxix-475.

JOHN RICHARDSON furnished the Augusta militia with four bundles of fodder, and two "diets," on their march to join General Green. Camp. cty, Va. 7 Mch 1782. i-9.

PATRICK ROBINSON petitions...was formerly in the war and received several wounds whereby he is now incapable to get his livelyhoode (also on account of age); is ordered tax free this year only. Som cty, Md. E. F. H. p. 2. Ct 2 Aug 1707.

WILLIAM RAGSDALE produces discharge from Col. Andrew Lewis, testifying that he (Ragsdale) served as a soldier in Capt. John McNeill's Company, expedition against the Indians in 1762, and makes oath that he served five years. Ordered certified. Pittsyl. cty, Va. iv. 319. May Ct 1780.

JOHN RICHARDSON, Gent. Comm'n as 1st Lieut. of Militia. Takes oath. Charl. cty. Va. Mch Ct 1780. Orders iv-209.

WILLIAM RUSSELL; makes oath that he served as a serjeant under Capt. James Gunn, Col. William Byrd, expedition against the Indians, 1760. Ordered certified. Pittsyl. cty. Mch Ct 1780. iv-293.

GEORGE ROWLAND; produces commission and is sworn as Captain of Militia. Pittsyl. cty, Va. 1767. Orders.

MORRIS ROBERTS, RICHARD TAYLOR, Mr. EDWARD CHILTON; were imprest in the Country's service to bring the corn &c., of the Rappahannock Indians to the River. Rappa., Va. 2 Apr 1684. Orders, p. 25.

THOMAS SMITH, a poor soldier in the service of the State; Cluverius Coleman, Gent., appointed to furnish Susannah Smith, the wife, with necessaries. Produces his account. Meckl. cty, Va. 13 Apr 1778. iv-499.

THOMAS SMITH makes oath that he served as a soldier three years in the 6th Va. Reg't. Ordered certified. Pittsyl. cty, Va. May Ct 1780. iv-319.

CHRISTOPHER SINGLETON; died in the service of the State. John Speed, Gent., makes oath that he has furnished Mary Singleton, the widow, with £15 for herself and children. Meckl. cty, Va. 13 Apr 1778. iv-499.

ISAAC SMITH; makes declaration for pension. Court declare opinion he was a Revolutionary soldier. Charl. cty, Va. 6 Nov 1832. Orders xxix-9.

GEORGE SOUTHWORTH; files declaration for pension. Court declare opinion that he was a Revolutionary soldier. Gchld, Va. 21 Aug 1832. p. 146 of Orders.

WILLIAM SHEPHERD. Order made in his favor in Mch 1791, concerning his pension, is amended. Jeff'n cty, Ky. 25 Oct 1791. Orders ii-275.

MARY CLINE SMITH [*sic.*] widow of Boltzer Cline Smith, shown by the record of the Court to have performed military service. Nthld cty, Penna. 2d vol. O. C. Docket.

ELIZABETH SANDERS, wife of Roger Sanders, who, by a ctf of Col. Thos. Price, appears to be a soldier for and during the war, in the Maryland line, makes application to the Court; it appearing that she needs assistance towards the support of fifteen young children, ORDERED, that the Clerk draw an order on the Treasurer of the Western Shore in her favor for the sum of fifteen pounds by way of assistance to her in the support of her family, for one year from this date. Fred'k cty, Md, Aug Ct 1782.

GEORGE SWAIN; files dealaration for pension. Court is of opinion he was a Revolutionary soldier. Bedford cty, Va. Ct. Aug. 1832.

JAMES STIFF; same; same.

DAVID SAUNDERS; same; same.

PHILIP SULIVAN, private, 7th Md Reg't; wounded battle of Camden, 16 Aug 1780. Court orders payment of £7–10sh. for six-months . . half-pay. Balto. cty, Md. 12 Feby 1789. Proc. ii-99. See also 14 Feby 1787. p. 2.

JAMES TEBBS, ; see Pr. Wm. cty, Va. 27 Feby 1762. Orders [4] p. 57.

RICHARD TOLER; makes declaration for pension. Court declare opinion he was a Revolutionary soldier. Gchld cty, Va. 21 Aug 1832.

JOHN TAYLOR; made proof of service on the frontiers in Capt. Dickerson's company of Rangers, raised in Va., in the last war, until disbanded. Bot. cty, Va. 13 Apr 1780. Orders

EMANUEL TOMBS; makes declaration for pension. Charl. cty, Va. 3 Dec 1832. Orders xxix-16.

FRANCIS THORNTON, Gent. Takes oath as 2d Lieut. Militia. Charl. cty, Va. Mch Ct 1780. Orders iv-209.

ABEL TUCKER; makes delaration of service, and Court declare opinion that he was a Revolutionary soldier. Charl. cty, Va. 1 Oct 1832. Orders xxix-5.

JOHN TREDWAY; served as private, Capt. Nathaniel Gest's Company, Va. Regt, War bet. Great Britain and France. Ordered certified. Charl cty, Va. Mch Ct 1780. Orders iv-210.

JAMES TAYLOR; makes oath that he served as a soldier under Capt. Chas. Scott, Col. Wm. Byrd's Reg't, expedition agt Indians, 1760. Ordered certified. Pittsyl. cty, Va. Mch Ct 1780. iv-297.

INTERCOUNTY AND INTERCOLONY

JAMES ALLEY, Rowan cty, N. C., to Edmund Alley, David Alley and Nathaniel Dennis of Henrico, Va., conveys 100 acres; consideration, £60. Hen. Va., Misc. vi-1991. 15 Mch 1767.

THOMAS ADAMS, of New Kent, Va., to William Accret [?] of Charles City cty; £155; 186 acres on "Chickomy" Swamp. Hen., Va. Misc. vi-1791. 2 June 1760.

JOHN ARCHDALE, of Wickham, Bucks county; Whereas he has executed a deed of gift to his grandson, Nevil Low, and to his father and mother, Em'll and Anne Low, all of Carolina, in America . . . he now gives power to Capt. John Robinson, of Carolina, to ackn. said deed. London, 2 Feby 1712. Pasquo. cty, N. C. A-12.

THOMAS BRATTEN, will. Father, John Bratten, of Drumlochen . . . neare Londonderry, Ireland. [When this will was recorded, the name of the parish was partly illegible.] Mr. John Hampton to dispose of his books and drects disposition of patent also. Wit: Waire, Carlyle, Skirven, Gordon. 26 Sept 1712. Wor. cty, Md. M. H. iii-106.

THOS. BUCKNER, Gent., of Caroline, to Rev. Mr. Rodham Kenner, Clerk, same; this is endorsed "*Acknowledged in Caroline Co., why is it in this office of Henrico?*" Hen. cty, Va. Misc. iii-855. 11 July 1733.

JAMES BRISTOW and wife Molley, of "Gait" cty, N. C.; Bartholomew Bristow and wife Nancy; and Josiah Bristow and wife Fanny, of Middlesex, to James Healy, Middlesex; 100 acres. 28 Dec. 1789. Middx, Va. 1785-1789, p. 172.

NATHANIEL DENNIS, Henrico, Va., to Burgis Harrelson, of Orange, N. C., 100 acres, psh and cty of Henrico; consideration, £50. Hen., Va. 9 June 1770. Misc. vii-2093.

PETER DUTOIT, of Moudon in *Suisse*, a dweller of King William psh, Henrico cty, Va. Will. About 1727. Hen. Va. Misc. ii-659.

MICHAEL GAWIN, N. C., to David Gavin [Gawin?] of Henrico; 400 acres, £40. John Gawin one of wit. 20 Mch 1765. Hen., Va. Misc. vi-1945.

MOSES HALL, of the upper psh of Nancymond cty, Va., to John Hubbard, of Chowan, N. C., tract of Woodland near the Rich Thicketts. 28 Jany 1734. Tyrrell cty, N. c. W-262.

JOHN LANE; had wife and chn in England; mentions cousin Elizabeth Mattux. Wit: Henderson, FrancisxLord, Sarah x Lord, Ann x Brend. 4 May 1712. Wor. cty, Md. M. H. iii-108.

WILLIAM MILWARD, mentions children in England. Wor. cty, Md. 16 Apr 1712. M. H. iii-101.

STEPHEN MONFORD, Goochland cty, Va., psh St. James, to Bertholeme Dupuy, of King William psh, Goochland; a tract of land in K. Wm psh. Hen cty, Va. 30 May 1728. Misc. iii-777.

Capt. WILLIAM MASSURY, of Salem, in the province of *Massatusets*, marriner, "Disceased" ....inventory his estate and account sales. Hyde cty, N. C. 2 June 1762 and 19 June 1762.

SAMUEL ROUND, Mcht in Maryland, now in Barbadoes, writes that he came in the ship *Herkonnell* [?] Estate in England to brothers and sisters. Wor. cty, Md. 15 Sept 1715. M. H. iii-118.

ANTHONY RAWLINGS and wf Catherine, and John Peirson and wf Rebeckah, and Rachel Dawson, of Dorchester county, Md., give power to James Thickpen and John Stepney, to convey to Isaac Wilson, a certain tract of land in Albemarle county, N. C. Wit: Rawlings, Taylor, Kennedy, Everden. Perq. cty, N. C. 3 Sept 1707. A-299.

PHILIP SMITH, of Bartie cty, N. C., to Francis Wilkinson, widow, tract in Henrico, Va., called Black Hall. Consideration, £30, 1sh. 23 Apr 1740. Hen., Va., Misc. iv-1123.

GEORGE TUCKER and MARY TUCKER, of the Island of Barbydos; referring to deed to Samuel Handy, Som. cty, Md., in which the said George and Mary Tucker conveyed 514 acres, give power to Capt. Isaac Handy to ackn. deed. Som. cty, Md. 26 Oct. 1747. xxi-299.

JOHN WORDIE, of Edinburgh, in Scotland, apothecary, only son and heir at law and devisee of Alexander Wordie, late of Worcester county, surgeon, deceased; gives power to Capt. Henry Lewes and John Williams. Som., Md. 18 June 1750. xx-159.

JOHN WOODWARD, 500 acres, Glouster cty, on Pyanketank River........" relinquished the rights to make good a pattent for Coll. Lee's children, viz. Wm. and Hancock Lee." S. L. O. Va. 17 May 1655. iii-337.

MOTTROM WRIGHT, of Milend psh, St. Dunstan's. Stepney, *als* Stebon Heath, Middlesex county [England] Mcht.........gives to his cousin, Jno. Wright, of Puttomack River in Virginia, £50. Also makes him residuary legatee. See will. 8 Oct 1700. Lanc. cty, Va. viii-103.

WILLIAM WILTON, of Philadelphia, going to live in Newbern, N. C., gives power to Aron Musgrove and Thos. Canby, of Philadelphia, Mchts. Wit: Henry Lish or Lisk, Wm. Harry, N. C. cty, Dela. 18 Aug 1764. Z1-161.

RICHARD WRIGHT, of Chickacone; will. Wf. Anne, one-half my land upon Machoatick and Patomack River, she taking the halfe that joins upon my brother Spencer and this land to have as long as she lives . . . reversion to son Francis. All the rest of my personal estate in Virginia and Maryland, to be divided into three parts; to son [illegible] land on Elke and 'Sassafras rivers; to daughter, land in the Patomack freshes; to Francis all my money in England. Brother Nicholas Spencer . . . brother Mr. Jno. Mottrom to be overseers; cousin Mathew Merriton of London, Mcht, one of the overseers for estate in England. Nthld, Va. 16 Aug 1663-10 Dec 1663. Vol. 1658-1666. Wf. Anne, makes oath to inv. 8 Mch 1663.

ANDREW WOODWARD, of Stafford county, Va., goes to Hampshire county. Stafford records.

STEPHEN WELLS of Edgecombe county, N. C. from Redmund [Redmon] Wells, of Craven city, S. C. Tract in Edgecomb, n. s. Tar river, 100 acres. Nash cty, N. C. About 21 Oct 1778. i-76.

RENUNCIATION OF FOREIGN ALLEGIANCE

MATHURIAN PERRIN, makes oath that he has resided in the U. S. previous to 29 Jany 1795; renounces allegiance to the French Republic; *has not been of any order of nobility.* Admitted to citizenship 20 May 1799. Same Court.

CHRISTOPHER ROBINSON and JOHN McLEOD, make oath as to residence, renouncing Great Britain, and *have not been of any order of Nobility.* 29 May 1799. Same Court.

JOHN RIDLEY makes oath; renounces King of Great Britain, and *is not of any order of Nobility.* 23 May 1799. Same Court.

DEDERICK SHEEKLE, makes oath as to residence, renounces allegiance to Prussia, and *has not been of any order of Nobility.* 23 May 1799. Same Court.

LUDWIG STHULE, renounces allegiance to the Kingdom of Hanover, and *has not been of any order of Nobility.* 24 May 1799. Same Court.

JOHN WATSON, oath as to residence; renounces Great Britain, and *has not been a member of any order of Nobility.* 27 May 1799. Same Court.

Reasonable price or two years' subscription will be given for numbers 1, 2, 3, 4, 6, and 7, COUNTY COURT NOTE-BOOK, 1921-1922. Address Editor.

Fifty cents will be paid for a copy of February 1927.

Printed at the Industrial School for Crippled and Deformed Children, 241 St. Botolph St., Boston, Mass.

INDEX TO COUNTY COURT NOTE-BOOK. VOLUME VII.

Abbott, Abbett, Abbert 5,10,25,39,48
Abdel 49
Ableck 10
Accret (?) 54
Acton 23
Acword, Ackword 51
Adair 29
Adams, Addams 9,10,13 19,29,31,54
Addison 49
Adkeson, (see Atkinson
Adkins, (see Atkins)
Aeshwin (?) 23
Aires 31
Alcock 15
Aldock 31
Alexander 11,18,26
Allen 1,10,11,18,23 31
Allerton 23
Alley 54
Alston 18
Ammons 13
Anderson 7,10,12,48
Anderton 31
Andrews 13,19,23,39, 41,49
Angell 23,29
Angulliott (?) 10
Appleby 10
Apriskett 23
Archdale 11,54
Areson, (see Aryson)
Arleson 23
Armor 31
Armstrong 11
Arnall 1
Arnold 1,10,48
Arsken, Arskins 26
Arsley 10
Arthur, Arther 6,9
Aryson 23
Ash 48
Ashby 12,17,37
Ashcroft 6,21
Ashdarne 23
Ashley 17,23
Atkins, Adkins 29,31 39
Atkinson, Adkeson 6, 21,23,29
Aughtry 13
Auld 6,21
Austin 23,30
Aydelott 47

BACHELDER 34
Bachelor 31,35
Back 10
Badwin 1
Bagwell 12
Baileinge 23
Bailey, Baile 10,41
Baker 30,31
Balance 11
Baldwin 16
Ball 23
Ballingall 23
Bandon 39
Banks 9,16,17,48
Bannister 10
Barber, Barbar, Barbour 10,41
Barclift 11
Barfield 17
Barfoot 13
Barker 39
Barks (?) 13
Barlow 21,38
Barnebe 47
Barnes 7,16,23
Barnett 6,39
Barrow, Barrows 9 23,35
Bartley 10
Bartram 11
Basnet 38
Bass 13,17
Batcholor 31,34
Bateman 23,31
Batson 12,22,25,38,49
Battle 11
Batts 10,48
Baxter 10,30,31
Bayley, Bayle, Baley 6, 9,10,21,23,31,34
Bazemore 17
Beach 31
Beadard 6,21
Beall 25,47
Beaman 46
Beauchamp 29
Beckett, Beckit 48,49
Becton 11
Beets 27
Beheathland 34
Bell 2,10,11,13,18,30 48,49
Bellamy 39
Bellfinn 10,47
Belvat 9,48,49
Bendon 10
Bennes 6
Bennett 16,17,30,31 34,39
Benson 39
Benston 25
Benthall 12,21,37,48,49
Berkeley 6,21
Berry 27,46
Berryman 34
Betts 31
Bevans 30
Bibby 38
Biggs 37
Billycate 22
Bingley 39
Birch 34
Bishop 30
Black 31,48
Blackburn 10,13
Blackman 13
Blades 18
Blake 30
Blanshard 17
Bley 34
Blithenborge 23

Blizard 30
Blossee 31
Blount 11,17
Boaten 23
Bodd (?) 48
Body 23
Boissanniere 11
Bold 13,38
Bolton 23,31
Bonyson 23
Boon 16,17
Boote 10,47
Booth 23,34
Boswell 23
Botson 25
Boulden 26
Bounds 51
Bowdoin (?) 1
Bowen 4,6,21,30
Bowling 34
Bowman 31
Boyd 11,18,35
Boykin 13
Bradford 23
Bradish 5
Bradley 27
Bradman 31
Bradshaw 13
Branch 4
Braswell 17
Bratten 54
Braybrooke 48
Breckinridge 41
Brend 54
Brent 23,33
Breriton 31
Brice 5
Brickell 6
Brickhouse 11,48
Bridgman 39
Brilson 5
Bristow 27,54
Britts 5
Broadwater 49
Broder 31
Brodhurst 39
Bromfield 10,37,48
Brooke 6,21
Brookes,Brooks 2,9,29
Broton 30
Brown 3,6,10,11,16,17
23,27,29,30,39
Browning 30
Bruce 31
Brumfield 37
Brunskin 1
Bryan 13
Bryant 3,16
Bryatt 31
Buchanan,Buckhannon
13,29
Buckhouse 11
Buckner 54
Bullen 39
Bullock 37
Bunbridge 10
Bunbury 34
Bunny 23
Bunting 10
Burd 10
Burdett,Burditt
13,37,45
Burkeloe 6,21
Burley 23
Burnell 23
Burnett 41
Burnham 11
Burns,Burnes 4,21
Burny 10
Burrough 39
Burt 10,11
Burton 13,41,47,48
Bushie 26
Bushop 37
Butler 10,13,18
Butt 10,48
Byard 6,21
Byers 5
Byrd 18

CABLE 3,12,38
Cafte 5
Cain 41
Cameron 27
Cammock 25
Campbell,Cambell
9,18,27
Campion 39
Camplin (?) 29
Canby 39,55
Caniel 10,48
Cann 42
Cannady 13,16
Cannon 5
Caple 10,37
Caps 30
Caraway 13
Carell 13
Carlyle 54
Carney 27
Carpenter 3,6,30,49
Carr 13
Carrell,Carrel 13
Carrington 26
Carter 10,13,16,19,31,
37,39
Carteris 5
Cartwright 6,31
Caruthers 42
Carwarding 5
Cason 13
Castle 3,39
Caswell 11
Catchmaid 11
Catts 39
Cavelery 31
Cawsey 23
Chaloner 5
Chambers 9,49
Chambey 48
Chamley 10
Champion 11
Chandler 11,30,34
Chappell 1
Charles 45
Charlton 41,45
Cheatham 18
Chees 37

Cherry 10
Cherryholm 16,17
Chestnutt 13
Chetwood 30
Chick 6,21
Chickley 10,48
Child 39
Chilton 29,53
Christian 22
Christopher 30
Clagett 42
Clare 2,10
Clarey 35
Clarke 37,38,46
Clarkey 23
Claughton 10,26
Clay 23,33,38
Cleaton 39
Clegg 49
Clement,Clements 10,27,48
Cliford 39
Clinton 23
Clotheire 10
Clowell 10
Clower 10
Coates 48
Cob 48
Cobbett 5,25
Cockayne 39
Cocke 11
Cockey 5
Cockshutt 21
Coffer 31
Cogar 27
Coggin 13
Coghan 41
Cole 5,13,19,23,31
Coleman 53
Colgan 4
Colley 1
Collins,Collings 6,10,21,30,41,47
Cone 23
Coniers 10,48
Conaway,Connoway 6,10,21
Conner 9,30,47
Consnes (?) 10
Cook 10,13,23,30 31,39
Cookman 10
Coon 27
Cooper 13,27,31,38
Coote 23
Copinn 23
Corbett 10
Cording 34
Cornan 2
Cornelius 6,47
Correld 10
Corsens 10
Coston,Costin,Costing 3,30,49
Cottingham 30
Cotton,Cotten 16,31
Coulson 17
Coulter 31
Cousins,Cossens 10,11
Coute 23
Covell (?) 10,48
Coward 2
Cowe (?) 31
Cowell 2
Coxe 11,31
Craghill 17
Crane 27
Cranfield 48
Crapper 51
Crawfield 10
Cray 23
Craycroft 6,21
Creaston 39
Creighton 23
Crosby 10,48
Crouch 6,21
Crumpler 13
Crussey (?) 29
Cudworth 16
Culpeper 23
Cuningham (?) 38,39
Cursitor 5
Custis 4,22,25,38,48
Cutter

DADE 34
Daily 1
Dainsy 23
Dallas 18
Dalton 27
Damsies (?) 48
Dangerfield 49
Daniel,Daniell 10, 13,18,38,48
Darby 42
Darden 13
Darken 23
Darling 31
Darr 41
Darril 33
Dashiell 30
Datsill 31
Dauge 11
Daughtry 13
Davenport 35
Davey,Davye 19,39
Davis 9,10,11,18,23,25, 29,30,31,34,41,46,47, 48,51
Davison 10,48
Daws 16
Dawson 10,54
Deane 5,31
Delamar 47
Delue 10,48
Denning 9
Dennis 47,54
Denny 48
Denston 47
Denwood 6,21
Deplaie (?) 50
Derman 23
Derrick 29,34
Derrickson,Dirickson 47,49
Devans 13
Devarr 48
Dew 17,31

Dewin 37
Dey 34
Dickenson 16
Dickins 31
Diggs 4
Dinely 26
Disney 5
Dixon,Dixson 16,37,48
Dobbins 39
Dodes (?) 1
Doget 16
Dollinge,Dollings 10,39
Dolby 48,49
Dolly 10,48
Donaldson 42
Donelson 6,15,40
Donnok 10
Doore 31
Dorman 2,23
Dorrow 31
Dorsett 6,21
Doss 27
Douglas 22,23,38
Douty 49
Dowin (?) 37
Downs,Downes 5,37
Drake 3,18,27,38
Dregors 30
Drewe 10,13
Drexel 41
Driggers 51
Drighouse 48
Drinan,Drinau 35
Drinkwater 30
Drummond 22,31,37,39
Duack 13
Duckel 6,21
Dudley 13,31
Duffell 10
Dunbar 31
Duncan,Dunkin 18,19
Duncomb 25
Dunfee 49
Dunn 10,48
Dunnahow 30
Dunton 13,22,37
Duparkes 38
Dupuy 54
Dutoit 54
Dyer 31

EARL 11
Eason 39
Easter 34
Eastmead 25
Eburn,Eborn,Ebern 9,11,35,41
Eccles 19
Edderman 10
Edgate 1
Edge,Edg 10,31,39
Edgcombe 39
Edmonds 31,49
Edward 10
Edwards 11,16,17,27,31
Efford 23
Egan 5
Elkins 31
Ellett 9
Elligood 13,37,48
Elliott 6,7,11,21,48
Elsbee 19
Else 16
Elson (?) 16
Eltonhead 45
Emerson 39
Emock 35
English 31
Ennis 51
Ensome,Eusome 10,48
Eskridge 51
Etheredge,Ethredge 9
Evans 2,3,5,16,22, 23,30,39,49
Everden 54
Everella 31
Evitt 6,21
Ewell 29

FAIRE 10,23
Faircloth 13
Fairpoint 10,48
Faison 13
Farine 31
Farmer 10,31
Farr 9
Farrell 11,30
Farwell,Farrwell 10
Faulkner 31
Fear 27
Feild 10,48
Feilding 26
Fellows 11
Felton 31,39
Fendall 39
Fenwick 6,21
Ferebe 46
Ferguson 35
Fevery 1
Feveryeare 1
Fier 10
Fishbrooke 23
Fisher 39
Fitchett 2,49
Fitzpatrick 30
Fitz Redmond 5
Fleming 10,29
Fletcher 2,12
Floring 31
Floyd 12,27,31,33,48
Fooks 33
Foland 10
Folley 34
Ford,Foord,Fourd 4,5,10
Forman,Foreman 9,21 35,49
Fornor (?) 31
Forrest,Farrast 10,31,48
Fortescue 9,35
Fossett 31
Foster 10,47
Fowke,Fouke 30,33
Fowler 27
Fox 18,48
Foxall,Foxhall 16,29

INDEX TO COUNTY COURT NOTE-BOOK. VOLUME VII.

Francis 7
Franklin 10,27,30,31
Frederick 13
Freeman 25,30
Freshwater 22,37
Freyer 13
Friday 18
Frisco 1
Froster 10
Frumpton 10
Furr 48

GADSBY 35
Gainey 13
Gallowell 9
Gammell 6
Ganaway 7
Ganey 13
Garlington 10
Garment 39
Garnett 26
Garrett,Garrat 12,31,37
Garterell 5
Gascoigne 22,49
Gaskins 11
Gatewood 26
Gault 49
Gavin 13,17,54
Gawin 54
Gay 23
Gelding 2,38
German 30
Gery 47
Gibbine 31,39
Gibbs 9,11
Gibson 10
Gilbert 5,6,29
Gilding 48
Gilhage 5
Gill 18,31
Gillard 31,39
Gilles 10
Gilmore 42
Gilson 10
Ginkins 13
Girringe 39
Githings 4
Givans,Givan 30,46
Glass 51
Glendon 6,21
Godale 23
Godfrey 17
Godlad 10,39
Godwin 13,48
Gogen (?) 30
Goldsborough 39
Goodman 18
Goodrich 10
Goodwin 9,10,12,31
Gordon 18,54
Gore 10,48
Gorein 31
Gosse 39
Gouch 39
Gower 23
Graffenreid,de 33
Grafton 48
Graham 29
Granbury 18
Grandy 11
Grant 23
Grantham 1
Gravat 34
Graves 10
Gray 1,10,23,41,48
Green 3,9,10,16,31 47,48,49
Greer 6
Gregory 13,35
Grey 23,33
Griffin 10,27,42
Griffith 16,38
Grigg,Grigges 10,31
Grigson 10
Grim 10
Grimes 23
Grimstead 7
Griskin (?) 48
Groome 1,6
Grove 11
Gruin (?) 10
Grum 39
Gugoll 39
Gulin (?) 31
Gunter 10,39,46
Gurganus 9
Gustinge 1
Guttery 42
Guy 48

HADDAWAY 5
Haggoman 49
Haies (see Hayes)
Haile,Hail 26,30
Haines 23
Hair,Heire 10,13
Hales 17
Hall 3,10,13,23,31,35, 39,47,54
Hallett 29
Halloway 31
Ham 10
Hamilton 7,34,42,43
Hammond,Hammon 10,17, 30,39,47
Hampton,Hamton 6,10 23,48
Hamsin 39
Hanby 37
Handy 30,39,55
Haney 13
Hankin 10
Hansford 10,48
Harding,Hardin 11,21 26,48
Hardy 10,48
Harford 31
Hargroves 13
Harma 31
Harmanson 12,22,38
Harnage 48
Harnett 29
Harper 10,38,48
Harrelson 54
Harrington 39
Harris 10,19,23,31,35 42,47,48

Harrison 25,39,42
Harry,Hary 23,55
Hart 17,22,31
Hartley 10
Harvey 9,23,34,35
Haswell 25
Hawkins 21,23
Hay 13,42,48
Hayes,Haes,Haies 10,38,41,42
Haynes,Heynes,Haines 23,48
Hazard,Hazzard 23,49
Heaberd 10
Heale,Healy 39,54
Hearitage 37
Hearny 39
Heath 49
Heather 30
Heaton 42
Heire,Hair 10,13
Hemsley 5
Henderson 17,18
Hendrick 11
Henfield 26
Henry 26
Henryfold 31
Henson 43
Henwell 23
Herman 6,21,39
Herring 13
Hewes 23
Hewett 2,10,23,37
Heynes (see Haynes)
Hickes,Hicks 21,31
Hickman 12,39
Hido 1
Higgens 47
Higginson 39
Higgison 31
Highway 29
Hill 2,6,10,11,16,21 23,25,33,39,51
Himley 48
Hines 1
Hinton 17
Hirton (?) 10
Hitchens 49
Hoard 10,42
Hobbs,Hobs 6,21,31
Hobson 17
Hoccaday 10
Hodges 43
Hoe (?) 10
Hoger (?) 10
Holbrook 48
Holcroft (?) 48
Holden 39,46
Holder 13
Holl 48
Holland,Hollon 10, 13,30,37,51
Hollaway 10,48
Holley 42
Holliday,Holladay 31,39,51
Hollingsworth 6,13,21
Hollis (?) 10
Holman 31
Holmes 13,31
Holt 13
Hocker 31
Hope 23,31
Hopewell 5
Hopkins 7,46
Hopton 13
Horne 42
Horsey 6,21
Horsington 30
Horsley 43
Hoskins 10
Hough 30
Houlsworth 10
Howard 23,31
Howe 10
Howell 31
Howes 31
Howgrave 31
Howkett (?) 31
Hubbard 54
Hubbell 35
Huber 35
Hudson 6,7,10,13,21 26,29
Hugh 31
Hughes,Heughes,Hues 7,10,23,34,35,48
Hughlett 23
Humphries 11,17
Hunt 12,22,23,31,37 38,42
Hunter 7,42
Hurd 26
Hurley 31
Hurstwell 48
Hutcheson 7
Hutton 5

IBSOM 31
Idolet 30
Ines or Ives 30
Ingle 45
Ingleton 10
Ingram 19,39
Innis 47
Irish 48
Irwin 43
Isbell 7
Isdell,Isdall 3,48,49
Isham 26
Israel 30
Ives or Ines 30
Ivey 13

JACKMAN 31
Jackson 11,13,15,17, 22,38,39
Jacobs,Jacob 5,6,10, 13,21,37,48
Jacocks 17
James 10,22,23,31,39,48
Jameson,Jamison, Jemmison 26,30,43,47
Jaquess 26
Jarman,Jarmin 30,34
Jarrett 6,21
Jarvis 10,35,38
Jarvy 31,39

Jasper 9,25
Jeane 43
Jefferys 1
Jeffrey 17
Jeffreys,Jeffress 1,16,26
Jenkins,Jinkins Ginkins 13,23,48
Jennings,Jenings 31,39
Jerman,Jernan, Jernew 48
Job 5,25
Johannes 23
Johnson 2,3,7,13,22, 23,25,26,30,31,37,38 48,49,51
Johnston 13,34
Jones 2,5,10,11,12,13, 16,17,18,23,30,31,34 35,38,39,43,47,48
Jordan 9, 10,11,22,34
Joy 30,31,48
Joyner 13,31
Joynes 37
Julian,Julyan 1
Jure 11

KEATING 35
Kedby 39
Keen 13
Keeve 49
Kellam,Kellum 30,38
Kelly 26,34
Kemp 35
Kendall 2,3,13,22,38
Kennedy 34,54
Kenner 54
Kennett 30
Kenningham 38
Kent 39
Kerton 31
Kiggs 48
Killman 39
King 13,18,31,38,43,51
Kipps 9
Kirke 39
Kirkpatrick 46
Knight 3,23,37,38
Kornegay 13
Kygan,Kygon 13,48
Kynnygam 39

LACOCK,LAYCOCK 1,29
Lake 13
Laman 1
Lamberson 4
Lancaster 4
Lane 5,7,30,46,54
Lange 12
Langley 9
Langsdale 46
Lanhan 47
Lanier 27
Lankford 46
Larimore,Larramore Larimer 46,51
Laughland, (see Loughland)
Law 10
Lawler,Lalor 2
Lawrence,Larrance 38,39,49
Layfield 47
Layward 10,48
Lazenby 47
Leatherbary 6,21
Le Baux 11
Le Breton 1
Lee 26,39,55
Leeke 5
Leeper 31
Lees,Loos 10,48
LeGrand 26
Leigh 11
Leirmont,Liermont 34
Leiry (?) 48
Lemoine 35
Lemon 38
Lendall 39
Lendy 48
Lennard 16
Leonard 11
Leprask 39
Lester 38
Letyn (?) 49
Lewellings 10
Lewes 55
Lewis 27,29,30,39
Libby 35
Lickey (?) 5
Light 39
Linch 38
Lindsey 15
Lingan 21
Linnee,Linny 10,39
Linquist 9
Lipscomb 43
Lipsey 2
Lish,Lisk 55
Liston 39
Littleton 2,12,40,46
Llewellins,Lewellings 5,10
Lobdenne 39
Lockett 18
Lockey 39
Lockhart 9
Logg 10,47
Loney 29
Long 7,11,12,23,39
Longo,Longoe 5,23
Looney 7
Loos,Lees 10,48
Lord 54
Lorry 48
Loughland 2,38
Loveing 31
Low 5,11,54
Lowdon (?) 35
Lowder 30
Loyd 10
Lucas 10,43,48,49
Luck 39
Luddington 46
Luke 49
Lullaman 39
Lumsdon 35

Lunderman 43
Lynch 7
Lyne,Lynes 29,52
Lyon 47

McCAMEY 26
McClanahan 43
Maclaney 47
McChester 47
McConnehay 43
McCormack 18,43
McCormaha 43
McCullam 18,43
McDaniel,Mack Daniell 10,17,21
McDearman 43
McDonald,McDonell 4,18,43
Mackdwell 48
Mackelmore 13
Mackhannin 48
McIlurner (?) 13
McInnish 15
Mack Loyd 48
Mackenny,Mackinny 2,16
Mackettrick 47
Maclaney 47
McLendon 13
MacLeod,McLeod,13 35,55
McLeran 15
McManus 49
MacMills 6
McNorvel 35
McSwain 9
Machell 47
Mackereel 31
Mackes 23
Madden 7
Maddison 26
Maddox,Maddux 2,38
Magee,Magoy 16
Magorene (?) 11
Magruder 6,21,47
Mahoones 1
Mahue 10,48
Mainwaring 29
Maior 30
Major 2
Malbury 18
Male 10,48
Malone 43
Malpus 16,17
Mandevill,Manduell, Mandowell 9,34,35
Manlove 2,47
Mann,Man 17,31
Manning 11
Mannington 2,38
Mapp 37
Margrett 10
Maris 39
Markes 23
Markhamson (?) 10
Marlett 47
Marley 13,31
Marlow 23
Marriot 3,13
Marsh 2,48
Marshall 12,22,33, 43,49
Martin 10,12,13,18, 23,35,39
Martyn 1
Mase 39
Maslin 2
Masman 12
Mason 2,19
Massey,Masey 16,34,48
Massury 19,54
Mathers 23
Mathis,Matthis 13
Mathew 23,31
Mathows,Matthews 3,30,38,39,49
Mathy 10
Mattux 54
Maxey 26
Maxwoll 35
May 10,31
Maybe (?) 10
Mayhew,Mahue 10
Maynard,Mainard Moygnard 16,25
Mayne 23
Mayner 16
Mayniadier 39
Mayo 5
Meador 43
Meadows 43
Mealy 43
Medley 10
Melling 46
Mells 39
Melton 16,47
Melvin 6,21,48
Mercer 49
Meredith 2,10,12,22
Merrell 30
Merriton 55
Merritt 13
Merry 49
Michael,Mickell 2,12,23,33,48
Micholls 10
Middleton 2
Milbourne,Milburn 43,47
Milby 2
Miles 2,47
Mill 10
Millard 13,48
Miller 11,12,17,23,49
Milliken 17
Mills 2,6,21,23,31, 37,43
Milward 54
Mines 31
Minor 47
Minstrell (?) 39
Mitchell 34,35,43,47
Moblay 13
Moffett 27
Mogbee 6,21
Molson 10,31
Monford 54
Monnette,Monet,Money 15,26,33,41,51
Montgomery 39
Moody 25
Mooro,Moor 2,12,13,16, 17,18,23,26,43,47,49

Moreaghen 2
Morfrey 39
Morgan,Morgans 2,26
31,48
Morisey 13
Morris 6,21,47,48,49
Morrison 47,48
Morter 10
Morton 26
Moseley,Mosely 2,41
Mote 30
Mottrom,Motrom 23,55
Mountney,Mounteney 2
Moygnard 25
Multis 31
Mumford 18,47
Munday 10,48
Mundeen 1
Munford 42
Murchison 19
Murphy 9,43
Muschet 26
Musgrove 55
Mutton 10,48

NAILOR 23
Natts 48
Navill 16
Neale,Neall 39,46
Nearne 47
Neeck 2
Needham 23
Needles 39
Nehon,Nehou,Nihen
10,48
Nelson 2,3,17,26,37
Nesham 47
Newcomb 10
Newell 30
Newman 7,34,35,39
Newsome 10,48
Nicholas,Nickolas
6,21,27
Nichols,Nicholls,
Neckolls 6,10,21,23
30,31,43,48,52

Nicholson,Nickolson
2,47,49
Nitter 31
Nixon 12
Noble,Nobles 6,21,47
Noele 49
Norman 23,31
North 52
Northam 3
Northington 19
Norton 23,31,39
Norvill 16
Nottingham 2,3,12
30,49
Novell (?) 49
Nowell 29
Nunelly 52
Nurse 31
Nutter 2,47

OATES 13
Oben 3
Ober 47
O'Bryan 52
O'Day 47
Odeere 3
Odon 9
Odell,Odel 5,25,47
Odom 13
Offut 6
Oldner 17
Oliver 16
O'Neil 35
O'Quin 16,17
Orley 26
Ormond 9
Orten 3
Osborne 46,49,52
O'Sullivan 23
Overton 31

PACE 17,52
Page 47
Pall 16
Paine,Pane 48
Palmer 1,3,5,31,39

Panewell 3
Panton 31
Parke 10,31
Parker 16,19,29,31
Parkes 33,39
Parnell 17
Parr 23,39
Parramore 3,47,49
Parrish 11
Parrott 52
Parry 23
Parsons 3,6,12,21,39,49
Parton 31
Partworthy 10
Pascall 10
Pashe 39
Patchitt 16
Pate 47
Patermacke 39
Paterson 34
Patrick 22, 37,48
Patton 26
Payne 31,42
Peate 31
Peed 34
Peeke 17
Peele 3
Peirson 54
Penn,Pen 48,52
Pennuel 46
People 39
Percey 39
Pere 11
Perkins 48
Perrin 55
Perry 11,23,31,48
Person,Persons 37,39
Peters 5,12
Peterson 31
Petres 23
Petti-John 38
Pettit 12,22,48
Petty 42
Pew 10
Phillips 6,21,30,39,47
Pigg 26

Pight 10,47
Pigott,Pigot 2,12,37,48
Pike 35
Pinson 10,48
Pinton 10,47
Pitt 47
Pitts 3,12,22,38,48,52
Pleasants 42,52
Plover 29
Pointer 47
Polk 4,51
Pollock 51
Polly 34
Poole 48
Poore 23,31
Pope 11,30,46
Port 39
Porter 12,23,30,31,46,
47,48,51
Postman (?) 31
Potter 18
Pouldson 12
Pounds 42
Powell 3,12,13,47,48
Poyner 11
Prather 47
Preeson 3,25,48
Presley 42
Prevett 10,48
Price 6,9,21,26
Prince 31
Prior 39
Pritchett 23
Pryor 52
Pugh 11
Pullings,Puttinge 48
Purnell 12,47,49
Pyett 10

QUARLES 48

RABOONE 12
Rabyshaw 12
Ragland 52
Ragsdale 53
Ralston 42
Ramsey 4
Randall 42
Randolph 26
Ransom,Rensum 31
Rasco,Rasko,see Roscoe
Raslin 10
Rawlins,Rawlings
31,54
Rayne 37
Read 9,10
Reckes 23
Redd 42,53
Redding 53
Reddish 34
Reed 53
Reese 7
Regan,Riggen,Regen
6,12,21,47
Reid 42
Rensum (?) 31
Respes,Respus 37,48
Rew 34
Reyland 31
Reynolds,Reynalds
31,48
Rhodes 1
Rice 12
Rich 39
Richards 1,12,31,51,52
Richardson 4,5,12,13
25,31,53
Richeson 39
Rickards 12,37
Ricks 15
Rickson (?) 39
Ricter 48
Riddle 52
Rider 1,31,39,48
Ridgers 49
Ridley 55
Rigg,Rige 10,26
Riggan (see Regan)
Right 5
Ring 1
Roads 3
Roah (?) 31
Roberson 18,19,22
Roberts 4,7,12,25,37
39,48,53
Robertson 11,49
Robeson, see Robison
Robins,Robbins 2,12,22,
35,37,39,41
Robinson 3,6,10,21,29
49,53,54,55
Robison,Robeson 29,33
Roch 39
Rockhold 5
Rogers 10,23,34,48
Rohocke,Rohoke,10,31
Rollett 31
Ronald 13
Roper 1
Roscoe,Rasko,Rascoe
2,48,49
Rose 10,17,31,53
Ross 53
Rosser 31
Roulhac 18
Round 54
Row 52
Rowan 5,11,42
Rowland 53
Ruferd 10,48
Rugleton (?) 39
Russell 1,12,25,53
Rutland 21
Ruyleton 39

SAFFIN 42
Salisbury 23
Salter 31
Sampson 13
Sanders 10,21,23,31,53
Sandeford 23
Sappinton 21
Satchell,Satchel
2,13,27,45
Sattathwaite 9,12
Saul,Sauls 12,15
Saunders 2,7,13,54
Savage 2,12,13,23,37

Savin 31
Scady (?) 12
Scarburgh 13,29,45,46
Scarf 17
Schin,Sckin 38
Schoolfield 4,30
Scott,Scot 2,13,16,21
22,29,30,37,39,42
Scottell 23
Scribner 34
Segar 22
Selby 12,30,47
Sellick 45
Serjeant 29
Serly 31
Seward 23
Sewell 39
Seymour 3,22
Shane 10
Sharp 23
Shaw 2,6,10,12,21
Sheekle 55
Sheely 30
Shelton 39
Shepheard,Shephard
37,46,53
Sheppard,Shepard
37,39,48
Sherly 31
Sherman 23
Shewell 51
Shipley 47
Short 48
Silverthorn 34
Silverton 39
Silvester 35
Simes 13
Simmons 15
Simons 11
Simpson 17,39
Sinclair 19
Singleton 53
Skame 10
Skinner 11,12
Skirwen 54
Slade,Sladd 9,34
Slater,Slatter
5,16,31,39
Sloe 10,48
Smart 13,22,23,31,46
Smawe,Smaw 23,37
Smay 48
Smith 2,5,9,10,12,13,
16,17,19,22,23,25,
27,31,34,39,47,48
49,51,53,54,55
Smithson 23
Smock 6,21
Smothers 22
Smyth 45
Snellinge 48
Snellings 10
Songo 5
Southern,Southrene
23,39
Southworth 53
Sowell 16
Spady 13
Spakeman 48
Spann 16
Sparker (?) 31
Sparrow 10
Speakman 22,37,48
Speed 53
Speir 16
Spence 12
Spencer,Spensor 13,23,
26,31,39,46,47,55
Spicer,Spicor 26,31
Spie 11
Spillman 2
Spratt 10
Spring 9
Spruce 31
Spruill 11,12
Stacy 12,17
Stallings 47
Stanford 39
Stanley 1
Stayton 22
Steed 48
Steele,Steale 48
Steer 22
Stelman 10
Stephens 23,30,31,
39,48
Stepney 54
Sterling 46
Sternell 10
Stevens 3,6,21,23,48
Stewart 27,31
Sthule 55
Stiff 54
Stiples 10
Stipley 47
Stith
Stobal
Stockley,Stokeley
22,37,45
Stone 5,31,45
Storke 34
Story 31
Stott 22,48,49
Stovall,Stoball 18
Strangwidge 42
Stratton 22,37
Stringer 2,12,13,22
Stripe 37,48
Strother 34
Stribbings 38
Studson 3
Sturgis,Sturges 3,48
Sue (?) 31
Sullivan,Sullivant
42,54
Sumner 17
Suran 10
Surfleete 39,48
Surlin (?) 31
Sutor,Surtor 31,39
Swain 53
Swindall 9
Symmes 11
Symmons 10,48
Sympson 29
Symson 10,48

TALBOTT 10
Tancred, Tankred 22,49
Tanner 2,23
Tappin 10
Tarbe 11
Tarrant 26
Tarte 34,35
Tasker 5
Tatum 3
Taylor, Talor 1,2,11, 12,22,30,35,37,45, 46,47,53,54
Tazewell 22
Teackle 22
Teague 22,49
Tebbs 54
Tegnall 30
Temple 27
Terrell 31
Thacker 31
Thatcher 25
Thickpen 54
Thirk 34
Thomas 10,22,25,42 48,49
Thompson 12,26,27 30,31
Thomson 31,48
Thoresby 1
Thornman 37
Thornton 34,54
Thorpe 31
Thoroughgood Thorowgood 9,22
Throop 12
Tibbott 29
Tidings 35
Tidman 17
Tier 48
Tillen 48
Tilney 2
Tilsby 31
Todd 10,48
Toft 46
Toler 54
Tolmon 37
Tombs, Toombs 4,54
Tompkins, Tomkins 22,39
Tompson 2,23,37,38
Tonnart (?) 39
Tonning 23
Towers 30,35
Townell 31
Townes 26
Townsend 39,49
Traveller 37
Traynum 4
Treadwell, Tredwell 13,18
Tredways 54
Trencher 10
Tressum 31
Treverson 39
Trevett 10
Trevin (?) 39
Trewett, see Truett
Trim 1
Trobury 10,48
Truett, Trewett 22,30,51
Trumbell 48
Tucker 39,47,54,55
Tuffes (?) 31
Tuley 9,34,35
Tulmarsh 48
Turberville 1
Turner 10,23,38,39,46
Turvill 30
Twyford, Twiford 22
Tye 23
Tyler 31

UNDERHILL 2,22
Underwood 41
Upshur 49

VADIN (?) 39
Vallette 3,4
Van Agthove 22
Vance 47
Vandulett 31
Vanhamell 22
Van Metre 4
Van Norcowe (?) 22
Van Soldt 2
Vanweker 22
Vaughan 10,48
Vernon 42
Vigerous 51
Vincent, Vinsent 10,47
Vodin, Vadin 39
Volly 31
Vorse 22
Vos 38
Vynes 22

WADE 29,39
Wadloe 31
Wagoman 38
Wainhouse 2
Waire 54
Wale 30
Waler 10,31
Walker 10,25,30,31 37,38,39
Wallace, Wallis, Wollis 9,31,39,47
Walls 34
Walter 48
Walthom 38
Walton 12
Ward 5,10,12,23,31,37
Ware 38
Warford 43
Warner, Wornor 10,39
Warren 12,16,22,31, 37,48
Waterfield 37
Waters 12,16,38,46
Waterson 2,22,38
Watkin 26
Watkins 7 ,31,33
Watkinson 23
Watson 10,23,35,37,55
Watt 23
Watton 39

INDEX TO COUNTY COURT NOTE-BOOK. VOLUME VII.

Watts,Wats 31,37
Weaver 4
Webb,Web 4,23,25
37,38
Webster 9,19,22,37
Weeks 11,12,23
Welburne 37,49
Welch 1,23,31,37
Wells 10,18,26,31
39,55
West 10,22,23,30,37,
38,48,51
Westerhouse 37,48,49
Westcott,Westcote 37
Weston 35,45,46
Wetherhorne 10
Wheeler 16
Whitaker 4
White 1,7,10,21,23,25,
29,31,34,37,39,49
Whitehead 5
Whiteneck 4
Whitfield 11
Whitby 1
Whitmarsh 38
Whitmell,Whitmill 17
Whittington 1,13,30
40,45,47,49
Wicks 12,31
Widgeon 38
Wild 23
Wilkins 12,22,37,38,48
Wilkinson 9,55
Will 39
Willett 22,23
William 23
Williams,Willyams 2,7,
9,10,12,16,18,23,25
26,30,31,37,38,42,
47,48,55
Williamson 16,17,38
Willis 9,10,31,37,38
48
Wills,Willes 3,31
Wilson,Willson 5,12,
23,27,31,37,38,48,
49,54
Wilton 55
Wimberley 17
Wimbleton 48
Windley,Windly 9,34,38
Window 6,21
Winfield 9,34
Winingham 18
Winn 23
Winter 6,21,23
Wise 12,23,38
Wite 48
Witty 23
Wood 10,23,26,31,48
Woodbridge 31
Woodford 31
Wooding 5
Woodliffe 31
Woodstock 39
Woodward 55
Woold 31
Wordon 31
Wordie 55
Worlock 31
Wormley 38
Worsham 4
Worth 39
Worthington 5
Wotton 23
Wressell 2,38
Wright 10,23,30,39,55
Wyatt 10,38

YARBROUGH 49
Yardley 2,12,23,38,46
Yeo 30
Yorke 48
Young 10,23,30,38,
39,47

More than one entry on the same page is indicated by underscoring.

The

County Court Note-Book

A Little Bulletin of History and Genealogy

February, 1929. Vol. VIII, No. 1

FAMILIES OF THE EASTERN SHORE
THE WHITTINGTONS

WILLIAM WHITTINGTON, son of WILLIAM (*see NOTE-BOOK for December, 1928*), commonly known as Colonel or Lieutenant-Colonel WHITTINGTON, was born about 1650. This is shown by the date on which he acknowledges receipt of his portion of his father's personal estate, being of age, according to his father's will (at eighteen). (N-n cty, Va. 29 June 1668. x-51.) Previous to this, the 20 Oct 1661, the records of the Virginia Land Office show that WILLIAM WHITTINGTON, son of Capt. WILLIAM WHITTINGTON, received a patent for 800 acres, beginning at the northern end of a dividend bought by Capt. WILLIAM WHITTINGTON from Capt. William Stone . . . at the head of Mattawambs main branch. This patent is the same as that issued the 11 Mch 1653, and, presumably, is a re-issue made necessary by the change of government in England. The 29 Oct 1669, Mr. WILLIAM WHITTINGTON receives a patent for 600 acres, between the seaboard on the east and 1800 acres on the east formerly sold by Capt. Stone to Capt. WILLIAM WHITTINGTON, deceased, father of said Mr. WILLIAM WHITTINGTON. There are 41 head rights. (S.L.O. vi-256.)

Mr. WILLIAM WHITTINGTON, son and heir to Capt. WILLIAM WHITTINGTON (who in 1655 had sold 400 acres to John Stockeley) confirms his father's deed in connection with a deed of sale and exchange with Lt. Col. William Kendall. (17 Jany 1670. N-n, xi-18.) The 28 Sept 1671, Mr. WILLIAM WHITTINGTON receives a patent for 600 acres in Northampton county, lying on the north and south of "Lovelong" Branch . . . the lands of Richard Bunduck and Mary Lewis mentioned . . . the 600 acres having formerly been granted to George Watson and by him deserted. 12 head rights. (S. L. O. vi-373.)

A patent for all of Jengoteague Island, containing 5800 acres, and lying on the seaboard side, it being the next island to the northward of Kekotanck Island, *als* Occocomson Island, and bounded on all sides by salt water, was granted to Mr. WILLIAM WHITTINGTON the 2 Oct 1672. 115 head rights. (S.L.O. vi-421.) And on the 11 Nov of the same year he obtains a patent for 2,850 acres at Hungers, in Northampton county, facing the bay, and also facing a parcel of 110 acres sold by Capt. Stone to James Davis, and 300 acres sold by Stone to Urmstone [Armstrong] Foster, and 390 acres, part of 1800 acres granted Stone and by him sold to WHITTINGTON'S father in 1653. . . "and now is descended to said WILLIAM WHITTINGTON as son and heir unto his father Capt. WILLIAM WHITTINGTON . . . and the remaining 1460 acres for the transportation of 30 persons." (S.L.O. vi-439.) This unusually detailed description enables the identification of Mattawombs Creek as the present Mattawoman Creek, and assists in the location of some historical estates.

In 1677, Gov. Berkeley assigns three servants to WILLIAM WHITTINGTON (John Millington, Richard Hill and Peter Grice) for the full time they have to serve for bearing arms under Bacon. (N-n, Va. xi-171.)

In 1678, WILLIAM WHITTINGTON gets a power from Thomas Jarvis, Mcht, of Elizabeth City cty, Va., to sell land in Somerset cty, Maryland. (Som. Md. 3 May 1678. v-305.) And in 1684, 19 Sept, he is found described as WILLIAM WHITTINGTON, of Somerset, Md., Mcht, when he buys from Henry Morgan, of New Castle cty, Territories of Pennsylvania, all that tract called Sandy Wharf, near the head of "Pocomek" River . . . 400 acres. (Som, vii-234.)

In 1685, however, he again receives a patent for Virginia land ...... 1300 acres on the seaboard side ... a neck or island...... Matchapungo river is mentioned. The patent recites that this tract was formerly granted Mr. Thomas Harmanson in 1654, and by him assigned to James Nevell (grant to the latter in 1662) but by them both deserted and granted to Capt. WILLIAM WHITTINGTON, 26 head rights. (S. L. O. vii-526.)

Somerset county, Maryland, records mention Capt. WILLIAM WHITTINGTON, of Accomack cty, Va., in a suit. (13 Mch 1687. A. W. p. 30.) And again in suits in the court records of 1687–1688. In one of these suits (or one of the entries concerning the same suit) WHITTINGTON appears against James Nevell, and it is shown that he was of Accomack cty, Va.; it is also shown that the debt goes back to 1681. The court orders that it be "paid conveniently in Northampton county, Virginia."

The 20 Jany 1687, ATTALANTA OSBORN, widow of Capt. JOHN OSBORNE, conveys to WHITTINGTON 1200 acres on the south side of a creek called Massiongo, the tract being called Choice, patented to Osborne and by his will devised to Attalanta. (Som. Md. vi-901.)

A record in the Virginia Land Office (23 Apr 1688. S. L. O. vii-633) shows that a patent was granted to WILLIAM WHITTINGTON for 250 acres in Charles City county, Bristoll parish. Five head rights. It is not certain that this was WILLIAM WHITTINGTON of Accomack, though it seems likely.

The date of WHITTINGTON'S actual removal into Maryland does not appear, but it was sometime before April 1689. As early as 6 May 1686, the Indians complain that Mr. WHITTINGTON and Capt. Osborne have taken up land within their [the Indians'] [bounds. (Md. Arch. v-479.) and in Nov 1688, Capt. WILLIAM WHITTINGTON (and Attalanta Osborne, admx of John

Osborne) sue John Swain concerning the building of a house. Swain is ordered by the Court to perform the conditions of obligation. (Som. Md. 14 Nov 1688. Vol. 1690-1691. p. 92.) WHITTINGTON appears in several court records in connection with this and other suits up to 1689. In April, 1689, the date mentioned above, it is entered in the Council Proceedings of Maryland that Capt. WILLIAM WHITTINGTON is to receive powder and ball when he shall call for it. (Md. Arch. viii-96.) In the same year, 1689, he is referred to as Capt. WILLIAM WHITTINGTON, Sheriff of Somerset, (under the "Associators'" Assembly.) See Md. Arch. xiii, p. 244.) There are now several entries in the Somerset records which are not at all clear but which seem to convey that charges had been made against WHITTINGTON as High Sheriff and that he was replaced. There is a letter from the Justices in effect demanding his appearance, and a confused letter from him explaining his astonishment [at the charges] and stating that he is ill. (Som. E. F. G p. 6. 29 Oct 1689.) He is replaced as Sheriff 13 Nov 1689. (Som. E. F. G.-19.) [As said above, nothing in this record relates what the trouble was, but as the Archives of the Province later show WHITTINGTON'S standing in the Assembly and with the higher authorities, the matter must have been capable of explanation.]

The 25 July 1690, WILLIAM WHITTINGTON buys from Peter Whaples and "now wife Frances", of the Indian River, a tract of land. The recital refers to a grant for a tract called Venture, north side Pocomoke river, and eastermost side of Dividing Creek. (Som. Md. vii-379.) He also buys Cedar Neck and Digges Point from Edward Digges of Prince George's cty, Md. (Som. Md. x-825.

Capt. WILLIAM WHITTINGTON, of Somerset, Gent., is appointed to collect a tax from all shipping. (16 Feby 1691. Som. Md. B. W. Z.-164.) But previous to that, the 19 July 1691 [it will be remembered that these dates are Old Style] a Committee report that Maj. WILLIAM WHITTINGTON is duly elected a Delegate [one of the four from Somerset] to serve for "Sum'r-sett." "Ord'r'd that he be called into the house . . "who enters." He takes the oaths ap pointed by Act of Parliament and subscribes the Test and Association and takes his place in the house. (See Md. Arch. xxii-439. See also Som. B. W. Z.-211. 28 Apr 1692, for county record of his election.) [There appears to be some lack of co-ordination in these dates and it is possible the Archives changed the dates from Old Style to New Style. The Editor will look this up and add a later note.]

(*To be continued*)

AUTHENTIC REFERENCES FOR INFERRED MARRIAGES

(*The following marriages are from Maryland records. See note in August Note-Book.*)

CHARLES RIDGELY and RACHEL HOWARD, before 1725. Md. Arch. xxxviii-378.

JOHN RAYMOND and SUSANNAH DYER, before 18 May 1713. Md. Arch. xxxviii-211.

RICHARD ROLLESON and MARGARET PIERPONT, admx of Thomas. Before 19 Aug 1804. A. A. cty, v-110.

HENRY REED and PARTHENIA, extx of John SMOCK. Before 31 Mch 1695. Wor. cty, J. W. xv-307.

.... RACKLIFFE and RACHELL WALE, dau. Edward. Before 21 Apr 1718. Wor cty, M. H. iii-143.

WILLIAM RICHARDSON and ELIZABETH SCARBURGH, dau. Mathew, Gent. About 1705. Som cty, A. B. (9)-52.

WILLIAM ROUNDS and MARTHA WOOD, dau. of John, of Dorking, Surrey, Eng., Clerk. Before 27 June 1713. Som. cty, x-1912.

JOHN SHEKELL and MARY BURGESS. Before 13 Aug 1800. Montg. cty. D-420.

ROBERT SMITH and ELIZABETH TOWNSEND, dau. John. Before 18 May 1698. Wor. cty, M. H. iii-43.

EZEKIEL SOMERS and NANCY ROACH, dau. Jonathan. Before 2 Mch. 1802. Som. cty, E. B. xxiii-58.

WILLIAM SEYMOUR and MARTHA, admx of William MILLWARD. See account returned 27 Aug 1714. Wor. cty, J. W. xv-324.

JONATHAN STURGIS prob. married dau. of John STOCKLEY. Before (?) 12 June 1716.

JOHN SCOTT and JANE PITTMAN, *extx of Peter Dent.* Before 3 June 1714. Som. cty, A. C. (12)-75.

JOHN SPEAK and WINIFRED WHEELER, dau. of John, of Chas. cty, Gent. About 11 Aug 1685. Md. Arch. xxxviii-380.

CHARLES STOAKLEY and COMFORT EWELL, of Acco. cty, Va. 1 Sept 1736. Som. cty, 1736-1738, p. 243.

JOHN STRAWBRIDGE and OLLIVE "FURNISH", admx of John. Before 11 Dec 1688. Som. cty, 1690-1691, p. 98.

WILLIAM STEVENS and the relict of Michael WILLIAMS. Before 20 Mch 1704. Som. cty, G. I. (8)-218.

ED: STOCKDELL probably married a dau. of WilliamBOYCE. Before 1723. Som. cty Rent Roll.

JOHN STITCHELL and JANNET FRASES (FRASER?) Before 27 July 1805. A.A. cty, v-220.

WILLIAM STONEM [?] and HANNAH COCKEY, wid. Before 13 Feby 1781. A. A. cty, ii-2.

WILLIAM SOUGHTON [?] and ANNE, the extx of Robert CATHERWOOD. Before Court 22 June 1716. Som. cty, 1715-1716, p. 298.

JOHN STERLING and ALCE BASSETT. Banns. 28 May 1667. Som. cty, B (1)-68.

RICHARD SHOCKLEY and BETTY TUCKER, Before 23 May 1793. Wor. cty, P-13.

THOMAS SHERMAN and MARGARET JAMISON, dau. of Alexander. Long before 17 Nov 1721. Som. cty, I. K.-174.

JOHN SMITH and MARY PORTER, admx of McKimmea Porter. Before 19 Sept 1791. Som. cty, E. B. xvi-481.

THOMAS TULL, of "Anomessicke," and MARY MITCHELL of Marumscoe. Banns. 4 Sept 1666. Som. cty, B (1)-29.

GEORGE TUCKER and the only dau. of Thomas HANDY. Before 26 Oct 1747. Som. cty, xxi-299.

LITTLETON TOWNSEND and SARAH KIRKE, dau. of John and Bridget. Before 3 May 1746. Som. cty, xxi-191.

.... TURVILLE and ELISABETH WALE, dau. Edward. Before 21 Apr. 1718. Wor cty. M. H. iii-143.

JAMES TRAIN and SARAH, admx of Barkley FISHER. Before 22 Mch 1738. Som. cty, E. B. xii.181.

THOMAS TRACEY, of A. A. cty, and SUSANNAH SEWICK, widow of John. Before 1711. Md. Arch. xxxviii-135.

WILLIAM TAYLOR and MARY DIRRICKSON. [Date not clear.] Som. cty, see C. H. -1. [Before 7 Sept. 1715, Wor. cty, M. H. iii-127.]

.... TORRENCE and MARTHA WHITE, extx of Capt. John WHITE. Before 12 Dec 1760. Fred'k cty, Al, inv. p. 466.

.... TINGLE and ELIZABETH POWELL, dau. of Walter. Before 18 Jany 1714. Som. cty, C. H. -155.

JOHN TARR and the widow of Thomas PROFFIT. Before 14 Aug. 1690. Som. cty, E. F. G. .168.

ANTHONY UNDERWOOD and MARTHA RIDGLEY, widow of Robert, of St. Marys', Gent. 4 Dec 1712. Som. cty, x-826.

VIRGINIA COLONISTS

(*From "Old Volume 5," S. L. O., Richmond.*)

COL. RICHARD LEE, no county given, but south of the Rappahannock, 1658.*

Head rights: Jno. Slattor, John Wornor, John Gibbinne[?] Robert Higgison, Rich. Kent, Timothy Gunter, Daniell Gugoll, Richard Watton, Wm. Boughton, Tho. Dollings, Jone Palmer, Mary . . . ., Sarah Hickman,

Eliza: Persey, Eliz: Holladay, Susanna Roberts, Jno. Parke[?] Peter Walker, Tho. Cooke, Peter Wade, Tho. Wade, Tho. Maw[?] Wm. Angell, Rob't Norton, Edward Barnett, Rich. Dobbins, Abraham Patermaster[?] Kath. Silverton, Rich. Albert;

Robert Girringe, Wm. Bingley, Hen. Billamy, Andrew Felton, Tho. Minstrell, Jno. Edgcombe, Walter Rich, Elias Port, Hugh Gouch, Samson Neale[?] Walter Rickson[?]

*This list as given in October, 1928, contained several errors or alternate readinge.

THOMAS LUCAS, JR., and VALENTINE ALLEN, 1657.

Head rights: Joane Hopkins, Elizabeth Hopkins.

JOHN LEWIS and ROBERT JONES, Westmoreland, 1658.

Head rights: Bernard Halliwell, John Nellson, Henry Hart, Alice Mercer. Andrew Stephenson, Symon Johnson, Mary Rosser, William Peynton, Philip Bayly, Jane Hughes, Edmond Price, Thomas Barker, William Treaton, Phillip Langham, Katherine Burditt, James Heyward;

Roger Hyde, Tho. Maye, Eliz: Morris, Jone Bennett, Wm. Cooper Tho. Coleman, Step: White, Mary Ayres, Walter Ray, Tho. Jenkins, Rich. North, Marmaduk Keibler, Edward Hall, Roger May, Joseph West, Richard Grey, Math. Harrison;

Peter Sherwood, Rebecca Major, Henry Mason, Tho. Joll [Jell ?] Charles Morley, Rich. Lawrence, Martha Robinson, Oct. 1672. (Marginal note: This Patt. relinquished & the 1st nine rites transferred to Thomas Merrit's Patt. by Mr. Jones' assigmt. 12.)

GILBERT MEDCALFE, "Gloster" cty. 1657.

Head rights: nine negroes and Mary Vaughan. (This land was renewed in the name of Maj. David Cant.)

JOHN MADDISON, New Kent cty. 1658.

Head rights: John Essome, Lewis Montaigne, John Folkes[?] John Durham, Mathew Nicholls, Tho. Bishopp.

Mr. PETER MONTAGUE, county not given, 1658.

Head rights: Peter Smith, Wm. Worrell, Jno. Sewell, Ann Bryan.

Mr. PETER MONTAGUE, Lancaster cty. 1658.

Head rights: Peter Smith, Wm. Worrall, Jno. Lowell, Ann Bryan. [Apparently a re-issue of the former patent. The name Sewell should perhaps be Lowell, or vice versa.]

LAMBATH MOORE and BARTHOLOMEW LINTON, Lancaster cty. 1658.

Head rights: Tho. OKelly, Henry Pollock, John Cramer, Sam'l Deluke [?] Jno. Savary, and two negroes.

THOMAS MERRIDITH, New Kent, 1658.

Head rights: Jone Nicholls, Nich. Hodge, Wm. Newman, Rich. Charlwood, Joane Rayman, Robert Peacocke, Ann Cloomer, Wm. Pottpowler, Joseph Morris.

THO. NOWELL, Warwick cty, 1658.

Head rights: Robert Kent [or Kents] Robert Hudgson, Wm. Porter, Silvester Patman, Tho: Bromsall, Georg Hancock, Peter Adams, Jno. Spiltimber, Jone Butler, Mary L.......... [?] Wm. Johnson, Richard Davis, Wm. Willis, Jno. Holdinge.

DAVID PALMER, county not given, 1658.

Head rights: MARY PALMER, RICHARD PALMER, Roger Shackleforth, Tho. Hall, Thomas Kibble, Guy Knight, Jane Annis. Renewed, same name, 1662.

JOHN PIGGE, New Kent. 1658.

Head rights: Roger Donne, Wm. Bowyer, James Spritt, Rees Hughes, Jno. Younge, Tho. Hardicke.

The County Court Note-Book

An every-other-monthly devoted mainly to abstracts from County Court Records, prior to 1800.

MILNOR LJUNGSTEDT, Editor and Publisher. Bethesda, Route 5, Maryland.

Published six times a year. Subscription, two dollars, in advance; must begin with the year.

February, 1929 **Whole**
Vol. VIII., No. 1 **No. 44**

VISITING

The Editor had the great good fortune to be able to make a little stay at the STATE LIBRARY of CONNECTICUT during a recent visit to New England. The Editor is too modest a person to make too much of the kindly courtesy with which she was received, or of the pains that the Librarian and his assistants took to show and explain the invaluable collections housed in the Library's most beautiful, dignified and *suitable* building..... this is so much the way of New England that the littlest searcher shares in it ..... if all accounts be true. But the Editor did hope to devote at least a column to the material in the Library and very specially to mention the exchange of courtesy between Massachusetts and Connecticut anent the TRUMBULL papers, and very certainly to say something about the wonderful collection of vital statistics and probate records..... the details of their acquisition and the manner in which they are preserved and indexed and made useful ....there is, however, too much to praise and the Editor can only recommend to the many who must be interested, that they read the report of the State Librarian for the two years ended the 22 June, 1922. Take the Editor's word, it is extremely interesting.

Who would dream that Connecticut has one hundred and fourteen probate districts, but only eight counties! Fancy having to hunt up those 114 probate courts! This curious arrangement reminds the Editor of the early South Carolina "Districts." It would seem advisable in the case of Connecticut, were it not for that wonderful storehouse in Hartford, to have a sort of war map with colored pins stuck in and little arrows pointing the road from one to another! But most of this trouble can be avoided by using the store in the storehouse, that is, in the Library. It is well arranged, and comfortably and readily accessible. It is, indeed, a pleasure to sit in the beautiful main reading-room.........it is a fine and noble hall, with a harmony of tone delightful to the eye and suitably subordinated to size and dignity and proportion.

The Memorial Hall is another beautiful room, and the arrangement for the safe preservation of its collection is excellent. This collection includes one of the two original charters, and also the original of the "Fundamental Orders," the first example in history of a frame of government drawn up by a popular assembly for its own Commonwealth.

The Editor's stay in beloved Boston was so largely taken up with the search for, and then the arrangement for photostating one certain letter written seventy-eight years ago (would you believe she found it, thanks to the New England Historic Genealogical Society and its helpful officers!) that she barely saw her own State Library......but did see the so-called "Log of the Mayflower," properly, Bradford's History. It lies in a glass case so that all may read at least two of the immortal pages, but every night it is wheeled into a treasure-house. This volume, it will be remembered, was returned to Massachusetts by our cousin-friends across the sea. The writing, the paper, the ink, are most remarkable in their preservation. This was also true of the Connecticut covenant. The ink of the Charter had not stood so well.

By the marked kindness of the Librarian of the N. E. H.-G. the Editor was permitted to have the letter she found photostated, as mentioned above, at the State Library. The Editor refrains from stating the very modest charge for most excellent work for fear the custodian of the photostat will be overwhelmed with requests.

There isn't room in this column for anything about Plymouth, nor about the so-delightful corner of a great library in Boston where afternoon tea is shared with the home-comer; nor of the fine Otis House with its really extraordinary collection . . . it seems impossible that the Editor's forbears and fellow-New Englanders could have died and left so much behind them! . . . but in spite of a possible appearance of irreverence the Editor must tell of what she is still smiling over. A search was on for an ancient grave in the crowded "village on the hill" at Plymouth . . . no other than one of the Editor's ancestors . . . an immigrant ancestor, indeed, though he didn't come because he wanted to, but because he had to. The amiable guide of the touring car helped; one or two others tried to help . . . *Francis Le Baron*, "phycitian" could not be found. So the guide out of the goodness of his heart went after the smallish boy who sells leaflets at the foot of the steps. The lad appeared suddenly. *"Did you want to find the grave of Francis Le Baron?"* *"Yes!"* *"There it is!"* He pointed a decided, almost an accusing finger at a stone nearby, and fled over the crowding graves. Didn't have time to have his picture taken, not he, he was pure business. The lady had a right to know where her ancestor lay and he felt the obligation to enlighten her. (N. B. She would have found it herself for had it not been upon a post card? But the Dames or the Daughters had framed the modest stone with its scallopy top in a much taller slab of granite. The Editor thinks it a pity.)

In Pilgrim Hall the same difficulty was encountered, but the guide and the custodian together helped, and "skied" on the wall in a corner found the etching of the ancestral marriage. The bridegroom, this same Dr. Le Baron, a French surgeon and prisoner of war, and shipwrecked, is attired in the most perfect of court costumes, if simple, and the lady, a daughter of Plymouth, is gowned with equal elegance. It is fortunate that the records really prove this marriage, the costumes might cause some doubt.

Several valuable volumes are in press or already published. A prospectus has been received from Mr. Dwelly [see page 8] for his address of "BRISTOL and AMERICA." This is the list of over 10,000 "Servants to America" . . . . persons sailing for the West Indies, Maryland and Virginia, mainly, and indentured for terms of years, which was found in the Bristol archives, England.

Mr. Nottingham has brought out his NORTHAMPTON REVOLUTIONARY SOLDIERS and the MARRIAGE LICENSE BONDS of the same county.

Dr. Stewart writes the Editor that the INDEX of VIRGINIA GENEALOGIES is in press, and Mrs. Nugent's VIRGINIA LAND PATENTS (the first number) is about ready to come out . . . . it has been delayed, in part, by the prepation of a very detailed index.

THE STANDING ADVERTISEMENT of Mr. MONNETTE, of Los Angeles, California, which will be found on page eight, is intended to cover all hitherto undiscovered material touching the MONNET FAMILY (the various spellings of the name are given by Mr. MONNETTE). Mr. MONNETTE'S work upon his family has been very far-reaching and thorough (see his published volume), but there still remain a few gaps which he is anxious to fill . . . perhaps it would be more correct to say that he desires to make his work even more comprehensive. For all new material he will be pleased to make full compensation. This statement also covers the allied families.

ERRATA :

The WEST-BARLOWE marriage given in the October NOTE-BOOK, 1928, is turned about and is erroneous. It should read: Mr. RALPH BARLOWE, Mcht., and KATHRYNE, dau. of Mrs. ANN WEST. Before 28 Sept 1653. [Barlowe was then deceased.]

In the issue for October, 1928, the item on page 41, a patent to "SUGAR CAIN," should have as a reference, Va.S.L.O. (Virginia State Land Office.)

Under the heading of "Church or Chapel at Diffical," the reference should be to the records of the *Welsh* Tract.

The first column on page 19 should have had the heading "MARYLAND'S NEXT OF KIN." In some way this was accidentally omitted.

It will be noted that the date of the Northampton tax-list in the December issue and in this issue has been changed from 1744 to 1742. The latter appears to be the correct date. This is an interesting list, recording as it does the taxable population of Northampton between the lists of 1704 (found in England) and the land books and personal property tax-lists of 1782, filed in Richmond. There are many tax-lists in existence in their original form, but in the course of years, as a result of much handling and many removals, and it can be added an almost universal lack of care, it is usually very difficult, even impossible, to decide whether any given list is complete. In this case, the papers through some happy accident had been kept together as originally filed and there is no reason to doubt their completeness. It may be added for the benefit of those who are interested that the very earliest lists, recorded in the minutes of the Court, are unquestionably complete, at least as to the heads of families.

OCCASIONAL

THOMAS HARWOOD, of the P'sh of *Charles als Poquoson*, Yorke. York cty, Va. 1683. vi-505.

JOHN LINKHORNE'S house mentioned. Rappa. cty, Va. 1683, Vol. 1677-, p. 22. ELLIS LYNCOLNE enters a caveat against the probate of her husband, Garritt Lincolne's will, "before she be cauled." Wmld cty, Va. 11 Apr 1684, 25 June 1684. 1676-1688, p. 334.

JAMES GIBSON; survey for 400 acres on the north fork of Clinch river, called the Flatheel[?] or "Old Hoosers Improvement;" divided by the "Kaintucky Road." Wash'n cty, Va. 8 July 1780. Surveys, iii.

AMBURROCOMICO: Grant to Edmond Scarburgh of 1450 acres, "scittuate in Accomack county at the seaboard side, being a neck of land formerly selected by Richard Bunduck and by him againe declined, called the Arcadia Neck. Bounded . . . by a Creeke and a branch thereof called by the Indians *Amburrocomico* now *Gargaphia*." Acco. cty, Va. 14 Mch 1664. ii-7.

"IRISH NECK" was in Westmoreland cty, Va. See will of James Butler. 1749-1752.

JOHN GREGSBY, supposed to be 107 years old; died 11 Oct 1728. [The year may be 1729 or 1730.] St. Paul's Psh Reg. K. Geo. cty, Va.

ELDERS OF THE PRESBYTERIAN CONGREGATION OF MONOKIN: Rev. William Stewart, John Turnstall, Robert King, John Gray, Robert Wilson, Mark Smith, Richard Wallace, Wm. Alexander, and James Strawbridge. Som. cty, Md. 19 Aug 1723. G. H. -71.

HENRY READ, patent for 673 acres, by assignment from Richard Read who obtained a grant for the land, found to escheat from William Read, son and heir of Mary Read. The land lies in the county of Accomack on Pocomoak Creek and branches, being a branch of Pongoteague Creek. S. L. O. Va. 10 Apr 1758 xxxiii-433.

CONTINUED articles COUNTY COURT NOTE-BOOK, and the dates on which they first appeared.

THE ANCESTRY OF COL. JOHN DONELSON. Began with February, 1927.

AUTHENTIC REFERENCES for INFERRED MARRIAGES (formerly called MARRIAGES BY INFERENCE). Began with May, 1922.

MARYLAND'S NEXT OF KIN. Began with July, 1922.

VIRGINIA COLONISTS. Alphabetized lists began with July, 1924.

MILITARY NOTES, both COLONIAL and REVOLUTIONARY, and later MILITIA NOTES. Began December, 1923.

INTERCOUNTY and INTERCOLONY (formerly called New Englanders and Others, &c., &c.). Began with March, 1922.

EASTERN SHORE FAMILIES. In the form of a one-page supplement, began with June, 1925.

SHIPS IN PORT and COLONIAL FORENAMES will appear in alternate issues or as space can be found for them.

THE TITHABLES OF NORTHAMPTON COUNTY, VIRGINIA, in 1742

(*See note on p. 4. From original lists*)

JOHN EVANS;
Reed Fletcher;
Peter Douty, Jacob Addison;
Rickards Dunton, Wm. Dunton;
Rich'd Hayes, John Hayes;
Kendall Jacob;
Rich'd Savage, Benj'n Warrenton;
Ezekiel Roberts;
Arthur Roberts;
Tho. and Jane Drighouse;
Nathan Drighouse;
Jno. Henderson;
Gardener Crosley, Henry Crosley;
Thos. Giddens, Danll Stott;
Henry Scott, Caleb Scott;
Nehemiah Stott, David Stott, Jr.;
Joseph Scott, Wm. Scott;
Nath'l Johnson;
Wm. Roan, Littleton Isdall;
Balmforth Salt;
Wm. Brickhouse;
Peter Brickhouse;
Posthumus Coar;
John Coar;
Edw'd Coar;
Jacob Waterfield, Wm. Waterfield;
Madox Fisher, Wm. Powel;
Philip Jacob;
John Roberts, Cooper;
Jno. Roberts, Sen'r, Isaac Roberts, Wm. Roberts;
Edw'd Roberts;
Jonathan Savage;
John Giddens;
Rich'd Jacob;
Sala'l Harrison, Joseph Elliot, Johnson Rice;
Andrew Pitts and Littleton Pitts;
Zorobabel Roberts;
Mr. Edw'd Robins, Robert Cooper;
Rich'd Brazier;
Stephen Fletcher;
Elija Edmonds;
James Brazier;
John Beloat;
John Dennis;
Sam'l Hardy;
Nath'l Pratt;
Charles Williams, of Hog Island;
Dan'l Scott;
Azel Benthall, Mathew Moore;
Thos. Elliot;
John Cormick.

(*Another District.*)

Mr. JOHN MARSHALL'S List of Tythables.
Robinson Custis;
Dingly [?] Gray; *Beniaman* Dingly Gray;
Daniel Eshon;
Jacob Abdel, Thomas Jacob;
Peal Andrews, Shephard Andrews;
Noah Belote;
Golding Fox;
Beary Floid, Charles Floid, Bearry Floid;
Ritchard Nottingham;
Sarah Widgen;
Abraham Smith, Jonathan Ware;
Southey Satchel;
David Bell;
Daniel Fisher, Thomas Fisher;
Thomas Edmons, Thomas Fisher;

(*To be continued*)

SERVICE AND SUPPLIES COLONIAL REVOLUTIONARY AND MILITIA

THOMAS CLARKE presents a duplicate of certificate from the Governor, stating him to be a pensioner entitled to £18 per annum. Sheriff ordered to pay two years' pension from 1st January last. Ffx cty, Va. Orders 1783-1788, p. 506. Court 22 Apr 1788.

JOHN FITZGERALD presents Commission as County Lieut. of Militia. Takes oath 22 May 1787. See also 22 June 1785. Ffx cty, Va. Orders 1783–1788.

CHARLES LITTLE, Gent. Takes oath as Colonel of Militia. 22 May 1787. Ffx cty, Va. Orders 1783-1788.

CHARLES SIMMS; commission from Governor appointing him Col. Commandant of Militia. 22 June 1785. Ffx cty, Va. Orders 1783-1788.

Major THOMAS STRECKLY, Captains JOSEPH BOHANNAM, and STRECKLY RENNOLDS; 2d Lieut. THOMAS SMITH, and Ensign RICHARD ROWZEE, qualify to their commissions. Oct Ct 1780. Essex cty, Va. xxix-486.

FREDERICK THOMPSON; stated that he served as a mounted gun man under Brig. Gen'l John Coffee, from 28 Sept 1814 to 9 Feby 1815. Davidson cty, Tenn. iv-384.

JOSEPH TERRY; makes oath that he served as serjeant under Capt. Wm. Phillips, Col. Andrew Lewis's expedition against the Indians in 1763. Ordered certified. Mch Ct 1780. Pittsyl. cty, Va. iv-253.

LEWIS THOMAS, an officer in the 7th Va. Reg't, came into Court and proved to the satisfaction of the Court that a pre-emp. ctf granted to him for 1000 acres in Kentucky, was mislaid or lost, Warrant issued 18 May 1782. S. L. O. Va. Pre-emptions, iii-205.

MARY TROUP. widow of Jacob, who died in the army in the year 1781. Three small children mentioned. Franklin cty, Va. Ct. Feby 1788.

JOHN TAYLOR, who has three sons in the regular service, is allowed £30 for his support. Oct Ct 1779. Essex, Va. xxiv-452.

MARK WALSH, a private, 7th Maryland; wounded at Germantown, 1777. To be paid £3-15 sh. for three months' half-pay. Balto. cty, Md. Proc. ii-21. 13 June 1787. See also 13 Feby 1787.

WILLIAM WALLACE; a poor soldier. His wife Elizabeth to be supplied with necessaries for herself and children. 8 Sept 1777. Mecklin. cty, Va. iv-370.

ROBERT WYNNE; appointed 2d Lieut. in Capt. John Wynne's Company of Militia. Pittsyl. cty, Va. June Ct, 1781. iv-371.

RICHARD WORSHAM; in Revolutionary service. See will of Watkins. Charl. cty, Va. 2 Apr 1781. i-365.

JOHN WATKINS, Gent. Takes oath as 1st Lieut of Militia. Mch Ct 1780. Charl. cty, Va. Orders iv-210.

JESSE WILL [or WILD], Sr.; applies for pension and files declaration. Court is of opinion he was a Revolutionary soldier. Aug. 1832. Bedford, Va. Ct. Orders.

JOHN YOUNG; makes oath that he served in the last war bet. Great Britain and France as a private in Capt. James Gun's company, 1st Va. Regt. Certificate ordered. Charl. cty, Va. Mch ct 1780. Orders iv-209.

DECEDENTS IN HYDE COUNTY, D. C. SHOWN BY INVENTORIES, &c. 1756-1761.

(*See August Note-Book.*)

THOMAS GOODWIN, Sr.; inventory. Thomas Goodwin, extr. 28 Aug 1761.

OLIVER SMITH; inventory. John x Far[?] extr. 1 June 1761.

JAMES DENNING, of Hyde county; inventory. Step'n Denning, admr. 1 June 1761.

WILLIAM CASON; inventory. Jane x Jason [Jason or Cason?] admx. 2 Dec 1761.

JOHN McHANRY; estate. John McHanry, extr. 2 Dec 1761.

ALEXANDER FOREMAN; inventory. John Foreman, admr. Mch 1762.

Mr. JAMES DENNING, Hyde county, List of sales. 14 Dec. 1761. Estate account [returned by] Step'n Denning. Mch 1762.

OLIVER SMITH; division his estate. Returned signed by Phillip Jolley. 6 Jany 1762.

Capt'n WILLIAM MASSURY, mariner, of Salem, in "Massatusets"; account sales his estate. June 1762. Another return as to his estate. Patrick Kennedy, admr. p. 60. Inventory, p. 57.

BENJAMIN SCOTT; inventory. Sarah Scott, extx. Recorded Sept Ct 1762. p. 60.

THOMAS HARVEY; account sales. 31 July 1762. p. 61.

JAMES CLAYTON; inventory. James Clayton, admr. 20 Mch 1762. p. 61. Account sales. p. 62.

THOMAS HARVEY; inventory. Thomas Fardon [?] admr. 1 June 1762. p. 62.

JOHN WRIGHT; inventory. Thom's Wright, admr. Ct Order Mch 1762. p. 62.

JAMES CLAYTON; account estate. Ct Order Mch 1763. Additional account; Richard Newman signs. Mch Ct 1763.

THOMAS BARROW, Esq.; inventory. Zechariah Barrow, extr. 26 Feby 1763. Additional inventory returned 27 May 1763. Account sales . . sale 5th April 1763.

THOMAS BANKS; inventory estate. Ann Banks admx. Returned 4 Mch 1763.

REBECCA SATTATHWAITE; inventory. Joseph x Sattatwhaite, admr. Taken 1 June 1763.

JOHN FOREMAN; estate account. [1763.] p. 70.

FRANCIS BANKS; account sales of his estate. Stephen Denning signs record. Mch Ct 1763.

JOHN SLADE; inventory. Jeremiah Slade and Elizabeth x Slade, extrs. Taken 10 Mch 1763. p. 72.

JOHN CHAMBERS; inventory. Mary Chambers, extx. 27 Nov 1762. Additional inventory. p. 72.

JOHN SLADE; account sales. 1 Apr 1763.

JOHN SPRING; inventory. Francis Gallaway, extr. Returned Sept Ct. 1763.

FRANCIS BANKS; account of debts against estate. Ann Banks signs. Returned Sept Ct 1763.

HENRY GIBBS, Sr. Henry Gibbs, Joseph Gibbs, extrs. Inventory. 30 Nov 1763.

ISRAEL WINDLE; inventory. Aaron Windly, extr, also Moses Windly. [The names are as given. Probably Windle.] Windle appears to have died 28 Nov 1763. Inventory returned at Dec Ct 1763.

JOHN SPRING; account sales. Sale 20 Sept 1763. Returned Dec 1763.

JOHN MANDOWELL; inventory. Taken by Samuel Mandowell, 3 Dec 1763. Account sales returned Mch Ct 1764. p. 84.

THOMAS BARROW; further account sales. Sale 20 August 1763.

ABRAHAM WILKINSON; inventory. Thos. Jordan, extr. Returned Mch Ct 1764. p. 84.

JOHN ARTHUR; inventory. Taken by Richard Harvey, Esq., admr. Returned Mch Ct 1764. Additional inventory, returned June Ct 1764. p. 88. Sale of estate 23 Mch 1764. Returned June Ct 1764. p. 89.

ISRAEL WINDLEY; additional inventory. Aaron and Moses Windley extrs. Returned June Ct 1764. p. 88.

NATHANIEL DAVIS; inventory. William Davis, extr. Returned June Ct. 1764.

RICH'D WILKINSON; inventory.

WILL'M FEN.........[?] Account of the administration by Joseph Adams. p. 91. [This entry is somewhat obscure, as to name, at least.]

This is the end of the obverse of this volume. The reverse, an Orphan's Court record, begins 25 Sept 1755.

Printed at the Industrial School for Crippled and Deformed Children, 241 St. Botolph St., Boston, Mass.

The

County Court Note-Book

A Little Bulletin of History and Genealogy

April, 1929. Vol. VIII, No. 2

FAMILIES OF THE EASTERN SHORE
THE WHITTINGTONS

In spite of the compiler's intention to restrict these notes largely to those records of county courts which touch upon marriages, deaths, wills, comings of age, acquisition of property, &c., &c., in the case of a man like Lieut. Col. WILLIAM WHITTINGTON it is very difficult to do so. WHITTINGTON held many offices, and, in Maryland, at least, was always more or less a public man. There is a great deal about him in the Maryland Archives and some of these records throw a quaint light upon the ways of legislative assemblies. And, although these records are published they are not within reach of all. So, perforce, here follow some.

Maj'r Wm. WHITTINGTON, for example, and Mr. Tho: Greenfeild and Mr. Jacob Moreland are ordered to "*inspect the Rules for the Clerk of the Inditements to walk by in their place of the Crowne and some other matters.*" (Md. Arch. xxii-440. 19 July 1691.) The 10 May 1692, Capt. WILLIAM WHITTINGTON takes the oath together with other members of the House. (Md. Arch. xiii-252.) He is appointed one of the Committee to examine the "*Body of the Laws of the Province.*" (p. 254.) And one of the Committee on Accounts. (p. 384.) With other members, Capt. WHITTINGTON is fined fifty pounds of tobacco for remaining "out Dores during the sitting of the House." June 1692, p. 405.
As one of the Burgesses he is appointed to collect the levy in Somerset (p. 465.) He signs addresses with others, in June and September. The 14 Oct 1692, the Indians complain that WHITTINGTON and one John Gillan encroach upon their land. (Md. Arch. viii-385.)

The 10 Aug 1693, Capt. WILLIAM WHITTINGTON enters his assent to the Court House to be at Dividing Creek. (Som. Md. L. D. -24.) He is appointed to the Quorum [higher grade of justices of the commission] the 16 Oct 1694. (Arch. xx-138.) However, on page 110, 30 July 1694 he is referred to as already of the Quorum "State of Somersett County."

In a list of military officers of the county he is mentioned as "of the foot." (Arch. xx-10. 30 July 1694.) He takes the oath as to transubstantiation the 21st Sept 1694. (Arch. xix-30.) And, returned as a Burgess, the same month, takes other oaths. (25 Sept 1694.)

A record of the 9 Oct 1694 (Arch. xx-153) refers to Capt. WILLIAM WHITTINGTON as Major for *Dorchester* county. [Nothing in the context explains this.]

Capt. WILLIAM WHITTINGTON gives 1000 lbs. tobacco towards the building of the free school as one of the several burgesses who make this gift. Acceptance recorded. (Arch xix-98. 18 Oct 1694.) He is elected chairman of the Committee of Accounts for 1695. (Arch. xix-193. 10 May 1695.) A resolution passed 3 Oct 1695, for the election of delegates from Talbot and Somerset states that Maj. WHITTINCTON is now Sheriff of Somerset. (Arch. xix-242.) The same year he was Treasurer for the Eastern Shore. (Arch. xxxviii-51.) He is ordered to render his account and does so. (Arch. xix-246 and 252.) An interesting item (p. 263) is that his "Itenerant" expenses as delegate in May were 2380 lbs tobacco......which are allowed. He is still High Sheriff of Somerset in March, 1695, and on the 27 Apr 1696, he prays continuance of his Sheriff's place ......to which his Excellency is pleased to answer that it is "*a thing of course.*" (Arch. xx-406.) The same date he is sent for to give what account he is able to the house concerning the "Devisionall" line and the bounds "betwixt this Province and Pensilvania," so that "some end might be put to the dispute." (Md-Arch. xix-511.) He receives his commission for the Sheriff's office 1 June 1696. (Som. Md. DD. 17-41.)

16 Dec 1696 (Arch. xx-579.) various officers in the counties are called to account for remissness in returns, including Maj. WHITTINGTON; in his case, for "*not returning an Acc't of the Justices Sitting and of the Ord'r about the Non Ests.*" In the following June, 1697, George Layfield, Esq, and Mr. Thomas Dixon of Somerset, set forth a complaint against Maj. WHITTINGTON. The grand jury, however, pray he may be continued. The petition is referred to the Somerset Court and they are directed to return names of two men whom they think most capapble for the office of Sheriff to the "end that the said P'sons may be Commissionated." (Arch. xxiii-134). WHITTINGTON files a petition in response to these charges [which do not appear in any definite shape] and requests investigation. (Arch. xxiii-157. 10 July 1697.) [The records show that the 9 Nov 1697 he was still Sheriff.] For want of space the compiler must now follow the simpler records of the County Court. If found interesting, notes from the archives will be added later.

WILLIAM WHITTINGTON, of Somerset, from William Parkes of Accomack, "some time of Somerset, Maryland", and wife Elizabeth, 300 acres, called "Winter Quarter." (Som. vii-577. 26 Aug. 1699.) Lt. Col. WILLIAM WHITTINGTON was administrator of William Montieth. (Som. Feby 1700. L. F.-468.) (See also Annap. T. P. xixA-194. 1703.) He was commissioned as High Sheriff 25 May 1704, and gives bond. John Bozman and James Dashiel, sec. (Som. G. I.-130. See also 15 June 1704.) A series of conveyances are shown in a deed from William Duncan and "now" wife Elizabeth, of Somerset, planter, to WILLIAM WHITTINGTON . . . including the sale by Parker to WHITTINGTON of "Winter Quarter", and a conveyance by WHITTINGTON and wife HANNAH, 16 Sept 1703. to William Duncan. (Som. viii-103. 22 Mch 1704.) WHITTINGTON was the administrator of Richard Warren. (Annap. T. P. xxi-102. Apr 1709.)

Several tracts are surveyed for WHITTINGTON: Ambrose Security, 92 acres; Summerfield, 64 acres (assigned to WILLIAM WHITTINGTON, Jr. and patented to the latter); Neglect, 50 acres, assigned to Richard Holland; "Mumford's Addition", assigned to Mumford; "Jericho", 109 acres, assigned to WILLIAM WHITTINGTON, Jr, and patented to him. These will be found in the Somerset and Dorchester Rent Rolls and in the Somerset Rent Rolls.

The 27 June 1713, WHITTINGTON buys from William Round and "now" wife Martha, 165 acres. (Som. x-1912.) and the 25 Mch 1715 he buys from Rounds, Gent., (wf Martha) a tract called "Amee Down," 300 acres, and "Mulberry" with a long recital of descent. (Som. xii-379.) The 16 Aug same year Hon. Col. WILLIAM WHITTINGTON of Somerset and wife ELIZABETH, convey to Charles Ramsy, Diggs' Point on the seaboard side, southeast side of Rehoboth Bay, "als Baltimore River" which tract descended after the death of Col. William Diggs to his son and heir, Mr. Edward Diggs, who conveyed to WHITTINGTON. (Som. xii-295.)

About 1716, WILLIAM WHITTINGTON approved the inventory, either as "Kin" or creditor, of John Lane, of Somerset. (Wor. Md. J. W. xv-72.) He was executor of Stevens White the 17 June 1719. (Som. C. H. p. 57.), and was security (called WILLIAM WHITTINGTON, Senior) with Robert Nearne and Isaac Piper. (Annap. xxiii-326. 3 Apr 1719.)

The will of WILLIAM WHITTINGTON, Esq., is to be found in several sets of records. He is called of Coventry parish, Somerset county. The following abstract is taken from the record in Worcester county, Md. (M. H. iii-172.) It was signed the 28 Feby 1719; codicil, 13 Mch 1719; probated 11 Apr 1720. [The will is very long. For want of space only a brief abstract can be given.]

To Jones Rickard as much land as he has paid for. To trustees for the maintenance and teaching of six poor children at a time, "to reade and learn the fundamentals of the Christian Religion," he gives part of his Cedar Neck and his Sandy Wharf tracts. To his two kinsmen, Edmond and Whittington Bayley, sons of Richard Bayley, of Accomack, in Virginia, by his wife Ursula, he gives his land at Rokiawawkin, called "New Haven." Tract called "Baltimore's Gift" to sons and daughters. To Andrew Spence, tract called "Middle Moor" provided he pay for it. The land at Cape Henlopen, patented to himself and Mr. Charles Carroll, he gives to his sons. Tract called "Woodman's Folly" to be sold. To his son SOUTHEY WHITTINGTON, he gives "the plantation on which I now live" called "Choice." Also adjoining tract called "Refuse." Land and houses in "Askimmecompson, Indian Town," to daughter ESTHER WHITTINGTON. To daugher HANNAH WHITTINGTON, tract called "Somerfield," together with the upper part of the beach called "Upper Pines." Mentions that the whole beach was a grant to Madame Elizabeth Digges, and by her son, Mr. Edward Digges, sold to him [WHITTINGTON.]

Personal estate to sons WILLIAM and SOUTHEY, and daughters ESTHER and HANNAH;

After bequeathing certain slaves and after "my wife has received such "a Pte of my negroes as was agreed on by a certain writing at or before marriage between us." all the rest of his slaves, excepting Daniel (whom he gives to his wife during her widowhood and then to be set free), to his daughters. A provision is attached to the legacy of Daniel to the effect that his wife is to remit to his daughters her interest in one of the three negroes "I am obliged to leave her during her life by the aforesaid instrument between us"; should she refuse to do this, further directions as to Daniel. All the estate which belongs to his wife in severalty to be hers.

"Whereas there is a certain instrument in writing, said to be signed . . . by me at the day of my marriage with my late deare wife ESTHER, wch is in possession of one of my sons" if sons shall claim any other portion of his estate than that which is given by his will, then such son or sons are debarred from any benefit by the legacies in the will, and such legacies are to fall to his daughters.

Grandson WILLIAM, son of WILLIAM WHITTINGTON mentioned.

Referring to his being executor of Stevens White, directs that Mr. John Watts and Robert Nearn, who are overseers under White's will take charge of White's estate and preserve and keep it for the use of his [White's] son, William White. Sons and daughters are to make a payment to the Justices for the use of the poor Brother-in-law, Mr. Samuel Hopkins. A ring to Mr. John Caldwell [that is, money to buy a ring.] The same to Francis Allen. Appoints his daughters as executors. Brother-in-law, Mr. Samuel Hopkins; friend, Mr. John Caldwell and Francis Allen to aid and assist daughters in the execution.

The witnesses were: John Morrough, Petter Robinson, Samuel Derickson, Littleton Bowen.

The codicil makes his sons executors with his daughters, and revokes gift to grandson.

WHITTINGTON'S inventory covers over five pages of the record book. "Ginina" Long signs first, then Sam: Hopkins and Nath'l Hopkins as kin. [This implied blood relationship is very difficult to explain.] The inventory was taken in April, 1720. (Wor., Md. J. W. xv-83.) The testamentary bond by WILLIAM WHITTINGTON [Jr.], SOUTHEY WHITTINGTON, ESTHER WHITTINGTON, HANNAH WHITTINGTON, his extrs, with Wm. Faucet, Adam Spence and Nath'l Hopkins as sec., was for £3,000 ster. (Annap. T. P. xxiv-206. 11 Apr 1720.) The Annapolis Testamentary Proceedings show that the inventory was returned 6 Nov. 1722. [This may have been a second inventory.] (Annap. T. P. xxv-47?] An additional inventory was filed 9 Sept 1726. Sa: Hopkins signs as one of the nearest of kin. (Wor. Md. J. V. xv-114.)

Lt. Col. WILLIAM WHITTINGTON married five times.

(1) TABITHA SMART, dau. of John Smart and his wife Tabitha Scarburgh. [See NOTE-BOOK for October and December, 1926.]
Chn: SMART [probably died young];
TABITHA, m. Edmond Custis.

(2) ESTHER LITTLETON, dau. of Col. Southey Littleton; born about 1665. [See further notes for proof.]
Chn: WILLIAM, born *circa* 1681; died about 1756; married Elizabeth Taylor.
ESTHER, married (1) William Skirven; (2) Isaac Morris.
HANNAH, married Edmond Hough.
SOUTHEY (or SOUTHY) called Senior, of Maryland; died bet. 1769 and 1773; married Mary Fassitt [various spellings] who died about 1775.

(3) ATTALANTA OSBORNE, daughter of Ann Toft of Accomack, and widow of John Osborne. This marriage was before the 3 June 1688. ATTALANTA died before 9 Nov 1691. [For proof of this marriage, see further notes.]

Chn: ATTALANTA, who married Stevens White.

(4) HANNAH [HOPKINS]. She was WHITTINGTON'S wife in 1703. No exact statement has been found anywhere that her family name was HOPKINS, yet it seems that it must have been.

(5) ELIZABETH . . . who outlived him and married (2) Rev. Samuel Davis, the grandfather of Col. JOHN DONELSON. She was WHITTINGTON'S wife in 1714.

It is very uncertain who was the mother of the two daughters, ESTHER and HANNAH. It is possible they were the children of HANNAH [HOPKINS].

(*To be continued*)

AUTHENTIC REFERENCES FOR INFERRED MARRIAGES

(*From York county, Virginia*)

DAVID ALEXANDER and ANN MORGAN. dau. of Mr. Francis Morgan. Before 23 May, 1698. x-82.

JOHN ANNESLEY, of West . . .[?] in Middlesex, Gent., and FRANCIS THORPE, relict and admx of Major Otho THORPE, dec'd. 26 Sept 1698. xii-103.

WILLIAM AYLETT and the relict of Mr. Jerom HAM and of Mr. Mathew HUBARD, dec'd. Before 24 Mch 1681. vi-397.

JAMES ARCHER and ELIZABETH HUBERD, dau. Mr. John HUBERD. Before or about 18 June 1678. vi-53.

WILLIAM BLACKEY and MARGARET GYBSON (sister of Thomas.) Before 28 Mch 1652. i-37.

THOMAS BUCKNER and SARAH MORGAN, dau. of Mr. Francis MORGAN. Before 23 May 1698. x-82.

WILLIAM BARBER and the widow of JOHN DENNETT. Before 20 Oct 1646. ii-180.

WILLIAM BRISTOE and the relict of WILLIAM PACE. Before 10 Dec 1683. vi-537.

WILLIAM CALVERT and MARGARET HAYWARD, relict of John. 24 June 1661. iii-120.

Mr. EDMUND CHEESEMAN[?] and . . . . TILLEY, widow. Before 20 Oct 1646. ii-180.

EDWARD CHALLIS and the relict of Daniel FOLEY, dec'd. Before 24 Apr 1678. vi-36.

JOHN CLIFFORD and the relict of Henry FREEMAN, Before 24 June 1680. vi-225.

JOHN CATTON[?] and the relict and extx of Mr. Chas. DUN, dec'd. Before 24 Feby 1679. vi-194.

NATHANIELL CROSSE and ANN MORELAND, dau. of Thomas. 13 Nov 1678. vi-58.

EDMUND COBB and FRANCES PEIRCE, widow of Matthew. Before 24 June 1695. [xi]-171. Note: she married (3) John Steward. The order of her first two marriages is not certain.

Mr. WILLIAM CAREY and MARTHA SCASBROOK, one of the daus. of Lt. Col. John SCASBROOK. Before 10 Dec 1683. vi-539.

Mr. DAVID CONDON and ELIZ SCASBROOK: dau. of John. Before 24 June 1679. vi-19.

Mr. DAVID CONDON and the extx of Col. Jno. SCASBROOK. Before 24 Jany 1683. vi-546. [These two entries would seem to call for further examination of records.]

CHARLES DUNNE and the relict of Thomas HARWOOD, dec'd. Before 17 Nov 1658. iii-40. (About Oct 1658. iii-36.)

JOHN DREWIT and DEBORAH CARROLL, dau. David. Before 24 Feby 1672. v-43.

ARTHUR DICKESON and the widow of Stephen PAGE. About 24 Jany 1659. iii-70.

.... DUKE and JANE SCASBROOK, dau. John. Before 24 June 1679. vi-19. [Her father was Lt. Col. SCASBROOK. She m. (2) Thomas Mountfort.]

BARTHOLOMEW ENALDS and the relict of Mr. Francis HEYWARD. Before 10 Sept. 1661. [iii]-131.

Mr. JOHN EDLOW and REBECCA HUBBARD, dau. of Mr. Matthew HUBBARD. Before 26 Mch 1683. vi-479. See also vi-400. Before the 8 May 1682.

DAVID FOX and the widow of............ CLARK and of .... MUNDAY. Before 20 Oct 1646. ii-180.

Mr. JOSEPH FRYTH and the relict of John WISDOM. Before 24 Oct 1679. vi-134.

THOMAS FEERE and ELIZABETH HURD, eldest dau. of Morris. Before 24 Mch 1683. vi-565.

WILLIAM FELLOWS [?] woodmonger, of London, and MARGARET x CHESLEY, widow of Phillipp, late of Queen's Creek, York river. Before 22 Aug 1677. vi-33.

THOMAS FEER and ELIZABETH THOMPSON, eldest dau. of Henry. Before 24 Jany 1683. vi-544.

PETER GOODWIN and REBECCA TIPLADY dau. of John. Before 25 Mch 1700. x-306.

Mr. EDWARD GRIFFITH and the widow of Capt. Henry JACKSON. About 1659. iii-65.

Mr. JOHN GRIGGS and the relict of Dr. Peters "Plver" [*sic.*] Before 27 Aug 1678. vi-46. [Note: These York volumes are copies.] A later reference gives this name as Peter PLOVEER, 10 Dec 1683. vi-537.

GEORGE GLASCOCK and the relict of Ambrose COBBS, dec'd. Before 24 July 1684. vi-605.

The County Court Note-Book

An every-other-monthly devoted mainly to abstracts from County Court Records, prior to 1800.

MILNOR LJUNGSTEDT, Editor and Publisher.
Bethesda, Route 5, Maryland.

Published six times a year. Subscription, two dollars, in advance; must begin with the year.

April, 1929 Whole
Vol. VIII., No. 2 No. 45

THE UNCERTAINTY OF DOUBTFUL THINGS

Reprinted by permission of Mr. Speake from the Washington, D. C., STAR.

Some kind friend has sent to me the *Star's* issue of the 18th ultimo, containing an interesting article concerning the "Jerry" Sullivan garages at "Kalorama." The narrator may have recounted an accurate history of the garages, but is far astray on the details concerning the old home and the Holmead family, and as the story is related as one of particular interest in this connection I am prompted to request space for these corrections.

This property was *not* Kalorama, nor was it a grant from the King of England to Anthony Holmead, nor was it inherited by a nephew of the same name from an uncle who would not avail himself of the patent.

From the settlement of Maryland to the War of Independence that colony had a proprietary form of government, excepting for a very few years at the beginning of the eighteenth century.

The Holmeads and their holdings in this section are historically interesting, but details are rapidly becoming lost in obscurity and inaccuracies. To be brief, and so avoid waste of space in genealogical history, it suffices to state that the Holmead name first appears in the records in 1718, when James Holmeard [*sic*] secured a patent for land from the government of Lord Baltimore. He later patented many additional tracts lying in the section from Cabin John (Captain John's Run) to beyond the limits, on the east, of the present District of Columbia, and generally north of Boundary street, now Florida avenue.

In 1741, James Holmead, sr., conveyed by deed to his nephew, James Holmead, jr., one of these tracts. Dying intestate in 1753 or 1754, all of his lands descended to James Holmead, jr. Senior and junior at that time did not necessarily mean father and son. The rent rolls of Maryland show the properties a year later in the possession of James Holmead, junior's, heirs and in another year or two in that of Anthony Holmead. This is the Anthony of the *Star's* story. The relationship of Anthony to the two James has not yet been determined, but he probably was also a nephew of the elder.

Anthony Holmead was primarily possessed, by inheritance and purchase, of about two or three thousand acres of land. He sold much of this, for, despite a patent to him in 1800 of the tract called Pleasant Plains of something in excess of five hundred acres, he bequeathed, mainly to his two sons, John and Anthony, but approximately one thousand acres.

The *Star* has heretofore published interesting articles on the history of Kalorama, which was the home of Anthony Holmead prior to its sale to Augustus Scott in 1794. The old place at 2201 S street is likewise referred to as Rock Hill. The correct name was Canton Rock Hill, a fact established by several references to it in an old Bible of my grandfather, Lieut. Josias Milbourne Speake, U. S. N., whose wife was Sarah, daughter of Anthony Holmead.

Please allow me further short space to refute other erroneous stories which have appeared at intervals.

The bricks of which this old house was built were, without doubt, not brought from England. Interesting statements have frequently been made about Colonial homes constructed of English brick. This is held to have been seldom, if ever, true.

Anthony Holmead did not bid the Indians farewell from the porch of the old home, as has been told. The house was not built until 1795 and Indians had departed from that section many years before.

Last, but not the least, Anthony Holmead was not a Tory. Of one hundred and eleven signers of Oaths of Fidelity, recorded at Rockville, Md., before Justice Burgess, I think it was, his name appears as number 27. His descendants are for this reason, I am informed, eligible for admission to the Sons, or Daughters, of the American Revolution, other requirements being met. I am pleased to have the opportunity to deny this false tradition which has brought chagrin to all Holmeads.

ALFRED HOWARD SPEAKE.

That indifference to fact which so greatly exasperates some of us, was never more clearly set forth than in the "traditional account" of famous "Kalorama" which this writer answers from the fullness of his interest and his information. Although the matter concerns only a tract now within the City of Washington, unfamiliar to many of the NOTE-BOOK'S readers, change of locality and name would make the article apply in a general way to hundreds of the so-called family traditions which pester the searcher. Old wives' tales of one sort or another have been lying around loose, so to speak, always. Bricks have been "brought from England" . . . enough to sink the entire merchant fleet; elderly aunts have produced from old bureau drawers ambrotypes or daguerreotypes of fresh-faced youngsters in Revolutionary uniform;* royal patents in the form of personal gifts from Majesties who had long before passed on the right to give to some high lord or other; pioneers of the 1770's, dead in the west before the declaration of peace between motherland and colony were identified in portraits of high-stocked and deep-collared gentlemen of 1810 to 1820; and as for the "three brothers" . . . it is a hopeless case to discuss them. A friend of the Editor once wrote in a

*A fact.

moment of exasperation, "Why not let people believe what they want to believe?"

And then came the Philadelphia Centennial, and the Daughters and the Dames and the Colonial Wars. No one except a few born-to-search searchers had ever doubted these hoary tales, so why begin? Few had been trained to doubt logically; reverence for old age and far-spreading family branches made the demand for proof almost an impertinence; and the march of inquiry by producing thousands of letters which flew from Maine to Texas and very specially from Virginia to California, simply spread "reliable accounts." And so they continued on.

ATTENTION is again invited to the publication of the marriages of CECIL COUNTY, MARYLAND. See advertising page.

Also to the unusually valuable and well arranged publications by Mr. STRATTON NOTTINGHAM, of Onancock, Virginia, of the MARRIAGE LICENSE BONDS and the REVOLUTIONARY SOLDIERS and SAILORS of NORTHAMPTON COUNTY, VIRGINIA. Both of these volumes contain more than the brief titles here given; one includes some marriage returns and the other the roster of a militia regiment of the county. Mr. NOTTINGHAM is now at work on an index of wills and administrations of Accomack county, which will be more than equal in value to his other work. The Editor knows these records.

Some time ago Mr. CHARLES KNOWLES BOLTON, of Boston, Librarian of the *Boston Athenaeum*, published a very interesting dictionary catalogue of the coats-of-arms in use in the United States. (BOLTON'S AMERICAN ARMORY.) Without direct permission the Editor has to state that Mr. BOLTON is still collecting this material with the possibility of a second and enlarged edition of his work in the future. It is a splendid little volume, containing several valuable indices and a glossary. The thing to do with a book like that (and it is certainly worth it) is to have your copy interleaved and then extra-illustrate it to suit your taste. Mr. Bolton's own interleaved copy would be an interesting study. The story of one plate is rather unusual. The Editor was in the office of a Virginia Clerk of the Court, who brought in to show her a rather large and ornate water-color of arms which had been brought from England to America by an ancestor of the Clerk, who had made a visit to his home land. By a happy accident the Clerk had found this water-color at the house of an old cousin to whom it had been lent years before by some one in the Clerk's direct line. The Clerk was a little "rubbed the wrong way" but also a little amused because some one had insisted that his heirloom was "just a piece of old wall-paper!" The Editor persuaded Mr. T.......... to have the painting restored and also to allow Mr BOLTON to list it.

Errata:

Under "Renunciation of Foreign Allegiance," the reference should be to the records of Prince William County, Virginia. See NOTE-BOOK for December, 1928.

A MATTER OF IMPORTANCE

The Editor of the NOTE-BOOK will pay ten dollars ($10) for a copy of the WILL of WILLIAM FLOYD, or a copy (in full) of the administration of his estate.

WILLIAM FLOYD was living in 1783; had wife ABADIAH, and probably living sons ROBERT, CHARLES and NATHANIEL. He was also the father of Col. JOHN FLOYD. WILLIAM FLOYD may have died in one of the frontier counties of Virginia, in Kentucky, or in one of the Territories northwest of the Ohio. He was about 56 years old in 1783 and owned land in the upper Valley of Virginia. He had removed to the frontier, but was driven back by the uprising among the Indians. Where he then settled is unknown.

PROBATES AND ADMINISTRATIONS KING GEORGE COUNTY, VIRGINIA

(*From the second Order Book. See NOTE-BOOK. for August, 1925*)

GEORGE HARRISON; will presented by Benjamin Marshall, his extr. Proved by Isaac Arnold and Richard Green. William Marshall and Isaac Arnold, sec. 3 Mch 1749. p. 610.

(SARAH STONE, widow and relict of FRANCIS STONE, declares dissent to husband's will. 2 June 1749. p. 618.)

CHARLES PAYNE; Barbary Payne relinquishes right to administer and letters of administration are granted to Thomas Turner, Gent. Harry Turner, sec. 2 June 1749. p. 619.

WILLIAM SIMPSON; will presented by Dianna Simpson, his extx. Proved by Simon Tomison, Edward Pilcher and James Hewett. 4 Aug 1749. p. 622.

CHARLES HOLDSWORTH; will presented by James Kay, his extr. Proved by Daniel Taylor and Lot Hackley. 1 Sept 1749. p. 624.

HENRY BERRY; will proved by John Siers. 1 Sept 1749. p. 626.

JOSHUA FARGUSON; will presented by Ann Farguson, one of his extrs, Joseph Farguson, the other extr, refusing. Proved by witnesses. Joshua Farguson, sec. 5 Jany 1749. p. 642.

JEREMIAH BRONAUGH; will presented by David Bronaugh, his extr. Proved by John Champe, Gent., and Anderson Doniphan.

MARGARET FRENCH; will presented by Burket Pratt and Thomas Pratt, her extrs. Proved by William Flood and Alexander Grant. 5 Jany 1749. p. 163.

JOSEPH BERRY; administration to Joseph and Benjamin Berry. James Stigler, sec. 5 Jany 1749. p. 643.

ALEXANDER SIMPSON; his nun-cup. will presented by William Bruce. 5 Jan 1749. p. 643.

STEPHEN BOWEN; will presented by William and Mathew Bowen, his extrs. Proved by wit. 5 Jany 1749. p. 643.

HONOUR RICHARDSON; adm'n granted to Joseph Pitcher. 2 Mch 1749. p. 644.

ABRAHAM KENYON; will presented by John Carter, his extr. Proved by wit. 2 Mch 1749. p. 644.

ELIZABETH DUFF; will presented by Benj. Rush, one of her extrs. Proved by wit. 2 Mch 1749. p. 645.

SAMUEL REID; will presented by William Underwood, his extr. Proved by wit. 2 Mch 1749. p. 645.

ISAAC CALL; admn granted to Sarah Call, who gives bond. William Marshall and Robert Ball, sec. 4 May 1750. p. 655.

RICHARD PORCH; will presented by Mary Porch and William Porch, extrs. Proved by wit. 4 May 1750. p. 655.

SARAH JAMES; admn granted to Francis James; Richard Fry and James Cash, sec. 4 May 1750. p. 655.

JOSEPH TUTT; admn granted to Martha Tutt. Richard Fry and Richard Tutt, sec. 4 May 1750. p. 656.

PETER NUGENT; Admn to John Elkin; Benj Elikin, sec. 4 May 1750. p. 656.

JOSEPH FARGUSON; admn granted to Isaac Farguson; John Taliaferro, Gent., sec. 4 May 1750. p. 656.

SAMUEL WITHERS; admn granted to Sarah Withers; John Elkin, sec. 4 May 1750. p. 656.

SARAH WORDEEL [WORDELL, WORSDAL?] Will presented by Catherine Cowley (late Worsdal). Proved by wit. 4 May 1750. p. 657.

CLAPHAM RICHARDSON, will; presented by Thomas Richardson, extr. Proved by wit. 4 May 1750. p. 657.

ANN DEANE; will presented by Charles Deane, extr. Proved by wit. 1 June 1750. p. 658.

WILLIAM TILLER; admn to John Tiller. Charles Deane, sec. 1 June 1750. p. 658.

JUDATHAN BALL; admn to John Champe, Gent. Henry Turner, sec. (Elizabeth Ball, widow, relinquishes.) 1 June 1750. p. 659.

EDWARD HOYLE; will presented by Margaret Hoyle, extx. Proved by wit: 1 June 1750. p. 659.

DANIEL WHITE; will presented by Thomas White, extr. Proved by wit. 7 Sept 1750. p. 660.

RICHARD GOLDING; admn to Harry Turner. Mary Golding, wodow, relinquishes. 7 Sept 1750. p. 663.

HENRY BERRY; admn, with will annexed, to Joel Berry, the extrs named in will refusing. Isaac Farguson, sec. 8 Sept 1750. p. 667. Will proved by one of wit.

JOHN DODD; will presented by Christopher Collins and Henry Drake, extrs. Proved by wit. 5 Oct 1750. p. 671.

THOMAS WILLIAMS; will presented by Bathias [ ] his extx, and provided by wit. 5 Oct 1750. P. 671.

JOHN MORISON, an infant; admn granted to Thomas Turner, his gdn. John Champe and Harry Turner, sec. 5 Oct 1750. p. 671.

JOHN WRENN; will presented by widow and extx, Hannah Wrenn. Proved by wit. 2 Nov 1750. p. 674.

HENRY WARE; will presented by John Ware, one of his extrs. Proved by wit., William and Benjamin Marshall. 7 Dec 1750. p. 676.

HENRY TAYLOR; admn granted to John Nichols, Ann Taylor, widow, relinquishing. Charles Deane, sec. 1 Mch 1750. p. 689.

JOHN BARKLEY; will presented by Elizabeth and William Barkley extrs. Proved by wit. 1 Mch 1750. p 690.

THOMAS THATCHER; will presented by Catherine Thatcher, his widow and extx. Proved by wit. 1 Mch 1750. p. 690.

NEWMAN BROWN; will presented by Martha Brown and William Marshall; proved by wit. 2 Mch 1750. p. 695.

JOHN ARMSTRONG; will presented by Margery Armstrong, widow and extx. Proved by wit. 1 Apr 1751. p. 705.

JOHN PAYNE; admn with the will annexed to Tabitha Payne. Proved by wit. 1 Apr 1751. p. 705.

MARIDITH PAYNE; admn to Tabitha Payne, his widow. Henry Turner, sec. 1 Apr 1751. p. 705.

WILLIAM GROVES; admn to William Rowley, Barbary Groves, widow, relinquishing. Rowland Thornton, sec. 1 Apr 1751. p. 705.

INTERCOLONY AND INTERCOUNTY

ELIZABETH BATSIL, age 42; "gone to Virginia." West St. Mary's Manor, Md. (Mss. at Md. Hist. Soc.) Before 1768.

JOHN BATSEL, age 25. Of the same Manor. Before 1768.

ANNE x CARMALL, late of Maryland, but now of Stafford county, Virginia, widow; for divers good causes binds one of her children to her loving friend, Edward Barton, of Stafford, "in this my great want and necessity . . . therefore for the more and better Christian care of my son John Carmall . . . he being now eleven years of age." Also binds her son and daughter, Henry and Bridget Carmall, for the same reasons to Burr Harrison. Staff, Va. 19 Oct. 1699. Z-2.

SAM'L DEASON, age 63; WILLIAM DEASON, Jr. [prob. senior?] age 60; JOHN DEASON, age 50; "Gone to Virginia about fifteen years ago." Gunpowder Manor, Balto. cty, Md. 1767. (Mss. at Md. Hist. Soc.)

MARY HERNLEY, age 40; DARBY HERNLEY, age 35; EDMUND HERNLEY, age 33; "All gone to Carolina." 1767. Same Manor as the foregoing.

WILLIAM DAWKINS; removed to South Carolina. Gives power to Thomas George Dawkins. Pr. Wm. cty, Va. 1 Oct 1766. Q-455. (Note: George Dawkins, prior to 26 Oct 1767, left 100 acres to Mary Edwards. Will not found.)

HENRY FULLER, age 50; NEHEMIAH FULLER, age 48; "All gone to Carolina." 1767. Gunpowder Manor, Balto. cty. Md. (Mss at Md. Hist. Soc.)

JAS. DEMMIT, age 60; ATHALIAH DEMMIT, age 29; ELIZA: DEMMITT, age 27; "All gone to Carolina." Same record. as above. WILLIAM DEMMITT, age 56, also mentioned, but it is not clear whether he also removed to Carolina.

JOHN HANSON, of St. Martin's in the Fields, and THOMAS PATMAN, of St. Katherine's, mariner; said John HANSON with the consent of his father and grandfather apprentices himself "as servant to the said Thomas to serve him and his assigns in the Plantation of Maryland beyond the seas for the space of seven years . . . at the time of the Ensealing hereof is of the age of 15 years, a single person." Wit: Mary x Bradford, Thos. Bells. Staff. cty, Va. 1698. Z-4.

JOHN HENN (or HEM); had a "lease for lives,' the lives being Sarah Henn, 48; Elizabeth Hems or Henn, 28. In Carolina 16 years." 1768. Monocacy Manor, Fred'k cty, Md. (The lease was made 1 Oct 1742.) Mss. at Md. Hist. Soc.

DARBY HERNLEY, 63; ANN HERNLEY, 42: MARY HERNLEY, 40. "All gone to Carolina." 1767. Gunpowder Manor, Balto. cty, Md. (Mss at Md. Hist. Soc.)

THE TITHABLES OF NORTHAMPTON COUNTY, VIRGINIA, IN 1742.

(From original lists)

JOHN ROBERTS;
William Smith;
Arthur Roberts, Gilburd Henderson;
Mager Goynes [Joynes];
Jacob Henderson;
John Downing, John Downing [*sic*];
Hennery Blare, John James;
Thomas Fox, Jonathan Butler;
Nicolas Laler;
William Mager [Major];
Robert James;
John Johnson, Southy Cob;
Kelly Johnson, Jonathan Johnson;
Nottingham Abdel, Edmon Johnson;
Holowil Buntin, Jonathan Buntin,
Wm. Marshall Stakes;
Andrew Turner, Obedience White;
William Glover;
John Bennet;
Peter Kellim;
Obedience Johnson;
Thomas Rose;
John Wesket;
Thomas Clark;
John White, John Kellem;
John Milby;
Jonathan Tilney;
Jeptha Johnson, Robinson Johnson, Elija Johnson, Thomas Knite [?]
Nathaniel Rodgers, Frances [probably Francis] Richardson;
Isaac Smith, const.;
Edward Turner;
Moses Turner;
Thomas Bental, William Jacobs, John Bentall, William Bentall;
William Dunston;
John Bull;
John Downing, John Downing, Jr.;
John Cob;
Mager Pits, Abraham Turner;
Stratton Cob;
Thomas Abdel (Const.), Jacob Abdel;
Stephen Wesket;
Thomas Harris, Thomas Garris;
Sarah Turner, Madux Turner;
Jonah Jackson;
Mary Johnson, Jeptha Johnson;
Robert Heat;
Spencer Johnson;
Mikel Ward;
Thomas Conley;
Thomas James;
Robencon Savage, Abel Savage;
Arthur Dowing, James *Mackmehorn*, Wilcoks Johnson, Hanery Clark;
John Darby, James Petygrew, Thomas Jacob, Eliga Darby, *Beniaman* Darby;
Thomas Goynes [Joynes], Watkens Goynes;
Charles Goynes;
Edmond Core;
Hennery Stakes;
Joseph Green, William Green, Hillery ...... [?] Joseph Green, Jr.;
John Rigs;
John Johnson;
John Pits, Hillary Pits;
Edward Hitchens;
Robert Jones;
John Smith, George Wilson;
Thomas Addison; Thomas Addison, Jr.;
Obedience Parimore;
John Larance;
Samuel Coward;
Thomas Savage, Thomas Savage, Jr.;
Moses Johnson, Abdel Turner;
Daniel Twiford;
Henery Bryan;

(To be continued)

Printed at the Industrial School for Crippled and Deformed Children, 241 St. Botolph St., Boston, Mass.

The

County Court Note-Book

A Little Bulletin of History and Genealogy

June, 1929. Vol. VIII, No. 3

FAMILIES OF THE EASTERN SHORE THE WHITTINGTONS

(*Fourth instalment*)

As stated in the April NOTE-BOOK, Lt. Col. WILLIAM WHITTINGTON, first of Virginia, then of Maryland, married five times. While pretty nearly every statement concerning the WHITTINGTONS has been more or less reasonably questioned, the Editor believes that these five marriages are established by the records of the courts.

The proof of the marriage to TABITHA SMART, daughter of John Smart and Tabitha Scarburgh, is fully set out in the October and December issues of the NOTE-BOOK, for the year 1925. For want of space it will not be repeated here.

Col. WHITTINGTON must have been very young at the time of his first marriage, but had large property interests and was, evidently a "promising" young man, so that he was acceptable to the dominant Scarburghs and the prominent Custises, who were closely associated. By his next marriage to ESTHER LITTLETON he allied himself with a family which, while not so much in the public eye of the court record, was most evidently a leading family socially and politically, and as shown by the will of Ann Littleton, grandmother to the young wife, a family not only of wealth but refinement. It is doubtful if any family on the Eastern Shore stood higher than the Littletons and Southeys. Ann Littleton's will cannot be given here, but an abstract will be published later, with some account of her family.

The marriage of WILLIAM WHITTINGTON to ESTHER LITTLETON is shown by the following records.

WILLIAM WHITTINGTON Humbly shewith that he married ESTHER, the daughter of Col. SOUTHY LITTLETON, deceased......... and is entitled to her share of his estate to be divided amongst his children .... [that she] hath attained to the age appointed by her father's will this two years or thereabouts. (Acco., 16 July 1683. vi-345.) The will referred to will be given in more detail in connection with the LITTLETONS, but it is sufficient to show here that Littleton gave to his daughter "Ester" a tract upon Magoty Bay and a neck of land at Jengoteague called King's Neck. Other lands were left to his four daughters. Daughter Ester to be kept at "my sister Robins"......... Concerning his personal estate he says "All the rest of my personal Estate I doe give to my Seven Children......... whom I doe hereby make my Execut'rs to be equally divided amongst them when they shall be come to age......... my Daughters [to be at age] at Sixteen to enjoy all their Estates Reall & Psonall.........." This will was signed in Albany, New York, where the testator died, and is recorded in Accomack the 18 Dec. 1679. (vi-171.)

There is not space at this time to show the later disposition of the lands left to ESTHER LITTLETON, though it may be necessary to do so, to prove the parentage of her sons.

A record under date of 15 Jany 1686 (Acco. v-443) mentions John Osborne, Gent. of Somerset cty, Md. "as marrying Attalanta one of the daughters of Ann, wife of Daniel Jenifer of Accomack County, in the Dominion of Virginia, Gent." A record of the previous 6 Sept 1686 (Acco. vi-441), is of the conveyance by Lt. Col. Daniel Jenifer, of Gargaphia, Acco., Gent., and wife Anne, to John Osborne, of Somerset, Gent., and wife Attalanta "......and whereas the afsd John Osborne had......married with Attalanta one of the afsd daughters of the sd Anne......."

The 20 Jany 1687, WILLIAM WHITTINGTON (as heretofore noted) buys from ATTALANTA OSBORNE, widow of Capt. John Osborne, 1200 acres on the south side of a Creek called Massiongo, a tract called Choice...... by will of Osborne devised to ATTALANTA. (Som., Md. vi-901.)

In 1688, at the June court of Somerset county, Md., Jno. Swain is cited in the matter of some suit, to answer unto WM. WHITTINGTON who intermarried with ATTALANTA OSBORNE, the extx of Capt. Jno. Osborn. (Som. Md. A.W.-40.) In 1690, 12 Feby, Capt. WILLIAM WHITTINGTON and ATTALANTA, his wife, extx and admx of Capt. Jno. Osbourne appear in a suit versus Matthew Scarbrough. (Som. Md. 1690-1691-p. 54.)

WILLIAM WHITTINGTON and wife, extx of Tho. Osborne, dec'd, are cited to appear. [This should probably be John Osborne. Thomas Osborne d. bet. 28 Dec 1687 and 9 June 1688. His wife was Elizabeth.] (Annap. T. P. xivA-14.)

ATTALANTA (TOFT) (OSBORNE) WHITTINGTON died about November, 1691. A letter from Thomas Welburne is recorded the 9 Nov. 1691. (Som. Md. BWZ-119) In this letter Welburne excuses himself for absence from court on account of his wife [another daughter of Ann Toft] being "dangerous sick"......his attendance at the court being necessary and "occasioned by Sister WHITTINGTON'S decease, once the Relict and widdow of Capt. Osborne." Welburne states that he proposed to Capt. WHITTINGTON to be equally concerned with him [Welburne] concerning the Osburne orphans, but that WHITTINGTON desires either to be "wholly concerned or not at all." [For details as to the difference between WHITTINGTON and Welburne, reference may be had to the court record.]

" No Result by this Court was given to sd Letter."

By his wife ATTALANTA, WHITTINGTON had, apparently, one child only, a daughter. At least only one child who lived.

WILLIAM WHITTINGTON to his "sonn-in-law," Stevens White, Gent., and to his daughter ATTALANTA, wife to the sd Stevens......consideration 5 shillings, conveys Springfield and Faire Meadow......924 acres. (Som. Md. 7 June 1710. 10-602.)

Of WHITTINGTON'S next wife all that the Editor has found is that in 1703, a wife HANNAH joins in a conveyance.

When Lt. Col. WHITTINGTON died his wife, was ELIZABETH. Her maiden name so far unknown. She is identified as being later the wife of Rev. Samuel Davis by the clauses in WHITTINGTON'S will concerning the negroes left to her and the reference to a contract between them (himself and wife.) As ELIZABETH DAVIS she refers to this contract in her will.

AUTHENTIC REFERENCE FOR INFERRED MARRIAGES

(*Maryland records*)

LUKE VALENTINE and JANE BOZMAN, admx of George. Before June Court, 1707. Som. cty, A. B. (9)-354.

Dr. JOHN VIGEROUS and ANN SMITH, dau. of Edward. Before 14 Apr 1687. Wor. cty, M. H. iii-13. See also page 22, will of Edward Smith.

OTHO-HOLLAND WILLIAMS probably m. MARY SMITH, dau. of William SMITH. [Smith was Williams' father-in-law.] Before 5 June 1794. Fred'k cty, G. M. iii-38. [The lateness of this date pre-supposes that Smith was father-in-law and not step-father.]

HEBER WHITTINGHAM, B. in Chester cty, England, and MARY HORSEY, of Som. cty, Md. Dep'n of Rev. Alex. Adams. See record 16 Nov. 1724, Som. cty, xxvi-102.

WILLIAM WALKER and ANN WALLACE, dau. of John. Before 7 Sept 1764. Som. cty, C-234.

THOMAS WARD and ANN PRICE, dau. James. Before 31 Oct. 1699. Som. cty, L. F. -225.

CORNELIUS WARD and MARGARETT PRICE, dau. of James. Before 31 Oct 1699. Som. cty, L. F. -225.

JOHN WILLIAMS and ESTHER, admx of William WHITE. Before 17 Jany 1736. Som. cty, E. B. xii-154.

JESSE WEATHERLY and SARAH PORTER, dau. McKimmea PORTER. Before 7 Jany 1790. Som. cty, E. B. xvii-97. See also E. B. xvi-648. Also E. B. xvi-636.

WILLIAM WALKER and ANN WALLACE, dau. of John. Before 7 Sept 1764. Som. cty, C-234.

ROBT (?) WEER and BRIDGET KIRKE, wid. of John. "Bonds of Matrimony." 10 May 1720. Som. cty, I. K. -20.

GEORGE IVORY WILLIS and FRANCES TALBOT. Before Oct. Court 1804. A. A. cty, v-129.

PETER WATSON and .... CLIFTON, dau. of Thomas. Before 1723. Chas. cty, i-133.

THOMAS WHITE and ELIZABETH, extx of William WILSON. Before1735 [?] Som. cty. E. B. xii-116.

THOMAS WHALEND and MARY, extx of George KIBBLE. Before 22 Sept 1776. Som. cty, E. B. xi-214.

JOHN WHEELER and ELIZABETH KENCKIN, both of Coventry Psh. "Bonds of Matrymony." 13 Apr 1720. Som. city, I. K.-16.

SOLOMON WOODLAND and BETSY GOOTEE. Before 25 Mch 1799. Dor. cty, H. D. xiii-243.

(*York County, Va., records*)

JOHN HAYWARD and the relict of Capt. William HAY, dec'd. Before 3 Apr 1672. v-15. (She was BRIDGET HAYES, extx of Capt. Wm. HAYES, of New Poquoson. vi-466.) (See also vi-77.)

MICHAELL HARTFIELD and ELIZABETH DYER, dau. of William. Before 24 May 1699. x-161. (MIKILL HARFIELD, See 24 June 1698. xii-72.)

WILLIAM HILL and ANNE HOLLMAN, dau. of Thomas. About Sept 1660. [iii]-89.

Dr. FRANCIS HADDON and the widow of Dr. GILLIS MODE[?] About 1659. iii-63. [This name is perhaps MAUDE.]

BARRINGTON [?] HOWLES and MARY DANIELL, widow of John. Before 3 Oct 1694. i-272. Another references gives this as BARENTINE[?] and spells DANIELL, DANNELL. 24 July 1689.

THOMAS HEYNES and the widow of Robert CLARKE. About 12 Nov 1660. iii-94.

CHARLES HANSFORD and ELIZABETH MOODY, relict of Josias. Before 23 Feby 1688. Vol. 1687-1691, p. 225.

WILLIAM HEWITT and MARY HANSFORD one of the "orphants" of Thomas. Before or about 18 Dec 1689. Vol. 1687-1691, p. 349. [viii-349.]

JOSEPH HAM and MARY PEAD. Before 3 Mch 1639. [i]-11.

Mr. HENRY HARTWELL and the admx of Col. William WHITE. Before 24 Apr 1683. vi-499.

THOMAS HARCOCK [HANCOCK?] and DOROTHEA WADE, dau. of Edward. Before 9 Nov 1675. vi-12. [It is almost impossible to decide what this copyist meant the name to be. Probably could not read the original.]

CHRISTOPHER HURT and the relict of John EVANS. Before 10 Oct 1679. vi-127.

RANDOLPH HOLT and ELIZABETH HANSFORD, oldest dau. of John. Before 24 Oct 1663. iv-66. [She was ELIZABETH WILSON, widow of Mr. Christian WILSON and perhaps of another.]

THOMAS HARWOOD and Mrs. LYDIA CHISMANDE[?] Before 24 Feby 1678. vi-77.

JAMES HARRISON and JANE BURLEY, widow of George. Before 12 Nov 1694. xi-54.

CHARLES HANKINS and SARAH STANNOP. dau. of Capt. John. 15 June 1694. xi-12.

MARYLAND'S NEXT OF KIN

(The abstracts in this list are taken from the records of inventories in the State Land Office at Annapolis, Maryland. They represent the decedents in the Colony of Maryland who left personal estate, with the exception of those returns in which the name of no relative can be found. If the record, however, explicitly states that there are no kin, or that none can be found, then that statement is copied and given here. The omissions of any mention are rather numerous and this list should not be relied upon by those who wish complete inventorial data.)

The first nine are reprinted with some corrections.

DOROTHY EASON, lately called DOROTHY HARRISON, makes oath; "The Greatest Creditors are WM. HARRISON Kindred." Inv. Francis Harrison, Talbott. 17 June 1722. viii-14.

CHARLES TUCKER, JOHN x TUCKER; inv. James Tucker, St. Stephens' Parish, Talbott cty. 9 June 1722. viii-15.

WILL. MATHEWS, ELIZ. MATHEWS; inv. Wm. Mathews of [Talbott cty.] 15 Mch 1721. viii-16.

ELIZA: TONNARD [?] EDWD NEEDLES; inv. Joseph Turner, "Carpinter," St. Peter's Parish [Talbott?] 2 Aug 1722. viii-19.

ROBT. GOLDSBOROUGH, R. GOLDSBOROUGH; Inv. Thomas Robins, Talbott cty. 14 Aug 1722. viii-22.

ELIZABETH CRESTON makes oath to inv. of Robt. *Creaston*, of St. Mary's cty. "Noe Kindred." 8 Mch 1722. viii-30.

THOMAS COCKAYNE, SAM'LL COCKAYNE; inv. Mr. Wm. Cockayne, of Talbott. 3 Feb 1721. viii-31.

JOHN NEALL, THOMAS KIRKE; inv. Dennis Roch, of Talbott cty. 14 May 1722.

THOS. MARTIN, HANAH MAYNIADIER; inv. Wm. Martin of Talbott cty. 5 Oct 1722. viii-35.

JANE PINDER, "The Nearest Kind"; inv. John Yewing. 11 Apr 1722. viii-38. County not given.

JOHN FISHER, JOSEPH FISHER; inv. Capt. Thos. Fisher of Q. A. cty. Date not found. viii-40.

MATTHEW GUIBERT, JOHN GUIBERT; inv. Mrs. Elizabeth Guybert. County not given. 1 Mch 1722. viii-54.

MARY HEMSLEY [this is uncertain]; inv. Daniel Lark. County not given. 26 Apr 1722. viii-56.

ORIAH [?] "her x mark," Wm. x Jenkinson; inv. Frances Lofting of Charles county. 24 Nov 1722. viii-60.

FRANCIS x ADAMS "No other kindred of age." Inv. George Godfrey of Charles cty. 4 Jany 1722. viii-60.

JOHN TINGLE, HUGH TINGLE; inv. Samuel Tingle. No county given, no date, viii-63.

JOHN CORDWRAY, EDW'D CORDWRAY; inv. John "Cadrey." County not given. 9 Nov 1722. viii-63.

No kin mentioned; "Widdow having all the Estate left to herself." Inv. William Drigours. 9 June 1722. viii-65.

.... HARRIS (her mark) [perhaps kin?] Inv. Elizabeth Bishop. 11 Aug 1722. viii-65.

NATH. DARE; inv. Robert Widdrington of Calvert cty. 26 Nov 1722. viii-69.

DOROTHY SMITH proves inv. of Jone Smith; no kin mentioned. 1 Mch 1722. viii-70.

ANN DYALL proves inv., as admx of Stephen Dyall of Calvert cty. No kin given. 20 Mch 1722. viii-71.

JOHN x STRICKLAND, JOSEPH STRICKLAND; inv. of Joseph Strickland of Calvert. 29 Jany 1722. viii-73.

The Kin of Thomas Billingsley of Calvert county "refused to be present." 9 Jany 1722. viii-75.

JOHN SHERWOOD, JAMES SMITH; inv Absalom Thrift of Talbott cty. 26 Sept 1722 viii-78.

ROBERT MONEY; inv. Thomas Walms of Cecill cty. 23 Nov. 1722. viii-80.

B. HARRIS; inv. Mr. Thomas Burne of Calvert cty. 14 Feby 1722. viii-81.

JOHN GARDNER, ROBERT GARDNER [Kin?] Inv. John *Garner* of Calvert cty. 28 Apr. 1722. viii-87.

ROBERT SANDERS, HENRY FRAME [Kin?] Inv. Walter King of Pr. Geo's cty. 28 Apr 1722. viii-87.

ALEX'R MAGRUDER, "Father-in-law," signs additional inv. of Mr. Thos. Letchworth of Pr. Geo's cty. 15 Mch 1722. viii-87.

SUSANNAH WILES, and GRACE HATTON, sisters, sign inv. of Timothy Cockling of Talbott cty. Date not given. viii-90.

RICHARD HARLINGTON, Jr.; inv. Thomas "Harlinton", of Talbot. Date not given. viii-91.

JOHN x TEBULS, ROBERT x TEBULS; inv. Abraham Tibbells of Talbot cty. 25 Jany 1720. viii-93.

WILLIAM SEWELL; inv. Mark Sewell. 18 Aug 1722. viii-95.

The County Court Note-Book

An every-other-monthly devoted mainly to abstracts from County Court Records, prior to 1800.

MILNOR LJUNGSTEDT, Editor and Publisher. Bethesda, Route 5, Maryland.

Published six times a year. Subscription, two dollars, in advance; must begin with the year.

June, 1929 **Whole**
Vol. VIII., No. 3 **No. 46**

Will the subscribers who intend to subscribe kindly forgive the Editor's sins as an Editor and Publisher, and also the delay of her very nice printers, and pay up? The Editor always did hate uncertainty, and she would like to know whether she can afford to go to Annapolis and even to Richmond for certain material.

Also and furthermore, if a few subscribers would gather in another few, the Editor could so much more enjoy the voice of the turtle in the scrub pine, or the energy with which the mocking-bird and the thrushes are attacking the apples set out for them on the front porch. Of course, this has nothing whatever to do with the case, nor have the lilacs waiting to be frosted, and the dogwood blooms getting bigger and bigger every day until they are as big as saucers (tiny ones), but the Editor *would* like to sit on the edge of the porch and lean against the post (that ought to be painted) and take in the very pleasant world of spring without knowing all the time that the NOTE-BOOK has to be paid for even if some dear correspondents do seem to think that it gathers like the gentle dew . . . paper and ink and postage.

"Quit?" Not on your life! But if there were twenty-five more subscribers there might be three issues a year of twelve pages each, and a free index.

"Bristol and America" is somewhat disappointing. It has no index, and not more than one-third of the apprenticed persons, bound out and bound for years, some few, let us hope, nominally only, give their "home town." The Editor has read the lists and if the whole ten thousand aren't Welsh perhaps one third are. Why? Will somebody please explain.

"Cavaliers and Pioneers," (Mrs. Nugent's first number is out,) is so extremely valuable that one wonders why everybody doesn't subscribe. Lots of people buy the Encyclopaedia Britannica and perhaps never look at it again. [The Editor was recently housed in a "Y." A volume of the Encyclopaedia was right heavy to carry up stairs, but it was mighty good reading.] I am sure that subscribers to the Virginia patents would read them many times. But there is one fact that the Editor is sadly accepting. . . . "lady readers" don't often care for encyclopaedic work. They much prefer two volumes about the Z . . . family . . . even if one volume isn't true.

A well-known Welsh family is said to claim descent from a witness of the Norman invasion. This is regarded as conclusive evidence that the Norman invasion really occurred. This may prove encouraging to several American families.

London Punch. 6 Feby 1929.

CONTINUED articles COUNTY COURT NOTE-BOOK, and the dates on which they first appeared.

THE ANCESTRY OF COL. JOHN DONELSON. Began with February, 1927.

AUTHENTIC REFERENCES for INFERRED MARRIAGES (formerly called MARRIAGES BY INFERENCE). Began with May, 1922.

MARYLAND'S NEXT OF KIN. Began with July, 1922.

VIRGINIA COLONISTS. Alphabetized lists began with July, 1924.

MILITARY NOTES, both COLONIAL and REVOLUTIONARY, and later MILITIA NOTES. Began December, 1923.

INTERCOUNTY and INTERCOLONY (formerly called New Englanders and Others, &c., &c.). Began with March, 1922.

EASTERN SHORE FAMILIES. In the form of a one-page supplement, began with June, 1925.

SHIPS IN PORT and COLONIAL FORENAMES will appear in alternate issues or as space can be found for them.

OCCASIONAL

BOHEMIA LANDING IN MARYLAND, was the most important Shipping port south of New York. Records of Holy Trinity, Wilmington, Dela. p. 1924.

"LANDLADY," Elizabeth Abbott was the Landlady of John Patrick; she had a son William Crippen. Acco., Va. 5 Aug 1736. ii-242.

ALEXANDER; Order certified that Robert Alexander is the eldest son of Gerrard Alexander, dec'd. and heir-at-law to Dr. George Alexander, dec'd. Ffx cty, Va. 18 May 1784. Orders 1783-1788, p. 64.

JOHN JOHNSON, negro, the sonne of Arth. Johnson, negro, complains that Jno. Johnson, Sr., detayneth a patent of his for 150 acres. N-n cty, Va. 8 Aug 1653. iv.200.

JOHN x FIRKETTLE intending to marry Dorothy Wilkinson binds his intended wife to serve in satisfaction of a debt to William Spencer should he not meet the obligation. N-n, Va. 10 Aug 1660. ix-85.

THOMAS SWEARINGEN, Gent., at a Court continued and held for Fayette cty, Ky., came into court and made satisfactory proof that the ctfs lost by Daniel Boone, and granted to Abraham Chaplin, were properly assigned to him for the purpose of procuring the pre-emtion Warrants in his name. S. L. O. Va. Pre-emp. iii-268.

IN SAVANNAH, Ga. Searcher: "This is the *worst* ink I ever struck. Why don't you have decent ink in a big office like this?" Deputy, amiably: "That ink? Oh, that's *election ink.*" "*Election ink?*" "Yeah, used in the booths, you know, and after the voting they collect what's left and turn it over to us."

A limited number of the CUSTIS family notes as published in 1925, will be sent with subscriptions for 1929, for fifty cents additional. These are supplements. The CUSTIS notes for 1926 are included in the body of the NOTE-BOOK. These notes include references to many Eastern Shore residents.

A MATTER OF IMPORTANCE

The Editor of the NOTE-BOOK will pay ten dollars ($10) for a copy of the WILL of WILLIAM FLOYD, or a copy (in full) of the administration of his estate.

WILLIAM FLOYD was living in 1783; had wife ABADIAH, and probably living sons ROBERT, CHARLES and NATHANIEL. He was also the father of Col. JOHN FLOYD. WILLIAM FLOYD may have died in one of the frontier counties of Virginia, in Kentucky, or in one of the Territories northwest of the Ohio. He was about 56 years old in 1783 and owned land in the upper Valley of Virginia. He had removed to the frontier, but was driven back by the uprising among the Indians. Where he then settled is unknown.

PROBATES AND ADMINISTRATIONS FROM STAFFORD COUNTY, VA., ORDERS 1689 TO 1693

(As shown by index. See note below as to later wills.)

COL[D]STREAM'S administration;
CULLEY, will;
FOLIS or FOLIO, admn;
HANKES, will;
HEWITT, will proved;
HASSELL, will proved;
KING, probate of will;
LUTHER GERRARD, will proved;
MINITHORN, admn;
MASON, will proved;
MILEMAYO [?] will proved;
MASSIE, will proved;
VINCENT YOUNG, will proved.

The same from a page to page reading of Orders, 1664 to 1667.

JACOB PORTER; admn to Ann Porter, widow. 15 June 1664.

Mr. Henry ADDAMS; Mr. John Townsend, atty for Mr. Brown, a creditor, granted admn. 15 Nov 1664.

HENRY RAMSEY; admn. to Edward Bullock; John Colclough, sec. 15 Nov 1664.

Mr. ROBERT WILLIAMS; Frances Williams, admx. 6 June 1665.

JOHN GILES; a reference shows that his will was proved by Mr. Francis Hales. See Court "9th 20ber 1665."

DANIEL COLLINGS; will proved by extrs. Before 27 June 1666.

Mr. HENRY PICTOE [?] Col. John Catlett and Maj. Andrew Gilson. extrs, get probate. 28 Nov 1666.

NICO: BRULY; probate of his will to Jane *Burley*, relict and extx. 12 June 1667.

[The volumes containing these wills evidently lost before 1721.]

A LIST OF WILLS WHICH WERE IN THE LOST RECORD BOOKS OF STAFFORD COUNTY, VIRGINIA

(Stafford county has lost the greater part of its records; some during the civil war and some during previous fires. An index now in existence begins in 1721 and probably covers all the probate records then in existence. It is thought that a list from this index may be of value as showing such persons were of Stafford county ai the time of making the will. A few of these missing wills are probably to be found in the records of the Superior Court of Law and Chancery which functioned over several of these counties.)

Will Book K. 1721-1730.

George Astery; .... Arrington; John Allen; John Adams.

Robert Brent; John Ball; John Bryand; .... Bevins; .... [Ba]lston; Henry [Bu]tler; .... Bunbury; Abram Baxter.

John Cave; Robert Curry, administrator's account; .... Carefoot; John Catlett.

Benony Darrell; .... Davis; .... Doniphan; Roger Day; Owen Dial, adm'n account; John Dagg, the same;

Thomas Edge; Thomas Elzey; .... English; .... Finning; . ... Foot; William Fenwick;

John Goin; John Gowry; *Jones* Gregg; .... Gowry; Stephen Gray; Charles Gwarkin [?]; Thomas Garner; William Good.

Mary Heath; Martin Howlet; Christian Hawkins; .... Hooper; .... Harrison; .... Hall; William Hopkins; Rice Hooe; Thomas Harrison; Ann Harrison; [Edward] Humston, adm'r's bond; Richard Herdman; William Halling.

James Johnson; James *Jewer;* Thomas James; .... Kent; Mary Kent [probably the same]; Joseph King.

.... Linch; .... Leitch; John Linton; John Linton's division; (this division gives the names of Ann, William, Moses, Ann, Jr., Francis, Constant, John and Letice Linton). Moses Linton; Andrew Leitch [probably same as above].

Patrick Murray; .... Moss; .... Murphey; .... Massey; David McGill; George Mauzy; George Mason; Thomas Marshall.

William Overhall; William McDaniel; Phillip Payton; Stephen Pilcher.

John Quarles' inventory; ...... Rhymes; John Rutland, admr's account; John Rutler [?] Thomas Raily.

Joseph Summers; John Short; John Sharpe; Amos Shadburn. Mary Shield; John Scott.

Samuel Todd; Raw. Traverse; ...... Timmons.

Elias Vickar.

William Ward; ...... Waddington; ...... Wilson; John Wats; Joseph Waugh; .... Wayman; Henry Washington's bond.

The next volume of wills was "M", 1729 to 1748. The list of testators from that volume will be given in AUGUST or OCTOBER.

PROBATES AND ADMINISTRATIONS KING GEORGE COUNTY, VIRGINIA

(From the Second Order Book.
See NOTE-BOOK for July, 1924.)

HENRY JONES; l. a. to Ann Jones, his widow. [1735. Page no. and date damaged.]

HENRY SWEET; will presented by Wm. Thornton, Gent., and proved by Henry Lock and Elizabeth Lock. 3 Oct 1735. p. 32.

JOHN NAYLOR; will presented by ...... Naylor and Hannah Naylor; dau. to be summoned, to show cause, if any, why probate should not be granted. 3 Oct 1735. p. 32.

JOHN WHITEMAN; will presented by Robert Doniphan and proved by wit. 3 Oct 1735. p. 33.

THOMAS TRAVERSE; will presented by John Champe, Gent., his extr. Proved by Wit. 3 Oct 1735. p. 35.

ROBERT STROTHER; will presented by Elizabeth, his widow, who makes oath. Proved by wit. 3 Oct 1735. p. 35.

RUSH HUDSON; administration to Edward Turbeville and wife, Sarah. 3 Oct 1735. p. 36.

RICHARD PRICE; l. a. to William Mumford and wife Katherine; sd William and James Stigler, sec. 5 Dec 1735. p. 39.

JOHN NAYLOR, will. [See before.] The atty for John Simpson, who married a daughter, makes objections. The Court are of opinion that the said will shall be established. Naylor stated to have died the 8 June 1735. Anne, his widow, and Hannah Bronaugh, a dau., take oath as executors, and the will is admitted to record. 6 Dec 1735. p. 44.

WILLIAM HUDSON; admn his estate to John Tiller; John Triplett, sec. 6 Feby 1735. p. 47.

ISRAEL ILLINGSWORTH; admn his estate granted to Thomas Turner; Samuel Skinker, sec. 6 Feby 1735. p. 47.

RICHARD ROSSER; will presented by Sarah Rosser, widow and extx, and proved by wit. 5 Mch 1735. p. 52.

JOSEPH TUCKER; admn his estate to Rosamond his widow. John Champ, sec. 5 Mch 1735. p. 53.

RICHARD GILL; admn his estate to widow, Margaret; Robert Elliston, William Taylor, James Jones, sec. 5 Mch 1735. p. 53.

DANIEL FRENCH; will presented by Hugh French, and proved by wit. 5 Mch 1735. p. 54.

THOMAS DICKESON; will presented by widow, Alice. Proved by wit. 31 Mch 1736. p. 61.

DANIEL FRENCH; will presented by Hugh French, extr. [See before.] 31 Mch 1736. p. 62.

JOHN WHARTON; will presented by Tabitha Wharton, Samuel Wharton and William Wharton, his widow and extrs, and proved by wit. 31 Mch 1736. p. 62.

WILLIAM GRANT; admn to Margaret, his widow; John Glendening, sec. 7 May 1736. p. 63.

WILLIAM LINTON, will; presented by Thomas Turner and Jonathan Gibson. Proved by wit. 7 May 1736. p. 67.

SARAH GIBSON; admn her estate to Jonathan Gibson. Thomas Turner, sec. 7 May 1736. p. 68.

PETER KERR; admn his estate to widow, Sarah. Joseph Berry, sec. 7 May 1736. p. 70.

ELIAS POWELL; admn to Mary Butler, late Mary Powell. James Hackley, sec. 2 July 1736. p. 76. [See also p. 79.]

JOHN JONES; admn to Sarah Jones, his widow. Thomas Bartleet, sec. 6 Nov 1736. p. 86.

THOMAS HARPER; will presented by widow, Margaret, extx and proved by wit. 1 Apr 1737. p. 102.

JOHN STRIBLING; admn on his estate to widow, Ann. Edward Hoyl, sec. 6 May 1737. p. 108.

THOMAS EVENS; will presented by Humphrey Evens, Benj. Stribling, extrs . . who refused. Honour Tinsley, late widow, relinquishes her right to administer but testifies to signature of will, and administration is granted to Humphrey, he being heir-at-law. 6 May 1737. p. 109.

JOSEPH WING; admn his estate to Agatha Wing, widow. George Pain, sec. 1 July 1737. p. 117.

ROBERT JONES; will presented by Phillis Smith, his extx. Proved by wit. 2 Sept 1737. p. 127.

JOHN BROWN; admn his estate to widow Elizabeth Brown; Stephen Bowen and Francis Stone, sec. 4 Nov 1737. p. 135.

THOMAS KING; will presented by George Hall and proved by wit. Widow, Elizabeth King, refuses to stand to the will. 3 Feby 1737. p. 138.

THE TITHABLES OF NORTHAMPTON COUNTY, VIRGINIA, IN 1742

(From original lists)

MIKEL DUNTON, Jeames Rasco, John Sweten;

Thomas Tatum, Henery Spratlen;

Bartholomew Pettet, Ritchard Jacob;

John Smith Turner [this is very possibly John Smith, *Turner*];

Joseph Dolby;

Thomas Johnson;

Arter Roberts, John Twiford;

William White;

John Waterfield;

Littleton Eyre, Peter Cleag, Jr., William Thomas, Edmon Joyner, William Hood, Thomas Rendan;

John Caple, *Beniaman* Dunton, Leaven Dunton;

Obedience Roberts, Obedience Roberts, Jr., Isaac Robert;

Gawton Young, Henery Young;
Nicolas Williams, James Sanders;
John Gill;
Hezekiah Addison;
Elener Dolby, Stephen Dolby;
John Evans;
Tatom Scott;
Pear[c]e Davis;
Dent Gascoine, John Hanes;
Jonah Belote.

Col. JOHN CUSTIS' list.
John Marshall, Thomas Marshall;
Cpt. R'd Nottingham, Isaac Nottingham;
John Custis, Robert Kirby, Thos. Gibbons, James Johnson;
John Frazier, Patroller;
Geo Holt;
Addison Nottingham, Patroller;
Wm. Monk, Patroller, Daniel Esham;
Edw'd Caple, Patroller;
Jacob Nottingham, Thomas Nottingham;
Jno. Fathery;
John Haggoman, Const.; John Haggoman, Jr.;
Abel Powell, Const.; Howson Mapp, Thomas Hay;
Adam Fisher;
Jos: White;
Laban Stott;
Hen: Jacob;
Patrick McGuy;
Benja. Fathery;
Rich'd Nottingham, Jr.;
Joanna Stott, Evan Jacob;
Peter Clegg, Isaac Clegg, Hollaway Clegg;
Rob't Nottingham, Jr., Jos. Nottingham;
Eliza: Nottingham, Joshua Nottingham;
Elias Dunton;
Jona. Battson, William Battson, Luke Battson.

(*To be continued.*)

SERVICE AND SUPPLIES COLONIAL, REVOLUTIONARY AND MILITIA

WILLIAM ALLEN: will: "A Soldier being Join'd in the Army but of parfect mind and memory." Ldn cty, Va. 14 Mch 1776-10 Feby 1777. B-327.

GEORGE BROKER [BROKES?] killed in the Continental service; Simon Triplett ordered to furnish the widow with necessaries. Ldn cty, Va. 14 Apr 1778. G-82.

JOHN CLEARKE testifies that he carried fifteen Gall. of Tarr aboard the *Admiral* for his Majestie's service. Acco. cty, Va. 19 Feby 1677. vii-114.

CHARLES ESKRIDGE, Gent. Commissioned Lt. Col. Militia and takes the oath. Ldn cty, Va. 13 Apr 1779. G-158.

JOHN FARNSWORTH's widow ordered supplied with necessaries. He probably died in Continental service. Ldn cty, Va. 14 Apr 1778. G-82.

THOMAS GUNNELL; commission as ensign of militia. Takes oath. Ffx, Va. Orders [3] 21 May 1770.

TIMOTHY HIXON, Gent. Commission as Captain militia. Takes oath. Ldn cty, Va. 13 Oct 1782. G-456.

ENOCH INNIS produces Captain's commission, Upper Foot Company, this county, and takes oath. K. Geo. cty. Va. Orders ii-77. 2 July 1736. See also p. 80, 2 July, 1736.

EDWARD KINKER, in Continental service; wife to be furnished with necessaries. Ldn cty, Va. 14 Apr 1778. G-82.

WHEREAS by the late recommendation, Colo. LEVEN POWELL was omitted in the Commission of the Peace by his being in the Continental Army, but as he has not resigned, ordered that it be recommended to his Excellency to put the said LEVEN POWELL in the same place he was before. Ldn cty, Va. 9 Feby 1779. G-141.

HENRY PAYNE commissioned as 1st Lieut militia and takes the oath. Ldn cty, Va. 14 June 1779. G-171.

SHAMACK PINKSTONE, soldier in the Continental service; wife in Loudoun cty. Ldn cty, Va. 9 Mch 1779. G-149.

PHILIP PATTERSON, soldier of cavalry; warrant for land to Susan Moun[?] who was Susan Hardie, only heir of Elizabeth Hardie, who was Elizabeth Patterson, the only heir of John Patterson, dec'd, who was the only heir-at-law of Philip Patterson, who died before 1787. S. L. O. Va. 22 Aug 1835 and 4 Aug. 1836. iii-428.

MOURNING ROBERTS; three years' service as private, Continental line. Ctf by James Pleasant, Jr., Gov'r. 8 June 1824. S. L. O. Va.

FRANCIS SUMMERS takes the oath "pursuant to his military comm'n." Ffx cty, Va. Orders [1]-64. 20 Mch 1754.

JOHN TALIAFERO, Gent. Presents commission to be Captain of the Upper Troop of the County. K. Geo. cty, Va. Orders ii-566. 1 Apri. 1748.

WILLIAM THORNTON, Jr., and Joseph Berry; oaths as Captains for this county. K. Geo. cty, Va. Orders ii-33. 3 Oct 1735.

FRANCIS THORNTON; commission to be Capt. of the Middle Troop of the County. K. Geo. cty, Va. Orders ii-p. 33. 3 Oct 1735.

CHRISTOPHER THOMSON; served under his Captain 14 days himself and horse in the "publique Service in the Late Rebellion......." Ctf granted him to the next Assemcly. Acco. cty, Va. 19 Feby 1677. x-112;

WILLIAM CHACE sets forth that he served in the Country's service under the command of Capt. William Whittington, 30 days. Ctf granted him for the next Assembly. Acco. cty, Va. 20 Feby 1677. vii-120.

Printed at the Industrial School for Crippled and Deformed Children, 241 St. Botolph St., Boston, Mass.

The
County Court Note-Book

A Little Bulletin of History and Genealogy

August, 1929. **Vol. VIII, No. 4**

SOME NOTES FROM NORTH CAROLINA RECORDS

THIS MAY CERTIFY that ELIZABETH daughter of JOB and ELIZ'H BRADFORD was baptized when an infant in the New North [Church] July first day year of our Lord one thousand seven hundred and fifty-nine. DORCAS [dau.] of the said JOB and ELIZABETH the twenty-second of June in the year following 1760. SAMUEL of the said JOB and ELIZABETH the ninth of the yr following viz: 1761. WILLIAM BREWER BRADFORD of the sd JOHN and ELIZABETH August Eighth 1762. ABIGAIL of the sd JOB and ELIZABETH July Twenty Fourth 1763, SAMUEL of the said JOB and ELIZABETH March Seventeenth 1765. JOB of the said JOB and ELIZABETH October 18th 1767. RUEFUS of the said JOB and ELIZABETH June 18th 1769. JOSEPH NASH of the sd JOB and ELIZABETH Sep'r 30th 1770.

"A TRUE COPPY from the Records of the New North Church in Boston. Transcribed Febry 11th 1792 by John Elliot pastor."

[I] SAMUEL PARKMAN of Boston......... having for near 30 years a particular acquaintance with the family of Capt. JOB BRADFORD late of sd Boston, dec'd, do now at the request of Mr. WILLIAM BOWES BRADFORD adm'r of the estate of his brother RUFUS dec'd, certifie that DORCAS NOYES wife of SILAS NOYES ABIGAIL ALLYN, wife of Rev. JOHN ALLYN, WILLIAM BREWER BRADFORD and JOSEPH NASH BRADFORD are the only children of sd JOB and ELIZABETH BRADFORD now living and they are as I believe the only legal Heirs to their late Brother RUFUS BRADFORD who Died in North Carolina all the other children of the sd JOB and ELIZABETH BRADFORD as Recorded in the Book of the New North Church in this town of which the foregoing is a Copy Sign[ed] by Rev. John Abot are dead and without issue. Dated at Boston Febry 13th 1792.

SAMUEL PARKMAN.

This may certify that SILAS NOYES and DARCAS BRADFORD were Mariade......"on the Evening of the month of February year of our Lord one thousand seven hundred and ninety by John Eliot Pastor New North Church."

That the Rev. JOHN ALLYN and ABIGAIL BRADFORD were married on the Evening of July Twentieth One thousand seven hundred and ninety one by John Eliot Pastor said Church. A True Copy from the Records. N. B. the Rev'd JOHN ALLYN is pastor of the Church in Dunbury [Duxbury?] Massachusetts.

Certificate that JOB BRADFORD and ELIZABETH PARKMAN were married.........on the 26th Day of January in the Year 1758 by the Rev'd Andrew Elliott at that time pastor of the New North Church......John Eliot pastor sd Church. Boston Febry 11th 1792.

A copy of the record shows that administration on the estate of RUFUS BRADFORD of Boston Massachusetts, was granted 13 Feby 1792 to WILLIAM BOWS BRADFORD of Boston. [This name Bows or Bowes is spelled in several ways, but appears to be *Bowes.*]

The foregoing are followed by a power from WILLIAM BOWES BRADFORD of Boston, to Samuel Lowder, of Wilmington, N. C. to act for said BRADFORD who is the adm'r of RUFUS BRADFORD, formerly of Boston, but late a resident in *Cape St. Francois* in the Island of Hispaniola and who deceased in the State of North Carolina. RUFUS BRADFORD is called a merchant. Witnesses: Edward Oliver, Joseph Foster 30 Feby 1792.

FAMILIES OF THE EASTERN SHORE
THE WHITTINGTONS

(Fifth Instalment.)

In the last issue of the NOTE-BOOK reference was made to the will of ELIZABETH DAVIS, who was the fifth and last wife of Lt. Col. WILLIAM WHITTINGTON, and after his death married the Rev. SAMUEL DAVIS, who was the grandfather of Col. JOHN DONELSON, of Maryland, Virginia and Tennessee. An abstract of ELIZABETH DAVIS' will follows......that is, of that part which refers to the WHITTINGTONS.

..................To "Easter Morris the mulatto Will, farmer, being one of the slaves that I am to leave to some of Coll. WHITTINGTON'S children as by an instrument of writing between us made." Also legacies to Esther [Morris], to Hannah Hough, Elizabeth Whittington, to Mary Whittington, &c., &c. Three-fourths of her estate to be divided between Isaac Morris, Edmund Hough, and SOUTHY WHITTINGTON; the other fourth to WILLIAM WHITTINGTON, Jr., SOUTHEY WHITTINGTON, EASTHER WHITTINGTON, and BETTY WHITTINGTON, the sons and daughters of WILLIAM WHITTINGTON, Sr., provided the said Edmund Hough "shall by an instrument from under his hand and seal wholly acquit his right and interest of the three negroes above mentioned, Simon, Will and Sam, but if he refuses, to have no benefit of this my will and the legese[sic] and the one-fourth of the remainder of my estate to him mentioned to be equally divided [between] Isaack Morris, Southey Whittington and William Whittington." Wor. Md. M. H. iii-320. 22 Nov 1734-14 Jany 1734.

As heretofore stated, in 1703, WHITTINGTON'S wife was HANNAH. In a deed in Somerset cty, (A. C.-298, 30 Aug 1715) reference is made to his wife Mrs. HANNAH WHITTINGTON of the earlier date. In 1714, his wife was ELIZABETH.

It is commonly supposed that HANNAH WHITTINGTON was a HOPKINS. This is because WHITTINGTON in his will mentions his brother-in-law Mr. SAMUEL HOPKINS, and also because the elder SAMUEL HOPKINS calls WHITTINGTON his son-in-law. An inventory filed in April 1720 (Wor. Md. J. W. xv-83) is signed by "GIMIMA" LONG, SAM: HOPKINS, NATH'L HOPKINS, all, apparently as next of kin. There seems no possible way in which the HOPKINSES could have been "next of kin," unless they sign as nephews of his former wife, or unless they are his own nephews. Some chance record will probably clear this up.

There are a number of records touching the estate of Lt. Col. WILLIAM WHITTINGTON ......they are mostly interesting because of further problems as to the age of his daughters and the dates of their marriage. The 11 Apr 1720, a testamentary bond is filed by WILLIAM WHITTINGTON, SOUTHEY WHITTINGTON, ESTHER WHITTINGTON, HANNAH WHITTINGTON, his executors. The bond was for £3,000 sterling, and Wm. Faucet, Adam Spence and Nath'l Hopkins were securities. (Annap. T. P. xxiv-206.) Another inventory was returned 6 Nov 1722. (Annap. T. P. xxv-47.) And an additional inventory 9 Sept. 1726. (Wor. Md. J. W. xv-114.) To this inventory SA: HOPKINS signs as one of the nearest of kin.

The 31 May 1725, WILLIAM WHITTINGTON, SOUTHY WHITTINGTON, ESTHER SKIRVIN, EDMOND HOUGH and wife, extrs of Col WILLIAM WHITTINGTON, dec'd, petition against Richard Bennett, Esq. The petition is dismissed at the request of plaintiffs. (Annap. 4 I. R. p. 141.) ESTHER SKIRVIN, as she was then, is shown by the records to have married probably before her father's death, although he calls her ESTHER WHITTINGTON, and the compiler believes that WHITTINGTON'S will was made some years before he died, the internal evidence of the difference with the sons, and their subsequent appointment as joint executors in a codicil, appears to prove this .....that is, that the will was written, though not signed until long after it was made.

Lt. Col. WHITTINGTON left two sons, WILLIAM AND SOUTHY.

WILLIAM WHITTINGTON, Jr., first appears in an estate account, that of Mr. John Edgar. (Wor. Md. J. W. xv-24. Oct. 1705.) [It is to be noted that all of these dates before 1742 relate to *Somerset* county. The persons living in what became Worcester county seem to have insisted on having copies of their records filed in the Worcester court; as a consequence similar records will be found in Worcester, in Somerset and in Annapolis. Those in Worcester are the simplest and easiest of access.] The same year, but a little earlier, 27 June, he buys from Thomas Pemberton, of Sussex county, territories of Penna, 900 acres called *Pemberton*. (Som. cty, viii-120.)

The Somerset and Dorchester Rent Roll, No. 1, p. 243, shows that the 26 June 1706, *Whittington's Chance*, 300 acres, northwest side of Rokiawaukin river was surveyed for WILLIAM WHITTINGTON, Jr., and that he conveyed 200 acres to Lane the 26 Feby 1719; and 300 acres to Pemberton, from himself and wife, 14 Mch 1722.

WILLIAM WHITTINGTON, Jr. Gent., of Somerset, buys of John German and wife Anne, Som., part of 2300 acres called *Durham House*, (Som. cty, x-890. 23 June 1713.) The recital of descent shows that *Durham House*, which was bounded by "Bockatenorton Creek" and Dividing Creek, &c., was the property of Anne Bishop, wife of German.

In I. K. L, Som. cty, 11 Jany 1714, WHITTINGTON signs himself "Jr."

WILLIAM WHITTINGTON, Jr., petitions that he hath bought part of a piece of land called *Durram house*, formerly belonging to Henry Bishop; that the bounds are uncertain, &c. &c. Commissioners appointed to establish bounds. The Comm'rs met and Mr. John Purnall reports: "The sd Com'rs Making a Clear and Nice Scrutene in Relation to the bounds of the sd land they find that the head of Poquetenorton Creek in the Pattent Resited......is Turned into Marsh by the *Salts* therefore the said Com'rs Ordered a Ceader State to be Sett in the marsh as near as Could be thought......that a tree Ever did Stand to the head of the sd Creek......" Thomas Selby, Sr., and Daniel Patrick, who appear to have settled on the disputed land, are ordered to deliver possession to WHITTINGTON. (Som. Md. 18 Nov 1719. A-47.)

Willett's Discovery was surveyed for WILLIAM WHITTINGTON the 23 Nov 1721. (See Som.-Dor. Rent Roll 2. p. 282.) It was on the south side of Pocomoke river......50 acres. And in 1722, 14 Mch, WILLIAM WHITTINGTON of Maryland, and wife ELIZABETH, convey to Joseph Pemberton of the Island of Nevis, now of Maryland, a messuage &c., called *Pemberton's*. (Som. Md. G. H.-38.) WILLIAM WHITTINGTON, Gent. Som., buys from John Bishop, Jr., son and heir of Henry, son and heir of John, Sr. pltr, a tract called *Bishop's Purchase* in "Boggete Norton," seaboard side. (Som. Md. xv-112. 22 Feby 1723.) And from John Bishop, son of Henry, *Durham House*, already conveyed by John "Jarmin" and wife Anne Bishop, dau. of Henry, Jr. (Som. Md. xvi-39. 7 Aug 1726.)

As late as 1730, 29 Jany, WILLIAM WHITTINGTON, SOUTHEY WHITTINGTON, Isaac Morris and Edmond Hough, extrs, [Morris and Hough evidently acting for their wives] petition against Thomas Johnson. (Annap. T. P. xxix-60.)

WILLIAM WHITTINGTON, as guardian of JNO. DONELSON, is sued by Samuel Hopkins, this being some matter concerning the property of Donelson. [The entry seems to establish the death of Capt. JOHN DONELSON, the father, before 20 Mch 1735.] (Som. cty, 1736-1738, p. 73. 20 Mch 1735.)

WILLIAM WHITTINGTON and wife ELIZABETH, Som. cty, to William Bishop, conveyance. (Som. cty, xix-161. 21 June 1737.) WILLIAM WHITTINGTON, Som., Gent., to Isaac Morris and Edmund Hough, Mchts, conveys slaves. (Som. cty, xix-296. 7 July 1738.) WILLIAM WHITTINGTON, Som. cty, Gent. lately called WILLIAM WHITTINGTON, JR., to Thomas Slingoe, Carp., land called *Summerfield*, on southermost side of Pocomoke river. (Som. cty, xix-316. 29 July 1738.)

WILLIAM WHITTINGTON, Gent., Som. Md., wife ELIZABETH, to Moses Challie, Jr. All that tract called *Spring Garden*, about two miles from Pocomoke river; reference to patent in 1734. (Som. cty, xx-143. 18 Apr 1740.) Another conveyance to John Ayres, mariner, in which wife ELIZABETH joins, conveys part of *Durham House*. (Som. cty, xx-286. 15 Mch 1741.) The 10 Mch 1741, WILLIAM WHITTINGTON, Som., Gent, conveys to Edmund Hough, Mcht, a lot in Snow Hill, of which Coll. WILLIAM WHITTINGTON, late of this county, dec'd, was seized, after whose death WILLIAM WHITTINGTON, Jr., son and heir-at-law is now seized. (Som. cty, xx-284.)

WILLIAM WHITTINGTON is now found in Accomack county, Virginia. This is proved by a deed of 1748, but before that WILLIAM x WHITTINGTON, of Accomack, Gent, conveys to SOUTHY WHITTINGTON, of Accomack, for £79-12-1, certain slaves heretofore mortgaged to Isaac Morris and Edmund Hough, Gent. Witnesses: Geo. Douglas, Tabitha Douglas, Esther x Isdale. (Acco. cty, Deeds i-390. The date of this is after the 21 Feby 1742.) The deed of the 26 Aug 1748, (Wor. cty, B-104) recites that WILLIAM x WHITTINGTON, formerly of Somerset and now of Accomack, Gent., conveys to John Williams of Pocomoke, consideration £20 gold, a tract called *Repentance*, on "Chessipeek Bay" so'most side of Pocomoke river, patented to WHITTINGTON 15 Apr 1736. Wife ELIZABETH joins. There are probably other records in Accomack touching WILLIAM WHITTINGTON, third of the name, but the compiler finds only this: which shows that he died intestate.

The inventory of WILLIAM WHITTINGTON, following a court order of 26 May 1756, is returned 26 Jany 1757, by SOUTHY WHITTINGTON, administrator. Wm. Beavens, Charles Stockly, John Watts, appraisers. (Acco. cty, xxvW-385.) And the 27 Apr 1757 (Acco. xxvO-185), it is ordered that Wm. Beavans, Charles Stockly, and John Watts, or any two of them, audit and settle SOUTHY WHITTINGTON'S accounts of his administration on the estate of WILLIAM WHITTINGTON, and make return to the Court. Another and similar order is entered under the date of 30 Dec 1762. (Acco. xxvO-508.)

AUTHENTIC REFERENCES FOR INFERRED MARRIAGES

(*Virginia records, at large*)

Capt. WILLIAM FOX and ANNE CHINN, dau. of Alice Streckley [wife of John] who had been the widow Chinn. Before 29 Aug 1701. Lanc., viii-105.

Mr. ARTHUR FORBES and the admx of Capt. Tho: GOLDMAN, of Rappa. cty. Before 7 Apr 1686. Rappa., Orders, p. 219.

ROBERT GIBSON, Christ Ch. psh, Lanc., and Mrs. RUTH WRIGHT, wid. of Mr. Molt. Wright, of Va. Mar. agreement. 11 Dec 1701. Lanc., ii-455.

GEORGE HARWARD and MARY LAWSON, widow. Before 5 Jany 1703. Lanc., viii-121.

WILLIAM HILL and CLARA DAVIS. Before 20 Feby 1804. Essex, xvi-267.

BENJAMIN HAYNIE and a dau. of Joseph ROBERSON, Before 17 Mch 1756. Nthd, iv-283.

MATTHEW HARRISON, Pr. Wm cty, and ELIZABETH WEBB, Richmd cty. Mar. contract. About 6 Apr 1774. Richmd, ii-266.

Dr. MOSES HUBBERT and the Relict and Extx of John BARROW. About 4 Nov 1685. Rappa., Orders, p. 174.

JOHN HUGHES and WINEFRET HARWOOD, Sp. William Walker, sec. Wmld, 20 Aug 1791. M. L. B.

RICHARD HEWES and MARY JOHNSON, wid. Before 1 Oct 1723. Nthld, Va., 1718-1726, p. 177.

WILLIAM HARDING, of Rappa cty, and MARTHA BULLEN. Before 12 Oct 1687. S. L. O. Va. vii-624.

RALPH HUDSPEATH and MARGARET EYRES, dau. Joseph, and gr. dau. William Humphreyes, Before 20 Aug 1692. Hen., Va., 1677-1739, p. 32.

ANDERSON JOHNSON and NANCY GEORGE, a legatee of William George. Prob. about or before 1820. Gchld, Va. Orders, p. 173.

WILLIAM JOHNSON, Esq., and MARY COBB. Mar. contract. 9 Aug 1788. Han., Va. [ii], 323.

OWEN JONES and RACHEL FEILDING, dau. and heir of John. Before 17 Oct 1716. Nthld, Va. 1713-1719. p. 182.

JOHN JONES and ANNE ROWING [?] dau. Henry. Before 20 Aug 1680. Hen., Va., Orders 1677-1739, p. 6.

Mr. RICHARD KENDALL and .... SHIPPEY, dau. Thomas. Before or about 20 Aug 1706. Hen., Va. 1677-1739, p. 48.

RICHARD LEAKE and SOPHIA T. ANDERSON. Before Sept, 1832 (about which time she died.) Gchld, Va. Orders, p. 156.

Mr. MATHEW MASON, of Maryland, and .... SPENCE, dau. Alexander. Before 23 Feby 1709. Nthld, Va. 1710-1713, p. 319.

Mr. RICHARD NEALE and .... SPENCE, dau. Alexander. Before 23 Feby 1709. Nthld, Va. 1710-1713, p. 319.

JOHN L. POWERS and LUCY W. BAILES. Before 16 July 1832. Gchld, Va. Orders, p. 131.

JOHN PEARCE and ESTHER WALKER, dau. Col. John Walker. Before 25 Jany 1705. S. L. O. Va. iii-123.

WILLIAM PAYNE and SUSANNAH FEILDING, relict of John. Before 19 Sept 1715. Nthld, Va. 1813–1719, p. 182.

Mr. WILLIAM PRATT and MARY STRATTON, dau. Mr. Edward Stratton. Before 20 Aug 1706. Hen., Va. 1677–1739, p. 48.

JOHN SAUNDERS and SARAH COX, dau. Nicholas. About 10 June 1735. Gchld, Va. ii-129.

WILLIAM SMITH and ELIZABETH DOWNING, dau. William Downing, Jr. Before 20 Oct 1712. Nthld, Va. 1710-1713. p. 304.

The County Court Note-Book

An every-other-monthly devoted mainly to abstracts from County Court Records, prior to 1800.

MILNOR LJUNGSTEDT, Editor and Publisher. Bethesda, Route 5, Maryland.

Published six times a year. Subscription, two dollars, in advance; must begin with the year.

August, 1929 **Whole**
Vol. VIII., No. 4 **No. 47**

JUST SUPPOSING

Suppose somebody said to you, "Why not throw away two dollars on this small paper and help keep it going. Whether you are interested or not, it's a good thing and a helpful thing. Of course, you have your own line all the way back to Charlemagne and......one of his wives, or else you haven't and don't care a darn, but here's a bit of history from some scrambled old record, or a forgotten Revolutionary, or somebody's frontier great-great-great, and why not help the cause along?"

And then supposing you did subscribe and after a look or two you cast the NOTE-BOOK aside with the Saturday Evening Post and the Cosmopolitan, and all the parts of the Sunday paper you have no use for (which is most of them......always excepting about two-thirds of the NEW YORK TIMES) and by and bye the Salvation Army truck gathering the flotsam and jetsam gathered also the Sunday papers and the thin little NOTE-BOOK, as thin as a dieted lady. But somehow it came on top the pack, and the assistant to the driver of the truck was or were (I've lost my subjunctive of late) a broken down fellow who once had an education, not to say a family, both of them long laid by, but he happened to see a name on the only visible page of the COUNTY COURT NOTE-BOOK. So he picks the sheet up (let us drop into the journalist indicative) and there he reads "JOHN SMYTHE.....York County, Virginia......1663" or it may have been Rhode Island or South Carolina, hardly 1620, Massachusetts, because the Editor is far from home and because she knows that better work than hers has long been done up that-a-way, anyhow, this broken-down victim of his habits or of just plain inertia, feels a sort of stir within him. That was a long, long time ago, but those were his folks, and he dimly remembers that they had a social and political standing, and he recalls his own parents and his grandparents......it was all so different. All so different, and he raises his head and looks over the truck, then he raises his head a bit more, "*Why is he here?*"

"Why?" Let us suppose that was the beginning, and the mired machine makes a last effort and gets up on the hard-surfaced road again, and with an ancestry behind him and a sort of a vision before him, pulls into the procession. It may be that all the old ideals are gone and the dollar is now the shining mark, but family pride sparks the engine, and personal pride keeps it going.

Well, why not suppose?

Speaking of Charlemagne, the Editor is assured by an Authority that at least one of her lines goes back to that *truly* monarch. But, since reading a recent article, the Editor is very much bothered as to which of the Madame Charlemagnes she must ascribe her ancestry. The Editor quite understands now why there has been a certain amount of argument on the lineages which meander back to the great Charles and is inclined to ask "Can anything be proved?"

The second of Mrs. Nugent's bulletins of Virginia patents (with full index) has been received. This is fine work and difficult work, and should be encouraged by plentiful subscription. Nobody knows better than the Editor (who has read 805 pages of the massive "Old Five" from cover to cover) what such compilation means in the way of labor and expense. It should be in every library and in the hands of all those who delight in reference libraries of their own.

The index of Virginia genealogies is well under way and it is hoped it will be out this fall. This will be another valuable work. While not a compendium of "source" material like the patent index, it will be just exactly as necessary to those who desire thorough research and who find clues, of occasion, in the meanders of others. Every pedigree that has been worked out to at least three generations will be included.

The STONE and WEBSTER JOURNAL, published in Boston, contains in its June issue advanced chapters from a new book by Mr. Charles Knowles Bolton, the Librarian of the Athenaeum. The volume will be called "Mr. BLAXTON COMES TO SHAWMUT," those who are interested in old Boston will know what the title means, and those who don't know but are interested in *all* our beginnings, will both find this a wonderful book. The Editor thinks there must never have been such a book, so readable and so full of information and historical data. It makes the Editor wish that the old, old print of *Bostonia Condita* which hung in the front "entry" could be included among the many other illustrations, and that some conveyance will record the site of her birthplace with a nice little footnote: "This is the well that stayed in the cellar of the house that......somebody built!"

OCCASIONAL

From the will of ANN x SMITH, of Somerset cty, Md; wife of EDWARD SMITH: "I bequeath to the sd RICHARD HILL [her son] ......upon condition that he give to SAMUEL DAVIS min[ister] a mare. Brother SAMUEL SHEWELL......dau. MARTHA HILL...... my bible or small Sermen booke writt by Increase Mather of Boston." Wit: Samuel Davis, John Howson. An additional memorandum mentions sons-in-law Dr. John Vigerous, Samuel Ennis, Richard Hill and dau. Elizabeth. 13 and 21 Aug 1688. M. H. iii-22. [This will is recorded in Worcester cty, Md., although in 1688 the county was Somerset. An explanation of this may be found in an earlier NOTE-BOOK.]

HENRY SELMAN, will: ......Directs that a "letter be sent on bard Sum Ship bound to London derected to Fransis Selmon or his heirs at old foard two miles from Long Acre in London giving the sd Selmon an Acc't of this my will." Acco., Va. 6 Dec 1725. 7 Dec 1726. xvi-265.

The INDEX for vol. VII is ready. About 1300 names. Price 50 cents.

MARYLAND'S NEXT OF KIN

THOMAS HARWOOD, REUBEN ROSS (son); inv. Reuben Ross of Pr. Geo's. 4 Mch 1722. viii-99.

ABRAHAM BOOTH, ISAAC x BOOTH; inv. Isaack Booth of St. Mary's. No date. viii-102.

ISAAC LEMASTER, RICHARD LEMASTER; inv. Abraham "Limaster" of Charles cty. 21 Mch 1702-3. [Probably 1722-3.] viii-104.

MARGARET x WARE, BENJ. GAITHER; inv. Capt. Edward Burgess. viii-107.

PHILL x COPPIDGE, JOHN x RALEY; inv. Phill Coppidge of Q. A. cty. 26 Dec 1721. viii-108.

ELIZABETH BROWN [Kin?] Inv. Mr. Benjamin Corby of Q. A. cty. 20 Nov 1722. viii-110.

MARGARET HUDSTERS; inv. Lawrence Everit, Sr., of Kent Island Q. A. cty. 3 Oct 1722. viii-111.

MARY BENTON; inv. John Dobs. No date, no county. viii-113.

JOHN HOSKINS, GEORGE x HOSKINS; inv. of William Hoskins of Sr. Mary's cty. 28 Jany 1722. viii-114.

WM. CARMAN, REBECCA x CARMAN; Edward Brown also signs and may be of kin. Inv. Thomas Carman of Q. A. cty. 9 Oct 1722. viii-115.

ROBT PHILLIPS, CHR'S PHILLIPS; inv. George Phillips, Sr. of Q. A. cty. No date. viii-116.

JOHN "LEDG"; inv. William Legg, of Kent Island, Q. A. cty. 2 July 1722. viii-118.

NATH'L CONNOR, THOS. HARRIS [Kin?] Inv. Daniel Harris of Q. A. cty. 13 Aug 1722. viii-121.

MARGET x ROE, ELLINOR x ROE; inv. Minto[?] Roe of Q. A. cty. 5 Oct 1722. viii-129.

MARY EMERY proves the inv. of Daniel Emery of Calvert cty. No kin mentioned as such. 3 May 1723. viii-129.

THOMAS x PEARCE, ELIZA: x PEARCE. [Uncertain whether these are kindred.] Inv. of Francis Sele [Sole?] of Cecil cty. 11 Aug 1722. viii-131.

PATRICK x KELLY, JAMES x PERDEW [?] xx Inv. Thomas Walmsley, county not given. viii-132.

B. ENNALLS, THOMAS ENNALLS; inv. John Hicks of Dor. cty. 23 Apr 1723. viii-134.

JOSEPH x THOMPSON, JOHN x THOMPSON, "Kindred and creditors." Inv. John Mackgowry of Dor. cty. 8 May 1723. viii-135.

WILLIAM x WARD, Sr., inv. Benjamin Ward. 16 May 1723. viii-139.

MARK PENN, BENJAMIN POSEY *or* JOHN PHILPOTT and JAMES LATIMER. [It is not clear which of these are kin and which creditors.] Inv. James Cottrill of Charles cty. 27 May 1723. viii-140.

RICH'D MITCHELL, ELIZABETH VICKERS; inv. Abraham Mitchell of Dor. cty. 13 Mch 1722. viii-145.

SUSANNA x NODEN, JONA x TIPTON, Sr. [Kin?] Inv. Samuel Noden of Baltimore cty. 7 July 1722. viii-147.

ELINOR CARLISLE makes oath; "Relations none." Inv. Jno. Rawlins, of Balto cty. 4 Mch 1722. viii-148.

HANNAH x KIMBLE, MARY x THOMAS. inv. John Thomas, of Balto. cty. 8 Mch 1722. viii-151.

BARBARA x CANNON, REBECCA x COLEGATE [Kin?] Inv. George Newport of Balto cty. 16 June 1722. viii-155.

GEORGE BALEY, JOHN x MAULAND; inv. Hector Maulain of Balto. cty. 9 Oct. 1722. viii-157.

JAMES COBBS, Sr. [Kin?] Inv. James Cobbs, Jr. County not given. No date. viii-159.

LANCE [?!] TODD, "JNO. ISRAELL, Children minors." Inv. of Darby Ragan of Balto. cty. 10 Dec 1722. viii-161.

JOHN x MILLER, MARY WINSON. Inv. John White of Som. cty. 12 Dec 1722. viii-162.

"No Kindred." Inv. Charles Colman of St. Mary's cty. 20 Apr 1722. viii-163.

WILLIAM FASSETT; inv. of John Fassitt. County not given. 23 Sept 1721. viii-164.

JOHN MERRITT, of Kin, would not attend, and "we know of no other." Inv. Sam'l Marrett of Kent cty. 12 Apr 1723. viii-165.

"We know of No Relations but two Children at Capt. Locker's." Inv. Nicholas Poor of Kent cty. 12 June 1723. viii-166.

MARY x BOOTS; inv. Thomas Boots. May, 1723. viii-167.

JAS. HEPBOURN, PHILLIP KANNARD; inv. Elizabeth Casely [?], of Kent cty. No date. viii-169.

PROBATES AND ADMINISTRATIONS KING GEORGE COUNTY, VIRGINIA

(*From the second Order Book.*)

JOHN SETTLE; will presented by Isaac Settle and proved by wit. 5 May 1738. p. 155.

HENRY LOCK; will presented by Elizabeth Lock his widow, and proved by wit. William Thornton, Jr., extr, refuses; admn granted to Elizabeth with this reservation, that she will not stand to her said husband's will. 7 July 1738. p. 163.

Same will. Elizabeth Lock resigns admn with will annexed, to William Thornton, Gent. Rowland Thornton, sec. 6 Oct 1738. p. 170.

JOSEPH MINTON; will presented by William Robinson, Gent., extr. Proved by Thomas Monroe and Catherine Taylor. 3 Nov 1738. p. 171.

GEORGE WHITE; will; presented by Jane White, his extx and proved by a witness. 3 Nov 1738. p. 172.

T. EDRINGTON; his will. Presented by William Edrington and John Edrington, his extrs, and proved by one of the wit. 3 Feby 1738. p, 178.

ROBERT WILSON; admn to Ann Wilson, his widow. Thomas Highlander and Richard Goulding, sec. 2 Mch 1738. p. 189.

WILLIAM DODGIN, will; presented by Samuel Moon and Benjamin Strother, his extrs. Proved by wit. Codicil also proved. 6 Apr 1739. p. 197.

GEORGE FISHPOOL; will presented by Mary Fishpool and William Brockenbrough, extrs. proved by wit. 7 Sept 1739. p. 213.

WILLIAM STONE; admn his estate to William Bates and his wife Catherine. 7 Mch 1739. p. 221.

EDMUND JENNINGS; admn his estate to Elizabeth Jennings his widow. John Fox, sec. 6 June 1740. p. 226.

ANN GLENDENING, will; presented by John Armstrong, her extr. and proved by wit. 6 June 1740. p. 227.

ANN GRIFFIN; admn her estate to James White and wife Ann. William Alsup, sec. 1 Aug 1740. p. 233.

JOHN HALL; Mary Hall presents his will; proved by John Percy, Richard Hall and Mary Hall. Admn with will annexed granted to widow, Mary Hall. 5 Sept 1740. p. 241.

JAMES GREECION[?] admn his estate to William Row and wife Mary. Christopher Robinson and James Lewis, sec. 5 Dec 1740. p. 245.

ELLEN SHIPPEY; will presented by James Hackley, extr. Proved by wit. 6 Mch 1740. p. 247.

SUDRACH COLLIFOR[?] Admn to John Wren. Francis Balthrop, sec. 6 Mch 1740. p. 247.

JOSEPH BAYLEY; admn to William Annadall. William Thatcher, sec. 6 Mch 1740. p. 247.

(The foregoing list completes the probates and administrations of the second volume of King George Orders. The first volume will be listed before long.)

INTERCOUNTY AND INTERCOLONY

PETER BOWDOIN; Custis Kendall and wf Elizabeth, extx of Bowdoin, present account of his estate. Finishing the new house at King's Creek mentioned. Begins 1756, but includes 1747 and 1748. *Henrico*, Va., Misc. papers. [Kings Creek is in Northampton county, and this record though found in Richmond, Va., very plainly belongs to the records of Northampton county, Va.]

URSULA x BROWNE, of Accomack, widow of Mr. Jno. Browne; gives power to Capt. Peter Wraxall of Bristoll. [Browne's will, 1654-1655.] N-n cty, Va. 22 Apr 1656. v-89.

SAMUEL COOPER, of Somerset. Ackn. bond to John Woodside of Ireland, Mariner. Som. Md. 22 June 1686. BWZ-196.

JOHN RILEY, Jr., of Barton cty, South Carolina. Conveyance to Moses Simpson, Ffx cty, Va. Ffx, 22 Oct 1773. L-88.

WILLIAM SIMS, of North Carolina, and wf Susannah, convey 200 acres to Zacharias Tait, of Hanover, Va. Hen., Va. 10 Nov 1758. S. L. 1928. p. 101.

"BLESSED" [?] Surveyed 1694 for ROWL'D THORNBURY; n. e. branch Jones Fall, Balto. cty, Md. Possessed by the orphans of sd Thornbury. The Orphans at Age and Gone into Virginia. Annap. records. Balto. R. R. 1723.

THOMAS SHEILDS, of Wicocomoco on the Eastern Shore, in Maryland, pltr, sells to Edward Sanders of Wicocomake in Northumberland, Va., pltr, 100 acres...... said land devised to Sheilds by John Smyth, dec'd. [This land seems to have been given to pay Smyth's debt for physic. Ed.] Wit: Tho: Meech, John Wancklin[?] Nthld, Va. 1658-1666. fo. 174. 4 Mch 1664.

JOHN SHELTON and wf Eleanor, of the Colony of Virginia, convey to Henry Hill, of Fred'k county, pltr, tract called Park's Hall, 113 acres. Fred'k, Md. 18 Nov 1761. G-310.

JOHN SYME, of St. Martin's psh, and wf Sarah, to John Warden, of King William county, Va., atty-at-law ...... "Whereas Adam Hoops late of the Falls, county of Bucks, Penna., father of the said Sarah Syme."......&c., &c. Hanover, Va. Deeds, 18 Aug 1790.

THO: SPEARE, of Boone [?] in Old England; power to Charles Ballard. Som. cty, Md. U-135. 1 Apr 1761.

JOHN SPEAKE, of the City of Bathe, in the county of Somersett, Gent.; power to Wm. Presly of Northumberland, Va., Mcht. Wmld, Va. 1668-1677, fo. 104. 26 Oct. 1668.

JOHN SIMPSON, Stafford, Va., to James Holley, Ffx, Va., tract of land in Powel's Run, Pr. William. The land was left by Henry Thompson to the three eldest sons of John Simpson, Staff, Va. 10 June 1755. B-29.

SAMUEL SIMPSON, of Albemarle county, Va., eldest son and heir of William Simpson, late of K. Geo., dec'd. Samuel conveys land to William Hewett. The deed shows that William Simpson's wife was Diana, and that he had a dau. Margaret Dafton and two sons-in-law, James and Evan Peyton. Diana died Feby 1773. K. Geo. Va. 12 May 1773. i-1038.

HENRY SMITH of Stafford, Va., to John Kerr, of Fauquier, eldest son to my dau. Sarah Kerr, a negro girl. Mentions son-in-law John Kerr. Staff. Va. 11 Feby 1785. S-172.

BENNET SCARBOUROUGH, Gent., of Accomack, one of the sons of Coll. Charles Scarburgh, dec'd, by Elizabeth his wife, now lately also deceased, who was the dau. of Major Richard Bennett of "Nanximan" River, in Virginia, also dec'd, and Temperance his wife; and Henry Scarburgh, of Acco., Gent., another of the sons of sd Charles and Elizabeth, and Winnifred his wife; and Mary Leatherbury of the said county of Accomack, Widdow, one of the daughters; and John Bagwell and Tabitha his wife, another of the daughters; and William Black of the said county, Clark, and Sarah his wife, another of the daughters of said Charles and Elizabeth; and Scarburg Drummond, son and heir of Elizabeth, who was the wife of Capt. Richard Drummond now both lately deceased, another of the daughters; and George Parker, Jr., son and heir of Ann, lately dec'd. who was the wife of Major George Parker, another of the daughters of the said Charles and Elizabeth; and ELIZABETH his wife, to George Dashiell. of Som. cty, Gent......conveyance of rights to Bennett's Adventure. Som., Md. 2 Oct 1721. IK-192.

JOHN STONE, Charles cty, Md. Will. Bro. Thomas; bro. Josias; bro. William; bro-in-law, Jeremiah Gray; sister-in-law. Betty Stone, mentioned, wife of William. Som. Md. Probate 29 Mch 1783. i-176.

MARY TAYLOR, wife of Richard, Jr., living in Stafford cty, Va. Power to my father, Richard Taylor, Sr., Balto. cty. Md. pltr, to make over her right to Stone's Delight, 100 acres, on a run descending into Herring Run, Balto., Md. 10 June 1723. I. S., G-401.

BENJA. TERRILL, and wife Sarah, Pittsylvania cty, Va., to John Kennon of Louisa county, 150 acres on Cawthan's Run, Louisa cty. Louisa, Va. 13 Jany 1800. i-715.

FRAN: WEEKS, widow; gives Ann Barlow her whole estate in England as well as in Virginia. Lanc. Va. 1662. ii-233.

EDWARD WYATT, of Gloucester cty, Va., ackn himself indebted to James Mills of Surry cty, and Capt. Joh: Scott of Ashforde on Long Island, Esquires. [Note: the matter appears to concern the assignment of one Edmund Conquest, to be instructed in the rudiments of navigation.] Surry, Va. 29 May 1665. i-267.

Mr. WILLIAM WINDER, his nun-cup will. Deposition that he discoursed concerning his land on the Eastern Shore, in Maryland (reference being made to a will of the 8 September, the Thursday before, this nun-cup. will appearing to be intended for a codicil) and touching his said land he devised the half part to Collo. Peter Hack, he having obliged himself to make a deed to the said Collo. Peter Hack. [Before the new will could be written, the testator died.] Nthld, Va. 1 Oct 1701. 1710-1713. p. 49.

WILLIAM YOUNG had sisters-in-law, Hannah Dawkins, Alice Pike, Johanna Pike, then living in Devonshire, England. Staff., Va. 2 Apr 1699. Z-21.

GOLIATH WILLIAMS, of Gloucester in the county of Providence in the Colony of Rhode Island, &c., in New England, yeoman, gives power to wife SUSANNA WILLIAMS, of same place, Wit: Timothy Hopkins, Charles Harris. 16 Feby 1756.

SUSANNA conveys land, consideration £1000, to DAVID ROSS, Jr. and THOMAS THORNTON, both of Gloucester, yeomen, at a place called New River, at the mouth of sd River...... 200 acres. Onslow cty, N. C. 3 Dec 1762.

JOHN NUTT of Wilmington, New Hanover, cabinet maker, and ELIZABETH WIMBLE, of Boston, Suffolk cty, Massachusetts, widow of WILLIAM, late of sd Boston, marriner, dec'd, to GILLAM BASS of sd Boston, Mcht, and REBECCA BASS, his wife, LEWIS MARREQUILLE of *Dracut* in Middlesex cty, Massachusetts, Gent. and KATHERINE MARRESQUILLE, his wife, and ELIZABETH BASS of said Boston and granddaughter of said ELIZABETH WIMBLE, on the other part; consideration £300, grant, bargain and sell to sd ELIZABETH WIMBLE ......a certain lot in Wilmington, which was conveyed by ELIZABETH WIMBLE *et al* the day before the date of these presents to the sd JOHN NUTT......Joshua Potts, Henry Hopkins. GILLAM BASS acknowledges receipt of £50 as attorney to the heirs of WILLIAM WIMBLE deceased. [This appears to be a mortgage.] New Hanover cty, N. C. I-236. 8 May 1789.

SERVICE AND SUPPLIES COLONIAL, REVOLUTIONARY AND MILITIA

BENJAMIN WOODWARD, a resident of Goochland. Age 73 in October last. Enlisted in the Army of the U. S. 1776, for two years, with Lieut. Nath'l Morris. Served in the 9th Va. of the Continental Line under Col. Thomas Fleming and others. Left the service in 1778. Enlisted in Gchland in which he resided when he entered the service. Was in the Battle at Brandywine. Court declare opinion that he was a Revolutionary soldier. Gchld, Va. Orders 1831-1836. p. 136. 20 Aug 1832.

THOMAS WRIGHT, of Goochland cty. Age 73 10 Oct last. Enlisted about 1777 and served in the 4th Regt, Continental Line. That he resided in the county of Orange when he entered the service. Was in no battles, but was at White Plains. Court declare opinion that he was a Revolutionary soldier. Same record,. p. 134. 20 Aug 1832.

THOMAS WITTEN, a Revolutionary soldier, resident of Tazewell cty, Va. Aged 80, next January, makes oath to statement of his service as ensign and scout, in a company commanded by Capt. Thomas Martin and Lieut. James Maxwell at the time he first entered the service in June, 1776. Histy Tazewell cty, Va. p. 223. [While this is not taken by the Editor from source material, there is no reason to doubt that it is a Court record.]

JOHN WILSON, volunteer soldier in 1777, in a company from Hampshire cty, West Va. Report, Dept Archives and History, W. Va. Vol. iii-47.

Printed at the Industrial School for Crippled and Deformed Children, 241 St. Botolph St., Boston, Mass.

The County Court Note-Book

A Little Bulletin of History and Genealogy

October, 1929. Vol. VIII, No. 5

THE STRANDED BETSEY AND OTHER SHIPS IN PORT

HENRY WARREN complains of LABAN PETTIT......of a plea of trespass......for that whereas the said Henry on the first day of July ......MDCCLXV at the county aforesaid being then and still owner of a certain sloop or Sea Vessel called the *Betsey* and bound on a voyage to the Port of New York the said Laban being or taking upon himself to [be] a mariner or person capable of navigating and commanding such a a Ship or vessel then and there in Consideration of the sum of three pounds ten shill. monthly wages shipped himself on baird the said vessel as master or Commander thereof for that voyage and having so shipped himself and taken upon him the charge of that Vessel afterwards to wit the first day of July in the year af'd at the County af'd......then and there undertook and then and there to the said Henry then and there faithfully did promise that he would......do his duty as a master or Commander of a vessel ought to do ......Yet the said Laban his promise and Assumption af'd in form af'd not regarding......after the said Vessel being then laden and only waiting for a Wind to proceed on her said Voyage, after he had shipped himself as a master as af'd......Carelessly and contrary to his Duty as master or Commander of the said Vessel, left the Vessel af'd insufficiently moored with an insuff. no. of Hands and continued on shore......the space of twenty days, by means of which forsaking and insufficient mooring the said Vessel was cast on shore and vessel and cargo much hurt. Whereupon the said Henry says he is damnify'd......&. therefore brings suit, &c., &c. N-n cty, Va. Chancery and other records. Oct. 1765.

The *Chester Merchant*, Robert Browning, Commander; now riding in Upper Machoduck; power from Browning to Rawley Travers. Staff. cty, Va. Z-11. 15 May 1699.

Ship *Dolphin*, of Chester; John Spurstow of the City of Chester, and for Company thereof, gives power to William Woodbridge of Richmond cty. Richmd cty, Va. v-135, 21 Aug1709.

The *Henry and Anne*; Thos. Arnoll, captain, York cty, Va. 1675-1684, p. 68. Ct 25 Jany 1678.

Ship *Duke of York*; Thomas James Commander. Lanc. cty, Va. ii-295. 2 Sept 1663.

Ship of War *Enterprise*; Mich. Smith, Com'dr. Va. St. Papers. i-141. 1710

Shipp *Expedicon*; sold by Henry Goodriche to Mr. William Carver. L. Norf., Va. D-420. 15 Feby 1664.

Barque *Expedicon*; Henery Hudson "now of Maryland", Mcht, owner. L. Norf., Va. D-401. 13 Apr. 1663.

The *Eagle Wing*; See Presbyterian Mags. viii-558. 1636.

Pinnace *Elizabeth*; George Wright, master. [The boat belonged to Mr. Charlton.] N-n, Va. ii-306. 28 May 1644.

Sloop *Elizabeth and Ann*, from Barbadoes. Lost. Capt. John Ellegood and Col. Geo. Newton, owners of two-thirds. Mr. John Britt, master. Norf., Va. G-55, 20 Jany 1727.

Ship *Federalist*; John Pratt, captain; from Charleston but now in London. Chatham cty, Ga. R-(30 ?) 1797.

Shipp *Farewell*; "Skipp'r" John Clawse de Boll "Mayster." Agreement between de Boll and Skipp'r Jno. Johnson and Jno. Macheele. N-n, Va. iv-94, 3 June, 1652.

FAMILIES OF THE EASTERN SHORE
THE WHITTINGTONS

(*Sixth instalment*)

The Archives of Maryland mention WILLIAM WHITTINGTON, IIId of the name, quite frequently as a delegate to the Assembly from Somerset county, he serving in the Lower House at the same time that his father was a Member of the Council. As early as October, 1713, Mr. WILLIAM WHITTINGTON, Jr., is referred to as present in the Assembly. (Arch. xxix-259.) Other references can readily be found in the published volumes. In vol. xxix-238, Mr. WILLIAM WHITTINGTON, Junior, is added to the Commission of Somerset county. That he was again returned as a delegate, or served at the same time in the two capacities, is shown by references in vol. xxxiv, pages 344 and 417. The compiler regrets that in endeavoring to identify this WILLIAM, later of Virginia, as the son of Lt. Col. WILLIAM of Somerset, those records of Accomack county, Virginia, which would give his political record, if any, were passed over for the more condensed wills and deeds.

WILLIAM WHITTINGTON (3), son of William, son of William, married ELIZABETH TAYLOR, the eldest daughter of Elias Taylor and wife Comfort, of Accomack, Comfort being one of the daughters of William Anderson, Gent. The date of this marriage is not known, but it was before 1725. (See Acco. xvi-237.)

This marriage is shown by various records, among them the following:

William Whittington, of Accomack, Gent., and wf Elizabeth, late Eliz: Taylor, eldest dau. of Elias Taylor, Gent., dec., by Comfort his wife, one of the daus. of William Anderson, Gent., dec., to Isaac Morris, Gent, of Somerset county, Md.,...love and affection to son Southy Whittington and the other issue of sd William Whittington and the sd Elizabeth, consideration five shillings, all that tract where they now dwell at Ockokonson...400 acres.....being one-third of the tract devised by William Anderson to his three eldest granddaughters......William and Elizabeth to have the use and profit, &c., during life and after death to the use and behoof of Southy Whittington and his heirs, and for the want of such heirs to John Whittington, another son, and for want of heirs to sd JOSHUA [*sic*] to the heirs and assigns of Elizabeth. Wit: Wishart, Douglas, Stockly. Acco. Va. (21 Feby 1742. Di-344.)

Previous to this [and no explanation is given of the change, but it is probable WILLIAM, the son, died] WILLIAM WHITTINGTON, of Som. cty, Gent.; love and affection to *eldest son and heir apparent,* WILLIAM WHITTINGTON, the younger, in Accomack, conveys several negroes and all "my right to my plantation near Occakanson where my son now lives." Wit: Wishart,Stockley,SOUTHY WHITTINGTON. Acco. Di-40. 31 May 1738. And in 1743, 22 Feby, WM. WHITTINGTON, of Acco., Gent., in consideratin of £79-12-1, Md. money (£84 in gold) conveys to Southy Whittington slaves heretofore mortgaged to Isaac Morris and Edmund Hough, Gents., with certain provisions. (Acco. Di-390.)

As late as 24 Sept 1765, John Watts and John Milligan return the division of the estate of WILLIAM WHITTINGTON [III], pursuant to order of the Court. (xxviiW-530.) The account shows payments to Southy, Joshua, the widow, William, Eliza: Ardis, Betty Faires. *Southey also gets cattle due from grandmother's legacy to him.* [The compiler has not been able to find a record of that legacy.] Division of the estate is made among the foregoing, the widow omitted [being dead.] Acco. xxviW-527, 528.

ELIZABETH WHITTINGTON died in 1762. Her will follows:

To grandson William Whittington, son of William, one half of my one-third "part of my Deceased Husband which Belongs to me." To the children of my son Joshua Whittington, viz: William and Esther Whittington; To Elizabeth Whittington all the rest of my estate. Son Joshua, extr. Wit: Elizabeth Wishart, Jacamon Wishart. (Acco. xxviiW-144. 25 Apr 1756-30 Nov 1762.) The will was proved by Jacamon Wishart, "now Jacamon Milligan," one of the wit. Joshua Whittington releases, and William gets extrship. Littleton Dennis, sec. John Watts, John Milligan, Washburn Tunnell and Wm. Ewell to appraise. (Acco. xxv0-488, 30 Nov. 1762.) Inventory returned, same vol., page 504. (See also xxviiW-156.) The amount of the inventory was £16-0-1.

The return of the administration is made by William Whittington, and shows payments to William, son of Joshua; one-third; to Esther Whittington, one-third; to Eliza; Whittington one-third. (Acco. xxixW.227. Returned 29 Nov 1768. Court order of 28 June 1763.)

As WHITTINGTON left no will the only list of his children which we have is made up from the will of the widow and this division of the property. As shown by these records they are:

WILLIAM, m. ELIZABETH......; (evidently married and died early, before or about 1742).

SOUTHY, m. ANN.....;

JOSHUA, m. ELIZABETH NAIRN; Joshua d. about 1761 [?]

ELIZABETH, m. ......ARDIS;

For the present the compiler will leave the Accomack WHITTINGTONS and take up the cadet branch, which remained in Maryland, and at the head of which is SOUTHY WHITTINGTON (son of William, son of William), brother of WILLIAM WHITTINGTON of Accomack, Virginia.

As early as 1717 SOUTHY WHITTINGTON approves the inventory of John Johnson, of Somerset county, Md., which would seem to show that he was of age. (Wor. Md. J. W. xv-79.) He was Surveyor for the county in 1720. (A-72. Som.) He is the owner of *Choyce*, a tract of 1950 acres, surveyed for him 5 Apr 1723., and lying on the north side of Pocomoke river, and on the north side of Bennefield, and by a landing of Nasseangoe creek called the Shallop Landing. (In 1735 he conveys part of this tract and of another called *Dull Folly* to Edmund Hough and wife.) The 29 June 1725, he buys from Joseph Summers, one-third of "*Emessex*"......250 acres in Annamessex, also *Little Worth*. (Som. xv-258.) In 1737, 22 June, SOUTHY WHITTINGTON and wf MARY, convey to Joseph Porter, a tract called *Adventure,* on the Seaboard side, beginning at a fork of a creek issuing from Assateague Baye or Sound northermost end of Cropper's Island, called Forked Creek. 150 a. (Som. E. I.-168.) [It is to be noted that on the Eastern Shore the creeks run *up* from the sounds and bays into the land!]

Various conveyances follow on the part of SOUTHY and wife MARY; the 6 June 1737 (Som. xix-147) land called *Choice* to Joshua Atkinson. The same date to John Bennett, tract called *Choice* "made up of several parcels," (Som. xix-174.) The 2 Feby 1738, to John Wildman, all that tract called *Spring Garden* and *Water Mills,* upon Nasaongoe Creek. (Som. xx-68.) To John Jenckin, Carpenter, part of *Choice.* 22 June 1739. (xx-69.)

These conveyances, as well as others, are also shown by the Somerset-Dorchester Rent Roll, No. 2. fo. 307. (Annap. Records.)

SOUTHY WHITTINGTON, Som. Gent, buys of Littleton Townsend and wf Sarah, tracts called *Recovery*, *Brigit's Lot*, and *Puzzle.* 3 May 1746. (Som. xxi-191.) And from Joshua Atkinson and wf Elizabeth, tract called *Canaan*, which seems to be made up of *Scott's Folly* and part of *Scotland.* (Som. xix-172.) In the settlement of a land dispute, WHITTINGTON conveys to Kirk Gunby tracts in Annamessex. Gunby's own patent is called *Middle Ridge.* (Som. Md, 20 Aug 1746. xxi-210.) The 16 Nov 1752 there was a further agreement as to bounds between WHITTINGTON and Gunby, at that time WHITTINGTON had *Gilead* and *Chance.* (Som. xxii-272.) The 28 Mch 1757, SOUTHEY WHITTINGTON. Gent, wife MARY, convey to Lazarus Lankford, pltr, a tract in Annamessix called *Chance*; the line of *Middle Ridge* is mentioned. (Som. xxiii-186.)

SOUTHY WHITTINGTON, Sr., of Somerset, to William Whittington the same; love and good will to his son, conveys *Puzzle*, part of *Recovery*, part of *Chance*, and mentions Goshen. 14 Apr 1763. (Som. xxiv-170.) And again, the 22 June,

1763, SOUTHY WHITTINGTON, Sr., to SOUTHY WHITTINGTON, Jr., of the same county, pltr. ......three tracts, *Canaan*, *Goshen*, *Gilead*, part of *Recovery*, part of *Chance*, in Annamessex. (Som. xxiv-178.)

The will of SOUTHY WHITTINGTON [Sr.], of Somerset, My. is recorded in Somerset (iv-171). Dated the 20 Feby 1769 and proved the 17 Mch 1773. He mentions his wife MARY; his son SOUTHY; son STEVENSON; son ISAAC; son WILLIAM; granddau. MARY COX. Also mentions friend George Hayward, of Worcester county. Makes son SOUTHY executor. Wit: Elijah Coulbourne, Jeffery Long, Samuel Long.

The account of his estate is returned by his wife MARY and SOUTHY WHITTINGTON, extr. 10 Oct 1775. (Som. E. B. xi-192.)

AUTHENTIC REFERENCES FOR INFERRED MARRIAGES

(*From the records of Accomack county, Virginia*)

EDMUND ALLEN, Gent. and ANNE CUSTIS, relict and extx of Henry. Acco. See xxiiO-226. 30 Jany 1739.

EDMUND ALLEN and TABITHA GILCHRIST, extx of Andrew. Acco. xxviiW-51. See acc't returned 30 Mch 1762. [TABITHA had probably also been the wife of Samuel Burton.]

GEORGE ABBOTT and SARAH JUSTICE, widow of James. Before 29 Nov 1774. Deeds iv-384.

ARON ACCOR and CATHERINE [KELLAM,] dau. of Frances Kellam. Katherine's surname is not certain. Before 2 Aug 1737. xx-287.

.... ABBOT and ELIZABETH MICHAEL. Before 16 June 1769. Diii-632.

NATH'L ANDREWS and ELIZABETH PITT, widow of Robert. Before 6 Mch 1716. xv-26. [This supplies the date missing in previous publication. See also xix-243. And xviii-47.]

WILLIAM ANDREWS and MARY GORE, widow of Daniel. About 4 Apr 1722. xvii-41. [Correction of previous note. See also Deeds ii-454. And xx-9.]

WILLIAM ARBUCKLE and KATHERINE SNEAD, dau. of Robert. Before 7 July 1766. Diii-435.

NATHANIEL BRADFORD and ELIZABETH PARKER, dau. of George. Before 1 Dec 1724. xvi-218. Before 4 Mch 1711. See xiv.36, 61.

JOHN BURROCK and ELEANOR JENKINS. Before Aug 1734. xx-170. (Before 31 Dec 1687. See vi-462. She was dau. of John. See also xv-258. "Captain" John Burrock.)

JOHN BURROUGHS and ESTHER BEBBEE. Burroughs was of the county of Sussex, and Gov't of the Three Lower Counties. Deeds iii-67. 18 Jany 1759.

THOMAS BURTON and SINAH [dau. of Abel Roberts?] xxviW-441. Ret. 24 Nov. 1761.

GEORGE BUNDICK and ELIZABETH ABBOTT, dau. of John, Sr. Before 1706. xi-387.

JAMES BYSWICK and PRUDENCE JERVIS, dau. of Robert. Before 19 May 1766. iii-422.

THOMAS BLAIR and ANNE McKEMIE, dau. Francis. Before 3 Oct 1721. xvi-287. [Former reference incorrect as to vol.]

GEORGE BONWELL and ELIZABETH HALL, dau. of Michael. Before 28 Oct 1767. Diii-530.

WILLIAM BAGWELL perhaps m. ELIZABETH PARKER, widow of William? See 3 Oct 1700. xi-261. (See also xii-117.)

WILLIAM BAKER and PATIENCE BUNDICK. Before 26 Nov 1805. L. C. 1773-1805. p. 313.

JONATHAN BAKER and MARY COE, widow of Benjamin. See 4 Jany 1725. xix-44. (Before 5 Sept 1723. See xviii-65.)

.... BAKER and RACHEL BUNDICK, sister of Elias. Before 26 Nov 1805. L. C. 1773-1805, p. 313.

ROBERT BAYLY and MARY MASSEY, coheir of John. Before 10 Jany 1770. Deeds iii-704.

THOMAS BARRAT and DIANA HICKMAN. About 1700. xi-263.

JOHN BARNES and FRANCES SACKER, widow. About 3 May 1672. vi-102. Marriage agreement.

.... BEAVANS and MARY STOCKLEY, widow of Eyre Stockley: Before 28 July 1761. Deeds iii-154. (At this date she was a widow again.)

WILLIAM BEAVANS and ELIZABETH DAVIS, dau. of Samuel and Naomi. See record 10 Apr 1769. Deeds iii-666.

CHARLES BAYLEY and MARY, one of the coheirs of John SIMPSON. Before 27 Mch 1765. Deeds iii-369. [The name of the wife has been previously published as *ANNE*, N. — B. for July 1924. This seems to call for further research.]

WILLIAM BEAVANS and MARY LANE, dau. of Walter, of Som. cty, Md. Before 1 Jany 1714. xi-642.

FRANCIS BENSTON and EDEAH [Edith? Adah?] NEWTON, dau. of Joseph. Before 18 Feby 1695. x-182.

SAMUEL BENSTON and JOANNA WATSON, dau. of Robert, Sr. Before 24 July 1702. xi-308.

MASSEY BENSON and TABITHA BENSON, dau. of Ambrose. Before 22 Jany 1763. Deeds iii-216.

JOHN BETTS and ELIZABETH ROBINSON, widow. Before or about 17 Mch 1679. vi-204.

ELIAS BLAKE prob. m. BRIDGET PRICE, sister of Elias. Before 1 May 1708. xi-488.

WILLIAM BLACK, Clerk, and SARAH SCARBURGH, dau. of Elizabeth. Before 2 Nov 1726. xix-66.

The County Court Note-Book

An every-other-monthly devoted mainly to abstracts from County Court Records, prior to 1800.

MILNOR LJUNGSTEDT, Editor and Publisher. Bethesda, Route 5, Maryland.

Published six times a year. Subscription, two dollars, in advance; must begin with the year.

October, 1929 **Whole**
Vol. VIII., No. 5 **No. 48**

STRAIGHT TALK

"Faithful are the wounds of a friend." Friendly Clerks will please forgive that which follows.

The condition of the invaluable minutes of the court of the ancient and honorable county of Somerset, Maryland, is disgraceful. If the county cannot afford their repair, which, after all, in the hands of expert commercial firms would not call for an unreasonable outlay nor take unnecessary time,.........then the State or some wealthy society should take the matter up.

Several immensely valuable records of Accomack county, Virginia, are in even worse condition. The first three volumes of deeds, after the differentation of the records.........well, the Editor must hunt up Roget and find a new batch of adjectives to make impressive any statement of their condition. A large and most important record of early wills is rapidly disintegrating......... this volume could be restored. It is not necessary to copy it. N. B. Accomack claims to be the richest county per capita in the United States. Anyhow, it is old enough to know better than to allow colonial records to go to waste. Both Accomack and Somerset date back to the 1660's.

Charles county, Maryland, has some pride. Its records are cared for, but it has one volume......... searchers take notice!.........that is so rotten it can't be handled. It is put away and supposedly invisible. Who will pay for the restoration?

Frederick county, Maryland, an up-to-date modern county without any great show of sentiment, deserves mention here. It has actually had several great bookbinders' "crabs" cut in two and nicely rebound. It was almost impossible to handle these volumes, and the searcher of any sensitiveness hated to impose the task of lifting them on a deputy. Why can't the State Land Office follow copy? Such books are seriously injured by being stood on end. Frederick, it should be added, has placed these old volumes on patent roller shelves.

A Maryland or Virginia county is practically governed by its County Commissioners or Supervisors, or its political boss. These are not always gentlemen of fine discrimination as to values, when it is not a question of corn or wheat, strawberries, apples or POTATOES!

Vale!

A MATTER OF IMPORTANCE

The Editor of the NOTE-BOOK will pay ten dollars ($10) for a copy of the WILL of WILLIAM FLOYD, or a copy (in full) of the administration of his estate.

WILLIAM FLOYD was living in 1783; had wife ABADIAH, and probably living sons ROBERT, CHARLES and NATHANIEL. He was also the father of Col. JOHN FLOYD. WILLIAM FLOYD may have died in one of the frontier counties of Virginia, Kentucky, or in one of the Territories northwest of the Ohio. He was about 56 years old in 1783 and owned land in the upper Valley of Virginia. He had removed to the frontier, but was driven back by the uprising among the Indians. Where he then settled is unknown.

VARIA

DISBURSEMENTS for Funerall Charges of WILLIAM WILLIS [evidently a minor.] John Dillecoat presents account.

To 2 Weathers [wethers].........0-10-0
To 1 1-2 gallons of rum.........0-3-0
To 4 pd Suger.........0-2-0
To 1-2 bushel of wheat flower.........0-2-0
To 2 pd butter 2 do. fatt.........0-1-6
To 6 Dunghill fowll.........0-2-3
To 1-2 bushel indian meal.........0-0-10
To a Coffin and small sheett.........0-7-0
To the trowbel of my house att the sd funerall.........
To Digging the grave.........0-1-3
[Total] £1-8-10. Sept'bre 1723. (Northampton cty, Va.)

HEZEKIAH FISHER, DANIEL FRAISE, JOSEPH JOHNSON, PETER KELLAM, JOHN ABDEEL, STRATTON COB, ROBERT PHINEY, JOHN HOW, were drafted by the Constable for the expedition against the French on the Ohio. The Constable reports that Nathaniel Savage refused to assist him with a deserter. N-n, cty, Va. Chancy, &c. records. 14 Jany 1755.

ABRAHAM SMITH humbly prays that he should be permitted to take young ROBERT MILLIKIN, "the *alfin* of Robert Millikin and Susanna his wife." "Your petitioner Stood for the Child & the child having no Estate your petitioner Is willing to take cear of the child." N-n, Va. Chancy records, May, 1735.

WHEREAS JOHN LEONARD, late of the County of Cape May in the State of New Jersey, dec'd, by his last will, 10 Feby 1771, did after the death of his wife ANN LEONARD give unto NATHAN GOFF the plantation where the testator lived on the Condition that the sd NATHAN GOFF should in about six months after the death of the said ANN LEONARD pay to JOHN LEONARD first above named [presumably in a statement before this] by the name and description of his cousin JOHN LEONARD, £16 and other sums to other persons being relations of the testator and living in Carolina, and whereas ANN LEONARD the widow of the Testator departed this life on or about the 10th day of September 1779, and the sd NATHAN GOFF was possessed of the sd plantation and ceder

Swamp devised to him.........[Now] SAMUEL LEONARD administrator and heir-at-law of sd JOHN LEONARD, intestate, quit-claims to NATHAN GOFF. J. Leonard a witness.

This is followed by the release of SAMUEL LEONARD, son of SAMUEL of Brunswick cty, N. C. Reference to the will of JOHN LEONARD is made and provision for payment to cousin [of JOHN] SAMUEL LEONARD. New Hanover cty, N. C. H-606. 4 Sept 1787.

Mr. ARTHUR MOSELEY was naturalized bet. Nov. 1689 and 16 Sept 1692. Norf., Va. 16 Sept 1692. v-84.

HENRY WASHINGTON, an head right under [Mrs.] Tabitha Smart. Acco., Va. 17 Nov 1664. 1-81.

THE DEPUTY COMMISSARY'S GUIDE WITHIN THE PROVINCE OF MARYLAND

(*Continued from December, 1928*)

ADMINISTRATION D. B. N. (*"De bonis non administratris."*) These are granted only in the following cases. First, upon the death of a former executor or administrator before he hath fully administered...............In case of "testacy" ......a person so appointed is called an administrator *de bonis non*, with a copy of the deceased's will annexed. Secondly, upon complaint of "male-administration;" or upon conviction of "fraud or covin."

Other forms of administration are those granted during the minority of a child of the deceased, or other person having a prior right to such administration, or during the minority of an infant executor, which minority is by the common law limited to twenty-one years, in case of intestacy, and to seventeen for an infant executor. "But by our [Maryland] acts of assembly the infant administrator is declared to be within like law with infant executors, that is, shall be of full age to administer when he arrives at the age of seventeen years."

Another form of letters of administration of temporary character is granted during the absence of such child, or other person, not a minor, having a prior right to administer.

Another is granted during the continuance of a contest, concerning right to administer.

"Note, that in all administrations *out of the Statute* the deputy commissary may, at his discretion, grant administration to whom he pleases."

There are also letters *"Ad colligendum bona defuncti"*...to collect the debts and effects of the deceased and return an inventory.

[The next subject which Eli Vallette handled was Wills and Testaments.]

A LIST OF WILLS WHICH WERE IN WILL BOOK "M" (LOST) STAFFORD COUNTY, VA. (1729-1748.)

Robert Alexander, William Allen, John Allenthorpe;

James Butler, Nathaniel Bryant, Thomas Botts (2), Samuel Bowman, William Brent, Thomas Butler, Mary Burrass, John Buckner, John Baylis;

Joseph Count, George Crosby, John Chadwell, John Cook, John Craford, Henry Conyers, Edward Clement, Mary Collingworth, John Calmers, Georg Crosby, William Cave, James Carter, George Crosby [*sic*];

Thomas Duncan, Mattox Derrick;

Charles Elliott;

John Fitzhugh, Hugh French, Hugh French [one of these probably a copy of the will, the other some record concerning it]; Chandler Fowke;

John Grigsby, Lucy Gregg, Ann Grant, Nicholas George, Charles Griggsby, Thomas Griggsby;

Elias Hore, Abraham Harrod, Bryant Handly, John Higgerson, Robert Hewett, John Hurst, John Hay;

Thomas Jeffrice, Swan Jones, John Jones;

John Kirk, Matthew Keene, Anthony Ketching [twice];

John Lehore, Anthony Linton, Edward Layer;

William Matharty [McCarthy ?], William Mason, Dade Massey, [again]; Thomas Masters, Ann Marshall, Ann McPhearson, Daniel Mealy, Edward Maulpiss [Mallpiss ?], William Moss, Mary Meese;

Timothy O'Neal;

Thomas Prestredge, John Parsons, Simon Pearson, Gratis [?] Powell, James Penny, Thomas Porter, Edward Ponton;

James Reddish, Thomas Reed;

Alexander Scott, William Scott, James Seaton;

John Toward, Richard Todd;

William Wigginton, Henry Wigginton, William Whitson, John Warner, John Washington, John Waugh, Town[s]hend Washington, John West, James Withers, John Wheeler, Joseph Waugh.

(*To be continued later*)

CERTIFICATES FOR LAND GIVING HEAD RIGHTS. FIRST PART, FIRST ORDER BOOK, STAFFORD COUNTY, VIRGINIA

To JOHN COLELOUGH, for 200 acres, for four persons: Robert Jones, George Griffith, Henry Lane, Nicholas Rawlins. 6 June 1665.

To SAM'L HAYWARD, for 250 acres, seven persons: JOSEPH HAYWARD, SARAH HAYWARD, Rowland Phillips, Thomas Bates, John Henen, Mary Wells, *Rebecai Methew*. 6 June, 1665.

To CHRISTOPHER LUND, 100 acres, for two persons: Henry Pate, Elizabeth Pate. 6 June 1665.

To HENRY WATTER [WALLER ?] for seven hundred acres for fourteen persons: Mathew Fearson, Anthony Royley, Alice Figg, John Wells, Jane Fish, John Hibbett, Anne Sheppard, John Causen, John Prebit[?], Anthony Stanton, Luse[?] Bully, Henry Paure, William Glumper. 6 June 1665.

To ROBERT MOSELY for five hundred acres, ten persons: ROBERT MOSELEY, THOMAS MOSLEY, Edward Fisher, Lucy Heaberd, Prisella Porter, William *Sipson*, Edward Wooiridge, Humpr. Boone, William Cross, Henry Butterfeill. 9 Dec 1665.

To HENRY HUDSON, for forty persons: Jno. Robinson, William *Kingt*, Jno. Edwards, Nich. Chapman, Jno. Robinson, William Edwards, Mich. Humphries, Moris Fitzgr., Ann Chapman, Ann Martin, Sha...... Kelly, Den's Cragh, John Caddell, Wm. Arkill, John Collings, Robt Foster, Alice Lee, Ric'd Lee, Tho. Grogery [?], Ann Askill [or Arkill], Wm. Fryer, John Bell, John Wallis, Thos. Key, Wm. Aviec, Jo. Foster, An Hart, Jas. Allen, Ric'd Griggs, Thos. Griffin, Ellen Collings, Thos. Crafford, Edwd Waller, Dinnis Magtaugh, Edmd Power, Robt Brunston, Robt Shelton, Wm. Martin, Edwd Bragget, John Richards. 29 Aug. 1666.-

To WILLIAM THOMAS for twenty-eight persons: Thomas Greene, William Floyd, John Hares, William Hoells, Jane Abbe, Mary File, James Farmer, Sam'l Jones, Mary Johnson, Thos. Fletcher, Timothy Stacy, William Brortt[?], Brigitt Bron, Nicho. White, Nath'l Bride, George Hanes, Mary Merse, Beth Inkson[?] 10 Oct 1666.

(*Will be continued later*)

SOME FORE-NAMES IN USE IN THE COLONIAL PERIOD

ARGALIS (ARGALUS) MERRILL, son of William. Wor. Md, 23 Jany 1709. M. H. iii-97.

ARGUIL THOUROUGOOD: will. Hyde cty, N. C. 19 Mch 1768. i-33.

ARCHALEUS HUGHES, ESQ., appointed Comm'r of the Taxes. Was previously a member of the Court. Henry cty, Va. 19 Oct 1778.

ARCHELAUS MOON, recommended for Lieut. of Militia. Camp. cty, Va. 1782. i-10.

ARCHELUS BAILY; account of his estate returned. Hyde cty, N. C. Nov. 1786. i-444.

ARGALUS POYNTER, son of Thomas. Wor., Md. 15 Feby 1802. M. H. iii-58.

ARCHELUS SURTREE, will. Currituck cty, N. C. 6 May 1802.

ATHALIAH ARBUCKLE, wf of William. Acco., Va. 24 June 1767. Diii-494.

DELILAH DEAN, dau. of Levin and Betty Dean. Dor. Psh, Md. b. 9 Oct 1748.

DELILAH HARDING, wf of Henry. Shenan. cty. Va. 1795. K-13.

DELIVERANCE VEIL, was wife of John Veil. Wmld wills (Crozier). 1718.

DEVOTION HASTINGS, deed. Camden, N. C. 15 Mch 1780. B-65.

DEVOTION WHITE, wit. to will of Jesse Cartwright. Pasq. cty, N. C. May 1797. M-20.

DRUSILLOW DAY, dau. of Wm. and Mary. Piscataway Psh, Md. Bap. 14 June 1767.

EPAPHRODITUS BRINCKLEY, deed. Tyrrell cty, N. C. 1 Nov 1734. W-232.

EPAPHRODITUS GILLIAM. St. Peter's Psh Reg., New Kent cty, Va, 1768.

EPEPHRODITUS WHITE was orphan of Daniel. Elbert cty, Ga. 2 Mch 1807.

EPAPHRODITUS HAWLE [HOWLE?] St. Peter's Psh, New Kent cty, Va.

FEREBY ROUNTREE was wife of Obed. Pitt cty, N. C. 25 Feby 1778 F-512.

[This name is spelled several ways and appears as a surname in early Surry, Virginia, spelled Ferrebe. Other times it is spelled Phereby or Pheriby. A county nurse recently in Northampton county, spelled her baptismal name FEREBA.]

GRIEF BARKSDALE, see will of Samuel Goode. Pr. Edwd, Va. 19 Aug 1796. iii-87.

GRESSELL POWELL, dau. of Samuel N-n, Va. 1 Aug 1666. vii-4.

GRIZZLE WADE, wf of Richard Wade, Sr, of Goochland. 1748. v-436.

HAMUTAL KNIGHT, wf of Henry. N-n, Va. Chancy records. 26 Sept 1758.

HANANIAH LINCOLN was in Northumberland cty, Penna. Penna. Archives. iii-219. 25 Nov. 1778.

HEROD GRIZZLE, enters 400 acres, line of William Grizzel mentioned. George Grizzle also enters 200 acres. Nash cty, Tenn. The former 1798 [?], the latter 1790.

JACOBAH (YACOBAH) SPIRES, wf of John. Acco., Va. 6 Sept 1715. xv-10.

JOCASTA SIMMS was wf of Ignatius, see his will. Ohio cty, W. Va. 1806. i-75.

JOSEBED PRITCHETT, wf of William. Dor. Psh, Md. About 1761.

LAMENTATION THOMPSON d. about 5 Nov 1798. Abbeville, S. C. i-224.

MICHOLL HUIT, wf of Robert. N-n, Va. 29 July 1658. ix-14. Also Acco., about 1676. vi-44.

METHUSALEM EVANS. Shenan, Va. 1787. G-11.

ONESEPHORIS DAMERON. See bond. Nthld, Va. 11 May 1750. i-4.

ONESIPHORUS DAMERON, "State of Virginia," carpenter and joiner, sells land on Sutton's Creek, for $1000 Spanish Milled dollars to Caleb White. 155 1-2 acres. Perq. cty, N. C. 8 Jany 1796. L-129.

ORIGINAL BROWN was son of David. There was also a grandson of the name. Wmld wills (Crozier) p. 37. 1729-1729.

ORIGINAL HIGDON, son of John. Same refs. p. 69. 1770-1771.

PELATJA [*sic*] CROFFORD, dau. of Philip and Pelatja Crofford. St. Paul's Psh Reg. K. Geo. cty, Va. Bap. 4 May 1718.

PELLATHYIA WALKER, dau. of Richard and Elizabeth. Same refs. Bap. 23 Mch 1735.

PALATHIA GRAFFORD m. Joseph Bowling. Same refs. 15 July 1738.

THE TITHABLES OF NORTHAMPTON COUNTY, VIRGINIA, in 1744

(From original lists. The date given in June, 1929, should have been 1744. An erroneous heading was inadvertently used.)

ELIZA: DUNTON, Henry Perry, John Moore; Rickets Dunton, Jr.;

John Sanders;

Ann Batson, Nehemiah Batson, Sol'n Batson, Hugh Hamilton Brown [?] Lawrence Driskell;

Matt. Harmanson, John Harmanson, Littleton Joyns, Ric'd Chambers, Will Rascoe, Jona Stevens;

Thomas Daulby, John Daulby;

Custis Kendall;

Solomon Esham;

Tankard Joyner [Joynes ?]

Maj. PETER BOWDOIN'S list;

Peter Bowdoin, Richard Cornelius;

William Bulford;

Culpepper Pigott, William Pigott;

Alex'r Kemp, George Robinson;

Luke Smaw;

John Willson, John Willson, Jr.;

Abiga: Williams, James and Thomas Willson and Thos. Warren;

John Burton;

Robert Trowers [?]

William Tazewell, William Tazewell, Jr.;

Eben: Tolman;

John Hanby;

Thomas Elliott, Thos., Wm. and James Elliott;

John Pigott, Lazarus Lewis;

William Jones, Richard Davis;

Nicholas Coffee;

Edward Mills, Nathan Mills, Wm. Tompson;

John Fathry;

Isaac Moor; Fra's Costen; Matt: Costen;

William Griffeth;

Peter Batson;

John Webb;

And's [?] John Phebin, Thomas Batson;

Matt: Freshwater, Mark Freshwater;

James Spady, Wm. Short;

Stephen Costen, Peter Costen;

Stephen Clements;

Clear [?] Fitchett, Selathiel Fitchett, Joshua Fitchett;

Hugh Bear;

John Jones, Benja. and Isaac Clays;

Thomas Jarvis, Jack, Hannah and Harrison Banks;

John Fitchett;

Thomas Spady, Thomas Willett;

Thomas Goffagon, John Goffagon, Wm. Young;

Tilney Dixon and William and Tilney Dixon;

John Dixon;

George Lynch;

Daniel Dennis, Thomas Moor;

Wise Hill, Mark Roberts;

Thomas Griffeth, Nathan Griffeth;

Fra's Stockley, Const.;

Robert Watson, Patr., William Pattern;

Matt. Floyde (Great);

John Groves;

James Goffogon;

John Roberts, Smith;

Phillip Jacobs, Thos. Tompson;

John Hall, John Hall, Jr.;

Fran's Hawkins, wid. Dorman Loffland;

Arthur Evans;

Matt: Floyd, Jr.;

Jacob *Coster* [*sic*], John Savage, Benoni Clay;

Thomas Dixon;

William Graves;

John Freshwater;

Jacob Elliott;

Moses Warren;

John Roberts, Jr., [of] Magotty Bay;

Robert Warren, Jr.;

Thomas Clay;

Benjamin Griffeth;

Richard Dreskell;

Joseph O'Dear;

Jerom Griffeth;

Southy Mills, Bowman Mills;

Isaac Elliott;

Luke Griffeth;

Jonathan Porter;

Capt. JOHN SAVAGE'S list;

William Bushop, Thomas Delaney;

Edward Widgeon;

John Savage, William Tomson;

Thomas Du Parks, John Du Parks, and Jacob Pettit.

Elick White;

Michael Waterfield [?], William Furketel;

P. Norley Ellegood;

Degby Seymour, Michael Christeen;

John Dolbe, Wm. Dolbe and Richard Sanders;

Moses Hall, Samuel Concle [?]

Degby Davis, Speakman Luker and Thos. Luker;

Richard Sanders [Sandes?]

Amey [?] Underhill [?]

Henry Serrin [?] Deverix Worrin;

George Winget;

Thomas Widggen, Jacob Batson;

Robert Widggen and S......... Widggen;

Jacob Lewis;

Thomas Cable, William Slaughter, Frances Sampton [?] Thomas Mercham [?]

Ezekiah Turley [?] Nicklas Cambell;

Daniel Call, Sr., Joseph Call;

(*To be continued*)

Printed at the Industrial School for Crippled and Deformed Children, 241 St. Botolph St., Boston, Mass.

The

County Court Note-Book

A Little Bulletin of History and Genealogy

December, 1929. **Vol. VIII, No. 6**

VIRGINIA COLONISTS

(From Old Volume 5, S. L. O. Richmond, Va.)

Mr. EDWARD LOCKEY, New Kent cty, 1658.
Head rights: John Emerson, Rich. Cheaton, John Cole, Tho. Evans, William Campion, Edmond Richeson, Wm. Lawrence, Wm. Shepard, Abraham Canby, Edward West, Tho. Feverstone [?] Rich'd Bennett. John Lobdenne, Jno. White, Abra. Preston, Wm. Hall, John Walker [perhaps Walter], Thomas Hill [?] Jno. Townsend, Edmond Gosse, Clemotine Smith;
James Morfrey, Georg Fendall, Peter Fisher, Richard Lucke, Richard Lendall, Xpher Edy, Rob't Montgomery, Richard Jones, Henery [?] Mells [Mills?] Wm. James, John Clifford.

NICHOLAS MERYWETHER, "James City Island," 1661.
Head rights: Thomas Dorr, Richard Ellis.

EDMUND MACHEN, New Kent cty, 1662.
Head rights: Susan Alcock, Sam'll Hoocks, Fran. Glover, Dorothy Glower [Glover?] Rich. Bullock, Thomas Man, Edw'd Evans, Tho: Poore, Joseph Hill, Edw'd Suckett [or Luckett] Wm. Clarke, Tho. Hyde [?] James White, Jno. Gilloe, Tho. Hayly, Tho. Wood, Wm. Wood, Edw'd Morris, Wm. Salmon, Edw'd Younge, Wm. Hay, Tho. Maples.

Mr. RICH. MAJOR, Sr., New Kent cty. 1659.
Head rights: Jone Cooke, John Wheeler, Jno. Drumon, Mary Rigby, Mary Butler, Tho. Goldsmith, Mary Harris.

JOHN MADDISON, Westmoreland cty, 1658.
Head rights: Symon Bowman, Sarah Bowman, Grace Bowman (three times), James Bowman.

GEORGE MORRIS, Rappahannock cty. 1667.
Head rights: Wm. Young, John Marsh, Edw. Turner, John Carty, Jno. a negro, Wm. Marley, Fra: Freke, Fra: Hart, Edw. Muth, John Scot, John Bathis [?] Edw. Marle [?] Jos: Stratton, Wm. Wigg, Tho. Coniers, Ed: Marten, Mary Jackson, Wm. Satom [?] Tho. Young, Wm. Fear, Wm. Joyner, Tho. Dooly, Tho. Wars, Jaco. Jones, Wm. Max;
John Tooke [Fooke?] Edw. Ditty, Wm. Sorle, Noah Turner, Nath. Haddon, Wm. Marster [?] Jno. Shaw, Tho. Fuell, Wm. Harvey, Tom, a negro, Frank, a negro; Jno. Darby, Wm. Swann, Edw. Muth, Tho. Tarvy, Wm. Fluell, Josiah Jackson, Mary Luell, Tho: Parker, Edw. Luell, Fra: Carson, Em'll negro, Tho. Collings, Cha: Mary, Tho. Blare, Edw: Williamson.

JOHN PIGGE, New Kent, 1658.
Head rights: Ann Beiry, Henry Wills, Margarett Reynolds, Wm. Blease, Wm. Harmar, Robert Florence, Wm. She [? perhaps Shea] Alexander Gregory, Alice Potter, Elias Barkamore, James Sanders, Tho. Meares, Alexander Baker, Tho. Dickson.

JOHN PETEETE, New Kent, 1658.
Head rights: Sarah Richeson, Jane Cole, Elianor Richeson, Richard Halliway, Owin Mason [?] James Collins, Phillip Prosser, Jeremiah Lewar [Lewis?] John Gouteer and one negro.

JAMES POPE, Northumberland cty, 1659.
Head rights: Edmond Taylour, Wm. Partlett, Robert Middleton, Eliz: Clemens, Georg Watson, Wm. Maninge, and five negroes.

JAMES POPE, Northumberland cty, 1659.
Head rights: Nine negroes, Thos. Loveday, Tho. Williams, Mary Witchall [Mitchell?] Hamond Franklin, Sarah Wikell [Michael?]

JOHN PHIPS, James City cty. 1656.
Head rights: Eliz: Leichfeiles [?] Jonas Page.

Mr. CUTHBERT POTTER, "on the north and south sides of a great Swampe or Pocoson which devides the Countyes of Lancaster and Glousester and about two miles above the horse path." 1659.
Head rights: 108 persons but no names given. [This item is given here on account of the unusual wording of the location.]

EDMOND PETERS, Gloucester cty. 1659.
Head rights: Wm. Peane [probably Paine] Henry Waller [or Haller] Henry Waltons, John Robison, Nicholas Chashey. [?]

Capt. MARTIN PALMER, New Kent cty. 1660.
Head rights: John Tasker, Margaret Jones, Edward Cooke, Daniel Parker, Tho. Scafe, Henry Pott, Tho. Luty, Jno. Sympson.

THOMAS ROBBISON, FRANCIS GOWER, ROBERT SISSON and JOHN DE YOUNGE, Rappa. cty. 1658.
Head rights: John Fisher, Thomas Gray, John Ackerson, Mary Johnson.

SYMON RICHARDSON, Northumberland, 1662.
Head rights: Five negroes, Jno. Bateman, Symon Carpenter, ...Wimboll.

EDWARD REVELL, Northampton cty. 1661. [See also patent 1652.]
Head rights: Five negroes; Mary Wiggins, Andrew Gadstone, Ann Morris, Wm. Stephens, Walter Jones.

Col. ROBT SMITH, 1669.
Head rights: Peter Jennings, Jno. Riggs, Eliz: Ellinore, Jno. Green, Wm. Wood, Wm. Bann, An Raignelt, Eliz: Ellis, Wm. Covenant, Mathew Morris, Abell Glover, Alex. Davis, Jno. Hawkshead, Jno. Palm[er] Jno. Hawkenett, Eliz: Turner, David Roch, Ralph Parr.

LITTLETON SCARBURGH, JOHN ALEXANDER and TABITHA SMART, Northampton cty. 1659.

Head rights: John Watts, Jeffery Cooke, Edm'd Cantwell, Thos: Stacy, Hugh Bowin, Sarah Huitt, Susan Fletcher, Jane Gardner, Mary Hues, Sarah Gardner, Alice Roberts, Joseph Huitt, Nicholas Letchey, John Hapworth, Morris Savatt [?] Jane Gethinge, Tho. Davis, Darby Ennis, John Davis, Edward Banbury, Robert Fookes, Jane Rogers;

Ann Lertch, Tho. Warren, Henry Robins, James Hayes, Timothy Jones, Charles Hackworth [Nackworth?] Mary Williams, Tho. Morris.

ROBERT THOMAS and WM. MOSSE, Rappahannock cty. 1660.

Head rights: George Johnson, Wm. Wilson, Elizabeth Turry, Wm. Smithson, Cornelius Clynton, Derrick Arrison.

Mr. WM. THOMAS, Northumberland. 1661.

Head rights: Phill: Harwood, Roger Pinner, Thomas Panton, Jno. Wray, Rob't Salter, Edw. Plaice [?]

THOMAS WOODWARD, I. W. cty. 1659.

Head rights: Jane Price, Mary Grimes.

JAMES WILSON, New Kent cty, "on Mount Folly path." 1661.

Head rights: Wm. Lewis, Thomas Wood, Lyddy How, Wm. Badger, Jno. Grisser [perhaps Griffen] Dan'll Merick, Jno. Jones, Edward Sier [? Sear], Mary Williams, Edw. Webb, Abell Jason, Wm. Richardson, Ann Robbinson.

Capt. JOHN UNDERWOOD, 1661.

Head rights: Tho. Barnhouse, Eliz: Bacons, Rob't Hill, Rich. Barns, Tho. Agnes, Tho. Graggs, Vane............, Jno. Dare, Fortune Perrin, An Dawe, negro; Wm. Hill, James Hill.

EDWARD VAHANE, county not given. 1662.

Head rights: Ann James, Mary Stephens, Wm. Shuite [?] Peter Mills, Stephen Norman.

FAMILIES OF THE EASTERN SHORE
THE WHITTINGTONS

(*Seventh instalment*)

(CONTINUING the cadet line.) As stated in the October NOTE-BOOK, SOUTHY WHITTINGTON, Senior, the first of that fore-name, died between the 20 Feby 1769 and the 17 Mch 1773. He was born before 1688, but presumably after 1682. (See the dates of the second and third marriages of his father, Lt. Col. WILLIAM WHITTINGTON.) So that he seems to have lived to be unusually old.

SOUTHY WHITTINGTON, Senior, married MARY FAWCETT, or, as usually spelled, FASSITT, daughter of WILLIAM FASSITT, of Somerset county, Maryland. (See Fassitt's will, Wor., Md., M. H. iii-322. 22 Jany 1734-30 May 1735.)

Some questioning has arisen over the fact that WILLIAM FASSITT in his will, mentions his grandson LITTLETON WHITTINGTON, son of his daughter, MARY WHITTINGTON, while SOUTHY WHITTINGTON does not mention any son of that name. There *was* a LITTLETON WHITTINGTON, son of ISAAC, son of SOUTHY. The very early date of FASSITT'S will makes it likely that SOUTHY and MARY (FASSITT) WHITTINGTON did have a son LITTLETON, who died, and that ISAAC WHITTINGTON either named his son after his brother, or because of the importance of the name. While the compiler has ever been of the opinion that the artifices of commentators, as some one says, but focus attention on and make the more glaring what one might call the absenteeism of facts, yet it would really be going out of one's way and "hunting for trouble" not to accept the simple and only records in this case.

The account of WHITTINGTON'S estate mentions wife MARY, and SOUTHY WHITTINGTON [his son], executor. (Som. Md. E. B. ii-192. 10 Oct 1775.)

The children of SOUTHY and MARY (FASSITT) WHITTINGTON were:

SOUTHY, m. Esther Nairne;
STEVENSON;
ISAAC, m. Elizabeth............;
WILLIAM m. Priscilla Polk;
HANNAH, m. John Cox. (See adm'n accounts.)

MARY (FASSITT) WHITTINGTON seems to have died about 1775.

SOUTHY WHITTINGTON, IId of the name, called "Junior," (son of Southy, son of William, son of William) was probably born before 1732. It has already been shown that he received from his father the tracts of *Canaan*, *Goshen*, *Gilead*, part of *Recovery*, part of *Chance* in Annamessex, while his brother WILLIAM received parts of the same tracts as well as other lands ......but during SOUTHY'S life he received (and by his will conveyed) a tract called *Cedar Hall*. on the Poeomoke, and this in a rather peculiar way.

A tri-partite deed on record in Worcester county, Maryland (G-72, 18 Apr 1767), recites the conveyance by JANETT PITT, who was formerly "JANNETT NARN" [NAIRN], as the party of the first part, LITTLETON DENNIS being the party of the second part, and JOHN NEARN, ELIZABETH NUTTER [she had been the wife of JOSHUA WHITTINGTON of the elder branch] and ESTHER WHITTINGTON, wife of SOUTHY WHITTINGTON, "all children of the aforesaid JENNETT," parties of the third part, to whom JENNET conveys [presumably through DENNIS as trustee] 250 acres of *Cedar Hall*, which was devised to her by the last will of Francis Drummond, and of which she has, by her marriage contract, full disposition...... the consideration being love and affection and five shillings.

Further than this, SOUTHY'S son SOUTHY, by will of John Nairn (1771-1771, Annap. xxxviii-640), receives one-half of *Cedar Hall*. This was the John Nearn referred to above, who was son of Janet Pitt. It is probable, though no direct explanation appears, that WILLIAM WHITTINGTON, son of her first husband, JOSHUA WHITTINGTON, inherited ELIZABETH NUTTER'S interest in *Cedar Hall* and probably conveyed it, as will be shown later, to one of the SOUTHYS.

In John Nairn's will (referred to previously), he devises to WILLIAM WHITTINGTON, son of JOSHUA (who was the first husband of

ELIZABETH NAIRN, afterwards NUTTER), his part of *Cedar Hall*. And this WILLIAM (son of JOSHUA) in 1772, 25 Dec., (Wor. Md. I-221), conveys to SOUTHY WHITTINGTON, for four hundred and six pounds, five shillings, so that the whole tract of *Cedar Hall* finally rested in the family of SOUTHY WHITTINGTON, "Junior," though how the devise to his son was handled the compiler has never quite understood.

One other note appears in the land records touching SOUTHY WHITTINGTON, "Junior." The 3 Aug 1762 (Som. Md. xxiv-135). "SOUTHEY WHITTINGTON, the younger," receives from Aaron Sterling of Somerset, consideration five shillings, as trustee for the Sterling heirs, tracts of land called *Hap Hazard*, *Barnitt*, 6 acres of *Johnson's Lott*, *First Oration* and *Sterling's Good Luck*......all in Annemessix.

SOUTHY WHITTINGTON, "Junior," died in 1785 or 1786. Abstract of his will follows.

SOUTHY WHITTINGTON, of Wor. cty. Md.
Wife ESTHER; son JOHN-NAIRN WHITTINGTON; son SOUTHY WHITTINGTON; daus. JEANNET; ESTHER; ELIZABETH; LEAH; KATHARINE WHITTINGTON; MARY MARSHALL; SARAH GILLETT;
Wit: Henry Dennis, Sam'l Handy, John Teackle, David Long. (J. W. xiii-107. 15 Jany 1785-29 Dec 1786.)

JANNET WHITTINGTON, one of the daughters, of Worcester cty, died in 1803, and as her will mentions her mother and others of the family it is given here.

JANNET WHITTINGTON (Wor. Md. J. B. R. vi-75. 9 May 1803-14 June 1803.)
Mother ESTHER WHITTINGTON; Brother JOHN N. WHITTINGTON; brother SOUTHY WHITTINGTON; sister ELIZABETH GUNBY, reversion to HESSEY SELBY; Sister LEAH LONG; nephew James Gillett; niece Leah Long; mentions Robert N. Marshall, Polly Marshall. Brother JOHN N. WHITTINGTON, extr.
Wit: William Huston, Betsy Gunby.

SOUTHY WHITTINGTON, " junior," m. ESTHER NAIRN, the daughter of ROBERT and JANET NAIRN. See will of ROBERT NAIRN, pltr, of Worcester cty, Md., in which he mentions his daughter ELIZABETH WHITTINGTON, and his daughter, ESTHER WHITTINGTON. (Wor. Md. J. W. iii-88. 21 Jany 1761-3 Feby 1764.) See also the will of JOHN NAIRN, brother of ESTHER. (Wor. cty, 11 Dec 1771. Annap. wills, xxxviii-640.)

The will of ESTHER WHITTINGTON, widow of SOUTHY (abstracted) is as follows: (Wor. Md. J. B. R. vi-4. 6 Sept 1805-11 Feby 1806.)
Dec'd dau. JANE WHITTINGTON; dau. BETSY GUNBY; son JOHN WHITTINGTON; dau. CATHARINE POWELL; grandaus. Eliza Gunby, Leah Long; gr. sons, John-Nairne Whittington; George Washington Powell; Robert Nairn Marshall; Levin Selby; Southey Whittington Gillett. Sons SOUTHEY WHITTINGTON and JOHN WHITTINGTON, extrs.
Wit: Littleton Dennis, James Merrill.

(*To be continued*)

AUTHENTIC REFERENCES FOR INFERRED MARRIAGES

(Accomack county, Virginia)

WILLIAM BLAKE, Jr., and ELIZABETH FOSTER, widow of Thomas. About Dec. 1685. vi-421. See also ix-49 and 77.

PETER BOWDOIN and SUSANNAH PREESON. Before 5 Nov 1734. Land Causes.

JAMES BRAUGHTON and ANNE BAYLY, dau. of Charles. Before 31 Oct 1775. Deeds iv-346.

JOHN BRITTINGHAM and LEAH MASSEY, coheir of John Massey. Before 10 Jany 1770. Deeds iii-704.

ISAAC BRITTINGHAM and MARY TAYLOR, wid. Elias. Before 3 May 1738. xii0-56.

Maj. EDMUND BOWMAN and Mrs. CATHERIN SCARBROW [widow?] Before 11 Mch 1685. ix-85.

Capt. EDM. BOWMAN and the widow of .... LEATHERBERRY. Before 19 June 1677. vii-55.

EDWARD BENSTONE and MARY MERCY [MASSEY.] Before 20 Dec 1742. xxiiiW-1.

PETER COLLIER and ELIZABETH WATTS, dau. of John and Priscilla Watts. Before 2 Jany 1724. See xvi-246 and xx-53. [This has been previously published, but the present note is more complete.]

COLIN CAMPBELL, of Nthld cty, Va., and MARY SNEAD, dau. of Robert. Before 7 July 1766. Diii-436, 437.

THOMAS CHAPWELL and MARY EBORNE, widow of William. Before 19 June 1677. vii-62.

...... COLONY and ELIZABETH SCARBURGH, widow. Before 11 Mch 1789. x1W-30. [She must also have married ...... Smith.]

WILLIAM CUSTIS and PATIENCE ALLEN [or BAGWELL?] sister of Stephen. [Allen's mother m. a Bagwell and he had "brothers and sisters" Bagwell.] Before 23 Sept. 1738. xxivW-172.

JOHN COLEBURN and ELIZABETH SCARBURGH, sister of Charles. Before 27 May 1756. Deeds ii-384 and 654. See also xxiii0-618, which shows that the marriage was before 27 Aug 1752.

Mr. ROBERT COLBURNE and REBECCA REVELL. Before 18 Sept. 1689. ix-192.

THOMAS CADE and SARAH MASSEY, coheir of John. Before 10 Jany 1770. Deeds iii-704.

JAPHET COOKE and ELIZABETH PARAMORE, before 26 Aug 1669. iii-157. [She was deceased before this date.]

GILES COPES and ELIZABETH PARKER, See xi-651. Before 1 Jany 1710.

THOMAS COPES and MARY PARKER, See the same references.

HENRY CHANCEY and JOAN FRANCKLIN, widow. Before 20 Feby 1688. ix-150. See also x-29.

The County Court Note-Book

An every-other-monthly devoted mainly to abstracts from County Court Records, prior to 1800.

MILNOR LJUNGSTEDT, Editor and Publisher.
Bethesda, Route 5, Maryland.

Published six times a year. Subscription, two dollars, in advance; must begin with the year.

December, 1929 **Whole**
Vol. VIII., No. 6 **No. 49**

EIGHT years......and the last issue of the year. The Editor feels as if she should say something of weight......but as the Swedish peasant replied to her pastor when catechized as to the Ten Commandments......"what could be said?" Besides, the Editor got so beautiful a letter the other day...... she (yes, it was a "female correspondent") she, this lady of eminent discrimination and wide understanding, she said "the editorials are worth the price of the book".....and that she had received full measure from those alone. And to think there were forty-three of them! Would you believe it? But the Editor did so need just that beautiful flattery.

Yet, here is the result, the Editor can't think of a thing to say. You all remember the man who made the perfect paper of needles. The Editor feels that this subscriber and a few others are to read this and she should at least live up to half a reputation. But nothing presents itself to her mind or her fingers but a bunch of facts. Some of them are right interesting.

For example, after wandering from Harrisburg, Pennsylvania, to Georgetown, Delaware (which Maryland thinks should be Maryland), to Dover, Delaware, and the Historical Society of Pennsylvania, the Editor discovers that the *original minutes of the old court of Deale County, Delaware,* are in the Pennsylvania Historical Society. And for this information she has to thank Mrs. Richardson of Baltimore, who in her interesting volumes ("*Side-Lights of Maryland History*") gives a reference to Dr. Turner's "*Some Records of Sussex county, Delaware,*" who, in his turn, wrote the Editor that these original records are to be found in Philadelphia. The Editor is perfectly frank when she says they ought not to be. The greater part of the Delaware papers have, the Editor understands, been turned over by Pennsylvania to Delaware; Massachusetts has given Connecticut the Trumbull papers, and England has given Massachusetts the so-called "Log of the May-flower." Why should one look for the records of the good little "Blue Hen" state in Pennsylvania?

The State Library of Virginia is listing the marriage license bonds of Amherst county, Virginia, so that the Clerk of the Amherst Court will be free of that worry. And numerous records of the older counties are in Richmond and will ......in course of time......be photostated. That is the trouble......*the course of time.* The uninformed searcher goes to an ancient county at some expense and more trouble...... and the records are not there. As this sort of thing is going on for some time, it is advised by the Editor that information as to the whereabouts of any and all Virginia records be secured before a visit is made to the courthouses.

The lighting at the State Land Office in Annapolis is so much improved, and the Editor under so many obligations to the executive head of that most interesting office, that she feels she really should not "grouch" about the shelving. But nobody else will do so (aloud), so she has to, in the spirit of her New England ancestry, who always seem to have felt they were born to set the rest of the world right. It's the State of Maryland that's at fault. Like some other States, it is so satisfied with the "*status quo.*" (And if that Latin isn't correct, the executive head will tell the Editor next time she goes over there.)

And that reminds the Editor that three of us being left alone for a few seconds in the Virginia Archives, the two others and the Editor promptly agreed that it is the worst ventilated room of the kind we had ever been in. But nobody but the Editor says anything for publication.

Dr. Stewart's most excellent and readable "RESEARCHER" has "quit." It is a great pity. But Dr. Stewart has in hand the proofs of Fairfax Harrison's fine contribution to Virginia publications......the *Index of Genealogies.* It should be out within a few months.

Mrs. Nugent's fourth bulletin of Virginia Patents......which is now called "*Cavaliers and Pioneers,*"......is about ready and will be out before this reaches its subscribers......those who also take the NOTE-BOOK, that is. The Editor and some others think it was a mistake to change the title, but it seems that there was occasionally a certain confusion with strictly official matters, which involved explanations and correspondence. Mrs. Nugent's work, though thoroughly approved by the authorities, is entirely personal. The Editor is very glad to say that "Cavaliers and Pioneers" is so well received that it will continue on. It should be in every library, for nothing so good of the kind has hitherto been put out. The "Virginia Colonists" running in the NOTE-BOOK, while useful as to names taken from a volume very few have read, does not cover the ground as fully as Mrs. Nugent's work.

Mr. Burgess' third volume of the records of Virginia Revolutionary Soldiers is about ready. It will contain most valuable material, heretofore unpublished. A fourth volume is well under way. This will cover a class of records quite untouched except as to individual searches.

CONTINUED articles COUNTY COURT NOTE-BOOK, and the dates on which they first appeared.

THE ANCESTRY OF COL. JOHN DONELSON. Began with February, 1927.

AUTHENTIC REFERENCES for INFERRED MARRIAGES (formerly called MARRIAGES BY INFERENCE). Began with May, 1922.

MARYLAND'S NEXT OF KIN. Began with July, 1922.

VIRGINIA COLONISTS. Alphabetized lists began with July, 1924.

MILITARY NOTES, both COLONIAL and REVOLUTIONARY, and later MILITIA NOTES. Began December, 1923.

INTERCOUNTY and INTERCOLONY (formerly called New Englanders and Others, &c., &c.). Began with March, 1922.

EASTERN SHORE FAMILIES. In the form of a one-page supplement, began with June, 1925.

SHIPS IN PORT and COLONIAL FORENAMES will appear in alternate issues or as space can be found for them.

STAFFORD COUNTY INDICES began in June, 1929.

A MATTER OF IMPORTANCE

The Editor of the NOTE-BOOK will pay ten dollars ($10) for a copy of the WILL of WILLIAM FLOYD, or a copy (in full) of the administration of his estate.

WILLIAM FLOYD was living in 1783; had wife ABADIAH, and probably living sons ROBERT, CHARLES and NATHANIEL. He was also the father of Col. JOHN FLOYD. WILLIAM FLOYD may havs died in one of the frontier counties of Virginia, in Kentucky, or in one of the Territories northwest of the Ohio. He was about 56 years old in 1783 and owned land in the upper Valley of Virginia. He had removed to the frontier, but was driven back by the uprising among the Indians. Where he then settled is unknown.

ERRATA: The heading on page seven, NOTE-BOOK for February, 1929, "DECEDENTS IN HYDE COUNTY" should read N. C. (*North Carolina*) and not "D. C."

In June, 1929, in the list of Northampton tithables, HOWSON MAPP and THOMAS HAY were not with ABEL POWELL, Constable, but formed another household and should be listed in a separate line.

VARIA

"IT was I Suppose a house pig for [I] could not keep it from the doore." Northampton cty, Va. 1718-1725.

INDEPENDENT GIST and STATES GIST. Patent for 1000 acres in Ohio county. Va. S. L. O. lviii-342. 12 June 1809.

ROBERT EDMUND, in his will, gives his dog to John Thompkins. N-n cty, Va. 27 Dec 1633. i-40.

The BUSINESS of a GRAND JURY in 1751. Presentments: A. B. for profane swearing one Oath; C. D. for profane swearing one Oath; E. F. for being drunk on the Sabbath Day; G. H., I. J., K. L., M. N., for Sabbath breaking in fiddling, dancing and fireing Guns, and for profane Swearing four Oaths, each; O. P. Sr., for Profane Swearing one Oath; Q. R. for profane Swearing..................N-n cty, Va. 12 Nov 1751. xxixO-23. [Not Connecticut, but Virginia.]

INDENTURE between ALEXANDER REID, latèlie in Inndrury in the Sherrefddome of Aberdeene and Kingdom of Scotland and now in North Fevriel[?] or Dunde within the Shirrifdome of Forfar and Kingdome foresaid only son, child and Heire of the deceased Alexander Reid in Inndrury who was brother German and of the whole Blood and heir in Law of the deceast George Reid, late of the province of Maryland in America Gentleman, and John Gaudy [Gandy?] of the City of London, Mariner. Annap. Md. T. L. ii-794. 23 Aug 1703.

DAVID x MORGAN "hath lately Imported himselfe, his wife and foure children into the [Lower parish of Northampton] and gives bond of indemnification against any charge, trouble, costs or incumbrances due to his residing there." N-n cty, Va. 5 Nov 1683. Original bond.

Note: In June, 1927, under "Occasional," is a paragraph "SHARP to RAZOR," the name being Rason, however, in the body of the bond, but the backing by the Clerk gives RASOR. It is an actual fact the name RASOR is in the early records, and it is probable that the Clerk's endorsement is correct. When the Editor finds the former reference, it will be given.

THE TITHABLES OF NORTHAMPTON COUNTY VIRGINIA, in 1744

(*From original lists*)

DANIEL CALL, Jr., William Munk, Jr.;
Nehemiah Fitchett, Constable;
Joanna Campbell, John Roberts;
Thomas Church *and wf Susanna*;
Samuel Mapp;
William Ellegood;
Jonathan Isham;
John Widggen;
Sarah Powell, Joseph Powell, John Powell;
Susanna Powell, Deverix Godwin;
David Ryen [prob. Rippen];
Hillary Stringer, Ann Mackenney;
John Kendall, Charles Satchell, Abraham Jacob;
Elizabeth Harmanson, George Kendall;
Bembridge [spelled Bemlidge], Web, negro;
Thomas Frost;
Roling [?] Floyd;
John Roberts of Smith Island;
James Delpech;
Stephen Dunton;
Wenneford Major, William Fletcher, Rob't Fletcher, Thomas Griffen, Bob Tapley;
Thomas Cowdry, John Sutherland;
Frances Pettit, William Jacob;
John Goffigon, Thomas Tatum;
John Stringer, George Griffen and Sary Ayrs;
John Lun;
Samuel Church *and wf. Elizabeth*;
George Munk and Nottingham Munk;
Matthew Worrin, Nichlas Powell;
Michal Benteley;
Josefas Mearare Johnson; [this is in reality *Josephus Maria Johnson.*]
Ester Savage, John Jones, Thomas Wilkins, Henry Trower;
Cornelius Berry;
William Young;
John Jones. (*End of list.*)

A LIST OF WILLS WHICH WERE IN WILL BOOK "N" (LOST) STAFFORD COUNTY, VIRGINIA (1767-1783)

JOHN ALEXANDER, William Allen, David Anderson, John Alexander [probably the same as above], James Allen, Adam Atchison;

WILLIAM BUNBURY, Peter Byram, William Byram, Samuel Bridwell, William Bowling, Abram Bridwell [see former note], Seth Botts, George Brent, John Bell, Sr., John Bell, Josiah Brown, William Brent; Matthew Bowen;

JOHN CARTER, Elisabeth Chinn, Benjamin Clift, Thomas Carver, Mary Carter, John Carpenter, Elisabeth Chinn [see above] John Cox, James Chinn;

ALEXANDER DONIPHAN, Francis Dade, Samuel Dunaway, Mott Doniphan, Peter Daniel;

WILLIAM EDRINGTON, Sr., Enoch Ennis, Sr.

GERRARD FOWKE, Thomas Fitzhugh, Richard Foot, Richard Fristoe, William Fant;

JOHN GRIGGSBY, William Griggsby, Thomas Gough, Christian Gallaway;

BURR HARRISON, Thomas Harwood, Elizabeth Heath, Thomas Hoard, Charles Harding, Peter Hansbrough, William Horton, Jessee Humphrey;

.... INNIS, Sr., Robert Jackson;

ANN KIRK, John Knox, Anthony Kitching, William Kendall, James Kenny, Ann Kenny;

FRANKLIN LATHAM, Joseph Lewis, William Lumley, Dianna Lunsford, Richard Lewis, Thomas Lee, Mary Lewis;

WILLIAM MILLS, Frances Moss, John Mercer William Matthews, Ann Mercer, John Matthews, William Mountjoy, John Mawsay, James Martin, Gerrard Messingo [?]

JOHN PAYNE, Jr., Steven Pilcher, Benjamin Porter, Nathaniel Price, Evan Peyton:

WILLIAM ROGERS, Patrick C. Rowen, William Rose, John Robertson, John Ralls, Jr., John Ralls, John Ratcliff;

HENRY SMITH, William Samuels, John Steth [*sic*], Charles Stuart ...... Stulcoat (non-cup.) Charles Stuart inv., John Stuart, Thomas Seddon, Sr., John Stark, William Sturdy [?] [damaged] Elizabeth............ther;

THOMAS THATCHER, Henry Tyler, Mary Tyler, Samuel Tayloe;

GEORGE WALLER, John Wheeler, Walter Williamson, John Waugh, Nathaniel Washington, Alexander Woodrow, Ben. Woodrow, Charles Walden, Allen Waller, Carty Wells, Sr., Morgan Williams;

WILLIAM YOUNG, Robert Yates.

VOLUME "T," DEEDS AND WILLS (LOST) 1789-1793

(Wills only are noted.)

LOW BAGDALL, Thomas Brooks, Aaron Botts, William Bridwell (indexed twice) Jeremiah Burnes;

JAMES CLOW, Joseph Cooper;

RACHEL FLETCHER, Patrick Fines, Jonathan Fennel, William French;

PHILIP GARNER, William Guy;

ELIZABETH HEWITT, Thomas Heath, John Horton;

WILLIAM JACOBS;

SIMON LYNN;

WILLIAM NEWTON;

JOHN POLLARD, Mason Pilcher, Calvert Porter;

WILLIAM ROSS, Joseph Reddish [Reddick ?]

JOSIAH STONE;

JOHN WALTERS, James Wallace, George Williams.

MARYLAND'S NEXT OF KIN

JOHN HEPRON, JAS. HEPBOURN; inv. of Joseph *Hebron* of Kent cty. No date. viii-170.

GEORGE SKIRVEN, MARY BROWN; Inventory of that part of Docter Wm. Skirven's Estate Deceas'd that Came by his last wife. County not given. 25 June 1723 and 5 July 1723. ix-1.

THOS. x DRANE, "Relation;" Inv. Anthony Drane of Pr. Geo's. Ret. 20 Sept 1723. ix-5.

JNO. x LIMAISTER, JOS. x SCOTT; inv. James Williams, Carpenter. County not given. 30 Sept 1723. ix-8.

ANDREW WILLIS, JOHN WILLIS; inv. Thos. Wallis, Dor. cty. 15 Oct 1722. ix-9.

JONAS x DORSON, JOHN DORSON; inv. Daniell Cronene, of Dor. cty. 11 Dec 1722. ix-12.

THOS x CISELL; inv. John Cissel, Sen'r, of St. Mary's cty. 12 Nov 1722. ix-14.

JOHN x WOLLSON, THOS. HEBB, Jr. [Kin?] Inv. John Wolson, of St. Mary's cty. 14 Dec 1722. ix-18.

CLEM'T SEWALL, ANN SEWALL; inv. Mr. Henry Sewall, of St. Mary's cty. 30 Aug 1722. ix-19.

WILLIAM LOCK, PHILLIP LOCK; inv. Phillip Lock of St. Mary's cty. 16 Nov 1722. ix-21.

ELEANOR LOWE, MARY LOWE [presumably kin;] inv. Bennitt Lowe of St. Mary's cty. 27 Dec 1722. ix-22.

SOLL: WRIGHT "daughter's husband" and Ann x Horney, dau. Inv. Jno. King of Talbott cty. 22 June 1722. ix-29.

RICH'S ALETERN [ALLERTON], JNO. VALLIANT, "Kindred and creditors." Inv. Mr. John Valliant of Talbot cty. 3 Sept 1722. ix-35.

SOPHIA x RICHARDSON, Daughter, WM. HARRISON, MARY WRIGHTSON, "Relations and Creditors." [It is not clear which are which.] Inv. Mr. Dan'l Richardson of Talbot cty. 1 Aug 1722. ix-37.

JOHN and THOS. SANDERS; inv. Richard Townroe[?] of Talbot cty. 1 Aug 1722. ix-44.

The administrators know of no relation to Robt. Flouracres, of Talbot cty. 9 Aug. 1722. ix-45.

TABITHA x HILL, SARAH x HAMBLER; inv. Mr. Stevens White. County not given. 9 Jany 1719, 27 Dec 1719 and 21 Dec 1720. ix-16.

SAM'LL HOPKINS, NATH'LL HOPKINS; inv. of Hon. Wm. Whittington, of Somerset cty. Apr 1720. ix-55.

"There is no Cred'rs nor Relations appears Though Notice given." Inv. James Hern of Kent cty. 12 Mch 1722. ix-63.

PETER GREEN, ROB'T GREEN; Inv. Dan'l Duffey of Kent cty. 3 Apr 1722. ix-63.

JOHN WILSON, MARY x WILSON, SARAH JONES [Kin?] Inv. Michaell Willson of Kent cty. 24 Nov 1721. ix-67.

MARY x RICAUD; inv. John Maxwell of Kent cty. 22 Nov 1722. ix-73.

WM. DEANE; inv. William Roberts of Kent 6 June 1722. ix-76.

CHRISTOPHER BROOKS, REBECCA BROOKS; inv. Gregory Brooks of Kent cty. 3 Dec 1722. ix-79.

CORNELIUS HURLEY, DANIEL HURLEY [probably kin.] Inv. Timothy Hurly of Kent cty. 7 Dec 1722. ix-80.

BENJ'N x RICAUD, ELIZ'TH x MAXWELL; inv. Thos. Ricaud of Kent cty. 25 July 1722 ix-84.

WILLIAM x BURROWS, JANE BURROWS; inv. Benjamin Ellis. County not given. 1 Dec 1722. ix-88.

R. BENNETT, MARY HEMSLEY sign, but a note follows: "This Inventory is not to be Rec'd because it is not Signed by the Credi'rs or Relations of the Decased as the Act of Assembly Directs." Add'l inv. Mr. Philemon Hemsley of Q. A. cty. ix-89.

ANN x TANSEY[?], MARTHA x BECK; inv. John Green of Kent cty. 15 Aug. 1723. ix-95.

"No relations." Inv. Thomas Taylor of Balto. cty. 7 Nov 1722. ix-94.

"Kindred none." Inv. Capt. Wm. Farfarr of Balto. cty. 18 Aug 1722. ix-96.

"MAD'M RECECCA COLEGATE alias POWELL, extx," makes oath. Children minors and "no Creditors of any Value Relations None.,' Inv. Col. Richd Colegate. 23 May 1722. ix-102. Balto. cty.

MAD'M MARY MARSHALL, extx, makes oath; "Relations in Ireland." Inv. Mr. Wm. Marshall, late of Baltimore cty. 1 Aug. 1722. ix-110.

CHRISTOPHER RANDALL. Brother; HANNAH x TEALL [?] Sister; Inv. Mr. Thomas Randall of Balto. cty. 3 Aug. 1722. ix-118.

JABAZ MORRAY, LUKE x TROTTAN "Relations;" Inv. John Eager of Balto. cty. 15 Oct 1722. ix-127.

RICHARD BURROUGH, ELIZ'TH BURROUGH; inv. Margrett Dreu, widow, of Balto. cty. 26 May 1722. ix-130.

HENERY DONAHUE, son; JOHN x KECY [?] "maried the daughter of the dec'd." Inv. Henery Donnahue, of Balto cty. 10 Nov 1722. ix-132.

OWEN x MAC CARTY, THOMAS x MORRIS; Inv. Daniel Mac Carty of Balto cty. 10 Aug 1722. ix-131.

INTERCOUNTY AND INTERCOLONY

SAMUEL COOKE, of Wappinge, Carp. Bill to him of John Chandler of *Newports News*, pltr, and Samuel Chandler, Mcht, London. To be paid at Mr. Thos. Stone's "Hose in Cateadied strate." N-n, Va. 27 Feby 1639. i-158.

COLIN CAMPBELL and wife MARY, were of Northumberland cty, Va. See settlement of certain Snead property rights. Acco., Va. 7 July 1766. Diii-436.

WM. CHOAT, marriner, of "NEWENGLAND," power to John Hutchenson. Acco., Va. 27 Feby 1765. Diii-377.

ROBERT DRAKES, owner of a plantation in Accomack in Virginia, late in the Occupation of John Parramore, gives power to brother-in-law, Rich: Hill. N-n, Va. 6 Oct 1653. iv-3.

Capt. WILLIAM EPES of the Island of St. Christopher, gives power to [Wm. Stonne?] Henry Ouldham one of wit. N-n, Va. 18 July 1633. i-159.

ROBERT EVANS, of Philadelphia, power to Laban Simpson. Acco., Va. 1 June 1764. xxvO-303.

THOMAS HUDSON, of Charles cty, Md., was son of Henry, dec'd. See Northumberland records, 1738-1743, p. 106. 1703.

JESSY HUNT, late of New York, mariner, to Luke Luker, land on Ceeder Island. Acco., Va. 26 May 1767. Diii-476.

PATRICK McDOWALL, of Edgecombe cty, N. C., at present residing in Accomack; power to Levin Parker. Acco., Va. 20 Oct 1766. Diii-446.

ROBERT GARDNER, of the State of Carolina, to John Gardner, Jr., part of Johnson's Lott and Short Neck. Calv. cty, Md. 5 Dec 1785. Annap. Records.

WILLIAM x FITZHUGH, of Washington cty, Md., deed to John Fitzhugh of Calvert cty, Md. Annap. Records. 6 Mch 1794.

THOMAS BOURNE, of Calv. cty, Md., conveys to Francis Wheatly, of Charles cty, Md., tract in Nelson cty, Kentucky, on the north side Green river......part of a tract purchased of William May of Kentucky, by George Bourne of Calvert cty, Md. Contains 500 acres. Annap. records. 7 May 1796.

WILLIAM KNIGHT, of North Carolina, to Matthew Floyd. Land in Northampton cty, Va. N-n, Va. 12 Oct 1745. Dxviii-312.

DENIS x MORRICE (County of Accomack) and wife Elizabeth x Morrice......she was the daughter of Richard Starling, the elder. L. Norf., Va. 16 Nov 1670. E. 101-102.

RICHARD RANDALL, of Boston, in New England, Mcht; power to Henry Addams of Charles cty, Md., Gent. Chas. cty, 3 May 1665. B-226.

THOMAS WEBB; Mr. James Austen was grandfather to Thomas Webb, son of Thomas, and left him land in Somerset, Eastern Shore. Nthld cty, Va. 1706-1720, fo. 5.

Printed at the Industrial School for Crippled and Deformed Children, 241 St. Botolph St., Boston, Mass.

INDEX TO COUNTY COURT NOTE-BOOK. VOLUME V111.

ABBE 38
Abbot,Abbott 20,35
Abdel,Abdeel 6,15,36
Accor 35
Ackerson 41
Adams,Addams 3,7,18,19,21,47
Addison 6,15,23
Agnes 42
Albert 3
Alcock 41
Alexander 5,11,20,37,42,45
Allen 3,10,21,23,35,37,38,43,45
Allenthorp 37
Allerton 46
Allyn 25
Alsup
Andrews 6,35
Angell 3
Anderson 27,33,45
Annadall 30
Annesley 11
Annis 3
Arbuckle 35,38
Archer 11
Arkill 38
Armstrong 14,30
Arnold,Arnoll 13,33
Arrington 21
Arrison 42
Arthur 7
Askill 38
Astery 21
Atchison 45
Atkinson 34
Austen 47
Avias 38
Aylett 11
Ayres 3,45
(See also "Eyres")

BACONS 42
Badger 42
Bagdall 46
Bagwell 31,35,43
Bailes 27
Bailey,Baley 29,38,43
Baker 35,41
Ball 14,21
Ballard 30
Bathrop 30
Balston 21
Banbury 42
Banks 7,39
Bann 41
Barber 11
Barkamore 41
Barker 3
Barkley 14
Barksdale 38
Barlow 5,31
Barnes,Barns 35,43
Barnett 3
Barnhouse 42
Barrat 35
Barrow 7,27
Bartleet 22
Barton 14
Bass 31
Bassett 2
Bateman 41
Bates 30,37
Bathis (?) 41
Batsel,Batsil 14
Batson,Battson 23 29
Baxter 21
Bayley,Bayly 3,10,30,35
Baylis 37
Bear 39
Beavens 27,35
Bebbee 35
Beck 47
Beiry 41
Bell,Bells 6,15,38 45
Bellamy,Billamy 3
Belote,Beloat 6,23
Bembridge 45
Bennett 3,15,26,31,34,41,46
Benson 35
Benstone 35,43
Benthall,Bentall 6,15
Bentley 45
Benton 29
Berry 13,14,22,23,45
Betts 35
Bevins 21
Billingsley 19
Bingley 3
Bishop,Bushop 3,19,26,39
Black 31,35
Blackey 11
Blair,Blare 15,35,41
Blake 35,43
Blare 15,41
Blease 41
Boll de 33
Bolton 13
Bonhannon 6
Bonwell 35
Boone 20,37
Booth 29
Boots 29
Botts 37,45,46
Boughton 3
Bourne 47
Bowdoin 30,39,43
Bowen 10,13,22,42,45
Bowling 38,45
Bowman 37,41,43
Bowyer 3
Boyce 2
Bozman 9,18
Bradford 15,25,35
Braggett 18
Braughton 43
Brazier 6
Brent 21,37,45
Brickhouse 6
Bride 38
Bridwell 45,46
Brinkley 38
Bristoe 11

_Name occurs more than once on the page.

Britt 33
Brittingham 43
Brockenbrough 30
Broker,(Brokes(?) 23
Bromsall 3
Bronaugh 13,22
Brooks 46,47
Brort (?) 38
Brown 14,21,22,29,30,38,
39,45,46
Browning 33
Bruce 13
Bruly 21
Brunston 38
Bryan 3,15
Bryant,Bryand 21,37
Buckner 11,37
Bulford 39
Bull 15
Bullen 27
Bullock 21
Bully 37
Bunbury 21,45
Buntlin 15
Bundick,Bunduck 1,5,35
Burditt 3
Burgess 2,29
Burley (?) 19,21
Burn,Burns 19,46
Burrass 37
Burrock 35
Burrough,Burroughs,
Burrowes 35,47
Burton 35,39
Butler 3,5,15,21,22,37,
41
Butterfield 37
Bryam 45
Byswick 35

CABLE 39
Caddell 38
Cade 43
Cadrey 19
Cain 5
Caldwell 10
Call 14,39,45
Calmers 37
Calvert 11
Campbell,Cambell 39,43,
45,47
Campion 41
Canby 41
Cannon 29
Cant 3
Cantwell 42
Caple 22,23
Carefoot 21
Carey 11
Carlisle 29
Carneall 14
Carman 29
Carpenter 41,46
Carroll 10,11
Carson,Cason 10,11
Carter 14,37,46
Carty 41
Carver 33,46
Casely (?) 29
Cash 14
Catherwood 2
Catlett 21
Catton (?) 11
Causen 37
Care 21,37
Chace 23
Chadwell 37
Challie,Challis 11,26
Chambers 7,39
Champe 13,14,22
Chancey 43
Chandler 47
Chaplin 20
Chapman 38
Chapwell 43
Charlton 33
Charlwood 3
Chashey(?) 41
Cheaton 41
Cheesman (?) 11
Chesley 11
Chinn 27,46
Chismande (?) 19
Choat 47
Christian 39
Church 45
Chissell 46
Clarke,Clearke 6,11,
15,18,23,41
Clay,Clays 39
Cleag 22
Clemens 41
Clement,Clements 37,
39
Clifford 11,41
Clift 46
Clifton 18
Cloomer 3
Clough 46
Clynton 42
Cobb,Cobbs 11,15,27,
29,36
Cockayne 19
Cockey 2
Cockling 19
Coe 35
Coffee 6,39
Colclough,Colelough
21,37
Coldstream 21
Cole 41
Coleburn,Coulbourne
35,43
Colegate 29,47
Coleman,Colman 3,29
Collier 43
Collifor (?) 30
Collingworth 37
Collins,Collings 14,
21,38,41
Colony 43
Condon 11
Coniers 41
Conley,Conele 15,39
Connor 29
Conquest 31
Conyers 37
Cooke 3,37,41,42,43,
47
Cooper 3,6,30,46
Copes 43
Coppidge 29
Corby 29
Corduray 19
Core,Coar 6,15
Cormick 6
Cornelius 39
Costen 39
Coster 39
Cottrill 29
Count 37
Covenant 41
Coward 15
Cowdray 45
Cowley 14
Cox 27,35,42,46
Craford 37
Cragle 38
Cramer 3

Crawfurd,Crafford 38
Creston,Creaston 19
Crippen 20
Cronene 46
Crosby 37
Crosley 6
Cross,Crosse 11,37
Cully 21
Curry 21
Custis 6,10,21,23,35,43

DADE 46
Dafton 30
Dagg 21
Dameron 38
Daniell 18,46
Darby 15,41
Dare 19,42
Darrell 21
Dashill,Dashiell 9,31
Davis 1,3,&,11,18,21,23, 25,27,28,35,39,41,42
Dawe 42
Dawkins 15,31
Day,21,38
Deane 14,38,47
Deason 14
Delaney 39
Delpech 45
Deluke (?) 13
Demmit 15
Dennett 11
Denning 7
Dennis 6,34,39,42,43, 47
Derrick 37
Derrickson,Dirrickson 3, 10
De Young 41
Dickson,Dickeson 11,22, 41
Digges,Diggs 2,10
Dillecoat 36
Ditty 41
Dixon 9,39
Dobbins 3
Dobs 29
Dodd 14
Dodgin 30
Dolby 22,23,39
Dollingo 3
Donahue 47
Donelson 11,25,26
Doniphan 13,21,22,46
Donne 3
Dooly 41
Dorr 41
Dorson 46
Douglas 27
Douty 6
Dowing 15
Downing 15,27
Drake,Drakes 14,47
Drane 46
Drew 47Drewitt 11
Drighouse,Drigours 6, 19
Driskell,Dreskell 39
Drummond 31,41,42
Duff 14
Duffey 47
Duke 11
Dunaway 46
Duncan 9,10,37
Dunne,Dun 11
Dunston 15
Dunton 6,22,23,39,45
Du Parks 39
Durham 3
Duall,Dial 19,21
Dyer 2,18

EAGER 47
Eason 19
Eborne 43
Edgcombe 3
Edge 21
Edlow 11
Edmonds,Edmons 6
Edmund 45
Edrington 30,46
Edwards 15,38
Edy 41
Elkin 14
Ellegood 33,39,45
Ellinore 41
Elliot,Elliott 6,25, 37,39
Ellis 41,47
Elliston 22
Elzey 21
Emerson 42
Emery 29
English 21
Ennals,Enalds 11,29
Ennis 28,42
Epes 47
Esham,Eshon,Essome 3,6,22,39
Eskridge 23
Evans,Evens 6,18,22, 23,38,39,41,47
Everett,Everit 29
Ewell 2,37
Ewing,Yewing 19
Eyre,Eyres 22,27

FARDON (?) 7
Fant 46
Far (?) 7
Farfar 47
Farguson 13,14
Farmer 38
Farnsworth 23
Fathrey,Fathery 23, 39
Fawcett,Fassit, Faucet 10,26,29, 42
Fear,Feere 11,41
Fearson 37
Feilding 27
Fellows (?) 11
Felton 3
Fen 7
Fendall 41
Fennel 46
Fenwick 21
Feverstone (?) 41
Figg 37
File 38
Fines 46
Finning 21
Firkettle,Furketel 20,39
Fisk 37
Fisher 3,6,19,23, 36,37,41
Fishpool 30
Fitchett 39,45
Fitzgerald 6,38
Fitzhugh 37,46,47
Fletcher 5,6,38,42, 45,46
Flood 13
Florence 41
Floyd,Floid 6,13,21, 36,38,39,45,47
Flouracres 46

Fluell,Fuell 41
Foley 11
Folis,Folio 20
Folkes (?) 3
Fooke,Fookes 41,42
Foot 21
Forbes 27
Foreman 7
Foster 1,25,38,43
Fowke 37,46
Fox 6,11,15,27,30
Fraise 36
Frame 19
Franklin,Francklin 41,43
Fraser,Frazer 2,23
Freeman 11
Freke 41
French 13,22,37,46
Freshwater 39
Fristoe 46
Frost 45
Fry 14
Fryer 38
Fuel 41
Fluell 41
Fuller 15
Furnish 2

GLADSTONE 41
Gaither 29
Galloway,Gallaway 7,46
Gardner 19,42,47
Garner 19,21,46
Garris 15
Gascoine 23
Gandy 45
George 27,37
Gerrard 21
German,Jerman 26
Gethinge 42
Gibbons,Gibbine 3,23
Gibbs 7
Gibson,Gybson 5,11,22,
27
Giddens 6
Gilchrist 35
Giles 21
Gill,22,23
Gillan 9
Gillett 43
Gillian 38
Gilloc 41
Gilson 21
Girringe 3
Gist 45
Glascock 11
Glendenning 22,30
Glover 15,41
Glower 41
Glumper 37
Godfrey 19
Goff 36
Goffagon,Goffegon,39,
45
Goin 21
Golding 14
Goldman 27
Goldsborough 19
Goldsmith 41
Gonteer 41
Good 21
Goodrich 33
Goodwin 7,11,45
Gootee 18
Gore 35
Gosse 41
Gouch 3
Gough 46
Goulding 30
Gower 41
Gowry 21
Goynes 15
Grafford 38
Graggs 42
Grant 13,22,37
Graves 39
Gray 5,6,21,41
Greecion (?) 30
Green,Greene 13,15,38,
41,47
Greenfield 9
Gregg 21,37
Gregory,Grogery 38,41
Grey 3,31
Grice 1
Griffin 30,38,42,45
Griffith 11,37,39
Griggs 11,38
Grigsby,Gregsby 5,37,
46
Grimes 42
Grisser 42
Grizzle,Grizzel 38
Gugoll 3
Guilbert,Guybert 19
Gunby 34,43
Gunnell 23
Gunter 3
Guy 46
Gwarkin (?) 21

HACK 31
Hackley 13,22,30
Hackworth 42
Haddon 18,41
Haggoman 23
Hales 21
Hall 3,21,22,30,35,
39,41
Haller 41
Halling 21
Halliwell 41
Ham 3
Hambler 11,18
Hanby 46
Hancock 3,18
Handley 37
Handy 3,43
Hanes 23,38
Hanks 21
Hansbrough 46
Hansford 18,19
Hanson 15
Hapworth 42
Hardicke 3
Harding 27,38,46
Hardy,Hardie 6,23
Hares 38
Harlington 19
Harmanson 1,39,45
Harper 22
Harris 15,19,29,31,
41
Harrison 3,6,13,14,
19,21,27,46
Harrod 37
Hart 3,38,41
Hartfield,Harfield
18
Hartwell 18
Harvey 7,41
Harward 27
Harwood 5,11,19,27,
29,42,46
Hassell 21
Hastings 38
Hatton 19
Hawkenett 41

Hawkins 19,21,39
Hawkshead 41
Hawle 38
Hay 23,37,45
Hayes 6,18,42
Hayly 41
Haynie
Hayward,Heyward 3,11,18,
35,37
Heabberd 37
Heath,Heat 15,21,46
Hebb 46
Hebron 46
Hem,Henn 15
Hemsley 19,46
Henderson 6,15
Henen 37
Henn,Hem 15
Hepbourn 29,46
Hepron
Herdman 21
Hern 47
Hernly 14,15
Hewes 27
Hewett,Hewitt,Huitt 13,
18,21,30,37,38,42,46
Heynes 18
Hibbett 37
Hickman 3,35
Hicks 29
Higdon 38
Higgison,Higgerson 3,
37
Highlander 30
Hill 1,18,27,28,30,39,
41,42,46,47
Hitchens 15
Hixon 23
Hoard 46
Hodge 3
Hodgson,Hudgson 3
Hoells 38
Holding 3
Holdsworth 13
Holladay 3
Holland 10
Holley 30
Hollman 18
Holmead 12
Holt 19,23
Hoocks 41
Hood 22
Hooe 21
Hooper 21
Hoops 30
Hopkins 3,10,11,21,26,
31,46
Hore 37
Horney 46
Horsey 18
Horton 46
Hoskins 29
Hough 10,25,26,27,34
Howle 38
How 36,42
Howard 2,43
Howles 18
Howlett 21
Houson 28
Hoyle,Hoyl 14,22
Hubbard,Huberd 11
Hubbert 27
Hudson,Hudgson 3,22,
33,38,47
Hudspeath
Hudsters
Hughes,Hues 3,27,38,
42
Huit,see Hewitt
Humphrey,Humpries 27,
38,46
Humston 21
Hunt 47
Hurd,Hurt 11,18
Hurley 47
Hurst 37
Huston 43
Hutcheson 47
Hyde 3

ILLINGWORTH 22
Inkson (?) 38
Innis 23,46
Isdall 6
Isham(see also Esham)
39,45
Israell 29

JACKSON 11,15,41,46
Jacobs,Jacob 6,15,22,
23,39,45,46
James 14,15,21,33,41,
42
Jamison 3
Jarmin,German 26
Jarvis,Jervis 1,35,39
Jason,Jason 7,42
Jeffries,Jeffrice
37
Jenifer 17
Jenkins,Jenekin 3,
34,35
Jenkinson 19
Jennings 30,41
Jewer 21
Johnson 3,6,15,20,
21,22,23,26,27,
33,34,36,38,41,
42,45
Joll,Jell (?) 3
Jolley 7
Jones 3,15,22,27,
37,38,39,41,42,
45,47
Jordan 7
Joyner 22,39,41
Joynes,Goynes 15,39
Justice 35

KENNARD,29
Kay 13
Kecy (?) 47
Keene 37
Keibler 3
Kellam 15,35,36
Kelly 29,38
Kems 39
Kencken 18
Kendall 1,27,30,39,
45,46
Kennedy 7
Kennon 31
Kenny 46
Kent 3,21
Kenyon 14
Kerr 22,30
Key 38
Kibble 3,18
Kimble 29
King 5,19,21,22,38,
46
Kinker 23
Kirby 23
Kirke 3,18,19,37,
46
Kitching,Ketching
37,46
Knight,Knite 3,15,
38,47

Knox 45

LALER 15
Lane 10,35,37
Langford,Lankford 34
Langham 3
Larke 19
Latimer 29
Laurence,Larance 3,15,
41
Lawson 27
Layer 37
Layfield 9
Leake 27
Leatherbury 31,43
Le Baron 4
Lee,3,38,46
Legg,Ledg 29
Lehore 37
Leichfeiles (?) 41
Leitch 21
Lemaster,Limaister 29,
46
Lendall 41
Leonard 36
Lertch 42
Letchey 42
Letchworth 19
Lewar 41
Lewis 1,3,6,30,39,42,
46
Linck 21
Lincoln,Linkhorne 5,38
Linton 3,21,22,37
Little 6
Littleton 10,17
Lobdenne 41
Lock 22,29,30,46
Locker 29
Loffland 39
Lofting 9
Long 10,26,35,43
Loveday 41
Lowder 25
Lowe 46
Lowell 3
Lucas 3
Lucke 41
Luckett 41
Luell 41
Luker 39,47
Lumley 46
Lund,Lun 37,45
Lunsford 46
Luty 41
Lynch 39
Lynn 46

McCARTHY(?) 37
MacCarty 47
McDaniel 2
McDowall 47
McGill 21
Mackgowry 29
Magruder 19
McGuy 23
McHenry 7
McKemie 35
Mackenny 45
McMalion,Mackmehorn 15
McPheerson 37
Macheele 33
Machen 41
Maddison 3,41
Magtough 38
Major,Mager 3,15,41,45
Man 41
Mandowell 7
Manning 41
Maples 41
Mapp,Map 23,45
Marley,Marle 41
Marrequille 31
Marret 29
Marsh 41
Marshall 6,13,14,21,23,
37,43,47
Marster (?) 41
Martin,Marten 19,31,38,
41,46
Mary 41
Mason 3,21,27,37,41
Massey,Massie 21,35,
37,43
Massury 7
Mathews,Matthews,
Mathew 19,37,46
Maulain,Mauland 29
Maulpiss 37
Mauzy,Mawsay 21,46
Maw (?) 3
Max 41
Maxwell 31,47
May,Maye 3,47
Mayniadier 19
Mealy 37
Meares 41
Medcalfe 3
Meech 30
Meese 37
Mells 41
Mercer 3,46
Mercham (?) 39
Meredith,Merridith
3
Merrick 42
Merrill 38,43
Merritt 3,29
Merse 38
Merywether 41
Messingo (?) 46
Methew 37
Michael 35,41
Middleton 41
Milby 15
Milemayo (?) 21
Miller 29
Milligan 34
Milliken 36
Millington 1
Mills 31,39,42
Millward 2
Minithorn 21
Minstrell 3
Minton 30
Mitchell 3,29,41
Mode 18
Molt 27
Money 19
Monk,Munk 23,45
Monnet,Monnette 5,
8,24,32
Monroe 30
Montague 3
Montaigne 3
Montgomery 41
Moody 18
Moon,Moun 23,30,38
Moore,Moor 3,6,39
Moreland 9,11
Morfrey 41
Morgan 1,11,45
Morison 14
Morley 3
Morris,Morrice 3,

10,25,26,27,31,33, 34,41,42,47
Morrough 10
Moseley,Mosley 37
Moss,Mosse 21,37,42,46
Mountjoy 46
Mumford 22
Munday 11
Murphey 21
Murray 21
Muth 41

NACKWORTH 42
Nairn,Nearne 10,34,42, 43
Nash 25
Naylor 22
Neale,Neall 3,19,27
Needles 19
Nelson 3
Nevell 1
Newman 3,7
Newport 29
Newton 33,35,46
Nichols,Nicholls 3,14
Noden 29
Norman 42
North 3
Norton 3
Nottingham 6,13,15,23
Noyes 25
Nugent 14
Nutt 31
Nutter 42,43

O'DEAR 39
O'Kelly 3
Oliver 25
O'Neale 37
Osborne 1,2,11,17
Ouldham 47
Overhall 21

PAGE 11
Palmer 3,41
Panton,Ponton 37,42
Paramore,Parimore,etc. 15,43,47
Parke (?) 3
Parker 31,35,41,43,47
Parkes 9
Parkman 25
Parr 41
Parsons 37
Partlett 41
Pate 37
Patermaster 3
Patman 3,15
Patrick 20,26
Pattern 39
Patterson 23
Paure 37
Payne,Pain,Peane 13,14, 22,23,27,41
Payton,Peyton 21,30,46
Peacock 3
Pead 18
Pearce 27,29
Pearson 37
Peirce 11
Pemberton 26
Penn 29
Penny 37
Perdew (?) 29
Perrin 42
Perry 39
Persey 3
Peters 41
Pettit,Pettet 22,33,39, 41,45
Petygrew 15
Peynton 3
Peyton,Payton 21,30,46
Phebin 39
Phillips 6,29,37
Philpott 29
Phiney 36
Phips 41
Pictoe (?) 21
Pierpont 2
Pigge 3,41
Pigott 39
Pike 31
Pilcher 13,21,46
Pinder 19
Pinkstone 23
Piper 10
Pitcher 13
Pitt,Pitts,Pits 6,15, 35
Pittman 2
Plaice 42
Pleasant 23
Plover 11
Polk 42
Pollard 46
Pollock 3
Poor,Poore 29,41
Pope 41
Porch 14
Port 3
Porter 3,18,21.34, 37,39,46
Posey 29
Pott,Potts 31,41
Potter 41
Pottpowler 3
Powell 3,6,22,23,37, 38,43,45,47
Power,Powers 27,38
Poynter 38
Pratt 6,13,27,33
Prebit (?) 37
Preeson 43
Presley 30
Preston 41
Prestredge 37
Price 3,18,22,35,42, 46
Pritchett 38
Proffit 3
Prosser 41
Purnall 26

QUARLES 21

RACKLIFFE 2
Ragan 29
Raily,Raley 21,29
Raignalt 41
Ralls 46
Ramesay,Ramsey 10, 21
Randall 47
Rascoe,Rasco 22,39
Tasor,Rason 45
Ratcliff 46
Rawlins 29,37
Ray 3
Rayman 3
Raymond 2
Read 5
Reddish,Reddick 37, 46
Reed 2,37
Reid 14,45
Rendan 22
Revell 41
Reynolds,Rennolds 6, 41

Rhymes 21
Ricaud 47
Rice 6
Rich 3
Richards 38
Richardson 13,14,15,41,
42,46
Richeson 41
Rickard 10
Rickson (?) 3
Ridgely 2,3
Rigby 41
Riggs,Rigs 15,41
Riley,Royley 30,37
Rippen 45
Roach,Rooh 2,19,41
Roan 6
Roberson 27
Roberts,Robert 3,6,15,
22,23,35,39,42,45,47
Robertson 46
Robins 6,17,19,42
Robinson 3,10,30,35,38,
39,42
Robison,Robbison 41
Roe 29
Rogers,Rodgers 15,42,46
Rolleson 2
Rose 15,46
Ross 29,31,46
Rosser 3,22
Round,Rounds 2,10
Rountree 38
Row 30
Rowen 46
Rowing (?) 27
Rowley 14
Rowzey 6
Rush 14
Rutland 21
Rutler (?) 21
Ryen 45

SACKER 35
Salmon 28,41
Salt 6
Salter 42
Sampton (?) 39
Samuels 46
Sanders 19,23,30,39,41,
46
Sandes (?) 39
Satchell 6,45
Saton (?) 41
Sattathwaite 7
Saunders 27
Savage 6,15,36,39,45
Savary 3
Savatt 42
Scafe 41
Scarburgh,Scarborough
5,17,31,35,42,43
Scasbrook 11
Scott 2,6,7,12,21,23,
31,37,41,46
Sear (?) 42
Seaton 37
Seddon 46
Seers 13
Selby 26,43
Sele 29
Serrin (?) 39
Settle 29
Sewall,Sewell 3,19,46
Sewick 3
Seymour 2,39
Shackleford 3
Sharp 21,45
Shaw 41
Shea,She 41
Shekell 2
Shelton 30,38
Shepard,Sheppard 37,41
Sherman 3
Sherwood 3,19
Shewell 28
Shield,Shields 21,30
Shippen 30
Shockley 2
Short 21,39
Shuite(?) 42
Silverton 3
Simpson 13,22,30,35,41,
47
Sims,Simmes 6,30,38
Sipson 37
Sisson 41
Skinker 22
Skirven,Skervin 10,26,
46
Slade 7
Slattor 3
Slaughter 39
Slingoe 26
Smart 10,17,37,42
Smaw 39
Smith 2,3,5,6,7,15,
18,19,22,27,28,
30,33,36,39,41,
43,46
Smithson 42
Smock 2
Smythe 30
Snead 35,43,47
Sole (?) 29
Somers 2
Sorle 41
Soughton (?) 2
Spady 39
Speak,Speake 2,12,
30
Speare 30
Spence 10,26,27
Spencer 20
Spiltimber 3
Spires 38
Spratlen 22
Spring 7
Spritt 3
Spurstow 33
Stacy 38,42
Stakes 15
Stannop 19
Stanton 37
Stark 46
Starling 47
Stephens 41,42
Stephenson 3
Sterling 2
Steth 46
Stevens 2,39
Steward 11
Stewart 5
Stigler 13,22
Stitchell 2
Stockdell 2
Stockley,Stoakley
1,2,27,33,35,39
Stone 1,13,22,30,31,
46,47
Stonem (?) 2
Stradburn 21
Stratton 27,41
Strawbridge 2,5
Streckley,Streckly
6,27
Stribling 22
Strickland 19
Stringer 45

Strother 22,30
Stuart 46
Stulcoat 46
Sturdy (?) 46
Sturgis 2
Suckett 41
Summers 21,23,34
Surtree 38
Sutherland 45
Swain 2
Swann 41
Swearingen 20
Sweet 22
Sweten 22
Syme 30

TAIT 30
Talbot 18
Taliaferro 14,23
Tansey (?) 47
Tapley 45
Tarr 3
Tarvy 41
Tasker 41
Tatum 22,45
Taylor,Tayloe 3,6,10,13,14,22,30,31,33,41,43,46,47
Tazewell 39
Teackle 43
Teall (?) 47
Terrill 30
Terry,Turry 6,42
Thatcher 14,30,46
Thomas 6,22,29,38,_42_
Thompkins 45
Thompson 6,11,29,30,38
Thomson 23
Thornbury 30
Thornton 14,22,_23_,29,30,31
Thoroughgood 38
Thorpe 11
Thrift 19
Tibbells,Tebuls 19
Tiller 14,22
Tilley 11
Tilney 15
Timmons 21
Tingee 3,19
Tinsley 22
Tiplady 11
Tipton 29
Todd 21,29,37
Toft 11,17
Tolman 39
Tomson,Tompson,Tomison 13,_39_
Tonnard (?) 19
Tooke 41
Torrence 3
Toward 37
Townroe (?) 46
Townsend 2,3,21,41
Tracey 3
Train 3
Travers,Traverse 21,22,23
Treaton 3
Triplett 22,23
Trottan 47
Troup 6
Trower,Trowers 39,45
Tucker 2,3,19,22
Tull 3
Tunnell 34
Turberville 22
Turley (?) 39
Turner 13,_14_,_15_,19,_22_,_41_
Turnstall 5
Turville 3
Tutt _14_
Twiford 22
Tyler 46

UNDERHILL 39
Underwood 3,14,42

VALENTINE 18
Valliant 46
Vaughan,Vahane 3,42
Veil 38
Vickar,Vickers 21,29
Vigerous 18,28

WADDINGTON 21
Wade 3,18,38
Walden 46
Wale 2,3
Walker 3,_18_,_27_,38,41
Wallace 5,7,18
Waller 37,38,41,46
Wallis 38,46
Walms 19
Walmsley 29
Walsk 7
Walter,Walters 4,46
Waltons 41
Ward 15,_18_,21,29
Warden 30
Ware 6,14,29
Warner 3,37
Warren,Worren 10,33,_39_,42
Warrenton 6
Wars 41
Washington 21,_37_,46
Waterfield 6,22,39
Watkins 7
Watson 1,18,35,39,41
Watter 37
Watton 3
Watts,Wats 10,21,27,34,42
Wauoklin (?) 30
Waugh 21,_37_,36
Wayman 21
Weatherly 18
Webb 27,39,42,47
Weeks 31
Weer (?) 18
Welburne 17
Wells _37_,46
Weskett _15_
West 3,5,37,41
Whalend 18
Whaples 2
Wharton 22
Wheatly 47
Wheeler 2,18,37,41,46
White 3,10,11,14,_15_,_18_,22,23,29,_30_,_38_,39,_41_,46
Whiteman 22
Whitson 37
Whittingham 18
Whittington _1_,_9_,_10_,_17_,23,_25_,_26_,_27_,_33_,42,43,46
Widgeon,Widggen 6,_39_,45
Widdrington 19
Wigg 41
Wiggins 41
Wigginton 37
Wikell 41
Wilde 7

Wildman 34
Wiles 19
Wilkins 45
Wilkinson 7,20
Will 7
Williams 2,6,14,<u>18</u>,21,
<u>23</u>,31,39,41,<u>42</u>,<u>46</u>
Williamson 41
Willett 39
Willis 3,18,36,46
Wills 41
Wilson 5,15,18,19,21,30,
31,<u>39</u>,<u>42</u>,<u>37</u>
Wimble,Wimboll 31,41
Winder 31
Windle,Windly <u>7</u>
Wing 22
Winget 39
Winson 29
Wisdom 11
Wishart <u>34</u>
Witchell 41
Withers 14,37
Witten 31
Wolson,Wollson 46
Wood 2,<u>41</u>,42
Woodbridge 33
Woodland 18
Woodrow 46
Woodside 30
Woodward 31,42
Woolridge 37
Worrell,Worrall 3
Worrin 45
Worsdale,Wordeel 14
Worsham 7
Wraxall 30
Wray 42
Wren 14,30
Wright 7,27,31,33,46
Wrightson 46
Wyatt 31
Wynne 7

YATES 46
Yewing 19
Young 3,7,21,<u>23</u>,31,39,
<u>41</u>,45,46

The

County Court Note-Book

A Little Bulletin of History and Genealogy

February, 1930. **Vol. IX, No. 1**

PROBATES AND ADMINISTRATIONS ROCKINGHAM COUNTY, VIRGINIA

From the first Minute or Scratch Book of the Court. The Orders were lost during the Civil War.

HUGH DIVES [?] will; proved by James Bly and John Reli [? Riley?] William Dives, extr, takes oath. 27 Apr 1778.

GEORGE McVEY; admn his estate to James McVey, his brother. 28 Apr 1778.

SAMUEL MEGANT [MEYGERT?] admn his estate to his widow, Catherine. 28 Apr 1778.

ANDREW HULING; admn his estate to his widow, Catherine, and James Huling, his son. 28 Apr 1778.

CHRISTIAN MILLER; admn his estate to widow Catherine Miller. 25 May 1778.

BRYAN BREEDEN; admn his estate to widow, Elizabeth Breeden. John Breeden was son and heir-at-law. 26 May 1778.

ALEX. HERRING; will proved. Whereupon Abigail Herring, Alex'r and Jess Herring, the extrs, give bond. 22 June 1778.

JNO. RI.........[?] will proved by wit. William Dunlop and Ann Riffe [?] extrs obtain probate. 24 Aug 1778.

THO. WILMOT; will produced. Witnesses Geo. Hanmer and Mary his wife to be summoned to prove an administration of estate of John Cravens, to Mary Cravens widow and Robt Cravens his brother. [It would seem that there is a confusion here of two records.] 24 Aug 1778.

JOST HINCKLE; will. Proved by Joseph Cheveront, one of the witnesses. The other witness, Philip Harper, to be examined. 24 Aug 1778.

JOHN FULTON; will proved by John Hopkins, Jr. and James Brown. Jesse Harrison and John Fulton, extrs. 24 Aug 1778.

WILLIAM LEMARR; admn his estate to James Bair, creditor. 24 Aug 1778.

JOHN CLOVERFIELD. Admn his estate to Felix Gilbert, a creditor 24 Aug 1778.

ROBERT BELSHA; will. Proved by Jno. Davidson, one of the wit. 24 Aug 1778. Further proved by oath of Joseph Hancock. 28 Sept 1778.

JAMES MARSHALL. Will proved by wit. Elizabeth Marshall and John Thomas, extrs. 24 Aug 1778.

THOS. WILMOT. Will proved by George Hamner and Mary Hammer [Hamner]. Mary Wilmot, the extx refuses. Admn to Thos. Wilmot with will annexed. 29 Sept 1778.

FAMILIES OF THE EASTERN SHORE THE WHITTINGTONS

(*Eighth instalment*)

WILLIAM WHITTINGTON, Gent., "formerly of Somerset but now of Accomack" (Wor. Md. B-104, 26 Aug 1748) who has been shown in previous issues of the NOTE-BOOK to represent the senior line of the WHITTINGTONS, left several children, but his son WILLIAM WHITTINGTON (IV), evidently died early, before his father and his mother. (See deeds to land at Occacomson previously given.) His, the fourth WILLIAM'S wife was ELIZABETH, as shown by records mentioned hereafter, which refer to her second husband, BENTON HARRIS. Her family name has not been found by this compiler.

That WILLIAM (IV) was born before 1719, is shown by a record in Worcester, Maryland (M. H. iii-83) in which he is mentioned as a son of WILLIAM of Accomack, Va., and a grandson of Lt. Col. WILLIAM WHITTINGTON. The date of his death can only be approximated by the Accomack deeds which have been given.

WILLIAM (IV) left one son, WILLIAM (V) who is mentioned in the will of his grandmother, ELIZABETH (TAYLOR) WHITTINGTON, as shown heretofore. He was under age in 1756, or just at age, when BENTON HARRIS presents his account of guazdianship. (Acco. xxv0-151. 31 Aug 1756.) HARRIS' will may be found in a suit in chancery 10 Nov 1790. (Annap. Chanc'y xxi-400.) In this will he leaves legacies to WILLIAM WHITTINGTON, "son of WILLIAM my son-in-law"........."to my dear friend WILLIAM WHITTINGTON'S now deceased his son WILLIAM WHITTINGTON, being born after his said father's death." In the course of the suit Littleton Dennis deposes that in the latter part of July, 1788, JOHN-ROUSBY WHITTINGTON, son of WILLIAM of Worcester, died at the Warm Springs, Berkeley county, Virginia, and William Stevens deposes that HARRIS and wife have been dead above two years. Further testimony shows that JOHN-ROUSBY WHITTINGTON died unmarried.

Another record (1769), specifically refers to WILLIAM (V) as grandson and heir-at-law of ELIZABETH TAYLOR who married WILLIAM WHITTINGTON........."both now deceased." (Acco. Diii-666.)

WILLIAM WHITTINGTON (V) married MARY KING.

Curiously enough this marriage and the previous one of WILLIAM WHITTINGTON (IV) are proved after the deaths of the two WILLIAMS, one by the stepfather's gifts, and the other by a gift from the mother, and by her validation of the conveyance of a negro girl, whom WILLIAM (V) then called of Worcester, had given bond to Samuel Hopkins. MARY-KING WHITTINGTON, as widow and executrix releases. (Wor. Md. 20 Feby 1770. H-208.)

WILLIAM WHITTINGTON (V) died between May 1768 and December 1769. The time between the making and the probate will be noted, and it will be seen that the infant unnamed was one of two sons, the second of whom was born after his father's death.

WILLIAM WHITTINGTON, of Worcester cty, Md. Will.

- Wife Mary-King, one-third of Double Purchase, Addition to Double Purchase, and Whittington's Meadow;
- Son JOHN-ROUSBY WHITTINGTON, not yet baptized;
- Step-father Benton Harris;
- Mother Betty Harris;
- Cousins Thomas Martin, son of James, and John Martin, son of John;
- Cousin Southy-Littleton Whittington, or Littleton Whittington, son of Southy-Littleton Whittington, who now lives in Virginia, lands called Sandy Wharf, Baltimore's Gift, and part of Sikes' Island;
- Cousin Nancy Martin, father "W. W.," Dolly Martin, Esther Hall, wife of Richard, mentioned;
- Wife, executrix. (Annap. xxxvii-537. 15 May 1768-13 Dec 1769.)

Wit: Neil McMullen, Sam'l Smyly, Polly Richardson, John Jenkinson.

[In the Annapolis record the date of probate appears to be 13th of December. In the Worcester record the name of the wife of Richard Hall is illegible.]

SOUTHY-LITTLETON WHITTINGTON, referred to in this will, appears in Accomack in a suit, in 1768. (Acco. xxx0-115.)

MARY-KING WHITTINGTON files the will and gives bond, 13 Dec 1769. (Annap. T. P. xliii-463.) Littleton Dennis and George Hayward, securities. Bond £1500 ster. The 3 Jany 1775, (Wor., Md. I-539) she makes a deed of gift, consideration love and affection, to son WILLIAM, "an infant born after the death of his father, WILLIAM WHITTINGTON, and not provided for by his father's will." And the court of Worcester county, the 14 Oct 1778, makes William Handy guardian of JOHN-ROUSBY WHITTINGTON, about ten years old, and of WILLIAM WHITTINGTON, about eight years old. (J. W. xv-36.)

An additional return of the inventory of WILLIAM WHITTINGTON, of Worcester, dec'd, is made by WILLIAM HANDY and wife MARY, extrs of WILLIAM WHITTINGTON. "Then came WILLIAM HANDY who inter. married with the executrix of WILLIAM WHITTINGTON, late of Worcester, dec'd." (Wor-Inv. 1762-1783, p. 359. Inv. ret'd 24 Feby 1781.)

WILLIAM WHITTINGTON (V), is shown, therefore, to have left two sons:

JOHN-ROUSBY WHITTINGTON and
WILLIAM WHITTINGTON (VI).

JOHN-ROUSBY WHITTINGTON lived to be only 20 or 21, for we have his will, made 29 Feby 1788 and probated 9 Jany 1789, as well as the deposition as to his death in Virginia. And he died unmarried.

His will provides that land which his father, WILLIAM WHITTINGTON, devised to him by will, should go to his brother WILLIAM WHITTINGTON. To his father-in-law, William Handy, he gives part of a legacy "*bequeathed to me by Benton Harris, deceased.*" To his mother, MARY-KING HANDY, wife of said William, the residue of the legacy. Mentions the children of William and MARY-KING HANDY, Robert, Samuel, Levin, Gertrude, makes "father-in-law" William Handy, extr. Wit: Anne Dennis, Nancy x Butler, John Done [?] (Wor. J. W. xiii-232.)

The compiler has not carried out the line of WILLIAM (VI) the brother, and does not, at this writing, know if he survived and married.

The second son of WILLIAM WHITTINGTON (III) and ELIZABETH TAYLOR, was JOSHUA WHITTINGTON, but this line has also not been carried out. His marriage to ELIZABETH NAIRN or NAIRNE, dau. of ROBERT, is shown by the latter's will..........To "daughter ELIZABETH WHITTINGTON, debt of £20 due me by her husband, JOSHUA," also gives her a sum of money beside this. (Wor., Md. J. W. iii-88. 21 Jany 1761-3 Feby 1764.) The same will mentions his daughter ESTHER WHITTINGTON. It is known by the will of JOHN "NEARN", brother to ELIZABETH and ESTHER, that JOSHUA had children WILLIAM, ESTHER, BETTY and MOLLY. This was previous to 1771. (Annap. records, xxxviii-640.)

The third son of WILLIAM WHITTINGTON (III) of Accomack, and wife ELIZABETH TAYLOR, was SOUTHY. He remained in Accomack, having received the estate as shown heretofore, which would have belonged to his elder brother WILLIAM. A record of 1 Oct 1765, to SOUTHY WHITTINGTON, of Accomack, son of WILLIAM WHITTINGTON and wife ELIZABETH, dec'd, recites possession by said WILLIAM and wife, in right of wife, to 400 acres at Ockohonson [*sic*] where they lived, being one-third of a tract devised by William Anderson to his three eldest granddaughters.........and being so seized said WILLIAM and ELIZABETH conveyed to Isaac Morris in trust for the use of themselves, the said WILLIAM and ELIZABETH, and then to and for the use of said

SOUTHY WHITTINGTON. This conveyance vests absolute estate in SOUTHY WHITTINGTON. (Acco. Diii.)

The will of SOUTHY WHITTINGTON, is dated 3 Aug 1789, and probated 27 Oct 1790.

He mentions wife Ann; son George, son Arthur, dau. Elizabeth Nicholson and her two eldest daus., Ann and Arcadia. Dau. Hannah Blake, dau. Gartrude Whittington. Wife and son George, extrs. Wit: Thos. Abbott, Wm. Ewell, Jr., Edward Taylor. (Acco. Va., xxxixW.)

The inventory of his estate was returned 7 Dec 1790. (xliiW-159.) And the account and settlement 27 Feby 1795. (See also xliiO-184.)

With this generation, then, the fourth from Capt. WILLIAM WHITTINGTON, of Northampton, Virginia, we come to at least a temporary break in the line of WILLIAMS and SOUTHYS of Virginia. As this collection of notes was made largely to disentangle the numerous WILLIAMS and SOUTHYS (about whom nobody agreed) the foregoing will only be followed by a few brief notes showing that these names continued to identify the family in Maryland.

AUTHENTIC REFERENCES FOR INFERRED MARRIAGES

(From the records of York county, Virginia)

Mr. THOMAS HARWOOD and LYDIA CHEESMAN, widow and admx of Capt. Edward CHEESMAN. Before 14 Apr 1683. vi-505. She is also mentioned as the daughter of Mrs. Eliz: Bushrod. (see vi-95. 24 June 1679.)

ROBERT HIDE and the *extx of Mrs. Mary Clapton*. Before Jany [?] 1679. vi-177.

Mr. HENRY HARTWELL and the admx of Col. Wm. WHITE. Before 24 Oct 1683. vi-524.

JOHN INSWORTH and ELIZABETH FIGG, widow. Before 27 Aug 1661. iii-128.

TOBIAS LOVE and .... DAVIS. dau. of Elias. Before 22 Nov 1688. 1687-1691, p. 334.

THOMAS LULLING [?] and the relict of John GRIGGS. Before 24 Mch 1678. vi-83.

JEREMIAH LAUNDY [?] and JANE WADE, dau. of Edward. Before 9 Nov 1675. vi-12.

MR. EDWARD LOCKEY and ELIZABETH HANSFORD, widow of John. Before 24 Oct 1663. iv-66.

ROBERT MARTIN and ELIZABETH REYNOLDS, widow of Thomas. Before 24 Jany 1682. vi-444.

WILLIAM MANSFIELD and MARY, the relict of Charles ALLEN. About or before 1691 or 1692. i-145.

JAMES MOORE and ELIZABETH GRIGGS, dau. of John, dec'd. Before 24 July 1689. viii-298.

DAN'LL MACKENTOSH and the extx of Francis KISTON. Before or about the 24 Mch 1696. xi-375.

THOMAS MEEKINS of James City cty, and FRANCES HURD, one of the daus. of Maurice AURD. Before 23 Sept 1701. x-329.

ALEXANDER MACKDANIELL and ELLINOR PRICKETT, widow of Henry. Before 24 October 1701. xii-520.

JOHN MATTHEWS and the relict of Thos. ISLES, dec'd. Before 24 Apr 1678. vi-36.

Mr. THO: MOUNTFORD and JANE, the surviving extx of Col. John SCASBROOK. Before 10 Dec 1683. vi-539.

WILLIAM PATTISON and the extx of Edward JENKINS. Before 24 Jany 1683. vi-544.

JAMES PARDOE and MARY the relict of Tho: BEMINS [?] Before 24 Feby 1680. vi-291. See vi-223. Before 24 June 1680.

Capt. MARTIN PALMER and the relict of Capt. Wm. CORBEN. Before 14 Jany 1677. vi-37.

Mr. MARTIN PALMER and the widow of Capt. William COCKER. Before 26 Aug 1678. vi-45. See vi-36. COCKE?

Capt. MARTIN PALMER and the relict of Capt. Richard CROWSHAW. Before 10 Dec 1677. vi-27.

Capt. MARTIN PALMER and the admx of Dr. Thomas ROBINS. Before the 26 Aug 1678. vi-45, 69, 78. [Note: It is probable that these widows were all one person and that Capt. Palmer was her fifth venture.]

.... PRICE and MARY HUDSON, widow. Before 26 Oct 1670. 1664-1672, p. 261.

SEMOR POWELL and ELIZ'TH TIPLADY, dau. John. Before 25 Mch 1700. x-306.

WILLIAM PATTISON and ANN ROW, dau. of Micheall. Probably before 27 June 1684. vi-624.

WILLIAM PATTISON and Mrs. HANNAH JACKSON, widow of Henry, Before or about 24 April 1683. vi-501.

THOMAS REYNOLDS, of Queen's Creek, and SUSAN SNEAD, dau. of Samuell. Before 28 Mch 1652. i-35.

THO: ROGERS and ANN DENNET, one of the daus. of Thomas, dec'd. Before 24 Aug 1680. ii-236.

ROBERT ROBERTS and the relict of Edward PAYNE. Before or about 1679. vi-151.

ROBERT ROBERTS and ....MAN, widow. [She had dau. Eve.] Before 10 Dec 1683. vi-534.

SAMUEL SMITH and JOANE GARLINGTON, admx and relict of Mr. Christ. GARLINGTON, of Northumberland cty. 10 Jany 1679. vi-200.

JOHN SCASBROOK prob. m. Mrs. ELIZABETH BUSHROD, widow. [Uncertain from this record.] Before 24 June 1679. vi-96.

Lt. Coll. SCASBROOK and ELIZABETH, oldest dau. of Mrs. ELIZ: BUSHROD. Before 24 June 1679. vi-19. [Note previous record.]

.... SEABRIGHT and ANN UDALL, widow of Thomas. Before 24 Jany 1683. vi-548.

The County Court Note-Book

An every-other-monthly devoted mainly to abstracts from County Court Records, prior to 1800.

MILNOR LJUNGSTEDT, Editor and Publisher. Bethesda, Rural Route 5, Maryland.

Published six times a year. Subscription, two dollars, in advance; must begin with the year.

February, 1930 **Whole**
Vol. IX., No. 1 **No. 50**

IN this issue begins a list of probates and administrations from the rough minute or scratch books of the Rockingham Court, Virginia. These were taken from a photostat copy of a very roughly and, naturally, hastily written volume, and it was at times impossible to make out what the Clerk intended as to some of the names. Corrections will be accepted.

There is much information of this character in the oourts, and in the cases where the copied records have been destroyed by the "Act of God," or the clash of war, patient reading would fill many gaps.

The signature which heads the eighth instalment of the WHITTINGTON family, is taken from an original paper, the administration bond of DOROTHY GRANGER, for whom WHITTINGTON was the first bondsman. As the date of this paper is 1679, when Capt. WILLIAM WHITTINGTON, the immigrant, was dead, and as the third WILLIAM was not yet born, it remains that this was an early authograph of Lt. Col. WHITTINGTON, later of Maryland, second of the name. The thanks of the editor are due the Clerk of the Court for his assistance in obtaining this excellent cut.

In setting up some additional book shelves and so re-arranging a number of volumes, the Editor is quite unhappy over finding several volumes to which she fears she has forgotten to give suitable attention in the NOTE-BOOK.

One of these is Mr. J. Adger Stewart's DESCENDANTS of VALENTINE HOLLINGSWORTH, Sr., an excellent and most valuable book. The generations are well arranged and the volume contains two charming prints, one of Hollingsworth Hall, England, and the other of the English parish church of the clan. Quite a gorgeous print of the Hollingsworth arms serves as a frontispiece.

If Mr. Stewart knew the patient research the Editor spent on those Delaware HOLLINGSWORTHS, just because they foregathered and intermarried with ROBINSONS! All the ROBINSONS in America, excepting those on Cape Cod, and those in tide-water Virginia appear to have flocked to Delaware Bay! "Three brothers" were as nothing to them, one of them was one of SEVEN! And a HOLLINGSWORTH married a daughter.

Another volume is that concerning JACOB CLARK, of Abbeville, South Carolina, and some of his descendants. Compiled by Mrs. Eva Turner Clark. This little volume (on such satisfactory paper) shows the fine hand of experienced and patient searching. It has some excellent cuts, and, above all, a map, a map of the Abbeville District as it was in 1820. If there be anything the Editor likes better than early court records, it is maps.

Going over the newly arranged volumes the Editor finds, as heretofore at intervals, two depressing gaps. Two books lent to two forgetful friends. The second volume of Jungle Stories (an early edition if not, maybe, a first) and, even worse, The NAMELESS NOBLEMAN. Why did the Editor insist on somebody borrowing that beloved book, for it is the story, very much enlarged and embroidered, of that François Le Baron who is part of her reason for being. And it was given to her by an aunt, now passed over, and the Editor doesn't know where she can get another. It has quite an explanatory inscription on a fly-leaf, and if any of the NOTE-BOOK'S readers happen on it, please, will that reader send an airplane special?

François Le Baron was a gentleman and somewhat of a scholar, a surgeon and an officer......... at least he was in the French navy. He did not live very long in the rigorous climate of Plymouth, where the fathers of the town persuaded him to "locate," for he was but a few years beyond thirty when he died. If he had not named his eldest son Lazarus, the Editor would feel happier about him. Perhaps Lazarus was so named because of some terrific tragedy in the father's life.........tradition says he escaped from Jesuit control. There is little to base this on, if anything. And I think the New Testament has more inspiring names.

Maj. J. B. CALVERT NICKLIN, has discovered through his experienced and patient search and comparison, that all the deeds and wills in Westmoreland county, Virginia, between certain dates for perhaps twenty years, are missing. He has found that the absentee records were presented to the court in due form, for the acknowledgments and probates are in the Order Books. Maj. Nicklin thinks that the originals were mislaid when the court took possession of the present building.........but this was a long time ago. It seems to the Editor, this is a mere notion, that as the earlier records were copied about 1835 [Major Nicklin gives this date] it is possible the old volumes, that is from 1671 to 1693 were "borrowed out" to be copied.........and perhaps there was a fire. Nothing is more aggravating to the modern searcher than to find that a record volume has been lent to some influential "party" ....how often it must have been done in the olden time!

QUERIES:

ELIZABETH O'DELL who married REUBEN FARLOW was born in Randolph county, N. C. in 1793. Her mother said to have been a BOWDOIN. Who were her parents? P. E. Haynes, East Aurora, N. Y.

ARCHIBALD GIBSON, died at Jamestown, Indiana, 1855; lived in Kentucky in 1821 and came from North Carolina (probably Wilkes county). Said to have had nine sons. His wife was VESHTA. (Surname unknown.) Information concerning any of this family desired. P. E. Haynes, East Aurora, N. Y.

A MATTER OF IMPORTANCE

The Editor of the NOTE-BOOK will pay ten dollars ($10) for a copy of the WILL of WILLIAM FLOYD, or a copy (in full) of the administration of his estate.

WILLIAM FLOYD was living in 1783; had wife ABADIAH, and propably living sons ROBERT, CHARLES and NATHANIEL. He was also the father of Col. JOHN FLOYD. WILLIAM FLOYD may have died in one of the frontier countries oJ Virginia, Kentucky, or in one of the Territories northwest of the Ohio. He was about 56 years old in 1783 and owned land in the upper Valley of Virginia. He had removed to the frontier, but was driven back by the uprising among the Indians. Where he then settled is unknown.

In response to this query several kindly persons, wishing to be helpful, have been at some pains to send published material which the Editor has already collected. What the Editor wants is something nobody seems to know about.

CONTINUED articles COUNTY COURT NOTE-BOOK, and the dates on which they first appeared.

THE ANCESTRY OF COL. JOHN DONELSON. Began with February, 1927.

AUTHENTIC REFERENCES for INFERRED MARRIAGES (formerly called MARRIAGES BY INFERENCE). Began with May, 1922.

MARYLAND'S NEXT OF KIN. Began with July, 1922.

VIRGINIA COLONISTS. Alphabetized lists began with July, 1924.

MILITARY NOTES, both COLONIAL and REVOLUTIONARY, and later MILITIA NOTES. Began December, 1923.

INTERCOUNTY and INTERCOLONY (formerly called New Englanders and Others, &c., &c.). Began with March, 1922.

EASTERN SHORE FAMILIES. In the form of a one-page supplement, began with June, 1925.

SHIPS IN PORT and COLONIAL FORENAMES will appear in alternate issues or as space can be found for them.

STAFFORD COUNTY INDICES began in June, 1929.

THE DEPUTY COMMISSARY'S GUIDE WITHIN THE PROVINCE OF MARYLAND

(Continued from October, 1929)

WILLS AND TESTAMENTS. . . . If an executor be named in a will, it is more properly called a testament; if no executor is named, "It is then no testament but only retaineth the name of a will; from which ariseth the position, that every testament is a last will, but every last will is not a testament."

Wills are of two kinds, written wills and nuncupative or verbal wills. A written will made in the lifetime of the testator, must be signed, sealed, acknowledged anddelivered by the testator himself, in the presence of three credible witnesses. (Then follows reference to the statute of 29 Car. 2 ch. 3. concerning devices of lands or tenements.) Wills conveying lands, tenements or hereditaments, are not revocable, otherwise than by some other will or codicil in writing, declaring the same, "or by burning, cancelling, tearing or obliterating the same by the testator himself, or in his presence, and by his direction and consent." . . . . . .

A nuncupative (or verbal) will is made when the testator without any writing, "doth declare his will before a sufficient number of witnesses, who put the same in writing after his death; such a will properly evidenced . . . . . is of force and effect for the personal estate only; lands, tenements, and hereditaments not being devisable by it."

And it is further quaintly provided that no nuncupative will shall be good "where the estate bequeathed shall exceed the value of thirty pounds . . . . . . unless such will were made in the time of the last sickness of the deceased, and in the house of his or their habitation or dwelling, or where he or she hath been resident for the space of ten days, or more, next before the making of such will, except where such person was surprised or taken sick, being from his own home."

Provision is also made that the nuncupative will [that is] it's substance, "must be committed to writing within six days." . . . . . . And no letters testamentary or probate of any nuncupative will "shall pass the seal of any court, till fourteen days at the leaste, after the decease of the testator; and the widow or next of Kindred shall be called in to the end that they may contest the same, if they please." And no written will shall be repealed, attested or changed, by any will by word of mouth only.

Nuncupative wills of personal estate, under thirty pounds, may be admitted at any time within six months of the making of such will on the oath of two credible witnesses at least; *"for one witness only in matters merely ecclesiastical, is as no witness at all."* If committed to writing, within six days, it my be admitted, after the expiration of six months.

(To be continued.)

Mr. STRATTON NOTTINGHAM'S Index of the Wills and Administrations of Accomack county, Virginia, is nearly ready for publication. This will be by far the most important of Mr. Nottingham's many valuable compilations. It is a great piece of work, for it wiil not only be a complete list of wills up to 1800, but will include notices of probates and of the appointment of administrators.

The Editor is advised that Mr. LOUIS A. BURGESS' third volume of Virginia Soldiers of 1776, is ready. It is said to contain the names of a greater number of soldiers than either of the previous volumes.

Volume four is ready for printing and only awaits enough advance orders to ensure financing. The returns from publications of this class seldom, if ever, equal their value to those who use them.

VIRGINIA COLONISTS

(From "Old Vol. 5" S. L. O. Richmond, Va.)

Mr. THOMAS HAMPTON, James City cty, 1658.
Head rights: Eliz: Sanders, Elizabeth Dallinge, Tho. Gibson, Mary Loyd, Susan Duffell [?] John Raslin, Wm. Skance, James Cooke.

CHARLES HILL, county not given. 1658.
Head rights: Roger Smith, Tho. Allen, Wm. Jordan.

CHARLES HILL, county not given. 1658.
Head rights: James Hill, Wm. Rogers, Mary Jones.

NICKO: JERMEN, "head of a creeke in Petomeck freshes, beyond the Doeg's Island"......... 1657. [This name was probably wrongly listed in an early NOTE-BOOK.]
Head rights: Peter Lefebur, Margaret Lefebur, Isaack Lefebur, Jacob Lefebur, Thomas Williams, Gilbert Coop, Anne Burton, Patrick Crispe, John Woodnightonhouse [?? Woodringtonhouse seems possible] Hen. Hawkins, Jno. Reade, Phillip Wadden, Jno. Giles.

THOMAS JONES, Rappahannock cty. 1658.
Head rights: Thomas Pyper, Tho. Reddinge, Katherine Browne, James Clerke, Eliz: Jones, Thomas Gill, Wm. Boulin, Jno. Smith, Robert Abraham, Thomas Jones, Jno. Morgan, Wm. Corman.

ROBERT JONES, New Kent, 1658.
Head rights: Jno. Clay, Jno. Norman, Jo. Parker, Wm. Luck, Robert Goswine, Ann Colchester, Wm. Florriday [note later Flowerdews, etc.] Daniel Roberts, Gregory Nash, James Rounds.

WILLIAM JACOB, L. Norf cty, 1656.
Head rights: Wm. Andrewes, Darby Kelly, Ann Breakes, Christian Christianes [?] Margarett Sibill, Wm. Hall.

RICE JONES and ANTHONY JACKMAN, Rappahannock county. 1658.
Head rights: Edward Howgrave, John Anderton or Anderson, James Payne, Christian Gowin, James Fossett, Tho. Bowman, Bressilea Holloway, Alice Kinge, Mary Floyd, Mary ...., Eliz: Farme, Edward Allen, Tho. Gill, Robert Doore, John Cox, Fran: Overton, Susanna Nurse, Wm. Mathewes, Fran. Morgans, Dous [?Dons] Williams, Adam Higgison.

LEONARD JONES, Rappahannock county. 1662.
Head rights: Wm. JONES, ANN JONES; Maria and Jeny, negroes.

WILLIAM KNOTT, "bounding n. easterly upon Petomeck River in the freshes above Anacosta." 1657.
Head rights: Edmond Ayres (twice), Nicholas Meger, Peter Orfle, Wm. Ewbanke, Jno. Squire, Jno. Colis, Darby Stanlin [?] Ann Burkett, Ri: Harman.

FORENAMES OF COLONIAL USAGE

MARIAM RAMEY m. William Hillings. 21 May 1789. Winchester, Va. Rev. Alex. Balmain's Register.

MIRIAM WILSON was dau. of Joseph. See his will, 1789-90. N. C. H. G. iii-197. Another MIRIAM WILSON was dau. of Jacob. See same vol.

MIRIAM SOUTHWARD m. Thomas Wright, 18 Oct 1789, both of King's co., N. Y. See records N. Y. Presbyt. Ch. N. Y. B. & G. xii-139.

MIRIAM MURDAU[G]H HUNNICUTT, dau. of James, of Gchland co., Va., m. Timothy Terrell, son of Thomas, of Caroline co., at Geneto Mtg, 10-6-1798. See records of Cedar Crk Mo'ly Mtg, Hanover Co. Va.

MIRIAM DEANS, Windham, Conn, 1797.

MIRIAM PRICE and Michael McKeel. M. L. B. 13 Dec 1799. N. C. H. G. i-246.

MIRIAM SECRIST, dau. of Elijah Davis. Hamp., W. Va. Will Book 1809-1813, p. 417. 1813.

MIRIAM R. GRIFFITH, dau. of Thomas and Rachel. Gunpowder Mo'ly Mtg, Md. Born 1816.

MERIAM REDD, dau. of George, and Samuel Devoe. Fred'k, Va. M. L. B. 21 Sept 1813.

MARIANN ANDS; wit. to mar. of Chas. Robinson, Philada. 1830.

MARIANNA DEFORD, dau. of John and Anna. Born 1751. St. Luke's, A. A. cty, Md.

MIRIAM BUTLER m. William Eager, son of William. He was born *circa* 1731. Histy Orange cty, N. Y. p. 301.

MIRIAM WALTER, grandaughter of MIRIAM RICHARDSON, Fred'k, Md. Wills A-1. 1767.

MIRIAM LEWIS, daughter of David, and wife Mary (McGrath) Hart (widow of Dr. Hart of Philada.) m. Gabriel Madison, probably before or *circa*1779. Histy Albemarle cty, Va. Woods. p. 255.

MIRIAM HALL, sister of Robert; founded a scholarship at Princeton. Histy Orange cty. N. Y. p. 255.

MERIAM HUNNICUTT, wife of .... HUNNICUTT. Sussex, Va. She signed in one place "Hunncutt."

MIRIAM LOUGE, dau. of David and Ann. St. Martin's Psh. Wor. cty, Md. Born 1750-1-2. Her mother was Ann Lockwood.

MIRIAM BURR m. Alpheus Brown. 1771. Bloomfield, Conn. Conn. Mar.

MERRIAM PEALE, was a dau. of Charles Wilson Peale. Old Kent, Md. p. 335. (Peale was born in 1741.)

MERIAM MORGAN, mentioned in will of James x Fitzgerrald. Kent cty. Dela. 1727. G-2.

MIRIAM HARTFIELD was wife of Matthew. St. Peter's Psh, New Kent cty, Va. Living 1738.

MARRIAM PERRY m. Peter Coffin. Nantucket Mar. p. 164. Vol. xli, N. E. H. and G.

MARRIAM MAGOUNE was wife of James. Nthld. cty, Va. 9 Oct 1742. 1738-1743, fo. 210.

MIRIAM TATUM m. James Egerton of Maryland. Crozier, vi-102. 31 July 1717.

MIRIAM BUCKINGHAM a wit. to a marriage. Tred Avon Mtg, Md. 6th 12th 1780.

MIRIAM TRUEBLOOD, a wit. at a marriage. Symons Creek records of the Quakers of Pasquotank. 5th 9th mo. 1811.

MIRIAM ROBINSON, Register of Friends, Pasquotank, &c. Born 6-1st mo, 1743-44.

MIRIAM HILL, dau. of Aaron and wf Miriam, "his second wife." Register of Friends, Pasquotank, &c. Born 13-3d mo. 1754.

MIRIAM BUNDY, dau. of Caleb and wife Mary [or Miriam?] Same record. Died 13th 2d mo. 1762.

SERVICE AND SUPPLIES COLONIAL, REVOLUTIONARY AND MILITIA

THOMAS GREEN enlisted in the Continental Army for three years and was killed at the battle of Brandywine. JOHN GREEN, heir-at-law. Fauq. cty, Va. May Court, 1783.

JAMES WRIGHT, a Captain in the Virginia line certifies that JOHN MORGAN enlisted in the Continental Army for three years and died in the service. CHARLES MORGAN, heir-at-law. Fauq. cty, Va. May Court, 1783.

GEORGE LEACH, serjeant, Virginia State Regiment of Artillery produced discharge from Col. Thomas Marshall, S. A. Ordered certified. Fauq. cty, Va. May Court, 1783.

WILLIAM HERRING appointed 2d Lieut., and Joseph Dictam [?Dickens] Ensign, Capt. Robert Craven's company. Rock'm cty, Va. Court 27 Apr 1778. [See note elsewhere as to this writing.]

RICH'D READER, apptd 2d Lieut, JOSEPH SMITH, Ensign, Capt. Daniel Smith's company. Same record, same date.

BRIDGET FOWLER, the distressed wife of JOHN FOWLER, a soldier in the Continental Army; Daniel Smith to lay out £12 for her. Court 25 May 1778. Rock'm cty, Va.

ANTO. RYDER, GAWIN HAMILTON, THO. HEWETT, THOS. BAGG, REUBEN HARRISON, and DAN'L SMITH, Jr., appointed Captains of Militia. Took the oath. Rock'm cty, Va. Court 25 May 1778.

JOSEPH SMITH, JOHN RICE, NICOLAS CARN [KERN?] appointed Lieutenants of Militia, take the oath. Same record, same date.

WILLIAM SMITH and CHRISTOPHER PANTER [?] Ensigns, take the oath. Same record, same date.

JOSIAH HARRISON, appointed Lieut. Militia takes oath. Same record, same date.

ELIZABETH PENNIRY, wife of THOMAS, a soldier in the army, is ill and in a very distressed condition. Ordered that Abraham Smith have £20 for her support. Rock'm cty, Va. Court 26 May 1778.

BRIDGET FOWLER and children to be assisted [as before.] Court 24 Aug 1778.

JOSEPH SMITH, oath as Ensign Militia. Court 28 Sept 1778.

FREDERICK KEISTER, commissioned as Lieut. Militia, and takes oath. Rock'm cty, Va. Court 28 Sept 1778.

JOHN HARDMAN. sworn 2d Lieut. Militia, and WILLIAM MORRIS, same. Rock'm cty, Va. Court 28 Nov 1778.

MARY, wife of NICOLAS ROPE, a soldier in the Continental Army, is in need, has seven children. Allowance made. Rock'm cty, Va. Court 28 Nov 1778.

MARY SYBERT, widow of Chas. Fred: Sybert, a soldier who died in the service of the Commonwealth, appearing to be in indigent circumstances, with one helpless child, is allowed £30. Rock'm cty, Va. Court 22 Mch 1779.

ELIZABETH SHULENGER, widow of George, late a soldier in the Continental service, is also allowed £30.

RACHEL CASH, wife of JOHN, a soldier; has two small children, is to be allowed £30. Rock'm cty, Va. Court 23 Mch 1779.

ROBT. DAVIS, ROBT CRAVENS, ANDREW JOHNSTON and JOHN RUSH, commissioned captains of Militia. JOSEPH DICTAM or DICTURN sworn Ensign. Rock'm cty. Va. Court 23 Mch 1779.

FRANCIS FOX, aged about 72, a resident of Wilkes county testifies that he served in the Revolutionary War, that he enlisted for three years in Duplin county, North Carolina, about 1773, in the company of Capt. Welsh in the 8th Reg't., N. C. line, commanded by Col. Armstrong; was marched to Halifax town, thence to the north, where he joined the main army under Gen. Washington . . . was discharged near Wilmington, N. C., by Capt. Robert Finney [?] who was then his Captain, he having been transferred to the 2d Reg't., N. C., commanded by Col. Clarke. . . . His wife's name is Catherine, aged about thirty, and he has three small children: Jesse about seven; Jackson, about four; Elizabeth about eighteen months. Knows no person who can prove his service, but one Charles Wood of Orange County, N. C.

Printed at the Industrial School for Crippled and Deformed Children, 241 St. Botolph St., Boston, Mass.

The

County Court Note-Book

A Little Bulletin of History and Genealogy

April, 1930. Vol. IX, No. 2

VIRGINIA COLONISTS

(From Old Volume 5, S. L. O. Richmond, Va.)

WM. WRIGHT, Nansimond cty, 1665.
Head rights: George Banton, Doll Dugraw.

Mr. JOHN WHETSTONE, 1665.
Head rights: Thomas Holmes, Alexand'r Wright, Humphry Thomas, Alice Grey, Lucy Hollis.

JOHN WILLIAMS, Accomack, 1666.
Head rights: Jno. Browne, Jno. Chester, Jno. Armiger, Wm. Davies, Rog'r Nappar, Wm. Warden, Step. Tompson, Wm. Swazy [?]

JOHN WALLOP *als* WADLOW, Accomack, 1666.
Head rights: Tho. Mackrell, Edgar Halsey, Marg't Hill, Roger Draper, John Cotswell, Robt Horton, Jean Stanly, Jno. Huberd, Luke Roe, Abraham Willett, Jno. Golding, Jeames Weatly, Ed Long, Walter Booth.

THOMAS WYATT, on Mockjack Bay, 1666.
Formerly granted to Richard Wyatt, Dec. 20 Aug 1645, and now due to Thomas, sonn and heire of Richard. No head rights given.

JOHN WILLIAMS, Accomack cty, 1666.
Head rights: Jude Morgan, Peter Scott, Benj. Pride, Wm. Seward, Arthur Shore, Wm. Jennett, Mary Pye, Peter Scott, Ann Morgan, Judith Smart, Wm. Stevens.

JOHN WALLOP *als* WADLOW, Accomack cty, 1666.
Head rights: Mary Jones, Susan Trott, Wm. Evans, Jno. Evans, Marg'tt Johnson, Peter Plummer.

DAVID WILLIAMSON, Accomack cty, 1666.
Head rights: Richard Combs, William Maston, Robt Sadler, Thomas Oxton, John Bristoll, *Algernell* Cecill, Thomas Cotton, John Cotrop, Robt Apre......? Nicholas Pedly, Jno. Heron, Robt Paine, Richard Naylor, Richard Ashley, Maurice Digg, Thomas Harless, Rich'd Masters, Jno. Marsh, Nicholas Tooke, Jno. Zouch, Wm. Flu[d?] Jno. Smith, Jno. Mason, Francis Twisden, Thomas Breader;

Christopher Allinson, Robt. Olivier, Francis Baston, Henry Pettis, Thomas Hortsee [?] Edward Mator [?], Richard Masters, Jacob Eason, Jno. Sacker, Jeremy Stanfor, James Pashly, Robt Watson, Tho. Brett, George Middleton, Roger Bradshaw, Jno. Nowell, James Beache [Beacke?] Jno. Bowes, Anto. Fowte [Fowke?] Wm. Rooke, Robt Larker, Thomas Beloir, James Albester, George Curtis; James Troutt, Rich'd Manly, George May [?] Peter Peps [?] Edward Wyatt, James Newman, Jno. Cason, Hortree Stephen [perhaps Stephen Hortree?] Herbert Randall, Thomas Peale, James West, Lewis Price, Ri: Amherst, Ri: Duck, Thomas Hindman, James Brooke, Edw. Marlington, Walter Gisson [Gilson?] Roger Wye, Ralph Massey, Thomas Stanory [?] Wm. Burford, 9 negroes;

Susan Williams, Jane Cole, Ann Jones, Peter Plumer, Arth. Edw'd, Wm. Stone, Stephen Cher [?] Pater Store [Peter Stone?] Susan Hunt, Henry Cary, Henry Williams, Jno. James, Jno. Johnson, James Stoner, Perter Corton, Edw'd Wattross, Sarah Jackson, Jno. Talton, Jno. Tard, Edm'd Williams, Peter Norton, Thomas Norton, Thomas Coulson;

Edward Gay, William Sayer, Norton Phillips, Jno. Evans, Robe Coleman, Henry Creeke, Peter Plumer, Eliz: Hart, Mary Jones, Wm. Tony. Susan March, Alex. Mecanter Edw'd Seward, Thomas West, Thomas Nord [?] Thomas Coleby, Thomas Pewter, Edward Jones.

Maj. THOMAS WALKER, "Gloster" cty, 1665, "Mattapony fort."
Head rights: Will Carvill, And. Jenkin, Thomas Holt, Mary Castle, Jno. Norcott, Andrew Jones, Susan Carry, Mary Tye, Wm. Crump, Antho. Longman, Marg'tt Twisdon, Ann Lagston, Ann Bray, Peter Scott, Jno. Evans, Wm. Castle, Jno. Parson, A......... Jones, Arthur Washott, Marg'tt Light, Wm. Tompson, Edward Vrott [probably Trott], Edward Williams;

An Longman, Edm. Pratt, Wm. Senior, James Store, William Hasser [Harser?] David Williams, Jno. Harris, Arthur Cort, Wm. White, Mary Strang, Edd. Trotham, Norton Williams, Phillip Langstone, Marg'tt Hart, Susan Strong, Edward Williams, Marg'tt Jones, Edward Walker, Jno. White, Susan Williams, Ann Toft, Wm. Strong, An Lowell, Susan Sparshott.

ROBERT WILLIAMSON, Isle of Wight cty, "on the greate Swampe of the Blackwater," 1666.
Head rights: JOANE WILLIAMSON, Herbert Richardson, Edw. Robbinsonn, Ann North, Connise [?] Tonge, Tristram Estan, Luke Mansens, Merrick Edwards, Jane Edwards, Nathaniell Simonds, Rich. Morgon, Hester Northern, George ...., John Johnson, Edw. Sanders, Edw. Morgan, Edward Toner [or Jones], Henry Baker, Katherine Langford, Ri...... Jenkins, Simon ...., Robert Lampton;

Merlin Cant, Joseph Baker, Wm. Downham, Silvester Hill, Winifie Evans, Jane Wheler, Mary ...., Wm. Stephens, John Williams, Peter "Jnoson," Jno. Jenkins, James Leyel, Mary Estwood, Wm. Carpenter, Emanuell ...., Fran: Reppington, Ann Chew, Ann Thomas, Wm. Tucker, Jno. Browne, Jno. Wilson, Wm. Athum [?] Sarah ...., Peter Nickolls, Peter Harris, Susan Hunt, Charles Dennison;

Mary Wannan, Jno. Sheppard, Peter Laster [probably Lassiter], four negroes; Abigall Cownter, Grace Hallock, Wm. Love, Eliz: Hill, Jno.

Barnes, Jno. Hilliard, Wm. Stone, Edward Jones, William Thomas, Jno. Williams, David Johs [Johns?]

CHRISTOP'R Wade, Isle of Wight cty, 1665. Head rights: John Williams, Walter Grimes, Mary Stone, Hannah Watson, Peter Store, Jno. Gore.

WILLIAM WHITEHURST, Lower Norfolk cty, head of Indian Creek, 1665. Head rights: Alexander Rose, Donagh Conah, Mag'tt Sonteman or Souleman, Daniell Maswello [?] Jno. Stephens, Peter Edwards.

COLL, FRANCIS WILLIS, Esq., "Gloster" cty, 1666.
Head rights: Jno. Bryant, Wm. Bush.

PHILLIP WADDING, "in the forest, n. side Rappahannock cty, about a mile and one-half from the head of "Pope's Creek," 1666. Head rights: Thos. Dally, Mary Wallett, Jane Davis, Henry Wilton, Francis Dumott, Charles Goach.

AUTHENTIC REFERENCES FOR INFERRED MARRIAGES

(York county, Virginia. Continued from February, 1930.)

HENRY x SAFFERY and ISBILL x MUCKENREE, the late wife of John MUCKENREE. Before or about 24 Nov 1679. vi-152.

BRYAN SMITH and DOROTHY TUCKER, dau. of Daniel. Before 3 Oct 1694. i-271

HUMPHREY STREET, and ANNE PEALE, dau. of Francis. Before 10 Sept 1658. Vol. 1657-1662. p. 34.

Mr. THOMAS SUMNER and the relict and extx of Jno WHISKIN, before 24 Nov 1680, vi-268.

Mr. WM. SOAMS and the relict and extx of Sr. John HALL [?] Before 24 Oct 1681. vi-344.

SAM'L TOMKINS and ELIZA: CLARKE, wid. of John. About 25 Apr 1681. vi-302.

Mr. SAMUEL TOPLADY and the relict of Mr. Chas DUN dec'd. Before 24 Aug 1680. ii-234.

Mr. RICHARD TROTTER and the relict of Jno. MURRY, dec'd. Before 24 Oct 1679. vi-130.

ABRAHAM TURNER and HANNAH BENNETT, dau. Samuel, the 11 Dec 1644, by Parson Cluverius, late minister of Hampton psh, Yorke cty; HANNAH being the widow of TURNER and is sythence married HUMPHREY TOMPKINS with whom she now liveth, Dep'n of John Hunt, John Nosworth, Armiger Wade, Anthony Rooksby, Augustine Warner, and Francis Willis. 22 Dec 1661 [Date of this reference] iii-159.

OTHO THORPE and ELIZABETH THORPE, widow of Richard. About June 1660. [iii]-93.

HENRY THOMPSON and MARY HURD, dau. Morris. Before 24 Mch 1683 vi-565.

PETER TEMPLE, Clerk, of Essex cty, and MARY LUDLOW, relict of Lt. Col. THOMAS LUDLOW. Before 24 Mch 1683. vi-570. Before or about 24 Feby 1678. vi-78.

Mr. HENRY TYLER and ELIZABETH CHILES. Before 24 Apr 1683. vi-499.

ALEXANDER VINES and the gr. dau. of Susanna Perkins. Before 23 May 1698. x-83.

WILLIAM WATKINS and REBECCA TIPLADY, relict of John. Before 25 Mch 1700. x-306.

HENRY WEBB and the relict of Edw'd WENTWORTH. Before 10 Sept 1661. iii-131.

WILLIAM WEATHERELL and ELIZABETH, dau. of Anne Davis, widow. Before 24 Nov 1673. v-66.

Mr. DANIEL WILD and the relict and extx of William STEPHENS, late of Warwick cty, dec'd. Before 10 Sept 1659. 1657-1662 p. 64. [Probably about 1659.]

End of York marriages.

The following marriages are from Accomack cty, Va.

JAMES DARMAN [DORMAN?] and SUSANNAH WILLIS, dau. of Peter. Before 23 Feby 1768. Diii-541. Her mother was Rose. See p. 546.

GEORGE DRUMMOND and SUSANNAH, admx of George PARKER. Before 28 Feby 1759. xxviW-113.

PETER DOLBY and SARAH, one of the extrs of Argol YARDLY. Before 6 Aug 1684. ix-48.

ROBERT DUKES and FRANCES GILLETT, dau. of Jarman GILLETT. Before 31 Dec 1706. xi-403.

WILLIAM DARTER and MARGARET HUDSON, dau. of William. Before 1705. xi-488.

JOHN DOWNING and FRANCES ROBERTS, dau. of Francis. Before 22 Oct 1697. xi-184.

RALPH DOE and the widow of John JAMES. Before 8 Feby 1672. iv-162.

JOHN DICKSON and ELIZABETH STOTT, dau of Mary STOTT (who was a dau. of Elizabeth Abdell.) See 25 Sept 1753. Dii-461.

WILLIAM DRUMMOND and BRADHURST SCARBURGH, dau. of John. See 27 May 1752. Dii-384. See Dii-236. Record 26 Dec. 1749. Also xxiiiO-618.

ISAAC DASHIEL and HANNIRETTA SCARBURGH, dau. of Henry, son of Charles. Before 28 Apr 1767. Diii-466.

FAMILIES OF THE EASTERN SHORE
THE WHITTINGTONS

Further and additional notes.

The second son of SOUTHY WHITTINGTON, Sr. (see NOTE-BOOK for December, 1929), was STEVENSON. No individual record of this son is found, and it is supposed he died unmarried.

The third son of SOUTHY, Sr., was ISAAC, his will follows.

ISAAC WHITTINGTON, of Somerset cty, Md. Wf ELIZABETH; dau. Nancy Cox; dau. Hannah Handy; gr. son Joshua Reece Handy; gr. son John Handy; gr. dau. Sally Handy; son THOMAS; son JAMES; son WILLIAM; son JOSHUA; son LITTLETON; son JAMES, extr.

Witnesses: Elisha Gunby, Southy Whittington, Benj. Conner. 17 Nov 1813-27 June 1815. (Som. xxiii-230.)

The fourth son of SOUTHY, Sr., was WILLIAM. WILLIAM married PRISCILLA POLK, dau. of James and Betty Polk. (This can be shown by records which cannot, at present, for want of space, be gone into.) WILLIAM probably died in 1819, as shown by his will.

WILLIAM WHITTINGTON, of Somerset cty, Md. Wf PRISCILLA one-half my lands during life, and the other half to my son JAMES; at death or marriage of wife, all lands to son JAMES. Negroes to son JAMES; mentions grchn. Jane S. Porter, Nelly Porter, Betsy Porter, Henry Porter, Juliana Porter; also gr.son WILLIAM WHITTINGTON; gr. son THOMAS WHITTINGTON; gr. dau. Mary Whittington; gr. dau. Peggy Whittington. Balance estate to wife PRISCILLA and son JAMES. JAMES to be extr.

Wit: Joshua Bratton, Benson S. Lowes, James Whittington, Elisha Gunby. 29 Dec 1815-11 May 1819. (Som. J. P. xxiii-271.)

PRISCILLA WHITTINGTON, the widow, desires that JAMES should not be compelled to furnish inventory, provided he gives bond. (Som. J. P. iv-248.) 19 May 1819.

SOUTHY WHITTINGTON, Jr., brother of ISAAC and WILLIAM above given, it will be recalled, had two sons by his wife ESTHER NAIRN.

The eldest son SOUTHY married MARY COULBOURN, 8 July 1804. (See Somerset list of marriage licenses.) His will was signed the 16 Apr 1842 and probated 26 Dec 1843. (Som. J. P. v-94.) In it he mentions son SOUTHY F. (whom the records show went to New Jersey), sons JOHN, STEPHENSON, ROBERT and LUTHER A. WHITTINGTON. Also daughter Hester-Ann. LUTHER A. WHITTINGTON appears to have been the youngest child and Hester-Ann the next.

The 18 Oct 1832, this SOUTHY WHITTINGTON (so far as he can be identified) and wife MARY, of Somerset county, convey to Elisha Gunby, for one hundred and fifty dollars, one-half of a parcel of marsh, &c., and the whole of a "hammock" situated in sd marsh that lies farthest to the south and west, called "Planting Hammock"...... with permission to gather and haul away any manure around and without the enclosures of another "hammock" called "Cedar Hammock," situated on said marsh......the privilege agreed upon that WHITTINGTON and his heirs may water and shelter their stock on "Planting Hammock;" the boundaries given mention "Indian Hammock Creek," also JAMES WHITTINGTON'S land, and a small "gutter" emptying into East creek. Wit: John H. Cohoon, Levi Daugherty. Ackn. in person. (Som. lvi-470.)

In 1737, 6 June, SOUTHY WHITTINTON, Somerset, Gent., and wife MARY, convey to Joshua Atkinson, a tract called *Choice* (with reference to a patent in 1726.) (Som. xix-147. And again the 2 June 1737, he and his wife MARY quit-claim to Joseph Porter all his (SOUTHY'S) right to a tract called *Adventure*, on the seaboard side, at the north end of Cropper's Island. (Som. xix-168.) And in the same month and date on which he conveys to Atkinson above, he and his wife MARY, sell to John Brunett (with reference to a patent in 1726) a tract made up of several parcels called *Choice*, on the north side of Pocomoke and bounded in part by *Benefield*. The whole amount of land is 450 acres, and it is "*now called Bennetts Purchase.*"

The same SOUTHY WHITTINGTON and wife MARY, 2 Feby 1738, convey to John Wildman, for £74, all that tract called *Spring Garden*, and water-mills upon Nasaongoe creek. (Som. xx, 68.) And again, 22 June 1739, wife MARY, to John Jenckins, Carpenter, for fifty pounds, part of a tract called *Choice*, laid out for 1950 acres on the north side of Pocomoke, on Nasseongo creek. In this deed the land of Whittngton Johnson is mentioned. (Som. xx-69.)

Included in the above deed is a "*warrant against any person Laying any claim or title thereto the Indians excepted.*"

In 1835, 24 Dec. SOUTHY WHITTINGTON, now calling himself "Senior," and wife MARY, of Somerset cty, convey to SOUTHY F. WHITTINGTON of the same, all that tract beginning the south side of George H. Johnson's land; Tull's land also mentioned. The witnesses are W. H. Whittington and W. H. Lankford. (Som. lviii-195.)

There is another deed in 1828, but no wife appears to identify the grantor. It may be that the wife's release is further on in the volume. But the 20 June 1827, SOUTHY WHITTINGTON, of Somerset, wife Mary releasing, conveys to James Burnett of Worcester cty, for $2,000 Maryland money, part of three tracts, one called Long's Chance, one Boston's Adventure, and the other called Convenience, adjoining each other . . . "It being the whole of the land I own on Morumpsko creek formerly belonging to Turpin and Jenkins." Wit: Wm. Roach and Wm. Coulbourn. (Som. liii-454.)

There are two other deeds from SOUTHY WHITTINGTON, one in 1840 and one in 1841. In neither of these does the wife appear, yet the tracts apnear to identify the grantor as the same SOUTHY. The first is to Bejamin Lankford . . a marsh and hammock on the west side of East Creek, called "Cedar Hammock," excepting so much of sd marsh as was conveyed to Elisha Gunby by the sd SOUTHY WHITTINGTON, (See Som. lx-38.) And the other is to STEPHENSON WHITTINGTON and is a farm-lease of a parcel of land beginning "near the gate at the county road" . . . and mentioning a direct course for Nathan T. Hull's house . . also a line to LITTLETON WHITTINGTON, and a lot of ground in the "Cedar Hammock" "during my life." This is signed with a mark and the matter is not clear.

The will of JOHN-NAIRN WHITTINGTON, who was the second son of SOUTHY WHITTINGTON, Jr., and wife ESTHER NAIRNE, is dated 31 Jany 1825, and was probated 5 April 1826. It will be noted, if the identification of these SOUTHYS is correct, that he died nearly twenty years before his brother and this recalls the varying lengths of life of the earlier WHITTINGTONS.

JOHN-NAIRN WHITTINGTON married SARAH .... who is sometimes called SARAH-ANN. In his will she is called SARAH. He mentions his dau. Elizabeth, son SOUTHY, son CHARLES, son JOHN, and dau. Sally Melbourn. After specific legacies, the balance of the estate is to be divided between Sally, Elizabeth, SOUTHY and CHARLES. Son JOHN and friend Dr. John Stevenson extrs. Wit: Levin Henderson, William Henderson, Charles Henderson. Wor. cty M. H. xxvii-217.

ISAAC WHITTINGTON, as shown in these notes, had sons THOMAS, JAMES, WILLIAM, JOSHUA and LITTLETON.

THOMAS WHITTINGTON married SARAH CONNER, 4 Nov 1789. See Registry of Coventry parish, Md. The Register shows that he had a son JOSHUA, b. 11 Oct 1790. THOMAS made his will 28 May 1818; probated 7 July 1818. Mentions wife SARAH and dau. Nelly-Conner Whittington. The witnesses were Beauchamp, Betsy Benson, and Betsy [T?] Lankford. As the abstract does not mention son JOSHUA, and as there were two THOMAS WHITTINGTONS, the compiler is not satisfied with the identification of this one. (See Som. J. P. 23-266.)

JAMES WHITTINGTON married SARAH COULBOURN. Som. M. L. 18 Dec 1799. He is set down as having sons WILLIAM and THOMAS, and daughters Betsy, Mary and Peggy. But, as in the case of THOMAS WHITTINGTON, JAMES had a cousin JAMES, and at present, proof is lacking as to which was which.

The compiler finds no information as to JOSHUA WHITTINGTON. LITTLETON WHITTINGTON is shown as purchasing land of SOUTHY F. WHITTINGTON (who removed to New Jersey). A conveyance in 1839 shows that MARY W. WHITTINGTON was wife of SOUTHY F.

WILLIAM WHITTINGTON, who married PRISCILLA POLK, had one son James, as shown by WILLIAM'S will. Nothing is known by the compiler as to this JAMES unless he be the one referred to above.

The compiler has many records of this family and of intermarried lines, as they appear in the records of the early 1800's. The foregoing notes have been set down in a rather informal fashion simply to be of use ot those who care to carry the search further. Each William and Thomas, John and James *et al* can probably be identified by their holdings of land. The Editor collected these incidentally to the identification of the earlier generations and did not carry them out with her accustomed minute and detailed search. They are to be accepted with limitations.

A PARTIAL LIST OF EARLY ADMINISTRATIONS IN CUMBERLAND COUNTY, NORTH CAROLINA

(From Minute Books of the Court.)

JOSEPH HARE; Anne Hare gets l. a. on his estate. John Hust [?] and Thos Frederick. security. 20 July 1756.

GILBERT SMITH, blacksmith; Katherine Smith gets l. a. as his widow. Alex. McKay and Duncan Browne, security. 20 July 1756.

DANIEL SMITH; David Smith gets l. a. Hector McNeal and Samuel Howard, Esq's security. 21 June 1757.

ANGUS McEACHRAN [?]; Duncan McClearen gets l. a. on his estate. Hugh Brown and Malcolm Smith security. 21 June 1757.

ROBERT HOWARD; Ruth Howard, widow, and Samuel Howard his son, get l. a. 19 Apr 1757.

MARY JONES; William Robards as greatest creditor, gets l. a. on her estate. 18 Oct 1757. Another entry makes his name Roberts, and gives George Roberts and John Stephens as his security.

THOMAS JONE; Tamer Jone, widow gets l. a. Wm .Dawson, Esq., and John Hust [Hurt?] security. 17 Jany 1758.

MATTHEW CAMBELL; caveat is entered by Hector McNeil, Esq., on behalf of Jane Cambell, to letters of administration granted to Matthew Cambell. 17 Apr. 1759.

JOHN CAMPBELL; Matthew Campbell gets l. a. on his estate. 17 July 1759.

JACOB AUSTIN; Mr. William Hodges asks l. a. on his estate. Rejected because the widow was not notified. 17 July 1759.

WILLIAM HOLTON; John Holton granted l. a. on his estate. 15 Jany 1760.

ROBERT STANTFIELD; Sarah Stantfield, his wife, gets l. a. Duncan McNeill and Stephen Gardner, security. Feby Ct 1761.

ARCHIBALD CLARK; Margaret Clark his wife granted l. a. Dushie Shaw and Hector McNeil security. Feby Ct. 1761.

ALEXAND'R CLARK; Archibald and Daniel his sons, get l. a. Wm. Dawson and Gilbert Clark, security. Feby Ct 1761.

JOHN HOLTEN; Patience Holten, his wife, granted l. a. James Simpson and Wm. Lomax, security. Feby Ct 1761.

CHARLES CAMPBELL; Elinor Campbell, his wife, gets l. a. on estate. Matthew and Alexander Campbell, security. Ct 18 Aug 1761.

WILLIAM HALL; Stephen Gardner gets l. a. on his estate. Joseph Adams and Sarah Blocker (?) security. Ct 18 Aug 1761.

SARAH PATCHET; David Tantham granted l. a. on her estate. Arthur Dannelly and Martin Trantham, sec. Ct. 18 Aug 1761.

DUGAL McMULLEN; Neill McNias granted l. a. on his estate, being married to the widow of sd. Dugall, Duncan McCleron and Hugh Brown, security. Ct. 18 Aug 1761.

JOHN WILSON; Thomas Killen to have l. a. on his estate. Nov. Ct 1761.

INTERCOUNTY AND INTERCOLONY

RALPH GORRELL, in his will gives to son Ralph living in Ireland the freehold "I purchased of my brother Robert in the county of Donegall on the waters of Yorick Swolly [?] called the Crannock freehold, named Lurgy Brach Down Hazel and Corouch Lea." [It should be noted that this volume has been copied, which probably explains these curious spellings.] His oldest dau. mentioned, Elizabeth Forbis; his daus. Mary Maxwell and Agness Stewart and Ann Tom. 5 Aug 1812. Guilford cty, N. C. A-141.

GEORGE JUDE and wf ANN, of Goochland cty, Va., to Edmond Brewer, of Guilford cty, N. C., convey 500 acres. 10 Oct 1781. Guilford cty, N. C. 2-126.

JACOB LASH, of Nazareth, Tshp of Bethlehem. Northampton cty, Penna., yeoman. His will. Surry cty, N. C. 21 Feby 1774–18 Nov 1782.

JOHN McBRIDE. of Lorrence [?] cty, Indiana Will. 2 Oct 1821. Surry cty, N. C. iv-155.

HENRY LYNE, of Granville cty, N. C., Will. Gives his grandson the tract whereon he formerly lived in King and Queen city, Va. Also to grandson Edmund Lyne land where his mill stands in King and Queen cty, Va. Mentions his grandson William Penn, his granddau. Lucy Taylor, and the daughters of my dau. Lucy Lyne, and to her granddau., dau. of her dau. Lucy Carter, dec'd. To Betsy Kemp Macon, to Seigniora Macon . . . their mother, he explains, is his step-dau. Grandson James Lyne, extr. Wit: Nath'l Macon, Wash'n Norwood, Samuel Smith. 10 Oct 1797–May Ct 1798. Granv. cty. N. C. iv-205.

THOMAS RAINEY, Caswell cty, N. C., to William Rice, of Hallifax cty, Va. Conveys land on waters of Cain creek, Caswell cty. 22 Feb 1796. Person cty, N. C. B-248.

JOHN BAIRD [?] of Pr. Geo. cty, Va., to Dan'l Hughes, of Person cty, N. C. Conveys tract in Person cty. 29 Sept 1792. A-99.

PHILLIP WEBBER and wife Tappanes [?] of Cumberland cty, Va. love and affection to our sister Catharine Brown wife of William Brown of Caswell cty, N. C., conveys to the children of our sister, certain negroes. 7 Jany 1792. A-18.

JOHN COWPER, of Gates cty, N. C., to John Lewis of Fredericksburg, Va., Whereas Cowper is indebted to Lewis for £600 Va. cur., which he desires to secure in the most satisfactory manner . . . WITNESSETH, consideration 5 sh., conveys to Lewis four tracts which were transferred by a deed of 17 May 1791 . . the sd John Lewis attorney in fact of George Washington and executor of Fielding Lewis, dec'd . . . . &c., &., 18 May 1791. Gates cty, N. C. ii-334.

ENEAS LYON, formerly of the City of Cadiz in the Kingdom of Spain, but now a transient person in the county of Perquimans, North Carolina. Will. Wife Mary Lyon, who I left in the City and Kingdom aforesaid, all my estate. Two friends Wm. B Bennett, of Edenton, and Fred'k Norcom, of Perquimans county and my wife, extrs. Wit: Rich Whedbee and Thomas Stevenson. 29 July 1780. Chowan cty, N. C. A-261.

JOHN S. WEST, Esq., Marshal of the U. S. A., for the North Carolina District, to John Lee of Southampton cty, Va., conveys lots. 29 Aug. 1800. Chowan cty, N. C. B (2) -84.

JOHN WILLIMOTT, psh St. Dunstant [*sic*] Stepney, cty of Middlesex, Marriner, now in the River of Gambia. Father and mother Willimott extrs, 22 Oz. and half of Gold and the Profitt of nine slaves when sold at "Forgena" [?] or Jamaica, and my wages and servants that shall be due to me on board the Ship Mary and Elizabeth . . . . To wife Radygon Willimott all my plate goods and Chattels, &c.. &c. Nath'll Davis, among others, to take charge of his personal property, and one of his wit. Wit: Will Courteray, Nat. Davis, Francis Wood, Wm. Moulton. Codicil: Whereas I stood obligated in England to find Nath'l Davis my second mate one slave and James Denison my Doct'r one slave and have brought each of them a slave which is now on Board . . . . &c., &c. 6 July 1712. 5 Nov 1712. Richmond cty Va. iii-108.

THOMAS GUIBERT and wf. REBECCA, of St. Mary's cty, Maryland; power to Thomas Grigsby of Stafford cty Va . . Sam'l Burton, one of wit. 30 Apr 1722. K. Geo. cty, Va. i-61.

PROBATES AND ADMINISTRATIONS ROCKINGHAM COUNTY, VIRGINIA

From the original minutes of the Court.

JOHN STEVENSON. Will proved by witnesses. Dan'l Smith, Gent., and Felix Gilbert, extrs, give bond. 28 Nov 1778.

ROB'T SCOTT. Will proved by Rob't Denniston and Andrew Hudlow, two of witnesses, Robert Hoop [Hook?] and James Scott, extrs. 28 Nov 1778.

DAN'L CALAHAN; administration his estate to Chas. Calahan, his son. 22 Mch 1779.

CHAS. FREDERICK; administration his estate to Nicolas Mildeberger. 22 Mch 1779.

GEO. SCHULENGER. Will proved by Chas. Rushone [?] and James Fraser.........Jno. Hetrick, extr, refusing, administration with will annexed granted to Elizabeth Schulenger, widow. 22 Mch 1779.

ANTHONY LEWIS. Will proved by Robert Denniston, one of the witnesses. 23 Mch 1779.

HENRY LING [?] Will proved by Philip Kite and Lawr. Runckle. The extr refusing. 27 Apr 1779.

JOST HINCKLE. Will further proved by deposition of Philip Harper. 24 May 1779.

The County Court Note-Book

An every-other-monthly devoted mainly to abstracts from County Court Records, prior to 1800.

MILNOR LJUNGSTEDT, Editor and Publisher. Bethesda, Rural Route 5, Maryland.

Published six times a year. Subscription, two dollars, in advance; must begin with the year.

April, 1930 **Whole**
Vol. IX., No. 2 **No. 51**

REMINISCENCES AND REGRETS

The Editor has always the most excellent intentions, that is, creative and collective intentions, but somehow she can't catch up with them.

In the old days at home the washing was done on Monday. . . Monday of a marning, it was, and in the afternoon the nice Irish maid in a clean calico gown sat in the pleasant kitchen doing her own sewing. Monday night the clothes were brought down from the "shed" (the top of the woodshed arranged for a drying-place) and shaken and flapped and flopped and slapped and sprinkled and rolled and put away . . . and what a delight it was to hang about and grab at the flying sheets!

Of a Tuesday the ironing was done, and it there was anything left over, of coorse it could be done on Widnesday, in the marning, and the silver could aisily be polished of an afternoon. Thursday the sweeping of the house began . . . Thursday must have had the afternoon out. Friday the sweeping continued, and there was Saturday for the kitchen. And so we come to Sunday and breakfast arranged so that the maid could go to early Mass and the minister be down at his church long before half after ten, the then hour of service. To tell the honest truth the child of the house *much* preferred flapping and folding sheets to going to church, but if you had to go to church, you had to go and that was all there was of it. Besides, there were mitigations. The old streets were so wonderful; one passed not only the "Boston Stone" but a small old eating-place with a round of beef in the window and the appetizing accompaniments round about it. (Was it there that the vegetables were cut into flower-shapes? Or was it in old New York?) And even at church, if one grew tired of studying the perspective of the painted chancel, and the dove overhead, were there not those wonderful chapters at the back of the prayer-book, with white horses, and cherubim and seraphim and beasts with eyes?

Sunday afternoon was difficult, to be sure, but if the girl child should write sermons and rig a visiting boy cousin up in a sort of surplice, one could play church and give out merit cards to the only available congregation, a younger girl cousin who looked like an angel, and, compared with the child of the house, was one, indeed.

But, so as it was, that was the week. An orderly week with never a Monday mixed up with a Tuesday and nothing left over.

Alas, in time the child of the house began housekeeping of her own, in another world, so different it was. The amiable Sarah, always smiling, impossible to systematize, impossible to bring to schedule, always "*Yas'm.*" Monday's washing slipped along, ironing followed suit, silver had to go over. Yet still she never got through! Urged to finish up and have some time of her own, it never "phased" her. Easy, unfinishing work quite satisfied her. All she wanted was her nights and Sunday afternoons and Thursdays out. The house mistress turned to occasionally and on "Thursdays out" scoured the pots and pans. But she sighed for the sunny kitchen with the great clothes boiler and the bread oven on the other side, the servant's table with its pretty checked cloth folded and put away in the drawer, the great ironing-board down which she used to slide, and the mysterious row of bells along the cornice. If she could only find out just which bell was which! And being a terribly irregular person herself she longed for the days when somebody made things go and go punctually and beautifully in order.

But that was quite some years ago. And now theEditor having long given up the Monday, Tuesday, and here it is Wednesday week, and nothing done, finds that week after week slips by and here it is April, and the next month will be May, and then it will be June and the year half over and nothing done.

THE ENGLISH OF IT.

On a fifty-three mile cross-country drive recently, from one county-seat to another, the Editor stayed the taxi long enough at a small town drugstore to have an ice cream. The chauffeur declined the ice cream but what he did accept the Editor leaves the reader to guess. She listened to the attendant giving the order to another and this is what he said: "*Ice cream and smopas!*" Just as a clue it is added that the "smopases" were wrapped up and could be carried out to the car.

There is something rather pleasantly homely about "*Did you want off?*" which is quite common over a large section.

There are a number of interesting publications either out or promised. Of these many will enjoy JUDGE ROBERTSON'S historical notes of Northampton County, Virginia. Some of these are reprints of valuable notes which appeared in an Eastern Shore paper......the local files of the paper were destroyed by fire some years ago with many of JUDGE ROBERTSON'S collected records. These are only a small part of the volume, however, for the author is an indefatigable researcher as well as an historian, and as a lawyer (he is the Judge of the Hopewell Corporation Court) he has been able to make something of more understandable value than some others of us out of the early local court records of our country.

The book is being published by the William-Byrd Press of Richmond. The Editor regrets that she has not the full title at hand.

Mr. STRATTON NOTTINGHAM is at work on his index of ACCOMACK WILLS AND ADMINISTRATIONS. It may be unoriginal to say so, but this volume will most surely "fill a long-felt want."

Since this paragraph was written, Mr. Nottingham's REVOLUTIONARY [and other] SOLDIERS OF LANCASTER County, and the perfectly invaluable LAND CAUSES OF ACCOMACK COUNTY, have been received. Comment will appear later.

Miss MARY DENHAM ACKERLY, of Lexington, Virginia, in association with Mrs. GEORGE F. PARKER, has completed a volume called "OUR KIN." This book contains genealogical data relating to many old families of Bedford County, Virginia, and is so comprehensive in its scope (it has more than 800 pages) it will be greatly in demand. The price is $15. The edition limited.

A MATTER OF IMPORTANCE

The Editor of the NOTE-BOOK will pay ten dollars ($10) for a copy of the WILL of WILLIAM FLOYD, or a copy (in full) of the administration of his estate.

WILLIAM FLOYD was living in 1783; had wife ABADIAH, and probably living sons ROBERT, CHARLES and NATHANIEL. He was also the father of Col. JOHN FLOYD. WILLIAM FLOYD may have died in one of the frontier counties of Virginia, Kentucky, or in one of the Territories northwest of the Ohio. He was about 56 years old in 1783 and owned land in the upper Valley of Virginia. He had removed to the frontier, but was driven back by the uprising among the Indians. Where he then settled is unknown.

In response to this query several kindly persons, wishing to be helpful, have been at some pains to send published material which the Editor has already eollected. What the Editor wants is something nobody seems to know about.

CONTINUED articles COUNTY COURT NOTE-BOOK, and the dates on which they first appeared.

THE ANCESTRY OF COL. JOHN DONELSON. Began with February, 1927.

AUTHENTIC REFERENCES for INFERRED MARRIAGES (formerly called MARRIAGES BY INFERENCE). Began with May, 1922.

MARYLAND'S NEXT OF KIN. Began with July, 1922.

VIRGINIA COLONISTS. Alphabetized lists began with July, 1924.

MILITARY NOTES, both COLONIAL and REVOLUTIONARY, and later MILITIA NOTES. Began December, 1923.

INTERCOUNTY and INTERCOLONY (formerly called New Englanders and Others, &c., &c.). Began with March, 1922.

EASTERN SHORE FAMILIES. In the form of a one-page supplement, began with June, 1925.

SHIPS IN PORT and COLONIAL FORENAMES will appear in alternate issues or as space can be found for them.

STAFFORD COUNTY INDICES began in June, 1929.

VARIA

EMBELLISHING A DAUGHTER.

Case of Lightfoot vs Lightfoot.........Francis Lightfoot (certain contingencies provided for) ...."to my Daughter Elizabeth 2500 £ current money of Virginia".........the attorney commenting on this bequest argues "There is nothing unkind or unreasonable in this. A very ample Portion is provided for the Daughter So as to make her a Suitable match to any Estate in the Colony. P. R88 of Virginia Colonial Decisions. Vol. i.

FROM THE CALENDAR OF [BRITISH] STATE PAPERS COLONIAL SERIES.

Of Plymouth........."a good silent people, never venemous in the Rebellion." [Was this *our* Plymouth?]

FAUQUIER COUNTY, VIRGINIA.

In the record of a suit in that county, [or in that judicial district] the following appears:

As to Germantown........."all the parties were German born beyond Sea of the Allegiance of our Sovereign Lord the King and none of them had never been Naturalized........ except John Hoffman, John Fishback, and Jacob Holtzclaw." Then follows an agreement as to how the patents should be taken out and the tracts leased. The original patent, it appears, was granted in 1724.

ALSO FAUQUIER COUNTY.

"For reasons appearing to the Court it is ordered that no person be inoculated for the small pox in this county for the future." Ct. 28 Apr 1771. Orders 1775-1783. But this is followed on the 26 May 1777 by this: "Leave is granted to any of the Inhabitants of this County to inoculate their families with the small pox where any of them shall have taken the disorder in the natural way."

AGAIN FAUQUIER. From the 1st vol. of Land Causes, p. 4.

Testimony in a case. "Jamie this is the line between you and I and if there should be a tree cut down on either side there shall be no suing between us.........if you cut one of mine I will cut two of yours." (Stone v. Stephenson.)

A NORTH CAROLINA WILL.

ELIZABETH SCOLLAY, of Bertie county, North Carolina, widow: Desires to be buried beside her late husband Samuel Scollay, and that a Genteel Tombstone be Provided; mentions son Thomas Pollock, son Cullin Pollock; Should son Thomas die without issue, reversion of negroes and plate provided to children of Tully Williams and the children of Richard Saunders. Negroes and plate given to son Thomas to be in care of Dr. Robert Lenox until otherwise ordered by sd Thomas. Mrs. Fannie Lenox, wf of Dr. Robert Lenox; Dr. Robert Lenox, John Scollay of Boston to have a negro and two bonds in consideration of a debt she owes him. One of the bonds is of Joseph Robinson of Perquimans county, and the other of Hon. John Rutherford.) Mentions Peggy Cathcart, dau. of Dr. William Cathcart; Sarah Blount, daughter of Joseph Blount; to Sophia Rasor. daughter of Edward; Fanny Cathcart daughter of Dr. William Cathcart; Thomas Blount son of Joseph; Cullin and Thomas Pollock to pay Mrs. Sarah Vaughan eight pounds a year. Remits money due her from Tully Williams; mentions former husband Mr. Thomas Pollock; Certifies that none of the negroes she has given to kindred and friends belong to Pollock. Thomas Pollock, Dr. Robert Lenox, Richard Sanderson, and Joseph Blount, extra. Wit: Hardy Hardison, Fred'k Hardison. 1 Dec 1776-4 Feby 1767. P. 90 of wills.

(The legacies are mostly of negroes.)

THE "FORTIES"

Perhaps others, as well as the Editor, have wondered what the "Forties" were, reminding some of spaces of the sea, and others of Scottish uprisings. This following is copied from a photostat of an old Northumberland county, Virginia, record.

Each of the names in this list is followed by a figure, Arthur Lynton, "5", Wm. Hill, "2", &c., &c. These, perhaps, represent the "tithes" of the gentlemen, or the "mates" of the workingmen. Possibly there were no workingmen in the list but all were independent landholders, calling themselves "planters." The record fails to discriminate. Perhaps Arthur Lynton counted as a fifth of a "forty." The term "supernumeraries," following "Vizt." and heading the list is puzzling. A search of Hening would probably make it clear, but there are always good people who enjoy explaining things, so the Editor throws herself upon the country with a frank confession of ignorance.

Att a Court for Northumberland County the 7th of June 1679......The Court haveing according to Act of Assembly in that Case made, received the Lyst of the Tythables in this County, & divided them into forties doe Order that each forty fitt out forthwth an able man & horse & p'vide for him a Case of pistolls, a Carbine, a Sword, eighty pounds of dryed porke or Bacon or one hundred pound of dryed Beefe, two Bushells of meale, & five Bushells of Indian Corne, & that the Sd p'vision be forthwith brought to the house of Mr. Thomas Mathew, the rest of Bow parish to the house of Mr. Richard Kenner, Necoman's Neck [?] and that Constables P'cincts to the house of Mr. Peter Presley, Senior, Little Wiccocomoco, & the North side of Great Wiccocomoco River as high as Mr. William Wildeyes to the house of Maj'r Thomas Brereton, the rest of Fairefeild parish to the house of William Downing Junior; all Wiccocomoco Parish to the house of Capt. William Downing, the p'visions to be brought in by the 14th of this Instant And the men fitted as aforesd to meet in Adam Yarratt's feild, on the twenty third Instant The Inhabitants ordered to Send out their men Apportioned as follows (VIZT:) Supernumeraries

Arth. Lynton, Wm. Hill, Jno. Knott, Jno. Roach, Dr. Pemberton, Adam Booth, Tho. Hickman, Jno. Bird, Steph. Wells, Sam'll Churchill, Rich'd Wells, Rich'd Bradly, Ph. Norgate, Rob't Bradly, Tho. Evans, Thos. Hopper, Wm. Hayward,......Claughton, ...Johnson,[......illegible] Jno. Claughton, Phill. Drake, Barth. Leazure' Tho. Hall;

Tho. Perryn, Jas. Crean, Geo. Hutton, Dan'll Beacham, Tho: Short, Phill. Boggus, Edw. Barnes, Edw. Williams, Ja. Seabury, Ja. Blewsone [?] Wm. Keen, Fra. Boon, Fra. Little, Hen. Boggus, Wm. Joeb [?] Wm. Owen, Mr. Tho. Mathew, Coll. Griffin, Jno. Rogers, Hen. Metcalfe, Ralph Stephens, Dom. Rice, Jno. Mitchell, Mr. Opie, Tho. Miller;

Jno. Waters, Abra. Joice, Geo. Courtnell, Wm. Dawson, Wm. Beane, Rich'd Flynt, [Peterf. ?] Alnerson, Jno. Stanly, Walter Grady, Wm. Garner, Tho. Simmons, Jno. Oldham, Cloud Tullos, Tho. Towdry, [Cowdry?] Walter Syms, Will. Taylor, Jno. Sanders, Tho. Shirly, Jno. Greensted, Jno. Beaz or Boaz [final letter cannot be made out] Robt Shepard, Jno. Powell.

(To be continued)

SERVICE AND SUPPLIES, COLONIAL, REVOLUTIONARY AND MILITIA

BENJAMIN x PHIPPS, a resident of Grayson city, Va., age 70. Was living at the house of Capt. John Cox on New River in Montgomery cty, now Grayson, about 1779 or 1780, engaged in making a crop of corn, when Col. Roberts at the head of a company of tories came and made prisoners of himself, Wm. Craig and Beverly Watkins......[This is very interesting but too long for a full abstract.] PHIPPS says he was born in Guilford cty, N. C. in 1761 or 1762, as he believes. Grayson cty, Va. Orders. 24 Sept 1832.

TIMOTHY SPENCER, a resident of Grayson cty, age 74. Entered the service of the United States, he believes in the fall of 1776, being drafted under Capt. Smith, of Salem, N. C., and marched against the Cherokee Indians. [Long account follows in detail.] Court declare that he was a Revolutionary soldier. Grayson cty, Va. Orders. Aug. Ct 1832.

WILLIAM CLOUD, resident of Grayson cty, aged 82. Entered under Capt. James Lyon in the fall of 1766, as a volunteer private soldier, then being a resident of the present county of Patrick, then being the county of Henry. Marched in a company with an expedition commanded by Col. Wm. Christian of Botetourt, against the Cherokee towns, 300 miles through the wilderness. On this expedition many of the Indian Towns and Crops were destroyed, and a Mrs. BEANE, who had been taken by the Indians was recovered and restored to her friends......[Many details given.] Grayson cty, Orders. 30 Aug 1832.

BENJAMIN BEASLY, resident of Grayson cty. Aged 70. Entered the service a year or two before the capture of Cornwallis, being then a resident of King and Queen county, under Capt. John Pollard......Grayson cty, Orders. 30 Aug. 1832.

DENNIS FIELDER, resident of Grayson, aged 76. Entered as a volunteer under Capt. John Clark, in May 1776 or 1777. At the time he volunteered he resided in Prince Edward cty, and continued to live there until 1789. Was born in Goochland, 21 Apr 1756. Grayson cty, Orders. 24 Sept 1832.

WILLIAM VAUGHN, a resident of Grayson cty. Entered service before Battle of Guilford as a substitute for William Vaughn the elder. [Long account of service.] Born in Hanover cty 1760. Lived in Bedford cty when he entered service. Grayson cty, Orders. 24 Sept 1832.

STEPHEN CLARK, Grayson cty, aged 70. Entered service while residing in Goochland. Was called upon to assist in guarding prisoners. Born Goochland cty, 1762, and resided there until 1805. Grayson cty, Orders. 24 Sept 1832.

The following are from the Minutes of Montgomery County, in the form of a "scratch book," beginning 7 Apr 1778.

JAMES MOORE, apptd Capt. Militia on the waters of Blue Stone. 8 Apr 1778.

BENJA. BAILEY, 1st Lieut., Capt. Bobbett's Co. Same date.

JOHN ALLCORN, ensign, Capt. Montgomery's Company. Same date. He took the oath of the Ensign of the militia. 5 May 1778.

JNO. HAYES, 2d Lieut. Same date.

JNO. KING, Ensign. Same date.

WILLIAM DOAK to be recommended for Captain in the bounds laid off by Mr. Davis and Mr. Buchanan. Same date.

JAMES DOWNING, takes oath as 1st Lieut Militia. Same date.

JAMES MOORE, Gent., oath as Captain of Militia. Same date.

JAMES MAXWELL, oath as Captain. Same date.

ROBERT MOFFETT, oath as 1st Lieut. Same date.

WILLIAM DOAK (see above) takes oath. Same date.

GEORGE PEARY, recommended for 1st Lieut.. Capt. Moore's Company, WILLIAM McGuire as 2d Lieut., and DAV'D INGLIS as Ensign. 1 Sept 1778.

WILLIAM WARD sworn as a Lieut. in Capt. Doak's Company. 2 Feby 1779.

CHRISTIAN SNIDE, recommended for Ensign, Capt. Lucas' Company of Militia. 3 Mch 1779.

CHARLES CAMPBELL, Ensign Capt. Buchanan's Company. 3 Mch 1779.

JEREMIAH PAYTE is excused from Military duty, being upwards of fifty years of age. 8 Apr 1778.

SAMUELL BRUMETT, and WM. ROBERTSON, are both unfit for service and so exempted. 8 Apr 1778.

ANDREW STEEL, who was "Drayghtyed", produced a Certificate of taking a deserter and is discharged for sd service. 8 Apr 1778.

EDMOND BROOKS was hired as a substitute. 8 Apr 1778.

JACOB KETTERING fined and imprisoned [apparently a sincere "Tory.] 6 Jany 1778.

HENRY FRANCIS is apptd Captain of Militia in the room of ANDREW THOMPSON, who is about to remove out of this State. 3 Mch 1778.

JAMES MONTGOMERY, recommended for Captain of Militia in the room of Capt. William BUCHANAN, who is in the "Kantucky" service. 8 Apr 1778.

SAMUEL CAMPBELL produced commission from the Committee of Safety appointing him Lieut. of Militia, and takes the oath. 21 Oct 1775.

GILES THOMAS, aged 68. Entered the service of the United States in the Maryland State Regiment, 26 July 1780, in Charles county, Regiment commanded by Alexander Smith, Edward Giles, Maj., Chas. Smith, Captain. Was in the service three years, until 26 July 1783. Was at Battle of Guilford, Camden and siege of "96.".........The Regiment on Continental establishment was commanded by Col. Gunby...Captain named Bruff; Brigadier Gist. Court declare opinion that THOMAS was a Revolutionary soldier. Orders, 1829-1832. Mont. cty. Ct. 6 Aug 1832.

SAMUEL CADDALL [*sic*] aged 73, makes declaration. Volunteered 1780 with Capt. Paxton in the 2d Va. Regt. of the line in Rockbridge cty, Va. Joined the regiment under Capt. Samuel Lasly, Colo. Haws commanding, and continued until 1782. After Col. Haws left the service from ill health, Col. Campbell took the command and was killed at the battle of Eutaw. Other officers mentioned. Was at the siege of "96." Court of opinion he was Revolutionary soldier. Orders 1829-1832. Ct. 8 Aug 1832.

HENRY MEYSER [or WEIZER?] a resident of Montgomery cty, aged 78. Enlisted in the U. S. Army in 1776, under Capt. Berry, in Frederick cty, Va. Served in the 8th Va. Regt. Gives his route to Sullivan's Island, S. C. Was there when attacked by British shipping. Was sick in Sunsberry, Ga., furloughed home and then ordered to Philadelphia.........Discharged Feby, 1779, at the White Horse in Penna. Returned home, married and lived in Frederick cty until 1781, when he was drafted. Was at the taking of Cornwallis. Court of opinion he was a Revolutionary soldier. [Name seems to be Wyser.] Orders 1829-1832. Ct. 3 Sepr 1832.

PETER CLINE, a resident of Pike cty, Kentucky. Aged 76. Enlisted in the army of the U. S. in 1774 [*sic*] with Capt. Henry Miller and served in the 12th Regt of the Penna line. Gives names of officers. Left service in Sept. 1777. ....At the time he entered service resided in *Redingtown* Barracks, *county* and State of Penna. Peter x Cline. Court declare opinion he was a Revolutionary soldier. 3 Sept 1832. Same record.

MARRIAGE REFERENCES FROM NORTH AND SOUTH CAROLINA

JOACHIM BODLEY and JAIME [perhaps meant for Jeanne?] HENRIETT DAMERY. Mar. settlement (in French). Chowan cty, N. C. S1-116.

JOSEPH BUNDY and ELIZABETH HENLEY, permission to marry. Pasquotauk, N. C. Mo'ly Mtg. 18-1-1786.

JOHN CATE and the widow of JAMES BENTON. Before 20 Mch. 1780. Ct. Minutes, Person cty, N. C.

EPHRAIM COOK, planter, and MEHETABEL BLACKWELL, 30 Apr 1798. Georgetown Dist. S. C. Grants. III-270.

Rev. JOSEPH B. COOK, of Beaufort, S. C. and ELEANOR S. WALKER, of Georgetown, S. C. [Probably before] 6 June 1801. Grants. IV-87.

.........CRITTENDEN and LUCY COX, dau. of Philip. Caswell cty, N. C. deeds. Before Jany court 1826.

STEPHEN COLEMAN and POLLY WILLIAMS. Before 1822.. Rockin cty, N. C Equity Ct. records.

LEWIS DILLARHERTY and LUCINDA JOHNSTON. Before 1822. Rockin cty, N. C. Equity Court records.

TOWNSEND DENT and MARY HEIGHTOUR. Cabarrus cty, N. C. M. L. B. 12 May 1792.

ABRAHAM DAVENPORT and ELIZABETH BOLSHANNON. 1797. Tryon and Lincoln counties, N. C. Abstract of M. L. B.

SOLOMON ELLIOTT and RACHAEL GRIGORY. 28 May 1797. Chowan cty, N. C. B2-303.

JOEL EMERY and EVE FITE. Rowan cty, N. C. M. L. B. 17 Mch 1828. [This bond is signed *Hembre.*]

HENRY FROLEY and CATHARINE CHARLES. Mar. contract. Rowan cty, N. C. 10 May 1763. VI-45.

GEORGE GIBSON and MARGARET HOUSTON, extx of George HOUSTON. Before July or Sept 1783. Ct. Minutes, Mecklenburg cty, N. C.

JOSEPH GENTRY and ELIZABETH GALLAWAY, wid. of James. About 1800. See Equity Court Record. Rock'm cty, N. C.

ROBERT GALLAWAY and POLLY GALLAWAY, only child of Charles. Probably before 1800. See Equity Court Records, Rockin Cty, N. C.

JOHN B. GRIFFIN and Mrs. CHARITY NEWLY, widow of Wyke Newly, 30 Oct 1779. Chowan cty, N. C. B 2 — 293.

AARON HOGGATT [HACKETT ?] and TABITHA HAMBLETON, Rowan cty, N. C. M. L. B. 25 July 1798.

BERRY x HUNT and MARY STARKEY, Orange cty, N. C. M. L. B. 18 May 1792.

JOHN HANKS and MARY JANE ARMSTRONG. Orange cty., N. C. M. L. B. 8 Oct 1795.

JOSEPH HENDERSON and WINNIE HUSBANDS, N. C. M. L. B. 3 July 1811.

THOMAS HUNTER and SARAH NORFLEET. Marriage agreement. Gates cty, N. C. Nov. 1797. IV-225.

THOMAS HILL and ANN HASKILL, permission to marry. Pasquotank Mo'ly Mtg, N. C. 16-3d-1785.

JOHN HOLLAND and CHRISTIANA ROBISON, Rowan cty, N. C. M. L. B. 26 Aug 1783.

JESSE HILL and MARY PRITCHARD; marriage approved. Pasquotank Mo'ly Mtg, N. C. 15-2-1786.

FREDERICK JACKSON and NANCY GOODWIN, extx of Sampson Goodwin. Union cty, S. C. Ct. Minutes. Before 2 Oct 1809.

THOMAS JACKSON and ESTHER [HAMOND?] [Esther was admx of Clement Hamond.] Inventories, &c. Bertie cty, N. C. Before 10 May 1736.

JOHN JORDAN and ELIZABETH TROTTER, widow of Thomas. (She d. 27-9th mo. 1788.) Pasquotank and Little River Register. Guilford College, N. C.

.... KING and RACHEL PERKINS, dau of Jesse. Before 11 Oct 1814. (She was then a widow.) Caswell cty, N. C. deeds.

ALBRIGHT LYDIE (?) and MARGARET COONE, eldest dau. of Michael. Before May, 1777. Rowan cty, N. C. Minute Book.

OWEN LINDLEY and SARAH THOMPSON, dau. of James. Orange cty, N. C. Before 7th mo. 1794. C-21.

MAXIMILIAN NORRIS and TAMAR SMITHSON. 22 Jany 1740. Pasquotank cty, N. C. records, Births, &c. p. 44.

JOHN PRYOR and BETSY PERKINS, dau. of Peter. (She m. (2) Henly Stone.) See Rock'm cty, N. C. Equity Court Records. [The date is not clear — but before 1822.]

JOHN PALMER, Jr., Esq., St. Stephen's Psh, and MARY ANN JERMAN, St. James' Psh. S. C. [Probably before] 5 May 1795. Grants II-379.

LEMUEL PRICE and CHARITY BUCKHANNON. 17 Sept 1795. Chowan cty, N. C. B 2-299.

WILLIAM REED and ELIZABETH DOUGLAS, marriage settlement. Orange cty, Minute Book I-13. 14 Mch 1753. A License from the President of Pensylvania & certificate of marriage between William Reed & Elizabeth Douglas, signed by Peter Tranburge, Missionary, of Wilmington in said Province was exhibited in open court . . and ordered to be Registered.

WILLIAM ROBINSON and MARY ABERNANTHIE, wid. of Thomas. Grants, S. C. II-458. 25 Dec 1795.

JAMES SAMPLE and MARTHA ROBINSON. 14 June 1802. Meckl. cty, N. C. M. L. B.

WILLIAM SAMPLE and SALLY SMITH. 17 Jany 1804. Meckl. cty, N. C. M. L. B.

JOSEPH SAMPLE and ELIZ: ROBINSON. 4 Feby 1801. Meckl. cty, N. C. M. L. B.

WILLIAM SCOTT and LUCY JOHNSON. 1 Jany 1800. Meckl. cty, N. C. M. L. B.

JOSEPH SCALES and ANN WILLIAMS, dau. of Nathaniel. Before 1 Dec 1803. Rock'm cty, N. C. A-26.

JOHN SANDERS and MARTHA WHITE, permission to marry. Pasquotank Mo'ly Mtg. N. C. 16-3d-1785.

FREDERICK SIMPSON and LYDIA ELLIOTT. 2 May 1796. Chowan cty, N. C. B2-303.

JOSEPH B. TUCKER and a dau. of Joseph BROCK Union cty, S. C. Before 14 Sept 1807. Ct minutes.

A BRIEF LIST OF THE MOST IMPORTANT SUBJECTS IN THE NOTE-BOOK, 1921-1929.

To simplify references and save space the issues of the NOTE-BOOK are referred to by number. The December copy is 49. Just number your NOTE-BOOK forward, or backward, if you choose, and the rest is easy.

Abbreviations, No. 17.
Accidents and findings, 25.
Accomack county, Va. See Marriages.
Accomack county notes (Gale-Littleton marriage), 21. (See Genealogical Blunders.)
Annapolis records, 4.
Anne Arundell orphans, 18 to 23.
Ashland, Ky. graveyard, 13.
Berkeley county, W. Va., notes, 38.
Bertie county, N. C., records, 39.
Bourbon county, Ky. Early pioneers, 9-11.
Brook Family chart, 26.
Calendar, 37.
Custis Family, 22-25, 29-32.
Custis-Tomkins, 16.
Day heirs, 13.
Deputy Commissary's Guide (Maryland), 38, 40, 42, 43, 48.
Donelson ancestry, 32-37, 42.
English records, 5-8, 40.
Fauquier county, Va. Land Causes, 10.
Floyd-Stewart book, 1.
Frederick county, Md Revolutionary, &c., 12.
Orphans, 12-17, 32.
Marriages, 25.
Friends, banished, 19-25, 29, 31.
Meetings, 1.
Memorials and records, 1, 7, 13, 15, 20.
Gale-Littleton, 21, 32.
Genealogical blunders, see Scrambled families, Custis-Tomkins, also Gale-Littleton. Also Kennedy-Wilson.
Georgia Archives, 16.
Marriages, 24.
Hyde county, N. C. Notes, 41, 44.
Kennedy-Wilson, 8.
Kentucky records, (mainly) persons born in Virginia, 14-17.
Court of Appeals, lists from, (mainly) persons born in Virginia. 27-30.
King George county, Virginia.
Bonds, 8.
Probates, &c. 17, 19, 20-23, 45-47.
Library (early private), 2.
Marriages, 4-16, 17 (2), 18-24, 25 (2), 26-34, 36-45, 47, 48, 49.
Mirandas, 1.
Eves, 25.
Smiths, 30.
Maryland counties, 31.
Inventories (Next of Kin), 5-11, 13-17, 19, 20, 24-28, 30, 32, 33, 35, 38, 40, 42, 46, 47, 49.
Marriages (and note), 41, 43, 44, 46.
Notes, 43.
Monongalia county, West Va. 19. (See also Revolutionary.)
Moses (pedigree), 3.
Mourning, a name, 2-4.
Names, 1-4, 9, 10, 13, 15, 16, 18, 24, 27, 29, 35, 41, 43, 48.
Naturalizations, 8, 10, 12, 14, 15, 17, 19, 20.
North Carolina counties, 28.
Northampton county, Va. notes, 15, 28. (See also marriages.)
Tithables, 42-46, 48, 49.
North Carolina notes, 39, 47.
Wills, 39. (See also marriages.)
Notes referring to two or more counties or colonies (now called Intercolony and Intercounty, formerly New Englanders and others, &c.), 3, 4, 6, 8, 10, 12, 15, 19, 23-26, 28, 29, 31-33, 37, 39, 40, 42, 43, 45, 47, 49.
Ohio county, West Va. 20.
Tax-lists, 10, 14, 24, 26.
Old houses, 3.
Paris postman, 3.
Pirates, 30.
Presbyterians, 16.
Prince William county, Va., probates, &c. 9-13, 18-21, 23. Bonds, 1-6.
Queen Victoria's ancestry, 41.
Renunciation of allegiance, 41, 43.
Revolutionary, &c. 11-15, 17-34, 36, 38-40, 42-44, 46, 47.
See also Frederick, Md., Monongalia county, West Va., and West Virginia.
Richmond county, Va., probates, &c. 21, 22, 24, 25.
Sampson county, N. C., wills, 39.
Scrambled families (Scarburgh-Smart-Whittington-Custis), 30, 31.
Ships mentioned in court records, 7, 9, 11, 16, 17, 20, 22, 24, 26, 29, 38, 41, 48.
Sixteen hundred and eighty script, 18.
Smith marriages, 30.
Somerset county, Md., records in Worcester county, Md. 11.
South Carolina districts and counties, 21.
Stafford county, Va., probates, &c. 46.
Ctfs for land, 48.
Lost wills as shown by index, 46, 48, 49.
Tennessee counties, 27.
Virginia counties, 25.
Patents, State Land Office, head-rights, 16-28, 33, 39-44, 49.
Records, 1, 2.
State Library, manuscript material, 14.
Webbs, 1-14.
West Augusta District, Va., records, 23.
Westmoreland county, Va., marriages, 26-28, 34.
West Virginia, revolutionary, &c. 11.
Whittington family, 43-49.
Williams family (notes), 26-33, 35, 37, 38, 40.
Wisconsin, 12.
York county, Va., marriages, 45.

Printed at the Industrial School for Crippled and Deformed Children, 241 St. Botolph St., Boston, Mass.

The

County Court Note-Book

A Little Bulletin of History and Genealogy

June, 1930. Vol. IX, No. 3

ROBERT WADE'S LEGACY

[Very direct family tradition states that WILLIAM PENN when he landed at Upland (now Chester) was received by ROBERT WADE at his home, and that he stayed there his first night in America. In addition, very interesting Pennsylvania records show that WADE bought this tract and that it had a previous history in connection with the Swedish and Dutch governments of the colony. The little old record book showing Wade's purchase is in Harrisburg. The brick mansion stood near the river front in Chester until some time in the last century.]

The following Deed of Exchange was found by a friendly correspondent after many years' unavailing search by the Editor.

It is given here with the hope that there may be among the readers of the NOTE-BOOK, by some happy chance, a descendant of either THOMAS or JOHN WADE, brothers of ROBERT, or the descendant of some other brother, unknown to the colonial court records. ROBERT WADE left no children, and there seem to have been very few left of the Chester county Wades.........though all of the name in that county are thought to be of the same family. Quite reliable tradition has it that several of the generation living in 1775, young men, and unmarried, were lost in the Revolutionary service. Capt. JOHN WADE, who must have died shortly before 1782, is thought to have been a great-nephew, perhaps a nephew of ROBERT. He was not, it seems, of the Society of Friends, and his line may have been disowned for departing and differing at least a generation before. Unfortunately, there are few other church records.

This list of names may be of value to others than WADE descendants; only two names in the list are known to belong to the WADES through marriage; ELISHA PRICE and MARY OLIVER.

This conveyance is dated 27 Dec. 1770, and was recorded [in spite of missing acknowledgments] 13 Mch 1771.

Grantors: Henry Hale (party of the first part, does not sign or acknowledge); John Salkeld, Edward Russell, Jonas Preston, David Cowpland, Eleanor Hanby, Samuel Shaw, Joseph Ashbridge, Joseph Howell, Samuel Howell, Isaac Howell, Joshua Howell, Joshua Howell, Elisha Price, George Spear, Mary Oliver, David Ogden, John Morgan, Thomas Pedrick, James Mather (parties of the second part, do not sign or acknowledge);

Grantees: Israel Pemberton, John Reynall, Samuel Preston Moore, James Pemberton, Hugh Roberts, Owen Jones, Joseph Morris, Richard Wistar, Samuel Rhoads, Isaac Greenleaf, Thomas Clifford, Henry Drinker, Joshua Howell, Abel James, Jacob Shoemaker, Jr., the present overseers of the Public School Founded by Charter in the Town and City of Philadelphia. (Parties of the Third part.)

Recital:

Will of ROBERT WADE, dated May 9, 1698, to the Free School at Philadelphia and 5£ yearly towards maintaining same forever and thereby charged his plantation in Chester called "ESSEX HOUSE" containing 360 acres with payments as to such times as set forth in the will duly proved and in the Register General's Office at Philadelphia, the devisees have sold the said plantation called "ESSEX HOUSE" to the party of the first part and parties of the second part.

The "Recital" continues: "WHEREAS great inconveniences have arisen as to the owners and possessors of the said plantation called 'ESSEX HOUSE' as to the said Overseers in proportioning collecting and receiving the said Yearly Rent of 5£ for preventing of which for the future and to the end and intent that all controversies disputes difficulties inconveniences might be amiably settled and the good intentions of the said ROBERT WADE more easily executed and performed and that the owners and possessors of the plantation aforesaid might hold and enjoy their several and respective parts and shares thereof free and clear of the same it was sometime heretofore mutually agreed by and between the said parties of the third part and owners and possessors of said plantation that they the said parties of the third part would accept in lieu or change thereof, one Annuity or Ground Rent in Philadelphia payable by one person only, and chargeable upon such a lot or tenement as in all probability would not be divided for which end and purpose the said party of the first part as well by and with the direction and approbation of the said Overseers as of the said owners and possessors of said plantation called 'ESSEX HOUSE' and with his and the owner's proper monies purchased the said Annuity or Ground Rent of 5£ 5s. hereinafter described.........in exchange for the said Yearly Rent of 5£ per annum and of one year's arrears of the said Yearly Rent now due and remaining unpaid as above set forth."

Under the heading of "GRANT" a description of the ground rent follows, the piece of ground being in Mulberry street (commonly called Arch Street) in Philadelphia, 19 ft 4 inches broad, and 107 ft long. Bounded by lands of Joshua Howell, Jacob Cooper, Frederick Hailer, and Mulberry or Arch street. "It being the same Ground Rent or Annuity which party of the first part purchased.........of and from Peter Knight of the Township of Northern Liberties in the City of Philadelphia merchant, and Elizabeth his wife by Indenture dated July 12th last."

The several paragraphs which follow merely release all persons having an interest in "ESSEX HOUSE" from the payment of any further annual charge for the benefit of the Philadelphia School, with the usual clauses as to repossession, &c., should this agreement not be followed out.

It is remarkable that neither the party of the first part or the parties of the second part acknowledged this paper. There was, at the time, running upon the most valuable heart of the property, a lease which the records, as examined, show to have been for 999 years. This may have complicated matters. It may be further noted that MARY OLIVER is known to have been a daughter of one of the WADES. And MIRIAM WADE, who in 1771 or 1772 was the wife of SAUL ROBINSON, was the daughter of another WADE and in all probability grand-niece of ROBERT, the testator. Tradition, with great particularity, says that a sister (?) or an aunt (?) of MIRIAM signed a "quit-claim." MIRIAM WADE could have had no interest in the property unless she descended from one of ROBERT'S brothers.

AUTHENTIC REFERENCES FOR INFERRED MARRIAGES

(Accomack county, Virginia)

MARK EWELL and COMFORT HOPE (probably). She was dau. of George HOPE. Before 20 Jany 1721. xvi-169.

SOLOMON EWELL and COMFORT TAYLOR. Before 5 June 1733. xx-134.

THOMAS *EVERGEN* and JOAN EDGE, widow. About 2 Mch 1702. xii-141.

.... FOSQUE probably m. SARAH JAMES, dau. of William. Before 13 Aug 1766. Diii-427.

JOSEPH FITZGERRALD probably m. SUSANNA CHANDLER, dau. of Solomon. Before 22 Feby 1757. xxvW-396.

SALATHIEL FIRCHETT and MARGARET HALL, dau. of Michael. Before 30 Aug 1774. Div-365.

DANIEL EASOM and GERTRUDE CROPER. About 22 Mch 1692. x-99.

JAMES EAST and RACHEL TURLINGTON. After 3 Jany 1785 and before 29 May 1796. 1773-1805, p. 154.

JOHN EYRE and ANN UPSHUR, dau. Abel. Before 30 May 1803. L. C. 1773-1805, p. 253.

COVENTON EWELL and MARY MATHEWS, oldest dau. John. Before 23 Aug 1777. xx-153.

JOHN GILLET of Som. cty, Md and ESTHER-ANNE-FRANCES AYRES, dau. Richard-Hill AYRES. Before 7 Oct 1735. xx-216.

CHRISTOPHER GLASS of Som. cty, Md. and PARTHENIA FOSTER, dau. of Thomas. Before 4 Mch 1706. xi-423. See also xx-233.

MATHIAS GALE and MARGARET GORDON, dau. of William of Middx cty., Va. Before 22 Feby 1755. ii-572.

JAMES GIBSON probably m. SARAH PREESON. Before 5 Nov. 1734. L. C. p. 16.

THOMAS GITTING and ELIZABETH [BELL] dau. of Thomas [?] About 10 Sept 1674. v-191.

MAXMILLIAN GORE and the widow of John SMITH. About 16 Dec 1678. viii-41.

JOHN GIBSON, of Glasgow, and CHRISTIAN ANDERSON. Long before 6 July 1728. xvi-340.

WILLIAM GROTEN and MARY KELLAM, dau. of Edward. Before or about 6 Sept 1720. xvi-127. See also ix-303.

LEVIN GALE and SARAH CUSTIS, sister of *Levin* CUSTIS. See the latter's will, 1733-1735. xx-212.

JOSEPH GLADING probably m. ANN EWELL, sister of George. Before 24 Apr 1728. xvi-310; xxi-147.

THOMAS GASCOYNE and MARY SNEAD, dau. of Robert and Mary. Before 8 Nov 1727. xvi-293.

LEVIN GALE and LEAH LITTLETON. Before 24 Aug 1725. xvi-244.

JOSEPH GONTEE, of Dor. cty, Md. and ELIZABETH JOHNSON, dau. of Alexander. Before 8 Oct 1756. Dii-719. Before 1719. (See ix-215.)

JAMES GOOTIE and LETITIA RUSSELL, dau. Robert, Sr. Before 1836. See L. C. 1831, p. 22.

ANDREW GILCHRIST probably m. TABITHA BURTON, wid. of Samuel. See record 30 Mch 1762. xxviiW-61.

WILLIAM HOPE and JOANNA-MARY CUSTIS, dau. Col. William CUSTIS. Hope was the son of George. Before 6 Aug 1718. xvi-55.

.... HANCOCK and TABITHA FLETCHER, sister of John, who d. 1811. See L. C. 1812-1821, p. 39. [No approx. date.]

WILLIAM HINMAN and TABITHA BUNDICK, sister of Elias. Before 26 Nov. 1805. See L. C. 1773-1805, p. 313.

GEORGE HAMBLING and ELIZABETH RODOLPHUS, widow of William. About May 1665. ii-14. See also 1-124.

JOSEPH HOLSTON and ELIZABETH NEWTON, wid. of Sterling. Before 6 June 1710. xiv-5.

HENRY HEWBANCK and MARY BONEWELL, widow of James. About 6 Oct 1702. xii-132.

WILLIAM HUGHS of Stafford cty, Va., and ELIZABETH SULLIVANT, widow of Dorman, of Acco. Before 30 Aug 1708. xi-456.

ALLEX'R HARRISON and ANN QUINTON, widow. Before 17 Dec 1708. xi-467. See also xi-596.

ARNOLD HARRISON and MATILDA SELVEY [also written SELBEY], dau. of Tobias. Before 1 Dec 1704. xi-357.

THOMAS HARMANSON, Jr. and GRACE ANDREWS, dau. of Maj. Wm. ANDREWS. Before 24 July 1673. See will. xi-259.

JOHN HINMAN and SARAH SMITH, widow of Thomas. About 28 Nov. 1657. ii-187.

THOMAS HARDING and SCARBURGH WEST, dau. Col John. Before 4 Oct 1706. xiii-81. See also Diii-539 and 652.

NATHANIEL HOLLAND probably m. ANN WEST, widow of John. Before 7 Apr 1731. xix-235.

.... HIX and TABITHA JONES, widow of Aaron. Before 27 Sept 1752. xxiiiO-630.

JOHN HUNT and MARY TANKRED, dau. of John. Before 4 Dec 1716. xvi-17.

WILLIAM HOPKINS and SARAH BRITTINGHAM, widow of Samuel. About 6 June 1728. xix-109. See also xx-fo. 20.

.... HARPER probably m. MARY JONES. [Henry Jones, her son had half-sister Sarah Harper, and half-bro. Robert Harper.] Before 8 Feby 1664. ii-5.

JAMES HALL and the widow and admx of Alex'r DANIEL. Before 29 Apr 1760. xxvO-336.

BENJAMIN HALEY probably m. ELIZABETH CHANDLER, dau. of Solomon. Before 22 Feby 1757. xxvW-396.

HENRY HALL and MARY SHAE, dau. of John and Tabitha. Before 26 June 1749. Diii-634.

WALTER HARGES and the widow of Edward SMALLEY. About 16 July 1679. viii-96.

.... HUGHBANCK and MARY WATSON, dau. of Robert, Sr. Before 24 July 1702. xi-308.

Mr. GEORGE HACK and MARGARET TEACKLE, dau. of Thomas. Before 21 July 1769. xxixW-347.

ALEX. HARRISON and SUSANNA ANDREWS. [This is somewhat uncertain.] See dep'n 16 Apr 1673. iv-196.

TWIFORD HILLARY and ROSANNA BALY, widow of Henry. Before or about 25 April, 1749. Dii-203.

JAMES HENRY and SARAH SCARBURGH, sister of Charles. Before 24 Feby 1761. Diii-137.

JOHH HARMONSON, Gent., of Northampton cty, and ELIZABETH SHEPHERD, dau. of John, Gent. Before 30 Sept 1755. ii-610.

THOMAS HICKMAN and LEAH FOOKS, dau. of Daniel. Before 30 Sept 1721. Diii-159.

HENRY HICKMAN and the widow of JOSEPH CUSTIS. Before 21 Feby 1770. Diii-683.

.... HICKMAN and PEGGY FOSTER, dau. of Joshua. Before 1773. xxviiW-109. [Hickman's name appears to have been either Custis or Eustis.]

FENIX [*sic*] HALL and HANNAH MELICHOP, widow of Nicholas. Before 27 Sept 1757. xxvO-214.

JAMES HAMILTON and GRATIANA x MICHAEL, dau. of John. Before 1729. xx-31.

GEORGE HENDERSON and MARGARET WATSON, widow of Benjamin. Before 9 June 1767. Diii-527.

JACOB HILL and MARY KNIGHT. About 1677. vii-48.

PETER HACK [d. 1708] and MATILDA WEST [d. 17 Oct 1742], dau. of Anthony [d. 1717], who was eldest son of John WEST, the Elder. Before 1708. See L. C. 1773-1805, p. 33.

GEORGE HOPE and TEMPERANCE ANDERSON, sister of William. Before 3 July 1698.

NEHEMIAH HOLLAND and SCARBURGH MARSHALL, dau. of Peter. Before 27 Apr 1762. Diii-178.

STEPHEN HORSEY of Som. cty, Md. and ELIZABETH REAVELL, dau. of John. Before 31 Aug 1726. xvi-274.

RICHARD JUSTICE and a dau. of Griffith SAVAGE. [This is possibly uncertain.] Before 5 Feby 1739. xxiiW-157.

EDWARD JOYNER and SARAH TANKRED, dau. of John. Before 4 Dec. 1716. xvi-17.

ISAAC JACOB and SARAH TILNEY, dau. Col. John TILNEY. Before 14 Apr 1675. v-274.

WILLIAM JETTE, afterwards of Rappahannock cty, and ELIZABETH HOSKINS, dau. of Anthony. Before 17 May 1681. vi-262.

WILLCOCK JOHNSON and REBECCA PRATT. Before 23 June 1725. xvi-239. [Before 3 June 1720.]

JOHN JUSTICE and MARY HOWELL. Before 1 Jany 1727. xvi-293.

DANIELL JENIFER and Mrs. ANNE TOFT. Before 5 Mch 1671. iv-78.

ISAAC JACOB and Sarah TILNEY, second dau. of Col. John TILNEY. Before 14 Apr 1675. v-274

THOMAS JARVIS and ANNE-SENIOR BELL, sister of Thomas. Before 1802. L. C.

THOMAS JACOB and ANNE HURTLY, dau. of William and Mary HURTLY. Before 29 May 1758. Diii-42.

EDWARD JOYNE and SARAH TANKARD, dau. of John. See record 4 Oct 1721. xvi-154. [These names also given as Joyner and Tankred. See record 4 Dec. 1716. vol. ix. See also Di-104.] The names probably Joynes and Tancred.

THOMAS JACOB and BETTY BAYLY, widow of Richard. Marriage contract. 14 Feby 1710. Diii-711.

.... JOHNSON and ELIZABETH JUSTICE, dau. of Ralph. Before 17 Sept 1729. xx-25.

DANIEL of St. THOMAS JENIFER and ELIZABETH MICHAEL. Before 1747. ii-55.

ABEL JANNEY and ELIZABETH BURDETTE, widow of William. Before 10 Feby 1786. L. C. 1773-1805, p. 87.

.... JOHNSON and DORITHY WASHBURNE, dau. of John. Before 8 Mch 1721. xvi-143.

SAMUEL INGASON and CATHERINE, the dau. of Rachel SAUNDERS. Before 2 Nov 1766. xxviiW-157.

HEZEKIAH JAMES probably m. SABRA SIMPKINS, dau of "SARABRA." Before 28 Mch 1770. Diii-692. [Simpkins was her mother's then name.]

THOMAS JACOB and BETTY HALL, widow of Michael. Before 8 Sept 1770. Diii-710.

JOHN JUSTICE and MARY HOWELL. Before 1 Jany 1727. xvi-293.

The County Court Note-Book

An every-other-monthly devoted mainly to abstracts from County Court Records, prior to 1800.

MILNOR LJUNGSTEDT, Editor and Publisher. Bethesda, Rural Route 5, Maryland.

Published six times a year. Subscription, two dollars, in advance; must begin with the year.

June, 1930 **Whole**
Vol. IX., No. 3 **No. 52**

PLEASANT COURTS AND OTHER PLACES

It is very quiet in the old Clerk's office. One hundred years have passed and left no noise behind. No electric fan disturbs the contemplative atmosphere; no jarring engine shakes the walls with its constant, deadly vibration. Later in the day the lawyers, one or two, the Commonwealth's Attorney, probably the old Sheriff or the County Agent for this or that will drop in and exchange politics and anecdotes and the last prohibition mix-up, sprawled in chairs or leaning on desk tops, each one touching his hat to the visitor as he enters,......smoking, yes, but the visitor grows "usened" to them and enjoys the joke which now and then brings out a guffaw and a slap on the next fellow's knee. At present only the Clerk is there for company; the old State Senator went home for dinner and hasn't come back. A fine old fellow, that Senator. Only one foot usable, not old enough fcr the Civil War, perhaps a Spanish Veteran, perhaps lost it hunting. But not easy for him to get about, so the visitor knowing the records and the shelves assists him with a chain of title. These are worth while people to meet. People of mind and manner, of experience......the kind of experience which smiles easily at red tape......and cuts it.

But the Clerk and the fire are now the hosts, a cheerful open fire, which, it is true, isn't the dustless form of heat, but good to lock at, and books and people don't altogether dry up by it. The Clerk, having offered his services and started the visitor on the indices, settles down to his mail. The visitor rests her eyes a moment and looks up at a wall of volumes......records of so many dead-and-goners......and some have been so long dead! She has but to reach up to this or that volume and follow the departed citizen through life in the courts, or as the owner of lands; to another volume to read his will......the list of his household goods, the names of his children, and the cost of his funeral. Sometimes in the more ancient books all this in one.

Outside the window the sun shines or the rain falls; the early robin calls cheerily or the redbird whistles.

The other picture is of a super-steam heated hall. A window or two is open and the draft sweeps across; the old ladies and the old gentlemen who sometimes have lumbago sigh and long for home. Even the younger ones shift their seats if they happen to object to the later fan unnecessarily scouring the bases of their brains. The electric lights are far above the tables and their illumination none too good.

The tables themselves are high and no provision is made to elevate the seats for the unfortunates who sit down short! And of all the trials of condemned bi-focals the worst is to use them at an improper angle. Bent upon the dim ink of a badly and awkwardly bound tax-list, the contents arranged rag carpet fashion, some long, some short, the longest far above the above said bi-focal vision if upright, but possible if flat, the visitor forgets the Powers That Be.

An attendant appears, representative of the Powers, grabs with the hand of autocracy the volume before the searcher and erects it upon a rack..... with some remark as to the law.

* * * * *

The searcher gives it up and hires younger eyes. In her *mind's* eye she sees the friendly Clerk and the hospitable if not over-clean county office. County offices may be slack, but centralization has a way of cutting out both friendliness and *common sense.*

Since receiving the ROBERT WADE record and trying to make "head and tail" out of it with reference to the Editor's personal interest, she has read a very carefully written account of Madame Papegoya's holdings; as the Editor recollects, Madame Papegoya was the daughter of the Dutch Governor Printz who built for her a mansion which she sold to ROBERT WADE. The Editor had supposed this to be ESSEX HOUSE, but has to admit that she is now very uncertain and would be glad of exact information. ESSEX HOUSE did stand directly on the bank of the Delaware, not many yards, the Editor would say, back from the spot where William Penn landed. It seems a pity that the house should not have been preserved and that the spot where the monument still remains, should not be in a cleared and open space.

ERRATA:

On page 17, of the APRIL issue, the Montgomery county referred to is in Virginia, and it should have been so stated.

In the second column on page 18, paragraph 11, the name Abernanthie should probably be Abernathie.

In the first column, same page, "Rockin" county, should be Rock'm, that is, Rockingham.

On page 10, first column, the item was intended to be "Coll. [Col.] FRANCIS WILLIS, Esq." CHRISTOP'R WADE was the patentee in the previous paragraph.

These errors crept in through the loss of a galley proof containing corrections.

HISTORICAL EPISODES AND TRADITIONS OF NORTHAMPTON COUNTY [Virginia]. The Honorable Thomas B. Robertson, now Judge of the Hopewell Court, Virginia, is the author of a very valuable and interesting volume which is about to come from the press. The fifteen chapters cover a vast amount of ground, and cover it in a reliable fashion......something that cannot be said of certain earlier Eastern Shore publications. Judge Robertson begins with the earliest settlements, and as early as 1623 gives lists of the settlers and the location of their homes. Carrying the story of the county on he gives the tithables immediately after the division, when the upper part became Accomack and the lower part retained the name of Northampton; touches upon the history of the churches, the building of the courthouse......probably one should write courthouses, for there have been several......gives some account of the prominent families, and all in all, has prepared what Northampton county should appreciate, a worth while story of a county that has been particularly blessed by nature and by location and also in possessing a court record of its history from 1632.

Judge Robertson has included in his book a very valuable list of marriages, adding to his own material from those collected by the Editor of the NOTE-BOOK, so that he writes that his list, with the one published by Mr. Nottingham, "will give nearly three hundred years of marriages in the county."

One of the most valuable publications ever brought out in the colonial states, but one that will escape recognition except by the better read class of searchers, has recently come to the Editor from Mr. STRATTON NOTTINGHAM of Onancock, Accomack county, Virginia. Mr. Nottingham is known for his painstaking and accurate rendition of revolutionary and marriage records of the counties about the Chesapeake Bay. In the volume now commented upon he has taken up and copied with meticulous care one of the most important sources of genealogical information to be found in Virginia ...... the LAND CAUSES of Accomack county. These "CAUSES" are in reality the record in their entirety of chancery suits touching land before usually heard before some sort of a higher, or chancery court, probably in this case, a "District Court" for several counties.

It is impossible to explain in a brief paragraph the substance and value of these suits. It can be said, however, that without them many family links now known would never have been discovered. At times they cover several generations with marriages, brothers and sisters of the full and the half-blood, and set out wills, patents, and conveyances of land.

Other counties sometimes have these "CAUSES," but Accomack has an unusually complete series.

Virginia having lost the greater part, if not all those chancery records which reached the General Court when Richmond was burned at the evacuation in 1865, records of this class when found in the counties have a value which cannot easily be estimated.

The GENEALOGY of the HARRIS AND ALLIED FAMILIES by Pauline Myra Jones, of Huntsville, Alabama, has been brought to the Editor's attention by a notice from the author. Not having seen the volume in question, comment cannot be made.

VARIA

John Lomax is ordered to sell the arm chair belonging to the Court house to the highest bidder and account to the Court for the same. Ffx cty, Va. Orders iii-167. 19 Dec 1770.

The Colonial Inn (Virginia):
To a night's Lodging with clean sheets......6d. otherwise nothing. All soldiers and expresses on his Majesty's service paying ready money shall have one fifth part deducted. Ffx cty, Va. Orders [2]. 28 Feby 1760.

Col. Nicholas Smith's estate account, returned by Mrs. Elizabeth Smith. Col. Smith left two orphans......"To Cash Paid for De graffenreidts Order in favour of Donne for your Dancing... £2." "To Cash Paid for Altering Stays. 3sh. 9d." K. Geo. cty, Va. (iii-16. Ab. 3 Sept 1742)

Stafford Courthouse, Va.
"Courthouse for the said county being burnt down in or about the year one thousand seven hundred and eighteen." (Staff. cty Deeds, P-7. 11 Mch 1755.)

"Sharp to Rasor."
Several years back the NOTE-BOOK published a marriage license bond on the Clerk of the Court had endorsed "Sharp to Rason", while the bond itself read, if the Editor remembers, *Rasor or Razor*. Later the Editor discovered that the name was, correctly, Razor or Rasor. Now it turns up in Culpeper county, Virginia, with three spellings, (George) Raisor, (Christopher) Rassor, and (Jacob) Raxor [?]. It was probably a German family name, of which there are so many in early Virginia records, but became twisted in its spelling as it travelled.

QUERIES:

MARY FINCH, daughter of Francis Finch and .... his wife, married ISAAC CALKE before 1692. Would like the name of Mary's mother.

ISAAC CAULK, Jr., (died 1749) left a widow TEMPERANCE. Would like the name of the parents of Temperance. C.

THE DEPUTY COMMISSARY'S GUIDE WITHIN THE PROVINCE OF MARYLAND

(Continued from February, 1930)

Continuing WILLS AND TESTAMENTS, the next paragraph in Eli Vallette's little volume touches upon codicils, giving the definition of a codicil, and explaining that executors cannot regularly be appointed in a codicil, "but yet they may be therein substituted," that is, they may be appointed in the room of the executor instituted in the first will in case the same should die or renounce the executorship; such a codicil must be made with all the solemnities required in the making of a will.

Then follows the oath of the executor touching belief in the identity of the will after being examined as to how it came into his hands. This to be followed by the examination of the witnesses as to the testator's and their signatures, &c., which testimony they cover with their oaths. And if representatives of the deceased are present, the deputy commissary must so certify, and that they did not object to probate......the widow and heir-at-law being specifically mentioned.

The will being thus proved, and legally established, the executor is called upon to declare his acceptance......if he refuse, or if "after a convenient time given him for deliberation" he neglects or refuses to take out letters testamentary, or doth not appear, being legally summoned ......then letters of common administration, with a copy of the deceased's will thereto annexed, must be granted to such person or persons as would have been entitled to administration had the deceased appointed no executor..........In every case, where executors enter their renunciation, *all* executors named in such will (if more there be) must do the same. Nor can one executor only out of several receive letters testamentary unless every other executor named in the will, renounces.

A widow must renounce or elect to accept the will within forty days from the probate. According to the wording of the form given she "quits her claim to the several bequests and devises......and elects in lieu thereof her dower, or third part of the deceased's estate, both real and personal"......or she makes "her election to stand to and abide by the several legacies...... with regard to the personal estate only, and claims her dower, or third part in the real estate."

"THE FORTIES"

(*See NOTE-BOOK for April, 1930.*)

Continuation of the list of "Supernumeraries."

ROBERT BRYERLY, Rich'd Tomson, Clem't Aldrige, Tho. Adams, Tho. Mallard, Rich'd Cox, Gilbert Harrold, Hugh Harris, Jno. Clewes, Hen. Proverb [?] Rich'd Jones, James Moore;

Mr. Farnefold, Capt. Rogers, Wm. Rogers, X'pher Neale, J. Kenner, Robt Wilson, Phill, Evans, Wm. Bershaw, Hen. Dawson [Davoson?] Mr. Robt Such;

Capt. Mottrome, Mr. Pet. Presly, Sen'r, Mr. Wm. Presly, Mr. Pet. Presly, Jr., Mr. Jno. Cotancean, Jacob Cotancean, Jno. Parker, Jno. Freeman;

Dan'll Neale, Ja: Hadwell, Walter Dunn, Jno. Warner, Rich'd Smyth, Jona. Roston, Jos. White, ThoroughGood Pate, George Carthouse [?] Walter Curtis, Tho: Sadler, Wm. Cornish [?] Rich'd Lamprey, Jno. Corbell, Tho. Barnes, Edw. Algood, Josias Harrison, Adam Garratt, Jno. Webb, Jno. Graham, Edmond Nesby, Walter Moore, Jno. Hull;

Pet. Maxwell, Wm. Cammell, Edw. Jones, Arth. Roper, Nicho. Lancaster, Jno. Paine, Jno. Courtney, Fra. Beckley, Sylas Duke, Howell Williams, Ralph Waddington. Tho. Harwood, John Bayles, Robt. Eldige, Jno. [This name very doubtful . . . . . Rich'd Hull, Hen. Rose, Geo. Pickens, Arth. Marsh, Wm. Allen, Jno. Higginson;

James Hopper [?] Mr. Hughlett, Mr. Edges [Eyes?] Den. Conoway, Rich'd Ro . . . ? Jno. Bryant, Hen. Franklyn, Jas. Southerby, Ar: La . . . shard [?] Capt. Haynie, Rich'd Haynie, Geo. Hamilton, Tho. Gilbert, Jno. Craford, Robt Hobbs. Jno. Edwards, Geo. Dawkins, Jno. Bysick, Jno. Palmer, Jno. Browne, Jno. Hallum. Jno. Bridgman, Hen. Hudnall, James Taylor, Wm. Wrotten [?] Cha: Paule;

Augt Kneton, Jas. Bee, Geo. Crosby, Tho. Howell, Wm. Walker, Tho. Kesterson, Mrs. [?] Thomas, Jno. Wood, Jno. Rotheram, Mr. Wm. Smyth, Tho. Gill, Jno. Howell, Wid .[?] Jones, Tho. Thorp, Jno. Atkins, Wm. Blundell, Jno. Robyson, Mr. Wildey, Wm. Downing, Jr., Jno. Downing, Mr. Nelmes, Jno Hudnall;

Mrs. Typton, Mrs. Signor [?] Jno. Nicholls, Jno. Reason, Widow Way, Jno. Cockrill, Dr. Harcum, Wm. Smyth, Wm. Hutt, Mr. Edward Coles, Jno. Read, Rich'd Williams, Mrs. Watts, Rich'd Lugg, Jno. White;

Maj. Bereton, Mr. Tho. Hobson, Jno. Wornam, Jno. Symons, Edward Bennett, Tho. Webb;

Col. St. Legerfeld [the name is blotted and illegible] Lieut. Colo. Smyth, Mrs. Shapleigh, Maj. Allerton, Mr. Jas. Austen, Tho. Clarke;

Mr. Erasmus Withers, Mr. Wm. Jones, Tho. Brewer, Mr. Eustas, Walter Jenkins, Azricam [?] Parker, Tho. High, Rich'd Linchfeild, Geo. Bledsoe, Mr. Tho. Winter, Kath. Ingram, O. Foulk, Jno. Swaine;

Mr. Jno. Harris, Mr. Jno. Waddy, Mr. Tho. Waddy, Rich'd Lewis, Jno. Pinckard, Jno. Nicholls, Barth, Dameron, Law. Dameron, Mr. Xpher Garlington, Josias Gascoyne, Geo. Dameron, Wid. Dennis, Jno. Atkins;

Tho. Fearn, Jno. Swanson, Abraham Sheares, Henry Huske, Wm. Cuminges, Mr. Tho. Williams, Rich'd Underwood, Jno. Mottoon, Sam'll Goushe (Gouche), Jno. Ordan [?], Anth. Stepto, Mrs. Petigrew, Stephen Sallowes, Clem't Lattimore, Wm. Barry [Bazy?], Jno. Lynn, Anth. Morris, Alex. Mullranie;

Capt. Knight, Mr. Rich'd Nutt, Mr. Feilding, Mr. Tho. Bancke, Cha. Easlond [?], James Hill, Edmond Bazey [?], Hen. Mayse, Hen. Gaskins, Joseph Palmer, Xpher Kyrk, Jno. Taylor, Sen'r, Mr. Jno. Taylor, Jr., Geo. Everard, Tho. Burborough, Wm. Hartland;

Jno. Champton, Jno. Bowen, Sam'll Mahew, Wm. Coppage, Wm. Byes [?], Jno. Bayles, Capt. Howson, Mr. Han: Lee, Capt. Wm. Downing, Will Flowers, Ezekiell Gennis.

(*End of list*)

INTERCOUNTY AND INTERCOLONY

JAMES ANDERSON, of Halifax county, Va., power to son John Anderson of Augusta county, Va., to demand and receive rents, &c., in Somerset. Som. cty, Md. 24 Feby 1758. B-204.

GEORGE KNIGHT, a shoemaker; Thomas Richards, master of a brigantine arrived from N. E., in Pongoteague river or creek, Acco., about thirty-two years before, brought Knight with him. Acco., Va., 1748. iiD-128.

SAMUEL PHILLIPS of London, Mcht; deed of land by John Soar as his atty, to George Davonport, William Davonport, and Fortunatus Davonport Bond for performance passed by *Sibilla* Hall of Limehouse and Samuel Phillips of London, to the Davonports; ackn. by the atty, John Soar. [The connection bet. Sibilla Hall and Samuel Phillips is not explained.] Richm'd cty, Va. Orders ii-216. [About 1697, April Court.]

JOHN MAKENRY [?] of the Island of Barbadoes, in a suit by his atty, Richard Green. Richm'd cty. Va. 7 Feby 1694. v-40.

THOMAS PRATT, of Stafford cty, Va., will; To John Bowen [under 21]; my son John-

Burket Pratt; my son Thomas Pratt; wf Margaret Pratt; land where bro. Burket Pratt lives, mentioned; sister Hungerford, living in King George cty, the tract called the Forrest Quarter and tract called Chapman's; extrs to sell Chapman's. Wife and Robert Brooking, Vivion Brooking and Thomas Bunbury, extrs. Appts Vivion Brooking gdn to two sons, John-Burket and Thomas Pratt. 8 Mch 1766-Oct 1766. K. Geo. Orders iv-295. [From Liber O, fo. 513 Stafford.]

JOHN DOYLE, of North Carolina, to Isaac Arnold, of Hanover psh, K. Geo. cty, Va., tract granted John Doyle, Sen'r, late of Richmond cty, Va., dec'd, father of this John Doyle. K. Geo., Va. A1-215.

ROBERT WICKLIFF, of Fairfax cty, Va., had property in "Monongohaly" county. Ffx, Va. D1 p 366.

WILLIAM SCOTT'S will mentions his brother Gustavus Scott of Dorchester cty, Md. 4 July 1785. Ffx cty, Va. E1-232.

CHARLES B. FENLEY, of Pr. Geo's cty, Md., mariner. Will. Estate to Michael Thorn [Thorm?] and makes him extr. Wit. Benchan, Blunt, Fenley. 13 May 1787-20 July 1789. Ffx. cty, Va. E1-324.

THOMAS MARSHALL, of Charles cty, Gent., to Sarah Marshall, dau. of sd Thomas; love and affection and one sh......all the remaining part of that tract conveyed to Marshall by Mr. Zephaniah Wade...... in Fairfax cty, Va....... exclusive of what Marshall hath given to his daughters Mary Macubbin and his nephew Samuel Marshall...... 5557 acres. Ffx cty, Va. C-537. 26 Feby 1753.

JOHN RILEY, Jr., of Barton county, S. C. to Moses Simpson of Fairfax cty; conveys land. 22 Oct 1773. L-88.

DAVID HERBERT, Sr., and wife "Marthew", of Surry county, N. C., to William Herbert of Montgomery county, Va., conveys land during life-time of David Herbert and wife. Montg. cty, Va. A-405.

WILLIAM WATERSON, otherwise lately called William *Waters*, of Augusta county, Va., in a suit agt Andrew Lightle. Amherst cty, Va. 6 Sept 1768. Orders, p. 403.

SERVICE AND SUPPLIES COLONIAL REVOLUTIONARY AND MILITIA

JOHN BLAIR, allowance as a soldier, December, 1783. Also the 14 Dec 1784. Orphans' Court Minutes, Montg. cty, Md.

JAMES BOWLING, a Revolutionary soldier, files declaration and the Court declare opinion that he served as he states. Amherst cty, Va. 20 Aug. 1832. Orders, p. 83.

JAMES CURRENT, allowance as a soldier. Montg. cty, Md. O. C. Min. P. 52. 9 June 1789.

WILLIAM HEALEY, allowance as a soldier. Same reference, p. 31. 14 Dec 1784.

WILLIAM HURLEY, allowance as a soldier. Same reference, p. 53. 14 Aug 1789.

WILLIAM HARRIS, aged 70, declares that he served in the Revolutionary War in the 10th Va. Reg't. Continental Line, commanded by Edward Stevens; in the company commanded by Capt. John Gillison; that he enlisted Jany, 1776, and served until Jany, 1779, when he was discharged at Morristown, N. J., having been transferred to the company of Washington's Life Guards, commanded by Maj. Gibbs of N. E.; that he was at the battle of Brandywine but not engaged, being detached as one of the guard to the General's baggage waggons. Being discharged from the regular service was in the Virginia militia and was at the siege of "Little York," and the capture of Lord Cornwallis. States that his original declaration was made Sept, 1819 . . . . . His wife Sarah is about 58 or 59, has been afflicted with sickness for 17 years. Has one son about 18 years old living with him, and a daughter named Mary, about 30. Wilkes cty, N. C. 31 Oct 1820. iii-244.

JAMES KERN, allowance as a soldier. Montg. cty, Md. O. C. Minutes. p. 31. 14 Dec 1784. Also in Apr 1783.

Court is satisfied that Elizabeth Weeks, Margaret Lunsford, and Sally Delany are the lawful heirs of WILLIAM LUNSFORD, who served as Cornet and Quartermaster in the Partizan "Legan" during the war, as proved by certificate from Henry Lee, Esq., commander of said army, and that LUNSFORD died in said service. Staff. cty, Va. Ct Rec. 1790-1793, p. 332. Oct 1792.

JAMES MURPHY, allowance as a soldier. Montg. cty, Md. O. C. Min. Dec 1783 and 14 Dec 1784.

CLEMENT REED, allowance as a soldier. Montg. cty, Md. O. C. Min. p. 30. 14 Dec 1784.

CHRISTOPHER READ, allowance as a soldier. Same reference, same date.

JAMES WHITE, allowance as a soldier. Same reference, same date. Also in Dec 1783.

SAMUEL B. WHITE; served in 1st Md. Reg't, under Capt. John Smith. Wounded at Camden. Montg. cty, Md. O. C. Min. p. 52. 9 June 1789. Also see 25 Apr. 1781.

The following were merely listed as applicants for pension, no details being found. Court record of Stokes county, N. C. Sept. 1832 and Dec. 1832.

JAMES LARRIMORE,
WILLIAM YOUNG,
BENJAMIN MARSHALL,
EDWIN HICKMON,
BENJAMIN JONES,
HOWELL HARTGROVE,
PETER SMITH,
SAMUEL STROUP,
JOSEPH DARNAL,
CHRISTOPHER EATON,
EPHRAIM LANDS,
JOSEPH WELSH,
EPHRAIM BANNER,
JAMES LOWE,
JOSEPH BANNER.

Printed at the Industrial School for Crippled and Deformed Children, 241 St. Botolph St., Boston, Mass.

The

County Court Note-Book

A Little Bulletin of History and Genealogy

August, 1930. Vol. IX, No. 4

THE MIGRANT HAYS, HAYES, HAISE, HAZE. SOME OF THEM.

(*First alphabet*)

ARCHIBALD HAYS; inv. his estate returned by Reubin x Hays. Wilkes cty, N. C. Feby 1807. [2]-199.

ANDREW and GEORGE HAYES, dec'd. Bond of John Hayes as admr. ANDREW HAYES and JAMES WALLACE, sec. Rock'm cty, Va. Wills. 6th mo. 1781. Vol. i......

ANDREW HAYS, will. Eldest son John; son Charles; son James; dau. Prudence Brownlee, 5 sh.; son Joseph; son David; dau. Mary Hays. Wit: John Moore, John Walker, James Moore. Rock'm cty, Va. 9 Feby 1786-2 May 1786. i-258.

ANNE x HAYES; had sons Nathaniel and Adam. She was widow of Robert. She also had sons *Thos. and Jno. Workman.* L. Norf. cty, Va. 1650. B-141.

ALICE HAYES is granted admn estate of Nathaniel, her late husband. L. Norf cty, Va. 15 Dec 1664. D-414.

ADAM HAYES. L. Norf cty, Va. 1663.

ANN HAYES [same as above], see petition of Nathaniel Hayes. They were married [she was the widow of Workman] about 15 Jany 1656. L. Norf. cty, Va. D-49. See also D-63.

ANTHONY HAY, son of Nathaniel and Anne. Born 20 June 1737. Also James, son of do. born 13 Sept 1738. York-Hampton Psh Reg.

CHARLES HAYSE married ELIZABETH ATKINS. 1788. Montg. cty, Va. M. L. B.

CHRISTOPHER HAYES, son of Robert, is mentioned in the will of Christopher Stribling. N-n cty, Va. 22 Apr 1669-28 June 1669. x-69.

CHARLES x HAYS, wife Jane, Wythe cty, Va., to James Paris of Montg. cty, Va. Tract of 232 acres on branch of New river. Montg. cty, Va. 5 Oct 1791. B-78.

DAVID HAY, heir-at-law, of Joseph Hay, dec'd, who was a soldier in the Cont. Army in Capt. Ball's company of Col. Grison's regiment. Ordered certified that Court believe he served as claimed. Rock'm cty, Va. 7 Aug 1783. Orders.

DANIEL HAY, a Presbyterian. A number of persons give notice that they intend to make use of [certain meeting-houses?] Lunenb. cty, Va.

DAVID HAY, Davidson cty, Mero District, Tenn. Gives power to Maj. John Hays, John Carruthers, and James Carruthers of Rockbridge cty, Va., to convey land in Lexington, Rockbr. cty, to Andrew Reid, Davidson cty, Tenn. 16 Apr 1791. i-203.

ELIZABETH HAY, head right under Rob't Windly in Northampton cty, Va. 1660.

FRA: HAYS, head right under John Watson. Henrico cty, Va. 1 Aug 1689. ii-307.

FREDERICK HAYS in a suit. Amherst, Va. 3 May 1768. Orders [1] p. 334.

FRAN'S HAYS, Pr. Edwd cty, Va. 1776. See Va. Mags. xviii-40.

FRANCIS HAYS, an appraiser with Obadiah Woodson, Henry Walker and "Mannen" McReiley, of the estate of William Hill, dec'd. Pr. Edw'd, Va. 16 May 1774. Orders D-433.

GEORGE x HAYES, sjt; was a resident of Hawkins cty, Tenn. Served in N. C. in the Rev. War. Went into the service in "Birk" cty, N. C. See Pension Office records. Appl'n in 1833.

GEORGE and THOMAS HAYS; dfts with others in a suit. 4 July 1768. Amherst cty, Va. Orders.

GODFREY HAYES. Northampton cty, Va. 28 Jany 1645. iii-14. See also 1-112. 13 Aug 1638. A witness to Evans-Bowin agreement. iv-133.

HENRY HAYES, late of this county, having departed and left behind him a poor orphant child named Rebecca, the child is apprenticed. York cty, Va. 25 Jany 1699. 1694–1702. p. 299.

HENRY HAYS, his inventory. Keziah x Hays, admx. Wilkes cty, N. C. Returned Feby 1805. [2]-145. Account sales, p. 147. Mentions Jonathan Hays, Hartwell Hays, Keziah Hays, Joshua Souther.

HUGH HAYS in a suit. 8 Dec 1767. Amherst Orders.

HUGH HAYSE, age about 27. Northampton cty, Va. 16 June 1635. 1-38.

ISABELLA HAYES (widow of Thomas). Mentioned in a deed by Wm. Robinson, Gent. L. Norf. 16 Aug 1687. v-41.

ISBELL HAYES and others, summoned as wit L. Norf., Va. 15 Apr 1646. A (pt 3) p. 57.

ISABELL HAYES m. Thomas Coffin, before 9 Nov 1683. N-n, Va. xiv-85. She was dau. of Robert.

JAMES HAYES; Hugh Hays, admr. Wilkes cty, N. C. Nov 1816. iii-136. Acc't sales, iii-138. Inv. Apr. 1816. iii-115.

JOHN HAYSES, age about 32. N-n, Va. 16 May 1636. 1-52.

JOHN HAYES, age about 26. N-n, Va. 23 Oct 1634. i-23.

JOHN HAY married Mary Garret. 12 July 1724. K. Geo. cty, Va. St. Paul's Psh. Reg.

Capt. JOHN HAYS married Nancy Christian, dau. of Michael. N-n cty, Va. 1777. M. L. B.

JOHN HAYES, killed by Indians about 16 or 17 years before. Widow petitions concerning estate; children Ruth and Hanna Hayes mentioned. N-n, Va. 30 Jany 1654. v-79.

JOHN HAY, York cty, Va., Charles parish. Will. Land to be sold and payment made of such sums as my children are entitled to under will of their grandfather, Daniel Preeson. Wife Frances; two daus. Elizabeth and Rebecca; sons James and John [under 21]; wife and friends Robert Shield and John Moss, extrs. Wit: John Russell, Henry Bonhanon, Wm. Davenport. 31 Mch 1788-15 Sept 1788. York cty, Va. xxiii-165.

AUTHENTIC REFERENCES FOR INFERRED MARRIAGES

JAMES ATKINS and MARY WARD, widow of David. Before 22 June 1699. Nthld, Va. Orders iv-26. See also iv-39.

JOHN ADAMS and SUSANNAH HUMPHREYS, dau. of Hannah, wf of Joseph HUMPHREYS. [It is not altogether clear that she was HUMPHREYS' daughter.] Staff., Va. Before 26 Mch 1783. S-102.

WILLIAM AYLETT, Gent. and ELIZABETH ESKRIDGE, dau. of George ESKRIDGE, Gent., dec'd. Before 26 June 1744. Wmld, Va. Fid. Acts [1]-296.

Capt. WILLIAM AYLETT, Jr. and ANN ASHTON, dau. Henry. Before 26 Feby 1730. Ffx, Va. L. C. p. 57.

JOHN ASHTON and HANNAH WEST, dau. John. Before 27 Mch 1776. Ffx, Va. D (1)-26.

HENRY ASHTON, and ELIZABETH HARDIDGE, dau. of William. Before 31 Oct 1711. Wmld, Va. v-12.

JOHN AUBREY and HANNAH TANNER, one of the daus. of Thomas. Before 23 Sept 1719. Wmld, Va, vi-556.

JOHN ASHTON and the widow of Sam'l SWILLIVANT. Before 22 Feby 1722. Wmld, Va. viii (1)-110.

WILLOUGHBY ALLERTON and ....BUSHROD, widow of John. See Va. Col. Decisions, p. R57. [The case which gives this information was of Apr 1731.]

SPENCER BALL and MARY PATTERSON. 31 July 1788. Greenbr., W. Va. M. L. B.

SPENCER BALL and BETSY-LANDON CARTER. Before 1823. Ffx, Va. L. C. p. 125.

SAMPSON BALL and ROSANNA NORMAN. Before 14 Jany 1830. Culp., Va. L. C. p. 1.

JOHN BLACKMORE and LUCY CARTER, relict and admx of Charles CARTER. Before 8 Nov 1768. Amherst Orders, Va.

............BERRYMAN and SARAH BUSHROD, dau. John. See Va. Col. Dec. p. R57. [Suit of Apr 1731.]

PIERCE BAYLY and MARY PAYNE, dau. William. Before 27 May 1782. Ffx, Va. D(1)-444.

THOMAS BURNITT and ANNE BELL, relict of Jeremiah. Nthld, Va. Before 18 Mch 1712. Orders iv-818.

ABRAHAM BARNES and SARAH, admx of Denis McCARTY. Before 16 July 1760. Ffx, Va. Orders [2]-496.

THOMAS BROOKE of St. Mary's cty, Md., and SARAH MASON, dau. of George. Before 1742. Ffx, Va. L. C.

ROBERT BERKELEY and JULIA CARTER. Before 1823. Ffx, Va. L. C. p. 125.

WILLIAM BARTON and the widow of William HUNGERFORD. Before 19 Apr 1661. Md. Arch. xli-455.

JOHN BATSON and GRACE SATCHELL, of N-n, Va. Before 7 Jany 1679 [?] Va. Col. Dec. p. R65.

JOHN BROWN and WINIFRED WALKER, relict and extx of George. Before 1 Sept 1747. Wmld, Va. Fid. Accts ii-37.

JOHN BAGGE and MARY BUTLER, widow. [See marriage contract of Caleb. She had a son Robert Vaulx, and also a son John Duddlestone. The record is lacking in details.] Wmld, Va. v-221. See 19 Dec. 1711, also her will 2 Feby 1712.

GEORGE BERRATT and ESTER, extx of Thomas HICKMAN, dec'd. Before 23 June 1699. Nthld, Va. Orders iv-31.

JOSEPH BELFIELD and JANE JONES. Before 1823. Ffx, Va. L. C. p. 125.

Col. THOMAS BLACKBURN probably m. CHRISTIAN SCOTT, sister of William. Before 4 July 1785. Ffx, Va. E (1)-232.

THOMAS BYRD and PATIENCE ELLZEY, dau. Lewis. Before 1 Oct 1785. Ffx, Va. E (1)-224.

MARMADUKE BECKWITH and SYBIL ELLZEY, dau. Lewis. Before 1 Oct 1785. Ffx, Va. E(1)-224.

THOMAS BLACKBURN and CHRISTIAN SCOTT, dau. Rev. James SCOTT. Before 21 May 1770. Pr. Wm, Va. R-352. [See Fairfax record above.]

BURGESS BECKLEY and STACY ELLZEY, dau. Lewis. Before 1 Oct 1785. Ffx, Va. E(1)-224.

JOHN BICKLY and the widow of Charles ELLIS. Before or about 7 Mch 1769. Amherst, Va. Orders.

GEORGE COLCLOUGH and ELIZABETH OVERZEE, widow of Simon. Probably before 21 Feby 1657. Md. Arch xli-425. "Tyme of her Siduity as adm'x" mentioned. [See also L. Norf, Va. D-305.]

Mr. GEORGE COLCLOUGH and the widow of Col. Jno. MOTTROM. [Her name was Ursula.] Nthld, Va. Before 30 Jany 1656. 1-124.

Dr. JOHN COOPER and HANNAH ALLERTON, widow of Col. Willoughby ALLERTON. Before 28 June 1727. Wmld, Va. Fid. Accts. [1]-65. See also Va. Col. Dec. p. R 57.

.... COOPER and ELIZABETH SPINKS,' dau. John. Before 21 Dec 1778. Ffx, Va. D(1)-100.

G. COOK and MARY A. M. HEETH. Before 3 May 1816. Pr. Wm, Va. M-101.

DAVID CURRIE, Clk, and ANN ALLERTON, Relict of Isaac. Before 26 Aug. 1746. Wmld. Va. Fid. Accts ii-4.

JOHN Y. CHINN and SARAH-FAIRFAX CARTER. Before 1823. Ffx L. C. p. 125.

JOHN CARLYLE and (1) SARAH FAIRFAX Before 5 Apr 1780. Ffx, Va. D(1)-203.

THOMAS COPPENHAVER and JULIANA SEEK[?]. Mar. agreement. About 13 Apr 1784. Montg., Va. A-333.

.... CONNOR and ELIZABETH LAWSON, dau. of Anthony, who d. 1701. Va. Col. Dec. p. R68.

CHARLES SAYER and MARGARET LAWSON, dau. Anthony. Va. Col. Dec. p. R68.

CHARLES CALVERT and MARY HOWSON, dau. Robert. Before 8 Jany 1699. Va. Col. Dec. p. R63.

BOWLER COCKE, Jr., Gent., and ELIZABETH TURNER. Widow of Maj. Harry TURNER. Before 10 Oct 1752. K. Geo., Va. iii-83.

RICHARD CONWAY and MARY WEST, dau. John. Before 27 Mch 1776. Ffx, Va. D (1)-26.

VIRGINIA COLONISTS

(*From "Old Vol. 5," S. L. O. Richmond, Va.*)

THOMAS GERRARD, Nthld, 1655.
Head rights: Mary Wesson, Christopher Peirce.

WILLIAM GRAVES, York cty, 1655.
Head rights: Bryan Coxon, Ellis Wheatly.

GERMAN GILLIOTT [record damaged], Acco· cty, 1666.
Head rights: Tho. Pettett, Rob't Satchell, Alice Granger, Jno. Collins.

JOHN HINMAN, Northampton cty, at Anancock creek, 16 [55].
Head rights: John Knight, Eliz: Johnson, Ro. Wright, Miles Gray, Jane Williams, Rich: Gardner, John Dye, Rich'd Gayney, Tho. Thorogood, Alex: Bromley, John Farman [Farmar?], Tho Collier, Rob. Rose, Mary Poole, Joane Willms, Joan Hodges.

JOHN HULETT, Nthld cty, 1655.
Head rights: John Hill, Tho. Holden, Wm. Pryor, John Evans, Nath. Jones, George Clearke.

RICHARD HAMLETT, James City, cty, 1655.
Head rights: Phill. Prenergrast, Rob. Andrew, Tho. Hawstone, Eliz. Sidney, Symon Hazleton, Wm. Andrew, Joshua [?] Downes, John Gryme, John Browne, Christopher Bowes.

Coll. EDWARD HILL, Freshes of Rappahannock, opp. Portobaccoe, 1655. Eighty persons; *Irish* assigned by Capt Barret. Names not given.

THOMAS HALE, Nthld cty, 1655.
Head rights: James Clere, Tho. Willis.

WILLIAM HALL, New Kent, 1655.
Head rights: Mary Ellise, And. Burchell, Barnes Staple, Martha Wright, Fra. Reinolls, Jno. Feild, Ro. Garland.

Doctor GEORGE HACKE, Northampton, 1661.
Head rights: . . . Yeomans, Anne Dooly, Mary Edwards, Wm. Skner [Skinner?] Mary Edger, Wm. Tomlin, Henry Willis, Tho: Browne, John Cary, Mary Williams, Johna. Shewell, Margt Purnell, Susan Foster, Jno. Martin, Howell Glading, Fra: Knight, Lucresa Pott, Kath. Smith, Walter Wood, Mary Griffeth.

Leift. RICHARD HILL, Acco. cty, 1666.
Head rights: Henry Korking, Francis Butler, Thomas Dyer, Sam'll Mountayne, Walter Vaux, Wm. Hudley, Francis Roberdam, Tho. Roles, Moses Stone, Tho. Bane, Rich. Harris, George Brigg, Edward Gill, Rich Spades, Rob't Carver. [List damaged.]

Mr. JAMES HURD, New Kent cty, 1660.
Head rights: Roger Barlow, James Mallinge, John Dromer, Patr'k Drunkee [?] Wm. Wilkin, Mary James, Jacob Johnson, Wm. Harris, James Payton, Rich: Scragg, Susan Higley, James Varley, Jeremy Revet, John Hardy, James Hill, Hugh Newitt, Mary Martin, Roger Lasley.

THOMAS HANSFORD, Yorke cty, 1662.
Head rights: Jno. Harris, William Whiteby.

THOMAS HODGKIN, *in a bay of Carolina river*, 1663.
Head rights: John Philpot, Jno. Tyler, Mary Lewis, Sam'll Burton, Math: Hwes, Wm. Bateman, Mich. Wills, James Rogers, Alex. Monts, Marke Allister, George Rayman, Roger Cleyton, Tho: Kintly, Robt Herne, Wm. Strood, Simon Allen, Jer. Ward, Rich: Card, Cutt. Fletcher, Ford: Downes.

WILLIAM JOHNSON, and STEPHEN HORSEY, Northampton cty, 1655.
Head rights: Tho. Denellin, Mary Denellin, Geo. Harrison, Ben. Sumer, Jno. Treddar, Wm. Jnoson [*sic*], Symon Brownely, Tho. Wilson, Rich'd Warren, Ellynor Walter.

THOMAS KEELE, in a bay of Paspetanke river, 1663.
Head rights: Wm. Badger, Jno. Gaffer, Dan'll Merick, Tho. Joanes, Ed. Seare, Margt Williams, Ann Robinson, Abell Jason, Rich. Bulloch, Tho: Mann, Rich: Evans, Edward Evans, Robert Evans, Jno. Sharpe, Ja: Fuller, John Carey.

(*Continued on page 35*)

The County Court Note-Book

An every-other-monthly devoted mainly to abstracts from County Court Records, prior to 1800.

MILNOR LJUNGSTEDT, Editor and Publisher. Bethesda, Rural Route 5, Maryland.

Published six times a year. Subscription, two dollars, in advance; must begin with the year.

August, 1930 **Whole**
Vol. IX., No. 4 **No. 53**

HAYS WITH VARIATIONS

The odds and ends of notes which begin in this issue of the NOTE-BOOK were collected, in part, for a friend who links North Carolina and New York. (He will note that I mention North Carolina first.) I think this friendly friend will have no objection to their publication.

The other object of the collection was to discover the ancestry of Col. ROBERT HAYS, of Tennessee, the well-known soldier of the Revolution. The family of Col. Hays seems to be utterly unknown. There is no record in existence of which the Editor is informed, which gives his origin, other than a letter from his son to Dr. Draper [I think this is where the statement is made] in which he says his father was born near Salisbury, North Carolina. The only HAYS in Rowan county, who seems to be available, is one PATRICK HAYS, and very little can be found concerning him. He seems to have been a land owner and a man of respectability.

The name PATRICK strongly suggests that PATRICK HAYS of Pennsylvania who came down into Virginia.

But the name SAMUEL . . . which was his son's name . . . certainly suggests that SAMUEL was "in the family."

Descendants in the South, who, unfortunately don't seem to have much information, claim that "it was an old Virginia family", and that Col. ROBERT was the son of a RICHARD HAYS.

That young ROBERT received an appointment as Ensign in the Revolutionary Army, and his further advance in military and civic rank, would seem to show that he was the son of a family of some standing, and yet his original appointment and his subsequent advancement may have been due entirely to his intelligence and his personality. It would be extremely interesting to clear the matter up.

CONTINUED articles COUNTY COURT NOTE-BOOK, and the dates on which they first appeared.
THE ANCESTRY OF COL. JOHN DONELSON. Began with February, 1927.
AUTHENTIC REFERENCES for INFERRED MARRIAGES (formerly called MARRIAGES BY INFERENCE). Began with May, 1922.
MARYLAND'S NEXT OF KIN. Began with July, 1922.
VIRGINIA COLONISTS. Alphabetized line began with July, 1924.
MILITARY NOTES, both COLONIAL and REVOLUTIONARY, and later MILITIA NOTES. Began December, 1923.
INTERCOUNTY and INTERCOLONY (formerly called New Englanders and Others, &c., &c.). Began with March, 1922.
EASTERN SHORE FAMILIES. In the form of a one-page supplement, began with June, 1925.
SHIPS IN PORT and COLONIAL FORENAMES will appear in alternate issues or as space can be found for them.
STAFFORD COUNTY INDICES began in June, 1929.

Some time ago the Editor published the late GILBERT COPE'S explanation of "Old Style" and "New Style." It did not seem at the time that there would be any confusion as to the "first month," but it seems that confusion does exist. The following table was given by Mr. COPE but not then used. From this it will be seen that when the Quakers wrote the "first month" before 1752, they meant MARCH.

OLD STYLE.		NEW STYLE	
Prior to 1752, the year began March 25th.		The year 1752 began with January 1st.	
March,	1st month.	Jan.	1st month.
April,	2d month.	Feb.	2d month.
May,	3d month.	March,	3d month.
June,	4th month.	April,	4th month.
July,	5th month.	May,	5th month.
August,	6th month.	June,	6th month.
Sept.	7th month.	July.	7th month.
Oct.	8th month.	Aug.	8th month.
Nov.	9th month.	Sept.	9th month.
Dec.	10th month.	Oct.	10th month.
Jan.	11th month.	Nov.	11th month.
Feb.	12th month.	Dec.	12th month.

VARIA

The two following paragraphs are contributed by Mrs. TALBOTT, of Rockville, Maryland. They are well worth preserving.

"I only need visit the graveyard of a community to know the character of the people." (Benjamin Franklin.)

"Show me the resting place of the dead, and I will judge the living." (Englehardt.)

GREEN BROWN and Susan Ragan. Mar. Li. Bond. Caswell cty, N. C. 25 Nov 1865.

PALLAS BLANKENBAKER, of Brumfield parish, Culp cty, Va. Conveys land to Adam Wyland and wife Elizabeth, her daughter. Culp. Va. 17 Dec. 1759. C-244.

"TOSCAPE DEATH *alias* HERMAN HUSBANDS." The "Land Book", or land tax list of Bedford county, Penna., includes this curious name. Date, 1774. In WHEELER'S HISTORICAL SKETCHES OF NORTH CAROLINA, vol. i, p. 60, it is stated that HERMAN HUSBANDS (concerned in the uprising in North Carolina in 1771, by the Regulators — the battle of Alamance) escaped and "settled in Pennsylvania near Pittsburgh." [There is much more about HUSBANDS on page 348, of vol ii.]

IN A CASE where one of the grand jury was not a freeholder, and the indictments were subsequently quashed, Hugh West, on behalf of the King prayed an appeal to the General Court, which the local Court refused, "*it appearing that no single fine* [in the cases quashed] *would exceed 10 or 2,000 lbs tobacco, and that the King was no party, and that no person offered security for the appeal*" [apparently for the County or the King's Attorney!]

THOMAS JENKINSON: will. Jenkinson had daughters Frances, *Mare, Naome,* Catherine and Elizabeth. He provides that his land shall forever be called the *Thomas Jenkinson Plantation*; if the name be altered the heirs are to be disinherited. Acco. cty, Va. 1720. xvi-202.

PROBATES AND ADMINISTRATIONS FROM THE ORDER BOOKS OF KING GEORGE COUNTY, VIRGINIA

(See previous abstracts)

RICHARD WHITE; Margaret White, widow, makes oath that he died intestate and gets ctf for l. a. John Glendening, sec. Orders i-126. 2 Aug 1723.

WILLIAM LAMPTON; Hester Lampton, widow, gets admn with will annexed. Hector Lampton, Wm. Skrine and James Kay, sec. 6 Dec 1723. Orders i-141.

GEORGE DOWNING and wf Ann, present will of Richard Smith and make oath. 8 Feby 1723. i-156.

FRANCIS JETT; Elizabeth Jett gets ctf for l. a. 8 Feby 1723. Orders 1-158.

RICHARD SMITH [see above]; his will presented by George Downing and wf Ann, extrs, and ctf for probate granted. 6 Mch 1723. Orders i-160.

MARGRETT DERMOTT; Robert Doniphan gets l. a. on her estate. John Clendening, sec. 1 Mny 1724. Orders i. 181.

JAMES LUMSFORD; Sarah Lumsford, extx, presents will, which is proved by Richard Standley and William Rowley. 5 June 1724. Orders i-194.

WILLIAM BRIDGES; Ann Bridges presents will and makes oath. Further proved by Francis Payne, John Payne, Robert Inglish. 7 Aug 1724. Orders i-201.

JOHN FRANKLIN; will presented by George Franklin, extr, and further proved by John Payne and William Hudson. 2 Oct 1724. Orders i-216.

JOHN PRATT; will presented by Evan Price and Margaret Pratt, extrs. Proved by John Kendall and Hellener Hughs. 1 Jany 1724. Orders i-232. Benjamin Berryman and William Harrison, sec.

NATHANIEL WILLIAMS; admn his estate to Thomas Williams. Henry Head, sec. 5 Feby 1724. Orders i-232.

PATRICK MAGGEE; will presented by Eliza: Maggee, the extx. Further proved by solemn affirmation of William Skrine. William Skrine and Wm. Duling, sec. 5 Feby 1724. Orders i-233.

PATRICK WHITE; will presented by John Savage, extr, and further proved by Peter Nugent and Thomas Tinpenny [?] Wm. Strother, Gent., and William Pattishall, sec. 8 May 1725. Orders i-251.

JOSHUA BUTLER; will presented by widow, and extx, Grace. Proved by John Bradford and James Warren. 3 Sept 1725. Orders i-271. Widow's sec. John Page and Thomas Welch.

THOMAS PRISE; will presented by Mary Prise his widow and extx and proved by George Stone and Elizabeth Scoffill, two of the wit. 3 Dec. 1725. Orders i-294.

GEORGE SEAGOOD, Clerk; Admn to Nicholas Smith, Gent. 3 Dec. 1725. Orders i-294.

SILVESTER THATCHER; admn his estate to William Underwood, nearest friend to Thomas Thatcher. John Fox, sec. 7 Jany 1725. Orders i-295.

DENNIS RAREDON; admn his estate to Jeremiah Bronaugh, Jr.; Jeremiah Bronaugh, sec. 7 Jany 1725. Orders i-296.

JOHN PAINE; admn his estate to William Jett. Chas. Seale, sec. 7 Jany 1725. Orders i-296.

JOHN BROWN; Sarah Brown, widow, gets admn. Jeremiah Brown and John Hardy sec. 4 Feby 1725. Orders i-297.

RICHARD PEARLE; admn his estate to widow Elizabeth. James Head and James Grant, sec. 4 Feby 1725. Orders i-297.

ADAM EDGAR; will presented by James Hackley, his extr. Proved by Peter Loud and John Hinshar. 4 Mch 1725. Orders 1-306.

JOHN GRIMSBY; will presented by Wealthy Grimsby, widow and extx. Thomas Grimsby, heir-at-law, consenting. Proved by Ralph Sise, wit. 5 Mch 1725. Orders i-307.

MARY COLLINGS; will presented by Catherine Pullein, extx. Proved by Thomas Dickenson and James Smith. 1 Apr 1726. Orders i-313.

JOHN HALL; admn his estate to Joseph Berry; Enoch Berry, sec. 1 Apr 1726. Orders i-314.

DAVID JONES; admn his estate to Martha Jones, his widow. Rush Hudson and Neal McCormack, sec. 6 May 1726. Orders i-318.

THOMAS ARNOLD; will presented by widow and extx, Grace. Also proved by Isaac Arnold. 6 May 1726. Orders i-319.

WILLIAM STROTHER; will presented by Margaret Strother, his widow and extx. Also proved by John Hardy and Martha Kendall. 1 July 1726. Orders 1-320.

(To be continued)

INTERCOUNTY and INTERCOLONY

CHRISTOPHER BEELER, now of Hampshire county, Va., Gent. Will. .... To his sister in the Cloisters in Lancaster county, in Pennsylvania, for taking care of my dau. Catharine when there, and in her sickness in Pennsylvania........... [Also] £100 to the sisters in the Cloisters. Ffx cty, Va. 30 Mch 1773-21 June 1779. D(1)-129.

JOHN BAIRD, of Pr. Geo. cty, Va., to Daniel Hughes of Person cty, N. C. Consideration 5 sh. specie; tract of land. Branch of Spoon water mentioned. Person, N. C. 29 Sept 1792. A-99.

MATHIAS BAKER, Sr., York, Penna. Impowers his son Mathias to bind him[self] as an apprentice to Godfrey [Boone?] of Fred'k, Md., for five years. Fred'k, Md. G-351, 26 Dec 1761.

JOHN BLOWER, of Spots. cty, Va., collier, to John Mercer of Stafford, Gent. 405 acres. Pr. Wm, Va. 16 May 1733. B-50.

ELIZABETH BUCHANAN, late of A. A. cty, Md., now of Alexandria, Ffx cty, Va. Will. Ffx, Va. D(1)-267. 13 July 1782.

BENJA. CHAPIN, of Alexandria, leaves house and lot in New London, Conn., to his son, Hiram GURDEN............Wf Margaret extx. Ffx, Va. 13 Aug 1781. D(1)-233.

JOHN CHRISTIAN, of Patrick cty, Va., conveyance from Benj. Cloud, late of Stokes cty. 3 Mch 1800. Stokes, N. C. iii-285.

ZACHARIAH COPLAND and WILLIAM PORTER, of Nancemond cty, Va., to William Goodman of Gates cty, N. C., a parcel of land which Copland and Porter were empowered by Joseph Porter's will to sell. 18 Nov 1786. Gates cty, N. C. i-240.

WILLIAM DUNBAR, upwards of 86, makes a deposition. In this he states that he had removed [from Fairfax county, presumably] to Pittsylvania county Virginia. Ffx cty, Va. 1804. L. C. p. 66. [The removal evidently at some much earlier date.]

JOHN FOX and wf MARY, of Spots. cty, Va., to William Pearce of King George cty, Hanover parish; convey land, part of a grant to Capt. William Underwood, and bequeathed by him to Mary Tutt. K. Geo., Va. 7 Feby 1745. iii-118.

ALLEN FORQUAR, of Maryland, farmer; to Martin Urner, of the Province of Pennsylvania, Chester county............conveyance of land. Fred'k, Md. 13 Apr 1761. F-1320.

JOHN GIBSON'S settlement (of his estate):...... "By cash from Wallace for a note on a man in Carolina supposed to be of slow payment if not Insolvent. $16.00." Rock'm, Va. 24 Feby 1724. v-376.

THOMAS GINBERT [or GUIBERT] and wf Rebecca, of St. Mary's cty, Md., power to Thomas Grigsby of Stafford cty, Va. Sam'l Burton one of wit. K. Geo. Va., 1-61. 30 April 1722.

HANNAH x HAWTHORNE, of Nottingham Tshp, Cecil cty, Md.......Will. ......To Josiah Watson, of Alexandria; to Jane Watson, his wife; to Margaret McElhatton; to Samuel Daff ...... Josiah Watson, extr. Wit: James Taylor, Moses Tandy. Ffx cty, Va. 12 Apr 1785-15 Jany 1787. (1E)-187.

THOMAS M., AMBROS W., and WM. H. JONES, of Dallas cty, Alabama; power to their father, Ambros Jones, of Person cty, in connection with the estate of the late Francis Ford. Raleigh, N. C. 1 Mch 1834. Person cty records, vol. xii.

GEORGE JUDE and wf ANN, of Goochland cty, Va., to Edmund Brewer, of Guilford cty, N. C. 500 acres, both sides Dann river. Guilford cty, N. C. 10 Oct 1781. ii-126.

JACOB LASH, yeoman, of Nazareth, tshp of Bethlehem, Northampton cty, Penna. Will. Surry, N. C. Wills. ii-8. 21 Feby 1774-18 Nov 1782.

JOHN McBRIDE, of "Lorrence" cty, Indiana. Will. Surry, N. C. 2 Oct 1821. iv-155.

MIRIAM MACY'S children by her first husband Tristram Macy, late of Nantucket. See Deep River Mo'ly Mtg records at Guilford Coll., N. C. p. 69. [Chn born 1766, 1771, 1774, 1776, 1779.]

Mrs. ANN MASON, dec'd. Inventory and appraisement her estate in Stafford cty, Va., and Charles cty, Md. Staff., Va. Returned 12 Dec 1763. O-456.

EDWARD MATHEWS, of Fred'k cty, Md., gives bond to convey land to Michael Runner, of Chester cty, Penna. Fred'k, Md. 30 Oct 1760. G-383.

JOHN POPE, of Minchin Hampton, Gloucester cty, G. B., mercer; power to Thomas Martin, of Bristol, Mcht, and Wm. Winstone, of Virginia, Mcht, to demand of Robert Burgis, late of Minchin Hampton, "coller maker"......... &c., &c. K. Geo., Va. 23 Feby 1721. 1-73.

SIMON PETER; will. He left musical instruments, notes and books. His brother was David Peter of Gardenhuetten, Ohio, and sister, Anna Peter, of Zeist, Holland. Friend Samuel Stotz warden of the Brethren's Congregation in Salem, Stokes cty, extr. Wit: Reichel and Huethin [?] Stokes cty, N. C. 7 Mch 1814. iii-36.

JOHN RABY, of Gates cty, N. C., to Kedar Raby, of the Upper Parish of Nancemond cty, Va. conveys fifty acres. 30 Oct 1786. Gates cty i-242.

THOMAS SCHLEY; of Fred'k cty, Md. Certificate of naturalization.........being a foreigner and having inhabited and resided for seven years in his Majesty's Colonies in America, and not having been absent out of some of the said Colonies a longer time than two months ....and having produced a certificate of having taken the Sacrament of the Lord's Supper within three months.........and subscribed to the oaths, &c., &c. Before Edward Shippen, Jr., Prothon. Supreme Court of Penna. Fred'k, Md. 24 Sept 1761. F-324.

Capt. WILLIAM SATERWHITE, and wf MELECENT, of Halifax cty, N. C., to Thomas Foster, yeoman; convey land in Parish of St. Luke, Rowan county, N. C. Rowan, N. C. 6 Aug 1764. vi-28.

JOSEPH TRIVELL [German signature] of York cty, Penna., conveys land to John Bryon of Fred'k cty, Md. Fred'k, Md. 9 Apr 1759. F-698.

WILLIAM WAITE, Bedford cty, Tenn., to Thomas Hallibarton of Person cty, N. C., conveys land. 10 mch 1810. Person cty, D-254.

Rev. ABNER WAUGH and wf PHILADELPHIA, late of King George, now of Caroline cty, Va. Commission to take release of wife's dower. K. Geo., Va. 19 Jany 1783. vi-341

SERVICE AND SUPPLIES COLONIAL, REVOLUTIONARY AND MILITIA

(The seventeen which follow were merely listed as applicants for pension. Court record of Stokes County, N. C. Sept. 1832 and Dec. 1832.)

MICAJAH FRANCIS,
JOHN WHITWORTH,
NOAH BAILY,
THOMAS JONES,
CHARLES DAVIS,
HARMON McGIE,
GEORGE KREIGER,
FREDIRIC BRINKLY,
CASPER STULTZ,
THOMAS FEARS,
ROBERT HILL,
FRANCIS STEELE,
EDMUND JONES,
JOHN WARD,
JACOB HELSAPECH (?)
CHRISTOPHER STANLY,
BENJAMIN CLEMENTS.

The following are taken from plats of surveys in Montgomery county, Virginia. Many of the warrants were sold or otherwise assigned to others. Service evidently proved as to the names here listed.

JOHN ARMSTRONG, serjeant "late war." 200 acres. 14 Mch 1774.

MATHEW ANDERSON, non-com. officer "last war." 200 acres. 11 Feby 1774.

NATHAN ABBOT, of Hanover county. "Corperol" Va. Reg't. 200 acres. 9 Mch 1774.

THOMAS BARNES, ctf that he served as Q. M. Sjt, Va. Reg't. 2,000 acres. 1 Mc. 1774.

RICHARD BLOXAM, served as drummer, Va. Regt. 200 acres. 24 Mch 1774.

JAMES ARMSTRONG; ordered certified that Mary Armstrong is his widow, he having been a soldier formerly in the Continental Army, and that she is in needy circumstances, with a considerable family of small children. K. Geo. cty, Va. 1 June 1786. Orders iv-299.

DAVID ALLEN; Susanna, his widow, allowed £10, maintenance. Allen died in Continental service. Granv. cty, N. C. Min. Book. 4 May 1786.

THOMAS CRADDOCK; fifer. 200 acres. Montg. cty, Va. Surveys. 2 June 1774.

WILLIAM CHRISTIAN, Gent. Captain, 2d Virginia. 3,000 acres. Montg. cty, Va. Surveys, 17 Feby 1785.

HENRY COLLINS, Esq. Lieutenant. 3,000 acres. Montg. cty, Va. Surveys. 21 Jany 1775.

WILLIAM DAINGERFIELD, Captain, Va. Reg't. 3,000 acres. Montg. cty Va. Surveys. 16 Dec 177...?

JOHN DRAPER; served as Ensign. 2,000 acres. Montg. cty Surveys. Mch 1774.

GEORGE FRAZER, dec'd. Entitled as a Lieut., Va. Reg't, under Col. Washington to 2,000 acres. Mr. Michael Robinson, the guardian of the only dau. and heir-at-law of Frazer, receives warrant. Montg. cty, Va. Surveys. 14 Mch 1774.

WILLIAM FINNIE is entitled to 6,000 acres ... to 2,000 as a Surgeon's Mate, Va. Reg't, under Col. Byrd, and two other thousand as heir to his father Alexander, who was a Lieut. same Reg't, as also 2,000 as heir to his bro. John, who was an Ensign same. Montg. cty, Va. Surveys. 10 Nov. 1773. (Rights assigned.)

HENRY HARRISON, son and heir of Capt. Henry Harrison 3,000 acres. Montg. cty, Va. Surveys. 31 Dec 1773.

GEORGE HIGHT makes declaration and Court declares opinion he was a Revolutionary soldier. Rock'm cty Va. Orders, p. 181 Dec 1832.

(*Continued from page 31*)

JOHN LAWSON, Lancaster cty, 1655.
Head rights: Henry Berry, Pa. Cleach, Sarah Turner, Eliz: Sethell, N. Motheringe, Wm. Nicholson, Geo. Godale, Jno. Mascale [?] Dan'l Cooper, Kath. English.

JOHN LEWIS, Acco., 1666.
Head rights: Grace Lais [this is probably meant for LEWIS ?] Indian Tom, Wm. Houlder, James Walker, An Ogden, *Sugar* Coleman, Ann Deacon, Tho. Wright, Rich: Stevens, Henry Michaell.

JOHN LEGGATT, New Kent, 1662.
Head rights: Barnaby Eaton, Wm. Jens [?] Sarah Rose, Tho: Jackson, Wm. Bayly, Jno. Vaughan, Tho: Harding.

JNO. LEWIS and THOMAS MICHELL, New Kent, 1662.
Head rights: Wm. Thornton, Rich: Boyne, Tho: Skugge, Law: Baker, Tho: Walder, Ellen Blarwood [?] Mary Stinson, Jane Mayson, Rich: Sanrow [?] Jno. Ellett, Geo. Castleton, Bryan Hazlewood, Ann Lislow [?] Eliz: Palmer, Joane Mudd, Hugh Davis, Jno. Gunne;
Wm. Colvert, Eliz: Gittins, James Ridly, Mary Taylor, Eliz: Smith, Ann Norton, Bridg: Black, Nich: Hart, Nich: Flower, Wm. Price, Rich: Overton, Ann Shelves, Tho: Hanson, Sarah Russell.

JOHN LAURENCE, westward side of the River of Chawanoke, 1663.
Head rights: Geo. Teague, Kath: Cornelius, Wm. Sharpe, Ann Bleach, Wm. Hare, Hen: Nathington [? perhaps Washington] Tho: Hill, Giles Wake, Hugh Farthy, Sar: H......... [?] Wm. Brithenton, Jane Doughting. A marginal note in a later writing says "Carolina."

Mr. ROBERT LAWRENCE, Jr., westward side of Chowanoke river. 1663.
Head rights: Wm. Gelding, Wm. Hart, Jno. Shaply, Tho. Turner, Ed: Morgan, Jno. Goffe, Ed: Stephens, Wm. Chester, Mary Cant, Tho: Stroud, Ja: Smith, Ed. Hawly.

Printed at the Industrial School for Crippled and Deformed Children, 241 St. Botolph St., Boston, Mass.

The

County Court Note-Book

A Little Bulletin of History and Genealogy

October, 1930.] **Vol. IX, No. 5**

SHIPS IN PORT

The *Antigoe Merchant*, Mr. Thomas Perry, master; arrived at the Cape of Virginia. Som. Md. 19 Jany 1676. L-174.

Ship *Ann and Taylor* [?]; Cavaliero Christian, master. Acco, Va. 1701. vii-276.

Shipp *Artillery*. See N-n cty, Va. 28 Apr. 1650. iii-210. Also 28 July 1653. iv-184.

The *Arcadia* was a sloop owned by David Derrick of Marcus Hook, Penna. Thos. Derrick, master.

Ship *Angell*. N-n, Va. 13 Nov 1656. vii-51.

Ship *Admiral*. See Acco, Va. 19 Feby 1677. vii-114.

Shipp *Ann*, of Dublin, Mr. William Thornton, master. Nthld, Va. 25 Oct 1702. Vol. 1699-1713.

Shipp *Anne*, of Jersey; Annie Daubergue & Compa. owners. Nthld, Va. 17 Sept 1702. 1699-1713, p. 224.

The good shipp *Amity*, of New Castle in England. Jirimiah Sympson, marriner and part owner. Wmld, Va. 18 June 1683. 1676-1688, p. 289.

The *Affrica* of Lyme was taken by the French; a boat which belonged to her was sold to Sam'll Maheu [?] by one John Freeman. Nthld, Va. 22 July 1708. Vol. 1699-1713.

Ship *Apollo*, of Glasgow. James Duncan, Commander. Wmld, Va. 29 June 1721. 1721-1731, fo. 3.

Shipp *Adventure*, of Bristoll; Thomas Cox, master. Wmld,Va. 26 Mch 1707. 1705-1721, fo. 46.

The *Batchelour's Delight*; difference bet. Robert Greenway, master, and Arthur Denis, concerning the sum of £12 for his and his wife's passage. Acco, Va. 1678-1682, p. 221. 18 May 1681.

Barque *The Blessing*; see N-n, Va. 29 Jany 1655. v-127.

The *Britania*; mentioned in the will of John Smith of Chippin [?] "John Scott lately of the Hill in Yorkshire, England, now on ihe *Britania*." Chester cty, Pa. A-479. 29 July 1699.

Sloop *Content*, from Bermuda (als Sumer Islands); Philip Hall, master. Wmld, Va. 26 Mch 1712. 1705-1721, fo. 178.

The *Essex*, Capt. Dausey [Dansey ?] Commander "Madam I have made Inquiry of your brother and can hear nothing of him but should be very glad to See him. I remain your humble Servant, Henry Atkinson" [who appears to be the Shipper of goods in the Essex.] To Mrs. Margarett Prieson. N-n, Va. Chancy, &. 1742.

Brigantine "*Friendship*," bound for Virginia. Thomas Eyres, master. 1691. Va. St. Pa. i-28.

Snow *Friendship*, of Ayrshire; Capt. John Aitken, Commander. [See will of John Reid.] Wmld Wills (Crozier.) p. 50. 1746.

The *Forward Friggot*, Daniel Russell, master. Mentioned in the will of Richard Walker, also the *Sarah and Mary*; also the *Princess Amelia*; and the *Mary*, James Hokins, master. Middx, Va. 1713-1734, p. 304. 1 Mch 1726.

The *Forward Gally*, of London; George Buckeridge, Commander, presents in court a power from Jonathan Forward, of London, Mcht. Wmld, Va. 25 Feby 1730. [2]-101.

Ship *Friendship*, of Kingston upon Hull; Jonathan Waterland, master. Acco, Va. 1674. v-193.

The *Grape*, of Liverpool; Thomas Preeson, master. 1690. Va. St. Pa. vi-24.

The Ship *Golden Lyon*; Capt. Anthony Guester; to Virginia about 1687. Middx, Va. See 3 Oct 1709. iv-453.

The Ship *Golden Lyon*, from Bristol, mentioned. Nthld, Va. 1666-1672, p. 43. 1 Feby 1667.

Ship *Golden Fortune*; John Storey was 1st mate; he petitions that one Morey be removed from pretended command......the master, Mr. Robert Arbuckle, having died, and that he (Storey) be allowed to succeed as master. 1680. Va. St. Pa. xx 1-13.

Ship *Goodwill*, Capt. John Lux, commander; from London to Maryland. Of fifty convicts shipt, nineteen "dyed." Annap., Md. P. L. v-337. 1720.

Sloop *Good Intent*, included in the inventory of Thomas Daily, marriner, late of London; "as she now stands." Hyde, N. C. Feby 1791. i-598.

Ship *Garland*; Capt. Arbuthnot. Va. St. Pa. i-251. 11 Apr 1756.

The Ship *Garland*, (Capt. Cook), was wrecked in Carolina. 1710. Va. St. Pa. i-139.

Shipp The *Golden Fortune*. Nthld, Va. 22 Feby 1655. i-65.

Shipp The *Golden Fortune*; Lewis Lewis, age 30, in 1655 was "upon a voyage at sea" on board this ship. Rappa, Va. 22 Feby 1655. i-70.

The *Golden Lyon*; Robert Ransom, commander, was aged 33. Deposition. York, Va, "12" -299. 4 Mch 1699.

"Ship *George Gally*;" Cornelius Serjant & Co., Bristol, Mchts, owners. K. Geo., Va. 7 June 1723. i-120.

Shipp *Harford Friggott*; Abraham Loyd & Co., Mchts, of Bristol, owners. Wmld, Va. 1705-1721, fo. 334. 30 Jany 1717.

Ship or pinke of Maryland, the *Grace*. N-n, Va. 1657. vii-54.

Ship *Henrietta*; came to Anchor 25 Nov. 1701. Capt. William Browning, commander. Wmld, Va. 1705-1721, fo. 9.

Their Majesties' hired ship the "*Henry Prize*;" Capt. Rich'd Finch. Va. St. Pa. About 1693. i-43.

The Good Ship *Henery and Ann*, of Monokin in Maryland; John Harrison, master, who gives power to Mr. Nath'l Littleton. Acco, Va. 20 Feby 1687. ix-227.

Shipp "*Honn'r*;" Capt. John Price, commander; granted an appeal to the High Court of Admiralty. England. York Va. 1657-1662, p. 133. 4 Apr. 1659.

AUTHENTIC REFERENCES FOR INFERRED MARRIAGES

(Virginia records)

JOSEPH DALY and ANN JENKINS, dau. of "Drewciller." Henrico papers. Before 1 Apr 1770.

ROBERT DOBIE and ....EPPES, a widow. Hen. Pa. Refers to will of October 1777.

THOMAS DRUMON [?] and MARTHA GEORGE, widow of Nicholas. Staff. Before 13 Oct 1737. M-249.

JESSE DOYNE (late of Charles county, Gent.) and ELIZABETH BRENT dau. of Robert, of Stafford, Gent. Staff. P-217. [They had a son Robert, born 26 Feby 1709.]

DANIEL DUNAWAY and JANE WALL, widow of John. Nthld. Before 21 Aug 1712. Orders iv-803.

WILLIAM DILLARD and MARY NORMAN, dau. of Joseph. Culp. Before 20 Nov 1783. L. C. p. 1.

ROBERT DOUGLESS and the widow of John PETTOCK [?] About or before 22 Aug 1780. Ffx, D (1)-201.

THO. EARTH and JANE SINGER widow of Edward. Before 18 Mch 1712. Nthld. Orders iv-817.

GEORGE ESKRIDGE and REBECCA, one of the children of Margarett Bonam. Before 28 Mch 1713. Wmld. v-151.

EDWARD FURNELL and LUCY, admx of RICH'D COX. See Court 28 Dec 1687. Nthld. Orders iii-419.

JOSEPH FRANKLIN and SUSANNA HUGHLETT extx of John. Before 22 June 1699. Nthld. Orders iv-28.

JOHN FITZHUGH and .... MACKARTY. Va. Col. Dec. p. R 112. [No date.]

WILLIAM FARIS, Jr. and MARTHA TRUEMAN, dau. Richard. Before 2 Sept 1765. Hen. Pa.

EDWARD FITZGARRELL and MARY LAURENCE, widow of William. Before 21 Apr 1656: Chas. city cty. 1655-1665, p. 52.

Capt. THOMAS FLETCHER and ELIZABETH HARRISON. Before 1793. Culp. L. C. p. 8.

ROBERT GREEN and MARY PRICKET. Va. Gen. Ct. Dec. About Feby 1678. p. B14.

ROBERT GREEN and MARY BALL, dau. of Samuel. Before 16 Aug 1751. Culp. A-60.

ANDREW GILES and MARY MALLICOTE, widow of Thomas. Before Apr 1738. Va. Gen. Ct. Dec. p. B.71.

ROBERT GORDON and the relict of Jno. NICKLESS. Before 18 June 1713. Nthld. Orders iv-842.

JAMES GODWIN and .... KINEHEN [?] sister of Matthew. Va. Gen. Ct. Dec. p. B68. Before 1738.

WILLIAM GARRET and MARY LUCAS, dau. of Thomas. Before 8 Apr 1718. Ffx. D (1)-81.

BENJAMIN GRAYSON and STACY ELLZEY, dau. of Lewis. [She had previously married Burgess Beckley.] Before 1 Oct 1785. Ffx. E (1)-224.

JOHN GRAHAM and ELIZABETH COCK. [Her will 7 Apr 1791] Soon after 19 Nov 1746. Pr. Wm. Dist. Ct. p. 405.

WENDLE GRAFF and ANNA-ELIZABETH BRIGHT, dau. of Wendall Bright. Before 1 Dec 1784. Ffx. E (1)-31.

.... HICKMAN probably married JANE JONES. Before 8 Feby 1664 Acco. ii-5. (There were three chn. Jane, Joan and Rachell.)

JOHN HOBBS, of London, and ELIZABETH GRIFFIN [probably also of London. She had evidently previously married......... Hewett.] Before 2 Feby 1702. Nthld iv-213.

ALEXANDER HANSFORD and ANN WREN, widow of John. Before 1 Mch 1759. K. Geo. iii-123.

JOHN HOPWOOD and HANNAH, dau. of Hannah Humphreys. Before 26 Mch 1783. Staff. S-102.

RICE HOE and ANN HOWSON, dau. of Robert. Before 8 Jany 1699. Va. Col. Dec. p. R63.

[See previous marriage list in which RICE HOOE is given as marrying MARY MASSEY, a widow of Sigismund, and also extx of Gerrard Lowther. Staff. Orders i-208. About 10 Feby 1691-2.]

JOHN HALL and AVERILLA GOSSE, dau. of Mathew, Sr. Before 20 Nov 1708. Staff. Z-468.

JOHN HACKLEY and JUDITH BALL, dau. of Samuel. Before 16 Aug. 1751. Culp.

Mr. WILLIAM HERBERT and SARAH CARLYLE. Before 5 Apr. 1780. Ffx. D (1)-203.

JOHN HARRIS and WINFRED [*sic*] BOGGESS. Before 1802. Ffx. L. C.

ANDREW HEISER and ANNA-MARY BRIGHT, dau. of Wendall. Ffx. Before 1 Dec 1784. E(1)-31. [See the marriage of ANNA ELIZABETH BRIGHT.]

JOHN JORDAN and DORCAS SPENCE, widow. See Va. Col. Dec. p. R61. [Sec also Westmoreland Wills.] Before 1700. Before 24 Aug 1685. See Wmld, Orders 1676-1681, p. 447.

Mr. ROBERT JONES and SARAH SALSBURY, relict of Thomas. Before 20 Apr 1699. Nthld Orders iv-10.

GEORGE JOHNSON appears to have married SARAH, extx of Denis McCarty. See also Abraham Barnes. Ffx. Before 20 Nov 1760. Orders [2], 541.

JOHN JAMES and DINAH ALLEN, dau. of William. Before 16 Aug 1738. Staff. M-309.

WILLIAM JEFFARS and ELIZABETH AUSTEN. Marriage contract. Nthld. 1 July 1656. Records i-89.

GEORGE JACKSON and ANN RANSHA, dau. of Argol. Before Oct 1738. Va. Gen. Ct. Dec. B78.

.... LETHERLAND and FRANCIS BARKER, widow of Mr. William. Before 12 Apr 1664. Chas. City cty. 1655-1665. p. 465. [She seems also to have married a Taylor.]

JOHN LOMAX and RACHEL, admx of Robert Jones, dec'd. Before 19 Aug 1771. Ffx. Orders [iii] p. 267,

GEORGE LYNES (m. about 48 years before) ELIZABETH WATKINS, also called RICHMOND [*she was a widow RICHMOND*]. (Dep'n of Eliza: Smith, of St. Mary's cty, Md., also of Thomas Gosling of the same county. Elizabeth would, at the time of the depositions, be "70 odd." She lived in Calvert county, Md.) Wmld, Va. Dep'ns 16 Aug 1731. Fid. Accts. i-fo. 131.

JACOB MARTIN and SARAH SCOTT, widow of John, Gent. Wmld, Va. Before 1664. i-127. See Fid. Accts, 1-127. (She had also married George Cross.)

THO: MAYZE and BARBARA SALISBURY, dau. of Thomas, dec'd. Nthld. Before 16 Feby 1692. iii-614.

RICHARD MARTIN probably married JANE RUSSELL, wid. Staff. Va. Before 24 Feby 1707. Z-409. Sea also Z-234.

Mr. WILLIAM MASON and the widow of Mr. Thomas HALLAM, of London. Before or about 14 Apr 1656. C. C. cty. 1655-1665, p. 58.

JOHN MERRYDITH and MARY BARRY, relict of William. Before 19 Apr 1693. Nthld, Orders iii-619.

JOHN MERRIDAY and Mrs. ANN NASH *als* MALLETT. Ctf of marriage. 11 Sept 1656. Nthld. Records i-90.

.... MALLETT and ANN NASH, widow of William. Before 20 May 1656. Nthld Orders i-47. (She afterward m. Merriday.)

RODERICK McCULLOUGH and ELIZABETH HORSLEY before 6 Mch 1769. Amherst Orders. [She was dau. of William.]

MARYLAND'S NEXT OF KIN

RICHARD BURROUGH, ELIZ'TH x BURROUGH; inv. Margrett Drew, of Balto. Widow. Taken 26 May 1722. ix-131.

HENERY DONAHUE, son of the deceased; JOHN x KECEY, married the daughter of the deceased; inv. Henery Donahue. Balto. Taken 10 Nov. 1722. ix-132.

OWEN MacCARTY and THOMAS MORRIS; inv. Daniel MacCarty, Balto. Returned 10 Aug. 1722. ix-p. 133.

ROB'T EYVE; inv. Ann Elizabeth Vause of Cisell cty. 24 June 1721. ix-138.

MICHAEL HOLLAND and MICHAEL HOLLAND, Jr. appear to be kin: inv. Capt. Wm. Bolitho of Som. cty. Taken 30 Apr 1722. ix-141.

ROBERT CARNEY, "one of the nearest of kin refused to sign and would not give any reason for it." Inv. John Smith of Som. cty. About 29 Mch 1723. ix-142.

WILLIAM LOCK may have been kin [doubtful]; inv. Joseph Owin, Jr. Calv. cty. Taken 15 Sept 1722. ix-143.

JNO. HELLEN and PETTER HELLEN; inv. Edmond Hongerford, late of Calvert cty. 30 Dec 1721. ix-145.

NAOMI x DORING, CHARLES x DORING; inv. James Willmot, Jr. of Calv. cty. Taken 27 Aug 1722. ix-150.

ALLEX'DR MAGRUDER signed as "father-in-law;" inv. Mr. Tho. Letchworth of Pr. Geo's. 26 Nov 1722. ix-150.

LEVIN x JONES signs, perhaps kin [uncertain]; inv. Phillip Lewing, Pr. Geo's cty. 15 Oct 1722. ix-153.

JAMES GILES may have been kin; inv. Edward Jones of Pr. Geo's. 15 June 1722. ix-154.

SAM'LL PEELE, one of nearest of kin; inv. John Maccubins Jr. of A. A. cty. 9 Apr 1722. ix-169.

ELIZ: WHITTINGTON; inv. Mr. John Whittington of Q. A. cty. 20 June 1723. ix-180.

JOHN TUCKER, MARY DOWNES; inv. Rich'd Powell, Q. A. cty. 18 Sept 1723. ix-184.

RICHARD WELLS, CHAR'S VANDERFORD; inv. John Brown, Q. A. cty. 3 July 1723. ix-185.

DENNIS x CONNER, SARAH x JENNET; inv. Sam'l Jennet, Q. A. cty. 17 Aug 1723. ix-187.

JEAN x GRIFFIN, JAMES x MURPHY, WM. RATCLIFFE [one or two of these are probably kin]; inv. Bernard Griffin, Q. A. cty. 15 July 1723. ix-189.

The County Court Note-Book

An every-other-monthly devoted mainly to abstracts from County Court Records, prior to 1800.

MILNOR LJUNGSTEDT, Editor and Publisher. Bethesda, Rural Route 5, Maryland.

Published six times a year. Subscription, two dollars, in advance; must begin with the year.

October, 1930 **Whole**
Vol. IX., No. 5 **No. 54**

THE SAVING GRACE

The dry-as-dustness of city courts, the lack of interest in anything but politics and the associated dollar, or the unassociated dollar, and in the editor's case, the utter indifference in a certain section of the country to the inherent rights of our poor relations, the "dumb animals," which always strikes her with astonishment, all these are occasionally relieved by a touch of that genial humor which Dickens knew so well in the average, or garden kind of man, and of that kindliness which notes a sparrow......or a starving cat deprived of the sparrow.

One is just naturally drawn to a man who feeds a kitten or pets a dog. "Ain't it?"

In the dismal and decidedly dusty basement rooms of the chattel mortgage division of the Baltimore Court used to be this sign writ large and plain and posted by the cellar steps.

"HOME OF MRS. MURPHY AND FAMILY. PLEASE KEEP THE DOOR CLOSED."

The notice is there no longer, for, alas, Mrs. Murphy had a serious accident of some kind, and the humane clerks had the S. P. C. A. take the last care of her. As for Mr. Murphy, whose red coat never appeared above the basement stairs, he probably hunted another mate. They will, you know. The little Murphys, wild and shy as their kin of the woods, or the first, original Murphy of that green and lovely isle across the water, "rampaged" about the cellar and the ancient desks of the record room until taken to some outside home. Perhaps one or two are carrying on at the old establishment. But no one would ever know why the clerks dubbed them with the family name of *Murphy*, for when the Editor tried to make their acquaintance, they were handsome darkgray and brindled.

The Editor is glad to have known those clerks.

VARIA

William Ownbread was a baker in Alexandria, Virginia. Ffx cty, Va. O-52. Oct. 1783. [The Editor is not responsible for the vagaries of contemporary spelling.]

David Williams and Jane Covington. "Bonds of Matrimony" published. Som. Md. 26 Nov 1667. B(1)-90.

"My Loving friend Strong Waters of Fairfax county," received by deed from Robert Foster, of Prince William, 100 acres; consideration, Love good will and affection and £10 ster. Fffx cty, Va. Ackn. 16 Apr 1745. A-354.

Thaddeus Dorgan and wife Joan, servants of Timothy Greenham, agree with their said master to Serve him one whole year above their Indenture time in consideration that he would keep them together. Nthld, Va. 8 Nov 1719. 1713-1719, p. 345.

William Robinson desireth this ensuing bill to be recorded by reson of the oldnes of the Paper and the naughtiness of the inke which is as followeth [then follows record.] Chas. cty, Md. Octpber 22th Ao. Doni 1655. i-162.

Probation was this day made in open Court of the Last will and Testament of William Smith by the corporall oathes of Mr. Tho: Browne and Mr. John Michaell, Jun'r & allowed of & Ordered to be Recorded & Whereas it appeares to this Court that there is a Young Child Borne named Sarah Smith which is not nominated nor inserted in the said will being Borne Since the Said will was made; Itt is the judgement of the Court that Said Child named Sarah Smith [have] a share of the Estate coequall with the Rest of the Children nominated & inserted in the said will. Acco., Va. 10 Sept 1674. v-177.

William Williams: Ruth Cole aged about thirty testifies as to his nuncupative will. "I am pretty well out of debt and what need I make a will. I leave my wife Executrix of all my estate to maintain her and the children," and further saith not. Richard Sutton, age about sixty-two, also deposes. Acco., Va. Proved 8 Sept 1686. ix-97.

THE DEPUTY COMMISSARY'S GUIDE WITHIN THE PROVINCE OF MARYLAND

(*Contined from June, 1930*)

Wills and Testaments.

It is interesting to note that of the two ways in which a will might be proved, either by common form, or in form of law......in which there is much more formality and citations of widow and kin, &c., "he that proved but in common "form may be compelled to prove again in form "of law......but being proved only in common "form the will may be questioned at any time "within thirty years after by common opinion, "before it works prescription."

The manner of proving wills within the province of Maryland, the writer (Eli Vallette) goes on to say, was, at the time of his writing, neither wholly in the one way or the other, but was a compound of both......"because all wills "here are proved in common form, that is by "the executor, to be the true will, and per *testes*, "by the witnesses thereto subscribed or of so "many of them as do appear......and most gen-"erally the widow, or other representatives of "the deceased are present at the time of probate "......and do acknowledge themselves to be con-"tent with, and that they have no objection to "the taking of the probate."

Regularly (that is by civil law) testaments were to be exhibited for probate to the commissary, within four months next after the testator's death; and [he quotes from authority] "the or-" dinary may sequester the goods of the deceased, " until the executors have proved the testament; " so may the metropolitan, if the goods be in " divers dioceses."

As to Lands.

By the common law of England, since the conquest, no greater estate in land than for years would be disposed of by will, except by special custom, in particular places. "A method " was, however, found out, by which lands in fee " simple were, in effect, disposed of by will; this " was by conveying the land to such uses, as " should be appointed by the owner of the land, " and an appointment made by will was good, " because, according to legal construction, the " person claiming under the appointment, took " under the deed."

But this method failed when under a statute of Henry VIII, "the use drew to it the land and could not be separated from it." By other statutes of Henry VIII, the power of disposing of lands by will was generally introduced, it being thereby enacted that all persons seized in fee simple, " except married women, infants, idiots and persons of *non sane* memory, might by will and testament in writing devise to another......all lands except copyholds."

"Bare notes, in the hand writing of another " person, were allowed to be good wills within " the statute......so, a letter written from beyond " sea which directed that the estate should go " in such a manner ....tho' not sealed...... " tho' in loose sheets ...... tho' in the form of an " indenture...... [or] where the lawyer only took " short notes, with a design to draw it in form, " which he did, but the devisor died before it " was read to him...... where written unknown " to the devisor, and afterwards read to, and ap- " proved by him......notes given to make a will, " and the devisor's memory failed him, these " not es being drawn into form [were] held to be " good."

But a statute under Charles II directed that all devises of *lands* should not only be in writing, but signed by the devisor, or some other person in his presence, and by his express direction, and be subscribed in his presence by three or four witnesses......and the same ceremony was necessary to revoke a will regularly made under this statute.

(To be continued)

THE MIGRANT HAYS, HAYES HAISE, HAZE, SOME OF THEM.

(First Alphabet.)

Mr. JOHN HAY'S additional inventory. Middx cty, Va. Jany 1713. 1713–1734. p. 5.

SARAH, dau. of JOHN and MARY HAY. Born 19 May 1725. St. Paul's Reg. K. Geo. cty, Va. She died 6 Sept 1728 [?]

MARGARET, dau. of same. Born 18 Oct 1732. Same reference.

JOHN HAYS. Amherst cty, Va. 3 July 1769. Orders [i] p. 510.

JOHN HAYES; was a resident of Newberry District, S. C. Born 30 Nov 1764. Lived in Granville cty until 1813. See Pension Records. 20 Nov. 1835.

JOSHUA x HAYS; Wash'n cty, Indiana, 1823. Aged 64; entered service 1781-1782 at Granville C. H., N. C. [Oxford.] Wife, Martha, aged 60. See Pension Records.

JOHN HAYS; De Kalb cty, Ga. Age 81. Born 8 Nov 1751, Bedford cty, Virginia. When he entered the service was a resident of Rutherford cty, N. C. [present name of county.] Afterwards volunteered in Wash'n cty, N. C. Had also lived in S. C. See Pension Records, 9 Apr. 1833.

JOHN HAYS. Hampshire cty, W. Va. Tax-list, 1783. Hardy cty, W. Va. Tax-list 1786.

JOHN HAYS, WILLIAM HAYS, ANDREW HAYS, CHARLES HAYS, LEWIS HAYS, LUKE HAYS. Montg. cty, Va. Pers. property tax-list. 1795.

JOHN HAYS, Montg. cty. Va., wife REBAKAH. to John Garwood of Culpepper cty, Va. Consideration £275; 220 acres, being a tract called Buffaloe Bottom, north branch of Indian otherwise Holstein river, first granted to Charles Campbell 1753, and by wills of said Charles and Margaret [Campell] cenveyed to JOHN HAYS by their executors. Wit: Davis, Davis, Atkins, Hezekiah Boone. Montg. cty, Va. 1 July 1786. A-400.

JESSE HAYS, Inventory. Allowance to widow ANN & family. Account sales; ROBERT HAYS and ANN HAYS adm'rs. Wilkes cty, N. C. Feby 1811. [2]-322. Also Apr 1811. [2] -324.

JOHN HAYS and Jenny Thompson, dau. of Adam. Mar. L. Bedford, Va. 2 Aug. 1779.

JONATHAN HAYS married Rachell Mitchell, one of the heirs of William Mitchell of Wilkes cty, N. C. Before 27 Apr. 1805. Wilkes cty, N. C. F-193.

JOSEPH HAYS and Jemimah Olley [or Alley.] Franklin cty, Va., M. L. B. 31 Mch 1788.

JAMES HAZE and Levina Gattey. Greenbr. cty, W. Va. M. L. B. 6 Dec 1784.

JAMES HAYS and Catherine Alexander. Greenbr cty, W. Va. M. L. B. 5 Nov 1790.

JAMES HAYS commissioned Ensign. Rock'm cty, Va. Orders. 7 Apr 1779.

JAMES HAYES, wit. to Robson deed from John Holland. Dor. cty, Md. 1725.

Maj. JOHN HAYES, granted l. a. on estate of ANDREW and GEORGE HAYES, dec'd. ANDREW HAYES and James Wallace, sec. Rock'm cty, Va. 6 Nov 1781.

JOAN HAIES, wife of ROBERT. Age about 30. Acco., Va. 22 Mch 1665-6. i-119.

MARY HAYES, age 15 years. Acco., Va. 3 Mch 1672. iv-173.

MARY HAYS, widow of JOHN. Age 85. JOHN was a private in the Rev. War. Married May, 1791. He died 15 July 1830. Had five chn. [Another statement says six chn.] Pension Records. 1 Feby 1849.

MOSES HAYS. Orange cty, Va. Mar. Li. 28 Oct 1780.

MOSES HAYS, mcht. Nthld, Va. 23 Nov 1706. 1699-1713. p. 413.

NATH'L HAIES. Estate. L. Norf, Va. 15 Oct 1666. E-9. Again mentioned 1661. Again 1663. D-410. Again 17 Nov 1656. D-43.

OWEN HAYES. Upper cty of New Norfolk, Va. About 1653. Again. L. Norf. 1662. D-351. Again, has 200 acres. L. Norf. 17 Oct 1664. D-407.

PATRICK HAYES, head right under Capt. John West. Acco, Va. 17 Nov 1671. iv-24.

PATRICK HAYS, HUGH HAYS, SAM'L HAYS. Augusta cty, Va. Land Book 1782. Also 1787.

PATRICK HAYS; funeral expenses, &c. Chas. cty, Md. 1662. i-242.

PATRICK HAIES ran away. Acco., Va. 17 Aug 1663. i-26.

PATRICK HAYS from Widow Elliott, Robert Elliott and wife Ann; Consideration $250, 49 1-2 acres, n. fork Anthonie's Creek, being the upper part of James Elliott's land, Elliott, dec'd. Sig. Widow Ann Elliott. Greenbr cty, W. Va. 11 Sept 1816. vii-153.

PATRICK HAIES an head right. Acco., Va. 17 Aug 1663. i-21.

INTERCOUNTY AND INTERCOLONY

JOHN ABINGDON, died in England. Letters of adm'n to James Crauford of Calvert county, Md. Adm'n in England shown to have been granted by the "Metropolytan" of England to Mad'm Mariel Parney [Barney?] and Mad'm Mariel Abington of London, extrs. Annap., Md. T. P. xvi-63. 21 May 1695.

Mr. THOS. BROUGHTON, of Boston in N. E., a mcht; sells land. Nthld, Va. 1658-1666, fo. 169. 1 Mch 1664.

THOMAS BROOKE, of St. Mary's cty, Md, Gent., to Robert Bogges of Prince William cty, Va. 320 acres s. w. side Pohick Run Pr. Wm, part of a patent in 1650 to Richard Normansel of Stafford, Gent.........descent related by various conveyances & heirship to Sarah Mason, wife of Brooke. Ffx, Va. L. C. 20 May 1742.

JAMES CRAIK and wife MARY ANNE, of Chas. cty, Md., to William Holladay of Winchester. Fred'k, Va. xix-382. 10 Feby 1783.

MARY CARROLL, widow and relict of Charles Carroll, Jr., of Duddington Manor, in Pr. Geo's cty, Md., gets 1. a. with will annexed. Ffx cty, Va., Orders 1772-1774, p. 265. 20 Sept 1773.

EDWARD CHILTON, of Charles cty, Md., Gent., to Lionel Copley of Maryland, Esq.; recites, Richard Wright, Mcht, and Nicholas Spencer, of London, Mcht, had a patent 2 May 1659, tract called Boulton. Annap. Md. (W. R. C. 1—). 4 Oct 1692.

ZACHARIAH COPLAND and WILLIAM PORTER, of Nancemond cty, Va., to William Goodman of Gates cty, N. C., a parcel of land which Copland and Porter were empowered by Joseph Porter's will to sell. 18 Nov 1786. Gates cty, N. C. i-240.

LOUIS DE SEGOUGNE and JULIE SEGOUGNE, his wife, of Middx cty, Va., to Hugh Walker, of Culpeper, and Anthony Gardner of King and Queen counties; £600... tract in Middx, 400 acres, purchased of Hugh Walker and whereon De Sigougne at present lives. Wit: Thomas Segar, William Bowden, John T. Walker. Middx, Va. 1785-1789, p. 157. 30 May 1789.

LEVIN GALE, Som. cty, Md., to Francis Corbin of Middx, Va. Tract of 750 acres bet. forks of Grange Creek.........followed by sale of slaves. Wit: Segar, Kemp, Kemp, Lumpkin, Ware. Middx, 1785-1789, p. 148. 4 Dec 1790.

WILLIAM HORE, City of London, Parish of Stepney, England, to Luke Raven, one negro boy. Wit: Methuen, Skelton. Balto., Md. Deeds, T. R. No. R. A. 9 Mch 1698-9.

NINEAN DANLAPS, late of New-Castle county, Penna., Delaware [*sic*], receives grant for a parcel of land called *Dunlap's Choice*. Som. Md. 25 Sept 1694. [Date of record.]

JOHN HUGGINS, of Bath cty, N. C.; power to Jacob Meizek. Som. Md., 20 Nov 1728. AZ-29.

BARNABAS HUGHES, of Lancaster cty, Penna., to William Allen of Philadelphia, Esq.; concerning a tract in Frederick cty, Md. S. L. O., Md. D. D. 2, p. 347. 8 May 1760.

MAHLON KIRKBRIDGE, of Bucks cty, Penna., from John Hough, Blacksmith, Fairfax cty, Va. 520 acres. Ffx, Va. 20 Nov 1752. C-376.

HENRY LEE and wife Matilda, of Westmoreland city, Va., to Samuel Adams, Henry Darne Simon Adams, and William Walters; conveyance of fish stands [in the river.] Ffx, Va. 11 Mch 1789. R-442.

RICHARD LEE leaves land at Cedar Point, Md., to son Phillip.........the land late in possession of Phillip Lynes; makes provision in case son should not win the lawsuit which it seems involves the tract.........also leaves land in Dorchester cty, Md., on the Nanticoke river. Wmld, Va. v-445.

SUSANNAH LEMAY, widow of Charles, of St. Paul's parish, Hanover cty, Va.; John Lemay, Meclinburg cty, and wife Christen, and Thomas Lemay, two sons of Charles Lemay of the parish of St. Paul, Hanover cty, to Thomas Ellett of the parish of St. John's, King William cty, Va..........362 acres in Hanover cty. Wit: Dugar, Ellett, Ellett Beal and Mary Ellett. Hanover cty, Va. 9 Dec1785. [ii]-151.

RICHARD MUDD about to go to Washington cty, Kentucky, the "place of my permanent residence," gives power to brother, Walter Mudd. Montg. cty, Md. 27 Oct 1812. i-180.

WILLIAM PARKER, citizen and draper of London, gives power to [brother] Philip Parker, Mcht., of Accomack. Wm. Allen, a wit. N-n, Va. 1659. ix-44.

MARGARET PLEASANTS, late of Goochland cty, Va., dec'd. William Henry Pleasants gets letters testamentary on her estate. Montg. cty, Md. 11 Dec. 1810. H.H. 2, 233.

THO: PAREMORE, of Acco., Va., Gent, and Jemima-Custes his wife to Joseph Stephenson; conveys Fookes Choyce, patented to Wm. Anderson, of Somerset, Md., decd, for 250 acres. William Hope died intest., so that the 250 acres became the right of his dau. Joanna Hope, and the aforesaid Joanna-Custes Hope is now intermarried with the afsd Thos. Paremore. Wit: Geo. Douglas and Robert Stevenson. Som, Md, Nov. 1733. E.I.39.

ELENOR x QUEEN, of Prince George's cty, Md., gives power to friend and brother-in-law, Philip Walsh, to receive of William Bruster [Brewster] of Fairfax cty, Va., her full proportional part of her deceased father's estate. Ffx, Va. 21 Oct 1746. B-195.

JAMES I. RYAN, late of Baltimore, Md., died in Kings cty, N. Y. at the residence of Elijah H. Kimball, in the town of Flatlands. Left legacies to Mrs. Ellen Coney [Couey?] of Savannah, Ga.; Ann Elizabeth Stanard, Lucilla Wallace, dau. of Mary; Susan Armstead, dau. of Agnes, all of Fredericksburg, Va; Betsy and Mary Voss of Fredericksburg; Charles Wallace of Fredericksburg. Wife Susan F. Ryan, extx. Balto., Md. Wills. 3 July 1852-23 Aug 1852. xxv-168.

JOHN RABY, of Gates cty, N. C., to Kedar Raby of the Upper Parish of Nancemond cty, Va. conveys fifty acres. 30 Oct 1786. Gates cty N. C, i-242.

SERVICE AND SUPPLIES COLONIAL, REVOLUTIONARY AND MILITIA

CHURCHILL BLAKEY, recommended for Ensign.* Middx, Va. 23 Sept 1782. vi-3.

WILLIAM CURTIS, recommended for 2d Lieutenant.* Middx, Va. 23 Sept 1782. vi-3.

JAMES CLARK; Lieutenant, Virginia Regiment. 2,000 acres.** Montg. cty, Va., Surveys. 28 Nov 1773.

CHARLES CURTIS, recommended for Ensign.* Middx, Va. 23 Sept 1782. vi-3.

FRANCIS DRAKE, a corporal, Virginia Regisment. 200 acres.** Montg. cty, Va. Surveys. 14 Dec 1773.

ROBERT DANIEL,* recommended for Captain in room of Thomas Segar, Gent., resigned, Middx, Va. 23 Sept 1782. vi-3. Takes the oath 28 Oct 1782. vi-7.

WILLIAM EDMISTON, Ensign. 2,000 acres.** Montg cty, Va. Surveys. 16 Dec 1773.

Capt. WILLIAM FLEMING, Captain 2d Virginia Regiment. 3,000 acres.** Montg. cty, Va. Surveys. 6 Nov 1773.

JACOB GRAY, a private in the Maryland line who lost his arm at the Storming of Stony Point, as appears by certificate of Richard Waters, Capt. of the Maryland Line, for an allowance, is ordered to receive half pay from 16 July 1779. Som. cty, Md. O. C. Proc. p. 65. 24 June 1783.

ANDREW GREEN; Ordered certified that from the wounds he received in the late war the Court are of opinion that he ought still to remain a pensioner. Ldn, Va. Orders H-482. 9 May 1785.

JOHN GEORGE, Gent. Produces commission as Lieut-Col. militia of this county. Middx. 23 Sept 1784. vi-3.

JOHN HILL, Sjt. 200 acres.** Montg. cty, Va. Surveys. 17 May 1774.

ELISHA HARRIS; was enlisted for two years and a half and died in the service of his country. His widow, MARY, is allowed five pounds for her maintenance the present year. Granv. cty, N. C. Old Minute Book. 2 May 1786.

THOMAS HEALY;* recommended for Captain in the room of William Murray, Gent., resigned. Middx, Va. 23 Sept 1782. vi-3.

JOHN KING, late a private soldier Maryland line, conveys land in Alleg. cty, Md. to Christopher Stump. Annap. J. G. 1-611. 12 May 1790.

WILLIAM INGLES; 2,000 acres for serving as an officer.** Montg. cty, Va. Surveys. Mch 1774.

FRANCIS JACKSON exhibits an account for arms taken from him for the use of the militia. Ordered certified. Pr. Wm., Va. Orders [4] Court October, 1761.

JOHN KINCAID; Conrade Fudge, and John Holloway, make oath and subscribe to his certificate and the Court declare opinion that he was a Revolutionary soldier. Alleg. cty, Va. Orders, p. 89. Mch 1833.

CHARLES KING'S declaration of service, taken in Court and ordered certified to the War Department. Alleg. cty, Va. Orders, p. 81. Jany 1833. Amended declaration, June, 1833. p. 118.

JAMES KELSON makes declaration and Court declare their opinion that he was a Revolutionary soldier. Rock'm cty, Va. Orders, p. 187. Jany 1833.

JOHN LOWRIE produces certificate from Maj. Alexander Roxburgh that he was a regular soldier in the 7th Maryland, and was wounded at Camden, S. C. Aug. 1780. Of which wound he lost his leg. Ordered to receive half-pay. Som. Md. O. C. Proc. p. 73.

WILLIAM MAXWELL served as a serjeant in the 35th Reg't in America, and has been an Inhabitant of Virginia for a number of years. Allowed 200 acres. Rock'm cty, Va. Orders 2 May 1780.

WILLIAM MOORE, Esq., makes declaration and the Court are of opinion that the applicant was a Captain in the Revolution and served as he states both as Captain and private. Rock'm, Va. Orders, p. 133. Aug. 1832.

* Presumably in the militia.

** Surveys under pre-emption and other warrants.

Printed at the Industrial School for Crippled and Deformed Children, 241 St. Botolph St., Boston, Mass.

The

County Court Note-Book

A Little Bulletin of History and Genealogy

December, 1930. Vol. IX, No. 6

MARYLAND'S NEXT OF KIN

JEAN x GRIFFIN, JAMES x MURPHY, WILLIAM RATCLIFFE; inv. Bernard x Griffin of Q. A. cty. 18 Sept 1723. ix-184. [Two of three given are probably kin.]

HELLENOR x EMPY, MATH. x COLLIER [probably kin]; inv. William Morris. Q. A. cty. 14 Feby 1722. ix-191.

JOHN x LEMAY; inv. John Lemey [Lemay] of Dor. cty. 18 Oct 1723 [In this inventory "cattail" beds are mentioned.]

MARY BECKWITH, GARY WARNER; inv. of Richard Fairbrother, of "Dorsett" cty. 13 Nov 1723. ix-194

ROBERT LUSBY, Sr., THOMAS LUSBY; inv. Robert Johnson of "Arundell" cty. 29 Nov. 1723. ix-201.

"No Relation;" inv. Jacob Garrett of Cecil cty' 14 Nov. 1723. ix-208.

"No relations in America." Inv. Martin Bence [?], of Cecil cty. 1 Nov. 1723. ix-212.

WILLIAM x WHITT, ANN x WHITT; inv. William White [Whitt?] of St. Mary's cty. 28 June 1723. ix-214.

JOHN GREEN, ELIZABETH GREEN; inv. Edward Miller of St. Mary's cty. 19 Nov. 1723. ix-215.

JOSEPH DOUGLAS, BENJ'N DOUGLASS, JAMES RUTHERFORD, THOS. x DOUGLAS. [Uncertain whether all are kin.] Inv. Jos'h Douglass, of Charles cty. 3 Nov. 1723. ix-217.

"No known kindred." Inv. Phillip Dove. County not given. 23 Nov 1723. ix-218.

LEWIS x JONES, FRANCIS x JONES; inv. Rich'd Daniel, Carpenter. [Probably of Pr. Geo's cty.] 12 Feby 1722. ix-222.

SUSAN'A x BOOKER, REBECCA BOOKER. inv. Andrew Booker, pltr, of Talbot cty 12 July 1722, ix-223.

HANNAH x SANDERS, BARNABY x STAPLEFORD; inv. William Peirce of Talbot cty. 5 Aug 1723. ix-224.

THOISON [?] LANGFORD (*her* mark) WILLIAM LANKFORD; inv. of Thos. Lankford of Talbot cty. 23 Oct 1723. ix-226.

ANNA COWARD; inv. Richard Coward of Talbot cty, Gent. Mrs. Sibilla Coward knows not any Relation the decceased has in this province except Anna Coward......25 Oct 1723. ix 227.

JOHN x EMERSON, ALICE x EMER$ON; inv. John Emerson of Talbot cty. 17 Oct 1723. ix-231.

Elinor, the wife of JOHN LINCH, and admx of James Hunter, her former husband, exhibited inventory and knew not of any Relations. Inv. of JOHN LINCH, returned 8 Nov 1723. ix-233.

JOHN STEVENS; inv. of Hannah Alcock of Talbot cty. 21 Oct 1723. ix-234.

JOHN BOREING, brother; inv. Thomas Boreing of Balto. cty. 16 May 1723. ix-237.

JOHN x EMERSON, ALICE x EMERSON; inv. John Emerson of Talbot cty. Taken 17 Oct 1723. ix. 237. [This is the same decedent as before. Probably an additional inventory.]

NOTES FROM THE PROBATE COURT OF SUSSEX COUNTY, DELAWARE. THE FIRST RECORD*

OTTO WOOLLGAST; Elizabeth Carter gets l. a. to her self and husband, William Carter, on the estate of her deceased husband. Court 8-9 Nov. 1681. p. 17.

JOHN HAGESTER; Ann Newcomb, his late wife, proves his will, of which she is extx, and l. a. are granted to Baptist Newcomb [her husband] and herself. 13 Sept 1682.

EDWARD BOODLE; John Kipshaven and John Depree get l. a. on his estate. [His will was proved by William Smith and Stephen Whetman. It was dated 7 Dec 1682.] Court 11th mo. 9-11, 1682. p. 101.

THOMAS GRUNDICK; Stephen Whetman, principal creditor, gets l. a. on his estate. Same court. p. 102.

EDWARD BOOTH, of "Deal County," will. To Mr. John Kipshaven son John one-half my land and pltn; if he dyes without wife or issue, to John Depree and his son Jacob, one-half his land; goods to Kipshaven; to Jno. Whittman, an old Sow; to Elizabeth Whittman, Martha Kipshaven, legacies; to Mr. Avery for surveying; to Wm. Emmett, Jr. He orders that his great Barrow be killed at his funeral...... *John Kipshaven and Jacob Depree shall pay something towards maintaining the widows and fatherless children of this County.* Wit: Summerfield, Whitman, Emmett [?] p. 143. Court 27-28, ed mo. 1683. [This must be the same person as "Boodle" above.]

ELIZABETH LEVERETT; nun-cup. will. Mentions son Richard Bracy. Wit: Jefry x Sumerford, Elisabeth x Johnson. p 154. Court 14th, 6th 1683. In another deposition it is affirmed that the testator said if a certain Bracy did refuse to make a certain payment, "*it would trouble her that would come again.*"

---

* See note on page 48.

JOHN PEARCE; Allexander Draper gets l. a. on his estate. p. 576. Court 4-6 of the 8th. 1687.

JOHN ROADES; Widow Comfort desires that it may not be proved until next Court. Ct 4th-6th of 8th 1687. p. 536.

HENRY SKIDMORE, his will published, and Richard Williams petitions for administration, which is granted. p. 63d. Court 8-9 Jany 1695.

DANIEL HILLIARD; William Clarke gets l. a. on his estate. p. 78d. Court 4 Mch 1695.

ROBERT BRACEE [?] Sr.; Robert Bracee asks l. a. on the estate of his father, upon a will made in open court 6 June 1694..... A former will is produced on the part of the widow, made in 1688. Continued. Court 4 June 1695. p. 41d.

JANE POTTER, widow, will; William Farmer presents her will which is probated and adm'n granted to Rich'd Dobson, extr. Dobson refuses and the Court appoints William Farmer. p. 67e. Court 8 Nov 1704.

AUTHENTIC REFERENCES FOR INFERRED MARRIAGES

(*The following marriages are all from Delaware*)

THO: BESANT and JANE KING, admx of John. Before 8 Aug 1695. Sussex cty reeords [1] p. 69d.

THOMAS BEDWELL and HONOUR, extr of William Clark, Esq. Before 3 Aug. 1709. Same record, p. 6 h.

BENJAMIN BROWN and HANNAH NOWEL, dau. of George. Before 26 May 1763. Kent cty. O. C. records.

...... CANNON and ANN STANLY, relict of Christopher. Before 19 Feby 1693. Kent cty. C-2.

JOHN CASEY and BRIDGETT, relict of Joseph Ayliff. Before 6 Nov 1702. Sussex cty records [1] p. 9e. See also 31e.

FRANCIS CORK [COCK? COOK?] and MARY CLAYPOOLE, admx of James Claypoole. [Uncertain as to her surname.] Before 2 June 1696. Sussex cty records [1] p. 83d.

JAMES COLEMAN and SARAH MANLOVE, dau. of Ebenezer. Before 1 Mch 1787. Kent cty O. C. records.

JOHN CORSE and MARY MANNERING, widow of John. Before 15 Feby 1813. Kent cty O. C. records.

ROBERT CLIFTON and the relict and admx of Capt. John AVORY. Before 11th of 1st mo. 1684. Sussex cty records [1] p. 197.

THOMAS COOK and SARAH NOWEL, dau. of George. Before 26 May 1763. Kent cty O. C. records.

ALLEX'R DRAPER and REBECCA MILLNER, widow. Before 6th of 10th mo. 1687. Sussex cty records [1] p. 79b.

THOMAS DAVOCK and ELIZABETH, extx of John STUART. Before 5 Feby 1705. Same record. p.8f.

WILLIAM FAUSITT and MARY, one of the extrs of Erasmus Harrison, late of Somerset, Md. Before 22 June 1696. Same record, p. 1e.

NEHEMIAH FIELD and RACHEL, admx of Norton CLAYPOOLE. Before 2 June 1696. Same record. p. 33d.

THOMAS FISHER and MARY DRIE [?] Before 8 Mch 1693. Same record. p. 10a.

RICHARD HINMAN and MARY, admx of Hercules SHEPHEARD. Before 9 May 1706. Same record p. 29f. See also 59f.

THOMAS HODGKINS and the relict and admx of Halm. WILTBANCK. Before 12th of 6th mo. 1684. Same record. p. 42a.

WILLIAM HAWLEY [HAWKEY?] and URSULA MARTIN, formerly wife to George MARTIN. Kent cty. Before 17 Mch 1702. B-47.

DANIELL ITHELL [?] and MARY, admx of John RICHARDS. Before 8 Aug 1695. Sussex cty records [1] p. 66d.

.... JORDAN probably m. MARY DAVIDS, widow. Before 8th Jany 1695. Same record. p. 65a.

ADAM JOHNSON and MARTHA JACOBS, relict and admx of Albertus. [She was the dau. of John Kipshaven, Sr.] Before 2 Feby 1702. Same record. p. 12e. See also p. 25e. Also 31e.

SAMUEL KNOWLES and JANE, widow of Thomas BESENT. Before 1 Aug 1704. Same record. p. 75e. See also p. 28f.

RICHARD LARRY and ESTHER COOSE [?] relict and admx of Richard, before 6 Nov 1702. Same record p. 8e.

WILLIAM MASON and MARGARET CLARKE, widow of James. Before 9 May 1706. Same record. p. 31f.

THOMAS MAY and a dau. of Maj. William SPENCER. Before 7 Dec 1694. [May's wife deceased before this.] Same record, p. 36a.

GEORGE MARTIN and URSILLA COLLIMER. Before 17 Mch 1702. (About 1686.) Kent cty. B-47.

EBENEZER MANLOVE and SARAH COOK, dau. of Thomas. Before 26 May 1763. Kent cty O. C. records.

EDWARD PARKER and PATIENCE, admx of William ORR. Before 7 May 1706. Sussex cty records [1] p. 24f.

.... PRITTYMAN and FRANCES INLOW, widow of Anthony. Before 4 Mch 1706. Same record. 59f.

.... PARRY probably m. ESTHER SMITH, widow. Before 4 Feby 1706. Same record. p. 55f.

MATHEW PARKER and the widow of Thomas PRICE. Before 5 May 1703. Same record. p. 33e.

RICH'D PAYNTER, Jr. and JANE, extx of William SWETNAM. Before 5 Sept 1694. Same record. p. 23a.

.... PENINGTON and DEBORAH CRAMER, widow of Thomas. Before 20 Dec 1726. Kent cty. F-20.

THURLOE SENIOUR and ANNE SMUT [?] a widow. Before 1 Aug 1704. Sussex cty. records [1] p. 75e.

.... STARR and KATHERINE VINES. Before 14th of 2dmo. 1685. Same record. p. 105a.

HARKLOS SHEEPARD [*sic*] and MARY AVERY, dau. of Capt. John. Same record. p. 117. Before 13th of 12th mo. 1682.

VIRGINIA COLONISTS

(*From "Old Vol. 5, S. L. O. Richmond, Va.*)

Dr. GILES MODE, New Kent, 1655.
Head rights: Dr. GILES MODE, twice: Mr. Tho. Bowler, four times; Jane Salmon, Roger Pidlers, Jno. Walker, Edward Phillips, Edw'd Waight, Wm. Griffin, Tho. Midleton, Wm. Angood, Henry Wilson, Wm. Morton, Joseph Tompson, one negro, Amy Edwards, Grace Davis;
Ellin Harmon [?], Jeremy Rawlings, Wm: Bradley, Kath: Burris, Rob. Smith, Richd Fincher [?] John Glan [?]

JOHN, SARAH and MARGARETT MACHILL, Northampton, 1660.
Head rights: JNO. MICHAELL, Sr., JNO. MICHAELL, Jr., Lawrence Jacob, William, a negro; Band, a negro; "Rowland Irish," Dorman Adonneway [O'Donneway?] John Flinte, Rachel Metkalfe, Elizabeth Bansley, Mary Teague, Abraham Rogers, Roberta Clewe, Jno. Jenings, Wm. Morgen, Jno. Cannedy, Ellis Appaie [?] Thomas Irish, Georg Sich, Mary Greenwood.

GEORGE MORRIS and JOHN PIGGE, New Kent. [This is from an old page inserted and date missing.]
Head rights: James Evans, Wm. Barby, Peter Arundell, David Hoskins, Evan Walker, Roger Batman, Wm. Warrey, Wm. Nicholas, Roger Peirce, Tho: Large, Tho: Hinkes, Rich'd Harvy, Katherine Prickett, M...... Collins, Ed. Tunstell, Tho. ...., Peter Grove, P......... E.........

WILLIAM MUNDAY, "in a small Creeke called Carratucke, falling into Kecoughancke River, which sd river falls into Carralina...", 1663.
Head rights: Wm. Edmonds, Joseph Gibson, Rob't Read, Rich: Smith, Sam'll Warren, James Bare.

JAMES MURDAH, west side Chowanoke river. 1663.
Head rights: Josias Pew, Jno. Boyce, Tho: Crafford, Wm. Morry, Nath: Bridges, Wm. Clarke, Hen: Kent, Ral: Bowles.

JOHN NICHOLLS, Northampton cty. 1655.
Head rights: Wm. Kendall, Mary Crumwell, John Haner [or Hane?] Rich'd Johnson, Tho. Sledwell, James Lynn, Wm. Stanton, Rob [?] Stanton.

ROBERT NICHOLSON, Charles City cty. 1655.
Head rights: Henry Seares, James Hukes, John Webber, Peeter Jackson, Arthur Slater, Henry Warner, Geo. Noble, Albin Thomas, "wronge entered."

THOMAS PAYNE and JOHN CHENLEY, Rappa. cty. 1663.
Head rights: Tho: Bacon, Will North.

THO: PAYNE and JOHN CHINLEY. 1663.
Head rights: Margery Atkins, Tho: Webb.

Capt. GEORGE PARKER, Acco. [1666.]
Head rights: Mordica Hammond, Jno. Forwood, Eliz: Branches, "Jno. a Scott."

THOMAS PINKEMAN, Yorke cty. 1662.
Head right: John Shaw.

HENRY PALIN, county not given. 1663.
Head rights: William Gailer, Tho. Giles, Hen: Sterne, Roger Simons, Isaac Scott, John Atkins, John Sheffield, Nich: Wilson, Ralph Sharpe.

SAMUELL SMITH, James City cty. 1655.
Head rights: John Walker, Henry Soare.

WILLIAM STEEVENS, Northampton cty. 1655.
Head rights: Robert Knowles, Jno. Hill, Rob Elles, Jno. Harris, Teague Owen, William South, John Gillet, Jno. Wilkes, William Stephens, Ann, his wife; Tho. Nockey, Jno. Robetton, Roger Roades, Tho. Howlett.

RICHARD SMITH, Northampton. [1660.]
Head rights: Joseph Harrison, Jas. Thomas, Katherine Harriss, Henry Scott.

ROBERT SIKES, Acco. 1666.
Head rights: Elianor Hooke. Sarah Naylor, Gartrid Iland.

EDMOND SCARBURGH, Acco. cty. 1663.
Head rights: Roger Noell, William Bannister, Henry Farrington, John Dickinson, William Ashley, Ralph: Castleton, Robert Drury, Edward Morris, Thomas Caros [Carr?] John Byrum, Henry Porter, Robert Fleetwood, William Weill, Nicholas Woodward, Thomas Crispe;
Richard Mills, James Jolly, Thomas Perry, William Pearle, Robert Drury, Francis Cranly, Elizabeth Bydolph, James Silverlocke, Thomas King, Peter Solm, Robert Parker, John Hodge, John Angel.

JNO. SHARPE, at the head of a creek issuing out of the s. w. side of Coratoman river. 1662.
Head rights: Tho: Wakerly, Rich: King, Jno. Gable, Wm. Lewin.

THO: SHERWOOD, n. side Carolina river. [1663.]
Head rights: Tho: Davis, Edward Sneath, Wm. Tanner, Robt Wheeler, Henry Weston, Wm. Lewis, Tho: Waad, Wm. Badger, Jno. Gafer [?] Eliz: Waad, Lidia Stow, Rich. Webb, Abell Jason, Sus. Alcocke, Sam: Francis, William Glover, Fr. Glover.

Mr. THOMAS STAMPE and ANNE NOAKES; n. side Carolina river. 1663.
Head rights: Hen: Leonord, Robt Flake, Rich: Baker, Eliz: Hancocke, William Preston. Duncomb Pantwell.

WILLIAM THOMAS, Nthld cty. 1655.
Head rights: John Gibbons, Eliz. Glissin, Joan, and Irishwoman; Jane Brocket.

GEORGE TREWETT, Northampton cty. 1660.
Head rights: John Tompson, Charles Barcroft, Alex. Mattrick, Wm. Branch, Tho. Moore, Tho. Musgrave, Jno. Young, Walter Lane, Jno. Watson, Robert Huntley.

The County Court Note-Book

An every-other-monthly devoted mainly to abstracts from County Court Records, prior to 1800.

MILNOR LJUNGSTEDT, Editor and Publisher, Bethesda, Rural Route 5, Maryland.

Published six times a year. Subscription, two dollars, in advance; must begin with the year.

December, 1930 **Whole**
Vol. IX., No. 6 **No. 55**

HAIL AND FAREWELL!

Hail to a New Year and farewell to an old year, and a difficult one, and, presently, farewell to this little bulletin. The NOTE-BOOK has touched some high spots this year......has found recognition in unexpected quarters, but, by-and-large, it has rested unknown upon the shelves. Why? Undoubtedly because of a lack in the Editor of the business capability which knows how to advertise. The enclosed card will give the Editor's plans for the coming year. A prompt decision on the part of her subscribers will greatly help.

Among the sadnesses of the year has been the loss by death of several old subscribers. Although the Editor had never met but one of them, they were really friends. . "mail order" friends, and the Editor feels their loss and misses their kindly interest.

The Editor never dreamed that she would be desolated by the death of a reader, but so it is, and this is truly one reason why she will presently close the last note-book and lay the last index slip face down upon the table.

One of the Editor's subscribers, who reads the NOTE-BOOK no more, was a charming letter-writer. The first cotrespondence was amusingly lively ...... the Editor had expressed herself too frankly as to lines running back to princes, potentates, and other importances who once sat in the seats of the mighty, and her (later) friend was indignant. But something in the letter made her new correspondent laugh, and although she was ill at the time, she wrote that the laugh did her good and she promptly got well and so forgave the Editor. As Christmas time came near this charming lady wrote and asked the Editor if she *smoked!* The Editor answered as became a person descended from the Mayflower and also from eminent Quakers, and then her friend wrote that she was going to send a twist of her own home-grown tobacco anyhow, maybe another member of the family would use it. The other member did ...... it is true he had long given up "rolling his own", but some suitable paper was found, part of the twist pulverized and smoked. And the Editor's opinion is, if you have got to smoke please use Kentucky tobacco!

And now her friendly subscriber is there no more; rides no more about her fields, rich with the weed America gave to the world to the world's detriment, some of us think ...... but we do not think as harshly of it as we once did.

The notes from Sussex county (the old county was at first called Whorekill and then Deale), are only a very small part of the general records of Sussex county which are to found more nearly in full in the published volumes of Dr. C. H. B. Turner, formerly Archdeacon of Delaware, and well-known as a distinguished antiquarian. It is thanks to Dr. Turner, however, that the Editor finally saw and read the original volume and from it abstracted such material as she needed. Dr. Turner's manuscript notes are now the property of the Pennsylvania Historical Society, a most valuable gift. His "Some Records of Sussex County" and other volumes are in the libraries of the country.

Since the last NOTE-BOOK, Mr. ROBERT ARMISTEAD STEWART'S INDEX to VIRGINIA GENEALOGIES has come from the printer. It may have been said before but can be repeated that this is a valuable, a long-needed volume. The work had been undertaken some years ago but completion had been delayed, and the real work of getting the material in shape, the indexing, &c., &c., as well as the collection of a vast amount of new references, was finally placed in the very able hands of Mr. Stewart. Some of us may differ as to the value of all of the authorities quoted, but no discrimination could be made in a work of so wide a scope.

The volume is of a beautifully convenient size, compact. but of good and clear type. The publishers are the Old Dominion Press, of Richmond, Virginia.

Mr. Stratton Nottingham's ABSTRACT of ACCOMACK WILLS and ADMINISTRATIONS is very nearly out......it will probably be on sale about the first of the year. This work and the one above are too good for any one to miss. Those searchers who have built heretofore on county histories, hit-or-miss abstracts, will find something here that every county should have, done in the thorough way in which Mr. Nottingham works.

A volume which is promised from Richmond will add another to the list of publications based upon reliable records......since they are official and contemporary......it is called WEST VIRGINIA REVOLUTIONARY ANCESTORS, and it is compiled by Miss ANNE WALLER REDDY, of Richmond, from the material in the Virginia Archives. It is an index of the public claims of the Revolutionary War, limited, as shown by the title, specifically to West Virginia. There is much information in these claims about persons whose records are hard to find, often lost. It is a good and unusual piece of work. Subscriptions may be sent to Miss Reddy at 1005, East Marshall street, Richmond.

The following was published as a supplement to the NOTE-BOOK for June, 1925. It was a loose leaf and seems to have escaped attention. As it is an important preface to the CUSTIS family notes, it is here reproduced.

CUSTIS OF VIRGINIA

The following is by way of a preamble to a considerable amount of early CUSTIS data which the Editor has gathered from those original records which are technically classified as *source* material, and which she hopes to publish from time to time as a supplement to the NOTE-BOOK.

BISHOP MEADE, page 262, of vol. i, Old Churches and Families of Virginia, says:

"A friend on the Eastern Shore, whose de- " light is in searching its ancient records, has sent " me a full account of the Custis family, which " so abounds in that part of the State. Its name " and blood are intermingled with those of most " of the families of Northampton and Accomack, " whether rich or poor. I give a brief statement " of it. The name JOHN CUSTIS first appears " on the record in 1640. It is probable that he " was the person of whom Colonel Norwood " speaks, in his account of his voyage to America " and shipwreck on the Eastern shore in 1649, " as having been a hotel keeper in Rotterdam " and a great favorite with English travellers. He " had six sons and one daughter. The daughter " married Colonel Argal Yeardley, son of Gov- " ernor Yeardley, of Virginia. His sons were " JOHN, WILLIAM, JOSEPH, who were in Vir- " ginia; THOMAS, who was in Baltimore, Ire- " land; ROBERT, who resided in Rotterdam; " and EDMUND, who lived in London. The " family is of Irish descent."

Bishop Meade further quotes his correspondent as saying that JOHN CUSTIS received Arlington by his first wife. Of this more anon. And that his second wife was daughter of Colonel Edmund Scarborough. This is an error, as she was his third, and last, wife, having outlived him and taken a fourth husband.

From the records:

JOHN CUSTIS; his certificate for 150 acres; head rights: John Smith, Joane Palmer, John Tully. N-n, Va., ii-35. 1640.

ELIAS HARTREE, deposition. This deposition is called forth by a case between two women concerning a cow. The wife of JOHN CURTIS is mentioned, called "Goody Curtis." The other party to the "difference" is the Widow Taylor, and she is ordered to pay JOHN CURTIS or any other, for his use, a pint of milk a day. JOHN CURTIS' plantation is referred to. N-n, Va. ii-86. 2 Aug 1641.

At this time, 1640-1641, JOHN CUSTIS, the head of the American family, was, perhaps, fourteen years old. There is no reason to suppose that his father, John Custis, of Rotterdam, who was known to be established in an important business over there, was in America. Certainly if he had come over at that date, and brought with him his son, his certificate would have included lands for himself and son, and there would have been some record concerning him in the old Accomack court proceedings, or in Lower Norfolk, where the son JOHN CUSTIS first appears.

It does appear from a record in 1655 (fourteen or fifteen years afterward) that two JOHN CUSTISES were temporarily in Northampton county; that is, JOHN, Senior, and JOHN, Junior, appear as members of a petit jury (not a grand jury). It seems possible that the elder JOHN was on this side of the water merely on a visit, probably on business......taking up land or "merchandizing."

Concerning this question of CUSTIS or CURTIS, the Editor has not only examined the original record herself, but has also used the very fine copy made by the late Mr. Upshur. There is probably no one now living, with one exception, who is as familiar with the early writing of the Eastern Shere records as was Mr. Upshur. Mr. Upshur makes the name CURTIS, as does the Editor. The Editor has also consulted two gentlemen who have made numberless examinations of these particular records, and both are willing to endorse the reading as CURTIS. Bishop Meade did what so many do, relied on some one else, who was unfamiliar with the meticulous exactness of the old scribes, especially of those of the very earliest days.

There is no record in Northampton county of any CUSTIS in the 1640's.

THE MIGRANT HAYS, HAYES HAISE, HAZE. SOME OF THEM.

(*First alphabet*)

PATRICK HAYS [Sig.] of Londonderry Township, Lancaster cty, Penna. Will. "Freal and infirm in body." Wf Jean; son David; son Patrick; son Robert; dau. Helener; son William; dau. Jean; son Samuel. A shilling to each of the children except that William gets a suit of clothes and Samuel is probably residuary legatee [?] Sons Robert and Patrick, extrs. Wit: David Wray, James Willson. Dauphin cty, Penna. 31 Aug 1781-27. May 1790. A-215.

RACHEL HAYS died 19 Jany 1703. York-Hampton Psh Reg. Va.

RICHARD HAYSE, JOHN HAYSE. Tithables. 1744. N-n, Va.

RICHARD HAIES' plantation in Isle of Wight, Va., is mentioned in original acts. 1639.

Mr. ROBERT HAYES, an appraiser, New Norf. cty, Va. 1641. A-46.

Mr. ROBERT HAYES; one of the members for Davidson cty; 1787. Col. Records of N. C. vol. xx-127 .... Nominated for Colonel of Cavalry, District of Mero. 1788. xx-565.

Col. ROBERT HAYS married the sister of Rachel (Donelson) (Robards) Jackson. *Andrew Jackson and Early Tenn.* p. 315.

Col. ROBERT HAYS; born near Salisbury, N. C., of highly respectable parenrs of Irish descent ...... entered service as an ensign; promoted to Lieutenant (reference to archives of War Department, he naving been a pensioner); among prisoners at Charleston. Returned to Salisbury after the war and became a surveyor and emigrated to Cumberland river. Married 27 Jany 1786, JANE DONELSON, dau. of Col. JOHN DONELSON. (The foregoing is from a letter by his son SAMUEL J.* HAYS, dated 16 Aug 1845, which is the Draper Collection of Mss.)

ROBERT HAYS; a certain Robert Hays, a cadet in the 4th Reg't. "I think he will make a good officer." ...... "Is recommended by a Board of officers." Col. Records of N. C. See vol. xi-p. 557. He is recommended for Ensign. 14 Aug 1777. vol. xi-p. 574. Promoted to Lieutenant 1 Jany 1778. (Appointed 16 Aug 1777.) Vol. xiii-p. 476.

ROBERT x HAY, wife Rachell x, of New Poquoson, York cty, Va., v. Samuell Singwell, same. WHEREAS Capt. William Hay, late of same county, by will 10 Jany 166-, gave lands to wife and his dau. Elizabeth, with provision that if a son should be born, &c. &c. And Samuel Singwell m. Elizabeth, the dau. and had issue who died young, Elizabeth is also dead, and Robert Hay, son of John, is heir-at-law, to whom all the lands descend after decease of Samuel Singwell tenant by "courtesy of England," ...... NOW, consideration £30, conveys all the lands in Yorke cty which Capt. William Hay possessed except tract upon which Robert lives which was given him by said will. York, Va. 18 Oct 1689. i-227.

ROBERT HAYES had an ordinary. Court to meet there. L. Norf. Va. 1645. A 3d pt. p. 15.

ROBERT x HAYES had son-in-law Thomas Coffin. Coffin seems to have married Isabell Hayes before 9 Nov 1683. There was also a dau. Anne, probably Anne Coffin. N-n, Va. xiv-85.

ROBERT HAYES, a juror. N-n, Va. 1666. Also in 1668.

PROBATES AND ADMINISTRATIONS FROM THE ORDER BOOKS OF KING GEORGE COUNTY, VIRGINIA

WILLIAM MILLER; admn granted to John Miller, with will annexed. 1 July 1726. Orders i-324. Will presented by John Miller, and proved by Simon Miller and Bloomfield Long. Robert Elliston, Henry Long and Bloomfield Long, sec.

JOHN TAYLOR; will presented by John Coburn, and proved by William Morrison. 1 July 1726. Orders i-325.

SARAH JONES; admn on her estate granted to David Jones, her brother. Benjamin Strother, Gent., sec. 2 Sept. 1726. Orders i-326.

ELIZABETH JETT; will presented by Thomas Thatcher, one of the extrs, and proved by Luke Tippet and Mathew Martin. 2 Sept 1726. Orders i-326.

JOHN TAYLOR [see above]; will presented by Bridget Coburn, extx, and proved by William Morrison and Elizabeth Sullivan. 2 Sept 1726. Orders i-326.

WILLIAM UNDERWOOD; will presented by Jaell, his widow and extx, and proved by William Pullein and James Smith. 2 Sept 1726. Orders i-327.

JOHN DINWIDDIE; will presented by Rose Dinwiddie, his widow, and proved by John Coburn and Bridget Coburn. Jeremiah Bronaugh, one of the extrs, refuses. 2 Sept 1726. p. 327.

WAUGH DARNELL; will presented by Elizabeth his widow and extx and proved by Charles Travers nad Thomas Stone. 7 Oct 1726. Orders i-329.

MORGAN DARNELL; will presented by widow and extx, Elizabethm and proved by Timothy Reading and Charles Morgan. 7 Oct 1726. Orders i-330.

FRANCIS THORNTON, will presented by widow Ann, extx, and proved by Thomas Turner and John Kendall. 7 Oct 1726. Orders i-330.

JEFFERY JOHNSON; will presented by Jeffery Johnson, his extr, and proved by Charles Morgan. 7 Oct 1726, Orders i-330.

JOHN PRINCE, Clerk; will presented by Samuel Skinker, Gent., and proved by Margaret Price and John Diskin. 7 Oct 1726. Orders i-330.

MARK ANDERSON; admn his estate to Charles Spoo, greatest Creditor; Mary, the widow, refusing. Daniel White and Charles Dean, sec. 7 Oct 1726. Orders i-331.

INTERCOUNTY AND INTERCOLONY

FRANCIS AWBREY, Parish of Truro, Prince William cty, Va., to John Tayloe of Lunenburgh Parish, Richmond cty, Va. Pr. Wm. Va. 20 Mch 1732. B-4.

WILLIAM EAST, one of the witnesses to will of Robert x Stevenson..."moved into Virginia" bet. 29 Oct 1760 and 3 June 1761. Wor. cty, Md. J. W. iii-39.

NICHOLAS HAILE, of Baltimore cty, Md., by attorney, conveys 52 acres in Pittsylvania cty, Va. Pitts. 15 Mch 1769. I-271.

JAMES JOHNSON had bro. Peter and Aunt Jane Johnson, in England. Wor. cty, Md. 10 Dec 1762. J. W. iii-55.

MARY KIRBY...leaves estate left to her by her grandfather, John Marshall, dec'd, late of Virginia. Wor. Md. 5 Dec 1763. J. W. iii-104.

CRAFORD MACELPINE (will); mentions estate left him by his great-grandfather, Robert "Caraffort" in Ireland. Wor. Md. 3 Jany 1763-3 Mch. 1763. J. W. iii-76.

JAMES PALMER, a minister of London, Eng. See petition for propagating the Gospel. About 1641. Va. Car. p. 9.

THOMAS RAINEY, of Caswell cty, N. C.. to William Rice, of Hallifax cty, Va. Conveys land on waters of Cain Creek. Person cty. N. C. 22 Feby 1796. B-248.

NATHANIEL SEIDEL, Clerk, of Bethlehem, N-n cty, Penna. (Will) All his lands in Penna., West Jersey, North Carolina or in the colonies of Ameriea in the West India Islands, to his friend Frederick Marshall of Salem, Rowan cty, Gent. Wit: Amadeus Pautinus Thrane, Christian Frederick Oerter, Andrew Weber, Jopson Fromett, John Bonn. Rowan cty, N. C. 20 June 1770. xii-380.

THOMAS SEED, of Bristoll, Cooper, and wife Elizabeth, one of the daughters and coheirs of Francis Barnard, late of Bristoll. Mcht, dec'd, and from Francis Brown, Cooper, Bristoll, son of Nathaniel Brown, Baker, also dec'd, and wife Mary, another daughter of Barnard......to Jeremiah Murdoch, of Virginia, Mcht. power to convey land purchased by Barnard from John Jones, of Bristoll, mariner. [Tract seems to be in Westmoreland.] K. Geo. cty, Va. 1732. A1-217.

"BLESSED" [?] surveyed 1694, for Rowl'd Thornbury, n. e. br. Jones' Fall, possessed per the orphans of sd Thornbury. "The Orphans at Age and Gon intoVirginia......" Annap. Balto. cty R. R. p. 373.

JOHN TAYLOR, of Acco. cty, Va., to Alex'r Linch, pltr, of Somerset cty, Md., part of Friends' Assistance, n. s. St. Martin's river. Som. Md. 17 Nov 1731. S. H.-356.

SQUIRE THOMSON, Blunt cty, Tenn., to John Howard, Rowan cty, N. C. Land on waters of Second creek, Rowan cty, 18 Dec 1811. xx-511.

RICHARD WILLIAMS, Bucks cty, Penna., farmer, from Edward Norton and wf Elizabeth, Ldn cty, Va. One hundred acres on the branches of Kittocton; also another tract above Kittocton Mtn, 400 acres. Ldn, Va. 15 June 1762. C-314.

ANTHONY WRIGHT (will), mentions his land on Staten Island, which he leaves to his son Zadok, also the "Pherry thereto belonging." Mentions bro. Hezekiah as owning land on Staten Island. Wor. Md. 15 June 1761. J. W. iii-42.

AMBROSE WHITE and wf Bathsheba, and Jacob White, of Sussex cty, Prov. of Penna., to Joseph Wyat, of Som. cty. pltr; 370 a. Windsor Forrest; consideration £47 "Lawful money of America." Som. Md. 14 Aug 1738. E. I.-307.

THO. WEBB (will); Eldest son Thomas my water grist mill with lands scituate in the Isle of *Weight* county on the south side of James river; youngest son John Webb, pltn where I live; dau. Elizabeth Webb, land on branch of Great Wiccocomoco river; mentions land devised to his son Thos. by his dec'd gr. fa. Mr. James Austen, also 300 acres in Somerset cty, Md., to sd Thomas. Bro. John Webb mentioned, also bro. Francis Webb, dec'd. To wife Anne, whatsoever she brought with her or did in any wise belong unto her before marriage or could lay any claims unto, and my youngest Horse. Friend Richard Wright and nephew Thomas Hobson, overseers. Son Thomas sole extr. Wit: John Spry, Thomas Hobson, Isabella x Fletcher. Nthld, Va. 11 Sept 1702-16 Sept 1702. Vol. 1706-1720, p. 5.

THACKER WASHINGTON, of K. Geo. cty, Va., and wife Harriott, to Hudson Muse of Middx cty, Va., 750 acres known as Hampstead, which came to said Washington from his father Henry Washington, dec'd. Middx, Va. 16 Dec. 1789. 1785-1789, p. 168.

MOTTROM WRIGHT, of Lanc. cty, Va., Gent, to Edward Chilton of Charles City cty, Va., Gent. £200 ster. all that tract called Bolton, e. s. Chessepeak Bay, n. side of Elke river; land called Turkey Point mentioned...1000 acres patented to Mr. Richard Wright, father of sd Mottrom, and Mr. Nicholas Spencer......and by will of Richard to son Mottrom. Annap. W. R. C. 1-588. 22 Apr 1692.

PHILLIP WEBBER and wife [Tappanes ?] of Cumberland cty, Va., love and affection to our sister Catherine Brown wife of William of Caswell cty, N. C....... give negroes to her chn. Person, N. C. 7 Jany 1792. A-18.

SERVICE AND SUPPLIES COLONIAL, REVOLUTIONARY AND MILITIA

ROBERT ADAM, Ensign; takes the oath. 17 June 1756. Ffx cty, Va. Orders [1] p. 549.

PATRICK ALLISON, a Lieutenant. Survey for 2,000 acres. 11 May 1774. (From the Montg. cty, Va., Surveys, as also the next nine in this list.)*

WILLIAM BLUNKALL; corporal in "last war." 200 acres. 12 May 1774.

WILLIAM BELL [of Fincastle county], serjeant "last war." 200 acres. 15 Mch 1774.

JOHN COFFEE, serjeant, Virginia Reg't, under Col. Byrd. 200 acres. 18 Mch 1774.

WILLIAM DUN, Corporal, Virginia Reg't, under Col. Byrd. 200 acres. 8 Mch 1774.

THOS. DUN, served as a serjeant, Virginia Reg't. EDWARD DUN his heir-at-law. 8 Mch 1774.

JOSEPH DAVENPORT, serjeant, Virginia Reg't, under Col. Byrd. 200 acres. Dec. 1773.

JOHN FULLER, a serjeant. 200 acres. 21 Apr 1774.

RICHARD HICKMAN was a Lieutenant. JAMES HICKMAN, his brother, entitled to 2,000 acres as heir. Also to 2,000 as heir to brother THOMAS HICKMAN, an ensign. 15 Mch 1774.

MARTIN HEWLETT, corporal, Virginia Reg't. 200 acres. 4 Apr 1774.

JOHN McCLAIN presents affidavits of William Moore, Esq., and John Davidson, and the Court declare opinion he was a Revolutionary soldier. Rock'm cty, Va. Orders, p. 131. Court Aug 1832.

DANIEL MORGAN, Ensign, 2,000 acres. Montg. cty, Va. Surveys. 10 Mch 1774.

THEODOSIUS McDONALD, Ensign, Virginia Regiment under Col. Byrd. His brother and heir-at-law, Mr. Daniel McDonald, 2,000 acres. Montg. cty, Va. Surveys. 5 Mch 1774.

SAMUEL MEREDITH, Captain, Virginia Reg't under Byrd. 3,000 acres. 9 Mch 1774. Montg. cty, Va. Surveys.

WILLIAM MUNELL, serjeant, Virginia Reg't. 200 acres. 26 Dec 1773. Montg. cty, Va. Surveys.

JACOB MORRIS, serjeant. Virginia service. 2 Apr 1774. Montg. cty, Va. Surveys.

THOS. MULLEN, corporal, Virginia Reg't, under Byrd. 200 acres. 10 Mch 1771. Montg. cty, Va. Surveys.

ULERICK [?] OSTETTER; makes declaration and presents certificate of Valentine N. Mason and Robert White. Court is of opinion he was a Revolutionary soldier. Rock'm cty, Va. Orders, p. 131. Aug. 1832.

WILLIAM PRESTON, Captain, Virginia Reg't. 3,009 acres, 17 Dec 1773. Montg. cty, Va. Surveys.

*Surveys under pre-emption and other warrants.

Printed at the Industrial School for Crippled and Deformed Children, 241 St. Botolph St., Boston, Mass.

INDEX TO COUNTY COURT NOTE-BOOK. VOLUME IX.

Abbott,Abbot 3,35
Abdell 10
Abernanthie 18
Abingdon 42
Abraham 6
Adams 12,26,30,42
Aitken 37
Albester 9
Alcock 45,47
Aldridge 26
Alexander 41
Algood 26
Allcorn 17
Allen 3,6,26,31,35,39,42
Allerton 26,30,31
Alley 41
Allison 51
Allinson 9
Allister 31
Alnerson 16
Amherst 9
Anderson 6,22,23,26,35,43,50
Anderton 6
Andrews,Andrew 6,23,31
Ands 6
Angel 47
Angood 47
Appraie (?) 47
Apre 9
Arbuckle 37
Arbuthnot 37
Armiger 9
Armstead 43
Armstrong 18,35
Arnold 33
Arundell 47
Ashbridge 21
Ashley 9,47
Ashton 30
Athum 9
Atkins 26,29,30,41,47
Atkinson 11,37
Aubrey
Aurd
Austin,Austen 12,26,39,51
Avery,Avory 45,46,47
Awbrey 50
Aylett 30
Ayliff 46
Ayres 6,22

BACON 47
Badger 31,47
Bailey,Bailly,Baly 17,23,35
Baird 13,33
Baker 9,33,35,47
Ball 30,38
Balmain 6
Banck 26
Bane 31
Banner 27
Bannister 47
Bansley 47
Banton 9
Barby 47
Bare,Bair 1,47
Barker 39
Barlow 31
Barnard 50
Barnes 10,16,26,30,35,39
Barrett,Berrat 30,31
Barry 26,39
Barton 30
Baston 9
Bateman 31
Batman 47
Batson 30
Bayles 26
Bayly 23,30,35
Bazey,Bazy 26
Beacham 16
Beache 9
Beal 42
Beane,Bane 16,31
Beasly 16
Beckley 26,30,38
Beckwith 30,45
Bee 26
Beeler 33
Bedwell 46
Belfield 30
Bell 22,23,30,51
Beloir 9
Belsha 1
Bemins (?) 3
Bence 45
Benchan 27
Bennett 10,13,26
Benson 12
Benton,Banton 9,17
Bereton 26
Berkeley 30
Berry 17,33,35
Berryman 30,33
Bershaw 26
Besant,Besent 46
Bickley 30
Bird 16
Black 35
Blackburn 30
Blackman 30
Blackwell 17
Blair 27
Blakey 45
Blankenbaker 32
Blarwood (?) 35
Bleach 35
Bledsoe 26
Blewsone (?) 16
Blocker 12
Blount 15
Blower 34
Bloxam 35
Blundell 26
Blunkall 51
Bly 1
Boaz,Beaz 16
Bobbett 17
Bodley 17
Bogge,Boggs,Boggess 7,16,30,39,42
Bohannon 30
Bolitho 39
Bolshannon 18
Bonam 38
Bonewell 22
Bonn 50
Boodle 45
Booker 45
Boone 16,33,41

_Name occurs more than once on the page

Booth 9,16,45
Boreing 45
Boulin 6
Bowden 42
Bowen 26
Bowes 9,31
Bowler 47
Bowles 47
Bowling 27
Bowman 6
Boyce 47
Boyne 35
Bracy,Bracee 45,46
Bradford 33
Bradley 16,47
Bradshaw 9
Branch 47
Branches 47
Bratton 11
Bray 9
Breader 9
Breakes 6
Breedan 1
Brent 38
Brereton 16
Brett 9
Brewer 13,26,34
Brewster,Bruster 43
Bridges 33,47
Bridgman 26
Briggs 31
Bright 38,39
Brinkly 35
Bristingham 23
Bristoll 9
Brithenton 35
Brock 18
Brocket 47
Bromley 31
Bronough 33,50
Brook,Brookes 9,17,30, 42
Brooking 27
Broughton 42
Brown 1,6,9,12,13,26, 30,31,32,33,39, 40,46,50,51
Browneley 31
Browning 38
Bruff 17
Brumett 17
Brunett 11
Bryan,Bryon 34
Bryant 10,26
Bryerly 27
Buchanan 17,18,34
Buckeridge 37
Buckingham 7
Bullock 31
Bunbury 27
Bundick 22
Bundy 7,17
Burborough 26
Burchell 31
Burdette 23
Burford 9
Burgis 34
Burkett 6
Burnett 11,30
Burr 6
Burris 47
Burrough 39
Burton 6,13,22,31, 34
Bush 10
Bushrod 3,50
Butler 6,30,31,33
Bydolph 47
Byes (?) 26
Byrd 30
Byrum 47
Bysick 26

CADDELL 17
Calahan 13
Calke,Caulk 25
Calvert 31
Campbell,Cambell 12, 17,41
Cammell 26
Cannedy 47
Cannon 46
Cant 9,35
Caraffort 50
Card 31
Carey,Cary 9,31
Carlyle 31,38
Carn 7
Carney 39
Caros (?) 47
Carpenter 9
Carroll 42
Carruthers 29
Carry 9
Carter 13,30,31,45
Carthouse 26
Carver 31
Carvill 9
Casey 46
Cask 7
Cason 9
Castle 9
Castleton 35,47
Cate 17
Cathcart 15
Cecill 9
Champton 26
Chandler 22,23
Chapin 34
Charles 18
Cheesman 3
Cher 9
Chester 9,35
Cheveront 1
Chew 9
Chiles 10
Chilton 42,51
Chinley 47
Chinn 31
Christian 16,30,34,35,37
Christianes (?) 6
Churchill 16
Clapton 3
Clark,Clerk,Clearck 4,6, 10,12,16,26,31,35, 43,46,47
Claughton 16
Clay 6
Claypoole 46
Clayton,Cleyton 31
Cleach 35
Clements 35
Clendening 33
Clere 31
Clewe,Clewes 26,47
Clifford 21
Clifton 46
Cline 17
Cloverfield 1
Cloud 16,34
Cluverius 10
Coburn 50
Cocke 3,31,38,46
Cocker 3
Cockrill 26
Coffee 51
Coffin 6,29,50
Cohoon 11
Colchester 6

Colclough 31
Cole,Coll 9,10,40
Coleby 9
Coleman 9,18,35,46
Coles,Colis 6,26
Collier 45
Collimer 46
Collins,Collings 31,33, 35,47
Colvert
Combs
Coney
Connor,Conner,Conah 9, 11,12,31,39
Conway,Conoway 26,31
Cooke 6,17,18,31,37,46
Coone 18
Coop 6
Cooper 21,31,35
Coore (?) 46
Copland 34,42
Coplay 42
Coppage 26
Coppenhaver 31
Corbell 26
Corbin,Corben 3,42
Cork 46
Corman 6
Cornelius 35
Cornish 26
Corse Coose 46
Cort 9
Corton 9
Cotancean 26
Cotropp 9
Cotswell 9
Cotton 9
Coney (?) 43
Coulbourn 11,12
Coulson 9
Courteray 13
Courtnell 16
Courtney 26
Covington 40
Coward 45
Cowdry 16
Cowper 13
Cownter 9
Cowpland 21
Cox 6,11,16,18,26,37, 38
Coxon 31
Craddock 35
Craig 16
Craik 42
Cramer 47
Cranly 47
Craven,Cravens 1,7
Crawford,Crauford,Crafford 26,42,47,50
Crean 16
Creeke 9
Crispe 6,47
Crittenden 18
Croper 22
Crøsby 26
Cross 37
Crowshaw 3
Crump 9
Crumwell 47
Cumminges 26
Current 27
Currie 31
Curtis 9,26,43,49
Custis,Custes 22,23,43, 48,49

DAFF 34
Dangerfield 35
Dallinge 6
Dally 10
Daly,Daily 37,38
Dameron 26
Damery 17
Daniels 23,43,45
Danlaps 42
Dannelly 12
Darman 10
Darnall,Darnal 27,50
Darne 42
Darter 10
Dashiel 10
Daubergue 37
Daugherty 11
Dausey 37
Davenport 26,28,30,51
Davids 46
Davidson 1,51
Davies 9
Davis 3,6,7,10,13,17, 35,41,47
Dawkins 26
Dauson 12,16,26
Deacon 35
Dean,Deans 6,50
Death 32
Deford 6
Denellin 31
Dennet 3
Dennis,Denes 1,2,26,37
Dennison,Denison 9,13
Denniston 13
Dent 18
Depree 45
Dermott 33
Derrick 37
De Segougne 42
Devoe 6
Dickenson 33,47
Dickson 10
Dictam,Dicturn 7
Digg 9
Dillaherty 18
Dillard 38
Dinwiddie 50
Diskin 50
Dives 1
Doak 17
Dobie 38
Dobson 46
Doe 10
Dolby 10
Donahue 39
Done (?) 2
Donelson 49
Doniphan 33
Dooly 31
Doore 6
Dorgan 40
Doring 39
Dorman 10,22
Doughting 35
Douglas 18,38,43,45
Dove 45
Downes 31,39
Downham 9
Downing 10,16,17,26, 33
Doyle 27
Doyne 38
Drake 16,43
Draper 9,35,45,46
Drew 39
Drie (?) 46
Drinker 21
Dromer 31
Drummond 10,38
Drunker 31
Drury 47

Duck 9
Duddlestone 30
Duffell (?) 6
Dugar 42
Dugraw 9
Duke,Dukes 10,26
Duling 33
Dumott 10
Dunaway 38
Dunbar 34
Duncan 37
Dunlap,Dunlop 1,42
Dunn,Dun 10,26,51
Dye 31
Dyer 31

EAGER 6
Earth 38
Easland (?) 26
Eason,Easom 9,22
East 22,50
Eaton 27,35
Edgar,Edger 31,33
Edge,Edges 22,26
Edmiston 43
Edmonds 47
Edwards,Edward 9,10,
26,31,47
Egerton 7
Eldige 26
Elliott 18,42
Ellett 35,42
Ellis,Elles,Ellise 30,
31,47
Elliston 50
Ellzey 30,38
Emerson 45
Emery 18
Emmett 45
Empy 45
English 35
Eppes 38
Eskridge 30,38
Estan 9
Estwood 9
Eustas 26
Evans 9,16,26,31,47
Everard 26
Evergen 22
Ewbank 6
Ewell 3,22
Eyre,Eyres 22,37,39

FAIRBROTHER 45
Fairfax 31
Farington 47
Faris 38
Farlow 4
Farman 31
Farme 6
Farmer 46
Farnefold 26
Farthy 35
Fausitt 46
Fearn 46
Fears 35
Feilding 26
Fenley 27
Field,Feild 31,46
Fielder 16
Figg 3
Finch 25,38
Fincher 47
Finney,Finnie 7,35
Firchett 22
Fishback 15
Fisher 46
Fite 18
Fitzgerald,Fitzgarrell
6,22
Fitzhugh 38
Flake 47
Fleetwood 47
Fleming 43
Fletcher 22,23,31,
34,40
Flinte,Flynt 16,47
Florriday 6
Flower,Flowers 26,
35
Floyd 5,6
Flu -- 9
Fooks 23
Forbes 13
Ford 34
Forquar 34
Forwood 47
Fosque 22
Fossett 6
Foster 22,23,31,34,
40
Foulk 26
Fowler 7
Fowte 9
Fox 7,33,34
Francis 17,35,47

Franklin,Franklyn
26,33,38
Fraser,Frazer 13,35
Frederick 12,13
Freeman 26,37
Froley 18
Fromett 30
Fudge 43
Fuller 31,51
Fulton 1
Furnell 38

GABLE 47
Gaffer 31,47
Gailer 47
Gale 22,42
Galloway 18
Gardner 12,42
Garland 31
Garlington 3,26
Garner 16
Garrett,Garratt 26,
30,38,45
Garwood 41
Gascoyne 22,26
Gaskins 26
Gattey 41
Gay 9
Gayney 31
Gelding 35
Gennis 26
Gentry 18
George 38,43
Gerrard 31
Gibbons 47
Gibson 4,6,18,22,34,
47
Gilbert 1,13,26
Gilchrist 22
Giles 6,17,38,47
Gill 6,26,31
Gillett 10,22,47
Gilliott 31
Gilson 9
Gisson 9
Gist 17
Gitting,Gittins 22,
35
Glading 22,31
Glass 22
Glen (?) 47
Glendening 33
Glissin 47

Glover 47
Goach 10
Godale 35
Godwin 38
Goffe 35
Golding 9
Goutee 22
Goodman 34,42
Goodwin,Godwin 18,38
Gootie 22
Gordon 22,38
Gore 10,22
Gorrell 13
Gosling 39
Gosse 38
Goswine 6
Gouche,Goushe 26
Gowin 6
Grady 16
Graff 38
Graham 26,38
Granger 4,31
Grant 33
Graves 31
Gray,Grey 9,31,43
Grayson 38
Green 7,26,38,43,45
Greenham 40
Greenleaf 21
Greensted 16
Greenway 37
Greenwood 47
Gregory,Grigory 18
Griffin 16,18,38,39,45,
47
Griffith 6,31
Griggs 3
Grigsby 13,34
Grimes 10
Grimsby 33
Groten 22
Grove 47
Grundick 45
Gryme 31
Guester 37
Guibert 13,14
Gunby 11,17
Gunne 35
Gurden 34

HACK,HACKE 23,31
Hackley 33,38
Hadwell 26
Hagester 45
Haile 50
Hailes 21
Hale 21,31
Haley 23
Hall 2,6,10,16,22,23,
26,31,33,37,38
Hallam,Hallum 26,39
Hallibarton 34
Hallock 9
Halsey 9
Hambleton 18
Hambling 22
Hamilton 7,23,26
Hamlett 31
Hammond 18,47
Hampton 6
Hanby 21
Hancock 1,22,47
Handy 2,11
Hane,Haner 47
Hanks 18
Hanmer 1
Hansford 31,38
Hanson 35
Harcum 26
Hardidge 30
Harding 22,35
Hardison 15
Hardman 7
Hardy 31,33
Hare 12,35
Harges 23
Harless 9
Harman,Harmon 6,47
Harmanson 22,23
Harper 1,13,23
Harris 1,2,9,25,26,27,
31,43,47
Harrison 1,7,22,23,26,
31,33,35,38,46
Harrold 26
Hart 6,9,35
Hartfield 6
Hartgrove 27
Hartland 26
Hartree 49
Hartwell 3
Harvy 47
Harwood 3,26
Haskill 18
Hasser 9
Hawkins 6
Hawley 35,46
Haws 17
Hawstone 31
Hawthorne 34
Hayes,Hay,Haze,17,29,32,40,
49
Haynie 26
Hayward 2,16
Hazleton 31
Hazlewood 35
Head 33
Healy,Healey 27,43
Heeth 31
Heightour 18
Heiser 39
Hellen 39
Helsapeck (?) 35
Henderson 12,18,23
Henley 17
Henry 23
Herbert 27,38
Herne 31
Herring 1,7
Heron 9
Hettrick 13
Hewbanck,Hughbanck
22,23
Hewett 7,38
Hewlett,Hulett,Hugh-
lett 26,31,38,51
Hickman 16,23,27,30,
38,51
Hide 3
Higginson 26
Higgison 6
High 26
Hight 35
Higley 31
Hill 6,7,9,16,18,23,
26,29,31,35,43,47
Hillary 23
Hilliard 10,46
Hillings 6
Hilman 9
Hinckle 1,13
Hinkes 47
Hinman 22,31,46
Hinshar 33
Hix 23
Hobbs 26,38
Hobson 26,51
Hodge 47
Hodges 12,31
Hodgkin,Hodgkins 31,
46
Hoe,Hooe 38

Hoffman 15
Hoggatt 18
Hokins 37
Holden 31
Holladay 42
Holland 18,22,23,39,41
Hollingsworth 4
Hollis 9
Holloway 6,43
Holmes 9
Holston 22
Holt 9
Holton,Holtun 12
Holtzclaw 15
Hook 47
Hoop 13
Hope 22,23,43
Hopkins 1,2,23
Hopper 16,26
Hopwood 38
Hore 42
Horsey 23,31
Horsley 39
Horton 9
Hortree 9
Hortsee (?) 9
Hoskins 23,47
Houlder 35
Hough 42
Houston 18
Howard 12,21,51
Howell 21,23,26
Howgrave 6
Howlett 47
Howson 26,31,38
Huberd 9
Hudley 31
Hudlow 13
Hudnall 26
Hudson 3,10,33
Huethin 34
Huggins 42
Hughes 13,22,31,33,42
Hukes 47
Huling 1
Hull 11,26
Humphrey,Humphreys 9, 30,38
Hungerford 27,30,39
Hunnicutt 6
Hunt 9,10,18,23
Hunter 18,45
Huntley 47
Hurd 3,10,31
Hurley 27
Hurtley 23
Husbands 18,32
Huske 26
Hutt 26
Hutton 16

ILAND 47
Ingason 23
Inglis,Ingles 17,43
Inglish 33
Ingrave 26
Inlow 46
Insworth 3
Irish 47
Isles 3
Ithell (?) 46

JACKMAN 6
Jackson 3,9,18,35, 39,43,47,49
Jacob,Jacobs 6,23,46, 47
James 9,10,21,22,23, 31,39
Janney 23
Jarvis 23
Jason 31,47
Jeffars 39
Jenifer 23
Jenkins,Jenkin 3,9,11, 26,38
Jenkinson 2,32
Jennet 9,39
Jennings,Jenings 47
Jens (?) 35
Jerman,Jermen 6,18
Jett,Jette 23,33,50
Johns 10
Johnson,Jnoson 9,11, 16,18,22,23,31,39, 45,46,47,50
Johnston 7,18
Joice 16
Jolb (?) 16
Jolly 47
Jones,Joanes,Jone 6, 9,10,12,21,23,26, 27,30,31,33,34,35, 38,39,45,50
Jordan 6,18,39,46
Joyne,Joyner 23
Jude 13,34
Justice 23

KAY 33
Kecey 39
Keele 31
Keen 16
Keister 7
Kellam 22
Kelly 6
Kelson 43
Kemp 42
Kendall 33,47,50
Kenner 16,26
Kent 47
Kern 7,27
Kesterson 26
Kettering 17
Killen 13
Kimball 43
Kincaid 43
Kinchen 38
King 2,6,17,18,43,46, 47
Kintly 31
Kipshaven 45
Kirby 50
Kirktridge 42
Kiston 3
Kite 13
Kinton 26
Knight 21,23,26,31
Knott 6,16
Knowles 46,47
Korking 31
Kreiger 35
Kyrk 26

LA ---shard 26
Lagston 9
Lamprey 26
Lampton 9,33
Lancaster 26
Lands 27
Lane 47
Langford,Lankford 9, 11,12,45
Langston 9
Large 47
Larker 9
Larrimore 27
Larry 46
Lash 13,34
Lasly,Lasley 17,31
Laster,Lasseter 9
Lattimore 26
Laundy 3

Laurence 35,38
Lawrence 38
Lawson 31,35
Lead 7
Leazure 16
LeBaron 4
Lee 13,26,27,42
Lefebur 6
Lemarr 1
Leggett 35
Lemay,Lemey 42,45
Lenox 15
Leonard 47
Letchworth 39
Letherland 39
Leverett 45
Levin 2,39
Lewin,Lewing 39,47
Lewis 6,13,26,31,35,
37,47
Leyel 9
Light 9
Lightfoot 15
Lightle 27
Linch 45,51
Linchfield 26
Linaley 18
Ling (?) 13
Lislow (?) 35
Little 16
Littleton 22,38
Lloyd,Loyd 6,38
Lock 29
Lockey 3
Lockwood 6
Lomax 12,39
Long,Longe 6,9,50
Longman 9
Loud 33
Love 3,9
Lowell 9
Lowe,Lowes 11,27
Lowrie 43
Lowther 38
Luck 6
Ludlow 10
Lugg 26
Lulling (?) 3
Lumpkin 42
Lumsford 33
Lunsford 27
Lusby 45
Lux 37
Lydie (?) 18
Lynes 39,42
Lynn,Lyne,Ling 13,26,
47
Lynton 15
Lyon 13,16

MacALPIN,MacElpin 50
McBride 13,34
McCarty 30,38,39
McClain 51
M'Clearen,M'Cleron 12
McCormack 33
Macubbin,Maccubins 27
39
McCullough 39
Mackdaniell 3
McDonald 51
McEackran 12
McElliston 34
Magee,McGie 33,35
McGill,Mackill 47
McGrath 6
Magruder 39
McGuire 17
MacHenry 26
McKay 12
McKeel 6
McMullen 2,12
McNeal,McNeill 12
McReilly 29
Mackrell 9
McVey 1
Machill 47
Macon 13
Macy 34
Madison 6
Magee 23
Magoune 7
Maken 37
Mallard 26
Mallet 39
Mallicote 38
Mallinge 31
Manlove 46
Manly 9
Mann,Man 3,31
Mannering 46
Mansfield 3
Mansens 9
March 9
Marlington 9
Marsh 9,26
Marshall 1,7,23,27,50
Martin 2,3,31,34,39,46,
50
Mascale (?) 35
Mason,Mayson 9,30,34,
35,39,42,46,51
Massey 9,39
Masters 9
Maston 9
Maswells (?) 10
Matthew,Mathew,Matt-
hews 3,6,16,22,34
Mator (?) 9
Mattrick 47
Maxwell 13,17,26,43
May 9,46
Mayze,Mayse 26,39
Mecanter 9
Meekins 3
Megant 1
Meger 6
Meizek 42
Melbourne 11
Melichop 25
Mercer 34
Meridith,Merrydith
39,51
Merick 31
Merriday 39
Methuen 42
Meygert 1
Meyser (?) 17
Michael,Machill,Mich-
ell,Mackrell 9,23,
35,47
Middleton 9,47
Mildeberger 13
Miller 1,16,17,45,50
Millner 46
Mills 47
Mitchell,Michell 16,
35,41
Mode 47
Moffett 17
Montgomery 17
Monts 31
Morgan,Morgans 6,8,
9,21,35,47,50,51
Moore 3,17,21,26,29,
43,47,51
Morey 37
Morris 7,21,26,39,45,
47,51
Morrison 50
Morry 47
Morton 47
Moss 30

Motheringe 35
Mottoon 26
Mottrom 26,31
Moneton 13
Mountayne 31
Mountford 3
Mudd 35,42
Mullen 51
Mullranie 26
Munday 47
Munell 51
Murdak 47
Murdock 50
Murphy 27,39,45
Murray 10,43
Muse 51
Musgrave 47

NAIRNE 2,11
Nappar 9
Nask 6,39
Naylor 9,47
Neale 26
Nelme 26
Nesby 26
Newcomb 45
Newitt 31
Newby 18
Newman 9
Newton 22
Nicholas,Nickless 38, 47
Nicholls,Nickolls 9, 26,47
Nicholson 3,35,47
Nicklin 4
Noakes 47
Noble 47
Nockey 47
Noell 47
Norcom 13
Norcott 9
Nord (?) 9
Norfleet 18
Norgate 16
Norman 6,30,38
Normansel 42
Norris 18
North 9,47
Northern 9
Norton 9,35,51
Norwood 13
Nosworth 10
Nowell,Nowel 9,46

Nugent 33
Nurse 6
Nutt 26

ODELL 4
O'Donneway 47
Oerter 50
Ogden 21,35
Oldham 16
Oliver,Olivier 9,21,22
Olley 41
Osie 16
Ordan (?) 26
Orfle 6
Orr 46
Ostetter 51
Overzee 31
Overton 6,35
Owen,Owin,Own 16,39,47
Ownbread 40
Oxton 9

PAGE 33
Paine 9,26,33
Palin 47
Palmer 3,18,26,35,49,50
Panter 7
Pantwell 47
Pardoe 3
Paremore 43
Paris 29
Parker 6,10,26 42,46,47
Parney 42
Parry 46
Parson 9
Pashley 9
Patchet 12
Pate,Payte 17,26
Patterson 30
Pattishall 33
Pattison 3
Paule 26
Payne 3,6,30,33,47
Paynter 46
Payton 31
Paxton 17
Peale 6,9
Pearce 34,46,47
Pearle 33
Peary 17
Pedley 9
Pedrick 21
Peele 39
Peirce 31,45,47

Pemberton 16,21
Pennington 47
Penn 13,21
Penniry 7
Peps (?) 9
Perkins 18
Perry 6,37,47
Perryn 16
Peter 34
Petigrew 26
Petis 9
Pettitt 31
Pettock 38
Pew 47
Pewter 9
Phillips 9,26,47
Philpot 31
Phipps 86
Pickens 26
Pidlers 47
Piggs 47
Pinckard 26
Pinkeman 47
Pleasants 43
Plummer,Plumer 9
Polk 11,12
Pollard 16
Pollock 15
Poole 31
Pope 34
Porter 11,34,42,47
Pott 31
Potter 46
Powell 3,16
Pratt 9,23,26,31
Preeson,Prieson 22, 30,37
Prenergast 31
Presley,Presly 16,26
Preston 45,51
Prettyman 46
Price 3,6,9,18,21,33, 35,38,46,50
Prickett 3,38,47
Pride 9
Prince 50
Pritchard 18
Proverb 26
Pryor 18,31
Pullein 33,50
Purnell 31
Pye 9
Pyper 6

QUEEN 43
Quintin 22

RABY 34,43
Ragan 32
Rainey 13,50
Ramey 6
Randall 9
Ransha 39
Ransom 37
Raredon 33
Raslin 6
Rasor,Razer Raisor 15, 25
Ratcliffe 39,45
Raven 42
Rawlings 47
Rayman 31
Reade 6,26,27,47
Reader 7
Reading 50
Reason 26
Reavell 23
Redd 6
Redding 6
Reed 18,27
Reid 29,37
Reppington 9
Revet 31
Reynolds,Reinolds 3,21
Rhodes,Roades,Rhods 21, 46
Rice 7,13,16,50
Richards 26,46
Richardson 2,6,9
Richmond 39
Ridly 35
Riffe (?) 1
Riley,Reli 1,27
Roach 11,16
Robards 12
Roberdam 31
Roberts 3,6,10,12,16, 21
Robertson 17
Robetton 47
Robins 3
Robinson 4,6,7,9,15, 18,22,29,31,35,40
Robyson 26
Rodolphus 22
Roe 9
Rogers 3,6,10,16,26,31, 47
Roles 31
Rooke 9
Rooksby 10
Rope 7
Roper 26
Rose 10,26,31,35
Roston 26
Rotheram 26
Rounds 26
Row 3
Rowland 47
Rowley 33
Roxburgh 43
Runcle 13
Runner 34
Rush 7
Rushone (?) 13
Russell 21,22,30,35,37, 39
Rutherford 15,45
Ryan 43
Ryder 7

SACKER 9
Sadler 9,26
Saffery 10
St Legerfield (?) 26
Salisbury,Salsbury
Salkeld 21
Sallowes 26
Salmon 47
Sample 18
Sanders 6,9,16,18,45
Sanderson 15
Sanro (?) 35
Satchell 30,31
Saterwhite 34
Saunders 15,23
Savage 25,35
Sayer 9
Scales 18
Scarborough,Scarburgh 10,23,47,49
Scasbrook 3
Schley 34
Schulenger 13
Scoffil 33
Scollay 13
Scott 9,13,18,27,30, 37,39,47
Scragg 31
Seabright 3
Seabury 16
Seagood 33
Seale 35
Seare,Seares 31,47
Secrist 6
Seed 50
Seek (?) 31
Segar 42,45
Seidel 50
Selby,Selvey 22
Senior 9,47
Serjeant 38
Sethell 35
Seward 9
Shae 23
Shapleigh,Shaply 26, 35
Sharp 31,35,47
Shaw 12,21,47
Sheares 26
Sheffield 47
Shelves 35
Shepard,Sheppard, Shepherd,Shepheard 9,16,23, 46,47
Sherwood 47
Shewell 31
Shields 20
Shirly 16
Shoemaker 21
Shore
Short
Shulenger,Schulenger 7,13
Sibell 6
Sich 47
Sidney 31
Signor (?) 26
Sikes 47
Silverlocke 47
Simon 47
Simonds 9
Simmons 16
Simpson 12,18
Simpkins 23
Singer 38
Singwell 50
Sise 33
Skance 6
Skelton 42
Skidmore 46
Skinker 50
Skinner 31
Skrine 33
Skugge 35

Slater 47
Sledwell 47
Smalley 23
Smart 9
Smeath 47
Smith 3,6,7,10,12, 13,17,18,22,25,27, 31 33,35,37,39,40, 45 46,47,49,50
Smithson 18
Smut (?) 47
Smyly 2
Smyth 26
Snead 3,22
Snide 7
Soams 10
Soare,Soar 26,47
Solm 47
Souleman 10
Souteman 10
South 47
Souther 29
Southerby 26
Southward 6
Spades 31
Sparshott 9
Spear 21
Spence 39
Spencer 16,42,46,51
Spinks 31
Spoo 50
Spry 51
Squire 6
Stampe 47
Stanard 43
Stanfor 9
Standley 33
Stanley 9,16,35,46
Stanlin (?) 9
Stantfield 12
Stanton 47
Staple 31
Stapleford 45
Starkey 18
Starr 47
Steele,Steel 17,35
Stephens,Stephen 9, 10,12,16,35,47
Stepto 26
Sterne 47
Stevens 2,9,35,45,47
Stevenson 12,13,15,43, 50
Stewart 13
Stinson 33
Stone 9,10,15,18,31,33,50
Stoner 9
Store 9,10
Storey 37
Stott 10
Stotz 34
Stow 47
Strang 9
Street 10
Stribling 29
Strong,Strang 9,27
Strother 33,50
Stroud,Strood 31,35
Stuart 46
Stump 43
Stultz 35
Such,Such 26,47
Sullivan,Sullivant, Swillivant 22,30,50
Sumer 31
Summerfield 45
Summerford 43
Sumner 10
Sutton 40
Swaine 26
Swanson 26
Swazy (?) 9
Swetnam 46
Swillivant 30
Sybert 7
Symons 26
Syms 16
Sympson 37

TALTON 9
Tandy 34
Tankred 23
Tanner 30,47
Tard 9
Tatum 7
Taylor,Tayloe 2,3,13,16, 22,26,34,35,39,49,50, 51
Teackle 25
Teague 33,47
Temple 10
Terrell 6
Thatcher 33,50
Thomas 1,9,10,17,26,47
Thompson,Tompson 9,10,17, 18,41,47
Thomson 51
Thorn 27
Thornbury 51
Thornton 33,37,50
Thorpe 10,26
Thorogood 51
Thrane 50
Tilney 23
Tinpenny (?) 33
Tiplady,Toplady 3, 10
Tippet 50
Toft 9,23
Tom 13
Tomkins 10
Tomlin 31
Tomson,Tompson 9,26, 47
Toner 9
Tonge 9
Tony 9
Tooke 9
Toplady,Tiplady 3, 10
Towdry 16
Tranburge 18
Trantham 12
Travers 10
Treddar 31
Trewett 47
Trivell 34
Trotham 9
Trott 9
Trotter 10,18
Troutt 9
Trueblood 7
Trueman 38
Tucker 9,10,18,39
Tullos 16
Tully 49
Tunstill 49
Turlington 22
Turner 10,31,35,50
Turpin 11
Tutt 34
Twisden,Twisdon 9
Tye 9
Tyler 10,31
Typton 26

Udall 9
Underwood 26,33,44, 50
Upshur 22
Urner 34

VALLETTE 40
Vanderford 39
Varley 31
Vaughan 15,16,35
Vause 39
Vaux,Vaulx 30,31
Vines 10,47
Voss 43
Vrott 9

WARD 47
Wade 3,10,21,24,27
Wadden 6
Wadding 10
Waddington 26
Waddy 26
Wadlow 9
Waight 47
Waite 34
Wake 35
Wakerly 47
Walder 35
Walker 9,18,26,29,
30,35,37,42,47
Wall 38
Wallace 29,41,43
Wallett 10
Wallop 9
Walters,Walter 6,31,
42
Wannan 9
Ward 17,30,31,35
Warden 9
Ware 42
Warner 10,26,45,47
Warren 31,33,47
Warrey 47
Washburn 23
Washington 35,51
Washott 9
Waterland 37
Waters 16,27,40,43
Waterson 27
Watkins 10,16,39
Watson 9,10,25,29,34,
47
Wattross 9
Watts 26
Waugh 34
Way 26
Weatherell 10
Weatly 9
Webb 10,26,47,51
Webber,Weber 13,47,50,
51
Weill 47
Wells 16,39
Welsh,Welch 27,33
Wentworth 10
Wesson 31
West 9,13,22,23,30,31,
32,42
Weston 47
Wheatly,Weatly 9,31
Whedbee 13
Wheeler,Wheler 9,47
Whetman 45
Whetstone 9
Whiskin 10
White 3,9,18,26,27,33,
45,50,51
Whiteby 31
Whitehurst 10
Whitman 45
Whittington 1,2,4,10,11
39
Whitworth 35
Wickliff 27
Wild 10
Wildey,Wildeyes 16,26
Wildman 11
Wilkes 47
Wilkin 31
Willett 9
Williams 6,9,10,15,16,18
26,31,33,40,46,51
Williamson 9
Willimot 13
Willis 10,24,31
Wills 31
Wilimott,Willimot 1,13,
39
Wilson 6,9,13,26,31,47,
49
Wiltbanck 46
Wilton 10
Windly 29
Winstone 34
Winter 26
Wistar 21
Withers 26
Wood 7,13,26,31
Woodnightonhouse 6
Woodson 29
Woodward 47
Workman 29
Wornam 26
Wray 49
Wren 38
Wright 6,7,9,31,33,
42,51
Wotten 25
Wyat, Wyatt 9,51
Wye 9
Wyland 32
Wyser, Weiser 17

YARDLY,YEARDLEY 10,
49
Yarratt 16
Yeomans 31
Young 27,47

ZOUCHE 9

The
County Court Note-Book

A Little Bulletin of History and Genealogy

February, 1931. Vol. X, No. 1

MARRIAGE LICENSES FROM PROCEEDINGS, OFFICE OF REGISTER OF PROBATES, RICHMOND COUNTY, GEORGIA

(*See note on page 4.*)

JOHN KENNADY, of Richmond cty, and ELISABETH WEBSTER, widow. 12 Aug 1791.

ISAAC PEARCE, pltr, and HENRIETTA GRUBBS, Sp. 6 Aug 1791.

MICAJAH WILKERSON, pltr, and MARY KENNADY, Sp. 8 Aug 1791.

HENRY OSBORNE and CATHARINE HOWELL, Sp. 20 Aug. 1791.

JOEL HILL and ANNY WATSON, Sp. 11 Oct. 1791.

JOHN MOORE, blacksmith, and CATHERINE THOMPSON, widow. 16 Nov 1791.

JOHN WILSON, pltr, and MARGARET BAKER, widow, of S. C. 24 Nov 1791.

WILLIAM DEARMOND, of Augusta, Ga., and ANN PEARRE, of Columbia cty, Sp. 20 Dec 1791.

HARDY RICE JERNIGAN, pltr, Richmond cty, and REBECCA LEE, same cty, Sp. 22 Dec 1791.

T. DICKENS, of Augusta, Ga., and MARY HICKS, same, Sp. 19 Jany 1792.

JESSEE RICE, Richmond cty, and SUSANAH JONES, Columbia cty, Sp. 23 Jany 1792.

NOAH KELSY, and SALLY HAWKINS, both of Augusta. 4 Feby, 1792.

WILLIAM CALHOON and RACHEL TRIPLETT, both Richmond cty. 8 Feby 1792. (Hope Hull was the minister.)

MICHAEL BURKE, M. D., and ANNE FISHBOURNE, widow; both of Richmond cty. 12 Mch 1792.

THOMAS JONES and ...... BOYD, widow, Richmond cty. 24 Mch 1792.

HENRY ARRINGTON, pltr, and MARY BUGG, widow; both Richmond cty. 12 Apr. 1792.

JNO. POWELL, M. D., and ANN WILKINSON, [widow?] 4 June 1792.

NATHAN HILLS and SUSANNAH REILY, Richmond county. 10 June 1792.

GEO. WISENGER and WINNY ANDERSON, Richmond cty. 30 June 1792.

JAMES JONES and MARY DARLING, Richmond cty. 3 July 1792.

JOEL JONES and NANCY MIDDLETON, 3 July 1792.

HEZEKIAH JONES and OBEDIENCE MITCHELL. 4 Aug. 1792.

RICHARD CHILD DAVIS and ELIZA NETTLES. 21 Aug 1794.

REUBEN ELKINS and ELIZABETH DAVIS. 23 Jany 1797.

SHIPS IN PORT.

"*Omnibus Christe fidelibus.*" The Protest of Capt. William Barker agt the Sea. Whereas I Wm. Barker Command'r of the Shipp *William* of London was distressed by Extremity of weather the 16th February anno 1654 on the Latitude of 52 degrees & 160 Leagues westward from the Lizard or thereabouts where wee lost our main Mast [the goods he had aboard being damaged.] And I the sd William Barker, P'ferred to deliver the said goods at Accomack in Virginia, but the owner would not receive them I being afterward forced to put them on Shoare into Coll. Jno. Mottroms Store at Chicacoan whoe is now deceased. [*sic.*] Rich: Covell, Stephen Allen also made oath. 21 May 1656. Nthld Records i-84.

Ship *Happy*. John Copeland, Comm'd'r. Letter of Marque, &c. Va. St. Pa. i-236. 13 Aug 1742.

Ship *Happy Adventure*. BRIDGET NEALE left this ship at Isle of "White;" she was a free passenger. See Acco., Va. i-58.

Sloop *Hunter*; Edward Robinson devises two-thirds interest in her. Philada., Penna. 7 Sept 1699. A-299.

Good Shipp *Industrie*, of Plimouth; Edward Blagg, of Plimouth, marriner, was master (under God) ...... and shortly bound forth in a voyage into Virginia. Thomas Hunt mentioned as of Plimouth, and Samuel Brett as the owner of the *Industrie*. [Henry Brett, whose widow Col. Washington married, was also of Plymouth.] Wmld. Orders 1662–1664, fo. 100. 31 May 1671.

Ship *Indiana*; Jno. McClallen supercargo and agent to Batavia, now on a voyage there. His will signed on board near the mouth of the river Severn, *Virginia*. Mr. James Calhoun, Jr. his extr. Balto., Md. Wills. 25 Sept 1807–11 Jany 1809. viii–368.

Ship *Jeffery*; One thirty-second part belonged to Maximilian Robinson. Va. Mags. xxii-22. 28 Oct. 1694.

The *John and Barbara*; concerning goods shipped in her. (Thomas Joynes mentioned.) N-n, Va. About 1 Feby 1640. i-48.

Shipped by the Grace of God in good order and well Conditioned by John Edmonds in and upon the good Ship called the *Jannie*, whereof is master under God for this present voyage John Steele and now at anchor in Rappohanock and by God's Grace bound for Port Glasgow to say Twenty Hhds Tob'o to be delivered in the like Good & Well conditioned ...... the danger of the Seas only excepted. Pr. Wm, Va. Bet. 1779 and 1784. U-545.

Ship *John and Mary*; Will'm Caswell, master. Chas. City cty, Va. 4 Dec 1665.

The *James* of Montrose; Walter Keith [?] Com'd'r. (Scotch servants imported.) York, Va. 24 Mch 1709. xiv-6.

The James and John; Capt. John Warner, comm'd'r. Lower Norf. Va. 15 May 1661. D-299.

The Good Schooner *Jene*; Patrick Dillon, owner; sells all the half to John Watts and William Nicholson. Acco., Va. 23 Nov 1759. iii-99.

Schooner *Lucretia*; John Guy, Gent., was engaged in partnership with Henry Guy in trading beyond the Seas to and from the West India Islands and elsewhere in the *Lucretia*, and that John by will (1760) gave wife Susanna all his personal estate and lands until son John should be 21. N-n, Va. Chancery Record. 1774.

His Majestie's Ships *Lincoln* and *Shoreham* to act as convoys. Va. St. Pa. 1701. i-13.

The Brigantine *Leah*, lying in Wickacomoco River takes Tobacco on board for Glasgow in North Brittain at Eight pound Sterling P[er] Ton and Liberty is given to all Freighters to consign to whom they please. Henry Lowes [?] signs. Som. Md. 12 Feby 1730. S. H. -298.

Shipp the *Lear Frigat*; Capt. William Norrington, Commander. His widow, Rebecka, received letters of administration at the Prerogative Court of "Canterberry" 9 July 1797. She gives power to Capt. Matthew Trim [?] Commander pf the Robert and Sam'll, now in London outward bound for Yorke River in Virginia. York, Va. xii-37.

Phillip Taylor understands that the Marylanders have taken his Pinnace, the *Longtayle*, with all her company and some other of his men, trading in other places. Given att the Isle of Kent. N-n, Va. 11 May 1635. i-149.

The *Mayflower*. Mr. Danell Hutt was Master. Wmld, Va. 17 Sept 1758. ii-38.

The *Morning Star*, of Liverpool. Bond of the Captain and owners. Va. St. Pa. 1693. i-47.

Shipp *Mary and Ellery*, of Jopson; Thomas Carpenter, Comm'd'r; from Newfoundland. Va. St. Pa. 1 May 1695. i-49.

Shipp *Mary and Sara*, of Bristoll. Wmld, Va. 28 Jany 1707. 1705-1721, fo. 77.

The *Barq Mary* of Carolina; Nathaniell Powell, mate, gets judgment for wages, £12-5-4 ster. Mr. George Barratt, Master, also gets judgment for his wages, Nthld. Va. 21 Jany 1679. iii-57.

The *Maryland Merchant*; Captain Miles Cook. Mr. Francis Dade came out of England in her, and falling sick, desired William Storke and Capt. Cook "to take notice and bear in memory" his last will, Wmld, Va. 1 May 1663. i-201.

AUTHENTIC REFERENCES FOR INFERRED MARRIAGES

(The following marriages are from Maryland records.)

WILLIAM AUSTIN and ANN WALKER. Before 1 Aug 1707. Pr. Geo's cty. C-210.

JOSHUA ATKINSON, of Wor. cty, and ELIZABETH SCOTT, dau. of William, late of Som. cty. Annap. E. I. 9-353. Before 5 Apr 1753. [They had son James, 18 or over.] See also Som. Md. xviii-74. Before 7 May 1733.

JNO. BENNETT and a dau. of William FURNISS. Som. cty. Before 13 June 1688. Vol. 1690-1691, p. 49. [This vol. also marked A.W.]

BENJAMIN BALL and MARTHA FREELAND, widow of Robert, of Calvert cty. Annap. Inv. and Acc'ts. xiiiB-95. Before 15 May 1696.

RALPH BRISCOE and SARAH, the extx of Lindsay DELASHMUTT. A. A. cty. Before 1 Apr 1796. Admn Accts. G. M. No. 1, p. 552.

JOHN BROOKS and JUDITH NEWMAN, widow of John of Dor. cty. Annap. T. P. xxiii-107. Before 17 Dec 1717.

ZEPHANIAH BEALL and KEZIAH, admx of Thos. ODELL. Before 16 Sept 1769. A. A. cty. Admn Accts B 2-90. [She was also extx of William Pritchett.]

.........BRITTINGHAM and MARY DAVIS, dau. of Charles. Before 31 Oct 1761. Wor. cty. J. W. iii-51.

"CHARLES BECKWITH who m. ELIZA: KEEN, "the extx of Fran's HILL, dec'd; CHARLES "BECKWITH who m. ELIZA: HOPEWELL, "admx of HUGH HOPEWELL; the same who "married ELIZA: KEEN, admx RICH'D "KEEN"......Citations [to be] Returned to the Last Thursday in April 1703. Annap. T. P. xixA-125. [St. Mary's cty.]

JOHN BURROUGHS and SARAH, extx of John SHEPHERD. Before 13 Dec 1769. A. A. cty. Admn Accts. B2-94.

SAMUEL PERRY and SARAH, extx of Meredith DAVIS. Before 4 June 1771. A. A. cty. Admn Accts. B2-162.

.........HENRY and SARAH OGLE, extx of Joseph. Before or about 18 Apr 1770. A. A. cty. Admn Accts. B2-106.

STEPHEN BORDLEY, of Kent cty, and HANNAH, widow of Thos. PERKINS. After 16 Feby 1768 and before July 1771. Annap. T. P. xliv-233.

.........BENSTON and ANN BLADS [?] dau. John. Before 9 Feby 1767. Wor. cty. J. W. iii-129.

.........BUTLER and ESTHER TURNER, dau. Samuel. Before 20 Feby 1752. Wor. cty. J. W. iii-16.

.........BLAIDS and LEVINAH HENDERSON, dau. of Charles. Before 3 October 1761. Wor. cty. J. W. iii-53.

.........BURNS and MAGDALENA BENSON, dau. of Henry. Before 19 June 1761. Wor. cty. J. W. iii-69.

ANDREW BROWN and GRACE COULBOURN, dau. John. Before 6 June 1752. Wor. cty. J. W. iii-115.

JOHN BEALL, of Pr. Geo's, Gent., and ELIZABETH FENDALL, dau. of John of Charles cty, Gent. Before or about 11 Apr 1728. Pr. Geo's. M-322.

WALTER BOSWELL and ELEANOR SMALLWOOD. Chas. cty. Md. 1779. Maryland Marriages at M. H. S.

KENDAL COLLIER and SARAH FASSITT, dau. of John, Sr., and Mary FASSITT. Before 12 Nov 1772. Wor. Md. J. W. iv-165. See also J. W. iv-238.

.........CLENCY[?] and ELIZABETH THOMAS, dau. of Daniel. Before 21 June 1742. Pr. Geo's cty. Y-516.

.........CRAWFORD and RACHEL MERRILL, dau. John. Before 21 Jany 1759. Wor. cty. J. W. iii-33.

.........CHRISTOPHER and SARAH SHOCKLEY, dau. of John, Sr. Before 19 Jany 1761. Wor. cty, J. W. iii-128.

THO. CARY, cooper, Som. cty, and RACHEL CROUCH, dau. of Robert. [and was presented by the grand jury, he having formerly married MARY CROUCH, sister of RACHEL.] 14 Nov 1706. Som. cty. A. B. (9)-214.

WILLIAM CANNEDAY and ANNE FISHER. "Bonds." Som. cty. 26 Apr 1668. B(1)-112.

JOHN COOPER and SUSANNA BRAYFIELD. "Bonds." Som. cty. 28 May 1667. B(1)-68.

.........CRAPPER [CROPPER?] and ESTHER CORD, dau. of William. Before 19 Nov 1759. Wor. cty. J. W. iii-19.

.........CUSTERS [CUSTIS?] amd SARAH CORD, dau. of William. Wor. cty. Before 19 Nov 1759. J. W. iii-19.

.........CORDRE[?] and ESTHER GODWIN, dau. of "Ceasar", Sr. Before 6 June 1761. Wor. cty. J. W. iii-26.

STEPHEN COOPER and SUSANNAH MORGAN, dau. of Robert. Before 14 May 1767. Cecil cty. x-481.

Dr. THOMAS CANNON and PEGGY PORTER, admx of John. Between 30 July 1787 and 20 June 1791. Som. cty. E. B. xvi-459.

WILLIAM COCKEE [*sic.*] of Seaverne, and FRANCES VINCENT. "Bonds of Matrimony." 29 Sept 1668. Som. cty. B (1)-137.

HENRY COSTON and ANN RIGGEN, dau. of Teague. Before 6 Jany 1807. Som. cty. R-111.

..... DIXON and GRACE TODVINE, dau. of Henry. Before 18 Oct 1756. J. W. iii-p. 1.

MAREEN DUVALL and SARAH, admx of Thomas MILES. Before 8 Apr 1769. A. A. cty. Admn Accts B2-57.

ANDRIAS DIRRICKSON and TEMPERANCE HOPKINS, dau. of Samuel. Before 1703. Som. cty. C. H.-1.

JOHN DISHAROON and MARGRETT, the admx of John STEVENS. Before June Court, 1707. Som. cty. A. B. (9)-355.

ZADOCK DICKERSON and a dau. of John COOKE. Before 28 Apr 1779. Fred'k cty.

NICHO [?] DAWSON and MARY DOYNE, sister of Robert and Charles. Before 2 Oct 1710. Som. cty. I.K.L.-60.

CHARLES EGARTON, Gent., of St. Mary's cty, and MARY NEALE, dau. of James. About or before 10 Apr 1702. Pr. Geo's cty. A-449.

SAMUEL ELLIOTT and MARGARET HAYWARD WAGGAMAN, 6 Mch 1793. Dor. cty Mar. Li.

BENJ. ELLIOT and MARY GRIFFIN. 16 Jany 1794. Dor. cty. Mar. Li.

PLANNER ELLIOTT and RHODA ELLIOTT. 4 Sept 1794. Dor. cty Mar Li.

JOSEPH ELLIOTT and LEAH ELLIOTT. 27 Oct 1782. Dor. cty Mar Li.

JOSEPH ELLIOTT and CHARLOTTE ELLIOTT. 15 Feby 1797. Dor. cty. Mar. Li.

EDWARD ELLIOTT and KESIAH ELLIOTT. 22 Nov 1796. Dor. cty. Mar. Li.

WILLIAM ENNIS and ELIZABETH JOHNSON, sister of Leonard. Before 7 Aug 1762. Wor. cty. J. W. iii-51.

SAMUEL ENNIS or INNIS and ...... SMITH, dau. of Edward and Ann. Before 14 Apr 1687. Wor. cty. M. H. iii-13 and 22.

ARTHUR EVITT and MARY GRAY. "Bonds." 26 Apr 1668. Som. cty. B (1)-112.

(The following marriages are from the records of Accomack county, Virginia.)

JONATHAN CHAMBERS and MARY, sister and coheir of Richard JONES. Before 3 Jany 1737. xx-294.

OWEN COLLONELL [?] and SUSANNA HARRISON, widow of Alexander. Before 16 Apr 1673. iv-196. [She was the sister of James Andrews, who lived at Hampton River, Virginia. See deposition.]

WILLIAM CLEVERDON and DEBORAH YEO, sister to Mr. Hugh YEO. Before 27 May 1796. viii-87.

THOMAS COPES and the widow of John HOOTTEN. Before 1720. xvi-135.

JOHN CHAMBERS and ELIZABETH TILNEY. Before 6 Aug 1723. [She was the daughter of William.] xviii-61.

DANIEL CUTLER and ANNE WEST, widow of John. About or before 19 Sept 1751. Deeds ii-389.

ISAAC COOPER and TABITHA MILBY, dau. of John. Before 7 Aug 1732. xx-112.

SEBASTIAN CROPPER and RACHEL PARKER. Before 2 Nov 1708. xi-65. Also xi-457. [There is some doubt in the compiler's mind as to whether this name is Parker or Parkes.]

THOMAS CRIPPING [CRIPPIN] and ELIZABETH WHITE, widow of William. Before 3 July 1683. vi-343. See also ix-13 or 14.

NATHAN CULLVER and MARY WILSON TAYLOR, dau. of Elias. Before 29 Mch 1757. Deeds ii-728.

HUMPHREY CHAPMAN and MARY MORRIS, widow of Gilbert. Before 25 Nov 1755. xiii-323.

.... COPES and RHODA SIMPSON. Probably before 1756. L. C. 1806-1829. p. 313.

MARYLAND'S NEXT OF KIN

JOHN EMERSON, ALICE EMERSON; inv. John Emerson, Talbot cty. 17 Oct 1723. ix-247.

MARGRETT HOLLIDAY. "No more Relations." Inv. James Holliday, Balto. cty, pltr. Returned 8 Aug 1723. ix-253.

FRANCIS and MARY OGG [probably] kin. Inv. William Beard. Returned 7 Nov 1723. ix-254.

JOHN WENMAN, JOHN GRAY; inv. Thomas Buttingshire, of Calvert cty. Taken .8 Apr 1723. ix-257.

JNO. GREVES, RACHELL ABBOTT; inv. Sam'll Abbott of Calvert cty. Taken 1 Aug 1723. ix-260.

WILLIAM WATTS, PETER RULE, THOMAS HEBB [HOBB?] Jr. [Not clear as to which are kin.] 22 Nov 1723. ix-264.

JEFFERY HORNEY, SOLOMON HORNEY; inv. John Horney of Talbot cty. 14 Oct 1723. ix-267.

"Know not of Any relations in this P'vince except ANN MEGROAH, who signed." Inv. Arthur Mackgraught of Talbot cty. Taken 23 Apr 1723. ix-270.

ROBERT COLLIER, THOMAS COLLIER. Inv. Elizabeth Collier, of Som. cty. 3 Dec 1723. ix-272.

JOHN EVANS, Sr., GEORGE COLLIER; inv. Coll. Nicholas Evans of Som. cty. Taken 13 Aug 1723. ix-275.

"No Kindred." Inv. Joseph Atkins of Som. cty. Returned 10 Aug 1723. ix-278.

WILLIAM x BOWIN, "one of the nearest of Kin." Inv. William Bowin, Jr., of Som. cty. 20 Nov 1723. ix-279.

JOHN MORE, JOHN MORE, Jr. Inv. James Smith of Som. cty. Returned 20 Dec 1723. ix-281.

"Know of no kin in America." Inv. Richard Michel, cordwainer, of Som. cty. Returned 20 Dec 1723.

ELIZABETH x WARD, GEORGE x WARD; inv. John Vaudry of Chas. cty. Taken 10 Oct 1723. ix-284.

JOHNxHIGTON, BENJA'N x HIGTON; inv. John "Hidgton" of Chas. cty. Returned 12 Dec 1723. ix-289.

JOHN STEWART, CURTIS EVANS; inv. John Trevelion, Jr., of Dor. cty. Taken 12 Aug 1723. ix-289.

WILLIAM MILLES, WILL: IRECK [this name very uncertain], JACOB x MILLES; inv. William Mills, Jr., of Dor. cty. Returned 10 Feby 1723. ix-293.

THOS. x CAUSEY, PHILLIP x CAUSEY; inv. William Causey, of Dor. Taken 17 Oct 1723. ix-295.

"Relations" MAJOR FRAME, RICH'D x BADLEY. [Uncertain.] Inv. Jno. Hicks of Dor. cty. Taken 5 Feby 1722. ix-296.

ANNE KELLY, THOS. JOCE. [Uncertain as to kinship.] Inv. William Kelly. 15 June 1723. ix-297.

"No known Kindred besides one of extrs and his wife." Inv. Thos. Marten of Chas. cty. Returned 8 June 1723. ix-299.

"No affinity." Inv. John Grafton. 9 Nov 1723. ix-305.

"No Kin in these parts." Inv. Daniel Jobson of Cecill cty. 24 Nov 1723. ix-309.

BEN: KEENE, EDWARD KEENE; inv. Capt. John Keene of Dor. cty. Returned 11 Mch 1723. ix-314.

EDWARD x MILLS, WALTER x FITCHEW; inv. Thomas Fitchew of Dor. cty. Returned 12 Mch 1723. ix-319.

"No Kindred in these parts." Inv. Thomas Dyas, of Dor. cty. Returned 6 Mch 1723.

"No Kindred at 'Age." Inv. Judith Avesse of Dorsett cty. Returned 12 Mch 1723. ix-320.

JAMES DOSSEY, REBEKA DOSSEY; inv. John Dorsey, of Calvert cty. Taken 12 Feby 1723. ix-321.

DANIEL WATTS, PETER RULE; inv. Coll. William Watts of St. Mary's cty. Returned 13 Apr 1724. ix-322.

THE MIGRANT HAYS, HAYES, HAISE, HAZE, SOME OF THEM.

REBECCA HAYS; petition agt. William Gordon. York, Va. 24 Mch 1709. xiv-7.

RICHARD HAYS, an head right under Mr. John Parker of Matapony. Acco., Va. 17 Mch 1681. viii-293.

ROBERT HAY, Died 12 Apr 1717. York-Hampton Psh Reg. Va.

ROBERT and ANNE HAY had dau. RACHEL, born 11 Dec. 1744. Also a son JAMES [son of ROBERT] d. 11 Mch 1701. York-Hampton Psh Reg. Va.

ROBERT and HANNAH HAY; dau. DORITHY. born 6 Feby 1713. York-Hamp. Psh. Reg. Va.

ROBERT and MARY HAY; son John born 4 Mch 1730; dau. Dorithy, 3 Nov 1732; dau. RACHEL, 29 Aug 1734; son ROBERT, 30 May 1736; dau. MARY, 18 June 1738; dau. RACHEL. 7 Dec 1740. York-Hamp. Psh Reg. Va.

ROBERT HAYS; in Orange cty. Orders 1743-1746, p. 110. 1743.

ROBERT HAYES, Lower Cty of New Norfolk. S. L. O. Va. about 1642.

ROBERT HAYES, a tithable. Northampton cty, Va. 1676. xii-148.

ROBERT HAY, had son John. Settlement of estate. York cty, Va. Returned 16 Feby 1789. xxiii-178.

ROBERT x HAYES; deposition. Age about 60. Northampton cty. 13 Nov 1680. xiii-109.

ROBERT HAYES, one tithe. N-n, Va. 1674, x-272.

ROBERT HAYES, cattle-mark. N-n, 1667.

ROBERT HAYES married Ann Draiton. N-n. 1660.

ROBERT HAYES gets ctf for land; eight persons; himself wife, Anne Workman, Mary Workman, Thos. Workman, Jno. Workman, Alex. Hayes, Nath'l Hayes. New Norf. cty, Va. 11 Juiy 1637. A-2.

ROBERT HAYES, age 44 years. New Norf. Va. 1637. A-4.

ROBERT HAY; estate appraised. York, Va. Returned 15 July 1754. xx-333.

ROBERT HAY; will. Dau. ANN HAY, mentioned. [Incomplete abstract.] York, Va. 1778.

ROBERT HAYES; surveyor of the highways. York, Va. 17 June 1712. xiv-170.

RICHARD HAYS and CHARLOTTE NORRIS, Fred'k cty, Md. Mar. Li. 11 Feby 1789.

RICHARD HAIES; one tithe. Acco., Va. 1685. vi-414.

SARAH HAY, relict of John. (Dower.) York, Va. Returned 15 Mch 1756. xx-395.

SARAH HAYES, widow of Adam Hayes. [Who was drowned.] L. Norf. Va. 1661.

STEPHEN HAYES, of Cecil county, Maryland. Buys land from the Robinsons, in Chester county, Penna. 100 acres on the Penna. line. 1806.

SIMON HAYES; Capt. Joseph Cloyd gets l. a. on his estate. Montg. cty, Va. Orders. 3 Nov 1788.

THOMAS HAYS and ANN WILEY. Fred'k cty, Md. Mar. Li. 11 Feby 1789.

THOMAS HAYES, Liverpool; power to Mr. Joseph Robinson. Acco., Va. 8 Mch 1685. vi-426.

Capt. THOMAS HAIES was a mariner. Acco., Va. 8 Feby 1686. ix-97.

THOMAS HAYES: head right under Edmund Scarburgh. Northampton, Va. 28 Apr 1651. iv-18.

THOMAS HAYES; mentioned in deed of William Robinson, Gent. L. Norf. 16 Aug 1681. v-41.

THOMAS HAYS, a constable. Amherst, Va. Orders. 7 Dec 1767.

THOMAS HAYES; one of the security for Bartho. Schrever, admr of Thomas Urquhart. Nthld, Va. 20 Feby 1711. Vol. 1710-1713, p. 154.

THOMAS HAYS; had part of "clean Drinking." Fred'k cty. Md. Debt Book. 1773.

WILLIAM HAYS; inventory and appr'm't his estate. Returned by Hood, Ward and Branch. Henrico, Va. 19 Nov. 1733. Vol. 1725-1737. p. 500.

WILLIAM HAYS in Henry cty, Va. 1781. St. Land Office.

WILLIAM HAY; son-in-law of Robert Sample [Semple.] Alleg. cty, Penna. 10 Aug 1808. [Date of will.] i-265.

WILLIAM HAYSE, farmer, will. Wife Nancy; children: James, Robert, Solloman, John, George, Jane, Nancy, Isabell, Elizabeth, Mary. Wife Ann and James and Robert Hayes administrators [?] James Hook mentioned. Wit: Rhodes, Hook, Smith. Wash'n cty, Penna. 22 Apr 1795-22 June 1795. i-266.

WILLIAM HAY, will. Wf Catherine; daus. Nancy and "Jain" Hay, 50 a. Son John, 500 acres. Balance of land to daus. as above. "I also wish that tract of or parcel of land in Ireland in the County of Londonderry left me by my father to be sold and the monies arising therefrom to be divided among my three children." Son John and friend Richard Harvey, extrs. Wit: Martin-Gardner-Clarkson. Campbell cty, Va. 4 Apr. 1822-13 May 1822. v-581.

WILLIAM HAYS, Warren cty, Ky. Aged 74, 10 Mch 1835. Enlisted in 1781 under McDowell. Was born Augusta cty, Va. 10 Mch 1761. Father moved from Augusta, Va., to Rutherford cty, N. C. See Pension records.

WILLIAM HAYS; had part of "Terry's Park" and other tracts. Fred'k cty, Md. Debt Book. 1773.

(To be followed by a second alphabet.)

The County Court Note-Book

An every-other-monthly devoted mainly to abstracts from County Court Records, prior to 1800.

MILNOR LJUNGSTEDT, Editor and Publisher, Bethesda, Rural Route 5, Maryland.

Published six times a year. Subscriptions must begin with the year.

February, 1931 **Whole**
Vol. X., No. 1 **No. 56**

COURTS, CLERKS, ROYALTY AND THE WEATHER

When the Editor, following modestly in the steps of Porte Crayon, began her Virginia explorations, the Clerks of the Courts, as one man, assured her that the law required the Clerks' Offices to be open every day in the year except Christmas, and one old Clerk now passed over, rather insisted that even Christmas was not excepted. Of course, every day in the year didn't mean Sunday. If the Clerks' clients did not go to church on Sunday they had to go to Court another day!

At the time the Editor started out she was in the habit of regarding GEORGE WASHINGTON......well, regarding him as every well-taught Northern child is apt to regard him, and that a Virginia Clerk's Office should pay no attention to the birthday of a Virginian like our first and immortal President seemed very strange, indeed. The Editor was moved to indignation and the purchase of two small United States flags which she flaunted as much as flags so small could be said to flaunt.

Since then, the law seems to have taken certain holidays into consideration......is George Washington's birthday among them? The Editor does not know.* She does know that in Maryland she is forever running into the Battle of North Point, or Easter Monday, or some other unexpected historical event.

But before George Washington was born, holidays do not seem to have been very official, unless something happened in a royal line, excepting that there was certainly at times...... maybe not often, a day of Thanksgiving. And while the courts ran into an occasional *dies non*, there were not many. Sometimes there was very bad weather, much like now, though it is doubtful if an Arctic current was then behaving in the perfectly uncalled for manner which is at present charged against it. An earthquake is recorded in one volume, but does not seem to have closed the Clerk's Office. In Westmoreland county, however, the very county of Washington, and in Northumberland, they appear to have had a time of it, as the following extracts will show. Sometimes royalty ...... sometimes weather.

Memorandum the Court did not sitt in January [1688-9] the Prince of Wales being then proclaimed. Northumberland, iii-452.

*It is.

The Court did not function "Extremity of the weather rendering it impossible to Sitt and doe the Counties Business." Westmoreland, 29 Dec 1694.

The day being appointed a Public Fast and Thanksgiving. ....Court adjourned until the next day. Northumberland, 18 Dec 1703.

"The Clerke being much disordered in his health & afflicted greatly with the gout doth adjourne the Court to the Third Wednesday in June." Northumberland, 18 May 1704.

The weather proving unseasonable, no Court met. Westmoreland, 25 Nov 1708.

A stormy day, so that the Clerke did not appear with the Records the Court is continued till the next Court in Course. "Die Mercury Vicesimo quinto." 1701.

Bad weather......noe court. Northumberland, 17 Mch 1709.

"It being Very Wett and Rainy Weather there was noe Court." Northumberland, 19 Aug 1813.

The Court Did not Sitt in October by reason of the Queen's death. Westmoreland, 30 Sept 1714.

"By meanes of Wett weather the Court did not meet in Aug't." Westmoreland, 1724.

The marriage licenses on page one are from a volume marked "*Proceedings of the Office of the Register of Probats*," in the office of the Richmond County, Georgia Court. They are very probably copied and recorded in the Georgia Archives, or have been published. They may be of interest to those who have not ready access to Georgia material. The list is not complete after page twenty, the Editor not having time for further copying.

After this volume of proceedings the licenses are to be found in specific books of license records.

The Editor regretfully records the death, last October, of the Reverend Charles H. B. Turner, D.D., antiquarian, historian and gentleman of the old school.

Also the death of Judge Conrad, Archivist of Delaware; like Dr. Turner, a gentleman and a scholar, a man of many parts, the memory of whose personal acquaintance will always be treasured by this writer.

Mrs. A. V. D. PIERREPONT, of Petersburg, Va., is preparing for publication the "Collected Records of Buckingham county, Virginia." This work might very properly be called the *History of a County without a record.* The Clerk's office was burned in 1869.

The Editor is in a position to say that Mrs. Pierrepont has succeeded in getting together a most remarkable collection of authentic data concerning the people of this county. An unusual and valuable book.

VARIA

RIVERS BANKS. This is a name in Abbeville, S. C. About 1790. Vol. i-257.

SCARLET RED, son of John Red. Spartanburgh, S. C. 1825. B-58.

CENSUS OF BOATS ordered. Wmld, Va. 28 Jany 1701. 1698-1705, fo.141.

JOHN EYRES, Gent., not being satisfied in his conscience of the lawfulness of an oath, would not take one as Justice. N.n, Va. 30 Dec 1792. xvii-220.

JOHN FAVER, a natural born subject of the French King, is naturalized. Richmond cty, Va. 14 Nov 1711; vi-19.

Mr. WILLIAM BURTON, church warden, presented persons for not abiding in the church during the time ofcommon prayer and preaching. Acco, Va. 5 Aug 1712. xiv.-45

JNO SUTTON and JOHN COLE, two strangers from Maryland, producing no certificate or other writing, nor making any probable circumstance appeare that they are freeman, are taken into custody. Nthld, Va. Orders iv-808. 17 Sept 1712.

"ORDERED for the future that noe P'son or P'sons w'tsoever (the Justices excepted who are confined to keep theire Station) Shall Smoak any tob'o in theCourthouse during the time the Court are sitting." Nthld, Va. iii-628. 22 June 1693.

PERSONS appointed by the Court to examine the Surveyor's Books report that they "could not do it, the surveyor being out of the County and having been as we are informed ever since last fall." Ffx, Va. Orders 1783-1788, p. 224. 17 May 1786.

ANTHONY RDBINSON pet'ns agt John Lawrence for an allowance for his the sd Anthony's wife's schooling, being late named Mary Dermott..... the sd Lawrence being bound to teach or cause her to be taught to Read and hath not performed the same. Nthld, Va. 1699-1713, p. 423. 18 Dec. 1706.

LYDIA SMART having given a paper Condemning her former taking an husband out of the Unity of friends, *hoping to be more Circumspect for the future.* (Lydia appears to be then intending to marry Thomas Pryor.) Friends, Mtg' Minutes. Phila. 28th of 2d 1699.

NOTES FROM GEORGIA RECORDS

WILL of PETER MASSIE, of Elizabeth Town, Essex cty. N. J. Wife Sarah's mother, Hannah Williams, mentioned. Leaves money for the education of poor children in Glynn county, Georgia, Savannah and Elizabeth Town, N. J. Also the rest of his estate after legacies, to the American Board of Commissioners for Foreign Missionaries. 19 Mch, 1839-31 Aug 1840. Glynn cty, Ga. 1st will and appraisement record, marked "D." p. 375.

Will of REYMOND DEMERE, of St. Simon's Island, pltr. To son Reymond Demere, an annuity of $200. To three grand-daughters, children of my son Reymond, my plantation in McIntosh [county] called Martens Hill; also lots in Darien. Whereas......my negro man Joy and my negro woman Rose ...... not only saved and protected a great part of my property during the time the British occupied St. Simons, but actually buried and saved a large sum of specie ...... I direct my executors to petition the Legislature to prepare an act for their manumission ...... and their two children. and any other children said Rose may have ...... for their faithful conduct during a period of Invasion when nearly all the negroes on St. Simons deserted and Joined the British ...... Should the Legislature refuse, Joy and Rose are to be sent to some other State where they can be freed .... Leaves legacies to them, one for Rose's son John, who is to be paid $1,000 when 21, and taught reading, writing and arithmetic, and be brought up to some mechanical profession.

Grandsons Joseph Demere and Lewis, and friend Thomas Little, Benjamin F. Cater, and John Couper, Jr.,: trustees in behalf of Joy, Rose and their children, Grandsons Lewis Demere, John Demere, and Paul Demere mentioned. Son Reymond Demere, grandson Joseph Demere, and grandson Lewis Demere, to be executors as they come of age, with friend Thomas Spalding, John Couper, Sen'r, and James Hamilton Couper. 29 Aug 1828.

Wit: Wm. Brown, R. Couper. A codicil provides should Rose's son John be freed, leaves to him two negro boys, and leaves to Rose his negro woman, Sally. 29 Aug 1828. 5 Jany 1829. Glynn cty, Ga. Vol. D. p. 158.

NATHANIEL TRACY, of Newbury Port, Essex cty, Massachusetts, and wife Mary, to William Scarbraugh, of Charleston, S. C., Esq. Consideration £12,000, S. C. money; plantation now annexed to the State of Georgia, but at the time of the grant was a part of South Carolina; original grant 3,000 but by a careful resurvey found to contain 3,446 acres, granted to William Haney, 21 May 1763; lying southward of Altamaha river ...... 10 Mch 1787. Glynn city, Ga. (Lease and release.)

THEODORE HOPKINS, CHARLES HOPKINS, THOMAS HOPKINS, STEPHEN AUSTIN and wife HULDAH; ASHBELL WELLS and wife MAY [MARY?] of Connecticut; ELISHA BUCKINGHAM HOPKINS and wife SARAH; and PETER WALLACE GALLAUDETT and wife JANE, of Pennsylvania;

to

ROBERT WATTS, of Georgia; WHEREAS JASON HOPKINS died seized of the premises hereinafter mentioned......in trust nevertheless for the sole use of aforesaid SARAH HOPKINS, as her separate estate; NOW, consideration one dollar, convey all that tract called Cabbage Bluff on Turtle River, near Brunswick, Glynn country, containing 1100 acres of live oak and rich pine hummock land......in trust......for the benefit of said SARAH, Glynn cty, Ga. 8 Mch 1800.

JOHN BEDINGFIELL, late of Richmond cty, Ga. William Stith, Jr. attorney for Agnes Bacon, grandmother and next of kin to Mary

Bedingfiell, age about ten, and John Bedingfiell, age about eight, orphans of John...... Thomas Carr appointed guardian.

WILLIAM FOSTER takes the oath which entitles him to citizenship. Richmond cty, Ga. July 1796. Minutes of the Inferior Court. p. 120.

SPICER CHRISTOPHER makes oath that his brother Spencer Christopher was born in April, 1795. Camden cty, Ga. B-C, p. 28. 15 Nov 1796.

ALEXANDER YOUNG, petitions to be made a citizen. 28 Oct 1793. Camden cty, G. B-C, p. 350. James Finley testifies that Alexander Young, now of the State of Georgia, told the Deponent that he was one of the Company of men called Ferguson's Men, and that he, the said Alexander Young, said also that he was with the said Ferguson at Kings Mountain in the Battle there, and there fought......and that said Young said he was taken prisoner by the Americans and that he soon found an opportunity to make his escape. 19 Nov 1794. Camden cty, Ga. B-C. p. 350.

Young's application to be made a citizen seems to be in the form of a letter, to which he adds "N. B. My Compliments to Mrs. King and Mrs. Harris. Gen'l Jackson has been here & has given orders for Lieut. Hunter & Eighteen men to keep Coleraine. Capt. McGillis at the Burnt Fort with eighteen men. No other [Stations]"......[The connection is not at all clear. Editor.]

JAMES CASHEN, an alien, desires his name enrolled this 22 Mch 1788. Camden cty, Ga. A-B, p. 33.

ROBERT STAFFORD and THOMAS STAFFORD, also desire their names enrolled. 4 Aug 1788. A-B, p. 33.

Oaths of THOMAS STAFFORD, A. J.[?] and N. Wright, A. J.[?] to support the Constitution of the United States. 15 Sept 1789. Camden cty, Ga. A-B, p. 16.

SOME NOTES FROM THE ORDER BOOK OF FAIRFAX COUNTY, VIRGINIA, 1756 TO 1763.

(This Order Book is much damaged and until lately has not been accessible. It is now repaired but many leaves are lost or broken up in small pieces. It had 909 pages, or more.);

EDWARD WASHINGTON was the guardian of Sarah and Margaret Berry. Ct 20 Oct 1756. p. 37.

GEORGE MASON, Gent. To be paid for keeping Occoquan Ferry, 2,000 lbs. tobacco. Same court. p. 37.

NICHOLAS GRIMES; Catharine Grimes gets l. a. on his estate. Nicholas Grimes and John Hunter her security. Ct 18 Jany 1767. p. 44.

BARNABY CURRY; Ann Curry gets l. a. on his estate. Sanford Remy and Robert Sanford her security. Same court. p. 44.

WILLIAM SMITH; John Bishop gets l. a. on his estate. Same court. p. 44.

JOHN WILKIE; Isabella Wilkie gets l. a. his estate. David Davis and Samuel Moxley, security. Same court. p. 47.

ELIZABET BOLLING [BOELING?]; John B...gets l. a on her estate. She was admx of William B......dec'd. Gerard B......her security. Court 16 Mch 1757. p. 49.

STEPHEN LEWIS; Elizabeth Lewis gets l. a. on his estate; Charles Broadwater and John Dalton, sec. Court 16 Mch 1757. p. 49.

DENNIS McCARTY, will; presented by Sarah Johnston, the extx therein named and proved by witnesses. George Johnston and James Hamilton, security. Court 18 May 1757. p. 110.

GEORGE DENT; Elizabeth Dent gets l. a. on his estate. Grafton Kirk, John Rhodes and Jeremiah Hampton, security. Court 17 Aug 1757. p. 155.

SARAH NELSON; William Gladin gets l. a. on her estate. Gerrard Boling and William Ashford, security. Court 22 Feby 1758. p. 194.

JOHN ADAM LONG; Christian Long gets l. a. on his estate. William Gladin, security. 19 Sept 1758. p. 303.

GILBERT SIMPSON, a sawyer, is added to the list of tithables. Court of 21 Nov 1758 [Probably.] p. 313. [Pages torn out.]

FRANCIS TRIPLETT; will presented by Elizabeth Triplett, extr. Proved by witnesses. Same court. p. 313.

JOHN LUMNLEY; l. a. on his estate to John Carlyle, Gent. Same court. p. 313.

RICHARD KENT; his will presented by William Kent, extr. Proved by witnesses. Extr gets probate. Court 19 Sept 1759. p. 413.

JOHN SPENCE; Elizabeth Spence gets l. a. on his estate. Court 20 Nov 1759. p. 420.

THOMAS and BURR HARRISON ordered bound to BURR HARRISON to learn the trade of carpenter and joiner. Court 22 Nov 1759. p. 425.

DAVID CRAIG; John Craig gets l. a. on his estate. Court 19 Feby 1760. p. 435.

WILLIAM GUNNELL; will presented. [Record damaged.] p. 436. Same court.

WILLIAM NATION died intest. L. A. granted. [Record damaged.] Same court. p. 436.

ELIZABETH DULIN; William and Edward Dulin get certificate for l. a. on her estate. Court 21 Oct 1760. p. 524.

NATHANIEL CHAPMAN; Constant Chapman gets l. a. on his estate. Court 19 Nov 1760. p. 537.

JOHN FARGUSON; his will presented by Joshua Farguson, extr, proved and Joshua gets ctf for probate. Court Dec 1760. p. 549.

DISTINCTIVE COLONIAL FORENAMES

ABIGAIL PARKER LUFBARRY[?] was the daughter of George Parker. Acco., Va. 1708. xi-602. See Parker's will. v-184.

ANABELLA WHITE, dau. of Henry. Rappa. cty, Va. 14 Feby 1683.

ANNABELLA LEE, late wife of Francis Lee of London, abiding in Accomac, conveys to John Marshall, pltr, 1666 acres at Chingoteague, given her and her sisters, in 1672, by Daniel Jenafer. Acco., Va. 15 June 1691. ix-204. See alo x-32.

ANNABELLA HOPE was wife of George. Acco., Va. 1761. iii-142.

ANNABELLA MARSHALL, was wife of John Marshall. Acco., Va. 1734. xx-193.

ARMENTHA DILWORTH, wf of John. Camden cty, Ga. 23 Apr 1795. B & C, p.11.

ABIGAIL LYNN, relict of Simon, returns inventory. Wmld, Va. Fid. Accts. i-210. -27 Mch 1739.

ARABELLAH WATERS, wife of John. Rappa., Va. 5 Mch 1678. 1677-1682. p. 242.

ABYGAIL ABBINGTON, dau. of Lydia Lawrence. Wmld, Va. 8 Nov 1670. 1668-1677. fo. 101.

AVERILLA CURTIS, was wife of Maj. Thomas Curtis. York, Va. 1657. iii-130.

ARCADA HAZARD was extx of. John. Annap. Bal. Bk. About 1754, 1-93.

ARCADIA DUNNAHOW was dau. of William Turvill. Wor., Md. 27 Feby 1691. M. H. iii-30.

AVARILLA LYNCH; William Allendor her extr. Annap. Records. 1769. D. D. ii-319.

AVARILLA CURTIS was dau. of James, who also had a son Christopher and a grandson Christopher Dudley. Middx, Va. 15 Nov 1720. 1713-1734, p. 154.

ARRALANTA ROBINS, was dau. of John Purnell. Wor. cty, Md. 8 Jany 1755. J. W. ii-148. She was wife of John Robins. See 3 Dec 1765. J. W. iii-125.

BEHETHLEN STROTHER m. Armistead Hubbard. Culp. Va. 27 Dec 1792. M. L. B.

BEHETHALEM OVERALL in a suit with others. Pr. Wm, Va. 3 Oct 1761. Orders [4]-1.

Mrs. BRIDGETT SEVERN. N-n, Va. 1638. i-124. She m. Charlton before 28 Aug 1648. iii-151.

BRIDGETT JOHNSON. Acco., Va. 8 Mch 1721. xvi-143.

BRIDGETT FISHER. N-n, Va. 1698. xvii-523.

BRIDGET REGAN. St. Paul's Register, K. Geo. cty, Va. Died 22 June 1733.

BRIDGET DIXON, wife of Jonah. N-n, Va. Chancery record. Aug 1730.

BRIDGET MURFIE was wife of John. See his will. Wor. Md. 3 Sept 1687. M. H. iii-20.

BRIDGETT HENLY, dau. of Bryant and Sarah. Born 1723[?] St. Paul's psh register. K. Geo. cty, Va.

BRIDGET MORRICE, was widow of Elias. Wmld, Va. 29 Mch 1727. Fid. Accts. i-52.

BRIDGET REGAN, dau. of William and Bridget. Born 22 June 1733. St. Paul's psh register. K. Geo. cty, Va. [See above.]

BRIDGET PARRAMORE was wife of John. 9 Mch 1750 or 1751. N-n, Va. xix-83.

BRIDGETT RASBERRY, wife of John. Tyrrell cty, N. C. 20 Oct 1713. W-7.

BRIDGET EALE. Old Rappa., Va. 1677-1682, p. 218. 1678.

BRIDGET PRIDUM, was wife of Christopher. Old Rappa. Va. 24 Nov 1678. 1677-1682, p. 219.

BRIDGETT SATCHELL, was wife of John. See his will. N-n, Va. 1749. xxviiR-385.

BRIDGET SOUTHWELL, a wit to a will. Rappa. cty, Va. 12 Mch 1682.

BRIDGET HALL, wit. to will of Richard Hill. L. Norf., Va. About 1685. iv-436.

BRIDGETT MOSS, wife of Will: Moss. 20 Oct 1664. Rappa. cty, Va. 1677-1682, p. 323.

BRIDGET EYRE, wife of Littleton Eyre, Gent. Acco., Va. 14 Feby 1753. ii-412.

BRIDGET CROWSON, wife of William. Acco., Va. 30 Sept 1762. iii-209.

BRIDGET DIX, wife of Isaac, Sr. Acco., Va. 30 Aug 1748. ii-168. [She was dau. of William Savage.]

BRIDGET CLARK, wife of James. Acco., Va. 1722. xvi-259.

BRIDGET WALTHOM, dau. of Stephen. Acco., Va. 1728. xiv-321.

BRIDGET PARRAMORE, wife and admx of Richard. There was also a dau. Bridget. N-n, Va. 14 July, 1761. xxxR-154.

BRIDGET SMITH, wife of John, of Somerset cty, Md. Acco., Va. 1708. xi-461.

BRIDGET WEST, wife of Thomas, Sr. Sussex, Dela. 13 Jany 1775. L(11) 458.

INTERCOUNTY AND INTERCOLONY

JOHN ADAMS, President, and his successors; a deed conveys to him an island called Grovers Island, Camden cty, Ga. 19 Dec. 1799. E-58.

THOMAS BYRNE, of County Kilkenny, Ireland, was an heir of Edmund Byrne of Spotsylvania cty, Va. Spots. Va. Abstracts. 17 Aug 1744. A-397. [These are the abstracts made by Rev. Mr. Torrence some years ago.]

CLAUDE BOREL [BOUL?] of St. Mary's, Esq., to Robert Cadman and Richard Proctor, both of Philadelphia, mill-wrights. They agree to erect a tide saw-mill[?] Camden, Ga. 8 July 1779. D-203.

WILLIAM BURNET, Jr., of New Ark, N. J., physician. Mentioned in deeds. Camden cty, Ga. 1785. D-120.

DANIELL BEDDLE; inventory. "Due for his wages last att New England." N-n, Va. About 1 Feby 1640. i-50.

JOHN BOWDOIN; power to brother James in Boston, also to wife Susannah. N-n, Va. 29 Mch 1708. xviii-396.

PAUL CARRINGTON, of the Island of Barbadoes, Mcht; suit agt Richard Hawkins, marriner, master of the Sloope *Elizabeth*, of the sd Island. York, Va. 25 Oct 1703. xii-145.

MARY CORIDON [Condon?], relict and extx of William; will. Directs that negro wench Violet and son George be sent as soon as possible to Matilda McMahan, wife to Thomas McMahan, in Bridge Town, Barbadoes, by reason that sd Violet was "lent me when I left Barbadoes by my sister, mother to afsd Matilda." York, Va. 5 Dec 1753. xx-310.

SILVANUS CHURCH, of Philadelphia, mariner, to Francis Sterling, of Camden cty, Ga. Camden, Ga. June, 1805. G-405.

JAMES CASHEN, of the Island of Amelia, in the Spanish Provence of East Florida, pltr, to David McCredie, Esq., of Charleston, S. C. (conveyance of land.) Camden, Ga. 9 June 1806. G-65.

WILLIAM COOKE, gdn [and father] of the chn of William and Eliza Cooke, late of this State and county, at present of St. Augustine, in East Florida......leases to Mrs. Anne Cunningham [*femme sole*) part of the Belvidere Tract at Clerk's Bluff. [The marriage contract of William Cook and Eliza Barrington is dated 17 Nov 1791, and is recorded after the above.] Glynn cty, Ga. 5 Apr 1804.

JAMES CRAIKE, was a citizen of Maryland in 1778, and previous thereto, and until 1780, when he removed into Virginia. [Suit about a slave.] Pr. Wm. Va., 28 May 1797. Superior Court, p. 116.

DAME MARY DOLLIFFE, Relict of Sir James Dolliffe, late of London, Knt, deceased; and admx of all his rights, &c.,......power to Tho: Lee of Potomack River in Virginia, Gent. York, Va. 19 Aug 1717. xv-157.

SIMON DILLINGHAM of Philadelphia, mariner; power to Luiss[?] Levy, of St. Mary's, Mcht. Camden, Ga. 1799. D-157.

JOHN EVERTON of North Carolina, Chowan county, mariner, love, good will and affection towards Cousin Phebe Reeves of New York and Town of Stephentown, Westchester cty. Gives negroes. Canden, Ga. 25 Apr 1799. E-15.

WILLIAM EATON, of "Blessland" psh., New Kent, Va., conveys 59 acres in Bruton psh. York, Va. 24 Aug 1705. xiii-348.

ANNE MARGARITE FRERE, wife of Leonard Henry Mussault, late of St. Domingo, but at present residing in South Carolina, manumits her mulatto slave, Suzette. Sig. FRERE MUSSAULT. Camden, Ga. 28 Mch 1798. G-33.

BENJ. FORDHAM'S will proved in Philadelphia. Fordham was of Annapolis, Md. Admn to James Parrock of Philada. Annap. T. P. xxiii-221. 16 May 1718.

THOMAS KILPATRICK, of Alexandria town and county, Va., conveyed (8-9 June 1774) to James Murray of Dorchester cty, Md., a tract in Fairfax, Va. James Murray having since departed this life leaving William Littleton Murray his only son and heir-at-law, to whom sd tract descended, and who conveyed to William Murray Robertson of Dorchester cty, Md. Pr. Wm., Va. Court Oct 1805. L. C. [2] p. 98.

JAMES McGIRTH, late of East Florida, now of Camden cty, Ga., to grandson John Robert McGirth, son of Daniel and Susan McGirth. Conveyance. Camden, Ga. 19 Apr. 1802. E-334.

RICHARD MUDD, about to go to Washington cty, Kentucky, "the place of my permanent residence "...gives power to brother Walter Mudd. Montg. cty, Md. 27 Oct 1812. i-180.

WILLIAM PAUL, of Fredericksburg, Va., had a sister Mary Young, of Abigton, psh Kirthbeen, Stewarty of Galloway, North Britain. Spots, Abstracts. 1772. E-97.

ISAAC POLOCK, to Littleton Dennis Teackle, Esq. of Princess Anne, Md. Land on that part of St. Mary's river that intersects the supposed Indian Boundary line as established bet. the United States in behalf of the State of Georgia and the Creek Indians, under the direction of Joseph Ellicot and commonly known as Ellicot's line. Camden cty, Ga. 17 Sept 1806. G-142.

Major PEYTON'S heirs in Gloucester cty, Va., own tract that was surveyed 1688 for William Layton. Som. cty, Md. Rent Roll. 1663-1723.

SERVICE AND SUPPLIES COLONIAL, REVOLUTIONARY AND MILITIA

LEWIS MORGAN; allowed 20 sh. specie for a hog furnished the militia under command of Capt. Joseph Cloyd, in 1779. Montg. Va. Orders [1] p. 187. 26 Apr 1785.

JAMES MORTIMER, of Grayson cty; aged 76. Served in New York Artillery. Grayson cty, Va. Orders 22 Oct 1832.

JOHN McDIFFIT; serjeant in the "last war." 200 acres. Montg. cty, Va. Surveys. 23 May 1774.

REV. Mr. CHARLES MYN THRUSTON; Lieut. Virginia Reg't under Col. Byrd. 2,000 acres. Montg. cty, Va. Surveys. 25 Nov 1773.

PATRICK MAHER, sometimes called PATRICK MAHONEY, makes oath that he has been an applicant for pension for several years; that he is given to understand that his name is entered on the roll filed in the War Office as PATRICK MAHONEY, instead of MAHER, under which name he made his declaration. He was called MAHONEY in the service and served in Capt. David Lynn's Company, 3d Maryland Reg't, Col. Howard; then of the State of Maryland. Thomas Wyndham was the orderly serjeant. Ordered certified to the War Department. Rock'm cty, Va. Aug. 1832. Orders, p. 130.

JOHN MAXWELL, heir-at-law of John Maxwell, who died in the service; to be allowed 200 acres for service as a serjeant in the train of Artillery in America. Rock'm, Va. 2 May 1780. Orders.

THOMAS MOUNTAGUE; recommended for First Lieutenant.* Middx, Va. 23 Sept 1782. vi-3.

HARRISON MANLY, Gent. Commissioned Ensign. Ffx, Va. 16 Apr 1770. Orders iii-2.

ROBERT MURRAY, Jr. Recommended for 1st Lieutenant.* Middx, Va. 23 Sept 1782. vi-3.

Mr. ROBERT NOURSE; Lieutenant in His Majesty's Navy in the late war in America. 3,000 acres. "Natural affection to my brother James Nourse." Montg. cty, Va. Surveys. 1 Mch 1775.

RICH'D OMOHUNDRO, serjeant. 200 acres. Montg. cty, Va. Surveys. 3 Mch 1774.

GRIFFIN PEART; ensign in Virginia Reg't under Col. Washington. 2,000 acres. Montg. cty, Va. Surveys. 17 Dec 1773.

AUDLY PAUL; Lieutenant. 2,000 acres. Montg. cty, Va. Surveys. 29 Jany 1774.

THOMAS POLLY; commissioned Ensign. Montg. cty, Va. Orders. 10 Jany 1782.

GEORGE PEARIS produces certificate signed by Hinson Gardenor, county commissary, for having furnished two spies with provisions, in 1782, and also for having furnished bacon to the militia of this county. Montg. cty, Va. 26 Apr 1785. Orders [1] p. 187.

THOMAS PRICE, Esq., Captain "in ye" Penna. Reg't under Col. Mercer. 3,000 acres. Conveys to Samuel Hughes of Frederick county, ironmaster, and John Swan of Elizabeth Town, Fred'k cty, Mcht. Montg cty Surveys. 28 Feby 1774.

MOSES PARRISH, a soldier in the "last war." 50 acres. Montg. cty Va., Surveys. 17 May 1774.

JACOB PERSINGER, resident of Allegany cty, Va., Aged 84. Enlisted in the Army of the Revolution in 1775, with Capt. Matthew Arbuckle, and served as a corporal. Andrew Wallace was 1st Lieutenant; ...... Wood, 2d Lieutenant; John Galloway, 3d Lieutenant, and Samuel Walker, Ensign, Virginia State Line. Reg't commanded by Major Newell. Left the service in 1776. Resided in Botetout, now Allegany county, when he entered the service. Was stationed at Pt. Pleasant; was in no engagement with the enemy during this service. The fort at Pt. Pleasant was attacked by Indians but he was not present at the time. Signed JACOB PERSINGER, Sr. Alleg. cty, Va. 16 Apr 1833. Orders, p. 94.

* Presumably militia.

WILLIAM ROWLISON; makes declaration with affidavits of James McDowell, Adam Hickman and William Miller. Court declare opinion that applicant was a Revolutionary soldier. Rock'm cty, Va. Sept 1832. Orders, p. 147.

DANIEL ROBINETT; a Lieutenant in Capt. William Davis' Company. Montg. cty, Va. Orders. 10 Jany 1782.

JOHN RICHARDSON; a Revolutionary soldier, makes declaration with certificate of Absolem and Charles Dupler [?]. Court is of opinion he served as stated. Alleg. cty, Va. Mch 1834. Orders, p. 171.

JOHN RILEY is allowed fifty acres for serving as a soldier in the old Virginia Reg't commanded by Coll Byrd. Ordered certified. Rock'm, Va. 2 May 1780. Orders.

WILLIAM SMITH; declaration made before Jesse Davis a Justice of the Peace. Archibald and John S. Kinkhead made oath and subscribed to certificate. Court of opinion he was a Revolutionary soldier. Alleg. cty, Va. Nov 1833. Orders, p. 68.

TURNER SOUTHALL; Lieutenant Virginia Reg't under Col. Byrd. 2,000 acres. Montg. cty, Va. Surveys. 13 Dec 1773.

BURRELL SPENCE, Grayson cty, Va. Aged 69. Lived in Montgomery county when he enlisted. Grayson cty, Va. 24 Sept 1832. Grayson cty Orders.

The officers of the Militia in Lancaster county, Virginia, in 1656, were
Coll. M. FANTLEROY, Lt. Coll. TOBY SMYTH, Major THO: GOODRICHE, Capt. WM. UNDERWOOD, Gapt. FRAN. SLAUGHTER, Capt. RICHARD LOES.
Lanc. Va. i-315.

HENRY VASS, Jr., takes the oath as 2d Lieut. Militia. Middx. Va. xiii A—p. 4.

THOMAS ROANE, oath as Major of Militia. (Same record.)

THOMAS HEALY recommended for captain in the room of William Murray, Gent. who has resigned (p. 3, same record.)

ROBERT MURRAY, Jr. for 1st Lieut. (Same record.)

CHURCHILL BLAKEY recommended for Ensign. (Same record.)

NICHOLAS GENTRY; wages due him as a soldier at Mattapony Garrison. York cty, Va VI-260. 24 Nov. 1680.

Lieut. EPAPHRODITUS SIDNOR takes the usual oaths. Richmond cty, Va. XI-42. 15 Nov 1739.

Printed at the Industrial School for Crippled and Deformed Children, 241 St. Botolph St., Boston, Mass.

The

County Court Note-Book

A Little Bulletin of History and Genealogy

April, 1931 Vol. X, No. 2

VIRGINIA MARRIAGES

These marriages are inferred from the court record for which the reference is given. The name of the county is followed by the volume and page of record. The exact date of the marriage is rarely shown by these miscellaneous entries. From the date of the recorded paper, or from some statement in the body of the paper, it is shown that the marriage must have occurred before the date as given in each reference.

Mr. JAMES ADAMS and JANE CUNNINGHAM, dau. of James. 18 June 1772. Charlotte. [Reference wanting.]

THOMAS ADDAMS and ELLEN HORNER, late the wife of George HORNER, dec'd. Before 15 Apr 1651. L. Norfolk. B-172.

.... ABBOTT [of King and Queen] prob. m. SARAH STRINGER, dau. of Daniel. Before 29 Oct 1789. Middlesex. 1785-1789.

EDWARD ADCOCK and ELIZABETH SMITH, sister of Henry SMITH, and dau. of Mrs. Phebe SMITH. Before 30 June 1677. Rappa. 1677-1682.

ARNOLD ADDISON and JOYCE DELOTT [?] widow of James. Before 12 Sept 1736. Northampton. Chanc'y papers.

JOHN ADOLPH prob. m. .... WEBB, a widow. Before 23 May 1701. Northampton, vol. iv.

JOHN AIRES and ANNE SMITH, widow of Robert. Before 16 June 1663. [At that date AIRES was dec'd.] Northumberland. 1658-1666, fo. 100.

JOHN ALEXANDER and SUSANNA PEARSON, dau. of Simon. After 7 Dec 1731. Pr. William. Land Causes.

JOHN ALLDIN and FRANCES WILLIAMSON. Before 23 Apr 1726. Middlesex. 1713-1734. p. 274.

JOHN ALDIN and JANE ORRILL, dau. of Laurence. Before 6 Mch 1748. Middlesex. D-87. [She seems to have m. (2) .... Meacham, before the above date. See also D-51.]

ROBERT ALLEN and SARAH GIVENS, widow [of Samuel ?] Before [?] May, 1756. Augusta Chronicles. i-316.

AR: ALLEN and CATHERINE BAKER, dau. of Laurence. Before 18 Mch 1681. Surry. i (2)-290.

JOHN ALLEN and a dau. of BENJ. WOODSON. Before [or about ?] 1762. Cumberland. iii-316.

.........ALEXANDER and SUSANNA PEARSON, dau. of Simon. Before 8 Oct 1773. Fairfax, 00-360.

[THOMAS ?] ALLISON and MARGARET SIMMONS, dau. of Lawrence. Before 1698. Westmoreland. Crozier Wills, pp. 11, 13.

ISAAC ALLERTON and the Relict and Admx of Maj. Geo. COLCLOUGH. Before 20 June 1663. Northumberland. 1658-1666, f. 101.

GEORGE ALVIS and the relict of Maj. Wm. HARRIS. Before Apr 1682. Henrico. ii-139.

Mr. HENRY ANDERSON and PRUDENCE STRATTON, dau. Mr. Edward STRATTON. Before or about 20 Aug 1706. Henrico. 1677-1737, p. 47.

ISAAC ANDERSON and SARAH GIBSON. Before 17 June 1794. Washington.

PATRICK ANGUS and MARY PORTER, widow of.........PORTER [Minister of Lynnhaven Parish.] Before 17 June 1684. L. Norfolk. iv..........(from Mr. Richmond's collection of data.)

JOHN APPLEWHAITE and ANNE MARSHALL, dau. of Humphrey. Before 18 Dec 1711. Isle of Wight. ii-533.

WILLIAM ARCHER and the relict and admx of William DUKE. Before 25 Jany 1678. Surry. i (2)-238.

ROGER ARCHER and MARY x CLAY, relict of Mr. John CLAY, Sr., of I. W. Before or about 31 May 1678. Surry. i (2)-241.

GEORGE ARCHER and.........HARRIS, sister of William. 1 June 1689. Henrico. ii-303.

JOHN ARNOLD and PATTY LEE, dau. of John. Before 1 Sept 1818. Campbell. v-131.

[HENRY] ARSKINS and JEAN THOMPSON, dau. of Joseph of [Cecil County, Maryland.] Before 27 Nov 1782. Henry. iii-275.

HENRY ASCOUGH and JOANE HUGHSON, widow of Robert. Before 20 Aug 1681. Henrico. 1677-1739-p. 7.

JOHN ASHWORTH and the Relict of Rich: SELBY. Before 16 Aug 1671. L. Norfolk. E-68.

WILLIAM ATKINSON and ELIZABETH PARKER, dau. of Richard. About or before 7 Jany 1716. Henrico i-89. (p. 143, W. and D. 1714.)

JOHN BOWEN, of Worcester County, Md. and SARAH FOOKS, dau. of Daniel. Accomack. Oct 1761. D iii-162.

PETER BOWDOIN and SUSANNA PREESON, dau. of Thomas and Elizabeth. Before 12 June 1733, and after 8 Sept 1732. Northampton. Land Causes 1754-1771, p. 47.

Maj. THOS. BOWLER and TABITHA EDLOE, sister of John. [County?] Cal. Va. State Papers. About 1670. i-4.

HENRY BOGGESS and JANE COX, posthumous dau. of Vincent COX. Before 27 May 1740. Westmoreland, Fid. Accts. i-233.

WILLIAM BRADLEY and HESTER BRIDGEWATER. relict of Thomas BRIDGEWATER Before 5 Oct 1725. Henrico. 1677-1737, p. 54.

NATHANIEL BRADFORD, Jr. and ALICE SMITH, dau. of Richard. (Bond of Nathaniel Bradford, Sr., to give to his son "my heire and the heire of the abovesd Smith 800 acres in consideration of the above marriage.") 18 Oct 1664. Accomack. i-77. See also deed 2 Mch 1724. xvi-231. See also ix-57.

NATHANIEL BRADFORD, of Accomack, and JONE FRANKLING, of Northumberland, sister of Henry. See deed 16 July 1713, from John Bradford the son. Northumberland. 1710-1713, p. 327. [Record damaged.] See also C. C. N-B. for June, 1923. See also Northumberland. 1710-1713, p. 335.

THOMAS BRANCH and ELIZA: ARCHER, dau. of George. Before 20 Oct 1681. Henrico. 1677-1737, p. 23.

CHARLES BRADSHAW prob. m. JEMIMA HENDRAKE, dau. of Adolfis [*sic*]. Before 23 Apr 1759. Cumberland. Orders.

GEORGE BRANCH, Jr., and a dau. of William CORKER. Before 5 Nov 1678. Sussex. i (2)-193.

WALTER BREWSE [?] and the widow of Thomas SAWYER. Before 15 Aug 1662. Lower Norfolk. D-350. See D-351. This name may be SAYER, it is probable that it is. See also D-307. Also D-438.

Mr. WALTER BRUER and the relict of Mr. THO: SAYRE. Before 18 June 1661. L. Norfolk. D-307.

.........BREWER and ABIGAIL WYCHE, dau. of Henry. Before 1735 [?] Brunswick. i-256.

[Rev. JOHN] BRUNSKILL, Jr., "Clerk," and E[dwina?] HUMSTON. Marriage contract, proved by witnesses. Mch 1756. Prince William. Orders [3] p. 50.

ROGER BRIANT and a dau. of Richard BOWLING. Before 16 Feb 1673-4. L. Norfolk. E-104.

ROB'T BRICE of Southton, mariner, and JUDITH HIX, widow of Stephen. Before 21 Dec 1652. L. Norfolk. C-30. [From a record 27 Dec 1651, A-203, JUDITH HICKES appears to have been the widow of *Michael.* See also B-202. Before 14 July 1650.]

BENJAMIN BRIDGES and SYBEL FARROW adm of Abraham. Before or about 4 Apr 1788. Prince William. G-343.

THOMAS BRIDGE, Gent., and the relict and admx of Mathewe PHILLIPE, dec'd. Before 30 Oct 1651. Lower Norfolk. B-188.* See also C-36. [See C. C. N-B. July, 1922.]

THO: BRIDGES [?] and [HESTER] BATEMAN, widow of George. Before 17 Dec 1660. Lower Norfolk. D-271.* See also record of 16 Jany 1660. [She was also the relict of John HOLMES.]

Mr. THOMAS BRIDGER [?] and HESTER HOLMES [widow; admx of John HOLMES.] Before 15 June 1664. Lower Norfolk. D-403.* Before 15 Aug 1663. D-376. [See earlier C. C. N-B. issues for previous notes of these marriages.*]

FRANCIS BRANSTON seems to have married .... DOLBY. Before 1708-9. Northampton. xix-66.

JOHN BRAWNER and MARY DAVIS, widow of Edward. Before 20 Sept 1770. Fairfax. Orders [3]-93.

ROBERT BROOKS and ELIZABETH HAYS, dau. of James. Before 6 Dec 1812. Albermarle. i-29.

THOMAS BROOKE, of St. Mary's, Md., and SARAH MASON, dau. of George. Before or about 1715. Fairfax. Land Causes.

RICHARD BRUCE and the widow of David THOMPSON. Before Aug 1771. See Alb. ii-272.

RICHARD BROWN and ANN x WARDER, widow of William. Before 2 Nov 1660. Northumberland. 1658-66, fo. 48.

JAMES BROWNE and the extx and relict of Capt. Tho: BROWNE. Before or about 15 Feby 1670-71. Lower Norfolk. E-60.

THOMAS BRERETON of Little Wickocomico, Mcht, and JANE CLAIBORNE, dau. of Coll. Wm. CLAIBORNE. Before 20 May 1671. Northumberland. 1666-1672, fo. 101.

JOHN BROCK and FRANCES ROBINSON, dau. Henry. Before 17 Oct 1671. Lower Norfolk. E-72.

HUGH H. BRACKENRIDGE, a preacher in Washington's Army, and SABINA WOLF. [County? Date?] Draper Mss. 11 CC-28 &c.

WILLIAM BRAWNER and JANE HUTCHISON. Before 11 May 1801. Loudoun. F-251.

Col. CARTER BURWELL and LUCY GRYMES, dau. of John. Before 4 Oct 1748. Middlesex. D-31.

ABRAHAM BURTON and ANNE FEATHERSTONE. About or before 1691. Henrico. 1677-1682, p. 405.

JAMES BURTON and NULLY [NUTTY?] GEST, dau. of George. Before 15 Apr 1749. Middlesex. D-155.

WILLIAM BURTON and ELIZABETH HARWOOD, extx [widow] of Thomas. Before Apr 1723. Henrico. Orders, p. 247.

WILLIAM BURTON and MARTHA FOLIO, widow of Thomas, before 11 Mch 1690. Stafford. i-125.

THOMAS BUTTEN and JANE JELLIOTT, [widow of John. She afterwards m. Watts.] See record 24 Jany 1671. Rappahannock. 1664-1673. p. 525.

THOMAS BUTTON and JANE GILLETT, widow of John. Before 10 Apr 1666. Rappahannock. ii-p. 23. [This is evidently the same as the previous marriage.]

WILLIAM BURGES, of Providence, Maryland, and ELIZABETH ROBINS, dau. of Mr. Edward ROBINS, Mcht, of Northampton. Before 25 Aug 1757. Northampton. vii-71.

PETER BUTLER and a dau. of George ROBERSON [ROBINSON.] Before 11 Jany 1739. Northampton. Chanc'y papers.

.... BURNS and MARGARET WRIGHT, widow of Arthur, Sen'r, who formerly lived in Dorset county, Maryland. Before 9 Oct 1728. Lancaster. xi-354.

BENJ. BULLINGTON and ELIZABETH KNIBB, widow of Samuel. Before 6 Oct 1718. Henrico. Misc. ii-383.

JOHN BUTLER [Chas. City county?] and MARY WALLAS, youngest dau. of Mr. James WALLAS. Before 24 Oct 1701. State Land Records ix-388.

Capt. JOHN BUCHANAN and MARTHA BUCHANAN, sister of Col. John BUCHANAN. Tazewell. See Hist'y Tazewell county, &c., p. 169. [This note not verified.]

RICHARD BUSH and ELIZABETH BIBEY, dau. of John. Before 2 Mch 1677. Rappahannock. 1677-1682. p. 163.

PAUL BUNTING and MARGARET OWENS. 5 Jany 1801. Norfolk, M. L. B.

WILLIAM TANEY BURRUS, of Orange county, and MARTHA SLAUGHTER. Before 24 Apr 1800. King William. "2" -25. [This name should perhaps be WILLIAM TANDY BURRUS.]

GEORGE BUTLER and ANN MACDANIELL, dau. of John. About or before 1754-55. Lunenburg, vol. iv.

LEVIN BUTLER and ALICE HOLMES. Before 15 Apr 1659. Lower Norfolk. D-204.

SIMON BUTT and NANCY BRESSIE, widow of Thomas. About 1804. Norfolk. Chanc'y records.

THOMAS BUTTERIS: MARY JOHNSON said to have been his wife "before God." Northampton. 28 July 1754. v-74. [The date is the date of the record.]

JOHN BURKETT and ANNA MILLS, sister of Peter. Before or about 30 June 1679. Rappahannock. 1677-1682, p. 231.

ABRAHAM BYRAM and .... CLAYE, widow. Before 20 June 1668. Northumberland. 1666-1672, p. 48.

Rev. JOHN CRAIG and MARY DONALDSON, dau. of Patrick. (She was born 20 May 1770. [Virginia?] Draper Mss. 1200-145 and 232. [See also p. 234. Patrick DONALDSON was killed in 1781.]

.... CABELL and ELIZABETH BURKS, dau. of Samuel. Albemarle. Before 6 Oct 1755. ii-23.

WALTER CALLOWHILL and the widow of Thomas HARDING. Before 17 Aug 1668. L. Norfolk. E-25.

MAXMILIAN CALVERT and Mrs. MARY SAVAGE. 28 July 1744. Norfolk. M. L. B. [From Misc. papers.] See also bonds.

NICHOLAS CAMPBELL and ANN PIGOT Before 1773 [1782?] Northampton. Chanc'y papers.

HENRY CAPS; intended marriage with the widow of James HAWKINGS. 14 Nov 1679. Norfolk. iv-69.

WILLIAM CAPP and FRANCES x [COX]. Before 26 June 1697. Princess Anne. i-144.

THOMAS CARDWELL and MARTHA PERRIN. Before 1 Apr 1717. Henrico. 1714-1718.

JOHN CARRAWAY and the relict of Roger WILLIAMSON. Before 15 Feby 1648. L. Norfolk. B-106. [It is uncertain whether this name was WILLIAMSON or WILLIAMS, and the date of the marriage is also given as about 15 Apr 1642. This date is also doubtful. See C-6.]

JOHN CARTER, Esq., and JANE GLYNN, dau. of Mr. Morgan Glynn. He also married ANN CARTER, dau. of Mr. Cleave CARTER, and SARAH LUDLOW, dau. of Mr. Gabriel LUDLOW. CARTER d. 10 June 1669. See Va. Colonial Churches, p. 234. (Churchyard inscriptions.)

CHARLES CARTER and MARY WALKER, dau. of Joseph WALKER, Esq. Before 10 Sept 1762. King George i-169.

JOB CARTER and "MILLIANT" TILLETT, widow of John. After 1733 and before 1749 [when she died.] Prince William. Orders [1] p. 184.

JOSIAH CARTER and MARY FURLONG, widow of Robert. Cumberland. 29 May 1796. Gdn's Accts, p. 172.

JOHN CARTER, Spotsylvania county, and SARAH KENYON, dau. of Abraham. Marriage settlement. 15 Feby 1741. King George ii-450.

LUCAS CARVERETTA [?] and the relict of Edward CANNON. Before 15 June 1664. Lower Norfolk. D-404.

PETER CARTWRIGHT and [probably] JEANE PATCH, widow. Before 15 Sept 1697 [about which time she died.] Norfolk. vi-103.

JOHN CATLETT and ELIZA: SLAUGHTER, relict of Capt. Francis SLAUGHTER. Before 5 Jany 1663. Rappahannock, 1656-1664, p. 326.

JOHN x CHAMPION and DIANA BARNES. Marriage contract, 4 Oct 1683. Isle of Wight. ii-235.

JOHN CHAMPION and JANE DUPRIEST. 15 Sept 1791. Goochland. xvi-34.

THOMAS CHETHAM, Jr. and the widow of Benjamin BRANCH, dec'd. Before 20 Aug 1711. Henrico. 1677-1737, p. 52.

THOMAS CHELEY probably m. .... RICKARDS, a widow. Before 23 Aug 1654. L. Norfolk. C-122. [One Thomas Cheley was 65 years old in 1653.]

MATHIAS CHETWOOD and MARY KEY, dau. and heir of Richard. Before 15 Feby 1725. Nocthumberland. 1718-1726, fo. 418.

RICHARD CHURCH and MARY SAWYER, dau. of Francis. Before 15 June 1666. L. Norfolk. E-3. [Another note makes her dau. of *Thomas*.]

WILLIAM CHURCHILL and ELIZABETH WORMELEY, widow of Ralph WORMELEY, Esq. Before 9 Nov. 1716. Middlesex. 1713-1734, p. 44.

WILLIAM CHURCHILL, of Middlesex, son of Armistead and BETTY CARTER, eldest dau. of Charles CARTER. Pre-nuptial settlement. 26 Apr 1751. King George. iii-413.

JOHN CLAY, of Hanover county, Va., and ELIZABETH HUDSON, dau. of George, of Hanover. Before 30 Nov 1770. See Durrett Mss. Univ. Chicago. Will of Geo. Hudson.

HENRY CLARKE and JANE HODWORTH. About or before 1 Jany 1677. Surry. i-186.

ROBERT CLARK and ELIZABETH RICE, widow of William. Before 6 Dec 1734 and after 26 Feby 1733. Westmoreland, Crozier, vol. vi, p. 20.

JOHN CLEERE and the widow of Jeremiah ROBINSON. Before 30 June 1673. Northampton. x-190.

WILLIAM CLEMENT and ELIZABETH EARLE, widow of John. Before 24 Apr 1662. Northumberland. 1658-1666, fo. 75 .

WILLIAM COFIELD of "Nansemun," and ELIZA: SHEPPARD. 5 Jany 1694-5. Elizabeth City. Mar. Li.

THOMAS CORKE [COCKE] and ELIZABETH MASON, dau. of Lemuel, Sr. Before June 1695. Norfolk, vi---

.... COLLINS and ANNE PRICE, dau. of Walter. Before 11 Jany 1680. Northampton. xiii-262.

SAMUEL COLLINS and POLLY HUGHES, dau. of Moses. Before 3 Jan. 1823. Amherst. C-174.

WILLIAM COLE and ANN GANTLETT, dau. of William, dec'd. Before 20 June 1699. Essex. 1695-1699, p. 158. [It is not clear from the record whether WILLIAM or his father JOHN m. ANN.]

HAWES COLEMAN and ANN OVERTON. Long before 26 Mch 1835. Amherst. F-137. [She was deceased at that date. Her will in Louisa was probated 25 Jany 1844.]

THO: COLLEY and SARAH ROPIER [RAPIER?] who came to Virginia about 1662. Before 20 Jany 1664. Northumberland. 1658-1666, fo. 149.

JACOB COLSON and .... DAVIS, dau. of John. Before Jany 1692. Henrico. 1677-1692, p. 463.

RICHARD CONQUEST and MARY SIBSEY, only dau. of Capt. John, dec'd. About 20 Apr 1653. L. Norfolk. C-47. See also D-284.

THOMAS CONNALY and MARTHA ADDISON, widow of John. Before 20 Nov. 1737. Northampton. Chanc'y papers.

LOUGHLY CONALIN and SARAH MOOR, widow of James. Bet. 1697 and 21 May 1707. Northumberland. 1706-1720, p. 148.

GEORGE CONWAY and ANN HEATH, dau. of Samuel. Before 8 Apr 1745. Northumberland. 1743-1749, fo. 66.

Mr. PETER CONWAY and a dau. of Richard LEE. Before 11 Aug 1740. Northumberland. 1738-1743, fo. 94.

JOHN CORNELIUS and the relict of HENDRICKE LIGHTHART. Before 15 Dec 1651. L. Norfolk. B-206.

JOHN CORBETT and the widow of Richard SMITH. Before 15 Feby 1668. L. Norfolk. E-31.

JAMES COTES and ELINOR WROE, dau. of John. Before 14 June 1783. Richmond. vii-428.

JOHN COTRELL and LUCRETIA NEALE, sister of Ebenezer and dau. of Daniel and Elizabeth. Before 16 Jany 1711. Northumberland. 1710-1713, p. 133.

JOHN COUNTS and ELIZABETH HARMANTROUT, widow of John. About 1753 or 1754. Augusta Chronicles. i–231.

ANDREW COURSES [?] a Spaniard, and HENDRICK HENDRICKSON [*sic*] set up their names as intending marriage, at the Court House door. 30 June 1660. L. Norfolk. D-260.

WILLIAM COWDREY and MARY SAVAGE, widow. (She was mother of Thomas SAVAGE.) 28 Feby 1689. Northampton. xvii–22.

WILLIAM COWDREY and MARY ROBINS, dau. of Col. Obedience and Grace ROBINS. Before 2 Mch 1683. Northampton. xiii-285.

Capt. EDMUND CRASK and ELIZABETH MOSS, widow of Thomas. Before 20 July 1683. Rappahannock. 1677-p. 12. See also p. 20. (She desired to be interred with her husbands.)

JOHN CRASKE and ELIZABETH MOSS, dau. of William. About 7 Dec. 1693 [?] Richmond. Deeds ii-2. (She was the youngest dau. of William MOSS, Sr. See Richmond Orders.)

MATTHEW CRASK, and a dau. of Robert CHOWNING, Before 5 June 1710. Middlesex. iv-225.

EDMUND CRICKMAN and JANE WOOD, whom he transported. About 12 Oct 1663, L. Norfolk. D. 383.

.........CROZIER and ANN PEARE, widow of Henry. About 16 Dec. 1673. Norfolk E-102.

ALEXANDER CUMMINS, of Stafford county, and SARAH MUTTON, coheir of John MUTTON, dec'd of Northumberland county. Before 4 Dec 1711. Northumberland. 1710-1713, p. 117.

HENRY CUSTIS and BETTY DOWNING. Before Feby 1765. Northampton.

JOHN DABNEY and PEGGY SMITH, dau. of Charles. Before 6 Sept 1773. Charlotte. Gdns' Accts, p. 1.

FRANCIS DADE and FRANCES TOWNSHEND, dau. of Robert. Before 10 Sept 1690. Stafford. i-98.

DAVID DALBY and SARAH (BANKS?) dau. [?] sister [?] of Thomas. Before14 Aug 1722. Northampton. Chanc'y papers.

ALEXANDER SPOTSWOOD DANDRIDGE (b. 1 Aug 1753, d. 1785) Hanover county, m. about 1780, ANN STEPHENS, only dau. of Gen'l Adam STEPHENS. Draper Mss. 8ZZ-77.

N. W. DANDRIDGE and DOROTHEA SPOTSWOOD, youngest dau. of Alex. SPOTSWOOD. [County?] Draper Mss. 8ZZ-38. [The date 18 June 1747 is given. It is not clear whether this is the date of the marriage or of the letter which gives this information.]

AUGUSTUS DARRELL and SARAH, extx of Dennis McCARTY. Before 19 May 1773. Fairfax. Orders 1772-1774, p. 211. Before 22 Nov 1770. See Orders [1].

BENJAMIN DARST or DURST and SALLEY PAYNE, 1 June 1796. Louisa. I-209.

THOMAS DAVENPORT and PERMELIA DAVENPORT, dau. of Dr. Henry DAVENPORT of Buckingham county. 28 Apr 1799. Washington. Mar. return.

JOHN DEVENPORT and NANCY BURNETT. 13 Mch 1796. Patrick. Mar. return.

BENJ. DAVENPORT and MARGARET S. CRAMER. 22 Feby 1807. Frederick. Mar. return.

THOMAS DAY, of Rappahannock, planter, and DOROTHY HUDSON. Marriage contract. About 1673 [?] Rappahannock, 1671-1676, p. 348.

ARTHUR DENWOOD and ESTHER ROBINS, dau. of John ROBINS, Sr. Before 1707. Northampton. xix-23.

SAM'LL DOWING and ELIZABETH SANDERS, dau. of Mr. Ebenezer SANDERS. Before 19 July 1710. Northumberland. 1710-1713, p. 55.

.... DIXON and EASTER PHILLIPS, dau. of James, of N. C. county, Delaware. Before 1771. Loudoun. L-73.

JACOB DIMIT and CATHERINE WILSON, dau. John. Before 7 Aug 1823. Ohio county [now West Virginia]. ii-249.

JOHN DONELSON and MARY PURNELL. 17 Aug 1779. Pittsylvania. Crozier, vol. ix. M. L. B.

WILLIAM DOULBY and ELIZA: LUCAS, extx of Charles. Before 14 Feby 1722. Northampton. Chanc'y papers.

WILLIAM DONALDSON and ANNE MASON [widow?] Before 17 July 1799. Fairfax. Orders [8]-149.

ADAM DOLLARD and the relict of John SOUSEY [?] Before 15 Nov 1665. L. Norfolk. D-431. [This name may be DOLLAR and the name SOUSEY appears to be spelled elsewhere "SOWSEY." See E-10.]

ADAM DOLLARD and EVE [?] SENSEY, relict of John. Before 15 Nov 1665. L. Norfolk. D-432. [This is the same marriage as the preceding.]

GREENBERRY DORSEY and CATHERINE GRIMES, admx of William. About 1768. Fairfax. [C] 23.

FRANCIS DOWNER and KATHERINE HOPKINS, widow of Robert. About [?] 6 Mch 1677. Rappahannock county. 1677-1682. p. 162. She had also been the wife of George SMITH. See p. 370 same vol.

JOHN DRAKE and MARY BROWNE, dau. of Samuel. Before 17 Oct 1739. Isle of Wight. viiiW-274.

ELIAS DUNTON and ABIGAIL STEAL. Before 11 Nov 1735. Northampton. Chanc'y papers. Her name is also given as STEEL, dau. of Francis. 9 Mch 1735. Same papers.

DAN x DUNWAY, probably m. JANE WALL, widow of John. Before 17 May 1711. Northumberland. 1710-1713. p. 48. See Orders iv. 803, where the name is given as DUNAWAY.

ROBERT DUDLEY and ELIZABETH [WHITE, dau. of Solomon.] Before 3 Mch 1728-1729. Princess Anne. ii-232.

JOHN DUKE and REJOICE DAVIS, dau. of John. Before 25 Sept 1751. Brunswick. iii-40.

WILLIAM DUCKWORTH, Burlington county, N. J., and MARY WRIGHT, same. 6 Dec 1731. See Frederick Land Records, p. 5. Copy of marriage license.

WILLIAM DUNN and LIDDY MUC[S]GROVE. 7 Oct 1788. Washington. Mar. return.

.... EATON and DEBORAH ALLENSON, widow of William. Before or about 10 Dec 1664. Northumberland. 1658-66, fo. 144.

JOHN EASLY and .... BENSKIN, dau. of Jeremiah. Before or about 20 Aug 1711. Henrico. 1677-1737, p. 53.

(Continued on p. 19)

The County Court Note-Book

An every-other monthly devoted mainly to abstracts from County Court Records, prior to 1800.

MILNOR LJUNGSTEDT. Editor and Publisher. Bethesda, Rural Route 5, Maryland.

Published six times a year. Subscriptions must begin with the year.

April, 1931 **Whole**
Vol. X, No. 2 **No. 57**

The Editor is sad and sorry over the delay in getting out the NOTE-BOOK. She finds it is as difficult to explain to herself why she has permitted herself to backslide in this way, as she does to those friendly readers who missed the NOTE-BOOK (and there are a few of them). Something happened to the Editor's will power ....the Editor doesn't know what.........but it seems to have evaporated for a space, along with surplus incomes, and to have become an intangible asset. No doubt any modern psycho-analyzer could have explained the matter, but the Editor cannot, with her heredity, humble herself sufficiently to be put on a sort of scientific (?) pin and be allowed to squirm. No......... it is like asking people into your bedroom.

Meanwhile the Editor believes that if her readers knew the very severe strain of at least twelve months of the last eighteen, much of it the result of the illness of a beloved member of the family, some of it the shadow of "economy," and some of it just plain red or yellow or blue or pink sun rays.........and too much of them, a few of them would try to excuse her......... even if somehow she can't excuse herself.

The present issue of the NOTE-BOOK, in order to hasten publication, contains nothing but "inferred Marriages." There are a lot of them, and the Editor thinks 98 percent are reliable. For the other two percent. she has supplied sufficient doubt to make them harmless. Not all the items are set forth exactly as they should be, a few references are lacking. It would take considerable time to look them up. If any reader would like to know more about this or that pair of pioneers, the Editor will be glad to make further search of her notes.

The next issue of the NOTE-BOOK, which will follow as soon as possible, will take up another subject.

I regretfully chronicle the death of a valued worker in colonial records, and a personal friend. Mr. STRATTON NOTTINGHAM died last winter. He was a comparatively young man and what he had done in the few short years he devoted to historical and genealogical research gives one to know the amount of invaluable work he would have done in later years.

I do not know any one *more* capable, and few, very few with Mr. NOTTINGHAM'S ability in this kind of research. He loved the work; he had a background of reading and education which is peculiarly lacking among many; he had patience and conscience. He had to satisfy himself before he satisfied a client. And he knew those old records as we knew our first primer in the days when we had primers. I would like to add that I think he had imagination...... but some would misunderstand that.

Mr. NOTTINGHAM'S last publication, The WILLS and ADMINISTRATIONS of ACCOMACK COUNTY, is a remakable compilation. Accomack is a small county, and with Northampton, off by itself, but many people came from that peninsula, and these are the records of their ancestry.

It is with hesitation and a real dislike that the Editor, having actual knowledge of the necessity of the warning, calls attention to the very general liability to error in the *copies* of records now in use in some Virginia courts...... that is to say, in the offices of the Clerks attached to these courts. Some of these copies are themselves very old. These are those copied by hand. Not every copyist was as frank as the Clerk of the Maryland Prerogative Court who wrote "*next subscriber being in Dutch is posponed.*" Probably it was only in Pennsylvania and Maryland, and New York (?), and a county or two in Virginia that the German script was a source of bewilderment.

The particular copied volumes that the Editor has in mind are, first, those type-written books in the office of the Clerk of the Court, Princess Anne county, Virginia. These contain unfortunate errors, and the originals should be asked for. In this case it is especially disagreeable to offer criticism, for the acting Clerk for years is a gentleman who takes a real interest in the old Court material, and has made a sincere effort to preserve the ancient records.

Few, indeed, are the readers who possess the marked ability of Mr. Nottingham to read with unquestioned accuracy the script of the seventeenth century.

Another person, whose name is used without her permission, another person who has what seems to be a natural gift for deciphering the quirks and quirls and abbreviations of the early colonial period, is Mrs. Nugent of the Virgiaia State Land Office. Her work, with which the Editor is personally familiar, is truly remarkable. No other Clerk in charge of these records has been able to so readily read such pages as those of "Old Volume Five."

In addition to the proceedings of the courts, there are many copied volumes of marriage license bonds here and there which should be subjected to close scrutiny by specialists. Your copyist may be a graduate of a dozen schools and yet not have the particular gift for this sort of thing. Attention might be called to the learned gentleman who some years ago mixed up things most badly by reading an "8" into an "0", or an "1" into a "7."

There is one rule which amateurs would do well to master.........and that is that the scribe knew exactly what he was doing, what he meant to write, and that what he wrote can be accurately read *only one way*. The editor has heard of two cases, both rather amusing, in which the lady searcher in each case insisted on a variant initial, or name, and in each case demanded (if recollection does not fail) a certified copy embodying the searcher's change of the reading.

The Editor has but now made acquaintance with a valuable and interesting addition to genealogical publications. It is the AMERICAN GENEALOGIST. Published and edited by Mr. Donald Lines Jacobus, of New Haven. This magazine succeeds the NEW HAVEN GENEALOGICAL MAGAZINE, of which there are already eight volumes. The AMERICAN GENEALOGIST is a fine piece of work, containing much source material and most valuable corrections of heretofore accepted genealogical errors. The printing and style are unusally good. The fine margins and clear type are delightful.........also the arrangement, spacing, and balancing of headings. The lack of "style" is so evident in many publications of this class ....the compilers not knowing the beauty of proportion, or believing it one of the unnecessary things.

CONTINUED articles COUNTY COURT NOTE-BOOK, and the dates on which they first appeared.

MARRIAGES BY INFERENCE. Began with May, 1922.

MARYLAND'S NEXT OF KIN. Began with July, 1922.

VIRGINIA COLONISTS. This alphabetized list began with July, 1924.

MARYLAND NATURALIZATIONS. Began with February, 1923.

KING GEORGE PROBATES, &c. Began with July, 1924.

The LIST OF BANISHED QUAKERS. Began with November, 1924.

MILITARY NOTES, both COLONIAL and REVOLUTIONARY, and some later MILITIA NOTES, will appear in every issue, if possible.

SHIPS IN PORT, NEW ENGLANDERS AND OTHERS, INTERCOUNTY and INTERCOLONIAL, and COLONIAL FORENAMES, will appear in alternate issues or as space can be found for them.

EASTERN SHORE FAMILIES, in the form of a one-page supplement, began with June, 1925.

Eight volumes of the COUNTY COURT NOTE-BOOK, bound or unbound, at a special price. Address the Editor.

(*Continued from p. 17*)

THOMAS EAST and ANN PERRIN. Before 1 Apr 1717. Henrico. 1714-1718.

CORNELIUS EDMUNDS and ANN BIRKET, dau. of John. Before 1 Dec 1721. King George. Oi-24.

COE EDMUNDS and ANNE BURKET, dau. of Mr. John BURKET. Before 9 Oct 1719. King George. i-51. [The same marriage as the preceding.]

.... EDWARDS and ELIZABETH PITMAN, dau. of Thomas. 19 Nov 1742. Northumberland. 1738-1743.

Mr. ANDREW EDWARDS and the widow of Cain WITHERS. About 1759. Stafford. P-281.

AMBROSE EDWARDS, Jr., and ANN SLAUGHTER. Before 24 Apr 1800. King William, "2"-25.

ISAKER EDWARDS and SARAH STACEY. 16 May 1757. Overwharton Parish Record.

THOMAS EDWARDS and the relict of William OLESS, dec'd. Before 1 May 1677. Surry, Oi-136.

Mr. THOMAS EDWARDS and the relict of Mr. Thomas OSBORNE, Sr. Before 21 Aug 1693. Henrico. 1677–1737, p. 34. [Note: OSBORNE m. *the relict of Mr. John* BRANCH.]

THOMAS EDWARDS, Psh Christ Church, Lancaster, Gent., and SARAH SWAN, widow, of John, Gent. Before 12 Mch 1753. Lancaster xiv-13.

WILLIAM EDWARDS and ELIZABETH SPAN [?] Before Sept 1740. Northumberland. 1738–1743, fo. 136. [There is some doubt as to this note.]

WILLIAM EDWARDS and ELIZABETH SPAN [?] Before 19 Sept 1716. Northumberland. 1706–1720. [See note above.]

FRANCIS ELDRIDGE and ELLIN HODGE. Before 26 Mch 1650. L. Norfolk. B-140.

MATHEW ELLIS and the dau. of Thomas x DAVIS. Before 11 Mch 1703-4. Surry. iii-297.

PHILLIP ELLIS and FRANCES AUBREY, dau. of John. Before 20 July 1767. Prince William. Land Causes, p. 143.

LEWIS ELLZEY and MARY GRIFFEN, widow of Walter. About 1743, Loudoun. A-193.

Mr. WILLIAM ELTONHEAD, of Maryland' and Mrs. JANE TAYLOR, widow of Capt. Philip TAYLOR. Northampton. Before Oct 1648. iii-147. (See also iv-27 and Va. Carolorum, pp. 410, 416.)

THOMAS ENDRIDGE, Jr., and the relict and admx of John BRIGHT. About 16 June 1671. L. Norfolk. E-66.

WILLIAM ESKRIDGE and ELIZABETH [SCOTT] heiress-at-law to William SCOTT, dec'd. Before 10 July 1789. Hampshire. [Now West Virginia.] S. L. O. T-561

MOSES ETHERIDGE and ELEANOR TUCKER, widow of William. About 1710. Norfolk, Misc. Papers.

JAMES EUBANKS and CLARKEY [?] MAYES. 5 Jany 1802. Charlotte, Va.

.... EVANS probably m. SUSANNA FOSTER, widow of "Vrinson." Before 29 Jany 1694, Northampton. xvii-297.

ISAAC EVANS and MARTHA WORTHINGTON, dau. of Robert. Before 31 Mch 1786. Yohogania. [Now in West Virginia.] S. L. O. W-260.

JOHN EVANS and ELIZABETH VEALE, dau. of William. Before 10 Dec 1681. Rappahannock. 1677-1682, p. 348.

THOMAS EVANS and SUSANNA COLE. widow of Joseph. 9 Nov 1736. Henrico. 1725-1737, p. 583.

THOMAS EVANS, Esq., of the Dominion of Ireland, m. MARY .... 1 Mch 1661. [About ?] L. Norfolk. D-364.

SOLOMON EWELL and COMFORT TAYLOR. Before 10 Apr 1769. Accomack. Deeds iii-666.

JOSEPH EYRES and MARGARET HUMPHREYS. [She m. (2) Maurice FLOYD.] Before 16 Jany 1685. Henrico. iv-32, i-436.

.... FAGAN and ELIZABETH GRIGSBY. dau. of Moses, dec'd. Before 13 Feby 1780, Stafford. S-7.

JOHN FAILE and the relict of Gilbert ELAM, Jr. Before 20 Aug 1702. Henrico. 1677-1737, p. 45.

JAMES x FAIRFAX and MARY HEWETH, dau. of Robert. Before 7 May 1728. Accomack. xvi-306. [A reference to Accomack, xx-137, states that she was the mother of John SMITH, and her father's name is given in various spellings. It was probably HEWETT.]

THOMAS FANSHAWE and MARY HORNE; permission granted her to marry. 15 Feby 1661. L. Norfolk. D-338.

Col. MORE FANTLEROY and MARY HILL, dau. of Thomas. Before 29 Aug. 1660. Westmoreland. ii-18. [See also Rappahannock, 1656-1664, 368. Court Order of 6 July 1664. FAUNTLEROY then dead. See also p. 369. Deed of Jointure. 20 Apr 1648. Also Court of 28 Mch 1664.]

WILL'M FANTLEROY, Gent., and Katherine .... 28 Feby 1681. Rappahannock. 1677-1682, p. 312. Marriage contract.

Mr. WILLIAM FAUNTLEROY and APPHIA BUSHROD, dau. of John. Before 26 Jany 1719. Westmoreland. See Crozier, p. 28, also p. 44. [She was also the daughter of Hannah COOPER. See Crozier, p. 44, and Westmoreland, ix-25.]

HENRY FARMER and the extx of William BASS. Before 20 Aug 1696. Henrico. 1677-1737, p. 39.

BENJAMIN FARROW and LUCY WILLIAMS, dau. of John SMITH. Before 1799. Fauquier. xiv-415.

Mr. JOHN FARRAR and the relict of Mr. Thomas BATTE. Before 21 Aug 1693. Henrico. 1677-1737, p. 34.

.... FAWCETT probably m. RHODA COULSTON, widow of John. 8 Jany 1673. [Probably before this date.] Accomack. v-25.

WILLIAM FEILDER and JANNEY [JANE ?] JACKSON, dau. of Francis. Before 10 Dec 1781. Prince William. G-142.

WILLIAM FERGUSON probably m. JANE SIMPSON, widow of Thomas. About 1734-35. Prince William. C-63.

Capt. PETER FIELD [FEILD] and Mrs. JUDITH [JUDAH] RANDOLPH, admx of Mr. Henry RANDOLPH. About 6 July 1680. Surry. i-307. (See also Henrico, 1688-1697, p. 8.)

JOHN FEREBEE and the relict and extx of William ELLIS, dec'd. About 16 June 1671. L. Norfolk. E-64.

JONATHAN FINLEY and ELIZABETH FINNIE. Before 18 Aug 1764. Accomack. iii-336.

WILLIAM FINNEY, Jr., son of William, and SARAH WATTS, dau. of Capt. John. 13 Oct 1720. Accomack. xvi-128. Marriage contract.

WILLIAM FINNEY, of Accomack, planter, and COMFORT TAYLOR, widow, same place. 4 May 1730. Accomack. xx-89. Marriage contract.

MOSES FITZPATRICK and HANNAH HUGHES, dau. of Moses. Before 3 Jany 1823. Amherst. C-174.

JOHN FIVEASH and JOYCE PETTWAY, dau. of Edward. Before or about 25 Aug 1682. Surry. i (2).

ALEXANDER FLEMING and URSULA BROWN, widow of John. Before 5 July 1658, Northampton. ix-18.

Capt. ALEXANDER FLEMING and JOYCE...... Before 7 Apr 1677. See record Rappahannock. 1677-1682, p. 129.

TARLTON FLEMING and MARY RANDOLPH. About 5 May 1760. Goochland. xii-133.

JAMES FLETCHER and MARY ATKINS, dau. of Richard. Before 13 Oct 1717. Prince George. Large vol. p. 230.

JOHN FLETCHER and ELEANOR HYNDMAN, sister of [Rev.] John HyndMAN. Before Nov. 1758. Augusta Chronicles, i-320.

ROBERT FLETCHER and .... SAVAGE, widow of Elkinton. Before 13 Jany 1727. Northampton. Chanc'y papers.

JOHN JAMES FLOURNOY and ANNE CARRINGTON CABELL. 26 May 1804. Amherst. M. L. B.

HUGHES FLANNAKIN and DRUCILLA HOLLOWAY, dau. of John. Before 27 Apr 1772. Cumberland. V-39.

WILLIAM FORMAN and CATHERINE X PARKER, dau. of JOHN. Before 11 May 1779. Hampshire. [Now West Virginia.] v-32. [FORMAN died before the date given.]

RICHARD FOSTER and ANNE JACKSON. [Before ?] 19 Nov 1640. New Norfolk. A-32.

SETH FOSTER probably m. ANN KING, extx of John. Before 1 Nov 1790. Dinwiddie. W. and M. xxiii-217.

JOHN FOSTER and ELIZABETH SHEPARD, dau. of John. Before 19 May 1716. Accomack. ix-150.

THOMAS FOSTURE and ELIZABETH BLACKLOCK, dau. of Thomas. Before 16 Mch 1682. Accomack. vi-328.

JOHN FOUKES and the widow of Thomas HALL. Before 15 Apr 1660. L. Norfolk. D-255.

THOMAS FOOKES and HICKMAN BONEWELL. Before 16 Mch 1679-80. Accomack. vi-202.

WILLIAM FOULKS, of Accomack, and MARY FOSTER, of Dorchester county, Md. 2d 6th 1704. Friends' Records. vi-5.

Mr. NICHOLAS FOUNTON and MARTHA PITT, dau. of Robert. Before 3 Apr 1722. Accomack. xviii-41.

Capt. ISAAC FOXCROFT and BRIDGET CHARLTON, dau. of Mr. Stephen CHARLTON. Before 18 June 1677. Accomack. vi-54.

ARTHUR FRAME and the widow of John GOSLING, 16 Dec 1691. Accomack. x-54.

PETER FRANCISCO and SUSANNAH ANDDERSON, dau. of James. Between 1782 and 1787. Cumberland. ii-432

JOHN FRAZER and ELIZABETH KELLY, widow of Charles. About 3 Sept 1736. Northampton.

Dr. GEORGE FRENCH and ANNE BRAYNE BENGER, dau. of John BENGER of Spotsylvania. Both of Fredericksburg. Before [?] 21 Feby 1780. Stafford, S-239.

WILLIAM FREEMAN and CATHERINE [WEST], probably widow of George WEST. Before 3 May 1710. Accomack. xiv-4.

WILLIAM FREEMAN and .... WILLIAMS, sister of Richard. Before 17 Apr. 1678. Accomack. vii-137.

GEORGE FRESHWATER and ELIZABETH, dau. of Bartholomew MEERS. Before 16 Dec 1682. Accomack, vi-323.

THOMAS FULCHER and the widow of Richard CONQUEST. Before 11 Nov 1662. L. Norfolk. D-327.

WILLIAM FULLEN and MARY GIBSON. 7 Mch 1796. Washington. Marriage returns.

CHARLES FORD and MARY WASHINGTON, widow of John. Before 1 Mch 1677. [At that date FORD was deceased.] Surry. i (2)-181.

SAVILL GASKIN and the widow of Mr. Christopher BURROWES. Before 16 June 1662. L. Norfolk. D-343.

HENRY GASKINS and MARY EDWARDS, dau. of John. [She was perhaps widow of Nathaniel FLOYD.] Before 26 Apr. 1742. Northumberland. 1738-1743, p. 201. See also p. 208.

DANIELL GAINES and MARGARET......... [It seems that she was the widow of Col. John CATLETT and also of John SMITH ?]

JAMES GALLOHOUGH and MARY RUSSEL, dau. of William. Before 10 Sept. 1690. Stafford. Orders i-100.

JOHN GALLAHUE and the widow of William BUTLER. Before 15 May 1766. Prince William, Q-390.

GILBERT GEE and KATHERINE ROBERTS, relict of John. Before 5 Oct 1725. Henrico. 1677-1737, p. 53.

JOHN GENTRY and NANCY SMITH, widow of Parke. Before 10 Mch 1785. Hanover. W. and M. xxii-114.

JAMES GIBSON and SARAH PREESON, dau. of Thomas and Elizabeth. After 8 Dec 1732. Northampton Land Causes.

JOHN GIBSON and CATHERINE CLOVERFIELD. Before 17 Sept 1799. Rockingham. " oo "-363.

THOMAS GIBSON and CHARLOTTE BEALE. 8 May 1782. Fauquier, M. L. B.

THOMAS GRIGSBY, of Stafford, and ROSE NEWTON, dau. of Gerrard NEWTON, late of Richmond county. Before 3 Oct 1729. King George. i-617.

JOHN GIBSON, Jr., and ANN EUSTACE. 24 Mch. 1783. Fauquier. M. L. B.

JOHN GIBSON and ELIZABETH HARRISON, 9 Mch 1795. Fauquier. M. L. B.

JOHN GIBSON, 6 Valley Va., 1 Jany 1775 d. 26 Aug. 1683; m. AMELIA CARTER CUMMINGS, dau. of Rev. Charles Cummings. Histy S. W. Va. p. 782.

ALEXANDER GIBSON and LUCY JEFFRIES. 28 Apr 1789. Fauquier. M. L. B.

WILLIAM GIBSON and HANNAH SETTLE, 31 Mch 1777. Fauquier. M. L. B.

MOSES GIBSON and BETSY WYNN. 7 Apr. 1795. Farquier. 30 Mch. M. L. B.

GEORGE GIBSON and ELENOR LOWERY. 4 Dec. 1798. Rockbridge. [She was dau. of Peter. The date of the M. L. B. is 29 Nov. 1798.]

WILLIAM GIBSON and ELIZABETH McCORMECK. 29 April 1794. Rockbridge.

SAMUEL GIBSON and CATY GRATNER. 14 Oct 1794. Washington, Mar. return.

WILLIAM GIBSON and SALLY WINN. 17 Dec. 1791. Fauquier. M. L. B.

JONATHAN GIBSON and LUCY SHUMATE. 12 Sept 1797. Fauquier. M. L. B.

BILLINGSLEY GIBSON and ELIZABETH McCROSKEY, widow of James. Before 10 Mch 1788. Washington. i-127. [GIBSON was formerly of Augusta county.]

HENRY GIBSON and SARAH HESTER GILBERT, 2 Dec 1782. Rockingham M. L. B.

JACOB GIBSON and SARAH KEMP. 11 Jany 1787. Frederick. Mar. returns.

JAMES GIBSON and SARAH PREESON. Before 1737. Northampton. Chanc'y papers.

JOHN GIBSON and ISABELLA ROBINSON. 8 Jany 1793. Campbell.

JOHN GIBSON and HANNA FITZGERRALL. 3 Dec 1789. Henry. Mar. return. [This date is given elsewhere as 8 Dec 1788.]

JOHN GIBSON and POLLY PEACH. 26 Sept 1796. Fauquier, M. L. B.

RICHARD GIBSON and the widow of Thomas HOLMES. 12 June 1690. Stafford. Orders i-65.

ROBERT GIBSON and SINAH NEWBY. 7 Dec. 1790. Fauquier, M. L. B.

SAMUEL GIBSON and SUSANNA SMITHERS. About 1794. Washington. Mar. return.

THOMAS GIDDENS and the widow and extx of Daniel STOTT. Before Mch Ct 1737. Northampton. Chanc'y papers.

.... GILDING perhaps m. ELIZEBETH WILLIT, dau. of William. Before 1704 [?] Northampton. See xix-91.

THOMAS GILL, Jr. and MARIAN BAILES, dau. of John, of St. Stephen's Psh. Before 16 July 1728. Northumberland. 1726-1729, fo. 100.

ARCHELUS GILLIAM and JUDITH TULEY. 15 Dec. 1781. Albemarle. M. L. B.

.... GILSON and BEHETHLAND SMITH, relic of John. See suit 11 June 1690. Stafford. i-53.

.... GLEDHILL m. MARY DAY or JOHNSON. She was the widow of James DAY and of John JOHNSON. See ii-543. 1712. Isle of Wight.

NATHAN GLENN and ELIZABETH LEGRAND, widow or dau. of John. [¿[Before 25 Dec 1800. Halifax, xviii-565.

WILLIAM x GLOW and CONSTANT TAYLER, dau. of Richard. Before 16 Feby 1679. Rappahannock. 1677-1682, p. 275.

Mr. WILL GLOVER and the relict of John DAVIS. Before 20 Aug 1685. Henrico. 1677-1737, p. 15.

JOHN GLOVER and MARY Johnson. Marriage contract. 17 July 1809. Cumberland. xi-264.

JOSEPH GOARE, of Middlesex, pltr, and MARY ALLISON, one of the daus. of David, late of Middlesex. Before 1 Feby 1692. Middlesex, ii-505.

JOHN HADEN and JENNY MOSELEY, dau. of John. Before 18 May 1747. Goochland.

THOS. HARDING and ELIZABETH PHILLIPS, dau. of Laur. PHILLIPS. Before 15 May 1655. L. Norfolk. C-151.

GEORGE HARDINGE and MARY ORLEY, dau. of Thos. and Anne, of London. Before 22 Sept 1664. Northumberland. 1658-1666, fo. 144.

SETH HATCHER and JANE PERRIN. Before 1 Apr 1717. Henrico. 1714-1718.

JOHN HARRIS and WINNIFRED BOGGESS. Between 1791 and 1812. Fairfax. Land Causes.

ROGER HAYWARD and KATHERINE, the widow of John REINE [?] Before 5 Nov 1666 L. Norfolk. D-266. (About 5 Nov 1660. D 273)

HENRY HARMANSON and ELIZABETH PATRICK. Before 25 July 1691. Northampton. xiv-26.

Mr. THOMAS HARMANSON, Sr., and [ELIZABETH] DANIEL, widow of John. (Roger Groves sets forth that in July, 1688, Mr. Harmanson on a bill from Groves to the sd Harmanson's pr'decessor John Daniell dec. obtained judgment.........&c.) Before 29 Sept 1692. Northampton. xv-440. Before 29 July 1689. See xv-440

WILLIAM HARMANSON and BRIDGET GASCOIGNE, granddaughter of William Gascoigne. About August 1688. Northampton. xviii-417.

GEORGE HARMANSON and ELIZABETH YARDLEY, eldest dau. of Argoll and Sarah (Michaell) YARDLEY. See 28 May 1702 Northampton. xvi-296. (Before 20 Mch 1694. See xvii-419. ELIZABETH is called the dau. of Sara MADDUX. Sarah had several husbands. YARDLEY was probably the father of ELIZABETH.)

THOMAS HARMANSON, Sr. and JANE ANDREWS. Before 1696. Northampton. xviii. 112.

WILLIAM HARMANSON and MARGARET MAPP, dau. of Robins MAPP. Before 1774. Northampton.

JOHN HARMANSON and SUSANNA x KENDALL, dau. of John. About 28 Mch 1690. Northampton. xvi-248. [Note: There were two SUSANNA KENDALLS. One could write, the other made her " x " mark.]

ISAAC HAGGAMOND and ELIZABETH ANDREWS, widow of Andrew, Gent. About 28 Mch 1700. Northampton. xviii-61. See also xviii-236.
[*It is probable that the date 1700 should be 1701.*]

WILLIAM HAGGOMAN and MARGARET MICHAEL, widow. 13 Jany 1755. Northampton. M. L. B. [She seems to have been the widow of Joachim MICHAEL. See Chanc'y papers.]

RICHARD HANBY and MARIA CHILCOTT. Northampton. Marriage contract. 20 Aug 1656. vii-8.

RICHARD HANBY probably m. SUSANNA DANIEL. Before 13 Mch 1664. Northampton. ix-212.

WILLIAM HARE and MARY CARTER, widow of George. Record of 8 Sept 1679. Surry i (2)-220.

WILLIAM x HARPER about to marry ELIZABETH HARPER, relict and extx of Francis HARPER. 22 July 1673. Northampton. xi, 85.

MARKE HAMMOND and ANNE DENNIS, who was servant of Thomas Powell. Before 16 July 1640. Northampton. i-3. [He m. (2) MARY CLARKE. Before 13 Dec 1641. ii-97.]

HARMANTROUT [d. 1753] and ELIZABETH HETRICK, dau. of Adam [then of Pennsylvania.]

WILLIAM HAINEY and ANN EDWARDS, widow. T. Edwards, her father, consents. in a letter to his son Thomas Edwards, 16 Oct 1747. Lancaster. M. L. B. (Wm. and Mary. xii-101.)

JAMES HAWARD, of KingSayle, *Upper parish of Nansemond*, and.........TITUS, dau. of Thomas. Before 20 Oct 1691. S. L. O. viii-178.

GEORGE NICHOLAS HACK, and ANNE WRIGHT, dau. of Mr. Richard WRIGHT, and neice of Mich: Spencer, Esq. Before 5 Feby 1694-5. S. L. O. ii-121.

GARRET HADEN and ELEANOR WOOD. 15 Apr 1803. Alexandria. M. L. B.

JONATHAN HALL and FRANCINIA FRANCIS. 19 Nov, 1790. Loudoun.

JOSIAS HALL and MARY NIXON. 13 Mch. 1793. Loudoun.

DANIEL ROLLS HALL and SUSANNA GUY, widow of John, Gent. Before 1774. Northampton. Chanc'y papers.

ABSALOM HALL and ANNE MARY POWELL, dau. of Samuel. Before 15 July 1752. Northampton. xxxix O-65. [A note from Chancery records makes her Ann Mary Jones, dau. of John Jones and wife Frances.]

RICHARD HALL and ELIZABETH STONE. 10 Nov 1791. Wythe. Mar. returns.

JAMES HAMBLETON and MARTHA MOSEBY, relict of John. Before 5 Oct 1725. Henrico. 1677-1737, p. 54.

GEORGE HAMLING and the widow of William RODOLPHUS. Before or about 18 Sep. 1666. Accomack. i-124.

SYMON HANCOCK and the admx. of GILBERT GUY. Before 5 July 1642. L. Norfolk. A-2. About 26 May 1642. See A-58.

SYMON HANCOCK Jr., of Princess Anne and APPHIA MALBONE. 29 Mch 1732. Norfolk. M. L. B.

WM. H. HARDING and ANN ALEXANDER BINNS, dau. of Charles. Before 2 Dec 1800. Loudoun. F-317.

NICOL. HARDING and ANN PAGET. Shenandoah. Mar. returns. [Son NICHOL. born 19 Apr 1773.]

GEORGE HARDING of Stafford cty, and NANCY BLAND, dau. of Thomas. Before or about 2 May 1785, Prince William. W -109.

JOHN HARTLY and ELIZABETH LAWRENCE, dau. of Susanna. See record 20 Sept 1737. Northumberland. 1638-1743-fo. 51.

ROBERT HARDIN and ELIZABETH DAVIS, dau. of Jonathan. Before 16 Aug 1787. See Lunenburg. iii-364.

WILLIAM HARDING and MARTHA BULLEN, sister and heir of John. Before 20 Oct 2687. [Rappahannock ?] S. L. O. vii-624.

WILLIAM HARDAGE and ELIZABETH BROWN, sister of George. Before 1724. Crozier, Westmoreland Wills. p. 32

DAVID HARPER and WILSON BUTT [??] 14 Apr 1784. Norfolk. M. L. B.

THOMAS HARPER and the relict of J. PIPER. Before 25 June 1707. Westmoreland. Crozier, p. 17.

THOMAS HARRIS and the rellict of John NELSON *als Isdale*. Before Nov 1727. Northampton. Chanc'y papers. (Harris removed to North Carolina.)

PETER HARRIS and EASTER GUNN, dau. of John. Before 4 Jany 1724. Henrico. Misc. p.583.

BURR HARRISON and the widow of Edw'd SMITH. She died before 12 Mch 1700. Stafford. "Z"-63.

SALATHIEL HARRISON and EDETH GODWIN, widow of Joseph. Before Aug 1740. Northampton. Chanc'y papers.

.........HARRISON and SARAH LANGHORNE, widow of John. [She was of Bourbon county, Kentucky.] Before 22 Nov 1779. Cumberland. viii-365.

THEOPHILUS HARRISON and MARY LOVE. Before 23 Nov 1790. Brunswick. Orders xv. 450.

MATT HARVEY and MAGDALENE HAWKINS, dau. of Benjamin. Before 12 Jany 1790. Botetourt. Orders, 1788-1792.

Capt. JOHN HASELWOOD, formerly of London. Mariner, [died about 1687] m. FRANCES COLE, dau. of Francis. Before 3 Oct 1709. Middlesex. iv-211: HASELWOOD m. (2) the widow of John CARTER, Esq. Before same date......... See same references.

GEORGE HASELWOOD, son of Capt. John HASELWOOD, and ANN ROBINSON, dau. of Richard. About 1705. Middlesex, iv-211. [See another deposition same page.]

MR. STRATTON NOTTINGHAM

of Onancock, Virginia.

died March 30, 1932.

A reference to his work and his great ability will be found elsewhere in this number. A list of his publications will be given later.

Printed at The Industrial School for Crippled and Deformed Children, 241 St. Botolph St., Boston, Mass.

The

County Court Note-Book

A Little Bulletin of History and Genealogy

June, 1931 **Vol. X, No. 3**

DELAWARE TAX-LISTS for 1776
NEWCASTLE COUNTY
Christiana Hundred

JAMES ADAMS, 12*; Arthur Anderson, 4; Wm. Anderson's Estate, 12; Jacobus Anderson, 8; Jac. Anderson, 3; Wm. Anderson, Jr. Est. 9; John Andrews, 8; Sarah Allison's Est. 4; Isaac Allen; Wm. Armor, 14; John Armstrong, 13; Rob't Armstrong, 12; John Armstrong, Junr, 7; Wm. Armstrong's Est. 25; Wm. Askew; John Augusta, 12; Allen's Est. 6.

STRANGE BACKHOUSE, 5; John Baldwin, 7; Francis Baldwin, 10; Samuel Barker's Est, "R'd"† 9; Joel Baylie's Est., 4; Peter Baker, 10; John Beaty, 7; Jos. Bennet, 12; Jos. Bennet, Junr, 5; Jacob Bennet, 12; John Bartram's Est. 6; Vincent Bonsall, 12; do. Brandewine Hd. 5; Wm. Brobson's Est. 12; James Breadan, 6; John Britten, 8; Rob't Britten's Est. 8; James Brindley, 8; David Brinten; Hanah Bonam's Est. "Rd." 6; James Broom, 13; Jacob Broom, 6; John Broom, 4; Abraham Brown, 4; Jas. Brown's Est. 8; Swen Brunburg, 9; Peter Brunburg; Jos. Buffington; David Busby, 8; Sam'l Bush, 3; Wm. Brown, 6; Moses Bryan, 4; David Boyd, 3; Rd. 6; Jas. Buckingham, 6.

WM. CAMBLE, 2; Wm. Camble, Junr. 4; Sam'l Camble, 8; Jas. Camble, 6; Benjamin Canby, 6; Jonas Canby, 6; Wm. Canby, 8; Sam'l Canby, 8; Rich'd Carson, 12; Wm. Carter, 5; Jer: Carter, 7; Caleb Chandler's Est. 8; Isaac Chandler, 4; Thos. Chandler, 18; Jesse Chandler, 6; Christ'r Chandler, 13; Swithan Chandler, 6; James Chandler, 10; Wm. Cleancy's Est. 12.

Thos. Clark, 9; John Clark, 5; Jacob Cling, 3; John Cloud, 10; Wm. Cloud, 8; Dan'l Cloud; 14; Wm. Cloud's Est. 3; Thos. Couch's Est. "Rd" 4; Geo. Cochran, 2; Jos. Coleman, 6; John Counsill, 10; do. Brandewine Hundred, 5; Geo. Craghead, 13; Watkins Crampton, 13; Matthew Crips, 16; Andrew Crips, 8; Thos.; Crow, 10; Geo. Crow's Estate, 4; Wm. Cumming's's Est. 4.

ALEX'R DAVIDSON, 2; Edw'd Dawes's Estate, 9; Jonth'n Dawes's Estate, 9; Josiah Dawes, 4; Neh: Delaplaine, 10; Wm. Derrickson, 8; Jacob Derickson, 12; Obediah Dingey, 7; Jacob Dingey, 7; Richard Denney, 4; Tho. Davis, 4; Jos. Dickiy, 4; Thomas Duff, 10; Bruce Dunn; lap, 2; Hannah Dixon's Estate, 8.

ROBERT EULES' Est. 4; William Elliott, 4; Jesse Eldridge, 9; John Ervin, 12; Charles Evans, 10; Do. Mill Creek Hd. 3; Jonathan Evans, 4; Oliver Evans.

JAS. FERGUSON, 3; David Ferriss, 18; Zach's Ferriss, 15; Ziba Ferriss, 12; John Ferriss, 10; Rob't Finney; Jas. Fletcher, 2; Abraham Ford, 7; Wm. Foot; Jacob Fussell, 7.

HENRY GILLIS, 4; ....Gamble, 6; John Garrett, 20; Do. Mill Creek Hd. Joshua Garret's Est. 4; Ab'm Garretson, 3; Jos. Garretson, 3, Henery Garretson, 15; Jas. Garretson, 3; Rob't. Galbreath, 8; Thos. Gilpin's Est. 9; Ann Gilpin's do. 9; David Gillaland, 3; Jas. Gilmore, 8; Jos. Gilpin; 9; Vincent Gilpin, 18; Geo: Gilpin's Est. 4; Thos. Gilpin, 10; Jos. Gilpin, Jr., 10; Thos. Gissing's Est. 6; Conrod Gray, 15; Sam'l Greave, 14; do. Mill Creek, Hd.; David Greave, 12; Jonathan' Greave, 7; Jacob Grea ve, 9; Joseph Green, 7; Sam'l Gregg's Est. 17; Harman Gregg's do. 12; Joseph Gregg, 15; Sam'l Gregg, 13; Ab'm Gregg, 8; Israel Gilpin, 10; Geo; Gothrope; John Gothrope, Geo. Gordon, 13; John Gyles Estate, 8.

ROB'T HERAGE, 4; John Harp, 3; Jas. Haveland; Timothy Hanson, 10; Barney C: Harriss, 9; Job Harvey; 13; Mary Harvey's Est., 12; John Hays, 9; John Hedge, 3; Do Brande, wine Hd. 2; Joseph Hedge, 3; Wm. Hemphill; 13; John Hendrickson, 17; David Hendrickson 12; Peter Hendrickson, 6; James Hicklin, 5; John Hill, 4; Susanna Hinton's Est. 4; John Hobson, 6; Isaac Hollingsworth, 13; Christ'r Hollingsworth, 13; Thos. Hollingsworth, 12; Amos Hollingsworth, 13; Jehu Hollingsworth's Est. 7; Sam'l Hollingsworth, 10; John Honn, 2; Barney Hanlon, 5; Wm. Hamilton, 5; Sam'l Heald, 5; Cornelius Heins, 6; Do. New Castle Hundred; John Horner; Henery Hyland's Est. 6; Sam'l Hogg, 3.

DAVID JAMSON, 6; Rich'd Jameson, 4; Matthias Jannet, 5; Pillip [*sic*] Jones, 6; Wm. Jones, 6; Jos. Jones, 6; Francis Johnson, 12; Simon Johnson, 13; Do. Brandewine Hd. 4; Rob't Johnson's Est. .8; John Johnson, 2; John Justice's Est, 15; Swen Justice's Est. 8; PeterJ ustice, James Jordan, 4; Griffith Jordan, 4.

THOMAS KEAN, 10; Rich'd Kean, 4; John Keen, 4; Sam'l Kelly, 6; John Kendall, 12; Adam Kirk, 7; Caleb Kirk, 13; Jonathan Kirk, 2; James Kirk, 2; Wm Kenady, 8; Wm. *Kirkparick's* Est. 10.

JAMES LAIRD'S EST. 6; John Langley, 4; Jas. Latimer, 30; Geo. Latimer, 12; Henry Latimer, 6; Jos. Lawson, 12; James Lea, 20; John Lea, 15; Do. Brandewine Hund. 11; Thomas Langley, 4; Rob't Lewis's Est., 9; Mich'l Lightbody, 4; Archibald Little, 12; Thomas Little's Est., 5; Joshua Litler's Est. 8;

John Litler, 9; Thomas Litler, 4; Joseph Lobb, 4; Andrew Lynam's Est., 13; John Lynam, 10; Phillip Lynam, 6; Andrew Lynam, 3; Sam'l Liitle, 4.

JOHN M'MISKAN, 9; Dan'l McBride's Est. R'd. 10; John M'Calmont's Est., 16; James M'Collom, 6; John M'Larry, 3; Jas. M'Comb's Est. R'd. 2; Sarah M'Dowel's Est. 4; John McKinley, Esq., 60; Do. New Castle Hund. 8; James McCorckle, 9; Wm. Marshall's 20; New Castle Hundred, 2; Matthias Marten, 4; James Marshall, 13:

Do. Mill Creek Hund. 6; Sam'l Means's Est. 10; Jesse Meriss's Est. 6; Stephen Mendinghall, 10; Benj'n Mendinghall, 9; Henery Metz, 4; Alex'r Miller, 16; John Millner, 12; Griffith Minshall, 20; Alex'r Moore's Est. 4; Wm. Moore, 8; Rebecca Morriss's Est. 5; Sam'l Morton's Est. 20; Thomas Musgrave, 4; Aaron Musgrave, 9.

HANU [?] NAST, 2; Hanu Nast, Jr., 4; Wm. Nash, 4; Wm. Niels, 16; David Nielson, 12; Alex'r Nielson, 7; Ellis Newlin, 15; Thos. Nickols, 12; Jos. Nickols, 12; Sam'l Nickols, 4; Hezekiah Niles, 13;

THOMAS OGLES, 12; Peter Osburn's Est. 6;

WM. PARKER, 4; John Parry & Son, 10; John Paulson, 10; Peter Paulson, 15; Charles Paulson, 10; Jacob Paulson, 5; Tobias Paulson, 2; Rob't Pierce, 20; Rob't Pierce, Jun'r., 6; Benja. Peterman, 7; Jonas Peterson, 2; And'w Peterson, 2; Peter Peterson, 5; Wm. Phillips's, Est. R'd. 18; Rob't Phillips, 20; Wm. Plughrite, 5; Wm. Poole, 12; Alex'r Porter, 10; John Porter, 5; Moles Paterson, 5.

HENERY REYNOLDS, 12; Henery Rice, 4; Richard Richardson, 65; Rob't Richardson's Est, 30; Rob't Robinson, 20; Wm. Robeson, 10; Jas. Robinson's Est. R'd. 10; Jonth'n Robinson, 13; Nich: Robinson, 14; Francis Robinson, 13; John Robinson, Lab'r, 3; Rich. & Jacob Robinson, 10; Do. Mill Creek Hundred; John Rogers, 4; Benja. Rodwell, 5; Jonth'n Rumford, 8; Jonth'n Rumford, Jun'r, 30;

CALEB SEAL, 15; Do. Brandewine Hund. 5; John Scothorn, 4; Wm. Shipley, 35; Thos. Shipley, 30; Wm. Shipley, Jun'r, 10; Sam'l Shipley, 10; Henery Sinnex, 6; John Sinnex, 10; Phillip Sliver, 3; Caleb Sharpless, 6; Francis Smith, 3; Wm. Smith, 7; Thos. Smith, 7; Jermiah Smith, 16; Isaac Smith, 4; Wm. Simmons, 6; Isaac Simmons; Jos. Shallcross, 18; Do. Brandewine Hund. 5; Geo. Spackman, 10; John Sperry, 4;

Peter Springer, 8; Jos. Springer, 10; Jacob Springer's Est. 9; Jos. Springer Jos. Son, 10; Jos. Springer Christ'r's Son, 8; Chas. Springer Jos. Son, 12; Chas. Springer Jas. Son, 12; Gab'l Springer, 12; John Springer, 4; Jonathan Stacy, 2; Thomns Stroud, 7; Peter Stalcop's Est. 20; John Stapler, 25; Isaac Starr, 8; Joseph Stedham, 12; Jonas Stedham, 18; John Stedham, 8;

Corn's Stedham, 16; Joseph Steel, 5; H...... [?] Stemcast, 4; And'w Stilley, 10; John Stilley, 8; Brandewine H'd, 1; John Stow, 6; Lewis Stone, 7; Geo: Stern, 4.

EDWARD TATNALL, 10; Geo: Taylor, 4; John Taylor, 2; Robert Taylor, 7; Wm. Taylor, 3; John Thelwell, 4; Seth Thomas, 7;...... Thompson, 5; Sam'l Templeton, 2; John Tomlinson's Est., 10; Joseph Towsend, 7; John Trip, 7; David Tryan, 5; Wm. Tussey, 6; Do. Brandewine H'd, 12.

JOHN VEAL, 4; Wm. Underwood, 14; Wm. Vaneman, 10; Do. Brandewine Hund, 5; Ab'm Vaneman's Est. 6; And'w Vaneman, 4; Frederick Vert, 7; Do, Brandewine Hund.

(Note: The U's and the V's were listed together as copied.)

JOHN WATT, 4; Ralph Walker, 10; Sam'l Walker, 3; And'w Walker, 3; James Walker, 3; Thomas Wallace, 5; Thomas Wallace, 18; Thomas Wallace, Jun'r, 6; Justa Walraven, 18; Jonas Walraven, 6; Jonas Walraven's Est. 6; Swen Walraven's Est. 6; Wm. Walter, 13; Jos. Warner, 10; New Castle Hundred, 5; Francis Way, 15; Caleb Way, 10;
Jos. Way's Est. 6; John Way's Est. 3; Nich. Way, 13; John Webster, 7; Charles West, 4; Joseph West, 10; John White's Est. 6; Isaac Whitelock, 9; Chas: Whitelock, 9; Wm. West, 6; Thos. Willson, 10; Do. Brandewine H'd, 5; Thomas Willson, Carter, 4; Wm. Willson, 9; Rich'd Willson, 4; Christ'r Willson's Est. 10; Capt. Willey, 5; David Windalls, 9; Nathan Wood, 6; Wm. Woodcocks, 6; Ben. Woodcock, 10; Mordeciah Woodard, 4.

JOHN YARNALL, 7; Nathan Yarnall's Est. 7; ...... Yarnells, 4; Andrew Yeatman, 18.

* *Although there is no headings to the columns in which these figures appear, it is evident from other sheets which have the pound mark ("£") that the figures represent the amount of tax.*

† *This abbreviation is either "2d" or "Rd"; apparently the latter.*

(*To be continued*)

ALBEMARLE, AMHERST AND BUCKINGHAM COUNTIES, VIRGINIA

Extracts from Albermarle Surveys

PETER SALLE, 400 acres, on Troublesome Creek of Slate River. 10 Dec 1745.

LAZARUS DAMRIL, 212 acres adj. north side Fluvanna River. 28 Mch 1746.

GEORGE DAMEREL, 147 acres, south side of Fluvanna.

JNO. DAMERON, 200 acres, on a branch of Woodson's Creek (adj. Richard Dameron.) 8 Nov 1746.

JOHN ROBINSON, Joyner, 250 acres north side of the Rivanna, touching the river. 17 Nov 1746.

JOHN HUGHES, 285 acres, north branch Willis' Creek. 27 Mch 1747.

JOHN HUGHES, 298 acres, east side of Willis' Mountain. 27 Mch 1747.

RICH'D POWELL, 283 acres, south side of Buffalo River. 4 Apr 1748.

HENRY MARTIN, Gent., 290 acres on a branch of Hardware. 10 Mch 1747.

JOHN GOOLDSBY, 400 acres on a branch of Hardware and Sotier. 21 Nov 1748. (Transferred to Handcock.)

GEORGE DAMERON, 400 acres north side of Hardware River and on Briery Creek. 16 June 1749.

ISAIAH BURTON, 1200 acres, north branch Slate River, surveyed by order of Council, 5 Dec 1749.

RICHARD POWELL, 200 acres on the branches of Puppies' Creek. 2 Apr 1750.

ISAIAH BURTON, Jr., 400 acres both sides Walton's Fork of Arthur's Creek of Slate River. 8 Mch 1749.

JOHN HAYES, 400 acres on the branches of Ballenger's and Mechum (?) creeks of Fluvanna. 4 Dec 1751.

The deeds which follow are thought to have conveyed land now in Buckingham. Buckingham records were destroyed by fire, 1869.

WILLIAM ALLEN, of Albemarle cty, Va., to William Hunt Allen, same. 650 acres on both sides Slate River. 9 Sept 1748. i-7.

WILLIAM DINGUID, Alb. cty, to Thomas McDaniel, parish of St. Anne, south side Fluvanna river. 156 acres. 1748. i-1.

WILLIAM ALLEN, Alb., to John Allen; 394 acres, both sides Slate River, and both sides Glover's Road, and both sides Horn Quarter Road, on the heads of the branches of Randolph's, Hatcher's and Joshua's creeks. 400 acres. 9 Sept 1748. i-9.

EDMUND WOOD, and wf Mary, Alb. cty. to Robert Thomson of Goochland, 595 acres, on the branches of Hatcher's Creek of Willis' river. 8 Sept 1748. i-10.

WILLIAM NOLAND, Alb., to Thomas Blakey, of Gchland cty, 200 acres on Arthur's Creek of Slate river. 8 Sept 1748. i-33.

(*To be continued*)

VIRGINIA MARRIAGES

(*Continued from April, 1931*)

REUBEN HAY and ELIZABETH FUQUA, John FUQUA, sec. 27 Oct 1788. Charlotte M. L. B.

THOMAS HAY and ELIZABETH HALEY. (Reuben HAY, sec.) 9 Dec 1768. Charlotte. M. L. B.

WILLIAM HAYES and ELIZABETH DENNIS, sister of Henry. Before 1726. Henrico. 1775-1737.

CHARLES HAYES probably m. JANE TILLEY a widow. Before 5 Apr 1755. Brunswick iii. 212.

JAMES HAYES [sig.] and MARTHA GRIGG, 7 June 1785. Charlotte. M. L. B.

ROBERT HAYES and JANE ERRISTALL. 17 July 1661. Northampton. ix-114.

ROBERT HAYES and ANN DRAITON. 20 Nov 1660. Northampton. ix-92.

THOMAS HAYS, of Nansemond cty. and JUDITH FRIAR, of Hertford cty, N. C. 18 Mch 1774. U. S. Pension Records.

ROBERT HAYS, Jr., son of Col. ROBERT HAYS and JANE COLLIER. U. S. Pension Records.

WILLIAM HAYS m. (in Franklin cty) ELIZABETH LEMON. 21 Aug 1785. U. S. Pension Records. [This marriage seems uncertain. Ed.]

JOHN HAYNIE and HANAH NEALE, sister of Ebenezer and dau. of Daniel and Elizabeth. Before 16 Jany 1711. Northumberland. 1710-1713, p.133.

WILLAM HEATH and the widow of John CARPENTER. Before Sept 1769. Northampton. Chanc'y papers.

ALEXANDER HENDERSON, Gent., and SARAH MOORE, 2d dau. of Henry. 19 Apr 1773. Fairfax. Orders 1772-1774, p.189. Marriage settlement.

JOHN HENMAM perhaps m. SARAH SMYTH, a widow. Before 18 Mch 1646. Northampton. iii-65.

PATRICK HENRY and DOROTHEA DANDRIDGE, sister of Alexander Spotswood DANDRIDGE, and dau. of N. W. and Dorothea DANDRIDGE. [When?] Draper Mss. 8ZZ-77.

RICHARD HEWES and Mary BALL, widow. Before 1 Oct 1720. Northumberland. 1718. 1726, p.177.

ROBERT HENLEY and ELIZABETH ENGLISH, widow of John. 15 Aug 1679. Rappahannock. 1677-1682, p. 242. Marriage Contract.

LITTLE BERRY [*sic*] HEWES and MARY WALKER dau. of William and Lucy. 3 May 1798. Prince Edward. See E5, p.59. [Another reference is to the Hughes Family.]

Mr. THO: HIGBY and Mrs. ANN Wilkins the widow of Jno. WILKINS. Before 29 Aug 1654. Northampton. v-27. Before 28 Feby 1650. See iv-10.

JOHN HIX and MOURNING WINN, dau. of Thomas. Before 1763 or 1764. Lunenburg. iii-75.

JOHN HODGE and the relict of Jno. COOPER. Before May 1 1677. Surry. Oi-136.

MATHEW HOGGSON and MARY BURCHER, dau. of George. Before 14 Jany 1660. i-164.

.........HOLDEN and AIME McKEMIE, dau. of Francis and Naomi. Before 10 Apr 1769. Accomack. Deeds iii-666.

HENRY HOLDEROST [?] and MARY WALKER, extx of Alexander. Before 1720 [?] Prince George. Order Book, p. 355.

THOMAS HOGG and JANE FORSITH, widow of John. [She was the dau. of George WILLIS.] Before 28 Feby 1665. Northampton, x-21. See also xi-68. Also xi-177.

THOMAS HODGE of Westmoreland cty, and MARY ROSE. Before 27 Feby 1797. King William, "11"-328. [At the date given HODGE was deceased.]

JONAS HOLLADAY and HANNAH HUTTON, widow of Capt. John. Before 15 Sept 1703. Norfolk. vii-7.

THORNE HORNE and JANE RIGLESWORTH, widow of Peter. About 16 Mch 1652. L. Norfolk. C-44.

ROBERT HOUSE, Jr., and MARTHA SPILTIMBER, dau. of Anthony. About 7 Mch 1681. Surry. Orders i-366.

WILLIAM HOGIN and ELIZABETH GRIFFEN. Before Aug 1743. Loudoun. A-193.

SAMUEL HOLMES and PRUDENCE COURTNEY, widow of Samuel. Before 11 Aug 1777. Mechlinburg. Orders, iv-367.

Omitted from list in April, 1931

[HENRY] ARSKINS and JEAN THOMPSON, dau. of Joseph of [Cecil County, Maryland.] Before 27 Nov 1782. Henry. iii-275.

HENRY ASCOUGH and JOANE HUGHSON widow of Robert. Before 20 Aug 1681. Henrico. 1677-1739-p. 7.

JOHN ASHWORTH and the Relict of Rich: SELBY. Before 16 Aug 1671. L. Norfolk. E-68.

WILLIAM ATKINSON and ELIZABETH PARKER, dau. of Richard. About or before 7 Jany 1716. Henrico i-89. (p. 143, W. and D. 1714.)

PATRICK ANGUS and MARY PORTER widow of........ PORTER [Minister of Lynn haven Parish.] Before 17 June 1684. L. Norfolk iv..........(from Mr. Richmond's collection of data.)

JOHN APPLEWHAITE and ANNE MARSHALL, dau. of Humphrey. Before 18 Dec 1711. Isle of Wight. ii-533.

WILLIAM ARCHER and the relict and admx of William DUKE. Before 25 Jany 1678. Surry. i (2)-238.

ROGER ARCHER and MARY x CLAY, relict of Mr. John CLAY, Sr., of I. W. Before or about 31 May 1678. Surry. i (2)-241.

GEORGE ARCHER and.........HARRIS, sister of William. 1 June 1689. Henrico. ii-303.

JOHN ARNOLD and PATTY LEE, dau. of John. Before 1 Sept 1818. Campbell. v-131.

MARYLAND'S NEXT OF KIN

(In some unexplained way the "Next of Kin" from p. 131, vol. ix, Maryland Inventories, have been omitted in these abstracts. The following list appears to "tie on" to the list in December, 1929.)

ROBERT EYVE [EYRE?]; inv. Ann Elizabeth Vause, Cisell[*sic*] cty. 24 June 1721. ix-138.

No kin mentioned. Add'l inv. Aquilla Paca, Balto. cty. No date. ix-141.

No kin mentioned. Inv. Charles Phillips Som, cty. 22 Oct 1723. ix-141

MICHAEL HOLLAND, MICHAEL HOLLAND, Jr. [Kin?] Inv. Capt. Wm. Bolitho. Som. cty. 30 Apr 1722. ix-141.

ROBERT CARNEY, "one of the nearest Kin refuses to sign and would not give Any Reason for it." Inv. John Smith, Som. cty. Mch 29 1723. ix-142.

Kin uncertain or not given. Inv. Joseph Owin, Jr. Calv. cty. 15 Sept 1722. iv-143.

Kin uncertain. Inv. Henery Clark, Calvert cty. 10 Nov 1722. ix-144.

JOHN HELLEN, PETER HELLEN; inv. Edmond Hunderford, Calv. cty. 30 Nov 1721. ix-145.

NAOMI x DORING, CHARLES x DORING; inv. James Willinot [Willmot?] Jr., Calv. cty. 27 Aug 1722. ix-150.

ALLEX'R MAGRUDER "signed as father-in-law." Inv. Mr. Tho: Letchworth, Pr. Geo's cty. 26 Nov 1722. ix-150.

LEVIN x JONES [Kin?] Inv. Phillip Lewing, Pr. Geo's. cty. 15 Oct 1722. ix-153.

JAMES GILES [perhaps kin?] Inv. Edward Jones, Pr. Geo's cty. 6 Nov 1722. ix-154.

No kin mentioned. Inv. Mr. Robert Levett, Pr. Geo's cty. 8 Aug 1722. ix-155.

SA'L MACKUBIN [extr?] SAM'LL PEELE [Kin?] [Very uncertain.] Inv. John Macubbins, A. A. cty. 9 Apr 1722. ix-169.

No kin mentioned. Inv. William Butterfield. A. A. cty. 14 Dec 1722. ix-171.

No kin mentioned. Inv. William Pearson, A. A. cty. 22 Mch 1721-2. ix-172.

PHILLIP BRADY; inv. Hugh Kennedy. County[?] 10 July 1722. ix-173.

No kin mentioned. Inv. Mr. John Whittington, Q. A. cty. 20 June 1723. ix-180.

MARY ROGERS, perhaps kin. [Uncertain.] Inv. Phillemon Hemsley. No date. ix-181.

No kin mentioned. Inv. John Murphy, Q. A. cty. 11 Feby 1722. ix-182.

JOHN RUCKER, MARY DOWNS; inv. Rich'd Powell, Q. A. cty. 18 Sept 1723. ix-182.

RICH'D WELLS, CHAR'S VANDERFORD; inv. John Brown, Q. A. cty. 3 July 1723. ix-185.

(*To be continued*)

SERVICE AND SUPPLIES COLONIAL, REVOLUTIONARY AND MILITIA

ISAIAH AUSTIN, aged 73; born 18 Feb'y 1759. [Probably deposes as to some one's service.] Grayson City, Va. Orders. 24 Sept 1832.

SAMUEL ARNBURN [?] of Grayson City; entered service 1776. [Seems to have lived in Philada. cty, Penna.] Aged 71. Grayson cty, Va. Orders. 27 Nov. 1832.

ANDREW BIRD, oath as Captain, Militia. Rock'm, Va. Minutes. 24 May 1779.

HOLLOWAY BUNTING, Esq. Commission as Major of the Militia. N-n Cty, Va. 14 Feby 1764. xxxii0. . .

JOHN BROWN, a serjeant and BENJAMIN FRY, a soldier, considered by the Court as pensioners. Amherst cty, Va. May Ct 1783. Orders, p. 116.

THOMAS CARPENTER, sold supplies, or furnished team, &c.* Amherst cty, Va. May Ct 1783. Orders, p. 108.

JOHN COMER, Grayson cty, Va. Age 79. Enlisted under Capt. Lewis Jones of Amelia. He was for awhile in the marine service. Grayson cty, Va. 22 Oct 1832. Orders.

DRURY, CHRISTIAN, see * Amherst cty, Va. May Ct 1783. Orders, p. 108.

JOEL CAMPBELL, see* Amherst cty, Va. May Ct 1783. Orders, p. 108.

SOLOMON CARTER, see* Amherst cty, Va. May Ct 1783. Orders, p. 118.

PETER CARTER, Commission as Lieut. of Militia. Amherst cty. 26 July 1782. Orders, p. 3.

JAMES COX, Grayson cty, Va. Age 69; 15 or 16 when he entered the service; served under his father Capt. John Cox and Maj. Wm. Love as an Indian spy. Was born in Fort Chisel [?] Wythe cty, then Botetourt, 24 Feby 1763. Orders, 24 Sept 1832.

DAVID CROUCH furnishes satisfactory proof that he is entitled to £3–10 for one beef cow and pasturage for 30 head of horses, two nights, at 6 [?] per night, &c., &c. Montg. cty, Va. Orders, p. 191. 28 June 1785.

ANDREW CROCKETT, commissioned 1st Lieut from 5 Apr 1781. Montg. cty, Va. Orders 10 Jany 1782.

MICHAEL KINSER, a pensioner; proved by oath of Samuel Sadler that Kinser was wounded at . . . [?] and that he belonged to Capt. Bently's Company. Surgeon ordered to examine him and certify to Governor. Montg. cty, Va. Orders. Ct 20 Nov 1786.

JAMES DOWNING: oath as 1st Lieut of Militia. Montg. Va. Orders. Ct 5 May 1778.

ALEXANDER EWING, entitled to pay for the use of a mare, 83 days, in the service of his country, at 1sh.-6 per day; also for some flour. Montg. cty, Va. [Fincastle cty records.] p. 191. Orders. 28 June 1785.

JOHN FOWKE. Will. "Now in the service of the United & Independent States of America" as Adjt, 10th Cont. Va. Regt. Dated at Newcastle Town, Delaware State. Spots. Abstracts. E-551. 22 Apr 1777.

JOHN FROST, a resident of Grayson cty, entered service in New Jersey a short time before the battle of Long Island. Was born 1756, Morris cty, N. J. Lived there when he enlisted. Grayson cty, Va. Orders. 24 Sept 1832

ANDREW FERGUSON, Corporal, Capt. Day Scott's Company, 1st Batt'n Md. Troops. A. A. cty, Md. Wills i-59. 6 July 1776–12 May 1778.

JAMES GIBSON qualified as 2d Lieut. (Chosen by the company.) Aug. cty, Va. 1-202 and 504. 20 Oct 1778.

JAMES GRISSHAM, recommended for Capt. Militia. Amherst cty, Va. Orders, p. 182. Ct 6 Oct 1783.

JOHN JONES, Grayson cty. 86 years old, 3 Apr 1832. Was born Morris cty, E. Jersey. Grayson cty, Va. Orders. 24 Sept 1832.

JOHN McCLAIN presents affidavits of William Moore, Esq., and John Davidson, and the Court declare opinion he was a Revolutionary soldier. Rock'm cty, Va. Orders, p. 131. Ct Aug. 1832.

THEODOSIUS McDONALD, ensign in the Va. Regt under Colo. Byrd, His bro. and heir-at-law, Mr. Daniel McDonald.........2,000 a. Montg. cty, Va. Surveys. 5 Mch 1774.

JAMES McALEXANDER, Jr. Produces commission as Captain of Militia Company. Amherst cty, Va. Orders, p. 142. Ct 4 Aug 1783.

JAMES MONTGOMERY. "For a large musket well fixt Brass Mounting Carried near an Oz Ball." Amherst cty, Va. Orders, p. 3. May Ct 1783.

DANIEL MORGAN, Ensign. Montg. cty, Va. Surveys. 10 Mch 1774.

JAMES NEVIL [?]* Amherst cty, Va. May Ct 1783. Orders, p. 108.

SAM'L POE, Sjt 1st Va. Reg't. 200 acres. Montg cty, Va. Surveys. 23 July 1774.

JAMES PATTISON (Infant); 760 barrels [?] of beef supplied. Amherst cty, Va. May Ct 1783. Orders, p. 118.

JOHN SAVAGE* Amherst cty, Va. May Ct 1783. Orders, p. 117.

WILLIAM STATON, for one canoe. (Lesley's Invasion.) Amherst cty, Va. May Ct 1783. Orders, p. 117. Also for a Rifle, Gen. Arnold's Invasion.

WILLIAM SUTHERLAND, Ensign, 95th Regt of Foot, under Col. Burton. 2,000 acres. Montg. cty, Va. Surveys. 24 Jany 1774.

JOHN STONE, to be Capt. in the room of William Boune [?] Montg. cty, Va. 26 Sept. 1786. Orders.

ARNOLD SHEALS, entitled to 200 acres. Served 1st Batt'n, Royal American Regt of Foot. Montg. cty, Va. Surveys. 4 July, 1774.

The County Court Note-Book

An every-other monthly devoted mainly to abstracts from County Court Records, prior to 1800.

MILNOR LJUNGSTEDT. Editor and Publisher. Bethesda, Rural Route 5, Maryland.

Published six times a year. Subscriptions must begin with the year.

June, 1931 Whole
Vol. X, No. 3 No. 58

The Editor was born with the scrapbook habit, inherited from ancestors who compiled "common-place" books, and others who treasured "Brilliants" from the Boston Transcript. The habit is the root of no end of trouble and worry, especially if you are also a kind of putting-off person, for the scraps increase even as the potato-bug or the grasshopper, and the state of mind of the scrapper is not always happy. If he or she be a person of great mental strength and will-power, the kind that says to himself or herself, "Why should I do this for posterity . . . what has posterity done for me?" and orders the general utility man to deposit the accumulation "on the place where you burn things up" . . . he or she will experience a great lightness of spirit, a marvellous lightness, but in after days will say "My! I wish I hadn't thrown away this or that!" and so never escape the worry cow after all.

The Editor only once, in desperation, did burn a bushel or two, and then returned to the ways of old . . . returned to find in the miscellany, here or there, something most consolingly worth while.

For example, here are some fragments from what I take to be the autobiography as published in a daily paper of a past Vice-President. I would call him a "sunshiny" man.

"So far as I know I am the only man of my "name who does not trace his origin directly or "collaterally to the great Chief Justice. Whether "some time in the past his blood and mine "mingled in somebody's veins I do not know, "and, with the utter recklessness of a Hoosier, I "do not care."

I regret to say that there then comes a tear in the clipping, but it seems that the then Vice-President was interviewed by an impecunious person of his name.

"He said there was no doubt whatever that "we could trace our origin back to William Earl "Marechal, who was in charge of the stables of "King John, and who saved the French King "from stealing the Magna Charta after it had "been wrested by the barons from an unwilling "sovereign. This gave me an idea, and I offered "to get him a job in the livery stable and let him "start the line anew on its illustrious career. "He disdainfully refused, borrowed ten dollars "and disappeared from my vision.

"Yes, ancestry is a great thing. Few people "can get along without it. It seems to be an "absolute household necessity. It softens the "blows of fortune and makes many a bow to "bend under the pull of adversity which other-"wise would break. . . . The City of Washing-"ton is full of ancestry. . . . 'Owners and occu-"pants of earlier days, from graves forgotten, "stretch their dusty hands and hold in mort-"main still their old estates!'"

The Vice-President continues humorously, but is there not a touch of bitter saneness behind his persiflage?

The last anecdote that the clipping records is that about that Marshal of Napoleon who, at a levee one morning, had listened to the bragging courtiers, until, when someone asked as to his ancestors, drew himself up and answered, "*I, myself, am an ancestor!*"

Our Vice-President runs down his branch of his family tree until he comes to a parting over slavery, and recalls that in the constant argument some one of his side repeated the words of Anne of Austria, which the Editor would like to record here, ephemeral as this paper is: "God does not pay at the end of every week, but He pays."

The Editor regrets to record the passing of a Virginia Clerk of the Court, whom she had known for a number of years. This is WILLIAM E. SANDIDGE, of Amherst county, whose father William Sandidge, was the last clerk under the old county system, and who is now succeeded by his son, William E. Sandidge, Jr. Mr. Sandidge spent most of his life in the Clerk's Office, having taken up the work when he was about fifteen years old, while just a boy attending Kenmore High School, near the courthouse town of Amherst. He served as deputy under various Clerks, including his father. In 1900, upon the death of his father he was appointed to fill the unexpired term. When the County and Circuit Courts were combined, he was elected Clerk and held the office until his death. The deputy, a lady the Editor holds as a friend, writes "*He went away on August 24th.*"

Mr. Sandidge, like many of the Clerks, was not easy to know offhand, but he was both friendly and helpful to the Editor . . who, like other searchers, was, no doubt, a good deal of a nuisance. Among the absolute necessities of existence she demanded to be kept warm . . . this is a northern failing. And the stove *was* "temperamental" and the wood wet, so that when the intermittent fire intermitted, the Clerk came to the rescue and with his own hands cajoled and argued with that fire. At a last visit, the courthouse and the Clerk's office had been vastly improved, even to the extent of steam heat, and it was with evident pride that the Clerk showed the roomy office and the new heat.

Many pleasant, some sad, some amusing memories come to the Editor in connection with the Virginia Clerk's Offices . . . not all to be told. She is glad to record those places and times where she was welcomed and invited to come back.

The Editor would like to call attention to the fact that it is probable that copies of Mr. Nottingham's later compilations can still be had, but that after a few years they will be "out of print." These books are so very valuable, especially the WILLS AND ADMINISTRATIONS OF ACCOMACK COUNTY, and the LAND CAUSES of the same county, that they should be in every public library and in every private library which includes historical, biographical as well as genealogical works.

Mr. Monnette has, it is now some little time ago, completed and published the fifth part of the FIRST SETTLERS OF THE PLANTATIONS in East New Jersey . . . in which he covers, in the work as completed, the fifty years from 1664 to 1714. This is a very remarkable compilation. The Pennsylvania Geneological Society's last magazine, in its reviews, refers to the wealth of genealogical and historical material gathered by Mr. Monnette. The volume is most beautifully and interestingly gotten up. Few genealogical books suit the Editor's over-critical eye . . . this does. When a man who has the means does this sort of a thing and does it well, it in part consoles those of us who have not the means.

Mrs. Hart's very excellent DELEWARE RECALL is filling a place that needed to be filled, and filling it in a close cut, compact style, suited to a publication of absolute fact. A systematic reading of the Delaware records was needed . . . a small State, but a trying one to the searcher.

The MARYLAND GENEALOGICAL BULLETIN, published by Mr. R. F. Hayes of Baltimore, is a worthwhile paper. If the Editor could induce Mr. Hayes to print the dates of his very valuable Bible records . . . that is to say, 'the date of the printing of the Bibles containing them . . . it would tend somewhat more to that scientific exactness which we are beginning to learn is necessary in this work. Mr. Hayes is making available material which otherwise, many would not know where to find.

Touching upon scientific exactness, the Editor calls attention to the excellent articles in recent issues of the AMERICAN GENEALOGIST, published by Mr. Donald Lines Jacobus, in New Haven. If the Editor could have said what Mr. Jacobus writes, that is the way she would have said it! The article in July, "*Interpreting Genealogical Records,*" is very, *very*, good, and the article in October, "*Is Genealogy an Exact Science*" is just as good and better. The Editor desires to publish here, her personal thanks. Besides these most readable essays, the Genealogist contains what the searcher craves, town records, family genealogies, critical comments on published errors, and a great deal more.

The list of "head-rights," under the title of VIRGINIA COLONISTS, will be continued in the NOTE-BOOK for August, and will be continued further in the issues for October and December, or in the possibly joint number for those months.

As will be noted by those familiar with the Virginia Land Office, the abstracts are extremely brief, the intention being merely to list the head rights under the patents issued from about 1655 to 1666, which were not copied from an early volume known as "Old Volume Five" when that volume was copied many years ago into two volumes of the regular series of patent records.

The Editor has just learned from Mrs. Nell Marion Nugent, the Clerk of the Land Office, that she has very wisely decided to include the original volume five in her forthcoming "Cavaliers and Pioneers," with notation to the copied volumes as well as to the original. So that when this valuable work appears upon the shelves of the libraries throughout the country the reader of the NOTE-BOOK who wishes more complete information can find it in Mrs. Nugent's complete abstracts.

The Editor further takes the opportunity of emphasizing the great scope as well as the great value of Mrs. Nugent's work. It will be, in effect, a complete abstract of the patent records up to the year 1800 . . . from the very beginning, which was about 1621 . . . although the patents of that time are not all of record. It is a remarkable piece of work, of unquestioned accuracy . . . . indeed, it will be more correct in details than the notes made by many sincere but inexperienced searchers.

The Editor knows that the compiler of the work regrets the delay in bringing this material out in printed form, and also that it has required a revision and re-printing of the parts previously published. Circumstances made it advisable to start again and enlarge upon the original plan. As now intended, the abstracts will fill four or five volumes, and with the index . . which will be one of those meticulously perfect things which everybody but the Editor demands . . . each volume will carry nearly 1,000 pages. (The index is a wonderful compilation but the Editor would rather read four hundred pages of the patents than one page of an index!)

The first volume of Cavaliers and Pioneers will be out, it is thought, within a few weeks.

The Editor has received a new style of genealogy . . . it is FRANCIS BURTON HARRISON'S BURTON CHRONICLE, and it is actually rather delightful reading. Perhaps that should not be said of a thorough piece of work like the CHRONICLE, which has a solid basis of fact as well as documentation. But it is an unusual book with a flexible style and a humorous undertone. The Editor does not know whether the subdued humor is due to the author or is the quite recognizable style of a very able genealogist . . Robert Armistead Stewart . . . . she suspects it is due to both.

The CHRONICLE has covered the BURTON ground wherever found in Colonial Virginia and Mr. Harrison has most carefully investigated the possible relationships of the many individuals of the name in that section. It is a pity that so valuable a book should be "privately printed," but there is no doubt that copies will be given to many libraries.

Information is received that Mr. STEWART'S HISTORY OF THE VIRGINIA NAVY OF THE REVOLUTION IS IN PRINT, or would be at the date this is written. The title has been wisely changed from "The Romance of Virginia's Navy" &c. The price is $3.50 and can be had of Mitchell and Hotchkiss, Richmond, Va.

See p. 34

vir, John C. Patterson, Myrtle R. MACE, et vir, Samuel V. Mace;

Marian J. BOGLEY, Arthur E, Rabbitt et ux, Bertie Rabbitt, Clara V. STUBBS, Agnes HARDY, Lee H. LONGLEY, John T. Hardy, et ux, Beulah Hardy, Blanche A. THOMPSON, Olive J. BREADY, Dorothy E. HEALY, infant, Charles B. Healy, infant, Doris L. Healy, infant, James D. Healy, infant, Ann M. Healy, infant;

Pauline C. SPLIEDT, et vir, Charles E. Spliedt, Margaret W. SUTTON, et vir, E. J. Sutton, the unknown heirs of Thomas Maurice Rabbitt, deceased, the unknown heirs of Mollie C. MAGRUDER, deceased, the unknown heirs of Thaddeus BALDWIN, deceased; the unknown heirs of Benjamin Franklin BALL, deceased;

Note: The amount of this land, which is desired for the improvement of one of the roads is ....seventeen one hundredths of an acre. Publication is made by the State Roads Commission of Maryland, who pay for the advertisement (which is over twice as long as the foregoing list); an interested "party" might ask who pays the Commission? The little foxes spoil the vines.

FORENAMES OF THE COLONIAL PERIOD

CHARITY MIDDLETON, mentioned in will of Richard Venitt, of Kent. 1710. Md. Wills. xiii-33.

CHARITY SMALLWOOD, wife of Bayne Smallwood, and dau. of Col. John Courts. 1709. Md. Wills. xii-208.

CHARITY THEOBALDS, dau. of John, of Charles county. 1712-1713. Md. Wills. xiii-540.

CHARITY BAILYE, dau. of John and wife of ....Thompson. She also had dau. CHARITY. 1712. Md. Wills xiii-582.

CHARITY BELT, dau. of John, A. A. cty. 1697-1698. Md. Wills vi-175. CHARITY Jordon was a wit to this will.

CHARITY COURTS, kinswoman of William Buttrune (?) of Charles county. 1692. Md. Wills vi-66.

CHARITY NORCROSS, dau. of William of Dorchester cty. 1694. Md. Wills vii-40.

CHARITY TIDINGS, daughter of Richard [She was under 16.] A. A. cty. 1687. Md. Wills vi-40. CHARITY CHESELL a witness.

CHARITY ATKINS, dau. of Joseph, of Somerset cty. 1722-1723. Wills xviii-136.

CHARITY JOHNSON, dau. of Leonard of Somerset. 1720. Wills xvi-273.

CHARITY JONES of Talbot cty. (Aunt of Absalom Thrift.) 1721. Wills xvii-91.

CHARITY POPE, dau. of John, of Somerset. 1719-1721. Md. Wills xvi-430.

CHARITY STORY, dau. of Walter of Charles cty. 1725-1736. Wills xviii-498.

CHARITY TIDINGS, wf. of Rich'd and dau. of Samuel Lockwood, of A. A. cty. 1722. Wills xvii-249.

CHARITY COURTS, [probably wife of John Rogers...or mother-in-law.] 1717. Wills xiv-521.

CHARITY GREEN, dau, of Thos. Haygoe[?] of Charles cty. 1714-1716. Wills xiv-213.

CHARITY HARVEY, wit. to will of Margret McClester of Somerset. 1715-1717. Wills xv-405.

CHARITY HEAD, dau. of William of Pr. George's. 1718-1719. Wills xv-140.

CHARITY JOHNSON, dau. of John Kellam, Sr., of Somerset. 1718. Wills xiv-726.

CHARITY JONES, will of Thomas Beswick, of Talbot cty. 1718. Wills xiv-726.

CHARITY WHITTINGTON, dau. of William, Sr., of Calvert. 1716. Wills. xiv-208.

MARYLAND NOTES

The first volume of the land records of Prince George's county, Maryland (A-1696) has the cattle-marks of the following persons recorded upon a fly-leaf.

Thomas Trueman Greenfield
David Small
Robert Tyler
Thomas Oanes [?]
William Offitt
Charles Tracy
Walter Evans
Jonathan Simmons
Richard Jaffy
Samuel Magruder
John Davis
Charles Davis
Richard Joanes
John Barrett
Joshua Hall
William Rayhus [?]
Matthew Maunbly
John Sprigg
Edmund Neell
Daniel Daniellson
Thomas Lucas
James Stoddert
William Selby
William Conley
Joseph Wells
Charles Walker
John Rigdon
Edward Phoney
William Rothery

A BOOK OF DISTRIBUTIONS, FREDERICK COUNTY, MARYLAND

This is a small, originally unbound record, which is now bound at the back of another collection of small unbound records, in the office of the Register of Wills, Frederick, Maryland. The dates are between 1777 and 1784. The first name is that of the deceased person; the other names are those of the distributees.

EDWARD RIPLEY; Widow Elizabeth and two children, Jacob and John. 11 Aug 1778.

DARIUS RUFE; Catharine Rufe, admx. [Distribution not given.] 11 Aug 1778.

JOHN KIMBOL; Lettice Kimbol, widow. [Distribution not given. No date.]

LETTICE KIMBOL; George Base [?] admr. [Distribution not given.]

ANN SELF; *Silos* Veatch, admr. [Distribution not given.] [No dates can be found for this and the two preceding.]

SAMUEL WICKHAM; Joseph Wood, Jr. extr. [Same note as above.]

JOHN WILLSON; Susannah Wilson, admx. [Same note.]

CONROD HEARSE; Harmon Hearse, admr. Distributees: Harmon Hearse, Catharine Lawrence, Christiana Winholtz; Mary Search[?] No date.

HENRY BRUNER; Magdalena and John, extrs. [Same note as above.]

ELEANOR MEDLEY; Leonard Smith, extr. To dau. Eleanor Medley. Feby Ct 1779.

NATHANIEL BARNARD; Mena Barnard, extx. Distributees: Widow; 9 chn: William, Luke, Mary, Phebe, Tobias, Jessee, Nath'l, Notley and Mina. Bond filed 20 Oct 1779.

CASPER DEVILBESS; Ann Cock, extx. Distributees: Casper Devilbess[?] Widow; 6 chn: George, John, Casper, Ann Remsburgh, Susanna Remsburgh, and Barbara Fleming. No date.

CHRISTIAN TLGNER[?] Anna Maria Tlgner, extx. Distributees: widow, and 3 chn: Catherine, Christian, John Jacob. Bond filed 12 Aug 1779. [This name is quite impossible to make out. It might be meant for Hagner. The German names and English Clerks in Western Maryland made difficult work for searchers.]

JACOB ECKMAN; Peter Bohrer and Peter Crebell, extrs. "Representatives"; Eve Elizabeth Eckman, Phillippina, Christina, Barbara, George, Peter and John Eckman. No date.

WILLIAM RIDGELEY; Mary Ridgeley, extx Widow and two chn: Martha and Sarah Ridgeley. No date.

CHARLES SPRINGER; Susannah Springer, admx. Widow and ten children: John S., Margaret Riddle, Rebeccah, Springer, Ann Silver, Chas. Springer, Edward, Peter, Susannah, Eliz'th and Levy Springer. Bond 20 Oct 1778.

WILLIAM CARMACK; Jane and William Carmack, extrs. No distribution, no date.

GEORGE HUTZELL (or HUTSELL); Magdalena Hutzell, admx. Widow and ten children: Margaret Miller, Susannah Engle, Geo. *Huzell*, John Hutsell, Peter Hutsell, Matthias, Lodewick, Mary, Mich'l and Gabriel Hutsell. Bond 12 Oct 1778.

PHILIP KEENER; Mary Keener, widow, and Mathias Mart [?] extrs. Balance to widow. No date.

PETER ERB; Judith Erb, Chris'r Erb and Charles Angel, extrs. Widow, six children: Peter, John, Catharine, Madelina, Lowisa and Eve Erb. No date.

JOHN BRICKER; Mary and John Bricker, extrs. Widow, and seven children: John, Eve, Jacob, Susannah, Christiana, Henry and Mary Bricker. No date.

CHRISTIAN THOMAS; Christian Thomas, extr. Distributees: Barbara Stoner, Mary Thomas, Barbara and Mary Zerich [Name uncertain.]) Four chn: Henry, Christian and Mary Thomas, Barbara Stoner. No date. [The repetition of names is in the record.]

PHILIP KING; Christiana Kennedy, admx. Widow and two children: David and John King. No date.

CONROD [HETULDY??] George Kurtz, admr. Three children: John, Henry and George. No date.

JACOB HUMMER; Jacob Hummer, extr. Five children: Mary, Elizabeth, Eve, John and Jacob Hummer. No date.

HENRY CARNUFF; admr. Widow and ten children: John, Peter, Henry, Adam, Jacob, Susannah, Catherine, Elizabeth, Mary and Ann. No date.

JACOB MIERS; Christiana Woolf, admx. Widow and two children: Elizabeth and Jacob Miers. No date.

VESTAL RIDGELEY; Urith Ridgeley, admx. Widow and eight children: Sarah, Jane, Urith, Vestal, Sophia, Martha, Richard and William. No date.

GABRIEL KETZENDANNER [this name was later written GETZENDANNER]; Adam Ketzendanner and Gilbert Kemp, extrs. Three children: Jacob, Henry and Margaret. No date.

(To be continued)

INTERCOUNTY AND INTERCOLONY

JOHN APPLING, of Nottoway psh, Amelia cty, Va. His will. Richmond cty, Ga. Will Book A-2. April 1783.

Col. WILLIAM BAILEY; special letters of administration on the interest of William Wells, late of Virginia, in this estate, granted to George R. Gilmer. 5 Mch 1827. Oglethorpe cty, Ga. Minutes of the Court.

[Mrs.] CATHERINE GREEN [widow] of Newport, R. I. . . her signature to a conveyance by Jeremiah Wadsworth [who first signs] [Records damaged and partly illegible, but CATHERINE appears to have been the widow of Maj.-Gen'l NATHANIEL GREENE, and this is a deed conveying part of his estate on Cumberland Island.] Camden cty, Ga. A-4. 9 and 31 Oct 1786.

JOHN HARDAWAY, now of Warren cty, Ga., but formerly of Dinwiddie cty, Va., gives power to Jno. Glass of Mecklinburgh cty, Va. 12 Aug 1795. Warren cty, Ga. A-95.

ETHELRED W. LANGSTON; State of Alabama . . . at an Orphans' Court . . . Cherokee cty, Ala. 5 Oct 1840, David C. Langston, a minor heir is shown to have property in Oglethorpe cty, Ga., and Chism [Chisholm] Daniel is appointed his guardian. Sept. Term, 1841.

DANIEL MELSON, of Sussex on Delaware, power to Daniel Melson, Jr., Hancock cty, Ga. 19 Aug 1791. A.B.-521.

By virtue of affidavits from Sussex and Maclenburg counties, Virginia, Ordered that the will of EDWARD POWELL be probated. 30 Mch 1798. From a loose leaf, Court Minutes. Oglethorpe cty, Georgia.

JOHN PETTY; Letters testamentary to William Petty. John Petty was late of Anne Arundel cty, Maryland. 17 Apr 1794. Minutes, Richmond cty, Ga. p. 40.

JOHN, son of JOHN PRYOR and ELIZABETH his wife, was Baptized May 12, 1778 [Copy from Wendron Baptisms]. ELIZABETH PRYOR, widow, and JOHN PRYOR, the son, and MARY PRYOR, the daughter of JOHN PRYOR, late of the parish of Wendrom, in the county of Cornwall. . . . England, make oath as to the marriage, and that JOHN PRYOR left home for America about eighteen years before. It is mentioned that there was another daughter called ANN. Edgefield cty, S. C. S-519.

JOHN PRYOR of this Parish [of Wendrom] and ELIZABETH CHEGWIDDEN [??] perhaps widow?] of this Parish married in the Church by Banns 26 Dec 1775, by Jacob Bullock, Vicar. "The above copy taken from the Wendron Marriage Register October ye 18th 1797." Edgefield, S. C. S-518.

LITTLETON REESE to David Rosser of Virginia; consideration, $1500, 287 1-2 acres on the waters of Fort Creek, Hancock cty, Georgia. Hancock cty, Ga. D-330. 10 Aug. 1729.

HENRY SWENEY, of East Florida; deed to John Duke of Camden cty, Georgia. 17 Sept 1788. Camden cty, Ga. A-B, p. 30.

JAMES THWEATT and wife BETSEY; John Mitchell and wife Sarah; John Hamilton and wife Tabitha; all of Hancock county, Georgia, to John B. Turne [Turner?] of Greensville cty, Virginia,; consideration $1200.........all our rights agreeable to the last will of Thomas Thweatt, deceased.........to 225 acres in Greensville cty, on Meheareng River, Joining Batts' land, the land that was Peterson Thweatt's...... and the sd Turner's land in Virginia [reference to will, dated 16 Oct 1783); to have and to Hold the said premises after the death of Betty Galt, wife of Thomas Galt, formerly wife of Thomas Thweatt, deceased. Wit: U. Thweatt, Joel Maybry, Jas. Mitchell. Hancock cty, Ga. 25 Jany 1800. C-297.

EDMUND WALSH, Hancock cty, Ga. Power to Cornelius O'Keef, of Carrick on Sine [?] in Tipperary county, Ireland, to receive from Michael Greene.........&c., &c. (Reference to house in Carrick in which Walsh lived.) Hancock cty, Ga. 19 Dec 1796. A. B.-307.

HUMPHREY WELLS, in his will, mentions a daughter Sibella. He leaves land in Maryland. Richmond cty, Ga. Will Book A-9. Aug. 1781.

"ET AL"

The land and probate records of the county courts often have the recording of causes containing extensive lists of heirs of varying degrees of kinship, but they cannot very often compete with the following list of persons covered by the "*et al*", who are joined in condemnation proceedings with TERESA RABBITT, of Montgomery county, Maryland. The case is a recent one, but the name RABBITT is an old one in the county. The names follow. The notice in the public press is addressed to

Teresa Rabbitt, Charles F. Rabbitt et ux, Mary Rabbitt, David T. Rabbitt, et ux, Mary C. Rabbitt, Sarah M. Rabbitt, George G. Rabbitt, Jr., James F. Rabbitt, Gertrude T. RICE, et vir, . . . Rice, Mary E. Rabbitt, John T. Rabbitt, Infant, Wade H. Rabbitt, et ux, Christine Rabbitt, Mary E. HALL, et vir, W, O. Hall, Joseph R. Rabbitt, et ux, Grace D. Rabbitt, Lucy Jane Rabbitt, William Frank Rabbitt, et ux, Mary Rabbitt, Annie H. Rabbitt, Irving E. Rabbitt;

Marie Pauline EARLE, Nora R. SHALLCROSS, et vir, Thomas Shallcross, George W. Rabbitt, et ux, Catherine Rabbitt, Ella G. Rabbitt, Harvey L. Rabbitt, et ux, Margaret Rabbitt, Murray L. Rabitt, et ux, Elizabeth B. Rabbitt;

Avis L. SHERMAN, et vir, Outran Sherman, Doris L. WEIKERT, et vir, Gerald Weikert, Marian V. FIELDS, et vir, Charles William Fields, Daniel C. KRAFT, Mary C. Rabbitt, et vir, Daniel T. Rabbitt, Henry J. T. Kraft, et ux, Minnie Kraft, Marian L. SHAW, et vir, Edwin F. Shaw, Edgar W. BOYLE, et ux, Mamie Boyle, Emory Boyle et ux, Delia Boyle, Elsie LAY, et vir, Augustus Lay;

Corrine WILSON, et vir, Thomas Wilson, Clara R. BALL, Albertus FIERY, Mabel C. EICHELBERGER, et vir, T. F. Eichelberger, Ward Fiery, William T. BALL, et ux, Nora C. Ball, Bernard M. Ball, et ux, Thalia V. Ball, Turner WILSON, Frank WILSON, et ux, Estelle Wilson, Amanda Wilson, Dolly Rabbitt, Leona COPPAGE, et vir, Hiram Coppage, William O. Rabbitt;

Myrtle R. BOPST, et vir, Lester Bopst, Ivy J. ZAUMEYER, et vir, William Zaumeyer, Warren Rabbitt, Eva Rabbitt, Alton Rabbitt, Isaac H. Rabbitt et ux, Annie Rabbitt, Maria V. O'NEAL, et vir, Daniel F. O'Neal, Mary C. PATTERSON et

UNCLASSIFIED PARAGRAPHS

William Maria Farthing, of St. Mary's county, to John Bradford, son and heir of John, deceased, of Prince George's county, Gent., consideration £30 . . . conveys a parcel of land about twenty miles higher than the falls of the Potomac, bordering on said River and called the Sugar Lands . . . adjoining a tract called Brightwell's Hunting Quarter and beginning at a "bounded" tree of Brightwell's Hunting Quarter, the land being originally granted to Edward Edloe of St. Mary's county, and known as Edloe's Adventure. . . . containing 300 acres . . . granted to Edward Edloe "derived" [devised ?] to John Noble, Jun'r of St. Mary's county, being Edward Edloe's sister's son, who d. s. p. It then "derived" to sd John Noble's sister, named Mary Noble, only survivor of sd John Noble, Jr. She also d. s. p. it "derived" to William *Spinse* [?] of St. Mary's county, planter, being first cousin of the whole blood by the father's side and heir-at-law to sd John and Mary; and "Spins" sold to William Maria Farthing, who sold to John Bradford, deceased, father of the present John Bradford, son and heir of said John Bradford . . . . . the deed made to sd John Bradford, deceased, being lost or mislaid or not recorded . . . . Wife, Ann Farthing. Pr. Geo's, Md. M-257. [The date of this was about 1727.]

William Eilbeck (or Eilbech), of Charles County, Gent., Thomas Stonestreet, and Peter Dent, of Prince George's county, Gent., give bond, £400, to John Wade and Sarah Edgar Wade and their executors. . . . Condition being that Eilbeck pay to sd John Wade and Sarah Edgar Wade, their executors, &c., &c., parts of John Edgar's estate. (Reference to Edgar's will.) Pr. Geo's cty, Md. Z-91. 26 Nov 1740.

(After the death of Robert Wade, of Chester, Penna., his heir and the heir of his wife, Lydia, a younger Lydia Wade, conveyed her lands to John Wade, who was a nephew of Robert and presumably cousin to the younger Lydia, who was a daughter of Thomas Wade, a brother of Robert. Lydia married one Philip Eilbeck, and a Maryland record refers to them as "languishing" in a Maryland jail . . . [for debt.] There are almost no Wade records of this line extant. It would be appreciated if some one coald and would supply the connecting threads. Editor.)

A Patriarch

John Sorrell, of Amherst county, Virginia, made a will the 25 Mch 1780, which was probated the 1 Sept 1783.

He had a grandson, Martin Dawson (who was a preacher.) and two grandsons, Thomas and William Dawson;

He also had a great grand-son, John Sorrell Dawson, "son of my grandson John Dawson, and his wife Sally;"

John Sorrell Dawson, as shown by the will, had a brother Pleasant Dawson, and a brother Benjamin Dawson.

There is also mentioned a great-granddaughter, Susannah Dawson, daughter of John and Sally, and two other great-granddaughters, Mary and Prissillah Dawson, also daughters of John and Sally, also Nancy and Betsy Dawson, sisters of Mary, and Prissillah.

Grandson John Dawson, son of Martin and wf Prissillah, must have been the brother of Martin, the preacher.

Grandsons John and Martin Dawson, and Peter Lyon are made executors.

Sorrell had also a daughter Katy Howard, and a granddaughter Mary Ann Sneed, he mentions the two oldest children, Frances and John Sneed.

His wife was Molly Coleman Sorrell.

Amherst, vol. ii, p. 140.

The will of Richard Simpson, of Frederick county, Md. mentions his four sons, Richard, Joshua, Charles and *Resin*, to whom he gives all his Frederick county lands; his daughter Delilah Simpson, to whom he gives 70 acres in *Pennsylvania and Fayette County* that fell to me by heirship at the decease of my brother Gaither Simpson and was bought by him of James Neill, Esq'r. . . Also gives her negroes, Pat, Betty and Hannah.

His four sons are to pay their sister, Delilah, five pounds each, and the daughter is to have the right to live "at my dwelling plantation that I have bequeathed to my son Rezin Simpson." Wf Sophia, extx. Wit: Ephraim Howard, John Maynard, Ephraim Maynard. 28 Jany 1796–21 May 1799. Montg. cty, Md. G. M. 3-292.

The will of Arre Simpson, mentions a sister Nancy Gaither, also a neice Arre Simpson Gaither. Leaves a family graveyard "to those of the family that has a desire to be buried within the wall." Negro Oston [Austin ?] to be free at 31. Mentions sister Sarah Middleton, nephew, Thomas John Hammond; niece Tomsey Pool; nephews Dennis Hammond, Johnsey, Denton and Nick Hammond, children of my dear sister Tomsey Hammond; niece Anne Williams and Harriet Worthington Griffith; niece Henrietta Simpson, Elizabeth Simpson; nephew, Francis Simpson, son of my dear Brother Basil Simpson; niece, Sarah Worthington Simpson; negro Rachel to be free at 25; nephew Basil Simpson, negro Ben, to be free at 25. Nephew Ephraim Simpson Gaither, niece Arre Simpson Gaither, a "Bofet", &c. Nephew Samuel West Burgess, mulatto Brow [?] Negro Jack and Wm., "Marrere," and others to be free at his death, and their children, (if any) to "respectfully go free" at 21. Negro "Marrere" being unable to support himself is to be cared for. Ephraim Gaither and testator's sister, Nancy Gaither, to be extrs. Wit: John Stoner (affirms), Henry Boocher, Char's Simpson. 7 Aug 1814– 11 Dec 1815. Fred'k cty, Md. R. H. S. 1-121.

Printed at The Industrial School for Crippled and Deformed Children, 241 St. Botolph St., Boston, Mass.

The
County Court Note-Book

A Little Bulletin of History and Genealogy

August, 1931 Vol. X, No. 4

VIRGINIA COLONISTS

(*From "Old Vol. 5," S. L. O. Richmond, Va.*)

WILLIAM JENNINGS, "in New Begin[?] creek," 1668.
Head rights: Sam'll Henrike, Steph. Peirson, Sam'll Moses, Tho: Peram, Tho. Richmond, Mich. Parram, Peter Janson, Sarah Marshall, Eliz: Jenner, Peter Dennis.

WILLIAM JOHNSON and STEPHEN HORSEY, Northampton cty. 1655.
Head rights: Tho. Denellin, Mary Denellin, Geo. Harrison, Ben Sumer, John Treddar, Wm. Jonson, Symon Brownely, Tho. Wilson, Rich. Warren, Ellynor Walter.

ROBERT KING, Northumberland cty. 1662.
Head rights: Tho: Pryse, Fra: Osborne, John Young, John Debford, Timo: Rosse.

THOMAS LUDWELL, Esq., Henrico cty, 1663.
Head rights: Phil: Ludwell, Wm. Broadrib, Wm. Drakeford, Wm. Hughlett, Robt. Jarrett, Rich: Crome, Rich: Talbot, Tho: Barton, James Durkett, Roger Heywood, Rob't Waid, John Venne, Dan: Cormacke, Hugh Berry, Ralph Parkson, Seth Dobson and two negroes.

ROBERT LAWEY[?] "in a Bay at the mouth of New Begin Creeke", 1663.
Head rights: ROB'T LAWRY, Jno. Major, Rich: Woodart, Jude Wilson, Geo. Preston, Jno. Turfe.

FENLAW [?] MACKWILLIAM, Accomack cty. 1663.
Head rights: James Mullins, Lewis Herbert, Jno. Hartfort, Francis Harwood, Jno. Smith, Tho: Mudge, James West, Jenkin Powell.

.... MICHELL [forename torn off], 1662. [County not found.]
Head rights: Wm. Appy, Tho: Irish, Geo. Stith, Mary Greenwood.

WILLIAM MOSELY, county not given, south side Rappahannock, parish of Sittingbourne, 1663.
Head rights: Jno. Richards, James Coop, Wm. Lee, Jno. Andrews, Joseph Doemy[?] Wm. Cross, James Read, Geo. Humphries, Richard Granger, Wm. Hickes, Thos. Powell, Dorothy Williams, Ralph Hunt, Alex. Dale, Mary Searle, Humphry Gibbons, James Sanders, Roger Dale, Thomas King, Wm. Gadd, Tho. Strang, Humphry Gressam, James Arnold.

GEORG MARISH, Rappahannock cty, 1664.
Head rights: Rachel Collings, Jno. Connagen, Ed. Boery, Do: Plummer, Hen. Pulman, Wm. Potter, Arthur Symons, Jno. Vaughan, George Price.

JOHN NICHOLLS, Northampton cty, 1655.
Head rights: Wm. Kendall, Mary Crumwell, John Haner [?] Rich'd Johnson, Thos. Sledwell, James Lynd, Wm. Stanton, Rob. Stanton.

ROBERT PEELE, county not given, 1663.
Head rights: Wm. Cornix, John Shard, Mary Carter, Jno. Sarmar[?] Wm. White, Mary Jones, Jno. Shalpe[??]

JOHN PAINE, Northumberland, [?]
Head rights: Wm. Young, Jno. Forby.

Coll. ROBT PITT and Mr. WM. BURGH, Isle of Wight cty, 1664.
Head rights: Henry Cray and wife, "Jno. et Richard et two children"; George Edwards, Jno. Carrell, Eliz: *Uxor.* [probably wife to Carrell], Richard Carrell, Jno. Carrell, Mary Carrell, Mary Soletree, Richard Wood, Wm. Bullock, Ema. Merchant, *Abrose* Boseman, John Watts, Roger Tarlton, Tho: Aladry[?] Jeremy Edmonds, Henry Coursie, Wm. Poope, twice, and his wife; Edm. or Edw. Tanner.

ROBT PITT and Wm. BURGH, Isle of Wight cty, 1664.
Head rights: Barniby Witwell, John Williams, Rob't Weir, Rich: Hinds, Henry Clerke, Wm. Ford, Jno. Bond, Wm. Willard or Hillard, Rich'd Horne, John ....[?] Rob. Floyd, Jno ....[?[Paul Bayly, Wm. Phillips, Henry Jones, James Haines[?] Mathew Culland, Francis Sibthrop, Thomas Hall, Rob't Lewis, Thomas Forecast, Tho: Clerke, Jane Jayes, George Wastell or Wartell.

EDWARD REVELL and JONAH JACKSON Accomack, 1663.
Head rights: Jno. Elver, Henry Loyd, Tho. Smith, Nich. Walbroke, Thomas Griffin, Mary Thomas, Christian Morris, Jos: Johnson, Mary Harwood, Edward Walsingham, Mary Sewell, Ann Heath, Ja: Wellfleet, Tho: Lazingby, Edw. Griffith, Mary Williams, Wm. Morgan, Jeane Shelley, Margt Powell, Joan Malford (Walford?)

Mr. THOMAS RELF, s. w. side Paspetanke river 1663.
Head rights: John Rouse, twice; Tho. Rouse, Step. Harris, Jno. Shorebury, Kath. Dolbin, Percy Whitty, Ann Maine [?] Ann Joanes, Mary Bayly, Tho. Reese, Wm. Black, Mary Belson, Jos. Rogers and his wife.

THOMAS RASON, Rappahannock cty, 1663.
Head rights: Jno. Smith, Tho. Smith, Rich'd Doefield, Elia Smith, Eliz. Smith, Henry Horton, Tho. Stone.

Mr. EDWARD SANDERS, [county?] 1662.
Head rights: (eighteen assigned by Hankes Dodson and Allen) Margtt Bassey, Francis Rosse

Mary Evans, Sumner Addams, Richard Harberd, Wm. Willis, Edward Peterson, Elizabeth Foy, Mary [?] Hunt, Jno. Bennett, David Jones, Mary Crow, Peter Brookes, Rich'd Foxon, Pêter Stone, John Goodwin, Abraham SANDERS, John SANDERS, Edwd Showdall, Tho: Arnall, Brown Hundrey, Simon Groves; George Edmunds, Wm. Thompson, Henry Hunt, Edward Web, Edward Parsly, Hug [Hugh?] Taylor, Wm. Palmer, John Edges, Wm. S.........[?] Mathew Aben[?]

THOMAS and ANTHONY STEPHENS, Rappahannock cty, 1662.
Head rights: (36 persons) Humph. Tompson, Wm. Garrett, Jos. Lambert, Tho: Briggs, James Baley, Christian Webb, Mary Brewer, James Hicks, Jno. Cheyney, Wm. Charlton, Susanna Smith, James Warner, Hen. Cobb, Grace Wilson, Ralph Pryce, John Grymes, Anth. Kenston, Aug: Withey, Sara: Watson, Margt Grey, "and 800 more rights by a relinquished patent." [Names not given here.]

JOHN SHARP, Rappahannock cty, 1664.
Head rights: Jno. Fookes, Anth. Webb, John Mullen, Peter Foster, James Diaz[?] Phil: Young, Mary Wilkinson, Jane Williams, Tho: Miles, Dorothy Ray, Martha Thornton.

JOHN SMITH, Rappahannock cty, [1664?]
Head rights: Jno. Irish, Nich. Corman, Wm. Mackinny, Watkin James, Arthur Cox, Jane Crillig, Jno. Martin. Jno. Carter, Michaell Hiland, Ellice Fletcher.

WILLIAM THOMAS, Notthumberland cty, 1655.
Head rights: John Gibbins, Eliz. Glissen, Joane, an Irishwoman, Jane Brocket.

GEORGE TREWETT, Northampton cty, 1660.
Head rights: John Tompson, Charles Barcroft, Alexander Mattrick, Wm. Branch, Tho. Moore. Tho. Musgrave, Jno. Young, Walter Lane, Jno. Watson, Robert Huntley.

Mrs. ANN TOFFT, Accomack cty, 1663.
Head rights: Even Jones, Mary Esthop, James Knowles, Mary Willis, Thomas Shandler [Chandler?] Owin Williams, Richard Porter, Morgan Mabri[?] Michaell Luey[?] Abraham Vincent, Peter Strong, Jeffry Wilkins, Mary Bridgmouth, Atlanta Hues, James Westgate, Tobias Dunsten, John Huntford, William Outred, John Jones, John Smith, Thomas Messenger, Margaret Roxby, Michaell White, Thomas Rouse.

ROGER WILLIAMS, n. s. Carolina river, 1663.
Head rights: Man: Rogers, Thos. Jones, Tho. Jefferies, John Rosse, Cha: Seward, Jno. Daniell, Jone Roper.

THO. WOODWARD, Jr., n. w. side Paspetanke river, 1663.
Head rights: Robt Chambers, Tho: Hamton, Ma: Lenox, Row: Denson, Rob: Shepard, Sil: Ward, Jno. Barker, Hum: Chapman; Tho. Bessie, Ja. Me......dah[?] Geo: Petit, Tho: Gilnett, Leo: Hathorne, Wm. Thomas, Rob, Walters, Jno. Simpson, Jno. Partride, Tho. Carner, Jeff. Mumford, Mary Croff, Jno. *Ceton*[?] Rich: Hamond, Rich: James, Mary Simons, Alex. Frizell, Wm. Hazelwood, Wm. Famill, Tho: Clements, A......... F.........[?] Dan. Finney.

WILLIAM WRIGHT, Gent., Nansemond cty, 1655.
Head rights: Dan: Gimblet, Nehemiah Lynch, Tho. Poole, Tho. Pinkard, Nich. Chapman, Jno. Walker, Jno. Norris, Arth. Holden, Enoch Hutchinson, Dorothy Westery[?] Aph[?] Cobin, Wm. Andrick, John Pryse, Edwd Russe, Martha Phillips, Jno. Wenec[?] Tho. Moore, Jno Eldes, Rob. *Jnoson*, Hen. Roberts, Fra. Davis, Jno. Smith, Raplh Bassill, Eliz. Hartly, Richard Harman, Mich. Lynge;
Mary Carter, Rob. Sapscoate (probably Prescoate, i. e. Prescott), Henry Prescoate, Roger Steward, Rich's Safrell, Marth. Roswell, Hester Barker, Kath. Hester, Mary Roberts, Eliz: Hartly, Mary Spencer, Anne Parker, Mich. Stallings, and his wife; Anth. Warren, Jno. Warren, Rob. Ewen, Leonard Strong, Jno. Browne.

JOHN WESTLOCKE, Northampton cty, 1655.
Head rights: Rose Lyna[?] Mary Lyna[?] Wm. Mees, Jno. Holmes, Arthur Lya [?] Jane Doe.

ABRAHAM WOOD, Charles City cty, 1663.
Head rights: "19 servants"; Henry Manneringe, Margaret Farrow, Nicholas Brookes, *Nichola* Overbey, Robt Harrison, Thom: Edwards, Rich'd Phillipps. Edw. Pleascock, Will'm Fleminge, John Blackshaw.

HENRY WHITE [?], Accomack, 1666.
Head rights: Hugh Piper, James Grinville [?] Jno. Billing, Marke Silly, Wm. Courtnay, Thos. Holin, Jno. Verman, Jno. Burgess, James Wery, Jno. Clarkfeild, Ridgeby North, Peter Courtney, Rich. Pridway, Charles Gells, Jno. Lawes, Rich. Arundell, Jo. Rashly, Fran. Buller, Jno. Elliot, Wm. Scawen, Wm. Cotton, Rob. Blaise [? list damaged.]

GEORGE WATSON, Accomack, 1666.
Head rights: Georg Greene, Mary Goodrick, Susan Poole, Wm. Greene, Jno. Waller, Jno. Clarke, Mary Jones, James Harlow, Jno. Carpenter, Luke White, James Garland, Marke Tomlin.

ST. MOUNT WELLS, westward side Chowanoake River, 1663.
Head rights: Tho. Poore, Jos: Hill, Ed: Suckett, Wm. Clarke, Tho: High. James White, Jno. Giloe, Tho. Bayly, Tho: Wood, Wm. Wood.

KATHERINE WOODWARD and PHILARETE WOODWARD, her daughter, westward side Paspetanky River, 1663.
Head rights: Fra. Est, Jno. Garnell, Mary Well, Alice Jeffry, John Newton, Christian Grene, Jno. Barnwell, Mary Taylor, Robt Cox, Ja: Johnson, Ja: Cocke, Rich. Harman, Tho: West, Jno. Smith, Tho. Turnell.

Mr. WILLIAM WEST, eastward side Pequimmin river, 1663.
Head rights: Jno. Mison, Tho: Cox, Wm. Camp, Wm. Jones, Mary Young, Tho: Carew, Edw. Frick, Wm. Stephens, Jno. Shaw, Marke Williams, Jno. Sarson, Tho: Cooly, Mary Carey[?] Jno. Sanders, Wm. Fewell, Marke L......[?] Wm. Capp, Tho: Stone "& 32 more."

THOMAS WOODWARD, Sr., and THOMAS WOODWARD, Jr. River of Chawanoke, 1663.
Head rights: Humph. Pawle, Tho. Pryer, Ann

Sutten, Robt. Black, Arth. Holder, Jacob Browne, Symon Pritchard, Ezekell Williams, Wm. Miller, Wm. Holden, Robt Conner, John Stevenson, Anth. Wyn, John Hamlin, Xpher Woodward, twice; Thomas Marshall, John Bird, Robt. Hancoke, Peter Dennis, twice; Eliza: Jemer[?] Sarah Marshall, Peter Janson, Ester Ruke, Mich. Talin[?] Tho: Richmond, Thos. Parin, Smith Moses, Steph. Persian, Sam'll Henry.

GEORGE WEADING, Westmoreland cty. 1664,
Head rights: John Watts, John Carpenter, John Hayle, Joane Charles, Tho. Floyd, Joane Powell, Sibill Press, Mary Smith, John Green, John Daby, Tho: Bigg, Martin Fisher.

HENRY WHITE, Sr., N. side Carolina river, 1663.
Head rights: Ann Donkaster, Geo: Jenkin, Edward Barrett, Dan'll Walker, Ann Jenkin.

HENRY WHITE, Jr., Corawtucke creeke, 1663.
Head rights: Peter Greene, Eliz: Howson, John Bench, Richard Rodds[?] Dan: Walker, Edward Morgan, Rich: Staples, Ann Dasor, Hester Morgan, Eliz: Emnes[?] Edw. Parrett, Sarah Wadman, Dan'll Walker, John Pine, James Rudder.

Mr. RICHARD WEBLEY, ROBT DAVIS and THOMAS FRESHWATER, Rappahannock and Northumberland counties, 1664.
Head rights: Sam'll Sparke, Jno. Dubb, James Temple, Fran: Potts, Wm. Salin, Peter Cramp, Joseph Cranfield, Xtopher Holmes, Wm. Hunter, Jno. Swan, Rich: Foster, Elnathan Tart, Jo. Cogginton, Peter Palmer, Ma: Hopewell, Wm. Hartwell, Hen: Williams, James Willis, Sam'll Furton, Barnab. Warhop, Elias Gurtford, Phillip Skotower, Tho: Parker, Rich: Doaford;

Wm. Burton, Mary Painter, Jane Gorge, Sarah Smith, Eliz: Whitfield, Susan Parrott, Rebecca Wolton or Wotton, Dorothy Cortrutt[?] Mary Fristo, Prudence Bishop, Sarah Bishop, Alice Baker, Fran. Webb, Katharine Simpson, Henry Frith, Jno. Finch, Tho: West, Richard Bateman, Pet'r Cottle, John Cottle, Ralph Cottle, Marmaduke Waterford, John Prince, Wm. Carpenter,

Fran: Marsh, Martyn Jones, Jenkin Powell, Harman Ruddock, Wm. Elder, Jno. Youngman, Dennis Culpepper, Lee Clemson, Stephen Wickes, Ferdinando Dew, Robt Hoskins, James Limproott[?] Tho. Hodkins, Hen: Mansfield, Jo: Clifton, Pet'r Chinly, Edw. Smith, Ann Borne, Tho: Broadhurst, Fran. Price, Rowland Walton, David Gressum, Jesper Wright, Rich'd Hampshire, Judith Hampshire, Morrice Vaughan, Pet'r Bagshaw, Rich: Lowdy;

Jno. Goodtry, Robt Stephens, Anth. Hudson, Sam'l Meader, Pet'r Scabroocke, James Tarpley, Martin Baxter, Wm. Thatcher, Sylvester Eales, Christo. Colly, Luke Foakes, Wm. Nicholls, Arthur Dawsey, Geo. Lane, Rich: Laffin, Jno. Turner, Miles Hobbs, Fran: Tablett, James Saunders, Pet'r Upton, Martin Hunt, Rich: Grandison[?] Fran: Posnett, Mary Paines, Jane Goose, Chas. Bryant, Sam. Pomphrett, Hannah Bacon, Susannah Martin, Constance Pullin, Fryzith[?] Collins, Thomas Hope;

Jno. Downes, James Parker, Mary Parker, Francis Parker, Em. Puddyford, Jno. Prat...... [?Prather] Robt Tompson, Luke Manton, Law. Jackman, Mary Shorbar, Jo. Griffin, Rich: Butlett, Jona. Colewright, Francis Palmer, Tymothy Forecaster, Jno. Beavin, Tho. Casse, Mary Cutfield, John Ellott, Sulvester Cartbolde, Tymothy Overcott. Eliz. Tatum[?] Jane Cullum, John Nelson[?Helson] Moses Buffolke, Rich: Howson, Jno. Armstrong, Jo: Peterson, Tho: Gardworth, Symon Culbertson; ;

Alex. Puly. Francis Courtman, James Bayly, Cornelius Clifton, Sam. Delaware, Jonathan Culverton, Elnathan Bray, Thomas Jennings, Frizwith Parsly, Ann Parsly, Robt Culpepper, Richard Welch, Elizabeth Dew, Samuel Hackett [Hachett?] Joseph Frith, Robert Catfeild, Sevillius Orange.

AUTHENTIC REFERENCES FOR INFERRED MARRIAGES

Maryland Records

THOMAS AUSTIN and SUSANNA POSEY, extx of John. About or before 13 Jany 1690. Chas. cty, Md. Q-24.

JOHN ABINGTON and MARY HUTCHESON, dau. of William, of Pr. Geo's, Gent. Before 1724. Md. Arch. xxxviii-343.

FRANCIS ALLEN and MARY, the admx of William BRADY. 7 Aug. 1750. Som. E. B. 12-52. (The Brady chn were Eunice, about 7, Phillis, 4; Sophia, 2.)

HENRY AYRES and COMFORT SCARBROUGH, dau. of Matthew. Before 11 Feby 1718. Wor. M. H. iii-240.

JAMES ARTIS and KEZIA FRYER, dau. of John. Before 10 Nov 1778. Montgy cty. A-102.

NEHEMIAH BECKWITH of Dor. cty, and FRANCES TAYLOR, same; Married at Transquaking. John Hudson, wit. 10th 5th 1712. Third Haven Mtg. iii-4.

PETER BOOTH and the admx of Thos. FURMAN. Before 23 Nov 1709. Som. cty. EFN-276.

.... BOWIN and RHODA FASSETT, dau. of William. Before 22 Jany 1734. Wor. M. H. iii. 322.

HENRY BONNER and ELIZABETH TAYLOR, widow of John. Before or about 1 Sept 1674. Chas. cty. [Reference wanting.]

WILLIAM BROWNE and MARY DAVIS, relict of Walter. Before 10 Aug. 1680. Chas. cty. H-330.

JOSEPH BULLETTT and ELIZABETH BRANDT, dau. of Rando. and wf Mary. Before or about 8 Sept 1685. Chas. cty. M-67.

JOHN BEALE and JOANE REID, widow. Before 6 June 1675. Annap. ii-346. (She also m. Robert Tyler.)

RICHARD BLUNT, of Cecil cty, and the widow of W. Howard. Before or about 14 Feby 1675 [1673?] Annap. T. P. vii-258.

WILLIAM BURGH and ELIZABETH BILLINGSLEY, widow of John. Before 4 Mch 1665. Annap. T. P. iF-1.

.... BURGH and MARGARET BILLINGSLEY, sister of George BILLINGSLEY of Virginia. Before 1724. Md. Arch. xxxviii-339.

WILLIAM BRITTINGHAM and the widow of Francis MARTIN. Before 1723. Som. cty Rent Roll 1723. p. 12.

JOHN BOOTH and DOROTHY PHILLIPS, dau. of Roger. Before 16 Nov 1715. Som. cty. 1715–1716. p. 10.

JOHN BRATHER and JANE, admx of John PEMBROKE. Before 10 June 1690. Chas. cty, R-9.

GEORGE BRENT probably [?] m. MARY CHANDLER. Before 10 June 1690. Chas. cty. R-15.

FRANCIS CHAPLIN and MARY WEBB. 14 Dec 1742. Talbot cty Md. (Mar. Li.)

AENEAS CAMPBELL and MARGARET HICKMAN, widow of Joshua. Before 27 Nov 1775. Montgy cty. A-52.

SAMUEL CHAMBERS and .... STEWART, sister of David of A. A. cty. Before 16 Aug 1744. Annap. Accts xx-313.

ROBERT CATHER and HANNAH WHITE. 31 Mch 1778. Cecil cty. Marriages.

JAMES CURTIS COULBOURNE and ZIPPORAH PARKER. 3 July 1819. Som. cty. Mar. Li.

ARTHUR CUNNINGHAM and BARBERY, extx of Joseph Kinney [or KENNING]. Som. cty. Before 27 Feby 1735. E. B. 12-137.

JOHN COTTMAN and MARY, extx of JOHN WATERS. Som. cty. Before 3 June 1714. AC(12)-75.

JO: DARDEN and MARY PORTER. 12 June 1745. Talbot cty. Mar. Li.

DANIEL DIES [b. ab. 1785, d. ab. 1855] and ESTHER PARKS, dau. of Toby who lived on Tangier Island. Md and Va. Boundary Line, p. 200.

THOMAS DENT of Chas. cty, and ANN BAYNE, dau. of John. Before Nov 1722. Md. Arch. xxxviii-315.

ROBERT DASHIELL and the dau. of Daniell HAFTS [?] Before 1723. Chas. cty, i-36.

GEORGE DISHAROON probably m. ALICE JUETT, admx of John. Before 9 Dec 1783. Som. cty. E. B. 2-158.

Capt. NICO. EVANS and SUSANNA WALKER, widow or sister of Thomas. Before 1723. Chas. cty. i-36. [See note previously published which gave the date as long before 1751.]

.... EVANS and MARY POWELL, dau. of Walter. Before 18 Jany 1714. Som. cty. CH-155.

.... EDWARDS and MARY SINDORFF, admx of Joseph. Before Apr Ct 1793. A. A. cty, iii-41.

CHARLES FITZ GEFERIES and ANN TOWNSEND. About 1688. Semmes Mss. M. H. S.

.... FREEBORN and RACHELL PROCTOR, widow of Robert of A. A. cty. Before 25 May 1694. Md. Arch. xxxvii-346.

.... FOWKE and ANN CHANDLER, widow. Before 10 Mch 1672. Chas. cty. E-101.

.... FORD and MARGARET St. CLAIR, dau. of William. Before 2 Apr 1796. A. A. cty. v-149.

ORLANDO GRIFFITH and KATHERINE HOWARD, dau. of John of A. A. cty. Before 1725. Md. Arch. xxxviii-378.

GEORGE GODFREY and MARY PAYNE, widow of John [who was her *first* husband.] Before 14 June 1681. Chas. cty. i-122.

MICHAEL GODDIN and MARY, admx of Nicholas CORNEWALLIS. Before June Court, 1707. Som. cty AB(9)-355.

RICHARD GREENE and MARGARETT HUMPHREY, dau. of Thomas and Mary. Before or about 8 Aug 1715. Som. cty. AC(12)-316.

Dr. JOHN HASWELL and SARAH BEALL, widow of James. Before Nov Ct 1726. Pr. Geo's cty. M-113.

ROBERT HILL and TABITHA WHITE, dau. of John. Before 12 June 1619. Som. cty. IK-188 and 209.

RICHARD HODGSHON and JOHANNAH KING, extx of Thomas King of Nanjemy. Before 15 Jany 1678. Chas. cty. H-106. See also K-36.

JOHN HOLSWORTH and ISABELLA MARTIN, widow of William. [She was also extx of *Geo. Abbott.*] Before 28 July 1694. Annap. Inv. and Accts. xiiiA-230.

RICHARD HILL and MILCAH CLARKSON, widow of Robert. Before 22 May 1666. Annap. T. P.lf-79.

HENRY HANDS and REBECCA FOOKS declare intention. 26th 1st mo. 1746. Third Haven Friends' Mtg. iii-87.

ADAM HITCH and ANNE BONDICK. [In Virginia this name is BUNDUCK, I think. Ed.] Before 3d Tuesday of Nov 1719. Som. cty. IK-19.

JOHN HAMBLETON and SARAH, admx of Mr. Thos. BROWN. Before May[?] 1750. Som. cty. E. B. 12-23.

LOT HAMMOND and ELIZABETH DAVIS. Before 13 Aug 1800. Montgy cty. D-420.

MICHAEL HOLLAND and PENELOPIE COULBOURNE, dau. of William. Before or about 18 June 1688. Som. cty. EFG-27.

JOHN HAMPTON and MARY, joint extx of Jno. HENRY. Before 18 Mch 1719. Som. cty. IK-29.

GEORGE HOWARD and the admx of Darby CONNER. Before 23 Nov 1709. Som. cty. EFN-277.

THOMAS HOLLINGSWORTH, of Q. A. cty and KATHRINE WELLS, dau. of Zorobabell. After 25 Mch 1696 and before 1712. Md. Arch. xxxviii-160.

ISRAEL HOLLAND, mariner, and ESTHER, admx of John HARRISTEY. See June Ct 1738. Som. cty. 1736–1738, p. 294.

WILLIAM HILLE and JUDY[?] HADLOWE. June 1667. Chas. cty. B-253.

EPHRAIM HEATHER and the admx of Daniel SELBY. Before 23 Nov 1709. Som. cty EFN-277.

JOHN INDRELL and ELINOR ABNATHAN. Banns of matrimony published. 12 Jany 1691. BWZ-147. Som. cty, Md. [This peculiar name, which appears to be made up of Abna-Nathan, cannot be explained.]

GILBERT ISRAEL and CHARITY CLARK, dau. of Richard. Before 2 Apr 1813. Balto. cty, ix-315.

.... JOHNSON and BRIDGET HOLLAND, dau. of Nehemiah. Before 2 Feby, 1758. Wor. cty. J.W. iii-15.

ANTHONY IVY, Q. A. cty, Gent. and ANNE SMITH, dau. of Robert, Esq. Before 2 Aug 1710. Md. Arch. xxxviii-211.

JOHN JERMAIN and dau. [ANN] of Henry BISHOP. Before 23 Nov 1709. Som. cty. EFM-276. [This marriage previously published. See Som. cty xvi-39. Only date then established, "Before 7 Aug 1726."]

.... JACOBS probably m. ELIZABETH DASHIELL, admx of Christopher. Before 12 July 1735. Som. cty E. B. 12-120.

[THOMAS] JORDAN and MARGARET BURGH, widow. Before 1724. Md. Arch. xxxviii-339.

WILLIAM JOSEPH, Gent. and ELIZABETH BROOKE, widow of James, of Pr. Geo's cty. Before Oct 1723. Md. Arch. xxxviii-326.

.... JACOBS and .... STEWARD, sister of David. Before 16 Aug 1744. Annap. Accts xx-313.

MOSES JONES and KATHERINE, extx of James Wheeler, dec'd. Before 13 Mch 1687. Chas. cty. O-65.

FRAS. KYLBORNE and ELIZA: JOHNSON. Between 14 Mch 1670 and Nov. 1672. Chas. cty. [Reference wanting.]

.... LABOLD and ANNA RACHINA[?] RAHM. Before Aug. Ct. 1785. A. A. cty. i-17.

JOHN MARSH probably m. .... EVANS dau. of Peter. [Date uncertain.] Md. and Va. Boundary. -p. 197.

WILLIAM MARTIN and ISABELLA ABBOTT, widow of George. [She was also widow of MARTIN and m. HOLSWORTH. See HOLSWORTH.] Before 28 July 1694. Annap. Inv. & Accts. xiiiA-230.

ALEXANDER MAGRUDER and ANN HUTCHISON, extx of Thomas, of Chas. cty. Before 21 Nov 1707. Pr. Geo's cty. J. B. 1-29.

ALEX. McDONALD and ANNASTASIA BURCH, extx of Edward. Before 1762. Pr. Geo's cty. DD6-359.

EDMOND MAJOR and ELIZABETH JOSEPH, widow of William, Gent. [See also JOSEPH.] Before Oct 1723. Md. Arch. xxxviii-326.

NATH'S OFFUTT and DEBORAH OFFUTT, dau. of Samuel. Before 17 June 1778. Montgy cty. A-96.

GEORGE OLDFIELD and PETRONELLA CARR, widow of John, of Cecill cty. Before 1728, after 30 Jany 1675. Md. Arch. xxxviii-421.

JAMES PORTER and ANNE RIPPEN. 21 Jany. 1744. Talbot cty. Mar. Li.

WILLIAM PALMER and MEMORY WALKER. Talbot cty. Md. Mar. "1780-1."

HENRY POPE and ANN BALMER, widow of Thomas. Before or about 11 Jany 1653. Md. Arch. x-307.

JOHN PAINE and MARIE WHITE. [About?] 23 Sept 1667. Chas cty. C-256. [See also p. 204. MARY WHITE. See also Q-3.]

ROBERT PROCTOR, of A. A. cty, and RACHELL......(who m. (2)............FREEBORN.) Before 25 May 1694. Md. Arch. xxxviii-346.

WILLIAM PILE and ELIZABETH HUTCHESON. Before 1724. Md. Arch. xxxviii-343.

GABRIEL PARKER and ANNE HUTCHESON, dau. of William, of Pr. Geo's cty, Gent. Before 1724. Md. Arch. xxxviii-343.

STEPHEN PAGE and BRIDGETT PARRAMORE, widow of Arnold. Before 12 May 1691. Som. cty. BWZ-199.

JOHN RENSHAW, Jr., and ANN ROBERTS, admr. of *Frances* ROBERTS. Before 2 Aug. 1710. Som. cty. EFH-413.

MOSES ROBERTS and MARY WEBB. 6 Apr 1795. Dor. cty. Mar. Li.

DAVID TRAIL and ELIZABETH FRYER, dau. of John. Before 10 Nov 1778. Montgy cty. A-102.

BASIL TRAIL and BARBARY DRYER, dau. of John. Before 10 Nov, 1778. Montgy cty. A-102.

.........TURNER [perhaps RICHARD] and ELIZABETH BEALL, dau. of Charles. Before 1812. Fred'k cty. R. B.-1.

[WILLIAM] THOMPSON and VICTORIA, the dau. of Jane Bread. Before 10 July 1688. Chas. cry. P. 15.

VAN SWEARINGEN and MILLY DAVIS. 1806. Montgy cty. Mar. Ret.

JAMES WHEELER and ELIZABETH, admx of Tho. CORKER. Before 11 Sept 1677. Chas. cty. [See also G-99.

The County Court Note-Book

An every-other monthly devoted mainly to abstracts from County Court Records, prior to 1800.

MILNOR LJUNGSTEDT. Editor and Publisher. Bethesda, Rural Route 5, Maryland.

Published six times a year. Subscription two dollars, in advance; must begin with the year.

August, 1931 **Whole**
Vol. X, No. 4 **No. 59**

The Editor intending soon to "quit" talking in a personal way and give you all a bulletin crammed with facts and nothing else (it will be a good bulletin and I hope you will take it) now grasps at an almost last opportunity to give advice . . . giving advice is evidently a trait descended from her forbears, they say we have a strong tendency that way in our section. The Editor has previously, perhaps, explained that it probably arises from a certain goodness of heart which desires that all the world should be as well informed as the folk in the neighborhood of parallel forty-two.

Well, whatever and why ever, one of the Editor's favorite maxims is this:

DO AWAY WITH THE UNNECESSARY THINGS.

It might be from Emerson but it is probably from M. A. Antoninus.

It is not necessary to start your line with CHARLEMAGNE or even William the Conqueror. Start with your great-grandfather, if you know who he was, and then work back from him. If you are among the innumerable descendants of Karl the Great or William of Normandy, or Egbert, or somebody of that set, sooner or later, along somebody's line you will strike your line tied into his.

The historical interest of such a descent, if it can be proved, is very great. I am not with those who hold that you may . . . must necessarily be infused with only a drop of that half of William which was entirely noble. One has only to line-breed hens to realize that something else than Mendels' law seems occasionally to take charge of heredity. You may be a good bit more like William than you would really enjoy, did you know him personally, or you may be like his mother. Possibly she was the saving grace of an ancient line. One does not like to think he got his cruelty from her.

But, anyhow and be that as it may, &c., &c., throw away in your search the *present* unnecessary things. Find the milestones . . . the gravestones, alas! from here to the sand upon which your immigrant ancestor's boat was beached, and then, if you can, cross the great water to his home. You may be very sadly surprised at the simplicity of that home and the lack of all the things your American fancy pictured, *yet the descent may be true.* It's the trueness that is interesting.

If an old-time friend from what was then a sort of frontier, is now alive, the Editor would like to recall to him his bit of a joke. Said he, "*Yes, we're Irish. My brother went over there once to find the ancestral castle, and sure enough he did. It was a most illigant and convanient place . . . you could reach your hand right down the chimbley and open the front dure!*"

(P. S. Perhaps the Editor should show more respect to Charlemagne, for learned genealogists have proved to their own satisfaction that both Carolus Magnus and William the Norman are her ancestors.)

.........The Editor desires not to be boresome, but occasionally some query makes it seem advisable to repeat earlier explanations as to the Inferred Marriages which have been published in the NOTE–BOOK since the early part of 1922.

These marriages are only occasionally set down in the public records in so many words as having occurred or being about to occur (as in prenuptial contracts); they are commonly inferred from some statement in a will or deed, or by the details of an estate account. The reference given is usually to the volume in which are recorded the wills or deeds or settlements, or Court orders, and to the folio or page upon which the record is found. [In spite of amateur searchers who delight in "libers" and "folios" .... *a page is not a folio!*] Few marriage records, as such, exist of the early dates. Those that are to be found are commonly parish records, sometimes recorded in the books of the Clerk of the Court. This is so in Northampton county, Virginia, and in Somerset county, Maryland. The so often referred to "D.B. I. K. L." of Somerset county [*Deed Book* IKL, properly], contains its "vital statistics" sandwiched in between the usual county court records, in quite an unusual way.

The Clerk of the Court in Virginia, or the Clerk or Register in Maryland, or the Register or Recorder in Pennsylvania, or the Surrogate or Recorder in New York; the Ordinaries, Recorders, &c., in the Carolinas and Georgia, will in most cases furnish *copies of the deed or will* (given as reference for the marriage) at a reasonable charge. It is suggested, however, that it is desirable to first inquire as to the record and have it perfectly identified.

In one case of which the Editor knows, there were two volumes marked "A". Without paying attention to the date or the individual names, the Clerk furnished a copy from a modern volume, which was not the one desired.

Whenever the Editor can assist by identification of the record and the order of a copy, she will do so. If the Clerk is not put to the trouble of search or identification his charges are usually (not always) very moderate.

CONTINUED articles COUNTY COURT NOTE-BOOK' and the dates on which they first appeared.
MARRIAGES BY INFERENCE. Began with May, 1922.
MARYLAND'S NEXT OF KIN. Began with July, 1922.
VIRGINIA COLONISTS. This alphabetized list began with July, 1924.
MARYLAND NATURALIZATIONS. Began with February, 1923.
KING GEORGE PROBATES, &c. Began with July, 1924.
The LIST OF BANISHED QUAKERS. Began with November, 1924.
MILITARY NOTES, both COLONIAL and REVOLUTIONARY, and some later MILITIA NOTES, will appear in every issue, if possible.
SHIPS IN PORT, NEW ENGLANDERS AND OTHERS, INTERCOUNTY and INTERCOLONIAL, and COLONIAL FORENAMES, will appear in alternate issues or as space can be found for them.
EASTERN SHORE FAMILIES, in the form of a one-page supplement, began with June, 1925.

It is understood that the DELAWARE RECALL, Mrs. Hart's very excellent periodical, will appear later this year as one enlarged number only.

Mr. ROBERT ARMISTEAD STEWART'S book, briefly mentioned in the last issue of the NOTE-BOOK, was originally advertised as the ROMANCE OF THE VIRGINIA NAVY IN THE REVOLUTION, it is now called The HISTORY OF THE VIRGINIA NAVY IN THE REVOLUTION, a much better title and more suited to Mr. Stewart's thorough work. The need of a volume of this kind is well-known to those who have searched for a record of a privateer, as the Editor has, and finally found all that appears to be known in a manuscript collection of official correspondence in the Library of Congress.

The Editor has just read an article written some years ago by Mr. DONALD LINES JACOBUS anent family tradition as opposed to facts. This case of the privateer was not merely family tradition, but family publication, for the supposedly glorious end of the privateer did not exactly fit its great mistake . . . which was that it attacked and captured the vessel of a neutral country, and there was quite a row over the matter. The gallant officer, however, that family tradition recorded, was *not* responsible, for he was not a naval man and so not in command. The only thing in the story that is true, is that there was a privateer and the young gentleman was aboard, but there is no apparent reason why he should be credited with the blunder.

Mr. STEWART'S account of the privateers will be not only valuable but interesting. It should have been written long ago.

There are some serious errors in the list of MARYLAND KIN in the JUNE NOTE-BOOK. Correction will be made in the number for October.

NOTES HERE AND THERE

This day (vizt) the 10th day of June Ano Dom 1708 Ordered that the New Meeting House built by Protestant dessenters at Rehoboth Town in Somerset County in the Province of Maryland be and is hereby appointed to be a house & place for the Publick Worship of Almighty God in; the Minister thereunto appointed having Qualified himself as Law required. . . . Som. Md. EFN-140.

A County Court called for the Electing and Chusing of Burgesses to serve at the next General Assembly at St. Maries. The precept then read directing public proclamation giving notice to all the freemen of sd County who have a seated plantation of 50 acres at the least or a visible personal Estate to the value of £40 sterling at the least requiring them to appear at a Special County Court to be suddenly called & held, for the Electing & chusing of four Deputies or Deligates to Serve . . . at a Gen'll Assembly holden at St, Maries the tenth day of May next. Som. Md. BWZ-205. 18 Apr 1692.

From PRINCE WILLIAM, Va., LAND CAUSES

MICAJAH HARRIS, born in Fairfax cty, Va., son of BURR HARRIS, who lived in Fairfax, Hon. Wm. Butler testifies; thinks BURR HARRIS died in South Carolina, He, BUTLER, was born in Virginia, near Bull Run and removed to South Carolina about 1769. MICAJAH HARRIS was then living in Newbury District, S. C. Pr. Wm cty, Va. 21 Feby 1807.

SOLOMON WARDER and ELIZABETH HOWELL, late of the Isle of Wight, declare intentions [of marriage] and produce certificate from Friends. "They might have accomplished their [marriage] had not the Ship come away before their next [Friends'] meeting . . . which certificate & also hers from London . . . . [were] read." Friends' Meeting Minutes. About 1699.

From the COURT, but modern. Deputy officer (game warden or sheriff): "Yeah... 16 year old flapper trappin' ducks. I'd a made him [some man] told on himse'f by arguing, but I couldn't argue with her and I was glad she didn't have any ducks. It would a' been kind of a pity, wouldn't it?" N-n cty, Va.

The old SUGAW CREEK PRESBYTERIAN CEMETERY, near Charlotte, North Carolina, is particularly interesting on account of its many finely cut stones, with unusual decoration. But the following inscription is also somewhat unusual.

To my Husband Silas servant of J. F. Irvin died July 31st 1856 Aged 36 years Left his wife Lidy Robson to morn his los. I am happy I have maid peace with God dont wep for me.

THE DEPUTY COMMISSARY'S GUIDE WITHIN THE PROVINCE OF MARYLAND

(*Continued from October, 1930*)

Witnesses: "The witnesses to a will . . . ought to be disinterested, to be *credible*, and therefore a legatee was not admitted to be a witness" (reference to a decision given.) And if the witness died before the testator, the witnesses' handwriting must be identified . . . or, rather, a proof would be admitted. But if any legacy is made to the witness, the devise, whatever it may be, is void, but, "he shall be admitted as a witness."

The compiler enjoys following Mr. Vallettes' setting forth of the law but it does seem a bit illogical that if a witness has been paid a legacy *he shall not refund, "tho' the will should be determined to be void."*. . .

Written wills of personal estate, need not any witness of their publication, and are good if in the testator's handwriting, and though written by another person, if by his instructions and approbation. Many cases are cited where informal wills have been held to be good.

Mr. Vallette then follows with quite a homile on "how indiscreet" it is for a man to put off making his will till he is on his death bed and says (this sounds very modern) that money cannot be better laid out, than in getting able assistance, *if not to be had without expence.*

It is not unusual to find that a man will provide in his will with the utmost particularity for the payment for land he has agreed to buy or to sell. The next paragraph explains that.

"Though a person ought to be seized, before "he can devise, . . . "and therefore. if he devise "land and purchase it afterward, the land shall "not pass, yet, if there be an agreement in *writ-"ing* for land, and the person agreeing to purchase "dies before conveyance, but devises the same, "the land shall pass in equity; *where that, which "is agreed to be done, is considered as done.*"

(The compiler did not know that anything so fine as that was in law.)

As to the age at which a minor can or could make a will: the age of discretion is fourteen, both in males and females . . . and neither male or female can make a will of chattels before fourteen years of age . . . and not oflands, for the devisor of land must be twenty-one years of age.

Idiots, lunaticks, and a man while he is drunk, cannot make a will. A traitor or a felon cannot make a will of his own chattels . . ." tho' he may of what he has as executor." A suicide cannot make a will devising chattels . . that is, such a will is void . . . but it is not void as to lands because lands are not forfeited. . . . And under a statute of Henry viii, wills of lands by married women shall not be good.

There are about three pages concerning the wills of married women . . . probably much of this has been changed, but it is, of course, applicable to the time. A wife had, generally, to have her husband's consent to the disposal of chattels by will, and her will made before marriage became void on marriage, even if she survived her husband. But with her husband's consent a married woman could make a will; "so of savings out of pin money or separate maintenance" she may make a will. . . . If a husband enter into bond before marriage to permit a wife to make a will, he shall be bound thereby . . . but a married woman could not dispose by will of any bequest to her as a legatee; for that belonged to her husband.

Should a married woman by settlement before marriage include the power to make a will, her will made in pursuance of such power or appointment, is good.

"Though I would strongly recommend to every "one, desirous of making an effectual will, and "who can afford to pay the inconsiderable ex-"pence, to get able assistance, and not leave his "family to scramble for his estate . . . and to be "inflamed by with an animosity destructive of "the harmony and good will, which family con-"nection ought to promote, yet, that those with "whom the consideration I have suggested will "not have their just weight, may have some rule "for their assistance, I have in the appendix, in-"serted some precedents for that purpose."

Thus, modestly, cutting in on the lawyer's fees, Eli Vallette finishes his chapter on wills.

The matters of Descent and Distribution which some of us find perplexing, will be taken up next in as brief form as possible.

DELAWARE TAX LISTS FOR 1776
NEWCASTLE COUNTY

Mill Creek Hundred

ARCH'D HOLMES, 11*; Alex'r Guthery, 12; Arch'd McDonald, 7; Arch'd McDonald, Jun'r, 6; Alex'r Montgomery, Esq., 6; Alex'r McMullen, 3; Aaron Mendinghall, 10; Alex'r McKim, 14; Andrew Poulson, 5; Alex'r Reynolds, 8; Abraham Richey, 6; Abel Haynor, 4; Alex'r Ford, 4; Andrew McIntier, Esq., 9; Alex'r Ogle, 5; Arther Patterson, 3; Adam Guthrey, 5; Andrew McClanon, 4;

Andrew Crosson, 2; Andrew McKee, 5; Alex'r Foreman, 5; Andrew Crosson, Jun'r, 5; Benjamin Foot, 5; Barbara Fulton, 4; Benjamin Huff, 5; Charles Black, 10; Chads Chaffin, 5; Charles Springer, 10; Chambers Hall, 5; Charles Springer, Jun'r, 15; Charles McGonigle, 2; Con Wolahan, 14; Cealob Harlen [*sic*], 9; "Ceabol" Barnes, 10; Christopher Springer, 3; Charles Williamson, 15; Charles Allen, 2; "Cathrian" McDonald And Sisters, 3;

DAVID CROSS, 3; David Henry, 6; Daniel Thompson, 16; David Twedy, 16; David Lewes, 4; Daniel Nickoles, 18; David Hollingsworth, 13; Daniel McGhee, 3; David Hughes, 14; David Montgomery, 16; David Mercer, 12; David Pyle, 5; David Hoopes, Est., 6; Daniel McGreger, 5; David Wilkin, 3; David Finney, Esq., 10; David Wolahan, 5.

EVAN RICE, Esq., Est. 12; Ephram Yarnel, 13; Evan Rice, 14; "Edart" Robinson, Est., 7; Elliot Hays, 3; Enoch Dinson, Est., 4; Evan Evans, Esq., Est., 2; "Edart" Stitt, 2; "Edart" Brearly, 6;

FRANCES GRAHAM, Est., 8; Fredrik Ford, 7; Forgis Cleaments, 4;

GEORGE WOLLASTON, 14; George Walker, 9; George Robinson, Est., 8; George Thomas, 2; George McKeay, 4; George Greyston [or Gregston] 3;

HUGH FORSYTH, 5; Hugh McWhorter, 12; Henry Bryan, 5; Hannah Jurdan, 9; Hugh Hueston, 14; Henry Brackin, 12; Hannah Bonham's Est., 3; Hugh McGreger, 7; Henry Brackin, Jun'r, 4; Heath John, 5. [Possibly this name should be *John Heath*.]

JOHN PARKS, 5; Jos. Hayns Est., 5; Jas. Thompson, 15; John Hadley, 15; Isaac Hughes, 14; John Mahon, 4; Jas. Boggs, 9; Jos. Barton, 6; John Nivin, 10; James McKever's Est., 3; Joseph England, 30; Jacob Wollaston, 8; Joseph Chambers, 13; John Cann's Est., 8; John Ferguson, 3; "Isah" Lewes, 8; John Ball, 13; John Reece Est., 8; James Moore, Jr., 4;

John Morgan, 13; James McDanald, 8; John McCormick, 4; James Miles, 4; John Herdman, 4; Jeremiah Wilston, 4; John Ways Est., 9; Jos. Way, 5; James Wilson, 14; John James, 13; John Watt, 12; John Jurdan Est, 4; John Bishop, 16; James Crosson, 12; Joseph Ball, 15; James Guthrey, 8; John Reece, Millright, 14; John Walker, 4; John McKnight, 2; Jacob

Moore, 10; James Walker, 3; James Phillips, 12; John Hays, 10;

John Johnston, "Coper", 3; Joseph Phillips, 8; John Bruce, 6; James Short, 7; John Thompson, 7; John Lockart, 9; James Jackson, 18; John Robinson, 5; James Fulton, 4; James Patterson, 3; John Dickson, 10; James Boggs, Jun'r, 5; James Robinson, Jun'r, 4; James Moore, 3; James Dixson, 9; John Mortons Est. 3; [this name may be *Marton.*]

John Robinson, Jun'r, 5; John Stewart, 2; John Pyle, 3; Joseph Rice, 5; Jean Rice, 8; John Reece, Jun'r, 5; John Way, 12; John Moore, 5; Joseph Miller, 5; John Connel, 5; John Beason, 14; James Hindman, 5; John McCannon, 5; Joseph Cannon, 9; John Hannah, 3; John McCombs, 5; James Blak, 20; Jess Logan, 5; John Burnside, 5; John Beal, 5; James McCroary, 3; Jacob Justis, 10; Joseph Deaver, 4;

John Anderson, 5; John Springer, 5; Isaac Allen, 3; John McCroary, 4; James Elder, 5; Jeanet English, 4; Isaac Dixson, 7;

LARANCE WOODS, 2;

MARGRET GRAY and "Cist[?] Corts Est., 8; Mathew Giffen, 5; Mark Mellen, "0"; Michael Mardock, 3; Moses McKnight, 14; Morten Justis' Est., 6; Mary Spencer, 3; Mary Trayhorn, 3;

NATHEL BRYANS, 13; Nivin Cadwell, 8; Nathel Bryans, Jun'r, 6; Nichlos Springer, 4; Nathel Green, 3;

PHILLIP DIXSON, 9;

QUINTER SHANNON, 5;

ROB'T MORTLAND, 4; Rich'd Jamison, 4; Rob't Montgomery, 16; Robert Boggs, 10; Robert Craighton, 10; Robert Kirkwood, 16; Robert Johnston, 15; Robert Starret, 6; Rob't Montgomery, Jun'r, 4; Dr. Robert Henry, 6; Robert Boys, 15; Rob't McPharson, 13; Dr. Rob't Boyn's Est., 10; Robert Kenney, 4; Robert Colberson's Est., 7; Richard Grubb's Est., 7; Robert Crafort, 14.

SAMUEL HUESTON, 7; Samuel Young, 8; Swen Justis, 16; Samuel Paxton, 5; Simon Gregg's Est, 4; Samuel Gunn, 5; Samuel Cannon, 5; Samuel Nickoles Est., 10; Samuel Barker, 22; Samuel Crosson, 12; Samuel Wilson, 15; Smith's & Steple's[?] Est., 12; Solomon Hershey, 12; Samuel Wright, 3; Simon Poulson, 8; Samuel Montgomery. 13; Samuel Cantrel, 4; Samuel Mordock's Est., 6; Sarah and Rebeacka English, 7;

THOMAS RICE, Est., 8; Thomas Cochran, 11; Thomas Rice, 5; Thomas Wollaston, 11; Thos. Montgomery, 18; Thomas Donald, 7; Thomas Dixson, 4; Thomas Robinson, 5;

WILLIAM HORSON [this name is very uncertain], 4; William Wilcocks, 7; William Haynor, 5; William Jordan, 6; William Morrow, 3; William Marshewel, 12; William Phillips, Jun'r, 5; William Dixson, 5; William Nivin, 15; William Gilleher, 5; William Reynolds, 21; William Wollaston, 7; William McIlvee [this is apparently what this name was meant for, but it is difficult to make out], 8;

William Grubb, 4; William Teat, 15; William Wilson, 6; William Anderson, Est., 8; William Wright, 5; William Johnston, 14, William Barton, 9. William "Ranthrew", 5; Wm. Buckingham, 8; William Buckingham, Jun'r; 7; William Phillips, 22; William Roes Est., 3; William Stitt, 4; William Crosson, 12; William Addy, 6;

William Brackin, 8; William Noble, 5; Wm. Gregg's Est., 8; William Ogle, 4; William Foot, 14; Wakter Ferguson, 4; William Evans, 4; William Wilkin, 5; William Robinson, 5; William Carson, 3, [perhaps Corson]; William Hutchison, 5; William Gilmer, 5; William Smith, 5.

[Estates of Pencader taxables in other hundreds.]

SAMUEL WILSON'S Est in White Clay Creek Hundred, 4; Dav'd Finnery, Esq., same, 55; Wm. Phillips in Chrsteen Hundred, 10; Samuel Barker's in same, 9; Hannah Bonham's in same; 8; Swen Justises in same, 9; David Finney, Esq., in New Castle Hundred, 20.

Estates[?] for road tax: Charles Evans, 3; Thomas Ogle, 3; Wm. McMehen, 3; "C"? Frances Johnston, 6; John Garretts, 6; Ann Ogle, 6! James Marshell's 6; Samuel Greaves, 4; Rob't Morrison, 3.

(*To be continued*)

*See note in June NOTE-BOOK.

CERTIFICATES FOR LAND WITH NAMES OF HEAD RIGHTS

Lancaster county, Virginia (From original county records)

WM. CLAPHAM, Jr:
Head rights: Jno. Cooke, Franc. Sewell, Marga. Malle, Eliz: Cornish [?] Jno. Cornish, Sara. Cornish, X'r Harford. 6 June 1654.

Mr. TOBY SMYTH;
Head rights: Abig: Ridge, Tho. Crowde, Seath Edward, Tho. Bambridge, Wm. Swan, Wm. Talbot, Jno. Warner, Jno. Clower, Kath: Moroughew [?] 7 Aug 1654.

ABRAHAM MOONE (perhaps Moore);
Head rights: Wf AN, Jno. Brewton, Wm. Attaway, Ja: Allison, Eliz: Paine, Jno. Craford. 7 Aug 1654.

Mr. ANDREW GILSON;
Head rights: Anth. North, Jno. Smyth, John Stainingbrow, Hen. Packer [Parker?] Eliza. Mynshem [?] 6 Oct 1654.

Mr. GEO. TAYLOR;
Head rights: Geo. Adams, Eliza: Shaw, Columbus Cloyd, Angus Cloyd. 6 Oct 1654.

Mr. JOHN WEIR;
Head rights: Robert Chambers, twice; Rich: Williams, Ann Collins, Magda. Steephens, Mary Steephens, Wm. Hardinge, Daniell Elsmore, Jno. Marke, Marga. Allen. 6 Oct 1654.

Mr. THO. CARTER;
Head rights: SUSANA CARTER, Wm. Short, Mary Smyth, Ann Hughs, Jos. Maxy, Mark Smyth, Edw. L......... [?] 6 Feby 1654.

Mr. ROW. LAWSON;
Head rights: Hen: Berry, Patrick Cleashe [?] Sarah Turner, Eliz: Sachell, Wm. Wilkinson, Geo. Goodale, Jno. Marshall. Also two more, Daniell Cooper and Katherine English. [One name is illegible.] 6 Feby 1654.

VINCENT STANFORD; David Dennis, Mary Marshall, Hen. Baker, Thomas Langford, Tho. Tilsley. 6 June 1655.

JO: EYERS:
Head rights: John Taylor, JOAN EYERS, Eliner Gill, Hen: Peeters. 6 Aug 1655.

Mr. THO: HAWKINS;
Head rights: John Humphreys, Peeter Hamlin, Ral. Parrey, Richard Cooper, Eliz. Warner, Francis Atkins, John Corriches [?] Wm. Crispe. 6 Aug 1655.

TOBYE HORTON [this very likely is NORTON]
Head rights: Robt. ...., Thos. Stevenson, John Ackson. 6 Aug 1655.

Mr. TOBY SMITH; [*He was "brother-in-law" to Moore Fauntleroy. See record* 4 Oct 1657.]
Head rights: Mr. Tho. Prettiman, Rich. Reding, Eliz: Howman [?] 6 Aug 1655.

JA. PAINE;
Head rights: JOHN PAINE, Jr., MARY PAINE, Wm. Emson, Marie Williams, Eliza: Pusie [?] 6 Aug 1655.

Mr. . . . KEMP;
Head rights: ANN KEMP, Sary Greene, Marie Sullivan, Daniell, an Irish boy. 5 Oct 1655.

THOMAS GRIFFITH;
Head rights: Reginald Johnson [?] Eliz: Roberts, John Penzance, John Paine, Anne Garrett, P[eter?] Ellys, George Minefrey. 6 Jany 1655.

WALTER DICKSON;
Head rights: Rich [?] Thyrold [?] John Williams, James Bradman, Mary Smith [?] 6 Feby 1655.

DAVID PHELPS;
Head rights: Himself, Hugh Maydes, Edward Porter, William Smith. 15 Apr. 1656.

EDWIN CONNOWAY;
Head rights: Richard Cartricke [perhaps meant for Cartwright?] Susan Warren. 15 Apr 1656.

VINCENT STANFFORD;
Head rights: Peter, a negro; MARY STANFORD, Edward Stevens, John Riggens, David Voyse, Jo: Wells, Barbery Shackells, Ann Tompson, Tho: Bond, Robert Thompson. 15 Apr 1656.

JON SHHERLOCK;
Head rights: Sam: Salizbury, Anne Cartwright June 1656.

Mr. HUMPHREY BOOTH;
Head rights: Himself, twice; Mathew Hoare, Anne Giddinge[?] Edward app Lewys, Abraham Stevens, John Suckett, Thomas Freshwater, Gowyn Younge, Mary Fisher, Jacob, a negro. June, 1656.

Lt. Col. MOORE FANTLEROY;
Head rights: Abraham Collins[?] John Lathbury, Dorothy Dansar, Thomas Newman, Joseph Webster, Peter, a negro; Kate, a negro. June 1656.

Mr. JAMES WILLIAMSON;
Head rights: Maudline Thomas, John Roberts, Rob't Smith, Fran: Settle, Daniel Hunter, John Stray or Stor, Matthew Whaite, Henry Carpenter, Thomas Stevenson, Alice, a maide servant; John Hull, Rob't Hull, Tho: Chittwood, thrice; Xpofer Browning, Mr. JA. WILLIAMSON, Anne Lonton, Will'm Gostell, Nicholas Redferne, Richard Walker, Stephen C......l[?] Zach ...., Mich: Filliott, Jeremy Hobert, Jo. Gossell. [This name is apparently the same as the one above, and is probably meant for Gosnell.] June 1656.

Mr. DAVID FOX:
Head rights: Glenham Drury, Jo: Henderson, Francis Hugan, Michaell Bayly, Jo: Kinge, Roger Gibson, Valentine Painter, Jo: Waight, Mary Taylor, Marg't[?] Axon, 6 negroes. 6 Aug 1656.

Sr. HEN: CHICHELY, Kt.
Head rights: Abraham Appleton, his wife Eliz:, Gabriell Littleton, Tho. Breweton, Dennis Downinge, Tho: Tomlyn, Tho: July, James Cadwallider, Robt. ....[?] Tho: Billby, Geo. Gudloe, Wm. Cushew, Jo: Reyley, Tho. Loe, John Harrys, Philip Kirby, Margarett Gudloe, Margarett Arnoll, Mary Savory, Joan Burley, Thomas Walgrave, Tho: Minnie, Roger Smith, Tho: Hubbet, two negroes. 6 Aug 1656.

Note: The early Lancaster books are extremely difficult to read. Many of these names are doubtful, they were, however, customarily recorded, upon receipt of the certificate and patent, in the land records now at Richmond, and as these particular years will be covered, the Editor understands, by Mrs. Nugent's forthcoming first volume of *Cavaliers and Pioneers*, checking and comparison can be made with those lists.

A BOOK OF DISTRIBUTIONS, FREDERICK COUNTY, MARYLAND

(Continued from June NOTE-BOOK)

NICH'S KEMP; Peter and Jacob Kemp, extrs. Widow and five children (distributees): Mary, Elizabeth, Peter, David and Jacob Kemp. No date.

JAMES MACKELL; Lydia Dawson, admx. Widow and two children: Benjamin and Susannah Mackell. No date.

JACOB UBRY or ULRY, Elizabeth U . . . extx. No distribution. 1779.

JOHN SETTLE or LITTLE, Agnus Settle or Little, admx. Widow and heirs. No list. No date.

LODOWICK WISINGER; Catherine Wisinger, extx. Seven children: Peter, Balser, Barbarah. George, Catherine, Lodowick, Jacob, No date.

LODEWICK PRINTZMAN [PRUTZMAN?] John P . . . extr. Widow and seven children: Mary, John, Lawrence, Catherine, Justina, Nathaniel, Henry. No date.

SAMUEL STEWART; Mary Stewart and William Tucker admrs. No distribution given.

PETER FOUT; Ursley Fout adms. No list. No date.

PHILIP KELP or KULP; Margaret K . . . extx. Widow and the heir-at-law, Philip Culp [*sic*] the only child. Bond 26 Oct 1779.

SNOWDEN BEYER; Margaret Collebarges extx. No list. No date.

CHRISTIAN SHUTTER; Mary Shutter, admx. Widow and six children: John, Jacob, Christiana, Catharine, Susuanah, Solomon. No date.

JOHN JEREMIAH MYERS; Barbarah Myer and Peter Huffman, extrs. Widow and four children: Jacob, Mary, Catherine, John Jeremiah. No date.

WILLIAM SARGEANT; Sarah Sargeant, admx. No list. No date.

HIGGENSON MOCKEBOY; Rebekah Mockeboy, admx. Widow, four children: Marean [?] Sarah Price, Priscilla and Thos.-Higgenson, No date.

THOMAS JOHNSON; John Johnson and Edw. Thomas, extrs. No list. No date.

WILLIAM ORBISON; Isabel McGlochlin, extx. Two children: Elizabeth and Mary Orbison. No date.

JOSEPH BURNESTON; William Burneston, extr. Widow; William Burneston a legacy; ten children: Wm., Sarah, Thos., Mary, Anne, Ann [*sic*] Rebeccah, Eliz'th, Joseph, Isaac. No date.

SERVICE AND SUPPLIES COLONIAL, REVOLUTIONARY AND MILITIA

JOHN BLAND, "Patroler." Pr. Wm, Va. Orders. 23 Nov 1756.

WILLIAM BASE, the same. Same reference.

JOHN, OBED and GEORGE CALVERT, the younger, Patrolers. Pr. Wm, Va. Orders. 22 Nov 1756.

WILLIAM BUCHANAN, oath as military officer. Pr. Wm, Va. Orders [3]. 23 Aug 1756.

GEORGE CALVERT, the Younger, makes oath to services for his Majesty. Ordered certified. Pr. Wm, Va. Orders [3], p. 46. 17 Mch 1756.

PRESLEY COX, Gent. Took oath of Lieut. of the Troop of Horse, commanded by Capt. George Lee. Wmld, Va. Orders, fo. 20. 29 Feby 1743.

GEORGE FOSTER, Jr. Patroler. Pr. Wm, Va. Orders. 23 Nov 1756.

JOHN FARROW, Patroler. Pr. Wm, Va. Orders. 22 Nov 1756.

ROBERT HAMRICK, Patroler. Pr. Wm. Va. Orders. 23 Nov 1756.

FRANCIS FOX, Revolutionary soldier. Wilkes cty, Ga.

WILLIAM HUGHES; ctf that he made oath that he had served as Lieut. and Adjt, Va. Reg't of Regulars, commanded by Col. Adam Stephen, which was raised in the year 1762. Ctf assigned to John May. S. L. O. Va. M. and I. Warrants. ii-37. 10 Jany 1780.

THOMAS HAZILRIGG, Patroler. Pr. Wm, Va. Orders. 23 Nov 1756.

WILLIAM JOHNSON and WALTER GWEAST[?] were soldiers at St. Inego's Fort, also JAMES LINDSEY "of the same province of Maryland", was a soldier. Prov. Court Records, Annapolis, Md. ii-201. 1 May 1647.

AUGUSTINE JENNINGS; oath as military officer. Pr. Wm, Va. Orders [3] -197. 25 Aug 1756.

SIMON MILLER; oath as military officer. Pr. Wm, Va. Orders. 23 May 1757.

THOMAS McCLANAHAN; sworn captain. Pr. Wm, Va. Orders [3]-308. 27 May 1757.

Edward McDonald, frontier soldier, Augusta County, Va. Hening vii-192. 1758.

HENRY O'KELLY, *alias* HENRY KELLY, states that he served in Col. Henry Lee'w Partizan Legion and has never received any pay since 1 Apr 1780. Power to Thomas Wells to claim pay that is due him. Kent cty, Dela. B(2)-232. 1 Mch 1791.

THOMAS RESPESS; to be recommended for Captain; GUNNELL SANDERS for Lieut., and JOHN SANDERS for Ensign . . . all of militia Ldn cty, Va. G-8. 13 Jany 1777.

DAVID SHEPHERDSON; makes usual declaration for pension, and Court declares opinion he was a Revolutionary soldier. Rock'm cty, Va. Dec 1832. Orders p. 181.

WILLIAM TURNER, Gent., produces comm'n and takes oath as Ensign. Ffx cty, Va. Orders [2] p. 665. 17 Nov 1761.

JONATHAN THOMAS, residing Grayson, aged 69. Born Orange cty, N. C. 29 Nov 1762. Grayson, Va. 23 Oct 1832. Orders.

ELIAS TAYLOR was Sjt of the 11th Va. Regt. Disch. 6 Jany 1780. Kentucky cty, Va. Court 3 Oct 1780.

ZACHARIAS TALIAFERO. See* Amherst cty, Va. May Ct 1783. Orders p. 108.

JOSEPH TUCKER produces comm'n as Captain of Militia company. Amherst cty, Va. 26 July 1782. Orders, p. 1.

WILLIAM TURREY; Court orders it to be Certified as their opinion that he should be continued on the list of pensioners. Ldn cty, Va. 14 June 1785. Orders i-44.

THOMAS VINES makes declaration and Court declare their opinion he served as a Revolutionary soldier. Rock'm cty, Va. Nov 1832. Orders, p. 166.

ZACHARY TAYLOR; 200 acres for service late war. Montg cty, Va. Surveys. 12 Feby 1774.

SHADRACK VAUGHAN, served as Lieut. Va. Regt under Col. Byrd. 2,000 acres. Montg cty, Va. Surveys. 2 Apr 1774.

HENRY VASS, Jr. recommended for 2d Lieut. Middx cty, Va. 23 Sept 1782. vi-3. Takes oath 28 Oct 1782. vi-4.

ROGER WEST, Gent., takes oath as Captain of Militia; WM. POWELL, Gent., as Lieut., and JAMES CRAKSENT, as Ensign. Ffx cty, Va. July 1787. Orders 1783-1788, p. 425.

Printed at The Industrial School for Crippled and Deformed Children, 241 St. Botolph Street, Boston

The

County Court Note-Book

A Little Bulletin of History and Genealogy

October, 1931 Vol. X, No. 5

MARYLAND'S NEXT OF KIN

"No kindred at age;" inv. Judith Avess, Dorset cty. 12 Mch 1723-4. ix-320.

JAMES DOSSEY, REBECKA DOSSEY; inv. John Dossey of Calvert cty. 12 Feby 1723. ix-321.

DANIEL WATTS, PETER RULE; Inv. Coll. William Watts of St. Mary's cty. 13 Apr 1724. ix-322.

JAMES x THOMPSON, ELIZ'TH x GRIGGES; inv. John Thomson of St. Mary's cty. 22 Feby 1723-4. ix-325.

CHARLES NEALE, WILL: CHANDLER; inv. Mr. Anthony Neale of Charles cty. 31 Oct 1723. ix-327.

JOHN SMALLWOOD, WILL'M x SMALLWOOD; inv. James Smallwood of Charles cty. 27 Feby 1723. ix-337.

JOHN x LEMASTER, JOHN SCOTT, "Kin and Cred'r Both"; inv. James Williams of Charles cty. 26 Mch 1724. ix-340.

EDW'D TRIPPE, WILLIAM TRIPPE; inv. Henry Trippe, of Dor. cty. 3 Apr 1724. ix-341.

THO: ROLPH, GLANVILLE x ROLPH; inv. Jno. Rolph of Kent cty. 16 Oct 1723. ix-357.

ELIZ'TH x COCKLEY, MARY x GRANGER; inv. William Rook of Kent cty. 25 Nov 1723. ix-361.

No kin given; add'l inv. Nicholas Power of Kent cty. 8 Apr 1724. ix-362.

SARAH COVINGTON, W. TURBUTT; inv. Samuel Turbutt of Talbot cty. 6 Feby 1723. ix-362.

Apparently no kin signed; inv. Rich'd Holmes of Talbot cty. 24 Jany 1723. ix-365.

JAMES HOPKINS, JOSEPH HOPKINS [very doubtful whether these are kin]; inv. Nathaniel Peck of Talbot cty. 20 Jany 1723. ix-366.

JOHN x DONNELLAN "relation," the adm'x Eliz'th "knows not of any relation......Except JOHN DONNELLAN;" inv. Thos. Donnellan. 20 Nov 1724. ix-367.

WM. WHITE, GEORGE ROBINS; inv. Hezekiah Mackey of Talbot cty. 21 June 1723. ix-368.

JOHN TURNER; inv. John Turner, Sr., of Prince George's cty. 13 Feby 1733. ix-371.

No kin recorded; inv. William Smith of Prince George's cty. 13 Feby 1723-4. ix-372.

JNO. HARPER; inv. Thomas Harper of Q. A. Cty. 19 Mch 1723-4. ix-372.

THOS. DASHIELL, LEVIN COVINGTON [probably kin]; inv. Sam'll Covington of Som. cty. 25 Nov. 1723. ix-373.

JNO. CONNER, JOB SHARRY, CHAS. COTTINGHAM [probably kin]; inv. of Chas. Cottingham of Som. cty. 10 Jany 1723. ix-374.

ALEXANDER WORDIE, BENJAMIN x HENDERSON, JOHN HENDERSON, SAM x DORMAN [these are both "kin and creditors", cannot be said which are which]; inv. Joseph Henderson of Som. cty. 17 Jany 1723. ix-374.

WM. CARY [Kin ?]; inv. Thomas Cary of Som. cty. 28 Jany 1723-4. ix-375.

ANN WHEELER; inv. Roger Wheeler of Calvert cty. 23 Mch 1723-4. ix-376.

Kin "None in the county to be had nor Cred." Inv. Mrs. Johanna Dansey of St. Mary's cty. 17 Mch 1723-4. ix-379.

Kindred none. Inv. Thomas Clapham of (? county). 18 Mch 1723. ix-380.

NICHOLAS RICHARDSON, ANNE x RICHARDSON; inv. Mrs. Bridgett Richardson of St. Mary's cty. 20 Apr 1724. ix-380.

AND'W EATON, FRAN'S HOPEWELL [these are either kin or creditors]; inv. Barbary Wilson of St. Mary's cty. 19 Mch 1723-4. ix-381.

PATRICK FORREST; inv. Richard Forrest of St. Mary's. 13 Feb 1723-24. ix-382.

BENJ'N DAVIS, ROBERT PORTER; inv. Moses and Sarah Davis of Cecill cty. ix-384.

EDWARD x SMITH, CHARLES BAKER, JOS. [MIDDLEMORE ?] FRAN. HOLLAND; "Kin and Creditors" inv. John Walker of Balto. cty. 5 May 1724. ix-384.

JOHN DURBIN, JAMES PRESTON; inv. Mr. Daniel Scott, Jr., of Balto. cty. 17 Apr 1724. ix-387.

Do not find kin; inv. Selah Dorman of Balto. cty. 25 Mch 1724. ix-390.

Add'l account of John Boone of Balto. cty. Do not find kin. 5 June 1724. ix-392.

MARY x NOBLE, REBECA x NOBLE; inv. Adam Noble of Cecill cty. 25 Mch 1723-4. ix-392.

MARY KIMBER "*Affinity*"; inv. Thomas Kimber of Cecill cty. 19 Dec 1723. ix-393.

"No Kin and the Widow not in this Province;" inv. Edward Williams of Cecill cty. 20 July 1721. ix-395.

EDWARD BESTIN; inv. William Beaston of Cecill cty. 20 Feby 1723. ix-396.

JOHN x LONGE, LEAH x KELLEY; inv. John Kelley of Cecill cty. 15 Feby 1723. ix-397.

No kin; inv. John Pigg of Q. A. cty. 11 Jany 1723. ix-399.

THOMAS x HINDS, SARAH x HOLLINGSWORTH; inv. Nathaniell Hynes of Q. A. cty. 11 Jany 1723. ix-400.

No kin appear; inv. Charles Warner of Q. A. cty. 10 Feby 1723. ix-401.

Find no kin; inv. Murto Roe of Q. A. cty. 10 July 1723. ix-402.

No kin. Inv. David Deen of Q. A. cty. 10 July 1723. ix-403.

ANDREW ORAM, ARTHUR RIGBY; inv. Thomas Oram of Talbott cty. 1 June 1724. ix-404.

Find no kin; inv. Thomas Evins of Talbott cty. 13 May 1724. ix-405.

Kin doubtful; inv. Wm. Larkins of Talbott cty. 4 June 1724. ix-405.

JAMES x WAYT or WAGGYT [?] inv. Nich's Linch of Kent cty. 13 May 1724. ix-406.

FRANCIS x KINEY; inv. Mr. Sam'l Wallis of Kent cty. 29 May 1724. ix-408.

CATHERINE x COLL, PETER COLL [probably should be COLE], GEORGE HALL [doubtful whether the latter is kin]; inv. John Cole of Kent cty. 1 Apr 1724. ix-410.

JNO. JAMES, "all the Kindred Except Minors"; inv. Mich'l Lassell of Kent cty. 16 May 1724. ix-414.

"No relations but what lives in Pensilvania"; inv. Henry Parmane of Kent cty. 17 June 1724. ix-415.

BENJ. SUTTEN, SAMUEL SUTTEN; inv. John Sutten of Kent cty. 4 Dec 1723. ix-416.

DELAWARE TAX-LISTS for 1776 NEWCASTLE COUNTY

Pencader Hundred

JOHN AIKEN, Francis Alexander, Isaac Alexander, William Adair, Sr., Alex'r Adair, Robt Armstrong, Arthur Austin, James Allen;

JOHN BOWEN, Jesse Bowen, Nathan Boulden, John Barr, Archibald Boyd, James Bolden, Elijah Bolden, Jesse Biddle, John Boggs, Elisha Bolden;

THOMAS CUMBERLAND, John Clark "Gone," James Conway, "Gone," Henry Clark, John Cochran "Gone" [a name here which is illegible on account of the folding of the paper, but ends in "version"], John Cornegey "Gone," James Cochran "Do," Wm. Culbertson, John Cazier, Williams Clark, John Cazier, Junr, Jas. Conway, Weaver; John Curlet; Thomas Cooch, Esq.*

DAVID DAVIS, John David Rees [this name is listed with the "D's"], Thomas David, James Dunlap, James Davidson, John David, Evan Davis, Benjamin David;

JOHN EDWARDS, John Evans, Sr., John Evans John Elder, Joel Evans, William Ellis, Jinkin Evans "gone;" *William Eynon* is listed with the "J's," possibly on account of some Welsh equivalent of his name;

ANDREW FISHER, Alex'r Faires, Sen'r, Jacob Faires, James Faires, William Faires, John Faires, Alex'r Faires, Jr.;

JOHN GRIFFITH, David Griffith, Griffith Griffith, Matthew Greaves "gone," Wm. Gallocher, Sen'r, Wm. Gallocher, Charles Graham, "gone," John Garretson, Wm. Gardiner "gone";

DAVID HOWELL, John Holland, Taylor; John Holland, William Haughey, Thomas Haughey, Abel Holland, Joseph Howell, James Hinman, Daniel Hughes, Daniel Hatton;

JOHN JAMES, James John, David John, Charles Johnston, Christopher Jones, James Johnston, Samuel Jones, Hugh Jackson, Shem James, Thomas Jenkins, Enoch Jones, John Jamison, Alex'r Jamison, Joseph Jamison, John Jack, Andrew Jones; Thomas James, Esq.*

JAMES KENNEDY, James Kelley, James Kinkead, Nathaniel Kerr, David Kirkpatrick;

ISAAC LEWIS [assessor of the hundred and compiler of this list], David Llewellyn, John Long, Alexander Law, Samuel Long, William Linsey, Caleb Laurence;

ALEXANDER MOORE, Francis Moore, Evan Morgan, John McWhorter, David McKinley, Hugh Muldroch, Andrew Muldroch, Hance Miller, Jeremiah Morgan, Robert McCoy, Thomas McCrea, John Moore, David Martin, Thomas McKinley "gone," Moses Minor, Wm. Milligan, David McFann, George McKinley "gone," James McKewin, Alex'r Moore, Jr., James McMullan, Robert McMullan, Christ'r McCallister, Peregrine Moore, Thomas Morgan, "gone";

JOHN NIVINS, "gone";

JAMES PORTER, James Price, William Price, Joseph Pritchard, Archibald Phillips, Thomas Pusey;

DAVID REES, Jehu Rees [John David Rees is listed with the "D's"], James Reaper, William Robinson, Hugh Riley;

JOHN STUART, Moses Scott, Wm. Scott, weaver; Hugh Smith, James Simpson, Benjamin Steuart, William Scott, Robert Sprowl;

ALEXANDER THOMPSON, John Tarrance, David Tweedy, Joseph Thomas, Thomas Thomas, William Thompson, John Thompson, John Townsend, Ephraim Thompson, Josiah Thomas;

JOHN UNDERWOOD, Solomon Underwood, Nathan Underwood;

*At the head of this list

WILLIAM WILLIAMS, Sen'r, William Williams, David Williams, Isaac Williams, Roger Williams, Thomas Williams, Thomas Watson, William Whann, Thomas Whitelock, William Weir, Jacob Welsh.

ESTATES: Nathaniel Evans, Wm. McMechen, Wm. Black, Hugh Reynolds, John Faires, Alex'r Porter, Benjamin Evans, Zachariah Jones, Mary Muldroch, John Jones, Robert McCreary, Joseph Griffith, Joseph Oburn, Jonathan Booth, Richard Biddle, Edward Armstrong, Benj. Bravard, John Hill, Wm. Johnston, David Thomas, Rich'd Thomas. [For easier typing and printing, the possessive "s" which is attached to each of these names in the original, is omitted.]

ADDITIONAL LIST OF ESTATES: Alex' Walker, John Robinson, David Barr, John Dickinson, Esq., John Evans, Esq., Richard Griffith, Samuel Kirkpatrick, James James, Abel Davis, Thos. Cooch, Esq., estate in White Clay Hundred; do. in Christiana Hundred.

The names of James Grimes and Andrew Allison appear at the end of the first part of the list, no figures being set against them. Possibly signed as witnesses.

In August, 1931, p. 45, 2d column, line 15, Pencader should read Mill Creek.

Newcastle Hundred

ALEXANDER AIKEN, 15; Rob't Aiken, 10; Samuel Aiken, 10; William Aiken, 15; Lucas Alricks, 9; Sigfreedes Alrichs, 8; Peter Alrichs, 7; John Anderson, 5; William Aiken, Taylor, 4; Joseph Allen, 2; Veazy Alexander, 4; Benjamin Alrichs, 4; William Anderson, 6; Williams Addams, 3; William Anderson, N. C. 8; Rich'd Adair, 6.

GUNNING BEDFORD, 16; Robert Bryan, 16; Robert Bryan, Ju'r, 16; Samuel Barr, 8; Robert Bail, 8; John Booth, 4; William Buchanan, 4; Charles Bryson, 4; Philip Belocal, 3; Hugh Brown, 3; Peter Belocal, 3; James Boyd, 2; Archabald Boyd, 3; James Booth, 5; Joseph Booth, 4.

ABRAHAM CANNON, 20; Thomas Cooch, 16; John Clark, Esq'r, 15; Jacob Colsberry, 10; William Clark, 8; Thomas Clark, 8; Thomas Clay, 8; Henry Colsberry, 8; James Creed, 6; William Colsberry, 6; John Chambers, 4; Isaac Cannon, 4; Joseph Carson, 3; John Clawson, 3; Swen Colsberry, 2; Michael Casey, 2; William Coffey, 6; James Crawford, 4.

FREDERICK DEVOU, 26; Aaddam Dyat, 4; John Dougherty, 4; John Donnel, 3; Hugh Dougherty, 3; Anthony Dougherty, 3; Dennis Doyle, 3; William Dennis, 2; Cornelius Dushane, 5.

JAMES EVES, 28; Joseph Enos, 16; John Enos, 6; Samuel Eves, 6; Richard Enos, 2; John Evans, 4.

ROBERT FURNIS, 14; James Faith, 3; William Fryar, 2.

ISAAC GRANTHAM, 30; James Garretson, 4; Rob't Gilmer, 3; John Garretson, 3; Peter Galagher, 3; Robert Gless, 2; Isaac Griffith, 4.

FREDERICK HILL, 10; Jacobus Hayns, 2; John Hinsey, 6; Jacobus Hayns, Jun'r, 5; Henry Haynes, 5; William Hazlet, 4; Hance Harman, 4; David Harp, 3; Samuel Hanna, 3; Isaac Hayns, 3.

HANCE JAQUET, 9; Francis Janvier, 8; Richard Janvier, 8; Peter Jaquet, Ju'r, 4; Isaac Justice, 6; David Irvin, 6; Joseph Isreal, 5; Phillip Janvire, 5; John Jordan, 5; Thomas Janvier, 4; John Jaquet, 2; Samuel Janvier, 3; George Johnston, 2; John Jaquet of Swan Hook, 8; David Irvin, weaver, 4.

JAMES KIRKPATRICK, 10; Michael King, 9; Joseph Kirk, 3; John Kirk, 5; John Kirk, Taylor, 4; James Kinneer, 3; Robert Kerr, 4.

JOHN LEWDEN, Jun'r, 60; John Lewden, Tanner, 24; James Lafever, 10; Daniel Lewis, 4; John Lafferty, 3; Michael Livingston, 2.

RICHARD McWILLIAM, Esq., 60; John Malcolm, Esq'r., 35; Theodore Mawrice, Esq'r, 25; Daniel McLonen, 28; Morton Morton, 18; Matthias Morton, 14; Thomas Moore, 13; Thomas Morton, 12; Joseph Moore, Strand [this is a street or frontage of Newcastle] 12; Jacob Morton, 10; Alexander Montgomery, Esq'r, 10; Daniel Murphy, 8; James McCalla, 8; Robert Mears, 8; John Miller, 6; Patrick Morgan, 4; William McKenney, 4; Andrew McCahan, 4; Andrew Morton, 4; William McGinnis, 4; John McGinnis, 4; Alex. Montgomery, 4; Thomas Montgomery, 4; Henry Montooth, 4; Edward McCreaden, 2; John McKee, 3; Rob't McIlheron, 3; James McDonald, 2; Patrick McCormick, 3; Daniel McRea, 2; Hugh Martin, 2; Charles McCreaden, 3; Archabald McIlroy, 3.

WILLIAM NORRIS, 6.

ALEX. PORTER, 62; John Pasmore, 20; Alex'r Porter, Jun'r, Esq'r, 15; David Porter, 15; John Powel, 15; John Powel, 5; William Pike, 3; James Partridge, 20; William Post, 2; John Post, 2; William Price, 2.

GEORGE READ, Esq'r, 32; Samiel [sic] Ruth, 12; Joseph Rhoads, Jun'r, 10; James Read, 10; John Reynolds, 10; James Rezous [?] Joseph Rhoads, 8; Richard Rhoads, 6; William Rhoads, 6; Andrew Reany, 4.

JONAS STIDHAM, 46; Peter Stalcup, 30; Peter Stidham, 28; Robert Shealds, 16; Abraham Short, 15; John Stewart, 14; Do'r Stephen Spencer, 10; William Stidham, 8; John Silsbee, 6; James Stewart, 6; Abraham Sankey, 6; William Scott, 6; Joseph Silsbee, 5; John Stafford, 3; Ephraim Stoops, 3; Benjamin Stoops, 3; Jasper Smith, 3; William Shannon, 3; Joshua Storie, 2; John Simmons, 2; Sampson Smith, 2; Morgan Stoops, 2.

JOSEPH TATLOW, 14; Thomas Turner, 12; Peter Turner, 16; John Titus, 3; Morgan Thompson, 2.

JOSEPH VANDEVIER, Zach'a Vanluvenigh, 32; John Vangezee [?] 22; Isreal Vanluvenigh, 3; Abraham Vandigrift, 2.

MORRIS WILLIAMS, 15; Do'r John Watson, 12; James Wilson, 10; Jacob Wirt, 8; Jacob Wirt, Jun'r, 6; Joseph Woodward, 5; Joseph Wilson, 4; Robert Wiley, 4, Christopher Wilson, 4; William Wood, 4; Lucas Walraven, 4; Robert Watson, 2.

JOHN YEATES, 10.

Estates in New Castle Hundred:

SAMUEL ALRICH 30; William Bedford, 10; William Blackburn, 5; Slater Clay, 24; Benjamin Devou, 18; Jacob Grantham, 12; Jediah Garretson, 4; Walter Delany, 3; Peter Jaquet, L. H., 13; John King, 20; William Land, 18; Sykes and Maxwell, 23; David Miller, 13; Morton Morton, 4; Robert McLonen, 8; John Porter, 10; Thomas Sankey, 10.

John Ross, Esq'r, 4; Joseph Richardson, 4; William Spencer, 5: William Smith, 6; Nathaniel Silsbee, 6; Samuel Wharton, 10; Donaldson Yates, 6; John Eves, 30; John Rankin, 18; John Kettle, 15; William Lear, 4; John McClay, 6; Do'r John Finney, 30; Thomas McKean, Esq'r, 15; Esther Mackey, 5; Benjamin Swett, 6; Addam Guyars, 15; Alexander Harvey, 15; Thomas Jaquet, 15.

Estates in NewCastle Hundred that belong to persons residing within the County:

DAVID FINNEY, Esq'r, 20; John Thompson, Esq'r, 15; Peter Jaquet, 28; Jobe Harvey, 15; George Monro, 10; Mary Hills, 4; Cornelious Hayns, 3; John Elliot, 10; William McMechen, 4; Sam'l Patterson, Esq'r, 8; John McKinly, Esq'r, 8; Joseph Warner, 5; William Marshal, 2; John Richardson, 2.

Estates in other Hundreds belonging to persons Residing in this:

RICHARD McWILLIAM, Esq'r in Christeen Hundred, 4; do. in Appoq'k, 12; Peter Stalcup in Christeen Hundred, 20; Jonas Stidham in do., 4; do. in Brandywine, 5; James Read in White Clay Creek Hundred, 4; Abraham Cannon in Red Lyon Hundred, 4; William Anderson in do. 4; James Kirkpatrick in do. 4; William Lea in do. 4; Alex'r Porter in do. 30; Alex'r Porter, Jun'r, Esq'r, do. 25.

This assessment was returned 26 Nov. 1776, by Robt Bryan, the Assessor. It is the last of the lists that were found in the Delaware folder in the Mss. Division of the Library of Congress.

(The figures are, as explained before, the amount of the assessment in pounds sterling.)

AMHERST PROBATES AND ADMINISTRATIONS, 1773 to 1777

From a recently found Order Book.

RICHARD POWELL; his will presented by Wiatt Powell, extr, and proved by Thomas Powell and Jacob Smith. Thomas Powell and Edmund Powell also appear to be executors, Jacob Smith their security. p. 35. 4 April 1774.

JAMES POWELL, grandson and heir-at-law to RICHARD POWELL, summoned to contest will if he think proper. p. 36. 4 April 1774.

WILLIAM CABELL; his will, produced by Nicholas Cabell and proved by John Horesby. p. 101. 4 July 1774.

THOMAS EVANS; his will presented and proved. Margaret, Ann and William Gatewood witnesses. Charles Evans, son and heir-at-law summoned. p. 107. 5 Sept 1774.

ELEANOR GILLILAND, John Gilliland, heir-at-law, gets admn of her estate. p. 110. 3 Oct 1774.

MOSES PENN, Jr.; Will presented by George and Gabriel Penn, extrs. Ctf for probate granted.

COSBY AYERS; Ctf of proof of non-cup. will presented by Leonard Philips, Jr., legatee, and admn granted to him. p. 116. 7 Nov 1774.

JAMES MARTIN; will presented by Wm. James and Azeriah Martin, extrs, and proved. p. 124. 6 Mch 1775.

JONATHAN JOHNSON; Ann Johnson gets admn; Charles Burras and Thomas Lumpkin, sec. p. 124. 6 Mch 1774.

CORNELIUS THOMAS; will presented by extrs and proved. p. 137. 2 Oct 1775.

BENJAMIN CHILDERS; will presented by three of the extrs and proved. p. 138. 2 Oct 1775.

WILLIAM LAVENDER; Milly Lavender, his widow, gets admn on his estate, Edmund Wilcox and George Gillaspie, security. p. 147. 5 Feby 1776.

RICHARD LAMASTER; will presented by Abraham Lamaster and proved by David London. p. 152. 3 June 1776.

JOHN LAVENDER; widow summoned to declare whether she will take administration of his estate. p. 152. 1 July 1776.

RICHARD LAMASTER; Abraham Lamaster granted admn on his estate; John Christian [of ?] Buffalo, sec. p. 154. 1 July 1776.

MARY MILLS; heir-at-law of William Mills to be summoned to declare whether he will take admn of her estate. p. 154. 1 July 1776.

JOHN LAVENDER; William Lane gets admn of his estate. p. 154. 1 July 1776.

JOHN WATERS; Francis Waters gets administration his estate. p. 154. 1 July 1776.

MARY MILLS; Ambrose Mills, son and heir-at-law of William Mills, summoned to declare whether he will admr her estate. p. 157. 1 July 1776.

BATTAILE HARRISON; his will presented by Reubin Harrison, the son and heir-at-law (John and Richard Harrison the other executors renouncing), whereupon the will was proved and probate granted to Reubin Harrison. p. 162. 7 Oct 1776.

SAMUEL STAPLES; Charles Irving gets admn his estate, John Staples, son and heir-at-law, consenting. p. 165. 4 Nov 1776.

WILLIAM JOHNS; Thomas Johns granted adm his estate. p. 167. 6 Jany 1777.

BENJ'N CASH; his will presented by Richard Ballenger and Robert Cash, two of the executors, Nancy Cash, widow, and other executors refusing execution. Will proved. p. 169. 3 Feby 1777.

NEILL CAMPBELL; his will presented and proved. p. 173. 3 Mch 1777.

AUGUSTINE WRIGHT, Alce Wright, widow ordered to appear and show cause why she does not prove his will. p. 176. 3 Mch 1777.

GEORGE CAMPBELL; will presented by Margaret Campbell and Charles Patrick, extrs, said Charles Patrick renouncing, ctf is granted Margaret Campbell, who renounces and demands her thirds, according to law. p. 181. 5 May 1777.

DAVID DUNCAN; John Duncan gets admn his estate. p. 182. 5 May 1777.

BENJAMIN WILSHER; Joseph Wilsher gets admn his estate. p. 185. 5 May 1777.

MOSES LONDON; James London, heir-at-law, to be summoned to declare whether he will take upon himself the admn of the estate. p. 190. 2 June 1777.

WILLIAM PENN; will presented by George and Gabriel Penn, extrs, who are granted ctf for probate. p. 190. 2 June 1777.

BENJAMIN CLARK; his will presented by William Clark and Joseph Roberts and proved. p. 190. 2 June 1777.

AUGUSTINE WRIGHT; Alcey Wright, his widow, granted admn on his estate. p. 191. 2 June 1777.

JESSE BOULWARE; will presented by John Rose, Gent., and ordered to lie for further proof. p. 192. 2 June 1777. Elizabeth Boulware, the widow, renounces. Further proved. p. 199. 1 Sept 1777.

MERRITT MAGANN; Joseph Magann granted admn his estate. p. 195. 4 Aug 1777.

MOSES LONDON; Alexander Chisnal granted admn on his estate. p. 196. 4 Aug 1777.

JESSE BOULWARE; John Rose, gentleman, extr, granted execution. p. 199. 1 Sept 1777.

REUBIN GRIFFIN; will presented by the extrs, who refused execution. Will proved. p. 201. 1 Sept 1777. John Griffin, heir-at-law, summoned to take execution. Gets execution. p. 204. 6 Oct 1777.

ITEMS FROM AN EARLY MINUTE BOOK OF PRINCE GEORGE COUNTY, VIRGINIA

Including marriage references.

The volume begins with the Court before that of May, 1715. Three items belong to the previous Court.

FRANCIS CLEMENTS and LYDIA, admx of George BLEIGHTON [?] Before the previous Court.

JAMES BELL and MARTHA, admx of Edward MARKS. do. do.

ROBERT WYNNE was the son of Major JOSHUA WYNNE.

JOHN WILLIAMS, wife REBECCA, was extx in *Barbadose* of Robert MINNET, mcht, lately deceased. 10 May 1715.

JOHN DAVIS, unlawfully departed. 10 May 1715.

JAMES BELL and MARTHA, admx of Edmond MARKS. 10 May 1715.

CHRISTOPHER DAVIS petitions to be levy free. Not granted. 14 June 1715.

JAMES SEEVEAR [looks more like SWEEAR] and SARAH VAUGHN, extx and relict of William, deceased. Before 13 Sept 1715. p. 33.

WILLIAM HOBB'S wife was SARAH, dau. of Thomas SMITH. Court 10 Apr 1716. p. 55.

JOHN DEW probably m. ELIZABETH SMITH, widow of Thomas. [Uncertain.] Before 10 Apr 1716. p. 55.

.........AVERY m. ELIZABETH NOWLIN [?] extx of Richard. Before 8 May 1716. p. 58.

MARY DANIELL, gets l. a. on estate of John. Benj. Foster, sec. 12 June 1716. p. 59. Returns inv. 10 July 1716.

.........AVERY m. ELIZABETH OSBORN, extx of Elias. Before 10 July 1716. p. 69.

ROBERT BURCHET presented for turning away his wife, &c. 14 May 1717. p. 123.

THOMAS WEBB was the surviving extr of Giles Webb, 11 June 1717. p. 131.

WILLIAM TOMLINSON probably m. JANE TAPLEY, widow. Before 13 Aug 1717. p. 141.

DANIEL CRAWLEY m. ELIZABETH, extx of Bryan FARRELL, dec'd. Before 12 Aug 1718. p. 201.

JOSEPH GOFFE, of the City of Boston, in the Province of New England, Mcht; suit agt Edward Wyatt. 11 Aug 1719. p. 280.

THOMAS ADAMS was father-in-law to Alexander Tapley. 14 Mch 1720, p. 355.

HANRY HOLDCROFT m. MARY, the surviving extx of Alexander Walker. Before 14 Mch 1720. p. 355.

ABRAHAM ODIUM, *non est inv.* 10 Nov 1719. p. 294.

Will of RICHARD BLAND; Wm. and Richard Randolph, extrs. 12 Apr 1720. p. 314.

HENRY THOMPSON; his will presented by Sarah his Relict and extx; proved by wit: Robert Richardson and Sampson Merredeth. Widow gets ctf for probate, John Jackson, sec. 10 May 1720. p. 318.

The Court record ends on p. 356, with the Court of 14 Mch 1720. Then follows a return of executions, &c.

The foregoing notes are incomplete, being only part of the matters recorded, the work of abstracting unfinished.

The County Court Note-Book

An every-other monthly devoted mainly to abstracts from County Court Records, prior to 1800.

MILNOR LJUNGSTEDT. Editor and Publisher. Bethesda, Rural Route 5, Maryland.

Published six times a year. Subscription two dollars, in advance; must begin with the year.

October, 1931 Whole

Vol. X, No. 5 No. 60

I am afraid the Editor is given to harping on Facts. Facts are such comfortable things...... once established, they are like the gold basis we used to believe in, for our money. No argument is required, nothing can happen to them, once proved they are as changeless as the sea. Suppose for instance that you walked down the right side of a street. You know that you did and other people know it. But suppose you did not know which side of the street you walked on, and never would know, because the thing happened so long ago it couldn't be proved. What possible satisfaction could there be in your next-door neighbor who had just moved in from Kalamazoo, what satisfaction could there be in her statement that you walked on the left side? And when the neighbor on the other side, a young thing, quoted her mother as saying that *her* mother always claimed that you walked on the right side, how intensely irritating to realize that *you* didn't know anything about it, and knew that they didn't know anything about it ......and nothing was left to prove it but the street!

It seems to be the turn of many minds to be satisfied with the street. The street was there at such and such a time, and the house was there and you were there......therefore......

There was a learned professor (like some others) on the Western Shore, some times called the Continent of Virginia. He wrote things about the Eastern Shore. Among various matters, possibly some were true, he wrote: "Capt. Daniel Jenifer married Miss Annie Toft, who was reputed the wealthiest and prettiest woman then living on the Eastern Shore of Virginia. She owned an immense landed estate in the eastern part of Accomac. They had a numerous family of children [doesn't this sound like the old family write-ups?] among whom were three daughters named Arcadia, Annabella and Atlanta."

Mistress Anne Toft [not Annie] was a mysterious and interesting personality. She was about sixteen when she came to Virginia, probably from the West Indies, and she did not marry Jenifer until 1670......when she was between twenty-four and thirty. Her daughters were not the daughters of Jenifer, records of gifts by Jenifer and wife to the daughters of Ann Toft plainly prove this. They were the offspring of a previous alliance.

Other statements have been made, including the creation of a Henry Toft, of whom we might say "not proven."

Publications like this, presumably by a man of high intelligence and honesty, are copied and relied upon here and there, and not the face of the records will shake the belief of many good people not only in mythical estates......but in mythical parents.

Professor Brent's article appeared under the heading of "Some Unpublished Facts Relating to Bacon's Rebellion on the Eastern Shore of Virginia."

THE DEPUTY COMMISSARY'S GUIDE WITHIN THE PROVINCE OF MARYLAND

(*Continued from October, 1930.*)

The extracts from the "Guide" closed in a recent number with the chapter upon wills and the intention was to continue with the laws of descent as being particularly useful to the intelligent searcher. There are, however, so many quaint and interesting paragraphs touching Legacies that the compiler is tempted to give the "gist" of a few of them.

The question as to whether the children of negro slave women were included in a devise of the mother seems to have been settled in this manner:

"Where female negroes have been bequeathed "to one for life, and a limitation over to another "on the death of the first legatee, it seems to be "a settled point, that the children of the negroes "bequeathed, belong to the first legatee, as part "of the use, or profit of the negroes bequeathed, "and do not go with the negroes bequeathed, to "the second legatee; but if the children or in- "crease be bequeathed over, then they shall go "according to the directions of the will."

Concerning the right of the wife in a lease for years belonging to her, "tho' the husband may dispose of it by *deed*, [it] does not belong to his executors or administrators, nor can he bequeath it; but it will belong to the wife."

Moveables, this exposition of the law says, "com- "prehend as well such goods as are passively "moveable, or removeable; things that have not "life; as such as are actively, and by their own "accord move themselves......But money arising "from land devised to be sold is not a moveable; "nor are, in favour of the heir, fish in a pond, "pidgeons belonging to a dove-cote, or deer in "a park." *Immoveables, or chattels real*, are, such "as a lease and the *natural* fruits of the soil." [It would seem that if there were a persimmon tree on your place, neither the tree nor the persimmons could be disposed of!]

The paragraph upon "*Household stuff*" is particularly interesting, especially as it is stated that formerly nothing of gold or silver was included under this head, but at the time of this digest vessels of silver, gold and precious stones...... "passed under the description of household stuff "or furniture......but if the testator...... used "them for pomp rather than for the ordinary "service of his house, they will not pass" as such household stuff or furniture.

Of Descent. The *first* rule of descent is, that inheritance shall lineally descend to the issue of the person last actually seized, *in infinitum;* but shall never lineally ascend. No person can properly be an ancestor, from whom an inheritance in lands or tenements can be derived, unless he hath had actual *seisin* of the land, by his own entry, or by the possession of his own, or his ancestor's lease for years......or hath what is equivalent to corporal seisin, such as the receipt of rent.

The *second* rule of descent is, that the male issue shall be preferred before the female...... yet daughters are to be preferred before any collateral relations.

The *third* rule is that when there are two or more *males,* in equal degree, the eldest shall inherit; *but if two or more females, they shall all inherit together.*

The *fourth* rule of descent is, that the lineal descendants, *in infinitum,* of a person deceased, shall represent their ancestor......shall stand in the same place as the ancestor would have done, had he been living. Thus the child, grandchild, or great grandchild of each sex, of the eldest son, shall be preferred before a younger son......This taking by representation is called a succession in *stirpes* according to the roots, since all the branches inherit the same share, that their root, whom they represent, would have done.

The *fifth* rule of descent is, that, on failure of lineal descendants, or issue of person last seised, the inheritance shall go to the blood of the first ......person that acquired the estate to his family ......by any method except only by *descent.* Wherefore, if lands come to a person by descent from his father, no relation of his mother can inherit; so if from his mother, no relation of his father can be the heir to inherit.

This, Vallette writes, is the great and general principle.

The next rule touches: the matter of collateral heirs and will be taken up at another time.

AUTHENTIC REFERENCES FOR INFERRED MARRIAGES

(The following marriages are from Maryland records.)

WILLIAM LOKER [LOCKER] and ELIZABETH PARROT, dau. of James Smith, of St. Mary's cty. Before Apr 1772. Annap. DDxviii-275.

.... LANE and LYDIA MASON, extx of William *Townsing.* Before 13 Apr 1796. A. A. cty. Minutes O. C. p. 26.

.... LAWS and SARAH COTTINGHAM, dau. of Jonathan. Before 7 Oct 1760. Wor. cty. J. W. iii-49.

HENRY LOWE and SUSANNA DARNALL, of Calv. cty., widow of John, Esq. Mar. contract. 18 May 1686. Annap. Province. Ct. W. R. C. i-728.

.... LATHBERY and MARY AYDELOTT, dau. of John. Before 15 Nov 1754. Wor. cty J. W. iii-9.

.... LEE, probably m. Mrs. MARY BUTLER, a widow. Before 11 June 1800. Minutes O. C. p. 111. Fred'kcty, Md.

SOLOMON LONG and COMFORT, extx of Stevens WHITE. Before 7 Nov 1772. Anap. Bal. Books.

.... LOTT and SARAH GOSLEE, dau. of Richard. Before 18 Oct 1762. Wor. cty. J. W. iii-53.

HEZEKIAH LINTHICUM and ELIZABETH WELSH, dau. of Capt. John. Before 23 Nov 1752. Semmes Mss. M. H. S.

ZADOCH LONG and LEAH WHITTINGTON. 13 Oct. 1796. St. Martin's Psh Reg.

HENRY LAKE and MARY COOK, svts to Thomas Cottingham. 13 Nov 1683. Som. cty. L [07] p. 11.

JOHN MERRYMAN and SARAH SMITH, extx of John Addison SMITH. Before 8 Oct 1782. Balto. cty. Adm'n Accts, viii-92.

WILLIAM MERRIKEN and SARAH TALBOT, widow of Benj. Before 16 Oct 1789. A. A. cty. Distributions, p. 13.

MATHEW MACKBEE and a dau. of Capt. BROCK. He m. (2) JANE.........Before 28 Mch 1710. Pr. Geo's cty. D-276.

HENRY MITCHELL and GRACE MOLDEN. About Oct. 1659. Md. Arch. xli-337.

Mr. RICE MADDOOKES and ANN DANDY, widow of John. Before 1 Jany 1657. Md. Arch. xli-13.

THOMAS MEARES and......... FREEMAN, a widow. Before 2 Aug 1659. Md. Arch. xli-317.

THOS. MACKELL and CHARLES POWELL'S widow, who was GARY'S dau. Dor. cty. Rent Roll, 1707.

.... MOMFORD and MARY COLLINGS, dau. of John, Sr. Before 26 Sept. 1759. Wor. cty. J. W. iii-19.

.... MORE and BETTEY HOLLAND, dau. of Nehemiah. Before 2 Feby 1758. Wor. cty, J. W. iii-15.

.... MACNAMARE and MARY STEWART, dau. of John. See his will. Dor. cty. Annap. Distributions i-150. 23 July 1751.

.... McELWAINE and SAPPHIRA AYDELOTTE, dau. of John. Before 15 Nov 1754. Wor. cty. J. W. iii-9.

JOHN x MASSEY and MARGARET McDANIEL, a widow. Before 11 Jany 1759. Wor. cty. J. W. iii-5.

HUGH MONTGOMERY and KATHERINE PARKER, widow of George. Before 5 May 1761. Annap. W. T. No. 3, p. 651.

DAVID MURRAY and HANNAH HOPKINS. Before 15 Sept 1745. See his will. Wor. cty. J. W. ii-37.

THOMAS MORRIS and MARY SMITH, dau. of Edward. Before 25 Mch 1728. Som. cty. S. H. 29.

.... MARSHALL and SARAH PEALE, dau. of Thomas. Before 13 Feb 1742. Wor cty.

JOHN McBROOM and KARINHAPPA ELLIOTT. Before [?] 31 Jany 1782. Balto. cty.

JOHN MOUNFORD [MUMFORD] of Wor. cty. and NEOMA [NAOMI] AYDELOTTE, dau. of Benjamin. Before 9 Dec 1749. Wor. cty. B-203.

THOMAS MORRIS and MARY INNIS, relict of Samuel. Before or about 1690. Som. cty. BWZ, p. 60.

.... MORRIS and CATHERINE BURTON, dau. of WILLIAM and FRANCES BURTON, Before 17 April 1744. Wor. cty. J. W. ii-29.

.... BURTON probably m. ELIZABETH MORRIS, dau. of the above. [The proof of this is not clear at the moment.] Wor. cty. J. W. ii-29.

EDWARD NEALE and .... LOWE, sister of Nicholas LOWE of St. Mary's cty. Before 28 Jany 1728. Annap. T. P. xxviii-311.

.... NOBLE, of St. Mary's cty, and .... EDLOE. Before [1727.] Pr. Geo's. cty. M-257.

JAMES NEALE probably m. ELIZABETH CALVERT, dau. of William. [The wording of the record is obscure.] Before 10 Apr 1702. Pr. Geo's cty. A-449.

JOHN NUTWELL and ELINOR HILLARY, widow of Thomas. Before 9 Sept 1741. Pr. Geo's cty. Y-395.

CHARLES NEALE and MARY SMITH, dau. of Maj. Walter Smith. Before 9 Sept 1741. Pr. Geo's cty. Y-395.

HENRY NICHOLLS and ELIZABETH, admx of William ROACH. Before 30 Mch 1724. Annap. T. P. xxvii-212.

.... NICHOLSON and MARY COTTINGHAM, dau. of Jonathan. Before 7 Oct 1760. Wor. cty. J. W. iii-49.

BENJAMIN NELSON and MARGARET HEDRICK. Before July, 1766. Annap. T. P. xli-348.

CHARLES NEALE and ELIZABETH DAVIS, widow of Thomas, late of Frederick cty., Md. About 1754. Annap. Accts. xxxvi-503. Semmes Mss. M. H. S.

JAMES NICHOLLS and MARTHA POPLEY [?] Banns published. Ctf. 30 Aug 1671. Som. cty. DT-151.

.........NELSON and COMFORT PEALL, dau. of Thomas. Before 13 Feby 1742. Wor. cty. J. W. ii-15.

.........NEWTON and ABRILAH [?] PEALL, dau. of Thomas. [Perhaps meant for AVARILLA?] Before 13 Feby 1742. Wor. cty. J. W. ii-15.

PHILIP NOLAND and MARTHA GIBSON. 4 May 1798. Fred'k. cty. Mar. Ret.

RUDY NOFFSINGER [HOFFSINGER?] and SUSANAH KAINS [KARN?] extx of Michael, late of Fred'k cty. Before 10 Apr 1787. Fred'k cty. "Judgment Records."

.........OUTTEN and RHODA PEALL, dau. of Thomas. Before 13 Feby 1742. Wor. cty. J. W. ii-15.

WILLIAM P. PALMER, of Mont. Cty., Md., son of Moses and Hannah, of Dela. cty, Penna., m. MARTHA GRAY, of Philada., at Darby Mtg House. 9-26-1822. Darby Mtg Records. (P. G. S. Collections.)

WILLIAM PURNELL and MARY ROBINS, dau. of Thomas. 3 Dec. 1765. Wor. cty. J. W. iii-125.

.... PRUITT and SARAH DAVIS, dau. of Charles. Before 31 Oct 1761. Wor. cty. J. W. iii-51.

.... PRICE and TABITHA HOLLAND, dau. of Nehemiah. Before 2 Feby 1758. Wor. cty. J. W. iii-15.

JOHN POTTER and RHODA TURVILL, sister of John. Before [?] 7 Mch 1753. Wor. cty. J. W. iii-20.

.... PARKER and ABIGAIL TURNER, dau. of Samuel. Before 20 Feby 1752. Wor. cty. J. W. iii-16.

JOHN PEACOCK and MARY JENKINS, admx of William, of Baltimore. Before 28 May 1771. Annap. vi-20.

JOHN PURNELL probably m. .... BAILEY. [Uncertain.] Before 15 Apr 1741. Annap. Wills. xxiii-177.

ERASMUS PERRY and ELIZABETH HARDING, Montg. cty. 13 Jany 1778. (By Rev. Thos. Reed.)

WILLIAM PORTER and NAOMI STURGES. 4 Jany 1796. Wor. cty. St. Martin's Psh Reg.

CHAS. PICKERING and MARY CARVIN. 28 Feby. 1748. Talbot cty. Mar. Li.

HEROD REAMS and ELIZA: PORTER. 15 June 1746. Talbot cty. Mar. Li.

WALKER x REDMAN and MARY TULLY, widow of John. After 28 July 1669. Som. cty. EFV-18.

JOSEPH RICHARSON and AMELIA BOWEN, dau. of Isaac. Before Nov. Term 1833. Som. cty. Court Proc. iv.

.... RYLE and RACHEL PEALL, dau. of Thomas. Before 13 Feby 1742. Wor. cty. J. W. ii-15.

STANLEY ROBINS and SARAH GOLDSBOROUGH. 6 Jany 1741. Talbot cty. Mar. Li. [Judge Goldsborough makes a note: that the only dau. of this marriage, Elizabeth, married Harry Nicols. Also that Geo. Robins, silk weaver, of Buckinghamshire, and Thomas Robins, "with a large family", immigrated to Talbot cty. in 1670.

THOMAS ROBINS and ARRALANTA PURNELL, dau. of John. Before 8 Jany 1755. Annap. Wills. xxix-407.

ISAAC SHERMON and SARAH LINCH. 28 May 1740. Som. cty. Stepney Psh Reg.

GEORGE STICHCOMB and AVARILLA ANDREWS. Before 15 Apr 1784. Balto. Cty. Proceedings, I-146.

ARCHIBALD SMITH and TURNER SMITH, dau. of Samuel. [This name is difficult to make out and should probably be TAMAR ...... but her father calls her TURNER SMITH, and her husband, in his will, says "wife, TURNER SMITH."] Before 20 Feby 1752. Wor cty. J. W. iii-16.

The following marriages are from the DELAWARE records.

JACOB KOLLOCK and MAGDALEN ROYALL. Mar. ctf. Sussex cty. Vol. I. [Date lacking in note.]

FRANCIS LAVERDY and MARGARET WHITE, Bans. 26 Jany 1788. Immanuel Ch. Records. Newcastle cty.

RICHARD McWILLIAMS and MARY CURTIS, dau. of Jehu. About 1751. [She d. 6 May 1757.] Immanuel Ch. tombstones. N. C. cty. and town.

NEIL MORRISON and ANNABELLA JOHNSON, dau. of William. Before 1768. N. C. cty, Surveys, p. 221.

JOSEPH MORRIS and PHEABE TOWNSEND, dau. of Solomon, Sr. Sussex cty. Before 1773. B2-467.

ROBERT MAXWELL, of Lancaster cty, Penna., and MARY SMITH, dau. of William. See Orphans' Ct. 6 Apr 1784. N. C. cty. F-301.

BAPTIST NEWCOMB and ANN, widow of John HAGESTER, dec'd. Before 13 Sept 1682. Sussex [Deale] cty, record, p. 75.

JOHN OWENS and ELIZABETH STAATS, wid. and admx of Peter. Before Oct. 1750. N. C. cty.

HENRY O'HARA and MARY REAH, dau. of Matthew. Before 1 July 1783. N. C. cty. F2-127.

MOSES PALMER and SARAH PHILLIPS, dau. of William, Sr. Before 15 Nov 1789. Dela. Wills. N. Y. cty.

WILLIAM READ, Shff N. Y. cty, and JANE JANE SPAULDING. She was b. in London. Died 5 July 1732. Married about 1714. Immanuel Church tombstones, N. C. town and cty.

JOSH, ROYALL, of *Lewis*, and MAGDELAN KOLLUCK, Ctf. of Mar. 21 Dec 1718. Sussex cty. Vol. marked "Ear Marks!" p. 137.

STEPHEN RICHARDSON and SARAH HOLDEN, dau. of Joseph. Prob. before 1700. N. C. cty. E-64.

JOHN REDMAN and JANE JONES, widow of Enoch. Before 16 Aug 1811. N. C. cty. M8-324.

JACOB READ and MARY HOLDEN, dau. of Joseph. Prob. before 1700. N. C. cty. E-64.

HARKLOS SHEEPART and MARY AVERY, dau. of Capt. AVERY. Before 13 Feby 1682. Some Records Sussex cty. Dr. Turner. p. 93.

CERTIFICATES OF MARRIAGES PERFORMED: AMHERST COUNTY, VIRGINIA

JAMES POLLOX to ELIZABETH PHILLIPS; return made 5 Aug 1782;

ANTHONY CAMPBELL to ANN WARE; same date;

DAVID ANDERSON to ELIZABETH HARDY, same date;

JOHN CARR to CHRISTIAN PHILLIPS, same date;

all by Benjamin Burger.

NICHOLAS JONES and AMMARETTAR CAMBLIN, by Rev. Benj. Coleman; married 26 July 1782.

ANGUS FORBUS marriage contract with MARY LEE, proved and recorded. 1782.

JAMES WARE, Bach. and MARY VEALE. Mar. 24 Oct 1782, by Rev. Chas. Clay.

DANIEL HARVEY, Batch. and SALLY TALLIAFERRO, Sp. 1 Nov 1782. By same minister.

GEORGE GILBERT, Batch. and MARTHA COLE WEST, Sp. Same minister.

ROBERT CHILDRESS and NANCY PRYOR, 27 Mch 1783.

JOSEPH HIGGENBOTHAN to RACHEL HIGGENBOTHAN. 16 Apr 1783.

THOMAS HASLEP and JANE LACKLAND. 21 Apr 1783.

All by Rev. Mr. Coleman.

GEORGE FULCHER and FANNY PENN, 15 Apr 1783. By Rev. Joseph Ballenger.

RICHARD BOND and SUSANNAH MAYS, 15 May 1783. By the same.

WILLIAM MAYS and MARY BROWN. 15 May, 1783.

JAMES RUSSELL and MARY GILMER, 15 May 1783.

GEORGE PENN, widower, and MARY WALDEN, widow, by Rev. Chas. Clay. 29 May 1783.

GEORGE TAYLOR, Batch., and ANN WATERS, Sp. 22 May, 1783, by same minister.

ZEDEKIAH SHOEMAKER and ELIZABETH HOGG, by Rev. Benj. Coleman, 12 June 1783.

WILLIAM SANDIDGE and TAMSEY CASH, by the same. 31 Aug 1783.

Note: The Editor is not certain as to some of the foregoing dates, whether they are the date of the marriage or of the return made by the minister. The ministers' returns are often very far from clear, especially those made by a reverend sir who is behindhand in complying with the law. Sometimes several months or a year are listed together.

FREDERICK COUNTY, MARYLAND DISTRIBUTIONS

JONA. MORRISS; Mary Morriss, admx. Distributees; Widow and ten children: Sarah, Isaac, Jonathan, William, Samuel, Joseph, Mary, David, Betty, Jessee. No date.

GEO. MICH'L ELLER; Henry Eller and Martin Gower [?] extrs. Distributees; Widow, Peter Eller, Leonard Eller, Elizabeth Ripp [or Kipp] and "six youngest children": Jacob, Geo., John, Eve, Catharine, Mary. No date.

WILLIAM PENNABAKER; Lod. Mouse [?] and Mary Jacobina Mouse.

JOHN GREGG; Jane Evans, admx. Distributees: Widow and 6 chn., Nathan, Ann, Sarah, James, William, Samuel. No date.

PETER BALSELL; Mary Balsell, admx, Jacob Balsell, sec. Distributees: Widow and ten children: Barbara, Catherine, Mary, Henry, Peter, Jacob, Elizabeth, Modelin, Margaret, Juliana. No date.

JACOB SNIDER; Mich'l Snider, admr. Distributees: Widow and ten children: John, Jacob, Abraham, Elizabeth, Magdalen, Daniel, Christiana, Lodewick, Ann-Mary, Barbara. No date.

ENOCH DAVIS: Abraham and Elizabeth Davis, admrs. Distributees: Widow and three children: William, Samuel, David.

BEN. NORRISS; Priscilla Norriss, admx. Distributees: Widow and ten children: Mary, Benjamin, Ann, Elizabeth, Priscilla, Keziah, John, Sarah, Susannah, Eleanor.

JOHN YENGLIN; Marg't Lenora Yenglin and Charles Angel, extrs. Distributees: Widow, Frederick Yenglin, and 14 children: Susana, Catharine, Elizabeth, Frederick, Maudlin-Anna [Uncertain] Maria, John, Jacob, Abraham, Margaret, Louisa, Christiana, Peter, Hanah.

GEORGE AUSTOTT; Henry Austott and Mich'l Kible, extrs. Distributees: Henry, Mary, Margaret, John, George, Nicholas, Modelina.

SAMUEL BUSSARD [?] Catharine Bussard, admx. Distributees: Widow and six children: Jacob, Samuel, Mary, David, Catharine, Susanah.

EDW. BURY or BUSY; Chas. Bury or Busy, admr. Distributees: not given.

SAMUEL FLEMMING; Barbara Flemming, admx. Distributees: Widow and daughter, Allice. No date.

FRANCIS ISDON; Normand Bruce, admr. No distribution. No date.

ROBERT SHIBBY; Bedwell Parnell, admr. Distributees: Brothers and sisters of deceased: Elizabeth Kiber, Sarah Henderson, Ruth Parnell, Mary Eason, Eleanor Eason, John Eason. No date.

HENRY STONER; John Stoner, admr. Distributees: Widow, son John. No date.

JAMES BROWN; Ann Brown and Joseph Gosnel, extrs. Distributees: James Brown, Ann Brown, Sarah Gosnell, Mary Fitzgerald, Ruhel [?] Prinkstone [?]. No date.

REBEKAH SMITH; William Smith, admr. Distributees: Three children: William, George, David Smith. No date.

MARG'T KNOUFF; John Knouff, admr. Distributees: Ten children: John, Susanah, Peter, Henry, Adam, Catharine, Jacob, Elizabeth. Mary, Ann. Receipt presented 10 June 1783,

ADAM WAGGONER; Sophia Waggoner, admx. Distributees: Widow, and William and Christ'r Waggoner. No date.

PETER APPLE; Catharine Apple, Henry Matthews, extrs. Distributees: Susannah Apple, Eve Horsey, Charlotte Myers, Mary Mathews, Magdalena Baily [?] No date.

JACOB AMBROSE; Cath. Ambrose and Peter Shover, admrs. Distributees: Widow and ten children: Sophia, Fanny, Catharine, Jacob, Mathias [?], John, Mary, Eliza'th, Eve, Lodewick. Bond, 10 June 1783.

JOHN MIDDAH; Mary King, extx. No list.

CASPER SMITH; Chris'a Smith and Jacob Smith, extrs. Distributees: Widow, [and children] Jacob, Chris'r, Dan'l, Mathias, Peter, Elizabeth Smith, Mary Carnhart. No date.

THOS. WALLACE; Andrew Hines, extr. Distributees: William and Elizabeth Wallace. No date.

WILLIAM PATTISON or PATTERSON; Margaret Pattison and Adam Hope, extrs. Distributees: Margaret, Rebekah, Mathew, and Samuel of Samuel Patterson; Robert Shields, Samuel Patterson, son of John, Sarah Patterson, dau. of John, Samuel Tweed, Elizabeth Tweed, Marg't Daniell of Hugh Daniel, James Betty of Robert, and Samuel Patterson of Samuel. No date.

JOHN BARRUK; John Barruk, admr. Distributees: Seven *children*; Charity Hover, John *Burruk*, William *Burruk*, Catharine Steel, Jacob Burruk, Marg't Smith, Mary Crum. No date. [The varied spellings are clues to pronunciation.]

MARTIN GRAWMER [?] Charles Angel and Chris'r Erb, admrs. Distributees: Widow, Balser and Elizabeth Grammer *or Cranmer.* [In Virginia, just across the Potomac, this name is Grammar or Grammer.]

(End of the volume. Other small series follow.)

SERVICE AND SUPPLIES COLONIAL, REVOLUTIONARY AND MILITARY

ANDREW WILEY makes declaration and Court declare opinion he served in the Revolutionary War. Rock'm cty, Va. Oct 1832.

SAMUEL WALLACE bequeathes warrants for land for military service. Rock'm, Va. 20 Mch 1786. I-256.

NATHANIEL WHEELER, soldier, 2d Md Regt, produces ctf from Capt. James Ewing that he [Wheeler] was wounded at the battle of Eutaw Springs, of which wound he lost his leg. Ordered that Wheeler receive half pay from 1 Jany 1783 to 1 Dec 1784, at 37-6 per mo. Som. cty, Md. O. C. Proc. p. 75.

JOHN WRIGHT'S declaration with ctf of Thomas Sanders presented & sworn to, and Court declare opinion he served in Revolutionary Army. Alleg. cty, Va. Sept 1833. Orders, 138.

JOHN WRIGHT, resident of county, aged 76; Enlisted for three years, Oct 1778, in Va. in the company commanded by Col. Taylor of the Continental Establishment; was discharged at Winchester. Thomas Sanders testifies that he was in the service in same Regt with Wright and both were discharged at Winchester. Alleg. cty, Va. 16 July 1832. Orders, p. 40.

JAMES WILLIAMSON gives satisfactory proof that he is entitled to £3 for a steer for the use of his country. Montg. cty, Va. Fincastle Order Book, p. 191. 28 June 1785.

JAMES WREN, Gent. Apptd Lieut. Militia; takes oath. Ffx cty, Va. Orders [iii] p. 3. 16bApr 1770.

Capt. THOMAS WAGENER; was Captain in Va. Regt under Col. Washington. 3,000 acres. Montg cty, Va. Surveys. 7 Mch 1774.

ROBERT WRIGHT;* "For a Smooth Gun, a Good Barrell, Indifferent Stock, Tollerable Lock." Amherst cty, Va. May Ct 1783. Orders p. 3.

ISAAC WRIGHT; See * Amherst cty, Va. May Ct 1783. Orders, p. 118.

Bond of RICHARD NOTTINGHAM & JOHN WILKINS (B. Smith), Northampton, to Thomas Davis, late of the ninth regiment in connection with an attachment agt Davis' estate in a suit: "The Cunteray Dr. to Richard "Notingham To Rum served to the fitague "partey at Severall Times 12 Gals at 15sh. per "Gal'n...... £9-0-0. N.B. The Same Quan- "tity of Rum will be Accepted as pay. G. E. "Rich'd Nottingham. The within 12 Gallons "Rum was furnished by Mr. Nottingham for "the fitague before Mr. Renold's Rum came "down. [Capt.] Thos. Davis [weaver.]"

Davis certifies that he was quartered in Mr. Rich'd Nottingham's for 32 weeks and 6 days and that he was to have 10sh. Pr weake for his Room & the use of his Kitchin.

N-n, Va. Chancery records, 17 Oct 1776.

PER CONTRA:

PHILIP AKERT and JOB REYNOLDS, accused of complotting and conspiracy. Rock'm cty, Va. Minute Book. 22 Mch 1779.

HENRY PENNINGER; for speaking disrespectful words of the Congress, and words tending to depreciate the Continental Currency .... Ordered that he be indicted. Gives security: Sebastian Hoover or Hover, and Henry Stone. Rock'm cty, Va. Minute Book. 22 Mch 1779.

* *Supplies, &c.*

DISTINCTIVE, INTERESTING OR CURIOUS FORE-NAMES OF THE COLONIAL PERIOD

ARCHELOUS LEWIS and Jemima Norman. Culpeper cty, Va. M. L. B. 10 Dec. 1793.

ARCHELAUS COX, taxed for 200 acres. Amherst cty, Va. 1782.

ARGULUS WILLIAMS, recovery of a debt due him. Som. Md, "Judgments". 1736-1738, fo. 308. 7 Aug 1738.

ARCHELAUS FERREL, in Greene cty, Ga. List of Mar. Li. About 1795.

ARCHELAUS POPE and NANCY EASON. Oglethorpe, Ga. Mar. Li. 30 Dec 1796.

ARCHELAUS AUSTIN, in a suit. Cumb. Va. Orders, 174. 26 Apr 1774.

ANGEL BALES was wife of John. Nthld, Va. 1699-1713, p. 370. 19 Jany 1705.

ANGEL MORNINGSTAR, had part of Sandy Run and Dry Meadow. *Jacob* Morningstar had part of "Keepstrite!" Annap. Fred'k cty Debt Book. 1773.

ANGELO ATKINSON, had son Angelo. Wor. Md. 3 Feby 1766. J. W. 3-109.

BEHETHLAND, wife of William Stark [Stock?] Wmld, Va. 1705-1721, fo. 61. 30 July 1707.

BEHETHLEM POLLY, dau. of John and Mary. St. Paul's Psh Reg. Va. Born 30 Mch 1728.

BEHETHLAND STEPHENS. dau. of James, Sr. Amherst M. L. B. 27 Sept 1796.

BEHETHLAND GIBSON; will probated by William Strother. Wmld, Va. 1705-1721, fo. 386. 30 Mch 1720.

FLORENTAYNE PAYNE, age about 36. N-n cty, Va. i-66. 27 Mch 1637.

FORTUNE MITTFORD, admx of Bulmer Mittford. Annap. Prov. Ct. 25 Mch 1666. FF No. 3.

FORTUNE BAGLEY was the orphan of Richard. Chas. City cty, Va. Ct. 15 Sept 1665. 1655-1665, p. 588.

FORTUNATUS CRUTCHFIELD assigns warrant. Va. S. L. O. About 1783.

FORTUNATUS x GREEN and Martha Mullins. Charl. Va. M. L. B. 1797.

FORTUNE MILLS and ROGER RAWLINGS, wife and attorney of James Mills, to Capt. Francis Gray. Surry, Va. 25 June 1661. i-170. See also p. 182.

Mrs. FORTUNE MILLS .... had son Walter Flood. 30 May 1671. Surry, Va. i-386.

FORTUNE SEMMES, widow of Marmaduke. Annap., Md. Inv. and Accts. xiiia-257. 1695

FORTUNE MILLS [see above] was a head right under James Mills, presumably his wife. Acco., Va. 16 Oct 1673. v-1.

FORTUNE COSSINETT, dau. of Susanna. N-n, Va. 1689. xiv-227.

FORTUNE CASSINETT mentioned in the will of Thomas Wade. She was his "daughter-in-law." [Probably step-dau.] N-n, Va. 3 Sept 1696. xvii-391.

Printed at The Industrial School for Crippled and Deformed Children, 241 St. Botolph Street, Boston

The

County Court Note-Book

A Little Bulletin of History and Genealogy

December, 1931 **Vol. X, No. 6**

SHIPS IN PORT

Being references to sea-going vessels as found in the early court records of Maryland, Virginia and other colonies.

Ship *Amelia*, Michael Higgins, Master; riding at anchor in Patuxent river. Pr. Geo's cty, Md. 28 July 1741. Y-457.

Ship *Anne*; Robert Avent, master; notification as to freight for London. Pr. Geo's cty, Md. 19 Sept 1720. M-148.

The *Arcadia* was a sloop owned by David Derrick, of Marcus Hook, Penna. Thos. Derrick, master. 1756. Penna. Arch. vol. xxv-571.

Ship *Amity* [salvaged?] L. Norf. cty, Va. 1661. See Va. State Papers, 411. 24 Nov. 1653. JOHN TULLY, master of the *Amity*......order ....to Virginia.

Ship *Beginning*, of Bristol. Acco. cty, Va. 1679.

The "*Alexander Brigantine*", John Turner, Commander. Pr. Geo., Va. Minutes. 13 Oct 1719.

Ship *Crown Frigot*, Cornelius Sarjant & Co., of Bristol, Mchts, owners. K. Geo. cty, Va. 2 Aug 1723. Orders i-129.

Ship *Friendship*, Anthony Marshal, master; now in Severn river, gives public notice of tobacco freight rate. A. A. cty, Md. 15 June 1749. R. B. iii-126.

Ship *Friends' Supply*, Thomas Hooper, master. Publishes rate of tobacco freight. A. A. cty, Md. 10 June 1749. R. B. iii-126.

Ship *Josiah*, of London; Stephen Robins, master. Pr. Geo. Va. 14 June 1720. Minute Book. p. 326.

The *Joseph and Daniel*, of London in Old England; John Harrison, master, gives bond to Peter Ellzey. Som. Md. 1 June 1706. GI (8) p. 298.

Sloop *Kingsales*, mentioned in the will of Josias x Seaward......not to be sold as long as bro. George Seaward will sail [?] in her......he to have third part of her hire and to keep her in repair. Also gives bro. a Shallop called the *Flying Hound*. Som. cty, Md. 27 Sept 1689. BWZ-p. 23.

Sail boat, *the Lady Hammond*; John Dilworth, Camden cty, pltr, love and affection to son James, gives a sail boat, now lying in a small creek leading to Cumberland Island. Camden cty, Ga. 11 May 1795. B and C, p. 27.

Brig *Margaret*, now a wreck on the Sand Bar off Cumberland Island. Alexander Chesholm, Master; Wm. Wilson, Mate, and Joseph Atkins, John Jackson and other seamen sign. [This is a "protest" against weather conditions.] Camden cty, Ga. 28 Oct 1790. B and C, page 311.

Barque *Mayflower*, John Speres, Master, an inhabitant of Virginia, deceased at Evan Thomas his house 25th 5 month [1655 at the head of opposite page.] p. 51, 9th Report, Record Comm'rs, Boston. (*Contributed.*)

Sloop *Marygold*, mentioned in will of Edward Robinson, bound for Providence. Sam'l Penly [?] master. Philada. 7 Sept 1699. A-299.

Good Ketch *Maryland Merchant*, Mr. Isaac Hull, master. Receipt by James Dashiell, Jr., of .... and for the use and proper acc't of Capt. John Higginson, of Salem, and James Barton, of Boston, New England, the particulars following........ including nine pound of powder in Cask the Tare unknown.........received in behalf of Sampson Walters, mariner, of Boston, New England. Som. cty, Md. 9 May 1692. BWZ-p. 212.

Ship *Merchants Adventure*; Leonard Somersett to be satisfied for attendance, &c. on Anthony Riggs [com'dr] who died on board. *8 guns were shot at his burial.........whether to be paid or not paid for* (and at what rate?) Chas. City cty, 12 Apr 1664. vol. 1655-1666, p. 449. (Va.)

The King's Ketch the *Noe*; Mr. Robert Hawkins, master. 24 Mch 1697. York cty, Va. Vol. "12", page 2.

Brigeten [brigantine] *Northampton*, Mr. John Bowdoin, Comm'd'r. N-n cty, Va. 28 Jany 1707-8. xviii-375.

Sloop *Perfect*; Antoine Suraez "gives peaceful possession to John Dilworth.........in Philadelphia". Bond for £350 ster. The *Perfect* was then lying in the River St. Mary's. Camden cty, Ga. 3 Apr 1795. B and C, p. 5.

The Catch [*sic*] *Prudence* of N. E. Samuel Treworgie [?] gives power to Capt. Edm. Lyster, Nthld cy, Va. 27 Mch 1669. Vol. 1666-1672, fo. 89.

Ship *Pearle* of Liverpool. Wm. Trenow, master. 28 Oct. 1691. Va. St. Pa. i-30.

Ship *Presly Merchant* Edward Collins, master. 30 Jany 1716. Wmld, Va. Vol. 1705-1721, fo. 304.

Sloop called the *Polly*, now on a voyage to New York; James Craven of Accomack cty, Va., mortgages one-half to William Andrews. 31 Aug 1765. Acco., Va. Diii-393.

The Shipp *Providence*, John Estes, master. This shipp was seized upon by Capt. Thomas Allen, Commander of His Majesties Ketch *Quaker* ....being supposed to have imported contraband goods.........10 Apr 1685. Wmld, Va. Vol. 1676-1688, p. 402.

Ship *Prince Royal*, of London; Thomas Boyd. commander; brought over convicted felons. See Wmld, Va. 2 Feby 1721. vol. 1721–1734, p. 40.

The *Reall Friendshipp*, James Cuttiford, Commander; now riding at anchor in the river of Lower Machodock, in Westmoreland cty, Va. 4 June 1673. Wmld. Va. vol. 1676–1688, p. 288.

Capt. Thomas Hasted [?], commander of the Shipp *Recovery*; Rich'd Willis bound to him. 18 Apr 1682. Middx cty, Va. ii–72.

The Shipp *Speedwell*, John Hine [?] master or commander. Wmld cty, Va. 29 May 1706. Vol. 1705–1721, fo. 23.

Ship *Spotswood*; Jeremiah Turney, Master and Commander. Pr. Geo. cty, Va. Minute Book. Ct 10 Sept 1717.

The *Saint George*, Jacob Waters, Captain; James Stone of Bishopgate street, London, *Oilman & Colourman*, gives power to Jonathan Plowman, Mcht, Baltimore, as to merchandize shipped to Capt. John Parker. Annap. Md. 16 Mch 1761. DD4–330.

Ship Washington: At the request of William Deakins Junior Agent for Wallace Johnson and Muir, the following instrument of writing was recorded this 25 day of November, 1789, To Wit: We the Subscribers Naval Commissioners Commanders [in the record the word Commissioners is underscored probably to call attention to an error?] being called on by Capt. Andrew White of the Ship Washington and Col. William Deakins this 25 Day of November 1789 to examine the State of the rigging and Sails of the Said Ship do find that the fore-rigging was Entirely *unserviceable* and Most of the Other Rigging is in a very Bad condition and that most of the Sails do require greater repairs as Witness our hands. Robt Bowezy, Master og the Ship Change, Richard Johns Leonard Mackall. Test: John Mountz . . . to the last two names. Montg. county, Md. D-308. [At that time the port of Georgetown was in Montgomery county,]

These are to give notice to all Persons that I the Subscriber am bound away in the *Bermuda Slope* if any Person hath anything to Claime of me Lett them Repaire to the house of John Robins and they shall be paid, Cornelius Slater. Sett up at Court dore the above Said date. N-n. cty, Va. 17 July 1711. xix-285. [A legal notice.]

THE MIGRANT HAYS and HAYES.

ALEXANDER HAYS; admn his est. to ROBERT HAYS. Stephen Hall and Frederick Verner, sec. 8 Apr 1789. Wmld cty, Penna. P. G. S. Pub'ns.

ANNE HAYES, head right under John Derman; also ELIZABETH HAYES. 28 Aug 1653. N-n, Va. iv-199.

ANTHONY HAY probably m. dau. of Thomas Penman. Before 12 Aug 1759. York cty, Va. xx-527.

BRIDGET HAY, wf of Capt. WILLIAM HAY. Daughter born 4 Nov 1667. York-Hampton Psh Reg.

CHARLES HAYS and SARAH HILTON; 12 Jany 1802. Fred'k, Md. Mar. Li.

DAVID HAYS, Sr., Wash'n cty, Penna. Will; 3 Apr 1792. Chn: Thomas, Joseph, William, Andrew, David, James, Moses, Prudence, Elenor, Elizabeth, Mary and Ann. Possibly also Phyllis and Rankin. Extrs, Edgar and Lyle and Thomas HAYS. Wit: Wilkin, McKenny, P. G. S. Pub'ns.

DANIEL HAYS' line is mentioned in will of Samuel Cobbs. 27 June 1757. Amelia cty, Va. 1-127.

EDMOND HAY and SARAH WHITACRE. 7 Apr 1797. Fred'k, Md. Mar. Li.

ELIZABETH HAY was Relict and widow of ANTHONY. 18 Jany 1772. York cty, Va. viii-229.

FRANCIS HAYS, an appraiser of Wm. Hill"s estate. 16 May 1774. Pr. Edwd cty, Va. Orders D-433.

FRANCES HAY, will; Son James, tract formerly my father's; Daniel Preeson mentioned; reversion to two daus. Husband, John Hay, dec'd; youngest son John Hay; friends John Moss and Bale [BALL?] Tabb, extrs. Wit: John Russell, Damaris Smith, Hanah x Russell. 11 Feby 1790. York cty, Va. xxiii:646. [It appears probable that Preeson was her father.]

FRANCIS HAY, psh St. Mary's, Essex, to Nicholas Ware. Conveyance. 19 Feby 1727. Essex cty, Va. xix-334.

FRED'K CHRISTOPHER HASE and ELIZABETH BECKERBACK. 25 July 1801. Fred'k, Md. Mar. Li.

GEORGE HAYS and ELIZABETH RIDGLEY. 9 Mch 1797. Fred'k cty, Md. Mar. Li.

GILBERT HAYS' will; presented by two of the extrs, William and Charles Hays. 3 Nov 1783. Amherst cty, Va. Orders, p. 184.

HENRY HAYES m. MARY PAYTON. 1 Oct 1783. Granv. cty, N. C. M. L. B. [This seems to be from a record in the U. S. Pension Office.]

HUGH HAYS in a suit. 8 Dec 1767. Amherst cty, Va. Orders.

JAMES HAY, will; mother Anne Spurr, sister Mary Spurr, father-in-law, Samuel Spurr. Probate 20 Aug. 1759. York, Va. xx-524.

JAMES HAYES, in a suit. 7 July 1773. Montg. cty, Va. Orders.

JOHN HAYS m. JENNY THOMPSON. 2 Aug 1779. Bedford cty, Va. M. L. B.

JOHN HAY, will; wife, son Robert. [Incomplete.] 25 Nov 1771 [?] York, Va. xxii-391.

JOHN HAY, admr. of ROB'T HAY. Gives bond. 17 June 1717. York, Va. xv-134.

JOHN HAY m. Martha Andrews, dau, of William. Balto. Md. Proceedings. Before 15 Apr 1784. I-146.

JOHN HAYSE and wf Rebecah. Conveyance proved by wit. 24 Oct 1786. Montg cty, Va. Orders, p. 270.

JOHN and MARGARET HAYS, orphans. Estate sworn to by Susanna, wf. of Jonathan Stott. 10 Aug. 1762. N-n cty, Va., Orders xxxiiO.

JOHN HAIES, head right. Nthld cty, Va. 10 Jany 1650. Vol. 1650-1652, fo. 46.

JOHN HAYES, son of JOHN (who departed this country) bound to Joseph Holt and wf Anne. 16 May 1711. Nthld city, Va. Vol. 1693-1713, p. 724.

JONATHAN HAYS; owner of *Good Luck* and part of *Brothers' Love*. Debt Book, Fred'k cty (at Annapolis), 1773.

JOHN HAYS and SUSANNA HOWARD. 29 Jany 1796. Fred'k cty, Md. Mar. Li.

JOSEPH HAYS and DEBORAH WIMMER. 7 Feby 1761· Fred'k, Md. Mar. Li.

LEONARD HAYS, owner of *Forced Hobson's Choice*. 1773. Fred'k cty, Md. Debt Book. (At Annapolis.)

MORRIS HAYES; Morris Fitzgerrald gets an attachment agt him. Nthld, Va. Vol. 1699-1713, p. 437.

MORRIS HAYES, a merchant. Nthld. cty, Va. 23 Nov 1706. p. 413. same volume as before.

NOTLEY HAYS and SARAH RAWLINGS. 29 Dec 1788. Fred'k cty, Md. Mar. Li.

PATRICK HAYES. in Richmond cty. Ga. Minutes Inferior Ct. 24 Sept. 1794.

ROBERT HAY; Chn: Dorothy, William "and a female child". Died 1 Mch, 5 Jany and 8 Feby, 1713. York-Hampton Psh Reg. Va.

ROBERT HAYS was son of JOHN HAYS. Wmld cty, Salem Tshp. [Penna.?] Will 1789. 1789. i-94. ROB'T HAYS also a wit. to the will.

ROBERT HAYES of Lynhaven, Lower Norf., Pltr. Upon petition of [a Frenchman]....... .. ordered that a certificate be granted to whom it may concern in England that the sd Frenchman is married to one Anne Claye.........N-n, Va. 14Dec 1647. iii, 128.

THOMAS HAYES, an head right. Acco., Va. 1664.

THOMAS HAYES, New Norf. Va. 6 July 1640. A-19.

THOMAS HAYES. L. Norf. 1644.

THOMAS HAYS. Amherst, Va. Orders. 8 Dec 1767.

WILLIAM HAYS was extr of THOMAS HAYS' Ffx, Va. 22 May 1754. Orders [1] p. 97.

WILLIAM HAYS, will. Jonathan Johnson, extr. N-n, Va. Orders xxxii. 13 Dec 1763.

WILLIAM HAYES. Ffx. cty, Va. 22 May 1761. Orders [2].

ZILPH [A] HAYS, wife of SAMUEL. See his will. N-n, Va. 24 Apr· 1741. 1-54.

SOME UNPUBLISHED WILLS

SOMERSET COUNTY, MARYLAND

In the very early records of the county courts of Virginia, all classes of records appear, due in part to the fact that the Clerk of a Virginia Court had all matters pertaining to the Court under his general care.........in the absence of the Judge he could even probate wills. In Maryland, however, there was a "Commissary" and a "Deputy Commissary", whose duties corresponded to those of the present Probate Judges, Registers, &c., or of the Surrogates and Ordinaries of other colonies. In Pennsylvania the official who probated the wills took the wills themselves to Philadelphia.........it was a sort of prerogative court, and the wills of Chester county, the earliest wills, that is, may now be found in Philadelphia.

In Maryland, Deputy Commissaries were located in the counties as early as 1665 or 1670, and after the usual proving and probate, the original wills were taken to Annapolis for record, and from Annapolis returned to the counties. So that we find in Annapolis the record of wills, of inventories, &c., &c., and we also find duplicates of these records, to a certain extent, in the counties. The published abstracts, usually called the "Baldwin Wills", were made from the records in Annapolis. No effort was made by the compiler to cover the colony for any omitted testaments. The only exception to this statement is that a few wills found in Baltimore were included in the published volumes.

However, some wills, for what reason no one now living can definitely state, were never recorded in Annapolis.........possibly they were never completely probated. A certain number of such wills are now in the Somerset records, and they are not in the records of the Register's office, although they have been long known to exist, but they are in the general records of the Court, in the care of the Clerk of the Court, who knows all about them.

These wills, are of course, very early. A few of them are given herewith, also some administrations, and at least one inventory.

From volume B. W. Z. Deeds. 1690-1692.

ANN SMITH, extx of EDWARD. (An account.) "To John Vigerous Admr." Son Edward mentioned. "To severall Cordialls for fainting fitts at the old plantation."
"Y' or son Joseph Smith."
"To a Large Cord: poition for divers takeings for fainting fitts." (&c., &c.) 1688. p. 40.

WILLIAM BRERETON, Gent. Of Som. cty Will.

Wf Sarah to have plntn called Brereton's Chance during life, with remainder to son William; second son John Brereton, tract called Mile End. 3d and 4th sons Thomas and Henry, tract called Middle Neck. [These sons are under 18.] Wf, extx. Francis Jenckins, Gent., overseer and to look after my papers & books. Wit: John x Parsons, Samps'n Power, Robert Crouch, Nicoholas Tyler.

Letters Test'y to widow Sarah. 4 Sept 1690-11 Nov 1690. p. 54.

ISAAC x NOBLE, of Wiccocomoco, Somerset cty, planter. Will.

Wf Mary; two sons, Isaac and John; dau. Mary Noble; wf, extx. Wit: William Brereton, Benjamin Nesham, Alex. x Michael. Henry x Freak. 15 Sept 1685. Date of proof not given. Recorded 14 Jany 1690.

SARAH SAUNDERS, Somerset. Will. [p. 79.] To her kinswoman Margery Beazely living with "my cossin Thomas Oxford, one cow calf, with the consent and approbation of my husband, John Saunders."

RICHARD BRITTIAN; administration his estate to THOMAS TULL, on behalf of his son JOHN TULL. Bond shows that BRITTIAN died intest. yet made a "nuncupitive" will. Refs. to A. W. p. 65. 10 Mch 1690. p. 81.

RICHARD HILL, will.

Wf [Frances]; 2 sons [under thirteen]. Wf. extx; John Emmet and Sampson Allen, overseers. Wit: Robert x Catlin, Anne x Catlin, William Walstone, John Heath. 9 June 1691. [p. 84.]

BENJAMIN KEIZER, of Pocomoke, Somerset cty. Will.

Bro. Eliazer Keizer's second sonn or second dau., one-third part of what my father George Keizer hath left me. To bro. John's second son or second dau., one-third do. To sister Mary Mould's second son or second dau. one-third do. To Jane Cooper and her two daus.; to Martha Gregory; to Lawrence Crawford, 300 acres left to me in Col. Stevens' will; to Mr. George Layfield, balance of £1000 left to me by do.; to Mr. George Layfield. 300 acres [with provisions]; mentions Cousins William White, Tabitha White, Priscilla White, Sarah White, Stevens White, William White [again]; Laurence Crawford and John Emmett, extrs. *Sig.* BENJAMIN KEYZER.

Wit: John Starrett, Edward Stockdell, Sarah Crawford, James x Henderson, David Browne. 26 Mch 1691–10 June 1691. p. 89.

ABRAHAM HEATH, will.

Eldest son, William; son Thomas, son Jacob; Wf Ursula, Heath's Quarter during life; dau. Mary; son Abraham.........land left testator by will of John Shipley. Wit: John Franklyn, John Miller, John Bowen, Thomas Bromley. 9 June 1691. p. 91.

JOHN GALBRAITH, Som. cty, Mcht, Will.

To Mr. Samuel Davis, Minister at Snow Hill, 5,000 lbs porke; to Mr. Francis Makemie, Minister of the Gospel at Rehoboth Towne, 5,000 lbs of porke; to Mr. Thomas Wilson, Minister of the Gospell at Monokin, 5,000 lbs porke; to friend Robert Nearn of Monokin, 10,000 lbs of porke; the rest of my goods as well elsewhere as in this afsd Province both at home and now abroad, to my friend Maj'r Robert King of Monokin, and appoint him extr. Wit: Adrian x Marshall, John Vigerous, William Robbeson, Allexander Cillock, Robert Nearn. 12 Aug 1691–8 Sept 1691. p. 94.

WILLIAM HEARNE [Gent.], Somerset; Will.

Wf Mary; sonn William [under 21]; expected child; wf to be extx, and Mr. Francis Jenckins and Mr. John Cornish, Overseers. Wit William Mead, Katherine x Trubshaw, Peter Dent. 28 Mch 1691–10 Nov 1691. p. 109.

EDMUND BEAUCHAMP, Mercer of London; county clerk of Somerset; Will.

Wf Sarah, furniture, &c.........land where she now lives during widowhood; Son Thomas, all the fees due me, &c., as concerning the Clerk's place, before Mr. John West and myselfe were concerned as partners together [mentioned later as Deputy]; Son Edmund; Son John; dau. Alice Beauchamp; son *Doget* [?] son Edward; son Robert; son Thomas; Patience Beauchamp; "all my children herein named", [in a list Patience is not mentioned.] Son Thomas, extr. Wit: Stephen Horsey, John Roach, Jr., John West. 10 Apr 1691–12 Nov 1691. p. 115.

[Note: the foregoing are taken from the apparent beginning of the volume, but at the end of the above pages it was discovered that a number of pages had been bound at the back, about twenty-four of them, and that the last page of all, as now arranged, had been pasted in upside down. The items which follow are, therefore, from the true first pages and are of earlier date than those above.]

WILLIAM COULBOURBE, of Annamessex, Somerset. Will.

Eldest son, William, extr; to have land and negroes Emanuel, Betty and Abraham; son Robert, land called Hart's Content and negro Jack; dau. Ann Taylor and John Taylor and the heirs of negro Hill, (mentions land formerly given dau. Penellopie); granddau. Dorothy to have first mare colt of the mare he gives dau. Ann Taylor; gives four granddaus. Ann, Jone, Dorothy and Mary Taylor calves, and to Dorothy an ewe lamb; dau. Penelope Holland; son William my house that is in Towne, &c., gr. dau. Ann Coulbourne one yearling *heafer;* cousin John West, two sons and dau., viz.: William, Robert & Ann; son Robert & John Taylor. Wit: Thomas Everndon, William Murton, Lancelott James, Georg: Madux, John West. 20 Jany 1689–11 Mch 1689. p. 5.

JAMES PRICE, Will.

Dau. Margaret Price, dau. Ann Price; remainder to cossin James Price and his [evident omission]; wife Mary; "For the tutition of my children I leave it to my well beloved wife Mary Price to doe with them as she thinks convenient." Wit: John Tyler, James Price, Patrick Mitchell. 2 Sept 1688. No date of probate. Letters, 11 Mch 1689. p. 28.

HENRY [probably meant for that] x OGLAMMIN, of Spittlefield, Somerset cty, Md. Will:

Eldest son Henney [?]; son Thomas and son John (all under age) land lately taken up called Gallaway; wife Ellen; to have her Life's right; mentions sons as wife's; dau. Ellen; dau. Elizabeth. Wit: Thomas Lucass, William Foster. 14th of the 6th Mo called August, 1689. Letters, 11 Mch 1689. p. 30.

WILLIAM JONES, Will. Of Manny Hundred, Somerset.

Son William, 20 sh. to buy him a ring; son Daniell, same; son John, all that plantation upon Little Manny Creek, Somerset. Wf Jane, to occupy plantation whereon I now live during life if she continue a widow. After wife's death gives plntn to son George; son Robert land on Poplar Branch; dau. Margaret Jones; Godson William Hayman; dau. Elizabeth Jones; Wf extx. Bro. George Mitchell and bro. George Betts to be overseers. Wm X Jones. Wit: John Winder, Thomas Winder, Livin Denwood, Jr., Wm. Brereton. 13 Aug 1689–10 June 1690 p. 17.

SAMUELL COOPER, Will

Wf Jane Cooper all estate (only desiring her to remember what I have desired of her) and makes her extx. Wit: Edm: Howard, Margaret Howard, Samuel Parker. 1 October 1681. 26 July 1688. Francis Jenckins gets administration. 10 June 1690.

[*This ends the wills of the reverse.*]

In the fourth volume of the NOTE-BOOK the Editor published considerable Custis material. At that time, the epitaph which follows was apparently not at hand. *Wilsonia*, the home of JOHN CUSTIS, II, is not easy to reach, and it was only through the courtesy of the father of the late Stratton Nottingham that the Editor was able to visit the once fine estate. Nothing remains of the house but part of the brick foundation. The condition of the graveyard is abominable. The long inscription reads:

Here lyeth the Body of JOHN CUSTIS, Esq., One of the Councill of Virginia, Colonel and Commander in Chief of the Militia of the Eastern Shore of the Colloney. He was the Son of the Honourable JOHN CUSTIS of Arlington and departed this Life the 26th of January 1713 and in the Sixtieth Year of his Age, his first Wife was MARGARET the Daughter of Mr. John Michaell, by whome he had 7 [so the copy reads] Sons and 2 Daughters who with 3 of their Sons lies near him his Second Wife was Sarah the Daughter of Colonel Southy Littleton and widow of Mr. Adam Michaell who survived him, but hopes to be Buried by him when She dies as was his desire. Which Accoɹdingly, Now Shee is and Departed this Life the 18 day of Aprill Anno Domini 1720, and in the Fifty-first Yeare of her Age.

An early Custis note:

The following agreement, signed in London, is recorded in Northampton cty. (xiv-92.) WHEREAS . . . a controversy is depending at Law undecided att Rotterdam . . . [as to] the proportion of the estate left by Mrs. JOANE CUSTIS which her son EDMUND, as also her son JOHN do individually lay claims to, and EDMUND renounces his title . . . being satisfied with my propostion by that gift of our said mother duringe her life in £200 sterling paid by Mr. John Smithier many yeares past. Sig. EDMO. CUSTIS. 5 Jany 1675. Wit: Isaac Key, Oliver Hering.

ERRATA:

In the list of MARYLAND KIN for February, 1931, the first item should read p. 237, not 247.

In December, 1930, first item, same subject, the date should be 15 July, vol. ix, p. 189.

The list in June, 1931, is an unintentional repitition of that in October, 1930, with the following errors:

Edmund Hunderford, should be Edmund Hongerford; John Macubbins, should be John Maccubins; John Rucker, should be John Tucker, and Downs should be Downes.

In the NOTE-BOOK for October, 1928, are a number of regrettable errors. See VIRGINIA COLONISTS, p. 39.

MARY HAMSIN, should be MARY HANSON;
MR. LOCKEY, should be Mr. EDWARD LOCKEY;
JOHN WALKER should be JOHN WALTER;
THOMAS WILL should be THOMAS HILL;
RICHARD LENDALL is possibly FENDALL;
THO. TREVERSTONE should be THO. FEVERSTONE;
Col. RICHARD LEE is of Rappahannock cty;
ROBERT HIGGISON should be ROBERT HIGGISON;
RICHARD ABBERT should be RICHARD ALBERT;
JOHN BELLAMY should be HEN BELLAMY.

THE DEPUTY COMMISSARY'S GUIDE WITHIN THE PROVINCE OF MARYLAND

Collateral heirs:

The *sixth rule of descent* [*see NOTE-BOOK for October*] is that the collateral heir of the person last seized, must be the next collateral relation of the whole blood, either personally, or by representation. ["Representation" in the sense as used here refers to heirs of the collateral relation.] This is to be reckoned by canonical degrees. Vallette explains that the relation by the whole blood excludes even any nearer relation by the half-blood. A relation of the whole blood, he goes on to say, is derived from the same couple of ancestors.

The *seventh rule of descent*, as touching collateral inheritance, is that the male stocks are to be preferred before the female, that is, kindred derived from the blood of the male ancestor, shall be admitted before those of the blood of the ancestress .... unless the lands have actually descended from a female.

Inheritances, it is further explained, "shall not ascend." a father shall not be entitled as heir to his son .... this is repeated as illustrating the first rule already given. And the further very simple illustration follows: "A man hath a "brother of the whole blood, ... and a son "by a first, and also a son by a second wife, ... "the son by the first (or by the second wife), "purchases land in fee, and dies without issue "......... the surviving brother is excluded, be- "cause only of the half-blood .... the father "cannot be heir, because an inheritance cannot "lineally ascend, ... but the *uncle* is heir. "Suppose the uncle .... then to die without "issue, ... if the father be alive, tho' he could "not claim by lineal ascent from the son, yet he "may claim as heir of the uncle. .... If the "father should die before the uncle, the brother "of the half-blood .... may claim as heir to "the father."

Consanguinity: this is the relation of persons descended from the same stock, or common ancestor. .... Every generation in direct lineal consanguinity, constitutes a different degree .... the father is related to his son in the first degree; the grandfather and grandson, reciprocally, in the second degree .... and so on. This natural way of reckoning the degrees in the direct line, obtains as well in the civil, and in the canon, as in the common law.

Vallette gives a beautifully engraved table, which the Editor wishes she could afford to reproduce, it is so clear as to the degrees of lineal and collateral relationship. The rule as to this which is quoted at length from Coke is rather difficult to follow .... too technical for this running abstract. Those who so desire will find the table referred to opposite page 102 of Vallette's Guide. (*A photostat can be furnished for a small sum.*)

The *rules of distribution* are taken from a statute of Charles II, and also from an Act of the Maryland Assembly of 1715. These rules are extremely interesting and the Editor regrets that there is not space for them at this time. Even if this rare little volume be not at hand, the English and Maryland statutes may be found in any large library.

The County Court Note-Book

An every-other monthly devoted mainly to abstracts from County Court Records, prior to 1800.

MILNOR LJUNGSTEDT. Editor and Publisher.
Bethesda, Rural Route 5, Maryland.

December, 1931 Whole
Vol. X, No. 6 No. 61

This is the last issue of the NOTE-BOOK. I am very sorry that this is so. I am fond of the NOTE-BOOK, and I have become attached to some of my subscribers. I know that quite a number of them will be sorry not to find this little paper in the mail.........somewhat irregularly, to be sure.

The NOTE-BOOK has not been a good financial "proposition".........that is not why I am giving it up, though I will admit that had I had sufficient subscribers to keep the worry cow from following me around, I might have held on a while longer. I think the underlying reason, however, for discontinuing, is the futility of trying to reach the understanding of many of those I have tried to help by the publication of my collected material. The folk who write, as did one subscriber, in the face of my very direct statements, "*You must be making a good income out of the NOTE-BOOK, for I know you are too good a business woman to keep it going otherwise.*" Incidentally, I think that is the first and only time I have ever been credited with any business sense whatever. I feel kind of sorry for that kind of person.........it is clear that they do not understand the joy of turning up a marriage here and there, or the migration of an immigrant, which marriage or migration solves some long unsolved puzzle of some personally unknown reader. Their standard of measurement is not that of the Editor.

So you see it is the failure of understanding to meet understanding that makes nothing seem quite worth while.

Then there is another side — the lack of recognition. Habitués and employees of large historical libraries do not in some cases know that the NOTE-BOOK is on their shelves. In one case the head of the reading-room of a well-known State library advised the Editor to ask the Librarian to subscribe. It had been in the private office of that Librarian for about two years! (Literally so.)

There is also the error the Editor has made from the beginning, the error of assuming that the usual searcher would understand the commoner proceedings of a court, and have some familiarity with abbreviations, also the fact that an "every-other" monthly could hardly carry more than six issues to the year.

Touching the second matter an example is given below.

But now I must turn the leaf and write here my gratitude and appreciation to those who have heartened me by their commendation and their understanding.........there are many of them, but I cannot mention them here......... their names are well known in their own lines of bibliography, literature and research. They have realized, I am sure, that I have been trying to be of use, and they have subscribed and paid their dues and said encouraging things, and they have my thanks and remembrance for the years that are left us.

To them, especially, and I hope to other readers, I am about to offer twenty-four pages (or more).........with no "Editorials".........to be published at intervals and to be known as ANCESTRAL PROOFS AND PROBABILITIES. The "Probabilities" are pretty safe ones, anyhow they will be interesting and appeal to that curiosity all searchers have. The first issue will appear as soon as I have enough subscribers to pay the printer. It will contain some 600 MARRIAGES, and several hundred of MARYLAND'S KIN. For further information please send a card to The F. W. FAXON COMPANY, 83, Francis street, Boston, Mass.

. . . .

In one of the paragraphs of MARYLAND'S KIN *published some little time ago, I mentioned the name of the decedent and his next of kin, as they gave their names in signing the inventory from which I got the information. I received the following from a reader residing in Washington.*

"I am writing up the history of the X.........family ....What does the W.........will mean? Was it his will? What also does it mean by Christopher R.........and James L.........sec.?" And later from the same person........." Several years ago we had some correspondence about the L.........family, occasioned by an item in the County Court Note-Book, which stated that L.........'s will of March 1702-3 mentioned Isaac and Richard of Charles County. I saw that record in Annapolis and it did not *mention and Richard a Joseph I think and it was 1702,"* [*Sic, as written.*]

My correspondent was evidently somewhat at sea in her deductions, and it seemed a pity to allow her to continue her mis-statements as to my abstracts. So I wrote, after reference to my notes, "The item referred to was NOT A WILL, *but a reversed abstract of an* inventory, *a listing of the persons who signed as nearest relatives.........I do not hesitate to say that what I published is correct."*

In reply I received a letter which came very close to violating the postal laws, the most abusive letter it has ever been my lot to receive.

In an issue of the NOTE-BOOK several years ago, the Editor called attention to the beautiful work of the EMERY RECORD RESTORING COMPANY in repairing various records and documents, private as well as public. Since then the Editor has had an opportunity to examine certain Chinese or Japanese silk panels (the sides of an unusually fine lantern). These panels, painted with birds and foliage, had become quite rotten as a result of the damp and perhaps the heat of a country house. They were sent to the Emery people to be restored by their process, and they are now hanging in the lantern, quite firm and strong, and clear as to the light, and, in fact, except for the natural wear and tear and fading of time, quite as good as ever.

Note has been made heretofore of Mr. MONNETTE'S valuable and beautiful books .... The First Settlers of New Jersey. There is not space here to comment in detail as to their contents but they are recommended to all interested, especially for the large number of historic records thus made available.

The AMERICAN GENEALOGIST, Donald Lines Jacobus, Editor and publisher is among the few very best periodicals of its kind. The October number recently received has so much of value that there is not space to review it here.

Mr. CHARLES KNOWLES BOLTON has followed up his American ARMORY, with a "Bulletin" containing additional matter. Catalogues of this kind are wonderfully useful and this is particularly recommended to searchers who may thus, by means of a tombstone or a simple ring or bookplate, tie on to some unknown relationship.

EDWARD WASHINGTON and his KIN. Miss Cordelia Jackson, of Washington, D. C., daughter of the historian of Georgetown, has recently published an interesting and valuable contribution to Washingtoniana. It is the result of a number of years of painstaking research and Miss Jackson says: "*I have almost made connection with George Washington.*" This she expects to do some day.

Curiosities of Certain
Historical Literature

In a volume entitled King and Queen County Virginia, by Alfred Bagby, the following is found on page 66.

"There is a tradition that this place, now "known as the Mount, was the residence of "Henry *Edmond Washington* (see Thackeray's "'The Virginians') and called by him 'Fanny's "Mount,' after his wife who was Fanny Moun- "tain." [Some one must have been "stuffing" the author!]

VARIA

"The point of research may occupy a long time to be expressed at last in brief phrase." Savage. 1-10.

The adjectives of early days were vigorous and comprehensive, a record in Surry county, Virginia, bears testimony to "an Orthodox, faithfull & painful minister." (1674. Vol. ii-73.) Another record in Accomack, Virginia, 1726, mentions the "advice & assistance of one indifferent & skillful & honest Person;" while ROSE YARDLEY, Gentlewoman, daughter of Argoll Yardley, Esq., buys from Obedience Robins, "one sufficient cowe." (N-n cty, Va., 1642. ii-205.)

Mable Robinson was to be fined according to Rules of Court for Smoaking in the Court. Som. cty, Md, G (1)-59. 13th of 7th, 1703.

In 1662, 15 Feby, the *County* of Lower Norfolk was presented by the grand jury for breach of the Sabbath. D-368.

Mary Case was presented for not enlisting herself as a Tithable on the 10 June 1751...... being a housekeeper in this county & marryed to Bristol a Negro Slave belonging to Daniel Cutler as it is said. "No True Bill." Acco. Va. 26 May 1752. xxiii0-588.

Tho: Cooler, Dorchester, county of Dorsett, makes over to Giles Russell of Weymouth & Melcombe Regis of Dorsett county, mariner, 15 persons convicted of felonies & other crimes, and who received judgment of transportation. Northumberland cty, Va. 1718-1726, fo. 72. 8 June 1719.

Mary Johns, the admx of ROBERT JOHNS, dec'd, and THOMAS JOHNS heir-at-law, are defts in a suit in Chancery in 1786, brought by Wm. Booth and wife Judith, John Richardson and wf Mary; Robert, William, Jesse Johns; Nathaniel Booth and wf Elizabeth; Martha Johns, an infant, by next friend; John Richardson; Frances, John, Alexander, Nancey, Salley. and Bartlett Johns, infants, by William Boothe, their next friend. From "Rule Order Book", Amherst cty, Va.

Found on the fly leaf of an old book in the Circuit Court for Somerset county, Md. "*Memorandum in perpetua; Fabricator hujus papyri aut stultus aut ignavus fuit.*" (Perpetual memorandum: The maker of this paper was either a fool or a knave.) Contributed by the Clerk of the Court.

Overheard in Clerks' Offices:

"Best way is as good as any......Want to be in the position to put the blame on the other fellow."

"Anything going on at the Courthouse today?" "Yes, sir! Expenses!"

William Micheel declares himself a citizen and renounces allegiance to any prince or other state. Ffx, Va. 17 Apr 1786. Orders, 1783-1788, p. 204.

William Byrd (*first*); "I returne you many "thankes for your care of my children and "hope you'l endeavor to put out the Girls for "their most advantage wth out any unnec- "essary charge; & for my Son I hope hee "may bee so imployed, as (at least) not to "loose anything hath been bestowed on him. "I cannot advise at this distance, but desire "he want nothing (in reason) for his necessary "accomplishm't." Va. Mags. xxviii, p. 12. 3 June 1691.

CONCERNING A PRONOUN, THE MISUSED SECOND PERSON PLURAL

"*Ye*" and "*folio*" and "*liber*" sound very learned and give an air of authenticity to many a copy or partial copy made from ancient records. The following timely article by SAMUEL ELLIOT MORISON which recently appeared in OLD-TIME NEW ENGLAND, the Bulletin of the Society for the Preservation of New England Antiquities, is part of a contribution to the Bulletin entitled "Mistress Glover's Household Furnishings at Cambridge, Massachusetts, 1630-1641."

Mr. Morison begins: "This little paper re- "volves about two documents, important in the "social history of New England. They give the "memories, under oath, of two domestic servants "as to the household possessions of their former "mistress, in the early years of the Bay Colony. "They afford striking testimony to the fact, not "often appreciated, that the Puritan settlers of "New England included no small number of "gentry, who were used to the finer things of "life, and who had both the wealth and the "taste to surround themselves in their New "England homes, with many of the luxuries and "the elegancies they had enjoyed in Old Eng- "land."

Then follows an historical note as to the widow of the Reverend Jose Glover, her second marriage to the President of Harvard, her death and the re-marriage of her second husband, who was sued by one of the Glover children for certain parental property.........in the course of this suit the documents referred to were filed in the Middlesex County Court, where they still remain.

Mr. Morison states that these documents have been printed heretofore, but upon examination of the originals, which he proposed to use in his History of Harvard College, he found that spelling, punctuation and text differed very seriously from the original.........such as when "4 winne cupes" became "4 mugs and a pot!" And then he devotes a column to that much argued over "ye" and "yat", &c. What he has to say is so very illuminating that the Editor has asked permission to print an abstract in the NOTE-BOOK, hoping that Mr. Morison may convince a reader or two that the "upside-down h," and the old form of "th" are neither of them "y."

Mr. Morison says: "there are several methods "of printing old manuscripts. Years ago, when "printing was far cheaper than it is now, the "*Massachusetts Bay Records* were printed with "special type to represent the tailed p's, curious "ampersands, and various curleycues that seven- "teenth century writers used as abbreviations. "The *Colonial Society of Massachusetts* does not "go in for such expensive refinements, but retains "all the superior letters and abbreviations, such "as &, ye, yt, wch, which can be rendered in "ordinary type. The *Massacusetts Historical "Society,* on the other hand, spells out such ab- "breviations as "and", "the", "that," "which," "while respecting the original spelling, punctua- "tion capitalization, and the contemporary usage "of i and j, u and v. Personally, I prefer this last "method, as it makes old texts intelligible to "modern readers. If, for instance, we printed "ye wife" thus, or even "ye wife" readers would "be apt to pronounce the first word as if it were "the antique second person plural; whereas "ye" "is merely an abbreviation for "the" and should "so be read. The apparent "y" is not really "a "y", but a corrupt runic representing "*th.*" "This misunderstanding is responsible for the "eruption of "*Ye cosie gift shoppe*" along New "England Highways."

With some further comment the author of the article then gives the very interesting depositions and for those who are not familiar with the finery that some colonial ladies indulged in .... both in furniture and dress .... the reading of these lists is recommended. To a researcher who has a fancy for definition and exactness, the setting down of that mis-matched, mis-mated, misused, unfortunate "*ye*" as it should be, the article is invaluable.

VIRGINIA COLONISTS

(From Old Volume 5, S. L. O. Richmond, Va.)

JOHN AYRES, north side Rappahannock river, 1653.

Head rights: Barnaby Johnson, James Parson, Thomas Hart, Elnor Hart———.

JOHN ADDISON, "towards end of Parrott's Creeke upon Rappahannock river," 1655.

Head rights: Jno. Bincks, Jno. Anderson, Theo Peele, Izable Huber,.........Greene, Wm. Reeves.

JOHN ATKINSON, Accomack cty, 1663.

Head rights: Edw. Hepworth, Jane Mosely, Tho. Jenings, Ed. Rawlings, Wm. Eping, Anth. Wyatt, Jeffry Compton, Ann Morris, Mary Joanes, Ed. Caraway.

MR. JOHN APPLETON, Lancaster, 1664.

Head rights: Richard West, Eliz: Wright, Ed. Perkensen, Geo. Pririe or Priece, Mathew White, Margett Would, Eliz: Paine, Rich. Hanford.

DANIEL BOUCHER, Isle of Wight cty, 1655.

Head rights: Richard David or Davie, Mathew Harby, Vereto Hugon [?] John MackMacols [?]

From another entry it appears that the patentee's name is DANIELL BOUSHE, and the name as the last head right is probably John Macknaroe [?]

Mr. ROBERT BOURNE and Mr. DANIELL PARKE, Yorke cty, 1655.

Head rights: DANIELL PARKE, his wife, Peeter French, his wife, Theo. Bayly, Thomas Hayward, Richard Palner, Jno. Newnham, Isabell Fletcher, Eliz: Conaway and two negroes.

WILLIAM BOTHAM, Westmoreland cty, 1655.

Head rights: Peirce Morris, Abagaill How, Mary Tanner, Jno. Ball, Wm. Huyse [?] Geo. Dalley, Nath. Jones, Wm. Thrush, Anne Bosnell, Jone Har.........[?]

WILLIAM BLAZE, Lancaster cty, Va.

Head rights: Jno. Lockey, Robt Bake, Anne Townsend, Ed. Ranshaw, Wm. Wickenfield, Eliz: Jnoson, Jno. Harris.

NATHANIELL BRADFORD, Accomack cty, 1664. (1400 acres formerly belonging to Edmond Scarburgh and assigned to Bradford.)

Head rights: John Evans, John Smith, John Dry, John Cashew, Robert Cashew, John Courtney, Robert Tremgoe [?] Samuell Short, Thomas Coles, John Carrick, John Hancock, John Wells, Robert Masters, Jonathan S...... [?] John Tyraud, Jenkin Morgan, John Disneth [?] John Sparkes, Ezard Paine, Ann Paine, Damaris Worthy, Ellno'r Puckett, Anne Found, Christenn [?] Wenters, Joane Orrett, Agnes Payle, Joane Mares [Morris?]

JOHN BATTLE, Westward side of Paspetanke river, 1663.

Head rights: John Garey, Ed: Maurice, Jno. Curtain, Tho: Cooley, Tho: Mary, Wm. Crow, Wm. Hutton, Sam'll Cornix, Abra: Travers, Wm. Fowler, Jacob Carew, Wm. Hughes, Mary Stevens.

Mr. RICHARD BULLER, "New Begin Creeke," 1663.

Head rights: Math: Smither, Artick Slatter, Joane Risding, Richard Ward, John Carey, Hester Sarkett, Robt Mason, James Cranedge, Thomas Horne, Robt Marson, Henry Warner, Thomas Turvor, John Mathews, John Pargetor, [?] S......[?] Johnson, And. Armstrong, Dorothy Bankes, Tho: Rich, Edward Mosby, Tho: Read, Mary M......h [?] Sarah Read, John Taft or Tapt, Wm. Sacum.

JOHN BARROW, 1662.

Head rights: Edw'd Gooch, Mary Powell, Ann Williams, Tho. Carew, Jno. Martin, Edw'd Fouch.

Mr. JOHN BEAUCHAMP, Henrico cty, 1664.
Head rights: Anthony Bridgman, Wm. Tomkins.

THOMAS BUTLER, Westmoreland cty, 1664.
Head rights: Wm. Cymber, Jno. Vincent, Tymothy Benett, Mary Blackman, Daniell Atway.

ROBERT BAYLY, Rappahannock river, 1663.
Head rights: Sarah Gunny, Jno. Smith, Rich: Reekes, Henry Michaell, Jno...... ?

WILLIAM BROOK, Lower Norfolk cty, 1664.
Head rights: Dennis Cragh, John Berwick, John Keene or Kerne, Owen Kerne, Darby Kenland, John Codall, Wm. Edwards, Denis Denby, Edm: Power.

WILLIAM BROOK, Lower Norfolk, 1664.
Head rights: Dennis Murragh, Alice Martin.

Mr. WM. BASNETT, Lower Norfolk cty, 1664.
Head rights: Robert Powes, Sen'r, John Powes, Jr., Mary Tudman [?] Richard Hopham, Wm. Jeremie, John Warton, Martha Fennell, Penelope Burt, Wm. Basnette wife, James Miller, Will Griffin.

WILLIAM CARDWELL, Stafford cty, 1664.
Head rights: WM. CARDWELL, Sr., [or CORDWELL] MARGARET CORDWELL, WILLIAM CARDWELL, Jr., GRACE CARDWELL, Henry Janes, Jno. Ossett, Jno. Twiggs.

NICH: and MAURICE COCKE, Lancaster cty, 1663.
Head rights: 6 persons, two names given. Ellin Franklin, Eliza: King.

CHRISTOPHER CALVERT, Northampton county, 1655.
Head rights: D......... [?] Cox [?] Rob. Harper, Jno. Owins, Mary Owens, Teague Shone, Mary Shone, John Doza, Mary Mackero, John Mackeri, Wm. Mackery [these are evidently all the same name.........its exact form doubtful] Tho. Jonas, Wm. Coarde, Tho. Owens, Rich'd Dyers, John Dyers, Mary Dyers.

JOHN COALE, James City cty, 1655.
Head rights: Fra: Salter, Tho. Edes, Ger. Bysam, Jer. Thorne, Jno. Fowler, Tho. Fay, James Wrie [Urie?] Bob. Worthy, Jeffry Speed, Bar. Stilt, Hugh Jeffers.

RICHARD COALE and DAVID ANDERSON, Westmoreland, 1655.
Head rights: Fra: Thomas, Jno. Frizzer, Anne Perry.

ROBERT CHUNING, Lancaster cty, 1662.
Head rights: Wm. Young, Jno. Tanner, Wm. Murry, Jno. Silvester, Mary Jones, Jno. Farling.

Capt. JOHN CHEESMAN [County?] 1662.
Head rights: Richard Watts, Geo. Billops, Geo. Cable.

HENRY CORBYN, Esq., Machoatick Creeke, 1664.
Head rights: Wm. Gantlet, Jno. Young, Mary Farmer, Thos. Jones, Wm. Hardish, Fra. Parker, Tho: Tanto [?] Jacob Cotteen, Em'll Frisby, Nath: Frisby, Rich: Baldin, Rich: Partner [?] Jacob Leech, Geo. White, Richard Martin, Tho. Wilkinson, Mary Fuell, Simon Sanders.

Mr. JOHN CUSTIS, Accomack cty, 1664.
Head rights: Mary Knight, Jno. Norgood, Jno. Abram, Wm. Bigge, Tho. Somersett, Jno. Watts, Tho. Coleman, and a negro.

JOHN CANNIDA, Rappahannock cty, 1663.
Head rights: Jno. Golding, Ed. Reeves, Ann Blandon, Wm. Griffin.

SAMUELL DAVIS, n. s. Carolina river, 1663.
Head rights: Robt. Smith [very uncertain] Jno. Blete, Oliv: Williams, Tho: Soare, Eliz: Jones, Eliz: Smith, Eliza: Williamson, Eliz: Kitchin, Wm. Turner, Jane Doughting, Geo. Oakley, Hen: H......... [?] Luke Lunn, Morg. Williams, Edw. Cole, Robt. Hughes, Tho: Holder, Ma: Carr.

GILBERT DEACON, 1655. [County?]
Head rights: GILBERT DEACON, Joseph Bowene, Geo. Burcher, Rich'd Delabere, Dan. Ruse, John Bagly, Eliz: Davis, Tho. Webs, Rich: Larrom or Larcom, Alex. Somers.

JOHN EARLE, Northumberland cty, 1655.
Head rights: Two persons, Wm. Thomas only name given.

PHILLIP EVANS, "New Begin Creeke," 1663.
Head rights: Richard Whitty, Henry Catchmaid, Dina Farnes, Jno. Scott, Mary English, and a negro.

Capt. GEORGE FLOID, New Kent, 1655.
Head rights: Mary Joyner, Rich'd Harper, Henry Hoffeild, Rich'd Hancock, Arthur Cammeck, Anne Renolls, James Plunket, Jno. King, Denock Hearne.

Mr. ALEX. FLEMING, n. side Rappahannock river, 1662.
Head rights: Tho. Stone, Jno. Mason, Wm. Taylour, Eliz: Weekes, Ann Stokes, Roger Reeve, Roger Read, Wm. Jones.

GEORGE FRIZELL and THOMAS MOORE, Northampton cty, 1655.
Head rights: Tho. Bosnell, Owen Read, Jno. Collins, Teague Row, Rich'd Scot, Wm. Dennis, Rich'd Drane, Rob. Downer, Jane Downer, Jno. Francis, Wm. Thompson, Charles Briscet[?]

Mr. DAVID FOX, Gent, Lancaster cty, 1663.
Head rights: three negroes.

Mrs. MARY FORTSON, west side Paspetanke river, [1663.]
Head rights: Wm. Welldon, Hen: Benns, Wm. Carne, Jno. Robinson, Ed. Hawley, Geo. Warter, Tho. Roberts, Amosse Dansy, Jno. Wright, Tho: Steward, Tho: Mountfort, Ben: Percy, Susan Johnson, Roger Stroake, Mary Adams, Robt M.........[?] Stephen Brewer, Edward Barrett, Mary Young, John Peelers, Tho: Starpe [Harpe?] Wm. Frizzell, Tho. Marmaid, Thomas Hawley, Edward Moulson, Sarah Samwayes[?] Wm. Howard, Fra: Chalke, Tho: Baxton, "*twice and his two wives,*" Tho: Harper, Jane Allen, Ro. Brer[?] James Perry, Eliz: Steel, Abiather Flarrell, Marg't Thurlot, Eliz. Newcomb.

THOMAS GERRARD, Northumberland cty, 1655.
Head rights: Mary Wesson, Xpr Peirce.

WILLIAM GRAVES, Yorke cty, 1655.
Head rights: Bryan Coxon, Ellis Wheatly.

RALPH GREENE, New Kent, 1662.
Head rights: .... Baker, Ann King, Carey Fitts, Jno. Burton, Dan: Macoy, Jno. Browne, Jno. Hills.

GEORGE GILBERT and RICHARD SCRUDY, Chickahomany River, 1663.
Head rights: Tho. Batt, Tho. Cromson, Edw. Markham, Mary Wood, Hen. Dennis, Hen, Wood, Rich. Steed, Jno. Stroud, Wm. Crensher. Jno. Owin, Geo. Stanly, Wm. Carlot, Geo. Brigg, Kath. Jones, Wm. More, Mary Hart, Edw. Malin, Jno. Shaw, Wm. Tarp, Jno. Wood.

Mr. JOHN HARVEY, "in a small Creeke called Carrawtucke" .... 1665.

Head rights: James Harvy, Hump. Evans, Ann Wombwell, Jos. Poole, Steph. Farrell, Tho: Elmes, Tho: Poole, Wm. Basse, John Davis, Rich: Blunt, ;Sam: Jenkins, Art Brown, Chas. Sawell[?]

Mr. JOHN HARVEY, River of Carolina, 1663.

Head rights: Vergis [?] Smith, Steph: Johnsey, Geo. Moore, Jane Parnell, Tho. Poole.

JOHN HULES, Wicocomoco Creeke, 1655.

Head rights: John Hill, Tho. Holden, Wm. Pryor, John Evans, Nath. Jones, George Clark.

RICHARD HAMLETT, James City cty, "north side of Chickahominy river and on the east side of Warrney Necke alias Tyasons Soundinge."

Head rights: Phill: Prendergrast, Rob. Andrew, Tho. Hawthorne, Eliz. Sidney, Symon Hazleton, Wm. Andrew, Joyce Downer, John Gryme, John Browne, Xph. Bones.

SAMUEL HUBY and JOHN CARTER, Surry. cty, 1655.

Head rights: Eliz: Duber [?] Jno. Henry, Fra: Hostier [?] Mary Holland, Dorothy Kew.

WILLIAM HARPER, Rappahannock cty, 1662.

Head rights: Wm. Jones, Jno. Jarman, Wm. Kid

THOMAS HODGKIN, "in a bay of the Carolina River", 1665.

Head rights: John Philpot, Jno. Tyler, Mary Lewis, Sam'll Burton, Math. Hewes, Wm. Bateman, Mich. Wills, James Rogers, Alex. Monts, Marke Allister, Geo. Rayman, Roger Cleyton, Tho: Kintley, Robt. Herne, Wm. Strood, Simon Allen, Jer. Ward, Rich: Card, C.........[?] Fletcher, Fard: Downes.

OWEN HAYES, Lower Norfolk, 1664.

Head rights: Joseph Milbee, Johnes Bay, Rich. Wright, John Fewes, George Benton, Will: Russell, Jane Greenfeild, Jane Addison, Mary Holyday, and a negro.

PATENTEE'S NAME ILLEGIBLE: 1660.

Head rights: Peter Cole, Wm. Chilturne, Jno. Gwinn, Bryan Clarke, Geo. Chidrene [?] Fran Knight, Tho. Edwards, Francis Garland, Wm. Reeves, Edward Yeow [?]

Head rights: Beniamin Jones, Margarett Palmer, Elizabeth Davis, Mary Johnson, Alice Wattson, Tho. Tull, Ann Smith, Margarett Moyne, Abraham Taylour, Wm. Hemseley. (1660.)

Head rights: Tho. Stone, Jno. Mason, Wm. Taylour, Eliz: Weekes, Ann Stokes, Roger Reeves, Roger Read, Wm. Jones. (1662.)

VIRGINIA COLONISTS will not be continued, even if the Editor is enabled to carry out her present intention of publishing a twenty-four page occasional bulletin, after the close of this volume of the NOTE-BOOK. The reason for the discontinuance of this material is that Mrs. Nugent of the Virginia State Land Office will include all the records in "Old Five" that are not shown by the volumes of the regular patent series. Mrs. Nugent's abstracts are far more extensive than the brief notes in the NOTE-BOOK, and cover such matters as patent lines, &c.

Up to Mrs. Nugent's work the Editor does noknow of any one but herself who has systematit cally taken up the publication of *all* the head rights in the years covered by "Old Five." The omissions in Greer's book are pretty well recognized.

INTER-COUNTY AND INTER-COLONY

THOMAS ARNOLD and wife MARY, of Albemarle county, to Robert Johns, of Albemarle, land in Cumberland county. Cumb. cty, Va. 22 Feby 1758. Deeds ii–368.

JOSIAH BURTON, went to Northampton cty, N. C. Cumb. cty, Va. Orders. 27 Aug. 1750. p. 147.

MATHIAS BAKER, Sr., of Yorke cty, Penna., to son Mathias to bind himself apprentice. Fred'k cty, Md. 26 Dec 1761. G–351.

WILLIAM BOON, late of Darby, now of Charleston, S. C., cabinet-maker, eldest son and heir of Swan Boon, late of Darby, by his attorney, conveys land in Darby. Chester cty, Penna., 30 June 1772. T–68.

CLAUD BOREL, late of Saint Domingo, now of Camden cty, pltr. Camden cty, Ga. 29 Jany 1796. B–C, p. 235.

JOHN BORLAND, of Boston in N. E., Mcht; power to Capt. David Browne of Somerset ..... particularly for a cargo of goods imported into the said county of Somersett in or about September 1685, in the Ketch *Friendship*, Andrew Elliott, master. Som. cty, Md. 18 Nov 1687. A. W. p. 7.

THOMAS BUTLER, Pr. Geo's cty, Md., to Thomas Nicholls; lease for lives to Thomas, wf Ann and son Thomas......land in Frederick cty, Md. Fred'k cty, 23 May, 1739. *Recorded* 31 Oct 1763. H-657.

WM. BUCKNER of York Town, Va., power to Francis Coney, late of York Town, now removing to Stafford cty. Staff. cty, Va. 21 Mch 1699. Z-23.

ZACHARIAH COPLAND and WILLIAM PORTER of Nancemond cty, Va., to William Goodman of Gates cty, N. C., a parcel of land which Copland and Porter were empowered by Joseph Porter's will to sell. 18 Nov 1786. Gates cty, N. C. i-240.

JOHN CHISWELL, Gent., Psh St. Martin's, Hanover cty, to Lawrence Small, Psh St. Anne; 200 acres Albemarle cty, branches of Corbin's creek, of Rockfish, near the Blue Mountains. Alb. cty, Va. 1748. I-13. Other deeds by Chiswell to land in Albemarle, to John Wright, Francis Wright, James Armor.

Col. JOHN CHISWELL, of St. James Psh, Hanover cty, to Edward Stenson, planter, psh St. Ann's, Albemarle cty, 280 acres in the forks of Lynch's and Taylor's Creeks, branches of Rockfish river. Alb. cty, Va. 10 Feby 1748. I-11.

MICHAEL CATTERTON, from Maryland, a few years after 1779, settled in Albemarle, with Willis, Turner, Ward and Elliott. Histy Alb. cty, Va. by Woods. p. 351.

MARY x CHAPMAN, wf of Edward Chapman, of Acco, was the dau. and heir of RICHARD HARRIS, of Albemarle county, N. C.; she gives power to John Evans to sell Albemarle land. Acco., xi-603. 7 July 1713.

WILLIAM DAWSON, of Edgefield cty, S. C., to William Dallas, of St. Mary's. Conveys land. 20 Oct 1795. Camden cty, Ga. B–C,–p. 235.

SAMUELL ELDRIDGE, of the Parish of St. Michael, Island of Barbadoes; power to James Gibson, Gent., at present of Barbadoes, to collect from Peter Norley Ellegood, Marriner. Acco. 6 July 1728. xvi-340.

JOHN FASSITT, in his will, leaves son Thomas land in Dubuque, Ty of Iowa, purchased of John's bro. James, Wor. cty, Md. 22 Mch 1842. M. H. 27-320.

HEN. x GOARING [GOING?] late of Rappahannock river, Va., now a resident in Calvert cty, Md., conveys land. Richmond cty, Va. 1 Apr 1691. I-60.

FREDERICK GRAMMER, a native of Wertenburg, departed this Life on the 15th day of October, 1818. Westminster Psh. Reg. Md.

ADIN GRAY (of Montg. cty) bro. of Jeremiah, went to Pittsylvania cty, Va. about 1789. Montg. cty, Md. D-182.

BARTHOLOMEW GREENE, of Charlestowne, in N. E., marriner; power to Maj. Thomas Tabirer [sic] of I. W. Co., Va. Wit: Ja. Daye, John Pitt. I. W. iv-18. 8 Apr 1689.

SARAH HOUSTON, of the Province of East Florida, buys a lot in St. Mary's, of Thomas Norris, Camden cty, Ga. A–B, p. 78. 10 Dec 1792.

STEPHEN HULL, of the Colony of Rhode Island, v. Davenport and others. Cumb. cty, Va. 28 Mch 1774. Orders, p. 80.

ABRAHAM HILL, upper Psh of Nansemond cty, Va. See Tyrrell cty, N. C. 30 Jany [1720.] Vol. C.

WILLIAM HUGHES, attorney for John Watson, of S. C. to John Smith, Sr., of Louisa cty, Va., 193 acres. Louisa cty, 12 Nov 1792. G-246.

GRIFFITH JONES and wife Mary, of Paspetank in N. C., power to Mr. John Scott, Somerset cty, Md., to ask conveyance of tract called Monmouth. Som., Md. 11 Oct 1721. I. K.-175.

WALTER JACKSON, of Washington cty, Ga., pltr, conveys to John Hall, of Phila., Esq., 75,000 acres on the Great and Little Satilla. Consideration, £5 sterling. Camden cty, Ga. 3 Jany 1795. A–B, p. 219.

EVAN JONES brings ctf from monthly meeting at Great Choptank river, Md. Now resident of Philadelphia. Phila. Mtgs. 31st 5th 1724. (P. G. S. Collections.)

EZEKIEL KING, of Phila., from John Garrett, of Augusta, Richmond cty, Ga., by his atty, Stephen Garrett. 7 Feby 1795. Camden cty, Ga. B–C, p. 153.

JOHN LANGLEY, of Newport, R. I., from Thomas Norris, of St. Mary's, Camden cty, Ga., a lot in St. Mary's, Camden cty. 17 June 1795. B–C, p. 32.

DANIEL MAXWELL, of N. C., late of Accomack cty, Va., but now of N. C., and wf Patience. Acco., Va. 28 Aug 1765. Diii-390.

Will of JAMES MATTHEWS, Stokes county, N. C.

.... Son TANDY MATTHEWS, tract he now lives on, in Town Fork, Stokes county, also 600 acres, and 100 acres on *Belew*creek, late the property of John Thompson; also 900 acres in Virginia.........Also to JOSEPH HOLLINGSWORTH in trust for JAMES HOLLINGSWORTH, 600 acres including mountain [?] house called Stone Chimneys.........to AQUILL [?] HOLLINGSWORTH, dau. of JOSEPH and MARY HOLLINGSWORTH. Mentions their son TANDY HOLLINGSWORTH (an infant); mentions dau. BETSY JAMES and her eldest dau. (an infant.) To son TANDY MATTHEWS in trust for my dau. BETSY'S children, 900 acres called Powell Cove. Powell's Valley mentioned. To JOSEPH HOLLINGSWORTH in trust for the children of my son, WILLIAM MATTHEWS, 230 acres at the east end of the Great Pea Vine in Amherst.........400 acres to son JOHN MATTHEWS on the waters of Little Yadkin. To Obediah Branham 235½ acres called Blackburres [?].........To Irwin Bran dan 300 acres ....to be liberally educated. 2 Oct 1902. Amherst cty, Va. B-18.

JOHN MITCHELL, Fred'k, Mcht, will.

To wife Elizabeth one-half his estate after debts are paid; "that is to say in America." Bro. William extr with testator's wife. Other half of estate in America, together with whatever belongs to him in Scotland, also mentioned. Wit: Reuben Paxson [Person?] DuncanxO'Gullion, Ed. Wyatt. Fred'k cty, Md. 22 Mch 1749—8 May 1750. A1-36.

WILLIAM NORMENT, of Savannah, Chatham cty, Ga., gentleman, by his atty, John Grayson, conveys 10,000 acres to Thomas Ruston, of Philada., physician, Camden cty, Ga. B-C, p. 1481; 17 Oct 1794.

SAMUEL NUCKOLLS, of Louisa cty, Va., to William Johns, psh. Southam, Cumb. cty, Va., land in Cumberland cty. Cumb. cty, 26 Nov. 1750. I-236.

GIDEON DAVIS PENDLETON, of Savannah, atty-at-law, to John Collins of Rhode Island, Esq., consideration £50 sterling, tract of land ....1150 acres on St. Mary's river. 13 Mch 1793. Camden cty, Ga., B-C, p. 233.

ROBERT PIGOTT, late of Toulouse, France. John Mason, Montgomery cty, Md., adm. A. A. cty, Md. 5 Apr 1800. Orphans' Ct records.

JOHN PARKER, of Accomack cty, Va., in suit. Nthld cty, Va. 18 July 1707. 1699-1713, p. 472.

JOHN RABY, of Gates cty, N. C., to Kedar Raby, of the Upper Parish of Nancemond cty, Va., conveys fifty acres. 30 Oct 1786. Gates cty i-242.

DANIEL ROBERDEAU, now of Philada., but lately of St. Christopher, W. I. is over 14 and asks for a guardian. Chooses Jno. Wilcox. Philada. Orphans' Ct Records. 10 Oct 1744. H. S. 9-97.

Mr. JAMES RICHARDS, an alien born within the Dominions of France, appointed Sheriff of Baltimore cty. Committee reports that he is not qualified. 19 May 1747. Md. Arch. xliv-508.

SARAH RANDALL, of Philada., buys part of a lot in St. Mary's, Georgia, from Antoine Suarez. Camden cty, Ga. 20 July 1798. B and C. p. 499.

ROBERT RISDON, late of N. E. Acco. cty Va. 4 Mch 1672. iv-191.

SOUTH CAROLINA; the following warrants for survey in Georgia are recorded.

For Ann Rogers, 5 Apr 1763. For George Noddings, 400 acres south of the Altamaha. Place or tract called Dover Bluff, for William Rogers. Camden cty, Ga. Field Notes.

Printed at The Industrial School for Crippled and Deformed Children, 241 St. Botolph Street, Boston

Abanathan, 41
Abbington, 9, 39
Abbott, 4, 13, 40, 41
Aben (?), 38
Abram, 69
Ackson, 46
Acton, 61
Adair, 50, *51
Adams, 9, 25, 45, 53, 69
Adcock, 13
Addams, 13, 38, 51
Addison, 13, 16, 68, 70
Addy, 45
Adolph, 13
Aiken, 50, *51
Aires, 13
Akert, 59
Aladry (?), 37
Albert, 65
Aldin, 13
Alexander, 13*, 50, 51
Alldin, 13
Allen, 1, *13, *25, *27, 37, 39, 44, *45, 50, 51, 62, 64, 69, 70
Allendor, 9
Allenson, 17
Allerton, 13
Allison, 13, 22, 25, 45, 51
Allister, 70
Alrich, 52
Alricks, *51
Alvis, 13
Ambrose, 58
Anderson, 1, *13, 21, *25, *45, *51, 52, 57, 68, 69
Andrew, *70
Andrews, 3, *22, 25, 37, 56, 62, 63
Andrick, 38
Angel, 33, *58
Angus, 13, 28
Apple, 58
Appleton, 46, 68
Applewhaite, 13, 28
Appling, 33
Appy, 37
Arbuckle, 11
Archer, *13, 14, *28
Armor, 25, 70
Armstrong, *25, 39, 50, 51, 68
Arnall, 38
Arnburn, 29
Arnold, 13, 28, 37, 70
Arnoll, *46
Arrington, 1
Arskins, 13, 28
Artis, 39
Arundell, 38
Ascough, 13, 28
Ashford, 8
Ashworth, 13, 28
Askew, 25
Atkins, 4, 20, 32, 46, 61
Atkinson, *2, 13, 28, 59, 68
Attaway, 45
Atway, 69
Aubrey, 19
Audley, 11
Augusta, 25
Austin, 2, 7, 29, 39, 50, 59
Austott, 58
Avent, 61
Averse, 49
Avery, *53, 57
Avesse, 4
Axon, 46
Aydelotte, *55, 56
Ayres, 39, 52, 68

Backhouse, 25
Bacon, 7, 39
Badley, 4
Bagley, 59
Bagly, 69
Bagshaw, 39
Bail, 51
Bailes, 22
Bailey, 33, 56
Baily (?), 58
Bailye, 32
Bake, 68
Baker, 1, 13, 25, 39, 46, 49, 69, 70
Baldin, 69
Baldwin, 25, 32
Bales, 59
Baley, 38
Ball, 2, 27, 32, 34, *44, 68
Ballenger, 53
Balmer, 41
Balsell, 58
Bambridge, 45
Banke, 68
Banks (?), 17
Barcroft, 38
Barker, 1, 25, *38, *45
Barnard, 33
Barnes, 16, 44
Barnwell, 38
Barr, 50, *51
Barratt, 2, 32, 39, 69
Barrington, 10
Barrow, 68
Barruk, 58
Barton, 37, 44, 45, 61
Bartram, 25
Base, 33, 47
Basnett, 69
Basnette, 69
Bass, 20
Basse, 70
Bassey, 37
Bassill, 38
Bateman, 14, 39, 70
Batt, 69
Batte, 20
Battle, 68
Batts, 34
Baxter, 39, 69
Bay, 70
Bayley, 46
Baylie, 25
Bayly, *37, 38, 39, 68, 69
Bayne, 40
Beal, 45
Beale, 21, 39
Beall, 2, 3, 40, 41
Beard, 4
Beason, 45
Beaston, 50
Beaty, 25
Beauchamp, 64, 69
Beavin, 39
Beazely, 63
Beckerback, 62
Beckwith, 2, 39
Bedford, 51, 52
Bedingfell, 8
Bedingfiell, 7
Behethland, 22
Bell, *53
Bellamy, 65
Belocae, 51
Belson, 37
Belt, 32
Bench, 39
Benger, 21
Bennet, 25
Bennett, 2, 38, 69
Benns, 69
Benskin, 17
Benson, 3
Benston, 3
Bently, 29
Benton, 70
Berry, 8, 37, 46
Berwick, 69
Bessie, 38
Beswick, 32
Betts, 64
Betty, 58
Beyer, 47
Bibey, 15
Biddle, 10, 50, 51
Bigg, 39
Bigge, 69
Billing, 38
Billingsley, *40
Billops, 69
Bincks, 68
Binns, 23
Bird, 29, 39
Birket, 19

Bishop, 8, 39, 41, 44
Black, 5, 37, 39, 44, 51
Blackburn, 52
Blacklock, 21
Blackman, 69
Blackshaw, 38
Blads (?), 3
Blagg, 1
Blaids, 3
Blaise (?), 38
Blak, 45
Blakey, 11, 27
Bland, 23, 47, 53
Blandon, 69
Blaze, 68
Bleighton, 53
Blete, 69
Blunt, 39, 70
Boery, 37
Boggess, 14, 22
Boggs, 44, *45, 50
Bogley, 32
Bohrer, 33
Bolden, *50
Bolitho, 28
Bolling, *8
Bonam, 25
Bond, 37, 46, 57
Bondick, 40
Bones, 70
Bonewell, 21
Bonham, 44, *45
Bonner, 39
Bonsall, 25
Boocher, 35
Boon, *70
Boone, 49
Booth, 39, 40, 46, *51, 67
Bopst, 34
Bordley, 2
Borel, 10, 70
Borland, 70
Borne, 39
Boseman, 37
Bosnell, 68, 69
Boswell, 3
Botham, 68
Boucher, 68
Boul (?), 10
Boulden, 50
Boulware, *53
Boune (?), 29
Bourne, 68
Boushe, 68
Bowdoin, 10, 14, 61
Bowen, 14, 50, 56, 64
Bowene, 69
Bowezy, 62
Bowin, 4, 39
Bowler, 14
Bowling, 14
Boyd, 1, 25, 50, *51, 62
Boyle, 34
Boyn, 45
Boys, 45
Brackenridge, 14
Brackin, 44, 45
Bradford, *14, 35, 68
Bradley, 14
Bradshaw, 14
Brady, 28, 39
Branch, 5, *14, *16, 19, 38
Brandt, 39
Branham, 71
Branston, 14
Brather, 40
Bravard, 51
Brawner, *14
Bray, 39
Brayfield, 3
Bread, 41
Breadan, 25
Bready, 32
Brearly, 44
Brent, 40
Brer (?), 69
Brereton, 14, *63, 64
Bressie, 15
Brett, *1
Brewer, 14, 38, 69
Breweton, 46
Brewse, 14
Brewton, 45
Briant, 14
Brice, 14
Bricker, 33
Bridge, 14
Bridgemonth, 38
Bridges, 14*
Bridgewater, 14
Bridgman, 69
Brigg, 69
Briggs, 38
Bright, 19
Brindley, 25
Brinten, 25
Briscet (?), 69
Briscoe, 2
Britten, 25
Brittian, 64
Brittingham, 2, 40
Broadrib, 37
Broadwater, 8
Broahurst, 39
Brobson, 25
Brock, 14, 55
Brocket, 38
Bromley, 64
Brook, *69
Brooke, 14, 41
Brookes, *38
Brooks, 2, 14
Broom, *25
Brown, 3, 14, 20, 23, 25, 28, 29, 40, 51, 57, 58, 70
Browne, 14, 17, 38, *39, 64, 69, *70
Brownely, 37
Browning, 46
Bruce, 14, 45, 58
Bruer, 14
Brunburg, *25
Bruner, 33
Brunskill, 14
Bryam, 15
Bryan, 25, 39, 44, 51, 52
Bryans, *45
Bryson, 51
Buchanan, 15, 47, 51
Buckingham, 25, 45
Buckner, 70
Buffington, 25
Buffolke, 39
Bugg, 1
Bullen, 23
Buller, 38, 68
Bullett, 39
Bullington, 15
Bullock, 37
Bundick, 40
Bunting, 15, 29
Burch, 41
Burcher, 27, 69
Burchet, 53
Burger, 57
Burgess, 15, 35, 38
Burgh, 37, *40, 41
Burke, 1
Burkett, 15, 19
Burks, 15
Burley, 46
Burnet, 10
Burnett. 17
Burneston, 47
Burns, 3, 15
Burnside, 45
Burras, 52
Burroughs, 2
Burrowes, 21
Burrus, 15
Burt, 69
Burton, 7, *14, 15, *27, 29, 39, *56, 69, 70
Burwell, 14
Bury, 58
Busby, 25
Bush, 15, 25
Bushrod, 20
Bussard (?), 58
Busy (?), 58
Butler, 3, *15, 21, 43, 55, 69, 70
Butlett, 39
Butt, 15, 23
Butten, 15

Butterfield, 28
Butteris, 15
Buttingshire, 4
Button, 15
Buttrune, 32
Byrd, *11, 29, 47, 67
Byrne, 9
Bysam, 69

Cabell, 15, 20, 52
Cable, 69
Cadman, 10
Cadwell, 45
Calhoon, *1
Callowhill, 15
Calvert, 15, *47, 56, 69
Camble, *25
Camblin, 57
Cammeck, 69
Camp, 38
Campbell, 15, 29, 40, *53, 57
Canby, 25
Cann, 44
Canneday, 3
Cannida, 69
Cannon, 3, 15, *45, *51, 52
Cantrel, 45
Capp, 15, 38
Caps, 15
Caraway, 68
Card, 70
Cardwell, 15, 69
Carew, 38, *68
Carey (?), 38
Carlot, 69
Carlyle, 8
Carmack, 33
Carn, 69
Carner, 38
Carney, 28
Carnuff, 33
Carpenter, 2, 27, 29, 38, *39, 46
Carr, 8, 41, 57, 69
Carraway, 15
Carrell, 37
Carrick, 68
Carrington, 10
Carson, 25, 45, 51
Cartbolde, 39
Carter, *15, 16, *23, 25, 29, 37, *38, 45, 70
Cartricke, 46
Cartwright, 15, *46
Carveretta, 15
Carvin, 56
Cary, 3, 49
Case, 67
Casey, 51
Cash, 53, 57
Cashen, 8, 10
Cashew, 68
Casse, 39
Cassinett, 59
Caswell, 2
Catchmaid, 69
Cater, 7
Catfield, 39
Cather, 40
Catlett, 15, 21
Catlin, 64
Catterton, 70
Causey, 4
Cazier, *50
Ceton (?), 38
Chaffin, 44
Chalke, 69
Chambers, 3, 4, 38, 40, 44, 45, 51
Champion, *16
Chandler, *25, 38, *40, 49
Chaplin, 40
Chapman, 4, 8, *38, 70
Charles, 39
Charlton, 21, 38
Cheesman, 69
Chegwidden, 34
Cheley, 16
Chesell, 32
Chesholm, 61
Chetham, 16
Chetwood, 16
Cheyney, 38
Chichely, 46
Chidrene (?), 70
Chilcott, 23
Childers, 52
Childress, 57
Chilturne, 70
Chinley, 39
Chisnae, 53
Chiswell, *70
Chittwood, 46
Chowning, 17
Christian, 52
Christopher, 3, 8
Chuning, 69
Church, 10, 16
Churchill, *16
Cillock, 64
Claiborne, 14
Clapham, 45, 49
Clark, 9, 16, 25, 28, 41, *50 *51, 53, 70
Clarke, 16, *38, 70
Clarkfeild, 38
Clarkson, 5, 40
Clay, 13, 16, 28, 52
Claye, 15, 63
Cleaments, 44, 53
Cleancy, 25
Cleashe (?), 46
Cleere, 16
Clement, 16
Clements, 38
Clemson, 39
Clency (?), 3
Clerke, *37
Cleverdon, 3
Cleyton, 70
Clifton, *39
Cling, 25
Cloud, *25
Cloverfield, 21
Clower, 45
Cloyd, 5, 10, 45
Coale, *69
Coarde, 69
Cobb, 38
Cobbs, 62
Cobin, 38
Cochran, 25, 45, *50
Cock, 33
Cocke, 16, 38, 69
Cockee (sic), 3
Cockley, 49
Codall, 69
Coffey, 51
Cofield, 16
Cogginton, 39
Colberson, 45
Colclough, 13
Cole, see Coll
Cole, 7, 16, 20, 23
Coleman, 16, 57, 69
Coleraine, 8
Coles, 68
Colesberry, *51
Colewright, 39
Coll, 50, 69, 70
Collebarges, 47
Colley, 16
Collier, 3, *4, 25, 27
Collings, 37, 55
Collins, 16, 39, 45, 46, 62, 69, 71
Collonell (?), 3
Colly, 39
Colson, 16
Comer, 29
Compton, 68
Conalin, 16
Conaway, 46
Condon (?), 10
Coney, 70
Conley, 32
Connagen, 37
Connaly, 16
Connel, 45
Conner, 39, 40, 49
Conquest, 16, 21
Conway, *16, *50
Cooch, 50, *51
Cook, 2, 55
Cooke, 3, 10, 45

Cooler, 67
Cooly, 38, 68
Coop, 37
Cooper, *3, 4, 20, 27, *46, *64
Copeland, 1
Copes, 3, 4
Copland, 70
Coppage, 34
Corbett, 16
Corbyn, 69
Cord, 3
Cordre (?), 3
Cordwell, 69
Coridon, 10
Corke, 16
Corker, 14, 41
Cormacke, 37
Corman, 38
Cornegey, 50
Cornelius, 16
Cornewallis, 40
Cornish, *45, 64
Cornix, 37, 68
Corriches (?), 46
Corson, 45
Cortright, 39
Cortrutt, 39
Corts, 45
Cossinett, 59
Coston, 3
Cotes, 16
Cotrell, 16
Cotteen, 69
Cottingham, 49, *55, 56
Cottle, 39
Cottman, 40
Cotton, 38
Couch, 25
Coulbourn, 3
Coulbourne, *40, 64
Coulston, 20
Counsill, 25
Counts, 16
Couper, 7
Courses (?), 16
Coursie, 37
Courtman, 39
Courtnay, *38
Courtney, 28, 68
Courts, *32
Covell, 1
Covington, *49
Cowdrey, *16
Cox, 14, 15, 29, *38, 47, 59, 69
Coxon, 69
Craford, 45
Crafort, 45
Cragh, 69
Craghead, 25
Craig, 8, 15
Craighton, 45
Craike, 10
Craksent, 47
Cramer, 17
Cramp, 39
Crampton, 25
Cranedge, 68
Cranfield, 39
Cranmer, 58
Crapper, 3
Crask(e), 16, 17
Craven, 62
Crawford, 3, 51, *64
Crawley, 53
Cray, 37
Crebill, 33
Creed, 51
Crensher, 69
Crickman, 17
Crillig, 38
Cripping, 4
Crips, 25
Crispe, 46
Crockett, 29
Croff, 38
Crome, 37
Cromson, 69
Cropper, 3, 4
Cross, 37, 44
Crossen, 45
Crosson, *44, 45
Crouch, 3, 29, 63
Crow, *25, 38, 68
Crowde, 45
Crowe, 38
Crowson, 9
Crozier, 17
Crum, 58
Crumwell, 37
Crutchfield, 59
Culbertson, 39, 50
Culland, 37
Cullner, 4
Cullum, 39
Culp, 47
Culpepper, *39
Culverton, 39
Cumberland, 50
Cummings, 21, 25
Cummins, 17
Cunningham, 10, 13, 40
Curlet, 50
Curry, 8
Curtain, 68
Curtis, *9, 57
Custers, 3
Custis, 3, 17, 65, 69
Cutfield, 39
Cutler, 4, 67
Cuttiford, 62
Cymber, 69

Dabney, 17
Daby, 39
Dade, 2, 17
Dalby, 17
Dale, *37
Dallas, 70
Dalley, 68
Dalton, 8
Damerel, 26
Dameron, 26, 27
Damril, 26
Dandridge, *17, 27
Dandy, 55
Daniel, 22, 23, 34
Daniell, 38, 53, 58
Daniellson, 32
Dansar, 46
Dansey, 49, 69
Darden, 40
Darling, 1
Darnall, 55
Darrell, 17
Darst, 17
Dashiell, 40, 41, 49, 61
Dasor, 39
Davenport, *17, 71
David, *50, 68
Davidson, 25, 29, 50
Davie, 68
Davis, 1, *2, 8, 11, 14, 16, 17, 19, 22, 23, 25, 32, 38, *39, 40, 41, 49, *50, 51, *53, *56, 58, *59, 64, *69, *70
Dawes, *25
Dawsey, 39
Dawson, 3, 35, 46, 70
Day, 17, 22
Daye, 71
Deacon, 69
Deakins, 62
Dearmond, 1
Deaver, 45
Debford, 37
Deen, 50
Delabere, 69
Delany, 52
Delaplaine, 25
Delasmutt, 2
Delaware, 39
Delott, 13
Demere, 7
Denby, 69
Denellin, 37
Dennis, 23, 27, 37, 39, 46, 51, *69
Denny, 25
Denson, 38
Dent, 8, 35, 40, 64
Denwood, 17, 64
Dereckson, 25
Derman, 62
Dermott, 7

Derrick, 61
Derrickson, 25
Devilbiss, 33
Devon, 51, 52
Dew, *39, 53
Diaz, 38
Dickens, 1
Dickerson, 3
Dickinson, 51
Dickiy, 25
Dickson, 45, 46
Dies, 40
Dillingham, 10
Dillon, 2
Dilworth, 9, *61
Dimit, 17
Dingey, *25
Dinguid, 27
Dinson, 44
Dirrickson, 3
Disharoon, 3, 40
Disneth (?), 68
Dix, 9
Dixon, 3, 9, 17, 25, *45
Dixson, 45
Doaford, 39
Dobson, 37
Dodson, 37
Doe, 38
Doefield, 37
Doemy (?), 37
Dolbin, 37
Dolby, 14
Dollar, 17
Dollard, *17
Dolliffe, 10
Donald, 45
Donaldson, 15, 17
Donelson, 17
Donkaster, 39
Donnellan, 49
Doring, 28
Dorman, *49
Dorsey, 4, 17
Dossey, 4, 49
Dougherty, *51
Doughting, 69
Doulby, 17
Dowing, 17
Dowinge, 46
Downer, 17, 69, 70
Downes, 39, 65, 70
Downing, 17, 29
Downs, 28
Doyle, 51
Doyne, 3
Doza, 69
Draiton, 5, 27
Drake, 17
Drakeford, 37
Drane, 69
Drury, 29, 46
Dry, 68
Dryer, 41
Dubb, 39
Duber (?), 70
Duckworth, 17
Dudley, 9, 17
Duff, 25
Duke, 13, *17, 28, 34
Dulin, 8
Dunaway, 17
Duncan, 53
Dunn, 17, 25
Dunnahow, 9
Dunnlap, 25, 50
Dunsten, 38
Dunway, 17
Dupler (?), 11
Dupriest, 16
Durbin, 49
Durkett, 37
Durst, 17
Dushane, 51
Duvall, 3
Dyas, 4
Dyat, 51
Dyers, 69

Eale, 9
Eales, 39
Earle, 16, 34, 69
Easly, 17
Eason, 58, 59
East, 19
Eaton, 10, 17, 49
Eckman, 33
Edes, 69
Edges, 38
Edloe, 14, 35, 56
Edmond, 2
Edmonds, *19, 37, 38
Edward, 23, 45
Edwards, *19, 21, 37, 38, 40, 50, 69, 70
Egarton, 3, 34, 35
Elam, 20
Elder, 39, 45, 50
Eldes, 38
Eldridge, 19, 25, 71
Elkins, 1
Ellegood, 71
Eller, 58
Ellicott, 10
Elliot, 3, 38, 46, 52
Elliott, *3, 25, 56, 70
Ellis, *19, 20, 50
Ellot, 39
Ellys, 46
Ellzey, 19, 61
Elmes, 70
Elsmore, 45
Eltonhead, 19
Elver, 37
Emerson, 4
Emmet, *64
Emnes, 39
Emson, 46
Endridge, 19
England, 44
Engle, 33
English, 27, *45, 46, 69
Ennis, *3
Enos, *51
Eping, 68
Erb, 33, 58
Erristall, 27
Ervin, 25
Eskridge, 19
Est, 38
Estes, 62
Esthop, 38
Etheridge, 20
Eubanks, 20
Eules, 25
Eustace, 21
Evans, 4, 20, *25, 32, 38, *40, 41, *45, 50, *51, 52, 58, 68, 69, *70
Everndon, 64
Everton, 10
Eves, *51, 52
Evins, 50
Evitt, 3
Ewell, 20
Ewen, 38
Ewing, 29, 59
Eyers, *46
Eynon, 50
Eyre, 9, 28
Eyres, 7, 20
Eyve, 28

Fagan, 20
Faile, 20
Faires, 50, 51
Fairfax, 20
Faith, 51
Famill, 38
Fanshawe, 20
Fantleroy, 11, 20, 46
Farguson, 8
Farling, 69
Farmer, 20, 69
Farnes, 69
Farrar, 20
Farrell, 53, 70
Farrow, 14, 20, 38, 47
Farthing, 35
Fassitt, 3, 71
Fauntleroy, 20, 46
Faver, 7
Fawcett, 20, 39
Fay, 69
Featherstone, 14

Feilder, 20
Fendall, 3
Fennell, 69
Ferebee, 20
Ferguson, 20, 25, 29, 44, 45
Ferrel, 59
Ferriss, *25
Feverstone, 65
Fewell, 38
Fewes, 70
Field, 20
Fields, 34
Fiery, 34
Filliott, 46
Finch, 39
Finley, 8, 20
Finney, 20, 25, 38, 44, 45, *46, *52
Finnie, 20
Fishbourne, 1
Fisher, 3, 9, 39, 50
Fitchew, 4
Fitts, 69
Fitz Geferies, 40
Fitzgerald, 58, 63
Fitzgerrall, 22
Fitzpatrick, 30
Fiveash, 20
Flannakin, 20
Flarell, 69
Fleming, *20, 33, 69
Fleminge, 38
Flemming, 58
Fletcher, *20, 25, 38, 68, 70
Floid, 69
Flood, 59
Flournoy, 20
Floyd, 20, 21, 37, 39
Foakes, 39
Folio, 15
Fookes, 21, 38
Fooks, 14, 40
Foot, 25, 44, 45
Forbus, 57
Forby, 37
Ford, 21, 25, 37, 40, *44
Fordham, 10, 44
Forecast, 37
Forecaster, 39
Forman, 21
Forrest, 49
Forsith, 27
Fortson, 69
Foster, 8, 20, *21, 38, 39, 47, 53, 64
Fosture, 21
Fouch, 68
Foukes, 21
Foulks, 21
Found, 68
Founton, 21
Fout, 46
Fowke, 29, 40
Fowler, 68, 69
Fox, 46, 47, 69
Foxcraft, 21
Foxon, 38
Foy, 38
Frame, 4, 21
Francis, 23, *69
Francisco, 21
Franklin, 69
Frankling, 14
Franklyn, 64
Frazer, 21
Freak, 63
Freeborn, 40, 41
Freeland, 2
Freeman, *21, 55
French, 21, 68
Frere, 10
Freshwater, 21, 39, 46
Friar, 27
Frick, 38
Frisby, 69
Fristo, 39
Frith, 39
Frizell, 38, *69
Frizzer, 69
Frost, 29
Fry, 29
Fryar, 51
Fryer, 39, *41
Fuell, 69
Fulcher, 21, 57
Fullen, 21
Fulton, 44, 45
Fuqua, 27
Furlong, 15
Furman, 39
Furnis, 51
Furniss, 2
Furton, 39
Fussell, 25

Gadd, 37
Gaines, 21
Gaither, 35
Galagher, 51
Galbraith, 65
Galbreath, 25
Gallaudett, 7
Gallocher, 50
Gallohough, 21
Gallohue, 21
Galloway, 11
Galt, 34
Gamble, 25
Gantlet, 69
Gantlett, 16
Gardenor, 11
Gardiner, 50
Gardner, 5
Gardworth, 39
Garey, 68
Garland, 38, 70
Garnell, 38
Garretson, 50, *51
Garrett, 38, 45, 46, 71
Garrettson, *25, 52
Gascoigne, 22
Gaskin(s), 21
Gatewood, 52
Gay, *23
Gee, 21
Gells, 38
Gentry, 11, 21
Gerrard, 69
Gessing, 25
Gest, 14
Getzendanner, 33
Gibbons, 37, 38
Gibson, 13, *21, 22, 29, 46, 56, 59, 71
Giddens, 22
Giddinge, 46
Giffen, 45
Gilbert, 22, 57, 69
Gilding, 22
Giles, 28
Gill, 22, 46
Gillaland, 25
Gillaspie, 52
Gilleher, 45
Gillett, 15
Gilliam, 22
Gilliland, 52
Gillis, 25
Gilmer, 33, 45, 51, 57
Gilmore, 25
Gilnett, 38
Giloe, 38
Gilpin, 25
Gilson, 22, 45
Gimblet, 38
Givens, 13
Gladin, *8
Glass, 34
Gledhill, 22
Glenn, 22
Gless, 51
Glissen, 38
Glover, *22
Glow, 22
Glynn, 15
Goare, 22
Goaring, 71
Goddin, 40
Godfrey, 40
Godwin, 3, *23
Goffe, 53
Going, 70
Golding, 69
Goldsborough, 56

Gooch, 68
Goodale, 46
Goodman, 70
Goodriche, 11
Goodtry, 39
Goodwin, 38
Gooldsby, 27
Goose, 39
Gordon, 5, 25
Gorge, 39
Goslee, 55
Gosling, 21
Gosnel, 58
Gossell, 46
Gossnell, 46
Gostell, 46
Gothrope, *25
Gower, 58
Grafton, 4
Graham, 44, 50
Grammar, 58
Grammer, 58, 71
Grandison (?), 39
Granger, 37, 49
Grantham, 51, 52
Gratner, 21
Graves, 69
Grawmer, 58
Gray, 3, 4, 25, 45, 56, 59, 71
Grayson, 71
Greave, *25
Greaves, 45, 50
Green, 25, 32, 39, 45, 59
Greene, *34, 38, 39, 40, 46, 68, 69, 71
Greenfield, 32, 70
Greenwood, 37
Gregg, *25, *45, 58
Gregory, 64
Grene, 38
Gressam, 37
Gressum, 39
Greves, 4
Grey, 38
Griffin, 3, 19, 28, 37, 39, 53, *69
Griffith, 35, 37, 40, 46, 50, *51
Grigg, 27
Grigges, 49
Grigsby, 20, 21
Grimes, 8, 17, 51
Grinville (?), 38
Grissham, 29
Groves, 22, 38
Grubb, *45
Grubbs, 1
Gryme, 70
Grymes, 14, 38
Gudloe, 46
Gunn, 23, 45
Gunnell, 8
Gunny, 69
Gurtford, 39
Guthrey, *44
Guy, 2
Guyars, 52
Gweast (?), 47
Gwinn, 70
Gyles, 25

H—— (?), 69
Hachett, 39
Hack, 23
Hackett, 39
Haden, 22, 23
Hadlowe, 41
Hafts (?), 40
Hagester, 57
Haggamond, 22
Haggoman, 22
Haines (?), 37
Hainey, 23
Haley, 27
Hall, 9, 21, *23, 32, 34, 37, 44, 50, 62, 71
Halloway, 20
Hambleton, 23, 40
Hamilton, 8, 25, 34
Hamlett, 70
Hamlin, 39, 46
Hamling, 23
Hammond, 23, 35, 40
Hamond, 38
Hampshire, 39
Hampton, 8, 40
Hamrick, 47
Hamton, 38
Hanby, *23
Hancock, *23, 68, 69
Hancoke, 39
Hands, 40
Haner (?), 37
Haney, 7
Hanford, 68
Hanks, 37
Hanlon, 25
Hanna, 51
Hannah, 45
Hanson, 25, 65
Har—— (?), 68
Harberd, 38
Harby, 68
Hardage, 23
Hardaway, 34
Harden, 23
Harding, 15, 22, *23, 56
Hardinge, 22, 45
Hardish, 69
Hardy, *32, 57
Hare, 23
Harford, 45
Harlen, 44
Harlow, 38
Harman, *38, 51
Harmanson, *22
Harmantrout, 16, 23
Harp, 25, 51
Harpe, 69
Harper, *23, 49, *69, 70
Harris(s), 8, 13, 22, 23, 25, 28, 37, 43, 68, 70
Harrison, 3, 8, 21, *23, 37, 38, 52, 61
Harristey, 41
Hart, 68, 69
Hartfort, 37
Hartly, 23, *38
Hartwell, 39
Harvey, 5, 23, *25, 32, *52, 57, *70
Harwood, 14, *37
Haselwood, *23
Haslep, 57
Hasted (?), 62
Haswell, 40
Hatcher, 22
Hathorne, 38
Hatton, 50
Haughey, 50
Haveland, 25
Haward, 23
Hawkings, 15
Hawkins, 1, 10, 23, 46, 61
Hawley, *69
Hawthorne, 70
Hayes, Haise, Hase, Hay, Haies, Hays, Hayse, *5, 14, 25, *27, 44, 45, 62, 63, 70
Haygoe (?), 32
Hayle, 39
Hayman, 64
Haynie, 27
Haynor, 44, 45
Hayns, 44, *51, 52
Hayword, 22, 68
Hazard, 9
Hazelton, 70
Hazelwood, 38
Hazilrigg, 47
Hazlet, 51
Head, 32
Heald, 25
Healy, 11, 32
Hearne, 64, 69
Hearse, 33
Heath, 16, 27, 37, 44, *64
Heather, 41
Hebb, 4
Hedge, *25
Hedrick, 56
Heins, 25
Hellen, 28
Helson, 39
Hemphill, 25
Hemsley, 28, 70

Henderson, 3, 27, 46, 49, 58, 64
Hendrake, 14
Hendrickson, 16, *25
Henley, 27
Henly, 9
Henman, 27
Henrike, 37
Henry, 27, 39, 40, 44, 45, 70
Hepworth, 68
Herage, 25
Herbert, 37
Herdman, 44
Hering, 65
Herne, 70
Hershey, 45
Hester, 38
Hetrick, 23
Hetuldy, 33
Hewes, *27, 70
Heweth, 20
Heywood, 37
Hickes, 14, 37
Hicklin, 25
Hickman, 11, 40
Hicks, 1, 4, 38
Higby, 27
Higgenbothan, 51
Higgins, 61
Higginson, 61
Higgison, 65
High, 38
Higton, 4
Hiland, 38
Hill, 1, 2, 9, 20, 25, 38, *40, *51, 62, 64, 65, 70, 71
Hillard, 37
Hillary, 56
Hille, 41
Hills, 1, 52, 69
Hilton, 62
Hindman, 45
Hinds, 37, 50
Hine (?), 62
Hines, 58
Hinman, 50
Hinsey, 51
Hinton, 25
Hitch, 40
Hix, 14, 27
Hoare, 46
Hobb, 4
Hobbs, 39, 53
Hobert, 46
Hobson, 25
Hodge, 19, 27, 28
Hodgkin, 70
Hodgshon, 40
Hodkins, 39
Hodworth, 16
Hoffield, 69
Hoffsinger, 56
Hogg, 25, 27, 57
Hoggson, 27
Hogin, 28
Holdcroft, 53
Holden, 27, 38, 39, *57, 70
Holder, 39, 69
Holderost, 27
Holin, 38
Holladay, 28
Holland, 28, 40, *41, 49, *50, 55, 56, 64, 70
Holliday, 4
Hollingsworth, *25, 41, 44, 50, 71
Holmes, *14, 15, 22, 28, 38, 39, 44, 49
Holsworth, 40, 41
Holt, 63
Holyday, 70
Honn, 25
Hood, 5
Hook, 5
Hooper, 61
Hoopes, 44
Hooten, 3
Hoover, 59
Hope, 9, 39, 58
Hopewell, 2, 39, 49
Hopham, 69
Hopkins, 3, *7, 17, 49, 55
Horesby, 52
Horne, 20, 28, 37, 68
Horner, 13, 25
Horney, 4
Horsey, 37, 58, 64
Horson, 45
Horton, 37, 46
Hoskins, 39
Hostier (?), 70
House, 28
Houston, 71
Hover, 58, 59
How, 68
Howard, 11, 35, 39, 40, *63, 64, 69
Howell, 1, 43, *50
Howman (?), 46
Howson, *39
Hubbard, 9
Hubbet, 46
Huber, 68
Huby, 70
Hudson, 16, 17, *39
Hues, 38
Hueston, 44, 45
Huff, 44
Huffman, 47
Hugan, 46
Hughes, 16, 20, *26, 27, *44, 47, 50, 68, 69, 71
Hughlett, 37
Hughs, 45
Hughson, 13, 28
Hugon (?), 68
Hules, 70
Hull, 46, 61, 71
Hummer, 33
Humphrey, 40
Humphreys, 20, 46
Humphries, 37
Humstom, 14
Hunderford, 28, 65
Hundrey, 38
Hungerford, 65
Hunt, 1, 37, *38, 39
Hunter, *8, 39, 46
Huntford, 38
Huntley, 38
Hutcheson, 39, *41
Hutchinson, 14, 38
Hutchison, 45
Hutsell, 33
Hutt, 2
Hutton, 28, 68
Hutzell, 33
Huyse (?), 68
Hyland, 25
Hyndman, 20
Hynes, 50

Indrell, 41
Innis, 3, 56
Ireck, 4
Irish, 37, 38
Irish boy, Daniel, 46
——An Irishwoman, 38
Irvin, 43, *51
Irving, 52
Isdon, 58
Israel, 41, 51
Ivy, 41

Jack, 50
Jackman, 39
Jackson, 8, 20, 21, 37, 45, 50, 53, 61, 71
Jacobs, *41
Jaffy, 32
James, 37, *38, 44, *50, 51, 52, 64, 69, 71
Jameson, 25
Jamison, 45, 50
Jamson, 25
Jannet, 25
Janson, 37, 39
Janvier, *51
Janvire, 51
Jaquet, *51, 52
Jarman, 70
Jayes, 37
Jeffers, 69
Jeffries, 21, 38
Jeffry, 38

Jelliott, 15
Jemer (?), 39
Jenafer, 9
Jenckins, 63, *64
Jenings, 68
Jenkin, *39
Jenkins, 50, 56, 70
Jenner, 37
Jennings, 37, 39, 47
Jeremie, 69
Jermain, 41
Jernigan, 1
Jnoson, 68
Joanes, 32, 37, 68
Jobson, 4
Joce, 4
John, 50
Johns, 52, 62, 67, 70, 71
Johnsey, 70
Johnson, 3, 9, 15, *22, *25, *32, *37, 38, *41, 46, 47, 52, 57, 60, 62, 62, *68, 69
Johnston, 8, *45, *50, *51
Jonas, 69
Jones, 1, 3, 23, *25, *28, *29, *32, 37, 38, 39, 41, *50, *51, *57, 64, 68, *69, 70, *71
Jonson, 37, 38
Jordan, *25, 41, 45, 51
Joseph, *41
Joyner, 69
Joynes, 2
Juett, 40
July, 46
Jurdan, *44
Justice, *25, 51
Justis, *45

Kains, 56
Karnes, 56
Kean, *25
Keen, *2, 25
Keene, 4, 69
Keener, 33
Keith, 2
Keizer, 64
Kellam, 32
Kelley, *50
Kelly, *4, 21, 25, 47
Kelp, 47
Kelsy, 1
Kemp, 22, 33, *46
Kenady, 25
Kendall, 22, 25, 37
Kenland, 69
Kennady, *1
Kennedy, 28, 33, 50
Kenney, 45
Kenning, 40
Kenston, 38
Kent, 8
Kenyon, 15
Kerne, 69
Kerr, 50, 51
Kettle, 52
Ketzendanner, 33
Kew, 70
Key, 16, 65
Keyzer, 64
Kiber, 58
Kible, 58
Kid, 70
Kilpatrick, 10
Kimber, 49
Kimbol, *33
Kiney, 50
King, 8, 33, *37, 40, 51, 52, 64, *69, 71
Kinge, 46
Kinkead, 50
Kinkhead, 11
Kinneer, 51
Kinney, 40
Kinser, 29
Kintley, 70
Kipp, 58
Kirk, 8, *25, *51
Kirkpatrick, 25, 50, *51, 52
Kirkwood, 45
Kitchin, 69
Kollock, *57
Knibb, 15
Knight, 69, 70
Knouff, 58
Knowles, 38
Kraft, 34
Kulp, 47
Kurtz, 33
Kylborne, 41

Labold, 41
Labold, 41
Lackland, 57
Lafever, 51
Lafferty, 51
Laffin, 39
Laird, 25
Lake, 55
Lamaster, *52
Lambert, 38
Land, 52
Lane, 38, 39, 52, 55
Langford, 46
Langhorne, 23
Langston, 34
Langley, *25, 71
Larcom, 69
Larkins, 50
Larrom, 69
Lassell, 50
Lathbery, 55
Lathbury, 46
Latimer, *25
Laurence, 50
Lavender, *52
Laverdy, 57
Lawes, 38
Lawey, 37
Lawrence, 7, 9, 23, 33
Lawry, 37
Laws, 55
Lawson, 25, 46
Lay, 34
Layfield, 64
Layton, 10
Lazingby, 37
Lea, *25, 52
Lear, 52
Lee, 1, 9, 13, 16, 28, 37, *47, 55, 57, 65
Leech, 69
Legrand, 22
Lemaster, 49
Lemon, 27
Lenox, 38
Levett, 28
Levy, 10
Lewden, 51
Lewes, *44
Lewing, 28
Lewis, 8, 25, 37, 50, 51, 59, 70
Lewys, 46
Lightbody, 25
Lighthart, 16
Limproott (?), 39
Linch, 50, 56
Lindsey, 47
Linsey, 50
Linthicum, 55
Litler, 25, 26
Little, 7, *24, 26, 46
Littleton, 46
Livingston, 51
Llewellyn, 50
Lobb, 26
Lockart, 45
Locker, 55
Lockey, 65, 68
Lockwood, 32
Loes, 11
Logan, 45
Loker, 55
London, 52, 53
Long, 8, *50, *55
Longe, 50
Longley, 32
Lonton, 46
Lott, 55
Love, 23, 29
Lowdy, 39
Lowe, 55, 56
Lowery, 21
Lowes, 2

Loyd, 37
Lucas, 17, 32
Lucass, 64
Ludlow, 15
Ludwell, 37
Luey (?), 38
Lufbarry (?), 9
Lumnley, 8
Lumpkin, 52
Lunn, 69
Lya, 38
Lyna (?), 38
Lynam, *26
Lynch, 9, 38
Lynd, 37
Lynge, 38
Lynn, 9, 11
Lyon, 35
Lyster, 61

M——(?), 69
M—h, 68
Mabri (?), 38
McAlexander, 29
McBride, 26
McBroom, 56
McCahan, 51
McCalla, 51
McCallister, 50
M'Calmont, 26
McCannon, 45
McCarty, 8, 17
Mace, 32
McClain, 29
McClallen, 1
McClanahan, 47
McClanon, 44
McClay, 52
McClester, 32
McCollum, 26
M'Comb, 26
McCombs, 45
McCorckle, 26
McCormeck, 21
McCormick, 44, 51
Macoy, 69
McCoy, 50
McCrea, 50
McCreaden, 51*
McCreary, 51
McCredie, 10
McCroary, *45
McCroskey, 22
Macubbin, 65
McDaniel, 55
MacDaniell, 15
McDiffit, 10
McDonald, 29, 41, *44, 47, 51
M'Dowel, 26
McDowell, 5, 11
McElwaine, 55
McFann, 50
McGhee, 44
McGillis, 8
McGinnis, 51
McGirth, 10
McGlochlin, 47
McGonigle, 44
McGregor, *44
McIlheron, 51
McIlroy, 51
McIlvee, 45
McIntier, 44
Mackall, 62
Mackbee, 55
McKean, 52
McKee, 44, 51
McKemie, 27
McKenny, 62
McKever, 44
McKewen, 50
Mackell, 46, 55
Mackeri, 69
Mackero, 69
Mackery, 69
Mackey, 49, 52
Mackgraught, 4
McKim, 44
McKinley, 26, *50
McKinly, 52
McKinney, 51
Mackinny, 38
McKnight, 44, 45
Mackubin, 28
Mackwilliam, 37
M'Larry, 26
McLonen, 51, 52
Mack Macols (?), 68
McMahan, 10
McMechen, 51, 52
Macknaroe, 68
McMehen, 45
M'Miskan, 26
McMullen, 44, 50
Macnamre, 55
McPharson, 45
McRea, 51
McWhorter, 40, 44
McWilliam, 51, 52, 57
Maddookes, 55
Maddux, 22
Madox, 64
Magann, 53
Magruder, 28, 32, 41
Maher, 11
Mahoney, 11
Mahoon, 44
A maide servant, 46
Maine (?), 37
Major, 37, 41
Makemie, 64
Malbone, 23
Malcom, 51
Malford, 37
Malin, 69
Malle, 45
Manley, 11
Manneringe, 38
Mansfield, 39
Manton, 39
Mapp, 22
Mardock, 45
Mares, 68
Marish, 37
Marke, 45
Markham, 69
Marks, 53*
Marmaid, 69
Marsh, 39, 41
Marshal, 37, 52, 61
Marshall, *9, 13, *26, 28, *39, *46, 56, 64
Marshell, 45
Marshewell, 45
Marson, 68
Mart, 33
Marten, 4, 26
Martin, 5, *26, 38, 39, *40, 41, 50, 51, 52, 68, *69
Marton, 45
Mason, 8, 14, 16, 17, 55, 68, 69, 70, 71
Massey, 55
Massie, 7
Masters, 68
Mathews, 68
Matthews, 58, *71
Mattrick, 38
Maunbly, 32
Maurice, 68
Mawrice, 51
Maxwell, 11, 52, 57, 71
Maxy, 45
May, 47
Maybry, 34
Maydes, 46
Mayes, 20
Maynard, 35
Mays, *57
Me——dah (?), 38
Mead, 64
Meader, 39
Means, 26
Meares, 55
Mears, 51
Medley, 33
Meers, 21
Mees, 38
Megroah, *4
Mellen, 45
Melson, 34
Mendinghall, 26, 44
Mercer, 11, 44
Merchant, 37

Meriss, 26
Merredeth, 53
Merriken, 55
Merrill, 3
Merryman, 55
Messenger, 38
Metz, 26
Michael, 22, 63
Michaell, 22, 65, 69
Micheel, 67
Michel, 4
Michell, 37
Middah, 58
Middlemore, 49
Middleton, 1, 32, 35
Miers, 33
Milbee, 70
Milby, 4
Miles, 3, 38, 44
Miller, 11, 26, 33, 39, 45, 47, 50, 52, *64, 69
Milles, *4
Milligan, 50
Millner, 26
Mills, 4, 15, *52, *59
Minefrey, 46
Minnet, 53
Minnie, 46
Minor, 50
Minshall, 26
Mison, 38
Mitchell, 1, *34, 55, *64, 71
Mittford, 59
Mockeboy, 47
Molden, 55
Momford, 55
Monro, 52
Montgomery, 29, *44, *45, *51, 55
Montooth, 51
Monts, 70
Moone, 45
Mordock, *45
More, 4, 55, 69
Morgan, 3, 10, 29, 37, *39, 44, *50, 51, *68
Moringstar, 59
Moor, 16
Moore, 1, 26, 27, 29, *38, 44, *45, *50, 51, 69, 70
Moroughew, 45
Morrice, 9
Morris, 4, 37, *56, 57, 58, *68
Morrison, 45, 57
Morriss, 26
Morrow, 45
Mortimer, 10
Mortland, 45
Morton, 26, 45, *51, 52
Mosby, 23, 68
Mosely, 22, 37, 68
Moses, 37, 39
Moss, 9, 16, 62
Mould, 64
Moulson, 69
Mounford, 56
Mountagne, 11
Mountfort, 69
Mountz, 62
Mouse, 58
Moxley, 8
Moyne, 70
Mucgrove, 17
Mudd, 10
Mudge, 37
Muir, 62
Mulatto, 35
Muldroch, 50, 51
Mullen, 38
Mullins, 37, 59
Mumford, 38, 56
Murphy, 9, 28, 51
Murragh, 69
Murray, 10, *11, 55
Murry, 69
Murton, 64
Musgrave, 26, 38
Musgrove, 17
Mussault, 10
Mutton, 17
Myers, 47, 58
Mynshem (?), 45

Nash, 26
Nast, 26
Nation, 8
Neale, 1, 3, 16, 27, 32, *49, *56, *64
Negroes, 7, *10, *35, 37, *46, 64, 67, 68, *69, 70
Nelson, 8, 23, 39, *56
Nesham, 63
Nettles, 1
Nevil, 29
Newby, 22
Newcomb, 57, 69
Newell, 11
Newlin, 26
Newnham, 68
Newman, 2, 46
Newton, 21, 38, 56
Nicholls, 37, 39, *56, 70
Nicholson, 2, 56
Nickoles, 44, 45
Nickols, 26, 56
Niell, 35
Niels, 26
Nielson, 26
Niles, 26
Nivin, 44, 45
Nivins, 50
Nixon, 23
Noble, 35, 45, 49, *56, 63
Noddings, 71
Noffsinger, 56
Noland, 27, 56
Norcross, 32
Norgood, 69
Norman, 59
Norment, 71
Norrington, 2
Norris, 5, 38, 51, *71
Norriss, 58
North, 38, 45
Norton, 46
Nottingham, 59
Nourse, 11
Nowlin, 53
Nuckolls, 71
Nully, 14
Nutty, 14
Nutwell, 56

Oakley, 69
Oanes, 32
Oburn, 51
Odell, 2
Odium, 53
Offitt, 32
Offutt, 41
Ogg, 4
Oglammin, 64
Ogle, 2, 44, *45
Ogles, 26
O'Gullion, 71
O'Hara, 57
O'Keef, 34
O'Kelly, 47
Oldfield, 41
Oless, 19
Omohundro, 11
O'Neal, 34
Oram, 50
Orange, 39
Orbison, 47
Orley, 22
Orrett, 68
Orrill, 13
Osborne, 1, 19, 37
Osburn, 26, 53
Ossett, 69
Outred, 38
Outten, 56
Overall, 9
Overbey, 38
Overcutt, 39
Overton, 16
Owens, 15, 57
Owin, 28, 69
Owins, *69
Oxford, 63

Paca, 28

Packer, 45
Page, 41
Paget, 23
Paine, 37, 39, 41, 45, *46, *68
Painter, 39, 46
Palmer, 38, *39, 41, 56, 57, 68, 70
Pargetor, 68
Parin, 39
Parke, 68
Parker, 4, 5, 9, 13, 21, 26, 28, 38, *39, 40, 45, 55, 56, 62, 64, 69, 71
Parkes (?), 4
Parks, 40, 44
Parkson, 37
Parmane, 50
Parnell, 58, 70
Parram, 37
Parramore, *9, 41
Parrett, 39
Parrey, 46
Parrish, 11
Parrock, 10
Parrot, 55
Parrott, 39
Parry, 26
Parsly, 38, 39
Parson, 68
Parsons, 63
Partner (?), 69
Partride, 38
Partridge, 51
Pasmore, 51
Patch, 15
Paterson, 26
Patrick, 22, 53
Patterson, 32, 34, 44, 45, 52, 58
Pattison, 29, 58
Paul, 10
Paulson, 26
Pawle, 38
Paxson, 71
Paxton, 45
Payle, 68
Payne, 17, 40, 59
Payton, 62
Peach, 22
Peacock, 56
Peale, 56
Peall, *56
Peare, 17
Pearis, 11
Pearre, 1
Pearson, 13*, 28
Peart, 11
Peck, 49
Peele, 28, 37, 68
Peelers, 69
Peeters, 46
Peirce, 69
Peirson, 37
Pembroke, 40
Pencader, 45
Pendleton, 71
Penly (?), 61
Penman, 62
Penn, 52, 53, *57
Pennabaker, 58
Penninger, 59
Penzance, 46
Peram, 37
Percy, 69
Perkenson, 68
Perkins, 2
Perrin, 15, 19, 22
Perry, 2, 56, *69
Persian, 39
Persinger, *11
Person (?), 71
Peterman, 26
Peterson, 26, 38, 39
Petit, 38
Pettway, 20
Petty, 34
Peyton, 10
Phelps, 46
Phillips, 14, 17, 22, 26, 28, 37, *38, 40, *45, 50, 52, *57
Philpot, 70
Phoney, 32
Pickering, 56
Pierce, 26
Pigg, 50
Pigot, 15
Pigott, 71
Pike, 51
Pile, 41
Pine, 39
Pinkard, 38
Piper, 23, 38
Pitman, 19
Pitt, 21, 37, 71
Pleascock, 38
Plowman, 62
Plughrite, 26
Plummer, 37
Plunket, 69
Poe, 29
Pollox, 57
Polly, 11, 59
Polock, 10
Pomphrett, 39
Pool, 35
Pook, 26, 88, *70
Poope, 37
Poore, 38
Pope, 32, 41, 59
Popley, 56
Porter, 3, 13, 26, 28, 38, 40, 41, 46, 49, 50, *51, *52, 56, 70
Posey, 39
Posnett, 39
Post, 51
Potter, 37, 56
Potts, 39
Poulson, 44, 45
Powel, 51
Powell, 1, 2, 23, 26, 27, 28, 34, *37, *39, 40, 47, *52, 55, 68
Power, 49, 63, 69
Powes, 69
Prat—, 39
Prather, 39
Preeson, 14, 21, 22, 62
Prendergast, 70
Prescoate, 38
Prescott, 38
Press, 39
Preston, 37, 49
Prettiman, 46
Price, 11, 16, *37, 39, 50, 51, 56, 64
Pridum, 9
Pridway, 38
Priece, 68
Prince, 39
Prinkstone (?), 58
Printzman, 46
Pririe, 68
Pritchard, 39, 50
Pritchett, 2
Proctor, 10, 40, 41
Pruitt, 56
Prutzman, 46
Pryer, 38
Pryor, 7, *34, 57, 70
Pryse, 37, *38
Puckett, 68
Puddyford, 39
Pullin, 39
Pulman, 37
Puly, 39
Purnell, 9, 17, *56
Pusie (?), 46
Pusey, 50
Pyle, 44, 45, 56

Rabbitt, *32, 34
Raby, 71
Rachina (?), 41
Randall, 71
Randolph, *20, 53
Rankin, 52
Ranshaw, 68
Ranthrew, 45
Rapier, 16
Rasberry, 9
Rashly, 38
Rason, 37
Rawlings, 59, 63, 68
Ray, 38

Rayhus (?), 32
Rayman, 70
Read, 37, *51, 52, *57, *68, *69, 70
Reah, 57
Reams, 56
Reany, 51
Reaper, 50
Red, 7
Redferne, 46
Reding, 46
Redman, 56, 57
Reece, *44, 45
Reekes, 69
Rees, *50
Reese, 34, 37
Reeve, 69
Reeves, 10, 68, 69, *70
Regan, *9
Reid, 39
Reily, 1
Reine (?), 22
Relf, 37
Remsburgh, 33
Remy, 8
Renold, 59
Renolls, 69
Renshaw, 41
Respess, 47
Revell, 37
Reynolds, 26, 44, 45, *51, 59
Rezous (?), 51
Rhoads, *51
Rhodes, 5, 8
Rice, 1, 16, 26, 34, *44, *45
Rich, 26, 68
Richards, 16, 37, 71
Richardson, 11, 26, 49, *52, 53, 57, 67
Richarson. 56
Richey, 44
Richmond, 37, 39
Riddle, 33
Ridge, 45
Ridgeley, *33
Ridgley, 62
Rigby, 50
Rigdon, 32
Riggin, 3
Riggins, 46
Riggs, 61
Riglesworth, 28
Riley, 11, 50
Ripley, 33
Ripp, 58
Rippen, 41
Risding, 68
Risdon, 71
Roach, 56, 64
Roane, 11
Robbeson, 64
Roberdeau, 71
Roberson, 15
Roberts, 21, *38, 41, *46, 53, 69
Robertson, 10
Robeson, *26
Robinett, 11
Robins, 9, 15, 16, 17, 49, *56, 61, 62, 67
Robinson, *1, *5, 7, 14, 15, 16, 22, 23, 26, 44, *45, 50, 51, 67, 69
Robson, 43
Rodds (?), 39
Rodolphus, 23
Rodwell, 26
Roe, 50
Roes, 45
Rogers, 26, 28, 32, 37, 38, 70, *71
Rolph, 49
Rook, 49
Roper, 38
Ropier, 16
Rose, 28, *53
Ross, 52
Rosse, 37, 38
Rosser, 34
Roswell, 38
Rothery, 32
Rouse, 37, 38
Row, 69
Rowlison, 11
Roxby, 38
Royall, 57*
Rucker, 28
Rudder, 39
Ruddock, 39
Rufe, 33
Ruke, 39
Rule, *4, 49
Rumford, *26
Ruse, 69
Russe, 38
Russel, 21
Russell, see Fussell
Russell, 57, 62, 67, 70
Ruston, 71
Ruth, 51
Ryle, 56

S—— (?), 68
Sachell, 46
Sacum, 68
Sadler, 29
Safrell, 38
St. Clair, 40
Salin, 39
Salizbury, 46
Salle, 26
Salter, 69
Sample, 5
Samwayes (?), 69
Sanders, 17, *37, *38, 39, 47, *59, 69
Sandidge, 57
Sankey, 51, 52
Sapscoate, 38
Sargeant, 47
Sarjant, 61
Sarkett, 68
Sarmer (?), 37
Sarson, 38
Satchell, 9
Saunders, 63, 64
Savage, 9, 15, 16, 20, 29
Savory, 46
Sawell (?), 70
Sawyer, 14, 16
Sayer, 14
Sayre, 14
Scabroocke, 39
Scarbraugh, 7
Scarbrough, 39
Scarburgh, 5, 68
Scawen, 38
Schrever, 5
Scot, *69
Scothorn, 26
Scott, 2, 19, *49, *50, 51, 71
Scrudy, 69
Search (?), 33
Searle, 37
Seaward, 61
Seevar, 53
Selby, 13, 28, 32, 41
Self, 33
Semmes, 59
Semple, 5
Sensey, 17
Seton, 38
Settle, 21, *46
Severn, 9
Sewall, 37
Seward, 38
Sewell, 45
Shackells, 46
Shallcross, 26, 34
Shalpe, 37
Shandler, 38
Shannon, 45, 51
Shard, 37
Sharp, 38
Sharpless, 26
Sharry, 49
Shaw, 34, 38, 69
Shealds, 51
Sheals, 29
Sheepart, 57
Shelley, 37
Shepard, 21, 38
Shepherd, 2

Shepherdson, 47
Sheppard, 16
Sherlock, 46
Sherman, 34
Shermon, 56
Shibby, 58
Shields, 58
Shipley, *26, 64
Shockley, 3
Shoemaker, 57
Shone, 69
Shorbar, 39
Shorebury, 37
Short, *45, 51, 68
Shover, 58
Showdall, 38
Shumate, 21
Shutter, 47
Sibsey, 16
Sibthrop, 37
Sidney, 70
Sidnor, 11
Silly, 38
Silsbee, *51, 52
Silver, 33
Silvester, 69
Simmons, 13, 26, 32, 51
Simons, 38
Simpson, 4, 8, 20, 35, 38, 39, 50
Skotower, 39
Slater, 62
Slatter, 68
Slaughter, 11, *15, 19
Sledwell, 37
Sliver, 26
Small, 32, 70
Smallwood, 3, 32, 49
Smart, 5
Smith, 3, 4, 5, 8, 9, 11, 13, 14, 16, *17, 20, *21, 23, *26, 28, 33, *37, *38, *39, 41, *45, *46, *49, 50, *51, *52, *53, *55, 56, *57, *58, 59, 62, 63, *68, *69, 70, 71
Smither, 68
Smithers, 22
Smyth, 11, 27, *45
Sneed, 35
Snider, 58
Soare, 69
Soletree, 37
Somers, 69
Somersett, 61, 69
Sorrell, 35
Sousey, 17
Southhall, 11
Southwell, 9
Sowsey, 17
Span, *19
Sparke, 39
Sparkes, 68
Spaulding, 7, 57
Speed, 69
Spence, 8, 11
Spencer, 23, 38, 45, 51, 52
Speres, 61
Sperry, 26
Spiltimber, 28
Spinse (?), 35
Spliedt, 32
Spockman, 26
Spotswood, 17
Sprigg, 32
Springer, *26, 33, *44, *45
Sprowl, 50
Spurr, 62
Staats, 57
Stacey, 19
Stacy, 26
Stafford, *8, 51
Stainingbrow, 45
Stalcop, 26
Stalcup, 51, 52
Stallings, 38
Stanfford, 46
Stanford, 46
Stanly, 69
Stanton, 37
Stapler, 26
Staples, 39, 52
Stark, 59
Starpe, 69
Starr, 26
Starret, 45
Starrett, 64
Staton, 29
Steal, 17
Stedham, *26
Steed, 69
Steel, 17, 26, 58, 69
Steele, 1
Steephens, *45
Stemcast, 26
Stenson, 70
Stephen, 47
Stephens, 17, *38, 39, 59
Steple, 45
Sterling, 10
Stern, 26
Steuart, 50
Stevens, 3, *46, 64, 68
Stevenson, 39, *46
Steward, 38, 69
Stewart, 4, 40, 41, 45, 46, *51, 55
Stichcomb, 56
Stidham, *51, 52
Stilley, 26
Stilt, 69
Stith, 7
Stitt, 44, 45
Stock, 59
Stockdale, 64
Stoddert, 32
Stokes, 69, 70
Stone, 23, 26, 29, 37, *38, 59, 62, 69, 70
Stoner, 33, 35, 58
Stonestreet, 35
Stoops, *51
Stor, 46
Storie, 51
Storke, 2
Story, 32
Stott, 22, 63
Stowe, 26
Strang, 37
Stratton, 13
Stray, 46
Stringer, 13
Stroake, 69
Strong, *38
Strood, 70
Strother, 9, 59
Stroud, 26, 69
Stuart, 50
Stubbs, 32
Sturges, 56
Suckett, 38, 46
Sullivan, 46
Sumer, 37
Suraez, 61*
Sutherland, 29
Sutten, 39, 50
Sutton, 7, 32
Swan, 11, 19, 39, 45
Swearingen, 41
Sweear, 53
Sweney, 34
Swett, 52
Sykes, 52
Symons, 37

Tabb, 62
Tabirer (?), 71
Tablett, 39
Taft, 68
Talbot, 37, 45, 55
Taliafero, 47
Talin (?), 39
Talliaferro, 57
Tanner, 37, 68, 69
Tanto (?), 69
Tapley, *53
Tapt, 68
Tarlton, 37
Tarp, 69
Tarpley, 39
Tarrance, 50
Tart, 39
Tatlow, 51
Tatnall, 26
Tatum, 39

Taylor, 2, 19, *20, 22, 26, *38, *39, 45, *46, *47, 57, 59, 64
Taylour, 69, *70
Teat, 45
Temple, 39
Templeton, 26
Thatcher, 39
Thelwell, 26
Theobalds, 32
Thomas, 3, 26, *33, 37, *38, 46, *47, *50, 51, 61, *69
Thompson, 1, 13, 14, 26, 28, *32, 38, 41, *44, 45, *46, 49, *50, 51, *52, 53, 62, 69, 71
Thomson, 27
Thorne, 69
Thornton, 38
Thrift, 32
Thrush, 68
Thruston, 10
Thurlot, 69
Thweatt, 34
Thyrold, 46
Tidings, *32
Tillett, 15
Tilley, 27
Tilney, 4
Tilsley, 46
Titus, 23, 51
Tlgner (?), 33
Todnine, 3
Toft, 38
Tomlin, 38
Tomlinson, 26, 53
Tomlyn, 46
Tompkins, 69
Tompson, 39
Townsend, 26, 40, 50, 57, 68
Townshend, 17
Townsing, 55
Tracy, 7, 32
Trail, *41
Travers, 68
Trayhorn, 45
Treddar, 37
Tremgoe (?), 68
Trenow, 61
Trevelion, 4
Trewett, 38
Trewor'gie, 61
Trim, 2
Trip, 26
Triplett, 1, 8
Trippe, 49
Trubshaw, 64
Tryan, 26
Tucker, 20, 46, 47, 65
Tudman (?), 69
Tuley, 22
Tull, 64, 70
Tully, 56, 61
Turbutt, 49
Turfe, 37
Turnell, 38
Turne(r), 34
Turner, 3, 39, 41, 46, 47, 49, 51, 56, 61, 69, 70
Turrey, 47
Turvill, 9, 56
Turvor, 68
Tussey, 26
Twedy, 44, 50
Tweed, 58
Twiggs, 69
Tyler, 4, 39, 63, 64, 70
Tylet, 32
Tyraud, 68

Ubry, 46
Ulry, 46
Underwood, 11, 26, 50
Upton, 39
Urie, 69
Urquhart, 5

Vanderford, 28
Vandergrift, 51
Vandevier, 51
Vaneman, *26
Vangezee (?), 51
Vanluvenigh, *51
Vass, 11, 47
Vaudry, 4
Vaughan, 37, 39
Vaughn, 47, 53
Vause, 28
Veale, 20, 26, 57
Veatch, 33
Venitt, 32
Venne, 37
Verman, 38
Verner, 62
Vert, 26
Vigerous, 63, 64
Vincent, 3, 38, 69
Vines, 47
Voyse, 46

Wade, 35, 59
Wadman, 39
Wagener, 59
Waggaman, 3
Waggoner, 58
Waggt (?), 50
Waid, 37
Waight, 46
Walbroke, 37
Walden, 57
Walford, 37
Walgrave, 46
Walker, 2, 11, 15, *26, *27, 32, 38, *39, 40, 41, 44, 45, 46, 49, 51, 53
Wall, 17
Wallace, 11, 26, *58
Wallas, 15
Waller, 38
Wallis, 50
Walraven, *26, 52
Walsh, 34
Walsingham, 37
Walstone, 64
Walter, 26, 37, 65
Walters, 38, 61
Walthom, 9
Walton, 39
Ward, 4, 5, 38, 68, *70
Warder, 14, 43
Ware, *57, 62
Warhop, 39
Warner, 2, 26, 38, 45, 46, 50, 52, 68
Warren, 37, 38, 46
Wartell, 37
Warter, 69
Warton, 69
Washington, 1, 8, 11, 21, 59, 67
Wastell, 37
Waterford, 39
Waters, 9, 40, 52, 57, 62
Watson, 1, 38, 51, *52, 71
Watt, 26, 44, 49
Watts, 2, 4, 7, 15, 37, 39, 69
Wattson, 70
Way, 26, 44, 45
Ways, 44
Wayt, 50
Weading, 39
Web, 38
Webb, 13, *38, 39, 40, 41, 53
Webley, 39
Webs, 69
Webster, 26, 46
Weekes, 69, 70
Weikert, 34
Weir, 37, 45, 51
Welch, 39
Welldon, 69
Wellfleet, 37
Wells, 7, 28, 32, 33, 34, *38, 41, 46, 47, 68
Welsh, 51, 55
Wenec (?), 38
Wenman, 4
Wenters, 68
Wery, 38
Wesson, 69
West, 4, 9, 21, *26, 37, *38, 39, 47, 57, *64, 68

Westery, 38
Westgate, 38
Westlocke, 38
Whaite, 46
Whann, 51
Wharton, 52
Wheatly, 69
Wheeler, *41, 49, 59
Whitacre, 62
White, 4, 9, 17, 26, 37, *38, *39, *40, 41, 49, 55, 57, 62, 64, 68, 69
Whitelock, 26, 51
Whitfield, 39
Whittington, 28, 32, 55
Whitty, 37, 69
Wickenfield, 68
Wickes, 39
Wickham, 33
Wilcocks, 45
Wilcox, 52, 71
Wiley, 5, 52, 58
Wiliston, 44
Wilkerson, 1
Wilkie, 8
Wilkin, 44, 45, 62
Wilkins, 27, 38, 59
Wilkinson, 1, 38, 46, 69
Willaid, 37
Willey, 26
Williams, 7, 15, 20, 21, 35, *37, *38, *39, 45, *46, 49, 50, *51, 52, 53, 59, 68, *69
Williamson, 13, 15, 44, *46, 59, 69
Willimot, 28
Willinot, 28
Willis, 27, 33, *38, 39, 62, 70
Willit, 22
Wills, 70
Willson, *26, 33
Wilsher, 53
Wilson, 1, 17, 34, *37, 38, 44, *45, 49, *52, 61
Wimmer, 63
Windalls, 26
Winder, 64
Winholtz, 33
Winn, 21, 27
Wirt, *52
Wisenger, 1
Wisinger, 46
Withers, 19
Withey, 38
Witwell, 37
Wolahan, *44
Wolf, 14
Wollaston, *44, *45
Wolton, 39
Wombell, 70
Wood, 11, 17, 23, 26, 27, 33, 37, *38, 52, *69
Woodart, 37
Woodcock(s), 26
Woods, 45
Woodson, 13
Woodward, 26, *38, 39, 52
Woolf, 33
Wordie, 49
Workman, 5
Wormeley, 16
Worthington, 20
Worthy, 68, 69
Wotten, 39
Would, 68
Wren, 59
Wrie, 69
Wright, 15, 17, 23, 38, 39, *45, *53, 59, 68, 69, *70
Wroe, 16
Wyatt, 53, 68, 71
Wyche, 14
Wyn, 39
Wyndham, 11
Wynn, 21
Wynne, 53

Yardley, 22, 67
Yarnall(s), 26
Yarnel, 44
Yates, 52
Yeatman, 26
Yenglin, 58
Yeo, 3
Yeow (?), 70
Young, 8, 10, *37, *38 45, *69
Younge, 46
Youngman, 39

Zaumeyer, 34
Zerich, 33

Ancestral Proofs & Probabilities

An Occasional Bulletin

Number One

ADVERTISEMENT

Some twelve years ago I found that I had accumulated a great amount of material in the form of brief abstracts from the records of the circuit or county courts, and from archival and other respositories. There was so much of this material and it was doing so little good to any one, especially to the collector, that it seemed a pity not to give it out in some form. Of course, after the collector's death it would be open to limited research, but it looked as if even that might be rather far ahead. So I started the COUNTY COURT NOTE-BOOK, sincerely desiring to be of some use to my countrymen, three-quarters of whom____or at least their sisters, or their cousins or their aunts____appeared to be extremely desirous to know more about their ancestry.

So I started the NOTE-BOOK. It was a foolish thing to do, and it began wrong with its name. For its editor had no idea that the old county court, so real to her, with its friendly Clerks, its terribly dusty volumes, its open fires and its draughty doors, but with so priceless a mass of records____the editor had no idea that this meant nothing to many readers, unless it might be a suggestion of criminal causes or mortgages upon their real estate.

There were other mistakes, but in spite of them the NOTE-BOOK came into existence and has been kept going for ten yeaers____ counting by volumes. It was hard work, and if "financial returns" are a measure of success, there was no success. But I, the editor (and everything but the printer) grew very fond of my NOTE-BOOK and there have been quite a number of subscribers who have written to me so encouragingly, that *sometimes* I thought my work was quite worth while. Besides, there was no easy way to stop off. Thousands of marriage references, testimony as to Revolutionary service, hundreds of references to the migrations of our restless colonials, and many quaint items from the county courts illustrating so clearly the mind and manners of our early days.

However, the difficulty of publication became too great, so the C. C. N-B. has been withdrawn from circulation. But as much material remains as has been published, and it still seems in the compiler's considerate judgment, to be as valuable as ever, so this Occasional Bulletin is projected in order to use up that surplus. If my readers are willing to pay for publication this first number will be followed by others, not only of the two thousand marriages which remain, but a really important ALPHABET OF DAVISES. Your approval is awaited.

For details of subscription, see page 20.

MARRIAGE REFERENCES

(*See explanatory note on page* 20.)

WILLIAM ADAMS and ANN LAWYER. Before 19 Aug 1755 and after Jany 1739. Staff., Va. P-71. (See also p. 68.)

WILLIAM ADAMS, son of John of Frederick cty, Va., and LYDIA MALIN, dau. of Isaac, same cty, at Hopewell Meeting, Va. 7-18-1771, Mtg records, p. 26.

Capt. WILLIAM AYLETT and ANN ASHTON, dau. of Henry, of Cople Psh, Wmld. Before 26 Feby 1730. Ffx, Va. L. C.

MOSES BALL, Jr. and MARY ANN HARDEN, dau. of William. Before 29 Jany 1791. Ffx, Va. T-148.

Capt. RICHARD BALL and SARAH, extx of Capt. Wm. *Howson*. Before 13 Mch 1702. Nthld, Va. 1699-1713, p. 244.

______BALL and REBECCA HUGHES, dau. of Thomas. Before 30 Nov 1778. Alb, Va. ii-371.

BENJAMIN BALLARD (of Spots, Va.?) and ELIZABETH STRAUGHAN. Prob. before 1800. U. S. Pension W6162.

Mr. JOHN BALLENDINE and MARY BLACKBURN, dau. of Richard. Before 12 July 1757. Pr. Wm, Va. L. C. [2]-361.

JAMES BANKS and MASON CALVARY. 6 Nov 1797. Ogleth. cty, Ga.

ROBERT BARRETT and the relict and admx of RICHARD BANKES, late of Md. Before 11 Feby 1691. Staff, Va. Orders i-218.

Mr. JOHN BAYLIS, of Pr. Wm, and JANE BLACKBURN, dau. of Richard. Before 12 July 1757. Pr. Wm., Va. L. C. [2]-361.

JAMES BELL and MARTHA MARKS, admx of Edward. Before 14 June 1715. Pr. Geo. cty, Va. Orders, p. 16.

JAMES BELL prob. m. MARTHA SANTOM, sister of William. It is also probable that she m. MARKS. See 31 Dec 1716. Pr. Geo. cty, Va. Large vol. p. 162.

______BENNETT and ANN McCARTY, dau. of Daniel, of Lincoln cty, N. C. Before 14 Aug 1782. Richm'd, Ga. Wills A-33.

WILLIAM BENTON and CHARITY ROCHESTER, dau. of Francis. Before 31 Oct 1783. Q. A., Md. O. C. Minutes.

FRANCIS BERRYMAN and ELIZABETH-NEWTON BARR, dau. of William. Before 10 July 1794. Pr. Wm, Va. Y-603.

THOMAS BEVILL and ELIZABETH CUNNINGHAM. 26 Nov 1807. Elbert, Ga. Reg. Book B.

HENERY BEWFORD and MARY OSBORNE, eldest dau. of Henry. [The signature of BEWFORD is *"boford."*] 5 Apr 1708. Middx, Va. iv-179.

CHARLES BINNS, Gent., of Ldn, and ANN ALEXANDER, dau. of John, "the Eldest." Before or about the 7 Apr 1760. Ldn, Va. B-49.

RICHARD BLACKBURN, Sr., Pr. Wm, and MARY ASHTON, wid. of Henry of Wmld, Gent. Before 11 Dec 1754. Pr. Wm, Va. L. C. p. 128.

JOHN BLAIR and NANCY THORNHILL. 2 June 1798. Bourbon, Ky. M. L. B.

HUGH BLAIR and JEMIMAH McCARTY, dau. of Dan'l of Lincoln cty, N. C. Before 14 Aug 1782. Richmd cty, Ga. Wills A-33.

JACOB BLITHE, St. Paul's Psh, Hanover cty, and MARY ANN PARKER, widow, same. 8 May 1787. Mar. contract "in solemn conformation." Hanover, Va. [ii] p. 221.

SION BOONE and GILLY HAWKINS. Prob. 1802. Greene cty, Ga. Mar. List.

JAMES BRAY and MOURNING PETTUS, wid. of Thomas. Before 24 May 1698. York, Va. 1694-1702, p. 31[?]

JOHN BRENTON and ANN SHAD. 1788. Mercer, Ky. M. L. B.

SAMUEL BRENTON and MARGARET COOLEY. 5 Aug 1789. Mercer, Ky. M. L. B.

WILLIAM BRENTON and FANNY WILEY. 7 June 1794. Bourbon, Ky. M. L. B.

WILLIAM BRINTER [BRINTON?] and FANNY WILLEY. 9 June 1794. Bourbon, Ky. Mar. Ret. [*This is very evidently the same two persons as in the preceding item, but from another record.*]

ROBERT BURTON and LYDIA CLABORN. 13 Mch 1798. Ogleth., Ga.

ROBERT BURTON of Edgefield, S. C., and PARTHENA GREEN, of Richmond cty, Ga. 4 Nov 1794. Richmd, Ga. Minutes A-47. (Mar. Li.)

WILLIAM BURTON and NANCY HUGHS. 25 Aug 1804. Ogleth, Ga.

______BUSH prob. m. ELIZABETH FEW, dau. of Wm. FEW, Sr. Before or about 16 Aug 1792. Wilkes, Ga. KK-135.

WILLIAM BUTLER and PRISCILLA COBB, both of Richmd cty. 4 Jany 1796. Richmd, Ga. Minutes A-187.

THOMAS BUTLER, Mcht, and MARGARET COOPER, dau. of Annanias COOPER Mcht, of Augusta. 3 Apr 1794. Richmd, Ga. Minutes A-165.

Mr. JOHN CAREY of GLOUCESTER cty, and ANN BLACKBURN, dau. of Richard. Before 12 July 1757. Pr. Wm, Va. L. C. [2]-361.

HENRY CARTER, of Kent cty, and SARAH, "relique" of John EVANS. Before 25 Aug 1684. Kent, Md. "K"-75.

JNO. CARTRIGHT and MARTHA McHAY[?] 23 June 1800. Greene, Ga. Mar. Li.

PETER CARTRIGHT, Jr., and BETSY SHAW. 29 Jany 1801. Greene, Ga. Mar. Li.

WILLIAM CHESNUT and CATHERINE CALLAHAN, dau. of Daniel. See Ct 27 Apr 1779. Rock'm, Va. Minute Book.

EDWARD COALMAN, of Westbury, Glouc, cty, founder, and ELIZABETH GWYNNE, of Bristol, widow. About 4 Dec 1726. Essex, Va. xx-241.

WILLIAM COLBERT and MARTHA CLARK. 24 Jany 1813. Elbert, Ga. Mar. List.

PETER COOKE, of Fleet street, London, Tinman, and MARY WELCH. Before 24 Feby 1735. Essex, Va. xxi-190.

ROBERT COOK and RACHEL COOK. 1802. Bulloch, Ga. Mar. Li.

______COOPER and ELIZABETH ARRELL, dau. of Richard. Before Oct Ct, 1805. Pr. Wm, Va. [2]-106.

CHARLES W. CHRISTIAN and NANCY RUFF. 6 June 1806. Elbert, Ga. Mar. Reg.

ISHAM CLEMENTS and HANNAH MORROW. 20 Dec 1796. Ogleth, Ga.

JNO. COLEMAN and POLLY WALKER, dau. of Henry G. WALKER. Before 1 Nov 1804. Elbert, Ga. Inventories, &c.

JAMES COLLINS and PENELOPE BAZEMORE. 11 Nov 1801. Bulloch, Ga. Mar. Li.

"ANGIS" DAGGS and MARY HILL. About 1807. Kanawha, W. Va. Mar. Ret.

DENTON DANIEL and LYDDY JONES. 10 Feby 1806. Greene, Ga. Mar. List.

SANDARS DARBY and NAOMI [WOOLF] sister of William. Before 16 Sept 1759. Sussex, Dela. B2-194.

WAUGH DARNALL prob. m. ANNA PRICE, dau. of Calem. Before 23 June 1777. See S. L. O. Va. Q-153.

WILLIAM DAVENPORT and MARGARET TAYLOR. 10 May 1785. Jeff'n, Ky. Mar. Li.

OBEDIAH DAVISSON and MARY WEBB, dau. of Thomas. Before 17 June 1780. Hamp., W. Va. ii-346.

JACOB DAWS and MARY McGUIRE. 20 Dec 1800. Chowan, N. C. H-316.

JOSEPH "D BIGNON" and MARIE C. A. DUGAS. 24 Apr 1810. Richmond, Ga. Mar. Li. (Mar. 26 Apr 1810.)

NATHANIEL DEEBLE, Jr., of Plymouth, G. B., Joyner and JUDITH PICKAS, dau. of Isaac, late of Plimouth, Grocer. Before 4 Nov 1727. Essex, Va. xviii-363.

MATTHIAS DENMAN (b. Springfield, N. J., 19 Feby 1751), and PHEBE BALDWIN. [*Circa* 1772] Wis. Hist. Soc. Draper 8CC-19.

______DENNIS and ANN, the extx of Thos. BANKS of Calv. cty. 19 Mch 1686. Annap. T. P. xiii-465.

JOHN DENTON and the widow of Richard LOCKHART. Before 1 Jany 1811. Hancock, Ga. Gdn's Bk B-29.

VALENTINE W. DEVORIX and MARY BUTCHER, admx of James. Before 7 June 1828. Q. A. Md, O. C. Records.

JONAS DEVENPORT and MARY THEOBALD. Nov 1788. Bourbon, Ky. Mar. Ret.

RICHARD DAVENPORT and ELIZABETH TADLOCK. 21 Jany 1798. Mercer, Ky. M. L. B.
JOHN DEVINPORT [sig. DEAVEPORT] and JOANNA CRUTCHFIELD. 18 Apr 1800. Mercer, Ky. M. L. B.
WILLIAM DAVENPORT and ELIZABETH McAFEE. 16[13?] May 1796. Mercer, Ky. M. L. B.
ISAAC DEVOU and SARAH LAIRD. Before July 1788. N. C. cty, Dela. 1A-1779.
WILLIAM DILLWIN and SARAH FULLER. Before or about 1692. Penna. Arch. Ser. 3, i-45.
ANDRIAS DIRRICKSON prob. m. TEMPERANCE HOPKINS, dau. of Samuel, Sr. Before 6 June 1719. Som., Md. CH-2.
JOHN DIXON and MARGARET JAQUET. Before Jany 1789. N. C. cty, Dela. A1____.
JOHN DIXSON, of Mill Creek, and REBECCA COX, at Hockessing Mtg. 1742. Chester cty, Penna., Mtgs. iii-26.
WILLIAM DOUGHTER and MARTHA NORSWORTHY. 3 Sept 1806. Greene, Ga. Mar. Ret.
______DOWELL and ELIZABETH, admx of John ANDERSON. Before 23 Nov 1761. Pr. Wm, Va. Orders [4]-33.
MATTHEW DRIGGON and MARY CRAFFORD. 18 June 1795. Bulloch, Ga. Mar. Li.
EDWARD DUDDLESON and MARY VAULX, extx of Robt. Before 31 May 1688. Wmld, Va., Orders 1676-1688, p. 650.
ISHAM DUKE and ELIZABETH SHERREL. Oct 1806. Greene cty, Ga. Mar. Li.
NATHAN DUNGAN and LUCY JONES. 3 Oct 1798. Mercer, Ky. M. L. B.
WILLIAM DUNLAP and KATHARINE WALLACE, dau. of Thomas. Before 28 Mch 1755. Wor, Md. C-302.
BROWN DYE and POLLY MARTIN. 23 Apr 1809. Elbert, Ga. Mar. List.
AARON EBORN and a dau. of John SATCHWELL, Sr. Before 23 Mch 1820. Beaufort, N. C. A-304. [The spelling of this man's name varies and should be looked for also under "A".]
MELCHIOR EBRIGHT and HANNAH DERRICK, dau. of Zacheriah. Before 6 Mch 1822. Dela. cty, Penna. R2-7.
JOHN ECKLEY and SARAH BURGE, wid. of John. After 1681 and before 5th mo. 23d 1705. Penna. Arch. ser. 2, xix-459.
ARNOLD EDGAR and HILLARY WALLACE, dau. of Aaron. Before 27 Mch 1799. Dor., Md. Proc. H. D. xiii-257.
JOHN EDWARDS and MARY COMBS, Wash'n cty, Md. 25 Apr 1799. Semmes Mss. M. H. S.
______ELISON and ISABEL [ISEABLE] BIRD, wid. of Thomas. [Her signature ("cross mark") is ELIZABETH.] Before 28 Sept 1750. Cecil cty, Md. vii-260.
JOS. EDWARDS and MARY HICKMAN. Before 28th 11th 1705. Penna. Arch. Ser. 2. xix-458.
ISRAEL ELLIOTT and NANCY SHORT. Before 1793. N. C. cty, Dela. N1-349.
JOSEPH ELSBURY and ANN SMITH. 9 Feby 1797. Ogleth., Ga. Mar. Li.
Mr. WILLIAM ELIZEY, Pr. Wm, and ALICE BLACKBURN, dau. of William. Before 12 July 1757. Pr. Wm, Va. L. C. [2] p. 361.
ENOCH EMBRY and BECKAH HARTSFIELD. 7 Nov 1798. Ogleth., Ga.
M______EMBRY and VINEY HOWARD. 1 Dec 1804. Ogleth., Ga.
CORNELIUS ENNIS and ELIZABETH SMITH, dau. of Edward. Before 25 Mch 1728. Som., Md. S.H.-29.
JAMES ENSOR and REBECCA DARNALL, wid. of John. Before 9 July 1666. Semmes Mss. M. H. S.
ISAAC EVANS and MARTHA WORTHINGTON, dau. of Robert. Before 31 Mch 1786. S. L. O. Va. W-260.
SAMUEL EVANS and MARY FORMAN. 1793. Bourbon, Ky. Mar. Ret.
______EVERETT and MARY JONES, dau. of Bridges JONES. Before 20 Apr 1819. Bulloch, Ga. B-42.
JOSHUA EVERITT and JANE CARTER. 7 Oct 1797. Bulloch, Ga. Mar. Li.
JOSEPH FARES [FERRISS?] and JUDY JOHNS. 26 Jany 1778. Cumb., Va. Orders, p. 423.
SAMUEL FARME [FARMER] and MARY WOOLEN, wid. of Joseph. Before 31 July 1741. Philada. O. C. 1716-1755, p. 222. P H. S.
JOHN FENDALL, Gent., Chase. Cty, Md. and ELIZABETH MARSHALL, widow of William. Before 3 May 1728. Semmes Mss. M. H. S.
BARNARD FEILDER and ELIZABETH, ext of John MARREAN. Before 30 Jany 1733. Wmld, Va. Orders, fo. 124.
BENJAMIN FIELDS and MARY STAATS. Before 3 May 1833. N. C. cty, Dela. Q4-234.
MICHAEL FINLEY and AGNES KENNEDY, dau. of David. Before 9 Mch 1773. Chester cty, Penna. Abstracts of will at P. H. S.
JOHN FISHER and SARAH PARKER, dau. of Anderson FISHER. Before 9 May 1759. Sussex, Dela. B2-299.
CHARLES FITZGEFERIS *went over St. Mary's River, to "St. Enegoes" to be married to one* ANN TOWNSEND. About 1695. Annap. Md. P. L. 6-265.
JOHN T. FITHUGH and MARGARET FOOTE. Before 30 Oct 1799. Pr. Wm, Va. Lup'r. Ct, p. 249.
JOHN FLEMING and LUCY DONALDSON. 16 Jany 1783. Fayette, Ky. Entries.
HENRY FLETCHER and SARAH EVERITT. 10 Mch 1804. Bulloch, Ga. Mar. Li.
RICHARD FLINT and MARY, relict and admx of John REMY. Before or 28 May 1745. Wmld, Va. Orders, fo. 73.
______FOOKS and SARAH ROACH, dau. of William. Before 4 Mch 1767. Wor., Md. J. W. iii-162.

WILLIAM FORMAN and CATHERINE PARKER, dau. of John. 11 May 1779. Hamp. W. Va. v-32.

______FOSSETT and RODIAH, admx of John CROPPER. Before 12 Jany 1687. Som, Md. A. W.-26.

WILLIAM FOOKS of Acco., Va., and MARY FOSTER, Jr., of Dor., Md. 2-6th-1704. Third Haven Friends' Mtg. iii-4.

ROGER FOUNTEYNE transp. MARY WHITE, his, wife, about 15 June 1658. L. Norf, Va. D-149.

ARCHIBALD FOWLER and REBECCA GOODING, dau. of John, Esq. Before 1767, N. C. cty, Dela. Y1-581.

GEORGE FISHPOOL and MARY, extx of John SPICER, Gent. Before 7 Apr 1739. K. Geo, Va. Oii-150.

______FRANKLIN and TABITHA PEALL, dau. of Thomas. Before 13 Feby 1742. Wor, Md. J. W. ii-15.

BARNET FRANKLIN and MARY CLEAVELAND, dau. of Col. CLEAVELAND Before 1800. Wis. Hist. Soc. Draper XNN-110.

SAMUEL FRAZER and ELEANOR ROBINSON, dau. of Andrew. Before 25 Aug 1812. Ohio cty, W. Va. Wills ii-37.

JAMES FRENCH and KEZIAH CALLAWAY, at Boonesborough, Vy. 27 June 1783 W.H. S. Draper 12CC-201-10.

EDWARD FRETWELL and MARY HOWARD, dau. of John. Before 29 Jany 1728. Philada. O. C. p. 38. (P. H. S.)

RICHARD FRY and CHRISTIAN MONROE, relict and admx of Andrew. Before or about 30 Aug 1743. Wmld, Va. Orders, fo. 2. Before 28 Apr 1741. See Orders, fo. 97. Also fo. 26. [*Note: There are several references as to the FRY marriage and it is uncertain whether he married the widow of Andrew or the widow of Spence. See Fid. Accts, i-299 and Orders fo. 282. The latter makes the marriage before 29 Aug* 1738.]

JOHN FULLERTON and SUSANNAH SMITH. About 1796. Kanawha, W. Va.

MOSES GALLOWAY and PAMELIA OWINGS. Before 13 Feby 1788. Admn Accts, Balto, Md. ix-153.

WILLIAM GARNETT and SARAH BYRNES, dau. of James. Before 17 May 1778. Q. A., Md. T. W. i-33.

RICHARD GASLE and TABITHA, the extx of John VENNABLE. Before 19 Jany 1736. Som, Md. E. B. 12-153

GEORGE GELASPIE and HANNAH JONSON, dau. of William. Before 1768. N. C. cty, Dela. Surveys, 221.

JOHN GIBSON and MARY CONNER. 7 Jany 1808. Fayette, Ky. Mar. Ret.

SAMUEL GIBSON and ISABELLA ROGERS, dau. of Hamilton and "Ezebel." 25 July 1796. Bourbon, Ky. M. L. B.

ISAIAH GIBSON and LYDIA WHITE. 20 Nov Prob. 1802. Greene cty, Ga. Mar. List.

DAVID GIBSON and POLLY MORROW. 4 Jany 1805. Fayette, Ky.

GEORGE GIBSON and ELIANOR ELLIOT, of Octorora. 17 Aug 1792. Presbyt. Hist. Soc. Journal, viii-343.

THOMAS S. GILKEY and GRACE FORMAN. 19 Nov 1798. Bourbon, Ky. Mar. Ret.

WILLIAM GLASS and SALLY WHITE, dau. of Joseph. Before 17 Aug 1801. Greene cty, Ga. D______.

______GODWIN and MARY WEST, dau. of George. Before 25 Jany 1755. Wor, Md. J. W. iii-17.

WILLIAM GOFF and NAOMI CARTER. 30 Nov 1807. Bulloch, Ga. Mar. Li.

HOWES GOLDSBOROUGH, of Cambridge Town, Md., Prsct's in Physick, and MARY McMULLAN, one of the daus. of James. 23 Mch 1797. Kent. Dela. F-71.

THOMAS GOLDSBOROUGH of Duck Crk, hd, and RACHEL CLARK, dau. of David. Before 30 Jany 1775. N. C. cty, Dela. B2-390.

JAMES GOOLSBY and NANCY MATTHEWS, by Rev. Benj. Coleman. 18 Apr 1782. Amherst, Va.

THOMAS GORE prob. m. ANN OSBOURN, dau. of John. Before 30 Sept 1786. Ldn, Va. Will C-244.

ALEXANDER GORGES and MARY VAULX, widow of Robert. Before 24 Nov 1686. Wmld, Va. 1676-1688, p. 525. She was also widow of Edward Duddleston, and seems to have also m. Caleb Butler!

WILLIAM GOTT and MARY TURVILL, sister of John. Before 7 Mch 1753. Wor, Md. J. W. iii-20.

SAMUEL GOULD and CHARLOTTE HACKETT, dau. of James. Before 5 Nov 1803. Q. A. W. H. N. iv-240.

SILAS GRACE and ELIZABETH LOCKHART, dau. of Richard. Before 20 May 1826. Hancock, Ga.

ROBERT GRAHAM and ELIZABETH COX, widow of Zachariah. 19 Sept 1744. Philada. O. C. Records, p. 222. (P. H. S.)

JOHN GRANT and MARGARET, extx of William STROTHER. Before 7 Apr 1739. K. Geo, Va. ii-150.

Mr. GEORGE GRAY nad MARY [STROTHER], sister of James STROTHER. Before 5 Feby 1764. Staff, Va. O-464.

PHILLEMON GREEN and ELIZABETH HACKETT, dau. of Thomas. Before 1 Feby 1760. Q. A., Md. W. H. N. i-235.

JACOB GREEN and ANN STAATS, dau. of Jacob. Before 1809. N. C. cty, Dela. Hiii-407.

THOMAS GREEN, of Eliz. River, L. Norf, Pltr. and JANE HARVEY wid. of Nicholas, of Patuxent, Md., pltr. Before or about 20 Aug 1657. Md. Arch ix-291.

RICHARD GREEN and MARGARETT HUMPHREY, Sr., dau. of Thomas and Mary. Before or about 8 Aug 1715. Som, Md. A. C. (12) 316.

WILLIAM GREENE and ELIZABETH MANLOVE, relict of Marke MANLOVE. Before 13 June 1677. Som, Md. L (7) p. 115.

DAN'L GREEN and MARY CHAMBERLAIN, dau. of Robert. Before 1 Apr 1786. Chester cty, Penna. Will Abstracts. P. H. S.

WILLIAM GREENSTED and ELIZABETH KEY. Published intention of mar. [She was perhaps widow of John.] 21 July 1656. Rappa, Va. 1st vol, p. 85. [For interesting data as to who she was, see record.]

JOHN GREGG and ANN HUGHES. 1787. Bourbon, Ky. Mar. Ret.

WILLIAM GREGORY and CAROLINE MUSE, dau. of George Augustine MUSE. Before 14 Nov 1792. K. Geo, Va. vii-418.

WILLIAM GRIGSBY and ELIZABETH SMITH, widow. Before 23 Apr 1828. Fauq., Va. x-386.

WILLIAM x GRIGSBY, Overwharton psh, Staff., and URSLEY [URSULA] MANN, dau. of James. Before 16 Dec 1640. Pr. Wm, Va. E-265.

THOMAS GRINAN and MARY HACKLEY, widow of Joseph. Before 27 Nov 1752. Pr. Wm, Va. Orders [i] p. 75.

WILLIAM GROVE and ELIZABETH DUNN, dau. of John and Jane. Before 30 Aug 1738. Wmld, Va. Orders, fo. 285.

BENJAMIN GRUBB and LYDIA LARKIN, dau. of John. Before 23 June 1786. Chester cty, Penna. Wills. iii2-42. P. H. S.

EDWARD GUPHILL [?] and ELIZABETH FORMAN, wid of Banj. the younger. Before 22 June 1769. Berkeley, W. Va. 11-156.

GEORGE NICHOLAS HACK and ANNE WRIGHT, dau. of Mr. Richard WRIGHT. Before 5 Feby 1694-5. S. L. O. Va. ii-121.

JAMES HAILES and BETSEY HAILES. 13 Aug 1802. Ogleth, Ga.

CHRISTOPHER HAILES and BETSY OR BETEY BORGAN. 7 Apr 1794. Ogleth, Ga. M. L. B.

JOHN HAILES and POLLY MARTIN. 9 Feby 1802. Ogleth, Ga.

OBED HAILES and MILLY HAILES. 3 Dec 1801. Ogleth, Ga.

WILLIAM HASLE and the relict of Thomas SHORT. About 2 Sept 1685. Essex, Va. Orders, p. 160.

JOSEPH HADNOT and ELINDER WHITEHURST. Mar. contract. 24 Nov 1792. Onslow, N. C. Loose leaf of deed book.

CHARLES HAIRSHAW and REBECAH, extx of Hampton ROBINSON. Before 6 Feby 1776. S. L. O. Va. Files.

WILEY HALES and JANE BUCKHANNON. 15 Mch 1810. Elbert, Ga. Mar. List.

HENRY HALL and LEVITY ROYALL. 5 Mch 1816. Elbert, Ga. K-310.

JOSEPH HALL and MARY FISHER, widow of Joseph. Before 11 June 1734. Philada. O. C. 1716-1755, p. 246. P. H. S.

AQUILA HALL, Gent. and ______ PHILLIPS, wid. of James, the younger. Before 8 Oct 1724. Md. Arch. xxxv-93.

SAMUEL HALL and SARAH WARNER, widow of John, son of Isaac. Before 7 Dec 1753. Philada. O. C. 1716-1775, p. 348. P. H. S.

WILLIAM HALL and SALLY SASNETT, dau. of Rich'd; niece of Benj. I. I. Borden and gr. dau. of Joseph Borden. Before 31 Jany 1816. Hancock, Ga. B-47.

JOHN HAMMON and POLLY HARRINTON. 26 Jany 1808. Lincolnton, Ga. Mar. Ret.

ANDREW HAMPTON and MARY DASSEY or DESSY. About 4 Apr 1797. Jefferson cty, Ga. p. 20 of damaged volume.

PRESTON HAMPTON and ELIZABETH CONNER, wid. of Charles. Before 11 Jany 1796. Ldn, Va. [Pckge of old papers.]

GEOR. HANKES and JANE BARECROFT. Before 25 Oct 1702. Nthld, Va. Orders iv-225.

______ HANSON and ELIZABETH WARREN, widow. Before 1763. S. L. O. Va. D. D. 2, p. 409.

JOSHUA HARP and SARAH NEWSOM, widow of John. About 1805. Warren, Ga. Minutes.

JOHN HARPER and MARY CUNNINGHAM. Mar. contract proved by the affirmation of James Lownes. Ct. 19 July 1790. Ffx, Va. Orders, 1789-1791.

GIDEON HARRINGTON and ANN MERRICK. Before 28 May 1772. Annap. Accts. lxvi-355.

NATHAN HARRINGTON and ELIZA: HARRINGTON, dau. of William of Q. A. Before 28 May 1772. Annap. Accts. lxvi-355.

HENRY HARRIS and LUCINDA PITMAN. 28 Apr 1814. Madison, Ga.

JOHN HARRIS and MARY BENNETT. Before 14 Nov 1691. Som, Md. B. W. 2-144.

MATTHEW HARRIS and NANCY COLEMAN, dau. of Clayton. Before 3 July 1797. Richmond, Ga. F2-539.

JOHN HARRIS and POLLY HARRIS COLEMAN, dau. of Clayton. Before 3 July 1797. Richmond, Ga. F2-539.

WILLIAM LEA HARRIS and ELIZABETH COLEMAN, dau. of Clayton. Before 3 July 1797. Richmond, Ga. F2-359.

WILLIAM HARRIS and *Madea* NORTCUTT [Probably this name is incorrectly written.] 2 Feby 1796. Ogleth, Ga.

JESSE HARRIS and RACHEL PENDLETON. 12 Dec 1789. Greene, Ga. Mar. Li.

WILLIAM HARRIS and HAN. HOGG. 23 Aug 1786. Greene, Ga. Mar. Li.

Capt. S. B. HARRIS and PATIENCE WILLIAMS. 9 Dec 1794. Green Ga. Mar. Li.

JOHN HARRIS and JOANNAH GRAGG [prob. GREGG.] 22 Jany 1809. Elbert, Ga. Reg. Bk B.

ANDREW HARRISON, Washington psh, Wmld, and MARY ROSIER, widow of John. Before 25 May 1715. Wmld, Va. v-455.

GEORGE HARRISON and BRIDGETT RUST, widow of Samuel. Before 27 May 1746. Wmld. Va. Fid Accts i-332.

CUTHBERT HARRISON and the widow of Thomas OSBORNE. Before 22 Oct 1750. Pr. Wm, Va. L-119.

JAMES HARRISON and MARY TOLSON, admx of James. Before or about 19 Jany 1828. Q. A., Md. O. C. Minutes.

JOHN HARRISON and JUDITH GODFREY. Bans of matrimony. 3 Feby 1668. Som, Md. D. T. (7)-68.

Mr. RICHARD HARRISON and MARY MORRIS, extx of Thomas. Before 5 Feby 1788. A. A cty, Md. Distributions, p. 1.

ROBERT HARRISON and the relict of John DISHMAN. Before Ct of 25 Oct 1743. Wmld, Va. Orders, fo. 3.

JAMES HARROD and ANN McDONALD. Before 23 Feby 1780. Fayette, Ky. Preemption Bk i-398. [About 1778?]

MOSES HART and ZILLY HORN. 22 Aug 1812. Bulloch, Ga. 22 Aug 1812. Mar. Li.

RICHARD HARRISON and ELIZABETH HALL, widow of Richard. 7-3-1695. Cliffe's Mtg, Md. p. 20.

RICHARD HARRISON and ELIZABETH PENN of Chas. cty. Before 4 Mch 1758. S. L. O. Md. T. P .xxxvii-48.

JOHN HART prob. m. SARAH HINCKLEY, dau. of Elnathan. Before 7 May 1754. Sussex, Dela. See I9-34.

Mr. ARCHIBALD HATCHER and the widow of Henry ARINTON. Dept 1795. Richmond, Ga. Minutes. She seems to have been MARY BUGG, a widow, who m. Henry ARRINGTON in 1792.

WILLIAM HARWOOD and REBECCA, the admx of Francis MORECOCK. Before 17 Nov 1740. York, Va. xviii-652.

ANDREW HAYNES and "ANNIE" EATON, dau. of William. Before 19 Feby 1759. Raleigh, N. C. Wills.

______HAYNIE and MARGARET DISKIN, dau. of John. Before 4 May 1762. Pr. Wm, Va. [4]-1762.

WILLIAM HAYS and SUSAN BOONE, dau. of Daniel. See Draper 12CC-44. Wis, Hist. Soc.

______HAZARD and ANN CORD, dau. of William. Before 19 Nov 1759. Wor, Md. J. W. iii-19.

URIAH HEADY and SCARBOROUGH ("SCARBRAY") COPES, dau. of Sarah. Before 24 Oct 1803. Cartaret, N. C. O-377.

NICHOLAS HEDRICK and RACHEL HOLDEN, dau. of Joseph. Prob. Before 1700. N. C. cty, Dela. E-64.

THOMAS HELM and JANE, dau. of WARDEN POPE. See record 23 Feby 1762. Wmld, Va. Inv. iv-183.

JOHN HAMMONS and ELIZABETH [LEATHERBURY?] dau. of Diana. Before 8 Oct 1773. Sussex, Dela. B2-506.

PETER HENDRICKSON and MARY LAIRD, admx of James. Before July 1788. N. C. cty, Dela. A1.

SAM HENDERSON and BETSY CALLOWAY. About 1776. Draper Mss. NN10. Wis. Hist. Soc.

JOHN HENDLEY and ELIZABETH COWARD. 16 July 1798. Bulloch, Ga. Mar. Li.

JOHN HENDRICKSON, of Philada., shipwright, and FRANCES BEZOR, dau. of John. Before 26th 12th 1704. Penna. Arch Ser. 2, xix-449.

PHILEMON HEMSLEY and MARY CONTEE, extx of Col. John. Before 10 May 1715. Md. Arch xii-139.

JOHN HENRY of Poco., Som. and MARY, extx and admx of Col. FRANCIS JENCKINE. [Date?] Som, Md. C. D. (10)-614.

HENEAGE HERRITAGE, Gent. and ELIZABETH LOVICK, dau. of Thomas and Sarah. Before 18 Mch 1767. Cartaret, N. C. H-229.

JOHN HESELIUS and MARY WOODWARD, extx of Henry, of A. A. cty, Md. Before Mch Ct 1765. A. A. cty records, p. 16.

Magister HESSELLIUS and SARAH WALRAVEN, dau. of Jonas. 3 May 1713 [?] Wmton, Dela. Records of Holy Trinity. [*As Magister is a title, meaning school teacher, this is probably his title and not his name.*]

WILLIAM HICKMAN and HANNAH CHAMBERLAINE dau. of Robert. Before 1 Apr 1786. Chester cty, Penna.

RICHARD HILL and CATHARINE BRAMMETT. 21 May 1798. Bourbon cty, Ky. Mar. Ret.

ROBERT HILL and MARGARET ANGLE. 16 Sept 1799. Bourbon, Ky. Mar. Ret.

JOHN HILL and ELIZABETH CHAMPION. 5 Feby 1797. [?] Richmond, Ga. See A-197.

NATHAN HILLS and SUSANNAH REILEY. 10 June 1792. Richmond, Ga. Mar. Li.

HENRY HILL and ALLEY BROWN. 10 Sept 1805. Kanawha, W. Va. Mar. Ret.

GEORGE HILL and ELIZABETH NANCE. 5 Mch 1807. Kanawha, W. Va. Mar. Ret.

RICHARD HILL and HANNAH DELAVALL, declare intention [of marriage] he having a ctf from a meeting in London and also a ctf for West River in Md. 24th of 4th 1687. Minutes Philada. Mtg, p. 265. P. H. S.

RICHARD HINMAN and MARY, dau. of Phillip MEREDITH. Before Oct 1672. S. L. O. Va. vi-430.

DAVID HOFFMAN and EVE MARGARET HECK, extx of Balser HECK. Before or about 13 Aug 1797. Fred'k, Md. G. M. I-pp. 617, 618.

KEMP HOLLAND and JANE MURRY, dau. of Henry. Before 5 Dec 1804. Davidson cty, Tenn.

WILLIAM HOLLIDAY and ELIZABETH NEIL. 13 Aug 1789. Greene, Ga. Mar. Li.

Mr. RICE HOOE, of Stafford cty, and FRANCES WITHERS, relict of Capt. John WITHERS. 8 Sept 1699. Staff, Va. Z-5. See also Z-12. [She was also widow of Francis Dade.]

MATHEW HOOPER and MARGARET ASSHETON, dau. of Robert. Before 7 Feby 1728. Philada, O. C. 1716-1755, p. 69. P. H. S.

JOSEPH HOPEWELL and CATHERINE DUBOIS. Before 13 Feby 1707. Philada. O. C. 1716-1755, p. 40. P. H. S.

PHILIP HORNBY and ______GOLDSMITH, widow of Thomas, Jr. Before 10 Feby 1787. Ga. Rev. Records, 1-621.

DANIEL HORSMAN and ELIZABETH STOCKLEY, dau. of Benjamin. Before 30 Nov 1762. Sussex, Dela. B2-299.

MOSES HOUSTON and the widow of David BARRY. Before or about 7 Jany 1734-5. Onslow, N. C.
GREEN HUFF and MARTHA LOCKHART, dau. of Richard. Before 7 Jany 1826. Hancock, Ga. Gdn's Book B-29.
HOLEMAN HUMPHREY and POLLY PADGETT. Before 10 Jany 1814. Shenan, Va. v-188.
JOHN HUNTT, of Albemarle cty, Province of Carolina, and the relict of Anthony HASE of same province. Before 16 Oct 1689. L. Norf, Va. v-135.
WILLIAM HUNTER and KITTY ARRELL, dau. of Richard. Before Oct Ct 1806. Pr. Wm, Va. L. C. [2] p. 106.
WILLIAM HUTCHISON, of Pr. Geo's Md. and SARAH DOYNE, sister of Robert and Charles. Before 2 Oct 1710. Som. Md. I. K. L. No. 60.
DANIEL IRVIN and PEGGY COMPTON. 1796. Kanawha, W. Va. Mar. Ret.
______ISHAM and HURSLEY [URSULA?] TULEY, dau. of John. Before 15 Nov 1747. Alb, Va.
ANGEL JACOBUS and ELIZABETH [aunt to the orphans of Fran: GOURE.] Before 2 Nov 1692. Richm'd, Va. Orders.
ROBERT JACKSON and MARY, extx of Robert DOWSING. Before 17 Nov 1740. York, Va. xviii-654.
GEORGE JACKSON and ANN RANSHAW [RENSHAW?] dau. of Argol. Before Oct 1738. Va. Gen. Ct. Dec B78. See also S. L. O. Va. viii-186. Before 20 Oct 1691. [Warwick cty?]
Mr. ANDREW JACKSON and DORATHY LISTER, a widow. Before 1709. Lanc, Va. viii-139.
Capt.______ JACKSON and ELIZ: CUTTS, dau. or widow of Baker CUTTS. Before 17 Aug 1719. S. L. O. Va. v-217.
RALPH JACKSON and ELIZABETH PALMEH, dau. of George [of Chester cty, Penna?] Before 25th 11th 1702. Penna. Arch. Ser. 2, xix-356.
DAVID JAMESON and MARGARET BELL [BEEL?] 12 Nov 1805. W. H. S. Draper Mss. 17CC-42 &c.
JAMES JAMESON and REBECCA BUCKINGHAM, Woodford cty, Ky. 22 July 1797. Same refs as above.
Dr. DANIEL JENIFER and the widow of John ROGERS. Before 11 May 1743. M. H. S. Semmes Mss.
______JENKINS and PRISCILLA HORN, widow of Jesse. About July 1798. Richm'd cty, Ga. Min. Inf. Ct $. 208.
______JENKINS and MARY ARRELL, dau. of Richard. Before 8 Oct 1806. Pr. Wm, Va. L. C. [2] p. 106.
F St. THOMAS JENIFER of St. Mary's cty and ELIZABETH, one of the daus. of Nathaniel ASHCOM, Calv. cty. Before April Ct, 1722. Annap. T. P. xxv-110.
HARDY-RICE JERNIGAN, pltr, Richmd cty, and REBECCA LEE, sp., same. 22 Dec 1791. Richmd, Ga. Mar. Li.
ENOCH JOB and ABIGAIL GATCHEL. Ser. 2. Penna. Arch. xix-763.
N MICHAEL JOBSON and MARY NAYLOR widow of Thomas. Before 8 July 1706. Chester cty, Penna. C-43.
ISAAC JOHNSON and SUSANNAH EMBREY, dau. of William. Before 24 July 1819. Ogleth., Ga. C-78.
Mr. JA: KAY and Mrs. GRACE ASHTON, widow of Capt. JOHN ASHTON. See record 1676-1688, pp. 155, 156; Ct 28 May 1679 and 30 July 1679. Also 8 Oct 1679. p. 165. Wmld, Va.
______KEMP and NAOMIE MAKEMIE, wid. of Rev. Francis. See record 7 Apr 1709. Acco., Va. xi-483.
CUSTIS KENDALL and ELIZABETH BOWDOIN, dau. of Peter. Before 14 Aug 1753. N-n, Va. xxviiiR-453. Before 9 Jany 1753. See xxxixO-213. See also Henrico Misc. Rec'ds, p.1721. In that she is called the extx of Peter.
WILLIAM KENDALL and NANNY BALEY, one of the daus. of Jane BALEY. Before 27 Nov 1770. Wmld, Va. Order Book.
______KENNEDY and LEVICIA SIMPSON, widow of William. Before 18 Feby 1797. Davidson cty, Tenn.
JOHN KENNADY, of Richmd cty, and ELIZABETH WEBSTER, widow. 12 Aug 1791. Richmd, Ga. Mar. Li.
______KENNEDY and RACHEL CLARK, dau. of Thomas, of West Caln, Chester cty, Penna. Before 1767. Chester cty, Penna. Wills.
JOHN KERR, of Fauquier, and SARAH SMITH, dau. of Henry. Before 11 Feby 1785. Staff, Va. S-172.
GEORGE KEY and DELILAH EMBRY, dau. of John. Before 11 Dec 1843. Madison, Ga. B-10.
TALBOT KEY and ELIZABETH, dau. of John EMBRY. Before 11 Dec 1843. (She was then deceased.) Madison, Ga. B-10.
WILLIAM KILGOAR and ANNE HIGINGBOTHAM. 19 Dec 1791. Greene, Ga. Mar. Li.
JOS. KILGORE and MARGARET STIT. 30 Nov 1795. Draper 12ZZ-330. W. H. S. [It is uncertain whether this reference is to Mason cty, Ky, or to Ohio.]
EPHRAIM KING, son of Capell, and MARY STOUGHTON, dau. of Will'm. About 6 July 1739. Som. Md. M. F.-75.
JOHN KING perhaps m. URSULA WHITTINGTON, dau. of Andrew. This is not proved. Before 20 Aug 1716. Som, Md. 1715-1716, p. 1.
PETER KINTELO and MARG'T UNSEL, widow. Before 2 Nov 1778. Ohio cty, W. Va. Minutes i-31.
GEORGE KIRKMAN and MARY THOMPSON, widow of John. 1 Apr 1788. Surry, N. C. Wills ii-40.
JOHN KIRTON, late of Kensington [England], and DAMERIS SANDERS, dau. of Thomas. Before 1738. Penna. Arch. Ser. 3, i-106.

DAVID LACY and SARAH PANCOAST, dau. of Israel. Before 22 May 1795. Ldn, Va. A-9.

SAMUEL LACY and MARY PANCOAST, dau. of Isreal. Before 22 May 1795. Ldn, Va. A-93.

JOHN LAKE and AMY HALL____*"Now supposed to be married to John Lake."* See Ct 2 Jany 1779. Pr. Wm, Va. L. C. [2].

WILLIAM LAKE and the relict of Thomas HARPER. Before 2 Oct 1684. Rappa., Va. Orders, p.61.

SCHOOLFIELD LAMBERSON and ARRA BOWEN, dau. of Isaac. Before Nov Ct 1833. Som. Md, Ct Proc. iv.

______LAMDEN and CATHERINE NEVIL, dau. of John. Before 7 Jany 1777. Q. A., Md. Wills. T. W. 1-22.

LEWIS LAMKIN, son of James, and a dau. of Lewis ap Lewis LEWIS. Before 30 June 1740. Nthld cty, Va. 1738-1743, p.85.

Capt. JAMES LANE and CATHARINE JETT, widow of William. Before or about 14 Apr 1763. Ldn, Va. A-90.

THO: LANE and MARTHA MORRIS, widow of Nicholas. Mar. agreement. 25 July 1665. Nthld, Va. 1658-1666, fo. 158.

Mr. BIRD LANIER and Miss ELIZABETH DIXSON. 22 Dec 1793. Effingh. Ga. Mar. Li.

THOMAS LANIER and ANNE MACLIN, dau. of William. Before 3 July 1735. Bruns. Va. i-189.

THOMAS LARAMORE and the extx of Robert Hopkins, Sr., late of Som, Md. Before 14 July 1710. Md. S. L. O. Inv. and Accts. 31-276.

JAMES LAUGHLIN and NANCY FRANCE [FRAME?] dau. of James. Before 14 Jany 1796. Fayette, Penna. B-337.

GEORGE LAYFIELD, Esq., and ELIZABETH STEVENS, widow of Col. William. Before 21 Feby 1692. Acco, Va. x-95.

JOHN LEAR and ELIZABETH SWANN, relict of Maj. Thomas SWANN. Before 20 Nov 1711. Surry, Va. iii-95.

HANCOCK LEE and MARY KENDALL, dau. of Lt. Col. Wm. KENDALL. [See his will.] N-n, Va. xv-224.

RICHARD LEE and MARY KENDALL, dau. of Col. Wm. KENDALL. 17 Apr 1731. Acco. xx-68.

RICHARD LEE and MARY DAVENPORT. 30 Sept 1795 Wash'n cty, Va. Mar. Ret.

JOHN LEE and ELIZABETH MURRY, dau. of Thomas. Before 27 Aug 1740. I. W. Va. viiiW-316.

______LEE and MARTHA MOORE, widow of Thomas. (She is called late of Mansel St., Goodman's Fields, psh of St. Mary Magdalen, *alias* White Chapel. Middx cty, G. B.) Before 26 Apr 1725. Wmld, Va. x-39.

CHARLES LEE, Gent., of Nthld, and MARY SPENCE. Before 6 Nov 1715. Wmld, Va. v-506.

JOS: LEE and the widow of James GREEN. Before 29 Nov 1733. Wmld, Va. Orders, fo. 116.

RICHARD LEE and GRACE ASHTON, a dau. and heir of Elizabeth ASHTON. Before 25 Feby 1734. Wmld, Va. Orders, fo. 162. See also fo. 174.

RICHARD HENRY LEE and ANNE, one of the daus. of William AYLETT, Gent., dec'd. Before 28 Aug 1758. Wmld, Va. Inv. iv-81.

PETER LESAD[E] and MAGDALENE *Lenude* [? perhaps Leonard?] Before or about Nov 1739. Charleston, S. C. A-10.

HENRY LEWIS and NANCY EDWARDS. 30 Dec 1806. Greene, Ga. Mar. Li.

JAMES C. LEWIS and MARCEY DAVIS. 1 June 1820. Bulloch, Ga.

JAMES LEWIS and a dau. of Cornelius THOMAS. Before or about 4 Oct 1779. Amherst, Va. Orders, p. 378.

WILLIAM LIGON and ANNE ROGERS. Before 1743. Goochld, Va. iv-155.

______LILES and MILTRET [*sic*] GREEN, widow of William. Before 6 July 1782. Newberry, S. C. A-84. [Evidently questioned as to a will "She declared she does not know what has become of the sd will but as the Brittish has Destroyed a good many of their Effects & papers," &c., &c.]

______LILEY and SARAH RILEI, widow, prob. of Thomas. Before 1707. Acco, Va. vii-427. [Her son's name was Thomas Rilei.]

JOHN LINN and SALLY FARIS. 22 June 1796. Clark cty, Ky. M. L. B.

EDW. LINTHICUM and MARY TERRILL. 8 Sept 1773. Cumb., Va. Mar. Li. Fee book.

THOMAS LINTHICUM and SARAH, extx of Rice BENNET. Before 28 Feby 1774. Cumb, Va. Orders, p. 5.

EDMUND LISBRO[?] and ANN LEE, relict of Col. Rich'd LEE. About 1666. Cal. Va. St. Pa. i-7.

WILLIAM LITTLETON and JOHANNAH SMITH, dau. of Simon. See Smith's will, 1721, also see 6 Aug 1723. Acco, Va. xvi-150, 192.

______LOSH and JANE McINTIRE, extr of Alex. Before 6 May 1791. Va. S. L. O. Ky. Mil. Dist.

JOHN LOW and FRANCES PECK of Henrico. About 25 Jany 1734. Henrico. See W. & M. xxi-58.

PETER LOVE and MARY EDEN. 17 Apr 1802. Balto. cty, Md. Mar. List.

JOHN LOWE and CATHERINE RUFF, both of Newberry Dist. Mar. contract. 17 Dec 1807. Charleston, S. C. K-276.

GAVIN LOWRY and BETHETHLAN NEWSOM. 13 Dec 1745. Lanc, Va. M. L. B.

GEORGE LUMPKIN and NACY RUTLEDGE [NANCY?] 28 Jany 1782. Pittsylv, Va. M. L. B.

MOORE LUMPKIN and ANNE WOODSON. 14 Apr 1773. Cumb., Va. Mar. Li. Fee Book.

JAMES LYNCH and SARAH ROLPH, admx of John. Before 2 Feby 1829. Q. A. Md. O. C. Minutes.

FRANCIS LORD and the relict of William STINTON [STENTON?] of J. C. cty. Before 5 July 1681. Surry, Va. 1(2)-296.

JOHN LOVEL and MARY DANIEL. Before 4 Nov 1789. Gchld, Va. iii-386.

THOMAS LOVICK, Esq., prob. m. SARAH SHEPARD, dau. of David[?] Before 18 Mch 1767. Carteret, N. C. H-229.

GEORGE LUKE and the widow and admx of Dr. Ralph SMITH. Before 12 Dec 1689. Staff, Va. Orders i.

PAUL LUKE and SARAH LLEWELLIN, widow of Thomas. Before 9 Nov. 1664. I. W. iii-26.

______LYNES and ELIZABETH WATKINS [apparently of Maryland]. [Long] before 27 Apr 1732. Wmld, Va. Orders, fo. 21. See also Ct 31 May 1733, fo. 89. Fo. 131, of Fid. Accts i, gives LYNES' name as GEORGE, and states that he had been married about 48 years: that ELIZABETH was of Calvert cty, Md, that she would now be about 70; also that she was a widow RICHMOND. These depositions are dated 16 Aug 1731.

SAMUEL McCALL and ISABELLA ROBINSON, widow of John. Mar. contract. 13 Dec 1799. Wmld, Penna. v-145.

JOHN McCARLE and MARY McKNIGHT. Before 30 Apr 1789. Cumb, Penna. E-148.

DANIEL McCARTEE, Gent., and ELIZABETH PAINE, widow of William. Before 26 Feby 1700. Wmld, Va. 1698-1705.

DANIEL McCARTY and ANN FITZHUGH, widow of William, Esq. Before 3 May 1723. K. Geo, Va. Oi-120. See also Wmld, Va. 8(1)-52. [She was gr. dau. of John Corbin who m. Lettice Lee.]

DANIEL McCARTY, Gent. and ELIZABETH SMITH, admx of Nicho., Gent. Before 25 Nov 1735. Wmld, Va. Orders, fo. 184. See also K. Geo, Va. Orders ii-33. Marriage prob. about 7 Nov 1735.

DANIEL McCARTY, [Sr.] and PENELOPE HIGGINS, dau. and sole heir of Augustine, Gent. Before 24 June 1735. [At this date she was deceased.] Wmld, Va. Orders, fo. 173. See also Wmld, Va. 8(1)-538. Before 26 July 1732. [Note: Va. Colonial Churches, p. 227, says that McCarty was the second son of Daniel, Esq. that his wife, Penelope, was the dau. of *Christine Higgens,* Gent, and that she died the 26 Mch 1732, aged 18.]

______McCLAYLAND [*sic*] and HANNAH RHODES. Orange, Va. v-327. [No date.]

GERRARD McCLANNAHAN and SALLY RUST. 5 May 1796. Fauquier, Va. 21 Apr 1796. M. L. B.

CORNELIUS McCONMEY and GARTRUDE GOODING, dau. of Abraham. Before 1767. N. C. cty, Dela. V-1-581.

JOHN McCLANAHAN and SALLY ELLIOTT. 5 Nov 1795. Fauquier, Va.

JOHN McCLESTER and MARY BAYLY, prob. widow of Charles. About 8 Dec 1725. Acco, Va. xix-42.

STEPHEN McCOY and NANCY McCALL. 27 Jany 1796. Bullock, Ga. Mar. Li.

WILLIAM McCORD and AGNES McKIMMEY, dau. of Joseph. Before 2 Feby 1785. Cumb., Penna. E-34.

JOHN McCREA and MARY GIBSON. 29 Apr 1788. Rockbr., Va.

JOHN McCULLOCH and SARAH WILSON, dau. of John. Before 7 Aug 1823. Ohio cty, W. Va. ii-249.

______McDONALD and SARAH DICKERSON. Before 7 Oct 1748. K. Geo., Va. Orders, 1735-1751, p. 591.

SAM'L McGEEHEE and ELIZABETH ELLITT[?] dau. of Susan ELLITT. Before 15 July 1735. Hanover cty, Va. [W. & M. xxi-63.]

______McGRITT and SUSANNAH ASHLEY, dau. of Jean. Before 1 May 1799. Camden cty, Ga. D-144.

JOHN McKEE prob. m. MARGARET McKNIGHT. Before 30 Apr 1789. Cumb, Penna. E-148.

DANIEL McKENNY and FRANCES, a dau. of Daniel CARRELL. Before 30 May 1733. Wmld, Va. Orders, fo. 80. See also fo. 105.

LAWRENCE McNEMARRA and SUSANNAH HOLLAND, widow. Before 24 Feby 1735. Wmld, Va. Orders, fo. 189. See also fo. 192 and 201.

Mr.______McNICOL and BETTY CRAWFORD, sister of William. Before 20 June [?] 1809. Glynn cty, Ga. D-1.

SAMUEL McPHERSON and the widow of WILLIAM BENNETT. Before 1 Nov 1779. Pr. Wm, Va. U-109.

WILLIAM MAFFITS and REBECCA ROBERTSON, dau. of James. Before 5 Dec 1790. Dauphin cty, Penna. A-282. [She had land in Kentucky from her father.]

RICHARD MAGRAW prob. m. ELIZABETH, admx of Thos. PHILLIPS. Before 1 July 1737. K. Geo, Va. Oii-118.

FRANCES MAKEMIE and NAOMI ANDERSON, dau. of William. Before 10 Apr 1769. Acco, Va. Deeds iii-666.

RICHARD MALDON and ELIZABETH MOORE. 6 Feby 1798. Bulloch cty, Ga. Mar. Li.

JOHN MANETT [also spelled MANNAT] and HANNAH MANLOW [MANLOVE]. 25 June 1667. Som., Md. I. K. L.

______MARCEY and BRIDGET CONNER. About 6 Mch 1722. Acco, Va. xviii-40.

RICHARD MARIS [MORRIS?] and ELIZ'TH HAYES, dau. of John [Jonathan?] Before the 29th 2d 1720. Penna. Arch. Ser. 2 xix-670.

PAUL MARSH and ELIZABETH MEREDITH, dau. of Phillip. Before 9 Oct 1672. S. L. O. Va. vi-430.

JOSEPH MARSHALL and ELIZABETH WALKER, dau. of Jeremiah. 31 May 1804. [She died before this date.] Elbert, Ga. Inv. &c.

ABRAHAM MARTIN and ELIZABETH PHILLIPS, dau. of William, late of J. C. cty, Va. Before 24 June 1709. York, Va. xiii-227.

FRANCIS MARTAIN and BETHIAH McCLENELSON[?] 19 Dec 1806. Greene, Ga. Mar. Li.

DANIEL MARSHAL and SARAH WELBOURN, widow of Daniel. Before 31 Oct 1749. Acco, Va. Deeds ii-223.

JOHN MARTIALL and ANNABELLA LEE, widow of ______Lee. Before 1724. Acco, Va. xvi-203.

CLUF [CLIF?] MARTIN and MARTHA VAUGHN. 8 Sept 1808. Elbert, Ga. Reg. Bk B.

DADE MASSIE and PARTHENIA ALEXANDER, dau. of Robert. Before 28 Apr 1735. Pr. Wm, Va. L. C. p. 96.

JOHN MEANS, of Fairfield cty, S. C., and MARY MILLING, one of the two daus. of David. Before or about 6 Dec 1788. Richmd, Ga. G-387.

ISAAC MEASON and CATHERINE HARRISon. 27 Apr 1778. Yohogania cty [then Va.] Minutes ii-3 [See Carnegie Museum Annals.]

Col. HOMER N. MELTON and ELIZA ROBINSON, dau of Jane. Before 18 Feby 1813. Jefferson cty, Ga. Wills.

JOHN MICHAEL and ELIZABETH THOROUGHGOOD, sister of Capt. Adam. Before 16 May 1666. N-n, Va. ix-242.

DANIEL MIFFLIN and ANN WALKER, dau. of John. Before 26 June 1771. Acco, Va. L. C. 1773-1805, p. 8.

ZACHARIAH MILES and MARY HALLEY, eldest dau. of Francis. Before 22 Oct 1741. Pr. Wm, Va. E-495.

NATH'L MILLER and Mrs. MARY SLADE, widow of Joesph. About 19 Mch 1796. Richmd, Ga. A-190.

EDWARD MILLS and ANN BARNES, dau. of John, Sr. 7 Dec 1697. Acco, Va. xi-184.

HENRY MILLER and SUSANNAH TEAKEL. 10 Jany 1806. Bulloch cty, Ga. Mar. Li.

WILLIAM MINOR and MARY DAVIS, widow of John. About[?] Jany, 1745. Orange, Va. iv-456.

DAVID MINITREY and BRIDGET INCE[?] relict of John. Before 24 Feby 1709. York, Va. xiv-1. See also p. 8.

______MITCHEL and MARTHA JORDAN, dau. of Josiah. About Nov 1825. Ogleth, Ga. Minutes.

GRIFFIN MIZELL and SUSANNAH CARTER. 29 May 1797. Bulloch, Ga. Mar. Li.

HENRY MOLER and ELIZABETH ZIRKLE. 15 Aug. 1797. Shenan., Va. Mar. Reg.

PETER MONETT and CHARLOTTE FIELDS. 8 July 1816. Guilford, N. C. M. L. B.

CHRISTOPHER MONNETT and CHARLOTTE HANNER. 20 Oct 1842. Guilford, N. C. M. L. B.

SPENCE MONROE prob. m. MARGARETT, a dau. of Nathaniel GRAY. Before 29 Feby 1744 [or about that time.] Wmld, Va. 1743-1746, fo. 57. See also fo. 37.

RICHARD MOORE, of Charleston, printer, and ANN WEBB, dau. of Mathew Webb, Butcher, and his wife Elizabeth, both of Charleston, they being free colored people. 27 May 1790. Charleston, S. C. 1787-1791, p. 213. [This is shown by a ctf of one Isaac Smith, and is duly recorded in the Office of the Probate Judge. Its formality is somewhat unusual and interesting.]

EDMOND MORAN and CATHRENE BLAIR, dau. of Andrew. Before 20 May 1782. Cumb, Penna. D-115.

ALEXANDER MORROW and BETTY STEELE. Before 18 Jany 1821. Alleg., Penna. xi-230.

WILLIAM MOSS and MARY JONES [probably a widow.] Before 3 Feby 1803. K. Geo, Va. viii-558.

DONALD MOXLEY and ANN MUSGROVE, dau. of John, Gent. Before 1 Oct 1744. Ffx, Va. A-182.

JEREMIAH MUNNETT and ELEY SLAGLE. 2 May 1805. Alleg, Md. Mar. Li. [In Hamp. cty, W. Va. Order Book 1795-1798, Isaac Monett is recommended to be Ensign in Capt. Slagle's Co.]

SIMON MUNRO and ELIZABETH WEST, St. Andrew's Psh, Mar. contract. 7 Mch 1768. Liberty, Ga. A-14.

JAMES MURPHY and DELIVERANCE BRINNON, relict of Owen BRENNON. Before 29 Nov 1743. Wmld, Va. Orders, fo. 6. [This name is still in the northern Neck of Va., but now is BRENNAN.]

ROGER MURPHY, Q. A., Md, and MARGARET JONES, youngest dau. of John. Before or about Apr Ct. 1722 Annap, Md. T. P. xxv-103.

JAMES MURPHY and HONOR, relict and admx of Thomas CURTIS. Before 26 JULY 1739. Wmld, Va. Orders, fo. 280.

JOHN MUSGROVE[?] and MARY BARKER. 26 Aug 1795. Bourbon, Ky. M. L. B.

DANIEL MUTCHLER and ELIZA x PANCOAST, dau. of John. Northumb, Pa. Before 1839. iii-328.

JAMES NEALE, of Charles cty, Md., Esq., and ELIZABETH LORD, dau. of John. About 28 Nov 1687. Wmld, Va. i-95.

JOSEPH NEALE, of Lanc., Gent., and HANNAH BUSHROD, dau. of HANNAH COOPER. Before 26 Dec 1738. Wmld, Va. ix-25. See also Fid. Accts, i-215.

THOMAS NAYLOR and MARY KING, widow of John. Before 8 July 1706. Chester cty, Penna. C-43.

JAMES NEALE and ELIZABETH CALVERT, dau. of William. Before 22 Nov 1707. Semmes Mss. M. H. S. See also iv-96, Wmld, Va.

JAMES NEALE and ANN GILL, dau. and heir of Benjamin. Before 9 Mch 1658. Annap., Md. T. P. i-53.

DANIEL NEALE and ELIZABETH HOLLAND, dau. of Daniel and Joyce. Before or about 12 June 1672. Nthld, Va. 1710-1713, p. 133.

CHRISTOPHER NEALE and HANNAH RODHAM, dau. of Matthew. Before 17 Dec 1666. Nthld, Va. 1666-1672, p. 24. See also p. 52.

Mr. RODHAM NEALE and a dau. of Mr. Robert CLARKE. Before 4 Apr 1748. Nthld, Va. 1743-1749, p. 78.

NATH'L NEAL of London, and the only dau. and heir-at-law of Mr. Thomas MATTHEWS. Before 6 Sept 1744. Nthld, Va. 1743-1749.

Mr. ROBERT NORTON and FRANCES CHAMBERS, widow of Jonathan. Before 3 Feby 1702. Acco. xii-137. See also Acco. xi-589. Capt. ROBERT NORTON and the widow of JOHN[?] CHAMBERS. [It is possible she was FRANCES WEST.]

ANDREW OBANNON [O'BANNION] and MARY SMITH, widow of Joseph. About 1779. Fauq, Va. i-394.

PHILIP O KAHANE and JOANE TAYLOR, widow of Walter. 17 Sept 1672. Acco, Va. iv-129.

TURLO "HOBRYANT" and LISHIA BROADWATER [ELISHABA?] dau. of William. Before 1725. Acco, Va. xvi-250.

PHILLIP OCAHONE and JANE TAYLOR, widow of Walter, of Watts Island. Before 11 Jany 1676. Acco, Va. vii-27. [This is undoubtedly the same as the above Phillip O Kahane.]

JAMES ODOM and MARY THOMAS. 24 Feby 1817. Bulloch cty, Ga.

CONSTANTINE O'DONNAL and FRANCES GIBSON, of Md. 4 Sept 1761. York, Penna. Christ Evan. Luth. Church.

JAMES V. OLIVER and CHARLOTTE PERSONS, dau. of Thomas. About 1820. Warren cty, Ga. Minutes.

JOYCE OLLIFFE and ISAAC MARRIOTT. 3 Sept 1681. Burl., N. J. Cty Ct Records.

GABRIEL O'MAHAR and ANN HUSE, widow of Robert. Before 12 Jany 1709. Cecil cty, Md. Deeds ii-136.

THOMAS OSBORN and ANN ENGLISH, dau. of Walter the Elder. See deed 23 July 1711. Wmld, Va. v-50. [She had a son Edmund Owen.]

RICHARD OSBOURNE, of Pr. Wm, Gent., and PENELOPE HIGGINS, dau. of John and sister of Augustine. Before 29 May 1733. Wmld, Va. viii-11.

Mr. THOMAS OSBORNE, Sr., and the relict of Mr. John BRANCH. Before 21 Aug. 1693. Hen, Va. 1677-1737, p. 34. [Osborne then dec'd.]

GEORGE OWEN and CATHERINE PARKS. 21 Nov 1796. Ogleth., Ga.

MANN PAGE and MARY SELDEN (gr. dau. of Ann Mason.) See her will about 1762. Pr. Wm, Va. L. C. pp. 22, 23.

WILLIAM PALMER and MEMORY WALKER. 7 July 1780. Dor, Md. Mar. Li.

EDWIN F. PALMER and JOSEPHINE E. MANN, by Rev. D. L. Buttolph. 7 Feby 1865. Lib. cty, Ga. Records.

SAMUEL PALMER and JANE BARCLAY, widow of Thomas. Before or about Dec 1749. Philada. O. C. 1716-1755, p. 221. P. H. S.

WILLIAM PANNILL and ANN MORTON, dau. of Jeremiah. See April 1763. Orange, Va. vi-716.

ELI S. PARDEE and SUSAN ELLIOTT, extx of John. Before or about 19 Jany 1828. Q. A., O. C Minutes. Md.

JOHN PARK and AGNES STERN. Before 6 Nov 1832. Charl., Va. Orders xxix-10.

______PARK and REBECCA CLARK, dau. of Thomas, of West Caln, Chester cty, Penna. Before 1767. Chester cty, Penna. See Clark's will.

JOHN PARKER and MARY DOE. (Intentions.) 29th of 9th 1700. Phila. Mtg Minutes, p. 281. P. H. S.

RICHARD PARKER and PRISCILLA LOVE. (Intentions). 29th of 4th 1705. Same refs. as above, p. 449.

JOHN PARKER of S. C., pltr, and MARY DANIEL (a minor), dau. of John. Bet. 12 July 1747 and 30 May 1755. Charleston, S. C. P2-619.

JOHAN PARKER and MARIA REES, at Newcastle. 27Nov 1723. Records H. T., Wilmington, Dela. P. 298.

RICHARD PARKER and the relict of Nichol. PERKINS. Before 20 Aug 1656. C. C. cty, Va. 1655-1665, p. 67.

JONATHAN PARKER and the widow and extx of Richard MILDMAY. Before 11 Nov 1691. Staff, Va. Orders i-185. About 6 Oct 1691. See p. 166.

EDWARD PARIS and SUSANNAH MOLTON. 6 May 1719. Kent cty, Dela. P. G. S. vii-159.

ANSEL PARRISH and NANCY HOLLAWAY. 26 Feby 1814. Bulloch cty, Ga. Mar. Li.

JOHN PAWLEY[?] and MARGARET STANDLEY. She was b. Penna., 28 Feby 1753, d. 1841. Emigrated with family to Greenbrier settlement, Va. Draper, ZZ-30. 1777. [She m. (2) Capt. Michael Erskine, from Penna., who d. 1812.]

FRANCES EDWARDS and GEORGE PAYNE. 13 Oct 1729. M. L. B. Lanc, Va.

JOHN PAYNE and MARY COLES, dau. of William. Before 3d 10th 1781. Hanover, Va. Deed Book, p. 566.

JOHN PEARCE and ESTHER WALKER, dau. of John. Before 25 Jany 1705. Va. S. L. O. N. N. iii-123.

SAMUEL PERKINS, Mcht of Charles Town, and SARAH CARTWRIGHT, of same, widow. Mar. contract. 15 Apr 1743. Charleston, S. C. HH-4.

ANTHONY PEYTON probably[?] m. ANN CARNABY, dau. of Anthony. Before 26 Sept 1746. K. Geo, Va. iii-157.

WILLIAM PHILLIPS and ANN STONE, dau. of Barton STONE. Before 28 July 1785. Staff, Va. S-302.

SAMUEL PLEASANTS, of Henrico, Va., Mcht, son of John and Margaret, and MARY PEMBERTON, dau. of Israel and Sarah, of Philada., 5th mo. 13th-1762. Philada. Mo'ly Mtg. p. 267. P. H. S.

______PLUNKET and LIDIA WALKER, widow of Thomas. Before 27 Sept 1732. Wmld, Va. Orders, fo. 40.

Col.______POLLOCK and ESTHER WILKINSON, widow of William, of N. C. Before 10 July 1716. Va. Gen. Ct Dec. p. B4.

LAURENCE POPE and DORCAS SPENCE, widow of John. Before 23 Oct 1700. Va. Col. Dec. See p. R61.

JOSEPH PORTER and MARY PATRIDGE, dau. of Jonathan. Before 18 Apr 1804. Dor, Md.

THOMAS PORTER and CATHERINE SWAN. 1765. Lanc, Pa. M. L. B.

CHARLES BINGLEY PORTER, of Orange cty, Va., and Miss MARY SCOTT of Haywood cty, Tenn. Bet. 1826 and 1832. Tenn. Hist. Mags. v-137.

SAMUEL Y. POTTS and MARGARET SWINTON. 24 Dec 1816. Sumter, S. C. M. L.

GABRIELL x POWELL and______LAURENCE, dau. of William. Before 11 Oct 1679. N-n, Va. Old bonds, &c.

WILLIAM PRESTON, b. 1730, son of John, and SUSANNA SMITH. Draper Mss. 1QQb. 1761. Preston d. 1783.

MEREDITH PRICE prob.[?] m. ELIZABETH SCOT, a widow. Before 5 Jany 1721. K. Geo, Va. O1-36.

WILLIAM PRICE and RACHEL ROE, widow of James, who d. 1768. Before Feby 1788. Q. A. O. C., Minutes. Md.

GEORGE PRIMROSE and HANNAH HACKETT, dau. Thomas. Before 1 Feby 1760. Q. A., Md. W. H. N. 1-235.

THOMAS PRYOR of Burlington, N. J. son of Thomas of Bucks cty, Penna., and HANNAH WHITE, at Mt. Holly, N. J. 12th mo. 1762. Burl. and Mt. Holly Mtgs. P. H. S.

______PUCKLE and ANN JOBSON. Before 8 July 1706. Chester cty, Penna. C-43.

______PYLE and ABIGALL BUSHALL, dau. of Joseph, of Chester cty. Before 12th mo 8th 1703. Chester cty, Penna. C-101.

JONATHAN PUGH and SUSANNAH ROGERS, dau. of William. She was *baptized,* age 22, about 12 July 1775. Shenan, Va. Mar. Ret.

BENJAMIN QUARLES and FRANCES L. PANNILL. Before 1805. K. Wm, Va. "9"-89.

WHARTON QUARLES and MOURNING SLAUGHTER. Before 17 Mch 1800. K. Wm, Va. "13"-493.

JAMES QUARLES, Sr., of Bruns. cty, Va., prob. m. CATHARINE READ, dau. of Elizabeth Before 11 Sept 1784. Bruns, Va. Wills, p. 400.

JACOB RAZOR and ELIZABETH SHARP. About 1791. Alb., Va. M. L. B.

JOSEPH READ and HENRIETTA HARDWICK, one of the extrs of James. Before 3 Aug 1742. Wmld, Va. Fid. Accts. i-269.

WILLIAM RICE and SUSAN SHANKS. Before 1800. Draper Mss. 12CC-251, 254. W. H. S.

WHARTON RANSDELL and SARAH, widow of William STURMAN. Gent. About 1739. Wmld, Va. Fid. Accts i-210, 155. Before 28 Nov 1738. See Orders, fo. 298. Also fo. 304.

EDWARD RANSDELL and ELIZABETH STURMAN, eldest dau. of William STURMAN. Same refs. as above. See additional refs. as above.

RICHARD ROSE, of St. Mary's cty Md. and ELIZABETH BATEMAN, one of the daus. of William, of Wmld, Va. Before 31 May 1737. Wmld, Va. Orders, fo. 229.

PRICHETT ROSE and RHODA WRIGHT. 2 Oct 1797. Car. cty, Md. Mar. Li.

ANDREW RUSSELL and PENELOPIE, admx of Francis SPENCER, and late the relict of William Manley. Before 31 Mch 1725. Wmld, Va. 1721-1731, fo. 86.

MATTHEW RUST and WINIFRED COX, dau. of Vincent [Vinson] COX. Before 27 May 1740. Wmld, Va. Fid. Accts, i-233. Before 26 Aug 1735. See Orders, fo. 179. See also fo. 201 and 285.

PETER RUST and SARAH NEWTON, dau. of William. Before 26 Feby 1733. Wmld, Va. Orders, fo. 126. See also fo. 138.

WILLIAM RUST and "MATILDAY" widow of Samuel EARLE. Before 27 June 1706. Wmld, Va. Orders, fo. 28.

______RUTLEDGE, and NANCY ECHOLS, dau. of Obadiah. Before 17 June 1800. Ogleth., Ga. Minutes.

EDWARD RICHARDSON, bricklayer, of Charles Town, and ELIZABETH FLY "intended spouse." Oct 1752. Charleston, S. C., 1754-1758. (Records.)

ROBERT RUDULPH, of St. Mary's, married MARY MICKLER, sister of Jacob. *Articles of separation.* Before 8 Nov. 1806. Camden, Ga. G-310. [Note: this very unusual record also proves a previous marriage.]

CHARLES READ, of Philda., Mcht, and AMY CHILDS, of Hertford, cty Hertford, Sp. Before 29th 10br 1701. Penna. Arch. Ser. 2, xix-459.

JNO. ROBINET and MARGARET NESBITT. Robinett and Samuel Miller give bond. 27 Jany 1801. Spartanb. S. C. Orders B6. [As it is claimed that South Carolina had no mar. licenses, it is possible, at least it has been suggested, that this was a bond given by the minister, permitting him to perform the marriage.]

JACOB RODRUCK and REBECCA WOOD, dau. of Enoch. Before 6 Sept 1831. Fayette, Penna. i-332.

JOSEPH ROGERS and ELIZABETH GIBSON, dau. of John. Before 25 May 1823. Fayette, Penna. i-234.

JOHN ROSSER and ELIZABETH MURPHY, prob. widow of Edward. Before or about 1807. Warren cty, Ga. Minutes.

SAM'L ROBINET and MARY TAYLOR, dau. of William. Before 21st 3d 1705. Penna. Arch. i-477.

______REED and PARTHENIA SMOCK, widow of John. Before 7 Nov 1705. Som, Md. A. B.-26.

PEYTON RANDOLPH and BETSEY HOLLAND. 15 Jany 1789. I. W, Va.

JOHN RANDOLPH and ANNE OSBORNE, one of the daus. and coheirs of Thomas, late of Pr. Wm, Gent. Before 20 Oct 1750. Pr. Wm, Va. L-117.

WILLIAM RAWLINS and JANE FITZGERRARD, widow of John. About 16 Dec 1690. Acco, Va. x-9. In another record (ix-212) the name is given at Catherine FITZ JARRELL.

______RAWLINE and CATHERINE FITZJARRELL, widow. Before 15 Sept 1691. Acco, Va. ix-212. [This item and the preceding one require further study. Tradition makes Catherine Fitz-Gerald an orphan immigrant.]

Capt. ROBT RANDOLPH and ANNE POWELL, widow of Col. James POWELL. Before 9 June 1693. I. W., Va. iv-75.

JOSIAH REDDITT and SARAH WILLIAMS, dau. of Arthur, of "Society." Before May 1775. Bertie, N. C. B-33.

______REDD and FRANCES ANDERSON, dau. of Charles. Before 1783. Cumb, Va. ii-391.

COLLEN REDDOCK and JANE W. BEVERLEY. Mar. settlement. Mch 1786. K. Wm. "11" 305.

Mr. PETER REVERDY and ELISHEBA ANDREWS, dau. of William. Before 24 July 1673. N-n, Va. x-210. [She was gr. dau. of Lt. Col. William Andrews, and also granddaughter of George Traveller. See N-n, xi-10.]

JAMES ROCKETS and JANE CURLE, wid. of Nicholas. E. C. cty, Va. Va. Col. Dec. p. R97. [No date.]

WILL x RICHARDSON, staff., and the relict of John CREECHLEY. Before 21 Oct 1699. Staff, Va. Z-20.

ROBERT RICHARDSON and SUSAN SMITH, dau. of Richard. Before 28 Mch 1667. N-n, Va. vii-231. See also Acco, Va. 149. Richardson was a "cordwayner", and Susan was Susanna. In Acco, ii-85, the name is given as RICHARDS.

THOMAS RICE prob. m. a sister of Jeremiah BALL. Long before 1783. Wmton, N. C. cty, Dela. L-405.

EVAN RICE, Esq., Mill Crk hd., N. C. cty, Dela, and ELIZABETH GRAHAM, dau. of Francis. Before 1783. Same refs.

JOHN ROADS and the admx of Ambrose WHITE. Before 14 July 1681. Acco, Va. x-247. From the several references for this marriage it seems safe to assume that the widow of White was COMFORT, formerly COMFORT PARKER, dau. of William. See Acco, Va. viii-247, ix-21, xi-502, and xvi. 70 and 71.

JOHN ROADS and MARY SAVAGE, dau. of Rowland. Before 5 Nov 1717. Acco, Va. xvi-32. [They were in Sussex, Dela. in Apr 1717.] Before 23 Aug 1709. See xvi-32.

JOHN ROADS and MARY LECATT, widow. Before 1 Dec 1702. Acco, Va. xi-294.

JOHN ROADES, Gent. and ALICE COE, widow of John. Before 30 May 1728. Acco, Va. xvi-314.

THOMAS-READE ROOTES and SARAH-RING BATTAILE (niece of Mary Robinson of Caroline cty, Va.) Before 19 Feby 1785. Hanover cty, Va., records.

WILLIAM ROBERTS and ELIZABETH DEAN, dau. of William. Before 13 Jany 1722. Kent, Md. i-255. [She had then m. (2) Henry DAVIS.]

WILLIAM ROBERTS and ANN PANNILL. Before 1805. K. Mm, Va. "9"-89.

JOHN ROGERS and ELIZABETH TOWLES, widow. Before 6 Oct 1724. Acco, Va. xvi-221.

NATHANIEL ROGERS and JEANE x WEST, dau. of Anthony. Before 26 Sept 1722. Acco, Va. xvi-173.

DANIEL ROYALTY and MARGARET WAUGH, widow of William. Before 5 Feby 1752. Pr. Wm. M-233.

WILLIAM ROWLEY and ANN GRIGSBY. Mar. contract. 18 Mch 1773. K. Geo, Va. i-1129.

JAMES RULE and AGNESS DOUGLAS, dau. of George. Before 13 Dec 1760. Acco, Va. Deeds iii-130. See also iii-262.

REUBEN RUTHERFOTD and ANNE, widow of Henry[?] HUNT. About July 1743. Orange, Va. From a list of administrations.

Mr. ROBT RUFFIN and ELIZABETH the extx of Capt. George WATKINS. Before 3 July 1677. Surry, Va. Orders i-143. Before 7 Sept 1675. See Oi-98.

JOHN RUST and MOLLY McCLANAHAN. 22 Dec 1796. Fauq, Va.

JORDAN SANDERS and Miss Ann NETTLES. 10 Oct 1805. Darlington, S. C. Mar. Li.

LITTLETON SAVAGE and MARGARET BURTON. 14 Jany 1768. N-n, Va. Mar. Li. Bond.

EDWARD SANFORD and ELIZABETH, one of the daus. of Patrick SPENCE. [the elder.] Before 27 Jany 1746. Wmld, Va. Fid. ii-27.

EDWARD SANFORD and MARGARET x MANLEY, widow of Harrison MANLEY. After Dec 1773. Ffx, Va. L. C. [She was the dau. of Mr. Edward Barry, see L-51. Her mother, a widow m. Edward Washington.]

RICHARD SANFORD and ELIZABETH PRICE, dau. of John. Before 7 Jany 1786. Ffx, Va. E(1)-127. See also K. Geo, Va. vii-174.

SAMUEL SAMFORD prob. m. ELIZABETH JADWYN, dau. of Jeremiah, Gent. Before 21 Nov 1704. Richm'd, Va. iii-172.

NATHANIEL SAVAGE and SARAH BOLES, widow of Henry "which SARAH was extx of William Parker, dec'd." About 1 Dec 1724. Acco, Va. xix-9. A N-n, Va., chancery record gives her name as BOLD.

NATHANIEL SAVAGE and MARGARET JAMES, dau. of Thomas. Before 11 Dec 1820. N-n, Va. L. C. 1815-1834. p. 82.

THOMAS SAVAGE and ESTHER LITTLETON. Before 1719. Acco, Va. xvi-253. A record (xvi-254) makes this Thos. SAVAGE, Jr.

WILLIAM SAVAGE and MARGARET, extx of Charles GREEN, Clerk. 21 May 1771. Ffx, Va. Orders [iii]-218.

WILLIAM SAVAGE and PHEBE SEAWARD, dau. of Josias. Before 6 Sept 1710. Acco, Va. xiv-12.

JEREMIAH SCOTT and COMFORT ROADES, widow of John. Before 17 Feby 1691. Acco, Va. x-58. [From a record, x-76, she seems to have been about 40, 17 Feby 1691-2.]

SAMUEL SCOLLAY and ELIZABETH POLLOCK, widow of Mr. Thomas POLLOCK. About 1766 or 1767. Bertie, N. C.

GEORGE SCHNEIDER and ELIZABETH REIGAL, dau. of William. Before 11 Jany 1779. Northumb, Pa. O. C. i-18.

THOMAS SCOTT and NANNY CROTHERS. Before 1800. Draper Mss. 11CC-224, 227. W. H. S.

WILLIAM SCOTT and GRIZELLA CROTHERS. Before 1800. Draper Mss. 11CC-224, 227. W. H. S.

HUGH SEAMOR [SEAMAN?] and MARY STEELE. Before 18 Jany 1821. Alleg. cty, Penna. ii-230.

WILLIAM SEARS and ANNA CONDEN. 1780. Cecil cty, Md. Mar. Reg.

NEVIL SEENEY and MARY ROCHESTER, dau. of Francis. Before 31 Oct 1783. Q. A. Md. Minutes.

SOLOMON SELLERS and REBECCA JACKSON. 20 July 1810. Bulloch cty, Ga. Mar. Li.

BRIG.-GEN'L. JOHN SEVIER and SARAH HAWKINS, of Aug. or Rock'm cty, Va. He m. (2) Katherine Sherrill. 14 Aug 1780. See Tenn. Hist. Mags. v-156.

Col. VALENTINE SEVIER and NAOMI DOUGLAS. About 1767. In Shenan, Va. Draper Mss. 3DD-265. W. H. S.

VALENTINE SEVIER and JOANNA GOOD. Before 1745, in Aug. cty, Va. Tenn. Hist. Mags. v-156.

THOMAS SISON [Bucks cty] and PRISCILLA PURCHASE, dau. of Samuel. Before 14 Dec 1699. Penna. Arch. i-440.

JAMES SHARKLAND and SARAH PARSLEY, at St. Paul's, Philada. 2 May 1761. Penna. Arch. Ser. 2, ix-445.

JACOB SHAHAN and RACHEL MANLOVE, widow of John. Kent, Dela. O. C. records. Before 21 Feby 1812.

HERCULAS [*sic*] SHEPARD and MARY AVERY, dau. of Capt. John. Before 13th 12th 1682. Sussex, Dela. A1-18.

PETER SHERWALT and CATHERINE REIGEL, dau. of William. Before 11 Jany 1779. Northumb. cty, Penna. O. C. Docket 1-18.

JOHN SHOEMAKER and EVE SAUL. 3 Jany 1772. N. Y. Mar. Li.

ALEXANDER SHEAPEARD and ______ BARRET, dau. and "heyre" of Francis. Before 10 July 1658. Va. S. L. O. v-175.

______SHORT and FRANCES HARRISON. Before 1778. [See wills of Cuthbert and Anne HARRISON.] Pr. Wm, Va. G-70.

JOHN SIMONTON and HANNAH JAQUAT, dau. of Paul. Before 1768. N. C., Dela. Surveys.

JAMES SIMPSON and ELIZABETH JOHNSON, dau. of William. Before 1768. Dela. Surveys. N. C. cty, p. 221.

LEONARD SMITH and CHARL[OTTE] LAIN. 29 Dec 1807. Elbert, Ga. Reg. Bk B.

JOSEPH SMITH and MARY ANN HARRIS. 30 Dec 1821. [1824?] Elbert, Ga. L-488.

JOHN SMITH and AMELIA SHELY (b. 24 July 1777.) 1 Jany 1804. Draper Mss. 17CC-53. From Roche family Bible. W. H. S.

JAMES SMITH and MARTHA CLASBY, dau. of Col. CLASBY. Before 1800. Draper Mss. XNN-110. W. H. S.

RICHARD SMITH and ANN STANTON, dau. of Stephen. Before Nov 1759. Kent, Dela. Chanc'y Proceedings.

WILLIAM SMITH and ELIZABETH WEBSTER. See record 18 Feby 1789. N. C. cty, Dela. E-64.

BENJAMIN SMITH and ANN LOUGHTON, prob. dau. of David. Before 3 May 1740. Charleston, S. C. T-602.

WILLIAM SMITH and ISABEL FOSTER. 16 Jany 1796. Ogleth. Ga. Mar. ctf.

JAMES SMITH and POLLY HARRIS. 1802. Bulloch cty, Ga. Mar. Li.

JOHN SMITH and PRISCILLA AUBRY. 23 Jany 1797. Ogleth. Ga. M. L. B.

JOHN SMITH and NANCY STEPHENS. 19 Dec 1798. Ogleth., Ga.

THOMAS SNEAD and SERANA WARD. Mar. contract. 10 Feby 1791. Onslow, N. C.

_____ SODOWSKY [SANDUSKY] and ______ VAUSE, a dau. of Col. VAUSE. Before 1800. Draper Mss. 11CC2-7-21. W. H. S. [This statement is made by the dau., Mrs. Shanklin, of Jessamine cty, Ky.]

THOMAS SORRELL and ELIZABETH, one of the daus. of John ARIES. Before 26 Apr 1737. Wmld, Va. Orders, fo. 227. See also fo. 236 and 244.

EDMOND SOUTHARD and SARAH THORNTON, dau. of the Rev'd Thos. THORNTON. After 1791. Filson Club, xxii-180.

SANDERS SOUTHERLAND and MARTHA DAVIS, dau. of Samuel. Before 15 Dec 1777. Fluvanna, Va. i-63.

JOHN SOUTHWELL prob. m. MARY HILTON, dau. of Thomas. Before 20 Apr 1819. Bulloch, Ga. B-41.

HENRY SPELLER and MARTHA KITTRELL, widow, relict of Dempsey KITTRELL. Mar. contract. 28 Jany 1807. Bertie, N. C. T-527.

HENRY SPARROW and LUCY HANKS. 3 Apr 1791. Mercer, Ky. M. L. B.

JOSEPH SIMONS and ANN WILLIAMS [dau. of Arthur.] Before May 1775. Bertie, N. C.

ROBERT SIMS and POLLY MARSTON. 22 Dec 1791. Culp. Va. M. L. B.

WILLIAM SKINNER and HARRIETT KEITH. 26 Dec 1796. Fauq, Va. M. L. B.

JOHN SLOAT and CATHERINE HENDRICKS, widow of John. Before 1814. See Dutchess cty, N. Y. xxiv-46.

THOMAS SPENCE and MARY MURPHY, widow of John. About 30 Oct 1744. Wmld, Va. Fid. Accts, fo. 302. See also Orders, fo. 46. Before the above date.

WILLIAM SPURGEON and JANE FORMAN. 1794. Bourbon, Ky. Mar. Ret.

EBENEZER SPENCER and BETTY TOWNSEND, dau. of Stephen. Before 10 Jany 1759. Sussex, Dela. B2-190.

JOHN STARR and HANNAH JAMES, admx of Daniel. See Ct 25 May 1792. N. C. cty, Dela. E-346.

ELISHA START [STAAT?] and HESTER HANSON, dau. of John and Hester. Before 1 May 1816. N. C. Dela. V3-254.

JONATHAN STARGES [STURGIS?] and HONOR KIPSHAVE, widow of John *Kipshaven*, Sr. Before 2 Feb 1702. Sussex, Dela. Early records. p. 18E.

ABRAHAM STAATS, Sr. and AMY BARBER, dau. of John. Before 1758. N. C. cty, Dela. N-331.

GEORGE STONEMITZ, of Salem, N. J., and ANN TUSSEY, dau. of Elias. Before 4 Nov 1769. N. C. cty, Dela. Z-631.

EDWARD STRETCHER, of Philada., prob. m. BETTY DAVIS, sister of Henry. Before 9 May 1765. Sussex, Dela. B2-283.

JOHN STURGIS and SARAH FITZGARALD, widow of James. Before 20 Dec 1770. Archives, Dover, Dela.

CHRISTOPHER STAIR and DOROTHEA DOUDEL, dau. of Jacob. Before 24 Mch 1785. York, Penna. O. C. E-267.

Mr. JOHN STATON and Miss PENELOPY SELLERS. 4 Aug 1794. Effingham cty, Ga. Mar. Li. [See Effingham List also.]

THOMAS STEEL and RESTITUTE WHISTON [WILSON?] dau. of RESTITUTE HALLOWS and her husband.[?] Va. Gen. Ct. Dec p. B26.

MARKEES [MARCUS or MARQUIS?] STEPHENSON and AGNES HINKSON. 11 Aug 1791. Bourbon, Ky. Mar. Ret.

JAMES STEPHENSON and HANNAH WATSON. 9 Jany 1775. Shenan., Va. Mar. Li.

______STEVENS and JUDITH EVANS, widow of Thomas. Before or about 11 May 1780. Botetourt, Va.

CLEMENT W. STEVENS, Lt. U. S. N., prob. m. SARAH J. FAYSSOUX [FAISSON?] Before 1822. Inscription, graveyard of Church of the Advent, Greenv, S. C.

MONTFORD STOKES and RACHEL MONTGOMERY, dau. of Hugh. Before 3 Feby. 1812. Wilkes, N. C. iii-28.

DAVID STONE and ELIZABETH JENIFER, dau. of Dr. Daniel JENIFER. Before 11 May 1743 Semmes Mss. M. H. S.

THOMAS STONE and JAMIMA STURMAN, "own sister" to William STURMAN. Before 31 May 1732. Wmld, Va. Orders, fo. 26. [The record says "Thomas Stone run away." Jamima was dead at the time of the record.]

WILLIAM STONE and CARAH[?] COBERT. 27 Oct 1812. Elbert, Ga. K-32.

ENOCH STORY and SARAH CARPENTER, dau. of Joshua. Before 1720. Philada. Wills. Abstracts. p. 431. P. H. S. See also Wills D-325.

JAMES STRANGE [perhaps STRONG?] and MARY BRADY, dau. of Samuel. Before 31 Mch 1785. Onslow, N. C. Wills, p. 35.

JAMES STRODE and MARTHA FORMAN. 21 Oct 1791. Bourbon, Ky. Mar. Ret.

FRANCIS STROTHER and ANNE HUGHES, prob. dau. of Thomas. Before 3 Sept 1744. K. Geo., Va. iii-261.

WILLIAM STROTHER and MARGARET, extx of William PATTISHALL. Before 4 June 1737. K. Geo, Va. Oii-116.

WILLIAM STROTHER and the widow of George WEEDON. Before 25 Feby 1746. Wmld, Va. Fid. ii-46.

WILLIAM STROTHER and MARGARET WATTS, dau. of Richard, Gent. Before 26 Mch 1718. Wmld, Va. 1705-1721. fo. 339.

WILLIAM STROUD and RACHEL HUGINS, of Jamaica. 2 Dec 1712. At Jamaica. N. Y. G. & B. xix-53.

JOHN SWINEFORD and BARBARA RUPLEY, dau. of Jacob. Before 6 July 1789. Cumb., Penna. E-284.

HARDY SUMMERLIN and PENELOPE COLLIN. 23 Nov 1801. Bulloch, Ga. Mar. Li.

______SWINEY and JANE RICKETS, widow of James. [E. C. cty, Va. Va. Col. Dec. No date.]

ROBERT SWINEY and JANE ARMSTRONG, dau. of Thomas and Rachel. Before 15 May 1724. Penna. Arch, Ser. 3. i-25.

JOHN SYMES, St. Martin's Psh, Hanover, and SARAH SYME, dau. of Adam HOOPES, of the Falls, Bucks cty, Penna. Before 18 Aug 1790. Hanover, Va. Deeds.

JAS. A. TABB and DOROTHY MERRICK. Mar. contract. About 22 Mch 1787. N. Hanover, N. C. H-470.

______TARR and SARAH HOLLAND, dau. of Nehemiah. Before 2 Feby 1758. Wor. Md, J. W. 3-15.

PETER TAYLOR and ANN SWANN, widow of John, Esq. Mar. contract. N. Hanover, N. C. E-104. 17 Oct 1764.

JOHN TAYLOR and ELIZABETH FISSELL, dau. of Frederick. Before 22 Mch 1785. York, Penna. O. C. E-243.

ABRAHAM TAYLOR and MARY MITCHELL. 4 Sept 1792. Richm'd, Ga. Mar. Li.

Col. RICHARD TAYLOR, b. 1744, and SARAH STROTHER. 1779. Draper Mss. W. H. S. 8zz-66.

JOHN THEOBOLD and the admx of Dr. Daniel JENIFER. Before 11 May 1743. Semmes Mss. M. H. S.

WILLIAM THOMPSON and "MELENIOUM" GRIMES. 25 Sept. 1812. Bulloch cty, Ga. Mar. Li.

JOHN TWIGS and ELINOR THOMAS, dau. of Paul. Before 1737-8. N. C. cty, Dela. M1-57.

WILLIAM TEBBS and MARY POPE, relict and admx of Thomas. Wmld, Va. Before 30 Apr 1745. See Orders, fo. 67; also 77 and 80. About 1741-2. See i-317. See also Fid. Accts p. 32, See Inv. iii-63.

JOHN TEW [TOW?] and GRACE x BALDRIDGE, widow of Maj. Thomas B. Before or about 21 Aug 1654. Wmld, Va. i-27. "Mrs. GRACE TOW als ISHAM." See i-47 1655.

JACOB THOMAS of Chester cty, and SARAH, sister of Joseph RUSSEL. Before 3 Dc 1768. Sussex, Dela. B2-346.

JESSE THOMAS and AVICE STANTON, dau. of Benj. Before 31st of 3d mo 1803. Carteret, N. C. O-366.

PRICE THOMAS and MARY MONROE. Before 29 May 1781. Wmld, Va. vii-158.

THOMAS THOMPSON and PENELOPE, relict of Patrick Spence. Before 3 Sept 1703. Wmld, Va. 1698-1705, fo. 202.

JOHN THOMPSON and AGNESS VIN LEER [VAN LEAR]. Before 7 Apr 1801. Dauphin cty, Penna. B-55.

THOMAS THOMSON, of Salem, W. Jersey. and REBECCA BRASSEY, dau. of Thomas. Before 5th mo, 23d, 1703. Penna. Arch. Series 2. xix-458.

SAMUEL THOMPSON and MARY LOGUE, sister of Ephraim. Before 30 Apr 1780. Caswell, N. C. Deeds A-116.

MOSES THOMPSON and REBECCA HUGHES, dau. of John. Before 15 Jany 1768. Rowan cty, N. C.

LUKE THORNTON and MILLESANT, the Relict of Wm. Longworth. [Thornton moved to "Oringe" cty.] Before 29 July 1735. Wmld, Va. Orders, fo. 177. Also Inv. i-156.

RICHARD TODD and NANCY ELLIT. Before 29 Sept 1734. Stafford Va. Wills. p. 163.

Gen. ROBERT TODD and NANCY TODD, dau. of John. Draper Mss, W. H. S. 13CC-167-69.

ADAM TURNER and LUCY KERR. [Mason cty, Kentucky?] Draper Mss. W. H. S. 12ZZ-330. 2 Mch 1796.

WILLIAM TURNER and COMFORT OXFORD, dau. of Thomas. Sussex, Dela. B-43. 1747.

ARD[?] JOHNSON VAN KIRK and GRACE BUNDOCK. 28 July 1681. By William Clark, Justice. Sussex [Deale] cty, Dela. Ancient Records. p. 4.

JOHN CORNELIUS VAN DER VER and MARIA STALCOP, dau. of Peter. Before 1714. Records of Holy Trinity, Wilmington, Dela. p. 169.

WILLIAM VAUGHAN and BETTY [WAPLES?] sister of Derickson. Before 23 Feby 1775. Sussex, Dela. B2-541.

[JOHN] WADDINGTON and FRANCES GILL, dau. of Thomas. Before 10 Feby 1707-8. Nthld, Va. 1706-1720.

______WADY and JANE SPENCE, dau. of John. Before 23 Oct 1700. Va. Col. Dec. p. R61. [*There is considerable doubt as to the identity of this JANE, as the early date of this marriage does not fit in with the date of her birth.*]

THOMAS WARD prob. m. ARCADIA WELBOURNE, widow of Thomas. Before 3 Apr 1816. Acco., Va. xv-18.

BENJAMIN WALTON and MARY SWIFT. Mar. contract. Bucks, Pa. Penna. No. 38.

EDWARD WASHINGTON and ______BARRY, widow of Edward. Before 16 June 1772. Ffx, Va. L-51.

JOHN WASHINGTON and MARY MUMPASS, widow of William. Before 29 Jany 1791. Caswell, N. C.

JOHN WASHINGTON and MARY FLOOD, widow. Contract of marriage______"in trust for Tho: Blunt sonne of sd Mary"______ Two of the wit. to this contract were Jno. Flood and Tho: Flood. 15 Oct 1658. Surry, Va. i-126. MARY next married Charles Ford. For further interesting notes, see Surry, i-207 and "2"-64.

JOSIAS WASTCOATE and MARY, admx of Francis CORNWALL. Before 2 June 1696. Sussex, Dela.

LEVI WALKER and ANN, dau. of Miriam REDD. Before 1838. N. C. cty, Dela. U1-50.

PAUL WAPLES and BATHSHEBA [LEATHERBURY?] dau. of Diana. Before 8 Oct 1773. Sussex, Dela. B2-506.

WILLIAM WAPLES and ABIGAIL STOCKLEY, dau. of Benjamin. Before 30 Nov 1762. Sussex, Dela B2-299.

WILLIAM WATERS and ISABELL HARMANSON, dau. of Thos., Sr. Before 29 Sept 1702. N-n, Va. xviii-112.

WILLIAM WATKINS, Jr, and RUTH POPE. 15 May 1806. Elbert, Ga. Reg. Bk B.

Capt. LUKE WATSON and SARAH PAYNER [?] widow of Richard, Sr. Before 9 May 1706. Sussex, Dela. p. 29f.

______WELBURNE and MASON WATT, extx of James. About 1 Oct 1717. Acco, Va. xvi-31.

______WATTS prob. m. KATHARINE WALTON, dau. of Col. Thos. About or before 1742-3. I. W., Va. D-264.

______WEBB and MARY WIGGINS [possibly a widow.] About 1802. Bulloch cty, Ga. Mar. Li.

BURRILL WEBB and SARAH BOOTH. 18 Oct 1806. Elbert, Ga. Reg. Bk B.

JAMES WEBB, of Orange cty, N. C. and NANCY DABBS, widow of Joseph, late of Goochland, Va. Before 8 July 1762. Cumb. Va. iii-279.

WILLIAM WEBB and MARTHA ORD. 1 June 1775. Penna. Mar. Li. Penna. Mgs. xli-492.

JOHN WEBB [who died 18 Oct 1774] m MARY BOONE, who was b. 23 Sept 1699 and d. 16 Jany 1774; she was dau. of Geo. and Mary. County not given. Draper Mss W. H. S. B-23.

TIMOTHY WEBSTER and ELIZABETH HOLDEN, dau. of Joseph. N. C. cty, Dela. E-64. [Joseph Holden d. about 1684.]

JAMES WELBORN and REBECAH MONTGOMERY, dau. of Hugh. Before Feby 1812. Wilkes, Ga. iii-28.

JAMES WELLS and CATHERINE OWENS, Apr 1789. Bourbon, Ky. Mar. Ret.

WRIXHAM WEST and ANN STOCKLEY, dau. of Benjamin. Before 30 Nov 1762. Sussex, Dela. B-2-299.

WILLIAM WEST, Sr., and SUSANNAH CHICHESTER, dau. of William Chichester, the pilot. West lived at Perquimans, N. C. He was deceased at the date of this record. Before 6 June 1722. Pr. A., Va. 1-412.

WRIXHAM WEST and ANN STOCKLEY,dau. of Benjamin. Before 30 Nov 1762. Sussex, Dela. B2-299.

ROBERT WHARTON and RACHELLIS, dau. of Thomas. Before 11th 11th 1702. Penna. Arch. Ser. 2. xix-348.

______WHISTON [WILSON] and RESTITUTE HALLOWS, dau. of John, "late of Rochdale in the County Palatine of Lancaster." [No date.] Va. Gen. Ct. Dec. p. B26.

RICHARD WHITAKER, psh of St. Martin in the Fields, Middx, Eng., peruke maker, and ABIGAIL WELCH. Before 24 Feby 1735. Essex, Va. xxi-190.

HAZLEWOOD WILKINSON and ANNA GRANT, dau. of Daniel. Before or about 11 Jany 1792. Wilkes, Ga. MM-42.

______WILLIAMS prob. m. ANNA HAGISTER, a widow. Before 2 Feb 1702. Sussex, Dela. p. 18E. See also 58f. [Early records.]

JOHN WILLIE, tallow chandler, of London, and ELIZABETH PITT, widow of Robert, late of London, mariner. Before 14 Apr 1675. Acco, Va. v-277.

RICHARF WILLIS and ANN GRIGGS, widow of Michael. Before 7 Aug 1691. Lanc. cty, Va. S. L. O. i-77.

JO. WILLIAMS and POLLY BROWN. [a list without year date______. prob. 1802.] Greene cty, Ga.

THOMAS WILLIAMS and MARY LOCKHART, dau. of Samuel S. Before 22 Oct 1831. Bulloch, Ga. B-377.

SAMPSON WILLIAMS and the widow of John INGLIS. Before Aug. Ct 1765. Cumb, N. C.

JONATHAN WILLIAMS and REBEKAH WILLIAMS. 17 May 1806. [Mar. 18 May 1808? This is prob. an error on the part of the clerk of the copysist.] Greene cty, Ga. Mar. Li.

ENOCH WILLS and NANCY LACKEY, dau. of Andrew. Before 1789. Kent, Dela. A2-110.

SAMUEL WILLSON and MARY LACKEY, dau. of Andrew. Samé refs.

ADAM WILSON and JEAN JAQUAT, dau. of Paul. Before 1768. N. C. cty, Dela. Surveys. p. 221.

ROBERT WILSON and POLLY RUSSELL. 102. Kanawha, W. V. Mar. Ret.

JAMES WILSON and PATSY RASIL. About 1796. Kanawha, W. Va.

CALEB WILSON and MARCY[?] FLOYD, dau. of Halsy. Before 28 Dec 1828. Perq. N. C. F-200.

JOHN WINTERS prob. m. MARY GILLILAND, dau. of Thomas, the Elder. 26 June 1778. Wilkes, Ga. i-47. [They had a son Thomas Winters.]

NATHAN NORRIST WRIGHT and TABITHA DAVIS, dau. of Samuel and Hannah. Before 22 Aug 1790. Kent, Md. vii-294. See also viii-162.

RICE WOLFE and MARY CORNEWALL, dau. of Francis. Before 4 Mch 1706. Sussex, Dala. Early records, 60F.

JOHN WRIGHT and SARAH WRIGHT. 24 June 1714. Records Holy Trinity, Wmton, Dela. p. 219.

THOMAS WYATT and SARAH POPE, dau. of John DAVIS. Before 1700. Pasquotank, N. C. A-329.

RICHARD WAYNE and ELIZABETH CLIFFORD, the younger, spinster, of St. Bartholomew's Psh. Mar. settlement. 14 Sept 1769. Charleston, S. C. TT-130.

SAFFORD or HAFFORD WALDRON and HANNAH WEBB. Before 2 July 1829. Northumb. Penna. iii-239.

JOHN WALLACE and MARGARET ANDERSON, dau. of Allen. Before 24 Mch 1785. York, Penna. O. C. E-261.

THOMAS WALKER and Mrs. ELIZABETH [GREGORY] THORNTON__"an old sweetheart." 14 Jany 1781. Draper Mss. W. H. S. 5QQ-92. See also B5-11.

FELIX WALKER and ISABELLA HENRY. 10 Jany 1780. Draper Mss. W. H. S. 24C-5.

THOMAS WAKEFIELD, of Eversham Tshp, Burl. cty, N. J. and KATHARINE SULAVAN, widow of *Thurlas*. Before 1 Aug 1702. E. Jersey Records. xxl-539.

JAMES WEST and JANE SCOGGIN, dau. of John. Before 24 Mch 1785. York, Penna; O. C. E-256.

JOSEPH WHITE and SUSANNA McCORD, dau. of Richard. Before 4 Feby 1786. York, Penna. O. C. E-355.

ALEXANDER WILLEY and the widow of Benajah DOTY. Before 20 Aug 1787. Onslow, N. C.

ALEXANDER WILSON and MARY ORBISON [?] widow of Thomas. Before 28 Nov 1782. Cumb, Penna. O. C. ii-313.

DAVID WOOD and RUTH GREGG, dau. of Thomas. Before 16 June 1821. Fayette, Penna. i-214.

JOSEPH WAY and PRUDENCE LARKIN, dau. of John. Before 23 June 1786. Chester cty, Penna. Will Abstracts. P. H. S. iii-242.

FRANCIS WORLEY, of Chester cty, Penna; and MARY BRASSEY. Before 5th mo. 23d. [1703.] Penna. Arch. Ser. 2. xiv-458.

BENJAMIN WILLIAMS and COMFORT WELSH, dau. of Capt. John Welsh. Before 23 Nov 1752. Semmes Mss. M. H. S.

______WHITE and CATHERINE WILLIAMS, widow of Moragn. Before 25 Jany 1705. S. L. O. iii-123. White was then deceased. [Catherine had also been a widow Stewart.]

ROGER WIGGINTON and the relict of John CLEMENTS. Before 29 Aug 1716. Wmld, Va. v-622.

JAMES WHITE and ELIZABETH, admx of Hugh FENIX, late of Q. A. Before 5 Dec 1829. Q. A., Va. Minutes. O. C.

ROBERT WHYTHELL, of Chas. cty, and ELIZABETH THEOBOLD, widow of John. Before 11 May 1743. Semmes Mss. M. H. S.

BENJAMIN WICKER prob. m. FRANCES BAILY, dau. of John and Susan. About or before 21 Mch 1789. Hanover cty, Va. W. & M. xxi-152.

CHRISTOPHER WILSON and DINAH GREGG, dau. of DINAH. Before 3-8-1763. Chester cty, Penna. Wills. P. G. S.

HENRY WINCOOP and SARAH DUBOIS, dau. of Isaac. Before 13 Feby 1707. Philada. O. C. 1716-1755; p. 40. P. H. S.

Mr. RICHARD WRIGHT prob. m.______the sister of Mich: SPENCER, Esq. Before 6 Sept 1665. Va. S. L. O. ii-121.

______WOODLIFE (of Chas. City cty) and ELIZA: WALLAS, eldest dau. of Mr. John Wallas. Before 24 Oct 1701. Va. S. L. O. ix-388.

JAMES WOOLFORD, of Somerset, and GRACE STEVENS of Dorchester, at the meeting-house near Choptank river. 3d of 9th 1698. Third Haven Friends' Records, v-395.

PHILLIP YEISSER and CATHERINE DOUDEL, dau. of Jacob. Before 24 Mch 1785. Yor. Penna. O. C. E-268.

JOHN YOPP prob. m. ANNE STEWART, widow and admx of James. Before 9 Feby 1746. Nthld, Va. 1743-1749. fo. 91 & 171.

GEORGE YOUNG and MARY SOUTHRINE. Before 6th of 10th 1687. Sussex, Dela. Early records. p. 79b.

GEORGIA:

The following references are to *Marriage Licenses* which will be found in a volume of miscellaneous records in the office of the Ordinary, in Effingham county, Georgia. Some of these marriage licenses have been published in the COUNTY COURT NOTE-BOOK.

Mr. CHRISTIAN BECHTLY and Miss ELIZABETH RIESSER. 16 Aug 1799.

JONOTHAN BECHLY and MARY RIESSER, dau. of Benj. and Catharine Rieser. Mar. before 12 Apr 1799. B-93. The marriage license for this record is dated 21 Feby 1795, and the names are given as BECKLEY and REASER.

Mr. William BIRD and Miss ELIZABETH STINER. 27 Apr 1798.

Mr. CHRISTIAN BIEDENBACH and Mrs. FREDERICA FOY. 25 Apr 1798.

JAMES BOSTON and Miss ELIZABETH BRIGGS. 18 Nov 1794.

Mr. WILLIAM CRAWFORD and Miss PATSEY BAILEY. 26 July 1794.

Mr. JOHN COWARD and Miss LIDIA ROLLISON. 18 Jany 1800.

Mr. MATTHEW CANBY and Mrs. LIDDIA FORD. 11 Dec 1793.

ABRAHAM COLSON and Miss MARGARET MOTT. 13 Dec 1793.

Mr. JOSIAH DANEL and Mrs. SARAH CAMPBELL. 18 Feby 1795.

Mr. NOAH DIKES and Miss SALLY STATON. 4 Feby 1797.

DAVID EWING and Miss MARY CONWAY. 30 Dec 1794.

Mr. GOTTLIEB ERNST and Miss CATHERINE FIELDS. 18 Sept 1798.

MICHAEL EXLY and CATHERINE EXLY. 12 Apr 1799.

JOHN FOLK and Miss MARY SHEELY. 5 May 1795.

Mr. CHARLES GACHET and Miss MARY GOBERT. 9 Feby 1795.

Mr. JAMES GREENHOUSE, Jr., and Miss ABEGAIL SCRUGGS. 12 Mch 1794.

Mr. TIMOTHY GNANN and Miss [Mrs.?] CATHARINE LEIMBERGER. 6 Nov 1799.

Mr. JAMES GARRISON and Miss MARTHA DYKES. 4 July 1799.

Mr. JAMES GOLDWIRE and Miss SARAH KING. 27 Dec 1796.

Mr. JOHN GARNETT and Miss MARY BOSTICK. 30 July 1794.

Mr. DAVID GROOVER and Miss HANNAH SHEROUS. 13 Nov 1798.

Mr. WALDIN GRIFFIN and Miss ESTHER RAWLESON. 20 June 1795.

Mr. HENRY LEWIS GRABENSTINE and Mrs. JUDITH BUSH. 19 Oct 1797.

Mr. CHRISTOPHER HUDSON and Mrs. HANNAH HEERSSEN. 6 Mch 1798.

JOHN HECK and Miss AGNES POULIDGE. 17 Sept 1775.

Mr. GEORGE HEITE and Miss SALLY REMSHART 2 July 1795.

Mr. JAMES HOLLEN and Mrs. HANNAH GREENHOW. 21 Mch 1798.

Mr. JACOB HINELY and Miss ELIZABETH MICK[?] 16 Jany 1799.

Mr. JOHN IVY and Miss NAOMY WOODLIEF. 4 Aug 1795.

Mr. JOHN KEEBLER and Miss ROSANNA STOCKMAN. 9 May 1797.

Mr. JACOB KETTLES and Miss AMEY GARNETT. 11 Mch 1795.

Mr. JOHN F. LOCKNER and Miss HANAH HEISLER. 30 Mch 1799.

JOHN LUCAN and Miss CLARESEY DUNMARKS. 20 Dec 1794.

Mr. DAVID LITTERAUER and Miss ELIZABETH IHLY. 24 Jany 1797.

Mr. ISRAEL LEIMBERGER and Miss MARY CATHERINE SNIDER. 2 May 1799.

Mr. MINIS LAMLEY and Miss POLLY HINES [?This name uncertain, it may be HUES.] 28 May 1799.

DAVID METZGER and Mrs. MARY REASOE. 1 Nov 1794.

Mr. JOHN MICHAEL and Miss ELIZABETH GROOVER. 22 Feby 1794.

ISAAC MOTT and Miss POLLY COLSON. 7 Dec 1793.

Mr. BENJAMIN MOREL and Miss SUSANNA GINDRAT. 28 Dec 1798.

WILLIAM MORGAN and Miss SARAH BAILIE. 4 May 1795.

Mr. DANIEL O'NEEL and Miss ANN CLYATT. 31 Mch 1793.

Mr. JOHN PORTER and Miss HENRIETTA RAVOT. 16 Jany 1795.

Mr. DAVID PORTER and Miss SALLY BOSTICK. 29 July 1797.

Mr. TRYON PACE and Miss MARY DYKES. 16 Aug 1798.

Mr. WILLIAM PORTER and Miss RACHEL GARNET. 14 Jany 1795.

Mr. ANTHONY PITTS and Miss ANN RAWLESON. 24 May 1794.

MATTHEW RALM, Wheelwright, and Miss HANNAH ELIZABETH DOLWICH, sp same. Mar. contract. 23 Jany 1802. B-155.

Mr. THOMAS ROBERTS and Miss ELIZABETH PINNINGER 18 Sept 1795.

BENJ. REISER and CATHARINE MICHALER, dau. of John. Before 12 Apr 1799. B-93. [This is a marriage.]

Mr. DAVID REISER and Miss MARY GROVENSTINE. 16 Apr 1792.

Mr. JOSEPH RAHN and Miss NAOMY SETLER. 25 Apr 1794.

JONATHAN SNIDER and Miss ELIZABETH GNANN. 18 Aug 1794.

Mr. DAVID SNOOK and Miss ELIZABETH PORTER. 1 Jany 1794.

Rev'd JAMES SWEAT and Miss SUSANNAH ANDERSON. 16 Jany 1795.

Mr. JAMES SHARBROUGH and Mrs. MARY LEWIS. 26 July 1797.

Mr. SAMUEL SNIDER and Miss CATHERINE ZIEGLER. 20 June 1798.

Mr. THOMAS SCHWEIGHOFFER and Miss SALOME ZANT. 10 June 1797.

Mr. JOSHUA STAFFORD and Mrs MARY LANE, relict of Thomas. 21 Apr 1794.

Mr. JOHN STATON and Miss PENELOPY SELLERS. 4 Aug 1794.

Mr. RICHARD TOUCHSTONE and Mrs. MARTHA CRAWFORD. 3 July 1798.

Mr. HENRY WHITE and Miss SARAH BUTTS. 25 Mch 1795.

Mr. ELIAS WINKLER and Mrs. MARY PINNINGER. 11 July 1796.

Mr. DANIEL WEITMAN and Mrs. ANN CATHERINE KRAMER. 8 July 1794.

Mr. JESSE WILSON and Miss ELIZABETH COOK. 10 Aug 1799.

Mr. HENRY W. WILLIAMS and Miss SARAH McCALL. 21 Apr 1794.

Mr. JOHN WILLIAMS and Miss RHEETEE [perhaps meant for RITA?] LONDON. 24 Mch 1794.

Mr. JOSHUA ZANT and Miss CATHERINE STEINER. 9 May 1796.

Mr. GIDEON ZETTLER and Miss MATILDA WILSON. 16 Apr 1799.

INITIALS and ABBREVIATIONS: some of these may need explanation. Alb is Albemarle; N, Northampton; Nthld, Northumberland; Wmld, Westmoreland; Mddx, Middlesex; Ldn, Loudoun; N. C., New Castle or North Carolina; Wor, Worcester; Q. A. Queen Anne's; O. C., Orphans' Court; S. L. O., State Land Office; M. H. S., P. H. S., W. H. S. &c Maryland Historical Society, Pennsylvania Historical Society, Wisconsin Historical Society or Library; &c., &c., M. L. B., Marriage License Bonds; L. C., Land Causes. I. K. L. is the curious lettering of an old Somerset, Md., volume. Nearly all the references are to county records, and the proper names with such references refer to counties.

PLEASE NOTE

the list of important Virginia publications on page 24. Information as to price, &c., can be had from Mrs. Nottingham, Onancock, Virginia.

If any researcher is interested in the publication of 2,000 additional marriage references, sufficiently to underwrite the expense (temporarily) of such publication, please address the Editor of this bulletin, Bethesda. R. R. 5, Md. About $100 is required.

EXPLANATORY

It is to be understood that the "inferred marriages" which begin upon the first page of this pamphlet are only in a small percentage based upon actual marriage returns, either by ministers or as occasionally given in records of the county courts-------more properly called Circuit Courts. Usually these references are taken from wills, settlements of estates, administration accounts, conveyances of land, or from marriage licenses or marriage license bonds. These last two sources are not to be considered as actual proof of marriage, though with rare exceptions the marriage may be considered to have occured after the filing of the bond and the issuance of the license.

The question of a license being proof of a marriage was strongly impressed upon the then somewhat inexperienced compiler by a gentleman high up in both law and genealogy. The compiler was seated upon a most uncomfortable high stool in the record room of the Clerk of the Court of Baltimore county, probably after hours, and was "paging" a thick volume of marriage licenses. Mr. Story, the gentleman referred to, came up to her and said *"You know these are not really marriages"* . . . . explaining that they were only proof that a marriage was intended.

But the exceptions are very few, at least in the earlier years.

The notation "before" is usually the best that can be done as to the date of the marriage. The "before" may cover a generation or a few months. This should be kept in mind.

In order to save space, the distinction "Deed Book" or "Land Record" or "Will Record", &c., has not usually been made. "A" or "B", &c., may refer to one of two or more series of records. The volumes are not difficult of identification (except in the numerous classifications of the early Orphans' Court) and the compiler of this list will be willing at any time to refer to her note-books and enlarge upon any reference. (Kindly, however, send postage.)

A few of these items have been hereofore published in the COUNTY COURT NOTE-BOOK. Sometimes accidental, occasionally a new and better reference has been found, or an error is corrected.

Spelling of names----the variations in spelling, are not, as a rule of great importance, and need not be enlarged upon; there is hardly a name which has travelled down the generations before 1800, which has not had its mutations. ROBINSON may be ROBERTSON, (and often should be) or ROBISON, ROBERSON, ROBBISSON, or ROBESON, &c. STERLING and be STARLING, and the initial "H" is subject at times to local aspiration or non-aspiration. In the matter of fore-names much of interest could be said. The compiler in some recent exploration on the Eastern Shore of Maryland, discovered the the original name of PEREGRINE (quite common in that section) had become condensed to *Pere*, pronounced *Perry* and possibly it settled down to that in some localities.

THE NEXT OF KIN

As shown by the Inventories recorded at Annapolis, Maryland.

BENJ: SUTTEN, SAMUEL SUTTEN; inv. of John Sutten, of Kent cty, Md. 20 Apr 1724. ix-416.

No kin mentioned; inv. of John Donkine, of Kent cty. 17 June 1724. ix-417.

"As for relations *there's* not any known of belonging to the Dec'd." Inv. of Thos. Cooke, of Kent cty. 22 May 1724. ix-418.

"Nearest akinn are HANAH WALTHAM & HANNAH x WALTHAM, Jr." The following list of kin is also given: Wm. Waltham, ab. 23 yrs; Hannah Waltham, ab. 20 yrs; Betty Waltham, ab. 17 yrs; Jno. Waltham, ab. 14 yrs. [These are apparently the heirs.] Inv. of Mr. Jno. Waltham, of Kent cty. Taken 7 Jany 1723 .ix-424.

"No Kindred." Inv. of Harbert Pagan, of Blackwater, Dor. cty. 25 Jany 1723-4. ix-421.

CHARLES WHEELER; inv. of John Pitts, of Dor. 23 May 1724. ix-422.

JOHN ELLIOTT and JANE HURLY; inv. of Jane Elliott, of Dor. cty. 3 June 1724. ix-423.

No kin given; inv. of Patrick Dyer, of Pr. Geo's cty. 11 July 1724. ix-424.

No kin given; inv. of Wm. Newgan, of Pr. Geo's cty. 11 July 1724. ix-424.

EDWARD KNOT, WILL'M KNOT; inv. of Francis Knot of St. Mary's cty. 6 June 1724. ix-424.

CHARLES KING and JANE KING; inv. of Edward King, of St. Mary's cty. 4 June 1724. ix-426.

PRISCILLA GRESHAM, dau. of THOMAS GRESHAM, son; inv. of John Gresham, Esq., of A. A. cty. 15 June 1724. ix-427.

The same; additional inventory in A. A. cty. Kent cty. ix-430.

The same; additional inventory in A. A. cty. ix-433.

Find no kin; inv. of Mr. Cuthbert Sawell[?] of St. Mary's cty. 4 June 1724. ix-443.

RICH'D MOY, ELIZ. CARTER; inv. of Anne Taylor of St. Mary's cty. 30 May 1724. ix-445.

MARGARET x NEAVETT, JNO. REALLY; inv of Mr. Francis Neavett, of St. Mary's cty. 5 June 1724. ix-446.

No kin mentioned; inv. of John Ross. [County?] ix-449.

Kin uncertain; inv. of Thomas Campbell, of St. Mary's cty. 8 Feby 1723. ix-450.

ROBERT FORD, JOHN FORD, Jr. Inv. of John Drewry of St. Mary's cty. 2 June 1724. ix-451.

ELIZABETH x HASTIE; inv. of Margaret Melone, of St. Mary's cty. 2 June 1724. ix-453.

"No relations but 2 daus. of Mr. James Greenfiell, who are minors." Inv. of Mrs. Martha Dansey. 21 July 1724. x-1.

RICH'D MOYE and GRACE TAYLOR; inv. of Darby Carter. 2 June 1724. x-7.

No Kin; inv. of Wm. Huddlestone, of St. Mary's cty. 17 June 1724. x-8.

JO'N GREENWELL, WM. GREENWELL; inv. of James Greenwell. [County?] 13 July 1724. x-9.

"No Kinn;" inv. of Patrick Lurty, of St. Mary's. 16 July 1724. x-11.

MARY LATIMAR, JAMES LATIMER; inv. of Edward Gardner, of Chas. cty. 19 May 1724. x-12.

"No Kin;" inv. of Geo: Middleton, Gent., of St. Mary's cty. 5 Aug 1724. x-15.

MARY x VOWLES, JOHN VOWLES; inv. of Rich'd. Vowles, Sr., of St. Mary's cty. 4 Aug 1724. x-15.

Find no kin; inv. of Mary Smith, of Annapolis, A. A. cty. 1 Jany 1723-4. x-27.

Find no kin; Inv. of Thomas Thorberr, of [county?] 25 Apr 1724. x-27.

Find no kin; add'l inv. of Sparrow Carter. 13 Apr 1724. x-28.

Kin uncertain; inv. of Rob't Eade, Chyrurgeon. 28 Oct 1723. x-28.

[The next entry is a list of debts of Aquila Paca, of Baltimore cty.]

HENRY HOSIER, "Near of Kin;" inv. of Miss Martha Smith, of Kent cty. 16 Aug 1724. x-31.

ROBERT CUTCHART; inv. of Thomas *Cuthcart,* of Talbot cty. 17 July 1724. x-45.

Find no kin; inv. of Jane Blackwell, of Talbot cty. 2 July 1724. x-46.

WILLIAM CLAYTON, SOLOMON CLAYTON; inv. of Capt. Wm. Finney, of Talbot cty. 14 July 1724. x-48.

Find no kin; inv. of James Blair of Talbot cty. 22 June 1724. x-54.

SAM'L DORMAN, ROBERT McCUEN; inv. of John Dorman, of Som. cty. x-57.

Find no kin; inv. of Sarah Grindles, of Som. cty. 1 Aug 1724. x-57.

THOMAS FOLER, MARY x FOULER, "the Sister of John Colens;" inv. of John Collins, od Som. cty. 14 May 1724. x-59.

"No Kindred." Inv. of Stephen Hall, of Som. cty. 7 June 1724. x-61.

WILLIAM RUSSELL, ESTHER x SMITH; inv. of Thomas Smith, of Som. cty. 8 June 1724. x-33.

JNO. JONES, MARGRITT NUTTER; inv. of Rob't Jones, of Som. cty. 7 July 1724. x-64.

WILLIAM BROWNE and WILLIAM STEWART [*it is uncertain whether these are kindred or not*]; inv. of Jno. Brown. [County?] 11 June 1724. x-66.

STEPHEN HORSEY, JOHN HORSEY, JOB SHARRY, and REMUEL HORSEY sign; it is probable that two of these are creditors. Inv. of Mr. Stephen Horsey. [Hannah Horsey makes oath.] 29 June 1724. x-67.

Find no Kin; inv. of Dennis O'BRYAN, of Cecil cty. 14 Aug 1724. x-69.

Find no Kin; inv. of John Heathcoate, of Cecil cty. [Date?] x-70.

FRANCIS HARPER, WILLIAM HARPER; inv. of John Harper, of Dor. cty. 11 Aug 1724. x-72.

THOMAS x CAWSEY, PHILIP x CAWSEY; inv. of William Cawsey, of Dor. cty. 14 July 1724. x-74.

THOMAS x CAUSEY, PHILIP x CORSEWAY; inv. of John Corseway. [Cawsey.] [County?] 24 July 1724. x-75.

Find no Kin; inv. of John Manning, of Calvert cty. 17 June 1724. x-76.

JOHN x COSTER[?] Inv. of William Coster, of Calv. cty. 11 July 1724. x-78.

MARG. COLBORT, MICHAELL x DEVOUE [?] Inv. of Robert Coverthought of Calv. cty. 25 Aug 1724. x-80.

ABRAHAM BIRCKHEAD and ANN BIRCKHEAD; inv. of Susanna Gover, of Calv. cty. 27 June 1724. x-81.

JOHN TUCKER, BENJA. TUCKER; inv. of Ann Tucker, of Calv. cty. 4 July 1724. x-84.

Find no Kin; inv. of William Johnson, of Kent cty. 13 Aug 1724. x-86.

HENRY WARD x WARD; inv. of Sarah King, of Kent cty. 29 Aug 1724. x-86.

THO. WILLIAMS, BENJA. BERRY; inv. of Baruch Williams, of Pr. Geo's cty. 15 Mch 1724. x-88.

Kin uncertain; inv. of Henry Bows of Pr. Geo's cty. 5 Sept 1724. x-90.

W. BEANES, SARAH x TANYHILL [perhaps kin?] Inv. of Benj. Gale of Pr. Geo's cty. 5 Sept 1724. x-91.

Do not find kin; inv. of John Rudderford. 28 May 1724. x-92.

ELIZ. x EMSOR [EMERSON] and JACOB HURD; inv. of Tobias *Emirson* [Emerson] of Balto. cty. 27 June 1724. x-93. [Elizabeth was administratrix.]

Find no kin; Inv. of Phill Pitslow of Balto., cty. 7 Sept 1724. x-96.

Find no kin; inv. of Wm. Lenox, of Balto. cty. 27 Aug 1724. x-97.

Find no kin; inv. of Wm. Wright, of Balto. cty. 7 Sept 1724. x-100.

JOHN x TAYLOR, ABRAHAM x TAYLOR; inv. of William Dawtridge, of Balto. cty. 7 July 1724. x-103.

WILLIAM x ARNALL [probably?] Inv. of Anthony Arnold of Balto. cty. 13 June 1722. x-105. [Charles Wells m. Sarah, the extx.]

WILLIAM COOPER and JOHN COOPER; inv. of Philip Cooper of Chas. cty. 31 Aug 1734. x-106.

"No Kinn." Inv. of Robert S. Stanfield, of Chas. cty. 25 Aug 1724. x-108.

Find no kin; Inv. of Sarah Lyfoly, of Annap. Q. A. cty. Taken 25 May 1723. x-109.

Find no kin; inv. of Stephen Gill, Jr., of Balto. cty. Taken 18 Dec. 1721. Ackn. 9 Sept 1724. x-11.

MATTHEW PUNPHREY, LANCE T ODD, ALEXANDER MITCHELL, EBENEZER PUMPHARY, *all these sign, but probably two are creditors, it is uncertain.* Inv. of Mrs. Marcey Pumphrey, of Balto. cty. 10 Sept 1724. x-112.

JOHN STEVENS and ALEX. TOWLSON; inv. of Charles Stephens, of Q. A. cty. 23 Sept 1724. x-115.

CUTHBERT x FENWICK, CUTHBERT FENWICK, Jr. Inv. of Mrs. Dorathy Fenwick, of St. Mary's cty. 11 Sept 1724. x-117.

JOHN ROBSON, ISAAC MUUKINS [MEEKINS?] Inv. of Rice Williams, of Dor. cty. 29 Aug 1724.

JOHN NEVETT, a brother, signs as *witness.* Inv. of Richard Nevett, of Chas. cty. 30 Sept 1724. x-120.

BEN: POSEY, Jr., BELAINE POSY, *brothers;* inv. of John Cole, of Chas. cty, Carpenter. Taken 19 Aug 1724. x-122.

MARGETT MILLER, "greatest creditor and nearest of Kin." Inv. of Thomas Hungerford, of Chas. cty. 22 Sept 1724. x-123.

MARY LANE, WILLIAM KIRKHAM; inv. of James Kirkham, of Q. Anne's. 5 Aug 1724. x-124.

"No Kin." Inv. of Dennis Connor, of Q. A. cty. 12 Aug 1724. x-27.

MARY EAGLE, WILLIAM BANNINE; inv. of Thomas *Bandee,* of Q. A. cty. 8 Aug 1724. x-128.

THOMAS x SPRY, EAVIES x SPRY [? Kin?] Inv. of Wm. Walkes, Q. A. 15 Aug 1724. x-132.

ABIGAL x CONNER [probably kin.] Inv. of Samuel Jemmett, of Q. A. cty. 18 Aug 1724. x-133.

CICILIUS Q. BUTLER, JOHN LEIGH. Inv. of Johanni Deheneyosia, of Q. A. cty. 28 Sept 1724. x-133.

Do not find kin; Inv. of Patrick Cavinan, of Q. A. cty. 24 Sept 1724. x-134.

MARY x HINES; inv. of Joseph Hine, of Q. A. cty. 24 Sept 1724. x-135.

THOS. x HINDS, bro., VINCENT HINDS, bro., JOHN x HINDS; inv. of John Hinds, of Q. A. cty. 10 Sept 1724. x-135.

MICHIL x KERBY, WM. x KERBY; inv. of Mich'll Kerby, of Talbott cty. 14 Aug 1724. x-136.

SAM'LL DUDLEY [extr?] ELIZABETH HANKIN[?] Inv. of Capt. John Needles, of Talbott cty. 30 Sept 1724. ix-138.

JOHN ROBSON, JAMES x ROBSON; inv. of Peter Pendleton, of Talbott cty. 2 Oct 1724. x-140.

Find no kin; inv. of Elias Cohale [?], of Som. cty. 22 Sept 1724. x-140.

"No relations that can be found." Inv. of Daniell Mullicane, of Kent cty. 12 Sept 1724. x-141.

SAMUELL BURWELL; inv. of John Beach, of Kent cty. 10 July 1724. x-144.

ELIZ'BTH x COUSINS, ANN x JACKSON; inv. of Thos. Taylor, of Kent cty. 12 Sept 1724. x-146.

"No Relations for to sign"; inv. of Margarett Brooks, of Kent cty. 12 Sept 1724. x-147.

JOHN RILEY, NICHOLAS RILY; inv. of Henry Channell. [Date?] x-149.

ABRAHAM CLARK, RICH'D JONES; inv. of Abraham Clark, of Pr. Geo's cty. 12 Oct 1724. x-149.

Find no kin; inv. of Daniel Macha of Calv. cty. 9 Oct 1724. x-150.

SAMUEL VINES, WM. HOLLOWAY, kin; KENSEY JOHNS, B. MACKALL. These names are headed "kin and creditors," and it cannot be said which are which. Inv. of James Douglas [Douglass], of Calv. cty. 9 Oct 1724. x-151.

ELIZABETH x WHEELER, ANN WHEELER, inv. of Roger Wheeler, of Calv. cty. 2 Oct 1724. x-152.

Kin not found; inv. of Mr. Anthony Drew. [County?] 16 Oct 1724. x-153.

Do not find kin; inv. of Roger Lee of Chas. cty. 22 Oct 1724. x-154.

"No Relations in Maryland." Inv. of John Gould, Taylor, of Galv. cty. 26 Oct 1724. x-154.

GEORGE BALEY, THOS. CROMWELL; inv. of Thomas Cromwell. [County?] 3 Nov 1724. x-156.

WILL'M x BURTON, WILLIAM PINDER; inv. of William *Ponder,* of Q. A. cty. 22 Oct 1724. x-159.

CHARLES x NEALE, CHARLES SETH; inv. of Rich'd Watts, of Q. A. cty. 29 Oct 1724. x-159.

"No Kindred at Age." Inv. of Thomas Wealch, of St. Mary's cty. 23 Sept 1724. x-162.

THOMAS x BANISTER, HUGH x WILLIAMS, "kin and creditors"; inv. Wm. Banister, Jr., of St. Mary's cty. 4 Nov 1724. x-164.

MARY x HOWARD, WILL'M x HOWARD; inv. of Thomas Melton, of St. Mary's. 3 Nov 1724. x-165.

JOHN GREENWELL, STEPHEN GREENWELL; inv. of Ignatius Greenwell, [county?] x-168.

WILLIAM ROACH "as the only person of kin ______ except my Mother who is admx." Inv. of WILLIAM ROCHE, of St. Mary's. 4 Nov 1724. x-169.

The next of kin are the sisters, but the names are not found. Inv. [Col.] Mr. James Phillips, of Balto. cty. 6 Nov 1724. x-174.

ELB. x MONSERE, MARGRETT x JOHNSON; inv. Thos. Mountseer [Mountsear], of Q. A. cty. 5 Aug 1724. x-191.

JOHN x SWEANY [kin?] Inv. of Darby Sweany, of Pr. Geo's cty. 10 Sept 1724. x-194.

MORGAN x ADAMS; inv. Martin Cole, Dor. cty. 26 Oct 1724. x-194.

LUCINDA THOMPSON; inv. of Daniel Thompson of A. A. cty. (Annapolis.) 23 Dec. 1724. x-195.

WILLIAM PHELPS, CHARLES PHELPS; inv. John Phelps, of A. A. cty. 20 June 1724. x-199.

JOHN HALL, brother[?] EDW HALL, uncle; brother-in-law; MARY SMITHERS; inv. Aquila Paca, of Balto. cty. [22 Aug 1722.] x-200.

JOSEPH MARRIOTT, EMAN'LL MARRIOTT; inv. of Sarah Marriott, of A. A. cty. 10 Nov 1724. x-214.

WM. x PRICHETT, GERARD x JORDAN; inv. of Jane Butterworth, of St. Mary's cty. 1 Dec 1724. x-215.

JOHN GWINN, JOSEPH GWINN; inv. of James Bayley, of Chas. cty. 4 Nov 1724. x-217.

WM. x HOLT; (Mary Miller, admx.) WM. HOLT, of Chas cty. 13 Oct 1724. x-218.

MATH. DAY, ANN x DAY, HUMPH'Y x YOUNGER, ROBERT x MEAKS, GEORGE x WEATHERLY, "kin and Creditors;" Inv. of Mr. John March of Kent cty. 20 Sept 1724. x-220.

JAMES x WILLIAMS, ELIZABETH x BALLCHER; inv. of John Henricks, of Talbott cty. 24 Nov 1724. x-231.

FRANCIS NEALE, JEREMIAH x NEALE, "Creditors and Kin." Inv. of SAMUEL NEALE, of Talbott cty. 2 Dec 1724. x-234.

"Noe Kindred." Inv. of John Christian, of Balto. cty. 30 Oct 1724. x-235.

Find no kin; inv. of John Hastings, of Balto. cty. 4 Nov 1724. x-236.

"Noe Kindred;" inv. of Simon Floyd, of Balto. cty. 29 Dec 1724. x-237.

Do not find kin, possibly MARY ORRELL *is intended to be listed as such.* Inv. John Orrell, of Dor. cty. Taken 22 Apr 1724. x-238.

JOHN x LEMAY; inv. of JOHN LEMEY, Jr., of Dor. cty. Taken 25 June 1724. x-242.

Kin not given; inv. of James Kirkham, of Q. A. cty. 18 Aug 1724. x-242.

Find no kin; inv. of Robert Lazenby, of Calv. cty. 19 Oct 1724. x-242.

"No kindred." Inv. of John Vogler, of Calv. cty. 2 Jany 1724-5. x-243.

THOS. x EUBANKS, GEORGE x EUBANKS; inv. of Thos. EUBANKS, of Q. A. cty. 30 Nov 1724. x-244.

ARKADA TURVILL makes oath, WM. TURVILL and HENRY JARMAN also sign, but it is not clear whether they are kin or creditors; inv. Capt. James Givan, of Som. cty. 17 Nov 1724. x-246.

HUMPHRY x CHAPMAN, JOHN CAPMAN [*sic*] *These are probably kin, but it is uncertain.* Inv. of Silas Chapman, of Som. cty. 20 Nov 1724. x-250.

NATHA. HOPKINS, JOHN SCARBROUGH; inv. Henry Aires, Som. 23 Sept 1724. x-251.

CATHERINE x STIMPSON, mother; inv. of Edwd Turner, of Pr. Geo's cty. Taken 18 Dec 1723. x-252.

BARTON WARREN, JOHN x HARRIS; inv. of John Duely, Chas. cty. 22 Dec 1724. x-253.

WM. x SISSELL, MATTHEW SISSELL; inv. of Thos. Cissell, of St. Mary's. 23 Nov 1724. x-254.

THOMAS DAVIS, JOHN COX; inv. of Wm. Davis, of Cecill cty. 4 Dec 1724. x-257.

PETER VAN BEBBER (son); inv. of Isaac V Bebber, of Cecill cty. 23 Nov 1724. x-258.

Do not find kin; Inv. of Richm'd Kimston, of Cecill cty. 10 Nov 1724. x-260.

ARTHUR x MUNDAY, MARY x LARRSEY [?] Inv. of Catherine Munday. [County?] 26 Oct 1724. x-262.

EDWD EVANS; inv. of Jonathan Jones, of Cecill cty. 25 Nov 1724. x-263.

JAMES KIDDER, MARY GWINN; inv. of Thos. Gray, of Dor. cty. 1 Dec 1724. x-264.
BENEDICT BOREMAN, JOHN PARNHAM; inv. of Joseph Pile of Chas. cty. 1 Jany 1724. x-265.
PETER HARWOOD, SOLOMON HORNEY; inv. of John Harwood, of Dor. cty. 18 Jany 1724. x-267.
EDMUND x BENTON; inv. of Mark Benton, of Q. A. cty. 3 Feby 1724-5. x-270.
JOHN x TRILBORT [?] THOMAS x SMITH; inv. of William Merricks, of Chas. cty. 25 Jany 1724. x-272.
SARAH x LOWDER, ROBERT x LOWDER; inv. of Robert Lowder, of Talbott cty. 19 Jany 1724. x-276.
MARY x COHEE, JAMES x COHEE; inv. of Thomas Lockwell, of Talbott cty. 5 Feby 1724. x-276.
CHARLES x LEWIS, WM. x LEWIS; inv. of Robert Jones, of Talbott cty. 11 Feby 1724. x-278.
JOAN x COOPER, GABRIEL SAILE "for FOSTER CUNLIFFE" [?] inv. of Ambrose Ford, of Talbott cty. 19 Feby 1724. x-280.
"No kin to either herself or her Dec'd husband but two small children"; inv. of Alan Cookoo, of Talbott cty. 13 Feby 1724. x-282.
THOMAS RICHARDSON, JAMES MERRICK, JOHN x TAYLOR, THOMAS x WILLS; inv. of John Barron, of Talbott. 13 Feby 1724. x-283.
SOLOMON WRIGHT, Jr., JOHN PARR; inv. of John King, of Talbot cty. 22 Jany 1724. x-283.
Find no kin; inv. of Abraham Clanage, of Q. A. cty. 17 Feby 1724-5. x-284.
WILLIAM x RAIBITS, ROEBUKE x RAIBITS [?] Inv. of James Morgan, of Q. A. cty. 14 Feby 1724-5. x-285.
HENRY x BREDLOE [?] JOHN HILLOCK [probably kin]; Inv. of John Dod, of Dor. cty. 28 Jany 1724. x-286.
Do not find kin; inv. of Mad'm Martha Smith, of Kent cty. 13 Mch 1724. x-288.
THOS. x BOWDEL, JAMES HOPKINS; inv. of Eve Homes of Talbott cty. 2 Mch 1724. x-289.
ARTHUR CONNOR, JAMES x SHEPARD, JOHN MEARS, ELIZ. x ABBOTT, "Kin and Creditors." Inv. of Wm. Gilbert, of Talbott cty. 2 Mch 1724-5. x-291.
ROSWELL NEALE, ROBERT MASON; Inv. of Mr. John Blackiston, of St. Mary's cty. 5 Feby 1724. x-292.
CATHA. BARKSTON, CATHARINE DARE; inv. of Clement Barkston, of Cecill cty, inv. holder. Taken 13 July 1723. x-296.
BENJAMIN RICAUD and MARY COOPER; inv. of Mr. Thos. Ricaud, of Kent cty. 10 Dec 1724. x-298.
ROBT x LOVE, THOMAS x LOVE [?] Inv. of John Bradshaw, of Balto. cty. 12 Jany 1724. x-298.
ANN HILL; inv. of Francis Hill, of Kent cty. 27 Oct 1724. x-299.
JAMES ANGELL, ANN x CARMICHELL; inv. of John Aingell, of St. Mary's cty. 19 Mch 1724. x-300.
Find no kin; inv. of Morris Nordike, of Kent cty. 1 Dec 1725. x-301.
MARY x GRINDIGE, WM. BROWN, Jr. Inv. of Jacob Davis, of Kent cty. 31 Jany 1724-5. x-301.
JOHN RYLEY, NICHOLAS RYLEY; inv. of James Ryley, of Kent cty. 20 Dec 1724. x-303.
CATHERIN x COLL, PETER COLL; inv. of John Cole, of Kent cty. Taken 11 May 1724. x-305. [*Note: in a case like this there is little question but that the name of the kindred is the same as that of the decedent.*]
JAMES HYND, "Nearest Relation in this county." Inv. of James Froud, of Cecill cty. 23 Oct 1724. x-307.
PENELOPE x LARKIN, JEREMIAH x LARKIN; inv. of Jeremiah Larkins. 2 Feby 1724. x-308.
[*Uncertain which are kin.*] PHILL. LOYD, R. BENNETT, MARGARET WARD. Inv. of James Loyd, of Talbott cty. 3 Mch 1724-5. x-309.
"No kindred." Inv of John Clarke, of Dor. cty. 11 Mch 1724-5. x-331.
EDW'D TRIPPE, WILLIAM TRIPPE; inv. of Henry Trippe, of Dor cty. 12 Apr 1725. x-331.
SARAH x ZOW, JOHN ELLIOTT, G. NICHOLLS "Greatest creditors and nearest of Kinn". Inv. of Thos. Noble, of Dor. cty. 29 Mch 1725. x-332.
"No Kinn." Inv. of John Coale, of Dor. cty. 22 Mch 1724-5. x-334.
Kin uncertain. Inv. of Tho: Thompson, son of Anthony, of Dor. cty. 29 Mch 1725. x-335.
JOHN x LANHAM, Jr., ELL x HUNTER [probably kin.] Inv. of Thos. Dickeson, of Pr. Geo's cty. 27 Feby 1724. x-336.

Printed by COBLE PRINTING CO.
OXFORD, N. C.

A N C E S T R A L P R O O F S & P R O B A B I L I T I E S

An Occasional Bulletin

Number Two
Containing 800
Marriage References

"The Point of Research may Occupy a long Time to be Expressed at length in Brief Phrase."

The MARRIAGE REFERENCES which follow on the next page are mainly from the courts of record of Maryland and Virginia. As has been explained in the first bulletin of this series, a very large part, probably the greater part, are taken from the records of wills, deeds of conveyance, and the miscellaneous details to be found in the probate courts and in the papers connected with chancery proceedings. For want of space and in order to curtail the expense of publication, it has been necessary to make the "documentation" extremely brief. Experienced searchers will know that "A-20" means volume A, page 20, and will note it down, perhaps to follow with their own reading of the original record; or they will call upon the Clerks of the Courts, who sometimes "sit up and take notice"... and sometimes don't.

Other readers will be perfectly satisfied with the mere fact that the statement is in print, while still others may find themselves in difficulties when the registrar or registress asks "Where did you get this?" so that it is advisable to carefully note the reference, county and volume and page. Those who choose to follow up the search in person may or may not find it enjoyable to visit...say, Grayson county, Virginia; Stokes county, North Carolina, or Liberty county, Georgia. It is in these treks that the real tang of research lies for some of us.

These references are intended as a guide for your help, and as possibly pointing the way to some obscure paragraph touching an ancestor, especially an ancestress.

For explanation of abbreviations, see Page 38.

JAMES ALIXANDER and ..... BURTON, a widow. Bef. 14 Jany 1708. Acco, Va. xi-463. See also xi-56.

EDMUND ALLEN, Gent. and ANNE CUSTIS, relict and extx of Henry Custis. (She had previously been the wid. of Thomas Custis.) Bef. 30 Jany 1739. Acco, Va. xxii0-226, 237, Dii-327. See also N-n, Va. Court papers.

EDMUND ALLEN and ANNE BAGWELL, wid. John. Bef. 29 Dec 1687. N-n, Va. xv-324.

JOHN ALLEN and URSILLA WITHERS, dau. James. Bef. 1 June 1746. Staff. Va. M-469.

...... ALLEN m. a dau. of John DRUMMOND. Bef. 10 Oct 1713. Acco, Va. xi-615.

ARCHIBALD ALLEN and PENELOPE, relict of Peter SKINNER, dec'd. Bef. 27 May 1724. Wmld, Va. 1721-1731, fo. 68.

ROBERT ALLEN and SARAH GIVENS, widow [of Samuel?] Bef. [?] May 1756. Aug. Va. Chron. i-316.

SAMUEL ALLEN and JENNY GIBSON. 11 Oct 1798. Wash'n cty, Penna. Mar. Ret.

WILLIAM ALLAN and BRIDGET WITHERS, dau. James. Bef 1 June 1746. Staff, Va. M-469.

WILLOUGHBY ALLERTON and ...... BUSHROD, wid. John. Va. Col. Decisions, p.R57. The case which gives this information was of Apr 1731. See next item.

WILLO: ALLERTON, Gent., and HANNAH, extx of Jno. BUSHROD, Gent. Bf 2 Mch 1721. Wmld,Va.1721-1731, fo. 14.

HEZEKIAH ALLFREE and AMEY HOLDEN, dau. Joseph. (Joseph d. abt 1684.) N.C. cty, Dela. E-64.

...... ALRICHS and MARY TURNEUR, extx of Thos. TOURNEUR or TOURNIER. Bf 29 Mch 1716. N.C.cty, Dela. C-35.

GEORGE ANDERSON and MARY MATHEWS, dau. John. [Long] bf 11 Dec 1707. Staff, Va. Z-392. [They had a dau. Rosannah. There are two records which do not entirely agree. See deed 12 Apr 1709.]

WHITTINGTON ANDERSON prob. m. JOANNA MARY BRADFORD, dau Bayley. [Uncertain.] Bf 1753. Acco, Va. ii-

Rev. JAMES ANDERSON m. 1712-13, SUIT GARLAND, dau. Sylvester of "the Head of Apoquinimy." She d. 24 Dec 1736, and ANDERSON m. (2) 27 Dec 1737, RACHEL WILSON, dau. of Peter CHEVALIER of Phila. Eagle's Notes, &c. I-380.

WILLIAM ANDREWS and MARY SELBY, dau. Daniel. Bf 3 Oct 1740. Som, Md. M.F.G.-177.

...... ANDRAS [ANDREWS] and REBECKAH PEALL, dau. Thos. Bf 13 Feby 1742. Wor. cty, Md. J.W.ii-15.

WILLIAM ANDREWS, Sr., and MARY LYNCHFIELD. Bf 15 Apr 1784. Balto., Md. Proceedings. I-146.

WM. ARBUCKLE and BRIDGET CUSTIS, wid. William. Bf 27 May 1729. Acco, Va. ix-12.

CLEMENT ARLEDGE and MARY EYES, relict of Dennis. Bf 18 Aug 1703. Nthld, Va. 1699-1713, p. 257. See also p.266.

ANTHONY ARMISTEAD and HANNAH ELLYSON, dau. Robt. Bf 18 July 1698. E.C. cty, Va. Records.

...... ARMITRADER and ELIZABETH BENSTON, wid. Bf 1765. Acco., Va. Orders 1764-1765. p.485.

JAMES ARMSTRONG and HANNAH RICHARDSON. Prob. bf 1740. N.C. cty, Dela. E-64. See record 18 Feby 1789.

JEREMIAH ASHBY and RACHEL ABDELL, dau and coheir of Elizabeth, wid. John. Bf 25 Sept 1753. Acco, Va. Deeds i-462.

JOHN ASHBY, of Fred'k cty, Va., and JANE COMBS, dau. of Joseph the Elder. 11 Sept 1756. Staff, Va. P-126.

CHARLES ASHTON, of Wmld, Gent., and the relict and surv. Extx of Capt. John WASHINGTON. Richmd Cty, Va. Orders iii-254.

CHARLES ASHTON "intending by the sufferance of God Almighty the said MARGARET HART to Espouse Marry & take to wife." 7 July 1706. Staff, Va. Z-232.

CHARLES ASHTON and SARAH, a dau. of Laurence BUTLER, Gent. Bf 25 Sept 1733. Wmld, Va. Orders, fo. 101.

HENRY ASHTON, of Cople psh, Wmld, Gent. and ELIZABETH HARDIDGE dau and sole heir of William. Bf 31 Oct 1711. Richmd, Va. cty vi-44.

WILLIAM ATKINS and MARY NICOLAS, dau James. Bf 12 Jany 1752. Wor, Md. J.W. ii-96.

...... ATKINS and a dau. of Edmund BOWMAN. Bf 1690 [?] Acco, Va. ix-236.

WILLIAM ATKINS and SARAH RUSSEL, dau. John. Bf 15 Nov 1761. Sussex, Dela. B2-239.

SAMUEL ATWELL and MARTHA, relict of Wm. DAVIES. Bf 31 Aug 1736. Wmld, Va. Orders fo. 216.

FRANCIS ATWELL and SARAH SORRELL, one of the daus of Thomas, Gent. 1736. Wmld, Va. Orders, fo.220. See also fo. 234.

JOHN ATWELL and WINNIFRED, admx of Walter ENGLISH, Jr. Bf 29 July 1696. Wmld, Va. 1690-1698. fo. 208.

THOS. ATWELL and MARY McFARLANE, dau. Thos. Bf 5 Jany 1763. Wmld, Va. Inv. iv-185.

FRANCIS AWBREY, Jr., [ABREY] and ROSE, relict of Samuel DEMONVELL. [She was perhaps a dau. of John Erwin.] Bf 27 Sept 1737. Wmld, Va. Orders, fo. 242. See also fo 278. Also Inv. i-187. Bf. 30 June 1737.

GEORGE AUSTEN and ANN CHILTON, dau. Stephen. See Cant. Eng. Mar. Li. 23 Apr 1621.

JOSEPH AYDELOTT and FRANCES STOCKLEY, admx of Cornelious. Bf 4 Feby 1778. Dela. Arch. (Sussex cty.)

...... AYMES and ESTHER GRAY, dau. James. Bf 1719. Acco, Va. ix-229.

JOHN AYRES and MARY DRAPER. Bf 7 Aug 1700. Richmd cty, Va. Orders iii-46.

JAMES BABICOME and KATHERINE MILNER, admx of John. Bf 1687. Henrico, Va. ii-252.

...... BAGBY and ELIZ: JOHNSON, dau. Isaac. Bf 28 Aug 1816. Cumb, Va. v-303.

NATHAN BAGNALL and ANN WILKINSON, dau. Richard. Bf 13 Apr 1741. I.W., Va. viiiW-418.

LAURENCE BAKER and the Relict of William GRIFFIN. Bf or abt 5 Mch 1701. Richmd cty, Va. Orders iii-144.

THOMAS BAKER and ANN CHRISTIAN, dau. Thomas and Sarah. Bf 18 Oct 1736. Cecil, Md. v-257.

WILLIAM BAKER prob. m. SARAH BAILY, dau. Susan and John. Bf 21 Mch 1789. W. & M. Hanover cty, Va. xxi-153.

[DAVID? BENJ.?] BALL and HANNAH SMITH, dau. Joseph. Bf 6 Jany 1793. Fauq., Va. ii-263.

...... BALL perhaps m. MARY JOHNSON, sister of John. See his will. Nthld, Va. 1718-1726. 129. Bf 1 Oct 1720.

SPENCER BALL, Jr., and ELIZA G. LUKE, wid. John. Bf 1 June 1816. Ffx, Va. 00-360.

BENJA. BALL, of Kent Island, and ELIZA: dau of Wm. and Mary Richardson. 8th of 5th, 1714. Friends' Mtgs, Md.

JOSEPH BALLENGER and TABITHA BALLEW, by Rev. Mr. Benj. Coleman. 4 Apr 1782. Amherst, Va. Mar. List.

BASIL BALLENTINE and ANN CAWSON, 16 Nov 1735. Norf, Va.M.L.B.

THOMAS BALLEW, son of William, and JANE THOMAS, dau Henry Hugh Thomas. [Date?] Merritt, Histy Tenn. iii-761.

WILLIAM BALLEW and DOROTHY PARKER, [Date?] Same refs as above.

WILLIAM BALLEW and JANE PERRIN, Bf or abt 1 Apr 1717. Hen., Va. 1714-1718.

...... BALTHROP prob. m. MARG'T JONES, dau of Nathaniel. Bf 30 Mch 1705. Staff, Va. Z-261.

WM. BARBER and MARGARET, wid. of Robert WRIGHT. Bf 25 Feby 1700. Staff, Va. Z-30.

JOHN BARBER and ELIZ'TH LANGHURST, dau John. Bf 29th 2d 1720. Penna. Arch. xix-670. 2d Series.

THOMAS BARCLAY and JANE PALMER, dau Anthony, Esq. Bf Dec 1749. Philada. O. C. 1716-1755, p. 221.

THOMAS BARDETT, Jr., and MARG'T WILSON, wid. Intend marriage. 3-9-1704. Cliffs Mtg, Md. p.34 of Minutes.

LEONARD BARKER and LYDIA FARROW, dau Abraham. Bf 9 June 1731. Staff, Va. M-31.

Capt. WM. BARKER and JOYCE, dau Samuell BAYLEY. Bf 8 Feby 1709. Richmd cty, Va. Wills iii-7.

LAWRENCE BARKER and the Relict of Wm. GRIFFIN. Bf 5 Mch 1701. Richmd Cty, Va. Orders iii-144.

JOHN BARNETT and ALCE TAYLOR, Banns of marriage. 13 Nov 1683. Som, Md. L(07)-11.

GEORGE BARNES and SARAH [LEATHERBURY?] dau Diana. Bf 8 Oct 1773. Sus, Dela. B2-506, p.36.

THOMAS BARNS prob. m. JANE WILKINS, wid. Bf 17 Nov 1703. Nthld, Va. 1699-1713, p.273.

PAUL BARNES, turner, m. WILLIAMPE[?] VANDERVEULEN, dau Reneer Vanderveulen. Bf 1713. N.C. cty, Dela. H2-95.

PAUL BARNS, of St. Geo's Hd, N. C. cty, Dela, and CATHERINE BAXTER, dau Edward. Bf 1758. N.C. cty Dela. W-1-502.

GEORGE BARRET and a dau of Sam'll SMITH. Bf 6 Nov 1740. Nthld, Va. 1738-1743, fo. 103.

THOMAS BARTLETT and ELIZABETH JONES, wid Lewis. Abt 1722. K. Geo., Va. i-92.

EDWARD BARTON and ANN, dau of Ann SCARLET. Bf 15 Oct 1700. Staff, Va. Z-103. [This is not proof that Ann Barton was Ann Scarlet, as her mother very likely had more than one husband.]

...... BASFORD prob. m. ANN CALVERT. Bf 10 July 1712. See Middx, Va, Wills A.

SIMON BASHFORD and GRACE ...... Abt 30 years before 1712. Nthld, Va. 1710-1713, p. 254.

WILLIAM BASNETT and the wid of George HAWKINS. Bf 15 Apr 1664. L. Norf, Va. D-400.

WILLIAM BASNETT and the wid of Thomas ALLEN. Bf 15 Aug 1662. L. Norf, Va. D-351. [It is probable that both these widows were the same person.]

JOHN BASS and AGNESS LAY, dau Thomas. Bf 28 Aug 1773. Dela. Arch. (Sussex cty.)

GEORGE BATEMAN and ESTHER HOLMES, wid John. Bf 18 Apr 1659. L. Norf, Va. D-242, 282.

WILLIAM BATES and ROSANNA MEADOR. Bf Sept 1832. Cumb, Va. Orders, p. 432. She was then deceased.

...... BAYLIS prob. m. SARAH SUGGITT, widow. Bf 8 Mch 1699. Richmd cty, Va. Wills ii-61.

ROBERT BAYLIS and ELLEN, one of the daus of Dennis McCARTY. Bf 13 July 1719. Rchmd cty, Va. vii-4, 483.

RICHARD BAYLEY, of Acco, Va., and URSULA SCARBURG. Bf 1719-1720. Annap. Md Wills xvi-105.

PHIL: BAUGUS [?] and a dau of Philip COOMES. Bf 28 Sept 1732. Wmld, Va. Orders, fo. 41.

PHILIP BAUGUSS [?] perhaps m. PRISCILLA CANNON, wid John. Bf 30 May 1738. Wmld, Va. Orders. fo. 262. [The order of Priscilla's marriages is difficult to make out. In 1738 she seems to have had three husbands: Hamilton, Bauguss and Cannon.]

STEPHEN BEADON, Joyner, and MARY CALLAHAN, dau Dan'll, and wf Honora, of Port Royal, in Granville cty. Abt 2 Feby 1712. Columbia, S. C. Hist. Com. Vol. 1712-13.

ARCHIBALD BEALL and JANE EDMONSTON, dau James. Bf 10 Sept 1785. Montg, Md. B-348.

REUBIN BEALE, and "Mrs." FRANCIS ROBINSON. 9 Mch 1749. Richmd, Va. M.L.B.

JOHN BEALE and MARY ROE. 9 Feby 1729. St. Luke's, Q.A., Md.

JOHN BEALL seems to have m. a dau of Elizabeth MARSHALL. Bf 13 Aug 1735. Semmes Ms. M. H. S.

WILL'M DENT BEALL and MARY BEALL, 2 Apr 1713. Montg cty, Md. See Md Marriages. M.H.S.

BENJ. BEAN and RECCA [sic] EVANS. 9 Dec. 1779. Pr. Geo's,Md.

DUNCAN BEARD and JUDITH WEBSTER. See record 18 Feby 1789, N.C.cty, Dela. E-64.

Dr. JOHN M. BEATTY and VIOLETTA MARSHALL, dau Robert of Chas. cty, Md. Bf 10 Nov 1802. Semmes Ms.

MATHEW BECK and ANN HORNER. 10 Feby 1740. St. John's Psh,Md.

RICH. BECK and ELIZABETH, svt of John Farnihaugh. Bf 15 Feby 1648. L. Norf, Va. B-106.

DANIEL BECKER and EVA HAMAEN. 28 Apr 1784. Evan. Luth. Church, Fred'k, Md. Wit: Johannes Hamann, Philipp Hoff. "Pub. three times in London." [The copyist has given this woman's name with the German feminine termination in.]

JOSEPH BELFIELD and MARY, extx of Alvin MOUNTJOY. Bf 2 Nov 1721. Rchmd cty, Va. Orders ix-28.

THOMAS WRIGHT BELFIELD and MARY COLSTON, wid. William. Bf 18 Sept 1733. Richmd cty, Va. viii-64.

...... BELL m. MARY PARRAMORE. Bf 13 Nov 1687. Wor, Md. M. H. iii-24. She was sister of Arnoll Parramore, see his will, Somerset and Worcester counties, Md. Also Md Wills, p.37. [It is possible that she was Arnoll's half-sister and born PARRAMORE.]

JOHN BELL and JOANNA PETTIT, extx of Laben. Bf 29 May 1773. Dela. Arch. Sussex cty.

HENRY BELL and REBECCAH [?] HARRISON [or HANSON.] 10 June 1773. Cumb, Va. Fee Book. Mar. Li.

SAMUEL BELLAMY and ANN LOGGINS. 21 July 1664. St. Benet, Paul's Wharf, London, Eng.

HUMPHREY BELT and MARGERY CRAGGES. Abt 1 Oct 1649. L.Norf, Va. B-123.

CHRISTOPHER BENN, of Nansemond, Va. and ELIZABETH SPEIGHT, Bf 1760. N. C. H. & G. i-446.

...... BENSON and MARY WILSON, dau Thomas. Bf 15 Nov 1734. N-n, Va. xviii-213.

...... BENSTON and SARAH WILSON, dau Thomas. Bf 15 Nov 1734. N-n, Va. xviii-213.

JOHN BENSTON and RACHELL MOODY, Bans of matrimony. 3 Feby 1668. Som, Md. D.T.(7)p.68. "But John Walker Freeman in the behalfe of Rachill Moody underwrites in these words Rachell Moody hath nothing to Say to John Walker in the way of Matrimony therefore is of no Effect."

WILLIAM BERRY and a dau of William (x) JACKSON. Bf 4 Mch 1793. Middx, Va. G-308.

BENJAMIN BERRYMAN and SARAH NEWTON, dau Willoughby. Bf 7 Dec 1766. Wmld Wills, Va.(Crozier) p.66.

CHARLES BETTS and MARY ROSTEN [?] dau of Mary ROSTEN, wf of Jonathan. Bf 20 May 1703. Nthld, Va. 1699-1713,p.249.

ABRAHAM BICKLEY, of E. N. J., and ELIZABETH GARDNER, of Burlington, N. J. At Burlington Mtg. 4 mo. 11, 1695. Burl. & Mt. Holly Mtgs p.20.

JOSEPH BIGNON and MARY LEGARD. 26 Apr 1811. Rchmd, Ga.Mar.hi.

FRANCIS BINNEY[?] and JANE STARAIT [STARRETT?] Long bf 1742. Wor, Md. A-30. [She was in Onslow cty, N.C. in 1742.]

ERICUS BIORK and CHRISTINA STALCOP, dau Peter. Bf 1714. Wmton, Dela. Holy Trinity Rec'ds, p.169.

DAVID BISHOP and SARAH PERSELL. Bans pub. Ctf 30 Aug 1671. Som, Md. D.T. 151.

HENRY BISHOP, pltr, of Som. cty, Md, and SARAH...... ab 1720. Sus, Dela. K-253, [They removed to N.C. abt 1736, New Hanover cty. BISHOP d. abt 1758 leaving five sons and three daus... Greer, Henry, William, Charles, Littleton, Temperance, Naomi, Mary.]

...... BLACK and MARY STOCKLEY. Bf 7 Sept 1787. Dela. Arch. Sus. cty.

EDWARD BLACKBURN and a dau of George HARRISON. Bf 19 June 1760. Ffx, Va. D-737.

RICHARD BLACKBURN, Sr., Pr. Wm, and MARY ASHTON, wid Henry of Wmld, Gent. Bf 11 Dec 1754. Pr. Wm, Va. L.C. p.128.

JOHN BLACKFORD, Whiteland Tshp, Chester cty, Penna. and ANNE HUNTER. Bf 1 May 1760. Chester, Penna. L2-221.

SAM'LL BLACKWELL, psh St. Stevens, Nthld, Va. and MARGERY x DOWNING, dau William, Dec'd. Bf 20 Mch 1710. Nthld, Va. 1710-1713-p.12.

EDMUND BLADES and MARY BOUNDS, wid Jacob, Jr. Bf[?] 6 Apr 1787. Dela. Arch. Sus. cty.

JAMES BLAISE and MILLICENT JONES, wid Mr. John JONES. After 13 Feby 1692. Essex, Va. vol i-abt p.175.

CHARLES BLAKE (alias PRICE) and MARY RATCLIFFE, dau of Charles of Som cty, Md. Bf [1752] Acco, Va. ii-400.

JOHN BLAKE and SARAH LANE. Bf 6 May 1749. Wor,Md.J.W.ii-82.

JOHN BLAKE and SARAH RACKLIFFE. Bf 3 July 1728. Acco, Va.h.c. 1721-1723, p.2.

NERI[?] BLESSING and MARY THOMAS. Bf 17 Apr 1743. Fred'k,Md. G.M.E. 2-747.
ABRAHAM BLETSOE [BLEDSOE] and CATHERINE BALL, dau Thomas. Bf 13 Mch 1702. Nthld, Va. 1699-1713,p.243. See also p.299.
WILLIAM BLOXSON and MARY JOHNSON, wid Robinson JOHNSON. N-, Va. 3 Aug 1790. M.L.B.
THOMAS BLUT [?] and ELIZABETH DAVIS. Bf or abt 1696 Hen, Va. 1677-1699.
...... BOGGASS and MARY ANN LINDSAY, dau Robert. Bf 11 Sept 1784. Ffx, Va. E(1)-31.
HENRY BOGGESS, of Pr. Wm, and JANE COX, one of the daus of Vincent. Bf 30 Aug 1738. Wmld, Va. Orders, fo. 285. See also Fid. Accts i-233.
HENRY BOGGESS and a dau of George HUMPHRIES. Bf 9 May 1757. Nthld, Va. iv-63.
[This name Boggess, in one place spelled Baugust, is evidently the same as Baugus and Bauguss listed on a previous page.]
JOHN BOLTON, Clerk, and FRANCES lately called FRANCES SPENCER, wid. Bf "Tricessimo" Nov 1693. Wmld, Va. [5]-219.
STEPHEN BONWELL and PEGGY TOPPING. 21 May 1796. Acco, Va. M.L.B.
ARNOLD BOONE, of Montg cty, Md. son of Josiah and wf Hannah, and BETSY SHOEMAKER, dau Jonathan and wf Hannah, of D.C. 28-9-1808. West River Mtg.
HUMPHREY BOOTH, Rappa, Va. Gent. and MARGARET ...... Bf 1 Aug 1663. Essex, Va. Wills, &c. ii-313.
THOMAS BOOTH and MARGARET THOMAS, wid Isaac. See Ct 25 May 1792. N.C. cty, Dela. E-333.
GEORGE BOSSMAN and JANE JONES. Abt or bf 10 June 1690. Som, Md. B.W.Z.
VALENTINE BOST and MARIA ELIZABETH ERBOUGH [?] wid Balser, bf 13 Apr 1790. See that Court. Fred'k, Md.
Mr. THO. BOTTE and AMY BEVILL, wid. Bf 2 June 1690. Hen,Va. ii-332.
MORDECAI BOUDEN [BOWDEN?] and the relict and extx of Thos. TOULEY, Sr. Bf 17 Feby 1673. L.Norf, Va. E-104. [In the right of his wife Bouden or Bowden gets land for his predecessor, for his wife (then Touley's wife) and six other Touleys, presumably children of Touley, Sr.]
JOHN BOUGHER and one of the co-heirs of Alex. THOMAS. Bf 1723. Som. R.R. Md.
Mr. RICHARD BOUGHTON and VERLINDA BURDET, wid Mr. Thomas BURDET. Abt 20 June 1668. Semmes Ms. M.H.S.
JOHN BOWRING and the Relict of ...... MERRITT. Bf 16 Apr 1673. L.Norf, Va. E-93.
JOHN BOULTON and NANCY RUSSELL, dau William. 22 Oct 1816. Charl, Va. M.L.B.

WILLIAM BOWDEN of Middx, Va, and JANE DUDLEY, same. Mar agreement, 15 Apr 1794. Middx, iv-173.

JOHN BOWEN, of Charleston Neck, psh St. Philip. S.C. and ELIZABETH MAY. 13 Feby 1788. Cha'ston,S.C. 1787-1795, p.82. See also 10 Sept 1788.

Rev. ADAM BOYD and JANE CRAIGHEAD, dau Rev. Thos. CRAIGHEAD. Prob bf 1740. Men of Mark, Cumb. Valley, Penna. p.61.

AUGUSTINE BOWYER and REBECCA CHRISTIAN, dau Thomas and Sarah. Bf 18 Oct 1736. Cecil, Md. v-257.

SAMUEL BURTON and PRISCILLA EYRE, dau Capt. John. Bf 14 Sept 1719. N-n,Va. xxiiiR-36.

JOHN CALAHAN and ESTHER STAATS, admx of John. Bf or abt 6 Apr 1784. N.C. cty, Dela. F-305.

DENNIS CAMERON and JANE, relict and extx of Walter WELSH. Bf 3 Jany 1693. Richmd, cty, Va. Orders i-159.

JOHN CAMPBELL and ESTHER FASSET, extx of Rous FASSET of Wor, Md, who was one of the extrs of Wm. Fasset of Sussex cty, Dela. Bf 14 Sept 1768. Dela Arch.

OVERTON [?] CANALEY [CONNELLY?] and PHILLIS COTTMAN wid Ebenezer. Bf 13 June 1766. Som cty, Md. E.B. 6-176.

BENJAMIN CANNON and SUSANNA WALTERS, dau John. Bf 1 Jany 1731. Hen Papers, Va. p.829.

ANDREW CANNON and VERONICA GOODING, dau Jacob. Bf 1767. N.C. cty, Dela. Y1-581.

THOMAS CANNON and PEGGY PORTER, admx John. Bet 30 July 1787 and 20 June 1791. Som, Md. E.B. xvi-459.

Mr. MATHEW CANTEY and Mrs. LIDDIA FORD. 11 Dec 1793. Effingham, Ga. Mar. Li.

WILLIAM P. CARHATT [?] and ROZANA, admx [?] of Jacob STAFFORD. Bf or abt 4 Sept 1764. Dela Arch. Sus.

JOHN CARLILE and ABIGAIL TOWNSEND, dau Solomon, Sr. Bf 4 Jany 1772. Sus, Dela. B-489. See also B2-487.

ZACHARIAH CARLISLE and REBEKAH WILLIAMS, eldest sister of William WILLIAMS. 9 Mch 1779. Dela Arch. Sus. cty.

EDWARD CARNABY and MARY, relict and admx of Thomas GEARING. Bf 1 June 1738. Wmld, Va. Orders fo. 267.

JOHN CARR and ALLICE TAYLOR, admx of Isaac. Bf 25 Sept 1733. Wmld, Va. Orders, fo. 100.

THOMAS (x) CARR, A. A. cty, Md, and ELIZABETH (x) PRICE, dau Mordecai and Mary. 22 Nov 1705. Friends' Mthgs, Md.

Rev. SAMUEL CARRICK and Miss ANNIS McCLELLAND. 30 Jany 1794. Tenn.Hist.Mags. (Carrick was b.17 July,1760;d.5 Aug 1709.)

CORNELIUS CARTY and MARY GOODING, dau Abraham. Bf 1767, N.C. cty, Dela. Y-1-581.

WILLIAM CATHER and ANN SWEENY. 4 June 1791.Cecil,Md. Mar.List.

JOHN CIRWITHIN and SARAH HALBUT, dau Samuel. Bf 27 Mch 1773. Dela. Arch. Sus. cty.
JAMES COWARD and MARY COLLIDGE, wid Hezechia. Bf 3 Jany 1693. Richmd cty, Va. Orders. 1-155. [Name may be CAWARD]
GEO. CHAMBERS and ELLINER JILL, dau William. Bf 24 Mch 1697. York, Va. 1694-1702.
...... CHANCE and MARY DRUMMOND, dau John. Bf 10 Oct 1713. Acco, Va. xi-615.
JOHN CHANCELLOUR and ABIGAIL HARRINGDON, of Wicomoco hd. 24 Oct 1676. Som. Md. L-60.
WILLIAM CHANDLER and DELIVERANCE VEALE [prob. a widow] Bf 26 July 1722. Wmld, Va. 1721-1731.
CHARLES CHARLESON and DOROTHY MUSGROVE, wid. 14 Nov 1689. Chas. cty, Md. Records.
JOHN CHASE and MARY COLLINS, dau John. Bf or abt 7 May 1718. Acco, Va. xvi-50.
JNO. CHILD and ELIZ'TH EVANS, sole dau and heiress of Nathaniel Evans. Bf 26th 12th 1704. Penna. Arch 2d series. xix-448.
...... CHILTON and MARY WATTS, wid Richard. Bf 25 Feby 1731. Wmld, Va. Orders, fo. 13. See also Orders 1705-1721, fo. 339. Bf 26 Mch 1718. Both CHILTON and WATTS were "Gents".
MICHAEL CHRISTIAN and a dau of John and Sarah POWELL. Bf 13 Feby 1722. N-n, Va. See also N-n, Va. xxivR-3. Bf 11 May 1725. The name of the dau was ROSE.
WILLIAM CHRISTIE and SARAH HAYS, dau Robert. Prob. bf 8 Sept 1794. Wmld, Penna. O. C. A-82.
JOHN CHRISTOPHER and ANNE DAVIS. Bf 23 May 1793. Wor, Md. P-13.
WILLIAM CHURN [?] and the wid of John ARMSBY [ORMSBY?] Long bf 1715. Wmld, Va. v-629.
ISAAC CLARK and RACHEL, one of the admrs of William SMITH. Bf 1 Mch 1768. Dela Arch. Sus. cty.
LARDNER CLARK and ELIZABETH BOWEN. 22 July 1784. Davidson cty, Tenn. M.L.B. Tenn. Hist. Mags.
ROBERT CLARKE and a dau of Joseph BENTHALL, Sr. Prob. MARY BENTHALL. Bf 30 Mch 1691. N-n, Va. xiv-286. See also xix-105.
DAVID CLASBEY and ELIZABETH CLASBEY, dau of Col. CLASBEY. Bf 1800. Draper Ms. XNN-110. Wis. Hist. Soc.
JOHN CLAYPOOL and MARY HARDY. Bf 26 May 1756. Wor, Md. J.W. ii-171.
SAMUEL CLEVELY and ELIZABETH MARSHALL, wid of William, of Calvert cty. Bf 1688. Annap. Mar. Ref. T.P. xiv-85, 86.
WILLIAM COATS and RACHEL DUBOYS, wid Isaac. Bf 13 Feby 1707. Philada. O.C. 1716-1755. p.40. P.H.S.
ROB'T COBGUTT [?] and the relict of Richard BAGLY. Bf 15 Sept 1665. C.C. cty, Va. 1655-1665- p.588.

...... COBOURN and ELIZABETH LARKIN, dau John. Bf 23 June 1786. Chester cty, Penna. Abstr. Wills iii-242.

FRANCIS COFER and ELIZABETH WITHERS, dau Oliver. Bf 18 Sept 1702. Staff, Va. "Z"-206.

PETER COLLIER and ELIZABETH LAYFIELD, dau George and Priscilla. Bf 19 June 1728. Som, Md. xvii-31.

BENJ. COLLINS and THANKFUL SERGEANT. 1768. Mansfield (Windham) Conn. Mar.

...... COLLINS and ELIZABETH OWEN, dau Jonathan. Bf 12 May 1717. Acco, Va. xvi-32. See also ix-82.

WILLIAM COLLINS and RACHEL BEAL. 1757. St. Luke's psh,Q.A.Md.

...... COLLINGS and SARAH TINGLE, dau Hugh. Bf 28 Apr 1723. Wor, Md. M.H. iii-311.

JOHN COLLINSWORTH, Jr., and MARY CHANDLER, dau Joseph. Bf 5 Jany 1763. Wmld, Va. Inv. iv-186. See also fo. 214.

ABRAHAM COLSON and Miss MARGARET MOTT. 13 Dec 1793. Effingham, Ga. Mar. Li.

ROBERT COLVERT and SUSANNA YOUNG. 20 July 1785. Cecil, Md. Mar. Li.

PHILLIP COMBS and KATHERINE, Relict of John SOUTHERLAIN. Bf 31 Aug 1720. Wmld, Va. 1705-1721, fo. 394.

JESSEY COMEGYES and MARY EVERIST. [Abt 1777-1779] Cecil, Md. Mar. Li.

STEPHEN COMPTON and MARY WARREN. Bf 1763. Annap,Md.DD2-409.

JAMES CONGLETON and the wid of Sam'l BIRCH. Bf 6th Xbr-1737. Penna. Arch. 3d ser. i-95. She was the dau of John THOMAS.

LOCKLEY CONOLLIN and the Relict of Rich'd TYDWELL. Bf 25 Mch 1696. Wmld, Va. 1690-1698, fo. 199.

SAM'LL COOPE and the Relict of John BOWLER. Bf 24 May 1698. York, Va. 1694-1702.

JOHN COOPER prob. m. ELIZ: CURTICE, wid. Bf 19 Mch 1643. N-n, Va. ii-232.

JOHN COOPER, Gent. and HANNAH BUSHROD, wid John, Gent. After 26 Jany 1719, bf 26 Mch 1734. Wmld, Va. Orders, fo. 131. See also viii-279.

Doctor JOHN COOPER and HANNAH ALLERTON, wid Col. Willoughby ALLERTON. Bf 28 June 1727. Wmld, Va. Fid. Accts i-65.

JOHN COOPER and the widow of John HIGGINS. Bf 2 Feby 1712. Wmld, Va. Wills v-138.

JOHN COOPER and SUSANNA BRAYFIELD. 28 May 1667. Som,Md.1-68.

WILLIAM COPELAND and MARY SAVAGE, dau Thomas. Bf 26 Aug 1726. N-n, Va. xxivR-130.

JONATHAN COPPOCK, of Chester, and JANE OWEN, dau Griffith. 10-27-1708. Ctfs Removal, Philada. Mo'ly Mtg. [This is probably not the date of marriage.]

GAWIN CORBIN and HANNAH LEE, dau Thomas. Bf 1749-50. Wmld Va. Wills (Crozier) p.53.

JOHN CORBIN, Essex cty, Va. Gent. and LETTICE LEE, dau Martha LEE, wid, of Middx cty, G. B. Bf 17 July 1744. Wmld,Va. x-39.

COVINGTON CORBIN and BARBARA, admx of Nehemiah WATT. Bf 10 Jany 1757. Acco, Va. Orders 1737-1744. p.28.

MICHAEL CORMERICK [?] and FRANCES MULLS [MILLS?] Bf 1697. N-n, Va. iv-243.

..... CORNWELL and ELIZABETH FOSTER, dau William. Bf 9 Sept 1780. Pr. Wm, Va. Z-167.

NEAL COULBOURN [?] and AILSE WILLISS. 10 Mch 1801. Som, Md. Mar. Li.

JOHN COURTS and a sister of Rich'd and Benjamin HARRISON. Bf 5 July 1729. Semmes Mss. M.H.S.

JAMES COWLES and ALICE EDWARDS. Bf 22 Oct 1782. Wmld, Va. vii-237.

THOMAS COWLES and MARY SERJANT EDWARDS. Bf 22 Oct 1782. Wmld, Va. vii-237.

CHARNOCK COX, Jr. and ELIZABETH, relict of William NEWTON. Bf 26 Feby 1733. Wmld,Va. Orders, fo. 126. See also fo. 138.

WILLIAM COXE and [MARY] the wid of Henry LANGFORD. Bf 6 Oct 1806. Greenv. S.C. Ct Record.

OSMAN CRABB and SARAH, dau Daniel OCCANY. Bf 30 Jany 1716. Wmld, Va. 1705-1721, fo. 304.

JOHN CRAIG and POLLY DONALDSON [dau Patrick?] Draper Mss. 12CC-232,234. M.H.S. (Patrick Donaldson killed 1781.) Another refs. same collection, 12CC-145, gives REV. JOHN CRAIG and MARY DONALDSON, and states that she was born 20 May 1770.

Rev. JOHN CRAIGHEAD and JENNY BOYD, dau Rev. Adam BOYD, in Lanc cty, Penna. Abt 1783. Men of Mark, Cumb. Valley, Penna. p.64.

JOHN CRASK or CRASKE and ELIZABETH MOSS, youngest dau William, Sr. Bf or abt 7 Dec 1693. Richmd cty,Va. Orders i-154. Deeds ii-2.

...... CREAN and JANE WEATHERSTONE, extx Alexander. Bf 17 June 1702. Nthld, Va. Orders iv-206.

...... CRIPPEN and ELIZABETH BAYLY, dau Edmund. Bf 6 Feby 1717. Acco, Va. ix-113.

JAMES CROUCH and ANNE, admx of John CHING, A.A.cty, Md. Bf 1 Sept 1711. Annap, Md. Balance Bks. 32C-146.

DAVID CROUCH, Nicholas cty, Ky, and a dau of John CASSIDY. 5 Dec 1786. Draper Mss. 12cc-225-229. W.H. S.

RICHARD CRUPPER and ANASTATIA..... "Marriage articles". Proved by James Triplet and Thomas Machen. 25 June 1753. Pr Wm,Va. Orders [1]-159.

...... CUNNINGHAM and ELIZABETH (x) WINEBIDDLE, wid Conrod. Bf 15 Oct 1803. Alleg cty, Penna. i-185. Bf 15 Oct 1803.

DAVID CUNNINGHAM and ANN FOGUSON. 28 June 1788. Cecil, Md. Mar. Li.
JOHN CUNNINGHAM and ELIZABETH CALDWELL. 18 Nov 1777. Cecil, Md. Mar. Li.
JOSEPH CUNNINGHAM and MARY TEMPLEN [TEMPLER?] 7 Jany 1794. Cecil, Md. Mar. Li.
JOSEPH CUNNINGHAM and ELIZABETH WATSON. 13 Feby 1799. Cecil, Md. Mar. Li.
DAVID CURRIE, Clk, and ANN ALLERTON, Relict of Isaac. Bf 26 Aug 1746. Wmld, Va. Fid. Accts ii-4.
PITTS CURTIS and JOANNA FLOKER. Bf 17 May 1704. Nthld, Va. 1699-1713, p.294.

...... DADE and SARAH BERRYMAN, wid Gilson BERRYMAN. [Beheth-land-Gilson Berryman was dau of Gilson.] Bf 9 Mch 1761. Staff, Va. P-297.
...... DADE and PARTHENIA MASSEY, wid Dade MASSEY. [Further proof desirable.] Bf 13 July 1736. Staff, Va. M-216.
Mr. HORATIO DADE prob. m. wid of Sigismond MASSEY. Bf 11 Sept 1753. Staff, Va. O-273.
JOHN DALTON and MARY, admx of Wm [?] BROCKENBROUGH. Bf 3 June 1703. Rchmd cty, Va. Orders iii-256.
SAMUEL DAMONVEL and ROSE BONAN or BONUM, late relict of Phil-pot BONAM. Bf 27 July 1732. Wmld, Va. Orders, fo. 32.
...... DAMRON and SALLY JOHNSON, dau Isaac. Bf 18 Aug 1816. Cumb, Va. v-303.
SIMON DARBE and JANE, admx of Will'm PILES. Bf 23 Jany 1768. Dela. Arch. Sus. cty.
HENRY DARNALL and ...... LOWE, sister of Nicholas, of St. M's cty. Bf 28 Jany 1728. Annap, Md. T.P. xxviii-311. Mr. HENRY DARNALL, of Portland Manor m. ELIZABETH LOWE, dau Henry. Semmes Mss. M.H.S. M7-4.
GEO. DASHIELL, Gent, and ELIZABETH, extx James FAIRFAX. Bf 14 July 1741. N-n, Va. xxvi0-444.
RANDALL DAVENPORT and MARY FORD, Relict and admx of Gerrard. Bf 28 Jany 1690. Wmld, Va. 1690-1698, fo 4. See also Staff, Va. Orders i-184. "FOORD".
JAMES DAVIDSON, Sussex, Dela, and ELIZABETH WOOD, dau John. Bf 22 Jany 1782. Wor, Md. K-406.
JOHN DEANE and ELIZABETH THATCHER, dau Sylvester. Bf 2 June 1697. Rchmd cty, Va. Orders ii-227.
EDWARD DEFORD and ESTHER TARBUTTON, wid Solomon. Bf 12 Dec 1801. Q.A. Md. Admns, p. 259.
...... DENT and ANNE WARREN, Bf 1763. S.L.O. Annap., Md. DD2-409.
JAMES R. DERMOTT and MARY GRAYSON, dau Spencer. Bf 2 Mch 1795. Pr. Wm, Va. Y-557.

JOHN DEVONPORT and LUCY HALL, dau Isham. 12 Dec 1791 Franklin, Va. M.L.B.

THOMAS DICKENSON and ELIZABETH BROCKENBROUGH, sister of Austin Bf 21 Feby 1716. Rchmd cty, Va. iii-326.

Mr. L. DICKMAN [or DISHMAN?] m. Miss NANCY TOMPKINS. Bf or abt 1783. Draper Mss. 52-J-75. [Prob in Kentucky.]

CHARLES DIGGES and ...... LOWE, sister of Nicholas, of St. M's cty, Md. Bf 28 Jany 1728. Annap, Md. T.P. xxviii-311.

...... DINGUID and ANN MOSS, dau Alex. Bf 10 Feby 1772. Cumb, Va. ii-53.

GERVASE DODSON and ISABELLA SALSBERRY, wid. Bf 20 Apr 1663. Nthld, Va. 1658-1666, fo. 96. [She also m. ANDREW PETTIGREW.]

JOHN DOE and FRANCIS COLE, dau John. Abt 1 Nov 1690 Acco, Va. ix-206.

WILLIAM DOUGLAS and ELIZABETH LEWIS, prob. dau Stephen. Bf 15 Mch 1764. Ldn, Va. Orders-287.

ALEX'R DOYLE, Mcht, Dumfries, Pr. Wm, Va. and ELIZABETH FOLSON [FOLSOM?] dau Israel. After 3 Nov 1771, bf 2 Feby 1778. Pr. Wm, Va. T-389.

JAMES DRUMMOND and ANN SMITH, wid George. Bf 29 Jany 1733. Wmld, Va. Orders, fo. 119. Bf 30 May 1733. See fo. 83. DRUMMOND "Has since run away".

SAMUEL EARLE, of Staff, Va. and ELIZABETH HOLDBROOK, dau Randal. Bf 8 Dec 1755. Staff, Va. P-84.

SAMUEL EARLE, Jr. and ANN SORRELL, dau of Thomas, Gent., dec'd. Bf 28 Nov 1733. Wmld, Va. Orders, fo. 111.

BENJ. EDWARDS and MARGARET, a dau of Ninian Beall. Abt 1777. Montg., Md. A-10. See A No. 1-12. 5 Aug 1777. [See Staff cty, Va.]

NATHANIEL ELLICOTT and ELIZABETH ELLICOTT, dau John of Balto cty, Md. Bf 18 Sept 1795. Pr. Wm, Va. Y-616.

RICHARD ELKIN and ELIZA: BRYANT, dau. Rich'd. bf 5 Apr 1703. Staff, Va. Z-228. [She may have been the widow Redmond.]

...... ELLEGOOD prob. m. MARY COULBOURNE, dau William. Bf 17 Nov 1761. Som, Md. E.B. iv-106.

JOHN ELLIOTT and SIBILLA HIGGINS [sister of Penelope (Higgins) McCarty.] Bf 29 May 1733. Wmld, Va. vii(2)-97. [Requires further verification.]

JOHN ELLIOTT and a dau of John HIGGINS. Bf 2 Feby 1712. Wmld, Va. v-138. [John Elliott who d. 1708, left widow <u>Sara</u>. See Orders, fo. 82.]

...... ELLMOOR and ANN LAMBERT, dau William. Bf 9 Jany 1715. Rchmd cty, Va. Deeds, iii-246.

...... ELLOTT prob. m. MARGARET BENNET, wid Stephen. Bf 17 Sept 1767. Dela Arch. Sus cty.

MALAND [prob. MAHLON] ELY and MARY LITTON [or SITTON]. Cecil, Md. 24 July 1779. Mar. Li.

HENRY EMANSON and MARY GULL ......? dau Charles. Bf 18 Jany 1714. N.C.H.G. Reg. i-145.

WALTER ENGLISH and BARBARY DAVIS, one of the daus of William. Bf 26 Sept 1738. Wmld,Va. Orders, fo. 290.

GEO. ERWIN and the admx of Anthony CARNABY. Bf 6 June 1700. Rchmd cty, Va. Orders iii-43.

GEORGE ESKRIDGE and HANNAH, one of the daus of Samuel DEMOVEL [DEMOVILE] dec'd. Bf 28 May 1 1745. Wmld, Va. Orders, fo. 75. See also Fid. Accts 1742-1789, p.32.

JOHN EUBANK and SARAH HENDRICK, dau Gustavus. 25 Jany 1783. Charl., Va., M.L.B.

THOMAS EVANS and the Relict of John WESTON. Bf or abt 25 Feby 1660. York, Va. iii-111.

THOMAS EVANS and ROSE WHITE, eldest dau of William. Bf 22 Nov 1723. Som, Md. xv-75.

MOUNTJOY EVELING and DOROTHY ROBINS, dau Obedience. Bf 29 Nov 1653. N-n, Va. iv-174.

THOS. EYRE, II, and JANE SEVERNE, "sole dau and heir" fo John SEVERNE. abt 1677. N-n, Va. xi-157. [Perhaps of 23 May 1668. iv-233.]

NEECH EYRE and ISBELL HARMANSON, widow. Bf 7 Jany 1737. N-n, Va. xviii-244. [Eyre's step-father (father-in-law) was William Burton.]

...... FARISS and JUDY JOHNS, dau Joseph. Bf 13 Jany 1775. Cumb, Va. ii-184. [See JOSEPH FARES in A.P. & P. No. 1.]

...... FARRAR and JUDITH JEFFERSON, dau Thomas. Bf 5 June 1732. Hen, Va. Misc. Records. p.857.

ABRAM FARRILL and PRESILLA, admr with FARRILL, of John NOBEL. Bf 3 Jany 1769. Dela Arch. Sus. cty.

WILLIAM FARSIT and NAOMI ROADS, wid John ROADS, the Elder, Gent. Bf 10 Nov 1769. Dela Arch, Sus. cty.

......FFOOLKS and AMY WADDELOW, wid Nicholas. Bf or abt 28 Feby 1660. N-n, Va. ix-85.

ABRAHAM FIELD and ELIZABETH WITHERS, dau James. Bf 1 June 1746. Staff, Va. M-469.

HENRY FILKINS and ROSE FARROW, dau Abraham. Bf 9 June 1731. Staff, Va. M-31.

...... FISHER and REBECCA STRATTON. [She was sister of Thomas.] 1658. N-n, Va. ix-12.

JOHN FITZHUGH, Staff, Gent. and ANNA BARBARA, the eldest dau of Dan'll McCARTY. Bf or abt 5 Dec 1715. Wmld, Va. v-510.

WILLIAM FITZHUGH, Staff, Gent. and LETTICE TURBERVILE, dau Maj. George and Martha TURBERVILE. Mar. settlement. & Mch 1743. Wmld, Va. Fid Accts i-293.

Col. WILLIAM FITZHUGH, Gent., and MARTHA, wid. of GEORGE TURBERVILLE. Bf 17 July 1744. Wmld, Va. X-39. See also Orders, fo. 26, fo. 73.

RICHARD FLINT, Jr. and one of the daus of John PERRY. 30 Sept 1747. Wmld. Va. Fid. Accts ii-41.

ANGUS FORBUS and MARY LEA, by Rev. Mr. Wm. Irvine. 20 Nov 1780. Amherst, Va.

JNO. FORD and FRANKY PIERCE [?] 25 Jany 1773. Cumb. Va. Mar. Li.

ALEX. FLEMING, Rappa, Va. Gent. and URSULA BROWN, wid. John. Bf 5 July 1658. N-n, Va. ix-18. See also Essex, Va. Wills &c. ii-174. BROWNE is then called of Acco, Va. She was his widow 29 May 1656. See also p.47.

ALEX'R FLEMING and SARAH KENNEDY, dau John. Bf 3 Jany 1692. Rchmd cty, Va. I-105.

ARCHIBALD FLEMING and the wid. of William STEWART. Bf 4 Mch 1788. Dela Arch. Sus. cty.

...... FLETCHER and RACHEL SEBASTIAN, admx of Isaac. Bf 11 July 1750. Staff, Va. O-112.

BRYANT FOLIO [FOLIS?] and MARY JONES, dau Evan and Anne. Bf 11 Dec 1707. Z-392. She was gr. dau. of John Mathews, whose dau Anne m. Evan Jones.

RICHARD FOOTE and the widow of Hugh FRENCH. Bf 14 June 1746. Staff, Va. M-475.

JOHN FOSAKER and ELIZABETH MOTT, eldest dau Mr. George MOTT. Bf 16 Apr [1692] Rchmd cty, Va. Deeds I-36.

...... FOSQUE and SARAH JAMES. Bf 13 Aug 1766. Acco, Va. iii-73.

WILLIAM FOULKS, of Acco, Va. and MARY FOSTER of Dor, Md, at Transquakin, Dor cty. 2d 6th 1704. Tred Avon Mtg, Md.vi-5.

CHARLES FOWLER, Calv. cty, Md. and SARAH HUNTON, dau Mordica. Bf Oct 1700. Annap,Md. W.T.No.3-454.

WALTER FRANCIS and ANN PRICE, extx Edward. Bf 8 Oct 1696. Rchmd cty, Va. Orders ii-173.

...... FRANKLIN and CATHERINE STEUART [STEWARD] dau William. Bf 2 Aug 1721. Rchmd cty, Va. viii-58.

MASON FRENCH and KATHRINE, late Relict of Cossom BENNETT. Bf 17 Feby 1733. Wmld, Va. Orders fo. 128.

PARISH GARNER and ELIZABETH PARKER, dau William. Bf 17 Mch 1703. Nthld, Va. 1699-1713, p.284.

WILLIAM GARRISON and JANE ASBURY. Bf 3 May 1774. Amherst,Va. Orders, p.73.

JNO. GASSAWAY and "PATEY" WOODSON. 14 Apr 1773. Cumb,Va. Mar. Li. Fee Book.

...... GIVIN and MARGARET STEEL, dau Rev. John STEEL. Bf 20 Nov 1782. Cumb, Penna. O.C.2-314.

JAMES GENETT and SUSANNA CHAPMAN, wid Thomas. Bf 5 May 1795. Pr. Wm, Va. Y-599.

THOS. GILBERT and the relict of John BROOME. Bf [1649?] N-n, Va. iii-176.

THO. GITTING prob. m. ELIZABETH BELL, dau Thomas BELL, Sr. and his wife Mary. Abt 10 Sept 1674. Acco, Va. v-191. [Note: it is possible that ELIZABETH was dau of Mary Bell but not of Thos.]

MICHAEL GLENN and MARTHA-ANN DAVIS, dau Thomas. Bf 26 Mch 1832. Kent, Md. xi-245.

...... GODWIN and ANN RICKARDS, dau Michael. Bf 4 Jany 1687. N-n, Va. xv-370.

JOHN GODFREY and ...... MALBONE, a widow. Bf 1 Mch 1660. L. Norf, Va. D-293.

THOMAS GOODACRE prob. m. ELIZABETH THATCHER, dau Alice THATCHER. 10 May 1662. [Note: on account of the almost universal re-marriage of widows, the surname of a daughter of a widow is never taken for granted.]

...... GOFFE and MARY, wid of Lieut-Col. John JARBOE, of St. Mary's cty, Md. Bf 29 Dec 1676. Annap. T.P. viii-349.

CHARLES GOODMAN and ELIZABETH HORSLEY, dau Rowland. 1760, Alb, Va. iii-92.

BENJAMIN GOODRICH and TABITHA HICKS. Mar. contract. 25 May 1789. Bruns, Va. Oxv-159.

PETER GOODWIN and REBECKA TIPLADY, dau John. Bf 24 May 1699. York, Va. 1694-1702. p.159.

Mr. JOHN GOOKINS and SARAH THORROWGOOD, wid Capt. Adam THORROWGOOD. Bf 2 May 1641. L.Norf, Va. A-39.

PETER GOODWIN and MARY, admx of ELIMALICH CALTHROP. Bf 17 Nov 1746. York,Va. xviii-471.

THOMAS GORDON and JANE (x) BUTTON, wid. Thomas. [She was also wid of John GILLETT.] Bf 25 Jany 1678. Rappa, Va. 1677-1682. p.203.

CHARLES GORING and ELLYNOR ALLAMBY, dau Capt. Thomas ALLAMBY. E.C.Cty, Va. [Date?]

SAMUEL GOULD and CHARLOTTE HACKETT, dau James. Bf 5 Nov 1803. Q.A.,Md. W.H.N. iv-240.

JOHN GOWTEE and BRIDGET MAJOR, dau John. Bf 28 Apr. 1767. Acco, Va. Diii-470.

JOHN GRANT and MARGARET, extx William STROTHER. Bf 7 Apr 1739. K.Geo,Va. ii-150.

JOHN GRAY (son of Henry), Surry cty, and HANAH WARD day Thomas. Contract of marriage. 5 Jany 1684. Surry,Va."2"-22.

Mr. JOHN GRAY and the widow of HENRY BRAKE. Bf 18 June 1661. L.Norf,Va. D-312. [The name may be BRAKER.]

ROBERT GREEN and the relict of BARTH. BURREY. Bf 2 Sept 1695. Hen, Va. 1677-1737, p.38.

PHILLEMON GREEN and ELIZABETH HACKETT, dau Thomas. Bf 1 Feby 1760. Q.A.,Md. W,H,N, i-235.

Mr. SAMUEL GREEN and ELIZA: extx of John JENKINS, of Chas.cty, Md. Annap. Bal.Bks,vi-291. Bf or abt 1773.

GEORGE GREGG and ELIZAB. WILSON. 8 Nov 1800. Ldn cty,Va. Mar. Li.

THOMAS GREGG and NAOMIA WHITACRE[?] 26 Aug 1803. Ldn, Va.

SAMUEL GREGG and SARAH RATTICAR. 6 Dec 1802. Ldn, Va.

AARON GREGG and MARY HIXON [?] 7 Jany 1804. Ldn, Va.

ROBERT GREEN and ELINOR BURROUGHS, wid of Bartholomew. Bf 21 Aug 1693. Hen,Va. 1677-1737, p.34.

JAMES GRESSAM and MARY CLARK. Abt Dec 1720. K.Geo.,Va.01-35.

JOHN GRIFFIS prob. m. KATHERINE TULLY, widow. Abt 15 June 1677. L.Norf,Va. iv-19.

RICHARD GRIMSTED and ELIZABETH JACKMAN, dau of Anthony. Abt 7 Apr 1681. Rappa,Va. 1677-1682. p.203.

WALTER GRIFFIN and MARY BAXTER, wid and admx of Thomas. Bf 11 Feby 1691-2. Staff,Va. Orders i-217. See also Z-50.

JEREMIAH GRIFFIN and the widow of Charles WEBB. Bf 14 Mch 1737, N-n, Va.

WILLIAM GROTEN and MARY KELLAM, dau Edward. Bf 1720. Acco,Va. ix-303.

JOHN GUE and PEGGY WHITTEN, by Rev. Benj. Coleman. 9 Apr 1782. Amherst, Va.

MATTHEW GUIBERT or GINBERT and ELIZABETH NEWTON, dau Gerrard. Bf 3 Oct 1729. K.Geo,Va. i-617.

Mr. FRANCIS HADDON and JANE, the relict of Dr. Giles MODE, dec'd. Bf 1662. York, Va. [iii]-56.

GEO. HAMLING, of Md, and the widow of William RODOLPHUS. Bf 13 Dec 1669. Acco,Va. ii-140.

...... HAMBY and JUDITH JOHNSON, widow of William. Bf or abt 25 Sept 1802. Cumb, Va. iii-211.

PRESTON HAMPTON and ELIZABETH CONNER, widow of Charles. Bf 11 Jany 1796. Ldn,Va. Pckge old papers.

JAMES HAMELTON and PRISCILLA, relict of Philip BAUGUSS. Bf 30 May 1738. Wmld,Va. Orders, fo. 262. See also fo 294. James was son of James.

JAMES HART and ELIZABETH HOPKINS. 1773. Rockbr.Va. [Contributed]

THOMAS HARMANSON, Sr, Gent. and ELIZABETH DANIEL, the "hr and extx" of JOHN DANIEL. Bf or abt Dec 1690.N-n,Va.xiv-278.

OLIVER HARRIOT and ANN, admx Laurence RICHARDSON, of Balto. Bf 15 July 1711. Annap,Md. 320-135.

Capt. S. B. HARRIS and PATIENCE WILLIAMS. 9 Dec 1794. Greene cty, Ga. Mar. Li.

WM. HARRIS and HAN. HOGG. 23 Aug 1786. Greene cty,Ga.Mar.Li.
JESSE HARRIS and RACHEL PENDLETON. 12 Dec 1789. Greene cty, Ga. Mar. Li.
JAMES HARRIS prob. m. ...... DAYNES, a widow. Bf 16 Aug 1662. L.Norf,Va. D-352.
ISAAC [?] HARRIS and ANN DINGUID. 7 June 1773. Cumb, Va. Mar. Li. Fee Book.
THOMAS HARRISON and MARY SANDERS, extx of William. Bf or abt 21 Sept 1704. Nthld,Va. 1699-1713, p.311.
MICHAEL HARTFIELD and ELIZABETH DYER, dau William. See Ct 24 May 1699. York,Va. 1694-1702. p.160.
WILLIAM HAY and NANCY LUMPKIN. 18 May 1796. Ogleth,Ga.
...... HAYES and DOROTHY GRIFFETH, dau Jerome. Bf 1707-8, N-n,Va. xviii-420.
PATRICK HAYS of Londonderry tshp, Land cty,Penna, and ANN McCALLISTER. 23 May 1780. Lanc, Penna. M.L.B.
ANTHONY HAYNIE and SARAH HARRIS, dau John. Bf 23 Feby 1709. Nthld,Va. v-318.
JOSEPH HELVENS and Miss SARAH FRESH. 6 June 1792. Eff,Ga. Mar. Li.
...... HENRY and JANE [JEAN] STAFFORD, wid Ralph. Abt 13 Dec 1803. Montg,Va. Orders.
ROBERT HILL and RABITHA WHITE, dau John. Bf 12 June 1719. Som.,Md. I.K. -188 and 209.
EDMOND HOLMES and SIBELLA HALLEY, dau Francis. Bf 22 Oct 1741. Pr. Wm,Va. E-495.
CHARLES HOLDSWORTH and ...... PHILLIPS, wid of William. Bf 24 June 1709. York,Va. xiii-227.
STEWART HOLT and ANN JOHNSON, dau Benjamin. Bf 1773. N-n, Va. Chencery records.
JOHN HOPEWELL prob. m. HANNAH KING, dau John. Bf 21 Mch 1766. Ldn,Va. A-146.
THOMAS HOPKINS and ELIZABETH HAIRR[?] 24 July 1716. St.Paul's Psh Reg. K.Geo,Va.
WILLIAM HOPKINS and PATSEY PATTON. Jany 1805.Rockbr,Va.
JOHN BOOKER HOY and "MODLIN" MOSBY, wid of Micajah. Bf 25 Apr 1774. Cumb,Va. Orders, p.161.
RALPH HUDSPATH and MARGARET EYRES, dau Joseph and Margaret. ab 4 Aug 1693. Hen,Va. iv-32.
...... HUGHS and MARY, dau. of Honour RICHARDSON. Bf 5 Dec 1735. K.Geo,Va. A1-341.
JOHN HUGHS and MARGARET WILLIAMS, widow. Bf 6 Sept 1776. Staff,Va. L-270.
FRANCIS HUNT and ISABEL DERRICKE, dau Thomas. Bf 11 Feby 1691-2. Staff,Va. Orders 1-214.
THOMAS HUNT and FORTUNE JORDAN, dau Lt.Col.Geo JORDAN. 2 June 1665.Surry,Va.1-216. [HUNT died bf 5 Mch 1671.]

THOMAS HUNT and ANN HUNT, wid Azariah. Bf or abt Mch 1736. N-n,Va. Chanc'y records.

THOMAS HUNT and ANNE WILKINS, dau John. Mar. contr. 1 Aug 1666, N-n, Va. vii-4.

THOMAS HUNT and JOANE, the wid of Robert DRAKE. Abt 29 Mch 1641. N-n, Va. ii-35, See also ii-60.

JOHN HUTCHINSON and ANN TAYLOR, wid Elias. Abt or bf 20 Sept 1641. N-n,Va. ii-100. See also ii-102.

...... HUTCHESON and MARY NEEDLES, dau William. Bf 7 June 1720. Middx,Va. iv-510. [She prob. m. (2) Henry Gilpin. In 1719 she was a wid HUTCHESON.]

JOHN HUX (age abt 46) and JONE GRAY, dau Tho: GRAY Sr. Bf 9 May 1659. Surry,Va. i-131.

THOMAS IVY and ANNE ARGENT, dau George, of near London. Bf 1662. [Both then dec'd.] L.Norf,Va. D-398.

...... JACKSON and GRACE, dau Edward MAULPIS. Bf 13 Oct 1743. Staff,Va. M-381.

...... JACKSON and MARY MARTIAL, sister of John. Bf 1 May 1765. Acco,Va. Diii-374.

JOHN JAMES and ANNE TRENT, dau James. Bf 1 Dec 1727. K.Geo, Va. I-467.

FRANCIS JAMES and MARY GOOD, Relict of John. Bf 5 Oct 1725. Hen,Va. 1677-1737, p.54.

ROBERT JAMES and SARAH TILNEY, admx Jonathan. Bf 13 Nov 1751. N-n,Va. xxxix0-37.

THOMAS JAMES and MARY WILLIS, dau John, Sr. Bf 1715. Rchmd Cty,Va. iii-214.

JOHN JAMES and DINAH ALLEN, dau William. Bf [1741] Staff,Va. M-309.

WILLIAM JAMERSON [JAMISON] and FLOREANA THOMPSON, dau Joseph [of Cecil cty,Md] Bf 27 Nov 1782. Henry,Va. iii-275.

EDMUND JAMESON and NANCY SCOTT, dau Francis. 23 Dec 1806. Charl,Va. M.L.B.

WILLIAM JARRETT and ANN BURCH, dau Joseph. Bf 16 May 1685. L.Norf,Va. iv-201.

WILLIAM JEFFARS and ELIZAB: AUSTEN. Mar. contract. 7 July 1756. Rappa,Va. vol.i-89.

RICHARD JOHNS, preacher among Friends, b. Bristol, Eng. 1645, m. ELIZABETH KENSEY, wid Thomas SPENCER. N.Y. Mar. Li, vol. viii-95. [Date?]

WILLIAM JETTE, ~~afterwds~~ of Rappa cty,Va. m. ELIZABETH HOSKINS, dau Anthony. Bf 17 May 1681. Acco,Va. vi-262.

OBEDIA JUDKINS and OBEDIENCE JENNER, "she coming lately from England". Laid before the meeting. 1678. Minutes Women's Mtg of Friends in Virginia [or Barbadoes?]

Mr. EDWARD KEELING and MARY WARRINER, dau Ralph. Bf 27 Feby 1676. Rappa,Va. 1677-1682. p.121.

Mr. JAMES KEMP and NAOMIE MAKEMIE, wid Mr. [Rev] FRANCIS MAKEMIE. Bf 3 Aug 1710. Acco,Va. xiv-9. See also xi-483.

WILLIAM KIRKPATRICK and ELIZABETH KAIN, dau Patrick. Bf Feby 1815. [She d. bf this date.] Wmld,Penna. O.C.D-80.

EDMOND KELLY and JANE GRIGGS, wid George. Bf 12 July 1737. Staff,Va. M-244.

JOHN KENDALL and SUSANNA SAVAGE, dau Capt. John. Abt 4 June 1667. N-n,Va. xii-169.

WILLIAM KENDALL, Jr. and JOAN PARKS, dau Charles. Bf 21 Feby 1709. N-n,Va. xix-143.

RICHARD KENNER and ELIZABETH RHODEN[?] dau Matthew. Abt 20 Sept 1665. Nthld,Va. 1658-1666, fo. 155.

Mr. RODHAM KENNER ["ROHAM"] and HANNAH FOX, dau David. Bf 22 June 1702. Lanc,Va. viii-112.

WALTER KEY, Shipmaster, Kirkaldy [cty Fife] and ISOBELL OSWALD, dau Thomas, Shipmaster, Kirkaldy. [She was sister of Dr. Henry OSWALD of Va.] Bf 6 Jany 1729. K.Geo,Va.I-599.

ROBERT KIRBY and MARY MILLER, dau John. Bf 3 Aug 1750. Wor, Md. J.W.ii-77.

THOMAS LARAMORE and the extx of Robert HOPKINS, Sr. Bf or abt 14 July 1710. Som,Md. E.B. xiii-43.

JOHN LAWRENCE prob. m. widow of John STRATTON. Bf 15 Nov 1665. L.Norf,Va. D-431.

THOMAS LAYFIELD and NAOMI FARSIT, widow William. Bf 10 Nov 1769. Dela. Arch. Sus. cty.

Col. JOHN LEAR and REBECCA MORYSON, wid Charles. Bf 1697. E.C.cty,Va. 1704-1730. p.64.

JACOB LEAR and a dau of Thomas TAYLOR. Bf 8 Feby 1726.Acco, Va. xix-71.

FRANCIS LEE, of London, Gent. and ANNABELLA, dau of Ann TOFFT. Bf 6 Sept 1686. Acco,Va. vi-443. [Annabella was b. bet 1664 and 1670.]

HUGH LEE and the relict of ...... HUETT. Bf or abt 1651? Isle of Kent cty,Md. Early Rent Roll.

Mr. PHILIP LEE and MARY SMITH, dau Rev. Thomas SMITH. Bf 14 Dec 1788. Wmld Wills (Crozier) p.83.

...... LEE and MARY KENDALL, dau Col. Wm. KENDALL. See Acco, Va. xx-71. [They had son Richard, whose wf was Judith.]

RICHARD LEE and MARY KENDALL, dau Col. Wm. Kendall. Bf[?] 17 Apr 1731. Acco,Va. xx-71. [They had son Richard whose wife was Judith.]

GEORGE LEWIS and MARY JAMES, wid. Bf 2 July 1800.Ldn,Va.A-115.

...... LEWIS prob. m. SARAH BEAVANS, dau Roland. Bf 28 Apr 1709. Wor,Md. M.H. iii-74.

JOHN LIDFORD and the Relict of Peter BAGLYE. Bf 7 Jany 1678. Surry, Va. I(2)-279.

RICHARD H. LIGON, and REBECCAH PALMER, dau Elisha. Bf 26 Nov 1810. Halifax,Va. viii-389.

EDWARD LITTLETON, presumably m. Mrs.* SARAH DOUGLAS, dau Col. Edward Douglas. 26 Jany 1657. N-n,Va. ix... "Joynter" to her from Littleton. *A courtesy title.

WILLIAM LLOID and MARY FAUNTLEROY, wid Col. Moore FAUNTLEROY. Bf 2 Jany 1666. Rappa,Va. ii-57.

[RICHARD?] LOCK and WINNEFORD WEST, dau Thomas. Bf 14 Sept 1747. Nthld,Va. 1-57.

...... LOWERY and MARY POINTER, dau Edward. Bf 17 Jany 1751. Wor,Md. J.W. ii-97.

JAMES LUTTON and MARGARET KAIN, dau Patrick. Bf Feby 1815. Wmld,Penna. D-80.

JOHN MACCUDDY and MARY FLEMING, dau John. Bf 25 Apr 1751. Wor,Md. J.W.ii-102.

JAMES McDANIEL and MARTHA WITHERS, dau James. Bf 1 June 1746. Staff,Va. M-469.

TIMOTHY McDANELL and KATHERINE, one of the daus of Denis McCARTY. Bf 13 July 1719. Rchmd cty,Va. vii-483.

JOHN MACKITTRICK and MARY ALLEN, wid. Banns. "Bonds". 28 May 1667. Som,Md. 1-68.

EDWARD MADDOCK and MARGERY STONE. Bf 12 Nov 1678. Semmes Mss. M.H.S.

Dr. EDWARD MADDOCKS and FRANCES MASON, wid and Relict of Col. George MASON, [and who was formerly the widow and extx of Capt. John Norgrave.] Staff. Orders I-105. 12 Nov 1690.

WM. MANLY and PENELOPE, a dau of John HIGGINS. Bf 12 Feby 1712. Wmld,Va. v-138. [PENELOPE was the admx of Francis SPENCER and late the relict of William MANLEY, and in 1725, or before. Had m. Andrew RUSSELL.]

HARRISON MANLEY and MARGARET BARRY, dau Edward. Bf 16 June 1772. Ffx,Va. L-51.

WILLIAM MARCEY and PATIENCE DRUMMOND. Bf 18 Nov 1736. Som, Md. xix-110. [This name may be MERCY or MASSEY.]

...... MARSHALL m. MASON WATT, dau Nehemiah. Bf 30 Sept 1766. Acco,Va. Diii-109. See also Diii-545, and 479. This name is also spelled MARTIAL.

PETER MARTIALL and ELIZABETH WARD, dau Thomas, Gent. Bf 19 Feby 1757. Acco,Va. Deeds iii-

PETER MARSHALL and the wid of Daniel TOWLE. Bf 28 Aug 1764. Acco,Va. Orders 1764-1765, p.213.

PETER MARSHALL, of Acco, and PATIENCE TAYLOR, wid John. Bf 30 July 1765. Acco, Va. Diii-384.

JOHN MARTIALL prob. m. ANNABELLA LEE, dau of Ann Tofft. 2 June 1724. Acco, Va. See xvi-202. [The record of this marriage is extremely interesting, as at the time it took place LEE, her first husband was living, but was supposed to have been lost at sea. A previously published note calls her "widow".]

JOHN MARTIAL, Acco, and MARY RICHARDSON, Mar, contract. 28 Apr 1721. Acco,Va. xvi-191. See also Acco,xx-152.

Mr. ALEXANDER MARSHALL "lately" m. Mrs. ELIZABETH LIGON. Bf 20 Aug 1706. Hen,Va. 1677-1737. p.48.

ROBERT MARSHALL and MARY PENNY, dau Richard. Bf 14 Apr 1693. I.W.,Va. 2-344.

WILLIAM MARSHALL and MARY PORTER. N-n,Va. 1660.

HENRY MARTIN and MARY DIXON, wid Thomas. Bf or abt 24 June 1670. I.W.,Va. ii-24.

ROBERT MASON and TEMPERANCE WADDELOWE, dau of Nicholas. Bf 7 Jany 1673. Acco,Va. v-66. See also vi-96.

THOMAS MASON, Gent. and MARY NEWTON, sole dau and hr of Capt. Nathaniel NEWTON. Bf 24 May 1737. Norf,Va. xii-226.

Col. GEORGE MASON and FRANCES NORGRAVE, wid Capt. John NORGRAVE. After 23 Jany 1669, bf 13 Nov 1690. Staff,Va. Orders i-110.

MIDDLETON MASON prob. m. RACHEL BIRD, dau Daniel. Bf 1751. Acco, Va. xxviW-40.

Mr. MATTHEW MASON, of Maryland, and ELIZABETH SPENCE, dau Alexander. Bf 27 May 1712. Nthld,Va. v-319. See also Wmld,Va. v-53, and viii-33. ELIZABETH d. bf 4 May 1724. She may first have married Robert Sanford[?] SPENCE was of St. Mary's cty,Md. See Wmld,Va. v-530.

NICHOLAS MASON and the wid. of Robert FOWLER, dec'd. Bf 12 Apr 1651. L.Norf,Va. C-67.

...... MATTHEWS and ELIZABETH ADDAMS, dau Phillip. 6 Jany 1767. Som,Md. E.B. 5-13.

JOHN MOORE, Esq., and Miss MARCEY McCALL. 14 June 1792. Effingham,Ga. Mar.Li.

JAMES NEALE, son of Capt. James NEALE, and ELIZABETH LORD. Abt 1694-5. Semmes Mss.M.H.S. [See note in Bulletin No.1 A.P. & P.]

JOHN NEAL and MARGARET WHITE, dau John. Bf 6 Jany 1762. Som, Md. iv-91.

DANIEL NEECH and MARGARET SAUNDERS, wid Eustace. Abt 1667. N-n,Va. xi-87.

DANIEL NEECH and the wid of Mathew GETHING. Bf or abt 1668. N-n iv-233. See also xi-197. [NEECH'S marriages and the various relationships brought about by them, are not at all clear, and it is the compiler's impression that the late

Mr. Nottingham - who was the authority on these records of the Virginia Eastern Shore - was himself in doubt about them.]

Mr. THOMAS NELSON and MARGARET READE, dau Robert. Bf 30 Dec 1712. York,Va. xiv-241.

JOHN NELSON and one of the daus of John BURCH. Bf 22 Feby 1736. Wmld,Va. Orders, fo.222.

THOMAS NELSON and Mrs. FRANCIS TUCKER. 1723. L.Norf,Va.M.L.B.

JOSHUA NEWBERRY and CATHERINE, dau and hr of Sarah ANSLOW, wife of James. Bf 4 Feby 1768. Acco,Va. iii-547 [Uncertain]

ROBERT NEWSON and BEHETHLEN JONES. 25 Oct 1738. Lanc,Va. M. L.B. W.&M. xii-100.

...... NEWTON prob. m. ELIZABETH BEAVANS, dau Roland. Bf 28 Apr 1709. Wor,Md. M.H. iii-74.

JOHN NICKOLS and MARY LEGRAND, dau John. Bf 25 Dec 1800. Hal, Va. xviii-565.

WILLIAM NICHOLASSON prob. m. BARBARA ROBINS, wid Capt. Arthur ROBINS. Bf 1697. N-n,Va. 1718-1725 p.47.

...... NOBLE and ELIZABETH PORTER [wid of William]. Bf 12 July 1718. Som,Md. E.F.V.-167.

DANIEL NUNNALY and SUSANNA WORMACK, Relict of Wm. Bf 5 Oct 1725. Hen,Va. 1677-1737, p.54.

Mr. DANIEL O'NEEL and Miss AN CLYATT. 31 Mch 1793 Effingham, Ga. Mar. Li.

JAMES OGILVIE and MARGARET, extx of Wm. NAPIER, late of the City of Glasgow, Mcht. Bf 28 June 1738. Wmld,Va. Orders, fo. 274.

...... OGLESBY and ELIZABETH PRICE, dau Daniel, Sr. Bf 21 Feby 1767. Hen,Va, Papers.

JOHN OSBORNE and ATTALANTA, dau of Ann TOFFT. Bf 6 Sept 1686. Acco, Va. vi-439. [She afterwards m. Lt.Col. Wm. Whittington. See County COURT NOTE-BOOK, for Whittington line.]

ROB'T PAINE prob. m. a sister of Mr. Henery WILLIAMSON. Bf 16 Mch 1716. Rchmd,Va. iii-304.

ELISHA PALMER and ANN LEGRAND, dau John. Bf 25 Dec 1800. Hal, Va. xviii-565.

ELIAS PALMER and HANNAH LEGRAND, dau John. Bf 25 Dec 1800. Hal,Va. xviii-565.

JEFFRY PALMER and SUSANNA LEGRAND, dau John. Bf 25 Dec 1800. Hal,Va. xviii-565.

MOSES PALMER and MARY EASTHAM. Bf 2 Dec 1803. Hal,Va.xx-234.

THOMAS PALMER and MARY, dau of Elizabeth ELLIOTT, Cecil cty, Md. Bf 28 Nov 1763. Annap,Md. T.P. xli-332. [The surname of MARY is not certain, it may have been Hedrick.]

Mr. ROB'T PARKE and the admx of Peter DALE, dec'd. Bf 4 July 1676. Surry,Va. O i-127.

RICHARD PARKER and JUDITH HUNTT, relict of William. Abt Feby 1667. I.W.,Va. ii-15.

JOHN PARAMORE, Jr., Som cty, pltr, and ABIAH PARAMORE, alias MANLOVE. Date? Som, Md. S.C.(3) p.1.

...... PARRAMORE and ...... JUSTICE, dau Ralph. Bf 17 Sept 1729. Acco,Va. xx-25.

THOMAS PATTY and CATHERINE GARTON, one of the daus of John, Dec'd. Bf 4 Mch 1701. Rchmd cty,Va.

WALTER PAVEY and (2) ANN NEWGENT. Abt [1682?] Rchmd cty,Va. Accts No.1, p.15.

WESLEY PAVEY, son of Walter, and SARAH TROCK. Abt [1702?] Rchmd, cty, Va. Accts No. 1, p.15.

EDWARD PAYNE and ANN-HOLLAND CONYERS. Bf 7 Sept 1758. Staff, Va. p.192.

...... PAYNE and ALICIA JONES, dau Edward. Bf 2 Sept 1715. Rchmd cty, Va. Deeds iii-224.

BENJAMIN PEARCE and MARY, extx of John HINSON, late of Cecill cty. Bf 16 July 1711. Annap,Inv. and Accts,32C-89.

FRANCIS PEART and ELIZABETH BLACKBURN. Draper Mss. 11CC-286. W.H.S. 22 Jany 1801. [From an inscription on tombstone... where?]

ROBERT PECK[?] and ELIZA: the only dau of St. John SHROPSHIRE, dec'd. Bf 1 Mch 1721. Wmld,Va. 1721-1731, fo.12.

NICHOLAS PERCY of Chas. City cty, Va., and ELIZABETH HUTTON, dau Daniel, dec'd. Bf 11 Mch 1671. Surry,Va. ii-8.

JOHN (x) PERKERSON and SUSANNA (x) SMITH, wid James, and dau of Ollive Watson, of Norfolk-Shire G.B. Abt 1791. Shenan, Va. H-67.

...... PETTIT prob. m. MARY CUSTIS, wid. [She had son Henry CUSTIS of Metompkin.] Bf 28 Feby 1769 Acco,Va.iii-626.

BARTHOLOMEW PETTIT and LEAH, dau of Leah MILBY. Bf 17 Sept 1776. N-n,Va. Chanc'y records.

FRANCIS PEYTON and FRANCES DADE, dau Henry. Bf 25 Oct 1756. Staff,Va. P-198,156.

ANTHONY PEYTON and ANN CARNABY, dau of Anthony [and Agathy?] CARNABY, of Hanover psh, K.Geo. Bf 26 Sept 1746. K.Geo, Va. iii-157.

PHILIP PEYTON and MARY RUSH, dau William. Abt 1678 [?] Wmld, Va. viii(1)-553.

CHARLES RACKLIFFE and MARY PURNELL, dau Thomas. 24 June 1768. Wor,Md. J.W. iii-198.

...... RACKLIFFE and RACHEL WALE, dau Edward. Bf 21 Apr 1718. Wor,Md. M.H. iii-143.

...... RACKLIFFE and MARTHA FASSITT, dau John, Sr. Bf[?] 28 Aug 1787. Wor,Md. J.W. xiii-43.

Mr. JOSEPH RAHN and Miss NAOMY SETLER. 25 Apr 1794. Effingham, Ga. Mar. Li.

MATTHEW RAHN, of Eff. cty, Wheelwright, and Miss HANNAH-ELIZABETH DOLWICH, spinstress, same. Mar. contract. 23 Jany 1802. Eff. cty, Ga. B-155. [It should be noted that "spinstress" was merely the original term for "spinster."]

JOSHUA RAINEY and ANNE WROE, dau John. Bf 14 June 1783. Rchmd cty, Va. vii-428.

...... RAINE and KEZIA ANDERSON, dau Charles. Bf 17 1783

JOHN H. RANSOME and ELIZABETH McKINNEY. Bf 1819. Cumb,Va. vi-164.

THOMAS READ, Jr. and ANN HASKINS, dau Thomas. Charl,Va. 10 Nov 1790. M.L.B.

JOHN NASH READ and ELIZABETH JULIA SPENCER. 27 Mch 1786. Charl,Va. M.L.B.

EDWARD READ and Mrs. ELIZ: GEORGE, wid Thomas. Bf or abt 4 Jany 1692. Rchmd cty, Va. Orders.

ALEXANDER READ and ELIZABETH PHIPPEN, admx of Lot PHIPPEM, yeoman. Bf 2 Feby 1779. Dela Arch.Sus.cty.

JAMES READ and the wid of William KING. Bf or abt 12 Feby 1707. Staff, Va. Z-393.

NICHOLAS REGAN and ELIZABETH SPENCE, admx John. Bet 1759 and 23 Oct 1765. Ffx,Va. B-411.

LEWIS REMSBURG and BARBARA THOMAS. Bf 17 Apr 1843. Fred'k, Md. G.M.E.2-747.

DANIEL RIGGS and SARAH DAVIS. 10 Feby 1794. Cecil,Md.Mar.Li.

Mr. DAVID REISER and Miss MARY GROVENSTINE. 16 Apr 1792. Eff. cty, Ga. Mar. Li.

JOHN REMEY and MARY SANFORD, wid Robert, Jr. Bf 14 May 1740. Wmld,Va. Fid.Accts i-232. See also Orders, fo.70.

...... REVELL, prob. m. AGNES BURTON, dau William. Bf 5 Jany 1695. N-n,Va. xi-101.

DAVID REVIL and ESTHER LANKFORD. 15 Feby 1804. Som,Md.Mar.Li.

WILLIAM RICE and MARY PAYNE. Abt 1739? Wmld,Va. Orders, fo.311.

JOHN RICE, of Virginia, Mcht and REBECCA TRAVERS, wid Col. Wm. TRAVERS. Mar. contract. 14 Nov 1679. Rappa,Va. 1677-1682, p.289. See also p.116. Also Orders 1676-1688,p.206.

ZOROBABEL RICE prob. m. ANN HOLLON, dau Symon. Bf 26 Sept 1733. Wmld,Va. Orders, fo.103.

JOHN RICE and ISABELLA GARLAND, dau William. Bf 29 Apr 1708. Wmld,Va. 1705-1721, fo.85.

......, RICKARDS and MARY AYDLOTT, wid. Bf 9 May 1787. Dela. Arch, Sus,cty.

...... RICKARDS and SARAH AYDLOTT. Bf 21 Feby 1752. Wor,Md. J.W.ii-95.

JOHN RICORDS and NAOMI LAY, dau Thomas. Bf 28 Aug 1773. Dela. Arch, Sus.cty.

GEORGE RIDING, Gent. and WINNEY SMITH, dau Thomas. Mar. contract. 5 Dec 1778. K.Geo,Va. I-1188.

...... ROACH and SUSANNA ANDERSON, wid of "Sciprean". Bf 6 Dec 1659. K.Geo,Va. iii-121.

STEPHEN ROACH prob. m. SARAH JONES, wid. Bf Nov 1841. Som, Md. J.P.v-64.

WM. M. SATTERFIELD and ANN DUKES. Bf 10 May 1798. Kent cty, Dela. O.C. Pet'ns. [At the date noted. Satterfield was dead.]

WILLIAM SAUNDERS and ANNE CRAWLEY, wid Robert. Bf 21 July 1761. York,Va. xxi-66.

...... SAUNDERS and LUCY GOOLSBY, dau Thomas. Bf 6 July 1766. Alb,Va. ii-307.

JOHN SAUNDERS and ANNE STOVALL, Relict of Bartholomew. Bf 5 Oct 1725. Hen,Va. 1677-1737,p.54.

THOMAS SAUNDERS and ANNE ADAMS, dau Robert. Abt 25 Sept 1736. Gchld,Va. ii-257.

JESSE SAUNDERS and MARY LAVILLIAN, dau Anthony. Bf 16 Dec 1736. Cum,Va. vii-515. See also iii-520, and iv-471.

DANIEL SAUNDERS and SARAH HOLLOWAY, dau John. Bf 27 Apr 1772. Cumb,Va. v-39.

JOHN SAVAGE and BETTY PARKER, wid George..."formerly widow and now dowager of-" Bf 1 Aug 1762. Acco,Va. iii-197.

THOMAS SAVAGE, Jr. and ESTHER LITTLETON (sister of Sarah Littleton Custis) Bf 11 Nov 1726. N-n,Va. xxiv-R-63.

...... SAVIN and MARY MOSS, admx John. Bf 13 Apr 1737. Staff, Va. M-238.

Capt. MARTIN SCARLETT and the relict and extx of William GREENE. Bf 13 Mch 1689. Staff,Va. Orders p.251 [p.25?]

ROBERT SCOTT and JUDITH TAYLOR, wid Elias (moved to Maryland) Bf 25 Aug 1748. Acco,Va. xx-288.

CHARLES SCOTT and FRANCES SWENY. Mar. contract. 24 Feby 1762. Cumb,Va. iii-267.

JNO. SCOTT and JANE PITTMAN, Relict Peter DENT, Gent. Bf or abt 8 Apr 1712. Som,Md. E.B.xiii-59. [This needs explanation.]

JAMES SCRIBNER and BEHETHLAND BEACH. 7 Nov 1773. K.Geo,Va. St. Paul's Psh Reg.

JAMES SCROSBY of Mddx cty, and ELIZABETH LEE, of Lanc. Wid of Thomas. Mar contract. 15 Apr 1737.Lanc,Va. xiii-35.

...... SCURLOCK and a dau of Abraham FARROW. Bf 9 June 1731. Staff, Va. M-31.

JAMES SEATON and FRANCES DISHMAN, dau John. Bf 25 Oct 1743. Wmld, Va. Orders, fo. 3.

JOHN SEAYERS, Essex cty, Gent. and KATHERINE BANNERMAN, wid Mark. Bf 13 Dec 1739. Acco,Va. "Vol. 1" p.173.

PARKER SELBY and MARY WATTS, dau Jno. and Priscilla. 13 Oct 1724. Som,Md. xv-198.

JOHN SETTLE and MARY STROTHER, sister of the half-blood and heir of William STROTHER. Bf 28 Sept 1693. Wmld,Va. 1690-1698, fo. 107.

ROBERT SHARP and NANCY BAKER, dau Nancy and Thomas. K.Wm,Va. abt 17 Feby 1794. "i"-297.

THO: SHARP and ELIZA: one of the daus of Francis GRAY. Bf 29 July 1691. Wmld,Va. 1690-1698,fo.34.

CHARLES SHEPHARD and DAMARIS WARD, wid John. Bf 25 Jany 1695. [Prob. much earlier.] Semmes Mss,M.H.S. [County or colony?]

JAMES SHIPP, cooper, of Essex, Va. and ELIZ:BROOKS, only dau and hr-at-law of Thomas BROOKS of Essex. Bf 24 May 1698. York, Va. 1694-1702, p.29.

...... SHOCKLY and SARAH DAVIS[?] dau of Sarah DAVIS, Sr. Wor. Md. J.W. xviii-57.

WILLIAM SHOARES and ELIZ: TINGEY. Mar. agreement. 26 Jany 1668. Nthld,Va. 1666-1672,p.45.

WILLIAM SHORES and SUSANNAH TOWNSEND. Bf 3 Sept 1787. Dela. Arch, Sus.cty. [They had son John.]

PHILIP SIDALL and ADDOSIA LINTON, Pr. Geo's cty. 9 Apr 1789. Md. Mar. M.H.S.

SAMUEL SIMSON and SARAH PARKER. Bf 1 Jany 1710. Acco,Va. xi-651.

JOHN SIMPSON and ELIZABETH NAYLOR, dau John. Bf 6 Dec 1735. K.Geo,Va. Orders ii-44.

JOSEPH SIMPSON and Mrs. MARY SKINKER. Mar. settlement. 23 May 1749. K.Geo,Va. I-514.

THOMAS SKIDMORE and ELIZABETH COSTON, wid Benton. Bf 9 Mch 1779. Dela Arch, Sus. cty.

JAMES SMITH and SARAH HARTLEY, dau John. Bf 27 Mch 1733. Wmld,Va. Orders fo.66.

JOSEPH SMITH and ANN BROWN, dau Joseph. Abt or bf 14 Mch 1785. Staff, Va. S-173,174.

GEO. STOVALL SMITH and ...... LAND. 26 July 1773. Mar. Li. Cumb, Va. Fee Book.

WILLIAM SMOOTE and ...... WOOD, a widow. Bf 1651. Chas.cty, Md. Early Rent Roll.

...... SMYTH and ELIZABETH, dau Henry WIGGINTON. Bf 28 Jany 1735. Staff,Va, M-220.

NICHO: SMYTH and AGGATHA STERNE, relict and extx of David.Bf or abt 5 May 1692. Rchmd cty, Va. Orders.

WILLIAM SPATES prob. m. PRISCILLA ALLISON...sister of Benjamin. Bf 4 Aug 1795. Montg,Md. C-219.

Capt. THOMAS SPENCER and ANNE WOODWARD, dau William. Bf 1695. J.Wm, Va. "5"-37.

...... SPENCER and FRANCES, extx of Mr. John SCRIMGEOUR,Clk. (He died Oct 1691, at Frances Spencer's on Nomony River.) Bf 22 Feby 1692. Wmld, Va. 1690-1698,fo.88.

THOMAS SPILMAN and LETTICE, prob. widow of Evan JONES. Bf 20 Sept 1704. Wmld,Va. 1698-1705.

ANTHONY SPILTIMBER, of Surry,Va. and MARY HARRIS dau Mr. Robt HARRIS, fr I.W. Abt 1663-4. I.W., Va. iii-4.

GEORGE WILSON SPOONER and JANE ASHTON, wid Henry. Bf 25 Aug 1763. Wmld,Va. Inv iv-191.

THOMAS STALY and the Relict of Henry DURANT. Bf 25 June 1684. Wmld,Va. Orders 1676-1688,p.342.

Mr. JOHN STATON and Miss PENELOPY SELLERS. 4 Aug 1794.Eff.Ga.

WILLIAM STEAL and RACHEL POINTER, dau Edward. Bf 17 Jany 1751. Wor,Md. J.W,ii-97.

JAMES STEPTOE and the Relict of Wm. AYLET, Gent. Bf 29 July 1746. Wmld,Va. Fid.Accts ii-9.

JOHN STONE and ELIZABETH GREGORY. 31 May 1809, Balto cty,Md.

EDWARD STAPLEFORD and MARY, admx of Joseph SPENCER. Bf 29 May 1773. Dela Arch,Sus.cty.

PRITTYMAN STOCKLEY and ELIZABETH PRITTYMAN. Bf 15 Aug 1770. Dela. Arch,Sus.cty.

THOMAS STONEHOUSE and ELIZA: who, with St. John Shropshire was admx of the senior SHROPSHIRE'S est. Bf 1 Mch 1721. Wmld,Va. 1721-1731,fo. 12.

BENJAMIN STONER and BARBARA THOMAS, dau Christian. Bf 14 May 1777. Fred'k, Md. G.M. 1-19.

GEORGE STOVALL and ELIZABETH EASTHAM, dau Robert. Bf 2 Dec 1803. Halifax,Va. xx-234.

JOHN STRATTON and ESTHER HARMANSON. Bf 11 Sept 1732. N-n,Va. xviii-284.

ISAAC STREET and RHODA CUNNINGHAM, dau James. Bf 21 May 1791. Cumb,Va. vii-141.

...... STRINGER and GRACE ROBINS. Bf 19 May 1731. N-n,Va. xviii-371.

JOSEPH STRICKLAND, Pr. Geo's cty and VERLINDA PAGE. 22 Jany 1789 Md. Mar. M.H.S.

THOMAS STUMP and ...... BOOTH, dau Robert. Bf 21 Sept 1759. Ldn, Va. A-

RICHARD SUTTON (will proved 25 June 1684) and SUSANNA BURKLEY, wid of Thomas; [She had also been the wid of John Cozier(?)] Bf 25 June 1684. Wmld,Va. 1676-1688,p,351.

VAN SWEARINGHAM and LUCY DAVIS, dau William, Sr. Bf 22 July 1775. Montg cty, Md. A-222.

VANN SWEARINGEN, Ohio cty,Va. and ELENOR VIRGIN. Bf 5 Nov 1793. Wash'n cty, Penna. 1-220. (P.G.S. Pub'ns.)

DANIEL TALBUT and ANN WEST "first dau" of John WEST. Bf 27 Mch 1776. Ffx,Va. D(1)-26.

JOHN TAIT and the relict of Capt. John Wall[WALK?] Bf 3 Feby 1665. C.C.cty,Va. 1655-1665,p.620.

JOHN TANKRED and ELIZABETH DRUMMOND, extx Robert. Bf 29 Nov 1744. Acco,Va. Deeds i-435.

JOHN TANKRED and SARAH SMART, dau William of Gloucester cty, Va, bf 28 Mch 1687. N-n,Va. xiv-152. See also N-n,xviii-437; Acco,Va. xi-431.

JOHN TARPLEY and ELIZ: NEWMAN, wid Capt. Alex'r NEWMAN. Contract of marriage. 10 Aug 1699. Rchmd cty,Va, Wills iii-32.

JOHN TARPLEY and ELIZA: admx of Wm. BRUCE. Bf 15 Apr 1702. Nthld,Va. 1699-1713.p.194. Orders iv-196.

JOHN TAVERNER and ELIZABETH COLE, wid. Pre-nuptial gift to her son Walter Cole. 20 Nov 1678. Rappa cty,Va. 1677-1682,p.211.

Mr. ELIAS TAYLOR and COMFORT, one of the daus of Mr. William ANDERSON. Bf 3 July 1696. N-n,Va. xi-209. See also Acco, Va, xii-84; Deeds iv-344; 1-344; Deeds ii-318.

...... TAYLOR and MARY JUSTICE, wid Abbott JUSTICE. 4 Feby 1724. Acco,Va. xix-18.

Mr. CHARLES TAYLOR and the wid of Mr. SKINNER WALL LOP. Bf 7 Mch 1726. Acco,Va. xix-72. Her name was ELIZABETH. See Acco xx-25.

CHARLES TAYLOR and ELIZABETH HUGHES, wid Robert. Abt 26 Aug 1740. Acco,Va. xxii0-285.

FRANCIS TAYLOR and ELIZABETH SNEAD, dau Charles. Abt Jany 1681. Rappa,Va. 1677-1682, p.331. See Rchmd cty,Va.I-67.

MICHAEL TAYLOR and DORCAS VAULTON, Relict of John-James VAULTON. Bf 5 Oct 1725. Hen,Va. 1677-1737 p.54.

WALTER TAYLOR and MARY HARRIS, dau Richard. Bf or abt 1672. Surry,Va. ii-25.

WILLIAM TAYLOR and ELIZABETH TEACKLE dau Thomas. Bf or abt 1 Feby 1731. Acco,Va. xx-91.

WILLIAM TAYLOR, Carpenter, prob. m. ...... OSBURN, a wid. [Mother of Thomas] Bf 5 Dec 1659. N-n, Va. ix-86.

JAMES TAYLOR and the extx of Capt. John LORD. Bf 3 Aug 1694. Wmld,Va. 1690-1698, fo. 149.

Capt. GEORGE TAYLOR and the Relict of Capt. William MOSELEY. Bf 2 Oct 1684. Rappa,Va. Orders, p.61.

...... TAYLOR and MARY TULEY, dau John. Bf 15 Nov 1747. Alb, Va. 1-14.

Rev. THOMAS TEACKLE and ISABEL DOUGLAS, wid Lt. Col. Edward DOUGLAS, 3 June 1658. Mar. contract. N-n,Va. ix-10. [TEACKLE was b. abt 1629.]

LEVIN TEACKLE and ANN ARBUCKLE. Mar. contract. 19 Apr 1760. Acco,Va. Deeds iii-228. Also xxviiW-707.

THOMAS TEACKLE [son of John] and ELIZABETH CUSTIS, dau Thomas. Bf or abt 1751, Acco,Va. Dii-327. [In King William Homes and Families,p.103, ELIZABETH is said to be the dau of John CUSTIS. This is incorrect.]

ANTHONY TERRICK prob. m. a dau of Christian THOMAS. Bf 14 May 1777. Fred'k,Md. G.M.1-19.

HEZEKIAH THIRK and BEHETHLAND BENNET. 10 Feby 1778. L.Geo, Va. St. Paul's Psh Reg.

HENRY THOMAS and MARGARET RAMSBURG, dau Geo. Sr. Bf 28 Sept 1826. Fred'k,Md. G.M.E.ii-419.

JOHN THOMAS and ELIZABETH RAMSBURG, dau Geo.,Sr. Bf 28 Sept 1826. Fred'k,Md. G.M.E.ii-419.

GABRIEL THOMAS and MARY RAMSBURG, dau Geo,Sr. Bf 28 Sept 1826. Fred'k,Md. G.M.E.ii-419.

ROBERT THOMAS, of Ldn. and FRANCES REMEY, the eldest dau of Jacob. Abt 21 Dec 1762. Ldn,Va. c-471.

THOMAS THORNBERRY and PRUDENCE COLLINS, admx Jacob. Bf 13 Apr 1790. Fred'k,Md. See Court that date.

[PRESLY??] THORNTON and WINNIFRED PRESLY, dau Peter. Nthld, Va. i-97. Bf 12 Aug 1748.

Mr. JOHN THORNTON and BEHETHLAND GILSON. Bf 12 Dec 1763. Staff,Va. O-462.

JACOB VALK, Gent, of Charles Town and ANN ROBERTS, wid William, Pract'r of Physic. Bf 17 May 1781. Charleston,S.C. TT-64.

VINCENT VASS and JUDITH BALL, wid. 27 Nov 1755. Rchmd cty, Va. M.L.B.

VINCENT VASS and JANE MOUNTAGUE, wid William. Bf 7 Feby 1758. Mddx,Va. D-432.

ROBERT VAULX and ELIZA: one of the daus of Rodham Kenner, Gent. Bf 21 Aug 1712. Nthld,Va. Orders iv-803.

...... VIGEROUS and ANNE SMITH, dau Edw'd. Bf 14 Apr 1687. Som,Md.

WILLIAM VIGORS and JOICE CARTER, Relict of James. Bf 3 July 1747. Wmld,Va. Fid.Accts, ii-38.

Mr. HENRY VOSS and Mrs. ANNE HIGBY. [Abt?] 3 Apr 1656. N-n, Va. viii-127.

...... WADDY and JANE SPENCE, dau John. Bf 23 Oct 1700. Va. Col. Dec. p.R61.

[JOHN] WADDINGTON and FRANCES GILL, dau Thomas. Bf 10 Feby 1707. Nthld,Va. 1706-1720.

ANDREW WADE and ANN HENRY RICHARDSON, dau ANN, wf of Wm. RICHARDSON. Bf 17 Jany 1814. K.Wm,Va. "15"-317.

JOHN WADE and MARY WILLIAMS, dau of Samuel. Bf or abt 15 June 1752. Gehld,Va. vi-211.

...... WADE and SUSANNA CAIN, dau James. Bf 1765. Sus,Dela. E-239.

CH'S WADE and ELIZA:ANDERSON. 27 Sept 1773. Cumb,Va. Fee Book. Mar.Li.[See was dau Charles..see ii-391.]

HENDRICK WAGOMAN, carpenter, a Dutchman of the City of Amsterdam; mar. contract with Mrs. WINIFRED SCHIN [SCKIN] dau of Margaret Westerhouse. 9 May 1660. N-n, Va. ix-70.

FRANCIS WAINHOUSE and PATIENCE FISHER, wid Thomas. Ab 30 May 1710. N-n,Va. xviii-533. Prob. abt the earlier date of 28 July 1709. See xviii-488.

BRIAN(x) WAID and the wid of ...... BARBER. Abt 4 Dec 1679. Rappa,Va. 1677-1682. p.246.

THOMAS WAKEFIELD of Eversham Tshp, Burlington cty, N.J. and KATHERINE SULAVAN, wid Thurlas. Bf 1 Aug 1702. E.Jersey records. xxi-539.

SAFFORD or HAFFORD WALDRON and HANNAH WEBB. Bf 2 July 1829. Nthld, Penna. iii-239.

THOMAS WALKER and FRANCES HILL, dau John, Gent. Bf 1 Apr 1797. K.Wm,Va. "8"-194. Walker was deceased at the date of this record.

THOMAS WALKER and Mrs. ELIZABETH [GREGORY] THORNTON, "an old sweetheart". 14 Jany 1781. Draper Mss.5QQ-92. See also B5-11. W.H.S.

FELIX WALKER and ISABELLA HENRY. 10 Jany 1780. Draper Mss. 24C-5. W.H.S.

WILLIAM WALKER and ...... JEFFARS, who had a bro. William. Bf 20 Mch 1655. Nthld,Va. 1658-1666. fo.86.

WILLIAM WALKER and JEAN [PIPER], sister of Harry PIPER. Bf 21 Mch 1774. Ffx,Va. D(1)-162.

...... WALKER and MARY SHARPE, wid Robert. Bf 20 Jany 1655. Nthld,Va. 1652-1658, fo.64.

WILLIAM WALKER and MARY JEPHS [?] sister of William who removed to Maryland [1658 or 1659] Wmld,Va. see record 24 Sept 1707. iv-40.

SAMUEL WALKER and ANN STUART, wid William. Bf 30 Mch 1736. Wmld,Va. Orders,fo.193. [ANN a dau of Elizabeth Muse?]

EDMOND WALKER and MARTHA, admx of Arthur HARRIS. Bf 30 Nov 1743. Wmld,Va. Orders,fo.9. See also fo.32.

WILLIAM WALKER and ELIZABETH NETHERTON, dau Henry. Bf 30 May 1733. Wmld,Va. Orders, fo.83.

JOHN WALLACE and MARGARET ANDERSON, dau Allen. Bf 24 Mch 1785. York, Penna. O.C. E-261.
GEORGE WALLER and ELIZABETH ALLEN, dau William. Bf 16 Aug 1738. Staff, Va. M-309.
JOHN WALLER and ENNIE [ANNIE? EUNIE? EUNICE?] dau John SPENCE Esq. Bf 19 Jany 1769. Dela Arch. Sus. cty.
SKINNER WALLOP and ELIZABETH DOUGLAS, dau George. Bf 25 May 1762. Acco,Va. Deeds iii-182.
JNO. WALTERS and MARY HORNER. 22 Feby 1767. St. John's psh, Md. His second wife.
THOMAS WALTERS prob. m. the admx of Gerrard NEWTON. Bf 11 Nov 1737. Staff,Va. Z-392.
BENJ. WALTON and MARY SWIFT. Bucks cty, Penna. xxxviii-408.
THOMAS WARD prob. m. ARCADIA WELBOURNE, wid Thomas. Bf 3 Apr 1716. Acco,Va. xv-18.
THOMAS WARD and ALICE HOLMES, dau John. Bf 16 Feby 1652. L. Norf,Va. C-40.
WILLIAM WARE and BARBARA BATSON, wid Jacob. Bf 6 Feby 1723 N-n,Va. xxiiR-193.
...... WARRINGTON and SARAH ROACH, admx William. Bf 2 Nov 1779. Dela Arch. Sus cty.
THOMAS WARRINGTON and ELIZABETH MORRIS, dau Joseph. Bf 5 June 1736. Som,Md. El-66.
FRANCIS WARRINGTON [WADDINGTON] and the admx of James MONK. Bf 14 Aug 1700. Staff,Va. Z-40.
WILLIAM WARING, Jr. and SARAH GREEN, dau George. Bf 17 Aug 1778. Essex,Va. xii-297.
JOHN WARRIN and wid of John MUSSAY [MASSEY?] Mar. contract. 22 July 1687. Acco,Va. vi-456.[This name may be NUSSAY.]
LUND WASHINGTON, Jr., and SUSANNA GRAYSON, dau Spence. Bf 2 Mch 1795. Pr. Wm, Va. Y-556.
JOHN WASHINGTON and MARY MASSEY, dau Dade MASSEY. Bf 16 Apr 1735. Staff,Va. M-172.
AUGUSTINE WASHINGTON, Gent., and ANNE AYLET, dau William, Gent. Bf 27 Nov 1744. Wmld,Va. Orders,fo.49. "Estate of their Grandfather Henry Ashton and Wm. Aylet Gent, de'c'd" referred to as well as the estate of "their deceased father."
JOSIAS WASTCOAT and MARY, the admx of Francis CORNEWALL. Bf 2 June 1696. Ancient Records of Sus. cty, Dela. at P.G.S., Phila. p.81d. See also p.60f and 8h.
ANDREW WATSON and the "Relict & Execution" of Robert MAPHEE[??] Bf 11 Dec 1667. Staff,Va. Orders i-93.
SILAS WATKINS and P.....[?] WATKINS. 26 Apr 1773. Cumb,Va. Fee Book. Mar. Li.
CHARLES WATTS and MARY DICKERSON, wid. Bf 5 Jany 1762. Wor, Md. J.W.iii-68.

JOHN WATTS and PRACILLA, extx George LAYFIELD. Bf 15 Aug 1706. Wor,Md. J.W.xv-321. See also Som,Md. C.D.-5.

THOMAS WATSON and ELIZABETH [sister to Nehemiah DAVIS' wife.] Bf 5 May 1741. Sus,Dela. G-7-342.

JOHN WATTSON and SARAH, dau Capt. John WALLOP. Bf 21 Mch 1694. Acco,Va. x-151.

Mr. JAMES WAUGH and a dau of Nathaniel BRITTINGHAM. Bf 30 Sept 1740. Staff,Va. M-475. [There is some doubt as to this...another entry seems to make Hugh French m. the dau of Brittingham.]

JOSEPH WAUGH, late of Stafford, and MILLION TRAVERSE, dau Giles. 20 Jany 1675. Pr. Wm,Va. L.C.p.345.

RICH'D WEBB and ELIZABETH SMITH, Relict of Henry. Bf 10 Mch 1702. Staff,Va. Z-163.

JAMES WEBB, of Orange cty, N.C., and NANCY DABBS, wid of Joseph, late of Goochland, Va. Bf 8 July 1762. Cumb,Va. iii-279.

JNO. WEBSTER and CHLOE, dau Nancy JOHNSON. Bf 8 Oct 1823. Pr. Wm,Va. M-105.

JORDAN WEEDON and MARTHA ELLIOTT, one of the daus of John, Gent. Bf 29 Aug 1711. Wmld,Va. 1705-1721,fo 168. See also fo. 181.

JOHN WEEDON and JANE SHEIRES, dau Alexander. Bf 25 July 1705. Wmld,Va. 1698-1705. fo.268.

JOHN WELCH and ELIZABETH FREEMAN, wid John. Bf 24 Sept 1754. Pr.Wm,Va. Orders [2]-141.

CALEB WELLING and the extx of John VAUS. Abt 1 June 1692. Rchmd cty,Va. Orders.

FRANCIS WEST and ELIZABETH BRANSFORD, dau John. Bf 1 May 1769. Hen. Papers, Va.

GEORGE WEST and PENELOPE PAYNE... she was his "last beloved wife". Bf 13 Apr 1786. Ffx,Va. E(1)-134. WEST also had a "beloved wife Ann Fowke," whose father was "the late Townshend of Fairfax". He mentions also a "first wife".

JOHN WEST prob. m. KATHERINE REVELL. Bf 11 Feby 1690. Som, Md. 1690-1691.

WRIXAM WEST and BETTEY [MILBY?] West and wf were admrs of Nathan Milby. Bf or abt 5 Sept 1769. Dela Arch.Sus.cty.

JAMES WEST and JANE SCOGGIN, dau John. Bf 24 Mch 1785. York, Penna. O.C. E-256.

PETER WEST and COMFORT, extx [?] of Thomas PRITTYMAN. Bf 7 Sept 1763. Dela Arch. Sus. cty.

JOHN WEST, Jr. and CATHERINE COLVILL, dau John. Bf 11 Aug 1767. Ldn,Va. C-85.

JOHN WEST, Jr. prob. m. the widow RIDGWAY. [This is uncertain.] Bf 15 Mch 1704. Staff,Va. Z-259.

WILLIAM WEST and MARY ELLZEY, dau Lewis. Bf 1 Oct 1785. Ffx, Va. E(1)-224.

THOMAS WHEELER, "Shoomaker", and ELIZABETH GREGORY, sister of John. Bf 20 June 1677. Rappa,Va. 1677-1682,p.283. See also p.134.

ROBERT WHARTON and RACHEL ELLIS, dau Thomas. Bf 11th 11th 1702. Penna Arch 2d ser. xix-348.

JOHN WHIDON and JANE YATES, dau Richard. [Date early but uncertain. L. Norf.Order B'k.]

JOHN WHISTON and the wid & extx of Nathaniel JONES. Bf 27 Apr 1664. Wmld,Va. 1662-1664,fo-26.

JOSEPH WHITE and SUSANNA McCORD, dau Richard. Bf 4 Feby 1786. York, Penna. O.C. E-355.

...... WHITE and ANN TULEY, dau John. Bf 15 Nov 1747. Alb, Va. 1-4.

...... WHITE and CATHERINE WILLIAMS, wid Morgan. Bf 25 Jany 1705. S.L.O. Rchmd,Va. iii-123. WHITE was then dec'd. CATHERINE had also been a widow STEWART.

JAMES WHITE and ELIZABETH, admx of Hugh FENIX, late of Q.A. Bf 5 Dec 1829. Q.A.,Md. Minutes O.C.

WILLIAM WHITE and MARTHA SMITH, of Curatoman; intentions of marriage. [Abt 26th 3d 1683.] Friends' Mtgs,Md.

GEORGE WHITE and ELIZABETH BURKET, dau Mr. John BURKET. Bf 9 Oct 1719. K.Geo, Va. 1-51.

Mr. GEORGE WHITE and Mrs. SYBELLA CODD. Bf 15 Dec 1646. L. Norf, B-23.

JOHN WHITE, L. Norf,pltr., and EDEY LLEWELLIN, dau Thomas. Bf 9 Nov 1664. I.W., Va. iii-26.

SHADRICK WHITE and SARAH GIBSON. 11 Apr 1799. Wash'n cty,Va. Mar. Ret.

JOHN WHITE and MARGARETT, extx of Leroy GEORGE. Bf 6 Nov 1702. Rchmd cty, Va. Oiii-195.

...... WHITE and TABITHA GRINALLS, dau Richard. Bf 7 Jany 1715. Acco,Va. xvi-2.

JOHN WHITE and SARAH...... They were extrs of Thomas BEAUCHAMP, was she his widow? Bf 24 Feby 1722. Som,Md. See E.B. xiii-153.

STEVENS WHITE and ATTALANTA WHITTINGTON, dau William. [Whittington gives them Springfield and Fair Meadow.] Bf or abt 7 June 1710. Som,Md. X-602.

STEVENS WHITE and CATHERINE, admx of Geo. HOPE. Bf 7 Aug 1717. Acco,Va. xv-35.

JOHN WHITE and MARY ELLETT. Bf 1705-6. K. Wm,Va. "2"-46.[It is possible WHITE was step-son to Thomas Ellett, father of Mary. Joseph Brown also makes gift to John WHITE, his "son-in-law" and wf Mary.]

THOMAS WHITBY and MARY, extx of Thomas COLLIER. Bf 24 Mch 1704. York,Va. xiii-60.

JOHN WHITESIDE and JEAN HOPKINS. 29 July 1788. Rockbr,Va.

JEREMIAH WHITNEY and SUSANNAH ROGERS, wid Robert. Bf 1743. Gchld,Va. iv-155.

JAMES WHITLOE and EDITH COX, dau Richard,Sr. Bf 5 June 1732. Hen,Va. Papers.

JOHN WHITEING and HANNAH PRICE, relict of William. [She was dau of William WEBB] Bf 25 Mch 1702. Wmld,Va. 1698-1705. fo.151.

ROBERT WHYTELL, of Chas. cty,Md. and ELIZABETH THEOBALD, wid John. Bf 11 May 1743. Semmes Mss. M.H.S.

BENJAMIN WICKER prob. m. FRANCES BAILY, dau John and Susan. Abt or bf 21 Mch 1789. Hanover cty, Va. xxl-152. W.& M.

ROGER WIGGINTON and the relict of John CLEMENTS. Bf 29 Aug 1716. Wmld, Va. v-622.

THOMAS WILD and HENRIETTA POWELL, wid William. Mar. agreement. 15 Apr 1776. Middx,Va. viii-505.

...... WILKINS and MARY WARREN, dau Argill[?] Waren. Bf 24 Sept 1721. N-n,Va. xxivR-123.

JOHN WILKINS and CATHERINE CUSTIS, "Gent", extx of Edmund. 23 June 1750. Acco, Va. Deeds ii-275.

RICHARD WILKINSON and SUSANNAH ELLETT, dau Thomas. Bf 28 Feby 1799. K.Wm,Va. "9"-30.

HAZLEWOOD WILKINSON and ANNA GRANT, dau Daniel. Bf or abt 11 Jany 1792. Wilkes, Ga. MM-42.

ALEXANDER WILLEY and the wid of Benajah DOTY. Bf 20 Aug 1787. Onslow, N.C.

...... WILLIAMS and CHARLOTTE WALKER. Bf 11 Apr 1797. Q.A., Md. Admns,p.89.

EDW'D WILLIAMS, of Chas. cty, Md, and MARY WOOD, dau John, Sr, Bf 12 Dec 1705. Staff, Va. Z-321.

ANTHONY WILLIAMS and the widow SHARP. [Uncertain] Bf 29 Dec 1699. Staff, Va. Z-42.

JOHN WILLIAMS and SARAH TOWER, dau Thomas. Bf 21 June 1699. Nthld, Va. Orders iv-24.

BENJAMIN WILLIAMS and COMFORT WELSH, dau Capt. John WELSH. Bf 23 Nov 1752. Semmes Mss. M.H.S.

JO. WILLIAMS and POLLY BOON. Prob. 1802. Greene cty, Ga. Mar. [A list without year date.]

DAVID WILLIAMS and JANE COVINGTON. "Bonds of Matrimony", published 26 Nov 1667. Som,Md. Bl-90.

JONATHAN WILLIAMS and REBEKAH WILLIAMS. 17 May 1806. Mar 18 May [1808?] Greene cty,Ga. Mar Li.

WILLIAM WILLIAMSON and JANE, the admx of John HALL, dec'd. Bf 17 June 1760. Ffx,Va. Orders [2] p.477.

JOHN WILLIE, tallow chandler, of London, and ELIZABETH PITT, wid of Robert, late of London, mariner. Bf 14 Apr 1675. Acco,Va. v-277.
HENRY WILLIS and MILDRED GREGORY. Bf 15 Dec 1738. Mr. Torrence's Spots. cty Abstracts, Va. p.150.
RICHARD WILLIS and ANN GRIGGS, wid Michall GRIGGS. Bf 7 Aug 1691. S.L.O.Lanc,Va. 1-77.
NATHANIEL WILLIS, of Som cty, and MARY LONGO, dau James. Bf 27 Oct 1736. Acco,Va. xx-259.
JAMES WILLS and REBECCA BARNABE. 13 Mch 1679. Som,Md.
...... WILSON and SARAH GREEN, dau Philemon. Bf 12 Dec 1774. Q.A.,Md. Wills, T.W.1-4.
ALEXANDER WILSON and MARY ORBISON[?] wid Thomas. Bf 28 Nov 1782. Cumb,Penna. O.C. ii-313.
CHRISTOPHER WILSON and DINAH GREGG, dau of Dinah. Bf 3-8-1763. Chester cty, Penna. Wills. P.G.S.
NICHOLAS WILSON and ELIZ: COCKER [?] wid William. Bf 7 May 1678. Surry,Va. Orders i-198.
JOHN WILSON, Jr., and the relict of William CHAMBERS. Bf 20 Aug 1707. Hen,Va. 1677-1737, p.49.
JAMES WILSON, Jr., and GRACE DUKE. 1743. Norf,Va.
HENRY WINCOOP and SARAH DUBOIS, dau Isaac. Bf 13 Feby 1707. Philada.O.C. 1716-1755. p.40. P.G.S.
WILLIAM WINDO and MARGRETT ALLISON, wid and admr of Thomas. Bf 26 July 1704. Wmld,Va. 1698-1705,fo.232.
MICHAELL WINDER and SUSANNA, relict of Henry BRUCE, Jr. [She was SUSANNA STEWART.] Bf or abt 5 Sept 1722. Richmd cty, Va. Orders ix-68.
HARRISON WINN and FRANCIS HAILE, dau Thomas. Bf 24 Oct 1816. ... Mech,Va. Wills,viii.
Capt. MINOR WINN and BETTY WITHERS, dau Thomas. Bf 5 Nov 1794. Fauq,Va. ii-251.
WILLIAM WINSTON and REBECCA BOBBY, dau Thomas BOBBY. Bf Jany 1733. Hanover cty,Va. xxi - W. & M.
JAMES WINSTON of Louisa and SARAH MARKS, dau Hastings MARKS. Bf 4 Apr 1787. Hanover,Va. xxiii-121. W. & M.
JOHN WINTERS prob. m. MARY GILLILAND, dau of Thomas, the Elder. 26 June 1778. Wilkes,Ga. i-47. [They had son Thomas Winters.]
CONROD WIRT and RACHEL, dau of Israel FOLSOM. By 20 July 1781. Pr. Wm,Va. W-191.
GEORGE WISE and HULDAH AYRES, dau Edmund. Bf 2 Oct 1736.Acco, Va. xx-246. [This name also spelled EYRES.]
JOHN WISE, Jr., and PEGGY DOUGLAS, dau George, Gent. Bf 26 Dec 1763. Acco,Va. iii-262. See also Diii-630.
JOHN WISE and MATILDA WEST, dau Col. John WEST. Bf 4 Dec 1706. Acco,Va. xiii-81.

TULLY ROBINSON WISE and TABITHA DOUGLAS, dau George and Tabitha. Bf 13 Dec 1760. Acco,Va. Deeds iii-130. See also Acco, xxvii-433.

Mr. JOHN WISTEN[?] and the Relict of Mr. Jugh DOWDING. Prob. bf or abt 7 Aug 1667. Staff,Va. Orders i-80.

...... WITHERS and MARY LITTLEJOHN, dau Oliver. Bf 18 Sept 1702. Staff, Va. Z-206.

JAMES WITHERS and ELIZABETH KEEN, dau Mathew. Bf 21 July 1723. Staff,Va. M-26.

WILLIAM WOFFENDALL and JANE, extx of Charles TYLER. Bf 27 Feby 1733. Wmld,Va. Orders fo.129. Records, Sus,Dela.60f.

RICE WOLFE and MARY CORNEWALL, dau Francis. Bf 4 Mch 1706. Early note.

JOHN WOOD and MARGARET MADDUX. Mar.contract. Oct Ct, 1793. Fauq.,Va. Orders, p.473.

DAVID WOOD and RUTH GREGG, dau Thomas. Bf 16 June 1821. Fayette, Penna. i-214.

JOHN WOOD, Sr., of Chas. cty [Md?] perhaps m. ..... RIGING, a widow. Bf 13 Dec 1705. Staff,Va. Z-323.

JOHN WOOD and ANNA, extx Josiah JENKINS, Fred'k cty, Md. Bf 28 Sept 1766. Annap. Bal. Bk v-8.

...... WOOD and ELIZABETH BRANSON, dau. John, Sr., of St. Mary's, Md.Bf 11 Jany 1770. Annap.Wills, xxxvii-654.

JAMES WOODLAND, of Kent cty, and SARAH HACKETT, dau Thomas. Bf 23 May 1796. Q.A.,Md. W.H.N. iii-124.

...... WOODLIFE, of Chas City cty,Va. and ELIZA: WALLAS, eldest dau. Mr. John WALLAS. Bf 24 Oct 1701. S.L.O.Rchmd,Va. ix-388.

JAMES WOOLFORD, of Som,Md, and GRACE STEVENS, of Dor,Md. at mtg house near Choptank river. 3d of 9th 1698. Third Haven Friends Records, v-395.

FRANCIS WORLEY, Chester cty, Penna, and MARY BRASSEY. Bf 5th 23d 1703 Penna. Arch. Ser 2. xiv-458.

JOSEPH WRIGHT and MARY FARQUHAR, dau William. Bf 7 Nov 1771. Fred'k, Md. G-78.

---oOo---

The abbreviations of the names of the counties and of the titles of the record volumes in the preceding list are the same as those used in the COUNTY COURT NOTE-BOOK, and the first number of ANCESTRAL PROOFS & PROBABILITIES, by this compiler. It may be as well to set them down here for the benefit of those who are unfamiliar with those publications. They are roughly classified geographically.

On the Eastern Shore of Virginia, Acco and N-n are Accomack and Northampton; on the same side of the Bay, but in Maryland, Dor is Dorchester; Wor, Worcester; Som, Somerset;

Talb, Talbot; Car, Caroline; Q. A., Queen Anne's; Kent and Cecil are not abbreviated. Northerly are Balto, Baltimore; Harf, Harford. Across the Bay A. A. is Anne Arundell; Chas, Charles, St. M's, St. Mary's. In northern and western Maryland are Montg, Montgomery; Fred'k, Frederick (also in Virginia); Wash'n, Washington (also in Virginia); Cumb, Cumberland (also Virginia), and Alleg, Allegheny. Pr. Geo's or P. G., Prince George's, on the Potomac. In Virginia the county is called Prince George.

Delaware, on the ocean side of the Eastern Shore, has N. C., Newcastle; Sus, Sussex, and another Kent.

In the Northern Neck of Virginia are Ldn, Loudoun; Fauq, Fauquier; Pr. Wm, Prince William; Staff, Stafford; K. Geo., King George; Wmld, Westmoreland (also in Pennsylvania); Nthld, Northumberland; Lanc, Lancaster; and Rchmd, Richmond. In Tide-Water Virginia and about the James, are Middx, Middlesex; York and Essex; E. C., Elizabeth City county; Norf, Norfolk [in early records Lower Norfolk]; Surry and Sus, Sussex, also Pr. A., Princess Anne; S-n, Southampton; on the north of the James, K. Wm, King William; J. C. City, James City county, and New Kent. C. C., Chas City county; Hen, Henrico, and westerly Fluv, Fluvanna; Louisa; Gchld, Goochland; Alb, Albemarle; Amherst. [Other counties of this general section: Camp, Campbell; Pow, Powhatan; Amelia; Chest, Chesterfield; P. E., Prince Edward. Less familiar are Pits or Pitsyl, Pitsylvania; Lunen, Lunenburgh; Meckl, Mecklinburgh; Henry and Frank, Franklin.

The Valley counties, or thereabouts, are Shenan, Shenandoah; Rock'm, Rockingham; Rockbr, Rockbridge; Aug, Augusta, Or, Orange; others can be easily identified. In the far corner is Gray, Grayson.

From the foregoing examples it is thought that the abbreviated names of the counties of West Virginia, Kentucky, Tennessee, the Carolinas and Georgia will be readily understood.

---oOo---

Emphasis must again be placed upon the fact that the dates given are merely (in most cases) the date of the record from which the marriage is inferred. Touching the variations in the spelling of names, it need hardly be said that the compiler is not responsible.

There are some repetitions in this list, some are accidental, others are given an additional reference. A dozen or two were wrongly alphabetized in Bulletin No. 1, and have been re-arranged in this.

AYDLOTT-Richards (2)
Anderson-Roach
Adams-Saunders
Arbuckle-Teackle
Anderson-Wallace
Allen-Waller
Aylet-Washington
Allamby-Goring
Argent-Ivy
Allen-James
----- Mackittrick
----- Basnett
----- Bagwell
Addams-Matthews
Austen-Jeffars
Abdell-Ashby
Asbury-Garrison
Allerton-Currie
----- Cooper
Armsby (Ormsby?)-Churn
Addison-Doughty
Ashton-Blackburn
Ayres-Wise
Allison-Window
Anderson-Raine

BAGWELL-Dix
Ballew-Ballenger
Baker-Dunkin
Bayly-Barker
Baily-Wicker
----- Baker
Berryman-Dade (2)
Bagwell-Allen
Baxter-Barns
Benston-Armitrader
Broome-Gilbert
Bell-Gitting
Brown-Fleming
----- Smith
Burrey-Green
Bonam-Damonvel
Brockenbrough-Dalton
----- Dickenson(2)
Bayly-Crippen
Boyd-Craighead
Brayfield-Cooper
Bagley-Cobgutt(?)
Beal-Collins
Birch-Congleton
Benthall-Clarke
Bowen-Clark
Bushrod-Cooper
Bowles-Coope
Beall-Edwards
Bryant-Elkin
Bennet-Ellot
Burch-Jarrett
Baglye-Lidford
Beavans-Lewis
----- Newton
Barry-Manley
Bird-Mason
Burch-Nelson
Blackburn-Peart
Burroughs-Green
Baxyer-Griffin
Branson-Wood
Brassey-Worley
Barnebe-Wills
Bobby-Winston
Boon-Williams
Bruce-Winder
Burton-Revell
----- Alexander
Beach-Scribner
Bannerman-Seayers
Baker-Sharp
Brooks-Shipp
Bennet-Thirk
Ball-Vass
Barber-Waid
Batson-Ward
Beauchamp(?)-White
Brittingham-Waugh
Bransford-West
Burket-White
Bauguss-Hamelton

*The second name is that of the man.

Button-Gordon
Brake-Gray
Bennett-French
Black-Dodd
Bevill-Botte
Brickhouse-Bowker
Bost-Erbough[?]
Burdit-Boughton
Beloat[Belote]-Bloxsom
Ball-Bletsoe[Bledsoe]
Bounds-Blades
Beall-Beall
Bernard-Butler
Bagge-Butler
Bayley-Bunting
Bagge, Butler, Vaulx, Duddletone, see Butler
Brown-Brenton
Buckner-Brazier
Bonan-Damonvel
Bowman-Atkins
Bradford-Anderson
Bushrod-Allerton
Butler-Ashton
----- Bagge

CALVERT-Basford
Chilton-Austen
Christian-Baker
Coe-Baker
Combs-Ashby
Cox-Disharoon
Crabb-Dunbar
Curtis-Barrett
Cox-Boggess(2)
Christian-Boyer
Craighead-Boyd
Cricther-Berry
Cragges-Belt
Cox-Bennett
Colston-Belfield
Cannon-Bauguss
Coomes-Baugus[?]
Caldwell-Cunningham
Ching-Crouch
Cole-Doe
Coulbourne-Ellegood
Carnaby-Erwin
Curtice-Cooper
Chapman-Genett
Calthrop-Goodwin
Clarke-Gressam
Covington-Williams
Cornewall-Wolfe
Cocker[?]-Wilson
Chambers-Wilson
Custis-Wilkins
----- Teackle
----- Pettit
Collier-Whitby
Cox-Whitloe
Custis-Bagwell
----- Allen
----- Arbuckle
Clements-Wigginton
Crawley-Saunders
Coston-Skidmore
Collins-Thornberry
Carter-Vigors
Cain-Wade
Cornewall-Wascoat
Colvill-West
Codd-White
Conner-Hampton
Clyatt-O'Neel
Conyers-Payne
Carnaby-Peyton
Chandler-Collinsworth
Clasbey-Clasbey
Collins-Chase
Collidge-Coward
Cottman-Canaley
Church-Bazey[?]
Critcher-Butler
Craig-Butcher
Coward-Bunting
Coomes-Brown
Chance-Bradley
Clay-Brantly
Callahan-Beadon
Cawson-Ballentine

DAVIS-Glenn

Daniel-Harmanson
Dyer-Hartfield
Daynes-Harris
Dinguid-Harris
Douglas-Wise
Dowding-Wisten[?]
Douglas-Wise
Dubois-Wincoop
Duke-Wilson
Doty-Walley
Dolwich-Rahn
Davis-Riggs
Dukes-Satterfield
Dishman-Seaton
Davis[?]-Shockly
Douglas-Teackle
----- Wallop
Dabbs-Webb
Dickerson-Watts
Derricke-Hunt
Drake-Hunt
Douglas-Littleton
Drummond-Marcey
Dixon-Martin
Dale-Parke
Dade-Peyton
Davis-Davison
----- Blut[?]
Dudley-Bowden
Downing-Blackwell
Drighouse-Beckitt
Donaldson-Craig
Davis-English
Demovel-Eskridge
Dubois-Coats
Drummond-Chance
Davis-Christopher
Dixon-Browne
Drummond-Bayly
----- Allen
----- Bagwell
Duddletone-Butler
Doyne-Brown
Demonvell-Awbry
Draper-Ayers
Dunkin-Bayley
Dyel-Dyer
Davies-Atwell

ENGLISH-Atwell
Ellett-Wilkinson
----- White
Elliott-Weedon
Ellzey-West
Ellis-Wharton
Eyres-Hudspath
Eastham-Palmer
Elliott-Palmer
Edwards-Buckley
----- Cowles(2)
Ellicott-Ellicott
Everist-Comegyes
Evans-Bean
----- Child
Ellyson-Armistead
Edmonston-Beall
Eyre-Burton
Edmunds-Bunting
Eyes-Arledge

FAIRFAX-Dashiell
Farrow-Barker
Ford-Davenport
Folson-Doyle
Fell-Dorsey
Farquhar-Wright
Folsom-Wirt
Fassitt-Rackliffe
----- Campbell
Farrow-Scurlock
Fisher-Wainhouse
Freeman-Welch
Fenix-White
Folson-Doyle
Farrow-Filkins
French-Foote
Foster-Cornewell
----- Foulkes
Floker-Curtis
Fresh-Helvens
Fox-Kenner
Farsit-Layfield

Fauntleroy-Lloid
Fleming-Maccuddy
Fowler-Mason
Foguson-Cunningham
Ford-Cantey
Farnihaugh-Beck
Fisher-Baily
Foord[Ford]-Davenport

GARLAND-Anderson
Gawton-Drake
Gregg-Wood
Gregory-Willis
Griggs-Willis
Gregg-Wilson
Green-Waring
----- Wilson
Gilliland-Winters
Grant-Wilkinson
George-White
----- Read
Grovenstine-Reiser
Garland-Rice
Goolsby-Saunders
Greene-Scarlett
Gray-Hux
----- Aymes
----- Sharp
Gilson-Thornton
----- Waddington
Grayson-Dermott
----- Washington
Gregory-Wheeler
Gibson-White
Grinalls-White
Gearing-Carnaby
Gooding-Carty
----- Cannon
Griffeth-Hays
Good-James
Griggs-Kelly
Gething-Neech
Garton-Patty
Goode-Burson
Gardner-Bickley
Gascoine-Benthall
Gayson-Browne

Gibson-Allen
Givens-Allen
Griffin-Barker
----- Baker

HARDIDGE-Ashton
Hart-Ashton
Hawkins-Basnett
Holden-Allfree
Hack-Boat[Boot]
Humphries-Boggus
Hunt-Benthall
Harrison-Blackburn
Hunter-Blackford
Horner-Beck
Haemenin[Hamaen]-Becker
Hopkins-Beckley
----- Laramore
----- Hart
----- Whiteside
Harris-Haynie
----- Taylor
----- Walker
Harrison[or Hanson]-Bell
Hartley-Smith
Hollon-Rice
Henry-Walker
Hill-Walker
Higby-Voss
Horner-Walters
Holloway-Saunders
Holmes-Ward
Hughes-Taylor
Hackett-Green
----- Gould
----- Woodland
Hall-Williamson
Haile-Winn
Hope-White
Haskins-Read
Horsley-Goodman
Horsey-Bruff
Hicks-Goodrich
Hogg-Harris
Halley-Holmes
Hairr[?]-Hopkins
Hunt-Buckner

Hunt- Hunt
Hoskins-Jette
Huett-Lee
Higgins-Elliott(2)
----- Cooper
----- Manly
Hedrick[?]-Palmer
Huntt-Parker
Hinson-Pearce
Harrison-Courts
Holdbrook-Earle
Hunton-Fowler
Hendrick-Eubank
Harmanson-Eyre
Hall-Devonport
----- Bayly
Holmes-Bateman
Harlin-Briscoe
Hatton-Brooke
Harbeson-Briscoe
Hardy-Claypool
Hays-Christie
Harringdon-Chancellour
Halbut-Cirwithin
Hancock-Brewer
Howell-Brett
Holmes-Bradford
Hudson-Dod
Humphreys-Bagshaw
Hutton-Percy

JENKINS-Wood
Johnson-Bagby
Jones-Bossman
Johnson-Bloxson
Johns-Fariss
Jefferson-Farrar
Jenkins-Green
Johnson-Hamby
----- Holt
----- Ball
----- Damron
Jordan-Hunt
Jenner-Judkins
James-Lewis
Jones-Newson
----- Payne
Jones Roach
----- Folio[?]
----- Whiston
----- Bartlett
----- Bayly
----- Balthrop
----- Blaise
Justice-Taylor
----- Parramore
Jarboe-Goffe
Jackman-Grimsted
Jeffars-Walker
Jephs-Walker
Johnson-Webster
James-Fosque
Jackson-Berry

KENNEDY-Fleming
Kellam-Groten
King-Hopewell
Kensey-Johns
Kain-Kirkpatrick
----- Lutton
Kendall-Lee
Keen-Withers
King-Read
Kenner-Vaulx

LAYFIELD-Watts
Llewellin-White
Lumpkin-Hay
Lee-Martiall
----- Corbin
Layfield-Collier
Lissumm[?]-Butler
Lay-Bass
Lake-Burdett
Lyson-Butler
Lovell-Bryan
Long-Bridgeman
Lane-Brickey
----- Brice
Langhurst-Barber
Leatherbury-Barnes
Lee-Ball
Lowe-Digges
----- Darnall

Luke-Ball
Lynchfield-Andrews
Langford-Cox

MATHEWS-Anderson
Marshall-Beall
----- Beatty
----- Clevely
McFarlane-Atwell
Malbone-Godfrey
Massey-Dade (2)
----- Washington
Major-Gowtee
Mode-Haddon
Moss-Savin
----- Crask
----- Dinguid
McCarty-Baylis
----- McDanell
----- Fitzhugh
McAllister-Hays
Makemie-Kemp
Miller-Kirby
Moryson-Lear
Mason-Maddocks
McCall-Moore
Mulls[Mills?]-Cormerick
Mott-Colson
Musgrove-Charleson
Maddux-Wood
Marks-Winston
McKinney-Ransome
Moseley-Taylor
Mountague-Vass
Morris-Warrington
Monk-Warrington[Waddington]
Mussay-Warrin
Maphee-Watson
Milby-West
McCord-White
Mott-Fosaker
McKomb-Brabon[?]
McClelland-Carrick
Massey-Dade (2)
Milner-Babicome
Milby-Pettit
Merritt-Bouring

May-Bowen
Moody-Benston
Meador-Bates
Mills-Burkett
Milling-Buchanan
Morgan-Buckner
Marson-Bryant
Moss-Browne
Mitchel-Brinson
Martial-Jackson
Maulpis-Jackson
Mosby-Hoy
Mothershead-Brinham
Mountjoy-Belfield
Monroe-Bankhead

NEWTON-Berryman
----- Walters
----- Guibert
----- Cox
Nash-Bragg
Neal-Bruce
Nicolas-Atkins
Nobel-Farrell
Needles-Hutcheson
Newgent-Pavey
Newton-Mason
Norgrave-Mason
Newberry-Anslow
Naylor-Simpson
Netherton-Walker
Napier-Ogilvie

OSWALD-Key
Overton-Butler
Occany-Crabb
Orbison-Wilson
Osburn-Taylor
Owen-Coppock
----- Collins
Orr-Dodd

PERRY-Flint
Pierce-Ford
Pitt-Willie
Price-Whiteing
Powell-Wild

Prittyman-West
Purnell-Rackliffe
Phippen-Read
Payne-Rice
Palmer-Ligon
----- Barclay
----- Dingee[?]
Parker-Savage
----- Simson
Presly-Thornton
Piper-Walker
Payne-West
Price-Oglesby
----- Carr
----- Francis
Piles-Darbe
Pendleton-Harris
Phillips-Holdsworth
Patton-Hopkins
Parks-Kendall
Pointer-Lowery
Penny-Marshall
Porter-Marshall
----- Noble
Paramore (alias Manlove)-
Paramore
Parker-Garner
----- Ballew
Persell-Bishop
Powell-Christian
Porter-Cannon
Pettit-Bell
Powell-Butler
Peall-Andras [Andrews?]
Perrin-Ballew
Phillips-Bennett
Parramore-Bell

RICHARDSON-Armstrong
----- Ball
----- Hughs
----- Harriot
Roach-Warrington
Richardson-Wade
----- Martial
Reade-Nelson
Ramsburg-Buckey
----- Thomas (3)
Rush-Peyton
Richards-Godwin
Ratticar-Gregg
Riging-Wood
Rogers-Whitney
Remey-Thomas
Roberts-Valk
Revell-West
Ridgway-West
Rosten-Betts
Robertson-Bird
Rust-Bennett
Robinson-Beale
Roe-Beale
Ragan-Butler
Rowland-Browne
Robins-Nicholasson
----- Eveling
Rogers-Brickhouse
Ratcliffe-Blake
Russell-Boulton
----- Atkins
Roads-Farsit
Riging-Durram
Rogers-Dunton
Rutter-Bloomfield
Rodolphus-Hamling
Rhoden-Kenner

SELBY-Andrews
Staats-Calahan
Sarrell-Barnes
Scarlet-Barton
Shelpman-Dobb
Spencer-Read
----- Bolton
Shoemaker-Boone
Spence-Mason
----- Waller
Stalcop-Biork
Starait [Starrett?]-
Binney
Stockley-Black
Speight-Benn
Savage-Kendall
----- Copeland

Sanders-Bell
Stockley-Beavans
Scarburg-Bayly
Saunders-Neech
Sanders-Harrison
Smith-Ball
----- Barret
----- Drummond
----- Clark
----- Perkerson
----- Lee
----- White
----- Webb
----- Vigerous
----- Riding
Stafford-Henry
Suggitt-Baylis
Savage-Bayly
Smith-Butler
Scamell-Bulloch
Sheires-Brown
Stowers-Brown
Simmons-Banks
Skinner-Allen
Steel-Givin
Strother-Grant
Stevens-Woolford
Strother-Settle
Sorrell-Atwell
Sharp-Williams
Setler-Rahn
Spence-Waddy
Spence-Regan
Sanford-Remey
Stovall-Saunders
Sweny-Scott
Skinker-Simpson
Snead-Taylor
Schin[Sckin]-Wagoman
Sulavan-Wakefield
Sharpe-Walker
Stuart-Walker
Swift-Walton
Sheires-Weedon
Scoggin-West
Scott-Jameson
Stratton-Lawrence

Stone-Maddock
Shropshire-Peck[?]
Steuart-Franklin
Southerlain-Combs
Sergeant-Collins
Sweeny-Cather
Stafford-Carhart
Salsbury-Dodson
Sorrell-Earle
Severn-Eyre
Stratton-Fisher
Steward-Fleming
Sebastian-Fletcher
South-Drummond
Starr-Drake
Sterling-Bagwell
Stockley-Aydelott

TAYLOR-Barnett
Thatcher-Deane
Terry-Dodd
Thomas-Ballew
Tarbutton-Deford
Thatcher-Deane
Tydwell-Conollin
Templen-Cunningham
Tingle-Collings
Taylor-Carr
----- Butler
----- Marshall
----- Lear
----- Hutchinson
----- Scott
Townsend-Carlile
Thatcher-Goodacre
Tiplady-Goodwin
Thomas-Blessing
----- Booth
----- Bougher
----- Terrick
----- Remsburg
Thorrowgood-Gookins
Tully-Griffis
Tyler-Woffendall
Town-Williams
Traverse-Waugh
Travers-Rice

Tuley-White
----- Taylor
Town-Williams
Theobald-Whytell
Thornton-Walker
Tompkins-Dickman
Tingey-Shoares
Townsend-Shores
Teackle-Taylor
Trent-James
Tilney-James
Thompson-Jamerson
Tofft-Lee
Towle-Marshall
Tucker-Nelson
Tofft-Osborne
Trock-Pavey
Turbervile-Fitzhugh(2)
Topping-Bonwell
Touley-Bouden[Bowden?]
Tilman-Bush
Tucke [Tucker?]-Brown
Turneur-Alrichs

VAULX-Butler
Vanderveulen-Barnes
Vaulton-Taylor
Vaus-Welling
Veale-Chandler

WATSON-Cunningham
Winebiddle-Cunningham
Weatherstone-Crean
Ward-Gray
----- Martiall
Whitacre-Gregg
Whitten-Gue
Williams-White
----- Wade
----- Williams
----- Carlisle
----- Hughs
----- Harris
Wilkins-Hunt
----- Barns
----- Baldwyn
Warriner-Keeling
Watt-Marshall
White-Evans
----- Neal
----- Hill
Waddelowe-Mason
Wormack-Nunnaly
Williamson-Paine
Woodson-Gassaway
West-Burton
----- Wise
----- Lock
Williss-Coulbourn
Watt-Corbin
Watts-Chilton
Warren-Compton
Weston-Evans
Waddelow-Ffoolkes
Wallas-Woodlife
Withers-Field
----- Cofer
----- Winn
Walker-Williams
Welsh-Williams
Webb-Waldron
----- Griffin
Wood-Williams
Warren-Wilkins
Wale-Rackliffe
Wilson-Benson[Benston]
----- Bardell
----- Gregg
Wroe-Rainey
Watts-Selby
Wood-Smoote
Wigginton-Smyth
Wallop-Taylor
Welbourne-Ward
Watkins-Watkins
Wallop-Wattson
Whittington-White
Warren-Dent
Wood-Davidson
Walters-Cannon
Withers-Allen
Wood-Davidson
Wootten-Durkee
Wright-Barber

in the Preceding List.

Welsh-Cameron
Warren-Dent
Washington-Ashton
Waugh-Dawson
----- Doniphan
Weeds-Baily
Wilkinson-Bagnall
Webster-Beard
Wilkins-Baldwyn
Waterson-Batson
Wigginton-Butler
Woodier-Bryant
Wallace-Briscoe
Withers-McDaniel

Yates-Whidon
Young-Colvert

Incomplete: Gull ----- Emanson (name illegible); ----- Beck; ----- Bashford; ----- Booth; ----- Crupper; ----- Watson.

---oOo---

This Bulletin is for sale by

The F. W. FAXON COMPANY
83 Francis Street,
Boston, Massachusetts.

Price $1.50 Milnor Ljungstedt, Editor and Compiler.

NOTTINGHAM'S RECORDS OF THE EASTERN SHORE OF VIRGINIA

A number of copies of these valuable compilations are still to be had.

Address Mrs. H. R. Nottingham, Onancock, Virginia.

CAVALIER and PIONEERS, by Nell Marion Nugent,
State Land Office, Richmond, Virginia.

Any attempt to praise this outstanding Virginia work (of which volume two is about ready) would be but faint praise, indeed. There is nothing in southern publications to equal it.

The HISTORY of the VIRGINIA NAVY of the REVOLUTION
By Robert Armistead Stewart, Richmond, Virginia.

Another scholarly volume, carefully thought and worked out, of which there have not been over many in the period.

If you have books or papers to be restored, write to the - EMORY RECORD PRESERVING COMPANY, Taunton, Massachusetts, leaders in this work.

Errata in Number 1, A.P. & P.

p. 2 - Denman refs. should be Draper Mss. 8CC-9.
p. 3 - MARY WOOLLEN not WOOLEN.
Mr. WILLIAM ELZEY - not Elizey.
JOHN T. Fitzhugh (Par. 20-col.2.)
JUDY JOHNS, dau of William. (Par. 12-col.2.)
p. 4 - Boonesborough, Ky.
HOWES GOLDSBOROUGH, Pract'r [Practitioner] in Physic.
p. 5 - BETSY or BETEY MORGAN and CHRISTOPHER HAILES.
p. 6 - Sept, 1795. (Par. 9, col.1.)
p. 7 - 24 July, 1829. (Par. 3, col. 2.)
ANGELL JACOBUS.
ELIZABETH PALMER (and RALPH JACKSON)
JENKINS - p. 208, Inf. Court.
JAMES BAILEY, not JANE.
p. 9 - Rev. FRANCIS MAKEMIE. Further refs. to this marriage is N-n, Va. xi-209. Bf 3 July 1698.
----- McDONALD and SARAH DICKENSON.
p.15 - WILLIAM SKINKER, not Skinner.
JONO. not JOHN KIPSHAVEN.
MARY BUMPASS (and JOHN WASHINGTON) not MUMPASS
WADDY, not WADY m. JANE SPENCE.
p.17 - RACHEL ELLIS m. ROBERT WHARTON.
POLLY BROWN should be POLLY BOOWN.
Dr. THOMAS WALKER.

A N C E S T R A L   P R O O F S

& P R O B A B I L I T I E S

An Occasional Bulletin

Number Three
Military Service

"The Point of Research may Occupy a long Time to be Expressed at last in brief Phrase."

MILITARY SERVICE from Court Records:

This list of officers and soldiers of the Colonial wars, the war of the Revolution, and of the county militia, with accompanying brief abstracts, is made up entirely from original court records, mainly of Virginia. These names, in the greater number of cases occur elsewhere in various Government bureaus, in State Archives, &c., &c., but in the volumes now in the probate offices and the clerks' offices of the counties, are occasionally found names omitted from official and approved lists, probably because the service in which the Court signified belief, did not pass the higher authorities, or for some other good reason was not officially recorded. Also, the large official volumes are often not available, and these brief and informal notes may be helpful, or at least interesting to many.

The spelling of the names must be taken "ad. lib."... uniform spelling came slowly, the variations which have survived to our time are a study in themselves, and call to a sceptical mind the insistence with which a modern American, of occasion, vigorously claims a letter more or less as proving his descent.

NATHAN ABBOT, of Hanover cty, Va, "Corperol",Va. Regt. 200 acres,Record of Plotts.9 Mch 1774.Montg.cty,Va.

WILLIAM ABBOTT; soldier under Col. Geo.Slaughter. Jas. Wheatley purchased and lost Abbott's ctf. Fauq, Va. Orders, Mch 1784, p.164.

JOHN ACUFF[?] served as sjt under Capt. Rob't Mumford in 1760. Col. Wm.Byrd's Reg't. Henry,Va.Ct.Min.27 Apr 1780.

FRANCES ADAMS; comm'd Ensign Mil. Ldn,Va. 12 Mch 1781. G-320.

HENRY ADAMS; makes declr'n of service; Court is of opinion he was a Revolutionary soldier. Bedford,Va. Ct Feby 1833. Orders, p.98.

WM. ADAMS; comm'd 2d Lieut.Mil.Henry,Va. 25 Jany 1781. Ct.Min. 2d Lieut. Hamon Critz[?] company,[who] resigned same date.

HENRY ADAMS makes declr'n of service and Court is of opinion he was a Revolutionary soldier.Bedford, Va. Sept Ct, 1832. p.45.

SAMUEL ALCOCK; comm'd Ensign, 4 May 1778. Amherst,Va. Orders, p.233. Recom. 2d Lieut, 2 Nov 1778. p.333. Produces comm'n 1 Feby 1779. p.340.

RICHARD ALCOCK; recom. 2d Lieut. Amherst,Va. 2 Nov 1778. Orders,p.333. Produces comm'n 1 Feby 1779. p. 340. Comm. Ensign 4 May 1778. Orders, p.233.

..... ALDICK, a soldier in Cont. service; wife Barbara to be allowed 20 pounds for her support for the year. Bkly, W.Va. 21 Sept 1779. Orders iv-43.

JOHN ALEXANDER, apptd Capt. Mil. in room of John Fontaine, Esq., resigned. Henry,Va. Ct.Min.6 May 1782.

JOHN ALEXANDER, Gent. Comm'd Lieut-Col. Mil.and sworn Ldn,Va. 9 Apr 1781. G-329. Recom. to be Capt. 13 May 1777. G-42.(In room of Henry Vanover.) Comm'd Major Mil. Ldn, Va. 9 Feby 1779. G-142.

MARK ALEXANDER; Promoted[?] to 2d Lieut. Patriotic Marylander, iii-111.

SAMUEL ALLEN, served as Capt. under Col. Byrd, 1760. Henry, Va. Ct. Min. 27 Apr 1780.

JAMES ALLEN; John Allen, representative; 2,000 acres Montg cty, Va. Proclamation of 1763. Record Plotts.

JOHN ALLGOOD.*

SPENCER ALLGOOD.*

JOHN ALSOP, private 7th Regt, wounded on board the Barges. Receives allowance, Fred'k cty, Md. Min.G.N.ii. 14 Dec 1784. See also courts of April and October, 1786.

..... ALSTON; widow GILLY.*

MATHEW ANDERSON, non-com. officer "last war".200 acres 11 Feby 1774. Record of Plotts. Montg. cty, Va.

JOHN ARMSTRONG, sjt in the late war. 200 a surv. 10 July 1776. Also 14 Mch 1774. Record of Plotts. Montg. cty, Va.

WILLIAM ARTHUR; makes declr'n of service and Court is of opinion he was a Revolutionary soldier. Bedford,Va. Ct Feby 1833. Orders, p.98.

THOMAS ATHEY, age 72; declares he enlisted Fairfax cty, Va. Capt. Wm. Patterson's Co., in 1777. In June or July, he thinks; was attached to 16th Va. and served bet. 2 and 3 years. Discharged at Middlebrook, Jersey, in consequence of severe hurt. Ordered ctfd. Hamp, W.Va. Orders. 18 Aug 1818.

FRANCIS ATWELL, Gent., recom. to be Captain in the room of Capt. Chs. Bell. Fauq, Va. Orders, 24 Nov 1777.

JOHN AUBER, serg't, 2d Regt. Wounded at Eubank[?] Allowed £11-10sh. Apr Ct 1787. See also Apr and Oct. courts, 1786. Fred'k, Md.

HOWARD AUSTIN; makes declr'n of service; Court is of opinion he was a Rev. soldier. Bedford, Va.Sept 1832. Orders, p. 45.

..... BAILEY; soldier in Continental Army; widow Catherine to have supplies. Fauq,Va. Sept 1782.Orders, p. 71.

RICHARD BAILEY proves enlistment in 1760, in a Virginia Regt. Amherst,Va. 6 Mch 1760. Orders, p.104.

JAMES BAIRD proves service in Capt. Dickerson's Co. of Rangers, last war. Bot,Va. 11 May 1780. Orders.

LEVY BALDOCK proves service in late war in a Virginia Regt. Ctf ordered to Reg. Land Office. Amherst,Va. 7 Feby 1780. Orders, p.396.

RICHARD BALDOCK; served as sjt in late war; Levy Baldock, heir-at-law. Ctf ordered to Reg. Land Office. Amherst, Va. 7 Feby 1780. Orders, p.396.

FARLING BALL, Gent., comm'd Captain. 13 May 1777. Ldn, Va. G-42.

NICHOLAS BALL [or BOLD] makes oath, Fauq, Va. Sept 1782. Orders p. 67. [See HUBBARD.]

WM. BALL; Captain in the room of John Webb, dec'd; Fauq, Va. 24 Mch 1777. Orders.

RICHARD BALLENGER; recom. to be Capt., Mil. Amherst,Va. 4 May 1778. Orders, p.228. Comm. same date.

WILLIAM BANKS; comm. Ensign. Amherst,Va. 3 Aug 1778. Orders, p. 242. Recom. to be 2d Lieut. 1 May 1780, p.421

LINN BANKS; proof that he served in 1759 as a soldier, and as a sjt in 1760, Va. troops. Ctf ordered. Amherst, Va. 7 Feby 1780. Orders, p.397.

JOHN BARKSDILL; apptd 1st Lieut Mil. Henry, Va.26 Apr 1781. Ct. Min. Apptd Captain of Co. formerly comm. by Bruce Martin, 30 Mch 1782.

THOMAS BARNES; ctf that he served as Q. M. Sjt, Va.Regt. 2,000 acres. Record of Plotts. Montg. cty, Va. 1 Mch 1774.

JOHN BARNETT; recomm. to be Captain. Amherst,Va. 6 May 1782. Orders, p.503.

WILLIAM BARNETT; recomm. to be Ensign. Amherst, Va. 6 July 1778. Orders, p. 236.

JAMES BARR makes declr'n of service; ordered ctfd to War Department. Bkly,W.Va. Orders. 9 Oct 1832.

WILLIAM BARTEE; makes oath. Served as sjt under Capt. John Smith, 1760, under Hon.Wm. Byrd,Esq. Has never rec'd land bounty. Henry,Va. 23 Mch 1780. Ct. Min.

DAVID BARTON; produces comm'n as 2d Lieut. Mil. of the county of Henry, Va. 22 Apr 1779. Ct. Min.

PIERCE BAYLY, Gent. Oath of allegiance. Ldn,Va. 8 May 1780. G-242.

RICHARD E. BEALE, upwards of 72; enlisted in 3d Va. Regt, Feby 1776, under Capt. John Chilton (who was killed at the battle of Brandywine.) John Blackwell was 1st Lieut. Served full term (two years); left service at Valley Forge, 1778. Lived in Stafford cty, Va. when he enlisted. Fauq,Va. 28 Aug 1832. Orders, p. 113.

JAMES BEARD, Jr.; James Beard, heir-at-law, proves decedent's service in Capt. Dickerson's Co. of Rangers, last war, until disbanded, and that he was afterward killed by Indians. Bot,Va. Orders. 11 May 1780.

..... BECK; widow SARY.**

JAMES BECKNALL; "inlisted" Cont. Army and died in service. (Son of Thomas and Elizabeth Becknall.) Amherst, Va. 4 Mch 1782. Orders, p. 469.

THOMAS BECKNALL; "inlisted" Cont. Army and died in service. (Son of Thomas and Elizabeth Becknall.) Amherst, Va. 4 Mch 1782. Orders, p. 469.

Maj. HENRY BEDINGER; Court certifies he was an officer in the War of the Revolution, and that he is a credible person, &c. Bkly, W.Va. 15 Aug 1832.

JOHN BELL, Gent.; oaths as mil. officer, including test oath. 26 June 1753. Pr.Wm,Va. Orders [1]-168.

JOHN BELL, Esq., oath as Colonel. Fauq,Va. 23 Apr 1761. Orders [1]-155.

HENRY BELL, Capt. of a "Patrol",to be paid. 4 Mch 1777. Amherst,Va. Orders, p.178. Was Capt. of a "Patrol" 1 July 1776. p.155.

ROBERT BELL, Lieut. Mil., takes oath. Ldn,Va. 11 Mch 1767. C-241.

..... BELL; widow ELIZABETH.*

JAMES BLEWES. ***

ESME BELOTE; died in Cont. service. His children received supplies from Hungar's Psh, N-n,Va. 8 Dec 1778. xxxvO-124. Also in 1779.

JOHN BENHAM; produces comm'n from his Excellency the Governor as Ensign Mil., and is sworn. Ldn,Va. 12 June 1780. G-249.

WILLIAM BERRY, Q.M. sjt in the Horse in the Rev. War; admn his estate granted to John R. Wallace "he being the same person whose name appears in the roll of Officers reported by a Board of officers assembled under a resolution of the General Assembly reported entitled to one-half pay for life." Fauq,Va. 24 Oct 1832. Orders, p.166.

CHRISTOPHER BEST proved that he served in the last war until discharged. 13 Apr 1780. Bot,Va. Orders.

WILLIAM BIBB; recomm. for 1st Lieut. 4 May 1778. Amherst, Va. Orders, p. 228.

BENJAMIN BIGGS; was in the Cont. service in 1776; claims land on which he made improvements in that year. Ordered ctfd. Jeff'n cty, Ky. 5 Aug 1783. Orders A-69.

JOHN BIGGS, Jr.; soldier Cont.Army;wf Mary & 3 children to receive supplies.Amherst,Va. 3 Sept 1781. Orders p. 455.

JOSEPH BRADBURY; makes oath; served under Capt John Lightfoot in Col. Byrd's Regt in 1760. Never proved same before. Henry,Va. 25 May 1780. Ct. Min.

..... BRADY; a soldier in the service; wife MILDRED allowed six pounds. Fauq,Va. 24 Nov 1777. Orders.

JOHN BRAND; soldier in the Ill.Regt; entitled to preemption in Kentucky Dist. Ordered ctfd. Jeff'n cty Ky. 8 Apr 1784. Orders A-11.

GEORGE BROCKER; killed in Cont. service; widow to be furnished necessaries. Ldn,Va. 14 Apr 1778. G-82.

WILLIAM BROUGHTON; ctf of Edm. Randolph that BROUGHTON, aged about 82, late a sjt-maj. in the 12th Va. was disabled at the battle of Brandywine by a bayonet; he is allowed £12 yearly com. 1 Jany 1785. Is ordered ctfd. 1 Dec 1787. Deeds, i-202. Hardy, W.Va.

JOHN BROWN; aged 56; enlisted at Leedstown, Wmld,Va. in Capt. John Mazzarett's [?] Co. about the spring of 1779 marched to Hampton, Va. thence to Wmsburg. Served in the 5th Va., Col. Thos. Marshall. Was in the battle of Camden and returned to town of "Glouchester" during siege of York, and was present at "capture of Cornwallis." Afterwards was discharged. Ordered ctfd. 19 Oct 1818. Hamp,W.Va. Orders.

JAMES N. BROWN.*

JOHN BROWN, formerly soldier in Maryland line. Receives allowance. See Minute Book G.M.ii, 12 Oct 1784. See also April Court 1786. Fred'k, Md.

..... BROWN, enlisted with Capt. Polson. His wife was ISABELLA, from Carlisle. Brown deserted her. Fred'k cty,Md. June Ct. 1755.

COLEMAN BROWN; recom. for Ensign Mil.9 Sept 1777.Ldn, Va. G-60.

JOHN BROWN; Sargt, Wash'n cty, 6th Regt, Wounded at Camden. Allowed £11-5sh. 12 Oct 1784. Fred'k, Md. Min. B'k G.M.ii.

LOW BROWN; aged 76; makes declr'n for pension; enlisted in the Ill. Regt of the "U.S.A." 1779, with Capt. Jesse Evans, and served under Col. George Rogers Clark and Lieut-Col. John Montgomery, in the company of Capt. Evans. Left service 1 Aug 1790, when the time of his enlistment expired; when he enlisted he resided in Montg. cty. Marched through the present States of Tennessee and Kentucky, by water from the mouth of big creek and then to Kaskadia in Illinois by water.Tazewell cty,Va. 21 Aug 1832.Orders,p.58.

THOS. BRONAUGH; recom. in the room of Jno. Blackwell (Militia). Fauq.,Va. 24 Nov 1777. Orders.

WILLIAM BRONAUGH, Colonel; produces comm'n and takes oath. 9 Feby 1779. Ldn,Va. G-143.

ZACHARIAH BRYANT, son of Benjamin; enlistment declared illegal, he being but 15 years old 4 last June. Enlisted under James Warren. Amherst,Va. 4 Oct 1779. Orders, p.381.

JAMES BUCK, "lives now in Frederick." ***

MORDECAI BUCKNER, Capt. in the Virginia Regt. 3,000 a. Assigned. Surv.16 Dec 1773. Record of Plotts, p.2, Montg.Va.

CHARLES BUCKLIFF [BURKELUP, BUCKLUP]. Private, 1st Regt; wounded at Eutaw Springs. Allowance ten pounds. Minutes G.M.ii, 8 Feby 1785. See also courts of April 1786 and April 1787, Fred'k, Md.

DAVID BUFFINGTON makes declaration. Is 55 years of age, enlisted at Cumberland C. H.,Va. July 1782, in a company comm. by Capt. Fitzpatrick,2d Va. Thinks his colonel was Freebecker. Was discharged at Winchester at the end of the war; was at the taking of Cornwallis. Ordered certified. 19 Aug 1818. Hamp, W.Va. Orders.

..... BULLARD; widow ANN. **

JOHN BULLER or Baller; proves service late war. Bot, Va, 14 Apr 1780. Orders.

JOHN BURFIN; oath to service in Rev. War. Court accepts declaration. 28 Aug 1832. Monon cty, W.Va. x-300.

JOHN BURNETT; soldier Cont. Army. Wf MARY to receive provisions. 5 Oct 1778. Amherst,Va. Orders,p. 322.

CHARLES BURRASS[?] Recom. to be Captain, Amherst,Va. 4 May 1778. Orders, p. 229. Commissioned, p. 232.

LUKE BURNES; maimed soldier, Maryland line. ***

JAMES BURK [BUCK] Private 2d Regt, wounded at Cowpens. Minutes G.M.ii, 14 Dec 1784. See also April and October courts, 1786. Receives allowance. Fred'k cty, Md.

BENJAMIN BURBRIDGE; declaration by his widow,MARY. He entered the army in Mch or Apr 1776 as a wagonmaster; remained with army until some time in 1777, when he died. Left chn: John, Patsy Cockaine, Philadelphia Burns, Sarah Johnston. 20 Sept 1819. Hamp, W. Va. Orders.

THOMAS BURTON. *

CLAUDEOUS BUSTER; recom. 1st Lieut. 5 July 1779. Amherst, Va. Orders, p. 365.

JOHN BUTCHER. ***

PATRICK BUTLER. *

ROBERT BUTLER; in Cont. service; wife to be furnished with necessaries. Ldn, Va. 14 Apr 1778. G-81.

Hon. WM. BYRD, Esq., Col. of the Va. Regt. 1,000 acres. 1 June 1774; 1,000 acres, 3 June 1774. Montg. Va. Record of Plotts.

NICHOLAS CABELL; Court certifies that early in this present contest with Great Britain CABELL did Actual Service as Captain of a Minute Company, and has since received a Colonel's Comm'n. and that this Court hath lately Recom. him for Col. of the 1st Batt'n; and that in the Different Public Capacities afsd in which he has acted, this Court Entirely approve of his conduct. Amherst,Va. 4 Sept 1780. Orders, p.431.

Recom. Col. Mil. 4 Oct 1779. Amherst,Va. Orders, p. 380. Comm'n, 7 Feby 1780. Orders, p.398. Recom. Col. 1st Batt'n, Mil. 5 June 1780. Orders, p.42.

JOSEPH CABELL; comm'd County Lieut. Amherst,Va. 6 July 1778. Orders, p.234.

WILLIAM CABELL, Jr., Gent. Recom. Maj. 1st Batt'n. Amherst,Va. 7 May 1781. Orders, p.446. Comm. Major Lower Batt'n, 7 May 1781. p. 480. Recom. Lieut-Col. 1st Batt'n, 6 May 1782. Orders, p.504.

JAMES CANDY[?] recom. for Lieut. 18 Apr 1796. Hamp,W. Va. Orders, p. 185.

JOSEPH CANTERBERRY; a poor soldier,Cont. Army; his wf RUTH furnished provisions. Amherst,Va. 3 Aug 1778. Orders, p.243. (See also p.322.)

DANIEL CARLAN; produced comm'n as Captain, Mil. Takes the oath. Henry,Va. 20 Apr 1778. Ct. Min.

BAILEY CARTER; was soldier under Col. Adam Stephens, 1762, and never rec'd land bounty. Henry,Va. 27 July 1780. Ct. Min.

PETER CARTER; recom. for Ensign. Amherst,Va. Orders,p. 374. Comm'd Ensign,6 Nov 1780. Orders, p.437. Recom. Lieut. 3 June 1782. Orders, p.509.

..... CARTER; widow ELIZABETH. *

HENRY CARTMILL; oath as Lieut. Mil. 14 Apr 1780. Bot, Va. Orders.

JNO. CARTMILL; oath as Captain Mil. Bot, Va. 11 May 1780. Orders.

THOS. CASADAY; proves service late war. 14 Apr 1780. Bot, Va. Orders.

DAURETT[?] CAVEY or COVEY; a soldier; wife MARY to be allowed twenty pounds for her support for the year. Bkly, W.Va. 21 Sept 1779. Orders iv-42.

WILLIAM CECIL, age abt 83; entered service 1776 under Capt. Thomas Martin, Lieut. James Maxwell, and Ensign Thomas Witten; company belonged to a Va. State Line Regt, comm'ded by Col. William Preston and Maj. Walter Crockett; applicant then resided in Tazewell cty, then called Montgomery. The company to which he belonged was never required to perform any other duty than as Indian spies to protect the western frontier of Virginia, and consisted of men mostly residents of border country and were kept in continual readiness and never regularly discharged or called out for any definite period. During the winter were permitted to return home. Thomas Witten (or Wotten) testifies for him; Joseph Oney also testifies he was with CECIL. Court doclare opinion that CECIL was an Indian spy. Taze, Va. Oct Ct, 1832. Orders, p.78.

Capt. WILLIAM CHERRY, of Jefferson cty, Va. Maj. Bedinger make oath as to his service. Bkly, W.Va. 15 Aug 1832.

THOMAS CHEWNING comm. 1st Lieut. Mil. Henry, Va. 26 Apr 1781. Ct. Min.

ELIHU CHILCOTT; It appears to the satisfaction of the Court that LIDIA CHILCOTT is the widow and relict of ELIHU, deceased, who was a pensioner of the United States, and departed this life some time in last May. Ordered ctfd. 19 June 1833. Hardy, W. Va.

JOHN CHILDS. *

CHAS. CHILTON, Gent. Recom. for 1st Lieut. Fauq, Va. 24 Nov 1777. Orders.

CHARLES CHRISTIAN; recom. Ensign. 1 May 1780. Amherst, Va. Orders, p.418. Comm'n, 5 June 1780. p.421.

DRURY CHRISTIAN; recom. Ensign. 1 May 1780. Amherst, Va. Orders, p.232.

ELIJAH CHRISTIAN; recom. for Ensign. Amherst,Va. 5 Oct 1778. Orders, p.323. Comm'n,5 Oct 1778.p.324. Recom. 2d Lieut. 5 Feby 1781. Orders, p.442.

HENRY CHRISTIAN; recom. for Captain. Amherst, Va.5 Oct 1778. Orders,p.323. Comm'n, 5 Oct 1778. p.324.

JOHN CHRISTIAN; comm'd Captain. Amherst,Va. 4 May 1778. Orders,p.232. Recomm. in place of James Christian, resigned. 7 Apr 1775. Orders, p.223.

IS. CHRISTIAN; proved that he served in 1759 as Commissary to the Batt'n com. by Col. Peachey, until discharged, and afterwards occasionally for the troops of the 1st Va. Regt, in the last war. Bot,Va. 13 Apr 1780. Orders.

ROBERT CHRISTIAN; recom. to be Ensign Mil. 7 Apr 1778. Amherst,Va. Orders, p.223. Comm. Ensign 4 May 1778. Orders, p.232. Recom. 2d Lieut. 1 May 1780. p.418. Comm'n, 4 Sept 1780. p.429.

A.... CHURCHILL, Gent. Recom. for Col. 2d Batt'n Mil. Fauq,Va. 24 Nov 1777. Orders.

WILLIAM CLARK; makes declr'n of service and is ordered ctfd. Bkly, W.Va. Orders 1829-1834.

HEZEKIAH CLARK; a regular enlisted soldier in the 13th Va. Regt; wife SARAH to be allowed £15 for her own support and two children for one year. Ohio cty, W. Va. May 1778. Court rec'ds.

LARKIN CLARK. *

..... CLARK; widow REBECCA. *

JAMES CLEVELAND, Gent.; comm'n Capt. Mil. Ldn,Va. 14 Feby 1780. G-220.

BURDIT CLIFTON; oath as Ensign. Fauq,Va. 27 Aug 1761. Orders 1-198.

..... COLBERT; widow SUSANNA. *

JAMES COLEMAN, Gent. Recom. for Major Mil. 13 Jany 1777 Ldn,Va. G-10. Sworn as Major; produces Comm'n. 10 Mch 1777. G-17. Comm. Lieut-Col. Mil. and takes oath. 8 June 1778. G-101. Oath of allegiance to the State, 11 Oct 1779. G-203.

LINDSEY COLEMAN; Comm'd 2d Lieut. Amherst,Va. 6 July 1778. Orders, p.235. Recom. 1st Lieut, 1 May 1780. p.418. Comm'n 5 June 1780. Orders, p.421.

JAMES CONNER. ***

JOHN COOK. *

..... COOK; widow MARY. **

JOHN COLLENN [COLLESON?] died in Cont. service; widow to receive necessaries. Ldn,Va. 14 Apr 1778.

JOHN CRAWFORD; Recomm. to be Ensign. Amherst,Va. 1 Nov 1781. Orders, p.458.

Col. WILLIAM CRAWFORD; killed by Indians at Sandusky; HANNAH CRAWFORD, his relict, states that she is still a widow and prays further allowance of pension. So ordered. Fayette, Penna. Aprl 1814. O.C. Docket ii-145.

GIDDION CREWS; Recomm. for 2d Lieut Mil. Amherst,Va. 5 Oct 1778. Orders,p.323. Comm'd 7 Dec 1778. p.337.

Capt. JOSEPH CREWS; resignation. Amherst,Va. 5 Oct 1778. Orders, p.323.

WILLIAM CROSS; served in last war. Bot,Va. 13 Apr 1780. Orders, p.323.

PETER CUNNINGHAM; private 7th Regt, wounded in South Carolina. Allowed £7-10sh. Apr Court, 1786. See also October Court. Fred'k, Md.

CORNELIUS DARNEL, of Tennessee; was b. Charles cty,Md. 15 Apr 1762; drafted 1781 in the Revolutionary service from Wash'n cty, Penna. Draper Mss.W.H.S. 26V 192.

JAMES DAUGHERTY; John Evans,Sr., makes oath that DAUGHERTY served as Captain under him in 1778, during McIntoshes[?] Campaign. Ordered ctfd. 1811. Monon. cty, W.Va. Orders.

BENJAMIN DAWSON; soldier in 16th Virginia; produces discharge from Col. Comm. Christian Febiger, 2d Va. Regt. Ordered ctfd. Fauq,Va. Sept 1782.Orders,p.85.

HENRY DAWSON; proves enlistment 1760, in Va. Regt,late war. Amherst,Va. 6 Mch 1780. Orders, p.404.

PLEASANT DAWSON; recomm. 2d Lieut. Amherst,Va. 7 May 1781. Orders, p.446.

Lt. HENRY DEARING; was an officer Va. State Regt, commanded by Col. Joseph Crockett. Bkly,W.Va. 15 Aug 1832.

WILLIAM DEBELL, Gent. Comm. Lieut. Mil. and sworn. Ldn, Va. 14 May 1781. G-356.

JOSHUA DEERING[?], a lieut. 25 Aug 1777. Fauq,Va.Orders.

JOHN DENNARD.*

JAMES DENT.***

PETER DICKERSON, to be 2d Lieut, Capt. John Mapp's Co. N-n,Va. 12 Aug 1777. xxxvO-11.

JAMES DILLARD.* [This may have been James Dillard who resigned in Amherst, Va. 1775. See CHRISTIAN.]
MICHAEL DUFFY.***
..... DYE; widow MARY.**
BROWN DYE; his orphans.*
JAMES DYRE.***

THOMAS EARLE; served as sjt Capt. Gist's Co., Col. Byrd's Regt. 1760. Henry, Va. 27 Apr 1780. Ct. Min.
JOHN EASTER; produces declr'n and Court declare opinion he was a Rev. soldier. Morgan, W.Va. Nov.Ct, 1832.
ELIAS EDMOND; formerly of Fauquier; Ordered ctfd that he d.15 Dec 1800; that he was the same ELIAS who belonged to the Regt of State Artillery in the War of the Revolution; that he was Lieut-Col. of Col. Thomas Marshall's Regt, and was the same officer to whom the State of Virginia paid $4500 by special Act; that he left a widow, FRANCES, now living, and the following chn: OCTAVIA E. m. George Grayson, who are both dead, leaving one dau. the wife of Richard H. Foote; ELIAS EDMONDS, now living and of age; BETSEY who m. Joseph Blackwell who d. intest. leaving wife and 4 chn, and that these are his heirs-at-law and distributes of sd Lt. Col. ELIAS EDMOND of the Regt of State Artillery. Fauq, Va. 24 Sept 1832. Orders, p. 143.
ROB'T EDMONDS, recomm. for 1st Lieut, 4 May 1778, Amherst, Va. Orders, p. 228.
JOSEPH EDWARDS. Amherst, Va. Recomm. for 2d Lieut. Mil. 5 Oct 1778. Amherst, Va. Orders, p.323. Comm'd 6 Nov 1780. p.437. See also p.374.
THOS. EDWARDS; Ensign under Capt. Atwell, Mil.Fauq.Va. 24 Nov 1777. Orders.
FRANCIS ELGIN; comm'd Ensign and takes oath. Ldn, Va. 9 Aug 1779. G-180.
GUSTAVUS ELGIN: sworn 1st Lieut. Mil. Ldn, Va. 10 Aug 1778. G-115. Presents Comm'n and is sworn Captain 13 Oct 1782. G-454.
WILLIAM ELLIOTT; produces comm'n as Ensign Mil. Ldn, Va. 12 Apr 1779. G-152.
CHARLES ELLIS; recomm. 2d Lieut. Amherst, Va. 7 Sept. 1778. Orders, p.291. Recomm. 1st Lieut, 1 May 1780. p.418. Comm'n, 5 Feby 1781. p.440.

JOSIAH ELLIS [JOSIAS?] Recomm. Captain.Amherst,Va. 1 May 1780. Orders,p.418. Comm'd 7 Aug 1780. p.426.

Capt. EZEKIEL ELDREDGE; Captain Mil. Co. at Cape May, N.J. 23 June 1709. P.G.S. Pub'ns, vii-67.

CHARLES ELLISON; served until disbanded. [Service not given in detail.] Bot,Va. 13 Apr 1780. Orders.

ANTHONY ESHELL; aged 75; entered service as volunteer Sept, 1775, under Capt. Simon Triplett, in Ldn cty and marched to Hampton and "saw a remnant of the fire of the burning of Norfolk by Lord Dunmore... performed guard duty at the old light house which was burned down before he left there". Born Ldn cty, Feby 1757. Court declare opinion that he was a Revolutionary soldier. Fauq,Va. 29 Aug 1832. Orders p. 117.

CHARLES ESKRIDGE; Ensign mil. Ldn,Va. 11 Aug 1761. A-484. Takes oath as Lt. Mil. 11 May 1762. A-588.

JOHN EUSTACE, dec'd; late a Captain,Va. Line. William Eustace, heir-at-law. Ordered ctfd. Fauq,Va. Sept 1783. Orders, p.175.

WILLIAM EUSTACE, Esq.; oath as Major. Fauq, Va. 23 Apr 1761. Orders [i]-155.

WILLIAM EUSTACE; oath as Mil. Officer. Pr.Wm, Va. 27 June 1753. Orders [i]-180.

WILLIAM EVANS.***

..... EVANS; widow ELIZABETH.**

JOHN EVANS, Sr.; David Scott makes oath that EVANS served in McIntosh's Campaign as a Lt.-Col. in 1778; that he also served in Dunmore's Campaign in 1774. Ordered ctfd. Monon, W.Va. 1811. Orders.

JOHN EVANS; files declr'n of service and is ordered ctfd. Monon,W.Va. 27 Mch 1833. 11[?]-357.

THOMAS EWERS; 2d Lieut. Recomm. Amherst,Va. 6 Sept 1779. Comm'd. 5 June 1780. Orders, p.375 & 421.

FREDERICK EYRE [IRE?].***

HENRY FARNSWORTH; produces comm'n Lieut. Mil. Ldn,Va. 14 Sept 1778. G-120. Is sworn, same date.

JOHN FARNSWORTH; killed in Cont. service, Ldn,Va. Orders 14 Apr 1778. G-82.

JACOB FARIS; Rev. soldier, ordered ctfd. Cumb,Va. Sept Court, 1832.

THOMAS FARRAR; Recomm. Ensign. Amherst,Va. 5 July 1779 Orders,p.365. Recomm. 2d Lieut. 1 May 1780. p.418.

JOHN FRAZER; died in Continental army. Ordered ctfd that BENJAMIN FRAZER is heir-at-law. Mch Ct 1784. Fauq, Va. p. 358.

ROBERT FRUER, Gent.; produces Comm'n and takes oath. Ldn,Va. 9 Feby 1779. G-143. Takes the new oath to the State. 12 Oct 1779. G-206.

MATTHIAS FUNER or FINNER[?]***

CALEB FURBEE; makes declr'n Revolutionary service and Court accepts. Monon, W.Va. 28 Aug 1832. x-300.

WILLIAM FULTON[?] Dead.***

DANIEL GAINES, Gent.; Recomm. Major Mil. Amherst, Va. 4 Oct 1779. Orders, p.380. Recomm. Col. 2d Batt'n Mil. 5 June 1780. Orders, p.422.

JULIAS GALDON, a soldier in the Continental Army, being charged with a breach of the peace, is delivered into the custody of James Dillard, Jun., one of the Continental officers. Amherst,Va. 6 Apr 1778. Orders, p. 221.

DAVID GALLOWAY, Jr. proved service late war. Bot, Va. 14 Apr 1780. Orders.

DAVID GALLOWAY, Sr., the same. Same refs.

WILLIAM GALLOWAY; the same. Same refs.

JAMES GARTH; private 4th Regt; wounded at the siege of Ninety-Six. Minutes G.M.ii, Court 14 Dec 1784. See also courts of Apr and Oct 1786. Received allowance. Fred'k cty, Md.

EDW'D GILL; Proved that he served in last war. 13 Apr 1780. Bot, Va. Orders.

DAVID GIRDWOOD; affidavit as to Rutherford's plntn, mentions it as being at Ashe's Creek, N.C. Ordinary's Records, iii-115. Charleston, S.C. 19 Feby 1782.[See GRAHAM.]

MOSES GOING; soldier in Capt. James Gunn's Co., Col. Byrd's Regt. 1760. 27 Apr 1780. Henry,Va. Ct. Min.

JOHN GOMBARS[?]; private in Flying Camp; wounded on "York Island". Fred'k, Md. Court June, 1789.

JOSIAH GOSLING petitions that he "did gitt his Damage [physical injury] in King George the first Servis on bord the Lenox man of war an was alowed by the Chest of Chatham Six pounds a year....Humbly Begs ....former allowances." It is ordered that the Petitioner be Allowed Six hundred pounds of Tab'o.in the next County Levy. Nov Ct. 1759. Fred'k,Md. H-1120.

MICHAEL GRAHAM; makes declr'n and Court is of opinion that he was a Rev. soldier. Bedford, Va. Dec Ct 1832 Orders, p.77.

SAMUEL GRAHAM, at present of the King's Yard as a[___?] at Charles Town, did formerly live with John Rutherford, at Ashe's Creek, in New Hanover County, in North Carolina; makes affidavit as to the Rebels taking possession of the plantation....refers to the British Troops coming to Wilmington and taking possession of Cape Fear River in Jany, 1781, and states that there were then upon the plntn 150 slaves, and that John Rutherford's waiting Man Sandy was murdered by the Rebels for having been a Pilot in Lord Cornwallis' Army....Charleston, S.C. Orders ii,p.113. [See DAVID GIRDWOOD.]

JOHN GRANTHAM; to be apptd an Ensign in a Co. of Mil. comm. by Capt. John McCormack[?] BKLY, W.Va. 20 Sept 1780. Orders iv-198.

WILLIAM GRANTHAM; Apptd Lieut. Mil. Co. comm. by Capt. John McCormack. Bkly, W.Va. 20 Sept 1780. Orders iv-198.

WILLIAM GRAVES; Comm. Ensign, Capt. Cowder's Co. Henry Va. 26 Apr 1781. Court Min.

.....GRAY; widow SUSANNAH.**

RICHARD GRAY; in the Cont. service. Col. Weltner's Regt. Court orders payment to his wife, Mrs. ANN GRAY, and her two chn. Fred'k, Md. Mch Ct 1779.

BENJAMIN GRAYSON; Lieut. Mil takes oaths. Ldn,Va. 13 Feby 1759. A-190.

DANIEL GREENWOOD; soldier under Col. Geo. Slaughter. James Wheatley purchased and lost Slaughter's ctf. Fauq, Va. Mch 1784. Orders, p.164.

JAMES GRESHAM; Recomm. Ensign. Amherst,Va. 5 Feby 1781. Orders, p.442.

JOHN GRIFFIN; ctfd for Carpenter's work. Amherst, Va. 7 May 1781. Orders, p.447.

MARTIN GRIFFITH; a pensioner; in consideration of his wounds Court is of opinion pension should be continued. He produces discharge signed by Richard Campbell, Lt. Col., and Hezekiah Morton, Capt. Fauq, Va. Oct 1781, and July 1783. Orders, p.22 & 151.

WILLIAM GRIGSBY; takes oath as Capt. Mil. Fauq, Va. Apr Ct 1779. Orders, p.364.

CALEB HAYLE [HAYLE?]***

WILLIAM HEATH; makes oath to service in one of the Va. Regts... in the war bet. the King of Great Britain and the French King..Assigns his claim for land to Thomas Hanson.Essex,Va. Feby Ct 1780.Orders xxix-.

WILLIAM HEATH; resident of Hardy cty, W.Va., aged 74; declares that he was drafted for six months, Aug. 1778, under Capt. John Harress and was marched across the Alleghany mtns...served six months and returned home 24 Dec 1778; served as volunteer ag't the tories in western part of Hampshire cty [now W. Va.] Court is of opinion he was a Rev. soldier. Hardy cty, W.Va. 22 Aug 1832. Min. B'k E, p.211.

JAMES HENDERSON; comm'd Ensign. Amherst, Va. 7 Aug 1780. Orders, p.245. See also 6 Sept 1779. p.375.

SAMUEL HENNISS; private in militia; marched in service of U. S. and was wounded. Allowed £7-10. Minutes G. M.ii, Ct 14 Dec 1784. See also Oct Ct 1786. Fred'k Md.

NICHOLAS HENRY; produces his declr'n, and Court declare opinion he was a Rev. soldier. Morgan, W.Va. July Ct. 1832. Orders, i-5.

JOHN HENRY; sworn Captain Mil. Ldn, Va. 10 Aug 1778. G-115.

Rev'd CHARLES ADOLPH HESSE; Oath of allegiance. 11 May 1778. Ldn, Va. G-89.

RICHARD HICKMAN; a Lieut. 2,000 acres under proclamation of 1763; assigned to bro. JAMES HICKMAN. Surv. 29 May 1775. Montg. Va, Record of Plotts. JAMES HICKMAN also gets 2,000 acres, as representative of his bro. THOMAS, who also served in the late war. Surv. 1174, p.240.

JACOB HIGGINBOTHAM; Recomm. to be 2d Lieut. Amherst,Va. 5 June 1780. Comm'd same date. Orders, p.420, 421. Recomm. to be Lieut-Col. Mil. 7 Apr 1778. Amherst. Comm'd 6 July 1778. Orders, p.224, 234.

CALEB HIGGINBOTHAM; Recomm. to be Ensign. Amherst, Va. 1 May 1780. Orders, 418.

JOHN HILL; Recomm. Captain. 5 June 1780. Comm'd 4 Sept 1780. Amherst, Va. Orders p.423,429.

CASMER HILL; soldier in Col. Weltner's Regt. Court orders payment to wife. (Two chn.) Mch 1779. Fred'k,Md.

SWINFIELD HILL; Apptd Captain Mil. in the room of Ed.

Short, who hath resigned to the sd HILL. Henry, Va. 25 Mch 1779. Ct. Min.

GEORGE HILTON; Comm'd 2d Lieut, Mil. Amherst,Va. 6 July 1778. Orders, p.235. Recomm'd to be 1st Lieut, 7 Apr 1778. p.223.

THOMAS HITCHCOCK [HITCHACOCK] makes oath to service in one of the Va. Regts in the war bet. the King of Great Britain and the French King. Assigns his land claim to Taylor Noell. Essex,Va. Feby Ct. 1780. Orders xxix-.

JAMES HOPKINS; Recomm. Lieut. Mil. Yohog.,Va. abt 25 Mch 1778.

JOHN HOPKINS; Ensign, Baxter's Co. Aug. Va. 1783.ii-370.

JAMES HOPKINS, Pittsylvania cty,Va. Age 67. Pension declr'n. Enlisted as a substitute for JAMES HOPKINS, Sr. in 1780.

JOHN HORSLEY; Recomm. 2d Lieut. 2 Nov 1778. Produces comm'n 1 Feby 1779. Amherst,Va. Orders p.333, 340. Comm'd 2d Lieut, 6 July 1778. p.235. Recomm. 1st Lieut, 2 Nov 1778. p.333.

WILLIAM HORSELEY, Gent. Comm'd 2d Lieut. 4 May 1778.Recomm. 1st Lieut, 1 May 1780. Comm'n 5 June 1780. Amherst, Va. Orders, p.232, 418, 421.

ROBERT HORSELEY; Recomm. Ensign. 1 Nov 1781. Recomm. Lieut. 3 June 1782. Amherst,Va. Orders, p.457, 507.

EPAPHRODITUS HUBBARD; Makes oath that he was an inhabitant of Virginia at the time he enlisted in 4th Regt Light Dragoons. Fauq,Va. Sept 1782. Orders, p.67.

THOMAS HUGART, heir-at-law of WILLIAM HUGART, a Lieut. in the Virginia service. Survey of 13 June 1775 for lands due (assigned) Montg,Va. Record of Plotts.

FRANCIS HUNTER; Makes declr'n and Court declare opinion he was a Rev. soldier. Bedford,Va. Dec Ct 1832. Orders, p. 76.

GEORGE HOWELL; JEMIMA HOWELL, his widow, is ordered paid a pension of £10 the 1st Jany 1795, and after that £10 a year. HOWELL was a private in the army of the U.S. and died in the service thereof, a prisoner within this county[?] Hamp, W.Va. Orders, p.419. [The date of this order seems to be 19 June 1797, and it is probable the pension was ordered paid from 1795.]

..... HOWARD, killed in the Rev. War. Widow JEMIMA is entitled to pension. 16 June 1818. Hamp,Va. Orders. [It is probable this is the same man as above.]

FREDERICK IMHOFF, late a Revolutionary War pensioner, d. 5 Jany 1832, leaving a widow or child. Richard Beall makes oath as to this. Ordered ctfd. Bkly, W.Va. Ct 15 Aug 1832. "Minutes" 1829-1834.

JAMES ISAACS.***

CHARLES ISON; Recomm. for 2d Lieut. Mil. 4 May 1778. Amherst, Va. Orders, p.228. Comm'd same date.Recomm. 1st Lieut, 5 June 1780. p. 420.

..... JACK; widow MARGARET.**

JOS. JAMES; Recomm. in the room of Samuel Blackwell (Mil.) Fauq, Va. 24 Nov 1777. Orders.

ALEXANDER JEFFRIES; aged 70. Makes declr'n; entered service 1 Mch 1781, under Capt. William Jennings. Born K. Geo. cty,Va. 1762; parents moved to Fauq. Charles Kemper certifies he served with JEFFRIES. Court declare opinion he was a Rev. soldier. Fauq. Va. 1 Sept 1832. Orders, p. 136.

BERRYMAN JENINGS; Ensign under Capt. Bronaugh. Fauq, Va. 24 Nov 1777. Orders.

AUGUSTINE JENNINGS; oath as Mil. officer, Pr.Wm, Va. 27 June 1753. Orders [1]-180.

WM. JETT, Jr. Q.M. Mil. Ldn, Va. 11 Aug 1761. A-484.

BENEDICT JOHNSON.***

OBEDIAH JOHNSON; Revolutionary soldier; makes declr'n for pension. Ordered ctfd. Sept Court, 1832. Cumb, Va. Orders, p. 439.

JAMES JOHNSON; served in Capt. Throgmorton's Co. of Regulars, last war. Bot, Va. 14 Apr 1780. Orders.

GEORGE JOHNSON; makes oath. Fauq,Va. Sept 1782. Orders p. 67. (See HUBBARD.)

WILLIAM JOHNSON; makes oath. Same refs.

WILLIAM JOHNS; to be Lieut. in a Mil. Co. commanded by Alexander Porterfield. Bkly, W.Va. 17 Aug 1780. Orders iv-184.

JOSEPH JONES; Ensign Mil. Takes oath. Ldn, Va; 11 Mch 1767. C-241.

STEPHEN JONES; makes declr'n and Court declare opinion he was a Rev. soldier. Bedford,Va. Oct,1832. Orders p. 52.

THOMAS JONES; Apptd 1st Lieut. Henry, Va. 22 Apr 1779.
JOSEPH JONES; Apptd 2d Lieut. Henry, Va. 22 Apr 1779.
THOMAS JONES; soldier in Cont. army. Wife to receive supplies. Amherst, Va. 5 Oct 1778. Orders, p. 322.
CHARLES JONES; Recomm to be Ensign. Amherst,Va. 6 May 1782. Orders, 503.
JAMES JONES; Resident of Culpeper; age 74; declr'n for pension; Born Fauq, 1758, 20 Apr. Court declare opinion he was a Rev. soldier. Fauq,Va. 26 Sept 1832. Orders, p. 151.
REWBIN JORDON; Recomm for Captain. Amherst, Va. 1 Nov 1781. Orders, 458.

JACOB KATON; Recomm. and produced comm'n as Ensign Mil. and takes oath. Ldn, Va. 14 June 1779. G-171.
WILLIAM KEATH; Died in Cont. service; vestry of Hungar's Psh, furnished supplies to widow ANNE, and two chn. N-n, Va. 8 Dec 1778. xxxv0-124. Also in 1779.
JACOB KEATON; Comm'd 2d Lieut. Mil. Henry, Va. 26 Apr 1781. Ct. Min.
DANIEL KEITH. *** ("Discharge eaten up by rats.")
Capt. ABRAM KELLER; was an officer Ill. Regt. His wid. MARY in indigent circumstances. Court decides she comes with propriety under pension law. Jeff'n, Ky. 3 May 1786. Orders ii-3.
GEORGE KELLER; makes declr'n service in Revolutionary War and Court orders ctf. Monon, W.Va. 28 Jany 1833 xi-344.
JAMES KELLY. ***
CHARLES KEMPER; ctfd copy of declr'n for pension, opinion, &c., transmitted to Sec'y War. Fauq,Va. 25 Sept 1832. Orders, p. 148.
HOWSON KENNER, Gent. Oath as Captain of a foot company of which Gawin Corbin,Esq., is Cty Lieut. Pr.Wm, Va. 27 June 1753. [1]-173. Oath as Captain. Fauq,Va. 26 Sept 1760. Orders i-114.
THOMAS KENNON, Gent.; Comm'd Captain Mil. Ldn, Va. 14 May 1787. G-356.
RICHARD KENNY; a soldier in the Cont. service; wife ELIZABETH to be allowed twelve pounds, ten shillings for her support for the year. Bkly,W.Va. Aug 1779. Orders iv-3.
..... KERLIN; widow ELIZABETH. **

WILLIAM KERNAL; Assigns his claim for land for service in war bet. King of Great Britain and the French King, to John Spindle, Essex, Va. Feby Ct. 1780. Orders xxix--.

ROBERT KERNS; Sjt 2d Regt; wounded at York. Allowed £11-5. See Minutes G.M. ii, 12 Oct 1784. Also October and April courts, 1786. Fred'k,Md. Another entry possibly same man, 12 Oct 1784, reads KUNS or KEENS.

WILLIAM B. KEY.*

JOSHUA KINCAID; produces disch. from John Mazaret, Maj. Comm. Va. Regt State Artillery. Ordered ctfd. Fauq, Va. Mch 1781. Orders, p.2.

JAMES KINCAID, same.

SMITH KING, Gent. Comm'd 2d Lieut Mil. and sworn. Ldn, Va. 14 May 1781. G-356.

EDWARD KINKER; in Cont. service; wife to be furnished with necessaries. Ldn, Va. 14 Apr 1778. G-82.

LEWIS KINSELL; a soldier in the Cont. service; wife MARY to be allowed 30 pounds for her support for the year. 16 Nov 1779. Bkly, W.Va. Orders iv-84.

JOHN KING, late a private soldier, Maryland Line, conveys land in Alleg. cty. to Christopher Stump. Annap, Md. 12 May 1790, J.G.1-611.

GEORGE LAMBERT; makes declr'n for pension and Court is of opinion he was a Rev. soldier. Bedford, Va. Dec Ct, 1832. Orders, p.74.

CHARLES LAMBERT; same; same refs.

YOUNG LANDRUM; Comm'd 2d Lieut. Amherst,Va. 7 Sept 1778. Recomm. 1st Lieut. 6 July 1778. Comm'd 5 July 1779. Recomm. Captain, 1 May 1780. Comm'd,5 June 1780. See Orders, pp. 293,236, 367, 418, 425, 365.

JOHN LAWRENCE; in Cont. service; £25 allowed wife MARY, for necessaries. 15 Feby 1779. Henry, Va. Ct. Min.

JOHN LEE; died in Cont. service; James Lee his heir-at-law. Fauq, Va. Mch 1784. Orders, p.358.

JOHN LEMAN or LEMON; late a soldier in the Ill. Regt; unable to procure a livelyhood and so ctfd. Jeff'n Ky. Orders A-165.

CHRIS'R LAMBERT, private 3d Regt. Disabled by fire in Carolina. Receives allowance. Minutes G.M.ii. 8 Feby 1785. Also Apr and Oct Cts, 1786. Fred'k, Md.

ROGER LANDIS; in Cont. service; wife ELIZABETH and 5 chn to receive £200 for one year. Ct.Min.Fred'k,Md.

DAVID LEVY; soldier, Col. Weltner's Regt. Court orders payment to wife. (6 chn.) Mch Ct 1779. Fredk, Md.

DAVID LINDSEY; soldier in the Cont. service; Court orders that wife CATHERINE be allowed One Hundred Pounds "for her support and four chn for the present year." Bkly,W.Va. 16 May 1780. Orders iv-129.

Dr. THOMAS LLOYD; Engaged in Co. of Rangers July 1755 under Capt. Preston and until discharged in June 1756, acted as surgeon in that and other companies as well as among such of the inhabitants who had been wounded by the enemy. Engaged a second time in another company under Preston and continued on frontiers of Augusta until May 1759, when Co. was disbanded. Acted as surgeon and without fee or expense of medicines to the County. Bot,Va. 14 Apr 1780. Orders.

PETER LOONEY; Proved that he served in Capt. Smith's Co. of Rangers last war..as a sjt until he was taken prisoner by the French and Indians in 1756, and that he did not return from them for near two years. Bot, Va. 13 Apr 1780. Orders 1776-1783.

JAMES McALEXANDER, Jr.; Recomm. to be 2d Lieut, Amherst, Va. 4 May 1778.Comm'd 6 July 1778. Orders, pp. 229, 235.

DAVID McANALLY; Recomm. to be Ensign; Amherst, Va. 5 July 1779. Orders, p. 365.

CHRISTOPHER McCANNON; Sjt 1st Va. Regt. Produces discharge from Brig-Gen'l Mughlenberg and makes oath, &c. Ordered ctfd as Rev. soldier. Fauq,Va. Oct 1781. Orders, p. 22.

WILLIAM McCLANAHAN; sworn Captain Mil. Ldn,Va. 10 Aug 1778. G-115. Declr'n for pension. Court is satisfied as to service and orders copy of declr'n &c. to be ctfd. 25 Sept 1832. Fauq,Va. Orders, p. 148.

WILLIAM McCLELAN; Oath as Capt. Mil. Ldn,Va. 10 Aug 1778. G-115.

RODERICK McCULLOCK; resigns Captaincy. Amherst, Va. 6 Sept 1779. Orders, p. 374.

JAMES McCUTCHEON; makes oath to service under Capt. John Blagg in Col. Byrd's Regt in 1760; has not received his land bounty. Henry,Va. 25 May 1780.Ct.Min.

ALEX'R McDONALD; proved service in Capt. Preston's Co. of Rangers, last war, until legally disch. 1758.

Bot, Va. 14 Apr 1780. Orders.

ISAAC McDONALD; soldier under Maj. John McNeall in 1762; Adam Stephens was Colonel. Henry,Va. 25 Mch 1780. Ct. Min.

JOHN McDONALD, a soldier; wife MARY to be allowed 30 pounds for her support for the year. Bkly, W. Va. 17 Nov 1779. Orders iv-85.

JOHN McGEACH; Comm'd Capt. Mil. Sworn. Ldn,Va. 13 Mch 1781. G-328.

CHARLES McKNIGHT, hospital surgeon. Allowed £15. June 1789. Fredk, Md.

JOHN McLAUGHLIN; Aged abt 76; testifies as to his service. [See JOHN PREWETT.] Declr'n ctfd by the Court. Taze, Va. Nov Ct, 1832. Orders, p.87.

HUGH McLEOD. ***

ALEXANDER McMAHON; to be recomm. Maj. Mil. Ldn,Va. 13 Mch 1781. G-328. Probably same man as ALEXANDER McMAKEN, Gent., comm'd Major and sworn. 9 Apr 1781. G-329.

JOHN McMULLEN; proved service late war. Bot,Va. 14 Apr 1780. Orders.

EDWARD McMULLEN; same. Same refs.

ALEX. McMUNN; entitled to pre-emption 1000 acres. (Improvements 1776.) Was in the service at the time the land Comm'n sat. Jeff'n,Ky.7 May 1784.Orders A-41.

MICHAEL McNEELY; Recomm. 2d Lieut. Amherst,Va. 6 July 1778. Orders, p.236. Comm'd, p.239. Comm'd 1st Lieut 4 June 1781. p.449. See also p. 375.

NICHOLAS McNEMARA. ***

THOMAS MAGEE. ***

HENRY MYERS; Aged 76; makes declr'n for pension: that in 1776, thinks it was April, enlisted in regular service, in York Town, York cty,Penna. in a company commanded by Capt. Christian Stakes, Regt commanded by Col. Swoope, and remained in service 9 mos; was not engaged in any battle but only in some skirmishes with scouting parties; Marched from York to Philadelphia, from thence to Trenton; from thence to Princeton; thence to Ft. Lee not far from Ft. Washington. At the surrender of Ft. Washington, 16 Nov 1776, his company officers were captured, the Regt broken up and most of them made prisoners. He was then transferred to a corps comm. by Gen. Putnam and assisted in capture of Hessians at Trenton, 26 Dec 1776. Was then sent as one of the guards with wounded Prisoners to Philada;..his time having expired, returned home. Subsequently "performed" in two tours in Militia service, the first under Capt. Duncan of Bkly cty, Va., the second under Capt. Linder. Was present and "assisted at the Capture of Lord Cornwallis at York Town." Has no documentary evidence of service; recollects no one except Maj. Henry Bedinger who can testify as to his service, and his brother Teter [probably PETER] MYERS, who served with him one tour. Was born Bkly cty, Va. 15 Mch 1756. Submits record of age. Lived in Bkly cty since the war. Recollects Col. Meriwether, an officer of the Regular service. Never rec'd a discharge. Refers to Archibald Sherer, a Justice, & John Kisinger. Bedinger swears that MYERS entered Capt. Christian Stakes' Co...that he served in sd Co. until Col. Swoope, Capt. Stake, Lieut. Holsinger and Ensign Barnett were captured at the surrender of Ft. Washington, on York Island, 16 Nov 1776. Teter Myers and John Meyers, brothers, testify. Court declare opinion MYERS was a Rev. soldier. Bkly, W.Va. Orders 1829-1834. Ct 15 Aug 1832.

..... NASH; widow FRANCES. **

MAXWELL NASH; served as sjt under Capt Gunn, Col. Byrd's Regt, 1763. Henry, Va. 27 Apr 1780. Ct. Min.

THOMAS NOTTINGHAM, Jr. Oath as Ensign. N-n, Va. 9 Sept 1777. xxv0-11.

JAMES F. NUNNELER. *

THOMAS O'BANNON; age 76; entered service 4 Sept 1780, under Capt. James Winn; was Q.M. Sjt. Disch. last day Feby 1781. Born Fauq, Va. 1757. Fauq,Va. 31 Aug 1832. Orders, p. 131.

JAMES O'HARA.***

BAZEL O'NEAL; Recomm. Ensign Mil. Henry, Va. 30 Mch 1782. Ct. Min.

EDWARD O'NEIL, of Middletown Tshp, Cumb cty, Penna. A pensioner. Was discharged from service 1 Nov 1783. Cumb, Penna. O.C.Docket, ii-379.

RICHARD O'QUIN, ***

JAMES OGLE; a mil. soldier, killed in the service of

the United States; widow MARY to be allowed £25 to enable her to support herself and six small chn for the ensuing year. Ohio cty, W.Va. Ct, May 1778.

WILLIAM PATTIE; aged 71; makes declr'n...entered "minute service" 1777; lived in Caroline cty when he entered; details as to ships; mentions many names. Court declare opinion he was a Rev. soldier. Fauq, Va. 26 Sept 1832. Orders, p.150. [A long declaration, too long for these abstracts.]

Capt. WILLIAM PAYNE; resident of Fauquier; aged 78; was living in town of Falmouth, Stafford cty,Va., in 1776 and had the comm. of a militia company. Continued to live there from 1776 to 1780 and to command same company. In 1780 removed to Westmoreland and was made Captain of company of militia, and was at the siege of Yorktown...."I have a letter of invitation requesting me to meet General Lafayette, on which I am addressed as Captain and styled his Brother in Arms"...also another from citizens of Fauquier. Was born in Westmoreland, 1755. Court is of opinion he was a Captain in the Rev. service. Fauq.,Va. 31 Aug 1832. Orders, p. 125.

AUGUSTINE PAYNE; age 70; entered service under Capt. John Obannon in Nov 1780 and served until last of May, 1781. Born 1762, Fauquier. Court declare opinion he was a Rev. soldier. Fauq,Va. 31 Aug 1832. Orders, p. 129.

HENRY PAYNE; to be recomm. 1st Lieut. Mil. Ldn,Va. 9 June 1777. G-60. Comm'd and sworn. 14 June 1777. p. 171.

WILLIAM PAYNE; age 73; enlisted 1775. Born Fauq. 1758 Gives detail of service. Court declare opinion he was a Rev. soldier.Fauq,Va. 29 Nov 1832.Orders p.183.

REUBEN PAYNE; apptd Ensign Mil. Henry,Va. Ct 6 May 1782.

JOHN PEARMAN; proof of service as a soldier in the Cont. army "at the time the comm'rs were setting to do business in the County." [Probably commission to settle land claims.] Claims improvements made in 1776, Also claims as heir-at-law of ELISHA and THOMAS PEARMAN, both dec'd. Ctf ordered. Jeff'n, Ky. 3 Sept 1783. Orders A-72.

ARON PENWELL[?] of W. Pennsborough Tshp; a private, 7th Batt'n Mil. Wounded and pension granted. Cumb,

Penna, O.C. Docket ii-381.

MARTIN PICKETT; allowed for use of his storehouses. Fauq, Va. Sept 1783. Orders, p.200. Fur. supplies. Ctfd. Feby 1781. Recomm. Lieut-Col. 1st Batt'n Mil. 24 Nov 1777.

WIATT POWELL; Recomm. 2d Lieut. 4 May 1778. Amherst, Va. Orders, p.229. Apptd. p. 232.

JOHN PREWITT; makes declr'n; age 72. Entered service 1775, under a recruiting officer and named Edmanson; Gen. McIntosh comm. Regt. (Campaign called McIntosh's Campaign.) Gen. Gray, the other field officer, and Capt. Miceal Daugherty and Lieut. Joseph Pryor, officers of his company. Resided in Washington cty when he entered; marched to Anderson's Ferry at James River, where he remained about three months; then marched to the light levels in Greenbrier... marched to mouth of Elkhorn where the army camped until 1 Mch 1756. Here joined Gen'l Broudhead... [This is a long declaration with much detail. Do not find court ctf of approval.] John McLaughlin testifies for PREWITT. Taze,Va. Nov Ct. 1832. Orders, p. 87.

GEO. PURVIS; Ctf for setting up 8 Flower Barrells. Amherst, Va. 7 May 1781. Orders, 447.

DAVID RANDLE; killed on the field of battle; BATHSHEBA RANDLE, heiress-at-law, proves that RANDLE served as a Lieut. in the regular service in 1763. Ohio cty, W.Va. Court 6 Mch 1780.

FRANCIS RAVENSCRAFT declares that he is 58 years old; enlisted in that part of Bkly cty, now Jefferson, in Capt. Francis Willis' Co., 16 Va. Regt, Continental Establishment 3 Apr 1777 and served 3 yrs and 3 mos. Was disch'd at Charleston,S.C.; was at the battle of Monmouth, &c. Ordered ctfd. Hamp, W. Va. 18 Aug 1818. Orders.

JOHN REABURNE; proved that he served in Capt. Peter Hog's Co. of Rangers, last war...until disch'd in 1759. Bot,Va. 14 Apr 1780. Orders.

WILLIAM READ; proved that he furnished his two sons with a rifle and gun when they entered the service in 1776, and that they both died in the service and the "guns never returned." Bedford,Va. 25 Feby 1782. Court of Public Claims.

JOHN REASONER; a soldier in the Cont. service; wife ELEANOR to be "allowed her eighty pounds for support and two children for the present year." Bkly, W.Va. 16 May 1780. Orders iv-131.

RICHARD REAGEN; takes oath as Lieut. Mil. Rock'm, Va. Minutes, Ct 27 Apr 1779.

THOMAS READ, formerly of Wiltshire in England, late a servant to Gen'l John Ashe..with whom he had lived chiefly at Rocky Point...,states that he was with Major Manson (with whom he at present lives as an hired servant) in June and July last, when he commanded a large Detatchment up the North East of Cape Fear and remained encamped about fourteen days at Rutherford's Saw and Grist Mills; and that when the Army under Major Cray's command marched for Newburn, that he was there also with Major Manson with the said Army when on their Return from Newburn they halted at Mr. Rutherford's Mills four days... That he verily believes that from July (excepting for these four days last mentioned) that the Rebels have been in possession of the said John Rutherford's Mills and plantations ever since Wilmington has been evacuated, have got all the Negros likewise excepting about Six now in Charles Town. [Charleston, S.C.] Signed this 23 Feby 1782.

Followed by a note: That during the last four Days as mentioned that the British Army were at Rutherford's Mills, five head of fatt Cattle belonging to the said Rutherford were Killed for their Use. Vol. TT, p.115, Office of the Ordinary, Charleston, S.C.

JACOB RIPLEY; produces declr'n for pension; Court is of opinion he was a Rev. soldier. Morgan, W.Va. Oct Ct 1832. Orders ii-5.

SOLOMON ROGERS; died in Continental service; widow SARAH receives supplies from Hungar's Psh. vestry. N-n,Va. 8 Dec 1778. xxxv0-124. Also in 1779.

WILLIAM ROGERS. ***

CHRISTOPHER RYNOL. ***

JOHN SALE; Asks ctf for bounty land; was serjant-major in Va. Regts in the late war bet. the British King, France and Spain. Gabriel Penn, Gent., says SALE was Sjt-Maj. in 1760 under Col. Byrd. Amherst, Va. 4 Oct

1779. Orders, p. 381.
THOMAS SANDERS; testifies he was in the service in the same Regt with John Wright, Col. Taylor Comm'd'r and was discharged at Winchester. Alleg,Va. 16 July 1832. Orders, p. 40.
WILLIAM SANDY; served two years as a gunner in the Corps of Artillery and four years in the Cavalry as a Q.M. sjt, during Rev. War. Enlisted with John Mouzard as Capt. of the Artillery,&c.,&c. Hamp, W. Va. 18 May 1818. Orders..... A second record under the Court date of 17 Nov 1818, gives his age as 58 and says he enlisted at Leedstown, Wmld cty,Va. in an Artillery Co. commanded by Capt. John Mazarett[?] about 13 Feby 1778. They marched to Hampton, &c. At Williamsburg "reinstated myself in Major John Nelson care of horse" [company of horse?] in Capt. Wm Armstrong's Co. "enduring the war from thence." Marched with Col. Porterfield's Lt. Inf. to Hillsborough, N.C., thence to New Providence and there joined Col. Washington's Regt of Horse, and was present at the taking of Ridgeley's Fort 6 miles of Camden..."I returned to Petersburgh in Va., and there joined Gen'l Mechlinburght and met the Enemy. From thence we marched to the seige of York." Was discharged in 1783. Ordered ctfd. Hamp.W.Va. Orders.
GEORGE SAVAGE; to be captain of a new company to be raised. N-n,Va. 9 Sept 1777. xxxv0-11.
..... SAXTON; widow ELIZABETH M. *
ALEXANDER SAYERS; makes declr'n for pension. Ctfd by Court. [See PREWITT.] Taze,Va. Nov Ct 1832. Orders p. 87.
GEO. SCOTT; recomm. with others to be comm'd Lieut. Mil. for Mercer cty. Mercer, Ky.24 July 1787.Orders.
JAMES SCOTT; makes declr'n of service in Rev. Court accepts declr'n. Monon,W.Va. 28 Aug 1832. x-300.
DAVID SCOTT, Sr.; John Evans, Sr., makes oath that SCOTT served as Capt. in Dunmore's War in 1774. Ordered ctfd. Monon, W.Va. 1811. Orders.
..... SEALS; widow ELIZABETH. **
JACOB SHANLEY. ***
JOHN SHAW. ***
ELIPHAZ SHELTON; Apptd Capt. Mil. in room of James Lyon Henry, Va. 15 Feby 1779. Ct. Min.
JACOB SHEPHERD; makes declr'n for pension; Court de-

clare opinion he was a Rev. soldier. Bedford, Va. Ct. Jany 1833. Orders, p. 89.

WILLIAM SKELLERN[?] served as Ensign in a Co. of enlisted men under Capt. Robert Breckinridge raised in Augusta cty, by order of Col. Wm. Byrd to garrison Fort Chiswell in the absence of the Army on the Expedition agt the Cherokees in 1761. SKELLERN continue to serve until the Co. was disbanded. Bot, Va. 13 Apr 1780. Orders. (It appears that two of the Justices dissented to these orders....because "it did not appear to them that they [the claimants] served in any other corps than militia.")

WILLIAM SLYE. ***

Col. JOHN SMITH proves that he served as Capt. of a Co. of new levies in 1760, under Col. Byrd, on the expedition against the Cherokees and was legally disbanded, for which he rec'd a warrant from Lord Dunmore for 3,000 acres. It further appears that SMITH had been Capt. of a Co. of Rangers, Aug 1755; that he raised sd Co. in Augusta cty and continued on duty until ordered on an expedition agt the Shawnees under Maj. Andrew Lewis and incorporated with a detatchment of the Va. Regt...served until expedition was at an end. He further continued on duty until 4 June 1756, when the fort he then com. was attacked by a body of French and Indians and the Garrison made prisoners and taken to Canada, and that he did not return to his family until 1758. Has been an inhabitant of Virginia ever since he returned from Captivity. Bot,Va. 13 Apr 1780. Orders.

JAMES SMITH. ***

JOSEPH SMITH. ***

..... SNELING; widow REBECKA. *

NINIAN STEEL; killed in the service of his country; his widow recommended to the General Assembly to obtain an annuity. Rowan, N.C. 7 Aug 1783. Min. p. 372.

ROBERT STOCKTON; produces ctf under the hand of Elijah King, a Lieut. in Col. Washington's Light Draggoons that he had impressed a horse in the sd service from him, which horse appears to the Court to be "5 ft high, 10 yrs old, and almost full blooded", and to be worth £150 specie. Henry,Va. 29 Mch 1782. Ct. Min.

..... TATE; widow ELIZABETH. *

ENOS TATE, Sr. *
JERE TATOM. *
WILLIAM TAYLOR; takes oath; was a soldier under Thomas Fleming in Gen'l Forbus' camphain in 1758, and never rec'd land bounty. Henry, Va. 27 July 1780. Ct. Min.
ZACHARIAS TAYLOR; Recomm. Ensign. Amherst, Va. 7 Sept 1778. Orders, p.291. Recomm. 2d Lieut. 1 May 1780. Orders, p.418. See also 1 Feby 1779. p.340. [This name is also given as ZACHARIAH.]
JOSEPH TERRILL. *
SAMUEL TINDEL. ***
JOHN THOMPSON; declr'n of service; was 2d Lieut of Co. under Capt. Robert Breckinridge. Bot, Va. 13 Apr 1780. Orders. (Two Justices dissent.)
WILLIAM TOMLIN, Sr. resident in Fauquier; aged 74; makes declr'n. Enlisted 1776 with Capt. John Chilton; disch. in Lancaster, Penna, latter part 1780; enlisted as Sjt and acted as such for 3 years. Court declare opinion he was a Rev. soldier. 24 July 1832. Fauq, Va. Orders 1832-1833, p. 97.
WILLIAM TRACY; files declr'n of service and Court is of opinion he was a Rev. soldier. Bedford, Va. Aug Ct, 1832. Orders, p. 31. Another entry of a man of the same name is recorded in Jany, 1833. Orders p.87.
Lt. JOHN TRUMAN. ***
JESSE TUCKER, son of MATTHEW; enlisted by John Woodroof, an officer, is discharged, he being just past his 14th year when enlisted, and the enlistment being, therefore, illegal [father not consenting.] Amherst, Va. 6 Sept 1779. Orders, 374,
GODFREY TUCKER. *
MATTHIAS TURNER [?]***

AUGUSTINE WADE; produces proof that he was a private soldier in the 6th Md. Regt and was wounded. Pension ordered. Wash'n, Md. O. C. 12 June 1787.
GEORGE WADE; makes oath to service in Rev. War and Court accepts declaration. Monon, W.Va. 28 Aug 1832. x-300.
WILLIAM WADDELL; soldier, Va. State Regt, produces dischge from John Mazaret, Maj. Comm. Ordered ctfd. Fauq, Va. May 1781. Orders, p. 8.
MICHAEL WALTMAN; private 7th Regt, wounded at Guilford.

Paid £13. Minutes G.M. ii. Court 14 Aug 1784. See also Courts of April and Oct 1786. Fred'k, Md.

CHARLES WARREN; 2,000 a. for his service as an Ensign in the Penna. Regt. Survey 1 June 1774. Montg, Va. Record of Plotts, p. 165.

JOHN WARD; ctf by Capt. R. Crockett that he served as a soldier in Crockett's company of Va. militia. Ctf dated 4 Dec 1793. Original paper.

JOSEPH WASSON; wounded in the service of his country; recommended to the General Assembly for an annuity. Rowan, N.C. 7 Aug 1783. Minutes, p. 372.

ISAAC WELSH; aged 65; enlisted at Fauquier C. H., Va. with Lieut. Alex. Keith and was attached to Capt. Thos. Blackwell's Co. 27 Jany 1776; thinks that he enlisted in the Continental Establishment under Col. Edward Stephens. Was in the battles of Brandywine, Germantown, Monmouth, &c. Captain resigned and he was left under the command of Lieut. Evans; transferred to 6th Va...the Regts reduced after battle of Monmouth, Disch. at Trenton, N.J. by Gen. Frebecker in Feby 1779. Ordered ctfd. 16 Aug 1819. Hamp. W.Va. Orders.

SYLVESTER WELCH, Sr.; aged 77; Enlisted 8 Feby 1777; served in 1st Va. Artillery; mentions Edward Shacklett, John Roach, Dale Carter, James Bailey, John Hopper, William Foster, Gideon Johnson, as serving with him. Court declares opinion he was a Rev. soldier. Fauq,Va. 1 Dec 1832. Orders, p. 189.

William Mott, age 68, and William Welch, age 72, declare they knew of Welch's enlistment in Northumberland.

In an additional statement WELCH gives his age as 70; states that he enlisted in 1777, and then resided in Northumberland cty, 23 July 1832. See p. 97.

THOMAS WELCH; a soldier in the Cont. army; supposed to be dead. Rachel Gaunt, widow of James, proves that her husband kept at his own expense an infant child of sd WELCH, and that since her husband's death she has kept the infant at her own expense. Bot, Va. 14 Apr 1780. Orders.

HENRY WILKINS; oath as 2d Lieut of a new company. N-n, Va. xxxv0-11. 9 Sept 1777.

SPENCER WITHERS, now of Mason county...enlisted at Warrenton, Fauq., in 1780, under Capt. Francis Triplett. JAMES WITHERS, a clergyman in Culpeper, and JESSE WITHERS in Fauq., are well acquainted with applicant, and believe him to be 66 years of age, and a Rev. soldier. Court declare opinion that WITHERS was a Rev. soldier. Fauq, Va. 30 Aug 1832. Orders, p. 123.

THOMAS WITTEN; age 80 in Jany following; makes declaration for pension. Entered service under Capt. Thos. Martin and Lieut. James Mawell, in June 1776. Comm'd Ensign and was attached to the State Regt comm. by Col. Wm. Preston and Maj. Walter Cockrell. His company had to perform frequent scouting expeditions as Indian spies along the Valley of the Clinch River, from the headwaters of Blue Stone to the forks of Clinch, within the now limits of Russell cty. Does not remember whether he was drafted or not; thinks he was called out by Col. Wm. Preston. Continued to act as Ensign until close of war; thinks he was engaged as an Indian Spy fully six months in each year...does not know what became of his commission. William Cecil, Nanny Cecil and Joseph Oney can testify to his service. Court declare opinion he was an Indian Spy. Taze, Va. 15 Oct 1832. Orders, p. 75.

Notes:

* The State of Georgia had two or more land lotteries; the Editor is not familiar with the details of the legislation connected with the lotteries, or with the processes by which they were carried out. In the county courts there are lists of the persons entitled to draw in these lotteries; the Editor's recollection is that they are to be found in the offices of the Ordinary or Probate Judge. Those that the Editor examined were arranged (at least in one Court) in double columns, covering two drawings. The soldiers of the War of the Revolution and their widows, the Editor is informed, were entitled to make two drawings, and in that way can be identified. It was at one time published that all the persons listed as entitled to draw, were veterans of the war. This is not so.

The list given in this bulletin is from Elbert cty.

** Indicates widows who had re-married.

*** In Annapolis, Maryland, in the office of the Register of Wills for Anne Arundell county, is a list of disabled soldiers, made in Feby, April, Sept, and Oct, 1784. They are indicated by three stars.

READERS of previous bulletins of this series, or of the COUNTY COURT NOTE-BOOK, will recognize the abbreviations of county names. A few, perhaps, have not been often used, such as Bot, for Botetourt; Taze for Tazewell; Monon for Monongahela; Hamp for Hampshire; Yohog for Yohogania; and Jeff'n for Jefferson.

The list of soldiers covered by this bulletin does not include all the material the Editor has collected, but it is all that can be put out at present. A search of a card index will be made for a moderate fee.

Milnor Ljungstedt.

A B A Electric Typed Letters Company, Washington, D. C.

A N C E S T R A L P R O O F S

& P R O B A B I L I T I E S

An Occasional Bulletin

Number Four
Next of Kin from
Maryland Inventories

"The Point of Research may Occupy a long Time to be Expressed at last in brief Phrase."

This list of the "Nearest of Kin," two of whom were required to sign each inventory, is taken in brief form from the inventories recorded in Annapolis, Maryland, where the various proceedings before the Deputy Commissaries of the Prerogative Probate Court were required to be returned.

The work of compiling the kindred of deceased Marylanders for publication was begun for the COUNTY COURT NOTE-BOOK by Mrs. George W. Hodges, who labored for years so faithfully and so intelligently in the archives in the State Land Office, as it was then constituted. After Mrs. Hodges' death, the present compiler continued the work.

At first it seemed sufficient to list only those entries which gave the names of the kindred, but later this compiler realized that there is as much information in "Noe Kinn in this Country" and similar entries, as when the known relatives signed, and the list now contains every reference to an inventory, except occasionally the omission of some small additional inventory not usually signed by the relatives.

It is not possible in these booklets, at the moderate price fixed, to make a complete index. The names of the decedents, however, as well as those in No. 1 of this series, will be found in a reference alphabet following page 17. The reference is to the original volume and page of the Annapolis record, which will be found following in consecutive order the names of the "Next of Kin."

BENJAMIN POSSEY, BELEAN POSSEY; inv. of Mary POSEY [county not given], no date. x-336.

GRIFFITH BEDDOE, nephew, and the "only Relation in the County." Inv. Mr. Edward Griffith [county not given.] 11 May 1725. x-337.

DOROTHY LEIGH, OWEN GUYTHER; inv. Mr. Nicholas Guyther, of St. Mary's cty. 9 Feby 1724-5. x-338.

PHILIP BRISTOE, Jr., EDWARD BRISTOE; Inv. Philip Bristoe, Sr., of Charles cty. 4 Feby 1724-5. x-342.

"Noe Kinn or known Creditors." Inv. George Bellows, of Charles cty. 13 Jany 1724. x-346.

JOHN SCOTT, Jr., WILLIAM SCOTT; inv. John Scott, Sr. of Charles cty. 13 Jany 1727. x-347.

ELIZA: DAVIS, ROBERT DAVIS; inv. Thomas Davis, of Calvert cty. 11 Feby 1724. x-350. [Arthur Jones and Robert Roberts also sign; not clear as in what capacity.]

ELIZABETH x HUNTER, JOSEPHxHUNTER; inv. Sam'll Hunter of Q. A. cty. 13 Oct 1724. x-351.

CHARLES x SNODEN, WILLIAM PRATT; inv. Henry Snoden, Q. A. cty. 12 Apr 1725. x-353.

Uncertain as to kin. Inv. John Gregory, Q.A. cty. 6 May 1724. x-354.

WILLIAM x DYER; inv. Patrick Dyer, Pr. Geo's cty. 12 Feby 1724. x-355.

JOHN RODERY, ELIZA: x SMITH, widow, signs. Inv. John Smith, Pr. Geo's cty. 2 Jany 1724-5. x-355.

"Noe Kinn Except one Infant." Inv. Andrew Rose. 11 May 1724. x-356.

ANN x SIMMS, HANAH x SIMMS; inv. Michael Brown, St. Mary's cty. 4 Mch 1724. x-357.

THOMAS KIRBY, HUGH HOPEWELL; inv. Mr. William Kirby, St. Mary's cty. 30 Mch 1725. x-357.

"Noe Kinn." Inv. William Evans, Cecill cty. 29 Mch 1725. x-359.

JOHN DORSEY, son of E. Dorsey, JANE DORSEY, EDWARD HALL [the latter may be a creditor]; inv. Mr. Sam'll Dorsey, Balto. cty. 20 May 1725. x-360.

NATH'LL HOPKINS, Sr., MATHEW HOPKINS; inv. Mathew Scarborough, Som. cty. 9 July 1724. x-361.

DANIEL HILLYARD, ANN x HILLYARD[?] inv. Henry Hillyard Additional inv. No date. x-363.

JOHN x HOLLOCK, WILLIAM x PAINE; inv. John Dodd, Dor. cty. 23 Apr 1725. x-363. (Bridgett Dodd, extx.)

to be Expressed at last in brief Phrase."

MARY x SEMMS, CHARLES x HIGDON [?] Inv. Benjamin Higdon, Charles cty. No date. x-363.

WILLIAM THRONE, R'D x SUITE; inv. John Ellis, Charles cty. No date. x-364.

ELIZABETH x GLASS; "Noe other Kinn known." Inv. John Glass, Charles cty. 18 Feby 1724-5. x-364.

ADAM WEAVOR[?] WILLIAM x COMPTON; inv. William Compton, Sr. Charles cty. 30 Mch 1725. x-366.

JOHN x SHAW, Sr., JNO. x SHAW, Jr. Inv. John Gibson, Charles cty. 23 Feby 1725. x-368.

EDW'D PHILLPOTT, CHARLES PHILLPOTT [PETER HARRAUT, Creditor?] Inv. Eleanor Phillpott. 10 Mch 1724. x-369.

"Noe Relations save the Deceased's Widow who is gone for England. "Rev'd Sam'll Skippon, Annapo., A.A. cty 5-6 Jany 1724. x-370.

MARY TOBIE als Monrow, his admx, makes oath. Walter Tobie, Annap., A.A. cty. 16 Feby 1724. x-373.

"Noe Relations." Inv. Alex'r Mitchell, Balto. Chirurgeon. 13 Mch 1724, x-374.

ABRAHAM REDGRAVE, Sr. "All the Relations." Inv. Robert Vance [Vause?] Kent cty. 26 Jany 1724-5. x-375.

GEORGE CLIFF, JAMES WHITE; inv. John Cliff, Talb cty. 17 Nov 1724. x-378.

WM. x ELSTON, ROGER x ELSTON; inv. Ralph Elstone, Tab. cty. 3 Oct 1724. x-381.

RICH'D HILL. LEVIN HILL. JOSEPH HILL; inv. Joseph Hill, Gent., A. A. cty. 14 Apr 1725. x-382.

"Noe Relations." Inv. John Wood, Kent cty. 14 Aug 1724. x-390.

Find no kin. Inv. John Harvey. Kent cty. 7 May 1725 x-390.

FRANCIS ARMSTRONG, JOHN PRICE; inv. George Nix, Talb, cty. 12 May 1725. x-391.

DAN'LL MAYNADIER, LOFTUS BOWDLE; inv. Wm. Marten, Talbot cty. 8 May 1725. x-392.

MICHAEL x KERBEY, WILLIAM x KERBEY; inv. Mich'll Kerbey. Talb. cty. 21 May 1725. x-398.

"No Kinn known Capable of Signing"; inv. Ann Garrett, Charles cty. 22 Mch 1724. x-393.

Find no kin; inv. Richard Coe. 1 May 1725. x-394.

GEORGE THOMAS, CHARLES x ADAMS; inv. Susannah Thomas, Charles cty. 4 May 1725. x-395.

THOMAS MATTHEWS, IGNA DOYNE; inv. William Mathews, Charles cty. 26 May 1725. x-396.
ELINOR x MACKENY; inv. Katherine Edwards, Charles cty. 19 Mch 1724-5. x-398.
SAM'LL WICKES, PETER PELLETEAR, JOS. WICKES; [uncertain whether all are kin.] Inv. Mrs. Mary Wickes, Q.A. cty. 20 May 1725. x-399.
Mr. DAN'LL SCOTT, admr, probably kin. Inv. Dan'll Scott, the Elder. Balto cty. 9 June 1725. x-402.
WM x BOWENS, MARY x BOWENS; inv. Edward Hammond, Som cty. "This appr'm't was made in 1719 & the extr has been dead 4 years. Brought to the office the 13 July 1723." x-403.
CATHERINE DRISKILL, DENNIS DRISKILL; inv. Dennis Driskill. 28 June 1722. "Winifritt Driskill d. about twelve months after this Inventory was drawn and never brought in till the 13th of July 1725, and now nobody will Swear to itt." x-405.
JOHN SMART (son); inv. John Smart, Cecill cty. 10 Sept 1722. x-406.
PETER HELLEN, RICHARD HELLEN; inv. David Hellen, Calv cty. 7 June 1725. x-407.
JOHN DERUMPLE [?] WALTER SMITH; inv. Rob't Spickernall, Calv cty. 27 May 1725. x-408.
"Noe kindred;" James Durham, Balto. 14 Apr 1725. x-410.
TAMER x LINEY [?] PHILIP JONES, Jr.[?] Inv. Philip Pitstow, Balto. 15 Feby 1724-5. x-411.
Uncertain as to kin. Inv. David Hagan, Balto cty. 15 Sept 1724. x-412.
Find no kin. Inv. William Wootten, A. A. cty. 8 Oct 1722. x-413.
STEPHEN MIRES; inv. John Miers, Kent cty. 14 June 1723. x-413.
"Noe Kindred;" inv. James Wildman, St. Mary's cty. 20 Apr 1725. x-414.
HERBERT x THOMAS, LUKE THOMAS; inv. Fadery, St. Mary's cty. 31 Mch 1725. [This peculiar name appears later as Fathery, I believe. Ed.] x-416.
"In the behalfe of my two sons," JOHN BULLOCK, MARGARET x BULLOCK; inv. Mr. James Vowles, St. Mary's. 22 Mch 1724. x-418.
"Noe Kindred." Inv. Wm. Hutchins, St. Mary's cty. 17 Jany 1723-4. x-421.

to be Expressed at last in brief Phrase."

ELIZABETH x BRIDGER; inv. John Bridger, St. Mary's cty. 19 June 1725. x-422.
EDW'D TIPPENS, MARY x POOLE; inv. Edward Tippens, Q.A. cty. 28 Apr 1725. x-422.
FRANCIS WATTSON, CHARLES x LOWDER; inv. Wm. Parsons, Q. A. 17 Apr 1724. x-425.
LEWIS DEROCHEBRUNE, MARY x BAXTER; inv. Thos. Baxter, Kent Island, Q. A. cty. 6 May 1721. x-426.
SARAH x SHIPHERD, WILLIAM x SHEPPARD; inv. John Mears, Talb cty. 14 Apr 1725. x-427.
JAMES SUTTON, JAMES x WALKER; Inv. Dan'll Walker, Schoolmaster, Talb. cty. 7 July 1725. x-429.
No kin sign; inv. (add'l) John Manning, Calv. cty. 23 Apr 1725. x-430.
Find no kin; Inv. David Richards, A. A. cty. 20 Mch 1724-5. x-431.
WM. HANDY, JOHN SCOTT; inv. Mr. Stephen Handy, Som. 13 Feby 1725. xi-1.
Find no kin; Charlston Smith, Som. cty. 10 June 1724. xi-3.
JOSHUA x HARTLEY; "No other Relations but Minors." Joseph Hartley, St. Mary's cty. 3 Aug 1725. xi-5.
"No Kinn but Minors." Inv. John Buttler, St. Mary's cty. 4 May 1725. xi-7.
SARAH x PERRY, MARY x BADSON; inv. Rob't Perry, St. Mary's. 8 July 1725. xi-9.
LAWRENCE x AMBROSIE; inv. John Calvin, Charles cty. 1 July 1725. xi-11.
HANNAH x MADKIN, SARAH x TALL, AGATHY TALL; inv. Anthony Tall, Som. cty. 9 June 1725. xi-12.
WM. WILLIAMS. SUSANNAH x WILLIAMS; inv. Katherine Montgomery, Calv. cty. 12 Nov 1724. xi-13.
JOHN MADDOX; inv. Samuel Maddox, St. Mary's. 11 June 1725. xi-17.
TUBMAN x MANKIN, JOAN x MANKIN; inv. Thomas Taylor, Charles cty. 20 Aug 1725. xi-20.
JAMES x JONES; inv. John Noe, Sr., Charles cty. 11 May 1725. xi-21.
Find no kin. Inv. Richard Smith, Charles cty. 17 Aug 1725. xi-22.
Find no kin. Inv. (add'l) Mr. John Atkinson, County? 22 Jany 1722-3. xi-23.
ELIZ: x LOMAX, MARY x ANDERS; inv. Aaron Loman. County? xi-25.

Find no kin. Inv. Timothy McQueen [MacQueen] Pr. Geo's cty. 21 July 1725. xi-26.

HEN:BARNES "near Related", WM x WEBSTER, "related." Inv. James Gibbs, Pr. Geo's cty. 19 June 1725.xi-27.

"No Kindred." Inv. Markham Mackfarson, Pr. Geo's cty. xi-28.

JNO. x MILLS, JACOB x MILLS; inv. Wm. Mills, Dor cty. 13 June 1725. xi-29.

"Adm'x knows of Noe Relations." Inv. Cornelius Flinn. Talb. cty. 20 May 1725. xi-31.

MARY x LORD, ROSANAH x LORD; inv. John Lord, Talb. cty 2 Aug 1725. xi-35.

Not clear as to kin. Inv. Francis Oden, Charles cty. 20 May 1725. xi-35.

MARGARET MARKLAND, formerly wf of David Jones, requested to sign inv. as being the nearest of Kinn, but she refused to sign without giving any reason. Inv. David Jones, Pr. Geo's cty. 22 June 1721. xi-37.

JOHN WARD, JOHN PRICE [doubtful whether kin]; inv. Jacob Caulk, Cecill cty. 18 Feby 1724. xi-39.

MARGARETT x WHEELER, SARAH x BILITER. Inv. Thomas King, Q. A. cty. 5 Aug 1725. xi-40.

J. DEMPSTER, THOS. HACKETT; inv. Capt. John Hackett, Q. A. 8 June 1725. xi-41.

REBECKAH CLARK, AARON PARROTT; inv. Benjamin Parrott, Talb cty. 10 Aug 1725. xi-45.

WILLIAM PARRISH, son of the dec'd, signs with Edward Fell as Creditor; WILLIAM PARRISH, bro. of the dec'd also signs. Inv. John Parrish, Balt. 28 June 1725. xi-48.

Find no Kin. Inv. Joseph Presbury, Balto. cty. 27 May 1725. xi-51.

JOHN MAGRAUGH, WM. x MAGRAUGH; inv. Richard Magraugh, Som. cty. 30 Mch 1725. xi-56.

J. DONELSON, KATH: DONELSON; inv. Rev. Mr. Sam'll Davis, Som. cty. 3 Apr 1725. xi-57.

"Noe Kindred to be found." Inv. Hon. Sam'll Cox, Som. cty. 7 July 1725. xi-59.

BETTY GALE, LEVIN GALE; inv. John Denwood, Som. cty. 12 May 1725. xi-60.

SARAH x ELGATE, MARY MACCLAMERY; inv. Edw'd McGlamery, Som. cty. 3 Jany 1723-4. xi-62.

WILLIAM STEWARD, J. DONELSON; inv. Mrs. Joan McKean, Som. cty. 4 Feby 1724-5. xi-63.

JOHN GOSLIN, RICHARD GOSLIN; inv. John Goslin, Som. 8 Nov 1722. xi-66.
JOSEPH PEMBERTON, JAS. CALDWELL; inv. John Relph, Stepney Psh, Som cty. 17 Sept 1724. xi-68.
ELIZA: x PERREMORE, MARVEN[?] [MARIAN?] x KING; inv. Thos. Relph. Som. cty. ---1723. xi-68. [Perremore, is probably Paramore, a name of that section.]
CATHERINE DIALL, DENNIS DRISKELL; inv. Winifritt Driskill, Som. cty. 14 Nov 1724. xi-71.
BETTY DENWOOD, MARY DENWOOD; inv. Esther Denwood, Som cty. 2 Oct 1724. xi-73.
CHARLES BALLARD, JARVIS x BALLARD; inv. Charles Ballard, Som. cty. 24 Feby 1724-5. xi-80.
WILLIAM x STOKES, PHILLIP x PHILLIPS; inv. Thomas Cooke, Dor. cty. 26 Apr 1725. xi-82.
"Noe Kindred." Inv. Abraham Loyd, Dor. cty. 5 Apr 1725. xi-83.
THOS. MOOTH, RACHEL ELSTON; inv. Darby Dulany, Talb. cty. 21 July 1724. xi-85.
MATY x JONES, "noe other Kinn." Inv. John Jones, Innholder. St. Mary's cty. May 1725. xi-89.
JOHN SPALDING, MARY x SPALDING; inv. Edward Field St. Mary's cty. 13 Nov 1724. xi-91.
Find no kin. Inv. Mich'll Devan, Calv. cty. 6 May 1725. xi-92.
"The ex'rs sayes there is No Kindred to the Dec'd." Inv. John Clegg, Balt. cty. 8 Dec 1723. xi-93.
CHARLES x MERRYMAN, MARY x MERRYMAN; inv. Jacob Cox, Balto cty. 4 Oct 1725. xi-94.
Find no kin. Inv. John Downs. County? 4 June 1725. xi-96.
Find no kin. Inv. Thomas Cutcart, Talb. cty. 19 Aug 1725. xi-97.
THO. TURNER, SARAH TURNER; inv. Charles Climer, Q. A. cty. 20 Aug 1725. xi-98.
CASSANDRA RIGBIE, ANN COALE; inv. Philip Coale, A. A. cty. 17 Oct 1725. xi-101.
DEBORAH HAWKINS; GRUNDY PEMBERTON; inv. James Pemberton, Gent. Q. A. cty. 27 Oct 1725. xi-103.
JAMES EARLE, "a Relation," CARPENDER EARLE; inv. Mr. Carpender Lillingston, Q. A. cty. 4 Sept 1725. xi-109.
WALTER TAYLOR, NATH: HORSEY, "The near Kind;" add'l inv. Capt. Wm. Bolitho, Som cty. 13 July 1725. xi-114.

JOHN WEBB, JAMES TAYLOR; inv. Richard Webb, Som. cty. 29 July 1725. xi-115.

RICHARD x BADDERD, NICHO'S x WARREN; inv. William Badderd, Som cty. 21 July 1725. xi-116.

THOMAS x GREER, SARAH x DENISTON; inv. John Greer, Som. cty. 30 July 1725. xi-117.

"There is no Kindred to the Dec'ed in this part of the World." Inv. Alex'r Serment. [County?] 23 Jany 1724. xi-118.

JAMES MARTIN, GEO. DASHIELL; inv. Mr. Robert Martin, Som. cty. 12 July 1724. xi-120.

No kin sign. Add'l inv. Mr. Stephen Handy, Som cty. 2 Sept 1725. xi-121.

ISABELL STEVENS; inv. Weybure Evans [Weyborough] Som. cty. 8 Sept 1725. xi-121.

SAM'LL HANDY, SARAH TULL; inv. Mr. Sam'll Handy, Som. cty. 16 June 1725. xi-122.

THOS. COLLIER, GEO. COLLIER; inv. Rich'd Phillips, Som. cty. 30 July 1725. xi-124.

"Liked on by us as Kindred." HAST: DASHIELL, MITCHELL DASHIELL; inv. Robert Dashiell, Jr. 23 Aug 1725. Som. cty. xi-124.

WILLIAM POINTER, CORNELIUS x ENNIS; inv. Charles Ennis, Som. cty. 8 Sept 1725. xi-127.

JOHN x RICARDS, JOHN ACWORTH, "Nearest of Kind." Inv. Mary Carter, Som. cty. 18 Jany 1723. xi-127.

WILLIAM x LUKES, Jr., JOHN x LUKES; inv. James Murphy, St. Mary's cty. 26 Apr 1725. xi-128.

JESSE DOYNE, EDW. ALOYSIUS DOYNE; inv. Ethelbert Doyne St. Mary's cty. 1 July 1725. xi-130.

JOSEPH CHUNN, CATHERINE CHUNN; inv. Thomas Morris [prob. St. Mary's cty.] 25 Aug 1725. xi-135.

RICHARD SMITH, LAWRENCE x BATEMAN; inv. John Smith, St. Mary's cty. 29 Oct 1725. xi-138.

RICHARD WIMSETT, JOHN x WIMSETT; inv. Richard Winsett St. Mary's cty. 28 Oct 1725. xi-139.

ISAAC LANSDALE; inv. Richard Lancaster, Pr. Geo's cty 18 June 1724. xi-139.

ELIZABETH x MILLER, ELIZABETH x RAKESTRAW; inv. Rich'd Rakestraw. [County not given.] 10 Nov 1725. xi-142.

Kin uncertain. Inv. Wm. Blinkinship. [County?] 10 Nov 1725. xi-144.

Kin uncertain. Inv. John Poulton, A. A. cty. 15 July 1725. xi-146.

MARY POWER, CLEM'T GARDINER; inv. Mr. Joseph Power, St. Mary's cty. 24 July 1725. xi-146.

JEAN x PEARNS[?] sister, JOHN NICHOLSON; inv. Wm. Weyatt. Q. A. cty. 17 Sept 1725. xi-148. [Thomas Weyatt, a brother, and William Weyatt also sign.]

WILLIAM VERNON, THOS. VERNON, "Relations and Creditors; inv. Christopher Vernon, A. A. cty 29 June 1725. xi-150.

CASSANDRA TALBOTT, SARAH TALBOTT; inv. John Talbott, A.A. cty. 18 June 1785. xi-152.

ROBERT HEIGHE, "nearest of kin." Inv. Mr. Sam'll Heighe, Calv. cty. 11 Aug 1725. ["Some of them Kindred & Cred'rs refused to bothere."] xi-155.

WILLIAM EVANS, ZEBULON PRITTCHET; inv. William Evins, Sr., Dor cty. 20 Oct 1725. xi-157.

PEREGRINE FRISBY, SARAH KNIGHT; inv. Mr. William Frisby, Cecill cty. 12 Apr 1725. xi-159.

THO: JAMESON; inv. Ann Jameson, St. Mary's cty. 19 May 1725. xi-162.

JESSE DOYNE, EDW'D ALOYSIUS DOYNE; inv. Ethelbert Doyne, St. Mary's cty. 17 Nov 1725. xi-163.

ANN CRAGER, BINCH[?], Jr. [Uncertain that these are kin.] Inv. William Watkins, Charles cty. 4 Oct 1725. xi-169.

WM. MACKDOWELL, JNO. x MACKDOWELL; inv. John Macdowell Calv. cty. 10 Aug 1725. xi-170.

"The deced has noe kindred." Inv. John Spencer, Calv cty. 23 Dec 1725. xi-171.

JNO. CAUSEEN, JNO. HAMITT [Uncertain.] Inv. John Wilkinson, Charles cty. 4 Oct 1725. xi-171.

JAMES HALL, HENRY x HALL, WILL'M x HALL; inv. Henry Hall, Balto. cty. 5 Feby 1725-6. xi-173.

MARTHA COPPIDGE, ELIZABETH WILKES, apparently kin; inv Jane Copedge. [County?] 29 Jany 1725-6. xi-175.

ROWLAND x FLOYD [Creditor?] ROBERT BEAUCHAMP, WILLIAM ROBB, MARY FOUNTAIN [uncertain that all are kin.] Inv. John Beauchamp, Gent. Dor cty. 4 Dec 1725. xi-176.

GRACE WOODCOCK, "No more Kindred." Inv. Elizabeth Edwards, Dor cty. 8 Dec 1725. xi-179.

ARTHUR RICH WHITELY, PETER RICH; inv. William Hatfield Dor. cty. 14 Dec 1725. xi-180.

ANTHONY THOMPSON, JOSHUA KENNERLY [probably kin.] Inv Thomas Thompson, son of Anthony Thompson, Dor. cty

Add'l inv. 8 Dec 1725. xi-184.

ANDREW x BANNING, W. BANNING; inv. Thomas Baning, Q.A. cty. 26 Jany 1725. xi-185.

MARTHA x MACKAMBLE, "Kind to the Deced." Inv. Thomas Pratt. Q.A. cty. 2 Aug 1725. xi-185.

WILL. WILKINSON [probably.] Inv. Mr. Francis Wilkinson. Calv. cty. 10 July 1725. xi-187.

ELINOR x TOMLIN; Inv. Edw'd Tomlin. Q. A. cty. 19 Sept 1724. xi-191.

JOHN HASKINS, KATHERINE BOND; inv. George Haskins, St. Mary's cty. 23 Aug 1725. xi-191.

Find no kin. Add'l inv. Mr. [Col.] Rob't Grundy, Talb. cty. 5 Mch 1725-6. xi-192.

SUSANNA ORRICK, KATTREN HAMOND, daughters. Inv. Tho: Hammond, Balto. cty. 5 Feby 1725-6. xi-196.

Find no kin. Inv. John Frizell, Balto. cty. 21 Feby 1725-6. xi-198.

MARY x TOMKINS, ELIZABATH FERSON [uncertain as to kin.] Inv. John Oakley, Charles cty. 2 Dec 1725. xi-200.

ROBERT HEIGHE, SARAH HEIGHE; inv. Mr. James Heighe, Calv. cty. 16 Jany 1725. xi-201.

GEO: HARRIS, WM. HARRIS; Inv. Joseph Harris, Calv. cty. 21 Dec 1725. xi-207.

CATHARINE x BRACKINGHAM, RACHELL x ATKINSON, "Kin by affinity." Inv. John Maccarty, Talb. cty. 14 Mch 1725. xi-211.

ALEX'R BEALE, JOHN BEALE, Sr. [SARAH BEALE, widow, also signs.] Inv. James Beall, Sr., Pr. Geo's, Gent. 23 Nov 1725. xi-213.

"No Kindred." Inv. Gilbert Marsh, Pr. Geo's cty. 1 Mch 1724. xi-221.

"Knows of no Kindred." Inv. John Green, Pr. Geo's cty. 1 Mch 1724. xi-222.

"No Kindred known." Inv. Jonathan Lewis, Pr. Geo's cty. 13 Feby 1724. xi-222.

"No Kinn known." Inv. Michaell Daniell, Pr. Geo's cty. 2 Feby 1725-6. xi-223.

PATRICK SINN, ROB'T ORME [probably.] Inv. Sarah Tannihill, Pr. Geo's cty. 16 Feby 1725-6. xi-224.

"No Kindred but Minors." Inv. Mary Miller, St. Mary's cty. --Feby 1725-6. xi-224.

"No Kin." Inv. Simon Hall, St. Mary's cty. 9 Sept 1725. xi-226.

BENEDICT BOARMAN, JOHN BOARMAN; inv. Dr. Richard Shirburn, St. Mary's cty. 3 Feby 1725. xi-227.

JOHN x CAMBELL, MARY x CAMBELL; inv. John Mackentosh, St. Mary's cty. 7 Mch 1725-6. xi-230.

WILLIAM MARCHMENT, MARY MARCHMENT; inv. Richard Wharton, Som cty. 10 May 1725. xi-231.

JOHN RIDER, [prob. ADAM MUIR]; inv. William Howsley, Dor. cty. 25 June 1726. xi-232.

WILLIAM WEST, MARY WEST; inv. Catrine West, Som. cty. 19 Feby 1723-4. xi-235.

RICHARD x BEATHARD, TOM'S x COLLINS. Inv. Thomas Powel, Som. cty. 7 Mch 1722-3. xi-238.

GABRIEL POWELL, JOHN WHEELER; inv. Garell Powell, Som. cty. 2 Nov 1725. xi-239.

BENJAMIN TRUITT, JOHN x BISHOP; inv. George Truitt, Som. cty, 3 Sept 1725. xi-239.

EDWARD x FOWLER, THO: DASHIELL; inv. Thomas Fowler, Som. cty. 20 Nov 1725. xi-241.

LEWISH DISHARUNE, THOMAS COX; inv. Solomon Early, alias Turpin, Som. cty. 11 Sept 1725. xi-242.

"Noe Kindred." Inv. Edward Flatt, Som. cty. 19 Jany 1725. xi-243.

Find no kin. Inv. Rodger Phillips, Som, cty. 1 Apr 1725. xi-244.

JAMES LAW, WM. McGRAW; inv. Marg'tt Macgrah, Som. cty 29 June 1725. xi-245.

WILLIAM x DEAN, JOHN x DEAN; inv. George Sleicome, Dor. cty. 5 Mch 1725-6. xi-247.

"No Kinn." Inv. Giles Procter, Dor. cty. 9 Dec 1725 xi-249.

"No Kindred." Inv. Joan Bacon, Dor. cty. 8 Mch 1725-6. xi-250.

PETER DICKESON, MARY x MATHIAS [uncertain.] Inv. John Mathews, Dor. cty. 1 Mch 1725. xi-251.

PHILL LOYD, MARGARETT WARD; inv. James Lloyd, Talb. cty. 3 Mch 1725, (Add'l.) xi-251.

MARY x ARNELL [uncertain.] Inv. John Right, of Balto. cty. 29 Oct 1723. xi-255.

SAM x FEARSON, JOHN x NEWMAN; inv. Charles Deane, Charles cty. 12 Apr 1726. xi-256.

CHARLES PHILLPOTT, JNO. PHILLPOTT [probably]. Inv. Edward Philpott, Charles cty. 25 Feby 1725-6. xi-258.

"There is not any Relations to the Deceased." Inv. John Thomas, Q. A. 28 Mch 1726. xi-259.

Kindred not given. Inv. Mr. Wm. Frisby, Cecill cty. 1 Mch 1725. xi-260.
JOHN MIDLAY, Jr., REBECCA x THOMPSON; inv. Wm. Medley St. Mary's cty. 9 Dec 1725. xi-260.
ELINOR BRISCOE, MARY KEECH; inv. James Somerhill, St. Mary's cty. 3 Mch 1725-6. xi-262.
JOHN POLLARD, MARY HOWELL; inv. Rev. Thomas Howell, Dor cty. 28 Feby 1726. xi-263.
JOHN SMITH, SAM'LL SMITH; inv. John Smith, Pr. Geo's cty. 28 Mch 1726. xi-266.
No kin given. Add'l inv. John Maccarty, Talb. cty. 2 May 1726. xi-267.
"We know of noe Kindred .... in this Country." Inv. John Gardiner, Cecill cty. 31 Jany 1725-6. xi-268.
"Noe Kinn." Inv. Elizabeth Wadlington, Cecill cty. 23 Dec 1725. xi-269.
JOHN BELL, "No other Relations but Minors." Inv. Richard Bell, Cecill cty. 1 Jany 1725-6. xi-269.
STEPH'N DARDEN, JOSEPH DARDEN; inv. Dr. John Carr, Talb. cty. Exhibited 31 Mch 1726. xi-272.
JEFFRY x COX, MARY x COX; inv. William Shaw, Talb. cty. 17 Aug 1724. xi-277.
THOMAS BRADSHAW, JOHN LENANZ; inv. John Bradshaw, Talb. cty. 2 May 1726. xi-279.
DEN'S HOPKINS, RALPH HOLMES; inv. William Holmes, Taylor, Talb. cty. 5 May 1726. xi-281.
"No Relation." Inv. Benjamin Bond, Kent cty. 24 Oct 1725. xi-285.
"No Relations." Inv. David Reed, Kent cty. 22 Jany 1724-5. xi-287.
JNO. TILDEN, "a kinn," CHARLES SCOTT, "a Kinn." Inv. Coll. Edward Scott, Kent cty. 20 Jany 1725. xi-289.
"No Relations to the Deceased that Appeared." Inv. Richard Scaggs, Kent cty. 7 Apr 1726. xi-304.
JNO. HAMBLETON, JOHN LEEDS. Inv. William Hambleton, Talb. cty. 25 Oct 1725. xi-306.
JOHN LARON[?] ISRAELL, GILBERT TALBOT ISRAELL; inv. Mr. John Israell, Balto. 19 Apr 1725. xi-308.
JOHN MERRIMAN, SAM'LL MERRYMAN; inv. Charles Merryman Balto. cty. 5 Feby 1725-6. xi-311.
Find no kin. Inv. Joseph Presbury, Balto. cty. 18 Feby 1725-6. xi-313.
Find no kin. Inv. Thomas Read, A. A. cty, 10 Nov 1725. xi-314.

to be Expressed at last in brief Phrase."

JOHN x RAWLINGS, WILLIAM RIDGLEY; inv. Mr. Jehosaphat Ridgeley, A. A. cty. 30 Mch 1726. xi-315.

JAMES HOWARD, PHILIP HOWARD; inv. Samuel Howard, A. A. cty. 14 Aug 1724. xi-318.

"Know of no Relations." Inv. John Abbercrombie, A. A. cty, 31 Mch 1726. xi-321.

THOMAS HOMEWOOD, SARAH EAGLE; inv. Mr. Saladine Eagle, A. A. cty. 30 Mch 1726. xi-325.

Find no kin. Inv. Mary Thompson, of Annapolis. 15 Nov 1725. xi-330.

ROBERT x GOULDSBERRY, JOHN x GOULDSBERRY; Inv. William Goldsberry, St. Mary's cty. 8 Apr 1726. xi-331.

HOW'D x WILLIAMS, JOHN x JERBO, ELABATH x WILLIAMS; inv. William Bannister, St. Mary's cty. 27 Apr 1726. xi-336.

JANE x GOUGH, SARAH x GREENWELL, [probably kin.] Inv. Robert Clark, St. Mary's cty. 9 Apr 1726. xi-337.

THO. BOULS, Senior, JO'N BOULS; inv. William Pritchet, St. Mary's cty. 7 Mch 1725-6. xi-339.

MARY LINSAR[??] Inv. John Lambeth. [County?] 27 Apr 1726. xi-343.

GEORGE THOMAS, MARY x MILER [uncertain.] Inv. John Baker, Jr. Charles cty. 22 Feby 1725. xi-344.

SARAH x NELSON, RICH'D WADE; Inv. Thomas Rockwood, Charles cty. 21 May 1726. xi-343.

WILLIAM ROBY x RICHARD ROBY; inv. John Robie, Sr., Charles cty. 23 Apr 1726. xi-346.

Find no kin. Inv. Henry Evans, Charles cty. 26 Mch 1726. xi-347.

JOHN ROUSE, JOHN x GALLAWAY; inv. William Rouse, Chas. cty. 21 May 1726. xi-348.

No kin listed. Add'l inv. John Calvin, Charles cty. 22 Apr 1725. xi-351.

"No Relation but Minors." Inv. Joseph Chrismond, Chas. cty. 24 Apr 1726. xi-352.

GEORGE DENT, SAMMUEL x TURNER; inv. Mary Dent, Charles cty. 2 June 1726. xi-356.

DANIEL x McDANIELL, ANN x PECOCK; inv. John Hammons, Charles cty. 5 Apr 1726. xi-357.

"Two nighest of Kin refused to sign." Inv. Thomas Brashier, Q. A. Town, Pr. Geo's cty. 3 Feby 1725. xi-359.

SOLOMON x TURNER, MARGARET x TURNER; inv. Philip Turn-34, Pr. Geo's cty. 11 Apr 1726. xi-361. [See note.]

Do not find kin. Inv. Samuel Howell, Pr. Geo's cty. 29 Jany 1725-6. xi-361. [See note.]

MARY x MOSSELL, SARAH x STRUCKLAND; inv. Ann Morsell, Calv. cty. 30 Dec 1725. xi-362.

GEORGE HARRIS, WILLIAM HARRIS; inv. Mr. Benj. Harris, Calv. cty. 15 Dec 1725. xi-364.

BENJA. WOOD, JOHN WOOD; inv. John Wood, Calv. cty. 9 Apr 1726. xi-370.

GRACE x MACKGILL, ELIZABETH FINWICK; inv. Mrs. Grace Brook, Calv. cty. 18 Nov 1725. xi-372.

JAMES HULSE, MARY LOCH; inv. William Hulse, St. Mary's cty. 10 June 1726. xi-374.

"No Kindred." Inv. Michael Early, St. Mary's cty. 18 Feby 1725. xi-376.

MARY HASKINS, SARY BARNS [uncertain.] Inv. Elizabeth Barnes, St. Mary's cty. 25 Apr 1726. xi-377.

JOS. CHUNN, JOHN BRANSON; inv. John Price, St. Mary's cty. 5 Apr 1726. xi-377.

"No Kindred." Inv. Thomas Parsons, Som. cty. 20 Jany 1725-6. xi-379.

NEHEM x HUGGINS, MARGRIT x SMITH; inv. Edmond Huggins Som. cty. 16 June 1726. xi-380.

J. DONELSON, KATHRIN STEWARD; inv. Mr. Patrick Donelson, Som. cty. 5 Feby 1725. xi-383. Jean Donaldson makes oath. [See note.]

"No Kindred." Inv. Dr. John Bannister, Som. cty. 29 Nov 1725. xi-385.

WILLIAM x RUSSELL; inv. Edward Wheatly, Som. cty. 23 Apr 1724. xi-387.

SARAH x HOUGIN[?] Inv. James Bradey, Som. cty. 20 Apr 1723. xi-389.

"No Kindred in the Country." Inv. Jas. Chalmer, Som. cty. 11 June 1726. xi-390.

GEORGE JARMAN, HENRY JARMAN; inv. Wm. Jarman, Som. cty. 7 July [year not given.] xi-391.

"No Kindred to be found." Inv. Jeremiah Veney, Som. cty. ----- 1721. xi-392.

CHARLES WHEELER, JOHN STEWART; inv. Henry Wheeler, Dor. cty. 9 June [year?] xi-393.

PHILIP FAIE or FALL - "No more." Inv. Mary Warner, Dor. cty. 8 Nov 1725. xi-395.

JOHN x PEIRESON, EDWARD x CAFFE; inv. Francis Bickham, Dor. cty. 22 June 1726. xi-396.

DAN'L COX, BETTY CANNER [CONNER?] Inv. Margaret Willis Dor. cty. 4 July 1726. xi-399.

Find no Kin. Inv. Philip Reyley, A. A. cty, Blacksmith. 2 Jany 1724-5. xi-402.

OSBORN SPRIGG; EDWARD SPRIGG refused to sign; Inv. Mr. Thos. Sprigg, Pr. Geo's cty. 28 May 1726. xi-405.

"No Kinn. Inv. Angnis Mackley, Charles cty. 15 May 1726. xi-412.

ELIZABETH x PARRANDER [PARRANDIER], MARY x SANDERS; inv. Matthew Sanders, Jr., Charles cty. 15 May 1776. xi-413.

THOMAS SMOOT, SAMUEL x LOVE; inv. Wm. Kingland, Chas. cty, 28 Apr 1726. xi-414.

MARMADUCK x SIMS, ANNA x OUKEE[??] Inv. John Simms, Charles cty. 1 Feby 1724-5. xi-418.

"No Kinn." Inv. Timothy Carter, Charles cty. 28 Feby 1725-6. xi-419.

THOMAS THOMPSON, WM. THOMPSON; inv. Cuthbert Thompson Charles cty. 17 Dec 1725. xi-420.

WM. HOWARD, JNO. HOWARD; inv. Thos. Howard, Charles cty. 23 Mch 1726. xi-421.

JNO. BRISCOE, Sr., SUSANNA BRISCOE, Sr.; inv. Edward Briscoe, Charles cty. 17 Mch 1725. xi-424.

"No Kinn." Inv. George Tate, Charles cty. 11 Apr 1726. xi-426.

"No Relations." Inv. James Ellery, Charles cty. ----- 1726. xi-427.

PERSEFUL x FERSON, GRACE SNOWMAN; inv. Samuel Ferson, Charles cty. 4 Apr 1726. xi-428.

"Know of No Kindred." Inv. Anguish Mackermitt, Pr. Geo's cty. ----- 1726. xi-430.

SETH HYATT, PETER HYATT; inv. Charles Hyatt, Pr. Geo's cty. 25 June 1726. xi-433.

JOHN SWEARINGEN, THOMAS SWEARINGEN [probably kin.] Inv Thomas Swearingen, Pr. Geo's cty. 16 June 1726. xi-434.

"Noe Kinn." Inv. X'r Bolton, Talb. cty. 9 July 1726. xi-436.

PETER SHARP, PETER STEVENS; inv. Edmond Stevens, Talb. cty. 10 June 1725. xi-438.

Kin not given. Add'l inv. Mr. John Valliant, Talb. cty. 8 July 1726. xi-440.

JAMES MERRICK, ELIZABETH x MERRICK; inv. Joseph Barron, Talb. cty. 2 June 1726. xi-441.

"No Kin Known" Inv. George Rickards, Waterman; Talb. cty, 30 June 1726. xi-442.

HEZ'H MACKEY; "No other Kinn but Minors." Inv. Henry Bullen, Talb. cty. 23 Mch 1726. xi-443.

JOHN x CROUCH, ANN x CROUCH; inv. John Crouch, Som. cty 31 July 1725. xi-444.

WM. HEARN, JAMES SMITH [uncertain]. Inv. Mr. Thomas Cox, Som cty. 27 Dec 1725. xi-446.

HAN'H DAVIS, JEAN DAVIS; inv. John Davis, Som. cty. 24 Mch 1722. xi-448.

"No Kindred." Inv. Relph Danvy, Balto, Md. 10 May 1726. xi-448.

JAMES x FRIZELL, JOHN x FRIZELL; Inv. Mary Frizell, Balto cty. 29 May 1726. xi-450.

SUTTON x THRIFT, JOHN x THRIFT; inv. Richard Thrift, Balto. 29 Jany 1726. xi-452.

PETER SHIPLEY, brother, ROB'T x SHIPLEY; inv. Richard Shipley, Balto cty. 30 Nov 1725. xi-454.

ANN x RICKARDS, GODFREY WATTERS [WALTERS?] Inv. Thomas Guinn, Balto cty. 23 June 1726. xi-457.

MELCHE'D MORRAY, NATHANIEL GILES; inv. John Giles, Balto cty. 19 July 1726. xi-458.

Some corrections in the list of Kin in Ancestral Proofs and Probabilities, No. 1.

Inventory of JOHN GRESHAM, Esq. The 1st additional inventory should read "Additional inventory in Kent county." Also Priscilla & Thomas, dau. and son (kin, not of age). p.21. of bulletin.

MARGARET x NEAVETT and JOHN REALY (not Really) were next of kin to Mr. Francis Neavett. 1st col., same page as above.

ESTHER SMITH, should be ESTER SMITH. 2d col. same page.

HANNAH HORSEY should be HANNA HORSEY.

HENRY x WARD; inv. of Sarah King, of Kent cty. 29 Aug 1724. x-86. p.22. of bulletin.

ROBERT STANFIELD, not Robert S. Stanfield. p. 20, 1st col.

Wm. WALKES, should read Wm. Walker. p. 22, 2d col.

The reference for the WALTHAM kin, p. 21, should be vol. ix-p. 420.

PHILL. LOYD, R. BENNETT, MARGARET WARD; [uncertain which are kin.] Inv. of James Loyd, of Talbott cty. 3 Mch 1724-5. x-309.

SARAH x ZOW, JOHN ELLIOTT, G. NICHOLLS, "Greatest creditors and nearest of Kinn"; inv. of Thos. Noble, of Dor. cty. 29 Mch 1725. x-335.

Inv. of JOSEPH COOKOO, not Alan. p. 24, col. 1. A.P. & P. No. 1.

The same page, col. 1, CLEMENT BARKSTON, of Cecill cty, inn-holder.

ABBERCROMBIE, xi-321
Atkinson, xi-23

BEALL, xi-213
Bacon, xi-250
Bond, xi-285
Bradshaw, xi-279
Bell, xi-269
Baker, xi-344
Bannister, xi-336
Brashier, xi-359
Barnes, xi-377
Brook, xi-372
Brady, xi-389
Bannister, xi-385
Bickham, xi-396
Bolton, xi-434
Briscoe, xi-424
Ballard, xi-80
Badderd, xi-116
Bolitho, xi-114
Blinkinship, xi-144
Baning, xi-185
Beauchamp, xi-176
Bullen, xi-443
Barron, xi-441
Baxter, x-246
Bridger, x-422
Buttler, xi-7
Brown, x-357
Bristow, x-342
Bellows, x-346

COALE, xi-101
Carter, xi-127
Copedge, xi-175
Cox, xi-446
Crouch, xi-444
Cox, xi-94
Clegg, xi-93
Coale, xi-101
Climer, xi-98
Cox, xi-59
Cutcart, xi-97
Compton, x-366
Caulk, xi-39
Calvin, xi-11
Cliff, x-378
Coe, x-394
Collins, xi-238
Carr, xi-272
Clark, xi-337
Chrismond, xi-352
Carter, xi-419
Conner, xi-399
Cooke, xi-82
Calvin, xi-351
Chalmer, xi-390

DOYNE, xi-163
Dashiell, xi-126
Doyne, xi-130
Daniell, xi-223
Deane, xi-256
Dent, xi-356
Donelson, xi-383
Downs, xi-96
Devan, xi-92
Dulany, xi-85
Denwood, xi-60
Davis, xi-57
Denwood, xi-73
Driskill, xi-71
Dashiell, xi-124
Danvy, xi-448
Davis, xi-448
Denwood, xi-60
Dodd, x-363
Driskill, x-405
Dyer, x-355
Dorsey, x-360
Davis, x-350
Durham, x-410

EVINS, xi-157

preceding list of Maryland Kin.

Ellis, x-364
Edwards, x-398
Elstone, x-381
Evans, x-359
Ennis, xi-127
Evans, xi-121
Early, xi-242
Eagle, xi-325
Evans, xi-347
Early, xi-376
Ellery, xi-427
Edwards, xi-179
Earle, xi-109

FRISBY, xi-159
Frizell, xi-198
Fowler, xi-241
Flatt, xi-243
Frisby, xi-260
Ferson, xi-428
Field, xi-91
Frizell, xi-450
Flinn, xi-31
Fadery, x-416

GREEN, xi-222
Grundy, xi-
Gardiner, xi-268
Goldsberry, xi-331
Goslin, xi-66
Greer, xi-117
Giles, xi-458
Guinn, xi-457
Grundy, xi-192
Gibbs, xi-27
Garrett, x-393
Glass, x-364
Gibson, x-368
Griffith, x-337
Guyther, x-338
Gregory, x-354

HEIGHE, xi-155
Handy, xi-122
Handy, xi-121
Howsley, xi-232
Harris, xi-207
Hall, xi-226
Heighe, xi-201
Hammond, xi-196
Haskins, xi-191
Hambleton, xi-306
Holmes, xi-281
Howell, xi-263
Howard, xi-318
Howell, xi-361
Hammons, xi-357
Huggins, xi-38
Hulse, xi-374
Harris, xi-364
Hyatt, xi-433
Howard, xi-421
Hall, xi-173
Hatfield, xi-180
Hall, xi-173
Hackett, xi-41
Hutchins, x-421
Hartley, xi-5
Handy, xi-1
Higdon, x-363
Hillyard, x-363
Hagan, x-412
Hammond, x-403
Hellen, x-407
Hill, x-382
Harvey, x-390
Hunter, x-351

ISRAELL, xi-308

JAMESON, xi-162
Jarman, xi-391
Jones, xi-89
Jones, xi-37

KINGLAND, xi-414

Kerbey, x-398
King, xi-40

LEWIS, xi-222
Lloyd, xi-251
Lambeth, xi-343
Loyd, xi-83
Lancaster, xi-139
Lancaster, xi-140
Loman, xi-25
Lord, xi-35

MAGRAUGH, xi-56
Murphy, xi-128
Marsh, xi-221
Mackentosh, xi-230
Maccarty, xi-211
Miller, xi-224
Mathews, xi-251
MacGrah, xi-245
Maccarty, xi-267
Medley, xi-260
Merryman, xi-311
Morsell, xi-362
Mackley, xi-412
Mackermitt, xi-430
Macdowell, xi-170
McKean, xi-63
McGlamery, xi-62
Martin, xi-120
McQueen, xi-26
Miers, x-413
Maddox, xi-17
Montgomery, xi-13
Mills, xi-29
Morris, xi-135
Mackfarson, xi-28
Manning, x-430
Mears, x-427
Marten, x-392
Mitchell, x-374
Mathews, x-346

NIX, x-391
Noe, xi-121

OAKLEY, xi-200
Oden, xi-35

POSEY, x-336
Phillips, xi-124
Powel, xi-238
Powell, xi-239
Procter, xi-249
Phillips, xi-244
Presbury, xi-313
Pritchet, xi-339
Parsons, xi-379
Price, xi-377
Presbury, xi-51
Pemberton, xi-109
Power, xi-146
Poulton, xi-146
Pratt, xi-185
Pemberton, xi-103
Parrott, xi-45
Parrish, xi-48
Parsons, x-425
Perry, xi-9
Phillpott, x-369
Pitstow, x-411

RIGHT, xi-255
Reed, xi-287
Ridgeley, xi-315
Read, xi-314
Robie, xi-346
Rockwood, xi-343
Rouse, xi-348
Reyley, xi-402
Relph, xi-68 (2)
Rakestraw, xi-142
Richards, xi-442
Rose, x-356
Richards, x-431

SHIRBURN, xi-227
Sleicome, xi-247

Scaggs, xi-304
Scott, xi-289
Shaw, xi-277
Smith, xi-266
Somerhill, xi-262
Simms, xi-418
Sanders, xi-413
Sprigg, xi-405
Swearingen, xi-434
Spencer, xi-171
Serment, xi-118
Smith, xi-139
Stevens, xi-438
Shipley, xi-456
Smith, xi-138
Smith, xi-22
Smith, xi-3
Smart, x-406
Spickernall, x-408
Scott, x-402
Smith, x-355
Scarborough, x-361
Scott, x-347
Snoden, x-353
Skippon, x-370

TALBOTT, xi-152
Tannihill, xi-224
Truitt, xi-239
Thomas, xi-259
Thompson, xi-330
Turner, xi-361
Tate, xi-426
Thompson, xi-420
Tomlin, xi-191
Thompson, xi-184
Thrift, xi-452
Taylor, xi-20
Tall, xi-12
Thomas, x-395
Tobie, x-373

VERNON, xi-150
Veney, xi-392
Valliant, xi-440
Vowles, x-418
Vance [Vause?] x-375

WEYATT, xi-148
West, xi-235
Wharton, xi-231
Wadlington, xi-269
Wood, xi-370
Warner, xi-395
Wheeler, xi-393
Wheatly, xi-387
Wilkinson, xi-171
Watkins, xi-169
Webb, xi-115
Wilkinson, xi-187
Winsett, xi-139
Walker, x-429
Wootten, x-413
Wickes, x-399
Wildman, x-414
Wood, x-390

ARNOLD, x-105
Aires, x-251
Aingell, x-300

BLACKWELL, x-46
Brown, x-66
Blair, x-54
Bows, x-90
Bandee, x-128
Brooks, x-147
Beach, x-144
Banister, x-164
Bayley, x-217
Butterworth, x-215
Benton, x-270
Barron, x-283
Barkston, x-292
Blackiston, x-292
Bradshaw, x-298
Bebber, x-258

COOKE, ix-418
Carter, x-7
Carter, x-28
Campbell, ix-450
Cuthcart, x-45
Collins, x-59
Cawsey, x-74
Corseway [Cawsey], x-75
Coverthought, x-80
Coster, x-78
Cooper, x-106
Connor, x-127
Cole, x-122
Cavinan, x-134
Clark, x-149
Channell, x-149
Cohale [??] x-140
Cromwell, x-156
Cole, x-194
Christian, x-235
Chapman, x-250
Cissell, x-254
Cookoo, x-282
Clanage, x-284
Cole, x-305
Clarke, x-331
Coale, x-334

DONKINE [Duncan?] ix-417
Dyer, ix-424
Dawtridge, x-103
Drew, x-153
Douglass, x-151
Dod, x-286
Dansey, x-1
Drewry, 9-451
Dorman, x-57
Deheneyosia, x-133
Davis, x-257
Duely, x-253
Davis, x-301
Dickeson, x-336

ELLIOTT, ix-423
Eade, x-28
Emerson, x-93
Eubanks, x-244

FINNEY, x-48
Fenwick, x-117
Floyd, x-237
Ford, x-280
Froud, x-307

GRESHAM, ix-427
Gresham, ix-430
Gresham, ix-433
Gardner, x-12
Greenwell, x-9
Grindles, x-57
Gover, x-81
Gale, x-91
Gill, x-111
Gould, x-154
Greenwell, x-168

Gray, x-246
Givan, x-246
Gray, x-264
Gilbert, x-291

HUDDLESTONE, x-8
Hall, x-61
Harper, x-72
Heathcoate, x-70
Horsey, x-67
Hungerford, x-123
Hinds, x-135
Hune, x-135
Henricks, x-231
Holt, x-218
Hastings, x-236
Harwood, x-267
Homes, x-289
Hill, x-299

JONES, x-64
Johnson, x-86
Jemmett, x-133
Jones, x-263
Jones, x-278

KNOT, ix-424
King, ix-426
King, x-86
Kirkham, x-124
Kerby, x-136
Kirkham, x-242
Kimston, x-260
King, x-285

LURTY, x-11
Lenox, x-97
Lyfoly, x-109
Lee, x-154
Lemey, x-242
Lazenby, x-242
Lowder, x-276
Lockwell, x-276
Larkins, x-308
Loyd, x-309

MIDDLETON, x-15
Manning, x-76
Macha, x-150
Mullicane, x-141
Melton, x-165
Mountsear, x-191
Marriott, x-214
March, x-220
Munday, x-262
Merricks, x-272
Morgan, -285

NEWGAN, ix-424
Neavett, ix-446
Nevitt, x-120
Needles, ix-138
Neale, x-234
Nordike, x-301
Noble, x-332

O'BRYAN, x-69
Orrell, x-238

PAGAN, ix-421
Pitts, ix-422
Pitslow, x-96
Pumphrep, x-112
Pendleton, x-140
Ponder [Pinder?] x-159
Phillips, x-174
Paca, x-200
Phelps, x-199
Pile, x-265

ROSS, ix-449
Rudderford, x-92
Roche, x-169
Ricaud, x-298
Ryley, x-303

SUTTEN, ix-416
Smith, x-27
Sawell[?] ix-443
Smith, x-31
Smith, x-33
Stanfield, x-108
Stephens, x-115
Sweany, x-194
Smith, x-288

THORBERR[?] x-27
Taylor, ix-445
Tucker, x-84
Taylor, x-146
Thompson, x-195
Turner, x-252
Trippe, x-331
Thompson, x-335

VOWLES, x-15
Van Bebber [See also Bebber[x-258
Vogler, x-243

WILLIAMS, x-188
Waltham, ix-424
Wright, x-100
Williams, x-
Walkes, x-132
Wheeler, x-152
Wealch, x-162

Compiled and edited by MILNOR LJUNGSTEDT, Editor of the COUNTY COURT NOTE-BOOK, Contributing Editor to the AMERICAN GENEALOGIST, and Honorary Member of the Pennsylvania Genealogical Society.

No. 1. Contains marriage references and Maryland Next of Kin. Price $2.00.
No. 2. Contains marriage references only. 800. Mainly from Delaware, Maryland & Virginia. Price $1.50.
No. 3. Contains nearly 500 alphabetized records of soldiers of the Colonial and Revolutional Wars. Price $1.00.
No. 4. This bulletin, containing the "Next of Kin" from Maryland Inventories. Price $1.00.
The COUNTY COURT NOTE-BOOK, 1920 - 1931, nine years of this available at a special price.

The F. W. FAXON COMPANY,
83 Francis Street,
Boston, Massachusetts.

Are selling and subscription agents for the above. Address all orders to them.

GENEALOGICAL RESEARCH - IMPORTANT PUBLICATIONS

Mrs. MILNOR LJUNGSTEDT, Researcher,
Beech Avenue, Bethesda Station, Washington, D. C.
Specializes in the records of the Middle and Southern Colonial States. Marriage and military indices.

CAVALIERS and PIONEERS, compiled and edited by
Mrs. NELL MARION NUGENT,
of the State Land Office,
Richmond, Virginia.
These volumes make accessible to every searcher the names of patentees of land, and of the thousands of immigrant ancestors.

NOTTINGHAM'S RECORDS OF THE EASTERN SHORE OF VIRGINIA
Address Mrs. H. R. Nottingham,
301 N. Sheppard Street, Richmond, Virginia.

The EMERY RECORD RESTORING COMPANY,
Taunton, Massachusetts.
Their work in this line has never been excelled.

A B A Electric Typed Letters Company, Washington, D. C.